AF505816

The Praeger Handbook of Veterans' Health

Volume I
History, Eras, and Global Healthcare

Volume II
Programs of Care and Groups with Special Needs

Volume III
Mental Health Treatment and Rehabilitation

Volume IV
Future Directions in Veterans' Healthcare

THE PRAEGER HANDBOOK OF VETERANS' HEALTH

History, Challenges, Issues, and Developments

Volume I: History, Eras, and Global Healthcare

Thomas W. Miller, Editor

AN IMPRINT OF ABC-CLIO, LLC
Santa Barbara, California • Denver, Colorado • Oxford, England

Library of Congress Cataloging-in-Publication Data

The Praeger handbook of veterans' health : history, challenges, issues, and developments / Thomas W. Miller, editor.
   v. cm.
 Includes bibliographical references and index.
 ISBN 978-0-313-38349-6 (hardcover : alk. paper) — ISBN 978-0-313-38350-2 (ebook)
1. Veterans—Health and hygiene—United States. 2. Veterans—Care—United States. 3. Veterans—United States—History. I. Miller, Thomas W., 1943– II. Title: Handbook of veterans' health.
 UB369.P73 2012
 362.1086'97—dc23
                         2012025159

ISBN: 978-0-313-38349-6
EISBN: 978-0-313-38350-2

16 15 14 13 12   1 2 3 4 5

This book is also available on the World Wide Web as an eBook.
Visit www.abc-clio.com for details.

Praeger
An Imprint of ABC-CLIO, LLC

ABC-CLIO, LLC
130 Cremona Drive, P.O. Box 1911
Santa Barbara, California 93116-1911

This book is printed on acid-free paper ∞
Manufactured in the United States of America

It is the VETERAN, not the preacher, who has given us freedom of religion.

It is the VETERAN, not the reporter, who has given us freedom of the press.

It is the VETERAN, not the poet, who has given us freedom of speech.

It is the VETERAN, not the campus organizer, who has given us freedom to assemble.

It is the VETERAN, not the lawyer, who has given us the right to a fair trial.

It is the VETERAN, not the politician, who has given us the right to vote.

It is the VETERAN, who salutes the Flag, It is the VETERAN, who serves under the Flag.

—Author Unknown

Contents

VOLUME I
HISTORY, ERAS, AND GLOBAL HEALTHCARE

Acknowledgments ix

Foreword xi
Jacob B. Gadd

Editor's Foreword xv

Part I History of Veterans' Healthcare **1**

1 Historical Contributions to Veterans' Healthcare 3
Rodney R. Baker

2 Administration and Veterans' Healthcare: A View from
the Top 25
James W. Holsinger Jr.

3 The Academic Mission of the Department of Veterans Affairs 53
*Stuart C. Gilman, Barbara K. Chang, Robert A. Zeiss,
Mary B. Dougherty, William J. Marks Jr.,
Deborah A. Ludke, and Malcolm Cox*

4 Veterans' Healthcare: Legislative Initiatives 69
*Thomas W. Miller, with assistance from Jacqueline D. Rychnovsky
and Corina M. Barrow, through the Congressional
Office of Senator Daniel Inouye*

Part II   Healthcare for Veterans from Various Eras   83

5   Healthcare for Veterans of World Wars I and II   85
        Thomas W. Miller

6   Veterans of the Korean War Era   105
        Thomas W. Miller

7   Healthcare for Veterans of Vietnam   121
        Robert J. Fitz

8   Veterans' Healthcare for Operations Enduring Freedom, Iraqi
        Freedom and New Dawn   157
        Delilah O. Noronha, John Chardos, Laura Gomez, Samina Iqbal,
        and Steven Lindley

Part III   Global Healthcare for Veterans   191

9   Veterans' Healthcare in Other Countries: Australia,
        Canada, China, Russia, and the United Kingdom   193
        Thomas W. Miller

10 Suicide in the Ex-service Community: Australian Research and
        Prevention Efforts for Veterans' Healthcare   207
        David Dunt, Jo Robinson, Colleen Doyle, Gennady Baksheev,
        and Suganya Selvarajah

11 The Evolution of Healthcare Programs for Canadian Veterans   237
        David Pedlar and Stewart Macintosh

12 Forgotten Heroes? Health and Well-being Issues and
        Resources for UK Veterans and Their Families
        in the Twenty-first Century   257
        Dai Williams

About the Editor   295

About the Contributors   297

Index   305

Acknowledgments

An endeavor of this magnitude has taken several years and the efforts of numerous colleagues and friends in the Department of Veterans Affairs and others interested in the health and well-being of our veterans and their families in the general public. It is to those in the Department of Veterans Affairs Central Office in Washington, D.C., their regional Veterans Integrated Service Networks (VISNs), and regional as well as local Veteran Affairs medical centers, that I am extremely grateful. Their efforts have addressed contacting the right people, gaining access to important information, manuscript preparation completion, reviews, and providing detailed guidance in the final chapters and volumes.

Special appreciation is expressed to the efforts of the Department of Veterans Affairs, Office of Communications, and in particular Mr. Daniel Bruneau, Director of Communications; Christine A. Pons, Regional Office of Public Affairs, Department of Veterans Affairs; and Charles F. Castner, Staff Attorney, Department of Veterans Affairs.

The assistance of Darlene Richardson, the Department of Veterans Affairs historian, has been helpful in completing several of the chapters, as have external organizations committed to the care and treatment of our veterans, including the American Legion, Veterans of Foreign Wars, and Paralyzed Veterans of America.

To a cadre of former and current colleagues and friends within the Department of Veterans Affairs, and to some beyond this system, for their support and encouragement, special appreciation is extended, including but

not limited to John Booss, MD; Rodney Baker, PhD; Malcolm Cox, MD; Robert Gresen, PhD; James McCormick, MD; James Holsinger, MD; Herb Spencer, MD; Robert Kraus, MD; Steve Kraman, MD; William Green, PhD; Pat DeLeon, JD, PhD; Brenda Frommer; Neil Carey, MSW; Skip Lowe, PhD; Jeffrey Fisher, PhD; Alla Moeller; Walter Penk, PhD; Ed Nighingale, PhD; Ed Kisarskis, MD; Jill Livingstone, MLB; Deborah Kessler, MLB; Desti Stimes; Joanna Hawthorne; Chesley Jaracz; Tom Martin; Ginny Hamm, JD; Joseph Fox, PhD; Donna K. Jacobs; Steve Campbell, MSW; Steve Nisenbaum, PhD, JD; Terry Clark, MSW; and Maureen Charles, ED, MSN, APRN, Military Nurse Fellow, Lieutenant Colonel, Air Force Nurse Corps.

Appreciation is extended to Praeger publishers as well and their staff and Debbie Carvalko, senior acquisitions editor, psychology, health, and social work, and Alicia S. Merritt, consultant, for their guidance and support.

I express my sincere appreciation to my family, especially my father who served our country in World War II in General Patton's army in the European theater, and friends, who have been so supportive of this effort. And I extend my sincere gratitude and appreciation to each and every contributor for the chapters in these volumes. They come from the several Department of Veterans Affairs facilities, from our major universities, and from both within and beyond our borders. The reader will meet each and every one of them in their chapters as well as in the short biographies that summarize their backgrounds, training, experiences, and expertise. May these volumes provide the reader with a detailed look at veterans' healthcare in the twenty-first century!

Foreword

For the past fifty years, the Department of Veterans Affairs (VA) has provided high-quality care to America's veterans, and it is recognized today as the largest integrated healthcare system in the United States. Its mission, as stated eloquently by President Abraham Lincoln during his second inaugural address, is "to care for him who has borne the battle, his widow and orphan." Currently there are more than twenty-five million veterans across the country. Eight million are enrolled in VA and about 5.5 million are seen at 1,300 Veterans Health Administration (VHA) facilities annually. The VHA has 153 medical centers, 800 community-based outpatient clinics (CBOCs), and 260 readjustment counseling centers (vet centers), with an operating budget of $1 billion dollars and close to 270,000 employees.

There are more than 107 VA medical centers conducting research to improve the health and wellness of veterans. Over the years, this research has led to breakthroughs including development of the CAT scan, the cardiac pacemaker, and the nicotine patch, as well as the first liver transplant. One of the VA's most successful recruitment tools is its medical school affiliations program, which helps trains thousands of medical practitioners each year.

In the 1990s the Department of Veterans Affairs began its transformation from an inpatient to an outpatient system of care. Dr. Kenneth Kizer, then under secretary of health for the VHA, and the VA leadership developed CBOCs to enable the VA to see patients closer to their communities and provide needed outpatient and primary care to veterans who were previously forced to travel hundreds of miles to receive care in veterans' medical centers. In addition, during that period the VA established a defined medical benefits

package for enrolled veterans as well as long-term care for veterans rated 70 percent or higher disabled for service-connected injuries and illnesses from their military service.

In 1998 Congress directed the VA to establish eight priority groups to prioritize and rationalize healthcare for veterans based on the most injured and poorest veterans. In 2003 then Secretary of Veterans Affairs Anthony Principi suspended enrollment for Priority Group 8 veterans due to the VA's limited budget and the increasing numbers of veterans enrolling for VA healthcare. In order to enroll, veterans were required to take a means test, or financial assessment, to determine if they qualified for one of the priority groups and if they could make copays. In 2008 the VA relaxed its enrollment by 10 percent higher than the original means test cut-off income restriction, which allowed an additional 240,000 veterans previously ineligible for VA healthcare to enroll.

Today the Priority Group 8 restriction still exists, but combat veterans who have served after September 11, 2001, in a combat theater of operations (i.e., Operation Enduring Freedom, Operation Iraqi Freedom, and Operation New Dawn), are eligible for five years of veterans' healthcare for any injury or illness related to their military service. Veteran service organizations, such as The American Legion, believe that any veteran should be entitled to use the VA, which is a system designed to meet their unique and complex war-related injuries. In 1997 the VA was given the authority to bill, collect, and retain third-party reimbursements for treatment of non-service-connected medical conditions. Veterans, regardless of level of income or injury, should be authorized to bring their private insurance to the VA for treatment of their non-service medical conditions, which would be an alternative budget stream to offset the demand for services. Another concern is that veterans are not allowed to use their Medicare benefits within the VA. Veterans pay into Medicare their entire working lives and are essentially penalized because they cannot use their earned Medicare benefits in the VA and are forced to use those benefits in the private sector. In the future, the VA must continue to try to improve access to care for any veteran and take advantage of the cost savings to the government of veterans using their Medicare benefits in the VA system rather than the private sector.

Today there is an unprecedented number of returning veterans from Iraq and Afghanistan with traumatic brain injury (TBI) and post-traumatic stress disorder (PTSD). The term *polytrauma* was coined by the VHA to describe the many returning service members with complex, multiple injuries that required a new and holistic way of providing care. Over the last several years, the VHA has developed a polytrauma system of care with four levels.

Level 1 is the lead polytrauma rehabilitation centers, network or Veteran Integrated Service Network (VISN) sites, facilities (VA medical centers), and clinic or polytrauma points of contact. The lead polytrauma centers in the country are located in Palo Alto, California; Tampa, Florida; Richmond, Virginia; and Minneapolis, Minnesota. A new center is being built in San Antonio, Texas. From the battlefield, service members are evacuated through Landshuhl, Germany, to one of the military treatment facilities in the United States. The VHA has nurse liaisons and social workers who help transition severely injured veterans from military treatment facilities to the polytrauma system of care.

If a service member is involved in an improvised explosive device (IED) blast and develops a TBI, it is very likely that the veteran will also develop PTSD. If left untreated, the TBI and PTSD symptoms could lead to substance abuse, depression, and suicide. The VA conducts mandatory screens for veterans when they first enter a VA medical facility for TBI and PTSD. If the screening is positive, those veterans are referred for a secondary evaluation. Veterans' healthcare has also developed a crisis intervention line, formerly known as the Suicide Prevention Hotline, to assist any veteran in crisis. The hotline is open 365 days a year and 24 hours a day and is staffed by licensed counselors. The hotline has been credited for saving over 16,000 lives, and the VA has suicide prevention coordinators in each VA medical center to ensure veterans in crisis receive the assistance they need. The Department of Defense (DoD) and the Department of Veterans Affairs have also led the effort to destigmatize mental health conditions in our returning service members by having mental health practitioners embedded in primary care and through antistigma campaigns such as the "Real Warriors Campaign" in the Department of Defense and "Make the Connection" campaign in the Department of Veterans Affairs.

The VA continues to work with the DoD to develop a joint medical record, which will assist transitioning veterans in obtaining their earned veterans' benefits and services. Both agencies are working on a virtual lifetime electronic record (VLER), which will help connect the DoD and the VA information technology (IT) platforms to follow a service member from the day he or she joins the service to the day that person is laid to rest. The DoD and the VA are continuing to conduct research to improve the prevention, screening, diagnosis, and treatment of TBI and PTSD.

Veteran service organizations were founded to assist veterans by helping them file claims for their earned benefits and services. Veteran service organization service officers are professionally trained and accredited by the VA to file claims for veterans. In addition, Veteran service organizations provide

advocacy and assistance to veterans as well as lobbying the administration, Congress, and senior officials in the VA to make recommendations for continuous improvements for all veterans.

The chapters that follow reflect the many contributions that have been made to veterans' healthcare as well as the key healthcare issues facing our nation's veterans in the twenty-first century. Our nation has a moral obligation to take care of our service members when they return home. George Washington once said, "The willingness with which our young people are likely to serve in any war, no matter how justified, shall be directly proportional to how they perceive the veterans of earlier wars were treated and appreciated by their nation." It is our nation's responsibility to ensure that the Department of Veterans Affairs continues to provide timely, quality healthcare for our nation's veterans.

Jacob B. Gadd
Deputy Director for Health Care,
The American Legion;
Former Hospital Corpsman Third Class,
United States Navy (1998–2003)

Editor's Foreword

This four-volume set focusing on veterans' healthcare provides a unique and valuable contribution to our understanding of veterans' healthcare in the first decade of the twenty-first century. As a professor emeritus and retired VA career service chief from Lexington Veterans Affairs Medical Center, I have enjoyed a forty-year career in veterans' healthcare. I was first contacted in 2005 by Praeger Publishers to serve as editor of a handbook on this topic and then contacted some colleagues from the Department of Veterans Affairs both past and present and several colleagues nationally to explore the level of interest in accepting the invitation from Praeger to produce a positive reference book focusing on veterans' healthcare. It is to this cadre of professionals that I am indebted; they have contributed their knowledge and expertise in the chapters comprising this handbook.

We must be reminded of not only the macro events, but also the micro transitions that have contributed to the finest model of healthcare for veterans in the world. The reader is about to begin an extraordinary journey into the spectrum of healthcare offered through the Veterans Health Administration (VHA). Volume I offers the reader an understanding of the history of veterans' healthcare. Rodney R. Baker provides an overview of the historical contributions to veterans' healthcare. James W. Holsinger Jr., the first under secretary for veterans' affairs, offers a "View from the Top," addressing the administration and VA healthcare. VHA's academic mission is presented by Stuart C. Gilman, Barbara Chang, Robert Zeiss, Mary Dougherty, William Marks Jr., Deborah Ludke, and Malcolm Cox. Recognizing the important role of legislative initiatives for veterans' healthcare, with the assistance of Corina M. Barrow, Jacquie Rychnovsky, and Patrick DeLeon of Senator Inouye's office, I provide a historical review of key legislation that has benefited veterans' healthcare.

I also examine healthcare for veterans from various eras, covering veterans of World Wars I and II and the Korean conflict. Robert J. Fitz discusses healthcare for veterans of the Vietnam era, and Delilah O. Noronha, John Chardos, Laura Gomez, Samina Iqbal, and Steven Lindley provide a discussion of healthcare for veterans of Operations Enduring Freedom, Iraqi Freedom, and New Dawn.

In an effort to examine global healthcare for veterans, provided is a comparative look at veterans' healthcare in other countries: Australia, Canada, China, Russia, and the United Kingdom. Professor David Dunt and his team examine a critical issue for veterans, focusing on suicide in the ex-service community in Australian research and prevention efforts. Dr. David Pedlar and Stewart Macintosh provide a closer look at veterans affairs in Canada. Finally, Professor Dai Williams takes a closer look at healthcare for British veterans.

Volume II examines programs of care and veterans' special needs. James W. Anderson, a pioneer in clinical care and research, explores healthcare programs for veterans with diabetes in primary care. This is followed by a discussion of neurological healthcare for veterans by Mitchell Wallin and John Kurtzke. David Booth then examines cardiology care for veterans, followed by Philip DeSimone's acknowledgment of veterans' sacrifices made in the quest for cancer treatment. Robert C. Gresen provides a first look at mental health care in VHA. Chiropractic care in veterans' healthcare is reviewed by Bart Green and a team of colleagues from the Naval Medical Center in San Diego and at the VA medical center in Buffalo, New York. Healthcare for veterans with infectious diseases is examined by Cynthia L. Gibert, and end-of-life care for veterans in the VA healthcare system is addressed by Betty L. Gillespie, James L. Ford, and Kye Y. Kim.

Many veterans have special needs. To examine these needs, we asked Dr. Hayden B. Bosworth to assess the lifestyles and health behaviors of veterans. Noting the special needs of amputees and the guidance of Fred Downs, I examined orthotics and prosthetics healthcare for veterans. The challenges faced by Native American veterans and their solutions are addressed by Joseph Stone of the Indian Health Service, and healthcare for women military veterans is addressed by Monica Roy. Prisoners of war have always been a special population and have had special needs; Brian Engdahl and Charles Stenger take a close look at serving America's former prisoners of war. Drs. Beth Hudnall Stamm, Susan L. Blampied, and Kirstina Beck examine a

special population of caregivers in their chapter on assistance dogs and their use by veterans with disabilities.

Volume III takes a closer and more detailed look at mental health treatment and rehabilitation. Delilah O. Noronha begins by examining primary care and mental health integration in providing veterans' healthcare. This is followed by a chapter that examines alcohol and substance abuse programs, by Susan R. Tate, Jennifer Mrnak-Meyer, and Jessica C. Tripp. Smoking has been critical in veterans' healthcare, and Carol A. Malte, Andrew J. Saxon, Kim Hamlett-Berry, and Miles E. McFall investigate integrating smoking cessation into mental health care for post-traumatic stress disorder.

Clinician researchers Mark S. Kaplan, Bentson H. McFarland, and Nathalie Huguet take a close look at suicide risk among veterans. VA healthcare for women veterans experiencing trauma is the focus of Carole A. Goguen. Stephen Tracy, Sara Tavakoli, Simona Stolpner, and Jodie Trafton discuss the treatment of substance use disorders; and the social context of adjustment in combat veterans is examined by Bradley Belsher, Josef Ruzek, and Matthew Cordova. Polytrauma care and treatment in veterans' healthcare is covered by Jeanne M. Bennett. Military traumatic brain injury and the postconcussive syndrome is addressed by colleagues in the Department of Defense led by Louis M. French, Victoria C. Anderson-Barnes, Katherine Brazaitis, and Aditya Bhagwat. Healthcare and issues of racial and ethnic diversity are carefully examined by Kathleen M. McNamara.

With special attention on rehabilitation care and treatment for veterans, colleagues Walter Penk, Dolores Little, and Nathan Ainspan address trauma-focused psychosocial rehabilitation. This is followed by a chapter on psychosocial rehabilitation and recovery services by Samantha Kettle, Loretta E. Braxton, Valerie Fox, and Josh Tiegreen. Next Ann D. Kirkwood, Beth Hudnall Stamm, and Chandra R. Story address eradicating mental illness stigma for active military personnel and veterans. Finally, Thomas P. O'Toole provides an in-depth assessment of how VA is engaging homeless veterans in primary care.

Volume IV provides an examination of some of the future directions for veterans' healthcare, first examining dedicated centers for veterans' healthcare. The first chapter reviews VHA centers of excellence. Then Drs. Katerine Osatuke, Jill Draime, Scott C. Moore, Dee Ramsel, Andrew Meyer, Sharon Barnes, Linda Belton, and Sue R. Dyrenforth examine the latest in organization development in VA.

Joseph F. Murphy, public affairs officer, VA NCPS, and James P. Bagian explore for the reader the VA National Center for Patient Safety. The significance of post-trauma stress is addressed by Matthew J. Friedman, the national

director of the Department of Veterans Affairs National Center for PTSD. Leading the way in pain-related disorders, Drs. Kathryn LaChappelle, Samantha Boris-Karpel, and Robert D. Kerns provide a detailed review of the efforts to address pain management in VHA.

Dr. K. Kizer, who is responsible for a major reorganization of VHA, provides a closer view of lessons learned about clinical integration from VA's experience with VISNs. The veterans' healthcare system is seen as a potential model for a national plan by Said A. Ibrahim, David Macpherson, and Michael E. Moreland.

New technologies are helping to create easier access to healthcare for veterans who live in rural and underserved areas of the country. Jennifer A. Wood, Thomas W. Miller, and Russell Hagy discuss telehealth applications to underserved veterans. Miller and Janet Kemp then explore the topic of suicide prevention through a national hotline. The Academy of Spinal Cord Injury is an organization outside VA that offers new directions in addressing the needs of spinal cord–injured veterans. The chapter on this topic is authored by the director, Terrie Price. VA has developed and implemented an Office for Preventative Ethics. Examining ethicolegal issues in VA healthcare are Steve Nisenbaum, Tom Miller, Sheila O'Keefe, and Dennis Norman. An organization external to VA that is meeting the needs of veterans, Give an Hour™, is described by its founder, Barbara Van Dahlen. Edmund J. Nightingale provides a very detailed and up-to-date summary of the efforts to provide quality, competent, and thorough veterans' healthcare in the final chapter, "Good to Great: The Veterans' Health Care System's Path to Excellence."

The comprehensive nature of this four-volume set offers the reader an in-depth examination of veterans' healthcare through the first decade of the twenty-first century. More than two hundred invitations were extended to present and past members of the Department of Veterans Affairs as well as aligned agencies, veterans' organizations, and healthcare facilities associated with veterans' healthcare. What is provided are the comprehensive and dedicated work and contributions of more than one hundred scientists and practitioners, researchers, and clinicians both within the Department of Veterans Affairs and those in academically affiliated universities and public and private institutions. An effort is made to provide a glimpse of veterans' healthcare internationally. This handbook is not meant to cover every topic related to veterans' healthcare thoroughly, but rather to offer to the reader an excellent reference point from which to start a journey toward a better understanding of the complexity of providing quality healthcare to our military veterans.

This compendium provides the opportunity for dialogue on improving our understanding of veterans' healthcare, and each of the authors deals with a

part of this complex whole. As editor I trust it offers the gestalt that will increase our understanding of veterans' healthcare and the transitions we face in providing a twenty-first-century focus on healthcare for veterans worldwide.

Thomas W. Miller, PhD, ABPP,
Professor Emeritus & Senior Research Scientist,
University of Kentucky; Veterans Affairs Medical Center (Retired),
Lexington, Kentucky; Center for Prevention Research,
University of Connecticut

Part I

History of Veterans' Healthcare

Historical Contributions to Veterans' Healthcare

Rodney R. Baker

Introduction

Providing benefits for disabled U.S. veterans who served their country in war began early on in the American colonies. In 1636 the Pilgrims of Plymouth Colony were at war with the Pequot Indians and promised to care for any man sent into battle who returned "maimed." That promise followed a tradition of providing benefits to veterans established in previous societies. On September 9, 1789, the First Congress of the United States took over the pensions paid to disabled veterans previously administered by the states. In this legislation, according to the Veterans Administration's 1967 report on medical care of veterans, submitted to the House Committee on Veterans Affairs, "Congress had now become, for the first time, the guardian of the disabled veteran, his widow, and his orphan—a right which it has jealously guarded ever since" (Veterans Administration 1967, 30). From these early beginnings, a benefit and healthcare system for veterans emerged in the Veterans Administration, renamed the Department of Veterans Affairs (VA) in 1989, to become the largest healthcare system in the world. Given that they have an almost 400-year history, any summary of the benefits provided to veterans must necessarily be limited in scope. The history of non-healthcare benefits is described in Baker (2008).

This chapter chronicles the historical contributions leading to today's healthcare system for U.S. veterans. Three major sources of contributions are identified, starting with a listing and brief description of significant federal healthcare legislation through 1946. Next is the development and impact of the Veterans Administration's affiliations with medical schools and universities, generally credited with the most sweeping contributions to the quality of healthcare for veterans after World War II. The chapter concludes with an introduction to the Veterans Administration's early medical research programs and their impact on healthcare.

Early Federal Healthcare Legislation for Veterans

Public Law 90, October 6, 1917

Magnuson (1951) has noted that prior to 1917, federal medical care for veterans was mostly incidental to domiciliary and similar residential care programs. Examples of that medical care date from 1811, when the federal government established the first domiciliary and medical facility for veterans in Philadelphia. Following the Civil War, Congress established the National Asylum (later called Home) for Disabled Volunteer Soldiers in 1865 to provide domiciliary and general medical care for veterans. Public Law 90, passed in 1917, was the first federal legislation designed purely to provide medical care to veterans. The law authorized the United States Public Health System (USPHS) to offer both healthcare and hospital services for World War I veterans.

Public Law 194, April 20, 1922

Because Public Law 90 limited USPHS medical services to World War I veterans, new legislation was needed to cover veterans of other wars. Public Law 194 closed that gap and was the first of a series of legislative actions to expand hospital and medical services to veterans.

The Veterans' Bureau had been created by Congress in 1921 to combine the functions of the Bureau of War Risk Insurance (established in 1914), the Rehabilitation Division of the Federal Board of Vocational Education (established in 1917), and the Public Health Service (established in 1902 from the former Marine Hospitals system). Public Law 194 authorized the Veterans' Bureau to expand healthcare benefits to veterans of the Spanish-American War, the Philippine insurrection, and the Boxer Rebellion. The legislation further authorized new hospital construction and gave the Veterans' Bureau authority to expand medical/hospital benefits to veterans with tuberculosis (TB) and neuropsychiatric illnesses.

Figure 1.1. General Frank T. Hines, Director, Veterans' Bureau, March 1923–July 1930; Administrator, Veterans Administration, July 1930–August 1945. *Source: Veterans Administration (1967).*

Public Law 536, July 3, 1930

The creation of the Veterans' Bureau in 1921 left two other agencies also administering benefits for veterans: the Bureau of Pensions and the National Home for Disabled Volunteer Soldiers. General Frank T. Hines (see figure 1.1), appointed the director of the Veterans' Bureau by President Warren G. Harding in 1923, soon became concerned about the negative impact on veterans of having several agencies administering their benefits. The need for veterans to deal with multiple agencies mirrored the experience of World War I veterans, who were irritated by sometimes confusing choices of where to seek information or whom to ask about applying for benefits.

In 1929 Hines asked President Herbert Hoover to explore legislation to combine all federal veterans' benefit agencies. In spite of strong opposition from the Department of the Interior (which administered the Bureau of Pensions) and representatives of the National Home for Disabled Volunteer Soldiers, strong support from most veterans' organizations eventually led to the passage of Public Law 536, which authorized the consolidation of all veterans' benefit programs into one agency. President Hoover issued Executive Order 5398 on July 21, 1930, establishing a single agency, called the Veterans Administration. (The apostrophe after "Veterans" in the agency's name in the Executive Order was later dropped and, with the exception of quoted material, is not used in this book.) Following is the text of Executive Order 5398 (Department of Veterans Affairs, Office of Public Affairs n.d.):

Executive Order 5398

Consolidation and Coordination of Governmental Activities Affecting Veterans

WHEREAS section 1 of the act of Congress entitled "An Act to authorize the President to consolidate and coordinate governmental activities affecting war veterans," approved July 3, 1930, provides:

"(a) That the President is authorized, by Executive order, to consolidate and coordinate any hospitals and executive and administrative bureaus, agencies, or offices, especially created for or concerned in the administration of the laws relating to the relief and other benefits provided by law for former members of the Military and Naval Establishments of the United States, including the Bureau of Pensions, the National Home for Disabled Volunteer Soldiers, and the United States Veterans' Bureau, into an establishment to be known as the Veterans' Administration, and to transfer the duties, powers, and the functions now vested by law in the hospitals, bureaus, agencies, or offices so consolidated and coordinated including the personnel thereof, and the whole or any part of the records and public property belonging thereto to the Veterans Administration.

"(b) Under the direction of the President the Administrator of Veterans' Affairs shall have the power, by order or regulation, to consolidate, eliminate, or redistribute the functions of the bureaus, agencies, offices, or activities in the Veterans' Administration and to create new ones therein, and, by rules and regulations not inconsistent with law, shall fix the functions thereof and the duties and powers of their respective executive heads."

NOW, THEREFORE, by virtue of the authority vested in me by said law, the United States Veterans' Bureau, the Bureau of Pensions, and the National Home for Disabled Volunteer Soldiers are hereby consolidated and coordinated into an establishment to be known as the Veterans' Administration, and duties, powers, and functions vested by law in the United States Veterans' Bureau, the National Home for Disabled Volunteer Soldiers, and in the Bureau of Pensions, and the personnel of the United States Veterans' Bureau, the Bureau of Pensions, and the National Home for Disabled Volunteer Soldiers, and the records and papers pertaining to the work thereof, and the public property belonging thereto, are hereby transferred to the Veterans' Administration.

THE WHITE HOUSE
HERBERT HOOVER
JULY 21, 1930

With the establishment of the new agency, fifty-four hospitals of the Veterans' Bureau and National Homes for Disabled Volunteer Soldiers were subsequently designated VA hospitals. Because TB was a major illness among veterans at the time, many of these hospitals were converted into TB hospitals or had large TB treatment programs. The new agency also made it possible for veterans to use any office or hospital of the Veterans Administration as a point of contact to obtain information or apply for benefits for which they were eligible.

Public Law 2, March 20, 1933

The passage of Public Law 2 and its subsequent amendments gave the Veterans Administration broad authority to provide medical care to veterans discharged from military service in any war (past or future) for disabilities and illnesses incurred in the line of duty. With some exceptions, the legislation also included health benefits for any medical care or domiciliary needs of veterans, whether or not those needs arose from their military service. The only limitations to this latter provision were that a veteran must have been honorably discharged and must be unable to pay for the care needed, and that the care provided must be within the resources of existing VA facilities (Magnuson 1951).

Public Law 346, June 22, 1944

Public Law 346, titled the Servicemen's Readjustment Act of 1944 and more commonly referred to as the G.I. Bill of Rights, is generally known for the many important non-healthcare veterans' benefits it provided for, such as its education and home loan programs. The legislation, however, contained two very important provisions to assist the Veterans Administration's healthcare mission. Section 100 designated the Veterans Administration "to be an essential war agency and entitled, second only to War and Navy Departments, to priorities in personnel, equipment, supplies" (Veterans Administration 1967, 170). Section 101 authorized $500 million for acquisition and construction of new VA hospitals.

The first provision giving the Veterans Administration priority for resources meant that military physicians could be assigned to help it provide patient care to veterans. Physicians involved in the army and navy special training programs could also stay with the Veterans Administration for two years to pay back the medical education they received from the government. This helped the Veterans Administration with its staffing shortages at the time but, as noted later, this provision presented a special problem. As of June 30, 1945, 1,700 of its 2,300 physicians were on active duty and on loan to the Veterans Administration (Veterans Administration 1947). It was believed that many of these physicians would be leaving the Veterans Administration when discharged from the military at the end of World War II.

Affiliations and Teaching Programs in the Veterans Administration

The Need for and Development of Public Law 293 and VA Affiliations

With the end of World War II, more than sixteen million discharged veterans would overwhelm the VA healthcare system with their eligibility for medical care. The construction of many authorized hospitals had been delayed due to the war effort. Many doctors and nurses had left to enter military service. The Veterans Administration had difficulty recruiting physicians not in the military because of cumbersome Civil Service hiring procedures. The quality of care for veterans deteriorated due to staffing shortages, and medical care was poorly organized, with the Veterans Administration's medical director included in the office of construction supply and real estate. As noted previously, almost three-fourths of VA physicians were on loan from the military, and physician staffing problems would become critical if the military physicians left the Veterans Administration, as anticipated, when discharged from their military commitment at the end of the war.

President Harry S. Truman chose General Omar N. Bradley to lead the Veterans Administration out of this disarray. Bradley (see figure 1.2) had been a popular general in the European theater of the war, given the nickname the "doughboys' general" because of his organizational skills and his compassion for and ability to understand others. He was known for never raising his voice in anger and never forgetting to be polite. Ernie Pyle, a famous war correspondent, wrote, "If I could pick any two men in the world for my father, except my own dad, I would pick General Omar Bradley or General Ike Eisenhower. If I had a son, I would like him to go to Bradley or Ike for advice" (Veterans Administration 1967, 189).

Bradley, aware of the challenges facing him, accepted Truman's invitation to serve as the new administrator of veterans' affairs and was sworn into office on August 15, 1945. He immediately began to identify people to help him and sought recommendations for improving healthcare in the Veterans Administration. Bernard M. Baruch, advisor to a number of presidents, had done a study of the problems of returning veterans and was asked by Bradley to brief him on what he had found and make recommendations. One of

Figure 1.2. General Omar N. Bradley, Administrator, Veterans Administration, August 1945–November 1947. *Source: Veterans Administration (1967).*

several recommendations given Bradley was to establish affiliations with medical schools and their residents to improve the quality of care in the Veterans Administration. Bradley wrote in the *Congressional Record* of September 11, 1945, that he had reached many of the same conclusions as Baruch, including the importance of affiliations with medical schools.

One of the first appointments to the Veterans Administration that Bradley envisioned was that of General Paul R. Hawley (see figure 1.3), who had been chief surgeon in the European theater. Bradley knew that in addition to his medical credentials, Hawley supported the idea of affiliations with medical schools. The affiliations of the medical units in the army with medical schools were generally recognized as helping the military to offer exceptional care to soldiers on the battlefield. Hawley would be a strong advocate for the affiliation legislation that Bradley would be seeking. Hawley accepted Bradley's offer to go to Washington in September 1945, and agreed to serve Bradley in a position that soon would be designated the Veterans Administration's chief medical director.

Hawley in turn knew about Paul B. Magnuson's (see figure 1.4) interest in medical school affiliations with the Veterans Administration, and he asked Magnuson to assist him and Bradley in improving VA healthcare. Magnuson was a highly respected surgeon in the Chicago area and would bring his

Figure 1.3. General Paul R. Hawley, Chief Medical Director, Veterans Administration, September 1945–December 1947. *Source: Veterans Administration (1967).*

influence with medical schools to the plan for affiliations. Magnuson agreed and was first appointed as a consultant to the Veterans Administration and then given the position as VA chief of research and education. (He would later succeed Hawley as the second chief medical director in the Veterans Administration when Hawley left in 1947.)

In the only reorganization available to Bradley under existing law, he removed the medical director position from construction and supply in September 1945. He designated Hawley as acting surgeon general, reporting directly to him. In his new position, Hawley again announced his support for affiliations and made the commitment to ensure that returning veterans would receive medical care "second to none" in the world (Veterans Administration 1967, 209).

Legislation was needed to put in place the changes Bradley, Hawley, and Magnuson wanted for the Veterans Administration, and they began drafting a legislative package to accomplish their goals. Their plan to reorganize medical care in the VA Central Office by creating a number of professional departments to help oversee medical care in the Veterans Administration would present no problems for legislation. However, two aspects of the legislation they proposed were especially problematic for congressional support. The idea of affiliations with medical schools and their training programs had been raised a number of times but had not received support because of congressional

Figure 1.4. Paul B. Magnuson, MD, Chief Medical Director, Veterans Administration, January 1948–January 1951. *Source: Veterans Administration (1967).*

concerns that medical residents would conduct risky experiments in their treatment of veterans. To combat this perception, in November 1944 Magnuson had joined with J. Roscoe Miller, dean of the Northwestern College of Medicine, to make a presentation to General Hines, then administrator of the Veterans Administration, to convince Hines of the improvements in veterans' care that would follow affiliations. Hines's concern about "guinea pig" experiments on veterans outweighed their arguments, and no action was taken.

The other problem with the legislation that Bradley and Hawley sought was special recruitment authority to hire doctors, dentists, and nurses in the Veterans Administration without using the cumbersome and lengthy Civil Service procedures. The authority they wanted would enable the Veterans Administration to more quickly hire these healthcare professionals and to pay them salary bonuses for special credentials. This provision would be strongly opposed by the Civil Service Commission.

With the advocacy of Bradley and Hawley, Congress passed H. R. 4717 on December 20, 1945, and the bill, which contained provisions for the new recruitment authority and affiliations with medical schools, was sent to President Truman. Bradley, however, heard that Truman was considering a veto of the bill on the recommendation of the Civil Service Commission.

Bradley and Hawley met with a presidential assistant to argue for Truman's signature on the bill, and when it appeared their arguments might be ignored, both Bradley and Hawley threatened to resign if the Civil Service recruitment process prevented them from quickly hiring the physicians they needed. That message was presumably given to Truman, who subsequently signed the bill, now Public Law 293 of the 79th Congress, on January 3, 1946.

Magnuson had been talking with deans of medical schools to explain what Bradley and Hawley were proposing. The day after passage of Public Law 293, Northwestern and the University of Illinois placed fifty-six medical residents at the Veterans Administration in Hines, Illinois.

With Magnuson's help, Hawley wrote VA Policy Memorandum Number 2, published January 30, 1946, which outlined the Veterans Administration's affiliation and training programs. Both Hawley and Magnuson subsequently traveled extensively, explaining the provisions of the memorandum to medical schools. By the end of 1946, sixty-three of the nation's seventy-seven medical schools had developed affiliations with the Veterans Administration. Rarely seen in publications, the full text of Policy Memorandum Number 2 (Department of Veterans Affairs, Office of Academic Affiliations n.d.) appears in the appendix at the end of this chapter.

Impact of Public Law 293

Public Law 293 created the Department of Medicine and Surgery within the VA Central Office, headed by a chief medical officer, a position Bradley gave to Hawley. Professional departments were organized under the Department of Medicine and Surgery, representing the major medical disciplines involved in the care of patients at the time, such as medicine, surgery, psychiatry and neurology, and physical medicine and rehabilitation. The chief medical officer maintained responsibility for all medical care in the Veterans Administration, but the department heads would help oversee the patient care activities of their disciplines in VA facilities. This new organization helped strengthen the management and quality of patient care throughout the Veterans Administration.

The approval of a special recruitment authority for physicians, dentists, and nurses (generally referred to as Title 38 recruitment) also had its intended effect. By the end of fiscal year 1946, the 2,300 doctors in the Veterans Administration (1,700 on active military duty) had been increased to more than 4,000 full-time physicians on VA employment rolls. Fewer than 400 of these physicians were still on military duty, and the Veterans Administration retained almost 1,200 additional army and navy physicians who were assigned to VA hospitals to complete their two-year obligation for the medical education they had received (Veterans Administration 1947).

In the Veterans Administration's 1967 special report on medical care for veterans, Public Law 293 was referred to as the "Magna Carta" of the newly formed Department of Medicine and Surgery (Veterans Administration 1967, 212). The reorganization of medical care authorized by Public Law 293 has undergone name changes over the years but still retains its basic structure.

Impact of Policy Memorandum No. 2

Important as were the previously noted improvements for patient care, the authority of Public Law 293 for Policy Memorandum No. 2 is generally credited with the most significance. The previous isolation of VA physicians from mainstream medicine was drastically changed through their interactions with the teaching and research missions of medical schools in the new affiliations.

Bradley left the Veterans Administration in November 1947 after only twenty-seven months to return to the army as its chief of staff. His second (and final) annual report to Congress was prepared only six months following the changes he had started in January 1946, and it was too soon to provide statistics about the affiliations. However, it is known that within fourteen months after the passage of Public Law 293 and the publication of Policy Memorandum No. 2, the Veterans Administration had 1,635 medical residents in training (Puestow 1947). The VA annual report to Congress for fiscal year 1949 indicated that there were 2,200 physicians receiving residency training in the Veterans Administration in eighteen specialties and subspecialties at sixty-eight VA hospitals and thirteen mental hygiene clinics (Veterans Administration 1950).

One early report on the training and quality care impact of affiliations in the Veterans Administration came from Puestow (1947), who described the affiliations at the VA hospital in Hines, Illinois, the first to receive medical school residents. He noted an increase in all admissions at the hospital, from 11,118 in 1945 to 17,748 in 1946. He attributed this increase to the additional staffing by medical school faculty and 144 residents. In his own area of specialty, Puestow reported that surgical admissions almost doubled from 1945 to 1946, with a 73 percent increase in operations performed.

Public Law 293 technically authorized affiliations and training programs only with medical residents, dentists, and nurses, but other healthcare professionals providing care in the Veterans Administration found entry into the

Veterans Administration's affiliation and training programs. One of the first was the clinical psychology program in the Department of Psychiatry and Neurology. Its first chief, James G. Miller, found language in Public Law 293 that would permit the employment of psychology graduate students as part-time staff with a training assignment delivering psychological services to patients (Baker & Pickren 2007). Miller convinced Bradley of this interpretation and, in the fall of 1946, 215 clinical psychology graduate students from twenty-two universities began their training in the Veterans Administration. Other nonmedical resident health professionals followed suit, and students from forty health disciplines were being trained in the Veterans Administration by 1973, when it consolidated all training in a newly established Office of Academic Affiliations (Moore 1992).

Magnuson assumed the position of chief medical director when Hawley resigned in December 1947. When Magnuson himself left the Veterans Administration in 1951, he summarized his impression of the impact of the affiliations:

> In addition to its own full-time staff in hospitals, clinics, and domiciliaries, the Veterans Administration has utilized the services of outstanding consultants and attending physicians. Many of these specialists are men of professional rank attached to the medical schools. . . . A huge reservoir of high-grade medical talent has thereby been made available in providing hospital and medical care for the disabled veterans. (1951, 78)

Impact of Research on Patient Care in the Veterans Administration

Early VA Medical Research

In 1924 General Hines had appointed a medical council to advise him on patient care matters in the Veterans' Bureau. The first recommendation he received was to adopt a policy of research, and he subsequently established a medical research section in the medical service. With the establishment of the Veterans Administration in 1930, several research units were started at VA facilities, including units in cancer research (the VA hospital at Hines, Illinois, in 1933), cardiovascular research (the VA hospital in Washington, D.C., in 1936), and neuropsychiatric research (the VA hospital at Northport, New York, in 1941) (Veterans Administration 1967). However, the end of World War II presented the Veterans Administration with several challenges that would be met by an expanded medical research program.

A significant number of veterans sought care from the Veterans Administration after the war for amputations resulting from combat. The magnitude of the need for physical rehabilitation for these veterans required the Veterans Administration to develop its own expertise in this area, especially in the use of prosthetics and sensory aids, instead of its previous dependence on contract work. In November 1945 the Veterans Administration created the Prosthetic Appliance Service, and legislation passed the following month (Public Law 268, December 28, 1945) gave the Veterans Administration wide latitude in providing prosthetic aids to veterans through contracts or whatever means the Veterans Administration believed appropriate. After the formation of the Department of Medicine and Surgery, one of the first major research efforts to receive budgeting by Congress was in the field of prosthetics and sensory aids (Public Law 729, June 19, 1948). That legislation provided the Veterans Administration with an annual budget of $1 million for prosthetic and sensory aid research. Although the Veterans Administration's research efforts sooned received congressional funding in other areas, Public Law 729 enabled the Veterans Administration to conduct pioneering research in the development and use of prosthetic and sensory aids. The Veterans Administration became a leader in the prosthetics field, guiding other organizations in this area of medical care (Veterans Administration 1967).

Another major problem for the Veterans Administration after the war was the use of two-thirds of its beds for the care of TB and neuropsychiatric patients, who were hospitalized for lengthy periods. By June 30, 1946, 58 percent of the Veterans Administration's hospital beds were being used to care for psychiatric patients, with an average stay of 180 days. An additional 9 percent of beds were occupied by TB patients, with an average stay of 174 days. The remaining beds were used to treat general medical and surgery patients, who had an average stay of 31 days (Veterans Administration 1947).

Although the Veterans Administration formed a number of advisory councils from the military and civilian sector in 1946 to guide its care of these patients, the private sector had never previously encountered the extent of these problems. Even the expertise brought to the Veterans Administration by affiliations with medical schools, especially in psychiatry, was insufficient. Medical school faculty in psychiatry were largely unfamiliar with the treatment of patients with long-term psychosis, the largest diagnostic category of psychiatric patients in the Veterans Administration (Baker & Pickren 2007). The Veterans Administration had to rely on the development of its own resources to deal with this problem.

The VA Cooperative Study Program

The Veterans Administration found a unique solution to the enormity of the problem of treating large numbers of psychiatric and TB patients. It developed a new research paradigm, first used with TB patients (see following subsection), in which patients would be enrolled in research projects at multiple VA sites using centrally designed research protocols. The advantages of these "Cooperative Studies" were many. A large data pool could be formed with huge datasets and increased statistical power of analyzed data. The use of multiple sites across the country would also reduce the influence of local or regional differences on research conducted at one site.

The first Cooperative Studies were focused on chemotherapy treatments. The large-scale Cooperative Studies in neuropsychiatry focused on the use of a number of psychotropic medications and, within a short time, the research findings translated into clinical usage that enabled the Veterans Administration to treat twice as many psychiatric patients with the same number of beds (Baker & Pickren 2007; Veterans Administration 1967).

The Cooperative Study paradigm was utilized by the Veterans Administration in studying treatment for a wide range of diseases and medical conditions, including hypertension, diabetes, lung cancer, and neuropsychiatric problems. By 1967 more than forty-seven Cooperative Studies were underway in the Veterans Administration, which had a worldwide reputation for developing the Cooperative Study approach; this approach was adopted by other medical research programs (Veterans Administration 1967). The example of the VA Cooperative Research Program in action, discussed in the next subsection, more fully illustrates the impact of research on patient care.

The VA Cooperative Research Program in Pulmonary TB

Pulmonary TB was a serious problem among veterans after World War II, requiring a major allocation of personnel and funding. More than 8,000 veterans were being treated for TB in VA hospitals or in non-VA hospitals providing care to veterans under contract when the Department of Medicine and Surgery was created in 1946. As noted previously, that was 9 percent of all hospitalized veterans under care in the Veterans Administration. That number was expected to grow; only three years later it had reached 14,000 beds (Veterans Administration 1950).

To address this problem, the Veterans Administration developed a series of TB research projects starting in 1946, using the Cooperative Study paradigm. Tuberculosis was a major problem for not only the Veterans Administration but also army and navy hospitals. For the first TB cooperative research study

(1946–1949), the army and navy were invited to join the Veterans Administration in a study of a chemotherapy treatment of TB that showed promise at the time. Five VA hospitals were chosen for that study, with the army and navy each adding one hospital. Under the leadership of the Veterans Administration, the number of hospitals participating in subsequent TB cooperative research projects eventually grew to sixty (Veterans Administration 1967).

The leadership of the Veterans Administration in these projects—especially with the use of streptomycin in the treatment of TB in the first study, together with the study and use of other antibiotics in subsequent projects—was responsible for a dramatic improvement in patient care and a reduction in resource use. Although the number of TB patients in the Veterans Administration continued to climb and reached a peak of 15,940 on June 30, 1954, the length of stay had been reduced because many patients could take their TB medications on an outpatient basis (Veterans Administration 1967). Seven years later, the Veterans Administration was treating an average daily load of 7,000 fewer hospitalized patients, and eight of the Veterans Administration's former twenty-one TB hospitals had been redesignated as general medical and surgical hospitals, with many other hospitals reducing or dropping their TB treatment units (Veterans Administration 1961). By May 31, 1966, the number of TB hospitals in the Veterans Administration had been reduced to two, with just over 4,000 hospitalized veterans (Veterans Administration 1967).

Throughout the course of the TB Cooperative Studies, the Veterans Administration issued a number of technical bulletins to provide guidance to its hospital personnel on the chemotherapy treatment of TB. Although prepared for distribution only in the Veterans Administration, the technical bulletins soon became widely used in military and civilian hospitals, with similar results in improving the treatment of TB as in the Veterans Administration.

Summary

The historical contributions to veterans' healthcare described in this chapter demonstrate the commitment U.S. society has made to veterans. Even the problems faced in meeting that commitment served to challenge Congress and early VA leaders to find ways to overcome obstacles to the care deserved by those who served their country.

The remaining chapters in this book tell a similar story of the healthcare problems of veterans and the commitment of the Veterans Administration to finding solutions and developing programs to treat those problems from the post–World War II era through the present day. The programs of the Veterans Administration are a central focus in this story, but the problems of veterans resulting from their sacrifice to their country is an even more remarkable story that needs to be told—and remembered.

References

Baker, R. R. (2008). Benefits for veterans: A historical context and overview of the current situation. In N. D. Ainspan & W. E. Penk (Eds.), *Returning wars' wounded, injured, and ill* (pp. 1–12). Westport, CT: Praeger Security International.

Baker, R. R. & Pickren, W. E. (2007). *Psychology and the Department of Veterans Affairs: A historical analysis of training, research, practice, and advocacy.* Washington, DC: American Psychological Association.

Department of Veterans Affairs, Office of Academic Affairs. (n.d.). *Policy Memorandum No. 2.* Retrieved June 19, 2009 from http://www.va.gov/oaa/Archive/PolicyMemo2.pdf.

Department of Veterans Affairs, Office of Public Affairs. (n.d.). *Executive Order 5398.* Retrieved June 18, 2009, from http://www1.va.gov/opa/feature/history/index.asp.

Magnuson, P. B. (1951). Medical care for veterans. *The Annals of the American Academy of Political and Social Sciences* 273, no. 1: 76–83.

Moore, D. L. (1992). The Veterans Administration and the training program in psychology. In D. K. Freedheim (Ed.), *History of psychotherapy* (pp. 776–800). Washington, DC: American Psychological Association.

Puestow, C. D. (1947). Graduate training in surgery in Veterans Administration hospitals. *Annals of Surgery* 126: 500–508.

Veterans Administration. (1947). *Administrator of Veterans Affairs annual report for fiscal year ending June 30, 1946.* Washington, DC: U. S. Government Printing Office.

Veterans Administration. (1950). *Administrator of Veterans Affairs annual report for fiscal year ending June 30, 1949.* Washington, DC: U. S. Government Printing Office.

Veterans Administration. (1961). *Administrator of Veterans Affairs annual report for fiscal year ending June 30, 1960.* Washington, DC: U. S. Government Printing Office.

Veterans Administration. (1967). *Medical care of veterans.* Washington, DC: U.S. Government Printing Office.

Author's Note

Much of the Veterans Administration's rich history is contained in internal documents not generally available outside the organization. Two of those document sources were used in this chapter to bring that history to the reader. The first is the Veterans Administration's 1967 report *Medical Care of Veterans*, submitted to the House Committee on Veterans Affairs of the 90th Congress (Veterans Administration 1967). This 400 + page report was compiled by Robinson Adkins, who served as an executive officer in the Department of Medicine and Surgery from May 1946 until his retirement in February 1963. His report used a variety of original sources available to him and those who assisted him in preparing the report, including firsthand experiences. Unless otherwise noted, much of the story of the development of VA affiliations in this chapter comes from this report. The photos included in this chapter were also taken from that report. Readers interested in a more detailed history of VA healthcare and benefit programs up to 1967, including a description of the social forces and legislative actions leading to the creation of the Veterans Administration, should read this report. It has limited availability but can be found in the VA Central Office Library in Washington, D.C., and in the Library of Congress.

The other internal source of material for this chapter is the Veterans Administration's annual reports to Congress. The reports beginning in 1946 and for the next two decades provide a wealth of information on the many rapid changes occurring in the Veterans Administration in the post–World War II era. Brief narratives in these reports prepared by VA Central Office staff are literally supplemented with dozens of statistical tables far exceeding the page length of the narratives; they track hospital utilization, diagnoses, and outpatient care in the Veterans Administration over the years. The raw data in these tables, with careful attention to footnotes, allow readers to form their own hypotheses about what was happening in the Veterans Administration. The reports also contain information on the Veterans Administration's loan programs, insurance claims, and other benefit programs and track annual legislative actions. These annual reports can also be found in the VA Central Office Library and in the Library of Congress.

Appendix: Full Text of VA Policy Memorandum Number 2

January 30, 1946 POLICY MEMORANDUM NO. 2

SUBJECT: Policy in Association of Veterans' Hospitals With Medical Schools.

1. GENERAL CONSIDERATIONS

a. Necessity for Mutual Understanding and Cooperation. The Department of Medicine and Surgery of the Veterans' Administration is embarking upon a program that is without precedent in the history of Federal hospitalization. It would, therefore, be most unusual if numerous problems did not arise for which no fully satisfactory solution were immediately apparent. Such problems frequently can be solved only by trial and error; and, until workable solutions are found, both parties in the program must exercise tolerance if the program is not to fail.

b. There can be no doubt of the good faith of both parties. The schools of medicine and other teaching centers are cooperating with the three-fold purpose of giving the veteran the highest quality of medical care, of affording the medical veteran the opportunity for post-graduate study which he was compelled to forego in serving his country, and of raising generally the standard of medical practice in the United States by the expansion of facilities for graduate education.

c. The purpose of the Veterans' Administration is simple: affording the veteran a much higher standard of medical care than could be given him with a wholly full-time medical service.

d. The purposes of both parties being unselfish, and there being no conflict of objectives, there can be no serious disagreement over methods. It will be recognized that the Veterans' Administration is charged with certain legal responsibilities in connection with the medical care of veterans which it cannot delegate, if it would. Yet the discharge of these responsibilities need not interfere with the exercise by the schools of their prerogatives in the field of education.

e. All medical authorities of the Veterans' Administration will cooperate fully at all times with the representatives of associated schools and other centers. It is the earnest desire of the Acting Chief Medical Director that our relations with our colleagues be cordial as well as productive.

f. General Division of Responsibility: The Veterans' Administration retains full responsibility for the care of patients, including professional treatment, and the school of medicine accepts responsibility for all graduate education and training.

2. THE VETERANS' ADMINISTRATION

a. Operates and administers the hospital.

b. As rapidly as fully qualified men can be had, will furnish full-time chiefs of all services (see par. 5 below) who will supervise and direct the work of their respective staffs, including the part-time attending staff furnished from the School of Medicine, insofar as the professional care of patients is concerned. Nominations by Deans' Committees for such full-time positions will be welcomed; and, unless there be impelling reasons to the contrary, will be approved wherever vacancies exist. These service chiefs are fully responsible to their immediate superior in the Veterans' Administration.

c. Will appoint the consultants, the part-time attending staff and the residents nominated by the Deans' Committee and approved by the Veterans' Administration.

d. Will cooperate fully with the Schools of Medicine in the graduate education and training program.

3. THE SCHOOLS OF MEDICINE:

a. Will organize a Deans' Committee, composed of senior faculty members from all schools cooperating in each project, whether or not furnishing any of the attending or resident staff.

b. Will nominate an attending staff of diplomates of specialty boards in the numbers and qualifications agreed upon by the Deans' Committee and the Veterans' Administration. (See 6e)

c. Will nominate, from applicants, the residents for graduate education and training.

d. Will supervise and direct, through the Manager of the hospital <u>and the Consultants</u>, the training of residents.

e. Will nominate the consultants for appointment by the Veterans' Administration.

4. HOSPITAL MANAGERS:

a. Are fully responsible for the operation of their hospitals.

b. Will cooperate with the Deans' Committee, bringing to its attention any dereliction of duty on the part of any of its nominees.

5. CHIEFS OF SERVICE:

1. Are responsible to their superior in the Veterans' Administration for the conduct of their services.

2. Will bring to the attention of their superior, for his action, such cases as they are unable to deal with personally of dereliction of duty or incompetence on the part of any full-time or part-time staffs under their control.

3. Will, <u>together with the part-time attending staff,</u> under the direction of the Manager, supervise the education and training program.

4. When full-time employees of the Veterans' Administration, will be diplomates of their respective boards and will be acceptable to the Deans' Committee and to the specialty boards concerned. It is the urgent purpose of the Veterans' Administration to place full-time fully qualified and certified chiefs of service for all services in each hospital associated with a School of Medicine. Except in cases where the chief selected has local affiliations, which might embarrass or prejudice his relations with one or another of the associated schools, his initial assignment may not be cleared through the Deans' Committee. In all cases, when it has been conclusively demonstrated that a chief of service cannot cooperate with a Deans' Committee, he will be transferred (if efficient otherwise) and replaced by another. Until this purpose can be fully accomplished, however, in order that a hospital may obtain approval for resident training by one or another specialty board, it may be necessary to appoint part-time chiefs of services who meet the requirements of the boards. This will be done; but it will be done with the understanding that the part-time chiefs will be replaced with qualified full-time chiefs as rapidly as they become available. The duties and responsibilities of part-time chiefs will be the same as those of full-time chiefs.

6. PART-TIME ATTENDING STAFF:

a. Will be responsible to the respective chiefs of service.

b. Will accept full responsibility for the proper care and treatment of patients in their charge.

c. Will give adequate training to residents assigned to their service.

d. Will be veterans unless approval in each case has been given by the Chief Medical Director.

e. Will be diplomates of their respective boards and acceptable to such boards for direction of resident training. Exception may be made in the case of a veteran who has completed the first part of his board examination, but whose completion of the examination was interrupted by the exigencies of the military service.

f. Will hold faculty appointments in one or another of the associated Schools of Medicine, or will be outstanding members of the profession of the caliber of faculty members.

7. CONSULTANTS:

a. Will be veterans unless approval in each case has been given by the Chief Medical Director.

b. Will be members of the faculty, of professorial rank, of one or another of the associated Schools of Medicine.

c. Will, as representatives of the Schools of Medicine, direct and be responsible for the educational training of residents.

d. Will afford to the Manager and the proper Chief of Service the benefit of their professional experience and counsel.

e. Will conduct their duties through, and in cooperation with, the Manager and the proper Chief of Service, <u>and also, in matters of education and training, with the part-time Attending Staff</u>—always, however, coordinating with the Chief of Service.

Source: U.S. Department of Veterans Affairs, Office of Academic Affiliations, "Policy in Association of Veterans' Hospitals with Medical Schools." Available at http://www.va.gov/oaa/Archive/PolicyMemo2.pdf/

Chapter 2

Administration and Veterans' Healthcare: A View from the Top

James W. Holsinger Jr.

On March 15, 1989, the Department of Veterans Affairs (VA) was established by P.L. 100-527 as the fourteenth cabinet-level department in the executive branch of the U.S. government. Within VA, the legislation redesignated the Department of Medicine and Surgery as the Veterans Health Services and Research Administration. This agency inherited a fourfold mission from its predecessor: (1) providing quality care to America's veterans, (2) training healthcare providers, (3) conducting healthcare research, and (4) providing support to the Department of Defense during war or national emergency (P.L. 97-174, 1982). In 1990 the Veterans Health Services and Research Administration's name was changed to the Veterans Health Administration (VHA). VHA's fourth mission would be developed and tested during the early days of its existence. Cabinet status for VA brought with it significant changes, including markedly enhancing the visibility of the organization's programs. With the onset of departmental status, the modern era of VA began.

Nominated by President George H. W. Bush on May 14, 1990 (Bush 1990; *The nominations* 1990), James W. Holsinger Jr. took the oath of office on August 6, 1990, as the first presidentially appointed and Senate-confirmed chief medical director (see figure 2.1).[1] Only hours before, on August 2, 1990, the Republic of Iraq had invaded Kuwait, an event that would trigger the fourth mission of VHA for the first time. The new chief medical director not only faced fighting VA's first war, but met a firestorm of criticism based on the inspector general's report on the surgical service of

Figure 2.1. Dr. James W. Holsinger Jr., Under Secretary for Health; Lt. Gen. D'Wayne Gray, Under Secretary for Benefits; and Ms. JoAnne Webb, Director of the National Cemetery Service, with President George H. W. Bush. *Source: Official photograph by White House photographer.*

the North Chicago VA Medical Center. In addition to these several crises, he faced the daunting task of developing an organization for the newly established VHA. Through resignations and retirements, all three of VHA's senior leadership positions were vacant. During his first several months in office, the chief medical director reorganized the old Department of Medicine and Surgery structure into the new Veterans Health Administration (see figure 2.2) and recruited new leaders, largely from field units of the VA system.

Management Style and Leadership Philosophy

Management style and leadership philosophy are key elements for a leader of VHA. During an interview in late 1990, the chief medical director described the new VHA leadership team: "Each of the people I chose is a leader in his own right and that's what I was looking for, not 'yes' men. . . . Part of my fun is trying to figure out how to lead a team of leaders. It's easy to lead a team

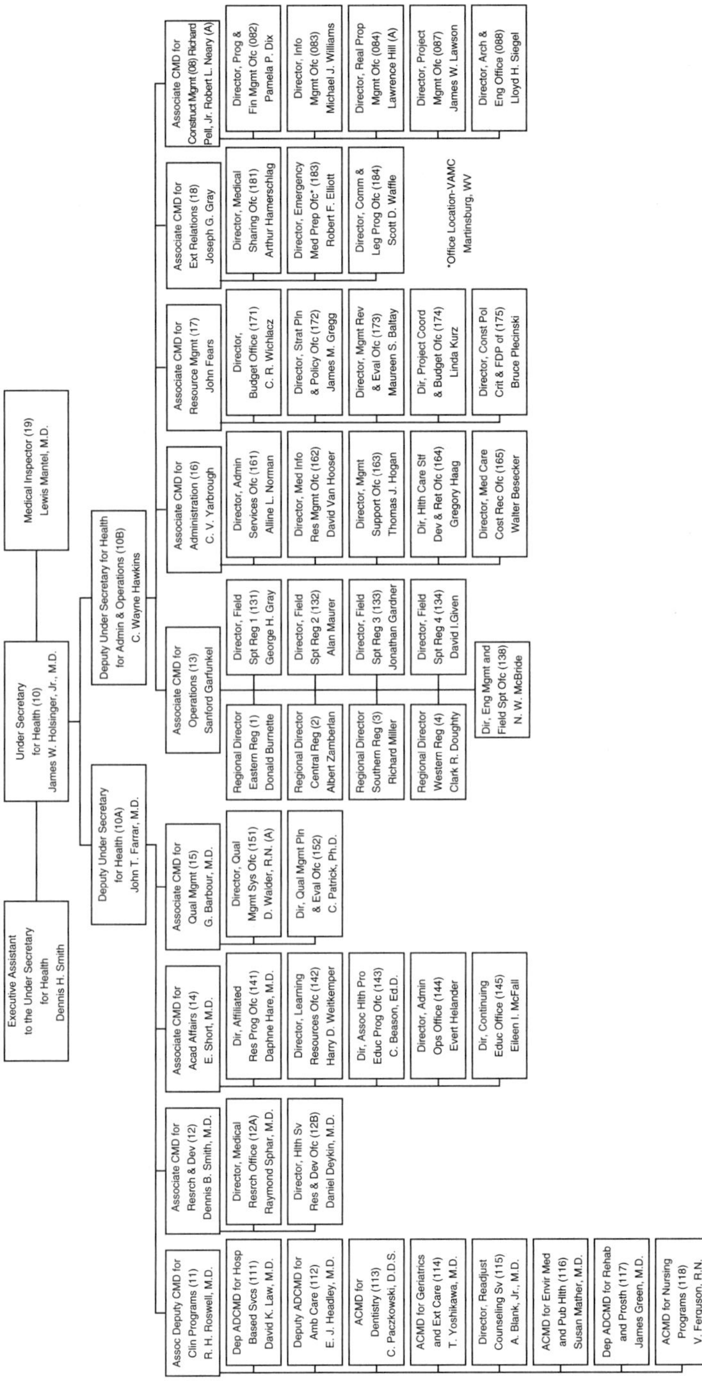

Figure 2.2. VHA Organizational Chart. *Source: Veterans Health Administration (1992a).*

of followers, but there is not a follower in the bunch" (Tobler & Silberman 1991). The chief medical director's management style and leadership philosophy were clearly identified in the *VA Practitioner* interviews with VHA's new senior leadership team. Concepts enunciated included (1) stressing that the team is greater than the sum of its parts; (2) power sharing between physicians and administrators; (3) a clean, well-demarcated organizational structure that enhances communication both within the Central Office and with the field; (4) daily team meetings to deal with current operations; (5) development of crisis action teams; (6) taking a proactive stance and being adept at correcting things in a political environment; (7) the ability to make decisions, assertiveness, and experience; and (8) seeking perfection in healthcare. As one senior leader remarked: "You seldom get a chance to join a new group from scratch and be on the ground floor of the implementation process" (Tobler & Silberman, 1991). The chief medical director's management style can be summed up as delegating day-to-day decision making to VHA's top management team, while expecting no surprises.

Central Office Reorganization

The chief medical director's management philosophy guided the reorganization of VHA's Central Office:

> The cornerstone of the changes was to build an organization that more completely represented the full spectrum of individuals involved in the health care delivery team—both at the clinical and administrator level. Central to this new management philosophy was the need to clarify the role of senior managers, to delegate responsibilities commensurate with authority, and to hold all managers accountable for performance. Particular emphasis in the new organization was placed on quality management as a basic tenet within VHA [Veterans Health Administration] and on the philosophy of continuous improvements to encourage improved communications, team building, and organizational risk taking. Also central to the changes was recognition of the critical importance in Central Office of program management and policy development. (Veterans Health Administration 1992a)

As a career VA physician, the chief medical director turned to individuals in the field, medical center directors and chiefs of staff, to fill the roles described in the organization. Dennis M. Smith, associate medical center director at Jackson, Mississippi, was assigned as executive assistant/chief of staff to the chief medical director, giving associate directors a voice on the senior leadership team. Mirroring the medical center organizational structure, a senior physician, Dr. John T. Farrar, chief of staff at Richmond, Virginia, was appointed deputy chief medical director and C. Wayne Hawkins, medical center director at Dallas, Texas, was appointed deputy chief medical director for administration and operations. All clinical, academic, and research programs reported to the deputy chief medical director, whereas all administrative and operational activities were overseen by the deputy chief medical director for administration and operations.

A major part of the VHA reorganization took place in the field:

> Commensurate with this major reorganization of VHA [Veterans Health Administration] Central Office, the elimination of the Medical Districts and reduction of the number of Regional Offices from seven to four was ongoing and represented one of the most far-reaching and complex changes ever undertaken by VHA [Veterans Health Administration]. . . . Twenty-seven Medical District Offices were closed, as well as Regional Offices in Dallas, Durham, Gainesville, Albany, and St, Louis. New Regional Offices were established in Jackson, MS, and Fort Howard, MD, and they, along with existing/expanded offices in San Francisco and Ann Arbor, make up the new four region configuration. (Veterans Health Administration 1992a)

The reduction from seven to four regional offices was already under way when the chief medical director was confirmed. Secretary Edward J. Derwinsky believed that a reduction in the number of regional offices would improve control and coordination of the medical centers. This configuration remained in place until 1995, when VHA reorganized into twenty-one Veterans Integrated Service Networks. The chief medical director firmly believed that a more balanced span of management control would provide improved control and coordination of the medical centers. He considered twelve "field management units," each overseeing approximately thirteen medical centers, to be ideal. With four regional offices, each regional director was responsible for forty or more medical centers with a commensurately greater span of control. As would be expected, the associate chief medical director for operations closely monitored the four regional directors.

Quality Management

The revamping of the VHA quality management program became a priority for the chief medical director. In 1990 he stated his vision: "VHA [Veterans Health Administration] will be the leader in quality health care by 1995" (Veterans Health Administration 1992a). Fortunately, prior to becoming chief medical director, Dr. Holsinger had served as the chair of the search committee for an assistant chief medical director for quality assurance and a medical inspector. As a result he inherited a quality management team.

Dr. Galen Barbour became the associate chief medical director for quality management and Dr. Lewis Mantel continued in his role as medical inspector.

As noted previously, following a June 1990 review of allegations presented to the secretary of veterans affairs, the inspector general issued a draft report detailing specific quality concerns in the Surgery Service of the North Chicago VA Medical Center and in its affiliation with the Chicago Medical School. This report was on the desk of the new chief medical director as he took office. In November 1990 he appointed a review team of clinicians, both surgeons and internists, including senior physicians such as Dr. David C. Sabiston, chair of the Department of Surgery at Duke University. Pending the review team's report, surgery at North Chicago was suspended. The report of the review team substantiated the complaints noted by the inspector general in his report. The review team recommended that subspecialty surgical procedures be eliminated, the general surgery program be maintained providing that caseload increased, documentation of house staff supervision should be improved, and the medical center's quality management program and credentialing and privileging processes should be enhanced at all levels (U.S. Department of Veterans Affairs, Office of the Inspector General 1991c). On March 25, 1991, the chief medical director responded to the inspector general, informing him that "[t]he North Chicago VAMC [Medical Center] will undergo a major mission change effective April 1, 1991, being redesignated as a Primary Care and Chronic Disease Center, placing emphasis on primary care, extended care, geriatrics, ambulatory care, and chronic disease care including psychiatry and neurology" (U.S. Department of Veterans Affairs, Office of the Inspector General 1991c). The North Chicago VA Medical Center issue placed quality management efforts clearly at the top of VHA's agenda.

In addition to the North Chicago VA Medical Center issue, the secretary of veterans affairs challenged the chief medical director early in his tenure to deal with the long-standing inspector general and Government Accounting Office (GAO) complaints about the credentialing and privileging of physicians and dentists in VHA. In February 1991 the inspector general issued a report, *Audit of VA's Control System for Credentialing and Privileging Physicians*, which was the eighth inspector general or GAO report in eleven years determining that problems existed in VHA's system (U.S. Department of Veterans Affairs, Office of the Inspector General 1991a). The chief medical director accepted the secretary's challenge, stating that VHA would solve the problem within one year, and challenged the secretary to instruct the inspector general to resurvey the system at that time. Utilizing his knowledge of, and the synergy of, the VHA system, the chief medical director directed that all medical centers implement a revised policy requiring that all physicians and dentists be credentialed and privileged utilizing a standardized template and credentialing folder (Veterans Health Administration 1992a). Using a systems approach:

> VA's current credentialing and privileging requirements exceed those of the Joint Commission on Accreditation of Healthcare Organizations (JCAHO) and help ensure that the physicians and dentists delivering care to our nation's veterans are both qualified and competent to do so. VHA [Veterans Health Administration] can be extremely proud of the recent IG [Inspector General] audit, "Implementation of Veterans Health Administration Policy for Credentialing and Privileging Physicians and Dentists." VA facilities were found to be in substantial compliance (greater than 96%) with credentialing and privileging policies and procedures. (Veterans Health Administration 1992a)

A year after the effort began, the inspector general's audit demonstrated a system in full compliance and brought to a close a twelve-year saga of failure.

In addition to developing policies and procedures to correct outstanding deficiencies, VHA, through the Office of Quality Management under the guidance of Dr. Galen Barbour, undertook a broad array of quality management endeavors (Barbour et al. 1996). By the middle of 1991, *Blueprint for Quality: A Solid Foundation* had been published, "a tool designed to coordinate, integrate and ultimately streamline the quality management programs at the national level of Veterans Health Administration (VHA) of the Department of Veterans Affairs (VA)....As Chief Medical Director, it is my vision that the Blueprint for Quality will serve as a foundation that will enable Veterans Health Administration to uphold the highest standards in providing quality care to our veteran patients" (U.S. Department of Veterans Affairs 1992). Initiated by a request from the secretary of veterans affairs (June 1991), the Office of Quality Management developed the *Quality Improvement Checklist (QUic) Version 1.0* in October 1991, and *Version 2.0* followed in May 1993. "The purpose of the checklist is to provide solid, verifiable data on the current level of quality, and the change over time, in various measures of health care quality. Directors will use the checklist to determine which areas need improvements and to document improvement with repeated measures using the same instrument" (Holsinger 1992). The *Quality Improvement Checklist* (1) emphasized clinical outcomes and processes, (2) provided information easily to those who could use it for improvement, (3) was data driven, (4) was relatively short, and (5) was interpreted as a whole and not through individual analysis of each question and answer (Barbour 1996). Other major programs also initiated during 1991 included the development and opening of the Quality Management Institute, designed to deal with quality assurance research, education, innovations development, and data development and computer support. In an effort to develop belief in the quality of the VHA system, the chief medical director implemented an external peer review system in early 1992 with the objective of providing VA medical centers with diagnosis and procedure-specific quality of care information and to establish a national database for comparison of individual medical center patterns. In addition, this system was designed to identify and pursue opportunities for improvement at all levels and to recognize and acknowledge the quality of care provided to veterans (Holsinger 1992). Thus throughout his tenure, the chief medical director worked not only to demonstrate the quality of care in the VA system, but to enhance it as well in order to provide care second to none for America's veterans.

Persian Gulf War

The onset of the Persian Gulf War following the invasion of Kuwait by Iraq created the second major issue facing the chief medical director following his Senate confirmation. Operation Desert Shield, the buildup phase of the Persian Gulf War, took place from August 7, 1990, through January 17, 1991, when the operational phase of the war (Operation Desert Storm) began. Prior to his appointment, the chief medical director, while serving as an Army Reserve officer on the Joint Staff and as the director of the Richmond VA Medical Center, had undertaken the task of developing the Department of Veterans Affairs/Department of Defense Contingency Hospital System, at the direction of the then chief medical director, Dr. John Gronvall, and the director for logistics (J-4), Lieutenant General Edward Honor. As a result, with the onset of Operation Desert Shield a basic plan was in place to implement VHA's fourth mission, to support the Department of Defense in time of war or national emergency. At the outset, grave concerns existed that the coalition forces would encounter high rates of casualties once the ground war ensued. As a result, VHA undertook to expand the Department of Veterans Affairs/Department of Defense Contingency Hospital System in such a manner as to enable VHA to provide up to 25 percent of its staffed operating hospital beds to the Department of Defense within seventy-two hours of implementation of the plan:

> In response to the Persian Gulf War, over 20,000 VA, DoD [Department of Defense] and civilian personnel were trained in VA-sponsored workshops and

teleconferences in such subjects as chemical injuries, infectious diseases, trau-
matic stress, contingency operations, and bed availability reporting.... VHA
[Veterans Health Administration] established an automated VA-DoD
[Department of Veterans Affairs/Department of Defense] Contingency
Planning System for the collection, analysis, and assembly of bed status and
mobilization data. (Veterans Health Administration 1992a)

Thus VHA had readied itself to meet the projected needs of the armed
forces in the Persian Gulf.

However, on January 9, 1991, the chairman of the Senate Veterans'
Affairs Committee expressed concern about VHA's preparations for providing medical services to the armed forces under the terms of Public Law 97-
174, the Veterans' Administration and Department of Defense Resources
and Emergency Operations Act of 1982. On January 18, 1991, only two
days after the onset of ground combat in the Persian Gulf, the inspector general determined that "VHA [Veterans Health Administration] was effective
in its preparations for providing medical services to members of the armed
forces under terms of the agreement reached with the Department of
Defense (DoD) for the provision of such services" (U.S. Department of
Veterans Affairs, Office of the Inspector General 1991b). The report also
stated that: "VHA's [Veterans Health Administration's] policy of providing
25 percent of staffed operating beds within 72 hours is essentially
met.... Therefore, we believe that VHA [Veterans Health Administration]
could reasonably meet its obligations to DoD [Department of Defense] in
terms of overall system capacity" (U.S. Department of Veterans Affairs, Office
of the Inspector General 1991b). Thus, although VHA was fully prepared to
fight its first war, the success of the Persian Gulf War ground combat resulted
in the Department of Defense not requiring its beds. However, VHA's
response to Hurricane Andrew demonstrated that its contingency planning
effort for the Persian Gulf War would continue to produce dividends.

Hurricane Andrew

In developing contingency plans for responding to national emergencies and
as an integral part of the National Disaster Medical System (NDMS), VHA
developed the Emergency Medical Preparedness Office at Martinsburg,
Maryland. On August 24, 1992, Hurricane Andrew struck south Florida.
Within hours, President George H. W. Bush had dispatched his personal
representative, Secretary of Transportation Andrew Card, to south Dade
County, Florida. On August 28, 1992, the chief medical director received a
direct request from the White House asking for any assistance that VHA

could provide, particularly in terms of mobile clinical facilities. VHA immediately arranged

> the deployment of three new mobile clinics located at the VAMCs [Medical Centers] in Prescott, AZ, Fayetteville, NC, and Spokane, WA. The three mobile clinics were designed by VHA [Veterans Health Administration] to provide primary health care to veterans living in remote rural areas, but had not yet begun those operations when called upon to support disaster relief efforts. They proved themselves to be a significant asset for disaster medical assistance. Due to the urgent requirement, the mobile clinics from Spokane, WA, and Prescott, AZ, were airlifted by Air Force C-5As to Opa Locka Airport in Miami. The Fayetteville, NC, clinic was driven to Miami, leaving Friday, August 28, and arriving Saturday, August 29. (Veterans Health Administration 1993b)

These three mobile clinics, during the period from August 31 to September 19, 1992, treated 5,681 men, women, and children for a variety of medical issues and injuries, including providing care to individuals from a migrant camp where there were no healthcare providers. Through its extensive emergency medical preparedness, VHA demonstrated its capability to engage in humanitarian and medical relief in the disaster area.

Planning for the Future

In 1991 the chief medical director projected that by the year 2000 VHA could become a model national healthcare system (Holsinger 1991). To make his vision a reality, three major initiatives were undertaken: (1) a response to the *Report of the Commission on the Future Structure of Health Care*, (2) VHA's *National Health Care Plan*, and (3) eligibility reform. The need to provide both continuity of care and a full spectrum of care created a requirement to reform veterans' eligibility for care within the system:

> At present, veterans' eligibility for health care is fragmented, resulting in the care of veterans being determined to some extent by administrative requirements rather than by the health care needs of the patient. Eligibility reform would provide a single eligibility requirement for all types of care, which would ensure that veterans' treatment could be based on their total health care needs. Such changes would result in a defined population of veterans being eligible for care rather than all veterans being "eligible." (Holsinger 1991)

In the aftermath of World War II, veterans' healthcare followed an inpatient model, which had become a major issue by the early 1990s. In the decades following World War II, as hospital lengths of stay decreased and medical care became progressively outpatient-based, the veterans' eligibility requirements became more and more onerous as physicians attempted to care for chronic diseases while their veteran patients possessed only a one-year post-hospital outpatient eligibility. Appropriate eligibility changes would offer VHA the opportunity to develop truly coordinated care for enrolled eligible veterans.

Early in his tenure at VA, Secretary Edward Derwinsky understood the need to realign the facilities of VHA. Initially he requested legislation to create a legal basis for the realignment along the lines of the Base Realignment and Closure Act (BRAC) being used successfully by the Department of Defense. However, when Congress did not approve such legislation, he appointed the Commission on the Future Structure of Veterans Health Care. Although the new chief medical director had not yet been confirmed (the first commission meeting was held on the same day as his Senate confirmation hearing), the secretary engaged him in the process of selecting commission members, particularly those with healthcare expertise as well as an understanding of the VA healthcare system.

On June 19, 1990, at the first commission meeting, Secretary Derwinsky stated:

> This is the first time in over 25 years that we've asked that someone take a good hard look at the entire VA health care system. As you know, it's a sprawling, maybe awkwardly-structured, national system. If we had to construct the VA from start today, the locations and mix of services would be quite different. But we have to deal with the reality. The reality is the VA as we see it today, and the direction in which we'd like to go. (U.S. Department of Veterans Affairs 1991a)

Secretary Derwinsky clearly understood the difficulties facing the commission, in that each VA medical center represented jobs in a congressional district and in all fifty states. However, he also clearly understood that all VA medical centers had the desire to be all things to all people and to be tertiary-care referral centers affiliated with university schools of medicine. But he also understood that the system needed to be right-sized and right-structured to succeed in the future. The chief medical director strongly supported the secretary's effort to develop a VA system that would, as the VA motto stated, be second to none. To do so would require courage, grit, and determination to set the VA healthcare system on a path to the twenty-first century.

The recommendations of the commission formed the basis for a number of VHA initiatives in the 1990s. Following are some of the most significant recommendations:

Recommendation 1a: The Commission recommends that the Administration and Congress change the law, removing differences in eligibility for inpatient, outpatient and long-term care.

Recommendation 1b: The Commission recommends that veterans with service-connected disabilities and poor veterans receive the full range of needed health-care services.

Recommendation 1e: The Commission recommends that VA health-care resources be redistributed to match veterans' needs.

Recommendation 3a: The Commission recommends a reorganization of the health-care system, granting Central Office the role of setting national policy and delegating operational authority to geographic service area managers.

Recommendation 4a: The Commission recommends that VA implement a "blueprint for quality." (U.S. Department of Veterans Affairs 1991b)

From these recommendations, VHA established several initiatives and continued others: (1) to develop a national plan for veterans' healthcare; (2) to develop proposals for reform of veterans' eligibility for care; (3) to develop a blueprint for quality; (4) to develop a new resource allocation model; and (5) to continue the Central Office and field reorganization under way prior to initiating the commission.

In his report to the commission, the chief medical director stated that the commission was facing an incredibly difficult task:

> First, you have the problem with trying to determine the future 20 years from now; and looking into a crystal ball was not always easy. And second, you have the problem of determining the present at a time…when our present situation in VHS&RA [Veterans Health Services and Research Administration] is at a time of great fluidity…and third, you don't have a lot of time to get the job done. (U.S. Department of Veterans Affairs 1991a)

The massive reorganization taking place literally as the commission met compounded its difficulty in determining the current organization of VHA. As VHA's Central Office reorganized, a significant number of individuals entered into new positions in the organization. In the field, twenty-seven medical districts had been abolished and seven regions were being reorganized into four. As the chief medical director stated:

> I am faced with the need to provide leadership and direction to an organization that's undergoing a period of controlled chaos. With both VHS&RA [Veterans Health Services and Research Administration] central office and the regional field reorganizations occurring simultaneously, our new team

coming together at this time must move rapidly to exert control, reduce tension and [un]certainty in our system and provide leadership required to keep [the Veterans Health Services and Research Administration] moving toward 2010. (U.S. Department of Veterans Affairs 1991a)

As indicated in the minutes of the commission, the chief medical director inherited the field reorganization. Thus establishing an organizational baseline would be difficult for the commission.

Early in his tenure, the chief medical director moved expeditiously to develop a national plan for veterans' healthcare, which became a key element in the commission's proposals. He was clearly cognizant of the issues pertaining to the delivery of care to veterans in the field facilities, having served for twenty-two years in local VA medical centers. He recognized that VHA needed to operate a fully integrated system of veterans' healthcare based not on a regional model, but a national one. Such a fully integrated national healthcare system included primary, secondary, and tertiary care, as well as a full spectrum of extended care programs, including nursing home care. Every modality of care required a national plan for its provision to determine where overlapping services occurred as well as gaps in service. In concept the national plan for veterans' healthcare required primary service areas for each modality based on veteran demographics. In developing such a system, overlapping services and gaps in the system of veterans' care would be determined and patient care services between medical centers would be realigned.

The chief medical director, in concert with the VHA Planning Review Committee, established the conceptual framework for the *National Health Care Plan*. This framework included the following provisions: (1) equal access for veteran patients through availability of an array of healthcare services in a network service area; (2) centralized direction for determining medical center missions; (3) a system for identifying gaps and overlaps in services and development of methods for distributing resources to fill gaps and reduce overlaps; and (4) design of a process for reviewing strategic plans and making decisions for program development and redistribution at the Central Office, region, network, and facility levels (Veterans Health Administration 1992b).

Based on the framework's provisions, the plan conceptualized seven key strategies: (1) The quality of VHA's healthcare will be second to none; (2) VHA will become a national leader in providing continuity of patient care; (3) VHA will build on its special strengths; (4) VHA will strive to develop progressive human resources management programs and achieve management excellence; (5) well-designed facilities and equipment are essential; (6) VHA will promote partnerships with the Department of Defense and the various communities through sharing and joint venture opportunities; and (7) VHA will be an active participant in national healthcare policy and reform. Based on these strategies, the plan determined medical center missions and required all facilities to provide primary care (basic clinical services units). The initial missions assigned to the medical centers reflected each facility's current capabilities, not necessarily its definitive role:

> The template differentiates between core and referral level services. Core services are provided locally and will be made available to veterans residing in each facility's catchment area. Referral services address less frequently occurring or more complex conditions for which specialized personnel, facilities, and support services are needed. Certain facilities will provide referral services to veterans in their own and other catchment areas. (Veterans Health Administration 1992b)

The plan, including a national healthcare planning process strongly endorsed by the commission, was presented to the new secretary of veterans affairs, Jesse Brown, on January 27, 1993. The secretary's briefing included both the *National Health Care Plan* and the proposed Geographic Service Area (GSA) concept designed to replace the four regions.

Field Reorganization

The GSA concept was a recommendation of the commission. Its purpose was to lessen the span of control, reduce competition for resources among facilities in a given area, reduce gaps and overlaps in services, reduce administrative overhead, and allow and stimulate flexibility and innovation among GSA facilities (*Geographic Service Area* 1993). Following the field reorganization from seven to four regions, it became evident that because of the vast geographic areas covered as well as the broad regional responsibilities, the span of control for the regions that included forty to forty-five medical centers was simply ineffective. Due to their broad span of management control, the regional directors focused heavily on those medical centers deemed to be in difficulty, rather than bringing greater centralized control to all the medical centers, as the secretary of veterans affairs had anticipated. Prior to the decision to reduce the number of regions to four, proposals had been considered for three or even two regions (Veterans Health Services and Research Administration n.d.). By the time the commission's report was issued in November 1991, it was becoming clear to all that the regions' span of control made the system unmanageable.

The secretary of veterans affairs accepted the recommendation of the commission, which entailed reorganizing the healthcare system. The role of setting national policy was assigned to VHA's Central Office, with operational authority delegated to the GSAs. As the William J. Clinton administration took office, a process of testing the concept of Geographic Service Areas was proposed to determine an optimal span of control. "The purpose of the GSA pilots is to establish an organizational framework that lessens the span of control of the regions, allows medical center directors more flexibility in resource allocation, deletes gaps and overlaps in services and will focus on patient care and program development issues" (Veterans Health Administration 1993c). It was anticipated that the GSAs would not only lessen the span of control and reduce gaps and overlaps in services, but would also reduce competition for resources among facilities in a given area, reduce administrative overhead, and stimulate flexibility and innovation among GSA facilities. The committee made three recommendations: (1) maintain an existing region as a control while dividing one region into three GSAs with a support office and piloting at least one GSA under the core services concept and one as a comprehensive services pilot; (2) create two core service and two comprehensive services pilots; and (3) immediate or phased-in GSA implementation nationwide. "Under a core services pilot, the GSA would have approximately ten FTE [full-time equivalent positions] concentrating on patient care and program development issues and a support office would assume the non-direct patient care responsibilities. The comprehensive services pilot would act as a 'mini-region' but serve fewer medical facilities and cover a smaller geographic area" (Veterans Health Administration 1993c). VHA's intention once a decision was made was to implement GSAs in October 1993. However, the new administration refined the concept and over the course of the next two years, the GSA approach blossomed into the Veterans Integrated Service Network (VISN), replacing the four regions. Under the VISN approach, one of the most, if not the most, successful field organizations in VA history was developed, and with it a fully integrated healthcare system for veterans.

Resource Management

The Commission's recommendation that VA health-care resources be redistributed to match veterans' needs coincided with the chief medical director's interest in developing a new resource allocation methodology. For a number of years funds had been distributed to medical centers based on the Resource Allocation Methodology (RAM), a process utilizing Diagnosis-related

Groups (DRG). Difficulties plagued this methodology from its inception. In June 1990, during the transition briefings for the new Chief Medical Director, it was disclosed that "a transitional RAM [Resource Allocation Methodology] incorporating the changes in direction endorsed by the chief medical director will also be provided to the field in June 1990 with facility-specific cost and workload data. A supplemental display will also be provided to the field in June 1990 which will illustrate how each VA medical center would fare if the Health Care Financing Administration (HCFA) DRG [Diagnosis-related Groups] weights were used in the RAM [Resource Allocation Methodology] instead of VA weights" (Veterans Health Services and Research Administration 1990). The new Central Office management team quickly moved to support the commission's recommendation to develop a new resource allocation model to be known as the Resource Planning and Management (RPM) System. The new system was based on the chief medical director's vision of "a significantly strengthened budgeting process, one in which national-level planning ensures the most appropriate distribution of scarce resources" (Veterans Health Administration 1992a).

The development of the Resource Planning and Management process began with the tenure of the new chief medical director in August 1990. Testing of the new system began in 1992, with further development and any needed corrections to be in place for fiscal year 1993 and full implementation in fiscal year 1994. "In conjunction with implementation of the National Health Care Plan (NHCP), RPM [Resource Planning and Management system] is expected to improve significantly VHA's [Veterans Health Administration's] planning and budgeting process" (Veterans Health Administration 1992a). The essential features of the process included producing a balance between Central Office and field oversight. VHA developed a state-of-the-art workload forecasting model as well as real-time, event-driven reporting integrated with the patient database. The combination of the National Health Care Plan and the Resource Planning and Management System became the keystone to the new, fully integrated veterans' healthcare system designed to fully implement the commission's recommendations.

Eligibility Reform

In November 1991 VA submitted an eligibility reform proposal to the Office of Management and Budget (OMB), but the fiscal year 1993 budget passback did not include eligibility reform (Veterans Health Administration 1993c). Following the commission's recommendation for reform of veterans' eligibility for healthcare, the secretary of veterans affairs directed the VA healthcare system to: "a) modernize, restructure and plan for the future, and b) to define VA's role in the Federal and U. S. health care communities. Further, [the deputy secretary] requested a study of how VA can: 1) simplify veteran eligibility for VA care; and 2) provide a comprehensive continuum of care" (*Executive summary* 1992). During the succeeding two years, the VA Health Care Eligibility Reform Task Force developed a variety of possible scenarios for redefining eligibility and securing the continuum of care for all eligible veterans. A key to understanding the work of the task force centered on the then current 1990 eligibility laws, rules, and regulations. The eligibility requirements for veterans had grown and changed over a number of years, with the result that VA met "the needs of those veterans with the highest SC [service connected] ratings and is a safety net for the poorest of veterans who may have no other resources with which to obtain health care. For other veterans, receiving VA care may be sometimes uncertain for all conditions in all settings" (*Eligibility reform* 1992). Incompatible with sound medical practice and encouraging fragmented care, the 1990 eligibility structure was an obstacle to providing continuity of care and a continuum of care; in addition, veterans and their families found it simply too complicated to understand (Veterans Health Administration 1993c).

The 1990 structure of veteran eligibility limited access to certain levels of care and encouraged overutilization of inpatient care when admission to a nursing home or the use of outpatient care would be the most appropriate level of care. In order to provide care to the whole person, physicians admitted veterans to the inpatient setting. The ensuing contradiction resulted in the most accessible level of care being the most expensive, while the least accessible level was the least expensive. As a consequence the eligibility system not only limited access to the least expensive programs, but it served as a major obstacle to reforming the entire system. Interestingly, access to all healthcare services would produce simplification because it would eliminate the complicated system of determining veteran eligibility for healthcare services. In 1990, because all types of impatient care were available to service-connected and poor non-service-connected veterans, any change in the eligibility system must provide all required outpatient care to such veterans.

As the task force undertook its work, eligibility requirements presented statutory barriers to outpatient care, in that 0–40 percent service-connected and non-service connected veterans were authorized for only one year of post-hospital outpatient care. A major reason for eligibility reform was to rectify this untenable situation. VA physicians often felt the need to flout the law in order to meet the needs of veterans. Physicians feared that veteran patients with chronic illnesses who had completed their statutory year of outpatient eligibility would no longer have access to the medications required to maintain their health. As a result, the continuum of care required by their patients would be interrupted. Only service-connected veterans rated greater than 50 percent and non-service-connected means-tested veterans with an income not greater than twice the pension level were eligible for continuing outpatient care, as well as certain other special categories of veterans based on period of service, age, disease, need, or other special category.

In the 1991 version of eligibility reform, veterans were divided into five categories:

- Category I: Health care was mandated in all VA patient care programs for veterans with service-connected conditions and for non-service-connected conditions for veterans who were service-connected at greater than 50 percent. Treatment of all other non-service-connected conditions was subject to a financial means test.

- Category II: Mandated care for veterans with an income less than the VA pension level but with a $2.00 prescription copayment.

- Category III: Still mandated care for veterans with an income between the pension level and twice the pension level but with the payment of deductibles and copayments.

- Category IV: Discretionary care for veterans with an income twice to three times the pension level with required copayments and deductibles.

- Category V: Veterans determined to be ineligible for VA care with an income equal to or greater than four times the pension level. (Veterans Health Administration 1993c)

VHA crafted a variety of proposals for eligibility reform that used as a framework "two eligibility categories—service-connected status and non-service-connected status combined with income (as compared to need or disease, age, period of service, or other special category)" (*Eligibility reform* 1992). The proposals ranged from no change to a full continuum of care for all veterans. The twelve alternatives ranged in cost from a low of $10.8 billion to a high of $49.9 billion at a time when the VHA budget was approximately $16 billion.

Providing a continuum of care for all eligible veterans became a major component of the cost of eligibility reform. In considering the continuum of care, the task force determined that "[c]urrent eligibility for VA care is complex to interpret and varies across patient care settings. Moreover, veterans are not treated as a whole person, but often can receive care only for certain service-connected conditions" (*Eligibility reform* 1992). The basic premise was determined to be that a certain population of veterans would be identified as eligible for VA care. Those veterans so identified would have all their healthcare needs met by the VA system. Thus such eligible veterans would be treated for all conditions and not just for service-connected conditions. The least restrictive, most appropriate, and most efficient care settings would be utilized considering several significant requirements: veteran preference, desired outcomes, quality of care, and quality of life. Ensuring that healthcare provided to eligible veterans was "determined by medical need and not the structure of the VA healthcare system, the structure of the laws governing the Department of Veterans Affairs, or any other reason unrelated to patient need and clinical considerations" (*Comprehensive continuum of care* 1992) became a major challenge. The comprehensive continuum of care, as defined by the task force, stated:

> It was conceived to include both medical and health related services and social support services to promote, maintain, or restore an individual's health, well-being, or maximum level of independence. These general types of services may be found in traditional institutional settings such as hospitals, outpatient clinics and nursing homes and in non-institutional settings such as day treatment centers and homes or various congregate living situations. Similarly, these types of services may involve short-term treatment and long-term care depending on the condition of the veterans. (*Comprehensive continuum of care* 1992)

The first major outside review of the task force's work occurred at a hearing on VA healthcare eligibility reform before the House Committee on Veterans' Affairs on May 20, 1992. At a November 4, 1992, briefing of the secretary of veterans affairs, the concept of a comprehensive continuum of care providing for the medical and healthcare-related needs of veterans became the basis for all future efforts to rationalize the eligibility requirements for VA healthcare. Without the impetus provided by the commission and the diligent work of the task force, appropriate care for America's veterans may well have been delayed for years.

Lessons Learned at the Top

During his more than three years serving as the thirteenth and last chief medical director of VA and as the first individual to hold the title "Under Secretary for Health," Dr. James Holsinger learned a variety of lessons (see figures 2.3 and 2.4). Various personal attributes may be appropriately employed in such a position, not least of which are honesty, integrity, transparency, and a sense of humor. It also helps not to take oneself too seriously. The latter is particularly useful when dealing with members of the

Figure 2.3. Artist's rendering of photograph of Dr. James W. Holsinger Jr., Under Secretary for Health, which hangs in the Department of Veterans Affairs Headquarters Building, Washington, D.C. *Source: Official photo by Department of Veterans Affairs photographer.*

congressional staff, many of whom take themselves far too seriously. They all too often assume a form of referred power, acting as though they possess the power of their senator or congressman. The under secretary for health (chief medical director) serves at the pleasure of the president of the United States and holds the executive level III grade. Basically only the secretary of veterans affairs stands between the under secretary and the president. Yet GS-14 congressional staffers subsume the power of their principal in an effort to control leaders in the executive branch of the U.S. government. Consequently, it helps to not place too high a value on pride of place and to instead maintain a sense of humor and simply recognize the source.

Although the position of under secretary is filled through the nomination of a search commission, since the creation of the Department of Veterans Affairs, the position has become highly politicized. Clearly, under secretaries should recognize going into the position that they serve at the pleasure of the president. This became clear in early 1993 when the new administration arrived in Washington, D.C. Although the position is statutorily four years in duration, its duration is clearly bounded by a change in administration, which may result in the appointment of a new secretary of veterans

James W. Holsinger, Jr., M.D.

Under Secretary for Health
Veterans Health Administration
Department of Veterans Affairs

James W. Holsinger, Jr., M.D., was the first Chief Medical Director appointed by the President of the United States on August 6, 1990. In October 1992 the title of the position was changed by legislation to Under Secretary for Health, to make it more reflective of VA's cabinet status.

Dr. Holsinger focused his leadership on priority issues such as quality management and improvement, enhanced women and homeless veterans programs, Persian Gulf War veterans care and preventive medicine. His vision was for the Veterans Health Administration to be a health care model for the nation under national health care reform.

Dr. Holsinger was born in Kansas City, Kansas, in 1939. He graduated from Duke University Medical School in 1964; then completed a surgical internship, residency in general surgery and fellowships in thoracic surgery and anatomy at Duke University. In 1968 he completed a Ph.D. with a major in anatomy and minor in physiology at Duke University. He also completed a residency in general surgery and a fellowship in cardiology at the Gainesville, Florida, VA Medical Center and the University of Florida. In 1981 he completed a master's degree in hospital management at the University of South Carolina.

Dr. Holsinger was appointed director of McGuire VA Medical Center, Richmond, Virginia, in 1981. He also served as professor of medicine and professor of health care administration at the Medical College of Virginia. In 1985, Dr. Holsinger was appointed assistant vice president for health services at Virginia Commonwealth University.

Dr. Holsinger retired from the U.S. Army Reserve with the rank of major general in 1992.

After serving as Under Secretary for Health, Dr. Holsinger was director of the VA Medical Center, Lexington, Kentucky. In July 1994, he became chancellor at the University of Kentucky Chandler Medical Center.

Figure 2.4. Plaque associated with artist's rendering of Dr. James W. Holsinger Jr.

affairs. Consequently any person accepting the nomination to the position of under secretary should contemplate an early exit from it. However, it is important for the secretary of veterans affairs and president to recognize that between the decision to make a change and a new appointee taking the oath of office a year or more may pass while the various required steps in the process take place: determining who will be appointed as members of the search commission, the call for nominations, the deliberations of the commission, the determination of whom to recommend to the president, the background check and clearance of the candidate, and the confirmation process by the U.S. Senate. On the last point, one hopes that no holds are placed on the nomination. In the current era, it may be wise for an under secretary to tender a letter of resignation to a new president to be either accepted or declined.

Persistence is another personal attribute that benefits an under secretary. At the close of the Persian Gulf War, returning combat zone veterans complained of a variety of symptoms, which became known as Gulf War Syndrome. The chief medical director had had extensive experience dealing with the Agent Orange issue from the Vietnam War. As Gulf War Syndrome manifested itself, in an effort to care for returning combat veterans, he issued a directive requiring all Persian Gulf War veterans complaining of unusual symptoms to be entered into a register and offered the identical physical examination and care as a Vietnam War veteran claiming exposure to Agent Orange. VA's deputy general counsel immediately took exception to the directive, recommending to the secretary of veterans affairs that it be rescinded regardless of the importance it had for the care of Gulf War veterans. His rationale was simple: There was no legislation authorizing the chief medical director to take such steps regardless of whether it was the right thing to do or not. While the deputy general counsel was making his point to the secretary, Congressman Sonny Montgomery, chair of the House Committee on Veterans' Affairs, telephoned the chief medical director to compliment him on his effort to care for those who had borne the battle and offering to obtain legislation should it be necessary. When the deputy general counsel was confronted by the chief medical director in the secretary's office, the issue was resolved by the former agreeing to "write a rule" until legislation could be obtained. As Chairman Montgomery noted at a hearing before his committee on September 16, 1992: "I want to commend the Department of Veterans Affairs for...getting ahead of the curve on this issue" (*Possible adverse health effects* 1992). The chief medical director's persistence paid off, with congressional action ratifying his directive giving primacy to the care of veterans. At a hearing before the House Committee on Veterans' Affairs ten years later, the chief medical director detailed a key lesson learned from this series of events:

> But what lesson did we learn from this experience? I believe we were hampered in our efforts to provide health care for Persian Gulf War veterans by not having stand-by legislation available when we needed it. What do I mean? While

waiting for the full support of Congress, we had to spend months waiting to get our expanded program initiated since enabling legislation was required. My one recommendation today is that this committee should see that legislation is enacted that will establish stand-by authority for the Secretary of Veterans Affairs to develop and implement the examination of veterans of the current as well as future conflicts who may have unusual symptoms or complaints, establish specialized treatment programs for these veterans, as well as establish the appropriate registry for tracking purposes. (*Ten years after* 2002)

Although the chief medical director learned his lesson, the Congress has yet to enact legislation providing standby authority for the secretary of veterans affairs.

Having the courage of one's convictions was another lesson learned. A clear example of this attribute was demonstrated in the final decision to make all VHA acute care facilities smoke-free on January 7, 1991. Prior to this point, some facilities, particularly those in states requiring healthcare institutions to be smoke-free, had banned smoking. However, those facilities with American Federation of Government Employees (AFGE) bargaining units had not been allowed to move ahead with such a policy. The chief medical director had his first contact with VA as a medical student at the Durham, North Carolina, VA Medical Center in the summer of 1962, at a time when volunteers provided free cigarettes to America's veterans. When he made the final smoke-free policy decision, the 25–45 percent incidence of smoking among veterans was higher than that of an age-matched, general male population.

As would be expected under these circumstances, a variety of potential barriers occurred in implementing a smoke-free policy. These barriers "included perceived violations of smokers' rights, management of nicotine-dependent patients, consideration of exceptions for patients with psychiatric and substance-use disorders, and labor disputes" (Joseph & O'Neill 1992). The national policy prohibited smoking by patients, visitors, and employees in all VA acute-care facilities. By 1991 VA prohibited the free distribution of cigarettes to patients and no longer sold such products at below market prices in Veterans Canteen Service stores. By October 1, 1991, VA prohibited all such stores from selling tobacco products. The Veterans Canteen Service had significant difficulty in implementing the policy because of the "profit" made on the sale of tobacco products, particularly following the decision made earlier to increase the sales price to local market levels. However, "[p]rogress toward the complete elimination of tobacco product sales from VA medical facilities [had] been hindered by congressional oversight committee concerns and apparent pressure from tobacco company lobby groups"

(Joseph & O'Neill 1992). As an example, in a hearing before the Senate Committee on Veterans' Affairs, the chief medical director commented:

> Mr. Chairman, before closing, I want to bring to the Committee's attention a matter of serious concern to the VA. H.R. 5192 was recently amended in committee to include a requirement that VA reinstitute sales of tobacco products in its canteens and provide indoor smoking areas within all VA hospitals. In effect, this legislation would negate the smoke-free policy of VA. Secretary Derwinski and I want you to know that we are very, very strongly opposed to this legislation. The VA smoke-free policy is a sound one based on an impressive aggregate of data that proves that smoking is the most devastating preventable cause of disease and premature death in this country.... We must also continue to encourage nonsmoking behavior which will lead to a longer, healthier life for the individual veterans that we serve. (*Health-Care legislation* 1992)

The chief medical director and the committee chair noted that each knew where the other stood on the issue, and that they agreed with the chief medical director's statement. By holding firmly to his position, the chief medical director prevailed as the nation's largest healthcare system enforced his smoke-free policy.

One of the most agonizing decisions facing an under secretary is the decision to close a VA facility. Clearly the veterans served by a facility that must be closed feel a certain sense of betrayal, as do the employees. Following a major San Francisco Bay area earthquake in August 1991, the secretary of veterans affairs determined to close the major clinical care building at the Martinez VA Medical Center due to seismic and safety issues. Because of the age and mechanical structure of the building, examination of the structure determined that if the earthquake had continued for an additional twenty to thirty seconds, the building would have collapsed. As a consequence "major design and structural deficiencies in the building were determined to present an intolerable risk to patients and staff" (Veterans Health Administration 1992a). For many years the perceived wisdom within the VA system was that there was no reason to close a facility because it would take at least two years to complete. The chief medical director had long believed that such a timetable was unreasonable, simply because clinicians would not continue to serve at a facility without patient admissions. With the shortened lengths of stay, complete turnover of the inpatients occurs within a very short period of time. A plan was rapidly developed, guided by clinical input, which resulted in patients, program, and staff members being transferred to adjacent VA medical centers. Staff members requested and received priority placement at any VA facility in the system.

Within sixty days, closure of the major clinical care building at Martinez occurred, verifying the chief medical director's insight. VA rapidly constructed new outpatient and long-term care facilities, with an 80,000-square-foot VA outpatient clinic opening only a year after the main hospital facility had been closed. Although virtually no VA facilities have been closed (many have been replaced with newly constructed facilities), had the commission's recommendations been fully implemented and VA facilities closed where excess capacity occurred, expeditious closure could have been achieved. Indeed, clinicians will not continue to work where their skills cannot be utilized. It should be remembered in an era of healthcare reform that the status of every healthcare system may change, which in the case of VHA could result in facility closures.

Another important lesson the chief medical director learned was how to work effectively with the secretary of veterans affairs. As the leader of one of the three operational units of VA, he worked directly for and with the secretary (see figure 2.5). The need for developing a process for deliberating with the secretary concerning the issues confronting VHA and working through them in a thoughtful manner became apparent early in his tenure. Obtaining the time and finding the opportunity for the two of them to work together became a major goal. Normally when meeting with the secretary, a number of individuals were present, including VHA staff, assistant secretaries, and staff from the Office of the Secretary, all of whom had a variety of agendas. In addition, attendees often worked hard to advance their points of view to keep from losing "face." The meetings often took the form of briefings, with several alternatives presented, and reaching agreement could be difficult because of competing interests.

The chief medical director discovered that following the end of the normal workday, he could engage the secretary in a productive discussion in his office. During these sessions the two worked through issues and developed decisions, knowing that when an issue was not clear-cut they could return to it at future meetings; thus they were able to reach consensus on the issue at hand. As a result of these sessions the chief medical director was able to maintain a consistent approach for keeping the secretary abreast of VHA issues and requirements while at the same time significantly reducing the occurrence of any "surprises" for the secretary. During the more than two years that they worked together, they solved in this manner a number of problems and finalized many important decisions. Understanding the need to develop a method allowing the secretary and chief medical director to work together for the good of America's veterans was a key lesson learned.

The lessons learned during the more than three years of service as the chief medical director for VHA can best be summarized by understanding

Figure 2.5. Dr. James W. Holsinger Jr., chief medical director, at his swearing-in ceremony with Secretary Edward J. Derwinski and Dr. Holsinger's spouse, Dr. Barbara C. Holsinger. *Source: Official photo by Department of Veterans Affairs photographer.*

that change is extremely difficult and that perceived wisdom is not necessarily the most effective wisdom. Change is particularly difficult in the federal government, because the perceived wisdom is often "this is just the way we do things." Congressional staff members in particular expect that new senior executive branch leaders will understand the way things are done, which often entails rapidly determining which issues are important to the members of Congress. Thus a new senior leader may misunderstand or misinterpret the way things are done and thus violate the perceived wisdom of congressional staff. Another item of perceived wisdom was that engaging the secretary of veterans affairs was best accomplished through the use of briefings, which often involved a fairly large and diverse group of individuals. The chief medical director discovered exactly the opposite. Effective use of one-on-one meetings with the secretary resulted in changing the way things were done.

Likewise, the perceived wisdom for many years had precluded even an attempt at closing outmoded and ineffective VA facilities. The chief medical director refuted this perception when the Martinez VA Medical Center was closed in sixty days due to safety issues. Standing firm on the decision to ban smoking in all VA medical centers was another example of a difficult change that enabled VA to move into the forefront of smoking cessation efforts nationally. In this situation, effective wisdom entailed taking a firm position and maintaining it, thus producing a beneficial change for veterans, staff, and visitors to VA facilities. The chief medical director learned that change, although difficult, can be accomplished with initiative, effort, and persistence and that effective wisdom can, and does, make a difference.

Note

1. On October 9, 1992, the title was changed to "Under Secretary for Health." To avoid confusion, "chief medical director" is used throughout this chapter.

References

Barbour, G. L. (1996). *Redefining a public health system: How the Veterans Health Administration improved quality measurement.* San Francisco: Jossey-Bass.

Barbour, G., Malby, L., Lussier, R. R., Thomale, R. W. & Lerner, J. A. (Eds.). (1996). *Quality in the Veterans Health Administration.* San Francisco: Jossey-Bass.

Bush, G. H. W. (1990, May 14). Nomination of James Wilson Holsinger, Jr., to be chief medical director at the Department of Veterans Affairs. In *Public papers of President George H.W. Bush.* http://bushlibrary.tamu.edu/research/public_papers.php?id = 1879&year = 1990&month = all (accessed July 1, 2010).

Comprehensive continuum of care. (1992, December). House and Senate Veterans Affairs committee staffs meeting on VA health care eligibility reform.

Eligibility reform. (1992, November). Secretary of Veterans Affairs briefing.

Executive summary. (1992, December). House and Senate Veterans Affairs committee staffs meeting on VA health care eligibility reform.

Geographic Service Area. (1993, January). Secretary of Veterans Affairs briefing.

Health-Care legislation and oversight: Hearing before the Committee on Veterans' Affairs, Senate. (1992). 102nd Cong., 1st sess.

Holsinger, J. W., Jr. (1991). The Veterans Health Care Administration: A health care model for the nation. *Academic Medicine* 66: 674–675.

Holsinger, J. W., Jr. (1992). Concern for quality overriding at VA. *U.S. Medicine* 28, nos. 1 & 2: 25.

Joseph, A. M. & O'Neill, P. J. (1992). The Department of Veterans Affairs smoke-free policy. *JAMA* 267: 87–90.

The nominations of Dr. James W. Holsinger Jr., to be chief medical director, and Stephen A. Trodden, to be inspector general, Department of Veterans Affairs: Hearing before the Committee on Veterans' Affairs, Senate. (1990). 101st Cong., 1st sess.

The possible adverse health effects of service in the Persian Gulf; and H. R. 5864, to establish a Persian Gulf War Veterans Registry: Hearing before the Subcommittee of Hospitals and Health Care of the Committee on Veterans' Affairs, House of Representatives. (1992). 102nd Cong., 1st sess.

Ten years after: Lessons from the Gulf War: Hearing before the Subcommittee on Health of the Committee on Veterans' Affairs, House of Representatives. (2002). 107th Cong., 1st sess.

Tobler, N. & Silberman, S. (1991). VHSRA's new team: Esprit at the core. *VA Practice* 8: 23–27, 31–34, 39–40, 43.

U.S. Department of Veterans Affairs. (1991a). *Proceedings of the Commission on the Future Structure of Veterans Health Care* (Parts 1–4). Washington, DC: Author.

U.S. Department of Veterans Affairs. (1991b). *Report of the Commission on the Future Structure of Veterans Health Care.* Washington, DC: Author.

U.S. Department of Veterans Affairs. (1992). *Blueprint for quality: A solid foundation.* Washington, DC: Author.

U.S. Department of Veterans Affairs, Office of the Inspector General. (1991a). *Audit of VA's control system for credentialing and privileging physicians.* Report No. 1AB-A99-023. Washington, DC: Author.

U.S. Department of Veterans Affairs, Office of the Inspector General. (1991b). *Review of the Veterans Health Administration's contingency planning for Operation Desert Storm.* Report No. 1AB-A99-065. Washington, DC: Author.

U.S. Department of Veterans Affairs, Office of the Inspector General. (1991c). *Special review of VA Medical Center North Chicago, Illinois.* Report No. 1QA-A28-021. Washington, DC: Author.

Veterans Health Administration. (1991). *Quality improvement checklist (QUIC) version 1.0.* Washington, DC: Author.

Veterans Health Administration. (1992a). *Mid-term report from the under secretary for health.* Washington, DC: Author.

Veterans Health Administration. (1992b). *National health care plan.* Washington, DC: Author.

Veterans Health Administration. (1993a). *Quality improvement checklist (QUIC) version 2.0.* Washington, DC: Author.

Veterans Health Administration. (1993b). *Hurricane Andrew after-action report.* Washington, DC: Author.

Veterans Health Administration. (1993c). *Briefing Information.* Washington, DC: Author.

Veterans Health Services and Research Administration. (1990). *Chief medical director transition program, vols. 1–2.* Washington, DC: Author.

Veterans Health Services and Research Administration. (n.d.). *Region concept white paper.* Washington, DC: Author.

Chapter 3

The Academic Mission of the Department of Veterans Affairs

Stuart C. Gilman, Barbara K. Chang,
Robert A. Zeiss, Mary B. Dougherty, William J. Marks Jr.,
Deborah A. Ludke, and Malcolm Cox

Introduction

As described in chapter 1, a defined academic mission was essential to the ability of the Veterans Administration to meet the challenges of the post–World War II era. Close relationships with schools of medicine were an ideal strategy to facilitate recruitment of well-trained physicians on the large scale then needed to ensure that veterans' healthcare was consistent with the best standards of care and to establish an environment in which research and education specific to issues in veterans' health could flourish.

On January 3, 1946, Public Law 79-293 provided statutory authorization for the Veterans Administration to affiliate with the nation's medical schools. Later in the same month, Policy Memorandum No. 2 (Veterans Administration Policy Memorandum No. 2 1946) ushered in the agency's long-standing and productive collaborative relationship with U.S. medical schools. Policy Memorandum No. 2 provided the framework upon which all of the subsequent expansion of academic affiliations was based, including the broad provisions that the agency would retain full responsibility for care of beneficiaries while its medical school partners would accept responsibility for education and training in VA hospitals. As a result, as VA hospitals expanded in the 1960s and 1970s, many were deliberately co-located close to their medical school affiliates. In 1989, VA became the cabinet-level Department of Veterans Affairs, but continues to use the abbreviation "VA."

Healthcare delivery and health professions education have changed dramatically since 1945. The most prominent changes in education include vastly different financing mechanisms, an explosion in the numbers of recognized physician specialties, the shift of nursing education from hospital- to university-based programs, and the emergence of many other health professions as indispensable components of the provision of quality healthcare. In many instances, VA has spawned or led these changes to support its patient care mission.

VA now hosts the largest health professions training program in the United States, and arguably the world. In fiscal year 2010 the agency's trainee education budget was approximately $1.5 billion, which supported the training of over 115,000 trainees in more than forty health professions. This includes about $697 million in direct costs (stipends and benefits) and another $794 million in indirect costs.

Academic affiliations are often considered synonymous with the agency's health professions training programs, but this extensive network of training programs is only the most visible aspect of the agency's statutory academic mission. The seminal importance of VA's academic mission to fulfill the nation's promise to its veterans is all too often insufficiently emphasized and rarely well understood by the general public.

Health professions education: VA provides trainees from academic affiliates access to clinical environments, patients, and teachers and supports trainee and faculty salaries and benefits in proportion to time spent in patient care, education, and research activities that benefit veterans. Health professions training enhances the agency's clinical mission in several ways. Supervised practice amplifies clinical productivity, allowing more patients to receive care. As shown in table 3.1, trainees constitute a considerable portion of VA's health professions workforce, including 37 percent of physicians and nearly 20 percent of clinical psychologists. Trainees foster a spirit of inquiry and learning, thereby promoting evidence-based standards of care. Finally, training experiences in the agency's hospitals and clinics prepare future health professionals to recognize clinical disorders relatively unique to military medicine, thereby facilitating the treatment of the many veterans who receive healthcare outside VA.

Recruitment and retention of clinical staff: Having clinical staff with faculty appointments at affiliated academic institutions allows VA to bring new and unique modalities of care directly to veterans. The opportunity to engage in teaching and research as well as clinical practice distinguishes VA from most other healthcare employment options. Many local, regional, and national VA leaders were initially drawn to the agency because of the opportunity for

Table 3.1. Residents as a Percentage of the VA Workforce in Selected Disciplines

Discipline or Occupational Category	Total Employee FTEE May 2009	Resident FTEE AY2008-2009	Total FTEE	Resident FTEE as a % of Total FTEE
Physicians	15,969	9,553	25,522	37
Psychologists	2,844	635	3,479	18
Dentists	847	356	1,203	30
Pharmacists	5,860	405	6,265	7
Podiatrists	328	186	514	36
Optometrists	532	151	683	22

engagement with affiliated academic programs. Providing health professions training is also an important factor in enhancing recruitment to VA clinical staff positions. Surveys of trainees and staff consistently demonstrate that persons who had clinical educational experiences in VA are more likely to seek employment with the agency following completion of training including VA experiences.

Leveraging VA's research program: Unlike extramural research programs such as those sponsored by the National Institutes of Health, VA has long relied on intramural funding, supporting its investigators directly rather than providing grants to university-based investigators. The excellence and productivity of this research program would not be possible without the agency's close relationship with the broader academic community and is an important factor in the agency's ability to recruit and retain outstanding clinicians.

Collaborative clinical program development: Academic affiliations have facilitated VA's role in the development of physician specialties and other health disciplines essential to veterans' healthcare. Geriatrics, addiction psychiatry, spinal cord injury, palliative care, clinical psychiatry, and prosthetics are notable examples of the agency's impact on the formation of formally recognized clinical specialties. Similarly, academic affiliations make possible the agency's Geriatric Research and Education Clinical Centers, Mental Illness Research and Education Clinical Centers, Mental Health Centers of Excellence, Health Services Research and Development Centers of Excellence, Veterans Engineering Resource Centers, and many other joint programs.

National health professions policy: The veterans' healthcare system exists within the broader context of healthcare provision, education, and research in the United States. Where such standards exist, VA is subject to national clinical, educational, and research accreditation standards. It is also subject to general cultural trends that shape all aspects of professional activity. VA recognizes that in many cases these interrelationships are manifested through academic affiliations and that the maintenance of these affiliations requires near daily interactions between the agency and a wide variety of licensing, accreditation, and other regulatory stakeholders locally, regionally, and nationally. These interrelationships provide important opportunities for the agency to lead changes in the broader regulatory environment and to advocate for veterans' healthcare.

The initial vision of creating educational and research missions for VA, seamlessly integrated with its (primary) clinical care mission, has proven to be an enduring positive force. The ensuing years have seen considerable expansion of the number and types of academic institutions with which the agency partners, but the benefits to the agency, its affiliates, and the nation are as great as ever. This is perhaps best evidenced by a recent survey reporting the high value placed by both sides on the partnership between VA and the nation's medical schools (Report of the Blue Ribbon Panel 2009).

VA's Office of Academic Affiliations has recently taken several steps toward systematically reexamining and refreshing the agency's academic mission. For example, a federal advisory committee has issued a series of recommendations to improve the operations of academic affiliations (Report of the Blue Ribbon Panel 2009). At the same time, the agency is undertaking a major redesign of fundamental aspects of how health services are provided to veterans, including primary, secondary and extended care. Expanding the role of academic affiliations in clinical care delivery will ensure that the benefits introduced by Policy Memorandum No. 2 are sustained.

Though it is difficult to overestimate the importance of the external expertise provided by academic affiliations, it is also important to recognize that academic affiliations are no longer sufficient to assure that the agency's statutory academic mission is fully realized. Unlike the situation in 1946, VA's healthcare can no longer be brushed aside as inferior and is frequently superior in quality, safety, and cost to care provided in the private sector (Trivedi et al. 2011; Longman 2010). The present challenge for VA is to ensure that clinical trainees participate in care in ways that advance its renowned quality and safety programs, a particularly acute challenge at a time when the agency's healthcare delivery systems are being redesigned.

To address this challenge, the agency has recognized the importance of the "linked aims of improvement" of professional development, patient care, and system performance described by Batalden and Davidoff (2007) and has developed the model of patient-centered clinical education, which describes the integral relationship between caring for patients and educating healthcare professionals. Veterans' healthcare systems are being redesigned to advance goals supported by the Institute of Medicine (Health professions education 2003), among others, to provide patient-centered care, work in interprofessional teams, practice in an evidence-based fashion, and engage in continual quality improvement. Because many health professions education programs do not sufficiently emphasize such issues in their curricula, VA has recognized that it needs to promote greater engagement of trainees in these activities and focus broader attention on these issues in health professions education programs.

The remainder of this chapter describes the present scope of VA's educational programs and how they are projected to develop in the future.

Medical and Dental Education

Medical Education

VA is currently the second largest single funding source for graduate medical education (the Centers for Medicare and Medicaid is first). More than 98 percent of the agency's medical residency programs are sponsored in the name of academic affiliates, including about 112 of the nation's 133 allopathic and 15 of the nation's 26 osteopathic medical schools.

Annually more than 36,000 physician residents (approximately one-third of all U.S. physician residents) rotate through approximately 10,000 VA-funded positions (representing approximately 9 percent of all U.S. graduate medical education positions). Overall, 80 percent of VA's 153 hospitals host more than 2,000 accredited graduate medical education training programs. The agency is also a major site for undergraduate medical education, hosting over 20,000 medical students annually. Some 70 percent of all U.S. medical students report having trained in VA, and currently approximately 60 percent of the agency's staff physicians report having obtained part of their medical training in a VA healthcare setting.

Dental Education

VA is also an important site for dental training, with more than 600 dental residents and 650 dental students rotating through sixty-five VA facilities annually. Thus, the agency trains about 8 percent of all U.S. dental residents. Unlike graduate medical education, about one-third of VA dental residencies are directly sponsored by the agency itself rather than by an academic

Table 3.2. Approved Additional Resident Positions by Request for Proposals (RFP)

	Graduate Medical Education Positions Awarded (2006–2010)						
Request for Proposal	2006	2007	2008	2009	2010	Totals	%
Critical Needs & Emerging Specialties	300	294	212	147	212	1,165	78
New Affiliations & New Sites	42	41	50	76	48	257	17
Educational Innovation	(N/A)	21	7	10	8	46	3
Rural Health Training	(N/A)	(N/A)	(N/A)	21	(N/A)	21	2
Totals	342	356	269	254	268	1,489	100

affiliate. It is noteworthy that 80 percent of the agency-sponsored programs are in general-practice dentistry.

Graduate Medical Education Enhancement

Despite the looming shortage of physicians and the need to expand medical residency positions to accommodate increasing numbers of medical school graduates, VA is the only federal payer presently increasing funding for graduate medical education. The last five years have seen a major investment by the agency in expanding support for graduate medical education. The Graduate Medical Education Enhancement initiative was designed to add approximately 2,000 positions to the agency's preexisting 8,900 physician resident positions and to increase the agency's share of U.S. resident positions from a nadir of 8.5 percent to about 10–11 percent.

By the initiative's fifth year (2010), nearly 1,500 new physician resident positions had been added, as detailed in table 3.2. These new positions were awarded to 90 VA facilities in 73 different specialties and 1,052 individual training programs. Although most of the additional positions have been in traditional and emerging subspecialties, 20 percent have been in generalist specialties and 17 percent have been used in the development of new medical school affiliations or community-based training sites. About 80 percent of the new positions have been distributed to areas of the country (primarily the Southeast and West) to which veterans are moving in large numbers. More recently, emphasis has begun to shift toward supporting innovations in medical education, with particular interest in enhancing the primary care curriculum and learning environment and developing a viable educational infrastructure in rural sites of care.

Associated Health Professions Education

VA is an important site of associated health professions[1] education. For example, it is estimated that 50 percent of psychologists presently in practice in the United States received all or part of their clinical training in VA. These training programs are a major source for recruitment of associated healthcare clinicians, with as many as 70 percent of the agency's optometrists and psychologists receiving part or all of their clinical education in VA facilities (Report of the Blue Ribbon Panel 2009).

VA's associated health training programs have undergone considerable expansion over the past decade, with a 45 percent increase in funded positions and stipend expenditures. Among other factors, this has been driven by increased recognition of the critical role of associated health professions in the delivery of comprehensive healthcare and by the agency's strong commitment to enhancing mental health services for veterans, especially those returning from the wars in Iraq and Afghanistan.

Mental Health Education Enhancement

Since 2006 VA has committed to a major expansion of its mental health services and its mental health staffing. Coincident with the 50 percent increase in size of its mental health workforce, VA has also expanded its commitment to training of the mental health professions, particularly in psychology and social work, which have seen greater than 30 percent increases in funded training positions. Many of the agency's more than 7,000 new mental health professionals have come from its own training programs. This has allowed the agency to recruit professionals not only with demonstrated skills but also with known sensitivity to the complex mental health needs of veterans.

Nursing Education Enhancement

In recent years VA's innovative nursing policies and programs have addressed major challenges to the future of nursing. Nursing practice, education, and research have evolved in synchrony with trends in inpatient and outpatient care. The increasing need for clinically proficient and academically credentialed nurses to provide the complex care needed by veterans is amplified by the demographics of the profession. Sixty-six percent of currently employed VA nurses are baby boomers, and nearly 8,000 nurses were eligible for retirement in fiscal year 2011 alone. Although the state of the U.S. economy has caused many to postpone retirement, the agency still anticipates

Table 3.3. VA Nursing Academy (VANA) Partnership Sites

VA Facility	Affiliated School
2007 Partnerships	
Gainesville	University of Florida
Salt Lake City	University of Utah
San Diego	San Diego State University
West Haven	Fairfield University
2008 Partnerships	
Charleston	Medical University of South Carolina
Hines	Loyola University of Chicago
Michigan Consortia (Detroit and Saginaw)	University of Detroit Mercy/Saginaw Valley State University
Oklahoma City	University of Oklahoma Health Sciences Center
Providence	Rhode Island College
Tampa	University of South Florida
2009 Partnerships	
Asheville	Western Carolina University
Birmingham	University of Alabama at Birmingham
Honolulu	University of Hawaii at Mānoa
New York Harbor (Manhattan and Brooklyn)	Pace University
Pittsburgh	Waynesburg University

the need to hire approximately 41,000 registered nurses through fiscal year 2014 (*Workforce succession strategic plan* 2009).

A national survey conducted by the American Association of Colleges of Nursing found that in 2004 alone approximately 33,000 eligible nursing school applicants could not be admitted due to capacity constraints. Nearly 50 percent of the responding schools identified a shortage of faculty as the primary reason for the inability to admit students (Faculty shortages in baccalaureate and graduate nursing programs 2005). In 2007 the VA Nursing Academy was founded to address the nursing shortage by enhancing affiliations between the agency and the nation's nursing schools.

The major goals of this bold program are to expand nursing faculty and practice development, increase nursing student enrollment, provide opportunities for education and practice innovation, and increase VA nurse recruitment and retention. Initially begun at four sites, there are now fifteen partnerships across the country (table 3.3). College-based nursing faculty increased by 176 and VA-based faculty by 264 in 2.5 years. In fiscal year 2010, the partnerships accommodated more than 500 nursing students, and the program is on target to produce close to 1,760 graduate nurses by 2012. Following formal evaluation of this fifteen-site demonstration project, it is anticipated that the essential elements of this innovative program can be adopted nationwide.

Advanced Fellowships and Special Programs

Advanced Fellowships

In 1978 VA recognized that accredited educational programs were necessary but not sufficient to meet the agency's clinical and educational missions. There are two principal reasons to support nonaccredited educational programs. First, emerging clinical disciplines of importance to veterans' healthcare may not be sufficiently mature to merit recognition by professional regulatory groups, and therefore may require special sources of financial support. Second, some important fields of inquiry (for example health policy, research, informatics, patient safety), though not recognized clinical disciplines, profoundly affect VA and veterans' health.

The agency's first two nonaccredited fellowship programs, at the time called "special fellowships,"[2] were started in 1978. One program was geriatrics, representing a clinical field of importance to veterans' healthcare, but not at the time a medical specialty recognized by the American Board of Medical Specialties or the Accreditation Council for Graduate Medical Education. The agency's commitment to geriatrics fellowships had a profound impact on the development of the field, and professional recognition emerged ten years later (Warshaw et al. 2003). Other "special fellowships" likewise matured into recognized clinical specialties, including geriatric psychiatry, addiction psychiatry, palliative care, and spinal cord injury.[3] At the same time, advanced fellowships in these fields have been continued to provide even more advanced experiences and leadership development opportunities.

The second "special fellowship" initiated in 1978 was the collaborative development of the Robert Wood Johnson Foundation's Clinical Scholars Program, which continues to this day. From this nationally prestigious program's inception VA has funded close to 200 fellows, representing nearly one-fifth of participants. The proportion of fellowship positions supported by the agency has increased over time and reached approximately 30 percent in academic year 2011–2012 (27 outstanding young physicians 2010).

In addition to funding fellow stipends and benefits, the agency also provides significant in-kind contributions, including access to agency databases and research resources.

The advanced fellowship portfolio is dynamic, constantly adapting to emerging needs. Recently developed programs address health conditions such as polytrauma and epilepsy, as well as health system management issues such as health systems engineering, clinical informatics, and patient safety. The portfolio has nimbly adapted to various instructional designs, periodically rethinking program purposes and target audiences. In recognizing that most care is provided by teams of health professionals, advanced fellowships no longer solely support physician development but now frequently include support for interprofesssional learning. A case in point is the VA Quality Scholars Program (Splaine et al. 2009). Jointly supported by VA and the Robert Wood Johnson Foundation's Quality and Safety Education for Nurses Initiative, this program provides postresidency physicians and postdoctoral nurses with an integrated two-year curriculum for improving quality of care and patient safety. (See table 3.4.)

Advanced fellowship alumni have made important contributions to VA's research program as well. For example, approximately 20 percent of the agency's Health Services Research and Development Career Development Award recipients were prior advanced fellows. In addition, alumni have held countless leadership positions in VA; in other federal agencies; and in a variety of local, regional, and national professional organizations.

Special Programs

VA also sponsors several training programs that focus on the special needs of veterans. Among these are clinical training programs in orthotics and prosthetics and blind rehabilitation. Though small, these specially targeted programs have seen significant growth in recent years. The orthotics and prosthetics residency has more than doubled in size, while blind rehabilitation training positions have increased by nearly 30%.

Pre- and Postdoctoral Fellowships

To support the development of doctorally prepared social workers and nurses, VA sponsors pre- and postdoctoral fellowships directed at enhancing clinical leadership and research capacity for both the agency and the nation in these important disciplines. In collaboration with the Hartford Foundation and the Gerontological Society of America, postdoctoral VA social workers engaged in research on aging also have the opportunity to participate in the prestigious

Table 3.4. VA Advanced Fellowship Participant Completion 1995–2009

Program	1995	1996	1997	1999	1999	2000	2001	2002	2003	2004	2005	2006	2007	2008	2009	Grand Total
Advanced Geriatrics (GRECC)									3	6	9	3	3	8	7	39
Advanced Psychiatry (MIRECC)									1	2	8	5	5	8	4	33
Advanced Psychology (MIRECC)									4	9	6	9	1			29
Ambulatory Care		25	26	22	19	20	18	13	19	12	22	15	14	5		221
Clinical Pharmacolog		3	3	1	1											6
Dental Research		3	3	3	3	4	2	2	3	0	0	0	0	2	0	27
Geriatric Neurology		8	3	2	5	5	1	2	3	1	3	5	1	5	0	44
Health Issues of Women Veterans		4	6	4	5	3	6	8	4	3	6	8	5	7	3	72
Health Services Research		2	4	1	4	4	4	3	2	3	2	3	9	16	14	71
Medical Informatics (MD		2		5	6	3	5	2	4	4	6	1	3	2	4	48
Medical Informatics (PhD)								1	0	0	0	2	5	3	0	11
Medical Toxicology				1	5	3	4									13
Multiple Sclerosis											1	1	1	1	2	6
National Quality Scholars							7	7	7	6	8	9	7	8	12	71
Neurosci/Traumatic Brain Injury		1	4	9	2	0	1	3	0	1	0	1	0	0	1	23
Palliative Care										9	7	12	9	9	29	75
Parkinson's Disease (PADRECC)								1	3	6	4	5	4	6	6	35
Patient Safety														8	4	12
Psychiatric Research		1	3	4	2	3	5	1	3	3	5	1	2	4	3	40
RWJ Clinical Scholars		6	9	5	8	7	7	8	4	6	8	9	8	7	9	101
Schizo. Research	0	1	1	0	3	2	2	2	1	2	1	13	0		1	20
Spinal Cord Injury Med.	1	8	3	4	9	6	9	0	0	2	2	2	4	2	3	55
Substance Abuse Treatment	0	5	5	8	4	2	7	4	3	2	2	2	3	2	0	49
War Related Injury												2	3	4	0	9
Grand Total	1	65	73	68	72	64	77	61	55	77	100	96	89	110	102	1110

Hartford Faculty Scholars Program. The nursing predoctoral fellowship program provides opportunities for nurses to conduct dissertation studies at VA facilities nationwide in topics relevant to the care of veterans. The postdoctoral nurse fellowship program is designed to provide nurses who have already earned doctoral degrees with an opportunity to broaden their academic background or to extend their potential for clinical research in nursing.

Learning Organization Transformation

In 2007 the Office of Academic Affiliations partnered with the Employee Education System, National Center for Organization Development, and Office of Nursing Services with the goal of transforming VA into a leading learning organization. Specific objectives included creating a more flexible, adaptable, and productive organization that could excel in an environment of rapid change; driving toward excellent individual and system performance; striving for high quality; rapidly adopting innovation and best practices; and motivating its employees to be curious and excited about learning.

Every VA and Veterans Integrated Service Network (VISN) facility was required to appoint a designated learning officer to serve as the focal point for local learning efforts for both staff and trainees. The Learning Organization Transformation Workgroup of the Human Resources Committee of VA's National Leadership Board was constituted to formulate strategy and measure progress in the learning organization journey.

New collaborative efforts with the academic community and private sector have been important components of this effort. In particular, joint projects with the Harvard Business School and the Masie Organization have led to the creation of innovative tools to determine and monitor the state of organizational learning. Drawing on findings from a variety of instruments (including the VA All Employee Survey, the Harvard Learning Organization Survey, the Masie Voice of the Learner Survey, and an Inventory of Educational/Learning Assets and Resources), a picture of VA as a learning organization and national benchmarks for healthcare organizations are being constructed. Goals include the creation of uniform methodologies to inventory and track learning resources on an enterprisewide basis coupled with the deployment of new strategies to enhance the effectiveness of learning.

This broad-based educational initiative complements and amplifies parallel work in clinical redesign and system transformation. Through systematic changes in areas such as primary care, care coordination, mental health programs, quality and safety programs, and many others, veterans' healthcare continues to distinguish itself from healthcare provided in other settings

(Longman 2010). In response to the need to ensure that health professions education in VA is "the best education anywhere," the agency is investing in sponsorship of an increasing array of innovative educational programs (e.g., the Graduate Medical Education Enhancement initiative, the VA Nursing Academy, Rural Health initiatives, and Primary Care Education Centers of Excellence, noted later in this discussion) that also support broader transformational goals (e.g., the agency's national adoption of patient-aligned care teams, modeled on the concept of the patient-centered medical home).

It is becoming increasingly apparent that the agency can no longer rely solely on educational evaluation strategies provided by the broader academic community. Therefore it has begun to invest in expanding its own educational evaluation capability. VA's Learners' Perception Survey has provided a robust tool to measure the satisfaction with and perceptions of the educational experience of health professions trainees (Cannon et al. 2008; Keitz et al. 2003). Irrespective of discipline, trainees are very satisfied: in 2010, for example, trainees offered an overall score of 87 on a 100-point scale expressing their level of satisfaction, and 88 percent stated that their VA training was as good as or better than their training experiences at other clinical sites.

The Learners Perception Survey is currently (in 2012) being used to *directly* contrast VA training with training at academic affiliates, from which important quality benchmarks are likely to emerge. However, additional evaluation strategies are needed to assess processes and outcomes of new educational programs and their relationship to clinical processes and outcomes. Much of this work will take place in VA's new Centers of Excellence in Primary Care Education, which began training in 2011. Another area of particular interest is the development of quantitative methods for assessing the quality of trainee supervision and the relationship between supervision and learning and patient outcomes (Byrne et al. 2010; Kashner et al. 2010a, 2010b).

Health Professions Education in the Twenty-First Century

The fundamental benefits of a strong academic mission for a largely hospital-based twentieth-century healthcare system have been well recognized and appropriately lauded (Gronvall 1987; Petersdorf 1987). Although many of the healthcare needs of veterans endure across conflicts (Hawley 1945; Magnuson 1951), the twenty-first century has presented new challenges that VA has risen to meet (Statement of the honorable Eric K. Shinseki 2009). At the same time, the vital role of VA's educational programs in the development and recruitment of health professionals with new or unique clinical expertise (e.g., mental health, polytrauma) will only increase.

There is a pressing need to redesign VA's overall healthcare system to enhance services to all veterans. It is fortunate that the agency is not constrained by some of the factors faced by other sectors of the U.S. healthcare system, including health insurance eligibility, fragmentation or limitation of insurance benefits, and misaligned financial incentives, to name but a few examples. Instead, VA is in an excellent position to seize the opportunity presented by national healthcare reform to focus on redesigning its healthcare system to achieve the goal of personalized, high-quality care delivered efficiently when and where needed.

In the same way that VA has recognized that healthcare systems need not be dictated by those in the private sector, it is also true that health professions education need not be confined by the professional structures and processes that emerged nationally out of the patchwork of financial and other forces over the past century. A new vision is emerging in which VA, as the nation's largest health professions educational system, has a voice equal to that of its academic affiliates in determining both the content and process of health professions education. Such voices have already been raised, perhaps starting in 1978 with the agency's sponsorship of advanced fellowships and more recently with the expansion of mental health training programs and nurse training capacity.

Notwithstanding these important developments, it may be that the agency's loudest "educational voice" will come from its recent investment in Centers of Excellence in Primary Care Education, an unprecedented initiative to fund curriculum development and evaluation at up to six VA medical facilities to foster the integration of patient-centered, interprofessional primary care education for physician residents and advanced practice nursing students. Though this program is being developed in close collaboration with local schools of medicine and nursing, VA itself has established the parameters within which these pilot projects will function, including carefully defined curriculum requirements. In 2011 each of these sites was provided with up to $1 million annually to support curriculum development and evaluation efforts over a five-year period.

Despite ever-present challenges to academic development, with forward-thinking initiatives such as these and continued strengthening of the agency's commitment to the foundational clinical goals of interprofessionalism, patient-centeredness, and systemwide quality and safety, VA will continue to play a leadership role in health professions education far into the future, thereby fulfilling its primary mission of maintaining and improving the health of those who have served their nation so well.

Notes

1. VA uses the term "associated health" rather than the more commonly used "allied health" to refer to all healthcare professions other than medicine and dentistry. The associated health professions encompass about forty specialties, among them audiology, dietetics, laboratory technology, nursing, occupational and physical therapy, optometry, pharmacy, podiatry, psychology, and social work.
2. To more accurately identify the nature of these programs, in 2005 the name of this training portfolio was changed to "advanced fellowships."
3. It is important to emphasize that advanced fellowships never compete with accredited clinical programs. In those cases where training has subsequently become accredited, the agency requires participants to have completed the relevant accredited training as an eligibility requirement for the advanced fellowship.

References

Batalden, P. B. & Davidoff, F. (2007). What is "quality improvement" and how can it transform healthcare? *Quality and Safety in Health Care* 16: 2–3.

Byrne, J. M., Kashner, T. M., Gilman, S. C., Aron, D. C., Cannon, G. W., Chang, B. K., et al. (2010). Measuring the intensity of resident supervision in the Department of Veterans Affairs: The resident supervision index. *Academic Medicine* 85, no. 7: 1171–1181.

Cannon, G. W., Keitz, S. A., Holland, G. J., Chang, B. K., Byrne, J. M., Tomolo, A., et al. (2008). Factors determining medical students' and residents' satisfaction during VA-based training: findings from the VA Learners' Perceptions Survey. *Academic Medicine* 83. no. 6: 611–620.

Faculty shortages in baccalaureate and graduate nursing programs: Scope of the problem and strategies for expanding the supply. (2005). American Association of Colleges of Nursing. http://www.aacn.nche.edu/publications/pdf/05FacShortage .pdf (accessed October 24, 2010).

Gronvall, J. (1987). The VA-medical school partnership: The VA perspective. *Journal of Medical Education* 62, no. 3: 158–162.

Hawley, P. R. (1945). Address to the House of Delegates, AMA. *JAMA* 129, no. 17: 1192–1194.

Health professions education: A bridge to quality. (2003). Institute of Medicine. http://books.nap.edu/openbook.php?record_id=10681&page=R1# (accessed October 24, 2010).

Kashner, T. M., Byrne, J. M., Chang, B. K., Henley, S. S., Golden, R. M., Aron, D. C., et al. (2010a). Measuring progressive independence with the resident supervision index: Empirical approach. *Journal of Graduate Medical Education* 2, no. 1: 17–30.

Kashner, T. M., Byrne, J. M., Chang, B. K., Henley, S. S., Golden, R. M., Aron, D. C., et al. (2010b). Measuring progressive independence with the resident supervision index: Theoretical approach. *Journal of Graduate Medical Education* 2, no. 1: 8–16.

Keitz, S. A., Holland, G. J., Melander, E. H., Hayden, B. B., Pincus, S. H. & Group, V. L. P. W. (2003). The VA Learners' Perceptions Survey: The foundation for educational quality improvement. *Academic Medicine* 99, no. 9: 910–917.

Longman, P. (2010). *Best care anywhere: Why VA health care is better than yours.* 2nd ed. Sausalito, CA: PoliPointPress.

Magnuson, P. B. (1951). Medical care for veterans. *The Annals of the American Academy of Political and Social Science* 273, no. 1: 76–83.

Petersdorf, R. (1987). The VA–medical school partnership: The medical school perspective. *Journal of Medical Education* 62, no. 3: 153–157.

The report of the Blue Ribbon Panel on VA–Medical School Affiliations: Transforming an historic partnership for the 21st century. (2009). Veterans Health Administration. http://www4.va.gov/oaa/archive/BRP-final-report.pdf (accessed September 27, 2010).

Splaine, M. E., Ogrinc, G., Gilman, S. C., Aron, D. C., Estrada, C. A., Rosenthal, G. E., et al. (2009). The Department of Veterans Affairs National Quality Scholars Fellowship Program: Experience from 10 years of training quality scholars. *Academic Medicine* 84, no. 12: 1741–1748.

Statement of the honorable Eric K. Shinseki. (2009). http://veterans.house.gov/hearings/Testimony.aspx?TID=53305&Newsid=382&Name=The%20Honorable%20Eric%20K.%20Shinseki (accessed September 24, 2010).

Trivedi, A. N., Matula, S., Miake-Lye, I., Glassman, P. A., Shekelle, P. & Asch, S. (2011). Systematic review: Comparison of the quality of medical care in Veterans Affairs and non–Veterans Affairs settings. *Medical Care* 49, no. 1: 76–88.

27 outstanding young physicians selected for prestigious national fellowship. (2010). Robert Wood Johnson Foundation. http://rwjcsp.unc.edu/resources/pressreleases/2011-13_CSP_New_Scholars.pdf (accessed July 15, 2010).

Veterans Administration Policy Memorandum No. 2. (1946). http://www4.va.gov/oaa/Archive/PolicyMemo2.pdf (accessed September 19, 2010).

Warshaw, G. A., Bragg, E. J., Shaull, R. W., Goldenhar, L. M. & Lindsell, C. J. (2003). Geriatric medicine fellowship programs: A national study from the Association of Directors of Geriatric Academic Programs' longitudinal study of training and practice in geriatric medicine. *Journal of the American Geriatrics Society* 51, no. 7: 1023–1030.

Workforce succession strategic plan. (2009). Veterans Health Administration HPDM National Program Office.

Chapter 4

Veterans' Healthcare: Legislative Initiatives

Thomas W. Miller, with assistance from
Jacqueline D. Rychnovsky and Corina M. Barrow,
through the Congressional Office of Senator Daniel Inouye

Introduction

This chapter examines the public laws, congressional testimony, and congressional reports that have produced relevant legislation for veterans' healthcare in the U.S. Congress. The chronology of laws affecting compensation for injured and disabled veterans and their dependents through veterans' healthcare is the primary focus. The chapter highlights some of the significant legislation that has been the basis for understanding the healthcare benefits for which veterans are eligible. It is not intended to be all-encompassing, but rather an overview. Details and more complete legislative chronology are available through the Department of Veterans Affairs (VA) and veterans' organizations that have crafted such legislation. The focus is on the key enacted legislation affecting disability care and compensation from World War I through the first decade of the twenty-first century.

Early Healthcare Legislation for War-Wounded

VA reports that the United States has the most comprehensive system of assistance for veterans of any nation in the world. These benefits can be traced back to 1636, when the Pilgrims of Plymouth Colony were at war with the Pequot Indians. The Pilgrims passed a law stating that disabled soldiers would be supported by the colony. The Continental Congress of 1776 encouraged enlistments during the Revolutionary War by providing pensions for soldiers who were disabled. Direct medical and hospital care given to veterans in the early days of the Republic was provided by the individual states and communities. In 1811 the first domiciliary and medical facility for veterans was authorized by the federal government. In the nineteenth century the nation's veterans' assistance program was expanded to include benefits and pensions for not only veterans, but also their widows and dependents.

Following the Civil War, many state veterans' homes were established throughout the country. Because domiciliary care was available at state veterans' homes, incidental medical and hospital treatment was provided for all injuries and diseases, whether or not of service origin. Indigent and disabled veterans of the Civil War, Indian Wars, Spanish-American War, and Mexican border conflicts, as well as discharged regular members of the armed forces, were cared for at these homes. Congress established a new system of veterans' benefits when the United States entered World War I in 1917. Among the legislative initiatives were programs for disability compensation, insurance for servicepersons and veterans, and vocational rehabilitation for the disabled. Healthcare of veterans became one of the critical targets for such legislation. In the 1920s the various benefits were administered by three federal agencies: the Veterans' Bureau, the Bureau of Pensions of the Interior Department, and the National Home for Disabled Volunteer Soldiers.

Contemporary healthcare for veterans began in the twentieth century. Veterans' healthcare legislation in 1917 included the model for an initial rating schedule for assessing the degree of injury experienced by veterans during military action. Congressional efforts to recognize veterans' healthcare needs and support for rehabilitation of injured veterans were realized in 1918 through vocational rehabilitation for veterans provided by the War Risk Insurance Act. In 1924 Congress provided for a rating schedule recognizing the effects of disability on the preservice occupations of the veterans injured during combat. A major step in healthcare provision was taken by legislative initiatives in 1930, when the Veterans Administration and a hospital system to serve veterans' postmilitary healthcare needs were created.

Creating the Veterans Administration

The Veterans Administration was established in 1930 when Congress authorized the president to "consolidate and coordinate Government activities affecting war veterans" (U.S. Department of Veterans Affairs 2008). The three component agencies became bureaus within the Veterans Administration. Brigadier General Frank T. Hines, who directed the Veterans' Bureau for seven years, was named as the first administrator of veterans' affairs, a job he held until 1945. The VA healthcare system has grown from 54 hospitals in 1930 to 173 medical centers; more than 350 outpatient, community, and outreach clinics; 126 nursing home care units; and 35 domiciliary facilities. VA healthcare facilities provide a broad spectrum of medical, surgical, and rehabilitative care. The responsibilities and benefits programs of the Veterans Administration grew enormously during the following six decades. World War II resulted not only in a vast increase in the veteran population, but also in a large number of new benefits provided by Congress for veterans of the war.

The G.I. Bill, signed into law on June 22, 1944, is said to have had a greater impact on the American way of life than any law since the Homestead Act in 1862. Further educational assistance acts were passed for the benefit of veterans of the Korean conflict, Vietnam Era, Persian Gulf War, and All-Volunteer Force.

Through the efforts of veterans' advocates, congressional legislation generated in 1933 provided for those veterans who qualified a cost of living index as the basis for valuing disability compensation. This was followed in 1937 by legislation that provided for veterans who lose both eyes, both feet, both hands, or any combination to be labeled "totally disabled," a term that had not been previously used, and tied it to compensation and care. Anticipating a draft, congressional legislation led to disabled veterans' benefits guaranteed to service members disabled in the line of duty. With the beginning of the American involvement in World War II, disability pensions were provided at "wartime rates" for veterans injured in action.

The G.I. Bill of Rights

After considerable efforts on the part of advocates for veterans and a spectrum of veterans' organizations, including the American Legion and Veterans of Foreign Wars, Congress passed legislation that provided for a new rating and compensation schedule, which provided 10 percent increment ratings for disability. Harry W. Colmery, a World War I veteran and the former Republican National Committee chairman, wrote the first draft of the G.I. Bill. Senator Ernest McFarland was actively involved in the bill's passage and is known, with Warren Atherton, as one of the "fathers of the G.I. Bill." Edith Nourse Rogers (R-Mass.), who helped write and who cosponsored the legislation, might be called the "mother of the G.I. Bill." Like Colmery, her contribution to writing and passing this legislation has been obscured by time. The bill was introduced in the House on January 10, 1944, and in the Senate the following day. The G.I. Bill was created to prevent a repetition of the Bonus March of 1932 and a relapse into the Great Depression after World War II ended.

This congressional legislation became the basis for future rate increases through the Servicemen's Readjustment Act of 1944, also known as the G.I. Bill of Rights. It was congressional intent that this series of benefits provide assistance and compensation to help veterans in their transition to civilian life. The G.I. Bill (P.L. 78-346, 58 Stat. 284m) was an omnibus bill that provided not only healthcare benefits but also college or vocational education for returning World War II veterans, who were commonly referred to as G.I.s, as well as one year of unemployment compensation. This legislation further provided many different types of loans for returning veterans to buy homes and start businesses. Since the original act, the term has come to include other veterans' benefit programs created to assist veterans of subsequent wars as well as those who served in peacetime. By the time the original G.I. Bill expired in July 1956, 7.8 million World War II veterans had participated in an education or training program, and 2.4 million veterans had home loans backed by the Veterans Administration. For veterans in the twenty-first century, the legacy of the original G.I. Bill lives on in the congressional efforts known as the Montgomery G.I. Bill.

Congressional legislation initiated in 1946 determined that veterans could not receive both institutional care and full disability compensation at the same time. In 1948 the Veterans Administration was authorized to pay up to 50 percent of special adaptive housing costs, and in 1954 disability compensation rates were increased by 5 percent.

All laws concerning veterans' benefits were updated in the Veterans Benefits Act of 1957. In 1960 Congress provided through legislation for extension of benefits for some non-service-connected disabilities and benefits for veterans first returning from Vietnam, finally realized in the Veterans Readjustment Benefits Act of 1966.

Veterans Readjustment Benefits Act of 1966

Whereas the G.I. Bills of 1944 and 1952 were designed to compensate veterans for wartime service, the Veterans Readjustment Benefits Act of 1966 changed the nature of military service in America by extending benefits to veterans who served during times of war and peace. At first there was some opposition to the concept of a peacetime G.I. Bill. President Dwight Eisenhower had rejected such a measure in 1959 after the Bradley Commission concluded that military service should be "an obligation of citizenship, not a basis for government benefits" (U.S. Department of Veterans Affairs 2008). President

Lyndon B. Johnson believed that many of his Great Society social programs negated the need for sweeping veterans' benefits. But prompted by unanimous support given the bill by Congress, Johnson signed it into law on March 3, 1966. Veterans of the Vietnam War disliked the fact that the bill did not provide them with the same educational opportunities that their World War II predecessors had received. Consequently, during the early years of the program, only about 25 percent of Vietnam veterans used their education benefits. Compensation categories for POWs were developed in congressional legislation introduced in 1970.

Congress raised funding levels during the next decade, resulting in increased numbers of veterans entering higher education. By the mid-1970s, ten years after the first veterans became eligible, the highest numbers of Vietnam-era veterans were enrolled in colleges and universities. By the end of the program, proportionally more Vietnam-era veterans had used their benefits for higher education than any previous generation of veterans. The Veterans' Disability Compensation and Survivors' Benefits Act of 1978 and the Former Prisoner of War Act of 1981 provided for veterans' care.

Veterans Educational Assistance Program (VEAP)

In 1973 the U.S. military became an all-volunteer force, and veterans continued to receive benefits in part as an inducement to enlist, under the Veterans Educational Assistance Program (VEAP) and the Montgomery G.I. Bill (MGIB). Congressional efforts led by Congressman Gillespie V. "Sonny" Montgomery expanded the G.I. Bill. The Montgomery G.I. Bill replaced the Veterans Educational Assistance Program for those who served after July 1, 1985. This was an entirely voluntary program in which participants could choose to forfeit $100 per month from their first year of pay. In return, eligible veterans received a tuition allowance and a monthly stipend for up to thirty-six months of eligible training or education. With Vietnam veterans struggling with a variety of disorders, in 1984 Congress generated the Veterans' Dioxin and Radiation Exposure Compensation Standards Act. Toxic defoliants used in Vietnam have had a negative effect on veterans. Additional legislation addressing these problems are the Radiation Exposed Veterans' Compensation Act of 1988 and the Agent Orange Act of 1991.

Both the Americans with Disabilities Act of 1990 and the Omnibus Budget Reconciliation Act of 1990 include benefits for veterans' healthcare.

VA was established as a cabinet-level agency on March 15, 1989. President George H. W. Bush hailed the creation of the new department, saying, "There is only one place for the veterans of America, in the Cabinet Room, at the table with the President of the United States of America" (U.S. Department of Veterans Affairs 2008). James C. Holsinger (see chapter 2) was appointed the first under secretary for veterans' health. Restoration of Disability Compensation Rights (P.L. 76-179) was approved with the passage of the Veterans Benefits and Health Care Improvement Act of 2000 (P.L. 106-419).

The Veterans Mental Health and Other Care Improvements Act of 2008

Senator Daniel K. Akaka (D-Hawaii), chairman of the Veterans' Affairs Committee, expressed great satisfaction with Senate passage of S. 2162, a sweeping veterans' mental health care bill: "S. 2162, the Veterans Mental Health and Other Care Improvements Act of 2008, passed the Senate today by unanimous consent. The bill makes various improvements to veterans' mental health care and other forms of health care, and is a tribute to Iraq war veteran Justin Bailey. Justin's story is far too common: he survived the war in Iraq only to be lost to post traumatic stress disorder and substance abuse-related suicide. An effort to educate the congress and the public about the mental health needs of military veterans was realized with this legislation. The 'invisible wounds of war,' including post traumatic stress disorder, are an injury—and an enemy—that many veterans face when they return home from war." This bill provided for better mental health support for wounded warriors facing mental health as well as physical health needs.

This legislation focused on improvements to veterans' mental health care and included

- setting a standard minimum level of care for substance use disorder and creating innovative enhancements to treatment;

- improving treatment to veterans with multiple disorders, such as post-traumatic stress disorder (PTSD) and substance use disorder;

- mandating the Veterans Healthcare Administration's (VHA) residential mental healthcare facilities, to ensure that they are adequately staffed;

- creating a research program on PTSD and substance use disorder, in cooperation with the National Center for Posttraumatic Stress Disorder; and

- enabling VHA to provide mental health services to veterans' families and setting up a program to aid the families of returning service members.

This legislation also made significant improvements in other areas of veterans' healthcare. The needs of rural and underserved veteran populations were recognized. Access to healthcare was essential. The legislation more than doubled the beneficiary travel mileage reimbursement (from 11 to 28.5 cents per mile) that eligible veterans can receive for travel to receive VA care; permanently set the deductible to $3 each way for such travel; created a pilot program on the use of peers to enhance outreach to rural veterans; and encouraged coordination between VHA facilities and rural, community-based resources.

Among the concerns for veterans' healthcare was emergency care. The legislation adjusted several procedures used by VA to reimburse community hospitals for emergency care provided to eligible veterans.

VHA created the VA Epilepsy Centers of Excellence. Recognizing the link between traumatic brain injury (TBI), a signature wound of the current conflicts in Iraq and Afghanistan, and epilepsy, the legislation established the foundation and dollars for six VHA Epilepsy Centers of Excellence focused on research, education, and clinical care for epilepsy.

Pain experienced by veterans also became an important focus of this legislation. Provisions in the legislation required a pain care program for all VHA inpatient facilities for long-term mental health and substance abuse care to prevent long-term chronic pain disability. It also expanded VHA healthcare staff to enroll in education programs on pain assessment and treatment and increased funding for VHA research targeting pain care and treatment.

Caregivers for veterans who have experienced invisible wounds of war were also addressed in this legislation. Authority was extended for VHA to provide institutional and noninstitutional long-term care and caregiver assistance. Authorized by this legislation was a series of major medical facility construction projects and outpatient clinic leases. The legislation created targeted programs to assist low-income veterans and increased funding capacity for the successful VHA grant and per diem program, which assisted community-based organizations that serve homeless veterans.

Perhaps one of the most significant aspects of this legislation was the healthcare to be provided for female veterans. Special attention was given in this legislation to special reviews of all veterans' medical facilities to ensure that they are providing the necessary healthcare and treatment for female veterans. It further emphasized psychosocial rehabilitation for returning veterans and expanded a program to help formerly incarcerated veterans reintegrate into society through employment counseling and other services. S. 2162 provided the foundation for present-day healthcare for women veterans and their children. The bill was passed by the Senate Committee, then by the full Senate unanimously before being amended in the House and passed by that body, then forwarded for signature by the president on October 10, 2008.

Veterans' Emergency Fairness Act of 2009

The Veterans' Emergency Fairness Act of 2009 was viewed by veterans and the veterans' organizations as very important legislation that amended existing statutes to allow VHA to reimburse eligible veterans for portions of emergency treatment that are not covered by their private insurance. Before this change in the law, VHA could only pay outside hospitals directly or reimburse veterans in cases where they did not have private health insurance. Veterans enrolled in VA healthcare had limited private health insurance, and this legislation helped to correct previous inequities in the law and to ensure that a trip to the emergency room doesn't cause financial ruin for those who honorably and selflessly served this nation. American Legion National Commander Clarence Hill strongly supported this legislation. The American Legion appreciated Congress recognizing the need for this legislation and the president for acting quickly to sign it into law. This legislation, introduced by Senator Daniel Akaka (D-Hawaii), also allowed VA to reimburse veterans retroactively for emergency care received before the bill's passage.

The Post-9/11 G.I. Bill

In 2010 Congress passed the Post-9/11 Veterans Education Assistance Improvements Act of 2010. This legislation, often referred to as G.I. Bill 2.0, expands eligibility for members of the National Guard to include time served on Title 32 or in the full-time Active Guard and Reserve (AGR). It does not, however, cover members of the Coast Guard Reserve who have served under Title 14 orders performing duties comparable to those performed by National Guard personnel under Title 32 orders. In addition to special veterans' healthcare provisions, the bill also provides for housing, tuition, and fees for educational study, with an annual cap on such coverage. These changes went into effect in August and October 2011.

The Caregivers and Veterans Omnibus Health Services Act of 2010

The Caregivers and Veterans Omnibus Health Services Act expanded mental health counseling and services for military veterans from Afghanistan and

Iraq, including National Guardsmen and Reservists. This legislation directed VHA to utilize hospitals and clinics outside its system to serve more wounded warriors with TBI. It increased support to veterans in rural and underserved areas with transportation and housing while they receive healthcare treatment and rehabilitation at VHA hospitals and clinics. It also made improvements in healthcare for women veterans to meet their unique needs, including maternity care for newborn children. Furthermore, this legislation provided the funding for launching a pilot program to provide child care for veterans receiving intensive medical care. The legislation eliminated copays for veterans who are catastrophically disabled. The legislation further expanded support to homeless veterans and supported a five-year effort to eliminate homeless veterans by providing domiciliary care for eligible veterans. Finally, this legislation marked a major step forward in America's commitment to families and caregivers who tend to wounded warriors every day. This includes spouses, parents, and sons and daughters of veterans. Much of this was accomplished by the collaborative efforts of veterans' organizations, which fought for this legislation, and it is a tribute to those who provided the leadership in Congress, including World War II veteran Senator Daniel Akaka, Senator Richard Burr, and Representatives Mike Michaud and Bob Filner.

The Caregivers and Veterans Omnibus Health Services Act of 2010 directed the secretary of veterans affairs to establish a program of comprehensive assistance for family caregivers of any veteran who (1) is undergoing medical discharge from the armed forces; (2) has a serious injury that was incurred or aggravated in the line of duty on or after September 11, 2001; and (3) is in need of personal care services. Included among such assistance are personal care services instruction and training, ongoing technical support, counseling, and lodging and subsistence while accompanying the veteran for VHA medical care. The legislation also made family caregivers of veterans eligible for VHA counseling and mental health services. Accountability for healthcare for women veterans became a priority. This legislation authorized VHA to furnish care to a newborn child of a woman veteran receiving VA maternity care for up to seven days after the birth of the child.

This legislation further required the secretary to establish a three-year pilot program on financial incentives for VHA physicians who assume and maintain inpatient responsibilities at community hospitals in health professional shortage areas. It directed the secretary to compensate participating physicians for such responsibilities carried out for which the physician would not otherwise be compensated by VHA. The legislation required a written agreement between VA and the physician with respect to compensation amounts and directed the secretary to report annually to Congress on the pilot program.

In Section 307 of this legislation Congress directed the secretary to make grants to state veterans' service agencies and to veterans' service organizations to provide innovative transportation options for veterans in highly rural areas. This effort was to improve access to healthcare for rural veteran populations who resided in underserved areas. Section 308 amended the Veterans' Mental Health and Other Care Improvements Act of 2008 to revise eligibility requirements for participation in a pilot program of enhanced VA contract of care for the healthcare needs of VHA-enrolled veterans residing at substantial distances from VA facilities providing primary, acute hospital, and tertiary care.

Improved Veterans' Mental Healthcare

Veterans' mental healthcare needs were also addressed by this legislation, which directed VHA to provide mental healthcare to any veteran serving in Operations Iraqi Freedom or Enduring Freedom who is eligible for readjustment counseling and related mental health services through the Veterans Health Administration's Readjustment Counseling Service, regardless of whether the member is on active duty at the time of receipt of such counseling and services. In addition, this legislation required (1) studying the number of veterans who died by suicide between January 1, 1999, and the date of enactment of the act and (2) reporting the study results to the veterans' committees. It repealed the requirement for annual reports on (1) pay adjustments for registered nurses and (2) VA long-range health planning. It authorized disclosure of VA medical information to a representative of a patient who lacks decision-making capacity.

The legislation further required (1) VHA's under secretary of health to designate a national quality management officer for VHA quality assurance programs; (2) each Veterans Integrated Service Network regional director to appoint a quality management officer; and (3) each VHA medical facility director to appoint a quality management officer. Also, the legislation authorized the secretary to utilize non-VHA facilities for the care and treatment of veterans suffering from TBI. Notably, the legislation gave veterans who have been awarded the Medal of Honor the same priority in VHA provision of hospital care and medical services as had been provided for veterans who were former prisoners of war or were awarded the Purple Heart.

Recognizing the distinctions among VHA's programs that provide disability benefits was important. VA has two basic disability benefits programs—compensation and pension. The Disability Compensation Program pays monthly benefits to qualifying veterans who have service-connected disabilities (injuries or diseases incurred or aggravated while on active service in the military not due to willful misconduct, either in wartime or peacetime). Compensation amounts are based on the veteran's degree of disability, regardless of whether the veteran is employed or how much he or she earns. In contrast, the Pension Program assists permanently and totally disabled wartime veterans under age sixty-five who have low incomes and disabilities that are not service-connected or are sixty-five or older with low incomes. The payment amount is determined on the basis of financial need. The law also required its budgetary effects, for purposes of compliance with the Statutory Pay-As-You-Go Act of 2010, to be determined by reference to the latest statement titled "Budgetary Effects of PAYGO Legislation," provided that such statement has been submitted prior to the vote on passage.

One of the challenges of this report on the history of veterans' disability benefits has been to distinguish between these two programs in the early years, before a clear distinction was made. Legislation from around the time of World War I often and repeatedly used the word *pension* to refer to service-connected disability compensation. Therefore, in analyzing legislation, Congress had to be mindful of this use of terminology to determine whether or not a given legislative provision applied. The law is much clearer beginning in 1946 (P.L. No. 79-494), when Congress legislated that under the laws administered by the Veterans Administration, monetary benefits, other than retirement pay, for service-connected disability or death, are to be designated "compensation," not "pension." Legislation affecting the Veterans' Disability Compensation Program impacts a number of topics. There are two apparent trends: the high frequency of legislation on the impact of economics on disability payments through the 1950s decreased, whereas the frequency of legislation on presumptions increased.

Veterans Organizations: Advocacy for Veterans' Healthcare

Various veterans' organizations have played critical roles in framing the needed healthcare over the past several decades. The American Legion, Paralyzed Veterans of America (PVA), Veterans of Foreign Wars (VFW), AmVets, and other veterans' organizations have been necessary and essential contributors to initiating the legislation that has provided healthcare to our veteran populations. Centers of Excellence in research, education and clinical treatment of multiple sclerosis (MS) was an idea long championed by the PVA. Two MS centers were to be created at the Baltimore VA medical center and jointly at the Portland and Seattle medical centers. Both facilities were to coordinate current MS programs at other VA locations. PVA tenaciously pursued a coordinated system of care within VHA, with the goal of ensuring veterans with MS the highest quality of healthcare, the most advanced therapies and rehabilitation services possible.

The PVA's determination to make the MS centers a reality required an ongoing advocacy effort with VA, where agency officials were persuaded of the need for coordinated MS care. Because funding was required to implement the Centers of Excellence concept, PVA staff worked with Sen. Barbara Mikulski (D-Md.), chair of the VA, HUD and Independent Agencies Subcommittee of the Senate Appropriations Committee, to secure the funding for the centers; she inserted language in the FY 2001 VA appropriations bill. Currently, MS afflicts more than 22,000 veterans, and of these, about 7,000 receive care in VHA facilities each year. Nationally, MS affects 350,000 people.

VA notes that each MS center is to conduct research on biomedicine, rehabilitation, health services delivery, and clinical trials. Taking advantage of the advances in telemedicine, the centers will offer their expertise to VHA staff and patients around the country. PVA, which was chartered by Congress, has for more than fifty-five years served the needs of its members, all of whom have catastrophic paralysis caused by spinal cord injury or disease. To learn more about PVA, visit its Web site at http://www.pva.org.

The American Legion has long been vigilant on recurring budget and funding issues. These include VA funding—support for mandatory funding for a large part of the VA budget so that it can function without having to go through the budget process each year; Department of Defense funding—support for adequate funding for our military's daily salaries, housing, and the equipment they need to complete their mission; state veterans' homes—support for adequate funding for veterans in these facilities; and Department of Housing and Urban Development and Department of Labor funding—support for adequate funding for initiatives related to affordable housing and job training and placement and transition assist programs (TAP).

Current areas of focus in veterans' healthcare are the Wounded Warrior Act, which will provide support for returning wounded soldiers; and long delays in processing VA claims—supporting legislation aimed at reducing the backlog within the VA system. Another critical issue is the need for the veteran to prove that health issues are combat-related—the burden of proof should be placed more on the military record. The classifications and effects of PTSD and TBI can cause serious problems for returning military and should be given special attention. Funding is needed for studies and care for veterans with these conditions.

Women veterans' issues include PTSD and military sexual trauma (MST). They are among the highest priority for veterans' organization as women have a greater presence in the active military. Those who support the Women Veterans Health Care Improvement Act note that the VA system has historically been a male-oriented system. It is time to look carefully at health issues faced by women in the military, now 15 percent of total personnel. Homeless veterans are still another priority, and these include both male and female veterans. Continuing efforts focus on minimizing the VA claims backlog, decreasing veteran unemployment, and improving VA healthcare. Legislative history and information on activities are available at www.vfw.org.

AMVETS veterans organization joined Rep. John Carter (R-Tex.) and Rep. Michele Bachmann (R-Minn.) to advocate for the Veterans for Equal Treatment of Service Dogs Act, or VETS Dogs Act, a critical piece of legislation that will permanently close a loophole in VA policy that has created hurdles to care for disabled veterans. Under current VA policy, only seeing-eye and guide dogs are offered unrestricted access to VA healthcare facilities. Veterans who utilize service dogs as VA-sanctioned prosthetic devices for other physical injuries can still be denied access at the discretion of each VA medical center director. VA made an effort to close this loophole through a directive on service dog access, but veterans' advocates say the legislative solution will offer the permanent equality in access that veterans deserve. Representatives John Carter, John Stone, and Fred Downes have said that they are not trying to be critical of VA, which has made a concerted effort to rectify an unfortunate situation for affected veterans, but that the purpose of the legislation is to ensure that VA has the requisite policies in place to ensure veterans and their service dogs will not be denied care in the future. AMVETS legislative efforts are listed at www.amvets.org/.

Concluding Thoughts on Veterans' Legislation

Legislation drives the system of providing veterans with the healthcare they deserve. In recent years the number of patients served by the medical system of VA has increased substantially. At the same time, VA's ratings for the quality of care and customer satisfaction have apparently improved. Many people both within and outside the department have pointed to several factors as being key to achieving those results: organizational restructuring designed to share decision-making authority among officials in the central office, regional managers, and key personnel at dispersed medical facilities; performance measurement targeted toward improving the quality of care; and extensive use of health information technology. Without advocacy through the recognized veterans' organizations, the leadership provided in both the Senate and House of Representatives of the Congress of the United States, and a supportive president working together with the veterans' organizations and Congress, the healthcare benefits that exist in the first decade of the twenty-first century would not be available to eligible veterans. Continued vigilance in passing and implementing legislation is a necessity for the system of healthcare provided for veterans of the U.S. military.

References

Congressional Budget Office. (2009). Quality initiatives undertaken by the Veterans Health Administration. Congressional Budget Office Report, August. http://www.cbo.gov/publication/20928 (accessed March 19, 2012).

Department of Veterans Affairs. (2011). History of the Department of Veterans Affairs. http://www.va.gov/about_va/vahistory.asp (accessed July 7, 2011).

DePledge, Derrick. (2011). The "right time." *Honolulu Star-Advertiser*, March 3. http://www.staradvertiser.com/news/20110303_The_right_time.html (accessed March 3, 2011).

Jha, A. J., Perlin, J. B., Kizer, K. W. & Dudley, R. A. (2003). Effect of the transformation of the Veterans Affairs Health Care System on the quality of care. *New England Journal of Medicine* 348: 2218–2227.

Khuri, S. F., Daley, J. & Henderson, W. G. (2002). The comparative assessment and improvement of quality surgical care in the Department of Veterans Affairs. *Archives of Surgery* 137, no. 1: 20–27.

Longman, Phillip. (2005). The best care anywhere. *Washington Monthly*, January/ February, 1–8.

U.S. Department of Veterans Affairs. (2008). *Archives of the Department of Veterans Affairs: Fact sheet.* Washington, DC: Library Archives.

Part II

Healthcare for Veterans from Various Eras

Chapter 5

Healthcare for Veterans of World Wars I and II

Thomas W. Miller

Historical Review

In 1919 President Woodrow Wilson proclaimed November 11 as the first commemoration of Armistice Day, recognizing World War I veterans for their contribution to world peace. The Treaty of Versailles officially ending World War I between the Allied nations and Germany was not signed until June 28, 1919, but the armistice, or temporary cessation of hostilities in World War I, went into effect on the eleventh hour of the eleventh day of the eleventh month. It is therefore recognized that it was on November 11, 1918, that the end of "the war to end all wars" was declared. Efforts to provide some benefits for veterans of the war were primarily monetary and healthcare was through military facilities.

President Wilson proclaimed the first Armistice Day with the following words: "To us in America, the reflections of Armistice Day will be filled with solemn pride in the heroism of those who died in the country's service and with gratitude for the victory...because of the opportunity it has given America to show her sympathy with peace and justice in the councils of nations" (U.S. Department of Veterans Affairs 2008). Armistice Day is set aside to honor all veterans of World War I. In 1954 President Dwight Eisenhower signed legislation changing the name of Armistice Day to Veterans Day. Thus November 11 of each year became a day to honor all veterans who served America as airmen, marines, sailors, or soldiers. Veterans

85

Day continues to be observed on November 11 (Veterans Oral History Project Act 2000).

The observance of Veterans Day on this date not only preserves its historical significance, but helps focus attention on the important purpose of Veterans Day: "A celebration to honor America's veterans for their patriotism, love of country, and willingness to serve and sacrifice for the common good" (U.S. Department of Veterans Affairs 2008). In the 1930s President Herbert Hoover and Republican congressmen opposed observing Veterans Day because it would negatively affect the federal government's budget and Depression-era relief programs. The emerging veterans' organizations pressed the federal government to allow the early redemption of their military service certificates.

Veterans of World War II were recognized with the declaration of Memorial Day, which commemorates the final battles of the European Theater and the German surrender in May 1945. The practice of wartime military bonuses began with the Revolutionary War in 1776, as payment for the difference between what a soldier was paid and what he could have earned had he not enlisted. The creation of the American Legion in 1919 was accompanied by a drive for additional benefits for veterans of the war. In 1924, overriding President Calvin Coolidge's veto, Congress enacted compensation for veterans in recognition of their service to their country and health-related issues they faced upon their return. Each veteran was to receive a dollar for each day of domestic service, up to a maximum of $500, and $1.25 for each day of overseas service, up to a maximum of $625. Those owed $50 or less were issued their due in that amount, but larger amounts were issued as certificates of service, which would mature in twenty years. Healthcare was limited to U.S. government military hospitals. With congressional legislation and presidential approval, 3,662,374 military service certificates with a face value of $3.638 billion were approved and issued. Congress subsequently established a trust fund to receive twenty annual payments of $112 million that, with interest, would finance the $3.638 billion owed to the veterans in 1945 (VandenHeuvel 1989; LaVerda, Vessey & Waters 2006).

Legislative Policies Focused on Healthcare

Each year Congress introduces and passes bills that address active military and veterans' healthcare needs. Post-traumatic stress disorder (PTSD), traumatic brain injury (TBI), suicide prevention and suicide response, as well hospice care, medical services, and nursing home care for any mental illness attributed to wartime service, are all issues the federal government is addressing with the bills discussed in this section, for military service members in need.

The Compensation Owed for Mental Health Based on Activities in Theater Post-traumatic Stress Disorder Act (COMBAT PTSD; H.R. 952), introduced February 10, 2009, recognized that PTSD is a serious issue affecting many military service members and veterans. The federal bill clarifies what the syndrome is, so that veterans may receive the healthcare needed to support them. The definition stipulates "combat with the enemy" to give military service members with service-connected disability compensation.

"Combat with the enemy" is defined as service performed while on active duty, in combat operations during war or in combat against a hostile force during a hostile period. The PTSD/TBI Guaranteed Review for Heroes Act (H.R. 1701), introduced March 25, 2009, charges a review board, under the secretary of defense, to reexamine the discharge or dismissal of a military service member if he or she was discharged dishonorably or has been diagnosed with PTSD or TBI.

The review process may be requested up to fifteen years after a military discharge, by the military service member, a surviving spouse, a legal representative, or a member of Congress. After a review, the board may change the discharge or dismissal of the military service member to an honorable discharge.

The Embedded Mental Health Providers for Reserves Act of 2010 (S. 3425), introduced May 26, 2010, guarantees military Reserves performing inactive duty access to on-site mental health assessments by a licensed professional. In addition, military service members are required to have access to behavioral health support programs that include suicide prevention, suicide response, and psychological health programs. The act also sets standardized privacy and security rules for all mental health services provided to military veterans.

Another legislative initiative, the Veterans Mental Health Accessibility Act (H.R. 1544), introduced March 17, 2009, opens up eligibility to veterans of U.S. wars for hospice care, medical services, and nursing home care for any mental illness attributed to wartime service. Eligible veterans are those who were active duty service members during World War II, the Korean conflict, the Vietnam War, the Persian Gulf War, Operations Iraqi Freedom or Enduring Freedom, and any war after the Persian Gulf, or who faced hostile forces during a period of hostilities. Introduced in 2009, the Caring for Veterans with Traumatic Brain Injury Act of 2009 (H. R. 1546) charges VA to create the Committee on Care of Veterans with Traumatic Brain Injury within the Veterans Health Administration (VHA). The goals of the committee are to continually assess the treatment and rehabilitation needs of military veterans with TBI and evaluate whether VHA is meeting their mental health needs.

A System Dedicated to Veterans' Healthcare and Benefits

With the development of the Veterans Administration in 1930, legislation was passed by Congress authorizing the president to "consolidate and coordinate government activities affecting war veterans." (Previous chapters in this volume address this period in more detail.) The earlier veterans' agencies became bureaus within the Veterans Administration under the leadership of Brigadier General Frank T. Hines, who had directed the Veterans' Bureau for seven years and was named as the first director of the Veterans Administration (U.S. Department of Veterans Affairs 2001).

The VHA healthcare system grew from the establishment of 54 hospitals across the country in 1930, to more than 170 medical centers and 350 outpatient clinics nationally. In addition, the healthcare system represented medical and healthcare specialties in community outreach clinics, nursing home care units, and domiciliary care. This system of VA healthcare facilities provided a broad spectrum of medical, surgical, psychiatric, and rehabilitative care. The responsibilities and benefits programs of the Veterans Administration grew enormously to provide benefits and healthcare to veterans of all wars. With the close of World War II, a considerable increase in the veteran population resulted in more benefits for military veterans through the G.I. Bill. This legislation, signed into law on June 22, 1944, resulted in a system of healthcare benefits across the United States. Veterans of the Korean conflict, the Vietnam War, the period of an "all-volunteer force" in 1973, and the Persian Gulf War, as well as those who served in Iraq and Afghanistan, reap their benefits and healthcare through the Department of Veterans Affairs (VA) (Damron-Rodriguez et al. 2004).

Historical Veterans' Healthcare in the United States

The Continental Congress of 1776 encouraged enlistments during the Revolutionary War by providing benefits through pensions for soldiers who were injured during the war. Direct medical and hospital care given to veterans in the earliest days of the United States was provided by the individual states and communities. In 1811 the first domiciliary and medical facility for veterans was authorized by the federal government, but it was not opened until 1834. During the nineteenth century the veterans' assistance program was authorized to include benefits and pensions not only for veterans, but for widows and dependents of these veterans. After the Civil War many states established veterans' homes for the healthcare needs of veterans. Through the efforts of the state governments, domiciliary care was made available at all state veterans' homes, and incidental medical and hospital treatment was provided for all injuries and diseases, whether or not they were connected with military service. These facilities provided the bases for care for indigent and disabled veterans of the Civil War, Indian Wars, Spanish-American War, and Mexican border conflicts as well as discharged regular members of military service in the United States.

In 1917 Congress established a new system of veterans' benefits when the United States entered World War I. Included were programs for disability compensation, insurance for servicepersons and veterans, and vocational rehabilitation for the disabled. By the 1920s the various benefits were administered by three federal agencies: the Veterans' Bureau, the Bureau of Pensions of the Interior Department, and the National Home for Disabled Volunteer Soldiers.

Healthcare Needs of Veterans of the World Wars

The healthcare needs of veterans have varied by the wars that have been waged. World War I and World War II veterans' needs for healthcare were based on the geographic locations of these wars, the types of wars fought, the weapons used, and the consequences of such experiences on their lives. Dr. Nancy LaVerda and a team of colleagues have provided a summary of the perceptions of World War II veterans' healthcare needs in two major areas. The first focus of this study was their military experiences and the resulting healthcare needs. The second focus was the veterans' perceived impact of their wartime experiences on their physical and mental health. Dr. LaVerda, Andrea Vessey, and Dr. William F. Waters have published much of this information (see LaVerda, Vessey & Waters 2006).

This qualitative research study evaluated the attitudes, perceptions, and opinions of veterans regarding the health impact of their military service. The study design involved adding relevant health questions to the interview format developed by the ongoing Veterans History Project (VHP), a military oral history depository directed and maintained by the U.S. Library of Congress, for which audiotaped interviews conducted with individuals and a focus group were coded and evaluated. Key informants provided background information (Veterans Oral History Project Act 2000). The results obtained in this study are summarized elsewhere (LaVerda, Vessey & Waters, 2006) and include a general consensus among participants that military healthcare during their wartime experiences was beneficial. Preventive health practices were instilled as lifelong habits, as were feelings of self-confidence and independence.

Special Needs for Former Prisoners of War

Perhaps the veterans group who had the most physical and mental health needs after their war were prisoners of war in World Wars I and II. These veterans endured very cruel and devastating experiences, including the extended deprivation of nutrition and social contact, with considerable healthcare consequences. Engdahl, Page, and Miller (1991) and Miller (1992, 1993, 1994) reported on prisoners of war and the consequences of captivity as prisoners of war of the Germans and the Japanese during World War II. Among the atrocities faced by prisoners of war of the Germans and the Japanese were malicious and aggravated assaults; a deliberate policy of fostering starvation; various forms of both physical and mental torture; deprivation of and limited information, contact with family, and social contact; burning with lighted cigarettes and inserting a can opener into a prisoner's open wound; starvation; experimental medical procedures and surgical interventions; and coerced indoctrination. Much of this has led to a lifetime of depressive symptoms, adaptation difficulties, and medical problems.

The results of their study suggest that VA was viewed positively by respondents but was not used to any great extent by veterans. The LaVerda, Vessey, and Waters (2006) study concluded that current good health and feelings of patriotism, duty, and selflessness may underlie expressed positive attitudes about the health impact of service during World War II. Research on the attitudes and perceptions of U.S. veterans suggests that they share an experience that uniquely shapes their lives. Research on the health of older adults often focuses on the impact of advancing age and its biological influences, rather than on the impact of historical events such as war. Such events can cause psychological trauma and social dislocation, but also can offer new opportunities and potential for personal growth. Legacies are a compelling reason for studying the effects of military experiences on health. To understand the potential effects, studies of veterans' life histories and their perceptions of the impact of their service on their health are needed, and efforts to collect such information are part of the VHP, supported by VA.

National Recognition for World War II Veterans

Renewed interest in the needs of World War II veterans was stimulated by the fiftieth anniversary of the end of that war in 1995. Public desire to recognize the veterans and to learn from their experiences led to the erection of a World War II memorial in Washington, D.C. In addition, considerable interest and congressional support for the VHP, a large-scale, long-term, storage and cataloging endeavor that was established by an act of Congress and signed into law by President Bill Clinton on October 27, 2000, continues today with a collection of oral histories of veterans and their healthcare providers. The overall purpose of this is to establish a depository of audio-taped and videotaped oral histories and other relevant supporting documents for U.S. war veterans, so that future generations can learn from the past and have a comprehensive resource for the study and understanding of veterans' healthcare in the twenty-first century.

Study Using VHP Guidelines

The shared recollections of veterans from both wartime military experiences and post-wartime experiences were acquired through multiple means. Among the initial efforts were the research and subsequent work of Taft and others (2004) to gain an understanding of the personal recollections of veterans who were interviewed as nursing home residents and elderly outpatient veterans through the VA. In addition, healthcare professionals have provided oral histories as an intervention for meeting health needs in older aged veterans and enhancing the quality of life of nursing home residents.

Analysis of the completed oral histories identified themes of patriotism, loss, tension, makeshift living, self-sufficiency, and uncertain journey. Conversations with VHA officials confirmed that they were not aware of other published research literature based on the VHP. Within the conceptual framework of renewed interest in World War II veterans because of the recent sixtieth anniversary of the end of the war; the opening of the World War II Memorial in Washington, D.C., in May 2004; the existing literature on the health impact of World War II service; and a desire to participate in the VHP, this research study was developed to answer the following question: What are the perceived health effects of military service among U.S. veterans during World War II and since then? This question was designed to provide a conceptual understanding of the perceived nature and meaning of the experiences of World War II veterans and the health impact of military service. The analysis is based on the framework of grounded theory in qualitative research developed by Strauss (1987).

The LaVerda, Vessey, and Waters (2006) study involved the use of semi-structured individual interviews, a focus group interview, and key informant interviews to collect an array of data, to allow the development of a coherent, robust understanding of the perceived health impact of World War II service. Although the VHP did not sponsor or actively participate in this research study, it was the impetus. Therefore, data collection guidelines established by the VHP were used, including a list of suggested questions, from which the researchers selected those most likely to be of common interest to participants and to elicit a well-formulated oral history of each respondent's wartime experience. To incorporate interest in the health impact of wartime service, questions were added to the standard VHP oral history interview (see box 5.1). Data were collected through audiotaped individual interviews with six veterans of World War II and a focus group discussion with ten veterans of World War II. In addition, four key informants—individuals who were knowledgeable about the health impact of military service on World War II veterans—provided background information for the study (LaVerda, Vessey & Waters 2006).

Box 5.1. Veterans History Project Interview Questions

1. What impact do you think your military service had on your health at the time you were actually serving during World War II, including, but not limited to, any direct injuries you sustained as a result of the war or any mental stress that you endured?

2. Do you remember any particular things you did, or were instructed to do, to try to keep healthy while serving during the war?

3. Do you remember any health examinations that you underwent while serving in the military during the war, including the circumstances surrounding those examinations and any results?

4. If you had a particular concern about your physical or mental health while serving during the war, how did you go about getting more information?

5. How did your military service during World War II impact your physical or mental health since the end of your service during that war (in particular, any events or exposures you had during the war that might have impacted your health, physically or mentally, at any point since your wartime service was completed)?

6. Do you remember any particular things you did, or were instructed to do, in response to any health concerns related to your wartime military experience since the end of the war?

(continued)

7. Do you remember any health examinations that you underwent after your wartime service that included discussions of how your military experiences might have impacted your health, including the circumstances surrounding those examinations and any results?

8. If you have a particular concern about your physical or mental health that you think may be related to your wartime service, how do you go about getting more information?

A noted limitation of these interviews was that among the focus group participants, all were retired military officers, but most were not officers during World War II. None were enlisted veterans. There were two nurses, one of the individual interviewees was a radiological technician, and one man who participated in the focus group had received some training as a medic. There was no overlap between those who completed individual interviews and those who participated in the focus group. Key informant interviews provided valuable information about the historical perspective on healthcare provided during World War II, background information on why certain healthcare policies were instituted at that time, and changes in military healthcare since the 1940s. All four key informants were middle-aged Caucasian males trained as physicians; two were high-ranking officials at the headquarters of VA.

Results of the Study

There was consensus among respondents about the impact of military service on their health during World War II (LaVerda, Vessey & Waters 2006). That was considered to be a healthy time in their lives, principally because the military provided a healthy environment based on regular exercise and meals. Military service was also thought to have contributed to healthy lifestyle changes that remained with respondents throughout their lives. Any negative impact that military service might have had was heavily downplayed. As one participant stated, "Well, I actually think I was quite healthy. You know, except for being tired. . . . But basically I was healthy during World War II."

Several respondents defended the military even in the presence of what might be construed as negative health effects. "Well of course there was yellow fever and we had Atabrin for that and we had your canteen water . . . you would always put your Clorox material in there and everyone watched themselves and did the proper health things that were required." In short, according to most respondents the military provided for their every need; sanitation procedures, digging of slit-trenches, and the general provision of water and food were seen in a very positive light (LaVerda, Vessey & Waters 2006).

Being with the unit was perceived as important to both physical and mental health, in large part because of the care and structure provided by the military. Examples given summarize how veterans saw their care and treatment. Respondents recognized that the war had negative effects on their mental health at the time, but they downplayed the ultimate importance of this aspect of their wartime experience. Rather, the general perception was that being in stressful situations produced fatigue. This perception was corroborated by key informants, who confirmed that most units were constantly moving and often went with little sleep, which in turn made soldiers less effective and more prone to increased feelings of fatigue and depression. Many participants mentioned the sense that one was thankful to be alive even though there was sadness at witnessing the deaths of friends. The consensus was that there were times when the war seemed to last for a very long time in the minds of those veterans who were interviewed. The stresses of war were associated with specific situations faced by veterans and were superseded by a sense of greater need to care for the injured soldiers on the battlefield (LaVerda, Vessey & Waters 2006).

It was noted in the detailed summary of the project that the nurses interviewed reported a sense of shock at seeing the inpatients suffering from mental distress and venereal diseases. Additional stressors noted by the nurses came from learning everything quickly and not being treated seriously because they were women. One respondent told of being unable to even get a call patched through to another naval facility although she was a lieutenant. They were also frustrated with the primitive technology. Yet many believed that they received the best healthcare available at the time. Former nurses and medics were frustrated with what they had to work with, yet had a sense of pride in what they accomplished and the role they played in providing a spectrum of care and service to veterans in need. Some respondents who worked in or near the hospitals and healthcare facilities reported having limited memories of seeing casualties. When reported at all, the impact was downplayed, as indicated by the researchers (LaVerda, Vessey & Waters 2006). There was also a consensus among those interviewed that the military was not to be blamed for the mental anguish they may have encountered. Few participants admitted in their interviews that their military service might have contributed to later alcoholism and substance abuse. Most respondents did indicate that they used alcohol when it was available during military service. Respondents also recognized that, in addition to severe mental stress, there were physical effects of their wartime experiences. Nevertheless, this impact was perceived as being related to specific injuries or wounds, which were generally downplayed. An example noted by LaVerda, Vessey, and Waters (2006) involved respondents downplaying the seriousness of their wounds or injuries. Further questioning, however, sometimes produced reluctant revelations of hospitalizations and the seriousness of their injuries. Nevertheless, respondents praised the type and quality of healthcare they received. Some praised the military for the evacuation of wounded being fairly quick and the evacuation hospitals being placed close to the front or as close as they could get to the frontlines and battlefields. In general most of the reported respondents thought the medical healthcare and service was positive.

The perceptions of respondents about health information and physical care and examinations received during the World War II era were that they were minimal. Although there was a sense that good general information on diet and regular exercise was provided and that this was sufficient for general healthcare, most participants pointed out that they were given an examination before entering the military and received annual examinations thereafter. These examinations were often seen as being very brief and hurried. Even former nursing personnel noted that the haste with which entrance physical examinations were given provided minimal screening, and almost everyone passed. Some respondents mentioned the "short-arm" inspection, the very mention of which was greeted with laughter. Further elucidation involved checking for various sexually transmitted diseases, including gonorrhea and syphilis (LaVerda, Vessey & Waters 2006).

The perceived silliness of the short-arm inspection in confronting the seriousness of venereal disease was corroborated by key informants, who noted that sexual education films created by the military during that time were poorly done and just entertaining. However, respondents noted that the message was received for the most part. In addition to general health information and examinations, all respondents received examination and education with respect to foot care. This interest was a well-learned lesson from earlier wartime experiences and was explained by key informants as a significant concern from military healthcare during World War I, in which many soldiers lost their lives due to "trench foot." LaVerda, Vessey, and Waters (2006) noted this as a "lesson learned" by the military in the first world war; from that point on, military medicine emphasized the proper care of feet, which was overwhelmingly emphasized by the study participants.

Obtaining Health Information during World War II

When asked where they obtained health information if they had a concern, most of the veterans involved in the study indicated that they had not attempted to obtain such information. There was a general sense that the appropriate information would have been provided if it was sought by going on sick call, and that the appropriate source of information was a military physician. However, most respondents suggested that this would be a "waste of time," because medical examinations initiated because of self-admitted health concerns were given minimal attention (LaVerda, Vessey & Waters 2006).

Health Needs since World War II

Most respondents thought that, because they were healthy during the war, their current poor health was mostly attributable to their advanced age. Engdahl, Page, and Miller (1991) concluded in their research study of World War II prisoners of war that symptoms of depression and what has come to be known as post traumatic stress disorder (PTSD) were present in several of the former prisoners of war being studied more than forty years after these veterans were held prisoner. Furthermore, they recognized that certain problems (for example, pain from old wounds and hearing losses) were related to their involvement in the war. In these cases, the majority of the participants were happy with VA's response and the disability payments they received (LaVerda, Vessey & Waters 2006). The one exception to this general sense of well-being was frustration with hearing loss from military life. An interesting note on hearing loss was that most veterans seemed to have such loss, but unless it was caused by a specific wound, little was done initially. Respondents complained that they could not get disability because the VA claimed it was not directly caused by military life.

Respondents had different views on the quality of VA healthcare. One noted that, even after receiving care through the veterans' healthcare system, his complaints did not go away and other problems were not fully addressed (LaVerda, Vessey & Waters 2006). Another perception was that military service had taught them healthy habits that followed the veterans throughout their lives, including the importance of caring for themselves and looking out for their fellow veterans. In addition, respondents recognized the importance of early health screening examinations and said that this habit was instilled into veterans during their military experience. Some respondents noted the impact of combat experience on mental health, but this relationship was downplayed when seeking healthcare. Unlike in today's veterans' healthcare, veterans were encouraged "to live with it."

LaVerda, Vessey, and Waters (2006) report that in terms of postwar healthcare related to wartime service, most respondents reported being happy with the care and level of treatment provided by the VA. Even when VA was not the primary caregiver (many respondents had private health care and insurance), there was a sense of confidence that, if needed, one could always go to the VA hospital for care and treatment for life. Respondents also noted that during annual examinations they were strongly encouraged to give up smoking, a habit that many admitted having picked up during their active duty during World War II. The military dispensed cigarettes to active military and to veterans in VA hospitals after the war as part of rations. It is interesting to note that, even without more recent information, it was common knowledge then that smoking was bad for one's health.

Aside from advice on smoking, most participants could not identify or recall any health education information that they received after the war related to their health and military service. The general view was that health problems should not be dwelled on or complained about. In many cases, it appeared that the participants' general good health at the present time was despite potentially hazardous exposures in their past. For example, one of the participants might have been exposed to radiation in Japan, because he was there soon after the nuclear bombings. When asked if this potential exposure to radiation worried him, he replied in the negative (LaVerda, Vessey & Waters 2006).

The results obtained from respondents showed that the perception of most veterans was that the health education information they might need would be available if requested; several even reported receiving information from VA without having requested it, and this was viewed in very positive terms by respondents. Although the availability of VA medical services was clearly recognized among veterans interviewed, many stated that they did not use those services because they had their own private insurance, so they used private doctors and facilities.

Future Directions in Understanding Veterans' Healthcare

The strengths of these noted findings include the use of the Veterans History Project as an impetus for evaluating the health impact of wartime service by obtaining oral histories and triangulation through the use of three data collection techniques: individual and focus group interviews and collection of background information from key informants. Relying on one data collection technique would have been unlikely to provide the required breadth and depth of understanding or the different ways of looking at the research question that were provided by the three techniques combined. Furthermore, data analysis based on the systematic review of transcripts is methodologically concomitant with the grounded-theory approach based on the development of core concepts, processes, and theories that are generated by integrating characteristics, conditions, causes, antecedents, and consequences of events or responses. The use of in-depth individual and focus group interviews, plus discussions with key informants, allowed for an understanding of participants' perceptions expressed in their own terms, with an opportunity to immediately follow up and probe for clarification, to better understand the nuances of military culture and formulate hypotheses in a flexible manner (Taft et al. 2004).

As with many research studies, there are limitations to the efforts of LaVerda, Vessey, and Waters (2006) to gain a better understanding of military veterans and their postmilitary healthcare needs. These include the study's dependence on the cooperation of a small group of people and on their openness and honesty, as well as potential observer effects and reliance on the ability of the researchers to be resourceful, systematic, and honest. Despite these limitations, the results appear to be a valid and reliable picture of a selected group of military veterans from World War II.

Contrasting viewpoints that did not fit the emerging model were explored and analyzed in the context of emerging patterns and served to modify them. This study was also limited by the fact that the respondents who participated were not a random sample of World War II veterans; they were long-term survivors and many were career military veterans, who might therefore have more positive views about their military experience than those who served only during the war. In addition, two were nurses and two were medical technicians, and such training most likely affected their attitudes about the impact of military experiences on health. Indeed, various factors can influence veterans' health during service, including selective survival, specific war experiences, and psychological benefits. Surviving military service means that physical and mental fitness is maintained during service (Hunt & Robbins 2001). Selection factors influence decisions about promotions because the military places a premium on physical fitness. Military service can also be beneficial because it represents an antidote to past socioeconomic deprivation (e.g., poverty) by providing regular food and exercise and, in psychological terms, by providing opportunities to gain maturity and self-confidence, positive role models, and opportunities to consider a wide range of life options.

Finally, postservice influences on veterans' health include access to quality healthcare and education and pension benefits, which positively influence health (Taft et al. 2004). The beneficial effect of military service was corroborated in the analysis, because it was revealed that participating veterans viewed their military service as a healthy experience. Although this perception was recounted years after the fact and may represent a post hoc judgment of a period of relative youth, it is also likely that, even today, these elderly veterans were able to view the healthy environment (especially regular exercise and meals) in comparison with less healthy environments they had experienced before their service. Because military service personnel learn, among other lessons, to view their circumstances in the most positive light possible; it is not surprising that the veterans downplayed any negative effects of their experience. It is likely that this is the result of the stoicism that the military expects and the sense of duty and selflessness demonstrated by these veterans. Positive aspects of military service were focused in three areas, namely (1) information on diet, (2) an emphasis on exercise and physical fitness, and (3) regular examinations. Respondents reported that these three preventive measures were instilled during military service and were maintained as a matter of habit throughout their lives. Interestingly, when respondents were asked for specifics about diet, exercise, and examinations, conflicting perceptions were evidenced regarding the specific nature of the type and quantity of food and the quality and quantity of health examinations. Nevertheless, there was a very positive general perception of the role of the military in this regard, particularly in comparison with what was available to civilians at the time. Respondents thought that the military had taken good care of them while they were in the service, and there was a strong sense that the military did the best it could under difficult circumstances. It seems that respondents did not expect much from the military in terms of healthcare services at the time, so any services that were provided were seen in a positive light. In particular, appreciation was expressed for the care provided by medical staff and healthcare providers, particularly in view of the constraints under which they had to work, such as the limited availability of helicopters for evacuation of the wounded.

Most respondents recognized that as a major life event, World War II inevitably affected their lives and their physical and mental health. Here again, the perception of respondents was that the source was the very nature and stress of war, rather than the role of the military itself. The impact on mental health tended to be minimized through the use of euphemisms; reference was often made to feelings of fatigue. This finding is supported by other studies that noted that, at least for PTSD, physical ill health exacerbates mental ill health. Most of the participants in this study reported that they enjoyed good physical and mental health. It may be that, because of the age of these participants (seventy-seven to ninety years old), mental health stressors related to wartime service must have diminished. As Fontana and

Rosenheck (1994) showed, lower levels of post-traumatic stress disorder symptoms were associated with increasing age. It was still possible for veterans in this cohort to demonstrate some form of mental distress and psychological distress attributable to war experiences identified for World War II and Korean War veterans one-half century after wartime service. Interestingly, a positive mental health aspect was noted, i.e., self-confidence (Fontana & Rosenheck 1994).

The consensus was that military service, and surviving the wartime experience, instilled a sense of self-confidence and independence that might not have developed otherwise. In discussing the health impact of military service since the war, respondents recognized that certain health conditions were directly related to their time in the service, although they also acknowledged the difficulty of determining whether symptoms originated in their wartime experience or were simply age-related.

There was also a sense of irony with respect to changes in healthcare. For example, the provision of cigarettes during the war meant that many soldiers started smoking during the war, only to be told years later that they should quit. Nevertheless, there were recognition and a sense of pride that military service had resulted in behavioral changes that were perceived as resulting in better health than that of the average civilian. The emphasis placed on physical fitness and annual examinations by the military was especially noteworthy (Hunt & Robbins 2001). Perceptions related to postwar health problems reflected a sense of resignation. Respondents generally expressed appreciation for services received from the VA through healthcare benefits, as well as other services, such as TRICARE. Although discontent was expressed by some regarding the quality of service received from VA, most respondents stated that they would recommend the VA healthcare system for the needs of veterans.

At the same time, there was also an apparent disconnection between awareness of and positive views of the VA and actually using its services. Most respondents relied on other forms of health insurance and used general care facilities rather than VA medical facilities. Nevertheless, they recognized that VA medical and healthcare services are available as an alternative. Among respondents, the use of private services reflects a sense of individual responsibility, as well as the desire to avoid the appearance of accepting what might be viewed as charity or welfare, instead of making use of a privilege earned. This dichotomy is supported by a focus-group-based study of veterans that revealed a consistently high value placed on veteran status but varying views on the quality and availability of veterans' health benefits and a divergent attitude toward VA, based on conviction of service entitlement and a fear of welfare stigma (Veterans Oral History Project Act 2000).

What is clear is that the casualties of World Wars I and II led to advances in prosthetic healthcare for veterans. Advances in orthotic and prosthetic devices included the use of aluminum for leg prostheses and externally powered prosthetic limbs, which were originally built in Germany. A suction socket for above-knee prosthesis, a major advancement in the attachment of lower limbs, was introduced toward the end of World War II in Europe. The early 1950s witnessed electrically and pneumatically powered devices for veterans in need of prosthetics and for the general public. In the last half of the twentieth century several breakthroughs occurred, including the development of artificial arms powered by carbon dioxide as an advancement toward improved movement of prostheses.

A below-the-knee prosthesis that improved the utility of conventional artificial limbs and contoured adducted trochanteric-controlled alignment method sockets, which tightly hold a limb into place and distribute the weight evenly, were invented in the last quarter of the twentieth century. The first use of a microprocessor in an external prosthesis occurred around the turn of the century and led to several innovative prosthetic advancements, including the iLimb Hand, which uses electric signals from existing muscles, enabling users to open and close lifelike fingers; the C-leg for above-knee amputees controlled by a microprocessor; the Power Knee, which synchronizes itself to the motion of the intact leg; Proprio Foot for below-knee amputees, with a motorized ankle controlled by sensor technology; and PowerFoot, with a self-sustained robotic system.

For veterans of World War I and II who have the need for prosthetic healthcare, the VA healthcare system provides twenty-first-century prosthetics, including electric arms that use a small battery; others controlled by a tiny switch; and myoelectric prostheses, which use electrical impulses detected by small electrodes placed on the skin over the remaining arm muscles. Newer devices have taken advantage of plastics and fiberglass for enhanced strength and comfort of the veteran. Those in need of artificial legs can be fitted with spring-loaded feet, artificial feet constructed with toes, synthetic coverings made to match skin tone and hair patterns, and electrodes in the artificial limb leading to the natural skin, which allows the brain to register feeling in the prosthesis.

Veterans' perceptions of their healthcare have been the focus of healthcare providers, researchers, and governmental agencies. This reported study shows that the health effects of the military experience of veterans of World War II and after are perceived as generally positive by most elderly veterans, who think that military service provided healthy habits and taught them the importance of caring for themselves. In contrast, negative perceptions are minimized and placed in the context of the benefits of military service. Previous studies showed that military experience can provide both psychological gains in developmental maturity and losses through the long-term impact of wartime anxieties and trauma, with different life outcomes being related to resilience. Respondents in this study perceive military service as being beneficial because of the personal growth it afforded, perhaps alongside their own resiliency (LaVerda, Vessey & Waters 2006). Future efforts to understand veterans' postmilitary experience and their healthcare needs should clearly examine the role that feelings of patriotism, duty, and pride among veterans have played in their perceptions of the impact of military service and the healthcare needs of transitioning from military to civilian life.

References

Damron-Rodriguez, J., White-Kazemipour, W., Washington, D., Villa, V.M., Dhanani, S. & Harada, N.D. (2004). Accessibility and acceptability of the Department of Veteran Affairs health care: Diverse veterans' perspectives. *Military Medicine* 169: 243–250.

Engdahl, B., Page, W.W. & Miller, T.W. (1991). Age, education, maltreatment and social predictors of chronic depression in former prisoners of war. *Social Psychiatry and Psychiatric Epidemiology* 38, no. 9: 178–182.

Fontana, A. & Rosenheck, R. (1994). Traumatic war stressors and psychiatric symptoms among World War II, Korean, and Vietnam War veterans. *Psychological Aging* 9: 27–33.

Hunt, N. & Robbins, I. (2001). The long-term consequences of war: The experience of World War II. *Aging Mental Health* 5: 183–190.

LaVerda, N., Vessey, A. & Waters, W.F. (2006). Use of the veteran's history project to assess World War II veterans' perceptions of military experiences and health. *Military Medicine* 171, no. 11: 1076–1082.

Miller, T. W. (1992). Long-term effects of torture in former prisoners of war. In M. Basoglu (Ed.), *Torture and Its consequences*. Cambridge, UK: Cambridge University Press.

Miller, T. W. (1993). The assessment of stressful life events. In L. Goldberger & S. Breznitz (Eds.), *Handbook of stress*. 2nd ed. New York: The Free Press.

Miller, T. W. (1994). Prisoners of war: Captivity and its consequences. In D. Miller (Ed.), *Handbook of post traumatic stress disorder*. New York: Plenum Publishers.

Strauss, A. (1987). *Qualitative analysis for social scientists*. Cambridge, England: Cambridge University Press.

Taft, L. B., Stolder, M. E., Briolat-Knutson, A., Tamke, K., Platt, J. & Bowlds, T. (2004). Oral history: Validating contributions of elders. *Geriatric Nursing* 25: 38–43.

VandenHeuvel, A. (1989). Mortality and morbidity trends among American veterans: Explanatory perspectives. Carolina Population Center Paper 89-8. Chapel Hill: University of North Carolina, Carolina Population Center.

U.S. Census Bureau. (2011a). American Community Survey Office main page. January 11. http://www.census.gov/acs/www/ (accessed January 21, 2011).

U.S. Census Bureau. (2011b). American FactFinder main page. January 11. http://factfinder.census.gov/servlet/ACSSAFFPeople (accessed January 21, 2011).

U.S. Census Bureau. (2011c). Table comparisons: ACS 5-year estimates and Census 2000 SF3. American Community Survey Office, January 11. http://www.census.gov/acs/www/table_comparisons/ (accessed January 21, 2011).

U.S. Department of Veterans Affairs. (2001). *Veterans History Project: How-to guide; helpful guidelines for conducting and preserving interviews and other project materials.* Washington, DC: Veterans History Project; Library of Congress, American Folk Life Center.

U.S. Department of Veterans Affairs. (2008). *Archives of the Department of Veterans Affairs: Letter document.* Washington, DC: Library Archives.

U.S. Department of Veterans Affairs. (2010). Office of Budget. Fiscal year performance and accountability report. November 15. http://www.va.gov/budget/report/ (accessed January 25, 2011).

Veterans Oral History Project Act. (2000). P.L. 106-380, 114 Stat. 1447–1449, 106th Cong., October 27.

Chapter 6

Veterans of the Korean War Era

Thomas W. Miller

The Korean conflict involved the U.S. military in some of the most brutal and hostile experiences of wartime. This period is also referred to as the Korean War. Hostilities began on June 27, 1950, and a final cease-fire was agreed upon on July 27, 1953. However, occupation forces remain in a divided Korean peninsula well into the twenty-first century. The U.S. Congress designated an extended period of eligibility for veterans to include the period of uneasy peace negotiations following hostilities, through January 31, 1955.

Historical Background

On June 25, 1950, the North Korean People's Army, without provocation or warning, attacked the Free Republic of South Korea. During the ensuing three years of warfare, the communist enemy committed a series of war crimes against U.S. and United Nations personnel that constituted one of the most heinous and barbaric epochs of recorded history. When the American people became aware war atrocities had been committed against American troops, thousands of letters were sent to members of Congress by parents, spouses, friends, and relatives of servicemen, requesting the investigation of the atrocities.

Korean War era veterans number more than 6.8 million military men and women who served on active duty during that period, making them veterans of the war, the war era, or both. Some 997,000 served during World War II,

347,000 during the Vietnam War, and 291,000 in all three wars (U.S. Census Bureau 2011). During the three-year period of actual hostilities in Korea, nearly two million Americans served in the Korean theater. Roughly four million military men and women served elsewhere in the world during this period. Some 36,940 service members died in theater during the Korean conflict era: 33,665 from battle wounds and 3,275 from causes unrelated to battle. Of the 33,665 battle dead, 23,898 were determined killed in action, 2,536 died from battle wounds, 4,793 died while missing in action, and 2,438 died while held as prisoners of war by the North Koreans. In addition, 17,320 U.S. military service members died elsewhere in the world during the Korean War era.

Military records reveal that more than 92,100 U.S. military service members were wounded in the Korean theater, some multiple times, accounting for more than 103,200 incidents in which American military personnel were wounded. Of these 8,176 are listed as missing in action, meaning that these veterans' bodies were not recovered from the Korean peninsula. This number continues to be subject to change as the remains of former American military service members are recovered and identified.

In the Korean conflict there were some 7,140 prisoners of war, of whom almost 4,418 were returned to the U.S. military; according to military records 2,701 died in captivity. A final count of former prisoners of war showed that 21 American military personnel refused repatriation to the United States at the end of the war and became citizens of North Korea. Military records also reveal that 131 prisoners of war have been recipients of the Medal of Honor since their repatriation in the United States.

At the turn of the current century, the database of the Department of Veterans Affairs (VA) revealed that there were approximately 3.9 million Korean War era veterans in the United States and Puerto Rico, down about 21 percent from the nearly 5 million still living in the previous decade. In 2000, Korean War era veterans made up nearly 16 percent of the 24.4 million total living veterans. Of this number, approximately 86,000 were women. Some 848,000 military personnel also served in other wartime periods, including World War II and the post-Korean conflict era. In the year 2000 the median age of Korean War era veterans was seventy-eight, with 336,500 under age seventy-four, 3.25 million aged seventy to seventy-nine, and 363,600 aged eighty or older. According to 2000 Census data, the five states with the most Korean War era veterans were California (431,000), Florida (294,000), Texas (243,000), New York (220,000), and Pennsylvania (201,000). These numbers reflect the geographic distribution of the overall general veteran population (U.S. Census Bureau 2011).

About 18 percent of Korean War era veterans had less than a high school education, and nearly half had at least some college. For male nonveterans ages sixty-five to seventy-four, the comparable percentages were 33 and 37 percent, respectively (U.S. Census Bureau 2011). Approximately 30 percent of male Korean War era veterans had gainful employment, but the remainder were no longer in the labor force. Among male nonveterans ages sixty-five to seventy-four, 20 percent had gainful employment and 80 percent were no longer in the work force between July 1999 and June 2000.

Department of Veterans Affairs data for fiscal year 2000 reveals that of all unique inpatients discharged from VA medical centers, 58,400, or 16 percent, were Korean War era veterans. Of all VA hospital inpatient discharges at that time, 95,000 were Korean War era veterans. Of those being treated on an outpatient basis through VA outpatient clinics, 466,700, or 15 percent, were Korean War era veterans. There were about 35 million visits to VA outpatient facilities during fiscal year 1999. Of these, 5.1 million, or 15 percent, were by Korean War era veterans. U.S. Census Bureau data for the year 2000 reveal that nearly 75 percent of Korean War era veterans possessed some kind of private health insurance coverage; only 3 percent had no health insurance, and 22 percent had only Medicare or Medicaid coverage. Three-fourths of the Korean War era veterans described their health as "good," "very good," or "excellent," compared to 66 percent of male nonveterans ages sixty-five to seventy-four. Some 10 percent of Korean War era veterans described their health as "poor," compared to 11 percent of their nonveteran counterparts (U.S. Census Bureau 1999).

Korean War Era Veterans' Healthcare Benefits

The U.S. Congress awarded veterans of the Korean conflict a spectrum of benefits, including medical care and education, through the Readjustment Assistance Act of 1952 (also known as the Korean Conflict G.I. Bill). Some 2.3 million veterans have received service-connected compensation; 172,600 were Korean War era veterans. Such benefits provide for extensive medical and health-related care for this veterans' group. Of the 370,200 veterans receiving non-service-connected pensions at the end of March 2000, 86,300 were Korean War era veterans. Of the nearly 605,900 dependents of veterans receiving survivors' benefits at the end of March 2000, 71,000 were survivors of Korean War era veterans. More than 90 percent of these were surviving spouses. By the end of fiscal year 1999, a cumulative total of about 2.4 million Korean War era veterans had received education and training under the Korean Conflict G.I. Bill. Of these, 1,213,000 received training in institutions of higher learning; 860,000 were trained in other schools; 223,000 received on-the-job training; and 95,000 received institutional on-farm training (U.S. Census Bureau 1999, 2010).

More than 1.8 million Korean War era veterans have used VA's home loan program to purchase homes, for which VA guaranteed more than $32 billion in mortgage loans (U.S. Department of Veterans Affairs 2010). Some 79,000 disabled Korean War veterans have received vocational rehabilitation training through VA, which helped them find new jobs when their disabilities prevented them from resuming their former jobs. There are more than 803,000 veterans' special life insurance (VSLI) policies for Korean War era veterans, with a "face value" (death benefit) of $7.4 billion. Currently there are some 234,000 VSLI policies in force, with a face value of $2.7 billion. VA paid $184 million to VSLI beneficiaries in 1999.

During fiscal year 1999, 9,800 Korean War veterans were interred in VA national cemeteries, representing 18 percent of all VA interments of veterans that year.

The Korean War Era Calendar

The Korean conflict has lasted for more than half a century and has created an ongoing need for healthcare services for veterans of this era. The extended time period (to July 27, 1955) designated by Congress defined a period of eligibility to include the period of uneasy peace negotiations following hostilities. That uneasy peace and hostilities continue to exist well into the twenty-first century.

During the first decade of the twenty-first century there were two main developments in U.S.–North Korean relations. First, North Korea says it is enriching uranium for a civilian power plant at a new, modern facility. Second, North Korea has initiated unprovoked hostilities by firing more than 100 artillery shells into Yeonpyeong Island off the west coast, killing two South Korean marines and wounding twenty-one people. More than 6.8 million active American military personnel have served on active duty in the Korean War era, some veterans of the war, some of the following war era, and some of both.

War Crimes Committed against American Military Prisoners of War

The era of the Korean conflict involved brutality and torture for some 7,140 veterans who were POWs, of whom 4,418 returned, 2,701 died in captivity, and 21 refused repatriation. Among this group were 131 recognized veterans of the war who have been recipients of the Medal of Honor (U.S. Government Printing Office 2003; U.S. Department of Veterans Affairs 2010). The evidence before the subcommittee conclusively proves that American prisoners of war who were not deliberately murdered at the time of capture or shortly afterward were beaten, wounded, starved, tortured, molested, displayed, and humiliated before the civilian populace and/or forced to march long distances without benefit of adequate food, water, shelter, clothing, or medical care to North Korean prison camps; once there they experienced further indignities. Prisoners of war faced cruel and unusual experiences with devastating healthcare consequences during the Korean War. Detailed discussion of the consequences of captivity for prisoners of war is provided by Engdahl, Page, and Miller (1991) and Miller (1992, 1994). Evidence before the subcommittee showed that American war prisoners who were not killed at the time of capture, or shortly thereafter, were forced to participate in what was uniformly described by survivors as death marches. It was determined that the usual procedure was to march the American prisoners of war from the point of capture to a temporary collecting point. The stay at these points varied from two weeks to five months, and then another march would be undertaken to a more permanent prisoner-of-war camp. Shortly after capturing the Americans, the North Koreans confiscated their heavy outer garments and combat boots, forcing them to march barefoot. Their suffering was intense because the weather was extremely cold, and many prisoners' feet were frozen. The average food ration consisted of one rice ball a day and little or no water. Many died from malnutrition, dysentery, beri-beri, and pneumonia. The combination of beatings, lack of food, and inadequate medical attention to wounded prisoners resulted in numerous deaths. Some prisoners were forced to parade through towns and villages to be displayed to the civilian populations. Prisoners who were too exhausted to continue the marches were killed. Many suffered considerable weight loss during their captivity. It is estimated that more than a thousand Americans died on these death marches, the exact figure being impossible to establish.

A group of medics and chaplains were surprised by the North Korean military and slaughtered, along with approximately twenty seriously wounded American soldiers, on July 17, 1950 (S. Rep. 83-848 [1954]).

The massacre on Hill 303 occurred August 14, 1950. Twenty-six American soldiers were surprised and captured by North Koreans, who the Americans thought were reinforcements. The men were stripped of their combat boots and personal belongings and their hands were tied behind their backs. Two days later several other American prisoners joined their group, bringing the total to approximately forty-five. On the third day all of the prisoners were led to a ravine, and without warning, their hands still tied, were shot in cold blood. Only four survived and subsequently testified before the U.S. congressional committee hearings on Korean conflict war atrocities.

Recognized as one of the most grueling of the death marches was the Seoul-to-Pyongyang death march, involving 376 American servicemen. These men, who had been assembled at Seoul, commenced their march to Pyongyang on September 26, 1950. After marching approximately 250 miles over a period of three weeks, suffering the indignities described previously, fewer than 300 survived this match.

On September 27, 1950, approximately sixty American prisoners who had been confined in Taejon prison were taken into the prison yard in groups of fourteen, with their hands wired together. These men were forced to sit hunched in hastily dug ditches and then were shot by North Korean troops at point blank range, with American M-1 rifles, using armor-piercing ammunition. Of the two seriously wounded survivors, only one lived to recount the gruesome details. Civilians, estimated at between 5,000 and 7,000, as well as soldiers of the Republic of Korea, were also slaughtered at Taejon, between September 23 and September 27, 1950.

Another painful atrocity was the Sunchon tunnel massacre, which occurred in October 1950 (S. Rep. 83-848 [1954]). Approximately 180 American prisoners of war were loaded into open railroad cars for transport northward. These men were survivors of the Seoul-Pyongyang death march and were weak from lack of food, water, and medical care. They rode unprotected in the raw climate for four or five days, arriving at the Sunchon tunnel on October 30, 1950. Late in the afternoon the prisoners were taken from the railroad cars in groups of approximately forty to nearby ravines, ostensibly to receive their first food in several days. There they were ruthlessly shot by North Korean soldiers; 138 American soldiers lost their lives in this manner; 68 were murdered at the tunnel, 7 died of malnutrition while in the tunnel, and the remainder died of pneumonia, dysentery, and malnutrition. Complete details are available in *Korean War Atrocities: Report of the Committee on Government Operations . . .* (S. Rep. 848, 83rd Cong., 2nd sess., January 11, 1954) (see also Miller 1992). Box 6.1 contains information from this report.

Twelve American soldiers captured near Naedae on October 13, 1950, were imprisoned in a Korean hut and later shot without warning by

Box 6.1: Korean War Summary Statistics and Report on Atrocities

Official dates of conflict: June 25, 1950–July 27, 1953
Total who served in all armed forces: 5,720,000
Unique health risks: cold, injury
Lasting effects of war: war neurosis, trauma, brain injury
Risks for prisoners of war: malnutrition, war neurosis, trauma, brain injury
Battle deaths: 33,652
Medals of Honor: 131

KOREAN WAR ATROCITIES

REPORT OF THE COMMITTEE ON GOVERNMENT OPERATIONS MADE THROUGH ITS PERMANENT SUBCOMMITTEE ON INVESTI- GATIONS BY ITS SUBCOMMITTEE ON KOREAN WAR ATROCITIES

INTRODUCTION

On June 25, 1950, the North Korean People's Army, without warning, attacked the Free Republic of South Korea. During the ensuing 3 years of warfare, the Communist enemy committed a series of war crimes against American and United Nations personnel which constituted one of the most heinous and barbaric epochs of recorded history. When the American people became aware war atrocities had been committed against American troops, thousands of letters were sent to Members of Congress by parents, wives, and relatives of servicemen, requesting an immediate investigation.

Accordingly, on October 6, 1953, Senator Joseph R. McCarthy, chairman of the Senate Permanent Subcommittee on Investigations, appointed a special subcommittee, chaired by Senator Charles E. Potter, to inquire into the nature and extent of Communist war crimes committed in Korea.

The purpose of the investigation was to bring to the attention of the world in general and to the American people in particular, the type of vicious and barbaric enemy we have been fighting in Korea, to expose their horrible acts committed against our troops, and to foster appropriate legislation.

(*continued*)

> The War Crimes Division in Korea has already opened more than 1,800 cases of crimes committed by the enemy involving many thousands of victims, including American, South Korean, British, Turkish, and Belgian troops, as well as many civilians. The subcommittee limited its inquiry to atrocities committed against American personnel. When it became apparent numerous cases involving American servicemen were under current investigation, exclusive of hundreds of cases completely documented by evidence, the subcommittee decided to further limit its investigation to illustrative types of war atrocities.
>
> A total of 29 witnesses appeared before the subcommittee in public hearings on December 2, 3, and 4, 1953. . . . Of this number, 23 were American servicemen who were either survivors or eyewitnesses of Communist war crimes. The remaining witnesses were former Army field commanders in Korea and officials of the War Crimes Division. Corroborative evidence consisting of affidavits, statements, photographs, and other official records from the files of the United States Army, Judge Advocate General's Division, and from the official records of the War Crimes Division in Korea, was also received.
>
> *Source:* S. Rep. No. 83-848 (1954).

North Koreans. Although wounded, five managed to survive by feigning death.

In the well-reported Kaesong massacre, a patrol of thirteen American soldiers was ambushed and captured by a large force of North Koreans near Kaesong on November 6, 1950. The prisoners were stripped of their belongings and taken to a small hut, where they were confined for about three hours. They were then ordered to march, purportedly to a nearby prison camp. After traversing a distance of approximately two miles, they were shot without warning from behind. One survived by feigning death.

In another reported incident, in late December 1950, five American airmen in a truck convoy were ambushed by North Korean forces. Their bodies, discovered shortly afterward by a South Korean patrol, had been punctured in as many as twenty areas with heated, sharpened bamboo sticks. No single perforation was sufficient to cause death by itself.

The inhumane treatment of the American prisoners of war in various holding areas and camps by the North Koreans significantly challenged the physical and mental health of American captives. Some compared it to the brutalities and indignities suffered by the prisoners on death marches. The prisoners at these camps were survivors of marches and were in poor physical health. The deliberate plan of savage and barbaric handling of these men was a continuation of the policy employed on all the marches and violated virtually every provision of the Geneva Convention of 1929. They were denied adequate food, nourishment, water, clothing, and shelter. Not only were they denied medical care, but they were subjected to experimental monkey-gland operations. Housing conditions were horrible and resulted in widespread disease (S. Rep. 83-848 [1954]).

In the North Korean camps the prisoners were unable to practice their religion and on numerous occasions were beaten, humiliated, and punished for attempting to do so. Political questioning and forced indoctrination were constant, and the men were subjected to physical abuse and other punishment when they refused to be receptive to the communist propaganda. The American newspapers provided were the *Daily Worker*, published in New York, and the *People's Daily World*, published in San Francisco, copies of which appeared in the prisoner-of-war camps about two months after the date of publication. The North Koreans utilized prisoners on numerous occasions for propaganda purposes and took posed pictures purporting to show the comfortable life they were leading. At the end of hostilities, it was revealed that American prisoners died by the thousands, at the rate of some fifteen to twenty per day.

Treatment of the prisoners improved somewhat when the peace talks at Panmunjom occurred, as the Chinese adopted their so-called "lenient policy." Prior to the adoption of this policy, prisoners had lost as much as 100 pounds in weight. Subsequently, conditions improved slightly, although not to the extent necessary to meet the terms of the Geneva Convention. Prisoners often slept on the floor; they were covered with maggots and were suffering from dysentery, pellagra, and beri-beri. In the hospitals the Chinese had introduced an operation that they claimed was a cure-all for disease, which they referred to as a tissue operation. It involved making an incision under the arm and injecting into it a chicken liver, then sewing it up and letting it heal. Prisoners who survived this procedure testified that under these conditions the cut did not heal readily and became infected.

War Crimes in Korea

Initial summaries of war crimes committed by the North Korean armies against captured United Nations (UN) military personnel began to filter into General Headquarters, United Nations Command, early in July 1950. When the facts were disclosed, Gen. Douglas MacArthur, Commander in Chief, United Nations Command, initiated investigations of the reported atrocities. The initial responsibility for the investigations was assigned to the Army Staff Judge Advocate of the Far East Command. On July 27, 1950, field commanders were advised of the procedures to be followed. In early October 1950 the immediate responsibility for war-crimes investigations was transferred to the Commanding General, Eighth Army; on September 1, 1952, responsibility was transferred to the Commanding General, Korean Communication Zone.

The War Crimes Division

The purpose in establishing the War Crimes Division in 1954 was to avoid the difficulties experienced after World War II, when little effort was made to investigate the commission of a war crime until some time after the war had ended. To define and clarify the limits of the investigations in Korea, war crimes were defined as those acts committed by enemy nations, or those persons acting for them, that constitute violations of the laws and customs of war and general application and acceptance, including contravention of treaties and conventions dealing with the conduct of war, as well as outrageous acts against persons or property committed in connection with military operations.

The War Crimes Division in Korea was organized into several branches, the more important sections from an operational standpoint being the Case Analysis Branch (CAB), the Investigations Branch, and the Historical Branch, the latter containing statistical and order-of-battle sections. The Investigations Branch utilizes field teams conducting on-the-spot investigations. Thousands of enemy prisoners of war, as well as friendly personnel, have been interviewed, during which interrogations every effort was made to discover contributing and corroborating evidence to establish the facts surrounding the reported war crimes. Investigators collect evidence consisting of affidavits, photographs, and statements of participants and perpetrators, and they locate bodies of victims, effecting their identification wherever and whenever possible. The CAB is composed of attorneys, and they review and analyze the cases.

The documented case against the subject involved is then referred to the Command Staff Judge Advocate, Headquarters, Armed Forces, Far East, for possible prosecution. With the signing of the Korean armistice the War Crimes Division in Korea did not terminate its operations, but it is continuing to develop additional evidence as a result of interrogations of repatriated prisoners under operation "Big Switch."

North Korean military massacres and the wholesale extermination of prisoners of war were a calculated part of North Korean psychological warfare. The atrocities perpetrated in Korea against the UN troops by Chinese and

North Korean military are not unique in history, nor can they be explained away on the grounds that inhumanity is often associated with so-called civilized warfare. The forces in Korea flagrantly violated virtually every provision of the Geneva Convention of 1929, as well as Article 6 of the Charter of the International Military Tribunal at Nuremberg, Germany.

With the evidence presented to the Senate Subcommittee to Investigate the Administration of the Internal Security Act and Other Internal Security Laws of the Committee on the Judiciary, this investigative body clearly determined that the general North Korean policy governing the treatment of American prisoners of war emanated from a command level. This was evident in the mass slayings on numerous occasions, particularly during UN offensives. In virtually every instance, the killing of American prisoners was either ordered or performed by a North Korean or Chinese military officer.

The confiscation of clothing and footwear, the inadequate medical attention, withholding of food and water, and the beatings and torture of American prisoners were constant during all forced marches and in all prisoner-of-war camps up until the peace talks at Panmunjom. This deliberate communist policy to weaken prisoners was closely connected with their program of incessant political probing and forced indoctrination. As the peace talks progressed, the treatment of prisoners would improve or deteriorate depending on the Communists' gains in these negotiations.

Upon hearing the testimony of all witnesses and studying the documentary evidence submitted, the subcommittee advised that the North Korean and Chinese armies were guilty of the following war crimes and crimes against humanity, committed against American personnel during the conflict in Korea from June 25, 1950, until July 27, 1953: murder; attempted murder; malicious and aggravated assault; various acts of torture, that is, perforating flesh of prisoners with heated bamboo spears, burning prisoners with lighted cigarettes and inserting a can opener into a prisoner's open wound; starvation; a deliberate policy of fostering starvation; experimental medical operations; coerced communist indoctrination; and bayoneting prisoners of war.

It was therefore concluded that the government in China at the time was equally as responsible and guilty as the government in North Korea for war atrocities committed against Americans held in captivity. Virtually every provision of the Geneva Convention governing the treatment of war prisoners was purposely violated or ignored by the North Korean and Chinese forces at that time. More than 5,000 American prisoners of war died because of communist war atrocities, and more than a thousand who survived were victims of war crimes. Several thousand American soldiers who have not been repatriated were victims of war crimes, died in action, or are presently confined in communist countries. North Korean forces violated the "Little Switch" agreement by failing to repatriate the sick and wounded prisoners in accordance with the Panmunjom truce. The Chinese and North Korean military were found to have used false propaganda to inaccurately portray the treatment accorded by them to American prisoners of war.

Operation Little Switch (April 20–May 3, 1953) was the exchange of sick and wounded prisoners of the Korean War. The exchange was agreed to during the truce talks at Panmunjom on April 11, following UN Commander in Chief General Mark W. Clark's indirect approach to North Korean Premier Kim II Sung and Chinese General Peng Dehuai, which itself had developed from initiatives at the UN and the International Red Cross in Geneva. The communist side repatriated 684 UN sick and wounded troops, while the UN Command (UNC) returned 1,030 Chinese and 5,194 Koreans, together with 446 civilian internees. As with everything else concerning the POW issue, the exchange was marked by strong disagreement and controversy. Returning communist prisoners tried to embarrass their captors by rejecting rations and clothing issued to them, while sensational reports appeared in the Western press alleging that numbers of sick and wounded POWs were still being held by the communists in spite of the exchange agreements. The contentious issue that had prolonged the war for two years, that no UN POW would be forcibly repatriated, remained. The surprising acceptance of this exchange may well have come as a result of uncertainty over Soviet policies after the death of Soviet Premier Joseph Stalin.

The congressional investigatory committee recommended that a resolution be offered in the Senate of the United States proposing that the Senate express its grave concern over these military atrocities and recommend to the United States delegation to the United Nations the establishment of an impartial investigating commission of the United Nations. The purpose of said commission would be to inquire into and report on the facts of all war crimes committed by the North Korean and Chinese military forces in or near Korea since June 24, 1950, and the means of subjecting the criminals responsible to just and lawful punishment.

Congressional Efforts to Meet Korean Veterans' Healthcare Needs

Legislation that addresses veterans' healthcare needs is introduced yearly. Among the healthcare concerns for veterans of the Korean war are the needs of those who suffer from post-traumatic stress disorder (PTSD), traumatic brain injury (TBI), suicide ideation, and mental health issues, as well as hospice care, medical services, and nursing home care for any mental illness attributed to wartime service. Since the Korean War greater emphasis has been placed on the trauma of war and adaptation upon return from war (Miller 1991). The Combat Post Traumatic Stress Disorder Act of 2009 (H.R. 952) recognized that PTSD is a serious issue affecting many military veterans, including Korean War veterans. The federal bill clarifies the syndrome so that veterans may receive the healthcare they need. The Combat PTSD Act establishes a requirement of "combat with the enemy" in order to award military service members with service-connected disability compensation. Combat with the enemy is defined as service performed while serving on active duty, in combat operations during war, or in combat against a hostile force during a hostile period.

Recognizing the needs of aging veterans, the Veterans Mental Health Accessibility Act of 2009 (H.R. 1544) opens up eligibility to veterans of U.S. wars for hospice care, medical services, and nursing home care for any mental illness attributed to wartime service. Eligible veterans include those who were on active duty service during the Korean War. Finally, the Caring for Veterans with Traumatic Brain Injury Act of 2009 (H.R. 1546) charges VA to create the Committee on Care of Veterans with Traumatic Brain Injury within the Veterans Health Administration (VHA). The goals of the committee are to continually assess the treatment and rehabilitation needs of military veterans who have been diagnosed with TBI and evaluate whether VHA is meeting their mental health needs. This is just a sampling of the relevant legislation passed to address the continuing mental health care needs of Korean veterans.

Healthcare Needs of Korean Veterans

As the veterans of Korea age, their need for increased healthcare and mental health services increases. Many look to VA for that needed healthcare. Fontana, Rosenheck, and Desai (2010) provide research evidence that PTSD may increase the risk of physical illness among aging veterans. Posttraumatic stress disorder can be associated with increased likelihood of medical problems (Miller & Basoglu 1992). Further complications of aging, along with cardiopulmonary care, alcohol and substance abuse disorder, issues of obesity, and diabetes care are all present in veterans, and care for these conditions is essential to veterans and their eligible family members.

Mental healthcare continues to be a strong need for aging veterans who still face many of the issues faced by veterans of combat, including wartime atrocities and terms as prisoners of war. With the incidence and prevalence rates of PTSD among the veteran population of recent wars and the already strained mental health resources in use by veterans with persistent problems related to mild cognitive impairments, TBI, and PTSD from present military operations and previous wars, VA's mental health system is and will continue to be overloaded. Furthermore, recent research has noted an increased incidence of dementia and Alzheimer's syndrome in veterans with PTSD. Recent research suggests that good social support may enhance the outcome of PTSD treatment for patients (Thrasher et al. 2010).

Long-term care has become a critical concern for aging Korean veterans. VA's long-term-care facilities are faced with accommodating the needs of eligible veterans and providing supportive healthcare for Korean era veterans. Many of them need services for a spectrum of cognitive deficits consistent with aging, along with the complexity of physical problems. Many of these Korean era veterans can no longer be cared for independently and at home by family caregivers. They look to the promise that VA will be there for them when they need healthcare.

Summary

President Barack Obama addressed the needs of Korean veterans when he signed the Korean War Veterans Recognition Act (H.R. 2632) on Friday, July 24, 2009. He proclaimed July 27, 2009, as National Korean War Veterans Armistice Day. The act passed in the House of Representatives by a vote of 421–0 and the Senate by unanimous consent. The act added National Korean War Veterans Armistice Day to the list of days on which the flag of the United States is flown nationally. Korean War veterans were recognized on this day for their courageous actions in pursuit of freedom and democracy for the Korean peninsula. Korean War veterans were recognized as dedicated men and women who deserve their nation's unending respect and gratitude for their military service.

The Korean conflict is often referred to as America's "silent war." It has been like no other military action of recent times, extending more than fifty years, into the twenty-first century. On November 11, 2010, President Obama honored Korean War veterans with a ceremony in Seoul, South Korea. It is estimated that there are some two million World War II veterans still living. Many of the veterans of World War II also served their country during the Korean War. The World War II veterans have a memorial on the mall in Washington, D.C., erected too late for many of them to see and appreciate. Honor Flights are more often the medium by which the nation has offered these aging veterans a token of our appreciation. The memorial for the veterans of the Korean War was constructed after the Vietnam and World War II Veterans Memorials were built on the Washington mall.

References

Engdahl, B., Page, W.W. & Miller, T.W. (1991). Age, education, maltreatment and social predictors of chronic depression in former prisoners of war. *Social Psychiatry and Psychiatric Epidemiology* 38 no. 9: 178–182.

Fontana, A., Rosenheck, R. & Desai, R. (2010). Female veterans of Iraq and Afghanistan seeking care from VA specialized PTSD programs: Comparison with male veterans and female war zone veterans of previous eras. *Journal of Women's Health* 19: 1–7.

Miller, T. W. (1991). Clinical issues in readaptation for Persian Gulf veterans. *Psychiatric Annals* 21, no. 11: 684–689.

Miller, T. W. (1992). Long-term effects of torture in former prisoners of war. In M. Basoglu (Ed.), *Torture and its consequences*. Cambridge, UK: Cambridge University Press.

Miller, T. W. (1993). The assessment of stressful life events. In L. Goldberger & S. Breznitz (Eds.), *Handbook of stress*. 2nd ed. New York: The Free Press.

Miller, T. W. (1994). Prisoners of war: Captivity and its consequences. In D. Miller (Ed.), *Handbook of post traumatic stress disorder*. New York: Plenum Publishers.

Miller, T. W. & Basoglu, M. (1992). Post-traumatic stress disorder: The impact of life stress events on adjustment. *Integrative Psychiatry* 44: 209–217.

Thrasher, S., Power, M., Morant, N., Marks, I. & Dalgleish, T. (2010). Social support moderates outcome in a randomized controlled trial of exposure therapy and (or) cognitive restructuring for chronic posttraumatic stress disorder. *Canadian Journal of Psychiatry* 55: 187–190.

U.S. Census Bureau. (2011). American Community Survey Office main page. January 11. http://www.census.gov/acs/www/ (accessed January 21, 2011).

U.S. Census Bureau. (1999). Table comparisons: ACS 5-year estimates and census 2000 SF3. American Community Survey Office. htpp://www.census.gov/acs/www/table_comparisons (accessed March 2012).

U.S. Census Bureau. (2010). American FactFinder main page. http://factfinder.census.gov/servlet/ACSSAFFPeople (accessed February 28, 2011).

U.S. Department of Veterans Affairs. (2010). Office of Budget. Fiscal year 2010 performance and accountability report. November 15. http://www.va.gov/budget/report/ (accessed January 25, 2011).

U.S. Government Printing Office. (2003). Transcripts: Executive sessions of the Senate Permanent Subcommittee on Investigations. http://www.senate.gov/artandhistory/history/common/generic/McCarthy_Transcripts.htm (accessed December 11, 2010).

U.S. Senate. (1954). *Korean War Atrocities: Report of the Committee on Government Operations...*, S. Rep. 848, 83rd Cong., 2nd sess., January 11. Washington, DC: United States Government Printing Office. Available at http://www.loc .gov/rr/frd/Military_Law/pdf/KW-atrocities-Report.pdf (accessed January 27, 2012).

Chapter 7

Healthcare for Veterans of Vietnam

Robert J. Fitz

Congress has established that Vietnam veteran benefits apply to those veterans who served between August 5, 1964, and May 7, 1975. For those who served "in country" the starting date was extended back to February 28, 1961. Within these parameters over six million veterans served, more than three million of them in Southeast Asia. There were 58,156 casualties in service, and another 75,000 were considered severely disabled. Many combat veterans who in previous conflicts would have died on the battlefield were airlifted by helicopter (Department of Veterans Affairs n.d.-a). Through the nature of this warfare, 5,283 American soldiers lost limbs and 1,081 sustained multiple amputations (Gailey 2007). The quick return to the United States added a new dimension to veterans' psychological adjustment, whether they were physically injured or not. There was little time for processing, and the end of the tour of duty was on an individual rather than a group basis. The service members returned singly or in small groups. In conflicts prior to Vietnam, units returned in military transports, allowing time and comradeship for debriefing and reassessing (Doyle, Maitland & The Editors of Boston Publishing Company 1985). Vietnam veterans felt betrayed by their government, that the war was not to protect America or the freedom of the Vietnamese people but for the economic gain and promotion of a few. Their experience was that even the South Vietnamese hated them as American invaders instead of soldiers dedicated to the South Vietnam cause. Then, after performing their duty and putting their lives on the line, they came home to abuse and being associated with the government. Many reported a culture shock from the sudden and drastic change of jungle warfare to the streets of the United States:

> There I was, a week out of the jungle, flying from San Francisco to New York. I fell asleep and woke up yelling, probably a nightmare. The other passengers moved away from me—a reaction I noticed more and more in the months ahead. The country didn't give a shit about the guys coming back or what they'd gone through. The feeling toward them was, "Stay away—don't contaminate us with whatever you've brought back from Vietnam." (Karnow 1983, 27)

Civilian protestors, who had never had combat training, could not empathize with the problems of psychological readjustment that a soldier experienced when returning home from Vietnam. Former U.S. Marine Corps Major General Smedley Butler wrote in 1936:

> Boys with a normal viewpoint were taken out of the fields and offices and factories and classrooms and put into the ranks. There they were remolded; they were made over; they were made to "about face"; to regard murder as the order of the day. They were put shoulder to shoulder and, through mass psychology, they were entirely changed. We used them for a couple of years and trained them to think nothing at all about killing or being killed. Then, suddenly, we discharged them and told them to make another "about face!" This time they had to do their own adjusting, sans mass psychology, sans officers' aid and advice, sans nationwide propaganda. We didn't need them anymore. So we scattered them about without any speeches or parades. Many, too many, of these fine young boys are eventually destroyed, mentally, because they could not make that final "about face" alone. (quoted in Knox & Price 1996, 3)

Compare that description with the account of a former marine with combat experience at Khe Sanh about the long-lasting effects of Marine Corps boot camp:

> Boys are turned not into men, but beasts—beasts that will fight and destroy at a moment's notice, without any regard to what they are fighting or why they are fighting, but just fight.... When I came back home I was very much antiwar, and yet there was a hostility in me toward other people.... If someone irritated me, my first impulse was to kill the fucker.... I'd catch myself and I'd think of another alternative to deal with whatever the problem was.... Today there is still a lot of hate in me—a hatred that makes it difficult to form... relationships with anyone. I am working on that. (quoted in Lifton 1973, 140–141)

The ever-present conflict with the civilian turned soldier was intensified in Vietnam because of the inability to identify the enemy. "I had taken in certain moral values. One was that killing was wrong. A second was respect for women.... But there we were in the jungle, and told to shoot at anything that moved. We couldn't tell if the people we were killing were men or women let alone Communists or peasants.... Something got broken in me, and I'm still angry about that" (Doyle, Maitland & The Editors of Boston Publishing Company, 1985).

Upon returning home, Vietnam veterans were faced with the added conflict of dealing with strong antiwar sentiments that were often irrationally transferred to the soldiers, as if the soldier was responsible both for the political decision to engage in the conflict and the horrors inherent in war, and as if each and every soldier had engaged in atrocities. The first landing on American soil was often in California, where the antiwar demonstrations were particularly intense. The uniform was a magnet for protestors at airports and other public transportation hubs. Bob Greene documented numerous emotionally laden accounts of veterans' first encounters with the American protest movement in *Homecoming* (1989).

For those whose combat experiences did not end but were re-experienced in nightmares and flashbacks long after leaving Vietnam, there was little understanding and no ready treatment. Many saw the Veterans Administration hospital as an extension of the military and avoided it (Doyle, Maitland & The Editors of Boston Publishing Company, 1985). Those who looked for help there were housed with World War II and Korean veterans in programs designed for these older veterans. The early 1970s saw the rise of veterans' self-help centers. There was no official diagnosis for the basis of government-supported treatment for their symptoms or for compensation. Those who deigned to present at the Veterans Administration were likely to be prescribed some form of major tranquilizing medication. Legislation designed specifically to help Vietnam veterans with readjustment problems repeatedly failed to pass in the early 1970s (Nicosia 2001). Vietnam veterans instinctively turned to one another in rap groups for validation and help in understanding what was happening to them.

The Veterans Administration was also not prepared for the large number of those with physical ailments, including amputees and paralyzed veterans. This was publicized in a *Life* magazine article on May 22, 1970, with startling photographs of the physical conditions and reports of inadequate care (Doyle, Maitland & The Editors of Boston Publishing Company 1985). Then VA director Donald E. Johnson unsuccessfully tried to defend the system, and his attempt to meet with disabled veterans was notably counterproductive (Nicosia 2001). The priorities of the Nixon administration did not include an increase in funding for VA facilities. In 1973 Ralph Nader claimed that the Veterans Administration was failing to provide Vietnam vets with proper care because of its continued orientation to older veterans (*New York Times*, March 4, 1973). Facing continued criticism of his management, Johnson resigned in April 1974. Shortly after taking office, President Gerald Ford appointed Richard L. Roudebush as the new director, in August 1974. He was a World War II veteran and a former national commander of the Veterans of Foreign Wars (VFW). He had been deputy director under Johnson. Young veterans anticipated that all this did not augur well for improved benefits for them. Some of Roudebush's accomplishments were the opening of several new facilities and extending veterans' educational assistance benefits and benefits for home loans. Attention to other areas such as understaffed VA facilities, slow processing of compensation claims, inadequate supply of prosthetics, and neglect of readjustment services specifically for Vietnam era veterans was hampered by the administration's funding cuts to social programs, including veterans. The new director had been quoted as calling Vietnam vets "cry babies" and saying that their problems stemmed from the fact that they had lost their war (Nicosia 2001).

This prompted Jack Smith, with Gonzalo Orrega and Ellen Hawkins of the National Veterans Resource Project, to take more extreme measures to press their case. They confronted Roudebush in his office after nailing the door shut. The heart of their demands was a presidential commission on Vietnam veterans. To his credit, the director was able to see this as an unconventional attempt to influence national policy and action. He was forced to listen to them for hours before the General Services Administration (GSA) guards broke into the office (Nicosia 2001). Some indications that Roudebush had heard their grievances and made limited improvements in the Veterans Administration followed, but more significant changes in attitude and action awaited a new administration and a new director.

Post-Traumatic Stress Disorder (PTSD)

The Diagnostic and Statistical Manual II (1968) did not include a diagnostic category for PTSD. What had been called shell shock or traumatic war neurosis in prior wars was now labeled "Vietnam Stress Syndrome." There were many pressures to keep Vietnam veterans from receiving treatment and compensation for an anxiety disorder related to war trauma. The Nixon administration promoted the view that returning veterans were basically well adjusted to civilian life occupationally and socially, and the majority of them appeared to have done just that. However, there was strong denial by the administration that the war had lasting effects on many returning veterans.

Older veterans' groups such as the VFW and American Legion opposed programs specifically for Vietnam veterans, to save more of the finite appropriations for the veterans they represented. Gaining acceptance for the concept of PTSD as a response to combat trauma was a long struggle. There was another economic force driving this. Some feared that opening this door would create a liability for the government that it could not meet. The military feared that legitimizing PTSD would create an easy out for soldiers and devastate morale (Nicosia 2001). Some also reasoned that such reactions were normal and temporary and would abate without treatment. The cases of prolonged symptoms and disability were attributed to preexisting psychiatric conditions such as depression or a personality disorder.

In the relative vacuum of no official recognition of PTSD, no congressional mandate for funding for special treatment, and no suitable treatment modality at VA installations, troubled vets sought help from each other and together with some empathic professionals. One more publicized group emerged from the Vietnam Veterans Against the War (VVAW). It included psychiatrists Robert J. Lifton, Chaim Shatan, and Jan Barry (Lifton 1973). Group meetings were dubbed "rap groups" by the vets instead of group therapy. The process was more open, less directed, and less controlled by the professionals than traditional therapy. There was more respect for those who came to be helped. Mental health practitioners in these settings were successful when they acknowledged that they had much to learn from the veterans. A former colleague of mine eventually worked almost exclusively with Vietnam veterans. When our staff was informed of new requirements to document continuing education activities, he quickly asked if we could include the encounters with our clients as continuing education. This was in spite of the fact that he was well read, grounded in theory and published. The VVAW rap groups had a sense that they were creating a new model of treatment and recovery.

Lifton (1973) identified three essential guiding principles of the process. First was affinity, a commonality of experience and the feelings associated with that experience. Second was presence, being fully engaged in the process and open to the influence of others. Third was self-generation, owning the major responsibility for one's own journey. It was most appropriate that these rap sessions be conducted at a VVAW office. Early groups of this nature antedated the vet centers by about a decade. Ideally vet centers, separate from the hospitals, incorporated the features of these rap groups. The internal distress for these vets was not limited to symptoms of PTSD, including survival guilt, but was embedded in the feelings of betrayal by their government, dealing with perceived negative changes in themselves as trained killers, and an aversion to this war and war in general. Betrayal was more frequently and keenly felt by the soldiers but was also verbalized by civilians. Gus Wilson was mayor of Bardstown, Kentucky, throughout most of the Vietnam War. The town lost sixteen of its sons to the war out of a population of 7,000 (Wilson 1994). The mayor's comments after the war gave voice to both veterans and civilians: "I think we realized as we went along—maybe later than we should have—that the government was pulling a bit of a flim-flam. We weren't getting the truth. The Vietnam war was being misrepresented to the people—the way it was conducted, its ultimate purpose" (Karnow 1983, 21–22).

A few hours after he was sworn into office, President Jimmy Carter appointed Max Cleland Director of the Veterans Administration. Cleland, a former army infantry captain, had lost both legs and his right arm in Vietnam. He was not just a symbolic figurehead for the younger veterans, but an optimistic and tireless worker for substantive changes in VA services. The most important achievement for the director, with the support of the VVAW, was the passage of Public Law 96-22, the Vietnam Veterans Rehabilitation Counseling Program, on June 13, 1979. This was enacted even before official recognition of PTSD by the American Psychiatric Association in the Diagnostic and Statistical Manual III, published in 1980. The Vet Center Program was designed to be a nonmedical program providing outpatient readjustment counseling in storefronts or other buildings separate from the VA and other government buildings. The purpose was to make services more appropriate for Vietnam veterans available for those averse to seeking help at existing Veterans Administration healthcare centers. It started with an appropriation of $12 million for ninety such centers. When first initiated they were exclusively for Vietnam veterans. Vietnam veterans as well as others knowledgeable about that war and its effects on those who served there staffed these programs. Many, but not all, had appropriate advanced degrees in mental health. The operation of the centers was focused on the consumer, the Vietnam veteran, and less on the service provider. Thus there were fewer recordkeeping requirements that could interfere with utilization. Medical records at these centers were confidential and could not be released, even to VA medical centers, without the consent of the veteran. It was more common for veterans to drop in rather than make appointments. In addition to group and individual counseling. the centers were a referral source for other benefits, such as substance abuse treatment, employment, and education. The goal was broad-based and included social rehabilitation and reintegration. The services offered were targeted to the needs of the local population of these veterans. Group counseling was typically in the form of rap groups like those described previously. Vietnam veteran counselors were likely to experience the facilitation of instant rapport, and clients did not have to explain themselves to other vets. "Nobody laughs at me if I tell them I hit the ground when I hear a sudden noise; they say they do too" (Doyle, Maitland & The Editors of Boston Publishing Company 1985). Vet centers were no panacea. Some veterans went there and encountered active substance abusers; they knew they didn't need that environment. Still, this treatment was probably the best possible in an imperfect world.

A review of America's history of attempts at psychological rehabilitation of its veterans concluded: "The Vet Center system is described as an efficient and effective instrument of mental health delivery services for veterans, an institutional expression of the social contract that should continue to be available for current and future generations of American war veterans" (Knox & Price 1996). Many considered the system a lifesaver, and there was great enthusiasm for this breakthrough in recognition of the problems and an attempt to solve them. Unfortunately the good feeling was not to last. Abraham Lincoln's oft-quoted commitment of the U.S. government "to care for him who shall have borne the battle and for his widow and his orphan" (Department of Veterans Affairs n.d.-b) is forever dependent on congressional action to approve programs and funding for all aspects of medical care and other benefits. In a recession or a change of administration, what has been taken for granted can be sacrificed in the name of fiscal restraint. Reagan's plan for economic recovery included increasing military spending, lowering taxes, and cutting spending on social programs, including the Veterans Administration. David Stockman, Reagan's director of the Office of Management and Budget, said the vet centers were "dispensable expenditures" and that Vietnam veterans could get counseling "within the VA system" (Nicosia 2001, 398). This attitude ignored the very reason for the centers' creation and threatened to undo the many years of work of veterans' groups and legislators. Vet centers were to be sunsetted, but Congress voted to continue them. A report dated August 26, 1987, from the General Accounting Office to congressional committees recommended that the Veterans Administration have the leeway to decide on an individual basis whether to leave vet centers as freestanding entities or incorporate them into existing facilities. This was based on an extensive review of the activities and documentation at the vet centers (U.S. General Accounting Office 1987). Legislation passed in April 1994 extended vet center eligibility to veterans of the Persian Gulf, Lebanon, Grenada, Panama, and Somalia. There are currently 232 such centers, and the scope of the clients they serve was extended in October, 1996 to all veterans who have served in a combat zone.

Starting with Diagnostic and Statistical Manual III i (American Psychiatric Association, 1980), PTSD has been recognized as an anxiety disorder resulting from exposure to a traumatic event that results in intense psychological distress. The trauma is repeatedly re-experienced, and the person attempts to avoid any reminders of the trauma. Part of the anxiety is increased arousal. As with any disorder, there is a minimum duration (one month) and resulting significant interpersonal distress or impaired functioning. In the course of combat trauma, the disorder is typically long-standing, particularly in the area of internal distress. The veteran may become functional, but at best some remnants of the inner conflict remain indefinitely. Studies of Vietnam veterans have shown that the incidence and the severity of PTSD are related to the amount of exposure to trauma. The National Vietnam Veterans' Readjustment Study (Kulka et al. 1990) was a result of a congressional mandate (P.L. 98-160, November 21, 1983). Its objective was to obtain incidence rates for psychological problems in Vietnam era veterans. This would in turn be a basis for planning for present and future programs and appropriations needed for provision of healthcare. The study's conclusions were that the majority of Vietnam veterans had successfully adjusted to civilian life after their service, but a substantial minority had a wide variety of life-adjustment problems. The prevalence of PTSD was assessed by a multimethod approach using psychological test results, structured interviews, and other measures. This resulted in an estimated lifetime occurrence of 15.2 percent of male and 8.5 percent of female veterans overall and higher rates for those veterans who had served in war zones: 35.8 percent of male and 17.5 percent of women who were diagnosed with PTSD (Kulka et al. 1990). Other disorders that occurred frequently among Vietnam theater veterans were generalized anxiety disorder, alcohol abuse, and depression. The NVVRS reported that approximately 830,000 male and female Vietnam veterans had clinical symptoms of PTSD and related functional impairment at the time of the study. This was 26 percent of the Vietnam theater veterans. A reanalysis of the study (Schnurr, Lunney & Sengupta (2004) shed some light on factors that predispose one to combat-related PTSD and those that protect one from it. Not surprisingly, factors that can be classified as additional stressors predisposed to PTSD. Protective factors included maturity, being older when entering the war, and having more education. Conclusions were that exposure to combat trauma in itself is sufficient to result in PTSD and is "dose related," but rates are also higher in those with predisposing factors. The results give support to the interpretation that PTSD is not simply a preexisting condition, but not everyone exposed to combat suffers from PTSD. In addition to those with the full criteria for a diagnosis of PTSD, many veterans experienced partial symptoms of the disorder.

A legacy of the Vietnam War was awareness of PTSD resulting from both combat and civilian trauma. Having had to play catch-up with PTSD treatment for Vietnam veterans, the Department of Veterans Affairs (VA) sought legislation to ensure that veterans of later conflicts would have early access to treatment for PTSD. With this attention came more appropriate and timely treatment and efforts to inoculate soldiers before the experience of combat. In 2004 VA and the Department of Defense jointly released a publication covering best practices in diagnosis, treatment, and prevention of PTSD based on research up to May 2002 (Department of Veterans Affairs/Department of Defense 2004). From the relative vacuum of being unable to respond, the Veterans Health Administration (VHA) has emerged as the leader in research, education, and treatment of PTSD. Public Law 98-528 mandated that VA establish and operate the National Center for Post-Traumatic Stress Disorder, which was founded in 1989 within VA. Its mission is "to advance the clinical care and social welfare of America's veterans through research, education and training in the science, diagnosis, and treatment of Post Traumatic Stress Disorder and stress related disorders." It collaborates with others in VA and with other government agencies as well as academic institutions. The center has grown immensely in its twenty plus years and devotes itself to all aspects of traumatic stress disorders except providing direct clinical treatment. It is at the forefront of research in understanding, preventing, and treating traumatic stress disorders. Training programs range from a basic introduction in an online module to a thirty-five-hour course and internships and postdoctoral fellowships. In-house, the center trains and certifies clinicians and trainers in various evidence-based treatments for stress related disorders (National Center for PTSD 2011).

Post-Traumatic Stress Disorder Treatment Programs in VA

Since the beginnings of the vet centers the preferred modality of treatment has been group therapy. "A group of peers provides an ideal therapeutic setting, because trauma survivors are able to risk sharing traumatic material with the safety, cohesion, and empathy provided by other survivors. It is often much easier to accept confrontation from a fellow sufferer who has impeccable credentials as a trauma survivor than from a professional therapist who never went through those experiences first-hand" (Post-Traumatic Stress Disorder Support Services 2010).

Individual treatment often focuses on some form of exposure therapy in which the traumatic experience is re-presented and re-experienced with the help of an experienced clinician. Although this can be very effective, it is counterintuitive and requires considerable preparation in information and rapport building. Even the well-trained therapist must be cautious not to retraumatize the patient. A VA study with women veterans found that exposure therapy was more effective than supportive counseling without the inclusion of trauma recall. Cognitive-behavioral therapy is also frequently used either in individual or group settings. The patient learns more effective ways of coping with the events that trigger the anxiety by cognitive restructuring of negative thoughts associated with the onset of anxiety.

Medications: Depending on the individual case, an antidepressant or an anxiolytic is sometimes a useful adjunct to the behavioral therapy. Many patients with PTSD also have some depressive symptoms, and an antidepressant is helpful in these cases. A relatively newer class of antidepressants, selective serotonin reuptake inhibitors (SSRIs), has been found to be more effective in PTSD. Prazosin, a medication prescribed for hypertension, has a use in the treatment of PTSD because it can lessen trauma nightmares. Drug therapy can also reduce anxiety to a level where the patient can tolerate treatment. Drugs used to treat anxiety that are related chemically to alcohol (benzodiazepines) are used carefully or avoided totally because of the danger of addiction and the tendency to train the patient to totally avoid the anxiety rather than learning to cope with it. It is very common for persons suffering from a stress disorder to become addicted to alcohol. There are other disorders frequently associated with PTSD, but alcohol is the most common comorbidity. For successful treatment any comorbid condition has to be treated along with PTSD. Thus VHA has developed programs specifically for the dual diagnosis of alcoholism and PTSD.

Health Issues Related to PTSD

The National Center for PTSD has summarized research linking PTSD to health issues (Jankowski 2007). Studies that controlled for other possible factors such as alcohol and tobacco use, age, socioeconomic status, and exposure to combat found PTSD was related to general health and some specific health problems. This was true using physician diagnosis and laboratory tests, not just patient-reported symptoms. Boscarino (2008) reported that PTSD in Vietnam veterans was predictive of early-age heart disease. He has found PTSD in Vietnam veterans to be related to autoimmune diseases such as rheumatoid arthritis, hypothyroidism, and psoriasis (Boscarino 2004). The resulting recommendations from the National Center for PTSD are that it is important to screen for PTSD in medical settings and to integrate PTSD and medical treatment.

Specialized Treatment Programs

Another provision of Public Law 98-528 established the first medical-center-based PTSD program. It authorized twelve special inpatient PTSD units. The concept has expanded, and now there are nearly 200 inpatient and out-patient specialized PTSD treatment programs in VA nationwide. The National Center for PTSD provides a program locator so that veterans can find which of these programs are offered near where they live. Its Web site also briefly describes these programs (PTSD treatment programs in the U.S. Department of Veterans Affairs 2007).

Specialized Intensive PTSD Programs (SIPPs)

These programs provide PTSD treatment within a "therapeutic community." Many are residential programs. They provide counseling, social, recreational, and vocational activities:

1. PTSD Day Hospitals (DH) are outpatient programs. They provide one-on-one and group treatment for four to eight hours each visit, daily or several times a week.
2. Evaluation and Brief Treatment of PTSD units (EBTPUs) provide PTSD treatment for a period of fourteen to twenty-eight days.
3. PTSD Residential Rehabilitation Programs (PRRPs) provide PTSD treatment and case management. The goal is to help the trauma survivor return to healthy living in the community. Length of stay in these programs tends to be twenty-eight to ninety days. Specialized inpatient PTSD units (SIPUs) provide trauma-focused treatment. Hospital stays last from twenty-eight to ninety days.
4. PTSD Domiciliary (PTSD Dom) programs provide live-in treatment for a set period of time. The goal is to help the veteran improve and move to outpatient mental healthcare.
5. The Women's Trauma Recovery Program (WTRP) was opened by VA in Palo Alto, California, in 1992. This live-in program focuses on war-zone-related stress as well as military sexual trauma. In the program veterans can

work on skills needed to deal comfortably with other people. The program is sixty days long.

Specialized Outpatient PTSD Programs (SOPPs)

1. PTSD Clinical Teams (PCTs) provide group and one-on-one treatment.
2. Substance Use PTSD Teams (SUPTs) treat the combined problems of PTSD and substance abuse.
3. Women's Stress Disorder Treatment Teams (WSDTTs) provide women veterans with both one-on-one and group treatment.

In addition to these specialized programs, other outpatient treatment options include vet centers and community-based outpatient clinics (CBOCs), which provide primary care in a local setting rather than at the large, centralized VA facilities. Some of these clinics provide mental healthcare. The vet centers operate under the VA Readjustment Counseling Service.

Health Issues Related to Agent Orange

A Congressional Research Service report (Panangala 2008) provides historical information on Agent Orange. Fifteen herbicides were used in Vietnam to defoliate areas of jungle that otherwise provided cover for enemy troops. The most commonly used of these was called Agent Orange because of the identifying orange stripes on the containers. The manufacture of this herbicide resulted in small amounts of dioxin, and this was part of the composite that was sprayed from January 1965 to April 1970. Other agents were used prior to 1965 and were reported to contain higher levels of dioxin, but were used in a more limited area. Veterans reported various delayed illnesses starting in the 1970s, which they attributed to prior Agent Orange exposure. Other than various illnesses caused by higher concentrations of dioxin in laboratory animals, there was no scientific proof that Agent Orange was causative, particularly because those disorders occurred in the civilian population. The burden of proof was on the veteran. However, some of the illnesses that occurred were rare in persons so young. Some soldiers who were exposed to higher concentrations of Agent Orange exhibited serious symptoms even while in country. For others the reaction of chloracne was also more immediate. Even the claims of delayed effects of Agent Orange were for each veteran convincing enough evidence. The Veterans Administration's reaction was slow and there were increasing angry demands by veterans to receive recognition and appropriate treatment (Doyle, Maitland & The Editors of Boston Publishing Company 1985).

Agent Orange Registry

The Veterans Administration established the Agent Orange Registry in August 1978. The purpose was to evaluate the number of cases and have a list of veterans who might need treatment and be considered for compensation. The Veterans Administration ordered that Vietnam veterans (later expanded to other areas of service in which defoliants were used) were to have a detailed history, physical exam, and laboratory tests. Three years after the registry was initiated there were 60,000 names on it, but no one had been compensated. The Veterans Administration said it was awaiting the results of scientific studies to determine what medical problems might be associated with Agent Orange exposure. One of these was the Air Force's Ranch Hand Study, which compared air force personnel who were involved in aerial spraying of Agent Orange to those who flew in those planes but were not involved in the spraying. Another was a study mandated by Public Law 96-151, signed into law on December 20, 1979, "to require the Veterans Administration to conduct an epidemiological study regarding veterans exposed to Agent Orange." The Veterans Administration entered into an agreement with the Centers for Disease Control (CDC) to conduct the epidemiological study. A third study, which the CDC also conducted, focused on the relationship between veterans' Agent Orange exposure and birth defects in their children. In determining eligibility for treatment and compensation for disorders resulting from herbicides, the VA assumes that all who served in Vietnam were exposed to Agent Orange. In 1981 Congress authorized (P.L. 97-22) the Veterans Administration to give priority medical care to Vietnam veterans for any health problems whose cause might be related to Agent Orange exposure. Congress went further in 1984, requiring the Veterans Administration, despite scientific uncertainty, to develop regulations to determine the service connection for disabilities of veterans exposed to dioxin in Vietnam.

The Office of Public Health and Environmental Hazards in VA has a research division, the Environmental Epidemiological Service. It conducts its own research studies on the health of veterans and collaborates with other researchers. It creates and maintains databases and registries of health utilization to support research on veterans' health. One of these sources is the Agent Orange Registry, which now includes 240,000 Vietnam veterans (Department of Veterans Affairs 2010). The Agent Orange Act of 1991 (P.L. 102-4) required VA to enter into an agreement with the National Academy of Science (NAS). In addition to its own research, VA has asked the Institute of Medicine of the NAS to provide independently an evaluation of the scientific literature on the health effects of Agent Orange and other herbicides that were used in Vietnam. The Institute of Medicine updates its report to the Secretary of the Department of Veterans Affairs every two years. VA relies on this information to help in its decisions about which disorders will be considered as presumptively resulting from Agent Orange exposure. Public Law 104-262 (1996) directed that a veteran did not have to prove the link between a listed health condition and exposure to Agent Orange. Over the years VA has expanded the list of disorders that are presumed to be a result of this exposure. Most are delayed in their manifestations. Currently the list includes chloracne and porphyria cutanea tarda (must occur within one year of exposure), transient peripheral neuropathy that occurs within two years after exposure, seven listed types of cancer, type 2 diabetes, and spina bifida in children of Vietnam veterans. A number of other birth defects of veterans' children are recognized as related to service in Vietnam but not to herbicide exposure.

Education

In November 1982 the Veterans Administration published its first Agent Orange review. It provided information to veterans about the status of research in this area and procedures to follow for evaluation and treatment. Between that first review and the most recent in August 2008 there have been forty-seven updates.

VHA developed and administers a program titled Veterans Health Initiatives. VA healthcare providers can use their independent study courses to increase their knowledge of diagnosis and treatment of various service-related conditions. One of these is an online course and study guide for VA employees to assist them in diagnosing and treating their Vietnam veterans who have possible exposure to Agent Orange.

Women Veterans Issues in the Vietnam Era

History

VA has provided a history of the service of women in the armed services that is a useful background for noting the achievements of women veterans during the Vietnam era (Department of Veterans Affairs. Office of Policy and Planning 2007). From the earliest years of American history, women have participated in the armed services. Without formal recognition, they followed family members into battle. Women served as nurses in the Spanish-American War. Shortly afterward, in 1901, Congress formally established the U.S. Army Nurse Corps. Although their importance was recognized, they did not have the military rank and benefits of their male counterparts until 1943, with the establishment of the Women's Army Corps. Between World War I and World War II, the civilian workforce saw an increase in the number of women in clerical positions. This change also occurred in the military, and in World War I there were additional roles for women in the military as draftsmen, translators, and recruiters. Women helped to fill the need for additional armed forces personnel during World War II, and the number and types of positions for women increased. At the end of the war there were approximately 280,000 women (2.3 percent) of a total of 12 million in the armed services. Recruitment during subsequent conflicts has seen a substantial rise in this proportion of females. In 2007 the VA reported that the proportion of women veterans rose from 4 percent in 1980 to 6 percent in 1990. Projections were for 8 percent (or 1.8 million) by 2010 and 10 percent by 2020. By October 31, 2009, that number had been exceeded; at that time there were 1,824,198 female veterans. Recent data on active military indicate that the proportion of female veterans will continue to rise. Of the total active duty armed forces reported as of September 30, 2009, there were 208,829 women or 14.3 percent. Perhaps more important than the growth in numbers is the increase in the breadth of functions of females in the armed services. "They've climbed from being cooks, laundresses and nurses with no rank to generals, admirals, astronauts, pilots, ships' captains, heavy equipment operators, administrators and much more" (Sunderland 2004). The changes have occurred gradually and against opposition and are considered to be still incomplete by women leaders in the military.

A significant change during the Vietnam era was passage of Public Law 90-130 in 1967. This removed promotion restrictions for women officers, and the 1970s saw many "firsts" as a result. "In 1970 Brigadier General Anna Mae Hays, head of the Army Nurse Corps, became the first woman to attain star ranking in nursing. In 1972 Rear Admiral Alene B. Duerk, head of the Navy Nurse Corps, became the first woman admiral; also in 1972, E. Ann Hoefly became a brigadier general in the Air Force Nurse Corps" (Department of Veterans Affairs. Office of Policy and Planning 2007). Also in the 1970s three women were appointed to star ranking who were not nurses.

Along with increased numbers and nontraditional roles for women came increased problems to be addressed by the Veterans Administration's healthcare. From 1962 until withdrawal of troops in 1973, officers in the Women's Army Corps served on the ground in Vietnam and were subject to shelling; they were ruled exposed to Agent Orange. The Veterans Administration system, used to caring for primarily males, had to examine its resources and plan for the health needs of an increasingly large number of women with separate issues. This was addressed in a series of congressional actions. The Veterans Health Care Act of 1983 (P.L. 98-160) established the Advisory Committee on Women Veterans. Since 1984 it has been charged with reviewing the adequacy of VA programs to meet the needs of women veterans. It makes a yearly report to the secretary for administrative and legislative changes. In recent years VA has added programs to treat female veterans diagnosed with PTSD resulting from combat exposure or sexual trauma. The Veterans Health Care Act of 1994 (P.L. 102-585) made specific provisions for women's health and included within the realm of PTSD treatment care for the aftermath of sexual trauma associated with military duty. As mentioned previously, there are women's stress disorder treatment teams within the VA system that are outpatient programs specifically for women dealing with the effects of traumatic stress. P.L. 102-585 also authorized VA to provide gender-specific services such as pap smears, breast examinations, management of menopause, mammography, and general reproductive health services to eligible women veterans. Public Law 103-446 established the Center for Women Veterans. Its mission is to ensure that (1) women veterans receive benefits and services on a par with male veterans; (2) VA programs are responsive to gender-specific needs of women veterans; (3) outreach is performed to improve women veteran's awareness of services, benefits, and eligibility criteria; and (4) women veterans are treated with dignity and respect. The center also promotes awareness of VA services and benefits and promotes research on issues related to female veterans.

A 2007 VA report on the history of women veterans concluded with the following paragraph:

The important role of women in our nation's defense and as part of the veteran population over the years cannot be overstated nor covered adequately in these few short pages. Their history is a glorious one and sadly not always acknowledged or appreciated. With time, however, has come deserved recognition, both for women in the military and for women as veterans. And with their projected larger numbers, with full integration in all branches, including combat units, and with greater ethnic and racial diversity in the armed forces, women will change the face not only of our military, but of our veteran population as well. Women will make up a larger share of the veteran population, add to its diversity, and require veteran services geared to their specific needs. The debt owed to all our veterans and to women in particular demands nothing less than full attention and action. (Department of Veterans Affairs. Office of Policy and Planning 2007)

Homeless Vietnam Veterans

A definition of homeless was provided by Public Law 100-77 (July 22, 1987). This definition is commonly used because it controls federal funding. According to this act a homeless individual is

(1) an individual who lacks a fixed, regular, and adequate nighttime residence, and (2) a person who has a nighttime residence that is:

A. a supervised publicly or privately operated shelter designed to provide temporary living accommodations (including welfare hotels, congregate shelters, and transitional housing for the mentally ill);

B. an institution that provides a temporary residence for individuals intended to be institutionalized; or

C. a public or private place not designed for, nor ordinarily used as, a regular sleeping accommodation for human beings. (P.L. 100-77, as reported in Perl 2007, 3)

History

Homelessness became more evident in the public's awareness during the 1970s and 1980s. Changes in family structure made it less likely that families would accommodate homeless relatives, low-rent temporary housing for transients declined, public drunkenness and vagrancy were no longer a crime and a reason for arrest, and mental hospitals no longer housed the chronically and seriously mentally ill for long periods of time (Perl 2007). Not surprisingly, studies on homeless veterans found that the chronically homeless often suffer from mental illness, have substance abuse disorders, and have limited social connections for emotional and financial support. The first federal program to help homeless veterans was the Veterans Administration's Homeless Chronically Mentally Ill Veterans Program, begun in May 1987 with authorization by Public Law 100-6 and funding of $5 million. This initiative has continued, though it changed its name to Healthcare for Homeless Veterans (HCHV) in 1992. It currently operates under Public Law 109-461. From the beginning of this effort to the present day, essential elements of this intervention have been medical and psychiatric care, including substance abuse treatment, coordination with other local resources, and outreach. The homeless typically do not just show up at a facility.

A report from the National Health Care for the Homeless Council (Zerger 2002) stated that: "Substance abuse is both a precipitating factor and a consequence of homelessness." Zerger stresses that a large proportion of the homeless have need of treatment for substance abuse complicated by a dual diagnosis with another psychiatric disorder, while they also encounter great barriers to accessing this care. This review reports that the homeless typically have access to inpatient treatment only for detoxification, and outpatient treatment is limited to twelve-step programs. In contrast, research points to therapeutic communities modified for the homeless as an effective treatment modality. The HCHV focuses on outreach to those most vulnerable and not in treatment and offers placement in VA treatment and rehabilitation programs. Part of Healthcare for Homeless Veterans' function is to administer VA's Homeless Providers Grant and Per Diem Program. Within the funding limits for each year, it provides to community agencies a grant to help in acquiring buildings used for transitional housing or service centers for veterans. Such programs can also receive a per diem payment up to $35.84 per day for each veteran housed.

Other Current VA Programs

The Department of Housing and Urban Development and VA's Supported Housing (HUD-VASH) Program is a cooperative effort of these two agencies. The VA provides case management and services needed to sustain physical and mental health to veterans who are homeless and eligible for VA healthcare, and HUD provides section 8 vouchers to public housing authorities. The goal is to promote and sustain recovery and permanent housing.

The Domiciliary Care for Homeless Veterans Program takes its origin from Public Laws 100-71 and 100-6. It is a time-limited residential treatment program started in 1987 that assesses each veteran's needs and provides an individualized treatment plan, typically for multiple deficits, that draws on a broad range of services, including medical treatment and psychiatric treatment. Social and vocational rehabilitation services are available. Modalities include group and individual counseling and recreational and occupational therapy.

Stand downs: This term is borrowed from the military, where it refers to a time of rest for exhausted troops who are removed to a relatively safe area for recovery. In regard to efforts to intervene in the lives of the homeless, it refers to a one- to three-day community-based intervention program to give some immediate relief to the basic needs of those on the street, typically food, clothing, showers, and medical and dental care. For longer-term benefits, there are booths for information on veterans' benefits, employment counseling, twelve-step meetings, and counselors to help veterans access services. Vietnam veterans organized the first stand down in 1988 in San Diego. There were approximately 127 stand downs scheduled in cities across the United States during 2010.

The Veterans Justice Outreach Initiative (VJO) was started June 11, 2008, when VHA published Handbook 1160.01. Uniform Mental Health Services in VA Medical Centers and Clinics. It states that the "VA is committed in principle that when veterans' non-violent offences are products of mental illness, veterans and their communities are often better served by mental health treatment than incarceration." To that end, VA medical centers have VJO specialists to conduct outreach, assessment, and case management for veterans involved in the justice system and to refer them to the appropriate VA or community services. (Department of Veterans Affairs 2009, 2).

Healthcare for Reentry Veterans Services and Resources (HCRV)

VHA Handbook 1160.01 requires that each Veterans Integrated Service Network (VISN) have a specialist assigned to this program to ensure that veterans in prison have prerelease assessments and appropriate referrals for medical, psychiatric, social, and employment services and short-term case management upon release. The objective is to reduce the likelihood of homelessness and reincarceration by addressing medical and psychiatric problems that could interfere with successful community reentry.

Supportive Services for Low-Income Veterans

This initiative was authorized by Public Law 110-387 on October 10, 2008. Its purpose was to "facilitate the provision of supportive services for very low income families in permanent housing." It stipulated that "the Secretary shall give preference to entities providing or coordinating the provision of supportive services for very low income veteran families who are transitioning from homelessness to permanent housing." The "entities" referred to include private nonprofit organizations and consumer cooperatives. They provide to these veteran families case management and assistance in accessing VA and other benefits such as healthcare, financial planning, transportation, and legal and housing counseling services. The aim is to make more sustainable the tenuous hold that such families have on permanent housing.

Homeless Veterans Dental Program

VA began this program in 1992. Homeless veterans report that dental care is one of their three top unmet needs. Veterans' own assessment is that dental care improves not only oral health, but also general health and self-esteem. VA sees it as an important element in vocational rehabilitation and in overall homeless rehabilitation. This program operates under directives in Public Law 107-95.

There is no means of recording the exact number of homeless people, but the estimates are useful enough for comparisons and noting trends, and independent estimates are reasonably consistent. The U.S. Interagency Council on the Homeless reported on December 8, 1999 that 23 percent of the homeless population were veterans, and that among the veterans 47 percent had served during the Vietnam era. Using data from the following census year (2000), VA's National Center on Homelessness Among Veterans reported that 10 percent of the adult population of the United States were veterans, but veterans accounted for 15 percent of the homeless. A VA report to Congress in 2007 listed major factors that contribute to homelessness in veterans and may help to account for the higher representation of veterans in the homeless populations. Poor social support after discharge, psychiatric disorders (but not PTSD), substance abuse, and not being married were the direct and major contributing factors. Combat exposure and PTSD were not found to be direct causes of homelessness but were indirect causes as a result of their strong relationship to the four main direct causes. Many veterans report problems with occupational readjustment, citing the lack of opportunity to use infantry training in civilian life. Nonetheless, the average level of education is noted to be higher among the veteran homeless than the non-veterans. VA initiated Project CHALENG (Community Homelessness Assessment, Local Education and Networking Groups) in 1994 to coordinate services provided by local VA centers with the community resources available in their area to provide a continuum of care to help homeless veterans become productive members of the community. The legislative authorization for this was contained in Public Laws 102-45, 103-446 and 105-114. Project CHALENG estimates show a consistent decline in veterans who are homeless in recent years: 195,000 in 2006, 154,000 in 2007, 131,000 in 2008, and 107,000 in 2009.

Substance Use Disorders

There was significant use of marijuana in civilian life in the United States during the Vietnam era. Soldiers on the ground in Vietnam found marijuana more accessible than in the States, and there was no Vietnamese governmental ban on it (Brush 2002). It was said to be the drug of choice for these soldiers whether they had experimented with it prior to being in the service or not. Alcohol abuse has always been linked to military service, and it was regarded by some as the more dangerous substance to interfere with adequate functioning in Vietnam. In the later years of the Vietnam conflict heroin became more available. In Vietnam it was most typically smoked, snorted, or used orally, but rarely injected. There were other drugs of abuse used less frequently, such as other opioids, barbiturates, and amphetamines. In the early 1970s heroin use among the military in Vietnam was estimated at 10 to 25 percent, and it was termed epidemic. The American public grew increasingly concerned about the rise in drug abuse, including heroin, in this country and about returning veterans with addiction problems. In 1970 President Richard Nixon signed into law the Drug Abuse Prevention and Control Act (P.L. 91-513). This changed the federal government's role from solely a punitive one to making efforts at treatment. In 1971 the first federal program for the treatment of opiate addiction with methadone maintenance was ordered by President Nixon. In the same year he ordered the Department of Defense to increase efforts to deal with drug use in the military. In response, urinalysis drug screens were initiated, and detoxification was provided for those who tested positive. The president further ordered that "The Department of Defense will provide rehabilitation programs to all servicemen being returned for discharge who want this help, and we will be requesting legislation to permit the military services to retain for treatment any individual due for discharge who is a narcotic addict" (quoted in Brecher 1972, 1). However, many servicemen were returned to the United States and discharged while still addicted, and few presented at the Veterans Administration for treatment. The National Center for PTSD reports that 60 to 80 percent of veterans applying for help for PTSD also have an alcohol use disorder. Researchers have tried to determine whether one is a cause of the other or both are the result of the same factor, most likely traumatic stress. Exposure to combat is a recognized high-intensity stress that frequently results in PTSD, and alcohol and other substance use disorders are more prevalent in those sustaining traumatic life events (International Society for Traumatic Stress Studies 2005). What researchers and clinicians readily agree on is that when there is comorbidity, as with PTSD and substance abuse, both must be addressed to have any hope of treatment effectiveness. One of the VA programs listed under the PTSD section of this chapter, SUPTs, addresses this very common comorbidity and treatment challenge.

VHA Program Guide 1103.3 (Department of Veterans Affairs 1999) provides guidelines for all mental health treatment in the VA. Each VA facility should have a substance abuse treatment modality, and there must be a full continuum of care for substance use disorders within each geographical region (VISN). An inspector general's report dated June 25, 2009, stated that all but one of the VISNs had a specialized residential program for substance use disorder. There are twenty-one VISNs in the VHA system across the nation. VA's description of the continuum of care for substance use disorders includes

first-time screening for alcohol or tobacco use in all care locations;

short outpatient counseling, including focus on motivation;

intensive outpatient treatment;

residential (live-in) care;

medically managed detoxification (stopping substance use safely) and services to get stable;

continuing care and relapse prevention;

marriage and family counseling;

self-help groups; and

drug substitution therapies and newer medicines to reduce craving.

The continuum of care also refers to the range of intensity of treatment and the degree of restrictions in the environment of care, from inpatient treatment in a locked ward to traditional outpatient services. The creation of the VISN was part of a major restructuring of VA care started in 1995. Managed care principles were instituted by planning for specialized programs to be provided on a regional basis—one within each VISN—rather than a duplication of these services within each VA medical center. The change also included a shift from hospital-based inpatient services to outpatient services and primary care settings. Like other services, substance use disorder treatment moved largely to outpatient settings. When this was not appropriate, the emphasis was on intensive outpatient treatment or residential rehabilitation sites rather than the added and presumably unnecessary cost of traditional inpatient treatment. Inpatient beds were still used, but at a greatly reduced level. A study of this transformation chronicled the number of VA substance abuse programs and patients in three categories of treatment, inpatient, residential, and outpatient, between 1990 and 1997 (Humphreys et al. 1999). Between 1990 and 1994 there was an increase in the total number of substance abuse treatment programs because of significantly increased funding during those years. The largest part of that growth was in outpatient programs, which increased from 98 to 177. The period between 1994 and 1997 showed a decline in the total number of programs (389 to 304) when VA's plan called for a reduction in inpatient services. To some extent the inpatient programs were replaced by residential rehabilitation programs, which require lower staffing ratios than inpatient programs. The Humphreys and colleagues' study reported that there were 2,960 inpatient beds lost and only 560 beds in residential treatment added by 1997. The other compensation for lost inpatient treatment was the increase in the number of intensive outpatient programs, from nineteen to eighty-five, in the same period.

The National Institute on Drug Abuse (2009) lists thirteen principles of effective treatment for substance use disorders, which it gleaned from the body of research into drug treatment. With the continuum of care listed previously, VA is well positioned to provide most of these important aspects of successful treatment of drug abuse. Two areas in which VA treatment may fall short of the ideal are in length of treatment and delay in starting treatment. The National Institute on Drug Abuse principles (2009) address the issue of retaining the patient in treatment for an adequate period of time: "Research indicates that most addicted individuals need at least three months in treatment to significantly reduce or stop their drug use and that the best outcomes occur with longer durations of treatment" (sec. 5), and "Because drug-addicted individuals may be uncertain about entering treatment, taking advantage of available resources the moment people are ready for treatment is critical" (sec. 3). Zerger (2002) echoes these concerns in regard to substance use disorder treatment with the homeless. She lists eight recommended strategies to encourage retention in substance abuse treatment. The first is to eliminate or at least decrease the waiting time between enrollment and admission. Her attention is focused on retention in treatment rather than comparison of programs of different lengths. Shavelson states: "If there is a single consistent finding that has come out of rehab research it is that the longer clients can be maintained in the programs the more likely they are to emerge clean and sober and stay that way" (quoted in Zerger 2002, 19). Unfortunately these are two of the important features that were jeopardized by VA's adoption of managed care procedures. From 1994 to 1997 the average length of stay in substance abuse programs in VA decreased, for inpatient programs from 24 to 20 days and for residential programs from 110 to 65 days. In 1994, 58 percent of residential programs had a waiting list, and in 1997, 74 percent did. Among inpatient programs 68 percent had waiting lists in both 1994 and in 1997. The authors express a specific concern about the waiting lists because many veterans live far from treatment sites, and many are homeless. They recommend an increase in the number of residential settings of treatment (Humphreys et al. 1999).

In June 2009 the inspector general issued a report on a review of residential mental health care facilities in VHA. Data were from fiscal year 2008 (Department of Veterans Affairs. Office of Inspector General 2009). The data

Table 7.1. Review of Residential VA Mental Healthcare Facilities, FY 2008

Cumulative percentages of time between application and screening:	
Within 24 hours	26%
< 3 days	54%
< 1 week	79%
< 2 weeks	90%
< 1 month	92%
Cumulative percentages of time between acceptance and starting the program:	
Within 24 hours	10%
< 3 days	21%
< 1 week	50%
< 2 weeks	67%
< 1 month	84%

on residential substance use disorder treatment in this report indicate an increase in number of programs and number of beds compared with the data from 2007. The number of programs increased from 57 to 67 and of beds from 1,750 to 2,160. Despite these increases, the inspector general's report again expressed concern about waiting lists. Delays occur between application for admission and screening and again between acceptance and starting the program. Table 7.1 shows the report's findings for fiscal year 2008.

The acting under secretary for health agreed with the inspector general's recommendation that this area needs attention. He cited VA's handbook on this issue and stated that veterans who have need of these programs should have timely access to them.

Effectively treating substance use disorder is an important task in itself for the welfare of veterans and society in general. Its treatment is vital to successful treatment of PTSD and in reducing homelessness. Another area of importance for the treatment of substance use disorder was explored in a study of healthcare utilization by Vietnam veterans (Virgo, Price & Ji 1997). The study compared a group of Vietnam veterans who had drug and/or alcohol problems immediately before their service, during their service, or immediately following their service with a group of Vietnam veterans who did not have substance abuse problems. Using several methods of measuring healthcare utilization, the study found that the group with substance use disorder had higher utilization in the twenty years following their service than did the control group. This appears to be added motivation to effectively treat substance abuse in veterans and a possible way to reduce overall VA healthcare costs.

Prosthetics

There were 5,283 amputations and 1,081 soldiers with multiple amputations in the Vietnam War (Gailey 2007). The percentage of soldiers surviving limb loss was much higher (70 percent) than in previous wars because of quick helicopter medivac. Vietnam veterans had the advantage of prior years' research and development of improved prostheses. There were nearly 15,000 soldiers in World War II who suffered amputations. They protested the poorly fitted prostheses that the government provided from the lowest bidder. General Omar Bradley, the administrator of the Veterans Administration in 1945, was noted to have revolutionized the agency. One of the changes he initiated was the establishment of the Prosthetics and Sensory Aids Service. Research in this organization resulted in improvements in prosthetics, orthotics, and aids for the hearing and sight impaired (Downs 2008). From this period on, VA has provided major support to prosthetic research at such facilities as the University of California at Los Angeles, New York University, and Northwestern University. The Veterans Administration began publishing the *Bulletin of Prosthetic Research* in 1968, which continued under that title through 1982. It continued publication of studies in this field from 1983 to the present in the *Journal of Rehabilitation Research and Development* (Wilson 1992).

The Veterans Administration partnered with private investigators, the Department of Defense, and manufacturers of prostheses to improve the quality of prosthetic care for veterans. One such collaboration in the Vietnam era was the Prosthetic Research Study (PRS) at the Seattle Veterans Administration Medical Center. From May 1964 to September 1965 it investigated the advantages of immediate postsurgical fitting of lower extremity prostheses and early ambulation. Although common in Poland and France, it was not yet widely used and accepted. The procedure promoted quicker healing and less postoperative pain. The principal investigator, Ernest M. Burgess, MD, PhD, had an illustrious and dedicated career in the development of new surgical procedures and prosthetic limbs. He is credited with making "prosthetic limbs more functional, life-like and affordable" (Finklea 2008, 2). One of the accomplishments of Dr. Burgess and the Prosthetic Research Study is the development of the Seattle Foot. Amputees were not satisfied with basic ambulation but desired full sport participation. To that end, in 1980 Dr. Burgess began studying the motions involved in running for an amputee.

The device he developed was the first energy-storing prosthesis involving a lightweight spring that is first activated when the person steps down and then releases to assist in the step off. The completion of this project involved local engineering expertise and local manufacturing as well as financial support from the Veterans Administration in the development and testing of the final product. The Seattle Foot won the Presidential Design Achievement Award in 1984 and was released for use in the following year. It was the beginning of the design of a complete Seattle limb system. The Prosthetics Research Study continues to this day as a nonprofit corporation with the stated mission "to create a path for the highest quality of life for people with limb loss."

The ideal of prosthetic research is to develop artificial limbs to the point where they may be thought of as replacement limbs. Vietnam veterans would have to wait for many of the advancements in replacements for limbs. In the 1980s computer-aided design and computer-aided manufacturing (CAD/CAM) of prosthetics was supported financially by the Veterans Administration but was still regarded as experimental. As late as 1992 a history of prosthetics (Wilson 1992) described it as impractical in its level of development at that time. VA provided equipment and training for the development of CAD/CAM at thirty-seven sites in 1993 and 1994. One of the early successful CAD/CAM systems was the Automated Fabrication of Mobility Aids, developed by Ernest Burgess at PRS in association with VA medical centers in New York and Chicago. By 2000 this system was used in more than 150 prosthetic centers (Finklea 2008).

A group of Vietnam veterans who were Dr. Burgess's patients had seen many Vietnamese who were amputees and had not been fitted with any prosthesis. Mostly a result of land mines, there were a reported 300,000 amputees in that country. Upon returning home those veterans asked him to find a way to provide these men, women, and children with prostheses. Dr. Burgess was known not only as an eminent scientist and innovator but also as a humanitarian. He started the Prosthetic Outreach Foundation (POF) in 1989 and opened a Prosthetic Outreach Center in Hanoi in 1990. Because it would create a burden on continued contributions to have prosthetic devices be fabricated in the United States and shipped, he established a fabrication workshop in Ba Vi, Vietnam. Through these efforts, the Vietnamese-staffed clinic and prosthetics factory became self-reliant, and more than 10,000 Vietnamese have become able to walk. The POF has provided prosthetics in many countries to people unable to afford them or who would have no other access to such rehabilitation. Through Dr. Burgess's foresight, dedication, and generosity as well as the loyalty of his associates, his work has continued following his death in 2000. Earlier that year he was honored by U.S. Senate

Resolution 278 for his lifetime achievement in global service to prosthetic medicine, one of many awards and honors (Finklea 2008).

Improvement in the quality of prosthetic devices was not the only challenge VA faced. There were inconsistencies from one VA medical center to another in the availability of prosthetics. When faced with budget cuts, some facilities cut some of their spending in this area, and veterans were faced with delays in needed equipment. On March 15, 1989, under President George H. W. Bush, the VA became a cabinet-level agency, the Department of Veterans Affairs. With this change VA and veterans now had a "seat at the table." In the early 1990s, under pressure from a coalition of veterans' groups, funding for prosthetics was moved to VHA's Central Office Prosthetics Service (Downs 2008).

The VA released an independent study course on traumatic amputation and prosthesis in May 2002 (Department of Veterans Affairs 2002). It begins with a very moving and detailed self-account of a Vietnam veteran, Frederick Downs Jr., describing traumatic injuries, including the loss of his left arm, as a result of a land mine explosion in Vietnam in 1968. After rehabilitation, he completed his master's degree and had a relatively brief service in industry. For about the past thirty-five years he has worked for VA. Fred Downs was named national director of the Veterans Administration's Prosthetic and Sensory Aids Service in 1980. He has been chief prosthetics and clinical logistics officer in VHA since that office was established on September 8, 2005. Among the duties of this office is the procurement of high-quality prosthetics in the most cost-effective manner. VA's volume of purchasing gives it leverage in keeping costs contained. Despite this a VA inspector general report in 2004 found continued inefficiencies in the system, including VA medical centers purchasing from local suppliers at higher cost. The House Committee on Veterans Affairs (2009) reaffirmed the government's commitment to quality of prosthetic care and increased control of expenditures, stating that changes in procedures and even legislation may be required to achieve these ends.

Of special note is that Mr. Downs was one of the first volunteers to conduct a two-week, take-home study of a new advanced, upper-extremity prosthesis funded by the Defense Advanced Research Projects Agency (DARPA). Since 1968, Mr. Downs had used a body-powered, split-hook prosthesis patented in 1912 and modified at the end of World War II. Figure 7.1 shows the revolutionary new arm and innovative socket system that provides Mr. Downs with a greater range of motion than his hook. In an interview with *60 Minutes*, Mr. Downs described his take-home experience with the arm system as providing him with the feeling of being

Figure 7.1. DARPA Upper-Extremity Prosthesis. Courtesy of VA Office of Research and Development.

bilateral again for the first time in over forty years. The arm provides six user-selectable grips that enable, among other things, operation of power hand tools and the ability to pick up small, fragile items (personal communication from Defense Advanced Research Projects Agency, December 22, 2010).

Future Directions

New Developments in Agent Orange Research

On March 25, 2010, VA published a proposal to include the following as presumptive diseases when associated with Agent Orange exposure: B-cell leukemias, including hairy cell leukemia; Parkinson's disease, and ischemic heart disease. There is also before the U.S. Congress proposed legislation to extend the definition of Vietnam veterans who are eligible for benefits relating to Agent Orange exposure. Currently a veteran has to have a record of serving on the ground in the Republic of Vietnam or on inland waterways. The Agent Orange Equity Act of 2009 (H.R. 2254 and S. 1939) would extend the eligibility to all combat veterans who served in the blue water surrounding Vietnam and in the air force over the Republic of Vietnam during the period of the Vietnam War.

Recent Developments in Women Vietnam Veterans' Health

The Secretary of the Department of Veterans Affairs announced on November 18, 2009, that VA was about to conduct a Cooperative Studies program to evaluate the long-term mental and physical health consequences of military service on women veterans during the Vietnam era. The study included 10,000 women veterans, contacted by mail and telephone interview, and for some a review of medical records. Purposes include gaining a greater understanding of the health needs of these women veterans and gathering necessary information for planning for future budgetary needs to provide anticipated programs and needed staffing.

VHA released the updated handbook on health services to women veterans on May 21, 2010. It provides new standard requirements for healthcare to women veterans that must be provided at each VA medical center and CBOC. It gives details on minimum standards and procedures, including timeliness requirements. Included are requirements for breast cancer and cervical cancer screening, gynecological care, maternity care, infertility, breast and reproductive oncology, mental health, and care for conditions related to military sexual trauma.

Recent Developments in Helping Homeless Veterans

On November 3, 2009, at the VA National Summit Ending Homelessness among Veterans, Secretary of Veterans Affairs Eric K. Shinseki stated: "President Obama and I are personally committed to ending homelessness among veterans within the next five years. Those who have served this nation as veterans should never find themselves on the streets, living without care and without hope.... This is not a summit on homelessness among veterans, it's a summit on ending homelessness among veterans" (Department of Veterans Affairs. Public and Intergovernmental Affairs 2009). There is reason to hope that this is more than political hyperbole. The significant reduction in the numbers of homeless veterans each year from 2006 to 2009 is evidence that existing initiatives are effective. Mr. Shinseki reported at the summit that VA would spend a total of $3.2 billion in the following year in areas related to preventing and reducing homelessness among veterans. Of that sum $2.7 billion is for medical services and over $500 million is for specific homeless programs.

On March 22, 2010, the House of Representatives unanimously passed the End Veterans Homelessness Act of 2010 (H.R. 4810). On May 3, 2010, the secretary announced the establishment of a telephone hotline to provide emergency support and resources to homeless veterans.

Future Directions in Prosthetics

The VA has been working closely with DARPA under a 2008 memorandum of agreement and plans to leverage the DARPA program to accomplish lofty goals. Already VA has sponsored an optimization study of one of the DARPA prosthetic arms that gave twenty-six subjects an opportunity to provide design feedback to DARPA; the study logged more than 1,000 use hours on patients from ages nineteen to eighty-two and at all levels of amputation. VA also plans to incorporate a DARPA arm into another ongoing study that would determine how well the arm can be controlled by signals recorded directly from the brain (personal communication from Defense Advanced Research Projects Agency, December 22, 2010). This passage from a VHA publication hints at VA plans:

> Researchers at the Center for Restorative and Regenerative Medicine—a collaboration among VA, Brown University and MIT—are working to improve function for people who have lost limbs. Their overarching goal is to develop high-tech "biohybrid" limbs that merge biological and non-biological materials and work in a natural, lifelike manner. The effort involves investigators with expertise in orthopedics, tissue engineering, neurotechnology, prosthetic design, and rehabilitation. One project involves a brain-computer interface that may allow people to control prosthetic devices and other devices using only their thoughts. (Veterans Health Administration 2010, 23)

Beyond the "biohybrids," VA has helped support the hand transplant study at the University of Pittsburgh Medical Center (UPMC). Its participation in funding this study is through the Armed Forces Institute of Regenerative Medicine. The innovative protocol at UPMC includes both antibody treatment and bone marrow cell therapy that changes the way the immune system functions. This has shown promise as a superior way to prevent organ rejection. The purpose is to reduce the risks associated with antirejection drugs. The first hand transplant at UPMC (the sixth in the nation) was done on March 14, 2009. The recipient was a former marine who lost his right hand during military training (University of Pittsburgh Medical Center 2009). On March 3, 2010, a retired female veteran was the tenth person in the United States to receive a hand transplant. It was the first such transplant performed on a woman in the United States and the first at a Defense Department facility (Lackland Air Force Base).

Colonel Dr. James Ficke, chairman of orthopedic surgery at Brooke Army Medical Center, reported that as yet no active duty serviceperson has had this procedure, but there are about fifty injured service members who might be eligible for it (Young 2010).

Research

It is apparent from the presentation of the major topics in this chapter that VA has been involved in a major and leading way in research in PTSD, substance abuse, Agent Orange, women veterans' issues, homeless veterans, and prosthetics. It is clinical research with important practical results, aimed at understanding these issues facing Vietnam veterans and finding the most effective treatment. In 2010 VA celebrated eighty-five years of Veterans Affairs Research and Development. The occasion was commemorated by National VA Research Week, April 26–30, and the publication of a magazine that highlighted some of the accomplishments of VA research. In addition to the areas previously named, it briefly described research accomplishments in cardiovascular disease, cancer, Alzheimer's disease, traumatic brain injury, chronic obstructive pulmonary disease, genomics, and improvements in laboratory diagnosis and more accurate hospital monitoring devices among other innovations. VA boasts research scientists who have won Nobel prizes for their accomplishments.

The Department of Veterans Affairs report on the proposed 2010 budget for VA included the following statements about continuing research:

> The research program will support 3,345 FTE (Full Time Employees) through direct appropriation and a total of 15,000 research staff through all funding sources.... [The] VA is uniquely positioned to move scientific discovery from investigators' laboratories to patient care. In turn, VA clinical investigators identify new research questions for the laboratory at the patient's bedside, making the research program one of the VA's most effective tools to improve the care of veterans. Embedding research within an integrated healthcare system with a state-of-the-art electronic healthcare record creates a national laboratory for the discovery of new medical knowledge and the translation of that knowledge into improved health. (Department of Veterans Affairs 2009, 1028)

References

American Psychiatric Association. (1980). Diagnostic and statistical manual of mental disorders. 3rd ed. Washington, DC: American Psychiatric Association.

Boscarino, J. (2004). Posttraumatic stress disorder and physical illness. Results from clinical and epidemiological studies. *Annals of the New York Academy of Science* 1032: 141–153. http://www.cfids-cab.org/cfs-inform/Ptsd/boscarino04.pdf (accessed December 29, 2010).

Boscarino, J. (2008). A prospective study of PTSD and early-age heart disease mortality among Vietnam veterans: Implications for surveillance and prevention.

Psychosomatic Medicine 70: 668–676. http://www.psychosomaticmedicine.org/cgi/content/abstract/70/6/668 (accessed December 29, 2010).

Brecher, E. M. (1972). Chapter 20: Heroin on the youth drug scene—and in Vietnam. In *The Consumers Union report on licit and illicit drugs. From the Schaffer Library of Drug Policy.* http://www.druglibrary.org/schaffer/library/studies/cu/cu20.html (accessed December 6, 2010).

Brush, P. (2002). Higher and higher: Drug use among U.S. forces in Vietnam. http://www.library. vanderbilt.edu/central/Brush/American-drug-use-vietnam.htm (accessed December 7, 2010).

Department of Veterans Affairs. (n.d.-a). VA history in brief. http://www1.va.gov/opa/publications/archives/docs/history_in_brief.pdf (accessed December 7, 2009).

Department of Veterans Affairs. (n.d.-b). Mission statement. www.va.gov/landing2_about.htm (accessed July 26, 2011).

Department of Veterans Affairs. (1999). VHA program guide 1103.3. http://www.va.gov/vhapublications/ViewPublication.asp?pub_ID = 1094 (accessed December 29, 2010).

Department of Veterans Affairs. (2002). Traumatic amputation and prosthesis. Independent study course. May. http://www.publichealth.va.gov/docs/vhi/traumatic_amputation.pdf (accessed December 6, 2010).

Department of Veterans Affairs. (2009). Medical and prosthetic research: Veterans Health Administration federal funds. www.navref.org/newsletter/pdf/FY2010 BudgetRequest.pdf (accessed December 7, 2010).

Department of Veterans Affairs. (2010). VA Environmental Epidemiology Service research on Vietnam veterans. Updated October 5. http://www.publichealth.va.gov/exposures/agentorange/health_effects.asp#EESresearch (accessed January 14, 2011).

Department of Veterans Affairs/Department of Defense. (2004). Clinical practice guideline for the management of post-traumatic stress. http://www.healthquality.va.gov/ptsd/ptsd_full.pdf (accessed January 4, 2011).

Department of Veterans Affairs. Office of Inspector General. (2009). Healthcare inspection: Review of Veterans Health Administration residential mental health care facilities. http://www.va.gov/oig/54/reports/VAOIG-08-00038-152.pdf (accessed December 27, 2010).

Department of Veterans Affairs. Office of Patient Care Services. (2009). VA services for veterans involved in the justice system: The Veterans Justice Outreach (VJO) initiative. http://www1.va.gov/HOMELESS/docs/VJO/vjofactsheet.doc (accessed December 27, 2010).

Department of Veterans Affairs. Office of Policy and Planning. (2007). Women veterans: Past, present and future. Rev. and updated September. http://www.va.gov/womenvet/docs/womenvet_history.pdf (accessed December 1, 2010).

Department of Veterans Affairs. Public and Intergovernmental Affairs. (2009). Press release: Secretary Shinseki details plan to end homelessness for veterans.

November 3. http://www.va.gov/opa/pressrel/pressrelease.cfm?id = 1807 (accessed December 1, 2010).

Doyle, E., Maitland, T. & The Editors of Boston Publishing Company. (1985). The Vietnam experience: The aftermath, 1975–1985. Boston: Boston Publishing Company.

Downs, F., Jr. (2008). Prosthetics in the VA: Past, present and future. *Proceedings Magazine* 134, no. 2: 1,260. http://www.usni.org/magazines/proceedings/2008-02/prosthetics-va-past-present-and-future (accessed December 6, 2010).

Finklea, L. (2008). Commending Ernest M. Burgess, MD, PhD with Senate Resolution 278 for his unwavering global service to prosthetic medicine. http://www.rehab.research.va.gov/jour/00/37/4/ed374e.htm (accessed December 6, 2010).

Gailey, R. (2007). Guest editorial. *Journal of Rehabilitation Research and Development* 44, no. 4. http://www.rehab.research.va.gov/jour/07/44/4/pdf/gailey.pdf (accessed December 30, 2010).

Greene, B. (1989). *Homecoming.* New York: G.P. Putnam's Sons.

House Committee on Veterans Affairs. (2009). Clear need for procurement reform at VA: A hearing by the House Veterans' Affairs Oversight and Investigations Subcommittee on December 16, 2009. http://veterans.house.gov/news/PRArticle.aspx?NewsID = 518 (accessed December 6, 2010).

Humphreys, K., Huebsch, P., Moos, R. & Suchinsky, R. (1999). Alcohol and drug abuse: The transformation of the Veterans Affairs substance abuse treatment system. Psychiatric Services 50. http://psychservices.psychiatryonline.org/cgi/content/full/50/11/1399 (accessed December 28, 2010).

International Society for Traumatic Stress Studies. (2005). Traumatic stress and substance use problems. http://www.aaets.org/article187.htm (accessed December 7, 2010).

Jankowski, K. (2007). PTSD and physical health. National Center for PTSD. http://www.ptsd.va.gov/professional/pages/ptsd-physical-health.asp (accessed December 29, 2010).

Karnow, S. (1983). Vietnam: A history. New York: The Viking Press.

Knox, J. & Price, D. (1996). Healing America's warriors: Vet centers and the social contract. Paper presented at Vietnam symposium, After the Cold War: Reassessing Vietnam, Texas Tech University, April 18–20. http://www.vietnam.ttu.edu/events1996_Symposium/96papers/healing.htm (accessed December 7, 2010).

Kulka, R. A., Schlenger, J. A., Fairbank, R. L., Hough, R. L., Jordan, B. K., Marmar, C. R. & Weiss, D. S. (1990). *Trauma and the Vietnam War generation: Report of findings from the National Vietnam Veterans Readjustment Study.* New York: Brunner/Mazel.

Lifton, R. (1973). *Home from the war.* New York: Simon & Schuster.

National Center for PTSD. (2011). Training programs. http://www.ptsd.va.gov/about/training/training-programs.asp (accessed January 13, 2011).

National Institute on Drug Abuse. (2009). Principles of drug addiction treatment: A research based guide. Revised April. http://nida.nih.gov/PODAT/ Principles.html (accessed December 28, 2010).

Nicosia, G. (2001). *Home to War*. New York: Crown Publishers.

Panangala, S. V. (2008). Veterans Affairs: Healthcare and benefits for veterans exposed to Agent Orange. CRS Report for Congress. February 11. http:// www.fas.org/sgp/crs/misc/RL34370.pdf (accessed December 29, 2009).

Perl, L. (2007). Veterans and homelessness. CRS Report for Congress. www.fas .org/sgp/crs/misc/RL34024.pdf (accessed December 27, 2010).

Post-Traumatic Stress Disorder Support Services. (2010). www.ptsdsupport.net/ ptsd_treatments.html (accessed December 29, 2010).

PTSD treatment programs in the U.S. Department of Veterans Affairs. (2007). National Center for PTSD. http://www.ptsd.va.gov/public/pages/va-ptsd-treatment-programs.asp (accessed December 4, 2010).

Schnurr, P. P., Lunney, C. A. & Sengupta, A. (2004). Risk factors for the development versus maintenance of posttraumatic stress disorder. *Journal of Traumatic Stress* 17: 85–95.

Sunderland, S. K. (2004). The lady is a general: Coral Wong Pietsch. Career Kokua. Department of Labor and Industrial Relations, State of Hawaii. www.careerkokua.org/career/article/?id = 90 (accessed May 3, 2011).

University of Pittsburgh Medical Center. (2009). Former Marine is first to receive hand transplant at UPMC. http://www.upmc.com/MediaRelations/NewsReleases/2009/ Pages/marine-hand-transplant.aspx (accessed December 6, 2010).

U.S. General Accounting Office. (1987). Vietnam veterans: A profile of VA's Readjustment Counseling Program. Report to the Ranking Minority Member, Committee on Veterans' Affairs, U.S. Senate. http://archive.gao.gov/d28t5/ 133705.pdf (accessed December 29, 2010).

Veterans Health Administration. (2010). Research advances, prosthetics/amputations. http://www.research.va.gov/resources/pubs/docs/Prosthetics.pdf (accessed December 7, 2010).

Virgo, K., Price, R. & Ji, T. (1997). Substance abuse as a predictor of VA medical care utilization among Vietnam veterans. http://gateway.nlm.nih.gov/Meeting Abstracts/ma?f = 102233465.html (accessed December 6, 2010).

Wilson, B. (1992). History of amputation surgery and prosthetics. In H. K. Bowker & J. W. Michael (Eds.), *Atlas of limb prosthetics: Surgical, prosthetic, and rehabilitation principles*. 2nd ed. Rosemont, IL: American Academy of Orthopedic Surgeons.

Wilson, J. (1994). The sons of Bardstown: 25 years of Vietnam in an American town. New York: Crown Publishers.

Young, V. (2010). Transplant recipient sees potential for wounded warriors. March 3. http://www.defense.gov/news/newsarticle.aspx?id=58169 (accessed December 6, 2010).

Zerger, S. (2002). Substance abuse treatment: What works for homeless people? National Healthcare for the Homeless Council. Prepared for Translating Research into Practice Subcommittee National HCH Council & HCH Clinicians Network Research Committee. http://www.nhchc.org/Publications/ SubstanceAbuseTreatmentLitReview.pdf (accessed December 6, 2010).

Chapter 8

Veterans' Healthcare for Operations Enduring Freedom, Iraqi Freedom and New Dawn

Delilah O. Noronha, John Chardos, Laura Gomez, Samina Iqbal, and Steven Lindley

Operation Enduring Freedom (OEF) in Afghanistan and Operation Iraqi Freedom (OIF) are the U.S.-led military campaigns that are part of the ongoing global war on terror (GWT). Although the name of the operations was changed to Operation New Dawn (OND) on September 1, 2010, this chapter refers to this era of veterans as OEF/OIF/OND. The name change was made mainly to reflect a change of mission and to recognize the evolving relationship with the government of Iraq. Operation Enduring Freedom began in October 2001, and Operation Iraqi Freedom began on March 20, 2003. Approximately 1.64 million U.S. service members have been deployed for OEF and OIF campaigns (Tanielian & Jaycox 2008). Both combat- and non-combat-related factors associated with deployments to these military conflicts have impacted both the physical and emotional health of service members, which in turn has affected their social functioning and their utilization of healthcare. This chapter provides a review of salient health and social issues most relevant to this era of service members. It also provides an overview of actions the Veterans Health Administration (VHA) has taken to address the needs of returning OEF/OIF/OND service members. Though OEF/OIF/OND service members experience a broad range of issues related to their service, this chapter focuses on the most pertinent and commonly recognized ones.

Introduction

As with other war eras, OEF/OIF/OND campaigns have unique characteristics and produce a pattern of health and social problems common in those deployed that differ from other service eras. With regard to recruitment, OEF/OIF/OND consists of 100 percent volunteer, highly trained professional forces. Compared to previous conflicts, the OEF/OIF/OND deployments have been considerably more rapid, involved a higher proportion of the armed forces, been longer, involved frequent multiple deployments, involved exposure to repeated intense combat missions, and tended to have shorter and/or infrequent breaks between deployments (Belasco 2007; Bruner 2006; Hosek, Kavanagh & Miller 2006).

Nearly 26,000 service members have been wounded in action (WIA) or killed in OEF and OIF. Although obviously tragic for those affected, these conflicts have produced historically lower casualty rates of killed or wounded service members when compared to earlier wars. This higher survival rate is likely due in part to both improvement in protective military equipment such as body armor and advances in medical technology (Regan 2004; Warden 2006). Although the higher survival rates are a very positive outcome, there can be significant physical and emotional consequences in those surviving combat injuries. OEF/OIF/OND service members may have a broad range of exposures, which may result in problems with physical and emotional health. For example, a survey by Hoge and others (2004) of 894 army soldiers deployed to Iraq found that 95 percent of those surveyed observed dead bodies or human remains, 93 percent were shot at or received small-arms fire, 89 percent were attacked or ambushed, 65 percent observed injured or dead Americans, and 48 percent were responsible for the death of an enemy combatant. Hoge and colleagues (2004) highlighted that cognitive and behavioral changes may be related to improvised explosive devices (IEDs). Just as alarming is that the physical and emotional injuries and cognitive impairments may not be easily identified in a timely manner.

History: Measures to Address the Problem

The President's New Freedom Commission on Mental Health, announced in April 2003, provided support for taking steps to address the mental health needs of returning service members. Later VHA developed the Mental Health Strategic Plan (MHSP), which specifically set forth recommendations for providing care to OEF/OIF/OND service members. On March 6, 2007, President George W. Bush created the Task Force on Returning Global War on Terror Heroes. Its purpose was to improve the delivery of federal services and benefits to GWT service members and veterans (Department of Veterans Affairs 2007).

The Department of Defense (DoD), VHA, Congress, and president of the United States have supported research that focuses on illness and injury management, quantifying the problems faced by returning service members, and formulating policy solutions (Tanielian & Jaycox 2008). On a local level, Department of Veterans Affairs (VA) facilities have implemented post-deployment integrated care teams.

Overview of Common Health Outcomes of OEF/OIF/OND Deployments

In the months and years following deployment, service members may experience symptoms or functional impairments that lead to a diagnosis of a physical and/or mental health condition. Table 8.1 depicts the frequency of possible diagnoses among OEF/OIF/OND services members that may or may not be deployment-related. While conditions listed in Table 1 are all of concern, the three that fall in the "Mental Disorder" category have received the most attention: post-traumatic stress disorder (PTSD), major depression, and traumatic brain injury (TBI). Tanielian and Jaycox conducted a comprehensive study of the postdeployment health-related needs from 2007 to 2008 associated with PTSD, major depression, and TBI among OEF/OIF/OND service members. Results revealed that approximately one-third of those previously deployed have at least one of those conditions, and approximately 5 percent report symptoms of all three (Tanielian & Jaycox 2008).

Physical Conditions

Service members may sustain deployment-related physical injuries and also acquire infections and/or diseases specific to the area of deployment. They may sustain injuries that result in traumatic or partial limb amputation, nerve damage, burns, wounds, fractures, vestibular damage, vision and hearing loss, physical pain, and mental health and adjustment problems (Department of Veterans Affairs. Quality Enhancement Research Initiative 2009).

Amputation

Amputations due to blast injuries are complicated by significant injury to soft tissue due to the kinetics of the blast, which increases the risk of

Table 8.1. Frequency of Possible Diagnoses among OEF and OIF Veterans

Diagnosis (Broad ICD-9 Categories)*	Frequency	Percent[†]
Infectious and Parasitic Diseases (001-139)	90,069	14.4
Malignant Neoplasms (140-209)	7,816	1.3
Benign Neoplasms (210-239)	35,520	5.7
Diseases of Endocrine/Nutritional/Metabolic Systems (240-279)	182,208	29.1
Diseases of Blood and Blood-Forming Organs (280-289)	20,064	3.2
Mental Disorders (290-319)	313,670	50.2
Diseases of Nervous System/Sense Organs (320-389)	262,878	42.0
Diseases of Circulatory System (390-459)	123,845	19.8
Disease of Respiratory System (460-519)	153,036	24.5
Disease of Digestive System (520-579)	219,342	35.1
Diseases of Genitourinary System (580-629)	85,003	13.6
Diseases of Skin (680-709)	123,985	19.8
Diseases of Musculoskeletal System/Connective System (710-739)	339,575	54.3
Symptoms, Signs and Ill-Defined Conditions (780-799)	304,400	48.7
Injury/Poisonings (800-999)	170,673	27.3

* These are cumulative data since FY 2002, with data on hospitalizations and outpatient visits as of September 30, 2010; veterans can have multiple diagnoses with each health care encounter. A veteran is counted only once in any single diagnostic category but can be counted in multiple categories, so the above numbers add up to greater than 625,384; percentages add up to greater than 100 for the same reason.

[†] Percentages reported are approximate due to rounding.

VA Office of Public Health and Environmental Hazards, December 2010: Cumulative from 1st Quarter FY 2002 through 4th Quarter FY 2010

complications and prolongs healing (Amputee Coalition of America n.d.). The Army Office of the Surgeon General reported that between September 2001 and January 2009 there were approximately 1,286 amputations in OEF/OIF/OND and unaffiliated conflicts. Fifty percent of these amputations were the result of IEDs (Fischer 2010).

Auditory and Vestibular Damage

The incidence of auditory and vestibular damage has risen dramatically in OEF/OIF/OND conflicts because of the increase in blast injuries. Service members may sustain such injuries due to noise, vibration, and other physical exposures during military service. Simply being in a battle zone increases the risk of hearing loss fifty-twofold (Helfer et al. 2005). Auditory dysfunction has been found to be one of the most prevalent service-connected disabilities (Department of Veterans Affairs. Veterans Health Administration n.d.-c). Approximately 60 percent of those with TBI have associated hearing loss and tinnitus (Lew et al. 2007). Air-filled organs like the ear are particularly vulnerable to blast injuries. Blast injuries can lead to hearing loss, tinnitus, central auditory processing deficits, and vestibular impairment (Fausti et al., 2009). Inner ear complications can lead to long-term vestibular problems that can manifest as positional vertigo or oscillopsia, the illusion that static objects are moving. Diagnosis can be challenging and can be missed because vestibular and auditory damage has significant symptom overlap with PTSD and TBI (Cohen et al. 2002). A comprehensive, multidisciplinary evaluation is usually necessary to determine appropriate diagnosis and management. Treatments for auditory and vestibular injuries vary, but may include surgical procedures and/or prosthetic devices.

Ocular Injuries

From 2001 to 2006, more than 1,000 service members were medically evacuated from overseas due to eye injuries (VeteransEyeCare.com 2009). In Iraq and Afghanistan, ocular injuries are most commonly due to IEDs, which can cause barotraumas or damage due to pressure differences between the air space inside or near the body and the surrounding fluid. Improvised explosive devices can also cause eye trauma via projectile debris resulting from the blast. Furthermore, the positive pressure wave from a blast can lead to conditions such as optic neuropathy and retinopathy. Because IEDs are frequently buried in the ground, dirt and rock further complicate surgical management (Mader et al. 2006). Thermal factors can also contribute to injury of the eye. Long-term consequences of thermal eye injury can be subtle and easily overlooked. Signs of problems can include light sensitivity, headaches, difficulty reading, and visual spatial abnormalities. Two-thirds of combat ocular trauma are associated with TBI while roughly 20 percent of TBI have associated ocular problems (Weichel et al. 2009).

Comprehensive screening and evaluation may help in identifying ocular problems. In previous conflicts, many service members would have had the eye removed, but more recent advances have led to many eyes being saved and recovery of eyesight (Mehta et al. 2007). It is recommended that patients with eye injuries be seen by an ophthalmologist for a detailed eye exam. The Defense Authorization Act includes provisions of the Military Eye Trauma

Treatment Act, which creates a Center of Excellence within the DoD to collaborate with VHA on a comprehensive approach to the prevention, diagnosis, alleviation, treatment, and rehabilitation of eye injuries and trauma. Furthermore, it creates a joint DoD/VHA program to coordinate on all aspects of visual dysfunction related to TBI (National Alliance for Eye and Vision Research 2007).

Concussion/Traumatic Brain Injury (TBI)

Blasts are the most common cause of injury in the GWT and are commonly associated with brain injuries. Traumatic brain injury (TBI) has been a "signature wound" of the OEF/OIF/OND era due to the use of IEDs in the combat zone, increasing service members' risk (Uomoto & Williams 2009). A TBI is a disruption of the normal brain function that occurs from a blow and/or jolt to the head, which may also be referred to as a concussion. According to the Defense Veterans Brain Injury Center, approximately 2,700 U.S. service members have suffered a traumatic brain injury (Hoge et al. 2007, 2008). It has been reported that 60 percent of injured military personnel have some degree of TBI (Defense and Veterans Brain Injury Center n.d.).

Because some concussions/TBIs do not penetrate the skull, they may go undiagnosed for long periods of time and may only surface after the service member has experienced a decline in functioning. Concussions/TBIs among service members vary in severity, ranging from mild, when a person is briefly unconscious or mentally unstable, to severe, when a person is unconscious for a long period of time and/or develops amnesia. The more severe levels of TBI may result in a broad range of symptoms, such as problems with cognition (e.g., memory, attention, and concentration), motor, perception, sleep, and behavior (see Vasterling et al. 2006). Although concussions/TBIs may be diagnosed, they do not always result in adverse symptoms. Thus, screening and further evaluation may be useful in identifying the presence of adverse symptoms, diagnosis of concussion/TBI, and emotional conditions (e.g., PTSD), and in treatment planning.

VHA and DoD have established systemwide screening and assessment procedures to identify concussions/TBIs. Screening of service members occurs upon entry into the VHA system, using a TBI clinical reminder tracking system (Schwab et al. 2007). Though the screening procedures are helpful in identifying service members with TBI, they do have limitations and may yield false positive results. Thus, follow-up evaluations are useful. Treatment for concussion/TBI is guided by evaluation results and may be provided through polytrauma programs.

Pain

As a result of strenuous training exercises, life-threatening missions, environmental exposures, and infectious diseases, OEF/OIF/OND service members may sustain injuries and conditions that result in skeletal, burn, amputation, muscular, neuropathic, and other types of pain. The results of a preliminary study by Gironda, Clark, Massengale, and Walker (2006) found that among 970 OEF/OIF/OND veterans, 47 percent had mild levels of pain and 28 percent had moderate to severe levels of pain. Haskell and others (2009) reported that among the 91,414 service members who were assessed for pain, 63.2 percent reported some type of pain and 43.3 percent reported moderate to severe pain. The results of Clark's (2004) examination of summary medical data for 619 service members who were deployed to Iraq and/or Afghanistan who were enrolling in a VA medical center indicate that of 553 who had documented pain scores, 42.7 percent reported some level of pain. Musculoskeletal injuries are the most common during deployment and often result in chronic pain (Owens et al. 2008). Kalra and others (2008) found that 52 percent of ninety-nine OEF/OIF/OND former service members admitted the presence of headaches when asked. Pain management is an important issue for VHA to consider, given that many service members may seek treatment at VA facilities.

The postdeployment pain literature indicates that the prevalence of pain among recent service members may surpass rates observed following the Persian Gulf War (Clark 2004; Gironda, Clark, Massengale & Walker 2006). Studies conclude that early identification, treatment, and consideration of comorbid conditions is necessary in facilitating improved quality of life and psychosocial functioning (e.g., Clark 2004; Kerns & Dobscha 2009). There are various methods and levels of pain care provided by VHA's facilities, including non-opioid pharmacotherapy, outpatient medical procedures, physical interventions, cognitive-behavioral therapy, and complementary alternative medicine interventions. When such remedies are not effective, opioid medication therapy and/or more invasive medical procedures may be considered.

VHA addresses postdeployment pain through research, policy, and practice. In November 1998 VHA's National Pain Management Strategy was launched by the former undersecretary for health for VA, Dr. Kenneth Kizer. The overall goal of this strategy was to develop a comprehensive, multidisciplinary, integrated, system-wide approach to acute and chronic pain management (Kerns & Dobscha, 2009). In the last decade VHA has seen progress in meeting the goals of the National Pain Management Strategy.

VHA and DoD have published the *Clinical Practice Guideline for the Management of Opioid Therapy for Chronic Pain* (Department of Veterans Affairs/Department of Defense Working Group 2003). Because of the multitude of organ systems impacted, polytrauma pain care can be complex. Clark's (2004) commentary on postdeployment pain reports the following implications for pain assessment and intervention: 1) need for community healthcare providers to assess for the presence of pain, 2) need for timely pain interventions, 3) need for multidisciplinary and cognitive-behavioral interventions, and 4) need for a knowledge base regarding treatment of pain and other comorbid conditions. Practice and policy will continue to evolve as VHA gains a better understanding of the prevalence of pain, variations in the pain experience, and the treatment of pain. VHA has met this challenge by establishing the National Polytrauma Pain Subcommittee (Clark et al. 2007).

Polytrauma

Polytrauma is defined as two or more injuries to physical regions or organ systems, one of which may be life-threatening, resulting in physical, cognitive, psychological, or psychosocial impairments and functional disability (Department of Veterans Affairs. Quality Enhancement Research Initiative 2009; Sigford 2008). There are frequent comorbid conditions that may be overlooked that can further complicate recovery (e.g., vestibular problems) (Chandler 2006). Pain, PTSD, TBI, and substance use disorders often co-occur and interact (Shipherd et al. 2007; Ruff, Ruff & Wang 2008; Lew et al. 2007; Villano et al. 2007). Given this, treatment planning and diagnosis may be complex, especially when considering that concussive/TBI symptoms can sometimes be difficult to distinguish from emotional symptoms (e.g., decreased concentration, irritability). Thus when considering symptom overlap among polytrauma conditions (e.g., PTSD and TBI), it is important to focus on symptom management rather than diagnosis, because etiology and diagnosis are not always clear.

Given that such injuries account for 65 percent of combat injuries, task forces, commissions, and review groups have been developed to identify multiple challenges arising from these complexities. These challenges guide activities focused on improving care, processes, and procedures in both the DoD and VHA. Given the potential for mental health and functional impairment, an interdisciplinary approach is useful in addressing physical, psychological, social, and economic problems. VHA and DoD have developed multiple clinical practice guidelines for polytrauma rehabilitation that highlight long-term management, which includes adequate management of pain, mental health, medical comorbidities, and the residual limb (Department of Veterans Affairs/Department of Defense 2009). VHA's polytrauma system of care is the result of improvement activities and was developed in response to the new multiple and complex demands brought on by the GWT.

The polytrauma system of care includes one of four VA polytrauma rehabilitation centers (PRCs) and/or its respective polytrauma network site (PNS). The polytrauma system of care coordinates services across a continuum of care. These programs have developed the necessary expertise to provide coordinated interdisciplinary care. Treatment of brain injury sequelae best occurs before, or in conjunction with, rehabilitation of other disabling conditions. The level of impairment guides the course of treatment. Though the polytrauma system of care is equipped to handle multiple injuries, it has a particular focus on the assessment and treatment of mild TBI (Belanger, Uomoto & Vanderploeg, 2009). Operating under a national memorandum of agreement (MoA) with the DoD, VHA has provided rehabilitation care to the majority of the severely combat-injured requiring inpatient rehabilitation. There are a variety of polytrauma treatment options that integrate use of medical technology such as personal digital assistants (PDAs). VHA and DoD have developed clinical practice guidelines for management of concussion and mild TBI (Department of Veterans Affairs/Department of Defense 2009).

Environmental Exposures

Multiple environmental and occupational exposures that occur during deployment may impact health. OEF/OIF/OND combat service members may have been exposed to a wide variety of environmental hazards during their service in Afghanistan or Iraq. These hazardous exposures may or may not impact health functioning. Service members may be at increased risk of various multiple environmental exposures (e.g., air, water, susceptibility to insect bites, chemical agent resistant coating [CARC] paint, chromium, cold and heat injuries, depleted uranium, and toxic embedded fragments) or undergo routine military procedures (e.g., bioterrorism vaccinations, prophylactic drugs such as Lariam [mefloquine]). (Department of Veterans Affairs/Department of Defense 2009).

VHA has mandated screening for those who have returned from Iraq and/or Afghanistan who may have had such exposures. These screening tools are part of primary care clinical reminders, which help providers deliver higher quality care to patients for both preventive healthcare and management of chronic conditions, and also help ensure that timely clinical interventions are initiated (Department of Veterans Affairs 2006). The OEF/OIF/OND clinical reminders specifically screen for dermatological symptoms, fever, gastrointestinal symptoms, and other symptoms that have lasted three months or longer and have interfered with activities of daily living. (Department of Veterans Affairs. Veterans Health Administration n.d.-d). Service members may have also sustained injuries from bullets and debris from IED blasts. VHA established the Toxic Embedded Fragment Surveillance Center (TEFSC) at Baltimore Veterans Affairs Medical Center to follow OEF/OIF/OND service members who have fragments lodged or embedded in their bodies. It also provides early identification and treatment of potentially related health problems. Identification is facilitated through use of VHA's embedded fragments clinical reminder. Once identified, service members may participate in testing for chemicals that may have been released by fragments. Service members identified as having had a fragment removed or who still have fragments in their bodies are included in a registry (Department of Veterans Affairs. Veterans Health Administration n.d.-e).

It is important to note that an exposure does not necessarily mean that it has an impact on health functioning. Service members who report exposures that occurred during their deployment may be referred to an environmental exposures clinic to be assessed, provided with treatment if needed, and registered in a national registry.

Infectious Diseases and Sexually Transmitted Infections

Service members may acquire infectious diseases (ID) or sexually transmitted infections (STIs) through lifestyle choices (i.e., sexual practices, IV drug use, and tattoos) or via combat exposures (i.e., contact with infected blood) or emergency medical procedures (i.e., blood transfusions). Therefore it is important to screen and educate new returnees about ways to treat and manage their symptoms and prevent reinfection and infection of others.

Sexually transmitted infections are a cause of morbidity in the active-duty military population. After skin infection, STIs were the most common infection for which OIF/OEF service members sought care at VA (Dau, Oda, & Holodniy 2009). Female service members of reproductive age are especially vulnerable to infectious diseases (Wright et al. 2006). For example, in a study of female U.S. soldiers in Kuwait from 2003 to 2004, STIs were found in about 2.5 percent of gynecologic office visits. The most prevalent STIs were genital herpes (29.5 percent), *Condyloma acuminata* (25.0 percent), and *Chlamydia trachomatis* (20.5 percent) (Wright et al. 2006). In 2008 more than 3,000 cases of chlamydia, gonorrhea, or syphilis were diagnosed among active-duty navy sailors and Marines. Although the incidence of human papilloma virus (HPV) is unknown, 205 active-duty female sailors and Marines were diagnosed with cervical cancer from 2001 to 2005 (Navy and Marine Corps Public Health Center 2009).

More alarming are findings about HIV and AIDS infection among service members. Scott (2007) found that twenty-one soldiers acquired HIV infection during deployment between October 2001 and July 2005. In 2008, 102 active-duty sailors and Marines became infected with HIV. Furthermore, from 1985 through 2007, at least 5,375 active-duty navy sailors and Marines were infected with HIV (Navy and Marine Corps Public Health Center 2009).

Contraction of sexually transmitted infections and infectious diseases can have serious consequences for physical health, emotional health, military performance, postdeployment health, and overall functioning (Wright et al. 2006; Department of Veterans Affairs n.d.-a). Preventative interventions and education and policies focused on safe sex practices, environmental risk factors, physical consequences, and the role of substances are important in health promotion and disease prevention. The military has initiated educational programs that address these issues for active-duty service members (Marine Corps Community Services n.d.; Navy and Marine Corps Public Health Center 2001); however, VHA continues to provide usual care methods for screening, providing education for and treating IDs/STIs.

Several policies have been developed for the uniform health services. For example, the DoD's HIV/AIDS prevention program's mission is to reduce the incidence of HIV/AIDS among service members who are deployed overseas. VHA also has an HIV/AIDS program and is the largest single provider of medical care to people with HIV in the United States (Navy and Marine Corps Public Health Center n.d.). Education about IDs/STIs and continued focus on prevention are an important aspect of the overall healthcare provided, especially among service members returning from deployment.

Medically Unexplained Physical Symptoms

Many environmental, occupational, and psychosocial factors may contribute to a complex symptom profile. Such complex symptom profiles may have unidentifiable etiology and are referred to as medically unexplained symptoms. Symptoms may include headaches, fatigue, memory loss, unexpected weight changes, sleep problems, joint pain, skin rash, and digestive problems. It is still not understood why some returning military members experience medically unexplained symptoms, but if reported to or identified by a healthcare provider, the service member's symptoms may be at least evaluated (Department of Veterans Affairs 2009b). VHA created War-Related Illness and Injury Study Centers (WRIISC) to serve combat veterans with unexplained illnesses. It is imperative that even if symptoms are unexplained, providers are sensitive to patients' concerns.

Mental Health

In addition to the physical injuries associated with OEF/OIF/OND deployment, there are aspects of OEF/OIF/OND conflicts that have resulted in problems in mental health functioning. Studies in OEF/OIF/OND populations have demonstrated high rates of positive PTSD, depression, and substance abuse screens. The rates of mental health illnesses are significantly higher than in nondeployed veterans, although the reported rates have varied from 18.5 to 42.7 percent (Hoge, Auchterlonie, & Milliken 2006; Milliken, Auchterlonie & Hoge 2007). High rates have been observed in active duty as well as in veteran populations. For example, Lapierre, Schwegler, and LaBauve (2007) found that of 3,000 active-duty soldiers who were deployed for at least one year and were anticipating another deployment, 44 percent reported clinically significant levels of depressive symptoms, PTSD symptoms, or both. Hoge and others (2004, 2006) reported that among 1,700 returning army soldiers and Marines from Iraq, 15 to 17 percent met criteria for major depression, generalized anxiety disorder, or PTSD, and 24 to 33 percent admitted to using more alcohol than they intended. Active duty service members younger than twenty-five years old had higher rates of PTSD, alcohol, and drug use disorder diagnoses compared with active-duty service members older than forty (Seal et al. 2009). Table 8.2 shows the frequency of possible mental disorders among OEF/OIF/OND Veterans since 2002.

Post-traumatic Stress Disorder (PTSD)

Combat exposure, as well as other aspects of the military experience, are associated with a high rate of developing PTSD. According to a RAND study by Tanielian and Jaycox (2008), nearly 20 percent of Iraq and Afghanistan service members screen positive for PTSD or depression.

There have been significant advances in treatment of PTSD. The primary interventions with the strongest amount of empirical support are cognitively based psychotherapies. Among pharmacotherapies, selective serotonin re-uptake inhibitor medications have also been shown to be effective in some populations. In keeping with VHA's commitment to provide the best care possible for PTSD, the Office of Mental Health Services has launched a national program to train providers in the two psychotherapies with the

Table 8.2. Frequency of Possible Mental Disorders among OEF/OIF Veterans since 2002[1]

Disease Category (ICD 290-319 code)	Total Number of OEF/ OIF Veterans[2]
PTSD (ICD-9CM 309.81)[3]	167,295
Depressive Disorders (311)	122,175
Neurotic Disorders (300)	102,767
Affective Psychoses (296)	72,952
Alcohol Dependence Syndrome (303)	33,660
Nondependent Abuse of Drugs (ICD 305)[4]	27,714
Specific Nonpsychotic Mental Disorder due to Organic Brain Damage (310)	21,533
Special Symptoms, Not Elsewhere Classified (307)	20,026
Sexual Deviations and Disorders (302)	17,034
Drug Dependence (304)	16,799

[1] These are cumulative data since FY 2002. ICD diagnoses used in these analyses are obtained from computerized administrative data. Although diagnoses are made by trained health care providers, up to one-third of coded diagnoses may not be confirmed when initially coded because the diagnosis is provisional, pending further evaluation.

[2] A total of 313,670 unique patients received a diagnosis of a possible mental disorder. A veteran may have more than one mental disorder diagnosis and each diagnosis is entered separately in this table; therefore, the total number above will be higher than 313,670.

[3] This row of data does not include information on PTSD from VA's Vet Centers or data from veterans not enrolled for VA health care. Also, this row does not include veterans who did not receive a diagnosis of PTSD (ICD 309.81) but had a diagnosis of adjustment reaction (ICD-9 309).

[4] This category currently excludes: 85,671 veterans who only have a diagnosis of tobacco use disorder (ICD-9CM 305.1); 20,834 veterans who only have a diagnosis of alcohol abuse (ICD-9CM 305.0); and 15,939 veterans who have diagnoses of both tobacco use disorder and alcohol abuse (ICD-9CM 305.1 and 305.0), but no other ICD-9CM 305 diagnoses.

VA Office of Public Health and Environmental Hazards, December 2010: Cumulative from 1st Quarter FY 2002 through 4th Quarter FY 2010

greatest amount of evidence support, prolonged exposure (PE) (Foa et al. 2005) and cognitive processing therapy (CPT), and to ensure that treatment is available to all veterans in need of these interventions (Monson et al. 2006). It is well known from Vietnam and other combat era service members how untreated PTSD may impact a service member's ability to adjust to civilian life for many, many years. Thus it is imperative to continue screening, treatment, and monitoring procedures.

Depression

Onset of depression following a deployment may be due to several factors, such as grief and loss related to lost comrades, health consequences of war, and transitioning from military culture back to U.S. civilian culture. Tanielian and Jaycox (2008) suggest that major depression is highly associated with combat exposure and should be considered as being along the spectrum of postdeployment mental health consequences. One study indicated that among 289,328 Iraq and Afghanistan service members, 17.4 percent were diagnosed with depression (Seal et al. 2009). Another study found that among 103,788 Afghanistan and Iraq service members deployed between September 2001 and September 2005, 5 percent had a diagnosis of depression (Seal et al. 2007).

Compared to PTSD, there are a much larger body of evidence for effective depression treatments and many more available evidenced-based treatments. Effective treatments for major depression include cognitive behavioral therapy and interpersonal therapy (Department of Veterans Affairs n.d.-b). One consideration is that service members of this era have some ways of coping that may be different than veterans of other eras. For example, they may be more action-oriented and thus at least initially, relaxation, mindfulness, and cognitive techniques may not be well received. Interventions such as behavioral activation and/or computer-based applications may be more helpful. There is also an array of pharamacotherpy treatments in addition to the SSRIs, including other classes of antidepressants and certain anticonvulsants and antipsychotics. VHA offers annual depression screening and risk assessment in addition to screenings for PTSD and alcohol use. If a service member is found to be appropriate and motivated to participate in mental health services, VHA offers a variety of evidence-based treatments such as cognitive-behavioral interventions. As with psychotherapies for PTSD, VHA has launched a national training effort to ensure a sufficient number of providers are appropriately trained in CBT for depression and anxiety.

Substance Misuse

Service members may have substance misuse that occurred before, during or after military service. One study found that among OEF/OIF/OND veterans who received care from VA facilities between 2001 and 2005, approximately 1/5 were diagnosed with a substance use disorder (Seal et al. 2007). The National Survey on Drug Use and Health (2007) reported that 7.1 percent of veterans aged 18 or older met criteria for a substance use disorder in the past year. Substance use contributes to decreased health functioning, decreased psychosocial functioning, legal problems, and morbidity from medical disorders (e.g., HIV).

Today's generation of service members has been reported to have greater access and exposure to substances at earlier ages. For example, among teenagers in the United States, 18 percent have abused Vicodin, 20 percent tried Ritalin or Adderall without prescription, 9 percent abused over-the-counter cough syrup to get high, and more teenagers had abused a prescription painkiller in 2004 than Ecstasy, cocaine, crack, or lysergic acid diethylamide (LSD). Eggleston, Straits-Troster, and Kudler (2009) report that stimulants and sedatives are used by service members to alleviate boredom, manage stress, and enhance performance. Anecdotal evidence indicates that although service members may be deployed to countries where alcohol and drugs are illegal, they are still widely accessible locally or via the postal service.

Alcohol Abuse

Alcohol misuse, abuse, and dependence have been found to be common among OEF/OIF/OND service members and related to combat experiences. The Millennium Cohort Study found that OEF/OIF/OND reserve and national guard personnel who experienced combat were significantly more likely to experience new-onset heavy weekly drinking, binge drinking, and alcohol-related problems compared to nondeployed personnel (Jacobson et al. 2008). Milliken, Auchterlonie, and Hoge (2007) reported that alcohol use was a self-reported problem for 12 percent of active-duty soldiers six months after deployment and for 15 percent of reservists or those in the National Guard. Calhoun and others' (2008) findings included that 1) hazardous alcohol use is prevalent among OEF/OIF/OND service members seeking VA healthcare; 2) 40 percent engage in "risky" potential hazardous drinking, and 22 percent possibly suffer from alcohol use disorder; and 3) 23 percent engage in binge drinking. VHA is conducting mandated screens for alcohol misuse and abuse and providing brief interventions in the primary care setting.

Illicit and Prescription Drug Use

Drug use in addition to alcohol is another problem found among OEF/OIF/OND service members. Thirty-eight percent of 46,571 OEF/OIF/OND service members surveyed abused illicit drugs. The abused drugs include cannabis, opiates, amphetamines, stimulants, and inhalants (Department of Defense 2002). The rate of illicit drug use in the month before the annual survey, including prescription drugs, increased from 5 percent in 2005 to

12 percent in 2008. The rate of drug use, excluding prescription drugs, has been unchanged at 2 percent from 2002 to 2008 (Military Health System 2009).

OEF/OIF/OND service members may also become physically and or psychologically dependent on prescribed or over-the-counter medications such as opiates and benzodiazepine medications (Department of Veterans Affairs/Department of Defense Working Group 2003; Edlund et al. 2007; Hermos, Young, Gagnon & Fiore 2004). An October 22, 2009 Substance Use Disorders QUERI reported that 26,818 service members treated were at VHA for opioid dependence (Department of Veterans Affairs 2009a). Zoroya (2009) noted that prescriptions for opiates for injured or wounded service members had jumped from 30,000 a month to 50,000 a month since the beginning of the Iraq war.

The DoD Survey of Health Related Behaviors Among Active Duty Military Personnel, which includes surveys from 2005 to 2008, surveyed more than 28,500 U.S. active-duty service members about their health behaviors (Bray et al. 2009). The survey results revealed that about 20 percent of Marines had also abused prescription drugs, mostly painkillers, in that same period.

The 2008 Health Related Behaviors survey found that the rate for illicit and prescription drug use in the past month was 12 percent, an increase since the 2005 survey. However, illicit drug use remained unchanged between the 2002 and 2008 surveys, at 2 percent (Military Health System 2009). The 2005 survey showed that 4 percent of soldiers had abused painkillers in the previous thirty days, compared with 13 percent in 2008. Abuse within the previous year was 10 percent in 2005, compared with 22 percent in 2008 (Bray et al. 2009).

There are several other substances that may be commonly abused by service members but may be unrecognized. OEF/OIF/OND service members have been found to be at risk of abusing nonprescribed steroids and consuming excessive caffeine. Though primarily anecdotal, there is limited empirical literature regarding this prevalence. Service members may use steroids to stay physically fit, improve body image, enhance performance, and increase levels of aggression, which may have been adaptive in the field (Eggleston, Straits-Troster & Kudler 2009). Steroid use may be harmful and may cause physical, emotional, and behavioral problems (Corcoran & Longo 1992).

Another commonly overlooked class of drugs among service members is inhalants. Inhalants are accessible, low cost, and rarely screened, which may lead to underdiagnosis or misdiagnosis (Lacy & Ditzler 2007). Inhalants can be attained because they are in products (e.g., compressed air cans) needed to maintain military weapons, computers, and other equipment. Service members may use inhalants recreationally to cope with stress and boredom. Inhalants can have lethal consequences.

The utility of caffeine in the war zone and the availability of various forms of caffeine (e.g., in popular energy drinks, caffeine pills, and supplements) enable OEF/OIF/OND service members to be at risk for using excessive caffeine and potentially developing caffeine-related disorders. Caffeine in excess may result in behavioral issues and contribute to sleep disabilities and headaches.

Clinicians often fail to screen and identify steroid abuse and excess caffeine intake until the consequences of use become obvious. Screening procedures and focusing on prevention will assist in reducing problematic use and its consequences. If a service member is identified as having difficulty with these substances, education may be useful, and, if needed, treatment may be directed by medical or mental health providers. VHA offers both inpatient and outpatient evidence-based treatments for illicit and prescription drug use. Furthermore, VHA has begun efforts to address legal consequences of substance use. For example, veterans' treatment court programs are becoming more accessible (Drug Policy Alliance 2009). Problems with alcohol may be managed in primary care, outpatient specialty care, inpatient, and residential settings. Evidence-based interventions such as motivational interviewing, as well as pharmacological treatments, are provided. VHA also offers inpatient residential programs for alcohol use.

Reintegration

As discussed previously, the variety of physical, mental health, and other social issues that OEF/OIF/OND service members may struggle with upon their return from deployment often makes it difficult to transition to civilian life, access VA facility's services, and navigate within the VA healthcare system. Service members go through extensive military training for months and sometimes years to acculturate to military culture and to learn/adjust to survival skills and procedures. Those who are at the end of their deployment period may have as little as seventy-two hours to prepare to return to the United States. The combination of health consequences, military experiences, and the acculturation to military ways of life may impact the reintegration process. Service members return home with no or limited training in how to transition back into civilian life. Civilian life presents as a setting in which many of the skills they have learned are irrelevant, inappropriate, harmful, and even illegal. Reintegration is the process that service members go through to readjust to the pace and lifestyle of U.S. civilian life. Though not all OEF/OIF/OND service members will experience significant difficulty reintegrating back into civilian life, after being overseas for an extended period of time it is often difficult for some. Things that were once simple may now appear difficult, frustrating, and/or monotonous. Military life during deployment to a combat zone is very different from civilian life in the United States, often making coming home a challenge (Department of Defense. Deployment Health Clinical Center n.d.).

Reintegration issues may transition to clinical mental health diagnoses if not addressed (e.g., depression and PTSD). Reintegration issues may manifest in functional impairments that may not be immediately identified and addressed. One key to positive reintegration is the ability for service members to adapt some military skills, combat experiences, and military culture to civilian life. Readjustment counseling and self-management programs (e.g., battle mind) may facilitate positive reintegration.

The ability to reintegrate into civilian life may also be dependent on the service member's developmental stage at entry into service, during active duty, and at military discharge. This is a particularly salient issue when considering service members who joined the service as teenagers. For these service members, their critical developmental years may have been spent emerged in the military culture. Their sense of identity may be anchored to their military role (i.e., to honor, protect, and defend). While assessing the service member it may be beneficial to consider his or her developmental stage prior to providing interventions. Early identification of problems with reintegration, education, and intervention may help facilitate an adaptive reintegration process and decrease the risk of developing mental health problems.

Extending Service Period

Sometimes after a service member is discharged from the military and returns to civilian life, he or she may begin considering extending the service period. There are various reasons for considering reenlistment, including continued commitment to serve one's country, feelings that the military is where one belongs, feelings that the military meets certain personal needs that civilian life cannot offer, and as a career choice. For some service members, extending the service period may be a difficult decision; for others it may be even more complex when considering the challenge of weighing in the costs and benefits of reenlistment, such as family obligations, financial issues, academic plans, and career goals. Making this decision may be stressful for service members and their families.

Redeployment Approximately 75 percent of OEF/OIF/OND service members have been deployed two or more times to Iraq and/or Afghanistan (Tanielian & Jaycox 2008). Redeployment may be stressful because it may trigger anxieties about characteristics of the deployment (e.g., location, threat, length of deployment, etc.). However, it can also be stressful for reasons not associated with the previous deployment. Service members may have to quickly make plans for their families and/or also work out more practical issues such as home care and/or pet care. Upon a return from deployment, service members typically have to reestablish themselves in civilian life and resume civilian routines. When notified of a recall, some service members may become burdened by the worry of having to do it all over again. Finally, service members' mental health symptoms may be triggered by actual re-experiencing the deployment process. Multiple military deployments may cause a service member and his or her family to experience a cycle of emotions, physical changes, and social adjustments. Contact with a mental health provider prior to redeployment, if possible, may assist with its related stressors.

Family functioning Service members' families are also impacted by combat deployment and reintegration. Unique characteristics of the military culture, such as deployments, separations from friends and family, changes in family roles, and relocations, increase the risk of family-related stress. Combat service members experience a high rate of marital instability and are at increased risk for domestic violence (Kessler 2000; Renshaw, Rodrigues & Jones 2008). Between 2001 and 2004, divorce rates among active-duty army officers and enlisted personnel nearly doubled (Crary 2005). In one study, 75 percent of married/cohabitating OEF/OIF/OND service members reported some type of family problem in the previous week (Sayers et al. 2009). This is of concern because research has found that distressed partners are less likely to provide support to their spouses (Beach & Tesser 1993), which may in turn further stress the service members. Thus there is need to provide family members access to medical information/education; information on physical, cognitive, and emotional changes; and instrumental support. VA facilities offer some level of family services, but it is likely that these programs will expand.

Unemployment Returning service members from Iraq and Afghanistan have been hit by a struggling economy and skyrocketing unemployment rates. New service members face a grim economic picture. The unemployment rate for all post-9/11 service members is 11.6 percent, compared with 10 percent for the general public. Unemployment rates are particularly high for veterans younger than twenty-four, more than 20 percent. The unemployment rate among female service members jumped to 11.2 percent in January from 6.6 percent a year earlier. Similarly, there has been an increase for male service members from 7.5 to 9.4 percent. In the general population, the trend has been much different. Over the same period, the unemployment rate for women and men rose from 6.9 to 8.4 percent and from 8.5 to 10.8 percent, respectively (Bureau of Labor Statistics 2010). In addition, according to a 2005 congressional analysis of census figures, about 1.5 million service members, 6.3 percent, had incomes below the federal poverty line. Service members may seek unemployment resources independently or with assistance from VA facilities.

Academic performance   School may be difficult for returning service members because of mild TBI or emotional symptoms. For many people who have a head injury, going back to school is one of the toughest things they are going to face. A number of head injury factors make this difficult. First, difficulties with attention, concentration, and short-term memory make it very difficult to learn new material. Second, participation in academic activities can be tiring and limit energy needed to do tasks such as studying. An already challenging academic schedule may be further complicated by the presence of mild TBI or emotional distress. Third, returning to school involves social skills that may be impaired by TBI. This is important not just for being able to work with others but to build social support. Fortunately many academic settings have student counseling services that can complement services provided by VHA.

Homelessness   Economic and other factors increase the risk of homelessness for OEF/OIF/OND service members. After Vietnam, it generally took nine to twelve years for service members' circumstances to deteriorate to the point of homelessness (Congressional Research Service 2005). OEF/OIF/OND service members, though, are seeking housing services much earlier after military discharge, some just months after returning from Iraq. According to VA, as of 2009 more than 3,000 Iraq and Afghanistan service members had sought housing assistance in the past four years, up from 1,800 in 2008. The number of female service members who are homeless has doubled in the past decade. The risk factors during service include extended deployment, multiple deployments, combat exposure, disrupted family status, injury, and diminished function.

Many of the homeless service members who were in the regular forces are very young. These individuals entered the service as teenagers, leaving their homes for the first time, never having been responsible for their own housing.

Upon their return, the family home may not be available or available only in the short term. In addition, young veterans who were exposed to childhood risks, unstable housing, and marginal family status are returning to the same unstable environments, with the added stress of combat experience. Veterans Health Administration officials say getting an accurate number of younger Iraq and Afghanistan service members who have become homeless is difficult because many are too embarrassed to seek help or avoid the streets by "house-surfing" with friends and family (Fairweather 2006).

VHA offers a broad range of special programs and initiatives specifically designed to help homeless veterans and service members. These programs promote self-sufficiency and independent living. VHA is the only federal agency that provides substantial hands-on assistance and is considered the largest integrated network of homeless treatment and assistance services in the country (Department of Veterans Affairs n.d.-c).

Special Issues

Suicide and Suicide Prevention

The worst possible outcome of emotional problems is suicide. Kang and Bulman (2008) found that suicide risk among OEF/OIF/OND service members was increased for former active-duty veterans and for veterans diagnosed with a mental disorder. In 2007 there was evidence of a 21 percent increase in suicides among OEF/OIF/OND veterans when compared to that of the United States general population, with adjustment for age, sex, race, and calendar year (Veterans Health Administration, Office of Environmental Epidemiology, cited in Department of Veterans Affairs 2010). Mental health education, screening, and access to suicide prevention coordination programs are useful in preventing suicides among service members.

Female Service Members

To date, the largest group of women service members has served in the OEF/OIF/OND. Between 2002 and 2009 more than 200,000 female personnel served in the OEF/OIF/OND (Department of Veterans Affairs. Veterans Health Administration n.d.-b). Several factors make assessing and treating these female service members unique. In FY 2008 and FY 2009, PTSD, hypertension, and depression were the top three diagnostic categories for female service members treated by VHA (VSSC Women Veterans Health Workload Report 2009). Of the 200,000 female personnel, 110,906 have separated from the military and 51,344 have received care at a VA facility. Fifty-five percent of those that served were active duty, and 45 percent were reservists/guards. Sixty-four percent served in the army, 18 percent in the air force, and 15 percent in the navy. Fifty-three percent were Caucasian, 30 percent African American, and 10 percent Hispanic. Eighty-eight percent were enlisted, and only 12 percent were officers (Department of Veterans Affairs. Veterans Health Administration 2009).

Women, just as men, were exposed to rocket-propelled grenades (RPGs), IEDs, mortars, etc. Similar to their male counterparts, female service members wear heavy protective gear, carry heavy packs, are exposed to extreme temperatures, and may experience emotional stress. Some issues that are unique to female service members are significant hygiene challenges, dietary deficiencies, and immersion in a male-majority military culture (Ritchie 2001).

Some 51,000 female service members seen at VA facilities experience a broad range of health concerns. Musculoskeletal disorders were diagnosed in 50 percent of the female service members; the most commonly diagnosed conditions were joint disorders that included hips, knees, and ankles; low back disorders; and disorders of the cervical region. Mental health disorders were seen in 44 percent of the women. Digestive system disorders were found in 36 percent of the female service members, with dental (gingival and periodontal) and esophageal conditions being most common. Genitourinary disorders were diagnosed in 35 percent of women; menstrual disorders, diseases of the cervix, vagina, and vulva, and urethral disorders were most common. Nervous system disorders were diagnosed in 35 percent of female patients. Respiratory disorders were seen in 29 percent of female service members, and 28 percent were found to have endocrine disorders. Female service members were less likely to report any pain. Among those with pain, female service members were more likely to report moderate to severe pain and less likely to report persistent pain (Haskell et al. 2009). VA facilities offer specialized services to meet the needs of returning female service members. These services may be embedded in an existing postdeployment clinic and may include gender-specific specialty care if needed.

Postdeployment Clinics

Milliken, Auchterlonie, and Hoge (2007) reported that rates of mental health issues increased from three to six months after deployment. Military outprocessing assessment may have differing assessment results than postdeployment assessments conducted after service members have been separated from the military and are back home state-side. Tanielian and Jaycox

(2008) described gaps in the healthcare system and the costs associated with these conditions and with providing quality healthcare to all those in need. The study suggested that treatment engagement within the first year after deployment is imperative. It also reported that military service members with probable PTSD or major depression seek care at about the same rate as the civilian population, and, just as in the civilian population, many of the afflicted individuals were not receiving treatment. Studies have found that approximately half of service members who screened positive for mental health symptoms or who met the criteria for current PTSD or major depression had sought and/or received help from a physician or mental health provider (Hankin et al. 1999; Tanielian & Jaycox 2008).

Many OEF/OIF/OND–era service members fail to initiate or complete a mental health treatment due to barriers such as features of their injuries/conditions (e.g., TBI), practical and logistical concerns, and stigma (Pietrzak et al. 2009). Untreated mental illness threatens to produce functional and occupational disability. Given the dynamic variety of health risks, injuries, exposures, functioning, and family dynamics, the OEF/OIF/OND population is best served with an integrated care approach. Furthermore, failure to engage in VA facilities may deprive service members of five-year postseparation health benefits, time-limited dental benefits, as well as other benefits that may have a limited enrollment window (Department of Veterans Affairs n.d.-a).

VHA has expanded its existing comprehensive healthcare services to meet the needs of the OEF/OIF/OND population. In doing so, it has moved away from a "one size fits all" approach to healthcare. Service members may access VHA services upon discharge from the military. At some facilities, many OEF/OIF/OND service members present or report service-related physical and emotional complaints or screen positive for depression, PTSD, alcohol misuse, TBI, Iraq/Afghanistan conditions, and embedded fragments at their initial VA primary care appointments.

Nationally, many VA facilities have adapted OEF/OIF/OND postdeployment clinics that function using one of three methods of service delivery for care: consultative postdeployment services, independent postdeployment clinic, and integrated postdeployment services. Consultative postdeployment care clinics provide usual care through primary care, but specialty postdeployment-related services (e.g., mental health, social work) are provided through consultation. Independent postdeployment clinics have dedicated space and primary care staff. These clinics only provide services to OEF/OIF/OND service members. Fully integrated postdeployment clinics may consist of primary care medical providers, co-located mental health providers, and OEF/OIF/OND social work case managers who are all embedded in the primary care clinic. Regardless of what model of care is utilized, primary care remains the typical first point of access to postdeployment services.

Postdeployment clinics and services may provide interventions focused on identification of health issues, prevention, and treatment. OEF/OIF/OND service members may present clinically to primary care providers with multiple physical and psychological issues that occur as a result of their deployments and military experiences. An example of such a program is Palo Alto Veterans Affairs Healthcare System, which implemented and integrated postdeployment clinics across the healthcare system. The Palo Alto Veterans Affairs Health Care System utilizes all three models of postdeployment clinics based on differing resources across nine primary care clinics. It provides a collaborative interdisciplinary approach to postdeployment health and in some cases utilizes mental health resources from the primary care–mental health integration teams. New returning service members have the opportunity to meet with their primary care provider, behavioral health provider, and OEF/OIF/OND case manager at their first primary care visit. This visit provides a medical examination, a behavioral health postdeployment assessment, and an OEF/OIF/OND social work assessment. A close collaborative relationship between providers offers the most comprehensive approach to care treatment planning and services. Each discipline brings a unique perspective to ensure all of the patient's physical, mental health, and social needs are met. Whether months or years after the deployment, it is critical that service members have access to healthcare services where their concerns can be comprehensively addressed.

Challenges and the Future

There is still much work needed to address barriers to access and help those requiring VA mental health services. Improving access to mental health services for OEF/OIF/OND service members will require reaching beyond the traditional methods of the DoD and VHA. VHA continues to develop innovations to engage/help service members, including multimedia marketing and education. Service members are not likely to take in information that is quickly told to them in large quantities or provided in hard copies. Today's returning service members vary in their choice of media for education and intervention (e.g., paper, Web, audiovisual); thus they should be provided with options for accessing education and treatment.

Access

Even though VHA has come a long way in increasing access to healthcare, it continues to develop ways to provide access to veterans who live in rural areas. Given the geographic diversity of the OEF/OIF/OND veteran population, other options for providing health services, including vet centers, non-medical centers that offer supportive counseling, and other services and community-based providers must be considered.

Stigma and poor understanding of conditions may be a problem for some OEF/OIF/OND service members. Mental health or medical condition stigma may be present due to fear of job loss, inability to attain work, or more commonly, fear of judgment by others. Further, poor understanding of the prognosis of conditions may serve as a barrier to recovery. Educating veterans and providers about realistic recovery expectations, goals, and social impacts is important. Given some service members' reluctance to utilize mental health services for fear of occupational consequences, VHA and DoD need to consider changes to policies and procedures to decrease those concerns and increase the likelihood that service members will receive needed care.

Cultural differences among this new era of veterans are prominent. VHA providers now more then ever should be aware of the military culture (i.e., understanding ranks, structure, values, processes and procedures, characteristics of combat). Furthermore, healthcare providers should be familiar with generational characteristics of this population. For example, these service members are more technologically savvy, more primed than previous service eras about mental health, and more action-oriented, and their reintegration experience upon return is unique when compared to other service eras. More common cultural diversity issues among this group of service members are age, ethnicity, gender, sexual orientation, and religion.

More training is needed to prepare VHA providers for this new generation of service members. VHA has increased access to postdeployment cultural awareness training. Awareness of this high-profile military generation assists with building rapport with these service members and also with better understanding the service member as a whole. Such training will help VHA providers to become acculturated not only to the OEF/OIF/OND military but also to the generational culture.

Help Seeking

Healthcare has transformed in the past several decades. VHA is in the lead in utilizing evidence-based treatments and interventions; however, engagement in such treatments is up to the service member. Only 37 percent of those service members eligible for VA services have actually received such care. Continued efforts to provide outreach to these service members are imperative.

One frustration among service members is the inability of VA facilities to quickly and efficiently access DoD medical records. Service members express dissatisfaction with having to repeat their histories, some of which involve trauma. Furthermore, inability to access DoD records may delay allocation and/or resources, benefits, and service connection ratings. VHA is currently working to better bridge DoD and VHA records.

Polytrauma is a relatively new concept that has been brought to light by the OEF/OIF/OND campaigns. There are still several unanswered questions about its impact on future functional status, emotional resilience, and overall physical health. Belanger, Uomoto and Vanderploeg (2009) describe the complexities associated with blast-related TBI and acknowledge the need for further research on TBI outcomes and the mechanisms of the injury. Efforts to investigate the impact of polytrauma interventions and programs that have been put in place will continue and shape future innovations in polytrauma. Finally, feedback regarding TBI needs to be phrased in a way that does not inhibit patients' efforts toward recovery.

Given continued U.S. military engagement in Operation New Dawn, there may be a sustained need for VHA services that are further tailored for service members returning from deployment. As VHA enrolls more OEF/OIF/OND service members and identifies deployment-specific needs, it is expected that there will be an increase in need for respective resources. Continued post-deployment research and program development will maximize healthcare outcomes of these veterans.

References

Amputee Coalition of America. (n.d.). The military amputee and the unique characteristics of war injuries. http://www.amputee-coalition.org/military-instep/war-injuries.pdf (accessed February 1, 2012).

Beach, S. R. H. & Tesser, A. (1993). Decision making power and marital satisfaction: A self-evaluation maintenance perspective. *Journal of Social and Clinical Psychology* 12: 471–494.

Belanger, Heather G., Uomoto, Jay M. & Vanderploeg, Rodney D. (2009). The Veterans Health Administration system of care for mild traumatic brain injury: Costs, benefits, and controversies. *Journal of Head Trauma Rehabilitation* 24, no. 1: 4–13.

Belasco, A. (2007). *The cost of Iraq, Afghanistan, and other global war on terror operations since 9/11.* Washington, DC: Congressional Research Service.

Bray, R. M., Pemberton, M. R., Hourani, L. L., Witt, M., Rae Olmsted, K. L., Brown, J. M., Weimer, B. J., Lane, M. E., Marsden, M. E., Scheffler, S. A.,

Vandermaas-Peeler, R., Aspinwall, K. R., Anderson, E. M., Spagnola, K., Close, K. L., Gratton, J. L., Calvin, S. L. & Bradshaw, M. R. (2009). 2008 Department of Defense Survey of Health Related Behaviors among Active Duty Military Personnel. Report prepared for TRICARE Management Activity, Office of the Assistant Secretary of Defense (Health Affairs) and U.S. Coast Guard. http://www.tricare. mil/2008HealthBehaviors.pdf (accessed February 2012).

Bruner, E. F. (2006). *Military forces: What is the appropriate size for the United States?* Washington, DC: Congressional Research Service.

Calhoun, Patrick S., Elter, John R., Jones, Everett R., Jr., Straits-Tröster, Kristy & Kudler, Harold. (2008). Hazardous alcohol use and receipt of risk-reduction counseling among U.S. service members of the wars in Iraq and Afghanistan. *Journal of Clinical Psychiatry* 69, no. 11: 1686–1693.

Chandler, C. (2006). Blast-related ear injury in current U.S. military operations: Role of audiology on the interdisciplinary team. *The ASHA Leader*, July 11.

Clark, M. E. (2004). Post-deployment pain: A need for rapid detection and intervention. *Pain Medicine* 5, no. 4: 333–334.

Clark, M. E., Bair, M. J., Buckenmaier, C. C., III, Gironda, R. J. & Walker, R. L. (2007). Pain and combat injuries in soldiers returning from operations Enduring Freedom and Iraqi Freedom: Implications for research and practice. *Journal of Rehabilitation Research & Development* 44: 179–194.

Cohen J. T., Ziv, G., Bloom, J., Zikk, D., Rapoport, Y. & Himmelfarb, M. Z. (2002). Blast injury of the ear in a confined space explosion: Auditory and vestibular evaluation. *Israel Medical Association Journal* 4, no. 7: 559–562.

Congressional Research Service. (2005). "Issues for Congress 2005." Author Shirley Cranston prepared this Congressional Research Service (CRS) report: Congressional Research Service, "Issues for Congress," 2005. "http://china.usc.edu/(x(1)A(bdqdBrVwygEkAAAAY2lwMDg5YzQtMThiyi00MGY4LThmNTgtZWlxMjM2NGJmYmNmloLXzsrXny3ksAT4RRfz8Vhc1yc1)S(f543ur45xu4p3f45fl2pqq55))/ShownArticle.aspx?articleID=760".

Corcoran, J. P. & Longo, E. D. (1992). Psychological treatment of anabolic-androgenic steroid-dependent individuals. *Journal of Substance Abuse Treatment* 9: 229–235.

Crary, D. (2005). Army divorce rates rising since 2001. Associated Press.

Dau, Birgitt, Oda, Gina, & Holodniy, Mark. (2009). Infectious complications in OIF/OEF service members with traumatic brain injury. *JRRD* 46, no. 6: 673–684.

Defense and Veterans Brain Injury Center. (n.d.). http://www.dvbic.org/ (accessed September 2010).

Department of Defense. (2002). *2002 Department of Defense Survey of Health Related Behaviors among Military Personnel.* Research Triangle Park, NC: RTI International. http://www.tricare.mil/main/news/2002wwfinalreport.pdf (accessed January 2006).

Department of Defense. Deployment Health Clinical Center. (n.d.). Emerging health concerns. http://www.pdhealth.mil/ehc/default.asp (accessed January 29, 2012).

Department of Labor. Bureau of Labor Statistics. 2010. March 12.

Department of Veterans Affairs. (n.d.-a). Returning service members (OEF'OIF). http://www.oefoif.va.gov (accessed January 29, 2012).

Department of Veterans Affairs. (n.d.-b). Depression: Therapy. http://www. health wise.net/myhealthevet/Content/StdDocument.aspx?DOCHWID = hw30709 &SECHWID = ug5179 (accessed July 2010).

Department of Veterans Affairs. (n.d.-c). Homeless veterans. http://www1.va.gov/ homeless/ (accessed June 1, 2010).

Department of Veterans Affairs. (2007). Task Force on Returning Global War on Terror Heroes. http://www.va.gov/op3/Docs/GWOTTaskForce/GWOT_TF_ Report_042407.pdf.

Department of Veterans Affairs. (2009a, October). Quality Enhancement Research Initiative (QUERI), SUD-Opioid Agonist Therapy: Implementing opioid agonist therapy. October 22. http://www.queri.research.va.gov/sud/wwd/oat/

Department of Veterans Affairs. (2009b, December). Medically unexplained symptoms. http://www.warrelatedillness.va.gov/docs/mus-veterans.pdf (accessed July 13, 2010).

Department of Veterans Affairs. (2010). VA suicide prevention program: Facts about veteran suicide. Office of Patient Care Services. Office of Mental Health Services. (Available at www.erie.va.)

Department of Veterans Affairs. Quality Enhancement Research Initiative (QUERI). (2009). Polytrauma/blast-related injuries QUERI Center strategic plan.

Department of Veterans Affairs. Veterans Health Administration. Office of Public Health and Environmental Hazards. (2009). Women veterans health' care: Facts and statistics 1st quarter. http://www.publichealth.va.gov/womenshealth/ facts. asp (accessed March 2009).

Department of Veterans Affairs. Veterans Health Administration. Office of Public Health & Environment Hazards. (n.d.-a). Women veterans' health care. www.publichealth.va.gov/womenshealth/index/asp (accessed February 2010).

Department of Veterans Affairs. Veterans Health Administration. Office of Public Health and Environmental Hazards. (n.d.-b). Women veterans' health care: Facts and statistics. http://www.publichealth.va.gov/womenshealth/facts.asp (accessed August 5, 2010).

Department of Veterans Affairs. Veterans Health Administration. Office of Public Health & Environment Hazards. (n.d.-c). Noise, vibration and other physical exposures. http://www.publichealth.va.gov/exposures/physical/index.asp (accessed July 2, 2010).

Department of Veterans Affairs. Veterans Health Administration. Office of Public Health & Environment Hazards. (n.d.-d). Operations Enduring Freedom and Iraqi Freedom (OEF/OIF/OND) hazardous exposures. http://www.public health.va.gov/exposures/oefoif/index.asp (accessed January 29, 2012).

Department of Veterans Affairs. Veterans Health Administration. Office of Public Health & Environment Hazards. (n.d.-e). Toxic embedded fragments: Toxic Embedded Fragment Surveillance Center. www.publichealth.va.gov/exposures/ toxic_fragments/surv_center.asp (accessed April 28, 2010).

Department of Veterans Affairs. VistA HSD&D. (2006). VistA clinical reminders version 2.0 patch PXRM*2*4: Clinician guide. http://www.va.gov/vdl/documents/Clinical/CPRS-Clinical_Reminders/pxrm_2_4_um.pdf (accessed February 29, 2012).

Department of Veterans Affairs/Department of Defense. Clinical Practice Guideline Working Group, Veterans Health Administration, Department of Veterans Affairs and Health Affairs. (2001). *Management of substance use disorders in primary and specialty care.* Office of Quality and Performance Publication No. 10Q-CPG/SUD-01. Washington, DC: Department of Defense.

Department of Veterans Affairs/Department of Defense. (2009). Clinical practice guideline for management of concussion/mild traumatic brain injury m(TBI) version 1.0. http://www.healthquality.va.gov/mtbi/concussion_full_1_0.pdf (accessed April 7, 2010).

Department of Veterans Affairs/Department of Defense Working Group. (2003). *VA/DoD clinical guidelines for opioid therapy for chronic pain.* Washington, DC: The Office of Quality and Performance, VA & Quality Management Directorate, United States Army MEDCOM.

Drug Policy Alliance (2009). *Healing a broken system: Veterans battling addiction and incarceration* (pp. 1–23). New York: Drug Policy Alliance.

Edlund, M., Steffick, D., Hudson, T., Harris, K. & Sullivan, M. (2007). Risk factors for clinically recognized opioid abuse and dependence among veterans using opioids for chronic non-cancer pain. *Pain* 129: 355–362.

Eggleston, A. M., Straits-Troster, K. & Kudler, H. (2009). Substance use treatment needs among recent veterans. *North Carolina Medical Journal* 70, no. 1: 54–58.

Fairweather, A. (2006). Risk and protective factors for homelessness among OIF/OIF veterans. http://www.nchv.org/news_article.cfm?id=273 (accessed March 15, 2010.

Fausti, S., et al. (2009). Auditory and vestibular dysfunction associated with blast-related traumatic brain injury. *Journal of Rehabilitation Research & Development* 46, no. 6: 797–810.

Fischer, H. (2010). U.S. military casualty statistics: Operation New Dawn, Operation Iraqi Freedom, and Operation Enduring Freedom. Congressional Research Service, September 28. http://www.fas.org/sgp/crs/natsec/RS22452.pdf (accessed April 9, 2012).

Foa, E. B., Keane, T. M., Friedman, M. J. & Cohen, J. A. (2005). *Effective treatments for PTSD: Practice guidelines from the International Society for Traumatic Stress Studies.* 2nd ed. New York: Guilford Press.

Gironda, R. J., Clark, M. E., Massengale, J. P. & Walker, R. L. (2006). Pain among veterans of Operations Enduring Freedom and Iraqi Freedom. *Pain Medicine* 7, no. 4: 339–343.

Hankin, C. S, Spiro, A., III, Miller, D. R. & Kazis, L. (1999). Mental disorders and mental health treatment among U.S. Department of Veterans Affairs outpatients: The veterans health study. *American Journal of Psychiatry* 156, no. 12: 1924–1930.

Haskell, S. G., Brandt, C. A., Krebs, E. E., Skanderson, M., Kerns, R. D. & Goulet, J. L. (2009). Pain among veterans of Operations Enduring Freedom and Iraqi Freedom: Do women and men differ? *Pain Medicine* 10, no. 7: 1167–1173.

Helfer, T. M., Jordan, N. N. & Lee, R. B. (2005). Post-deployment hearing loss in U.S. Army soldiers seen at audiology clinics from April 1, 2003, through March 31, 2004. *American Journal of Audiology* 14: 161–168.

Hermos, J., Young, M., Gagnon, D. & Fiore, L. (2004). Characterization of long-term oxycodone/acetaminophen prescriptions in veteran patients. *Archives of Internal Medicine* 64: 2361–2366.

Hoge, C., Auchterlonie, J. & Milliken, C. (2006). Mental health problems, use of mental health services, and attrition from military service after returning from deployment to Iraq or Afghanistan. *JAMA* 295, no. 9: 1023–1032.

Hoge, C. W., Castro, C. A., Messer, S. C., McGurk, D., Cotting, D. I. & Koffman, R. L. (2004). Combat duty in Iraq and Afghanistan, mental health problems, and barriers to care. *New England Journal of Medicine* 351: 13–22.

Hoge, C. W., McGurk, D., Thomas, J. L., Cox, A. l., Engel, C. C., & Castro, C. A. (2008). Mild traumatic brain injury in U.S. soldiers returning from Iraq. *New England Journal of Medicine* 358: 453–463.

Hoge, C. W., Terhakopian, A., Castro, C. A., Messer, S. C. & Engel, C. C. (2007). Association of posttraumatic stress disorder with somatic symptoms, health care visits, and absenteeism among Iraq war veterans. *American Journal of Psychiatry* 164: 150–153.

Hosek, J., Kavanagh, J. & Miller, L. (2006). *How deployments affect service members.* Santa Monica, CA: RAND Corporation. http://www.rand.org/pubs/monographs/MG432/ (accessed March 13, 2008).

Jacobson, I., et al. (2008). Alcohol use and alcohol-related problems before and after military combat deployment. *JAMA* 300, no. 6: 663–675.

Kalra, R., Clark, M. E., Scholten, J. D., Murphy, J. L. & Clements, K. L. (2008). Managing pain among returning service members. *Federal Practitioner* 25: 36–45.

Kang, H. K. & Bullman, T. A. (2008). Risk of suicide among U.S. veterans after returning from the Iraq or Afghanistan war zones. *JAMA* 300: 652–653.

Kerns, R. & Dobscha, S. (2009). Pain among veterans returning from deployment in Iraq and Afghanistan: Update on the Veterans Health Administration Pain Research Program. *Pain Medicine* 10, no. 7: 1161–1164.

Kessler, R. C. (2000). Posttraumatic stress disorder: The burden to the individual and to society. *Journal of Clinical Psychiatry* 61, supp. 5: 4–12.

Lacy, B. W. & Ditzler, T. F. (2007). Inhalant abuse in the military: An unrecognized threat. *Military Medicine* 172, no. 4: 388.

Lapierre, C. B., Schwegler, A. F. & LaBauve, B. J. (2007). Post-traumatic stress and depression symptoms in soldiers returning from combat operations in Iraq and Afghanistan. *Journal of Traumatic Stress* 20: 933–943.

Lew, H. L., Jerger, J. F., Guillory, S. B. & Henry, J. A. (2007). Auditory dysfunction in traumatic brain injury. *Journal of Rehabilitation Research & Development* 44, no. 7: 921–928.

Mader, T. H., Caroll, R. D., Slade, C. S., George, R. K., Ritchey, J. P. & Nevilee, S. P. (2006). Ocular war injuries of the Iraqi insurgency, January–September 2004. *Ophthalmology* 113: 97–104.

Marine Corps Community Services (MCCS). n.d. Military life: Fitness and health promotion. http://www.usmc-mccs.org/healthpromotions/index.cfm?sid = ml (accessed January 29, 2012).

McCarty, M. (2005). Homelessness: Recent statistics, targeted federal programs, and recent legislation. Washington, DC: Congressional Research Service.

Mehta, S., Agarwal, V. & Jiandani, P. (2007). Ocular injuries in survivors of improvised explosive devices (IED) in commuter trains. *BMC Emergency Medicine* 7: 16.

Military Health System. (2009). Department of Defense Survey of Health Related Behaviors among Active Duty Military Personnel: 2008 survey summary as Q&A. http://www.tricare.mil/2008SurveyQ&As.pdf (accessed January 29, 2012).

Milliken, C. S., Auchterlonie, J. L. & Hoge, C. W. (2007). Longitudinal assessment of mental health problems among active and reserve component soldiers returning from the Iraq War. *JAMA* 298, no. 18: 2141–2148.

Monson, C. M., Schnurr, P. P., Resick, P. A., Friedman, M. J., Young-Xu, Y. & Stevens, S. P. (2006). Cognitive processing therapy for veterans with military-related posttraumatic stress disorder. *Journal of Consulting and Clinical Psychology* 74: 898–907.

National Alliance for Eye and Vision Research. (2007). Defense appropriations and authorization bills address combat-related eye injuries and include vision research funding opportunities. http://www.eyeresearch.org/leg_updates/12.20.07.html (accessed June 1, 2010).

National Survey on Drug Use and Health. (2007, November 1). Serious psychological distress and substance use disorder among veterans. Office of Applied Studies, Substance Abuse and Mental Health Services Administration. http://www-nehc.med.navy.mil/healthy_living/sexual_health/military_std_policy.aspx.

Navy and Marine Corps Public Health Center. (2001, September 9). Uniformed services sexual health policies. http://www-nehc.med.navy.mil/healthy_living/sexual_health/military_std_policy.aspx.

Navy and Marine Corps Public Health Center. (2009, December). Ensuring Navy and Marine Corps readiness through leadership in prevention of disease and promotion of health. Sexual Health and Responsibility Program (SHARP). Promoting Sexual Health. http://www-nehc.med.navy.mil/healthy_living/sexual_health/military_std_policy.aspx.

Navy and Marine Corps Public Health Center. (n.d.). Uniformed services sexual health policies. http://www-nehc.med.navy.mil/healthy_living/sexual_health/military_std_policy.aspx (accessed February 29, 2012).

Owens, B. D., Kragh, J. F., Wenke, J. C., Macaitis, J., Wade, C. E. & Holcomb, J. B. (2008). Combat wounds in Operation Iraqi Freedom and Operation Enduring Freedom. *Journal of Trauma* 64: 295–299.

Partnership for a Drug Free America. 2005. 17th annual study of teen drug abuse (Partnership Attitude Tracking Study).

Pietrzak, R. H., Johnson, D. C., Goldstein, M. B., Malley, J. C. & Southwick, S. M. (2009). Brief report: Perceived stigma and barriers to mental health care utilization among OEF-OIF service members. *Psychiatric Services* 60: 1118–1122.

Regan, T. (2004). Report: High survival rate for US troops wounded in Iraq. *Christian Science Monitor*, November 29.

Renshaw, K. D., Rodrigues, C. S. & Jones, D. H. (2008). Psychological symptoms and marital satisfaction in spouses of operation Iraqi Freedom veterans: Relationships with spouses' perceptions of veterans' experiences and symptoms. *Journal of Family Psychology* 22, no. 3: 586–594.

Ritchie, E. C. (2001). Issues for military women in deployment: An overview. *Military Medicine* 166, no. 12: 1033.

Ruff, L., Ruff, S. & Wang, X. (2008). Headaches among Operation Iraqi Freedom/Operation Enduring Freedom veterans with mild traumatic brain injury associated with exposures to explosions. *Journal of Rehabilitation Research & Development* 45: 941–952.

Sayers, S. L., Farrow, V. A., Ross, J. & Oslin, D. W. (2009). Family problems among recently returned military veterans referred for a mental health evaluation. *Journal of Clinical Psychiatry* 70, no. 2: 163–170.

Schwab, K. A., Ivins, B., Cramer, G., Johnson, W., Sluss-Tiller, M., Kiley, K., Warren, L. & Warden, D. (2007). Screening of traumatic brain injury in troops returning from deployment in Afghanistan and Iraq: Initial investigation of the usefulness of a short screening tool for traumatic brain injury. *Journal of Head Trauma Rehabilitation* 22, no. 6: 377–389.

Scott P. (2007). HIV-1 infections among U.S. Army soldiers deployed to combat operations in Iraq and Afghanistan. In *Proceedings of the 45th Annual Meeting of the Infectious Diseases Society of America, October 4–7, San Diego, CA.* Arlington, VA: IDSA.

Seal, K. H., Bertenthal, D., Miner, C. R., Sen, S. & Marmar, C. (2007). Bringing the war back home: Mental health disorders among 103,788 US veterans returning from Iraq and Afghanistan seen at Department of Veterans Affairs facilities. *Archives of Internal Medicine* 167, no. 5: 476–482.

Seal, K. H., Metzler, T. J., Gima, K. S., Bertenthal, D., Maguen, S. & Marmar, C. R. (2009). Trends and risk factors for mental health diagnoses among Iraq and Afghanistan service members using Department of Veterans Affairs health care, 2002–2008. *American Journal of Public Health* 99, no. 9: 1651–1658.

Shipherd, J. C., Keyes, M., Jovanovic, T., Ready, D. J., Baltzell, D., Worley, V., Gordon-Brown, V., Hayslett, C. & Duncan, E. (2007). Veterans seeking treatment for posttraumatic stress disorder: What about comorbid chronic pain? *Journal of Rehabilitation Research and Development* 44: 153–166.

Sigford, B. J. (2008). "To care for him who shall have borne the battles and for his widow and his orphan" (Abraham Lincoln): The Department of Veterans Affairs polytrauma system of care. *Archives of Physical and Medical Rehabilitation* 89: 160–162.

Tanielian, T. & Jaycox, L. H. (Eds.). (2008). *Invisible wounds of war: Psychological and cognitive injuries, their consequences, and services to assist recovery* (pp. 87–115). Santa Monica, CA: RAND Center for Military Health Policy Research.

U.S. Bureau of Labor Statistics. (2010). Bureau of Labor Statistics Data—Databases, Tables. Retrieved at: data.blsgov/timeseries/LASST060000032010 Jan: 18208603(F) 15964791(F) 2243812(F) 12.3(F) 2010 Feb: 18255058(F) 15999510(F).

Uomoto, J. M. & Williams, R. M. (2009). Post-acute polytrauma rehabilitation and integrated care of returning veterans: Toward a holistic approach. *Rehabilitation Psychology* 54, no. 3: 259–269.

Vasterling, J. J., Proctor, S. P., Amoroso, P., Kane, R., Heeren, T. & White, R. F. (2006). Neuropsychological outcomes of army personnel following deployment to the Iraq War. *JAMA* 296, no. 5: 519–529.

VeteransEyeCare.com. (2009). Eye disease and disorders. AND Federal legislation improves tracking, diagnosis and treatment of military eye trauma. http://www.aao.org/veterans/news/eye_trauma_law.cfm (accessed April 5, 2010).

Villano, C., Rosenblum, A., Magura, S., Chunki, F., Cleland, C. & Betzler, T. (2007). Prevalence and correlates of posttraumatic stress disorder and chronic severe pain in psychiatric outpatients. *Journal of Rehabilitation Research & Development* 44, no. 2: 167–178.

VSSC Women Veterans Health Workload Report. (2009, October). http://www.womenshealth.va.gov/facts.asp (accessed August 5, 2010).

Warden, D. (2006). Military TBI during the Iraq and Afghanistan wars. *Journal of Head Trauma Rehabilitation* 21, no. 5: 398.

Weichel, E., et al. (2009). Traumatic brain injury associated with combat ocular trauma. *Journal of Head Trauma Rehabilitation* 24, no. 1: 41–50.

Wright J., Albright, T. S., Gehrich, A. P., Dunlow, S. G., Lettieri, C. F. & Buller, J. L. (2006). Sexually transmitted diseases in Operation Iraqi Freedom/Operation Enduring Freedom. *Military Medicine* 171, no. 10: 1024–1026.

Zoroya, G. (2009). U.S. service members admit abusing prescription drugs. *USA Today*, December 16. http://www.usatoday.com/news/military/2009-12-16-milhealth_N.htm. (accessed January 30, 2010).

Part III

Global Healthcare for Veterans

Veterans' Healthcare in Other Countries: Australia, Canada, China, Russia, and the United Kingdom

Thomas W. Miller

Introduction

Historical documentation of healthcare for the military can be traced to anecdotal accounts from ancient Greek, Roman, and Egyptian military records. The Romans in particular demonstrated concern about public health issues, which led physicians of the day to cleanse and sanitize wounds and to promote hygiene by members of the military to reduce disease. Hippocrates of Thessaly, Greece, was also a major influence on the medicine of ancient Rome. Hippocrates is given credit for spreading the use of what has come to be known as the "scientific method" in studying disease, originally credited to a Greek physician named Pythagoras. Based on his use of the scientific method, which introduced a research framework to medicine, Hippocrates promoted the belief that the human body was composed of four humors. Both Greeks and Romans developed a strong interest in injury repair. Repairing wounds of war led to the use of the medical techniques traced to a Hindu surgeon, which led the Romans to adopt a medical procedure called the "pedicle flap." This procedure became a significant contribution to military medicine; it involved removing a piece of skin from one part of the body and sewing it onto a damaged area on the warrior.

The focus of these volumes on veterans' healthcare is to address the care and treatment of veterans of the U.S. armed forces. However, other nations also have programs of healthcare and are committed to the health and well-being of their military veteran population. Among the countries that have specialized programs for veterans are Australia, Canada, China, Israel, Russia, and the United Kingdom. A summary of their veterans' healthcare programs follows, with Australia, Canada, and the United Kingdom covered in more detail in separate chapters.

Australia

The Australian Department of Veteran Affairs (DVA) is a separate and independent governmental organization within Australian healthcare. Minister for Veteran Affairs Alan Griffin has reassured the veteran and ex-military service community that the government has no plans to merge the DVA with any other agencies, although discussion of such a move emerged during the first decade of the twenty-first century. The Australian government understands that veterans and the ex-service community have many special needs. Delivering an appropriate level of healthcare for military veterans requires a DVA with a discrete budget and awareness of the special circumstances that exist within this community. The DVA works closely with both Centrelink and Medicare in the Australian healthcare system.

Gradients of services and healthcare benefits are provided to veterans based on their level of eligibility. Entering the second decade of the twenty-first century, the DVA Healthcare Services requires one of the following designated cards to provide services: a Gold Repatriation Health Card, which entitles the veteran holder to treatment for all conditions, or a white card, whose holders are entitled to treatment for conditions accepted by the DVA. (Additional information is available at http://www.dva.gov.au.) Orange cards are for pharmaceuticals only. Some service restrictions apply for residents in aged-care facilities.

The Australian government, through the Department of Health and Aging, sets national health policies and subsidizes health services provided by state and territorial governments and the private sector to military veterans. Total expenditures on health by all levels of government and the private sector account for about 10 percent of Australia's gross domestic product. Within Australia, the state and territorial governments provide a variety of direct health services, including most acute and psychiatric hospital services. State and territorial governments also provide community and public health services, including school health, dental health, maternal and child health, occupational health, disease control activities, and a variety of health inspection functions.

As are several other countries with universal healthcare, Australia is facing growing pressures on health funding because of technological changes, increasing patient expectations, and an aging population. The Australian government funds universal medical services and pharmaceuticals and gives financial assistance to public hospitals, residential aged-care facilities, and home and community care for the aged. It is also the major source of funds for health research and provides support for training health professionals and financial assistance to tertiary students. The main health responsibilities of local government are in environmental control such as garbage disposal, clean water, and health inspections. Local governments also provide home care and personal preventive services, such as immunization.

Public Sector Health Financing

During the early 1980s and by legislation in 1984, a comprehensive healthcare system, known as Medicare, was introduced. Medicare facilitates access by all eligible Australian citizens to free or low-cost medical, optometric, and public hospital care, while leaving them free to choose private health services. This includes veterans of military service. Veterans' financial contributions to the public healthcare system are based on their income and are made through a taxation levy known as the Medicare levy or tax.

By law, Australia's public hospital system is jointly funded by the Australian government and state and territorial governments and is administered by state and territorial health departments. People admitted to public hospitals as public patients covered by Medicare services receive treatment by physicians and specialists nominated by the hospital. They are not charged for care and treatment or after-care by the treating physician or healthcare professional.

Private patients in public or private hospitals can choose their physicians. Medicare will pay 75 percent of the Medicare schedule fee for services and procedures provided by the treating physician or healthcare professional. For patients who have private health insurance, some or all of the outstanding balance may be covered. Private patients are charged for hospital accommodation and items such as surgical room fees and medicine. These costs may also be covered by private health insurance but are not covered by Medicare in Australia.

The entity known as "Medicare Australia" is the agency within the Department of Human Services responsible for processing and paying Medicare benefits for approved services. Medicare Australia also pays pharmaceutical benefits under the Pharmaceutical Benefits Scheme (PBS), which subsidizes an agreed-upon list of prescription medications. For both medical and pharmaceutical services, safety net arrangements exist to make sure patients who need a high level of treatment or medication do not incur significant out-of-pocket expenses. Out-of-pocket costs are the difference between the Medicare benefit provided and what the patient is actually charged for healthcare services.

The Australian government also provides medical, pharmaceutical, and hospital services for military war veterans, war widows, and their eligible dependants under legislation administered by the DVA. The Australian government provides about two-thirds (67 percent) of public sector expenditure on health, and state, territorial, and local governments provide the remaining reimbursement (Organisation for Economic Co-operation and Development 2011).

Nongovernmental Health Sector Financing

Private hospitals in Australia provide about one-third of all the hospital beds in the country. Private medical practitioners provide most out-of-hospital medical services and, along with salaried doctors, perform a large proportion of hospital services. Private practitioners provide most dental services and allied health services such as physiotherapy. About half of all Australians have private health insurance. About 40 percent of the population, some nine million people, is covered by hospital insurance for treatment as private patients in both public and private hospitals. A similar percentage of the population has ancillary coverage for nonmedical services provided out of hospital, such as physiotherapy, dental treatment, and the purchase of prescription eyeglasses.

New Directions in Healthcare for Australian Veterans

The Australian government is seeking to achieve a better balance between public and private sector involvement in healthcare by encouraging all citizens to take out private health insurance, while it also preserves Medicare as the universal safety net. The government helps to make private health insurance more affordable by offering a 30 percent rebate for the cost of private health insurance premiums. Senior Australians and some veterans meeting certain eligibility criteria would receive higher rebates. Safety nets for medical services and pharmaceuticals assist people facing high annual out-of-pocket health costs. An Extended Medicare Safety Net, introduced in 2004, provides further assistance by meeting 80 percent of the out-of-pocket cost of medical services provided outside the hospital, once an annual threshold is reached.

Private sector expenditure on health accounts for about one-third of total health expenditure. The majority of this is the recipients' out-of-pocket expenses and the remainder is expenditure covered by private health and other insurers such as workers' compensation and third-party motor vehicle insurers.

Global Veterans' Healthcare

International collaboration allows Australia and other countries to learn from combined experience and enables Australia to contribute to international and regional health policies. Australia continues to collaborate with health ministries in other countries, international organizations, and health and medical institutes on a range of international health issues. Cooperation with these bodies also helps Australia to set international health standards and support health promotion (Organisation for Economic Co-operation and Development 2011).

Australia places particular emphasis on the Asia-Pacific region, which involves collaboration with ministries of health in China, Indonesia, and Vietnam as well as Pacific Island countries. Australia also works with regional international organizations such as the World Health Organization (WHO), Asia-Pacific Economic Cooperation, and the Organisation for Economic Co-operation and Development on issues that affect the region's and Australia's public health. Issues include the prevention and control of emerging and reemerging infectious disease, pandemic preparedness, health system strengthening, and health and medical research and trade. Australia also participates in international research and health policy exchange programs and contributes to research foundations such as the Commonwealth Fund and the Nuffield Trust.

Medicare Australia works with the World Bank, AusAID, and the WHO to provide international consultancy services in a range of areas, including the development and management of secure online health business solutions, health system financing, health insurance administration, health information systems, pharmaceutical systems design and operations, and training and institutional development.

Foreign Veterans Visiting Australia

Several countries internationally have agreements that allow for healthcare services for their veteran populations and the general public. The Australian government has signed reciprocal healthcare agreements with the governments of the United Kingdom, the Netherlands, Norway, the Republic of Ireland, Finland, Italy, Malta, New Zealand, and Sweden. Veterans from those countries can expect to receive reciprocal healthcare and services as mandated by this agreement. Visitors from these countries are eligible for Medicare assistance for medically necessary treatment. If hospital treatment is required, such visitors are eligible for treatment only as Medicare patients, not as private patients. The agreements between Australia and these countries vary slightly. Foreign visitors who are not named in the agreement are not eligible for Medicare and must arrange for health insurance to cover their stay in Australia.

Royal Flying Doctor Service

The Royal Flying Doctor Service was founded in 1928 by the Reverend John Flynn and is unique to Australia. Veterans in Australia and visiting veterans may also receive healthcare benefits through the Flying Doctor Service. It provides a 24-hour-a-day, 365-days-a-year aeromedical emergency and healthcare service to people who live, work, or travel in Australia's remote areas, including veterans. The Royal Flying Doctor Service reports that it has contact with some 242,000 patients each year, about 35,000 of whom are medically transported to other sites to receive needed healthcare. From its twenty-one bases, the service's forty-seven aircraft fly over its "territory" of 7,150,000 square kilometers and cover almost 22 million kilometers annually in service to direct patient care.

Best known for its emergency evacuation services, the Royal Flying Doctor Service conducts some 12,000 healthcare clinics each year, treating about 127,000 patients. It is continuing to build on its primary healthcare role for people in remote areas. A large proportion of its work also involves telephone and radio consultations by doctors and nurses with people at remote outposts. The Royal Flying Doctor Service receives grants from the federal, state, and Northern Territory governments, but also relies on funds donated by the business sector and the general public.

The Australian government has fully funded the delivery of the Royal Flying Doctor Service's traditional services: aeromedical evacuations, primary and community healthcare clinics, telehealth consultations, and general healthcare. The state and Northern Territory governments will continue to be responsible for funding the transportation of patients between hospitals. The Australian government reports that over the last few years it has provided nearly $150 million in recurrent and capital funding for the provision of healthcare services to its veterans and the general public. A more thorough discussion of veterans healthcare and benefits is accessible at the Australian DVA Web site (http://www.dva.gov.au).

Canada

Veterans' healthcare in Canada is provided through the Department of Veterans Affairs, which is a federal department of the Canadian government. Although life-threatening cases are dealt with as an emergency, some specialist services needed are nonurgent, and patients are seen at the next available appointment in their locally chosen facility. Although the services of their physicians and hospitals are included in Canadians' benefit packages, they do have to pay for the cost of prescription medications. Many purchase insurance to cover the costs of other services, but this is not required. Some veterans do meet some expenses themselves out of pocket. Chapter 11 discusses healthcare for Canadian veterans in detail.

China

Veterans' healthcare in China has been based for some time primarily on a socialized medicine system, in which most Chinese, including urban and rural residents, enjoy low-priced medical and healthcare services. In the early 1980s China began several economic reforms, which dismantled the socialized medicine model and began to embrace a modified economically driven healthcare model to ease the government's burden of healthcare costs for the Chinese population (French 2006). At the turn of the twenty-first century, China adopted a market-driven healthcare system for all Chinese, including veterans. Insufficient government funding resulted in deficits for public health institutions, thus opening the door for hospitals to generate their own revenue by raising fees and aggressively selling medications. Growing public criticism of soaring medical fees, lack of access to affordable medical service, poor doctor-patient relationships, and low medical insurance coverage compelled China, beginning in 2006, to consider a new round of reforms (see Davis & Schoen's study of the comparative performance of healthcare internationally [2007]).

By the end of 2008 the Chinese government had published its reform plan, clarifying the government's responsibility by saying that it would play a dominant role in providing public health and basic medical services. It declared that both central and local governments should increase healthcare funding. The percentage of the government's input into total health expenditure would be increased gradually so that the financial burden of individuals could be reduced. The plan listed public health, rural areas, city community health services, and basic medical insurance as four key areas for government investment. It also promised to tighten government control over medical fees in public hospitals and to set up a "basic healthcare system" to address public complaints about rising costs of medication and healthcare.

A healthcare plan was approved by the Chinese cabinet in January 2009. This effort to remodel and reform the Chinese medical system of healthcare delivery was estimated to cost more than 850 billion yuan by 2011 to provide universal medical and healthcare coverage, thus providing basic medical healthcare on the national level for all Chinese citizens, including veterans.

Israel

Israel has maintained a system of socialized healthcare since its establishment in 1948, although a national health insurance law has provided national health insurance coverage for all citizens and military only since January 1, 1995. The state of Israel is responsible for providing health services to all residents of the country, who can register with one of the four health service funds. To be eligible for healthcare services and medication, a veteran of Israel must pay a health insurance tax. Healthcare coverage in Israel includes medical diagnosis and treatment; preventive medicine and healthcare options; hospitalization in general; and specified services including maternity delivery and healthcare, psychiatric care and chronic healthcare, surgery and transplants, preventive dental care for children, first aid and transportation to a hospital or clinic, medical services at the workplace, treatment for drug abuse and alcoholism, necessary medical equipment and appliances, obstetric healthcare and fertility treatment, medication, treatment of chronic diseases, and paramedical services such as physical therapy, occupational therapy, and other allied healthcare services (Organisation for Economic Co-operation and Development 2011).

Russia

Veterans' healthcare in the Soviet Union and then under Perestroika alerted Russians to the need for reform in their healthcare delivery system. Russia has a history of providing healthcare to veterans through its socialized medicine model and healthcare benefits to the general population nationally. In addition to this level of care, there were special private hospitals for the healthcare of military officers and war heroes, some of which were located in remote areas of Russia, with access to these hospitals limited by selection through the Russian military.

Veterans of the military in Russia receive healthcare and treatment services through a universal healthcare services model. During the Soviet period between 1917 and the early 1990s, the country had a healthcare model based on a totally socialist model of healthcare. This reflected a centralized, integrated, hierarchical organization in which the government provided free healthcare to all citizens and veterans. Initially successful at controlling communicable diseases, the effectiveness of the healthcare delivery model declined with economic problems throughout the country. Healthcare policy and planning also suffered because of poor governmental initiatives. The National Mental Health Research Center in Moscow had a strong interest in collaborative clinical research and care for veterans with post-traumatic stress disorder with other countries, including the United States. Veterans of various wars and military experiences had suffered the same or similar reactions to combat as had been the focus of study in the United States and other Western countries. (Miller et al. 1992; Miller et al. 1993). Despite the Soviet government's efforts between 1950 and 1990 to double the number of hospital beds available to the public, including veterans, and to increase access to physician healthcare, the quality of care began to decline throughout the 1980s, and medical care and health outcomes fell below Western benchmarks, resulting in patient dissatisfaction with available healthcare, access difficulties in some regions, and limited financing for healthcare services.

As Russia approached the twenty-first century, new healthcare policy and planning switched to a mixed model of healthcare coverage for veterans and the general public of private financing and national financing functioning alongside state financing and provision of healthcare services. The OECD (Organisation for Economic Co-Operation and Development 2011) reported that unfortunately, none of this has worked out as planned, and the reforms have in many respects made the system worse. The population's health has deteriorated on virtually every measure. The resulting system across the Russian Federation in 2006 was an overly complex and very inefficient system of healthcare. It has little in common with the model envisaged by the Russian Federation reformers. Although there are more than 300 private insurers and numerous public ones in the market, real competition for patients is rare, leaving most patients with little or no effective choice of insurer, and in many districts and regions, no choice of healthcare provider. The insurance companies have failed to develop as active, informed purchasers of healthcare services. Most are passive intermediaries, making money by simply channeling funds from regional funding to healthcare providers across the Russian Federation (Organisation for Economic Co-Operation and Development 2006).

In 2010 *Itar-Tass* noted that the Russian government continues to seek reform of the national healthcare model, with Prime Minister Vladimir Putin acknowledging the importance of healthcare reform for the general public and veterans, especially those associated with the Great Patriotic War (World War II) and other military conflicts in Afghanistan and Chechnya. Recognizing the needs of healthcare professionals and citing the need for improved training and educational institutions; treatment programs; prosthetic care for veterans' qualitative medical care; and cutting-edge methods of diagnostics, treatment rehabilitation, and prevention (Zhuraleva 2010), Putin defined a new direction for Russian Federation healthcare. He announced a large-scale healthcare reform in 2011 and pledged to allocate more than 300 billion rubles ($10 billon) over the next few years to improve healthcare in the country. He also said that obligatory medical insurance tax paid by companies for compulsory medical insurance will increase from current 3.1 to 5.1 percent (Fedorenko 2011).

United Kingdom

Veterans' healthcare in the United Kingdom is provided through the National Health Service (NHS) system and until recently through the Haslar Naval Hospital in Southampton, England (Miller 1992). The current delivery system of healthcare is the result of the National Insurance Act of 1911, which created a system of medical and unemployment insurance for all male workers sixteen years of age or older (Järvelin 2002). The system, funded by a tax of four pennies per week from the employee, three from the employer, and two from the government, was at first received with some concern by the medical profession but was eventually seen to have advantages in providing standardized healthcare to both the general public and veterans across the United Kingdom.

In 1948 the national healthcare system was extended to the entire population and a new service, the National Health Service (NHS), was established. Today it is the world's largest publicly funded health service. It was set up on July 5, 1948, to "provide healthcare for all citizens, based on need, not the ability to pay." It is funded by the taxpayers, and in England it is managed by a government department, the Department of Health, which sets overall policy on health issues which, for the English NHS, are summarized in the NHS Constitution for England. There are four separate health services, one each for the three constituent nations (England, Scotland, and Wales and Northern Ireland). In practice, they work closely together and provide a seamless service based on the same core principles. The NHS is committed to providing quality care that meets the needs of everyone, is free at the point of service, and is based on a patient's clinical need and not ability to pay for healthcare services, whether a veteran or civilian (Berwick 2010; English National Health Service 2008).

Choice in Healthcare

Every citizen in the United Kingdom has the right to register with any general physician of his or her choice practicing in that area, district, or region. If the general practitioner has contracted to provide NHS services, as virtually all have done, then all consultations with the general practitioner will be free of charge to the patient. An NHS general practitioner is usually not allowed to refuse to register a patient, and patients usually choose to maintain a relationship with that general practitioner over a long period to maintain continuity. All treatments are offered on the basis of the informed consent of the patient and, when a referral is made to a specialist at a hospital, the patient can choose which hospital to be referred to. A Web site informs patients which NHS hospitals in their area offer the referred service and provides details about the quality, service indicators (such as number of procedures each year and percentage of successful outcomes), as well as details about the wait times for that service. NHS patients have a choice of providers, including at least one private provider, all of which receive the standard NHS fee for the standard NHS level of care. The patient can make the appointment at home using the Internet or obtain assistance from the general practitioner or staff members to make the booking. However, the patient cannot access medical services such as specialists without a referral from the general practitioner (Davis & Schoen 2007).

Some citizens of the United Kingdom choose to be treated in private hospitals. Most private treatment options are at the patient's own expense, but sometimes the NHS may subcontract work to a private operator, in which case the NHS offers to pay for care in a private facility. Veterans who choose to go fully private for a particular health care episode must pay for it on their own, including the cost of follow-up care and medications, or obtain funding through an insurance policy.

Veterans receive their general healthcare services through the general practitioners or family doctors who are responsible for the care of patients registered with them. General practitioners are mostly self-employed doctors who choose to contract with the NHS to provide services to patients commissioned by primary care trusts. Some have employment contracts with general practitioner practices, and a few are directly employed by the local primary care trust. Self-employed general practitioners have considerable freedom in the way that they choose to provide clinical care and services.

Only general practitioners (NHS or private) can refer their patients to a hospital (NHS or private) for acute care. Most patients choose to be treated in NHS-run hospitals. Private hospitals mostly specialize in routine surgery and do not have the range of equipment that is available in NHS general hospitals. (A more thorough discussion of veterans' healthcare benefits in the United Kingdom is accessible through the Web site, http://www.nhs.uk/aboutnhs/ nhshistory/Pages/NHSHistorySummary.aspx.) See also chapter 12.

Comparative Healthcare Analysis across Countries

In an international comparative study of the healthcare systems in six countries (the United Kingdom, Australia, Canada, Germany, New Zealand, and the United States), the British healthcare system was ranked in first place for quality of care. It also gained first-rank position for equity and efficiency and a top place ranking for performance overall. Contrary to opinion sometimes expressed in the United States, citizens, seniors, and veterans in the United Kingdom are well cared for by their NHS system (Glied 2008).

For greater detail and discussion of veterans' healthcare in Canada, Australia, and the United Kingdom, see chapters 10, 11, and 12. Dr. David Dunt, from the Centre for Health Policy, School of Population Health at the University of Melbourne, and Jo Robinson and others have studied critical issues related to suicide in veterans and provide an important look at Australian research and prevention efforts for veterans' healthcare in chapter 10. Dr. David Pedlar and Stewart Macintosh examine Veterans Affairs Canada in greater detail in chapter 11. Finally, healthcare for British veterans is examined by researcher and scholar Dai Williams in chapter 12.

References

Berwick, D. (2010). Transcript: Dr. Donald Berwick's speech to the British National Health Service. *Kaiser Health News*. http://www.kaiserhealthnews .org/Stories/2010/July/07/berwick-british-NHS-speech-transcript.aspx (accessed January 20, 2010).

Davis, K. & Schoen, C. (2007). Mirror-mirror on the wall: An international update on the comparative performance of American health care. *The Commonwealth Fund*. http://www.commonwealthfund.org/usr_doc/1027_Davis_mirror_mirror_inter national_update_final.pdf (accessed March 8, 2009).

English National Health Service. (2008). A practical guide to NHS Connecting for Health. http://information.connectingforhealth.nhs.uk/prod_images/pdfs/ 31556.pdf (accessed March 8, 2009).

Fedorenko, Vladimir. (2011). Putin calls for large-scale health care reform starting 2011. *RIA Novosti*. http://en.rian.ru/russia/20100420/158666502.html (January 17, 2011).

French, Howard W. (2006). Wealth grows, but health care withers in China. *New York Times*, January 14. http://www.nytimes.com/2006/01/14/international/asia/14health.html (accessed May 23, 2010).

Glied, Sherry A. (2008). Health care financing, efficiency, and equity. National Bureau of Economic Research Working Paper no. 13881, March.

Järvelin, Jutta. (2002). Health care systems in transition. The European Observatory on Health Care systems. http://www.euro.who.int/document/e74071.pdf (accessed February 25, 2009).

Miller, Thomas W. (1992). Long-term effects of torture in former prisoners of war. In M. Basoglu (Ed.), *Torture and its consequences*. New York: Cambridge University Press.

Miller, T. W., Kraus, R. J., Kamenchenko, P. & Krasnianski, A. (1992). Assessment of PTSD in Soviet and American veterans. *International Journal of Psychology* 27, nos. 3/4: 546–547.

Miller, T. W., Kraus, R. F., Krasnianski, A. & Kamenchenko, P. (1993). Post-traumatic stress disorder in U.S. and Russian veterans. *Hospital and Community Psychiatry*, 44, no. 6: 585–589.

Organisation for Economic Co-operation and Development (OECD). (2006). Economic Survey of the Russian Federation 2006: Executive summary. http://www.oecd.org/document/63/0,3746,en_2649_201185_37722111_1_1_1_1,0 0.html.

Organisation for Economic Co-operation and Development (OECD). (2011). Health care reforms in Russia.

Reid, T. R. (2009). *The healing of America: A global quest for better, cheaper, and fairer health care.* New York: Penguin Press.

Relman, Arnold S. (2006). Crisis of abundance: Rethinking how we pay for health care. *New England Journal of Medicine* 355: 1073–1074.

U.S. Census Bureau. (2011). American Community Survey Office, January 11. http://www.census.gov/acs/www/table_comparisons/ (accessed January 21, 2011).

U.S. Department of Veterans Affairs. (2010). Fiscal year 2010 performance and accountability report, Office of Budget, November 15. http://www.va.gov/budget/report/ (accessed January 25, 2011).

Zhuraleva, V. (2010). Teaching history of medicine in Russia.

Suicide in the Ex-service Community: Australian Research and Prevention Efforts for Veterans' Healthcare

David Dunt, Jo Robinson, Colleen Doyle,
Gennady Baksheev, and Suganya Selvarajah

Suicide is recognized as a major public health problem that affects all sectors of society. Although rates of suicide are lower among those currently serving in the military than in the general population, this effect fades over time, so that some years after service, rates of suicide have been found to be higher among veterans of military service than in the general population.

This chapter explores the rates of, and risk factors for, suicide among war veterans and discusses some approaches that may be implemented to address these. It begins with an overview of the rates of suicide in the general population to provide a context for the problem of suicide among war veterans. This is followed by an investigation of the rates of suicide among war veterans in the wider international literature and the literature specific to Australia. Risk factors for suicide are then considered, both in the general population and among war veterans. This is followed by a discussion of a range of prevention programs that may go some way toward reducing suicide rates among war veterans.

Defining Suicide

The continuum of suicide ranges from ideas or thoughts (suicidal ideation) and gestures to suicide completions, but this chapter focuses primarily on completed suicides. In the absence of an internationally accepted definition of suicide, this chapter uses a definition that was proposed by the National

Institute of Mental Health Center for the Studies of Suicidal Prevention meeting in 1972–1973 and further refined by O'Carroll and colleagues (1996). For the purposes of this chapter, *suicide* refers to "death from injury, poisoning or suffocation where there is evidence (either explicit or implicit) that the injury was self-inflicted and that the decedent intended to kill himself/herself" (O'Carroll et al. 1996). The section on prevention programs also refers to suicide attempts. *Suicide attempt* has been defined as "a non-fatal, self-inflicted destructive act with explicit or inferred intent to die" (Goldsmith et al. 2002). Suicide attempts occur at approximately twenty times the rate of completed suicides and are a key risk factor for suicide; hence they are often used as proxy indicators of the effectiveness of suicide prevention programs. *Suicidal ideation* is more common still and has been defined as any thoughts, images, beliefs, voices or other cognitions reported by the individual about intentionally ending his or her own life (Wenzel, Brown & Beck 2009).

Rates of Suicide in the General Population

Suicide is a major public health problem and is a leading cause of death both in Australia and internationally. In 2005 in the United States alone, more than 30,000 lives were lost to suicide, a rate of 11.1 per 100,000, and approximately 1 million were lost worldwide. In 2004 more than 2,000 lives were claimed by suicide in Australia, corresponding to a suicide rate of 10.55 per 100,000, while more than 4,000 lives were claimed in the United Kingdom in 2007, corresponding to a rate of 6.45 per 100,000. Suicide rates vary significantly from one geographical region to another; however, this may reflect variable data collection procedures, with less accurate reporting from less-developed countries (see table 10.1).

Table 10.1. Suicide Rates per 100,000 for Selected Countries

Country	Year	Total	Males	Females
United States	2005	11.0	17.70	4.50
United Kingdom	2009	6.9	10.9	3.0
Australia	2006	8.2	12.8	3.6
China (selected rural and urban areas)	1999	13.9	13.00	14.80
Azerbaijan	2007	0.6	1.00	0.30
Belarus	2007	27.4	48.7	8.8

Source: Most recent data from the World Health Organization (WHO 2009, 2012).

Not only do suicide rates vary by country, but they also vary within each country. In the United States, for example, higher rates have been reported in the western states than in central and eastern states and higher in rural than in urban areas (Goldsmith et al. 2002). In Australia between 2001 and 2005, the highest suicides rates were seen in the Northern Territory, followed by Tasmania, Queensland, and South Australia. These states had higher suicide rates compared to the national average. In contrast, New South Wales, Victoria, and the ACT had suicide rates below the national average (Australian Bureau of Statistics 2007). Consistent with findings from the United States, suicide rates are higher in rural areas than in metropolitan areas, and men ages twenty to twenty-nine in rural areas have particularly high suicide rates (Caldwell, Jorm & Dear 2004).

Suicide rates also vary according to gender and age. Generally male suicides outnumber female suicides at a ratio of 3–5:1 in most Western countries, such as the United States, Australia, and the United Kingdom. These ratios are lower in most Asian countries. China is the sole country for which rates of suicide are higher for females than males (World Health Organization 2009).

Suicide is a leading cause of death among young adults, being ranked among the top three causes of death for those fifteen to thirty-four years of age (World Health Organization 2001). In Australia in 2008, the highest age-specific suicide rate for males was for those in the forty- to forty-four-year-old age group (26.4 per 100,000) and for females in the fifty- to fifty-four-year-old age group (8.6 per 100,000) (Australian Bureau of Statistics 2010). Internationally, however, of all the age groups the elderly have been shown to have the highest rates of suicide, particularly among males ages seventy-five and older (see figure 10.1) (World Health Organization 2002).

Suicide rates also vary according to other factors, such as race and ethnicity, sexual orientation, and incarceration status. In the United States in 2006, across all age groups and both males and females, the rates of suicide are reported to be highest among non-Hispanic whites (12.48 per 100,000) and Native Americans/Alaskan natives (11.98 per 100,000). The suicide rates are lower among Asian/Pacific Islanders (5.7 per 100,000) and non-Hispanic blacks (4.96 per 100,000). Homosexual youths are more likely to attempt and complete suicide (Lebson 2002). Suicide rates have also been shown to be approximately eleven to fourteen times higher among jail inmates than in the general population (Hayes 1989).

A range of suicide methods is used in the general population. In Australia, in 2009, the most common method was found to be hanging, which accounted for approximately half (52 percent) of all deaths. Other

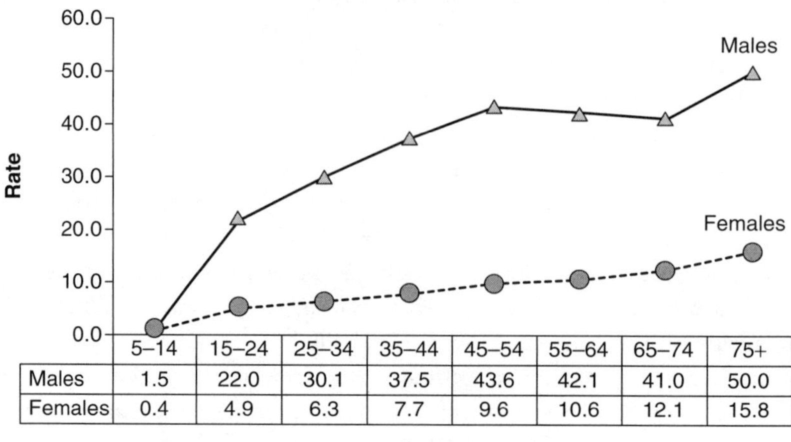

	5–14	15–24	25–34	35–44	45–54	55–64	65–74	75+
Males	1.5	22.0	30.1	37.5	43.6	42.1	41.0	50.0
Females	0.4	4.9	6.3	7.7	9.6	10.6	12.1	15.8

Figure 10.1. Distribution of Suicide Rates. *Source: World Health Organization (2002).*

methods included poisoning by drugs (15 percent); poisoning by other methods, including by alcohol and motor vehicle exhaust (12 percent); and the use of firearms (7.7 percent). The remaining suicide deaths comprised drowning, jumping from a high place, and "other" methods (Australian Bureau of Statistics 2011). In the United States, firearms are the most commonly used method of suicide, with over half (50.7 percent) of the individuals who died by suicide in 2006 using this method (American Association of Suicidology 2006). The most common method of suicide used in more rural countries, such as China, India, Sri Lanka, and Vietnam, is the ingestion of pesticide (World Health Organization 2004).

Rates of Suicide among War Veterans

Although war veterans have not been cited as a high-risk group for suicide (Living is for Everyone Framework 2007; National Strategy for Suicide Prevention 2001; National Suicide Prevention Strategy for England 2002), there is emerging evidence of elevated rates of suicide among this population compared to the general population. People recruited into the armed forces are subject to an intense physical and mental health screening process and thus represent a healthy subgroup of the total population. Due to this screening process, it is likely that rates of physical and mental problems would be lower compared to the general population. However, this "healthy worker" effect may be counterbalanced by the deleterious effects of exposure to war combat, so that war veterans may eventually report poorer health in the long term than does the general population.

The studies of morbidity and mortality among veterans have been well documented, with many including suicide rates as an indicator of health. Although the focus of these studies has been primarily the physical health of veterans, there have been an increasing number of studies on mental health status, and suicide in particular, among this population. Veterans of a number of major deployments since World War II have been studied, with Vietnam War veterans receiving the majority of this attention.

"Evidence" cited in various media reports suggests that suicide rates are elevated among war veterans. A five-month investigation undertaken by CBS News (2007) found that in 2005, American veterans were more than twice as likely to commit suicide as were nonveterans. These reporters obtained suicide data from forty-five of the fifty states and found that the rate of suicide among war veterans was between 18.7 to 20.8 per 100,000, compared to a rate of 8.9 per 100,000 among the general population (CBS News 2007). Further media reports go so far as to suggest a suicide "epidemic" among war veterans, some claiming that suicides among military veterans increased by as much as 25 percent from 2005 to 2007 (IPS News 2010).

A number of international empirical studies more significantly have investigated suicide among war veterans, primarily in the United States (see table 10.2). The majority of these studies concluded that the rate of suicide is elevated among veterans in comparison to the general population. For example, Kaplan, Huguet, and McFarland (2007) used data from the National Health Interview Survey to estimate the risk of mortality from suicide among American male veterans. Their sample comprised 104,026 veterans and 216,864 nonveterans. They found that over a twelve-year period, veterans were twice as likely to die by suicide than male non-veterans in the civilian population. The risk of death from natural or external causes (accidents and homicides) did not differ between veterans and nonveterans after adjusting for confounding factors. This study, however, did not examine factors that may have increased the risk of suicide among veterans, such as the presence of underlying psychiatric conditions (Kaplan, Huguet & McFarland 2007).

A further study, the U.S. Veterans Health Study, was conducted by Zivin and colleagues (2007) and studied 807,694 veterans. These researchers

Table 10.2. Selected International Studies of Suicide among War Veterans

Authors	Location	Description of Method	Results/Suicide Rates
Zivin et al. 2007	United States	VA National Registry for Depression linked to Data Merge Initiative and National Death Index N = 807,694	88.25 per 100,000 people. 1,683 committed suicide during study period (0.21%).
Thoresen, Mehlum & Moller 2003	Norway	Norwegian men who served one or more 6-month terms with a UN or NATO peacekeeping or peace-enforcement operation N = 22,845 males, linked with general population and cause of death registries	Standardized mortality ratio for suicides was 1.41 (95% CI 1.1–1.8). SMR reduced to 1.1 and not significant when marital status was controlled for.
Thoresen & Mehlum 2004	Norway	Norwegian male veterans of peacekeeping operations who served during 1978–1995 N = 22,275	73 suicides and 68 accidental deaths. There are common risk factors for alcohol-related fatal accidents and suicide—increased level of unemployment, problems in social network, negative life events in their last year, suicidal communication, major depression, alcohol or substance abuse, and psychiatric treatment (also of borderline significance, increased rate of living alone).
Thoresen, Mehlum, Roysamb & Tonnessen 2006	Norway	45 interviews with next of kin for deceased suicide subjects from cohort (n = 22,275) of Norwegian male	Peacekeeper veterans who committed suicide had significantly more parental psychosocial problems in their childhood, and had

(continued)

Table 10.2. (*continued*)

Authors	Location	Description of Method	Results/Suicide Rates
		veterans; questionnaire data from random n = 888 male veterans	experienced 3 out of 11 negative life events. Involuntary repatriation was a major risk factor for completed suicide.
Kaplan, Huguet, McFarland et al. 2007	United States	1986–1994 National Health Interview Survey linked to National Death Index N = 104,026	Veterans represented 15.7% of the NHIS sample but accounted for 31.1% of the suicide decedents. Over time, veterans were twice as likely (adjusted HR 2.13, 95% CI 1.14–3.99) to die of suicide compared with male nonveterans in the general population.
Kang & Bullman 2008	United States	Veterans of Operation Iraqi Freedom and Enduring Freedom (OIF/OEF) N = 490,346	SMR = 1.15, 95% CI 1.03–1.69 overall; Risk of suicide for former active duty veterans, SMR = 1.33 (1.03–1.69); Risk of suicide for veterans diagnosed with a selected mental disorder, SMR = 1.77 (1.01–2.87)
Bullman & Kang 2000	United States	1,545 Navy recruits exposed to mustard gas chamber tests compared with 2,663 Navy veterans who served at the same location and time but were not exposed to mustard gas	Crude suicide rate for overall group was 32 suicides out of 4,208 veterans. Crude suicide rate per 10,000 person-years for exposed group was 1.44 and not exposed group was 1.86.
Desai, Dausey & Rosenheck 2008a	United States	N = 119,159 All patients discharged with a diagnosis of major affective disorder,	1,057 patients died by suicide (0.89%). High rate compared to general population but

(*continued*)

Table 10.2. (*continued*)

Authors	Location	Description of Method	Results/Suicide Rates
		bipolar affective disorder, PTSD, or schizophrenia from psychiatric inpatient units in VA	comparable to other studies of suicide in samples of psychiatric patients.
Desai, Rosenheck & Desai 2008b	United States	Three cohorts of VA mental health outpatients, 1995, N = 76,105; 1997, N = 81,512; 2001, N = 102,184 and National Death Index data	1995—13.18 per 10,000 person-years 1997—11.41 per 10,000 person-years 2001—10.32 per 10,000 person-years
Macfarlane, Thomas & Cherry 2000	United Kingdom	N = 53,462 Gulf War veterans and a comparison group who were not deployed (era cohort)	MRR for all external causes was 1.18 (0.98–1.42), with 254 deaths due to external causes in the Gulf cohort and 216 in era cohort. Number of suicides was the same in the two groups: 51 in Gulf cohort and 50 in era cohort. Although Gulf War veterans report higher levels of current morbidity than those who were not deployed, there is only a very small (non-significant) increase in mortality.

suggested that veterans may be particularly susceptible to suicide, due in large part to the high prevalence of depressive disorders and comorbid psychiatric conditions among this population. Zivin and colleagues found that the prevalence of depressive symptoms among veterans was two to five times higher than in the general U.S. population. Further, the overall rates of suicide were seven to eight times higher among the depressed veteran population (88.25 per 100,000) than in the general population (13.5 per 100,000) (Zivin et al. 2007).

Further support for the notion of an elevated risk of suicide among a vulnerable subgroup of war veterans was suggested by Kang and Bullman (2008). They found that although the rate of suicide did not differ between Iraqi war veterans and the general U.S. population at that time, there were elevated rates of suicide for former active duty veterans and for those veterans who were diagnosed with a selected mental disorder (Kang & Bullman 2008). Previous studies of Vietnam War veterans conducted by the same authors (Bullman & Kang 1994; Bullman & Kang 1996) also found that the risks of suicide were elevated among veterans who experienced severe physical or psychological trauma during the war.

A recent review examined the relevant literature that investigated suicides among current and former U.S. military personnel (Kang & Bullman 2009). Published studies suggest that Vietnam War veterans did not have elevated risks of suicide when compared to Vietnam-era veterans or the general U.S. population. However, increased risks of suicide were found among specific groups of veterans, in particular those who had a diagnosis of post-traumatic stress disorder (PTSD) and those hospitalized after a combat wound or wounded more than once. Veterans from the Gulf War were also found to have rates of suicide similar to the general population. An increased risk for suicide was found for those veterans who were deployed as part of the Iraqi Freedom war, with rates significantly higher than the general population. Similarly, veterans from the Iraqi Freedom war diagnosed with a mental disorder had a higher risk of suicide than the general population.

Other international studies have reported mixed results regarding the relationship between war veterans and suicide. For example, in a retrospective cohort study of all UK armed forces who served in the Gulf War between September 1990 and June 1991, Macfarlane, Thomas, and Cherry (2000) found that suicide rates did not differ between deployed Gulf veterans and nondeployed military personnel. They did find, however, a slightly higher rate of external causes of death (e.g., accidental) among those who had served in the Gulf War.

In contrast, a study of Norwegian peacekeepers by Thoresen, Mehlum, and Moller (2003) found elevated suicide rates among a sample of 22,275 veterans. The standardized mortality ratio was highest in veterans who were more than ten years away from their peacekeeping service. Over half (55 percent) of the completed suicides occurred with firearms. However, the authors attributed their results to a selection effect. Former peacekeepers were less frequently married than would be expected in the general population (a known risk factor for suicide), and when marital status was taken into account, the elevated suicide risk disappeared.

A number of studies have also been conducted in Australia. The Mortality of Vietnam Veterans Study, conducted by the Department of Veterans' Affairs (Crane et al. 1997a), examined rates of mortality among the three branches of the armed forces: the army, air force, and navy. The mortality rate for all male military personnel and individual service branches was compared to the mortality rate for the general male Australian population between the years 1980 and 1994. Both the overall mortality rate (SMR = 1.07; 95 percent CI = 1.02–1.12) and the suicide rates (SMR = 1.21; 95 percent CI = 1.02–1.42) were significantly higher among ex-military personnel than the general population. Among the individual service branches, navy veterans had the highest mortality rate, elevated by 37 percent, with significant elevations in mortality from external causes, including suicide. Army and air force veterans did not have higher mortality rates than the Australian general population.

In a supplementary study, the Mortality of National Service Vietnam Veterans study (Crane et al. 1997b) extended the period of data collection by a further seven years and was undertaken specifically to compare mortality rates among national service veterans who saw combat in Vietnam with those who did not. The study had a follow-up period of between twenty-two and twenty-nine years. While the mortality rate from all causes (RR = 1.28; 95 percent CI = 0.97–1.70) and suicide rates (RR = 1.13; 95 percent CI = 0.77–1.67) were slightly higher among Vietnam veterans than those who did not serve in Vietnam, they were not significantly different.

Similar findings were reported by The Morbidity of Vietnam Veterans Study, conducted by the Australian Institute of Health and Welfare (1999), which comprised a series of studies about the health of Vietnam army veterans and their families. The sample included a retrospective cohort study of 46,166 Australian national servicemen. This study compared the mortality of national service veterans who served in Vietnam to national service personnel who remained in Australia. It found no significant increase in mortality among veterans who served in Vietnam compared to those who did not, and both groups demonstrated significantly lower mortality rates than expected for a similar aged cohort of Australian males (Australian Institute of Health and Welfare 1999).

In addition to inquiring about the health of army veterans, this study also inquired about the health of their children. Veterans were asked to report on deaths in their children according to three categories of causes: accident/ other, illness, and suicide. Despite the relatively low rates of mortality among veterans reported by this study, it was found that children's death rates as reported by their veteran fathers were higher than those of the general

Australian community for all three categories. Notably, the rate of suicide from 1988 to 1997 was more than three times higher among children of war veterans (46.6 per 100,000) than the general population (14.8 per 100,000) (Australian Institute of Health and Welfare 1999).

The Third Australian Vietnam Veterans Study (Wilson, Horsley & van der Hoek 2005) was a retrospective cohort study of male Australian personnel who served in Vietnam between May 1962 and July 1973. The study examined all deaths identified during the period from completion of Vietnam service to December 31, 2001, and compared the mortality rates of male Australian Vietnam veterans with those of Australian males in the general population. Overall, Australia's Vietnam veterans had lower rates of mortality than the general population. Although suicide was among the more common causes of death in this population, the rate was no higher than in the general population. The healthy worker effect, that is, the selection of men who were fit at the time of service, at least in part was thought to account for this overall lower mortality. However, the manifestation of the healthy worker effect diminishes over time, and when the follow-up period was broken down into three distinct time periods, the mortality rate for some causes of death, including suicide, increased.

Veterans from the Korean and Gulf Wars have received less attention in the Australian literature. A study conducted by Harrex and colleagues (2003) found that Korean War veterans had a 21 percent higher mortality rate than an equivalent Australian male population, and an increase by 31 percent for deaths from suicides. These rates varied for veterans from the army, navy, and air force. Army veterans had a 53 percent higher suicide rate than the general Australian male population, but there did not appear to be elevated suicide rates in the other forces. Those who completed their service by 1952 (which marked the end of the offensive/counteroffensive phase of the conflict) had a significantly lower suicide rate than the general population, whereas those who served in Korea after 1952 had a higher suicide rate than the general population. Almost 9 percent of Korean War veterans had also participated in the Vietnam War, and at least 30 percent of Korean War veterans had also participated in World War II. The impact of this fact on suicide rates is unclear.

Although Sim and colleagues (2003) did not find elevated mortality rates among Gulf War veterans compared to veterans who were not deployed, it was found that veterans were at an increased risk of developing psychological disorders and were more likely to rate for persistent psychiatric symptomatology, placing them at an increased risk of suicide in the future (see table 10.3).

Table 10.3. Selected Australian Studies of Suicide among War Veterans

Authors	Location	Description of Method	Results/Suicide Rates
O'Toole & Cantor 1995	Australia	19,430 served in Vietnam theater and 27,081 served at home in Australia, called "Vietnam era veterans." Random sample of 727 veterans and 1,059 era veterans	91 of 1,650 died by suicide. Those who scored low on intelligence test scores, post-school education, AWOL charge during service, and history of diagnosis and treatment of psychological problems had a higher rate of suicide.
O'Toole et al. 1996a; 1996b	Australia	Vietnam era draftees; examined 1,000 army veterans whose service had been completed more than 20 years previously; did not examine suicide or mortality specifically	Veterans at increased risk of health problems when compared to community norms: such as alcohol abuse and dependence, PTSD and somatization diagnosis; significantly related to combat exposure.
Sim et al. 2003	Australian Gulf War Veterans Health Study	Compared health and mortality of Gulf War veterans from all three service divisions, with random sample of Australian Defense Force (ADF) members who were deployed compared to those who were not deployed; deaths from 1991 to 2000 were included.	Mortality rates from all external causes, including intentional self-harm, were similar between the two groups; of deaths due to external causes, one-third were due to intentional self-harm in both groups. Veterans were at increased risk of developing psychological disorders and persistent psychological symptomatology. Suicide rates were not specifically reported.

(continued)

Table 10.3. (*continued*)

Authors	Location	Description of Method	Results/Suicide Rates
Wilson et al. 2005	Third Vietnam Veterans Mortality Study	All deaths among male Australian Vietnam veteran cohort from the time of completing Vietnam service to December 31, 2001, compared with number of expected deaths based on mortality of the Australian community	Overall SMR for suicide was 1.03 (0.93–1.13). Over time there was an increase in mortality from suicide. SMRs for 1963–1979 were 0.86 (0.7–1.02); for 1980–1990, 1.06 (0.89–1.23); and 1991–2001, 1.15 (0.97–1.33).

Research findings indicate that the most common method of suicide among war veterans in the United States is by using firearms. A recent study from the United States found that among 28,534 suicide decedents across all age groups, male and female veterans had higher firearm suicides than nonveterans (Kaplan, McFarland & Huguet 2009).

Limitations of Current Research

Thus there appear to be conflicting findings about suicide rates among veterans when compared to the general population. A number of factors may explain this. For example, biases may exist in the way in which veteran status is determined on death records, and there may be misclassification biases and unadjusted demographic differences (Blue Ribbon Report 2008). In the United States, studies that rely on death certificates and other death records may overestimate the number of veterans, as anyone who has served in the U.S. Armed Forces may be counted as a veteran. People who have not completed basic or advanced training due to misconduct, personality disorders, legal problems, adjustment reactions, alcohol and drug-related problems, and other administrative reasons for discharge may still be classified as veterans. Similarly people who trained in the Reserve component but did not serve in active duty can also be misclassified as veterans.

Another reason for the apparent differences in suicide rates across studies may be misclassification biases. For example, in the study by Kaplan and colleagues (2007), the rate of death due to suicide was higher among veterans, but deaths due to external causes, such as accidents and homicides, were higher among nonveterans. Further, undetermined deaths were higher among nonveterans than veterans. There are several possible misclassification biases that may account for this. First, it may be possible that suicide among veterans is correctly classified due to the more common use of firearms, compared to self-inflicted deaths by other mechanisms among nonveterans, such as overdoses, which may be misclassified as an undetermined cause of death. Second, it may be possible that suicides among veterans are classified correctly compared to suicides among nonveterans given the availability of more accurate information for the death certificates of veterans. As a whole, veterans have access to more varied and higher quality care than do nonveterans, information that can be used to determine the cause of death. Finally, implicit societal beliefs about a higher suicide rate among veterans may bias the determination of death (Blue Ribbon Report 2008).

Differences in suicide rates may also emerge as a result of unadjusted demographic differences. Studies generally adjust for age and gender; however, it has been shown that suicide rates in the general population also vary by other factors, such as race and ethnicity. Given the higher proportion of white/non-Hispanic individuals who are war veterans compared to the general population, this may serve to increase the apparent difference between veterans and nonveterans, because suicide rates are higher among white individuals. Therefore, although there is some evidence to suggest that suicide rates among veterans are higher than in the rest of the population, the evidence is by no means conclusive, and there is some doubt about the reliability of these findings.

A further limitation relates to the selection of a comparison group. Some studies have compared suicide rates among veterans with those of the general population. However, given the possibility of an initial "healthy worker" effect, together with differences in other socio-demographic factors that may place people at increased or decreased risk of suicide, this may not be appropriate. Other studies have compared veterans who were engaged in active combat with those who were not. Thus there is some inconsistency regarding the comparison groups employed.

Finally, the International Classification of Diseases (ICD-10) classifies suicide under death due to external causes, including purposely self-inflicted poisoning and injury and suicide (attempted). However, in many cases the level of suicide intent can be difficult to determine reliably, and some under-reporting of suicide is to be expected because of misclassification of a suicide as an accident or disease-related death, or due to reporting delays. Misclassification may also be more common in the deaths of older people. There may also be misreporting because of stigma, sociocultural norms, insurance reasons, or location (De Leo and Krysinska 2008).

Summary of Suicide Rates among War Veterans

Overall there is some evidence to suggest that suicide rates among veterans are higher than among the general population; however, this is by no means conclusive. Some of the studies cited here suggest that the elevated suicide rates might be a result of specific risk factors that have also been identified in the general population, such as psychiatric disorder and marital status. The elevated suicide rates among war veterans may also reflect factors specific to the veteran population, such as exposure to combat. The following sections discuss the risk factors for suicide that have been identified in the general population and among war veterans specifically.

Risk Factors for Suicide in the General Population

This section presents a description of the risk factors for suicide in the general population, to provide a context for the following discussion on the risk factors for suicide among war veterans.

The pathways to suicide are complex and multi-factorial, and studies examining risk factors are often hampered by small sample sizes and varying definitions of suicide risk. Further, suicide is a low base rate event, and many of the risk factors lack specificity and thus have relatively poor predictive values. For example, known risk factors for suicide include being male and unemployed. Although it is certainly the case that many people who die by suicide are unemployed males, it is also true that most males and most unemployed people do not commit suicide.

Given these limitations, research has demonstrated that some risk factors have a strong association with suicide, which can be of use when planning prevention strategies. This evidence was classified by De Leo and Krysinska (2008), who ranked the strength of evidence for risk factors associated with suicide in the general population from Level A—those with the strongest evidence—through to Level D—those that are associated with suicidal ideation/thinking and/or nonfatal suicidal behavior but for which more research is required to establish a relationship with completed suicide (De Leo & Krysinska 2008). Box 10.1 presents the risk factors that fall into the category of Level A. Other risk factors include self-mutilation (Level B: good evidence of association with suicide); religion; a lack of sanctions against suicide; migration (where high suicide rates exist in the country of origin); acculturation stress; social isolation; language barriers and neurobiological factors (Level C: some evidence of an association with suicide, but more research needed); and aborted suicide attempts and sexual orientation (homosexuality) (Level D factors).

> **Box 10.1. Level "A" Evidence of Strong Risk Factors for Suicide**
>
> **Demographic factors**
>
> - Male
> - Aged 30–34 years
> - Of indigenous descent
> - From rural and remote areas
> - Divorced, widowed, or separated marital status
> - Low socioeconomic status, unemployment
> - Physical illness, chronic physical pain
> - Social isolation and lack of social support
> - Negative life events and low coping potential
> - Family history of psychopathology and suicidal behavior
>
> **Psychiatric/psychological factors**
>
> - Diagnosis of a mental disorder: affective disorders, substance abuse, anxiety disorders, personality disorders, and psychiatric comorbidity
> - Psychiatric hospitalization
> - Previous nonfatal suicidal behavior and suicidal ideation
> - Hopelessness
> - High aggression and impulsivity
> - Lack of reasons for living
> - Cognitive rigidity
> - Poor problem-solving skills
> - Perfectionism
> - Psychological pain
> - Neurobiological activity: hypo-activity of the serotonergic system
>
> **Easy access to and availability of lethal means of suicide**
> **Inappropriate media reporting**

Although it is expected that these risk factors will also apply to the veteran population, it may be that there are additional risk factors specific to that population, or particular combinations of risk factors that make veterans particularly susceptible to suicide.

Risk Factors for Suicide among War Veterans

Suicide risk factors among veterans have been classified into the following subgroups: socio-demographic factors, psychiatric and psychological factors; access to and availability of means of suicide; and exposure to combat.

Socio-demographic factors

As in the general population, several demographic factors appear to be associated with elevated suicide risk. In particular, male veterans have been found to have higher suicide rates than females. In a review of the risk factors for suicide among war veterans, Lambert and Fowler (1997) found that male gender was more strongly associated with risk for suicide than female gender, at a ratio of approximately 3:1. Although women made more frequent suicide attempts and engaged in more frequent self-injurious behavior (itself a risk factor for completed suicide), completed suicide was more common among men (Lambert & Fowler 1997). This has been further supported by Zivin and colleagues (2007), who found rates of suicide to be as high as 89.6 per 100,000 and 28.9 per 100,000 for male and female veterans respectively.

Differences in ethnicity and age have also been cited as risk factors for suicide among war veterans. Increased suicide rates were observed among male, younger and non-Hispanic white veterans. Veterans ages eighteen to forty-four had a suicide rate of approximately 95 per 100,000, compared to a rate of 78 per 100,000 among veterans ages forty-five to sixty-four, and 90 per 100,000 for those ages sixty-five and older (Zivin et al. 2007). In contrast, Lambert and Fowler (1997) found that men over the age of sixty-five were at the highest risk of suicide. They suggested that as the veteran population ages, suicide risk may increase, postulating that older veterans may fit the profile of those most at risk of suicide, citing poor health, diminished psychosocial support, high frequency of depression, and substance abuse problems as characteristics of this group.

A study of suicide risk factors among Australian Vietnam era draftees further identified low intelligence, as measured by the Australian Army General Classification test, to be related to risk of death from suicide as well as death from other external causes (O'Toole & Cantor 1995). A more recent study has supported this notion, showing that poor cognitive functioning was related to both passive and active suicidal ideation (Ayalon et al. 2007).

Being unmarried has been demonstrated to be a risk factor for suicide, as well as being divorced or separated, unemployed, and living alone. Other risk factors that have been identified comprised social problems, negative life events in the previous year, expression of suicidal ideation, and poor psychosocial support, such as inadequate family income, lack of marital support, and lack of a stable place to live (Lambert & Fowler 1997; Thoresen & Mehlum 2006; Thoresen et al. 2006; Thoresen & Mehlum 2004). Notably, Thoresen and Mehlum (2006) found that living alone and the breakup of a close relationship were still predictive of suicide even after controlling for mental health problems, such as depression and psychotic disorders, arguably the strongest risk factors for suicide.

Psychiatric Disorders

As in the general population, the presence of psychological or psychiatric disorders, such as substance abuse, has been found to increase the risk of suicide among war veterans (Tanielien & Haycox 2008; Zivin et al. 2007; Ayalon et al. 2007; Thoresen & Mehlum 2006; Thoresen & Mehlum 2004; Lambert & Fowler 1997). Depression, PTSD, and traumatic brain injury (TBI) have been demonstrated to increase the risk of suicide among veterans (Tanielien & Haycox 2008). For example, suicide rates among a population of veterans undergoing treatment for depression were seven to eight times higher than the general population (Zivin et al. 2007). Not all studies, however, have found an association between suicide and PTSD. Zivin and colleagues (2007) reported that the presence of PTSD was associated with lower rates of suicide. This finding may be explained by the fact that those with PTSD may have received more care through PTSD programs (Hampton 2007). Although a diagnosis of PTSD may reduce suicide risk in some cases, clusters of specific PTSD symptoms may be predictive of suicidal ideation among veterans, in particular re-experiencing symptoms (Bell & Ney 2007). Borderline personality traits have also been found to be associated with suicide attempts among a veteran outpatient population (Reich 1998).

Substance abuse has also been associated with an increased risk of suicide (Zivin et al. 2007). Those veterans with a diagnosis of substance abuse had suicide rates of 119.73 per 100,000 compared to rates of 72.63 per 100,000 among veterans without a diagnosis of substance abuse. However, the authors found that veterans with a service-connected disability had lower rates of suicide than those without. They suggested that these results may be explained by veterans with service-connected disabilities having greater access to Department of Veterans Affairs health services and regular compensation payments to bolster their income. They concluded that as a group, veterans may be particularly susceptible to suicide because of a high prevalence of depressive disorder and comorbid psychiatric conditions (Zivin et al. 2007).

Treatment factors have also been implicated in the risk for suicide. Among a sample of 226,866 veterans who received a diagnosis of depression in 2003 and 2004, rates of suicide attempts were lower for those who were treated with antidepressants than for those who were not, in particular among those treated with selective serotonin reuptake inhibitors (SSRIs) and tricyclic antidepressants. Among those treated with SSRIs, this effect was seen in all adult age groups. Not surprisingly, suicide attempt rates were higher prior to treatment and decreased with the commencement of treatment. Thus, SSRI antidepressant treatment may have a protective effect (Gibbons et al. 2007).

Access to Means of Suicide

Ready access to means of suicide has been consistently shown to increase the risk of suicide in the general population and may be more important among war veterans, given that they frequently have ready access to firearms (Lambert & Fowler 1997). Indeed, veterans who died by suicide were more likely to have done so using a firearm than their nonveteran counterparts (Kaplan et al. 2007).

In a further study of the correlates in the use of firearms in suicide, Desai, Dausey, and Rosenheck (2008) surveyed a sample of 119,159 veterans who had been discharged from a psychiatric inpatient unit from 1994 to 1998. The suicide rate among this sample was 0.89 percent, a rate much higher than that of the general population but comparable with other studies of suicide among psychiatric patients. Patients who were male, Caucasian, had a diagnosis of PTSD or substance abuse, and lived in states with less restrictive gun ownership laws were more likely to use a firearm than another means to commit suicide (Desai, Dausey & Rosenheck 2008).

Exposure to Combat

Higher levels of suicidal ideation have been associated with the experience of war zone violence and with functioning as an agent of death. In addition, greater exposure to atrocities was associated with higher levels of re-experiencing PTSD symptoms, which in turn has been associated with suicidal ideation (Bell & Ney 2007). Involuntary repatriation and conflict with the military system have also been shown to increase the risk of suicide (Thoresen et al. 2006). People who experienced involuntary repatriation may have done so because of their inability to comply with conduct codes or to cope with the demands the military service placed on them, but repatriation itself can be perceived as a major traumatic event with problems of social

---

Box 10.2. Risk and Protective Factors among Veterans

Risk Factors	Protective Factors
• Being male	• Having service connections
• Being younger or older (not middle-aged)	• Receiving regular compensation payments, a good income
• Being white	• Using antidepressants
• Being a high school graduate	• Having psychosocial support
• Living in a rural area	
• Being unemployed	
• Having poor psychosocial support or social network, including being unmarried, separated, divorced, homeless	
• Experiencing negative life events before military service	
• Having a psychiatric disorder, including depression and substance abuse	
• Undergoing psychological treatment during service	
• Being involuntarily repatriated, in conflict with military service system	
• Having poor cognitive functioning or low intelligence	

---

stigma. A related risk factor was a charge of being "absent without leave" (AWOL) during service (e.g., Ayalon et al. 2007).

Summary

Although research has provided some evidence regarding the risk factors for suicide among war veterans, it is evident that these are not significantly different from the risk factors that have been delineated for suicide in the general population. To determine with certainty the differences between suicide rates and risk factors among the veteran and general population, better controlled studies are required. Box 10.2 presents the identified risk and protective factors for suicide among war veterans. It is these factors that need to be targeted to develop effective suicide prevention strategies for this population.

Approaches to Suicide Prevention

Suicide prevention approaches have been classified into universal, selective and indicated interventions (Silverman & Maris 1995). Universal interventions target whole populations, such as a nation, state, or neighborhood, with the aim of reducing risk factors and enhancing protective factors. Suicide risk factors are reduced by removing barriers to care and increasing public education about what to do and say to help suicidal individuals. Protective factors are enhanced by strengthening social supports and coping skills. Examples of programs that use universal interventions include public education campaigns; restricting access to means; and educating the media industry to report suicide issues responsibly, accurately, and sensitively. Gunnell and Frankel (1994) argued, for example, that the greatest potential way to reduce rates of suicide was to restrict the availability of means. This included the likely decrease in suicide rates following the introduction of catalytic converters in cars to reduce the lethality of car exhausts and reducing the quantity of medications that can be bought over the counter (Gunnell and Frankel 1994). Further, Hawton and colleagues (2001) demonstrated that the annual number of deaths from paracetamol poisoning decreased by 21 percent, and the number of deaths from salicylates dropped by 48 percent following legislation that restricted pack sizes of these drugs being sold in the United Kingdom.

Selective interventions target subsets of the total population, paying particular attention to at-risk groups that have a greater probability of becoming suicidal. These interventions aim to prevent the onset of suicidal behaviours among at-risk groups, such as young people and those living in rural and remote areas. Examples of programs that use selective prevention interventions are screening programs to identify and assess at-risk groups, gatekeeper training for frontline adult caregivers, support and skills training and increasing access to crisis services and referral sources. The Gotland program is an example of the gatekeeper training intervention. Rutz and colleagues (1989) implemented a program that educated general medical practitioners to recognize and treat depressive disorders, with the aim of increasing responsibility of these physicians for treating these disorders. It was found that this program led to marked decreases in referrals to psychiatry for depression, inpatient care, and an increase in antidepressant prescriptions. There was also a significant decrease in the rates of suicide after physician training compared to the suicide rates of the preceding four years (Rutz, von Knorring & Walinder 1989; Rutz et al. 1989).

Indicated interventions specifically target those people already known to be at risk for suicide and showing early signs of suicidal behavior. Examples include the pharmacological treatment of underlying psychiatric disorders such as depression, using antidepressants (MacGillivray et al. 2003) or antipsychotic medication for people with psychotic disorders (Meltzer et al. 2003), and psychotherapy-based interventions, such as cognitive behavioral therapy (Slee et al. 2008), dialectical behavioral therapy (Turner 2000), group-based therapy (Wood et al. 2001), and contact-based interventions such as letters or postcards (Carter et al. 2005; Motto & Bostrom 2001).

Given that the pathways to suicide are complex, it is widely accepted that suicide prevention strategies need to encompass the full range of intervention approaches. People who commit suicide usually do so one at a time and therefore have individual states or traits that require targeted and specific interventions. However, although much is known about the epidemiology of suicide among various populations, less is known about effective interventions (Robinson et al. 2008), in particular among war veterans.

Suicide Prevention Programs for War Veterans

Reviews of suicide prevention strategies in the general population identify interventions that have been shown to be effective and others that show promise that could be readily tested and applied in military settings (Mann et al. 2005). Further, knowledge about risk factors for suicide in this population gives us some idea about where interventions would be best targeted.

The U.S. Army and Air Force have both instigated large-scale suicide prevention programs that combine universal, selective, and indicated approaches. The Air Force Suicide Prevention Program sought to reduce the number of suicides among active Air Force officers by reducing suicide risk and promoting mental and physical health. The program is based on eleven initiatives that comprise community education and training, increasing command's responsibility as gatekeepers to make seeking assistance acceptable and delivery of community preventive services. After implementation of the suicide prevention program, Knox and colleagues (2003) demonstrated that there was a 33 percent relative risk reduction for suicide.

The U.S. Army has also taken a comprehensive approach toward the prevention of suicide among its personnel. The U.S. Army Center for Health Promotion and Preventive Medicine, together with the American Association of Suicidology, produced a suicide prevention resource manual, *The Army Suicide Prevention Program* (ASPP), which incorporates universal, selective, and indicated approaches. The program comprises universal community programs delivered by chaplains, social workers, or other professionals; screening personnel who may be encountering distress; gatekeeper training, whereby potential gatekeepers, such as professional counselors or chaplains are trained to provide more in-depth screening, supportive counseling, and risk assessment where required; and finally indicated, or tertiary, prevention when an individual is actively suicidal and referred for professional psychiatric treatment (see http://www.medtrng.com/suicideprevention/suicide_prevention.htm).

In 2010 a comprehensive report entitled *Health Promotion, Risk Reduction, Suicide Prevention* was also published by the U.S. Army, building on the previous work. The report includes information about rates of and risk factors for suicide plus a detailed description of the army's approach to suicide prevention. The report can be found at http://www.military.com/military-report/army-suicide-prevention-program.

In addition, the Joshua Omvig Veterans Suicide Prevention Act was signed into law on November 5, 2007 (Cvetanovich & Reynolds 2008), requiring the Department of Veterans Affairs to establish a suicide prevention program. This program comprises a national suicide prevention lifeline, a suicide prevention coordinator at each Department of Veterans Affairs medical center, training staff to recognize risk factors for suicide, educating veterans and their families about suicide risks, and the establishment of a Mental Health Center of Excellence (see http://www.mentalhealth.va.gov/suicide_prevention/index.asp).

However, not all veterans make use of the healthcare services provided by the Department of Veterans Affairs, with only 33 percent, or 7.8 million veterans, having been registered in 2007 (Kaplan et al. 2009). Therefore most veterans use primary care services, making it imperative that healthcare services outside the Department of Veterans Affairs healthcare sector be aware of the suicide risk among war veterans and the risk factors that need to be monitored. A number of important clinical implications can therefore be drawn from knowledge of suicide rates among war veterans, the factors that heighten the risk for suicide among veterans, the protective factors against suicide, and the suicide prevention strategies that may likely be used with this population. For example, primary care services need additional education regarding the suicide risk factors among war veterans. These primary care services can then serve as gatekeepers and possibly provide specific interventions to address presenting clinical concerns, such as PTSD. War veterans identified as needing further treatment in this gatekeeper strategy can also be referred to other appropriate services and agencies. Gatekeeper training for primary care services and Department of Veterans Affairs services can include assessing whether veterans have access to firearms, their intentions about acquiring a firearm, and assessing whether females have any military experience.

The use of indicated interventions for veterans with clinical conditions such as depression and PTSD is also warranted. Sher (2009), for example, argued that these conditions are often co-morbid among war veterans and this often serves to increase the risk for suicide. A recommended suicide prevention approach for what Sher terms "post-traumatic mood disorder" (PTMD) should focus on (1) improvement in recognizing PTMD, (2) treating PTMD symptoms, (3) preventing a relapse when the patient is in remission, (4) treating suicidal ideation, (5) treating co-morbid psychiatric conditions including alcohol and drug abuse, (6) treating medical and neurological disorders including TBI, and (7) provision of social support. Interventions can also address risk factors that are specific to suicide among war veterans, such as exposure to combat.

Universal strategies can also be employed to address the suicide rates among war veterans. Given the previous success of restricting the packet sizes of paracetamol and the decline in suicide rates in the United Kingdom (Hawton et al. 2001), it may be possible that restricting access to firearms would be an effective approach to reducing suicides among war veterans. This must be addressed both by clinicians, to ensure that individuals at risk of suicide have limited access to means, and also by policy makers, to ensure that access to firearms is limited in the general population. Also, war veterans need to be educated and encouraged to store unloaded firearms in locked locations. This may serve to increase the amount of time between feeling the desire to commit a suicidal act and accessing a firearm, during which time the intent to commit suicide may subside.

It may also be possible that suicide prevention programs for people currently serving in the military may have further flow-on effects as these personnel retire as veterans. However, further research is required to establish the effectiveness of such programs for retired, as well as currently serving, military personnel.

Summary: Suicide Prevention Programs for Veterans

Both the U.S. Army and Air Force have developed large-scale suicide prevention programs. To the best of our knowledge, the effectiveness of the army program is to date untested; however, the air force program appears to have led to a significant reduction in the risk of suicide (Knox et al. 2003). Both programs have adopted a multifaceted approach, which incorporates a range of universal, selective, and indicated strategies.

However, because not all veterans make use of healthcare services provided by the Department of Veteran Affairs, this population can also benefit from primary care–based suicide prevention interventions such as enhanced GP training. In addition, because of the relationship between psychiatric morbidity, in particular PTSD and depression, veterans will also benefit from the effective treatment of these disorders.

Finally, the reduction of access to means of suicide has been shown to have an effect on suicide rates (Beautrais et al. 2007; Mann et al. 2005; Gunnell & Frankel 1994), and is a key component of the suicide prevention strategies of several countries, including the U.S., England and Australia (National Strategy for Suicide Prevention 2001; National Suicide Prevention Strategy for England 2002; Living Is for Everyone Framework 2007). As most suicides by veterans involve the use of firearms, there may be some benefit to programs that restrict access to these weapons.

Summary

This chapter has considered the literature on suicide rates among war veterans. There is some evidence to suggest that rates of suicide may be elevated among this population when compared to community norms, and further evidence to suggest that this elevated risk may be mediated by factors such as an increased risk of health problems that could lead to elevated mortality, such as physical health problems and psychological disorders such as PTSD. The most common method of suicide among this population is use of firearms.

Risk factors for suicide among veterans can be categorized as socio-demographic factors; psychiatric and psychological factors, in particular PTSD; access to and availability of means of suicide; and exposure to combat.

There is some evidence to suggest that a multifaceted approach can lead to reduced rates of suicide among air force personnel. In addition, the U.S. Army has established a comprehensive suicide prevention program that incorporates various components and is based on best available practice and evidence. However, further, well-designed studies are required to examine suicide rates among war veterans and to assess rates of suicide among veterans who do not access DVA healthcare services. Further work is also required to evaluate the effectiveness of suicide prevention interventions for this population, including specific indicated interventions for conditions such as PTSD, especially when it occurs in combination with major depression.

References

American Association of Suicidology. (2006). http://www.suicidology.org/c/document_library/get_file?folderId = 232&name = DLFE-159.pdf (accessed July 2, 2011).

Australian Bureau of Statistics. (2007). Suicides Australia 2005. Canberra. http://www.abs.gov.au/AUSSTATS/abs@.nsf/Lookup/3309.0Main + Features12005? OpenDocument (accessed December 1, 2009).

Australian Bureau of Statistics. (2010). Causes of death, Australia, 2008. http://www.abs.gov.au/ausstats/abs@.nsf/0/6B3EE404901565F8CA2576F600124E28? opendocument (accessed July 2, 2011).

Australian Bureau of Statistics. (2011). Causes of death, Australia, 2009. http://abs.gov.au/AUSSTATS/abs@.nsf/mf/3303.0/ (accessed July 11, 2011).

Australian Institute of Health and Welfare. (1999). *Morbidity of Vietnam veterans: A study of the health of Australia's Vietnam veteran community: Volume 3 validation study*. Canberra: AIHW.

Ayalon, L., Mackin, S., Area, P. A., Chen, H. & Herr, E. C. (2007). The role of cognitive functioning and distress in suicidal ideation in older adults. *Journal of the American Geriatrics Society* 55: 1090–1094.

Beautrais, A., Fergusson, D., Coggan, C., et al. (2007). Effective strategies for suicide prevention in New Zealand: A review of the evidence. *New Zealand Medical Journal* 120: U2459.

Bell, J. B. & Ney, E. C. (2007). Specific symptoms predict suicidal ideation in Vietnam combat veterans with chronic post-traumatic stress disorder. *Military Medicine* 172: 1144–1147.

Blue Ribbon Report. (2008). Report of the Blue Ribbon Work Group on suicide prevention in the veteran population. http://www.mentalhealth.va.gov/suicide_prevention/Blue_Ribbon_Report-FINAL_June-30-08.pdf (accessed June 30, 2011).

Bullman, T. A. & Kang, H. K. (1994). Post-traumatic stress disorder and the risk of traumatic deaths among Vietnam veterans. *Journal of Nervous and Mental Disorders* 182, no. 11: 604–610.

Bullman, T. A. & Kang, H. K. (1996) The risk of suicide among wounded Vietnam veterans. *American Journal of Public Health* 86, no. 5: 662–667.

Bullman, T. A. & Kang, H. K. (2000). A fifty year mortality follow-up study of veterans exposed to low level chemical warfare agent, mustard gas. *Annals of Epidemiology* 10: 333–338.

Caldwell, T., Jorm, A. & Dear, K. (2004). Suicide and mental health in rural, remote and metropolitan areas in Australia. *Medical Journal of Australia* 181, no. 7 Supp.: S10, S14.

Carter, G. L., Clover, K., Whyte, I. M., et al. (2005). Postcards from the Edge project: Randomised controlled trial of an intervention using postcards to reduce repetition of hospital treated deliberate self poisoning. *British Medical Journal* 331: 805–809.

CBS News. (2007). http://www.cbsnews.com/stories/2007/11/13/cbsnews_investigates/main3496471.shtml (accessed June 30, 2011).

Crane, P., Barnard, D., Horsley, K. & Adena, M. (1997a). *Mortality of Vietnam veterans; the Veteran Cohort Study: A report of the 1996 retrospective cohort study of Australian Vietnam veterans*. Canberra: Department of Veterans' Affairs.

Crane, P., Barnard, D., Horsley, K. & Adena, M. (1997b). *Mortality of national service Vietnam veterans: A report of the 1996 retrospective cohort study of Australian Vietnam veterans.* Canberra: Department of Veterans' Affairs, 90.

Cvetanovich, B. & Reynolds, L. (2008). Joshua Omvig Veterans Suicide Prevention Act of 2007. http://www.harvardjol.com/wp-content/uploads/2009/08/619-640_Cvet-Reynolds.pdf (accessed July 2, 2011).

De Leo, D. & Krysinska, K. (2008). Appendix D: Review of suicide risk factors. In *Living is for everyone: Research and evidence in suicide prevention* (pp. 64–69). Canberra: Commonwealth of Australia, Department of Health and Ageing.

Desai, M. M., Rosenheck, R. A., & Desai, R. A. (2008). Time trends and predictors of suicide among mental health outpatients in the Department of Veterans Affairs. *Journal of Behavioral Health Services and Research* 35: 115–124.

Desai, R. A., Dausey, D. & Rosenheck, R. A. (2008). Suicide among discharged psychiatric inpatients in the Department of Veterans Affairs. *Military Medicine* 173: 721.

Gibbons, R. D., Brown, C. H., Hur, K., Marcus, S. M., Bhaumik, D. K. & Mann, J. J. (2007). Relationship between antidepressants and suicide attempts: An analysis of the Veterans Health Administration data sets. *American Journal of Psychiatry* 164: 1044–1049.

Goldsmith, S. K., Pellmar, T. C., Kleinman, A. M., et al. (2002). *Reducing suicide: A national imperative.* Washington, DC: Committee on Pathophysiology & Prevention of Adolescent & Adult Suicide, Board on Neuroscience and Behavioral Health. Institute of Medicine.

Gunnell, D. & Frankel, S. (1994). Prevention of suicide: Aspirations and evidence. *British Medical Journal* 308: 1227.

Hall, W. D., Mant, A., Mitchell, P. B., et al. (2003). Association between antidepressant prescribing and suicide in Australia, 1991–2000: Trend analysis. *British Medical Journal* 326: 1001–1011.

Hampton, T. (2007). Research, law address veterans' suicide. *JAMA* 298: 2732.

Harrex, W. K., Horsley, K. W., Jelfs, P., et al. (2003). *Mortality of Korean War veterans; the Veteran Cohort Study: A report of the 2002 retrospective cohort study of Australian veterans of the Korean War.* Canberra: Department of Veterans' Affairs.

Hawton, K., Townsend, E., Deeks, J., et al. (2001). Effects of legislation restricting pack sizes of paracetamol and salicylate on self poisoning in the United Kingdom: Before and after study. *British Medical Journal* 322: 1203.

Hayes, L. M. (1989). National study of jail suicides: Seven years later. *Psychiatry Quarterly* 60: 7–29.

IPS News. (2010). http://ipsnews.net/news.asp?idnews=49971 (accessed June 30, 2011).

Kang, H. K. & Bullman, T. A. (2008). Risk of suicide among US veterans after returning from the Iraq or Afghanistan war zones. *JAMA* 300, no. 6: 652–653.

Kang, H. K. & Bullman, T. A. (2009). Is there an epidemic of suicides among current and former U.S. military personnel? *Annals of Epidemiology* 19: 757–760.

Kaplan, M. S., Huguet, N., McFarland, B., et al. (2007). Suicide among male veterans: A prospective population-based study. *Journal of Epidemiology & Community Health* 61: 619–624.

Kaplan, M. S., McFarland, B. H. & Huguet, N. (2009). Firearm suicide among veterans in the general population: Findings from the national violent death reporting system. *Journal of Trauma* 67: 503–507.

Knox, K. L., Litts, D. A., Talcott, G. W., et al. (2003). Risk of suicide and related adverse outcomes after exposure to a suicide prevention programme in the US Air Force: Cohort Study. *British Medical Journal* 327: 1376.

Lambert, M. T. & Fowler, D. R. (1997). Suicide risk factors among veterans; risk management in the changing culture of the Department of Veterans Affairs. *Journal of Mental Health Administration* 24: 350–358.

Lebson, M. (2002). Suicide among homosexual youth. *Journal of Homosexuality* 42: 107–117.

Living Is for Everyone Framework. (2007). Research and evidence in suicide prevention. http://www.livingisforeveryone.com.au/IgnitionSuite/uploads/docs/LIFE_research-web.pdf (accessed July 2, 2011).

Macfarlane, G. J., Thomas, E. & Cherry, N. (2000). Mortality among UK Gulf War veterans. *The Lancet* 356: 17–21.

MacGillivray, S., Arroll, B., Hatcher, S., et al. (2003). Efficacy and tolerability of selective serotonin reuptake inhibitors compared with tricyclic antidepressants in depression treated in primary care: systematic review and meta-analysis. *British Medical Journal* 326: 1014–1019.

Mann, J. J., Apter, A., Bertolote, J., et al. (2005). Suicide prevention strategies: A systematic review. *JAMA* 294: 2064–2074.

Meltzer, H. Y., Alphs, L., Green, A. I., et al. (2003). Clozapine treatment for suicidality in schizophrenia: International Suicide Prevention Trial (InterSePT). *Archives of General Psychiatry* 60: 82–91.

Motto, J. A. & Bostrom, A. G. (2001). A randomized controlled trial of postcrisis suicide prevention. *Psychiatric Services* 52, no. 6: 828–833.

National Strategy for Suicide Prevention. (2001). http://www.sprc.org/library/nssp.pdf (accessed June 29, 2011).

National Suicide Prevention Strategy for England. (2002). http://www.dh.gov.uk/prod_consum_dh/groups/dh_digitalassets/@dh/@en/documents/digitalasset/dh_4019548.pdf (accessed June 29, 2011).

O'Carroll, P. W., Berman, A. L., Maris, R. W., et al. (1996). Beyond the tower of Babel: A nomenclature for suicidology. *Suicide & Life Threatening Behavior* 26: 237–252.

O'Toole, B. I. & Cantor, C. (1995). Suicide risk factors among Australian Vietnam era draftees. *Suicide and Life Threatening Behaviour* 25: 475–488.

O'Toole, B. I., Marshall, R. P., Grayson, D. A., et al. (1996a). The Australian Vietnam Veterans Health Study II: Self-reported health of veterans compared with the Australian population. *International Journal of Epidemiology* 25: 319–330.

O'Toole, B. I., Marshall, R. P., Grayson, D. A., et al. (1996b). The Australian Vietnam Veterans Health Study III: Psychological health of Australian Vietnam veterans and its relationship to combat. *International Journal of Epidemiology* 25: 331–340.

Reich, J. (1998). The relationship of suicide attempts, borderline personality traits, and major depressive disorder in a veteran outpatient population. *Journal of Affective Disorders* 49: 151–156.

Robinson, J., Pirkis, J., Krysinska, K., et al. (2008). Research priorities in suicide prevention in Australia: A comparison of current research efforts and stake-holder-identified priorities. *Crisis* 29: 180–190.

Rutz, W., von Knorring, L. & Walinder, J. (1989). Frequency of suicide on Gotland after systematic postgraduate education of general practitioners. *Acta Psychiatrica Scandinavia* 80: 151–154.

Rutz, W., Walinder, J., Eberhard, G., et al. (1989). An educational program on depressive disorders for general practitioners on Gotland: Background and evaluation. *Acta Psychiatrica Scandinavia* 79: 19–26.

Sher, L. (2009). A model of suicidal behavior in war veterans with posttraumatic mood disorder. *Medical Hypotheses* 73: 215–219.

Silverman, M. M. & Maris, R. W. (1995). The prevention of suicidal behaviors: An overview. *Suicide & Life Threatening Behavior* 25: 10–21.

Sim, M., Abramson, M., Forbes, A., et al. (2003). Australian Gulf War Veterans Health Study. http://www.coeh.monash.org/gwvhs.html (accessed July 3, 2011).

Slee, N., Garnefski, N., van der Leeden, R., et al. (2008). Cognitive-behavioural intervention for self-harm: Randomised controlled trial. *British Journal of Psychiatry* 192: 202–211.

Tanielien, J., & Haycox, L. (2008). Invisible wounds of war: Psychological and cognitive injuries, their consequences, and services to assist recovery. Rand Center for Military Health Policy Research.

Thoresen, S. & Mehlum, L. (2004). Risk factors for fatal accidents and suicides in peacekeepers: Is there an overlap? *Military Medicine* 169: 988–993.

Thoresen, S. & Mehlum, L. (2006). Suicide in peacekeepers: risk factors for suicide versus accidental death. *Suicide and Life Threatening Behaviour* 36: 432–442.

Thoresen, S., Mehlum, L. & Moller, B. (2003). Suicide in peacekeepers: A cohort study of mortality from suicide in 22,275 Norwegian veterans from international peacekeeping operations. *Social Psychiatry and Psychiatric Epidemiology* 38: 605–610.

Thoresen, S., Mehlum, L., Roysamb, E. & Tonnessen, A. (2006). Risk factors for completed suicide in veterans of peacekeeping; repatriation, negative life events, and marital status. *Archives of Suicide Research* 10: 353–363.

Turner, R. M. (2000). Naturalistic evaluation of dialectical behavior therapy-oriented treatment for borderline personality disorder. *Cognitive and Behavioral Practice* 7: 413–419.

Wenzel, A., Brown, G. K. & Beck, A. T. (2009). *Cognitive therapy for suicidal patients: Scientific and clinical applications.* Washington, DC: American Psychological Association.

Wilson, E. J., Horsley, K. W. & van der Hoek, R. (2005). *Australian Vietnam Veterans Mortality Study.* Canberra: Department of Veterans' Affairs.

Wood, A., Trainor, G., Rothwell, J., et al. (2001). Randomized trial of group therapy for repeated deliberate self-harm in adolescents. *Journal of the American Academy of Child & Adolescent Psychiatry* 40: 1246–1253.

World Health Organization. (2001). The world health report: Suicide. http://www.who.int/whr/2001/chapter2/en/index6.html (accessed July 1, 2011).

World Health Organization. (2002). Distribution of suicide rates (per 100,000) by gender and age, 2000. http://www.who.int/mental_health/prevention/suicide/suicide_rates_chart/en/index.html (accessed July 1, 2011).

World Health Organization. (2004). Pesticides and health. http://www.who.int/mental_health/prevention/suicide/en/PesticidesHealth2.pdf (accessed July 11, 2011).

World Health Organization. (2009). Suicide rates per 100,000 by country, year and sex (table). http://www.who.int/mental_health/prevention/suicide_rates/en/ (accessed July 2, 2011).

Zivin, K., Kim, M., McCarthy, J. F., et al. (2007). Suicide mortality among individuals receiving treatment for depression in the Veterans Affairs health system: Associations with patient and treatment setting characteristics. *American Journal of Public Health* 97: 2193–2198.

Chapter 11

The Evolution of Healthcare Programs for Canadian Veterans

David Pedlar and Stewart Macintosh

Introduction

Canada has a historic commitment to its sons and daughters who donned military uniforms to serve their country during World Wars I and II (1914–1918, 1939–1945), the Korean War (1950–1953), and military operations since then in the cause of national defense and international peace and security. More than 600,000 Canadians enlisted in World War I, over a million during World War II, and approximately 27,000 in the Korean War. Today there are approximately 700,000 Canadians who have had some type of military service (MacLean et al. 2010). Canadians enjoy a legacy of peace and prosperity, free from the specter of world war, free to raise their families in a nation that is the envy of the world. Canadian Forces (CF) peacekeepers continue to carry on Canada's legacy of peacemaking throughout the world today (Mogan 2002).

One of the fundamental responsibilities of the government of Canada is the provision of essential care and support to veterans of military service. Veterans Affairs Canada (VAC) is the department charged with delivering on this obligation. VAC provides benefits and services to veterans and their families, survivors, and eligible members of the Canadian Forces (CF). It also keeps the memory of veterans' achievements and sacrifices alive through commemoration and remembrance programs. Since its establishment in 1944, the department has enjoyed a strong performance record.

This chapter considers the evolution of veterans' benefits in Canada, paying particular attention to two major milestones: the introduction of the Veterans Independence Program (VIP) in 1980 and the launch of the New Veterans Charter (NVC) in 2006. Both VIP and NVC came at points in time when significant demographic shifts in Canada's veteran population demanded innovative solutions to meet their changing needs.

The Early Years of Veterans' Benefits in Canada

The evolution of veterans' benefits in Canada began even before Confederation (1867). Demobilized soldiers of New France as well as the veterans of the Revolutionary War, the War of 1812, and the Fenian Raids were given land grants as a means of helping them to establish themselves in civilian life. Disability pensions were first authorized at the time of the Fenian Raids. In August 1866, an Order in Council was passed providing the granting of pensions "to the militia men wounded or disabled or who may be hereafter wounded or disabled in encountering any hostile invasions of Canada, and to the widows and children of those who have been killed in battle or have lost their lives from actual service in the field." After the Northwest Rebellion in 1885, the terms of the earlier authority were extended to include the officers and men who had taken part (Veterans Affairs Canada 1986). This approach continued until Canada had to consider the grim realities of mounting casualties from World War I.

In 1915 the government responded to an urgent need for hospital care and treatment by establishing the Military Hospitals Commission to deal with the illness and injuries of soldiers returning from World War I. The seriousness of veterans' circumstances resulted in a recognition by the government of the inadequate assistance then available for injured soldiers and their families. This realization led to the creation of a modest range of demobilization benefits, including the War Service Gratuity, a cash payment based mainly on length of service. There was a push to retrain even the seriously injured and get them gainfully employed in the labor market. Reestablishment benefits for returning soldiers included a clothing allowance, vocational training, insurance, preference in civil service employment, and farming assistance. Programs were criticized for being hastily designed, and many were unhappy with them. Over the years, enhancements were made to the disability pension scheme to better meet client needs.

The War Veterans Allowance (WVA) was introduced in 1930. The intent of this social assistance benefit was to keep aged and unemployed veterans off the provincial welfare rolls. Often referred to as the "burnt-out pension," the WVA targeted the permanently unemployable. Many amendments have been made over the years to extend the WVA to new groups. It was also enhanced to provide recipients with access to emergency funds to meet basic needs (the Assistance Fund). In 1943 the WVA was extended to widows after an intensive lobbying effort by veterans' organizations.

Having learned from the astonishing social disruption that emerged after World War I, when returning veterans found very little compensation available to them, the Canadian government formed a cabinet committee in 1940, only months after the outbreak of World War II. This committee led to a huge change in the Canadian government's attitude toward those who served their country. It was responsible for producing the "Post-Discharge Re-Establishment Order," which promised that everybody who served in the Canadian military in World War II would be eligible for rehabilitation benefits. Following World War I, such benefits had been restricted to disabled veterans (Neary and Granatstein 1998). From 1939 to 1945 Canada was on a war footing—one million people served in uniform, but a greater number of the population-at-large, especially females, worked in industry in support of the war. Support to veterans was accepted by society as a key component of social policy (Veterans Affairs Canada 1986).

The compendium of legislation designed for World War II veterans became known collectively as the Veterans Charter. This compendium described federal responsibilities, services to be provided, and specific client groups. Walter S. Woods, "chief architect of the program devised for Canadian veterans of the 1939-45 conflict," believed that most Veterans would rather work than receive government assistance (Veterans Affairs Canada 1986). Woods said that veterans wanted "opportunity with security" and that most needed a short-term program to help them return to civilian life (Neary 2000).

The Veterans Charter also had a major positive impact on the education and healthcare of the civilian population. University education provided to veterans helped expand Canada's university system tremendously. The comprehensive healthcare provided to veterans helped to establish a model for Canada's 1957 Hospital Insurance Act and, in 1968, Medicare, Canada's universal healthcare program. Organizations formed to provide services to veterans with disabilities became strong lobbyists for improved care for others with disabilities, for example, the War Amputations of Canada, the Sir Arthur Pearson Association of War Blinded, and the National Society of the Deaf and Hard of Hearing. VAC also began providing rehabilitation for civilians and, in 1951, cosponsored the First National Conference on the Rehabilitation of Physically Handicapped in Canada, thereby laying the foundation for a national rehabilitation program for civilians.

A demobilization program provided support to military personnel integrating into civilian society. In addition to the standard veterans' programs, which continue to evolve to this day (e.g., disability benefits and survivors' pensions, healthcare, income support, and burial assistance), veterans could choose from one of three programs:

- a reestablishment credit for purposes such as a down payment for a mortgage or reduction, home repair, furniture, business start-up, acquisition or investment, insurance, or buy-back of wartime superannuable time;
- educational assistance, including rehabilitation allowances; or
- farming under the Veterans' Land Act.

Other postwar demobilization programs included a war service gratuity, a clothing allowance, temporary unemployment insurance, veterans' business and professional loans, and access to insured healthcare for one year after discharge.

In 1948 VAC began adjudicating disability pensions for the Royal Canadian Mounted Police. In the 1950s the needs of Canadian veterans of the Korean War were addressed through various orders in council, and through the passage of the Veterans Benefits Act, which provided Korean War veterans with Veterans Charter benefits.

The Canadian government had made a commitment in the 1930s to the long-term care of permanently disabled veterans and those not able to reintegrate successfully into civilian society (often referred to as "burnt-out" veterans). The care aspect took the form of institutional chronic and domiciliary care. Initially, eligibility was restricted to war service pensioners, but as the demand for acute care declined after both world wars, unused institutional capacity in veterans' institutions resulted in expanding eligibility to all veterans with a war disability or with service overseas. By the mid-1960s about 200,000 World War I and 600,000 World War II veterans became eligible for care at departmental expense in its eighteen hospitals across Canada.

Recommendations by the Royal Commission on Government Organization (the "Glassco Commission"), which found that most veterans in departmental hospitals required chronic or nursing home care as opposed to acute hospital care, resulted in the transfer of seventeen of the eighteen veterans' hospitals to provincial authorities. The sole exception was Ste. Anne-de-Bellevue Hospital in the province of Quebec, which remains under VAC authority. With the hospital transfers, contracts were negotiated with each of the provinces for priority access to a certain number of beds for veterans, contributions to facility maintenance, and more appropriate response to the long-term-care needs of residents.

Today, VAC's long-term-care program consists of nursing home care and chronic care provided at Ste. Anne-de-Bellevue Hospital, or in priority access beds (beds in the community to which veterans have priority access). This includes access to a full range of healthcare, such as prescription drugs, vision care, and dental and audiology services) throughout Canada, as well as chronic care in community facilities. Eligible war service veterans and certain civilians may qualify for intermediate care or chronic care at the department's contract facilities or at more than 1,900 community facilities across the country, some of which have contractual arrangements with the department. In addition, they may qualify for long-term care at Ste. Anne-de-Bellevue Hospital. Canadian Forces pensioners may qualify to receive intermediate or chronic care in a community facility if the need for this care is related to a pensioned condition. Allied veterans who have lived in Canada for ten or more years after their period of service may be eligible for long-term care in community facilities.

Caring for Aging War Veterans and the National Healthcare System

With the passage of the postwar years, VAC gained extensive expertise and skill in developing services and benefits for an aging veteran population. In so doing, the department established an excellent track record of consulting experts in the fields of gerontology, rehabilitation, and mental health to develop programs responsive to the changing needs of veterans and in line with cutting-edge treatment and program design. Such consultations led to a comprehensive review of long-term-care needs of veterans in the early 1980s, resulting in the development of a program that to this day remains North America's only national self-managed home-care program—the Veterans Independence Program (VIP) (discussed later in this chapter).

The provision of veterans' benefits has been influenced over time by the evolution of the Canadian healthcare system. Today, healthcare is delivered by Canada's provinces and territories based on the provisions of the Canada Health Act of 1984 (CHA). The CHA provides universal coverage for medically necessary healthcare services based on need, rather than on ability to pay. Canada's publicly funded healthcare system is best described as an interlocking set of ten provincial and three territorial health insurance plans. Known to Canadians as "Medicare," the system provides access to universal, comprehensive coverage for medically necessary hospital and physician services (Health Canada 2010). Most Canadians receive their care through their provincial/territorial system, but there are some exceptions, one of which is the responsibility retained by the federal government for treating disabilities due to military service. This exception means that VAC assumes the cost of treating veterans for their service-related disabilities, as well as for other programs such as rehabilitation and those not covered under the CHA (e.g., dental care and prescription drugs outside of a hospital setting). VAC does not generally deliver services directly; rather, it pays the provincial system or registered service providers for the required services. In addition, VAC tops up provincial services to better meet veterans' needs, as is the case with VAC's home-care program.

Veterans Independence Program

In the early 1980s VAC faced the prospect of having to provide some form of care to over half a million aging World War II veterans. Canadian veteran eligibility rules had evolved in such a way that a majority of these veterans' only eligibility was for a long-term-care bed. In their younger years, this was not a significant issue; however, as the population began moving into their sixties, the cost of long-term care and bed accessibility (i.e., wait lists) became increasingly problematic, with VAC looking at enormous cost increases to place this population in long-term-care beds (Pedlar, Lockhart & Macintosh 2009). As a result, VAC was forced to explore program options, other than institutional care, to meet the needs of aging war service veterans.

VAC's considerations were strongly influenced by a growing body of research that promoted maintaining people in their homes as both cost-effective and better for their quality of life. This approach had already been partially developed in what was then a departmental hospital (Deer Lodge Hospital) in Winnipeg, Manitoba. In 1967 a staff geriatrician, Dr. Jack MacDonnell, developed a geriatric day hospital for veterans and their caregivers. MacDonnell's philosophy had developed in the 1950s from the influences of British geriatricians such as Anderson, Warens, and Cozins. The basic principle was that older people were happier and healthier in their own homes when provided with care from a multidisciplinary team. Elements that would be central to VIP emerged in Winnipeg: assessments, support to caregivers, meals, and interventions based on the specific needs of the individual (Struthers 2004).

While the philosophy of integrated home care was being developed, there was much discussion among policy makers and veterans' organizations about how best to proceed. Veterans' organizations were lobbying for additional bed construction; the federal government's central agencies were expressing concern about costs; and VAC was trying to develop a workable approach that considered service and cost. In 1979 VAC's then Deputy Minister Bruce

Brittain stated that "DVA policy towards aging veterans simply 'ignores reality.'" Brittain went on to state that then current VAC policy was badly outmoded, expensive, and not cost-effective; that, to a large degree, it ignored the severe plight of many aged veterans and their spouses; and that many veterans were in expensive hospital beds because there were no viable alternatives (Struthers 2004). It is noteworthy that veterans' organizations were initially skeptical of what they saw as a "trade-off" for bed entitlement. Government analysts were also doubtful about the policy merits of this new program (Mogan 2002).

On April 1, 1980, the Aging Veterans Program (AVP) was announced in the House of Commons, with a start date of April 1, 1981. The program would provide financial aid so that eligible veterans could purchase the services necessary to continue to live independently and comfortably in their own homes. When this was no longer possible, the department would assist veterans to meet costs of care in nursing homes in their communities so that they would be near family and friends. Originally the AVP was provided to veterans with overseas service and a VAC disability pension. Embedded in the program was Dr. MacDonnell's philosophy, which included multidisciplinary healthcare team assessments and a range of benefits designed to meet health and social needs, such as groundskeeping, housekeeping, friendly visiting, respite care, homemakers, meals-on-wheels, and access to health professionals such as physiotherapists and occupational therapists (Struthers 2004). While the program and eligibility requirements would undergo modifications over the years, its key principles remain unchanged (Veterans Affairs Canada 2010b):

- preventative community care approach to continuing care;
- concepts of dignity and independence;
- comprehensive continuum of care;
- early intervention;
- home support;
- a self-managed approach to care (if the client is capable), which promotes consumer choice, family control, and independence;
- managed care transitions to assist clients as they move to or through different care settings; and
- supplementary provincial/territorial and community programs.

From the beginning, the AVP recognized the importance of a veteran's spouse in providing care to the veteran. Many AVP services assisted with tasks that would traditionally have fallen to the spouse, recognizing that the veteran's spouse was aging and that the spouse's role in providing care was critical.

Benefits would be provided based on an assessment of the veteran, the spouse, and their living environment. The VAC Case Manager and the Healthcare Team would follow the veteran and make sure that services would be provided to match current needs. Veterans would be followed on an ongoing basis and case plans would be adapted as needed. Although changes would be made over the years, the basic suite of benefits and the philosophy of service have remained unchanged.

In 1986, under the direction of then Minister of Veterans Affairs George Hees, the program's name was changed to the Veterans Independence Program (VIP).

Program Expansion

From its commencement in 1981, the program was designed to adapt to the changing needs of veterans and their spouses. Indeed, throughout the program's history, many incremental eligibility changes have been made to VIP. Several proposals for comprehensive eligibility changes were rejected based on current fiscal pressure (Struthers 2004), but the dilemma remained of having an aging population whose sole eligibility was for a long-term-care bed. This was leading to significant financial liability over the longer term. Recent internal VAC estimates show that annual home-care costs per client average $5,000 to $6,000, whereas annual nursing home bed costs range from $45,000 to $60,000, depending on provincial/territorial jurisdiction. Given these costing realities, the department resorted to a series of small, incremental changes, resulting in a gradual expansion of program eligibility to more and more veterans.

Some of those changes had to do with survivors. In 1990 the department included the provision to allow VIP services to remain in place for one year following the death of the veteran (Veterans Affairs Canada 2006). Recognizing that both the veteran and spouse were aging and were relying on VIP benefits to remain healthy and independent, the department introduced further program changes in 2003 to allow for the lifetime continuation of some VIP benefits to survivors. With the 2003 change, survivors remained eligible to receive housekeeping and grounds maintenance benefits until their own deaths or until the benefits were no longer needed due to institutionalization.

Overall, six major eligibility changes (outlined below), implemented between 1988 and 2003, resulted in VIP client numbers increasing from

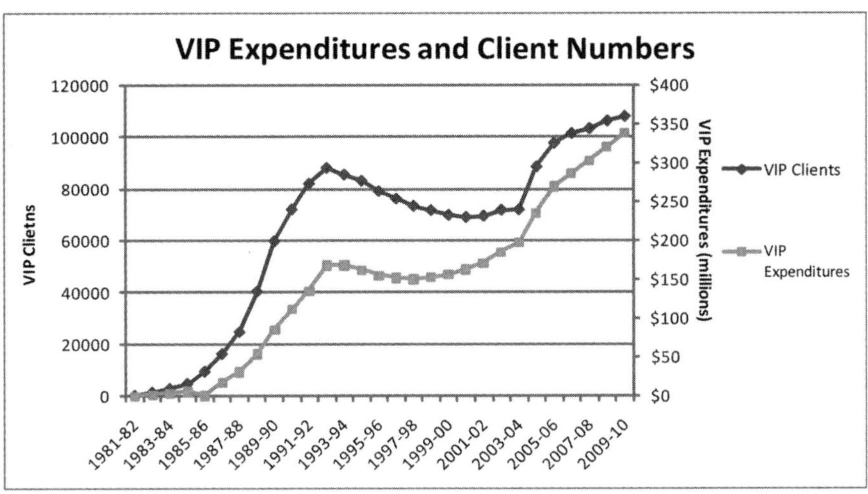

Figure 11.1. War Service Veterans and Canadian Forces Veterans (Actuals to 2010). *Source: Veterans Affairs Canada (2011).*

16,250 in 1986–1987 to 101,270 in 2006–2007 as shown in figure 11.1 (Veterans Affairs Canada 2011):

- 1987—extension of VIP eligibility based on income qualification (i.e., low-income) to most War Service Veterans
- 1989—extension of VIP eligibility to veterans with wartime service in Canada only (Canada Service Veterans)
- 1990—extension of VIP benefits to survivors for one year following the death of the VIP client, in recognition of their reliance on those services
- 1991—extension of the VIP to some CF members for their service-related disability
- 2001—broader extension of the VIP to CF members for their service-related disability
- 2003—lifetime continuation of the VIP to survivors after the death of the veteran

The changes in 1987 and 2003 represent significant shifts in VIP program philosophy. Where VIP benefits were originally provided in relation to a service disability, the extension of benefits based on income represented a move to provide benefits based on recognition that the war service population was special. Similarly, lifetime continuation of the VIP for survivors was a more formal recognition by the department of the central role of the caregiver in supporting the VAC client. Program costs have tended to generally follow increases in client numbers; rising from $18 million in 1986–1987 to $287 million in 2006–2007 (Veterans Affairs Canada 2011).

Service Delivery Model

Today, the VIP is delivered through a national service delivery network. This involves the coordinated use of healthcare identification cards, centralized call centers, and multidisciplinary healthcare teams. Direct, face-to-face case management services are provided through local VAC offices, often in the veteran's home. For clients with higher care needs, the assessment in a client's home is very important, so that VAC is able to assess both the veteran and the spouse, to ensure that appropriate services are in place and to determine frequency of follow-up. At a minimum, VIP clients have annual contact with the department, with more frequent contact provided if needed. One of the key functions of local VAC staff is to ensure that VIP services are coordinated with any available provincial/territorial programs.

The VIP was designed to be integrated into provincial/territorial home-care programs, with the VIP augmenting those existing programs. While the federal government has responsibility for care related to veterans' disabilities, the overall responsibility for healthcare in Canada rests with the provinces/territories. As such, VIP recipients are expected to access those services first. In practice, VAC case managers work with provincial/territorial home-care staff to coordinate benefits. Provincial/territorial home-care services are not standardized in Canada. Major discrepancies exist among the programs, with some providing post-acute home care only, others having programs for the elderly or disabled, and some with income qualification required. One of the VIP objectives is to ensure a relatively standard level of care for veterans regardless of where they live. This means that VIP service usage can vary considerably across the country depending on the availability of local services.

As the VAC case manager assesses the veteran and the family, a range of VIP options is available, from minor interventions to the provision of institutional care. To illustrate, following is a common trajectory for service utilization:

a. When the veteran and spouse are still fairly independent, approval may be given for some housekeeping and grounds maintenance to assist the veteran. These benefits might gradually be increased as more assistance is required.

b. As autonomy becomes more of an issue, personal care services are included. These services may include bathing and changing, thereby helping both the veteran and the caregiver.

c. If food preparation becomes an issue, access to services such as meals-on-wheels can be provided.

d. If the veteran's health deteriorates to the point where he or she cannot drive, social transportation is provided to assist in getting out for meals or attending social activities, and assistance is provided to get to medical appointments.

e. To facilitate socialization and assist and perhaps reduce stress on caregivers, coverage for adult day care can be provided.

f. As care needs climb, the caregiver may find providing care overly burdensome. In addition to housekeeping or personal care, respite care can be provided.

g. If the client's health deteriorates to the point where institutionalization is required, the veteran has access to intermediate care services in a long-term-care facility. When placement is required, the goal is to place the client in a bed in the community so as to ensure proximity to friends and family.

h. End-of-life care can be provided to allow the veteran to die at home in comfort and dignity.

i. When the veteran dies, housekeeping and grounds maintenance services are continued for the surviving spouse to help him or her remain independent.

Each case varies, but VIP flexibility is well-illustrated. It is able to adapt to the changing health needs of veterans and their spouses over time. The program "changes" along with the individual needs of each veteran.

A key component of the VIP is the client's ability to choose service providers. As part of the assessment process, VAC staff determine the specific benefits and hours of care approved for the client. For housekeeping and grounds maintenance, the client and/or the family will then choose who provides the service(s). For other VIP elements, the client has input into who provides services based on departmentally developed service provider criteria.

In 2003 VAC automated its claims processing system to include the VIP. Up until that point, the VIP had been administered by VAC staff on stand-alone systems. This process was labor-intensive for staff and could be burdensome for clients in that they had to maintain receipts to verify that services had been provided. As World War II veterans aged, these administrative requirements were becoming increasingly difficult for some. Automation allowed for registration and direct payment of service providers. This change meant that veterans no longer had to maintain receipts for review by VAC staff. Some veterans continue under the old scheme, but more and more are opting for direct payment to registered service providers.

Program Observations

Four primary program observations can be made regarding the VIP:

- cost effectiveness,
- the role of the caregiver,
- aging in place, and
- the need for ongoing improvements.

The debate about the cost effectiveness of home care versus institutional care is long-standing. It is a very complicated issue because it is difficult to consistently measure all of the components in a healthcare system. From VAC's perspective, based on a strict comparison between an institutional care bed and the average cost of VIP services, cost effectiveness was apparent but did not consider any other input costs. Although client satisfaction surveys and advocacy by veterans' organizations showed that the program was popular, there was little empirical evidence relating to effectiveness. This debate is not new and is not restricted to VAC. Initially, research conducted primarily in the United States found that home care was not a cost-effective alternative to institutionalization. The challenge with this thesis was that it compared costs associated with the introduction of a new home-care service to existing community services and did not include existing resources in the equation. Beginning in the late 1990s, however, new research emerged in both the United States and internationally that considered home care to be a cost-effective alternative to institutional care when direct comparisons between the home-care services and institutional costs are made (Miller et al. 2008).

In 2008 VAC and the Province of Ontario conducted a study that showed home care is a lower-cost alternative to long-term facility care, and that the VIP has encouraged considerable substitution of home care for facility care for clients with comparable care needs. The advantage was even more evident when broader societal costs such as replacement wages and out-of-pocket expenses were included (Hollander et al. 2009). A VAC pilot project that extended VIP services to veterans on long-term-care wait lists further supported this analysis. Although the primary goal was to relieve pressure on limited bed spaces, the choice to remain at home showed the potential for cost savings when comparing VIP costs with the cost of institutional care (Pedlar & Walker 2004). This evidence supports the thesis that home care is a cost-effective alternative to institutional care. The pilot proved to be so successful, both in terms of managing bed spaces and for veterans' quality of life, that it has since been formally integrated into the VIP as one more service option.

The role of the caregiver in providing support to a spouse is not unique to veterans. Unpaid caregiving is a fundamental component of home care. The VIP has shown that the role of the caregiver is critical to ensuring healthy aging and aging at home. Most World War II veterans are male, and the VIP was modeled on the then traditional belief that caregiving was a normal expectation of a wife. As such, caregiver costs were not recognized. However, though program eligibility is derived from the veteran, when a VAC case manager visits a veteran's home, the assessment includes both the veteran and the spouse. This approach explains why housekeeping is the largest program element despite the fact that very few veterans would have been doing the housework themselves.

The extension of housekeeping and grounds maintenance to surviving spouses is seen by some as a significant step toward recognizing the efforts of unpaid caregivers, which has been an ongoing subject of debate in policy and academia in Canada and internationally (Struthers 2007). What is certain is that VAC understood that the spouse and veteran had to be considered as a unit when assessing benefits and services. As the couple aged in place, the spouse also came to depend on the benefits to support his or her independence. VAC's Gerontological Advisory Council (GAC) stated that the decision to extend certain VIP benefits to surviving spouses, initially for one year (1990) and then for their lifetimes (2003), indicated that VAC understood the concept of linked lives and the important role primary caregivers play in providing care for veterans (Gerontological Advisory Council 2006).

The VIP has shown that aging in place is an effective policy approach. Client satisfaction surveys and commentary from veterans' organizations strongly demonstrate a high level of support for the VIP. Advocacy by veterans' organizations has been for program expansion. The Senate of Canada, in its 2009 report on aging in Canada, recommended that a national home-care program, a "Seniors Independence Program," be developed, based on the VIP (Senate of Canada 2009). Leading Canadian gerontologists who are members of the GAC have also strongly endorsed the VIP and have called for broader expansion. They see the VIP as an integral part of an expanded program for veterans, which they refer to as "Veterans Integrated Services," which they recommend should be designed to promote health and independence for veterans through the life course. Their main criticism of the VIP was that program eligibility restricted access (Gerontological Advisory Council 2006). The range of benefits and services available through the VIP and the program's flexibility mean that veterans with a wide range of disability are able to remain at home and to be as independent as possible. A VAC pilot project, since included as a program component, also showed that those veterans on a wait list for institutional care can be safely cared for at home with VIP services in place.

VAC is rightly proud of the VIP, both because it so effectively meets departmental needs and because it is so popular with clients. This does not mean that the program is perfect. A key challenge, raised by the same academics and veterans' organizations who praise the program, is program eligibility. There is always pressure to expand program eligibility; this pressure becomes stronger as effectiveness is demonstrated. The VIP also faces challenges with today's housing alternatives, an issue pointed out by the GAC (Gerontological Advisory Council 2006). In 1981 the choices were primarily home or institution. Today there is a range of options from condominiums to assisted living, and it can be challenging to match VIP benefits with client needs in different environments. Finally, as VAC's population changes, with a growing and younger population of CF veterans with disabilities, the department has to assess VIP services and objectives with this group in mind. It may be that a program designed for maintaining the independence of aging clients does not work for those younger veterans who need support in transitioning from military to civilian life.

Benefits for the Twenty-first Century

The early 1990s saw a dramatic increase in the tempo of peacekeeping operations. Canadian Forces members were increasingly being deployed in civil wars in the defense of human rights to protect civilian populations. During this same period, the CF was undergoing a period of strength reduction. Maintaining Canada's international commitments meant that the same CF personnel were redeploying overseas with increasing frequency and were deploying into settings where combat was likely. This combination of factors inevitably resulted in increased casualties and increasing pressure on the department to respond to the needs of a younger population of CF veterans.

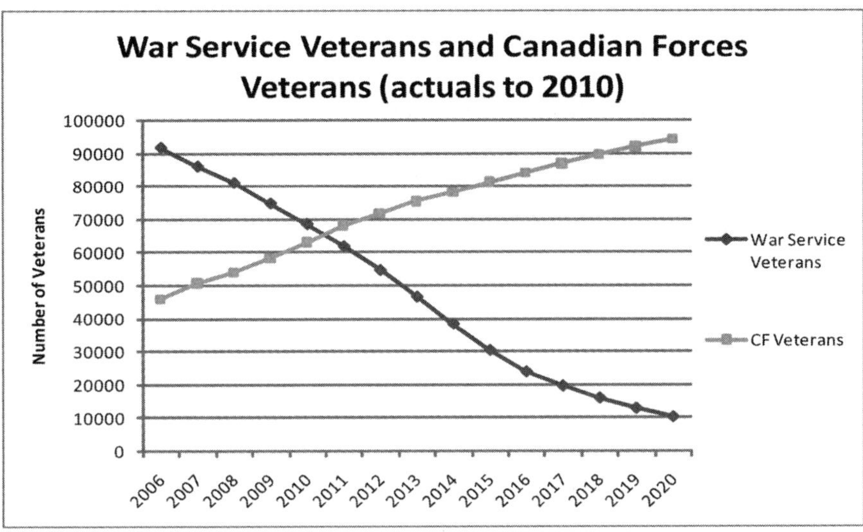

Figure 11.2. War Service Veterans and Canadian Forces Veterans (actuals to 2010). *Source: Veterans Affairs Canada (2011).*

The broad suite of reintegration benefits available through the Veterans Charter for those returning from World War II and Korea had gradually been discontinued as this population aged—the department's focus shifted from reintegration to maximizing health and independence. For the majority of CF veterans, eligibility was restricted to disability benefits and treatment related to their military service. There were no educational programs available once a member left the military. A considerable number were being released from the military and were having a difficult time reintegrating into civilian life. Many injured members faced the prospect of being released before they were eligible for a retirement pension, meaning that they faced significant income shortages. Given the existing programs, veterans essentially had to use disability benefits as income replacement, which was not their purpose. To increase this income source, the veteran had to prove that he or she was more seriously injured to receive higher levels of disability benefits. It was apparent that benefits had to once more evolve to meet the needs of this younger population of veterans, a group that was becoming a significant percentage of VAC's client population. As can be seen in figure 11.2, Canadian veterans were forecast to become the majority of VAC clients by 2011 (Veterans Affairs Canada 2011). This combination of emerging need in younger veterans and changing demographics forced VAC to review its programs and look to the future.

The New Veterans Charter

In 2004 the then Minister of Veterans Affairs and the Department of National Defence (DND) jointly announced the government's plans to modernize programs to better serve CF clients and their families. The necessity of responding to CF veterans' needs in a way that fulfilled the government's responsibility to take care of injured personnel by promoting health and wellness was paramount. An internal VAC task force was created to design programs and services tailored for the CF population. In the meantime, both VAC and the DND had been and were continuing to make concerted efforts to improve the transition to civilian life for CF members and families. Although this work established a solid foundation for modernization, it was clear that improvements at the policy level had been maximized and that fundamental change was needed for VAC to fulfill its reestablishment mandate.

Underpinning the redesign was the desire to promote wellness and well-being for CF members and their families in the transition from military to civilian life. This translated into a new scheme of programs and services that became known as the New Veterans Charter. The New Veterans Charter, launched in April 2006, represented the most sweeping changes to veterans' benefits since the end of World War II. It offers a range of programs to assist CF members, veterans, and their families in successfully reestablishing in civilian life. Developed in consultation with CF members and veterans, a main feature is an emphasis on "wellness" rather than disability. A "dual award approach" to compensation recognizes separately the economic and noneconomic impacts of a service-related or career-ending disability. Programs available are discussed in the following subsections.

Rehabilitation

The Rehabilitation Program helps disabled CF veterans who need support to reenter civilian life. Its purpose is to restore the capability and functioning of CF veterans and their families and to remove barriers to successful reestablishment. In most cases, the Rehabilitation Program is provided through a network of local experts and resources. There are three components: medical rehabilitation to stabilize physical and psychiatric conditions and restore basic functions, psychosocial rehabilitation to restore independence and adapt to disability, and vocational rehabilitation to identify and achieve vocational goals.

Rehabilitation needs tend to first become apparent during a transition interview, which VAC conducts with each member being released. Case management is key to the Rehabilitation Program. A VAC case manager works with the client to develop his or her "case plan," which incorporates the client's goals and objectives, with an agreement on services and benefits that will be needed to assist him or her in meeting these objectives; outlines timelines for monitoring and review; and can involve multiple service providers from various agencies, organizations, and the private sector. The case manager takes a lead role in coordinating service providers and benefits. VAC's case managers work with the CF case managers (when the member is still serving) to allow for a smooth transition to civilian life.

Financial Benefits

CF veterans who have been approved for VAC's Rehabilitation Program may have access to the following:

- Earnings Loss Benefit—A monthly benefit that ensures the veteran's income does not fall below 75 percent of his or her gross prerelease military salary while taking part in the Rehabilitation Program.
- Permanent Impairment Allowance—A monthly benefit, payable for life, to CF veterans who suffer from lost job opportunities as a result of being permanently and severely impaired and who have a rehabilitation need due to a Disability Award condition.
- Supplementary Retirement Benefit—A one-time, lump sum benefit, payable to veterans who, because of their disability, were unable to benefit from vocational rehabilitation and were not capable of holding suitable gainful employment, to compensate for the lost opportunity to contribute to a retirement fund after releasing from the forces.
- Canadian Forces Income Support (CFIS)—A monthly tax-free, income-tested benefit to help CF veterans who have completed the Rehabilitation Program and are considered able to work, but have not been able to find a job or have a low-paying job. This benefit is also available to those who had been receiving the "Earnings Loss Benefit," which is available until age sixty-five.

Health Benefits Program

This program provides postrelease access to the Public Service Healthcare Plan (PSHCP) for CF veterans and their families who would not otherwise qualify for PSHCP benefits after they release. It is open to those eligible for the Service Income Security Insurance Plan (a program available through the CF that provides income security and rehabilitation for those medically releasing from the CF) or those who are eligible for VAC's Rehabilitation Program. It is also available to survivors when the death of the CF member or veteran is service-related. The Health Benefits Program offers group health insurance through the PSHCP at an affordable cost. This coverage may include items such as prescription drugs and vision care.

Disability Award

The Disability Award is meant to recognize and compensate CF members and veterans (and their families) for the noneconomic impacts of a service-related disability. The Disability Award is a tax-free, lump sum payment. The amount depends on the extent of the disability. The maximum amount, in 2011, was $285,319.47. It is adjusted annually based on the cost-of-living index.

Death Benefit for Survivors

The Death Benefit is a tax-free, lump sum payment. It is paid to a spouse or common-law partner, and dependent children, if a CF member is killed while in service or injured while in service and dies within thirty days of the injury. The Death Benefit in 2011 was $285,319.47 and is adjusted annually based on the cost-of-living index.

Career Transition Services

The New Veterans Charter also provides assistance to those who release from the CF without disability and to reservists who require assistance in obtaining a civilian job after completing service in a Special Duty Area or Special Duty Operation or after having served full-time for twenty-one out of twenty-four consecutive months. Career Transition Services provide practical help in finding a job. The program focuses on three key services: job-search training, career counseling, and job-finding assistance.

Other Benefits

Other benefits under the New Veterans Charter include a clothing allowance related to disability, reimbursement for financial advice related to the management of a Disability Award or Death Benefit, and a detention benefit.

Family Support

When a CF member leaves the Canadian Forces, it can affect the whole family. This is why the New Veterans Charter offers more support to families than ever before. This support may include benefits such as healthcare, family counseling, rehabilitation services, case management, and educational grants for dependants.

Conclusion

Veterans' programming in Canada has evolved along with the veteran population. Programs were developed following World War I to provide care to injured soldiers. The immediate decades following this war showed that more comprehensive programming would be required if reintegration was to succeed. Following World War II, Canada spent massively to reintegrate returning veterans to civilian society—they were educated, housed, and treated for illness. As this population aged, VAC programs evolved to meet their needs, gradually moving to focus on independence and long-term care—the hallmark is the VIP. Today, although this group gets smaller with each passing month (traditional veteran clients are forecast to decrease from 75,000 in 2010 to 54,000 in 2013), the needs of those remaining continue to increase.

Between 1955 and 1995 Canada considered the men and women who served in the CF not so much as veterans but as people choosing the military as a career—they may have to act as peacekeepers around the world, but the average person considered this to be a "safe" job. Veterans' programming focused almost exclusively on treatment for disability in the event that injury occurred while on duty. In the later stages of the 1990s and beyond, Canada began to recognize that peacekeeping was actually peacemaking, and that deployments in Rwanda, Bosnia, and Afghanistan were very dangerous. Although on a smaller scale, many of the reintegration needs seen after World War II were becoming relevant once again. With the number of CF veterans in receipt of VAC benefits forecast to increase from 58,000 in 2009 to 75,000 in 2013 (Veterans Affairs Canada 2010a), Canada's veterans' programming had to once again evolve to meet this group's unique needs—the result being the New Veterans Charter. In all likelihood, the New Veterans Charter is but the latest evolutionary stage in nearly 100 years of veterans' programming in Canada.

References

Gerontological Advisory Council—Veterans Affairs Canada. (2006). *Keeping the promise: The future of health benefits for Canada's war veterans.* Charlottetown, PE: Author.

Health Canada. (2010). Canada's healthcare system (Medicare). http://www
.hc-sc.gc.ca/hcs-sss/medi-assur/index-eng.php (accessed November 15, 2010).

Hollander, M., Miller, J., MacAdam, M., Chappell, N. & Pedlar, D. (2009).
Increasing value for money in the Canadian healthcare system: New findings and
the case for integrated care for seniors." *Healthcare Quarterly* 12, no. 1: 38–47.

MacLean, M. B., Van Til, L., Thompson, J. M., Pedlar, D., Poirier, A., Adams, J.,
Hartigan, S. & Sudom, K. (2010). *Life After Service Study: Data collection methodol-
ogy for the Income Study and the Transition to Civilian Life Survey*. Charlottetown,
PE: Veterans Affairs Canada.

Miller, J., Hollander, M., Corbett, C. & van der Valk, J. (2008). *The Continuing
Care Research Project for Veterans Affairs Canada and the government of Ontario.
Study 1: A case study for the OSV/VIP initiative*.

Mogan, W. D. (2002). The Veterans Independence Program: A second legacy to
the people of Canada. Submission to the Commission on the Future of
Healthcare in Canada. Unpublished report.

Neary, P. & Granatstein, J. L., eds. (1998). *The Veterans Charter and post–World
War II Canada*. Montreal: McGill-Queen's University Press, 1998, 6.

Neary, Peter. (2000). The Veterans Charter. Lecture presented to Veterans Affairs
Canada, Charlottetown, PE, February 25.

Pedlar, D. & Walker, J. (2004). The overseas service veterans at home pilot: How
choice of care may impact use of nursing home beds and waiting lists. *Canadian
Journal on Aging* 23, no. 4: 367–369.

Pedlar, D., Lockhart, W. & Macintosh, S. (2009). Canada's Veterans
Independence Program: A pioneer of "aging at home". *Healthcare Papers* 10, no.
1: 72–77.

Senate of Canada. (2009). Special Senate Committee on Aging report. *Canada's
aging population—seizing the opportunity*. Ottawa, ON: Senate of Canada.

Struthers, J. (2004). *Comfort, security, dignity: The Veterans Independence Program, a
policy history*. Charlottetown, PE: Veterans Affairs Canada.

Struthers, J. (2007). They suffered with us and should be compensated: Entitling
caregivers of Canada's veterans. *Canadian Journal on Aging* 26, no. 1: 117–131.

Veterans Affairs Canada. (1986). *A historical perspective of veterans legislation*.
Charlottetown, PE: Veterans Affairs Canada.

Veterans Affairs Canada. (2006). *Evaluation of the Veterans Independence Program—
departmental audit and evaluation report*. Charlottetown, PE: Veterans Affairs
Canada.

Veterans Affairs Canada. (2010a). *Client and expenditure forecast 2011-12 VAC
forecast cycle*. Charlottetown, PE: Veterans Affairs Canada.

Veterans Affairs Canada. (2010b). *Veterans program policy manual, Section 3.1.1:
Overview of the VIP and of its principles and objectives*. Charlottetown, PE:
Veterans Affairs Canada.

Veterans Affairs Canada. (2011). *Official departmental statistics from VAC Statistics
Unit, Finance Division*. Charlottetown, PE: Veterans Affairs Canada.

Forgotten Heroes? Health and Well-being Issues and Resources for UK Veterans and Their Families in the Twenty-first Century

Dai Williams

Military service in the UK armed forces plays a vital role in preserving the power of the state over external military threats, internal dissent, emergency and disaster response, and promoting international trade and influence. The media report on current military operations, and films sometimes celebrate war heroes. The sacrifices of generations of UK service personnel killed or wounded in action are remembered once a year.

The health and well-being of military veterans and their families involve an industry of medical, social, and other services. These are provided by state, medical, commercial, and charitable organizations. However, the achievements and ongoing contributions of the veteran community to the UK economy and society are rarely recognized.

If you are a veteran, in a veteran's family, or working with veterans, what are your experiences? What have you given and learned from military service? What has it cost you or your family? Do you feel valued and listened to? What does the United Kingdom do well for our veteran community? What could we do better?

Why the Veteran Community Is Important, and Who Cares?

In the twentieth century, the United Kingdom had veterans from two world wars, national service, internal conflict in Northern Ireland, and frequent international operations. They have been a major source of practical, technical, organizational, and leadership skills in the UK economy. This resourceful community provides talented support to many local and national organizations.

The numbers of active service personnel in the UK have fallen in recent years to approximately 191,000 plus 210,000 reserves in 2011, but there are more than 3.7 million veterans. The wider veteran community, including families, is likely to exceed ten million, one in six of the UK population.

Military selection creates a relatively fit, well-trained, and resilient workforce. However, military service can make extreme demands on personnel and families, with consequences for long-term health and well-being. So who cares about the veteran community?

The health and well-being of the veteran community are monitored by veterans' charities like the Royal British Legion, Combat Stress, and many medical and social research projects. Some of the most comprehensive UK studies of serving personnel and veterans are based at Kings College in London University. The work of the independent King's Centre for Military Health Research (KCMHR) is described in its *15 Year Report of Research into the Health of the UK Armed Forces*. Established as the Gulf War Illnesses Research Unit in 1996 and renamed in 2004, KCMHR works closely with the Academic Centre for Defence Mental Health (ACDMH), the Ministry of Defence (MoD), and military communities.

This chapter explores key features of the veteran community in the United Kingdom, some of the physical and mental health issues for veterans, plus social and economic well-being issues for veterans and their families. It outlines services and resources available to veterans in the United Kingdom and positive aspects of their contribution to society.

There are significant differences in policy, practice, and research perspectives among organizations serving the needs of the veteran community. Many needs are well recognized. Some old problems persist, and new problems are emerging, in the early twenty-first century. Some are medical. Many are practical social and economic issues like housing and employment for veterans and their children. There may be room for nonmedical, nonpatronizing initiatives enabling veteran communities to develop their own resources and potential.

Several questions arise when comparing the services, views, objectives, and priorities of agencies serving the veterans' community, including the military, government, health and community services, and charities:

• How can veterans and their families manage the transition from the structure and support of service life to uncertain housing and employment prospects in an economic recession?

- What extra resources are available or needed for veterans and their families, compromised by injury, trauma, or other long-term health hazards?

- How different are the physical and mental health needs of veterans and their families from the needs of civilian communities coping with rapid change, migration, insecurity, and violence? In some regions, these may be similar.

- What talents do veterans have for living in an uncertain world?

- How can state systems in the United Kingdom be encouraged to revise twentieth-century attitudes about health and well-being issues for veterans in the twenty-first century?

After World Wars I and II the huge needs of the UK veteran community led to the development of major charities, such as the British Legion. Many veterans have created more charities to cover unmet needs. The government provides good medical (not dental) services free, barely adequate financial benefits, and insufficient housing. Accessing state benefits has become increasingly complex and bureaucratic. In recent years there have been attempts to rationalize some of these support systems. The Service Personnel and Veterans Agency (SPVA) combines administration and advice across a range of areas from pensions and compensation to welfare and special support programs.

The Internet is helping veteran and community support organizations like the UK Citizens Advice Bureau Advice Guide (CAB) by providing links for veterans, reservists, and dependents to major agencies that deal with physical health, mental health, allowances, compensation, and so forth.

Some of these services cover essential social and economic well-being needs of many veterans: availability of housing, opportunities for employment, and access to financial support or compensation. Many refer to mental health issues, most frequently to post-traumatic stress disorder (PTSD). Others concern obvious physical health issues like recovery from severe injuries.

From a work psychology perspective, there may be relevant comparisons between leaving military service and the challenges faced by individuals, families, and communities coping with redundancies (layoffs) and industrial closures in other sectors of the UK economy since the 1980s. Life span development (Hopson & Adams 1976, Sugarman 1986, 2001) and transition psychology (Williams 1999, Miller et al. 2010) processes used in career counseling practice can highlight hazards and opportunities for veterans' career events and consequences for the lives of their families. Some of these frameworks may be unfamiliar to policy makers and researchers who mainly focus on military or medical perspectives. However, they have been important in my work with individual veterans and their partners, widows, or children, as reflected in several parts of this chapter. They may be relevant to other practitioners and researchers working with the veteran community.

There are some veterans' issues that successive governments or the Ministry of Defence seem reluctant to recognize or resolve, for security, legal, financial, or political reasons. In some of these areas, the integrity of sponsored research, taking legal action against veterans, or delaying legal appeals by them may be in doubt.

The UK Veteran Population, Community, and Cohorts

The health and well-being of veterans and their families are ongoing national issues in many countries. The UK veteran population in 2007 was estimated to be between 3.7 and 5 million (Woodhead et al. 2009). These are made up of successive cohorts of Army, Royal Navy, Royal Air Force, Royal Marines, Special Forces, and Reserve personnel from the last eighty years of UK military operations (see figure 12.1). The total veteran population is gradually falling; UK armed forces numbers are now much lower than during World War II and the period of compulsory National Service that continued until the mid-1960s.

The wider UK veteran community includes the immediate families of ex-service personnel and other special groups. A recent British Legion study includes partners (including widows and separated or divorced spouses or

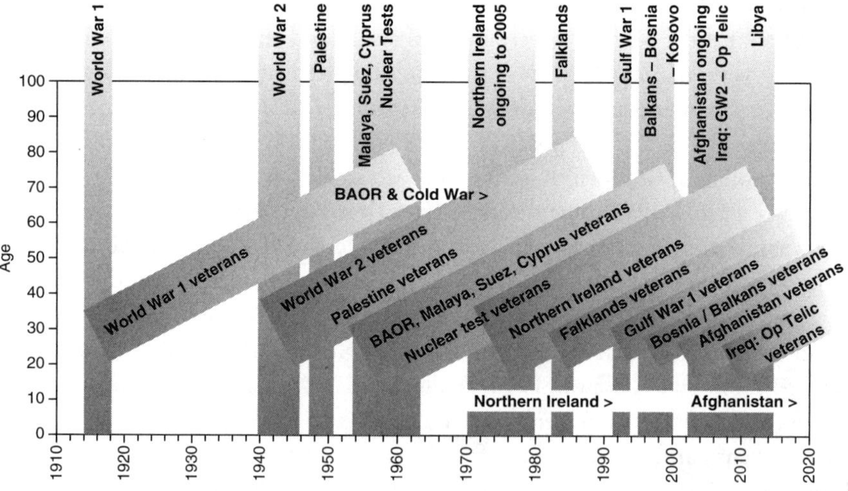

Figure 12.1. UK Armed Forces Operations and Veteran Cohorts 1910–2020.

partners) and children, as well as Gurkhas and Commonwealth soldiers discharged from the Armed Forces in the last five years.

When service personnel have died or have left service with long-lasting physical or mental health disabilities, parents, siblings, or other kin may be deeply affected. These people should be considered in wider enquiries about the health and welfare of the veteran community. In some cases, when veterans have been exposed to genetic damage from toxic or radiological hazards, the health and welfare of grandchildren as well as children are of long-term concern.

Various military roles and assignments have involved different physical occupational health hazards related to evolving military technology and deployment environments. This is another reason to recognize that the veteran population includes many distinct cohorts: military personnel who served in specific campaigns, in different arms or forces, and in different geographical regions.

For occupational health purposes, these cohorts may have been exposed to different types of physical or mental challenges during their service that may have adversely affected their long-term health, such as long-term hearing damage among aircrews or asbestos exposure among naval personnel.

Over many decades there have also been widely differing types and lengths of service. Regular service personnel may have served for many years, in several campaigns, and sometimes in more than one force. Many were called up for several years' full-time military service during World War II or long-term regular service contracts. Some of these people continued in reserve service. Many were involved in shorter contracts during national service or short-service contracts. Typically, five to ten years' military service may be followed by forty to fifty years as a veteran.

The number of veterans who have experienced active service in combat zones or other hazardous environments has varied in recent decades. Many service roles have potential occupational risk factors in training or normal operations without being directly exposed to lethal combat risks, such as ground crew decontaminating aircraft after observation sorties for nuclear tests.

Some of these veterans' cohorts have only emerged as organized networks long after their military service was over, brought together by common experiences of long-term health problems. The best known are veterans of the Persian Gulf War in 1991 and possibly veterans of Operation Telic in Iraq since 2003. Others, like the Atomic and Nuclear Test Veterans and Porton Down (chemical and biological warfare research) volunteers, were involved in secret operations that could not be revealed for thirty years. Many veterans or surviving family members have formed campaign groups to claim compensation for health consequences of their military service after being denied war pensions.

Policy, Practice, and Research Perspectives

The needs and qualities of the UK veteran population (over 3.7 million people) and the wider veteran community (over 10 million) can be seen from several perspectives. Of particular interest are the experience and evolving needs of individual veterans and their families. Government and military priorities and perspectives are different from those of veterans' organizations, and from medical or other social support organizations serving the veteran community.

Successive governments (regardless of political party) and the defense establishment (the Ministry of Defence, senior officers of each force, and possibly former senior officers now in the House of Lords) acknowledge varying levels of responsibility for veterans and their dependents as matters of public policy and financial commitments. But successive governments have been reluctant to put the "Military Covenant" into law. This would formalize Britain's duty of care to its armed forces, an unspoken pact between society and the military (BBC News 2011b). Governments put tight financial constraints on military expenditure, to the point where military operations may be compromised or public opinion may jeopardize future election prospects.

However, there have been significant improvements in provision of in-service medical care by the Defence Medical Services (DMS) in cooperation with the National Health Service (NHS). The DMS has fifteen regional rehabilitation units (RRUs) across the United Kingdom and Germany, five MoD hospital units (MDHUs) embedded in NHS acute trusts, the Royal Centre for Defence Medicine (RCDM) in Birmingham, and fifteen military-run Departments of Community Mental Health (DCMH) in the United Kingdom with five DCMHs at the major permanent overseas bases (Defence Medical Services 2011).

In the current economic climate, UK armed forces are expected to make major financial savings. This will include redundancies, adding to the veteran community, and will continue pressure on the MoD to minimize any avoidable expenditure.

Veterans' issues have little political value to governments unless they compromise morale in the serving forces (e.g., facing redundancy from budget cuts) or risk public anger (e.g., the recent campaign on behalf of Gurkha veterans). In addition, some veterans' issues may raise questions about the legality of certain weapons systems or military operations (past, present, or future). Researchers may be cautioned that full disclosure (e.g., of health data) could compromise national security or international relations. The default position for government-funded research into health and well-being issues for military personnel and veterans appears to be to minimize legal or financial liability for the state. Researchers and organizations that rely on government(s), the defense industry, or the North Atlantic Treaty Organization (NATO) for future funding tend to avoid controversial conclusions about the health implications of military operations and equipment (e.g., reports by the UK Royal Society and World Health Organization about the hazards of depleted uranium weapons in 2001).

Veterans' organizations may represent them on a wide range of issues, offering practical support, individual advocacy, and occasional campaigns on single issues. These organizations may undertake more controversial research, but they have nothing like the financial or technical resources available to the government. Occasionally joint research projects with veterans and civilian specialists, as well as military representatives, have produced interesting results with high standards of technical quality and transparency, such as the Depleted Uranium Oversight Board (Ministry of Defence, DUOB 2007) project for Gulf War 1 veterans from 2001 to 2007. However, it was not permitted to continue its monitoring for Gulf War 2 (Op Telic) veterans after 2007.

Medical and other community services may recognize special needs for the veteran population and their families. Some excellent medical support services have been developed for in-service personnel who have suffered physical injury or mental trauma. Professional practitioners, for example in NHS Health Trusts, have developed ongoing action research projects with medical professionals in the military and emergency services to pilot new procedures (Kitchener 2009). Some of these offer long-term treatment, therapy, or rehabilitation for ex-service personnel in the veteran community.

The degree of specialist medical support and community resources available to veterans may vary widely depending on their geographic location, age, and special needs. Public medical and social services in the United Kingdom have increasing standards for individual practitioners and organizations, subject to government funding constraints. These can provide good individual services. However, they may not have resources for coordinated research. In addition, they may be strictly limited in potential advocacy roles on behalf of individuals or groups of veterans with shared issues.

Therefore, there are several research perspectives on the health and well-being of the UK veteran community. These vary widely in motivation and resources depending largely on the sponsors of the research investigations. Some military medical research has long been motivated by the need to understand the limits of effective human performance and endurance under extreme operational conditions (e.g., short-term resilience to nuclear weapons or air combat). Restoring injured or traumatized personnel to combat effectiveness is a high priority. In addition, some research aims at reassuring and maintaining the confidence and morale of military personnel.

However, some medical research into potentially adverse long-term health effects of military service may be controversial (e.g., exposure to external or internal radiation). This has raised complex legal, financial, and ethical issues such as those identified by the Redfern Inquiry, published in 2010. The Redfern Inquiry examined the analysis of human tissue taken from individuals who had worked in the UK nuclear industry, including samples from UK nuclear test veterans. Michael Redfern QC looked at the processes and practices involved in the analysis of human tissue that was carried out in UK nuclear facilities from 1955 to 1992. This was not a military project, but it raised serious issues about covert medical research into civilian and military nuclear hazards.

Some health and environmental research is sponsored by veterans, independent researchers, or other organizations. This provides independent scientific evidence for legal actions by, or on behalf of, veterans claiming war pensions or other compensation.

In view of the size of the total veteran population and of specific cohorts (e.g., 3,000 surviving of the 20,000 military personnel involved in nuclear testing in Australia and the Pacific in the 1950s and early 1960s), medical research findings could have major financial implications for the MoD and future governments. If research indicates adverse long-term health consequences of new weapon systems, these may affect civilians in conflict zones as well as troops, and the children and grandchildren of veterans. They may also affect complex legal, commercial, and political relationships with other countries and alliances. In such areas, national security interests may be invoked to minimize adverse research outcomes, such as those identified by Redfern. These cases raise important legal and ethical issues for scientific researchers and health practitioners.

On a more positive note, some military and veteran health issues, such as mental health consequences of trauma, affect many people and have attracted significant interest, cooperation, and consensus from a wide range of agencies in the United Kingdom. Trauma Risk Management (TRiM) was pioneered in the Royal Marines and has been adopted by the Army, Royal Navy, and RAF Regiment. It is "a novel system of post incident management which intends to allow commanders to provide appropriate support to their subordinates in the aftermath of traumatic events" (Greenberg, Langston & Jones 2008).

Some of these pioneering projects have acted as prototypes for improving health and well-being research and services. The TRiM approach has also been used to improve trauma support in nonmilitary settings, for example, for paramedics in the London Ambulance Service. Similar prototype projects may be useful for other health issues that require cooperation among veteran communities, health professionals, and government agencies in the United Kingdom.

Health and well-being research for military personnel and veterans may have important spin-offs for civilian health and well-being studies in occupational and community health settings. Local and regional dialogue in the United Kingdom is connected to national and international levels by networks like the International and European Societies for Traumatic Stress Studies, ISTSS and ESTSS.

Differing policy, practice, and research perspectives are to be expected from different organizations working with the veteran community, and given the diverse range of ages, military roles, and operations involved. The size of the total veteran community makes large-scale studies very expensive. But the gradual trend toward increasing collaboration among the various perspectives of military, medical, veterans, and other professions and disciplines should produce deeper insights into veterans' health and well-being and more practical and cost-effective support for veterans and their families.

Health Hazards and Resilience from Military Service

Military service can involve multiple traumas, stress, change, hostile environments, separation, and loss experiences, with short- and long-term mental health and well-being consequences. These affect in-service personnel, veterans, and their families. During and after major wars, and during many years of conflict in Northern Ireland, these trials were shared with the wider civilian population. In the twenty-first century, the challenges faced by veterans and military families may not be appreciated by the public or politicians in England, except in locations where major terrorist attacks have occurred, for example in London and Manchester.

Military personnel are likely to face most of the health and safety hazards encountered by the general population, such as infectious diseases, age- or gender-related health disorders, accidents, injuries, and psychological issues associated with loss, relationships, and so forth. In general, military personnel may represent a fitter, healthier segment of the national population because of rigorous selection procedures.

In addition, several aspects of military life may increase an individual's resilience to everyday stresses and civilian life events in his or her postservice (veteran) careers, such as confidence, skills, discipline, teamwork, and motivation.

However, military service can involve a wide range of hazards to physical and/or mental health not often faced by civilians in the United Kimgdom. Some may have rapid or early onset effects, such as wounds or other injuries. Others may not display adverse physical or mental health symptoms for several months or years. Sometimes these may be hard to distinguish from, or triggered by, other events that may affect most of the population, such as midlife health, employment, or relationship issues.

There are major overlaps between health and well-being issues for in-service personnel and their families, and for the veteran community (e.g., diagnosis and treatment for the effects of trauma). These are covered by excellent in-service military medical organizations (refer to the DMS previously discussed), sometimes working in triservice teams and, where they are based in the United Kingdom, in conjunction with civilian National Health Service (NHS) specialists.

Medical priorities vary among conflicts, weapons technology, and long-distance medical evacuation resources. In the nineteenth century military hospitals like Haslar near Portsmouth were built to give easy access for ships carrying military casualties home from wars in Europe. Recent wars have had far fewer casualties than those in the nineteenth and twentieth centuries. Air-evacuated troops may survive severe injuries, such as those from IEDs in Iraq and Afghanistan. They may go to specialist DMS treatment and rehabilitation centers within NHS hospitals like the Royal Centre for Defence Medicine (RCDM) at Queen Elizabeth Hospital in Birmingham, Frimley Park near Aldershot, or specialist rehabilitation facilities like Headley Park. Some of these have become modern legends for treating extreme injuries, reminiscent of surgeon Sir Archie McIndoe's pioneering work on skin grafts for burns suffered by aircrew in the RAF during World War II.

Severe injuries may require extended medical support and rehabilitation for personnel and families during treatment, usually from state-run and -funded NHS healthcare facilities. This may continue years after leaving service, so some NHS medical practitioners have long experience of healthcare for veterans, particularly in areas with local military communities. However, there can be wide regional variations in the specialist skills and experience needed to treat some of the physical and mental health needs of military veterans.

Certain occupational health hazards from past eras of military service are recognized by civilian NHS medical services and may occur in some civilian occupations. Hearing damage or loss and tinnitus used to have military and industrial causes, though these have been reduced by modern health and safety precautions. Ironically, these problems are now emerging from other sources like high-volume entertainment systems. Other physical injuries are occurring in extreme work conditions or high-performance equipment (e.g., long-term physical effects of spinal injuries from ejector seats and decompression from high-altitude ejection or sub-sea diving emergencies).

More complex physical health and military medical research issues arise from potential exposure of troops to unconventional chemical, biological, radiological, or nuclear (CBRN) weapons used by enemy or allied forces.

Toxic exposures may arise from deliberate or accidental dispersal of industrial chemicals or other toxins, for example, oil fires in Kuwait and Iraq, sulfur fires, and detonation of chlorine tankers. Radiological hazards may occur from fires of munition supplies (e.g., 1,500 kg of depleted uranium shells burned in the Doha fire after the war in 1991) and from contamination of vehicles destroyed by uranium weapons then moved to military scrap yards (UNEP 2005).

In short but intense military operations like the first Persian Gulf War in 1991, troops may be exposed to multiple toxic hazards. These may have brief early onset effects such as flu-like symptoms indicating immune system responses, or more disabling conditions, referred to as "Gulf War Syndrome":

> Some veterans developed unexplained illnesses following their service in the Gulf two decades ago. Reported symptoms range from chronic fatigue, headaches and sleep disturbances to joint pains, irritable bowel, stomach and respiratory disorders and psychological problems. Twenty years on, though, there is still disagreement over why rates of ill health are twice as high among Gulf War veterans than troops deployed elsewhere. (BBC News 2011a)

The KCMHR 15 Year Report (2010) summarizes its research into many possible causes of Gulf War illnesses, but found no single specific cause for the increase in ill health after 1991 operations: "Plausible candidates for the increase in symptoms therefore include medical counter measures, stress/ fear of chemical weapons, media/social influences.... No Iraq War Syndrome was reported after operations in 2003."

However, enough UK veterans from the first Gulf War were affected to set up their own campaign organizations. Large numbers of troops in the United States seemed to have similar health problems in the 1990s. After serving in the Balkans in 1995 and 1999, significant numbers of troops from

Italy and Spain suffered severe and unexplained health problems developing from 1999 onward.

Statistically these incidents may appear insignificant when compared to national populations. But when correctly compared to equivalent, fit-soldier comparison groups, the incidence of leukemia was eleven times higher than expected. It seems likely that smaller groups of (mainly Mediterranean) troops within the total NATO force may have been exposed to unknown hazardous materials (suspected uranium weapons) in relatively local areas. UNEP surveys did not study bomb or missile targets, only A10 antitank airstrikes with DU (deplated uranium).

Episodes of severe illness among small groups of military personnel are likely to carry over into the veteran population, possibly after a period of deteriorating health in-service. In many cases, these lead to disputes about whether the cause of chronic illness or incapacity was military service. This has important financial consequences for veterans who may then be denied war pensions or compensation, or only be able to obtain them after many years of litigation. This is not good for the morale or mental health of veterans or their families, or longer term for the confidence of serving personnel.

Exposure to radiation, and research to estimate short-term operational performance and survival during or after radiation exposures, were major issues during atomic and nuclear testing programs in the 1950s and 1960s and still are in 2012. The primary reasons for the atomic and nuclear tests in Australia and Christmas Island were to test and demonstrate the tactical effects of nuclear weapons. However, an important parallel agenda was to test their health effects on the operational capacity of military personnel, with and without radiation protection. Most of the 20,000 military personnel involved have since died, but about 3,000 remain alive: the nuclear test veterans cohort.

These human guinea pig experiments have caused ongoing physical and mental health problems for some veterans past and present, including early onset illnesses such as skin disorders and later leukemia and multiple cancers. These are lucidly reported by affected veterans and relatives. However, they appear to have curiously little statistical significance in military medical research in the United Kingdom or Australia. Veterans report both physical and mental health consequences for children and grandchildren.

In the United Kingdom, many nuclear test veterans or their families have been denied compensation for chronic health effects because the MoD's default position is that most veterans were not exposed to hazardous levels of radiation during the tests. The MoD also holds that they applied for compensation too late (they were forbidden to discuss these concerns publicly for at least thirty years as military secrets). These are the subject of ongoing legal action, in which more than 1,000 UK veterans are seeking compensation and/or pension entitlements. Further hearings are scheduled for 2012, well over fifty years after the atomic and nuclear tests were conducted.

It is perhaps surprising that any veterans exposed to nuclear tests in the late 1950s and early 1960s have survived for more than fifty years. Resilience is a recurring—and optimistic—theme in the history of health and well-being for many UK veterans. The nuclear test veterans were a very fit and well-trained workforce at that time. As with most regular service personnel, they were relatively fitter than the general population. However, in some cases children and grandchildren have suffered cancers or birth defects characteristic of genetic damage caused by radiation exposure.

In the past, most medical research into military radiation exposures has focused on the effects of high doses of external, gamma radiation. In recent years, investigations have been considering the long-term health effects of ongoing internal alpha radiation, which may create more long-term chromosome damage than brief exposure to higher levels of external radiation. This is important if the potential health effects of nuclear or nonfissile uranium weapons are to be investigated (e.g., ingested fallout from nuclear tests or airborne dust from uranium-enhanced conventional weapons).

The KCMHR 15-Year Report drew these conclusions about depleted uranium (DU) exposure:

> After the conclusion of the 2003 invasion of Iraq, we were able to launch a direct study looking for evidence of DU exposure, concentrating particularly on those most at risk, which were those in the armoured brigades and those involved after the end of active war fighting in cleaning up knocked out Iraqi tanks. DU is excreted by the kidneys, but we found no traces of DU in 341 at-risk Army and Royal Marines personnel who had taken part in the invasion of Iraq. (2010, 46)

This interpretation of the isotopic analysis of urine samples did not take into account accumulating evidence since 1999 that some enhanced weapon systems are using undepleted or low-enriched uranium. Anomalies do exist in the Op Telic population data, reported in the DUOB final report (Ministry of Defence 2007, 65–66). Mean contamination levels of almost-natural uranium were three times higher than the UK control group, and not natural. A normative study of uranium levels in British forces for the MoD (Miller et al. 2007) found significant variations in uranium ratios and in concentration levels between army personnel from other recent operations (excluding Iraq) and RAF and navy personnel. These, and other UK and United Nations

(UN) studies, have assumed that uranium weapons only use depleted uranium, and only involve ammunition.

Major advances have been made in military medical research studies of uranium and other potential CBRN exposures. But many interpretations about exposures and health effects for troops and veterans need urgent review in the United Kingdom, NATO, and UN. Invalid assumptions about weapon types, novel materials, and targets have compromised sampling, test methods, analysis, and interpretation because of groupthink errors (e.g., all uranium is depleted) and ignorance or concealment of new weapons technologies.

Ongoing health surveillance for veterans of all recent conflicts where new weapons have been used may be increasingly important over the next ten to twenty years, including rates of miscarriage and possible genetic or genomic instability effects on children. Epidemics of cancers and birth defects occurred among civilian populations in Iraq after the 1991 conflict and are increasing in areas worst affected by combat operations between 2003 and 2005, such as Fallujah, Baghdad, and Babil province. Whether these are due to oil fires, uranium dust, or other genotoxic sources is an urgent research question (Alaani 2011). Hopefully troops in recent conflict zones had lower exposures to combat toxins than civilians who continue to live in contaminated areas with reported increases in cancers, leukemias, or birth defects (e.g., the Balkans and Iraq).

If serving personnel or their families are affected by genotoxic combat exposures, military medical personnel and the MoD should already be aware of delayed onset health problems. For veterans and their families it is not clear whether any long-term health monitoring programs are planned. The Redfern Inquiry (2010) showed how successive governments have been reluctant to publish potentially adverse radiation-related health studies for economic and military reasons. The veteran community may be wise to commission its own health-monitoring research.

New weapons technology is likely to create new physical health hazards for troops, with long-term consequences for recent and future veterans. New forms of explosive are being developed to deal with different kinds of threat, such as new thermobaric (high temperature, high pressure) weapons ranging in size from small infantry-launched RPGs to missiles and larger bombs. These can create severe internal organ damage and extreme burns if personnel survive the initial blast.

New high-velocity ammunition can cause complex internal injuries. New high-density explosives (e.g., DIME) can cause survivable but untreatable injuries, embedding hundreds of particles of micro-shrapnel in the victim.

New focused-blast weapons are designed to cause lower limb amputation. In recent conflicts, most of these highly sophisticated, sublethal weapons have been developed and deployed by allied forces. UK personnel injuries should be rare, except in blue-on-blue/friendly fire incidents.

One example of a new combat-related health hazard reported by KCMHR is mild traumatic brain injury (mTBI). Whether this is related to thermobaric weapons or other sources seems unclear:

> When we started our main study in 2003, mTBI was not an issue, and it was only later that it became labeled as the "signature injury" of the war. However, we were able to look at the symptoms that made up the post concussional syndrome. We found that these were indeed associated with self-report of blast injury, which is what was being predicted. But the same symptoms were also associated with exposures that had nothing to do with blast injury, such as exposure to depleted uranium munitions, or with problems at home during deployment. And finally they were strongly associated with PTSD, which had already been reported by the Walter Reed team. So it seemed that post concussion symptoms were not a specific consequence of blast injury. (Fear et al. 2009)

Some of these new weapons may contravene the principles of the Inhumane Weapons Convention of 1980 as weapons of indiscriminate effect. For example, do thermobaric weapons constitute new types of incendiary weapons, and are uranium-enhanced weapons tacitly radiological weapons?

Arms control protocols lag decades behind new weapons technology. In the interim troops, future veterans, and potentially veterans' children and grandchildren face an increasingly unpleasant range of severe injury and early and delayed onset chronic health hazards (Williams 2008).

Physical health issues for armed services personnel may also include endemic biological hazards overseas, such as hepatitis plus malaria and other tropical diseases. Ironically, pesticides and vaccinations intended to mitigate these risks were two of the potential hazards that may have contributed to Gulf War illnesses. Some tropical diseases can be effectively controlled by modern medicines, so they are rarely mentioned. However others, like hepatitis, can have long-term health consequences for veterans and veterans' healthcare. Brief reports of mystery illnesses with skin or internal bleeding symptoms like leishmaniasis and CCHF (Crimean Congo hemorrhagic fever) have been reported by WHO in communities in Bosnia (1995), Afghanistan (2001–2002), and Iraq (2003) soon after allied bombing in the local area. A mystery illness that affected UK troops in Bagram in May 2002 was finally described as winter vomiting sickness. Natural and combat-related health hazards may be hard to differentiate.

Mental Health Issues from Recent Conflicts

The mental health of armed service personnel can be as important a concern as physical injury or illness. Mental health issues that develop during service may have longer-term consequences for veterans and their families. Other mental health issues may emerge after leaving service. Some cases may be a delayed reaction to past trauma. Other mental health problems may emerge as part of the transition from the services to civilian life. In addition, other mental health issues may develop years after leaving the services, whether or not attributable to military service.

The Mental Health Foundation (MHF) summarizes the mental health outlook for UK military personnel as follows:

> Most British military personnel do not experience mental health problems while they are in service, or afterwards in civilian life. However they face unique risks in service and, if they do experience mental health problems, they may require particular treatments and particular mental health services.
>
> The mental health problems experienced by military personnel are the same as the general population, although experiences during service and the transition to civilian life mean that their mental ill health may be triggered by different factors. PTSD, depression, anxiety and substance abuse affect a significant minority of service personnel and veterans.

Staff at the Institute of Psychiatry, Kings College (Fear et al. 2010) are engaged in an extensive research program studying the mental health and well-being of military personnel serving in Iraq and Afghanistan. In their recent study of 10,000 serving personnel, including 83 percent regulars and 17 percent reservists, their main findings were that

- 4 percent reported probable PTSD,
- 19.7 percent reported other common mental disorders,
- 13 percent reported alcohol misuse,
- regulars deployed to Iraq or Afghanistan were significantly more likely to report alcohol misuse than those not deployed,
- reservists were more likely to report probable PTSD than those not deployed,
- regular personnel in combat roles were more likely than those in support roles to report probable PTSD, and
- experience of mental health problems was not linked with number of deployments.

There have been many studies of PTSD in military and civilian contexts in recent years and significant progress in the United Kingdom in diagnosis and treatment. The development of cognitive behavioral therapy (CBT) and techniques like eye movement desensitization and reprocessing (EMDR) have been valuable resources for supporting traumatized military and police personnel in Northern Ireland.

Where there is a carryover of PTSD symptoms from military service to civilian life, both the NHS and organizations like Combat Stress offer specialist support to veterans.

There may be long overlaps between mental health issues for veterans and families during and after leaving service. Serving personnel who have a severe physical injury, mental trauma, or both are likely to experience a period of hospitalization, medical care, or therapy before being discharged from service. The tragic event of suicide may be diagnosed or recorded as a mental health crisis, but for some veterans it became the only escape from prolonged and intolerable physical distress from service-related injuries or illnesses, or from cumulative mental distress. Advances in treatment, more enlightened approaches to mental health, and access to social support and other enabling factors for transitions (discussed later in the chapter) may ease severe distress for veterans.

Resources for Mental Health Support

The Service Personnel and Veterans Agency (SPVA), part of the MoD, acts as a single point of contact to provide advice for serving military personnel, ex-service personnel, and their dependents. The SPVA is responsible for the War Pensions Scheme and Armed Forces Compensation Scheme for armed forces personnel who experience illness as a result of service. The NHS provides medical support.

The MHF summarizes recent mental health projects set up by the MoD with the NHS and with veterans' charities recognizing the needs of veterans to access mental health support with expertise in understanding military mental health issues:

> The Medical Assessment Programme (MAP), based at Guy's and St Thomas' in London, offers help and treatment to any veteran of any conflict, no matter how long ago, and their carers.
> There is also a Reserves' Mental Health Programme (RMHP) open to anyone who has seen active service as a volunteer or reservist since 1 January 2003 and is now demobilized, and has mental health problems that might be linked to service on operations. (Mental Health Foundation n.d.)

Since 1998 the MoD and NHS have run six Veterans Mental Health pilot projects across the United Kingdom. These were assessed by Sheffield University in 2010. These projects aim to increase knowledge and understanding of veterans' mental health needs among mainstream NHS staff, to improve access to mainstream NHS services. The projects provide treatment and referrals to community mental health services, social services, and specialist assessment and treatment elsewhere, including the residential centers run by the voluntary sector veterans' support organization Combat Stress. Each project has a community veterans' mental health therapist, and the projects also have links with local veterans' organizations to reach out to people who may need help, as these notes about the Wales project explain:

> The *All Wales Veterans Health and Wellbeing Service* launched in April 2010 after a 2-year pilot project. The service offers information, advice, therapy, and appropriate onward referral for veterans who are experiencing Post Traumatic Stress Disorder (PTSD), Depression or Anxiety and those who are having difficulties with alcohol and other substance misuse.
>
> The service is delivered by the NHS in Wales. Local Health Boards appoint an experienced clinician as a Veterans Therapist (VT) with an interest or experience of military health problems. This VT will accept referrals from health staff, GP's, veteran charities and self-referrals from ex-service personnel. Following the assessment, the veteran may be offered treatment by the VT or referred onto other NHS teams or departments for further treatment. The VT will also refer to veteran charities for help with debt management, benefits and war pension/armed forces compensation claims as indicated. (Veterans Wales n.d.)

Another recent example of joint mental health projects for veterans in the United Kingdom is the South Central Regional Forum on Veterans' Mental Health and Wellbeing, held in June 2011, with representatives from the South Central Strategic Health Authority, the MoD, and veterans' organizations, including Combat Stress and the British Legion. The range of topics covered and quality of cooperation can be seen in presentations available online (Berkshire NHS Trust 2011).

Outside the NHS, Combat Stress and other charities provide specialist residential and community outreach mental healthcare for veterans.

Health and Well-being Issues for Veterans' Families

The needs of families of serving armed forces personnel are covered by several organizations within the MoD, within each major force by welfare and support organizations, and by Army, Navy and Air Force Family Federations. For example, the Army Families Federation (AFF) offers advice on housing, health and additional needs, education and child care, TA and reserve forces, deployments, money matters, employment and training, and family life. The Service Families Task Force (SFTF) deals with all family issues that are outside the scope of an individual Service.

This in-service infrastructure is important to veterans and their families because it offers essential support during the transition to ex-service life. Whereas services for individuals tend to depend on the force they have been in, many needs of veterans are common to all. There is a balance between maintaining individual service identity and loyalty and providing efficient and consistent services. The Service Personnel and Veterans Agency (SPVA) coordinates these services. They are explained on the Veterans UK Web site. The Internet is a valuable tool for veterans and families to navigate through the labyrinth of issues and services available to them.

Similar health and well-being issues for veterans and their families are identified by various organizations within the MoD and service organizations, charities providing services, and advocacy and research organizations. Some are very practical day-to-day issues like housing, relocation, employment, and continuity of education for children.

Special issues arise immediately for coping with wounded or traumatized veterans or bereaved families. Other physical or mental health or social issues may emerge over longer periods. These may include subtle differences when moving from a military back to a civilian culture and social environment: some better, some worse. These involve psychological as well as administrative transitions.

Some of these issues are not unlike those faced by civilian families forced to relocate or emigrate when faced with mass redundancies or widespread economic recession. Other postservice health and well-being issues may be specific to particular types of injury or trauma, or in rare cases to long-term health hazards.

The practical issues are well recognized by the charities with long experience of supporting veterans and their families, such as the British Legion. Longer-term health or well-being issues may be less obvious because of time delays, or because veterans from specific campaigns may become widely dispersed by redeployment to new operations and after leaving military service. These may be detected by diligent research projects, such as studies of military families by French and Dandeker (2005).

For families the practical and psychological consequences of injury, trauma, or death of their partner, parent, child, or sibling are likely to be a major life event either during or after military service. If the incident is remote, the loss may not cause PTSD, but it may cause complex issues of denial. In some cases family members may have the direct trauma of witnessing suicide, with potential for PTSD effects like witnessing death in action. The impacts of trauma or loss on veterans' families may have some similarities to the experience of civilian communities in combat zones.

Because the experiences of military families coping with bereavement or other serious trauma may overlap in service and post-service periods, a recent study by the British Legion included both situations. *Health, Welfare and Social Needs of the Armed Forces Community: A Qualitative Study* (Royal British Legion 2011) covered six groups. Many issues were shared with the general UK population (e.g., financial hardships, including lack of employment and difficulties accessing state benefits). Common social problems included loneliness, adjusting to civilian life, social isolation, and difficulties with new or existing relationships. But the study found that

> some of these needs are compounded by the peculiarities of active Service and Service family life. The most frequently cited concerns related to the nature of modern combat which leads to such traumatic injuries and death, the unique pressures exerted on relationships and parenting and the frequent changes of location impacting on ... Employment, Childcare, Schooling, Healthcare and proximity [or remoteness] of other family members.

Certain groups appeared to exhibit problems specific to their situation:

- **Those seriously injured by service, and their family members** reported physical and cognitive difficulties caused by their injuries. Impacts on participation in sport, interaction with children and on employment opportunities were all cited.

- **Veterans with a long-term health condition or disability not caused by service, and their family members** reported physical restrictions arising from their condition leading to social isolation, difficulty with home and garden maintenance and the impact on their "well" partner.

- **Serving Armed Forces family members** faced particular challenges with employment opportunities, childcare, schooling, continuity of healthcare and establishing social networks—mainly due to the frequent changes of location and absence through active service of the husband.

- **Family members of service personnel who have died** reported excellent short-term, practical support but exhibited a need for longer-term, emotional support. Bereaved single, lonely parents with a poor relationship with the deceased's spouse appeared particularly needy.

- **Estranged spouses or partners of service personnel** felt particularly unsupported by the services once their relationship had broken down and un-informed about available assistance. Their problems included loss and lack of social networks and difficulties in adapting to civilian life (housing, schooling, employment).

- **Gurkhas and Commonwealth soldiers discharged from the Armed Forces within the last five years** had experienced difficulties with transferring their skills and qualifications to employment in Civvy Street and with securing opportunities to further their qualifications. Commonwealth soldiers experienced particular difficulties with accommodation at the time of discharge, understanding the British way of life, having few social or family contacts and language barriers.

The study came up with some important risk factors for people getting into difficulties. They exhibited one or more of the following:

- Inability to secure alternative employment
- Few transferrable skills or qualifications
- Lack of a partner
- Complicated injuries or illnesses
- Having little contact or support from family
- Low income or financial insecurity
- Ongoing depression or mental health problems
- Social isolation, limited social network, change of location or accommodation
- Lack of awareness of available support
- Difficulty coping with absent partners
- Lack of preparation for transition to civilian life

The report recommended that "identification of those at particular risk, combined with enhanced services to meet their needs, could help to prevent them from falling into a downward spiral."

These are useful checklists for family support agencies involved in preparing families for the transition from military to civilian life. They are also useful for community agencies, including schools and social services, and NHS healthcare services, who support veterans and their families. The risk factors overlap with several resilience factors for civilians coping with transitions after redundancy and other major life events in the 1990s (Williams 1999 and discussed later in this chapter).

Intergenerational Effects of Military Service

A special aspect of the health and well-being of veterans and their families emerged while compiling the UK veteran cohorts chart in figure 12.1 (p. 260). This was adapted from a chart of twentieth-century life influences used for briefing clients in career and personal development programs. Studies in the field of life span development psychology (e.g., Sugarman 1986, 2001; Sheehy 1995; Neugarten 1996) encouraged reflection on an individual's life and family history to identify social and genetic influences, and historical context, on the early development of core values, deeply held beliefs, personality, and talents.

Several hundred autobiographical reviews with career development clients have highlighted the importance of family circumstances in early childhood, including work roles and behavior of parents, grandparents, and teachers. Significant early life events include relocation; change of schools; and traumatic events including illness, separation, injury, or death of parents. In normal circumstances these significant adults, and older siblings, may act as key role models for dealing with trauma, stress, and change.

Vicarious trauma may affect children when a parent suffers separation or bereavement of his or her parents or siblings (grandparents, uncles, or aunts). Although these may not affect the child initially, the predictable distressed behavior of parents will affect children sooner or later. A parent's trauma may become a crisis several months later without the child having any way to understand distressed or hostile parental behavior.

However, stable parenting relationships in the first five years seem to give children a degree of emotional resilience for coping with future periods of loss or change, including relocation, and even separation of parents years later.

Career counseling programs with adults who had been children of civilian or military expatriate families have illustrated significant developmental issues. Families that have several local or international relocations may model effective adapting behavior (transitions skills) to children who later develop talents for international careers. But some children of service personnel who experienced multiple relocations among several countries suffered fragmented education and lacked stable identity or social support outside the family. This had serious social, employment, and mental health consequences during late adolescence and early adult life.

Some of the potential intergenerational effects of military service are illustrated in figure 12.2, which is based on detailed life review interviews I conducted with veterans, their partners, widows, and children of veterans. Positive effects include role modeling and emotional support. Potential negative effects include psychological trauma and sometimes physical health effects of genetic damage from toxic or radioactive exposures. The figure indicates that a relatively short period of military service may have powerful positive influences between generations or potentially damaging effects. One family may be affected by the past military service of grandparents up to

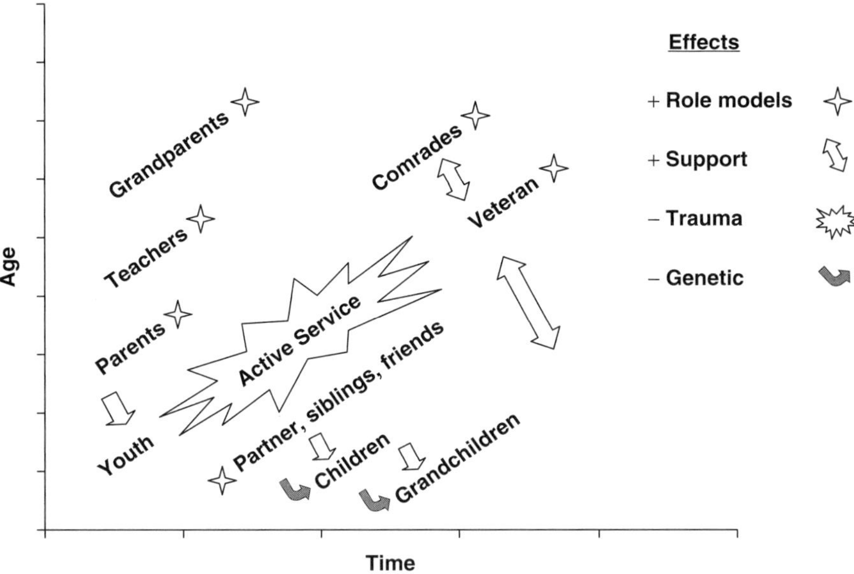

Figure 12.2. Intergenerational Effects of Military Service.

eighty years earlier, and from current serving personnel up to forty or fifty years into the future.

Until 1980 many UK families had parents or grandparents who had done military service in World Wars I or II or compulsory national service until the 1960s. Whether these relatives had positive or negative experiences, or long-term health consequences, from military service had direct effects on the psychological well-being of partners, children, and often grandchildren.

These intergenerational effects have been recognized in a series of outstanding and very detailed studies in Australia of families of troops sent to Vietnam and other major military operations (Centre for Military and Veterans Health 2007).

In the United Kingdom and United States there has been some concern about tough parenting behavior by fathers in active service. This is one of the issues monitored in the study by KCMHR funded by the U.S. Department of Defense:

> We are also aware that the subject of military families has received less attention than it merits. With this in mind, in 2010 we started a large-scale epidemiological study to systematically examine mental health outcomes for children across the age ranges 3–16 years. Data will be collected from fathers, mothers, children themselves (11 +) and their teachers and care-givers. (Kings Centre for Military Health Research 2010)

The Transition from Service to Ex-service Life

The term *transition* is widely used in current policy statements and research projects associated with the process of leaving military service and returning to "civvy street" or civilian life. From a career psychology perspective, the term *transition* is entirely appropriate in this context. The Career Transition Partnership (CTP) is a flagship project serving 20,000 personnel who leave military service each year. It is a partnering agreement between the MoD and Right Management, global career development and outplacement specialists.

However, from the sources explored in this article it appears that UK military and medical policy analysts, researchers, or service providers seem unaware of transition psychology research and practice, which explores the psychological processes that can enable individuals to adapt effectively to major life events, good or bad, including severe trauma (Hopson & Adams 1976; Sugarman 1986; Williams 1999; Miller et al. 2010).

Transition psychology is not only relevant to the leaving-service transition, but also to the post-trauma transition period experienced by veterans or serving personnel and/or their families after injury or death, usually only described in terms of medical pathologies like PTSD or depression. It is a key process enabling psychological resilience in the face of trauma or change, including positive events like birth of a child or a new work assignment (see figure 12.3).

Transition psychology may offer some additional insights into the transition period needed for ex-service personnel and their families to adapt to postservice life. This transition period may be partially eased by transfer to

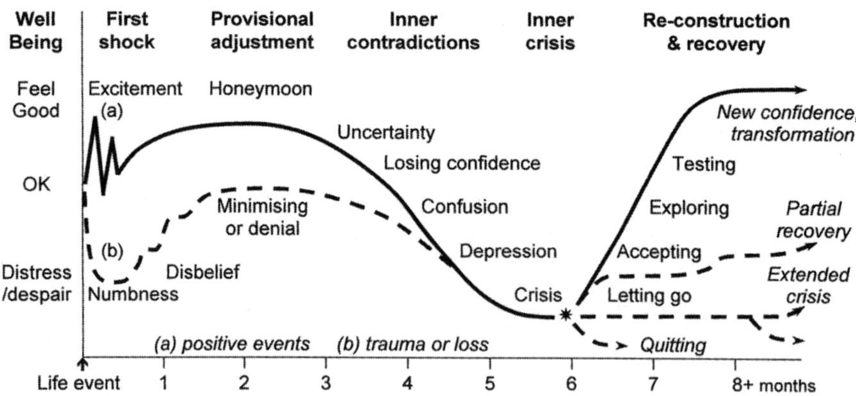

Figure 12.3. Phases and Features of the Transition Cycle (Williams 1999, adapted from Hopson & Adams 1976).

reserve forces status. However, leaving full-time military service with a clearly defined occupational identity, organizational support, and economic security (financial and often housing) would rate as a major transition trigger event in almost any employment context.

The leaving service transition deeply affects the individual and his or her family across the life-work boundary, because it will usually involve significant geographic relocation, or at least relocation to a different neighborhood and community even if staying in a garrison area. These changes are likely to impact social support networks for partners and children, and often require a change of schools and friends for children.

In these circumstances, the leaving service transition may need transition support for the whole family, individually and as a social group. Ideally, this support recognizes the natural stages and timing of the psychological transition process and its healing and growth potential even after extreme trauma.

Transition support should involve transition awareness by healthcare, community services, and educational professionals who may assist the family during the transition period, or who may become involved if one or more family members develop distressed behavior during the predictable transition crisis period. This crisis period typically develops five to six months after a key trauma, loss or other change event. In favorable conditions (see later discussion of *enabling factors*), the crisis phase may be resolved within a few weeks. Otherwise, recovery may be delayed or crisis behavior may involve quitting.

Unfortunately, quitting loss events like redundancy or bereavement may not be an option. There is also a risk of quitting another life role simply to escape internal distress (e.g., quitting a relationship several months after redundancy or leaving military service), or quitting a job after separation or bereavement.

The potential problems of post-trauma and postservice transitions are fairly well recognized both in the military and in community and veteran support organizations. The risk factors identified in the recent British Legion study (discussed previously) are similar to the inhibiting factors reported by many civilian career-advice clients recalling extended transition crisis periods.

However, none of the veterans' well-being studies, or support services reviewed here refer to the natural underlying processes of transition psychology. Instead, temporary distress may be described as "poor mental health." The practical external tasks of readjustment, relocation, and job search seem obvious to salaried administrators or researchers in secure employment. However, they are not easy for individuals working through, and trying to survive, a profound internal identity crisis.

This psychological transition period is likely to affect most personnel, of all ranks, from all branches, during the first six to twelve months after leaving active service. Unfortunately, researchers who are unaware of the transition process may pathologize symptoms of distress with a psychiatric diagnosis. Symptoms of anxiety, distress, emotional exhaustion, out-of-character behavior, tense relationships, and depression are typical in the transition crisis phase, provided they do not last more than a few weeks.

Experienced practitioners may describe this distressed behavior as reactive depression, recognizing it as a temporary phase of disturbed behavior likely to occur to most normal individuals several months after a major life event. This crisis phase is a normal, possibly even necessary, feature of transition while individuals build up the courage, or sufficient angst, needed to let go of deeply held beliefs or assumptions about themselves and their world. This letting go is a precursor to the task of reconstruing their values, beliefs, and assumptions, needed to adapt to their new circumstances, a nonmilitary environment (Williams 1999).

There is scope for more dialogue between medical specialists or therapists and occupational or counseling psychologists about the causes and stages of transition. At what point can a temporary crisis (or nervous exhaustion) situation become a pathological psychiatric condition, with risks to self or others? With prior transition briefing and awareness, many individuals will work through this period in a few weeks. In acute cases, medical intervention with drugs or CBT may be appropriate to alleviate severe distress, dangerous behavior, or an extended crisis period of several months. However, premature therapy or medication may impede an individual's natural capacity to reconstrue his or her world as needed to reach the growth phase of transition.

Several nonmedical factors can be important in enabling or inhibiting individuals to adapt to major life transitions. Some might be assisted during the leaving service transition period, for example, by guaranteeing suitable housing for the first twelve months. Other factors like offering stable alternative employment may be difficult in the current unstable economic environment.

Enabling Factors in Transitions

A number of conditions appear to enable successful transitions (Williams 1999):

- **Economic security:** surplus resources, no debt, stable income, own home, low commitments, multiple-income household

- **Emotional security:** supportive partner, stable childhood, support networks, openness on emotional and mental health issues
- **Good health:** good physical fitness, prudent lifestyle, quality time for leisure
- **Prior transition skills:** positive transition experiences, clear goals
- **Supportive work environment:** high respect/low control culture, good team morale, clear role and contract terms, life-work boundaries respected
- **Transition support:** briefing, monitoring issues, practical support, life-career planning, tolerance, dignity, valuing the past, time off before illness, confidential counseling, freedom/recognition for new ideas

Positive outcomes: Minimizing severity of distress in the crisis phase, minimizing risks of quitting or extended crisis, optimizing recovery time, high innovation, personal transformation, healing old wounds, "rejuvenated" staff, high group morale and synergy, and enabling organizational transformation.

Inhibiting Factors in Transitions

- **Economic insecurity:** low income; debt; high financial commitments; fear of job loss; unemployment; a temporary, ambiguous, or onerous work contract
- **Emotional insecurity:** no partner, few friends, dependent relatives, secret grief (lost lover or child), sense of guilt, unresolved issues or regrets, multiple transitions, anxiety over being diagnosed and stigmatized as mentally ill
- **Poor health:** chronic or undiagnosed conditions, low fitness, fatigue, lifestyle
- **Hostile work environment:** work overload, unrealistic demands, insufficient resources, abuse of life-work boundary (e.g., excessive time demands affecting relationships, leisure, fitness), low respect/high control culture, no time off except for sickness, discipline for absence, scapegoating of weaker members by stressed teams, harassment or abuse by an aggressive or stressed manager, change of manager, rigid agendas
- **Poor transition management:** no support, no preparation for change, unrealistic time scales, no monitoring of key issues before the crisis, no opportunity for fresh insights, past achievements ignored or disparaged

Negative outcomes: increased risk of severe crisis (e.g., extended absence, quitting, breakdown, suicide); high risk of errors (e.g., accidents at work, driving or at home); indiscretions or poor strategic decisions; poor, broken, or abusing relationships; poor team morale; high turnover; delayed recovery; insubordination; unused insights; dissent; and conflict.

In civilian settings, opportunities for medical practitioners (including physicians, psychiatrists, and occupational or mental health nurses) to discuss suspected transition crisis cases with psychologists or counselors have been helpful. This has saved high-value staff from being disciplined or dismissed for performance issues in a temporary transition crisis period. Two-way transition-review discussions can also alert "talking therapists" and others who support veterans or their families to understand when medical treatment may be important.

Most adults may experience ten to twenty significant transition events and subsequent delayed crisis and recovery periods. Awareness of previous psychological transitions and coping strategies are useful life skills (e.g., using a personal lifeline exercise). Transition awareness also has much wider significance for leaders, managers, and politicians involved in planning or managing organizational change, or dealing with mass traumas from wars or other disasters (Williams 2010).

Social and Economic Well-being of Veterans

Many ex-service personnel make smooth and successful transitions back to civilian life. Finding employment and finding suitable accommodation are essential to economic well-being for veterans and their families. Some are coping with physical or mental health concerns. Some may have got into internal discipline problems before leaving. KCMHR researchers have done a series of studies into social outcomes for successful and vulnerable service leavers. Iverson and colleagues (2005) looked at 4,000 people who had left the UK armed forces at some time between 1991 and 2001; 87.5 percent had found employment: "probably a healthy worker effect." They also looked at 500 of the vulnerable leavers:

> Six months post-discharge, over half had indeed not done well, as might have been predicted from the factors identified at MCTC. Half were in debt and half did not have proper housing. 10% had experienced homelessness.
>
> Just over half had a mental health problem, the commonest being alcohol dependence. Looking back, participants reported that they now recognized the need for targeted advice and guidance at the point of transition so that immediate assistance could be given to tackling the multitude of resettlement difficulties they faced.

The KCMHR 15-Year Report (2010) identified the following key outcomes for veterans since 1991:

- The same dataset suggests that service in the Armed Forces is not associated with overall increase in psychiatric disorders

- Most people who leave the Armed Forces do well and get jobs quickly
- Service leavers with poor mental health in service are more likely to leave and less likely to get jobs after leaving
- Poor outcomes are clustered in early service leavers and [tend] to be multiple (debt, antisocial behavior, substance misuse, mental health problems, unemployment, marital difficulties and unstable housing)
- Those with psychiatric problems have difficulties accessing appropriate NHS services and rarely obtain the best psychological treatments. This is not unique to the Armed Forces
- The main barriers to care remain stigma and reluctance to access services, but this is also not unique to Armed Forces
- For the minority most at risk of poor social outcomes, interventions need to be broad based and given before or as soon after separation as possible.

These problems are likely to increase for veterans leaving UK military service in 2012 because of rising unemployment in the nation. The UK Government is concerned about the paradox of needing to maintain morale for military personnel on active service in Afghanistan and Libya, then having to announce major reductions in manpower and other MoD budgets. Some of these defense spending cuts may fall directly on personnel leaving service without a job to go to. They may also involve cutbacks in services for veterans and their families.

From an occupational psychology perspective, new veterans are likely to have many positive qualities that could give them an advantage in job search situations during a recession, provided they can get at least temporary work within five to six months of leaving active service, i.e., before they enter a potential transition crisis phase.

Even if he or she is injured, UK military service suggests that an individual has started adult life with above-average physical fitness and an ability to accept structure, organization, and self-discipline. Depending on an individual's service records and postings, he or she may have significant overseas experience, operating in different climates and cultures and sometimes in hostile environments.

Depending on personality and assignments, veterans may be well suited for operational roles using advanced technologies and diverse logistics within formal command and control structures. Many have experience of training and supervising colleagues and sometimes training overseas personnel with limited literacy (e.g., to learn security and policing roles). If they have held officer or NCO rank, then they have probably had more leadership training and experience than most civilians have. The Career Transition Partnership is likely to have a very attractive portfolio of candidates for UK and overseas employers.

However, during an economic recession veterans are likely to face similar challenges and disappointments that many civilian job searchers do. In this environment, they could benefit by forming their own networks and self-help groups, using the networking and team-building skills they may have learned during military service.

Self-help, unemployed support groups developed spontaneously in parts of the United Kingdom during the early 1990s recession. Leaders and facilitators from one network in Surrey pooled their experiences to compile a *Handbook for Unemployed Support Group Leaders and Helpers* (CSGU 1994), which is available online. There was no single perfect model, but several approaches that depended on the people involved. Their notes could be adapted to many similar situations in which self-reliance is vital because official support services may be overloaded or downsizing to comply with further government cuts.

Self-help groups can be a first step to locating potential coworkers with sufficient rapport to form a new business or social enterprise, starting with low-cost, low-risk prototype projects. An ability to maintain self-motivation in adverse conditions is a fundamental aspect of military culture in the United Kingdom. This may be the attitude needed to launch a new era of businesses and other organizations needed to restart economic growth in the United Kingdom and to export products, goods, or services overseas. Despite grim employment prospects, the UK veteran community may give courage, hope, and resilience to civil society in the United Kingdom.

Restoring Trust between the Veteran Community and Governments

This chapter has tried to illustrate the diversity of the UK veteran population, made up as it is of several generations of past and recent service men and women, also identifiable as cohorts from different military campaigns by land, sea, and air. The UK veteran community has normal access to generally good public health and social services programs, plus additional state and charity-funded programs. But when veterans have suffered death or severe health consequences from unconventional military operations, their grievances have often been silenced with secrecy. A major breakdown of care and trust has followed for tens of thousands of UK veterans and their relatives.

When the state recruits or conscripts a citizen for military service, it takes on a lifetime obligation to maintain that individual and his or her dependents with dignity and respect. In time of war, the state may make extreme demands that may cost lives and traumatize veterans and their families. The United Kingdom exists as a nation because of the sacrifices of past and present generations of veterans. War pensions and compensation in the United Kingdom try to be fair with sliding scales for loss and injury. However, the amounts are small compared with civilian compensation.

The military training and experience of the wider veteran community have been an outstanding investment in technical, organizational, and leadership skills for the UK economy over decades. After leaving military service, veterans may be active workers and taxpayers for another twenty to forty years. How are the UK educational and employment systems planning to replace this valuable input as the UK armed forces and veteran populations get smaller? Where will future leadership training be developed?

The media image of veterans in the United Kingdom sometimes suggests a declining population of weak and sick or traumatized people and families who need heavy subsidies from taxpayers. The reality is rather different: a diverse population of resilient and capable people who have saved our country from invasion and then rebuilt it after leaving military service.

Governments regard war pensions and compensation as a drain on current taxes. Is it possible that the MoD sees serving forces as assets and the veteran community as a liability? If this is the mindset in some corners of government and the Civil Service, it needs to be questioned. The nation is indebted to service personnel and veterans who sacrifice their lives and physical health for the nation, and to their bereaved or traumatized families.

However, many of these veterans and their families have become Britain's forgotten heroes. The price they and their families have paid has been hidden for decades behind a shroud of secrecy. No compensation can be enough for these sacrifices.

So how have heroes become scapegoats? One result of this moral and financial debt may be a large shadow of guilt over the unfulfilled covenant to the veteran community. In organizational theory, the concept of *shadow* in an organization represents a potentially dangerous and malicious energy that seeks to divert attention from its dark secrets, usually projecting its guilt onto scapegoats within or outside the organization—blaming the victims.

Gerard Egan (1994), Bill Tate (2009), and others have described the concept of organizational shadow. Egan suggested that "the shadow side [of organizational life] deals with the covert, the undiscussed, the undiscussible, and the unmentionable."

Within the UK veteran community there are several cohorts of veterans and their families whose lives have been blighted by past decisions, ignorance, or grave incompetence. These include the nuclear test veterans from UK, Australia and New Zealand. They include troops exposed to radioactive or some other genetically toxic contamination from new weapons used by allied forces in Iraq, the Balkans, and Afghanistan. Bereaved families of crew and security experts killed in the Mull helicopter crash in 1994 had to wait until September 2010 for an independent review to begin that cleared the pilots of blame in July 2011. Gurkha veterans who have campaigned for decades for equal pensions as UK troops and UK residency finally obtained qualified recognition in 2009 after a major public campaign.

A common factor among these groups of veterans or their families is that claims for compensation or justice—on behalf of some of the bravest UK military personnel—have been consistently denied or rejected by successive governments and senior MoD personnel advising governments. The response to many veterans' cases appears to be a cheap way to save money, by refusing pension or compensation claims or delaying them for decades.

Some disputes about veterans' health have involved systematic cover-ups and deception about critical information. These include lost or destroyed records, for example about radiation doses, secret biopsy sampling of corpses (Redfern 2010), suspected strategic purchasing errors, and misleading information to conceal the existence of new weapons with indiscriminate effects that may contravene the Geneva Conventions (Williams 2008).

Why do UK veterans have to resort to legal action in the courts to get facts, truth, justice, recognition, and compensation for occupational health consequences of military service? Which Government departments are blocking their cases, and why?

There is a paradox between the annual display of respect for UK veterans on Remembrance Day and what appears to be the ongoing organizational shadow that abuses some of the most vulnerable members of the veteran community. In some cases thousands of veterans and their families have been or still are involved. This might have been justified for a few years for interests of national security, for example, to conceal the hazards of radiation from nuclear testing during the Cold War in the 1950s and 60s.

However, the apparent inability of several *generations* of senior military staff and politicians to apologize to veterans or their families for the past actions, or inaction, of their predecessors suggests a long-established tradition of using delays, denials, deception, and the Official Secrets Act to cover up many embarrassing incidents.

The result appears to be a culture of contempt in parts of the UK defense establishment and government departments for veterans or their families with just cause for complaint. This culture appears to hold past as well as current defense operations to be above question. Extensive legal, scientific and political resources are used against veterans who question it. This long-standing practice is completely at odds with the military covenant and has blighted many lives in the veteran community for decades. Whether a symptom of organizational shadow, or of self-justifying groupthink, this culture appears to be as endemic and insidious as the culture of institutional racism reported in parts of the London Metropolitan Police in 1999.

These contradictions in the treatment of veterans by senior levels within the MoD, Armed Forces and successive governments may suggest a different perspective for trying to rebuild trust with the UK veteran community. Dysfunctional behaviour in organizations can be due to internal structural issues, e.g., conflicting roles and objectives.

There are fundamental conflicts of interest within the MoD and governments between priorities for current military personnel and operations and long-standing legal, financial, and moral obligations to the veteran community. Both come under the Minister for Defence Personnel, Welfare and Veterans. Would UK veterans be treated more fairly if they were represented, funded and administered by a separate ministry for veterans' affairs, independent from the MoD?

The ongoing contribution and dignity of the UK veteran community deserve our nation's gratitude and respect. The energy and commitment in many organizations that support veterans and their families show amazing determination and loyalty. Only a few have been mentioned here, but all deserve recognition. The complexity of military, medical, and charity organizations that have evolved to support the veteran community is confusing, but several agencies and their internet sites act as valuable guides.

I am concerned that parts of the UK state have consistently failed certain groups of veterans who seek truth and justice. I have highlighted particular concerns that some veterans and current personnel have been, or may be, exposed to genotoxic contamination from new weapons. In a cover-up culture that controls most military medical research in the United Kingdom, it could be decades before past and current health hazards for troops and veterans are accurately identified and published. Genetic damage cannot be repaired. How can military medicine safeguards and research into the long-term health of veterans and their families be improved?

Excellent research and best practice cooperation occur between Defence Medical Services (DMS) and the NHS for physical injuries, rehab, and mental health for serving personnel.

However, things go badly wrong when the best interests of the health and well-being of serving personnel, veterans, or their families may jeopardize the reputation of political leaders, the commercial interests of major corporations, or covert agreements with other states or alliances. Successive UK governments and the defense establishment have a poor record for truth, fairness, and scientific or legal integrity.

Veterans and their families require far stronger advocacy, independent access to the highest quality scientific resources, faster dispute resolution, and full transparency about weapons technology and its human and environmental effects. On these matters, there can be fundamental conflicts of interest between the veteran community, the arms industry, the MoD and governments. In theory, the UK Health Protection Agency (HPA) might have the authority, funds, and technology to represent the veteran community in these matters. In practice, the HPA relies on close collaboration with both the defense establishment and nuclear industries.

Full respect and accountability for the long-term health and well-being of the UK veteran community seems elusive. It must be an essential part of the future "Military Covenant." However, UK military and government institutions must recognize how their shadow culture has for centuries treated troops as disposable and veterans as liabilities. These recurring breaches of trust are unlikely to be reformed until British veterans, and their families establish a new, independent, and representative veterans' organization, or a more powerful alliance of existing organizations, with the resources and independent authority of military unions in parts of Europe.

A lot of good work is done by and for veterans and their families in the United Kingdom. They have been a resilient and resourceful population for centuries. Successive cohorts of veterans will continue to be a massive strategic asset to the civilian economy and international relations in the twenty-first century. However, many veterans and their families continue to pay a high price in loss, pain or distress for their military service to the nation. Britain's forgotten heroes deserve far more recognition, support, and respect.

References

Alaani, S., et al. (2011). Uranium and other contaminants in hair from the parents of children with congenital anomalies in Fallujah, Iraq. *Conflict and Health* 5: 15. http://www.conflictandhealth.com/content/5/1/15 (accessed September 2011).

Army Families Federation (AFF). www.aff.org.uk.

BBC News. (2011a). Two decades on, battle goes on over "Gulf War syndrome." January 16. www.bbc.co.uk/news/uk-12195884.

BBC News. (2011b). Talks over military covenant legal status. May 14. www.bbc.co.uk/news/uk-13397909.

Berkshire NHS Trust. (2011). Veterans' mental health and wellbeing regional forum. www.berkshirehealthcare.nhs.uk/news_item.asp?fldID = 406; Outcomes pack. www.berkshirehealthcare.nhs.uk/_store/documents/regional_forum_veterans_mental_health_wellbeing_14062011_outcomes_pack.pdf (accessed September 2011).

Bland, D., et al. (2007). Urinary isotopic analysis in the UK Armed Forces: No evidence of depleted uranium absorption in combat and other exposed personnel in Iraq. *Occupational and Environmental Medicine* 64: 834–838.

Bridges, W. (1995). *Managing transitions: Making the most of change.* Wokingham: Addison-Wesley.

CAB: Citizens Advice Bureau. (n.d.). Advice guide: Healthcare for people injured in the armed forces and veterans. www.adviceguide.org.uk/ . . . health_index_ew/healthcare_for_people_injured_in_the_armed_forces_and_veterans.htm (accessed September 2011).

Centre for Military and Veterans' Health (CVMA). (2007). The intergenerational health effects of service in the military. www.dva.gov.au/aboutDVA/publications/health_research/effects_of_service/Pages/index.aspx (accessed September 2011).

Combat Stress. (n.d.). www.combatstress.org.uk.

CPT: The Career Transition Partnership. (n.d.). www.ctp.org.uk.

CSGU. (1994). *Handbook for unemployed support group leaders and helpers part 1.* www.eoslifework.co.uk/pdfs/CSGU2005pt1.pdf.

Defence Medical Services (DMS). (2011). Overview. www.mod.uk/DefenceInternet/MicroSite/DMS/WhatWeDo (accessed September 2011).

Egan, G. (1994). *Working the shadow side: A guide to positive behind-the-scenes management.* San Francisco: Jossey-Bass.

EMDR Association UK & Ireland. (n.d.). www.emdrassociation.org.uk.

ESTSS: European Society for Traumatic Stress Studies. (n.d.). www.estss.org.

Fear, N. T., et al. (2009). Symptoms of post-concussional syndrome are nonspecifically related to mild traumatic brain injury in UK Armed Forces personnel on return from deployment in Iraq. *Psychological Medicine* 39: 1379–1387.

Fear, N. T., Jones, M., Murphy, D., et al. (2010). What are the consequences of deployment to Iraq and Afghanistan on the mental health of the UK armed forces? A cohort study. *The Lancet* 375, no. 9728: 1783–1797.

French, C. & Dandeker, C. (2005). UK military families and the deployments to Iraq: Preliminary findings from a pre-, during-, and post-deployment study of the British Army. Paper presented at Inter-University Seminar on Armed Forces and Society, Chicago.

Greenberg, N., Langston, V. & Jones, N. (2008). Trauma risk management (TRiM) in the UK armed forces. *Journal of the Royal Army Medical Corps* 154, no. 2: 123–126. www.kcl.ac.uk/kcmhr/information/publications/articles/screening/123TraumaRisk.pdf.

Hopson, B. & Adams, J. (1976). Towards an understanding of transition. In J. Adams, H. Hayes, and B. Hopson (Eds.). *Transition: Understanding and managing personal change.* London: Martin Robertson.

International Society for Traumatic Stress Studies. (n.d.). www.istss.org.

Iversen, A., Nicolaou, V., Greenberg, N., Dandeker, C., Ross, J. & Wessely, S. (2005). What happens to UK veterans when they leave the Armed Forces? *European Journal of Public Health* 15: 175–184.

Kings Centre for Military Health Research (KCMHR), King's College, University of London. (2006). A ten year report. www.kcl.ac.uk/kcmhr/publications/10yearreport.pdf (accessed September 2011).

Kings Centre for Military Health Research (KCMHR), King's College, University of London. (2010). 15 year report into the health of the UK Armed Forces. www.kcl.ac.uk/kcmhr/publications/15YearReportfinal.pdf (accessed September 2011).

Kitchener, N. (2009). A community NHS mental health service for veterans of the armed forces. Cardiff & Vale NHS Trust. Paper presented at ESTSS Seminar, September.

Mental Health Foundation (MHF). (n.d.). Armed forces and mental health. http://www.mentalhealth.org.uk/help-information/mental-health-a-z/A/armed-forces/ (accessed September 2011).

Miller, B. G., Colvin, A. P., Hutchison, P. A., Tait, H., Demsey, S., Lewis, D. & Soutar, C. A. (2007). A normative study of levels of uranium in the urine of British Forces personnel. *Occupational and Environmental Medicine* 65: 398–403.

Miller, T. W., et al. (2010). *Handbook of stressful transitions across the lifespan.* New York: Springer.

Ministry of Defence, DUOB. (2007). Final report of the depleted uranium oversight board. www.mod.uk/NR/rdonlyres/CABAB04E-3584-4234-A62E-C6034E543B6C/0/final_report_feb2007.pdf (accessed September 2011).

Murphy, D., Iversen, A. & Greenberg, N. (2008). The mental health of veterans. *Journal of the Army Medical Corps* 154, no. 2: 136–139.

Neugarten, B. L. (1996). *The meanings of age: Selected papers of Bernice L. Neugarten.* Edited by D. A. Neugarten. Chicago: University of Chicago Press.

Redfern, M. (2010). *The Redfern Inquiry into human tissue analysis in UK nuclear facilities.* House of Commons papers 571-I,II 2010-11. London: TSO (The Stationery Office).

The Royal British Legion & Compass Partnership. (2011). Health, welfare and social needs of the armed forces community: A qualitative study. marhttp://www.britishlegion.org.uk/media/1642552/welfare2010qualitativestudy.pdf.

Schlossberg, N. K., Waters, E. B. & Goodman, J. (1995). *Counseling adults in transition.* New York: Springer.

Sheehy, G. (1995). *New passages.* New York: Ballantine Books.

SPVA: The UK Service Personnel and Veterans Agency. (n.d.). www.veterans-uk.info.

Sugarman, L. (1986). *Life-span development: Concepts, theories and interventions.* London: Methuen.

Sugarman, L. (2001). *Life-span development: Frameworks, accounts and strategies.* Hove, UK: Psychology Press.

Tate, W. (2009). *The search for leadership: An organisational perspective*. Axminster: Triarchy Press. (See chapter 13, Leadership and the shadow.)

UNEP. (2005). Assessment of environmental "hot spots" in Iraq. www.unep.org/disastersandconflicts/portals/155/dnc/docs/iraq/Iraq_ESA_hotspots_2003.pdf (accessed September 2011).

Veterans Wales: The All Wales Veterans Health and Wellbeing Service. (n.d.). www.veteranswales.co.uk.

Williams, D. (1999). Life events and career change: Transition psychology in practice. In *BPS Occupational Psychology Conference, Blackpool 1999, proceedings* (pp. 288–293). www.eoslifework.co.uk/transprac.htm (accessed September 2010).

Williams, D. (2008). Under the radar: Identifying third-generation uranium weapons. UNIDIR Disarmament Forum 2008 no 3. www.unidir.org/pdf/articles/pdf-art2759.pdf.

Williams, D. (2010). Surviving and thriving: How transition psychology may apply to mass traumas and changes. In T. W. Miller et al. (Eds.), *Handbook of stressful transitions across the lifespan*. New York: Springer.

Woodhead, C., et al. (2009). An estimate of the veteran population in England: Based on data from the 2007 Adult Psychiatric Morbidity Survey. *Population Trends* 138, no. 1: 50–54. www.ons.gov.uk/ons/rel/population-trends-rd/population-trends/no–138–winter-2009/an-estimate-of-the-veteran-population-in-england–based-on-data-from-the-2007-adult-psychiatric-morbidity-survey.pdf (accessed September 2011).

About the Editor

Thomas W. Miller, PhD, ABPP, is Professor Emeritus and Retired Career VA Chief, Psychology Service, at the VA and University of Kentucky College of Medicine. He has been a Senior Research Scientist, Master Teacher, and University Teaching Fellow through his forty-year career and tenure at the University of Kentucky and University of Connecticut. He has served on several national and regional professional and VA task forces and committees. A graduate of the State University of New York, he is a diplomate of the American Board of Professional Psychology, and Fellow of the American Psychological Association, the Association for Psychological Science, and the Royal Society of Medicine. He is a Distinguished Alumnus from the State University of New York and recipient of the APA Distinguished Professional Contributions to Clinical Practice Award. He honors his veteran patients and his father, William J. Miller, a veteran of Patton's Army in World War II and the Korean conflict.

About the Contributors

Rodney R. Baker, PhD, retired as chief of psychology at the San Antonio VA Medical Center in 2004 after an almost forty-year career serving veterans. His publications include a number on the history of the treatment of veterans and the history of psychology in VA; he coauthored *Psychology and the Department of Veterans Affairs* and edited *Stories from VA Psychology.* Prior to contributing the introductory chapter for this book, he also wrote an introductory chapter on benefits for veterans for *Returning Wars' Wounded, Injured, and Ill* (Praeger Security International, 2008).

Gennady Baksheev, BA (Hons), PhD, is a research fellow at Orygen Youth Health Research Centre, Centre for Youth Mental Health, The University of Melbourne. Gennady's interests are in the functional recovery of young people experiencing a first episode of psychosis. He has a particular interest in the relationship between mental illness and violence and reducing violence risks among patients presenting for treatment at youth mental health services.

LTC Corina M. Barrow, RN, MSN, is a commissioned Army Nurse Corps Officer and has proudly served for more than eighteen years. She holds a BS in nursing from the University of Cincinnati and a dual master's degree in nursing informatics and nursing administration from the University of Pittsburgh. LTC Barrow has been assigned to numerous medical treatment facilities throughout the army and has served honorably in various capacities. LTC Barrow participated in the Army Training with Industry Program in

Miramar, Florida, and is currently assigned as the Military Nurse Detailee for Senator Daniel K. Inouye.

Barbara K. Chang, MD, MA, is Director, Medical and Dental Education, Department of Veterans Affairs, where she oversees VA's physician and dentist residency training, including policy-related issues. Previously she served as senior consultant to the CARES project; Chief of Staff, NM Veterans Healthcare System; Associate Dean, UNM School of Medicine; and Associate Chief of Staff/Education, Augusta VAMC, Medical College of Georgia. Currently she is Professor (Emeritus) of Medicine, UNMSOM. The Department of Veterans Affairs awarded her the David M. Worthen Award for Academic Excellence, its highest honor in education. Dr. Chang serves as VA representative to AAMC's Group on Resident Affairs Steering Committee, COGME, and ACGME.

John Chardos, MD, is an Assistant Clinical Professor of Internal Medicine at Stanford and works full time at the VA Palo Alto Healthcare System. After completing his internal medicine training at the University of California at San Diego, he was Chief Medical Resident. In 2004 he became Director of Telemedicine for the VA San Diego Healthcare System. He supervised the implementation and development of several telemedicine programs, including Home Telehealth, Telemental Health, and Teleretinal Imaging. He also was a champion for Quality Improvement and System Reengineering. In 2008 he joined the VA Palo Alto Healthcare System as Associate Chief of Staff for Ambulatory Care. He has been particularly interested in delivery of care for recently returned veterans and is the clinical champion for postcombat care for his region of VA.

Malcolm Cox, MD, is Chief Academic Affiliations Officer for the Department of Veterans Affairs, where he oversees the largest health professions educational program in the United States. Previously he was Chief of Medicine at the Philadelphia VA Medical Center, Associate Dean for Clinical Education at the University of Pennsylvania, and Dean for Medical Education at Harvard Medical School. Dr. Cox currently serves on the National Leadership Board of the Veterans Health Administration, the National Board of Medical Examiners, the Accreditation Council for Graduate Medical Education, and the National Advisory Committee of the Robert Wood Johnson Clinical Scholars Program.

Mary B. Dougherty, DNSc, MBA, RN, is National Director of the Veterans Affairs Nursing Academy. Previously she held Vice President of Patient Care Services and Vice President—Hospital positions in academic medical centers. Her teaching has included undergraduate and graduate nursing positions as well as graduate business faculty positions.

Dr. Colleen Doyle, PhD, is a research psychologist with a special interest in evaluation of health services. Her current research interests are the relationship between dementia and post-traumatic stress disorder in veterans, treatment of apathy in people with dementia, evaluation of dementia services, and treatment of chronic disease. Her current research is funded by the Australian Department of Veterans' Affairs, Victoria Department of Health, and Beyondblue. She has written and published more than sixty-five academic and technical papers in the area of aged care. She directed the national evaluation of the Dementia Initiative from 2006 to 2010.

David Dunt, MBBS, PhD, FFPH, is Professor and Founding Director of the Centre for Health Policy, Programs and Economics (CHPPE), School of Population Health at the University of Melbourne. He is a medically trained epidemiologist with additional postgraduate training and major interests in the social sciences. This background informs his disciplinary area of health services research and the evaluation of health programs. His main work has involved the evaluation of complex, multidimensional government initiatives and related programs. He has recently completed two invited ministerial reviews for the Australian government: a review of mental health services in the Australian Defence Forces through transition to discharge and an independent study of suicide in the ex-service community.

Robert J. Fitz, PhD, earned his doctorate in clinical psychology from the Catholic University of America. He retired from VA in 1995 after thirty years of service. For over twenty years he provided psychotherapeutic services to veterans, including Vietnam veterans in the Day Hospital Unit in Lexington, Kentucky. He taught psychology courses at the University of Kentucky, University of Delaware, and Harford Community College. In retirement he provides disability examinations for the commonwealth of Kentucky and has served in the Stephen Ministry.

Stuart C. Gilman, MD, MPH, is Director, Advanced Fellowships and Professional Development, Office of Academic Affiliations, in the Veterans Health Administration. He holds the title of Professor of Clinical Health Sciences, University of California, Irvine.

Laura Gomez, LCSW, is a social worker and OEF/OIF/OND Program Manager with the VA Palo Alto Healthcare System. She has more than twelve years' human/social service experience, including direct clinical practice, organizing and managing social service programs as specified. The OEF/OIF/ OND program provides case management for the severely injured veterans in our healthcare system and assists in transitioning active duty and recently discharged veterans into the VA healthcare system.

James W. Holsinger Jr., MD, PhD, currently serves as the Charles T. Wethington Jr. Endowed Chair in the Health Sciences at the University of Kentucky. His faculty appointments include Preventive Medicine and Health Services Management in the College of Public Health. Dr. Holsinger served for twenty-six years in the Department of Veterans Affairs, retiring on July 13, 1994. His career culminated in his appointment by the president of the United States as Chief Medical Director of the Veterans Health Administration on August 6, 1990. In 1992 he became Under Secretary for Health, Department of Veterans Affairs.

Samina Iqbal, MD, is the Medical Director of the Women's Health Program at the VA Palo Alto Healthcare System, a position she has held for the past eight years, and she is also Clinical Assistant Professor at the Stanford University School of Medicine. An internist, she joined VA and Stanford University in 1994 as a fellow in general internal medicine and health services research and policy. In October 2008 she was appointed Senior Clinical Consultant to WVHSHG. She found her niche and has since continued to work at the VA Palo Alto. She enjoys teaching and is involved in teaching medical students and residents from Stanford University. She has been closely involved, together with her team, in developing programs for women veterans through the Women's Health Center at Palo Alto. Most recently she and her team received the award for clinical excellence in women's health, the first of its kind.

Steven Lindley, MD, PhD, is Director of Outpatient Mental Health Services for the VA Palo Alto Healthcare System and is Assistant Professor of Psychiatry at the Stanford School of Medicine. Dr. Lindley has been a psychiatrist with VA Palo Alto for sixteen years. As a psychiatrist with doctoral training in pharmacology/neuroscience, Dr. Lindley has considerable expertise relating to the biopsychosocial aspects of mental disorders, including PTSD. His research interests include investigating the efficacy and adverse effects of treatments for PTSD. He has recently been working with his colleagues to develop informatics solutions to monitor treatment efficacy and adverse effects.

Deborah A. Ludke, MHA, is Administrative Officer for Advanced Fellowships and Professional Development in the Office of Academic

Affiliations for the Department of Veterans Affairs, where she oversees administrative operations.

Stewart Macintosh, BS, MS, has worked with Veterans Affairs Canada since 1992. He has had the opportunity to work in most areas of the department, including a year in a district office. He has experience in administration, service delivery, policy design, program development, and project management. His bachelor's degree is from Carleton University and his master's from Dalhousie University.

William J. Marks Jr., MD, is Director of Learning Initiatives, Evaluation, and Analytics in the VA Office of Academic Affiliations. In this role, Dr. Marks has forged collaborations between multiple program offices within the Veterans Health Administration and extramural academic partners to conduct systems-level research focused on organizational learning and health professions education. Dr. Marks is also Associate Professor of Neurology at the University of California San Francisco (UCSF). A graduate of the Johns Hopkins University School of Medicine, Dr. Marks completed residency and fellowship training at UCSF.

Delilah O. Noronha, PsyD, is Program Manager of the Primary Care–Behavioral Health Program (PCBH) at the VA Palo Alto Healthcare System. She completed a clinical psychology internship at the James A. Haley VA in Tampa, Florida, and a postdoctoral fellowship at the University of Oklahoma Health Sciences Center–Oklahoma City VA Consortium. The focus of her pre- and postdoctoral clinical training and experience is the areas of primary care–mental health integration, postdeployment health, and behavioral medicine. Her VA appointments include staff psychologist for the PCBH program and program manager. She has been responsible for the development and implementation of several primary care–behavioral health clinics within the VA Palo Alto Healthcare System. She also serves on the VA Palo Alto integrated postdeployment clinic leadership committee. She was appointed the clinical champion for the implementation of the MyhealtheVet: My Goals Internet protocol for patients. Dr. Noronha's major areas of interest include primary care–mental health integration, OEF/OIF postdeployment health, and innovations in mental health service delivery.

David Pedlar, PhD, is Director of Research at the Veterans Affairs Canada Head Office in Charlottetown (2000–present). He was a Rotary Foundation Scholar at the University of Southern California, a Fulbright Scholar at Case Western Reserve University, and a corecipient of an International Psychogeriatric Association/Bayer Research Award in Psychogeriatrics.

He has held university affiliations in medicine at Dalhousie University and in nursing at the University of Prince Edward Island. He has completed more than forty research studies conducted at Veterans Affairs Canada on veterans' health topics and has been an investigator in a number of Canadian Institutes of Health Research (CIHR)–funded studies. He was a codirector of the Prince Edward Island Centre on Health and Aging for two waves of the Canadian Study of Health and Aging. He conducts applied research and publishes and speaks on military and veterans' health and continuing care for seniors.

Jo Robinson, MSc, BSc (Hons), is a research fellow at Orygen Youth Health Research Centre at the University of Melbourne, where she leads a research program specializing in youth suicide prevention. She has a particular interest in testing interventions that use modern forms of technology to deliver psychological intervention to people at risk. She also has an interest in the development of early detection models. She is currently developing a randomized, controlled trial testing a Web-based intervention with school students at risk and a peer support project for young people with first-episode psychosis. Jo also has significant experience in suicide prevention policy development and has worked with the government in the United Kingdom and Australia.

Jacqueline D. Rychnovsky, PhD, RN, CPNP, is a Captain, Nurse Corps, U.S. Navy Nurse Corps Detailee to Senator D. Inouye (D-HI) in Washington, DC.

Suganya Selvarajah, MS, MD, is a public health researcher with a background in medicine. She obtained her doctor of medicine degree in Russia in 2003, following which she worked as a medical officer in Sri Lanka in both clinical and public health settings. She discovered her passion for public health research and the contribution that research can make to the betterment of society. She went to Australia in 2006, where she then completed double masters in public health and health promotion at Deakin University in 2008. Since then she has worked extensively in public health research in various projects for the National Ageing Research Institute, University of Melbourne, and La Trobe University. She is currently working for the Centre for Eye Research Australia. Project areas in which she has worked include geriatrics (ageing), mental health, chronic diseases, and psychosocial determinants of health. Her publications and presentations include a conference abstract in the *Australasian Journal on Ageing,* a poster presentation for the Australian Association of Gerontology, a technical report for Beyondblue, a poster presentation for Beyondblue's Victorian Centre of Excellence Awards, and a paper published in the *International Journal of Mental Health Promotion*. She is currently awaiting publication of papers on her recent and current projects. She was awarded a full scholarship and will be commencing a PhD program in the Faculty of Medicine, Dentistry and Health Sciences, at the University of Melbourne in 2012. Her research interests include mental health, international health programs, human rights, and public health practices.

Dai Williams is a Chartered Occupational Psychologist and has been an independent practitioner in the United Kingdom since 1986. As part of his previous work with Shell, he set up an occupational health–monitoring program in Vancouver. He works with clients on career and personal development programs, including management of trauma, stress, and change for individuals and organizations. He applies work and transition psychology methods to community psychology settings, including economic and political crises, wars, and natural disasters. In 1999 reports of DU weapons in the war in the Balkans interested him in studying physical as well as mental health hazards for troops and civilians in recent conflict zones.

Robert A. Zeiss, PhD, is Director of Associated Health Education for the Office of Academic Affiliations in the Department of Veterans Affairs. Dr. Zeiss, a clinical psychologist, was previously Co-Director of Inpatient Psychiatry at the VA Palo Alto Healthcare System. A Fellow of the American Psychological Association, Dr. Zeiss was on the Clinical Faculty of the Department of Psychiatry and Behavioral Sciences of the Stanford University School of Medicine from 1985 to 2006, after which he relocated from California to the VA Central Office.

Index

academic mission of the Dept.
    of Veterans Affairs, 53–69
advanced fellowships, 61–62
advanced participant completion
    1995–2009, 63 (table)
approved additional resident
    physicians by request for
    proposal (RFP), 58 (table)
associated health professions
    education, 59–61
Centers of Excellence in Primary
    Care Education, 66
collaborative clinical program
    development, 55
dental education, 57–58
graduate medical education
    enhancement, 58
Hartford Faculty Scholars
    Program, 64
health professions education, 54,
    65–66
introduction to, 53–57
Learners Perception Survey, 65

learning organization
    transformation, 64–65
medical education, 57
mental health education
    enhancement, 59
national health professions policy,
    55–56
Nursing Academy (VANA)
    partnership sites, 60
nursing education enhancement,
    59–61
pre-and postdoctoral fellowships,
    62–64
Public Law 79-293, 53
Quality Scholars Program, 62
recruitment and retention of clinical
    staff, 54–55
research program leveraging, 55
residents as a percentage of
    VA workforce in selected
    disciplines, 55 (table)
"special fellowships," 61–62
special programs, 62

administration and veterans' health care
   Agent Orange, 46
   central office reorganization,
      28–29
   chief medical director, 43–51
   Commission on the Future
      Structure of Veterans Health
      Care, recommendations of,
      35–36
   eligibility reform, 40–43
   field reorganization, 38–39
   Gulf War Syndrome, 46
   Hurricane Andrew, 33–34
   lessons learned at the top, 43–51
   management style and leadership
      philosophy, 26–28
   medical center closures, 48–49, 51
   National Health Care Plan,
      conceptual framework
      for, 37–38
   Persian Gulf War, 32–33
   planning for the future, 34–38
   quality management, 29–32
   reorganization, 35–37
   resource management, 39–40
   VA smoke-free policy, 48–49
   Veterans Integrated Service
      Networks, 29
   VHA organizational chart, 27
Advisory Committee on Women
     Veterans, 136
Agent Orange, 46
   Agent Orange Act of 1991, 73
   Agent Orange Equity Act of
     2009, 148
   Agent Orange Registry, 133–134
   developments in research, 148
   health issues related to, 132–134
Akaka, Daniel K., 74, 77
American Legion, 79, 80, 86
Americans with Disabilities Act
     (1990), 73
AMVETS, 79, 81

The Army Suicide Prevention Program
    (ASPP), 228
Audit of VA's Control System for
    Credentialing and Privileging
    Physicians, 30
Australia, veterans' healthcare in,
    194–199
   directions in healthcare for
      Australian veterans,
      196–197
   foreign veterans visiting, 197–198
   global veterans' healthcare, 197
   Medicare Australia, 197
   nongovernmental health sector
      financing, 196
   overview of, 194–195
   public sector health financing,
      195–196
   Royal Flying Doctor Service,
      198–199

Bachmann, Michele, 81
Baker, Rodney R., 297
Baksheev, Gennady, 297
Barbour, Galen, 31–32
Barrow, Corina M., 297–298
Barry, Jan, 125
Batalden, P. B. & Davidoff, F. (2007),
    56, 67
Blueprint for Quality: A Solid
    Foundation, 31
Bradley, Omar N., 8–9
Brittain, Bruce, 242–243
Burgess, Ernest M., 145–147
Burr, Richard, 77
Bush, George H. W., 25, 26 (image),
    33, 73–74
Bush, George W., 158

Canada, veterans' healthcare in, 199
Canadian veterans, evolution of
     healthcare programs for,
     237–256

Aging Veterans Program (AVP),
243–244
aging war veterans, caring for,
241–242
benefits for the 21st-century,
250–251
Bruce Brittain and, 242–243
Canada Health Act of 1984
(CHA), 241–242
conclusion concerning, 255
demobilization program, 240
disability pensions, 240
early years of veterans' benefits,
238–241
family support, 254–255
introduction to, 237–238
Jack MacDonnell and, 242, 243
Medicare, 241–242
New Veterans Charter, 252–255
New Veterans Charter benefits,
253–255
Public Service Healthcare Plan
(PSHCP), 253
Ste. Anne-de-Bellevue Hospital,
240–241
Veterans Charter (NVC),
238, 239
Veterans Independence Program
(VIP), 238, 242–250
Veterans Independence Program
(VIP) expansion, 244–246
Veterans Independence Program
(VIP) expenditures and client
numbers, 245 (fig.)
Veterans Independence Program
(VIP) observations, 248–250
Veterans Independence Program
(VIP) special delivery model,
246–248
Walter S. Woods and, 239
war service veterans and Canadian
forces veterans (actuals to 2010),
251 (fig.)

War Veterans Allowance (WVA),
238–239
Caregivers and Veterans Omnibus
Health Services Act of
2010, 76–79
Caring for Veterans with Traumatic
Brain Injury Act of 2009,
87, 117
Carter, Jimmy, 126
Carter, John, 81
Center for Women Veterans, 136
Chang, Barbara K., 298
Chardos, John, 298
China, veterans' healthcare in,
199–200
Cleland, Max, 126
*Clinical Practice Guideline for the
Management of Opioid Therapy
for Chronic Pain* (Department of
Veterans Affairs/Department
of Defense Working Group
2003), 164
Clinton, Bill, 91
Colmery, Harry W., 71
Committee on Care of Veterans with
Traumatic Brain Injury, 117
comparative healthcare analysis across
countries, 204
Compensation Owed for Mental
Health Based on Activities in
Theater Post-traumatic Stress
Disorder Act (COMBAT
PTSD), 87
Coolidge, Calvin, 86
Cox, Malcolm, 298

Derwinsky, Edward J., 29, 35, 50
(image)
Desai, M. M., Rosenheck, R. A., &
Desai, R. A. (2008), 225, 233
Diagnostic and Statistical Manual III i
(American Psychiatric
Association, 1980), 128

disability benefits (basic), 78–79
Disability Compensation Program, 79
Domiciliary Care for Homeless
　　Veterans Program, 138
Dougherty, Mary B., 298–299
Downs, Frederick Jr., 81, 147–148
Doyle, Colleen, 299
Drug Abuse Prevention and Control
　　Act, 141
Duerk, Alene B., 135
Dunt, David, 299

Egan, G. (1994), 287, 291
Eisenhower, Dwight D., 72, 85
eligibility reform, 40–43
Embedded Mental Health Providers
　　for Reserves Act of 2010, 87
Emergency Medical Preparedness
　　Office, 33
End Veterans Homelessness Act
　　of 2010, 149
Engdahl, B., Page, W.W. & Miller,
　　T. W. (1991), 90, 96, 102
Euerk, Alene B., 135

Farrar, John T., 28
federal healthcare legislation for
　　veterans (early), 4–8
　　Executive Order 5398, 6
　　Public Law 2, March 20, 1933, 7
　　Public Law 90, October 6, 1917, 4
　　Public Law 194, April 20, 1922, 4
　　Public Law 346, June 22, 1944,
　　　7–8
　　Public Law 536, July 3, 1930,
　　　5–7
female veterans and healthcare, 75, 81
　　Advisory Committee on Women
　　　Veterans, 136
　　Center for Women Veterans, 136
　　OEF/OIF/OND and, 177–178
　　promotion restrictions, 135

PTSD, 128, 136
　　recent developments in, 149
　　Vietnam era, 134–136
Ficke, James, 150
Filner, Bob, 77
Fitz, Robert J., 299
Fontana, A. & Rosenheck, R. (1994),
　　99–100, 102

G.I. Bill of Rights, 71–72, 88
Gilman, Stuart C., 299
Gironda, R. J., Clark, M. E.,
　　Massengale, J. P. & Walker,
　　R. L. (2006), 163, 185
Gomez, Laura, 299–300
GSA concept, 38–39
Gulf War Syndrome, 46
Gunnell, D. & Frankel, S. (1994),
　　227, 233

Hawkins, C. Wayne, 29
Hawkins, Ellen, 124
Hawley, Paul R., 9, 10, 12
Hays, Anna Mae, 135
health care for veterans of World Wars
　　I and II, 85–103
　　future directions in understanding
　　　veterans' healthcare, 97–102
　　health needs since World War II,
　　　96–97
　　healthcare needs of veterans of the
　　　World Wars, 89–90
　　historical review, 85–86
　　historical veterans' healthcare in the
　　　U.S., 88–89
　　legislative policies, 86–88
　　national recognition of World War
　　　II veterans, 90–91
　　prosthetic healthcare, 101
　　special needs for former prisoners of
　　　war, 90
　　study using VHP guidelines, 91–97

study using VHP guidelines, results
of, 93–95
Veterans History Project
interview questions, 92–93 (box)
*Health Promotion, Risk Reduction,
Suicide Prevention*, 229
Healthcare for Homeless Veterans
(HCHV), 137, 138
Healthcare for Reentry Veterans
Services and Resources
(HCRV), 139
Hines, Frank T., 5, 70–71, 88
Hoefly, E. Ann, 135
Holsinger, James W., Jr., 25–26,
29–30, 43–45, 300
image of, 26, 50
homeless Vietnam veterans, 137–140
current VA programs, 138–139
definition of homeless, 137
Domiciliary Care for Homeless
Veterans Program, 138
history of, 137–138
Homeless Chronically Mentally Ill
Veterans Program, 137
homeless veterans dental program,
139–140
Project CHALENG, 140
Reentry Veterans Services
and Resources (HCRV)
healthcare, 139
stand downs, 138
support services for low-income
veterans, 139
Hoover, Herbert, 5–6, 86
Executive Order 5398, 6
Hurricane Andrew, 33–34

Iqbal, Samina, 300
Israel, veterans' healthcare in, 200

Johnson, Lyndon B., 73
Joshua Omvig Veterans Suicide
Prevention Act, 229

Kang, H. K. & Bullman, T. A. (2008),
215, 233
Kaplan, M. S., Huguet, N.,
McFarland, B., et al. (2007),
211, 219, 234
Kizer, Kenneth, 163
Knox, K. L., Litts, D. A., Talcott,
G. W., et al. (2003), 228, 234
Korean War era veterans, 105–120
Congressional efforts to meet
Korean veterans' healthcare
needs, 117
healthcare benefits, 107–108
healthcare needs of, 117–118
Hill 303 massacre, 109–110
historical background to, 105–107
Kaesong massacre, 112
Korean War era calendar, 108
Korean War era veterans today,
117–118
Korean War summary statistics
and reports on atrocities,
111–112 (box)
Korean War Veterans Recognition
Act, 118–119
memorial for, 119
Operation Little Switch, 116
Seoul to Pyongyang death
march, 110
Sunchon tunnel massacre, 110
war crimes committed against
American POWs, 108–113
War Crimes Division, 114–116
war crimes in Korea, 113–114

LaVerda, N., Vessey, A. & Waters,
W. F. (2006), 90, 91, 92, 95, 97,
98, 102
LaVerda, Nancy, 89
legislative initiatives for veterans'
healthcare, 69–82
Agent Orange Act, 73

legislative initiatives for veterans'
    healthcare (*continued*)
  Caregivers and Veterans Omnibus
    Health Services Act of 2010,
    76–78
  creation of the Veterans
    Administration, 70–71
  disability benefits (basic), 78–79
  Disability Compensation
    Program, 79
  Disability Compensation Rights
    (P.L. 76-179), 74
  early healthcare legislation for war
    wounded, 69–70
  female veterans and healthcare, 75
  G.I. Bill of Rights, 71–72
  improved veterans' mental
    healthcare, 78–79
  introduction to, 69
  Montgomery G.I. Bill, 72, 73
  pensions, 79
  Post-9/11 G.I. Bill, 76
  Radiation Exposed Veterans'
    Compensation Act, 73
  Treatment of Service Dogs Act, 81
  Veterans' Dioxin and Radiation
    Exposure Compensation
    Standards Act, 73
  Veterans Educational Assistance
    Program (VEAP), 73–74
  Veterans' Emergency Fairness Act
    of 2009, 76
  Veterans Mental Health and Other
    Care Improvements Act of 2008,
    74–76, 78
  veterans organizations, 79–81
  Veterans Readjustment Benefits
    Act of 1966, 72–73
Lifton, R. (1973), 125, 153
Lindley, Steven, 300
low-income veterans, support services
  for, 139
Ludke, Deborah A., 300–301

MacDonnell, Jack, 242
Macfarlane, G. J., Thomas, E. T
    Cherry, N. (2000), 215, 234
Macintosh, Stewart, 301
Magnuson, Paul B., 9–10,
    11 (image), 12
Marks, William J., Jr., 301
McFarland, Ernest, 71
McIndoe, Archie, 266
Medicare Australia, 197
Mental Health Strategic Plan
    (MHSP), 158
Michaud, Mike, 77
Mikulski, Barbara, 80
military bonuses, 86
military sexual trauma (MST), 81, 136
Miller, J. Roscoe, 11
Miller, Thomas W., 90, 102, 295
Milliken, C. S., Auchterlonie, J. L. &
    Hoge, C. W. (2007), 178, 187
Montgomery, Gillespie V. "Sonny,"
    46, 73
Montgomery G.I. Bill, 72, 73

National Center for Post-Traumatic
    Stress Disorder, 129
National Institute on Drug Abuse, 143
National Vietnam Veterans'
    Readjustment Study, 128
Nixon, Richard, 141
Noronha, Delilah O., 301
North Chicago VA Medical Center
    issue, 30

Obama, Barack, 118–119
Omnibus Budget Reconciliation Act
    (1990), 73
Operation Desert Shield, 32
Operations Enduring Freedom, Iraqi
    Freedom and New Dawn:
    veterans' health care for,
    157–189
  academic performance, 176

access to, 180–181
alcohol abuse, 171
amputation, 159–160
auditory and vestibular damage,
    160–161
concussion/traumatic brain injury
    (TBI), 162
depression, 170
environmental exposure, 165–166
extended service period, 174
family functioning, 175
female service members, 177–178
frequency of possible diagnoses
    among OEF and OIF veterans,
    160 (table)
frequency of possible mental
    disorders among OEF/OIF
    Veterans since 2002,
    169 (table)
help seeking, 181–182
homelessness, 176–177
illicit and prescription drug use,
    171–173
infectious diseases and sexually
    transmitted infections, 166–167
introduction to, 158
medically unexplained physical
    symptoms, 167–168
mental health, 168
Mental Health Strategic Plan
    (MHSP), 158
ocular injuries, 161–162
overview of common health
    outcomes of OEF/OIF/OND
    deployments, 159–180
pain, 163–164
physical conditions, 159
polytrauma, 164–165
postemployment clinics, 178–180
redeployment, 175
reintegration, 173–174
substance misuse, 170–171
suicide and suicide prevention, 177

Task Force on Returning Global
    War on Terror Heroes,
    158–159
unemployment, 175–176
Orrega, Gonzalo, 124

Paralyzed Veterans of America
    (PVA), 79, 80
Pedlar, David, 301–302
pensions, 79
Persian Gulf War, 32–33
    Gulf War Syndrome, 46
Policy Memorandum No. 2, 12,
    13–14, 19–23, 53
Post-9/11 Veterans Education
    Assistance Improvements Act
    of 2010, 76
Post-Traumatic Stress Disorder
    (PTSD)
    Combat Post Traumatic Stress
        Disorder Act of 2009 (H.R.
        952), 117
    Compensation Owed for Mental
        Health Based on Activities in
        Theater Post-traumatic Stress
        Disorder Act (COMBAT
        PTSD), 87
    Diagnostic and Statistical Manual
        III i (American Psychiatric
        Association, 1980) and, 128
    female veterans and, 81, 128, 136
    frequency of possible mental
        disorders among OEF/OIF
        Veterans since 2002,
        169 (table)
    health issues related to, 130–131
    Korean War veterans, 117–118
    medications, 130
    National Center for Post-
        Traumatic Stress Disorder, 129
    National Vietnam Veterans'
        Readjustment Study, 128
    official recognition of, 126

Post-Traumatic Stress Disorder
      (PTSD) (*continued*)
   Operations Enduring Freedom,
      Iraqi Freedom and New Dawn,
      168–169
   prevalence of, 128
   PTSD/TBI Guaranteed Review for
      Heroes Act (H.R. 1701), 87
   Public Law 98-528 and, 129, 131
   Specialized Intensive PTSD
      Programs (SIPPs), 131
   Specialized Outpatient PTSD
      Programs (SOPPs), 132
   suicide and, 224, 229–230
   treatment programs in the VA,
      129–130
   UK veterans and, 272–273
   Vietnam veterans, 124–129
   Vietnam Veterans Rehabilitation
      Counseling Program, 126
   World War II and, 96, 99
Project CHALENG, 140
prosthetic healthcare, 101, 145–148
   DARPA performer, 147,
      148 (image)
   Ernest M. Burgess and, 145–147
   future directions in, 150
   Prosthetic Appliance Service, 15
   Prosthetic Outreach Foundation
      (POF), 146
   Prosthetic Research Study
      (PRS), 145

Quality Improvement Checklist
      (QUic), 31

Radiation Exposed Veterans'
      Compensation Act of 1988, 73
Redfern, Michael, 264
Resource Allocation Methodology
      (RAM), 39–40
Robert Wood Johnson Foundation's
      Clinical Scholars Program, 61, 62

Robinson, Jo, 302
Rogers, Edith Nourse, 71
Roudebush, Richard L., 124
Russia, veterans' healthcare in,
      200–202
Rutz, W., von Knorring, L. &
      Walinder, J. (1989), 227, 235
Rychnovsky, Jacqueline D., 302

Selvarajah, Suganya, 302–303
Shatan, Chaim, 125
Sher, L. (2009), 229, 230, 235
Shinseki, Eric K., 149
Sim, M., Abramson, M., Forbes, A.,
      et al. (2003), 217, 235
Smith, Dennis M., 28
Smith, Jack, 124
stand downs, 138
Statutory Pay-As-You-Go Act of
      2010, 79
Stockman, David, 127
Stone, John, 81
suicide in the ex-service community
   access to means of suicide, 225
   in Australia, 216–219
   defining suicide, 207–208
   exposure to combat in suicide risk,
      225–226
   International Classification of
      Diseases (ICD-10) and, 220
   Joshua Omvig Veterans Suicide
      Prevention Act, 229
   limitations of current research on,
      219–221
   methods used, 209–210
   misclassification of, 220
   Post-Traumatic Stress Disorder
      (PTSD), 224, 229–230
   psychiatric disorders and suicide
      risk, 224–225
   rates of suicide, distribution of
      by gender and age (2000),
      210 (fig.)

rates of suicide in the general
  population, 208–210
rates of suicide, per 100,000 for
  selected countries, 208 (table)
risk and protective factors among
  veterans, 226 (box)
risk factors for suicide among war
  veterans, 223–226
risk factors for suicide in the general
  population, 221–222
risk factors for suicide, level "A"
  evidence of, 222 (box)
socio-demographic risk factors,
  223–224
suicide prevention, approaches
  to, 227–228
suicide prevention programs for
  veterans, summary of, 230–231
suicide prevention programs for war
  veterans, 228–230
summary concerning, 226
war veterans, rates of suicide among,
  210–219
war veterans, selected Australian
  studies of suicide among,
  218–219 (table)
war veterans, selected international
  studies of suicide among,
  212–214 (table)
war veterans, summary of suicide
  rates, 221
Supported Housing (HUD-VASH)
  Program, 138
supportive services for low-income
  veterans, 139

Tanielian, T. & Jaycox, L. H. (Eds.).
  (2008), 159, 168, 170, 178, 189
Task Force on Returning Global War
  on Terror Heroes, 158–159
Tate, W. (2009), 287, 293
Thoresen, S. & Mehlum, L. (2006),
  224, 235

Thoresen, S., Mehlum, L. & Moller, B.
  (2003), 215, 235
Truman, Harry S., 8, 12

UK, veterans' healthcare in, 202–204
  choice in healthcare, 203–204
  comparative healthcare analysis
    across countries, 204
  general practitioners, 203
  Internet addresses concerning, 204
  National Health Service
    (NHS), 202
  private hospitals, 203–204
  private treatment options, 203
UK veterans, health and well-being
  issues and resources for,
  257–293
  15 Year Report of Research into the
    Health of the UK Armed Forces
    (KCMHR), 258, 267, 269, 271,
    279, 284–285
  Career Transition Partnership,
    285–286
  Defence Medical Services (DMS),
    262, 289
  endemic biological hazards, 271
  Gulf War illnesses, 267–268
  Handbook for Unemployed Support
    Group Leaders and Helpers
    (CSGU 1994), 286
  health hazards and resilience from
    military service, 265–271
  Health Protection Agency
    (HPA), 290
  importance of veteran community,
    257–260
  intergenerational effects of military
    service, 277–279
  the Internet and, 259
  King's Centre for Military Health
    Research (KCMHR), 258
  mental health issues from recent
    conflicts, 272–273

UK veterans, health and well-being
  issues and resources for
  (*continued*)
  mental health support resources,
    273–274
  Michael Redfern and, 264
  new weapons technology and,
    270–271
  policy, practice, and research
    perspectives, 262–265
  radiation exposure, 268–270
  Service Personnel and Veterans
    Agency (SPVA), 259, 273
  social and economic well-being
    of veterans, 284–286
  transition, enabling factors in,
    282–283
  transition, inhibiting factors in,
    283–284
  Trauma Risk Management
    (TRiM), 264–265
  UK Armed Forces Operations and
    Veteran Cohorts 1910–2020,
    260 (fig.)
  UK Citizens Advice Bureau Advice
    Guide (CAB), 259
  veteran community and
    governments, restoring trust
    between, 286–290
  veterans' families, health and
    well-being issues for, 274–275

VA as cabinet-level agency, 73–74
VA Epilepsy Centers of Excellence, 75
VA medical center closures, 48–49, 51
VA mental healthcare facilities,
    review of residential (FY 2008),
    144 (table)
VA smoke-free policy, 47–48
Vessey, Andrea, 89
Veterans Administration, affiliations
    and teaching programs in, 8–14
  H. R. 4717, 11–12

Policy Memorandum No. 2, full
    text of, 19–23
Policy Memorandum No. 2, impact
    of, 12, 13–14, 53
Public Law 293, impact of, 12–13
Public Law 293, need for and
    development of, 8–12
Veterans Administration, creation of,
    70–71
Veterans Administration, impact of
    research on patient care, 14–17
  amputation, TB, and psychiatric
    patients, 15
  Cooperative Research Program in
    pulmonary TB, 16–17
  Cooperative Studies Program, 16
  VA medical research (early), 14–15
Veterans Day observance, 85–86
Veterans Educational Assistance
    Program (VEAP), 73–74
Veterans' Emergency Fairness Act
    of 2009, 76
Veterans for Equal Treatment of
    Service Dogs Act, 81
Veterans Health Care Act of 1983
    (P.L. 98-160), 136
Veterans History Project (VHP), 89,
    92–93, 97
Veterans Integrated Service Network
    (VISN), 39
Veterans Justice Outreach Initiative
    (VJO), 139
Veterans Mental Health Accessibility
    Act, 87
Veterans Mental Health and Other
    Care Improvements Act of
    2008, 74–76
Veterans of Foreign Wars (VFW), 79
veterans organizations, 79–81
Veterans Readjustment Benefits Act
    of 1966, 72–73
VHA Epilepsy Centers of
    Excellence, 75

VHA Program Guide 1103.3, 141
Vietnam, healthcare for veterans of,
    121–155
  Advisory Committee on Women
    Veterans, 136
  Agent Orange education, 134
  Agent Orange, health issues related
    to, 132–134
  Agent Orange, new developments in
    research, 148
  Agent Orange Registry, 133–134
  Center for Women Veterans, 136
  Domiciliary Care for Homeless
    Veterans Program, 138
  End Veterans Homelessness Act of
    2010, 149
  Healthcare for Homeless Veterans
    (HCHV), 137, 138
  Healthcare for Reentry Veterans
    Services and Resources
    (HCRV), 139
  Homeless Chronically Mentally Ill
    Veterans Program, 137
  homeless veterans dental program,
    139–140
  homeless veterans, recent
    developments in helping, 149
  homeless Vietnam veterans,
    137–140
  overview of, 121–124
  Post-Traumatic Stress Disorder
    (PTSD), 124–129
  Post-Traumatic Stress Disorder
    (PTSD) and the VA,
    129–130
  Post-Traumatic Stress Disorder
    (PTSD), health issues related
    to, 130–132
  Project CHALENG, 140
  promotion restrictions, 135
  prosthetics, 145–148, 150
  prosthetics, future directions in, 150
  research and, 151
  stand downs, 138
  substance use disorders, 140–145
  supportive services for low-income
    veterans, 139
  VA mental healthcare facilities,
    review of residential (FY 2008),
    144 (table)
  Veterans Justice Outreach Initiative
    (VJO), 139
  Vietnam Veterans Rehabilitation
    Counseling Program, 126
  women veterans issues, 134–136
  women Vietnam veterans' health,
    recent developments and, 149
Vietnam Veterans Against the War
    (VVAW), 125, 126
Vietnam veterans and PTSD,
    124–129
Vietnam Veterans Rehabilitation
    Counseling Program, 126

Waters, William F., 89
Williams, Dai, 303
Wilson, Woodrow, 85
Women Veterans, Center for, 136
Women's Army Corps, 135
Woods, Walter S., 239

Zeiss, Robert A., 303
Zerger, S. (2002), 143, 155
Zivin, K., Kim, M., McCarthy, J. F.,
    et al. (2007), 211, 223, 224, 236

The Praeger Handbook of Veterans' Health

Volume I
History, Eras, and Global Healthcare

Volume II
Programs of Care and Groups with Special Needs

Volume III
Mental Health Treatment and Rehabilitation

Volume IV
Future Directions in Veterans' Healthcare

THE PRAEGER HANDBOOK OF VETERANS' HEALTH

History, Challenges, Issues, and Developments

Volume II: Programs of Care and Groups with Special Needs

Thomas W. Miller, Editor

PRAEGER

AN IMPRINT OF ABC-CLIO, LLC

Santa Barbara, California • Denver, Colorado • Oxford, England

Library of Congress Cataloging-in-Publication Data

The Praeger handbook of veterans' health : history, challenges, issues, and developments / Thomas W. Miller, editor.
    v. cm.
 Includes bibliographical references and index.
 ISBN 978-0-313-38349-6 (hardcover : alk. paper) — ISBN 978-0-313-38350-2 (ebook)
1. Veterans—Health and hygiene—United States. 2. Veterans—Care—United States. 3. Veterans—United States—History. I. Miller, Thomas W., 1943– II. Title: Handbook of veterans' health.
 UB369.P73 2012
 362.1086'97—dc23

                  2012025159

ISBN: 978-0-313-38349-6
EISBN: 978-0-313-38350-2

16 15 14 13 12   1 2 3 4 5

This book is also available on the World Wide Web as an eBook.
Visit www.abc-clio.com for details.

Praeger
An Imprint of ABC-CLIO, LLC

ABC-CLIO, LLC
130 Cremona Drive, P.O. Box 1911
Santa Barbara, California 93116-1911

This book is printed on acid-free paper ∞
Manufactured in the United States of America

It is the VETERAN, not the preacher, who has given us freedom of religion.

It is the VETERAN, not the reporter, who has given us freedom of the press.

It is the VETERAN, not the poet, who has given us freedom of speech.

It is the VETERAN, not the campus organizer, who has given us freedom to assemble.

It is the VETERAN, not the lawyer, who has given us the right to a fair trial.

It is the VETERAN, not the politician, who has given us the right to vote.

It is the VETERAN, who salutes the Flag, It is the VETERAN, who serves under the Flag.

—Author Unknown

Contents

**VOLUME II
PROGRAMS OF CARE AND GROUPS WITH SPECIAL NEEDS**

Acknowledgments   ix

Foreword   xi
Jacob B. Gadd

Editor's Foreword   xv

Part I   Healthcare Programs   1

1 Veterans with Diabetes in Primary Care   3
James W. Anderson

2 Neurological Healthcare for Veterans   45
Mitchell T. Wallin and John F. Kurtzke

3 Cardiology Care for Veterans in VA Healthcare   63
David C. Booth

4 Veterans' Sacrifices Made in the Quest for Cancer Treatment   81
Philip A. DeSimone

5 Mental Healthcare in the Veterans Health Administration   93
Robert C. Gresen

6 Chiropractic in Veterans' Healthcare   135
Bart N. Green, Claire D. Johnson, and Andrew S. Dunn

7   Healthcare for Veterans with Infectious Diseases   157
Cynthia Livingstone Gibert

8   End-of-Life Care for Veterans in the VA Healthcare System   195
Betty L. Gillespie, James L. Ford, and Kye Y. Kim

Part II   Veterans with Special Needs   217

9   Lifestyles and Health Behaviors of Veterans   219
Hayden B. Bosworth

10   Orthotics and Prosthetics Healthcare for Veterans   243
Thomas W. Miller

11   Native American Veterans and Post-traumatic Stress Disorder:
Issues, Challenges, and Solutions   255
Joseph B. Stone

12   Healthcare for Women Military Veterans   313
Monica Roy

13   Serving America's Former Prisoners of War: Getting It "Right"   343
Brian Engdahl and Charles Stenger

14   Service Dogs and Their Use for Veterans with Disabilities   353
Beth Hudnall Stamm, Susan L. Blampied, and Kirstina Beck

About the Editor   381

About the Contributors   383

Index   391

Acknowledgments

An endeavor of this magnitude has taken several years and the efforts of numerous colleagues and friends in the Department of Veterans Affairs and others interested in the health and well-being of our veterans and their families in the general public. It is to those in the Department of Veterans Affairs Central Office in Washington, D.C., their regional Veterans Integrated Service Networks (VISNs), and regional as well as local Veteran Affairs medical centers that I am extremely grateful. Their efforts have addressed contacting the right people, gaining access to important information, manuscript preparation completion, reviews, and providing detailed guidance in the final chapters and volumes.

Special appreciation is expressed to the efforts of the Department of Veterans Affairs, Office of Communications, and in particular Mr. Daniel Bruneau, Director of Communications; Christine A. Pons, Regional Office of Public Affairs, Department of Veterans Affairs; and Charles F. Castner, Staff Attorney, Department of Veterans Affairs.

The assistance of Darlene Richardson, the Department of Veterans Affairs historian, has been helpful in completing several of the chapters, as have external organizations committed to the care and treatment of our veterans, including the American Legion, Veterans of Foreign Wars, and Paralyzed Veterans of America.

To a cadre of former and current colleagues and friends within the Department of Veterans Affairs, and to some beyond this system, for their support and encouragement, special appreciation is extended, including but

not limited to John Booss, MD; Rodney Baker, PhD; Malcolm Cox, MD; Robert Gresen, PhD; James McCormick, MD; James Holsinger, MD; Herb Spencer, MD; Robert Kraus, MD; Steve Kraman, MD; William Green, PhD; Pat DeLeon, JD, PhD; Brenda Frommer; Neil Carey, MSW; Skip Lowe, PhD; Jeffrey Fisher, PhD; Alla Moeller; Walter Penk, PhD; Ed Nighingale, PhD; Ed Kisarskis, MD; Jill Livingstone, MLB; Deborah Kessler, MLB; Desti Stimes; Joanna Hawthorne; Chesley Jaracz; Tom Martin; Ginny Hamm, JD; Joseph Fox, PhD; Donna K. Jacobs; Steve Campbell, MSW; Steve Nisenbaum, PhD, JD; Terry Clark, MSW; and Maureen Charles, ED, MSN, APRN, Military Nurse Fellow, Lieutenant Colonel, Air Force Nurse Corps.

Appreciation is extended to Praeger publishers as well and their staff and Debbie Carvalko, senior acquisitions editor, psychology, health, and social work, and Alicia S. Merritt, consultant, for their guidance and support.

I express my sincere appreciation to my family, especially my father who served our country in World War II in General Patton's army in the European theater, and friends, who have been so supportive of this effort. And I extend my sincere gratitude and appreciation to each and every contributor for the chapters in these volumes. They come from the several Department of Veterans Affairs facilities, from our major universities, and from both within and beyond our borders. The reader will meet each and every one of them in their chapters as well as in the short biographies that summarize their backgrounds, training, experiences, and expertise. May these volumes provide the reader with a detailed look at veterans' healthcare in the twenty-first century!

Foreword

For the past fifty years, the Department of Veterans Affairs (VA) has provided high-quality care to America's veterans, and it is recognized today as the largest integrated healthcare system in the United States. Its mission, as stated eloquently by President Abraham Lincoln during his second inaugural address, is "to care for him who has borne the battle, his widow and orphan." Currently there are more than twenty-five million veterans across the country. Eight million are enrolled in VA and about 5.5 million are seen at 1,300 Veterans Health Administration (VHA) facilities annually. The VHA has 153 medical centers, 800 community-based outpatient clinics (CBOCs), and 260 readjustment counseling centers (vet centers), with an operating budget of $1 billion dollars and close to 270,000 employees.

There are more than 107 VA medical centers conducting research to improve the health and wellness of veterans. Over the years, this research has led to breakthroughs including development of the CAT scan, the cardiac pacemaker, and the nicotine patch, as well as the first liver transplant. One of the VA's most successful recruitment tools is its medical school affiliations program, which helps trains thousands of medical practitioners each year.

In the 1990s the Department of Veterans Affairs began its transformation from an inpatient to an outpatient system of care. Dr. Kenneth Kizer, then under secretary of health for the VHA, and the VA leadership developed CBOCs to enable the VA to see patients closer to their communities and provide needed outpatient and primary care to veterans who were previously forced to travel hundreds of miles to receive care in veterans' medical centers. In addition, during that period the VA established a defined medical benefits

package for enrolled veterans as well as long-term care for veterans rated 70 percent or higher disabled for service-connected injuries and illnesses from their military service.

In 1998 Congress directed the VA to establish eight priority groups to prioritize and rationalize healthcare for veterans based on the most injured and poorest veterans. In 2003 then Secretary of Veterans Affairs Anthony Principi suspended enrollment for Priority Group 8 veterans due to the VA's limited budget and the increasing numbers of veterans enrolling for VA healthcare. In order to enroll, veterans were required to take a means test, or financial assessment, to determine if they qualified for one of the priority groups and if they could make copays. In 2008 the VA relaxed its enrollment by 10 percent higher than the original means test cut-off income restriction, which allowed an additional 240,000 veterans previously ineligible for VA healthcare to enroll.

Today the Priority Group 8 restriction still exists, but combat veterans who have served after September 11, 2001, in a combat theater of operations (i.e., Operation Enduring Freedom, Operation Iraqi Freedom, and Operation New Dawn), are eligible for five years of veterans' healthcare for any injury or illness related to their military service. Veteran service organizations, such as The American Legion, believe that any veteran should be entitled to use the VA, which is a system designed to meet their unique and complex war-related injuries. In 1997 the VA was given the authority to bill, collect, and retain third-party reimbursements for treatment of non-service-connected medical conditions. Veterans, regardless of level of income or injury, should be authorized to bring their private insurance to the VA for treatment of their non-service medical conditions, which would be an alternative budget stream to offset the demand for services. Another concern is that veterans are not allowed to use their Medicare benefits within the VA. Veterans pay into Medicare their entire working lives and are essentially penalized because they cannot use their earned Medicare benefits in the VA and are forced to use those benefits in the private sector. In the future, the VA must continue to try to improve access to care for any veteran and take advantage of the cost savings to the government of veterans using their Medicare benefits in the VA system rather than the private sector.

Today there is an unprecedented number of returning veterans from Iraq and Afghanistan with traumatic brain injury (TBI) and post-traumatic stress disorder (PTSD). The term *polytrauma* was coined by the VHA to describe the many returning service members with complex, multiple injuries that required a new and holistic way of providing care. Over the last several years, the VHA has developed a polytrauma system of care with four levels.

Level 1 is the lead polytrauma rehabilitation centers, network or Veteran Integrated Service Network (VISN) sites, facilities (VA medical centers), and clinic or polytrauma points of contact. The lead polytrauma centers in the country are located in Palo Alto, California; Tampa, Florida; Richmond, Virginia; and Minneapolis, Minnesota. A new center is being built in San Antonio, Texas. From the battlefield, service members are evacuated through Landshuhl, Germany, to one of the military treatment facilities in the United States. The VHA has nurse liaisons and social workers who help transition severely injured veterans from military treatment facilities to the polytrauma system of care.

If a service member is involved in an improvised explosive device (IED) blast and develops a TBI, it is very likely that the veteran will also develop PTSD. If left untreated, the TBI and PTSD symptoms could lead to substance abuse, depression, and suicide. The VA conducts mandatory screens for veterans when they first enter a VA medical facility for TBI and PTSD. If the screening is positive, those veterans are referred for a secondary evaluation. Veterans' healthcare has also developed a crisis intervention line, formerly known as the Suicide Prevention Hotline, to assist any veteran in crisis. The hotline is open 365 days a year and 24 hours a day and is staffed by licensed counselors. The hotline has been credited for saving over 16,000 lives, and the VA has suicide prevention coordinators in each VA medical center to ensure veterans in crisis receive the assistance they need. The Department of Defense (DoD) and the Department of Veterans Affairs have also led the effort to destigmatize mental health conditions in our returning service members by having mental health practitioners embedded in primary care and through antistigma campaigns such as the "Real Warriors Campaign" in the Department of Defense and "Make the Connection" campaign in the Department of Veterans Affairs.

The VA continues to work with the DoD to develop a joint medical record, which will assist transitioning veterans in obtaining their earned veterans' benefits and services. Both agencies are working on a virtual lifetime electronic record (VLER), which will help connect the DoD and the VA information technology (IT) platforms to follow a service member from the day he or she joins the service to the day that person is laid to rest. The DoD and the VA are continuing to conduct research to improve the prevention, screening, diagnosis, and treatment of TBI and PTSD.

Veteran service organizations were founded to assist veterans by helping them file claims for their earned benefits and services. Veteran service organization service officers are professionally trained and accredited by the VA to file claims for veterans. In addition, Veteran service organizations provide

advocacy and assistance to veterans as well as lobbying the administration, Congress, and senior officials in the VA to make recommendations for continuous improvements for all veterans.

The chapters that follow reflect the many contributions that have been made to veterans' healthcare as well as the key healthcare issues facing our nation's veterans in the twenty-first century. Our nation has a moral obligation to take care of our service members when they return home. George Washington once said, "The willingness with which our young people are likely to serve in any war, no matter how justified, shall be directly proportional to how they perceive the veterans of earlier wars were treated and appreciated by their nation." It is our nation's responsibility to ensure that the Department of Veterans Affairs continues to provide timely, quality healthcare for our nation's veterans.

Jacob B. Gadd
Deputy Director for Health Care,
The American Legion;
Former Hospital Corpsman Third Class,
United States Navy (1998–2003)

Editor's Foreword

This four-volume set focusing on veterans' healthcare provides a unique and valuable contribution to our understanding of veterans' healthcare in the first decade of the twenty-first century. As a professor emeritus and retired VA career service chief from Lexington Veterans Affair Military Center. I have enjoyed a forty-year career in veterans' healthcare. I was first contacted in 2005 by Praeger Publishers to serve as editor of a handbook on this topic and then contacted some colleagues from the Department of Veterans Affairs both past and present and several colleagues nationally to explore the level of interest in accepting the invitation from Praeger to produce a positive reference book focusing on veterans' healthcare. It is to this cadre of professionals that I am indebted; they have contributed their knowledge and expertise in the chapters comprising this handbook.

We must be reminded of not only the macro events, but also the micro transitions that have contributed to the finest model of healthcare for veterans in the world. The reader is about to begin an extraordinary journey into the spectrum of healthcare offered through the Veterans Health Administration (VHA). Volume I offers the reader an understanding of the history of veterans' healthcare. Rodney R. Baker provides an overview of the historical contributions to veterans' healthcare. James W. Holsinger Jr., the first under secretary for veterans' affairs, offers a "View from the Top," addressing the administration and VA healthcare. VHA's academic mission is presented by Stuart C. Gilman, Barbara Chang, Robert Zeiss, Mary Dougherty, William Marks Jr., Deborah Ludke, and Malcolm Cox. Recognizing the important role of legislative initiatives for veterans' healthcare, with the assistance of Corina M. Barrow, Jacquie Rychnovsky, and Patrick DeLeon of Senator Inouye's office, I provide a historical review of key legislation that has benefited veterans' healthcare.

I also examine healthcare for veterans from various eras, covering veterans of World Wars I and II and the Korean conflict. Robert J. Fitz discusses healthcare for veterans of the Vietnam era, and Delilah O. Noronha, John Chardos, Laura Gomez, Samina Iqbal, and Steven Lindley provide a discussion of healthcare for veterans of Operations Enduring Freedom, Iraqi Freedom, and New Dawn.

In an effort to examine global healthcare for veterans, provided is a comparative look at veterans' healthcare in other countries: Australia, Canada, China, Russia, and the United Kingdom. Professor David Dunt and his team examine a critical issue for veterans, focusing on suicide in the ex-service community in Australian research and prevention efforts. Dr. David Pedlar and Stewart Macintosh provide a closer look at veterans affairs in Canada. Finally, Professor Dai Williams takes a closer look at healthcare for British veterans.

Volume II examines programs of care and veterans' special needs. James W. Anderson, a pioneer in clinical care and research, explores healthcare programs for veterans with diabetes in primary care. This is followed by a discussion of neurological healthcare for veterans by Mitchell Wallin and John Kurtzke. David Booth then examines cardiology care for veterans, followed by Philip DeSimone's acknowledgment of veterans' sacrifices made in the quest for cancer treatment. Robert C. Gresen provides a first look at mental health care in VHA. Chiropractic care in veterans' healthcare is reviewed by Bart Green and a team of colleagues from the Naval Medical Center in San Diego and at the VA medical center in Buffalo, New York. Healthcare for veterans with infectious diseases is examined by Cynthia L. Gibert, and end-of-life care for veterans in the VA healthcare system is addressed by Betty L. Gillespie, James L. Ford, and Kye Y. Kim.

Many veterans have special needs. To examine these needs, we asked Dr. Hayden B. Bosworth to assess the lifestyles and health behaviors of veterans. Noting the special needs of amputees and the guidance of Fred Downs, I examined orthotics and prosthetics healthcare for veterans. The challenges faced by Native American veterans and their solutions are addressed by Joseph Stone of the Indian Health Service, and healthcare for women military veterans is addressed by Monica Roy. Prisoners of war have always been a special population and have had special needs; Brian Engdahl and Charles Stenger take a close look at serving America's former prisoners of war. Drs. Beth Hudnall Stamm, Susan L. Blampied, and Kirstina Beck examine a

special population of caregivers in their chapter on assistance dogs and their use by veterans with disabilities.

Volume III takes a closer and more detailed look at mental health treatment and rehabilitation. Delilah O. Noronha begins by examining primary care and mental health integration in providing veterans' healthcare. This is followed by a chapter that examines alcohol and substance abuse programs, by Susan R. Tate, Jennifer Mrnak-Meyer, and Jessica C. Tripp. Smoking has been critical in veterans' healthcare, and Carol A. Malte, Andrew J. Saxon, Kim Hamlett-Berry, and Miles E. McFall investigate integrating smoking cessation into mental health care for post-traumatic stress disorder.

Clinician researchers Mark S. Kaplan, Bentson H. McFarland, and Nathalie Huguet take a close look at suicide risk among veterans. VA healthcare for women veterans experiencing trauma is the focus of Carole A. Goguen. Stephen Tracy, Sara Tavakoli, Simona Stolpner, and Jodie Trafton discuss the treatment of substance abuse disorder; and the social context of adjustment in combat veterans is examined by Bradley Belsher, Josef Ruzek, and Matthew Cordova. Polytrauma care and treatment in veterans' healthcare is covered by Jeanne M. Bennett. Military traumatic brain injury and the postconcussive syndrome is addressed by colleagues in the Department of Defense led by Louis M. French, Victoria C. Anderson-Barnes, Katherine Brazaitis, and Aditya Bhagwat. Healthcare and issues of racial and ethnic diversity are carefully examined by Kathleen M. McNamara.

With special attention on rehabilitation care and treatment for veterans, colleagues Walter Penk, Dolores Little, and Nathan Ainspan address trauma-focused psychosocial rehabilitation. This is followed by a chapter on psychosocial rehabilitation and recovery services by Samantha Kettle, Loretta E. Braxton, Valerie Fox, and Josh Tiegreen. Next Ann D. Kirkwood, Beth Hudnall Stamm, and Chandra R. Story address eradicating mental illness stigma for active military personnel and veterans. Finally, Thomas P. O'Toole provides an in-depth assessment of how VA is engaging homeless veterans in primary care.

Volume IV provides an examination of some of the future directions for veterans' healthcare, first examining dedicated centers for veterans' healthcare. The first chapter reviews VHA centers of excellence. Then Drs. Katerine Osatuke, Jill Draime, Scott C. Moore, Dee Ramsel, Andrew Meyer, Sharon Barnes, Linda Belton, and Sue R. Dyrenforth examine the latest in organization development in VA.

Joseph F. Murphy, public affairs officer, VA NCPS, and James P. Bagian explore for the reader the VA National Center for Patient Safety. The significance of post-trauma stress is addressed by Matthew J. Friedman, the national

director of the Department of Veterans Affairs National Center for PTSD. Leading the way in pain-related disorders, Drs. Kathryn LaChappelle, Samantha Boris-Karpel, and Robert D. Kerns provide a detailed review of the efforts to address pain management in VHA.

Dr. K. Kizer, who is responsible for a major reorganization of VHA, provides a closer view of lessons learned about clinical integration from VA's experience with VISNs. The Veterans' healthcare system is seen as a potential model for a national plan by Said A. Ibrahim, David Macpherson, and Michael E. Moreland.

New technologies are helping to create easier access to healthcare for veterans who live in rural and underserved areas of the country. Jennifer A. Wood, Thomas W. Miller, and Russell Hagy discuss telehealth applications to underserved veterans. Miller and Janet Kemp then explore the topic of suicide prevention through a national hotline. The Academy of Spinal Cord Injury is an organization outside VA that offers new directions in addressing the needs of spinal cord–injured veterans. The chapter on this topic is authored by the director, Terrie Price. VA has developed and implemented an Office for Preventative Ethics. Examining ethicolegal issues in VA healthcare are Steve Nisenbaum, Tom Miller, Sheila O'Keefe, and Dennis Norman. An organization external to VA that is meeting the needs of veterans, Give an Hour™, is described by its founder, Barbara Van Dahlen. Edmund J. Nightingale provides a very detailed and up-to-date summary of the efforts to provide quality, competent, and thorough veterans' healthcare in the final chapter, "Good to Great: The Veterans' Health Care System's Path to Excellence!"

The comprehensive nature of this four-volume set offers the reader an in-depth examination of veterans' healthcare through the first decade of the twenty-first century. More than two hundred invitations were extended to present and past members of the Department of Veterans Affairs as well as aligned agencies, veterans' organizations, and healthcare facilities associated with veterans' healthcare. What is provided are the comprehensive and dedicated work and contributions of more than one hundred scientists and practitioners, researchers, and clinicians both within the Department of Veterans Affairs and those in academically affiliated universities and public and private institutions. An effort is made to provide a glimpse of veterans' healthcare internationally. This handbook is not meant to cover every topic related to veterans' healthcare thoroughly, but rather to offer to the reader an excellent reference point from which to start a journey toward a better understanding of the complexity of providing quality healthcare to our military veterans.

This compendium provides the opportunity for dialogue on improving our understanding of veterans' healthcare, and each of the authors deals with a

part of this complex whole. As editor I trust it offers the gestalt that will increase our understanding of veterans' healthcare and the transitions we face in providing a twenty-first-century focus on healthcare for veterans worldwide.

Thomas W. Miller, PhD, ABPP,
Professor Emeritus & Senior Research Scientist,
University of Kentucky; Veterans Affairs Medical Center (Retired),
Lexington, Kentucky; Center for Prevention Research,
University of Connecticut

Healthcare Programs

Chapter 1

Veterans with Diabetes in Primary Care

James W. Anderson

Introduction

Diabetes is emerging as a major health problem in the United States (Anderson & Pasupuleti 2008). This increase is affecting veterans; the prevalence of diabetes in U.S. adults in 2007 was approximately 10.7 percent, whereas the prevalence of diabetes in persons over sixty years old was 23.1 percent. Over the past forty years Veterans Administration/Department of Veterans Affairs (VA) staff members have provided high-quality care for veterans and served as pacesetters for applied clinical research related to the treatment of diabetes. VA staff physicians have developed and conducted many applied clinical research projects that have guided the management of all individuals with diabetes. Many VA staff physicians have served as presidents of the American Diabetes Association.

The following VA staff physicians have made outstanding contributions to the clinical management of diabetes: C. Abraira (Abraira et al. 2003a), J. D. Brunzell (Brunzell et al. 2008), J. A. Colwell (Colwell et al. 1989), W. Duckworth (Duckworth et al. 2009; Duckworth et al. 1998), R. R. Henry (Henry & Gumbiner 1991), F. Q. Nuttall et al. 1983), J. M. Olefsky (Henry, Wallace & Olefsky 1986), D. Porte Jr. (Porte 1991), G. M. Reaven (Reaven 1988), and R. H. Unger (Unger 1976; Unger 1983). VA has encouraged and supported investigator-initiated research and cost-effective and focused Cooperative Studies to examine diabetes, its complications, and comorbidities.

This chapter reviews clinical and basic research supported by VA and performed at the Lexington VA Medical Center (VAMC) to show how focused and cost-effective research support from VA has improved the clinical care of veterans with diabetes at this medical center and provided guidance for other healthcare providers worldwide. VA Cooperative Studies (VACS) related to diabetes are also reviewed. These studies have led to development of *evidence-based guidelines* for management of diabetes to replace *experienced-based guidelines* that have been used for decades.

Advances in Nutritional Management of Diabetes

Nutrition Guidelines for Persons with Diabetes in the Twentieth Century

The old wives' tale that "eating sugar causes diabetes" has guided much of nutritional management of diabetes over the last two millennia. Changes in recommendations for a weight-maintaining diet for individuals with diabetes are summarized in table 1.1. Only in the last quarter of the twentieth century did scientific *evidence-based* data emerge to support the current recommendations that a generous carbohydrate, high-fiber diet is the most effective approach for nutritional management of diabetes (American Diabetes Association 2004; Anderson et al. 2004). VA investigators in Seattle (Brunzell et al. 1974) and Lexington (Kiehm, Anderson & Ward 1976; Anderson & Ward 1979) provided the lead in laying to rest the old "carbohydrate restriction for management of diabetes" concept. While these higher carbohydrate, higher fiber diets have the strongest clinical research basis and international consensus *evidence basis* for management of all persons with diabetes (Anderson et al. 2004), *experience-based* recommendations for carbohydrate restriction, without strong clinical research support, are still found in recommendations of the American Diabetes Association (2010) and from the Joslin Clinic (Hamdy et al. 2008).

I review here work leading to the hypothesis that a high-carbohydrate, high-fiber diet is the most effective nutritional approach to management of type 1 and type 2 diabetes. My and my colleagues' clinical research studies (Anderson, Herman & Newcomer 1969; Anderson & Herman 1972; Anderson, Herman & Zakim 1973) and animal feeding experiments (Anderson & Zakim 1970; Tyrrell & Anderson 1971; Anderson & Tyrrell 1973; Murphy & Anderson 1974; Anderson 1974a, 1974b) supported the hypothesis that low-carbohydrate diets were associated with insulin resistance and that high-carbohydrate

Table 1.1. Macronutrient Content of Diets Recommended for Individuals with Diabetes in the Twentieth Century*

Nutrient	1930	1955	1970	1990	2004**
Carbohydrate (g/d)	70	176	225	290	**295**
Percentage energy (%)	14	35	45	58	**59**
Simple (g/d)	40	71	112	130	**115**
Complex (g/d)	30	105	113	160	**180**
Fat, total (g/d)	153	99	82	60	**60**
Percentage of energy (%)	69	45	37	27	**27**
Saturated (g/d)	87	46	35	14	**16**
Monounsaturated (g/d)	50	37	31	26	**28**
Polyunsaturated (g/d)	9	11	13	17	**16**
Cholesterol (mg/d)	1,060	690	550	< 200	**<200**
Protein (g/d)	85	101	90	75	**70**
Percentage of energy (%)	17	20	18	15	**14**
Dietary fiber (g/d)	8	15	20	40	**35**

*Values in grams or mg per day are for 2,000 kcal diet.

**These evidence-based nutrition recommendations are consistent with those strongly recommended by national nutrition advisory panels from Canada, Europe, India, Japan, South Africa, and the United Kingdom.

Source: Modified from Anderson et al. (2004); Anderson (2006)

consumption improved insulin sensitivity and glucose tolerance in nondiabetic and diabetic subjects. This hypothesis was also supported by the reports of Singh (1955) and Viswanathan (1968) as well as the emerging work of Brunzell and colleagues at the Seattle VAMC (Brunzell et al. 1971; Brunzell et al. 1974).

Development of the High-Carbohydrate, High-Fiber (HCF) Diet

Our research at the Lexington VAMC provided support and guidance for the development of improved nutritional management of diabetes. In 1974 the VAMC in Lexington, Kentucky, opened the ten-bed Special Diagnostic and Treatment Unit (SDTU) with a metabolic kitchen staffed by research dietitians and cooks. This unit was one of the SDTUs opened by VA to provide support for research related to diabetes and other metabolic conditions. My colleagues and I began testing the efficacy and safety of the HCF diet. Based on our preliminary research (Anderson, Herman & Newcomer 1969; Anderson & Herman 1972; Anderson, Herman & Zakim 1973), the report of Kempner (Kempner, Peschel & Schlayer 1958), and studies reported from India (Singh 1955; Viswanathan 1968), we postulated that an HCF diet would enhance insulin sensitivity and improve glycemic control and serum lipoprotein risk factors for persons with type 1 or 2 diabetes.

The first HCF diets that we began testing in 1974 provided approximately 75 percent of energy from carbohydrate (114 g/d oligosaccharides and 300 g/d polysaccharides), 16 percent from protein, and 9 percent from fat, with approximately 70 g/d of dietary fiber. The HCF diet was compared to a representative American Diabetes Association (ADA) diet providing energy from the following sources: carbohydrate, 43 percent (109 g/d oligosaccharides and 125 g/d polysaccharides); protein, 23 percent; and fat, 34 percent, with 14 g/d of dietary fiber. Diabetic patients were admitted to the hospital and fed a weight-maintaining ADA diet for one week and then fed the HCF diet for two to three weeks. Plasma glucose values were monitored fasting at 8:00 a.m. and before the evening meal. Finger-stick blood glucose monitoring was not available, so quantitative urine glucose values were monitored with dipstick measures four times daily (Anderson 1974c; Kiehm, Anderson & Ward 1976).

Lean and obese individuals with type 1 or type 2 diabetes participated in these studies. While our endocrinology colleagues were concerned about treating "insulin-dependent" diabetic patients with these high-carbohydrate diets, the results were surprising. Without changes in insulin doses, glycosuria increased during the first few days and then decreased, requiring reductions in insulin doses. The first patient we treated was a thirty-nine-year-old farmer who was lean and fit; he had been insulin-treated for type 1 diabetes for twenty years. He had maintained good glycemic control taking a total of 65 units of insulin daily. Over three weeks on the HCF diet, we decreased his insulin dose to 35 units/day. He was instructed in a high-carbohydrate, high-fiber maintenance diet before discharge and followed this diet rigorously, with quarterly visits to our diabetes clinic for the next thirty years. On his last visit to my VA diabetes clinic in 2004, he was at the same body weight, had good glycemic control on 35 units of insulin daily, and had no evidence of macrovascular or microvascular (i.e., retinopathy, albuminuria, or neuropathy) complications.

The responses of patients with types 1 and 2 diabetes are summarized in table 1.2. Most of our studies were fixed-sequence, controlled studies, and outcomes were well documented in the scientific literature (Kiehm, Anderson & Ward 1976; Anderson & Ward 1978b, 1979; Anderson 1980a, 1980b; Anderson et al. 1980). For lean individuals with type 2 diabetes, weight-maintaining HCF diets allowed us to discontinue oral anti-diabetes medication more than 80 percent of the time and even discontinue insulin therapy in more than 70 percent of those taking less than 30 units/day. In addition to

Table 1.2. Responses of Lean Diabetic Patients to Weight-Maintaining HCF Diets*

Treatment Group	No.	Dose/d (mg or U)		Glucose		Cholesterol		Triglycerides	
		Control	HCF	Control	HCF	Control	HCF	Control	HCF
Sulfonylureas, mg/d	12	750 (89)	68 (48)**	143 (12)	130 (8)	212 (11)	159 (6)**	153 (6)	140 (7)
Discontinued, %			83%						
Insulin: Low dose, U/d	18	17 (1)	1 (1)**	149 (14)	137 (7)				
Range		14 20	0 2						
Moderate dose, U/d	12	28 (1)	7(2)**	178 (11)	168 (14)				
Range		22 32							
High dose (Type 1), U/d	6	43 (3)	31 (7)	180 (17)	167 (17)				
Range		40 55							
All Insulin, U/d	36	26 (3)	11(3)**	164 (9)	152 (7)	206 (10)	147 (5)**	142 (5)	134 (8)

*Values are means (SEM).

**Values differ significantly from control diet values.

Source: Anderson & Ward (1979); Anderson (1980a).

improvements in glycemic control with lower doses of medication, serum cho-
lesterol values decreased more than 25 percent with introduction of HCF diets.
These results surprised many nutritionists and diabetologists, but were con-
firmed by many other research centers (Anderson, Akanji & Randles 2001).
This clinical research, initially funded from clinical care services at the Lexing-
ton VAMC, was subsequently funded by VA Merit Review and National
Institutes of Health (NIH) funding (Kiehm, Anderson & Ward 1976;
Anderson & Ward 1979; Anderson et al. 2004).

Diet advocates and popularizers who visited Lexington to learn more details
about our diets in the mid-1970s included dietary fiber pioneers Denis Burkitt
(Burkitt & Trowell 1975) and Hugh Trowell (Trowell & Burkitt 1981); diet
advocate Nathan Pritikin (Pritikin & McGrady 1979; Barnard et al. 1983);
and international nutrition and diabetes experts Mohan Viswanathan and his
son and son-in-law (Viswanathan 1968; Ramachandran & Viswanathan
1997); as well as David Jenkins (Jenkins, Leeds & Gassull 1976; Goulder,
Alberti & Jenkins 1978; Jenkins et al. 2003). Jenkins and I established a long-
term collaborative relationship that still functions (Anderson et al. 2004;
Jenkins et al. 2003; Stephenson et al. 2005; Wong et al. 2008).

With the growing interest in our approach to nutritional management of
diabetes and its effectiveness, our patients wanted detailed guidelines,
exchange lists, etc. Many health professionals also requested our exchange
lists, practical guidelines, and information. As an outgrowth of this research
at the VAMC, we established the HCF Nutrition Research Foundation in
1979 and were then able to begin distributing educational material to consumers and health professionals (Anderson & Ward 1978a; Anderson, Sieling
& Chen 1981; Anderson 1984, 1986). Because accurate estimates of total
dietary fiber content of common foods were not available (Kiehm, Anderson
& Ward 1976), our laboratory developed techniques to measure dietary fiber
content of widely used foods (Chen & Anderson 1981; Anderson & Bridges
1988; Anderson et al. 1989); our publications of these dietary fiber measurements by the HCF Nutrition Research Foundation (Anderson 1990) were
widely cited in the scientific literature for almost ten years, until standardized
measurements became available.

Studies with the Artificial Pancreas and Insulin Clamp Techniques

To rigorously assess the comparative effects of low-carbohydrate, low-fiber
(LCLF) diets and high-carbohydrate, high-fiber (HCHF) diets, we conducted a randomized, crossover trial involving twelve nonobese individuals

Table 1.3. Insulin Requirements of Patients with Type 1 Diabetes Estimated with the Artificial Pancreas on Low-carbohydrate, Low-fiber (LCLF) and High-carbohydrate, High-fiber (HCHF) Diets

	LCLF Diet	HCHF Diet
Hemoglobin A1c, %	8.1 (0.4)	8.0 (0.3)
Artificial pancreas: Total insulin, U	37.1 (3.0)	32.9 (3.3)*
Artificial pancreas: Basal insulin, U	21.6 (3.1)	18.5 (2.7)
Artificial pancreas: Meal-related insulin, U	11.9 (1.2)	12.0 (2.0)
Carbohydrate: Insulin Ratio, grams/U	5.6 (0.5)	11.9 (1.1)*

*Values are mean (SEM)

Source: Anderson et al. (1991d)

with type 1 diabetes (Anderson et al. 1991d). An artificial pancreas (Biostator Glucose Controller, Miles, Inc., Elkhart, IN) was used to quantitate insulin requirements over an eighteen-hour period. Volunteers were hospitalized in the SDTU or the General Clinical Research Center at the University of Kentucky Hospital, where all food was provided. After seven days on a control diabetes diet (similar to the LCLF diet), subjects were randomized to either the LCLF or HCHF diet for twenty-eight days. After a six-week washout period, subjects reentered the research ward to receive the other diet intervention. The control and LCLF diets were similar to the ADA-recommended diet, and the HCHF diet was similar to the HCF described previously (Anderson & Ward 1979). Baseline artificial pancreas studies were performed for an eighteen-hour period between 12:00 noon and 8:00 a.m. at the end of the seven-day control diet period and after twenty-eight days on each test diet. The diagnosis of type 1 diabetes was confirmed by measurements of urinary C-peptide values. Nine men and one woman completed the study. The HCHF diet was associated with significant reductions in total insulin requirements while connected to the artificial pancreas despite a 64 percent increase in total carbohydrate consumption (see table 1.3). After meals, these diabetic individuals utilized twice as much carbohydrate per unit of insulin (the carbohydrate:insulin ratio) with the HCHF diet as with the LCLF diet. This study was supported by SDTU, VA Merit Review, and NIH funding (Anderson et al. 1991d).

The effects of HCF diets were further examined in healthy college students and older volunteers at the Massachusetts Institute of Technology while I was on sabbatical there from 1983 to 1984 (Fukagawa et al. 1990).

Six healthy young men and six healthy older individuals (sixty-seven to eighty-six years old) volunteered for euglycemic insulin clamp procedures. This technique is still considered to be the most accurate procedure for assessing insulin sensitivity. Measurements were performed while volunteers were consuming their usual "American" diet and our HCF diet. Carbohydrate (percent of energy) and fiber (g/d) for the usual and HCF diets, respectively, were: 42 percent and 69 percent and 17 g/d and 69 g/d. Fasting glucose and insulin values were significantly lower on the HCF than on the usual diet. Mean glucose disposal increased 43 percent ($P < 0.02$) with the HCF compared to the usual diet. These studies in nondiabetic individuals support those in diabetic individuals, indicating that higher carbohydrate, higher fiber diets enhance insulin sensitivity and would serve to protect from developing diabetes and slow its progression. Prospective cohort studies and clinical trials point to the protective effect of high-fiber intakes for slowing progression of prediabetes to overt clinical diabetes (Anderson et al. 2009; Lindstrom et al. 2006).

Long-term Studies with the HCF Maintenance Diet

Because diets providing 70 percent of energy from carbohydrate and 65 grams of dietary fiber per day did not seem practical for long-term use for the average American, we modified the diets to be more consumer-friendly for our veteran population. Our preliminary results were encouraging using the high-fiber maintenance (HFM) diet that provided 55 to 60 percent of energy from carbohydrate and 50 grams of dietary fiber per day (Anderson & Ward 1978b). Long-term follow-up of nonobese diabetic subjects confirmed these observations. Insulin-treated, nonobese male veterans with type 1 (n = 3) or type 2 (n = 11) diabetes were followed for an average of forty-nine months. Insulin treatment was discontinued for all type 2 individuals and reduced from 44 to 30 units/day for type 1 individuals. After an average follow-up period of four years, insulin therapy averaged 36 units/day for the type 1 individuals and was not reinitiated for any of the type 2 individuals. Weights and glycemic control did not differ significantly between baseline, HCF diets on the SDTU and at four years of follow-up. Serum cholesterol values were 199 mg/dl at baseline, 147 mg/dl on the HCF diet and 177 mg/dl on the HFM diet at four years (p < 0.05 vs. baseline). Fasting serum triglyceride values were 133 mg/dl at baseline, 136 mg/dl with the HCF diet, and 101 mg/dl on the HFM diet at four years (p < 0.05 vs. baseline). Adherence to the HFM diet was assessed in eleven of the patients and was excellent (n = 3), good (n = 6), fair (n = 1), and poor (n = 1). These studies indicated that the HFM diet was effective and acceptable for long-term management of diabetes and that the diet also favorably affected lipoprotein risk factors (Story et al. 1985).

Comments

Studies at the Lexington and other VAMCs paved the way for development of strong *evidence-based* nutritional management plans for individuals with type 1 and 2 diabetes. These dietary recommendations are generous in carbohydrate and fiber, moderate in protein, and restricted in saturated fat and cholesterol. These dietary interventions improve glycemic control and reduce risks for cardiovascular disease. These nutrition recommendations are consistent with those strongly recommended by national nutrition advisory panels from Canada, Europe, India, Japan, South Africa, and the United Kingdom (Anderson et al. 2004).

Management of Obese Diabetic Individuals

HCF diets had a low-energy density, and our patients were challenged to consume adequate volumes of food to maintain their weights. Even though our research dietitians carefully calculated the energy requirements for each individual and adjusted the menus almost daily in an attempt to maintain stable weights, most patients—lean or obese—tended to lose weight with HCF diets. Because very-low-energy diets (VLED, < 800 kcal/d) were gaining popularity for obesity management in the mid-1970s (Genuth 1979; Anderson & Konz 2005), we began testing VLED and low-energy HCF-type diets (LED, >800 kcal/d) for management of obese diabetic individuals (Anderson & Sieling 1980). Although we could provide adequate protein intakes with VLED, we learned that LED were much better tolerated and safer while providing similar efficacy to VLED. The results of these clinical trials are summarized in table 1.4.

With high-fiber VLEDs diabetic patients lost weight faster but had a higher frequency of side effects, such as neuropathy. Even mildly energy-restricted diets (e.g., 1,600 kcal/day) led to substantial reductions in insulin requirements. Overall, our experience indicates that reductions in oral antidiabetic medications and insulin doses were similar for obese diabetic individuals treated with high-fiber, 1,600 kcal/day diets as with high-fiber VLED; insulin was discontinued in the following percentages of patients: 1,600 kcal/day diets, 86 percent; 1,000 kcal/day LED, 86 percent; and 600 kcal/day VLED, 88 percent (Anderson & Sieling 1980; Anderson 1985).

Table 1.4. Response of Obese Diabetic Individuals to Energy-restricted, High-fiber Diets

Measurement	1,600 kcal diets		1,000 kcal diets		600 kcal diets	
	Initial	Final	Initial	Final	Initial	Final
No. of patients	7		7		8	
Weight, pounds	211	206	206	195	249	230
Insulin dose, Units/day	29	12	34	5	59	1
Insulin discontinued, %		86		86		88
Fasting plasma glucose, mg/dl	178	158	282	153	238	153

Source: Anderson & Sieling (1980); Anderson (1995).

The mean changes in insulin doses for 15 obese men treated with high-fiber, energy-restricted diets were as follows. In thirteen of fifteen patients we were able to discontinue insulin at these intervals: ten days, six patients (all taking 25 U/d or less); twenty days, three additional patients; thirty days, one additional patient; and forty days, three additional patients. The most dramatic reduction in insulin dose was seen in one patient with an initial insulin dose of 110 U/d, with reduction to 40 U/d in ten days and discontinuation of insulin by twenty days; however, one patient had an initial insulin dose of 40 U/d that increased to 45 U/d despite a weight loss of eight pounds in three weeks. Thus, this experience on the SDTU indicated that although weight loss dramatically decreases mean insulin doses for obese individuals with type 2 diabetes, the time course is variable, and a small percentage of patients do not have reduced insulin requirements despite sizable amounts of weight loss (Anderson & Sieling 1980; Anderson 1985).

Research from other VAMCs reinforced the recommendations that we developed for management of obese diabetic individuals (Henry, Schaeffer & Olefsky 1985; Henry, Wallace & Olefsky 1986; Henry & Gumbiner 1991). We summarized these recommendations (Anderson, Kendall & Jenkins 2003) and they were reinforced by the ADA (Klein et al. 2004).

Treatment of Obese Individuals without Diabetes

Guided by our experience in obesity management in the SDTU at the VAMC in Lexington, the University of Kentucky established a partnership with Health Management Resources (HMR®) to initiate the HMR® Weight Management Program at the University of Kentucky in 1985.

I served as medical director of this Program from 1985 through 2007. From 1985 to 1995 the HMR® program predominantly utilized VLED using meal replacement shakes (i.e., five HMR 500 shakes daily), but since 1995 we have primarily recommended LED using shakes and shelf-stable entrees (Anderson et al. 1991c; Anderson, Brinkman & Hamilton 1992; Anderson, Hamilton & Brinkman-Kaplan 1992; Anderson et al. 1994; Anderson et al. 1999c; Anderson, Conley & Nicholas 2007; Furlow & Anderson 2009). Our ongoing clinical trial experience at the VAMC guided our development of a very effective, intensive behavioral obesity treatment program.

Comments

Nutrition management strategies for obese nondiabetic individuals have paralleled those for obese diabetic individuals over the past three decades. VLED and LED diets, proven effective and safe for diabetic individuals with appropriate medical monitoring, have been made available to obese individuals without diabetes and with significant risk factors (Anderson et al. 2001; Anderson & Konz 2005). In addition to emphasis on caloric restriction, our VA-supported research has documented the effectiveness of higher fiber intakes for weight management (Anderson & Bryant 1986; Anderson et al. 2009).

Reductions of Cardiovascular Risk Factors

Lipoprotein Responses to the HCF Diet

HCF diets were associated with dramatic reductions in serum total cholesterol, low-density lipoprotein (LDL) cholesterol, and triglyceride values (Kiehm, Anderson & Ward 1976; Anderson & Ward 1978b; Anderson & Ward 1979). Although the HCF diets were much lower in saturated fat and cholesterol content than the control ADA diets, reductions in total and LDL cholesterol values were much larger than expected using the Mensink and Katan calculations (Mensink & Katan 1992).

These studies at the Lexington VAMC paved the way for more rigorous studies of the effects of high-fiber, low-fat diets (similar to the HFM diet) on serum lipoproteins that were funded by the NIH (Anderson et al. 1992) as well as the VAMC. Men and women with moderate hypercholesterolemia (n = 177) were randomized to a usual diet, the American Heart Association (AHA) step 2 diet, or the high-fiber, low-fat diet. The AHA diet and the high-fiber diet were similar in macronutrient content, but the high-fiber diet had significantly more total and soluble dietary fiber. Approximately fifty individuals completed each diet. At twelve months changes in serum LDL cholesterol values were control, −10.0 percent; AHA diet, −13.6 percent; and high-fiber diet, −17.9 percent (P < 0.05 vs. AHA diet). These studies documented that soluble fiber that has viscous properties has significantly greater hypocholesterolemic effects than similar diets that have similar reductions in saturated fat and cholesterol (Anderson et al. 1992).

High-carbohydrate diets—low in dietary fiber—have well-recognized hypertriglyceridemic effects (Parks & Hellerstein 2000). However, we saw consistent reductions in fasting serum triglyceride values with HCF diets (Anderson 2000). The triglyceride responses of 54 hypertriglyceridemic patients to HCF diets on the SDTU and to follow-up with the HFM diet are summarized as follows. None of these patients received pharmacotherapy for dyslipidemia. Patients with increasingly higher initial serum triglycerides had progressively greater reductions in values. The fifteen men with initial triglyceride values of 175 mg/dl had reductions of 11 percent with the HCF diet and sustained reductions of 37 percent over six to twenty-four months of follow-up on the HFM diet. The seven men with the highest initial values (2,913 mg/dl) had reductions of 81 percent with the HCF diet and sustained reductions of 92 percent with the HFM diet. Overall, the fifty-four hypertriglyceridemic patients had reductions of serum triglyceride values by 75 percent with the HCF diet and sustained reductions of 83 percent with the HFM diet. One patient had an initial fasting serum triglyceride value of >22,000 mg/dl and had a reduction of ~50 percent in twenty-four hours. After two weeks on the SDTU consuming a weight-maintaining HCF diet, his fasting triglyceride values were < 500 mg/dl. These observations led me to counsel hypertriglyceridemic patients in my VA Diabetes and General Internal Medicine Clinics that they were "allergic to fat" and should pursue a diet rich in dietary fiber and very low in fat content (Anderson 1995).

Clinical Studies with Oat Bran, Beans, and Psyllium

The substantial reduction in serum cholesterol and LDL cholesterol concentrations for diabetic patients noted with HCF diets (see table 1.2) prompted us to use our rodent model to examine the effects of different dietary fibers on serum lipids in rats (Lin & Anderson 1977; Anderson & Chen 1979; Chen & Anderson 1979a, 1979b). These studies were performed in our biochemistry laboratory at the VAMC and funded by VA Merit Review Grants. Earlier studies by Keys (Keys, Grande & Anderson 1961) using pectin, and by deGroot (deGroot, Luyken & Pikaar 1963) using oatmeal suggested that soluble (viscous) dietary fibers appeared to have hypocholesterolemic effects, while insoluble dietary fibers such as wheat bran and cellulose did not affect serum cholesterol values. In the fall of 1976 I obtained oat bran from the Quaker Oats Co. and concurrently began testing it in animals and humans (Chen, Anderson & Gould 1981; Gould, Anderson & O'Mahouny 1980). Our clinical studies in the SDTU and of outpatients helped establish the efficacy and safety of oat bran as a hypocholesterolemic food (Kirby et al. 1981; Anderson et al. 1984b; Anderson et al. 1984a; Anderson & Chen 1986; Anderson & Gustafson 1988; Wood et al. 1989; Anderson et al. 1990a and 1990b); many of the ninety publications from our group that related to oat bran were supported by clinical and research funding from VA. These observations strongly supported the health claim approved by the FDA in 1997 that oat bran, as part of a low-fat, low-cholesterol diet, may reduce risk for heart disease (U.S. Department of Health and Human Services, FDA 1997). This was the first food to obtain approval for a health claim in this area.

Encouraged by the favorable effects of oat bran on serum lipoproteins, we examined other foods rich in viscous soluble fibers. A series of studies with beans indicated that their soluble fibers had similar favorable effects on serum lipoproteins and operated through similar mechanisms (Anderson et al. 1984b; Anderson & Gustafson 1988; Anderson et al. 1990a). These studies documented that consumption of oat bran or beans as part of a diet served on the SDTU was associated with a reduction of LDL cholesterol values of 25 to 30 percent. After instructing patients in use of two servings of oat bran daily (as cereal or muffins) or a generous serving of beans (1 cup pinto, navy, or other beans daily), they sustained reductions of serum LDL cholesterol for up to two years. In this way we were able to spare many of our patients the risks and side effects related to hypocholesterolemic drugs such as statins. A novel observation we reported was that serum HDL cholesterol values, after an initial decrease, increased steadily over time and achieved and sustained values averaging 20 percent higher than initial values over the two years of follow-up (Anderson & Gustafson 1988).

In 1984 we began studies to examine the hypocholesterolemic effects of psyllium. Psyllium is a widely available supplement that is a soluble dietary fiber with viscous properties. As recently summarized, different dietary fibers have different health-promoting properties, with oat bran being a food that delivers the largest range of these beneficial physiologic effects and psyllium being a supplement that has the broadest range of health-promoting effects (Anderson et al. 2009; Anderson 2009). Our series of clinical trials (Anderson et al. 1988; Anderson et al. 1991a; Anderson et al. 1992b; Anderson et al. 2000b) and meta-analyses (Olson et al. 1997; Anderson et al. 2000a) documented the important serum LDL cholesterol–lowering effects of psyllium and the benefits for persons with diabetes (Anderson et al. 1999a). Studies from our laboratory indicated that psyllium has the largest hypocholesterolemic effects of commonly used supplements in the rat model (Anderson, Jones & Riddell-Mason 1994). This research, supported by clinical and research funds from VA, contributed to the base of knowledge that led the FDA to approve a heart health claim for psyllium in 1999—the first such claim for a dietary fiber supplement (U.S. Department of Health and Human Services, FDA 1998).

Dietary fibers have a number of physiologic effects that reduce risk for atherosclerotic cardiovascular disease (Anderson et al. 2009; Anderson 2009). Many of these beneficial effects of dietary fiber—lowering of blood pressure, favorable effects on weight loss and management, improvement in postprandial glycemia, and favorable effects on lipoproteins—have been documented with clinical studies in the Lexington SDTU. Our early observations indicated that HCF diets lowered blood pressure of diabetic men (Anderson 1983). Subsequent studies have confirmed these effects, and different types of dietary fibers—both soluble and insoluble—appear to provide these health benefits (Anderson et al. 2009; Anderson 2009). Dietary fiber supplementation enhances the effects of hypocaloric diets and enables overweight or obese individuals to lose significantly more weight than similar individuals randomized to hypocaloric diets with nonfiber placebos (Anderson et al. 2009). Soluble, viscous fiber consumption lowers postprandial glycemia in normal and diabetic individuals (Anderson et al. 1999a). and preliminary data suggest that chronic consumption of certain soluble fibers may slow the progression of pre-diabetes to diabetes (Anderson et al. 2009; Andon & Anderson 2008).

Dietary fiber intake has favorable effects on the three major cardiovascular serum lipoprotein risk factors, namely LDL cholesterol, HDL cholesterol, and triglyceride-rich very-low density lipoproteins (VLDL). HCF diets lower serum triglycerides, but the dietary components—low fat, high complex carbohydrate, or type of dietary fiber—responsible for this favorable effect are unclear (Anderson et al. 2009). Insoluble as well as soluble dietary fibers appear to contribute to the hypotriglyceridemic effects. Soluble dietary fibers with viscous properties have the capacity to reduce serum LDL cholesterol concentrations, as discussed previously (Anderson et al. 2009). We have examined the mechanisms for these hypocholesterolemic effects in our biochemical laboratory (Chen, Anderson & Gould 1981; Anderson, Jones & Riddell-Mason 1994) and with human volunteers on the SDTU (Anderson et al. 1991b). The efficacy of different dietary fibers related to these LDL-cholesterol-reducing effects was recently compared (Sirtori, Anderson & Arnoldi, 2007). Oat bran intake may specifically decrease the more atherogenic, small, dense LDL particles while increasing the less atherogenic, larger, less dense LDL particles and may also decrease LDL oxidation (Andon & Anderson 2008).

Laboratory Studies of Mechanisms and Lipoprotein Effects

VA Merit Review Program funding allowed us to perform dose-ranging studies and examine mechanisms of action of different dietary components. With our cholesterol-fed rat model we could feed different fibers and assess their hypocholesterolemic potential. In this manner we determined that an array of insoluble fibers did not have hypocholesterolemic effects, and nonviscous, soluble fibers also were not efficacious (Anderson & Chen 1979; Lin & Anderson 1977; Chen, Anderson & Gould 1981; Jennings et al. 1988). Later we compared the hypocholesterolemic effects of ten different fibers with the rat model (Anderson, Jones & Riddell-Mason 1994) and noted that the relative rank of hypocholesterolemic effects in this model was similar to that documented in human studies (Anderson, Jones & Riddell-Mason 1994; Anderson et al. 1984a). In vitro studies with perfused rat livers and hepatocytes indicated that propionate, a major short-chain fatty acid resulting from fermentation of certain soluble fibers, appears to mediate some of the hypocholesterolemic effects of soluble fibers (Anderson & Bridges 1984; Chen, Anderson & Jennings 1984; Wright, Anderson & Bridges 1990). Later we reported serum levels of short-chain fatty acids in humans that were correlated with the hypocholesterolemic effects of oat bran (Bridges et al. 1992). Early clinical studies from our laboratory documented that increased bile acid excretion contributed to the hypocholesterolemic effects of oat bran for humans (Anderson et al. 1984b). Thus, being able to perform biochemical studies in a VA-based and -supported laboratory provided guidance and support for the clinical studies related to lowering LDL cholesterol concentrations and ultimately led to improved nutrition management of dyslipidemia for veterans in our clinic and the general population.

The Lexington VAMC provided a milieu that supported excellent research scientists and graduate students. Using our animal models and human veteran volunteers, we were able to explore the potential antioxidant benefits of vitamin E and soy protein on lipoprotein oxidation. Oxidation of LDL appears to contribute importantly to the pathogenesis of atherosclerosis (Steinberg et al. 1989). With the rat model we documented that administration of vitamin E or soy protein decreased all parameters of lipoprotein oxidation, specifically decreasing LDL oxidation by approximately 30 percent (Anderson, Diwadkar & Bridges 1998). Extending these observations to the diabetes clinic, we documented that the LDL particles from diabetic patients were more extensively oxidized than those of nondiabetic control volunteers (Diwadkar et al. 1999; Anderson et al. 1999b). Furthermore, providing vitamin E supplementation significantly decreased LDL of diabetic patients (Anderson et al. 1999b). These research observations led me to recommend that my diabetic patients take vitamin E supplementation and guided my recommendations for diabetic patients (Anderson & Geil 1994; Anderson 2006) and other adults (Anderson & Breecher 1996) about the use of vitamin E and reduction of risk for cardiovascular disease.

Abnormally low serum HDL cholesterol values are a significant risk factor for coronary heart disease (Anderson & Konz 2001; Rubins & Robins 2000). In addition to the common occurrence of low HDL cholesterol values, the chemical composition of HDL is altered in diabetes (Gowri et al. 1999). Using in vitro techniques and sophisticated measurements, we documented that HDL particles from diabetic subjects have a variety of function and chemical abnormalities that reduce their ability to protect from atherosclerotic processes compared to nondiabetic controls (Gowri et al. 1999). Although we do not have specific interventions documented to reverse these abnormalities, they have prompted us to encourage our diabetic patients to follow an array of lifestyle procedures (diet and physical activity), antioxidant supplementation, and pharmacotherapy (Rubins et al. 2002) to reduce their risks for cardiovascular disease.

Comments

The Lexington VAMC and the VA Merit Review Program have supported our activities to examine effective therapeutic approaches to lipoprotein risk factors for cardiovascular disease and potential mechanisms of actions of these interventions. These studies indicate that viscous soluble fibers—such as oat bran, beans, and psyllium—effectively decrease serum LDL cholesterol values. Diets rich in dietary fiber from insoluble (e.g., wheat bran) and soluble fiber (e.g., citrus pectin) coupled with decreased dietary fat act to significantly decrease fasting serum triglycerides. High-carbohydrate, high-fiber diets coupled with increased physical activity increase serum HDL cholesterol concentrations; these effects are enhanced by weight loss.

Mechanistic studies indicate that increased fecal excretion of bile acids contributes importantly to the hypocholesterolemic effects of soluble fiber; propionate resulting from fermentation of soluble fibers in the colon is absorbed into the portal circulation and acts to inhibit hepatic cholesterol synthesis. Abnormally high oxidation of LDL particles appears to contribute to accelerated atherosclerosis in diabetic individuals and can be attenuated by vitamin

E supplementation. We have documented chemical and functional abnormalities of HDL particles from diabetic individuals and explored therapeutic approaches to improve HDL function for diabetic individuals. The ability to explore functional abnormalities of diabetic patients at our VAMC and test interventional strategies for these individuals on the SDTU research ward and in our biochemistry and animal laboratories has enhanced our primary care delivery to our veteran patients.

Assessing the Role of Dietary Protein and Monounsaturated Fats for Diabetic Individuals

Glycemic Effects of Protein Intake

Nuttall at the Minneapolis VAMC has made important contributions to our understanding of the beneficial effects of protein intake in reducing postprandial glycemia and insulinemia (Nuttall et al. 1983; Nuttall et al. 1984). The Minneapolis VA team documented that higher protein intakes led to short-term improvement in glycemic control for patients with type 2 diabetes (Gannon et al. 2003; Nuttall & Gannon 2006). This laid the foundations for further work indicating that protein intake had important satiating effects that are probably mediated by the response of gut hormones involved in regulation of appetite and satiation (Lomenick et al. 2009). While Nuttall has documented that providing up to 30 percent of energy from protein does not have adverse effects on renal function for diabetic individuals with normal renal function (Gannon et al. 2003; Nuttall & Gannon 2006), he has noted slight increases in serum creatinine values (Nuttall & Gannon 2006). Our research team has expressed concern about chronic intake of high protein diets, because these are usually associated with high intakes of atherogenic fat and cholesterol and may enhance the risk for renal failure (Anderson 1993; Anderson et al. 1998).

Benefits of Soy Protein for Diabetic Patients with Nephropathy

Soy protein foods have many beneficial effects on kidney function. Soy protein intake slows or prevents development of renal disease in several different animal models, has favorable effects on renal blood flow and glomerular filtration rate in humans, and improves renal function of diabetic individuals with nephropathy (Anderson 2008). Based on this prior work, we began pilot studies in the Lexington SDTU with diabetic patients with proteinuria or impaired renal function. Our preliminary work led to the "soy-protein hypothesis," suggesting that substitution of soy protein for animal protein in the diet of diabetic individuals would result in less hyperfiltration and glomerular hypertension, leading to prevention or reversal of diabetic nephropathy (Anderson et al. 1998). Further observations in a controlled clinical trial of diabetic individuals with type 1 diabetes who had abnormally high glomerular filtration rates (hyperfiltration) supported this hypothesis, but longer-term studies are required (Stephenson et al. 2005). For ten years we have used this guidance from the VA studies to manage diabetic individuals who develop microalbuminuria, the first signs of diabetic nephropathy.

Effects of Substituting Monounsaturated Fats for Saturated and Polyunsaturated Fats

Garg, Grundy, and Unger from the Dallas VAMC have proposed that substitution of monounsaturated fats for carbohydrate in the diet of diabetic individuals may improve glycemic control and improve dyslipidemia (Garg et al. 1988; Garg, Grundy & Unger 1992). These recommendations have not been widely implemented in the nutritional management of diabetes, but may have a specific role for certain types of dyslipidemia. This group has also reported the beneficial effects of a high-carbohydrate, high-fiber diet for individuals with type 2 diabetes (Chandalia et al. 2000). Thus from Seattle to Lexington and from Minneapolis to Dallas, there has been a good dialogue between VAMCs related to the macronutrient composition—carbohydrate, protein, and fat—of the nutrition plan to be recommended for diabetic individuals.

Comments

Studies from multiple VAMCs have examined the nutritional composition of the diet for diabetic patients and presented data on total protein content, soy protein intake, and use of monounsaturated fats. Each of these areas of investigation has contributed to our tailoring of the nutrition prescription in the care of our veteran patients. Increased protein intake offers benefits during weight loss because of the satiating effects of protein as part of a hypocaloric diet. Soy protein intake has many health benefits for diabetic patients by preserving renal function, favorably affecting major lipoprotein risk factors—serum LDL cholesterol, HDL cholesterol, and triglycerides (Anderson, Johnstone & Cook-Newell 1995)—and lowering blood pressure. Substituting monounsaturated fats for saturated and polyunsaturated fats favorably affects serum LDL-cholesterol levels; substituting monounsaturated fats for a small percentage of carbohydrate, especially simple carbohydrate, has a favorable or neutral effect on glycemic control. Again, clinical research studies from various VAMCs have provided direction as we tailor the nutrition prescription for the veteran with diabetes.

Contributions of VA Cooperative Studies to Diabetes Management

Antiplatelet Agents for Diabetic Patients

Colwell from the Charleston, SC VAMC initiated and led an early VA Cooperative Study (VACS) called "VACS on Anti-platelet Agents in Diabetic Patients after Amputation for Gangrene." Because blood platelets were suspected to have a role in the pathogenesis of atherosclerosis and because platelet function is altered in diabetes, the hypothesis being tested was that anti-platelet therapy would reduce progression of atherosclerosis in diabetic individuals. This study assessed major outcome variables for 231 men with type 2 diabetes who presented with gangrene or had had amputations for gangrene. The primary endpoints were death from atherosclerotic disease or amputation of the opposite extremity for gangrene. The effects of aspirin (325 mg) plus dipyridamole (75 mg), each given three times daily, were compared to placebo (Colwell et al. 1984). The study concluded that anti-platelet agents had no effect on the primary vascular endpoints, vascular deaths and/or amputation of the opposite extremity (Colwell et al. 1986). Further analyses indicated that sudden deaths were significantly more common in the aspirin plus dipyridamole group (p = 0.001), but the total deaths from atherosclerotic vascular disease and deaths from all causes did not differ significantly between the two groups (Colwell et al. 1989). Although this study was not associated with the expected favorable outcome, it did identify a group of VA staff physicians who would participate in a series of further VACS.

Implanted Insulin Pump Study

Duckworth from the Omaha VAMC played a major role in the VA Implantable Insulin Pump Study (Duckworth et al. 1998). Since about one-third of type 2 diabetic individuals are treated with insulin, this study compared the efficacy and safety of implantable insulin pump (IIP) therapy with multiple daily insulin (MDI) injections. This was the first randomized, controlled study to evaluate IIP compared to MDI. After enrolling 121 men with type 2 diabetes, they were randomized to IIP or MDI arms. The major objectives were to compare glycemic control, frequency of hypoglycemia, weight change, quality of life, and adverse events over a one-year period (Saudek et al. 1996).

The insulin pumps were 2 cm by 8 cm in diameter and 2 cm in thickness with a weight of 220 grams; they were implanted subcutaneously in the abdomen under local or general anesthesia. Subjects used an external telemetry system to regulate basal insulin infusion rates and premeal bolus doses of insulin. The IIPs were refilled with insulin every four to twelve weeks transcutaneously. Mean values for fasting blood glucose and hemoglobin A1c values were lower with IIP than with MDI therapy, but these differences were not significant. Self-monitored blood glucose values were significantly lower with IIP than with MDI (P < 0.001). Patients with IIP had significantly fewer hypoglycemic episodes than those with MDI therapy. While patients using MDI had a significant weight gain (>3 kg) in one year, those using IIP therapy had no weight gain (P = 0.003 for difference in weight gain) (Saudek et al. 1996). Of additional interest, IIP therapy was associated with slightly lower systolic and diastolic blood pressure values and with a lower requirement for antihypertensive medications (Duckworth et al. 1998). This study developed the diabetes management strategy and collaborative effort between VAMC investigators that was used extensively in the Veterans Affairs Diabetes Trial (Duckworth et al. 2009).

HDL Intervention Trial

Drs. Sander and Robins, of the Boston VAMC, and Hanna Rubins, of the Minneapolis VAMC, codirected the VA HDL Intervention Trial (VA HIT) (Rubins et al. 1999). This was the first study to critically examine the question of whether therapy aimed at increasing HDL cholesterol concentrations for persons with low values would affect coronary heart disease events. Though not focused specifically on diabetic individuals, this study enrolled a large number of diabetic subjects and enrolled subjects with low HDL cholesterol values, a dyslipidemia that is common among diabetic individuals (Rubins et al. 2002). This landmark study recruited 2,531 men with coronary heart disease at twenty VAMCs. Men with fasting serum HDL-cholesterol values of 40 mg/dl or less, LDL cholesterol values of 140 mg/dl or less, and triglyceride values of 300 mg/dl or less were randomized to placebo or gemfibrozil, an agent that selectively increases HDL cholesterol while decreasing triglyceride values. After one year, in the gemfibrozil group average HDL cholesterol values were 6 percent higher and triglyceride values were 31 percent lower, while LDL cholesterol values were unchanged compared to baseline values. Throughout the five-year follow-up period, these differences from baseline were maintained, while values in the control group did not change significantly. Major cardiovascular events were reduced by 21 to 24 percent in the gemfibrozil group compared to the placebo group. Specifically, nonfatal myocardial infarcts, strokes, and deaths from coronary heart disease or stroke were all significantly lower in treatment than in placebo groups (Rubins et al. 1999). A subgroup analysis of diabetic patients included in this study indicated that they had an even greater reduction in events, with a 41 percent reduction in events for those in the gemfibrozil group compared to those in the placebo group (Rubins et al. 2002). This impactful study indicated that intervention in persons with low HDL cholesterol and high triglyceride values to reverse these lipoprotein abnormalities was as effective in reducing cardiovascular events as are interventions with statin drugs to manage individuals with abnormally high LDL cholesterol values (Rubins et al. 1999).

Diabetes Control and Cardiovascular Complications

The recently completed Veterans Affairs Diabetes Trial (VADT) addressed the controversial question of whether intensive glycemic control reduces risk for cardiovascular events for veterans with type 2 diabetes (Abraira et al. 2003a; Duckworth et al. 2009). Drawing on the experience and expertise from previous VACS, Duckworth and Abraira recruited nineteen VAMC sites for this intensive study, which randomized 1,791 veterans and followed them for up to eight years (median, 5.6 years). The primary outcome was the time of occurrence of a cardiovascular event. Poorly controlled diabetic patients, with a mean age of sixty years, were randomized to standard or intensive glucose control with the intention to equivalently control nondiabetic risk factors such as weight, blood pressure, and serum lipoproteins. An impressive 86 percent of patients completed the study or reached an endpoint. As planned, equivalent blood pressure and serum lipoprotein values within the target range were achieved in both groups. Weight gain in the intensive glycemic control group (18 pounds) was significantly greater than in the control group (9 pounds, P = 0.01). Hemoglobin A1c values decreased initially in both groups and stabilized between six and seventy-eight months. With regular coaching and encouragement from the staff at the Coordinating Center, physicians and nurses at the VAMC sites were able to achieve and sustain the targeted difference in hemoglobin A1c values of 1.5 percent between groups after the first six months. Median hemoglobin A1c values were 8.4 percent in the control group and 6.9 percent in the intensive treatment group. The rates of cardiovascular events did not differ significantly between groups, and the hazard ratio (intensive to control group) was 1.07 (P = 0.62). There were no observed differences between groups for microvascular events. Adverse events, predominantly hypoglycemia, were 17.6 percent in the standard-therapy group and

24.1 percent in the intensive-therapy group (Duckworth et al. 2009). Thus, this persuasive study indicated that, for middle-aged diabetic subjects with type 2 diabetes, intensive glycemic control neither increased nor decreased risk for cardiovascular events over a six-year period of follow-up.

Comments

VA has been fortunate to be able to establish a milieu to attract and retain multitalented staff physicians who have made important contributions in laboratory science, clinical research, VACS leadership, being presidents of national societies, and chairing nutrition advisory committees. Colwell and Nuttall are examples of physicians who have provided leadership in all these areas. This may be related to the provision of research laboratories and Merit Review funding, SDTUs at some facilities, hospitals and medical clinics where physicians can bring their laboratory findings to the bedside, and, conversely, where they can take their patient-induced questions to the research ward or the laboratory. The VACS program seems to have been especially cost-effective, as three of the four VACS described above have had major impacts on clinical care for persons with diabetes. Based on my experience as principal investigator in more than 200 clinical trials, serving as site principal investigator for the four VACS described above, as site principal investigator on several NIH-funded clinical trials, and on many NIH review panels, my assessment is that the VACS program has been conducted at a fraction of the cost per subject compared to large, multisite NIH clinical trials. Thus, VA has established a model to very efficiently address clinical care issues related to diabetes management.

VA's Contribution to Evidence-Based Medicine Related to Diabetes

Much of medical practice is based on experience and a consensus among practitioners regarding the best approaches to management of specific problems. *Experience-based medicine* has guided most areas of medical practice for millennia. However, bias can affect these practices. Many advocates with vested interests—pharmaceutical companies, technology companies, the food industry, insurance companies, hospital practices—as well as reimbursement issues affect medical practice. For example, if someone presents in the emergency room with chest pain and there are electrocardiogram changes or blood chemistry abnormalities, a cardiac catheterization may be justified by *evidence-based* practice (Hemingway et al. 2008; Faxon 2008; Patel et al. 2010). If cardiac catheterization shows significant coronary atherosclerosis, one or more drug-eluting stents may be inserted. All of these procedures are justified by current *experience-based* guidelines. However, this decision-making process is affected by "education" from stent manufacturer representatives, reimbursement considerations, and, sometimes, consultancy arrangements. Recent reports indicate that only one-third of patients without known disease who underwent coronary angiography had obstructive coronary heart disease (Patel et al. 2010). *Evidence-based medicine* guidance is required to make optimal decisions related to patient welfare and healthcare costs (Ho, Peterson & Masoudi 2008; Cope & Allison 2010). Some of the recent VA-based studies addressing issues related to care of diabetic patients will be reviewed.

Cardiovascular Disease

As technology developed for balloon angioplasty, coronary artery stents, and then drug-eluting stents, these procedures were adopted and became widely used. Because these were very remunerative procedures for invasive cardiologists and their use had a good safety profile, their use spread widely and was implemented earlier and earlier in the treatment of coronary artery disease. An estimated 1 million stents are inserted in the United States annually (Winstein 2010). Their use was *experience-based*; *evidence-based* guidelines are still evolving and being debated. Obviously, it is difficult for the experts— invasive cardiologists—to reach unbiased decisions regarding the *evidence basis* for their use and to implement these recommendations into firm practice guidelines (Weintraub 2007). Several VA studies have provided strong guidance in directing optimal care in this area (Ward et al. 2006; Boden et al. 2007). The "COURAGE" study, headed by VA physician William Boden, randomized VA patients with significant coronary artery disease to percutaneous coronary intervention (PCI with balloon angioplasty and/or stent placement) or optimal medical therapy. Patients were followed for a mean of 4.7 years. The results indicated that PCI did not reduce the risk of death, myocardial infarction, or other cardiovascular events compared to optimal medical therapy (Boden et al. 2007). It is estimated that the healthcare cost savings would exceed $5 billion per year in the United States if physicians followed the evidence presented in the "COURAGE" study (Winstein 2010).

Statin drugs are widely used for management of hypercholesterolemia in diabetic and nondiabetic patients. Many of my patients present with LDL cholesterol values of 30 to 60 mg/dl, values with which their cardiologists are pleased, but which put them at risk for neurologic complications. Recognition of statin-associated neuropathy, loss of cognitive function, and an amyotrophic lateral sclerosis–like syndrome is increasing (Golomb 2005; de Langen & van

Puijenbroek 2006; Edwards, Star & Kiuru 2007; Elias et al. 2005; Muldoon et al. 2004). The *evidence base* is strong for setting target LDL cholesterol values of approximately 70 mg/dl for individuals with established coronary heart disease under the age of seventy years (Grundy et al. 2004). However, there is no solid evidence that individuals over the age of seventy years derive benefits from lowering serum LDL cholesterol values below 100 mg/dl (Carey 2008; Golomb 2005). Rodney Hayward, MD, at the VAMC in Ann Arbor, has reviewed recommendations regarding statin use carefully and made stronger *evidenced-based* recommendations; however, the *experience-based* practice employed by many cardiologists and internists utilizes statin drugs and doses more heavily than supported by scientific evidence (Hayward et al. 2010; Mathews 2010). The VA-HIT Study provided a solid evidence base for using pharmacotherapy to increase serum HDL cholesterol values for individuals with suboptimal levels. (Rubins et al. 1999) Similar carefully designed, unbiased studies with rigorous monitoring of side effects are required to establish an evidence basis for achieving different target LDL cholesterol levels, especially in older individuals.

In the past two decades many new classes of pharmaceutical agents have been developed to manage hypertension, a common cardiovascular risk factor in diabetic individuals. Often newer brand-named agents replace equally effective generic agents because of successful "education" by pharmaceutical companies. As an example, in the last year I received prescriptions for brand-name drugs with monthly costs of $199 and $289 for two different conditions; with a little research I found that effective generic agents were available for $10 and $19 monthly. Recently a physician friend and therapist recommended that I get my prescriptions filled at his large multispecialty private clinic rather than at Wal-Mart or Walgreens, because his pharmacy was "more reliable." These are real-life examples of how ethical, principled physicians direct patients to choices that are more expensive for the patient or payer. The VA-led ALLHAT documented the efficacy of generic hydrochlorothiazide as an effective first line choice for treatment of hypertension and provided a strong evidence basis for this recommendation (Appel 2002).

Obesity

The prevalence of obesity in the VA population is slightly higher than in the U.S. adult population. Among 93,290 women American veterans, 68.4 percent were overweight (BMI >25 kg/m^2), 37.4 percent were obese (BMI >30 kg/m^2), and 6.0 percent were severely obese (BMI >40 kg/m^2). Among 1,710,032 male American veterans, 73.0 percent were overweight

(BMI >25 kg/m^2), 32.9 percent were obese (BMI >30 kg/m^2), and 3.3 percent were severely obese (BMI >40 kg/m^2)(Das et al. 2005). Steven Yevich, a VA physician, has spearheaded efforts to assess and improve weight management for these veterans with obesity and related comorbidities. Initially, a comprehensive survey of weight control practices at VA facilities was performed (Wang et al. 2005). In response to the needs, a comprehensive Weight Management Program for Veterans (MOVE!) was developed after consultation with an expert advisory panel, on which I served. After testing the program's feasibility at seventeen VHA sites, the program was refined and disseminated nationally in January 2006. By June 2008 more than 100,000 patients had participated (Kinsinger et al. 2009). This program provides another example of the VA system instituting well-designed, planned, and tested programs into the practical management of health problems.

Behavioral management of all obese individuals is the treatment of choice (Anderson et al. 2007; Anderson, Conley & Nicholas 2007; Furlow & Anderson 2009). Pharmacotherapy is the second treatment of choice, but effective agents are not available. Fenfluramine was approved by the U.S. FDA in 1973 but had to be withdrawn in 1997 because of cardiac toxicity (Roth 2007). Rimonobant, initially approved for use in eighteen countries, was extensively tested in the United States and submitted to the FDA, but approval was denied in 2007 (Fong & Heymsfield 2009). As a principal investigator at our clinical site, I am aware that the company aggressively resisted the reporting of adverse psychiatric events, and these effects were only documented when FDA auditors visited sites to collect this information.

Currently, as in other areas, pharmaceutical companies carefully control data published from clinical trials (Vedula et al. 2009). In 1997 I proposed a study to evaluate the efficacy and safety of sibutramine for long-term maintenance of weight loss; I served as coordinator investigator for this study, which recruited 460 subjects at twenty-six sites. The study was completed in 2003, and the final report was completed by the company in 2005. Subsequently, with access to all the data, I completed a draft manuscript in 2008 that has been reviewed multiple times by the company, and the final draft was essentially approved in mid-2009. However, the company has not allowed me to submit the manuscript. This important study, with unique follow-up data for more than 300 volunteers for three to seven years, has not been submitted for publication because of company decisions that are unclear to me. So pharmacotherapy is potentially the second treatment of choice for virtually all obese subjects, as it is for hypertension after lifestyle changes, but adverse effects of previous agents and lack of complete and accurate reporting of data have severely sensitized the FDA to the extent that it will be reluctant to approve any of the three agents under review now. When appropriate agents become available, it is likely that the VA physicians will evaluate them in a comprehensive and responsible manner, as they have done for diabetes, hypertension, and dyslipidemia, following the MOVE! model (Kinsinger et al. 2009).

Bariatric surgery has emerged as a widely used intervention for obese individuals; an estimated 220,000 procedures are currently performed annually (Blackburn, Hu & Hutter 2009). Although we have suggested that intensive behavioral management should be the initial intervention for severe obesity (Anderson, Conley & Nicholas 2007; Anderson et al. 2007), currently the *evidence-based* recommendations are that bariatric surgery is the treatment of choice for severely obese individuals and may be considered for moderately obese individuals: body mass index (BMI) values of 35.0 to 39.9 kg/m^2 (National Institutes of Health Consensus Development Panel 1991; Wadden & Tsai 2006). Roux-en-Y gastric bypass (RYGB) is the most effective and *evidence-based* procedure for effective and long-term management of severe obesity (Sjostrom et al. 2007). However, because laparoscopic adjustable gastric banding is much easier and quicker to perform and has lower morbidity and mortality, it is becoming the most popular procedure in the United States. Experimental procedures such as mini-gastrectomy (Armstrong 2005) and sleeve gastrectomies are growing in popularity, but there is minimal scientific data to support an evidence-based recommendation for performance of different bariatric procedures (Mechanick et al. 2009). Despite recent guidelines indicating that evidence-based information does not justify bariatric surgery for individuals with BMIs of < 32 kg/m^2, nonobese individuals (with BMI values as low as 23.4 kg/m^2) with type 2 diabetes in Brazil are undergoing gastric sleeve operations (DePaula et al. 2008). VA physicians are making important contributions to the bariatric surgery field by carefully and accurately assessing morbidity and mortality from various procedures (Lautz et al. 2007; Alami et al. 2005; Arterburn et al. 2009; Deveney 2009; Huerta et al. 2007). Unfortunately, anecdotal, self-reported adverse event rates based on case reviews of individual or groups of surgeons tend to substantially underestimate rates observed with controlled clinical trials and rigorous prospective studies carried out in line with FDA guidance for clinical trials (Lautz et al. 2007).

Diabetes

VACS related to diabetes and dyslipidemia carried out under VA leadership have provided comprehensive efficacy and safety evaluations and accurate reporting without evidence of bias from pharmaceutical companies

(Duckworth et al. 2009; Rubins et al. 1999). The role of a pharmaceutical company in selective reporting of clinical trial data was recently reviewed (Vedula et al. 2009). I have served as a consultant to Cargill related to glucosamine hydrochloride and its effects on glucose metabolism since 2003 and have carefully tracked studies related to the safety and efficacy of glucosamine, a popular nutritional supplement taken to relieve the symptoms of osteoarthritis (Anderson, Nicolosi & Borzelleca 2005). Because of its widespread use as a nutritional supplement, the NIH commissioned a clinical trial to assess the safety and efficacy of glucosamine for painful knee osteoarthritis. Because Pfizer, the largest pharmaceutical company in the world, distributed a branded drug—celecoxib (Celebrex®)—used to manage osteoarthritis, it persuaded the NIH to include celecoxib as a comparator. The results of the Glucosamine/chondroitin Arthritis Trial (GAIT) were reported in the *New England Journal of Medicine* in 2006 (Clegg et al. 2006). Of interest, eleven of the twenty physician authors acknowledged that they had received financial support from Pfizer. For all randomized patients, celecoxib offered significantly better pain relief than glucosamine or a combination of glucosamine/chondroitin. However, for patients with moderate-to-severe pain, the combination offered significantly better pain relief (P = 0.002) than celecoxib, which had a nonsignificant effect (P = 0.06). This lack of effect of celecoxib and the benefits of glucosamine/chondroitin were minimized in the final report (Clegg et al. 2006) and denied by Dr. Clegg, the senior author, at his presentation at the American College of Rheumatology in November 2005. Subsequently rheumatology experts have minimized the effects of glucosamine/chondroitin in later review articles (Lozada 2007; Hampton 2007). It seems likely that bias could have affected these unbalanced reports. This study highlights the challenges associated with clinical trials with pharmaceutical industry involvement and contrasts them with the unbiased reporting associated with the VACS clinical trials that I have participated in (Colwell et al. 1989; Duckworth et al. 1998; Rubins et al. 1999; Duckworth et al. 2009).

Comments

VA has played a leadership role in conducting rigorous randomized clinical trials to establish *evidence-based* data for the management of diabetes and its comorbidities, such as atherosclerotic cardiovascular disease, dyslipidemia, hypertension, and obesity over the past thirty years. These objective studies, which show little evidence of bias, have counterbalanced studies supported by pharmaceutical companies, device manufacturers, invasive cardiologists, and bariatric surgeons. These VA-based studies have reliably provided information on efficacy and adverse effects related to pharmaceutical, procedural, and surgical interventions.

Conclusions

In the last quarter of the twentieth century VA attracted and nurtured a rather unique group of gifted diabetologists who also had clinical trial skills and biochemistry laboratory experience. These physicians directed research teams that advanced knowledge in their own areas of research and also teamed with like-minded individuals to conduct important clinical trials. Ideally, medical practice should be based on *evidence-based guidance* rather than anecdotal information. Unfortunately, strong evidence-based guidelines are not available for most areas of clinical practice, so most therapeutic interventions are based on *experience-based guidance* rather than on strong scientific data. Unfortunately, food industry groups—such as beef and dairy advocates—strongly affect dietary guidelines, and the pharmaceutical industry strongly influences therapeutic decisions. The effects of accepting the "old wives' tale" that diabetic individuals should minimize consumption of carbohydrates are summarized above. The VA system has been instrumental in developing evidence-based guidances in several areas related to diabetes. These relate to diabetes diets, treatment of ischemic limbs, use of implantable insulin pumps, pharmacotherapy of dyslipidemia, pharmacotherapy of hypertension, comparisons of interventions for CHD, bariatric procedures, and intensive management of glycemia in type 2 diabetes. The VA system has a unique opportunity to continue to provide leadership in developing evidence-based guidelines for the management of type 2 diabetes and obesity.

References

Abraira, C., Duckworth, W., McCarren, M., Emanuele, N., Arca, D., Reda, D. & Henderson, W. (2003a). Design of the Cooperative Study on glycemic control and complications in diabetes mellitus type 2: Veterans Affairs Diabetes Trial. *Journal of Diabetes Complications* 17: 314–322.

Alami, R. S., Morton, J. M., Sanchez, B. R., Curet, M. J., Wren, S. M. & Safadi, B. Y. (2005). Laparoscopic Roux-en-Y gastric bypass at a Veterans Affairs and high-volume academic facilities: A comparison of institutional outcomes. *American Journal of Surgery* 190: 821–825.

American Diabetes Association. (2004). Nutrition principles and recommendations in diabetes. *Diabetes Care* 27: S36–S46.

American Diabetes Association. (2010). Standards of medical care in diabetes—2010. *Diabetes Care* 33: S11–S61.

Anderson, J. W. (1974a). Alterations in metabolic fate of glucose in the liver of diabetic animals. *American Journal of Clinical Nutrition* 27: 746–755.

Anderson, J. W. (1974b). Glucose metabolism in jejunal mucosa of fed, fasted, and streptozotocin-diabetic rats. *American Journal of Physiology* 226: 226–229.

Anderson, J. W. (1974c). Influence of high carbohydrate diets on glucose tolerance of normal and diabetic men. In *Proceedings of the International Sugar Research Symposium, Washington, DC.* Washington, DC: International Sugar Research Symposium.

Anderson, J. W. (1980a). High-fibre diets for diabetic and hypertriglyceridemic patients. *Canadian Medical Association Journal* 123: 975–979.

Anderson, J. W. (1980b). The role of dietary carbohydrate and fiber in the control of diabetes. *Advances in Internal Medicine* 26: 67–96.

Anderson, J. W. (1983). Plant fiber and blood pressure. *Annals of Internal Medicine* 98: 842–846.

Anderson, J. W. (1984). *User's guide to HCF diets.* 2nd ed. Lexington, KY: HCF Nutrition Research Foundation, Inc.

Anderson, J. W. (1985). High-fiber diets for obese diabetic men on insulin therapy: Short-term and long-term effects. In P. Bjoerntorp, G. V. Vahouny & D. Kritchevsky (Eds.), *Dietary fiber and obesity* (pp. 49–68). New York: Alan R. Liss, Inc.

Anderson, J. W. (1986). *Nutrition management of metabolic conditions: Professional guide to HCF diets.* Lexington, KY: HCF Nutrition Research Foundation, Inc., 1–139.

Anderson, J. W. (1990). *Plant fiber in foods.* 2nd ed. Lexington, KY: HCF Nutrition Research Foundation, Inc.

Anderson, J. W. (1993). Why do diabetic individuals eat so much protein and fat? *Medicine, Exercise, Nutrition and Health* 2: 65–68.

Anderson, J. W. (1995). *Professional guide to high fiber fitness plan.* Lexington, KY: HCF Nutrition Research Foundation, Inc.

Anderson, J. W. (2000). Dietary fiber prevents carbohydrate-induced hypertriglyceridemia. *Current Atherosclerosis Reports* 2: 536–541.

Anderson, J. W. (2006). Diabetes mellitus: Medical nutrition therapy. In M. E. Shils, M. Shike, A. C. Ross, B. Caballero & R. J. Cousins (Eds.), *Modern nutrition in health and disease,* 10th ed. (pp. 1043–1066). Philadelphia: Lea & Febiger.

Anderson, J. W. (2008). Beneficial effects of soy protein consumption for renal function. *Asia Pacific Journal of Clinical Nutrition* 17 (Supp. 1): 324–328.

Anderson, J. W. (2009). All fibers are not created equal. *Journal of Medicine* 2: 87–91.

Anderson, J. W., Akanji, A. O. & Randles, K. M. (2001). Treatment of diabetes with high fiber diets. In G. A. Spiller (Ed.), *Dietary fiber in human nutrition,* 3rd ed. (pp. 363–390). Boca Raton, FL: CRC Press.

Anderson, J. W., Allgood, L. D., Lawrence, A., Altringer, L. A., Jerdack, G. R., Hengehold, D. A. & Morel, J. G. (2000a). Cholesterol-lowering effects of psyllium intake adjunctive to diet therapy in men and women with hypercholesterolemia:

Meta-analysis of 8 controlled trials. *American Journal of Clinical Nutrition* 71: 472–479.

Anderson, J. W., Allgood, L. D., Turner, J., Oeltgen, P. R. & Daggy, B. P. (1999a). Effects of psyllium on glucose and serum lipid responses in men with type 2 diabetes and hypercholesterolemia. *American Journal of Clinical Nutrition* 70: 466–473.

Anderson, J. W., Baird, P., Davis, R. H., Ferreri, S., Knudson, M., Koraym, A., Waters, V. & Williams, C. L. (2009). Health benefits of dietary fiber. *Nutrition Reviews* 67: 188–205.

Anderson, J. W., Blake, J. E., Turner, J. & Smith, B. M. (1998). Effects of soy protein on renal function and proteinuria in patients with type 2 diabetes. *American Journal of Clinical Nutrition* 68: 1347S–1353S.

Anderson, J. W. & Breecher, M. M. (1996). *Dr. Anderson's antioxidant, antiaging health program*. New York: Carroll & Graf.

Anderson, J. W. & Bridges, S. R. (1984). Short-chain fatty acid fermentation products of plant fiber affect glucose metabolism of isolated rat hepatocytes. *Proceedings of the Society for Experimental Biology and Medicine* 177: 372–376.

Anderson, J. W. & Bridges, S. R. (1988). Dietary fiber content of selected foods. *American Journal of Clinical Nutrition* 47: 440–447.

Anderson, J. W., Bridges, S. R., Tietyen, J. & Gustafson, N. J. (1989). Dietary fiber content of a simulated American diet and selected research diets. *American Journal of Clinical Nutrition* 49: 352–357.

Anderson, J. W., Brinkman, V. L. & Hamilton, C. C. (1992). Weight loss and 2–year follow-up for 80 morbidly obese patients treated with intensive very-low-calorie diet and an education program. *American Journal of Clinical Nutrition* 56: 244S–246S.

Anderson, J. W., Brinkman-Kaplan, V., Hamilton, C. C., Logan, J. E., Collins, R. W. & Gustafson, N. J. (1994). Food-containing hypocaloric diets are as effective as liquid-supplement diets for obese individuals with NIDDM. *Diabetes Care* 17: 602–604.

Anderson, J. W. & Bryant, C. A. (1986). Dietary fiber: Diabetes and obesity. *American Journal of Gastroenterology* 81: 898–906.

Anderson, J. W. & Chen, W. J. (1979). Plant fiber: Carbohydrate and lipid metabolism. *American Journal of Clinical Nutrition* 32: 346–363.

Anderson, J. W. & Chen, W. J. L. (1986). Cholesterol-lowering effects of oat products. In F. Webster (Ed.), *Oats: Chemistry and technology* (pp. 309–333). Minneapolis, MN: American Association of Cereal Chemists.

Anderson, J. W., Conley, S. B. & Nicholas, A. S. (2007). One hundred pound weight losses with an intensive behavioral program: Changes in risk factors in 118 patients with long-term follow-up. *American Journal of Clinical Nutrition* 86: 301–307.

Anderson, J. W., Davidson, M. H., Blonde, L., Brown, W. V., Howard, W. J., Ginsberg, H., Allgood, L. D. & Weingand, K. W. (2000b). Long-term cholesterol-lowering effects of psyllium as an adjunct to diet therapy in the treatment of hypercholesterolemia. *American Journal of Clinical Nutrition* 71: 1433–1438.

Anderson, J. W., Diwadkar, V. A. & Bridges, S. R. (1998). Selective effects of different antioxidants on oxidation of lipoproteins from rats. *PSEBM* 218: 376–381.

Anderson, J. W., Ferguson, S. K., Karounos, D., O'Malley, L., Sieling, B. & Chen, W. J. (1980). Mineral and vitamin status on high-fiber diets: Long-term studies of diabetic patients. *Diabetes Care* 3: 38–40.

Anderson, J. W., Floore, T. L., Geil, P. B., O'Neal, D. S. & Balm, T. K. (1991a). Hypocholesterolemic effects of different bulk-forming hydrophilic fibers as adjuncts to dietary therapy in mild to moderate hypercholesterolemia. *Archives of Internal Medicine* 151: 1597–1602.

Anderson, J. W., Garrity, T. F., Wood, C. L., Whitis, S. E., Smith, B. M. & Oeltgen, P. R. (1992a). Prospective, randomized, controlled comparison of the effects of low-fat and low-fat plus high-fiber diets on serum lipid concentrations. *American Journal of Clinical Nutrition* 56: 887–894.

Anderson, J. W. & Geil, P. B. (1994). Nutritional management of diabetes mellitus. In M. E. Shils (Ed.), *Modern Nutrition in Health and Disease*, 8th ed. (pp. 1259–1286). Philadelphia: Lea & Febiger.

Anderson, J. W., Gilinsky, N. H., Deakins, D. A., Smith, S. F., O'Neal, D. S., Dillon, D. W. & Oeltgen, P. R. (1991b). Lipid responses of hypercholesterolemic men to oat-bran and wheat-bran intake. *American Journal of Clinical Nutrition* 54: 678–683.

Anderson, J. W., Gowri, M. S., Turner, J., Nichols, L., Diwadkar, V. A., Chow, C. K. & Oeltgen, P. R. (1999b). Antioxidant supplementation effects on low-density lipoprotein oxidation for individuals with type 2 diabetes mellitus. *Journal of the American College of Nutrition* 18: 451–461.

Anderson, J. W., Grant, L., Gotthelf, L., & Stifler, L. T. (2007). Weight loss and long-term follow-up of severely obese individuals treated with an intense behavioral program. *International Journal of Obesity (London)* 31: 488–493.

Anderson, J. W. & Gustafson, N. J. (1988). Hypocholesterolemic effects of oat and bean products. *American Journal of Clinical Nutrition* 48: 749–753.

Anderson, J. W., Gustafson, N. J., Spencer, D. B., Tietyen, J. & Bryant, C. A. (1990a). Serum lipid response of hypercholesterolemic men to single and divided doses of canned beans. *American Journal of Clinical Nutrition* 51: 1013–1019.

Anderson, J. W., Hamilton, C. C. & Brinkman-Kaplan, V. (1992). Benefits and risks of an intensive very-low-calorie diet program for severe obesity. *American Journal of Gastroenterology* 87: 6–15.

Anderson, J. W., Hamilton, C. C., Crown-Weber, E., Riddlemoser, M. & Gustafson, N. J. (1991c). Safety and effectiveness of a multidisciplinary very-low-calorie diet program for selected obese individuals. *Journal of the American Dietetic Association* 91: 1582–1584.

Anderson, J. W. & Herman, R. H. (1972). Effect of fasting, caloric restriction, and refeeding on glucose tolerance of normal men. *American Journal of Clinical Nutrition* 25: 41–52.

Anderson, J. W., Herman, R. H. & Newcomer, K. L. (1969). Improvement of glucose tolerance of fasting obese patients given oral potassium. *American Journal of Clinical Nutrition* 22: 1589–1596.

Anderson, J. W., Herman, R. H. & Zakim, D. (1973). Effect of high glucose and high sucrose diets on glucose tolerance of normal men. *American Journal of Clinical Nutrition* 26: 600–607.

Anderson, J. W., Johnstone, B. M. & Cook-Newell, M. E. (1995). Meta-analysis of the effects of soy protein intake on serum lipids. *New England Journal of Medicine* 333: 276–282.

Anderson, J. W., Jones, A. E. & Riddell-Mason, S. (1994). Ten different dietary fibers have significantly different effects on serum and liver lipids of cholesterol-fed rats. *Journal of Nutrition* 124: 78–83.

Anderson, J. W., Kendall, C. W. & Jenkins, D. J. (2003). Importance of weight management in type 2 diabetes: Review with meta-analysis of clinical studies. *Journal of the American College of Nutrition* 22: 331–339.

Anderson, J. W. & Konz, E. C. (2001). Obesity and disease management: Effects of weight loss on comorbid conditions. *Obesity Research* 9 (Supp. 4): 326S–334S.

Anderson, J. W. & Konz, E. C. (2005). The use of very-low-calorie diets (VLCDs) and meal replacement use for weight control. In D. Mela (Ed.), *Food, diet and obesity* (pp. 379–411). Cambridge, UK: Woodhead Publishing.

Anderson, J. W., Konz, E. C., Frederich, R. C. & Wood, C. L. (2001). Long-term weight-loss maintenance: A meta-analysis of US studies. *American Journal of Clinical Nutrition* 74: 579–584.

Anderson, J. W., Nicolosi, R. J. & Borzelleca, J. F. (2005). Glucosamine effects in humans: A review of effects on glucose metabolism, side effects, safety considerations and efficacy. *Food and Chemical Toxicology* 43: 187–201.

Anderson, J. W. & Pasupuleti, V. K. (2008). Future trends and directions. In V. K. Pasupuleti & J. W. Anderson (Eds.), *Nutraceuticals, glycemic health and type 2 diabetes,* 1st ed. (pp. 529–535). Ames, IA: Blackwell Publishing Professional.

Anderson, J. W., Randles, K. M., Kendall, C. W. & Jenkins, D. J. (2004). Carbohydrate and fiber recommendations for individuals with diabetes: A quantitative assessment and meta-analysis of the evidence. *Journal of the American College of Nutrition* 23: 5–17.

Anderson, J. W., Riddell-Mason, S., Gustafson, N. J., Smith, S. F. & Mackey, M. (1992b). Cholesterol-lowering effects of psyllium-enriched cereal as an adjunct to a prudent diet in the treatment of mild to moderate hypercholesterolemia. *American Journal of Clinical Nutrition* 56: 93–98.

Anderson, J. W. & Sieling, B. (1980). High fiber diets for obese diabetic patient. *Obesity & Bariatric Medicine* 9: 113.

Anderson, J. W., Sieling, B. & Chen, W. J. L. (1981). *A professional guide to HCF diets.* Lexington, KY: HCF Nutrition Research Foundation, Inc.

Anderson, J. W., Spencer, D. B., Hamilton, C. C., Smith, S. F., Tietyen, J., Bryant, C. A. & Oeltgen, P. (1990b). Oat-bran cereal lowers serum total and LDL cholesterol in hypercholesterolemic men. *American Journal of Clinical Nutrition* 52: 495–499.

Anderson, J. W., Story, L., Sieling, B., & Chen, W. J. L. (1984a). Hypocholesterolemic effects of high-fibre diets rich in water-soluble plant fibres. *Journal of the Canadian Dietetic Association* 45: 140–149.

Anderson, J. W., Story, L., Sieling, B., Chen, W. J., Petro, M. S. & Story, J. (1984b). Hypocholesterolemic effects of oat-bran or bean intake for hypercholesterolemic men. *American Journal of Clinical Nutrition* 40: 1146–1155.

Anderson, J. W. & Tyrrell, J. B. (1973). Hexokinase activity of rat intestinal mucosa: Demonstration of four isozymes and of changes in subcellular distribution with fasting and refeeding. *Gastroenterology* 65: 69–76.

Anderson, J. W., Vichitbandra, S., Qian, W. & Kryscio, R. J. (1999c). Long-term weight maintenance after an intensive weight-loss program. *Journal of the American College of Nutrition* 18: 620–627.

Anderson, J. W. & Ward, K. (1978a). *HCF diets: Guidelines for high carbohydrate, fiber diets.* 1st ed. Lexington, KY: University of Kentucky College of Medicine.

Anderson, J. W. & Ward, K. (1978b). Long-term effects of high-carbohydrate, high-fiber diets on glucose and lipid metabolism: A preliminary report on patients with diabetes. *Diabetes Care* 1: 77–82.

Anderson, J. W. & Ward, K. (1979). High-carbohydrate, high-fiber diets for insulin-treated men with diabetes mellitus. *American Journal of Clinical Nutrition* 32: 2312–2321.

Anderson, J. W. & Zakim, D. (1970). The influence of alloxan-diabetes and fasting on glycolytic and gluconeogenic enzyme activities of rat intestinal mucosa and liver. *Biochimica et Biophysica Acta* 201: 236–241.

Anderson, J. W., Zeigler, J. A., Deakins, D. A., Floore, T. L., Dillon, D. W., Wood, C. L., Oeltgen, P. R. & Whitley, R. J. (1991d). Metabolic effects of high-carbohydrate, high-fiber diets for insulin-dependent diabetic individuals. *American Journal of Clinical Nutrition* 54: 936–943.

Anderson, J. W., Zettwoch, N., Feldman, T., Tietyen-Clark, J., Oeltgen, P. & Bishop, C. W. (1988). Cholesterol-lowering effects of psyllium hydrophilic mucilloid for hypercholesterolemic men. *Archives of Internal Medicine* 148: 292–296.

Andon, M. & Anderson, J. W. (2008). The oatmeal-cholesterol connection: 10 years later. *American Journal of Lifestyle Medicine* 2: 51–57.

Appel, L. J. (2002). The verdict from ALLHAT—thiazide diuretics are the preferred initial therapy for hypertension. *JAMA* 288: 3039–3042.

Armstrong, D. (2005). A doctor's version of obesity surgery raises some bile. *Wall Street Journal*, January 14.

Arterburn, D., Livingston, E. H., Schifftner, T., Kahwati, L. C., Henderson, W. G. & Maciejewski, M. L. (2009). Predictors of long-term mortality after bariatric surgery performed in Veterans Affairs medical centers. *Archives of Surgery* 144: 914–920.

Barnard, R. J., Massey, M. R., Cherny, S., O'Brien, L. T. & Pritikin, N. (1983). Long-term use of a high-complex-carbohydrate, high-fiber, low-fat diet and exercise in the treatment of NIDDM patients. *Diabetes Care* 6: 268–273.

Blackburn, G. L., Hu, F. B. & Hutter, M. M. (2009). Updated evidence-based recommendations for best practices in weight loss surgery. *Obesity (Silver Spring)* 17: 839–841.

Boden, W. E., O'Rourke, R. A., Teo, K. K., Hartigan, P. M., Maron, D. J., Kostuk, W. J., Knudtson, M., Dada, M., Casperson, P., Harris, C. L., Chaitman, B. R., Shaw, L., Gosselin, G., Nawaz, S., Title, L. M., Gau, G., Blaustein, A. S., Booth, D. C., Bates, E. R., Spertus, J. A., Berman, D. S., Mancini, G. B. & Weintraub, W. S. (2007). Optimal medical therapy with or without PCI for stable coronary disease. *New England Journal of Medicine* 356: 1503–1516.

Bridges, S. R., Anderson, J. W., Deakins, D. A., Dillon, D. W. & Wood, C. L. (1992). Oat bran increases serum acetate of hypercholesterolemic men. *American Journal of Clinical Nutrition* 56: 455–459.

Brunzell, J. D., Davidson, M., Furberg, C. D., Goldberg, R. B., Howard, B. V., Stein, J. H. & Witztum, J. L. (2008). Lipoprotein management in patients with cardiometabolic risk: Consensus statement from the American Diabetes Association and the American College of Cardiology Foundation. *Diabetes Care* 31: 811–822.

Brunzell, J. D., Lerner, R. L., Hazzard, W. R., Porte, D. & Bierman, E. L. (1971). Improved glucose tolerance with high carbohydrate feeding in mild diabetes. *New England Journal of Medicine* 284: 521–524.

Brunzell, J. D., Lerner, R. L., Porte, D. & Bierman, E. L. (1974). Effect of a fat free, high carbohydrate diet on diabetic subjects with fasting hyperglycemia. *Diabetes* 23: 138–142.

Burkitt, D. P. & Trowell, H. C. (1975). *Refined carbohydrate foods and diseases: some implications of dietary fibre.* London: Academic Press.

Carey, J. (2008). Do cholesterol drugs do any good? *BusinessWeek*, January 28, 51–59.

Chandalia, M., Garg, A., Lutjohann, D., von, B. K., Grundy, S. M. & Brinkley, L. J. (2000). Beneficial effects of high dietary fiber intake in patients with type 2 diabetes mellitus. *New England Journal of Medicine* 342: 1392–1398.

Chen, W. J. & Anderson, J. W. (1979a). Effects of guar gum and wheat bran on lipid metabolism of rats. *Journal of Nutrition* 109: 1028–1034.

Chen, W. J. & Anderson, J. W. (1979b). Effects of plant fiber in decreasing plasma total cholesterol and increasing high-density lipoprotein cholesterol. *Proceedings of the Society for Experimental Biology and Medicine* 162: 310–313.

Chen, W. J. & Anderson, J. W. (1981). Soluble and insoluble plant fiber in selected cereals and vegetables. *American Journal of Clinical Nutrition* 34: 1077–1082.

Chen, W. J., Anderson, J. W. & Jennings, D. (1984). Propionate may mediate the hypocholesterolemic effects of certain soluble plant fibers in cholesterol-fed rats. *Proceedings of the Society for Experimental Biology and Medicine* 175: 215–218.

Chen, W. J. L., Anderson, J. W. & Gould, M. R. (1981). Effects of oat bran, oat gum and pectin on lipid metabolism of cholesterol-fed rats. *Nutrition Reports International* 24: 1098–1103.

Clegg, D. O., Reda, D. J., Harris, C. L., Klein, M. A., O'Dell, J. R., Hooper, M. M., Bradley, J. D., Bingham, C. O., III, Weisman, M. H., Jackson, C. G., Lane, N. E., Cush, J. J., Moreland, L. W., Schumacher, H. R., Jr., Oddis, C. V., Wolfe, F., Molitor, J. A., Yocum, D. E., Schnitzer, T. J., Furst, D. E., Sawitzke, A. D., Shi, H., Brandt, K. D., Moskowitz, R. W. & Williams, H. J. (2006). Glucosamine, chondroitin sulfate, and the two in combination for painful knee osteoarthritis. *New England Journal of Medicine* 354: 795–808.

Colwell, J. A., Bingham, S. F., Abraira, C., Anderson, J. W., Comstock, J. P., Kwaan, H. C. & Nuttall, F. (1986). Veterans Administration Cooperative Study on antiplatelet agents in diabetic patients after amputation for gangrene: II. Effects of aspirin and dipyridamole on atherosclerotic vascular disease rates. *Diabetes Care* 9: 140–148.

Colwell, J. A., Bingham, S. F., Abraira, C., Anderson, J. W., Comstock, J. P., Kwaan, H. C. & Nuttall, F. (1989). VA Cooperative Study of antiplatelet agents in diabetic patients after amputation for gangrene: Unobserved, sudden, and unexpected deaths. *Journal of Diabetes Complications* 3: 191–197.

Colwell, J. A., Bingham, S. F., Abraira, C., Anderson, J. W. & Kwaan, H. C. (1984). VA Cooperative Study on antiplatelet agents in diabetic patients after amputation for gangrene: I. Design, methods, and baseline characteristics. *Controlled Clinical Trials* 5: 165–183.

Cope, M. B. & Allison, D. B. (2010). White hat bias: Examples of its presence in obesity research and a call for renewed commitment to faithfulness in research reporting. *International Journal of Obesity (London)* 34: 84–88.

Das, S. R., Kinsinger, L. S., Yancy, W. S., Jr., Wang, A., Ciesco, E., Burdick, M. & Yevich, S. J. (2005). Obesity prevalence among veterans at Veterans Affairs medical facilities. *American Journal of Preventive Medicine* 28: 291–294.

de Langen, J. J. & van Puijenbroek, E. P. (2006). HMG-CoA-reductase inhibitors and neuropathy: Reports to the Netherlands Pharmacovigilance Centre. *Netherlands Journal of Medicine* 64: 334–338.

deGroot, A. P., Luyken, R. & Pikaar, N. A. (1963). Cholesterol-lowering effects of rolled oats. *Lancet* 2: 203–204.

DePaula, A. L., Macedo, A. L., Rassi, N., Machado, C. A., Schraibman, V., Silva, L. Q. & Halpern, A. (2008). Laparoscopic treatment of type 2 diabetes mellitus for patients with a body mass index less than 35. *Surgical Endoscopy* 22: 706–716.

Deveney, C. W. (2009). Possible lack of survival advantage for one group: Comment on "Predictors of long-term mortality after bariatric surgery performed in Veterans Affairs medical centers." *Archives of Surgery* 144: 920.

Diwadkar, V. A., Anderson, J. W., Bridges, S. R., Gowri, M. S. & Oelgten, P. R. (1999). Postprandial low-density lipoproteins in type 2 diabetes are oxidized more extensively than fasting diabetes and control samples. *Proceedings of the Society for Experimental Biology and Medicine* 222: 178–184.

Duckworth, W., Abraira, C., Moritz, T., Reda, D., Emanuele, N., Reaven, P. D., Zieve, F. J., Marks, J., Davis, S. N., Hayward, R., Warren, S. R., Goldman, S., McCarren, M., Vitek, M. E., Henderson, W. G., Huang, G. D., Anderson, J. W., et al. (2009). Glucose control and vascular complications in veterans with type 2 diabetes. *New England Journal of Medicine* 360: 129–139.

Duckworth, W. C., Saudek, C. D., Giobbie-Hurder, A., Henderson, W. G., Henry, R. R., Kelley, D. E., Edelman, S. V., Zieve, F. J., Adler, R. A., Anderson, J. W., Anderson, R. J., Hamilton, B. P., Donner, T. W., Kirkman, M. S. & Morgan, N. A. (1998). The Veterans Affairs Implantable Insulin Pump Study: Effect on cardiovascular risk factors. *Diabetes Care* 21: 1596–1602.

Edwards, I. R., Star, K. & Kiuru, A. (2007). Statins, neuromuscular degenerative disease and an amyotrophic lateral sclerosis–like syndrome: An analysis of individual case safety reports from vigibase. *Drug Safety* 30: 515–525.

Elias, P. K., Elias, M. F., D'Agostino, R. B., Sullivan, L. M. & Wolf, P. A. (2005). Serum cholesterol and cognitive performance in the Framingham Heart Study. *Psychosomatic Medicine* 67: 24–30.

Faxon, D. P. (2008). Assessing appropriateness of coronary angiography: Another step in improving quality. *Annals of Internal Medicine* 149: 276–278.

Fong, T. M. & Heymsfield, S. B. (2009). Cannabinoid-1 receptor inverse agonists: Current understanding of mechanism of action and unanswered questions. *International Journal of Obesity (London)* 33: 947–955.

Fukagawa, N. K., Anderson, J. W., Hageman, G., Young, V. R. & Minaker, K. L. (1990). High-carbohydrate, high-fiber diets increase peripheral insulin sensitivity in healthy young and old adults. *American Journal of Clinical Nutrition* 52: 524–528.

Furlow, E. A. & Anderson, J. W. (2009). A systematic review of targeted outcomes associated with a medically supervised commercial weight loss program. *Journal of the American Dietetic Association* 109: 1417–1421.

Gannon, M. C., Nuttall, F. Q., Saeed, A., Jordan, K. & Hoover, H. (2003). An increase in dietary protein improves the blood glucose response in persons with type 2 diabetes. *American Journal of Clinical Nutrition* 78: 734–741.

Garg, A., Bonanome, A., Grundy, S. M., Zhang, Z. J. & Unger, R. H. (1988). Comparison of a high-carbohydrate diet with a high-monounsaturated-fat diet in patients with non-insulin-dependent diabetes mellitus. *New England Journal of Medicine* 319: 829–834.

Garg, A., Grundy, S. M. & Unger, R. H. (1992). Comparison of effects of high and low carbohydrate diets on plasma lipoproteins and insulin sensitivity in patients with mild NIDDM. *Diabetes* 41: 1278–1285.

Genuth, S. (1979). Supplemented fasting in the treatment of obesity and diabetes. *American Journal of Clinical Nutrition* 32: 2579–2586.

Golomb, B. A. (2005). Implications of statin adverse effects in the elderly. *Expert Opinion on Drug Safety* 4: 389–397.

Gould, M. R., Anderson, J. W. & O'Mahouny, S. (1980). Biofunctional properties of oats. In G. E. Inglett & L. Munch (Eds.), *Cereal for food and beverages* (pp. 447–460). New York: Academic Press.

Goulder, T. J., Alberti, K. G. & Jenkins, D. A. (1978). Effect of added fiber on the glucose and metabolic response to a mixed meal in normal and diabetic subjects. *Diabetes Care* 1: 351–355.

Gowri, M. S., Van der Westhuyzen, D. R., Bridges, S. R. & Anderson, J. W. (1999). Decreased protection by HDL from poorly controlled type 2 diabetic subjects against LDL oxidation may be due to the abnormal composition of HDL. *Arteriosclerosis, Thrombosis, and Vascular Biology* 19: 2226–2233.

Grundy, S. M., Cleeman, J. I., Merz, C. N., Brewer, H. B., Clark, L. T., Hunninghake, D. B., Pasternak, R. C., Smith, S. C., Jr., & Stone, N. J., for the Coordinating Committee of the National Cholesterol Education Program (2004). Implications of recent clinical trials for the National Cholesterol Education Program Adult Treatment Panel III guidelines. *Circulation* 110: 227–239.

Hamdy, O., Goebel-Fabbri, A., Carver, C., Arathuzik, G., Shahar, J., Capleson, R., Beaton, J., O'Donnel, S., Elsayed, N., Mitri, J., Mentzelopoulis, V. & Abrahamson, M. J. (2008). Why WAIT Program: A novel model for diabetes weight management in routine clinical practice. *Obesity Management* 10: 176–183.

Hampton, T. (2007). Efficacy still uncertain for widely used supplements for arthritis. *JAMA* 297: 351–352.

Hayward, R. A., Krumholz, H. M., Zulman, D. M., Timbie, J. W. & Vijan, S. (2010). Optimizing statin treatment for primary prevention of coronary artery disease. *Annals of Internal Medicine* 152: 69–77.

Hemingway, H., Chen, R., Junghans, C., Timmis, A., Eldridge, S., Black, N., Shekelle, P. & Feder, G. (2008). Appropriateness criteria for coronary angiography in angina: Reliability and validity. *Annals of Internal Medicine* 149: 221–231.

Henry, R. R. & Gumbiner, B. (1991). Benefits and limitations of very-low-calorie diet therapy in obese NIDDM. *Diabetes Care* 14: 802–823.

Henry, R. R., Schaeffer, L. & Olefsky, J. M. (1985). Glycemic effects of intensive caloric restriction and isocaloric refeeding in noninsulin-dependent diabetes mellitus. *Journal of Clinical Endocrinology and Metabolism* 61: 917–925.

Henry, R. R., Wallace, P. & Olefsky, J. M. (1986). Effects of weight loss on mechanisms of hyperglycemia in obese non-insulin-dependent diabetes mellitus. *Diabetes* 35: 990–998.

Ho, P. M., Peterson, P. N. & Masoudi, F. A. (2008). Evaluating the evidence: Is there a rigid hierarchy? *Circulation* 118: 1675–1684.

Huerta, S., Kohan, D., Siddiqui, A., Anthony, T. & Livingston, E. H. (2007). Assessment of comorbid conditions in veteran patients after Roux-en-Y gastric bypass. *American Journal of Surgery* 194: 48–52.

Jenkins, D. J., Kendall, C. W., Marchie, A., Jenkins, A. L., Augustin, L. S., Ludwig, D. S., Barnard, N. D. & Anderson, J. W. (2003). Type 2 diabetes and the vegetarian diet. *American Journal of Clinical Nutrition* 78: 610S–616S.

Jenkins, D. J. A., Leeds, A. R. & Gassull, M. A. (1976). Unabsorbable carbohydrates and diabetes: Decreased postprandial hyperglycaemia. *Lancet* 2: 172–174.

Jennings, C. D., Boleyn, K., Bridges, S. R., Wood, P. J. & Anderson, J. W. (1988). A comparison of the lipid-lowering and intestinal morphological effects of cholestyramine, chitosan, and oat gum in rats. *Proceedings of the Society for Experimental Biology and Medicine* 189: 13–20.

Kempner, W. R., Peschel, R. L. & Schlayer, C. (1958). Effect of rice diet on diabetes mellitus associated with vascular disease. *Postgraduate Medicine* 24: 359–364.

Keys, A., Grande, F. & Anderson, J. T. (1961). Fiber and pectin in the diet and serum cholesterol concentration in man. *Proceedings of the Society for Experimental Biology and Medicine* 106: 555–558.

Kiehm, T. G., Anderson, J. W. & Ward, K. (1976). Beneficial effects of a high carbohydrate, high fiber diet on hyperglycemic diabetic men. *American Journal of Clinical Nutrition* 29: 895–899.

Kinsinger, L. S., Jones, K. R., Kahwati, L., Harvey, R., Burdick, M., Zele, V. & Yevich, S. J. (2009). Design and dissemination of the MOVE! Weight-management program for veterans. *Preventing Chronic Disease* 6: A98.

Kirby, R. W., Anderson, J. W., Sieling, B., Rees, E. D., Chen, W. J., Miller, R. E. & Kay, R. M. (1981). Oat-bran intake selectively lowers serum low-density lipoprotein cholesterol concentrations of hypercholesterolemic men. *American Journal of Clinical Nutrition* 34: 824–829.

Klein, S., Sheard, N., Pi-Sunyer, F. X., Daly, A., Wylie-Rosett, J., Kulkarni, K. & Clark, N. (2004). Weight management through lifestyle modification for the prevention and management of type 2 diabetes: Rationale and strategies. *Diabetes Care* 27: 2067–2073.

Lautz, D. B., Jackson, T. D., Clancy, K. A., Escareno, C. E., Schifftner, T., Henderson, W. G., Livingston, E., Rogers, S. O., Jr. & Khuri, S. (2007). Bariatric operations in Veterans Affairs and selected university medical centers: Results of the Patient Safety in Surgery Study. *Journal of the American College of Surgeons* 204: 1261–1272.

Lin, W. J. & Anderson, J. W. (1977). Effects of high sucrose or starch-bran diets on glucose and lipid metabolism of normal and diabetic rats. *Journal of Nutrition* 107: 584–595.

Lindstrom, J., Peltonen, M., Eriksson, J. G., Louheranta, A., Fogelholm, M., Uusitupa, M. & Tuomilehto, J. (2006). High-fibre, low-fat diet predicts long-term weight loss and decreased type 2 diabetes risk: The Finnish Diabetes Prevention Study. *Diabetologia* 49: 912–920.

Lomenick, J. P., Melguizo, M. S., Michell, S. L., Summar, M. & Anderson, J. W. (2009). Effects of meals high in carbohydrate, protein, fat on ghrelin and peptide YY secretion in pre-puberal children. *Journal of Clinical Endocrinology and Metabolism* 94: 4463–4471.

Lozada, C. J. (2007). Glucosamine in osteoarthritis: Questions remain. *Cleveland Clinic Journal of Medicine* 74: 65–71.

Mathews, A. M. (2010). A radical view on giving statins. *Wall Street Journal*, June 15.

Mechanick, J. I., Kushner, R. F., Sugerman, H. J., Gonzalez-Campoy, J. M., Collazo-Clavell, M. L., Spitz, A. F., Apovian, C. M., Livingston, E. H., Brolin, R., Sarwer, D. B., Anderson, W. A., Dixon, J. & Guven, S. (2009). American Association of Clinical Endocrinologists, the Obesity Society, and American Society for Metabolic & Bariatric Surgery medical guidelines for clinical practice for the perioperative nutritional, metabolic, and nonsurgical support of the bariatric surgery patient. *Obesity (Silver Spring)* 17 (Supp. 1): S1–70.

Mensink, R. P. & Katan, M. B. (1992). Effect of dietary fatty acids on serum lipids and lipoproteins: A meta-analysis of 27 trials. *Arteriosclerosis and Thrombosis* 12: 911–919.

Muldoon, M. F., Ryan, C. M., Sereika, S. M., Flory, J. D. & Manuck, S. B. (2004). Randomized trial of the effects of simvastatin on cognitive functioning in hypercholesterolemic adults. *American Journal of Medicine* 117: 823–829.

Murphy, E. D. & Anderson, J. W. (1974). Tissue glycolytic and gluconeogenic enzyme activities in mildly and moderately diabetic rats: Influence of tolbutamide administration. *Endocrinology* 94: 27–34.

National Institutes of Health Consensus Development Panel (1991). Gastrointestinal surgery for severe obesity. *Annals of Internal Medicine* 115: 956–961.

Nuttall, F. Q. & Gannon, M. C. (2006). The metabolic response to a high-protein, low-carbohydrate diet in men with type 2 diabetes mellitus. *Metabolism* 55: 243–251.

Nuttall, F. Q., Mooradian, A. D., DeMarais, R. & Parker, S. (1983). The glycemic effect of different meals approximately isocaloric and similar in protein, carbohydrate, and fat content as calculated using the ADA exchange lists. *Diabetes Care* 6: 432–435.

Nuttall, F. Q., Mooradian, A. D., Gannon, M. C., Billington, C. & Krezowski, P. (1984). Effect of protein ingestion on the glucose and insulin response to a standardized oral glucose load. *Diabetes Care* 7: 465–470.

Olson, B. H., Anderson, S. M., Becker, M. P., Anderson, J. W., Hunninghake, D. B., Jenkins, D. J., LaRosa, J. C., Rippe, J. M., Roberts, D. C., Stoy, D. B., Summerbell, C. D., Truswell, A. S., Wolever, T. M., Morris, D. H. & Fulgoni, V. L., III (1997). Psyllium-enriched cereals lower blood total cholesterol and LDL cholesterol, but not HDL cholesterol, in hypercholesterolemic adults: Results of a meta-analysis. *Journal of Nutrition* 127: 1973–1980.

Parks, E. J. & Hellerstein, M. K. (2000). Carbohydrate-induced hypertriacylglycerolemia: historical perspective and review of biological mechanisms. *American Journal of Clinical Nutrition* 71: 412–433.

Patel, M. R., Peterson, E. D., Dai, D., Brennan, J. M., Redberg, R. F., Anderson, H. V., Brindis, R. G. & Douglas, P. S. (2010). Low diagnostic yield of elective coronary angiography. *New England Journal of Medicine* 362: 886–895.

Porte, D., Jr. (1991). Banting lecture 1990: Beta-cells in type II diabetes mellitus. *Diabetes* 40: 166–180.

Pritikin, N. & McGrady, P. M., Jr. (1979). *The Pritikin program for diet and exercise*. New York: Grosset & Dunlap.

Ramachandran, A. & Viswanathan, M. (1997). Dietary management of diabetes mellitus in India and South East Asia. In K. G. M. M. Alberti, P. Zimmet, R. A. DeFronzo & H. Keen (Eds.), *International textbook of diabetes mellitus*, 2nd ed. (pp. 773–777). New York: John Wiley & Sons.

Reaven, G. M. (1988). Role of insulin resistance in human disease. *Diabetes* 37: 1595–1607.

Roth, B. L. (2007). Drugs and valvular heart disease. *New England Journal of Medicine* 356: 6–9.

Rubins, H. B. & Robins, S. J. (2000). Conclusions from the VA-HIT Study. *American Journal of Cardiology* 86: 543–544.

Rubins, H. B., Robins, S. J., Collins, D., Fye, C. L., Anderson, J. W., Elam, M. B., Faas, F. H., Linares, E., Schaefer, E. J., Schectman, G., Wilt, T. J. & Wittes, J. (1999). Gemfibrozil for the secondary prevention of coronary heart disease in men with low levels of high-density lipoprotein cholesterol. (Veterans Affairs High-Density Lipoprotein Cholesterol Intervention Trial Study Group). *New England Journal of Medicine* 341: 410–418.

Rubins, H. B., Robins, S. J., Collins, D., Nelson, D. B., Elam, M. B., Schaefer, E. J., Faas, F. H. & Anderson, J. W. (2002). Diabetes, plasma insulin, and cardiovascular disease: subgroup analysis from the Department of Veterans Affairs high-density lipoprotein intervention trial (VA-HIT). *Archives of Internal Medicine* 162: 2597–2604.

Saudek, C. D., Duckworth, W. C., Giobbie-Hurder, A., Henderson, W. G., Henry, R. R., Kelley, D. E., Edelman, S. V., Zieve, F. J., Adler, R. A., Anderson, J. W., Anderson, R. J., Hamilton, B. P., Donner, T. W., Kirkman, M. S. & Morgan, N. A. (1996). Implantable insulin pump vs multiple-dose insulin for non-insulin-dependent diabetes mellitus: A randomized clinical trial. (Department of Veterans Affairs Implantable Insulin Pump Study Group). *JAMA* 276: 1322–1327.

Singh, I. (1955). Low-fat diet and therapeutic doses of insulin in diabetes mellitus. *Lancet* 268: 422–425.

Sirtori, C. R., Anderson, J. W. & Arnoldi, A. (2007). Nutritional and nutraceutical considerations for dyslipidemia. *Future Lipidology* 3: 313–339.

Sjostrom, L., Narbro, K., Sjostrom, C. D., Karason, K., Larsson, B., Wedel, H., Lystig, T., Sullivan, M., Bouchard, C., Carlsson, B., Bengtsson, C., Dahlgren, S., Gummesson, A., Jacobson, P., Karlsson, J., Lindroos, A. K., Lonroth, H., Naslund, I., Olbers, T., Stenlof, K., Torgerson, J., Agren, G. & Carlsson, L. M. (2007). Effects of bariatric surgery on mortality in Swedish obese subjects. *New England Journal of Medicine* 357: 741–752.

Steinberg, D., Parthasarathy, S., Carew, T. E., Khoo, J. C. & Witztum, J. L. (1989). Beyond cholesterol: Modifications of low-density lipoprotein that increase its atherogenicity. *New England Journal of Medicine* 320: 915–924.

Stephenson, T. J., Setchell, K. D., Kendall, C. W., Jenkins, D. J., Anderson, J. W. & Fanti, P. (2005). Effect of soy protein-rich diet on renal function in young adults with insulin-dependent diabetes mellitus. *Clinical Nephrology* 64: 1–11.

Story, L., Anderson, J. W., Chen, W. J., Karounos, D. & Jefferson, B. (1985). Adherence to high-carbohydrate, high-fiber diets: Long-term studies of non-obese diabetic men. *Journal of the American Dietetic Association* 85: 1105–1110.

Trowell, H. C. & Burkitt, D. P. (1981). *Western diseases: Their emergence and prevention.* London: Edward Arnold.

Tyrrell, J. B. & Anderson, J. W. (1971). Glycolytic and pentose phosphate pathway enzymes in jejunal mucosa: Adaptive responses to alloxan-diabetes and fasting in the rat. *Endocrinology* 89: 1178–1185.

Unger, R. H. (1976). The Banting memorial lecture 1975: Diabetes and the alpha cell. *Diabetes* 25: 136–151.

Unger, R. H. (1983). The Berson memorial lecture: Insulin-glucagon relationships in the defense against hypoglycemia. *Diabetes* 32: 575–583.

U.S. Department of Health and Human Services, FDA. (1997). Health claims: Oats and coronary heart disease—Final rule. *Federal Register* 62: 3583–3601.

U.S. Department of Health and Human Services, FDA. (1998). Health claims: Soluble fiber from certain foods and coronary heart disease—Final rule. *Federal Register* 63: 8103–8121.

Vedula, S. S., Bero, L., Scherer, R. W. & Dickersin, K. (2009). Outcome reporting in industry-sponsored trials of gabapentin for off-label use. *New England Journal of Medicine* 361: 1963–1971.

Viswanathan, M. (1968). High carbohydrate diet and diabetes. *Journal of the Diabetic Association of India* 8: 353.

Wadden, T. A. & Tsai, A. G. (2006). Bariatric surgery: Crossing a body mass index threshold. *Annals of Internal Medicine* 144: 689–691.

Wang, A., Kinsinger, L. S., Kahwati, L. C., Das, S. R., Gizlice, Z., Harvey, R. T., Burdick, M. B. & Yevich, S. J. (2005). Obesity and weight control practices in 2000 among veterans using VA facilities. *Obesity Research* 13: 1405–1411.

Ward, H. B., Kelly, R. F., Thottapurathu, L., Moritz, T. E., Larsen, G. C., Pierpont, G., Santilli, S., Goldman, S., Krupski, W. C., Littooy, F., Reda, D. J. & McFalls, E. O. (2006). Coronary artery bypass grafting is superior to percutaneous coronary intervention in prevention of perioperative myocardial infarctions during subsequent vascular surgery. *Annals of Thoracic Surgery* 82: 795–800.

Weintraub, A. (2007). Heart trouble. *BusinessWeek,* October 29, 53–60.

Winstein, K. J. (2010). A simple health-care fix fizzles out. *Wall Street Journal,* February 11.

Wong, J. M. W., Josse, A. R., Augustin, A. R., Esfahani, A., Banach, M. S., Kendall, C. W. C. & Jenkins, D. J. A. (2008). Glycemic index and glycemic load: effects on glucose, insulin and lipid regulation. In V. K. Pasupuleti & J. W. Anderson (Eds.), *Nutraceuticals, glycemic health and type 2 diabetes,* 1st ed. (pp. 49–64). Ames, IA: Blackwell Publishing Professional.

Wood, P. D., Anderson, J. W., Braaten, J. T., Cave, N. A., Scott, F. W. & Vachon, C. (1989). Physiological effects of b-D-glucan rich fractions from oats. *Cereal Foods World* 34: 878–882.

Wright, R. S., Anderson, J. W. & Bridges, S. R. (1990). Propionate inhibits hepatocyte lipid synthesis. *Proceedings of the Society for Experimental Biology and Medicine* 195: 26–29.

Chapter 2

Neurological Healthcare for Veterans

Mitchell T. Wallin and John F. Kurtzke

History

The Development of Neurology in the United States

Within the United States, the field of neurology had its start in the latter 1800s. Three major forces were at work to spur its development: European scientific discoveries, medical specialty initiatives in the United States, and the American Civil War (Goetz, Chmura & Lanska 2003). The major teaching centers of neurology were located in large eastern U.S. cities. Many students were attracted to Philadelphia, New York, and Boston to train in neurology during this period.

Europe was the center for neurological study and training for much of the nineteenth century, with its leaders producing an explosive growth in clinical and basic neuroscience. Medicine had started to subdivide into specialty care disciplines wherever there was a sufficient knowledge base. The medical specialty movement started in Europe and slowly spread to America. Although there was initial resistance by generalists, it quickly proliferated in academia and specialty clinics. Discoveries by Jean-Martin Charcot, Hughlings Jackson, and Theodor Meynert, among others, allowed neurology to flourish as a specialty. In the United States at this time teaching and training in neurology were confined to a small number of medical schools. Practitioners trained in neurology advertised their specialty services in medical journals. The movement in neurological specialty care, like other medical specialties, was aided by the growing wealthy class produced by the Industrial Revolution, whose members were ready and willing to pay for specialized care.

The Civil War was arguably the most influential event shaping American neurology in the nineteenth century (Goetz, Chmura, & Lanska 2003). In addition to more than 600,000 human casualties, the Civil War produced a large number of devastating injuries to the central and peripheral nervous system. Combined with a cadre of physicians interested in studying neurological disorders, the postwar years were a ripe time for expansion of this knowledge base. William A. Hammond (1828–1900) was named the U.S. Surgeon General during the Civil War and in this role established Turner's Lane Hospital in Philadelphia. Hammond appointed Silas Weir Mitchell to a post at this facility. At Turner's Lane S. Weir Mitchell, George Morehouse, and William Keen performed their seminal work on nervous system injuries (Freemon 1993). Voluminous notes were taken on each case, and the clinical material obtained was divided among the three for analysis. The Civil War injuries provided the case material for the development of clinical neurology in the United States. Numerous journals published articles on peripheral nerve injury, post-traumatic epilepsy, malingering, and neurasthenia.

William Hammond and Edward Seguin introduced neurology to New York City and were key figures in the founding of the American Neurological Association (ANA) in 1875 (American Neurological Association 2011; Goetz, Chmura & Lanska 2003). The ANA was the first national neurological association in the world with a goal to form a small group of devotees to "the cultivation of Neurological Science." It was an academic society by nature and requirements. The first ANA meeting took place at the Young Men's Christian Association on 4th Avenue and 23rd Street in New York City on June 2, 1875, and was attended by eighteen of its thirty-five members. All the members were men and largely based in New York, Boston, Philadelphia, and Chicago; St. Louis was the westernmost city to be represented.

While the medical specialty movement flourished in the United States from the late 1800s, many so-called specialists had questionable training and oversight (Goetz, Chmura & Lanska 2003). This forced specialty movements to reevaluate their credentialing systems and align with other specialty groups to prevent isolation. Within neurology, this dilemma helped to solidify a relationship with psychiatry in the early twentieth century after initial efforts to keep the two fields separate. This relationship was a critical factor leading to the establishment of the American Board of Psychiatry and Neurology in 1934.

Neurology Care and Training in the Veterans' Healthcare System

Through these initial efforts by Hammond and Mitchell, a system of care for Civil War veterans was born. The National Homes for Disabled Volunteer

Soldiers were established in eleven locations throughout the United States. These, with the Naval Home in Philadelphia and the Soldiers' Home in Washington, D.C., were the sole federal resources for indigent or disabled veterans before World War I (Adkins 1967; Kurtzke 1997).

During that conflict 4.7 million Americans served, and a Bureau of War Risk Insurance was formed. Veteran medical care was the charge of the U.S. Public Health Service, which was reimbursed by the bureau (Adkins 1967). Both hospital space and staffing were limited.

"Neuropsychiatry" came to be formally recognized during World War I, with the American expeditionary forces establishing centers for treatment in France. "Neurologists" dealt with "neuroses" and "organic diseases"; "psychiatrists" dealt with "psychoses" (Bailey, Williams & Domora 1929; Salmon & Fenton, 1929)." Most "neurologists" were neuropsychiatrists, and many "psychiatrists" had been "alienists" or psychiatric hospital physicians.

To address and manage the medical needs of World War I veterans more formally, the Veterans' Bureau was created in 1921. The launch of this bureau combined the medical staff of the Public Health Service with civil service physicians employed by the bureau for a total of 1,455 physicians and 216 dentists (Adkins 1967). Brigadier General Frank Hines was appointed director of the Veterans' Bureau in 1923, a position he retained as administrator of the Veterans Administration when it was formed in 1930. In March 1923 the Veterans' Bureau was operating forty-five hospitals (fifteen tuberculosis, nineteen general medical and surgical, eleven neuropsychiatric) with 15,400 beds, plus a hundred or so dispensaries. There were 17,000 veteran patients in the Veterans' Bureau, Army, Navy and Public Health Service hospitals and 6,000 in private hospitals (Kurtzke 1997).

World War II was a watershed period for both neurology training and veterans' care. A total of 16.5 million veterans served between September 15, 1940, and July 25, 1947, the war period as designated by the Veterans Administration (Kurtzke 1978).

Physicians were obviously part of the massive World War II deployment. In the army, for example, their numbers increased from 1,574 in June 1940 to 47,938 in June 1945 (McMinn & Levin 1963). The navy (with a V12 program) and the army (with the Army Student Training Program [ASTP]) sent well over 20,000 students through medical school as enlisted men. Active duty army physicians were assigned to the Veterans Administration between January 1944 and May 1946 (McMinn & Levin 1963). In June 1945 physician staffing in Veterans Administration hospitals consisted of about 600 civilians and 1,700 army officers. By that time also some 1,200 ASTP and V12 graduates were assigned to the Veterans Administration for their two years of required active duty; these last were all released by July 1948 (Adkins 1967).

Virtually all academics in medicine as well as most male practitioners were either in service or served as civilian consultants during the war. Thus the quality of military medicine, and with it the Veterans Administration, was unsurpassed while the war lasted. World War II hostilities ceased in Europe in May 1945 and in Japan in August 1945. A precipitous demobilization took place for a year thereafter, which included medical personnel. To help with the medical care of World War II veterans, twenty-five Army General Hospitals were transferred to the Veterans Administration (see table 2.1).

Prior to 1946 neurologic medicine and research were not recognized by the Veterans Administration as specific disciplines within the field of medicine. That year Pearce Bailey Jr., on separation from his neurologic duties at the Philadelphia Naval Hospital, was asked to take charge of the neurologic program that was then under neuropsychiatry in the Division of Medicine and Surgery of the Veterans Administration (DeJong 1982).

Bailey's first act as chief of neurology was to procure a medical advisory committee selected by the council of the ANA. The ANA committee was of inestimable help in shaping the nascent Veterans Administration neurological program and guiding it along lines conducive to academic neurology and the better care of veteran patients. The Veterans Administration neurological training program breathed new life into residency training throughout the country, so that in two years 34.6 percent of the 170 neurological residents in the country were in Veterans Administration hospitals. In 1946 the patient census of neurologically disabled veterans from both world wars was large, constituting about 20 to 30 percent of the patient population in general medical and surgical hospitals and 10 percent in psychiatric hospitals. In 1947 the Veterans Administration Neuropsychiatric Division changed its name to the Psychiatry and Neurology Service. Bailey became the chief of the Neurology Section. In 1972 the Neurology Service in the VA Central Office (VACO) became a separate service under the directorship of Warren V. Huber (Bailey 1975).

Bailey was appointed the first director of the National Institute of Neurological Disorders and Blindness (NINDB) in the fall of 1951 (Bailey 1975). His position in the VACO was assumed by Benedict Nagler. Robert Ruff became VA director of neurology in 2006, based at the VA Medical Center (VAMC), Cleveland, rather than the Central Office at Washington. This pattern of "decentralization" was begun by his predecessor, John Booss, who was based at VAMC, West Haven. All neurology owes these two men a tremendous debt for their efforts.

Table 2.1. U.S. Army General Hospitals in the United States during World War II transferred to the Veterans Administration, November 1945–September 1946*

U.S. Army General Hospital	Location
Ashburn	McKinney, TX
Barnes	Vancouver, WA
Baxter	Spokane, WA
Billings	Indianapolis, IN
Birmingham	Van Nuys, CA
Crile	Cleveland, OH
Cushing	Framingham, MA
Deshon	Butler, PA
Finney	Thomasville, GA
Foster**	Jackson, MS
Kennedy**	Memphis, TN
LaGarde	New Orleans, LA
Lawson	Atlanta, GA
McCloskey	Temple, TX
McGaw	Walla Walla, WA
McGuire	Richmond, VA
Moore	Asheville, NC
N. D. Baker	Martinsburg, WV
Nichols	Louisville, KY
Oliver	Augusta, GA
O'Reilly	Springfield, MO
Schick	Clinton, IA
Thayer	Nashville, TN
Vaughan	Hines, IL
Winter	Topeka, KS

*Total USAGH hospitals = 64.

**Foster Kennedy was an eminent New York neurologist (Kurtzke 1977).

Neurology continued to be centered at medical schools until World War II, and most of the academics were neuropsychiatrists rather than "pure" neurologists. Established in 1934, the American Board of Psychiatry and Neurology granted certifications in either field or in both (Hollender 1991). Annual certifications in psychiatry (P) or neuropsychiatry (psychiatry and neurology, or P&N) were given in essentially equal numbers until 1945, when a striking increase occurred for psychiatry alone. This trend persisted unchanged through the early 1960s, and another surge plateaued in the late 1970s and later declined. Neuropsychiatry gradually disappeared in the 1950s when neurology began a progressive growth into the late 1970s (Kurtzke et al. 1986).

What was the cause of this increase in neurologists? In part it was the availability of additional residency positions, especially in the Veterans Administration. But mostly it was because of an increase in the awareness of neurology as a career choice. This was the result of the creation of the National Institute of Neurological Diseases and Blindness (NINDB).

During the tenure of Director Richard L. Masland at the NINDB (1959 to 1968) there was considerable proliferation of the training grants program, reaching sixty-two neurological programs in thirty states, twenty-three neurosurgical programs in fourteen states, eleven child neurology, and nine neuroradiological programs in six states. The growth and plateau in the numbers of neurologists at the time parallels these NIH developments closely. As DeJong stated: "American neurology would not have risen to its present peak had it not been for the NINDB and the institutes it spawned" (1982).

By the mid-1980s all adult neurology training programs were of three or four years' duration, and almost all were university-based. Child neurology programs were finally formally authorized, but they could be established only where there was an approved adult program. None of this growth would have occurred, however, if there were not a market for the output. The public soon perceived a need for neurologists in practice, which corresponded with their availability.

Several points were obvious in establishing effective neurology residency training programs, based on the experience we have had at the Georgetown University Neurology Residency Program in Washington, D.C. First, proper neurological care of patients required competent clinicians with teaching and research skills. They could only be attracted and retained in VA in a university-affiliated program. Second, the Residency Review Committee was phasing out partial and nonaffiliated programs in neurology. Third, Georgetown had neither the faculty nor the facilities to add appreciably to their numbers of residents. Therefore, to establish an academic neurology service we had to "buy" our own staff and residents, who would concurrently be both VA and Georgetown personnel, funded, however, by the VA.

Neurological Research and the Veterans' Healthcare System

Along with the expanding healthcare and residency training mission after World War II, the Veterans Administration also formed an effective biomedical research enterprise. Both laboratory-based and clinical research projects received funding in the research portfolio. Of immediate concern in 1946

was how to manage the 10,000 veterans with tuberculosis. A study was initiated by Drs. John Barnwell and Arthur M. Walker to evaluate the efficacy of
various drugs, including streptomycin (Barnwell, Bunn & Walker 1947).
This was the first multicentered therapeutic trial in the United States. The
results of this study both helped revolutionalize the care of tuberculosis and
served to launch the VA Cooperative Study Program (CSP). As of 2003,
VA has established five CSP Coordinating Centers, located at Hines, Illinois;
Palo Alto, California; West Haven, Connecticut; Perry Point, Maryland; and
Boston, Massachusetts.

During the later 1940s there was also concern about how best to manage
World War II veterans with multiple sclerosis (MS), the most common progressive neurological disease of young adults. Based on the apparent success
of an MS pilot trial with the tuberculosis drug isoniazid (Kurtzke & Berlin
1954), a larger trial was planned within the Veterans Administration neurol-
ogy system. The VA Central Office recruited eleven of its neurology centers
throughout the country to participate in a treatment trial of isoniazid and
MS. The trial was headed by Benedict Nagler, Director of Neurology
VACO, and Gilbert Beebe of the National Academy of Sciences Follow-up
Agency, with collaborative assistance from Leonard Kurland of the National
Institute of Health. The trial used the disability scale developed by Kurtzke
(Kurtzke 1955) for the pilot study, the forerunner to the Expanded Disabil-
ity Status Scale (Kurtzke 1983). The results showed no evidence of any treat-
ment effect in terms of relapses or MS morbidity on the Disability Status
Scale or other measures (Veterans Administration Multiple Sclerosis Study
Group 1957). This was the first-ever multicentered, randomized, placebo-
controlled, double-blind trial of therapy for MS in the world; its results were
in accord with the later experience of Kurtzke and Berlin (1957).

A number of other large clinical neurology trials were funded and published
by VA in the later twentieth century. The development of VA cohorts and
databases can be traced back to the work of the Medical Follow-up Agency,
National Academy of Sciences, which provided an infrastructure for the development of longitudinal studies for veterans after World War II (Kurtzke
1978, 2005). Some highlights include clinical trials of seizures, status epilepticus, and stroke (Hobson et al. 1993; Mattson et al. 1985; Treiman et al.
1998). Major epidemiological studies on MS (Kurtzke, Beebe & Norman
1979) and ALS (Horner et al. 2003) have been supported by the VA.

More recently, VA studies have evaluated cost and outcomes related to
neurological conditions (stroke and MS) (Bourdette et al. 1993; Winkler
et al. 2010). Large clinical trials continue to utilize the CSP program, which
is capable of providing statistical, pharmaceutical, and administrative support

for multisite studies. In 1998 three Epidemiological Research and Information Centers (ERICs) were established within the CSP to conduct observational population-based research. Smaller investigator-initiated trials and laboratory-based studies have relied on the VA Merit Review funding program and targeted requests for proposals.

New Directions

VA Neurology Training and Care Changes in the 1990s

The Veterans Administration attained U.S. cabinet status in 1989, increasing its political influence within subsequent presidential administrations. It was renamed the Department of Veterans Affairs (VA). Along with the addition of the new VA cabinet secretary, the last decade of the twentieth century brought swift and extensive changes for the VA healthcare system. These changes were under the direction of Kenneth W. Kizer, MD, MPH, who served as Under Secretary for Health between 1994 and 1999. Following are summaries of major policy initiatives (Booss 1997):

- **Veterans Health Information Systems and Technology Architecture (VISTA):** The development and deployment of health information technology in VA served to transform the communication between healthcare providers. The launch of the Computerized Patient Record System (CPRS) in the late 1990s was transformational in terms of providing access to information, and allowing efficiency and safety in the care of patients.

- **Outpatient focus:** For decades VA had focused its care delivery model on inpatients with large wards, and small clinics with limited staffing. Because Congress had changed the rules that govern access to various types of care, it allowed for more efficient use of outpatient services (Booss 1997).

- **Primary care:** A mandate to offer primary care to every veteran in VA was enacted in the mid-1990s. This shift led to the hiring of more primary care physicians and the release of specialists.

- **Residency reallocation:** The federally chartered Residency Realignment Committee, chaired by Robert Petersdorf, MD, made recommendations for the reallocation of residency slots away from specialty areas and toward primary care–based disciplines. In neurology training programs, this led to a loss of fifty residency slots over a three-year period.

- **Realignment of research:** A federally mandated commission made recommendations to align research activities in VA with the most common illnesses experienced by veterans and funding of designated research areas. Recruitment and training of junior investigators was also affirmed.

- **Eligibility reform:** The 104th Congress authorized more flexibility in outpatient care and contracting activities within VA. At the same time, it also mandated more intensive documentation and registration of eligible veterans and the services they could receive.

- **Resource allocation:** Through a law enacted by the 104th Congress, the distribution of appropriations was closely tied to the geographic location of veterans. Past VA appropriations were influenced by historical patterns. Generally, more funding for veterans' healthcare would move from the Northeast to the South and Southwest portions of the country.

- **Reorganization:** VA healthcare facilities were reorganized into twenty-two Veterans Integrated Service Networks (VISNs), which were given considerable autonomy and administrative authority that had traditionally resided with the VA Central Office in Washington. In the past a medical school was the primary collaborator with VA, and hospitals tended to be isolated from each other. The VISN concept provided a structure for facilities to collaborate in care and resources.

In 1994 a major change was made for all VA residency training programs, not only neurology. Whereas previously VA residents were paid directly by VA, from then on they were to be paid by the university (or other) medical center, with VA reimbursement directly to the medical center. VA Academic Affairs still controlled the number and type of VA residents allowed for each center.

Numbers of VA neurology residency positions currently authorized may be lower, a few programs cited no longer exist, some have consolidated, and a small number of new ones have been added, as is true nationwide. Beds and admissions per center correlate strongly with the size of the program. In 1985 there were 349 VA neurologists in pay status (144 full time, 205 part time), for a total full-time equivalent (FTE) of 254.4. As of September 1996 they numbered 438: 130 full time, 308 part time; the FTE number was not available (Kurtzke 1997).

"But anyone who believes the VA would maintain standards without tertiary hospital training centers should read (as I have) some pre–WW II medical records. Put kindly, they left much to be desired in diagnosis and management. Teaching affiliations have been the salvation of the VA. These affiliations and the quality of VA medical care, which is their direct result, are, I fear, in jeopardy" (Kurtzke 1997, 331). Iglehart recently summarized the planned restructuring of the VA system into "one that is rooted in primary care delivered in outpatient settings" (Iglehart 1996, 1408). "There is no question that there is enormous pressure to reduce specialty care by FIAT.... The current political atmosphere and corporate mentality that postulates that primary care physicians suddenly are experts in all fields of medicine and surgery is counterintuitive to what all of us understand has developed in medicine since the end of World War II. It is important for each specialty to continue to educate the public while demonstrating the validity of their own work" (Weiner & Shulman 1996, 1108).

This is especially the situation for neurology. No field of medicine of which we are aware requires any training in neurology during residency, except for neurosurgery. And there are still medical schools without obligatory neurology clerkships. Even in some of those that have such programs, the dedicated durations have recently been shortened. Thus, good physicians enter practice too often without even being aware of what they don't know about the nervous system and its disorders. Further, who is going to advance the many fields of medicine except the appropriate specialists? And specialists cannot only be consultants. They cannot properly advise others about appropriate treatment unless they are doing it themselves (Kurtzke 1997):

> During the first two decades of VA hospital development between 1925 and 1945, the AMA opposed government participation in the care of veterans. During the next three decades there was a reluctant acknowledgment by the American Medical Association (AMA) of the need for federally housed care of veterans with service-connected illnesses. At the same time, the AMA recognized the value of the mission of the VA in training specialists through postgraduate medical education. More recently, the AMA has been especially supportive of VA-medical school affiliations and VA activities in education and research....
> It appears to be a time of enhanced opportunity for the AMA to work more closely with the Department of Veterans Affairs.... [Adopted in 1993 in an AMA Policy Compendium Supplement was the statement that the] AMA will monitor and take appropriate action to ensure the tradition of joint responsibilities through dual medical school-VA appointments; and will monitor any changes in health systems to ensure that the successful relationships between VA academic medical centers and the nation's medical schools are maintained. (Kendall 1995)

Survival of a tertiary-cum-primary care system for eligible veterans is not only in the best interests of organized and academic medicine, it is also our duty as a nation. We believe VA should also include as class A veterans all military retirees. They, with their families, had come to expect total medical care for the rest of their lives. This has not happened. Retirees are being essentially forced into "Tricare" programs (contract civilian care maintained by military medicine), but once age sixty-five is reached, all retirees join the rest of Americans in being entitled only to Medicare. Very little care is available in military hospitals for retirees. Although at present VA can legally do little medically for veterans' families, it would certainly help to fulfill some of the promises that were made to retirees when they entered the services.

Specialty Centers for Neurological Disorders

Over the past ten years three specialized clinical centers in neurology have been launched in VA. The Parkinson's Disease Research, Education & Clinical Centers were created in 2001, the Multiple Sclerosis Centers of Excellence in 2003, and the Epilepsy Centers of Excellence in 2009. All three centers were driven by the new treatments made available for these disorders and the need to provide services to veterans in properly staffed and equipped facilities. In addition to providing state-of-the-art clinical care for veterans, these programs have been the nidus for training residents and fellows and providing infrastructure for research studies. All of these specialty centers provide educational training in their neurological disorder for veterans and their families.

- **Parkinson's Disease Research, Education & Clinical Centers** (http://www.parkinsons.va.gov): The Department of Veterans Affairs treats an estimated 40,000 veterans with Parkinson's disease each year. In 2001 VA expanded its commitment to veterans with PD and related movement disorders by establishing the Parkinson's Disease Research, Education and Clinical Center (PADRECC) network. This network supports six PD Centers of Excellence, located in Portland/Seattle, San Francisco, Los Angeles, Houston, Richmond, and Philadelphia. Each PADRECC is designed to deliver state-of-the-art clinical care, innovative research, and outreach and education programs to its surrounding region, also referred to as its "service area."

- **Multiple Sclerosis Centers of Excellence** (http://www.va.gov/ms): The MS Centers of Excellence (MSCoE), established by VA in 2003, are committed to serving the healthcare needs of approximately 40,000 veterans with MS. The Centers of Excellence are located in Seattle and Portland (MSCoE, West) and Baltimore and Washington (MSCoE, East). These cooperative centers are organized around four functional cores: 1) clinical care, 2) education and training, 3) research and development, and 4) informatics and telemedicine. The mission of the MSCoE is to improve services for veterans with MS and act as a resource for providers through a specialized and collaborative integration of clinical care, education, research, and informatics. The overall goals of the MSCoEs are to improve the quality and consistency of health services delivered to veterans across the country. The MS Centers of Excellence are influencing providers and veterans using a population-based management model. Essential elements of this model are the availability of a national registry of veterans who have been diagnosed with MS, the ability to impact services at the point-of-care with electronic medical record tools, and the development of face-to-face and distant education and training options for health professionals and veterans to facilitate evidence-based delivery of services. Integration of these elements permits short- and long-term assessment of interventions and modification to achieve goals.

- **Epilepsy Centers of Excellence:** In late 2009 VA initiated funding for the Epilepsy Centers of Excellence. These centers are divided into four geographic locations with key coordinating hospitals within each center as follows:

  - Northwest: Madison, Portland, and Seattle; polytrauma site, Minneapolis.
  - Southwest: San Francisco, West Los Angeles, Albuquerque, and Houston; polytrauma site, Palo Alto.
  - Southeast: Miami, Gainesville, FL, and Durham, NC; polytrauma site, Tampa.
  - Northeast: Baltimore and New Haven, CT; polytrauma site, Richmond, VA.

Initially there will be four multisite centers that leverage existing VA epilepsy resources. This network will push outward with a hub and spoke system that reaches other facilities and links the existing sites of strength with the Polytrauma Network. Overall the Epilepsy Centers of Excellence will enable VA to provide the most up-to-date care to veterans with complex epilepsy while minimizing outsourcing.

Specialty postgraduate residency training in neurology is available for neurology or medical residents and neuroscience graduate students. Table 2.2 lists the current neurology specialty areas of training available for postgraduates in VA. Programs are site-specific and typically linked with a university affiliate program.

Looking to the Future

There are 152 VA Medical Centers in the system and 784 Community Based Outpatient Clinics. In 2008 there were 23,440,000 veterans living in the United States, of whom 8,493,700 (36 percent) received VA benefits and

Table 2.2. Postgraduate Neurological Specialty Training within the Department of Veterans Affairs

Behavioral Neurology
Epilepsy
Multiple Sclerosis
Neurophysiology
Neuropsychology
Sleep Disorders
Spinal Cord Injury
Parkinson's Disease

services. Of the 126 neurology residency training programs in the United States, 63 are affiliated with VAMCs. These training programs bring faculty, house staff, and medical students from the nation's premier medical schools to care for veterans. Neurology care remains an important part of healthcare delivery through traditional specialty care services and as part of the multidisciplinary care being assembled for recently returning Operation Enduring Freedom/Operation Freedom veterans. Traumatic brain injury (TBI) is the signature injury from this conflict, and the Polytrauma Centers as well as the Epilepsy Centers of Excellence have been set up to better manage morbidity related to this condition.

Secretary Erik K. Shinseki has argued that serving "Veterans in the 21st [century] requires bold investment today for a transformed VA tomorrow." In 2009 he outlined a series of programs known as the T-21 initiatives (see table 2.3). The T-21 initiatives are intended to transform VA into an organization that is patient-centered, results-driven, and forward-looking.

The T-21 initiatives include developing a new model of care that is patient-centered and integrates both primary and specialty care services. The patient-centered medical home project was launched within primary care in 2010 and has been labeled the Patient Aligned Care Team (PACT). This project is set to quickly transform all VA primary care practices to conform to a primary care medical home model ("Joint Principles of the Patient-Centered Medical Home" 2008). The goal of PACTs for a patient-driven, team-based approach is the delivery of efficient, comprehensive care through active communication and coordination of healthcare services. A typical primary care PACT team will consist of a small group of medical, social service, and administrative staff who will have responsibility for the primary care needs of about 1,000 patients. Communication between providers and patients will be facilitated by the

Table 2.3. Department of Veterans Affairs T-21 Strategic Goals, 2009

1) Creating a "virtual lifetime electronic record" to ensure uniform registration of all military service members, in conjunction with the Defense Department
2) Accelerating a "telehealth" and home care initiative, primarily for older, chronically ill veterans to keep them out of hospitals
3) Eliminating homelessness among veterans
4) Self-service devices so veterans can improve interactions with VA staff, and an integrated "veterans relationship management" system
5) Developing a human capital plan for strategically managing VA's staff of nearly 300,000

well-developed information technology pathways in VA. These include the CPRS, electronic clinical reminders, an Internet-based patient Web portal (My HealtheVet), and a comprehensive telehealth program. Open access scheduling and remote visits will offer flexibility in the daily schedule of primary care clinics and will be a noted advantage for both patients and providers, with more real-time electronic encounters and fewer face-to-face visits.

Little is known about the extent to which specialty providers utilize patient-centered medical home principles. A recent national survey of internal medicine subspecialty practices by Casalino and colleagues (2010) attempted to address this issue. One question in the survey asked, "In some cases, specialists also serve as primary care physicians for their patients. To the best of your knowledge, for approximately what percentage of patients, if any, do the physicians in your practice serve as primary care physicians as well as specialists?" A total of 81 percent of practices reported that they served the primary care needs of 10 percent or fewer of their patients. Only 2.7 percent of the specialty practices surveyed served as the primary care providers for over 50 percent of their patients. These numbers provide evidence that few specialty practices in internal medicine are providing primary care.

Several private and public demonstration projects have been initiated to evaluate the patient-centered medical home model in recent years. In 2010 the U.S. Congress passed the Patient Protection and Affordable Care Act and the Health Care and Education Reconciliation Act, establishing a new Innovation Center to test novel patient-centered medical home (PCMH) models of care within Medicare, Medicaid, and the Children's Health Insurance Program. Concerns have been raised about adequate payment to support the PCMH and the difficulties of small practices in adopting the model. Another issue is how specialty medicine interacts with or becomes a patient-centered medical home. Kirschner and Barr (2010) argue that a specialty practice can serve as a patient-centered medical home for a subgroup of patients or function as a patient-centered medical home "neighbor" that interfaces with patient-centered medical home practices. For example, an endocrinology practice may function as a patient-centered medical home for patients with complicated diabetes mellitus by managing diabetic-related problems and providing care consistent with the joint principles just noted, which include first-contact and comprehensive care. A patient-centered medical home "neighbor" is a middle-ground approach in which the specialty clinic works along with PCMH practice to enhance coordination of care, improve consultation access, and create a seamless transition for patients with complicated chronic conditions. An integrated clinic for a chronic neurological condition such as MS could serve as a PCMH "neighbor" by providing principal MS care or care that requires special expertise but also meets many of the patient's general healthcare needs. Specialty models of care within the PCMH require further development in communication flow, accountability for care, and outcomes.

The current healthcare system in the United States has a suboptimal structure to provide comprehensive, cost-effective care for patients with neurological and other complex chronic diseases. Many specialty practices function as "silos," with limited incentives for coordination with other providers caring for the patient. Evidence-based medicine and decision support tools are underused. The result is a fractured healthcare experience with little care coordination on behalf of the patient. The patient-centered focus of the PACT within VA is a welcome paradigm shift in chronic care delivery that holds much promise for providers and patients alike.

The VA healthcare system is ideal to demonstrate a variety of care models. Its size, infrastructure, and ability to capture costs would make trials of various care models relatively easy to design and implement. Because it is a capitated system, it is not constrained by the fee-for-service model of health insurance or Medicare. Within neurology, models of care that employ the information technology systems in the home and smaller clinics could open up educational, diagnostic, and therapeutic delivery for patients that are separated from clinics by distance or disability.

References

Adkins, R. (1967). *Medical care of veterans.* House Committee Print No. 4. 90th Cong., 1st sess., April 17. Washington, DC: U.S. Government Printing Office.

American Neurological Association (ANA). 2011. www.aneuroa.org.

Bailey, P., Jr. (1975). Government organization of neurological research and development in the Veterans Administration and the National Institute of Neurological

Diseases and Blindness. In D. Denny-Brown, A. S. Rose & A. L. Sahs (Eds.), *Centennial anniversary volume of the American Neurological Association 1875–1975* (pp. 509–531). New York: Springer Publishing.

Bailey, P., Williams, F. & Domora, P. (1929). *Neuropsychiatry in the United States.* Washington, DC: U.S. Government Printing Office.

Barnwell, J., Bunn, P. & Walker, A. (1947). The effect of streptomycin upon pulmonary tuberculosis. *American Review of Tuberculosis* 56: 485–507.

Booss, J. (1997). Change in the Department of Veterans Affairs: What should be done? *Neurology* 49, no. 2: 338–340.

Bourdette, D. N., Prochazka, A. V., Mitchell, W., Licari, P. & Burks, J. (1993). Health care costs of veterans with multiple sclerosis: Implications for the rehabilitation of MS: VA Multiple Sclerosis Rehabilitation Study Group. *Archives of Physical and Medical Rehabilitation* 74, no. 1: 26–31.

Casalino, L. P., Rittenhouse, D. R., Gillies, R. R. & Shortell, S. M. (2010). Specialist physician practices as patient-centered medical homes. *New England Journal of Medicine* 362, no. 17: 1555–1558.

DeJong, R. (1982). *A history of American neurology.* New York: Raven Press.

Freemon, F. R. (1993). The first neurological research center: Turner's Lane Hospital during the American Civil War. *Journal of the History of Neuroscience* 2, no. 2: 135–142.

Goetz, C. G., Chmura, T. A. & Lanska, D. (2003). Part 1: The history of 19th century neurology and the American Neurological Association. *Annals of Neurology* 53 (supp. 4): S2–S26.

Health Care and Education Reconciliation Act of 2010. Pub. L. No. 111–152.

Hobson, R. W., II, Weiss, D. G., Fields, W. S., Goldstone, J., Moore, W. S., Towne, J. B. & Wright, C. B. (1993). Efficacy of carotid endarterectomy for asymptomatic carotid stenosis: The Veterans Affairs Cooperative Study Group." *New England Journal of Medicine* 328, no. 4: 221–227.

Hollender, M. (1991). *The American Board of Psychiatry and Neurology: The first fifty years.* Deerfield, IL: American Board of Psychiatry and Neurology.

Horner, R. D., Kamins, K. G., Feussner, J. R., Grambow, S. C., Hoff-Lindquist, J., Harati, Y., Mitsumoto, H., Pascuzzi, R., Spencer, P. S., Tim, R., Howard, D., Smith, T. C., Ryan, M. A., Coffman, C. J. & Kasarskis, E. J. (2003). Occurrence of amyotrophic lateral sclerosis among Gulf War veterans. *Neurology* 61, no. 6: 742–749.

Iglehart, J. K. (1996). Reform of the Veterans Affairs health care system. *New England Journal of Medicine* 335, no. 18: 1407–1411.

Joint principles of the patient-centered medical home. (2008). *Delaware Medical Journal* 80, no. 1: 21–22.

Kendall, J. W. (1995). The Evolution of American Medical Association policies concerning health care of veterans. *Military Medicine* 160, no. 10: 518–521.

Kirschner, N. & Barr, M. S. (2010). Specialists/subspecialists and the patient-centered medical home. *Chest* 137, no. 1: 200–204.

Kurtzke, J. F. (1955). A new scale for evaluating disability in multiple sclerosis. *Neurology* 5, no. 8: 580–583.

Kurtzke, J. F. (1978). Data registries on selected segments of the population: Veterans. *Advances in Neurology* 19: 55–67.

Kurtzke, J. F. (1983). Rating neurologic impairment in multiple sclerosis: An expanded disability status scale (EDSS). *Neurology* 33, no. 11: 1444–1452.

Kurtzke, J. F. (1997). On the role of veterans in the development of neurology in the United States: A personal reflection. *Neurology* 49, no. 2: 323–333.

Kurtzke, J. F. (2005). Epidemiology and etiology of multiple sclerosis. *Physical Medicine & Rehabilitation Clinics of North America* 16, no. 2: 327–349.

Kurtzke, J. F., Beebe, G. W. & Norman, J. E., Jr. (1979). Epidemiology of multiple sclerosis in U.S. veterans: 1. race, sex, and geographic distribution. *Neurology* 29, no. 9, pt. 1: 1228–1235.

Kurtzke, J. F., Bennett, D. R., Berg, B. O., Beringer, G. B., Goldstein, M. & Vates, T. S., Jr. (1986). Neurologists in the United States—past, present, and future. *Neurology* 36, no. 12: 1576–1582.

Kurtzke, J. F. & Berlin, L. (1954). The effects of isoniazid on patients with multiple sclerosis. Preliminary report. *American Review of Tuberculosis* 70, no. 4: 577–592.

Kurtzke, J. F. & Berlin, L. (1957). Isoniazid in treatment of multiple sclerosis. *Journal of the American Medical Association* 163: 172–174.

Mattson, R. H., Cramer, J. A., Collins, J. F., Smith, D. B., Delgado-Escueta, A. V., Browne, T. R., Williamson, P. D., Treiman, D. M., McNamara, J. O., McCutchen, C. B., et al. (1985). Comparison of carbamazepine, phenobarbital, phenytoin, and primidone in partial and secondarily generalized tonic-clonic seizures. *New England Journal of Medicine* 313, no. 3: 145–151.

McMinn, J. & Levin, M. (1963). *Personnel in World War II*. Washington, DC: U.S. Government Printing Office.

Patient Protection and Affordable Care Act of 2010. Pub. L. No. 111–148.

Salmon, T. & Fenton, N. (1929). *Neuropsychiatry in the American Expeditionary Forces*. Washington, DC: U.S. Government Printing Office.

Treiman, D. M., Meyers, P. D., Walton, N. Y., Collins, J. F., Colling, C., Rowan, A. J., Handforth, A., Faught, E., Calabrese, V. P., Uthman, B. M., Ramsay, R. E. & Mamdani, M. B. (1998). A comparison of four treatments for generalized convulsive status epilepticus: Veterans Affairs Status Epilepticus Cooperative Study Group. *New England Journal of Medicine* 339, no. 12: 792–798.

Veterans Administration Multiple Sclerosis Study Group. (1957). Isoniazid in treatment of multiple sclerosis. Report on Veterans Administration Cooperative Study. *Journal of the American Medical Association* 163: 168–172.

Weiner, W. J. & Shulman, L. M. (1996). Worth of neurologists. *Neurology* 47, no. 4: 1108.

Winkler, S. L., Vogel, B., Hoenig, H., Ripley, D. C., Wu, S., Fitzgerald, S. G., Mann, W. C. & Reker, D. M. (2010). Cost, utilization, and policy of provision of assistive technology devices to veterans poststroke by Medicare and VA. *Medical Care* 48, no. 6: 558–562.

Chapter 3

Cardiology Care for Veterans in VA Healthcare

David C. Booth

History

On a morning in September 1977 at the Washington, D.C., VA Medical Center, the enlivened discussion among the cardiology fellows and staff members concerned the publication in the *New England Journal of Medicine* of the five-year results of the Department of Veterans Affairs (VA; then the Veterans Administration) Cooperative Study Number 4: the first randomized trial comparing coronary artery bypass surgery to medical therapy in patients with stable angina pectoris and the first trial of a size sufficient to address the issue of survival benefit in patients with one or multivessel coronary artery disease (Murphy et al. 1977). In 1975 the same investigators had published randomized data demonstrating a survival advantage with surgery (Takaro et al. 1976) in patients with left main coronary disease, and from that point left main disease patients were excluded from the main trial. Foretelling the power of the randomized trial in cardiovascular medicine, the VA coronary bypass study group had previously carried out prospective randomized studies of the Beck procedure, in which powder was instilled into the pericardial sac (*Medical Research in the Veterans Administration* 1968), showing no benefit, and of internal mammary implantation, the Vineberg procedure (Bhayana, Gage & Takaro 1980), in which the internal mammary artery was buried in a trench in the left ventricular myocardium. Notwithstanding that Dr. Vineberg was well-intentioned and would eventually be knighted by the queen of England for his medical contributions, the VA bypass surgery study group conclusively demonstrated that the procedure would have a Class III indication in today's parlance: of no benefit and possibly harmful. Led by such formidable VA investigators as cardiologist Dr. Herbert Hultgren, cardiac surgeon Dr. Timothy Takaro, and stellar biostatistician Dr. Kathleen Detre, VA Coop Study No. 4 demonstrated in patients with stable angina pectoris that bypass surgery did not result in a survival advantage at five years, compared to medical therapy. As was also concluded in a subsequent meta-analysis of the large randomized trials of bypass surgery (Yussuf, Zucker & Chalmers 1994), with the exception of selected subgroups, subsequent long-term follow-up data (Veterans Administration Coronary Artery Bypass Surgery Cooperative Study Group 1984) from Study No. 4 would confirm the original hypothesis. Also, planted therein was the seed for important future trials in bypass surgery and percutaneous coronary intervention.

The VA Coop Study No. 4 perfectly captures the mission of the Cooperative Studies program: to address scientifically relevant clinical questions utilizing the power of multicenter randomization. Also, by adding to extant science, VA Cooperative Studies reflect one of the overall aims in veterans healthcare, which is to continuously improve the quality of care delivered to veterans. This chapter summarizes the history of cardiovascular care and clinical investigation in VA and discusses what services are available today in cardiovascular care for veterans.

The history of veterans' participation in human research is as long and decorated as the military careers served by these real American heroes. The scientific value of veterans in human cardiovascular research studies cannot be overestimated. Many of the investigators who have carried out human research in VA are or were responsible for the day-to-day delivery of care to the patients. An often cited example of best clinical practices in the combination of clinical care and research in the Veterans Health Administration (VHA) is the team of Dr. William Chardack, then chief of the Surgical Service at the Buffalo, New York, VA Medical Center; thoracic surgeon Dr. Andrew Gage; and Wilson Greatbatch, a Buffalo area electrical engineering consultant who developed the first implantable pacemaker, two and one-half inches in diameter and five-eighths inch in thickness (Chardack et al. 1965). In 1960 sixteen patients received the device. From the vantage point of current 6 French-size transvenous leads, one can only admire the determination and ingenuity that Chardack brought to the problem of early and frequent lead failures. Based on an intra-oral orthodontic spring, he developed a platinum-iridium helical coil model that could be inserted by the transvenous approach and is the basis for all modern-day pacemaker and defibrillator leads. Although perhaps not a direct connection, the pioneering work of

Chardack in VA leads inevitably to Dr. Ross Fletcher, now chief of staff at the Washington, D.C., VA Medical Center, formerly chief of the Cardiology Section, an internationally recognized expert in clinical electrophysiology and pacemakers, whose innovative methods of pacemaker follow-up are the basis for the trans-telephonic techniques employed throughout cardiology today. The author attests from personal observation that Dr. Fletcher's clinical efforts are single-minded, aimed solely at the well-being of his patients. To document the cardiovascular expertise available in the Veterans Administration dating from the mid-1960s, the cardiology staff at the Washington, D.C., VA Medical Center is representative. Early in Dr. Fletcher's career in the Cardiology Section, down the hall was renowned hypertension investigator Dr. Edward Freis (Frolich 2005), as well as Hubert Pipberger, electrocardiographer and one of the proponents of vectorcardiography and later computerized interpretation of the electrocardiogram. Also in the group was Dr. Jay Cohn, whose pioneering ideas regarding treatment of left ventricular systolic function must have benefited from the expertise of Dr. Freis.

The Cooperative Studies Program

Historical examples of therapeutic trials include, for example, the treatment of scurvy with citrus fruit, and even the "King's meat" trial in the Old Testament Book of Daniel, but the modern randomized clinical trial in medicine had its inception around 1950, with the publication of a trial of streptomycin in the treatment of tuberculosis designed by Sir Austin Bradford Hill (Streptomycin in Tuberculosis Trials Committee 1948), generally credited as the originator of the modern randomized clinical trial. Trials sponsored by the Department of Veterans Affairs Cooperative Studies Program have had a far-reaching beneficial effect in cardiovascular disease management, including one of the first Cooperative Studies sponsored by the Veterans Administration, an assessment of the impact of therapy in hypertension carried out by Dr. Freis and colleagues (Mohler & Freis 1960). Starting with the VA hypertension trial, arguably the first major randomized trial in cardiovascular medicine, and continuing through current clinical programs intended to improve cardiovascular care and the care process, an underlying tenet of VA is continuous improvement in care, and one implementation of this institutional aim has been in research and development. The Veterans Administration Cooperative Study on Effects of Treatment on Morbidity in Hypertension, organized prior to but among the inciting stimuli for the establishment of the VA Cooperative Studies Program, was a randomized, double-blind, placebo-controlled trial of drug therapy in hypertension. Although the effectiveness of treatment of malignant hypertension had been amply demonstrated by such noted investigators as Harriett Dustan, Pricilla Kincaid-Smith, Maurice Sokolow (not referenced here), and Freis himself (Mohler & Freis 1960), the first specific aim to be addressed by the VA hypertension study group, the impact of antihypertensive drug therapy on outcome, had not been demonstrated in a randomized clinical trial. At the time there was substantial skepticism that treating hypertension could have a long-term beneficial effect, but as did Freis, authorities outside the mainstream of hypertension research felt that data needed to be brought to bear on the question (Relman 1966). The VA medical centers participating in the trial included the Bronx; Brooklyn; Pittsburgh; Richmond; Salt Lake City; San Juan, Puerto Rico; Washington, D.C.; West Haven, Connecticut; and West Roxbury, Massachusetts. Listed as a consultant to the study, but also the site investigator at the Iowa City VAMC, was Dr. Walter M. Kirkendall, a faculty member in the Department of Internal Medicine at the University of Iowa, already an internationally respected authority in hypertension, who would eventually be this author's mentor in internal medicine. Antihypertensive therapy in the treatment arm included hydrochlorthiazide, reserpine, and hydralazine. Cardiovascular events were the driving endpoint of the trial, including death, nonfatal myocardial infarction, ischemic stroke, intracerebral hemorrhage, transient ischemic attack, congestive heart failure, severely elevated blood pressure, azotemia, atrial fibrillation, and antihypertensive drug toxicity. Notably, of the 143 patients with this severe degree of hypertension covered in the first publication of the hypertension coop study group, 77 were black and 66 white. The original report of the trial was published in 1967 (Veterans Administration Cooperative Study Group on Antihypertensive Agents 1967) and demonstrated a reduction in morbidity in patients with average diastolic blood pressures between 115 and 129 mm Hg, from data that were "unblinded" to the investigators by the study biostatistician Lawrence Shaw, AM, when he saw that the event rate had been lowered with a convincing degree of statistical significance. Although these results are virtually self-evident now, at that time the VA hypertension study was groundbreaking, showing for the first time in an appropriately powered study that treating hypertension improves outcome. The group continued to enroll patients with milder degrees of hypertension, diastolic blood pressure less than 114 mmHg, for an additional two years, with biostatisticians monitoring the unblinded data and sharing the results with Central Office officials. As described by Marguerite Hays (1980) in *A Historical Look at the Establishment of the Department of Veterans Affairs Research and Development Program*, working at his Central Office desk on a Saturday was the soon-to-be-renowned

Thomas Chalmers, MD, assistant chief medical director for research and education and already an authority on clinical trials. Looking at the latest statistical results from the hypertension study, Chalmers saw immediately the impact of therapy in milder hypertension and sent out instructions to all clinics to break the blind and place all patients on active treatment. Borrowing one of the three components of the Belmont Principles, Dr. Chalmers at the time acted beneficently, and as a forerunner of the modern Data Safety and Monitoring Board. Subsequent reports followed documenting effectiveness of drug therapy in milder degrees of hypertension (Veterans Administration Cooperative Study Group on Antihypertensive Agents 1970) and the impact comorbidities (Veterans Administration Cooperative Study Group on Antihypertensive Agents 1972). The successful conduct of the trial was the basis for the prestigious Albert and Mary Lasker Clinical Research Award given to Dr. Freis in 1971. Dr. James Taguchi (then chief, Cardiology Section, Dayton VAMC), and Dr. Freis reported an updated analysis in the *New England Journal of Medicine* (Taguchi & Freis 1972) on 380 hypertensive veterans with initial diastolic blood pressures of 90 to 114 mm Hg. Patients in the treatment arm were analyzed in two groups: subgroup A, in which blood pressures fell in response to therapy from an average of 105 mm Hg pretreatment to 98 mm Hg, and subgroup B, in which the average blood pressure decreased from 103 mm Hg to 76 mm Hg. Although the event rate was higher in subgroup A than in subgroup B, 14.9 and 9.7 percent respectively, both rates were significantly lower than the 28.9 percent in the placebo group. An ingenious urinary riboflavin fluorescence test was utilized throughout the trial to demonstrate that adherence to therapy was the same in the treatment and placebo arms. The results of the subsequent analysis suggested that benefit occurred even when blood pressure was not lowered to normal. Whereas today we still strive for Joint National Committee (JNC) blood pressure control as recommended in the JNC7 guidelines, the finding that partial blood pressure lowering is beneficial remains true (ALLHAT Officers and Coordinators 2002).

The VA randomized trials of hypertension and of bypass surgery for stable angina and unstable angina (Luchi, Scott & Deupree 1987) were followed by such investigations as

the aspirin in unstable angina trial (Lewis et al. 1983);

the Department of Veterans Affairs Vasodilator in Heart Failure Trial (Cohn et al. 1986), or VHeFT-1, led by Dr. Jay Cohn of the Minneapolis VA, the first randomized trial to demonstrate a survival advantage of afterload reduction in heart failure;

the ACME Trial (Parisi, Folland & Hartigan 1992), led by Drs. Alfred Parisi and Edward Folland of the West Roxbury VA, the first randomized trial of percutaneous transluminal coronary angioplasty;

the VANQUISH Trial (Boden et al. 1998), led by Dr. William Boden from the West Roxbury VA;

the AWESOME Trial (Morrison et al. 2001), led by Dr. Douglas Morris of the Denver and then the Tucson VA; and

the recent COURAGE Trial (Boden et al. 2007), initiated by Dr. Boden and the Cooperative Studies Program and named by the American Heart Association one of the ten most important research studies of the first decade of the twenty-first century.

These investigations underscore a continuing commitment by the Cooperative Studies Program and VA to the advancement of clinical cardiovascular knowledge.

Three of these trials deserve further discussion—VHeFT-1 (Cohn et al. 1986), ACME (Parisi, Folland & Hartigan 1992), and the COURAGE Trial (Boden et al. 2007)—for having a seminal and/or sustained impact on the management of the diseases that were studied. The VHeFT-1 trial was the first sufficiently powered, randomized trial to demonstrate that effective vasodilator therapy could have a favorable impact on left ventricular systolic function and survival in patients with chronic left ventricular systolic heart failure. A total of 642 patients with heart failure who were taking digoxin and a diuretic were entered in the trial from 1980 through 1985 at eleven VA medical centers. Patients were randomized to receive double-blind treatment with placebo, prazosin, or the combination of hydralazine (H) 300 mg daily and isosorbide dinitrate (I) 160 mg daily and were followed up for an interval of at least six months, with an average follow-up of 2.3 years. The results of the trial were published in the *New England Journal of Medicine* in 1986. Of the 642 patients, 284 (44.2 percent) had coronary disease and 385 (55.8 percent) had heart failure unrelated to coronary disease. A perhaps unavoidable weakness of the trial, but nevertheless a weakness, was that only men between the ages of eighteen and seventy-five were part of the study. Follow-up ended in December 1985 without early stopping. Mortality over the entire period of follow-up was lower in the H/I group, though the difference reached borderline statistical significance, but for the prespecified endpoint of mortality at two years, the risk reduction for the H/I group was 34 percent, $p < 0.028$. Mortality in the prazosin group was similar to that in the placebo group. Left ventricular ejection fraction rose significantly in the

H/I group, but not in the prazosin or placebo groups. Notably, in the VHeFT-2 trial (Cohn et al. 1991), the same VA Cooperative Study group confirmed the benefit demonstrated in VHeFT-1 for the H/I combination and demonstrated a survival benefit of angiotensin-converting inhibitors. In this trial, the benefit was in reduction in sudden cardiac death that was confined to NYHA Class I and II. A provocative recent reanalysis of VHeFT-1 suggested that the majority of the survival benefit was in African Americans, and has engendered the hypothesis that the H/I combination may be acting as an antioxidant (Taylor et al. 2004).

The Angioplasty Compared to Medicine (ACME) Trial (Parisi, Folland & Hartigan 1992) deserves mention because it is the first randomized trial of percutaneous transluminal coronary angioplasty. It was initiated in May 1987 and randomized patients over an interval of three years. Notably, the trial was also one of the first PTCA trials to include an economic analysis. The results of the trial were published in 1990 in the *New England Journal of Medicine*. Among VA investigators were Dr. Kenneth Morris at the Durham VA, Dr. John Giacomini at the Palo Alto VA, Dr. Eric Bates at the Ann Arbor VA, Dr. John Hodgson at the Richmond VA, and the author at the Lexington VA. We tested the hypothesis that angioplasty would result in better exercise tolerance and better angina status at six months following the procedure compared to medical therapy alone in patients with single-vessel coronary disease. Single-vessel disease patients were eligible for the trial if they had stable angina pectoris, a strikingly positive exercise tolerance test (ST segment depression ≥ 3 mm), or a myocardial infarction within the past three months. All patients had ≥ 1 mm of ST segment depression on exercise testing or evidence on thallium scanning of a reversible defect in the area corresponding to the qualifying lesion. One hundred and seven patients were randomly assigned to medical therapy and 105 to PTCA. The procedure was clinically successful in 80 of 100 patients in the PTCA group who actually underwent the procedure; two patients required emergency coronary artery bypass surgery, and by six months after the procedure 16 patients had had repeat PTCA. Myocardial infarction occurred in 5 patients assigned to PTCA and to 3 patients assigned to medical therapy. At six months 64 percent of patients (61 of 96) in the PTCA group were free of angina pectoris, compared to 46 percent (47 of 102) in the medically treated group, p < 0.01. The total duration of exercise on the Standard Bruce protocol increased by 2.1 minutes in the PTCA group, compared to 0.5 minute in the medicine group, p < 0.0001, and patients in the PTCA group were able to exercise longer on the treadmill without angina, p < 0.01. The use of medical resources, as measured by cumulative total of cardiac procedures and the number of hospital days at six months, was higher among patients in the PTCA group than in the medically treated patients, making PTCA the more costly treatment over the first six months. Thus, the ACME findings foreshadowed the tenor of many subsequent percutaneous coronary intervention trials: improved outcome in the variable assessed accompanied by a higher cost associated with the need for repeat procedures.

The Courage Trial was reported in 2007 in the *New England Journal of Medicine* (Boden et al. 2007). Organized between 1995 and 1998 by Drs. William Boden, Robert O'Rourke, and William Weintraub, and under the auspices of the VA Cooperative Studies Program and the redoubtable and nonpareil Pamela Hartigan, who had been biostatistician for the ACME study, the COURAGE Trial is the largest to date to investigate percutaneous coronary intervention. It addressed the question of whether PCI in combination with pharmacologic therapy and lifestyle intervention (optimal medical therapy) is superior to medical therapy alone in reducing cardiovascular events. The trial was multicenter and multinational, comprising 50 VA and non-VA U.S. and Canadian medical centers. Between 1999 and 2004 it randomized 2,287 patients with objective evidence of myocardial ischemia and significant coronary disease: 1,149 patients to PCI plus optimal medical therapy, and 1,138 to optimal medical therapy alone. The primary outcome was death from any cause and nonfatal myocardial infarction during a follow-up period of 2.5 to 7.0 years, median follow-up 4.6 years. In contrast to ACME, a single-vessel trial that assessed exercise tolerance and angina status, COURAGE evaluated outcomes, analogous to the VA Coop Study No. 4 some thirty years earlier. In the PCI + optimal medical therapy group there were 211 primary endpoint events, and there were 202 in the optimal medical therapy group: 4.6-year cumulative event rates of 19 and 18.5 percent, respectively; hazard ratio 1.05; and confidence interval 0.87-1.27, P = 0.62. There were no significant differences in the composite endpoint of death, myocardial infarction, and stroke; hospitalization for acute coronary syndrome; or myocardial infarction. Thus for the primary outcome of the trial, optimal medical therapy was as effective as PCI + optimal medical therapy, favoring an approach of medical treatment as the initial management of angina pectoris.

In addition to the primary outcome manuscript, the COURAGE Trial has spawned a wealth of meaningful substudy publications, and has pointed the direction for future study. One notable report in this regard is that of Shaw and colleagues, the COURAGE nuclear substudy (Shaw et al. 2008), which suggests that in patients with stable angina pectoris, there may be an extent of inducible myocardial ischemia as assessed by myocardial perfusion scintigraphy at or above which survival may be improved by revascularization, a hypothesis to be tested.

Available Cardiovascular Clinical Services in VA

The Department of Veterans Affairs operates the largest integrated healthcare system in the United States, including 154 hospitals in all fifty states and Puerto Rico. At this writing, 76 VA hospitals were operating cardiac catheterization laboratories (John Rumsfeld, MD, personal communication), 67 of which carry out percutaneous coronary interventions. From CART-CL uploads, VA averaged 10,216 cardiac catheterization procedures for 2008 and 2009. Ninety-three of the 145 VA hospitals carry out cardiac device implantation, of which 56 perform both pacemaker and ICD implantation.

Cardiac transplantation is performed at the Richmond VAMC, the Madison VA, the Palo Alto VA, and the Nashville VA. More stable patients identified as warranting evaluation for cardiac transplantation undergo testing at the referring VA medical center, and a dossier is uploaded to the VA Central Office in Washington, D.C. The patient's records are then evaluated by an ad hoc committee composed of transplant physicians from the transplant VA centers for transplant listing. The majority of patients listed for transplant in this manner would be likely to be active Status 2 on a transplant at one of the centers. In practice, the majority of hearts acceptable for donation go to patients with higher acuity status. When a higher-acuity heart failure patient is identified, the local judgment to refer the patient out must be made with accuracy and alacrity, as a patient with potential to be listed Status 1A, the highest level of acuity for transplant, also has the potential to deteriorate rapidly. Fortunately in these cases, our cardiac transplant colleagues readily accept the critically ill heart failure patient who meets criteria for transplant evaluation. In the past five years at the Lexington VA, two such patients were air-evacuated to the closest VA transplant centers and ultimately underwent successful cardiac transplantation. From 2005 to 2010, an average of approximately 90 patients per year were referred for evaluation, and approximately 25 per year had transplant surgery.

Ongoing Continuous Improvement Efforts

The randomized clinical trials previously discussed constitute the scientific basis for improvement in quality of care and are evidence of a commitment by VA to advancement of biomedical knowledge. Through present-day quality improvement efforts such as Time Is Life, led by Principal Deputy Under Secretary for Health Dr. Robert Jesse, MD, and the External Peer Review Program (EPRP), by which performance at VA hospitals in the care of myocardial infarction is assessed at arm's length by an independent reviewing body, cardiovascular specialists are working to continuously improve quality of care at the level of the patient. Open-heart surgery in VA has benefited from the same self-examination approach, as embodied by the VA National Surgical Quality Improvement Program (Khuri, Daley & Henderson 2002), NSQIP (now, the VA Surgery Quality Improvement Program), first organized by the late Dr. Shukri Khuri, chief of cardiac surgery at West Roxbury VA, with particular emphasis in cardiac surgery developed under the auspices of Drs. Fred Grover and Karl Hammermeister and others at the Denver VA, the VA Continuous Improvement Cardiac Surgery Program (Grover et al. 2001). The cardiac portion of NSQIP was the first multicenter quality improvement initiative in cardiac surgery, the model for the New York Department of Public Health heart surgery database (Hannan et al. 1994) and quality improvement endeavors later organized by the Society of Thoracic Surgeons (Grover et al. 2001). One advantage in VA, the most public healthcare maintenance entity in the United States, is that openness leads to improvement.

Another national VA quality endeavor is the Cardiovascular Assessment, Reporting, and Tracking, or CART project, under the auspices of Dr. John Rumsfeld at the Denver VAMC. CART is a database of cardiovascular procedure performance throughout the VA system. It is a clickable subroutine within the Computerized Patient Record System (CPRS), the VA electronic medical record, itself an effort to improve quality of care. The initial area of emphasis in the reporting and tracking system is CART-CL (Catheterization Laboratory), which is utilized for catheterization procedure reporting in virtually every VA cath lab. Modeled after the National Cardiovascular Database Registry of the American College of Cardiology, CART-CL permits systematic data input for report generation, and the database is surveillable for assessment of performance in individual labs and across the VA system.

Two quality improvement efforts deserving of more detailed discussion are NSQIP and the Time Is Life program. In the mid- to late 1980s VA came under scrutiny for perceived quality problems in surgical care in the veterans' hospitals, specifically perceived higher mortality rates than in the private sector. Although at that time the "norms in the private sector" were in fact unknown, the Veterans Administration responded by initiating the National VA Surgical Risk Study (NVASRS) in forty-four VA medical centers (Khuri et al. 1997). From preoperative, intraoperative, and thirty-day outcome variables in a total of over 117,000 major operations, the NVASRS developed risk models for thirty-day mortality and morbidity in nine surgical subspecialties. The success of the NVASRS program encouraged VA to create an ongoing program, and NSQIP was established. The mandatory NSQIP risk-adjusted database program went into operation in 1987. Each year more than 110,000 major surgical cases have been added to the database, and there are now more than one million surgical cases in the VA system (Khuri, Daley & Henderson 2002).

A similar voluntary risk-adjusted system was initiated by the Society of Thoracic Surgeons for cardiac surgery in 1989 (Grover et al. 2001). By 2001 more than 74,000 cardiac surgical patients had been entered into NSQIP, and 1.6 million cases into the STS database (Khuri, Daley & Henderson 2002). Among other findings, in 2001 both the VA cardiac surgery and the STS databases demonstrated a decrease in the risk-adjusted cardiac surgical death rate during the preceding decade despite increased patient risk factor profiles, the ratio of observed to expected deaths decreasing from 1.05 to 0.9 for VA and from 1.5 to 0.9 for the STS (Grover et al. 2001). Risk factors predicting surgical death following coronary artery bypass surgery were remarkably similar for the two databases. Within VA, the database findings produce actionable data: when the observed-to-expected mortality of a VA cardiac surgical center is above the VA average, an automatic audit of the center is triggered. Aspects of risk-adjusted reporting have been questioned, for example, indications in the New York State database that the observed mortality may have been lowered by referral of high-risk cases to other centers or even out of state, and that expected mortality rates may have increased as a result of an increase in risk factors (Hannan et al. 1994). In VA, reducing the observed mortality rate by referring the patient out is usually not an option. For VA medical centers with sharing agreements for surgery with academic medical centers, the academic center is required to participate in NSQIP. Rather than a rationing of surgery, one effect of NSQIP may be a more careful consideration of the patients on whom open-heart surgery should be performed. On the other hand, the importance of honest reporting of risk, and thereby an accurate expected mortality, cannot be overemphasized.

In 2003 Peterson and colleagues, from the Center of Quality of Care and Utilization at the Houston VA Medical Center, and other contributing bodies published findings (Petersen et al. 2003) demonstrating underutilization of coronary arteriography after acute myocardial infarction (AMI) in VA hospitals compared to Medicare patients presenting to traditional fee-for-service hospitals: 43.9 versus 51 percent, odds ratio 0.79, confidence interval 0.57-0.96. However, controlling for availability of on-site cardiac procedures at the admitting hospital, there was no significant difference in the underuse of angiography among VA patients as compared with Medicare patients (odds ratio, 1.02; 95 percent confidence interval, 0.82 to 1.26) or in one-year mortality (odds ratio, 1.08; 95 percent confidence interval, 0.89 to 1.28). In a study reported in 2004 from a random sample of nearly 600 patients receiving care from VHA in twelve communities between 1997 and 2000, Asch and colleagues (2004) found that healthcare was generally of higher quality on 294 measures than that received by nearly 1,000 patients enrolled in commercial managed care plans in the same communities. On the other hand, in an external study commissioned by VA and also reported in 2004, analyzing administrative data from patients hospitalized with AMI between 1996 and 1999, Landrum and colleagues (2004) reported that survival was significantly lower at one year compared to patients whose care was funded by Medicare. A subsequent study (Maynard et al. 2006) showed that the higher mortality reported by Landrum and colleagues was related to a higher proportion of VA patients sustaining an AMI after having been admitted for another medical problem than in the Medicare cohort. Nevertheless, VA used the Peterson and Landrum findings as the impetus to initiate a systemwide program of acute cardiac care improvement. Part of the response was the Time Is Life program, among aspects of which were two national-level, mandatory meetings for cardiology representatives from every VA hospital. The first meeting took place in 2004, the second in 2005. Discussion of the means of getting guidelines for management of AMI was one of the primary aims of the first meeting, and all hospitals were charged with implementing systems to meet standards of care in the management of acute ST segment elevation (STEMI) and non-ST segment elevation myocardial infarction (non-STEMI). The second meeting reinforced the first and included presentations by hospitals with innovative approaches to the problem, for example, the accreditation of the Gainesville VAMC by the Society of Chest Pain Centers, the first VA hospital to gain SCPC accreditation, accomplished by a hospital task force led by Mary Lynn Allen, MD, then director of the Gainesville emergency room, now ACOS for Ambulatory Care. Subsequent meetings aimed at identifying strategies for optimizing clinical performance in acute coronary syndromes and congestive heart failure management were held in 2006, 2007, and 2008.

In 2009 Fihn and colleagues evaluated outcomes in myocardial infarction dating from when the cardiac care improvement initiative was undertaken, using the Medicare population as the comparator. Two separate analyses were performed, one of the annual mortality rates in VHA following AMI, the second to compare patients treated in VHA hospitals with those whose healthcare was funded by Medicare. The time period for assessing trends in AMI mortality in VHA was January 1, 2004, through September 30, 2006, and the sample size was 11,609 patients $\geq$ age sixty-five who had been assigned ICD9 (International Classification of Diseases 9th Revision) codes 410.xx at 145 VHA hospitals. Data sources for the VHA review were abstracted from records in the External Peer Review Program (EPRP). Trained abstractors under contract to EPRP assessed outcome. Mortality status was obtained from the VA Vital Status File. Data demonstrated a significant decline in adjusted thirty-day AMI mortality from 16.3 percent in 2004 to 13.9 percent in 2006, relative risk reduction 15 percent, p = 0.011. Similar declines were identified for in-hospital and ninety-day mortality.

The VHA-Medicare comparison included 27,494 VHA patients aged sixty-five and older and 789,400 Medicare patients from January 1, 2000 to June 30, 2005, the same age range and ICD9 codes as in the VHA substudy, except 410.x2. The records for VHA patients in the comparison substudy were extracted from the VA Patient Treatment File (PTF), those of the Medicare cohort from the Medicare Provider Analysis and Review (MedPAR) File. Vital status for the VHA patients was gleaned from the VA Vital Status File, and that of the Medicare patients from the Social Security Administration death master file and the Medicare vital status file. The thirty-day mortality following AMI declined from 16.0 percent during 2000–2001 to 15.7 percent during 2004–June 2005 in VHA and from 16.7 percent to 15.5 percent in Medicare patients in private sector hospitals. Thus, the odds ratio of death in the VHA versus Medicare patients in the private sector was 1.02, 95 percent confidence interval 0.96-1.08 (p = 0.60).

The foregoing findings appear to lay to rest concerns raised in the earlier Peterson and Landrum studies indicating higher mortality in AMI. In the Fihn analysis, outcomes following AMI for the two medical systems were similar. Interestingly, the reduction in mortality observed in the two systems for the interval 2000 to 2005 was also similar. The reasons for the decrease in the VA population may include the cardiac care initiatives described previously. Another and possibly more likely explanation are VA data from 2006 showing that patients with a Class I indication for therapy received aspirin, statins, and beta blockers at least 95 percent of the time and that patients with a left ventricular ejection fraction of less than 40 percent received angiotensin-converting enzyme inhibitors 87 percent of the time, results exceeding the performance of all hospitals reporting to the Joint Commission on Hospital Accreditation (2006). It has been postulated that use of Class I-indicated pharmacologic therapies and rehabilitation during and after hospitalization is responsible for over 90 percent of the mortality reduction following AMI, and less than 10 percent from revascularization (Ford et al. 2007). This author believes that the computerized medical record accounts in some significant part for the improvement in the VA patients. Possible reasons for declining AMI mortality in Medicare patients in the private sector include success of guideline-based improvement initiatives by organizations such as the American Heart Association and the American College of Cardiology.

Future Directions and Policies

One can anticipate that the strategy in VA medical care, to quote Dr. Jesse, will be to find not just what works, but what works best (Department of

Veterans Affairs 2010), and to incorporate these emerging best medical practices and guidelines as the standard approach in the care of the veteran patient. An openness to change for the better, just openness plain and straightforward, should and will continue to be guidewords. Institutional candor in VA is exemplified by its policy on disclosure of adverse medical events, which was recently praised in the *New England Journal of Medicine* (Dudzinski et al. 2010), and the genesis of which is owed in at least significant part to my former colleague at the Lexington VAMC, past chief of staff Dr. Steve Kraman (2001). Not only in cardiology but in all aspects of VA healthcare, part of the reason for progress is that VA is in fact owned by the citizens of the United States and is therefore subject to the full scrutiny of the populace, which we in VA should only view as productive. The importance of research and development to the advancement of medical care cannot be overstated. For the author, participation with colleagues in VA Cooperative Studies continues to be a high point, the opportunity to be part of the "crown jewel" of the VA research program. In terms of clinical decision making, the late, plain-spoken Dr. Chalmers is reputed to have said, "You should always endeavor to enroll patients in clinical trials: that way, you'll be wrong only 50% of the time," and there may be no better endorsement of the impact of VA randomized cardiovascular trials than this succinct statement. Perusal of the participant appendices in the left main disease paper (Takaro et al. 1976) is instructive of physician quality in VA: Andrew Gage, Ross Fletcher, Alfred Parisi, William H. Barry, Henry Blackburn, and Park Willis III. The author hopes he has been able to reach the level of care provided by these exceptional doctors.

Acknowledgments: The author extends thanks and gratitude to Drs. Ross Fletcher, Frederick Grover, Robert Jesse, Henry Ooi, John Rumsfeld, Tim Takaro, and Joel Kupersmith, and to Dr. Kupersmith's wonderful assistant, Ms. Nazneen Mama, who so kindly provided information used in the writing of this chapter.

References

ALLHAT Officers and Coordinators for the ALLHAT Collaborative Research Group. (2002). Major outcomes in high-risk hypertensive patients randomized to angiotensin-converting enzyme inhibitor or calcium channel blocker vs. diuretics. *Journal of the American Medical Association* 288: 2981–2997.

Asch, D. A., McGlynn, E. A., Hogan, M. M., Hayward, R. A., et al. (2004). Comparison of quality of care for patients in the Veterans Health Administration and patients in a national sample. *Annals of Internal Medicine* 141: 938–945.

Bhayana, J., Gage, A. A. & Takaro, T. (1980). Long-term results of internal mammary implantation for coronary artery disease: A controlled trial by the participants of the Veterans Administration coronary artery bypass surgery Cooperative Study group. *Annals of Thoracic Surgery* 29: 234–242.

Boden, W. E., O'Rourke, R. A., Crawford, M. H., et al. (1998). Outcomes of patients with acute non-Q-wave myocardial infarction randomly assigned to an invasive strategy as compared with a conservative management strategy. *New England Journal of Medicine* 338: 1785–1792.

Boden, W. E., O'Rourke, R. A., Teo, K. K., Hartigan, P. M., Maron, D. J., Kostuk, W. J., Knudson, M., Dada, M., Casperson, P., Harris, C. L., Chaitman, B. R., Shaw, L., Gosselin, G., Nawaz, S., Title, L. M., Gau, G., Blaustein, A. S., Booth, D. C., Bates, E. R., Spertus, J. A., Berman, D. S., Mancini, G. B. J. & Weintraub, W.S., for the COURAGE Trial Research Group. (2007). Optimal medical therapy with or without PCI for stable coronary disease. *New England Journal of Medicine* 356: 1507–1516.

Chardack, W. M., Gage, A. A., Federico, A. J., Schimert, G. & Greatbatch, W. (1965). Five years' clinical experience with an implantable pacemaker: An appraisal. *Surgery* 58: 915–922.

Cohn, J. N., Archibald, D. G., Ziesche, S., Franciosa, J. A., et al. (1986). Effect of vasodilator therapy in chronic congestive heart failure: Results of a Veterans Administration Cooperative Study. *New England Journal of Medicine* 314: 1547–1552.

Cohn, J. N., Johnson, G., Ziesche, S., Cobb, F., et al. (1991). A comparison of enalapril with hydralazine-isosorbide dinitrate in the treatment of chronic congestive heart failure. *New England Journal of Medicine* 325: 303–310.

Department of Veterans Affairs. (2010). Web site: Public and governmental affairs, news releases, September 29–October 29.

Dudzinski, D. M., Hébert, P. C., Foglia, M. B. & Gallagher, T. (2010). The disclosure dilemma: Large-scale adverse events. *New England Journal of Medicine* 363: 978–986.

Fihn, Stephan D., Vaughan-Sarrazin, Mary; Lowy, Elliott; Poescu, Ioana; Maynard, Charles, et al. (2009). Declining mortality following acute myocardial infarction in the Department of Veterans Affairs healthcare system. *BMC Cardiovascular Disorders* 9: 44.

Ford, E. S., Ajani, U. A., Croft, J. B., Critchley, J. A., Labarthe, D. R., Kottke, T. E., Giles, W. H. & Capewell, S. (2007). Explaining the decrease in U.S. deaths from coronary disease, 1980–2000. *New England Journal of Medicine* 356: 2388–2398.

Frolich, E. D. (2005). In memoriam: Edward D. Freis, MD (1912–2005). *Hypertension* 45: 825.

Grover, F. L., Shroyer, L. W., Hammermeister, K., Edwards, F. H., et al. (2001). A decade's experience with quality improvement in cardiac surgery using the Veterans Affairs and Society of Thoracic Surgeons national databases. *Annals of Surgery* 234: 464–474.

Hannan, E., Kumar, D., Racz, M., et al. (1994). New York State's Cardiac Surgery Reporting System: Four years later. *Annals of Thoracic Surgery* 58: 1852–1857.

Hays, Marguerite. (1980). *A historical look at the establishment of the Department of Veterans Affairs Research and Development Program.* Baltimore, MD: Department of Veterans Affairs, R&D Communications, 232–233.

Joint Commission on Hospital Accreditation. (2006). Quality check.

Khuri, S. F., Daley, J. & Henderson, W. G. (2002). The comparative assessment and improvement of quality surgical care in the Department of Veterans Affairs. *Archives of Surgery* 137: 20–27.

Khuri, S. F., Daley, J., Henderson, W., Hur, K., Gibbs, J. O., Barbour, G., Demakis, J., Irvin, G., III, Stremple, J. F., Grover, F., McDonald, G., Passaro, E., Jr., Fabri, P. J., Spencer, J., Hammermeister, K. & Aust, J. B. (1997). Risk adjustment of the postoperative mortality rate for the comparative assessment of the quality of surgical care: Results of the National Veterans Affairs Surgical Risk Study. *Journal of the American College of Surgeons* 185, no. 4: 315–327.

Kraman, S. S. (2001). A risk management program based on full disclosure and trust: Does everyone win? *Comprehensive Therapy* 27: 253–257.

Landrum, M. B., Guadagnoli, E., Zummo, R., Chin, D. & McNeil, B. J. (2004). Care following acute myocardial infarction in the Veterans Administration Medical Centers: A comparison with Medicare. *Health Services Research* 39: 1773–1792.

Lewis, H. D., Davis, J. W., Archibald, D. G., et al. (1983). Protective effects of aspirin against acute myocardial infarction and death in men with unstable angina: Results of a Veterans Administration Cooperative Study. *New England Journal of Medicine* 309: 396–403.

Luchi, R. J., Scott, S. M. & Deupree, R. H. (1987). Comparison of medical and surgical treatment for unstable angina. *New England Journal of Medicine* 316: 977–984.

Maynard, C., Lowy, E., Rumsfeld, J., Sales, A. E., Sun, H., Kopjar, B., Fleming, B., Jesse, R. L., Rusch, R. & Fihn, S. D. (2006). The prevalence and outcomes of in-hospital acute myocardial infarction in the Department of Veterans Affairs Health System. *Archives of Internal Medicine* 166: 1410–1416.

Medical research in the Veterans Administration, FY 1968. (1968). Washington, DC: Government Printing Office, 85.

Mohler, E. R. & Freis, E. D. (1960). Five-year survival of patients with malignant hypertension treated with anti-hypertensive agents. *American Heart Journal* 60: 329–335.

Morrison, D. A., Sethi, G., Sacks, J., Henderson, W., Grover, F., Sedlis, S., Esposito, R., Ramanathan, K., Weiman, D., Saucedo, J., Antakli, T., Paramesh, V., Pett, S., Vernon, S., Birjiniuk, V., Welt, F., Krucoff, M., Wolfe, W., Lucke, J. C., Mediratta, S., Booth, D. C., Barbiere, C. & Lewis, D., for the Investigators of the Department of Veterans Affairs Cooperative Study 385, the Angina with Extremely Serious Operative Mortality Evaluation (AWESOME). (2001). Percutaneous coronary intervention versus coronary artery bypass graft surgery for patients with medically refractory myocardial ischemia and risk factors for adverse outcomes with bypass: A multicenter, randomized trial. *Journal of the American College of Cardiologists* 38: 143–149.

Murphy, M. L., Hultgren, H. N., Detre, K., Thomsen, J. & Takaro, T. (1977). Treatment of chronic stable angina. A preliminary report of survival data of the randomized Veterans Administration Cooperative Study. *New England Journal of Medicine* 297: 621–627.

Parisi, A. F., Folland, E. D. & Hartigan, P., on behalf of the Veterans Affairs ACME investigators. (1992). A comparison of angioplasty compared to medicine in the treatment of single-vessel coronary artery disease. *New England Journal of Medicine* 326: 10–16.

Petersen, L. A., Normand, S.-L. T., Leape, L. L. & McNeil, B. J. (2003). Regionalization and the underuse of angiography in the veterans affairs healthcare system as compared with a fee-for-service system. *New England Journal of Medicine* 348: 2209–2217.

Relman, A. S. (1966). Comment. *Controversy in Internal Medicine* 101–102.

Shaw, L. J., Berman, D. S., Maron, D. J., Mancini, G. B., Hayes, S. W., Hartigan, P. M., Weintraub, W. S., O'Rourke, R. A., Dada, M., Spertus, J. A., Chaitman, B. R., Friedman, J., Slomka, P., Heller, G. V., Germano, G., Gosselin, G., Berger, P., Kostuk, W. J., Schwartz, R. G., Knudtson, M., Veledar, E., Bates, E. R., McCallister, B., Teo, K. K., Boden, W. E. & COURAGE investigators. (2008). Optimal medical therapy with or without percutaneous coronary intervention to reduce ischemic burden: results from the Clinical Outcomes Utilizing Revascularization and Aggressive Drug Evaluation (COURAGE) Trial Nuclear Substudy. *Circulation* 117, no. 10: 1283–1291.

Streptomycin in Tuberculosis Trials Committee. (1948). Streptomycin treatment of pulmonary tuberculosis: A Medical Research Council investigation. *British Medical Journal* 2: 769–782.

Taguchi, J. & Freis, E. D. (1972). Partial reduction of blood pressure and prevention of complications in hypertension. *New England Journal of Medicine* 291: 329–331.

Takaro, T., Hultgren, H. N., Lipton, M. J. & Detre, K. M. (1976). The VA cooperative randomized study of surgery for arterial occlusive disease II: Subgroup with significant left main lesions. *Circulation* 54 (Supp.): III107–117.

Taylor, A. L., Ziesche, S., Yancy, C., Carson, P., et al. (2004). Combination of isosorbide dinitrate and hydralazine in blacks with heart failure. *New England Journal of Medicine* 351: 2049–57.

Veterans Administration Coronary Artery Bypass Surgery Cooperative Study Group. (1984). Eleven-year survival in the Veterans Administration randomized trial of coronary bypass surgery in stable angina. *New England Journal of Medicine* 311: 1333–1339.

Veterans Administration Cooperative Study Group on Antihypertensive Agents. (1967). Effects of treatment on morbidity in hypertension: Results in patients with diastolic blood pressures averaging 115 through 129 mm Hg. *Journal of the American Medical Association* 202: 1028–1034.

Veterans Administration Cooperative Study Group on Antihypertensive Agents. (1970). Effects of treatment on morbidity in hypertension, II: Results in patients with diastolic blood pressures averaging 90 through 114 mm Hg. *Journal of the American Medical Association* 213: 1143–1152.

Veterans Administration Cooperative Study Group on Antihypertensive Agents. (1972). Effects of treatment on morbidity in hypertension, III: Influence of age, diastolic blood pressure, and prior cardiovascular disease. *Circulation* 45: 991–1004.

Yussuf, S., Zucker, D. & Chalmers, T. C. (1994). Ten-year results of the randomized control trials of coronary artery bypass graft surgery: Tabular data compiled by the collaborative effort of the original trial investigators. Parts 1 & 2. *Online Journal of Current Clinical Trials* October 14. Doc. Nos. 14 & 15.

Chapter 4

Veterans' Sacrifices Made in the Quest for Cancer Treatment

Philip A. DeSimone

Introduction

War, as defined by the *New Oxford Dictionary* (2010), is a struggle between living beings or opposing forces. The struggle often results in both technical and scientific advances that help win the struggle or assuage human suffering. Examples of such advances are the blood transfusion, the femoral rod, and radar. The desire to win also results in advances not directly related to the immediate destruction that war causes. The effects may be so far-reaching that decades later a good can be found.

Erich Maria Remarque's *All Quiet on the Western Front* (1929) describes the horrors, inhumanities, and destructive powers of World War I as seen and experienced by the protagonist. The mental and physical sufferings of the individual soldiers on both sides of the conflict are vividly described in detail. Remarque paints a picture of "gas," nitrogen mustard gas, floating as clouds low to the ground and sinking into foxholes, seeking out the unprotected. The shouted word "gas" warned the soldiers of the horror of melting flesh and lungs. The winds over the battlefield, as winds of war, changed direction unexpectedly: the aggressor became the victim and the victim became the aggressor. Men scrambled to cover their skin and put on gas masks. The nitrogen mustard gas caused severe skin sloughing and pulmonary irritations, leading to respiratory failure.

After World War II, wounded servicemen were "rewarded" by the tobacco industry. The author remembers that on *The Arthur Godfrey Show* in the

1950s, one of the sponsors was the American Tobacco Company, the maker of Camel cigarettes, which gave away hundreds of cartons of cigarettes to veterans' hospitals throughout the United States. The servicemen's reward for their valor was the seed of addiction to nicotine and the long list of cancers caused by tobacco (lung, urinary bladder, head and neck, colon, etc.).

In the 1950s soldiers were "volunteered" to sit in bunkers close to nuclear test sites so that the destructive power of the atomic bomb could be assessed. The effects of radiation fallout were not known or fully understood. Also in the 1950s, the federal government developed a campaign called "Duck and Cover" (*Duck and Cover* 1951) as a means for civilians to "protect" themselves from radiation fallout. Schoolchildren had to practice hiding under a desk or placing paper over their heads to help protect themselves in case of a nuclear attack by the Soviet Union. As a young person, the feeling of the protection of a desk over my head or a piece of paper helped me not worry about any consequences of this invisible force. The soldiers in the vicinity of the explosion must have felt extremely safe in their bunkers.

War on Cancer

President Richard Nixon proposed the National Cancer Act of 1971, later to be known as the "war on cancer." It was an intensive campaign to find the cure for cancer. The U.S. Army's Fort Detrick, Maryland, was converted into a cancer research center, Frederick Cancer Research and Development Center. When it was proposed it was met with opposition from the National Institutes of Health (NIH) and the American Medical Association (AMA), because it funneled monies and resources into one specific area. Nixon was quoted as saying, "I hope in the years ahead we will look back on this action today as the most significant action taken during my administration."

The National Cancer Act gave the National Cancer Institute (NCI) a unique autonomy from the NIH, with a special budgetary authority. The Cancer Chemotherapy National Service Center (CCNSC) was developed to acquire new compounds for testing, with the awarding of acquisition and documentation of test agents. One of the act's major mandates was to support research and application of the results of that research to reduce the incidence of, morbidity from, and mortality from cancer. The Cancer Act now plays a strong role in the strategy of the Department of Veterans Affairs (VA) in its role in the treatment and management of cancer. Vincent T. DeVita, MD, former director of the NCI, commented on the positive effects of the National Cancer Act. It was predicted that cancer incidence and mortality would rise as a straight line until the year 2000. Starting in 1990, cancer incidence and mortality have declined every year by about 1.2 percent. The trend of rapidly escalating incidence of mortality has been reversed. Dr. DeVita stated that the NCI was reshaped in the way it was supposed to be by the Cancer Act.

Physicians Data Query (PDQ) is a comprehensive cancer database. Today it contains data from 8,000+ open, and 19,000 closed, cancer clinical trials, information on 1,200 agents used in the treatment of cancer and cancer-related disorders (National Cancer Institute n.d.). The information is peer-reviewed, evidence-based summaries of adult and pediatric cancers and treatments, supportive and palliative care, screening, prevention, genetics, and complementary and alternative medicine. All physicians in the world have access to PDQ (National Cancer Institute n.d.). The National Cancer Act not only changed cancer management, research, and education, but it helped change society's attitude toward the word *cancer*. It was no longer whispered as a dirty word and was brought into the light as something that must be dealt with openly, frankly, and forthrightly. Our society now wages a war on cancer.

The cancer surveillance arm of the NCI, through its nine SEER (Surveillance, Epidemiology, and End Results) regions, has demonstrated the falling incidence of cancer (National Cancer Institute 2008). Beginning in 1990, a decrease in the rate of cancers was observed, from 510 cases per 100,000 to 460 cases per 100,000 in 2005. The decreases were seen in both men and women. The greater rate of change occurred in men: from 660 to 540 per 100,000; for women the drop was from 435 to 410 per 100,000. All groups demonstrated a fall in the annual percent change from 2000 to 2006. Black men and women had the highest rate of change in mortality, 3.0 and 2.2, respectively. Similar changes, but less steep, were seen in white men and women. The falling rates for males have implications for the veteran population as it ages. Cancers in men, including prostate, lung and bronchus, and colon/rectum fell precipitately from 1990 to 2005. For all women, white and African American, only colorectal cancers had begun to decline before 1990. Bronchus/lung cancer showed only a slight change in incidence but a rise in the delayed–adjusted of .5 percent. As the number of women in the armed forces increases, the impact of this lack of change will greatly affect VA in years to come. The groundwork laid by the National Cancer Act of 1971 may have been the foundation for positively changing the trend by making the population much more socially aware of the word "cancer." It is no longer a dirty word; it now conjures up the response, "How can I fight to conquer this dreaded illness?"

The SEER data cited do not take into consideration the entire veteran population. A recent policy change by VA regarding sharing of cancer data has resulted in incomplete information on VA hospital cases. New data have been calculated to adjust for the undercounted cancer patients seen at VA hospitals. The United States is divided into seventeen SEER registries. All but four of these registries provide VA and non-VA case counts for the years 2000–2005. Data were stratified by year, diagnosis, gender, primary cancer, and five age groups. The VA counts were provided in tabular format, with no patient identifiers. For each SEER registry, the VA population proportion of patients was estimated by the year of diagnosis for 2000–2005, by gender and age. Based on these data, the conclusion was drawn that VA cases were underreported. The overall cancer burden was underestimated by 1.6 percent for males and .05 percent for females in 2005. Table 4.1 shows the estimated proportion of age-adjusted missing cases for the ten leading cancers. It clearly demonstrates that the percent missing ranges by site from 2.5 percent for hepatocellular to 0.4 percent for melanomas of the skin. Males were under-reported an average of .6 percent in SEER group 9 and 1.5 percent in SEER group 17 for the ten cancer sites. Table 4.2 shows correction factors for two SEER groups for the three leading cancers (prostate, lung/bronchus, and colorectal) in the VA hospital system when adjusted by age, sex, and race.

Table 4.1. Estimated Proportion of Missing Cancer Cases for 2005, and VA Adjustment Factor for Age-Adjusted Rate*

Rank Based on Counts	Cancer Site	Estimated Missing Cases (%) 2005†	VA Adjustment Factor for 2005 Age-Adjusted Rate‡
	All Sites Combined	1.6%	1.015
1	Prostate	1.4%	1.012
2	Lung and Bronchus	2.4%	1.023
3	Colorectal	1.5%	1.016
4	Urinary Bladder	1.0%	1.011
5	Head and Neck	2.4%	1.027
6	Melanomas—Skin	0.4%	1.005
7	Kidney and Renal Pelvis	2.0%	1.020
8	Leukemia	1.5%	1.015
9	NHL—Nodal	1.3%	1.013
10	Liver	2.5%	1.024

*Based on information for Atlanta, Connecticut, Iowa, New Mexico, San Francisco, Utah, San Jose–Monterey, Los Angeles, Rural Georgia, Greater California, Kentucky, New Jersey and projected to SEER-17 (excluding Louisiana).

†Difference between average proportion based on 2000–2003 and 2005.

‡Adjustment factors are generated for SEER-17 (excluding Louisiana) registry.

Table 4.2. Correction Factors for 2005 Age-Adjusted Rates by Race, Males Only

	White		Black	
Primary Cancer Site	SEER-9	SEER-17*	SEER-9^	SEER-17*
All Cancer Combined	0.93%	1.24%	4.22%	3.52%
Prostate	0.70%	1.00%		3.25%
Lung and Bronchus	1.37%	1.75%		5.36%
Colorectal	0.83%	1.36%		2.96%

*Louisiana is excluded from SEER-17.

^The site-specific numbers were too small for blacks in SEER-9 to estimate a correction factor.

SEER group 9 reported a decrease in whites of .93 percent, and SEER group 17 reported a decrease of 3.5 percent. Age was also taken into consideration for males, and it is surprising that ages forty though eighty-five plus make up the area of biggest discrepancy reporting in both SEER groups, as shown in table 4.3. The largest two age groups were fifty to fifty-four and sixty-five to sixty-nine. The underreporting ranged from 1.85 to 2.7 percent in the age group fifty to fifty-four and .32 percent in the age group sixty to sixty-four.

The Veteran Population

VA published a fact sheet in November 2008 tallying the veteran population for each war, from the American Revolution in 1775–1783 through the present conflicts in Iraq and Afghanistan. In World War II there were 16,100,000 total veterans; the Vietnam War had 8,700,000 veterans. The total number of Americans who have fought in wars is 41,800,000. There are presently 23,500,000 peacetime veterans or approximately 8 percent of the U.S. population. The veteran percentages of the population for World War II, Korea, and Vietnam are not available. The fact sheet also estimates the numbers of surviving World War II veterans and changes by year. In 2010 there were 1.7 million World War II veterans, and by 2020 only 233,000 World War II veterans will be alive. This information is needed for future cancer management. A National Service Veterans Organization survey conducted by VA from 2000 to 2005 provides a detailed assessment of the veteran population. Twenty-five million veterans were included. Overall, the average age of veterans is fifty-eight, with the largest group of veterans being between ages forty-five and sixty-four. A comparison to a 1990 survey demonstrated

Table 4.3. Correction Factors for 2005 Age-Specific Rates, All Cancer Sites Combined, Males Only, All Races

Age at Diagnosis	Correction Factor	
	SEER-9	SEER-17*
00 years	0.00%	0.00%
01–04 years	0.00%	0.00%
05–09 years	0.00%	0.00%
10–14 years	0.00%	0.00%
15–19 years	0.00%	0.00%
20–24 years	0.15%	0.24%
25–29 years	0.60%	0.44%
30–34 years	0.11%	0.23%
35–39 years	0.00%	0.23%
40–44 years	0.56%	0.64%
45–49 years	0.27%	1.05%
50–54 years	1.85%	2.70%
55–59 years	0.00%	0.90%
60–64 years	0.00%	1.32%
65–69 years	1.32%	2.06%
70–74 years	0.45%	1.51%
75—84 years	0.66%	1.51%
85+years	0.00%	0.26%

*Louisiana is excluded from SEER-17.

that the population is rapidly aging. The youngest cohort (under age forty-five) fell from 32 to 21 percent, and the oldest group (over age sixty-five) rose from 26 to 38 percent. These changes will affect planning for diseases of the aging population. Currently most veterans are white, married, and employed and have a combined household income of $50,000. A significant finding was the educational level achieved: only 11 percent of veterans had less than a high school education, 40 percent had high school diplomas or GED, and 49 percent had training or a bachelor's degree or higher. Our veteran population is well educated and possibly more sophisticated than the average American population. This population will be more prepared to discuss their future cancer needs in prevention, diagnosis, palliative care, hospice pain management, and treatment. The survey included an age and health conditions tabulation. It reported a 7.4 percent cancer incidence, with a range of 0.8 percent for the group under age thirty-five to 16.6 percent for veterans over age seventy-five. The six ten-year age groups showed a linear increase of cancer of 0.8, 1.4, 2.9,

6.5, 11.9, and 16.6 percent, respectively. The gender of the veterans was 77.6 percent males and 22.3 percent females. Cancer incidence follows high blood pressure, heart trouble, and lung problems in the survey's list of twenty-one maladies.

VA Cooperative Studies Program

The mission of the Cooperative Studies Program (CSP) is to advance the health and care of veterans through collaborative research studies that produce innovative and effective solutions to national healthcare problems (Department of Veterans Affairs. Cooperative Studies Program n.d.). The CSP is a division of the Clinical Science Research and Development Service of the VA Office of Research and Development. It was established in 1946 by Drs. Barnwell and Walker to evaluate the efficacy of various drugs in the treatment of tuberculosis. In 1972 it became a division of the VA Medical Research Services to evaluate and coordinate multicenter clinical trials. The CSP became the fourth independent research service within the VA Office of R&D in 1996. It has pandered to the desire of universities to be named centers of epidemiology, health economics, and a pharmacogenomics analysis laboratory to increase the stature of these lobbied university systems. An interagency agreement (IAA) between the VA and the NCI for a partnership in clinical trials for cancer was signed in 2000. The purpose of the partnership is to 1) increase the access of eligible veterans (as defined by P.L. 99-272 and P.L. 1101-508) to NCI-sponsored trials of new approaches to the diagnosis, treatment, and prevention of cancer; and 2) provide VA clinical investigators with expanded opportunities to participate in clinical cancer research. On the surface this is an excellent merger. The problem is that not enough patients or veterans are enrolled in cancer clinical trials. Only 5 percent of all cancer patients are entered in cancer trials. Future state-of-the art cancer treatment and management is based on a very highly motivated, selected patient population. Does this explain why 80 percent of cancer patients will die from their illness? Has the CSP been successful in its efforts to direct (conduct) clinical trials? The CSP has published a list of fifteen publications dating back to 2004, 2.5 articles per year. Only one publication was related to cancer. It described the accuracy of fecal occult blood testing by digital exam and was not a seminal study.

The National Cancer Strategy

Veterans Health Administration Directive VHA 2003-034 (Department of Veterans Affairs. Veterans Health Administration 2003) outlines the purpose of the strategy for the treatment of cancer and its maladies, providing background and objectives. The background cites American Cancer Society data that there would be 556,000 cancer deaths in 2003. VA estimated that 175,000 of these deaths would come from the VA hospital system. Approximately 35,000 new cases of cancer will occur in veterans yearly, and cancer is the second leading cause of death among veterans. Because the disease is often protracted, and treatment is quite demanding on resources, a strategy was developed to ensure the availability of the veterans' medical association for easy access to consistently high-quality care, cancer prevention, detection, and treatment. All the directive's objectives are important, and special emphasis should be placed on the clinical usefulness of prevention, screening, and early cancer detection, ensuring suitable, timely, patient-centered end-of-life care is made available when appropriate, and that the clinical research activities of VA contribute to the national research base and provide state-of-the-art prevention, diagnostic, and therapeutic interventions. The strategic elements are the heart of the policy. The directive covers prevention and education, screening, early detection and diagnosis, treatment, rehabilitation, clinical investigation and research (an area that has been expanded and is truly necessary to get good clinical research done in the VA hospital) (see appendix 2 of the IAA of January 1, 2000, between the VA and the NCI), tumor registry, and continuing and end-of-life care. The directive also outlines the specific duties of the chief patient care officer, which includes increasing participation in clinical trials in accordance with the interagency agreement. The VISN directors' responsibility is to designate comprehensive cancers to be included in the NCI cooperative cancer care program or in the Community Clinical Oncology Programs (COOPs). The medical director of each hospital is to ensure that there is a good tumor registry; provide hospice care; ensure that hospice services are available to every appropriate VA cancer patient when the need arises; provide and participate in palliative care (a very critical part); ensure a formal evidence-based protocol for pain management; and ensure the documentation of adequate patient pain relief is recorded in the patient record. This reflects VA's intention to define hospice as end-of-life care and palliative care as being pain management. Palliative care, as is the present vogue in hospitals, is delivered to patients before they are admitted to terminal care or truly end-of-life care in hospice. The medical directors must ensure that clinical trials, if clinical research in oncology is conducted, are NCI-sponsored, and that VA cooperative groups or all of the CCOP studies are given primary consideration over more limited local or regional protocols.

Attachment B of the national strategy (Department of Veterans Affairs. Veterans Health Administration 2003) recognizes malignancies as presumed to be service-connected based on hazardous exposures. The first exposure to mustard gases was full body exposure to nitrogen or sulfur mustard or to nitrogen mustard. The cancers related to nitrogen mustard included nasopharyngeal, larynx, lungs (except mesothelioma), squamous cell carcinoma of the skin, and acute lymphocytic leukemia. Exposure to ionizing radiation occurred before and during World War II and the occupation of Hiroshima and Nagasaki in Japan. The cancers secondary to ionizing radiation are all forms of leukemia; cancer of the thyroid, bone, brain, lung, ovaries, pharynx, esophagus, stomach, small intestine, pancreas, bile duct, gallbladder, salivary glands, and urinary tract; lymphomas except Hodgkin's disease; multiple myeloma; respiratory cancer including lung, larynx, trachea, and bronchus; and prostate cancer, with chronic lymphatic leukemia in the process of being added. This directive ended on June 30, 2008.

The VA National Care Strategy makes reference to two very important documents concerning cancer care and physician and patient education as it relates to the veteran and the veteran's family (Department of Veterans Affairs. Veterans Health Administration 2003). These are 1) the IAA of January 1, 2000, between the VA and NCI, and 2) the PDQ of the NCI (National Cancer Institute n.d.), available through the National Library of Medicine. The basic intent of the IAA is to form a new partnership between the NCI and VA with emphasis on new programs of preventive, diagnostic, and treatment innovations, and to provide VA clinical investigations with opportunities to participate in clinical research. The purpose of the IAA is to continue expanding the already productive relationship between VA and the NCI into a more formal and extensive partnership. Five major areas were considered in the agreement: 1) All eligible VA patients will have access to the full range of promising new approaches to the diagnosis, treatment, and prevention of cancer; 2) the NCI clinical trials will realize a potentially significant increase in accrual rates and shorten completion time of studies, providing earlier reporting; 3) VA investigators will expand opportunities to participate; 4) the cancer center cooperative group clinical trial program will be strengthened with the expanding pool of veterans and researchers, and 5) the involvement of the NCI and VA to improve the quality and the efficiency of planning of both agencies. This has an indirect effect on patients. The NCI will provide funding for the clinical cost of participation in the NCI programs so that it will not be the responsibility of the eligible veteran participating in a trial. The partnership directs that VA will receive access to user-friendly information systems through the PDQ, which provides quick access to comprehensive information on NCI-sponsored trials throughout the country. The NCI will provide PDQ for any VA facility or clinic lacking this process prior to such access. The Under Secretary of Health (see Attachment A of the national strategy; Department of Veterans Affairs.

Veterans Health Administration 2003) strongly encourages that patients with cancer be provided a patient version of the PDQ related to their disease so as to improve joint decision making. The directive also emphasizes that VA and the NCI will continue to jointly plan educational activities to expand the process of patients in the NCI-sponsored clinical cancer research. VA recognizes that excellence in cancer patient care is improved when the patient is well informed with the latest cancer knowledge. VA demonstrates its compassion and humanistic approach to cancer care in section 7, paragraph 1, under the heading "Care of Continual and Terminal Care Patients."

The professional and ethical obligations of VA providers do not end when it is clear that further therapeutic interventions do not hold the hope of cure. Indeed, it is then that the greater challenge to medical care begins. It is not appropriate to believe and never to state that there is no more that can be done for the patient. Although a cure may not be possible, care is always needed to provide a dignified and comfortable end-of-life, which should be as free as possible from anxiety, pain, and suffering. The national strategy also provides for a very formal relationship with organizations providing hospice care; pain management; and the foundation for continuing and terminal care needs to afford dignity, comfort, communication, and the company of loved ones during the patient's final days.

The IAA between VA and the NCI outlines a partnership in cancer clinical trials. The purpose of the agreement is to expand the relationship between VA and the NCI into a formal and extensive partnership. VA and the NCI will continue to jointly develop initiatives to inform veterans throughout the system of the opportunity to participate in clinical cancer research. The emphasis on research is very important in the field of clinical oncology. It is known that only between 3 and 5 percent of all patients are placed on clinical protocol. All the advances in cancer management, care, and therapy are based on a very small number of motivated, participating individuals in research protocols. If VA is to advance as well as any other Cooperative Study group, more patients are needed to increase accrual into cancer clinical trials. Clinical trials are the backbone for future cancer patient treatment involving the best approach to treatment, diagnosis, end-of-life care, pain management, screening, education, alternative care, and most important, prevention. VA has made bold advances in its strategy for cancer, which if followed should make it a world leader in the field of oncology.

Acknowledgments: Appreciation is extended to Brenda Frazier, Administrative Support in the Associate Division of Hematology, Oncology and Blood

& Marrow Transplantation, Department of Internal Medicine, University of Kentucky, Lexington, for her assistance in the completion of this chapter.

References

Department of Veterans Affairs. Cooperative Studies Program. (n.d.). http://www.research.va.gov/programs/csp/.

Department of Veterans Affairs. Veterans Health Administration. (2003). National cancer strategy. VHA Directive 2003-034. www1.va.gov/vhapublications/ViewPublication.asp?pub_ID=261 (accessed April 22, 2012).

Department of Veterans Affairs and National Cancer Institute. (2000). Interagency Agreement. January 1.

Duck and cover. (1951). Bert the turtle Civil Defense film. Can be viewed at http://archive.org/details/DuckandC1951 (accessed April 22, 2012).

National Cancer Act of 1971. Pub. L. No. 92-218.

National Cancer Institute. (2008). SEER cancer statistics review 1975–2008. http://seer.cancer.gov/csr/1975_2008/ (accessed April 22, 2012).

National Cancer Institute. (n.d.). PDQ®—NCI's comprehensive cancer database. http://www.cancer.gov/cancertopics/pdq/cancerdatabase (accessed April 22, 2012).

National Service Organization Survey. (n.d.). www.va.gov/vhapublications/viewpublications.

New Oxford American Dictionary. (2010). 3rd ed. New York: Oxford University Press.

Remarque, Erich Maria. (1929). *All quiet on the Western front.* London: G. P. Putnam's Sons.

VA fact sheet. 2008. www.va.gov/vhapublications/viewpublications.

Chapter 5

Mental Healthcare in the Veterans Health Administration

Robert C. Gresen

History

The Veterans Health Administration (VHA) is responsible for the provision of all medical services within the Department of Veterans Affairs (VA), including mental health. In fiscal year 2009 VHA had a budget of approximately $40 billion to deliver healthcare in over 1,400 unique locations, including 153 medical centers, more than 900 community-based outpatient clinics (CBOCs), 135 community living centers (formerly known as nursing homes), more than 200 mental health residential rehabilitation treatment programs, 232 vet centers, and 108 comprehensive home care programs. In 2008 alone, over five million veterans received care in VHA, with 773,600 episodes of inpatient care and over 60 million outpatient visits. As of September 30, 2008, VA had 278,565 employees, including 247,113 working for VHA (Department of Veterans Affairs, Office of Public Affairs and Media Relations 2009).

This chapter reviews the evolution of mental healthcare in VHA, starting in the mid-1990s. The focus of the present chapter does not include the Readjustment Counseling Service program, which is responsible for over 200 community-based vet centers and is separate from medical centers throughout the country. These centers have been in operation since the Vietnam era and have expanded their readjustment counseling services to veterans of all eras. This program provides services to a significant number of veterans, many but not all of whom also receive services through VHA's medical facilities and CBOC network. The vet center program is a critical component of the overall continuum of services provided by VHA. However, the creation, development, growth, and current status of this program are well beyond the scope of the present chapter.

In the mid-1990s a major reorganization and cultural shift was just beginning in VHA. VA healthcare was perceived by many as the worst example of what can result from "socialized medicine" (Longman 2007). Media coverage, both locally and nationally, portrayed VHA as outdated, inefficient, unsafe, expensive, and providing inconsistent care at best and poor quality care at worst. This degree of media attention, coupled with fewer elected congressional representatives who were veterans themselves, led to diminished political and budgetary support for VA and not infrequent calls for closing VA medical centers and vouchering veteran healthcare to the private sector. The number of veterans in the country was decreasing as well, which arguably contributed to diminishing political influence of veteran stakeholder groups, namely veterans' service organizations such as the American Legion, Disabled American Veterans, and Vietnam Veterans of America. Although efforts were being made within VA to address the many concerns being raised, a major overhaul was needed in order for VA to survive, much less thrive, going into the last several years of the twentieth century and beyond.

At this critical juncture in the history of VHA, Kenneth Kizer, MD, MPH, was appointed Under Secretary for Health, the top healthcare official in VHA. Dr. Kizer had a background of leading complex medical systems and a reputation for making major changes. Prior to his appointment, he served from 1985 to 1991 as the director of the California Department of Health Services and California's top health official. He had also served as California's chief of public health and before that, as director of the state's emergency medical services. Dr. Kizer served as VHA's Under Secretary for Health from 1994 to 1999 and was "widely credited as the chief architect and driving force behind the greatest transformation of VA healthcare since the system was created in 1946" (Robert Wood Foundation 2009). On July 24, 1997, he testified before the House Committee on Veterans Affairs' Subcommittee on Health and Subcommittee on Oversight and Investigations about his reorganization and transformational strategy (*VA's Treatment Facility Integration Strategy* 1997). He discussed the changes occurring in VHA in the context of changes occurring in the larger American healthcare system, with integrated service networks being a widely adopted model at the time. Such networks were being formed to pool and align resources to better serve patient needs. Kizer reported that VHA had developed its own version of a network integration strategy and had reorganized its facilities into twenty-two separate networks, or Veterans Integrated Services Networks (VISNs), based on regional utilization patterns. Further, he outlined five principles that were guiding the first forty facilities that had been approved for integration: increase access to care; increase the predictability and consistency of high-quality care; optimize the utilization of all resources including physical plant, capital assets, and personnel; modernize VA healthcare, including administrative practices, clinical and care management strategies, and physical assets; and reduce unnecessary costs and increase efficiency. Very importantly, Dr. Kizer was able to redirect any monies saved from these efficiencies to direct patient care needs rather than returning those monies to the Treasury, which was the usual process in the federal government.

Given the size of VHA and the scope of the change being implemented, the process outlined by Dr. Kizer, which was ultimately adopted by all facilities systemwide, required several years to accomplish. Nonetheless, Dr. Kizer was able to report preliminary results from these initial forty sites that were quite encouraging. By July 1997 facility integrations had produced savings of over $50 million, with significant additional gains expected. More than 1,000 staff had been reduced, with administrative staff decreasing and clinical staff being added. Even during a time of limited budgets, primary and specialty care were growing. Clinics were opened or enhanced at medical centers that had previously referred veterans to more distant facilities for care, resulting in improved access and reduced waiting times. Some of the reclaimed resources from these organizational efficiencies were used to open community-based outpatient clinics (CBOCs), replace needed medical equipment, and implement other facility capital improvements.

Prior to this time, virtually every VHA facility was organized in more or less the same way. Clinical services, for example, were typically organized by professional discipline, including those serving mental health needs. Psychiatrists were organized under a psychiatry service reporting to a chief psychiatrist, who reported to the facility's chief of staff. Psychology, social work, nursing, etc., had parallel structures. But in the spring of 1995, medical centers were given the flexibility to reorganize in order to respond to changing local and regional circumstances in their healthcare marketplaces. Organizational changes were subject to review and approval at higher levels, but over the next several years most VHA facilities reorganized into product or service line structures, with mental health often taking the lead. The new organizational structure in mental health was typically a mental health service line with mental health staff reporting to the chief of mental health regardless of professional discipline. Professional services (psychiatry, psychology, etc.) were sometimes retained as sections within the service line but often were eliminated completely. And as was the case for VHA's reorganization more globally, efficiencies were gained through staffing reductions over the next several years. For example, psychologist full-time employee equivalent (FTEE) was approximately 1,750 in fiscal year 1995. A steady erosion of psychologists occurred over the next several years, bottoming out at approximately 1,480 FTEE in fiscal year 2002 (Karlin 2007). This represented a decrease of 16 percent in a time period when the number of veterans being treated for mental health problems had increased by almost 35 percent, to 757,767 (Greenberg & Rosenheck 2003). By 2005 total mental health staffing was at approximately 14,000 FTEE, which was viewed by many as a low point, though the actual bottom may have occurred slightly earlier (Katz 2009)

The organizational changes set in motion by Dr. Kizer significantly impacted VHA's mental healthcare system in many ways. As a percentage of all veterans receiving VHA healthcare, users of mental health services declined from 18.3 percent in 1995 to 17.0 percent in 2001. The number of veterans receiving any inpatient mental health treatment declined 21 percent from 1995 to 2001 (76,798 to 60,990), and the total number of days of specialized inpatient mental healthcare fell 57 percent during this same period (3,520,314 to 1,501,265). Among those treated in an inpatient unit, the average number of stays per patient per year remained stable at 1.8. The average length of stay, however, fell from 25.4 days in 1995 to 13.5 days in 2001. The number of veterans receiving outpatient (nonpharmacy) mental healthcare services increased 37 percent during this time, resulting in a 21 percent increase in outpatient clinic visits (5,832,047 to 7,069,605). The absolute number of patients enrolled in residential treatment programs remained relatively small, increasing from 1,353 in 1995 to 5,757 in 1999, but then declining through 2001 (4453). The total days of residential care rose 237 percent from 1995 to 1999, followed by a 9 percent decline through 2001. Spending for VA mental health treatment increased 12.6 percent from 1995 to 2001, while total VHA health services spending increased 15.5 percent. Increasing expenditures for mental health residential and outpatient care were overshadowed by a larger decrease in spending on inpatient mental healthcare, leading to a 22 percent drop in the overall average mental health spending per VA user from 1995 to 2001. Spending for specialized inpatient mental healthcare fell 21 percent from 1995 to 2001, while spending for outpatient and residential care (excluding outpatient pharmacy) rose nearly 73 percent. Some of the monies saved were redirected to expand less expensive patient care services, primarily outpatient and residential care. This shift from inpatient to outpatient care also coincided with a rapid increase in medication spending. Outpatient medication costs for mental health rose 183 percent over this seven-year period. This major increase in mental health medication costs paralleled the national trend outside VA during this time. For example, from 1996 to 2006, medication expenditures for mental health in the United States increased over 350 percent, while expenditures for all other forms of mental healthcare remained essentially flat (Frank 2009).

In general, substance use disorder services may have been impacted more significantly and adversely than mental healthcare services during this time. Chen, Wagner, and Barnett (2001) examined substance use disorder services in VHA from 1993 to 1999. During this time VHA spending on all healthcare rose 10 percent, while monies available for substance use disorder treatment declined 41 percent. As a percent of all VA healthcare expenditures, substance use disorders accounted for 4.2 percent in 1993, compared to 2.3 percent in 1999. Similar to what was found for other mental health services, there was a significant shift from inpatient care to residential and outpatient services. Specialized inpatient costs fell more than 80 percent, while residential care, which treated a much smaller number of veterans, increased 133 percent, and outpatient treatment rose more than 50 percent. The number of veterans receiving inpatient substance use disorder treatment declined 75 percent, though the number of veterans receiving residential treatment increased by 300 percent, and those receiving outpatient care increased by 16 percent. Overall, the total number of VA patients receiving any type of healthcare rose 26 percent during this time, whereas the total number of veterans receiving care for substance use disorder increased less than 2 percent.

As noted by Chen, Wagner, and Barnett (2001), this disproportionate drop in mental health and substance use disorder services relative to other VHA healthcare was consistent with American healthcare trends in general during this time. VHA also mirrored broader healthcare system changes in regard to the venue in which services were being delivered, rapidly shifting from expensive inpatient care to less expensive residential and outpatient settings. As promised by Dr. Kizer, initially savings from downsizing of inpatient capacity were reinvested in other, less costly forms of mental health and substance use disorder care. Ultimately, only a percentage of those savings was made available for reinvestment purposes. Chen, Wagner, and Barnett (2001) specifically examined a variety of factors that could have accounted for the drop in substance use disorder services, such as demographics, changes in demand for care, prevalence, and severity of illness. They concluded that reduced funding was most likely accounted for by limiting treatment to only the most seriously ill and, in general, restricting veterans' access to these services.

Recalling Dr. Kizer's testimony from 1997, VHA's transformation of its healthcare delivery system was undertaken with five major goals in mind. Early results appeared to demonstrate that substantial progress was being made in at least four of the five areas: enhancing access to care, increased utilization of resources, modernizing the VHA healthcare system, and redirecting monies saved from efficiencies to serve additional direct patient care needs. However, the fifth goal, of increasing the predictability and consistency of high-quality care, was crucial to the ultimate success of Dr. Kizer's transformation of VHA. A primary method by which quality was to be evaluated was through a series of performance measures and monitors focused on key organizational and patient care variables. Specific organizational goals, as measured by these indicators, were incorporated into the performance contracts of network and facility leadership developed by top management in the VA Central Office. These measures included both process and outcome data covering various components of VHA's healthcare delivery system. In fiscal year 1998, performance measures specific to mental health included the percentage of patients discharged from an inpatient bed for mental healthcare who received outpatient care within thirty days of discharge; implementation of VHA's Guidelines for the Management of Major Depressive Disorder, Modules A and C; implementation of the Schizophrenia Module from VHA's Guidelines for the Management of Psychosis; the percentage of veterans discharged to independent housing from VHA homeless programs; and the percentage of veterans who secured employment following discharge from a VHA homeless program. Timeliness of scheduling outpatient appointments and other generic measures covering research, safety, and patient satisfaction were typically applied across all clinical programs, including mental health. Over the years, measures and monitors were added and subtracted depending on past performance, the emergence of new issues, and other factors.

As improvements were demonstrated through positive changes in performance measures and through favorable comparisons with other healthcare systems, VHA began to be recognized as providing high-quality healthcare services at a very good price (Longman 2007). This progress did not come easily, nor did it develop evenly across the system or within all sectors of VHA healthcare. In particular, questions and concerns were raised about the impact of VHA's reorganization and transformation on the mental healthcare system in particular. These questions were being raised by oversight committees responsible for monitoring the delivery of and recommending needed improvements to VHA mental healthcare, such as the Committee on the Care of Severely Chronically Mentally Ill Veterans (SMI Committee), a congressionally mandated group charged with monitoring VHA's capacity to care for its most vulnerable mental health patient population. Another outside stakeholder group, the National Alliance for the Mentally Ill (NAMI), provided testimony to the House Veterans Affairs Committee in 2001

(NAMI E-news 2001) that supported earlier concerns of the SMI Committee. NAMI noted issues with the current budgetary process utilized by VHA, which provided money to the VISN level but did not allocate specific funding amounts for the care of the mentally ill. This became of particular importance and concern given the major reorganization and decentralization that was occurring. NAMI opined that adequate assurances were not being provided that the needs of veterans with mental illness were being met, especially as budgets had been essentially frozen for the previous five years and staffing reductions, as noted previously, had occurred. NAMI testified that in fiscal year 1999, 191,606 veterans were treated with a severe mental illness, but only 33,531 (18 percent) received any form of treatment as an inpatient. Recognizing, and indeed supporting, the treatment of severe mental illness in the community to the greatest extent possible, NAMI was concerned that veterans were finding it increasingly difficult to obtain needed inpatient care due to the precipitous drop that had occurred in inpatient treatment capacity. Some of NAMI's concerns were validated and supported by an April 2000 Government Accountability Office (GAO) report (GAO HEHS-00-57, 2000), which concluded that between 1996 and 1998 inpatient services dedicated to the seriously mentally ill decreased by 19 percent and substance use disorder inpatient treatment beds decreased by 41 percent. Additional NAMI testimony emphasized the importance of providing a full array of evidence-based and best practice services to veterans, not merely demonstrating that the number of veterans being seen was increasing. Data were provided suggesting VHA may have been underserving the seriously mentally ill veteran population with evidence-based services such as intensive case management. NAMI was also concerned that integrated care of individuals dually diagnosed with a mental illness and a substance use disorder, another evidence-based modality, was not widely available in VHA. Despite VHA's commitment to enhance access to healthcare services, the majority of new outpatient clinics being opened were not providing any form of mental healthcare. NAMI also expressed concern that policies and procedures being implemented by VHA were raising barriers to veterans with serious mental illness against receiving the most appropriate and effective medications, including more recently developed and more expensive atypical antipsychotics. NAMI was an ardent supporter of the transition of mental health services to a psychosocial rehabilitation approach, including recovery-oriented care, which is discussed later in this chapter. During its testimony, NAMI recognized that an important paradigm shift within the VHA mental healthcare system would be needed to implement psychosocial rehabilitation and recovery-oriented care. Such a shift would require significant continuing education for existing VHA mental health staff, as many had not been trained in these approaches. Similarly, NAMI encouraged and supported a redoubling of efforts to establish consumer councils at the facility and network level to allow consumers, family members, veterans' service organizations, and community agencies to discuss services, policies, and issues of importance to veterans recovering from mental illness. NAMI was also acutely aware of the serious problem of homelessness among veterans, noting that over 250,000 veterans were estimated to be on the streets and homeless on a typical night. Given that 43 percent of these veterans were believed to have serious mental illness and 69 percent to have substance use disorders, VA was urged to increase its focus on this most vulnerable population.

In 2002 the American Psychiatric Association, along with the Chair of the SMI Committee, told the Senate Veterans Affairs Committee that VHA mental health services had been eroding since 1996. They noted that expenditures for the care of veterans with mental health disorders in VHA had declined 20.6 percent from 1995. Further, spending for substance use disorder services declined 41 percent from 1993 to 1999 despite an overall VA budget increase of 10 percent during that same period. They also testified to mental health service access shortfalls in areas such as CBOCs and mental health intensive case management (MHICM) programs, VHA's version of assertive community treatment (Mulligan 2002).

In January 2003 the SMI Committee made several recommendations supporting the theme of recovery-oriented services. Recommendations included the development and/or enhancement of services such as supported employment and housing, and family psychoeducation, an evidence-based intervention associated with positive outcomes for both patients and family members. In addition, the committee advocated for other standing recommendations that were highlighted in NAMI's testimony, including increased access to mental health services in CBOCs, expansion of MHICMs, and staff education focused on recovery-oriented principles and services. Actively involving veterans and their family members when planning and evaluating mental health services was viewed as an important step by the committee in reducing the stigma associated with mental illness and to promote recovery (Department of Veterans Affairs, Mental Health Consumer Council 2003).

Another congressionally mandated oversight group, the Special Committee on Post-Traumatic Stress Disorder (PTSD Committee), was also issuing annual reports, containing recommendations for improving VHA services to veterans with PTSD. PTSD, which can be a consequence of exposure to life-threatening events such as combat, is of particular interest to Congress and to VHA given its veteran population. Due to the special place of PTSD in

VHA, this committee was first mandated by Congress in the 1980s. The Honorable Lane Evans, ranking Democratic member of the House Veterans Affairs Committee, requested the GAO to assess VHA's implementation of the PTSD Committee's recommendations from its 2004 annual report (GAO 2005). This report contained thirty-seven recommendations as well as an assessment of VHA's response to the committee's recommendations from earlier years. The GAO ultimately studied twenty-four of the committee's prior recommendations, which were focused on the provision of clinical care. The GAO concluded that VHA had not fully implemented any of the recommendations, though progress had been made on at least fourteen of the twenty-four recommendations reviewed. It further concluded that VHA did not intend to fully implement twenty-three of the twenty-four recommendations until at least 2007, based on a review of VHA's planning documents at the time. Concerns were raised by the GAO about VHA's capacity to provide PTSD services to veterans who were already receiving care as well as to veterans returning from the ongoing conflicts in Iraq and Afghanistan. The GAO recommended that VHA prioritize the PTSD Committee's recommendations and develop a plan to expedite their implementation. VA strongly disagreed with these findings and any implication that adequate services were not being provided or that sufficient capacity did not exist to accommodate both current and newly returning combat veterans.

In November 2003 Secretary of Veterans Affairs Anthony Principi appointed a task force to review mental health and substance abuse services for all veterans, with an emphasis on those veterans who were homeless. The task force submitted a report to the secretary in March 2004 with four sets of recommendations: restore services for veterans with substance use disorders, establish case management services for homeless veterans with mental health or substance use disorders, provide a full continuum of mental healthcare to those veterans in need, and develop a full range of supportive services for veterans in a partnership with the community (Mellow 2006). The secretary called for a series of actions to be taken as a result of these recommendations and asked the task force to report on the progress of these actions over the next three years.

In 1999 the GAO issued a report (1999) asserting that billions of dollars were being spent to maintain a large number of unnecessary buildings throughout the VHA system. If this was true, it was thought that reducing those unnecessary capital expenditures would provide increased funding for direct patient care activities. As a result, VHA initiated a planning process to determine VA's capital needs for the provision of healthcare services over the next twenty-year period, using 2012 and 2022 as major years of analysis. The intent of the initiative was clear from its acronym, CARES: **C**apital **A**sset **R**ealignment for **E**nhanced **S**ervices. This initiative was first piloted in VISN 12, which included most of Illinois, Wisconsin, and Michigan's Upper Peninsula, to develop a methodology that would be applied to all other networks in VHA. A complete inventory of capital assets was conducted, including all buildings at all VHA facilities, and analyzed in relation to expected future demand for service. The average age of VHA facilities at this time was approximately fifty years, compared to ten years for medical facilities in the private sector. Therefore many VHA facilities required significant expenditures to meet service demands of the future and provide modern healthcare to veterans. Each facility's analysis included recommendations regarding the best means of bringing its capital asset structures up to needed levels, keeping the following major alternatives in mind: maintaining the status quo with no major changes in facility structures or services delivered; facility closure, which was among the most controversial alternatives for many stakeholder groups; changes in services being delivered at specific sites; increasing collaboration with other agencies both inside and outside the federal government; contracting services to non-VA providers, which would reduce the burden of capital asset expenditures; renovate or expand existing facilities; build new facilities; or consolidate services. VA hired a private consulting firm specializing in healthcare actuarial services to develop a model to predict future service needs and create a basis for estimating capital requirements. The work of the actuary relied heavily on a private sector model to project veterans' future demand for health services, including mental healthcare.

Given the concerns being raised about VHA's capacity to meet current mental health needs, there was a great deal of interest in early projections being generated in conjunction with CARES. As VA mental healthcare experts and other stakeholders began to examine the model's projections, they concluded that mental health service demand was being underestimated (Mulligan 2003). The main reason for this appeared to be the model's reliance on private sector healthcare systems, which treated a significantly different population than VHA. In contrast to the private sector, VA mental health patients were typically older, were more often homeless, and represented a significantly different case mix of patients. Veterans also tended to be sicker, with a greater number of comorbidities. A greater percentage of the VHA population is male than in the private sector, and VA does not treat children. It was also believed that veterans, compared to private sector cohorts, would typically have higher rates of reliance on VA mental healthcare relative to other healthcare needs, given the lack of adequate mental health services outside VA in many parts of the country. The private-sector-based projection model tended to assume that individuals in a certain age group would consume similar amounts and type of healthcare from one generation to another. This also appeared to be questionable in a VA population, in which, for example, Vietnam era veterans were likely to consume higher levels of mental health resources as they became older, compared with older veteran cohort utilization at that time. In addition, the prevalence of substance use disorders in Vietnam veterans suggested that addiction services would be needed at higher rates as that population aged compared to the utilization rates for those services by older veterans currently being seen. Upon closer analysis, it was also uncovered that approximately 35 percent of all mental health services provided by VA were absent in the private sector model and not accounted for in the model's future projections (e.g., compensated work therapy, PTSD programs, homeless programs). In reviewing mental health service availability in various markets nationwide, a great deal of variability was observed. Therefore, the uniform application of averages across the system appeared to be inappropriate. VHA was also in the very early stages of reviewing the report of the President's New Freedom Commission on Mental Health, which called for a complete transformation of mental healthcare in this country. Any retooling resulting from the commission's report was not accounted for in the initial demand model. Finally, future demand estimates did not include any increase resulting from the ongoing global war on terror, either in terms of the numbers of newly returning combat veterans who would require care or the types of service that might be needed.

Draft recommendations from the CARES Commission were published in the *Federal Register* in August 2003, and its final recommendations were presented to the Secretary of Veterans Affairs in February 2004. The CARES recommendations were ultimately approved in May 2004 by the Secretary of Veterans Affairs, the culmination of a three-year, intensive, and, at times, controversial process. Although efforts were made to address the model's inability to adequately predict future mental health needs, mental health projections were known to require additional development at the time the plan was finalized. Mental health providers and leadership were assured, however, that opportunities for fine tuning would be available and yearly revisions to the projection model would be possible. Planning based on approved CARES decisions began almost immediately, with networks identifying a variety of ways to begin closing the gap between current capacity and future projected need. Concurrently, a CARES–Mental Health Workgroup continued to refine mental health projections. Because private sector benchmarks were not available for approximately 35 percent of all VHA mental health services, a combination of VA data, expert opinion, and top leadership policy decisions was required to project future need. Due to varying utilization by cohort, a program-by-program analysis was conducted and expert opinion applied to estimate utilization rates and future projected need. Estimated veteran reliance on VA mental health services was raised to 85 percent, as fewer alternatives outside VA were thought to be available for veterans to address their mental health needs relative to other healthcare needs. Additional focus was dedicated to examining the impact of an aging veteran population as well as the distribution of mental health programs associated with beds, including the entire continuum from acute to long-term care as well as domiciliary and residential programs.

This work group was a collaborative effort with representation from the National CARES Office, the Mental Health Strategic Healthcare Group (now known as the Office of Mental Health Services), the SMI Committee, and Milliman, USA, the actuarial consulting group contracted by VA. The final product resulted in higher projections of need and larger gaps between actual and expected levels of capacity compared to the original CARES analyses. The original model estimated the outpatient mental health gap in service at 18 percent for fiscal year 2012 and 9 percent in fiscal year 2022. Under the revised scenario, the percentages were 30 and 16 percent, respectively. For inpatient care, the original gap estimates were 14 and -3 percent, whereas the modified projections were 14 and 15 percent for the same two target fiscal years. When revised projections were issued to the field, VISNs were required to incorporate them into their plans. Strategic planning reports at the VISN level were also required to document the progress in eliminating mental health service gaps. When CARES was folded into VA's budget and strategic planning processes, it was replaced by the Comprehensive Mental Health Strategic Plan (MHSP), discussed below.

Staffing resources consume a large percentage of the healthcare dollar, especially in mental health, which does not tend to utilize expensive medical equipment. Given this large investment in personnel, there has been a long-standing interest in developing a methodology to ensure that staffing resources were being properly utilized and productive. Developing an adequate and credible methodology, however, has turned out to be a challenging and somewhat elusive goal. VA commissioned a National Academy of Sciences (NAS) study to establish staffing guidelines. This study was completed in 1977 but failed to recommend any guidelines, because the NAS was unable to accurately estimate future VHA workload. In lieu of recommended staffing standards, the NAS recommended that VA establish productivity standards (Baker & Pickren 2006).

VA initiated an internal study of staffing guidelines following a 1981 GAO report criticizing VA for the lack of productivity standards. Several disciplines, including psychology, participated in this study, collected a large amount of data at pilot sites across the country, and drafted a tentative staffing guideline methodology. This methodology could have been utilized to construct staffing and productivity standards, but was never mandated and was left to local discretion. Given the lack of a national directive, these guidelines were never widely adopted in VHA and languished over time. The next significant effort to develop productivity guidance for mental health providers occurred in the early 2000s. A work group was convened by the Mental Health Strategic Healthcare Group, composed of national program officials and mental health representation from six VISNs that had been working on this issue. The work group reviewed existing methodologies being employed in VHA as well as published literature in professional, peer-reviewed journals. This effort ultimately resulted in a consensus statement that was reviewed and supported by the national mental health office and national leaders in psychiatry, psychology, social work, and nursing. A white paper was written that provided select inpatient, residential, and outpatient workload productivity guidelines for each of the four mental health disciplines (Gresen et al. 2003). Given the lack of consistent and reliable data, much of this work relied on expert opinion. In addition, the degree of certainty associated with the recommendations varied across disciplines and mental healthcare settings. Although it never received official approval as a policy-level document, the white paper was widely distributed throughout the system and became a primary source document on mental health productivity in VHA. In addition to providing specific productivity guidance, it also recommended a set of business rules to assist clinicians in reporting various types of workload.

During this same period VHA became interested in developing workload standards for all of its healthcare providers, especially physicians. The Office of Productivity, Efficiency and Staffing (OPES) was created and was charged with developing productivity and staffing standards for VHA healthcare providers while providing safe, efficient, effective, and compassionate care. In 2007 the OPES approached the Office of Mental Health Services (OMHS) to develop recommendations for mental health providers. A work group was established consisting of national and field-based mental health experts, national information management experts, and representatives from the disciplines under study: psychiatry, psychology, social work, physician assistants, clinical nurse specialists, and nurse practitioners. Similar to the 2003 group, a review of existing published literature was undertaken. In contrast to the 2003 work group, however, this group was charged with drafting an official policy directive mandating productivity standards. Another major difference between the two groups was the availability of VA national databases to inform their work of current productivity being reported in the system. In addition, national benchmark data from systems outside VA were available to compare with VHA experience. As national databases were very robust for outpatient workload, the group ultimately focused on developing a workload standard that applied to outpatient work only. Adding inpatient productivity would have to wait until VHA data were more reliably and consistently reported. This was likely to take several years to accomplish, as national policy requiring the collection and recording of all professional mental health inpatient workload was not put in place until January 2009. At the time of this writing, the work group was finalizing its draft recommendations for outpatient productivity standards in mental health for the review and approval of the VHA national leadership. Although the number of veterans seen (panel size) and the number of clinic encounters were also studied, it appeared most likely that work relative value units (wRVUs) would become the primary metric in the finalized policy document.

In addition to the major changes occurring in VHA healthcare and in the nation, another major influence on the future of mental healthcare was emerging. In April 2002 President George W. Bush established a presidential commission on mental health as part of his commitment to eliminate inequality for Americans with disabilities. The president directed the commission to develop recommendations that could be implemented by governments at all levels to maximize the use of existing resources, improve coordination of treatments and services, and promote successful community integration for adults with a serious mental illness and children with a serious emotional disturbance. The final report of the President's New Freedom Commission on Mental Health, *Achieving the Promise: Transforming Mental Healthcare in America* (2003), was released on July 22, 2003. It recommended a fundamental transformation of mental healthcare in the United States, delineating nineteen formal recommendations organized under six proposed national goals for mental health: 1) Americans understand that mental health is essential to overall health; 2) mental health is consumer and family driven; 3) disparities in mental health services are eliminated; 4) early mental health screening, assessment, and referral to services are common practice; 5) excellent mental healthcare is delivered and research is accelerated; and 6) technology is used to access mental healthcare and information.

Although the Substance Abuse and Mental Health Services Administration (SAMHSA) was designated as the lead federal agency to implement the recommendations of the commission, VA has been recognized as the one federal agency to receive the report most enthusiastically from the beginning (National Mental Health Association 2004). VA initiated action in a remarkably short period of time after the release of the commission's final report. On July 30, 2003, the Under Secretary for Health charged a work group to review the report "to determine the relevance of the Commission's goals and recommendations to veterans' mental health programs and to develop an Action Plan that is tailored to the special needs of the enrolled veteran population." The six goals of the commission and accompanying recommendations were translated into an eighty-two-item action agenda for VHA, designed to begin a transformation of its mental health delivery system to meet the mental health needs of veterans using a recovery model of treatment and support and achieve the commission's vision that every veteran at risk for acquiring or recovering from a mental illness should have the opportunity to participate fully in the community. *Action Agenda: Achieving the Promise, Transforming Mental Healthcare in VA* (2003) was approved on December 1, 2003.

In the end, this action agenda was the initial step in a much broader and ambitious five-year Mental Health Strategic Plan (MHSP) that was commissioned by Under Secretary for Health Dr. Jonathon Perlin. Dr. Perlin charged the Action Agenda Steering Committee to develop a strategic plan driven by the President's New Freedom Commission's principles and goals. This five-year plan was to be developed without regard to resources, because resource availability was not immediately apparent. The intent of developing such a plan was to identify what was needed to transform VHA's mental healthcare system without being constrained by resource realities of the moment. To accomplish this charge, the Action Agenda Steering Committee created nine work groups, focused on seriously mentally ill psychosocial rehabilitation, medical/surgical comorbidities, PTSD, substance abuse, VA/Department of Defense (DoD) transition, general psychiatry and crosscutting issues, homelessness, geropsychiatry, and women's mental health. Over 125 mental health experts from both within and outside VA were convened and began their work in early 2004 (Department of Veterans Affairs, Office of Inspector General, Healthcare Inspection 2007).

The work groups were charged with developing an action plan addressing the needs of their respective populations. Each group was supplied with a standard template so that their work could eventually be combined into a single, comprehensive plan for veterans' mental healthcare. Work groups were asked to keep the following three issues in the forefront of their minds as they developed their part of the plan: access to care should be the key driver, the final plan should incorporate as many of VHA's action agenda recommendations as possible, and the plan had to be linked to VHA and VA strategic goals and objectives. Each group was expected to evaluate the current status of VHA care in their assigned area of responsibility, relying on data as much as possible. This step took advantage of the work that had already been accomplished by CARES. Groups were expected to articulate aspirational goals relating to the ideal provision of mental health services and identify service gaps that currently existed. In addition to summarizing their work and findings, each group provided a set of prioritized recommendations, with a supporting rationale, and identified potential barriers to implementation. Integration and crosscutting issues were identified by all work groups. In addition, each group was asked to address issues of accountability, including who or what office should be tasked with implementation and monitoring of goal attainment and outcomes. Although groups were instructed to propose the ideal, independent of resource needs, they were also required to estimate the resource implications of their recommendations. Each group also had the freedom to address any other issues that were identified, including, but not restricted to, other needed or desirable collaborations that would facilitate the attainment of goals outlined in their reports. Each group provided a finished product consistent with their charge. All recommendations were reviewed, synthesized, and collated into a final strategic plan draft. Although the final plan would include only a summary of each work group's efforts, their individual reports remained available for later guidance and reference throughout the implementation process. These reports were extremely helpful, as they included detailed rationales, data analyses of need, the current status of VHA mental healthcare, and guidance regarding possible steps and sequencing that would serve as templates for addressing existing gaps in service.

The MHSP was completed and approved by the Under Secretary of Health in July 2004 (Department of Veterans Affairs 2004a). Approximately thirty pages long, the final report was formatted using an Excel spreadsheet organized in parallel with the President's New Freedom Commission. It was divided into six major sections, one for each of the commission's overarching goals. Each goal was further divided into subsections representing seventeen of the nineteen formal recommendations in the commission's final report. Only recommendations 4.1 and 4.2 were not included, as they covered promotion of mental health in young children and improving/expanding mental health programs in schools. In addition to remaining true to the President's Commission's report and VHA's action agenda, VHA also incorporated all outstanding recommendations of the SMI Committee, the PTSD Committee, and the Secretary's Task Force on Mental Health report into the final plan. Each recommendation was operationalized with one or more new initiatives, translating the plan into actionable, concrete milestones that were specific to and relevant for the mental healthcare of veterans. Further, these initiatives were prioritized on a timeline, indicating which areas would become an immediate focus and staging the other initiatives over the expected five-year life of the plan. This resulted in approximately 265 actionable initiatives. Over time, additional columns were added to the spreadsheet to document the current status of each item, identify the responsible party for overseeing each initiative, summarize concrete actions taken, and list outcomes achieved.

The six overarching goals of the plan and their operationalization had to be specifically tailored to the unique nature of VHA. For example, the first goal of the commission—"Americans need to understand that mental health is essential to overall health"—was refocused on the veteran population along with other stakeholder groups, including family members. This goal included specific milestones such as making efforts to destigmatize mental illness through national educational campaigns, reaching out to specific veteran populations such as newly returning combat veterans and their family members, educating VHA healthcare providers, promoting coping skills, resiliency and community support, promoting seamless transition of care from one level of service to another and one type of care to another, promoting the integration of primary care and mental healthcare, reducing suicide rates, developing an accurate projection model of mental health service demand, eliminating gender disparities in mental healthcare, organizationally aligning domiciliary programs under mental health (historically, domiciliaries were organized under extended and long-term-care programs), reducing geographic variation in mental health services availability, providing a full continuum of mental healthcare, restoring services to veterans with substance use disorders, enhancing services to homeless veterans with mental illness, developing a full range of supportive services in collaboration with the community, meeting the needs of the seriously mentally ill, and ensuring adequate access and availability of services throughout the continuum of mental healthcare.

The second goal of the President's Commission's report stated that mental healthcare is consumer and family driven. For VHA, this translated into objectives and strategies such as individualizing treatment plans and including family members in the process, seeking stakeholder input into mental health programming, educating staff on the recovery model, removing bureaucratic barriers to working with families, developing peer support programs, engaging Operation Enduring Freedom (OEF) and Operation Iraqi Freedom (OIF) veterans in transition planning and referrals/placement, increasing housing opportunities for the homeless and supported employment for the unemployed, and partnering with community agencies and stakeholder groups such as NAMI. Elimination of disparities in the provision of mental health services is the third goal.

VHA initiatives here included ensuring that VHA's workforce was culturally diverse, evaluating and eliminating potential disparities in the treatment of any minority group, supporting interagency relationships to address minority issues, ensuring that staff are culturally competent, enhancing the dissemination of new knowledge throughout VHA, and addressing rural veteran access challenges. The commission's fourth goal read as follows: "Early mental health screening, assessment, and referral to services are common practice." In support of this goal, VHA planned to implement screening instruments for mental health problems, educate primary care providers about mental health disorders, improve diagnosis and treatment of mental health disorders among newly returning combat veterans, elevate competencies of all mental health providers in the assessment and treatment of mental and substance use disorders, and identify effective prevention interventions for mental illness in combat veterans. VA's suicide prevention initiatives were highlighted and emphasized in this goal as well. The fifth goal of the commission is to accelerate research to promote recovery and resilience and ultimately cure and prevent mental illness. The VHA translation of this goal into action included emphasizing recovery and rehabilitation in both clinical care and research, developing a research agenda to identify prevention and early interventions for acutely traumatized individuals, sharing best practices, maintaining and updating clinical practice guidelines, expanding diversity in the workforce, ensuring that mental health providers are adequately compensated, establishing spiritual assessment as a routine practice, implementing collaborative care models, creating educational programs on mental health in the primary care setting, ensuring highly competent mental health and organizational leadership, evaluating the effectiveness of education and training in the specially funded psychosocial rehabilitation fellowship program, and developing an algorithm for the administration of atypical antipsychotics. The sixth and final goal of the commission focuses on technology and its application in distributing information and improving access to mental healthcare. VHA had already taken a leadership role in this area and was positioning itself to become even stronger in the twenty-first century. Initiatives listed here included expanding the charge of a Telemental Health Field Workgroup to areas such as homelessness; enhancing access to mental healthcare through technology by improving the exchange of information between VA and the DoD; expanding telemental healthcare to all medical centers, CBOCs, and vet centers; exploring the use of in-home messaging devices and other new technologies; exploring sharing and partnering with other agencies such as the Indian Health Service (IHS), DoD, and others; developing a mental health treatment planning tool; and creating a mental health component in MyHealtheVet, an innovative work in progress for veterans to access their records, obtain healthcare education, and get updates on their health status online.

The Secretary of Veterans Affairs approved the MHSP in November 2004, contingent upon the availability of future funding. Given the lack of funding to implement the plan, MHSP recommendations were initially identified that could be accomplished with existing resources. In the spring of 2004, SAMHSA (2005a) reported that VHA had implemented or was in the process of implementing several low and no additional cost initiatives. VHA kicked off a national mental health campaign to increase awareness of mental health as essential to overall health and to combat stigma. A national strategy for suicide prevention was created and collaborative care approaches for mental health disorders in primary care settings were promulgated. Other educational products were created with a focus on cultural competency. For instance, a videotape series of programs was created on PTSD in Native American, Asian American/Pacific Islander, African American, and Hispanic American veterans for VHA mental health providers, veterans, and their family members. VHA initiated a collaboration with DoD focused on newly returning combat veterans from Iraq. Each network was charged with participating in its respective state's mental health plans. VHA joined with other federal agencies through a Federal Partners consortium to identify best practices in rural mental healthcare. Other initiatives within available resources focused on direct patient care activities such as annual screening for depression, PTSD, and substance use disorders in primary care; piloting the use of peer support staff with veterans recovering from serious mental illness; introducing evidence-based practices across the system; and exploring the application of recovery-oriented care. Several technology-based initiatives were also identified early in the implementation process, including the expansion of telemental health services to enhance access and creating a mental health component in MyHealtheVet.

VHA was able to capture some monies to support the early implementation of the MHSP even though they were not specifically targeted for that purpose. Six million dollars for new supported employment mentoring sites and $10 million for compensated work therapy support were made available due to supplemental funding provided to VHA by Congress. Education and information dissemination regarding the MHSP was one of the highest priority early initiatives. The MHSP became a centerpiece of face-to-face meetings that occurred at all levels of the organization. The plan was discussed during national conference calls and presented on a televised satellite program to all VA facilities in April 2006. Web-based educational programs and DVDs were also developed to cover specific aspects of the MHSP during the early rollout phase.

To implement the plan more fully and within a five-year time frame, new monies were needed as well. Monies specific for MHSP implementation were provided for the first time in fiscal year 2005. During that fiscal year, the Under Secretary for Health allocated $100 million above fiscal year 2004 levels for initiatives specifically addressing unmet needs in the MHSP. This was followed by $200 million above fiscal 2004 levels in 2006, $100 million of which was to cover and maintain the newly funded services from fiscal year 2005. Most significantly, these monies were provided outside the established mechanism for funding VHA healthcare. At this time, VHA was distributing monetary resources using the Veterans Equitable Resource Allocation System (VERA), which was first implemented in April 1997. The core principle underlying the VERA was that monies should be allocated based on the workload being generated. This was calculated through an increasingly complex methodology to adjust for variables such as regional differences in cost, the priority level of the veterans being served, and other factors. At its core, however, it attempted to allocate funds based primarily on the number of veterans treated, weighted by the complexity of care required and the intensity of resources utilized. These calculations were made at the network level, and monies were budgeted at that level as well. Once the money was allocated to each VISN, it was their responsibility to determine how that money would be distributed and spent. This was intended to provide maximum flexibility to VISNs in responding to local needs while still operating within a national system that required attainment of certain overarching goals and objectives. Once the money left Washington, D.C., local administrators determined how monies were divided among each healthcare facility as well as which programs would be funded, and at what levels, within each facility. Although local leaders were not totally autonomous and were held accountable to national leadership, they nonetheless had a great deal of leeway and authority in the allocation of the resources made available to them. Allocating monies specifically targeted for mental healthcare was not always viewed as consistent with the VERA funding model, because it reduced local leadership control and discretion over those resources. This also seemed to be inconsistent with one of Dr. Kizer's major organizing principles, that all healthcare is local. Therefore, the department's decision to allocate this level of resource specifically for mental healthcare sent a strong and clear message regarding the national commitment to address the mental health needs of veterans.

The GAO examined how these targeted funds were actually utilized during the first few years of mental health enhancement (2006). According to the GAO, VHA was able to allocate approximately $88 million of the $100 million that had been targeted for MHSP initiatives in fiscal year 2005.

Approximately $53 million of these monies was awarded using a request for proposal (RFP) process. All networks were invited to submit proposals to fund initiatives in specifically identified areas from the MHSP. During a three-month period from October 2004 to January 2005, five separate RFPs were issued in the following areas: psychosocial rehabilitation services, services for veterans with PTSD, services targeting newly returning combat veterans, substance use disorder initiatives, and mental health domiciliary enhancement/expansion. Proposals were reviewed and ranked by panels of mental health experts, who submitted their recommendations for funding to VHA leadership. As funding decisions were made, monies were disbursed throughout fiscal year 2005. VHA also funded initiatives outside the RFP process to help close other identified gaps in service. For example, funding was provided to all networks to expand or include mental health providers at CBOCs in order to improve veterans' access to psychotherapy and psychiatric medications prescribed by a mental health professional. Funding was provided to add new and enhance existing mental health intensive care management (MHICM) teams as well as to increase services to homeless veterans and to veterans diagnosed with PTSD or substance use disorders. Funding was also made available specifically for newly returning combat veterans from OIF and OEF. Monies were provided to improve mental health services delivered in VHA nursing home care units. The remaining $35 million allocated during fiscal year 2005 was sent to networks through the usual resource allocation process. Presumably it was used to close additional gaps in mental health services as identified by the MHSP but outside of the RFP process. This was intended to provide some discretion at the local level in prioritizing other mental healthcare deficiencies. However, it was not entirely clear how those monies were ultimately utilized and what, if any, additional mental health service gaps were addressed. At the time of these initial allocations, it was anticipated that centralized, targeted funding would continue for a limited period, possibly one to three years. And in fact, these targeted funds were mostly folded into the mainstream funding process beginning in fiscal year 2010. However, facilities were required to hire staff permanently, because it was expected that all mental health enhancements would become part of the standard operating budget and plan.

VHA utilized a similar process in fiscal year 2006, allocating approximately $158 million of the budgeted $200 million. Approximately $92 million was used to fund new initiatives using RFPs and targeted funding mechanisms, similar to fiscal year 2005. In addition, $66 million was needed to support the recurring expenses of the initiatives that had been newly funded in fiscal year 2005. New initiatives funded in this second fiscal year included domiciliary expansion and increased and enhanced services for OIF/OEF veterans and veterans diagnosed with PTSD or substance use disorders. This included funding for veterans dually diagnosed with both substance use disorders and other psychiatric illnesses. Additional monies were allocated for mental health staff in CBOCs and to fund initiatives in newly developing areas such as psychosocial rehabilitation and recovery-oriented services. Technology enhancements were funded, similar to fiscal year 2005, for telemental health and Internet-based approaches. A variety of homeless outreach and support services was funded, both outpatient and residential, as was a pilot program for incarcerated veterans with mental health conditions. Additional MHICM teams were funded and monies were dedicated to suicide prevention. Several other targeted initiatives were supported due to special circumstances, such as the impact of Hurricane Katrina on VHA facilities in the Gulf Coast region of the country.

Notwithstanding VHA's strong commitment to closing mental health service gaps, the department was not able to spend all of the monies available that were specifically provided for that purpose during the first two years of the MHSP's implementation. As noted previously, VHA was not able to spend $12 million in fiscal year 2005 and could not be certain to what extent the $35 million distributed through the usual resource allocation process was used for that purpose. In fiscal year 2006, $42 million budgeted for closing mental health service gaps was never allocated for that purpose. In addition, $46 million of the $158 million allocated was ultimately returned to the VA Central Office because it could not be spent for the intended purpose within the time constraints imposed by federal regulation. Placing these monetary amounts in perspective, VHA was spending approximately $2 billion annually on mental healthcare at this time. Although the new monies that were provided to begin closing gaps were substantial, they represented slightly more than 5 percent of the total being spent on mental healthcare at the time. But even that amount of money was difficult to spend in a timely manner, in part because of federal regulation and in part because of inadequate existing infrastructure, both nationally and locally, to distribute and absorb such a large infusion of new monies that quickly.

The RFP process, though initially effective, was unlikely to result in an even distribution of resources and services throughout the country. Regardless of how carefully and thoughtfully the review process was conducted, proposals that were well written may have been somewhat more likely to be funded than other proposals that may have represented a greater need. Just as important, proposals were only being submitted for the types of program desired by each facility and network, even if other services were lacking relative to other parts of the system. As a result of these issues, several alternatives to the RFP process were employed for distributing additional new resources in fiscal year 2007. One approach was to review unfunded proposals that had been submitted during previous RFP cycles. As these proposals reflected a need in an area of importance, networks were asked to work with national program officials to make necessary changes to those submissions such that they would be suitable for funding.

A second approach was to fund MHSP priorities in a more directive manner, with the VA Central Office in Washington, D.C., allocating monies to networks to invest in specific areas. This approach was initiated in fiscal year 2007 and continued in 2008. This allocation strategy was used to support the integration of mental health services within the primary care setting from the national level. Substance use disorder services, which had been significantly underfunded in previous years, were enhanced. A variety of homeless initiatives was started or expanded, including a program focused on assisting incarcerated veterans' reentry into the community. High-priority areas such as veterans with PTSD, including military sexual trauma victims, and newly returning combat veterans received support through these monies. In addition to providing resources to MHICMs, a new intensive case management program developed specifically for rural areas was rolled out. New, full-time positions were created to coordinate and facilitate the development of services that were virtually nonexistent in the system at the time.

At least one full-time suicide prevention coordinator was hired at every major VHA facility to develop suicide prevention services. This individual was to serve as a first contact and liaison for suicide prevention services within their respective markets as well as with other facilities and the soon to be developed suicide hotline. The coordinator was also made responsible for the ongoing monitoring, support, and reporting of suicide prevention activities and outcomes at their facility.

Similarly, local recovery coordinators (LRCs) were hired on a full-time basis at every medical center in VHA. Each LRC was responsible for promoting, coordinating, and educating staff, veterans, family members, and other stakeholders about psychosocial rehabilitation and recovery-oriented care. As this was a new position in VHA covering new approaches that were not widely utilized, a list of expected responsibilities and milestones was distributed along with initial funding to help local leadership understand the importance of the position and its function in mental health. Expanding the use of telemental health was supported with these monies. New initiatives trained large numbers of mental health professionals in evidence-based care, including, but not limited to, cognitive behavioral therapy, motivational interviewing, prolonged exposure, and cognitive processing therapy for PTSD, interpersonal therapy, and social skills training for the seriously mentally ill. Money was also available for increasing training opportunities for mental health staff and to increase the number of trainee positions in psychology. Although most of these monies were used to support direct and indirect patient care in VHA facilities, a small portion was used to create three mental health Centers of Excellence throughout the country.

Additional new monies were made available through supplemental appropriations enacted by Congress in June 2007. Some $100 million was specifically designated by Congress to be spent on mental health services and $20 million for substance use disorder services. This allowed for other services to be supported, in addition to those mentioned previously, during fiscal year 2007. Substance abuse disorder services, both psychotherapeutic and medication based, were a primary focus. Other service areas that were directed for expansion with these supplemental funds included homeless veterans, residential rehabilitation, intensive psychosocial rehabilitation programs for veterans with serious mental illness, peer support, family psychoeducation, continued expansion of mental health services in CBOCs; added services for veterans with PTSD, and increased integration of mental health services in primary care.

After two years of mental health enhancement funding, each network was asked to conduct a thorough analysis of remaining mental health services gaps. These analyses were submitted in February 2007 and reviewed by an expert panel at the national level. This exercise provided a great deal of information about deficiencies in care that remained throughout the country. However, there was a great deal of variability in how the gap analyses were conducted and in the type of information and degree of detail provided. In the end, another round of funding did not result from this exercise. However, it did have the effect of building an increased spirit of cooperation and collaboration between national and local leadership as future implementation efforts proceeded.

New policies were also being issued during this time, sometimes with additional funding and sometimes not, to implement components of the MHSP and close gaps in mental health services. These policy statements, often issued in the form of a memorandum, were typically issued by the Deputy Under Secretary for Health for Operations and Management (DUSHOM). In June 2007, for example, the DUSHOM issued a memorandum outlining several initiatives to increase mental health service capacity and access. This memorandum required that veterans presenting for mental health and/or substance use disorder treatment obtain an initial evaluation within twenty-four hours. In order to comply with this policy, the evaluation had to determine the urgency of need, identify the appropriate setting for follow-up, arrange treatment, provide contact information for a mental health provider, provide information about emergency services, facilitate the veteran's engagement, and respond to questions. Follow-up was required within fourteen days of this initial evaluation to complete any additional diagnostic workup and initiate care. If there was an indication of a possible emergent mental health problem, further evaluation and appropriate intervention were required immediately. A second policy statement in this same memorandum focused on following up with patients who had missed appointments to ensure that they were not at risk of harming themselves or others, address any dissatisfaction with care, answer questions, and reinforce the importance of continuing with care. The third policy issued in this document expanded services beyond normal working hours by requiring clinics to offer outpatient services at least one evening per week and encouraged additional evening and weekend hours. Finally, emergency departments were required to provide mental health coverage on a 24/7 basis, and urgent care centers were required to have mental health coverage during their regular hours of operation. All policies and procedures in this memorandum were required to be implemented within sixty days. A follow-up memorandum in April 2008 clarified staffing requirements in order to meet the emergency department and urgent care mandate for mental health (Deputy Under Secretary for Health for Operations and Management 2008). To provide services for life-threatening mental health emergencies, emergency departments were required to provide mental health coverage with an independent, licensed mental health provider. The importance of providing mental health screening, evaluation, prevention, treatment, consultation, and referral services in all CBOCs was also discussed. Barriers to implementation that needed to be addressed at both the local and national levels included funding, time required to recruit and hire staff, and negotiating working condition issues with unions.

As individual policy documents were being disseminated, it was determined that a more comprehensive set of national standards was needed to ensure a consistent set of services were being offered and delivered throughout the country. Initially, the Office of Mental Health Services in the VA Central Office began to develop a set of "specifications" during the fall of calendar year 2007. This evolved into the *Uniform Mental Health Services in VA Medical Centers and Clinics* handbook (USH), which was issued in June 2008 and reissued with revisions three months later (Department of Veterans Affairs, Veterans Health Administration 2008). This document mandated the minimum level of mental healthcare to be provided by VHA on a national basis. By promulgating such standards, it was hoped that all veterans, regardless of their location, would have access to the mental health services they needed.

The standards were written to cover required mental health services at medical facilities as well as CBOCs. It delineated which services were required to be provided on-site and which services could be delivered via telemental health. It dictated which services were required to be provided directly as opposed to others that could be offered on a referral basis. Also, services were categorized on the basis of being required, encouraged, or strongly encouraged. Responsibilities of facility and VISN mental health leadership for implementing coordinated care were articulated. All veterans receiving mental healthcare were to be assigned a principal mental health provider responsible for ensuring that care was coordinated and that a treatment plan was developed, implemented, and revised as needed. Unless declined by the individual, all veterans receiving mental healthcare were expected to be enrolled in VHA primary care, emphasizing the importance of coordinating all healthcare services. Following the principles outlined by the President's New Freedom Commission, all mental health services were required to become recovery-oriented as defined and conceptualized by the National Consensus Statement on Mental Health Recovery (SAMHSA 2005b). Cultural competency was viewed as a crosscutting training issue, including military and veteran culture along with more traditional domains typically identified in this area. The handbook provided specific requirements in twenty-two sections covering approximately thirty-six pages. It covered the structure and governance of mental health services, community mental health issues such as coordination of services with local and community agencies, and reaching out to OEF and OIF veterans. This section also strongly encouraged the creation of Consumer-Advocate Liaison Councils composed of consumers of mental health services, their family members, and other stakeholders to facilitate input and feedback on the delivery of mental healthcare. Given the importance of access in the overall vision of mental health's transformation, there was a robust section on "24 Hour a Day, 7 Days a Week (24/7) Care." This section delineated requirements for mental health coverage in facilities and CBOCs, with specific language for emergency department and urgent care center capacity, emergency/involuntary hospitalizations, and other issues. Acute inpatient care was required to be available to all veterans in need of this level of care. Key issues highlighted in this section included environmental safety, staffing, privacy, integrated and coordinated care, and the overall philosophy of psychosocial rehabilitation and recovery-oriented care. The handbook also discussed potential barriers to its implementation, such as space, lack of clinician availability, information technology challenges, patient travel distances, lack of adequate community resources, and time needed to develop contracts with non-VA providers. The handbook also allowed for the possibility of VISN requests for variances and/or exceptions.

The handbook covered outpatient mental healthcare in detail and provided clear expectations regarding timelines for access into care and the initiation of treatment. Policy also recognizes that a large percentage of mental healthcare is delivered by primary care providers in addition to mental health professionals. Veterans who are placed on waiting lists to obtain outpatient treatment must be provided with interim services. Also, the handbook described when facilities and CBOCs must provide general rather than specialty mental healthcare, either on-site or by referral or using telemental health. Residential care, which grew in importance as other bedded programs downsized and new rehabilitative approaches emerged, was also addressed in the handbook. This increasingly important level of care provides more intensive treatment than would be possible in an outpatient venue but less intensive than acute hospitalization. Programs often target veterans with specific mental health problems, including substance use disorder, PTSD, serious mental illness, and others. In addition to the general information provided in the USH, a separate, free-standing handbook dedicated to this level of care was subsequently developed to provide more detailed information and guidance.

Separate sections of the handbook were devoted to substance use disorders, serious mental illness, homelessness, incarcerated veterans, specialized PTSD services, and military sexual trauma (MST). Other sections covered areas that were relatively new to VHA's mental health system and emphasized as high priorities for implementation. Rehabilitation and recovery-oriented services is an example of one such area. These services were a centerpiece in the President's New Freedom Commission report, embraced by VHA's MHSP and institutionalized in the USH. VHA took several unique steps to facilitate the rollout of rehabilitation and recovery services nationwide, which are described in the USH. A full-time LRC was required to be hired at every VHA facility with a mental health program to facilitate the transformation of VHA's mental health services into a recovery-oriented model of care. Facilities with at least 1,500 veterans on VHA's National Psychosis Registry were required to have a Psychosocial Rehabilitation and Recovery Center (PRRC). This outpatient program is designed as a primary locus of recovery-oriented services for seriously mentally ill veterans. This program was also anticipated to replace all existing day treatment centers, which had provided a traditional model of care for the seriously mentally ill for many decades in VHA. These centers were intended to help veterans with serious mental illness maintain their current level of functioning, minimize resource utilization including inpatient hospitalization, and provide a place for veterans to socialize with other veterans and remain active. The orientation of these programs was primarily supportive rather than rehabilitative. Other areas highlighted in this section of the handbook were family involvement, social skills training, peer counseling, and supported employment.

Another section of the handbook was dedicated to evidence-based treatments (EBTs). At the time of this writing, VHA had identified several EBTs for national dissemination, including cognitive processing therapy and prolonged exposure therapy for veterans suffering from PTSD, cognitive behavioral therapy, acceptance and commitment therapy, and interpersonal therapy for veterans with depressive or anxiety-related disorders and social skills training for veterans with serious mental illness. Evidence-based pharmacotherapy, when indicated, must be available for veterans with mood disorders, anxiety disorders including PTSD, psychotic disorders, substance use disorders, dementia, and other cognitive disorders. Access to electroconvulsive therapy was also discussed.

VA has a primary mission "to care for him who shall have borne the battle and for his widow, and his orphan," a motto taken from President Abraham Lincoln's second inaugural address and inscribed on plaques outside the VA's Central Office building in Washington, D.C. For VHA, this mission goes beyond the provision of direct healthcare services to include other benefits and humanitarian goals to help veterans maintain their highest level of functioning as productive members in their communities. Of course these additional services must be relevant to and consistent with the delivery of healthcare services and within regulatory and legislative authorities. The handbook described homeless services that are within VHA's purview, including outreach, referral, assessment, and treatment for mental health disorders. Because VA does not have authority to provide permanent housing, a strong emphasis is placed on collaboration with the community and other agencies. For example, VA's grant and per diem program provides monies to non-VA entities to establish homeless shelters, which can be staffed by VHA mental health professionals. VHA also collaborates with the Department of Housing and Urban Development, which can provide vouchers for community housing. In regard to incarcerated veterans, each VISN is required to have at least one staff person dedicated to supporting veterans being released from state and federal prisons. Although providing direct healthcare services is not authorized, VHA can play an important role in reaching out to incarcerated veterans with mental illness who will be seeking VHA mental health services when released from prison. These veteran coordinators are charged with contacting eligible veterans to begin prerelease planning and to collaborate with community agencies.

PTSD is a unique mental illness, in that the diagnosis requires exposure to a traumatic event involving actual or potential harm to an individual. It also has a unique place in VHA healthcare given the large number of veterans who have been exposed to combat-related stressors. This has become even more prominent in recent years, with the current cohort of newly returning combat veterans from Iraq and Afghanistan. VHA has necessarily placed a strong emphasis on PTSD-related services in the USH. All networks are required to have specialized residential or inpatient programs for veterans suffering from severe PTSD. Specialized outpatient services must be available in all medical centers and large CBOCs, including services for newly returning OEF and OIF veterans. Smaller CBOCs must have the ability to provide diagnostic and treatment planning services for veterans presenting with PTSD and referral mechanisms for treatment if not provided on-site.

VHA has also embarked upon a very significant and groundbreaking effort to address suicide risk among veterans. Every medical center and large CBOC is required to have a full-time suicide prevention coordinator. Coordinator responsibilities include the tracking and reporting of veterans identified as high risk; coordinating referrals from the VHA National Suicide Prevention Hotline; staff training, partnering with the community; and developing/enhancing assessment, early intervention, and treatment. Other sections in the handbook include gender specific care, care transitions, integrating mental health into medical care settings, integrating mental health services in services to older veterans, prevention and management of violence, disaster preparedness, and rural mental healthcare.

The USH was to be followed by a set of metrics to evaluate the level of compliance and implementation of the handbook across the system. These metrics will cover a variety of areas, ranging from the presence of required program elements described in the handbook to measures of patient function and outcomes.

The last major national distribution of funds specifically targeting mental health services was completed in January 2009. These funds were distributed to each VISN for the purpose of fully implementing the USH. Funding amounts were derived from planning documents requested from each VISN outlining their remaining needs in order to fully implement the USH. In addition, site visits were conducted to each network by a small team of national experts to help VISNs identify their needs and develop a plan of corrective action. The overall expectation with the release of these funds was that the USH would be fully implemented by the end of fiscal year 2009. Any exceptions to full implementation were required to be submitted to the national VHA office for prior approval. At the time of this writing, the major focus of the national office and of the VHA mental healthcare system more globally was the transition from building sufficient capacity within the mental healthcare system to sustaining this newly developed capacity into the future.

**Box 5.1. Implementation Status of the Uniform Services
Mental Health Handbook (USH) December 2009**

VHA facilities completed a checklist from the VA Central Office regarding the current status of USH implementation as of December 2009. This time frame preceded the date by which full implementation of the handbook was required. The checklist included ninety-seven distinct elements covering the following twelve mental health care domains: general requirements, emergency coverage, inpatient care, serious mental illness, substance use disorders, primary care integration, older adults, homelessness, PTSD, medical treatment settings, general ambulatory care, and residential rehabilitation (Zeiss 2010a).

Overall, VA medical centers reported 90 percent implementation of handbook requirements, with 17 of 139 reporting greater than 95 percent implementation. At the network (VISN) level, fourteen of twenty-one VISNs reported greater than 90 percent implementation with all networks reporting greater than 80 percent. VHA outpatient clinics (CBOCs) were surveyed on the following domains, whose requirements varied depending on clinic size: staffing, inpatient care, residential, basic mental health, general ambulatory care, emergency coverage, homelessness, PTSD, older adults, and mental health/primary care. Overall, very large CBOCs reported 91 percent implementation, with one area, primary care/mental health integration, reaching only 72 percent. In general, all CBOCs had a similar pattern of implementation rates for all other domains, with midsize clinics at 94 percent and small CBOCs at 90 percent.

Administrative data were utilized to cross-validate checklist reports for twenty programs at VA medical centers (VAMCs) and thirteen programs at very large CBOCs. For VAMCs, survey reports could be confirmed 78 percent of the time. For very large CBOCs, results were confirmed 51 percent of the time. In both cases, these data included both disconfirmations of positive survey reports as well as positive administrative reports for services not reported through the checklist. Further investigation was indicated to determine if these discrepancies were due to program implementation problems, coding errors, or both.

In general it appeared that substantial progress had been made by December 2009 to implement the requirements of the USH. Though most domains were well on their way to implementation, several areas were visibly lagging the others, namely services for the seriously mentally ill and primary care/mental health integration in very large CBOCs. In addition,

(*continued*)

significant variability in the implementation of specific programs across the system was noted. The Office of Mental Health Services in the VA Central Office had plans for continued monitoring of USH implementation and maintenance.

Current Status

In fiscal year 2008 (October 1, 2007–September 30, 2008), VHA treated approximately 5.1 million individual veterans in its medical centers and clinics. Of that total, over 1.6 million, or 31 percent, were diagnosed with at least one mental health condition, and 22 percent (1.1 million individuals) were seen in mental health specialty care. This compares to 565,529 veterans who received mental health services in 1995, representing 18.3 percent of all VHA users in that year (*Charting the U.S. Department of Veterans Affairs' Progress* 2009; Greenberg & Rosenheck 2006, 2009). The number of individuals obtaining care as inpatients dropped to 32,772 from 123,217 in 1995. The average length of stay dropped during this time from over twenty-seven days to slightly less than twelve. In fiscal year 1995, 545,004 veterans were treated in mental health as outpatients, versus 1,045,737 in 2008. Mental health residential care expanded rapidly as well during this time, increasing from 400 beds to 6,831 with a total of 33,251 veterans served in fiscal year 2008 versus 1,353 in 1995. Approximately 20,000 VHA employees provided mental healthcare in fiscal year 2008, a remarkable increase from 14,000 in fiscal year 2005. For fiscal year 2010, the VHA budget included $4.6 billion for mental healthcare, approximately 10 percent of VHA's total healthcare budget. In addition, over $3.2 billion was budgeted to assist veterans with homelessness, the majority of whom have one or more mental health and/or substance use disorder diagnoses (National Coalition for Homeless Veterans 2010). However, these dramatic increases, which combine mental health and substance use disorder services, mask the fact that substance use disorder services did not grow at a similar rate during this time. Comparing the two fiscal years, 55,308 veterans received inpatient substance use disorder treatment in 1995, versus 1,512 in 2008. These figures might have been expected given the transition from inpatient to other venues of care experienced by mental healthcare in general. However, 130,115 veterans obtained outpatient treatment for substance use related disorders in 1995, compared to 129,771 in fiscal year 2008. These data suggest that services to veterans with substance use disorders have not experienced the same level of enhancement and support over recent years as the mental health system more globally in VHA.

In its 2008 annual report, the Northeast Program Evaluation Center noted several important trends regarding VHA mental healthcare (Greenberg & Rosenheck 2009). It noted an 86 percent increase from 1995 through 2008 in the number of veterans receiving specialized mental health services. It also reported a 69 percent decrease in the number of occupied mental health beds (2,801) and an overall decline of 50 percent in the number of inpatient mental health episodes of care. The average length of stay in an inpatient mental health bed decreased almost 68 percent. Data also confirmed that VHA's transformation emphasizing an outpatient system of care has continued to the present. From 1995 through 2008, 92 percent of veterans who obtained mental healthcare were seen as outpatients, although the intensity of service decreased by almost 27 percent as measured by the number of clinic stops per year. There was a 98 percent decrease in the number of occupied substance abuse beds and a 12 percent decline in the number of veterans receiving specialized substance abuse services of any type (inpatient, outpatient, or residential). Fiscal data reflect similar trends for this time period. There was a 21 percent decrease from 1995 in total expenditures for mental health inpatient care and a 113 percent increase in expenditures for outpatient care, resulting in a net increase of 8.6 percent in total mental healthcare expenditures. Total per capita expenditures on mental health patients declined by 28 percent between 1995 and 2004 and increased almost 21 percent from 2005 to 2008 (a new accounting system introduced in 2005 precluded meaningful comparisons with 1995). Increases of over 31 percent in residential care expenditures, 47 percent in outpatient care expenditures, and 34.7 percent in total mental health expenditures were reported from 2005 to 2008. VA dedicated significant enhancement funds for mental health starting in FY 2005, increasing from $100 million in fiscal year 2005 to $557 million in fiscal year 2009. This clearly led to a significant expansion of mental health services, the number of veterans treated, and the number of mental health staff providing those services. In the past decade, total funding for VHA mental healthcare increased by 81 percent, from $2.1 billion in fiscal year 2001 to no less than $3.8 billion in fiscal year 2009.

VHA is the largest provider of mental health services in the country. It has the capacity to care for veterans with mental health disorders at virtually every medical facility and CBOC in the country, representing over 1,000 sites of care. VHA provides a significant amount of mental health services within primary care settings in addition to a full array of specialized care for veterans with mental health disorders, including substance use disorders. These services are intended to be provided in an integrated, coordinated manner and across a comprehensive continuum of care. Outpatient services are offered through mental health clinics and a variety of more focused and specialized programs, such as MHICM, Psychosocial Recovery and Rehabilitation Centers (PRRCs), and many other programs providing service and outreach to individuals such as homeless and incarcerated veterans. Services are also available to those in need of acute and longer term hospitalization as well as to veterans in need of residential rehabilitation services for a range of mental health disorders, including PTSD, substance use disorder, and serious mental illness. VHA has made a significant investment in state of the art, evidence-based services, including both psychotherapeutic and psychopharmacological interventions. It has also taken bold action with initiatives in a variety of areas, including incarcerated veterans, homeless veterans, and suicide prevention. It is on the leading edge of expanding services and access through tele-mental health initiatives and other technologies, including Internet-based interventions. Services provided to veterans suffering from the psychological aftermath of trauma and combat, including those veterans diagnosed with PTSD, rightfully remain one of the highest of all priorities within VHA. In fiscal year 2008, VA provided care in ambulatory, residential care, or inpatient settings to 442,000 veterans with a diagnosis of PTSD. Of the 400,304 OEF/OIF veterans who received care at VA medical centers and clinics through the end of fiscal year 2008, 178,493 (45 percent) had a possible mental health diagnosis, and 92,998 (23 percent) had possible PTSD.

Box 5.2. Training

Although the focus of the present chapter is on clinical services, it is important to acknowledge VA's commitment to increasing the number of mental health trainee positions during this same time period. As shown in figure 5.1, the number of trainee positions in psychiatry, psychology, and social work increased significantly from 2006 to the present time, with expected additional increases expected in fiscal year 2011.

VHA substantially increased its investment in mental health employee training as well. When new monies for the Mental Health Strategic Plan (MHSP) were identified, approximately $500,000 was specifically dedicated to mental health employee education on an annual basis and transferred to VA's Employee Education Service. These monies have been spent on a broad array of educational offerings covering many new

(continued)

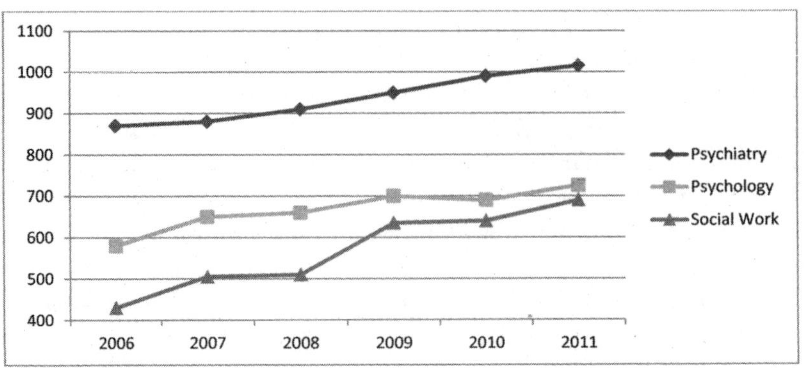

Figure 5.1 Total Number of VHA Trainees by Discipline, 2006–2011. From Zeiss (2010b)

initiatives, including psychosocial rehabilitation and recovery-oriented services (e.g., peer support, local recovery coordinators, psychosocial rehabilitation and recovery centers, consumer councils), suicide prevention, and reentry outreach. Program enhancements also required significant training resources in areas such as residential rehabilitation, homelessness, addiction services, PTSD services, and mental health/primary care integration. Of particular note, VHA initiated an ambitious effort to train VHA providers in evidence-based psychotherapies. To date, training has been funded for cognitive processing and prolonged exposure psychotherapy for PTSD and social skills training for the seriously mentally ill, with several other psychotherapies scheduled for training in the future.

Policy

As a department in the executive branch of the federal government, VA is authorized by law and its operation is governed by regulation and detailed VA policy. Federal law, regulation, and policy prescribe the details of what services may be provided, to whom, and under what circumstances. This section provides a brief overview of some of the key federal legislative and policy developments that have been important to the recent transformation of VHA services, especially in regard to mental healthcare.

Congress passed the Veterans Eligibility Reform Act of 1996, which liberalized eligibility rules and eliminated restrictions on outpatient care for low-income veterans. This bill was acknowledged by Dr. Kizer as critical to his transformation strategy (Kizer, Demakis & Feussner 2000). Prior to its passage, income eligible veterans qualified only for inpatient services or for outpatient care that was medically necessary to prevent a hospital stay. With the enactment of this law, veterans immediately became eligible for outpatient services, too. President Bill Clinton acknowledged the importance of this change when he signed the bill, proclaiming that it would allow VA to provide comprehensive healthcare services to all veterans (Longman 2007). Dr. Kizer also noted that this legislation gave inpatient and outpatient care the same standing under the law, so that VHA could provide the most appropriate care based on need rather than on eligibility criteria. This law also gave VA authority to contract with non-VA providers, which had not been previously allowed, another important change that helped to provide veterans with equal access to healthcare services. Other requirements of this legislation were extremely important and specific to mental healthcare in VHA. It mandated VHA to maintain the capacity to treat veterans with mental illness at levels that had been provided in 1996. This safeguard was inserted because of a concern that possible lapses could occur in caring for veterans with mental illness as a result of VHA's transformation. This legislation also charged the SMI committee with evaluating the care provided to veterans with serious and chronic mental illness. As discussed previously in this chapter, the advocacy of groups including the SMI Committee placed a critical focus on deficiencies within the mental healthcare system, which helped bring about the major enhancement/expansion effort that began in 2005.

In April 1999 Dr. Kizer signed VHA Directive 99-018, Filling Vacant Leadership Positions in Mental Health (Department of Veterans Affairs 1999a). This directive established a formal policy of recruiting and hiring the most qualified individuals for mental health leadership positions from among the major mental healthcare disciplines represented in VHA. It was issued after several years of experience with mental health service line organizational structures, highlighting the importance of strong, interdisciplinary leadership throughout the mental health continuum of care. Service lines have continued as the modal organizational structure within VHA, and this directive has remained in place, with several modifications, to the present time.

A second major directive specific to mental health was also issued in the same year: Authority for Mental Health Program Changes (Department of Veterans Affairs 1999b). This directive was thought to be needed because of the rapid changes occurring throughout the system and a national need to monitor the impact of these changes on mental healthcare in particular. This directive was one of the last to be signed by Dr. Kizer before ending his tenure as Under Secretary for Health. Eventually this directive was incorporated into a more comprehensive policy directive covering significant program changes in all VHA healthcare programs.

VHA also issued VHA Program Guide 1103.3, *Mental Health Program Guidelines for the New Veterans Health Administration* in June 1999 (Department of Veterans Affairs 1999c). Although several other program guides preceded 1103.3, this publication was the most comprehensive. These guidelines covered the provision of virtually all mental health services in VHA, highlighting special populations and providing an exhaustive listing of programs available within VHA's continuum of mental healthcare. Further, it included a brief synopsis of legislative authorities and very useful guidance on reporting mental health workload. Given the dramatic changes that occurred in the following ten years, a revised and updated version of 1103.3 was being contemplated at the time of this writing.

Over the next several years, other policy mandates were issued as VHA directives or as memoranda from the VA Central Office. Areas covered included but were not restricted to the Healthcare for Homeless Veterans program, the Homeless Providers Grant and Per Diem Program, MHICM, Encounter and Workload Capture for Psychosocial Rehabilitation Vocational Programs, military sexual trauma counseling, local recovery coordinators, and suicide prevention coordinators.

The MHSP and USH were clearly the two most important policy documents issued during this time and have been discussed in great detail. As promised by the USH, other handbooks were scheduled to be written and distributed at a later time to provide more detailed descriptions and guidance than was possible in the USH. At the time of the present writing, handbooks had already been distributed for the Grant and Per Diem Program and VHA's Mental Health Residential Rehabilitation Programs, with others in various stages of completion.

Finally, clinical practice guidelines covering various mental health populations began to be developed and disseminated during this time. These guidelines were developed by examining the professional literature in peer-reviewed journals and guidelines already created by other groups such as the American Psychiatric Association. An expert panel was convened to finalize each set of guidelines and develop consensus recommendations in areas where the empirical evidence did not provide adequate guidance. At the time of this writing, VA, typically in collaboration with the DoD, had issued four clinical practice guidelines specific to mental illness: major depressive disorder, substance use disorders, psychosis, and PTSD (Department of Veterans Affairs 2000, 2001, 2004b, 2004c).

New Directions

One of VA's highest priorities at the time of this writing was developing an even closer working relationship with the DoD. Precipitated to a large extent by the newest returning combat veterans, VA is committed to providing a seamless transition of veterans' care from their status as active duty service members to veterans.

It has been difficult for VHA to involve family members in the care of veterans because its legislative authority is restricted to providing care to veterans, not family members. As psychosocial rehabilitation and recovery-oriented services become more ingrained within the system, however, VHA is likely to find additional ways of including family members to a greater extent. Based on their experiences with DoD healthcare, which does not have VHA's restrictions on family member involvement, OEF/OIF veterans and family members expect VHA to include family members when their care is transferred from DoD. Recent legislation to hire marriage and family therapists in VHA may also facilitate further developments in this area (Pub. L. No. 109-461[2006]).

VHA, though a recognized leader in the electronic medical record, is focused on several areas to remain at the leading edge of computer-based technology in the twenty-first century. VHA has made a large commitment to telemental health as a way of enhancing veterans' access to service and ensuring veterans the same standard of care regardless of where they live. VHA is also pioneering Web-based technologies such as MyHealtheVet, which will provide veterans with their own healthcare information online, in addition to developing more interactive tools over time.

The integration of mental healthcare in primary care is in place, though a great deal remains to be done. There is also a great deal of interest in going beyond mental health and primary care to develop more robust programming in behavioral health. This would involve a more global integration of mental health and behavioral concepts applied across the entire continuum of medical care within VHA. In this context, psychological expertise is typically applied broadly in the healthcare system to help individuals manage their chronic medical illness, avoid and prevent medical disease, provide rehabilitation services to people with acute and chronic disease, and facilitate healthy lifestyles. Most recently, a full-time health behavior coordinator, typically a psychologist, was hired at every VHA facility to promote and coordinate these efforts.

At a 2009 VHA homeless summit, Secretary of Veterans Affairs Eric K. Shenseki announced VHA's goal to prevent and end homelessness among veterans within five years (Department of Veterans Affairs 2009). VHA has had homeless programs in place for many years, which have benefited greatly from the infusion of mental health enhancement funds. Nonetheless, the secretary's announcement represents one of the boldest new initiatives and directions taken by VA in recent times.

With an ambitious, aspirational plan in place to create a comprehensive continuum of mental health services across the country, VHA was in the early stages of developing a monitoring process to measure present status, ongoing progress, and, ultimately, the impact of mental health services on veterans. Using a combination of tools including administrative data and medical record review, VHA planned to create a set of metrics to monitor program development and maintenance and to ensure that sufficient mental health staffing resources are in place across the country. Other plans, in earlier stages of development, include the routine and periodic assessment of functional and symptomatic status of veterans receiving mental healthcare in VHA.

References

Baker, R. & Pickren, W. E. (2006). *Psychology and the Department of Veterans Affairs*. Washington, DC: American Psychological Association.

Charting the U.S. Department of Veterans Affairs' Progress on Meeting the Mental Health Needs of Our Veterans: Discussion of Funding, Mental Health Strategic Plan, and the Uniform Mental Health Services Handbook. (2009). House Committee on Veterans Affairs, April 30 (statement of Ira Katz).

Chen, S., Wagner, T. H. & Barnett, P. G. (2001). The effect of reforms on spending for veterans' substance abuse treatment, 1993–1999. *Health Affairs* 29, no. 4: 169–175.

Department of Veterans Affairs. (1999a). VHA directive 99-018: Filling vacant leadership positions in mental health. Veterans Health Administration directive. Washington, DC.

Department of Veterans Affairs. (1999b). VHA directive 99-030: Authority for mental health program changes. Veterans Health Administration directive. Washington, DC.

Department of Veterans Affairs. (1999c). *Mental health program guidelines for the new Veterans Health Administration*. VHA program guide 1103.3. Washington, DC: Department of Veterans Affairs.

Department of Veterans Affairs. (2000). *Management of depressive disorders in adults*. Veterans Health Administration, Office of Quality and Performance clinical practice guideline. Washington, DC: Department of Veterans Affairs.

Department of Veterans Affairs. (2001). *Management of Substance Use Disorders in Primary and Specialty Care*. Veterans Health Administration, Office of Quality and Performance clinical practice guideline. Washington, DC: Department of Veterans Affairs.

Department of Veterans Affairs. (2003). *Action Agenda: Achieving the Promise: Transforming Mental Healthcare in VA*. Washington, DC: Department of Veterans Affairs.

Department of Veterans Affairs. (2004a). *Comprehensive mental health strategic plan.* Washington, DC: Department of Veterans Affairs.

Department of Veterans Affairs. (2004b). *Management of psychosis.* Veterans Health Administration, Office of Quality and Performance clinical practice guideline. Washington, DC: Department of Veterans Affairs.

Department of Veterans Affairs. (2004c). *Management of post-traumatic stress.* Veterans Health Administration, Office of Quality and Performance clinical practice guideline. Washington, DC: Department of Veterans Affairs.

Department of Veterans Affairs. (2009). Secretary Shinseki details plan to end homelessness for veterans. Public and Intergovernmental Affairs press release. http://www1.va.gov/opa/pressrel/pressrelease.cfm?id=1807.

Department of Veterans Affairs, Mental Health Consumer Council. (2003). *Consumer Council News* 6, no. 8. http://www.mentalhealth.va.gov/cc/archival/pdf/012303.pdf.

Department of Veterans Affairs, Office of Inspector General, Healthcare Inspection. (2007). *Implementing VHA's MHSP initiatives for suicide prevention.* Report #06-03706-126. Washington, DC: Department of Veterans Affairs. http://www.va.gov/oig/54/reports/vaoig-06-03706-126.pdf.

Department of Veterans Affairs, Office of Public Affairs and Media Relations. (2009). *Facts about the Department of Veterans Affairs.* Fact sheet. Washington, DC: Department of Veterans Affairs. http://www.va.gov/opa/publications/factsheets/fs_department_of_veterans_affairs.pdf.

Department of Veterans Affairs, Veterans Health Administration. (2008). *Uniform mental health services in VA medical centers and clinics.* VHA handbook 1160.01. Washington, DC: Department of Veterans Affairs.

Deputy Under Secretary for Health for Operations and Management. (2007). Mental health initiatives. Department of Veterans Affairs memorandum. Washington, DC.

Deputy Under Secretary for Health for Operations and Management. (2008). Clarification of provider staffing requirements for emergency departments and urgent care clinics in VHA. Department of Veterans Affairs memorandum. Washington, DC.

Frank, Richard G. (2009). Balancing the treatment portfolio in mental health. Presented at 2009 Summit on the Future of Psychology Practice, American Psychological Association, San Antonio, Texas, May 16. http://www.reisman-white.com/associations/4888/files/Farley.pdf.

Government Accountability Office. (1999). Report no. GAO/T-HEHS-99-83. http://www.gao.gov/archive/1999/he99083t.pdf.

Government Accountability Office. (2000). Report no. GAO HEHS-00-57.

Government Accountability Office. (2005). Report no. GAO 05-287. http://www.gao.gov/new.items/d05287.pdf.

Government Accountability Office. (2006). Report no. GAO-07-66. http:// www.gao.gov/new.items/d0766.pdf.

Greenberg, G. & Rosenheck, R. (2003). *National Mental Health Program Performance Monitoring System: Fiscal year 2002 report.* West Haven, CT: Department of Veterans Affairs, Northeast Program Evaluation Center.

Greenberg, G. & Rosenheck, R. (2006). *National Mental Health Program Performance Monitoring System: Fiscal year 2005 report.* West Haven, CT: Department of Veterans Affairs, Northeast Program Evaluation Center.

Greenberg, G. & Rosenheck, R. (2009). *National Mental Health Program Performance Monitoring System: Fiscal year 2008 report.* West Haven, CT: Department of Veterans Affairs, Northeast Program Evaluation Center.

Gresen, R. C., Losonczy, M. F., Martone, L., Wolkin, A., Short, D., Dean, M. A., McGlawn, J. H., Ramsel, D., Breckenridge, J. N. & Kuttesch, D. A. (2003). Mental health provider workload guidelines, version 2. Unpublished manuscript. Department of Veterans Affairs, Veterans Health Administration, Patient Care Services, Mental Health Strategic Health Group, March.

Karlin, B. (2007). Personal communication to author, March 12.

Katz, I. (2009, July). Opening address: Meeting the diverse mental health needs of veterans: Implementing the Uniform Services Handbook. Department of Veterans Affairs, Veterans Health Administration, Patient Care Services, Office of Mental Health Services. Baltimore, MD.

Kizer, K. W., Demakis, J. G. & Feussner, J. R. (2000). VA's Quality Enhancement Research Initiative: Reinventing VA healthcare: Systematizing Quality Improvement and Quality Innovation. *Medical Care* 38, no. 6, supp. I: I-7–I-16.

Longman, P. (2007). *Best care anywhere: Why VA healthcare is better than yours.* Sausalito, CA: PoliPoint Press.

Mellow, A. (2006). *Mental health services in Veterans Healthcare Network (VISN) 11.* http://www.in.gov/fssa/dmha/files/veteranspresent1106.pdf.

Mulligan, K. (2002). VA allowing mental health services to erode, APA charges. *Psychiatric News* 37, no. 17: 2–35. http://pn.psychiatryonline.org/content/37/17/ 2.1.full.

Mulligan, K. (2003). VA's health system reform plans elicit concerned reactions. *Psychiatric News* 38, no. 22: 2–8.

NAMI E-news. (2001). *Dr. Frese testifies before the House Veterans' Affairs Committee.* April 4. http://www.nami.org/Template.cfm?Section=eNews_Archive&template=/ contentmanagement/contentdisplay.cfm&ContentID=6098&title=NAMI%20 Testimony%20on%20VA-HUD%20Appropriations.

National Coalition for Homeless Veterans (2010). *FY 2010 VA Budget Includes $3.2 Billion for Homeless Vets.* January 4. http://www.nchv.org/news_article.cfm ?id=650.

National Mental Health Association. (2004). President's 2003 report languishes a year later: No progress made on New Freedom Commission recommendations. *The Bell* (Fall): 7.

The President's New Freedom Commission on Mental Health. (2003). *Achieving the promise: Transforming mental healthcare in America.* http://store.samhsa.gov/shin/content//SMA03-3831/SMA03-3831.pdf.

Public Law 109-461. (2006). http://ftp.resource.org/gpo.gov/laws/109/publ 461.109.pdf.

Robert Wood Foundation. (2009). *Physician faculty scholars.* http://rwjfpfsp.stan ford.edu/nac/kizer.html.

Substance Abuse and Mental Health Administration. (2005a). Federal partners spotlight: U.S. Department of Veterans Affairs. *Mental Health Transformation Trends* 1, no. 2: 4. http://www.samhsa.gov/Matrix/MHST/TransformationTrends May05.pdf.

Substance Abuse and Mental Health Services Administration. (2005b). National consensus statement on mental health recovery. http://store.samhsa.gov/shin/content//SMA05-4129/SMA05-4129.pdf.

VA's treatment facility integration strategy. (1997). *Hearing before the Subcommittee on Health and Subcommittee on Oversight and Investigations.* Committee on Veterans Affairs, House of Representatives, July 24 (statement of Kenneth W. Kizer).

Veterans Eligibility Reform Act of 1996. Pub. L. No. 104-262, 110 Stat. 3177–3211.

Zeiss, A. (2010a). OMHS update FY2010. Presented at VA Psychology Leadership Conference, San Antonio, Texas, May 13.

Zeiss, R. (2010b). Update on psychology education in VA. Presented at VA Psychology Leadership Conference, San Antonio, Texas, May 13.

Chapter 6

Chiropractic in Veterans' Healthcare

Bart N. Green, Claire D. Johnson, and Andrew S. Dunn

Introduction

Chiropractic care in the Veterans Health Administration (VHA) is a national program under the Office of Rehabilitation Services and is included in the medical benefits package. Chiropractic was first offered to veterans at VHA facilities in 2004 (Veterans Health Administration 2009). This chapter provides a historical overview of the inclusion of chiropractic care in VHA, describes how this newest offering to veterans functions in the VHA system, and explains how veterans may access care. This chapter also discusses policies relevant to access to chiropractic care, future developments, and new directions.

Chiropractic Care

Complementary and alternative medicine (CAM) is commonly used in the United States. According to the U.S. Department of Health and Human Services, almost four out of every ten adults report using some type of CAM therapy, and Americans spent $33.9 billion out of pocket for CAM services in 2007 (Barnes, Bloom & Nahin, 2008; Nahin et al. 2009). Of the 42 percent of the U.S. population that uses CAM, approximately 30 percent of these visits are associated with chiropractic care (Coulter et al. 2002). Use of CAM by veterans and active duty military members has been studied as well. Approximately 50 percent of veterans report using CAM (Baldwin et al. 2002). Of these, the primary reasons for seeking CAM include back pain (56 percent) and musculoskeletal pain (22 percent) (Baldwin et al. 2002). Studies of military populations have shown similar findings. Over 37 percent of active duty personnel report using at least one CAM therapy in the past year (Smith et al. 2007). Higher levels of pain and lower satisfaction with conventional medical care were suggested as possible reasons for these patients seeking CAM (Smith et al. 2007).

A distinct health profession, chiropractic is the largest, most regulated, and most recognized CAM profession in the United States (Kaptchuk & Eisenberg 1998; Meeker & Haldeman 2002) and is the third largest healthcare profession in the United States (medicine and dentistry are first and second) (Christensen, Kollasch & Hyland 2010). It is duly licensed in all fifty states, Puerto Rico, Virgin Islands, and District of Columbia, and there are approximately 70,000 active chiropractic licenses in the United States (Christensen, Kollasch & Hyland 2010). Chiropractic is a healing profession that is sometimes incorrectly referred to as if it were a modality or procedure (Hawk 1998). For example, some may consider chiropractic equivalent to spinal manipulation; however, manipulation is only one of many procedures that can be incorporated into an overall chiropractic approach to health (Meeker & Haldeman 2002). Chiropractic provides nonpharmaceutical, conservative healthcare that uses a multimodal approach, including manipulation, to manage neuromusculoskeletal and other disorders. The majority (estimated to be at least 80 percent) of patients seek chiropractic care for neuromusculoskelatal conditions (Kaptchuk & Eisenberg 1998). Box 6.1 contains a definition of chiropractic from the American Chiropractic Association.

Chiropractic care offers safe and effective conservative management for a variety of neuromusculoskeletal complaints. The chiropractic approach aims to identify the cause of the problem, confirms that there are no "red flags" that may harm the patient, and then applies the most appropriate treatment methods to correct the problem and prevent it from returning. The chiropractic examination includes a history of the chief complaint and may include inspection, palpation, ranges of motion, orthopedic tests, neurological tests, spinal analysis, and possibly other diagnostic tests (e.g., diagnostic imaging, laboratory examinations), depending on the findings (Meeker & Haldeman 2002).

As stated in VHA Directive 2009-059, chiropractic treatment in a VHA facility will typically include "patient education, therapeutic exercise, lifestyle recommendations, and other interventions such as joint manipulation and mobilization, soft tissue therapies, and physical modalities" (Veterans Health Administration 2009). Therapeutic exercise may include stretching, strengthening, posture and balance exercises, and/or a full rehabilitation program.

Box 6.1. American Chiropractic Association Definition of Chiropractic

Chiropractic is a health care profession that focuses on disorders of the musculoskeletal system and the nervous system, and the effects of these disorders on general health. Chiropractic care is used most often to treat neuromusculoskeletal complaints, including but not limited to back pain, neck pain, pain in the joints of the arms or legs, and headaches.

Doctors of Chiropractic—often referred to as chiropractors or chiropractic physicians—practice a drug-free, hands-on approach to health care that includes patient examination, diagnosis and treatment. Chiropractors have broad diagnostic skills and are also trained to recommend therapeutic and rehabilitative exercises, as well as to provide nutritional, dietary and lifestyle counseling.

The most common therapeutic procedure performed by doctors of chiropractic is known as "spinal manipulation," also called "chiropractic adjustment." The purpose of manipulation is to restore joint mobility by manually applying a controlled force into joints that have become hypomobile—or restricted in their movement—as a result of a tissue injury. Tissue injury can be caused by a single traumatic event, such as improper lifting of a heavy object, or through repetitive stresses, such as sitting in an awkward position with poor spinal posture for an extended period of time. In either case, injured tissues undergo physical and chemical changes that can cause inflammation, pain, and diminished function for the sufferer. Manipulation, or adjustment of the affected joint and tissues, restores mobility, thereby alleviating pain and muscle tightness, and allowing tissues to heal.

Source: www.acatoday.org. Permission to reprint granted by the American Chiropractic Association.

Patient education and lifestyle recommendations may include many procedures, but typically will focus on ergonomics training, healthy diet and exercise advice, stress reduction exercises or counseling, nutritional testing or advice, and may include collaborative care from other providers.

Chiropractic's nonpharmacological and conservative approach to neuromusculoskeletal conditions may be especially beneficial under certain circumstances, which may include allergies or negative reactions to pharmaceuticals, multiple drug interactions, addiction to pain medication, and restrictions to activities if taking medication (e.g., driving a vehicle, operating heavy machinery). It has been suggested that interdisciplinary care, including CAM, may be helpful in assisting veterans suffering from chronic pain (Tan et al. 2010). Within an integrated healthcare setting, doctors of chiropractic work with other healthcare providers to maximize the possible health benefits of care and reduce any potential risks (Dunn, Green & Gilford 2009; Goldberg et al. 2009; Green, Sims & Allen 2006; Lisi et al. 2009; Meeker 2000; Smith, Greene & Meeker 2002).

History of Chiropractic

Although joint manipulation and bone-setting have existed for centuries and go back to the time of Hippocrates, the chiropractic profession in the United States began in 1895. At that time there were no antibiotics, modern analgesics, or physical therapy, and modern surgical methods had yet to be developed. Chiropractic's founders were searching for ways to address health and wellness and recognized the body's innate, homeostatic capacity to heal. Some say the focus of chiropractic healing is not on disease but on removing the barriers to health, which include physical, psychosocial, emotional, and/or spiritual components; thus, chiropractic has a holistic view of health (Hawk 2005). Fifty years after the beginning of chiropractic, the World Health Organization's definition of *health* contained similar characteristics to this holistic paradigm: "[a] state of complete physical, mental and social well-being, and not merely the absence of disease" (World Health Organization 1946). The first state to license chiropractors as health practitioners was Illinois, in 1905, and the first state to license chiropractic as a profession was Kansas, in 1913. As the chiropractic profession continued to grow, educational requirements and specifications became more rigorous. The GI Bill allowed many veterans returning from World Wars I and II to go to chiropractic college and earn a doctor of chiropractic (DC) degree. During this time, chiropractors and patients who were veterans saw the need for military members and veterans to have greater access to chiropractic care, because they witnessed how helpful chiropractic care was to their patients and themselves. As more people demanded chiropractic care, actions were taken to ensure access for military and veteran patients.

Chiropractic services have been integrated into the healthcare systems of the Department of Defense (DoD) and Department of Veterans Affairs (VA) through legislative action. As early as 1978, Congress authorized VA to provide chiropractic services to veterans (*Chiropractic service* 2000). Before integrating chiropractic care within VA, chiropractic services were provided

---

Box 6.2. Legislation Pertinent to Chiropractic Care in VA

a. Pub. L. 106-117, the Veterans' Millennium Health Care and Benefits Act (the Millennium Act), required the Under Secretary for Health to establish a VHA-wide policy regarding the role of chiropractic treatment in the care of Veterans.

b. Pub. L. 107-135, Section 204, requires VHA to carry out a program to provide chiropractic care to Veterans through Department of Veterans Affairs (VA) medical centers and clinics.

   (1) Pub. L. 107-135, Section 204, Subsection (c) states "the Secretary [of Veterans Affairs] shall designate at least one site for such program in each geographic service area of the Veterans Health Administration."

   (2) Pub. L. 107-135, Section 204, Subsection (d) states chiropractic care provided by VHA "shall include a variety of chiropractic care and services for neuro-musculoskeletal conditions, including subluxation complex."

   (3) Pub. L. 107-135, Section 204, Subsection (e)(1) states "the Secretary shall carry out the program through personal service contracts and by appointment of licensed chiropractors in Department medical centers and clinics."

---

under the DoD by the Military Health System. Beginning in fiscal year 1993, the National Defense Authorization Acts prompted chiropractic integration within the Military Health System, which led to a Chiropractic Health Care Demonstration Project in DoD. The demonstration project began in 1995 and served as a feasibility assessment for including chiropractic care throughout the Military Health System (Birch & Davis Associates 2000). Due to the project's success, including excellent patient satisfaction and good clinical outcomes, the chiropractic program was fully implemented. Ten pieces of legislation over seventeen years contributed to the current presence of chiropractic within the Military Health System of DoD (Dunn, Green & Gilford 2009) (see box 6.2). At the time of this writing, chiropractic care is available at more than sixty military hospitals or clinics, including the newest locations outside of the continental United States, in Okinawa and Germany (Dunn, Green & Gilford 2009).

Many active duty personnel have received chiropractic care as part of their healthcare regimen. As these active duty personnel retire from military service, they can do so with the expectation that chiropractic will continue to be a part of their healthcare as they transition to veteran status. Beginning in 1999, three pieces of legislation contributed to the delivery of chiropractic services in VHA medical facilities. These acts resulted in the provision of the initial twenty-six chiropractic clinics in VHA medical facilities (Dunn, Green & Gilford 2009).

Chiropractic Education

Currently there are fifteen accredited educational programs that grant doctor of chiropractic degrees at seventeen locations in the United States (see box 6.3). The accrediting body, the Council on Chiropractic Education (CCE), is recognized by the secretary of education for accreditation of programs and institutions. Doctors of chiropractic are required to undergo rigorous training before being able to take their licensure exams. Before someone may enter a chiropractic college, a minimum of three years (ninety units) of undergraduate education is required, and some colleges require a bachelor's degree. Chiropractic education is similar to other healing professions and covers many of the same subjects as other health professions programs (Coulter et al. 1998). These include domains such as the basic sciences (anatomy, physiology, pathology) and the clinical sciences (diagnosis, treatment, patient management, emergency procedures) (Coulter et al. 1998). The length of the typical chiropractic degree program is ten semesters, which includes a clinical internship. This is equivalent to five academic years and about 4,800 hours of training, comparable to medical programs (Coulter et al. 1998). Proper training and skill development is important for safe and effective care, especially joint manipulation. Although manipulation can be performed by various nonchiropractic licensed practitioners, DCs have the greatest number of curricular hours and the most focused training in manipulation of the spine and upper/lower extremities of all the professions (Coulter et al. 1998).

Chiropractic Licensure and Postgraduate Training

After graduating from an accredited chiropractic institution, candidates must pass additional exams prior to licensure. These exams require the candidates to demonstrate their knowledge and clinical competencies through several written and practical licensure examinations (Christensen, Kollasch & Hyland 2010). After licensure, some chiropractors choose to pursue additional specialty training. These specialties include radiology, sports medicine, rehabilitation,

---

**Box 6.3. Fifteen Doctor of Chiropractic Programs
in 17 U.S. Locations**

- Cleveland Chiropractic College—Overland Park, KS
- D'Youville College Doctor of Chiropractic—Buffalo, NY
- Life University College of Chiropractic—Marietta, GA
- Life Chiropractic College West—Hayward, CA
- Logan College of Chiropractic—Chesterfield, MO
- Southern California University of Health Sciences
    - Los Angeles College of Chiropractic—Whittier, CA
- Doctor of Chiropractic Degree Program in the College of Professional Studies of the National University of Health Sciences—Lombard, IL
- New York Chiropractic College—Seneca Falls, NY
- Northwestern Health Sciences University
    - Northwestern College of Chiropractic—Bloomington, MN
- Palmer College of Chiropractic
    - Palmer College of Chiropractic—Davenport, IA
    - Palmer College of Chiropractic West—San Jose, CA
    - Palmer College of Chiropractic Florida—Port Orange, FL
- Parker College of Chiropractic—Dallas, TX
- Sherman College of Chiropractic—Spartanburg, SC
- Texas Chiropractic College—Pasadena, TX
- University of Bridgeport College of Chiropractic—Bridgeport, CT
- University of Western States College of Chiropractic—Portland, OR

Source: http://www.cce-usa.org.

---

nutrition, and other areas, and each requires additional competency examinations in order to be board-certified (Christensen, Kollasch & Hyland 2010). Additional advanced degrees, such as a master's degree in public health or education or an additional doctorate degree that relates to chiropractic practice or academics, may also be pursued. Chiropractors must complete annual continuing educational requirements to maintain licensure, and additional training each year is typically required for chiropractors working in hospital systems.

Part of the Healthcare Team

With the increasing demand for chiropractic care, there has also been an increase in the number of chiropractors being included in healthcare teams. Doctors of chiropractic work in different capacities depending on the location. In the private sector, some will work in solo or group practices and others will work within larger healthcare settings. Those who are integrated may work in the role of hospital manager or within different departments such as orthopedics, neurology, or physical therapy. Others may be included in ambulatory (outpatient) diagnostic and treatment services or a separate physical medicine department. How chiropractic services are integrated often depends on the organization of the local facility and the particular needs of that location (Branson 2009; Goldberg et al. 2009; Grieves, Menke & Pursel 2009; Johnson 2009). The most efficient and effective way to offer chiropractic services is to integrate them in the healthcare system. This helps to ensure interprovider communications and provide more consistent and appropriate care for patients (Boon et al. 2009; Johnson 2009).

Benefits of Chiropractic Care

Back and neck pain are common in the U.S. population. According to exhaustive research conducted by numerous scientists and published in *The Burden of Musculoskeletal Diseases in the United States*, 43 to 60 percent of the adult population report having had back or neck pain in the previous three months, and the prevalence of back pain continues to increase with age (Andersson & American Academy of Orthopaedic Surgeons 2008). Direct medical costs associated with spine-related conditions are estimated at $193.9 billion for 2002–2004 and $14.0 billion for indirect costs (e.g., lost wages) per year (Andersson & American Academy of Orthopaedic Surgeons 2008). Back pain is common among veterans (Haskell et al. 2010) and more than 60 percent report chronic pain, especially in the back, knee, or hip (Butchart et al. 2009). Some subsets of the military population may have a higher prevalence of back pain than others. For example, Gulf War veterans had a higher prevalence of back pain (20–52 percent) than non–Gulf War veterans (15–49 percent) (Thomas et al. 2006).

Because inclusion of chiropractic services as a VA benefit is relatively new, research is just now evaluating the advantages of chiropractic care that are unique to conditions that veterans may experience (Green, Johnson & Lisi 2009; Green et al. 2009; Johnson et al. 2008). Studies have shown that chiropractic inclusion in VA facilities is feasible (Dunn, Green & Gilford 2009; Dunn & Passmore 2008; Dunn et al. 2006; Lisi et al. 2009). Recent publications on clinical benefits for veterans are also showing positive results (Dunn, Baylis & Ryan 2009; Dunn et al. 2009; Lisi 2010).

There is a considerable amount of scientific research on chiropractic care in the general population (Kaptchuk & Eisenberg 1998). Most of it has focused on clinical outcomes as they relate to neuromusculoskeletal conditions. The studies that have evaluated spinal manipulation for low back and neck pain have shown that chiropractic management is comparable to conventional medical care (Meeker & Haldeman 2002). Some clinical trials have shown that chiropractic care and/or spinal manipulation provided more favorable outcomes than placebo or other methods to treat back pain (Koes et al. 1996; Meeker & Haldeman 2002; van Tulder, Koes & Bouter 1997).

Clinical practice guidelines suggest that chiropractic care can be useful when addressing various conditions. The American College of Physicians' clinical practice guideline for low back pain recommends conservative procedures, such as those that chiropractors provide (e.g., spinal manipulation, exercise, myofascial treatment) (Chou et al. 2007). Guidelines have also been published in scientific journals specifically on chiropractic management for the following conditions: back pain and low back–related leg complaints (Globe et al. 2008; Lawrence et al. 2008), myofascial trigger points and pain syndromes (Vernon & Schneider 2009), fibromyalgia syndrome (Schneider et al. 2009), tendinopathy (Pfefer, Cooper & Uhl, 2009), extremity conditions (Brantingham et al. 2009), diagnostic imaging/X-ray use (Bussieres, Peterson & Taylor 2007, 2008; Bussieres, Taylor & Peterson 2007, 2008), terminology for acute conditions (Dehen et al. 2010), care of chronic spine conditions (Farabaugh, Dehen & Hawk 2010), and care of older adults (Hawk & Cambron 2009). These guidelines help to provide the best possible care for patients and consistent case management among healthcare facilities.

Patient Satisfaction

Patient satisfaction is one indicator of high-quality care. Chiropractic care has demonstrated high levels of patient satisfaction in various research studies for decades. One of the earliest studies evaluated injured workers with neck and back injuries and compared conventional medical care to chiropractic care. The patients receiving chiropractic care reported their ability to return to previous functional levels was the same as with medical care; however, patients receiving chiropractic care expressed significantly higher satisfaction regarding their interaction with their chiropractor compared to those receiving medical care (Kane et al. 1974). In a study conducted by Cherkin, patients seeing chiropractors for low back pain were three times more likely to report that they were very satisfied with care when compared to medical care. These patients reported they were more satisfied with the amount of information they were given and felt that the provider was concerned about them and was more confident in addressing their low back pain problem (Cherkin & MacCornack 1989). In a recent study reviewing research on satisfaction with chiropractic care, the author concluded that high patient satisfaction is consistent in the published literature over time and that a majority of patients report high satisfaction with chiropractic care (Gaumer 2006).

Adverse Events

Chiropractic has been shown to be relatively low risk for adverse events when compared to other treatments used to address pain. All healthcare therapies have some risk associated with them. Although chiropractic is considered a conservative approach, some risks are still present. In general, most adverse effects to treatment are mild and transient, such as soreness and stiffness (Hurwitz et al. 2004, 2005). Severe adverse events (disability/death) are rare. The occurrence of severe reactions is estimated to be approximately three to six events in ten million manipulations, but this is difficult to calculate because these events are so rare (Kaptchuk & Eisenberg 1998; Meeker & Haldeman 2002). Adverse events due to spinal manipulation are considered rare when compared to adverse events of other pain-related therapies, such as NSAIDS, which are reported to cause 107,000 hospitalizations and 16,500 deaths per year due to gastrointestinal complications (Singh 1998). Currently, identifiable factors for severe reactions to manipulation are not clear (Meeker & Haldeman 2002), and research continues to be conducted to attempt to find these factors and make spinal manipulation as safe as possible (Kawchuk, Herzog & Hasler 1992; Wuest et al. 2010).

Cost Effectiveness of Chiropractic

Recent studies of comparative cost effectiveness in the private sector have shown that chiropractic is cost effective when compared to other therapies. A study of patients with low back pain presenting for healthcare in a managed care organization showed that chiropractic management was less expensive than medical management of back pain when care extends beyond primary care (Grieves, Menke & Pursel 2009). A study evaluating patients with chronic low back pain found that chiropractic care appeared relatively cost-effective compared to medical care for the treatment of chronic low back pain and that chiropractic and medical care performed similarly for acute patients (Haas, Sharma & Stano 2005). As integrative healthcare environments become more commonplace, more cost effectiveness studies will need to evaluate what impact including chiropractic has on cost.

Inclusion of Chiropractic Care in VHA

Historical Overview

Chiropractic care in VA began under the Veterans Millennium Health Care and Benefits Act of 1999, which required the Under Secretary for Health of the Department of Veterans Affairs to establish a policy for the role of chiropractic treatment for veterans. Implementation of this policy was carried out in compliance with the Department of Veterans Affairs Health Care Programs Enhancement Act of 2001 (Department of Veterans Affairs 2001). Under this act, at least one site was selected in the year 2004 within each Veterans Integrated Service Network (VISN) of VHA to provide chiropractic care through the appointment of chiropractors in VA medical facilities and through personal service contracts. Thus, twenty-six chiropractic facilities were established by VA beginning in 2004 (Lisi et al. 2009).

Prior to 2004, chiropractic services were only available as a veterans benefit by means of a fee-basis referral from the veteran's primary care provider to a chiropractor outside of VHA. Chiropractic services became the first healthcare discipline to become integrated within VHA since optometry and podiatry were integrated in 1976.

Legislative History

Three pieces of legislation have contributed in a meaningful way to the landscape of chiropractic services in VHA. First, the Veterans Millennium Health Care and Benefits Act of 1999 established a policy for VHA regarding the role of chiropractic in the treatment of veterans and provided definitions for both *chiropractor* and *chiropractic treatment*. The Department of Veterans Affairs Health Care Programs Enhancement Act of 2001 then required VHA to provide chiropractic services at select medical centers. Finally, the Veterans Health Care, Capital Asset, and Business Improvement Act of 2003 clarified state licensure requirements for chiropractors within VHA. While legislative action served as the impetus for chiropractic integration within VHA, and additional legislation is anticipated, the expansion of chiropractic services beyond those facilities initially identified in 2004 has occurred in the absence of additional legislative driving forces.

Programmatic Growth of Chiropractic in VHA

The chiropractic program in the VHA had expanded from twenty-six to more than thirty-eight VA medical centers or community-based outpatient clinics facilities as of 2010. Veterans can locate VA locations and the services they provide at http://www2.va.gov/directory/guide/home.asp?isflash=1. A map of the current locations for VHA chiropractic care is presented in figure 6.1.

The majority of chiropractic clinics are aligned administratively with Physical Medicine and Rehabilitation Services (Lisi et al. 2009). A survey of VHA chiropractors and chiropractic clinics (Lisi et al. 2009) has identified some variation in employment and provider characteristics, clinical practice, and provider integration. Consistent with earlier published reports (Dunn & Passmore 2008; Dunn et al. 2006), the most common complaints reportedly seen by VA chiropractors are back pain, followed by neck pain, with consultation requests stemming mainly from primary care providers (Lisi et al. 2009). The majority of chiropractors are full-time employees in VA medical centers, serving as the only chiropractors at their facilities (Lisi et al. 2009). A small percentage of chiropractors within the VA system are considered "without compensation academic-affiliate appointees" and serve as chiropractic college faculty members, providing clinical services to veterans and supervising chiropractic students within the structure of an affiliation agreement. The addition of chiropractic college faculty as "without compensation" appointees represents a portion of the growth that occurred following the identification of the initial twenty-six VA medical centers at which chiropractic services were integrated.

Academic Affiliations

Academic affiliations between chiropractic institutions and VA medical centers were established starting in 2004. Information about the initial affiliation and integration and a subsequent survey of the initial four affiliations are published in the scholarly literature (Dunn 2005, 2007). Details guiding the supervision of chiropractic students, listed as fourth-year clerks, are included in the VHA handbook for supervision of associated health trainees (Department of Veterans Affairs 2008). Chiropractic students take part in supervised clinical training, contributing to veteran care through history taking, examination, and

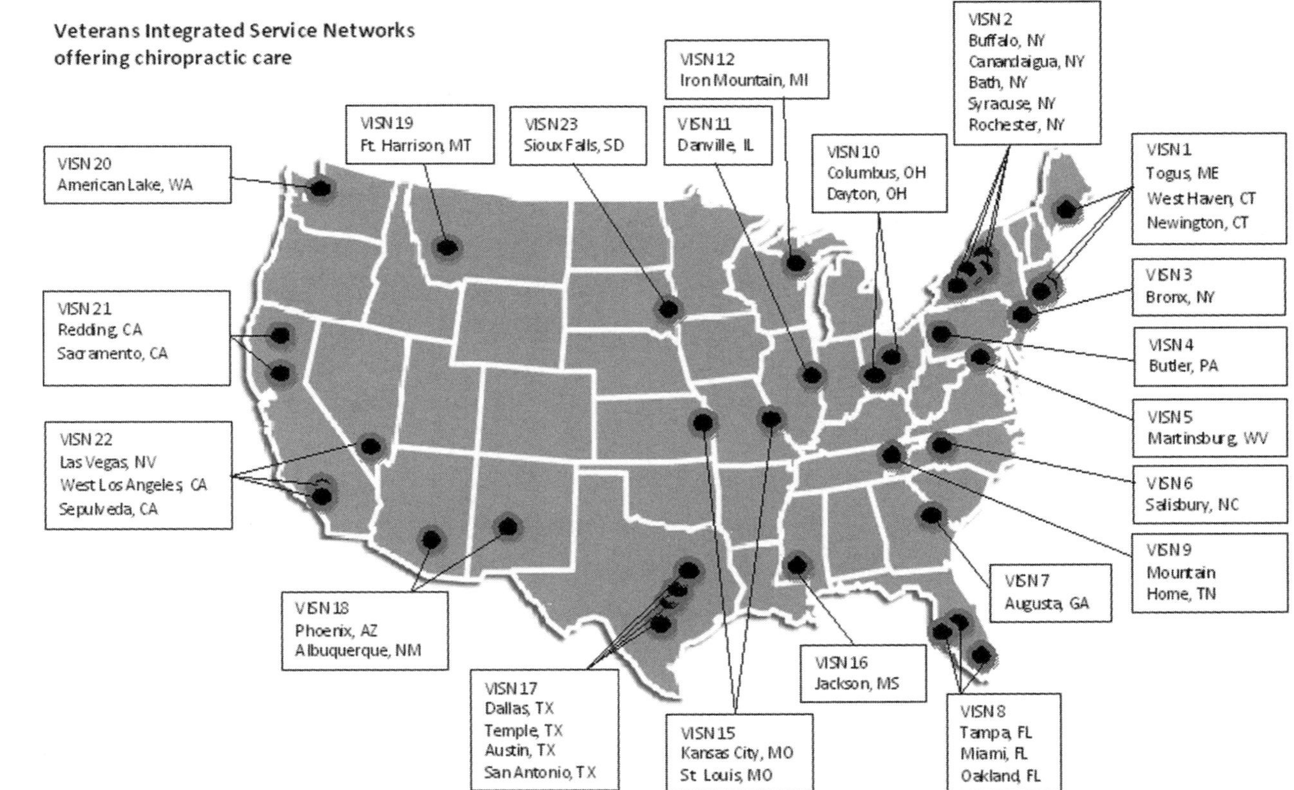

Figure 6.1. Veterans Integrated Service Networks Offering Chiropractic Care

treatment and assuming graduated levels of responsibility, as appropriate. Chiropractic students are exposed to a variety of complex care presentations, further develop their clinical skill and judgment with a patient-centered and evidence-based approach to patient care, and interact with a multitude of provider types in an integrated medical setting. A survey of VHA chiropractors reported that 42 percent were involved in the training of chiropractic students (Lisi et al. 2009). As of the end of 2010, there were twenty academic affiliations involving eleven chiropractic institutions and VA medical centers or community-based outpatient clinics where chiropractic students completed portions of their clinical education.

Research

A number of VHA chiropractors are actively engaged in research activities, serving as investigators for studies ranging from local, unfunded cross-sectional designs to multisite, funded, randomized clinical trials. Although the emphasis of this research has largely been on chiropractic management of musculoskeletal conditions, collaborative relationships with behavioral health providers, physical therapists, and health systems specialists have expanded the boundaries of investigation. A 2009 review of the state of the literature regarding chiropractic practice in military and veterans' healthcare identified thirteen publications stemming from various study designs, including commentaries, case reports, and descriptive studies, such as surveys and cross-sectional studies (Green et al. 2009). In at least two VA medical centers, VHA chiropractors contribute to the research proposal process through participation and leadership on facility research committees, including research and development committees and institutional review boards.

Leadership Structure

Subsequent to legislative mandate, an external Advisory Committee on Chiropractic Care Implementation was convened in 2002 to assist then VA Secretary Anthony Principi with the integration of chiropractic into VA. In January 2006 an Internal Chiropractic Field Advisory Committee was formed to replace the external advisory committee. While chiropractic services first became available to veterans within VA medical centers in 2004, chiropractic became an established program with a program director in September 2007. At that time, the chiropractic program became a fifth service within the VHA rehabilitation service along with audiology and speech pathology, blind rehabilitation, physical medicine rehabilitation, and recreation therapy. The director of the chiropractic program, serving under the Deputy Chief Consultant and Chief Consultant of Rehabilitation Services, serves as a field-based program director, with half of the time of this position being dedicated to the chiropractic program.

Policies and Practice

Chiropractic care in VHA is available to veterans. At present, dependents are not eligible for this service. Access to chiropractic care is through the standard consultation system used in VHA. Typically originating from primary care (Lisi et al. 2009), a VHA healthcare provider may make a consultation request for chiropractic care on behalf of the veteran patient. However, other providers in the VHA facility may also offer chiropractic care through a consultation request (Veterans Health Administration 2009).

If a veteran is considered to be too far from a VHA facility that has a chiropractor on station, the outpatient fee-basis care program may be used to provide chiropractic care through community doctors of chiropractic or through a memorandum of agreement with a DoD military treatment facility that provides chiropractic services (Veterans Health Administration 2009). Access to community chiropractic is on a fee basis or through a memorandum with a DoD facility and originates through a consultation from the veteran patient's primary care manager or other VHA specialist.

Scope of Chiropractic Care in VHA

The VA chiropractic job description reads as follosw:

> 0604—Chiropractor. Description: VA Chiropractors are responsible for providing the full range of clinical diagnoses and chiropractic treatment for neuro-musculoskeletal conditions. They collaborate with a diverse group of clinicians and administrative personnel within the facility. Chiropractors support established clinical practice guidelines, including those relating to immunization programs. Requirements: For positions within the VA healthcare system, Chiropractor applicants must have successfully completed the requirements for the chiropractic medicine program that lasts four years and leads to a Doctor of Chiropractic (D.C.) degree. The program has to also be accredited by the Council on Chiropractic Education. (http://www.vacareers.va.gov/vacareers_Occupations_results.cfm)

Chiropractors practicing in VHA facilities are independent licensed practitioners and provide examination, diagnosis, treatment, and management of musculoskeletal and neuromusculoskeletal disorders (Veterans Health Administration 2009). The most frequent problems for which chiropractors in VHA provide care are low back, neck, and midback complaints. However, headache, upper limb, and lower limb disorders are also treated by these providers (Lisi et al. 2009).

Chiropractors will use standard examination techniques to determine an appropriate course of treatment (Veterans Health Administration 2009). Clinical protocols such as taking a patient history, conducting an orthopedic and neurologic examination, postural assessment, and medical record review are routinely performed by VHA chiropractors, and diagnostic imaging, laboratory studies, and electrodiagnostic testing are ordered as appropriate (Lisi et al. 2009).

A variety of chiropractic services may be offered at a VHA facility, depending on the training of the doctor(s) of chiropractic working there. VHA Directive 2009-059 states that chiropractic treatment may include such interventions as "patient education, therapeutic exercise, lifestyle recommendations, and other interventions such as joint manipulation and mobilization, soft tissue therapies, and physical modalities." There is also some provision for chiropractors to provide other therapies, such as acupuncture, that may be considered complementary and alternative medicine, as long as they are properly trained and licensed to do so and the VHA facility determines that there is a need for such services (Veterans Health Administration 2009). As mentioned previously, in addition to joint manipulation procedures, VHA chiropractors nearly always provide some element of patient education or therapeutic exercise. Soft tissue mobilizations, such as acupressure and massage, are also frequent treatment methods used, as are a variety of physical modalities, such as electrical stimulation, hot or cold packs, and ultrasound (Lisi et al. 2009).

If a chiropractic doctor determines that another healthcare professional is better suited to manage a particular case or that the veteran patient would benefit from an additional form of care, the chiropractor may place a consultation request to another provider for such care. Such consultations may be to clinics such as orthopedics, pain management, neurology, or other service lines at the VHA facility.

On the Horizon

There are increasing numbers of veterans with polytrauma and musculoskeletal disorders with associated comorbidities. These cases of increasing complexity pose significant challenges for the veterans who have them, the providers who care for the veterans, and the systems that are in place (Goldberg et al. 2009). Caring for the veteran population requires a well-trained interdisciplinary team of healthcare professionals, peer and family support, and community integration to address the many important issues central to the health of America's former service members. Chiropractic care is an additional treatment option that is now part of this set of potential solutions.

At the time of this writing (2011), chiropractic care is available at approximately thirty-eight VHA sites. However, legislation is in process to provide chiropractic care to all veterans. In May 2010 the U.S. House of Representatives passed H.R. 1017, the Chiropractic Care Available to All Veterans Act. This would amend the Department of Veterans Affairs Health Care Programs Enhancement Act of 2001 and title 38 of the United States Code to require chiropractic care and services for veterans at all VA medical centers. At the time of this writing, H.R. 1017 was still waiting to be voted upon by the Senate and then signed by the president.

Conclusion

Chiropractic care is the most recent addition of musculoskeletal services to VHA and is rapidly growing in both the number of providers working for VHA and number of patients receiving care. VHA chiropractors are credentialed providers working at VHA hospitals and clinics. VHA chiropractic departments are involved in clinical care, education, and research.

References

Andersson, G. & American Academy of Orthopaedic Surgeons. (2008). *The burden of musculoskeletal diseases in the United States: Prevalence, societal, and economic cost.* Rosemont, IL: American Academy of Orthopaedic Surgeons.

Baldwin, C. M., Long, K., Kroesen, K., Brooks, A. J. & Bell, I. R. (2002). A profile of military veterans in the southwestern United States who use complementary and alternative medicine: Implications for integrated care. *Archives of Internal Medicine* 162, no. 15: 1697–1704.

Barnes, P. M., Bloom, B. & Nahin, R. L. (2008). Complementary and alternative medicine use among adults and children: United States, 2007. *National Health Statistics Report* 12: 1–23.

Birch & Davis Associates. (2000). *Final report: Chiropractic health care demonstration program.* Falls Church, VA: Author.

Boon, H. S., Mior, S. A., Barnsley, J., Ashbury, F. D. & Haig, R. (2009). The difference between integration and collaboration in patient care: Results from key informant interviews working in multiprofessional health care teams. *Journal of Manipulative and Physiological Therapeutics* 32, no. 9: 715–722.

Branson, R. A. (2009). Hospital-based chiropractic integration within a large private hospital system in Minnesota: A 10-year example. *Journal of Manipulative and Physiological Therapeutics* 32, no. 9: 740–748.

Brantingham, J. W., Globe, G., Pollard, H., Hicks, M., Korporaal, C. & Hoskins, W. (2009). Manipulative therapy for lower extremity conditions: Expansion of literature review. *Journal of Manipulative and Physiological Therapeutics* 32, no. 1: 53–71.

Bussieres, A. E., Peterson, C. & Taylor, J. A. (2007). Diagnostic imaging practice guidelines for musculoskeletal complaints in adults—an evidence-based approach: Introduction. *Journal of Manipulative and Physiological Therapeutics* 30, no. 9: 617–683.

Bussieres, A. E., Peterson, C. & Taylor, J. A. (2008). Diagnostic imaging guideline for musculoskeletal complaints in adults—an evidence-based approach. Part 2: Upper extremity disorders. *Journal of Manipulative and Physiological Therapeutics* 31, no. 1: 2–32.

Bussieres, A. E., Taylor, J. A. & Peterson, C. (2007). Diagnostic imaging practice guidelines for musculoskeletal complaints in adults—an evidence-based approach. Part 1: Lower extremity disorders. *Journal of Manipulative and Physiological Therapeutics* 30, no. 9: 684–717.

Bussieres, A. E., Taylor, J. A. & Peterson, C. (2008). Diagnostic imaging practice guidelines for musculoskeletal complaints in adults—an evidence-based approach. Part 3: Spinal disorders. *Journal of Manipulative and Physiological Therapeutics* 31, no. 1: 33–88.

Butchart, A., Kerr, E. A., Heisler, M., Piette, J. D. & Krein, S. L. (2009). Experience and management of chronic pain among patients with other complex chronic conditions. *Clinical Journal of Pain* 25, no. 4: 293–298.

Cherkin, D. C. & MacCornack, F. A. (1989). Patient evaluations of low back pain care from family physicians and chiropractors. *Western Journal of Medicine* 150, no. 3: 351–355.

Chiropractic service in the Department of Veterans Affairs: Hearing no. 106–51, before the House Comm. on Veterans' Affairs, 106th Cong. (October 3, 2000). http://www.Access.Gpo.Gov/congress/house/house18ch106.html (accessed January 17, 2011).

Chou, R., Qaseem, A., Snow, V., Casey, D., Cross, J. T., Jr., Shekelle, P., et al. (2007). Diagnosis and treatment of low back pain: A joint clinical practice guideline from the American College of Physicians and the American Pain Society. *Annals of Internal Medicine* 147, no. 7: 478–491.

Christensen, M. G., Kollasch, M. W. & Hyland, J. K. (2010). *Practice analysis of chiropractic 2010.* Greeley: National Board of Chiropractic Examiners.

Coulter, I., Adams, A., Coggan, P., Wilkes, M. & Gonyea, M. (1998). A comparative study of chiropractic and medical education. *Alternative Therapies in Health and Medicine* 4, no. 5: 64–75.

Coulter, I. D., Hurwitz, E. L., Adams, A. H., Genovese, B. J., Hays, R. & Shekelle, P. G. (2002). Patients using chiropractors in North America: Who are they, and why are they in chiropractic care? *Spine* 27, no. 3: 291–296; discussion 297–298.

Dehen, M. D., Whalen, W. M., Farabaugh, R. J. & Hawk, C. (2010). Consensus terminology for stages of care: Acute, chronic, recurrent, and wellness. *Journal of Manipulative and Physiological Therapeutics* 33, no. 6: 458–463.

Department of Veterans Affairs. (2008). *VHA handbook 1400.04: Supervision of associated health trainees.* Washington, DC: Veterans Health Administration.

Department of Veterans Affairs Health Care Programs Enhancement Act of 2001. Pub. L. No. 107-135.

Dunn, A. S. (2005). A chiropractic internship program in the Department of Veterans Affairs health care system. *Journal of Chiropractic Education* 19, no. 2: 92–96.

Dunn, A. S. (2007). A survey of chiropractic academic affiliations within the Department of Veterans Affairs health care system. *Journal of Chiropractic Education* 21, no. 2: 138–143.

Dunn, A. S., Baylis, S. & Ryan, D. (2009). Chiropractic management of mechanical low back pain secondary to multiple-level lumbar spondylolysis with spondylolisthesis in a United States Marine Corps veteran: A case report. *Journal of Chiropractic Medicine* 8, no. 3: 125–130.

Dunn, A. S., Green, B. N. & Gilford, S. (2009). An analysis of the integration of chiropractic services within the United States military and veterans' health care systems. *Journal of Manipulative and Physiological Therapeutics* 32(9): 749–757.

Dunn, A. S. & Passmore, S. R. (2008). Consultation request patterns, patient characteristics, and utilization of services within a Veterans Affairs Medical Center chiropractic clinic. *Military Medicine* 173, no. 6: 599–603.

Dunn, A. S., Passmore, S. R., Burke, J. & Chicoine, D. (2009). A cross-sectional analysis of clinical outcomes following chiropractic care in veterans with and without post-traumatic stress disorder. *Military Medicine* 174, no. 6: 578–583.

Dunn, A. S., Towle, J. J., McBrearty, P. & Fleeson, S. M. (2006). Chiropractic consultation requests in the Veterans Affairs health care system: Demographic characteristics of the initial 100 patients at the Western New York medical center. *Journal of Manipulative and Physiological Therapeutics* 29, no. 6: 448–454.

Farabaugh, R. J., Dehen, M. D. & Hawk, C. (2010). Management of chronic spine-related conditions: Consensus recommendations of a multidisciplinary panel. *Journal of Manipulative and Physiological Therapeutics* 33, no. 7: 484–492.

Gaumer, G. (2006). Factors associated with patient satisfaction with chiropractic care: Survey and review of the literature. *Journal of Manipulative and Physiological Therapeutics* 29, no. 6: 455–462.

Globe, G. A., Morris, C. E., Whalen, W. M., Farabaugh, R. J. & Hawk, C. (2008). Chiropractic management of low back disorders: Report from a consensus process. *Journal of Manipulative and Physiological Therapeutics* 31, no. 9: 651–658.

Goldberg, C. K., Green, B., Moore, J., Wyatt, M., Boulanger, L., Belnap, B., et al. (2009). Integrated musculoskeletal rehabilitation care at a comprehensive combat and complex casualty care program. *Journal of Manipulative and Physiological Therapeutics* 32, no. 9: 781–791.

Green, B. N., Johnson, C. D. & Lisi, A. J. (2009). Chiropractic in U.S. military and veterans' health care. *Military Medicine* 174, no. 6: vi–vii.

Green, B. N., Johnson, C. D., Lisi, A. J. & Tucker, J. (2009). Chiropractic practice in military and veterans health care: The state of the literature. *Journal of the Canadian Chiropractic Association* 53: 194–204.

Green, B. N., Sims, J. & Allen, R. (2006). Use of conventional and alternative treatment strategies for a case of low back pain in a F/A-18 aviator. *Chiropractic Osteopathy* 14: 11.

Grieves, B., Menke, J. M. & Pursel, K. J. (2009). Cost minimization analysis of low back pain claims data for chiropractic vs. medicine in a managed care organization. *Journal of Manipulative and Physiological Therapeutics* 32, no. 9: 734–739.

Haas, M., Sharma, R. & Stano, M. (2005). Cost-effectiveness of medical and chiropractic care for acute and chronic low back pain. *Journal of Manipulative and Physiological Therapeutics* 28, no. 8: 555–563.

Haskell, S. G., Mattocks, K., Goulet, J. L., Krebs, E. E., Skanderson, M., Leslie, D., et al. (2010). The burden of illness in the first year home: Do male and female VA users differ in health conditions and healthcare utilization? *Women's Health Issues* 21, no. 1: 92–97.

Hawk, C. (1998). Chiropractic: More than spinal manipulation. *Journal of Chiropractic Humanities* 8: 71–76.

Hawk, C. (2005). When worldviews collide: Maintaining a vitalistic perspective in chiropractic in the postmodern era. *Journal of Chiropractic Humanities* 12: 2–7.

Hawk, C. & Cambron, J. (2009). Chiropractic care for older adults: Effects on balance, dizziness, and chronic pain. *Journal of Manipulative and Physiological Therapeutics* 32, no. 6: 431–437.

Hurwitz, E. L., Morgenstern, H., Vassilaki, M. & Chiang, L. M. (2004). Adverse reactions to chiropractic treatment and their effects on satisfaction and clinical outcomes among patients enrolled in the UCLA Neck Pain Study. *Journal of Manipulative and Physiological Therapeutics* 27, no. 1: 16–25.

Hurwitz, E. L., Morgenstern, H., Vassilaki, M. & Chiang, L. M. (2005). Frequency and clinical predictors of adverse reactions to chiropractic care in the UCLA Neck Pain Study. *Spine* 30, no. 13: 1477–1484.

Johnson, C. (2009). Health care transitions: A review of integrated, integrative, and integration concepts. *Journal of Manipulative and Physiological Therapeutics* 32, no. 9: 703–713.

Johnson, C., Baird, R., Dougherty, P. E., Globe, G., Green, B. N., Haneline, M., et al. (2008). Chiropractic and public health: Current state and future vision. *Journal of Manipulative and Physiological Therapeutics* 31, no. 6: 397–410.

Kane, R. L., Olsen, D., Leymaster, C., Woolley, F. R. & Fisher, F. D. (1974). Manipulating the patient: A comparison of the effectiveness of physician and chiropractor care. *Lancet* 1, no. 7870: 1333–1336.

Kaptchuk, T. J. & Eisenberg, D. M. (1998). Chiropractic: Origins, controversies, and contributions. *Archives of Internal Medicine* 158, no. 20: 2215–2224.

Kawchuk, G. N., Herzog, W. & Hasler, E. M. (1992). Forces generated during spinal manipulative therapy of the cervical spine: A pilot study. *Journal of Manipulative and Physiological Therapeutics* 15, no. 5: 275–278.

Koes, B. W., Assendelft, W. J., van der Heijden, G. J. & Bouter, L. M. (1996). Spinal manipulation for low back pain: An updated systematic review of randomized clinical trials. *Spine* 21, no. 24: 2860–2871; discussion 2862–2863.

Lawrence, D. J., Meeker, W., Branson, R., Bronfort, G., Cates, J. R., Haas, M., et al. (2008). Chiropractic management of low back pain and low back-related leg complaints: A literature synthesis. *Journal of Manipulative and Physiological Therapeutics* 31, no. 9: 659–674.

Lisi, A. J. (2010). Management of Operation Iraqi Freedom and Operation Enduring Freedom veterans in a Veterans Health Administration chiropractic clinic: A case series. *Journal of Rehabilitation Research and Development* 47, no. 1: 1–6.

Lisi, A. J., Goertz, C., Lawrence, D. J. & Satyanarayana, P. (2009). Characteristics of Veterans Health Administration chiropractors and chiropractic clinics. *Journal of Rehabilitation Research and Development* 46, no. 8: 997–1002.

Meeker, W. & Haldeman, S. (2002). Chiropractic: A profession at the crossroads of mainstream and alternative medicine. *Annals of Internal Medicine* 136: 216–227.

Meeker, W. C. (2000). Public demand and the integration of complementary and alternative medicine in the US health care system. *Journal of Manipulative and Physiological Therapeutics* 23, no. 2: 123–126.

Nahin, R. L., Barnes, P. M., Stussman, B. J. & Bloom, B. (2009). Costs of complementary and alternative medicine (CAM) and frequency of visits to CAM practitioners: United States, 2007. *National Health Statistics Report* 18: 1–14.

Pfefer, M. T., Cooper, S. R. & Uhl, N. L. (2009). Chiropractic management of tendinopathy: A literature synthesis. *Journal of Manipulative and Physiological Therapeutics* 32, no. 1: 41–52.

Schneider, M., Vernon, H., Ko, G., Lawson, G. & Perera, J. (2009). Chiropractic management of fibromyalgia syndrome: A systematic review of the literature. *Journal of Manipulative and Physiological Therapeutics* 32, no. 1: 25–40.

Singh, G. (1998). Recent considerations in nonsteroidal anti-inflammatory drug gastropathy. *American Journal of Medicine* 105, no. 1B: 31S–38S.

Smith, M., Greene, B. R. & Meeker, W. (2002). The CAM movement and the integration of quality health care: The case of chiropractic. *Journal of Ambulatory Care Management* 25, no. 2: 1–16.

Smith, T. C., Ryan, M. A., Smith, B., Reed, R. J., Riddle, J. R., Gumbs, G. R., et al. (2007). Complementary and alternative medicine use among US Navy and Marine Corps personnel. *BMC Complementary and Alternative Medicine* 7: 16.

Tan, G., Dao, T. K., Smith, D. L., Robinson, A. & Jensen, M. P. (2010). Incorporating complementary and alternative medicine (CAM) therapies to expand psychological services to veterans suffering from chronic pain. *Psychological Services* 7, no. 3: 148–161.

Thomas, H. V., Stimpson, N. J., Weightman, A., Dunstan, F. & Lewis, G. (2006). Pain in veterans of the Gulf War of 1991: A systematic review. *BMC Musculoskeletal Disorders* 7: 74.

van Tulder, M. W., Koes, B. W. & Bouter, L. M. (1997). Conservative treatment of acute and chronic nonspecific low back pain: A systematic review of randomized controlled trials of the most common interventions. *Spine* 22, no. 18: 2128–2156.

Vernon, H. & Schneider, M. (2009). Chiropractic management of myofascial trigger points and myofascial pain syndrome: A systematic review of the literature. *Journal of Manipulative and Physiological Therapeutics* 32, no. 1: 14–24.

Veterans Health Administration. (2009). *VHA directive 2009–059: Chiropractic care.* Washington, DC: Veterans Health Administration.

Veterans Health Care, Capital Asset, and Business Improvement Act of 2003. Pub. L. No. 108-170.

Veterans Millennium Health Care and Benefits Act of 1999. Pub. L. No. 106–117, sec. 303.

World Health Organization. (1946). *Preamble to the constitution of the World Health Organization as adopted by the International Health Conference.* New York: World Health Organization, p. 200, http://www.who.int/about/definition/en/print.html (accessed January 3, 2011).

Wuest, S., Symons, B., Leonard, T. & Herzog, W. (2010). Preliminary report: Biomechanics of vertebral artery segments c1–c6 during cervical spinal manipulation. *Journal of Manipulative and Physiological Therapeutics* 33, no. 4: 273–278.

Disclaimer: The views expressed in this article are those of the authors and do not reflect the official policy or position of the Department of the Navy, Department of Defense, or the United States government.

Chapter 7

Healthcare for Veterans with Infectious Diseases

Cynthia Livingstone Gibert

Early History of the Veterans Affairs Hospitals and Tuberculosis

The Veterans Health Administration (VHA), the largest healthcare system in the United States, oversees the operation of 153 medical centers, 882 ambulatory care and community-based outpatient clinics, 136 long-term-care facilities, 207 veteran centers, 45 rehabilitation treatment programs, and 92 comprehensive home-based-care programs. In 2010, of the 22.6 million living U.S. veterans, over 5 million received medical care at Department of Veterans Affairs (VA) medical facilities. The establishment of this complex medical care system was certainly not foreseen in April 1922 when the Veterans' Bureau was established by President Warren Harding. Prior to that date the care of veterans was provided by the Public Health Service hospitals. At that time these hospitals were serving primarily veterans, so the transfer of the administration of these hospitals to the Veterans' Bureau was logical.

In 1917 legislation was passed authorizing the establishment of the Bureau of War Risk Insurance. At the end of World War I, unlike in the past, there were expectations that medical care for veterans would be provided in government hospitals. The bureau had no hospitals or doctors, so it looked to the Public Health Service Marine Hospitals to provide care to veterans being discharged from military hospitals. The two most common illnesses among these veterans were nervous and mental disorders and tuberculosis (Hayes 2010).

At the end of World War I, among the 178,000 service disability discharges, 12 percent had tuberculosis. Between 1920 and 1922 the number of veterans hospitalized with tuberculosis rose from 12,000 to a peak of 44,951. Given the recommendations of the American Thoracic Society that sanatoria should be located away from cities, VA hospitals were built in rural areas, often in the mountains. In that preantibiotic era, the care of veterans with tuberculosis was considered the best in the nation. In 1926 the first publication of the Veterans Administration's new Research Subdivision was a statistical analysis of veterans hospitalized with tuberculosis since 1919 who had a second disability. The majority of these 39,000 veterans were black (62 percent). The following year a VA study of outcomes among patients with tuberculosis concluded that climatic conditions did not influence the outcome (Hayes 2010).

Between 1922 and 1941 the number of veterans hospitalized with tuberculosis declined from 40 to 8 percent. In 1927 a number of clinical research articles on the management and diagnosis of TB appeared in the Veterans Administration's *Medical Bulletin*. By the end of World War II the care of veterans in the VA medical facilities had declined; some 12,000 veterans were hospitalized with tuberculosis. The number of veterans hospitalized with TB continued to increase over the coming years.

Beginning in 1946 a limited supply of streptomycin became available to treat veterans with tuberculosis. General Paul Hawley, the head of the VA medical department, persuaded Dr. John Barnwell, a professor at the University of Michigan, to come to Washington to head up the Veterans Administration's fight against tuberculosis. Dr. Barnwell was not only an authority on tuberculosis but had himself been treated for tuberculosis. Dr. Barnwell was appointed chair of the "Streptomycin Committee." Concerned with the management of veterans with tuberculosis, the first VA-Armed Forces clinical trial began that year under the leadership of Drs. John Barnwell and Arthur Walker. The study was conducted at seven VA and two military hospitals. After much debate a decision was made to not enroll control subjects in the study (Barnwell 1948a). This and two subsequent studies demonstrated that the clinical outcome was better in those treated with streptomycin than in those not treated (Barnwell 1948a, 1948b).

The controversies that surrounded these studies included their not being randomized placebo-controlled trials and the failure to provide informed consent for the patients. On the other hand, based on the experience gained in the conduct of these trials, in 1960 Dr. William Tucker, chairman of the first Cooperative Studies Evaluation Committee, published an article, "The Evolution of the Cooperative Studies in Chemotherapy of Tuberculosis of the

Veterans Administration and Armed Forces of the USA." This report defined the essential principles of a controlled clinical trial (Tucker 1960). These principles still serve as the foundation of VA's Cooperative Studies Program and of the conduct of all clinical investigations involving the participation of veterans.

Since these early studies in the Veterans Administration on tuberculosis, the clinical and research infectious diseases–related issues relevant to the care of veterans have substantially increased. Extensive basic science and clinical research in the areas of bacterial and viral diseases have been undertaken. In addition, there has been considerable interest in providing comprehensive care to veterans with a number of chronic infectious diseases, including human immunodeficiency syndrome and viral hepatitis B and C infections. VA clinical trials led to the approval of the preventive vaccines for pneumococcal infection and also shingles. Another area of interest in VA has been improvement of patient care. Systems have been developed for the collection of outcomes following surgical procedures and working in collaboration with the Centers for Disease Control and Prevention (CDC) on hospital-acquired infections.

The Infectious Diseases Program, working under the auspices of Patient Care Services in the VA headquarters in Washington, D.C., provides leadership and sets standards for infection-control practices across the VA medical system. With the increasing prevalence of infections caused by antibiotic resistant pathogens, VA has established policies for the management of certain conditions, such as methicillin-resistant *Staphylococcus aureus* infection and *Clostridium difficile*–related diarrheal illness. Efforts are ongoing to establish programs for improved antibiotic stewardship. The Public Health Strategic Health Care Group (PHSHG), also working from VA headquarters, oversees the programs and policies for HIV, viral hepatitis infections, and influenza prevention. In addition, the PHSHG works with the Department of Defense (DoD) on bioterrorism preparedness. The Office of the Medical Inspector, also located in the VA Central Office, has conducted several surveys related to the care of veterans residing in VA long-term-care facilities.

Thus the spectrum of infectious diseases–related issues for VHA and the veterans who receive care in VA medical facilities is not only broad but also reflects the ongoing efforts of the VA healthcare system to identify and meet the needs of an increasingly diverse veteran population—from those who served in World War II to those returning from the ongoing conflicts in Iraq and Afghanistan. This chapter reviews VA infectious diseases research, including viral infections—influenza, HIV, and viral hepatitis; immunizations; bacterial infections—surveillance, treatment, and pathogenesis; fungal infections; and infections in special populations.

Viral Infections

Influenza

During the 1918 influenza pandemic, the first cases in the United States were reported on March 4, 1918, among soldiers at Fort Riley, Kansas. The massive troop movements of World War I hastened the spread of the pandemic. It is estimated that more than 43,000 soldiers died from influenza. Influenza was responsible for more deaths in the military than war-related casualties during World War I (Crosby 1989). Similarly, the Hong Kong flu epidemic of 1968 is thought to have been brought into the western United States by U.S. soldiers returning from the Vietnam War (Starling 2006).

Concern for the rapid spread of influenza across the U. S. including military troops was again of great concern in the 2009 H1N1 influenza pandemic. It was speculated that the medical facilities in the United States would be overwhelmed (Executive Office of the President 2009). Preparedness for a pandemic in the United States included efforts of the DoD and VHA. Beginning in the 1990s a number of U.S. military hospitals were closed; accordingly, in 2009, the Department of Defense (DoD) looked to VHA for support in planning for this epidemic. The VHA Office of Public Health and Environmental Hazards (OPHEH) worked closely with the DoD and the CDC to track the spread of the epidemic and develop policies for preparing for, responding to, and recovering from pandemic influenza. This included an assessment of VHA bed capacity in the inpatient setting, long-term-care facilities, and intensive care units. In addition, the PHSHG updated VA medical facilities on a regular basis about these issues. Considerable effort was expended to ensure that the seasonal influenza vaccine was made available to both veterans and VA staff members as well as to provide the H1N2 vaccine to those persons identified as being most appropriate to receive the initially limited supply of this vaccine. Each year the OPHEH provides policy statements and educational materials on influenza to the VA medical community.

Human Immunodeficiency Virus/Acquired Immunodeficiency Syndrome

Unlike influenza, which causes acute illness, human immunodeficiency virus (HIV)/acquired immunodeficiency syndrome (AIDS) and hepatitis B and C virus infections are chronic illnesses that require ongoing, long-term medical care. The PHSHG in VA headquarters provides direction for the prevention and management of these infections.

It is now thirty years since the first cases of AIDS were reported by the CDC in the *Monthly Morbidity and Mortality Weekly* (Centers for Disease Control 2011). Young homosexual men in Los Angeles, New York City, and San Francisco had been diagnosed with *Pneumocystis jirovecii* pneumonia and Kaposi's sarcoma. Shortly thereafter, similar cases were reported among hemophiliacs, injection drug users and their partners, and recipients of blood transfusions. By 1983 a retrovirus had been isolated from patients with AIDS. By 1985 a laboratory test to detect infection caused by HIV had been developed and licensed.

HIV Treatment Trials

The VA medical system has cared for veterans with HIV/AIDS since the beginning of the epidemic. Several landmark studies were conducted under the auspices of the Veterans Affairs Cooperative Study Group on AIDS. In 1987 the Food and Drug Administration (FDA) approved the first nucleoside analogue for the treatment of HIV, zidovudine (ZDV/AZT). This approval was based on the results of a double-blind, placebo-controlled study begun in February 1986 and conducted by the AZT Collaborative Working Group. In this trial AZT was shown to significantly decrease mortality and AIDS-related opportunistic infections compared to placebo among AIDS patients (Fischl et al. 1987). Between January 1987 and January 1990 the VA Cooperative Study Group on AIDS enrolled 338 veterans with symptomatic HIV infection and CD4+ cell count between 200 and $500/mm^3$ in a multicenter, randomized, placebo-controlled study that compared early treatment with AZT to deferred therapy (i.e., an AIDS-defining illness or CD4+ cell count of $<200/mm^3$). The principal investigators for this study were John Hamilton and Michael Simberkoff (Hamilton et al. 1992). Similar to the earlier trial of AZT, this study also demonstrated benefits of earlier therapy. In 1989 Larder, Darby, and Richman reported the development of viral resistance to AZT. The potential for HIV resistance to AZT confounded decisions about when to start antiretroviral therapy. In 1990 the results of another study, conducted by the National Institutes of Health (NIH), National Institute for Allergy and Infectious Diseases (NIDA)-funded AIDS Clinical Trial Group showed that initiation of AZT therapy in asymptomatic HIV-infected patients with CD4+ cell counts of $<500/mm^3$ delayed progression to symptomatic illness (Fischl et al. 1990).

The introduction of highly active ART (HAART) in the late 1990s was viewed as a panacea for the treatment of HIV infection. As a result of the development of multiclass ART resistance because of nonadherence, coupled with the long-term effects of combination ART—changes in body fat, dyslipidemia, drug-induced hepatitis, and possibly increased risk of cardiovascular events—the question of when to start ART remained. It was thought that the interruption of ART in patients with a CD4+ cell count >350/ mm^3 would be safe and also decrease the side effects of long-term therapy.

The Strategies for Management of Antiretroviral Therapy (SMART) trial was conducted by the NIH, NIAID-funded Terry Beirn Community Programs for Clinical Research on AIDS (CPCRA). SMART enrolled 5,472 patients with a baseline CD4+ cell count >350/mm^3 beginning in January 2002 at 318 sites, including 232 HIV-infected veterans at 13 VA medical centers. Patients were randomly assigned to continuous or episodic use of ART. Patients randomized to episodic use were to stop ART at study entry, restart ART when the CD4+ cell count fell to <250, and discontinue therapy when the CD4+ cell count was greater than 350. The primary endpoint was the development of an opportunistic infection or death. Following the sixth Data Safety Monitoring Board meeting, the trial was prematurely interrupted because the risk of opportunistic disease or death was significantly increased among the patients randomized to episodic treatment (Strategies for Management of Antiretroviral Therapy Study Group 2006).

The question of when to start ART remains. Accordingly, the International Network for Strategic Intervention in Global HIV Trials (INSIGHT), an HIV/AIDS clinical trial network, an outgrowth of the original CPCRA, is now conducting the NIH, NIAID-funded Strategic Timing of Anti-retroviral Therapy (START) trial addressing this question in an antiretroviral treatment-naïve cohort of HIV-infected patients with a baseline CD4+ cell count greater than 500. Patients randomized to defer treatment are to initiate therapy when the CD4 cell count is <350, although earlier initiation of therapy is permitted. The goal of START is to determine if the risk of developing AIDS or other serious illness is less among HIV-infected asymptomatic individuals who begin ART earlier rather than later. The study is being conducted at 238 sites worldwide, and at this time two VA sites are enrolling patients into this important trial (Strategic Timing of Anti-Retroviral Treatment n.d.).

Another study on antiretroviral treatment interruption was the OPTions in Management with Antiretrovirals (OPTIMA) Trial, which was conducted as a collaboration among the VA Cooperative Studies Program, the Canadian HIV Trials Network, and the MRC Clinical Trials Unit in London. This 2x2 factorial, randomized, open-label, controlled study sought to determine if ART interruption and intensification was beneficial to patients with advanced multidrug resistant (MDR) HIV infection. From 2001 to 2006, 386 patients who had a CD4 count $\leq$300 cells/cc^3 and documented ART failure were randomized to two options: retreatment with either standard ($\leq$ 4 drugs) or intensive ($\geq$5 drugs) antiretroviral therapy, and either immediate treatment or deferral of therapy for a twelve-week, monitored treatment interruption. The majority of the patients, 288 (78 percent), were enrolled from twenty-five VA clinical sites. The primary endpoint was the time to developing a first AIDS-defining event or death from any cause. Interestingly, the trial did not show any clinical benefit or harm (Holodniy et al. 2011).

OPTIMA is the largest and longest study to investigate both ART intensification and interruption among patients with advanced HIV infection with limited treatment options. Since the initiation of this study, several newer ARTs have received FDA approval, and the practice is now to continue ART even in patients with multidrug-resistant HIV infection. The OPTIMA trial did suggest that with close clinical follow-up, for some patients with advanced HIV disease and limited therapeutic options, treatment intensification or interruption may be appropriate (Holodniy et al. 2011). It is unlikely that a clinical trial similar to this will be conducted.

HIV Care in VA

As of 2011, VA is the largest single provider of HIV care in the United States. More than 64,000 HIV-infected veterans have received care since the beginning of the HIV epidemic. In 2010, 24,000 HIV-infected veterans were in care. The PHSHG oversees the HIV program for VHA and as such fosters efforts to improve HIV care throughout the VA medical care system. There are a number of programs under the jurisdiction of the PHSHG that combine a clinical and research role. In December 2009 the PHSHG's *The State of Care for Veterans with HIV/AIDS* was published. This monograph presents data on care throughout the VA healthcare system. The data presented are intended to identify regional and local differences in care, as well as areas requiring changes in care delivery.

The PHSHG oversees and supports educational programs for clinicians and patients, HIV prevention efforts, expanded HIV testing with retention in care, policy development, and research. Many of these programs rely on the support of the PHSHG's National Clinical Public Health Program Office in Washington, D.C., and the Centers for Quality Management in Public Health (CQMPH), a component of the PHSHG, based at the VA Palo Alto Health Care System Medical Center. The CQMPH is responsible for the Clinical Case Registry (CCR). The initial Immunology Case Registry (ICR) included data only on patients with HIV/AIDS (Backus et al. 2001). The

ICR was expanded in 2006 to include data on veterans with hepatitis C virus infection as well. Many of these veterans are coinfected with HIV. The VHA electronic medical record (EMR) made possible the development of this centralized patient registry. The CCR software supports a registry at each VA facility to oversee and review care at the local site as well as providing a national clinical database. The CQMPH periodically provides reports based on the CCR data that serve to guide clinical and administrative activities to improve care to veterans living with HIV/AIDS.

The CCR also serves as a valuable resource for HIV research. A number of studies on HIV in VA have been conducted using CCR data. Following the more widespread use of ART, there was a concern that cardiovascular deaths were increased among HIV-infected patients on antiretroviral therapy. One of the earliest studies using data from the Immunology Case Registry (now the Clinical Case Registry) sought to determine the increased risk of cardiovascular events and deaths among HIV-infected patients on treatment. Between 1995 and 2001, Sam Bozette and his colleagues found that overall mortality, among the 36,766 HIV-infected veterans who had received care at a VA medical facility, had declined by more than 75 percent. This retrospective VA study also showed that the rate of cardiovascular disease was stable or had declined in this era (Bozzette et al. 2003). The results of several other studies on cardiovascular events in the HAART era have contradicted this study; thus the issue remains controversial (Sklar & Masur 2003).

HIV and Aging

It is now thirty years since the beginning of the HIV epidemic and fifteen years since the beginning of the HAART-era that followed the introduction of protease inhibitors. The life expectancy of those living with HIV/AIDS is now similar to that of people living without HIV infection, but there is increasing evidence that those aging with chronic HIV infection still express a different phenotype (Deeks 2011). One of the major studies being conducted to address this complex issue is the NIH, National Institute of Alcohol and Alcohol Abuse (NIAAA)–funded Veterans Aging Cohort Study (VACS). The study began in 2002 under the leadership of Amy C. Justice, the principal investigator.

The VACS is now the single largest cohort of HIV-infected patients in the world. The study is being conducted at eight VA medical centers (Atlanta, Baltimore, Bronx, Houston, Los Angeles, Manhattan/Brooklyn, Pittsburgh, and Washington, D.C.) and has enrolled 3,684 HIV-infected and 3,642 age, race, and gender-matched HIV-uninfected veterans. The VACS has also established a Virtual Cohort (VC) from national VA healthcare system data. The VC now includes 39,648 HIV-infected veterans matched 2:1 to 79,296 uninfected comparators. The aims of the VACS have been to ascertain if aging is different among those with HIV infection and to delineate the causes (Justice et al. 2006). In addition, the study seeks to assess the impact of alcohol use on HIV disease progression and on the comorbidities of aging, such as cardiovascular disease, liver health, renal disease, and endocrine and metabolic complications. The study gathers data not only from the EMR but also from patient and provider surveys. The surveys capture behavioral, overall health status, adherence, and functionality data that supplement the EMR patient information.

The VACS investigators have reported a number of studies comparing outcomes between those with and without HIV infection as well as specific to the HIV-infected cohort. One of the major accomplishments has been the development and verification of the VACS Risk Index—a combined prognostic index to predict survival in HIV infection. Using clinical and laboratory data that are routinely collected on HIV-infected subjects, the VACS Risk Index improves prediction of mortality when compared to using only HIV biomarkers (CD4+ cell count, HIV RNA, and AIDS-defining illnesses) (Justice et al. 2010).

Screening for HIV

In September 2006 the CDC published revised guidelines for HIV testing (Centers for Disease Control 2006). At that time estimates were that more than 1.1 million people in the United States were HIV-infected, there were more than 56,000 new HIV infections a year, and that over 20 percent of those living with HIV did not know they were infected. Part of the decision to change the recommendations for routine HIV screening was based on a study published by investigators from the Palo Alto VA Health Care System, Duke University, and Stanford University (Sanders et al. 2005). Using a Markov model of costs, quality of life, and survival benefit, it was shown that expanded testing would lead to increased life expectancy, earlier entry into care, decreased medical costs, and reduced HIV transmission.

In 1998, as part of a systemwide transformation to improve the quality of care across VA, the VA Health Services Research and Development Service launched the Quality Enhancement Research Initiative (QUERI). The overall goal of QUERI is to facilitate translation of research into routine clinical practice. One of the initiatives was the QUERI HIV-Hepatitis. Its mission is to improve the identification and care of veterans living with either chronic HIV or HCV infection (Goetz et al. 2008; Groom et al. 2008). In accordance with the 2006 CDC revised recommendations for routine HIV testing of all patients between ages thirteen and sixty-four unless the rate of HIV infection is less than one case in 1,000 persons tested in all healthcare settings, and the 2007 U.S. Preventive Services Task Force recommendation for testing all adults and adolescents at increased risk for HIV infection, in August 2009 VHA Directive 2009-036 mandated that routine HIV testing be conducted and removed the requirement for written informed consent. Because all VA facilities have rates of HIV infection of 0.1 percent, the directive essentially requires that all veterans in care have at least one HIV test. Implementation of this directive has been a major focus of the QUERI-HIV and the National Clinical Public Health Program Office.

In addition to working to support testing efforts throughout VA, the PHSHG has provided additional funding to several sites to implement expanded programs to support rapid HIV testing. These programs have increased HIV testing, but sustaining the success of such programs will require having clinicians, particularly in primary care clinics, continue to offer routine HIV testing. Rates of testing in VA have, however, increased since 2009. In 2010, 795,126 HIV tests were performed, of which 2,233 were positive, compared to 2009, when 1,739 HIV tests were positive of 524,267 tests completed (Halloran et al. 2012).

There are now more than 24,000 veterans with HIV in care at VA facilities. The PHSHG continues to oversee care and support programs to ensure entry into and maintenance in care. As patients with HIV are living longer, the burden of comorbidities and aging will increase the complexity of care and the demands for supportive services. VA investigators have also made significant contributions to HIV/AIDS basis science research.

HIV Basic Science Research

Chemokine Receptor 5 (CCR5) Predicts HIV Progression In 2007 Dr. Sunil Ahuja, at the VA Center on AIDS and HIV Infection of the South Texas Veterans Health Care System, in collaboration with an international team of investigators, reported that genetic variation in two genes, chemokine receptor 5 (CCR5) and CCL3L1, contributes to ultimate HIV progression to AIDS as significantly as HIV RNA level and CD4 cell count. CCR5 is the major coreceptor required for HIV entry into cells. These genetic markers may serve to predict outcomes of HIV infection (Dolan et al. 2007).

GB Virus-C Inhibits HIV Growth   At the Iowa City VA Medical Center, Drs. Jack Stapleton and Jinhua Xiang have been investigating the inhibition by GBV-C of HIV growth in cell models. HIV-infected patients coinfected with GBV-C have decreased mortality compared to those without coinfection (Williams et al. 2004). Patients with GBV-C infection have slower loss of T-cells. The researchers isolated a GBV-C–related protein, NS5A, which appears to decrease the number of binding sites on CD4 cells for the HIV virus. This protein has the potential to be developed into novel HIV therapies that would block HIV entry into cells and, unlike current antiretroviral therapy, not lead to drug resistance (Xiang et al. 2006).

AIDS Vaccine   Development of an AIDS vaccine that would confer sustained immunity would be the most significant contribution to the fight against HIV/AIDS. Thirty years into the epidemic, a vaccine has not been developed. Among those working on the development of an AIDS vaccine is Susan Zolla-Pazner, a researcher at the VA New York Harbor Healthcare System and New York University (NYU). In 1981, early in the AIDS epidemic, Dr. Zolla-Pazner initially participated in research on Kaposi's sarcoma. In 2006, with funding from the Bill and Melinda Gates Foundation, she became director of the NYU AIDS Vaccine Discovery Consortium. The consortium works to develop candidate vaccines that focus on the V3 loop of the gp120 protein. The V3 loop, through direct chemokine receptor interaction, is crucial to viral infectivity, and contains epitopes that are susceptible to neutralization by broadly reactive antibodies (Cardozo et al. 2007). The vaccine project will expand upon previous investigations in Dr. Zolla-Pazner's lab on neutralizing antibodies.

HIV Drug Resistance, Viral Load, and Viral Dynamics   Two VA researchers have achieved worldwide recognition for their contributions to the understanding of the pathogenesis of HIV, antiretroviral drug resistance, viral latency, and viral dynamics. They are Dr. Victoria A. Johnson, at the Birmingham VA Medical Center and the University of Alabama at Birmingham School of Medicine, and Dr. Douglas D. Richman, at the VA San Diego Healthcare System and the University of California San Diego. Both have participated at the national and international levels in the development of guidelines for HIV resistance testing and therapeutic options. In what was in retrospect truly a landmark study, Dr. Richman and Drs. Brendan Larder and G. Darby described the first report of antiretroviral therapy resistance, in viral isolates from patients taking zidovudine monotherapy. The clinical implications of this phenotypic resistance were not initially appreciated (Larder et al. 1989).

For more than twenty years, defining optimal HIV therapy and treatment of resistant HIV virus has been one of the major focuses of both clinical and basic science HIV research. Dr. Richman has also been interested in viral latency and viral replication in different body compartments—both of which appear to prevent HIV eradication (Havlir & Richman 1997). Dr. Johnson was instrumental in developing HIV RNA viral load testing and in educating clinicians about its significance, and in HIV genotypic and phenotypic drug resistance testing (Johnson et al. 2008). The research lab that she oversees is involved in the development and validation of virologic assays for HIV and viral hepatitis B and C, as well as HIV and viral hepatitis coinfection.

Viral Hepatitis C Infection

Many of the early landmark studies on viral hepatitis C were done by investigators in the VA Hepatitis Cooperative Studies Group (see "Viral Hepatitis B and C Disease" in the section "VA Infectious Diseases Research"). In1987 hepatitis C virus was identified as the causative agent of non-A non-B hepatitis. In May 1990 the FDA approved an enzyme immunoassay for HCV antibody, the first serologic test. Estimates are that 270–300 million people worldwide and 2.7–2.9 million in the United States have chronic hepatitis C infection. Veterans are recognized as being at greater risk for having acquired HCV infection, particularly in the Vietnam War era. In 2008 the CCR included 147,352 veterans with HCV viremia, of whom 6,753 had HIV coinfection or 28.8 percent of the 23,463 HIV-infected veterans in care. Long-term sequelae of HCV include cirrhosis and hepatocellular carcinoma (HCC). HCC is now a more frequent cause of death than colon cancer among veterans. In 2010 the PHSHG published the report "State of Care for Veterans with Chronic Hepatitis C," which summarizes the epidemiology, comorbid conditions, rates of cirrhosis, hepatocellular carcinoma, death, and treatment outcomes.

VA is the largest single provider of care to patients with chronic HCV in the United States. Recognizing the need to expand HIV care and related research, in 1999 VA established the Centers of Excellence in Hepatitis C at the Miami and San Francisco VA medical centers. In 2007 four VA Hepatitis C Resource Centers (HCRCs) received support from VHA—in Minneapolis, San Francisco, West Haven, and the Northwest HCRC at sites in Portland and Seattle. Working with the PHSHG, the HCRCs are considered an integral part of VA's National Hepatitis C Program. The centers are tasked to develop best practices for HCV prevention and clinical care, provide patient and clinician education, and perform ongoing evaluation of the HCV program across the VA healthcare system.

Injection drug use has been the major risk factor for acquisition of HCV among veterans, and most are infected with genotype 1 virus. Early response to HCV therapy and achievement of sustained virologic response is least among those with genotype 1 viral infection. Two novel proteases received FDA approval in 2011: boceprevir and telaprevir. Preliminary data suggest that the response to therapy will be greater when these agents are given in combination with ribavirin and pegylated interferon, including genotype 1 virus infections (Bacon et al. 2011; McHutchison et al. 2010). Plans for expanded HCV treatment in VA are underway, and VA guidelines for the management and treatment of HCV, cirrhosis, and hepatocellular carcinoma are being updated.

Overall the care of veterans living with chronic HCV, HIV, and HIV/HCV coinfection will remain a focus of the VA infectious diseases programs. Contributions of VA investigators to basic science and clinical research have been significant, and the support of VHA has been invaluable.

Immunizations

The two greatest advances for the prevention of infectious diseases and related disability and mortality have been immunizations and sanitation. Most immunizations have been used to prevent childhood-associated illnesses, such as poliomyelitis. There are, of course, many that are used in both children and adults. The VA healthcare system is well suited to the conduct of immunization trials in adults given the maintenance in routine care of most veterans.

It is known that the incidence and severity of herpes zoster infection, or shingles, increases with age, and may cause prolonged post herpetic neuralgia. Between November 1998 and September 2001, the VA Cooperative Studies Program No. 403 trial, the Shingles Prevention Study, enrolled 38,546 adults more than sixty years of age in a randomized, double-blind, placebo-controlled (RDBPC) trial of an investigational varicella-zoster virus (VZV) vaccine (Oxman et al. 2005). The zoster vaccine not only decreased the incidence of herpes zoster infection by 51 percent, but also reduced the burden of disease and post-herpetic neuralgia in this older veteran population. The study results contributed to the FDA approval of the Merck Zostavax® vaccine in 2006.

Pneumococcal disease is the leading cause of death among vaccine-preventable bacterial infections. Pneumococcal pneumonia remains the leading cause of community-acquired pneumonia in the United States today and is associated with considerable morbidity and mortality, particularly among the elderly and in those with underlying comorbid conditions. In 1981 a VA CSP was initiated to determine the efficacy of the 14-valent pneumococcal capsular polysaccharide vaccine. A cohort of 2,295 veterans over the age of fifty-five years with chronic medical conditions was enrolled in a RDBPC trial of the vaccine versus placebo. As was anticipated because of presumed poor immune response in older people, the vaccine did not prevent pneumonia or bronchitis (Simberkoff et al. 1986). Despite these findings, given the increasing rate of antibiotic resistance among pneumococcal isolates, routine use of pneumococcal vaccine is recommended.

Every year efforts to expand uptake of viral influenza vaccine are extended across the VA care facilities. Demonstrating therapeutic benefit increases the willingness of both veterans in care and VA healthcare providers to receive the flu vaccine. The VA CSP No. 448 was a RDBPC trial comparing the efficacy of trivalent inactivated influenza virus vaccine with or without intranasal live-attenuated, cold-adapted influenza vaccine in older veterans with underlying chronic obstructive pulmonary disease. The study showed no clinical benefit from the addition of the intranasal vaccine in the study population of 2,215 veterans over the age of fifty years. It was also found that it was difficult to distinguish laboratory-diagnosed cases of influenza from no influenza illness using clinical criteria (Gorse et al. 2003).

Infectious Diseases Surveillance and Prevention

VA has contributed significantly to improving outcomes among hospitalized patients and to improving surveillance of infections. VA programs initiated to improve quality of care have ultimately informed medical practice in the areas of surgical infections, device-related infections, surveillance of infectious pathogens, infections in long-term-care facilities, and nosocomial acquisition of methicillin-resistant *Staphylococcus aureus* colonization and infection.

Surgical Infections

In 1994 VA established the National Surgical Quality Improvement Program (NSQIP). All VA medical centers performing surgical procedures were mandated to participate (Khuri et al. 1998). Data are collected in a standardized manner at each site on both workload and risk-adjustment that includes forty-five preoperative, seventeen intraoperative, and thirty-three outcome variables. Data management is done at a national center. Logistic regression models predict the probability of death or complications within thirty days of the procedure in or out of the hospital. The NSQIP system is now endorsed by the American College of Surgeons, and the program has been adopted at most private hospitals. Since the inception of NSQIP by VA, thirty-day postoperative mortality following a major surgical procedure has declined by 27 percent, and thirty-day morbidity by 45 percent (Khuri, Daley & Henderson 2002).

For patients eligible for inclusion in NSQIP, pertinent demographic, pre-operative, intraoperative, laboratory, and postoperative patient information is collected. With respect to infectious diseases risks and complications, data are gathered on pneumonia, open wounds, gangrene, and sepsis. Perioperative data are gathered on surgical site infections, pneumonia, urinary tract infections, systemic sepsis, sepsis, and septic shock. Review of such data at both the local and national levels informing clinical care has led to improvements in outcomes and decreases in infectious surgery-related complications.

Healthcare-Associated Infections

It is well known that healthcare-associated infections (HAIs) contribute significantly to morbidity and mortality, increase cost of care, and lead to longer lengths of inpatient hospitalization. In 2002 the CDC estimated that 1.7 million HAIs occurred in U.S. hospitals. Each year such infections add $20 billion to healthcare costs and are tied to 100,000 deaths (Klevens et al. 2007). Many of these infections are preventable. Recognizing that changes in care practices may decrease such infections, many states have mandated public reporting of HAIs by individual medical facilities; local and national hospital groups and national infection-control groups, such as the Association for Professionals in Infection Control and Epidemiology, have initiated programs to decrease HAIs.

In October 2008 the Centers for Medicare and Medicaid Services defined conditions that would not be reimbursed. In 2009, ten condition categories were selected for Inpatient Prospective Payment System hospitals. These conditions included catheter-associated bloodstream infections; catheter-associated urinary tract infections; and surgical site infections among patients undergoing coronary bypass graft, certain orthopedic procedures, or bariatric surgery. Consideration was given to the inclusion of methicillin-resistant *Staphylococcus aureus* infections and *Clostridium difficile*–associated diarrheal illness. VHA is not impacted by many of these mandates. At the same time, however, because it is the largest healthcare system in the United States and political attention is frequently focused on outcomes among veterans in care, there is always interest among VHA leadership to improve care among veterans and to serve as a leader in the promotion of programs that will guide policy for patient care.

There are now several programs in place across the VA healthcare system that were implemented primarily to improve patient care, but have ultimately contributed to changes in standards of care for certain healthcare-associated infectious diseases. The data obtained from these programs have not only been used to inform policies relating to quality of care but have also served to guide research projects. These include the "Methicillin-resistant *Staphylococcus aureus* (MRSA)

Initiative," undertaken across the VA medical care system in compliance with a directive from then acting Under Secretary for Health Michael Kussman, MD.

MRSA Initiative

In 2001 the "MRSA bundle" was implemented at the VA Pittsburgh Healthcare System in collaboration with the CDC and the Pittsburgh Regional Healthcare Initiative. Within four years following the introduction of the "MRSA bundle" in this pilot project, there was a significant reduction in the rates of healthcare-associated MRSA infections in both a surgery ward and the surgical intensive care unit (ICU) (Muder et al. 2008). Based on these findings, in 2007 the "MRSA bundle" was rolled out in acute care VA hospitals. The bundle included screening the nares of all patients at the time of admission, transfer within a facility, and upon discharge for MRSA nasal carriage; using contact precautions for all patients colonized or infected with MRSA; hand hygiene; and a culture change to make infection prevention and control the responsibility of all hospital staff and a part of routine patient care. A centralized database was established to aggregate the data on adherence to the mandated surveillance screening, the prevalence of MRSA colonization and infection, and the transmission of healthcare-associated MRSA and related infections.

By October 2007 the MRSA Prevention Initiative had been fully implemented in all VA medical center ICUs and non-ICUs. In April 2011 the findings from this project were published in the *New England Journal of Medicine* (Jain et al. 2011). Between October 2007 and June 2010, there were 1,934,589 patient admissions or transfers and 8,318,675 patient-days of care. The rate of MRSA infections among the 365,139 ICU patients decreased by 62 percent ($P<0.001$ for trend) and among the 1,569,459 non-ICU patients by 45 percent ($P<0.001$ for trend). Given the widespread use of alcohol-based hand rub throughout the VA that overlapped this period, the introduction the previous year of guidelines for prevention of ventilator-associated pneumonia and central-line related bacteremias, and the provision of guidance for decolonization of MRSA-colonized patients six months following the implementation of the MRSA bundle, there has been controversy over the significance of the contributions of the various components of the MRSA bundle.

Accompanying the publication of the results of the MRSA Prevention Initiative in the *New England Journal of Medicine*, a cluster-randomized trial to study the effects of active surveillance for MRSA and vancomycin-resistant *Enterococcus* (VRE) colonization with expanded use of barrier precautions in ten ICUs compared to standard contact precautions in eight control ICUS was also published. In this study, Huskins and others (2011) found that the intervention did not reduce the transmission of MRSA or VRE. These studies serve to inform the ongoing debate about the relationship between clinical practice and research. To determine what is the best day-to-day practice to improve patient care and outcomes will require further study. Such efforts will need to examine the overlap of quality improvement and research, making the conduct of appropriate research studies less onerous, and determining ways to evaluate changes in care in the routine clinical setting.

HAIISS: Healthcare-Associated Infection and Influenza Surveillance System

Realizing the need to improve infectious disease–related outcomes across the VA healthcare system, the VHA, Public Health Strategic Health Care Group's Office of Public Health Surveillance and Research has laid the groundwork to establish a comprehensive, electronic surveillance system, HAIISS, the Healthcare-Associated Infection (HAI) and Influenza Surveillance System. HAIISS will extract data from both the VA VistA electronic medical record and the HAIISS Data Warehouse. Two software programs will be utilized: the QC PathFinder™ (QCP) electronic HIA detection application, and the Electronic Surveillance System for Early Notification of Community-based Epidemics (ESSENCE) biosurveillance application. HAIISS will support four "pillars of surveillance" (Oda 2011).

- **Pillar 1: CDC's National Healthcare Safety Network (NHSN) Healthcare-Associated Infection Surveillance.** ICU device-associated infection and surgical site infection surveillance are defined utilizing NHSN infection definitions and methodology. This system will allow VHA facilities to actively participate in NHSN surveillance activities and to create VHA benchmarks within NHSN utilizing electronic data collection and infection determination, with data transmittal to CDC via the NHSN web-based application. Aggregation of data will be provided for analysis to evaluate effectiveness of interventions and to compare infection control strategies VHA-wide.

- **Pillar 2: Biosurveillance/ Syndromic Surveillance.** Surveillance for influenza-like illness (ILI) and other conditions included in the seven syndrome groups characteristic of illnesses potentially caused by Category A bioterrorist agents or emerging pathogens:

  - Respiratory—cough, pneumonia, ILI, URI

  - Gastrointestinal—vomiting, diarrhea

  - Neurological—meningitis, botulism-like

  - Dermatologic—hemorrhagic

  - Dermatologic—vesicular (smallpox-like)

- Fever, malaise, sepsis
- Coma/sudden death

- **Pillar 3: Organisms/Infections of Epidemiologic Significance.** Includes surveillance for multidrug-resistant organisms such as MRSA, vancomycin-resistant *Enterococcus*, and multidrug-resistant gram negative organisms; clustering of organisms of epidemiologic significance such as *C. difficile*, group A streptococcus, *Legionella*, and tuberculosis; and infectious diseases/conditions reportable to the local, state, and national public health authorities. Allows VHA, at local facility and national levels, to monitor and detect trends in transmission of infection and to identify and report infections/conditions that require notification to public health authorities.

- **Pillar 4: Antimicrobial Usage and Decision Support Tools.** T Antimicrobial usage trends and organism resistance patterns will be tracked by specific antimicrobial agents, facility, and locations within the facility. The system will identify bacterial pathogen/antibiotic choice mismatch, and promote appropriate antimicrobial usage by allowing VHA, at the national level, and local facilities to monitor antimicrobial usage and resistance trends and recognize antimicrobial misuse. Aggregation of data will be available for analysis to evaluate effectiveness of interventions and to compare antimicrobial usage and ordering patterns across VHA medical facilities.

It is anticipated that HAIISS will greatly facilitate surveillance in these four settings for many different users across the VA healthcare system. In 2011 HAIISS was being tested in a prototype format using data from the VA Palo Alto Health Care System and the VISN 20 Data Warehouse. Following beta-site testing at selected VA medical centers, implement of HAIISS across all VA facilities is anticipated. HAIISS will serve as an invaluable resource to the VA healthcare system and also facilitate VA's participation in national surveillance systems (Oda 2011).

Users of HAIISS

- VHA healthcare professionals in the field and at VACO
- Infection preventionists, MRSA coordinators, ID physicians, pharmacists
- VHA National Program Offices

  - PHSHG, Office of Public Health Surveillance and Research
  - Patient Care Services, National Infectious Diseases Program Office
  - VA Pharmacy Benefits Management Services
  - Office of Research and Development

- Collaborators

  - Centers for Disease Control and Prevention
  - Department of Defense
  - Johns Hopkins University
  - Stanford University

For more than forty years the CDC has supported national systems for the surveillance of nosocomial infections. Beginning in 1970 with sixty-two participating hospitals, the CDC's National Nosocomial Infections Surveillance System (NNIS) began collecting data using standardized protocols on hospital-acquired infections (Richards et al. 2001). Ultimately there were 300 hospitals in 42 states included in NNIS, of which 17 were VA or military hospitals. Data were reported by type of ICU on device-related infections—urinary catheter–related urinary tract infections, central line-associated bloodstream infections, and ventilator-associated pneumonia. Surveillance of procedure-specific surgical site infections was also conducted. Antibiotic usage was tracked (NNIS 2004). In March 2000 the CDC reported that the 300 hospitals participating in NNIS had met or surpassed the ten-year national health objective to decrease by at least 10 percent the incidence of HAIs in ICU patients and of surgical wound infections (Centers for Disease Control 2000).

Building on the experience that voluntary surveillance and comparison to national benchmarks decreases healthcare-associated infections, in 2005 the CDC established the National Healthcare Safety Network (NNSH). The expanded program now includes 1,545 hospitals, 31 being VA hospitals, tracking device-associated infections, procedure-associated infections, and antimicrobial susceptibility data for selected organisms and/or antimicrobial usage (Edwards et al. 2009). Of the 463 hospitals reporting data on antimicrobial-resistant pathogens, twenty were VA facilities (Hidron et al. 2008). When HAIISS, the VHA surveillance system, begins tracking healthcare-associated infections, antimicrobial usage, and microorganism resistance patterns, VA will be positioned to enroll more of its medical centers into NNSH, facilitating improvement of patient care and also informing issues related to quality management and evidence-based clinical research.

VA Infectious Diseases Research

VHA's leadership has long recognized that VA research serves to not only expand knowledge but also to improve clinical care for veterans and to enhance the education of medical students, as well as residents and other healthcare professionals. The opportunity to be supported in the conduct of both laboratory and clinical research has attracted many distinguished scientists to spend their careers as VA researchers.

The first VA research studies in infectious diseases were on tuberculosis. For the past thirty years research related to HIV/AIDS has been a major VA focus. VA infectious diseases researchers have made significant contributions to advancing understanding of the diagnosis, pathogenesis, clinical manifestations, and treatment of many other infectious diseases.

Many of the VA investigators responsible for this research are recognized as leaders in their chosen fields. Their fields of interest have included studies on anaerobic bacteria, *Clostridium difficile* and *Clostridium difficile* associated disease (CDAD), multidrug-resistant Gram-negative organisms (MDROs), *Enterococcus*, *Legionella* and mycoplasma, unculturable pathogens, and hepatitis B and C viral infections. In addition, research has been conducted on endemic fungal infections that affected veterans, caused by *Blastomyces*, *Coccidiodes*, and *Histoplasmosis*.

Anaerobic Infections

In the 1960s there were advances in the study of anaerobic infections: the development of the GasPak system to easily create anaerobiosis, facilitating the isolation of anaerobes; the improved taxonomic classification of anaerobes; and the enhanced understanding of the benefits of appropriate anaerobic therapy. At the VA Greater Los Angeles Medical Center (formerly the Wadsworth VA Hospital), Dr. Sydney Feingold and others investigated antibiotics for the treatment of anaerobic infections including lincomycin and then clindamycin, metronidazole, cefoxitin, and other drugs (Gorbach & Bartlett 1974; Finegold 1993). Dr. Finegold has been at the VA medical center in Los Angeles for almost fifty years. He continues to direct his research laboratory and is internationally recognized for his contributions to the study of anaerobic bacteria and understanding the diseases caused by these bacteria and the role of intestinal bacteria in autoimmune diseases, autism, and chronic constipation. His studies on the effect of antimicrobials, such as cefoxitin, on intestinal flora contributed to understanding of the pathogenesis of *Clostridium difficile* colitis (Mulligan et al. 1984). In recognition of his contribution to the field of anaerobic infections, several bacteria bear his name—*Finegoldia magna*, *Alistipes finegoldi*, and *Bacteroides finegoldii*.

Clostridium difficile and *Clostridium difficile–associated Diarrhea*

The epidemiology and prevention of *Clostridium difficile* disease, and the pathogenesis and treatment of this anaerobic bacterium, have been a major research interest of Dr. Dale Gerding, the associate chief of staff for research and development at the Edward J. Hines VA Medical Center in Hines, Illinois. With the emergence in 2000 in North America and Europe of a hypervirulent strain of *C. difficile*, Dr. Gerding and his colleague at the Hines VA, Stuart Johnson, MD, have become recognized as leading experts in both the pathogenesis and treatment of *C. difficile*–associated diarrhea (CDAD). In an article published in December 2005 in the *New England Journal of Medicine*, in collaboration with investigators from the CDC, they described the widespread emergence of hypervirulent strains of *C. difficile*, resistant to fluoroquinolones, and responsible for outbreaks of CDAD across the United States (McDonald et al. 2005). Dr. Gerding has also investigated the in vitro activity of drugs for the treatment of CDAD, including rifaximin. His studies in the hamster model have advanced understanding of the role of antibiotic exposure to the development of CDAD (Merrigan et al. 2003).

As the VHA National Infectious Diseases Program Office works to expand molecular-based testing for *C. difficile* to all VA medical facilities, Drs. Gerding and Johnson will provide the expertise needed to improve outcomes for patients with CDAD and decrease nosocomial spread of this infection.

Multidrug-Resistant Organisms

Antimicrobial resistance is an increasing problem, particularly, but not only, in healthcare-associated infections. Understanding the mechanisms of resistance, which are increasingly complex, is essential both for drug development and tracking the spread of these frequently multidrug-resistant organisms. Drs. Mark Adams and Robert Bonomo at the Louis Stokes Cleveland VA Medical Center have been working to identify the genetic mechanisms of resistance of *Acinetobacter buamanii* and have shown that horizontal gene transfer is one of them. This bacterium has been identified as a pathogen in more than 30 percent of soldiers wounded in Iraq and Afghanistan. Even very closely related isolates of *A. baumanii* may have different genes. *Acinetobacter* can share resistance genes between bacteria by mechanisms including "horizontal gene transfer," and its antibiotic susceptibility can change during a hospital outbreak or within a patient (Adams et al. 2008).

Dr. Lou Rice, working in collaboration with Drs. Bonomo and Curtis Donskey at the Louis Stokes Medical Center, has investigated mechanisms of transfer of resistance genes in *Enterococcus faecium* and the regulation of antibiotic resistance (Rice et al. 1998). The researchers are also studying resistance in Enterobacteriaciae to beta-lactam antibiotics (Endimiani et al. 2009). Understanding these mechanisms is essential given the increasing incidence of infections resistant to all beta-lactam antibiotics, including the carbapemens. Should infections caused by "superbugs" carrying the plasmid-encoding carbapenemase-resistant metallo-beta-lactamase enzyme become endemic in U.S. hospitals, morbidity and mortality from healthcare-associated infections would increase, as well as associated costs of care.

Atypical Pathogens

Legionella

In 1976 an outbreak of pneumonia occurred at the Pennsylvania State American Legion convention in Philadelphia. In 1979 the causative agent was identified as *Legionella pneumophilia*. For more than twenty years, Dr. Victor Yu led a research team studying Legionnaire's disease at the Pittsburgh VA Medical Center. He and his colleagues proved that the reservoir for Legionnaire's disease was potable water (Stout et al. 1992). In addition, his lab team developed the media to culture both clinical and environmental samples. Dr. Yu also proposed that hospital outbreaks of Legionnaire's disease could be prevented by doing routine culturing of hospital water supplies (Yu 2000). Although initially not accepted, this is now standard environmental practice in hospitals and other facilities. Dr. Yu, Dr. Robert Muder, and other colleagues in Pittsburgh also isolated *L. micdadei*, the Pittsburgh pneumonia agent, defined its niche, and identified the associated clinical syndrome (Fang, Yu & Vickers 1989; Muder, Yu & Zuravleff 1983).

Mycoplasma and the Eaton Agent

The Eaton agent, the causative agent of cold-agglutinin atypical pneumonia, was originally described in the 1940s. In the 1960s it was identified as a species of mycoplasma, and in 1963 was named *Mycoplasma pneumoniae*. Dr. Maurice A. Mufson, who at that time was on staff at the VA West Side Hospital in Chicago, worked on the identification of this pathogen (Mufson et al. 1962).

Gulf War Veterans' Illness and Mycoplasma fermentens

Another mycoplasma, *Mycoplasma fermentans*, was imputed as the causative agent of Gulf War Veterans' Illnesses (GWVI). Of the 700,000 soldiers returning from the Persian Gulf following the 1990 to 1991 Gulf War, 15 percent developed unexplained symptoms of fatigue, pain, and neurocognitive problems that were termed GWVI. The Antibiotic Treatment Trial of

GWVI (VA CSP No. 475) was conducted to see if treatment with doxycyline for twelve months would improve the symptoms in 491 veterans with *Mycoplasma* DNA isolated from their blood. At the end of twelve and eighteen months of follow-up, there was no difference in the mental and physical findings between those who received doxycyline versus placebo. In fact, those treated with doxycycline had more side effects. In conclusion, the study found no benefit to treatment and some potential harm (Donta et al. 2004). The etiology of GWVI remains unknown.

The Search for Unculturable Pathogens

Recognized as one of the most creative and provocative infectious diseases researchers, David A. Relman is the chief of infectious diseases at the VA Palo Alto Health Care System and on the faculty at Stanford University School of Medicine. The major focus of his research has been identifying, using molecular and genomic techniques, previously unculturable pathogens that are the causative agents of diseases of infectious etiology (Relman 2002). He has also been interested in studying the endogenous microbes in humans both in the oral cavity and the gut—most of which have been previously unrecognized. Some of these organisms cause disease, but others have a symbiotic codependency. Dr. Relman and his colleagues believe that unraveling these complex relationships may shed light on how altering the gut flora potentially increases the risk for colon cancer, diabetes, and possibly autism, among other diseases. They have already shown that even a short course of therapy with an antibiotic such as ciprofloxacin may alter the gut flora indefinitely (Dethlefsen & Relman 2011).

Dr. Relman and his colleagues are credited with identifying several unculturable pathogens. In 1990 they reported that using PCR amplification of tissue from HIV-infected and organ transplant patients of specific DNA sequences, they had successfully found the causative agent of bacillary angiomatosis to be a rickettsia-like organism, closely related to *Rochalimaea quintana* (Relman et al. 1990). This organism was also reported to cause peliosis hepaticus, and fever and bacteremia in AIDS patients. In 1993 all *Rochalimaea* organisms were reclassified as *Bartonella* species, including *B. quintana* and *B. henselae*. In 1992 Dr. Relman and colleagues identified the unculturable bacillus responsible for Whipple's disease. Whipple's disease was known for over eighty-five years to be caused by an unculturable pathogen. Using 16S rRNA sequence amplification, the organism was detected in tissue specimens from patients with Whipple's disease and named *Tropheryma whippelii* (Relman et al. 1992). Dr. Relman's other areas of research, using molecular techniques, include the study of how *Bordetella pertussis*, the causative agent of whooping cough, invades human respiratory epithelial cells (Belcher et al. 2000; Ishibashi, Relman & Nishikawa 2001).

Dr. Relman continues to contribute to understanding the complex interactions of humans and microbes and to probe questions about what pathogens are causing diseases or maintaining health. To quote Dr. Relman, "Who is there?" "Who else—in addition to bacteria—are there?" "What precisely are they doing?" and "How are they doing it?" (DiGiulio & Relman 2009).

Viral Hepatitis B and C Disease

Dr. Relman is now world-renowned as a pioneer in using molecular technologies to push forward the horizons of microbiology. In 1965 Dr. Leonard B. Seeff began what was to be an equally distinguished VA career as a hepatologist, first at the Boston VA and then from 1971 to 1998 at the Washington, D.C. VAMC. Working with his mentor and teacher, Dr. Hyman J. Zimmerman, and with Dr. Kamal Ishak of the Armed Forces Institute of Pathology, he began his thirty-year VA career studying, in particular, the newly described virologic markers of viral hepatitis. In the 1970s serologic assays for hepatitis A virus and hepatitis B virus were developed, and it was thought that transfusion-associated non-A non-B hepatitis was caused by an as yet unrecognized virus.

As principal investigators for a series of VA Cooperative Studies on viral hepatitis, Drs. Seeff and Zimmerman studied transfusion-related viral hepatitis and treatments for viral hepatitis B infection with immune serum and hepatitis B immune globulin to prevent hepatitis B following needle stick injuries and blood transfusions. Working with Dr. Elizabeth Wright, an epidemiologist, and later with their assistant at the Washington, D.C. VAMC, Zelma Buskell-Bales, they defined the clinical course and natural history of non-A non-B hepatitis. It was not until the late 1980s that serologic tests for hepatitis C virus became available, and it was recognized as the causative agent of non-A non-B hepatitis (Choo et al. 1989).

Five prospective transfusion-associated hepatitis studies included two VA Cooperative Studies. In 1992 the study on long-term mortality among patients who acquired non-A non-B hepatitis following transfusion was published. After an average of eighteen years of follow-up, all-cause mortality was about 50 percent for those with non-A non-B hepatitis and matched, transfused non-hepatitis controls (Seeff et al. 1992). There was, however, a small increase in deaths from liver disease among those with non-A non-B hepatitis. In 2001 a study of the long-term mortality and morbidity of patients with non-A non-B hepatitis enrolled in three prospective transfusion studies begun in the 1970s was completed. Hepatitis C virus was shown to be the cause of transfusion-associated hepatitis in most patients. With approximately twenty-five years of follow-up, 17 percent initially infected with HCV progressed to cirrhosis; yet HCV infection was not associated with increased mortality (Seeff et al. 2001).

In another study completed in 2000, Dr. Seeff and colleagues conducted a retrospective cohort study of 8,568 military recruits from whom serum specimens were obtained between 1948 and 1954. Outcomes of HCV infection in healthy adults with forty-five-year follow-up were studied. Interestingly, only 17 (0.2 percent) persons had laboratory evidence of HCV infection. Among those one (5.9 percent) died of liver disease, compared to 119 (1.4 percent) of those without chronic HCV infection. The conclusion was that the risk for progressive liver disease with chronic HCV infection was less than previously thought (Seeff et al. 2000). The studies of Dr. Seeff and his colleagues advanced understanding of the natural history of HCV infection.

Dr. Seeff was also instrumental in completing two major studies of hepatitis B infection. In 1942 there was an epidemic of icteric hepatitis among U.S. army personnel. Over 51,000 soldiers were hospitalized with hepatitis. The outbreak was linked to the human serum used in the manufacture of yellow fever vaccine. In 1985 three groups of veterans were studied: those who had received the vaccine and developed jaundice; those who had received the vaccine and not developed jaundice; and those who had received a serum-free vaccine with no subsequent jaundice. Given that 97 percent of Group I, 76 percent of Group II, and only 13 percent of Group III had antibodies to hepatitis B virus, it was concluded that the epidemic in 1942 had been caused by hepatitis B. In addition, it was estimated that as many as 330,000 soldiers were exposed to hepatitis B following receipt of the contaminated vaccine. This follow-up study of healthy young white men with acute hepatitis B infection, as was the case with hepatitis C infection, found that the progression to chronic liver disease was lower than previously reported (Seeff et al. 1987).

Between July 1972 and August 1975, Dr. Seeff led a VA Cooperative Study to compare the efficacy of hepatitis B immune globulin (HBIG) to that of immune serum globulin (ISG) for prophylaxis against hepatitis B infection among medical and paramedical personnel accidentally exposed by needle stick or ingestion of blood products that were potentially infectious for viral hepatitis (mostly hepatitis B). The acquisition of hepatitis B infection was significantly less among those who received HBIG than ISG (Seeff et al. 1975). In a reanalysis of this study, the mechanism of action of HBIG and ISG was studied. This study showed that ISG contained antibodies against hepatitis B and so, like HBIG, provided some protection against infection. The rate of infection was the same in both groups but was more frequently subclinical in those who received HBIG (Hoofnagle et al. 1979).

Fungal Infections

There has been considerable interest in the study of fungal infections by VA researchers. The VA experience with the care of veterans with tuberculosis allowed the VA investigators to undertake the study of fungal diseases among veterans. Three fungal infections that were endemic to areas in which veterans were living were of particular interest—blastomycosis, coccidiomycosis, and histoplasmosis. The Cooperative Study Group on the Chemotherapy of Tuberculosis of the Veterans Administration–Armed Forces, having successfully completed studies on the treatment of TB, subsequently undertook studies on coccidiomycosis and histoplasmosis, and in 1957, on blastomycosis.

The first case of blastomycosis was described by Gilchrist in a patient in Baltimore, and the disease became known as Gilchrist's disease (Bradsher 1996). Early studies on blastomycosis were conducted under the auspices of the Blastomycosis Cooperative Study of the Veterans Administration in collaboration with other investigators, including the U.S. Public Health Service Cooperative Mycoses Study. The clinical manifestations and radiographic findings of blastomycotic infection were described by these investigators (Gehweiler, Capp & Chick 1970). The epidemiology of blastomycosis in Arkansas, Kentucky, and Mississippi, where blastomycosis is endemic, was reported by investigators from the University of Kentucky and the VA hospital in Lexington (Furcolow et al. 1966). A review of 198 cases of blastomycosis in VA hospitals was one of the earliest large studies of this disease (Busey et al. 1964). In the 1960s and 1970s, in Cooperative Studies done by VA and the U.S. Public Health Service, the treatment of blastomycosis with amphotericin B, azoles, and other agents was investigated (Lockwood et al. 1962). The National Institute of Allergy and Infectious Diseases Mycoses Study Group and the Infectious Diseases Society of America practice guidelines for the management of patients with blastomycosis were informed by these studies (Chapman et al. 2000).

Coccidiomycosis is a systemic fungal infection endemic to the southwestern United States. Interest in the study of coccidiomycosis increased just before World War II. It was recognized that there was a high rate of infection among people with no prior exposure who had recently moved to endemic areas, particularly in southern California. It is estimated that there were over 4,000 cases among soldiers stationed in the San Joaquin Valley between 1942 and 1945, particularly at the military airfields (Shelton 1942).

In 1955, following the isolation of amphotericin B, the VA-Armed Forces Cooperative Study of Coccidiomycosis was begun at the San Fernando, California VA hospital led by David Salkin, a chest physician, and John Steele, a surgeon. This study enrolled veterans diagnosed with coccidiomycosis. The interest of this Cooperative Study group was similar to the earlier tuberculosis study group. Between January 1955 and December 1958, 699 military and veteran patients diagnosed with coccidiomycosis were enrolled in the study. Among these patients there were 25 with meningeal involvement. Those patients without extrapulmonary dissemination other than to the meninges survived longer than those with both meningeal and extrapulmonary disease (Vincent et al. 1993). In 1972, an earthquake destroyed the medical center in San Fernando, but the work continued from the Sepulveda VA hospital, studying the pathogenesis, mycology, and clinical aspects of the disease. Interest in the study of coccidiomycosis is now continued under the auspices of the Coccidomycosis Study Group with participation by a number of VA investigators. Neal Ampel and John Galgiani, both at the Tucson VA Medical Center, have participated in studies of coccidiomycosis in patients with HIV/AIDS, among pregnant women, and in renal transplant patients. They have also investigated therapeutic antifungal agents—particularly, the azoles.

Like blastomycosis and coccidiomycosis, histoplasmosis is an endemic fungal pathogen, In the United States, histoplamosis is endemic in the Midwest and Southeast. In certain regions of the Mississippi and Ohio River valleys, where the fungus is present in the soil, histoplasmosis affects over 90 percent of residents. The first case of *Histoplasmosis capsulatum* was described by Darling in 1906 in a patient in Panama. It took several decades to understand that the histoplasmosis causes primarily lung disease. The severity of disease depends on the inoculum exposure and the immunity of the host. Patients may have an acute pulmonary syndrome that includes pneumonia, particularly in children. Older adults, especially male smokers with underlying chronic obstructive pulmonary disease, are more likely to develop chronic cavitary pulmonary histoplasmosis. More rarely, primarily in immunocompromised hosts, patients may present with disseminated histoplasmosis (Kauffman 2007).

Many of the early studies on chronic pulmonary histoplasmosis were done among inpatients in TB sanatoriums as well as in VA hospitals. These patients were initially thought to have tuberculosis, because the diseases may mimic each other. Chronic infection and severe acute infection require treatment. Between 1955 and 1975, a twenty-year prospective study of chronic pulmonary histoplasmosis was conducted at the Nashville VA hospital. Data from this study were combined with those from a mostly retrospective study at the Middle Tennessee Chest Disease Hospital, also in Nashville. This study described the natural history of chronic histoplasmosis and its pathogenesis (Goodwin et al. 1976).

The mainstays of treatment of histoplasmosis remain amphotericin B and the azoles. Several treatment studies of amphotericin B were undertaken in the 1950s and 1960s by the VA–Armed Forces Cooperative Study on histoplasmosis. These randomized studies defined amphotericin B as the curative therapy for chronic pulmonary histoplasmosis for more than the next twenty years (Sutliff et al. 1964; Putnam et al. 1968). In 1970 a follow-up study of eighty-nine cases of chronic histoplasmosis from four VA hospitals, in Memphis, Tennessee; Jackson, Mississippi; Little Rock, Arkansas; and Cincinnati, Ohio, was reported. This study confirmed the long-term benefit of amphotericin B therapy but also that relapses following therapy do occur (Baum, Larkin & Sutliff 1970).

As was the case with tuberculosis, VA investigators have contributed significantly to research on fungal infections. In the thirty years since the beginning of the HIV epidemic, VA researchers have advanced understanding of AIDS-defining fungal infections such as cryptococcosis, coccidiomycosis, and histoplasmosis.

Infections in Special VA Populations

Long-Term Care

VHA is the single largest provider in the United States of care to patients living in residential facilities. There are now more than 35,000 veterans in institutional long-term care. The VA Community Living Centers (CLCs), formerly VA Nursing Home Care Units, are usually located on the campus of a VA medical center or nearby. Despite the fact that over 40 percent of Americans over sixty-five years of age will receive care at some time in a nursing home, research on infectious complications in nursing home settings is limited. In 2005 and 2007 the VA Office of the Medical Inspector Taskforce to study infections in VA long-term-care facilities conducted Web-based, one-day point prevalence surveys of nursing home–associated infections. More than 10,000 residents in the 133 VA CLCs were included in these surveys. In both surveys patients with indwelling devices were more likely to have a nursing home–associated infection than those without (Tsan et al. 2008). The ability to conduct Web-based surveys to assess care in VA CLCs should serve to improve outcomes.

Dr. Larry Strausbaugh, while at the Portland VA Medical Center, studied infections in nursing homes, including MRSA infection and colonization, and the incidence and impact of infections among nursing-home residents. He was a leader in promoting research on infections in long-term-care facilities including antibiotic resistance among residents of long-term facilities, and infectious diseases outbreaks in this vulnerable population (Strausbaugh et al. 1996; Strausbaugh et al. 2003). Dr. Susan F. Bradley, at the Ann Arbor VA Medical Center, is another VA researcher with an interest in infections in long-term-care facilities. She participated in the development of Infectious Diseases Society of America (IDSA) guidelines on catheter-associated urinary tract infections (Hooton et al. 2010) and on the evaluation of fever and infection in older adult residents of long-term-care facilities (High et al. 2009). Her studies on infections, colonization, and antimicrobial resistance, particularly in nursing care facilities, have demonstrated the complexity of appropriate management and the difficulty of translating the data from related studies to policy (Mody et al. 2011).

Diabetic Foot Infections

With over 1,000,000 veterans in care with diabetes mellitus, the VA healthcare system is the single largest provider of care to diabetics. Some 15 percent of veterans with diabetes will develop foot ulcers, and there is significant associated morbidity, particularly amputation. Dr. Benjamin A. Lipsky, an infectious diseases physician at the VA Puget Sound Healthcare System, has contributed significantly to research to improve understanding of this complex disease. Dr. Lipsky and Dr. Warren S. Joseph, from the VA Medical Center, Coatesville, Pennsylvania, were among the authors of the IDSA guidelines for the diagnosis and treatment of diabetic foot infections (Lipsky et al. 2004).

Spinal Cord Injury

It is estimated that there are 200,000 people in the United States with spinal cord injury and/or disorder (SCI&D). The VA healthcare system, as the single largest provider of care in the world to those with SCI&D, serves the complex medical and long-term needs of more than 25,000 affected veterans. The VA Spinal Cord Injury and Disorders Services delivers care from twenty-four regional SCI & D centers. In 1998 the VA HSR&D established a SCI-QUERI to improve outcomes for veterans living with the long-term complications of such injuries. Infectious complications are common in such patients, including urinary tract infections, primarily associated with indwelling catheters; pressure ulcers; respiratory tract infections; nosocomial infections; and skin and soft tissue infections. Other issues have included rates of MRSA colonization and infection, particularly in CLCs, and also ensuring that SCI patients receive influenza vaccinations (for a listing of related publications and presentations, see http://www.queri.research.va.gov/sci/publications.cfm).

Conclusions

Since the early days of the Veterans Administration, the impact of infectious diseases on veterans has not changed, but the types of infections and their treatment, management, and diagnoses have changed considerably. Patients are no longer hospitalized for months at a time. Medical care of infectious diseases relies increasingly on rapid microbiologic diagnostic tests, frequently coupled with sophisticated radiographic studies. The electronic medical record has improved care while allowing enhanced surveillance for infectious pathogens.

The VA healthcare system, as the single largest provider of medical care in the United States, will increasingly be able to inform research questions regarding best practices. Many of the questions posed will be about improving care of patients who are frequently debilitated, require complex medical and surgical procedures, receive care in the intensive care setting, and have indwelling medical devices. Research studies combining syndromic surveillance with the most advanced genetic diagnostic tests will no doubt contribute to improved understanding of infections such as HIV/AIDS, influenza, viral hepatitis; drug-resistant bacteria and fungi; emerging infectious diseases; and agents of bioterror. Immunizations for prevention of infections such as MRSA will no doubt be developed. With deployment of U.S. soldiers across the globe, pathogens that may be challenges to diagnose, treat, and prevent should be a focus of VA research efforts. Vaccine research should be supported. There is every reason to believe that VA infectious diseases investigators will be at the forefront of advances in basic science and clinical research.

References

Adams, M. D., Goglin, K., Molyneaux, N., et al. (2008). Comparative genome sequence analysis of multidrug-resistant *Acinetobacter baumannii*. *Journal of Bacteriology* 190, no. 24: 8053–8064.

Backus, L., Mole, L., Chang, S. & Deyton, L. (2001). The Immunology Case Registry. *Journal of Clinical Epidemiology* 54 (Supp. 1): S12–S15.

Bacon, B. R., Gordon, S. C., Lawitz, E., et al. (2011). HCV RESPOND-2 Investigators: Boceprevir for previously treated chronic HCV genotype 1 infection. *New England Journal of Medicine* 364, no. 13: 1207–1217.

Barnwell, J. B. (1948a). Results of a co-operative study on the effects of streptomycin. *Journal—Michigan State Medical Society* 47, no. 11: 1220.

Barnwell, J. B. (1948b). Veterans Administration tuberculosis division, 1945–1947: Progress report. *American Review of Tuberculosis* 58, no. 1: 64–76.

Baum, G. L., Larkin, J. C., Jr. & Sutliff, W. D. (1970). Follow-up of patients with chronic pulmonary histoplasmosis treated with amphotericin B. *Chest* 58: 562–565.

Belcher, C. E., Drenkow, J., Kehoe, J., et al. (2000). The transcriptional responses of respiratory epithelial cells to *Bordettla pertussis* reveal host defensive and pathogen counter-defensive strategies. *Proceedings of the National Academy of Sciences USA* 97, no. 25: 1347–1352.

Bozzette, S. A., Ake, C. F., Tam, H. K., Chang, S. W. & Louis, T. A. (2003). Cardiovascular and cerebrovascular events in patients treated for human immuno-deficiency virus infection. *New England Journal of Medicine* 348, no. 8: 702–710.

Bradsher, R. W. (1996). Histoplasmosis and blastomycosis. *Clinical Infectious Diseases* 22 (Supp. 2): S102–S111.

Busey, J. F., Baker, R., Birch, L., et al. (1964). Blastomycosis, I: Review of 198 collected cases in the Veterans Administration hospitals. *American Review of Respiratory Disease* 89: 659–672.

Cardozo, T., Kimura, T., Philpott, S., Weiser, B., Burger, H. & Zolla-Pazner, S. (2007). Structural basis for coreceptor selectivity by the HIV type 1 V3 loop. *AIDS Research and Human Retroviruses* 23, no. 3: 415–426.

Centers for Disease Control (CDC). (2000). Monitoring hospital-acquired infections to promote patient safety—United States, 1990–1999. *Morbidity and Mortality Weekly Report* 49: 149.

Centers for Disease Control (CDC). (2006). Revised recommendations for HIV testing of adults, adolescents, and pregnant women in health-care settings. *Morbidity and Mortality Weekly Report* 55 (RR-14): 1–17.

Centers for Disease Control (CDC). (2011). Thirty years of HIV—1981–2011. *Morbidity and Mortality Weekly Report* 60: 689.

Chapman, S. T., Bradsher, R. W., Jr., Campbell, G. D., Jr., Pappas, P. G. & Kauffman, C. A. (2000). Practice guidelines for the management of patients with blastomycosis. *Clinical Infectious Diseases* 30: 679–682.

Choo, Q. L., Kuo, G., Weiner, A. J., Overby, L. R., Bradley, D. W. & Houghton, M. (1989). Isolation of a cDNA clone derived from a blood-borne non-A, non-B viral hepatitis genome. *Science* 244, no. 4902: 359–362.

Crosby, A. (1989). *America's forgotten pandemic: The influenza of 1918*. Cambridge: Cambridge University Press, 5.

Deeks, S. G. (2011). HIV infection, inflammation, immunosenescence, and aging. *Annual Review of Medicine* 62: 141–155.

Dethlefsen, L. & Relman, D. A. (2011). Incomplete recovery and individualized responses of the human distal gut microbiota to repeated antibiotic perturbation. *Proceedings of the National Academy of Sciences USA* 108 (Supp. 1): 4554–4561.

DiGiulio, D. B. & Relman, D. A. (2009). Majority rules? Tallying the microbial census in an abscess by means of molecular methods. *Clinical Infectious Diseases* 48: 1179–1181.

Dolan, M. J., Kulkarni, H., Camargo, J. F., et al. (2007). CCL3L1 and CCR5 influence cell-mediated immunity and affect HIV-AIDS pathogenesis via viral entry-independent mechanisms. *Nature Immunology* 8 no. 12: 1324–1336.

Donta, S. T., Engel, C. C., Jr., Collins, J. F., et al. for the VA Cooperative #475 Group. (2004). Benefits and harms of doxycycline treatment for Gulf War veterans' illnesses: A randomized, double-blind, placebo-controlled trial. *Annals of Internal Medicine* 141: 85–94.

Edwards, J. R., Peterson, K. D., Shailendra, B., et al. (2009). National Healthcare Safety Network (NHSN) report: Data summary for 2006 through 2008. *American Journal of Infection Control* 37: 783–805.

Endimiani, A., Hujer, A. M., Perez, F., et al. (2009). Characterization of blaKPC-containing *Klebsiella pneumoniae* isolates detected in different institutions in the Eastern USA. *Journal of Antimicrobial Chemotherapy* 63, no. 3: 427–437.

Executive Office of the President. President's Council of Advisors on Science and Technology. (2009). Report to the President on U.S. Preparations for 2009 H1N1 Influenza. August 7. www.whitehouse.gov/assets/documents/PCAST_H1N1_Report.pdf.

Fang, G. D., Yu, V. L. & Vickers, R. M. (1989). Disease due to the Legionellaceae (other than *Legionella pneumophila*): Historical, microbiological, clinical, and epidemiological review. *Medicine* (Baltimore) 68, no. 2: 116–132.

Finegold, S. M. (1993). A century of anaerobes: a look backward and a call to arms. *Clinical Infectious Diseases* 16 (Supp. 4): S453–S457.

Fischl, M. A., Richman, D. D., Grieco, M. H., et al. (1987). The efficacy of azidothymidine (AZT) in the treatment of patients with AIDS and AIDS-related complex: A double-blind, placebo-controlled trial. *New England Journal of Medicine* 317, no. 4: 185–191.

Fischl M. A., Richman, D. D., Hansen, N., et al. (1990). The safety and efficacy of zidovudine (AZT) in the treatment of subjects with mildly symptomatic human immunodeficiency virus type 1 (HIV) infection: A double-blind, placebo-controlled trial; the AIDS Clinical Trials Group. *Annals of Internal Medicine* 112, no. 10: 727–737.

Furcolow, M. L., Balows, A., Menges, R. W., Picker, D. & McClellan, Saliba A. (1966). Blastomycosis: An important medical problem in the central United States. *JAMA* 198 no. 5: 115–118.

Gehweiler, J. A., Capp, M. P. & Chick, E. W. (1970). Observations on the roentgen patterns in blastomycosis of the bone: A review of cases from the Blastomycosis Cooperative Study of the Veterans Administration and Duke University Medical Center. *American Journal of Roentgenology Radium Therapy & Nuclear Medicine* 108, no. 3: 497–451.

Goetz, M. B., Hoang, T., Bowman, C., et al. (2008). QUERI-HIV/Hepatitis Program Group: A system-wide intervention to improve HIV testing in the Veterans Health Administration. *Journal of General Internal Medicine* 23, no. 8: 1200–1207.

Goodwin, R. A., Owens, F. T., Snell, J. D., et al. (1976). Chronic pulmonary histoplasmosis. *Medicine* (Baltimore) 55, no. 6: 413–452.

Gorbach, S. L. & Bartlett, J. G. (1974). Anaerobic infections: 1. *New England Journal of Medicine* 290, no. 21: 1177–1184.

Gorse, G. J., O'Connor, T. Z., Young, S. L., et al. (2003). Efficacy trial of live, cold-adapted and inactivated influenza virus vaccine in older adults with chronic obstructive pulmonary disease: A VA Cooperative Study. *Vaccine* 21, nos. 17–18: 2133–2144.

Groom, H., Dieperink, E., Nelson, D. B., et al. (2008). Outcomes of a hepatitis C screening program at a large urban VA medical center. *Journal of Clinical Gastroenterology* 42, no. 1: 97–106.

Halloran, J., Czarnogorski, M., Dursa, E., et al. (2012). HIV testing in the US Department of Veterans Affairs. *Archives of Internal Medicine* 172, no. 1: 61-62.

Hamilton, J. D., Hartigan, P. M., Simberkoff, M. S., et al. (1992). A controlled trial of early versus late treatment with zidovudine in symptomatic human immunodeficiency virus infection: Results of the Veterans Affairs Cooperative Study. *New England Journal of Medicine* 326, no. 7: 437–443.

Havlir, D. V. & Richman, D. D. (1997). The role of viral dynamics in the pathogenesis of HIV disease and implications for antiviral therapy. *Springer Seminars in Immunopathology* 18, no. 3: 267–283.

Hayes, M. (2010). *VA Research: Improving veterans' lives, a historical look at the establishment of the Department of Veterans Affairs Research and Development Program.* Washington, DC: U.S. Government Printing Office.

Hidron, A. I., Edwards, J. R., Patel, J., et al. (2008). NHSN annual update: antimicrobial-resistant pathogens associated with healthcare-associated infections: annual summary of data reported to the National Healthcare Safety Network at the Centers for Disease Control and Prevention, 2006–2007. *Infection Control and Hospital Epidemiology* 29: 996–1011.

High, K. P., Bradley, S. F., Gravenstein, S., et al. (2009). Clinical practice guideline for the evaluation of fever and infection in older adult residents of long-term care facilities: 2008 update by the Infectious Diseases Society of America. *Journal of the American Geriatric Society* 57, no. 3: 375–394.

Holodniy, M., Brown, S. T., Cameron, D. W., et al. OPTIMA Team (2011). Results of antiretroviral treatment interruption and intensification in advanced multi-drug resistant HIV infection from the OPTIMA trial. *PLoS One* 6, no. 3: e14764.

Hoofnagle, J. H., Seeff, L. B., Buskell-Bales, Z., et al. (1979). Passive-active immunity from hepatitis B immune globulin. *Annals of Internal Medicine* 91: 813–818.

Hooton, T. M., Bradley, S. F., Cardenas, D. D., et al. (2010). Diagnosis, prevention, and treatment of catheter-associated urinary tract infection in adults: 2009 international clinical practice guidelines from the Infectious Diseases Society of America. *Clinical Infectious Diseases* 50: 625–663.

Huskins, W. C., Huckabee, C. M., O'Grady, N. P., et al. (2011). Intervention to reduce the transmission of resistant bacteria in intensive care. *New England Journal of Medicine* 364: 1407–1418.

Ishibashi, Y., Relman, D. A. & Nishikawa, A. (2001). Invasion of human respiratory epithelial cells by *Bordetella pertussis*: possible role for a filamentous hemagglutinin Arg-Gly-Asp sequence and alpha5beta1 integrin. *Microbial Pathogenesis* 30, no. 5: 279–288.

Jain, R., Kralovic, S. M., Evans, M. E., et al. (2011). Veterans Affairs initiative to prevent methicillin-resistant *Staphylococcus aureus* infections. *New England Journal of Medicine* 364: 1419–1430.

Johnson, V. A., Brun-Vezinet, F., Clotet, B., et al. (2008). Update of the drug resistance mutations in HIV-1: Spring 2008. *Top HIV Medicine* 16, no. 1: 62–68.

Justice, A. C., Dombrowski, E., Conigliaro, J., et al. (2006). Veterans Aging Cohort Study (VACS): Overview and description. *Medical Care* 44, no. 8 (Supp. 2): S13–S24.

Justice, A. C., McGinnis, K. A., Skanderson, M., et al. and the VACS Project Team. (2010). Towards a combined prognostic index for survival in HIV infection: The role of "non-HIV" biomarkers. *HIV Medicine* 11, no. 2: 143–151.

Kauffman, C. A. (2007). Histoplasmosis: A clinical and laboratory update. *Clinical Microbiology Reviews* 20, no. 1: 115–132.

Khuri, S. F., Daley, J., Henderson, W., et al. and the participants in the National VA Surgical Quality Improvement Program. (1998). The Department of Veterans Affairs' NSQIP: The first national, validated, outcome-based, risk-adjusted, and peer-controlled program for the measurement and enhancement of the quality of surgical care. *Annals of Surgery* 228: 491–507.

Khuri, S. F., Daley, J. & Henderson, W. G. (2002). The comparative assessment and improvement of quality of surgical care in the Department of Veterans Affairs. *Archives of Surgery* 137, no. 1: 20–27.

Klevens, R. M., Edwards, J. R., Richards, C. L., Jr., et al. (2007). Estimating healthcare-associated infections and deaths in U.S. hospitals, 2002. *Public Health Reports* 122, no. 2: 160–66.

Larder, B. A., Darby, G. & Richman, D. D. (1989). HIV with reduced sensitivity to zidovudine (AZT) isolated during prolonged therapy. *Science* 243, no. 4899: 1731–1734.

Lipsky, B. A., Berendt, A. R., Deery, H. G., et al. (2004). Diagnosis and treatment of diabetic foot infections. *Clinical Infectious Diseases* 39: 885–910.

Lockwood, W. R., Busey, J. F., Batson, B. E. & Allison, F., Jr. (1962). Experiences in the treatment of North American blastomycosis with 2–hydroxystilbamidine. *Annals of Internal Medicine* 57: 553–562.

McDonald, L. C., Killgore, G. E., Thompson, A., et al. (2005). An epidemic, toxin gene-variant strain of *Clostridium difficile*. *New England Journal of Medicine* 353, no. 23: 2433–2441.

McHutchison, J. G., Manns, M. P., Muir, A. J., et al. and the PROVE3 Study Team. (2010). Telaprevir for previously treated chronic HCV infection. *New England Journal of Medicine* 362, no. 14: 1292–1303.

Merrigan, M., Sambol, S., Johnson, S. & Gerding, D. N. (2003). Susceptibility of hamsters to human pathogenic *Clostridium difficile* strain B1 following clindamycin, ampicillin or ceftriaxone administration. *Anaerobe* 9, no. 2: 91–95.

Mody, L., Bradley, S. F., Galecki, A., et al. (2011). Conceptual model for reducing infections and antimicrobial resistance in skilled nursing facilities: Focusing on residents and indwelling devices. *Clinical Infectious Diseases* 52, no. 5: 654–661.

Muder, R. R., Cunningham, C., McCray, E., et al. (2008). Implementation of an industrial systems-engineering approach to reduce the incidence of methicillin-resistant *Staphylococcus aureus* infection. *Infection Control and Hospital Epidemiology* 29: 702–708.

Muder, R. R., Yu, V. L. & Zuravleff, J. J. (1983). Pneumonia due to the Pittsburgh pneumonia agent: New clinical perspective with a review of the literature. *Medicine* (Baltimore) 62, no. 2: 120–128.

Mufson, M. A., Bloom, H. H., Manko, M. A., Kingston, J. R. & Chanock, R. M. (1962). Eaton agent: A review. *American Journal of Public Health* 52, no. 6: 925–932.

Mulligan, M. E., Citron, D., Gabay, E., Kirby, B. D., George, W. L. & Finegold, S. M. (1984). Alterations in human fecal flora, including ingrowth of *Clostridium difficile*, related to cefoxitin therapy. *Antimicrobial Agents Chemotherapy* 26, no. 3: 343–346.

National Nosocomial Infections Surveillance (NNIS). (2004). System report: Data summary from January 1992 through June 2004, issued October 2004. *American Journal of Infection Control* 32: 470–485.

Oda, G. (2011). HAIISS: Detecting and monitoring healthcare-associated infections in VHA. *Public Health Matters: Public Health Strategic Healthcare Group* 7: 4–6.

Oxman, N. M., Levin, M. J., Johnson, G. R., et al. for the Shingles Prevention Study Group. (2005). A vaccine to prevent herpes zoster and posttherapeutic neuralgia in older adults. *New England Journal of Medicine* 352: 2271–2284.

President's Council of Advisors on Science and Technology. Executive Office of the President. Report to the President on U.S. preparedness for 2009-H1N1 influenza. 7 August 2009. Available at: www.whitehouse.gov/assets/documents/PCAST_H1N1_Report.pdf.

Putnam, L. R., Sutliff, W. D., Larkin, J. C., et al. (1968). Histoplasmosis Cooperative Study: Chronic pulmonary histoplasmosis treated with amphotericin B alone and with amphotericin B and triple sulfonamide. *American Review of Respiratory Disease* 97: 96–102.

Relman, D. A. (2002). New technologies, human-microbe interactions, and the search for previously unrecognized pathogens. *Journal of Infectious Disease* 186 (Supp. 2): S254–S258.

Relman, D. A., Loutit, J. S., Schmidt, T. M., Falkow, S. & Tompkins, L. S. (1990). The agent of bacillary angiomatosis: An approach to the identification of uncultured pathogens. *New England Journal of Medicine* 323: 1573–1580.

Relman, D. A., Schmidt, T. M., MacDermott, R. P. & Falkow, S. (1992). Identification of the bacillus of Whipple's disease. *New England Journal of Medicine* 327: 293–301.

Rice, L. B., Carias, L. L., Donskey, C. L. & Rudin, S. D. (1998). Transferable, plasmid-mediated vanB-type glycopeptide resistance in *Enterococcus faecium*. *Antimicrobial Agents and Chemotherapy* 42, no. 4: 963–964.

Richards, C., Emori, T. G., Edwards, J., Fridkin, S., Tolson, J., Gaynes, R. & the National Nosocomial Infections Surveillance System. (2001). Characteristics of hospitals and infection control professionals participating in the National Nosocomial Infections Surveillance System 1999. *American Journal of Infection Control* 29: 400–403.

Sanders, G. D., Bayoumi, A. M., Sundaram, V., et al. (2005). Cost-effectiveness of screening for HIV in the era of highly active antiretroviral therapy. *New England Journal of Medicine* 352: 570–585.

Seeff, L. B., Beebe, G. W., Hoofnagle, J. H., et al. (1987). A serologic follow-up of the 1942 epidemic of post-vaccination hepatitis in the United States. *New England Journal of Medicine* 316: 965–970.

Seeff, L. B., Buskell-Bales, Z., Wright, E. C., et al. & the National Heart, Lung, and Blood Institute Study Group. (1992). Long-term mortality after transfusion-associated non-A, non-B hepatitis. *New England Journal of Medicine* 327: 1906–1911.

Seeff, L. B., Lollinger, F. B., Alter, H. J., et al. (2001). Long-term mortality and morbidity of transfusion-associated non-A, non-B, and type C hepatitis: A National Heart, Lung, and Blood Institute Collaborative Study. *Hepatology* 33: 455–463.

Seeff, L. B., Miller, R. N., Rabkin, C. S., et al. (2000). 45-year follow-up of hepatitis C virus infection in healthy young adults. *Annals of Internal Medicine* 132: 105–111.

Seeff, L. B., Wright, E. C., Finkelstein, J. D., et al. (1975). Efficacy of hepatitis B immune serum globulin after accidental exposure. *Lancet* 2, no. 7942: 939–941.

Shelton, R. M. (1942). Survey of coccidiomycosis at Camp Roberts, California. *JAMA* 118: 1186–1190.

Simberkoff, M. S., Cross, A. P., Al-Ibrahim, M., et al. (1986). Efficacy of pneumococcal vaccine in high-risk patients: Results of a Veterans Administration Cooperative Study. *New England Journal of Medicine* 315: 1318–1327.

Sklar, P. & Masur, H. (2003). HIV infection and cardiovascular disease—is there really a link? *New England Journal of Medicine* 349, no. 21: 2065–2067.

Starling, A. (2006). *Plague, SARS and the story of medicine in Hong Kong.* Hong Kong: Hong Kong University Press, 55.

The state of care for veterans with HIV/AIDS. VA National HIV/AIDS Web site. www.hiv.va.gov/provider/state-of-care/acknowledgements.asp.

Stout, J. E., Yu, V. L., Muraca, P., Joly, J., Troup, N. & Tompkins, L. S. (1992). Potable water as a cause of sporadic cases of community-acquired Legionnaires' disease. *New England Journal of Medicine* 326, no. 3: 151–155.

Strategic Timing of Anti-Retroviral Treatment (START). (n.d.). NIH, NIAID, ClinicalTrials,gov Identifier NCT00867048.

Strategies for Management of Antiretroviral Therapy (SMART) Study Group (El-Sadr, W. M., Lundgren, J. D., Neaton, J. D., et al.). (2006). CD4+ count-guided interruption of antiretroviral treatment. *New England Journal of Medicine* 355, no. 22: 2283–2296.

Strausbaugh, L. J., Crossley, K. B., Nurse, B. A., Thrupp, L. D. & the SHEA Long-Term-Care Committee. (1996). Antimicrobial resistance in long-term-care facilities. *Infectious Control and Hospital Epidemiology* 17: 129–140.

Strausbaugh L. J., Sukumar S. R., & Joseph C. L. (2003). Infectious disease outbreaks in nursing homes: An unappreciated hazard for frail elderly persons. *Clinical Infectious Diseases* 36: 870–876.

Sutliff, W. D., Andrews, C. E., Jones, E. & Terry, R. T. (1964). Histoplasmosis Cooperative Study: Veterans Administration–Armed Forces Cooperative Study on histoplasmosis. *American Review of Respiratory Disease* 89: 641–650.

Tsan, L., Davis, C., Langberg, R., et al. (2008). Prevalence of nursing home-associated infections in the Department of Veterans Affairs nursing home care units. *American Journal of Infection Control* 36, no. 3: 173–179.

Tucker, W. B. (1960). The evolution of the Cooperative Studies in the chemotherapy of tuberculosis of the Veterans Administration and Armed Forces of the U.S.A: An account of the evolving education of the physician in clinical pharmacology. *Bibliotheca Tuberculosia* 15: 1–68.

Vincent, T., Galgiani, J. N., Hippert, M. & Salkin, D. (1993). The natural history of coccidiodal meningitis: VA–Armed Forces Cooperative Studies, 1955–1958. *Clinical Infectious Diseases* 16: 247–254.

Williams, C. F., Klinzman, D., Yamashita, T. E., et al. (2004). Persistent GB virus C infection and survival in HIV-infected men. *New England Journal of Medicine* 350, no. 10: 981–990.

Xiang, J., McLinden, J. H., Chang, Q., Kaufman, T. M. & Stapleton, J. T. (2006). An 85-aa segment of the GB virus type C NS5A phosphoprotein inhibits HIV-1 replication in CD4+ Jurkat T cells. *Proceedings of the National Academy of Sciences USA* 103, no. 42: 15570–15575.

Yu, V. L. (2000). Nosocomial legionellosis. *Current Opinion in Infectious Diseases* 13, no. 4: 385–388.

Chapter 8

End-of-Life Care for Veterans in the VA Healthcare System

Betty L. Gillespie, James L. Ford, and Kye Y. Kim

Introduction

Over the last forty years, the hospice movement and end-of-life (EOL) care have slowly and steadily entered mainstream medicine. Since Dame Cicely Saunders started the first hospice in London in 1967 (Warpole 2009), winning acceptance from the traditional medical community and the general public has been a gradual, incremental process. However, several recent events have accelerated that process. Healthcare legislation before Congress proposed financial incentives to reimburse physicians providing patients with EOL care information and increased Medicare and Medicaid reimbursement for facilities with accredited palliative care treatment programs (Warner 2009).

On August 7, 2009, former Alaska Governor Sarah Palin posted a now famous Facebook entry. She used the term "death panels" to describe physician-patient consultation to discuss patient and caregiver goals and options regarding EOL care (Weiner 2009), reawakening an impassioned debate between those who favor preservation of life at all costs (Annas 2005) and those who favor preservation of the individual's right to choose how to die (Gazelle 2007). Suddenly EOL care was thrust into the spotlight, being discussed and debated on popular talk shows, in Congress, and by people waiting in line at the grocery store.

In the wake of this political and social controversy, two things became immediately clear. First, there were many misconceptions about EOL care. People were confused about what it was and how it might apply to them or their loved ones. Second, EOL care provoked strong emotional reactions, which confirmed an underlying cultural anxiety about death (Yalom 2009).

Whether this debate was a boon or a bane to EOL care remains to be seen. Nonetheless, heightened interest in healthcare in general and EOL care in particular provided an opportunity to discuss and reevaluate EOL care as practiced in the United States, and more specifically within the Department of Veterans Affairs (VA) Medical Center (VAMC) system. Toward that end, this chapter 1) defines and clarifies EOL care, 2) reviews recent history and current VA initiatives, 3) explains existing VA policies, 4) explores quality and costs, 5) discusses EOL care challenges, 6) presents recent developments, and 7) previews new directions in EOL care.

Before defining relevant terms it is important to note that EOL care has become increasingly relevant because of changes in population demographics, timing of death, and the process of dying (Field & Cassel 1997). People are aging and dying in the United States in unprecedented numbers due to recent population and public health trends. Baby boomers are aging, and by 2030, 20 percent of U.S. citizens will be of retirement age (Field & Cassel 1997).

In addition, the way people are dying has changed dramatically over the last fifty years. Due to medical advances and the success of public health and safety initiatives, people are less likely to die from acute events, such as infections and accidents. Death tends to come later in life after a protracted course of physical decline (Emanuel, von Gunten & Ferris 2005). This protracted decline, necessitating long-term care, provides caregivers and patients a much greater array of care choices (National Cancer Institute 2002).

Many in our aging population are veterans. Veterans of the World War II, Korean, and Vietnam eras are now dying at an estimated rate of 1,600 per day (Beresford 2004). Deborah Grassman (2007) reported that 600,000 veterans died in 2006, comprising one-fourth of all deaths in the United States. Within the Veterans Health Administration (VHA), which administers the VAMC system, there is a recognized need to expand our ability to meet dying veterans' needs and expectations (Beresford 2004). VHA has demonstrated a firm commitment to meet that need through recent initiatives and policy changes designed to ensure high-quality EOL, palliative, and hospice care for all veterans (Veterans Health Administration 2005).

Defining End-of-Life Care

EOL care refers to medical, psychological, and spiritual treatment interventions to help patients who are dying. Palliative care, designed to improve patients' quality of life, often plays an important role in EOL care (Morrison

& Meier 2004). Hospice care refers to palliative care, provided by medical and psychosocial professionals, in either home-based or inpatient settings, which is specialized to meet the needs of patients with terminal illness: those who have an estimated life expectancy of less than six months (Connor 2009). Palliative EOL care differs from hospice care in terms of estimated remaining life span for the patient.

Palliative care includes medical, psychosocial, and spiritual treatments that seek to relieve pain and suffering in patients with advanced, but not necessarily life-limiting, illness (Steinhauser et al. 2000; Singer et al. 1998). Common symptoms targeted with palliative interventions include shortness of breath, insomnia, constipation agitation, pain, and nausea, as well as spiritual and emotional discomfort. Palliative care may be used in addition to curative treatments or in lieu of traditional and/or curative medical interventions, depending on patient needs and wants (Field & Cassel 1997).

Palliative EOL care is patient-centered (Connor 2009), with treatment teams acting as consultants to the patient. Treatment teams provide information about available interventions, possible intervention consequences, and when available, outcome data for various interventions. Then the patient or a medical proxy decides what course of treatment to pursue. This patient-centered approach reflects widely held expectations that medical providers need to satisfy the patient as an active consumer, rather than a passive recipient, of healthcare (CHCC 2010). Today's healthcare consumers are more likely to seek collaborative relationships with their care providers than their grandparents and great-grandparents were. Rather than the benevolent authority figure characterized by Robert Young as Marcus Welby, MD in the popular television series of the early 1970s, healthcare providers increasingly act as valued and knowledgeable consultants to patients who prefer to direct their own care.

In light of the current zeitgeist toward empowerment of patients as healthcare consumers (CHCC 2010), it is difficult to believe that U.S. President Franklin Delano Roosevelt was not told by his primary physician that he was dying (Smith 2008). The fact that his trusted physician kept this information from FDR may seem quaintly paternalistic or disturbingly irresponsible, depending on one's point of view. When viewed through the lens of postmodern sensibilities, the relationship between FDR and his physician vividly illustrates how expectations about physician-patient relationships have changed.

Advance care planning (ACP) has been defined as a process "whereby a patient, in consultation with health care providers, family members and important others, makes decisions about his or her future health care should he or she become incapable of participating in medical treatment decisions" (Singer, Robertson & Roy 1996, 1689). The purpose of ACP is to educate the patient about her or his illness and relevant medical care choices, thereby empowering patients to make informed decisions about current and future medical interventions (Singer, Robertson & Roy 1996). Typically this process produces advance directives that designate a substitute decision maker or medical proxy, named by the patient, to make medical care decisions should the patient become incapable of deciding. Ideally the medical proxy is an individual who knows and attempts to follow patient care preferences.

Effective advance care planning requires dedicated, competent medical staff and strong organizational commitment with supportive policies and procedures. Research demonstrates that despite the level of commitment and staff resources required, ACP improves outcomes for patients (Hammes & Rooney 1998; Briggs 2004), decreases anxiety and depression in family members of the deceased (Hammes & Rooney 1998), and results in higher quality of life near EOL (Detering et al. 2010; Lautrette et al. 2007; Wright et al. 2008).

Holistic, palliative EOL care, provided by multidisciplinary teams (Gazelle 2007), is designed to provide care for a broad spectrum of patient needs. Teams may consist of physicians, physician's assistants, nurses, nursing assistants, social workers, psychologists, chaplains or other spiritual practitioners, musical therapists, physical therapists, and volunteers. A team-based approach is essential in treating the patient as a whole person, rather than a set of symptoms (Mount 1993), addressing psychological (Morita et al. 2000), spiritual (Hampton et al. 2007), social, and physical needs with sensitivity to multicultural issues (Smith, Sudore & Perez-Stable 2009).

Palliative EOL care is patient-centered, emphasizing patient treatment in the context of social support networks (Connor 2009). Although there is only one identified patient, there is often an assortment of relatives and loved ones who are deeply impacted by the patient's illness. At times these persons play a decision-making role, as medical proxies, when the patient is incapacitated. Hospice and palliative EOL treatment teams seek to understand the needs of patients, their caregiver(s), and other social support systems (Patterson & Dorfman 2002). Casarett and colleagues (2003) surveyed caregivers; they requested that palliative EOL care treatment teams provide 1) symptom management for the patient; 2) regular communication regarding patient condition by phone or face-to-face; 3) consistent contact despite shift changes; and 4) education about specific signs and symptoms of impending death, so that family and loved ones know what to expect with regard to the course of the illness. Needs of significant others comprise an important part of multifaceted treatment issues addressed by palliative EOL care teams caring for dying patients.

When so many different individuals work together to help patients and their families, it is important to ensure mutual understanding among providers and recipients of care about what is being done, by whom, to whom, for what purpose, and with what outcome. Communication among the treatment team, patient, and family regarding goals of care is a critical component of palliative EOL care, necessary to coordinate services and ensure that patient needs are met and preferences honored. Dialogue among and between patient and providers is an iterative process encompassing specific treatment options and their affect on patient well-being.

For the treatment team the most important source of information is often the patient. In an extensive literature review, Kaldjian and associates (2009) provided a framework of six general goals of care for patients facing the end of life, to be used as a *starting point* in discussing patient preferences and priorities. Individual patients rank these overall goals in order of personal importance to elucidate their specific EOL care goals. Goals of care include 1) recovery/curing disease; 2) prolonging quantity of life; 3) positively impacting quality of life, such as level of control and independence; 4) providing palliation or relief from suffering; 5) assisting patients in achieving personal aspirations, such as attending a certain social event or mending relationship conflict; and 6) supporting the patient's family/caregivers during the dying process and after the patient has died.

When the patient identifies alleviation of suffering as a primary treatment goal, such as in the case of advanced, chronic, terminal illness deemed incurable, palliative EOL care becomes the primary treatment modality. However, goals of care may change, hence the need for open and ongoing dialogue among all participants in the patient's dying process, to ensure necessary responsiveness and flexibility.

In sum, the focus of palliative EOL care is on patient quality of life. EOL care allows the patient to pursue treatment for life-limiting illness with a focus on quality of life and comfort rather than cure, thereby benefiting from both traditional medicine and more holistic, alternative approaches, according to patient needs and preferences (Mount 1993). EOL care providers seek to restore dignity, comfort, and autonomy to the dying patient. The popularity of palliative medicine reflects a shift toward a collaborative process in which a multidisciplinary treatment team acts as consultant to the patient and the family, with an emphasis on restoring quality of life rather than prolonging quantity of life at all costs.

History and Current VA Initiatives

Stephen R. Connor, PhD, senior executive of the Worldwide Palliative Care Alliance (WPCA), wrote an excellent overview of palliative care development in the United States over the last three decades (Connor 2009). He traced palliative care from its beginnings in 1963 with lectures at the Yale School of Nursing to 1973, when hospice care was first delivered to patients in Branford, Connecticut. He pointed out the preference for in-home care in the United States versus inpatient preference in the United Kingdom, where the modern hospice movement began. Another milestone was the establishment of the Hospice Medicare Benefit in 1982, which provided much-needed fiscal support. He expressed the primary challenge of EOL care, to achieve "unfettered access to quality palliative care for all who need it" (Connor 2009, 98).

As recently as 2002 VA had not established a reliable way to meet hospice and palliative care needs of U.S. veterans (Edes, Shreve & Casarett 2007). At that time veteran deaths were near an all-time high. VA palliative care clinics were offering some unique approaches to improving EOL care for outpatients not enrolled for hospice care (Casarett et al. 2003). However, few VA hospitals offered inpatient palliative care services. Therefore, VA set in motion impressive changes that within three years instituted palliative care teams in all VA hospitals and established nationwide partnerships with community-based hospice agencies, to dramatically increase EOL care for veterans (Edes, Shreve & Casarett 2007).

These hospice partnerships provide care for older veterans in nursing homes, thereby reducing unnecessary prescription medication and the likelihood of adverse drug reactions and interactions (Suhrie et al. 2009). Given the significant increase in veterans receiving VA-sponsored or VA direct palliative care, there is a dire need to clarify trajectories and patterns of dying to improve EOL care plans and best utilize limited VA resources. VA is now established, through both delivery of services and research, as a leader in EOL care and has the potential to play a major role in the development of targeted interventions to address differing dying trajectories (Duffy et al. 2007). Recently VA researchers have developed a nationwide quality of care survey measure. The Family Assessment of Treatment at End of Life (FATE) survey provides an important source of data to improve EOL care for veterans, whatever the type of care and wherever delivered (Finlay, Shreve & Casarett 2008). Continued commitment to improved access to and quality of EOL care is further validated by innovative palliative care educational initiatives, relevant interdisciplinary literature, and research offered through the Veterans Integrated Service Network (VISN) (Howe & Sherman 2006).

Policy

Per national policy set by the Veterans Health Administration (VHA), hospice and palliative care are available to all veterans enrolled in the VA healthcare system as a paid benefit for their honorable service (VHA 2005). Each VAMC must 1) provide EOL care, including inpatient palliative and hospice care, and 2) make home hospice care available in the community with fee-based services depending on veterans' preferences and needs.

Each VAMC has a designated Palliative Care Consult Team (PCCT) available throughout the facility to provide education for providers and patients about EOL care. Another important mandate for the PCCT is to partner with community hospice agencies for a variety of purposes. First, the PCCT is able to offer referrals to community hospice when patients choose to spend their final days at home rather than in the hospital. Second, the PCCT is charged with educating home hospice providers about dying veterans' needs (Grassman 2007). Per policy, each VAMC must collect ongoing data regarding the demand for EOL care services so that each facility is able to adapt accordingly to meet the needs of dying veterans. Finally, hospice-veteran partnerships within national VAMCs are designed to develop and promote universal standards for EOL care throughout the VA hospital system (Beresford 2004).

The scope of EOL care covered though the VAMC is designed to be comprehensive and flexible. VHA-mandated EOL care benefits cover a wide array of interventions and services, including inpatient hospice and home or community-based services for both veteran and caregiver, with home visits by doctors, nurses, social workers, and volunteers. Additional covered benefits include medications; supplies; biological, durable medical equipment; ancillary services; and bereavement care. VHA has developed policies promoting program development, staff training, and education, national policy guidelines, and community partnerships to ensure systemwide integration of services so that all veterans can receive quality EOL care at the level they need. EOL care for veterans must be sufficiently flexible to meet a variety of veteran needs and preferences. Toward promoting continuity of care for veterans, each VAMC PCCT works in collaboration with community hospice providers by offering complementary services and facilitating veteran patients' movement among different treatment settings depending on level of care needed and desired. For example, transition to inpatient hospice from home-based care may occur when pain and other symptoms cannot be managed at home or when patients require hospitalization for reasons unrelated to their terminal diagnosis. VA inpatient care can be ongoing if the patient and family require it, or short-term until the patient's symptoms are stabilized, followed by a return to home hospice.

Partnerships between VAMC PCCTs and local non-VA providers represent an important opportunity to educate non-VA partners about the special needs of many dying veterans. Grassman (2007) reported that although one-quarter of people dying in the United States in 2006 were veterans, most veterans did not die in a VAMC. Instead they were cared for by healthcare providers outside the VA system, who may be unfamiliar with the unique needs of the veteran population. Grassman provided highly practical suggestions from PCCTs training local hospice providers to work with veterans, including identifying at the outset whether or not clients are veterans so that they may receive EOL care benefits from their preferred VA treatment provider. In addition, she advises determining whether the veteran has a history of combat and/or trauma. Such veterans, she cautions, may have developed an attitude of stoicism, which may complicate the dying process, especially if they underreport symptoms of pain or emotional distress or resist surrendering to the dying process. In addition, terminally ill veterans, with a history of causing death or loss to others as a result of their role in combat situations, may require intensive spiritual healing as well as a safe emotional environment in order to grieve. Finally, terminally ill patients who have suffered from anxiety related to combat trauma may need to retain "as much control as possible" over the dying process (Grassman 2007). Based on recent policy and ensuing changes in available EOL care in the VAMC system, VHA has demonstrated a strong commitment to providing an impressive range of quality care EOL options for dying veterans as part of their covered health benefits. There is also mounting evidence that palliative EOL care is both preferred by the majority of patients and more economical for healthcare institutions (Smith et al. 2003; Center to Advance Palliative Care 2010).

Quality and Cost

Data suggest that ACP encourages patients to choose less invasive and costly modes of care. When patients and their families have an opportunity to discuss EOL treatment options with a palliative care team before they are actively dying, they tend to make medical decisions that significantly shorten their subsequent stay in an intensive care unit, but not total length of stay in the hospital (Norton et al. 2007). These researchers report that patient mortality rates are not affected by palliative consult.

The Functional Living Index-Cancer was designed to be used by patients to assess general well-being across social, psychological, and somatic domains, and has demonstrated sound psychometric properties (Schipper et al. 1984). Support groups reduced stress and depression experienced by caregivers (Mittelman et al. 1996; Mittelman, Ferris & Shulman 1995). Undertreatment of symptoms remained a problem (SUPPORT Investigators 1995; Bernabei et al. 1998). However, Gelfman and associates (2008) demonstrated in their study that palliative care consultation is associated with improved satisfaction, attention to family concerns, and enhanced self-efficacy. Palliative care offered a unique approach by integrating family needs into patient care.

Research addressing the effectiveness of palliative EOL care and associated cost reductions suggests that palliative EOL care is better for patients and hospital budgets. Health care experts cite evidence that traditional medicine fails to meet the needs of dying patients suffering from untreated pain and other distressing symptoms (SUPPORT Investigators 1995; Bernabei et al. 1998), and often leads to long-term hospitalization involving unwanted, largely ineffective, and costly medical treatments, with low family satisfaction (Casarett et al. 2008; Morrison & Meier 2004; Hogan et al. 2001). After reviewing research into cost effectiveness of curative versus palliative medical treatment at the end of life, Emanuel (1996) concludes that ACP and hospice care saves between 25 and 40 percent in healthcare costs during the last month of life, decreasing to 10 to 17 percent over the last six months and further decreasing to 0 to 10 percent over the last twelve months of life. Clearly, time frame impacts cost savings. Based on these findings, he argues that EOL care, including hospice and advance care planning, should be available to patients in the final stages of life. Research confirms that palliative treatment costs less than traditional approaches and provides patients a say in what happens to them when so much else is beyond their control.

Theis and associates (2007) cited the importance of research assessing financial costs associated with various treatment options, specifically with regard to curative versus palliative interventions with the terminally ill. Existing comparative data tend to demonstrate the cost effectiveness of palliative treatment measures over treatment interventions designed to cure illness, while ensuring that patient and family needs are met.

More recently, Brumley and associates (2007) examined homebound, terminally ill patients, randomly assigned to either traditional medical care or in-home palliative intervention care in conjunction with traditional care. Palliative care included essential pain and symptom relief, family education and training, and psychosocial support. Patients in the intervention group reported greater satisfaction thirty to ninety days after enrollment, were more likely to die at home, were less likely to visit the emergency department, and were less likely to be admitted to the hospital. As a result of less-intensive services, care costs for the intervention group were significantly lower than for the control group. Morrison and colleagues (2008) studied cost of palliative versus traditional care in medical inpatients. They reported that among patients eventually discharged from the hospital alive, there was a savings of $1,696 in direct costs per admission. And for 2,630 out of 2,966 palliative care patients, matched with patients receiving traditional care, a $279 savings in direct costs per day was found. There was an even greater cost reduction among palliative care patients who died during their hospitalization. For these patients compared to the control group, there was an adjusted net savings of $4,908 in direct costs per admission and $374 in direct costs per day.

Challenges

Capacity Questions and Care Planning

The capacity of informal caregivers typically wanes over time, due to advancing age and physical or psychological circumstances. Therefore, challenges of planning for and providing quality EOL care increase. A longer-term perspective that considers short-term, mid-range, and long-term issues is recommended (Reuben 2009). Dr. Reuben suggests, after an assessment of life expectancy, an emphasis on restoration of health in the first year, preventative care and psychosocial support in year one through five, and beyond year five, on planning for decline and meeting EOL goals. This framework provides a means of segmenting the hospice and palliative patient population, and addresses some of the pressing problems of managing EOL care, given medical practitioner time constraints.

The clinical course of advanced dementia presents even more of a challenge in providing quality care and successful transitioning from attempts to cure toward providing palliative care (Mitchell et al. 2009). Mitchell and colleagues followed 323 advanced-dementia residents in twenty-two nursing homes for eighteen months. Over half of the residents died (54.8 percent), and although eating and infection problems were prevalent, the underlying cause of death was their major illness, dementia. The likelihood of receiving comfort care as opposed to questionable, aggressive care interventions was found to be a consequence of the quality of counseling provided to healthcare agents or proxies. When proxies understood poor prognoses, residents were less likely to experience aggressive, life-saving interventions near the end of life.

Ethical Issues

End-of-life situations often lead to ethical dilemmas for dying persons as well as their professional and informal caregivers (Werth & Kleespies 2006). Ethical decision making at the end of life has become more complex because of the capabilities of medical technology to sustain life, sometimes life of painful and questionable quality, when comfort care may be the better option (Mularski et al. 2009). Helping professionals providing psychosocial support for patients and families near the end of life requires specific training and preparation for dealing with and helping to resolve ethical issues (Werth & Blevins 2006).

The choice to terminate curative care and seek comfort or hospice (i.e., palliative) care "challenges courts, legislatures, health professionals, and bioethicists to discern humane and morally acceptable ways of assisting patients and their families as death approaches" (Young 1998, 267).

Some base their ethical reasoning on the Hippocratic principles of nonmalificence and beneficence, along with more recent principles of autonomy and justice (Hinshaw 2008). Others, at VA for example, focus on current and varying ethical priorities of managers concerned with equitable distribution of resources; clinicians worried about resource constraints impacting patient care; ethics committee emphasis on EOL care; and perhaps most important, patients' desire for what they consider fair and respectful care (Foglia et al. 2009). Renowned medical ethicist Edmund Pellegrino (2006) points to the moral centrality of the healing relationship. He states: "The physician cannot fully heal without giving the patient an understanding of alternatives such that he or she can freely arrive—together with the physician—at a decision in keeping with his or her personal morality and values" (2006, 65). Pellegrino expresses concern that our pluralistic society precludes universal agreement between physicians and patients in regard to ethical and moral issues.

However, the impetus to develop a "best practice" integrated or universal model of palliative care may be elusive for good reason. Recent analysis of palliative care ethical practices and statements of thirty-four health organizations, including seven international and twenty-seven national organizations operating in Australia, Canada, the United Kingdom, and the United States, found no clear integrated model of ethical practice:

> It might be argued that the lack of a fixed and coherent model is due to the relevance of unavoidable context issues in palliative care, such as specific cultural settings, patient-centered variables, and family specificity. The implication is that palliative care staff has continuously to adapt their model of caring to the specific needs and values of each patient, more than applying a fixed, although maybe comprehensive, care model. (Barazzetti et al. 2010, 1)

In contrast to these views, Casarett (2005) suggests there is an urgent need for research to define a standard of palliative care and improve access to quality care. Ethical concerns of palliative care research include presenting potential benefits or risks to future patients or study participants while considering decision-making capacity to ensure voluntary participation (Casarett 2005). Ethical outcomes are placed at risk when opportunities to understand patient and patient family perspectives and preferences are missed; opportunities to listen and respond to families, to acknowledge and discuss emotions, and to share key principles of medical ethics should not be overlooked (Curtis et al. 2005).

Ageism and Euthanasia

The ethical peril of ageism and the preference for providing sometimes limited resources to young patients rather than older ones is significantly reduced when research participants reflect on a broad range of moral principles (Johri et al. 2009). From a professional nursing perspective, dying patients remain a relatively vulnerable group in U.S. healthcare institutions, caught in the struggle to balance provision of palliative care with curative interventions (Robley 2008). A longitudinal study of attitudes toward physician-assisted suicide and euthanasia (Pacheco et al. 2003) shows how attitudes of terminally ill patients change as they approach the end of life. Although healthy persons tend to support their right to prematurely end their own lives, this study confirms that significant changes in the use of social-emotional support and religious resources actually lead patients to become less supportive of legalizing such options in spite of approaching death.

Recent Developments

Evolving Perceptions of Palliative Care (2000–2010)

Over the last decade interest in palliative care has increased in the United States (Byock et al. 2006) and internationally (Ahmedzai et al. 2004; Centeno et al. 2007). Attempts to understand and describe EOL care phenomena have produced numerous and sometimes conflicting research and care perspectives. Some have discussed quality of life in spite of approaching death, including calls for more comprehensive and generalizable research on care structures and clinical outcomes (Morrison 2005) and development of measures to evaluate quality of life at the end of life (Steinhauser et al. 2002). Others were more interested in quality of death and focused on the quality of care for patients in the process of dying (Bailey et al. 2005) and differences of opinion on the components of a good death (Gibson et al. 2008); some debated the futility or utility of such care (Rodriguez & Young 2006) and the place of hope near the EOL (Back, Arnold & Quill 2003; Kylmä et al. 2009).

Near the turn of the new millennium palliative care was proposed as an international human right (Ahmedzai et al. 2004; Gwyther, Brennan & Harding 2009). The fact that tens of thousands of veterans from World War II, Korea, and more recent conflicts were dying each month of the past decade meant that palliative care for veterans was an essential part of the conversation (Casarett et al. 2008; Hwang et al. 2003; Jones et al. 2006). The Casarett and associates study of 2008 pointed out that numerous aspects of EOL care for veterans of most concern to family members were not addressed in current survey instruments. In 2003 Hwang and colleagues conducted research that found racial and patient-perceived health status disparities among veteran cancer patients and suggested informed, veteran-rated health status as a potential explanatory variable for survival and EOL care trajectories. The Jones and colleagues study in 2006 confirmed continued underutilization of palliative care services despite the great strides in providing such care to veterans (Daratsos & Howe 2007).

Given the moral obligation and social mandate to provide quality EOL care for our aging veterans, VHA and partner organizations, both formal and informal, have a crucial part to play in refining and improving palliative care services (Chong et al. 2004; Duffy et al. 2007; Edes, Shreve & Casarett 2007). For that reason, among others, VA recently initiated a nationwide assessment of quality of care at the end of life. The first phase of this national initiative, entitled Family Assessment of Treatment at End of Life (FATE), was conducted six weeks after veterans' deaths and among other findings reported higher family members' satisfaction associated with palliative and hospice care consultation and referral (Finlay, Shreve & Casarett 2008).

Person-Centered Palliative Care

Promotion of ethics and excellence in palliative care may best be served by a person-centered perspective. Participants and persons of interest in palliative care include professional care providers, informal caregivers, often family members, and patients; the emphasis here is on veteran patients and their families. The Robert Wood Johnson Foundation recently funded twenty-two demonstration projects focused on promoting excellence in end-of-life care to develop models for delivering palliative care to patients and their families (Byock et al. 2006). These innovative projects demonstrated the feasibility of providing quality EOL care acceptable to patients, families, clinicians, funders, and administrators alike. Key factors essential to excellence were individual patient and family assessment and aligning current resources and services with specific patient and family needs, that is, centering attention on the persons/patients and families dealing with the realities of EOL care.

Current palliative care in developed countries seldom restricts care to incurable disease; therefore, the World Health Organization introduced an updated definition in 2002:

> Palliative care is an approach that improves the quality of life of patients and their families facing the problems associated with life-threatening illness, through the prevention and relief of suffering by means of early identification and impeccable assessment and treatment of pain and other problems, physical, psychosocial and spiritual. (Ahmedzai et al. 2004, 2193)

The emphasis of the definition is on patients and their families. Further, there is a need to consider individual trajectories in the dying process and the key role of VHA, given its extensive experience providing palliative care to dying veterans (Duffy et al. 2007). In fact, VA has been a leader in palliative and hospice care for several decades (Daratsos & Howe 2007). VA has also promoted serious consideration of ethical issues as viewed by various stakeholders, including managers' concerns about fair allocation of resources; clinicians' concerns about resource constraints on care; ethics committee chairpersons' concerns with EOL care; and perhaps most important from a person-centered perspective, patients' concerns with receiving treatment that is caring, respectful, and fair (Foglia et al. 2009). Further, when VAMC physicians need to refer a veteran patient to an outside hospice program, there is understandable concern about the quality of such care. One measure of importance is the degree to which a given program is patient- and family-centered. Although there are some validated tools to measure perceptions of the quality of hospice care from patient and family perspectives, improved definitions and measurements are necessary to guide preferred, person-centered care choices (Teno & Connor 2009).

Studies have consistently demonstrated that patients with life-threatening illness experienced untreated pain and other symptoms; lengthy hospitalizations, often involving unwanted low-yield and costly medical treatments; and low overall family satisfaction (Casarett et al. 2008; Morrison & Meier 2004; Hogan et al. 2001).

New Directions

Priorities set by the Centers for Disease Control and the National Association of Chronic Disease Directors include the need to adopt universal standards of care for EOL (Theis et al. 2007). However, EOL care must remain flexible and responsive to the changing needs of patients and their support systems. For example, at the time of diagnosis, a patient may begin treatment on an outpatient basis through a clinic. Depending on the course of the illness, subsequent inpatient hospice care, home-based primary care, home hospice care, and/or nursing home placement may be necessary to adequately treat this patient's illness and related problems. Improved continuity of care is needed to facilitate level of care transitions, ensure patient comfort, and prevent caregiver burnout.

EOL care and palliative treatment need to be a fundamental part of training for medical practitioners. There is a need to review the percentage of medical residency and nursing programs that offer or require training in EOL care. Specifically, medical training needs to increase provider sensitivity to EOL issues and the provider's personal responses to terminal illness. Healthcare providers need to be aware of possible bias toward heroic, lifesaving measures. To combat misrepresentation of palliative EOL care as treatment signifying physician failure to cure, palliative measures should be promoted as compassionate and highly valued services that practitioners provide their dying patients. Healthcare providers need to be familiar with criteria for referral for EOL care (Theis et al. 2007). Adequate understanding of the needs of dying patients and their families, as well as methods in palliative EOL care, may also enable practitioners to make more timely diagnoses and referrals for consultation with palliative care providers.

In addition to caregiver attitudes, physician-patient communication is an important part of provider skills training (Magauren & Brennan 2005; Curtis 2004; Larson & Tobin 2000; Ptacek & Eberhardt 1996). With regard to ACP and palliative EOL care, medical providers need to engage in collaborative prognostic decision making with patients (Knight et al. 1992). Toward this end, Alderman, Baishali & Fox (2008) describe a promising training program designed to increase medical residents' competence and confidence in assisting patients with advanced care planning. Medical training programs need to make such evidence-based curricula a fundamental part of provider education.

Some internal medicine programs do integrate palliative care content that is currently being tested as part of the American Board of Internal Medicine examination. Improved palliative care knowledge has been confirmed during internal medicine residency (Olden et al. 2009). Further, a palliative care course and subsequent evaluation of a cohort of Dutch residents in internal medicine not surprisingly found that engagement in more palliative cases and length of clinical experience has a positive influence on perceived EOL care competence (Mulder et al. 2009).

Conclusion

Despite recent controversy over "death panels," the impact of palliative and hospice EOL care perspectives is here to stay. Both national and international definitions have evolved, honoring voices of multiple medical care disciplines, patients, their caregivers, and loved ones. Historical and recent initiatives have improved quality of care for dying persons, supported by appropriate policies, sound economics, and ethical imperatives. Recent developments and new directions predict continued improvement in meeting dying patients' needs and care preferences.

Over the last decade the extensive VHA system has established clear palliative care policy initiatives, while VAMCs and clinics have provided care for tens of thousands of dying veterans. VHA has emerged as a leader among healthcare institutions in the necessary transformation of EOL care. Benefits of these efforts for dying veterans and their families are profound. Illness and death always involve loss, but untoward suffering is no longer acceptable. Though death remains a mystery, care of the dying need not be.

References

Ahmedzai, S. H., Costa, A., Blengini, C., Bosch, A., Sanz-Ortiz, J., Ventafridda, V., et al. (2004). A new international framework for palliative care. *European Journal of Cancer* 40, no. 15: 2192–2200.

Alderman, J. S., Baishali, N. & Fox, M. D. (2008). Resident training in advanced care planning: Can it be done in the outpatient setting? *American Journal of Hospice & Palliative Medicine* 25: 190–194.

American Society of Clinical Oncology. (1998). Cancer care during the last phase of life. *Journal of Clinical Oncology* 16: 1986–1996.

Annas, G. J. (2005). "Culture of life" politics at the bedside: The case of Terri Shiavo. *New England Journal of Medicine* 352: 1710–1715.

Back, A. L., Arnold, R. M. & Quill, T. E. (2003). Hope for the best, and prepare for the worst. *Annals of Internal Medicine* 138: 439–443.

Bailey, F. A., Burgio, K. L., Woodby, L. L., Williams, B. R., Redden, D. T., Kovac, S. H., et al. (2005). Improving processes of hospital care during the last hours of life. *Archives of Internal Medicine* 165: 1722–1727.

Barazzetti, G., Borreani, C., Miccinesi, G. & Toscani, F. (2010). What "best practice" could be in palliative care: An analysis of statements on practice and ethics expressed by the main health organizations. *BMC Palliative Care* 9: 1.

Beresford, L. (2004). VA transforms end-of-life care for veterans. http//www.1.va/gov/geriatricshg/docs/vatransform.

Bernabei, R., Gambassi, G., Lampane, K., et al. (1998). Management of pain in elderly patients with cancer. *Journal of the American Medical Association* 279: 1877–1882.

Briggs, L. (2004). Shifting the focus of advance care planning: Using an in-depth interview to build and strengthen relationships. *Journal of Palliative Medicine* 7: 341–349.

Brumley, R., Enguidanos, S., Jamison, P., Seitz, R., Morgenstern, N., Saito, S., McIl-wane, J., Hillary, K. & Gonzales, J. (2007). Increased satisfaction with care and lower costs: Results of a randomized trial of in-home palliative care. *Journal of the American Geriatrics Society* 55: 993–1000.

Byock, I., Twohig, J. S., Merriman, M. & Collins, K. (2006). Promoting excellence in end-of-life care: a report on innovative models of palliative care. *Journal of Palliative Medicine* 9: 137–151.

Casarett, D. (2005). Ethical considerations in end-of-life care and research. *Journal of Palliative Medicine* 8, supp. 1: S148–S160.

Casarett, D., Pickard, A., Bailey, F. A., Ritchie, C., Furman, C., Rosenfeld, K., et al. (2008). Important aspects of end-of-life care among veterans: Implications for measurement and quality improvement. *Journal of Pain and Symptom Management* 35: 115–125.

Casarett, D. J., Hirschman, K. B., Crowley, R., Galbraith, L. D. & Leo, M. (2003). Caregivers' satisfaction with hospice care in the last 24 hours of life. *American Journal of Hospice & Palliative Medicine* 20: 205–210.

Centeno, C., Clark, D., Lynch, T., Racafort, J., Praill, D., De Lima, L., et al. (2007). Facts and indicators on palliative care development in 52 countries of the WHO European region: Results of an EAPC Task Force. *Palliative Medicine* 21: 463–471.

Center to Advance Palliative Care. (2010). http://www.capc.org/building-a-hospice-based-palliative-care-program/financing/cost-savings.

Chong, K., Olson, E. M., Banc, T. E., Cohen, S., Anderson-Malico, R. & Penrod, J. D. (2004). Types and rate of implementation of palliative care team recommendations for care of hospitalized veterans. *Journal of Palliative Medicine* 7: 784–790.

Collins, L. G., Parks, S. M. & Winter, L. (2006). The state of advance care planning: one decade after SUPPORT. *American Journal of Hospice & Palliative Medicine* 23: 378–423.

Connor, S. J. (2009). *Hospice and Palliative Care: The Essential Guide/Edition 2*. New York: Routledge.

Consumers for Health Care Choices (CHCC). (2010). http://www.chcchoices.org/about.html.

Curtis, J. R. (2004). Communicating about end-of-life care with patients and families in the intensive care unit. *Critical Care Clinician* 20: 363–380.

Curtis, J. R., Engelberg, R. A., Wenrich, M. D. & Au, D. H. (2005). Communication about palliative care for patients with chronic obstructive pulmonary disorder. *Journal of Palliative Care* 21: 157–164.

Danis, M., Southerland, L. I. & Garrett, J. M. (1991). A perspective study of advance directives for life-sustaining care. *New England Journal of Medicine* 324: 882–888.

Daratsos, L. & Howe, J. L. (2007). The development of palliative care programs in the Veterans Administration: Zelda Foster's legacy. *Journal of Social Work in End-of-Life & Palliative Care* 3: 29–39.

Department of Veterans Affairs, Employee Education System and Durham Veteran's Affairs Medical Center. (2005). *Education for physicians on end-of-life care participant's handbook*. Washington, DC: Department of Veterans Affairs.

Detering, K. M., Hancock, A. D., Reade, M. C. & Silvester, W. (2010). The impact of advance care planning on end of life care in elderly patients: randomized controlled trial. *British Medical Journal* 340: c1345. http://group.bmj.com/group/media/press-release-archive-files/BMJ/bmj-2010/BMJ.

Duffy, S. A., Copeland, L. A., Hopp, F. P. & Zalenski, R. J. (2007). Diagnostic classifications and resource utilization of decedents served by the Department of Veterans Affairs. *Journal of Palliative Medicine* 10: 1137–1145.

Edes, T., Shreve, S. & Casarett, D. (2007). Increasing access and quality in Department of Veterans Affairs care at the end of life: A lesson in change. *Journal of the American Geriatrics Society* 55: 1645–1649.

Emanuel, E. J. (1996). Cost savings at the end of life. *Journal of the American Medical Association* 275: 1907–1914.

Emanuel, L. L., von Gunten, C. F., Ferris, F. D. (Eds.). (2005). *The education for physicians on end-of-life care (EPEC) curriculum.* EPEC Project. The Robert Wood Johnson Foundation.

Field, M. J. & Cassel, C. K. (Eds.). (1997). *Approaching death: Improving care at the end of life.* Washington, DC: National Academy Press.

Finlay, E., Shreve, S. & Casarett, D. (2008). Nationwide veterans affairs quality measure for cancer: the family assessment of treatment at end of life. *Journal of Clinical Oncology* 26: 3838–3844.

Foglia, M. B., Pearlman, R. A., Bottrell, M., Altemose, J. K. & Fox, E. (2009). Ethical challenges within Veterans Administration healthcare facilities: Perspectives of managers, clinicians, patients, and ethics committee chairpersons. *American Journal of Bioethics* 9: 28–36.

Gazelle, G. (2007). Understanding hospice: An underutilized option for life's final chapter. *New England Journal of Medicine* 357: 321–324.

Gelfman, L. P., Meier D. E., et al. (2008). Does palliative care improve quality? A survey of bereaved family members. *Journal of Pain and Symptom Management* 36: 22–28.

Gibson, M. C., Gutmanis, I., Clarke, H., Wiltshire, D., Feron, A. & Gorman, E. (2008). Staff opinions about the components of a good death in long-term care. *International Journal of Palliative Nursing* 14, no. 8: 374–381.

Grassman, D. (2007). *Veterans: An underserved population.* Washington, DC: American Hospice Foundation. http://www.americanhospice.org/_article/veteranunderserved.pdf.

Gwyther, L., Brennan, F. & Harding, R. (2009). Advancing palliative care as a human right. *Journal of Pain and Symptom Management* 38: 767–774.

Hammes, B. J. & Rooney, B. L. (1998). Death and end-of-life planning in one midwestern community. *Archives of Internal Medicine* 158: 383–390.

Hampton, D. M., Hollis, D. E., Taylor, J. & McMillan, S. C. (2007). Spiritual needs of persons with advanced cancer. *American Journal of Hospice & Palliative Medicine* 24: 42–48.

Hanson, L. C., Tulsky, J. & Danis, M. (1997). Can clinical interventions change care at the end of life? *Annals of Internal Medicine* 126: 381–388.

Hinshaw, D. B. (2008). Ethical issues in end-of-life care. *Le Journal Médical Libanais (The Lebanese Medical Journal)* 56, no. 2: 122–128.

Hirschman, K. B., Coffey, J. F. & Pierre, L. (2002). Does a palliative care clinic have a role in improving end of life care? *American Journal of Hospice and Palliative Care* 20, no. 3: 205–210.

Hogan, C., Lunney, J., Gavel, J. & Lynn, J. (2001). Medicare beneficiaries' costs of care in the last year of life. *Health Affairs* 20: 188–195.

Howe, J. L. & Sherman, D. W. (2006). Interdisciplinary educational approaches to promote team-based geriatrics and palliative care. *Gerontology & Geriatrics Education* 26: 1–16.

Hwang, S. S., Chang, V. T., Alejandro, Y., Osenenko, P., Davis, C., Cogswell, J., et al. (2003). Caregiver unmet needs, burden, and satisfaction in symptomatic advanced cancer patients at a Veterans Affairs (VA) Medical Center. *Palliative & Supportive Care* 1: 319–329.

Johri, M., Damschroder, L. J., Zikmund-Fisher, B. J., Kim, S. Y. H. & Ubel, P. A. (2009). Can a moral reasoning exercise improve response quality to surveys of healthcare priorities? *Journal of Medical Ethics* 35: 57–64.

Jones, D., Edes, T., Shreve, S. & Casarett, D. J. (2006). You won't know if you're improving unless you measure: Recommendations for evaluating hospice-veteran partnerships. *Journal of Pain and Symptom Management* 32: 488–496.

Kaldjian, L. C., Curtis, A. E., Shinkunas, L. A. & Cannon, K. T. (2009). Goals of care toward the end of life: A structured literature review. *American Journal of Hospice & Palliative Medicine* 25: 501–511.

Knight, C. F., Knight, P. F., Gellula, M. H. & Holman, G. H. (1992). Training our future physicians: A hospice rotation for medical students. *American Journal of Hospice & Palliative Medicine* 9: 23–28.

Kylmä, J., Duggleby, W., Cooper, D. & Molander, G. (2009). Hope in palliative care: an integrative review. *Palliative & Supportive Care* 7: 365–377.

Larson, D. G. & Tobin, D. R. (2000). End of life conversations: Evolving theory and practice. *JAMA* 284: 1573–1578.

Lautrette, A., Darmon, M., Megarbane, B., Joly, L. M., Chevret, S., Adrie, C., et al. (2007). A communication strategy and brochure for relatives of patients dying in the ICU. *New England Journal of Medicine* 356: 469–478.

Luce, J. M. & Rubenfeld, G. D. (2002) Can health care costs be reduced by limiting intensive care at the end of life? *American Journal of Respiratory and Critical Care Medicine* 165: 750–754.

Magauren, C. E. & Brennan, M. J. (2005). Patient-doctor communication and the importance of clarifying end-of-life decisions. *American Journal of Hospice & Palliative Medicine* 22: 335–336.

Mitchell, S. L., Teno, J. M., Kiely, D. K., Shaffer, M. L., Jones, R. N., Prigerson, H. G., et al. (2009). The clinical course of advanced dementia. *New England Journal of Medicine* 361, no. 16: 1529–1538.

Mittelman, M. S., Ferris, S. H. & Shulman, E. (1995). A comprehensive support program: Effect on depression in spouse-caregivers of advanced dementia patients. *Gerontologist* 35: 792–802.

Mittelman, M. S., Ferris, S. H., Shulman, E., Steinberg, G. & Levin, B. (1996). A family intervention to delay nursing home placement of patients with Alzheimer's disease: A randomized controlled trial. *JAMA* 276: 1725–1731.

Morita, T., Tsunoda, J., Inoue, S. & Chihara, S. (2000). Terminal sedation for existential distress. *American Journal of Hospice & Palliative Care* 17: 189–195.

Morrison, R. S. (2005). Health care system factors affecting end-of-life care. *Journal of Palliative Medicine* 8, supp. 1: S79–S87.

Morrison, R. S. & Meier, D. E. (2004). Palliative care. *New England Journal of Medicine* 350: 2582–2590.

Morrison, R. S., Penrod, J. D., Cassel, J. B., Caust-Ellenbogen, M., Litke, A., Spragens, L. & Meier, D. E. (2008). Cost savings associated with US hospital palliative care consultation programs. *Archives of Internal Medicine* 168: 1783–1790.

Mount, B. (1993). Whole person care: Beyond psychosocial and physical needs. *American Journal of Hospice & Palliative Medicine* 10: 28–37.

Mulder, S. F., Bleijenberg, G., Verhagen, S. C., Stuyt, P. M. J., Schijven, M. P. & Tack, C. J. (2009). Improved competence after a palliative care course for internal medicine residents. *Palliative Medicine* 23: 360–368.

Mularski, R. A., Puntillo, K., Varkey, B., Erstad, B. L., Grap, M. J., Gilbert, H. C., et al. (2009). Pain management within the palliative and end-of-life care experience in the ICU. *Chest* 135: 1360–1369.

National Cancer Institute (NCI). (2002). SEER cancer statistics review 1975–2002. http://seer.cancer.gov/csr/1975_2002/results_merged/topic_survival.pdf.

Norton, S. S., Hogan, L. A., Holloway, R. G., Temkin-Greener, H., Buckley, M. J. & Quill, T. E. (2007). Proactive palliative care in the medical intensive care unit: Effects on length of stay for selected high-risk patients. *Critical Care Medicine* 35: 1530–1535.

Olden, A. M., Quill, T. E., Bordley, D. & Ladwig, S. (2009). Evaluation of a required palliative care rotation for internal medicine residents. *Journal of Palliative Medicine* 12: 150–154.

Pacheco, J., Hershberger, P. J., Markert, R. J. & Kumar, G. (2003). A longitudinal study of attitudes toward physician-assisted suicide and euthanasia among patients with noncurable malignancy. *American Journal of Hospice & Palliative Care* 20: 99–104.

Patterson, L. B. & Dorfman, L. (2002). Family support and hospice caregivers. *American Journal of Hospice & Palliative Medicine* 19: 315–323.

Pellegrino, E. D. (2006). Toward a reconstruction of medical morality. *American Journal of Bioethics* 6, no. 2: 65–71.

Ptacek, J. T. & Eberhardt, T. L. (1996). Breaking bad news: A review of the literature. *JAMA* 276: 496–502.

Reuben, D. B. (2009). Medical care for the final years of life: "When you're 83, it's not going to be 20 years." *JAMA* 302, no. 24: 2686–2694.

Robley, L. R. (2008). From ethics to palliative care: a community hospital experience. *Nursing Clinics of North America* 43, no. 3: 469.

Rodriguez, K. L. & Young, A. J. (2006). Perceptions of patients on the utility or futility of end-of-life treatment. *Journal of Medical Ethics* 32, no. 8: 444–449.

Schipper, H., Clinch, J., McMurray, A. & Levitt, M. (1984). Measuring the quality of life of cancer patients: The Functional Living Index-Cancer: Development and validation. *Journal of Clinical Oncology* 2: 472–483.

Singer, P. A., Martin, D. K., Lavery, J. V., Thiel, E. C., Kelner, M. & Mendelssohn, D. C. (1998). Reconceptualizing advance care planning from the patient's perspective. *Archives of Internal Medicine* 158: 879–884.

Singer, P. A., Robertson, G. & Roy, D. J. (1996). Bioethics for clinicians: 6. Advance care planning. *Canadian Medical Association Journal* 155: 1689–1692.

Smith, A. K., Sudore, R. L. & Perez-Stable, E. J. (2009) Palliative care for Latino patients and their families. *JAMA* 301: 1047–1057.

Smith, J. E. (2008). *FDR*. New York: Random House.

Smith, T. J., Coyne, P., Cassel, B., Penberthy, L., Hopson, A. & Hager, M. A. (2003). A high-volume specialist palliative care unit and team may reduce in-hospital end-of-life care costs. *Journal of Palliative Medicine* 6: 699–705.

Steinhauser, K. E., Bosworth, H. B., Clipp, E. C., McNeilly, M., Christakis, N. A., Parker, J., et al. (2002). Initial assessment of a new instrument to measure quality of life at the end of life. *Journal of Palliative Medicine* 5: 829–841.

Steinhauser, K. E., Christakis, N. A., Clipp, E. C., McNeilly, M., McIntyre, L. & Tulsky, J. A. (2000). Factors considered important at the end of life by patients, family, physicians, and other care providers. *JAMA* 284: 2476–2482.

Suhrie, E. M., Hanlon, J. T., Jaffe, E. J., Sevick, M. A., Ruby, C. M. & Aspinall, S. L. (2009). Impact of a geriatric nursing home palliative care service on unnecessary medication prescribing. *American Journal of Geriatric Pharmacotherapy* 7: 20–25.

SUPPORT Investigators. (1995). A controlled trial to improve care for seriously ill hospitalized patients in the Study to Understand Prognoses and Preferences for Outcomes and Risk of Treatments. *JAMA* 274: 1591–1598.

Teno, J. M., Licks, S., Lynn, J., Wenger, N., Connors, A. F., Jr., Phillips, R. S., O'Connor, M. A., Murphy, D. P., Fulkerson, W. J., Desbiens, N. & Knaus, W. A. (1997). Do advance directives provide instructions that direct care? SUPPORT Investigators study to understand prognosis and preferences for outcomes and risks of treatment. *Journal of the American Geriatrics Society* 45: 508–512.

Teno, J. M. & Connor, S. R. (2009). Referring a patient and family to high-quality palliative care at the close of life: "We met a new personality... with this level of compassion and empathy." *JAMA* 301, no. 6: 651–659.

Theis, K. A., Rao, J. K., Anderson, L. & Thompson, P. (2007). End-of-Life content in comprehensive cancer control plans: A systematic review. *American Journal of Hospice & Palliative Medicine* 24: 390–398.

Veterans Health Administration. (2005). *VHA handbook 1140.5*. http://www.il-hpco.org/File/VA_Hospice_Referral_Handbook.pdf.

Veterans Health Care Eligibility Reform Act of 1996. Pub. L. No. 104-262. www.tavausa.org/PL%20104-262.pdf.

Warner, M. (2009). Senator Warner introduces legislation enhancing senior health care choices. Press release to the U.S. Senate. http://www.nhpco.org/i4a/pages/index.cfm?pageID=5923.

Warpole, K. (2009). *Modern hospice design*. New York: Routledge.

Weiner, R. (2009). Palin: Obama's "death panel" could kill my Down syndrome baby. *Huffington Post*, August 7. http://www.huffingtonpost.com/2009/08/07/palin-obamas-death-panel_n_254399.html.

Werth, J. L., Jr. & Blevins, D. (Eds.). (2006). *Psychosocial issues near the end of life: A resource for professional care providers*. Washington, DC: American Psychological Association.

Werth, J. L., Jr. & Kleespies, P. M. (2006). Ethical considerations in providing psychological services in end-of-life care. In J. L. Werth Jr. & D. Blevins (Eds.), *Psychosocial issues near the end of life: A resource for professional care providers* (pp. 57–87). Washington, DC: American Psychological Association.

Wright, A. A., Zhang, V., Ray, A., Mack, J. W., Trice, E., Balboni, T., et al. (2008). Associations between end-of-life discussions, patient mental health, medical care near death, and caregiver bereavement adjustment. *JAMA* 300: 1665–1673.

Yalom, I. (2009). *Staring at the sun: Overcoming the terror of death*. San Francisco: Jossey-Bass.

Young, E. W. D. (1998). Ethical issues at the end of life. *Stanford Law & Policy Review* 9: 267–288.

Veterans with Special Needs

Chapter 9

Lifestyles and Health Behaviors of Veterans

Hayden B. Bosworth

Overview

The Veterans Health Administration (VHA) provides a unique opportunity to evaluate programs to improve lifestyle and behaviors. This chapter provides a summary of VHA and how it has impacted programs on healthcare for veterans, with an emphasis on lifestyle and health behaviors. A brief overview of prior work examining prevalence and interventions to improve specific health behaviors and lifestyles such as obesity, physical activity, smoking, sleep behaviors, and medication adherence among veterans is provided. Specific issues that may impact lifestyle and health behavior, such as mental health, are presented. Finally, policy implications for health behaviors and lifestyle for veterans are discussed.

The Veterans Health Administration is the nation's largest integrated healthcare system; it operates 155 medical centers and 872 community and outpatient clinics. In 2010 it served 8.3 million patients and registered more than 80 million visits in its outpatient clinics (Department of Veterans Affairs, National Center for Veterans Analysis and Statistics 2010). Policy and programs are developed centrally, then disseminated through the twenty-one Veterans Integrated Service Networks (VISNs), within which all VHA medical centers and clinics are organized.

In response to ongoing pressure over the past decade to expand access to primary care (Kizer, Fonseca & Long 1997), VHA mandated a 200 percent increase in midlevel providers (Kizer, Fonseca & Long 1997; Lynn et al. 1999).

219

According to most estimates, approximately 30 percent of VHA primary care providers (PCPs) are midlevel (Department of Veterans Affairs/VHA 2006; Huang et al. 2004; Running et al. 2000) This increase in healthcare providers and the healthcare system itself is due to VA's being particularly concerned with chronic care as a result of the increasing numbers of aging veterans who are coping with multiple chronic diseases. VHA patients are complex, with poorer health status, more medical conditions requiring intensive management, and higher use of medical resources than the general U.S. population (Agha et al. 2000; Kazis et al. 1998; Mrus et al. 2006; Payne et al. 2005; Rogers et al. 2004). To help alleviate the increasing number of older and sicker veterans, VHA has implemented several initiatives to improve access to care, including the fast-growing community-based outpatient clinics (CBOCs) that were designed to improve access for veterans living far from VA facilities and/or in rural settings.

Although VHA offers a comprehensive set of chronic care services and has a strong tradition in primary care, a patient with multiple chronic conditions or other complex care needs often has to negotiate a multitude of healthcare providers, ancillary services, and administrative tasks to get optimal care. In addition, for many of VA's older patients, chronic care needs are further complicated by the dual use of both VA services and private sector healthcare available through Medicare benefits. Many of VA's patients have dual use of VHA and Medicare-sponsored private healthcare services. Challenges of continuity of care increase multiplicatively with dual healthcare insurance use. Devising the best possible patient-centered care for patients with complex chronic care needs requires substantive mechanisms for continual patient and caregiver input and feedback.

To address the increase in veterans and in the prevalence of chronic diseases, VA's Health Services Research and Development Service (HSR&D) works to identify and evaluate innovative strategies that lead to accessible, high-quality, cost-effective care for veterans and the nation. HSR&D pursues its goals through its key centers, including fourteen Centers of Excellence that cover an array of healthcare issues such as care of complex chronic diseases, healthcare disparities, mental illness, elder care, medical informatics, organization of care, primary care, and long-term care. HSR&D research also addresses critical issues for veterans returning home from Iraq and Afghanistan with conditions that may require care over their lifetimes. In addition, HSR&D oversees and facilitates VA's Quality Enhancement Research Initiative (QUERI), designed to improve care by facilitating the adoption of new evidence-based treatments, tests, and models of care into routine clinical practice. QUERI is a central component of VA's commitment to improving the quality of veterans' healthcare. The VHA National Center for Health Promotion and Disease Prevention

(NCHP) was developed in 1995 to encourage the planning, monitoring, and provision of preventive medicine services for veterans. The NCHP adopted the evidence-based criteria established by the U.S. Preventive Services Task Force (USPSTF) as the standard of care for the asymptomatic, average-risk veteran receiving primary care.

Providing quality healthcare to veterans is paramount in the VA healthcare system. VA has undergone a dramatic transformation and has emerged as a nationally and internationally known leader in quality improvement efforts. It supports a powerful electronic medical record, sophisticated systems of performance measurement, and patient safety—all of which contribute to quality of care.

VHA has made advances in information technology to improve access to care, such as telehealth, the delivery of health-related electronic information and services via telecommunication technologies that may include the telephone, the Internet, and videoconferencing. Planned telephone contacts by physicians, nurses, or health educators have been used successfully in VA health services interventions to improve chronic disease care (Clark et al. 2007; Piette et al. 2000; Simon et al. 2000; Weinberger et al. 1993); however, most telephone-based interventions focus on a single disease and represent a supplemental (rather than alternative) method of delivering care.

Healthcare costs are rising at an unsustainable rate and threaten not only the American healthcare system, but the economy as a whole (Orszag 2007). Now more than ever, innovations in healthcare must demonstrate their value based on both health outcomes and costs. Telemedicine enthusiasts have promoted telehealth innovations as a means of transforming healthcare delivery for the future (Jadad 2004); however, despite the range of possible applications and over thirty years' experience, there is still limited evidence that telemedicine is a cost-effective means of delivering healthcare (Whitten et al. 2002). In particular with the increased interest in technological advances in disease telemonitoring and videoconferencing, it is unclear how novel health technology will increase the quality of care without also significantly increasing costs (Bodenheimer 2005; Bodenheimer & Fernandez 2005). VA has reaped substantial benefits from its investments in health information technology, but must continue to evaluate the model for integrating telehealth in primary care to optimize its utility in healthcare delivery.

Interventions that target self-management skills among patients with chronic diseases have been growing in popularity recently and have been suggested as an integral part of improving the quality of chronic disease care (Powers et al. 2009). Self-management education goes beyond traditional patient education by seeking to motivate patient behavioral change, enhance patient confidence, and provide problem-solving skills to manage the day-to-day tasks in managing their chronic illness (Bayliss et al. 2007; Clark et al. 2003). Self-management education programs have sought to improve disease outcomes through improved adherence to medications, diet, and lifestyle; however, experts do not agree on what the essential elements of effective self-management education are. A systematic review of chronic disease self-management programs in older adults reported modest but clinically important reductions of glycosolated hemoglobin (with an average reduction of 0.8 percent) and systolic blood pressure (average reduction of 5 mm Hg) (Chodosh et al. 2005). Counseling and behavioral interventions to improve low-density lipoprotein cholesterol (LDL-C), however, have produced smaller benefits, with mean reductions ranging from 3 to 7 mg/dL (Brunner et al. 2007; Ebrahim et al. 2006). Most self-management interventions target a single chronic disease and focus on disease-specific outcomes (Chodosh et al. 2005; Ismail, Winkley & Rabe-Hesketh 2004; Schroeder, Fahey & Ebrahim 2004; Warsi et al. 2004). The principles and methods of self-management support in chronic disease interventions are similar across disease states, suggesting that the benefits of a self-management intervention may extend beyond the intended targets (Powers et al. 2009). Therapeutic interventions that can improve multiple cardiovascular risk factors simultaneously would be particularly valuable in light of the growing prevalence of multimorbidity and synergistic relationship between risk factors.

Adults receiving healthcare at Veterans Affairs Medical Centers (VAMCs) receive recommended services for preventive care, diabetes mellitus care, and inpatient management of acute myocardial infarction and heart failure at greater rates than adults covered by other insurance plans, including Medicare and managed care organizations (Ross et al. 2008). Better healthcare quality at VAMCs has been attributed to a nationally integrated healthcare system reform in 1995, which created organizational and structural differences between VAMC and non-VAMC sectors, including information technology implementation, performance measurement and reporting, service integration, and realigned payment policies (Ashton et al. 2003; Doebbeling et al. 2002).

Despite these quality improvements in the VAMC, there remains significant work. For example, whereas in the U.S. population as a whole, effective therapy for diabetes, hypertension, and hypercholesterolemia is available, a study using the Third National Health and Nutrition Examination Survey found that only 7.3 percent of patients with diabetes simultaneously achieve recommended goals of therapy for all three conditions (Saydah, Fradkin & Cowie 2004). Similarly, in VA, only 4 percent of patients with diabetes achieve targets of simultaneous control of all three risk factors (Jackson, Edelman & Weinberger 2006) and only 13 percent of patients with known cardiovascular disease achieve target blood pressure and cholesterol control (Johnson et al. 2006). The following section reviews recent work focusing on lifestyle and health behavior interventions among veterans.

Ongoing VA Work Addressing Lifestyle and Health Behavior

Factors Related to Lifestyle and Health Behaviors

The lack of focus on treatment adherence is a shame, given the clear relationships between health behaviors and outcomes. Despite advances in healthcare, all too often the benefits of these treatments are not fully realized because of patient nonadherence. Almost all medical and behavioral health treatments require at least some degree of adherence to treatment (e.g., coming to appointments, picking up medications, agreeing to have procedures performed, use of contraception, obtaining immunizations, attending follow-up appointments), and many treatments require significant behavioral change (e.g., following long-term demanding and complex medication regimens, improving diet and physical activity, reducing alcohol consumption and cigarette smoking). Adherence has been defined as the extent to which a person's behavior—taking medication, following a diet, and/or executing lifestyle changes—corresponds with agreed recommendations from a healthcare provider.

Despite the low levels of adherence to recommended health behaviors, there is growing evidence of the impact of adherence on health behaviors. The major causes of morbidity and premature mortality in the United States—heart disease, cancer, and stroke—are influenced by multiple health risk behaviors, including smoking, alcohol abuse, physical inactivity, and poor diet. The fifty-two-nation INTERHEART study identified tobacco use, obesity, lipids, and psychosocial factors as accounting for about 90 percent of the population-attributable risks for myocardial infarction (Lanas et al., 2007; Yusuf et al., 2004). In a recent study of 77,782 middle-aged U.S. women, never smoking, engaging in regular physical activity, eating a healthy diet, and avoiding becoming overweight were each associated with a markedly lower mortality during twenty-four years of follow-up. It was estimated that 55 percent of all-cause mortality, 44 percent of cancer mortality, and 72 percent of cardiovascular mortality during the follow-up could have been avoided by adherence to these four lifestyle guidelines (van Dam et al. 2008).

Several factors are important to fostering self-management in VHA: tool availability, ease of use, effectiveness, and cost. VHA has been a leader in health information technology. Simple devices, for example pedometers, have been shown to increase physical activity and reduce weight and blood pressure

(Bravata et al. 2007). Thus, VA facilities across the organization currently supply veteran patients with pedometers to foster behavioral modification when prescribed by the VA clinical provider. Similarly, home blood pressure monitoring has been well studied as a method to improve BP control (Bosworth et al. 2009b). Its main effect is thought to be on BP recognition, which may lead to improved adherence and better control. A decrease in BP may encourage the patient to continue treatment, whereas continued high BP readings may encourage appropriate changes in lifestyle or therapy (Stahl et al. 1984) and faster changes to medical regimens (Campbell et al. 1995). Subsequently, veterans may receive a home BP monitor if it is prescribed by their VA provider.

Another self-management support tool is My HealtheVet (MHV), the Internet-based personal health record created by VA for veterans to manage their care (Damush et al. 2010). MHV was introduced in 2003 to complement traditional services, improve comanaged care, and empower patients and their families to play a more active role in veterans' healthcare (Naditz 2008; Nazi 2010; Nazi et al. 2010). The My HealtheVet portal (http://www.myhealth .va.gov) enables veterans to create and maintain a robust personal health record (PHR) that includes access to trusted patient health education information, a comprehensive personal health journal, and electronic services such as online VA prescription refill requests. The My HealtheVet Program is based on the core belief that knowledgeable patients are better able to make informed healthcare choices, stay healthy, and seek services when needed. By October 2009 the number of registered users had increased to 850,000 (16 percent of VA patients receiving services), and the total number of visits to My HealtheVet since it was launched on November 11, 2003, had exceeded 32 million. Since online interactive ordering of VA prescription refills became available in August 2005, veterans have refilled more than 11 million prescriptions using My HealtheVet. Thus, support tools can extend the care of the healthcare organization to reach a larger portion of its consumers and provide self-management support during and in between medical visits (Nazi 2010).

Many veterans miss visits because of transportation problems or the financial burdens associated with paying for travel (Piette & Moos 1996; Schmitt, Phibbs & Piette 2003). On the health system side, burgeoning caseloads mean that VA clinicians are limited in their ability to meet patients' needs for self-management support during face-to-face encounters. Health information technologies (HIT) may improve VA patients' access to self-care support both during and between outpatient visits. Many HITs have very low incremental costs once the system is in place and may provide a partial solution to the challenge of meeting guidelines for self-management support within the constraints of limited staff time and budgets (Glasgow et al. 2004).

Obesity

Overweight and obesity are tremendous health problems for the U.S. population. Similarly, veterans who receive medical care in the VHA have a high prevalence of overweight and obesity. A study of 1.8 million veterans who received VHA care in 2000 found a prevalence of overweight/obesity of 73.0 percent among men (32.9 percent obese) and 68.4 percent among women (37.4 percent obese) (Das et al. 2005). According to the 2003 Behavioral Risk Factor Surveillance System, 72.2 percent of veterans who use the VHA for healthcare were overweight or obese (Nelson 2006). VHA-using veterans, who by definition are seeking medical care, may have different characteristics from people in general community samples. Furthermore, VHA users have more physical and mental health conditions than people in community healthcare settings (Rogers et al. 2004). Obesity-associated conditions, such as hypertension, diabetes, ischemic heart disease, and arthritis, are also highly prevalent in the VHA population (Yu et al. 2003).

Many diet and weight loss interventions have been proven effective over short durations. Even more difficult than initiating a weight loss diet, however, is maintaining weight loss once this onerous task has been achieved. Adherence to dietary interventions tends to wane over longer durations. Overall, patients who adhere to weight loss programs of various types typically lose approximately 10 percent of original body weight, but one-third to two-thirds of this weight is regained at one year, and nearly all of it is regained at five years (NIH Technology Assessment Conference Panel 1993). Because of these depressing statistics on long-term effectiveness, patients and health professionals are quick to discount these interventions.

Practitioners in VHA identified comprehensive weight management as a high priority in early 2001. The *MOVE!* Weight-Management Program for Veterans was developed on the basis of published guidelines from the National Institutes of Health and other organizations. *MOVE!* has been implemented at nearly all VHA medical centers. By June 2008 more than 100,000 patients had participated in *MOVE!* during more than 500,000 visits (Kinsinger et al. 2009).

In general, several trials indicate that weight loss can be achieved, and to some extent sustained. The most successful interventions for promoting and maintaining weight loss involve sustained personal contact; self-monitoring of weight, diet, and physical activity; goal-setting; social support; and motivational counseling (Perri et al. 2001; Ryan et al. 2003; Svetkey et al. 2008; Wadden, Butryn & Byrne 2004; Wing et al. 1998).

Although dietary adherence can be a daily struggle for many people, a number of practical points and strategies can assist clinicians when counseling patients on dietary modifications. Yancy and Voils (Yancy, in press) summarize a number of recommendations, including: recognizing that obesity is a chronic disease and that successful treatment often requires lifelong monitoring, therapy, and support. As with any chronic disease, dietary interventions require developing strategies to help motivate patients into making beneficial changes to their diet and designing specific goals that describe exactly what they plan to do, help patients to choose goals that are meaningful but also achievable, and recognize and congratulate patients for any success in dietary change or weight loss (i.e., positive reinforcement). Recognition of these issues can go a long way toward building a therapeutic alliance with patients and increasing their motivation to initiate and maintain dietary changes. Use of these simple strategies can make the difference between a patient following a diet temporarily with transient health improvement and a patient making a successful lifestyle change leading to sustained improvements in satisfaction and quality of life, decreased morbidity, and increased longevity.

Physical Activity

Physical activity is associated with many physical and psychological health benefits. Yet despite decades of effort to improve physical activity levels, many Americans do not meet physical activity (PA) recommendations, and this remains an important public health problem. In a recently completed study at one VA site among adults seventy years of age and older, approximately 400 veterans were randomized to twelve months of usual care (UC) or multicomponent physical activity counseling, consisting of baseline in-person and every other week and then monthly telephone counseling by a lifestyle counselor, one-time clinical endorsement of physical activity, monthly automated telephone messaging from the primary care provider, and quarterly tailored mailings of progress in PA. The investigators demonstrated improvements in rapid gait speed and minutes of moderate/vigorous physical activity relative to usual care. This study demonstrated that sedentary older adults with a range of functional states can be targeted to receive consistent, evidence-based counseling that, when integrated with endorsements from their primary care physician, result in significant improvements in physical activity and rapid gait (Morey et al. 2009).

Although time limitations and competing demands during healthcare visits are barriers to physical activity counseling, it should be considered that outcomes for many chronic health conditions can be substantially improved by increasing physical activity levels. Therefore, discussion of physical activity should be treated as a priority. Following are recommendations for incorporating physical activity screening and counseling into healthcare visits:

Ask patients about physical activity behaviors *routinely* during visits.

Clearly advise that patients become and remain physically active, and stress that physical activity is a key component to maintaining health and managing disease.

Provide written information on physical activity recommendations and advise that patients set a goal to achieve that amount of physical activity weekly.

Assist patients with specific plans for incorporating physical activity into their daily lives.

For physically inactive patients, ask about main barriers to physical activity and provide recommendations for dealing with these.

Physical inactivity should not be an acceptable lifestyle.

Smoking

Cigarette smoking is the leading cause of preventable death in the United States. It is known to cause cancer, heart disease, peripheral vascular disease, and chronic pulmonary disease. According to estimates, 25 percent of adults in the United States continue to smoke despite awareness of the causal association between smoking and disease (American Cancer Society 2000). Smoking cessation confers appreciable reductions in risk for cancer and cardiovascular disease, with risk reduced to that of a nonsmoker within twelve months after quitting (Peto et al. 2000; American Cancer Society 2000). Thus, encouraging smoking cessation is necessary to reduce incidence rates of cancer and other smoking-related health outcomes.

Smoking cessation has also been shown to reduce disease severity in patients diagnosed with cardiovascular disease and cancer. Among patients with coronary heart disease, a meta-analysis has found a 36 percent reduction in mortality for those who quit smoking compared to those who continued to smoke (Critchley & Capewell 2004). For patients who have been smokers and who experience a cardiac event, quitting reduces the risk of a recurrent event by 50 percent. Yet only 42 percent of current smokers hospitalized with heart disease report receiving counseling about smoking cessation (Houston et al. 2005).

Cigarette smoking is also a significant health problem in the U.S. military. The estimated costs of smoking among U.S. military healthcare system beneficiaries were more than $900 million per year in 1995 ($584 million in direct healthcare costs and $346 million in lost productivity among active duty personnel) (Helyer, Brehm & Perino, 1998). Recent data suggest the prevalence of smoking might be increasing among active duty military personnel (Bray et al. 2002). Data from the 2003–2007 Behavioral Risk Factor Surveillance System (BRFSS), a state-based, random-digit dialed telephone survey, were used to estimate the prevalence of current smoking among adults (aged $\geq$eighteen years) who reported ever serving on active duty in the U.S. Armed Forces. The age-adjusted prevalence of smoking during the period was 27.0 percent (standard error, 0.36) among veterans and 21 percent (0.12) among nonveterans. The prevalence of smoking was 43 percent (90 percent CI=39.0–47.6) among veterans with self-reported coronary heart disease (CHD), greater than that for nonveterans with CHD (31 percent; 90 percent CI = 28.6–33.1). Although the prevalence of smoking has declined among U.S. adults, there are opportunities to further reduce smoking among U.S. veterans, particularly young veterans, for whom the prevalence of smoking is similar to that of the U.S. adult population during the late 1960s/early 1970s (Brown 2010).

To date, the most successful interventions (cessation rates over 50 percent) incorporate multiple components (tailored print materials, telephone counseling, and nicotine replacement therapy) and target special populations such as those with a recent diagnosis of heart disease or cancer (Rohrer et al. 2011; Schnoll et al. 2003). Future interventions can attempt to promote cessation among specific target groups by utilizing multicomponent interventions.

Sleep

In the wake of recent military conflicts, postdeployment mental health has emerged as a central VA focus, and chronic disease prevention is similarly a primary focus. Sleep disturbance is one of the two most common complaints of recently deployed veterans with post-traumatic stress disorder (PTSD). Since military operations began in 2001, more than 1.5 million U.S. military personnel have been deployed to Afghanistan and Iraq (Hoge et al. 2008). Estimates suggest that 9.8 percent of troops deployed to Iraq and 4.7 percent of troops deployed to Afghanistan will screen positive for PTSD upon their return (Hoge, Auchterlonie & Milliken 2006) and most of these will report difficulty initiating or maintaining sleep (Maher, Rego & Asnis 2006).

Over the past ten years a significant body of research has emerged regarding the relationships between insomnia and sleep duration, and cardiovascular health. Bonnet and Arand (2007) prepared a comprehensive review and analysis of this literature. With respect to insomnia, they combined recent findings with a previous meta-analysis assessing the link with general cardiac outcomes.

The collective findings suggest an increased risk of heart disease in insomniacs of between 1.21 and 3.1 relative to good sleepers. Taylor and colleagues (2007) found a significant risk of both heart disease and hypertension in those with objectively assessed insomnia even after controlling for comorbid sleep disorders, depression, and anxiety.

Other studies have shown an association between insomnia and risk factors for the development of cardiovascular disease (CVD). In a large study of Japanese telecommunication workers, sleep maintenance insomnia was associated with an odds ratio of 1.88 for increased risk of hypertension after adjusting for confounding factors (Suka, Yoshida & Sugimori 2003).

Recent research also points to an association between short sleep duration and CVD risk factors. The combined findings of several studies of sleep deprivation in healthy adults showed an increase in both systolic and diastolic blood pressure following total sleep deprivation in healthy adults (Bonnet & Arand 2007). Regular physical activity is recommended for all Americans to improve health and prevent CVD (U.S. Department of Health and Human Services 2008). Regular physical activity also seems to be beneficial for improving sleep (Atkinson & Davenne 2007). Thus, interventions that include strategies for improved sleep *and* promote physical activity may have synergistic effects by affecting the underlying physiological processes that are shared across sleep disturbance and cardiovascular health in those with PTSD.

Internet-based interventions have been shown to be effective in both the treatment of insomnia (Strom, Pettersson & Andersson 2004) and cognitive-behavioral treatment for insomnia (CBTI) (Ulmer et al. 2008). Ongoing work is being conducted to identify simple methods for identifying sleep disturbance problems as well as brief but effective interventions for alleviating these prevalent problems.

Medication Adherence

A key component in the management of healthcare conditions is the use of prescribed medications. The effectiveness of medications and their long-term benefits depends on adherence to the prescriber's instructions (Sabate 2003). Medication nonadherence includes delaying filling prescriptions, failing to fill prescriptions, cutting dosages, and reducing the frequency of administration (Bosworth 2010).

Patients frequently do not adhere to essential medications, with substantial consequences to public health (Sabate 2003). Medication nonadherence is an enormous burden to the world's healthcare system. Half of the 3.2 billion annual prescriptions dispensed in the United States are not taken as prescribed (Osterberg & Blaschke 2005). Numerous studies have shown that patients with chronic conditions adhere only to 50–60 percent of medications as prescribed despite evidence that medication therapy improves life expectancy and quality of life (Avorn et al. 1998; Benner et al. 2002). Across different definitions of nonadherence, approximately 50 percent of patients do not take their prescribed medication as recommended (Feldman et al. 1998; Flack et al. 1996; Haynes, McKibbon & Kanani 1996; Mallion et al. 1998). The true rate of nonadherence may be higher, because patients with a history of nonadherence are likely underrepresented in outcomes research.

The recognition of the importance of medication adherence has been increasing. A World Health Organization report (Sabate 2003) states that because the magnitude of medication nonadherence and the scope of the sequelae are so alarming, more health benefits worldwide would result from improving adherence to existing treatments than any developing new medical treatments. Interventions that stimulate better adherence to essential medications, even slightly, may meaningfully improve public health.

While medication nonadherence is prevalent and a significant barrier to quality health care, enhancing medication adherence requires a combination of appropriate educational, behavioral, and communication strategies. Anticipating the most common adverse events as well as when they are likely to occur and what can be done to ameliorate them also can improve medication adherence. It is useful to ask patients what they already know and believe about the medications before and after explaining these points. The simplest adherence management available to clinicians is a time-efficient, problem-solving process based on questioning the patient. The process aims to determine if an adherence problem is present, define the problem, and design and test a solution by collaborative negotiation with the patient. Asking the patient open-ended questions to describe his or her adherence practices starts the process and the search for adherence problems. The questions must be asked in a manner that is nonjudgmental and nonthreatening to gain the patient's trust and truthfulness. Usually the patient's answers provide information that quickly makes the next logical question obvious to the clinician. The major obstacle to adherence management is getting the process started (Bosworth 2010).

Multiple Behavior Interventions

Self-management interventions often focus on multiple behaviors. As examples of some programs directed to improve multiple health behaviors among veterans, three recent studies conducted by VA are described in this subsection.

Less than one-half of the seventy-three million Americans with hypertension have adequate blood pressure (BP) control. The Veteran Study to Improve the Control of Hypertension (V-STITCH) examined the effectiveness of two interventions for improving patient BP control (Bosworth et al. 2009b). This was a two-level (primary care provider and patient) cluster randomized trial with two-year follow-up occurring among patients with hypertension enrolled from a VAMC primary care clinic. Primary care providers (n = 17) in the intervention received computer-generated decision support designed to improve guideline concordant medical therapy at each visit; control providers (n = 15) received a reminder at each visit. Patients received usual care or a bimonthly, tailored, nurse-delivered behavioral telephone intervention to improve hypertension treatment. Behavioral components that were addressed included smoking, exercise, and diet as well as issues such as hypertension knowledge, literacy, and side effects of hypertensive medications. The primary outcome was the proportion of patients who achieved a BP<140/90 mm Hg (<130/85 for diabetic patients) over the twenty-four-month intervention. Of the 816 eligible patients contacted, 190 refused and 38 were excluded. The 588 enrolled patients had a mean age of sixty-three years, 43 percent had adequate baseline BP control, and 482 (82 percent) completed the twenty-four-month follow-up. There were no significant differences in amount of change in BP control in the three intervention groups as compared to the hypertension reminder control group. In secondary analyses, rates of BP control for all patients receiving the patient behavioral intervention (n = 294) improved from 40.1 to 54.4 percent at twenty-four months (P = .03); patients in the nonbehavioral intervention group improved from 38.2 to 43.9 percent (P =.38), but there were no between-group differences at the end of the study. The brief behavioral intervention showed improved outcomes over time, but there were no significant between-group differences (Bosworth et al. 2009a).

In a large study involving over 1,300 veterans with poorly controlled hypertension cared for by 182 providers, investigators compared three interventions (Roumie et al. 2006). Providers who cared for eligible patients were randomly assigned to receive an e-mail with a Web-based link to the Seventh Report of the Joint National Committee on the Prevention, Detection, Evaluation and Treatment of High Blood Pressure (JNC 7) guidelines (provider education); provider education and a patient-specific hypertension computerized alert (provider education and alert); or provider education, hypertension alert, and patient education, in which patients were sent a letter advocating drug adherence, lifestyle modification, and conversations with providers (patient education). Patients of providers who were randomly assigned to the patient education group had better blood pressure control (138/75 mm Hg) than those in the provider education and alert or provider education alone groups (146/76 mm Hg and 145/78 mm Hg, respectively). More patients in the patient education group had a systolic BP of 140 mm Hg or less compared with those in the provider education or provider education and alert groups (adjusted relative risk for the patient education group compared with the provider education alone group, 1.31 [95 percent CI, 1.06 to 1.62]; $P = 0.012$). Similar to the V-STITCH, a multifactorial intervention including patient education improved blood pressure control compared with provider education alone.

In another study, health behaviors and lifestyle among veterans within the context of cholesterol were examined (Voils et al. 2009). Almost 50 percent of Americans have elevated low-density lipoprotein cholesterol (LDL-C). The behaviors required to lower LDL-C levels may be difficult to adhere to if they are inconsistent with spouses' health practices, and, alternatively, may be enhanced by enlisting support from the spouse. This trial extends previous trials by requiring spouse enrollment, teaching spouses how to provide emotional and instrumental support, allowing patients to decide which component of the intervention they would like to receive, and having patients determine their own goals and action plans. Veteran outpatients with above-goal LDL-C (N = 254) and their spouses were randomized, as a couple, to receive printed education materials only or the materials plus an eleven-month, nurse-delivered, telephone-based intervention. The intervention contains four modules: medication adherence, diet, exercise, and patient-physician communication. Patients decided which modules they complete and in which order; modules may be repeated or omitted. Telephone calls were to patients and spouses separately and occurred monthly. During each patient telephone call, patients' progress was reviewed, and patients created goals and action plans for the upcoming month. During spouse telephone calls, which occurred within one week of patient calls, spouses were informed of patients' goals and action plans and devised strategies to increase emotional and instrumental support. The primary hypothesis is that an eleven-month, telephone-based, patient-spouse intervention will result in a greater reduction in LDL-C as compared to printed education materials. Given the social context in which self-management occurs, interventions that teach spouses to provide instrumental and emotional support may help patients initiate and adhere to behaviors that lower their LDL-C levels. Moreover, allowing patients to retain autonomy by deciding which behaviors they would like to change and how may improve adherence and clinical outcomes (Voils et al. 2009).

Mental Health and Health Behaviors

A particular issue that needs to be addressed among veterans is the greater prevalence of mental health issues and their impact on health behaviors. For veterans, diagnoses of severe mental illness include schizophrenia-spectrum disorders, bipolar disorder, and PTSD. High rates of health risk behaviors are prevalent in this population (Carey et al. 2001) and may lead to increased use of health care services through associated medical illnesses (Bosworth et al. 2004; Calhoun et al. 2002). For example, heart disease (HD) is one of the leading causes of death among persons with mental disorders (Angst et al. 2002; Hennekens 2007), and it has been associated with twenty-five to thirty years of premature mortality among patients diagnosed with schizophrenia (Colton & Manderscheid 2006; Hennekens 2007). The impact of mental health and morbidities like heart disease is likely to be higher in the VA than in other healthcare systems.

Depression is related to nonadherence with medical treatment. It may increase nonadherence because positive expectations and beliefs in the benefits and efficacy of treatment have been shown to be essential to patient adherence (DiMatteo et al. 1993). Depressed patients often feel hopeless, and adherence might be difficult or impossible for a patient who has little optimism that any action will be worthwhile. In addition, depression might be associated with reductions in the cognitive functioning essential to remembering and following through with treatment recommendations (e.g., taking medication).

There are many reasons for the increased risk of medical illnesses and subsequent premature mortality in persons with mental disorders. Notably, a substantial percentage of those with severe mental illness have significantly higher rates of obesity (Casey et al. 2004), diabetes, and hypertension compared to the general population (Goff et al. 2005). The prevalence of negative health behaviors, including smoking (Hennekens et al. 2005) and limited physical activity (Kilbourne et al. 2007), is also higher among patients diagnosed with schizophrenia and other mental disorders than among the general population (Goff et al. 2005). Given that VA is in the vanguard for developing, evaluating, and implementing many mental health programs, these advances are likely to improve veterans' mental and physical health and subsequently support improved health behaviors and lifestyles.

Conclusion

Veterans are, on average, some of the sickest patients in the country. Addressing the complexity of these patients' care highlights some of the weakest links in processes critical to quality self-management support: treatment coordination, effective patient education, promoting and helping sustain health behavior changes, and ensuring effective communication between patients and their healthcare teams. As lessons are learned about implementing self-management programs focusing on improving health behavior and lifestyles in VA, resource allocation for providing patient access, facilitating self-management, and incorporating support tools to foster self-management will have to be refined by the healthcare organization. Redesigning the system to deliver and support health behaviors will be important as evidence-based self-management practices are translated into routine care and their impact on health-related quality of life of veterans living with chronic disease is evaluated.

Acknowledgments: This manuscript is supported by a grant from Veterans Affairs, Health Services Research and Development (IIR 04-426), a career scientist award from the Veterans Affairs, Health Services Research and Development (08-027) and an Established Investigator Award from the American Heart Association. The views expressed in this manuscript are those of the author and do not necessarily represent the views of the Department of Veterans Affairs.

References

Agha, Z., Lofgren, R. P., VanRuiswyk, J. V. & Layde, P. M. (2000). Are patients at Veterans Affairs medical centers sicker? A comparative analysis of health status and medical resource use. *Archives of Internal Medicine* 160, no. 21: 3252–3257.

American Cancer Society. (2000). *Cancer facts and figures 2000*. Atlanta, GA: American Cancer Society.

Angst, F., Stassen, H. H., Clayton, P. J. & Angst, J. (2002). Mortality of patients with mood disorders: Follow-up over 34–38 years. *Journal of Affective Disorders* 68, nos. 2–3: 167–181.

Ashton, C. M., Souchek, J., Petersen, N. J., Menke, T. J., Collins, T. C., Kizer, K. W., et al. (2003). Hospital use and survival among Veterans Affairs beneficiaries. *New England Journal of Medicine* 349, no. 17: 1637–1646.

Atkinson, G. & Davenne, D. (2007). Relationships between sleep, physical activity and human health. *Physiology & Behavior* 90: 229–235.

Avorn, J., Monette, J., Lacour, A., Bohn, R. L., Monane, M., Mogun, H., et al. (1998). Persistence of use of lipid-lowering medications: A cross-national study. *JAMA* 279, no. 18: 1458–1462.

Bayliss, E. A., Bosworth, H. B., Noel, P. H., Wolff, J. L., Damush, T. M. & McIver, L. (2007). Supporting self-management for patients with complex medical needs: Recommendations of a working group. *Chronic Illness* 3, no. 2: 167–175.

Benner, J. S., Glynn, R. J., Mogun, H., Neumann, P. J., Weinstein, M. C. & Avorn, J. (2002). Long-term persistence in use of statin therapy in elderly patients. *JAMA* 288, no. 4: 455–461.

Bodenheimer, T. (2005). High and rising health care costs. Part 2: Technologic innovation. *Annals of Internal Medicine* 142, no. 11: 932–937.

Bodenheimer, T. & Fernandez, A. (2005). High and rising health care costs. Part 4: Can costs be controlled while preserving quality? *Annals of Internal Medicine* 143, no. 1: 26–31.

Bonnet, M. H. & Arand, D. L. (2007). Cardiovascular implications of poor sleep. *Sleep Medicine Clinics* 2: 529–538.

Bosworth, H. B. (Ed.). (2010). Improving patient treatment adherence: A clinician guidebook. New York: Springer.

Bosworth, H. B., Calhoun, P. S., Stechuchak, K. M. & Butterfield, M. I. (2004). Use of psychiatric and medical health care by veterans with severe mental illness. *Psychiatric Services* 55, no. 6: 708–710.

Bosworth, H. B., Olsen, M. K., Dudley, T., Orr, M., Goldstein, M. K., Datta, S. K., et al. (2009a). Patient education and provider decision support to control blood pressure in primary care: A cluster randomized trial. *American Heart Journal* 157, no. 3: 450–456.

Bosworth, H. B., Olsen, M. K., Grubber, J. M., Neary, A. M., Orr, M. M., Powers, B. J., et al. (2009b). Two self-management Interventions to improve hypertension control: A randomized trial. *Annals of Internal Medicine* 151, no. 10: 687–695.

Bravata, D. M., Smith-Spangler, C., Sundaram, V., Gienger, A. L., Lin, N., Lewis, R., et al. (2007). Using pedometers to increase physical activity and improve health: A systematic review. *JAMA* 298, no. 19: 2296–2304.

Bray, R. M., et al. (2002). Department of Defense Survey of Health Related Behaviors among Military Personnel. Research Triangle Park, NC: Research Triangle Institute. http://www.tricare.mil/main/news/DoDSurvey.htm#3.2.1 (accessed October 13, 2009).

Brown, D. W. (2010). Smoking prevalence among US veterans. *Journal of General Internal Medicine* 25, no. 2: 147–149.

Brunner, E. J., Rees, K., Ward, K., Burke, M. & Thorogood, M. (2007). Dietary advice for reducing cardiovascular risk. *Cochrane Database System Review* 4: CD002128.

Calhoun, P. S., Bosworth, H. B., Grambow, S. C., Dudley, T. K. & Beckham, J. C. (2002). Medical service utilization by veterans seeking help for posttraumatic stress disorder. *American Journal of Psychiatry* 159, no. 12: 2081–2086.

Campbell, N. R., Abbott, D., Bass, M., Birkett, N. J., Chockalingam, A., Dagenais, G. R., et al. (1995). Self-measurement of blood pressure: Recommendations of the Canadian Coalition for High Blood Pressure Prevention and Control. *Canadian Journal of Cardiology* 11, supp. H: 5H–17H.

Carey, M. P., Carey, K. B., Maisto, S. A., Gordon, C. M. & Vanable, P. A. (2001). Prevalence and correlates of sexual activity and HIV-related risk behavior among psychiatric outpatients. *Journal of Consulting and Clinical Psychology* 69, no. 5: 846–850.

Casey, D. E., Haupt, D. W., Newcomer, J. W., Henderson, D. C., Sernyak, M. J., Davidson, M., et al. (2004). Antipsychotic-induced weight gain and metabolic abnormalities: implications for increased mortality in patients with schizophrenia. *Journal of Clinical Psychiatry* 65, supp. 7: 4–18; quiz 19–20.

Chodosh, J., Morton, S. C., Mojica, W., Maglione, M., Suttorp, M. J., Hilton, L., et al. (2005). Meta-analysis: Chronic disease self-management programs for older adults. *Annals of Internal Medicine* 143, no. 6: 427–438.

Clark, N. M., Barlow, J., Wright, C., Sheasby, J., Turner, A., Hainsworth, J., et al. (2003). Management of chronic disease by patients. *Annual Review of Public Health* 24, no. 2: 289–313.

Clark, R. A., Inglis, S. C., McAlister, F. A., Cleland, J. G. & Stewart, S. (2007). Telemonitoring or structured telephone support programmes for patients with chronic heart failure: Systematic review and meta-analysis. *Britich Medical Journal* 334, no. 7600: 942.

Colton, C. W. & Manderscheid, R. W. (2006). Congruencies in increased mortality rates, years of potential life lost, and causes of death among public mental health clients in eight states. *Preventing Chronic Disease* 3, no. 2: A42.

Critchley, J. & Capewell, S. (2004). Smoking cessation for the secondary prevention of coronary heart disease. *Cochrane Database System Review* 1: CD003041.

Damush, T. M., Jackson, G. L., Powers, B. J., Bosworth, H. B., Cheng, E., Anderson, J., et al. (2010). Implementing evidence-based patient self-management programs in the Veterans Health Administration: Perspectives on delivery system design considerations. *Journal of General Internal Medicine* 25, supp. 1: 68–71.

Das, S. R., Kinsinger, L. S., Yancy, W. S., Jr., Wang, A., Ciesco, E., Burdick, M., et al. (2005). Obesity prevalence among veterans at Veterans Affairs medical facilities. *American Journal of Preventive Medicine* 28, no. 3: 291–294.

Department of Veterans Affairs, National Center for Veterans Analysis and Statistics. (2010). Utilization. http://www.va.gov/vetdata/Utilization.asp.

Department of Veterans Affairs, Veterans Health Administration. (2006). Primary care direct patient care time. November 3. VHA directive 2006-060. http:/www1.va .gov/vhapublications/view/publication.asp?pub_id=1505 (accessed March 2010).

DiMatteo, M., Hays, R. D., Gritz, E. R. & Bastani, R. (1993). Patient adherence to cancer control regimens: Scale development and initial validation. *Psychological Assessment* 5: 102–112.

Doebbeling, B. N., Vaughn, T. E., Woolson, R. F., Peloso, P. M., Ward, M. M., Letuchy, E., et al. (2002). Benchmarking Veterans Affairs Medical Centers in the delivery of preventive health services: Comparison of methods. *Medical Care* 40, no. 6: 540–554.

Ebrahim, S., Beswick, A., Burke, M. & Davey Smith, G. (2006). Multiple risk factor interventions for primary prevention of coronary heart disease. *Cochrane Database System Review* 4: CD001561.

Feldman, R., Bacher, M., Campbell, N., Drover, A. & Chockalingam, A. (1998). Adherence to pharmacologic management of hypertension. *Canadian Journal of Public Health* 89, no. 5: 116–18.

Flack, J., Novikov, S. V. & Ferrario, C. M. (1996). Benefits of adherence to antihypertensive drug therapy. *The European Society of Cardiology* 17, supp. A: 16–20.

Glasgow, R. E., Bull, S. S., Piette, J. D. & Steiner, J. F. (2004). Interactive behavior change technology: A partial solution to the competing demands of primary care. *American Journal of Preventive Medicine* 27, no. supp. 2: 80–87.

Goff, D. C., Sullivan, L. M., McEvoy, J. P., Meyer, J. M., Nasrallah, H. A., Daumit, G. L., et al. (2005). A comparison of ten-year cardiac risk estimates in schizophrenia patients from the CATIE Study and matched controls. *Schizophrenia Research* 80, no. 1: 45–53.

Haynes, R. B., McKibbon, K. A. & Kanani, R. (1996). Systematic review of randomised trials of interventions to assist patients to follow prescriptions for medications. *Lancet* 348, no. 9024: 383–386.

Helyer, A. J., Brehm, W. T. & Perino, L. (1998). Economic consequences of tobacco use for the Department of Defense, 1995. *Military Medicine* 163, no. 4: 217–221.

Hennekens, C. H. (2007). Increasing global burden of cardiovascular disease in general populations and patients with schizophrenia. *Journal of Clinical Psychiatry* 68, supp. 4: 4–7.

Hennekens, C. H., Hennekens, A. R., Hollar, D. & Casey, D. E. (2005). Schizophrenia and increased risks of cardiovascular disease. *American Heart Journal* 150, no. 6: 1115–1121.

Hoge, C. W., Auchterlonie, J. L. & Milliken, C. S. (2006). Mental health problems, use of mental health services, and attrition from military service after returning from deployment to Iraq or Afghanistan. *JAMA* 295: 1023–1032.

Hoge, C. W., McGurk, D., Thomas, J. L., Cox, A. L., Engel, C. C. & Castro, C. A. (2008). Mild traumatic brain injury in U.S. soldiers returning from Iraq. *New England Journal of Medicine* 358: 453–463.

Houston, T. K., Allison, J. J., Person, S., Kovac, S., Williams, O. D. & Kiefe, C. I. (2005). Post-myocardial infarction smoking cessation counseling: Associations with immediate and late mortality in older Medicare patients. *American Journal of Medicine* 118, no. 3: 269–275.

Huang, P. Y., Yano, E. M., Lee, M. L., Chang, B. L. & Rubenstein, L. V. (2004). Variations in nurse practitioner use in Veterans Affairs primary care practices. *Health Services Research* 39, no. 4, pt. 1: 887–904.

Ismail, K., Winkley, K. & Rabe-Hesketh, S. (2004). Systematic review and meta-analysis of randomized controlled trials of psychological interventions to improve glycaemic control in patients with type 2 diabetes. *Lancet* 363, no. 9421: 1589–1597.

Jackson, G. L., Edelman, D. & Weinberger, M. (2006). Simultaneous control of intermediate diabetes outcomes among Veterans Affairs primary care patients. *Journal of General Internal Medicine* 21, no. 10: 1050–1056.

Jadad, A. R. (2004). A view from the Internet age: Let's build a health system that meets the needs of the next generation. *CMAJ* 171, no. 12: 1457–1458.

Johnson, M. L., Pietz, K., Battleman, D. S. & Beyth, R. J. (2006). Therapeutic goal attainment in patients with hypertension and dyslipidemia. *Medical Care* 44, no. 1: 39–46.

Kazis, L. E., Miller, D. R., Clark, J., Skinner, K., Lee, A., Rogers, W., et al. (1998). Health-related quality of life in patients served by the Department of Veterans Affairs: Results from the Veterans Health Study. *Archives of Internal Medicine* 158, no. 6: 626–632.

Kilbourne, A. M., Rofey, D. L., McCarthy, J. F., Post, E. P., Welsh, D. & Blow, F. C. (2007). Nutrition and exercise behavior among patients with bipolar disorder. *Bipolar Disorder* 9, no. 5: 443–452.

Kinsinger, L. S., Jones, K. R., Kahwati, L., Harvey, R., Burdick, M., Zele, V., et al. (2009). Design and dissemination of the MOVE! Weight-Management Program for Veterans. *Preventing Chronic Disease* 6, no. 3: A98.

Kizer, K. W., Fonseca, M. L. & Long, L. M. (1997). The veterans healthcare system: Preparing for the twenty-first century. *Hospital Health Services Administration* 42, no. 3: 283–298.

Lanas, F., Avezum, A., Bautista, L. E., Diaz, R., Luna, M., Islam, S., et al. (2007). Risk factors for acute myocardial infarction in Latin America: The INTERHEART Latin American Study. *Circulation* 115, no. 9: 1067–1074.

Lynn, M. M., Achtmeyer, C., Chavez, C., Zicafoose, B. & Therien, J. (1999). The evolving role of advanced practice nursing within the new Veteran's Health Administration. *Health Care Management Review* 24, no. 4: 80–93.

Maher, M. J., Rego, S. A. & Asnis, G. M. (2006). Sleep disturbances in patients with post-traumatic stress disorder: Epidemiology, impact and approaches to management. *CNS Drugs* 20, no. 7: 567–590.

Mallion, J. M., Baguet, J. P., Siche, J. P., Tremel, F. & de Gaudemaris, R. (1998). Compliance, electronic monitoring and antihypertensive drugs. *Journal of Hypertension Supplement* 16, no. 1: S75–79.

Morey, M. C., Peterson, M. J., Pieper, C. F., Sloane, R., Crowley, G. M., Cowper, P. A., et al. (2009). The Veterans Learning to Improve Fitness and Function in Elders Study: A randomized trial of primary care-based physical activity counseling for older men. *Journal of the American Geriatric Society* 57, no. 7: 1166–1174.

Mrus, J. M., Leonard, A. C., Yi, M. S., Sherman, S. N., Fultz, S. L., Justice, A. C., et al. (2006). Health-related quality of life in veterans and nonveterans with HIV/AIDS. *Journal of General Internal Medicine* 21, supp. 5: S39–47.

Naditz, A. (2008). Telemedicine at the VA: VistA, MyHealtheVet, and other VA programs. *Telemedicine Journal and E-Health* 14, no. 4: 330–332.

Nazi, K. M. (2010). Veterans' voices: Use of the American Customer Satisfaction Index (ACSI) Survey to identify My HealtheVet personal health record users' characteristics, needs, and preferences. *Journal of the American Medical Information Association* 17, no. 2: 203–211.

Nazi, K. M., Hogan, T. P., Wagner, T. H., McInnes, D. K., Smith, B. M., Haggstrom, D., et al. (2010). Embracing a health services research perspective on personal health records: Lessons learned from the VA My HealtheVet system. *Journal of General Internal Medicine* 25, supp. 1: 62–67.

Nelson, K. M. (2006). The burden of obesity among a national probability sample of veterans. *Journal of General Internal Medicine* 21, no. 9: 915–919.

NIH Technology Assessment Conference Panel. (1993). Methods for voluntary weight loss and control. *Annals of Internal Medicine* 119, no. 7, pt. 2: 764–770.

Orszag, P. (2007). *The long-term outlook for health care spending.* Washington, DC: The Congress of the United States, Congressional Budget Office.

Osterberg, L. & Blaschke, T. (2005). Adherence to medication. *New England Journal of Medicine* 353, no. 5: 487–497.

Payne, S. M., Lee, A., Clark, J. A., Rogers, W. H., Miller, D. R., Skinner, K. M., et al. (2005). Utilization of medical services by Veterans Health Study (VHS) respondents. *Journal of Ambulatory Care Management* 28, no. 2: 125–140.

Perri, M. G., Nezu, A. M., McKelvey, W. F., Shermer, R. L., Renjilian, D. A. & Viegener, B. J. (2001). Relapse prevention training and problem-solving therapy in the long-term management of obesity. *Journal of Consulting & Clinical Psychology* 69, no. 4: 722–726.

Peto, R., Darby, S., Deo, H., Silcocks, P., Whitley, E. & Doll, R. (2000). Smoking, smoking cessation, and lung cancer in the UK since 1950: Combination of national statistics with two case-control studies. *BMJ* 321, no. 7257: 323–329.

Piette, J. D. & Moos, R. H. (1996). The influence of distance on ambulatory care use, death, and readmission following a myocardial infarction. *Health Services Research* 31, no. 5: 573–591.

Piette, J. D., Weinberger, M., McPhee, S. J., Mah, C. A., Kraemer, F. B. & Crapo, L. M. (2000). Do automated calls with nurse follow-up improve self-care and glycemic control among vulnerable patients with diabetes? *American Journal of Medicine* 108, no. 1: 20–27.

Powers, B. J., Olsen, M. K., Oddone, E. Z. & Bosworth, H. B. (2009). The effect of a hypertension self-management intervention on diabetes and cholesterol control. *American Journal of Medicine* 122, no. 7: 639–646.

Primary Care Management Module (PCMM). 2003. *Enhancements for direct primary care: User's guide.* January. www.va.gov/vdl/documents/clinical/pri_Care_Mgmnt_Module(PCMM)/sd_53_277.um-final.doc (accessed March 2010).

Rogers, W. H., Kazis, L. E., Miller, D. R., Skinner, K. M., Clark, J. A., Spiro, A., III, et al. (2004). Comparing the health status of VA and non-VA ambulatory patients: The veterans' health and medical outcomes studies. *Journal of Ambulatory Care Management* 27, no. 3: 249–262.

Rohrer, L. D., Gierisch, J. M., Fish, L. J., Blakeney, J. K. & Bastian, L. A. (2011). A five-step guide for moving from observational studies to interventional research for women veterans. *Women's Health Issues* 21, supp. 4: S98–S102.

Ross, J. S., Keyhani, S., Keenan, P. S., Bernheim, S. M., Penrod, J. D., Boockvar, K. S., et al. (2008). Use of recommended ambulatory care services: Is the Veterans Affairs quality gap narrowing? *Archives of Internal Medicine* 168, no. 9: 950–958.

Roumie, C. L., Elasy, T. A., Greevy, R., Griffin, M. R., Liu, X., Stone, W. J., et al. (2006). Improving blood pressure control through provider education, provider alerts, and patient education: a cluster randomized trial. *Annals of Internal Medicine* 145, no. 3: 165–175.

Running, A., Calder, J., Mustain, B. & Foreschler, C. (2000). A survey of nurse practitioners across the United States. *Nurse Practice* 25, no. 6, pt. 1: 15–16, 110–116.

Ryan, D. H., Espeland, M. A., Foster, G. D., Haffner, S. M., Hubbard, V. S., Johnson, K. C., et al. (2003). Look AHEAD (Action for Health in Diabetes): Design and methods for a clinical trial of weight loss for the prevention of cardiovascular disease in type 2 diabetes. *Controlled Clinical Trials* 24, no. 5: 610–628.

Sabate, E. (2003). *Adherence to long-term therapies: Evidence for action.* Geneva, Switzerland: World Health Organization.

Saydah, S. H., Fradkin, J. & Cowie, C. C. (2004). Poor control of risk factors for vascular disease among adults with previously diagnosed diabetes. *JAMA* 291, no. 3: 335–342.

Schmitt, S. K., Phibbs, C. S. & Piette, J. D. (2003). The influence of distance on utilization of outpatient mental health aftercare following inpatient substance abuse treatment. *Addictive Behavior* 28, no. 6: 1183–1192.

Schnoll, R. A., James, C., Malstrom, M., Rothman, R. L., Wang, H., Babb, J., et al. (2003). Longitudinal predictors of continued tobacco use among patients diagnosed with cancer. *Annals of Behavioral Medicine* 25, no. 3: 214–222.

Schroeder, K., Fahey, T. & Ebrahim, S. (2004). Interventions for improving adherence to treatment in patients with high blood pressure in ambulatory settings. *Cochrane Database System Review* 2: CD004804.

Simon, G. E., VonKorff, M., Rutter, C. & Wagner, E. (2000). Randomised trial of monitoring, feedback, and management of care by telephone to improve treatment of depression in primary care. *BMJ* 320, no. 7234: 550–554.

Stahl, S., Kelley, C. R., Neill, P. J., Grim, C. E. & Mamlin, J. (1984). Effects of home blood pressure measurement on long-term BP control. *American Journal of Public Health* 74: 704–709.

Strom, L., Pettersson, R. & Andersson G. (2004). Internet-based treatment for insomnia: a controlled evaluation. *Journal of Consulting & Clinical Psychology* 72, no. 1: 113–120.

Suka, M., Yoshida, K. & Sugimori, H. (2003). Persistent insomnia is a predictor of hypertension in Japanese male workers. *Journal of Occupational Health* 45: 344–350.

Svetkey, L. P., Stevens, V. J., Brantley, P. J., Appel, L. J., Hollis, J. F., Loria, C. M., et al. (2008). Comparison of strategies for sustaining weight loss: The weight loss maintenance randomized controlled trial. *JAMA* 299, no. 10: 1139–1148.

Taylor, D. J., Mallory, L. J., Lichstein, K. L., Durrence, H. H., Riedel, B. W. & Bush, A. J. (2007). Comorbidity of chronic insomnia with medical problems. *Sleep* 30: 213–218.

Ulmer, C., Edinger, J., Means, M. K., Lineberger, M. D., Stechuchak, K. M., Olsen, M. K., Goodin, A. & Carney, C. E. (2008). Cognitive behavioral therapy for insomnia in veterans with PTSD. Paper presented at the Annual Meeting of the Association for Behavioral and Cognitive Therapies, Orlando, FL.

U.S. Department of Health and Human Services. (2008). 2008 physical activity guidelines for Americans. http://health.gov/paguidelines/.

van Dam, R. M., Li, T., Spiegelman, D., Franco, O. H. & Hu, F. B. (2008). Combined impact of lifestyle factors on mortality: Prospective cohort study in US women. *BMJ* 337: a1440.

Voils, C. I., Yancy, W. S., Jr., Kovac, S., Coffman, C. J., Weinberger, M., Oddone, E. Z., et al. (2009). Study protocol: Couples Partnering for Lipid Enhancing Strategies (CouPLES)—a randomized, controlled trial. *Trials* 10: 10.

Wadden, T. A., Butryn, M. L. & Byrne, K. J. (2004). Efficacy of lifestyle modification for long-term weight control. *Obesity Research* 12, supp.: 151S–162S.

Warsi, A., Wang, P. S., LaValley, M. P. & Avorn, J. S. D. (2004). Self-management education programs in chronic disease: A systematic review and methodological critique of the literature. *Archives of Internal Medicine* 164, no. 15: 1641–1649.

Weinberger, M., Tierney, W. M., Cowpar, P. A., Katz, B. P. & Booher, P. (1993). Cost-effectiveness of increased telephone contact for patients with osteoarthritis: A randomized controlled trial. *Arthritis & Rheumatism* 26: 243–246.

Whitten, P. S., Mair, F. S., Haycox, A., May, C. R., Williams, T. L. & Hellmich, S. (2002). Systematic review of cost effectiveness studies of telemedicine interventions. *BMJ* 324, no. 7351: 1434–1437.

Wing, R. R., Venditti, E., Jakicic, J. M., Polley, B. A. & Lang, W. (1998). Lifestyle intervention in overweight individuals with a family history of diabetes. *Diabetes Care* 21, no. 3: 350–359.

Yancy, W. S., Jr. & Voils, C. I. (in press). Improving dietary adherence. In H. B. Bosworth (Ed.), *Improving patient treatment adherence: A clinician guidebook*. New York: Springer.

Yu, W., Ravelo, A., Wagner, T. H., Phibbs, C. S., Bhandari, A., Chen, S., et al. (2003). Prevalence and costs of chronic conditions in the VA health care system. *Medical Care Research Review* 60, no. 3, supp.: 146S–167S.

Yusuf, S., Hawken, S., Ounpuu, S., Dans, T., Avezum, A., Lanas, F., et al. (2004). Effect of potentially modifiable risk factors associated with myocardial infarction in 52 countries (the INTERHEART Study): Case-control study. *Lancet* 364, no. 9438: 937–952.

Chapter 10

Orthotics and Prosthetics Healthcare for Veterans

Thomas W. Miller

Introduction

The Department of Veterans Affairs (VA) has become a world leader in prosthetics and rehabilitation through an integrated delivery system designed to provide prosthetic and sensory aids, devices, assistive aids, and repairs to disabled veterans to facilitate treatment of their medical conditions. Fred Downs, himself a person with a disability, has been a leader and instrumental in the development and direction of prosthetics in VA. Fred Downs is discussed in volume 1, chapter 7, devoted to healthcare for veterans of the Vietnam era.

History and Policies

Prosthetics have been a critical component of healthcare and military life for centuries. Initially crude replacements for missing limbs, prosthetics have advanced from the peg leg to computerized artificial limbs, joints, and more. The first extant document about prosthetics dates back to the Greek historian Herodotus, who wrote about a prisoner who had escaped his cell by cutting off his foot and replacing it with a wooden one. In 3000 BC the Egyptians pioneered prosthetic technology, creating limbs made of fiber. Archeologists have also discovered a bronze peg that served as a prosthetic leg. Leather peg legs and crutches made of wood, leather, or metal were created during the dark ages, and during the early 1500s a German mercenary, Gotz von Berlichingen, had a pair of technologically advanced iron hands made after he lost his right arm in battle. During this same period Ambroise Pare, a French surgeon, developed an artificial leg with a movable knee joint, a flexible foot operated with a spring, and an artificial hand with fingers that were moved by tiny internal cogs and levers. During the latter part of the seventeenth century Dutch surgeon Pieter Andriannszoon Verduyn developed the first nonlocking prosthesis for below the knee (American Orthotic & Prosthetic Association 2010).

At the dawn of the nineteenth century James Potts designed a prosthesis made of a wooden shank and socket, a steel knee joint, and an articulated foot, controlled by tendons from the knee to the ankle. In the mid-nineteenth century, Dr. Douglas Bly of Rochester, New York, invented a prosthetic leg with an articulated ankle made of an ivory ball in a vulcanized rubber socket. During the American Civil War (1861–1865) the government of the United States joined several states in paying for prosthetic devices for war veterans so that they could return to independent lives, and companies began to supply limbs made from wood, metal, and leather. During the nineteenth century interest in the use of suction devices led Dubois Parmlee to develop an advanced prosthesis with a suction socket, polycentric knee, and multi-articulated foot. Giuliano Vanghetti created a new procedure for using a patient's remaining tendons and muscles to allow movement within a prosthetic limb.

The first externally powered prosthetic limbs were built in Germany in the early twentieth century. Gustav Hermann created the first aluminum leg prosthesis in 1915. The world wars resulted in advances in both Europe and the United States in prosthetic science. Scientists at the University of California at Berkeley in the early 1950s researched the introduction of a suction socket for above-knee prosthesis and made major advances in the attachment of lower limbs with electrically and pneumatically powered devices, leading to advances veterans came to know in the last half of the twentieth century.

A microprocessor in an external prosthesis was introduced toward the end of the twentieth century. New prosthetic advances—including the C-leg for above-knee amputees, controlled by a microprocessor; the Power Knee, which synchronizes itself to the motion of the intact leg; Proprio Foot for below-knee amputees with a motorized ankle controlled by sensor technology; PowerFoot, with a self-sustained robotic system; and iLimb Hand, which uses electric signals from existing muscles, enabling users to open and close lifelike fingers—emerged at the dawn of the twenty-first century.

Modern limbs include electric arms that use a small battery, others controlled by a tiny switch, and the myoelectric prostheses, which use electrical impulses detected by small electrodes placed on the skin over the remaining arm muscles. Artificial legs can be fitted with spring-loaded feet; artificial feet can be constructed with toes; synthetic coverings are made to match skin tone and hair patterns; and electrodes in the artificial limb lead to the natural skin, which allows the brain to register "feeling" in the prosthesis. Artificial limbs use plastics and fiberglass for enhanced strength and comfort (Downs 2008).

Contemporary Policies of the Department of Veterans Affairs

Department of Veterans Affairs VHA Directive 2006-029 (May 15, 2006), entitled "Specific Purpose Funding for Prosthetics," outlines the procedures for managing this funding of the Prosthetics Program. Prosthetics is a Veterans Health Administration (VHA) special emphasis program and serves almost a quarter of the patients in the VHA system. As a result of eligibility reform in 1996, prosthetics workload and expenditures have increased dramatically each year. Prior to 1998, prosthetics funding was earmarked as "specific purpose." In 1998 the VA Central Office decided to place the funding for the Prosthetics Program under general purpose funds. As a result of this change, the level of care and the timely delivery of prosthetic appliances and services decreased significantly. For this reason, the Under Secretary for Health issued a memorandum on October 2, 2000, mandating that funding for prosthetics would once again be placed under "specific purpose."

The Patient Protection and Affordable Care Act became law on March 23, 2010, and is now in the process of being implemented. There is currently a rumor circulating that the act will require U.S. Veterans and service members to pay a tax on prosthetic limbs and other vital medical devices. The truth is that any veteran receiving healthcare in the VA system receives his or her prescribed medical devices and prosthetics at no charge. Any increase in price due to the new tax will be borne by VHA. Every veteran will continue to receive prescribed devices free of charge. (For information on the White House's response to this rumor see http://www.whitehouse.gov/blog/2010/07/07/how-affordable-care-act-helps-veterans.)

VHA brought about the merger of the Prosthetics and Sensory Aids Service (PSAS) and the Office of Clinical Logistics at the Central Office level; however, the specific purpose funding for prosthetics must not be affected by the merger of the two offices, and it must continue to be a mainstay in providing prosthetic devices and services to our veterans.

Developments and New Directions

The PSAS is the largest and most comprehensive provider of durable medical equipment and prosthetic devices in the world. Although the term "prosthetic device" may suggest images of artificial limbs, it actually refers to any device that supports or replaces a body part or function. As noted, a full range of equipment and services is available to eligible veterans through the PSAS. These range from items worn by the veteran, such as an artificial limb or hearing aid; to those that improve accessibility, such as ramps and vehicle modifications; to devices surgically placed in the veteran, such as hips and pacemakers.

Assistive and Adaptive Program

The number of veterans seeking prosthetic services from VHA exceeds two million at this writing, based on information provided by the Senate Committee on Veterans Affairs. As the demand for services increased, so did the budget to provide them, from $532 million in 2000 to $1.6 billion in 2008 (Senate Committee on Veterans Affairs 2008).

Although the number of veterans seeking services continues to rise, the primary reason for the increased spending is the escalating cost of the products and services provided, especially the costs of new technologies. Under the Home Improvements and Structural Alterations (HISA) program, veterans with service-connected disabilities or with non-service-connected disabilities may receive assistance for any home improvement necessary for the continuation of treatment or for disability access to the home and essential lavatory and sanitary facilities. An HISA grant is available to veterans who have received a medical determination indicating that improvements and structural alterations are necessary or appropriate for the effective and economical treatment of the disability. A veteran may receive both an HISA grant and either a Special Home Adaptation (SHA) grant or a Specially Adapted Housing (SAH) grant. The Automobile Adaptive Equipment (AAE) program permits physically challenged persons to enter, exit, and/or operate a motor vehicle or other conveyance. Veterans are trained, through the VHA Driver's Rehabilitation Program, how to safely operate their vehicles on our nation's roadways. VHA also provides necessary equipment such as platform wheelchair lifts, UVLs (under vehicle lifts), power door openers, lowered floors/raised roofs, raised doors, hand controls, left foot gas pedals, reduced effort and zero effort steering and braking, and digital driving systems. Furthermore, the VA program provides reimbursements for standard equipment, including, but not limited to, power steering, power brakes, power windows, power seats, and other special equipment necessary for the safe operation of an approved vehicle.

The PSAS provides items prescribed by appropriate VHA clinicians. Items may range from a $2 cane tip to a $100,000 microprocessor-controlled bionic knee that replaces muscle activity to bend and straighten the knee.

Regardless of cost, VA's mission is to provide the most appropriate technology to veterans in a timely manner.

Specialists, Services, and Training

One of the many avenues to providing the best devices for veterans is the VA's prosthetic and orthotic laboratories. As of August 2007, all sixty-three VA prosthetic and orthotic labs had earned certification by one of the two national accrediting organizations. Eight of these labs are also accredited by the National Commission on Orthotic and Prosthetic Education, enabling them to participate in residency programs of the nine prosthetic and orthotic programs in U.S. universities and colleges. One of those nine schools, California State University–Dominguez Hills, is relocating to the Long Beach VA Medical Center campus. This collaboration with the prosthetic educational system, which includes a contractual training program, will further strengthen clinical care by providing training courses for VA's orthotic fitters and specialists.

The PSAS has more than 100 board-certified prosthetists and orthotists working at its labs, a standard that far exceeds the private sector. After assessing a patient, an orthotist designs and fabricates a custom orthopedic appliance, such as a brace or splint, to meet the veteran's physical challenge, and fits it to the patient's extremity or spine. A prosthetist works with a veteran amputee to perform a mechanical assessment, design a custom prosthesis, fabricate custom sockets, order components, assemble the prosthesis, and perform an alignment process to ensure that the veteran can use the prosthesis to its highest potential.

Specialized equipment in the laboratories enables the prosthetist and orthotist to design, fabricate, repair, and adjust the veteran's appliances. VA is a leader in the use of the newest computer-aided design and manufacture (CAD/CAM) equipment. Prosthetic representatives, prosthetists, and medical specialists in various disciplines are part of VA medical centers' amputation care teams, responsible for assessing a veteran's prosthetic needs. The team prescribes a prosthesis based on the veteran's medical condition, needs, and stated goals, and evaluates its functionality after it is made and delivered to the veteran.

Whether provided by VA prosthetists or through one of more than 600 contracts with nationally accredited local prosthetists, VA pays the full cost of a limb as well as all repairs. This applies to all devices provided through prescriptions. Prosthetists in this healthcare system support all the specialty clinics that require a prosthetic device for a veteran, such as spinal cord injury, audiology, blind rehabilitation, and podiatry.

Special Programs for Veterans with Disabilities

In addition to providing devices, the PSAS also administers three unique programs to assist veterans with disabilities. An annual clothing allowance is available to veterans with a service-connected condition who, because of the disability, must wear a device or use a prescribed ointment that damages outer clothing. The HISA grant is available to alter the home of a veteran who needs access. Examples include ramps, railings, lowered countertops, flooring, widened doorways, and accessible bathrooms. The one-time maximum amount ($1,200 for non-service-connected veterans and $4,100 for service-connected veterans) depends on the veteran's service-connected rating.

In keeping with its dedication to providing equipment to address all the needs of veterans, the PSAS administers the Automobile Adaptive Equipment program. This program provides equipment and training that some service-connected patients need to enter, exit, and operate a motor vehicle once they have been awarded an automobile grant and completed driver's training with an approved driver evaluator. A patient who does not meet the criteria to operate a vehicle can still be approved for equipment to enter and exit a vehicle.

Iraq and Afghanistan: Healing the Wounds of War

This wide breadth of equipment and services the PSAS can provide is not limited to veterans of a particular period of service. VHA is sensitive to the needs of the Persian Gulf War veterans and the newest veterans, who comprise less than 5 percent of the patients working with its PSAS staff nationwide. At the end of fiscal 2008, VA had provided equipment to 89,152 veterans of Persian Gulf operations and Operation Enduring Freedom (OEF) and Operation Iraqi Freedom (OIF), in addition to millions of veterans from earlier periods. With the type of military operations in the Persian Gulf War, VHA realized the importance of prosthetic care in its veteran population (Miller 1991). With the use and introduction of IUDs in this combat arena, the need for orthotics and prosthetics has become a critical focus of veterans' healthcare. The VA research program is the only federal program that focuses on discovery in diseases and conditions that affect our growing veteran population.

Fundamental research through the VA Medical and Prosthetic Research Program is critical to the VA clinical mission, which excels at providing expert medical care for veterans, particularly those whose medical problems develop in the line of duty, through the Veterans Affairs Medical Centers (VAMCs). The VHA research program restricts awards to its employees, providing VA with a powerful tool for recruiting and retaining the highly qualified clinician-investigators who provide quality care to veterans, focus their research on conditions prevalent in the veteran population, and educate future clinicians to care for veterans.

Research efforts through VA have gained international recognition for their many contributions, including the development of innovative medical treatments, devices, and healthcare delivery systems that have served the specific needs of veterans and provided revolutionary health improvements to civilian patients nationwide. VHA research has played a key role in health innovations, including liver transplants, cardiac pacemakers, prosthetic limbs, and mental health treatments for alcoholism and addiction as well as post-traumatic stress disorder (PTSD). For their notable work, veterans' healthcare researchers have won three Nobel prizes, six Lasker awards, and several other recognitions.

Treating Soldiers and Pioneering Medicine

Department of Veterans Affairs researchers supported by federal funding have consistently developed healthcare solutions that address the specific needs of our veteran population, while also providing innovations and therapies that benefit the nation as a whole. In particular, VA research has been critical to the study of brain and spinal cord injury, development of limb prostheses, and understanding and treating PTSD and diabetes. Researchers supported by VA have recently demonstrated that infusion of bone marrow stem cells can protect against the brain trauma many soldiers suffer in combat. The ongoing development of ankle-foot prostheses and a flexible prosthetic wrist by VA researchers will promote greater mobility and more lifelike interaction with objects for veterans who have lost limbs. Veterans' health researchers have also demonstrated that linezolid, a new antibiotic, effectively treats diabetic foot infections, a leading cause of amputations. VA research has contributed to establishing new treatment for PTSD by uncovering the mechanisms involved in nerve transmission and brain circuitry when stressed or threatened and found that prazosin, an inexpensive generic drug for blood pressure and prostate problems, reduces nightmares for veterans with PTSD. In addition, VA researchers have identified seven genes that are associated with risk for diabetes, which may serve as important diagnostic tools, as well as providing targets for therapies and interventions. These innovations will continue to shape the care provided to our veterans. However, it is only through sustained investment through federal funding that VA scientists will be able to carry on their work.

Future Directions of Prosthetic Healthcare for Veterans

Veterans in the twenty-first century who are wounded in Afghanistan, Iraq, or elsewhere will encounter a new era of prosthetic healthcare. Even with all the wonders of modern medicine, building a robotic arm with a fully functioning hand has not been possible. One remarkable leap in technology is the DEKA arm, just one of the breakthroughs in revolutionizing prosthetics. Frederick Downs is the head of prosthetics for VHA and has been wearing the standard prosthetic arm since 1968, after he stepped on a landmine in Vietnam (Columbia Broadcasting System 2009). The prosthetics of World Wars I and II, Korea, or Vietnam were mechanical devices that allowed the veteran to rotate the hook and lock it, demonstrating the limited movement ability of any prosthetic device. Dr. Geoffrey Ling, an army colonel and neurologist, is leading the revolution in prosthetics through the development of new computer-based prosthetic devices that permit the mechanical use of the opposable thumb and independently moving, articulating fingers (Downs 2008).

Clinician-researchers, scientists, engineers, neuroscientists, and psychologists are exploring and developing treatments for a range of medical conditions. VHA investigators are studying chronic pain management, pioneering home dialysis techniques, developing new hearing loss prevention and treatments, and exploring the use of computer technology to assist patients with spinal injuries in everyday activities. Veterans' healthcare research is also addressing the needs of an aging veteran population, with research into diabetes, exploration of healthcare delivery effectiveness, and the identification of genes associated with various diseases and disorders. Frederick Downs, who serves as the PSAS chief consultant for prosthetic and sensory aids, stresses the need for research to develop new designs for upper-extremity prostheses that operate more like a hand and look less like a hook. Ideas raised for future investigation include conducting basic research on pain; looking at gender differences and other diversity issues among amputees; exploring ways to improve the "machine-body" interface between the prosthesis socket and the residual limb; evaluating various components using computer modeling; developing new ways to control prostheses, both through the internal neuromuscular impulses of the user and externally generated electronic signals; and testing how supplying external power to artificial limbs affects the body's metabolism.

Reiber and colleagues (2010) have provided some direction for the future through their research survey of traumatic limb loss veterans. Care of veterans and service members with major traumatic limb loss from combat theaters is one of the highest priorities of VA. Reiber and colleagues achieved a 62 percent response rate in our Survey for Prosthetic Use of 298 Vietnam War veterans and 283 service members/veterans from OIF/OEF who sustained major traumatic limb loss. Veterans surveyed reported their combat injuries; health status; quality of life; and prosthetic device use, function, rejection, and satisfaction. Despite their serious combat injuries, their health status was rated excellent, very good, or good by 70.7 percent of Vietnam War and 85.5 percent of OIF/OEF survey participants. However, many health issues persist for Vietnam War and OIF/OEF survey participants (respectively): phantom limb pain (72.2 percent/76.0 percent), chronic back pain (36.2 percent/42.1 percent), residual-limb pain (48.3 percent/ 62.9 percent), prosthesis-related skin problems (51.0 percent/58.0 percent), hearing loss (47.0 percent/ 47.0 percent), traumatic brain injury (3.4 percent/33.9 percent), depression (24.5 percent/24.0 percent), and posttraumatic stress disorder (37.6 percent/ 58.7 percent). Prosthetic devices are currently used by 78.2 percent of Vietnam War and 90.5 percent of OIF/OEF survey participants to improve function and mobility. On average, the annual rate for prosthetic device receipt is 10.7-fold higher for OIF/OEF than for Vietnam War survey participants. The clinical and research results from this cross-conflict survey identify much strength in prosthetic rehabilitation for those with limb loss and several areas for future consideration through the Department of Defense and VHA.

Wounded Warrior Project™ (WWP)

The Wounded Warrior Project™ exists to honor and empower wounded warriors who incurred service-connected injuries on or after September 11, 2001. Because of the advancements in battlefield medicine and body armor, an unprecedented percentage of service members are surviving severe wounds or injuries. For every U.S. soldier killed in World Wars I and II, there were 1.7 soldiers wounded. In OEF/OIF, for every U.S. soldier killed, seven have been wounded. Combined, almost 42,000 have been injured in the two conflicts: nearly 32,000 in OIF and nearly 10,000 in OEF.

With the mission to honor and empower wounded warriors, the WWP is clearly a hand extended to encourage them as they adjust to their new "normal" and achieve new triumphs. Offering a variety of programs and services, the WWP is equipped to serve warriors with every type of injury, from the physical to the invisible wounds of war. The Wounded Warrior Project (WWP) began when several veterans and friends, moved by stories of the first wounded service members returning home from Afghanistan and Iraq, took action to help others in need. What started as a program to provide comfort items to wounded service members has grown into a complete rehabilitative effort to assist warriors as they recover and transition back to their civilian lives.

With its name derived from Homer's epic poem about overcoming adversity and finding the way home, Project Odyssey™ helps veterans overcome combat stress through outdoor, rehabilitative retreats that encourage a connection with nature, peers, Project Odyssey staff, and trained counselors. Through outdoor, recreational activities, veterans will discover inner strength and find the courage to continue their journey to recovery. The experiences gained from Project Odyssey help veterans work through challenges related to combat stress and improve mental attitudes and outlook. The program continues for veterans beyond the retreat. For more information on Project Odyssey and how to apply, contact projectodyssey@woundedwarriorproject.org.

The Combat Stress Recovery Program (CSRP) addresses the mental health and cognitive needs of warriors returning from war. It provides services at key stages during a warrior's readjustment process. Although PTSD and combat/operational stress are common after wartime experiences, the WWP approaches these issues from the warrior's perspective. Assistance is offered to veterans in navigating mental health resources that help process their combat experience. The Wounded Warrior Project Restore™ is an online tool that teaches warriors more about the invisible wounds of war and the readjustment challenges that they may well face.

Efforts to enlist specialists from VHA to contribute further to this chapter were unsuccessful. The reader interested in more details about veterans' healthcare specifically related to orthotics and prosthetics and the PSAS are encouraged to see http://www.prosthetics.va.gov/. VHA has a special commitment to the mission of the PSAS in providing comprehensive support to optimize the health and independence of the veterans in need of such services. This vision is to be the premier source of prosthetic and orthotic services, sensory aids, medical equipment, and support services for veterans' healthcare.

References

American Orthotic & Prosthetic Association. (2010). History of prosthetics & orthotics. http://www.aopa.org.au/index.php?option=com_content&view=article&id=71:history-of-prosthetics-a-orthotics&catid=37:general&Itemid=58 (accessed December 20, 2010).

Columbia Broadcasting System. (2009) The Pentagon's bionic arm: Pentagon is working to develop a life-changing, high tech prosthetic arm. *60 Minutes.* http://www.cbsnews.com/stories/2009/04/10/60minutes/main4935509.shtml (accessed December 18, 2010).

Downs, Frederick. (2008). Prosthetics in the VA: Past, present, and future. U.S. Naval Institute. www.usni.org (accessed December 20, 2010).

Miller, T. W. (1991). Clinical issues in readaptation for Persian Gulf veterans. *Psychiatric Annals* 21, no. 11: 684–689.

Patient Protection and Affordable Care Act of 2010. Pub. L. No. 111-148.

Reiber, G. E., McFarland, L. V., Hubbard, S., Maynard, C., Blough, D. K., Gambel, J. M. & Smith, D. G. (2010). Service members and veterans with major traumatic limb loss from Vietnam War and OIF/OEF conflicts: Survey methods, participants, and summary findings. *Journal of Rehabilitation Research & Development* 47, no. 4: 275–298.

Senate Committee on Veterans Affairs. (2008). Assistive and Adaptive Devices Report to the Senate Committee on Veterans Affairs. Washington, DC: Senate Office Building.

Wounded Warrior Project™ (WWP). (2011). WWP program summary. http://www.woundedwarriorproject.org/programs.aspx (accessed September 12, 2011).

Chapter 11

Native American Veterans and Post-traumatic Stress Disorder: Issues, Challenges, and Solutions

Joseph B. Stone

Native American veterans encompass a wide variety of tribal communities across the United States and comprise the single most highly decorated racial subgroup of combat warriors who have fought for the U.S. military. We in our tribal communities honor our veterans and warriors in many ways. For example, at pow-wows, if an eagle feather drops to the arena floor, it is required that a veteran be the individual who picks it up. So this chapter is for you, my brother Native veterans and your families, caregivers, and relatives, and it is for all the young First Nations men and women who chose to take the path of the warrior. I hope that this attempt to try to understand this warrior's path, the outcomes of taking it, and the challenges of those outcomes honors you . . . all of you. I hope I am honoring those aboriginal veterans who have made the ultimate sacrifice through combat or through the often sad outcomes of combat that reoccur and reecho across decades and through families and communities. A Shawnee poet wrote about an elder, Horse Man, who had passed over:

> I have seen the rain speak and the wind dance. I have seen the lightning knife cut the sky. I have seen the hills at the first light of day whispering secrets in the Southwind People's ears. I am happy now. I am no longer thirsty. I dance a warrior's dance. I am not sick, I am free. This night, I dream a new dream. Now, I come to drink the stars! (Pierce Eyen 1997).

This chapter is dedicated to several specific Native veterans:

Richard K. Laughter, MD, a Navajo (Dine) marine who served in Iraq and is my spiritual brother

Daniel Foster, PhD, a Lakota (Sioux) army veteran who served in Vietnam and is my spiritual brother

Jerry Zamora, a member of a Montana tribe and a Vietnam veteran afflicted by disease related to Agent Orange and a medicine man and teacher

Joseph B. Stone Jr., an Aamskapipikuni (Blackfeet) World War II veteran shot at Bougainville and my beloved uncle; I carry your purple heart in my medicine box to this day.

In time, all my brother and sister Native veterans and I will dance that warrior's dance together.

Introduction

It is noteworthy that the aboriginal veteran is a member of a highly honored and decorated group of warriors and protectors called to service for this country who have served with distinction in a fine historical tradition. Armed forces' records detail brave exploits and deeds of Native fighting men and women. Of note, the actions of the Navajo (Dine) tribal code talkers during World War II are often referred to as significant.

When I was asked to approach this topic, I was both honored and overwhelmed, since I am primarily a practicing clinician and not an academic and write infrequently. But I was honored by the request to engage in this task and by the realization that issues important to me would be presented and examined. As a clinician in a remote rural location, my access to the fine libraries and literature bases is limited, and time is at a premium for direct clinical services to my tribal patients (I prefer the term *relatives* rather than *patients* and use it throughout this chapter), including those native relatives who are veterans of foreign expeditions and often have post-traumatic stress disorder (PTSD).

During a late evening I was writing about these issues after an Inuipi (sweatlodge) ceremony. Two of us who were in that ceremony (an Aamskapipikuni/Lakota and a Dine or Navajo) are expeditionary veterans and warriors ourselves and seek the healing of this sacred ritual for ourselves and others, nonveterans and veterans alike. After the Inuipi ceremony, I was home at the computer when my pager went off. The emergency room physician stated, in a panicked voice, "Could you please come in and evaluate a patient, she is really crazy—hollering and screaming and threatening." In the background, I could hear a female relative's voice screaming threats at the emergency room staff. So I asked, who is the patient? The emergency room doctor replied with a name I know well. She was a native woman veteran who had spent significant time in Iraq and was profoundly impacted and impaired by PTSD from her experiences there. So I went to the hospital and evaluated this native sister and arranged for a flight 500 miles to a nonveterans' residential psychiatric facility, with the hope that once the psychosis had cleared I could re-engage and help her find her path to a formal Department of Veterans Affairs (VA) treatment program. But even if this occurred, and even if she benefited from the many solid, evidence-based programs and methods that VA offers for PTSD evaluation and treatment that are explained in this volume, it is my opinion that as a native veteran, she will need more and will benefit from more, specifically the culture and spirituality of the local tribe and their healing ways. Later in this chapter I present a hypothetical case study comprised of my clinical impressions derived from several years of clinical work with a cross-section of native veterans and look at the cultural and spiritual recommendations and methods that are unique to native veterans. In addition, some of these cultural and spiritual methods might be good for treating veterans of other than indigenous background, race, and culture.

The History of Native Veterans

Historically, native veterans have played a vital role in the preservation and protection of freedom, from the American Revolution through the present. American Indians are distinguished by their traditions of courage, honor, and spirit and their warrior's orientation. Ranging from early exploits as trackers and scouts to modern service in various military specialties, the American Indian veteran has a rich history of military service (Brown 1997; Holiday et al. 2006; Mansfield 2004; Naval History and Heritage Committee 2011). The history of Native military service is briefly examined here, based on information from Brown (1997), Holiday and others (2006), and Mansfield (2004).

Throughout the Revolutionary War, the War of 1812, and the Civil War (on both sides of the conflict), natives were particularly active as scouts. In 1866 the Indian Scouts were formally established to make use of their skills in tracking and observation of the opponents. They served with General Pershing in Mexico in pursuit of Pancho Villa and with Teddy Roosevelt in Cuba as Rough Riders during the Spanish-American war.

In World War I approximately 12,000 Natives served, including 600 Oklahoma and Cherokee cited for bravery in the Texas 124th Infantry, which was active in France (four of these Natives were awarded the Croix de Guerre for valor, France's highest military honor). Native women also served during World War I, in the Army Nurse Corps. Finally, the Choctaw language was first used for code in World War I. U.S. citizenship was granted to American Indian soldiers and sailors in 1919, fully five years before the rest of the aboriginal population received citizenship through the Snyder Act in 1924. The Snyder Act also made American Indians subject to conscription through the draft.

In World War II a disproportionate number of tribal peoples or Natives joined the armed forces to defend the American homeland and values. Nearly 44,000 tribal service members enlisted for service in World War II, almost 13 percent of the total Native population of 350,000. An additional 40,000 tribal people worked in nonmilitary war efforts, so that almost 20 percent of the total Native population engaged as combatants or in support efforts. During World War II, the Navajo (Dine) language was used by more than 400 marines, the famous Navajo (Dine) Code Talkers, in the Pacific Theater.

Some 10,000 American Indians enlisted in the Korean conflict, including battle-seasoned troops from World War II. Subsequent military service by Natives has been a tradition in Vietnam (42,000 Indians at a volunteer rate of 90 percent), Grenada, Panama, Somalia, the Persian Gulf, and most recently the Balkans and Middle Eastern engagements in Iran and Iraq. Currently 24,000 of the 1.4 million active military members are American Indians, representing roughly 2 percent of the active duty force and fully 1 percent of the approximately 2.6 million Natives in the United States. Indigenous males in the U.S. military are more than 3 percent of all tribal members between twenty and forty-four years of age. Ubiquitously, fully one-half of active duty American Indians are in the U.S. Navy, and they are also overrepresented in the Marines (20 percent versus 13 percent in all other branches of the service). In general, the trend is that American Indian males serve in the military in greater proportion than the general population of eligible males. As noted in the Brown (1997), Holiday and colleagues (2006), and Mansfield (2004) reports, Native veterans have a rich history of service to the U.S. military in support of American interests. The next section examines the prevalence data for military service and the prevalence rates and incidence of PTSD.

American Indian Military Service: Prevalence and Incidence of PTSD

More than 383,000 veterans self-identify as American Indians, which is 1.5 percent of the more than twenty-six million veterans. In general, American

Indian veterans are younger than their nonveteran counterparts (81 percent of native veterans are younger than sixty-five, as opposed to 63 percent of non-native veterans). Thirty-seven percent of native veterans live in the West, and 36 percent live in the Southwest. The average family income for Native veterans is less than $30,000 and less likely to be in the $50,000 range than all other veterans (Holiday et al. 2004).

In the report *Wounded Spirits, Ailing Hearts Training Manual* (Manson 2000), prevalence data for American Indian Veteran PTSD is presented and compared to other relevant data for the general veteran population. For example, Kulka and colleagues (1990), in the National Vietnam Veterans Readjustment Study (NVVRS), reported that the lifetime PTSD prevalence in Vietnam theater veterans ranged from 14 percent of all white veterans to 22–26 percent of Natives of various tribes (Loo 2010), to 30.9 percent of non-native men and 26.9 percent of non-native women (Friedman et al. 1997). Compare these statistics to an overall rate of 45–57 percent for American Indian veterans reported by Loo (2010) and quantified further in the Matsunaga Vietnam Veterans Project (MVVP) (Friedman 1997). The MVVP found a lifetime prevalence rate of PTSD of 57.2 percent for Northern Plains Indians and 45.3 percent for Southwest tribal veterans (Beals et al. 2002) These high lifetime rates of PTSD are reflected by rates ranging from 27 to 31 percent at the time of interview in a study of 621 Native Vietnam combat veterans by Beals and others (2005). In that study 70 percent of the Native respondents were abusing or dependent on alcohol, which is two to six times greater than any other group of Vietnam combat veterans. In addition, nearly 9 percent of the veterans interviewed reported that they suffered from current depression, and 12 percent had suffered from depression at some point in their lives. Finally, over one-half of the Native veterans interviewed reported that they had attempted suicide, and others had succeeded prior to the project's initiation.

These prevalence rates of PTSD; alcohol abuse; and dependence, depression, and suicide indicate that something is clearly amiss in the lives or development of Native combat veterans. Although controversial, the recent emergence of the field of postcolonial stress and historical trauma might shed light on the predeterminants for vulnerability to developing PTSD among American Indian veterans. Three authors expressed concern about the possible relationships between intergenerational PTSD and historical trauma among indigenous people in general and the vulnerability to development of PTSD among aboriginal people (Cabaniss 2010; French 1992; Kawennano & Johnson 1996). I have long reflected on the issue of historical predeterminants of vulnerability to later development of PTSD and attendant issues among my relatives and myself. I examine the issue of predeterminants of PTSD and other psychiatric manifestations in the next section of this chapter and hope that this portion honors my relatives and our historical and contemporary experiences. I ask that no one accept these ideas without critical examination, but I do ask that you, the reader, make this critical examination.

Clearly, Indian Country presents even the most seasoned and careful researcher, clinician, administrator, or social worker with numerous professional issues and clinical challenges. It is critical to any competent treatise on the issues and challenges faced by indigenous veterans to understand that nothing in military service, combat-related or not, happens in the absence of a significant historical background of predetermining risk factors for tribal veterans. Our first dilemma in addressing the issues and challenges of Native veterans with PTSD is to describe the intergenerational and developmental precursors to their military service and experiences and the possible implications for resiliency versus risk of psychiatric disorders that might be the result of these predeterminants.

Two of the most salient of these issues represent complex and interwoven challenges: 1) appropriate understanding and acknowledgment of postcolonial stress in the tribal communities and 2) the provision of culturally competent clinical services (Brown & Tandon 1983; Brydon-Miller 1997; Duran 1984; Duran & Duran 1995; Locust 1995; Lewis, Duran & Woodis 1999; McTaggert 1991; Park 1999; Stone 2002; Walters & Simoni 1999; Weissberg & Greenberg 1998; Whyte, Greenwood & Lazes 1989; Wisner, Stea & Kruks 1991; Yellow Horse Brave Heart 1998).

Tribal Historical Trauma and Postcolonial Stress: A Theoretical Path Analysis

Tribal communities are impacted by a historical trend of violence perpetrated by the dominant or affluent Euro-American culture. This has included numerous systemic influences across history: 1) dispossession, 2) biological warfare, 3) disruption of culture, 4) Indian wars, 5) the federal and religious boarding schools (disruption of family and language), 6) termination of tribal identity, 7) relocation of natives, and 8) modern influences (gangs & drugs). Each of these influences has in turn predisposed parenting practices within the tribal communities and thus the neurodevelopment and developmental psychopathology of tribal people. Understanding this systemic intergenerational process affecting tribal communities and individuals gives the professional behavioral health worker insight into the depth and breadth of the underlying dynamic, often manifesting itself in the form of psychiatric disorders and addictive behaviors. Implications for reclaiming tribal identity and spirituality for recovery are described and recommended.

Although it is beyond the scope of this chapter to describe fully the postcolonial stress theoretical perspective, I must briefly acknowledge the issues of trauma and grief, which robustly impact tribal peoples across and within generations. This has led to Natives and tribal families being immersed in an intergenerational and intragenerational crucible of stress. Thus it follows that a higher level of post-traumatic stress in First Nation individuals, families, and communities, and also secondary consequences similar to those exhibited by Jewish Holocaust and Khmer Rouge survivors, exist as a result of postcolonial stress (Last & Klein 1984; Nadler, Kav-Venaki & Gleitman 1985; Rowland-Klein & Dunlop 1998; Sack, Clarke & Seeley 1995; Yehuda et al. 1998).

Consequently a high incidence and prevalence of psychiatric disorders and social problems, lateral violence, and high rates of substance abuse and dependence and depression that are likely secondary to post-traumatic stress are observed in indigenous peoples (Ball 1998; Gagne 1998; Nagel 1988; Weaver & Yellow Horse Brave Heart 1999). In 1992 Herman suggested that the symptoms of the sequelae of prolonged and complex trauma across time on psychological functioning might be very significant. The primary effects of this sort of stress in the lives of long-term sexual abuse survivors and combat veterans are a highly coherent description of many of the symptoms and issues faced by tribal people (Ford 1999; Ford & Kidd 1998; Zlotnick et al. 1996). Following is a discussion of the methodology for this chapter.

Review and Methodology Procedures

The primary task of this chapter was to review 123 articles, book chapters, and other documents pertaining to the history of and impacts of military service on tribal and Native veterans. The author reviewed the reference lists of recent books, review articles, and various other published studies and documents, and also manually searched several recent journals. Keywords included *posttraumatic stress, postcolonial, intergenerational trauma, unresolved historical grief, resiliency, attachment, neurodevelopment, developmental psychopathology, participatory action research, collaborative community research, native veterans, tribal veterans, American Indian Veterans, Indigenous Veterans, aboriginal veterans, veterans' health, veterans' affairs and native veterans, and the Indian Health Service, and native veterans.*

Numerous studies, articles, and books contained relevant information referenced in this chapter. The author used the postcolonial stress theory and the initial research findings as the basis for developing a coding instrument to analyze the reviewed articles, book chapters, books, and related documents. It is important to discuss Native veterans' issues and challenges in the context of a postcolonial stress theory.

Next I describe the general background of the postcolonial stress disorder theory as it applies to tribal people, and then move on to a brief discussion of my personal theoretical perspective and path analysis model on the predetermining origins and implications of postcolonial stress in tribal individuals, families, and communities.

Clearly, native people and tribes face numerous behavioral health challenges, including high frequency rates, incidence rates, and prevalence rates of substance abuse (alcohol and drug abuse and dependency), depression, anxiety, lateral violence (child maltreatment and domestic violence), and suicide. Historically, the context of these mental health and substance abuse behaviors for native individuals and in tribal communities is related to a long history of oppressive detrimental relationships and interactions with the dominant culture.

Several areas of concern related to these current issues in tribal behavioral health are examined here. I also turn my attention to healing efforts and methods. Integration (bringing together) of culturally relevant tribal coping and healing methods with modern Western methods is described and proposed.

Detrimental Systemic Influences

Unfortunately, native/tribal behavioral health service clients often exhibit diagnosable behaviors that are self-defeating, or toxic behaviors that cause problems to others (family members, other tribal members, employers, healthcare providers, or representatives of the criminal justice and court system) with whom the native person interacts. Often these problematic behavioral and substance abuse disorders are directly related to the tribal client's personal history, which was influenced by his or her parenting and thus indirectly by the experiences of that client's parents and grandparents. In many historical situations (some recent), tribal individuals, their parents, and their grandparents have been adversely impacted by various traumatic experiences.

Historical impacts on tribal families, in combination with a culture of poverty, lead to situations within which parents, grandparents, or other caregivers have not been able to provide adequate care. In some cases, situations evolved in which tribal clients were sexually or physically abused, resulting in the development of PTSD. This type of personal history has led to a higher than average incidence of depression and anxiety in parents and has contributed to various behavioral problems and disorders and acting out behaviors in Native communities: substance abuse, lateral violence, and suicide.

Tribal Intergenerational PTSD and Compromised Behavioral Immunity

It follows that members of each successive generation of tribal parents have experienced their own adverse impacts, roughly in the following order: 1) the introduction of disease into the system, for which there was no immunity; 2) dispossession of property and enforced removal to reserved lands typically of marginal value; 3) persecution and murder of natives during the various "Indian Wars"; 4) enforced assimilation and acculturation of tribal peoples through the General Allotment Act and the federal boarding school system; 5) oppression of and outlawing of religion, culture, and language (which is the carrier of culture); 6) introduction to vices such as alcohol and drugs; 7) inappropriate and inefficient management of governmental and healthcare systems by dominant culture bureaucrats; and 8) the acting out of internalized oppression through domestic violence and child sexual abuse of other tribal peoples, both within and outside the nuclear family, by Native people.

As a result, each successive generation of new, young tribal parents has been struggling with its own increased incidence, prevalence, and frequency of anxiety and depression. Because of this anxiety and depression, and the simultaneous loss of previously effective tribally based parenting and emotional coping mechanisms, each generation of young tribal parents has provided less than optimum parenting during the development period for its infants. This negatively affected those infants with respect to attachment, attachment disorder, and neurological development during critical periods of brain development. I regard this as compromised behavioral immunity; the individual impacted by compromised parenting is subsequently much more likely to develop and exhibit psychiatric and substance abuse disorders. This contrasts with behavioral immunity to such symptoms, the resiliency that is imparted by good adaptive parenting processes.

Therefore, not only were tribal/native people being affected by the gross social mechanisms listed in the preceding section, but also by incremental increases in compromised behavioral immunity imparted by the less than fully adequate parenting that is usually a consequence of parental anxiety and/or depressed mood. Successive generations of attachment disorder and its antecedent consequence to the developing infant, PTSD, have caused compromised behavioral immunity or lessened resilience, which underlies the current high prevalence, frequency, and incidence of psychiatric and substance abuse disorders in Native/tribal communities.

Theoretical Background

Clearly the literature in the scientific area of attachment and infant mental health is vast. It is not my goal here to offer a completed theoretical discussion of attachment, regulation, or infant mental health. Rather, I am providing a simplified version of this complex area as a heuristic mechanism to initiate further discussion of the issues central to attachment, self-regulation, and infant mental health as a possible mechanism to describe the occurrence of postcolonial stress in tribal peoples. It also is not my goal to suggest that this perspective on postcolonial stress is "right or correct," but rather to suggest that it might be considered and investigated for potential value as a possible correlate to postcolonial stress. It is possible that the description of tribal history might have a relationship with attachment, self-regulation, and infant mental health that has some role as an influencing factor in postcolonial stress. Further, perhaps researchers should consider taking postcolonial stress into account as an important variable in developing a participatory research agenda with tribal communities, even if this description of the possible relationships of attachment, self-regulation, and infant mental health ultimately fails the scientific test.

Recently, B. Perry (2002) asserted that the first four years of life are the most critical for brain development of the child. Borrowing from Perry, I provide a simplified description of brain development during the first four years of life. Initially the infant's cognitive abilities are limited by the not fully developed prefrontal cortex and nerve fiber system, which is involved with thinking and memory (representation of visual and verbal experiences). Neonates appear capable of storing and retrieving sensory information even delivered to them prenatally; however, lacking speech, they are unable for some months to engage in the type of inner speech that one might characterize as thought. During this initial period of time, the infant is capable of feeling arousal, because the limbic system is well enough developed to generate those feelings (Nieuwenhuys, Voogd & van Huijzen 1981; Papuz 1937).

I believe that one important goal of infant behavior is emotional regulation, which is the effort to find calmness through control, modulation, and mediation, when unmet needs or noxious environmental events cause an uncomfortable arousal state, thus achieving homeostasis or "emotional balance" (Post 2002a). Thus some of the reasons that infants cry include signaling their experience of painful arousal to the caregiver in order to be fed or cleaned, or when they are otherwise uncomfortable in order to signal to adult caregivers their high levels of arousal (Post 2002a). Self-soothing behavior is a complicated area to discuss and understand. Perhaps infants learn to self-soothe by recalling a representation of the caregiver, for example, via transitional objects such as blankets, stuffed animals, etc. They might be soothed by the caregiver's voice (prosodic verbal memory) and items of clothing that smell (olfactory memory) like the caregiver. Perhaps one critical aspect of the infant becoming capable of self-regulation of the internal limbic system-mediated arousal is that this capability is learned through the type of response that the infant receives from caregivers or parents to its signals of need (Schore 1994; Stern 1985; Greenspan 1981).

In general, although the range of caregiver responses to children's needs is quite wide, I would like to point out the effects of the two polar extremes of caregiver response to the infant's development of a capacity to control or modulate its own arousal. These polar extremes are the responses of *adequate caregivers*, who equitably meet the child's developmental needs for care that facilitates adaptive brain development, versus the responses of *inadequate caregivers*, who do not adequately meet the child's developmental need for care that facilitates adequate brain development. In addition, there are "difficult to soothe" infants who present temperaments that challenge adequacy in caregivers as well as reverse socialization processes that include "slow to warm" infants, who leave caretakers feeling rejected and gradually less willing to be involved in attachment and bonding behavior with the infant. The next section considers a simplified description of adequate caregivers and the implications for child brain development.

The Implications of *Adequate* Caregiver Behavior

Consistent caregiver response to a child's expressed needs and the caregiver's unconditional attention to the child are likely the most significant and important features of caregiver-child interaction underlying adaptive brain development of the child (Noshpitz & King 1991). For example, if a child cries when in an arousal state related to a basic need (food, comfort, safety, etc.), and the caregiver responds in an adaptive and beneficial manner, the child becomes calmer and over time more capable of self-regulation (soothing itself or modulating its own limbic system–mediated level of arousal). First, the caregiver provides the desired or needed items or care. It is likely that of greater importance to the child's adequately developing the capacity to regulate arousal (soothe itself) is the effect of the caregiver's contact and soothing behaviors during the interaction (Amini et al. 1996; Gazzaniga & LeDeux1978; Heineman 1998). A caregiver who consistently picks the child up and holds the child close and who is simultaneously in a relaxed and calm state will physically impart that regulated state to the child. The child will synchronize and regulate heart rate, breathing, and state of muscle tension to those of the caregiver. Thus, through the act of holding and soothing a child, the child's brain is repeatedly stimulated in the process of self-soothing or regulation of arousal that parallels the regulated state of the caregiver. Over time, with consistency, as the child's brain is developing, this process becomes second nature to the child (i.e., simultaneously, the brain of the child develops the capacity for self-regulation of arousal and the process of self-regulation of arousal is learned) (Schore 1994). Simultaneously, the development of the child's prefrontal cortex and the enervation (growth of nerve fibers connecting various areas of the brain) of the brain is occurring during the first few years of life. This process of brain development and enervation underlies the development of various areas of the brain communicating with and signaling to each other with biochemical neurotransmitters. Thus neurodevelopment leads to communication between the prefrontal cortex and the limbic system (Schore 1994; Birch 1999).

This is tremendously important, because concurrent with the capacity for self-regulation developing during consistent caregiver responses, the child is also developing the capacity to maintain a set of internal verbal, visual, and auditory images (stored and integrated in the prefrontal cortex). Clearly these processes are dependent on approximate ages and sequences of development. Receptive language precedes expressive language, sometimes by years, in boy infants. Therefore the question arises, how does understanding speech at ten months help in self-regulation? For example, a mother smiles and says "no" gently to a ten-month-old daughter and the baby clearly stops, smiles, and hesitates, watching the mother carefully. In this case the mother did not have to regulate the child herself bodily, and speech extended her range of interaction as well as the baby's ability to self-regulate via understanding of the verbal cue. How a child can develop the capacity to integrate and control self-regulation through improved communication between the prefrontal cortex and the limbic system, based on the growth of nerve fibers connecting these areas of the brain, is indeed a complex process that exceeds the scope of this chapter. Apparently all aspects of the caregiver and the context of the care become associated with increased capacity to self-regulate arousal. Thus the child can produce internal visual, verbal, and auditory representations of safety and care that are learned during interactions with the caregiver. The child integrates these representations in the prefrontal cortex and attaches meaning to them. This process becomes the basis of a biochemical and electrical message from the developing prefrontal cortex to the limbic brain through the newly developing connective nerve fibers. It is likely that a complex developmental process of caregiver-child interaction occurring simultaneously with brain development underlies a child's capacity to self-regulate arousal (Emde & Buchsbaum 1989; Fair 1992; van der Kolk & Fisler 1994). Two of the most critical aspects of the developmental process of self-regulation are that 1) the caregiver is consistent and available to facilitate the developmental process of self-regulation and 2) the caregiver is capable of self-regulation and is consistently and predictably self-regulating her or his arousal during this developmental process. Adaptive parenting is likely adequate facilitation of child attachment.

There exists a polar opposite in parenting style, the inadequate caregiver model, which contributes to development of deregulation of arousal. Perhaps chronic unregulated arousal in a child can be described as reactive attachment disorder, and the issues that surround the unregulated arousal might be a product of caregiver-child interaction.

The Impact of *Inadequate* Caregiver Behavior

The scientific literature is clear: Several types of caregiver behaviors are inadequate per se. Excessive anxiety, depression, substance abuse, and psychotic process in the caregiver underlie the expression of psychopathology in the child and developmental psychopathology as the child ages and grows (Post 2002b). Of course it is equally reasonable that within families affected by or functioning under stress, caregivers in stress act as the primary facilitators of the children's development. Therefore, I believe that in addition to caregivers with defined psychiatric conditions, such as those discussed above, the caregivers in families impacted by ongoing stress are also often rendered inadequate in their provision of developmental care by the stressful conditions impacting their families.

Caregivers experiencing anxiety, depression, or substance abuse are less consistent, are less capable of self-regulation, and thus are less capable of providing an adaptive developmental experience during the aforementioned critical period of child neurodevelopment. In families impacted by stress or wherein the caregiver is compromised or inconsistent, the child does not receive the type of consistent care needed for self-regulation of arousal. In addition, in many cases caregivers in this type of family are themselves not as capable of self-regulation. The child cannot directly experience an adult model of self-regulation while in direct contact with an adult who is incapable of self-regulation, and therefore the child's brain cannot fully develop a capacity for self-regulation of arousal.

I believe that inadequate caregivers cannot provide a child with a consistent experience in self-regulation because of depression, impairment by substance abuse, or extreme anxiety and concurrent incapacity to self-regulate arousal. Consequently the child experiences an inconsistent process of what it means to be soothed, and it follows that the child develops an inconsistent ability to regulate arousal. Often children with inadequate or inconsistent caregivers receive care in intermittent spurts of stimulation. These children often do not develop the capacity to regulate arousal in a consistent manner. These children's limbic systems actually do not develop the capacity to regulate arousal consistently as a result of inconsistent stimulation during child care.

Caregiver attention that comes in spurts of stimulation (positive but inconsistent and/or varying to negative) subsequently conditions the child to regulate arousal by engaging in a stimulation-seeking process. These children become indiscriminate in the types of stimulation that they might elicit to activate arousal-regulatory mechanisms in their limbic systems. Often children conditioned indiscriminately "act out" in a manner that elicits negative stimulation or punishment, because this is equally effective in helping them activate their capacity to regulate arousal. In these situations, the child acts out in order to be punished or abused, because even that type of response stimulates the brain to dampen uncomfortable levels of arousal (to self-regulate).

Of course if inconsistent caregiver attention creates a limbic response that is sensation-seeking as a means of stimulating regulation, there is an unfortunate additional effect to the developing prefrontal cortex and enervation. That is, the verbal, visual, and auditory images of the caregiver and environment that are integrated into meaning in the prefrontal cortex are disjointed and inconsistent (Brown 1991; Coen 1985; George 1996; Krystal 1990, 1991; Green 1995; Dubowitz et al. 1993). Furthermore, in addition to the fact that the images that stimulate the flow of chemical and electrical messages designed to control limbic arousal might exist in this disjointed manner, the actual set of nerve fibers is smaller and less robust. That is because the development of these nerve fibers is dependent, in part, on adaptive developmental care (Rakic 1991).

The child receiving inconsistent care develops a limbic system that regulates arousal based on stimulation that is both positive (adaptive behavior) and negative (maladaptive behavior). In addition, these children often have cognitive distortions about what represents appropriate stimuli for regulation of arousal. Finally, they often must seek intense stimulation in order to create a biochemical and electrical message of great enough magnitude to overcome the deficient nerve fibers connecting the prefrontal cortex and limbic system.

There is a second problem that children experience from care given by adults who cannot control their own arousal. These children cannot develop the process of self-regulation because they have no model or contact with another human who is self-regulated. These children must replicate the level of self-control and self-regulation experienced by their caregiver. If that is limited, the children's capacity to self-regulate arousal is limited. We are aware that this has long-term implications, because if the critical period of brain development passes, then it is likely that these children will always have greater difficulty with regulation of arousal. One model for understanding this is recent research on the children of depressed caregivers versus the children of nondepressed caregivers. On a brain scan study of infants of depressed caregivers, the infants had responses to depressed caregivers walking *toward* them similar to those of infants of nondepressed caregivers to their caregivers walking *away* from them. It was postulated that these infants might have experienced unregulated arousal during interactions with depressed caregivers (Post 2002b).

Obviously children with inconsistent caregivers or caregivers who could not regulate their arousal become adult clients with up-and-down behavioral phases across time of living well, not living well, living well, not living well. Relationship patterns, such as falling in love, falling out of love, falling in love, and falling out of love with very exciting and toxic people who are highly stimulating, occur. As adults they get themselves into risky situations as a mechanism to stimulate modulation of arousal. Perhaps they jump out of airplanes with parachutes for fun. Perhaps they engage in high-risk sexual escapades in order to have the type of stimulation that helps them regulate their arousal. Perhaps they engage in substance abuse in order to use the derivative chemical interactions secondary to substance abuse as a mechanism to regulate arousal.

Often when children have had inconsistent parenting in infanthood, as adults they seek stimulation, ride on this wave of stimulation, and must have stimulation in order to regulate arousal. But that stimulation is not necessarily provided by consistent, healthy, or adaptive behaviors. Furthermore, the child whose early capacity to self-regulate is compromised by inconsistent or unregulated developmental interactions with the caregiver is set up to be an adult susceptible to anxiety, depression, and consequently substance abuse. I call this result of developmental process *compromised behavioral immunity* (CBI).

Compromised Behavioral Immunity

I initially became aware of the phenomenon of CBI when I worked with war veterans and victims of violent sexual assault as adults. In both of these populations, I found that the impacted individual might have very similar experiences to those of his or her peers. However, some individuals responded well to treatment and improved rapidly, but others did not. As I became more aware of the clients' individual histories, I saw a trend emerging. Individuals who appeared to make good progress in therapy and to improve from treatment usually reported much more adaptive developmental experiences as children and adolescents. They usually had adequate caregivers and usually were not impacted by as many or as intensive a set of developmental insults as adolescents. On the other hand, individuals who reported experiencing inadequate caregivers as children usually exhibited a greater magnitude of psychiatric symptoms as a result of war experiences or adult sexual assault. Compromised behavioral immunity is the result of the impact of inadequate early developmental experiences on resiliency in adulthood.

Compromised behavioral immunity seems to reduce resiliency in adults and thus underlies the expression of psychiatric disorders of greater magnitude. The experience of families in stress (wherein the adults are not as available to facilitate child brain development) and families with caregivers who have psychiatric and substance abuse issues describes the milieu of development leading to unregulated arousal, reactive attachment disorders, and CBI. This was the crucible of child development for tribal families and their children across the past 500 years. I believe many psychiatric and substance abuse issues of postcolonial stress emerge from and are described by the following model of colonial impact on tribal communities, families, and individuals.

Postcolonial Neurodevelopment and Developmental Psychopathology

This theory of neurodevelopment is greatly simplified with respect to the large body of scientific literature that is available, and a complete description is clearly beyond the scope of this chapter. However, perhaps a simplified model of attachment, self-regulation, and infant mental health has some descriptive value when integrated into a postcolonial stress model. We need to marry our concepts of historical trauma, the postcolonial mechanisms that have shaped tribal communities and families, and the impact of these events and systems on the development of tribal children across generations. Understanding these interrelated phenomena and dynamics leads to understanding the neurological impact of what being a tribal person in this country has brought to each and every one of us who are tribal people.

This model describes a simplified version of neurological development and human development in the Native community across the past several generations. One must bear in mind that this postcolonial stress model demonstrates the tremendous resiliency and strength of survival demonstrated across the generations. Perhaps one reason that this resiliency and survival in the tribal community is evident is the strength of tribal spirituality.

The events discussed within the various generations in this section are examples of ongoing processes, so the reader must consider that the negative and oppressive dynamics described herein and experienced by our tribal ancestors are in many cases continuing for contemporary tribal people in the United States. It is important to note that this postcolonial stress model of intergenerational neurodevelopment and developmental psychopathology can likely be adapted and applied to other indigenous colonized populations, such as New Zealand Maori, Australian Aborigines, South American indigenous, and South African blacks.

This intergenerational postcolonial stress model of neurodevelopment and developmental psychopathology secondary to colonization and CBI in tribal communities is by no means representative of any given individual Native family. I initially thought about this model as it applied to understanding my personal tribal family history, for heuristic reasons. Following my professional training, I later integrated scientific aspects of the postcolonial stress model and generalized the theory. I think the generalized model is somewhat representative of most tribal people's developmental experiences, given the need for a more robust examination and subsequent integration of attachment, self-regulation, and infant mental health literature. Furthermore, it is clear that a growing number of studies support that idea that intergenerational transmission of attachment and attachment problems exists (van Ijzendoorn 1995a, 1995b; van Ijzendoorn & Bakermans-Kranenburg 1997; van Ijzendoorn, Juffer & Duyvesteyn 1995; Zeanah, Finley-Belgard & Benoit 1997).

Dispossession and Biological Warfare

Early in the colonization period of the 1500s–1600s on the East Coast of America, tribal people were dispossessed of property: the enforced movement of Native people from the prime country in which they lived. Tribal people were forcibly displaced from the places that they loved and were spiritually attached to. Dispossession was almost always enforced at musket point and with violence.

Beginning with early tribal dispossession, we can begin to see correlations with post-traumatic stress in the dispossessed Native communities, families, and individuals. I assume that the first generation of dispossession began inducing anxiety, in the form of post-traumatic stress, into the tribal community.

Occurring simultaneously with tribal dispossession was the "biological warfare" that began in that era. It also introduced anxiety in the form of PTSD into tribal communities, families, and individuals. The colonizers distributed blankets infected with smallpox and other foreign bacteria and viruses to decimate tribal communities. That type of biological warfare initially killed many Native people outright. It also made the communities, families, and individuals less capable of engaging in their customary economic and social processes. It destroyed our Native communities' capacity to engage in the economy, which was mainly gathering and hunting. If many gatherers and hunters of a group are down and sick and dying, they can't gather and hunt. If other tribal people are helping them, they can't gather and hunt while providing care to the sick.

This early biological warfare was very destructive to traditional child-rearing patterns and to the tribal knowledge base. It was very destructive of our tribal knowledge base because our Native "libraries" were the elders, who kept tribal knowledge in the form of oral histories. The elders were most susceptible to disease, and thus our historical knowledge, which stretched back as oral history for centuries, was devastated. The biological warfare also killed large numbers of children, because they were young and susceptible to infection.

In some tribes, when children were born, the parents took a whole year just to nurture them. Other tribal members hunted and gathered for them while the parents just took care of their children. Then at the end of the year the children were turned over to the tribal elders and raised to become who they would become. The tribal elders chose to teach the children what they would need to know to function optimally and support the tribe. One can imagine the effects of biological warfare impacting these two portions of our tribal community.

The most pernicious effect of this biological warfare was its impact on tribal spirituality. In our First Nation communities, the capacity to cope with difficult situations and/or health crises was enhanced or made greater by our Native spirituality. Our tribal spirituality was tied into the context within which it was practiced. Native spiritual practices, such as smudge, or whatever we burned; its smell; the chanting; the drumming; the use of tribal medicine; and the presence of tribal healers all occurred in an environment wherein indigenous people were confident that they influenced healing. When the spiritual ceremonies and practices that enacted healing occurred, of course healing would follow, because those ceremonies and practices would activate the tribal member's immune system. People were confident that they would get well. Their immune systems would be enhanced by a ceremonial, and they would get well. However, when a foreign microbe invaded the tribal community, the tribal member's immune system could not cope with that foreign microbe. Therefore, even if an enhanced immune function occurred in a tribal member secondary to a ceremony, the person still did not get well, because the immune system could not cope with the microbe. Even the most highly respected medicine people and healers could not help others or themselves. So we saw the abrupt and total failure of tribal spirituality to activate the immune system and help Native people deal naturally with the microbes introduced by the colonizers. Of course the same tribal spiritual practices were used to cope with emotional disturbances secondary to the trauma of illness and dispossession. Consequently, when their tribal spiritual practices were disrupted, what coping mechanisms would Native people turn to for emotional coping?

I think the entire process of tribal lifestyle, healthcare, oral history, child rearing, and emotional coping was violently disrupted by biological warfare about 500 years ago. In addition to these effects of biological warfare in the Native community, individual tribal people developed PTSD as a result of their family members dying around them.

Native Anxiety and Depression Secondary to Colonization

Of course PTSD is an anxiety disorder that exists on a continuum with depression (at the opposite polar extreme). Furthermore, subjectively speaking, anxiety feels very much like arousal. If one is anxious one feels as if one is experiencing a higher level of arousal most of the time. If one doesn't have a coping mechanism to help reduce or regulate that anxiety, one is susceptible to becoming depressed. For these anxious individuals, their experience with anxiety is like a dog sitting on a steel grating getting electrical shocks that it cannot escape. The dog jumps as a result of the electrical jolt and attempts to escape. I think that historically, following a jolt of anxiety tribal people used ceremonial community-based spiritual coping to reduce that anxiety. However, when tribal spirituality was disrupted, these Natives' subsequent experience was similar to that of the dog, receiving uncontrollable electrical shocks but unable to escape them. Every time something happened to the Native person, his or her anxiety rose with nothing to control it. Soon, no matter how hard electricity hits the dog, he just lies on the grate. In parallel, the tribal person continued feeling a lot of anxiety but could not regulate it with the accustomed spiritual practices. Tribal people began experiencing a shift in the anxiety-depression continuum. They developed depressed mood stemming from uncontrollable anxiety that was no longer ameliorated by use of tribal spiritual practices as coping mechanisms.

During the first generation of colonization, the first tribal people experienced anxiety and depression disorders manifested in families and in caregivers' behavior toward their children. Furthermore, these tribal families were in continual stress from other external factors predicated on colonization.

It is logical that parents in a crucible of family stress, such as oppression, racism, warfare, and other factors based on colonization, would be distracted from their children and child-raising practices. These tribal parents were distracted by anxiety and unavailable because of depression. Thus this generation of Native parents became less than optimal caregivers for their children's developmental processes. This was the first generation of colonized effects on tribal families (families within which ongoing stress, anxiety, and depression are manifested). The dispossession and biological warfare were ongoing processes across the Eastern seaboard, so it is highly likely that most tribal people were affected. If most tribal people were affected, then most young tribal people who married and had children became families in stress, with these new parents having their own issues from becoming the first generation of Natives manifesting anxiety and depression as a result of the effects of colonization.

This was the first generation of colonization-impacted Native parenting practice. We have already established that children who receive parenting from inadequate parents, families in stress, anxious parents, or depressed parents, are more likely to manifest reactive attachment disorder or a deregulation of arousal. This means the first generation of Native children began to have some deregulation of arousal, resulting in reactive attachment disorder and CBI. Postcolonial stress–impacted Native adults (anxious and depressed) were providing parenting within families under further continual colonization stress from external factors.

We have defined reactive attachment disorder as stemming from a high level of unregulated arousal, which sets up a child for CBI and greater susceptibility to developmental insult. Furthermore, the discrete generational events or occurrences we are discussing occurred across generations and are cumulative effects from one generation to the next generation. So it wasn't just this generation of tribal people experiencing dispossession and biological warfare. The next generation of Natives experienced the Indian Wars, and dispossession and biological warfare continued during the Indian War period.

Post-traumatic Stress Disorder and the Indian Wars

Envision Colonel Chivington on the hill overlooking Sand Creek in Colorado and his pony soldiers in a skirmish line across the bend in the creek. There is a camp of the Cheyenne in the bend of the creek, and it is dawn. Tribal people are getting up and preparing for the day. Older people (men and women) and adult women and children of the camp are getting up and breaking camp at dawn and getting water to start their day.

The fact that there are no Cheyenne men in the camp is why the U.S. Cavalry is here. Colonel Chivington sees this as a political opportunity to "put down an Indian insurrection." The Cheyenne men are off the reservation against the orders of the U.S. government. The Cheyenne men might be hunting because the rations provided to the tribe are not adequate and the people are hungry. Of course, oral historians suggest that the Cheyenne men might be off and engaged in the Ghost Dance religion, which is also against the government's rules.

Colonel Chivington is poised to attack the Cheyenne elders, women, and children at Sand Creek. It is politically expedient for him to prosecute the savages and will enhance his ability to be elected to office. Another famous pony solder, General Custer, tried that route to political office, and we know how that turned out, but that's another story.

We'll envision Chivington's mini-guns on top of the hill overlooking the Sand Creek Cheyenne camp because that's where the colonel, being a good military man, put his mini-guns. Mini-guns are small cannon that are easily hauled by horse teams. Of course the colonel, being frugal, loaded the mini-guns with grapeshot. Grapeshot was the stuff swept up off the floor of the blacksmith shop at the fort—bits of metal from shoeing horses, nails, and other chunks of material. It was mixed with large quantities of horse manure, so it was very, very dirty, and being hit with grapeshot, even in a nonlethal manner, could result in sepsis. So when shooting a mini-gun loaded with grapeshot at tribal people, it was not necessary to hit them directly. All that was required was a grazing wound or a scratch, which would result in infection (more biological warfare). A Native injured in such a manner might die or lose an arm or leg.

Colonel Chivington sets mini-guns up on the hill overlooking the Cheyenne camp down in Sand Creek. The Cheyenne warriors are gone. The Cheyenne's buffalo hide lodges are not invulnerable to shells and cannot turn away mini-gun grapeshot. The colonel has his pony soldiers in a skirmish line across the river, and he orders them to draw sabers because he wants to save on pistol cartridge rounds.

At dawn, when the Cheyenne people are breaking camp, Colonel Chivington orders the mini-guns fired. A round of grapeshot sprays through the camp at Sand Creek and knocks down tribal people immediately or wounds them with that deadly sepsis-inducing effect, so they may die or lose an arm or leg from infection later. Then the colonel sends his pony soldiers across the river with their sabers, and they start hacking folks up. The Sand Creek massacre is only an example of the type of aggressive attacks on tribal communities that occurred across the country over and over and over during the Indian Wars.

Consider two hypothetical young tribal people coming out of the first generation's postcolonial-stress-influenced parenting (tribal parents having some anxiety and depression). These two hypothetical young Native people, with some symptoms of unregulated arousal, reactive attachment, and resulting compromised behavioral immunity, develop post-traumatic stress as a result of their presence in the Indian Wars. We now have a second generation of young tribal parents facing continued externally generated stress, secondary to colonization, and developing internal anxiety and subsequent depression, secondary to the Indian War experiences, impacting their parenting. Since this hypothetical young tribal couple is anxious; depressed; in a social crucible of poverty, dispossession, and forced movement from their historical land base; and experiencing biological warfare, Indian warfare, and disruption of spirituality, culture, and religion, we can assume that they are not 100 percent invested in or capable of adequate parenting. When this hypothetical Native couple have their children, they are raising the next generation of tribal children who will develop with unregulated arousal, reactive attachment disorder, and CBI.

We are now two generations into this intergenerational process, so what is next on the colonial agenda for tribal people in this country? What is the next stage of colonial assimilation and acculturation? The next generation of postcolonial-stress-impacted tribal people experienced the impact of the boarding schools.

The Federal and Religious Indian Boarding Schools

Envision sending a young Native male into the federal Indian boarding school system. General Richard Pratt created the boarding school system for the express purpose of "killing the Indian to save the man" (Adams 1995; Stefon 1987; Utley 1964; Witmer 2002). When these Native children were sent to the federal Indian boarding school systems, the instructors and teachers of these impressionable young Native students were retiring pony soldiers, recruited by Pratt, himself a retired pony solder officer. So the largest group of teachers in the boarding school system was made up of retired lieutenants, sergeants, enlisted men, etc.

The era of the federal Indian boarding school system continues to have pernicious effects, often political in nature, in our Native communities, observable even today. For example, Indian policemen enforced attendance of tribal children at the boarding schools. Indian policemen would go to other tribal members' families and forcibly take their children. Of course in many cases, families resisted and serious fights resulted, often ending in the death of either the

Indian policemen or tribal family members. In most cases the Native children were ultimately taken to boarding school. Political effects of that period of enforced boarding school attendance linger three or four generations later in tribal communities. In some tribal communities, there are families with incredible animosities toward one another for no rational reasons. Tribal members who achieve political power often act out these animosities against one another within the political forum, rather than collaborating for the good of the tribe in general. Apparently they cannot overcome their historical hatred, derived from the boarding school era, when an ancestor from one family was an Indian policemen taking the child of another family's ancestor. This dysfunction split or atomized the effects of the larger culture, using one part of the tribe (the Indian police) against another part of the tribe (the families of students forced into the boarding schools). The old animosities still exist and are played out to the detriment of the functioning of modern Native society.

When tribal children arrived at the federal Indian boarding schools, their hair was cut and they were prohibited from speaking their language, even if that was the only language they knew. These children were put into regiments and units and forced to wear uniforms.

Around the former locations of the federal Indian boarding schools there are killing fields or vast unmarked cemeteries. These cemeteries contain the bones of the tribal children who died of broken hearts or illness because they had been brought together from around the country with no immunity to one another's diseases.

Tribal children in the boarding schools experienced their first exposure to large amounts of physical and sexual abuse. Physical abuse was a mainstay of discipline in the boarding schools. As a result, this first generation of individuals returned to their tribal communities trained in the boarding schools to use physical violence as a means of controlling children and spouses. Family domestic violence, a product of learned behavior from the boarding schools, became widespread in tribal communities. Lateral violence spread through the Native communities as an outgrowth of the violence practiced against tribal children in the boarding school system. Further, the literature indicates that situational molesters are usually previous victims of physical abuse and that they molest out of a need for power and control. Thus, a generation of situational molestation or sexual abuse was introduced into the tribal communities as yet another form of learned behavior, derived from the boarding school era.

So the experience of a hypothetical young tribal man in the federal Indian boarding school system was loss of culture, language (the carrier of culture), beliefs, values, etc., and the introduction to physical abuse and subsequent learning of physical abuse as a control mechanism for family functioning.

Finally, it is likely that the young tribal member who attended the federal boarding school experienced the devastation of identity that accompanies physical (and sexual) abuse. The loss of tribal identity and sense of personal power by these Native students led to the expression of powerlessness in the form of situational molestation within the tribal community and family. Situational molestation to achieve a sense of power and control was acted out in the Native community and family as a form of self-perpetuating, lateral violence.

Consider a hypothetical scenario which is close to the actual experience of many young natives in boarding schools. Envision a young Native woman being sent to a religious Indian boarding school. The religious boarding school was the equivalent of the federal boarding school in the amount of physical abuse used to control the children. One good example is a small reserve in Canada, in which three generations live, aged fifty-five to sixty-five years, forty-five to fifty-five years, and thirty-five to forty-five years. For many years each of these groups contains smaller groups in all the social and political arenas of tribal life, including the schools, the police, the legal system, the health system, and the political system. Never in the history of the tribe could Natives from one of these groups cooperate or collaborate with tribal members from the other groups. There has always been dissension and conflict, apparently without reason and certainly to the detriment of tribal functioning in general.

Members of the youngest group of Natives (thirty-five to forty-five) go into counseling and psychotherapy. In psychotherapy, members of the youngest group of tribal members remember and discuss sexual and physical abuse that they have experienced at the hands of the slightly older group of tribal members (forty-five to fifty-five). So then members of the youngest group of Natives begin to sue members of the middle group of tribal members.

As a result of the stress of the lawsuit, several members of the middle group of tribal members go for supportive psychotherapy. In psychotherapy, members of the middle group begin to think about their own abuse at the hands of members of the oldest group (fifty-five to sixty-five). The middle group of tribal members initiates lawsuits against the oldest group of tribal members.

So now a bunch of lawyers get into the fray in this Canadian reserve, helping tribal people sue each other and splitting the community. Of course all these lawsuits are high profile, so the Canadian government becomes involved and hires a Native psychologist to find out what is going on. The Native psychologist finds out that on that tribal reserve there was a religious Indian boarding school with a domicile. The domicile was a four-story building for the Native children and for the religious group that taught the children.

The religious group lived up on the fourth floor of the domicile. The oldest group of tribal people lived on the third floor, the second oldest group of tribal people lived on the second floor, and the youngest group of tribal people lived on the first floor. It was revealed to the consulting psychologist that as children, the tribal people on each floor were physically and sexually abusive to one another, the oldest children to the middle and youngest, and the middle children to the youngest children.

However, this process of tribal children abusing other tribal children has derived from and been set in motion by the actions of the religious teachers, who come downstairs and are sexually abusive to the children on all three floors. These religious teachers have done another thing that is very detrimental to the tribal children's future relationships with one another. They have used the oldest group of Native children to enforce their will on the second oldest group of tribal children, and have used the second oldest group of Native children to enforce their will on the youngest group. The religious leaders set these groups of Native children at one another's throats in order to control them.

As a result, when these tribal children grow up on that Canadian reserve, three distinct political factions have emerged in which the people hate one another, are unwilling to talk to one another, and cannot collaborate politically for the good of the reserve. In addition, many members of these three groups also act out in lateral violence: sexual molestation and physical abuse in the community as a result of what happened to them in the religious boarding school.

A huge social problem has evolved for the tribe. Tribal members are acting out lateral physical abuse and sexual molestation against the children of the next generation, they cannot cooperate or collaborate with one another at any level, and they are all suing one another. Probably the only good thing that has happened is that once this phenomenon is understood, everybody from the tribe does finally collaborate. The tribal people get together and sue the religious group. Unfortunately, healing isn't emphasized in this collaboration. Apparently the hurt is so great that when this tribe starts on the path to healing, they stop and step back and begin the process of disagreement and social disruption again. The tribe can't tolerate healing together, so they are stuck with this distinctly split-up community, as a result of the influence of their attendance at a tribal religious boarding school.

We have envisioned a hypothetical male tribal person from the federal Indian boarding school with some experience of physical abuse and possibly sexual molestation. Further, we envisioned a hypothetical female tribal member from a religious Indian boarding school with a history of sexual and physical abuse. Perhaps she attended a school similar to the religious boarding school in Canada. We know that people who have been sexually abused have difficulty protecting their children from being sexually abused. People who are physically abused often become situational molesters—not pedophiles, but molesters who use sexuality as a way of achieving power and control. So a generation of tribal people came home from boarding school with sexual abuse techniques because that is what they had been taught—they experienced physical abuse, so they have a need to cope with their own powerlessness, and they have histories of sexual abuse, so they can't protect their children.

These outside influences of learned behaviors (sexual and physical abuse) were subsequently acted out laterally within the First Nation communities, as happened on the reserve in Canada, and as happens in our political system today. We see the lateral expression and continuation of physical or sexual abuse in our Native families and communities. That is how the physical and sexual abuse, the political divisiveness, and the difficulties in collaborating socially with one another were introduced to Native people and perpetuated in the tribal community. And they perpetuate themselves.

Now there is a generation of Natives from the federal Indian boarding schools and religious boarding schools who have experienced physical and sexual abuse. This implies that tribal people in this generation experienced PTSD in the boarding schools, following a childhood characterized by unregulated arousal, reactive attachment, and CBI, and leading to adulthood with higher incidence and prevalence of psychiatric disorders.

These survivors raise and parent the next generation of tribal children with unregulated arousal, reactive attachment, CBI, anxiety, and depression (still within a crucible of ongoing postcolonial stress). A further complicating factor has been introduced to the tribal communities: lateral violence has become an issue in the Native community because tribal people bring this type of abusive tendency forward and act it out. This next generation of First Nations people goes forward with unregulated arousal, reactive attachment, CBI, and experiences of physical and sexual abuse. The next section examines the effects of overseas service and wartime PTSD in the tribal communities.

Wartime PTSD and Tribal Termination

Tribal people, as a subgroup, are the most decorated veterans of foreign wars in this country. Native warriors have joined the U.S. military and fought in overseas conflicts in battles for the United States with great ferocity, with the greatest incidence of being rewarded for being heroic. Furthermore, there is evidence in the *Congressional Record* that a much higher percentage of Native and other minority solders were placed in the frontlines in Vietnam (Walker 2002). Of course these warriors come home with PTSD, to a cultural and historical experience of combined loss of language, loss of culture, loss of spirituality, introduction of sexual abuse, introduction of physical abuse, loss of community, and dispossession. As previously discussed, their postcolonial childhood experiences in Native families in stress contributed to a higher potential of unregulated arousal and CBI. In turn, this predetermined a less than adaptive response to the war-induced post-traumatic stress experiences. In this case, our young Native war hero comes home to a terminated reservation.

Termination was a U.S. government experimental period between 1945 and 1961 during which several tribes were terminated by the passage of congressional resolutions and legislation (Deloria & Lytle 1983). The reason for this policy was to reduce and eventually eliminate the federal budget for Indian people and to manage the "Indian problem" by declaring that the reservation and tribal systems within which a given tribe lived or with which it was affiliated were null and void—that the tribe and all the tribal support systems were no longer recongnized by the federal government and thus no longer existed (Ball 1998). Subsequently, the tribal people's group holdings were "nationalized"; the Natives were given a few hundred dollars and told they were no longer Natives and that their tribes no longer exist. These First Nations people were then exhorted to go about their business. In 1998 Ball published a dissertation in which he examined the effects of termination with respect to causing post-traumatic stress among the members of one Native tribe. He carefully compared the effects of termination to other forms of PTSD-inducing experiences that members of this tribe had experienced, including deaths of tribal members and violence. Following termination as a tribe, these tribal people provided test scores indicating a rate of PTSD that was ten times that of the U.S. population at large.

As a result of tribal terminations, yet another source of tribal PTSD exists. Now there was a generation with two more sources of PTSD: overseas war service and tribal termination. Imagine the equal opportunity trauma to our hypothetical native couple. The man went to war, and the woman went through a tribal termination experience. Alternately, she went to war and he went through a tribal termination experience. It matters little what the mechanism of induction was for the developmental insults; what is critical is that these insults accrue in addition to the historical postcolonial stress and concurrent ongoing postcolonial stress effects on the family that forms when this couple marries.

Imagine yet another postcolonial-stress-inducing effect at this time to the tribal family: relocation. Before they actually meet, this young couple are sent through the U.S. federal relocation project, as individuals from two different reservations, to the city. The relocation program is designed to help young tribal people assimilate into the Western economy and culture by transporting them to the city and providing a small amount of money to live on as they become established. What happens is that when he returns from war he is given a bus ticket to the city and some "seed money" to begin a new life, while she leaves the reservation because, as a result of termination, she no longer has a tribal setting within which to live.

Relocation, Alcohol, and Alcoholism

Both of these hypothetical Native individuals go to Los Angeles or Minneapolis or Seattle; no one speaks their language, it is difficult to communicate, and they don't have the skills to interact adequately in the highly commercialized Western economy and market. But the young Native people meet, form a couple, and have a family in the city. Let's say they are now living in relocation in Los Angeles, a foreign country with respect to their history, beliefs, values, communication skills, etc.

What happens is that this young Native couple live in poverty, because of lack of job skills and language skills and ongoing racism and oppression. What coping mechanisms do they have in the city to deal with all of the internalized pain or to regulate arousal? Alcohol becomes the answer to internalized pain and unregulated arousal. A generation of tribal people is now living in the cities and is using alcohol excessively to cope with their pain and unregulated arousal (postcolonial stress). This young Native couple continues to bring forward into their family interactions and to their children the physical and sexual abuse from lateral violence that they have experienced, the trauma of termination, the trauma of war, the trauma of relocation, and the cumulative effects of postcolonial stress. As a result, this generation of Native children has unregulated arousal, reactive attachment, and CBI as a basis to combine with whatever developmental insults occur to them.

Because alcohol is being used extensively in this generation of tribal people, the first generation of Native adult children of alcoholics is created, their children. This underlies a further fragmenting of the psyches of tribal people. In addition, the first generation of Native people with alcohol-related neurological deficits secondary to maternal alcohol (and drug) abuse during pregnancy is born. Thus, another generation is created of Native people with unregulated arousal, reactive attachment, CBI, alcohol-related neurological effects, sexual abuse, physical abuse, and experience of complicated and subtle oppression. The dynamics of racism and oppression are becoming quite sophisticated, and as a result young tribal people begin internalizing that process and identifying with it as a self-image.

Implications for Contemporary Tribal Communities

The issues facing this generation of tribal people are gangs and gang membership, alcohol, drugs, and the biased dominant culture of child protection services and adoption. This generation of tribal people may have a four-year-old child who is reported into the child protective service system because the parents are substance-abusing. Substance abuse and parenting skills are an issue. But this young tribal family is carrying a lot of weight from the past in the form of postcolonial stress effects and concurrent ongoing oppression. These young Natives might be contending with a gang membership issue, wherein it is dangerous for them to withdraw from the gang, but legally they must do so to retain their child. Their ability to parent might be compromised by having to participate in a demanding temporary aid to needy families (TANF) system, while simultaneously completing an outpatient substance abuse treatment program that was never designed for Natives and is not a culturally appropriate route to abstinence and sobriety. These are the issues facing the current First Nation generation in the United States: poverty, substance abuse, psychiatric disorders, oppressive political and racial systems and agenda, culturally inappropriate child protection efforts and treatment methods, and the cumulative effects of several generations of postcolonial stress.

For purposes of this chapter, what is the value of discussing the theoretical historical path analysis of postcolonial stress and the cumulative effects of postcolonial stress and historical trauma in the tribal communities? Clearly Native veterans have measurably higher rates of lifetime and current rates of post-traumatic stress and the concurrent psychiatric and social problems secondary to those high prevalence and incidence rates. There must be a reason for this, especially when these prevalence and incidence rates occur independently of all other variables besides exposure to combat. This path analysis of historical trauma and postcolonial stress and the possible implications for risk versus resilience offers some insight into at least one possible theoretical rationale for the high levels of post-traumatic stress among Native veterans. It asserts that intergenerational effects across time have a predetermining and cumulative outcome of increasing vulnerability to post-traumatic stress among Native veterans. The next section discusses Native veterans' policies, issues and challenges, as well as possible solutions.

Native Veterans' Policies

In general, policy dictates that American Indian veterans receive any and all benefits that are available to all veterans. However, some specific policies provide for additional or different services specifically for Native veterans. Housing loans are available to aboriginal veterans under the Native American Veterans Home Loan Act of 2001 for home loans on federal trust land if a memorandum of agreement exists between the VA and the tribe (Baca 2011; Brown 1997; *Federal Benefits* 2010; Mansfield 2004). Guedel (2010) states that there is a new law supporting affordable housing by allowing for the exclusion of veterans' benefits from the definition of income. According to Mansfield (2004) management and advising on veterans' benefits are available and provided by Veterans' Benefits Activities outreach coordinators through tribal veterans' representatives, who help indigenous veterans with information and referral on services and benefits. In addition, the Native-American Cemetery Act of 2003 provides grants to tribes for establishment of veterans' cemeteries on public land.

Brown (1997) explained that as a result of the Matsunaga Vietnam Veterans Study findings, additional services were being implemented for Native veterans, including behavioral treatment for substance abuse, PTSD, homelessness, and other psychiatric disorders. Furthermore, vet center services for American Indian veterans will include treatment for PTSD by the Readjustment Counseling Service (RCS) and Mental Health and Behavioral Science (MHBS) with quality outreach and treatment processes, and through the Center for Minority Veterans, outreach efforts to aboriginal veterans will be extended and training provided. Specifically, the annual Camp Chaparral PTSD training was created and funded on the Yakima reserve to help VA employees better improve their understanding and treatment of indigenous veterans with PTSD. The Department of Veterans Affairs (2010) reported that President Barack Obama signed a memorandum of agreement promoting tribal consultation, which mandates that federal agencies such as VA coordinate services such as the treatment of post-traumatic stress with the tribes. VA also provides compensation and pensions to service-disability-connected Native veterans and the Service Member's Group Life Insurance programs. Finally, the VA healthcare system provides a broad spectrum of medical care for indigenous veterans, and a memorandum of agreement was signed in 2003 with the Indian Health Service to coordinate care for tribal veterans, including those with PTSD (Kramer et al. 2009b).

This brief and noncomprehensive review of policies regarding tribal veterans reveals fiscal support for housing, mandates for research and training specifically for Native veterans with PTSD, access to funds for veterans' burials, and outreach and treatment of secondary related behavioral disorders such as substance abuse and depression among tribal veterans.

Native Veterans' Issues and Challenges

Native veterans with post-traumatic stress face many challenges and issues, including socioeconomic disparities and lesser income; being located in rural areas far from VA facilities; difficulty navigating the dual treatment options of Indian Health Services (IHS)and VA services; specific issues of female Native veterans; co-occurring or comorbid behavioral diagnoses and physical diagnoses; confusion about whether to use traditional Native treatments, modern treatments, or both; and contemporary and historical trauma and postcolonial stress (Buckwald et al. 2005; Gurley et al. 2001; Libby et al. 2004; Sawchuck et al. 2006; Stone 2002).

In 2006 Holiday and colleagues reported that the average family income of Native veterans was more likely less than $30,000 and further less likely to be in the $50,000 range than the income of all other veterans. Native veterans often live on the reservation, which can be hundreds of miles from VA facilities, and often do not have reliable transportation (Johnson, Carlson & Hearst 2010). The 2003 memorandum of agreement between the IHS and VA does not guarantee access to the systems. A population of 64,746 Native veterans revealed that 25 percent used both VHA and the IHS; that the IHS only correctly identified 44 percent as veterans, which underestimates the total number of tribal veterans; that American Indian veterans presented with more complex needs for care; and that the majority of female dual users (68 percent) were nonveterans (Kramer et al. 2006, 2009a, 2009b). For female veterans, VA provided the most specialty care, including 84 percent of mental health services. In many cases of Native veterans 28 percent used the VA services exclusively, and 46 percent the IHS exclusively. The IHS is grossly underfunded, and few Native veterans reported having health insurance (Johnson, Carlson & Hearst 2010; Villa 2003). Many native veterans have additional serious physical health issues, such as diabetes, hypertension, and PTSD and chronic pain (Buckwald et al. 2005; Kramer et al. 2009a, 2009b). Childhood abuse, other developmental traumas, historical trauma, and postcolonial effects comprise predeterminants for Native veteran post-traumatic stress and complicate the assessment and treatment process. Women Native veterans, especially those with post-traumatic stress, are unlikely to receive robust and appropriate assessment and treatment services (Kramer et al. 2009b). The issues of modern versus traditional Native cultural and spiritual treatments are examined in more detail in the final section of this chapter, but here it is important to illustrate the issues and challenges facing tribal veterans afflicted with post-traumatic stress using a hypothetical case study, based on the case report structure developed and used by Manson (1996, 1997, 2000).

Hypothetical Case Study of a Female Native Veteran with PTSD

Patient Identification

L. is a twenty-nine-year-old Native woman, unmarried, divorced twice, and with no children. She lives with her mother (and recently has demanded that a male live-in partner move out because of his excessive alcohol abuse) in a small New Mexico town on a large reservation. Her mother works at a local health-care facility, and she is estranged from her father, who lives in a nearby community. L is a student at a local community college. She served in the navy during the Iraq conflict in 2002–2003. She is seen at the local IHS facility for psychiatric medication management and individual counseling, which at first she attended only intermittently but lately has attended regularly. At first the counseling rarely focused on her issues of post-traumatic stress, but that has become a focus as her symptoms have improved. She has frequently been seen in the IHS emergency room for suicidal ideation and was twice transported to residential psychiatric treatment for evaluation and stabilization. Methamphetamine use and abuse led to a stroke in 2009, resulting in a three-week hospitalization and permanent loss of some short-term memory capacity.

History of Present Illness

L. was recently placed in a residential psychiatric facility after a psychotic break during which she was aggressive, labile, attending to internal stimuli, and had poor reality testing. This was caused by a lack of sleep and an overdose of over-the-counter sleep medications. She had been admitted to the local IHS hospital previously for similar symptoms, including a toxic level of medications in her bloodstream. She characterized her lack of sleep as being caused by intrusive dreams and nightmares of her Iraq wartime experiences. Prior to her stroke, she struggled with drinking, drug abuse, and a series of dysfunctional relationships and marriages to men who drank and used drugs excessively and engaged in domestic violence and aggression. She would often engage in what she characterized as "runners," during which she would drink and use drugs excessively to black out, then wake up in distant towns or cities, often in the company of strangers. She was also arrested multiple times for public intoxication and was found with a small amount of methamphetamine in her possession, resulting in probation. Following her stroke, she spontaneously stopped all use of drugs and reduced her alcohol abuse significantly, but continued to have relationships with substance-abusing men who initiated domestic violence.

L. first began drinking heavily in Iraq, and her use of methamphetamines began when she came home, at which time she was briefly married to two servicemen, both of whom used methamphetamines. She reported that during her time in Iraq, she was continually fearful of being shot by a hidden sniper and also saw large numbers of Iraqi soldiers' bodies floating down a river, which was tinted red with their blood. She also stated that fellow soldiers called her a "rag-head" because of her dark complexion, similar to many Iraqis. During her counseling sessions at the IHS facility she reported intrusive thoughts and nightmares on a daily basis, avoided talking about her wartime experiences, and felt alienated and sought to withdraw from social contact unless drinking or using drugs. Her affect was blunted and she experienced a feeling of a foreshortened future, believing she might die or be killed at any time. Her nightmares correlated with awaking covered in sweat, and she was typically angry and irritated. In addition, she had unpredictable but frequent daytime flashbacks. L. said that these symptoms increased in frequency and intensity following her return from Iraq.

Psychiatric History and Previous Treatment

Prior to her most recent hospitalization, she had steadily refused to go to VA for dedicated PTSD treatment, stating that it was too far and that the non-natives didn't understand her. She also stated that the local VA group therapy was "run by white men" and consisted of all men, who would "hit on her following the sessions." She had a history of arrests for public intoxication and drug possession and was often sexually involved with men she had just met, who were substance abusers and perpetrated domestic violence. She stopped drug abuse and reduced alcohol consumption as the result of a stroke. She continued to have symptoms of PTSD and to refuse referral, relying on a regimen of antidepressants and superficial counseling sessions wherein she avoided deep-seated issues and was often flirtatious and coy with the therapist.

Social and Developmental History

L. was born in the local New Mexico IHS facility with no complications. She grew up in a small New Mexico town with her mother (because her father walked out on the family when she was six) and two siblings, both sisters. Both of her sisters and L. reported that their father had sexually abused them when they were small children. She characterized her mother as loving, but largely absent as an influence because she needed to work to support the family. During high school L. discovered marijuana and alcohol and began to use both regularly, often drinking and smoking to the point of intoxication with her friends. While in high school she discovered men and was soon well-known among her peers for overt sexual behavior and promiscuity. At age twenty she enlisted in the navy and was deployed to Iraq for one tour. When she returned, she was briefly married to one serviceman and started an affair with another, resulting in a divorce after six months of marriage and a subsequent remarriage within a month. Both of these men were substance abusers and both engaged in regular domestic violence toward her. The second marriage ended within six months after she was honorably discharged and returned to New Mexico without her husband. She has had a steady series of brief relationships with male companions since that time. L. has lived at home with her mother since her discharge and has frequently shuffled men into and out of their home as brief residents with her. She is very successful when college is in session and does well in her classes.

Family History

L. reported that her mother is "super responsible" but still works too many hours, as she always has since L. was a child. She is estranged from her father, who lives in a local community, and she has stated that, because of his sexual abuse of her, "he is a terrible man" and he "messed my head up." She has remarked that her father talked to her once about being a physical and sexual abuse victim himself as a child in boarding school, and also having nightmares from these experiences. Both of her sisters have also experienced significant problems with relationships, and both are divorced.

Assessment and Treatment Outcome

L. was referred to the closest VA Medical Center's PTSD program, where the diagnosis of post-traumatic stress was confirmed, but she left this program during the course of treatment, commenting that "the non-native staff did not understand her." Following this abortive PTSD treatment, she has attended a new post-traumatic stress group for natives co-led by a Native psychologist from the local IHS and a trained VA specialist in post-traumatic stress, where she was able to discuss openly with the group her desire to "not be hit on by the men." These Native men have treated her like a valued colleague and introduced her to other cultural and spiritual methods of treatment. In addition, she now sees the same Native psychologist for one-on-one counseling at the local IHS facility and is much more willing to discuss both her post-traumatic symptoms and options for relieving them, including cognitive-behavioral methods. Her nightmares and intrusive thoughts have diminished, and she is less irritable and angry than before. An additional focus of her ongoing treatment is resolution of her childhood sexual abuse issues, and she has also sought the mentorship of a local Native female elder "to learn her tribe's ways."

Diagnosis

AXIS I: 309.81 Posttraumatic Stress Disorder, 304.40 Amphetamine Dependence, Sustained Full Remission, 303.90 Alcohol Dependence, Sustained Partial Remission
AXIS II: Undetermined
AXIS III: Residual Effects from the Stoke, Herpes Simplex
AXIS IV: Current: Relational difficulties, moderate; Conflict with father, moderate; Past: Wartime trauma, extreme; Childhood sexual abuse, extreme; Poverty, moderate; Racial discrimination, moderate
AXIS V: Highest past year: GAF = 75; Current GAF = 80

Cultural Group

L. is a full blood (4/4 quantum) tribal member and an enrolled member of a Southwest American Indian tribe located in New Mexico. Her mother and father are members of the tribe, as are her sisters.

Language

She speaks English well, but is not fluent in her native language. Recently she has been learning some words and concepts from her tribal mentor and the other veterans in the PTSD group.

Cultural Factors in Development

Historically, her family has been rich with Native traditional healers and medicine people, including crystal gazers (diagnosticians) and singers (healers) among the men and hand tremblers (diagnosticians) among the women. Despite the desires of her extended family and grandparents that she learn her native language and participate in cultural and spiritual activities, her parents interdicted this. Her father was angry because of his experiences at the boarding school with sexual and physical abuse at the hands of "white men," because his native family had not protected him, and he wanted nothing to do with "Indian stuff," and her mother was a born-again Christian who stated that native cultural and spiritual practices were witchcraft. L. was not allowed much contact with her extended family and grandparents, who have all passed on, and she has only recently been active with her uncle's Native American church, a tribal peyote-based religion, which she espouses as being very helpful for her reduction in post-traumatic stress symptoms. Finally, she has begun attending a female sweat lodge (inuipi) ceremony on a weekly basis, which is also helpful for her PTSD symptoms. She felt very marginalized when fellow servicemen called her a "raghead" because of her dark coloring and is suspicious of the motives of non-natives. However, she also has had trouble forming a bonded relationship with a native male, secondary to her father's sexual abuse.

Cultural Perspectives on PTSD

The local tribal members and her family have long been dismayed by her behaviors and symptoms. Her mother has asserted that these cultural and spiritual ways are the real genesis of L's symptoms. Other tribal members believe that she is under the malign influence of "bad spirits" or nefarious medicine workers. Unfortunately, many of her symptoms are merely exaggerated aspects of what is normative in her community, where suicide, substance abuse, depression, child physical and sexual abuse, and behavioral acting out through sexually charged relationships is common. Her use of methamphetamines was to avoid sleep and nightmares, and she drank in order to sleep deeply enough not to dream. The local Native veterans assert that she and they are afflicted with a wounded spirit, which is a natural consequence of their participating in wars and combat or closely observing combat and battle casualties. These indigenous veterans are active in ceremonies designed to ameliorate the spiritual and emotional consequences of their PTSD symptoms. One of the local medicine men espouses the view that all things have a spirit, including drugs and alcohol, which a famous Native psychologist supports as being true, and also suggests that these spirits can be malignant in nature if invited into a person's life and can subjugate the addicted person's will (Duran 1984). Duran has also asserted that on many occasions he has successfully treated addictions in natives through use of this perspective as a teaching tool in conjunction with therapy, which was this author's clinical and personal experience as a recipient of traditional spiritual native treatments and ceremonies.

Tribal Explanations and Models

The local tribe, of which L is a member, endorses *sb'a naghai bik'e hozhiq*, a lifestyle philosophy. *Sb'a nagai* is the spirituality, a tribal member's desire to live this life in a good way and attain eternal life after death. Old age is *sb'a*, and *naghai* is the process of getting there. The beauty and harmony of this process of living well and attaining eternal life is called *Bik'e hozhiq*, which includes balance of male and female identity characteristics, necessary to maintain a positive self. When this is not in balance, a tribal member's harmony is upset, such as occurred with L's child sexual abuse and her father and mother restricting her access to Native language, culture, and spirituality. A consequence of this imbalance has been her PTSD and substance abuse, which has impeded her ability to pursue and obtain *sb'a naghai bik'e hozhiq* (Manson 2000).

Tribally Based Cultural and Spiritual Treatment

One aspect of L's treatment is her attending a local VA outpatient group comprised of Native veterans with post-traumatic stress, which is managed by a VA specialist in PTSD and incorporates a consulting Native psychologist from the local IHS as a co-facilitator. Within the group, L. is a fellow Native warrior, and the men are respectful and do not "hit on her." Also, they recommended and facilitated her access to a local Inuipi (sweat lodge) ceremony for women, which is held weekly at the IHS facility and is run by a female native healer. She is also attending her uncle's Native American church (peyote religion) meetings, which include native veterans on a regular basis, and she has gained insight and encouragement from fellow practitioners to remain abstinent and follow the path of *sb'a naghai bik'e hozhiq*. Recently L. has been considering attending a Sundance ceremony to dance and pray for veterans' issues.

Social Stress and Support

L. does not work steadily, due to poor economic conditions; however, she has been attending college and doing well. Her mother is a source of fiscal support, and she has access to a food bank. L. is increasingly interested in and involved in traditional tribal cultural and spiritual activities.

Functional Assessment

L. has been attending college successfully and is doing fine in classes, with some accommodations for issues arising from her stroke. She no longer uses drugs, and her use of alcohol is significantly reduced. Currently she is "taking a break" from men and plans on choosing more carefully in the future as her self-esteem rises and her self-image becomes more realistic. She is more deeply integrated into tribal activities than before and anticipates this trend continuing.

Her symptoms of PTSD have responded well to the VA Native veterans' PTSD group treatment and traditional tribal spirituality.

Cultural Elements of Treatment

Some aspects of majority culture PTSD treatment, such as an inpatient group and an outpatient group of non-native veterans, were not helpful. But L. responded well to the VA outpatient native veterans' group, especially since her individual therapist at the IHS facility is a co-facilitator and also works with her on other issues, such as childhood sexual abuse and relationship issues. According to L. the most critical aspect of her treatment has been reintegration into tribal cultural and spiritual values, beliefs, and practices.

Comprehensive Cultural Evaluation

L. is an indigenous patient (relative) with a complicated presentation of numerous problems: wartime combat-related trauma; discrimination and racism during her military service; alcohol and other drug dependencies; sexual abuse as a child; secondary effects of a stroke caused by methamphetamine abuse; and alienation and unfamiliarity with traditional tribal culture, values, beliefs, and spirituality. Only after she stopped other drug and methamphetamine use and abuse and significantly reduced her alcohol use was she able to consider and enter an inpatient PTSD program. Despite the failure of this level of treatment, she continued to seek help with a VA-sponsored Native veterans' group and enlisted the aid of the group's co-facilitator, a Native psychologist at the local IHS facility. As a result, she was able to enter individual therapy with this worker and address child sexual abuse issues and relationship issues, and even openly discuss PTSD problems. L. has also increased her understanding of tribal and cultural values, beliefs, and practices and participation in spiritual practices. The resultant recovery from PTSD, increasing abstinence from alcohol, and improved abilities to benefit from college are all related to a synergistic effect of combined Western and traditional therapies and lifestyle choices, all possible because of L's comfort in both cultures.

L. has never had any difficulty seeing the relationship between her combat and wartime experiences and resultant post-traumatic stress and her drug abuse, but required a significant life event, the stroke, to provide motivation to stop drug abuse and cut back significantly on drinking. The combination of VA Native group therapy and individual therapy with the group's co-facilitator has enabled her to further explore the links between her early childhood sexual abuse, later in life developmental insults during the war, and alienation from tribal cultural and spiritual traditions. She has gained a deeper level of camaraderie with men through functional relationships with male warriors from her Native treatment group, who accept her and treat her as a peer, and has increased trust in men in general. These fellow "wounded warriors" have been instrumental in her reintroduction to her local tribal traditions, culture, and spirituality. This has led her to various specific ceremonies helpful in treating her post-traumatic stress: Inuipi, Native American church, and soon, the Sundance. She has increased attention to the traditional roles and values of tribal women through mentorship with an adult female elder. She is now proud to be a warrior and has adopted the values and practices of the local "neotraditionalists" who are rescuing native ways and living them out in their lives. She credits the combination of Western group and individual therapies with a reawakened interest and participation in native and tribal ways for her recovery from many of the symptoms of PTSD.

L's PTSD symptoms are ameliorating, and she must continue to engage in self-development and self-actualization to optimize her future recovery. Seemingly mundane aspects of life, such as forming a loving and stable love relationship, are going to be challenges for L. She anticipates great benefits from the upcoming Sundance, which is a major yearly commitment and ceremony. The overall benefit of continuing Western therapies and tribal involvement should continue to help L. improve her symptoms and increase her adaptive functioning.

This hypothetical case formulation draws from both my professional clinical experience with many Native veterans with PTSD and my personal journey, as well as the personal and professional journeys of other Native professionals to a healthy *Amsapi Pikuni* way of looking at the world and living in it. For me, as a Native psychologist serving my relatives, the Western models of assessment and treatment are but the beginning of the path to wellness. That path, or "Red Road," is one of reclamation of culture, spirituality, language, beliefs, values, practices, and identity and self-hood. I leave the robust technical explanations of Western models to those experts in this volume and only touch briefly on them. I thank the workers in the field who developed the Western models of PTSD treatment and those who apply these methods with veterans, including my Native relatives. The next section discusses a specific level of Native methods and mechanisms for healing from post-traumatic stress.

Native Veterans' Solutions

Several authors cited in the previous sections suggested that knowledge about native culture, spirituality, values, beliefs, and practices is incredibly valuable in assessment and treatment of aboriginal veterans with PTSD. Other authors cited in this chapter have advocated for the provision of Western PTSD assessment and treatment. It is my contention that Native veterans often benefit most from an approach to treatment that coordinates both Western models and native cultural and spiritual methods, discussed in this section.

Native Healing Ways

Floerchinger (1991) suggested that unfamiliarity with bereaved clients' cultural beliefs and practices regarding death, dying, grief, and bereavement could undermine the therapeutic relationship, perhaps leading to poor outcomes. Indeed, lack of cultural familiarity or sensitivity among doctors, nurses, mental health practitioners, substance abuse counselors, and other helping professionals has been known to impact a wide range of clinical outcomes (Archambault 1997). For example, one physician repeatedly told a native patient diagnosed with diabetes, "You will die if you don't take your medication." In this patient's tribe, open discussion of death was thought to actually *invite* death. An expert in traditional tribal mores advised the physician to modify his comment as follows, "If you do take your medication, you will live." Subsequently the native patient began complying with this medical directive, which was interpreted as being health-promoting (Toelken 1994). In another case, a female Hopi tribal member who was residing in San Francisco was brought to an urban hospital after cutting her arms, pulling out her hair, and reporting that she was hearing the voice of a recently deceased relative. Although the interdisciplinary treatment team considered hospitalization, a psychologist familiar with Hopi people advised the treatment team that the woman was exhibiting culturally appropriate bereavement behavior. Rather than hospitalization, the intervention consisted of obtaining a bus ticket for her to return home to mourn the loss of her relative (Wheeler 1993).

The Value of Traditional Cultural Practices and Beliefs

Several authors have suggested that support of traditional cultural practices is critical to the maintenance of health in tribal communities. For example, 20 percent of Office of Substance Abuse (OSAP) high-risk-youth demonstration projects have been awarded to Native American grantees (Augustson 1990); cognizant of the importance of tribal beliefs, almost all grantees budgeted a portion of these funds for cultural enhancement activities. Indeed, DeJong (2008) reported that tribal members believe strongly that efforts aimed at increasing youths' knowledge of their cultural history, traditions, and values cultivate positive identity and pride. The restoration of traditional ceremonials has long been considered a health-promoting activity in native communities (Jilak 1982).

Two recent studies of recovery from heart disease among indigenous patients examined the correlates of the following activities: hobbies (beadwork and leatherwork), praying (peyote meetings, Inipi, and Wiwanyag Wachipi), and social activities (hand games, gourd dances, and pow-wows). Involvement in these traditional tribal activities was associated with a reduction in patient stress and improved recovery from heart problems (Miller, Johnson & Garrett 1982; Miller et al. 1985).

Tribal rituals and ceremonial practices have been utilized as intervention tools in some native mental health programs (e.g., Guilmet & Whited 1987; Mitchell & Patch 1986). For instance, Guilmet and Whited (1987) reported that at a tribal mental health center in Washington State, staff and clients used several traditional practices. These traditional practices included the use of cedar and sage smoke. Cedar and sage smoke (representing power) and prayers were considered useful in "spiritual" cleansing. Pipe ceremonies, traditional talking circles, Southwest shamanic practices, and the Inipi were also used in Washington tribal mental health programs. The integration of traditional healing practices appeared to be related to greater numbers of native clients completing therapy.

Despite evidence that clinicians' knowledge about native beliefs and spiritual practices may contribute to successful health, mental health, and substance abuse treatment of indigenous people, many traditionally important tribal beliefs and practices have not been adequately documented. Do mental health and substance-abuse professionals know what comprises culturally adaptive versus maladaptive ways of coping among native people?

The Importance of Cultural Knowledge and Sensitivity

Numerous authors have recommended that mental health and substance-abuse professionals intending to serve native clients develop cultural knowledge and sensitivity. It is my observation and belief that because of the lack of trained mental health workers in "Indian country," substance-abuse professionals often are the only professional helpers in a given community. Therefore, native clients often must turn to substance-abuse counselors in their communities to receive services commonly thought of as being within the domain of mental health professionals. Mental health professionals in dominant culture communities typically provide one of these services, PTSD counseling. The development of cultural knowledge and sensitivity in the provision of PTSD treatment is important because of the challenges of providing services, such as psychotherapy, across cultural boundaries. "Cross-cultural therapy implies a situation in which the participants are most likely to evidence discrepancies in their shared assumptions, experiences, values, beliefs, expectations, and goals" (Manson & Trimble 1982, 149).

An exhaustive review of the material recommending the development of cultural knowledge and sensitivity as the basis of effective clinical work with indigenous clients exceeds the scope of this chapter. However, it is important to summarize the central premise underlying this research: Cultural knowledge and sensitivity about tribal cultures may be a prerequisite for effective clinical practice with tribal clientele. Therefore, a brief review of the literature was conducted. This author located fifteen studies discussing various aspects of the importance of cultural knowledge and sensitivity to the practitioner of clinical services in Native communities. Several cultural arenas requiring knowledge and sensitivity of practice are discussed in this section: 1) gender stereotyping and other issues of Native women, 2) genuine versus pseudo indigenous spirituality, 3) use of tribal archetypes (Heyoka) in counseling, 4) understanding family and community variables, 5) becoming familiar with language differences, 6) recognizing Native methods of achieving social justice, 7) traditional models of tribal "group therapy," 8) identifying the healthy use of peyote rituals, and 9) observing the value of ceremonies for combat veterans.

Native Women

Medicine (1988) writes that Native women are usually portrayed in stereotypical fashion in the research literature, usually either as subservient drudges (the Plains Indian, male-dominated warrior culture) or as matriarchal matrons of an Eastern horticultural group. Furthermore Kramer and colleagues (2009a) found similarity in the PTSD assessment and treatment needs of Native women and disparities in the use of therapeutic systems, with Native women veterans more likely to use the IHS as the primary source of care and the VA medical system as a secondary source. Two studies also clearly identified significant differences between male and female Native veterans in various areas, including access to and use of healthcare and the effects of PTSD on their health. Noteworthy was that Native women with higher lifetime prevalence of PTSD had elevated cortisol levels compared to Native men with similar PTSD diagnoses (Kramer et al. 2009a; Laudslager et al. 2008).

The true diversity of the lives of female tribal relatives needing intervention into post-traumatic stress that exists beyond the stereotypical descriptions in the literature cannot be appreciated without cultural education. Though not as readily identified as the roles for men, the tribal social and work roles for Indian women are as individual and diverse as they are among women in any culture. Certainly practitioners can best serve female Indian clients if they take the time to learn more about this diversity. One area of importance when studying native people to develop cultural knowledge and sensitivity is spirituality.

Kasee (1995) explained that reclaiming a positive sense of tribal spirituality and incorporating it into one's daily life is critical for Native women recovering from mental health and substance abuse disorders. She lamented the difficulties caused by exploitation of tribal belief systems and ceremonials by charlatans and "plastic medicine men or women." Professionals working with tribal women must develop accurate cultural knowledge and sensitivity about the real versus ersatz types of indigenous spirituality to which female Native clients might be exposed. Such knowledge may strongly influence the social support resources clinicians may rely upon to assist these native clients.

Tribal Archetypes (Heyoka)

According to Herring (1994), understanding the meaning of various psychological archetypes, such as the clown or contrary figure (e.g., the trickster, a tribal archetype) might underlie the development of powerful mental health interventions for Native clients. Such archetypes may be represented in the thoughts and feelings of Indian clients and may be used by clinicians to illustrate points, make interpretations, etc. For example, historically the role or meaning of the contrary figure (or trickster) was to draw attention to the tendency of individuals or groups of tribal peoples to engage in "black and white" or overly polarized thinking or behavior. That is, the clown behaved in a satire or parody of the polarized thinking or behavior and called attention to it as a possible problem, in an indirect and nonthreatening manner. Clinicians may use their knowledge of this archetype to help tribal clients gain insight into maladaptive, dichotomous thinking.

Indeed, Herring (1994) strongly cautioned mental health workers to recognize that there is always an underlying, metaphorical message in the humor of the clown figure. He only included a few lines about the Lakota contrary figure or "Heyoka" in his writings. However, if Herring's views are correct, it would be important to learn more about the metaphorical meaning and relevance of the Heyoka in order to work effectively with Lakota clients. For example, telling a Lakota client a culturally appropriate story incorporating a Heyoka might be an effective means of providing an indirect and therefore nonthreatening confrontation.

Value of Tribal Affiliation and Spirituality

Garrett and Garrett (1994) suggested that mental health-substance abuse professionals must not separate Native clients from their spirituality or affiliation with their tribal group. Therefore, it is incumbent upon these professionals to understand as much as possible about the meaning of tribal affiliation and spirituality for their clientele.

For example, tribal individuals often belong to historical clans or groups, which once had numerous roles that have changed over time. However, a Native client may serve a traditional role in the tribe's historical clan system or be expected to participate in grieving according to a predetermined manner. Responsible clinicians would strongly support the client's full participation in these roles, particularly those who are clinically depressed because of bereavement.

Understanding Community and Family Variables

Horijsi, Heavy Runner-Craig, and Pablo (1992) described twelve situational, cultural, and community factors that might impact child protective services (CPS) providers working with indigenous families. Of these, three are important in this chapter: foster care, extended family structure, and living in a tribal community. First, it is doubtful that most clinicians in the dominant culture appreciate the fact that tribal cultures have no words for the concept of foster care (Cross 1987). The extended family among Indian people is essential to tribal economies and the social fabric. If uninformed professionals attempt to promote foster care, they may be offering recommendations that are offensive, because the concept is at odds with tribal and family values. Rather, clinicians must realize that the extended family can be used to support clinical interventions and compensate for inadequacies in parenting skills among biological parents.

Silence and Language Issues

The phenomenon of interpersonal silence is another area in which nonindigenous therapists likely need additional training. For example, therapists at a Seattle family therapy clinic were having difficulty communicating with a female Native client. Following an observation of their interviewing methods, a consultant familiar with the client's culture recommended that the practitioners add several more seconds of silence after posing a question. Additional silence following a query was more familiar to the Native woman, and she responded by becoming a more communicative and hard-working client

(Tafoya 1995). Several authors have written about the value of silence as a safe or culturally appropriate response by a Native client to unpredictable, uncontrollable, or unfamiliar situations such as counseling or psychotherapy (Guilmet 1976).

Promoting active verbal interaction with clients is a value held by many training programs in the dominant culture. Aggressive pursuit of verbal dialogue with Native clients may be counterproductive, however. Often there is a deeply held belief within Native communities that it is inappropriate to notice or discuss another person's problems or personal issues (Spindler & Spindler 1957). Such tribal beliefs call into question the common or general applicability of verbally based psychotherapy for this population (Guilmet & Whited 1987).

Tribal Judicial Systems

Often mental health–substance abuse professionals provide assessment reports and expert testimony to tribal courts. This occurs even though such assessment methods are not normed on particular tribes and are rooted exclusively in the judicial system of the dominant culture. Understanding the normative limitations of psychological tests and the value of tribal traditions in achieving social justice may be very important to practitioners working with tribal judicial systems.

Two articles in the early 1990s argued that native communities have age-old and effective, formal methods of dispensing justice (Bluehorse & Zion 1993; Mansfield 1993). For example, several traditional Northwest tribes recommend that traditional methods of justice (e.g., peacemaking) be formally reincorporated into the tribal court and used to supplant modern methods (Mansfield 1993). Also, Bluehorse and Zion (1993) recommend the reintroduction of the Hozhooji Naat'aanii or Navajo justice and harmony ceremony. Mental health practitioners who work with tribal courts might benefit tribal justice systems by shaping their recommendations and testimony so as to support tribal traditions and values, rather than those more typically associated with normative testing outcomes. Often Native veterans with post-traumatic stress come to the attention of tribal courts and legal systems through the commission of crimes when they are intoxicated, so referrals from these courts and judicial systems into PTSD assessment and treatment are critical.

Traditional Tribal "Group Therapies"

Within the dominant culture, practitioners regard group therapy as a popular, powerful method for effecting change in clients (Cohn & Osbourne 1992;

Corey 1990). Such methods can complement traditional native ceremonies and practices. For example, among the Lakota there are two tribal ceremonies that bear similarities to group counseling work: the Inipi (sweat lodge ceremony) and the "talking circle." The Inipi and talking circle are important ceremonies, which have elements in common with Western group therapy models (Stone 1994). It has been suggested that these ceremonies be studied and recommended, at appropriate times, by practitioners working with tribal clients (Garrett & Osbourne 1995).

Appropriate Tribal Use of Peyote Rituals

Even within the American military, the Native American church peyote religion has been accepted. For example, a recent general order allowed indigenous military personnel to practice the ritualistic use of peyote (*Peninsula Daily News* 1997). The ethno-psychedelic use of peyote as a preferred treatment for alcohol dependence among Native people has long been documented (Albaugh & Anderson 1974; Chuelos et al. 1959; MacLean et al. 1961; Smith 1958). However, such a Native practice might be viewed as unhealthy or destructive by clinicians adhering to a (dominant culture) Alcoholic's Anonymous model, which strongly advocates total abstinence from all drugs. It would be gravely irresponsible for dominant culture health practitioners to automatically interpret a Native client's use of peyote as an attempt to "escape or avoid reality" or responsibility for personal problems. However, given the fact that dominant culture training models shape the views of most mental health–substance abuse professionals, it might be difficult for these workers to attain the cultural sensitivity necessary to understand the relevance of the peyote ritual to Native people.

Traditional Treatment for Post-Traumatic Stress

According to Scurfield (1995) and Silver (1994), the outcome of treatment for PTSD manifested by tribal Vietnam veterans has been clearly improved by the addition of indigenous beliefs and rituals. Both of these authors stressed the importance of integrating traditional Native practices and beliefs into the treatment of indigenous Vietnam veterans exhibiting PTSD symptoms. For example, both Scurfield and Silver reported that the addition of the Native sweat lodge ceremony or Inipi benefited tribal veterans. Uniquely, beneficial effects of integrating the Inipi and other traditional tribal rituals into the formal treatment model also proved salutary for dominant culture Vietnam veterans.

Summary: Native Traditions and Spiritual Methods

In summary, there is sufficient documentation in the literature to justify the suggestion that mental health–substance abuse professionals need to develop cultural knowledge and sensitivity. Furthermore, it naturally follows that specific tribal veteran post-traumatic stress clientele would benefit from culturally specific knowledge and sensitivity among practitioners. Therefore, it was deemed important to conduct the present research project to inform professionals about contemporary and traditional Native/tribal and Western mental health and substance abuse treatment beliefs and practices. Many of the clinical practices of mental health workers in the dominant culture may or may not be consistent with the indigenous culture. Also, culturally sensitive clinicians may best help tribal clients by encouraging their involvement in particular Native ceremonies and practices.

Directions and New Developments for Native Veterans

There are significant developments in the assessment and treatment of PTSD among Native relatives. These developments include an increased professional understanding of the possible predeterminants and risk factors inherent in Native historical trauma, postcolonial stress, and current stress (French 1992; Cabaniss 2010; Kawennano & Johnson 1996; Stone 2002). This perspective is only one of many ways to view the effects of history and current stress on resilience and risk for PTSD, but it might be considered in case conceptualization.

Hamblen (2010) describes many modern Western methods of PTSD treatment, including cognitive behavioral therapy, exposure therapy, eye movement desensitization and reprocessing, group therapy, brief psychodynamic psychotherapy, family therapy, and medication management.

- Cognitive behavioral therapy helps the veteran understand and change his or her thinking about trauma and its aftermath.
- Cognitive processing therapy helps the veteran: 1) learn about PTSD symptoms, 2) become aware of thoughts and feelings, 3) learn skills in changing thinking, and 4) understand changes in beliefs (United States Department of Veterans Affairs. National Center for PTSD 2010a).
- Exposure therapy helps the veteran learn not to fear his or her memories and thoughts about trauma and consists of 1) education, 2) breathing, 3) real world practice, and 4) talking through the trauma (United States Department of Veterans Affairs. National Center for PTSD 2010b).

- Eye movement desensitization and reprocessing consists of talking about and thinking about memories combined with specific eye movements.

- Group therapy is talking with others who share similar experiences, becoming comfortable with symptoms, memories, and other aspects of life, and building interpersonal relationships.

- Brief psychodynamic psychotherapy facilitates identification of triggers for memories and other symptoms, ways to cope with intense feelings, self-awareness of thoughts and feelings, and increased self-esteem.

- Family therapy helps partners and children understand symptoms and behaviors caused by PTSD.

- Medication management includes the selective use of antidepressant, anti-anxiety medications and tranquilizers to ameliorate symptoms of PTSD.

Many authors suggested Native methods and ways of dealing with PTSD, including

- specific tribal training in the cultural ways of Native women for indigenous women coping with post-traumatic stress (Kasee 1995; Medicine 1988);

- the use of tribal archetypes as metaphors for living (Herring 1994);

- increased tribal affiliation and spirituality (Garrett & Garrett 1994);

- a better understanding of tribal community and family variables (Horijsi, Heavy Runner-Craig & Pablo 1992);

- increased understanding of PTSD and increased referral from tribal courts to appropriate assessment and treatment for Native veterans (Bluehorse & Zion 1993; Mansfield 1993);

- traditional tribal group therapies (Cohn & Osbourne 1992; Corey 1990; Garrett & Osbourne 1995; Stone 1994);

- the Native American church and peyote (Albaugh & Anderson 1974; Chuelos et al. 1959; MacLean et al. 1961; *Peninsula Daily News* 1997; Smith 1958); and

- traditional Native treatments such as the sweat lodge (Scurfield 1995; Silver 1994; Indian Country Today Media Network 2010).

It is my contention that a careful case formulation on an individual basis is critical to designing an intervention into PTSD for Native veterans. The Western and Native methods briefly described above comprise a smorgasbord of opportunity for clinicians to create effective integrated treatments for Native veterans. Some suggestions for future directions follow:

- Increased national and local collaboration between the IHS and the VA medical system for creating assessment and treatment options for Native veterans with PTSD.

  - This might include the establishment of a national policy, procedure, and advocacy office jointly funded and directed and staffed by a team of workers dedicated to improving the collaboration process.
  - This might include local level collaboration between the IHS and VA faculties, programs, and workers for direct clinical services and sharing resources.

- Increased use of telemedicine to improve access to PTSD outpatient assessment and treatment for rural aboriginal veterans with PTSD (Shore et al. 2007).
- Increased funding for and access to Camp Chaparral and similar programs designed to train VA PTSD professional staff in the specific methods and mechanisms of Native cultural and spiritual treatment of PTSD (Deconinck 2010; Olsen & Elliot 2010).

  - The creation and funding of programs like Camp Chaparral and the continuation of Camp Chaparral and those at Fort Carson (Deconinck 2010) teach the ancient and effective Native methods of healing post-traumatic stress (Holm 1995). Despite the success of this program, the VA system has cut funding and no longer sends as many staff to this type of program as previously, exactly at the time that many Native veterans are returning from combat-laden tours in Afghanistan and Iraq.

- Increased funding for research into understanding tribally specific healing mechanisms for post-traumatic stress and incorporation of these into best-practice models for the VA medical system; and state, regional, local, and tribally based mental health treatment programs.

  - The development of theoretical and practical Native PTSD treatment program models that facilitate integrated Western and traditional native cultural, spiritual, and ceremonial treatments (Holm 1995).

Conclusion

There are many Western PTSD assessments and treatments, and there are many Native traditional cultural and spiritual treatments available for Natives suffering from PTSD. Efforts to combine the resources and capacity of the

IHS and the VA system to conduct research to understand, model, and integrate these mechanisms to ameliorate post-traumatic stress among native veterans and to optimally share resources are critically needed. Increasing access for relatives located at rural sites through innovation methods such as telemedicine is also needed. Finally, a continued commitment of the IHS, VA medical system, and tribal entities is required to enhance, rather than cut away, training programs such as Camp Chappell. It has been an honor to briefly examine and present the needs and solutions available for friable veterans with post-traumatic stress and to recommend some mechanisms to enhance and continue these necessary services and create what we the *Aamskapipikuni* call *niipaitappyssin*, a way of life (Burns 2010).

Author's note: In this chapter important traditional native ceremonial practices are referred to by their tribal names out of respect for tribal cultures and spiritual beliefs of indigenous people and to familiarize the reader with these names and terms.

Among the Aamskapipikuni (Blackfeet) we say Aho for thank you; thus I say Aho or thank you to the editor of this book, Dr. Thomas Miller, and to the Native veterans who served or are serving this nation in a good way. My English name is Joseph B. Stone, or as my elders have said, among the Aasakapipipikuni tribal relatives, I am ómahkapi'si iniskim—Wolf Buffalo Stone.

References

Adams, D. W. (1995). *Education for extinction: American Indians and the boarding school experience, 1875–1928* (pp. 36–55). Lawrence: University of Kansas Press.

Albaugh, B. J. & Anderson, P. O. (1974). Peyote in the treatment of alcoholism among American Indians. *American Journal of Psychiatry* 131, no. 11: 1247–1251.

Amini, F., Lewis, T., Lannon, R., Louie, A., Baumbacher, G., McGuinness, T. & Schiff, E. Z. (1996). Affect, attachment, memory: Contributions toward psychobiologic integration. *Psychiatry* 59: 213–239.

Archambault, A. (1997). Personal communication to author, May 17.

Augustson, K. L. (1990). Memorandum to Thomas R. Burns, special assistant to the director, Alcoholism and Substance Abuse Branch, Indian Health Service, May 21.

Baca, J. (2011). Congressman Baca fights for Native Americans. www.house.gov/baca/legislation-native-americans.htm (accessed January 4, 2011).

Ball, T. (1998). Prevalence rates of PTSD and lifetime trauma in an adult American Indian sample. PhD dissertation, University of Oregon.

Beals, J. Holmes, T., Ashcraft, M., Fairbank, J., Friedman, M., Jones, M., Schlenger, W., Shore, J. & Manson, S. W. (2002). A comparison of the prevalence of post-traumatic stress disorder across five racially and ethnically distinct samples of Vietnam theater veterans. *Journal of Traumatic Stress* 15, no. 2: 89–97.

Beals, J., Manson, S. M., Whitesell, N. R., Spicer, P., Novins, D. K., Mitchell, C. M., et al. (2005). Prevalence of DSM-IV disorders and attendant help-seeking in two American Indian reservation populations. *Archives of General Psychiatry* 62: 99–108.

Birch, M. (1999) Attachment issues and attachment disorders in children: Clinical training for Port Angeles, Washington child protective service (CPS). Presented at training in Port Angeles, Washington, June 4 & 22 and July 13.

Bluehorse, P. & Zion, J. W. (1993). Hozhooji naat'aanii: The Navajo justice and harmony ceremony. *Mediation Quarterly* 10, no. 4: 327–337 (special issue: Native American perspectives on peacemaking).

Brown, J. (1997). *Statement of Jesse Brown, Secretary of Veterans Affairs, before the Committee on Indian Affairs, United States Senate.* www4.va.gov/OCA/testimony/other/nativeam.asp (accessed January 4, 2011).

Brown, L. D. & Tandon, R. (1983). Ideology and political economy in inquiry: Action research and participatory research. *Journal of Applied Behavioral Science* 19, no. 3: 277–294.

Brown, L. F., Bell, G., Klein, R. E. & Wells, M. R. (2006). *American Indian and Alaska Native veterans: Lasting contributions.* Washington, DC: Office of Policy Assistant Secretary for Policy, Planning, and Preparedness, U.S. Department of Veterans Affairs.

Brown, L. S. (1991). Not outside the range: One feminist perspective on psychic trauma. *American Imago* 48, no. 1: 119–133.

Brydon-Miller, M. (1997). Participatory action research: Psychology and social change. *Journal of Social Issues* 53, no. 4: 657–666.

Buckwald, D., Goldberg, J., Noonan, C., Beals, J. & Manson, S. (2005). Relationship between post-traumatic stress disorder and pain in two American Indian tribes. *Pain Medicine* 25: 72–79.

Burns, C. (2010). The long way back home: An incredible journey. Unpublished manuscript.

Cabaniss, M. (2010). *Post traumatic stress disorder: "A legacy" for Native Americans.* Santa Fe, NM: Institute of American Indian Arts Chronicle.

Chuelos, N., Blewett, D. B., Smith, C. M. & Hoffer, A. (1959). Use of d-lysergic acid diethylamide in the treatment of alcoholism. *American Journal of Studies on Alcohol* 20: 577–590.

Coen, C. W. (Ed.). (1985). *Functions of the brain.* Oxford: Clarendon Press.

Cohn, B. & Osbourne, W. L. (1992). *Group counseling: A practical self-concept approach for the helping professional.* Chappaqua, NY: LS Communications.

Corey, G. (1990). *Theory and practice of group counseling.* 3rd ed. Pacific Grove, CA: Brooks/Cole.

Cross, T. (1987). *Cross-cultural skills in Indian child welfare: A guide for the non-Indian.* Portland, OR: Northwest Indian Child Welfare Association, Inc.

Deconinck, T. (2010). Modern soldiers, ancient medicine, *AOLNews,* November 11. http://www.aolnews.com/2010/11/11/modern-soldiers-ancient-medicines/ (accessed January 5, 2011).

DeJong, David H. (2008). *"If you knew the conditions": A chronicle of the Indian Medical Service and American Indian health care, 1908–1955*. New York: Lexington Books.

Deloria, V. & Lytle, C. M. (1983). *American Indians, American justice*. Austin: University of Texas Press.

Dubowitz, H., Black, M., Harrington, D. & Verschoore, A. (1993). A follow-up study of behavior problems associated with child sexual abuse. *Child Abuse and Neglect* 17: 743–754.

Duran, E. (1984). *Archetypal consultation: A service delivery model for Native Americans*. New York: Peter Lang.

Duran, E. & Duran, B. (1995). *Native American post-colonial psychology*. Albany: State University of New York Press.

Emde, R. N. & Buchsbaum, H. K. (1989). Toward a psychoanalytic theory of affect: II. Emotional development and signaling in infancy. In S. I. Greenspan & G. H. Pollock (Eds.), *The course of life*. Vol. 1, *Infancy*. Madison, CT: International Universities Press.

Fair, C. M. (1992). *Cortical memory functions*. New York: Norton.

Federal benefits for veterans, dependents, and survivors. (2010). Chapter 5: Home loan guaranty. Washington, DC: Department of Veterans Affairs. www1.va.gov/opa/publications/benefits-book/benefits-chap05.asp (accessed January 4, 2011).

Floerchinger, D. S. (1991). Bereavement in late adolescence: Intervention on college campuses. *Journal of Adolescent Research* 6, no. 1: 146–156 (special issue: Death and adolescent bereavement).

Ford, J. D. (1999). Disorders of extreme stress following war-zone military trauma: Associated features of posttraumatic stress disorder or co-morbid but distinct syndromes. *Journal of Consulting and Clinical Psychology* 67, no. 1: 3–12.

Ford, J. D. & Kidd, P. (1998). Early childhood trauma and disorders of extreme stress as predictors of treatment outcome with chronic posttraumatic stress disorder. *Journal of Traumatic Stress* 11, no. 4: 743–761.

French, L. A. (1992). *Cultural disintegration perpetuated through substance abuse among American Indians*. Washington, DC: Annual Convention of the American Psychological Association.

Friedman, M. J., Ashcraft, M. L., Beals. J. L., Keane, T. M., Manson, S. M. & Marsella, A. J. (1997). *Matsunaga Vietnam Veterans Project (Volumes 1 and 2)*. Denver: National Center for Posttraumatic Stress Disorder and National Center for American Indian and Alaska Native Mental Health Research.

Gagne, M. A. (1998). The role of dependency and colonialism in generating trauma in First Nations citizens: The James Bay Cree. In Y. Danieli (Ed.), *International handbook of multigenerational legacies of trauma* (pp. 355–372). New York: Plenum Press.

Garrett, J. T. & Garrett, M. W. (1994). The path of good medicine: Understanding and counseling Native American Indians. *Journal of Multicultural Counseling and Development* 22: 134–144.

Garrett, M. W. & Osbourne, W. L. (1995). The Native American sweat lodge as metaphor for group work. *The Journal for Specialists in Group Work* 20, no. 1: 33–39.

Gazzaniga, M. & LeDeux, J. (1978). *The integrated mind*. New York: Plenum Press.

George, C. (1996). A representational perspective of child abuse and prevention: Internal working models of attachment and care giving. *Child Abuse and Neglect* 20, no. 5: 411–424.

Green, A. H. (1995). Comparing child victims and adult survivors: Clues to the pathogenesis of child sexual abuse. *Journal of the American Academy of Psychoanalysis* 23, no. 4: 6655–6670.

Greenspan, S. I. (1981). *Psychopathology and adaptation in infancy and early childhood*. New York: International Universities Press.

Guedel, G. (2010). New federal law boosts housing for Native American veterans. *Native American legal update: The resource for current legal developments*. www.nativelegalupdate.com/2010/10/articles/new-federal-law-boosts-housing-for-native (accessed January 5, 2011).

Guilmet, G. M. (1976). The nonverbal American Indian child in the urban classroom. PhD dissertation, Department of Anthropology, University of California, Los Angeles.

Guilmet, G. M. & Whited, D. L. (1987). Cultural lessons for clinical mental health practice: The Puyallup tribal community. *American Indian and Alaska Native Mental Health Research* 1, no. 2: 32–49.

Gurley, D., Novins, D. K., Jones, M. C., Beals, J., Shore, J. H. & Manson, S. M. (2001). Comparative use of biomedical services and traditional healing options by American Indian veterans. *Psychiatric Services* 52, no. 1: 68–74.

Hamblen, J. (2010). Treatment of PTSD. U.S. Department of Veterans Affairs National Center for PTSD. www.ptsd.va.gov (accessed January 4, 2011).

Heineman, T. V. (1998). *The abused child: Psychodynamic understanding and treatment*. New York: The Guilford Press.

Herman, J. L. (1992). *Trauma and recovery*. New York: Basic Books.

Herring, R. D. (1994). The clown or contrary figure as a counseling intervention strategy with Native American Indian clients. *Journal of Multicultural Counseling and Development* 22: 153–164.

Holiday, L. F., Bell, G., Klein, R. E. & Wells, M. R. (2006). *American Indian and Alaska Native veterans: Lasting contributions*. Washington, DC: U.S. Department of Veterans Affairs Office of Policy, Assistant Secretary for Policy, Planning, and Preparedness.

Holm, T. (1995). PTSD in Native American Vietnam veterans: A reassessment. *Wicazo Sa Review* 11, no. 2: 83–86.

Horijsi, C., Heavy Runner-Craig, B. & Pablo, J. (1992). Reactions by Native American parents to child protection agencies: Cultural and community factors. *Child Welfare* 71, no. 4: 329–342.

Indian Country Today Media Network. (2010). *Heavy heat*. indiancountrytodaymedianetwork.com/2010/12/heavy-heat-native-american-vets-religion (accessed January 5, 2011).

Jilak, W. G. (1982). *Indian healing: Shamanic ceremonialism in the Pacific Northwest today*. Surrey, BC: Hancock House Publishers.

Johnson, P., Carlson, K. & Hearst, M. (2010). Healthcare disparities for American Indian veterans in the U.S.: A population-based study. *Medical Care* 48, no. 6: 583–589.

Kasee, C. R. (1995). Identity, recovery, and religious imperialism: Native American women and the new age. *Women & Therapy* 16, nos. 2–3: 83–93 (special issue: Women's spirituality, women's lives).

Kawennano, D. & Johnson, R. (1996). Intergenerational multi-cultural PTSD: A Native American perspective. Presented at the 20th annual convening of crisis intervention, Chicago, Illinois. www.uic.edu/orgs/convening/proc20.htm. (January 4, 2011).

Kramer, B., Jouldjian, S., Washington, D. L., Harker, J. D., Sailbe, D. & Yano, E. M. (2009a). Health care for American Indian and Alaska native women. *Women's Health Issues* 19, no. 2: 135–143.

Kramer, B., Wang, M., Jouldian, S., Lee, M., Finke, B., & Sailbe, D. (2009b). Veterans Health Administration and Indian Health Service: Healthcare utilization by Indian Health Service enrollees. *Medical Care* 47, no. 6: 670–676.

Kramer, B. J., Wang, M., Hoang, T., Harker, J. D., Finke, B. & Saiba, D. (2006). Identification of American Indian and Alaska Native veterans in administrative data of the Veterans Health Administration and the Indian Health Service. *American Journal of Public Health* 96, no. 9: 1577–1578.

Krystal, H. (1990). An information processing view of object-relations. *Psychoanalytic Inquiry* 10: 221–251.

Krystal, H. (1991). Integration and self-healing in post-traumatic states: A ten-year retrospective. *American Imago* 48, no. 1: 93–118.

Kulka, R. A., Schlenger, W. A, Fairbanks, J. A., Hough, R. L., Jordan, B. K., Marmar, C. R. & Cranston, A. S. (1990). *Trauma and the Vietnam War generation: Report of findings from the National Vietnam Veterans Readjustment Study.* New York: Bruner/Mazel.

Last, U. & Klein, H. (1984). Impact of parental Holocaust dramatization on offspring's reports of parental child-rearing practices. *Journal of Youth and Adolescence* 13, no. 4: 267–283.

Laudslager, M., Noonan, C., Jacobson, C., Goldberg, J., Buchwald, D., Bremner, J. D., Vaccarino, V. & Manson, S. M. (2008). Salivary cortisol among American Indians with and without posttraumatic stress disorder (PTSD): Gender and alcohol influences. *Brain, Behavior, Immunity* 23, no. 5: 658–662.

Lewis, E. W., Duran, E. & Woodis, W. (1999). Psychotherapy in the American Indian population. *Psychiatric Annals* 29, no. 8: 477–479.

Libby, A. M. Orton, H. D., Novins, D. K., Spicer, P., Buchwald, D., Manson, S. M., et al. (2004). Childhood abuse and lifetime alcohol and drug disorders for American Indians. *Journal of Studies on Alcohol* 65, no. 1: 74–83.

Locust, C. (1995). The impact of differing belief systems between Native Americans and their rehabilitation service providers. *Rehabilitation Education* 9, nos. 2–3: 205–215 (special double issue: Spirituality, disability, and rehabilitation).

Loo, C. M. (2010). PTSD among ethnic minority veterans. www.ptsd.va.gov/profes sional/pages/ptsd-minority-vets.asp (accessed January 5, 2011).

MacLean, J. R., MacDonald, D. R., Byrne, U. P. & Hubbard, A. M. (1961). The use of LSD-25 in the treatment of alcoholism and other psychiatric problems. *American Journal of Studies on Alcohol* 22: 34–45.

Mansfield, E. (1993). Balance and harmony: Peacemaking in Coast Salish tribes of the Pacific Northwest. *Mediation Quarterly* 10, no. 4: 339–353 (special issue: Native American perspectives on peacemaking).

Mansfield, G. (2004). *Statement of Gordon Mansfield, Secretary of Veterans Affairs, before the Committee on Indian Affairs, U.S. Senate.* www4.va.gov/OCA/testi mony/other/nativeam.asp (accessed January 4, 2011).

Manson, S. M. (1996). Cross-cultural and multi-cultural assessment of trauma. *Culture, Medicine, and Psychiatry* 20: 469–498.

Manson, S. M. (1997). Cross-cultural and multi-cultural assessment of trauma. In J. P. Wilson & T. M. Keane (Eds.). *Assessing psychological trauma and PTSD: A handbook for practitioners.* New York: Guildford Press.

Manson, S. M. (2000). *Wounded spirits, ailing hearts training manual.* Washington, DC: U.S. Department of Veterans Affairs, National Center for PTSD.

Manson, S. M. & Trimble, J. E. (1982). Toward an understanding of American Indian concepts of mental health: Some reflections and directions. In A. Marsella & P. Pederson (Eds.), *Intercultural applications of counseling and therapies.* Beverly Hills, CA: Sage.

McTaggart, R. (1991). Principles for participatory action research. *Adult Education Quarterly* 41, no. 3: 168–187.

Medicine, B. (1988). Native American (Indian) women: A call for research. *Anthropology & Education Quarterly* 19: 86–92.

Miller, P., Garrett, M., McMahon, M., Johnson, N. & Wikoff, R. (1985). Coping methods and societal adjustment of persons with cardiovascular disease. *Health Values* 9, no. 4: 10–13.

Miller, P., Johnson, N. & Garrett, M. (1982). Health beliefs of and adherence to the medical regimen by patients with ischemic heart disease. *Heart and Lung* 11, no. 4: 332–339.

Mitchell, W. & Patch, K. (1986). Religion, spirituality, and the recovery of Native American alcoholics. *IHS Primary Health Care Provider* 11: 129.

Nadler, A., Kav-Venaki, S. & Gleitman, B. (1985). Transgenerational effects of the holocaust: Externalization of aggression in second generation holocaust survivors. *Journal of Consulting & Clinical Psychology* 53, no. 3: 365–369.

Nagle, J. K. (1988). Unresolved grief and mourning in Navajo women. *American Indian & Alaska Native Mental Health Research* 2, no. 2: 32–40.

Naval History and Heritage Committee. (2011). Native Americans and the U.S. military. www.history.nay.mil/faqs61–1.htm (accessed January 5, 2011).

Nieuwenhuys, R., Voogd, J. & van Huizen, Chr. (1981). *The human central nervous system.* 2nd rev. ed. Berlin: Springer.

Noshpitz, J. & King, R. (1991). *Pathways of growth: Essentials of child psychiatry.* Vol. I: *Normal development.* New York: Wiley.

Olsen, K. & Elliot, A. (2010). *Ancient traditions help mental-health professionals connect with American Indian veterans battling PTSD.* Spokane, WA: Spokesman Review.

Papuz, J. W. (1937). A proposed mechanism of emotion. *Archives of Neurological Psychiatry* 38: 725–743.

Park, P. (1999). People, knowledge, and change in participatory research. *Management Learning* 30, no. 2: 141–157.

Peninsula Daily News. (1997). U.S. military accepts service members' use of peyote, April 14.

Perry, B. (2002). Personal communication to author, May 1.

Pierce Eyen, Jennifer. (1997). Wuski A-Baw-Tan (A new dream)—A poem dedicated to our elder, Horse Man, who passed over to the land of the death dream one stormy night. In J. Harjo & G. Bird with P. Blanco, B. Cuthand & V. Martinez (Eds.), *Reinventing the enemy's language: Contemporary Native women's writings of North America* (pp. 149–150). New York: W.W. Norton & Company.

Post, B. (2002a). Education and the child of trauma. www.bryanpost.com/articles/edutrauma.htm (January 5, 2011).

Post, B. (2002b) Personal communication to author, June 25–26.

Rakic, K. (1991). Development of the primate cerebral cortex. In M. Lewis (Ed.), *Child and adolescent: A comprehensive textbook.* Baltimore, MD: Williams & Wilkins.

Rowland-Klein, D. & Dunlop, R. (1998). The transmission of trauma across generations: Identification with parental trauma in children of Holocaust survivors. *Australian and New Zealand Journal of Psychiatry* 32, no. 3: 358–369.

Sack, W. H., Clarke, G. N. & Seeley, J. (1995). Posttraumatic stress disorder across two generations of Cambodian refugees. *Journal of the American Academy of Child and Adolescent Psychiatry* 34, no. 9: 1160–1166.

Sawchuck, C. N., Roy-Bryne, P., Goldberg, J., Manson, S. M. & Buckwald, D. (2006). The relationship between post-traumatic stress disorder and cardiovascular disease in an American Indian tribe. *Psychological Medicine* 35: 1785–1794.

Schore, A. (1994). *Affect regulation and the origin of self: The neurobiology of emotional development.* Hillsdale, NJ: Lawrence Erlbaum.

Scurfield, R. H. (1995). Healing the warrior: Admission of two American Indian war-veteran cohort groups to a specialized PTSD unit. *American Indian & Alaska Native Mental Health Research* 6, no. 3: 1–22.

Shore, J. H., Savin, D., Orton, H., Beals, J. & Manson, S. M. (2007). Diagnostic reliability of telepsychiatry in American Indian veterans. *American Journal of Psychiatry* 164: 115–118.

Silver, S. (1994). Lessons from child of water. *American Indian & Alaska Native Mental Health Research* 6, no. 1: 4–17.

Slaby, A. E. (1991). Dual diagnosis: Fact or fiction. In M. S. Gold & A. E. Slaby (Eds.), *Dual diagnosis in substance abuse* (pp. 3–29). New York: Marcel Dekker.

Smith, C. M. (1958). A new adjunct to the treatment of alcoholism: The hallucinogenic drug. *American Journal of Studies on Alcoholism* 19: 406–417.

Spindler, G. & Spindler, L. (1957). American Indian personality types and their socio-cultural roots. *Annals of the American Academy of Political and Social Science* 311: 148–149.

Stefon, F. J. (1987). Richard Henry Pratt and his Indians. *Journal of Ethnic Studies* 15: 88–112.

Stern, D. N. (1985). *The interpersonal world of the infant.* New York: Basic Books.

Stone, J. B. (1994). The American Indian sweat bath ceremony: A brief description. Unpublished manuscript, Psychology Department, Utah State University, Logan.

Stone, J. B. (2002). Focus on cultural issues in research: Developing and implementing Native American post-colonial participatory action research. In *Work Group on American Indian Research and Program Evaluation Methodology (AIRPEM), Symposium on Research and Evaluation Methodology: Life span issues related to American Indians/Alaska Natives with disabilities* (pp. 98–132). Flagstaff: Northern Arizona University, Institute for Human Development, Arizona University Center on Disabilities, American Indian Rehabilitation Research and Training Center. http:// www4.nau.edu/ihd/airrtc (accessed January 5, 2011).

Tafoya, T. (1995). Personal communication to author, April 19.

Toelken, B. (1994). Personal communication to author, February 17.

United States Department of Veterans Affairs. National Center for PTSD. (2010a). Cognitive processing therapy. www.ptsd.va.gov/public/pages/cognitive-processing-therapy.asp (accessed January 5, 2011).

United States Department of Veterans Affairs. National Center for PTSD. (2010b). Prolonged exposure therapy. www.ptsd.va.gov/public/pages/prolonged-exposure-therapy.asp (accessed January 5, 2011).

United States Department of Veterans Affairs. Office of Government Relations. (2010). Native American Medal of Honor recipients. www.va.gov/tribalgovern ment/ (accessed January 5, 2011).

Utley, R. M. (Ed.). (1964). *Richard Henry Pratt, battlefield and classroom. Four decades with the American Indians, 1867–1904,* New Haven and London: Yale University Press.

van der Kolk, B. A. & Fisler, R. E. (1994). Childhood abuse and neglect and loss of self-regulation. *Bulletin of the Menninger Clinic* 58, no. 2: 145–168.

van Ijzendroon, M. H. (1995a). Adult attachment representations, parental responsiveness, and infant attachment: A meta-analysis on the predictive validity of the Adult Attachment Interview. *Psychological Bulletin* 117: 347–403.

van Ijzendroon, M. H. (1995b). Of the way we are: On temperament, attachment, and the transmission gap: A rejoinder to Fox. *Psychological Bulletin* 117: 411–415.

van Ijzendoorn, M. H. & Bakermans-Kranenburg, M. J. (1997). Intergenerational transmission of attachment: A move to the contextual level. In L. Atkinson & K. J. Zucker (Eds.), *Attachment and psychopathology.* New York: Guilford Press.

van Ijzendroon, M. H., Juffer, F. & Duyvesteyn, M. G. C. (1995). Breaking the inter-generational cycle of insecure attachment: A review of the effects of attachment-based interventions on maternal sensitivity and infant security from a contextual perspective. *Journal of Child Psychology and Psychiatry* 36: 225–248.

Villa, V. M. (2003). Determinants of VA ambulatory care use among Native American veterans. U.S. Department of Veterans Affairs. www.hardresearch.va.gov/research/abstracts.cfm?Project_ID= -1927724230 (accessed January 5, 2011).

Walker, D. (2002). Personal communication to author, June 27.

Walters, K. L. & Simoni, J. M. (1999). Trauma, substance abuse, and HIV risk among urban American Indian women. *Cultural Diversity & Ethnic Minority Psychology* 5, no. 3: 236–248.

Weaver, J. N. & Yellow Horse Brave Heart, M. (1999). Examining two facets of American Indian identity: Exposure to other cultures and the influence of historical trauma. *Journal of Human Behavior in the Social Environment* 2, no. 1: 19–33.

Weissberg, R. P. & Greenberg, M. T. (1998). Prevention science and collaborative community action research: Combining the best from both perspectives. *Journal of Mental Health* 7, no. 5: 470–492.

Wheeler, R. (1993). Personal communication to author, April 22.

Whyte, W. F., Greenwood, D. J. & Lazes, P. (1989). Participatory action research: Through practice to science in social research. *American Behavioral Scientist* 32, no. 5: 513–551.

Wisner, B., Stea, D. & Kruks, S. (1991). Participatory and action research methods. In E. H. Zube & G. T. Moore (Eds.), *Advances in environment, behavior, and design*. Edmonton, OK: Environmental Design Research Association.

Witner, L. F. (2002). *The Indian Industrial School, Carlisle, Pennsylvania, 1879–1918* (pp. 18, 50). 3rd ed. Carlisle, PA: Cumberland County Historical Society.

Yehuda, R., Schmeidler, J., Elkin, A., Wilson, S., Siever, L., Binder-Brynes, K., Wainberg, M. & Aferiot, D. (1998). Phenomenology and psychobiology of the intergenerational response to trauma. In Y. Danieli (Ed.), *Intergenerational handbook of the multigenerational legacies of trauma* (pp. 639–655). New York: Plenum Press.

Yellow Horse Brave Heart, M. (1998). The return to the sacred path: Healing the historical trauma and historical unresolved grief response among the Lakota through a psycho educational group intervention. *Smith College Studies in Social Work* 68, no. 3: 288–305.

Zeanah, C. H., Finley-Belgard, E. & Benoit, D. (1997). Intergenerational transmission of relationship psychopathology: A mother-infant case study. In L. Atkinson & K. J. Zucker (Eds.), *Attachment and psychopathology*. New York: Guilford Press.

Zlotnick, C., Zakriski, A. L., Shea, M. T. & Costello, E. (1996). The long-term sequelae of sexual abuse: Support for a complex posttraumatic stress disorder. *Journal of Traumatic Stress* 9, no. 2: 195–205.

Chapter 12

Healthcare for Women Military Veterans

Monica Roy

Historical Review

Women have served in various capacities in the U.S. military since America's War of Independence, often in roles that helped the day-to-day functioning of the servicemen. Women served as cooks, seamstresses, and launderers during the American Revolution. At times women have served in unconventional roles during different conflicts, such as spies, saboteurs, and couriers, as well as playing an important part in the execution of war. During the Civil War at least four hundred women on both sides of the conflict disguised themselves as men so that they could serve in more traditional roles in combat. Although women played a crucial role in the U.S. military, it wasn't until the early part of the twentieth century that their role was formalized.

In 1901, during the Spanish-American War, the Army Nursing Corps was institutionalized by an act of congress as an auxiliary of the army (Thomas 1978, 3). Soon afterwards the Navy Nurse Corps was established, in 1908. The turning point for women's status in the military occurred during World War I, and the number of women serving in the military grew. By the end of World War I about 34,000 women were serving as nurses in all of the armed forces, including the Marines, the Coast Guard, the army, and the navy. In 1917 the Navy Department authorized women to be in the Naval Reserve. Despite their growth in numbers in the military and the formalization of their contributions, women still did not have military rank or benefits due to the overwhelming sentiment that women should not be in the military.

Despite this sentiment, World War II marked another turning point for women in the military. There was a shortage of manpower, and the number of women serving in the military grew exponentially. Not only did the population of women serving in the military increase, but women were also no longer serving solely as nurses but also in a variety of roles such as clerical positions. By the end of the war, of twelve million members of the armed forces, close to 280,000 were women, and it was during this war that women were given full military status through the establishment of the Women's Army Corps (WAC), which was instituted by Congress in 1943.

The Women's Army Auxiliary Corps (WAAC) preceded the WAC. The WAAC was introduced in a bill by Massachusetts Congresswoman Edith Nourse Rogers. After the creation of the WAAC was approved by Congress, five training centers were opened within a year, at Fort Des Moines, Iowa; Daytona Beach, Florida; Fort Ogletherpe, Georgia; Fort Devon, Massachusetts; and Camp Ruston, Louisiana.

During this time several other organizations were created in the other branches of service, including the Women Accepted for Volunteer Emergency Service (the Navy WAVES, established in 1942), the Marine Corps Women's Reserve, the Coast Guard Women's Reserve (known as SPARS, established in 1942), and the Women Air Force Service Pilots (the WASPs, made up of civil service pilots). All of these groups contributed in World War II and had units stationed overseas.

After the war many women (as well as men) left the military, and Congress determined that the role of women in the military should be reduced. However, in 1947 General Dwight D. Eisenhower, who was a strong advocate for the legislation making the WAC a part of the regular army and reserve, recommended that President Harry Truman sign the Women's Armed Services Integration Act. This bill was signed on June 12, 1948, and made women permanent members of the regular and reserve forces of the U.S. Army, Navy, Marines and the newly created Air Force. Also at this time Truman's Executive Order 9981 ended racial segregation in the armed forces, marking changes within the military for those of minority status.

The Korean conflict marked continuing change for women in the military. There were 22,000 women in the armed forces, with one-third in nursing or health-related jobs. During this conflict the objective was to mobilize between one-half and one million women in the armed forces. It was during this conflict, in 1951, that Secretary of Defense George C. Marshall created the Defense Department Advisory Committee on Women in the Services (DACOWITS). This committee was created to provide advice and recommendations on policies related to the recruitment and retention, treatment, employment, integration, and well-being of professional women in the armed forces. Also in 1951, Congress approved funds so that the WAC could be given a permanent home at Fort McClellan, Alabama. The center opened in 1954 and was used for many purposes, including conducting basic training, training clerk-typists, teaching stenography, training personal specialists, leadership training, cadre courses for enlisted personnel, and basic and advanced courses for officers. Despite these changes and active efforts to recruit women, the military fell short of the goal to recruit more women. The number of women who served in the Korean conflict at its peak was 48,700, and the number declined to about 35,000 by the end of the war era in June 1955.

The next big push to recruit women into the military was during the Vietnam War. The Department of Defense (DoD) aimed to add 6,500 women to the military (Holm 1982, 187). The DoD met this goal, with nearly 7,000 women serving in the military in the Southeast Asian theater of operations, most as nurses.

The Vietnam era marked a period of change for many groups seeking equal status in society, including women. In 1967, Public Law 90-130 was passed, which aimed at removing any obstacles for women to become high-ranking military officers. The 1970s marked an era of gains by women in the military. In 1970 Brigadier General Anna Mae Hays, head of the Army Nurse Corps, became the first woman to attain star rank in nursing. In 1972 Rear Admiral Alene B. Duerk, the head of the Navy Nurse Corps, became the first woman admiral, and E. Ann Hoefly became the first brigadier general in the Air Force Nurse Corps. Soon women who were not nurses began to receive star rank, such as Army Brigadier General Elizabeth P. Hoisington and Air Force Brigadier General Jeanne M. Holm.

The creation of the All-Volunteer Force (AVF) in 1973 continued the trend toward greater gender equality. This led to the opening of occupational roles to women because of the need to fill positions in a volunteer force. Women played an important role in an AVF because personnel demands could not be met with male volunteers alone. This led to the need to find ways to further integrate women into the military. In 1978 the WAC was discontinued as a way to assimilate women in the army rather than continuing in a separate organization.

In 1979 Congress further acknowledged the role of women in the military by granting veteran status to women who had served in the WAAC during World War II. This was a way of acknowledging the crucial role that women played during World War II even though they had not been formally recognized as a part of the military during their service.

Other efforts have been made to increase recruitment and retention by making the military more "family friendly." Although these efforts still need to be improved, the number of women serving in the armed forces has increased dramatically from 1973, when 55,000 women made up only 2.5 percent of the armed services, to 2009, when more than 205,000 women made up nearly 14 percent of the military.

Today's Woman Veteran

Currently women represent a larger portion of U.S. military forces. Some 14 percent of the forces deployed in support of Operation Iraqi Freedom (OIF) and Operation Enduring Freedom (OEF) in Afghanistan have been women, which equals 180,000 deployed female troops (Department of Defense 2008). Female troops have comprised 2.1 percent of all troop deaths during Operating Enduring Freedom and 2.4 percent of all OIF troop deaths (Fischer 2009).

Not only have the numbers of women in the military increased, but their duties and roles have also changed, especially since the Persian Gulf War. After the Persian Gulf War, the DoD made more than 90 percent of military occupations available to women. The responsibilities of women in Iraq and Afghanistan have further changed from prior conflicts. Although they are still barred from positions related to direct combat (e.g., infantry in the Marines and army), given that the conflicts in Iraq and Afghanistan have less distinct frontlines, women are exposed to combat situations more now than ever before. Women serve in a variety of support positions that involve leaving military bases; working side-by-side with combat soldiers; and coming under direct fire in positions as military police, convoy transportation, intelligence agents, pilots, medics, and mechanics (Street, Vogt & Dutra 2009).

Given the increase in the number of women serving in the military and their changing roles, more women are being deployed overseas (e.g., in Iraq and Afghanistan) than ever before, and the new generation (OIF/OEF) of women veterans face unique family-related challenges. Women veterans are often the primary caregivers in their families; military mothers are three times more likely to be single parents and five times more likely to be married to a military spouse who is also eligible for deployment (Joint Economic Committee 2007). Military mothers also tend to be young ($<$ age twenty-five) and lower in socioeconomic status (Joint Economic Committee 2007). Some OIF/OEF military mothers are in the position of having to manage family responsibilities from overseas, which may expose them to dual stressors. This can be problematic in that family/relationship disruptions are more strongly associated with postdeployment mental health issues for women veterans than for male veterans (Vogt et al. 2005).

Services for returning women veterans will have to address their unique needs. This will include taking into account that a growing number of women veterans tend to be younger, are more highly educated, are less likely than male veterans to be employed or married, are faced with financial hardship, and are two to four times more likely to be homeless than their nonveteran counterparts (Frayne et al. 2006; Gamache, Rosenheck & Tessler 2003).

Demographics of Today's Woman Veteran

In general, women veterans are younger than their male counterparts. In 2007 the estimated median age of women veterans was forty-seven, whereas the estimated median age of male veterans was sixty-one (Holder 2007). The age difference reflects the periods of service in which men and women served. Women were more likely to have served in the later war periods (e.g., Persian Gulf War), whereas men are more likely to have served in the earlier war periods (e.g., Vietnam War). The Gulf War era had the greatest estimated number of women veterans in 2007 (763,000), followed by the Vietnam era (256,000), World War II (135,000), and Korea (71,000). More than 554,000 women have served in peacetime only. The greatest number of male veterans are estimated to have served during the Vietnam era, followed by the Gulf War, Korea, and World War II (Office of Policy and Planning 2007).

Geographic Distribution of Women Veterans

In general, the geographic distribution of women veterans is similar to that of their male counterparts. In 2007 the states with the highest estimated portions of the total women veteran population were California, Texas, Florida, Virginia, Georgia, New York, Pennsylvania, Ohio, and North Carolina. Half of the women veteran population resides in these nine states. The least number of women veterans in proportion to the population are in Wyoming, Vermont, North Dakota, and the District of Columbia, which parallels the distribution of male veterans. In planning for Department of Veterans Affairs (VA) services it was estimated that by 2010 the top five states where women veterans live would be California, Texas, Virginia, Florida, and Georgia (Office of Policy and Planning 2007). It will be necessary for VA medical centers in these states to have facilities that properly accommodate women veterans.

Race and Marital Status

Over the years the military has seen an increase in the proportions of women, racial and ethnic minorities, and women of racial and ethnic minorities, and these changes have been reflected in the veteran population. Women veterans have been more likely then their male counterparts to identify themselves as a racial minority, and the population of women from racial minority backgrounds is growing. Between 1990 and 2000 the proportion of white non-Hispanic women veterans has declined from 83 to 72 percent. Nearly 30 percent of women veterans identified themselves as a member of a racial/ethnic minority group. Specifically, 17 percent identified themselves as black, non-Hispanic. Approximately 1 percent identified themselves as Asian, less than 1 percent as Pacific Islander, and 2 percent of some other race or multiple race. The rise in women veterans from diverse backgrounds may have implications for use of Veterans Health Administration (VHA) services. For instance, studies of utilization of VA services have shown that women seeking outpatient services within VA were more likely to describe themselves as black (Wright et al. 2006).

The proportion of Hispanics among women veterans also increased, from 3 percent in 1990, to 6 percent in 2000, to 7 percent in 2007. The proportion of non-white, non-Hispanics among women veterans is projected to increase from 22 percent in 2000, to 25 percent in 2010, to 27 percent in 2020 (Office of Policy and Planning 2007).

The August 2005 Current Population Survey (CPS) indicated that women veterans were just as likely to be married as nonveterans (52 percent of women veterans were married; 53 percent of nonveterans were married). This similarity was observed for all age groups. The implications of marital status for health status are discussed later in this chapter.

Educational Attainment and Employment

The educational attainment of women veterans is comparable to their non-veteran counterparts. Approximately 72 percent of women veterans had at least some college experience, and 40 percent of those had at least a bachelor's degree. Four percent of women veterans had no high school diploma, and 24 percent had finished high school as the highest level of education (Office of Policy and Planning 2007). The high rate of graduation from high school may be accounted for by the military's minimal educational requirements for service.

Women veterans seem to attain higher educational achievement than male veterans: 57 percent of male veterans and 72 percent of female veterans had at least some college education; 11 percent of male veterans and 4 percent of female veterans had less than a high school diploma. This may be attributed to the fact that male veterans may have joined the military when the educational requirements were not as high as they have been in recent years (Office of Policy and Planning 2007).

Data from the U.S. Census in 2000 show that women veterans ages twenty-five to sixty-four were more than 70 percent employed. Only 2 percent were unemployed; 27 percent were not in the labor force, and 45 percent of those not in the labor force were more than sixty-five years old. These percentages are comparable to nonveterans. Employment status may have implications for the use of VHA services, in that studies of the use of VA services have shown that women seeking outpatient services in VA were more educated and were more likely to be employed and have service-connected status than their male counterparts (Wright et al. 2006).

Data from the 2007 Current Population Survey show that women veterans are less likely than their nonveteran counterparts to be at the low end of the family income distribution but are more likely to be at the high end of the family income scale. Approximately 10 percent of veterans had family incomes less than $15,000, compared to 14 percent of nonveterans, and 28 percent of female veterans had a family income of $75,000 or more, compared to 29 percent of female nonveterans (Office of Policy and Planning 2007). In general, women veterans who sought treatment through VA appeared to have higher incomes than their male counterparts (Wright et al. 2006).

Use of Veterans' Healthcare Benefits

Evaluation of the rates of service connection is important because there is some evidence that service-connected disability status is a positive predictor of VHA use (Vogt et al. 2006), which in turn may inform services that are required for women veterans. Service connection is a monetary benefit paid to veterans who are disabled by an injury or illness that was incurred or aggravated during active military service. At the end of fiscal year 2006, 193,112 women veterans worldwide received service-connected compensation, and 191,231 of these veterans lived in the United States and Puerto Rico. This represents 11.2 percent of the total estimated population of women veterans as of September 30, 2006 (Office of Policy and Planning 2007).

Differences exist between male and female veterans in the distribution of compensation by degree of disability. Female veterans tend to be compensated at the lower and middle levels of the rating schedule. For instance, when comparing female and male veterans' percentage of compensation, approximately 40 percent of women are under 30 percent disabled, compared to 45 percent of men. When compensation increases between 30 and 60 percent disabled, approximately 41 percent of women fall into this category, versus 34 percent of men. Finally, 19 percent of women are considered 70 percent disabled or greater, versus 21 percent of men (Office of Policy and Planning 2007, tables on compensation).

Non-service-connected pensions are given to veterans who served during wartime and are deemed to be in economic need. In September 2006, 10,307 women veterans received this pension, compared to 319,549 male veterans. Of these women, 42.1 percent had served during World War II.

Women veterans also qualify for the GI Bill, which was established in 1944. The bill provided that (1) the federal government would subsidize tuition, fees, books, and educational materials for veterans and contribute to living expenses incurred while attending college or other approved institutions; (2) veterans were free to attend the educational institution of their choice; and (3) colleges were free to admit those veterans who met their admissions requirements. As of March 2007, 242,590 women veterans made use of Chapter 30, the Montgomery G.I. Bill, available to veterans entering the military after June 30, 1985. The earlier program, Chapter 32 (the Post–Vietnam Era Veterans Educational Assistance Program, VEAP), was used by 21,688 women veterans as of March 2007. This program was available to veterans who entered the military between January 1, 1977, and June 30, 1985. Among women veterans, the 2001 National Survey of Veterans showed that 34 percent used at least one VA education benefit, which is somewhat lower than the 40 percent of male veterans who used such benefits.

In fiscal year 2006, 240,000 women veterans sought VA medical care. The majority of those (61.5 percent) were veterans from the more recent post-Vietnam and Gulf War eras. Approximately 45 percent were between forty-five and fifty-four years old. Women veterans who presented for medical care were younger than their male counterparts who sought treatment at the VA, more frequently used VA services in the prior year, and were more likely to be single and have better health than their male counterparts (Wright et al. 2006). The top three diagnostic categories that women veterans were treated for were post-traumatic stress disorder (PTSD), hypertension, and depression. Eight thousand women veterans were in Priority Categories 1 and 2, which includes veterans with service-connected disabilities. Approximately 71,017 women veterans were in Priority Category 5, which includes non-service-connected veterans who meet low-income criteria for eligibility (Office of Policy and Planning 2007).

VA offers vocational rehabilitation services to veterans. Of the 52,982 veterans who used vocational rehabilitation and employment services through VA (Chapter 31) in fiscal year 2006, 9,895 (19 percent) were women. Of these women veterans, 2,310 were considered successfully rehabilitated during the year and increased their income sixfold after completing rehabilitation.

One of the coveted benefits offered to veterans is the VA Home Loan Guaranty Program. Between 1944 and the end of FY 2006, VA guaranteed more than eighteen million home loans. During fiscal year 2006, 17,355 women veterans successfully used this program.

VA life insurance is available to veterans as a way for those who leave military service to maintain government life insurance after discharge. The 2001 National Survey of Veterans indicated that 11 percent of male and female veterans had VA life insurance coverage, with older veterans having a larger proportion (17 percent of females and 20 percent of males). Data show that 70 percent of female veterans have life insurance from a source other than VA (Office of Policy and Planning 2007).

VA offers veterans burial benefits as well. The VA National Cemetery Administration's memorial program honors veterans and eligible family members in many ways, including in-ground burial, cremation burial, grave markers and headstones, and presidential certificates. In 2006, 3 percent of the 129,444 veterans who used these benefits were women.

Changes for Women Veterans

The 1980 Census was the first time that American women were asked if they had ever served in the armed forces, and an unexpected 1.2 million answered "yes" to this question. This led Congress and the Veterans Administration to initiate efforts to recognize and inform women veterans of their benefits and entitlements, beginning with gathering information about the needs of women veterans. In 1982 the "Survey of Female Veterans: A Study of Needs, Attitudes and Experiences of Women Veterans" was conducted to gain a better understanding of women veterans (Veterans Administration 1985). Results showed that, disappointingly, 57 percent of women did not know they were eligible for VA services. Another notable difference between women veterans and women in the general adult population was that women veterans reported twice the rates of cancer, with gynecological cancers being the most common. This indicated that women veterans may require more access to medical care than their nonveteran counterparts; however, they were not aware of the benefits that would allow them to obtain these services.

In 1982 the National Advisory Committee on Women Veterans was created by Harry Walters, and in November 1983, soon after the first meeting of the committee, Congress passed Public Law 98-160, Veterans' Health Care Amendments of 1983, mandating VA to establish the Advisory Committee on Women Veterans to assess the needs of women veterans; make sure that VA programs such as compensation, rehabilitation, outreach, and healthcare are designed to meet the needs of women; and make recommendations for change to ensure the availability of gender-specific care.

Almost a decade later, in November 1994, the Center for Women Veterans was established by Congress as a result of Public Law 103-446. This center was created to further oversee the VA programs for women veterans. The director of the center acts as the primary advisor to the Secretary of Veterans Affairs on all matters related to policies, legislation, programs, issues, and initiatives affecting women veterans. The mission of the Center for Women Veterans is to ensure that (1) women veterans receive benefits and services on par with male veterans; (2) VA programs are responsive to gender-specific needs of women veterans; (3) outreach is performed to improve women veterans' awareness of services, benefits, and eligibility criteria; and (4) women veterans are treated with dignity and respect.

The goals of the Center for Women Veterans include (1) identifying policies, practices, programs, and related activities that are unresponsive or insensitive to the needs of women veterans and recommending changes, revisions, or initiatives to address these deficiencies; (2) fostering communication among all elements of VA on these findings and ensuring the women veterans' community that their issues are incorporated into VA's strategic plan; (3) promoting and providing educational activities on women veterans' issues for VA personnel and other appropriate individuals; (4) encouraging and developing collaborative relationships with other federal, state, and community agencies to coordinate activities on issues related to women veterans; (5) coordinating outreach activities that enhance women veterans' awareness of new VA services and benefits; and (6) promoting research activities on women veterans' issues.

The center works on regularly monitoring changes VA-wide and assessing the impact these changes may have on the delivery of services to homeless women veterans with children, rural and elderly women veterans, and minority women veterans. Activities at the center also include monitoring VA briefings during the Transition Assistance Program to ensure that active duty women are provided access to information about the benefits and services that are available to them as veterans prior to their discharge from active duty. The center also monitors VA's research agenda to ensure that women veterans and their issues are included in all VA studies as well as working as a liaison to establish relationships with state, county, and national departments of veterans' affairs (Department of Veterans Affairs).

The population of women veterans has continued to increase over the last decade, in contrast to the population of male veterans. This can be accounted for by (1) the increasing number and proportion of women entering the military; (2) a more favorable survival rate of women compared to men at any given age; and (3) the younger age distribution of women veterans compared to male veterans, which means relatively more women at younger ages, with lower mortality rates. In the 1990 Census there were 1.2 million women veterans; in the 2000 Census there were 1.6 million women veterans. This number stayed stable for the 2007 census projections.

Challenges Faced by Women Veterans

The Impact of Military Service on Women Veterans' Health

Women veterans' experiences are unique and can impact their physical and mental health. In general, most women veterans report good to excellent health even as they age, which may be expected because they are a group that was selected for the military based on their physical ability; however, they have high odds of developing a variety of conditions and illnesses related to their military service (Murdoch et al. 2006). The challenges faced by women who have served in the military are discussed below; for a more concise review see table 12.1, a brief review of challenges and the steps that have been taken to alleviate them.

Contextual factors, such as the era in which a female veteran served, may impact health status. Other factors to consider are that women who serve in the military make a nontraditional career choice in early adulthood and that this decision could have a lifelong impact on higher education, marriage, childbearing, employment, and connectedness to social networks and social support. All of these factors impact one's social, occupational, emotional, and physical well-being.

When evaluating the impact of military service on the well-being of women veterans, it is important to take into account the influence of military environmental exposures on physical health. For example, women who were deployed during the Persian Gulf War and were exposed to oil-well-fire smoke appear to be at greater risk of asthma than veterans who were not exposed. Some deployed Gulf War veterans' risk for amyotrophic lateral sclerosis may be increased if they were exposed to some unknown environmental trigger (Murdoch et al. 2006).

The Vietnam era involved different challenges. Nurses who were deployed to Vietnam have higher than expected rates of pancreatic and uterine cancer death than the general population. Even those who were not deployed and served stateside show differences in their physical health. For instance, nondeployed Vietnam era nurses have higher than expected lung cancer mortality (Murdoch et al. 2006).

Table 12.1. Challenges Faced by Women Veterans and Future Directions

	Challenge	Future Directions
The Impact of Military Service on Health	Many health problems in women veterans are specific to the era that they served. For example, women who were deployed during the Persian Gulf War who were exposed to oil-well-fire smoke are at greater risk for asthma. Women who were deployed during the Vietnam War have higher rates of pancreatic and uterine cancer death.	The Women Veterans Health (WVH) Strategic Health Care Group is redesigning the delivery of primary care to women veterans to include gender-specific care at every VA site. This includes increased awareness of the impact of military service on women veterans' health.
Military Sexual Trauma and Harassment	The experience of sexual assault and harassment is prevalent in all female veteran cohorts. Military sexual assaults have long-term implications for both mental and physical health.	• The Department of Defense has introduced new education and prevention programs and hired additional attorneys as a result of mandates by law and congressional hearings in 2008 and 2009. • VA medical centers are required to provide military sexual trauma treatment and services. They have military sexual trauma coordinators to help women veterans access the care they need. Those who screen positive for military sexual trauma are eligible for treatment regardless of their discharge type or length of service.
Combat-Related Trauma	In 1990 bans on women serving in combat roles were lifted, and in the conflicts in Iraq and Afghanistan 12 percent of women were classified as experiencing moderate levels of combat exposure. Combat exposure	VA medical centers provide both outpatient and residential treatment for combat-related trauma in women-specific programs. Every VA medical center has a women veterans program manager who is available as an advocate for women

(*continued*)

Table 12.1. *(Continued)*

	Challenge	Future Directions
	can lead to higher risk of substance use disorders, mental health problems, and somatic complaints.	veterans and to help them to connect with the appropriate services.
Substance Use	Women veterans are at higher risk of developing substance use disorders and related problems than their nonveteran counterparts as a result of working in a traditionally male-dominated environment and experiencing military-related stressors.	VA medical centers provide both outpatient and residential treatment programs for substance use disorders for both male and female veterans.
Barriers to Care	Women veterans have not been aware of services offered by VA medical centers and have received same or slightly worse care at these facilities than care offered at other facilities.	The Center for Women Veterans was developed in November 1994 as a result of Pub. L. No. 103-446. The primary goal of this center has been to improve the quality of care and remove barriers to care for women veterans.
Homelessness	Women veterans are up to four times more likely to be homeless than their nonveteran and male counterparts. In 2009 approximately 13,100 women veterans were homeless.	• In 2009 The Zero Tolerance for Veteran Homelessness Act of 2009 was created to work on providing more opportunities for housing for veterans with mental, emotional, and physical health problems and who have an extremely low income. • In 2009 The Homeless Women Veterans and Homeless Veterans with Children Act of 2009 was created to help fund programs to help with child care so single mothers and fathers can pursue employment and maintain long-term, stable housing.

Military Sexual Trauma and Harassment

The choice to serve in a predominantly male work environment may have significant implications for woman veterans' long-term well-being. Military settings may be more prone to increased sexual aggression toward women, given the high male-female ratios. Traditionally male environments. as well as the high rate of male supervisors, are factors that have been associated with the increased possibility of sexual harassment (Gutek 1985). Interpersonal stressors such as sexual assault, sexual harassment, and gender-based harassment are stressors that women in the military are at higher risk for experiencing during military service (Murdoch et al. 2006), and women veterans report experiencing stressful and traumatic events at a higher rate than either nonveteran women or their male counterparts (Vogt et al. 2006). Unfortunately the experience of both sexual assault and sexual harassment is prevalent in all female veteran cohorts, including World War II veterans. In-service sexual assaults and sexual harassment have several long-term health implications. Psychosocial complications of sexual assault include increased suicide risk, PTSD, major depression, alcohol or drug abuse, long-term sexual dysfunction, disrupted social networks, and employment difficulties. Medical conditions may include increased risk of breast cancer, heart attacks, obesity, and asthma (Murdoch et al. 2006).

The percentage of women reporting being a victim of sexual assault varies. In a study of 160 female returnees from Operation Desert Storm, it was found that 7 percent reported experiencing military-related sexual assault (Wolfe et al. 1998). In a study conducted by Hankin and colleagues (1999), it was found that 23 percent of the national sample participating in the study (N = 3,632) reported experiencing sexual assault while serving in the military. More recent population-based data indicate that 9 percent of military women reported experiencing some sort of sexual coercion within the previous year. A higher proportion of military women, 31 percent, reported experiencing some other form of unwanted sexual attention in the previous year. Over half of military women, 52 percent, reported experiencing other offensive sexual behaviors such as repeatedly being told offensive sexual stories or jokes or unwelcome attempts to be drawn into a discussion of sexual matters (Lipari et al. 2008).

Those who reported having experienced sexual assault were significantly younger than those who did not. They reported having served longer in active military duty, were more likely to be enlisted rather than an officer, and were more likely to have served in the army than those who did not report a sexual assault history (Hankin et al. 1999). Sexual assault that is experienced in the military may impact women differently than assault experienced in the general population. For instance, military sexual assaults are usually experienced within a compressed time period (during military duty), women are usually young when they are serving in the military, and they are more likely to know the perpetrators. These factors can significantly impact women's perception of their military experience and trust in others, in that unit cohesion serves as a strong protective factor for service men and women; if a woman is assaulted by another unit member, this can lead to feelings of isolation and possible difficulty readjusting to civilian life (Skinner et al. 2000).

Sexual harassment is defined as any deliberate or repeated sexual behavior that is unwelcome or other sex-related behaviors that are hostile, offensive, or degrading (Fitzgerald 1993). Prevalence rates vary for women in the general population; however, it is estimated that 13 to 20 percent may have experienced sexual harassment (Koss & Heslet, 1992), which differs from prevalence rates reported in the military. Studies have indicated that more than half (55 percent) of women have reported having been sexually harassed while in the military (Skinner et al. 2000), and that rate is as high as 90 percent for female veterans younger than fifty years old who have sought services at VA facilities (Murdoch & Nichols 1995). In-service sexual harassment may result in greater odds of depression, anxiety, and PTSD.

Significant differences have been found in occupational functioning after being discharged from the military for woman who report experiencing military sexual harassment and assault and those who do not. Women reporting assault more often were not working because of physical limitations or psychological reasons (Skinner et al. 2000).

Military sexual assault and harassment can have long-term impacts on physical health. Women who experienced sexual assault and harassment also report more sleep disturbances, nightmares, and difficulty staying asleep. Reproductive outcomes can also differ significantly, with those who report experiencing sexual assault or harassment being twice as likely to report that their military experiences interfered with their desire for children and that they were not satisfied with their current sex lives (Skinner et al. 2000).

Women who reported no history of military sexual assault reported fewer mean number of visits to a mental health specialist or other healthcare providers (e.g., physician's assistant, nurse practitioner, physical therapist, chiropractor), indicating that women with a history of sexual assault are more likely to seek mental and physical health treatment (Skinner et al. 2000), and they are more likely to seek services within VHA (Kelly et al. 2008). However, although they are more likely to seek services through VHA, they are also more likely to have poorer perceptions of VHA facilities and staff and more problems with services than women without a history of sexual assault.

Combat-Related Trauma

In 1990, long-standing bans on women serving in combat-related roles were lifted as a result of women's performance in the Persian Gulf War in 1990 and 1991. In the early 1990s, women flew combat aircraft, operated missile placements, served on ships in the Gulf, drove convoys in the desert, and assumed other roles that made exposure to combat more likely. In the 2001 National Survey of Veterans, 12 percent of women veterans reported having served in combat or war zones, and approximately one-quarter of those who served in combat reported having contact with dead, dying, or wounded compatriots during their military service (Office of Policy, Planning, and Preparedness 2003).

During the conflicts in Iraq and Afghanistan (through 2007), 12 percent of women were classified as experiencing moderate levels of combat exposure, and 3 percent were classified as having had high levels of combat exposure based on self-report (MHAT-IV 2008). Rona and colleagues (2007) conducted a study evaluating women veterans' exposure to combat in the UK armed forces who were deployed to Iraq. Approximately 16 percent of women reported that they came under small arms fire, 40 percent reported that they came under mortar/artillery fire, and 37 percent indicated that they saw seriously hurt personnel. Among OEF/OIF veterans seen at VA facilities minimal differences were found between women and men regarding risk for receiving a PTSD diagnosis (11 and 13 percent, respectively) (Seal et al. 2007).

Exposure to combat and combat-related trauma may lead to problems similar to those associated with sexual assault. Therefore deployed female veterans have been shown to be at greater risk of drug-related disorders, PTSD, accidental death, higher levels of general psychiatric distress, and more frequent somatic complaints than nondeployed female veterans (Murdoch et al. 2006), although reactions to combat exposure may involve less personal blame and distress when compared to the experience of sexual assault, given the impersonal nature of combat compared to sexual assault (Wolfe et al. 1998).

Research findings indicate that female service members experience lower rates of combat exposure than men (Tolin & Foa 2006). Among Vietnam veterans, combat exposure seemed to have an indirect association with post-traumatic stress disorder, through its influence on perceived threat, more so for women than for men (King et al. 1999).

Although exposure to combat may have been less for women than for men, this may be changing, as seen in Operation Iraqi Freedom (OIF) and Operation Enduring Freedom (OEF), where the frontlines are no longer as clear-cut as in prior conflicts. More women are being exposed to combat experiences, and recent studies have found that the female gender was associated with postdeployment PTSD in a population-based sample of OEF/OIF veterans, after accounting for preexisting differences in PTSD (Smith et al. 2008). Therefore, it will be important for VA medical centers to consider the potential impact that deployments to Iraq and Afghanistan may have on the experience of trauma-related symptoms in women veterans.

Women who experienced combat exposure differ from women veterans who present to VHA for care without combat exposure. They are more likely to have a service-connected disability and have a higher level of education than those without a history of combat exposure (Kelly et al. 2008). They do not have a different perception of VHA care from male veterans; however, a history of combat exposure has been associated with significantly more problems with VHA doctors/staff (Kelly et al. 2008).

Substance Use in Women Veterans

Women working in a traditionally male-dominated environment may be at higher risk for alcohol use disorders (AUD) (Ames & Cunradi 2004). This, in combination with the risk of experiencing unique military-related stressors—like the pressures of performing a traditionally male job, an increased risk for experiencing negative affective states such as depression, and increased risk of experiencing negative life events such as physical, sexual, or combat-related trauma—may result in more women serving in the military developing AUDs. In particular, the experience of military sexual assault may result in greater risk for women developing a substance use disorder (SUD). It has been found that those who report experiencing sexual assault in the military have been two to three times more likely to meet screening criteria for depression and alcohol abuse (Hankin et al. 1999).

A study completed by Wallace, Sheehan, and Young-Xu (2009) compared the prevalence of AUDs in the woman veteran population and in their civilian counterparts. They examined 28,083 alcohol treatment episodes for veterans and 1.5 million alcohol treatment episodes for civilians between 1992 and 2003 for female patients between the ages of twenty-five and forty-four years old. Results showed that annual treatment episodes were highest for female veterans aged thirty to thirty-four, with the peak in 1992 to 1993. Interestingly, by 2003 annual treatment rates for female veterans were lower than rates for civilians in all age groups. This decline may be attributed to several factors. For instance, over the past two decades the military has been promoting itself as a mainstream career choice for women. This change in recruitment strategy may be attracting a different type of woman with different drinking patterns.

Second, and more likely, in the 1980s the military adopted the twenty-one-year-old minimum drinking age and policies of zero tolerance for underage drinking and abuse of alcohol. Around this time intervention and prevention programs were also implemented. These changes in drinking policies may have led to a decline in abusive drinking for both men and women in the military.

Given that unique experiences of women in the military may lead them to be more prone to develop SUDs and that there are more women serving in the military than ever before, it will be important for providers working in the VA medical centers and other facilities that treat women veterans to be competent in assessment and treatment of SUDs.

Homecoming Readjustment

Women veterans tend to be the primary caregivers in their families. This, coupled with the stress of deployment, creates unique problems in readjustment after overseas deployment and after being discharged from the military. In a study conducted by Frayne and colleagues (2006) of 28,000 female veterans, findings showed that levels of social support were almost universally lower in women than in men, across age strata. They were more likely to be unmarried and have no one to take them to the doctor if they were unwell, and women over forty-five years old were more likely than male veterans to live alone.

Of women veterans ages seventy-five or older, 71.4 percent are not married, which is a significantly higher percentage than the 30.9 percent of men veterans who are not married. A higher percentage of women (52.5 percent) than men (22.1 percent) live alone, and 15.1 percent of women had no one to take them to the doctor, versus 9.6 percent of men (Frayne et al. 2006).

The association between indicators of social support and health status is complex. Being married or living with someone benefits the mental health status of male veterans but not female veterans, whereas having instrumental support (someone who could take the patient to the doctor when needed) benefits mental health status in both men and women. This may be because even when married, women tend to bear a heavier burden of caregiving and may receive less support than men. Given that instrumental support does benefit mental health in women, VA's efforts to reach out to vulnerable populations (e.g., with in-home care, transportation benefits, and satellite primary care centers) may prove particularly valuable to women.

When comparing women veterans' health with that of the general population of women, women veterans have consistently and markedly worse physical and mental health. This could be attributed to exposures during military service that distinguish women veterans from nonveteran women, adversely affecting their health. Although women report worse health status than their nonveteran counterparts, women veterans over the age of sixty-five have better mental health scores than male veterans. This may imply that women in this cohort have access to some types of social support less available to men or that women in this cohort (World War II and Korean era veterans) may have developed specific patterns of coping that distinguish them from men of their era.

In general, results of Frayne and others' (2006) study indicate that women veterans will require an intensity of services similar to that of their male counterparts. The VHA Office of Public Health and Environmental Hazards (2009) released similar data, indicating that 46 percent of all OIF/OEF female veterans have attended at least one outpatient appointment at VA, compared to 43 percent of male veterans. Approximately 44 percent of women veterans continued to receive ongoing care at VA (i.e., attended more than ten outpatient sessions), compared to 35 percent of male veterans. Given the increase in women utilizing VA care, and with the growing number of women in the military, an increase in VA services will be necessary in the future.

Homelessness

In 2009 VA Secretary Eric Shinseki created a five-year plan designed to decrease the number of homeless veterans. This plan includes expanding VA's partnership with federal agencies and community-based service providers.

The Zero Tolerance for Veteran Homelessness Act of 2009 was introduced by Senators Reed, Bond, Murray, Johnson, Kerry and Durbin. This act delineated the expansion of housing vouchers to 60,000 for veterans with serious mental and emotional illness and other disabilities. Given that data collected by the National Alliance to End Homelessness estimate there are approximately 63,000 chronically homeless veterans, this act should essentially end chronic homelessness among veterans (National Coalition for Homeless Veterans 2009).

In 2009 there were an estimated 13,100 homeless female veterans in the United States (Mulhall 2009). Women veterans have been found to be up to four times more likely to be homeless than their nonveteran and male counterparts (Gamache, Rosenheck & Tessler 2003). It has been found that homeless women veterans are more likely to have experienced severe forms of mental illness than men and higher rates of military sexual trauma (Williamson & Mulhall 2009). In general, women veterans possess many characteristics that are likely to be risk factors for homelessness, such as low income, high rates of childhood abuse, comorbid PTSD, self-rated poor physical health, and having lived in their cities for a shorter period of time than nonveterans (Gamache, Rosenheck & Tessler 2003).

In 2009 more than 5 percent of veterans requesting services from VA and community-based homeless veteran services were women, and more than half of these veterans were between the ages of twenty and tewnty-nine. More than 10 percent of these women had children who were dependent on them (National Coalition for Homeless Veterans 2009). The Homeless Women Veterans and Homeless Veterans with Children Act of 2009 was created to recognize the readjustment difficulties of single women with children. This act authorizes up to $10 million in grants to community- and faith-based organizations to provide critical, specialized support for deserving men and women as they work their way out of homelessness. One part of this specialized care is to add child care assistance so that women and men with children can pursue employment so they can maintain housing (National Coalition for Homeless Veterans 2009).

Barriers to Care

As previously noted, in the 1980 Census most women veterans were not aware of the services that they were eligible for, and the goal of the Center for Women Veterans has been to improve the quality of care and remove barriers to care for women veterans. Studies have been conducted to investigate the perceived quality of care for women veterans as well as to identify barriers to care. Most studies have looked at individual/personal barriers to care and have focused on factors such as socioeconomic status, gender, age, and disease status.

One study found that women who currently used VHA were less likely to be ethnic minorities, had fewer children, had served more time in the military, had lower rates of insurance coverage, had poorer health, had more PTSD symptomatology, had greater exposure to combat and assault, and were more likely to have a service-connected disability (Ouimette et al. 2003).

Vogt and others (2006) conducted a study of 942 women veterans (543 current VHA users, 399 former users) to document perceived and /or actual barriers to care in a nationally representative sample of women veterans who had accessed VHA care and examine associations between barriers to care and VHA use and the extent to which those barriers differ for women with and without service-connected disabilities. Findings indicated that women veterans reported that VHA care was about the same or slightly worse than the care offered at other facilities. Facility characteristics (e.g., hours, parking availability) were perceived to be similar for VHA and non-VHA facilities. The least positive ratings were for the availability of services and logistics of care. Women who had a service-connected disability reported a greater problem with ease of using VHA healthcare facilities. Significant negative associations were found for availability of services, physician sensitivity and skill, logistics of care, and facility/physical environment characteristics, which were maintained after accounting for previously documented background characteristics.

Findings indicate that additional attention should be given in two areas: 1) the availability of needed services, including especially women-specific services, and 2) factors related to the logistics of receiving care at VHA, such as the waiting time to obtain care and issues related to continuity of care.

Women Veterans' Satisfaction with Care

Literature reviews have shown that age, health status, and racial/ethnic status are associated with satisfaction with care in inpatient and outpatient treatment at VHA (Wright et al. 2006). Older veterans tend to report more satisfaction with healthcare, whereas sicker patients and veterans from minority backgrounds reported less satisfaction with care. Mixed results have been found when relating gender to satisfaction of care. Some studies find that women are more satisfied, some find that men are more satisfied, and some find that there is no difference. In general, satisfaction was higher for veterans receiving outpatient versus inpatient care. An area for further exploration may be whether this difference in satisfaction with inpatient care is related to gender or to being a minority in inpatient units. In outpatient clinics there is usually gender-specific care (i.e., women's clinics, etc.).

One significant gender-related difference has been found, that women involved in outpatient treatment were more satisfied with continuity of care than those in inpatient care. In a study examining the satisfaction of women veterans with VA healthcare, data were accumulated through a survey of VA consumers, who were asked to rate the quality of care that they received within the previous two months. Information about satisfaction with care was collected from women receiving outpatient services and from women who received inpatient services. Satisfaction was also evaluated related to access and continuity of care, visit coordination, courtesy, education, emotional support, involvement of family and friends in treatment, overall coordination, pharmacy by mail, pharmacy pickup, physical comfort, patient preference, specialist care, and transition from inpatient to outpatient (Wright et al. 2006). No other differences in satisfaction with care were found between men and women receiving services in VHA.

Information about satisfaction with care is important to take into account because of the increase in numbers of women veterans, indicating that more women may be seeking VHA services. Satisfaction data will provide important information about how to meet the needs of women veterans and inform new directions for healthcare.

New Directions for Women's Healthcare

The conflicts in Iraq and Afghanistan are exposing women to military situations that women were not exposed to in prior conflicts. This has led to women assuming different roles in the military and receiving different accommodations. In 2005 the first woman in history was awarded the Silver Star for combat action. In 2006 the Coast Guard appointed the first woman vice commandant, which made her the first woman ever to serve as a deputy service chief in any of the U.S. armed forces. In 2007 the first woman in the history of the navy took command of a fighter squadron, and in 2008 the first woman was promoted to the rank of four-star general. Women are serving in higher rank and larger numbers in the military, and the number of women veterans is increasing by the day. VA began providing medical and psychosocial services for women in 1988, when women represented 4.4 percent of all veterans. By 2010 women made up more than 14 percent of the total U.S. veteran population.

Data suggest that getting women in the doors of VA for services may be problematic because of perceptions about limited privacy and negative perceptions of the quality of VA healthcare (Washington et al. 2007). Difficulties related to logistics of care may also act as a barrier to seeking services at VA (Vogt et al. 2006). Women veterans who access VA care are more reliant on VA for inpatient treatment for mental health, SUDs, issues related to skin, subcutaneous tissue, and breasts, and are less likely to seek treatment for female reproductive system and nervous system problems (Mooney & Weeks 2007). Reasons for this may be related to the expertise in treatment for mental health and SUDs versus the lack of gender-specific medical services (e.g., gynecologic surgery). New directions in treatment may be added by evaluating gender-specific services offered through the private sector in order to increase the quality of care for women in VHA.

As part of VA's readiness for the entrance of new women veterans, in 2007 the Women Veterans Health Program was elevated to a Strategic Health Care Group within the Office of Public Health and Environmental Hazards. In 2008 VA facilities received $32.5 million in supplemental funding for investments in women's health equipment, training, and supplies (including DEXA scans, mammography machines, ultrasound, and biopsy equipment) (Office of Public Health and Environmental Hazard 2009). This funding will provide additional services for women veterans. In general, additional attention should be given to 1) the availability of needed services, including especially women-specific services, and 2) factors related to the logistics of receiving care at VHA, such as the waiting time to obtain care and continuity of care (Vogt et al. 2006).

Treatment and evaluation of military sexual trauma is an important facet to address, given that women who have experienced military sexual trauma are at greater risk of developing PTSD and may be in greater need of services through VHA. However, military sexual trauma has been associated with more difficulty in accessing women-specific services, problems with doctors and staff at VHA, and problems with the ease of using the VHA system. Findings from studies related to the impact of military sexual harassment and assault have shown that these experiences strongly impact readjustment to civilian life in interpersonal, physical health, mental health, and occupational functioning. The implication of these findings is that it is important for both VA and non-VA facilities to screen for assault and harassment when providing care to woman veterans, given the differences between the groups reporting sexual assault and those reporting no sexual assault.

In July 1992 hearings on women veterans' issues by the Senate Veterans Affairs Committee first brought the problem of military sexual trauma to policy makers' attention. In November 1992 Congress responded by passing Public Law 102-585, which authorized healthcare and counseling for women veterans to overcome psychological trauma resulting from sexual assault or sexual harassment during their military service. In 2005 these laws were expanded to benefit male veterans, and limitations on the required duration of service were changed and extended for receiving these benefits. Following the passage of these laws, VA directives mandated universal screening of all veterans for a history of military sexual trauma and mandated that each facility identify a military sexual trauma coordinator to oversee the screening and treatment referral process (Street & Stafford 2004).

Research on women veterans has been descriptive and observational in nature and has tended to address the impact of the stress of military life, the health and performance of women veterans, health services, and psychiatric conditions. There has been a gap in research on chronic diseases, women veterans' preferences and self-reported care needs, utilization patterns within and outside of VA, transitions from military to veteran status, and the quality of care delivered to women veterans and how to improve it (Goldzweig et al. 2006). These gaps are being addressed. In 2004, the VA Office of Research & Development gave the VA HSR&D Service the responsibility of overseeing the development of the first national VA Women's Health Research Agenda. A planning group was created and developed a four-step action plan to meet the needs of women veterans and lead VA to becoming a national leader in women's health research. VA Health Services Research and Development Services has published a new women's health solicitation and has been working on planning grants, pilot funds, and administrative supplements to add women to existing studies (Yano et al. 2006). New developments as a result of these efforts include the first VA survey of women veterans across the country to gather information on demographics, healthcare needs, barriers to healthcare in VA, and healthcare preferences.

Along with new directions in research, education related to women veterans' health is being increased in VA medical centers. The Women Veterans Health Strategic Health Care Group (WVHSHG) has partnered with the VA Employee Education Services to conduct mini-residencies in women's health. One round of training included 700 VA providers, who have now been trained in women-specific care, and more training is scheduled. For more information on future directions in research and trainings related to women veterans, refer to table 12.2.

Along with this training, the Women Veterans Health Center puts out monthly outreach campaigns for women veterans program managers, public affairs officers, and others who work in the field with women (http://www.publichealth .va.gov/womenshealth/campaigns.asp). These outreach campaign publications provide information on various topics, such as substance abuse, physical and mental health, and public health issues for women veterans. This attention to women's research and education will help to increase inclusion of women in VA healthcare planning, clinical care, and research, which will improve understanding of women veterans' needs and the quality of healthcare for women veterans.

Table 12.2. New Directions in Research and Training on Women Veterans

Steps Being Taken in Women's Health Research	VA Office of Research and Development (ORD) has a key role in documenting the healthcare needs and utilization of women veterans as well as their access to and quality of care. Valuable information can be gained through risk assessments conducted on epidemiological data from women who served in Operation Enduring Freedom and Iraqi Freedom (OIF/OEF) and through the OEF/OIF Cohort Study. For the first time in 25 years, VA surveyed women veterans across the country to (1) identify in a national sample the current status, demographics, healthcare needs, and VA experiences of women veterans of the U.S. armed forces; (2) determine

(continued)

Table 12.2. *(Continued)*

	how healthcare needs and barriers to VA healthcare use differ among women veterans of different periods of military service; and (3) assess women veterans' healthcare preferences in order to address VA barriers and healthcare needs. The interim report, released in summer 2010, informs policy and planning and provides a new baseline for program evaluation with regard to veterans' perceptions of VA health services. WVHSHG has partnered with the Women's Health Evaluation Initiative based in Palo Alto, CA, to develop a series of sourcebooks with key descriptive information about women veterans, including demographics, population growth over time, diagnoses, utilization, and cost of care.
VA Study on Women Vietnam Veterans	The study "Long-Term Health Outcomes of Women Veterans' Service During the Vietnam Era" otherwise known as HealthVIEWS (the Health of Vietnam Era Women's Study) is being sponsored by VA. This study seeks to contact approximately 10,000 women to participate in a mail survey, a telephone interview, and a medical records review. The study aims to determine the prevalence of lifetime and current psychiatric conditions, including PTSD, among women who served during the Vietnam era; the physical health of women who served during the Vietnam era; and the level of current disability in women who served during the Vietnam era. For more detailed information on the study, see the study Web site: http://www.research.va.gov/programs/csp/csp579.cfm.
Women's Health Education	The WVHSHG partners with VA Employee Education Services (EES) to conduct mini-residencies in women's health. To date, more than 700 VA providers have been trained. A second round of mini-residencies, covering additional women's health topics, got underway in late 2010, focused on more advanced women's health topics. Grants released to the field allow for the training of additional providers by facilities. In addition, VA facilities are recruiting new providers interested and proficient in women's health to meet the needs of the growing population of women veterans.

(continued)

Table 12.2. (*Continued*)

	Work is also ongoing in VA's Office of Academic Affiliations to support women's health fellowships and the Office of Nursing Service to provide advanced clinical training in women's health.
Women Veterans Forum Presentations and Toolkit	On July 28, 2010, the Secretary of Veterans Affairs hosted A Forum on Women Veterans at the Women's Memorial at Arlington National Cemetery. The purpose of the forum was to engage and educate veterans' service organizations and women veterans' advocates about enhancements in VA services for women veterans. An information marketplace, staffed by internal and external subject matter experts, allowed participants to build toolkits customized for their respective constituents at the local and regional levels. For further information see http://www1.va.gov/WOMENVET/Forum_on_Women_Veterans.asp.
Communication and Partnership	The WVHSHG is leading development of a VHA-wide communication plan to enhance the language, practice, and culture of VA to be more inclusive of women veterans. A national Women's Health Communications Workgroup was created to advise WVHSHG on communication strategies to reach women veterans and VA employees. Branding Women Veterans Health Care with a powerful identity, including a visual logo and tagline—You Served, You Deserve the Best Care Anywhere—has helped establish a consistent, nationally recognized symbol for high-quality services that women veterans should expect at every VA facility. WVHSHG also works closely with VA analysts and data specialists to ensure that women veteran populations are represented clearly in statistical data, including demographics, epidemiology, health status, and quality of care. Enhanced Web capabilities are continually being implemented to improve the transfer of information among field and leadership personnel.

References

Ames, G. & Cunradi, C. (2004). Alcohol use and preventing alcohol related problems among young adults in the military. *Alcohol Research and Health* 28: 252–257.

Bureau of the Census for the Department of Veterans Affairs and the Department of Labor. (2006). *Current Population Survey, Veterans Supplement.* http://www.census .gov/apsd/techdoc/cps/cpsaug05.pdf (accessed December 19, 2009).

Department of Defense. (2008). *Active duty personnel by rank/grade.* http://siadapp .dmdc.osd.mil/personnel/MILITARY/rg0809f.pdf (accessed December, 2009).

Department of Veterans Affairs. (n.d.). Center for Women Veterans. http://www1.va.gov/ womenvet/docs/CWV_Fact_Sheet_Final_August_2008.pdf (accessed December 10, 2009).

Fischer, H. (2009). *United States military casualty statistics: Operation Iraqi Freedom and Operation Enduring Freedom.* Washington, DC: Congressional Research Service. http://fas.org/sgp/crs/natsec /RS22452.pdf (accessed December 5, 2009).

Fitzgerald, L. F. (1993). Sexual harassment: Violence against women in the workplace. *American Psychologist* 48: 1070–1076.

Frayne, S. M., Parker, V. A., Christiansen, C. L., Loveland, S., Seaver, M. R. & Kazis, L. E., et al. (2006). Health status among 28,000 women veterans: The VA women's health program evaluation project. *Journal of General Internal Medicine* 21: 40–46.

Gamache, G., Rosenheck, R. & Tessler, R. (2003). Overrepresentation of women veterans among homeless women. *American Journal of Public Health* 93: 1132–1136.

Goldzweig, C. L., Balekian, T. M., Rolón, C., Yano, E. M. & Shekelle, P. G. (2006). The state of women veterans' health research: Results of a systematic literature review. *Journal of General Internal Medicine* 21: S82–92.

Gutek, B. (1985). *Sex and the workplace.* San Francisco: Jossey-Bass.

Hankin, C. S., Skinner, K. M., Sullivan, L. M., Miller, D. R. Frayne, S. & Tripp, T. J. (1999). Prevalence of depressive and alcohol abuse symptoms among women VA outpatients who report experiencing sexual assault while in the military. *Journal of Traumatic Stress* 12: 601–612.

Holder, K. A. (2007). *The educational attainment of veterans: 2007.* Washington, DC: U.S. Census Bureau. http://www.census.gov/hhes/www/laborfor/veterans/ veteranseducation.pdf (accessed December 12, 2009).

Holm, J. (1982). *Women in the military: An unfinished revolution.* Rev. ed. Novato, CA: Presidio Press.

Joint Economic Committee. (2007). *Helping military moms balance family and longer deployments,* Washington, DC: Author. http://jec.senate.gov/archive/Docu ments/Reports/MilitaryMoms05.11.07Final.pdf (accessed December 12, 2009).

Kelly, M. M., Vogt, D. S., Scheiderer, E. M., Ouimette, P., Daley, J. & Wolfe, J. (2008). Effects of military trauma exposure on women veterans' use and perception of Veterans Health Administration care. *Journal of General Internal Medicine* 23: 741–747.

King, D. W., King, L. A., Foy, D. W., Keane, T. M., Fairbank, J. A. (1999). Posttraumatic stress disorder in a national sample of female and male Vietnam veterans:

Risk factors, war zone stressors, and resilience-recovery variables. *Journal of Abnormal Psychology* 108(1): 164–170.

King, D. W., King, L. A., Gudanowski, D. M. & Vreven, D. L. (1995). Alternative representations of war zone stressors: Relationships to posttraumatic stress disorder in male and female Vietnam veterans. *Journal of Abnormal Psychology* 104: 184–195.

Koss, M. P., & Heset, L. (1992). Somatic consequences of violence against women. *Archives of Family Medicine* 1: 53–59.

Lipari, R. N., Cook, P. J., Rock, L. M. & Matos, K. (2008). *2006 Gender Relations Survey of Active Duty Members.* Arlington, VA: Department of Defense Manpower Data Center.

MHAT-IV (2008). Mental Health Advisory Team (MHAT) V: Operation Iraqi Freedom 06–08. Office of the Surgeon Multinational Force Iraq and Office of the Surgeon General United States Army Medical Command. http://www.armyme dicine.army.mil/reports/mhat/mhat_v/Redacted1–MHATV-OIF-4–FEB-2008 Report.pdf.

Mooney, S. E. & Weeks, W. B. (2007). Where do women veterans get their inpatient care? *Women's Health Issues* 17: 367–373.

Mulhall, E. (2009). *Women warriors: Supporting she "who has borne the battle."* New York: IAVA.

Murdoch, M., Bradley, A., Mather, S. H., Klein, R. E., Turner, C. L. & Yano, E. M. (2006). Women and war: What physicians should know. *Journal of General Internal Medicine* 21: 5–10.

Murdoch, M. & Nichols, K. (1995). Women veterans' experiences with domestic violence and sexual harassment while in the military. *Archives of Family Medicine* 4: 411–418.

National Coalition for Homeless Veterans. (2009). *Ending veterans' homelessness, testimony before the Senate Comm. on Banking, Housing, and Urban Affairs.* http://banking .senate.gov/public/index.cfm?FuseAction=Files.View&FileStore_id=71b2a12e-33ad-47c0–bf20–9c72a4878522 (accessed January 1, 2011).

Office of Policy and Planning. (2007). Women veterans: Past, present and future. http:// www1.va.gov/womenvet/docs/womenvet_history.pdf (accessed December 5, 2009).

Office of Public Health and Environmental Hazard, VA. (2009). Women veterans' healthcare. http://www.publichealth.va.gov/womenshealth/about.asp (accessed December 12, 2009).

Ouimette, P., Wolfe, J., Daley, J. & Gima, K. (2003). Use of VA health care services by women veterans: Findings from a national sample. *Women's Health* 38: 77–91.

Rona, R. J., Fear, N. T., Hull, L. & Wessely, S. (2007). Women in novel occupational roles: Mental health trends in the UK armed forces. *International Journal of Epidemiology* 36: 319–326.

Seal, K. H., Bertenthal, D., Mner, C. R., Sen, S. & Marmar, C. (2007). Bringing the war back home: Mental health disorders among 103,788 US veterans returning from Iraq and Afghanistan seen at Department of Veterans Affairs facilities. *Archives of Internal Medicine* 167: 476–482.

Skinner, K. M., Kressin, N., Frayne, S., Tripp, T. J., Hankin, C. S. & Miller, D. R., et al. (2000). The prevalence of military sexual assault among female Veterans Administration outpatients. *Journal of Interpersonal Violence* 15: 291–310.

Smith, T. C., Ryan, M. A., Wingard, D. L., Slymen, D. J., Sallis, J. F. & Kritz-Silverstein, D. (2008). New onset and persistent symptoms of post-traumatic stress disorder self-reported after deployment and combat exposures: Prospective population based US military cohort study. *British Medical Journal* 336: 366–371.

Street, A. & Stafford, J. (2004). Military sexual trauma: Issues in caring for veterans. In National Center for Posttraumatic Stress Disorder, *Iraq War clinicians guide*, 2nd ed. http://www.ptsd.va.gov/professional/manuals/manualpdf/wcg/iraq_clinician_guide_ch_9.pdf (accessed January 12, 2010).

Street, A. E., Vogt, D. & Dutra, L. (2009). A new generation of women veterans: Stressors faced by women deployed to Iraq and Afghanistan. *Clinical Psychology Review* 29: 685–694.

Thomas, P. J. (1978). *The role of women in the military: Australia, Canada, and the United States.* Special Report 78–10. San Diego: Navy Personnel Research and Development Center.

Tolin, D. F. & Foa, E. B. (2006). Sex differences in trauma and posttraumatic stress disorder: A quantitative review of 25 years of research. *Psychological Bulletin* 132: 959–992.

U.S. Department of Veterans Affairs. (2003). Office of Policy and Planning & Preparedness: Annual Report. Washington, DC: Veterans Affairs Central Office.

VA Center for Women Veterans (n.d.). http://www1.va.gov/womenvet/ (accessed November 14, 2009).

Veterans Administration. (1985). *Survey of Female Veterans: A study of the needs, attitudes and experiences of women veterans.* Washington, DC.: Louis Harris and Associates, Office of Information Management and Statistics.

Vogt, D., Bergeron, A., Salgado, D., Daley, J., Ouimette, P. & Wolfe, J. (2006). Barriers to Veterans Health Administration care in a nationally representative sample of women veterans. *Journal of General Internal Medicine* 21: S19–25.

Vogt, D., Pless, A. P., King, L. A. & King, D. W. (2005). Deployment stressors, gender, and mental health outcomes among Gulf War I veterans. *Journal of Traumatic Stress* 18: 272–284.

Wallace, A. E., Sheehan, E. P. & Young-Xu, Y. (2009). Women, alcohol, and the military: Cultural changes and reductions in later alcohol problems among female veterans. *Journal of Women's Health* 18: 1347–1353.

Washington, D. L., Kleimann, S., Michelini, A. N., Kleimann, K. M. & Canning, M. (2007). Women veterans' perception and decision-making about Veterans Affairs health care. *Military Medicine* 172: 812–817.

Williamson, V. & Mulhall, E. (2009). *Invisible wounds: Psychological and neurological injuries confront a new generation of veterans.* New York: IAVA.

Wolfe, J., Sharkansky, E. J., Read, J. P., Dawson, R., Martin, J. A. & Ouimette, P. C. (1998). Sexual harassment and assault as predictors of PTSD symptomatology among U.S. female Persian Gulf War military personnel. *Journal of Interpersonal Violence* 13: 40–57.

Wright, S. M., Craig, T., Campbell, S., Schaefer, J. & Humble, C. (2006). Patient satisfaction of female and male users of Veterans Health Administration services. *Journal of General Internal Medicine* 21: S26–32.

Yano, E. M., Bastian, L. A., Frayne, S. M., Howell, A. L., Lipson, L. R., McGlynn, G., et al. (2006). Toward a VA women's health research agenda: Setting evidence-based priorities to improve the health and health care of women veterans. *Journal of General Internal Medicine* 21: S93–101.

Chapter 13

Serving America's Former Prisoners of War: Getting It "Right"

Brian Engdahl and Charles Stenger

Introduction

American former prisoners of war (POWs) are exceptional individuals. As many as 110,000 were alive in the mid-1950s; at last estimate, less than 30,000 remained (Stenger 2006). They were subjected to an appalling spectrum of harsh abuse and suffered a myriad of insults, including malnutrition, exposure to environmental extremes, infections, and physical and emotional injuries. With few exceptions, they did not receive the special attention they deserved from the Veterans Administration until the passage of the Former POW Benefit Act of 1981, described later in this chapter.

Post-repatriation treatment was aimed at restoring their lost weight and treating their medical illnesses and physical injuries. Many were told that their ordeal would shorten their lifespan considerably, although the studies cited below showed increased illness and death rates only in the first postwar years. Beebe (1975) proposed a model to explain the persisting effects he observed among POWs he studied. It consists of two trauma types: one is physical and primarily short-term, caused by malnutrition, infection, and physical injury; the other is psychological and essentially permanent, leading to a loss of ego strength and lowered thresholds for both physical and psychological distress.

POWs with psychiatric problems were particularly underserved by the Veterans Administration and the Department of Defense (DoD). These systems were overburdened by returning soldiers requiring care for combat injuries. In general, POWs were told that they should return home and get on with their civilian lives, and that they would "get over" any emotional problems they were experiencing. This reflected psychiatry's then prevailing view that adult trauma did not lead to long-term effects, except among those who were emotionally disturbed before they went off to war. Psychological counseling was typically psychoanalytically oriented, aimed at exploring their childhoods, when in fact they were overwhelmed by their war experiences. POWs experiencing nightmares and flashbacks were diagnosed as hallucinating psychotics and subjected to the treatments of the day, including insulin coma therapy and some of the early psychotropic medications (Skelton 2002).

Many POWs suffer from what we now know as post-traumatic stress disorder (PTSD) (American Psychiatric Association 1994), which is defined by an enduring set of maladaptive symptoms that arise after exposure to one or more potentially life-threatening events. These symptoms include unwanted re-experiencing of persistent painful trauma memories through nightmares, daytime intrusive memories, and psychological distress or physiologic arousal when reminded of the trauma. Other symptoms include avoidance of trauma reminders, withdrawing from one's environment, and a general numbing of responsiveness. Persistent arousal through sleep disturbances, irritability, exaggerated startle response, and/or hypervigilance also contribute to the functional impairments of the disorder.

Until the publication of the third revision of the *Diagnostic and Statistical Manual of Mental Disorders* (DSM III) (American Psychiatric Association 1980), there was no diagnostic category to describe many of the POWs' most distressing psychological problems. Establishing the PTSD diagnosis enabled POWs to be properly assessed, treated, and compensated for their emotional injuries. It increased public awareness and families' understanding of problems the POWs had faced for decades, often suffering in silence and shame, convinced that they were alone and the problems they had were due to their own inability to cope with the aftermath of their traumatic wartime experiences.

The long-lasting effects of combat and imprisonment are not universally negative. Post-traumatic growth is an important but often overlooked aspect of functioning among trauma survivors. The mental health field tends to focus on negative effects, but this narrow focus diminishes our understanding of both the complexity of responses to trauma and the resilience that survivors exhibit. Sledge, Boydstun and Rabe (1980) found that 61 percent of American POWs held by North Vietnam perceived their imprisonment experience as beneficial. Most reported improvements in their self-concept and an increased appreciation of interpersonal relationships. Segal (1986) noted positive effects among American POWs who perceived some sense of control while held by North Vietnam.

Speed and colleagues (1989) observed that American World War II POWs attributed their increased appreciation for freedom, country, family, friends, and food to their traumatic war and captivity experiences. In another sample, World War II and Korean conflict POWS learned through their combat and prison camp trauma that they were stronger than they thought they were. They also came to have a greater appreciation of life, and many had positive growth in their spiritual lives. (Erbes et al. 2006).

The Facts

Those captured in the European theater during World War II are the largest group of POWs (93,000 repatriated; 1.2 percent died in captivity). Most were captured toward the end of the war (1944–1945), spending an average of a year in captivity. World War II POWs held by Japan include 16,300 who were repatriated. They were held an average of 3.2 years, and 40 percent died in captivity (Dawes 1994). The primary causes of death and chronic illness were starvation, untreated infectious diseases, hazards related to transportation to Japan, and environmental exposure, especially toward the end of the war when they were used as slave labor in northern Japan and Manchuria (Holmes 2001). Most suffered beatings and other abuse at the hands of their captors; many were intentionally killed, being viewed as cowards for surrendering or as war criminals for their participation in bombing raids on Japan (Hata 1996). Korean conflict POWs include 4,400 who were repatriated. They were held an average of 2.2 years, and 38 percent died in captivity. Over half of the Americans held by the North Koreans during the first twelve months of the war died. After the Chinese took over the camps, death rates declined. During the Vietnam War, 660 American POWs were repatriated, primarily in 1973. Their average length of captivity was 3.5 years; some were held for over 8 years; and 15 percent died in captivity. Interrogations and physical torture were extremely brutal in the early years of the war.

A Story

This POW suffered nearly fifty years with untreated PTSD until offered services authorized by the Former POW Act.

A seventy-four-year-old white male reported that he had experienced a normal childhood, leaving school after tenth grade to work and play semiprofessional baseball. His National Guard unit was activated in 1941 and sent to the Philippines. Japan attacked the Philippines on December 8, 1941. Following fierce combat with heavy casualties, mainland Allied forces were surrendered on April 9, 1942. The average weight loss among POWs *prior* to their capture was 15–20 percent, due to severe food shortages on Bataan and Corregidor. Some 70 percent of the men in the 31st Infantry on Bataan were on the sick list on the day of capture. Together with over 10,000 ill and underfed Americans, this POW was forced into the Bataan Death March. In his 100-mile trek from the southern areas of Bataan to the camps of O'Donnell and Cabanatuan, 650 Americans died, mostly from beheadings and shootings, and over 16,500 Philippine nationals, who had fought alongside the Americans were murdered.

As a POW, he witnessed senseless executions and endured beatings, death threats, malnutrition, and multiple untreated medical diseases. While laboring, his weight dropped from 155 to 80 pounds, until he was too ill to work. In December 1944 he and 1,600 other POWs were forced into the hold of one of the last Japanese ships to leave the Philippines. Only half survived transport to Japan. The unmarked freighter was sunk by American planes after leaving port; he swam to shore. He was recaptured and put on another ship that was hit by American planes near Formosa; he again swam to shore. The journey to Japan on these "hell ships" included forty-nine days of confinement in the overcrowded, intensely hot holds of three different ships with little food, water, or sanitation. Many POWs became delirious; some attacked fellow POWs and were killed.

In Japan he labored in a coal mine for twelve hours per day, ten days in a row, followed by one day off. Rations were about 1,000 calories per day. Anyone too ill to work was placed on half-rations. Camp officials made it clear that they were under orders to execute all POWs if America invaded Japan. However, the officials abandoned the camp following the bombings of Hiroshima and Nagasaki and the Japanese surrender. Some were later prosecuted for war crimes.

Throughout his captivity and postwar life he has maintained an inner posture of resistance. He returned home, married, recuperated from tuberculosis, and began working for the U.S. Postal Service, where he remained a clerk for thirty-six years, failing to be promoted because of his "personality." He and his wife raised three children.

His only Axis I disorder is PTSD, lifetime and current, for which he is now rated 100 percent disabled by VA. He recalled complaining of nervousness to several nonpsychiatric physicians after World War II but was not referred for mental health services; he reported being told he would "have to live with it." His records indicate he refused tranquilizers. He suffers a trauma-related phobia of closed spaces and from most of the PTSD symptoms, chiefly daily intrusive recollections, frequent nightmares, hypervigilance, and survivor guilt. His only friends are a few other POWs of Japan. He became obese and was incapable of dieting; hunger pangs are intolerable, because they remind him of being a prisoner.

Since participation in a POW Protocol Examination and a POW research study, he has joined a POW support group that meets twice monthly. Although at times he appears anxious and speaks rapidly, he describes decreased distress and has become more comfortable with discussing his POW experiences and his current concerns as a result of participating in the group.

The Research

POWs have high rates of disability when compared to age-matched, non-POW combat veterans (all POWs are combat veterans), as the following key studies show. VA sponsored five National Academy of Science (NAS) POW studies. Cohen and Cooper (1954) studied World War II POWs and age-matched controls, encompassing the years 1945 to 1951. Nefzger (1970) added Korean conflict POWs and covered the period 1953 to 1965. Beebe (1975) covered 1946 to 1965 in greater detail. Keehn (1980) encompassed 1965 to 1975. Finally, Page (1992) analyzed self-reports and POW Protocol Examinations.

Among POWs held by Japan, Cohen and Cooper noted increased deaths in 1945–1947, tapering off in 1947–1951. Tuberculosis, cirrhosis of the liver, and physical trauma were to blame. Tuberculosis was acquired while in prison camp or picked up after repatriation among those with decreased immunity; malnutrition and accompanying vitamin deficiencies were underlying causes. Cirrhosis was caused by a combination of alcohol abuse upon repatriation and chronic liver damage from prison camp malnutrition. Deaths due to trauma were primarily attributed to motor vehicle accidents, assaults, and suicides not officially recognized as such; mental health problems were the underlying causes. Hospital admission rates for POWs of Japan were greater than for controls in every disease category examined, including nervous system, circulatory system, genitourinary system, allergic disorders, psychiatric disorders, respiratory system, and infectious diseases.

Nefzger used VA service-connected disability ratings to summarize illnesses among POWs. POWs of Japan had higher illness rates in all categories than non-POWs who fought against Japan. Musculoskeletal, digestive, skin, and psychiatric disorders were more frequent among European POWs than non-POW European combat veterans. Eye problems; systemic diseases; and respiratory, digestive, skin and psychiatric diagnoses were all significantly higher for Korean conflict POWs than non-POW combat veterans.

Page, Engdahl, and Eberly (1997) followed this same cohort of POWs and controls. They found that depressive symptoms were still greatly elevated among the POWs twenty to forty years after repatriation. These symptoms were directly related to captivity maltreatment and inversely related to education, age at the time of capture, and the amount of social support received after repatriation. Depression appeared to be a consequence of prolonged anxiety/posttraumatic stress disorder (PTSD). In 2001 Port, Engdahl, and Frazier reported that PTSD symptoms were highest shortly after World War II, declined for several decades, and increased within the past two decades (1980–2000).

In a community of POWs (N = 426), Eberly and Engdahl (1991) found that anxiety disorders (particularly PTSD) and depressive disorders were more frequent among POWs than among the general population. Disorders less likely to be related to trauma exposure (e.g., schizophrenia and bipolar disorders) were not. In another community sample of POWs (N = 262) from World War II and the Korean conflict, over half met lifetime criteria for PTSD, and 30 percent met criteria for current PTSD, forty to fifty years after repatriation (Engdahl et al. 1997). The most severely traumatized group, POWs held by Japan, had lifetime PTSD rates of 84 percent and current rates of 58 percent. Few of these men had ever sought mental health treatment or compensation.

The Bottom Line

Findings from these and other studies, along with intense and persistent lobbying by Dr. Stenger (himself a combat medic who served in Europe during World War II and who was taken prisoner) and others, have helped establish a long list of "presumptive" service-connected disabilities for POWs. "Presumptive" disabilities, if found to be present, are automatically presumed to be related to the POW's military experience, without requiring historical written proof, qualifying the POW for care and disability benefits. Many medical records were never generated, or were lost, leaving the POW with no way to prove a connection between wartime service and present-day illnesses. The "presumptives" initially included arthritis due to injury, any disease due to malnutrition, chronic dysentery, frostbite, helminthiasis (parasitic worms), psychosis, panic disorder, PTSD and other anxiety disorders, depression, peripheral neuropathy (nerve damage), irritable bowel syndrome, and peptic ulcer disease. Subsequent research and congressional lobbying led to the addition of ischemic heart disease, cirrhosis, stroke, and osteoporosis.

Lessons Learned

The capacity to confront the emotional injuries these POWs sustained was variable and limited until the major boost for POW care, compensation, and research was provided by the passage of the 1981 Former POW Benefit Act. Prior to its passage, POWs were an invisible part of the veteran population, of no particular significance to Veterans Administration and DoD providers. The act offered health examinations and certain benefits to all POWs. Using repatriation records and help from veterans' service organizations, all locatable POWs were contacted, urged to undergo lengthy POW Protocol Examinations, offered compensation where warranted, and provided Veterans Administration care at high levels, including dental work, eyeglasses, and hearing aids. As outlined above, POW research mushroomed, helping to establish links between POW status and other conditions for which care and compensation have been provided. By their unselfish participation in research projects, these former POWs have taught us much about the costs of war, preparing the Department of Veterans Affairs (VA) to better serve veterans of all wars (Engdahl 2006). In a reciprocal fashion, POWs have benefited from the efforts of veterans of more recent wars. The activism of Vietnam veterans and their supporters led to the introduction of the PTSD diagnosis in 1980.

A vigorous outreach effort continued, and it was necessary because initially many POWs who could benefit were reluctant to participate. This was in part due to the effects of their captivity experiences, which often created a mindset of passivity and resignation, plus survivor guilt and feeling unworthy of benefits (Farber, Harlow & West 1957). Furthermore, many POWs felt abandoned by their government when taken captive ("we were expendable") and rejected offers of aid. Still others perceived that they were treated with indifference and even rejection upon return to civilian life, viewed as cowards who had "surrendered to the enemy," when in reality they almost never had a choice. Countering this, the Former POW Benefit Act established a "POW Medal" provided by the DoD, to recognize their status. It was slow to be accepted, in part because the then secretary of the Veterans Administration opposed it. A retired general, he was heard to say that "in my Army, we gave medals to men who fought, not those who surrendered." Nevertheless, the medal gained acceptance and has helped in a healing process for many POWs and their families. The outreach efforts resulted in widespread participation, leading to increased medical and mental healthcare plus compensation, "getting it right" at long last.

References

American Psychiatric Association. (1980). *Diagnostic and statistical manual of mental disorders.* 3rd ed. Washington, DC: Author.

American Psychiatric Association. (1994). *Diagnostic and statistical manual of mental disorders.* 4th ed. Washington, DC: Author.

Beebe, G. W. (1975). Follow-up studies of World War II and Korean War prisoners, II: Morbidity, disability, and maladjustments. *American Journal of Epidemiology* 101: 400–422.

Cohen, B. M. & Cooper, M. Z. (1954). *A follow-up study of World War II prisoners of war*. Veterans Affairs medical monograph. Washington, DC: U.S. Department of Veterans Affairs.

Dawes, G. (1994). *Prisoners of the Japanese: POWs of World War II in the Pacific*. New York: William Morrow.

Eberly, R. E. & Engdahl, B. E. (1991). Prevalence of somatic and psychiatric disorders among former prisoners of war. *Hospital and Community Psychiatry* 42: 807–813.

Engdahl, B. E. (2006). From WWII to Iraq to the community: Interplay of resilience, spirituality and posttraumatic growth. Symposium presented at the ISTSS annual convention, Los Angeles.

Engdahl, B. E., Dikel, T., Eberly, R. E. & Blank, A. (1997). Posttraumatic stress disorder in a community sample of former prisoners of war: A normative response to severe trauma. *American Journal of Psychiatry* 154: 1576–1581.

Erbes, C., Johnsen, E., Harris, J., Dikel, T., Eberly, R. & Engdahl, B. (2006). Posttraumatic growth among American POWs. *Traumatology* 11, no. 4: 285–295.

Farber, I., Harlow, H. & West, L. (1957). Brainwashing, conditioning, and DDD (debility, dependency, and dread). *Sociometry* 20: 271–285.

Former Prisoners of War Benefit Act of 1981. Pub. L. No. 97-37.

Hata, I. (1996). From consideration to contempt: The changing nature of Japanese military and popular perceptions of prisoners of war through the ages. In B. Moore & K Fedorowich (Eds.), *Prisoners of war and their captors in World War II*. Oxford, UK: Berg.

Holmes, L. G. (2001). *Unjust enrichment: How Japan's companies built postwar fortunes using American POWs*. Mechanicsburg, PA: Stackpole Books.

Keehn, R. J. (1980). Follow-up studies of World War II and Korean conflict prisoners. *American Journal of Epidemiology* 111: 194–211.

Miller, T. W. (1992). Long-term effects of torture in former prisoners of war. In M. Basoglu (Ed.), *Torture and its consequences: Current treatment approaches* (pp. 107–135). New York: Cambridge University Press.

Nefzger, M. D. (1970). Follow-up studies of World War II and Korean war prisoners: I. Study plan and mortality findings. *American Journal of Epidemiology* 91: 123–138.

Nice, D. S., Garland, C. F., Hilton, S. M., Baggett, J. C. & Mitchell, R. E. (1996). Long-term health outcomes and medical effects of torture among US Navy prisoners of war in Vietnam. *Journal of the American Medical Association* 276: 375–381.

Page, W. F. (1992). *The health of former prisoners of war: Results from the Medical Examination Survey of Former POWs of World War II and the Korean Conflict*. Washington, DC: National Academy Press.

Page, W. F. & Engdahl, B. E. (1994). A tradition of VA-supported research on POWs: Searching for scientific knowledge and benefit. *The VA Practitioner* (June).

Page, W., Engdahl, B. & Eberly, R. (1997). The persistence of PTSD in former POWs. In C. Fullerton & R. Ursano (Eds.), *PTSD: Acute and long-term responses to trauma* (pp. 147–158). Washington, DC: American Psychiatric Press.

Port, C., Engdahl, B. & Frazier, P. (2001) A longitudinal and retrospective study of PTSD among older POWs. *American Journal of Psychiatry* 158: 1474–1479.

Segal, G. (1986). Positive effects among American POWs held by North Vietnam. Washington, DC: APA Annual Meeting, August 7–10.

Skelton, W. P., III. (2002). *The American ex-prisoner of war.* http://www.public health.va.gov/docs/vhi/pow.pdf (accessed October 21, 2011).

Sledge, W., Boydstun, J. & Rabe, M. (1980). Self-concept changes related to war captivity. *Archives of General Psychiatry* 37: 430–443.

Speed, N., Engdahl, B., Schwartz, J. & Eberly, R. (1989). PTSD as a consequence of the POW experience. *Journal of Nervous and Mental Disease* 177: 147–153.

Stenger, C. A. (2006). *American prisoners of war in WWI, WWII, Korea, and Viet Nam.* Washington, DC: Veterans Administration Advisory Committee on Former Prisoners of War, Department of Medicine and Surgery, VA Central Office.

Veterans Administration. (1983). *POW: Study of former prisoners of war.* Washington, DC: VA Office of Planning and Program Evaluation.

Veterans Administration. (1984). Former POW medical history. VA Form 10-0048. Washington, DC: U.S. Government Printing Office.

Service Dogs and Their Use for Veterans with Disabilities

Beth Hudnall Stamm, Susan L. Blampied, and Kirstina Beck

A Short Tail

Rainbow looks like any other Labrador retriever, but she is not a pet. Trained by a prison inmate, her mission is to help Roland Paquette, an injured veteran of the conflict in Afghanistan, stay on his new feet, the ones he got after an explosion destroyed his legs. While veterans who lose their sight or hearing or must use a wheelchair have long had "service" dogs as companions, Rainbow is one of the first dogs in the country trained to work with someone who uses both a wheelchair and prosthetics to get around. Mr. Paquette's hope is that eventually Rainbow will allow him to abandon his canes altogether and rely only on the metal handle attached to the harness she wears around her torso. "I'd much rather be able to walk with her at my side than with the canes," said Mr. Paquette, who is 28. "It makes me less obvious.... I've got a feeling that lots of guys who see me with Rainbow are going to want a dog," he said. (Storm 2006)

History

The U.S. Department of Veterans Affairs (VA) has long supported the use of assistance animals for veterans who served in World War I and wars thereafter. There has been a long history of laws and other legal support for the use of assistance animals for military veterans. However, developing and implementing VA policy to address these laws has been difficult. In reality, the legal authority to provide assistance animals has superseded the VA's practice, a fact strongly underscored by the July 2010 Veterans Health Administration Audit of Guide and Service Dog Programs (Department of Veterans Affairs,

Office of the Inspector General, Office of Audits and Evaluations 2010) (hereinafter VA Audit 2010).

To understand the following history, a brief comment on the use of terms associated with assistance animals is warranted. The language of assistance animals is confusing because the same term may be used to mean different types of assistance animals. A full discussion of the language of assistance animals follows the history section. Very generally, *assistance animals* includes all animals that are trained to provide some type of assistance to mitigate a person's disability. Dogs are the most well known subset of assistance animals and are the focus of this chapter. Assistance dogs include guide dogs, which are trained to assist people who are blind; hearing dogs, which are trained to alert to specific sounds for people who are deaf or hard of hearing, and service dogs, which are trained to provide assistance with a variety of physical or psychological disabilities. In all cases, assistance animals are trained to perform specific tasks to assist their partners with their disabilities.

Origins of the VA Providing Assistance Dogs

On May 26, 1944, President Franklin Roosevelt signed into law the Blind Veterans' Guide-Dog Law, which authorized the Veterans Administration to provide guide dogs for blinded war veterans. The law called for an appropriation of $1 million to purchase and train guide dogs. After the passage of the law, Brigadier General Charles C. Hillman of the U. S. Army Medical Corps wrote in the *Journal of the American Medical Association* that misinformation was being promulgated and that there was no need for the guide dogs, because in Hillman's experience only about 10 percent of blinded servicemen would benefit from a guide dog (Hillman 1944). In an effort to fight the public perception that guide dogs were needed by veterans, Hillman included detailed information about the number of veterans who became blind or deafened as a result of serving in the war. While the article has the tone of an apologist for the Veterans Administration, the number of veterans who were blinded or deafened as a result of the war was in fact likely smaller than the public perception. The amount of money committed to training guide dogs probably exceeded what was needed to serve the veterans who had been blinded. However, this exchange between the Veterans Administration and Congress about the need for guide dogs was contentious.

Nonetheless, veterans of World War II were provided with guide dogs and at least some Veterans Administration offices recruited veterans of World War I to participate in the program. There was no discussion at that time about hearing dogs, because guide dogs were the assistance animals that people understood could provide help to a person with a disability. In 2001 a law was passed that provided VA with the ability to help veterans acquire service and hearing dogs. In 2009 a clarification to the law included psychiatric service dogs in the category of a service dog, which permitted veterans to receive help from an additional category of assistance dogs.

Policies

Translating law into administrative rules and then into policy is a tedious and perplexing process. For example, just the information about assistance dogs in the current schedule of veterans' benefits (38 U.S.C. §1714, as amended by P.L. 111-5, enacted February 17, 2009) incorporates six public laws enacted over a span of forty-five years, beginning in 1958 (American Recovery and Reinvestment Act of 2009). This schedule was amended yet again in December 2009 to include psychiatric service dogs. According to the VA Audit (2010), between October 2008 and July 2010, financial support was given to 230 veterans with impaired vision, but only 8 veterans were given support for service dogs.

VA, like most agencies and organizations, faces challenges implementing any law into practice. Moreover, there has been fluidity in the definition of an assistance animal in the United States. Many types of disabilities exist today, making it harder for government organizations and advocates to create precise definitions to fit the variety of assistance animals that could be trained to mitigate a person's disability.

Definition of a Disability under the Americans with Disabilities Act

The Americans with Disabilities Act of 1990 (ADA), as amended in 2008, defines disability to mean (1) a physical or mental impairment that substantially limits one or more major life activities of such individual; (2) a record of such an impairment, or (3) being regarded as having such an impairment (ADA Amendments Act of 2008 [ADAA]). General life areas include things like taking care of oneself, walking, breathing, learning, communicating, etc. The ADAA specified that an impairment that is episodic or in remission is a disability and that the determination of impairment must be made without regard to an ameliorating effect such as medication, assistive technology, reasonable accommodation, or learned or behavioral adaptations.

Definition of an Assistance Animal/Dog

An assistance animal, in this chapter the specific category of dog, is individually trained to provide assistance to a *qualified individual* with a disabling condition. The ADA defines an assistance animal "as any guide dog, signal dog, or other animal individually trained to provide assistance to an individual with a disability" (Americans with Disabilities Act of 1990). Task training to mitigate a person's disability differentiates assistance animals from animal companions. In 2010, the Department of Justice clarified the rules regarding assistance dogs, noting that the "work or tasks performed by a service animal must be directly related to the individual's disability (Department of Justice 2010).

A Short Tail

"Dango" matched with Brian Fountaine, a veteran who lost both legs when an IED exploded in Iraq. Dango walks quietly by his human partner's side; retrieving keys, picking up a dropped cell phone and his leash. He even brings the portable phone to Brian when it rings. As of late he has figured out how to bring Brian his prosthetic legs. (NEADS 2010)

One of the most frequently cited documents for understanding and identifying service animals is the U. S. government's "Commonly Asked Questions about Service Animals in Places of Business" (Department of Justice 2008). In this document the link between the person's disability and the animal trained to perform tasks to mitigate that disability is clearly made. In addition, the document clearly specifies that assistance animal partners are not required to provide documentation or certification of the assistance dog before allowing access to a public place of business.

VA generally uses the same definition for guide and service dogs as does the Department of Justice. "The Veterans Affairs Guide and Service Dog Frequently Asked Questions" (Department of Veterans Affairs 2010) states: "A guide dog is trained to assist blind and visually impaired people by avoiding obstacles. A service dog is trained to help those with physical or hearing disabilities by alerting deaf and hearing impaired individuals to a variety of household sounds or by assisting in the performance of a wide variety of tasks depending on need and training (e.g. balance, retrieving, or pulling a wheelchair)."

The Coalition of Assistance Dog Organizations (2005) offers this definition:

service animal means an assistance dog, and may include other animals specifically trained to perform physical tasks to mitigate the effects of an individual's disability. Assistance dogs include guide dogs that guide individuals who are legally blind; hearing dogs that alert individuals who are deaf or hard of hearing to specific sounds; and, Service dogs for individuals with disabilities other than blindness or deafness. Service dogs are trained to perform a variety of physical tasks including but not limited to pulling a wheelchair, lending balance support, picking up dropped objects or providing assistance in a medical crisis.

Table 14.1. Summary of Key Legal Definitions

Term	Source	Definition
Disability	ADAA	Having or a record of having or being regarded as having a physical or mental impairment that substantially limits one or more major life activities.
Service Dog	ADA, ADAA	Individually trained to do work or perform tasks for the benefit of an individual with a disability. The definition requires the person to have a disability. No dog is a service dog unless the individual has a disability and the dog is trained to mitigate that person's specific disability.
Emotional Support (ESA), Pet & Companion Dog ((P/C)	ADA, ADAA	Pet and companion dogs (P/C), emotional support dogs (ESA) provide "emotional support, comfort, therapy, companionship, therapeutic benefits, and the promotion of emotional well-being." P/C and ESAs are not service dogs and therefore do not qualify for public access. Under medical supervision ESAs do have some privileges not afforded P/Cs.
Therapy Animal/ Dog	ADA, ADAA	Usually the personal pets of their handlers, therapy dogs provide people with contact with animals. Therapy dogs are not limited to working with people who have disabilities. Therapy dogs are not service dogs and therefore do not qualify for public access.

Summarized from the U.S. Department of Justice ADAA-based code, 28 C.F.R. Pt. 35 CRT, 3a

At the core of both definitions is the aspect of *task training to mitigate a disability*: Is this dog specifically trained to mitigate that person's specific disability? An assistance dog is not a pet. Dogs that naturally provide comfort but are not task-trained to mitigate a disability are not assistance dogs. Dogs that are used for personal defense are not assistance animals, because this training does not qualify for mitigation of a person's disability. (See table 14.1 for a summary of key legal definitions.)

Eligibility Based on Discharge

Veterans may be eligible to receive a guide or service dog based on disability and discharge. Veterans must be honorably discharged or have a general discharge under honorable conditions. Veterans who are involuntarily separated but under other than adverse conditions and those separated for bad conduct may be eligible. Veterans dishonorably discharged are not eligible.

Guide Dog "Provided to Veterans Who Prefer"

For visually impaired veterans, guide dogs are available. VA policy stipulates that following orientation and mobility training, *those who are blind and prefer a guide dog* are referred to a qualifying non-VA school for a dog and training (Department of Veterans Affairs 2009).

Service Dogs: "Allowed but Not Required"

While the VA's policy toward providing guide dogs for veterans who are blind or have low vision is well established and based on the veteran's preference for a guide dog, the policies toward service dogs for hearing, mobility, or other chronic impairment are more restrictive. In 2001, Public Law No. 107-135 allowed, but did not require, VA to provide hearing and service dogs to veterans (Department of Veterans Affairs Health Care Programs Enhancement Act of 2001). The most updated U.S. statute, 38 U.S.C. § 1714, includes laws in effect as of January 3, 2007. This statute defines and allows for the provision of guide dogs for the blind, service dogs trained for the aid of the hearing-impaired, and service dogs for people with spinal cord injury or dysfunction or other chronic impairment that substantially limits mobility. In December 2009, the Consolidated Appropriations Act of 2010 (P.L. 111-117) added a category of "service dogs trained for the aid of persons with mental illnesses, including post-traumatic stress disorder." Thus, VA currently has legal authorization to provide guide dogs for the blind, dogs trained for the aid of hearing-impaired, and service dogs for people with spinal cord injury or dysfunction or other chronic impairment that substantially limits mobility, as well as service dogs for people with mental illnesses.

VA Struggles with Service Dogs

Even with legal permission to provide service dogs, granted beginning in 2001, and with popular sentiment and some congressional pressure for service animals, VA was not in favor of the practice. On January 14, 2008, Secretary of

Veteran Affairs James Peak approved a memorandum recommending against VA providing service dogs to eligible veterans who were mobility- or hearing-impaired (Kussman 2008). The decision not to provide hearing and service dogs to eligible veterans was based on VA's belief that there were multiple issues, including (1) a lack of research evidence on the effectiveness of service dogs, (2) costs saved by a decrease in paid assistance would be offset by the cost of care for the dog, (3) VA had alternative low-tech devices that serve the same purposes as a service dog, (4) a veteran's condition might worsen over time, making it difficult for the veteran to care for a dog, (5) service dogs require constant training and care, and (6) consistent clinical standards regarding the use of a dog have not been identified. In response to the memorandum, Lowery Heussler, a member of the board of directors of NEADS, Inc. (Dogs for Deaf and Disabled Americans), urged VA to rescind this decision. In his letter he "provided research based on experiential" information to refute each conclusion, saying that their interpretations were "dangerously close to scientific misrepresentation" (Huessler 2008).

On June 8, 2008, VA Chief Prosthetics & Clinical Logistics Officer Fredrick Downs Jr. discussed the decision with Brian Lamb on a C-SPAN program. During that dialogue, Dr. Downs said that VA would consider providing service dogs to veterans but also stated that it would have to develop standards, because there were currently no standards in the service dog industry (C-SPAN 2008). This demonstrates just one of the issues that led to the memorandum on providing service dogs. However, advocates pointed out that this was incorrect, because Assistance Dogs International, Inc., has set standards and provided accreditation to assistance dog agencies since 1987 (Assistance Dogs International 2010).

Current Service Dog Practice for Veterans

Although no formal data have been collected, it appears from informal sources that most veterans are being partnered with service dogs outside of the VA system. This is not inconsistent with VA's history with guide dogs. However, there is a distinguishing difference in that it appears most veteran and service dog partnerships are initiated outside of the VA channels, compared to guide dogs, for which referrals are made through VA. There are numerous organizations that serve specifically veterans (e.g. Freedom Service Dogs, America's Vet Dogs). Other long-standing organizations (e.g. NEADS, Dogs for Deaf and Disabled Americans, Canine Companions for Independence) have developed programs for veterans or put particular effort into recruiting veterans for partnering with service dogs. The International Association of Assistance Dog

Partners (IAADP) has disseminated the information that veterans partnered with service dogs may be eligible for things such as veterinary care, working equipment, and preventative medicine. The IAADP recommendation refers to dogs that are already partnered with a disabled veteran, not to veterans who were approved by the VA system prior to being partnered with a dog.

It is difficult to determine the validity of the popular perception that VA provides service dogs for two reasons. First, there is no publicly available information about the number of service dogs that have been qualified through VA. Second, because individuals, as well as VA, do refer to accredited service dog schools that are outside of the VA system, it is difficult to ferret out the precise source of an application to an agency for a service dog.

The information posted in April 2010 at the VA Web site states that veterans can apply for a service dog. Cases are evaluated based on the clinical need for assistive devices. VA notes that the assistive devices may include a service dog. The determination for the assignment of a dog is based on (1) the veteran's ability to care for the dog currently and in the future, (2) the goals that are accomplished through the use of the dog, and (3) the goals that are to be accomplished through other assistive technology or therapy (Department of Veterans Affairs 2010). Veterans are referred to an accredited agency, presumably accredited by Assistance Dogs International in the case of service dogs.

Comparison of VA Benefits for Service Dogs and Guide Dogs

Both guide dogs and service dogs are organizationally in the VA's Prosthetics & Sensory Aid Service (PSAS). Guide and service dogs, including hearing dogs, are classified as an assistive device. Based on current public information, VA views guide dogs as one of the array of assistive devices available for a veteran who is blind. Blind veterans may choose to use a guide dog. Service dogs are considered alternative assistive devices that are weighted against other assistive devices. There is an implication that provision of a service dog is not a choice of assistive devices, but that the case must be made that the service dog is a better alternative to a different type of assistive device.

When a veteran is qualified for an assistance animal, VA will pay for veterinary care, working equipment, basic preventative medicine, and prescriptions. The cost of training to be partnered with a guide dog is covered, but these costs are not covered for service dogs. While many guide and service dogs are made possible through donation and foundation funds, some agencies do require students to pay some expenses associated with partnering with a guide or service dog. For example, students may be required to pay for travel to and from the training facility and lodging during training. While the VA procedures for covering training and partnering expenses may be the same for guide and service dogs, the information available on the VA Web site does not specify that the policies are the same.

Types of Assistance Dogs to Mitigate a Qualifying Disability

A Short Tail

I am a traumatic brain injury survivor. TBI often affects multiple cognitive, physical, and psychological aspects. I have a body disregulation that causes my upper body to jerk and makes balance difficult. Sometimes I get lost and my dog helps me locate places following previously prescribed routes. Early in our partnership I used two canes and a lead for my dog Sophie. Some unfortunate "unbalancing" events caused my health team to think about other types of equipment for Sophie's and my partnership. We determined that a harness with a handle to grasp would be a good alternative for me since it would aid my balance and it would improve our navigation. Sometimes I hear people speaking loudly to each other saying, "Look at the lady with the dog, she does not look blind." While I appreciate the confusion regarding assistance dog equipment, because of the rude manner in which people speak as if I were not there, I am always tempted to reply, in a loud stage whisper, "and she's not deaf either." (B. H. Stamm, author)

Although the overall determination of an assistance animal revolves around the person's disability and an animal's trained ability to mitigate that disability, there are generally accepted understandings of the types of assistance animals. There has been, and remains, variability in the definitions and organization of the names for various types of assistance animals, even when one limits the discussion to dogs. We have adopted the terms used by the industry-wide coalition of nonprofit organizations working with assistance dogs, Assistance Dogs International (ADI) (2010). While the ADI does not specifically define the types of dogs, it does define the training standards across types of assistance that dogs provide. Other alternatives include calling all dogs trained to mitigate a person's disability service dogs, incorporating guide dogs into the service dog name. Some methods set apart guide dogs and then incorporate all non-guide dogs into a single service dog category. Another alternative is defining as service dogs all who are not guide or hearing dogs. Following are the preferred terms for assistance dogs drawn from ADI and the IAADP and incorporating legislative language where appropriate. Froling (2001, 2009) provides a very detailed discussion of various types of assistance dogs organized by tasks performed.

Guide Dogs

Guide dogs (GD) assist blind and visually impaired people. They are trained in obstacle avoidance, signaling changes in elevation, locating objects on command, and other tasks to serve their partners.

Hearing Dogs

Hearing dogs (HD) assist deaf and hard of hearing individuals. They may alert their partners to sounds around the home such as doorbell rings, alarm clocks, baby cries, and smoke detectors. Outside of the home, they may alert their partners when someone calls the person's name, alert to a honking horn, or distinguish between phones in a work setting, alerting their partners to their phones.

Service Dogs

Service dogs (SD) assist people with disabilities other than vision or hearing impairment. There are a variety of types of disabilities that SDs can be trained to help with based on the specific disability of the person with whom the dog is partnered. They may be trained to help people with mobility disorders, alert to seizures or other medical conditions including those regarding mental health, and do other things. Service dogs may carry or retrieve things for their partners; they may provide bracing, balance, or pulling tasks. They may call for medical assistance and even assist with chores like doing the laundry and taking out the trash for people whose disabilities make these tasks difficult.

Public Access Training and Task Training

A Short Tail

I have been partnered with a service dog for five years and I frequently travel by air. On one occasion the flight was long, very crowded, and delayed on the tarmac. My service dog patiently stayed under the seat in front of me like a piece of luggage with legs. At the end of the seven-hour flight, when I exited the window seat, the people who had been sitting in the middle and aisle seats beside me both cried out, "I didn't know there was a dog under there!" (B. H. Stamm, author)

While there are no federal regulations regarding the minimum standards or criteria for assistance dogs working in public, the associations and accrediting organizations in the assistance animal field have collaborated on several sets of standards. There are typically two types of training for which assistance animals are trained. The first is public access and the second is task training.

Public Access

Public access training includes basic obedience training and things such as controlled load and unload from a vehicle, walking calmly in a crowded space, not sniffing, remaining quiet, not soliciting or stealing food, urinating and defecating on command, and other attributes that keep a dog from being obtrusive or interrupting the normal course of business. These characteristics are not unique to assistance dogs. For example, show dogs learn the same behaviors. Some public access criteria are related to the partner, not the dog. These types of criteria include keeping the dog well groomed and not letting the dog have a foul odor. Typically, public access, skills training occurs over a four- to nine-month period depending on the dog. Dogs that have basic obedience skills may learn the other public access skills in a short time. Puppies may train for a year learning their basic obedience and public access skills.

Task Training

Task training is the second category of training for an assistance animal. This training refers to learning specific tasks to mitigate the disability of the dog's partner. There are multiple aspects of this training, including following the commands of the human partner. The animal must learn to perform its duties in public and become accustomed to being in public. Part of learning to work in a human-dog partnership is learning to stay with the partner in a way that it can perform its task but also stay out of the way of others. The dog must learn to stay within a close radius of its partner, typically within twenty-four inches, and must learn to lie quietly by its partner. Dogs are typically task-trained for six months to two years, depending on the tasks they need to learn and the individual dog.

Public Access Rights under the ADA of Persons with a Disability Using a Service Dog

Under the ADA, all organizations that serve the public must allow access to people with disabilities who have assistance animals to all areas of the facility where the general public normally has access. This federal law applies to all businesses and organizations open to the public, including restaurants, grocery and department stores, hospitals and medical offices, health clubs, hotels, taxis and shuttles, theaters, parks, and zoos.

In the United States and some other countries, civil rights are afforded to people with disabilities under national law. In the United States, the ADA covers the rights of all persons with disabilities along with those who use assistance animals. A good overview of the regulations regarding assistance animal access can be found in "ADA Business BRIEF: Assistance Animals" at the ADA's Web site. A person with a disability who has an assistance animal may be asked by the staff of the business what tasks the assistance animal performs; however, they may not ask for special certification or ID cards for the animal and may not ask about the person's disability. In addition, a person with a disability cannot be charged an additional fee because he or she is accompanied by an assistance animal. A person with a disability who is accompanied by an assistance animal must be admitted into all general public areas and may not be isolated, segregated, or treated less favorably than the general public.

Housing

While instances of being denied access to restaurants and stores do occur, housing is an area that is fraught with difficulties since so many people live in housing owned by someone other than themselves. Currently, the Fair Housing Amendments Act of 1988 addresses this issue for the majority of assistance animals.

This act requires that landlords allow assistance animal's access to all housing opportunities, including those for the elderly and locations that regularly uphold no-pet rules (Texas Hearing and Service Dogs 2003). This continues in the practice established by the ADA allowing those with disabilities who have assistance animals equal access to locations that are accessible to the general public. The landlord can require verification that the assistance animal is task-trained but cannot request specific information about the individual's disability and must accept written certification from the individual or family member that he or she has a disability (Texas Hearing and Service Dogs 2003). The law does not specify regulations regarding psychiatric assistance animals or emotional support animals, which are discussed further in the "Issues" section of this chapter. In addition, there is no mention of regulations for "assistance animals in training."

Transportation

One government agency that rapidly is responding to the assistance dog movement is the Department of Transportation (DoT), particularly in regards to the airline industry. The Air Carrier Access Act requires that airlines accommodate assistance animals when they accompany a person with a disability. Airline personnel must accept visual identification or verbal confirmation for an assistance animal. The act, which took effect May 13, 2009, includes *psychiatric service dogs (PSD)* in its definition of "any guide dog, signal dog, or other animal individually trained to provide assistance to an individual with a disability." If the animal meets this definition, it is considered a service animal regardless of whether it has been licensed or certified by a state or local government (Department of Transportation 2008).

There is, however, a distinction made in the regulations for psychiatric assistance animals versus other assistance animals. PSD dogs require current documentation from a licensed mental health professional if they are to travel in the cabin. Other exclusions include unusual or exotic assistance animals, or "assistance animals in training." In these cases it is up to airline personnel to determine if the assistance animal will be allowed to travel with the passenger in the cabin. If an assistance animal is not allowed to travel in the cabin, the reason must be explained to the passenger and documented in writing, with a copy provided to the passenger at the airport or within ten days (Air Carrier Access Act 2008).

Issues

Policies regarding assistance animals continue to change in an effort to address the emergence of different types of assistance animals. While agencies, including the VA, continue to try to find ways to address the changing world of assistance animals, there are still many issues that have not been resolved.

Types of Assistance Dogs

A Short Tail

Like any other golden retriever seeking a treat, Tuesday nudged his owner's hand with his snout one recent morning and waited expectantly. Luis Carlos Montalvan got up from a chair in his small Brooklyn apartment and walked to the kitchen. Tuesday followed close behind, eyes fixed on a white cabinet. The retriever sat alertly as Mr. Montalvan, an Iraq war veteran with severe post-traumatic stress disorder, reached for a vial of pills, lined a half-dozen on the table and took them one by one. The dog had gotten what he wanted: When the last pill was swallowed, he got up and followed his master out of the kitchen, tail wagging. Tuesday is a so-called psychiatric-service dog, a new generation of animals trained to help people whose suffering is not physical, but emotional. They are, effectively, Seeing Eye dogs for the mind. (Dreazan 2009)

PSDs

A PSD is a dog trained to perform tasks to mitigate disabling mental impairment. There are many tasks that a PSD can do to aid its partner, including assisting during a crisis by bringing medication, calling 911, turning on lights, etc. (Froling 2009). Like other assistance dogs, a PSD's tasks are specialized based on the psychiatric needs of its human partner. For example, a PSD for a person with PTSD may turn on lights and do a "perimeter check."

As mentioned in the policy section, the DoT has established that a PSD must have current documentation from a licensed mental health provider to be allowed access to an airplane cabin. This differs from other assistance animals, which are allowed based on visual clues such as the presence of a harness or vest and questions regarding task training. There are currently no policies providing access to housing for PSDs. These limitations may create obstacles for the many veterans who either have PSDs or are interested in obtaining one.

Nonassistance Dogs with Health-related Contributions

There are varieties of other types of roles that dogs can take on that provide health-related support but are not those of an assistance animal covered under the ADA's access guidelines. Perhaps one of the most confusing for the general public is what is known as a *comfort dog, a companion dog,* or an *emotional support dog* (ESA). The DoJ recognizes the benefits of pets and support animals, noting they can provide "emotional support, comfort, therapy, companionship, therapeutic benefits, and the promotion of emotional well-being," and that a "pet or support animal may be able to discern that the individual is in distress, but it is what the animal is trained to do in response to this awareness that distinguishes a service animal from an observant pet or support animal" (Department of Justice 2010). The difference between a PSD and an ESA is, as with other assistance dogs, the task training for the mitigation of a disability. Having a calming and focusing effect on a person with a mental disability may be a valuable innate quality, but does not require specific training. Another role that dogs can take on is as a *therapy dog* or *animal assisted therapy.* Depending on their location, therapy dogs may be seen in public settings or in particular health-related settings. However, they are not covered under the ADA public access criteria. Therapy dogs are increasingly seen in settings where people have long-term illnesses or are in rehabilitation and can benefit from interaction with a visiting dog. They may also make visits to schools. *Therapy dogs enjoy working with their handlers to provide affection and comfort to others.* VA defines animals that do therapy or activity assistance as those that "assist therapists to accomplish therapeutic goals or for general engagement of the patients" (Department of Veterans Affairs 2010).

Another type of helping dog that is trained to tasks normally associated with an assistance dog is a *facility dog*. Though at one time very rare, *facility dogs* are increasing in number. These dogs are trained to the same standards as service dogs but are not partnered with individuals. They may work in a healthcare facility providing service-dog tasks for several different people. They may work in schools to increase a student's social interaction and language by taking commands from the student. Some facility dogs specialize in working in courtrooms and with witnesses. They may accompany traumatized witnesses to the courtroom when they testify.

Conflicting Accessibility Regulations

Individual states may have their own laws regarding assistance dogs. Sometimes these laws can conflict with federal requirements established by the ADA and the ADAA. From a legal perspective, federal law sets the minimum standards, and state laws can enhance but not reduce the power of federal laws. Thus a state law, if it is contrary to the federal regulations, is not the higher authority. Nonetheless, it is not uncommon for local and state jurisdictions to call for behaviors that are more restrictive than those in the federal regulations.

School and Owner Training

One issue that remains contested for those who have assistance animals is the distinction between those animals that have been owner-trained versus school-trained. This also becomes an issue in locations that require school documentation for assistance animals.

A Short Tail

A well-known advocate who is partnered with a guide dog tells this story. The State Law in California required that guide dogs be trained in accredited schools to qualify to be covered as assistance animals for public access. The advocate was partnered with a privately trained guide dog. She and two other guide dog owners went to see an influential state legislative figure. They sat down, each with their dog quietly lying beside them. The advocate said, "which of these three dogs do you want to turn out? One of them is not school trained." The legislative figure brushed off the regulatory definition but in the end came to understand that the source of training was less important than the quality of and the specificity of the training for a person's disability. Corrective legislation followed closely on the heels of this conversation. (Eames 2010)

Discriminatory Belief Systems

Stigma

The personal isolation of those with disabilities is greatly increased by the impact of stigma (Kilbury, Bordieri & Wong 1996). For people with disabilities, stigma promotes and maintains negative effects on self-esteem (Corrigan et al. 2005; Stamm et al. 2006). A considerable body of research denotes stigma as one of the most important barriers to productive lives for people with disabilities. People learn from childhood through cultural influences stigma's negative attributions toward people with disabilities (Wahl 1995). These messages contain assumptions about people with disabilities, including that they are to be feared, trivialized, pitied, or ridiculed (Shapiro 1999; Wilson & Lewiecki-Wilson 2001). Language often stigmatizes a person with a disability and perhaps speaks to the VA's perception of rehabilitation as far back as World War II. In regard to soldiers who were blinded, Hillman wrote, "with a skillful used cane, they are inconspicuous" (1944). Although VA positively identifies the need for training and community integration, this is followed by the stigmatizing idea that if one is careful, his or her disability can be "inconspicuous," which implies that being blind should not be evident. For those with disabilities, stigma negatively affects their quality of life and self-esteem (Yanos, Rosenfeld & Horowitz 2001; Corrigan & Watson 2002; Link et al. 2001).

Research has shown that assistance animals can counteract the stigma associated with disabilities. They decrease the barrier between the general public and those with disabilities (Allen & Blascovich 1996; Eddy, Hart & Boltz 1988; Guest, Collis & McNicholas 2006; Lane, McNicholas & Collis 1998). This is accomplished both through a decrease in depressive symptoms in the human partner (Allen & Blascovich 1996; Collins 2005; Guest, Collis & McNicholas 2006) and an increase in the general public's willingness to acknowledge a person with a disability who is with an assistance animal (Eddy, Hart & Boltz 1988; Lane, McNicholas & Collis 1998). Assistance animals therefore can be helpful both in daily activities and by helping to break down the barriers created by stigma.

Stereotypes

The majority of the population still view assistance animals as helping those who are blind. With the increase in the number and types of disabilities that assistance animals can alleviate, the general public is faced with reinterpreting its view of assistance animals.

A Short Tail

A person with a service dog was called for jury duty. In the papers filed prior to the beginning of the jury duty period the handler dutifully had included information about being partnered with a service dog. When the person arrived to register for jury duty the clerk said, "What is the dog doing with you? Is he in training?...But you look..., ah...uh...so good." As the words came out of her mouth, the clerk had a stricken look on her face, realizing that she just had projected the stereotype that you have to look "disabled" to qualify.

Hidden Disabilities

With the increase in assistance animals who work with those who are hearing-impaired, have traumatic brain injury, or have psychiatric issues, the general public is no longer able to easily identify an individual's disability. Many in the general public do not know all of the disabilities that an assistance animal can help to mitigate, and when faced with a hidden disability, people may be unsure how to handle the situation. In addition, for those assistance-animal partners who are used to having their disabilities hidden, the presence of an assistance animal introduces their disabilities to the world, which can be uncomfortable for some.

Dog Size

The image of an assistance animal tends to be a golden retriever or a labrador retriever; however, there is more variety in the currently growing world of assistance animals. Among thirteen guide dog organizations that participated in the Guide Dog School Survey 2006, the breeds used include Australian shepherd, boxer, doberman pinscher, german shepherd, golden retriever, labrador retriever, labrador-golden cross, labrador-poodle cross, smooth coat collie, standard poodle, vizsla, and border collie. One organization exclusively used german shepherds, two other organizations used labrador retrievers at least 90 percent of the time, and another five schools used labrador retrievers between 50 and 75 percent of the time (Guide Dog Users 2006). These thirteen schools demonstrate that a wide range of breeds can be trained to become guide dogs. The variety of breeds is even greater when hearing dogs, service dogs, and psychiatric service dogs are included.

Many smaller breeds are now used to assist people with disabilities. For example, a hearing dog may be a smaller breed because it does not need to do many tasks requiring physical strength. The size of the dog depends greatly on what tasks its partner requires it to complete. This means that the typical image of an assistance animal no longer depicts the range of animals that are currently working to assist those with disabilities. With this change in the view of a "typical" assistance dog, it is necessary for the general public to accept the image of dogs of various sizes fulfilling the duties of an assistance animal.

Challenges

Many organizations have long waiting lists for receiving an assistance dog. Veterans must either wait long periods of time or be moved ahead of others who have been waiting for dogs. The thirteen schools that participated in the Guide Dog School Survey 2006 show that the wait time to receive a dog varies by organization. The range indicated by these thirteen schools is one month to one year. Three-, four-, and six-month wait periods were indicated most often, with the average wait time being 4.5 months (Guide Dog Users Inc. 2006).

Economics and Finance

There are many financial items to consider when planning to receive an assistance animal. First there are the costs involved with getting the dog from a school, including transportation to and from housing at the school's location when the partner is placed with the assistance dog. Of the thirteen guide dog organizations that provided responses to the survey, three offer in-home training, eleven offer facility-based training, and six offer a training program that uses a combination of home-based and facility-based training. Training periods range from fourteen to forty-two days, with the average being twenty-four days, and the most often used period being twenty-eight days (Guide Dog Users Inc. 2006). Although some schools are home-based, many require the human partner to travel to their site and stay in the area during the initial pairing and training with the assistance dog.

The process of getting a dog is different for each organization; an organization may require a small fee or a percentage of the cost to be paid; may request donations; or may provide the dog for free. Alternatives to school-trained assistance dogs are owner-trained dogs, and an issue then is what the difference in cost is between the two options. One cost involved is the transportation to the facility for training. The Guide Dog School Survey 2006 showed that 63.6 percent of the schools offer subsidized transportation to and from training, and an additional 18.2 percent of schools indicate that they can offer subsidized transportation on a case-by-case basis. There are also costs for the daily maintenance of the animal.

Many people with disabilities can also experience financial constraints, which make the maintenance of an assistance dog difficult. There are services and support available; for example, VA will assist in payment, and there are also benefits available through the IAADP. VA states that "Blind Veterans with working dogs are provided veterinary care and equipment through VA Prosthetics and Sensory Aids. VA does not pay for boarding, grooming, food, or any other routine expense associated with owning a dog" (2009). There is no stated position on financial assistance for those veterans who have service, hearing, or psychiatric service dogs.

Some schools offer financial support for veterinary services after the handler has completed training with the dog. The Guide Dog School Survey 2006 showed that 23.1 percent of the schools offer an annual veterinary care stipend while the dog is working; one school even provides the annual stipend after the dog retired. Four of the schools offer a stipend either on a case-by-case basis or only for a specified period of time. Heartworm, flea, and tick prevention medication, free or reimbursed, is provided by 30.8 percent of the schools, and an additional 30.8 percent offer the same medications at a reduced cost. Two of the schools provide dog food at a reduced cost to their graduates. In addition, 38.5 percent of the schools offer loans or grants to assist graduates with vet costs, while another 46.2 percent help graduates find organizations that may assist with veterinary costs (Guide Dog Users Inc. 2006).

Assistance dogs can also help to decrease the costs involved in paid assistance for people with disabilities. Allen and Blascovich (1996) noted that for those provided with assistance dogs, there was a decrease of 68 percent in the amount spent on paid assistance. Many people with disabilities also receive assistance from family members or friends. There was a decrease of 64 percent in the amount of assistance time needed from friends and family members (Allen & Blascovich 1996). Although there are some financial costs involved in acquiring an assistance animal, the presence of such an animal can also help to decrease the paid and unpaid human assistance needed.

Research on Service Dog Partnerships

As demonstrated by the limited literature review of articles in this chapter, there is insufficient scientific and social research on service dogs and service dog partnerships. Studies that have been published are small in size and often based entirely on qualitative data. Qualitative data contribute rich and important information to the research data, but alone are insufficient to fully understand the issues. Some money for research on and placement of service dogs was appropriated in the FY2010 Omnibus Appropriations Act (H.R. 1105 [2009]). In addition, bills forwarded by Senator Al Franken have recognized the issues associated with high rates of suicide and psychiatric illnesses among veterans of the current war in Iraq and Afghanistan and requested studies to understand if, and how, service dogs might provide the same sorts of support for community integration and other benefits to these veterans as do guide dogs to blind and low-vision veterans.

New Directions in Veterans' Healthcare

This chapter has attempted to provide information regarding all the relevant history, policies, issues, and challenges involved with the growing world of assistance animals and the role the VA plays. There are some issues in providing assistance animals to veterans that VA still needs to address.

VA's Policy Position on Assistance Animals

While VA has a clear policy regarding veterans receiving guide dogs, there is no clear position on the policies involved in providing assistance for veterans who wish to receive service, hearing, or psychiatric service dogs. VA is providing help for veterans receiving all types of assistance animals; however, without a clear written policy, there is still ambiguity about the role VA plays. It is necessary for VA to have a clear written policy about all types of assistance animals.

Assistance dogs continue to be featured in the news, and with the growing coverage, the demand for assistance dogs from veterans may increase. VA needs to develop clear policies to adequately address this growing demand from current and future veterans. In addition, VA needs to define the role that an assistance animal plays in a veteran's rehabilitation. Will an assistance animal be considered another form of assistive technology, or are they separate issues?

Clarifying Psychiatric Service Dogs' Role

There is an increasing demand for and prevalence of psychiatric service dogs being placed with veterans from Operation Enduring Freedom (OEF) and Operation Iraqi Freedom (OIF). Because of this demand, it is necessary to clarify the role of psychiatric service dogs and the tasks they perform for veterans. Psychiatric service dogs can be trained to turn on lights, remind their partners to take their medications, provide grounding in reality, perform perimeter checks, and put physical distance between their partners and the general public. These tasks are all necessary to assist many veterans with the symptoms of PTSD.

There are some tasks that, depending on the emphasis placed on them, can alter the perceptions of psychiatric service dogs. Many psychiatric service dogs perform perimeter checks or are trained to "guard the back" of their human partners by providing space for their human partner in a crowded location. The issue becomes when these commands meant to provide safety for the human partner lead to an attack function. Assistance animals are task-trained, but they cannot be trained to attack others and still be considered an assistance animal. It is therefore necessary to distinguish those psychiatric service dogs who provide safety through distance and alertness and those dogs who are trained to attack, as this is not a function of an assistance animal.

A distinction also needs to be made for the function involved in grounding a person in reality. This is an important task for psychiatric service dogs; however, if this is the only task the animal performs, then there is ambiguity in terms of the distinction between a psychiatric service dog and a comfort dog. This distinction should be clarified for those veterans seeking the services of an assistance animal.

Future Issues

The most important future issue is addressing VA's policy about and implementation of guide and service dogs for veterans with disabilities. The VA Audit (2010) directs, and the VA Under Secretary for Health agreed, to set and clarify policy and train personnel to apply it in regard to guide and service dogs. Implementing new policy, even when it is a revision of existing policy, sets into motion positive and negative unintended consequences. Moreover, policy created for large systems such as VA can work well for most people within the overall system but poorly for some individuals within that same system. Consequently, monitoring and adjustments will be important in the coming years to find ways for the policy to best suit the system and individuals within that system.

Clarification of VA Policy in Regard to Successor Dogs

While good progress in regard to identifying and placing dogs with veterans who can benefit from a guide or service dog is being made in response to the VA Audit (2010), congressional pressure, and advocacy, successor dogs will soon become an issue. Policies will be needed to address how VA will participate in a veteran's effort to find a successor dog. Successor dogs will be needed because of retirement or death of the original assistance dogs. In addition, as with the death of any animal and in this case a partner, it is essential to deal with the grief involved. VA should review what its position will be in regard to assistance for veterans who have experienced the loss of an assistance animal.

Burgeoning Service Dog Movement

In part due to the number of returning service members from the current conflicts, the number of working service dogs is rapidly increasing. One benefit of this is that the public is more aware of service dogs and how they can provide services and support to their human partners. How service dogs are trained and how they and their human partners work in public is an issue. There is a long tradition of service dogs being trained in multiple ways, including by accredited schools, private trainers, and owner-trainers. There is no reason to change this tradition. However, it is important for service dog partnerships to understand how their work in public is conducted and perceived.

Research on Service Dogs and Service Dog Partnerships

Research on service dogs themselves and on service dog partnerships must be undertaken. Most would not recognize the need for research on the dogs alone; however, there are many questions about how best to identify, train, and predict work outcome of service dogs. Research should also be done concerning how best to predict the success of a partnership from the side of the human partners. Other questions include issues of community integration, in particular how a person with a service dog can navigate life systems such as finding housing; meeting daily needs such as shopping, receiving healthcare, using public transportation; and understanding perceptions and stigmas that people may experience as part of a service dog partnership. Funding sources for research on dogs and on service dog partnerships are so insignificant that they are effectively absent. Many researchers exist who could conduct this research well but they simply do not have funding to conduct and publish their research.

Research on Dogs Themselves

Some accredited schools have their own breeding programs, which appears to increase the probability of any one dog being a good service dog. Other programs use shelter dogs and train them. Some individuals select dogs of their liking and either do owner training or hire an individual trainer. Some dogs come though programs like "Puppies Behind Bars," in which prison inmates train service dogs. All of these pathways have led to very successful service dog training. However, as many as 50 percent of dogs that commence training do not qualify for service dog work. The questions associated with this issue include trying to understand how to identify puppies and dogs that will not make good service dogs by comparing them to dogs that will. Temperament tests do exist (e.g. IAADP: Finding a Suitable Candidate for Assistance Dog

Work, http://www.iaadp.org/temperament.html), but they are not satisfactorily predictive. Other research on the dogs includes understanding the effect of work on them. There are two major issues here. First, dogs may work well for a period of time and suddenly stop working or perform their jobs poorly. One of the hypotheses about this work cessation is that the dogs may be "burned out," but there is no clear information about that. Another concern is the behavioral changes that a dog may experience during its working career. For example, some dogs may work well but suddenly become reactive to a particular stimulus, including being reactive to particular situations or to other dogs. Reactivity to other dogs is potentially dangerous and at a minimum a very difficult management problem for the human partner.

Issues in identifying the appropriate point for retiring a dog should be examined. Some dogs work up until the time of their deaths, either from disease or old age. Other dogs retire after six to eight years. What are the characteristics that identify the need to retire a dog? Finally, there are many questions that should be addressed about an animal's health. Nutritional research can provide important clues to how to maintain a dog's health and even its reactivity or hypervigilance. Some dogs have or develop what are known to be psychological problems that are well treated by medications such as antidepressants. Other dogs may develop problems such as seizures, which are well treated by anti-seizure medications. Do these dogs need to be retired out of service, or can they, if well maintained on medications, continue to work?

Research on Human–Service Dog Partnerships

What predicts the success of a service dog partnership? Some human partners are well suited to partner with a service dog, and others are not. What are the characteristics of humans that predict potentially successful partnerships? Do the variables include things such as a liking for dogs? Are the variables more related to desires for independence? Are they associated with a person's expectations of how the partnership will unfold? Are there variables associated with the type of dog placed with a person? How is the age of the veteran associated with partnership success? Do older or younger veterans fare better, or is age not a factor? Other human-partner-related concerns include the effect of predisability lifestyle and activity level, the fit with family and close other support, expectations, values, and beliefs.

What are the criteria for selecting the specific task training to mitigate a specific disability? Will, or can, the person maintain consistency in commands and training for the dog to continue to work well? Will a person choose to train new tasks to mitigate his or her disability as he or she works more with the canine partner and understands what assistance is needed? Other questions are related to health and mobility. Is a dog appropriate for someone who is not able to attend to all of the dog's routine physical needs, such as eating and toileting? For example, might a spinal-cord-injured person benefit from a dog even if he or she needs assistance from an attendant to meet the dog's needs?

Research on Partnerships

Perhaps the most important research question in regard to the establishment and maintenance of a good service dog–human partnership is the quality of the relationship itself. At the core of this question are the health, community integration, and stigma issues that may be decreased or improved by a human–service dog partnership. One burning question among those currently coming into the VA system is the effect of partnerships on potential suicides. Isolation is a significant risk factor for suicidal behavior. Do dogs reduce a veteran's sense of isolation?

What happens when a partnership is not particularly affectionate? There are situations in which the match does not work and a dog is returned to the trainer and replaced by another dog or even no dog. Do the partners have to like each other significantly to have a working relationship? Discussions with service dog handlers suggest that they may be very close to some of their dogs and not to others that they have had during their time of using a service dog. There are partnerships based on mutual respect or at least tolerance, while others are based primarily on affection. What stresses and strains can negatively or positively affect the partnership? Can the dog be close to people other than its human partner? What about family members with whom the partners live? If the dog is effectively a "dog" when not working, can it work well for the human partner?

Some humans in service dog partnerships choose not have a successor dog or retire a dog early. What is it that causes this to happen? Has the person gained sufficient independence that he or she feels confident without a canine partner, or is there something about being partnered that drives the desire not to be in partnership? One could hypothesize that barriers to community integration have contributed to the desire not to be in partnership with a dog. For example, are chronic issues associated with obtaining and maintaining housing so overwhelming that a person chooses not to have a service dog?

Notes

1. This research was supported in part by the Idaho Youth Suicide Awareness to Action Youth Suicide Prevention Project, Substance Abuse and Mental Health

Services Administration, United States Department of Health and Human Services, grant no. 1U79SM059188.

2. This chapter is dedicated to the memory of one of the greatest advocates worldwide for assistance dogs, Ed Eames, PhD (March 7, 1930–October 25, 2009).

References

ADA Amendments Act of 2008, 42 U.S.C. § 12102 (2008).

Air Carrier Access Act, 14 C.F.R. § 382 (2008).

Allen, K. & Blascovich, J. (1996). The value of service dogs for people with severe ambulatory disabilities: A randomized controlled trial. *JAMA* 275, no. 13: 1001–1006.

American Recovery and Reinvestment Act of 2009, 38 U.S.C. § 1714 (2009).

Americans with Disabilities Act of 1990, 42 U.S.C. § 12181 (1990).

Assistance Dogs International, Inc. (2010). http://www.assistancedogsinternational.org/ (accessed March 1, 2012).

Coalition of Assistance Dog Organizations (CADO). (2005). Service Animal Regulations under ADA, January 11. http://www.iaadp.org/CADO2005.html.

Collins, D. M. (2005). Functional, psychological, and economic benefits of service dog partnerships. PhD dissertation, University of Pittsburgh. Available from ProQuest Dissertations and Theses database. (UMI No. 3139662).

Consolidated Appropriations Act of 2010, 38 U.S.C. § 1714 (2009).

Corrigan, P. W. & Watson, A. C. (2002). The paradox of self-stigma and mental illness. *Clinical Psychology: Science & Practice* 9: 35–53.

Corrigan, P., Watson, A., Gracia, G., Slopen, N., Rasinski, K. & Hall, L. (2005). Newspaper stories as measures of structural stigma. *Psychiatric Services* 56, no. 5: 551–556.

C-SPAN. (2008). Interview with Frederick Downs Jr., Chief Prosthetics & Clinical Logistics Officer, Department of Veterans Affairs (Interviewer, Brian Lamb). *Q&A*, June 8. http://www.q-and-a.org/Transcript/?ProgramID=1183.

Department of Justice. (2008). Commonly asked questions about service animals in places of business. January 14. http://www.ada.gov/qasrvc.htm (accessed March 1, 2012).

Department of Justice. (2010). Nondiscrimination on the Basis of Disability in State and Local Government Services, 28 C.F.R. Pt. 35 CRT Docket No. 105; AG Order No. RIN 1190-AA46 as corrected by the 28 CRT Docket No. 105; AG Order No. 3180-2010, RIN 1190-AA46.

Department of Transportation. (2008). Nondiscrimination on the Basis of Disability in Air Travel. 14 C.F.R. Pt. 382. http://airconsumer.ost.dot.gov/rules/Part%20382-2008.pdf.

Department of Veterans Affairs. (2009). *Guide and service dogs.* June 17. http://www1.va.gov/health/ServiceAndGuideDogs.asp (accessed March 1, 2012).

Department of Veterans Affairs. (2010). Guide and service dogs: Frequently asked questions (FAQs). March 24. http://www.prosthetics.va.gov/ (accessed March 1, 2012). Guide_and_Service_Dogs_Frequently_Asked_Questions_FAQs.asp#FAQ1.

Department of Veterans Affairs Health Care Programs Enhancement Act of 2001, 38 U.S.C. § 1714 (2001).

Department of Veterans Affairs, Office of the Inspector General, Office of Audits and Evaluations. (2010). Veterans Health Administration audit of guide and service dog programs. http://www4.va.gov/oig/52/reports/2010/VAOIG-10-01714-188.pdf (accessed March 1, 2012).

Dreazen, Y. J. (2009). "Sit! Stay! Snuggle!": An Iraq vet finds his dog Tuesday. *Wall Street Journal*, July 11. http://online.wsj.com/article/SB124727385749826169.html?KEYWORDS=Sit+Stay+Snuggle (accessed March 1, 2012).

Eames, Toni. (2010). Personal communication to author, July 23.

Eddy, J., Hart, L. A. & Boltz, R. P. (1988). The effect of service dogs on social acknowledgement of people in wheelchairs. *Journal of Psychology* 122, no. 1: 39–45.

Froling, J. (2001). Assistance dog tasks. http://www.iaadp.org/tasks.html (accessed March 1, 2012).

Froling, J. (2009). Service dog tasks for psychiatric disabilities. http://www.iaadp.org/psd_tasks.html (accessed March 1, 2012).

Guest, C. M., Collis, G. M., & McNicholas, J. (2006). Hearing dogs: A longitudinal study of social and psychological effects on deaf and hard-of-hearing recipients. *Journal of Deaf Studies & Deaf Education* 11: 252–261 (accessed March 1, 2012).

Guide Dog Users Inc. (2006). Guide Dog School Survey 2006. Retrieved from http://www.gdui.org/schoolsurvey.html.

Hillman, C. C. (1944). The army rehabilitation program for the blind and the deafened. *JAMA* 125, no. 5: 321–323.

Huessler, L. (2008). [Letter to M. K. Kussman and J. B. Peake], April 16. http://www.psychdog.org/attach/VA_Letter_Denies_SD_Provision.pdf (accessed March 1, 2012).

Kilbury, R., Bordieri, J. & Wong, H. (1996). Impact of physical disability and gender on personal space. *Journal of Rehabilitation* 62, no. 2: 59–64.

Kussman, M. K. (2007). Decision memo concerning providing service dogs to eligible veterans, to J. P. Peake, December 11. http://www.psychdog.org/attach/VA_Letter_Denies_SD_Provision.pdf (accessed March 1, 2012).

Lane, D. R., McNicholas, J., & Collis, G. M. (1998). Dogs for the disabled: Benefits to recipients and welfare of the dog. *Applied Animal Behaviour Science* 59: 49–60.

Link, B. G., Struening, E. L., Neese-Todd, S., Asmussen, S. & Phelan, J. C. (2001). Stigma as a barrier to recovery: The consequences of stigma for the self-esteem of people with mental illnesses. *Psychiatric Services* 52: 1621–1626.

NEADS. (2010). Canines for combat veterans. http://www.neads.org/services_new/military_dog.shtml (accessed March 1, 2012).

Omnibus Appropriations Act, H.R. 1105, 111th Cong. (2009).

Shapiro, T. (1999). "Between empathy and judgment": Comment. *Journal of the American Psychoanalytic Association* 47, no. 2: 390–395.

Stamm, B. H., Kirkwood, A. D., Larsen, D., Piland, N. F., Spearman, R. C., Davis, K. S., Wolfley, D., Tivis, L., Tivis, R. L. & Parker, D. (2006). Final report: Idaho Systems Change Project. Pocatello: Idaho State University.

Storm, S. (2006). Trained by inmates, new best friends for disabled. *New York Times,* October 31. http://www.nytimes.com/2006/10/31/us/31dogs.html?pagewanted= 1&_r=1&sq=service%20dog%20veteran&st=nyt&scp=14 (accessed March 1, 2012).

Texas Hearing and Service Dogs. (2003). Legal rights of people using hearing and service dogs—Texas and U.S. laws. www.servicedogs.org/resources/LAWSUMM .doc (accessed March 1, 2012).

Wahl, O. F. (1995). *Media madness: Public images of mental illness.* New Brunswick, NJ: Rutgers University Press.

Wilson, J. & Lewiecki-Wilson, C. (Eds.). (2001). *Embodied rhetorics: Disability in language and culture.* Carbondale: Southern Illinois University Press.

Yanos, P. T., Rosenfeld, S. & Horowitz, A. V. (2001). Negative and supportive social interactions and quality of life among persons diagnosed with severe mental illness. *Community Mental Health Journal* 37, no. 5: 405–419.

About the Editor

Thomas W. Miller, PhD, ABPP, is Professor Emeritus and Retired Career VA Chief, Psychology Service, at the VA and University of Kentucky College of Medicine. He has been a Senior Research Scientist, Master Teacher, and University Teaching Fellow through his forty-year career and tenure at the University of Kentucky and University of Connecticut. He has served on several national and regional professional and VA task forces and committees. A graduate of the State University of New York, he is a diplomate of the American Board of Professional Psychology, a Fellow of the American Psychological Association, the Association for Psychological Science, and the Royal Society of Medicine. He is a Distinguished Alumnus from the State University of New York and recipient of the APA Distinguished Professional Contributions to Clinical Practice Award. He honors his veteran patients and his father, William J. Miller, a veteran of Patton's Army in World War II and the Korean conflict.

About the Contributors

James W. Anderson, MD, graduated from West Virginia University and Northwestern Medical School. He trained in internal medicine and endocrinology at the Mayo Clinic. After five years at the University of California in San Francisco, he moved to the University of Kentucky in 1973. He directed the Special Diagnostic and Treatment Unit at the Lexington VAMC, the Metabolic Research Group and more than 200 clinical research trials, the Health Management Resources Weight Management Program, and the Obesity Research Network. His biochemistry research related to diabetes and cardiovascular disease and his clinical research related to diabetes, obesity, cardiovascular disease, and nutrition. He has published approximately 400 peer- reviewed articles, books, book chapters, and education articles.

Kirstina Beck works in research support at Idaho State University Institute of Rural Health, with specialized work in graphic design and publication. Among her projects was the graphic design and layout editing for Idaho Suicide Prevention Hotline: Analysis of Options for Decision Making report. Beck was an editorial assistant for the *Journal of Rural Mental Health*. She provides ongoing research support for health-focused grants, publications, and organizations. Her work includes organization of service dog classes and supporting grants and publications specific to both traumatic brain injury and veterans' mental health.

Susan L. Blampied holds a bachelor's degree in international studies–political science from the University of California, San Diego. She is currently a graduate student in sustainable international development and women's and gender studies at Brandeis University focusing on gender-based violence. Blampied worked as an Assistant Case Manager and AmeriCorps VISTA member with the International Rescue Committee assisting people from Bhutan, Iraq, and Afghanistan with refugee resettlement. She also worked as an intern with Survivors of Torture International, San Diego. Her most recent position was at the Idaho State University Institute of Rural Health, where her work centered on suicide prevention research and secondary traumatic stress research.

David C. Booth, MD, trained in cardiology in the Georgetown University Affiliated Hospitals program and worked at the Washington, D.C., VA Medical Center from 1977 to 1979; has been Chief, Cardiology Section, Lexington VA Medical Center since 1984; is an endowed Professor of Medicine, Division of Cardiology, the Gill Heart Institute, University of Kentucky Medical Center; is an everyday working member of the UK-Lexington VA interventional cardiology group; is an assistant in the UK transplant program; and is director of services for pulmonary hypertension for the Lexington VA and the Gill Heart Institute. Both the author's parents were veterans of a foreign war, having served (and met) in the South Pacific in World War II. The author is grateful for the privilege of caring for his veteran patients and the opportunity to participate in randomized VA cooperative studies.

Hayden B. Bosworth, PhD, a health services researcher, focuses on patient and organization level factors to improve chronic care outcomes. He is the Associate Director of the Center for Health Services Research in Primary Care and Career Award Scientist at the Durham VAMC. He is a Research Professor in the Department of Medicine, Division of General Internal Medicine, Research Professor in the Department of Psychiatry and Behavioral Sciences, and Research Professor in the School of Nursing at Duke University Medical Center.

Philip A. DeSimone, MD, is Professor Emeritus, College of Medicine at the VA and University of Kentucky. He served as army helicopter flight surgeon in Vietnam and was awarded a Bronze Star and Flight Wings with oak leaf clusters. On return to the United States, he was assigned to the president's flight detachment in Washington, D.C. Dr. DeSimone became Chief of Medicine at the Lexington VA hospital from 1984 to 1999. He is the recipient of several teaching awards, the third-year clinical clerkship "Golden Apple," and a teaching excellence award from the Fellows of the American College of

Physicians in Internal Medicine. His publications include sixty articles in peer-reviewed journals and six book chapters. He was awarded the first NCI Cooperative Cancer Treatment grant at the University of Kentucky. He now serves as President and CEO of the Markey Cancer Foundation, University of Kentucky.

Andrew S. Dunn, DC, MEd, MS, is the lead chiropractor at the VA Western New York Healthcare System. He supervises an academic affiliation as an Adjunct Associate Professor with New York Chiropractic College. Within VA, he is the chair of the chiropractic field advisory committee, serving as a conduit between the VA chiropractic field and the chiropractic program office. The focus of his research has been VA chiropractic integration, chiropractic clinical outcomes, and post-traumatic stress disorder.

Brian Engdahl, PhD, has served veterans for thirty-two years as a rehabilitation psychologist at the VA Health Care System in Minneapolis, Minnesota. From 1997 to 2007, he provided clinical services to severely injured patients and their families at the VA Polytrauma Rehabilitation Center. He is a faculty member of the Brain Sciences Center at the Minneapolis VA, and an Associate Professor of Psychology at the University of Minnesota, where he earned his BA in psychology in 1975 and his PhD in counseling psychology in 1980. He interned at the Minneapolis VA. He has coauthored more than 100 articles, chapters, and presentations related to trauma: caregiver stress; the effects of combat, captivity and torture; post-traumatic growth; the role of prayer in recovery; and sleep disturbances and brain changes in PTSD.

James L. "Jim" Ford, PhD, LMFT, CSAC, is Assistant Research Scientist and Grant Projects Coordinator in the Family and Community Resilience Laboratory, Department of Child and Family Development, University of Georgia. Jim is a licensed Clinical Member of the American Association for Marriage and Family Therapy, Certified Addiction Counselor, U.S. Air Force Vietnam veteran, and U.S. Merchant Marine Captain. His doctoral dissertation, "Doing the Right Thing: Relational Ethics in Institutional Caregiving for Veterans," was awarded Virginia Tech's Outstanding Dissertation Commendation Award in Social Sciences and the Humanities. Recent publications include articles in the *Journal of Marital and Family Therapy* and the *Journal of Family Psychotherapy*.

Cynthia Livingstone Gibert, MD, MSc, FACP, FIDSA, is Professor of Medicine at the George Washington University (GWU) School of Medicine and Health Sciences and on the faculty of the GWU School of Public Health and Health Services, DC Developmental Center for AIDS Research. She is an attending physician in the Medical Service and Section of Infectious Diseases at the Washington, D.C., Veterans Affairs Medical Center. Dr. Gibert was the President of the VA Society for Practitioners of Infectious Diseases. For more than twenty years, Dr. Gibert has participated in HIV-related clinical research both nationally and internationally.

Betty L. Gillespie, PhD, is a Licensed Clinical Psychologist at Salem Veterans Affairs Medical Center, working with veterans with life-limiting illness and their families at an inpatient palliative care unit. Her current research interests include bereavement, specifically prolonged grief disorder, and the patient-practitioner relationship. She received her PhD in clinical psychology from Virginia Polytechnic Institute and State University in 1993.

Bart N. Green, DC, MSEd, DACBSP, is a chiropractic physician at the Naval Medical Center, San Diego. He serves as the Associate Editor of the Publications Department of the National University of Health Sciences and the Editor-in-Chief of the *Journal of Chiropractic Education*. Previous appointments include Associate Dean of Curriculum at Palmer College of Chiropractic West, adjunct faculty member for the Division of Medical Education at the University of Southern California, and Assistant Professor at the Los Angeles College of Chiropractic. Research interests include utilization of chiropractic among military members, nonsurgical/nonpharmacological methods for treating musculoskeletal pain in military aircrew, and the history of the chiropractic profession.

Robert C. Gresen, PhD, is a clinical psychologist who worked in the Department of Veterans Affairs his entire professional career. He has held various leadership positions, including Chief, Psychology Service; Mental Health Service line manager; and national VA mental health program official. He currently serves as a national consultant to VA Mental Health and is an Assistant Professor of Psychiatry at the Medical College of Wisconsin. Dr. Gresen has been active in several professional organizations and is a recipient of an American Psychological Association Presidential Citation and VA Under Secretary for Health Commendation for his long service to veterans.

Claire D. Johnson, MSEd, DC, DACBSP, is a Professor at the National University of Health Sciences and the Editor in Chief of the *Journal of Manipulative and Physiological Therapeutics, Journal of Chiropractic Medicine*, and *Journal of Chiropractic Humanities*. Previous appointments include Professor at the Southern California University of Health Sciences, Associate Dean of Student Assessment at Palmer College of Chiropractic West, and adjunct faculty member for the Division of Medical Education at the

University of Southern California. Research interests include utilization of chiropractic in integrated healthcare settings, public health issues related to neuromusculoskeletal health, safety of CAM practices, and history of the chiropractic profession.

Kye Y. Kim, MD, is a geriatric psychiatrist and Director, Memory Disorders Clinic/Dementia Unit at Salem Veterans Affairs Medical Center. He is also Professor in Psychiatry at Virginia Tech Carilion School of Medicine. His research interests include dementia care coordination, neuropsychiatric symptoms of dementing disorders, and end-of-life issues in dementia.

John F. Kurtzke, MD, FACP, FAAN (Rear Admiral, US Navy, retired), is Distinguished Professor of Neurology at the Uniformed Services University and Professor Emeritus at Georgetown University. He has written more than 500 publications. His awards include the Legion of Merit from the Navy (twice), the Department of Veterans Affairs Secretary's Distinguished Career Award, the Charcot Award from the International Federation of Multiple Sclerosis Societies, the Lifetime Achievement Award from the Consortium of Multiple Sclerosis Centers, and the John Jay Dystel Prize for Multiple Sclerosis Research from the National Multiple Sclerosis Society and the American Academy of Neurology. He was Consultant in Neurology to the Surgeon General of the Navy (1970–1996) and to the National Naval Medical Center in Bethesda (1966–2000). He received an honorary MD (2000) and Gold Medal and Diploma of Honor (2008) from the University of Ferrara, Italy, and is an Honorary Member of the Neurological Societies of Denmark, France, and Germany. Born in Brooklyn, New York, he attended Brooklyn Preparatory School (1940–1943); St John's University College, Brooklyn (1943–1944, 1946–1948, BS summa cum laude 1948); and Cornell University Medical College, New York (1948–1952, MD 1952). He served in the U.S. Navy (PhM2/c 1944–1946) and USNR (1944–1986, postretirement permissive orders 1986-2000). He interned in internal medicine at Kings County Hospital, Brooklyn (1952–1953); was resident in neurology at the VA Hospital in Bronx, New York (H. G. Wolff Director of Training, 1953–1956); was certified in neurology by the American Board of Psychiatry and Neurology (1958); was Chief of Neurology Service at the VAMC in Coatesville, Pennsylvania (1956–1963) and the VAMC in Washington, D.C. (1963–1995); and has been consultant in neurology and neuroepidemiology at the VAMC in Washington, D.C., since 1995.

Monica Roy, PhD, received her doctorate in clinical psychology from Nova Southeastern University in 2007. She is employed by the VA Boston

Healthcare System as the Program Manager of the Substance Abuse Residential Rehabilitation Treatment Program and outpatient substance abuse treatment program. She is an instructor through Boston University and has an active role in training through the Boston Consortium. She has special interests in the promotion of diversity and multiculturalism in psychology training settings. She is a member of several diversity committees and task forces both within her local VA Medical Center and nationally.

Beth Hudnall Stamm, PhD, holds degrees from Appalachian State University (BS, MA) and the University of Wyoming (PhD). She is a Research Professor at the Institute of Rural Health at Idaho State University. Her previous positions were at the VA National Center for Posttraumatic Stress Disorder and Dartmouth Medical School. She was recognized by the International Society for Traumatic Stress Studies for "fundamental contributions to the international public understanding of trauma." She specializes in traumatic stress, cultural trauma, and secondary traumatic stress. Stamm is a traumatic brain injury survivor.

Charles Stenger, PhD, entered the U.S. Army in 1943 and served as a combat medic with the 106th Infantry Division. He, along with thousands of other American soldiers, was taken prisoner by the German Army in December 1944 during the Battle of the Bulge. Following liberation in the spring of 1945, he resumed his college studies and eventually earned his PhD in clinical psychology. In 1964 he was brought into the Clinical Psychology Division in the VA Central Office as Chief of Psychology for Medical and Surgical Hospitals. In 1976 he became the Associate Director for Psychology in the VA Central Office. He was instrumental in helping VA prepare to serve returning Vietnam War combat veterans and POWs. Upon retirement in 1980, he became a legislative consultant and tireless advocate for POWs through his affiliation with the national service organization the American Ex-POWs. He was a driving force behind the passage of the 1981 Former POW Act, which established a wide array of designated benefits and services for American ex-POWs.

Joseph B. Stone, PhD, SAC III, ICADC, CADC III, is Chief, Gallup Indian Medical Center Behavioral Health Services. Dr. Stone is an enrolled member of the Blackfeet (Aamskapipikuni) and a descendant of the Sioux (Lakota), with Turtle Mountain Chippewa lineage. He was trained by the American Indian Support Project at Utah State University in the professional-scientific psychology program and holds multiple certifications in addictions counseling. Dr. Stone is an expeditionary veteran of the U.S. Navy.

Mitchell T. Wallin, MD, MPH, is an Associate Professor of Neurology at Georgetown University and the University of Maryland School of Medicine. He has written more than forty publications. His awards include the VA Mark Wolcott Award for Clinical Leadership and the Westra Fellowship. Dr. Wallin received his MD from the University of Minnesota–Minneapolis in 1990 and MPH from Johns Hopkins University in 1995. He completed residency training at Northwestern University, the University of Minnesota Hospitals, and Johns Hopkins University. Dr. Wallin is board certified in adult neurology and preventive medicine/public health. He serves as the Associate Director for Clinical Care at the MS Clinic of Excellence-East and Director of Neuroepidemiology and the MS Center at the VAMC-Washington, D.C.

Index

Abraira, C., 3
Achieving the Promise: Transforming Mental Healthcare in America (2003), 106
Action Agenda: Achieving the Promise, Transforming Mental Healthcare in VA (2003), 107
Adams, Mark, 177
Air Carrier Access Act, 364–365
Albert and Mary Lasker Clinical Research Award, 67
Allen, K. & Blascovich, J. (1996), 371, 377
Allen, Mary Lynn, 74
ALLHAT, 26, 76
American Board of Psychiatry and Neurology, 46, 49
American Neurological Association (ANA), 46
American Psychiatric Association, 100
Americans with Disabilities Act of 1990 (ADA), 355
America's former prisoners of war (POWs), 343–351

Diagnostic and Statistical Manual of Mental Disorders (DSM III), 344
facts concerning, 345
Former POW Benefit Act (1981), 349
introduction to, 343–345
POW Medal, 349
"presumptive" disabilities, 348
PTSD and, 344, 348, 349
research, 347–348
story concerning, 345–347
Ampel, Neal, 183
Anderson, James W., 383
angina, 67–68
Asch, D. A., et al., 73, 76
Assistance Dogs International (ADI), 361

Bailey, Pearce, Jr., 48
Barnwell, John, 51, 158
Barry, William H., 76
Bates, Eric, 69
Beck, Kirstina, 383
Beebe, Gilbert, 51

Beebe, G. W. (1975), 347, 350
behavioral health, 129
Behavioral Risk Factor Surveillance
System (BRFSS), 228
Blampied, Susan L., 383–384
blastomycosis, 182
Bluehorse, P. & Zion, J. W. (1993),
299, 305
Bly, Douglas, 244
Boden, William, 70
Bonnet, M. H. & Arand, D. L.
(2007), 228, 235
Bonomo, Robert, 177
Booss, John, 48
Booth, David C., 384
Bosworth, Hayden B., 384
Bradley, Susan F., 185
Brown, J. (1997), 284, 305
Brumley, R., et al. (2007), 203, 210
Brunzell, J. D., 3
Burkitt, Denis, 8
Bush, George W., 106

cancer treatment, veterans' sacrifices
made in quest for, 81–91
Cooperative Studies Program
(CSP), 87
correction factors for 2005
age-adjusted rates by race,
males only, 85 (table)
correction factors for 2005
age-specific rates, all cancer
sites combined, males only,
all races, 86 (table)
estimated proportion of missing
cancer cases for 2005, and VA
adjustment factor for
age-adjusted rate, 84 (table)
IAA of January 1, 2000, 89, 90
incidence of cancer, 83
introduction to, 81–82
National Cancer Act, 82–83
National Cancer strategy, 87–90

PDQ of the NCI (National Cancer
Institute), 89–90
Physicians Data Query
(PDQ), 83
SEER (Surveillance, Epidemiology,
and End Results) data,
83–85
veteran population and, 85–87
war on cancer, 82–85
cardiology care for veterans in VA
healthcare, 63–80
ACME Trial, 68, 69–70
AMI mortality in VHA, 74–75
angina, 67–68
angiography underuse, 73
Angioplasty Compared to Medicine
(ACME) Trial, 69–70
antihypertensive therapy, 66
aspirin in unstable angina trial, 67
available cardiovascular clinical
services in VA, 71
AWESOME Trial, 68
Cardiovascular Assessment,
Reporting, and Tracking, or
CART project, 72
Cooperative Studies Program,
65–70
Cooperative Study on Effects of
Treatment on Morbidity in
Hypertension, 65–67
COURAGE Trial, 68, 70–71
External Peer Review Program
(EPRP), 71
future directions and policies,
75–76
history, 63–65
Lawrence Shaw, 66
National Surgical Quality
Improvement Program, 72
National VA Surgical Risk Study
(NVASRS), 72
NSQIP risk-adjusted database
program, 72–73

ongoing continuous improvement
efforts, 71–75
open-heart surgery, 72
Time Is Life program, 71, 72, 74
VA Vasodilator in Heart
Failure Trial (VHeFT-1),
67, 68–69
VANQUISH Trial, 68
CARES: Capital Asset Realignment
for Enhanced Services,
102–104
CARES-Mental Health Workgroup,
103–104
Casalino, L. P., et al., 58, 60
Casarett, D. (2005), 205, 210
Casarett, D., et al. (2003), 198, 211
Casarett, D., et al. (2008), 206, 211
celecoxib (Celebrex®), 29
Chalmers, Thomas, 67, 76
Chen, S., Wagner, T. H. & Barnett,
P. G. S (2001), 97, 130
chiropractic in veterans' healthcare,
135–156
academic affiliations, 146–148
adverse events, 144
American Chiropractic Association
definition of chiropractic,
137 (box)
benefits of chiropractic care,
142–143
chiropractic care, 135–138
Chiropractic Care Available to All
Veterans Act, 151
chiropractic education, 140
chiropractic examination, 136
chiropractic treatment, 136
common complaints, 146
complementary and alternative
medicine (CAM), 135–136
conclusion concerning, 151
cost effectiveness of, 144–145
Council on Chiropractic Education
(CCE), 140

doctor of chiropractic programs in
the U.S., 141 (box)
expansion of, 146
future of, 150–151
GI Bill and, 138
historical overview, 145
history of chiropractic, 138–140
inclusion of chiropractic care in
VHA, 145–149
integrated service networks
offering chiropractic care,
147 (fig.)
integration into the VA, 138–139,
142
introduction to, 135
leadership structure, 148–149
legislation pertinent to chiropractic
care in VA, 138–139
legislative history of, 145–146
licensure and postgraduate training,
140–142, 146
patient education and lifestyle
recommendations, 136–137
patient satisfaction, 143–144
policies and practice, 149–150
programmatic growth of, 146
research, 148
scope of chiropractic care in
VHA, 149–150
therapeutic exercise, 136
VA chiropractic job description,
149
VHA Directive 2009-059 for, 136
Clinton, Bill, 127
Coalition of Assistance Dog
Organizations (2005), 356
coccidiomycosis, 182–183
Cohen, B. M. & Cooper, M. Z.
(1954), 347, 350
Cohn, Jay, 65
Colwell, J. A., 3, 24
Combat Stress Recovery Program
(CSRP), 252

Committee on the Care of Severely
	Chronically Mentally Ill
	Veterans (SMI Committee), 98
Conno, Stephen R., 199

Data Safety and Monitoring
	Board, 67
DeJong, David H. (2008), 294, 306
DeJong, R. (1982), 50, 60
depression, 233, 320, 348
DeSimone, Philip A., 384–385
Detre, Kathleen, 64
diabetes and veterans in primary
	care, 3–44
	antiplatelet agents for diabetic
		patients, 21
	artificial pancreas and insulin
		clamp techniques, studies
		with, 8–10
	cardiovascular disease, 25–26
	cardiovascular risk factors,
		reductions of, 13–19
	clinical studies with oat bran, beans,
		and psyllium, 14–17
	conclusions concerning, 30
	contributions of VA cooperative
		studies to diabetes management,
		21–24
	diabetes and evidence-based
		medicine, 28–29
	diabetes control and cardiovascular
		complications, 23–24
	dietary protein and
		monounsaturated fats for
		diabetic individuals, assessing
		the role of, 19–21
	evidence-based medicine related
		to diabetes, VA's contribution
		to, 24–30
	glycemic effects of protein intake, 19
	HCF maintenance diet, long-term
		studies with, 10–11
	HDL intervention trial, 22–23
	high carbohydrate, high-fiber
		(HCF) diet, development
		of, 5–8
	implanted insulin pump
		study, 21–22
	insulin requirements of patients
		with Type 1 diabetes estimated
		with the artificial pancreas on
		low-carbohydrate, low-fiber
		(LCLF) and high-carbohydrate,
		high-fiber (HCHF) diets,
		9 (table)
	introduction to, 3–4
	laboratory studies of mechanisms
		and lipoprotein effects, 17–19
	lipoprotein responses to the HCF
		diet, 13–14
	macronutrient content of diets
		recommended for individuals
		with diabetes, 5 (table)
	monounsaturated fats for saturated
		and polyunsaturated fats, effects
		of substituting, 20
	nutritional guidelines, 4–5
	nutritional management, advances
		in, 4–11
	obese diabetic individuals,
		management of, 11–12
	obese diabetic individuals, response
		to energy-restricted, high-fiber
		diets, 12 (table)
	obese individuals without diabetes,
		treatment of, 12–13
	obesity, 26–27
	responses of lean diabetic patients
		to weight-maintaining HCF
		diets, 7 (table)
	role of a pharmaceutical company in
		selective reporting of clinical trial
		data, 29
	soy protein for diabetic patients
		with nephropathy, benefits of,
		19–20

*Diagnostic and Statistical Manual of
    Mental Disorders (DSM III)*, 344
Downs, Fredrick, Jr., 359
Duckworth, W., 3
Dunn, Andrew S., 385

Eberly, R. E. & Engdahl, B. E.
    (1991), 348, 350
end-of-life care, 195–216
    Advance care planning (ACP),
        197–198
    capacity questions and care
        planning, 204
    conclusion concerning, 209–210
    defining end-of-life care, 196–199
    ethical issues, 204–206
    Family Assessment of Treatment at
        End of Life (FATE), 200
    Functional Living Index-Cancer, 202
    history and current VA initiatives,
        199–200
    hospice partnership, 200
    introduction to, 195–196
    new directions in, 208–209
    Palliative Care Consult Team
        (PCCT), 201
    palliative EOL care, 196–198
    person-centered palliative care,
        207–208
    policy, 200–202
    quality and cost, 202–204
    Robert Wood Johnson Foundation
        on, 207
    World Health Organization on, 207
Engdahl, Brian, 385
Epilepsy Centers of Excellence, 56
Evans, Lane, 101
External Peer Review Program
    (EPRP), 71

Feingold, Sydney, 176
female Native veteran with PTSD,
    hypothetical case study of,
    286–293

assessment and treatment
    outcome, 288–289
comprehensive cultural evaluation,
    292–293
cultural elements of treatment, 292
cultural factor is in development,
    289–290
cultural group, 289
cultural perspectives on PTSD, 290
diagnosis, 289
family history, 288
functional assessment, 291–292
history of present illness, 286–287
language, 289
patient identification, 286
psychiatric history and previous
    treatment, 287
social and developmental history,
    287–288
social stress and support, 291
tribal explanations and models,
    290–291
tribally based culture and spiritual
    treatment, 291
See also Native American veterans
    and post-traumatic stress
    disorder; post-traumatic stress
    disorder (PTSD)
Fihn, Stephan, D., et al., 75, 77
Fletcher, Ross, 65, 76
Floerchinger, D. S. (1991), 294, 306
Ford, James L. "Jim," 385
Former POW Benefit Act
    (1981), 349
Freis, Edward, 65, 66, 67
Froling, J. (2001, 2009), 361, 378
Functional Living Index-Cancer, 202

Gage, Andrew, 64, 76
Gainesville VAMC, 74
Galgiani, John, 183
Garrett, J. T. & Garrett, M. W.
    (1994), 298, 306

Gelfman, L. P., Meier D. E., et al. (2008), 202, 212
Gerding, Dale, 177
GI Bill, 138, 320
Giacomini, John, 69
Gibert, Cynthia Livingstone, 385–386
Gillespie, Betty L., 386
glucosamine/chondroitin Arthritis Trial (GAIT), 29
Grassman, D. (2007), 201, 212
Grassman, Deborah, 196
Greatbatch, Wilson, 64
Green, Bart N., 386
Gresen, Robert C., 386
Grover, Fred, 72
Gulf War Veterans' Illnesses (GWVI), 178–179

Hamblen, J. (2010), 301, 307
Hammermeister, Karl, 72
Hammond, William, 46
Hankin, C. S., et al. (1999), 326, 339
Hartigan, Pamela, 70
Hawley, Paul, 158
Hays, Marguerite. (1980), 66, 78
Health Care and Education Reconciliation Act, 58
Henry, R. R., Wallace, P. & Olefsky, J. M. (1986), 39
Henry, R. R., 3
Hermann, Gustav, 244
Herring, R. D. (1994), 297, 307
Hill, Austin Bradford, 65
Hillman, Charles C., 354, 368
Hines, Edward J., 177
histoplasmosis, 183–184
A Historical Look at the Establishment of the Department of Veterans Affairs Research and Development Program (Hays), 66
HIV/AIDS, 160–168

HMR® Weight Management Program, 12
Hodgson, John, 69
Homeless Women Veterans and Homeless Veterans With Children Act of 2009, 332
homelessness, 120, 129, 331–332
Hong Kong flu epidemic (1968), 160
Horijsi, C., Heavy Runner-Craig, B. & Pablo, J. (1992), 298, 307
Huber, Warren V., 48
Hultgren, Herbert, 64
Hwang, S. S., et al. (2003), 206, 213
hypertension management, 26

Iglehart, J. K., 53–54
infectious diseases, healthcare for veterans with, 157–193
  "The Evolution of the Cooperative Studies in Chemotherapy of Tuberculosis of the Veterans Administration and Armed Forces of the USA" (Tucker), 158–159
  AIDS vaccine, 167
  anaerobic infections, 176–177
  ART (HAART), 161–162
  atypical pathogens, 178–179
  AZT therapy, 161
  blastomycosis, 182
  Clostridium difficile disease, 176–177
  coccidiomycosis, 182–183
  conclusions concerning, 186
  diabetic foot infections, 185–186
  early history of the Veterans Affairs hospitals and tuberculosis, 157–159
  fungal infections, 182–184
  Gulf War Veterans' Illnesses (GWVI), 178–179
  HAIISS: Healthcare-Associated Infection and Influenza

Surveillance System,
173–175
healthcare-associated infections,
171–172
histoplasmosis, 183–184
HIV and aging, 164–165
HIV basic science research,
166–168
HIV care in VA, 163–164
HIV drug resistant, viral load, and
viral dynamics, 167–168
HIV screening, 165–166
HIV treatment trials, 161–163
human immunodeficiency virus
(HIV)/acquired
immunodeficiency syndrome,
160–161
immunizations, 169–170
infections in special VA
populations, 184–186
Infectious Diseases Program, 159
influenza, 160
Inpatient Prospective Payment
System hospitals conditions, 171
Legionella pneumophilia, 178
MRSA Initiative, 172–173
multidrug-resistant organisms,
177–178
Mycoplasma and the Eaton
agent, 178
National Healthcare Safety
Network (NNSH), 175
National Nosocomial Infections
Surveillance System
(NNIS), 175
National Surgical Quality
Improvement Program
(NSQIP), 170–171
OPTions in Management with
Antiretrovirals (OPTIMA)
Trial, 162–163
Public Health Strategic Health
Care Group (PHSHG), 159

QUERI HIV-Hepatitis initiative,
165–166
research, 175–184
Shingles Prevention Study, 169
spinal cord injury, 185–186
*The State of Care for Veterans with
HIV/AIDS*, 163
Strategic Timing of Anti-retroviral
Therapy (START), 162
Strategies for Management of
Antiretroviral Therapy
(SMART), 162
surgical infections, 170–171
surveillance and prevention,
170–175
unculturable pathogens search,
179–180
VACS Risk Index, 165
viral hepatitis B and C disease,
180–181
viral hepatitis C infection, 168–169
viral infections, 160–169
viral influenza vaccine, 170
insomnia, 229
International Association of Assistant
Dog Partners (IAADP),
359–360
Ishak, Kamal, 180

Jesse, Robert, 71
Johnson, Claire D., 386–387
Joseph, Warren S., 185
*Journal of the American Medical
Association*, 354
Justice, Amy C., 164

Kaldjian, L. C., et al. (2009), 199, 213
Kasee, C. R. (1995), 297, 308
Keehn, R. J. (1980), 347, 350
Kendall, J. W. (1995), 54, 60
Khuri, Shukri, 72
Kim, Kye Y., 387
Kirkendall, Walter M., 66

Kirschner, N. & Barr, M. S. (2010), 58, 60
Kizer, Kenneth, 94–95, 98, 127
Kramer, B., et al. (2009a), 296, 308
Kulka, R. A., et al.(1990), 259, 308
Kurtzke, J. F., 54
Kurtzke, John F., 387
Kussman, Michael, 172
Landrum, M. B., et al. (2004), 74, 78
Larder, B. A., Darby, G. & Richman, D. D. (1989), 161, 167, 190

Lexington VAMC, 17, 18
lifestyles and health behaviors of veterans, 219–241
    adherence to treatment, 223
    Behavioral Risk Factor Surveillance System (BRFSS), 228
    cardiovascular disease, 222–223
    conclusion concerning, 233–234
    diabetes and, 222
    factors related to, 223–224
    Health Services Research and Development Service (HSR&D), 220
    INTERHEART study, 223
    low-density lipoprotein cholesterol (LDL-C) intervention, 222
    medication adherence, 229–230
    mental and health behaviors, 233
    MOVE! Weight-Management Program for Veterans, 225
    multiple behavior interventions, 230–232
    My HealtheVet (MHV), 224
    obesity, 225–226
    ongoing VA work in, 223–232
    overview of, 219–223
    physical activity, 226–227
    Quality Enhancement Research Initiative (QUERI), 220
    self-management education, 221–222
    self-management support tools, 223–224
    sleep, 228–229
    smoking, 227–228
    telemedicine, 221
    Veteran Study To Improve The Control of Hypertension (V-STITCH), 231
    Veterans Affairs Medical Centers (VAMCs) and, 222
    VHA National Center for Health Promotion and Disease Prevention (NCHP), 220–221
Lipsky, Benjamin A., 185
local recovery coordinators (LRCs), 115

Manson, S. M. (1996, 1997, 2000), 285, 309
Masland, Richard L., 50
medication adherence, 229–230
Medicine, B. (1988), 296, 309
Mental Health Strategic Plan (MHSP), 107–109
mental healthcare, 93–133
    Achieving the Promise: Transforming Mental Healthcare in America (2003), 106
    Action Agenda: Achieving the Promise, Transforming Mental Healthcare in VA (2003), 107
    Action Agenda Steering Committee work groups, 107–108
    American Psychiatric Association and, 100
    CARES: Capital Asset Realignment for Enhanced Services initiative, 102–104
    CARES-Mental Health Workgroup, 103–104
    clinical practice guidelines, 128

Committee on the Care of Severely
Chronically Mentally Ill
Veterans (SMI Committee)
and, 98, 100
Comprehensive Mental Health
Strategic Plan (MHSP), 104
current status of, 123–126
DUSHOM memorandums,
116–117
evidence-based treatments
(EBTs), 120
expansion of, 115–116
Filling Vacant Leadership Positions
in Mental Health directive, 127
funding, 112–115
GAO 1999 report, 101–102
history of, 93–123
homeless services, 120, 129
incarcerated veterans, 120
Kenneth Kizer, 94–95, 98, 127
local recovery coordinators
(LRCs), 115
Mental Health Program Changes
directive, 127
*Mental Health Program Guidelines
for the New Veterans Health
Administration* (1999), 128
Mental Health Strategic Healthcare
Group, 105
Mental Health Strategic Plan
(MHSP), 107–108,
111–112
MyHealtheVet, 129
National Alliance for the Mentally
Ill (NAMI) and, 98–100
new directions for, 129–130
Office of Productivity, Efficiency
and Staffing (OPES), 105
performance measures and
monitors, 98
policy, 126–128
post-traumatic stress disorder
(PTSD), 120–121, 125, 126

post-traumatic stress disorder
(Special Committee on),
100–101
President's New Freedom
Commission, 106, 107–110,
118, 119, 133
Psychosocial Rehabilitation and
Recovery Center (PRRC), 119
reorganization of the VHA, 94–97
spending for VA mental health
treatment, 96–97
staffing reductions in the VHA, 96
staffing resources, 104–105
Substance Abuse and Mental
Health Services Administration
(SAMHSA), 107–108
substance use disorder services, 97
suicide prevention coordinator,
115, 121
telemental healthcare expansion,
110, 115
total number of VHA trainees
by discipline (2006–2011),
126 (fig.)
training, 125–126 (box)
*Uniform Mental Health Services in
VA Medical Centers and Clinics*
handbook (USH), 117–121
*Uniform Mental Health Services
in VA Medical Centers and
Clinics* handbook (USH),
implementation status of,
122–123 (box)
VA primary mission and, 120
Veterans Eligibility Reform Act
(1996), 126–127
Veterans Equitable Resource
Allocation System (VERA), 112
Veterans Integrated Services
Networks (VISNs), 94–95
VHA budget for, 93
workload standards, 105–106
Miller, Thomas W., 381

Montgomery G.I. Bill, 320
Morris, Kenneth, 69
Morrison, R. S., et al. (2008), 203, 214
Mufson, Maurice A., 178
multiple behavior interventions,
    230–232
Multiple Sclerosis Centers of
    Excellence, 55
My HealtheVet (MHV), 129, 224

Nagler, Benedict, 51
National Advisory Committee on
    Women Veterans, 321
National Alliance for the Mentally Ill
    (NAMI), 98
National VA Surgical Risk Study
    (NVASRS), 72
Native American veterans and
    post-traumatic stress
    disorder, 255–312
  adequate caregiver behavior,
    implications of, 265–267
  Center for Minority Veterans,
    284
  community and family variables,
    298
  compromise behavioral immunity
    (CBI), 269–270, 274
  conclusion concerning, 303–304
  contemporary tribal communities,
    implications for, 283
  cultural knowledge and sensitivity,
    295–296
  detrimental systematic influences,
    262–263
  Directions and new developments
    for, 301–303
  dispossession and biological warfare,
    271–273
  federal and religious Indian
    boarding schools, 276–280
  history of Native veterans,
    257–258
  inadequate caregiver behavior,
    implications of, 267–270
  introduction to, 256–257
  issues and challenges, 285
  Mental Health and Behavioral
    Science (MHBS), 284
  Native American Cemetery Act
    (2003), 284
  Native American Veterans Home
    Loan Act (2001), 284
  Native anxiety and depression
    secondary to colonization,
    273–274
  Native healing ways, 294
  Native veterans' policies, 283–284
  Native veterans' solutions, 293–300
  Native women, 296–297
  peyote rituals, appropriate tribal
    use of, 300
  postcolonial neurodevelopment and
    developmental psychopathology,
    270–283
  posttraumatic stress disorder
    and the Indian wars, 274–275
  prevalence and incidence among
    American Indian military service
    members, 258–259
  Readjustment Counseling Service
    (RCS), 284
  relocation, alcohol, and alcoholism,
    282
  review and methodology
    procedures, 261–262
  Sand Creek massacre, 274–275
  silence and language issues,
    298–299
  summary of, 301
  systematic influences on tribal
    communities, 260–261
  theoretical background,
    264–265
  traditional cultural practices and
    beliefs, value of, 294–295

traditional treatment for
PTSD, 300
traditional tribal "group therapies,"
299–300
tribal archetypes (Heyoka), 297
tribal historical trauma and
postcolonial stress, 260–261
tribal intergenerational PTSD and
compromised behavioral
immunity, 263–264
tribal judicial systems, 299
tribal spirituality, 272–273
value of traditional cultural practices
and beliefs, 294–295
value of tribal affiliation and
spirituality, 298
wartime PTSD and tribal
termination, 280–282
*Wounded Spirits, Ailing Hearts
Training Manual* (Manson
2000), 259
See also female Native veteran with
PTSD, hypothetical case study
of; post-traumatic stress disorder
(PTSD)
Nefzger, M. D. (1970), 347, 350
neurological healthcare for veterans,
45–61
development of neurology in the
United States, 45–46
future of, 56–59
neurological research and the
veterans' healthcare system,
50–52
neurology care and training in
the veterans' healthcare
system, 46–50
Patient Aligned Care Team
(PACT), 57
patient-centered medical home
(PCMH) models, 58–59
postgraduate neurological specialty
training, 57 (table)

specialty centers for neurological
disorders, 55–56
T-21 initiatives, 57–58
T-21 Strategic Goals, 2009,
58 (table)
traumatic brain injury (TBI), 57
U.S. Army General Hospitals in the
United States during WW II
transferred to the Veterans
Administration, November
1945–September 1946,
49 (table)
VA neurology training and care
changes in the 1990s, 52–55
New England Journal of Medicine, 67,
68, 69, 70, 76, 172
Nixon, Richard, 82
NSAIDS, 144
Nuttall, F., 19, 24

Obama, Barack, 284
obesity, 26–28
Office of Productivity, Efficiency and
Staffing (OPES), 105
O'Rourke, Robert, 70
orthotics and prosthetics healthcare for
veterans, 243–253
assistive and adaptive program,
246–247
Automobile Adaptive Equipment
(AAE), 246
Combat Stress Recovery Program
(CSRP), 252
contemporary policies, 245
developments and new directions
in, 245–246
Driver's Rehabilitation
Program, 246
HISA grants, 248
history and policies of, 243–245
Home Improvements and
Structural Alterations (HISA)
program, 246

orthotics and prosthetics healthcare for
    veterans (*continued*)
  Internet address, 252
  introduction to, 243
  Iraq and Afghanistan war wounded,
    248–249
  Patient Protection and Affordability
    Care Act, 245
  Persian Gulf War veterans, 248
  Project Odyssey™, 252
  prosthetic and orthotic
    laboratories, 247
  prosthetic healthcare for veterans,
    future directions of, 250–251
  Prosthetics and Sensory Aids
    Service (PSAS), 245, 246, 248
  Special Home Adaptation (SHA)
    grant, 246
  special programs for veterans with
    disabilities, 248
  specialists, services, and training,
    247
  Specially Adapted Housing (SAH)
    grant, 246
  specific purpose funding, 245
  treating soldiers and pioneering
    medicine, 249
  Wounded Warrior Project™,
    251–252
  Wounded Warrior Project
    Restore™, 252

Page, W., Engdahl, B. & Eberly, R.
    (1997), 347, 351
Parisi, Alfred, 76
Parkinson's Disease Research,
    Education & Clinical Centers, 55
Patient Aligned Care Team
    (PACT), 57
Patient Protection and Affordability
    Care Act, 245
Patient Protection and Affordable Care
    Act, 58

patient-centered medical home
    (PCMH) models, 58–59
Perlin, Jonathon, 107
Perry, B. (2002), 264, 310
pharmaceutical company in selective
    reporting of clinical trial data,
    role of, 29
physical activity, 226–227
Physicians Data Query (PDQ), 83
Porte, D., Jr., 3, 41
post-traumatic stress disorder (PTSD)
  prisoners of war (POWs) and, 344,
    348, 349
  Special Committee on Post-
    Traumatic Stress Disorder,
    100–101
  uniqueness of, 120–121
  VA research, 249
  women military veterans and,
    320, 335
  See also female Native veteran with
    PTSD, hypothetical case study
    of; Native American veterans
    and post-traumatic stress
    disorder
POW Medal, 349
President's New Freedom Commission,
    106, 107, 118, 119, 133
Principi, Anthony, 101
Pritikin, Nathan, 8
provider education, 231–232

Readjustment Counseling Service
    program, 93–94
Reaven, G. M., 3, 42
Reiber, G. E., et al. (2010), 250, 253
Relman, David A., 179, 180
Rice, Lou, 177
Robert Wood Johnson
    Foundation, 207
Roy, Monica, 387–388
Ruff, Robert, 48
Rumsfeld, John, 72

Salkin, David, 182
Scurfield, R. F. (1995), 300, 310
Seeff, Leonard B., 180, 181
Seguin, Edward, 46
service dogs and their use for veterans
    with disabilities, 353–379
  accessibility regulations, conflicting,
    367
  Assistance Dogs International
    (ADI), 361
  challenges, 370–372
  Coalition of Assistance
    Dog Organizations
    (2005), 356
  comparison of VA benefits for
    service and guide dogs,
    360–361
  current service dog practice,
    359–360
  definition of a disability, 355
  definition of an assistant animal/
    dog, 355–357
  discriminatory belief systems,
    368–370
  dog size, 369–370
  economics and finance, 370–371
  eligibility based on discharge, 358
  future issues, 373–376
  guide dogs (GD), 358, 362
  hearing dogs (HD), 362
  hidden disabilities, 369
  history of, 353–354
  housing, 364
  International Association of
    Assistant Dog Partners
    (IAADP), 359–360
  key legal definitions (summary),
    356
  new directions in, 372–376
  nonassistance dogs with
    health-related contributions,
    366–367
  organizations providing, 359
  origins of VA providing assistance
    dogs, 354–355
  policies, 355
  PSDs, 366
  psychiatric service dogs, 372–373
  public access rights under the ADA
    of persons with a disability using
    a service dog, 363–365
  public access training and task
    training, 362–363
  "Puppies Behind Bars," 374
  research on dogs themselves,
    374–376
  research on human-service dog
    partnerships, 375–376
  research on partnerships, 376
  research on service dog partnerships,
    371–372
  school and owner training, 367
  service dog movement, 374
  service dogs: "allowed but not
    required," 358
  service dogs (SD), 362
  stereotypes, 368–369
  stigma, 368
  task training, 363
  Transportation, 364–365
  types of assistance dogs, 365–367
  types of assistance dogs to mitigate a
    qualifying disability, 361–362
  VA policy in regard to successor
    dogs (clarification), 373
  VA struggles with, 358–359
  VA's policy position on assistance
    animals, 372–373
sexual trauma and harassment,
    326–327, 335
Shaw, Lawrence, 66
Shinseki, Erik K., 57, 129, 331
Silver, S. (1994), 300, 310
Sledge, W., Boydstun, J. & Rabe, M.
    (1980), 344, 351
sleep, 228–229

smoking, 227–228
Society of Chest Pain Centers, 74
Speed, N., Engdahl, B., Schwartz, J. &
    Eberly, R. (1989), 345, 351
Stamm, Beth Hudnall, 388
Steele, John, 182
Stenger, Charles, 388
Stone, Joseph B., 388
Strausbaugh, Larry, 184
Streptomycin Committee, 158
Substance Abuse and Mental Health
    Services Administration
    (SAMHSA), 106–107

T-21 initiatives, 57
Taguchi, James, 67
Takaro, Timothy, 64
telemedicine, 221
Theis, K. A., Rao, J. K., Anderson, L.
    & Thompson, P. (2007),
    203, 215
traumatic brain injury (TBI), 57
Trowell, Hugh, 8
Tucker, William, 158, 193

Unger, R. H., 3
*Uniform Mental Health Services in VA
    Medical Centers and Clinics*
    handbook (USH), 117–121
    implementation status of,
    122–123 (box)
U.S. Army General Hospitals in the
    United States during World
    War II transferred to the
    Veterans Administration,
    November 1945–September
    1946, 49 (table)

VA Coop Study No. 4, 64
VA Cooperative Study Program
    (CSP), 51
VA Home Loan Guaranty Program, 321

VA life insurance coverage, 321
VA Merit Review Program, 17, 18
VA primary mission, 120
VA residency training programs, 53
Veteran Study To Improve The
    Control of Hypertension
    (V-STITCH), 231
Veterans Eligibility Reform Act
    (1996), 126–127
Veterans Equitable Resource
    Allocation System (VERA), 112
Veterans Integrated Services Networks
    (VISNs), 94–95
VHA National Center for Health
    Promotion and Disease
    Prevention (NCHP), 220–221
VHA National Suicide Prevention
    Hotline, 121
Viswanathan, Mohan, 8
Vogt, D., et al. (2006), 341

Walker, Arthur M., 51
Wallace, A. E., Sheehan, E. P. &
    Young-Xu, Y. (2009), 329, 341
Wallin, Mitchell T., 389
Walters, Harry, 321
Weintraub, William, 70
Willis, Park III, 76
women military veterans, healthcare
    for, 313–342
    "Survey of Female Veterans: A
       Study of Needs, Attitudes
       and Experiences of Women
       Veterans," 321
    barriers to care, 332–333
    Center for Women Veterans, 322
    challenges faced by women
       veterans and future directions,
       324–325 (table)
    changes for, 321–323
    combat-related trauma, 328–329
    educational attainment and
       employment, 318–319

geographic distribution of women
veterans, 317
historical review, 313–316
homecoming readjustment,
330–331
Homeless Women Veterans and
Homeless Veterans With
Children Act of 2009, 332
homelessness, 331–332
impact of military service on women
veterans' health, 323
military sexual trauma and
harassment, 326–327
National Advisory Committee on
Women Veterans, 321
new directions for, 334–338
new directions in research and
training on women veterans,
336–338 (table)
population of women veterans,
322–323
Public Law 98-160, 321
Public Law 103-446, 322
race and marital status, 318
satisfaction with care, 333–334

substance use, 329–330
today's woman veteran, 316–317
today's woman veteran,
demographics of, 317
use of veterans' healthcare benefits,
319–321
VA Home Loan Guaranty
Program, 321
VA life insurance coverage, 321
Zero Tolerance for Veteran
Homelessness Act of 2009, 331
World Health Organization, 207
*Wounded Spirits, Ailing Hearts Training
Manual* (Manson 2000), 259
Wounded Warrior Project
Restore™, 252
Wounded Warrior Project™, 251–252

Yancy, W. S., Jr. & Voils, C. I.
(in press), 226, 241

Zero Tolerance for Veteran
Homelessness Act of 2009, 331
Zimmerman, Hyman J., 180

The Praeger Handbook of Veterans' Health

Volume I
History, Eras, and Global Healthcare

Volume II
Programs of Care and Groups with Special Needs

Volume III
Mental Health Treatment and Rehabilitation

Volume IV
Future Directions in Veterans' Healthcare

THE PRAEGER HANDBOOK OF VETERANS' HEALTH

History, Challenges, Issues, and Developments

Volume III: Mental Health Treatment and Rehabilitation

Thomas W. Miller, Editor

PRAEGER

AN IMPRINT OF ABC-CLIO, LLC
Santa Barbara, California • Denver, Colorado • Oxford, England

Library of Congress Cataloging-in-Publication Data

The Praeger handbook of veterans' health : history, challenges, issues, and developments / Thomas W. Miller, editor.
    v. cm.
 Includes bibliographical references and index.
 ISBN 978-0-313-38349-6 (hardcover : alk. paper) — ISBN 978-0-313-38350-2 (ebook)
1. Veterans—Health and hygiene—United States. 2. Veterans—Care—United States. 3. Veterans—United States—History. I. Miller, Thomas W., 1943– II. Title: Handbook of veterans' health.
 UB369.P73 2012
 362.1086'97—dc23
                                    2012025159

ISBN: 978-0-313-38349-6
EISBN: 978-0-313-38350-2

16 15 14 13 12   1 2 3 4 5

This book is also available on the World Wide Web as an eBook.
Visit www.abc-clio.com for details.

Praeger
An Imprint of ABC-CLIO, LLC

ABC-CLIO, LLC
130 Cremona Drive, P.O. Box 1911
Santa Barbara, California 93116-1911

This book is printed on acid-free paper ∞
Manufactured in the United States of America

It is the VETERAN, not the preacher, who has given us freedom of religion.

It is the VETERAN, not the reporter, who has given us freedom of the press.

It is the VETERAN, not the poet, who has given us freedom of speech.

It is the VETERAN, not the campus organizer, who has given us freedom to assemble.

It is the VETERAN, not the lawyer, who has given us the right to a fair trial.

It is the VETERAN, not the politician, who has given us the right to vote.

It is the VETERAN, who salutes the Flag, It is the VETERAN, who serves under the Flag.

—Author Unknown

Contents

VOLUME III
MENTAL HEALTH TREATMENT AND REHABILITATION

Acknowledgments   ix

Foreword   xi
Jacob B. Gadd

Editor's Foreword   xv

**Part I   Mental Health and Mental Illness Research,
Education, and Clinical Centers   1**

1   Primary Care–Mental Health Integration   3
Delilah O. Noronha

2   Alcohol and Substance Abuse Programs: History, Policies,
Challenges, Issues, Developments, and New Directions   51
Susan R. Tate, Jennifer Mrnak-Meyer, and Jessica C. Tripp

3   Integrating Smoking Cessation into Mental Healthcare for
Post-traumatic Stress Disorder: Transforming Treatment
Delivery in the Veterans Health Administration   79
*Carol A. Malte, Andrew J. Saxon, Kim Hamlett-Berry,
and Miles E. McFall*

4   Suicide Risk among Veterans of Military Service   123
Mark S. Kaplan, Bentson H. McFarland, and Nathalie Huguet

5 VA Healthcare for Women Veterans Experiencing Trauma   155
Carole A. Goguen

6 Treating Substance Use Disorders within the VA Healthcare
System   169
Stephen Tracy, Sara Tavakoli, Simona Stolpner, and Jodie Trafton

7 The Social Context of Post-trauma Adjustment in Veterans   199
Bradley E. Belsher, Josef I. Ruzek, and Matthew J. Cordova

8 Polytrauma Care and Treatment in Veterans' Healthcare   227
Jeanne M. Bennett

9 Military Traumatic Brain Injury and the Postconcussive
Syndrome   251
Louis M. French, Victoria C. Anderson-Barnes,
Katherine Brazaitis, and Aditya A. Bhagwat

10 Healthcare and Issues of Racial and Ethnic Diversity   279
Kathleen M. McNamara

**Part II   Rehabilitation Care and Treatment
for Veterans   305**

11 Trauma-focused Psychosocial Rehabilitation   307
Walter Erich Penk, Dolores K. Little, and Nathan D. Ainspan

12 Psychosocial Rehabilitation and Recovery Services   333
Samantha Kettle, Loretta E. Braxton, Valerie Fox,
and Joshua Tiegreen

13 Eradicating Mental Illness Stigma for Active Military
Personnel and Veterans   365
Ann D. Kirkwood, Beth Hudnall Stamm, and Chandra R. Story

14 Engaging Homeless Veterans in Healthcare   389
Thomas P. O'Toole

About the Editor   421

About the Contributors   423

Index   433

Acknowledgments

An endeavor of this magnitude has taken several years and the efforts of numerous colleagues and friends in the Department of Veterans Affairs and others interested in the health and well-being of our veterans and their families in the general public. It is to those in the Department of Veterans Affairs Central Office in Washington, D.C., their regional Veterans Integrated Service Networks (VISNs), and regional as well as local Veteran Affairs medical centers that I am extremely grateful. Their efforts have addressed contacting the right people, gaining access to important information, manuscript preparation completion, reviews, and providing detailed guidance in the final chapters and volumes.

Special appreciation is expressed to the efforts of the Department of Veterans Affairs, Office of Communications, and in particular Mr. Daniel Bruneau, Director of Communications; Christine A. Pons, Regional Office of Public Affairs, Department of Veterans Affairs; and Charles F. Castner, Staff Attorney, Department of Veterans Affairs.

The assistance of Darlene Richardson, the Department of Veterans Affairs historian, has been helpful in completing several of the chapters, as have external organizations committed to the care and treatment of our veterans, including the American Legion, Veterans of Foreign Wars, and Paralyzed Veterans of America.

To a cadre of former and current colleagues and friends within the Department of Veterans Affairs, and to some beyond this system, for their support and encouragement, special appreciation is extended, including but

not limited to John Booss, MD; Rodney Baker, PhD; Malcolm Cox, MD; Robert Gresen, PhD; James McCormick, MD; James Holsinger, MD; Herb Spencer, MD; Robert Kraus, MD; Steve Kraman, MD; William Green, PhD; Pat DeLeon, JD, PhD; Brenda Frommer; Neil Carey, MSW; Skip Lowe, PhD; Jeffrey Fisher, PhD; Alla Moeller; Walter Penk, PhD; Ed Nighingale, PhD; Ed Kisarskis, MD; Jill Livingstone, MLB; Deborah Kessler, MLB; Desti Stimes; Joanna Hawthorne; Chesley Jaracz; Tom Martin; Ginny Hamm, JD; Joseph Fox, PhD; Donna K. Jacobs; Steve Campbell, MSW; Steve Nisenbaum, PhD, JD; Terry Clark, MSW; and Maureen Charles, ED, MSN, APRN, Military Nurse Fellow, Lieutenant Colonel, Air Force Nurse Corps.

Appreciation is extended to Praeger publishers as well and their staff and Debbie Carvalko, senior acquisitions editor, psychology, health, and social work, and Alicia S. Merritt, consultant, for their guidance and support.

I express my sincere appreciation to my family, especially my father who served our country in World War II in General Patton's army in the European theater, and friends, who have been so supportive of this effort. And I extend my sincere gratitude and appreciation to each and every contributor for the chapters in these volumes. They come from the several Department of Veterans Affairs facilities, from our major universities, and from both within and beyond our borders. The reader will meet each and every one of them in their chapters as well as in the short biographies that summarize their backgrounds, training, experiences, and expertise. May these volumes provide the reader with a detailed look at veterans' healthcare in the twenty-first century!

Foreword

For the past fifty years, the Department of Veterans Affairs (VA) has provided high-quality care to America's veterans, and it is recognized today as the largest integrated healthcare system in the United States. Its mission, as stated eloquently by President Abraham Lincoln during his second inaugural address, is "to care for him who has borne the battle, his widow and orphan." Currently there are more than twenty-five million veterans across the country. Eight million are enrolled in VA and about 5.5 million are seen at 1,300 Veterans Health Administration (VHA) facilities annually. The VHA has 153 medical centers, 800 community-based outpatient clinics (CBOCs), and 260 readjustment counseling centers (vet centers), with an operating budget of $1 billion dollars and close to 270,000 employees.

There are more than 107 VA medical centers conducting research to improve the health and wellness of veterans. Over the years, this research has led to breakthroughs including development of the CAT scan, the cardiac pacemaker, and the nicotine patch, as well as the first liver transplant. One of the VA's most successful recruitment tools is its medical school affiliations program, which helps trains thousands of medical practitioners each year.

In the 1990s the Department of Veterans Affairs began its transformation from an inpatient to an outpatient system of care. Dr. Kenneth Kizer, then under secretary of health for the VHA, and the VA leadership developed CBOCs to enable the VA to see patients closer to their communities and provide needed outpatient and primary care to veterans who were previously forced to travel hundreds of miles to receive care in veterans' medical centers. In addition, during that period the VA established a defined medical benefits

package for enrolled veterans as well as long-term care for veterans rated 70 percent or higher disabled for service-connected injuries and illnesses from their military service.

In 1998 Congress directed the VA to establish eight priority groups to prioritize and rationalize healthcare for veterans based on the most injured and poorest veterans. In 2003 then Secretary of Veterans Affairs Anthony Principi suspended enrollment for Priority Group 8 veterans due to the VA's limited budget and the increasing numbers of veterans enrolling for VA healthcare. In order to enroll, veterans were required to take a means test, or financial assessment, to determine if they qualified for one of the priority groups and if they could make copays. In 2008 the VA relaxed its enrollment by 10 percent higher than the original means test cut-off income restriction, which allowed an additional 240,000 veterans previously ineligible for VA healthcare to enroll.

Today the Priority Group 8 restriction still exists, but combat veterans who have served after September 11, 2001, in a combat theater of operations (i.e., Operation Enduring Freedom, Operation Iraqi Freedom, and Operation New Dawn), are eligible for five years of veterans' healthcare for any injury or illness related to their military service. Veteran service organizations, such as The American Legion, believe that any veteran should be entitled to use the VA, which is a system designed to meet their unique and complex war-related injuries. In 1997 the VA was given the authority to bill, collect, and retain third-party reimbursements for treatment of non-service-connected medical conditions. Veterans, regardless of level of income or injury, should be authorized to bring their private insurance to the VA for treatment of their non-service medical conditions, which would be an alternative budget stream to offset the demand for services. Another concern is that veterans are not allowed to use their Medicare benefits within the VA. Veterans pay into Medicare their entire working lives and are essentially penalized because they cannot use their earned Medicare benefits in the VA and are forced to use those benefits in the private sector. In the future, the VA must continue to try to improve access to care for any veteran and take advantage of the cost savings to the government of veterans using their Medicare benefits in the VA system rather than the private sector.

Today there is an unprecedented number of returning veterans from Iraq and Afghanistan with traumatic brain injury (TBI) and post-traumatic stress disorder (PTSD). The term *polytrauma* was coined by the VHA to describe the many returning service members with complex, multiple injuries that required a new and holistic way of providing care. Over the last several years, the VHA has developed a polytrauma system of care with four levels.

Level 1 is the lead polytrauma rehabilitation centers, network or Veteran Integrated Service Network (VISN) sites, facilities (VA medical centers), and clinic or polytrauma points of contact. The lead polytrauma centers in the country are located in Palo Alto, California; Tampa, Florida; Richmond, Virginia; and Minneapolis, Minnesota. A new center is being built in San Antonio, Texas. From the battlefield, service members are evacuated through Landshuhl, Germany, to one of the military treatment facilities in the United States. The VHA has nurse liaisons and social workers who help transition severely injured veterans from military treatment facilities to the polytrauma system of care.

If a service member is involved in an improvised explosive device (IED) blast and develops a TBI, it is very likely that the veteran will also develop PTSD. If left untreated, the TBI and PTSD symptoms could lead to substance abuse, depression, and suicide. The VA conducts mandatory screens for veterans when they first enter a VA medical facility for TBI and PTSD. If the screening is positive, those veterans are referred for a secondary evaluation. Veterans' healthcare has also developed a crisis intervention line, formerly known as the Suicide Prevention Hotline, to assist any veteran in crisis. The hotline is open 365 days a year and 24 hours a day and is staffed by licensed counselors. The hotline has been credited for saving over 16,000 lives, and the VA has suicide prevention coordinators in each VA medical center to ensure veterans in crisis receive the assistance they need. The Department of Defense (DoD) and the Department of Veterans Affairs have also led the effort to destigmatize mental health conditions in our returning service members by having mental health practitioners embedded in primary care and through antistigma campaigns such as the "Real Warriors Campaign" in the Department of Defense and "Make the Connection" campaign in the Department of Veterans Affairs.

The VA continues to work with the DoD to develop a joint medical record, which will assist transitioning veterans in obtaining their earned veterans' benefits and services. Both agencies are working on a virtual lifetime electronic record (VLER), which will help connect the DoD and the VA information technology (IT) platforms to follow a service member from the day he or she joins the service to the day that person is laid to rest. The DoD and the VA are continuing to conduct research to improve the prevention, screening, diagnosis, and treatment of TBI and PTSD.

Veteran service organizations were founded to assist veterans by helping them file claims for their earned benefits and services. Veteran service organization service officers are professionally trained and accredited by the VA to file claims for veterans. In addition, Veteran service organizations provide

advocacy and assistance to veterans as well as lobbying the administration, Congress, and senior officials in the VA to make recommendations for continuous improvements for all veterans.

The chapters that follow reflect the many contributions that have been made to veterans' healthcare as well as the key healthcare issues facing our nation's veterans in the twenty-first century. Our nation has a moral obligation to take care of our service members when they return home. George Washington once said, "The willingness with which our young people are likely to serve in any war, no matter how justified, shall be directly proportional to how they perceive the veterans of earlier wars were treated and appreciated by their nation." It is our nation's responsibility to ensure that the Department of Veterans Affairs continues to provide timely, quality healthcare for our nation's veterans.

Jacob B. Gadd
Deputy Director for Health Care,
The American Legion;
Former Hospital Corpsman Third Class,
United States Navy (1998–2003)

Editor's Foreword

This four-volume set focusing on veterans' healthcare provides a unique and valuable contribution to our understanding of veterans' healthcare in the first decade of the twenty-first century. As a professor emeritus and retired VA career service chief from Lexington Veterans Affairs Medical Center, I have enjoyed a forty-year career in veterans' healthcare. I was first contacted in 2005 by Praeger Publishers to serve as editor of a handbook on this topic and then contacted some colleagues from the Department of Veterans Affairs both past and present and several colleagues nationally to explore the level of interest in accepting the invitation from Praeger to produce a positive reference book focusing on veterans' healthcare. It is to this cadre of professionals that I am indebted; they have contributed their knowledge and expertise in the chapters comprising this handbook.

We must be reminded of not only the macro events, but also the micro transitions that have contributed to the finest model of healthcare for veterans in the world. The reader is about to begin an extraordinary journey into the spectrum of healthcare offered through the Veterans Health Administration (VHA). Volume I offers the reader an understanding of the history of veterans' healthcare. Rodney R. Baker provides an overview of the historical contributions to veterans' healthcare. James W. Holsinger Jr., the first under secretary for veterans' affairs, offers a "View from the Top," addressing the administration and VA healthcare. VHA's academic mission is presented by Stuart C. Gilman, Barbara Chang, Robert Zeiss, Mary Dougherty, William Marks Jr., Deborah Ludke, and Malcolm Cox. Recognizing the important role of legislative initiatives for veterans' healthcare, with the assistance of Corina

M. Barrow, Jacquie Rychnovsky, and Patrick DeLeon of Senator Inouye's office, I provide a historical review of key legislation that has benefited veterans' healthcare.

I also examine healthcare for veterans from various eras, covering veterans of World Wars I and II and the Korean conflict. Robert J. Fitz discusses healthcare for veterans of the Vietnam era, and Delilah O. Noronha, John Chardos, Laura Gomez, Samina Iqbal, and Steven Lindley provide a discussion of healthcare for veterans of Operations Enduring Freedom, Iraqi Freedom, and New Dawn.

In an effort to examine global healthcare for veterans, provided is a comparative look at veterans' healthcare in other countries: Australia, Canada, China, Russia, and the United Kingdom. Professor David Dunt and his team examine a critical issue for veterans, focusing on suicide in the ex-service community in Australian research and prevention efforts. Dr. David Pedlar and Stewart Macintosh provide a closer look at veterans affairs in Canada. Finally, Professor Dai Williams takes a closer look at healthcare for British veterans.

Volume II examines programs of care and veterans' special needs. James W. Anderson, a pioneer in clinical care and research, explores healthcare programs for veterans with diabetes in primary care. This is followed by a discussion of neurological healthcare for veterans by Mitchell Wallin and John Kurtzke. David Booth then examines cardiology care for veterans, followed by Philip DeSimone's acknowledgment of veterans' sacrifices made in the quest for cancer treatment. Robert C. Gresen provides a first look at mental health care in VHA. Chiropractic care in veterans' healthcare is reviewed by Bart Green and a team of colleagues from the Naval Medical Center in San Diego and at the VA medical center in Buffalo, New York. Healthcare for veterans with infectious diseases is examined by Cynthia L. Gibert, and end-of-life care for veterans in the VA healthcare system is addressed by Betty L. Gillespie, James L. Ford, and Kye Y. Kim.

Many veterans have special needs. To examine these needs, we asked Dr. Hayden B. Bosworth to assess the lifestyles and health behaviors of veterans. Noting the special needs of amputees and the guidance of Fred Downs, I examined orthotics and prosthetics healthcare for veterans. The challenges faced by Native American veterans and their solutions are addressed by Joseph Stone of the Indian Health Service, and healthcare for women military veterans is addressed by Monica Roy. Prisoners of war have always been a special population and have had special needs; Brian Engdahl and Charles Stenger take a close look at serving America's former prisoners of war. Drs. Beth Hudnall Stamm, Susan L. Blampied, and Kirstina Beck examine a

special population of caregivers in their chapter on assistance dogs and their use by veterans with disabilities.

Volume III takes a closer and more detailed look at mental health treatment and rehabilitation. Delilah O. Noronha begins by examining primary care and mental health integration in providing veterans' healthcare. This is followed by a chapter that examines alcohol and substance abuse programs, by Susan R. Tate, Jennifer Mrnak-Meyer, and Jessica C. Tripp. Smoking has been critical in veterans' healthcare, and Carol A. Malte, Andrew J. Saxon, Kim Hamlett-Berry, and Miles E. McFall investigate integrating smoking cessation into mental health care for post-traumatic stress disorder.

Clinician researchers Mark S. Kaplan, Bentson H. McFarland, and Nathalie Huguet take a close look at suicide risk among veterans. VA healthcare for women veterans experiencing trauma is the focus of Carole A. Goguen. Stephen Tracy, Sara Tavakoli, Simona Stolpner, and Jodie Trafton discuss the treatment of substance use disorders; and the social context of adjustment in combat veterans is examined by Bradley Belsher, Josef Ruzek, and Matthew Cordova. Polytrauma care and treatment in veterans' healthcare is covered by Jeanne M. Bennett. Military traumatic brain injury and the postconcussive syndrome is addressed by colleagues in the Department of Defense led by Louis M. French, Victoria C. Anderson-Barnes, Katherine Brazaitis, and Aditya Bhagwat. Healthcare and issues of racial and ethnic diversity are carefully examined by Kathleen M. McNamara.

With special attention on rehabilitation care and treatment for veterans, colleagues Walter Penk, Dolores Little, and Nathan Ainspan address trauma-focused psychosocial rehabilitation. This is followed by a chapter on psychosocial rehabilitation and recovery services by Samantha Kettle, Loretta E. Braxton, Valerie Fox, and Josh Tiegreen. Next Ann D. Kirkwood, Beth Hudnall Stamm, and Chandra R. Story address eradicating mental illness stigma for active military personnel and veterans. Finally, Thomas P. O'Toole provides an in-depth assessment of how VA is engaging homeless veterans in primary care.

Volume IV provides an examination of some of the future directions for veterans' healthcare, first examining dedicated centers for veterans' healthcare. The first chapter reviews VHA centers of excellence. Then Drs. Katerine Osatuke, Jill Draime, Scott C. Moore, Dee Ramsel, Andrew Meyer, Sharon Barnes, Linda Belton, and Sue R. Dyrenforth examine the latest in organization development in VA.

Joseph F. Murphy, public affairs officer, VA NCPS, and James P. Bagian explore for the reader the VA National Center for Patient Safety. The significance of post-trauma stress is addressed by Matthew J. Friedman, the national

director of the Department of Veterans Affairs National Center for PTSD. Leading the way in pain-related disorders, Drs. Kathryn LaChappelle, Samantha Boris-Karpel, and Robert D. Kerns provide a detailed review of the efforts to address pain management in VHA.

Dr. K. Kizer, who is responsible for a major reorganization of VHA, provides a closer view of lessons learned about clinical integration from VA's experience with VISNs. The veterans' healthcare system is seen as a potential model for a national plan by Said A. Ibrahim, David Macpherson, and Michael E. Moreland.

New technologies are helping to create easier access to healthcare for veterans who live in rural and underserved areas of the country. Jennifer A. Wood, Thomas W. Miller, and Russell Hagy discuss telehealth applications to underserved veterans. Miller and Janet Kemp then explore the topic of suicide prevention through a national hotline. The Academy of Spinal Cord Injury is an organization outside VA that offers new directions in addressing the needs of spinal cord–injured veterans. The chapter on this topic is authored by the director, Terrie Price. VA has developed and implemented an Office for Preventative Ethics. Examining ethicolegal issues in VA healthcare are Steve Nisenbaum, Tom Miller, Sheila O'Keefe, and Dennis Norman. An organization external to VA that is meeting the needs of veterans, Give an Hour™, is described by its founder, Barbara Van Dahlen. Edmund J. Nightingale provides a very detailed and up-to-date summary of the efforts to provide quality, competent, and thorough veterans' healthcare in the final chapter, "Good to Great: The Veterans' Health Care System's Path to Excellence!"

The comprehensive nature of this four-volume set offers the reader an in-depth examination of veterans' healthcare through the first decade of the twenty-first century. More than two hundred invitations were extended to present and past members of the Department of Veterans Affairs as well as aligned agencies, veterans' organizations, and healthcare facilities associated with veterans' healthcare. What is provided are the comprehensive and dedicated work and contributions of more than one hundred scientists and practitioners, researchers, and clinicians both within the Department of Veterans Affairs and those in academically affiliated universities and public and private institutions. An effort is made to provide a glimpse of veterans' healthcare internationally. This handbook is not meant to cover every topic related to veterans' healthcare thoroughly, but rather to offer to the reader an excellent reference point from which to start a journey toward a better understanding of the complexity of providing quality healthcare to our military veterans.

This compendium provides the opportunity for dialogue on improving our understanding of veterans' healthcare, and each of the authors deals with a

part of this complex whole. As editor I trust it offers the gestalt that will increase our understanding of veterans' healthcare and the transitions we face in providing a twenty-first-century focus on healthcare for veterans worldwide.

Thomas W. Miller, PhD, ABPP,
Professor Emeritus & Senior Research Scientist,
University of Kentucky; Veterans Affairs Medical Center (Retired),
Lexington, Kentucky; Center for Prevention Research,
University of Connecticut

Part I

Mental Health and Mental Illness Research, Education, and Clinical Centers

Chapter 1

Primary Care–Mental Health Integration

Delilah O. Noronha

The Veterans Health Administration (VHA) has a mission to provide a gold standard of healthcare; thus it is no surprise the Department of Veterans Affairs (VA) is at the forefront in leading the largest primary care–mental health integration effort to date. VHA primary care–mental health integration (PCMHI) programs facilitate improved access to mental health services in primary care and promote quality of care across a broad range of illnesses. In recent years VHA has increased attention to the mental health needs of its veterans by supporting the expansion of PCMHI programs. As a result, VHA has become one of the largest U.S. healthcare systems to integrate primary care and mental health.

This chapter describes PCMHI; reviews the evidence leading to VHA PCMHI initiatives and implementation; retraces VHA's journey toward integrating mental health into primary care; demonstrates how VHA is applying the evidence to clinical practice; and presents a review of target outcomes of integrating mental health services in primary care for patients, clinical providers, administration, and the healthcare system as a whole. This chapter also discusses challenges, special issues, and implications of PCMHI. The information provided here focuses specifically on the mental health aspects of PCMHI in VHA.

Introduction

Prevalence

The Veterans Health Administration's population can be considered complex in terms of physical and mental health functioning when considering

Table 1.1.

Diagnosis (Broad ICD–9 Categories)	Frequency	Percent
Infectious and Parasitic Diseases (001–139)	68,569	13.5
Malignant Neoplasms (140–208)	5,809	1.1
Benign Neoplasms (210–239)	25,491	5.0
Diseases of Endocrine/Nutritional/Metabolic Systems (240–279)	135,250	26.6
Diseases of Blood and Blood Forming Organs (280–289)	14,342	2.8
Mental Disorders (290–319)	243,685	48.0
Diseases of Nervous System/Sense Organs (320–389)	202,298	39.8
Diseases of Circulatory System (390–459)	94,671	18.6
Diseases of Respiratory System (460–519)	116,308	22.9
Diseases of Digestive System (520–579)	172,462	33.9
Diseases of Genitourinary System (580–629)	63,421	12.5
Diseases of Skin (680–709)	93,635	18.4
Diseases of Musculoskeletal System/Connective System (710–739)	265,450	52.2
Symptoms, Signs, and Ill-Defined Conditions (780–799)	233,443	45.9
Injury/Poisonings (800–999)	130,300	25.6

Note: The data in this table are cumulative since FY 2002, with data on hospitalizations and outpatient visits as of September 30, 2009; veterans may have multiple diagnoses with each healthcare encounter. A veteran is counted only once in any single diagnostic category but can be counted in multiple categories, so the numbers add up to greater than 508,152; percentages add up to greater than 100 for the same reason.

comorbidities, level of severity, and other psychosocial needs. Treating veterans with such complex presenting problems is further complicated when the veteran's first point of entry to VA is through primary care. Primary care clinics are often the first point of entry for veterans with mental health issues. Patient concerns about mental health and/or psychosocial stressors are commonly presented to primary care physicians in conjunction with physical complaints. Seventy percent of primary care visits are related to psychosocial issues (Robinson & Reiter 2007). Findings from epidemiological studies have demonstrated that close to half of the primary care population will experience a mental disorder at some point in their lives (e.g., Kessler et al. 2003; Regier et al. 1993; Wang et al. 2006). One study found that 70 to 80 percent of all primary care visits are related to psychological distress (Kroenke, Arrington & Mangelsdorff 1990). During a one-year period, up to 30 percent of the U.S. population meets the criteria for one or more mental health diagnoses (Kessler

Table 1.2. Frequency of Possible Mental Disorders among OEF/OIF Veterans since 2002[1]

Disease Category (ICD 290-319 code)	Total Number of OEF/OIF Veterans[2]
PTSD (ICD-9CM 309.81)[3]	129,654
Depressive Disorders (311)	90,936
Neurotic Disorders (300)	74,559
Affective Psychoses (296)	52,982
Nondependent Abuse of Drugs (ICD 305)[4]	41,980
Alcohol Dependence Syndrome (303)	24,454
Specific Nonpsychotic Mental Disorder Due to Organic Brain Damage (310)	15,040
Special Symptoms, Not Elsewhere Classified (307)	14,531
Sexual Deviations and Disorders (302)	12,382
Persistent Mental Disorders Due to Conditions Classified Elsewhere (294)	12,029

Source: VA Office of Public Health and Environmental Hazards (February 2010)

[1] Cumulative from 1st Quarter FY 2002 through 4th Quarter FY 2009. ICD diagnoses used in these analyses are obtained from computerized administrative data. Although diagnoses are made by trained healthcare providers, up to one-third of coded diagnoses may not be confirmed when initially coded because the diagnosis is provisional, pending further evaluation.

[2] A total of 243,685 unique patients received a diagnosis of a possible mental disorder. A veteran may have more than one mental disorder diagnosis, and each diagnosis is entered separately in this table; therefore, the total number will be higher than 243,685.

[3] This row does not include information on PTSD from VA's vet centers or data from veterans not enrolled for VA healthcare. Also, this row does not include veterans who did not receive a diagnosis of PTSD (ICD 309.81) but had a diagnosis of adjustment reaction (ICD-9 309).

[4] This category currently excludes 67,172 veterans who have a diagnosis of tobacco use disorder (ICD-9CM 305.1) and no other ICD-9CM 305 diagnoses.

et al. 2005). Furthermore, mental health problems are two to three times more common in patients with chronic physical conditions (Katon 2003; Katon, Lin & Kroenke 2007). Such studies highlight the importance of providing mental health support in primary care.

The psychological distress presented to primary care providers may be a result of transient stressors or mental health diagnoses, or related to a medical condition. The most common mental health problems presented to primary care providers are related to depression, anxiety, and substance use. It has been estimated that 35 to 40 percent of veterans in a VA primary care setting have a diagnosis of depression, post-traumatic stress disorder (PTSD), and/or alcohol-related disorder (Hankin et al. 1999; VHA/DoD 2000). Thus, in addition to providing standard primary care medical services, psychological factors and behavior must be taken into account, especially when considering clinical outcomes. Providers in primary care are typically generalists, are juggling competing clinical and administrative demands, and often have a very limited amount of time to address the issues that served as the purpose of the primary care visit, let alone other issues that may spontaneously arise. Nevertheless, patients often disclose issues such as mental health complaints that need to be addressed in a timely manner. Integrating mental health into primary care addresses those mental health problems presented in primary care.

Anxiety

Anxiety has been reported as being a prevalent mental health problem among patients who seek general medical care (Stein et al. 2000; Calleo et al. 2009). Prevalence estimates for anxiety disorders range from 9 to 28.8 percent in the integrated care literature (Kessler et al. 2005; Taubman-Ben-Ari et al. 2001; Stein et al. 2000). Veterans are particularly vulnerable to having PTSD. When considering VHA's population it is important to note that although prevalence rates for PTSD vary, it has been reported that approximately 30 percent of Vietnam veterans, 10 percent of Gulf War veterans, and 11–20 percent of Operation Enduring Freedom/Operation Iraqi Freedom (OEF/OIF) veterans meet criteria for PTSD (e.g., Kulka et al. 1990; Tanielian & Jaycox 2008).

Depression

In VHA, major depressive disorder is the second most prevalent condition, and approximately 7 percent of veterans meet criteria for it (Yu et al. 2003). In fiscal year 2002, 542,075 veterans were diagnosed with a depressive disorder (QUERI 2009). Combined data from the Substance Abuse and Mental Health Services Administration 2004 to 2007 National Surveys on Drug Use and Health indicate that an annual average of 9.3 percent (312,000) of veterans twenty-one to thirty-nine years of age had experienced at least one major depressive episode in the previous year (http://www.oas.samhsa.gov).

Suicide Risk

Given the prevalence of various mental health disorders found in the primary care population, it is no surprise that suicide risk poses significant concern for healthcare providers. The prevalence of recent suicidal ideation is thought to be higher in patients who have screened positive for depression and even higher for patients who have been diagnosed with a depressive and/or anxiety disorder (e.g., Bruce et al. 2004; Nutting et al. 2005).

Substance Use

Substance use is a common problem either identified by healthcare providers or self-reported by patients. In VHA, more than 375,000 veterans seen in FY 2007 had a substance use disorder (SUD) other than nicotine dependence (McDermott, Dobson & Owen 2008). The Substance Abuse and Mental Health Services Administration's National Survey on Drug Use and Health found that in 2003 an estimated 56.6 percent of veterans had used alcohol in the previous month, compared to 50.8 percent of comparable nonveterans. Furthermore, an estimated 13.2 percent of veterans reported driving while under the influence of alcohol or illicit drugs in the previous year. This is slightly higher than comparable nonveterans (http://www.oas.samhsa.gov) who were estimated at 12.2 percent. Substance use may place veterans and nonveterans at increased risk of serious injury, legal problems, and even death.

Other Presentations of Psychological Distress

Although efforts to achieve PCMHI in VHA may have been made primarily to address depression, PTSD, and substance use, there are mental health issues that are subclinical, related to transient psychosocial stressors (Boone & Christensen 1997), and/or related to a medical condition (Barlow & Campbell 2000; Cummings & Follette 1968; Cummings, Kahn & Sparkman, 1962; Follette & Cummings 1967 cited in Haas & de Gruy 2005; Roy-Byrne et al. 1994) that may also be observed in primary care. Given the literature in this area, there has been a movement away from simply focusing on anxiety, depression, and substance use to addressing the behavioral components of disease state, process, and overall biopsychosocial patient functioning (Casciani 2004). This differs from the single diagnosis initiatives of the last fifteen years (Kessler, Stafford & Messier 2009). Patients with conditions such as coronary artery disease (Fleet, Lavoie & Beitman 2000; Sheps & Sheffield 2001), diabetes (Egede, Zheng & Simpson 2002) and coronary obstructive pulmonary disease (e.g. Kim et al. 2000; van Manen et al. 2002) are at risk for experiencing some level of psychological distress during the course of their physical illness. Psychological complaints may be directly related to a medical condition (e.g., hypothyroidism) or may cause or exacerbate physical symptoms and diagnoses (e.g., high blood pressure). Furthermore, psychological distress may be expressed through other behaviors, such as overutilization of primary care services (i.e., an increased number of same-day appointments). Mental health services have become necessary in improving chronic disease management in primary care and support PCMHI (Institute of Medicine 2006; Ng et al. 2007).

Defining Primary Care–Mental Health Integration

The primary care setting provides a unique opportunity to promote mental health awareness and engagement within a nonstigmatizing setting. There are various definitions of integration (Blount 2003; Butler et al. 2008a; Doherty, McDaniel & Baird, 1996; Haas 2004); however, the Institute of Medicine (1994, 2006) defines integrated treatment as the "interactions between clinicians to address the individual needs of the client/patient" and consists of "any mechanism by which treatment interventions for co-occurring disorders are combined within the context of a primary treatment relationship or service setting" (Institute of Medicine 1994, 2006, 213). Wagner and others' (1996) chronic care model framework is the basis of PCMHI. The core features of primary care—access, continuity of care, comprehensive approach to care, chronic disease management, and care coordination—parallel integrated mental health care. Primary care–mental health integration provides a breadth of healthcare that is patient-centered and fits patient care needs within an accessible, seamless system that promotes communication among providers and patients. As a result, PCMHI can improve clinical outcomes, clinical efficiency, and cost effectiveness and result in higher patient and provider satisfaction (Cummings, O'Donohue & Ferguson 2003; Felker et al. 2004; Strosahl 1996). Findings such as those by Pomerantz and colleagues (2008) demonstrated that integrated care interventions and services can have sustainable outcomes such as decreased wait times for mental health care, increased clinical productivity, and increased mental health evaluations for new referrals.

Primary Care–Mental Health Integration versus Specialty Mental Health

Primary care–mental health integration is a population-based, interdisciplinary, rather than multidisciplinary, approach to increasing access to mental health services in the primary care setting. It is not a specialty mental health clinic that is simply located in primary care and is not intended to replace specialty mental health. It is a unique approach that closes the gap between primary care patients and needed mental health services to overcome barriers to mental health services. It also provides services in primary care for patients who may not need the intensity of specialty mental health. Primary care–mental health integration is differentiated from specialty mental health in that it does not assume treatment for all patients with severe and chronic mental illness; rather, it facilitates the transition to specialty mental health clinics when appropriate. Primary care–mental health integration providers primarily serve a consultative role.

The Primary Care Setting

The primary care setting is fast-paced and ever-changing and often presents unique challenges. Just as the primary care provider is the generalist of medicine, the primary care psychologist is viewed as a generalist of mental healthcare. Because of the variations in VA's primary care clinics and emphasis on advanced access, an integrated care mental health provider may experience referral flow as "feast or famine." Nevertheless, even at times when referral flow may be slow, the primary care–mental health provider may engage in other clinical and administrative activities (i.e., clinical follow-up, clinical supervision, performance monitoring). Given that the primary care setting is dynamic, it requires flexibility, professionalism, a broad range of clinical skills, excellent interpersonal skills, a pragmatic approach, clinical efficiency, and the ability to handle complex patient conditions and concerns.

Benefits of Integration

Primary care–mental health integration increases access to a diversity of mental health services with the goal of achieving various objectives, including identification, normalization of mental health issues, patient choice in care setting, continuity of care across care episodes, treatment engagement and adherence, functional outcomes, and provider and patient satisfaction. Integrated care recognizes that health conditions do not always fit in one of two categories, physical or mental health (http://www1.va.gov/PrimaryCare/mhi, accessed 06/01/10). Furthermore, integrated care can enhance and/or complement mental health specialty services while also supporting primary care providers.

Improved Access

Data from VHA's National Registry for Depression (NARDEP) reveal that among veterans diagnosed with depression in 2002, 56 percent received the

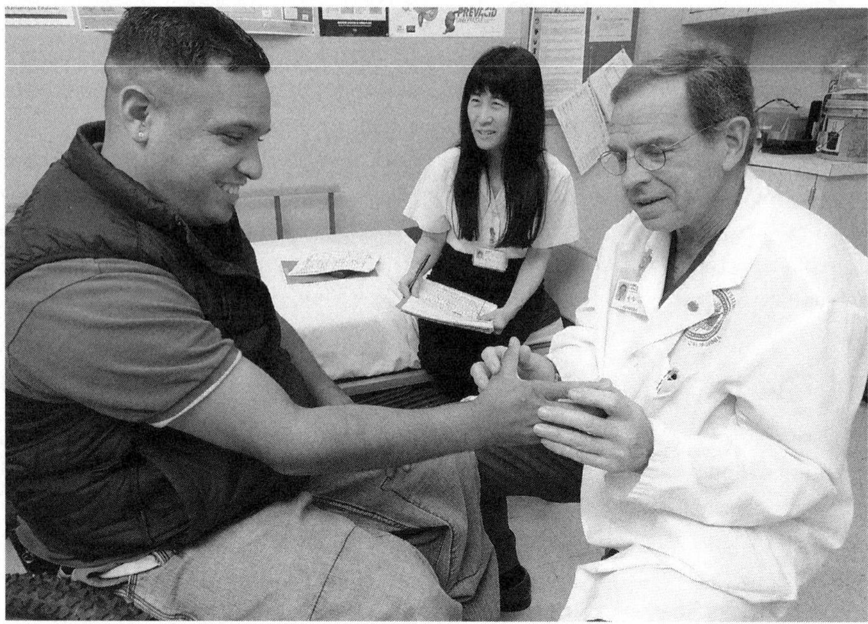

Figure 1.1. Primary Care-Mental Health Integration offers VA patients mental health care along with healthcare evaluations by a multidisciplinary team.

majority of their mental healthcare in specialty settings and 44 percent received all or the majority of their mental healthcare in the primary care setting (Blow et al. 2002). Improving access to mental health services in primary care is important for identifying patients who may benefit from mental health services and decreasing barriers to mental health treatment. Increased access is most relevant to patients who otherwise may not have been identified as having mental health concerns and/or patients who may not be comfortable with, or appropriate for, a specialty mental health referral. More important, increased mental health access through PCMHI may prevent patients from "falling through the cracks," that is, failing to make it to a needed mental health appointment between the primary care appointment and the specialty mental health appointment. This is accomplished by coordinating appointments and/ or increasing timely delivery of key mental health services during the primary care visit (i.e., mental health screening, triage, and treatment) and providing follow-up focused on increasing patient compliance with mental health referrals and recommendations.

At the most basic level, increase in access translates to an increase in exposure to available mental health services. Through having open mental health access, the primary care–mental health provider can be clinically flexible and have more opportunities to serve patients by providing unscheduled check-in on their progress and follow-up on missed appointments, and being available as needed before or after a medical appointment. Furthermore, increased mental health access may be helpful for primary care providers whose competing demands, time constraints, and focus on physical health make it difficult to address mental health issues in a fifteen- to twenty-minute primary care visit.

Reducing Mental Health Stigma

A patient's comfort level with acknowledging and/or disclosing mental health concerns and accepting a mental health referral is an important factor when considering acceptance and follow-through with mental health screening, assessment, and treatment. Research has found that individuals with more severe psychological symptoms had the greatest concerns about the stigma of receiving mental health care (e.g., Hoge, Auchterlonie & Milliken 2006; Hoge et al. 2004; Kessler et al. 2001). This highlights the fact that those who need mental health services the most may be the least likely to actually utilize mental health services. When looking only at the military population, Greene-Shortridge, Britt, and Castro (2007) found that mental health stigma was more pronounced in the military population than in the civilian population. Primary care providers develop a relationship with their patients that may foster engagement in a mental health treatment referral and treatment compliance when they have a mental health colleague who is working in the primary care setting. For co-located PCMHI providers, the personal introduction of the psychologist to the patient, also known as a "warm hand-off," assists in gaining patient buy-in to mental health services. In addition, this collaborative, interdisciplinary team approach normalizes mental health services provided in primary care.

Continuity of Care

Primary care–mental health integration provides services directed at enhancing and supporting continuity of care (Skultety & Zeiss 2006). The American Academy of Family Physicians (2010) defines continuity of care as the process by which the patient and the physician are cooperatively involved in ongoing healthcare management toward the goal of high-quality, cost-effective medical care. Furthermore, continuity of care improves the patient-provider relationship through having a continuous, sustained relationship. Continuity of care is useful for assessment and treatment planning purposes, and it has been associated with improved treatment compliance, healthcare outcomes, better healthcare utilization behaviors, increased patient satisfaction, and improved cost effectiveness. Although a PCMHI provider may terminate scheduled brief treatment or may only get as far as providing assessment and a same-day intervention, all primary care patients referred to PCMHI programs theoretically remain on the caseload because they are expected to return to primary care for at least an annual physical examination. Thus, if a mental health issue arises during the period of a patient's primary care appointment, he or she can be re-referred to the PCMHI program because there is open access. This is possible because most primary care patients are seen at least once a year for an annual checkup. Given this, patients may present with mental health concerns in which the primary care–mental health provider is accessible almost immediately. The primary care–mental health provider may opt to check in to monitor the mood of a patient who may have declined mental health treatment or with a patient who did not present with symptom severity that warranted mental health treatment. A primary care–mental health provider's placement in the primary care clinic facilitates interventions focused on follow-up on missed appointments and with specialty referrals. Primary care–mental health integration promotes multidirectional flow of information sharing in which each team member can remain abreast of patient progress. Patients may easily see that the entire primary care team is working together. Finally, continuity of care may lower healthcare costs by reducing unnecessary medical contacts and tests that are a result of contact with various new providers. Enhanced continuity of care leads the way to better quality of care and improved health outcomes.

Interdisciplinary Team Approach

Patients may benefit from having an entire team of clinicians working on their healthcare plans. Patients having difficulty managing or coping with several complex and comorbid conditions will benefit from having multiple perspectives from their healthcare team. An interdisciplinary team approach facilitates increased access because every team member may take responsibility for the patient's care and at least connect the patient with the discipline or resource that would meet his or her needs. Interdisciplinary collaboration may facilitate continuity of care, increased patient satisfaction, and improved outcomes.

Satisfaction Ratings

Primary care–mental health integration may improve patient and provider satisfaction ratings. Patient satisfaction has been found to be a key factor in successful mental health and substance abuse treatment, as well as quality of life (Chen et al. 2006). Provider satisfaction may strengthen team cohesion, enhance quality of care, and indirectly improve patient outcomes (Haas et al. 2000; Katz 1999).

Efficient Healthcare Utilization and Cost Effectiveness

Primary care–mental health integration programs decrease unnecessary over-utilization of medical services and medical costs. A patient with mental health problems can become a high utilizer of medical services, often presenting with unexplained physical complaints. In fiscal year 2002, 542,075 veterans diagnosed with depression accounted for 14.3 percent of VHA's total healthcare costs (QUERI 2009). Similarly, the National Alliance on Mental Illness (NAMI) (2009) reported that veterans diagnosed with depression account for slightly more than 14 percent of the total U.S. expenditures on depression. Primary care–mental health integration has been found to be the most cost-effective method of service delivery (Cummings, O'Donohue & Ferguson 2003; Katon et al. 2002; Liu et al. 2003). Considering the numbers of veterans who present with mental health issues, healthcare savings could be substantial.

History

Integrating mental health services into medical settings has been in progress since the 1960s (Earl & Kincey 1982; Coleman et al. 1979; Cummings 1997; Katon et al. 1992; Wiggins & Cummings 1998); however, due to the increase in the evidence base, discussed in the next section, it gained the most attention in the last decade. In 1999 *Mental Health: A Report of the Surgeon General—Executive Summary* was published. In this report, Dr. David Satcher, former surgeon general of the United States, emphasized the importance of increasing mental health access. Dr. Satcher's report stressed that referral to specialty mental health services is not an effective method of engaging those persons who can be considered "difficult to engage" in mental health treatment (U.S. Department of Health and Human Services 1999). The report described primary care as an important gateway for introducing patients to mental health treatment. This is most important for patients who experience barriers to accessing mental health services or who are unaware that they need them. After Dr. Satcher's report, the U.S. Preventive Services Task Force (2002) recommended depression, suicide, and alcohol use screening in clinical practices. On April 2003 President George W. Bush announced the President's New Freedom Commission on Mental Health. This was the first presidential mental health commission in twenty-five years and reaffirmed the president's support for mental health parity legislation (Hogan 2003). The report emphasizes that mental health and physical health problems are interrelated components of overall health and are best treated in a coordinated care system (Hogan 2003). The steps VHA has taken to address recommendations are discussed in a later section.

Evidence Base

Movement toward PCMHI in VHA and non-VHA care has been supported by the literature, which set the foundation for current integration models. Studies in the area of integration vary in types of models assessed, population samples, outcomes assessed, clinical settings, behavioral health services, and extent of implementation. Cummings developed one of the first integrative collaborative care models in 1962 at Kaiser Permanente Medical Center in San Francisco, California, where co-located mental health providers worked together with primary care providers to assist in mental health management (Cummings 1997). Over the years there has been mounting evidence supporting the use of similar integrated care models.

In the 1980s the Hawaii Medicaid Study, one of the first large-scale studies of its kind, implemented delivery of collaborative behavioral health services care. This randomly controlled prospective study of 36,000 Medicaid eligible patients and 90,000 federal employees identified and evaluated key components used in PCMHI models today (Cummings et al. 1993; Pallak et al. 1994). This study demonstrated that providing behavioral healthcare reduced medical utilization rates and total healthcare costs by 40 percent in eighteen months (Cummings 1997). The Hawaii Integrated Health Care Demonstration Project was conducted as a follow-up to the Medicaid study. The most noteworthy outcome of this follow-up study revealed high patient satisfaction and a 21 percent reduction in medical utilization following intervention (Cummings n.d.; Laygo et al. 2003).

The Partners in Care (PIC) project was a real-world trial conducted from 1995 to 2000, designed to improve the quality of care for depression in primary care. The PIC project was carried out in forty-six primary care clinics in six diverse, nonacademic managed care plans. The study evaluated two quality improvement (QI) programs. One directed quality improvement resources toward supporting medication treatment; the other directed resources toward supportive psychotherapy. Nurse care managers in the second program provided assessment and education, but then referred patients directly to cognitive-behavioral group therapy. Compared to a group receiving the usual care (what normally would have been provided without intervention), the PIC project groups improved in the areas of treatment adherence and symptom reduction. The two quality improvement programs, supported medication treatment and psychotherapy, had similar positive outcomes; thus, either model can be selected (http://www.rand.org; Wells et al. 2004; Miranda et al. 2003). The largest impact was among ethnic minority patients. A nine-year longitudinal analysis of PIC found that after five years, participants who received quality improvement interventions had improved mental health with fewer negative life events and with improved psychological well-being postintervention (Sherbourne et al. 2008). The Mental Health Awareness Project followed PIC as a continuous quality improvement (CQI) project at Kaiser and VA. This trial demonstrated an increase in patient satisfaction with care where the intervention care model was at least minimally evidence-based. Depression symptom scores significantly improved across all depressed patients who received the intervention (Butler et al. 2008a).

In 1999 the U.S. Air Force prioritized behavioral health–primary care integration as an initiative for Air Force Primary Care Optimization. Implementing the initiative led to increased patient and provider satisfaction, improved access to behavioral health services, and services that contributed to prevention of more severe mental health issues (Runyan, Fonseca & Hunter, 2003 cited in Cummings, O'Donohue & Cummings 2009). The U.S. military has developed integrated care systems that provide access to mental health providers, who are commonly referred to as behavioral health specialists.

The Improving Mood-Promoting Access to Collaborative Treatment (IMPACT) for late-life depression study was conducted from 1998 to 2003 and included 1,801 depressed older adults in eighteen primary care clinics across five states. Collaborative care is described in this trial as use of on-site mental health specialists and standardized treatment algorithms for brief psychotherapy and medication management. The IMPACT model more than doubled the effectiveness of depression treatment for older adults when compared to usual care. Specifically, IMPACT findings include at least a 50 percent reduction in depressive symptoms for the intervention group, compared to 19 percent of the usual care group. Intervention patients were found to maintain significantly less depressive symptoms than usual care patients at the twenty-four-month follow-up. In addition, the IMPACT intervention was significantly more cost effective than usual care. Several follow-up studies that utilized data derived from the IMPACT trial found better outcomes for collaborative care when compared with usual care among older adult patients (Hunkeler et al. 2006; Callahan et al. 2005; www.impact-uw.org).

The Prevention of Suicide in Primary Care Elderly: Collaborative Trial (PROSPECT) was conducted from 1999 to 2001. It was an effectiveness study designed to assess the effect of care management on reducing risk factors for late life suicide (Bruce et al. 2004). Results of the PROSPECT study revealed that suicidal ideation decreased among primary care participants at four and eight months in the intervention group.

One of the largest studies of its kind is Primary Care Research in Substance Abuse and Mental Health for Elderly (PRISM-E). This trial was conducted from 2000 to 2002 at community health centers, VA facilities, and other community primary care clinics. The trial examined two models of care for depression, anxiety, and at-risk drinking among older adults through either an integrated care (IC) or enhanced referral (ER) model. There were 23,828 participants aged sixty-five and older who were screened in primary care clinics from ten study sites throughout the United States. More than 2,200 of those who were screened met diagnostic criteria for depression, anxiety, and/or at-risk alcohol consumption, and 5 percent endorsed suicidal ideation. These patients were randomly assigned to either IC or ER models or "better than usual care." The first report of PRISM-E study results found that participants with depression who received integrated care had superior rates of engaging in mental health service when compared to rates for those who received enhanced referral to specialty care. Furthermore, quantity and frequency of alcohol consumption decreased over six months in both IC and ER groups. Finally, the study found that primary care providers preferred integrated care due to better communication between primary care and mental health providers, normalization of mental health services, and better care coordination (Levkoff et al. 2004). Several subsequent PRISM-E publications reported positive outcomes of the PRISM-E trial (Bartels et al. 2004; Gallo et al. 2004; Gallo et al. 2007; Oslin et al. 2006a).

The Re-Engineering Systems for Primary Care Treatment of Depression (RESPECT-Depression) project, developed by the MacArthur Initiative on Depression and Primary Care, explored the impact, dissemination, and sustainability of an evidence-based approach to enhancing depression management. It encouraged ongoing relationships among primary care providers, mental health providers, and care managers. In February 2002 and February 2003, researchers randomly assigned 400 patients diagnosed with depression to treatment using either the RESPECT-Depression approach or usual care practices. After six months of treatment, 60 percent of RESPECT-Depression patients had responded to treatment, compared with 47 percent in usual care. Depression remission rates for RESPECT-Depression patients were 37.3 percent versus 26.7 percent for usual care. Ninety percent of RESPECT-Depression patients rated their depression care as either good or excellent, versus 75 percent with usual care (Dietrich et al. 2004). The RESPECT-Depression Project has been modified as part of a collaborative effort between DoD's Deployment Health

Clinical Center and RESPECT-Depression developers to enhance the identification and quality management of PTSD and depression. This modified RESPECT-Depression project is known as Re-Engineering Systems of Primary Care Treatment in the Military (RESPECT-Mil) (http://www.pdhealth.mil/respect-mil). One article found the majority of the sixty-nine participants experienced clinically important improvement in PTSD and depression after a six-plus-week collaborative care intervention (Engel et al. 2008).

The VA Medical Center at White River Junction, Vermont, began a collaborative care clinic in 1997 after experimenting with various mental health service delivery models. This model provided immediate access to psychiatric services, regardless of psychiatric acuity, and emphasized that all mental health issues may not require the intensity of specialty mental healthcare. After revision of the program in 2004, a program evaluation revealed that persons with mental health concerns were identified, treatment was initiated, more intensive treatment needs were identified, "no show" rates dropped to zero, wait times dropped to minutes, and there were high ratings on patient and provider satisfaction surveys (American Psychiatric Association 2005). This model was supported nationally by VHA and served as an example of the co-located collaborative care model.

VA facilities across the nation were awarded a two-year grant, and efforts among Veterans Integrated Service Network (VISN) leadership began to decide how to implement the evidence base on collaborative care for depression throughout VHA (AHRQ 2008). This project became known as Translating Initiatives in Depression into Effective Solutions (TIDES); its care managers are typically registered nurses who provide guideline-based treatment support to primary care patients. This support includes monitoring mood, compliance, and treatment response of patients who were prescribed psychotropic medications by their primary care provider. Studies have found that this program improves quality of care and patient outcome. TIDES was continued as Regional Expansion of TIDES (ReTIDES) between 2006 and 2008, an ongoing evaluation that was based on performance measures derived from the electronic health record (EHR) and a provider survey. Its focus is on learning about regional sustainability, spread, and national implementation needs for departmental collaborative care. As a result of ReTIDES, TIDES spread to new VA facilities and clinics (McDermott, Dobson & Owen 2008). In 2006 the TIDES intervention received funding from the Office of Primary Care and Mental Health Integration, facilitating further implementation (AHRQ 2008).

Despite the variations in integrated care studies, a number of reviews of integrated care programs demonstrate positive outcomes (Blount 2003; Wulsin, Sollner & Pincus 2006; Druss & Newcomer 2007). One study that reviewed randomized controlled trials of integrated care and geriatric evaluation management (GEM) programs for primary care patients found improvements in depressive symptoms and patient outcomes for both programs (Skultety & Zeiss 2006). Gilbody and colleagues (2006) published a meta-analysis of thirty-seven randomized trials of collaborative care for depression among more than 12,000 patients. Results from this meta-analysis found collaborative care models to be more effective at six months of follow-up than standard care. The meta-analysis highlighted that there were three key factors associated with effective collaborative care programs: 1) improved treatment adherence to antidepressant medications, 2) use of case managers, and 3) supervision by psychiatrists. Given the evidence, it is clear that integrated models of care improve quality of care and various clinical and administrative outcomes for diverse patient populations in VA and managed care settings.

VHA's Journey Toward Integration

The Surgeon General's report and the President's New Freedom Commission on Mental Health guided and provided support for VHA's motion to prioritize mental health integration (Unutzer et al. 2006). This resulted in VA's Mental Health Action Agenda Steering Committee recommendation that VHA develop an adaptive, collaborative care model dissemination package (Mental Health Action Agenda Work Group 2003). Primary care–mental health integration in VHA is a shared responsibility of the Office of Mental Health Services and the National Primary Care Program. VHA began implementation of a PCMHI pilot program by requesting proposals in FY 2007 under the mental health enhancement initiative. Ninety-four facilities were funded for pilot co-located collaborative care or care management programs (Oslin & Post 2010). Other programs that did not receive enhancement funds were funded on the VISN and local level. In September 2008 further expansion of PCMHI was advocated through the *Uniform Mental Health Services Handbook*. VHA began annual national mental health integration conferences and efforts in primary care–mental health strategic planning and program development. By 2008 there were $32 million in mental health integration funds and approximately ninety-two integrated care programs.

The Mental Health Strategic Plan (MHSP) was developed by VHA and recommends restructuring and redesigning mental health service delivery. A primary goal of the MHSP was to develop a collaborative care model for patients with mental health concerns that equates mental healthcare with the

same level of urgency/intervention as medical healthcare (http://vaww1.va
.gov/pcmh). Zeiss and Karlin's (2008) article indicates that the MHSP has
265 action items to be completed over a five-year period. The 2008 article
identifies one of the five major components that capture most of the essential
elements of the action items, facilitation of the integration of mental health
services with primary care (http://vaww1.va.gov/pcmh). Implementation of
the MHSP began in 2005. The plans for implementation are outlined in
"Uniform Mental Health Services in VA Medical Centers and Clinics,"
issued in *Veterans Health Administration Handbook* 1160.01 in September
2008; it combines VA Central Offices (VACO) direction and VISN/facility
discretion and reestablished a unified funding stream. It expands beyond
funded sites to all VHA facilities (i.e., community-based outpatient clinics)
(UMHSP 2008). Today VHA's PCMHI is in practice with the support and
guidance of VA Central Office, VISN, and local VA facilities leadership.
VHA's commitment to PCMHI is in line with President Obama's healthcare
reform legislation. The Patient Protection and Affordable Care Act (PPACA,
Pub. L. No. 111-148), highlights the importance of integrating mental health
into primary care with the goal of prevention and health promotion, especially
for chronic illness.

VHA's PCMHICare–Mental Health Models

Individual VHA PCMHI programs have adapted one of three primary
care–mental health models: co-located collaborative care, care management, or blended models. Although the three models are different, they
share some commonalities. First, episodes of care are initiated by formal
consult or "curbside" consults, which may be prompted by mandated mental
health reminder screens or provider preference. Second, the mental health
providers offer screening, evaluation, treatment planning, mental health
interventions, triage, and monitoring of outcomes. Third, all three are
interdisciplinary and population-based models. Model selection is dependent on 1) guidance from leadership at VISNs and medical center levels, 2)
local patient needs, and 3) resources and staffing. Once selected, models can
be tailored to the facility.

Co-Located Collaborative Care Model

The co-located collaborative care model includes an embedded mental health
team that provides open access to in-person, same-day mental health services

(e.g., screening, triage, consultation, and evidence-based interventions). The co-located mental health team may include a prescribing provider and/or mental health provider(s) who can coordinate patients' access to mental health. Patients being followed in co-located collaborative care clinics may be scheduled for follow-up, asked to come for a same-day appointment, provided with telephone interventions, and/or provided with access to other forms of intervention.

One of the most recognized co-located collaborative care models was developed at the White River Junction VA Medical Center. One study by Watts and colleagues (2007) found that the co-located collaborative care model demonstrated significant increases in both the proportion of depression screen-positive patients receiving any treatment as well as the proportion of patients receiving guideline-concordant treatment for depression. In addition, investigators found an increase in utilization of guideline adherent depression treatment. In a 2008 article, Pomerantz and colleagues reported several improvements in outcome after implementing an integrated care model. Of these outcomes, improvements were found in the areas of attendance rates for the initial evaluation, wait times, improved capacity of specialty mental health services, productivity, and patient satisfaction.

Care Management Model

Care management is a strategy for coordinating and integating care among providers and systems to maximize patient clinical outcomes, reduce costs, enhance quality, and promote continuity (Miller 1997). The care management model consists of a mental health provider, usually a nurse, designated as a care manager and supervised by a psychiatrist or psychologist. The care manager provides primarily telephone-based evaluation, triage, screening, monitoring of adherence, algorithm-based use of medication, and referrals as necessary; support to primary care providers; and follow-up for mental health treatment plans that are generated and managed in integrated care (i.e., support for frontline psychotropic medications prescribed by a primary care provider). Care managers do not have to be physically located in the primary care clinic to provide substantial mental health services. Two care management programs have been adopted by VHA: TIDES and the Behavioral Health Laboratory (BHL).

Translating Initiatives for Depression into Effective Solutions (also discussed previously) is an evidence-based collaborative approach for depression management in which mental health providers and primary care providers work together. Felker and colleagues (2006) describe the impact of a telephone-based depression care management program that used a collaborative care work group three-phase process to enhance collaboration between mental health and primary care in management of depression. This study was supported by the TIDES initiative and found that use of collaborative care work groups facilitated increased rates of primary care providers who followed patients with depression (82 percent), attendance rates for specialty mental health services (88 percent), and primary care patients who receive antidepressants (76 percent).

The Behavioral Health Lab, developed by Oslin and colleagues (2006b), focuses on the management of depression, anxiety, and alcohol use using structured assessment, follow-up, algorithm-based treatment planning, and follow-up that integrates algorithm-based medication management. These treatments are guided by clinical software, which allows for data tracking and outcome review. Services include evaluation; psychoeducation; watchful waiting (monitoring symptoms, providing treatment options); depression monitoring (monitoring medication compliance and response); disease management protocols for depression, anxiety, alcohol use, and referral management; and follow-up protocols. One study found that implementation of the BHL led to a significant increase in the proportion of patients who screened positive for depression as well as identification of comorbid mental health disorders (Oslin et al. 2006b).

Blended Model

Given the value of both care management and collaborative/co-located models of care, VHA is now promoting the combination of co-located collaborative care with care management components, resulting in the blended model of care. This model incorporates the strengths of both models: telephone-based and face-to-face follow-up, diagnostic assessment, triage, crisis intervention, psychotropic medication management within primary care, and evidence-based psychotherapies. It also provides opportunities for PCMHI providers to collaborate across disciplines via co-location in primary care. It can be tailored to patient and provider needs, ultimately increasing patient access by considering individual differences among patients, clinics, and resources.

The VA Palo Alto Health Care System (VAPAHCS) utilizes a blended model of care that is tailored to the patient's access needs and the healthcare facility's size and structure. Components of both the co-located collaborative care and care management models were significantly beneficial to development and progression of the VAPAHCS integrated care program. This blended model is referred to as the Primary Care–Behavioral Health (PC-BH) program. It provides services across nine primary clinics. Six of the nine geographically diverse clinics have PC-BH teams located on-site, and the other three are covered remotely via telephone care. Palo Alto's blended model consists of clinical psychologists, consult psychiatrists, and psychology technicians (bachelor's and master's level providers). There are three major components of the PC-BH program: direct patient care, direct collaboration, and program evaluation. Program evaluation is a major component of this model, as it directs clinical care and program development.

Key Services of VHA PCMHI Models

Primary care–mental health providers address a broad range of clinical, professional, and administrative issues. These include providing screening, triage, assessment, curbside consultation, brief therapy, collaborative care medication monitoring, provider education and support, and research. All of the clinical services are possible because of increased mental health access, which normalizes mental health services and promotes mental health prevention.

Screening/Assessment

Mental health access in primary care is provided to patients who are self-identified and those who are identified by other means (i.e., primary care provider screening). However, for those who do not self-identify, mental health screening is useful. Despite evidence regarding the prevalence of psychological issues among primary care patients, up to two-thirds of patients meeting diagnostic criteria for mental illness are not identified by their primary care providers (deGruy 1996; Spitzer et al. 1994). Furthermore, Speer and Schneider's (2003) review of the need for interdisciplinary team approaches to mental health notes that primary care providers fail to detect and diagnose approximately 50 percent of their patients with mental health disorders. The answer is not to task primary care providers with having to be accurate mental health diagnosticians, as they are often overburdened with basic clinical demands, but rather to embed PCMHI providers in primary care clinics. Desai, Rosenheck, and Craig (2006) report that patients who were more likely to screen positive for mental health issues were less likely to be screened. Liu and colleagues (2006) found that among VA patients with severe depressive symptoms, 36 percent remained undiagnosed and untreated with antidepressants for over one year. Similar to most medical conditions, early identification of psychological symptoms may initiate treatment that prevents the condition from worsening.

Screening and identification of mental health is essential in optimizing patient care, and primary care is an ideal setting to identify patients with mental health needs. Pignone and colleagues' (2002) meta-analysis reveals that screening and feedback reduced risk for persistent depression. VHA implemented systemwide mandated screening for depression, PTSD, and substance abuse. Routine and standardized mental health screening parallels the annual routine medical examination wherein patients attend an appointment for check-up and prevention purposes rather than because they are in need of specific treatment or evaluation. Routine screening combined with nonscreen dependent referrals from primary care providers will better ensure that mental health issues are identified and addressed.

VHA-mandated mental health screening includes the Patient Health Questionnaire-2 item (PHQ-2), Primary Care–Posttraumatic Stress Disorder (PC-PTSD), and Alcohol Use Disorder Identification Test (AUDIT-C), which are screens used to identify veterans who may benefit from mental health services. The PHQ-2 is a two-item questionnaire that inquires about depressed mood and loss of interest over the previous two weeks (Kroenke, Spitzer & Williams 2003). The PC-PTSD is a four-item screen that was designed for use in primary care and other medical settings and is currently used to screen for PTSD in veterans at VA facilities (Prins et al. 2003). The AUDIT-C is an alcohol screen that can help identify patients who are hazardous drinkers or have active alcohol use disorders (including alcohol abuse or dependence) (Bush et al. 1998). Once veterans are identified as having a positive initial screen, they are provided with a required follow-up evaluation, which may yield both clinical and subclinical conditions. The PHQ-2 and PC-PTSD follow-up screenings at a minimum provide suicide risk questions, optional self-report inventories, and the opportunity for referral for mental health treatment (Kroenke, Spitzer & Williams 2001). The follow-up for an AUDIT-C consists of alcohol counseling and the opportunity for mental health treatment referral.

Assessment

Primary care–mental health assessment may be provided within the primary care setting and may be initiated by mandated mental health screen follow-ups or by primary care provider preference. Positive mental health screens initiate suicide screening questions and/or alcohol education. PCMHI assessment may also include the use of follow-up measures such as the Patient Health Questionaire-9 item (PHQ-9) (Hahn et al. 2000; Kroenke, Spitzer & Williams, 2001) and Posttraumatic Stress Disorder Checklist (PCL-C) (Weathers et al. 1993). Such measures may be used as part of the primary care–mental health assessment to guide diagnoses and treatment planning.

Triage/Referral

Primary care–mental health integration triage is a service typically provided when mental health issues are presented in a primary care clinic and after screening and assessment have been completed. Triage enables rapid assessment of the urgency of the mental health problems and problem-focused interventions and connects patients with an appropriate level of mental healthcare and/or local mental health resources. Once patients are identified as having mental health issues that need to be addressed, they are typically referred for some level of treatment. Usual care procedures would provide referral to specialty mental health, which may not be appropriate or efficient because of the mismatch of symptom severity and specialty referral. Instead, a more appropriate brief, nonintensive treatment may be offered. Primary care–mental health integration enables exploration of other treatment options such as brief intervention in primary care, referral to a community agency/resource, or referral to a VA center. As an example of the problem with always referring to specialty mental health, a patient who is experiencing mild symptoms or expectable levels of stress may not feel that he or she needs or wants to go to a specialty mental health clinic, resulting in that patient not getting any form of mental health service. Conversely, a flood of referrals for patients who actually may benefit from less intensive mental health services provided by primary care–mental health can overburden the specialty mental health system, resulting in increased wait times for patients with severe mental health conditions; put a strain on available resources; and limit the range, frequency, and intensity of treatment provided. Triage enables advance access to mental health services and coordinated, appropriate referrals. Primary care–mental health integration programs may help enhance specialty mental health services through providing appropriate referrals and increasing collaboration between primary care and specialty mental health.

Primary Care–Mental Health Brief Interventions

Patients who need assistance with behavior change, who are not better served by specialty mental health, may be managed by primary care–mental health services in the medical setting. Increasing overall access means providing more pragmatic interventions that are generalizable across a limited number of sessions. Brief episodes of care may range from same-day psychoeducation to brief therapy. Treatment planning and selected intervention are based on a stepped-care approach; that is, patients receive the lowest level of intervention needed to gain the optimum outcome. Nevertheless, all levels of stepped care

are selected according to screening/assessment results, patient preference, and the evidence base for the presenting problem. Monitoring of patient progress and interdisciplinary team collaboration are necessary to ensure that the level of the stepped-care approach selected is appropriate and effective.

Primary care–mental health integration services are provided in the primary care setting and include evidence-based interventions, self-management protocols, education, and therapy, which are implemented in a collaborated team approach. Primary care–mental health treatment includes brief, stepped, episodic behavioral interventions and primary care provider collaborative care medication monitoring rather than traditional individual or group therapies.

Nonpharmacologic Interventions

Nonpharmacological interventions are focused on addressing realistic functional goals that can be achieved in brief therapy. These interventions include care management (i.e., watchful waiting), motivational interviewing (Anstiss 2009), behavioral techniques, cognitive interventions, self-management interventions (Rollman et al. 2005), supportive techniques, psychoeducation, and care management interventions. Katon and colleagues (1996) found that most primary care patients will complete mental health treatment that is brief and pragmatic. Behavioral interventions have been found to increase medical compliance and life change (Cummings, O'Donohue & Cummings 2009). Whitlock and colleagues (2002) highlight the need for behavioral counseling in primary care to facilitate health-related behavioral change and promote self-management practices, continuity of care, health promotion, and disease prevention. Furthermore, Matalon and colleagues (2009) found improvements in functional status and self-perception of health among primary care patients who participated in integrated short-term cognitive-behavioral therapy, stress reduction techniques, and medication.

VHA has taken the lead in promoting evidence-based treatments. Primary care–mental health providers may use cognitive-behavioral therapies (CBT) or utilize specific cognitive and behavioral interventions to assist patients in meeting functional goals. Howell and colleagues (2008) describe a multimodal skills-based approach that incorporates a range of evidence-based psychosocial strategies, such as problem solving, referred to as "keeping the blues away" (KBA), which revealed among older patients that relapse rates were significantly reduced when compared with the control. Bertholet and colleagues' (2005) meta-analysis of outcomes of brief alcohol interventions in primary care found that they were effective in reducing alcohol consumption among primary care patients. After identifying that the patient may be a candidate for medication monitoring, the psychologist may discuss with the primary care physician and provide medication support if the primary care physician chooses to prescribe psychotropic medication. Patient self-management is another area of intervention that VHA is utilizing. Self-management interventions are important in the management of chronic conditions, making them ideal for the primary care setting. Healthcare outcomes are enhanced when patients collaborate with providers on the care plan. Self-management empowers patients, increases self-efficacy, and enables patients to play an active role in their care. Providers must be prepared to provide education and training to patients appropriate for self-management interventions. Furthermore, monitoring of patient progress and assessment of knowledge and practice are helpful in maximizing the outcomes of self-management interventions.

Collaborative Care Medication Monitoring

Patients are often treated by their primary care providers with frontline psychotropic medications. One study found that VHA patients who were receiving services that were not considered PCMHI for depression in primary care were found to be less likely to receive antidepressants than patients receiving some or most of their depression treatment in a specialty mental health setting (Blow et al. 2002). Roy-Byrne and colleagues' (2005) randomized, controlled trial of six sessions of cognitive-behavioral therapy in the primary care setting combined with algorithm-based pharmacotherapy found sustained and gradually increasing improvement in anxiety symptoms, as well as other health-related factors. In another study, only 54 percent of VHA patients started on antidepressants complied with the medication for the recommended time frame (Busch, Leslie & Rosenheck 2004). Patients may not take medications as recommended (Moncrieff, Wessely & Hardy 2001). In another study, only 31 percent of veterans treated with antidepressants had adequate follow-up care (Cully et al. 2008). Such studies support the need for PCMHI programs that offer first-line antidepressant medication. To increase access, address barriers to receiving and complying with psychotropic medications, and ultimately maximize use of specialty mental health services, PCMHI provides collaborative care medication monitoring.

Collaborative care medication monitoring consists of providing support to primary care providers and enabling patients to receive appropriate treatment in primary care rather than being referred to specialty mental health. This intervention provides quick access to first-line psychotropic medication for patients experiencing mild to moderate depression and anxiety. This treatment option may be more clinically appropriate and efficient than a referral to specialty mental health. Typically, the psychologist will consult with the primary care provider about whether or not the patient will benefit from a first-line antidepressant. The primary care provider may prescribe a medication if it is appropriate, and the psychologist or a care manager provides basic education about the medication and monitors and tracks compliance, side effects, and response. A primary care physician may choose not to write the prescription and instead refer the patient to specialty mental health. Collaborative care medication monitoring is not exclusive to patients who have never been referred to specialty mental health and may also include patients who have been managed by specialty mental health for mild to moderate noncomplex conditions that are now stable and can be discharged from specialty mental health and managed by their primary care providers. Collaborative care medication monitoring can be provided during the course of brief therapy. Katon and colleagues (1999) found that the collaborative care program in their study resulted in significant improvements in adherence to antidepressants, patient satisfaction, and treatment outcomes.

Special Issues

Chronic Pain

Pain is a common concern voiced by primary care patients (Bigos et al. 1994). Physicians often describe having difficulty managing these patients and may not have referral resources that are practical or appropriate for and/or accepted by patients. Primary care–mental health integration is ideal for complementing primary and secondary levels of medical care for patients suffering from chronic pain. Integration of medical and behavioral services that include assessment, interventions, and treatment planning can benefit both patients and their providers. Integrated pain assessment and treatment planning may identify key functional problems and promote more comprehensive, balanced recommendations. Primary care–mental health providers can provide assessment and support for concerns regarding medication misuse if a patient has a history of substance abuse. Assessment results may assist in appropriate triage and/or treatment planning by the primary care team (i.e., referral to pain clinic, referral to substance use program).

Behavioral interventions provided by primary care–mental health providers may complement pharmacotherapy and other medical procedures used for pain management. Dobscha and colleagues (2009) found significant improvements in outcomes with care management for chronic pain in primary care (i.e., depression scores, pain intensity, disability, use of antidepressants, and use of any opioids). Furthermore, findings from Stepped-Care for Affective

Disorders and Musculoskeletal Pain (SCAMP) found improvements in depression scores, pain scores, and antidepressant compliance (Kroenke et al. 2009). These studies provide support for the premise that pain management services can be beneficial and sustainable in an integrated care system. Providing integrated pain management services in primary care meets objectives of PCMHI.

Post-9/11 Service Members

Research indicates that post-9/11 Operation Enduring Freedom–Operation Iraqi Freedom/ Global War on Terrorism/ Operation New Dawn (OEF-OIF/GWOT/OND)–era service members have high rates of mental health and psychosocial issues (Seal et al. 2009; Tanielian & Jaycox 2008). Due to issues such as mental health stigma, these service members would not likely attend a "cold" scheduled mental health visit; thus, primary care is an ideal setting to identify needs and promote treatment engagement. In an effort to promote postdeployment mental health and prevent more complex mental health issues, OEF-OIF/GWOT/OND–era service members, at a minimum, are undergoing mandated postdeployment screening (e.g., screening for traumatic brain injury) during their first primary care visits. For other clinics with available resources, postdeployment clinic visits are being scheduled as part of the patient's first primary care appointment. During this visit the patient is seen by the primary care provider, a primary care–mental health provider, and an OEF/OIF social worker/case manager. Postdeployment clinics that are part of PCMHI programs can facilitate normalization of mental health issues by 1) establishing that mental health is part of physical health, 2) providing routine mental health screening, and 3) showing that mental health and medical providers collaborate in the same setting. Due to the needs of new returnees, access provided by PCMHI is imperative.

Diversity Issues

Primary care patients have become more diverse along with the general U.S. population. In 2006 in the general population there were 2.4 million African American/black veterans, 1.1 million Hispanic veterans, 292,000 Asian veterans, 169,000 American Indian or Alaska Native veterans, and 28,000 Native Hawaiian or Other Pacific Islander veterans (U.S. Census Bureau 2006). Given the numbers of culturally diverse groups and the research conducted by

VHA regarding mental health access of diverse groups, attention to the access needs of these groups is important. Uebelacker and colleagues (2009) found that minority groups were less likely to receive mental health care. A 2007 article describes how PCMHI is a means to overcoming ethnic disparities in access to mental health services. Specifically, the authors found that elderly African Americans in the integrated model were significantly more likely to have at least one mental health/substance abuse visit (77.5 percent), versus African Americans/blacks in the enhanced referral model (22 percent) (Ayalon et al. 2007). VHA has developed the Center for Minority Veterans, which is part of the Office of the Secretary. Its goal is to provide and promote utilization of VHA's services by minority veterans (http://www1.va.gov/centerforminorityveterans/). Although diversity issues and provider competencies generally remain constant across various mental health specialties and subspecialties, PCMHI programs offer an additional point of access.

Women are one of the fastest-growing groups in the veteran population. The U.S. Census reported that in 2006 there were 1.7 million female veterans (U.S. Census Bureau 2008a, table 505). Chatterjee and colleagues (2009) concluded that female veterans underutilized specialty mental health services when compared to male veterans. Regardless of whether a female veteran is seen in a VA women's health clinic or a mixed male and female primary care clinic, they will have access to PCMHI services. Primary care–mental health integration can facilitate better overall health outcomes in female veterans.

The U.S. Census also reported that in 2006 there were 9.2 million veterans who were age sixty-five or older (U.S. Census Bureau 2008b, table 506). Many of these veterans may experience mental health problems and psychosocial stressors, but for various reasons may not address them. Karlin and Fuller's (2007) article provides a review of geriatric mental health delivery that supports the need to provide enhanced identification and treatment of mental health conditions in older primary care patients. Furthermore, Arean and colleagues' (2002) survey found that 70 percent of older adult primary care patients in the sample reported that they would utilize mental services presented, and 46 percent reported that they would speak with a mental health provider or nurse about their mental health concerns. Although primary care clinics provide services to veterans of all ages, there are circumstances in which older veterans (i.e., World War II veterans with physical disability) cannot attend outpatient visits. VHA's home-based primary care (HBPC) clinics focus on providing integrated services to homebound veterans. These teams consist of physicians, nurses, social workers, a full-time mental health provider, and other providers who may contribute to treatment (e.g., physical therapists, pharmacists, and occupational therapists). The mental health provider is a core member of the team and provides evidence-based cognitive and psychological assessment, as well as psychological interventions to veterans, their families, and caregivers. A unique aspect of this program is that HBPC providers can gather valuable information about patients' functioning and progress by seeing their home environments and interacting with family members and caregivers. Although this program may not utilize any of the aforementioned PCMHI models, it provides a collaborative approach to primary care that integrates mental health assessment and treatment.

Patient Aligned Care Teams (PACT)

The "patient-centered medical home" has been in existence and has been refined since the 1960s, and, like PCMHI, it has been considered an approach that could improve primary care processes, clinical quality and patient experience, and cost efficiencies (American Academy of Pediatrics, Council on Pediatric Practice 1967). In 2007 the American Academy of Family Physicians, and American Academy of Pediatrics, and American College of Physicians published a joint statement on the principles of the medical home. These principles emphasize provider-patient relationships, team delivery of holistic care, care coordination across settings, quality improvement, open access to care, and affordable care. A salient objective of the patient-centered medical home is to engage patients in playing an active role in their healthcare. Many of the aforementioned principles are enhanced by new developments in healthcare information technology. The patient-centered medical home is a comprehensive approach that promotes direct patient-provider communication and when appropriate also involves the patient's family and community (Donaldson et al. 1996; Starfield, Shi & Macinko 2005).

In 2010 VHA implemented patient-centered medical homes to enhance continued efforts to improve healthcare quality, patient satisfaction, and efficiency. VHA later renamed the patient-centered medical homes the patient aligned care teams (PACTs). Many VA healthcare systems have already implemented components of PACTs with the goal of full implementation. A common question that has been presented is how the PACTs impact or interface with PCMHI. Although the answer to this question may evolve as PACTs are implemented throughout VHA, PCMHI does share several similarities with PACTs. Given that PACTs and PCMHI share several key principles, the two should complement one another. It can be expected that the PACTs may only enhance functioning of PCMHI programs by improving the quality of clinical services and healthcare efficiencies.

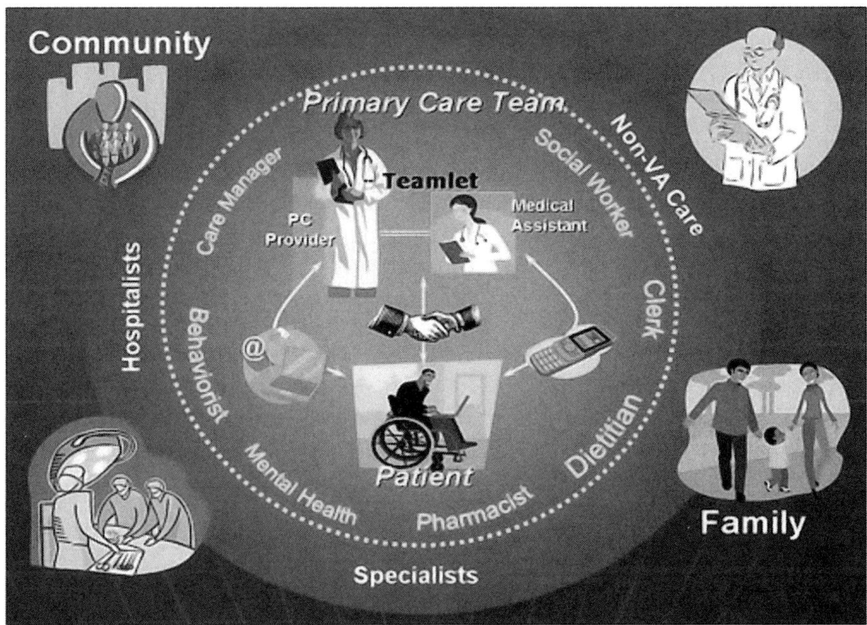

Figure 1.2. Primary Care–Mental Health Integration Model for VA Healthcare.

Challenges and Future Implications

Serving as a Bridge

A primary care–mental health provider in a VA facility is in a unique position in that many VA facilities house mental health and primary care clinics on the same campus, allowing for more interface between clinics. In a system that typically had disallowed care between departments, primary care–mental health providers can easily find themselves taking sides with either specialty mental health or primary care. The primary care–mental health provider's first obligation is to provide quality clinical care; thus it is important that a patient's providers, regardless of clinic, are working together at some level. Primary care–mental health providers should serve to facilitate communication and enhance relations between primary care and mental health facilities. They serve as both mental health and primary care representatives. One way to meet this challenge is to keep this role in mind, especially when being confronted with concerns from either clinic. It also helps to try to maintain well-balanced relationships between both services.

Collaborative Care Medication Monitoring

There are several challenges that may present when considering collaborative care medication monitoring intervention provided in some of the primary care–mental health models. Although collaborative care medication monitoring appears to be a valuable service, gaining buy-in from primary care physicians can be a challenge. Primary care providers may be accustomed to sending all patients with psychotropic medication needs to specialty mental health regardless of severity level and even if the patient may only need a first-line antidepressant. Reasons for this include physicians feeling over burdened by managing basic general medical issues and physicians having the perception that all psychotropic medication should be managed by psychiatrists. This may occur for several reasons, the most important being that primary care physicians are overwhelmed by other clinical management issues. One way to address such issues is by providing education, building the provider's confidence through excelling in other services, and including this process in a service agreement and gaining local leadership support.

Psychologists having prescription privileges continue to be an area for debate in many state legislatures (VandenBos & Williams 2000); however, regardless of local regulation, VHA PCMHI providers may be accustomed to supporting primary care providers in prescribing first-line psychotropic medications. Given this new role, it is important for a primary care–mental health provider to carefully manage expectations and clarify his or her role regarding medications. Providing medication monitoring services to prescribing primary care physicians may be beneficial in facilitating patient adherence and continuity of care.

Implementation

Although PCMHI has been supported by VHA, its implementation has encountered resistance. One of the initial challenges faced by those attempting to implement it has been facilitating a culture shift for medical staff as well as mental health staff. For mental health providers not trained in PCMHI, integration is a major shift from traditional mental healthcare services (i.e., fifty- to sixty-minute sessions). The spirit of PCMHI promotes access through interdisciplinary teamwork; in systems that are accustomed to multidisciplinary teams and/or siloed care, this shift may be more challenging. Primary care–mental health integration requires careful and collaborative organizational planning and attention to clinical, operational, logistical, and financial issues. It is not simply just placing a mental health provider in primary care, and Kessler (2008) cautions against this approach. Differences between mental and medical health providers can be overcome by building positive interpersonal relationships and improvements in patient care and outcomes.

Recruitment

Once programs receive funding, recruitment challenges may arise with regard to filling positions in rural locations and finding candidates with prior PCMHI training and experience. To date there are a limited number of psychology training programs that teach the principles of PCMHI and facilitate the skills needed to be successful in the primary care setting. Increasing PCMHI training opportunities in psychology graduate programs, internships, and postdoctoral fellowships may be helpful in preparing future primary care–mental health providers for the primary care culture and the broad range of administrative and clinical needs. Filling PCMHI positions in rural areas was particularly difficult during the early national implementation. To address this, VHA provided recruitment incentives for providers through Mental Health Enhancement Initiative Funding. Exploring other methods of announcing positions, such as posting to credible national listservs and announcing at mental health conferences and workshops, may be helpful.

Training

Because PCMHI is a relatively new program, upon its implementation mental health providers were asked to take on program management roles for programs that they were often unfamiliar with. In response to the need, VHA implemented training for PCMHI program managers. National, dynamic PCMHI education and training programs continue to be developed. In keeping with the spirit of integration, it would be beneficial to have national training that joins medical and mental health provider participants.

Evidence-based Psychotherapy

The Veterans Health Administration supports brief, evidence-based treatments. Currently, PCMHI providers offer patients a range of interventions such as psychoeducation, motivational interventions, and cognitive and behavioral techniques. As more PSMHI programs progress and further develop treatment protocols, more evidence may become available on standardized individual and group protocols that are tailored for primary care patients.

Program implementation at some facilities has been challenging for several reasons. An example is initiating the program at a facility without knowing how the program will be received by both medical and mental health providers. To better facilitate positive experiences when initiating a new PCMHI program, a controlled and gradual roll-out may be useful. Furthermore, larger VA healthcare systems may need to consider how multiple implementation sites within the same system can be individually tailored to meet site-specific needs while preserving core PCMHI principles and key standardized procedures. Support from both primary care and mental health leadership will facilitate implementation.

A common challenge that surfaced was the inability of facilities to provide appropriate office space for a new and growing PCMHI team. It should be noted that among co-located collaborative care and blended models it is imperative that space be provided that is co-located and embedded within the primary care clinic to ensure visibility and access, and to further normalize mental health services. Space may be shared, and the primary care provider may have to use an available exam room rather than a traditional office. As Kessler, Stafford, and Messier (2009) suggest, office space should be multipurpose in order to be financially viable. Flexibility and primary care administrative support are important factors in addressing this issue.

Sustainability

Sustainability has been of concern, and VHA is taking steps to ensure programs can be sustainable. One thing to consider regarding sustainability is reimbursement. Although VHA does not have to be concerned about fee-for-service, other issues are of concern for providers. For example, patient care is measured by productivity criteria that may not capture important services (e.g., team treatment planning, team meetings). Systemic redesign that matches the demand and expectations of PCMHI settings and practices and workload/workflow standards is necessary to ensure sustainability, efficiency, and satisfaction. Use of evaluation and management (E&M) codes specifically focused on integrated mental health services is important. Health and behavior codes used for behavioral treatment of medical issues and the code for consultation and treatment planning between psychologist and physician are ideal for use in PCMHI programs (Kessler, Stafford & Messier 2009).

There are challenges regarding cost to patient and reimbursement. For example, some patients may still encounter financial barriers (i.e., copays) for services such as chronic illness self-management groups. On a positive note, primary care–mental health assessment and triage may assist in reducing the numbers of patients unnecessarily referred to specialty mental health, ultimately reducing cost to patients, because specialty clinics are more costly than nonspecialty clinics (e.g., a $15 copay rather than a $50 copay). The Substance Abuse and Mental Health Services Administration (SAMHSA) and the Health Resources and Services Administration (HRSA) have published a document entitled *Reimbursement of Mental Health Services in Primary Care* (Kautz, Mauch & Smith 2008) that may help resolve issues related to PCMHI reimbursement.

Information Technology (IT)

The President's New Freedom Commission on Mental Health (Hogan 2003; U.S. Surgeon General 2003) set the goal to use technology to access mental health care information and to improve coordination and quality to all veterans, including those who are considered underserved. Technology focused on database management, tracking systems, decisional support tools, and Web-based registries can lead to quality improvement (Croghan et al. 2006). There are multiple modalities of technology that can enhance access and facilitate patient self-management and self-monitoring such as telephone, video, and secure e-mail messaging. VHA has embraced innovations in technology and can be considered the leader in health information technology. It enhances clinical practice and quality of care through use of the integrated computerized patient record system (CPRS), My HealtheVet, and telemedicine. Primary care–mental health integration models such as the BHL have used IT for program implementation and maintenance, as well as for increasing access to underserved areas. While advances in healthcare communication and technology provide increased access to underserved geographic locations, they bring with them a broad range of challenges and raise important legal and ethical questions that need careful consideration. Furthermore, primary care–mental health providers need to keep abreast of technological advances. Education and staff training will assist with addressing these challenges.

Outcome Monitoring, Quality Assurance, and Program Evaluation

In order to assess, monitor, and possibly revise procedures, the objectives of PCMHI programs are being met. These programs participate in evaluation at the VISN, facility, and programmatic level. In addition to mandated use of performance measures, facility programs may provide internal program evaluation, outcome monitoring, and patient tracking. The VHA's Office of Primary Care–Mental Health Integration also conducts national evaluation of PCMHI. Such evaluations facilitate program fidelity, accountability and provide information useful for policy development.

Performance measures are utilized to ensure quality of care and to monitor outcomes. However, some providers may feel that such measures add to their already busy schedules. There may also be concern about whether performance targets may not reflect the complexities of the veteran population. Efforts to improve measures and their targets will be useful in improving provider satisfaction and quality improvement methods. Meanwhile, providers may contribute to improvement of measures by providing feedback to their administrators regarding clinical utility and functionality of such measures. Nevertheless, program evaluation and use of performance metrics contribute to system redesign and program development.

Policy

Primary care–mental health integration impacts VHA policy and continues to shape resource allocations, funding, dissemination, implementation projects, and clinical mandates. Although new policy is often developed with the intention of enhancing patient care quality, it also presents challenges to providers. For example, providers who are already balancing multiple clinical demands may have additional demands added, with no adjustment to or consideration for current processes. Given this, more preparation, time to adjust, and input from front-line clinicians may assist in the overall implementation process. Future policy directed at providing reinforcement to providers that is based on qualitative clinical factors (e.g., use of patient-centered approach, patient satisfaction) would be helpful in not only building provider morale but also promoting overall quality.

Leadership and Support

Continued primary care–mental health leadership at the VISN level will be useful in evaluating outcomes, strategic planning, and systems redesigns and in providing guidance to facilities. As PCMHI outcome data become available, it is likely that programs will continue to evolve and progress. With changes, there will also be a need for continued implementation support to individual programs through teleconferences, VISN conferences, and national conferences. Program implementation, whether from a bottom-up or top-down development approach, requires attention to relationships at all levels. Program management training opportunities will facilitate strong leadership skills among VA PCMHI program leaders.

In conclusion, PCMHI is a major step toward enhancing VHA care quality and efficiency by bridging mental and physical health. As PCMHI programs evolve, there may be an increase in identified VHA best practices and continued transformation of U.S. healthcare.

References

AHRQ. (2008). *Evidence report/technology assessment* number 173: Integration of mental health/substance abuse and primary care. AHRQ Publication No. 09–E003.

American Academy of Family Physicians. (2010). Continuity of care, definition of. http://www.aafp.org/online/en/home/policy/policies/c/continuityofcaredefinition .html (accessed January 25, 2010).

American Academy of Family Physicians, American Academy of Pediatrics, American College of Physicians, American Osteopathic Association. (2007). Joint principles of the patient-centered medical home. http://www.aafp.org (accessed January 2010).

American Academy of Pediatrics, Council on Pediatric Practice. (1967). Pediatric records and a "medical home." In *Standards of child care* (pp. 77–79). Evanston, IL: American Academy of Pediatrics.

American Psychiatric Association. (2005). APA gold award: Improving treatment engagement and integrated care of veterans. *Psychiatric Services* 56: 1306–1308.

Anstiss, T. (2009). Motivational interviewing in primary care. *Journal of Clinical Psychology in the Medical Setting* 16: 87–93.

Arean, P. A., Alvidrez, J., Barrera, A., Robinson, G. S. & Hicks, S. (2002). Would older medical patients use psychological services? *The Gerontologist* 43, no. 3: 392–398.

Ayalon, L., Arean, P. A., Linkins, K., Lynch, M. & Estes, C. L. (2007). Integration of mental health services into primary care overcomes ethnic disparities in access to mental health services between black and white elderly. *American Journal of Geriatric Psychiatry* 15, no. 10: 906–912.

Barlow, D. H. & Campbell, L. A. (2000). Mixed anxiety-depression and its implications for models of mood and anxiety disorders. *Comprehensive Psychiatry* 41, no. supp. 1: 55–60.

Bartels, S. J., Coakley, E. H., Zubritsky, C., Ware, J. H., Miles, K. M., Areán, P. A. & Levkoff, S. E. (2004). Improving access to geriatric mental health services: A randomized trial comparing treatment engagement in integrated and enhanced referral care for depression, anxiety, and at-risk alcohol use. *American Journal of Psychiatry* 161: 1455–1462.

Bertholet, N., Daeppen, J., Wietlisbach, V., Fleming, M. & Burnand, B. (2005). Reduction of alcohol consumption by brief alcohol intervention in primary care. *Archives of Internal Medicine* 165: 986–995.

Bigos, S., Bowyer, O., Braen, G., Brown, K., Deyo, R., Haldeman, S., et al. (1994). *Acute low back problems in adults.* AHCPR Publication No. 95–0642. Rockville,

MD: Agency for Health Care Policy and Research, Public Health Service, U.S. Department of Health and Human Services.

Blount, A. (2003). Integrated primary care: Organizing the evidence. *Families, Systems & Health Summary* 21, no. 2: 121–133.

Blow, F. C., Owen, R. E., Valenstein, M., Austin, K., Khanuja, K., & McCarthy, J. F. (Serious Mental Illness Treatment Research and Evaluation Center (SMITREC)). (2002). Specialty care for veterans with depression in the VHA: 2002 National Registry for Depression (NARDEP) report.

Boone, J. L. & Christensen, J. F. (1997). Stress and disease. In M. D. Feldman & J. F. Christensen (Eds.), *Behavioral medicine in primary care: A practical guide* (pp. 265–276). Stamford, CT: Appleton and Lange.

Bruce, M. L., Tenhav, T. R., Reynolds, C. F., III, et al. (2004). Reducing suicidal ideation and depressive symptoms in depressed older primary care patients: A randomized controlled trial. *JAMA* 291, no. 9: 1081–1091.

Burman, M. L., Kivlahan, D., Buchbinder, M., Broglio, K., Zhou, X. H., Merrill, J. O., Mcdonell, M. B., Fihn, S. D. & Bradley, K. A. (2004). Alcohol-related advice for Veterans Affairs primary care patients: Who gets it? Who gives it? *Journal of Studies on Alcohol* 65: 621–630.

Busch, S. H., Leslie, D. & Rosenheck, R. (2004). Measuring quality of pharmacotherapy for depression in a national health care system. *Medical Care* 42, no. 6: 532–542.

Bush, K., Kivlahan D. R., McDonell M. B., Fihn S. D. & Bradley K. A. (1998). The AUDIT alcohol consumption questions (AUDIT-C): An effective brief screening test for problem drinking. *Archives of Internal Medicine* 158, no. 16: 1789–1795.

Butler, M., Kane, R. L., McAlpine, D., Kathol, R. G., Fu, S. S., Hagedorn, H. & Wilt, T. J. (2008a). Integration of mental health/substance abuse and primary care. *Evidence Report/Technology Assessment (Full Report)* 173: 1–362.

Butler, M., Kane, R. L., McAlpine, D., Kathol, R. G., Fu, S. S., Hagedorn, H. & Wilt, T. J. (2008b). *Integration of mental health/substance abuse and primary care.* Prepared by the Minnesota Evidence-based Practice Center under Contract No. 290–02–0009. AHRQ Publication No. 09–E003. Rockville, MD: Agency for Healthcare Research and Quality.

Callahan, M. C., Kroenke, K., Counsell, S. R., Hendrie, H. C., Perkins, A. J., Katon, W., Noel, P. H., Harpole, L., Hunkeler, E. M. & Unützer, J., for the IMPACT Investigators. (2005). Treatment of depression improves physical functioning in older adults. *Journal of the American Geriatric Society* 53, no. 3: 367–373.

Calleo, J., Stanley, M. A., Greisinger, A., Wehmanen, O., Johnson, M., Novy, D., Wilson, N. & Kunik, M. (2009). Generalized anxiety disorder in older medical patients: Diagnostic recognition, mental health management and service utilization. *Journal of Clinical Psychology in Medical Settings* 16, no. 2: 178–185.

Casciani, A. I. (2004). The practical application of health and behavior codes. Paper presented at the American Psychological Association annual meeting, Honolulu, Hawaii.

Chatterjee, S., Rath, M. E., Spiro, A., Eisen, S., Sloan, K. L. & Rosen, A. K. (2009). Gender differences in veterans health administration mental health service use: Effects of age and psychiatric diagnosis. *Women's Health Issues* 19, no. 3: 176–184.

Chen, H., Coakley, E. H., Cheal, K., Maxwell, J., Costantino, G., Krahn, D. D., Malgady, R., Durai, U. B., Quijano, L. M., Zaman, S., Miller, C. J., Ware, J. H., Chung, H., Aoyama, C., Van Stone, W. & Lekoff, S. E. (2006). Satisfaction with mental health services in older primary care patients. *American Journal of Geriatric Psychiatry* 14, no. 4: 371–379.

Coleman, J. V., Patrick, D. L., Eagle, J. & Hermalin, J. A. (1979). Collaboration, consultation and referral in an integrated health–mental health program at an HMO. *Social Work in Health Care* 5: 833–896.

Croghan, T. W., Schoenbaum, M., Sherbourne, C. D., et al. (2006). A framework to improve the quality of care for depression in primary care. *Psychiatric Services* 57, no. 5: 623–631.

Cully, J. A., Zimmer, M., Khan, M. M. & Petersen, L. A. (2008). Quality of depression care and its impact on health service use and mortality among veterans. *Psychiatry Services* 59, no. 12: 1399–1405.

Cummings, N. A. (1997). Pioneering integrated systems. In N. A. Cummings, J. L. Cummings & J. N. Johnson (Eds.), *Behavioral health in primary care: A guide for clinical integration* (pp. 23–35). Madison, WI: Psychological Press International Universities Press.

Cummings, N. A. (n.d.). Appendix 8B: Medical cost offset as a roadmap to behavioral entrepreneurship: Lessons from the Hawaii Project. In J. L. Thomas, J. L. Cummings & W. T. O'Donahue (Eds.), *The collected papers of Nicholas A. Cummings: The entrepreneur in psychology* (Vol. II, pp. 200–218). Phoenix, AZ: Zeig, Tucker & Co.

Cummings, N. A., Dorken, H., Pallak, M. S. & Henke, C. J. (1993). The impact of psychological intervention on health care cost and utilization: The Hawaii Medicaid Project. In *Medicaid, managed behavioral health and implications for public policy*, volume 2, *Healthcare and utilization cost series* (pp. 3–23). South San Francisco, CA: Foundation for Behavioral Health.

Cummings, N. A. & Follette, W. T. (1968). Psychiatric services and medical utilization in a prepaid health plan setting, part 2. *Medical Care* 6: 31–41.

Cummings, N. A., Kahn, B. I. & Sparkman, B. (1962). *Psychotherapy and medical utilization: A pilot study*. Oakland, CA: Annual Reports of Kaiser Permanente Research Projects.

Cummings, N. A., O'Donohue, W. T. & Cummings, J. L. (2009). The financial dimension of integrated behavioral/primary care. *Journal of Psychology in the Medical Setting* 16: 31–39.

Cummings, N. A., O'Donohue, W. T. & Ferguson, K. E. (2003). *Behavioral health as primary care: Beyond efficacy to effectiveness*. Reno, NV: Context Press.

Cummings, S. M., Neff, J. A. & Husaini, B. A. (2003). Functional impairment as a predictor of depressive symptomatology: The role of race, religiosity, and social support. *Health & Social Work* 28: 23–32.

deGruy, F. (1996). Mental health care in the primary care setting. In M. S. Donaldson, K. D. Yordy, K. N. Lohr, et al., *Primary care: America's health in a new era*. Washington, DC: National Academy Press.

Department of Veterans Affairs, Center for Minority Veterans. (n.d.). http://www1.va.gov/centerforminorityveterans/ (accessed February 5, 2010).

Department of Veterans Affairs, Quality Enhancement Research Initiative (QUERI), SUD-PTSD Work Group. (2008). Update: Co-occurring SUDs and PTSD. http://www.queri.research.va.gov/about/impact_updates/SUD-PTSD.pdf (accessed February 5, 2010).

Department of Veterans Affairs, VA Health Services Research and Development Service, Office of Research and Development. (2008). *Collaborative care for depression in the primary care setting: A primer on VA's Translating Initiatives for Depression into Effective Solutions (TIDES) project*. Boston: Center for Information Dissemination and Education Resources; Washington, DC: Department of Veterans Affairs.

Desai, M. M., Rosenheck, R. A. & Craig, T. J. (2006). Case-finding for depression among medical outpatients in the Veterans Health Administration. *Medical Care* 44, no. 2: 175–181.

Dietrich, A. J., Oxman, T. E., Williams, J. W., Jr., Schulberg, H. C., Bruce, M. L., Lee, P. W., Barry, S., Raue, P. J., Lefever, J. J., Heo, M., Rost, K., Kroenke, K., Gerrity, M. & Nutting, P. A. (2004). Re-engineering systems for the treatment of depression in primary care: Clustered randomized controlled trial. *British Medical Journal* 329, 7466: 602.

Dobscha, S. K., Corson, K., Perrin, N. A., Hanson, G. C., Leibowitz, R. Q., Doak, M. N., & Gerrity, M. S. (2009). Collaborative care for chronic pain in primary care: A cluster randomized trial. *Journal of the American Medical Association* 301, no. 12: 1242–1252.

Doherty, W. J., McDaniel, S. H. & Baird, M. A. (1996). Five levels of primary care/behavioral healthcare collaboration. *Behavioral Healthcare Tomorrow*, October: 25–28.

Donaldson, M., Yordy, K., Lohr, K. & Vanselov, N. (Eds.) (1996). *Primary care: America's health in a new era*. Washington, DC: National Academy Press.

Druss, B. G. & Newcomer, J. W. (2007). Challenges and solutions to integrating mental and physical health care. *Journal of Clinical Psychiatry* 68, no. 4: e09.

Earl, L. & Kincey, J. (1982). Clinical psychology in general practice: A controlled trial evaluation. *Journal of the Royal College of General Practitioners* 32: 32–37.

Egede, L. E., Zheng, D. & Simpson, K. (2002). Comorbid depression is associated with increased health care use and expenditures among individuals with diabetes mellitus. *Diabetes Care* 25, no. 3: 464–470.

Engel, C. C., Oxman, T., Yamamoto, C., Gould, D., Barry, S., Stewart, P., Kroenke, K., Williams, J. W., Jr. & Dietrich, A. J. (2008). RESPECT-Mil: Feasibility of a systems-level collaborative care approach to depression and post-traumatic stress disorder in military primary care. *Military Medicine* 173, no. 10: 935–940.

Felker, B. L., Barnes, R. F., Greenberg, D. M., Chaney, E. F., Shores, M. M., Gillespie-Gateley, L., Buike, M. K. & Morton, C. E. (2004). Preliminary outcomes from an integrated mental health primary care team. *Psychiatric Services* 55, no. 4: 442–444.

Felker, B. L., Chaney, E., Rubensein, L. V., Bonner, H. L., Yano, E. M., Parker, L. E., Worley, L. M., Sherman, S. E. & Ober, S. (2006). Developing effective collaboration between primary care and mental health providers. *Primary Care Companion Journal of Clinical Psychiatry* 8, no. 1: 12–16.

Fleet R., Lavoie K. & Beitman, B. D. (2000). Is panic disorder associated with coronary artery disease? *Journal of Psychosomatic Research* 48: 347–356.

Funderburk, J. S., Maisto, S. A., Sugarman, D. E., Smucny, J. & Epling, J. (2008). How do alcohol brief interventions fit with models of integrated primary care? *Families, Systems & Health* 26, no. 1: 1–15.

Gallo, J. J., Bogner, H. R., Morales, K. H., Post, E. P., Lin, J. Y. & Bruce, M. L. (2007). The effect of a primary care practice-based depression intervention on mortality in older adults: A randomized trial. *Annals of Internal Medicine* 146, no. 10: 689–698.

Gallo, J. J., Zubritsky, C., Maxwell, J., Nazar, M., Bogner, H. R., Quijano, L. M., Syropoulos, H. J., Cheal, K. L., Chen, H., Sanchez, H., Dodson, J., Levkoff, S. E. & PRISM-E Investigators. (2004). Primary care clinicians evaluate integrated and referral models of behavioral health care for older adults: Results from a multi-site effectiveness trial (PRISM-E). *Annals of Family Medicine* 2, no. 4: 306–309.

Gilbody, S., Bower P., Fletcher, J., et al. (2006). Collaborative care for depression: A cumulative meta-analysis and review of longer-term outcomes. *Archives of Internal Medicine* 166, no. 21: 2314–2321.

Greene-Shortridge, T. M., Britt, T. W. & Castro, C. A. (2007). The stigma of mental health problems in the military. *Military Medicine* 172, no. 2: 157.

Grossberg, P. M., Brown, D. D. & Fleming, M. F. (2004). Brief physician advice for high-risk drinking among young adults. *Annals of Family Medicine* 2, no. 5: 474–480.

Haas, J. S., Cook, E. F., Puopolo, R. L., Burstin, H. R., Cleary, P. D. & Brennan, T. A. (2000). Is the professional satisfaction of general internists associated with patient satisfaction? *Journal of General Internal Medicine* 15: 122–128.

Haas, L. J. (2004). *Primary care psychology*. Oxford: Oxford University Press.

Haas, L. J. & deGruy, F. V. (2005). Primary care, psychology and primary care psychology. In L. J. Haas (Ed.), *Handbook of primary care psychology* (pp. 5–19). New York: Oxford University Press.

Hahn, S. R., Kroenke, K., Williams, J. B. W. & Spitzer, R. L. (2000). Evaluation of mental disorders with the PRIME-MD. In M. Maruish (Ed.), *Handbook of psychological assessment in primary care settings* (pp. 191–253). Mahwah, NJ: Lawrence Erlbaum.

Hankin, C. S., Spiro, A., III, Miller, D. R. & Lewis, K. (1999). Mental disorders and mental health treatment among U.S. Department of Veterans Affairs outpatients: The Veterans Health Study. *American Journal of Psychiatry* 156, no. 12: 1924–1930.

Hedrick, S. C., Chaney, E. F., Felker, B., Liu, C., Hasenberg, N., Heagerty, P., Buchanan, J., Bagala, R., Greenberg, D., Paden, G., Fihn, S. D. & Katon, W. (2003). Effectiveness of collaborative care depression treatment in veterans' affairs primary care. *Journal of General Internal Medicine* 18, no. 1: 9–16.

Hogan, M. F. (2003). New Freedom Commission report: The President's New Freedom Commission: Recommendations to transform mental health care in America. *Psychiatric Services* 54, no. 11: 1467–1474.

Hoge, C. W., Auchterlonie, J. L. & Milliken, C. S. (2006). Mental health problems, use of mental health services, and attrition from military service after returning from deployment to Iraq or Afghanistan. *JAMA* 295: 1023–1032.

Hoge, C. W., Castro, C. A., Messer, S. C., McGurk, D., Cotting, D. I. & Koffman, R. L. (2004). Combat duty in Iraq and Afghanistan, mental health problems, and barriers to care. *New England Journal of Medicine* 351, no. 1: 13–22.

Horvitz-Lennon, M., Kilbourne, A. M. & Pincus, H. A. (2006). From silos to bridges: Meeting the general health care needs of adults with severe mental illnesses. *Health Affairs* 25, no. 3: 659–669.

Howell, C. A., Turnbull, D. A., Beilby, J. J., Marshall, C. A., Briggs N. & Newbury, W. L. (2008). Preventing relapse of depression in primary care: A pilot study of the "keeping the blues away" program. *Medical Journal of Australia* 188, no. 12: s138–s141.

Hunkeler, E. M., Katon, W., Tang, L., Williams, J. W., Jr., Kroenke, K., Lin, E. H. B., Harpole, L. H., Arean, P., Levine, S., Grypma, L. M., Hargreaves, W. A. & Unützer, J. (2006). Long term outcomes from the IMPACT randomized trial for depressed elderly patients in primary care. *British Medical Journal* 332, no. 7536: 259–263.

Institute of Medicine. (1994). *Defining primary care: An interim report.* Washington, DC: National Academy Press.

Institute of Medicine. (2006). *Improving the quality of health care for mental health and substance-use conditions.* Quality chasm series. Committee on Crossing the Quality Chasm: Adaptation to Mental Health and Addictive Disorders. Board on Health Care Services. Washington, DC: National Academy Press.

Karlin, B. E. & Fuller, J. D. (2007). Meeting the mental health needs of older adults: Implications for primary care practice. *Geriatrics* 62, no. 1: 26–35.

Katon, W. J. (2003). Clinical and health services relationships between major depression, depressive symptoms, and general medical illness. *Biological Psychiatry* 54, no. 3: 216–226.

Katon, W. & Gonzales, J. (1994). A review of randomized trials of psychiatric consultation–liaison studies in primary care. *Psychosomatics* 35: 268–278.

Katon, W., Lin, E. & Kroenke, K. (2007). The association of depression and anxiety with medical symptom burden in patients with chronic medical illness. *General Hospital Psychiatry* 29, no. 2: 147–155.

Katon, W., Robinson, P., Von Korff, M., Lin, E., Bush, T., Ludman, E., Simon, G., & Walker, E. (1996). A multifaceted intervention to improve treatment of depression in primary care. *Archives of General Psychiatry* 53(10): 924–932.

Katon, W., Von Korff, M., Lin, E., et al. (1992). A randomized trial of psychiatric consultation with distressed high utilizers. *General Hospital Psychiatry* 14, no. 2: 86–98.

Katon, W., Von Korff, M., Lin, E., Simon, G., Walker, E., Unutzer, J., Bush, T., Russo, J. & Ludman, E. (1999). Stepped collaborative care for primary care patients with persistent symptoms of depression: A randomized trial. *Archives of General Psychiatry* 56: 1109–1115.

Katon, W. J., Roy-Byrne, P., Russo J. & Cowley, D. (2002). Cost-effectiveness and cost offset of a collaborative care intervention for primary care patients with panic disorder. *Archives of General Psychiatry* 59: 1098–1104.

Katon, W., Russo, J., Von Korff, M., Lin E., Simon, G., Bush, T., Ludman, E. & Walker, E. (2002). Long-term effects of a collaborative care intervention in persistently depressed primary care patients. *Journal of General Internal Medicine* 17, no. 10: 741–748.

Katz, A. (1999). Better outcome means more job satisfaction: Pilot project in Winnipeg and Halifax to enhance physician-patient communication. *Canadian Family Physician* 45: 218–220.

Kautz, C., Mauch, D. & Smith, S. A. (2008). *Reimbursement of mental health services in primary care settings.* Rockville, MD: Center for Mental Health Services, Substance Abuse and Mental Health Services Administration.

Kessler, R. (2008). Integration of care is about money too: The health and behavior codes as an element of a new financial paradigm. *Families, Systems and Health* 26, no. 2: 207–216.

Kessler, R. & Stafford, D. (2008). Primary care is the de facto mental health system. In R. Kessler & D. Stafford (Eds.), *Collaborative medicine case studies: Evidence in practice.* New York: Springer.

Kessler, R., Stafford, D. & Messier, R. (2009). The problem of integrating behavioral health in the medical home and the questions it leads to. *Journal of Clinical Psychology in Medical Settings* 16: 4–12.

Kessler, R. C., Berglund, P., Demler, O., Jin, R., Koretz, D., Merikangas, K. R., Rush, A. J., Walters, E. E. & Wang, P. S. (2003). The epidemiology of major depressive disorder: Results from the National Comorbidity Survey Replication (NCS-R). *JAMA* 289: 3095–3105.

Kessler, R. C., Berglund, P., Demler, O., Jin, R., Merikangas, K. & Walters, E. E. (2005). Lifetime prevalence and age-of-onset distributions of DSM-IV disorders in the National Comorbidity Survey replication. *Archives of General Psychiatry* 62: 593–602.

Kessler, R. C., Berglund, P. A., Bruce, M. L., Koch, J. R., Laska, E. M., Leaf, P. J., Manderscheid, R. W., Rosenheck, R. A., Walters, E. E. & Wang, P. S. (2001). The prevalence and correlates of untreated serious mental illness. *Health Services Research* 36, no. 6, pt. 1: 987–1007.

Kim, H. F., Kunik, M. E., Molinari, V. A., et al. (2000). Functional impairment in COPD patients: The impact of anxiety and depression. *Psychosomatics* 41: 465–471.

Kosten, T. R. & United States Department of Veterans Affairs (VA), Quality Enhancement Research Initiative (QUERI). (2008). Substance use disorders QUERI strategic plan. http://www.queri.research.va.gov/about/strategic_plans/sud.pdf (accessed February 5, 2010).

Kroenke, K., Arrington, M. E. & Mangelsdorff, A. D. (1990). The prevalence of symptoms in medical outpatients and the adequacy of therapy. *Archives of Internal Medicine* 150, no. 8: 1685–1689.

Kroenke, K., Bair, M. J., Damush, T. M., Wu, J., Hoke, S., Sutherland, J. & Tu, W. (2009). Optimized antidepressant therapy and pain self-management in primary care patients with depression and musculoskeletal pain: A randomized controlled trial. *JAMA* 301, no. 20: 2099–2110.

Kroenke, K. & Mangelsdorff, A. D. (1989). Common symptoms in ambulatory care: incidence, evaluation, therapy, and outcome. *American Journal of Medicine* 86, no. 3: 262–266.

Kroenke, K., Spitzer, R. L. & Williams, J. B. (2001). The PHQ-9: Validity of a brief depression severity measure. *Journal of General Internal Medicine* 16: 606–613.

Kroenke K., Spitzer R. L. & Williams, J. B. (2003). The patient health questionnaire-2: Validity of a two-item depression screener. *Medical Care* 41: 1284–1292.

Kulka, R. A., Schlenger, W. E., Fairbank, J. A., Hough, R. L., Jordan, B. K., Marmar, C. R. & Weiss, D. S. (1990). *Trauma and the Vietnam War generation: Report of findings from the National Vietnam Veterans Readjustment Study.* New York: Brunner/Mazel.

Laygo, R., O'Donohue, W., Hall, S., Kaplan, A., Wood, R., Cummings, J., et al. (2003). Preliminary results from the Hawaii Integrated Healthcare Project II. In N. A. Cummings, W. T. O'Donohue & K. E. Ferguson (Eds.), *Behavioral health as primary care: Beyond efficiency to effectiveness* (pp. 111–144). Reno, NV: Context Press.

Levkoff, S. E., Chen, H., Coakley, E., Herr, E. C. M., Oslin, D. W., Katz, I., Bartels, S. J., Maxwell, J., Olsen, E., Miles, K. M., Costanino, G. & Ware, J. H. (2004). Design and sample characteristics of the PRISM-E Multisite randomized trial to improve behavioral health care for the elderly. *Journal of Aging and Health* 16: 3–27.

Linzer, M., Spitzer, R., Kroenke, K., et al. (1996). Gender, quality of life, and mental disorders in primary care: results from the PRIME-MD 1000 Study. *American Journal of Medicine* 101: 526–533.

Liu, C. F., Campbell, D. G., Chaney, E. F., Li, Y. F., McDonell, M. & Fihn, S. D. (2006). Depression diagnosis and antidepressant treatment among depressed VA primary care patients. *Administration and Policy in Mental Health* 33, no. 3: 331–341.

Liu, C., Hedrick, S. C., Chaney, E. F., Heagerty, P., Felker, B., Hasenberg, N., Fihn, S. & Katon, W. (2003). Cost-effectiveness of collaborative care for depression in a primary care veteran population. *Psychiatric Services* 54, no. 5: 698–704.

Matalon, A., Yaphe, J., Nahmani, T., Portuguez-Chitrit, N. & Maoz, B. (2009). The effect of a multidisciplinary integrative intervention on health status and general health perception in primary care frequent attenders. *Families, Systems & Health* 27, no. 1: 77–84.

McDermott, L., Dobson, A., & Owen, N. (2008). Smoking reduction and cessation among young adult women: A 7-year prospective analysis. *Nicotine & Tobacco Research*. 10: 1457–1466.

Mental Health Work Group. (2003). Summary notes. Department of Veterans Affairs.

Miller, L. (1997). *VHA Work Group on Case Management: Draft strategy on case management.* Washington, DC: Department of Veterans Affairs, VHA Headquarters.

Miranda, J., Duan, N., Sherbourne, C., et al. (2003). Improving care for minorities: Can quality improvement interventions improve care and outcomes for depressed minorities? Results of a randomized, controlled trial. *Health Services Research* 38, no. 2: 613–630.

Miranda, J., Schoenbaum, M., Sherbourne, C., et al. (2004). Effects of primary care depression treatment on minority patients' clinical status and employment. *Archives of General Psychiatry* 61, no. 8: 827–834.

Moncrieff, J., Wessely, S. & Hardy, R. (2001). Antidepressants using active placebos. *Cochrane Database of Systematic Review* 1 CD003012.

National Alliance on Mental Illness (NAMI). (2009). Depression and veterans. http://www.nami.org/Template.cfm?Section=Depression&Template=/Content Management/ContentDisplay.cfm&ContentID=88939 (accessed March 29, 2012).

New Freedom Commission on Mental Health. (2003). *Achieving the promise: Transforming mental health care in America, final report.* DHHS pub. no. SMA-03–3832. Rockville, MD: Department of Health and Human Services. www.mentalhealth commission.gov/reports/finalreport/fullreport-02.htm (accessed February 5, 2010).

Ng, T., Niti, M., Tan, W. C., Cao, Z., Ong, K. C. & Eng, P. (2007). Depressive symptoms and chronic obstructive pulmonary disease: Effect on mortality, hospital readmission, symptom burden, functional status, and quality of life. *Archives of Internal Medicine* 167: 60–67.

Nutting, P. A., Dickinson, L. M., Rubenstein, L. V., Keeley, R. D., Smith, J. L. & Elliott, C. E. (2005). Improving detection of suicidal ideation among depressed patients in primary care. *The Annals of Family Medicine* 3, no. 6: 529–536.

Oslin, D. & Post, E. P. (2010). Veterans Affairs' primary care–mental health integration. University of Michigan Depression Center colloquium series.

Oslin, D. W., Grantham, S., Coakley, E., Maxwell, J., Miles, K., Ware, J., Blow, F. C., Krahn, D. D., Bartels, S. J., Zubritsky, C. & PRISM-E Group (2006a). PRISM-E: Comparison of integrated care and enhanced specialty referral in managing at-risk alcohol use. *Psychiatric Services* 57, no. 7: 954–958.

Oslin, D. W., Ross, J., Sayers, S., Murphy, J., Kane, V. & Katz, I. R. (2006b). Screening, assessment, and management of depression in VA primary care clinics: The Behavioral Health Laboratory. *Journal of General Internal Medicine* 21, no. 1: 46–50.

Oslin, D. W., Ross, J., Sayers, S., Murphy, J. & Katz, I. (2005). Screening, assessment, and management of depression and alcohol misuse in primary care: Effects of the Behavioral Health Laboratory. Paper presented at the VA HSR&D National Meeting, February 17, Baltimore, MD.

Pallak, M. S., Cummings, N. A., Dorken, H. & Henke, C. J. (1994). Medical costs, Medicaid, and managed mental health treatment: The Hawaii Study. *Managed Care Quarterly* 2, no. 2: 64–70.

Pignone, M. P., Gaynes, B. N., Rushton, J. L., Burchell, C. M., Orleans, C. T., Mulrow, C. D. & Lohr, K. N. (2002). Screening for depression in adults: A summary of the evidence for the U.S. preventative services task force. *Annals of Internal Medicine* 136, no. 10: 765–776.

Pincus, H. A., Pechura, C., Keyser, D., et al. (2006). Depression in primary care: Learning lessons in a national quality improvement program. *Administration & Policy in Mental Health* 33, no. 1: 2–15.

Pomerantz, A., Cole, B. H., Watts, B. V. & Weeks, W. B. (2008). Improving efficiency and access to mental health care: Combining integrated care and advanced access. *General Hospital Psychiatry* 30: 546–551.

Pomerantz, A. S., Corson, J. A. & Detzer, M. J. (2009). The challenge of integrated care for mental health: Leaving the 50 minute hour and other sacred things. *Journal of Clinical Psychology in Medical Settings* 16: 40–46.

Post, E. P. & Van Stone, W. W. (2008). Veterans health administration primary care–mental health integration initiative. *North Carolina Medical Journal* 69, no. 1: 49–52.

Prins, A., Ouimette, P., Kimerling, R., Cameron, R. P., Hugelshofer, D. S., Shaw-Hegwer, J., et al. (2003). The primary care posttraumatic stress disorder screen (PC-PTSD): Development and operating characteristics. *Primary Care Psychiatry* 9: 9–14.

Quality Enhancement Research Initiative (QUERI). (2009). *Fact sheet.* Little Rock, AR: Mental Health. (QUERI currently focuses on nine conditions that are prevalent and high risk among veterans: chronic heart failure, diabetes, HIV/hepatitis, ischemic heart disease, mental health, polytrauma and blast-related injuries, spinal cord injury, stroke, and substance use disorders.)

Regier, D. A., Narrow, W. E., Rae, D. S., Manderscheid, R. W., Locke, B. Z. & Goodwin, F. K. (1993). The de facto US mental and addictive disorders service system: Epidemiologic Catchment Area prospective 1-year prevalence rates of disorders and services. *Archives of General Psychiatry* 50: 85–94.

Robinson, P. & Reiter, J. (2007). *Behavioral consultation and primary care: A guide to integrating services.* New York: Springer. http://www.amazon.com/Behavioral-Consultation-Primary-Care-Integrating/dp/0387329714.

Robinson, P. J. & Strosahl, K. D. (2009). Behavioral health consultation and primary care: Lessons learned. *Journal of Clinical Psychology in Medical Settings* 16: 58–71.

Rollman, B. L., Belnap, B. H., Mazumdar, S., Houck, P. R., Zhu, F., Gardner, W., Reynolds, C. F., III, Schulberg, H. C. & Shear, M. K. (2005). A randomized trial to improve the quality of treatment for panic and generalized anxiety disorders in primary care. *Archives of General Psychiatry* 62: 1332–1341.

Roy-Byrne, P. P., Craske, M. G., Stein, M. B., Sullivan, G., Bystritsky, A., Katon, W., Golinelli, D. & Sherbourne, C. D. (2005). A randomized effectiveness trial of cognitive-behavioral therapy and medication for primary care panic disorder. *Archives of General Psychiatry* 62, no. 3: 290–298.

Roy-Byrne, P. P., Katon, W., Cowley, D. S. & Russo, J. (2001). A randomized effectiveness trial of collaborative care for patients with panic disorder in primary care. *Archives of General Psychiatry* 58: 869–876.

Roy-Byrne, P., Katon, W., Broadhead, W. E., Lepine, J. P., Richards, J., Brantley, P. J., Russo, J., Zinbarg, R., Barlow, D. & Liebowitz, M. (1994). Subsyndromal (mixed) anxiety-depression in primary care. *Journal of General Internal Medicine* 9: 507–512.

Runyan, C. N., Fonsesca, V. P. & Hunter, C. (2003). Integrating consultative behavioral healthcare into the Air Force medical system. In N. A. Cummings, W. T. O'Donohue & K. E. Ferguson (Eds.), *Behavioral health in primary care: Beyond efficacy to effectiveness* (pp. 145–163). Reno, NV: Context Press.

Seal, K. H., Metzler, T. J., Gima, K. S., Bertenthal, D., Maguen, S. & Marmar, C. R. (2009). Trends and risk factors for mental health diagnoses among Iraq and Afghanistan veterans using Department of Veterans Affairs health care. *American Journal of Public Health* 99, no. 9: 1651–1658.

Sheps, D. S. & Sheffield, D. (2001). Depression, anxiety, and the cardiovascular system: the cardiologist's perspective. *Journal of Clinical Psychiatry* 62, supp. 8: 12–6; discussion 17–8.

Sherbourne, C. D., Edelen, M. O., Zhou, A., Bird, C., Duan, N. & Well, K. B. (2008). How a therapy-based quality improvement intervention for depression affected life events and psychological well-being over time: A 9-year longitudinal analysis. *Medical Care* 46, no. 1: 78–84.

Simon, G. E. & VonKorff, M. (1995). Recognition, management, and outcomes of depression in primary care. *Archives of Family Medicine* 4: 99–105.

Skultety, K. M. & Zeiss, A. (2006). The treatment of depression in older adults in the primary care setting: An evidence-based review. *Health Psychology* 25, no. 6: 665–674.

Speer, D. C. & Schneider, M. G. (2003). Mental health needs of older adults and primary care: Opportunity for interdisciplinary geriatric team practice. *Clinical Psychology: Science and Practice* 10: 85–101.

Spitzer, R., Williams, J., Kroenke, K., Linzer, M., deGruy, F., Hahn, S., Brody, D., & Johnson, J. (1994). Utility of a new procedure for diagnosing mental disorders in primary care: The PRIME-MD 1000 Study. *Journal of the American Medical Association* 272: 1749–1756.

Stanton, A. L., Revenson, T. A. & Tennen, H. (2007). Health psychology: Psychological adjustment to chronic illness. *Annual Review of Psychology* 58: 565–592.

Starfield, B., Shi, L. & Macinko, J. (2005). Contribution of primary care to health systems and health. *Milbank Quarterly* 83, no. 3: 457–502.

Stein, M. B., McQuaid, J. R., Pedrelli, P., Lenox, R. & McCahill, M. E. (2000). Posttraumatic stress disorder in the primary care medical setting. *General Hospital Psychiatry* 22, no. 4: 261–269.

Strosahl, K. (1996). Confessions of a behavioral therapist in primary care: The odyssey and the ecstasy. *Cognitive and Behavioral Practice* 3: 1–28.

Stuck, A. E., Siu, A. L., Wieland, G. D., Adams, J. & Rubenstein, I. Z. (1993). Comprehensive geriatric assessment: A meta-analysis of controlled trials. *Lancet* 342: 1032–1036.

Tanielian, T. & Jaycox, L. (Eds.). (2008). *Invisible wounds of war: Psychological and cognitive injuries, their consequences, and services to assist recovery.* Santa Monica, CA: RAND Corporation.

Taubman-Ben-Ari, O., Rabinowitz, J., Feldman, D. & Vaturi, R. (2001). Posttraumatic stress disorder in primary care settings: Prevalence and physicians' detection. *Psychological Medicine* 31: 555–560.

Uebelacker, L. A., Smith, M., Lewis, A. W., Sasaki, R. & Miller, I. W. (2009). Treatment of depression in a low-income primary care setting with co-located mental health care. *Families, Systems & Health* 27, no. 2: 161–171.

Uniform Mental Health Services Package (UMHSP). (2008). Issued as VHA handbook 1160.01. http://vaww1.va.gov/pcmh/ (accessed November 24, 2009); http://vaww1.va.gov/pcmh/ (accessed November 24, 2009).

Unutzer, J., Katon, W., Callahan, C. M., Williams, J. W., Hunkeler, E., et al. (2002). Collaborative care management of late-life depression in the primary care setting: A randomized controlled trial. *JAMA* 288, no. 22: 2836–2845.

Unutzer, J., Katon, W. J., Fan, M., Schoenbaum, M. C., Lin, E. H. B., Penna, R. D. D. & Powers, D. (2008). Long-term cost effects of collaborative care for late-life depression. *American Journal of Managed Care* 14, no. 2: 95–100.

Unutzer, J. (2006). Transforming mental health care at the interface with general medicine: Report for the President's Commission. *Psychiatric Service* 57(1): 37–47.

U.S. Census Bureau. (2006). American Community Survey. http://factfinder .census.gov (accessed February 5, 2010).

U.S. Census Bureau. (2008a). *Statistical abstract of the United States: 2008.* Table 505. http://www.census.gov/Press-Release/www/releases/archives/facts (accessed February 5, 2010).

U.S. Census Bureau. (2008b). Statistical abstract of the United States: 2008. Tables 506.

U.S. Census Bureau. (2009). *2009 statistical abstract, section 1: Population.* http:// www. Census.gov (accessed February 2, 2010).

U.S. Department of Health and Human Services. (1999). *Mental health: A report of the surgeon general.* Rockville, MD: U.S. Department of Health and Human

Services, Substance Abuse and Mental Health Services, National Institutes of Health, National Institute of Mental Health.

U.S. Preventive Services Task Force. (2002). Screening for Depression: Recommendations and Rationale. *Am Fam Physician* 66(4): 647–650.

U.S. Preventive Services Task Force. (2009). *Screening for major depressive disorder in children and adolescents.* Rockville, MD: Agency for Healthcare Research and Quality. http://www.ahrq.gov/clinic/uspstf/uspschdepr.htm (accessed February 5, 2010).

U.S. Surgeon General. (2003). The Surgeon General's report and the President's New Freedom Commission on Mental Health provided support for Veterans Health Administration (VHA). http://vaww1.va.gov/pcmh/ (accessed November 24, 2009).

van Manen, J. G., Bindels, P. J. E., Dekker, F. W., IJzermans, C. J., van der Zee, J. S. & Schadé, E. (2002). Risk of depression in patients with chronic obstructive pulmonary disease and its determinants. *Thorax* 57, no. 5: 412–416.

VandenBos, G. R. & Williams, S. (2000). The Internet versus the telephone; What is telehealth, anyway? *Professional Psychology: Research and Practice* 31: 490–492.

Veterans Affairs health care for women: Progress made in providing services to women veterans. (1999). Report to the Chairman, Subcommittee on Health, Committee on Veterans Affairs, House of Representatives. Publication GAO/HEHS-99–38. Washington, DC: U.S. General Accounting Office.

Veterans Health Administration/Department of Defense. (2000). *Clinical practice guideline for the management of major depressive disorder in adults.* Washington, DC: Department of Veterans Affairs. http://www.oqp.med.va.gov/cpg/MDD/ MDD_Base.htm (accessed February 5, 2010).

Wagner, J. R., & Carpenter, M. J. (1996). Does smoking reduction increase future cessation and decrease disease risk? A qualitative review. *Nicotine & Tobacco Research* 8: 739–749.

Wang, P. S., Demler, O., Olfson, M., Pincus, H. A., Wells, K. B. & Kessler, R. C. (2006). Changing profiles of service sectors used for mental health care in the United States. *American Journal of Psychiatry* 163: 1187–1198.

Watts, B. V., Shiner, B., Pomerantz, A., Stender, P. & Weeks, W. B. (2007). Outcomes of a quality improvement project integrating mental health into primary care. *Quality & Safety in Health Care* 16: 378–381.

Weathers, F., Litz, B., Herman, D., Huska, J. & Keane, T. (1993). The posttraumatic stress disorder checklist (PCL): Reliability, validity, and diagnostic utility. Presented at the Annual Convention of the International Society for Traumatic Stress Studies, San Antonio, TX.

Weisberg, R. B., Bruce, S. E., Machan, J., Dolan, R. T., Culpepper, L. & Keller, M. B. (2002). Non-psychiatric medical illness in primary care patients with trauma histories and post-traumatic stress disorder. *Psychiatric Services* 53: 848–854.

Wells, K., Sherbourne, C., Schoenbaum, M., et al. (2004). Five year impact of quality improvement for depression: Results of a group-level randomized controlled trial. *Archives of General Psychiatry* 61, no. 4: 378–386.

Whitlock, E. P., Orleans, T., Pender, N. & Allan, J. (2002). Evaluating primary care behavioral counseling interventions: An evidence-based approach. *American Journal of Preventative Medicine* 22, no. 4: 267–284.

Wiggins, J. G. & Cummings, N. A. (1998). National study of the experience of psychologists with psychotropic medications and psychotherapy. *Professional Psychology: Research and Practice* 29: 549–552.

World Health Organization. (n.d.). Depression. http://www.who.int/mental_health/management/depression (accessed November 12, 2009).

Wulsin, L. R., Sollner, W. & Pincus, H. A. (2006). Models of integrated care. *Medical Clinics of North America* 90, no. 4: 647–677.

Yu, W., Ravelo, A., Wagner, T. H., Phibbs, C. S., Bhandari, A., Chen, S. & Barnett, P. G. (2003). Prevalence and costs of chronic conditions in the VA health care system. *Medical Care Research and Review* 60: 146S–147S.

Zeiss, A. M. & Karlin, B. E. (2008). Integrating mental health and primary care services in the Department of Veterans Affairs health care system. *Journal of Clinical Psychology in Medical Settings* 15: 73–78.

Zeiss, A. M. & Steffen, A. M. (1996). Treatment issues with elderly clients. *Cognitive and Behavioral Practice* 3: 371–389.

Alcohol and Substance Abuse Programs: History, Policies, Challenges, Issues, Developments, and New Directions

Susan R. Tate, Jennifer Mrnak-Meyer, and Jessica C. Tripp

Introduction

Substance use disorders (SUDs) have devastating personal and familial effects, including interpersonal conflict, unemployment, and crime, as well as a host of mental and physical health consequences, such as premature mortality. In addition, significant societal costs are incurred (e.g., increased healthcare costs, increased expenditures for legal and criminal consequences, loss of productivity) because of SUDs. Unfortunately the number of veterans with SUDs continues to climb. Veterans are more likely to have used tobacco (18.8 percent), alcohol (56.6 percent), and marijuana (3.5 percent) in the previous month than comparable nonveterans (14.3 percent, 50.8 percent, and 3.0 percent respectively; Wagner et al. 2007). Research suggests that approximately half of veterans seen in mental healthcare settings, and more than a quarter of veterans seen in physical healthcare settings, meet diagnostic criteria for an SUD (Lambert, Griffith & Hendricksen 1996; Tracy et al. 2007; VA's Alcoholism Screening Procedures 1991). However, substance use disorders are frequently not detected in these settings (e.g., Kirchner et al. 1998; Tracy et al. 2007), and consequently, veterans with these addictive behaviors may not receive needed treatment.

Adding to underdetection by healthcare providers, stigma associated with substance use and other mental health disorders often reduces help-seeking by veterans. Negative beliefs about mental healthcare, specifically beliefs that "therapy is not effective for most people" and "therapy is a sign of weakness," are associated with decreased treatment utilization (both counseling and medication) by veterans (Pietrzak et al. 2009). Individuals who screen positive for a mental health disorder postdeployment were twice as likely to report concerns about stigmatization, most prominently the belief that they would be seen as weak, as those who screen negative for mental health disorders (Hoge et al. 2004). Soldiers have reported more distress associated with discussing psychological problems, relative to physical problems, upon return from deployment and a reduced likelihood of following through with a psychological referral than a medical referral (Britt et al. 2007). Together, these findings suggest that veterans may be hesitant to access substance treatment even if the need for such treatment has been detected.

Significant resources have been devoted to developing, evaluating, and providing addiction treatments for veterans, with results clearly supporting benefits of many interventions in terms of reducing alcohol and illicit drug use, improving personal health status and relationship functioning, and cost effectiveness (Pyne et al. 2006; Volk et al. 1997). The Department of Veterans Affairs (VA) has more than 200 substance disorder treatment programs to meet the ongoing needs of veterans experiencing addiction difficulties.

Rates and types of SUDs among veterans vary widely in different areas of the country (Wagner et al. 2007). Not surprisingly, SUDs have also historically differed across VA facilities (e.g., Ouimette, Finney & Moos 1997). To aid in the consistent, state-of-the-art delivery of services to veterans with SUDs, the Veterans Health Administration (VHA) and the Department of Defense (DoD) established a working group for the purpose of developing practice guidelines (Management of Substance Use Disorders Working Group 2009), with the overarching goal of improving substance use outcomes for veterans. The working group evaluated extensive research to establish the best methods for identifying and treating substance use disorders. This chapter includes information from this guideline and other resources relevant to SUDs and veterans. For clarification, throughout this chapter the term *substance* refers to both alcohol and illicit drugs. Although not the primary focus of this chapter, because of significant co-occurrence and health consequences, tobacco use is addressed in many sections, but is not subsumed under the term *substance*.

Policies

Screening

As noted previously, problematic substance use must first be detected in order to provide appropriate treatment. Screening procedures can be used to determine if there is a need for further evaluation or treatment. These measures are brief, extremely cost-effective assessments aimed at identifying unhealthy substance use along the entire continuum of substance use. Unhealthy use of alcohol, the most common substance in veteran samples, is defined as alcohol use above recommended limits or any drinking despite contraindications. Recommended maximum drinking levels differ by gender: a maximum of four drinks per occasion or fourteen drinks per week for men, and a maximum of three drinks per occasion or seven drinks per week for women. Contraindications for any level of alcohol use include pregnancy, liver disease, other medical or psychological conditions potentially exacerbated by drinking (e.g., pancreatitis, depression), and medications with alcohol interactions. Screening for unhealthy alcohol use is mandated annually for all veterans seen in VA general and mental healthcare settings.

Screening can be accomplished with one of two very brief methods: 1) the Alcohol Use Disorders Identification Test Questions (AUDIT-C), or 2) the Single-Item Alcohol Screening Question (SASQ). The AUDIT-C can be administered by interview or written self-report and consists of three questions that ask how often an individual drinks alcohol, how many drinks are typically consumed per occasion, and how often more than six drinks are consumed on a single occasion (Bush et al. 1998; Bradley et al. 2003). Scoring can be accomplished quickly and is automatically done in most computerized VA medical records. A positive AUDIT score is one that exceeds the recommended maximum drinking levels listed above. The SASQ requires two questions, first ascertaining if an individual drinks alcohol, followed by asking how many times in the past three months a person has consumed five or more drinks in a day for men and four or more drinks in a day for women. In VA settings, a positive screen on the SASQ is considered any positive response on the second question within the past three months (Seale et al. 2006; Williams & Vinson 2001), although the National Institute on Alcohol Abuse and Alcoholism (NIAAA) recommends using a full-year timeframe (2007). Although the SASQ is easier to recall for use in clinical interviews, the AUDIT-C provides some added information that can be helpful.

When using assessments that inquire about how many alcohol drinks are consumed, it is important for clinicians to communicate what a "standard drink" refers to: 12 ounces of beer, 5 ounces of wine, or 1.5 ounces of 80 proof alcohol. Many people underestimate alcohol consumption due to not knowing these definitions (e.g., pouring a "glass" of wine larger than 5 ounces, drinking a "double" in a single glass) or due to concerns of being negatively evaluated, compromising the screening process.

As described previously, screening for unhealthy *alcohol* use is recommended at least annually. However, broad-based screening in general healthcare settings for other illicit drug use has not been recommended, and instead is advised in specialized healthcare settings serving veterans with high risk for substance use (hepatitis C or HIV clinics). This difference in recommended screening is based on prevalence rates (alcohol is the most used substance, with other drugs used less frequently), the proven cost-effectiveness of alcohol screening and treatment, and rates of illness and death associated with alcohol (U.S. Preventive Services Task Force 2008).

If a veteran screens positive for unhealthy alcohol use, the provider should provide brief counseling that includes expression of concern about the veteran's health, personalized education on the connection between current alcohol use and the veteran's health, advice to reduce or abstain from drinking, and a referral for addiction treatment if appropriate. Brief alcohol counseling has been shown to be effective for many individuals in reducing alcohol use in numerous studies (for reviews, see Kaner et al. 2007; Moyer et al. 2002) and may also improve motivation for following through with referrals to specialized substance treatment clinics. Providing brief interventions in primary care settings may be particularly effective, because health concerns can provide a "window of opportunity" when individuals are more receptive to the benefits of reducing substance use (e.g., Monti et al. 1999; Tate, McQuaid & Brown 2005). Specifically, biological markers can be used to provide objective feedback on the negative consequences of problematic alcohol use on physical health (Tate et al. 2010).

Indications warranting a referral to specialized addiction treatment following a positive alcohol screen include difficulty in stopping or cutting down on one's own, lifetime diagnosis of alcohol or other substance dependence, or past addiction treatment. Although individuals may decline referral to addiction treatment, repeat monitoring and counseling is beneficial (e.g., Moyer et al. 2002).

In addition to screening for problem alcohol consumption, VA requires all veterans be asked about tobacco use. Current use of any tobacco warrants intervention, as any use poses risk and most tobacco users meet nicotine dependence criteria.

Diagnosis and Assessment

Assessment answers the questions: To what extent, and in what ways, are there problems related to substance use? What are the veteran's strengths, resources, motivations, weaknesses, and preferences that should be considered? Are diagnostic criteria met? Comprehensive assessment and collaboration with the veteran guides decision processes regarding intensity, duration, and modality of addiction treatment, as well as identifying possible benefits of adjunctive or integrative treatments.

Diagnostic criteria for SUDs as defined in the *Diagnostic and Statistical Manual of Mental Disorders* (DSM-IV; American Psychiatric Association 1994) includes substance abuse and substance dependence. Both disorders require "a maladaptive pattern of substance use, leading to clinically significant impairment or distress, as manifested by the presence of specified criteria occurring at any time in the same 12-month period." For abuse, a single criterion (of a possible four) is needed, and for dependence, three or more (of seven criteria) are required. Proposed revisions for SUDs in the DSM-V, anticipated for publication in 2013, include the elimination of qualitatively different criteria for abuse and dependence, and the addition of quantitative severity specifiers of moderate (two to three criteria positive) or severe (four or more criteria positive). Revisions to criteria include the addition of "craving or a strong desire or urge to use a specific substance" and removal of "recurrent substance-related legal problems." More information about proposed changes, background, and rationale related to addictive disorders are described on the DSM-V Web site (www.dsm5.org).

Treatment

A broad range of services is provided by VA with the aim of eliminating or reducing substance use as a contributing factor to physical, psychological, and social dysfunction and associated problems (e.g., employment, legal, financial). Treatment can include stabilization, brief interventions, assessment and diagnosis, psychotherapy interventions (outpatient, intensive day/partial hospitalization, and inpatient), and pharmacotherapy interventions. In addition, complementary services provided by many VA medical centers, such as marital/family counseling, anger management, and vocational rehabilitation, may improve substance use treatment outcomes. The following section describes specialized addiction interventions.

Stabilization

Emergency or urgent situations related to SUD treatment include acute medical problems (e.g., trauma, myocardial infarction), unstable psychiatric issues (risk of danger to self or others, delirium), and acute intoxication or withdrawal. Veterans presenting with these problems must first be provided appropriate care to achieve stabilization. Treatment may require emergency procedures, inpatient hospitalization, or pharmacological interventions. Alcohol or other sedative withdrawal, in particular, can be life threatening; and pharmacological assistance may be justified for alcohol, sedative-hypnotics, and opiate withdrawal. Following stabilization, evaluation and collaborative treatment planning with the veteran should be continued.

Psychotherapy Interventions

Fortunately a wide variety of interventions is available for treatment of SUDs. We provide brief descriptions of psychotherapy interventions that have been rigorously evaluated in multiple research studies and shown to be effective. These interventions are available in many VA facilities and may be offered alone or in combination (Ouimette, Finney & Moos 1997). Following psychotherapy interventions, brief descriptions of pharmacotherapy interventions with demonstrated benefits for treatment of some SUDs are provided. The diversity of treatment options allows treatment to be tailored to an individual's needs and preferences.

Twelve-step facilitation (TSF). Many addiction treatment programs provided to veterans encourage active participation in community-based Alcoholics Anonymous (AA) or other substance-related, twelve-step groups such as Narcotics Anonymous (NA). A significant body of research supports this practice, showing improved outcomes associated with engaging in these programs (see Humphreys et al. 2004 for a review). Twelve-step groups focus on abstinence as the only effective means of recovering from addictive disorders, with support provided by other group members, a sponsor, and written materials. A more structured, formalized AA/NA facilitation intervention was evaluated in the Project MATCH study (Nowinski, Baker & Carroll 1994). This twelve-session TSF intervention focuses on material from the twelve steps and encouragement of twelve-step activities (meeting attendance, acquiring a sponsor). In the large Project MATCH study, participants in all three types of treatment reduced their alcohol use, and no significant group differences in the percentage of days participants were abstinent were found. However, consistent with the twelve-step philosophy, individuals who received TSF therapy were more likely to be completely abstinent from alcohol use. Other studies have provided similar support, although to a more limited extent, for other substances (e.g., Carroll et al. 1998; Linehan et al. 2002). The wide availability of twelve-step community support groups represents an important ongoing resource for individuals initiating and maintaining abstinence. A limitation is that some individuals are less likely to participate and benefit from twelve-step self-help groups, particularly those with co-occurring mental health disorders (e.g., social anxiety, Book et al. 2009; depression, Kelly, McKellar & Moos 2003; schizophrenia or schizoaffective disorder, Jordan et al. 2002). Manuals for all treatments administered in the Project

MATCH study are available at http://pubs.niaaa.nih.gov/publications/match.htm.

Cognitive behavioral therapies (e.g., relapse prevention, coping skills training). Many addiction interventions utilize cognitive-behavioral strategies that share the common theme of teaching and practicing skills for altering thoughts and behaviors associated with substance use. Therapists work with individuals to collaboratively choose treatment goals, identify maladaptive thoughts, generate alternative cognitions, and rehearse thought-disputing techniques in situations that could lead to substance relapse, schedule and evaluate specific activities for managing pressure to resume substance use, and develop interpersonal skills including assertiveness and communication training aimed at successfully resisting social pressure to use. Skills are practiced during treatment sessions, and practice is also assigned outside of treatment sessions to provide opportunities for examining and problem solving any difficulties encountered. Cognitive behavioral therapy (CBT) interventions have been evaluated in numerous research studies and have been shown to be effective in reducing alcohol and illicit drug use (Dutra et al. 2008), including the large Project MATCH study (Kadden et al. 1994), wherein individuals provided with CBT had reductions in alcohol use similar to those of individuals receiving the other interventions (TSF, described previously, or a motivational therapy, described later). Advantages of CBT include acceptability to veterans, demonstrated effectiveness across many substances, flexibility in treatment delivery (individual, group, computer), and evidence of durability of treatment gains over time (Carroll et al. 2009; Lydecker et al. 2010). In addition, CBT interventions readily accommodate integration with interventions for other mental health disorders (anxiety, Kushner et al. 2006; depression, Lydecker et al. 2010; PTSD, Ouimette, Brown & Najavits 1998).

Two other interventions based on cognitive and behavioral principles have been developed and evaluated. Contingency management approaches involve providing either monetary or nonmonetary reinforcement contingent on abstinence from illicit drugs. Contingency management interventions have demonstrated effectiveness during treatment for opiate and stimulant dependence, although results are less certain after treatment (Dutra et al. 2008; Prendergast et al. 2006). Limitations of these approaches are that they are generally conceptualized as adjuncts to other psychotherapy or pharmacotherapy interventions and the additional cost and administration for contingent rewards. Community reinforcement interventions are more comprehensive, focusing on environmental factors influencing an individual's behavioral choices. Community reinforcement approaches often involve significant social supports with the goal of creating an environment offering greater reinforcement for abstinence relative to substance use. These interventions are complex, but have demonstrated effectiveness with alcohol (Miller & Wilbourne 2002) and to a lesser extent, cocaine (Higgins et al. 2003).

Brief motivational interviewing interventions (MI; Miller & Rollnick 1991) and *motivational enhancement therapy* (MET; Miller et al. 1992). MI involves a style that emphasizes empathetic, client-centered, and directive interactions focused on identifying ambivalence, increasing commitment, and improving self-efficacy for making behavioral changes. Motivational interventions aim to capitalize on an individual's unique strengths, knowledge, resources, and abilities for supporting change. A benefit of motivational interventions is the generally briefer duration relative to many other therapies, usually one to four sessions. MET is more structured, including alcohol-related assessment and personalized feedback over four sessions. MET has been shown to be an effective intervention for alcohol dependence as a stand-alone treatment (U.S. Project MATCH Research Group 1997), as an adjunct to treatment as usual (Ball et al. 2007), or integrated into other interventions (Anton et al. 2006). An additional advantage of MET is that in the Project MATCH study, MET was beneficial for alcohol-dependent individuals with high levels of anger relative to the other two interventions provided (TSF and CBT). However, the benefits of MI or MET for substances other than alcohol have limited support to date.

Behavioral couples/family therapy. Interpersonal conflict is often experienced among couples and families with a substance-abusing family member. However, family members can play an important supportive role in the process of changing addictive behaviors. Various behavioral couples therapy (BCT) interventions have been developed that share the common goals of reducing alcohol or illicit drug use and increasing relationship satisfaction. BCT utilizes behavioral principles that may involve contracts for substance-related behaviors (taking medication, drug testing, attending counseling or community meetings), communication skills building, and increasing pleasurable shared activities. As couples interventions have been shown to decrease substance use and improve relationship satisfaction (Shadish & Baldwin 2005), BCT is provided as an adjunct in some VA substance abuse treatment programs. Ongoing VA-provided trainings disseminating BCT to more therapists is occurring to increase the availability of this effective treatment option to more veterans.

Pharmacotherapy Interventions

Medications have been added to the arsenal of treatments for SUDs. It is important to note that pharmacotherapies for treatment of substance dependence are not "stand-alone" treatments, but are best provided in addition to addiction counseling. Although pharmacotherapies hold promise for improving addiction treatment outcomes, there are also challenges associated with prescribing these medications. In 2003 approximately 14 percent of substance-dependent veterans receiving treatment in specialty addictions clinics received a prescription specifically for treatment of their substance disorder. However, less than 5 percent of substance-disordered veterans who received care in psychiatric clinics and less than a quarter of 1 percent of substance-disordered veterans who received all of their healthcare in primary care clinics were prescribed medication for treatment of the substance disorder (Tracy et al. 2007). Thus, unless veterans with SUDs are identified and referred to specialty addiction treatment programs, the likelihood of receiving pharmacotherapy is low.

Pharmacotherapy for Alcohol Dependence

For treatment of alcohol dependence, three medications have been approved by the FDA and are available through VA: disulfiram, naltrexone, and acamprosate. Poor adherence to oral medication regimens is a significant challenge in the treatment of alcohol dependence, often reducing the efficacy of these interventions.

Disulfiram, also known as Antabuse, has been studied in relatively few clinical trials with placebo control comparison groups, but modest support for improved alcohol treatment outcomes has been documented (Fuller et al. 1986; Petrakis et al. 2005). Research findings also support the efficacy of disulfiram for the treatment of combined cocaine and alcohol dependence (e.g., Carroll et al. 1998; George et al. 2000). However, caution is warranted in the use of disulfiram, given the potential for serious liver toxicity and potential for life-threatening illness if alcohol is consumed in health-compromised individuals.

Naltrexone, an opioid antagonist, has been widely studied, and has demonstrated modest success in treating alcohol dependence. A meta-analysis of twenty-four randomized controlled trials (Srisurapanont & Jarusuraisin 2005) illustrated that daily naltrexone reduced the risk of relapse to alcohol by approximately 36 percent in twelve-week trials. However, use of naltrexone was also associated with side effects including nausea, dizziness, and fatigue when compared to placebo. More recent findings indicate that targeted use of naltrexone, that is, taking the drug in anticipation of high-risk drinking situations, may be more effective than daily use, particularly among men. Kranzler and colleagues (2009) found that men taking naltrexone on a targeted basis drank significantly less then men on a daily regime or placebo. The relationship between alcohol and the opioid system is complex and not fully understood. Researchers employing animal studies propose that competitive binding of opioid antagonists, such as naltrexone, may reduce the rewarding effects of alcohol by decreasing the dopamine released in the brain (Spanagel & Zieglgansberger 1997).

Acamprosate is another widely used drug in the treatment of alcohol addiction that has demonstrated modest effectiveness. A meta-analysis of seventeen randomized, placebo-controlled trials indicated that continuous abstinence rates among recently detoxified alcohol-dependent individuals were higher among individuals treated with acamprosate compared to placebo (Mann, Lehert & Morgan 2004). Mason and colleagues (2006) found similar results; acamprosate was associated with more abstinence relative to placebo. This effect is greater among individuals with an abstinence goal at baseline.

Pharmacotherapy for Opiate Dependence

For veterans meeting criteria for opiate dependence, opiate-agonist medications are a first-line treatment because they prevent withdrawal, reduce drug cravings, reduce effects of illicit opioids, and decrease likelihood of illicit opiate use (Farre et al. 2002; Mattick et al. 2008). Both methadone and sublingual buprenorphine/naltrexone have demonstrated benefits, with some evidence showing methadone to be more effective. However, these medications carry significant medical risks and require appropriate medical supervision. Opiate-agonist treatment programs are very structured, intensive programs that provide medications for very brief time periods, with limited take-home medications provided, as part of comprehensive treatment including counseling, mental health, and social services. This intensive care reduces risks associated with these medications, but such programs are not accessible to many veterans either geographically or for other reasons. Alternatively, buprenorphine is sometimes available in office-based programs with specially credentialed physicians. The determination of intensive methadone programs versus office-based buprenorphine pharmacotherapy takes many factors into consideration, including accessibility in a given area, physical health, and the veteran's preference for and ability to benefit in a less intensive office setting (Management of Substance Use Disorders Working Group 2009). In either case, veterans must be strongly warned about the risk of overdose and death if other substances are consumed (alcohol and other sedatives/anxiolytics) with opiate-agonist therapy.

There is limited evidence for use of naltrexone as an alternative to the two medications previously described for treatment of opiate dependence. Few individuals utilize naltrexone, because cravings may continue as naltrexone has no opioid-agonist effects. Abstinence from opiates is necessary for seven to ten days due to the opiate-antagonist effects of naltrexone causing withdrawal and the resulting negative reaction to any subsequent intervention efforts (Management of Substance Use Disorders Working Group 2009). Naltrexone is available orally and, within VA, as nonformulary injectable medication.

Tobacco Pharmacotherapies

Several nicotine and non-nicotine medications are effective for tobacco dependence. VA clinicians are informed by practice guidelines to encourage all veterans attempting to quit smoking to consider use of such medications, except in the case where there is nominal research supporting effectiveness, such as in pregnant women and smokeless tobacco users. VA relies on nicotine replacement therapies (nicotine gum, inhaler, lozenge, nasal spray, and patch), bupropion sustained release (SR), varenicline, or a combination of drug therapies in the treatment of nicotine dependence in veterans. Combination therapies typically involve a long-acting nicotine patch and a short-acting nicotine delivery system (i.e., inhaler, nasal spray) to be used as needed to manage breakthrough cravings and/or withdrawal symptoms. Varenicline is utilized only when nicotine replacement therapies, buproprion, or a combination therapy trial has failed, as the drug has been associated with violent thoughts, intent, or actions toward oneself or others, and therefore should not be utilized in individuals who express current suicidal or homicidal ideation or have a history of such thoughts. They should also be monitored closely for developing violent thoughts when taking varenicline (Fiore et al. 2009).

Challenges

Matching and Level/Intensity of Care (ASAM Criteria)

Determining what level and intensity of addiction treatment service to provide can be informed by the multidimensional assessment recommended by the American Society of Addiction Medicine (ASAM). The six ASAM dimensions are (1) acute intoxication and/or withdrawal potential; (2) biomedical conditions or complications; (3) emotional, behavioral, or cognitive conditions or complications; (4) readiness to change; (5) relapse and continued use potential; and (6) recovery environment. Clinicians then attempt to match the veteran to one of four ASAM-defined levels of care for his or her current level of substance use. Levels of care include (1) outpatient treatment, (2) intensive outpatient/partial hospitalization, (3) inpatient/residential treatment, and (4) medically managed intensive inpatient treatment (i.e. medical detoxification) (American Society of Addiction Medicine 2007). However, some research suggests that individuals correctly matched to treatment via ASAM dimensions do not have better treatment outcomes than those who are incorrectly matched. Further, research has found no support that individuals seeking treatment for alcohol problems who met ASAM criteria for inpatient treatment had better outcomes in inpatient treatment than intensive outpatient treatment (McKay et al. 1997). More research is needed within the veteran population to determine if this methodology for treatment placement is efficacious and cost-effective.

Attendance/Retention

Low attendance and early dropout are a pervasive challenge in addiction treatments (see review by Stark 1992). High dropout rates and attrition have been observed across treatment settings, different types of treatment, and substances of abuse (Dobkin et al. 2002; Sinha, Easton & Kemp 2003; Wickizer et al. 1994). This is a critical issue because there is a well-known relationship between greater treatment attendance and better outcomes following treatment (e.g., Dobkin et al. 2002; Hoffman et al. 1996; McKay et al. 1998; Simpson, Joe & Rowan-Szal 1997). Research has frequently shown that older patients (Laudet et al. 2003; Siqueland et al. 1998), males (McCaul, Svikis & Moore 2001; Sayre et al. 2002), and individuals using only alcohol (McCaul, Svikis & Moore 2001) generally remain in treatment longer, in contrast to younger patients, females, and individuals using illicit drugs, who more often leave treatment prematurely. As these factors are immutable patient characteristics, efforts to improve treatment retention and engagement should focus on aspects of treatment. Possible options include use of modern technology to reach younger veterans, providing support for women who may be responsible for child or elder care, and employing drug-specific interventions.

Comorbid Mental Health Disorders

Co-occurring mental health disorders are prevalent among individuals with substance disorders, estimated to be as high as 30 and 45 percent for those with alcohol and drug dependence, respectively (Farrell et al. 2003). Comorbidity estimates are even higher for individuals receiving addiction treatment, resulting in challenges for addiction treatment settings. In a nationally representative sample, the majority of patients receiving treatment for either alcohol (55 percent) or drug dependence (69 percent) had a concomitant psychiatric disorder (Kessler et al. 1996).

The most common co-occurring mental health disorders are depressive disorders (Grant 1995; Grant & Harford 1995; Kessler et al. 1996). Unfortunately, the co-occurrence of depression and substance disorders is frequently predictive of poorer treatment outcomes (Dodge, Sindelar & Sinha 2005; Kodl et al. 2008; McKay et al. 2002). Symptoms associated with depressive disorders, such as difficulty concentrating, loss of interest, and social isolation, may compromise treatment efforts. Substance-dependent individuals with co-occurring depression are also less likely to benefit from community resources, such as Alcoholics Anonymous (Kelly, McKellar & Moos 2003). Co-occurring substance disorders and depression are associated with more frequent and costly health service use compared to either of these disorders separately (e.g., Curran et al. 2003; O'Toole et al. 2007; Mark 2003).

Of particular importance in veteran populations, high rates of post-traumatic stress disorder (PTSD) are common among individuals receiving addiction treatment, with some estimates ranging from 30 to 59 percent (e.g., Stewart et al. 2000).

As with depression, symptoms resulting from PTSD (poor concentration, sleep difficulties, hypervigilance) may contribute to lack of benefit from treatment. Individuals with concomitant substance disorders and PTSD often have worse addiction treatment outcomes than individuals without both disorders (Driessen et al. 2008; Najavits, Weiss & Shaw 1997; Ouimette, Brown & Najavits 1998). However, substance-dependent individuals who receive treatment for their PTSD have better substance use outcomes (Ouimette, Moos & Finney 2003) than those who do not.

Among the many challenges associated with comorbid disorders are difficulties in assessment of psychiatric symptoms independent of substance use, concerns about medication management when substance relapse is a risk, and consideration of how to best address co-occurring disorders. Historically, treatment has been provided separately for each disorder, either sequentially (e.g., treatment for depression following completion of treatment for substance disorder) or in a parallel manner during the same time (with separate appointments, in different settings, by different providers). For example, Brown and colleagues (1997) added a separate cognitive behavioral therapy for depression to the usual addiction treatment in a parallel fashion, which resulted in better alcohol and depression outcomes than the addition of a relaxation training control condition.

Difficulties can occur with sequential and parallel interventions, such as the potential for conflicting treatment philosophies and recovery models (e.g., Drake et al. 1996). In addition, there are challenges for veterans receiving treatment in different locations and scheduling problems for separate appointments. To address these problems, integrated treatments have been advocated that provide treatment that is compatible in approach and philosophy, more efficient in terms of appointments and settings, and delivered by providers trained in interventions for both disorders.

Comorbid Physical Health Problems

Numerous negative physical health effects have been associated with alcohol dependence, including liver disease, cardiovascular disease, cancer, sexually transmitted disease, neuropsychological deficits, and accidental injuries (Blot 1992; National Institute on Alcohol Abuse and Alcoholism 1998, 2001, 2002; Vinson et al. 2003), as well as increased mortality from both natural and unnatural causes (Ojesjo, Hagnell & Otterbeck 1998). Although less well-studied, other illicit drugs have also been associated with negative consequences for physical health (e.g., Jovanovski, Erb & Zakzanis 2005) and mortality (Mokdad et al. 2004). In addition to direct effects, substance use also compromises physical health indirectly through decreased adherence to treatment regimens and decreased contact with healthcare professionals (Catz et al. 2001; Kunz 1997).

Although these co-occurring health issues increase difficulties for veterans, some research findings suggest that experiencing a health problem may have a beneficial impact for motivating change in addictive behaviors. One study that followed veterans for a year after addiction treatment found that those who experienced a recent acute health event were less likely to resume substance use and drank less alcohol than veterans without acute health problems (Tate, McQuaid & Brown 2005). Support for the premise that health events provide "teachable moments" for brief interventions promoting reductions in problematic alcohol use comes from a small but growing research literature (Kristenson 1987; Lieber et al. 2003; Monti et al. 1999; Tate et al. 2010). These findings suggest health issues may increase motivation for change and represent a promising new area for assisting veterans with SUDs in improving their overall health.

Not surprising given the physical health issues noted previously, SUDs are also associated with physical pain (e.g., Demyttenaere et al. 2007). In a recent study, 33.2 percent of veterans in outpatient addiction treatment reported persistent pain, and 47.3 percent reported intermittent pain (Caldeiro et al.

2008). Co-occurring chronic pain and SUD complicates assessment and reduces success of treatment for pain and addiction (e.g., Caldeiro et al. 2008; Currie et al. 2003). Individuals requesting treatment for chronic pain have been perceived as drug-seeking, and thus modalities of therapy in addition to medications (especially opioids) are needed. Including assessment and treatment of chronic pain in addiction treatment programs has been advocated to decrease substance use, increase functionality, and expand coping skills to reduce reliance on medications for pain management (Clark, Stoller & Bronner 2008). Results from an integrated cognitive behavioral intervention provide support for concurrent treatment of pain and SUDs (Currie et al. 2003). The intervention included ten sessions focused on education and relapse prevention for pain medications and substance abuse, relaxation training, pacing skills, stretching and body mechanics, sleep enhancement, nutrition, and stress management. Abstinence from alcohol and illicit drugs was required, and prescribed opiate medications were required to have a fixed-interval administration rather than "as needed" doses. Assessments in this small study of thirty adults documented reduced pain, decreased use of pain medication, and improved emotional functioning.

Suicidal Thoughts, Behaviors, and Attempts

Veterans are a population at high risk for suicide. One study documented that veterans are twice as likely to die by suicide than nonveterans in the general population (Kaplan et al. 2007). Veterans are also likely to have one or more of the general risk factors for suicide (male, elderly, diminished social support, medical and/or psychiatric condition associated with suicide, availability and knowledge of firearms; Kaplan et al. 2007; Lambert & Fowler 1997). Of the medical and psychiatric conditions associated with increased risk of suicide, substance use disorders play a prominent role. In one study, 4.5 percent of individuals with alcohol dependence attempted suicide, compared to 1.9 percent of the general population (Preuss et al. 2003). Further, 40 percent of individuals seen in a hospital emergency service for a suicide attempt had consumed alcohol within the prior six hours, compared to only 2 percent of all other patients seen in this setting (Lejoyeux et al. 2008). The presence of SUDs with other co-occurring disorders, such as PTSD or depression, puts patients at even greater risk for suicide compared to patients with only one of these disorders (e.g., Dhossche, Meloukheia & Chakravorty 2000; Waller, Lyons & Constantini-Ferrando 1999). Therefore, treatment providers must maintain vigilance in monitoring suicidal ideation among veterans with SUDs and have procedures in place for appropriately managing these crisis situations.

New Directions

Integrated Interventions

As previously noted, SUDs frequently co-occur with other physical and mental health disorders. Regrettably, the effectiveness of standard addiction treatments is often compromised for individuals struggling with these concomitant disorders (e.g., see Clark, Stoller & Bronner 2008; Dodge, Sindelar & Sinha 2005; Driessen et al. 2008; Kodl et al. 2008; Najavits, Weiss & Shaw 1997). Consequently, integrated treatments that address both the addiction and the co-occurring disorder(s) have been advocated (e.g., Clark, Stoller & Bronner 2008; Drake et al. 1996) and accepted as an essential evidence-based practice in treatment for substance disorders (Drake et al. 2001). While in the early stages of development and evaluation, these newer integrated interventions appear to hold promise for improving outcomes for the SUD, co-occurring disorder, and general quality of life. For example, an integrated intervention for pain management and substance abuse resulted in reduced pain, emotional distress, and reduced use of pain medications (Currie et al. 2003). In a veteran sample, an integrated cognitive behavioral intervention for co-occurring depression and substance disorders resulted in reductions in both depression and substance use during treatment, with improvements in substance use better maintained in the year following treatment for veterans in the integrated treatment relative to a comparison group (Lydecker et al. 2010). Individuals with co-occurring substance disorders and schizophrenia were retained in integrated treatment longer than parallel treatment (Hellerstein, Rosenthal & Miner 1995). Similarly, integrated interventions have demonstrated outcomes for individuals with concomitant anxiety disorders superior (Kushner et al. 2006; Morrissey et al. 2005) to treatment for addiction alone. In summary, the limited research evaluating integrated interventions for co-occurring substance and psychiatric disorders suggests these interventions yield improved outcomes and deserve continued attention for addressing this pressing treatment need.

Newer Technologies: Computer- and Web-based Interventions

An exciting new area is the development and testing of interventions utilizing computers and the Internet. These modalities offer benefits to both treatment providers and treatment users. For individuals accessing treatment, computer and Web-based interventions offer flexibility in time and place without the need to commute. Individuals can review information at their own pace and repeatedly access material as needed for gaining mastery over new concepts. Importantly, the privacy and anonymity associated with Web-based interventions may increase accessibility of treatment for individuals with concerns about stigma and negative evaluation. For providers, such interventions are a cost-effective means of providing treatment. Research focused primarily on screening and brief feedback interventions targeting problem alcohol use found that Web-based interventions are generally well received, although further research is needed to clearly document effectiveness (e.g., see the review by Bewick et al. 2008). However, early findings suggest such Web-based interventions are effective in reducing alcohol misuse among military personnel (Williams et al. 2009). Although it is in the early stages of development and testing, findings suggest that this new technology also holds promise for improving outcomes for individuals meeting diagnostic criteria for substance dependence. In one study, individuals randomized to receive computer-assisted cognitive behavioral therapy, as an adjunct to treatment as usual, had longer periods of abstinence than individuals who received treatment as usual during the eight weeks of treatment, and importantly, this difference was maintained for six months (Carroll et al. 2008; Carroll et al. 2009). In sum, computer interventions may provide a cost-effective means of prolonging treatment gains.

Continuing Pharmacotherapy Research

Continuing research guided by multidisciplinary teams, including molecular and behavioral genetics, is focused on the development and evaluation of new medications for treatment of substance use disorders. Ongoing trials are examining ondansetron, topiramate, sertraline, aripiprazole, quetizapine, and baclofen as pharmacotherapeutic interventions.

Baclofen, a $GABA_A$ receptor agonist, has demonstrated effectiveness in reducing alcohol consumption and craving for alcohol in dependent individuals when compared to placebo (Addolorato et al. 2002). Baclofen has also been found effective and safe in maintaining alcohol abstinence among alcohol-dependent individuals with liver cirrhosis (Addolorato et al. 2007). Baclofen treatment among chronic cocaine users has also shown preliminary effectiveness. Chronic cocaine users taking the drug were more likely to provide urine samples free of cocaine metabolites in the first eight weeks of treatment relative to placebo, suggesting benefits of baclofen in early phases of treatment (Shoptaw et al. 2003). However, a more recent study found no significant difference in cocaine use among dependent individuals treated with baclofen versus those taking the placebo (Kahn et al. 2009).

References

Addolorato, G., Caputo, F., Capristo, E., Domenicali, M., Bernard, M., Janiri, L., Agabio, R., Colombo, G., Gessa, G. L. & Gasbarrini, G. (2002). Baclofen efficacy in reducing alcohol craving and intake: A preliminary double-blind randomized controlled study. *Alcohol and Alcoholism* 37: 504–508.

Addolorato, G., Leggio, L., Ferrulli, A., Cardone, S., Vonghia, L., Mirijello, A., Abenavoli, L., D'Angelo, C., Caputo, F., Zamben, A., Haber, P. S. & Gasbarrini, G. (2007). Effectiveness and safety of baclofen for maintenance of alcohol abstinence in alcohol-dependent patients with liver cirrhosis: Randomized, double-blind controlled study. *The Lancet* 370: 1915–1922.

American Psychiatric Association. (1994). *Diagnostic and statistical manual of mental disorders*. 4th ed. Washington, DC: American Psychiatric Association.

American Society of Addiction Medicine. (2007). *ASAM PPC-2R patient placement criteria for the treatment of substance-related disorders*. Washington, DC: American Society of Addiction Medicine.

Anton, R. F., O'Malley, S. S., Ciraulo, D. A., Cisler, R. A., Couper D., Donovan, D. M. et al., for the COMBINE Study Research Group (2006). The COMBINE Study: A randomized controlled trial. *JAMA* 293: 2003–2017.

Ball, S. A., Martino, S., Nich, C., Frankforter, T. L., Van Horn, D., Crits-Christoph, P., Woody, G. E., Obert, J. L., Farentinos, C. & Carroll, K. M., for the National Institute on Drug Abuse Clinical Trials Network (2007). Site matters: Multisite randomized trial of motivational enhancement therapy in community drug abuse clinics. *Journal of Consulting and Clinical Psychology* 75: 556–567.

Bewick, B. M., Trusler, K., Barkham, M., Hill, A. J., Cahill, J. & Mulhern, B. (2008). The effectiveness of web-based interventions designed to decrease alcohol consumption—A systematic review. *Preventive Medicine* 47: 17–26.

Blot, W. J. (1992). Alcohol and cancer. *Cancer Research* 52, supp.: 2119–2123.

Book, S. W., Thomas, S. E., Dempsey, J. P., Randall, P. K. & Randall, C. L. (2009). Social anxiety impacts willingness to participate in addiction treatment. *Addictive Behaviors* 34: 474–476.

Bradley, K. A., Bush, K. R., Epler, A. J., Dobie, D. J., Davis, T. M., Sporleder, J. L., Maynard, C., Burman, M. L. & Kivlahan, D. R. (2003). Two brief alcohol-screening tests from the Alcohol Use Disorders Identification Test (AUDIT): Validation in a female Veterans Affairs patient population. *Archives of Internal Medicine* 163: 821–829.

Britt, T. W., Greene-Shortridge, T. M. & Castro, C. A. (2007). The stigma of mental health problems in the military. *Military Medicine* 172: 157–161.

Brown, R. A., Evans, M., Miller, I. W., Burgess, E. S. & Mueller, T. I. (1997). Cognitive-behavioral treatment for depression in alcoholism. *Journal of Consulting and Clinical Psychology* 65: 715–726.

Bush, K., Kivlahan, D. R., McDonell, M. B., Fihn, S. D. & Bradley, K. A. (1998). The AUDIT alcohol consumption questions (AUDIT-C): An effective brief screening test for problem drinking: Ambulatory Care Quality Improvement Project (ACQUIP)—Alcohol use disorders identification test. *Archives of Internal Medicine* 158: 1789–1795.

Caldeiro, R. M., Malte, C. A., Calsyn, D. A., Baer, J. S., Nichol, P., Kivlahan, D. R. & Saxon, A. J. (2008). The association of persistent pain with out-patient addiction treatment outcomes and service utilization. *Addiction* 103: 1996–2005.

Carroll, K. M., Ball, S. A., Martino, S., Nich, C., Babuscio, T. A., Gordon, M. A., Portnoy, G. A. & Rounsaville, B. J. (2008). Computer-assisted cognitive-behavioral therapy for addiction: A randomized clinical trial of CBT4CBT. *American Journal of Psychiatry* 165: 881–888.

Carroll, K. M., Ball, S. A., Martino, S., Nich, C., Babuscio, T. A. & Rounsaville, B. J. (2009). Enduring effects of a computer-assisted training program for cognitive behavioral therapy: A 6-month follow-up of CBT4CBT. *Drug and Alcohol Dependence* 100: 178–181.

Carroll, K. M., Nich, C., Ball, S. A., McCance, E. & Rounsaville, B. J. (1998). Treatment of cocaine and alcohol dependence with psychotherapy and disulfiram. *Addiction* 93: 713–727.

Catz, S. L., Heckman, T. G., Kochman, A. & DiMarco, M. (2001). Rates and correlates of HIV treatment adherence among late middle-aged and older adults living with HIV disease. *Psychology, Health & Medicine* 6, no. 1: 47–58.

Clark, M. R., Stoller, K. B. & Bronner, R. K. (2008). Assessment and management of chronic pain in individuals seeking treatment for opioid dependence disorder. *The Canadian Journal of Psychiatry* 53: 496–507.

Curran, G. M., Sullivan, G., Williams, K., Han, X., Collins, K., et al. (2003). Emergency department use of persons with comorbid psychiatric and substance abuse disorders. *Annals of Emergency Medicine* 41: 659–667.

Currie, S. R., Hodgins, D. C., Crabtree, A., Jacobi, J. & Armstrong, S. (2003). Outcome from integrated pain management treatment for recovering substance abusers. *Pain* 4: 91–100.

Demyttenaere, K., Bruffaerts, R., Leen, S., Posada-Villa, J., Kovess, V., Angermeyer, M. S., Levinson, D., de Girolamo, G., Nakane, H., Mneimneh, Z., Lara, C., de Graaf, R., Scott, K. M., Gureje, O., Stein, D. J., Haro, J. M., Bromet, E. J., Kessler, R. C., Alonso, J. & Von Korff, M. (2007). Mental disorders among persons with chronic back or neck pain: Results from the World Mental Health Surveys. *Pain* 129: 332–342.

Dhossche, D. M., Meloukheia, A. M. & Chakravorty, S. (2000). The association of suicide attempts and comorbid depression and substance abuse in psychiatric consultation patients. *General Hospital Psychiatry* 22, no. 4: 281–288.

Dobkin, P. L., De Civita, M., Paraherakis, A. & Gill, K., 2002. The role of functional social support in treatment retention and outcomes among outpatient adult substance abusers. *Addiction* 97: 347–356.

Dodge, R., Sindelar, J. & Sinha, R. (2005). The role of depression symptoms in predicting drug abstinence in outpatient substance abuse treatment. *Journal of Substance Abuse Treatment* 28: 189–196.

Drake, R. E., Goldman, H. H., Leff, H. S., Lehman, A. F., Dixon, L., et al. (2001). Implementing evidence-based practices in routine mental health service settings. *Psychiatric Services* 52: 179–182.

Drake, R. E., Mueser, K. T., Clark, R. E. & Wallach, M. A. (1996). The course, treatment, and outcome of substance disorders in persons with severe mental illness. *American Journal of Orthopsychiatry* 66: 42–51.

Driessen, M., Schulte, S., Luedecke, C., Schaefer, I., Sutmann, F., Ohlmeier, M., et al. (2008). Trauma and PTSD in patients with alcohol, drug, or dual dependence: A multicenter study. *Alcoholism, Clinical and Experimental Research* 32: 481–488.

Dutra, L., Stathopoulou, G., Basden, S. L., Leyro, T. M., Powers, B. & Otto, M. W. (2008). A meta-analytic review of psychosocial interventions for substance use disorders. *American Journal of Psychiatry* 165: 179–187.

Farre, M., Mas, A., Torrens, M., Moreno, V. & Cami, J. (2002). Retention rate and illicit opioid use during methadone maintenance interventions: A meta-analysis. *Drug and Alcohol Dependence* 65: 283–290.

Farrell, M., Howes, S., Bebbington, P., Brugha, T., Jenkins, R., Lewis, G., et al. (2003). Nicotine, alcohol, and drug dependence, and psychiatric comorbidity—results of a national household survey. *International Review of Psychiatry* 15: 50–56.

Fiore, M. C., Jaén, C. R., Baker, T. B., et al. (2009). Treating tobacco use and dependence: 2008 update. In *Quick reference guide for clinicians*. Rockville, MD: U.S. Department of Health and Human Services, Public Health Service.

Fuller, R. K., Branchey, L., Brightwell, D. R., Derman, R. M., Emrick, C. D., Iber, F. L., James, K. E., Lacoursiere, R. B., Lee, K. K., Lowenstam, I., et al. (1986). Disulfiram treatment of alcoholism: A Veterans Administration Cooperative Study. *JAMA* 256: 14449–14455.

George, T. P., Chawarski, M. C., Pakes, J., Carroll, K. M., Kosten, T. R. & Schottenfeld, R. S. (2000). Disulfiram versus placebo for cocaine dependence in buprenorphine-maintained subjects: A preliminary trial. *Biological Psychiatry* 47: 1080–1086.

Grant, B. F. (1995). Comorbidity between DSM-IV drug use disorders and major depression: Results of a national survey of adults. *Journal of Substance Abuse* 7: 481–497.

Grant, B. F. & Harford, T. C. (1995). Comorbidity between DSM-IV alcohol use disorders and major depression: Results of a national survey. *Drug & Alcohol Dependence* 39: 197–206.

Hellerstein, D. J., Rosenthal, R. N. & Miner, C. R. (1995). A prospective study of integrated outpatient treatment for substance-abusing schizophrenic patients. *American Journal on Addictions* 4: 33–42.

Higgins, S. T., Sigmon, S. C., Wong, C. J., Heil, S. H., Badger, G. J., Donham, R., Dantona, R. L. & Anthony, S. (2003). Community reinforcement therapy for cocaine-dependent outpatients. *Archives of General Psychiatry* 60: 1043–1052.

Hoffman, J. A., Caudill, B. D., Koman, J. J., Luckey, J. W., Flynn, P. M. & Mayo, D. W. (1996). Psychosocial treatments for cocaine abuse: 12-month treatment outcomes. *Journal of Substance Abuse Treatment* 13: 3–11.

Hoge, C. W., Castro, C. A., Messer, S. C., McGurk, D., Cotting, D. I. & Koffman, R. L. (2004). Combat duty in Iraq and Afghanistan, mental health problems, and barrier to care. *New England Journal of Medicine* 351: 13–22.

Humphreys, K., Wing, S., McCarty, D., Chapel, J., Gallant, L., Haberle, R., et al. (2004). Self-help organizations for alcohol and drug problems: Toward evidence-based practice and policy. *Journal of Substance Abuse Treatment* 26: 151–158.

Jordan, L. D., Davidson, W. S., Herman, S. E. & Bootsmiller, B. J. (2002). Involvement in 12-step programs among persons with dual diagnoses. *Psychiatric Services* 53: 894–896.

Jovanovski, D., Erb, S. & Zakzanis, K. K. (2005). Neurocognitive deficits in cocaine users: A quantitative review of the evidence. *Journal of Clinical and Experimental Neuropsychology* 27: 189–204.

Kadden, R., Carroll, K. M., Donovan, D. M., Cooney, N. L., Monti, P. M., Abrams, D., et al. (1994). *Cognitive-behavioral coping skills therapy manual.* Bethesda, MD: Project MATCH, National Institute on Alcohol Abuse and Alcoholism.

Kahn, R., Biswas, K., Childress, A-R., Shoptaw, S., Fudala, P. J., Gorgon, L., Montoya, I., Collins, J., McSherry, F., Li, S-H., Chiang, N., Alathari, H., Watson, D., Liberto, J., Beresford, T., Stock, C., Wallance, C., Gruber, V. & Elkashef, A. (2009). Multi-center trial of baclofen for abstinence initiation in severe cocaine-dependent individuals. *Drug and Alcohol Dependence* 103: 59–64.

Kaner, E., Beyer, F., Dickinson, H., Pienaar, E., Campbell, F., Schlesinger, C., Heather, N., Saunders, J. & Burnand, B. (2007). Effectiveness of brief alcohol interventions in primary care populations. *Cochrane Database System Review* CD004148.

Kaplan, M. S., Huguet, N., McFarland, B. H. & Newsom, J. T. (2007). Suicide among male veterans: A prospective population-based study. *Journal of Epidemiological Community Health* 61: 619–624.

Kelly, J. F., McKellar, J. D. & Moos, R. (2003). Major depression in patients with substance use disorders: Relationship to 12-Step self-help involvement and substance use outcomes. *Addiction* 98: 499–508.

Kessler, R. C., Nelson, C. B., McGonagle, K. A., Liu, J., Swartz, M. & Blazer, D. G. (1996). Comorbidity of DSM-III-R major depressive disorder in the general population: Results from the U.S. National Comorbidity Survey. *British Journal of Psychiatry Supplement* 30: 17–30.

Kirchner, J. E., Owen, R. R., Norquist, C., et al. (1998). Diagnosis and management of substance use disorders among inpatients with schizophrenia. *Psychiatric Services* 49: 82–85.

Kodl, M., Fu, S., Willenbring, M., Gravely, A., Nelson, D. & Joseph, A. (2008). The impact of depressive symptoms on alcohol and cigarette consumption following treatment for alcohol and nicotine dependence. *Alcoholism: Clinical and Experimental Research* 32, no. 1: 92–99.

Kranzler, H. R., Tennen, H., Armeli, S., Chan, G., Covault, J., Arias, A. & Oncken, C. (2009). Targeted naltrexone for problem drinkers. *Journal of Clinical Psychopharmacology* 29: 350–357.

Kristenson, H. (1987). Methods of intervention to modify drinking patterns in heavy drinkers. *Recent Developments in Alcoholism* 5: 403–423.

Kunz, J. L. (1997). Alcohol use and reported visits to health professionals: An exploratory study. *Journal of Studies on Alcohol* 58: 474–479.

Kushner, M., Donahue, C., Sletten, S., Thuras, P., Abrams, K., Peterson, J. & Frye, B. (2006). Cognitive behavioral treatment of comorbid anxiety disorder in alcoholism treatment patients: Presentation of a prototype program and future directions. *Journal of Mental Health* 15: 697–707.

Lambert, M. T. & Fowler, D. R. (1997). Suicide risk factors among veterans: Risk management in the changing culture of the Department of Veterans Affairs. *Journal of Mental Health Administration* 24: 350–358.

Lambert, M. T., Griffith, J. M. & Hendricksen, W. (1996). Characteristics of patients with substance abuse diagnoses on a general psychiatry unit in a VA medical center. *Psychiatric Services* 47: 1104–1107.

Laudet, A. B., Magura, S., Cleland, C. M., Vogel, H. S. & Knight, E. L. (2003). Predictors of retention in dual-focus self-help groups. *Community Mental Health Journal* 39: 281–297.

Lejoyeux, M., Huet, F., Claudon, M., Fichelle, A., Casalino, E. & Lequen, V. (2008). Characteristics of suicide attempts preceded by alcohol consumption. *Archives of Suicide Research* 12: 30–38.

Lieber, C. S., Weiss, D. G., Groszmann, R., Paronetto, F. & Schenker, S., for the veterans Affairs Cooperative Study 391 Group (2003). I. Veterans Affairs Cooperative Study of polyenylphosphatidylcholine in alcoholic liver disease: Effects on drinking behaviors by nurse/physician teams. *Alcoholism: Clinical and Experimental Research* 27: 1757–1764.

Linehan, M. M., Dimeff, L. A., Reynolds, S. K., Comtois, K. A., Welch, S. S., Heagerty, P. & Kivlahan, D. R. (2002). Dialectical behavior therapy versus comprehensive validation therapy plus 12-step for the treatment of opioid dependent women meeting criteria for borderline personality disorder. *Drug and Alcohol Dependence* 67: 13–26.

Lydecker, K. P., Tate, S. R., Cummins, K. M., McQuaid, J., Granholm, E. & Brown, S. A. (2010). Integrated treatment for depression and substance use disorders: Outcomes of a randomized clinical trial. *Psychology of Addictive Behaviors* 24: 453–465.

Management of Substance Use Disorders Working Group. (2009). VA/DoD clinical practice guideline for management of substance use disorders (SUD; version 2.0). www.healthquality.va.gov/sud/sud_full_601f.pdf (accessed September 1, 2010).

Mann, K., Lehert, P. & Morgan, M.Y. (2004). The efficacy of acamprosate in the maintenance of abstinence in alcohol-dependent individuals: Results of a meta-analysis. *Alcoholism: Clinical and Experimental Research* 28: 51–63.

Mark, T. L. (2003). The costs of treating persons with depression and alcoholism compared with depression alone. *Psychiatric Services* 54: 1095–1097.

Mason, B. J., Goodman, A. M., Chabac, S. & Lehert, P. (2006). Effect of oral acamprosate on abstinence in patients with alcohol-dependence in a double-blind, placebo-controlled trial: The role of patient motivation. *Journal of Psychiatric Research* 40: 383–393.

Mattick, R. P., Kimber, J., Breen, C. & Davoli, M. (2008). Buprenorphine maintenance versus placebo or methadone maintenance for opioid dependence. *Cochrane Database System Review* CD002207.

McCaul, M. E., Svikis, D. S. & Moore, R. D. (2001). Predictors of outpatient treatment retention: patient versus substance use characteristics. *Drug and Alcohol Dependence* 62: 9–17.

McKay, J. R., Cacciola, J. S., McLellan, A. T., Alternman, A. I. & Wirtz, P. W. (1997). An initial evaluation of the psychosocial dimensions of the American Society of Addiction Medicine criteria for inpatient versus intensive outpatient substance abuse rehabilitation. *Journal of Studies on Alcohol* 58: 239–252.

McKay, J. R., McLellan, A. T., Alternman, A. I., Cacciola, J. S., Rutherford, M. J. & O'Brien, C. P. (1998). Predictors of participation in aftercare sessions and self-help groups following completion of intensive outpatient treatment for substance abuse. *Journal of Studies on Alcohol* 59: 152–162.

McKay, J. R., Pettinati, H. M., Morrison, R., Feeley, M., Mulvaney, F. D. & Gallop, R. (2002). Relation of depression diagnoses to 2-year outcomes in cocaine-dependent patients in a randomized continuing care study. *Psychology of Addictive Behaviors* 16: 225–235.

Miller, D. R., Kalman, D., Ren, X. S., et al. (2001). *Health behaviors of veterans in the VHA: Tobacco abuse: 1999 Large Health Survey of VHA Enrollees.* Washington, DC: Office of Quality and Performance, Veterans Health Administration, Department of Veterans Affairs.

Miller, W. R. & Rollnick, S. (1991). *Motivational interviewing: Preparing people to change addictive behavior.* New York: Guilford Press.

Miller, W. R. & Wilbourne, P. L. (2002). Mesa Grande: A methodological analysis of clinical trials of treatments for alcohol use disorders. *Addiction* 97: 265–277.

Miller, W. R., Zweben, A., DiClemente, C. & Rychtarik, R. (1992). *Motivational enhancement therapy: A clinical research guide for therapists treating individuals with alcohol abuse and dependence.* Project MATCH monograph series, vol. 2. DHHS pub. no. (ADM) 92–1894. Washington, DC: Department of Health and Human Services.

Mokdad, A. H., Marks, J. S., Stroup, D. F. & Gerberding, J. L. (2004). Actual causes of death in the United States, 2000. *JAMA* 291:1238–1245.

Monti, P. M., Colby, S. M., Barnett, N. P., Spirito, A., Rohsenow, D. J., Myers, M., Wollard, R. & Lewander, W. (1999). Brief intervention for harm reduction with alcohol-positive older adolescents in a hospital emergency department. *Journal of Consulting and Clinical Psychology* 67: 989–994.

Morrissey, J. P., Jackson, E. W., Ellis, A. R., Amaro, H., Brown, V. B. & Najavits, L. M. (2005). Twelve-month outcomes of trauma-informed interventions for women with co-occurring disorders. *Psychiatric Services* 56: 1213–1222.

Moyer, A., Finney, J. W., Swearingen, C. E. & Vergun, P. (2002). Brief interventions for alcohol problems: a meta-analytic review of controlled investigations in treatment-seeking and non–treatment seeking populations. *Addiction* 97: 279–292.

Najavits, L. M., Weiss, R. D. & Shaw, S. R. (1997). The link between substance abuse and posttraumatic stress disorder in women: A research review. *American Journal on Addictions* 6: 273–283.

National Institute on Alcohol Abuse and Alcoholism. (1998). *Alcohol and the liver: Research update.* Alcohol alert, no. 42. Rockville, MD: U.S. Department of Health and Human Services.

National Institute on Alcohol Abuse and Alcoholism. (2001). *Cognitive impairment and recovery from alcoholism.* Alcohol alert, no. 53. Rockville, MD: U.S. Department of Health and Human Services.

National Institute on Alcohol Abuse and Alcoholism. (2002). *Alcohol and HIV/ AIDS.* Alcohol alert, no. 57. Rockville, MD: U.S. Department of Health and Human Services.

National Institute on Alcohol Abuse and Alcoholism. (2007). *Helping patients who drink too much: A clinician's guide.* NIH publication no. 07–3769. Rockville, MD: U.S. Department of Health and Human Services, National Institute of Health.

Nowinski, J., Baker, S. & Carroll, K. (1994). *Twelve-step facilitation therapy manual: A clinical research guide for therapists treating individuals with alcohol abuse and dependence.* National Institute on Alcohol Abuse and Alcoholism, Project MATCH monograph series, vol. 1; NIH publication No. 94-3722. Washington, DC: Superintendent of Documents, U.S. Government Printing Office.

Ojesjo, L., Hagnell, O. & Otterbeck, L. (1998). Mortality in alcoholism among men in the Lundby community cohort, Sweden: A forty-year follow-up. *Journal of Studies on Alcohol* 59: 140–145.

O'Toole, T. P., Pollini, R., Gray, P., Jones, T., Bigelow, G., et al. (2007). Factors identifying high-frequency and low-frequency health service utilization among substance-using adults. *Journal of Substance Abuse Treatment* 33: 51–59.

Ouimette, P. C., Brown, P. J. & Najavits, L. M. (1998). Course and treatment of patients with both substance use and posttraumatic stress disorder. *Addictive Behaviors* 23: 785–795.

Ouimette, P. C., Finney, J. W. & Moos, R. H. (1997). Twelve-step and cognitive-behavioral treatment for substance abuse: A comparison of treatment effectiveness. *Journal of Consulting and Clinical Psychology* 65: 230–240.

Ouimette, P., Moos, R. H. & Finney, J. W. (2003). PTSD treatment and 5-year remission among patients with substance use and posttraumatic stress disorders. *Journal of Consulting and Clinical Psychology* 71: 410–414.

Petrakis, I. L., Poling, J., Levinson, C., Nich, C., Carroll, K., Rounsaville, B. & VA New England VISN 1 MIRECC Study Group. (2005). Naltrexone and disulfiram in patients with alcohol dependence and comorbid psychiatric disorders. *Biological Psychiatry* 57: 1128–1137.

Pietrzak, R. H., Johnson, D. C., Goldstein, M. B., Malley, J. C. & Southwick, S. M. (2009). Perceived stigma and barriers to mental health care utilization among OEF-OIF veterans. *Psychiatric Services* 60: 1118–1122.

Prendergast, M., Podus, D., Finnery, J., Greenwell, L. & Roll, J. (2006). Contingency management for treatment of substance use disorders: A meta-analysis. *Addiction* 101: 1546–1560.

Preuss, U. A., Schuckit, M. A., Smith, T. L., Danko, G. P., Bucholz, K. K., Hesselbrock, M. N., Hesselbrock, V. & Kramer, J. R. (2003). Predictors and correlates of suicide attempts over 5 years in 1,237 alcohol-dependent men and women. *American Journal of Psychiatry* 160, no. 1: 56–63.

Pyne, J. M., Booth, B. M., Farahati, F., Tripathi, S., Smith, G. R. & Marques, P. R. (2006). Preference-weighted health status associated with substance use–disorders treatment. *Journal of Studies on Alcohol* 194: 436–444.

Sayre, S. L., Schmitz, J. M., Stotts, A. L., Averill, P. M., Rhoades, H. M. & Grabowski, J. J. (2002). Determining predictors of attrition in an outpatient substance abuse program. *American Journal of Drug & Alcohol Abuse* 28: 55–72.

Seale, J. P., Boltri, J. M., Shellenberger, S., Velasquez, M. M., Cornelius, M., Guyinn, M., Okosun, I. & Sumner, H. (2006). Primary care validation of a single screening question for drinkers. *Journal of Studies on Alcohol* 67: 778–784.

Shadish, W. R. & Baldwin, S. A. (2005). Effects of behavioral marital therapy: A meta-analysis of randomized controlled trials. *Journal of Consulting and Clinical Psychology* 73: 6–14.

Shoptaw, S., Yang, X., Rotheram-Fuller, E. J., Hsieh, Y-C. M., Kintaudi, P. C., Charuvastra, V. C. & Ling, W. (2003). Randomized placebo-controlled trial of baclofen for cocaine dependence: Preliminary effects for individuals with chronic patterns of cocaine use. *Journal of Clinical Psychiatry* 64: 1440–1448.

Simpson, D. D., Joe, G. W. & Rowan-Szal, G. A. (1997). Drug abuse treatment retention and process effects on follow-up outcomes. *Drug and Alcohol Dependence* 47: 227–235.

Sinha, R., Easton, C. & Kemp, K. (2003). Substance abuse treatment characteristics of probation-referred young adults in a community-based outpatient program. *American Journal of Drug and Alcohol Abuse* 29: 585–597.

Siqueland, L., Crits-Christoph, P., Frank, A., Daley, D., Weiss, R., Chittams, J., Blaine, J. & Luborsky, L. (1998). Predictors of dropout from psychosocial treatment of cocaine dependence. *Drug and Alcohol Dependence* 52: 1–13.

Spanagel, R. & Zieglgansberger, W. (1997). Anti-craving compounds for ethanol: new pharmacological tools to study addictive processes. *Trends in Pharmacological Science* 18: 54–59.

Srisurapanont, M. & Jarusuraisin, N. (2005). Naltrexone for the treatment of alcoholism: A meta-analysis of randomized controlled trials. *International Journal of Neuropsychopharmacology* 8: 267–280.

Stark, M. J. (1992). Dropping out of substance abuse treatment: A clinically oriented review. *Clinical Psychology Review* 12: 93–116.

Stewart, S., Conrod, P. J., Samoluk, S. B., Pihl, R. O. & Dongier, M. (2000). Post-traumatic stress disorder symptoms and situation-specific drinking in women substance abusers. *Alcoholism Treatment Quarterly* 18: 31–47.

Tate, S. R., McQuaid, J. R. & Brown, S. A. (2005). Characteristics of life stressors predictive of substance treatment outcomes. *Journal of Substance Abuse Treatment* 29: 107–115.

Tate, S. R., Mrnak-Meyer, J., Tripp, J. C. & Brown, S. A. (2010). Brief health focused motivational intervention for alcohol dependent veterans. *Alcoholism: Clinical and Experimental Research* 34, no. 6: 230A.

Tracy, S. W., Trafton, J. A., Weingardt, K. R., Aton, E. G. & Humphreys, K. (2007). How are substance use disorders addressed in VA psychiatric and primary care settings? Results of a national survey. *Psychiatric Services* 58: 266–269.

U.S. Preventive Services Task Force: Polen, M. R., Whitlock, E. P., Wisdom, J. P., Nygren, P. & Bougatsos, C. (2008). *Screening in primary care settings for illicit drug use: Staged systematic review for the U.S. Preventive Services Task Force.* Evidence synthesis no. 58, part I; AHRQ publication No. 08–05108–EF-1. Rockville, MD: Agency for Healthcare Research and Quality.

U.S. Project MATCH Research Group. (1997). Matching alcoholism treatments to client heterogeneity: Project MATCH posttreatment drinking outcomes. *Journal of Studies on Alcohol* 58, no. 1: 7–29.

VA's alcoholism screening procedures. (1991). Publication no. HRD-91–71. Washington, DC. United States General Accounting Office.

Vinson, D. C., Maclure, M., Reidinger, C. & Smith, G. S. (2003). A population based case-crossover and case-control study of alcohol and the risk of injury. *Journal of Studies on Alcohol* 64: 358–366.

Volk, R. J., Cantor, S. B., Steinbauer, J. R. & Cass, A. R. (1997). Alcohol use disorders, consumption patterns, and health-related quality of life of primary care patients. *Alcoholism: Clinical and Experimental Research* 21: 899–905.

Wagner, T. H., Harris, K. M., Federman, B., Dai, L., Luna, Y. & Humphreys, K. (2007). Prevalence of substance use disorders among veterans and comparable nonveterans from the National Survey on Drug Use and Health. *Psychological Services* 4: 149–157.

Waller, S. J., Lyons, J. S. & Constantini-Ferrando, M. F. (1999). Impact of comorbid affective and alcohol use disorders on suicidal ideation and attempts. *Journal of Clinical Psychology* 55, no. 5: 1999.

Wickizer, T., Maynard, C., Atherly, A. & Frederick, M. (1994). Completion rates of clients discharged from drug and alcohol treatment programs in Washington State. *American Journal of Public Health* 84: 215–221.

Williams, J., Herman-Stahl, M., Calvin, S. L., Pemberton, M. & Bradshaw, M. (2009). Mediating mechanisms of a military web-based alcohol intervention. *Drug and Alcohol Dependence* 100: 248–257.

Williams, R. & Vinson, D. C. (2001). Validation of a single screening question for problem drinking. *Journal of Family Practice* 50: 307–312.

Integrating Smoking Cessation into Mental Healthcare for Post-traumatic Stress Disorder: Transforming Treatment Delivery in the Veterans Health Administration

Carol A. Malte, Andrew J. Saxon,
Kim Hamlett-Berry, and Miles E. McFall

Our lack of greater progress in tobacco control is more the result of failure to implement proven strategies than the lack of knowledge about what to do.
—Surgeon General David Satcher, MD, PhD
(U.S. Department of Health and Human Services 2000).

Tobacco use remains the single most preventable cause of morbidity and mortality in the United States (Centers for Disease Control and Prevention Coordinating Center for Health Promotion 2007). Much of the burden of tobacco use falls on individuals with mental illness, who smoke at over twice the rate of the general population and are much less likely to successfully quit than non–mentally ill smokers (Lasser et al. 2000). As the largest provider of mental health care in the nation, the Veterans Health Administration (VHA) is on the front line of the fight to treat nicotine dependence in this population.

Posttraumatic stress disorder (PTSD) is highly prevalent in the VHA patient population (20 percent) (Hankin et al. 1999; Dobie et al. 2004) and is associated with a rate of smoking (31–60 percent) (Beckham et al. 1995, 1997;–Cohen et al. 2009) that far exceeds that of VHA enrollees in general (20 percent) (Department of Veterans Affairs 2009). Patients in VHA with PTSD smoke more heavily than those without PTSD (Beckham et al. 1997) and use tobacco in part to regulate mood states and psychiatric symptoms (Beckham et al. 2005, 2007). Tobacco dependence likely contributes to the higher prevalence of various physical health problems (Dobie et al. 2004; Boscarino 2004, 2008; Beckham et al. 1998) and use of medical services (Deykin et al. 2001; Schnurr et al. 2000; Calhoun et al. 2002, 2006; Ford et al. 2004) among veterans with PTSD, compared to those without the disorder.

Despite advances in pharmacological and behavioral treatments for smoking cessation, healthcare organizations, including VHA, still struggle to treat tobacco use disorder in individuals with mental illness. For veterans with PTSD, integrating smoking cessation treatment into mental healthcare offers an alternative to the standard method of delivering cessation care, referral to specialized smoking cessation clinics. Integrated care for smoking cessation is based on the therapeutic relationship between the veteran and his or her mental health provider, which allows for frequent and appropriate follow-up for both nicotine dependence and PTSD-related symptoms. This chapter focuses on the context of tobacco cessation within VHA in which integrated care developed, the unique issues faced by veterans with PTSD who smoke, the philosophy and specific interventions involved in the delivery of integrated care, and initiatives underway in VHA to spread the use of integrated care.

Tobacco Cessation and the Veterans Health Administration

Historically, smoking rates among veterans enrolled in VHA have been much higher than in the general U.S. population. As recently as 1999, the prevalence of smoking among veterans enrolled for care in VHA, at 33 percent (Office of Quality and Performance, Veterans Health Administration 2001), was well above the 23 percent in the U.S. population (Centers for Disease Control 2000). Such high rates are not surprising considering the relationship between tobacco use and U.S. military service. Although cigarettes are no longer included in rations as they were during World Wars I and II and the Korean and Vietnam Wars, tobacco use continues to be a major part of military culture and daily life. Military service is a risk factor for smoking even for those who did not smoke prior to age eighteen, a milestone associated with being a nonsmoker in the general population (Klevens et al. 1995). According to the Department of Defense (DoD), 30.6 percent of active military personnel reported cigarette use in 2008 (Bray et al. 2009); although this is a great improvement from the 51 percent reporting use in 1981, it is significantly higher than the 20.6 percent of users in the U.S. population in the same year. Veterans enrolled in VHA are more likely to smoke for reasons beyond military service. Enrollees in VHA are similar to adult smokers nationally in that they tend to be older (median age of sixty-three years) and financially disadvantaged (median income $30,000 per year), with a number of medical and psychiatric co-occurring disorders (Department of Veterans Affairs 2009).

History of Tobacco Cessation Efforts at the Veterans Health Administration

In recent years VHA has taken many steps to reduce tobacco use among its enrollees. The earliest systematic effort was in 1969, when VHA issued guidelines to reduce smoking (Veterans Administration 1969); these measures included environmental changes to discourage smoking, eliminating the sale of cigarettes in hospital stores, and developing clinical programs targeting "high-risk patients" who wanted to quit smoking. Since then, additional changes have included creating smoke-free indoor areas and smoking cessation specialty clinics at each facility, and availability of Federal Drug Administration–approved smoking cessation medications on the national VHA formulary (Hamlett-Berry 2004).

Although these changes have increased the availability of smoking cessation counseling and medications, this availability has not translated directly into utilization of the services. In 2002 the Veterans Health Administration Public Health Strategic Health Care Group and a group of healthcare professionals, researchers, and administrators, comprising the Veterans Health Administration Smoking and Tobacco Use Cessation Technical Advisory Group, began work to increase veterans' access to evidence-based tobacco cessation care. The group identified two primary barriers to treatment utilization: (1) national policy restricting prescriptions for smoking cessation medications to specialized cessation clinics, and (2) copayments for smoking cessation counseling that were required for many veterans, depending on their income level and disability status (Hamlett-Berry et al. 2009).

Prescription Restrictions

The 1999 Veterans Health Administration/Department of Defense Clinical Practice Guideline recommended that primary care providers prescribe nicotine replacement therapy or bupropion for patients who smoked (Office of Quality and Performance, Veterans Health Administration 1999), which conflicted directly with VHA's national policy requiring that cessation medications be prescribed only to patients enrolled in smoking cessation specialty programs. In 2003 the Public Health Strategic Health Care Group and Smoking and Tobacco Use Cessation Technical Advisory Group successfully advocated removing the prescribing restrictions on nicotine replacement therapy and/or bupropion, thereby increasing access to smoking cessation medications. This change also opened the door to allow psychiatrists and nurse practitioners working in VHA mental health clinics to prescribe cessation medications. Between 2004 and 2008 the number of patients receiving nicotine replacement therapy in VHA increased by 63 percent, after adjusting for growth in the number of unique patients, while bupropion prescriptions grew by 35 percent among all patients and 61 percent among patients who also received nicotine replacement therapy (Smith et al. 2010).

Copayment for Cessation Counseling

Also in 2003, the Public Health Strategic Healthcare Group and Smoking and Tobacco Use Cessation Technical Advisory Group argued for removal of the $15 copayment for cessation counseling, based on expert guideline recommendations to reduce or eliminate copayments for smoking cessation services (Fiore et al. 2000) and findings that healthcare plans that eliminated copays experienced greater utilization of services and, in turn, higher quit rates (Curry et al. 1998; Schauffler et al. 2001). As a result, cessation counseling was reclassified as a preventive service, moving it to a "no copayment" category of outpatient care previously reserved for publicly announced health initiatives such as health fairs, screenings, and immunizations (Department of Veterans Affairs 2006a).

Veterans Health Administration/Department of Defense Clinical Practice Guidelines

In an effort to summarize best practices in the field, VHA's Office of Quality and Performance and the DoD developed an evidence-based clinical practice guideline for treating tobacco use in 1999. At that time the guideline encouraged use of specialized smoking cessation programs based on evidence of treatment effectiveness. Unfortunately these specialized programs, despite their effectiveness, failed to reach a significant proportion of tobacco users, and tobacco use remained high (Hamlett-Berry et al. 2009). When the VHA/DoD guidelines were revised in 2004 (Office of Quality and Performance, Veterans Health Administration 2004), integration of tobacco cessation treatment into various clinical settings, including primary care and dentistry, was encouraged. Unlike specialized programs, primary care–based treatment, although less effective, provided a greater number of tobacco users access to treatments. Additional changes to the guideline included evidence that the chronic, relapsing nature of tobacco dependence responded best to ongoing care and multiple interventions, new findings regarding the efficacy of nicotine replacement therapy and telephone quitlines, and the cost-effectiveness of smoking cessation interventions. The clinical guideline work group concluded that "smoking cessation treatments should not be withheld from patients when other less cost-effective medical interventions are routinely delivered. Furthermore, access to tobacco treatment should be as easy as purchasing tobacco products" (Office of Quality and Performance, Veterans Health Administration 2004).

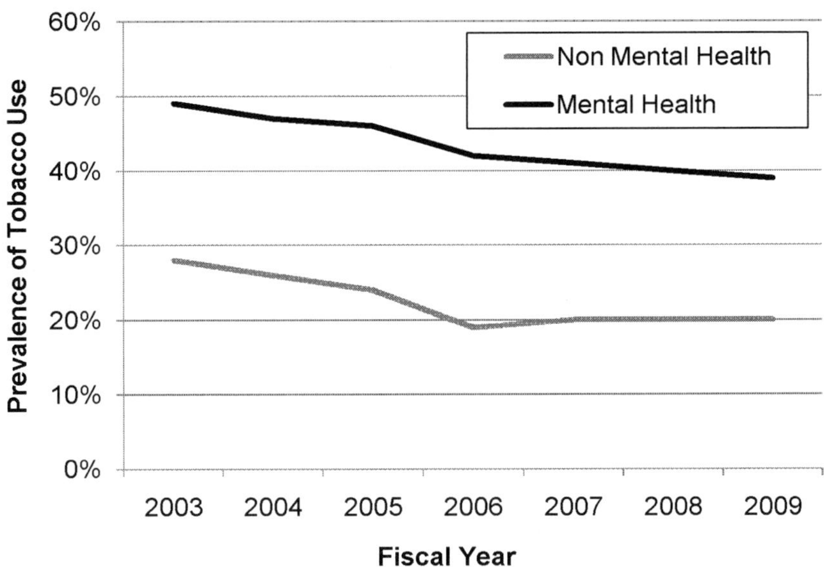

Figure 3.1. National Prevalence of Tobacco Use among VHA Enrollees. *Source:* VHA Office of Quality and Performance.

National Performance Measures

In accordance with systems-level evidence-based practice as outlined in the Public Health Service Clinical Practice Guideline, VHA also put clinical assessment and intervention requirements in place to ensure that all patients are screened for tobacco and that those who smoke are given brief counseling, offered cessation medications such as nicotine replacement therapy, and offered referral for additional services on an annual basis. In 2005 the delivery of smoking cessation interventions was quite low (20–26 percent) (Hamlett-Berry et al. 2009). A year after implementing the new intervention requirements, 76 percent of current smokers seen in mental health settings and 75 percent of those seen in nonmental health settings had received brief counseling to quit smoking and were offered a referral to a smoking cessation clinic. In addition, 75 percent of current smokers seen in mental health settings were offered smoking cessation medications to assist with quitting, as were 71 percent of those in nonmental health settings (Hamlett-Berry et al. 2009).

These efforts have led to improvements in cessation rates in recent years (see figure 3.1). In a 2007 survey, 19.7 percent of veterans enrolled in VHA reported smoking, a rate comparable to the general population (Department of

Veterans Affairs 2009). Such improvements likely are due both to societal factors (changing attitudes toward smoking nationally, smoking bans, increased taxes on cigarettes, numerous population level interventions) and systematic policy changes within VHA.

Psychiatric Disorders and Smoking

The Veterans Health Administration is the nation's largest provider of treatment for mental health and substance use disorders, enrolling over 1.5 million veterans with these conditions. Smoking cessation treatment is of particular importance with this group of veterans. Although overall smoking rates for veterans seen in VHA have declined significantly over recent years, the smoking rate among veterans with mental health disorders remains high, at nearly 40 percent (see figure 3.1). The high prevalence of smoking among individuals with a psychiatric disorder is well documented (Lasser et al. 2000; Grant et al. 2004; El-Geubaly et al. 2002), and the high rate of co-occurrence of smoking and mental illness has been observed for both male (Buckley et al. 2004) and female (Davis et al. 2003) veterans.

Smoking Is a Public Health Problem in Veterans with PTSD

One of the most prevalent of all mental disorders nationally (5–10 percent for males and 10–18 percent for females) (Kessler et al. 1994; Breslau et al. 1998; Breslau 1998) and among VHA enrollees (20 percent) (Hankin et al. 1999; Dobie et al. 2004), PTSD is highly associated with smoking (Lasser et al. 2000; Hapke et al. 2005) and nicotine dependence (Hapke et al. 2005; Cougle et al. 2010). A study of New York City residents following the September 11, 2001, terrorist attack (Vlahov et al. 2002) found that residents who increased their smoking following the attack were far more likely to have PTSD than were residents who did not exhibit increased smoking (24 percent versus 6 percent, respectively), illustrating a clear link between PTSD and smoking. Smoking rates among the over 400,000 enrollees in VHA with PTSD range from an estimated 31 percent in Iraq and Afghanistan veterans (Cohen et al. 2009), to 40 percent in female veterans (Davis et al. 2003), to 53–60 percent in male Vietnam combat veterans (Beckham 1995, 1997). In the general population, individuals with PTSD are more likely to be heavy smokers (Cougle et al. 2010). This finding holds among VHA enrollees as well; a greater proportion of VHA patients with PTSD smoke heavily (>25 cigarettes/day) than those patients without the disorder (48 percent versus 28 percent) (Beckham et al. 1997). Moreover, PTSD is associated with failed cessation attempts (Cougle et al. 2010, Zvolensky et al. 2008). Only 23 percent of smokers with PTSD have stopped smoking (Lasser et al. 2000), whereas half of all persons who have smoked have quit (Fiore, Hatsukami & Baker 2002). Tobacco dependence likely contributes to the higher mortality (Boscarino 2004, 2008; Beckham et al. 1998), morbidity (Boscarino 2006, 2008; Schnurr & Jankowski 1999), and healthcare utilization of veterans with PTSD (Beckham et al. 1998; Deykin et al. 2001; Schnurr et al. 2000; Calhoun et al. 2002, 2006; Ford et al. 2004) than those without PTSD.

Box 3.1. What Is Posttraumatic Stress Disorder?*

Post-traumatic stress disorder (PTSD) is an anxiety disorder that people may develop after directly experiencing or witnessing a traumatic event. Traumatic events include military combat, physical or sexual assault, natural disaster, or serious accident and involve death, serious injury, or a threat to physical integrity. Although most survivors of trauma do not develop PTSD, some people develop stress reactions that do not go away and may get worse over time. These individuals may develop PTSD.

Symptoms of PTSD: Individuals with PTSD experience three different types of symptoms: re-experiencing symptoms, avoidance and numbing symptoms, and hyperarousal symptoms:

1. **Re-experiencing symptoms:** Re-experiencing symptoms involve reliving the traumatic event through unwanted memories, dreams, or flashbacks. Reliving the event may cause intense feelings of fear, helplessness, and horror similar to feelings experienced when the traumatic event took place.

2. **Avoidance and numbing symptoms:** Avoidance symptoms involve efforts made to avoid thoughts and feelings, as well as places and people, associated with the traumatic event. Numbing symptoms are another way to avoid the traumatic event. Individuals with PTSD may feel detached or estranged from others and less interested in activities they once enjoyed. Some people forget, or are unable to talk about, important parts of the event. Numbing also may involve a belief that one will have a shortened life span.

3. **Hyperarousal:** Hyperarousal symptoms include feelings of being constantly alert after the traumatic event. This increased emotional arousal can cause difficulty sleeping, outbursts of anger or irritability, and difficulty concentrating. Individuals with PTSD may be constantly "on guard" and may startle easily.

(Continued)

> *How does PTSD develop?* Most people will experience some of the symptoms listed above after going through a traumatic event, but not everyone develops PTSD. The likelihood that someone will develops PTSD depends on
>
> - how intense the trauma was or how long it lasted;
> - whether the individual lost someone he or she was close to, or was hurt, in the event;
> - how close the individual was to the event;
> - how strong the individual's reaction (fear, horror, etc.) was;
> - how much the individual felt in control of events; and
> - how much help and support the individual got after the event.
>
> Many people who develop PTSD get better at some time. However, about one of three people with PTSD continue to experience symptoms to varying degrees over many years.
>
> *Based on information from Department of Veterans Affairs, National Center for Posttraumatic Stress Disorder, What is PTSD? http://www.ptsd.va.gov/public/pages/what-is-ptsd.asp.

Why is smoking so highly prevalent and difficult to manage in individuals with PTSD? Nicotine has been shown to promote analgesia (Zarrindast, Pazouki & Nassiri-Rad 1997), enhance cognition (Heishman, Henningfield & Singleton 2002) and mood (Kalman 2002), and relieve anxiety (Benowitz 1988). As a result of these properties, individuals with a variety of mental disorders, including PTSD, may smoke to regulate their moods and cope with symptoms (Kirch 2000; Hall et al. 1993; Beckham et al. 1996). Posttraumatic stress disorder is associated with smoking when experiencing PTSD symptoms, anxiety, and stress (Beckham et al. 2007, 2008) and with reducing negative affect (Feldner et al. 2007). The connection between PTSD and smoking goes further; veterans with PTSD report smoking in response to distressing military memories (Beckham et al. 1996) and experience nicotine withdrawal symptoms in response to trauma-related stressors that activate PTSD symptoms (Veterans Administration 1969). The perception that smoking reduces stress may reflect a temporary alleviation of withdrawal symptoms in nicotine-dependent individuals whose nicotine plasma levels have declined (Parrott 1995; Picciotto, Brunzell & Caldarone 2002). Given the role of smoking in regulating mental health symptoms, it follows that veterans with PTSD may be particularly sensitive to nicotine withdrawal and thus vulnerable to smoking relapse.

Smoking cessation in individuals with PTSD may be further complicated by the high co-occurrence of PTSD with depression (Roszell, McFall & Malas 1991; Brady et al. 2000), a disorder associated with excessive nicotine withdrawal symptoms (Breslau, Kilbey & Andreski 1992). Some prior studies have shown that patients with a history of major depression who quit smoking are more likely to develop a new episode of major depression than are patients with a similar history who fail to quit smoking (Covey, Glassman & Stetner 1997; Glassman et al. 2001). Others, however, have found that though a prior history of major depression predicted recurrence of major depression among smokers who attempted quitting, successful abstinence from smoking bore no relationship to depression recurrence (Tsoh et al. 2000). Regardless of their depression history, individuals who experience depressive symptoms during a quit attempt may return to smoking quickly (Killen et al. 2003). Further, Boden, Fergusson, and Horwood (2010), using data on a cohort of young adults followed from birth, recently concluded that smoking increased the risk of experiencing depressive symptoms, a finding that has important implications for smoking cessation. It is unclear how engagement in ongoing psychiatric care might affect the potential adverse impact on mental status of nicotine withdrawal. Taken together, this research suggests a dynamic relationship between PTSD and tobacco use disorder that argues for a coordinated approach to treatment of both conditions.

Treatment Barriers among Patients with PTSD

Limited access to tobacco cessation treatment is a barrier to quitting smoking for patients in both VHA and general healthcare settings. A 1999 nationwide survey of 875,000 veterans enrolled in VHA healthcare showed that 24 percent of smokers reported being treated or referred for tobacco use in the prior year, and only 17 percent of smokers actually received desired cessation services (Office of Quality and Performance, Veterans Health Administration 2001; Goldman & Craig 2004). Healthcare organizations and clinicians serving the general public also provide cessation treatment to only a fraction of their patients who smoke (Thorndike et al. 1998; Thorndike, Stafford & Rigotti 2001; Ockene et al. 1997; Goldstein et al. 1997). Smokers are infrequently referred to specialized cessation clinics (Ockene et al. 1997; Sherman et al. 2005; Vaughn et al. 2002), and patients who are referred often fail to attend (Sherman et al. 2005, 2006b; Thompson et al. 1988) or complete treatment (Sherman et al. 2006b).

Box 3.2. Standard Smoking Cessation Care Delivery in the Veterans Health Administration

Specialized Smoking Cessation Clinics. Traditionally, the standard of care for smoking at most VA healthcare system facilities was referral to a specialized smoking cessation clinic (Hamlett-Berry et al. 2009). A survey (Sherman et al. 2006a) of forty VHA smoking cessation clinics found that virtually all adhered broadly to recognized practice guidelines (Fiore et al. 2008) for smoking cessation. At a minimum, these clinics deliver (a) assessment of smoking history and nicotine dependence; (b) education about individual health risks, benefits of, and strategies for quitting smoking; (c) behavioral counseling to help patients overcome barriers to abstinence, develop problem-solving and coping skills, prevent relapse, and obtain social support; and (d) opportunities for follow-up visits. In addition, these clinics have the capacity to prescribe smoking cessation medications directly through smoking cessation clinic providers or an established liaison arrangement with veterans' primary medical care providers.

Primary Care. Although nearly all VA healthcare system facilities have specialized smoking cessation clinics, these clinics typically operate one day per week (Department of Veterans Affairs 2006b) and thus aren't able to accommodate all smokers who want treatment. Increasingly, smoking cessation care is delivered in primary care settings. Primary care clinics typically deliver brief treatments (screening, brief counseling advising quitting, cessation medications, referral to specialized smoking cessation clinics) per VHA mandates.

Although primary care providers screen for tobacco use (Goldman & Craig 2004; Thorndike, Regan & Rigotti 2007), they often do not provide cessation counseling or medications to aid quitting (Thorndike et al. 1998; Thorndike, Regan & Rigotti 2007; Goldstein et al. 1997; Vaughn et al. 2002; Ferketich, Khan & Wewers 2006). As discussed previously, VHA, in an effort to improve access to cessation care, recently lifted restrictions that prevented primary care providers from prescribing nicotine replacement medications (Hamlett-Berry et al. 2009). In addition, primary care clinics are largely responsible for screening all patients annually for tobacco use and offering brief counseling, medication and referrals per VHA. However, it remains undetermined whether such policies will lead to improved smoking quit rates among veterans with mental illness, given the very limited time that primary care practitioners can devote to cessation counseling and evidence that nicotine replacement therapy alone is ineffective (Joseph & Antonnucio 1999; Pierce & Gilpin 2002).

Historically, primary care clinics have struggled to provide the frequent follow-up contacts (Goldstein et al. 1997; Sherman et al. 2001) that appear to be needed for a quit attempt to be successful. Evidence-based guidelines (Fiore et al. 2008) recognize that tobacco dependence is a chronic, relapsing disorder that requires extended treatment contacts over time and encourage multiple quit attempts. Smokers who successfully quit typically make at least three quit attempts (Curry & McBride 1994); reapplication of treatment following initial failure improves quit rates (Gonzales et al. 2001). The relationship between treatment length and intensity and favorable outcomes has been established in non-psychiatrically ill smokers (Fiore et al. 2008) and has been observed to be proportionately greater for smokers with past histories of depression (Hall & Prochaska 2009). A chronic disease management model, which emphasizes relapse management, helps patients recover from a lapse and "recycle" by making additional quit attempts (Curry & McBride 1994) and may be particularly critical for patients with PTSD, because of the likely reemergence of psychological symptoms that were managed in part by nicotine (Cook et al. 2007).

In response to the evidence that smoking prevalence remains disproportionately high among individuals with mental illness, tobacco cessation guidelines (Fiore et al. 2008; Institute of Medicine 2009) have begun to strongly encourage delivery of cessation treatment within mental health settings; however, this charge has proven difficult to meet. Historically there has been a tendency for mental health and addiction treatment providers to ignore tobacco use as a significant clinical issue requiring attention (Substance Abuse and Mental Health Services Administration 2002; Center for Substance Abuse Treatment 2005; Ziedonis 2004). Surveys have found that psychiatrists (Himelhoch & Daumit 2003) and psychologists (Phillips & Brandon 2004) often miss opportunities to intervene with patients with respect to smoking. Part of this reluctance to take on tobacco cessation may be long-held beliefs about the impact of quitting smoking on psychiatric symptoms. In a recent survey, Weinberger and colleagues (2008) found that though the majority of mental health clinicians viewed smoking cessation treatment as very important, concerns remained that cessation would contribute to relapse or worsening of psychiatric symptoms.

Treatment Implications

Research findings to date have implications for smoking cessation treatment for smokers with PTSD. Smokers with mental illness, including PTSD, may need more assistance in quitting smoking and multiple quit attempts to achieve

Box 3.3.

Traditional Delivery of Cessation Treatment		Integrated Care
Limitations		Benefits
Brief, episodic tobacco cessation treatments are no match for chronic, relapsing disorders such as nicotine dependence.	→	An integrated disease management approach that provides extended treatment (Fiore, Hatsukami & Baker 2002; Cook et al. 2007; Okene et al. 2000; Hall et al. 2004; McFall et al. 2006; Ellerbeck et al. 2009; Fagerstrom & Aubin 2009) and encourages multiple quit attempts (Fiore et al. 2008; Curry & McBride 1994; Niaura & Abrams 2002) is more suitable than brief episodic interventions for the chronic relapsing disorder of tobacco dependence.
There is limited provider time for repeated monitoring of status, response to relapses, and pursuit of drop-outs.	→	Mental health providers are well positioned to monitor smoking relapses and reapply cessation treatment owing to the frequent, ongoing nature of psychiatric care for chronic PTSD.
There is limited time/training to address smoking complicated by PTSD. Most providers are unfamiliar with the dynamic interplay between PTSD symptoms and tobacco use.	→	Mental health professionals have advanced training and experience in treating behavioral and substance use disorders applicable to nicotine dependence, enabling them to tailor cessation interventions to address exacerbation of tobacco dependence by psychiatric symptoms (Cook et al. 2007; Fu et al. 2007; Carmody, Vieten & Astin 2007) as well as potential deterioration in mood states resulting from smoking quit attempts (Glassman et al. 2001; Killen et al. 2003; Aubin 2009).
Many patients referred to cessation treatment fail to initiate care or drop out early.	→	Integrated care overcomes barriers to care that are inherent in referring veterans with mental disorders to specialty smoking cessation clinics

(Continued)

Traditional Delivery of Cessation Treatment	Integrated Care
Limitations	Benefits
Limited resources (e.g., operating hours, provider availability) prevent many patients from receiving the treatment that they desire. $\rightarrow$	(e.g., scheduling delays, relating to unfamiliar providers) and better coordinates cessation interventions with ongoing mental healthcare. Integrated care expands access to care for VHA patients who currently do not receive desired cessation treatment services from existing resources.

long-term abstinence. In addition, reduction of PTSD symptoms and implementation of mood management may be especially important in increasing the probability of quitting smoking among smokers with PTSD (Aubin 2009).

Why Integrated Care?

Barriers that interfere with delivery of effective tobacco use treatment of veterans with PTSD may be overcome by integrating cessation interventions into routine PTSD care provided by mental health clinicians, so that both disorders are treated concurrently. Mental health programs provide an ideal platform for delivering smoking cessation interventions, for the reasons shown in box 3.3.

Goals of Integrated Care

Integrated care was designed to overcome barriers that may limit the effectiveness of specialized smoking cessation clinics for veterans with PTSD. The overall goal of integrated care is to create a clinic culture that prioritizes tobacco cessation care as a core responsibility of mental health providers. This shift in culture involves the following actions:

- Assess and treat tobacco use disorder in all willing patients undergoing mental health treatment

- Embrace tobacco cessation as part of all mental health providers' jobs.

- Provide cessation interventions on repeated occasions to veterans who smoke

Box 3.4. What Is Integrated Care?

Integrated care is guideline based, modeled after the U.S. Public Health Service clinical practice guideline entitled *Treating Tobacco Use and Dependence* (Fiore et al. 2008), manualized, and delivered by post-traumatic stress disorder (PTSD) mental health provider teams. Integrated care interventions address the five "A's" of smoking cessation treatment recommended by the Public Health Service guideline: (1) ask about tobacco use repeatedly, (2) advise patients to quit, (3) assess willingness to make a quit attempt (including another quit attempt after relapse), (4) assist in the quit attempt(s), and (5) arrange follow-up assessment and treatment. Clinicians delivering integrated care follow a treatment manual that details specific interventions for each session. Integrated care comprises three elements: (1) core interventions, (2) relapse prevention and management interventions, and (3) administrative interventions.

Core Integrated Care Interventions

Behavioral counseling. Five core individual behavioral counseling sessions, averaging thirty minutes each, are delivered on a once-weekly basis by PTSD providers who are responsible for providing ongoing mental healthcare for PTSD. These sessions provide guideline-concordant (a) education about tobacco use and health benefits of quitting, (b) behavioral and problem-solving skills for quitting smoking and coping with smoking urges, (c) encouragement to set a quit date, (d) strategies for securing social support, and (e) instruction in relapse prevention. These skills acquisition sessions are followed by three weekly follow-up visits designed to assess tobacco use status, reinforce abstinence, and manage smoking relapses. Ideally, these core sessions are delivered in individual, in-person sessions.

   Self-help work. Veterans receive a participant workbook containing assigned readings and exercises that correspond to session topics. The workbook is an important aspect of treatment, because it prompts patients to use coping strategies in between scheduled smoking cessation visits. The participant workbook consists of (a) basic information about the risks of tobacco use, the benefits of quitting smoking, and the addictive nature of smoking and (b) "homework" assignments to complete worksheets that correspond with treatment session topics (e.g., identifying smoking triggers, developing and practicing skills for coping with smoking triggers, preparations for the smoking quit date, identifying and using social support skills, and making lifestyle changes that

(Continued)

support smoking cessation). Similar patient education and self-help materials have been found to reduce smoking relapse rates (Brandon et al. 2000).

Pharmacotherapy. Integrated care encourages use of cessation medications in accordance with published practice guidelines (Fiore et al. 2008) while allowing PTSD medical staff latitude to make personalized prescribing decisions for each patient. Medications may be provided as monotherapy or combination therapy. Pharmacological interventions are initiated by PTSD medical staff within two weeks following a patient's first integrated care session, and ongoing care is incorporated into regularly scheduled medication management sessions for PTSD.

Relapse Prevention and Management

After delivering core integrated care interventions, mental health providers deliver brief, once-monthly booster sessions aimed at helping veterans to prevent relapses or recover from relapses. The relapse management strategy will involve reinstatement and/or adjustment of smoking cessation medicines, reapplication of appropriate behavioral counseling strategies, and reading assignments in the participant workbook.

Administrative Intervention

In order to be successful, implementing integrated care requires broadening providers' expectations to include tobacco use as an important issue that they should routinely treat. To promote tobacco cessation as a priority within the clinic culture and prompt providers to initiate integrated care, PTSD clinics incorporate discussions of veteran smoking status into regular weekly staff meetings. During these meetings, providers review the smoking status of new and existing clinic patients and implement a team-based strategy for intervention, using methods specified in the treatment manual.

Who Delivers Integrated Care?

The ideal provider for the behavioral counseling component of integrated care is the veteran's primary mental health provider. The primary mental health provider is the patient's main point of contact and coordinates his or her overall mental healthcare. Most important, this person provides ongoing continuous contact and a familiar relationship. As a result of this ongoing relationship, the primary mental health provider has the ability to monitor, detect, and respond to relapses over time.

In addition to a primary mental health provider, each veteran seen in a PTSD clinic typically sees a mental health prescriber. The prescriber may be a psychiatrist, physician's assistant, or nurse practitioner. As part of integrated care interventions, this prescriber must be able to work closely with both the veteran and the primary mental health provider to coordinate tobacco use cessation medications and to monitor and address changes in mental health symptoms that result from quit attempts.

Components of Clinical Interventions

As stated previously, integrated care interventions are designed to provide guideline-based care for smoking cessation within the context of regular PTSD care. The treatment manual walks providers through the following key components of smoking cessation care:

- Assessment of nicotine dependence and prior abstinence
- Education about benefits of quitting
- Personalized advice to quit

Box 3.5. Motivational Interventions

Not all veterans will be ready to quit smoking. If they are thinking about quitting but not ready to take action, or if they are ambivalent about quitting, motivational interventions can be used to help them get to the point where they're ready to engage in treatment. One strategy as part of integrated care is the 4 R's (Fiore et al. 2008):

- **R**elevance to particular smoker. Mental health providers help veterans to pinpoint personalized reasons for quitting.

- **R**isks of continued smoking. Providers work with veterans to identify risks of continued smoking that are personally relevant.

- **R**oadblocks to quitting smoking. Providers assist in identifying obstacles and provide education regarding strategies to overcome these obstacles.

- **R**epeat motivational intervention at each clinic visit until the veteran is either willing to engage in or refuses cessation treatment.

- Motivational interventions
- Behavioral counseling and problem solving
- Intra-session support and help in identifying extra-session support
- Pharmacological regimen

Breakdown of Integrated Care Sessions

The following descriptions detail the interventions delivered in each integrated care session.

Session 1

The focus of the first session is on assessing current tobacco use and prior abstinence attempts by the veteran, as well as identifying personalized reasons for quitting smoking. The clinician introduces the patient to behavioral counseling, smoking cessation medications, and guidelines for setting a quit date. A participant workbook is given to each patient, which provides session by session instruction and worksheets for completing assignments. Specifically, the mental health provider will

- assess tobacco use, abstinence attempts, and reasons for quitting smoking;
- use motivational enhancement interventions for an ambivalent smoker as appropriate;
- advise the patient to stop smoking based on a summary of known health risks and personalized reasons for quitting and provide empathetic support and encouragement for quitting smoking;
- orient the patient to the plan for behavioral counseling;
- provide information on smoking cessation medications, assess past medication use, and provide a rationale for medication use;
- present guidelines for setting a quit date;
- ask the patient to 1) read about negative physical and mental health consequences of smoking and 2) record reasons for quitting smoking and review these reasons daily before smoking; and
- coordinate care with the prescriber to ensure that the patient is seen to discuss cessation medications in advance of the quit date.

Session 2

The overall purpose of this session is to identify a quit date for the veteran and to begin developing coping skills for smoking triggers. Interventions include

- establishing a quit date for smoking cessation;
- assisting the patient in identifying smoking triggers (environmental or internal emotional or somatic cues that make one want to smoke, e.g., seeing others smoking, finishing a meal, feeling anxiety);
- discussing strategies for reducing smoking prior to the quit date (If the patient is interested in reducing smoking, the provider will set appropriate smoking reduction goals; the purpose of reducing smoking is primarily to give the veteran practice with not smoking for a period of time when there is a desire to smoke prior to an actual attempt at total abstinence.);
- introducing skills for coping with smoking triggers, such as controlled breathing, and identifying existing patient-generated coping skills; and
- asking the patient to 1) detail the smoking triggers, 2) utilize personalized coping skills to deal with smoking triggers, 3) start reducing smoking if appropriate, and 4) continue to review the reasons for quitting prior to smoking.

Session 3

The primary purpose of this session is to generate an action plan for coping with smoking triggers. In addition, the use of smoking cessation medications is reviewed. The provider will

- review the assignment to practice coping with smoking triggers;
- review the status of reduced smoking when applicable;
- teach the principles of coping with smoking triggers, including 1) avoiding external trigger situations, 2) altering trigger situations, 3) replacing smoking with substitute behaviors, and 4) mentally coping with internal emotional triggers;
- develop an action plan for coping with smoking triggers;
- assess the veteran's understanding of smoking cessation medications and check the status of the appointment with the mental health prescriber; and
- ask the patient to 1) practice resisting smoking in three trigger situations using personalized coping skills, 2) continue to reduce cigarette consumption if applicable, and 3) continue to review the reasons for quitting before smoking.

Session 4

In this session the mental health provider reviews the behavioral changes necessary to prepare for the quit date and helps identify sources of social support for quitting smoking. The provider will

- review the assignment to practice coping with smoking triggers and review the use of controlled breathing or other coping strategies;
- review the status of reduced smoking when applicable;
- discuss behavioral changes to prepare for the quit date;
- identify sources of social support and how others will help the patient stop smoking;
- assess the availability and use of smoking cessation medications; and
- ask the patient to 1) begin taking actions to prepare for the quit date, 2) identify people who will be supportive of the quit attempt and begin asking others for support, 3) continue to practice resisting smoking in trigger situations, using identified coping skills, 4) continue to reduce cigarette consumption if applicable, and 5) continue to review the reasons for quitting before smoking.

Session 5

Information presented in this session includes actions to be taken on the quit date and relapse prevention strategies. The provider will

- review the assignment to practice coping with smoking triggers and assignments to use social supports;
- review the status of reduced smoking when applicable;
- review preparations for the quit date assignment and discuss actions to take on the quit date;
- introduce relapse prevention and discuss how to respond if a smoking lapse occurs and how to identify high-risk situations;
- review the plan for using smoking medications; and
- ask the patient to 1) review the actions to take on and after the quit date and 2) review coping skills to plan for dealing with high-risk relapse triggers.

Follow-up and Booster Sessions

At each of the three weekly follow-up sessions and monthly booster sessions, providers will assess smoking status and discuss quit date experiences if applicable. Additional interventions will vary depending on whether the veteran continues to be abstinent or has relapsed to smoking:

- **Abstinent patients.** The primary focus with a veteran who successfully quit is to support continued abstinence by discussing positive experiences associated with quitting, assess problems encountered or anticipated threats to abstinence, and identify solutions to any anticipated difficulties in maintaining abstinence.

- **Patients who continue to smoke.** For a veteran who was unable to quit successfully, the provider aims to reframe relapse as a learning experience and renew the patient's commitment to abstinence. If the patient is willing, the provider will reinstate appropriate treatment by utilizing motivational interventions and readministering interventions from sessions 1–5 as needed.

Concurrent Treatment of PTSD

Veterans who enroll in PTSD care in VHA are typically seen for one visit per week, though many step down their visits to once or twice per month. Long-term treatment of one or more years is the norm, owing to the chronicity and severity of military-related PTSD. Standard treatments delivered in PTSD clinics include individual case management and/or group therapy, cognitive-behavioral treatment, coping skills and problem-solving training, educational and supportive interventions, prolonged exposure therapy, and medication management. Integrated care assumes that patients will receive concurrent mental healthcare for PTSD and other co-occurring disorders, such as depression. Hence, mood and anxiety symptoms that adversely affect smoking cessation efforts will be addressed responsively as a part of routine care. Integrated care does not prescribe how PTSD care is delivered, providing maximum flexibility to clinicians to address symptoms and issues as appropriate.

Preliminary Studies of Integrated Care

Two preliminary research studies were conducted to assess whether integrated care was associated with improved tobacco use outcomes and to determine the feasibility of conducting a larger randomized, controlled trial of integrated care.

Study 1: A Randomized Trial of Integrated Care versus Specialized Smoking Cessation Clinic (McFall et al. 2005)

Veterans enrolled in a PTSD outpatient clinic who smoked more than ten cigarettes per day were randomly assigned to integrated care (n = 33) versus referral to the specialized smoking cessation clinic (n = 33) for treatment. The integrated care treatment approach was similar to that described in box 3.4, with the exception that clinicians did not apply systematic, sustained follow-up treatment contacts. Veterans randomized to the smoking cessation clinic

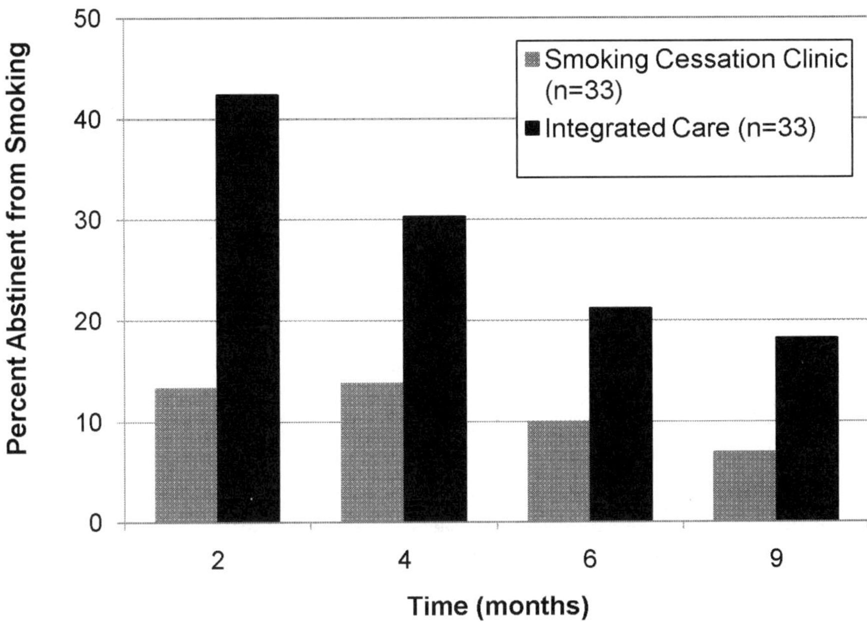

Figure 3.2. Point Prevalence Abstinence Rates for Veterans with PTSD.

received the usual standard of care for smoking cessation treatment. The primary outcome measure was abstinence from tobacco over the prior seven days (verified by a breath carbon monoxide reading) at two, four, six, and nine months after study enrollment.

It was highly feasible to recruit patients to participate, with only 3 percent of clinic patients who desired cessation treatment refusing to participate in the study. Of the sixty-seven randomized patients, 100 percent of integrated care patients and 88 percent of smoking cessation clinic patients attended at least one smoking cessation treatment session. Adherence of integrated care prescribers to guideline-recommended pharmacological interventions was high, with nearly all of the integrated care patients filling a prescription for nicotine patch and gum and 61 percent filling a prescription for bupropion. In addition, 80 percent of the integrated care counseling interventions were administered, as determined by medical record review.

Figure 3.2 presents seven-day abstinence data. Over the nine-month course of the study, veterans receiving integrated care were five times more likely to have been abstinent over the seven days prior to the assessment than those referred to the smoking cessation clinic (odds ratio 5.23, 95 percent confidence interval 1.76 to 15.54, p <.001).

Table 3.1. Medication Use by Treatment Condition

Variable	Integrated Care	Smoking Cessation Clinic
Bupropion	61%	48%
Nicotine Patch	94%	67%
Nicotine Gum	88%	42%
Total Treatment Sessions	5.2	2.6
Quit Attempts	4.29	3.25
Satisfaction with Amount of Treatment	3.9 (1-5 scale)	3.5

In addition, veterans assigned to integrated care were more likely to receive the nicotine patch and gum, had a greater number of treatment sessions, made more quit attempts, and were more satisfied with the amount and quality of their treatment (see table 3.1).

Study 2: An Open Trial of Practice-Based Integrated Care (McFall et al. 2006)

Fifty-eight veterans with PTSD who smoked more than ten cigarettes per day received integrated care for smoking cessation in an open clinical trial. As shown in figure 3.3, over 25 percent of patients achieved seven-day abstinence, verified by breath carbon monoxide readings, at two, four, six, or nine months.

Pooled Data from Studies 1 and 2

To increase the sample size, data from the two preliminary studies were pooled to include 124 veterans. The number of patients who achieved sustained abstinence, defined as seven-day abstinence at each of three time points (months 4, 6, and 9), was determined using the pooled data. As shown in table 3.2, results suggest that integrated care is capable of improving sustained smoking quit rates for veterans with PTSD by as much as 10 percent, compared to quit rates for the smoking cessation clinic.

Treatment Delivered

Veterans receiving integrated care attended nearly twice as many sessions as those assigned to the smoking cessation clinic (4.5 sessions for integrated care, 2.5 sessions for smoking cessation clinic, $p < 0.001$) in the pooled sample.

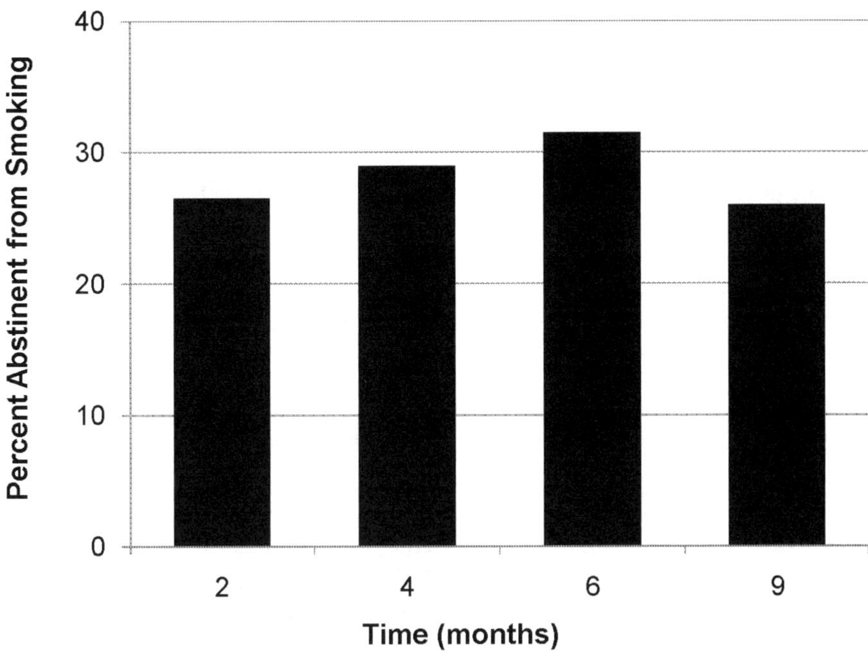

Figure 3.3. Point Prevalence Abstinence for Veterans with PTSD Receiving Integrated Care. *Source: Journal of the American Medical Association, 2010, 304(22): 2485–2493. Copyright © 2010 American Medical Association. All rights reserved.*

Table 3.2. Long-term* Abstinence Rates

Treatment Group	Randomized Trial (n = 66)	Open Clinical Trial (n = 58)
Integrated Care	12.1%	22.4%
Smoking Cessation Clinic	3.3%	

*Seven-day abstinence at each of 3 assessments (4, 6 and 9 months).

There was a clear relationship between the number of sessions received and success quitting smoking for both the integrated care and smoking cessation clinic patients. In both groups, none of the thirty-two patients attending two or fewer sessions achieved sustained abstinence (see table 3.3). Integrated care delivered more cessation treatment sessions than the smoking cessation clinic, which may explain its greater effectiveness.

Patients receiving integrated care did not differ significantly from those in the smoking cessation clinic in their likelihood of filling a prescription for

Table 3.3. Long-Term Abstinence by Treatment Received, Stratified by Number of Sessions Attended*

Treatment Group	Attended 2 or Fewer Sessions		Attended More Than 2 Sessions	
	Non-Smoker	Smoker	Non-Smoker	Smoker
Integrated Care	0	13	17	61
Smoking Cessation Clinic	0	19	1	11

*Analysis was based on pooled data for study 1 and study 2 ($n = 122$). Non-smoking status was defined as 7-day abstinence at each of 3 assessments (4, 6 and 9 months).

bupropion (integrated care = 60 percent; smoking cessation clinic = 52 percent) or nicotine patch (integrated care = 81 percent; smoking cessation clinic = 82 percent), but were more likely to receive nicotine gum (integrated care = 82 percent; smoking cessation clinic = 52 percent, $p < .0001$) and nicotine patch and gum in combination (integrated care = 73 percent; smoking cessation clinic = 48 percent, $p < .01$). Quitting smoking was not associated significantly with filling a prescription for bupropion, nicotine patch, or nicotine gum.

Change in Psychiatric Symptoms

Analysis of study 1 data showed that veterans receiving integrated care did not differ from those referred to a smoking cessation clinic in change on PTSD and depression measures over nine months of study enrollment. Although prior research shows that PTSD patients report smoking in order to reduce mental health symptoms (Beckham et al. 2007, 2008; Feldner et al. 2007), these two preliminary studies did not find that stopping smoking was related to worsening symptoms of PTSD or depression; when study 1 and study 2 data were combined, veterans who quit smoking ($n = 18$) did not differ from those who continued to smoke ($n = 104$) on change in PTSD or depression scores over the course of the study.

Conclusions from Preliminary Studies

Preliminary studies of integrated care demonstrated that veterans with PTSD who smoke are receptive to cessation treatment and are able to complete the full treatment course. Integrated care improved sustained smoking quit rates for veterans with PTSD by as much as 10 percent, compared to referral to specialized smoking cessation clinics. Veterans in integrated care attended more cessation treatment sessions than veterans referred to the smoking cessation clinic, which may explain its greater effectiveness. Mental health was not adversely affected by integrated care, as patients receiving integrated care did not differ from those referred to the smoking cessation clinic in change in symptoms of PTSD and depression over time. Further, associations were not detected between stopping smoking and worsening symptoms of PTSD or depression.

Multisite Effectiveness Trial

Based on results from preliminary studies, the Department of Veterans Affairs Cooperative Studies Program approved a ten-site, randomized clinical effectiveness trial (McFall et al. 2007) comparing integrated care to the usual standard of care (referral to the smoking cessation clinic) in order to replicate initial findings on a larger scale. One of the largest tobacco-cessation trials ever conducted in VHA and one of the very few tobacco cessation trials involving smokers with current mental illness, the study tested whether integrating smoking cessation treatment into mental healthcare for PTSD improved the rate of long-term abstinence from smoking in veterans with PTSD, compared to referral to the smoking cessation clinic. Further, the study examined treatment process variables, including the amount of smoking cessation counseling and medication received, that may explain differences in long-term abstinence between integrated care and the smoking cessation clinic, and assessed the long-term effects of smoking cessation on symptoms of PTSD and depression.

Between November 2004 and December 2007, veterans were recruited from outpatient PTSD clinics at ten VHA medical centers and followed for eighteen to forty-eight months. Veterans who enrolled in the study met diagnostic criteria for PTSD related to military trauma, were receiving treatment in participating PTSD outpatient clinics, smoked ten or more cigarettes per day on most days, and consented to receive cessation interventions. If veterans used noncigarette tobacco; met diagnostic criteria for current psychotic, bipolar, or substance dependence (other than nicotine) disorder; or were experiencing severe psychiatric symptoms, psychosocial instability, or cognitive impairment, they were not allowed to participate. Outcomes were assessed at three-month intervals through month 18 and every six months thereafter. At each assessment, daily use of cigarettes, other tobacco products, and cessation medications was determined.

Patients received initial cessation treatment within three months of study enrollment, with integrated care delivered by patients' primary mental health providers in the PTSD clinic and smoking cessation clinic care delivered by smoking cessation experts in on-site smoking cessation clinics.

Primary Outcome: Twelve-Month Prolonged Abstinence

The primary outcome was one-year prolonged abstinence from tobacco during the period from six to eighteen months after study enrollment. Tobacco use during the first six months of study participation was not considered in the primary outcome measure in order to allow for initial treatment episode completion and recovery from early relapses. Prolonged abstinence defined nonabstinence as 1) smoking for seven consecutive days or at least once a week for two consecutive weeks or 2) using non-cigarette tobacco for seven consecutive days or at least once a week for two consecutive weeks (Hughes et al. 2003). The Society for Research on Nicotine and Tobacco recommends prolonged abstinence as the most appropriate primary outcome for smoking cessation clinical trials (Hughes et al. 2003), because it more realistically reflects the process of quitting by allowing multiple quit attempts and not counting transient "slips" as failures.

Veterans assigned to integrated care were more than twice as likely as those referred to the smoking cessation clinic to achieve prolonged abstinence between six and eighteen months. Per self-report, seventy-three (15.5 percent) veterans assigned to integrated care and thirty-three (7.0 percent) to the smoking cessation clinic (p < 0.001) achieved prolonged abstinence. Prolonged abstinence rates as verified by carbon monoxide and/or cotinine were lower in both conditions (integrated care, 42; 8.9 percent; smoking cessation clinic, 21; 4.5 percent [p = 0.004]).

Secondary Smoking Outcomes

Secondary smoking outcomes included seven-day abstinence, verified by breath carbon monoxide and urinary cotinine monitoring, and for patients who quit smoking for at least twenty-four hours, time to relapse following the first quit attempt.

Seven-day abstinence rates between three and eighteen months are presented in figure 3.4. Differences in abstinence between integrated care and smoking cessation groups were largest at six months (16.5 percent vs. 7.2 percent, p < 0.001) and remained significant at eighteen months (18.2 percent versus 10.8 percent, p < 0.001). Veterans in integrated care were twice as likely as those referred to the smoking cessation clinic to achieve seven-day abstinence between three and eighteen months (p < 0.001).

For patients who quit smoking for at least twenty-four hours (integrated care, n = 361; smoking cessation clinic, n = 321), time to relapse following the first quit attempt was calculated. Consistent with the definition of prolonged abstinence (Hughes et al. 2003), relapse was defined as tobacco use on seven consecutive days or at any time during each of two consecutive weeks. As

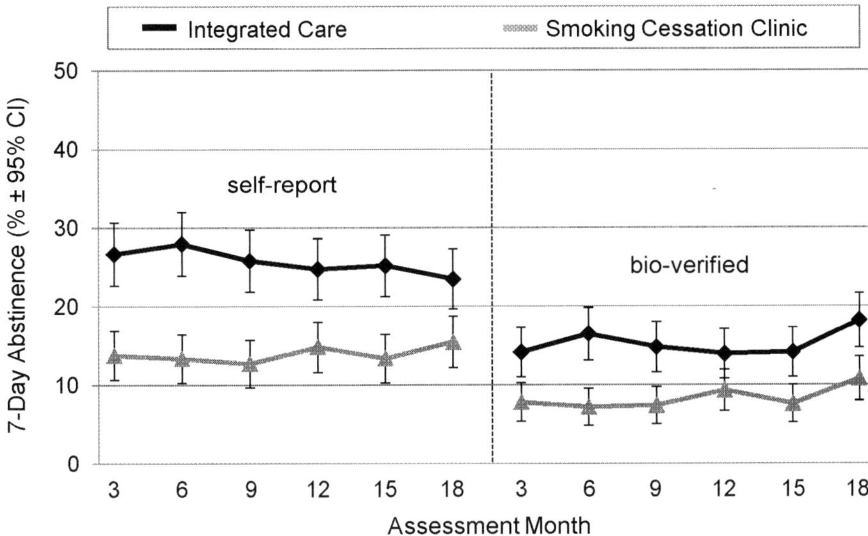

Figure 3.4. Seven-day Abstinence by Treatment Condition (n = 943). *Note:* Data reflect percentages of abstinent patients with 95% confidence intervals.

shown in figure 3.5, time to relapse was significantly longer for veterans in integrated care. Median time to relapse following the initial twenty-four-hour quit was twenty-nine days (interquartile range eighteen–forty-two days) for integrated care and eighteen days (interquartile range seven–twelve days) for smoking cessation clinic (p < 0.001).

Treatment Effect Mediators

Treatment process variables that may affect outcomes include number of smoking cessation counseling sessions delivered and type and amount of smoking cessation medications used over the study course. Identification of mediators of successful smoking cessation outcomes may enhance the understanding of how integrated care works and how it can be improved.

Treatment process variables are presented in table 3.4. Veterans in the integrated care group attended an average of six more cessation treatment sessions than did those in the smoking cessation clinic. They also were more likely to use bupropion, nicotine gum, and/or lozenges, and bupropion and nicotine replacement therapy in combination, although the proportion of patients using any cessation medication was similar in the two groups. Total counseling sessions received and self-reported medication use days explained 29.5 percent (95 percent CI: 26.6 to 32.5) and 9.6 percent (95 percent CI: 7.7 to 11.5) of

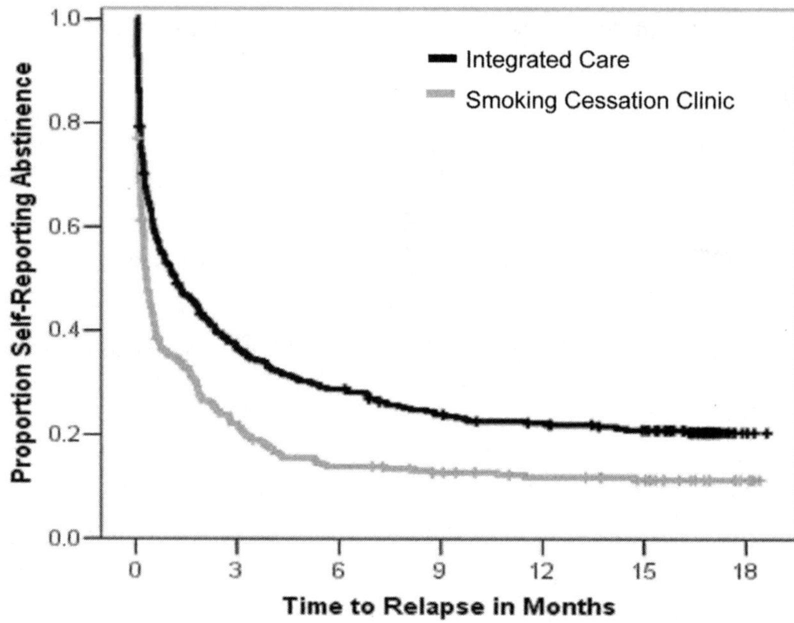

Figure 3.5. Months to Relapse Following Initial 24-Hour Quit between Randomization and 18-Month Assessment (n = 682). *Note:* A total of 261 Veterans (Integrated Care: n = 111, Smoking Cessation Clinic: n = 150) who did not quit for 24 hours between randomization and 18 months were not included in the analysis. Vertical marks represent censored observations.

the difference in prolonged abstinence rates between integrated care and smoking cessation clinic conditions, respectively.

Psychiatric Symptoms

The possibility that smoking cessation treatment participation and quitting smoking contribute to worsening psychiatric symptoms remains a major concern among mental health providers (Weinberger et al. 2008). A secondary aim of this study was to determine whether participation in integrated care and stopping smoking, regardless of treatment received, was associated with worsening of PTSD and depression symptoms. Evidence regarding the effects of smoking cessation on mental health symptoms is contradictory and inconclusive (Brown et al. 2001; Covey, Glassman & Stetner 1997; Glassman et al. 2001; Killen et al. 2003; Prochaska et al. 2008; Tsoh et al. 2000). If quitting smoking is associated with worsening mental health symptoms in patients with PTSD,

Table 3.4. Smoking Cessation Treatment Received from Randomization to Month 18.

Intervention	Integrated Care (n=472)	Smoking Cessation Clinic (n=471)	p-value
	n (%) or M$\pm$SD		
Total smoking cessation treatment sessions*	8.8 $\pm$ 6.4	2.4 $\pm$ 3.2	<0.001
Pharmacotherapy Received[†]			
Any cessation medication used			
Patients reporting use	383 (84.0)	364 (79.3)	0.07
Total days of use[‡]	164.8 $\pm$ 173.4	130.9 $\pm$ 156.2	0.005
Bupropion for smoking cessation			
Patients reporting use	188 (41.2)	134 (29.2)	<0.001
Total days of use[‡]	181.3 $\pm$ 159.3	185.1 $\pm$ 166.4	0.84
Nicotine Patch			
Patients reporting use	234 (51.3)	224 (48.8)	0.45
Total days of use[‡]	52.5 $\pm$ 65.3	50.8 $\pm$ 73.8	0.79
Nicotine Gum and/or Lozenge			
Patients reporting use	171 (37.5)	140 (30.5)	0.03
Total days of use[‡]	87.1 $\pm$ 111.7	61.6 $\pm$ 85.0	0.02
Bupropion plus any nicotine replacement medication			
Patients reporting use	100 (21.9)	60 (13.1)	<0.001
Total days of use[‡]	56.8 $\pm$ 81.4	44.2 $\pm$ 49.8	0.23
Varenicline[§]			
Patients reporting use	56 (12.3)	54 (11.8)	0.81
Total days of use[‡]	82.3 $\pm$ 68.9	67.0 $\pm$ 70.2	0.25

*Attendence data were not available for 7 integrated care patients and 5 smoking cessation clinic patients; [†]medication data were not available for 16 integrated care and 12 smoking cessation clinic patients; [‡]days of use were calculated only for patients who self-reported any use; [§]varenicline did not become available within the Veterans Health Administration until year 3 of the study and was used as a second line agent; thus it was not available to all patients.

clinicians can anticipate and make plans to address potential adverse consequences of cessation as part of treatment.

Symptoms of PTSD, as measured by the Clinician Administered PTSD Scale, improved for veterans in both integrated care and smoking cessation clinic conditions at eighteen months (p < 0.001), with a 7.5-point (10 percent) drop in scores in both conditions from baseline. Similarly, changes in PTSD severity, as measured by the Clinician Administered PTSD Scale and the PTSD Check-list, did not differ between those who achieved prolonged abstinence and those who did not, with both groups showing improvement over time. Over eighteen months, no significant differences were seen in depression measures between veterans in the integrated care and smoking cessation clinic groups. Those who did not achieve prolonged abstinence worsened slightly on the depression scores relative to those who did achieve abstinence ($p = 0.03$), whose depression scores did not change over time.

Significance

As one of the largest smoking cessation trials conducted with psychiatric patients, this multisite effectiveness trial demonstrated that mental health pro-viders can successfully integrate cessation treatment into routine mental healthcare for PTSD. Further, integrating rather than separating treatment for PTSD and nicotine dependence improves smoking quit rates. Integrated care doubled prolonged abstinence compared to smoking cessation clinic, was superior on seven-day abstinence at each assessment time point, and increased time to relapse.

Seven-day abstinence rates, confirmed by carbon monoxide and/or coti-nine, for integrated care were comparable to outcomes in studies of other smo-kers with mental illness, including those with depression (Hall et al. 2006; MacPherson et al. 2010), alcoholism (Prochaska, Delucchi & Hall 2004), and schizophrenia (George et al. 2000). However, quit rates from this study were lower than those typically found for non–mentally ill smokers (Fiore et al. 2008), likely because smokers with mood and anxiety disorders often are more nicotine dependent and more likely to relapse following treatment (Hall & Prochaska 2009; Piper et al. 2010).

As seen in preliminary work, the superiority of integrated care likely can be explained in part by its ability to get more treatment to the veterans who need it. Our results corroborate those of other studies indicating that treatment length and intensity are related to favorable cessation outcomes (Fiore et al. 2008; Cook et al. 2007). The fact that less than half of the treatment effect was explained by the number of treatment sessions and cessation medications received suggests that other factors contributed to the effectiveness of integrated care. These fac-tors may include qualitative aspects of the therapeutic relationship, such as mental health providers' ability to motivate patients and skill in managing the dynamic interplay between psychiatric distress and smoking urges.

The possibility that smoking cessation treatment participation (Killen et al. 2003) and quitting smoking (Glassman et al. 2001) contribute to worsening psychiatric symptoms remains a major concern among mental health providers (Weinberger et al. 2008). Veterans in this trial showed no overall deterioration in psychiatric status regardless of treatment assignment, and actually improved on measures of PTSD at eighteen months. This finding shows that integrated care participation did not detract from effectiveness of PTSD treatment. Slight improvements in PTSD and little change in depression symptoms were seen among those achieving prolonged abstinence, substantiating other reports of no adverse effects of smoking cessation in individuals with mental illness, including current PTSD (McFall et al. 2005), depression (Prochaska et al. 2008) or past histories of depression (Tsoh et al. 2000; Brown et al. 2001). Veterans in this study were engaged in ongoing psychiatric care, which may have attenuated the potential adverse impacts of nicotine withdrawal on mental status.

This large-scale clinical trial was designed as a practical clinical trial applicable to "real world" settings, using a clinically relevant comparison group, broad inclusion criteria to ensure that the sample reflects the population of VHA patients with PTSD, and practitioners from diverse healthcare settings who were not tobacco cessation experts (Tunis, Stryer & Clancy 2003). Such design features optimize translation of tobacco cessation treatments to practice-based mental health clinics (Glasgow, Lichtenstein & Marcus 2003). Further, use of a rigorous primary endpoint (one-year prolonged abstinence between months 6 and 18 following enrollment) ensures that outcomes are clinically meaningful, with known benefits to health and longevity.

Future Directions

Dissemination of Integrated Care within the Veterans Health Administration

One of the most challenging aspects of improving healthcare delivery is translating treatments proved efficacious in controlled trials into actual practice. The Veterans Health Administration has been very proactive in addressing this challenge in regard to integrated care for tobacco dependence and PTSD.

As a result of findings from preliminary studies indicating that integrating smoking cessation into routine mental healthcare for veterans with PTSD was superior to referral to a specialized smoking cessation clinic, in 2003 the Public Health Strategic Health Care Group funded the development of a clinical preceptorship for VHA mental health professionals on the practice of integrated care (McFall 2006). Its goal was broadly defined as "making it easy for providers to do the right thing" to help their patients stop using tobacco. Between 2004 and 2006 three training programs were held, resulting in 160 preceptors nationwide trained in evidence-based smoking cessation. The trainings were followed by regular conference calls with the program faculty to share best practices and address implementation barriers. In turn, the preceptors were charged to become tobacco cessation clinical "champions" within their local mental health clinics and promote cessation efforts in these settings.

As of 2005, 42 percent of VHA healthcare facilities reported having cessation programs tailored to veterans served in outpatient mental health clinics and 26 percent reported programs for inpatient mental health (Department of Veterans Affairs 2006b). Although it is not known if the preceptorship directly influenced development of these programs, it is clear that a conversation has been started regarding the unique treatment needs of smokers with mental illness.

In order to train providers in integrated care on a wider scale, in 2010 the Department of Veterans Affairs National Center for Posttraumatic Stress Disorder launched a presentation designed to provide instruction on the impact of smoking on veterans with PTSD and the reasons for integrating smoking cessation treatment into PTSD treatment and to introduce behavioral treatments and medications used in cessation care (Department of Veterans Affairs, National Center for PTSD 2010).

Additional dissemination efforts began in 2010, when the Public Health Strategic Health Care Group sponsored a learning collaborative to implement integrated care in six selected VHA outpatient PTSD clinics nationwide. The goals of this effort were to train mental health clinics in the delivery of integrated care and increase the number of patients receiving cessation services in PTSD clinics. Multidisciplinary teams worked together within and across medical centers to address barriers that interfered with the successful delivery of integrated care. Although PTSD clinics were involved in this dissemination project for only one year, the learning collaborative model endeavored to make integrated care a sustainable practice once the project was completed by working with clinic teams to put proper supports in place. As a result of this project, integrated care was implemented at all six sites, with 46 providers (range 5–11 per site) delivering care to 175 veterans (range 16–54). Significant changes in clinic practices included 1) altering intake procedures to assess smoking status/interest in quitting and offer integrated care to all new patients, 2) developing systems (psychiatric note templates, clinic surveys) to routinely assess smoking status/treatment interest among existing patients, and 3) training new staff in integrated care delivery. To encourage spread and sustainability, multiple teams began training providers outside of the PTSD clinic in integrated care delivery.

Because selected clinics were diverse in populations served (younger Iraq and Afghanistan veterans, women) and in primary treatment modalities (group versus individual, long-term versus time-limited therapies) used, their experiences and innovations in delivering integrated care are expected to be applicable to a wide variety of VHA settings. Further, integrated care was delivered alongside newly mandated, evidence-based treatments for PTSD, which require substantial training and are time-intensive to deliver. Project findings will be used to identify strategies for delivering integrated care in this new environment of PTSD care and to guide larger, systemwide implementation efforts in the future.

Challenges

The National Institute of Mental Health report on tobacco use in psychiatric patients recommends carrying out research on the integration of smoking cessation treatments into current mental healthcare (Ziedonis et al. 2008), emphasizing the potential helpfulness of frequent contacts in delivering interventions. At the same time, the report recognizes potential barriers to integrated care delivery, such as getting providers to adopt these treatments and incorporating cessation services into a variety of mental health programs.

In recent years, clinicians working in VHA PTSD clinics have experienced a substantial increase in the number of competing demands on their time. The wars in Iraq and Afghanistan have infused PTSD clinics with unexpected additional clinical workload, on top of the usual 8–10 percent annual increase in patients. In addition, national VHA roll-outs of evidence-based therapies for PTSD have led to increased training and documentation requirements for clinicians. Meeting these clinical demands imposes time constraints on clinic providers and may limit efforts to screen and treat tobacco use disorders. For PTSD programs that treat veterans primarily in group therapy, the individualized format of integrated care may prove difficult to accommodate within regularly scheduled treatment and may be seen as detracting from needed PTSD care.

Thus far, integrated care has been employed with predominantly older male Vietnam-era veterans with chronic PTSD and co-occurring depression. It is possible that this intervention will not be as successful with female veterans or veterans with other psychiatric disorders. In addition, younger Iraq and Afghanistan veterans appear more reluctant to engage in tobacco cessation treatment, perhaps because they have not yet experienced adverse health consequences of smoking. Testing integrated care in these populations and modifying interventions to fit the needs of other individuals with mental illness is an essential next step if the treatment is to have wide application. Alternative delivery methods, such as group, telephone, and Internet-based care, should be tested as part of overall efforts to treat an increasingly diverse veteran population.

Since 2002 VHA has made a number of systemwide changes to address tobacco use among veterans, including increasing access to smoking cessation medications, eliminating copayments for smoking cessation counseling, and developing evidence-based guidelines to guide treatment efforts. As the care provider for over 1.5 million veterans with mental illness, including more than 400,000 with PTSD, VHA is in a unique position to address smoking among those with mental illness. The Veterans Health Administration funded one of the largest trials of smoking cessation in mentally ill individuals and is actively taking steps to disseminate research results, thus demonstrating a desire to bridge the gap between research and clinical practice with respect to smoking cessation. The sustainability and spread of these efforts will depend on the long-term support offered to PTSD clinics, as well as investment in the translation of integrated care into other mental health settings with different populations of psychiatrically ill smokers. The work that VHA undertakes in coming years takes on particular salience with the cohort of younger Iraq and Afghanistan veterans with PTSD, for whom stopping smoking now could greatly impact their overall health and quality of life in years to come.

References

Aubin, H. J. (2009). Management of emergent psychiatric symptoms during smoking cessation. *Current Medical Research and Opinion* 25: 519–525.

Beckham, J. C., Dennis, M. F., McClernon, F. J., Mozley, S. L., Collie, C. F. & Vrana, S. R. (2007). The effects of cigarette smoking on script-driven imagery in smokers with and without PTSD. *Addictive Behaviors* 32: 2900–2915.

Beckham, J. C., Feldman, M. E., Vrana, S. R., Mozley, S. L., Erkanli, A., Clancy, C. P. & Rose, J. E. (2005). Immediate antecedents of cigarette smoking in smokers with and without PTSD: A preliminary study. *Experimental and Clinical Psychopharmacology* 13: 219–228.

Beckham, J. C., Kirby, A. C., Feldman, M. E., Hertzberg, M. A., Moore, S. D., Crawford, A. L., Davidson, J. R. & Fairbank, J. A. (1997). Prevalence and correlates of heavy smoking in Vietnam veterans with chronic PTSD. *Addictive Behaviors* 22: 637–647.

Beckham, J. C., Lytle, B. L., Vrana, S. R., Hertzberg, M. A., Feldman, M. E. & Shipley, R. H. (1996). Smoking withdrawal symptoms in response to trauma-related stressors among Vietnam combat veterans with PTSD. *Addictive Behaviors* 21: 93–101.

Beckham, J. C., Moore, S. D., Feldman, M. E., Hertzberg, M. A., Kirby, A. C. & Fairbank, J. A. (1998). Health status, somatization, and severity of PTSD in Vietnam combat veterans with PTSD. *American Journal of Psychiatry* 155: 1565–1569.

Beckham, J. C., Roodman, A. A., Shipley, R. H., Hertzberg, M. A., Cunha, G. H., Kudler, H. S., Levin, E. D., Rose, J. E. & Fairbank, J. A. (1995). Smoking in Vietnam combat veterans with post-traumatic stress disorder. *Journal of Traumatic Stress* 8: 461–472.

Beckham, J. C., Wiley, M. T., Miller, S. C., Dennis, M. F., Wilson, S. M., McClernon, F. J. & Calhoun, P. S. (2008). Ad lib smoking in post-traumatic stress disorder: An electronic diary study. *Nicotine and Tobacco Research* 10: 1149–1157.

Benowitz, N. L. (1988). Pharmacologic aspects of cigarette smoking and nicotine addiction. *New England Journal of Medicine* 319: 1318–1330.

Boden, J. M., Fergusson, D. M. & Horwood, L. J. (2010). Cigarette smoking and depression: Tests of causal linkages using a longitudinal birth cohort. *British Journal of Psychiatry* 196: 440–446.

Boscarino, J. A. (2004). Posttraumatic stress disorder and physical illness: Results from clinical and epidemiologic studies. *Annals of the New York Academy of Sciences* 1032: 141–153.

Boscarino, J. A. (2006). External-cause mortality after psychologic trauma: the effects of stress exposure and predisposition. *Comprehensive Psychiatry* 47: 503–514.

Boscarino, J. A. (2008). A prospective study of PTSD and early-age heart disease mortality among Vietnam veterans: Implications for surveillance and prevention. *Psychosomatic Medicine* 70: 668–676.

Brady, K. T., Killeen, T., Brewerton, T. & Lucerini, S. (2000). Comorbidity of psychiatric disorders and PTSD. *Journal of Clinical Psychiatry* 61, supp. 7: 22–32.

Brandon, T. H., Collins, B. N., Juliano, L. M. & Lazev, A. B. (2000). Preventing relapse among former smokers: A comparison of minimal interventions through telephone and mail. *Journal of Consulting and Clinical Psychology* 68: 103–113.

Bray, R. M., Pemberton, M. R., Hourani, L. L., Witt, M., Olmsted, K. L. R., Brown, J. M., et al. (2009). *2008 Department of Defense Survey of Health Related Behaviors among Active Duty Military Personnel*. Research Triangle Park, NC: Research Triangle International. http://www.tricare.mil/2008HealthBehaviors.pdf (accessed March 13, 2012).

Breslau, N. (1998). Epidemiology of trauma and PTSD. In R. Yehuda (Ed.), *Psychological trauma* (pp. 1–29). Washington, DC: American Psychiatric Press.

Breslau, N., Kessler, R. C., Chilcoat, H. D., Schultz, L. R., Davis, G. C. & Andreski, P. (1998). Trauma and PTSD in the community. *Archives of General Psychiatry* 55: 626–632.

Breslau, N., Kilbey, M. & Andreski, P. (1992). Nicotine withdrawal symptoms and psychiatric disorders: Findings from an epidemiologic study of young adults. *American Journal of Psychiatry* 149: 464–469.

Brown, R. A., Kahler, C. W., Niaura, R., Abrams, D. B., Sales, S. D., Ramsey, S. E., Goldstein, M. G., Burgess, E. S., & Miller, I. W. (2001). Cognitive-behavioral treatment for depression in smoking cessation. *Journal of Consulting and Clinical Psychology* 69: 471–480.

Buckley, T. C., Mozley, S. L., Bedard, M. A., Dewulf, A-C. & Greif, J. (2004). Preventative health behaviors, health-risk behaviors, physical morbidity, and health-related role functioning impairment in veterans with post-traumatic stress disorder. *Military Medicine* 169: 536–540.

Calhoun, P. S., Bosworth, H. B., Grambow, S. C., Dudley, T. K. & Beckham, J. C. (2002). Medical service utilization by veterans seeking help for PTSD. *American Journal of Psychiatry* 159: 2081–2086.

Calhoun, P. S., Bosworth, H. B., Stechuchak, K. A., Strauss, J. & Butterfield, M. I. (2006). The impact of PTSD on quality of life and health service utilization among veterans who have schizophrenia. *Journal of Traumatic Stress* 19: 393–397.

Carmody, T. P., Vieten, C. & Astin, J. A. (2007). Negative affect, emotional acceptance, and smoking cessation. *Journal of Psychoactive Drugs* 39: 499–508.

Center for Substance Abuse Treatment. (2005). *Assessment and treatment of patients with coexisting mental illness and alcohol and other drug use.* Treatment improvement protocol series. Rockville, MD: U.S. Department of Health and Human Services.

Centers for Disease Control. (2000). State-specific prevalence of current cigarette smoking among adults and the proportion of adults who work in a smoke-free environment—United States, 1999. *Morbidity and Mortality Weekly Report* 49: 978–982.

Centers for Disease Control and Prevention Coordinating Center for Health Promotion. (2007). Targeting tobacco use: The nation's leading cause of preventable death. http://www.cdc.gov/chronicdisease/resources/publications/AAG/osh.htm (accessed March 13, 2012).

Cohen, B. E., Marmar, C., Ren, L., Bertenthal, D. & Seal, K. H. (2009). Association of cardiovascular risk factors with mental health diagnoses in Iraq and Afghanistan war veterans using VA health care. *Journal of the American Medical Association* 302: 489–492.

Cook, J. W., McFall, M. E., Calhoun, P. S. & Beckham, J. C. (2007). Posttraumatic stress disorder and smoking relapse: A theoretical model. *Journal of Traumatic Stress* 20: 989–998.

Cougle, J. R., Zvolensky, M. J., Fitch, K. E. & Sachs-Ericsson, N. (2010). The role of comorbidity in explaining the associations between anxiety disorders and smoking. *Nicotine & Tobacco Research* 12: 355–364.

Covey, L., Glassman, A. H. & Stetner, F. (1997). Major depression following smoking cessation. *American Journal of Psychiatry* 154: 263–265.

Cromwell, J., Bartosch, W. J. & Mitchell, J. B. (1997). The cost-effectiveness of AHCPR's smoking cessation guideline. Waltham, MA: Health Economics Research, Inc.

Curry, S. J. & McBride, C. M. (1994). Relapse prevention for smoking cessation: Review and evaluation of concepts and interventions. *Annual Review of Public Health* 15: 345–366.

Curry, S. J., Grothaus, L. C., McAfee, T. & Pabiniak, C. (1998). Use and cost effectiveness of smoking-cessation services under four insurance plans in a health maintenance organization. *New England Journal of Medicine* 339: 673–679.

Davis, T. M., Bush, K. R., Kivlahan, D. R., Dobie, D. J. & Bradley, K. A. (2003). Screening for substance abuse and psychiatric disorders among women patients in a VA health care system. *Psychiatric Services* 54: 214–218.

Department of Veterans Affairs (2006a). Elimination of copayment for smoking cessation counseling: final rule. *Federal Register* 71: 2464.

Department of Veterans Affairs (2006b). *2005 smoking and tobacco use cessation report*. Washington, DC: Veterans Health Administration, Office of the Assistant Under Deputy for Health for Policy and Planning.

Department of Veterans Affairs (2009). *2008 Survey of Veteran Enrollees' Health and Reliance upon VA*. Washington, DC: Veterans Health Administration, Office of the Assistant Under Deputy for Health for Policy and Planning.

Department of Veterans Affairs, National Center for PTSD. (2007). What is PTSD? http://www.ptsd.va.gov/public/pages/what-is-ptsd.asp (accessed March 3, 2012).

Department of Veterans Affairs, National Center for PTSD. (2010). Integrated smoking cessation and PTSD treatment. http://www.ptsd.va.gov/professional/ptsd101/course-modules/smoking-cessation.asp (accessed March 3, 2012).

Deykin, E. Y., Keane, T. M., Kaloupek, D., Fincke, G., Rothendler, J., Siegfried, M. & Creamer, K. (2001). Posttraumatic stress disorder and the use of health services. *Psychosomatic Medicine* 63: 835–841.

Dobie, D. J., Kivlahan, D. R., Maynard, C., Bush, K. R., Davis, T. M. & Bradley, K. A. (2004). Posttraumatic stress disorder in female veterans: Association with self-reported health problems and functional impairment. *Archives of Internal Medicine* 164: 394–400.

El-Geubaly, N., Cathcart, J., Currie, S., Brown, D. & Gloster, S. (2002). Smoking cessation approaches for persons with mental illness or addictive disorders. *Psychiatric Services* 53: 1166–1170.

Ellerbeck, E. F., Mahnken, J. D., Cupertino, A. P., Cox, L. S., Greiner, K. A., Mussulman, L. M., et al. (2009). Effect of varying levels of disease management on smoking cessation: A randomized trial. *Annals of Internal Medicine* 150: 437–446.

Fagerstrom, K. & Aubin, H. J. (2009). Management of smoking cessation in patients with psychiatric disorders. *Current Medical Research & Opinion* 25: 511–518.

Feldner, M. T., Babson, K. A., Zvolensky, M. J., Vujanovic, A. A., Lewis, S. F., Gibson, L. E., Monson, C. M. & Bernstein, A. (2007). Posttraumatic stress symptoms and smoking to reduce negative affect: An investigation of trauma-exposed daily smokers. *Addictive Behaviors* 32: 214–227.

Ferketich, A. K., Khan, Y. & Wewers, M. E. (2006). Are physicians asking about tobacco use and assisting with cessation? Results from the 2001–2004 National Ambulatory Medical Care Survey (NAMCS). *Preventive Medicine* 43: 472–476.

Fiore, M. C., Bailey, W. C., Cohen, S. J., Dorfman, S. F., Goldstein, M. G., Gritz, E. R., et al. (2000). *Treating tobacco use and dependence*. Clinical practice guideline. Rockville, MD: U.S. Dept. of Health and Human Services, Public Health Services.

Fiore, M. C., Hatsukami, D. K. & Baker, T. B. (2002). Effective tobacco dependence treatment. *Journal of the American Medical Association* 288: 1768–1772.

Fiore, M. C., Jaén, C. R., Baker, T. B., Bailey, W. C., Benowitz, N. L., Curry, S. J., et al. (2008). *Treating tobacco use and dependence: 2008 update.* Clinical practice guideline. Rockville, MD: U.S. Department of Health and Human Services. Public Health Service.

Ford, J. D., Schnurr, P. P., Friedman, M. J., Green, B. L., Adams, G. & Jex, S. (2004). Posttraumatic stress disorder symptoms, physical health, and health care utilization 50 years after repeated exposure to a toxic gas. *Journal of Traumatic Stress* 17: 185–194.

Fu, S. S., McFall, M., Saxon, A. J., Beckham, J. C., Carmody, T. P., Baker, D. G. & Joseph, A. M. (2007). Post-traumatic stress disorder and smoking: a systematic review. *Nicotine & Tobacco Research* 9: 1071–1084.

George, T. P., Ziedonis, D. M., Feingold, A., Pepper, T., Satterburg, C. A., Winkel, J., Rounsaville, B. J. & Kosten, T. R. (2000). Nicotine transdermal patch and atypical antipsychotic medications for smoking cessation in schizophrenia. *American Journal of Psychiatry* 157: 1835–1842.

Glasgow, R. E., Lichtenstein, E. & Marcus, A. C. (2003). Why don't we see more translation of health promotion research to practice? Rethinking the efficacy-to-effectiveness transition. *American Journal of Public Health* 93: 1261–1267.

Glassman, A. H., Covey, L. S., Stetner, F. & Rivelli, S. (2001). Smoking cessation and the course of major depression: A follow-up study. *Lancet* 357: 1929–1932.

Goldman, R. & Craig, T. (2004). VHA smoking cessation treatment: findings from national patient surveys and medical record reviews. *National Association of VA Ambulatory Care Managers [Newsletter]* 15: 6.

Goldstein, M. G., Niaura, R., Willey-Lessne, C., DePue, J., Eaton, C., Rakowski, W. & Dube, C. (1997). Physicians counseling smokers: A population-based survey of patients' perceptions of health care provider–delivered smoking cessation interventions. *Archives of Internal Medicine* 157: 1313–1319.

Gonzales, D. H., Nides, M. A., Ferry, L. H., Kustra, R. P., Jamerson, B. D., Segall, N., Herrero, L. A., Krishen, A., Sweeney, A., Buaron, K. & Metz, A. (2001). Bupropion SR as an aid to smoking cessation in smokers treated previously with bupropion: A randomized placebo controlled study. *Clinical Pharmacology and Therapeutics* 69: 438–444.

Grant, B. F., Hasin, D. S., Chou, S. P., Stinson, F. S. & Dawson, D. A. (2004). Nicotine dependence and psychiatric disorders in the United States: Results from the National Epidemiologic Survey on Alcohol and Related Conditions. *Archives of General Psychiatry* 61: 1107–1115.

Hall, S. M., Humfleet, G. L., Reus, V. I., Muñoz, R. F. & Cullen, J. (2004). Extended nortriptyline and psychological treatment for cigarette smoking. *American Journal of Psychiatry* 161: 2100–2107.

Hall, S. M., Muñoz, R. F., Reus, V. I. & Sees, K. L. (1993). Nicotine, negative affect, and depression. *Journal of Consulting and Clinical Psychology* 61: 761–767.

Hall, S. M. & Prochaska, J. J. (2009). Treatment of smokers with co-occurring disorders: Emphasis on integration in mental health and addiction treatment settings. *Annual Review of Clinical Psychology* 5: 409–431.

Hall, S. M., Tsoh, J. Y., Prochaska, J. J., Eisendrath, S., Rossi, J. S., Redding, C. A., Rosen, A. B., Meisner, M., Humfleet, G. L. & Gorecki, J. A. (2006). Treatment for cigarette smoking among depressed mental health outpatients: A randomized clinical trial. *American Journal of Public Health* 96, no. 10: 1808–1814.

Hamlett-Berry, K. (2004). Smoking cessation policy in the VA health care system: Where have we been and where are we going? In S. L. Isaacs (Ed.), *VA in the vanguard: Building on success in smoking cessation conference proceedings, September 21, 2004*. San Francisco: Department of Veterans Affairs.

Hamlett-Berry, K., Davison, J., Kivlahan, D. R., Matthews, M. H., Hendrickson, J. E. & Almenoff, P. L. (2009). Evidence-based national initiatives to address tobacco use as a public health priority in the Veterans Health Administration. *Military Medicine* 174: 29–34.

Hankin, C. S., Spiro, A., Miller, D. R. & Kazis, L. (1999). Mental disorders and mental health treatment among U.S. Department of Veterans Affairs outpatients: The Veterans Health Study. *American Journal of Psychiatry* 156: 1924–1930.

Hapke, U., Schumann, A., Rumpf, H. J., John, U., Konerding, U. & Meyer, C. (2005). Association of smoking and nicotine dependence with trauma and PTSD in a general population sample. *Journal of Nervous & Mental Disease* 193: 843–846.

Heishman, S. J., Henningfield, J. E. & Singleton, E. G. (2002). Tobacco, nicotine, and human cognition. *Nicotine and Tobacco Research* 4: 3–4.

Himelhoch, S. & Daumit, G. (2003). To whom do psychiatrists offer smoking-cessation counseling? *American Journal of Psychiatry* 160: 2228–2230.

Hughes, J. R., Niaura, R., Ossip-Klein, D., Richmond, R. & Swan, G. (SRNT Subcommittee on Abstinence Measures). (2003). Measures of abstinence from tobacco in clinical trials: issues and recommendations. *Nicotine & Tobacco Research* 5: 13–25.

Institute of Medicine. (2009). *Combating tobacco use in military and veteran populations.* Washington, DC: The National Academies Press.

Joseph, A. M. & Antonnucio, D. O. (1999). Lack of efficacy of transdermal nicotine in smoking cessation [letter]. *New England Journal of Medicine* 341: 1157.

Kalman, D. (2002). The subjective effects of nicotine: Methodological issues: A review of experimental studies, and recommendations for future research. *Nicotine & Tobacco Research* 4: 25–70.

Kessler, R. C., McGonagle, K. A., Zhao, S., Nelson, C. B., Hughes, M., Eshleman, S., Wittchen, H. U. & Kendler, K. S. (1994). Lifetime and 12-month prevalence of DSM-III-R psychiatric disorders in the United States: Results from the National Comorbidity Survey. *Archives of General Psychiatry* 51: 8–19.

Killen, J. D., Fortmann, S. P., Schatzberg, A., Hayward, C. & Varady, A. (2003). Onset of major depression during treatment for nicotine dependence. *Addictive Behaviors* 28: 461–470.

Kirch, D. (2000). Nicotine and major mental disorders. In M. Piasecki & P. A. Newhouse (Eds.), *Nicotine in psychiatry: Psychopathology and emerging therapeutics* (p. 132). Washington, DC: American Psychiatric Press.

Klevens, R. M., Giovino, G. A., Peddicord, J. P., Nelson, D. E., Mowery, P. & Grummer-Strawn, L. (1995). The association between veteran status and cigarette-smoking behaviors. *American Journal of Preventive Medicine* 11: 245–250.

Lasser, K., Boyd, J. W., Woolhandler, S., Himmelstein, D. U., McCormick, D. & Bor, D. H. (2000). Smoking and mental illness: A population-based prevalence study. *Journal of the American Medical Association* 284: 2606–2610.

MacPherson, L., Tull, M. T., Matusiewicz, A. K., Rodman, S., Strong, D. R., Kahler, C. W., Hopko, D. R., Zvolensky, M. J., Brown, R. A. & Lejuez, C. W. (2010). Randomized controlled trial of behavioral activation smoking cessation treatment for smokers with elevated depressive symptoms. *Journal of Consulting and Clinical Psychology* 78, no. 1: 55–61.

McFall, M. (2006). Foreword. In *Integrating tobacco cessation treatment into mental health care: Proceedings of a tobacco cessation preceptor training program, May 4–5, 2006.* Washington, DC: Department of Veterans Affairs.

McFall, M., Atkins, D. C., Yoshimoto, D., Thompson, C. E., Kanter, E., Malte, C. A. & Saxon, A. J. (2006). Integrating tobacco cessation treatment into mental health care for patients with PTSD. *American Journal on Addictions* 15: 336–344.

McFall, M., Saxon, A. J., Malte, C. A., Chow, B., Bailey, S., Baker, D. G., et al. (2010). Integrating tobacco cessation into mental health care for PTSD: A randomized controlled trial. *Journal of the American Medical Association* 304, no. 22: 2534–2535.

McFall, M., Saxon, A. J., Thaneemit-Chen, S., Smith, M. W., Joseph, A. M., Carmody, T. P., et al. (2007). Integrating smoking cessation into mental health care for post-traumatic stress disorder. *Clinical Trials* 4: 178–189.

McFall, M., Saxon, A. J., Thompson, C. E., Yoshimoto, D., Malte, C., Straits-Troster, K., et al. (2005). Improving the rates of quitting smoking for veterans with PTSD. *American Journal of Psychiatry* 162: 1311–1319.

Niaura, R. & Abrams, D. B. (2002). Smoking cessation: progress, priorities, and prospects. *Journal of Consulting and Clinical Psychology* 70: 494–509.

Ockene, J., Lidsay, E., Hymowitz, N., Giffen, C., Purcell, T., Pomrehn, P. & Pechacek, T. (1997). Tobacco control activities of primary care physicians in the Community Intervention Trial for Smoking Cessation (COMMIT). *Tobacco Control* 6, supp. 2: S49–S56.

Office of Quality and Performance, Veterans Health Administration. (1999). *Veterans Affairs/Department of Defense clinical practice guidelines on tobacco use cessation in the primary care setting.* Washington, DC: Veterans Health Administration.

Office of Quality and Performance, Veterans Health Administration. (2001). *Health behaviors of veterans in the VHA: Tobacco use: 1999 Large Health Survey of Enrollees.* Washington, DC: Veterans Health Administration.

Office of Quality and Performance, Veterans Health Administration. (2004). *Veterans Affairs/Department of Defense clinical practice guidelines for the management of tobacco use.* Washington, DC: Veterans Health Administration.

Okene, J. K., Emmons, K. M., Mermelstein, R. J., Perkins, K. A., Bopnollo, D. S., Voorhees, C. C. & Hollis, J. F. (2000). Relapse maintenance issues for smoking cessation. *Health Psychology* 19, supp.: 17–31.

Parrott, A. C. (1995). Smoking cessation leads to reduced stress, but why? *International Journal of the Addictions* 30: 1509–1516.

Phillips, K. M. & Brandon, T. H. (2004). Do psychologists adhere to the clinical practice guidelines for tobacco cessation? A survey of practitioners. *Professional Psychology, Research and Practice* 35: 281–285.

Picciotto, M. R., Brunzell, D. H. & Caldarone, B. J. (2002). Effect of nicotine and nicotinic receptors on anxiety and depression. *Neuro Report* 13: 1097–1106.

Pierce, J. P. & Gilpin, E. A. (2002). Impact of over-the-counter sales on effectiveness of pharmaceutical aids for smoking cessation. *Journal of the American Medical Association* 288: 1260–1264.

Piper, M. E., Smith, S. S., Schlam, T. R., Fleming, M. F., Bittrich, A. A., Brown, J. L., Leitzke, C. J., Zehner, M. E., Fiore, M. C. & Baker, T. B. (2010). Psychiatric disorders in smokers seeking treatment for tobacco dependence: relations with tobacco dependence and cessation. *Journal of Consulting and Clinical Psychology* 78, no. 1: 13–23.

Prochaska, J. J., Delucchi, K. & Hall, S. M. (2004). A meta-analysis of smoking cessation interventions with individuals in substance abuse treatment or recovery. *Journal of Consulting and Clinical Psychology* 72, no. 6: 1144–1156.

Prochaska, J. J., Hall, S. M., Tsoh, J. Y., Eisendrath, S., Rossi, J. S., Redding, C. A., et al. (2008). Treating tobacco dependence in clinically depressed smokers: Effect of smoking cessation on mental health functioning. *American Journal of Public Health* 98: 446–448.

Roszell, D. K., McFall, M. E. & Malas, K. L. (1991). Frequency of symptoms and concurrent psychiatric disorder in veterans with chronic PTSD. *Hospital and Community Psychiatry* 42: 293–296.

Roy-Byrne, P., Sherbourne, C. D., Craske, M. G., Stein, M. B., Katon, W., Sullivan, G., Means-Christensen, A. & Bystritsky, A. (2003). Moving treatment research from clinical trials to the real world. *Psychiatric Services* 54: 327–332.

Schauffler, H. H., McMenamin, S., Olson, K., Boyce-Smith, G., Rideout, J. A. & Kamil, J. (2001). Variations in treatment benefits influence smoking cessation: Results of a randomised controlled trial. *Tobacco Control* 10: 175–180.

Schnurr, P. P. & Jankowski, M. K. (1999). Physical health and post-traumatic stress disorder: Review and synthesis. *Seminars in Clinical Neuropsychiatry* 4: 295–304.

Schnurr, P. P., Friedman, M. J., Sengupta, A., Jankowski, M. K. & Holmes, T. (2000). PTSD and utilization of medical treatment services among male Vietnam veterans. *Journal of Nervous and Mental Disease* 188: 496–504.

Sherman, S. E., Joseph, A. M., Yano, E. M., Simon, B. F., Arikian, N., Rubenstein, L. V. & Mittman, B. S. (2006a). Assessing the institutional approach to implementing smoking cessation practice guidelines in Veterans Health Administration facilities. *Military Medicine* 171: 80–87.

Sherman, S. E., Yano, E. M., Lanto, A. B., Simon, B., & Rubenstein, L. V. (2001). Veterans who smoke: Do they want to quit and are we helping them? Paper presented at VA Health Services Research and Development 19th annual meeting, Washington, DC, February 14–16, pp. 67–68.

Sherman, S. E., Yano, E. M., Lanto, A. B., Simon, B. F. & Rubenstein, L. V. (2005). Smokers' interest in quitting and services received: Using practice information to plan quality improvement and policy for smoking cessation. *American Journal of Medical Quality* 20: 33–39.

Sherman, S. E., Yano, E. M., York, L. S., Lanto, A. B., Chernof, B. A. & Mittman, B. S. (2006b). Assessing the structure of smoking cessation care in the Veterans Health Administration. *American Journal of Health Promotion* 20: 313–318.

Smith, M. W., Chen, S., Siroka, A. M. & Hamlett-Berry, K. (2010). Using policy to increase prescribing of smoking cessation medications in the VA health care system. *Tobacco Control* 19: 507–511.

Song, F., Raftery, J., Aveyard, P., Hyde, C., Barton, P. & Woolacott, N. (2002). Cost-effectiveness of pharmacological interventions for smoking cessation: A literature review and a decision analytic analysis. *Medical Decision Making* 22: S26–S37.

Stein, M. B., Katon, W., Sullivan, G., Means-Christensen, A. & Bystritsky, A. (2003). Moving treatment research from clinical trials to the real world: The design of a first-generation effectiveness study for panic disorder. *Psychiatric Services* 54: 288–300.

Substance Abuse and Mental Health Services Administration. (2002). *Report to Congress on the prevention and treatment of co-occurring substance abuse disorders and mental disorders.* Washington, DC: Substance Abuse and Mental Health Services Administration, US Department of Health and Human Services.

Thompson, R. S., Michnich, M. E., Friedlander, L., Gilson, B., Grothanus, L. C. & Storer, B. (1988). Effectiveness of smoking cessation interventions integrated into primary care practice. *Medical Care* 26: 62–76.

Thorndike, A. N., Regan, S. & Rigotti, N. A. (2007). The treatment of smoking by US physicians during ambulatory visits: 1994–2003. *American Journal of Public Health* 97: 1878–1883.

Thorndike, A. N., Rigotti, N. A., Stafford, R. S. & Singer, D. E. (1998). National patterns in the treatment of smokers by physicians. *Journal of the American Medical Association* 279: 604–608.

Thorndike, A. N., Stafford, R. S. & Rigotti, N. A. (2001). U.S. physicians' treatment of smoking in outpatients with psychiatric diagnoses. *Nicotine & Tobacco Research* 3: 85–91.

Tsoh, J. Y., Humfleet, G. L., Muñoz, R. F., Reus, V. I., Hartz, D. T. & Hall, S. M. (2000). Development of major depression after treatment for smoking cessation. *American Journal of Psychiatry* 157: 368–374.

Tunis, S. R., Stryer, D. B. & Clancy, C. M. (2003). Practical clinical trials: increasing the value of clinical research for decision making in clinical and health policy. *Journal of the American Medical Association* 290: 1624–1632.

U.S. Department of Health and Human Services. (2000). *Reducing tobacco use: A report of the surgeon general—executive summary.* Atlanta, GA: Department of Health and Human Services, Centers for Disease Control and Prevention, National Center for Chronic Disease Prevention and Health Promotion, Office on Smoking and Health.

Vaughn, T. E., Ward, M. M., Doebbeling, B. N., Uden-Holman, T., Clarke, W. T. & Woolson, R. F. (2002). Organizational and provider characteristics fostering smoking cessation practice guideline adherence: An empirical look. *The Journal of Ambulatory Care Management* 25: 17–31.

Veterans Administration, Department of Medicine and Surgery. (1969). Policy on smoking in medical care facilities. Circular 10–69–105. Washington, DC: Veterans Administration.

Vlahov, D., Galea, S., Resnick, H., Ahern, J., Boscarino, J. A., Bucuvalas, M., Gold, J. & Kilpatrick, D. (2002). Increased use of cigarettes, alcohol, and marijuana among Manhattan, New York, residents after the September 11th terrorist attacks. *American Journal of Epidemiology* 155: 988–996.

Weinberger, A. H., Reutenauer, E. L., Vessicchio, J. C. & George, T. P. (2008). Survey of clinician attitudes toward smoking cessation for psychiatric and substance abusing clients. *Journal of Addictive Diseases* 27, no. 1: 55–63.

Zarrindast, M. R., Pazouki, M. & Nassiri-Rad, S. (1997). Involvement of cholinergic and opioid receptor mechanisms in nicotine-induced antinociception. *Pharmacology and Toxicology* 81: 209–213.

Ziedonis, D. M. (2004). Integrated treatment of co-occurring mental illness and addiction: Clinical intervention, program, and systems perspectives. *CNS Spectrums* 9: 892–904.

Ziedonis, D., Hitsman, B., Beckham, J. C., Zvolensky, M., Adler, L. E., Audrain-McGovern, J., et al. (2008). Tobacco use and cessation in psychiatric disorders: National Institute of Mental Health report. *Nicotine & Tobacco Research* 10: 1691–1715.

Zvolensky, M. J., Gibson, L. E., Vujanovic, A. A., Gregor, K., Bernstein, A., Kahler, C., et al. (2008). Impact of posttraumatic stress disorder on early smoking lapse and relapse during a self-guided quit attempt among community-recruited daily smokers. *Nicotine & Tobacco Research* 10: 1415–1427.

Chapter 4

Suicide Risk among Veterans of Military Service

Mark S. Kaplan, Bentson H. McFarland,
and Nathalie Huguet

Concerns about the psychological toll of military service preceded the conflicts in Afghanistan and Iraq. Suicide in the various military branches is a topic of particular concern in today's political environment. In the late nineteenth century the French sociologist Émile Durkheim provided one of the earliest accounts of the risk of suicide in the military. In *On Suicide*, Durkheim (2006 [1897], 147) demonstrated that the risk among soldiers was substantially higher than the risk among the civilian population:

> It is a general fact in all the countries of Europe that the likelihood of soldiers committing suicide is much above that of the civilian population of the same age.... This is all the more surprising since at first sight many factors would seem to protect members of the army from suicide. First from the physical point of view, the men who make it up are the flower of their country's youth. They are carefully selected on the basis that they have no serious flaw. Moreover, the esprit de corps and communal life should have the protective influence that they exercise elsewhere.

This chapter presents an overview of current knowledge of suicide among veterans. In particular, after describing suicide in the general population, it provides a comprehensive review of the epidemiology and risk factors that are associated with suicide among veterans. It then discusses current military suicides. Finally, it describes suicide prevention efforts.

Table 4.1. Suicide Rates per 100,000, by Age and Gender

Age Group	5–14 Years	15–24 Years	25–44 Years	45–64 Years	65 Years and Over	All Age Groups*
Men	0.6	15.8	22.5	25.8	28.6	18.4
Women	0.3	3.2	6.3	8.2	3.9	4.7

*This rate is age adjusted using data from the 2000 census.

Sources: NCHS Vital Statistics System (2007) for the number of deaths and Bureau of Census (2000) for the population estimates.

Suicide in the General Population

Suicide in the general population remains a serious public health problem, and reducing suicide is a national imperative, according to the Institute of Medicine (Goldsmith et al. 2002). Approximately 37,000 people take their lives every year (Centers for Disease Control and Prevention 2009). Suicide ranks as the eleventh leading cause of death in the United States. As shown in table 4.1, suicide rates for women are much lower (in spite of the greater prevalence of major depressive disorder among women) than those for men (Brockington 2001). The suicide rate among white women nevertheless is double that of women in nonwhite ethnic/racial groups (Mann 2002). Suicide is the third leading cause of death among young people aged fifteen to twenty-four (Miniño, Heron & Smith 2006).

The highest suicide rates occur among elderly white men (Adamek & Kaplan 2000; Miniño et al. 2002), although rates among African American men are higher than those among white men in the younger age groups (Joe & Kaplan 2001, 2002). Indeed, the suicide rates of young African American men (aged twenty to thirty-five) are twice as high as those of young white men (Joe & Kaplan 2002).

A large body of published work exists on the epidemiology of suicidal behavior, with fairly consistent findings on demographic, psychiatric, psychological, and interpersonal variables that are associated with the risk of suicide. Studies of suicide decedents have consistently shown that the vast majority had major psychiatric problems, including previous suicidal behavior, depressive disorders, and substance abuse (Center for Substance Abuse Treatment 2008; Conwell 2001; Gould & Kramer 2001). Substance misuse is a substantial risk factor for suicide (Center for Substance Abuse Treatment 2008). Recent problematic substance use and a longer duration of substance use tend to show the most significant associations with suicidal thoughts and behaviors (Benda 2003; Ilgen et al. 2007; Price et al. 2004; Rodell, Benda & Rodell, 2003;

Thompson et al. 2006; Tiet et al. 2006). Personality traits, such as impulsivity and hopelessness, have been repeatedly shown to be associated with suicide (Goldsmith et al. 2002). Post-traumatic stress disorder (PTSD) has been associated with suicidality (Lehmann, McCormick & McCracken 1995; Freeman, Roca & Moore 2000), sometimes indirectly as a factor that contributes to other psychiatric disorders (Hendin & Haas 1991). Anxiety disorders other than PTSD are also related to suicidal behavior (Boden, Fergusson & Horwood 2007; Bolton et al. 2007; Sareen et al. 2005a; Sareen et al. 2005b). Suicidal thoughts, attempts, and completion have been linked to relationship problems (Benda 2005; Thoresen & Mehlum 2006; Thompson et al. 2006), and suicide ideation and attempts have been linked to family difficulties (Kausch 2003a; Porter, Astacio & Sobong 1997; Thompson et al. 2006). Childhood adversity, such as physical or sexual abuse, also elevates the risk of suicidal behaviors in later adulthood (Enns et al. 2006).

Suicidal Ideation and Suicide Attempts

Suicide morbidity (including ideation and attempts) is also a substantial public health problem (Goldsmith et al. 2002; Hawton et al. 1998; Kessler, Borges & Walters 1999; Mann et al. 2005; Skegg 2005). In the United States, it is estimated that roughly 0.6 percent of the population attempts suicide each year. In most cases, it is believed that suicidal ideation precedes both attempted suicide and death from suicide (Mann et al. 2005). Risk factors for suicide attempts include socioeconomic disadvantage and psychiatric illness—particularly major depressive disorder, substance abuse, and anxiety disorders (Skegg 2005).

Suicidal ideation is an important risk factor for suicide attempts (Goldsmith et al. 2002; Suominen et al. 2004b) and for suicide completion (Goldsmith et al. 2002; Suominen et al. 2004a). Operationally, suicidal ideation is defined as "thoughts of harming or killing oneself" (Goldsmith et al. 2002). Given this definition, approximately 3.6 percent of the U.S. adult population reports having suicidal thoughts in a twelve-month period (Brook et al. 2006). Among the social and psychological factors that have been associated with suicidal ideation are depressive symptoms (Goldney et al. 2000; Turvey et al. 2002), gender (female), being divorced or separated (Weissman et al. 1999), a decrease in income (Turvey et al. 2002), unemployment (Hintikka et al. 2001; Gunnell et al. 2004), and traumatic life events (Goldney et al. 2000). Nearly three-quarters of those with suicidal ideation have a psychiatric disorder (chiefly major depressive disorder) or substance abuse problems (Brook et al. 2006). Alcohol dependence is known to increase the risk of suicidal ideation, suicide attempts, and suicide deaths (Goldsmith et al. 2002). The risk is associated with numerous factors, including sociodemographic, clinical, treatment-related, and life situational characteristics, as well as current drinking status and the effects of inebriation (Hufford 2001; Pirkola, Suominen & Isometsä 2004). Dual diagnoses (of major depressive disorder and substance misuse) appear to be a considerable risk factor for younger age groups (Asgard 1990; Barraclough et al. 1974; Goldsmith et al. 2002; Rich, Young & Fowler 1986).

Suicide Risk in the Military

> We should be cognizant of the individuals who now "self select" and drive the makeup of the all-volunteer Army. (U.S. Army 2010, 40)

Suicidal behaviors and factors associated with suicide among current military personnel are a harbinger of future suicide trends in the veteran population. For example, PTSD, a risk factor for suicide, can persist for more than two decades (Centers for Disease Control and Prevention 1988; Kulka et al. 1990).

From 1994 to 2001, the suicide rate in the U.S. Army generally decreased (Allen, Cross & Swanner 2005). From 2001 to 2007, the suicide rate for active duty soldiers climbed and attained record levels. Suicides by soldiers continue to increase and have stimulated national concern (see figure 4.1). Alvarez (2009) reported that suicides among active duty soldiers rose from 2006 through 2008. For example, there were some 115 confirmed suicide deaths in the army or 18.1/100,000 soldiers during 2007 (Tyson 2008). There were at least 128 deaths of soldiers due to suicide in 2008, with another 15 deaths under investigation (Alvarez 2009). Suicide deaths of soldiers in the army in 2009 appeared to be occurring at similarly elevated rates, with 24 confirmed or suspected suicides in January and 18 suspected suicides in February (Levine 2009). The rate of suicides in the army is now approximately 20 per 100,000 soldiers per year and is higher than the age-adjusted civilian suicide rate (Alvarez 2009).

Given the extensive screening and selection procedures that precede entrance into the army, one may expect a "healthy worker effect" such that army suicide rates (other things being equal) would be lower than those for civilians (Mahon et al. 2005). Of course, other things are not equal. Regarding the recent rise in suicides, General Peter Chiarelli, former army vice chief of staff, was quoted as saying that "stress is a factor" (Alvarez 2009).

Stress, Mental Health, and the Suicide of Soldiers

Indeed, as combat operations have increased over the past few years, it should not be surprising that soldiers' mental health problems (presumably including

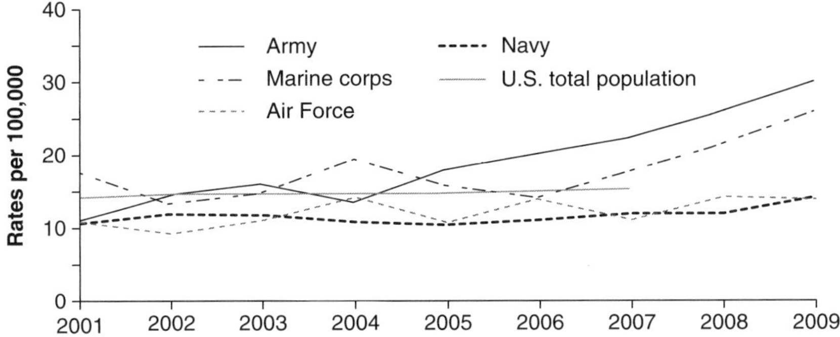

Figure 4.1. Military Suicide Rates, 2001–2009. *Note:* Suicide counts were obtained from the 2010 Final Report of the Department of Defense Task Force on the Prevention of Suicide by Members of the Armed Forces (2010). Population estimates derived from yearly September end-strength reports from the Defense Manpower Data Center (2010). Yearly age- ($\geq$20) and gender-adjusted suicide rates fro the total U.S. population were downloaded from Web-based Injury Statistics Query and Reporting System (CDC, 2007).

suicide) have increased (Ritchie 2007). In particular, during 2008 there were seven suicides of soldiers in Afghanistan and thirty-one in Iraq. Moreover, as army units move from Iraq to Afghanistan, there may well be further increases in mental health difficulties. For example, the army's Mental Health Advisory Team V report on Operation Enduring Freedom noted that combat levels in Afghanistan during 2007 were at least as great as those in Iraq (Office of the Surgeon Multinational Force 2008). Soldiers in Afghanistan in 2007 reported rates of mental health problems at least as high as those for troops in Iraq but had greater barriers to accessing behavioral healthcare than did those in Iraq (Office of the Surgeon Multinational Force 2008).

In addition to combat, deployment itself is a stressor. In Iraq, "multiple deployers reported higher acute stress than first-time deployers" (Office of the United States Army Surgeon General 2005, 3, and "[d]eployment length was related to higher rates of mental health problems and marital problems" (2006, 78). Unfortunately, long deployments (of twelve or more months) in combat zones are likely to persist indefinitely (Kaplan 2006), are the number one morale problem among U.S. troops in Iraq (Office of the U.S. Army Surgeon General 2005), and have come to be expected (Sullivan 2007). Kaplan (2006) pointed out that troop-rotation requirements suggest that almost all soldiers have been or will be deployed to Iraq or Afghanistan. Former defense secretary Robert Gates stated that extended tours are "exhausting" for both soldiers and their family members (Kaplan 2008). Tragically, orders to deploy again have been cited as precipitating death by police of a returned soldier (Barry 2007).

Longitudinal studies of troops who returned from Iraq and/or Afghanistan have heightened concerns about soldiers' mental health. For example, Milliken, Auchterlonie, and Hoge (2007) found that positive screening for PTSD rose from 6 percent at return to 9 percent among active duty soldiers and 14 percent for Reserve or National Guard troops six months thereafter. It is not surprising that early reports showed that more than 10,000 Iraq or Afghanistan veterans have been diagnosed with PTSD (Levin-Epstein 2005; Seal et al. 2007), and more than 50,000 Iraq or Afghanistan veterans have been seen in Veterans Affairs (VA) facilities for PTSD symptoms (President's Commission on Care for America's Returning Wounded Warriors 2007). Stecker and colleagues (2007) interviewed Army National Guard soldiers who were home from Iraq for a year and found that 57 percent screened positive for at least one major depressive disorder, panic disorder, generalized anxiety disorder, PTSD, or alcohol abuse. LaPierre, Schwegler, and LaBauve (2007) compared soldiers who returned from Iraq with those who returned from Afghanistan and found similar prevalences of clinically significant PTSD. With regard to Afghanistan and Iraq veterans, Jakupcak and colleagues (2007) reported that PTSD was highly correlated with anger, hostility, and aggression.

The level of exposure to combat presumably increases with the length of overseas deployment and is believed to be closely related to the chances that troops will develop subsequent mental health problems, such as PTSD (Callen et al. 1985; Hoge et al. 2004). A before-and-after study of troops who served in Afghanistan showed that the estimated prevalence of PTSD rose from 9 to 12 percent (Hoge et al. 2004). There were also high (estimated) prevalences of major depressive disorder (about 15 percent) and alcohol misuse (18 to 35 percent). A large population-based descriptive study of U.S Army soldiers and Marines found that 19 percent of those who returned from Iraq and 11 percent of those who returned from Afghanistan reported mental health problems that were often associated with combat experience (Hoge, Auchterlonie & Milliken 2006). Furthermore, mental disorders are highly correlated with discharge from military service (Hoge et al. 2002, 2005).

On the other hand, exposure to combat per se is far from the sole explanation for rising rates of suicide in the U.S. Army. From 2005 to 2008, some 30 percent of these suicides occurred during deployment, 35 percent occurred after deployment, and the remaining 35 percent were soldiers who had never deployed (Alvarez 2009). There were suicides of West Point cadets in December 2008 and January 2009 (Tyson 2009). Army officials were reported as saying that financial, personal, and legal problems, as well as job-related difficulties, were common factors among the suicides (Alvarez 2009).

A closely related concern is the deployment of a large number of Reserve and National Guard service members (Friedman 2005; Kaplan 2006; Reeves, Parker & Konkle-Parker 2005; Segal & Segal 2005). In contrast to Regular Army soldiers, Reserve and National Guard service members are unlikely to have lived in military communities prior to activation (Friedman 2005). Consequently, they may find themselves with few close resources to assist them in addressing the consequences of exposure to combat (Friedman 2005; Schumm 1999). Indeed, mental health concerns appear to be higher among Reserve or National Guard service members than among Regular Army forces (Levin-Epstein 2005; U.S. Department of Defense 2005).

Other pertinent issues include alcohol misuse (Stahre et al. 2009) and military-related sexual trauma (Kimerling et al. 2008). Stahre and colleagues (2009) found that the prevalence of binge drinking (more than five drinks on an occasion for men or four drinks for women) was 44 percent for active-duty military personnel versus 26 percent for comparable civilians. Kimerling and colleagues (2008) noted that the annual incidence of sexual assault among active-duty military personnel is 3 percent for women and 1 percent for men.

Taking a long-term perspective, it is important to appreciate that although suicide rates among soldiers have increased in recent years, suicide deaths are still rare in the army. Nonetheless, military service appears to confer an elevated risk of suicide among both current and former personnel.

Suicide Risk among Veterans of Military Service

According to the U.S. Department of Veterans Affairs Office of Inspector General (2007), 1,000 veterans who receive VA care and as many as 5,000 of all veterans die by suicide every year. Data from the 2007 Oregon Violent Death Reporting System (OVDRS) revealed that the age-adjusted suicide rate was 45.7 per 100,000 among male veterans but 27.4 per 100,000 among male nonveterans (Shen, Millet & Kohn 2007). In Oregon, suicide is the second leading cause of death among male veterans younger than forty-five. McCarthy and colleagues (2009) found that male (43 per 100,000) and female (10 per 100,000) VA patients had higher suicide rates than did nonveteran men (23 per 100,000) and women (5 per 100,000) in the general population.

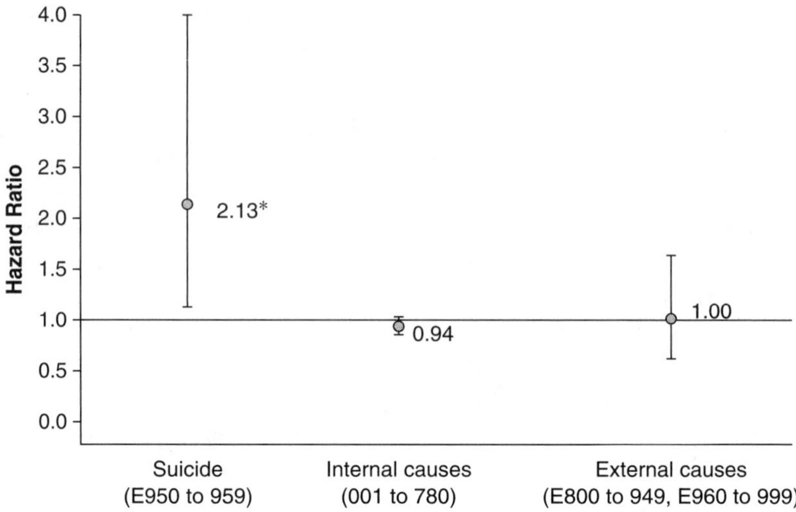

Figure 4.2. Suicide Risk among Male Veterans in the General Population. *Significant difference ($p<0.05$) between suicide and other causes of death using competing risk analyses. Error bars denote 95% CI. Risk coefficient adjusted for age, marital status, living arrangement, race, education, family income, employment status, region, interval since last doctor visit, self-rated health, and BMI. *Source.* Kaplan, Huguet, McFarland, and Newsom 2007.

In a landmark prospective study involving data from the National Health Interview Surveys from 1986 to 1994 linked to data from the National Death Index (NHIS-NDI) from 1986 to 1997, Kaplan and colleagues (2007) showed that men who served in the military were twice as likely as nonveterans to complete suicide even after adjustment for numerous established suicide risk factors (see figure 4.2).

Furthermore, exploratory work with the NHIS-NDI suggested that female veterans have an even higher relative risk of suicide (McFarland et al. 2007). It is not surprising that there has been growing interest in suicide among veterans in the media. For example, *CBS News* (2007) found that the rate of suicide among veterans was double that of their nonveteran peers.

However, not all studies have found that veterans are at an increased risk for suicide. On the basis of a review of thirteen studies on suicides among current and former military personnel, Kang and Bullman (2009) noted that veterans have historically had a lower risk of suicide than has the general population. Similarly, Miller and colleagues (2009) found no connection between military service and suicide in a large (but not nationally representative) longitudinal study of middle-aged and elderly men.

Epidemiology of Veterans' Suicides

According to the Centers for Disease Control and Prevention (CDC), veterans account for about one in five of all suicide deaths in the United States each year (Sundararaman, Panangala & Lister 2008). Studies of veteran populations have shown that those who contemplate, attempt, or complete suicide are more likely than are those who do not to be dependent on drugs and/or alcohol (Fontana & Rosenheck 1995a; Kausch & McCormick 2002, 2003a; Lehmann, McCormick & McCracken 1995). Veterans who live alone (Thoresen & Mehlum 2006), experience work problems (Benda 2005), are unemployed (Farberow, Kang & Bullman 1990; Porter, Astacio & Sobong 1997; Rodell, Benda & Rodell 2003; Thompson et al. 2006), are homeless (Benda 2003; Porter et al. 1997), or experience financial difficulties (Thompson et al. 2006) may be at an increased risk of suicide. Veterans who seek psychiatric or substance abuse treatment may be at an increased risk for suicide attempts if they have experienced lifetime or current physical or sexual abuse (Tiet, Finney & Moos 2006), particularly if they are homeless (Benda 2003, 2005; Rodell, Benda & Rodell 2003). The military branch, service era, service location, and combat exposure may affect the risk of suicide (MacLean & Elder 2007). Adams and colleagues (1998) found that U.S. Army personnel were more than seven times more likely to complete suicide than were individuals who served in the Marine Corps during the Vietnam War. Studies have also shown that veterans may be at a greater risk of suicide if they served in the Vietnam War than in World War II (Davidson et al. 1990), or if they served elsewhere during the Vietnam era compared to those who served in Vietnam (Breslin et al. 1998). In a comprehensive review of military service during the life course, MacLean and Elder (2007, 175) summarized a large body of literature by saying that "veterans exposed to combat have suffered worse outcomes than non-combat veterans and than non-veterans." Certain war zone traumas may be more strongly related than others to suicide attempts, including specific combat experiences, such as guilt over killing or failing to prevent death and injury (Fontana, Rosenheck & Brett, 1992), as well as intensive combat-related guilt (Hendin & Haas 1991).

Misclassification of Suicide Deaths

The Blue Ribbon Work Group on Suicide Prevention in the Veteran Population (U.S. Department of Veterans Affairs 2008) raised several concerns regarding the misclassification of deaths (for both veterans and nonveterans). Definitions are helpful to understand this issue. In particular, it is important to appreciate distinctions between the epidemiologic concept of misclassification and the medicolegal concept of undetermined death.

In this context, misclassification implies that a death that is due to intentional self-destruction (i.e., a true suicide) was inappropriately labeled as being other than suicide. For example, a review of all U.S. military deaths in 1998–1999 found that reporting and classification errors may account for 21 percent more suicides than are officially documented (Carr et al. 2004). It is also possible that a death that was due, say, to unintentional injuries could be mislabeled as intentional suicide. The epidemiologic concept of misclassification presupposes that a decedent can be assigned unambiguously to suicide (intentional self-destruction) versus nonintentional death. On the other hand, in the medicolegal domain, coroners and medical examiners label deaths as due to natural causes, unintentional injuries, suicide, homicide, or undetermined (Timmermans 2006). An example of an undetermined death is the situation in which it is unclear whether the deceased victim of a fall jumped (intentional suicide) or fell (unintentional death) or (rarely) was pushed (homicide presumably unintended by the victim). An example of a clear-cut suicide would be the death of a man by hanging himself. An example of a clearly unintentional fatality would be the death of a passenger that was due to a motor vehicle crash. Fatal poisonings or overdoses (of either licit medications or illicit drugs) are often undetermined as to intent (Ohberg & Lönnqvist 1998; Sorenson, Shen & Kraus 1997).

Indeed, suicide research has long been plagued by deaths that have been labeled as undetermined regarding intent (Baumert, Erazo & Ladwig, 2005; Ohberg & Lönnqvist 1998; Pfab et al. 2006). For example, in 2007 there were some 5,381 deaths with undetermined intent in the CDC Web-based Injury Statistics Query and Reporting System (WISQARS) database (Centers for Disease Control and Prevention, National Center for Injury Prevention and Control 2009). Of these deaths, some 3,770 (70 percent) were due to poisoning/overdose. It is not surprising that a fatal overdose can result in a classification of undetermined death, because there may well have been ambiguity with regard to suicidal intent at the time of the ingestion. Interviews with survivors of overdoses (conducted by the authors) showed that numerous reasons may be given for self-poisoning. For example, the survivors frequently stated that they "just wanted to sleep" or "wanted not to hurt anymore" or "forgot how many pills I took." On the other hand, some survivors stated, "yes, I wanted to die" or "I wanted to check out."

Pfab and colleagues (2006), who interviewed German opiate addicts who survived overdoses, classified 57 percent of the events as unintentional and the remainder as deliberate. The two groups differed on several characteristics, including previous overdoses and drugs used in the current overdose

(Pfab et al. 2006). Similarly, Donaldson and colleagues (2006) compared undetermined with unintentional (accidental injuries) and suicide deaths by poisoning in Utah using data similar to those available in the National Violent Death Reporting System (NVDRS) described subsequently. They found substantial differences among the groups, especially with regard to "suicidal behavior," which was defined as previously attempted suicide, leaving a suicide note, or declaring the intent to commit suicide. Using classification and regression tree analyses, Donaldson and colleagues (2006) showed that suicidal behavior was a powerful predictor of suicide versus unintentional death. Other predictors included evidence of a major depressive disorder, alcohol or drug problems, and physical health problems.

It is important to note that rates of undetermined deaths have been found to be higher in nonveterans than in veterans (Kaplan et al. 2007). Furthermore, it has been suggested that the deaths of veterans may be less likely than those of nonveterans to be classified as undetermined (U.S. Department of Veterans Affairs 2008). The death of veterans may be more likely to be classified as suicide for several reasons, including a higher use of firearms (more likely to be classified as suicide than other methods), the greater availability of accurate information for death certificates, and implicit societal beliefs that veterans are at elevated risk of suicide (U.S. Department of Veterans Affairs 2008). In epidemiologic terms, the suggestion is that misclassification bias (chiefly for nonveterans) in assigning undetermined deaths versus suicide as the manner of death may account for the apparently higher suicide rates found among veterans (U.S. Department of Veterans Affairs 2008). However, there have been few (if any) national studies comparing clinical features of veteran versus nonveteran undetermined decedents.

Risk Factors and Precipitating Circumstances

Risk factors specific to veterans include access to firearms, debilitating physical injuries, and mental health issues. Recent deployment also increases the risk of suicide because of complications, such as depression, alcohol or drug addiction and abuse, divorce, job loss, homelessness, poverty, and PTSD (Posey 2009).

The literature on veterans and suicide suggests risk factors that may make a veteran more susceptible to suicide, including those related to sociodemographic characteristics, substance abuse, mental health, and life events. In many studies, a combination of risk factors was correlated with veterans' suicides (Benda 2003, 2005; Desai, Dausey & Rosenheck 2005; Desai, Rosenheck & Desai 2008; Farberow et al. 1990; Ilgen et al. 2007; Kaplan et al. 2007; McCarthy et al. 2009; Rodell, Benda & Rodell 2003).

Demographic Characteristics

Many demographic factors have been linked to suicide in veterans. They include being male (Zivin et al. 2007), single (unmarried, separated, divorced, widowed) (Rodell, Benda & Rodell 2003; Thompson et al. 2006; Thoresen, Mehlum & Moller 2003; Thoresen et al. 2006), white (Bullman & Kang 1996; Desai et al. 2005; Desai, Rosenheck & Desai 2008; Kaplan et al. 2007; Lish et al. 1996) or African American (Price et al. 2004), younger (Desai, Rosenheck & Desai 2008; Kaplan, McFarland & Huguet 2009; Turner et al. 2006; Zivin et al. 2007) or older (Adams et al. 1998; Desai et al. 2005; Desai, Rosenheck & Desai 2008; Maynard & Boyko 2008); having more than twelve years of education (Kaplan et al. 2007), and residing in the southern or western United States (Zivin et al. 2007).

Kaplan and colleagues (2007; Kaplan, McFarland & Huguet 2009) made extensive use of data from the CDC to examine suicide among veterans. The National Violent Death Reporting System (NVDRS) collects standardized information on suicide deaths from several states, using information supplied by coroners or medical examiners plus numerous other sources. Using data from the NVDRS 2003–2006, the 2003–2006 American Community Surveys from the U.S. Census Bureau, and the 2003–2006 VA population estimates, Kaplan, McFarland, and Huguet (2009) computed rates of suicide among male veterans of various ages. Figure 4.3 shows that male veterans had higher suicide rates across the four age groups (18–34, 35–44, 45–64, and 65 +). There have been few studies about female veterans and suicide. Among them, McFarland, Kaplan, and Huguet (2010) showed that the suicide risk for military women was notably elevated, particularly for younger women.

Similarly, former VA secretary James Peake (2008) noted that female veterans had higher rates of suicide than did nonveterans. Moreover, Zivin and colleagues (2007) found a narrowing of the differential between male and female suicide ratios among depressed VA users compared to the general population. In addition, the Blue Ribbon Work Group noted that there are confusing results regarding the relationships between age and suicide. Researchers have found that younger and older veterans are at an increased risk of suicide (U.S. Department of Veterans Affairs 2008). The Oregon Violent Death Reporting System (Shen, Millet & Kohn 2008) found that the rates of suicide for younger veterans have increased since 2005, whereas those of older veterans have decreased. Several studies have shown the effects of time period on age variation in suicide rates (see, e.g., Stockard & O'Brien 2006). Therefore, it is important to assess age and period effects on the relative risk of suicide among veterans versus nonveterans.

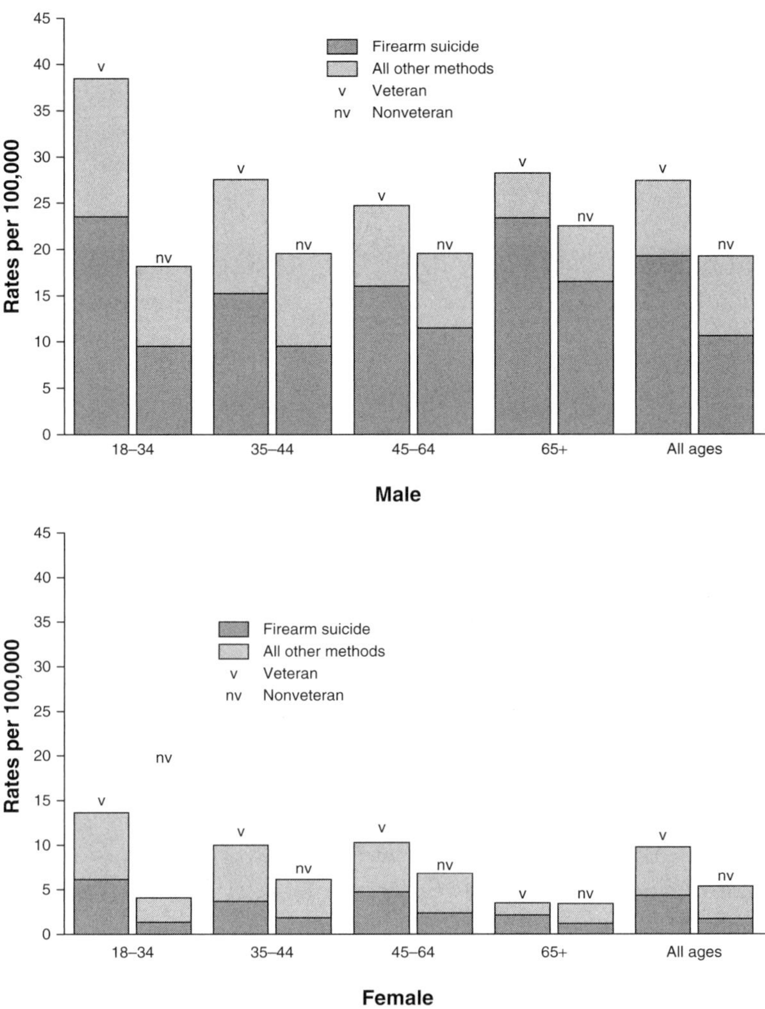

Figure 4.3. Male and Female Suicide Rates per 100,000 by Methods, Age, and Veteran Status, 2003–2006. *Source. Kaplan, McFarland, Huguet, 2009a. Used by permission.*

Addiction and Dependence

Studies of populations of veterans have found that those who contemplate, attempt, or complete suicide are more likely than those who do not to be dependent on drugs and/or alcohol (Fontana & Rosenheck 1995a, 1995b; Kausch 2003a, 2003b; Lehmann, McCormick & McCracken 1995; Zivin et al. 2007). In general, recent problematic substance use and the longer duration of substance use tend to show the most significant associations with suicidal thoughts and behaviors (Benda 2003; Ilgen et al. 2007; Price et al. 2004; Rodell, Benda & Rodell 2003; Thompson et al. 2006; Tiet et al. 2006). Although the association between specific types of drug abuse and suicidality is not clear, cocaine use has been linked to both suicidal ideation and attempts (Ilgen et al. 2007; Tiet et al. 2006). Alcohol or other drug disorders may amplify the effects of long-term sexual abuse (Rodell, Benda & Rodell 2003) and of psychiatric diagnoses, including schizophrenia (Strauss et al. 2006), depression (Zivin et al. 2007), and unipolar and bipolar disorders (Waller, Lyons & Costantini-Ferrando 1999) on suicidality. Only one study (Desai, Dausey & Rosenheck 2005) found that suicide rates were significantly lower among psychiatric inpatients with a diagnosis of drug abuse or dependence. High rates of attempted suicide in veterans have also been linked to pathological gambling, both with and without comorbid substance abuse (Kausch 2003a, 2003b). The acute use of alcohol is also associated with suicide (Hufford 2001). Kaplan and colleagues (2012) found that one-third of veterans aged eighteen to forty-four were intoxicated (blood alcohol level $\geq$.08 g/dl) at the time of death. Alcohol intoxication may have acted as an agent of emotional disinhibition by fostering impulsive behavior that facilitated the use of firearms among suicidal persons (Sher 2006; Gossop 2005).

Mental Disorders

Veterans who have made previous suicide attempts are at a greater risk of future attempts (Hartl et al. 2005; Thompson et al. 2006; Tiet et al. 2006) and completion (Farberow, Kang & Bullman 1990). A history of psychiatric hospitalizations has also been linked to veteran suicide and suicidal thoughts and attempts (Benda 2003; Desai, Rosenheck & Desai 2008; Farberow, Kang & Bullman 1990; Rodell, Benda & Rodell 2003; Thompson et al. 2006; Zivin et al. 2007). Current mental health problems are also significant risk factors for suicide. Veterans with mental health problems are more likely to complete suicide than is the general population (Hartl et al. 2005; McCarthy et al. 2009; Thompson et al. 2002; Thoresen et al. 2006; Zivin et al. 2007), and those who perceive their mental health as poor are more likely to experience suicidal ideation or attempts (Freeman, Roca & Moore 2000; Lish et al. 1996). General psychiatric symptoms have been associated with suicide in veterans (Farberow, Kang & Bullman 1990; Fontana et al. 1995b), as have specific symptoms such as anxiety (Hendin & Haas, 1991; Lish et al. 1996); hearing voices (Porter, Astacio & Sobong 1997); and mania, irritability, hallucinations, and paranoid delusions (Thompson et al. 2006). Some mental disorders show an association with suicidality in veterans. They include borderline personality disorder (Reich 1998), bipolar disorder (Desai, Rosenheck & Desai 2008; Waller, Lyons & Costantini-Ferrando 1999), and particularly unipolar depression (Benda 2005, 2003; Desai, Dausey & Rosenheck 2005; Farberow, Kang & Bullman 1990; Hartl et al. 2005; Reich 1998; Thompson et al. 2006; Waller, Lyons & Costantini-Ferrando 1999; Zivin et al. 2007). Post-traumatic stress disorder has also been associated with suicidality in veterans (Freeman, Roca & Moore 2000; Lehmann, McCormick & McCracken 1995), sometimes indirectly as a factor contributing to other psychiatric disorders (Hendin & Haas 1991). Evidence for a correlation between PTSD and suicidality in the presence of comorbid disorders is supported by studies of veterans who abuse substances (Benda 2005), suffer from a major depressive disorder (Campbell et al. 2007), and have schizophrenia or schizoaffective disorders (Strauss et al. 2006). There is limited evidence that PTSD may not be as important a risk factor as other psychiatric diagnoses (Fontana & Rosenheck 1995a, 1995b), or that it may even be protective (Desai, Rosenheck & Desai 2008) or protective in combination with other disorders (Desai, Dausey & Rosenheck 2005; Zivin et al. 2007), perhaps because veterans who suffer from comorbid PTSD receive more mental health treatment than do those who do not have the disorder.

Psychosocial Factors

Psychosocial and interpersonal factors have also been linked to suicide in veterans. Suicide risk is lower in states with higher social capital (Desai, Dausey & Rosenheck 2005). Suicidal ideation is associated with lower social support in VA patients with multiple sclerosis (Turner et al. 2006) and in substance-abusing homeless female veterans (Benda 2005). Suicidal thoughts, attempts, and completion have been linked to relationship problems (Benda 2005; Thompson et al. 2006; Thoresen et al. 2006), while ideation and attempts have been linked to family difficulties (Kausch & McCormick 2002; Porter, Astacio & Sobong 1997; Thompson et al. 2006). Veterans who live alone (Thoresen et al. 2006), experience work problems (Benda 2005), are unemployed (Farberow, Kang & Bullman 1990; Rodell, Benda & Rodell 2003; Thompson et al. 2006; Porter, Astacio & Sobong 1997), are homeless (Benda 2003; Porter, Astacio & Sobong 1997), or experience financial difficulties (Thompson et al. 2006) may be at an increased risk of suicide. Veterans seeking psychiatric or substance abuse treatment may be at an increased risk for suicide attempts if they have experienced lifetime or current physical or sexual abuse (Institute of Medicine 2008), particularly if they are homeless (Boehmer et al. 2004, Rodell, Benda & Rodell 2003; Thoresen, Mehlum & Moller 2003). Those who have fair or poor perceived physical health (Lish et al. 1996) or severe chronic pain (Porter, Astacio & Sobong 1997; Thompson et al. 2006), whose activity is limited (Kaplan et al. 2007), or who have high levels of physical disability (e.g., due to multiple sclerosis; Turner et al. 2006), may be at an increased risk of suicide or suicidal ideation. Kaplan and colleagues (2012) found that a physical health problem was the most prevalent circumstance associated with suicide among veterans aged sixty-five and older.

PTSD

A large body of research suggests that there is a connection between PTSD and suicide (Hudenko & Crenshae 2007). Currently, PTSD is defined in the *Diagnostic and Statistical Manual of Mental Disorders IV* (American Psychiatric Association 2000) as occurring after one experiences, witnesses, or confronts a traumatic event such as an actual or threatened death, a serious injury, or a threat to the bodily integrity of oneself or others that evokes fear, helplessness, or horror.

The prevalence of PTSD among current and former military personnel varies. Hoge and colleagues (2004) found that four months after deployment to Iraq, nearly 13 percent of U.S. Army soldiers and 12 percent of Marines met the screening criteria for PTSD. The rate increased to nearly 17 percent after one year among U.S. Army personnel (Hoge et al. 2007). According to a report from the RAND Corporation (Tanielian & Jaycox 2008), 14 percent of all returning service members deployed for Operation Enduring Freedom and Operation Iraqi Freedom (OEF/OIF) met the criteria for PTSD. Only half those suffering from PTSD seek mental healthcare. The stigma associated with mental illness and the potential consequences for the service member's career are major reasons for not obtaining mental healthcare.

Factors associated with PTSD among veterans include being female (Kang et al. 2003), being of black or Hispanic origin (Kulka et al. 1990; Kang et al. 2003), having lower socioeconomic status (Black et al. 2004), lower military rank (Kang et al. 2003), exposure to combat (O'Toole et al. 2009), early-life traumatic events (Fontana & Rosenheck 1994), having a history of psychiatric disorders (Black et al. 2004), and having a combat-related injury (Hoge et al. 2007).

The increased risk of death by suicide among wartime veterans may stem from the greater likelihood that these veterans suffered from PTSD (MacLean & Elder 2007; O'Toole et al. 2009). Traumatic events include physical assault, natural or man-made disasters, combat, and captivity (Cook and O'Donnell 2005). Symptoms of PTSD include reexperiencing (flashbacks or visceral responses), avoidance activities (such as drinking or drug use), and arousal or hypervigilance. Post-traumatic stress disorder is considered acute if the symptoms last less than three months and chronic symptoms continue for more than three months.

Many studies have shown that veterans who have PTSD are at an increased risk for suicide. For example, Jakupcak and colleagues (2007) found that OEF/OIF veterans who were diagnosed with PTSD were four times more likely to report suicidal ideation than were veterans without PTSD. Boscarino (2005) also found an association between PTSD and suicide among Vietnam veterans.

The Role and Importance of Firearms

Veterans have greater access to firearms than do members of the general population (Lambert & Fowler 1997). A survey of firearm use among combat veterans in a PTSD rehabilitation program (Freeman et al. 1994) found that 75 percent of veterans currently owned firearms, 59 percent had considered using their firearm to complete suicide, and 38 percent had loaded a firearm with suicide in mind while intoxicated. Considering veterans' greater access to firearms than those in the general population, it is surprising that few studies have examined the availability of firearms as a risk factor for veterans' suicide. Although only a limited number of studies have examined the means by which suicide was completed, those that did generally found that firearms accounted for upward of 50 percent of all suicides (Drescher et al. 2003; Kang & Bullman 2008; Kaplan et al. 2007; Kaplan, McFarland & Huguet 2009; Thompson et al. 2002; Thoresen et al. 2006; Thoresen, Mehlum & Moller 2003). A review of suicide risk factors in veterans found that the availability and knowledge of firearms is a risk factor for suicide in veterans who are treated in the VA healthcare system (Lambert & Fowler 1997). Suicidal veterans are more likely to own a gun than are nonsuicidal veterans (Thompson et al. 2006), and veterans are more likely to use a firearm to complete suicide than are members of the general population (Desai, Dausey & Rosenheck 2005; Kaplan et al. 2007; Kaplan, McFarland & Huguet 2009). Using the National Violent Death Reporting System 2003–2006, Kaplan, McFarland, and Huguet (2009) reported that the firearm suicide rate among male veterans was 81 percent higher than the rate among their nonveteran counterparts. The study also showed that both male and female veterans were more likely to die by suicide using a firearm (see figure 4.3). Veterans Affairs staff members are well aware that veterans have considerable experience with firearms. However, clinicians outside VA may have limited appreciation for the importance of firearms with regard to suicide by veterans.

Although policies on access to firearms raise numerous questions regarding civil rights, the importance of this topic merits discussion. Former military service personnel, by definition, have considerable experience with firearms. Therefore, a comprehensive suicide risk assessment must entail a thorough discussion of access to firearms, attitudes toward firearms as a means of suicide, clinical severity, intent to die, need for intensive care, and any other factor that is even remotely related to the individual's opinion about or familiarity with the use of a firearm for any reason, including a suicide attempt.

Prevention of Suicide among Current and Former Military Personnel

Numerous programs have been developed for the prevention of suicide among active duty military personnel (see Bagley, Munjas & Shekelle 2010 for a review). Before versus after studies (see, e.g., Knox et al. 2003) have suggested that programs may have had some impact on military suicide rates. However, Bagley, Munjas, and Shekelle (2010) noted that secular trends complicate the evaluation of prevention programs that are intended to influence rare phenomena such as suicide.

Given the complexity of suicide, it is not surprising that the strategies often include multifaceted approaches, such as the eleven-component U.S. Air Force program (Knox et al. 2003). The military programs typically emphasize education of troops about suicide risk factors and the availability of resources, combined with special instructions for leaders (Bagley, Munjas & Shekelle 2010). Recently the U.S. Army issued an extensive report on suicide among soldiers that included numerous recommendations for prevention with an emphasis on the role of leadership (U.S. Army 2010). This report also addressed stigma regarding mental health treatment (Greene-Shortridge, Britt & Castro 2007). It noted that though there may have been some improvement in attitudes toward behavioral healthcare, thanks to educational communication programs, about half the soldiers who were surveyed indicated that mental health treatment would be detrimental to their military careers (U.S. Army 2010). Along these lines, former army vice chief of staff General Peter Chiarelli admonished leaders: "We must identify our Soldiers who are at-risk, mitigate their stress, and, if necessary, personally intervene to assist them" (U.S. Army 2010, iii). However, the general also emphasized "firm enforcement of discipline, retention, and separation policies" and stated: "We must ensure that Soldiers who cannot adapt to the rigors and stress of this profession find sanctuary elsewhere" (U.S. Army 2010, iii). It is prudent, then, to anticipate that problems of suicide in the active duty military will be echoed in the veteran population.

In this regard, the Joshua Omvig Veterans Suicide Prevention Act of 2007 directed VA to undertake several activities that were designed to reduce suicide among people who have left the military (see box 4.1). Similarly, the Blue Ribbon Work Group on Suicide Prevention in the Veteran Population produced numerous recommendations in June 2008 (see box 4.2). Veterans Affairs has also addressed risks for the suicide of veterans who are hospitalized in VA mental health units (Mills et al. 2010). However, it is important to appreciate that only a small minority of veterans use VA programs. For example, the 2001 National Survey of Veterans (U.S. Department of Veterans Affairs 2001) found that only 23 percent of male veterans and 19.4 percent of female veterans used VA services in the year prior to the interviews. Conversely, some 76.4 percent of male veterans and 80.6 percent of female veterans exclusively used non-VA healthcare in the year prior to the interviews. The point is that healthcare providers outside VA need information about suicide among veterans.

At the individual level, early detection of mental health and/or substance abuse conditions can result in an increased willingness to begin behavioral health treatment with (it is hoped) a rapid resolution of symptoms (and presumably improved treatment outcomes). A key consideration is that many, if not most, people who complete suicide have had recent contact with a healthcare provider (typically in the primary care sector). Therefore, to ensure an earlier diagnosis, patients who enter medical treatment for reasons other than behavioral healthcare should be screened for mental health and/or substance

---

Box 4.1. Joshua Omvig Veterans Suicide Prevention Act

- Training all VA staff to recognize risk factors for suicide.
- Placing a suicide prevention coordinator at each VA medical facility.
- Operating a national suicide prevention lifeline (800-273-8255).
- Educating veterans and their families about suicide risks.
- Establishing a mental health center of excellence in Canandaigua, New York.

Source: The Library of Congress, H.R.327, March 2007

Box 4.2. Blue Ribbon Work Group on Suicide Prevention

- Resolve conflicting study results.

- Revise and reevaluate VA's current policies regarding mandatory suicide screening assessments.

- Ensure that suicide- and suicide-attempt-reporting use definitions consistent with broader VHA surveillance efforts.

- Ensure that specific pharmacotherapy recommendations related to suicide or suicide behaviors are evidence based.

- Pursue opportunities for outreach to enrolled eligible veterans and to disseminate messages to reduce risk behavior associated with suicidality.

- Clarify that the issue of confidentiality of the health records of OEF/OIF service members who receive care through VHA is ongoing.

- Evaluate the roles and workloads of the suicide prevention coordinators' positions.

Source. U.S. Department of Veteran Affairs (2008).

---

abuse issues. Safety should also be addressed, with an emphasis on minimizing access to firearms.

At the population level, there may be policies that could reduce suicide among veterans. Recognizing that financial distress and homelessness are risk factors for suicide, programs that are intended to address these issues for veterans may also reduce veteran suicide.

More challenging are policies and/or programs to address access to firearms and substance (especially alcohol) misuse among veterans. An innovative program may be to employ community-based behavioral economic approaches. One wonders, for example, what veterans would think about being paid to turn in their guns. Analogously, there may be value in financial encouragement for veterans to pledge abstinence from alcohol or other drugs. Obviously any such undertakings would need to be preceded by extensive involvement of veterans in program planning and implementation. The point here is that creativity will be needed to address the substantial (and presumably growing) problem of suicide among veterans.

Acknowledgments: Some of the studies reviewed in this chapter were supported by the National Institute of Mental Health (MH070520), American Foundation for Suicide Prevention, and Joyce Foundation. The views expressed in this chapter are those of the authors and should not be ascribed to the organizations that funded the research reported here.

References

Adamek, M. E. & Kaplan, M. S. (2000). Caring for depressed and suicidal older patients: A survey of physicians and nurse practitioners. *International Journal of Psychiatry in Medicine* 30: 111–125.

Adams, D. P., Barton, C., Mitchell, G. L., Moore, A. L. & Einagel, V. (1998). Hearts and minds: Suicide among United States combat troops in Vietnam, 1957–1973. *Social Science and Medicine* 47: 1687–1694.

Allen, J. P., Cross, G. & Swanner, J. M. (2005). Suicide in the Army: A review of current information. *Military Medicine* 170: 580–584.

Alvarez, L. (2009). Suicides of soldiers reach high of nearly 3 decades. *New York Times*, January 30.

American Psychiatric Association. (2000). *Diagnostic and statistical manual of mental disorders*. 4th ed., text rev. Washington, DC: Author.

Asgard, U. (1990). A psychiatric study of suicide among urban Swedish women. *Acta Psychiatrica Scandinavica* 82: 115–124.

Bagley, S. C., Munjas, B. & Shekelle, P. (2010). A systematic review of suicide prevention programs for military veterans. *Suicide and Life-Threatening Behavior* 40: 257–265.

Barraclough, B., Bounch, J., Nelson, B. & Sainsbury, P. (1974). A hundred cases of suicide. *British Journal of Psychiatry* 125: 355–373.

Barry, D. (2007). Asked to serve again, a soldier goes down fighting. *New York Times*, May 27.

Baumert, J. J., Erazo, N. & Ladwig, K. H. (2005). Sex- and age-specific trends in mortality from suicide and undetermined death in Germany 1991–2002. *BMC Public Health* 5: 61.

Benda, B. (2003). Discriminators of suicide thoughts and attempts among homeless veterans who abuse substances. *Suicide and Life-Threatening Behavior* 33: 430–442.

Benda, B. (2005). Gender differences in predictors of suicidal thoughts and attempts among homeless veterans that abuse substances. *Suicide and Life-Threatening Behavior* 35: 106–116.

Black, D. W., Carney, C. P., Peloso, P. M., Woolson, R. F., Schwartz, D. A., Voelker, M. D., et al. (2004). Gulf War veterans with anxiety: Prevalence, comorbidity, and risk factors. *Epidemiology* 15: 135–142.

Boden, J. M., Fergusson, D. M. & Horwood, L. J. (2007). Anxiety disorders and suicidal behaviours in adolescence and young adulthood: Findings from a longitudinal study. *Psychological Medicine* 37: 431–440.

Boehmer, T. K. C., Flanders, D., McGeehin, M. A., Boyle, C. & Barrett, D. H. (2004). Postservice mortality in Vietnam veterans: 30-year follow-up. *Archives of Internal Medicine* 164: 1908–1916.

Bolton, J. M., Cox, B. J., Afifi, T. O., Enns, M. W., Bienvenu, O. J. & Sareen, J. (2007). Anxiety disorders and risk for suicide attempts: findings from the Baltimore Epidemiologic Catchment area follow-up study. *Depression and Anxiety* 25: 477–481.

Boscarino, J. A. (2005). Posttraumatic stress disorder and mortality among U.S. Army veterans 30 years after military service. *Annals of Epidemiology* 16: 248–256.

Breslin, P., Kang, H. K., Lee, Y., Burt, V. & Shepard, B. M. (1998). Proportionate mortality study of U.S. Army and U.S. Marine Corps veterans of the Vietnam War. *Journal of Occupational Medicine* 30: 412.

Brockington, L. (2001). Suicide in women. *International Clinical Psychopharmacology* 16, 2 supp.: S7–S19.

Brook, R., Klap, R., Liao, D. & Wells, K. B. (2006). Mental health care for adults with suicide ideation. *General Hospital Psychiatry* 28: 271–277.

Bullman, T. A. & Kang, H. K. (1996). The risk of suicide among wounded Vietnam veterans. *American Journal of Public Health* 86: 662–667.

Callen, K. E., Reaves, M. E., Maxwell, M. J. & McFarland, B. H. (1985). Vietnam veterans in the general hospital. *Hospital and Community Psychiatry* 36: 150–153.

Campbell, D. G., Felker, B. L., Liu, C. F., Yano, E. M., Kirchner, J. E., Chan, D., et al. (2007). Prevalence of depression? PTSD comorbidity, implications for clinical practice guidelines and primary care-based interventions. *Journal of General Internal Medicine* 22: 711–718.

Carr, J., Hoge, C., Gardner, J. & Potter, R. (2004). Suicide surveillance in the U.S. military—Reporting and classification biases in rate calculations. *Suicide and Life-Threatening Behavior* 34: 233–241.

CBS News. (2007). Veteran suicides: How we got the numbers. November 13. http://www.cbsnews.com/stories/2007/11/13/cbsnews_investigates/main3498625 .shtml (accessed October 6, 2010).

Center for Substance Abuse Treatment. (2008). *Substance abuse and suicide prevention: Evidence and implications: A white paper.* DHHS pub. no. SMA-08-4352. Rockville, MD: Substance Abuse and Mental Health Services Administration.

Centers for Disease Control and Prevention. (1988). Health status of Vietnam veterans. I. Psychosocial characteristics: The Centers for Disease Control Vietnam experience study. *Journal of the American Medical Association* 259: 2701–2707.

Centers for Disease Control and Prevention, National Center for Injury Prevention and Control. (2009). Web-based Injury Statistics Query and Reporting System (WISQARS). www.cdc.gov/ncipc/wisqars (accessed March 14, 2012).

Conwell, Y. (2001). Suicide in later life: A review and recommendations for prevention. *Suicide and Life-Threatening Behavior* 31s: 32–47.

Cook, J. M. & O'Donnell, C. (2005). Assessment and psychological treatment of posttraumatic stress disorder in older adults. *Journal of Geriatric Psychiatry and Neurology* 18: 61–71.

Davidson, J. R. T., Kudler, H. S., Saunders, W. B. & Smith, R. D. (1990). Symptom and comorbidity patterns in World War II and Vietnam veterans with PTSD. *Comprehensive Psychiatry* 31: 162–170.

Defense Manpower Data Center. (2010). U.S. active duty military personnel by service by region/country 2001–2009. http://siadapp.dmdc.osd.mil/personnel/MILITARY/miltop.htm (accessed March 15, 2011).

Department of Defense Task Force on the Prevention of Suicide by Members of the Armed Forces. (2010). The challenge and the promise: Strengthening the force, preventing suicide and saving lives. http://www.health.mil/dhb/default.cfm (March 15, 2011).

Desai, M. M., Rosenheck, R. A. & Desai, R. A. (2008). Time trends and predictors of suicide among mental health outpatients in the Department of Veterans Affairs. *Journal of Behavioral Health Services & Research* 35: 115–124.

Desai, R. A., Dausey, D. J. & Rosenheck, R. A. (2005). Mental health service delivery and suicide risk: The role of individual patient and facility factors. *American Journal of Psychiatry* 162: 311–318.

Donaldson, A. E., Larsen, G. Y., Fullerton-Gleason, L. & Olson, L. M. (2006). Classifying undetermined poisoning deaths. *Injury Prevention* 12: 338–343.

Drescher, K. D., Rosen, C. S., Burling, T. A. & Foy, D. W. (2003). Causes of death among male veterans who received residential treatment for PTSD. *Journal of Traumatic Stress* 16: 535–543.

Durkheim, E. (2006). *On suicide.* New York: Penguin Group. (Original work published 1897).

Enns, M. W., Cox, B. J., Afifi, T. O., De Graaf, R., Ten, H. M. & Sareen, J. (2006). Childhood adversities and risk for suicidal ideation and attempts: a longitudinal population-based study. *Psychological Medicine* 36: 1769–1778.

Farberow, N. L., Kang, H. K. & Bullman, T. A. (1990). Combat experience and postservice psychosocial status as predictors of suicide in Vietnam veterans. *Journal of Nervous and Mental Disease* 178: 32–37.

Fontana, A. & Rosenheck, R. (1994). Posttraumatic stress disorder among Vietnam theater veterans: A causal model of etiology in a community sample. *Journal of Nervous and Mental Disease* 182: 677–684.

Fontana, A. & Rosenheck, R. (1995a). An etiological model of attempted suicide among Vietnam theater veterans: Prospective generalization to a treatment-seeking sample. *Journal of Nervous and Mental Disease* 183: 377–383.

Fontana, A. & Rosenheck, R. (1995b). Attempted suicide among Vietnam veterans: A model of etiology in a community sample. *American Journal of Psychiatry* 152: 102.

Fontana, A., Rosenheck, R. & Brett, E. (1992). War zone traumas and PTSD symptomatology. *Journal of Nervous and Mental Disease* 180: 748–755.

Freeman, T., Clothier, J., Thornton, C. & Keesee, N. (1994). Firearm collection and use among combat veterans admitted to a posttraumatic stress disorder rehabilitation unit. *Journal of Nervous and Mental Disease* 182: 592–594.

Freeman, T. W., Roca, V. & Moore, M. (2000). A comparison of chronic combat-related posttraumatic stress disorder (PTSD) patients with and without a history of suicide attempt. *Journal of Nervous and Mental Disease* 188: 460–463.

Friedman, M. (2005). Veterans' mental health in the wake of war. *New England Journal of Medicine* 352: 1287–1290.

Goldney, R. D., Wilson, D., Dal Grande, E., Fisher, L. J. & McFarlane, A. C. (2000). Suicidal ideation in a random community sample: Attributable risk due to depression and psychosocial and traumatic events. *Australian and New Zealand Journal of Psychiatry* 34: 98–106.

Goldsmith, S. K., Pellmar, T. C., Kleinman, A. M. & Bunney, W. E. (2002). *Reducing suicide: A national imperative.* Washington, DC: National Academies Press.

Gossop, M. (2005). Alcohol in suicide attempts and completions. *Psychiatric Annals* 35: 513–521.

Gould, M. S. & Kramer, R. A. (2001). Youth suicide prevention. *Suicide and Life-Threatening Behavior* 31s: 6–31.

Greene-Shortridge, T. M., Britt, T. W. & Castro, C. A. (2007). The stigma of mental health problems in the military. *Military Medicine* 172: 157–161.

Gunnell, D., Harbord, R., Singleton, N., Jenkins, R. & Lewis, G. (2004). Factors influencing the development and amelioration of suicidal thoughts in the general population: Cohort study. *British Journal of Psychiatry* 185: 385–393.

Hampton, T. (2007). Research, law address veterans' suicide. *JAMA* 298: 2732.

Hartl, T. L., Rosen, C., Drescher, K., Lee, T. T. & Gusman, F. (2005). Predicting high-risk behaviors in veterans with PTSD. *Journal of Nervous and Mental Disease* 193: 464–472.

Hawton, K., Arensman, E., Wasserman, D., Hulten, A., Bille-Brahe, U., Bjerke, T., et al. (1998). Relation between attempted suicide and suicide rates among young people in Europe. *Journal of Epidemiology and Community Health* 52: 191–194.

Hendin, H. & Haas, A. P. (1991). Suicide and guilt as manifestations of PTSD in Vietnam combat veterans. *American Journal of Psychiatry* 148: 586–591.

Hintikka, J., Pesonen, T., Saarinen, P., Tanskanen, A., Lehtonen, J. & Viinamäki, H. (2001). Suicidal ideation in the Finnish general population: A 12-month follow-up study. *Social Psychiatry and Psychiatric Epidemiology* 36: 590–594.

Hoge, C. W., Auchterlonie, J. L. & Milliken, C. S. (2006). Mental health problems, use of mental health services, and attrition from military service after returning from deployment to Iraq or Afghanistan. *JAMA* 295: 1023–1032.

Hoge, C. W., Castro, C. A., Messer, S. C., McGurk, D., Cotting, D. I. & Koffman, R. L. (2004). Combat duty in Iraq and Afghanistan, mental health problems, and barriers to care. *New England Journal of Medicine* 351: 13–22.

Hoge, C. W., Lesikar, S. E., Guevara, R., Lange, J., Brundage, J. F., Engel, C. C., et al. (2002). Mental disorders among US military personnel in the 1990s: Association with high levels of health care utilization and early military attrition. *American Journal of Psychiatry* 159: 1576–1583.

Hoge, C. W., Terhakopian, A., Castro, C. A., Messer, S. C. & Engel, C. C. (2007). Association of posttraumatic stress disorder with somatic symptoms, health care visits, and absenteeism among Iraq War veterans. *American Journal of Psychiatry* 164: 150–153.

Hoge, C. W., Toboni, H. E., Messer, S. C., Bell, N., Amoroso, P. & Orman, D. T. (2005). The occupational burden of mental disorders in the U.S. military: Psychiatric hospitalizations, involuntary separations, and disability. *American Journal of Psychiatry* 162: 585–591.

Hudenko, W. & Crenshae, T. (2007). The relationship between PTSD and suicide. http://www.ptsd.va.gov/professional/pages/ptsd-suicide.asp (accessed October 6, 2010).

Hufford, M. R. (2001). Alcohol and suicidal behavior. *Annual Review of Clinical Psychology* 21: 897–911.

Ilgen, M. A., Harris, A. H. S., Moos, R. H. & Tiet, Q. Q. (2007). Predictors of a suicide attempt one year after entry into substance use disorder treatment. *Alcoholism, Clinical and Experimental Research* 31: 635–642.

Institute of Medicine. (2008). *Gulf War and health*, volume 6: *Physiologic, psychologic, and psychosocial effects of deployment-related stress.* Washington, DC: National Academies Press.

Jakupcak, M., Conybeare, D., Phelps, L., Hunt, S., Holmes, H., Felker, B., et al. (2007). Anger, hostility and aggression among Iraq and Afghanistan war veterans reporting PTSD and subthreshold PTSD. *Journal of Traumatic Stress* 20: 945–954.

Joe, S. & Kaplan, M. S. (2001). Suicide among African American men. *Suicide and Life-Threatening Behavior* 31s: 106–121.

Joe, S. & Kaplan, M. S. (2002). Firearm-related suicide among young African-American males. *Psychiatric Services* 53: 332–334.

Kang, H. K. & Bullman, T. A. (2008). Risk of suicide among US veterans after returning from the Iraq or Afghanistan war zones. *JAMA* 300: 652–653.

Kang, H. K. & Bullman, T. A. (2009). Is there an epidemic of suicides among current and former U.S. military personnel? *Annals of Epidemiology* 19: 757–760.

Kang, H. K., Natelson, B. H., Mahan, C. M., Lee, K. Y. & Murphy, F. M. (2003). Post-traumatic stress disorder and chronic fatigue syndrome–like illness among Gulf War veterans: A population-based survey of 30,000 veterans. *American Journal of Epidemiology* 157: 141–148.

Kaplan, F. (2006). The army, faced with its limits. *New York Times,* January 1.

Kaplan, F. (2008). Defense Secretary Robert Gates is the anti-Rumsfeld: Cautious, courteous and conciliatory. But will that be enough to bring Washington together on Iraq and Iran? *New York Times Magazine,* February 10, 40–98.

Kaplan, M. S., Huguet, N., McFarland, B. H. & Newsom, J. T. (2007). Suicide among male veterans: A prospective population-based study. *Journal of Epidemiology and Community Health* 61: 619–624.

Kaplan, M. S., McFarland, B. H. & Huguet, N. (2009). Firearm suicide among veterans in the general population: Findings from the National Violent Death Reporting System. *Journal of Trauma* 67: 503–507.

Kaplan, M. S., McFarland, B. H., Huguet, N. & Valenstein, M. (2012). Suicide risk and precipitating circumstances among young, middle-aged, and older male veterans. *American Journal of Public Health* 102, supp. 1: S131–S133.

Kausch, O. (2003a). Suicidal attempts among veterans seeking treatment for pathological gambling. *Journal of Clinical Psychiatry* 64: 1031–1038.

Kausch, O. (2003b). Patterns of substance abuse among treatment-seeking pathological gamblers. *Journal of Substance Abuse Treatment* 25: 263–270.

Kausch, O. & McCormick, R. A. (2002). Suicide prevalence in chemical dependency programs: preliminary data from a national sample, and an examination of risk factors. *Journal of Substance Abuse Treatment* 22: 97–102.

Kessler, R. C., Borges, G. & Walters, E. E. (1999). Prevalence of and risk factors for lifetime suicide attempts in the national comorbidity survey. *Archives of General Psychiatry* 56: 617–626.

Kimerling, R., Street, A. E., Gima, K. & Smith, M. W. (2008). Evaluation of universal screening for military-related sexual trauma. *Psychiatric Services* 59: 635–640.

Knox, K. L., Litts, D. A., Talcott, G. W., Feig, J. C. & Caine, E. D. (2003). Risk of suicide and related adverse outcomes after exposure to a suicide prevention programme in the US Air Force: Cohort study. *BMJ* 327, no. 7428: 1376.

Kulka, R. A., Schlenger, W. E., Fairbank, J. A., Hough, R. L., Jordan, B. K., Marmar, C. R., et al. (1990). *Trauma and the Vietnam War generation: Report of findings from the national Vietnam veterans readjustment study.* New York: Brunner/Mazel Publishers.

Lambert, M. T. & Fowler, D. R. (1997). Suicide risk factors among veterans: Risk management in the changing culture of the Department of Veterans Affairs. *Journal of Mental Health Administration* 24: 350–658.

LaPierre, C. B., Schwegler, A. F. & LaBauve, B. J. (2007). Posttraumatic stress and depression symptoms in soldiers returning from combat operations in Iraq and Afghanistan. *Journal of Traumatic Stress* 20: 933–943.

Lehmann, L., McCormick, R. A. & McCracken, L. (1995). Suicidal behavior among patients in the VA health care system. *Psychiatric Services* 46: 1069–1071.

Levine, A. (2009). Army reports another month of high suspected suicides. CNN, March 5.

Levin-Epstein, M. (2005). Screening soldiers for mental health issues: Before, during and after. *Behavioral Healthcare Tomorrow*, December, 8–12.

Lish, J. D., Zimmerman, M., Farber, N. J., Kuzma, M. A. & Plescia, G. (1996). Suicide screening in a primary care setting at a veteran's affairs medical center. *Psychosomatics* 37: 413–424.

MacLean, A. & Elder, G. H. (2007). Military service in the life course. *Annual Reviews in Sociology* 33: 175–196.

Mahon, M. J., Tobin, J. P., Cusack, D. A., Kelleher, C. & Malone, K. (2005). Suicide among regular-duty military personnel: A retrospective case-control study of occupation-specific risk factors for workplace suicide. *American Journal of Psychiatry* 162: 1688–1696.

Mann, J. J. (2002). A current perspective of suicide and attempted suicide. *Annals of Internal Medicine* 136: 302–311.

Mann, J. J., Apter, A., Bertolote, J., Beautrais, A., Currier, D., Haas, A., et al. (2005). Suicide prevention strategies: a systematic review. *JAMA* 294: 2064–2074.

Maynard, C. & Boyko, E. J. (2008). Datapoints: Suicide rates in the Washington State veteran population. *Psychiatric Services* 59: 1245.

McCarthy, J. F., Valenstein, M., Kim, H. M., Ilgen, M., Zivin, K. & Blow, F. C. (2009). Suicide mortality among patients receiving care in the veterans health administration health system. *American Journal of Epidemiology* 169: 1033–1038.

McFarland, B. H., Kaplan, M. S. & Huguet, N. (2010). Self-inflicted deaths among women with United States military service: A hidden epidemic? *Psychiatric Services* 61: 1177.

McFarland, B. H., Kaplan, M. S., Huguet, N. & Newsom, J. T. (2007). Suicide among female veterans in the general U.S. population. Paper presented at the 116th Annual Meeting of the American Psychiatric Association, San Diego, CA, April 19–24, 2007.

Miller, M., Barber, C., Azrael, D., Calle, E. E., Lawler, E. & Mukamal, K. J. (2009). Suicide among US veterans: A prospective study of 500,000 middle-aged and elderly men. *American Journal of Epidemiology* 170: 494–500.

Milliken, C. S., Auchterlonie, J. L. & Hoge, C. W. (2007). Longitudinal assessment of mental health problems among active and reserve component soldiers returning from the Iraq war. *JAMA* 298: 2141–2148.

Mills, P. D., Watts, B. V., Miller, S., Kemp, J., Knox, K., DeRosier, J. M. & Bagian, J. P. (2010). A checklist to identify inpatient suicide hazards in Veterans Affairs hospitals. *The Joint Commission Journal on Quality and Patient Safety* 36, no. 7: 87–93.

Miniño, A. M., Arias, E., Kochanek, K. D., Murphy, S. L. & Smith, B. L. (2002). Deaths: Final data for 2000. *National Vital Statistics Reports* 50: 1–119.

Miniño, A. M., Heron, M. P. & Smith, B. L. (2006). Deaths: Preliminary data for 2004. *National Vital Statistics Reports* 54: 1–49.

Office of the Surgeon Multinational Force–Iraq & Office of the Command Surgeon. (2008). *Mental Health Advisory Team (MHAT) V: Operation Iraqi Freedom 06–08: Iraq, Operation Enduring Freedom 08: Afghanistan.* Arlington, VA: Walter Reed Army Institute of Research.

Office of the Surgeon Multinational Force–Iraq & Office of the Surgeon General, United States Army Medical Command. (2006). *Mental Health Advisory Team (MHAT) IV: Operation Iraqi Freedom 05–07. Final Report.* Arlington, VA: Office of the Surgeon, Multinational Force–Iraq and Office of the Surgeon General, United States Army Medical Command.

Office of the United States Army Surgeon General. (2005). *Operation Iraqi Freedom (OIF-II) Mental Health Advisory Team (MHAT-II) report.* Washington, DC: Office of the United States Army Surgeon General.

Ohberg, A. & Lönnqvist, J. (1998). Suicides hidden among undetermined deaths. *Acta Psychiatrica Scandinavica* 98: 214–218.

O'Toole, B. I., Catts, S. V., Outram, S., Pierse, K. R. & Cockburn, J. (2009). The physical and mental health of Australian Vietnam veterans 3 decades after the war and its relation to military service, combat, and post-traumatic stress disorder. *American Journal of Epidemiology* 170: 318–330.

Peake, James B. (Former Secretary of Veteran Affairs). (2008). *The truth about veterans' suicides. Hearing before the House Committee on Veterans Affairs.* 110th Cong., May 6.

Pfab, R., Eyer, F., Jetzinger, E., & Zilker, T. (2006). Cause and motivation in cases of non-fatal drug overdoses in opiate addicts. *Clinical Toxicology* 44: 255–259.

Pirkola, S. P., Suominen, K. & Isometsä, E. T. (2004). Suicide in alcohol-dependent individuals: epidemiology and management. *CNS Drugs* 18: 423–436.

Porter, L. S., Astacio, M. & Sobong, L. C. (1997). Telephone hotline assessment and counseling of suicidal military service veterans in the USA. *Journal of Advanced Nursing* 26: 716–722.

Posey, S. (2009). Veterans and suicide: A review of potential increased risk. *Smith College Studies in Social Work* 79: 368–374.

President's Commission on Care for America's Returning Wounded Warriors. (2007). *Serve, support, simplify.* Arlington, VA: President's Commission on Care for America's Returning Wounded Warriors.

Price, R. K., Risk, N. K., Haden, A. H., Lewis, C. E. & Spitznagel, E. L. (2004). Post-traumatic stress disorder, drug dependence, and suicidality among male Vietnam veterans with a history of heavy drug use. *Drug and Alcohol Dependence* 76S: S31–S43.

Reeves, R. R., Parker, J. D. & Konkle-Parker, D. J. (2005). War-related mental health problems of today's veterans. *Psychiatric Annals* 35: 930–942.

Reich, J. (1998). The relationship of suicide attempts, borderline personality traits, and major depressive disorder in a veteran outpatient population. *Journal of Affective Disorders* 49: 151–156.

Rich, C. L., Young, D. & Fowler, R. C. (1986). San Diego suicide study. I. Young vs old subjects. *Archives of General Psychiatry* 43: 577–82.

Ritchie, E. C. (2007). Commentary on the MHAT IV recommendations: An update. *Traumatology* 13: 55–58.

Rodell, D. E., Benda, B. B. & Rodell, L. (2003). Suicidal thoughts among homeless alcohol and other drug abusers. *Alcoholism Treatment Quarterly* 21: 57–74.

Sareen, J., Cox, B. J., Afifi, T. O., de Graaf, R., Asmundson, G. J., Ten Have, M., et al. (2005a). Anxiety disorders and risk for suicidal ideation and suicide attempts: a population-based longitudinal study of adults. *Archives of General Psychiatry* 62: 1249–1257.

Sareen, J., Houlahan, T., Cox, B. J. & Asmundson, G. J. (2005b). Anxiety disorders associated with suicidal ideation and suicide attempts in the national comorbidity survey. *Journal of Nervous and Mental Disease* 193: 450–454.

Schumm, W. R. (1999). Reserve component families. In P. McClure (Ed.), *Pathways to the future: A review of military family research* (pp. 109–133). Scranton, PA: Military Family Institute.

Seal, K. H., Bertenthal, D., Miner, C. R., Sen, S. & Marmar, C. R. (2007). Mental health disorders among 103,788 veterans returning from Iraq and Afghanistan seen at Department of Veterans Affairs facilities. *Archives of Internal Medicine* 167: 476–482.

Segal, D. R. & Segal, M. W. (2005). U.S. military's reliance on the reserves. http://www.PRB.org (accessed October 6, 2010).

Shen, X., Millet, L. & Kohn, M. (2007). *Violent deaths in Oregon: 2005*. Portland: Oregon Department of Human Services.

Shen, X., Millet, L. & Kohn, M. (2008). *Violent deaths in Oregon: 2006*. Portland: Oregon Department of Human Services.

Sher, L. (2006). Alcohol consumption and suicide. *Quarterly Journal of Medicine* 99: 57–61.

Skegg, K. (2005). Self-harm. *Lancet* 366: 1471–1483.

Sorenson, S. B., Shen, H. & Kraus, J. F. (1997). Undetermined manner of death: A comparison with unintentional injury, suicide, and homicide death. *Evaluation Review* 21: 43–57.

Stahre, M. A., Brewer, R. D., Fonseca, V. P. & Naimi, T. S. (2009). Binge drinking among U.S. active-duty military personnel. *American Journal of Preventive Medicine* 36: 208–217.

Stecker, T., Fortney, J. C., Hamilton, F. & Ajzen, I. (2007). An assessment of beliefs about veterans who served in Iraq. *Psychiatric Services* 58: 1358–1361.

Stockard, J. & O'Brien, R. M. (2006). Cohort variation in suicide rates among families of nations: An analysis of cohorts born from 1875 through 1985. *International Journal of Comparative Sociology* 47: 5–33.

Strauss, J. L., Calhoun, P. S., Marx, C. E., Stechuchak, K. M., Oddone, E. Z., Swartz, M. S., et al. (2006). Comorbid posttraumatic stress disorder is associated with suicidality in male veterans with schizophrenia or schizoaffective disorder. *Schizophrenia Research* 84: 165–169.

Sullivan, P. (2007). Post traumatic stress disorder and personality disorders: Challenges for the U.S. Department of Veterans Affairs. July 25. http://veterans.house.gov/hearings/hearing.aspx?NewsID=45 (accessed October 6, 2010).

Sundararaman, R., Panangala, S. V. & Lister, S. A. (2008). Suicide prevention among veterans. CRS report for Congress. http://i.a.cnn.net/cnn/2007/images/05/04/mhat.iv.report.pdf (accessed October 6, 2010).

Suominen, K., Isometsä, E., Ostamo, A. & Lönnqvist, J. (2004a) Level of suicidal intent predicts overall mortality and suicide after attempted suicide: A 12-year follow-up study. *BMC Psychiatry* 4, no. 11: 1–7.

Suominen, K., Isometsä, E., Suokas, J., Haukka, J., Achte, K. & Lönnqvist, J. (2004b). Completed suicide after a suicide attempts: A 37-year follow-up study. *American Journal of Psychiatry* 161: 563–564.

Tanielian, T. & Jaycox, L. H. (2008). Invisible wounds of war: Psychological and cognitive injuries, their consequences, and services to assist recovery. Rand Center for Military Health Policy Research. http://www.rand.org/pubs/monographs/MG720/ (accessed October 6, 2010).

Thompson, R., Kane, V., Cook, J. M., Greenstein, R., Walker, P. & Woody, G. (2006). Suicidal ideation in veterans receiving treatment for opiate dependence. *Journal of Psychoactive Drugs* 38: 149–156.

Thompson, R., Katz, I. R., Kane, V. R. & Sayers, S. L. (2002). Cause of death in veterans receiving general medical and mental health care. *Journal of Nervous and Mental Disease* 190: 789–792.

Thoresen, S. & Mehlum, L. (2006). Suicide in peacekeepers: Risk factors for suicide versus accidental death. *Suicide and Life-Threatening Behavior* 36: 432–442.

Thoresen, S., Mehlum, L. & Moller, B. (2003). Suicide in peacekeepers: A cohort study of mortality from suicide in 22,275 Norwegian veterans from international peacekeeping operations. *Social Psychiatry and Psychiatric Epidemiology* 38: 605–610.

Thoresen, S., Mehlum, L., Røysamb, E. & Tønnessen, A. (2006). Risk factors for completed suicides in veterans of peacekeeping: Repatriation, negative life events, and marital status. *Archives of Suicide Research* 10: 353–363.

Tiet, Q. Q., Finney, J. W. & Moos, R. H. (2006). Recent sexual abuse, physical abuse, and suicide attempts among male veterans seeking psychiatric treatment. *Psychiatric Services* 57: 107–113.

Tiet, Q. Q., Ilgen, M. A., Byrnes, H. F. & Moss, R. H. (2006). Suicide attempts among substance use disorder patients: Steps towards a decision tree. *Alcoholism, Clinical and Experimental Research* 30: 998–1005.

Timmermans, S. (2006). The fifty-one percent rule of suicide. In S. Timmermans (Ed.), *Postmortem: How medical examiners explain suspicious deaths* (pp. 74–112). Chicago: University of Chicago Press.

Turner, A. P., Williams, R. H., Bowen, J. D., Kivlahan, D. R. & Haselkorn, J. K. (2006). Suicidal ideation in multiple sclerosis. *Archives of Physical Medicine and Rehabilitation* 87: 1073–1078.

Turvey, C., Stromquist, A., Kelly, K., Zwerling, C. & Merchant, J. (2002). Financial loss and suicidal ideation in a rural community sample. *Acta Psychiatrica Scandinavica* 106: 373–380.

Tyson, A. S. (2008). Soldiers' suicide rate on pace to set record. *Washington Post*, September 5.

Tyson, A. S. (2009). Military investigates West Point suicides. *Washington Post*, January 30.

U.S. Army. (2010). Army health promotion, risk reduction, suicide prevention report. usarmy.vo.llnwd.net/e1/HPRRSP (accessed October 6, 2010).

U.S. Department of Defense. (2005). Pre- and post-deployment health assessments, US armed forces, January 2003–August 2005. *Medical Surveillance Monthly Report*, volume 11. Washington, DC: Army Medical Surveillance Activity.

U.S. Department of Veterans Affairs. (2001). National survey of veterans final report. http://www1.va.gov/vetdata (accessed October 6, 2010).

U.S. Department of Veterans Affairs. (2008). Report of the Blue Ribbon Work Group on suicide prevention in the veteran population. June 30. http://www.mentalhealth.va.gov/suicide_prevention (accessed October 6, 2010).

U. S. Department of Veterans Affairs, Office of Inspector General. (2007). *Implementing VHA's mental health strategic plan initiatives for suicide prevention.* Washington, DC: Department of Veterans Affairs.

Waller, S. J., Lyons, J. S. & Costantini-Ferrando, M. F. (1999). Impact of comorbid affective and alcohol use disorders on suicidal ideation and attempts. *Journal of Clinical Psychology* 55: 585–595.

Weissman, M. M., Bland, R. C., Canino, G. J., Greenwald, S., Hwu, H. G., Joyce, P. R., et al. (1999). Prevalence of suicide ideation and suicide attempts in nine countries. *Psychological Medicine* 29: 9–17.

Zivin, K., Kim, H. M., McCarthy, J. F., Austin, K. L., Hoggatt, K. J., Walters, H., et al. (2007). Suicide mortality among individuals receiving treatment for depression in the Veterans Affairs health system: Associations with patient and treatment setting characteristics. *American Journal of Public Health* 97: 2193–2198.

Chapter 5

VA Healthcare for Women Veterans Experiencing Trauma

Carole A. Goguen

Women in the Military

Women have served on the battlefields as members of the U.S. military since the founding of our country. Records from the Revolutionary and Civil Wars indicate that women enlisted using male pseudonyms and served in battle alongside the male soldiers. At the beginning of World War II women officially entered military service through the newly created Women's Army Auxiliary Corps (later the Women's Army Corps), the Women's Naval Reserve, and the Marine Corps Women's Reserve. Roles for women in the military were limited, yet many were exposed to combat (primarily as nurses) as a function of their military assignment. After the war the Women's Armed Services Act of 1948 allowed women serving in the Women's Naval Reserve and the Marine Corps Women's Reserve to be fully integrated into armed forces units. In 1978 the Women's Army Corps was disbanded as a separate entity of the U.S. Army. Since World War II, women military personnel have served in armed conflicts including Korea, Vietnam, and the Persian Gulf (e.g., Holm 1993; Thomas 1978; Trowell-Harris 2004).

In recent years the roles of military women have been expanded, including combat positions and combat-support positions located in combat zones. With women's increasing role in combat and combat-support positions, they are encountering greater exposure to combat-related traumas, including firefights, handling human remains, and explosions such as mortar attacks and improvised explosive devices (IED) (e.g., Trowell-Harris 2004; Vogt et al.

2011). However, a greater challenge to military women is exposure to military sexual trauma (MST).

Military sexual trauma is defined by Section 1720 D of Title 38 of the U.S. Code as "psychological trauma, which in the judgment of a VA mental health professional, resulted from a physical assault of a sexual nature, battery of a sexual nature, or sexual harassment which occurred while the veteran was serving on active duty or active duty for training." Sexual harassment, included in the definition of MST, is defined as "repeated, unsolicited verbal or physical contact of a sexual nature which is threatening in character."

In addition to being physically forced into sexual activities, as occurs in sexual assault, rape, etc., MST includes coercion into sexual activities using threats of negative consequences such as threats to safety or to professional position, as well as implied promises of better treatment or faster promotions in exchange for sex. Furthermore, sexual activities performed while unable to consent, such as while intoxicated, also constitute MST, as do unwanted sexual touching or grabbing, offensive remarks about a person's body or sexual activities, etc.

Department of Veterans Affairs Policies

The public as a whole became aware of MST in 1991 after it was reported in the media that eighty-three women (including officers) and seven men were sexually assaulted during the Tailhook Symposium (e.g., Borkowski 1994). Beginning in 1992, the U.S. Congress passed several laws directing the Department of Veterans Affairs (VA) to provide outreach and treatment for the psychological and physical aftermaths of MST. In addition, VA issued several directives addressing MST issues (see appendix A).

Challenges

Identification and Outreach

Once Congress provided the authorization for VA to offer outreach and treatment for MST, the first task was (and continues to be) to identify veterans who had experienced MST. VA has instituted a process by which every veteran is screened for MST (Department of Veterans Affairs 2010). However, many veterans are reluctant to report MST even after leaving the military. Also, the screening is conducted only once. This is problematic because a degree of trust is often required for a veteran to make such a sensitive disclosure, and the screening is conducted soon after the veteran begins receiving services at VA. In addition, VA is currently providing services to reservists who may be subjected to MST.

MST Sequelae

Common mental health problems encountered by women who had experienced MST include post-traumatic stress disorder (PTSD), panic disorder, generalized anxiety disorder, depressive disorders, eating disorders, and substance use disorders (e.g., Dutra et al. 2011). In addition, common medical problems include chronic pain (low back pain, headaches, etc.), irritable bowel syndrome, chronic fatigue, menstrual disorders, pelvic pain, obesity, smoking, and sedentary lifestyles (e.g., Suris & Lind 2008). If the treating clinician determines that a physical condition is MST-related, treatment for the condition is also provided at no cost to the veteran.

Unfortunately, features of common medical examinations often replicate aspects of the trauma and may trigger significant emotional reactions. Potential triggers include being in an enclosed examining room; exposure of the woman's body; pelvic, oral, or rectal examinations; medical personnel standing behind her; and physical/chemical restraints. These factors can cause women veterans to forgo necessary and potentially life-saving examinations or procedures.

Treatment

In 2008 VA issued a revision of the *Veterans Health Administration Handbook* to include the "Uniform Mental Health Services in VA Medical Centers and Clinics." With regard to MST, it specifies the following:

- Mental health–related services that must be available at every VA facility are described.

- Veterans who request treatment must be provided free care for mental and physical health conditions related to MST. Determination of whether the care is MST-related or not is made by the clinician providing care and is indicated by checking the MST box on the encounter form for the visit.

- Veterans may be eligible for free MST-related care even if they are otherwise ineligible for VA services.

- Every Veterans Integrated Service Network (VISN) must provide access to residential programs that can provide care for conditions resulting from MST.

- Non-VA medical care (known as fee basis) is permissible if clinical, resource, or geographic reasons make it not feasible to provide counseling in a VA facility.

- Every Veterans Administration Medical Center (VAMC) must have an MST coordinator, who monitors and ensures that national and VISN-level policies related to MST screening, education and training, and treatment are implemented at the facility; serves as a point person and a source of information and problem solving for MST-related issues at the facility; and establishes and monitors mechanisms to ensure that all veterans are screened for MST and have access to treatment for conditions related to MST.

- Evidence-based mental healthcare must be available to all veterans with mental health conditions related to MST.

- When clinically indicated, facilities are strongly encouraged to give veterans the option of being assigned a same-sex mental health provider (or opposite-sex provider if the MST involved a same-sex perpetrator).

In addition, VA's National Center for PTSD has established a national training program in evidence-based treatment for mental health issues, including post-traumatic stress disorder (PTSD) and depression. Prolonged exposure therapy (PE) (see box 5.1) and cognitive processing therapy (CPT) (see box 5.2) are the evidenced-based treatments the National Center for PTSD is providing for the treatment of PTSD. Each program includes training materials with specific components on MST-related PTSD.

Box 5.1. Prolonged Exposure Therapy (PE)

Prolonged exposure (PE) is a . . . therapy that works for many people who have experienced trauma. It has four main parts:

- Education: PE starts with education about the treatment. You will learn as well about common trauma reactions and PTSD. Education allows you to learn more about your symptoms. It also helps you understand the goals of the treatment. This education provides the basis for the next sessions.

- Breathing: Breathing retraining is a skill that helps you relax. When people become anxious or scared, their breathing often changes. Learning how to control your breathing can help in the short term to manage immediate distress.

- Real-world practice: Exposure practice with real-world situations is called *in vivo exposure*. You practice approaching situations that are safe but that you may have been avoiding because they are related to the trauma. An example would be a veteran who avoids driving since he experienced a roadside bomb while deployed. In the same way, a sexual trauma survivor may avoid getting close to others. This type of

(Continued)

exposure practice helps your trauma-related distress lessen over time. When distress goes down, you can gain more control over your life.

- Talking through the trauma: Talking about your trauma memory over and over with your therapist is called *imaginal exposure*. Talking through the trauma will help you get more control of your thoughts and feelings about the trauma. You will learn that you do not have to be afraid of your memories. This may be hard at first, and it might seem strange to think about stressful things on purpose. Many people feel better over time, though, as they do this. Talking through the trauma helps you make sense of what happened and have fewer negative thoughts about the trauma.

With the help of your therapist, you can change how you react to stressful memories. In PE, you work with your therapist to approach trauma-related situations and memories at a comfortable pace. Usually, you start with things that are less distressing and move toward things that are more distressing. A round of PE therapy most often involves meeting alone with a therapist for about eight to fifteen sessions.

With time and practice, you will be able to see that you can master stressful situations. The goal is that YOU, not your memories, can control what you do in your life and how you feel. Therapy helps you to get your life back after you have been through a trauma.

PE has been shown to be one of the most effective treatments for PTSD. For this reason, VA's Office of Mental Health Services has rolled out a national PE training program. VA providers throughout the country will be trained in how to use PE treatment. The providers will at first be supervised as they use these treatments in actual cases. Then they will be asked to use PE in their routine clinical care. Others will be selected and trained as consultants.

From the National Center for PTSD Web site, ttp://www.ptsd.va.gov/public/pages/prolonged-exposure-therapy.asp.

Box 5.2. Cognitive Processing Therapy (CPT)

Cognitive processing therapy (CPT) helps by giving you a new way to handle these distressing thoughts and to gain an understanding of these events. By using the skills learned in this therapy, you can learn why recovery from traumatic events has been hard for you. CPT helps you

(Continued)

learn how going through a trauma changed the way you look at the world, yourself, and others. The way we think and look at things directly affects how we feel and act.

CPT has four main parts:

- **Learning about your PTSD symptoms:** CPT begins with education about your specific PTSD symptoms and how the treatment can help. The therapy plan will be reviewed and the reasons for each part of the therapy will be explained. You will be able to ask questions and to know exactly what you are going to be doing in this therapy. You will also learn why these skills may help.

- **Becoming aware of thoughts and feelings:** Next, CPT focuses on helping you become more aware of your thoughts and feelings. When bad things happen, we want to make sense of why they happened. An example would be a veteran who thinks to himself or herself, "I should have known that this would happen." Sometimes we get stuck on these thoughts. In CPT you will learn how to pay attention to your thoughts about the trauma and how they make you feel. You'll then be asked to step back and think about how your trauma is affecting you now. This will help you think about your trauma in a different way than you did before. It can be done either by writing or by talking to your therapist about it.

- **Learning skills:** After you become more aware of your thoughts and feelings, you will learn skills to help you question or challenge your thoughts. You will do this with the help of worksheets. You will be able to use these skills to decide the way YOU want to think and feel about your trauma. These skills can also help you deal with other problems in your day-to-day life.

- **Understanding changes in beliefs:** Finally, you will learn about the common changes in beliefs that occur after going through trauma. Many people have problems understanding how to live in the world after trauma. Your beliefs about safety, trust, control, self-esteem, other people, and relationships can change after trauma. In CPT you will get to talk about your beliefs in these different areas. You will learn to find a better balance between the beliefs you had before and after your trauma.

You and your therapist will work together to help you learn a new way of dealing with your trauma. In CPT you will work closely with your therapist to reach your goals. You will be meeting with him or her on a regular basis for twelve sessions. During your therapy you will also have the

(Continued)

chance to practice your new skills outside of your therapy meetings. The more you practice your new skills, the sooner they will begin working for you. By choosing to approach your experiences in a new and different way, you will be able to decide how your past affects your future.

From the National Center for PTSD Web site http://www.ptsd.va.gov/public/pages/cognitive_processing_therapy.asp.

MST Residential Treatment Programs

The sole purpose of MST or sexual trauma specific residential treatment programs is the treatment of sexual trauma; they include trauma programs with a specific sexual trauma treatment track and the availability of two or more staff members possessing sexual trauma treatment expertise. Although the majority of the MST residential programs are specifically residential/inpatient programs, others are located in outpatient facilities that have residential/inpatient beds available.

Following are locations of MST residential treatment programs:

Boston, MA (2)	Batavia, NY
Lyons, NJ	Baltimore, MD
Augusta, GA	Bay Pines, FL
Cincinnati, OH	Milwaukee, WI
North Chicago, IL	Topeka, KS
Temple, TX	Menlo Park, CA
Long Beach, CA (primary program + aftercare)	

Issues

Some women veterans, especially earlier-era women veterans, do not self-identify as being veterans. They may lack knowledge of their VA healthcare benefits, especially benefits related to MST. Many women are primary caregivers and are not able to find adequate childcare in order to seek treatment. They may perceive that VA healthcare provided to women is inadequate or substandard. And increasingly women veterans are dealing with homelessness.

Resources

Women's Mental Health Services: "There are far more men than women Veterans in the VA system. For this reason, many women Veterans are not aware of resources offered just for them. Many women Veterans prefer treatment with other women. Research shows that people often do better in treatment with others that are more like them. As a result, mental health services just for women are offered in many VA's across the country." http://www.ptsd.va.gov/public/pages/womens_mental_health_services.asp.

Women's Trauma Recovery Program (WTRP): "More than a decade ago, the Department of Veterans Affairs opened the National Women's Trauma Recovery Program (WTRP) as part of the National Center for PTSD at Menlo Park, CA. The WTRP, designed to treat women veterans with post traumatic stress disorder (PTSD), is the first residential program of its kind and is open to women across the country. Many of the women who are referred to the program were sexually assaulted during their military service and suffer what is now referred to as Military Sexual Trauma (MST)." http://www.womenvetsptsd.va.gov/.

PTSD Treatment Programs in the U.S. Department of Veterans Affairs: "Each medical center within VA provides treatment for Veterans with PTSD. Plus, the VA provides nearly 200 specialized PTSD treatment programs. Not all VA's offer the same programs, though. Your doctor can help you decide which program is best for you. This fact sheet describes the main types of VA programs that offer PTSD treatment."

Vet Centers: "Vet Centers provide readjustment counseling and outreach services to all veterans who served in any combat zone. Services are also available for their family members for military related issues. Veterans have earned these benefits through their service and all are provided at no cost to the veteran or family. No information about your treatment will be given to any person or agency (including VA) without your consent."

Brief description of VA benefits:

Directory of veterans' service organizations: http://www1.va.gov/vso/.

An MST coordinator or a women veterans program manager can be contacted through your local VA Medical Center.

References

Borkowski, M. (1994). Chronology of a scandal that tarnished the navy. *New York Times*, February 9. http://www.nytimes.com/1994/02/09/us/chronology-of-a-scandal-that-tarnished-the-navy.html.

Department of Veterans Affairs. (1995). Sexual trauma counseling, care, and services. *VHA Directive 10-95-030*. Washington, DC.

Department of Veterans Affairs. (1998). Extension of VA's authority to provide counseling services and treatment to veterans for sexual trauma. *VHA Directive 98-058*. Washington, DC.

Department of Veterans Affairs. (1999). Military sexual trauma software mandate. *VHA Directive 99-039*. Washington, DC.

Department of Veterans Affairs. (2000). Sexual trauma counseling section of the Veterans Millennium Health Care Act, public law 106-117 (RCN 10-0905). *VHA Directive 2000-008*. Washington, DC.

Department of Veterans Affairs. (2005). Military sexual trauma counseling. *VHA Directive 2005-015*. Washington, DC.

Department of Veterans Affairs. (2008). Uniform mental health services in VA medical centers and clinics. *VHA handbook 1160.01*. Washington DC.

Department of Veterans Affairs. (2009). Military sexual trauma counseling. *VHA Directive 2009-012*. Washington, DC.

Department of Veterans Affairs. (2010). Military sexual trauma (MST) programming. *VHA Directive 2010-33*. Washington, DC.

Dutra, L., Grubbs, K., Greene, C., Trego, L. L., McCartin, T. L., Kloezeman, K.,& Morland, L. (2011). Women at war: Implications for mental health. *Journal of Trauma & Dissociation* 12: 25–37. doi.org/10.1080/15299732.2010.496141.

Holm, J. (1993). *Women in the military: An unfinished revolution*. Rev. ed. Novato, CA: Presidio Press.

Suris, A. & Lind, L. (2008). Military sexual trauma: A review of prevalence and associated health consequences in veterans. *Trauma, Violence, and Abuse* 9: 250–269.

Thomas, P. J. (1978). *The role of women in the military: Australia, Canada, the United Kingdom, and the United States*. Special Report 78-10. San Diego, CA: Navy Personnel Research and Development Center.

Trowell-Harris, I. (2004). Women veterans: A proud heritage. In *Proceedings from the National Summit on Women Veterans' Issues*. http://www.va.gov/womenvet/docs/SUMMIT_04_web_copy.pdf.

Under Secretary for Health. (1997). Information letter IL-10-97-037.

Veterans Benefits. (2007, 2009). 38 U.S.C. § 1720D.

Veterans Health Care Act of 1992. Pub. L. No. 102-585, 106 Stat. 4943.

Veterans Health Programs Extension Act of 1994. Pub. L. No. 103-452, 108 Stat. 4783.

Veterans Health Programs Improvement Act of 2004. Pub. L. No. 108-422, 118 Stat. 2379.

Veterans Programs Enhancement Act of 1998. Pub. L. No. 105-368, 112 Stat. 3315.

Vogt, D., Vaughn, R., Glickman, M. E., Schultz, M., Drainoni, M., Elwy, R. & Eisen, S. (2011). Gender differences in combat-related stressors and their association with postdeployment mental health in a nationally representative sample of U.S. OEF/OIF veterans. *Journal of Abnormal Psychology* 120, no. 4: 797–806.

Appendix A: MST-Related Laws, Directives, and Policies

Note: Provisions that were changed in later public law, directives, or policies are struck through.

1992: Public Law 102-585

- Added section 1720D to Chapter 17 of Title 38 ("Veterans Benefits"; 38 C.F.R. 17), U.S. Code of Federal Regulations to authorize VA to provide outreach and counseling (up to December 31, 1995) to help ~~women~~ veterans overcome "psychological trauma" from a "physical assault of a sexual nature, battery of a sexual nature, or sexual harassment" that occurred while the veteran was serving on active duty.

- Sexual harassment was defined as "repeated, unsolicited verbal or physical contact of a sexual nature which is threatening in character."

- The Secretary was to "give priority to the establishment and operation of the program to provide counseling."

- The veteran was required to seek counseling within two years of discharge.

- Treatment could last for up to a year.

- Mandated education of "mental health professionals and... other health care personnel" on MST issues.

1994: Public Law 103-452

- Amended section 1720D of 38 C.F.R. 17 to extend VA's authorization to provide treatment through December 31. 1998.

- Repealed requirement that veteran seek counseling within two years of discharge.

- Expanded treatment to men.

- Expanded treatment to physical conditions resulting from MST.

- Changed outpatient sexual trauma counseling, care, and services to priority I.

- Repealed limits on length of treatment.

1995: VA Directive 10-95-030

- Implemented P.L. 103-452.

- Made MST-related "counseling, care, and services" free of charge. However, "medication copayments will be charged for services provided for non-service-connected conditions."

1997: Under Secretary for Health's Information Letter IL-10-97-037

- Based on a General Counsel Opinion (VAOPGCADV 17-97), clarified the eligibility rules for veterans seeking treatment for MST.

  - Persons are eligible for MST care and counseling services if they meet the definition of "veteran" in 38 U.S.C. § 1720D. This includes reservists and members of the National Guard who were activated to full-time duty status in the armed forces.

  - No minimum length of service requirements apply.

  - Veterans need not have filed a claim for service-connected disability.

1998: Public Law 105-368 [section 902 on Acrobat page 46 of this document]

- Amended § 1720D of 38 C.F.R. 17 to extend VA's authorization to provide treatment through December 31, 2001.

1998: VA Directive 98-058

- Notified VA healthcare personnel that VA's authority to provide treatment had been extended through December 31, 2001 (as per P.L. 105-368).

1999: Public Law 106-117 ("Millennium Bill") [section 115 on Acrobat page 14 of this document]

- Amended § 1720D of 38 C.F.R. 17 to extend VA's authorization to provide treatment through December 31, 2004.
- Changed wording from VA "may" provide care to "shall" provide care.
- Required outreach to veterans about the MST-related counseling and treatment available, particularly in collaboration with DoD.
- Required VA to submit reports to Congress on outreach activities specified in this public law and on the number of veterans receiving MST-related counseling.

1999: VA Directive 99-039

- Instituted a nationwide system ("MST software application") to "indicate a veteran's claim of MST; indicate if a veteran's treatment is related to MST; and generate statistical and demographic reports related to MST."
- Stated that it is "important" that all primary care and behavioral health providers screen for MST.

2000: VA Directive 2000-008

- Provided a definition for MST, based on P.L. 102-585: "The law defines sexual trauma as sexual harassment, sexual assault, rape, and other acts of violence. It further defines sexual harassment as repeated, unsolicited verbal or physical contact of a sexual nature, which is threatening in nature."
- Given the need for "confidentiality and sensitivity to the impact of MST on veterans," mandated that all staff receive education on MST-related issues.
- Mandated screening all veterans for MST.
- Per the Millennium Bill, required outreach, particularly in collaboration with DoD, to help overcome barriers to treatment.
- Required all facilities to designate an MST coordinator.
- Required all facilities to implement the "MST software" and "track MST patients."
- Required monitoring treatment rates for MST, aggregated by gender.

2004: Public Law 108-422 [section 301 on Acrobat page 4 of this document]

- Amended § 1720D of 38 C.F.R. 17 to make VA's authority to provide sexual trauma counseling to veterans permanent.
- Extended MST treatment to active duty for training (ADUTRA) service members.

2005: VA Directive 2005-015

- Specified that medical center directors are responsible for appointing a designated MST coordinator.
- Medical center directors must also ensure that a "MST Counselor(s) or Team" is available so that all enrolled veterans are screened for MST.
- Mandated "necessary staff education and training."
- Scheduling for outpatient MST-related care should be within 30 days, consistent with VHA performance standards of scheduling for special populations and mental health clinics.
- Required documentation of screening, referral, and treatment for MST-related care, aggregated by gender via use of the MST software and MST clinical reminder.
- Specified that even veterans who are otherwise ineligible for VA healthcare benefits based on length of military service may be provided MST-related care.

- Stated that veterans receiving MST-related counseling and treatment should not be billed for inpatient, outpatient, or pharmaceutical copayments.
- Veterans "need to be informed of their eligibility to file a claim for service connected disability compensation" and told how to learn more about how to do this.

2007: Code of Federal Regulations, Title 38, § 1720D

- Title 38 description of coverage of veterans' benefits related to MST, as last updated in 2007.

2009: VA Directive 2009-012

- Specifies that MST-related care is not subject to outpatient copayments

Reprinted by permission of Margaret Bell, PhD, Education, Resources, and Practices, Military Sexual Trauma (MST) Intranet Resources, VA Office of Mental Health Services.

Treating Substance Use Disorders within the VA Healthcare System

Stephen Tracy, Sara Tavakoli,
Simona Stolpner, and Jodie Trafton

Introduction

Drug and alcohol misuse, abuse, or dependence is a problem for a large proportion of veterans who seek care from the Department of Veterans Affairs (VA). Findings from the Substance Abuse and Mental Health Services Administration (SAMHSA) show that alcohol misuse and illicit drug use occur at greater rates among veterans than in the civilian population (Office of Applied Studies 2005). High levels of combat exposure, perceived threat to life, and experiences of abuse contribute to higher incidences of psychological problems, such as post-traumatic stress disorder (PTSD), depression, and alcoholism, in the veteran population (King et al. 1995).

The Department of Veterans Affairs operates the largest substance use disorder (SUD) treatment system in the United States, and every VA Medical Center (VAMC) offers a variety of SUD diagnostic and treatment services. The SUD treatment system offers services on a continuum, ranging from standard and intensive outpatient treatment to residential and inpatient services. To treat SUDs, VA utilizes various treatment modalities, including evidence-based psychosocial interventions and evidence-based pharmacological treatments. In addition, VA is equipped to provide screening, diagnosis, and treatment outside the specialty SUD treatment setting, in primary care and/or general mental health clinics.

Extensive research and development endeavors, clinical training practices, and recent funding opportunities have enabled VA to serve as a model for evidence-based SUD care. This chapter explores the detection and treatment of SUDs among veteran populations within VA. Specifically, the chapter summarizes (1) the history of specialized VA SUD treatment, (2) screening and initial assessment of substance use, (3) management of substance misuse and SUDs in primary care and general mental healthcare settings, (4) management of SUDs in specialty settings, (5) pharmacotherapy for substance dependence, (6) stabilization and withdrawal management, and (7) new directions in meeting the changing needs of the veteran population.

History of Specialized VA SUD Treatment

During the past twenty years, VA's SUD treatment system has changed substantially. Under the Anti-Drug Abuse Act of 1988 (Pub. L. No. 100-690) and the president's drug control policy, VA began receiving recurring funds in 1990 to enhance its SUD treatment program. From 1990 to 1994, the number of SUD treatment programs and specialty SUD treatment staff in VA grew to the highest number in its history. The majority of this SUD programming was delivered in an inpatient or residential setting.

In 1995 VA underwent a transformation of its vast healthcare system. It was reorganized into twenty-two Veterans Integrated Service Networks (VISNs), decentralizing the funding of services from VA headquarters to each VISN and its affiliated facility director (in FY 2002, two VISNs were consolidated, creating a total of twenty-one VISNs). Following the nationwide shift to managed care, VA was converted from a hospital-based specialty healthcare system to one focused on primary care delivered in outpatient settings (Iglehart 1996). The SUD services were reorganized in a parallel manner, with each VISN receiving the mandate and autonomy to shift its focus from hospital-based inpatient care to less expensive outpatient care (Kizer, Fonseca & Long 1997). This produced an uneven system of SUD treatment, with variation in the extensiveness of SUD treatment services provided across VISNs (Humphreys et al. 1997). Consistent with trends observed outside VA and a shift toward less costly outpatient care, spending on SUD treatment programming in VA decreased by 41 percent (Chen, Wagner & Barnett 2001).

Since 2000 VA has taken steps to increase SUD treatment services and ensure consistent availability of evidence-based treatments across facilities. In 2000 funds were allocated under the Veterans Millennium Health Care and Benefits Act with the specific purpose of hiring additional SUD treatment staff to increase treatment capacity. In an effort to improve the quality and availability of mental health services nationwide, the President's New Freedom Commission on Mental Health (2003) called for fundamental changes to the nation's mental health treatment system. In response to the commission's recommendations, VA formulated and disseminated central guidance and implemented broad policy changes in an effort to fill gaps in available treatment services and continue improving mental healthcare services, including SUD care for veterans. Specifically, VA Secretary Anthony Principi approved the Mental Health Strategic Plan (MHSP), which included over 200 initiatives (Greenberg & Rosenheck 2009).

To actualize the recommendations in the MHSP, VA undertook the Mental Health Enhancement Initiative (MHEI) in 2005. As part of this initiative, VA utilized recurring funds from 2005 to 2009 to expand and improve its SUD treatment system. Specifically, facilities received funds to hire additional SUD treatment staff. Funding from the MHEI had been authorized to provide enhancements in various capacities, including establishing evidence-based opiate agonist treatment, integration of SUD services into mental health and primary care settings, and establishing new outpatient and residential SUD treatment programs.

To ensure that all veterans have access to evidence-based clinical services for VA mental health and SUD treatment regardless of where they receive care, the Department of Veterans Affairs issued *Handbook 1160.01: Uniform Mental Health Services in VA Medical Centers and Clinics* (also referred to as the *Handbook*) in 2008. The *Handbook* translates the MHSP into an operational, point of service, programmatic package of approximately 400 mental health service guidelines. It clearly defines specific requirements for mental health and SUD-related services that must be *provided* (i.e., those services that must be delivered when clinically needed to patients receiving healthcare at a facility by appropriate staff located at that facility) and those that must be *available* (i.e., those that must be made accessible when clinically needed to patients receiving healthcare from VA). The overall objectives of the *Handbook* include expanding access and capacity, integrating mental health and primary care, transformation toward a recovery and rehabilitation model, and implementing evidence-based care in practice.

In 2009 VA collaborated with the Department of Defense (DoD) to revise the *Clinical Practice Guidelines for the Management of Substance Use Disorders* (*SUD Guidelines*). The purpose of these guidelines is to reduce current unwarranted practice variation and provide facilities with a structured framework to help improve patient outcomes, provide evidence-based recommendations to assist providers and their patients in the decision-making process, and identify outcome measures to support the development of evidence-based practice (Department of Defense & Department of Veterans Affairs 2009).

In an effort to facilitate access to treatment and improve quality of care for patients with SUDs, VA utilizes program evaluation, research, and quality improvement strategies to guide policies and clinical practices. One example of an entity engaged in such endeavors is the VA Office of Mental Health Services' Program Evaluation and Resource Center (PERC), which conducts evaluations of VA SUD services and monitors care received by VA patients who have SUDs within VA's national healthcare system. Another example is the Northeast Program Evaluation Center (NEPEC), which evaluates VA residential treatment services, including substance abuse residential rehabilitation treatment programs (SARRTP), substance abuse domiciliaries (SA Dom), and specialized SUD tracks in general mental health rehabilitation treatment programs. Two Centers for Excellence in Substance Abuse Treatment and Education (CESATE) conduct and evaluate demonstration projects, disseminate treatments, and conduct clinical training. The Health Services Research and Development Service (HSR&D) works to identify and evaluate innovative strategies that lead to accessible, high-quality, cost-effective care for veterans in various treatment settings. One HSR&D Center of Excellence, the Center for Health Care Evaluation (CHCE), focuses on health services research in areas of treatment of substance use and psychiatric disorders, clinical decision making, screening and diagnostic assessment, and organization and delivery of healthcare services. In addition, VA's SUD Quality Enhancement Research Initiative (SUD QUERI) works to improve detection and management of alcohol misuse in primary care, promote evidence-based specialty care for patients with SUD, and improve services for patients with SUD and co-occurring conditions.

Screening and Initial Assessment for Substance Use

Detection of substance misuse in patients is an important first step to high-quality SUD care. Although SUD specialty services focus on providing care for patients whose use of illicit drugs and/or alcohol meets diagnostic criteria for abuse or dependence, the full spectrum of care for substance-use-related problems begins with screening and includes identifying and providing empirically based brief interventions to patients who may not meet diagnostic criteria for SUD, but whose use of substances puts them at risk for developing a SUD or other health problems.

Screening for Alcohol Misuse in Primary Care and General Mental Healthcare Settings

Alcohol misuse, otherwise known as unhealthy alcohol use, ranges from drinking above recommended limits (i.e., "risky drinking") to severe alcohol dependence. The majority of patients with alcohol misuse are not alcohol dependent. Even so, there are such a large number of nondependent patients with unhealthy drinking habits that they account for most of the morbidity and mortality attributed to drinking (Institute of Medicine 1990).

The VA *Handbook* requires that veterans be screened for alcohol misuse during their initial medical visit and at least annually thereafter in primary care, mental healthcare, and other appropriate medical specialty care settings. Annual screening of all patients for alcohol misuse is recommended based on evidence that alcohol screening followed by brief alcohol counseling is effective for reducing drinking. The SUD guidelines recommend utilization of the three-item Alcohol Use Disorders Identification Test (AUDIT-C), a validated screening questionnaire, to identify past-year alcohol misuse. The AUDIT-C was evaluated in VA patients and has since been validated in other U.S. clinical populations (Bradley et al. 2007).

To prompt alcohol screening in all VA patients, in FY 2002 VA made the percentage of eligible patients screened annually for alcohol misuse with the AUDIT-C a performance measure affecting compensation of VISN and facility management (Bradley et al. 2006). In addition, VA developed an electronic medical record–based clinical reminder that reminds clinicians to conduct the AUDIT-C when they view the record of a patient who is due for screening. With this attention and systemwide support, annual screening for alcohol misuse is now conducted at rates well over 95 percent in VA facilities nationwide.

Screening for alcohol misuse in primary care and general mental healthcare settings offers an opportunity to identify those patients who may benefit from brief alcohol counseling interventions and patients for whom referral to specialty SUD care is warranted. For nondependent patients with alcohol misuse, early intervention may reduce the probability of developing dependence and reduce alcohol-related problems. Thus, screening ought to identify patients along the entire spectrum of alcohol misuse, from those who drink above recommended limits to those with severe alcohol dependence.

If patients screen positive for unhealthy alcohol use, they must receive further assessments to determine the level of misuse and establish a diagnosis. Diagnostic assessment can be conducted by primary care or other medical providers, mental health providers, or specialists in SUDs. Patients diagnosed with SUDs must receive a multidimensional bio-psychosocial assessment to guide patient-centered treatment planning for substance use and any coexisting psychiatric or medical conditions.

There are multiple challenges to identifying veterans who misuse substances. Comparisons with known rates of SUDs indicate that mental health providers may not detect these problems as much as one-third of the time, and that primary care practitioners may fail to detect SUDs in two-thirds of presenting patients (Tracy et al. 2007). These findings replicate other research conducted in VA and non-VA samples suggesting that SUDs are under-detected by healthcare providers (Kirchner et al. 1998). While providers may employ evidence-based screening questions to identify alcohol misuse in veterans, there is currently no equivalent set of questions to identify veterans who misuse drugs. Some veterans who use substances may not admit to substance use, and if they do, they may underreport the quantity and/or frequency of their use.

Efforts by VA to encourage screening appear to be improving the detection of alcohol misuse. The percentage of VA patients diagnosed with a SUD has increased since FY 2002, with the largest increases in the percentage of patients diagnosed with abuse of or dependence on a single substance. Specifically, there have been increases in the percentage of VA patients diagnosed with alcohol or cannabis use disorders without other substance use diagnoses. Use of these substances may be less likely to be identified without active efforts toward detection because patients and providers *may* consider use of these substances more normative.

Population-based screening for drug use disorders (nonalcohol substances) is not evidence-based and is not recommended in the *SUD Guidelines* or the *Handbook*. As an alternative to population-based drug screening, selective case-finding in high-risk populations is required to identify patients who use illicit drugs or misuse prescription or over-the counter agents. These methods must include evaluations of signs and symptoms of substance use in patients with other relevant conditions, such as other mental health disorders and HIV disease. The Department of Veterans Affairs has also developed a brochure for patients encouraging them to self-disclose use of illicit substances to their healthcare providers. According to the *Handbook*, patients who have an indication of an illicit substance-use problem must receive further assessments to determine the level of misuse in order for providers to establish a diagnosis if applicable.

Screening and Treatment for Nicotine Dependence

In recent years VA has taken great interest in screening and treating veterans who are nicotine dependent. Tobacco use screening must now occur during all new patient encounters and at least annually thereafter in primary care, medical specialty care, and general mental health or specialty SUD treatment settings. The recently revised *VA/DoD Clinical Practice Guidelines for Management of Tobacco Use* (2008) takes a public health approach to screening and treating tobacco dependence by recommending that care be provided to the entire population of smokers who seek care at VA.

Because treatment often requires repeated intervention and multiple quit attempts, the *SUD Guidelines* recommend that in addition to counseling and smoking cessation education, evidence-based pharmacotherapy must be made available in the most intensive treatment setting that the veteran is willing to attend. Specifically, nicotine replacement therapy (NRT) involves the use of long-acting nicotine treatment (patch) in combination with short-acting formulation (gum, lozenge, inhaler, or nasal spray). Treatment with NRT prevents severe withdrawal symptoms and controls breakthrough cravings that may lead to potential relapse situations. Based on the overwhelming evidence of the cost-effectiveness of smoking cessation treatment and the revised *VA/DoD Clinical Practice Guidelines for Management of Tobacco Use*, VA is focused on the development, implementation, and evaluation of interventions for increasing the use of evidence-based smoking cessation treatment.

Management of Substance Misuse and SUDs in Primary Care and General Mental Healthcare Settings

Through screening and early intervention, clinicians in primary care and general mental health can act as a gateway to encourage patients to seek appropriate care for substance use problems. The need for coordination of care for co-occurring disorders and patient reluctance to attend specialty SUD treatment because of SUD-related stigma highlight the importance of providing opportunities for SUD interventions in primary care and general mental healthcare settings. In addition to SUD screening, detection, and referral services, the management of SUDs in nonspecialty SUD settings may be beneficial for early intervention for less severe SUDs or chronic disease management for patients unwilling or unable to engage in specialty SUD treatment.

Brief Interventions and Motivational Counseling

Primary care and mental healthcare visits provide important opportunities for initiating interventions to address substance misuse, because providers in these settings are often the first to identify possible substance misuse. When a patient presents to one of these settings and alcohol misuse is detected, the *Handbook* requires that patients receive brief motivational counseling by a healthcare worker with appropriate training in this area, referral to specialty SUD care providers, or other interventions depending on the severity of the condition and the patient's preferences. A brief intervention for alcohol use can be a single session or multiple sessions that include motivational discussion focused on increasing insight and awareness of alcohol use and motivation in the direction of behavior change.

Brief alcohol interventions involve providing feedback to veterans on the medical problems associated with alcohol consumption and advice to either abstain from drinking or drink within recommended limits. Brief intervention for alcohol can be used as a stand-alone treatment and can serve as a conduit for engaging patients in need of more extensive levels of care. For patients who do not respond to brief interventions, comprehensive medical management and monitoring in addition to opportunistic referral to specialty SUD care is the emphasis of treatment. To encourage use of brief interventions in response to alcohol screening, VA has adopted a chart-review-based national performance measure that assesses delivery of brief motivational counseling following detection of alcohol misuse. In addition, VA has funded and is implementing several large-scale training initiatives to educate providers in evidence-based motivational counseling approaches.

Integration and Coordination of Care

Co-occurring disorders (CODs) are common with SUDs and are defined as subclinical or diagnosed medical and/or behavioral health conditions that occur with and influence SUD conditions. The CODs may complicate the treatment of SUDs and compromise the health of patients. Therefore, it is critical that providers identify and document any CODs in patients with SUD.

Traditionally, mental healthcare has been organized around a specific disorder rather than the treatment of CODs (Ridgely, Goldman & Willenbring 1990). A growing body of research demonstrates that integrated services produce better outcomes for individuals with CODs, particularly those with more serious or complex conditions. Integrated service is any process by which mental, medical, health, and SUD services are integrated or combined either at the level of direct contact with the patient or through collaboration between providers or programs serving patients with CODs.

The *Handbook* establishes service requirements enabling veterans to access a specific range of needed mental health and SUD treatment services, regardless of where they live. In 2008 VA allocated funds to address significant gaps in the provision of SUD services outside SUD specialty care settings as well as promote the integration of SUD and mental health treatment. To improve access to SUD services for at-risk or isolated veteran populations, VA has recently funded several initiatives. One such initiative provides a full-time SUD specialist for each "non-SUD" residential rehabilitation treatment program (RRTP) with an average census of at least forty patients; while VA offers care in programs designated as "SUD specific" RRTPs, many patients receiving care in "non-SUD" RRTPs also have SUDs and are at risk for relapse. Services provided by SUD specialists include SUD specific treatment while in the RRTP, relapse prevention services, and arrangement of SUD treatment follow-up services after discharge from the RRTP.

Considering the frequent co-occurrence of SUD problems with PTSD, VA has also assigned a full-time SUD specialist to each of its hospital-level PTSD services or teams. The specialist is an integral member of the PTSD clinical services team and works to integrate SUD care with all other aspects of PTSD care; including identification of veterans in the early stages of SUD or who are at risk for developing a problem and provision of services to prevent SUD.

A third SUD-related initiative assigned a full-time SUD specialist to large community based outpatient clinics (CBOCs) without specialty SUD treatment programming on-site and that are distant from VA medical centers with specialty SUD treatment programming. Specialists assigned to these CBOCs provide SUD treatment services and facilitate coordination among RRTPs, primary care, general mental health, and other SUD treatment programs. Specifically, they are tasked with providing evaluation, diagnosis, and treatment planning services, as well as conducting individual, group, and family treatment for veterans with SUDs and with CODs (Deputy Under Secretary for Health for Operations and Management 2008a).

In efforts to ensure coordination of care, the *SUD Guidelines* recommend that providers in nonspecialty care settings communicate regularly and integrate their care with specialty SUD care services whenever possible. The *Handbook* requires that facility and VISN mental health leadership work in collaboration to ensure integration or coordination in the care of SUDs, other mental health conditions, and other medical problems.

Management of SUD-Related Co-occurring Disorders

Substance use disorders are particularly prevalent in patients who seek care in mental health clinics; studies indicate that approximately 40 to 50 percent of all veterans seen in mental health clinics have a SUD (Timko et al. 2003; Tracy et al. 2007; Gifford, Jaszka & Tracy 2008). In accordance with the *SUD Guidelines*, Gifford, Jaszka, and Tracy (2008) found that a majority of mental health programs sampled conducted SUD screening and ongoing monitoring for alcohol misuse; in addition, almost half of the programs took primary responsibility for treating veterans with both mental health disorders and SUDs, while about a third indicated that their standard protocol is to treat the mental health disorders only and refer patients to other VA specialty programs to receive SUD treatment (Tracy et al. 2007).

To ensure that services are available to all veteran patients, the *Handbook* requires that SUDs must never be a barrier for treatment of patients with other mental health conditions and vice versa. When it is deemed appropriate to delay any specific treatment, other care or interim services must be provided to address the clinical needs of the patient.

Primary Care and Mental Health Integration

One goal of the MHSP was to develop a collaborative care model for mental health disorders that raises mental healthcare to the same level of importance as medical healthcare. In FY 2007 VA set out to integrate mental health into primary care in more than 100 pilot programs. The purpose of this initiative was to promote the effective treatment of common mental health and SUDs into the primary care environment and improve access and quality of care for veterans. To help track pilot program activities, a new DSS identifier code (a VA method to capture workload electronically) for primary care and mental health integration (PC-MHI) was made effective beginning in FY 2008. These pilot programs continued with funding during FY 2008 and FY 2009. Introduction of the *Handbook* in 2008 set further clinical expectations and structural requirements for primary care and mental health integration. The *Handbook* requires that all VAMCs and CBOCs with primary care clinics seeing over 5,000 unique veterans have full-time on-site integrated mental health services in the primary care clinics, utilizing a blended model that includes co-located collaborative care and care management.

Although many patients with a presumptive or possible SUD diagnosis are offered treatment and/or a referral to specialty SUD treatment and are monitored for unstable medical or mental health conditions, some patients may be managed effectively in nonspecialty care and will not require care in a specialty SUD program. In accordance with the *SUD Guidelines*, patients with suspected, presumed, or identified SUD should be provided with an explanation of their medical condition and an outline of their treatment options to allow them the opportunity to make informed decisions regarding their care.

Treating SUDs in VA's Specialty SUD Care Settings

For veterans with presumptive or possible SUD who are referred to specialty SUD care, assessment is the beginning of the therapeutic process. The *Handbook* requires a comprehensive and multidimensional assessment to evaluate the patient's strengths, needs, abilities, and preferences. It is also important to determine the patient's priorities so an initial treatment plan can be developed in a patient-centered manner. Ensuring appropriate housing and access to care is an essential part of the assessment process. The comprehensive intake assessment should include a diagnostic formulation, a summary of past treatment response, and an integrated summary of all clinically relevant information. In addition, the patient's motivational level and personal goals should be taken into consideration when selecting treatment goals and options.

Regarding the determination of patient level of care placement, the American Society of Addiction Medicine (ASAM) criteria (2001) are the most widely accepted placement system criteria. These criteria consider problem severity in seven domains in making recommendations for patient placement in specific levels of care. There is a fair amount of research that indicates patients with co-occurring problems such as mental health disorders and housing problems and patients with greater substance use severity will do better in more intensive levels of treatment. Those with lower levels of substance use severity will do as well or better in less-intensive forms of SUD treatment. It is important to note that there is little scientific evidence to support the validity of the ASAM placement criteria. The patient's preference in terms of selecting the appropriate level of treatment and goals of treatment has become an accepted best practice and should be approached in the context of a working collaboration between the treatment provider and the patient. When both the patient and the provider agree on what is to be accomplished and how it is to be accomplished, the odds of achieving a good outcome are enhanced (Putnam et al. 1994).

To accommodate patient needs for various levels of care, VA provides specialty SUD treatment services in a variety of settings. These settings include inpatient SUD programs that provide acute in-hospital care and possibly detoxification services for veterans experiencing urgent psychiatric or medical symptoms. "SUD specific" RRTPs (SA RRTPs) provide intensive SUD treatment and rehabilitation treatment services with supportive housing for those who require a more structured community environment. They generally have longer lengths of stay and lower staffing levels than hospital-based inpatient treatment programs. Consistent with ASAM, intensive outpatient treatment programs (IOPs) provide at least three hours of treatment services at least three days per week, and standard outpatient treatment programs provide less-intensive ambulatory services such as aftercare.

Every VAMC offers specialty SUD services for the treatment of alcohol and drug problems. The specialty SUD treatment programs implement evidence-based psychosocial and pharmacologic interventions. Psychosocial interventions include motivational enhancement therapy, contingency management, cognitive behavioral therapy for relapse prevention, twelve-step facilitation counseling, and SUD-focused behavioral couples counseling. A brief description of the aforementioned psychosocial interventions is provided later in this chapter. In addition to psychosocial treatment for SUDs, VA offers pharmacotherapies, such as methadone, buprenorphine, naltrexone, and acamprosate, also discussed in detail later in this chapter. Most specialty SUD programs also provide assessment and care for co-occurring mental health disorders and infectious diseases that may be acquired during drug use.

Expansion of VA SUD Services

Specialty SUD treatment services have evolved in recent years, and VA is currently implementing a number of improvements to SUD treatment services available to veterans. As envisioned in the MHSP and more recently in the *Handbook*, VA has reversed a long-term trend of decline in services for SUDs. Recent gains have been made in the number of SUD treatment programs and staff, number of beds available to patients receiving specialty SUD care, and intensity of SUD treatment services. In the last several years VA leadership has continued to make SUD treatment services a major focus of support and attention, which has helped increase the accessibility and quality of the system. Specifically, interest in improving VA SUD services led to supplementary funding initiatives allocated in 2005, 2006, 2007, 2008, and 2009. It appears that these supplemental funds, coupled with the guidance of the MHSP, *SUD Guidelines*, and *Handbook* have improved VA SUD treatment. Major initiatives and significant program improvements are outlined below and can be broadly categorized into initiatives that focus on increasing *access* to specialty SUD treatment services or enhancing the *quality* of specialty SUD care.

Increasing Access to Specialty SUDCare

The Department of Veterans Affairs has taken steps to increase veterans' access to specialized SUD services through the MHEI. As outlined in the *Handbook*, all VAMCs are required to offer coordinated and intensive SUD treatment programs to all veterans who require them to establish early remission from SUD. These coordinated and intensive SUD services can be offered through intensive outpatient treatment services in a designated program delivered by staff with documented training and competencies in addressing SUD. Otherwise, coordinated and intensive services can be offered in an RRTP, either in a facility that specializes in SUD services (i.e., SA RRTP) or a "SUD track," in another RRTP that provides a 24/7 structured and supportive residential environment as part of the SUD rehabilitative treatment regimen. In 2008 VA began establishing twenty-seven additional SUD IOPs. The locations for these new IOPs were selected based on the absence of existing intensive SUD services and the number of veterans with SUDs of such severity that treatment provided in a standard outpatient SUD care setting would likely be insufficient (Deputy Under Secretary for Health for Operations and Management 2008b). The new IOPs are expected to offer services such as SUD rehabilitation, pharmacotherapies to address SUDs, and care for other conditions. As of December 2009, twenty of the twenty-seven IOPs were in operation, with the remaining seven in various stages of implementation (U.S. Government Accountability Office 2010).

The *SUD Guidelines* and *Handbook* indicate that addiction-focused pharmacotherapy should be made available and offered to all patients with opioid dependence and/or alcohol dependence. To expand capacity of evidence-based pharmacotherapy for opioid dependence with buprenorphine, a recent initiative provided funding and guidance to establish buprenorphine treatment services at sites that do not have licensed DEA and Joint Commission accredited opioid substitution programs (e.g., methadone clinics). Addiction pharmacotherapy in the VA system is covered in more detail later in this chapter. Recent SUD enhancement initiatives have provided a tremendous opportunity to increase access to SUD services for veterans in need.

Improving the Quality of Specialty SUD Care

To meet the growing demand for SUD treatment and improve the quality of services provided, VA has initiated various quality improvement efforts in recent years. One such effort has focused on improving continuity of care (COC) during treatment transitions (e.g., following discharge from a residential or intensive treatment program) for veterans receiving SUD treatment services. The Institute of Medicine's (1990) recommendations identify COC as a critical component in high-quality SUD treatment. Improving COC involves practices such as instituting appointment reminders and joint discharge planning with outpatient staff coordinating ongoing care. In alignment with the Institute of Medicine's recommendations, VA designated SUD COC as an official national performance measure in 2003. Since 2003 national performance on VA's COC performance measure (i.e., ninety-day retention of patients beginning new episodes of SUD specialty care) has improved steadily.

More recently, efforts to increase the quality of VA SUD treatment services include promoting evidence-based treatment practices through the *SUD Guidelines* and the *Handbook*. In August 2009 VA completed an update of its *SUD*

Guidelines to assist providers in managing patients with SUDs. The *SUD Guidelines* used by VA reflect validated, evidence-based consensus standards developed by the National Quality Forum (2007). They include a detailed, step-by-step process for recommended clinical decision making in addressing SUDs, along with a brief discussion of the research supporting the rationale for those decisions. Policy changes and advances in evidence-based care for SUD are disseminated to providers in the field through national training conferences and Web-based seminars in conjunction with the Employees Education System, teleconferences, and e-mail announcements from the Office of Mental Health Services (OMHS) as well as through initiatives of the Centers of Excellence in Substance Abuse Treatment and Education (CESATE) in Seattle and Philadelphia.

The *Handbook* was designed, in part, to support VA's efforts to provide veterans with SUD services that are based on scientific evidence. With regard to evidence-based psychosocial treatments for SUDs, the *Handbook* requires multiple (at least two) evidence-based SUD treatments be made available to all veterans who need them. The treatment approaches delineated in the *Handbook* are (1) motivational enhancement therapy, which uses motivational interviewing techniques to help clients resolve their ambivalence about changing problem behaviors and to achieve lasting change; (2) cognitive behavioral therapy for relapse prevention, an approach that assumes that maladaptive behaviors can be unlearned and teaches patients to improve their cognitive and behavioral skills to change problem behaviors; (3) twelve-step facilitation, a brief, structured, and manual-driven approach to facilitating early recovery from alcohol abuse/alcoholism and other drug abuse/addiction; (4) contingency management, a method that uses positive reinforcement (such as vouchers, coupons, or cash) to encourage specific behavior change, such as negative urine screens, attending treatment, etc.; and (5) SUD-focused behavioral couples counseling or family therapy: SUD interventions that assume that intimate partners and family members can reward abstinence and that reducing relationship distress can lessen the risk of relapse. Challenges to implementing evidence-based psychotherapies include, but are not limited to, the time required for training, practicing learned techniques, travel funds for staff to participate in training, and time for providers to become proficient in delivering the new therapy.

SUD Treatment Staffing Challenges

Instability of the workforce exists at all levels in the national mental health and SUD treatment system. McLellan, Carise & Kleber (2003) found a 53 percent per year turnover rate among directors and a similar rate among counselors in a national survey of private and public sector SUD treatment programs. The Department of Veterans Affairs has attempted to ameliorate this problem by allocating additional funds to its SUD treatment programs.

Difficulty recruiting experienced and highly qualified staff to fill vacant positions in the SUD treatment setting is a common problem nationwide (Gallon, Gabriel, & Knudsen, 2003), as well as an issue for VA. Finding qualified applicants can be a challenge in itself, especially for high-profile positions (e.g., psychiatrists and nursing staff), about which candidates can be selective. This, coupled with high turnover rates, results in instability in the SUD treatment workforce in both the private and public sectors (Gallon, Gabriel & Knudsen 2003; McLellan, Carise & Kleber 2003). In the VA system, funding initiatives, coupled with monitoring to ensure backfilling of vacated positions, have helped to offset staff attrition.

Research into the reasons for ongoing attrition of SUD treatment staff and development of systems to retain staff and programming is essential to ensure the availability of SUD treatment services over the long term. Proactive solutions to retain and recruit staff, and staffing plans that include recognition of high staff turnover rates, are needed to maintain and improve access to specialty SUD treatment. The Department of Veterans Affairs is monitoring and requiring the maintenance of overall mental health staffing levels over the coming years, which should help in this regard.

Pharmacotherapy for Substance Dependence

Pharmacotherapy for Opioid Dependence

Opioid dependence is a chronic and relapsing SUD that is characterized by an individual's inability to stop using opiates, which include illicit drugs such as heroin, and prescription medications used to treat pain, such as morphine, oxycodone, and hydrocodone. Opioid dependence is characterized by repeated self-administration and usually results in opioid tolerance, withdrawal symptoms, and compulsive drug use, despite negative consequences (American Psychiatric Association 2000). Untreated, opioid dependence can contribute to premature mortality and increased utilization of healthcare and social services (Mark et al. 2001), use of other drugs, criminal activity, and morbidity from other medical disorders.

Opiate agonist treatment (OAT) for opioid dependence is an evidence-based treatment with a strong record of effectiveness (Marsch 1998; Krantz & Mehler 2004; Mattick et al. 2003) and consists of administering an opioid agonist medication, such as methadone or sublingual buprenorphine, in combination with a comprehensive range of supportive and psychosocial services. If administered properly, OAT can prevent withdrawal, reduce craving, and lessen the effects of opioids, allowing the patient to focus more readily on recovery. In addition, OAT has been associated with a reduction in drug-related criminal behavior and human immunodeficiency virus (HIV) risk behavior.

Methadone- and buprenorphine-based OAT is the evidence-based standard of care for treatment of opioid dependence (Neri et al. 2005; Schottenfeld et al. 2005; Mattick et al. 2003), and VA recommends adherence to clinical guidelines that have been shown to elicit more positive outcomes in opioid dependent patients (Humphreys, Trafton & Oliva 2008). Although naltrexone is an FDA-approved alternative to opioid agonist treatment for patients with opioid dependence, evidence of its usefulness in the treatment of opioid dependency has been limited (Johansson, Berglund & Lindgren 2006), and the number of individuals maintained on naltrexone in VA remains low. The *SUD Guidelines* provide specific guidance on effective practices for retaining patients receiving OAT. These guidelines include (1) providing adequate dosing, (2) providing psychosocial services and support, (3) having a maintenance rather than detoxification goal, and (4) using contingency management techniques.

Office-Based versus Specialty Program Treatment Settings for OAT

In VA, OAT can be delivered through an opioid agonist treatment program (OATP) or through office-based opioid treatment (OBOT) with buprenorphine. Regardless of the treatment setting, the *Handbook* requires that pharmacotherapy be accompanied by psychosocial treatment and support. Along with prescribing methadone, many OATPs also provide individual therapy, group therapy, and family counseling. Although OATPs have a long history in VA, several factors may limit incorporation of OAT into this treatment setting. The prescription and dispensing of methadone is highly regulated; in fact, methadone can only be dispensed in an OATP that is registered with the Drug Enforcement Agency (DEA). In addition, regulations limit dispensing take-home doses, thus requiring patients to make frequent clinic visits and attend mandated patient laboratory testing and assessments.

Whereas the provision of methadone is limited to patients receiving specialized care, buprenorphine is the only medication approved for office-based opioid treatment (OBOT) and can be provided by credentialed physicians in nonspecialized outpatient and residential settings. Although the cost of buprenorphine is higher than methadone, one advantage of OBOT is that it requires fewer resources than formal methadone clinics. Patients who have difficulty accessing an OATP (e.g., large geographical distances, lack of transportation) may be better treated in OBOT using buprenorphine. Some patients may prefer to be treated in a primary care setting rather than in a specialized OATP. In addition, providers determine whether to prescribe methadone or buprenorphine based on patient-level factors such as severity, coexisting pain, and pregnancy. Social and environmental factors (e.g., homelessness, marital discord, dangerous living environments) may prompt a provider to suggest an OATP rather than OBOT care, because OATPs generally have more access to services that may assist in the patient's recovery (e.g., vocational training, housing assistance, family counseling). Finally, the decision to place a patient on either methadone or buprenorphine may depend on the patient's response to either medication.

Continued Expansion of OAT Services in VA

Despite the historically high number of veterans with opioid dependence, proliferation of pharmacologic treatment for this disorder within the VA system has been gradual but has progressed in the last decade. Policy changes in regulating OAT in the United States have affected the diffusion of pharmacologic treatment within VA. The period from 2000 to 2003 brought significant changes to provision of OAT in the United States. First, regulations for methadone maintenance provision were modified in 2001 to accredit OAT clinics like other healthcare programs and ease restrictions on take-home dosing of long-term maintenance patients. Second, in 2002, Congress passed an amendment to the Drug Abuse Treatment Act that allowed physicians to prescribe OBOT (i.e., buprenorphine). Finally, the FDA's "black box" warning on LAAM, a commonly prescribed opiate agonist, led to its manufacturer discontinuing it in 2003.

Amid these transitions, VA expanded its capacity for providing OAT. Funding from the Veterans Millennium Health Care and Benefits Act of 2000 was used to open new OAT clinics and expand existing clinics. In 2003 VA nonformulary guidelines for buprenorphine were established, permitting the use of buprenorphine in general practice (Goodman et al. 2003). Considering that OAT was historically restricted to delivery in licensed OATPs, this allowed for the implementation of new and novel modes of providing OAT treatment to patients, such as the introduction of buprenorphine into general practice (Gordon et al. 2007). With the approval of medications allowing the provision of OBOT, it became possible to provide OAT to the many opiate dependent patients who do not live in proximity to a licensed OATP in the VA system.

Although the use of long-term methadone maintenance has remained stable in recent years, gains in OAT access have been attained through VA's expansion of buprenorphine maintenance treatment. Pharmacy Benefits Management data show increased use of buprenorphine in VA, from 300 patients in FY 2004 to 4,827 patients in FY 2009 (Gordon 2010). More recent data show that the number of patients treated with OBOT and the number of facilities offering this treatment have increased steadily. However, though buprenorphine use has increased, the implementation and adoption process has been gradual and highly variable across regions (Gordon et al. 2007).

Barriers to implementation include perceived economic concerns of treatment and practitioner resistance. To help improve the implementation of buprenorphine OAT in VA, the Buprenorphine Task Group (BTG), consisting of interdisciplinary addiction experts, was established in 2005. Among the goals of this task force were to identify barriers and facilitators to providing buprenorphine, enhance VA organizational readiness to provide buprenorphine treatment in specialty and nonspecialty settings, and motivate providers to prescribe buprenorphine. The BTG actively consulted VA facilities that received specialized supplemental funding in 2007 as part of an initiative to develop buprenorphine treatment capability for veterans with opiate dependence. The BTG provides ongoing assistance to sites that are implementing or have implemented buprenorphine for opioid dependence treatment, including regular in-service trainings, clinical mentorship, regular newsletters with updates on recent research and practice findings, monitoring of buprenorphine use rates at facilities, and a help line and listserv for questions.

Pharmacotherapy for Alcohol Dependence

For patients with alcohol dependence, pharmacologic treatment also has known efficacy and can serve as an effective adjunct to nonpharmacologic treatments to help patients reduce or eliminate alcohol consumption. Three drugs have been FDA approved for adjunctive therapy in alcohol dependence: naltrexone, acamprosate, and disulfiram. Evidence supporting the use of these medications varies by medication and is somewhat inconsistent. However, several systematic reviews have indicated that acamprosate and naltrexone are efficacious and cost-effective treatments for alcohol dependence (Anton et al. 2005; Bouza et al. 2004; Srisurapanont & Jarusuraisin 2005). There is a paucity of randomized placebo-controlled clinical trials supporting the use of disulfiram.

Despite the fact that research supports the use of pharmacotherapy for alcohol dependent patients, only a small proportion of such patients are treated with pharmacotherapy in VA. In 2006 and 2007, it was estimated that of the almost 300,000 VA patients with alcohol use disorders (AUDs), only about 3 percent received pharmacotherapy for this disorder overall (Harris et al. 2010). This underutilization of alcohol pharmacotherapy is not unique to VA. The proportion of Americans with AUDs who are treated with alcohol pharmacotherapy is also very small (Mark et al. 2009). However, discussing all treatment options is now considered the standard of care for patients with AUDs in VA. Further, the *Handbook* requires that all patients with these disorders have access to and be considered for treatment with alcohol pharmacotherapy.

A lack of awareness that effective pharmacotherapy options for alcohol dependence exist is a principal factor in low utilization of pharmacotherapy in clinical practice. Other possible explanations include clinician beliefs that medications may reduce motivation for psychosocial treatment, concerns about side effects, cost, perceived ineffectiveness, lack of sufficient time allocated for patient management, and patient reluctance (Kranzler et al. 2006; Ducharme, Knudsen & Roman 2006; Thomas et al. 2008). There is considerable variation in the provision of alcohol pharmacotherapy across VA facilities. This may be attributed to various factors, including hospital affiliation, educational level of administrators (Oser & Roman 2007), or patient demographics. Although not all patients with alcohol dependence warrant or want pharmacologic treatment, considering that patients with chronic and severe AUDs have high rates of relapse, readmission, and treatment attrition, wider use of these medications has been recommended and is being encouraged.

In an effort to increase use of alcohol pharmacotherapy, VA has taken strides to implement policies to increase use. Consistent with evidence-based treatment standards recommended under the *SUD Guidelines*, the *Handbook* requires the availability of FDA-approved alcohol pharmacotherapy and consideration of their use in treating alcohol-dependent veterans. Specifically, the *Handbook* indicates that pharmacotherapy with an evidence-based treatment for alcohol dependence must be offered and available to patients diagnosed with alcohol dependence and without medical contraindication. If prescribed, the *Handbook* requires that pharmacotherapy be provided in combination with psychosocial support and treatment. Because of the risk of significant toxicity and limited evidence of effectiveness, disulfiram should only be used when abstinence is the goal and when combined with SUD-focused counseling. The VA Office of Research and Development has funded projects to identify barriers to and facilitators of alcohol pharmacotherapy in hopes of determining effective targets for intervention to increase use of this evidence-based treatment.

Stabilization and Withdrawal Management

Untreated alcohol and other sedative-hypnotic withdrawal, in particular, can lead to severe symptoms such as seizures, delirium, or even death. Withdrawal from opiates poses little risk of mortality, but symptoms can be intense and protracted. In addition, there is considerable mortality risk from overdose for those who relapse after unsuccessful medically supervised withdrawal attempts due to loss of opioid tolerance. Proper withdrawal management can not only prevent morbidity and mortality associated with withdrawal from substances; it can also serve as a critical gateway for transitioning a patient from active use to sustained treatment for SUDs.

The Department of Veterans Affairs has made efforts to ensure that appropriate services are made available for intoxicated veterans who require withdrawal management services. Whether patients present to an emergency department requiring withdrawal management or require supervised withdrawal support services prior to entering a rehabilitation program, the *Handbook* requires that facilities make medically supervised ambulatory and inpatient withdrawal management available as needed at a VAMC or by a contract or fee-basis arrangement. A recent report by the VA Office of the Inspector General (OIG) indicated that 95 percent of VA facilities reported having inpatient withdrawal management services available to patients either in the medical unit, in the mental health unit, through referral to a nearby VAMC, or through a non-VA arrangement (Department of Veterans Affairs, Office of Inspector General 2009).

The need for withdrawal management and the level of intensity of treatment are determined in part by the particular substance(s) involved. Withdrawal from alcohol, sedatives, and opiates may require medical management to prevent severe complications, while other substances such as stimulants, hallucinogens, and cannabis may not require specific medications but rather require psychosocial supportive care. The *Clinical Practice Guidelines* encourage providers to use standardized measures to assess the potential severity of withdrawal symptoms. Withdrawal from alcohol or opiates can be assessed by utilizing the Clinical Institute Withdrawal Assessment for Alcohol Scale—Revised (CIWA-Ar) and the Objective, Subjective and Clinical Opiate Withdrawal Scales (OOWS, SOWS, and COWS), respectively (Sullivan, Sykora & Schneiderman 1989; Wesson & Ling 2003).

Medications typically used for alcohol or sedative withdrawal include benzodiazepines; however, the abuse potential of these medications has led some prescribers to use nonabused medications such as oxy-carbamazepine and valproic acid in ambulatory settings. In accordance with the *SUD Guidelines*, withdrawal from opiates is typically managed with buprenorphine; however, other options include clonidine or methadone. Due to the high relapse rate in heroin or other opioid-dependent patients, the *SUD Guidelines* recommend that withdrawal management not be used as a stand-alone treatment modality;

stabilization should be combined with psychosocial interventions. In addition to alleviating acute symptoms, treatment of opioid withdrawal should focus on encouraging and assisting patients to enter comprehensive long-term treatment.

Emphasis is placed by VA on establishing and promoting a clinical relationship of trust and compassion, particularly during the sensitive withdrawal and stabilization stages, in an effort to engage the patient in further clinical assessment and treatment. Although patients are encouraged to remain in observation until they are no longer intoxicated, they cannot be held against their will. However, consistent with a 2007 rapid response initiative for mental health services, all intoxicated patients must be evaluated for risk of harming themselves or others prior to discharge. Once the patient is stabilized, appropriate follow-up is conducted, which may include linkage to specialty SUD services.

Because social support is critical for successful ambulatory withdrawal management, the *SUD Guidelines* recommend that patients without adequate social support be monitored more closely and provided with temporary shelter if needed to enable access to outpatient care. Withdrawal management can often be the first step in long-term treatment; therefore it is critical that effective provision of inpatient and ambulatory withdrawal management and stabilization services with follow-up care be available to all veterans seeking help. In outlining specific policy and clinical practice guidelines for the provision, care, and management of veterans requiring withdrawal and stabilization services, VA has shown considerable progress in ensuring appropriate care is available.

New Directions

Secretary Eric Shinseki has the challenge of moving VA into the twenty-first century to meet the needs of the growing and changing veteran population. Veterans returning from the wars in Afghanistan (i.e., Operation Enduring Freedom or OEF) and Iraq (i.e., Operation Iraqi Freedom or OIF) are younger, many are women, and because advanced battlefield medicine has saved so many lives, OEF and OIF veterans often suffer from many injuries, both physical and mental.

OEF and OIF Veterans

About 1.5 million military personnel have been deployed to Afghanistan and Iraq, representing the largest cohort of veterans to see combat since the Vietnam era. High numbers of returning veterans are enrolling to receive VA healthcare, creating unprecedented demands on treatment services. Many OEF/OIF veterans are being diagnosed with a variety of mental health conditions, the most common of which is PTSD. This presents a concern for VA SUD treatment providers, because research shows that among men diagnosed with PTSD, the most common co-occurring disorder is alcohol misuse (Jacobson et al. 2008; Seal et al. 2007).

The number of OEF/OIF veterans requiring SUD treatment is expected to increase as more military personnel separate from active service and return to civilian life. The high co-occurrence between SUDs and PTSD in the OEF/OIF veteran population has prompted VA to offer more integrated services for these two conditions. To promote integration of SUD and PTSD treatment, VA established the SUD-PTSD Task Group, which is charged with developing a strategic plan to implement and support ongoing evidence-based screening, support improved access to effective PTSD treatment, promote coordination of care for SUDs and PTSD, train clinicians, adapt evidence-based therapies, and survey VA key informants on systemwide needs related to SUD-PTSD treatment. In addition, the Task Group is currently conducting studies on treatment for co-occurring SUD and PTSD, rates of untreated alcohol and PTSD problems in OEF/OIF veterans, and a VA adaptation of *Seeking Safety*, an evidence-based treatment manual for co-occurring SUD and PTSD.

Women Veterans

In OEF and OIF, for the first time women served alongside men in combat roles, exposing themselves to higher chances of military trauma and increasing their chances of developing trauma-related psychiatric disorders. Women who screen positive for PTSD have higher self-reported rates of substance abuse (Dobie et al. 2004; Nunnink et al. 2010). This presents a challenge, because historically VA has served mostly men.

A U.S. Government Accountability Office (GAO) report (2009) on women's healthcare in VA states that most of the evaluated VAMCs provide at least basic mental health services for women. To improve the provision of SUD treatment services for women veterans, the *Handbook* mandates that services provided to women veterans should be sensitive to their unique treatment needs. The Department of Veterans Affairs is continuing to further augment their services as more female veterans return to civilian life and seek healthcare at VA facilities.

Homeless Veterans

Homelessness is a pressing problem in the veteran population. Veterans are at greater risk for becoming homeless than their civilian counterparts (Perl 2009).

It is difficult to determine why veterans represent a disproportionate number of the homeless population. However, it is clear that substance misuse and SUD are major problems among the homeless: both in the general and veteran populations. An Office of Policy Development and Research (1999) study showed that over a one-year period, 58 percent of homeless veterans reported difficulties with alcohol misuse.

The prevalence of homelessness among veterans has prompted VA to expend greater efforts to treat mental health and SUD-related problems and provide stable living arrangements for homeless veterans. The *Handbook* states that if inpatient or residential treatment for SUD is not immediately available, facilities must provide interim services that ensure patient safety and promote treatment. In regard to homelessness specifically, the *Handbook* states that each facility must have collaborative relationships with community providers that offer shelter, temporary housing, or basic emergency services for homeless veterans.

In 2009 Secretary of Veterans Affairs Eric Shinseki introduced a comprehensive plan to end veteran homelessness in five years. The plan allocated $2.7 billion to treat health problems among homeless veterans. That same year, Congress passed the Homes for Heroes Act (H.R. 403), which provides $200 million to fund the Housing and Urban Development and VA Supportive Housing (HUD-VASH) program that provides 20,000 rental vouchers for homeless veterans. To be eligible for a voucher, the veteran must work with a case manager to establish a treatment plan that focuses on dealing with alcohol and drug problems; medical/mental health issues; and problems with employment, financial, and legal issues.

Monitoring and Metrics for SUD Treatment

The MHEI dramatically increased SUD treatment capacity at VA, and the development of the MHEI, the *Handbook,* and the *SUD Guidelines* have prompted the development of initiatives to improve the quality of SUD treatment services. The OMHS has made a commitment to maintain existing programs while at the same time assisting VISNs and VAMCs in meeting the new requirements outlined in the *Handbook.* The *Handbook* mandates that outcomes monitoring should be an integrated part of SUD treatment.

Previous efforts to monitor SUD treatment outcomes have yielded mixed results; assessments were often too lengthy; procedures were not well integrated into standard clinical care; there was undue burden on staff and patients and low follow-up rates; and the information gathered had no real clinical value. These factors prompted the Center of Excellence in Substance Abuse Treatment and Education (CESATE) at the Philadelphia VAMC to develop an improved SUD outcomes monitoring tool, the Brief Addiction Monitor (BAM).

The BAM is currently being studied in an implementation trial with the main objective of assessing its feasibility and acceptability for clinical use as a method to inform treatment planning using ongoing brief assessment and tracking of progress or problems in key domains. Once the initial implementation trial is completed, the CESATE will begin a staggered rollout of the BAM to other VAMCs.

In addition to the BAM, VA is developing other metrics to monitor the delivery of SUD services. First, to enhance clinical capacity to treat SUDs, VA has committed to hiring, credentialing, and training new staff. The OMHS will evaluate recruitment of SUD treatment staff and monitor increases in the number of positions. Second, the OMHS will monitor the utilization of services by tracking the number of unique veterans treated in mental health, the number of encounters, and the access times for specific services. Finally, VA will build on its current protocol of quality and performance metrics to ensure that evidence-based care meets the specifications of interventions that have been proven to be effective in the treatment of SUD.

Technology in SUD Treatment

The Department of Veterans Affairs is a pioneer in utilizing the Internet and other technologies to improve SUD treatment quality for its clients. The Internet enables the secure collection of self-reported data from clients with SUDs, which can facilitate activities including (1) patient assessment and feedback for brief motivational interventions, (2) provider assessment of individual-level data on outcomes for clients who are receiving treatment for SUDs, and (3) monitoring ongoing recovery for clients who have completed treatment. The Internet can also assist in training clinicians in the latest SUD treatment approaches (Cucciare, Weingardt & Humphreys 2009).

My HealtheVet, a secure, Internet-based personal health record, is available to all veterans. A system called My Recovery Plan is currently under development, which will be available through My HealtheVet. My Recovery Plan will provide veterans with interactive, Web-based tools to monitor their symptoms and their progress toward achieving recovery goals, and assist them in following through their individualized plans for coping with relapse triggers.

Technology also has the potential to improve healthcare for underserved veterans seeking treatment in rural areas. Because veterans living in remote areas often have difficulty traveling to a VAMC, VA operates approximately 700 CBOCs, which provide services closer to the patients' homes. However, many CBOCs do not have specialized mental health and SUD services. The Department of Veterans Affairs is attempting to ameliorate this problem by promoting the use of telehealth, consisting of video, digital pictures, and messaging devices to provide care for veterans who do not have convenient physical access to specialized treatment providers.

Conclusions

Refocused efforts in VA to improve SUD treatment services have led to supplementary funding initiatives allocated in 2005 through 2009. It appears that these supplemental funds, coupled with the guidance of the MHSP, *SUD Guidelines*, and the OMHS, have reversed a prior long-term trend of VA SUD treatment contraction and have expanded veteran access to evidence-based care for SUD. Further research, guidance, and policies should further strengthen VA's ability to provide SUD treatment services to an increasing number of veterans. Leadership in VA and the U.S. Congress has continued making SUD treatment services a major focus of support and attention, which should increase the accessibility and quality of VA's SUD treatment services in the coming years.

Acknowledgments: We are grateful to Dr. Ira Katz and Dr. John P. Allen for their careful review of and helpful comments on this chapter.

References

American Psychiatric Association (2000). *Diagnostic and statistical manual of mental disorders.* 4th ed. Washington, DC: American Psychiatric Association.

American Society of Addiction Medicine. (2001). Patient placement criteria for the treatment of substance related disorders. In D. Mee-Lee, G. D. Shulman, M. Fishman, D. R. Gastfriend & J. H. Griffith (Eds.), *ASAM patient placement criteria for the treatment of substance-related disorders,* 2nd ed., rev. Chevy Chase, MD: American Society of Addiction Medicine.

Anton, R. F., Moak, D. H., Latham, P., Waid, L. R., Myrick, H., Voronin, K., et al. (2005). Naltrexone combined with either cognitive behavioral or motivational enhancement therapy for alcohol dependence. *Journal of Clinical Psychopharmacology* 25: 349–357.

Bouza, C., Angeles, M., Muñoz, A. & Amate, J. M. (2004). Efficacy and safety of naltrexone and acamprosate in the treatment of alcohol dependence: A systematic review. *Addiction* 99: 811–882.

Bradley, K. A., DeBenedetti, A. F., Volk, R. J., Williams, E. C., Frank, D. & Kivlahan, D. R. (2007). AUDIT-C as a brief screen for alcohol misuse in primary care. *Alcoholism, Clinical and Experimental Research* 31, no. 7: 1208–1217.

Bradley, K. A., Williams, E. C., Achtmeyer, C. E., Volpp, B., Collins, B. J. & Kivlahan, D. R. (2006). Implementation of evidence-based alcohol screening in the Veterans Health Administration. *American Journal of Managed Care* 12: 597–606.

Chen, S., Wagner, T. H. & Barnett, P. G. (2001). Policy changes in the mid-1990s sent veterans to outpatient facilities for treatment, mirroring trends in the overall U.S. health care system. *Health Affairs* 20, 4: 169–175.

Cucciare, M. A., Weingardt, K. R. & Humphreys, K. (2009). How internet technology can improve the quality of care for substance use disorders. *Current Drug Abuse Reviews* 2: 256–262.

Department of Defense & Department of Veterans Affairs. (2008). *VA/DOD clinical practice guidelines for management of tobacco use.* http://www.healthquality.va.gov/Management_of_Tobacco_Use_MTU.asp (accessed May 25, 2010).

Department of Defense & Department of Veterans Affairs. (2009). *VA/DOD clinical practice guidelines for treatment of substance use disorders: Version 2.0.* http://www.healthquality.va.gov/sud/sud_full_601f.pdf (accessed June 6, 2010).

Department of Veterans Affairs. (2008). *VHA handbook 1160.1: Uniform mental health services in VA medical centers and clinics.* Washington, DC: Retrieved from http://www1.va.gov/vhapublications/ViewPublication.asp?pub_ID=1762.

Department of Veterans Affairs, Office of Inspector General. (2009). *Healthcare inspection implementation of VHA's Uniform Mental Health Services Handbook.* Report no. 08-02917-105. http://www.va.gov/oig/publications/reports-list.asp (accessed May 5, 2010).

Deputy Under Secretary for Health for Operations and Management (10N). (2008a). *Memorandum June 11, 2008: Mental health enhancement funding FY 2008.* Washington, DC: Department of Veterans Affairs.

Deputy Under Secretary for Health for Operations and Management (10N). (2008b). *Memorandum Aug 07, 2008: Implementing uniform mental health services in VA medical centers and clinics.* Washington, DC: Department of Veterans Affairs.

Dobie, D. J., Kivlahan, D. R., Maynard, C., Bush, K. R., Davis, T. M. & Bradley, K. A. (2004). Posttraumatic stress disorder in female veterans: Association with self-reported health problems and functional impairment. *Archives of Internal Medicine* 164: 394–400.

Ducharme, L. J., Knudsen, H. K. & Roman, P. M. (2006). Trends in the adoption of medications for alcohol dependence. *Journal of Clinical Psychopharmacology* 26, supp. 1: S13–S19.

Gallon, S. L., Gabriel, R. M. & Knudsen, J. (2003). The toughest job you'll ever love: A Pacific Northwest treatment workforce survey. *Journal of Substance Abuse Treatment* 24: 183–196.

Gifford, E., Jaszka, J. & Tracy, S. W. (2008). Substance use disorder treatment in VA mental health settings: The 2007 Program Evaluation and Resource Center Psychiatry Survey. Evaluation report to VA Mental Health Strategic Healthcare Group. VA Central Office.

Goodman, F., Gordon, A., Kivlahan, D., Dalack, G., Pope, J., McNichols, L. & Suchinsky, R. (2003). Criteria for non-formulary use of buprenorphine sublingual tablets for opioid dependence. In *Criteria for use monograph.* http://www.ahrn.net/library_upload/uploadfile/file2176.pdf (accessed May 27, 2010).

Gordon, A. (2010). *Models of care*—buprenorphine experience in the Department of Veteran Affairs (PowerPoint slides). http://buprenorphine.samhsa.gov/bwns/2010_presentations_pdf/18_Gordon_508.pdf (accessed May 27, 2010).

Gordon, A. J., Trafton, J. A., Saxon, A. J., Gifford, A. L., Goodman, F., Calabrese, V. S., McNichols, L. & Liberto, J. (2007). Implementation of buprenorphine in the Veterans Health Administration: Results of the first 3 years. *Drug and Alcohol Dependence* 90: 292–296.

Greenberg, G. A. & Rosenheck, R. A. (2009). An evaluation of an initiative to improve Veterans Health Administration Mental Health Services: Broad impacts of the VHA's Mental Health Strategic Plan. *Military Medicine* 174, no. 12: 1263–1269.

Harris, A. H. S., Kivlahan, D. R., Bowe, T. & Humphreys, K. (2010). Pharmacotherapy of alcohol use disorders in the Veterans Health Administration. *Psychiatric Services* 61, no. 4: 392–398.

Humphreys, K., Hamilton, E. G., Moos, R. H. & Suchinsky, R. T. (1997). Policy-relevant program evaluation in a national substance abuse treatment system. *Journal of Mental Health Administration* 24, no. 4: 373–385.

Humphreys, K., Huebsch Dearmin, P., Moos, R. H. & Suchinsky, R. T. (1999). The transformation of the Veterans Affairs substance abuse treatment system. *Psychiatric Services* 50, no. 11: 1399–1401.

Humphreys, K., Trafton, J. A. & Oliva, E. M. (2008). Does following research-derived practice guidelines improve opiate-dependent patients' outcomes under everyday practice conditions? Results of the Multisite Opiate Substitution Treatment Study. *Journal of Substance Abuse Treatment* 34: 173–179.

Iglehart, J. K. (1996). Reform in the Veterans Affairs health care system. *New England Journal of Medicine* 335, no. 18: 1407–1411.

Institute of Medicine. (1990) *Broadening the base of treatment for alcohol problems.* Washington, DC: National Academy Press.

Jacobson, I. G., Ryan, M. A. K., Hooper, T. I., Smith, T. C., Amoroso, P. J., Boyko, E. J., et al. (2008). Alcohol use and alcohol related problems before and after military combat deployment. *Journal of the American Medical Association* 300, no. 6: 663–675.

Johansson, B. A., Berglund, M. & Lindgren, A. (2006). Efficacy of maintenance treatment with naltrexone for opioid dependence: A meta-analytical review. *Addiction* 101, no. 4: 491–503.

King, D. W., King, L. A., Gudanowski, D. M. & Vreven, D. L. (1995). Alternative representations of war zone stressors: Relationships to posttraumatic stress disorder in male and female Vietnam veterans. *Journal of Abnormal Psychology* 104: 184–196.

Kirchner, J. E., Owen, R. R., Nordquist, C. & Fischer, E. P. (1998). Diagnosis and management of substance use disorder among inpatients with schizophrenia. *Psychiatric Services* 79: 82–85.

Kizer, K. W., Fonseca, M. L. & Long, M. L. (1997). The veterans healthcare system: Preparing for the twenty-first century. *Hospital and Health Services Administration* 42: 283–289.

Krantz, M. J. & Mehler, P. S. (2004). Treating opioid dependence: Growing implications for primary care. *Archives of Internal Medicine* 164, no. 3: 277–288.

Kranzler, H. R., Koob, G., Gastfriend, D. R., Swift, R. M. & Willenbring, M. L. (2006). Advances in the pharmacotherapy of alcoholism: Challenging misconceptions. *Alcoholism, Clinical and Experimental Research* 30: 272–281.

Mark, T. L., Kassed, C. A., Vandivort-Warren, R., Levit, K. R. & Kranzler, H. R. (2009). Alcohol and opioid dependence medications: Prescription trends overall and by physician specialty. *Drug and Alcohol Dependence* 99: 345–349.

Mark, T. L., Woody, C. E., Juday, T. & Kleber, H. D. (2001). The economic costs of heroin addiction in the United States. *Drug and Alcohol Dependence* 61, no. 2: 195–206.

Marsch, L. A. (1998). The efficacy of methadone maintenance interventions in reducing illicit opiate use: HIV risk behavior and criminality: A meta-analysis. *Addiction* 93, no. 4: 515–532.

Mattick, R. P., Breen, C., Kimber, J. & Davoli, M. (2003). Methadone maintenance therapy versus no opioid replacement therapy for opioid dependence. *Cochrane Database of Systematic Reviews* 2: CD002209.

McLellan, A. T., Carise, D. & Kleber, H. (2003). Can the national addiction treatment infrastructure support the public's demand for quality care? *Journal of Substance Abuse Treatment* 25: 117–121.

Mee-Lee, D., Shulman, G. D., Fishman, M., Gastfriend, D. R. & Griffith, J. H. (Eds.). (2001). *ASAM patient placement criteria for the treatment of substance-related disorders.* 2nd ed. rev. (ASAM PPC-2R). Chevy Chase, MD: American Society of Addiction Medicine.

National Quality Forum. (2007). National voluntary consensus standards for the treatment of substance use conditions: Evidence-based treatment practices. www.quality forum.org/WorkArea/linkit.aspx?LinkIdentifier=id (accessed May 14, 2010).

Neri, S., Bruno, C. M., Pulvirenti, D., Malaguarnera, M., Italiano, C., Mauceri, B., et al. (2005). Randomized clinical trial to compare the effects of methadone and buprenorphine on the immune system in drug abusers. *Psychopharmacology* 179, no. 3: 700–704.

Nunnink, S. E., Goldwaser, G., Heppner, P. S., Pittman, J. O. E., Nievergelt, C. M. & Baker, D. G. (2010). Female veterans of the OEF/OIF conflict: Concordance of PTSD symptoms and substance misuse. *Addictive Behaviors* 35: 655–659.

Office of Applied Studies. (2005). *Substance Survey on Drug Use and Health report: Substance use, dependence and treatment among veterans.* Washington, DC: Substance Abuse and Mental Health Services Administration.

Office of Policy Development and Research. (1999). *Homelessness: Programs and the people they serve: Findings of the national survey of homeless assistance providers and clients.* Washington, DC: U.S. Department of Housing and Urban Development.

Oser, C. B. & Roman, P. M. (2007). Organizational-level predictors of adoption across time: Naltrexone in private substance-use disorders treatment centers. *Journal of Studies on Alcohol and Drugs* 68: 852–861.

Perl, L. (2009). *Veterans and homelessness.* RL 34024. Washington, DC: Congressional Research Service.

President's New Freedom Commission on Mental Health. (2003). *Achieving the promise: Transforming mental health care in America.* DHHS pub. no. SMA-03–3832. Rockville, MD: Department of Health and Human Services.

Putnam, D. E., Finney, J. W., Barkey, P. L. & Bonner, M. J. (1994). Enhancing commitment improves adherence to a medical regimen. *Journal of Consulting and Clinical Psychology* 62, no. 1: 191–194.

Ridgely, M. S., Goldman, H. H. & Willenbring, M. (1990). Barriers to the care of persons with dual diagnosis: Organizational and financing issues. *Schizophrenia Bulletin* 16, no. 1: 123–132.

Schottenfeld, R. S., Chawarski, M. C., Pakes, J. R., Pantalon, M. V., Carroll, K. M. & Kosten, T. R. (2005). Methadone versus buprenorphine with contingency management or performance feedback for cocaine and opioid dependence. *American Journal of Psychiatry* 162, no. 2: 340–349.

Seal, K. H., Bertenthal, D., Miner, C. R., Sen, S. & Marmar, C. (2007). Mental health disorders among 103,788 US veterans returning from Iraq and Afghanistan seen at Department of Veterans Affairs facilities. *Archives of Internal Medicine* 167: 476–482.

Srisurapanont, M. & Jarusuraisin, N. (2005). Naltrexone for the treatment of alcoholism: A meta-analysis of randomized controlled trials. *International Journal of Neuropsychopharmacology* 8: 267–280.

Sullivan, J. T., Sykora, K. & Schneiderman, J. (1989). Assessment of alcohol withdrawal: The revised Clinical Institute Withdrawal Assessment for Alcohol Scale (CIWA-AR). *British Journal of Addiction* 84: 1353–1357.

Thomas, S. E., Miller, P. M., Randall, P. K. & Book, S. W. (2008). Improving acceptance of naltrexone in community addiction treatment centers: A pilot study. *Journal of Substance Abuse Treatment* 35: 260–268.

Timko, C., Lesar, M., Calvi, N. J. & Moos, R. H. (2003). Trends in acute mental health care: comparing psychiatric and substance abuse treatment programs. *Journal of Behavioral Health Services & Research* 30, no. 2: 145–160.

Tracy, S. W., Trafton, J. A., Weingardt, K. R., Aton, E. G. & Humphreys, K. (2007). How are substance use disorders addressed in VA psychiatric and primary care settings? Results of a national survey. *Psychiatric Services* 58, no. 2: 1–4.

U.S. Government Accountability Office. (2009). VA has taken steps to make services available to women veterans, but needs to revise key policies and improve oversight processes. GAO-10–287. http://www.gao.gov/new.items/d10287.pdf (accessed March 25, 2010).

U.S. Government Accountability Office. (2010). *VA faces challenges in providing substance use disorder services and is taking steps to improve these services for veterans.* GAO-10–294R. http://www.gao.gov/new.items/d10294r.pdf (accessed May 27, 2010).

Wesson, D. R. & Ling, W. (2003). The Clinical Opiate Withdrawal Scale (COWS). *Journal of Psychoactive Drugs* 35, no. 2: 253–259.

The Social Context of Post-trauma Adjustment in Veterans

Bradley E. Belsher, Josef I. Ruzek, and Matthew J. Cordova

Introduction

The stress of military deployment in general, and of combat exposure in particular, can have a profound negative impact on veterans and their families. It is estimated that 10–30 percent of combat veterans will develop post-traumatic stress disorder (PTSD) (Kulka et al. 1990; Tanielian & Jaycox 2008), along with depression (Kessler et al. 2005), substance abuse (Jacobsen, Southwick & Kosten 2001), and physical health problems (Friedman & Schnurr 1995; Schnurr & Jankowski 1999). Among returning veterans, family strain and other relationship difficulties, including elevated rates of divorce, domestic violence, and parenting problems, are common (Matsakis 2007; Sayer et al. 2010; Tanielian & Jaycox 2008). Post-traumatic stress disorder is associated with a variety of relationship difficulties (e.g., Cook et al. 2004; Galovski & Lyons 2004; Monson, Taft & Fredman 2009; Riggs et al. 1998; Ruscio et al. 2002; Sayers et al. 2009). Depression, PTSD, and traumatic brain injury (TBI) are all independently associated with divorce in Operation Enduring Freedom (OEF) and Operation Iraqi Freedom (OIF) returnees (Tanielian & Jaycox 2008). In addition, spouses/partners and other family members may experience depression, anxiety, and adjustment problems as they cope with the practical challenges of deployment and homecoming (Bowling & Sherman 2008) and attempt to support their veteran loved ones through their struggles (Dekel & Solomon 2007; Jordan et al. 1992). More broadly, combat veterans often struggle with social isolation, difficulty adjusting to civilian life, and a sense of not fitting in with and being accepted by society.

Thus, the social context of post-trauma adjustment for veterans is of central importance. Veterans who have stronger social support from family and friends may be less likely to develop psychiatric difficulties (Wilcox 2010), but veterans who experience greater family dysfunction and unsupportive partners report a relative increase in PTSD symptoms over time (Evans et al. 2010; Evans, Cowlishaw & Hopwood 2009). Although having practical help (e.g., transportation, financial assistance, aid in getting to appointments) may buffer veterans from some day-to-day demands that increase stress and complicate adjustment, having supportive others with whom to talk about current and past experiences may help veterans better understand their own reactions and adjust to what they have been through. When emotional problems do develop, veterans with greater support may be more likely to seek professional assistance (Pietrzak et al. 2009).

Veterans generally welcome family involvement in treatment. Eighty-six percent of veterans receiving treatment for PTSD through the Department of Veterans Affairs (VA) Veterans Health Administration (VHA) view their problem as a source of family stress, and 79 percent want greater family involvement in their treatment (Batten et al. 2009). Veterans often report that a primary motivation for seeking therapy is to improve their family relationships and/or maintain their marriages. The proximal reason for initiation of treatment is often persuasion or pressure by family members.

For these reasons, the VA healthcare system has strengthened its focus on veterans' social support system (VHA Directive 2006-041). Family involvement was identified as a central component of care in the Veterans Affairs Mental Health Strategic Plan (Department of Veterans Affairs 2004). Through Public Law 110-387, signed into law in October 2008, VA established marriage and family counseling as necessary provisions for veterans with service-connected conditions. The *Uniform Mental Health Services Handbook* (Department of Veterans Affairs, OMHS 2008), a document developed by the Office of Mental Health Services to delineate clinical requirements for VA mental healthcare, specifies that a range of family services must be available to veterans with mental health problems, including family engagement, education, involvement in treatment planning, and problem solving.

In line with this emphasis, evidence-based treatments are being disseminated nationally through attempts to foster social connection, communication, and support in veterans, their families, and their broader social networks. Programs are underway to train mental health providers in several family-related interventions (Cohen et al. 2008; Makin-Byrd et al. 2011) and family psychoeducation methods (Sherman 2006; McFarlane 2002). In addition, recovery-oriented care models emphasize increasing social connection between veterans and their broader support system, including family, friends, peers, and the community at large (Substance Abuse and Mental Health Services Administration 2010).

While these efforts attempt to bolster family involvement and social support among veterans, the specific ways in which social support enhances veterans' adjustment are not well understood. Theoretical frameworks that improve our understanding of the impact of social support on recovery following deployment to a war zone may help guide development and implementation of specific new intervention approaches and have policy implications. This chapter introduces one such framework and discusses its application and potential utility in veterans' mental healthcare.

This chapter has three primary objectives. First we introduce a conceptual framework, the Social Cognitive Processing Model (Lepore 2001), for understanding the impact of the social environment on adjustment following traumatic experiences. Second, we discuss the implications of this framework for veterans, their families, and their broader social support system. Finally, we discuss individual, family, group, healthcare system, military, and societal approaches that may enhance social support for veterans and their families.

Models of Post-traumatic Stress Disorder

Several theoretical frameworks focus on the development and maintenance of post-traumatic stress response symptoms and processes of recovery following a traumatizing experience. These models emphasize that the vast majority of stress reactions in the immediate aftermath of a traumatic event are normal and typically diminish over time. Post-traumatic stress disorder emerges when this recovery process is forestalled and the stress response symptoms persist and significantly interfere with functioning. Though there are differences among these theories, they all emphasize the function of emotional and cognitive processing of trauma-related information in successful recovery, and conversely, the role of avoidance in the development and maintenance of PTSD.

Mowrer's (1939) Two-Factor Conditioning Model was one of the first frameworks used to explain post-traumatic symptoms (Keane, Zimering & Caddell 1985; Kilpatrick, Veronen & Resick 1979). This model takes into account classical and operant conditioning mechanisms, as well as the process of habituation. Foremost, this theory posits that a neutral object (e.g., a pile of trash) becomes coupled with an aversive object (e.g., an extremely stressful experience such as an IED explosion) via classical conditioning, and subsequently the neutral object comes to elicit a set of fear-based responses (e.g., heart pounding, shaking, dissociation, fear) similar to those experienced at the time of the trauma itself. The individual then learns, through a process of operant conditioning, to avoid these coupled reminders and the intense distress they can elicit. This avoidance reduces trauma-related anxiety, consequently reinforcing the avoidance behaviors. Based on this model, post-trauma adjustment and recovery may be facilitated by exposure to the now-feared conditioned stimuli (e.g., a pile of trash) without the feared outcome (trauma), long enough and often enough that the association between the trauma reminder and the trauma is eliminated, and the fear-based emotional response diminishes (i.e., habituation).

Subsequent theoretical models have developed more comprehensive frameworks to explain the specific symptom constellations associated with trauma exposure. Emotional processing theory holds that survivors develop a fear network in memory during and following a traumatic experience (Foa, Steketee & Rothbaum 1989). This fear network consists of information regarding the trauma (e.g., IED explosion) and associated cues (e.g., pile of trash, hot weather, crowd of people), emotional responses during and after the event (e.g., fear, anger), and interpretations of these experiences (e.g., "I should have been watching more closely") (Foa & Kozak 1986). The survivor may generalize and incorporate similar objects, thoughts, feelings, images, and sensations in the present into the fear network (Foa, Steketee & Rothbaum 1989). Encountering one of these cues (e.g., driving by trash in a U.S. neighborhood) can activate the fear network, resulting in increased physiological activity (e.g., heart palpitations), thoughts that signal danger (e.g., "I need to evade"), and fight/flight behaviors (e.g., swerving, road rage) (Foa & Kozak 1986).

According to this theory, individuals who develop PTSD are hypothesized to possess easily activated fear structures that elicit a disproportionate amount of distress (Foa & Kozak 1986). Their fear structures are almost always activated and easily accessed, as these individuals generalize and incorporate a disproportionate amount of fear elements in their environment, both external and internal (Foa & Kozak 1986). Activation of any of these elements sets off the fear response system and elicits a cascade of interrelated responses and interpretations attached to the original trauma. As a result, considerable effort is exerted to avoid any stimuli that might activate the fear structure, including associated environmental cues, as well as trauma-related thoughts and feelings. As a result of pervasive avoidance, a limited amount of emotional processing and habituation takes place over time, preventing the individual from learning that these cues (both internal and external) are not accurate indicators of danger.

Like the Two-Factor Conditioning Model, emotional processing theory suggests that trauma recovery requires exposure to feared elements in the environment. Survivors must confront not only the environmental cues, but also the internal thoughts, emotions, and memories that make up the fear structure (Foa, Steketee & Rothbaum 1989). This includes exposure to the traumatic memory itself, so that new experiences discordant with a sense of threat and danger are experienced (Foa & Kozak 1986). Repetitive exposure to environmental triggers, as well as to the traumatic memory, in a safe context promotes emotional processing and trauma recovery (Foa & Kozak 1986).

Cognitive models of PTSD (Creamer, Burgess & Pattison 1992; Janoff-Bulman 1992; Resick & Schnicke 1992) posit that humans possess underlying, and largely unconscious, assumptions that "reflect and guide our interactions in the world and generally enable us to function effectively" (Janoff-Bulman 1992, 5). These beliefs develop out of previous events, influence ongoing experiences, and guide future behaviors (Hollon & Kriss 1984). At the core of these beliefs are fundamental assumptions about safety, trust, control, power, esteem, and intimacy (McCann & Pearlman 1990). Given the importance of these internal blueprints in organizing and understanding the world, individuals go to great lengths to interpret new experiences in a way that lets them preserve these assumptions. When traumatic events provide evidence that is incongruent with these assumptions, individuals actively attempt to incorporate and reconcile this new information with prior beliefs (Janoff-Bulman 1992). The cognitive processing framework suggests that traumatic events introduce highly discrepant and emotionally charged information that often runs strongly counter to older underlying beliefs about the self and the world (Epstein 1991). How the survivor encounters, interprets, and incorporates this new trauma-related information in light of previous beliefs will largely determine whether recovery will occur or post-traumatic distress will persist.

Trauma abruptly and directly challenges many personal assumptions resulting in cognitive disorganization and emotional distress (Janoff-Bulman 1992). As a result, survivors subsequently experience two conflicting needs following a traumatic experience: an urge to encounter and understand the trauma-based information and an opposing desire to avoid the distress that is associated with these memories and feelings (Horowitz 1986). Trauma-related information that is evaded through behavioral avoidance, mental suppression, and emotional numbing is not adequately reconciled with previous beliefs. Although these avoidance tactics temporarily decrease distress, the unprocessed information remains in active memory and continues to intrude into awareness via trauma-related thoughts, nightmares, and images. Individuals with PTSD experience a chronic avoidance/intrusion pattern, and due to the marked avoidance (both emotional and behavioral) do not fully integrate the trauma-based information.

Cognitive processing models posit that trauma recovery is facilitated through acceptance of the trauma, recognition of the implications of the event, and the modification of preexisting assumptions to incorporate this information while maintaining a realistic and useful blueprint of the world. In essence, survivors must come to recognize and accept the trauma and its implications while maintaining functional core assumptions about themselves and the world. Until the trauma-related information is adequately processed and integrated with current assumptions, this distressing information will continue to intrude into awareness, elicit distress, and engender avoidance.

Different trauma models emphasize specific mechanisms that underlie post-trauma adjustment, but they all focus on "processing" the traumatic experience and its effects. Furthermore, while emotional processing theory and cognitive processing models emphasize specific components (i.e., emotional, cognitive) of processing, they both incorporate concepts of emotional and cognitive processing in their description of trauma recovery. Trauma processing likely occurs through multiple, dynamic pathways (emotional, cognitive, and behavioral). Lepore and Helgeson (1998) define trauma processing as those "mental activities that help people to interpret traumatic events in personally meaningful terms, integrate threatening or confusing aspects of the experience into a coherent and nonthreatening conceptual framework, and reach a state of emotional acceptance" (90–91). It is likely that these outcomes are achieved via a range of mechanisms, including habituation to environmental and internal stimuli, processing of emotions, cognitive reappraisal, overt behavior change, development of more adaptive coping responses, and environmental changes.

Social Cognitive Processing

Lepore's (2001) social cognitive processing model of adjustment makes an important contribution by emphasizing that trauma processing often occurs within a social context. Individuals experience a natural tendency to want to talk following a stressful experience (Rimé 1995), and this social sharing may facilitate trauma processing and promote recovery (Lepore 2001). However, talking per se may not facilitate recovery (Rimé 1995). Rather, the benefit of discussing trauma-related experiences is largely contingent on the quality of the interpersonal context in which this sharing takes place (Lepore et al. 2004; Lepore, Ragan & Jones 2000; Lepore et al. 1996). Social cognitive processing occurs in the context of supportive social conditions that promote a sense of understanding, safety, acceptance, and openness for the survivor to engage in discussions. Subsequently, this supportive social environment encourages survivors to safely encounter, discuss, and make meaning of their distressing experiences (Burleson & Goldsmith 1998; Cohen & Wills 1985; Pennebaker 1995). The presence of this supportive environment further reestablishes a sense of safety and trust for the survivor, enabling exposure to the emotions, physical sensations, and thoughts that have been avoided, and validating many of one's previous assumptions that may have been challenged in the face of the traumatic event. This trauma-specific form of social support may be essential in facilitating adequate recovery for many survivors.

On the other hand, the presence of negative and critical social responses may limit interpersonal processing and serve to reinforce and perpetuate mal-adaptive and dysfunctional beliefs and behaviors (Lepore 2001). Social con-straints are defined as "any social condition that causes a trauma survivor to feel unsupported, misunderstood, or otherwise alienated from their social net-work when they are seeking social support or attempting to express trauma-related thoughts, feelings, or concerns" (Lepore & Ituarte 1999, 168). They are characterized by an unreceptive social environment that inhibits trauma discussion, promotes avoidance, and may serve to further stigmatize the survi-vor. Socially constrained individuals are met with unpredictable and negative social responses to trauma disclosure and subsequently learn that it is not acceptable to discuss their experiences and internal reactions with others. Con-sequently, these individuals may engage in less disclosure and processing and more mental suppression and behavioral avoidance. As a result, socially con-strained trauma survivors may experience a greater frequency of intrusions, develop more distorted and negative post-traumatic beliefs, and experience greater fear and distress when exposed to trauma reminders. As more perva-sive and dysfunctional symptoms develop, significant others may become more distant and critical, causing the survivor to experience greater psychological distress and stronger urges to engage in avoidance behaviors.

The social cognitive processing model has received empirical support through studies on healthcare populations that are adjusting to stressful and often traumatic events. For example, greater levels of social constraints have been associated with poorer psychological adjustment for a variety of cancer patients (Cordova et al. 2007; Cordova et al. 2001; Lepore & Helgeson 1998; Schmidt & Andrykowski 2004; Zakowski et al. 2003), HIV positive men liv-ing in rural areas (Ullrich, Lutgendorf & Stapleton 2002), bone marrow trans-plant recipients (Widows, Jacobsen & Fields 2000), and rheumatoid arthritis patients (Danoff-Burg et al. 2004).

Investigations of other traumatized populations also support the social cog-nitive processing model. In general, these studies indicate that social constraints are positively associated with PTSD symptoms following a traumatic experience (Bonanno, Rennicke & Dekel 2005; Cordova et al. 2005; Kliewer et al. 1998; Manne, Duhamel & Redd 2000). For instance, social constraints were positively correlated with PTSD symptoms at several points following the September 11, 2001, terrorist attacks (Bonanno, Rennicke & Dekel 2005). Social constraints were also found to be a significant predictor of PTSD severity following traumatic injury (Cordova et al. 2005). Studies on sexual and non-sexual assault survivors have indicated that negative, critical, and unreceptive social networks exert an important influence on the development of PTSD (Andrews, Brewin & Rose 2003; Davis, Brickman & Baker 1991; Davis & Brickman 1996; Ullman & Filipas 2001; Zoellner, Foa & Brigidi 1999).

Several studies help shed light on the mechanisms involved in social cognitive processing. Individuals who feel more restrained in talking about their stressful experiences develop a higher frequency of intrusive thoughts and more frequent attempts to avoid thinking and talking about their experiences (Cordova et al. 2001; Lepore & Helgeson 1998; Schmidt & Andrykowski 2004). Greater intrusion frequency is associated with more talking for those reporting low constraints, while greater intrusion frequency is actually associated with less talking for those experiencing social constraints (Lepore et al. 1996). Socially constrained individuals subsequently report greater distress and worse outcomes as a result of experiencing a high frequency of trauma-related intrusions in a critical and unreceptive social environment (Lepore et al. 1996; Lepore & Helgeson 1998; Manne, Duhamel & Redd 2000). On the other hand, individuals with fewer social constraints tend to engage in more discussions surrounding these intrusions, employ more adaptive coping strategies, and have better outcomes (Cordova et al. 2001; Lepore 2001). Thus, social constraints appear to limit cognitive-emotional processing and engender worse outcomes during recovery, while discussing trauma-related experiences in receptive environments promotes recovery.

While the influence of social relationships on recovery from trauma seems apparent, several caveats must be considered. First, social constraints may be perceived by the trauma survivor, independent of objective constraining responses from others. Second, social constraints may be elicited by the way the trauma survivor talks or interacts with others. Finally, social constraints may result from others' well-intended attempts to assist the survivor.

The perception of social support may be more important than objective responses from others (Haber et al. 2007; Prati & Pietrantoni 2010). For instance, psychological distress has shown a stronger relationship to perceived social support than actual, enacted support (Barrera 1986). Several factors may contribute to trauma survivors' negative interpersonal perceptions. Given trauma's impact on core beliefs surrounding self, others, and the world, trauma survivors may feel guilty, ashamed, and unacceptable to others. They may expect that others will judge them, not be able to understand, or be burdened by hearing about their difficulties. These negative beliefs may contribute to inaccurate perceptions and interpretations of others' behaviors and intentions. Further, relative to those without PTSD, individuals with PTSD experience greater difficulty recognizing and distinguishing certain emotions of others (Sta. Maria 2002) and are more vigilant and responsive to threat cues (Huppert et al. 2009). Inaccurate perceptions and hyperresponsiveness to threat may bias traumatized individuals to misread the social context and (inaccurately) experience interpersonal negativity in their environment. In addition, trauma survivors, due to their own difficulty in tolerating painful emotions and uncomfortable physical sensations related to anxiety, may be motivated to conclude that others can't understand, can't handle, or don't want to hear about their experiences; such judgments may represent avoidance behaviors that serve to reduce or avoid emotional distress.

Social constraints may not be a stable characteristic of the social environment, but rather may be a function of reciprocal interactions between the trauma survivor and the social network. Specific interpersonal behaviors may elicit greater rejection by others (Joiner & Metalsky 2001). For instance, individuals who excessively seek reassurance or conversely seek negative feedback from others experience diminished social support as a result (Borelli & Prinstein 2006; Starr & Davila 2008). Individuals with PTSD may engage in specific behaviors that elicit social constraints in their environments, including externalizing (i.e., anger, aggressiveness, irritability) and internalizing (i.e., withdrawal, emotional numbing, depression) behaviors endemic to post-trauma recovery (Renshaw, Blais & Caska 2011). Moreover, initially supportive others may become less supportive when symptoms do not resolve with the passage of time. Thus, PTSD symptoms may erode social support over time (King et al. 2006; Laffaye et al. 2008) and contribute to more negative social reactions when the symptoms are associated with maladaptive interpersonal behaviors.

Finally, significant others, seeking to help, may unintentionally promote avoidance behaviors that maintain PTSD. Examples of these types of interactions include treating survivors as helpless victims, telling them not to think about the trauma, encouraging distraction, and withdrawing to prevent further distress. While these behaviors may be intended to decrease the survivor's distress, an implicit message is conveyed that survivors should not think about or discuss their experiences. These types of interactions may reinforce avoidance coping behaviors and further stigmatize and disempower survivors.

The social cognitive processing model of adjustment highlights the importance of receptive social support networks and the negative implications of restraining social conditions. However, perceiving, receiving, and providing adequate social support in the presence of post-traumatic symptoms is a complicated process. This is particularly true for combat veterans, their families, and their broader social networks.

The Social Cognitive Processing Model and the Combat Veteran

Combat veterans are exposed to a range of potentially traumatic experiences that they may want and/or need to talk about and process. But while war exerts a significant toll on veterans, their family members also endure emotional hardships during these deployments (Orthner & Rose 2005; SteelFisher, Zaslavsky & Blendon 2008). Indeed, there is a higher prevalence of depression, anxiety, adjustment issues, acute stress reactions, and sleep problems among spouses of deployed soldiers (Mansfield et al. 2010). Upon returning from deployment, individuals comprising the veteran's social support network may struggle to redefine their relationship with the veteran. The task of communicating empathy while managing one's own psychological distress may be especially challenging. Though relieved that the veteran is home, family and friends may also experience a range of other emotions (e.g., anger, resentment, sadness, fear) as they attempt to once again readjust their lives. The veteran's new behaviors may cause uncertainty about how to interact with the changed individual. These complex challenges of social reintegration may lead to greater interpersonal friction and contribute to decreased social support, especially for veterans experiencing post-traumatic stress symptoms (Goff et al. 2006; Goff & Smith 2005).

For those in veterans' support networks, changes observed in the returnee may cause alarm. However, caregivers may dismiss or avoid acknowledging their concerns rather than directly addressing them, in hopes that the issues will recede with time. Potential supporters may also avoid discussions about the war because of their own discomfort. They may be unsure whether to raise the subject, afraid to upset the veteran, unclear about what to say, or uncomfortable in a helping role. Veterans' attempts to discuss their experiences may be further met with social reactions of horror, disgust, or fear that reinforce the guilt and shame that some veterans feel.

Social constraints may also be combined with internal constraints on disclosure. The veteran, especially in the face of PTSD symptoms, often feels emotionally distant from other people, different from civilians who have not served, emotionally numb, and/or irritable and angry; these internal experiences may inhibit self-disclosure. Veterans' own beliefs may also pose obstacles to talking about their experiences and distress. Often those with PTSD believe that others do not care, cannot help, or will seek to take advantage of them. This internal sense of constraint, coupled with intense symptoms, may hinder the veteran from expressing himself and engaging in dialogue with others and may also elicit more negative reactions from others. For instance, veterans with greater arousal symptoms tend to express considerable anger toward their spouses that erodes their support over time (Evans et al. 2003; Taft et al. 2005). Post-traumatic stress symptoms of avoidance and numbing are also strongly associated with greater marital dissatisfaction (Evans et al. 2003; Solomon, Dekel & Mikulincer 2008). In general, veterans with post-traumatic stress may have greater difficulty developing emotional intimacy with their partners (Riggs et al. 1998) and engage in less emotional expression and disclosure (Carroll et al. 1985). In essence, these symptoms and behaviors may push social support away and impair emotional intimacy, leading to a greater sense of estrangement. Family members on the receiving end of these behaviors will be less likely to provide emotional support and more likely to avoid dialogue with the veteran.

Combat veterans may experience pervasive feelings of guilt and shame and feel unable to discuss these intense feelings with others. In particular, involvement with killing in war (active killing or failing to prevent killing) is predictive of PTSD and associated with greater interpersonal problems upon return (Fontana & Rosenheck 1999; MacNair 2002; Maguen et al. 2010). Veterans who experience some type of moral injury in combat (Litz et al. 2009) may be less likely to discuss their experiences with others due to fears of disapproval, shame, and rejection. Simultaneously, these veterans may be overly (and inaccurately) sensitive to rejection cues from others that reinforce their negative self-concept. These fears of disclosure, combined with biased perceptions of social rejection by others, may further suppress communication and maintain avoidance behaviors.

The veteran, then, may learn to limit disclosure about the events of war and his or her internal experiences. As these negative interactions spiral, veterans may further withdraw and experience more severe symptoms, leading those in support networks to further distance themselves from them. Thus, a negative and self-perpetuating pattern emerges that significantly interferes with cognitive-emotional processing and hinders post-trauma adjustment and recovery for the returning veteran.

While the social cognitive processing model focuses on social constraints encountered during interactions with family and friends, broader social reactions in the form of societal constraints may also affect likelihood of disclosure. Historically, this was perhaps most clearly illustrated following the Vietnam War, when many returning veterans faced a culture steeped in antiwar sentiment and an unsupportive American public, many of whom disapproved of their actions and lacked empathy for their suffering. Societies continue to have difficulty reconciling what military combatants are required to do with acceptance of these acts once they have occurred. Veterans themselves are also trained within socially constrained military environments that reinforce stoicism, nondisclosure of perceived "weakness," and the suppression of personal needs for a greater good. Discharging from this environment into a mainstream society that does not want to hear about the traumas inherent in war, while attempting to reestablish emotional openness and intimacy with family, is an arduous task facing our returning soldiers.

In sum, the social cognitive processing model may help illustrate how social support influences veterans' adjustment and direct attention to specific mechanisms that promote or impede trauma recovery. Socially constraining environments, whether experienced, perceived, or elicited, inhibit trauma processing and forestall recovery for veterans experiencing post-traumatic symptoms. Given the high prevalence of soldiers returning with PTSD and experiencing family dysfunction, treatment interventions developed to reduce social constraints on trauma processing are timely. The social cognitive processing theoretical framework can inform development of these treatment approaches and is potentially consistent with a wide range of individual, familial, group, and social environmental therapeutic intervention strategies.

Models of Intervention

The social cognitive processing model has implications for intervention approaches and policy aimed at facilitating adjustment among combat veterans. Individual, family, and group counseling approaches may facilitate processing both intrapersonally and interpersonally. In addition, policy and systemic approaches in the VA healthcare system, the military, and society at large may set the stage for social processing and recovery.

Individual Psychotherapy

Individual PTSD treatment, though largely focusing on intrapersonal processes of recovery, often facilitates social cognitive processing. In treatment, veterans learn to disclose details of their traumatic experiences along with their personal reactions and symptoms. Trauma-focused interventions like prolonged exposure (Foa, Hembree & Rothbaum 2007) and cognitive processing therapy (Resick, Monson & Chard 2007) are among the most highly recommended PTSD treatments in the Department of Veterans Affairs–Department of

Defense (DoD) Clinical Practice Guideline Working Group joint *Clinical Practice Guideline for Management of Traumatic Stress* (2010).

Both prolonged exposure and cognitive processing therapy specifically encourage veterans to discuss with the therapist, in detail, the nature of their traumas and the feelings, thoughts, and meanings associated with those experiences. Therapists seek to avoid constraining disclosure and are trained to accept the content of their patients' trauma narratives. As part of these discussions between therapist and patient, cognitive-emotional processing is facilitated and trauma-related appraisals are reconsidered and, if appropriate, explored and challenged. Through these processes, veterans may come to better accept their traumatic event; fully experience the emotions associated with the trauma; and learn to tolerate trauma-related memories, emotions, and physical reactions. Veterans may emerge with more functional views related to themselves, others, and the world, and subsequently experience a decrease in negative emotions (e.g., guilt, shame) and dysfunctional behaviors (e.g., avoidance, hypervigilance). Successfully talking with someone else about trauma-related experiences may also promote a greater willingness and ability to talk with others in a way that is less likely to elicit social constraints and may thus further facilitate processing and adjustment.

In fact, following disclosure in the context of a clinician-patient relationship, many veterans go on to share aspects of their experience with spouses or other significant others, family, and other social supports. However, current evidence-based treatments for PTSD do not formally undertake to facilitate processes of disclosure and social support in the natural social environments of the trauma survivor, and little is known about the effects of treatment on social cognitive processing. It remains unclear whether clinicians might train trauma survivors and their significant others to engage in mutual support behaviors and target communication patterns that facilitate or disrupt disclosure of trauma-related content.

Family Interventions

As noted previously, family involvement in veterans' care is called for in the Department of Veterans Affairs *Comprehensive VHA Strategic Plan for Mental Health Services* (2004) and in the *VHA Handbook 1160.01: Uniform Mental Health Services in VA Medical Centers and Clinics* (2008). Treatment approaches that educate families about veterans' mental health issues, including PTSD, and that teach communication and coping skills, may reduce actual and perceived social constraints and promote processing and adjustment in veterans and their loved ones. Such programs may also facilitate access to other services through the VA healthcare system and the community.

Several family education and intervention programs are being disseminated and implemented nationally (Makin-Byrd et al. 2011) and have particular relevance to the social cognitive processing model. Support and Family Education (SAFE) (Sherman 2006) is a professionally led, eighteen-session program designed to educate families about PTSD; relevant resources; and useful skills to enhance communication, problem solving, and stress management. The National Alliance for the Mentally Ill (NAMI) Family-to-Family Education Program is a twelve-session program led by trained family member volunteers, designed to teach families about mental illness and its treatment, communication skills, community services, and self-care (Dixon et al. 2004; Pickett-Schenk et al. 2006, 2008). Multifamily Group Psychoeducation (McFarlane 2002; Jewell, Downing & McFarlane 2009) is a multiyear program that helps those with mental illness and their families build supportive relationships with other families struggling with similar issues, learn about mental illness and its treatment, strengthen coping strategies, develop problem-solving strategies, set goals, and increase integration into the community. Behavioral family therapy (Mueser & Glynn 1995) teaches veterans and their families about mental illness, available treatments, and communication (including empathetic listening) and problem-solving skills. Integrative behavioral couples therapy (IBCT) (Christensen et al. 2010; Christensen & Jacobson 2000) teaches communication and problem-solving strategies to couples while emphasizing acceptance of their differences and tolerance of emotional responses to problem situations.

In addition, researchers are beginning to develop couples' interventions that focus specifically on PTSD. Cognitive-behavioral conjoint therapy for PTSD (Monson & Fredman in press; Monson et al. 2004; Monson, Taft & Fredman 2009) is designed to both reduce symptoms and improve relationship functioning. The fifteen-session treatment includes psychoeducation about PTSD and relationship difficulties, conflict management, behavioral interventions to reduce avoidance and improve partner communication, and dyadic cognitive interventions to address maladaptive thinking patterns that maintain both PTSD symptoms and relationship distress. Strategic Approach Therapy (Sautter et al. 2009), a ten-session, manualized behavioral couples' therapy, targets PTSD avoidance and numbing symptoms through education, motivational enhancement, training in communication and problem-solving skills, increasing behaviors that promote intimacy and positive emotions, and partner-assisted anxiety reduction techniques. Cordova and colleagues (2003) described a one-session educational dyadic intervention aimed specifically at reducing social constraints, promoting disclosure, and removing barriers to cognitive-emotional processing after trauma.

Despite the variability of these approaches, their common attention to education, communication and problem-solving skills, and emotional tolerance is consistent with the social cognitive processing model. Orienting family members to common psychiatric symptoms in combat veterans and teaching them effective communication strategies may improve their awareness of these issues, reduce social constraints, facilitate more mutually beneficial exchanges between veterans and their families, increase trauma processing, and reduce caregiver burden and stress.

Group Interventions

Group treatments for PTSD also afford a significant social context that can facilitate processing of the traumatic experience. A core goal of group treatment is the development of mutual support and understanding among group members (Foy et al. 2000), and most group leaders take steps to establish a sense of emotional safety, trust, and cohesion among members (Shea et al. 2009). The group focus on interactions among members serves to improve communication and resolve conflicts and fosters a climate of group support that reduces the social isolation and interpersonal alienation that often accompanies PTSD. In effect, groups are structured to reduce constraints on disclosure and to actively promote greater willingness to discuss personal experiences. A particular strength of groups is their capacity for effective modeling of disclosure. When members observe one another disclosing aspects of their traumatic experiences and/or reactions to trauma in the absence of negative reactions from group leaders and peers, they will be more likely to do the same, both in the group and in day-to-day interactions with family and friends.

Trauma-focused groups attempt the same kind of processing that is undertaken in many individual PTSD treatments. Social cognitive processing of negative trauma-related appraisals may be especially enhanced when members provide feedback to one another. For example, a veteran who blames himself for killing a civilian who failed to stop at a checkpoint may receive feedback from peers who, being familiar with the situations he describes, can help him recognize the specific context in which the difficult choices were made (e.g., that failure to stop the civilian may have resulted in loss of life of military personnel; that there was limited time to weigh different options).

Healthcare System Interventions

The healthcare system itself provides a variety of treatment contexts that affect disclosure of traumatic experiences. Research indicates that veterans will often be unlikely to disclose their post-traumatic-related problems, and those experiencing higher levels of symptoms may be especially unlikely to seek help (Maguen & Litz 2006). Rather than talking to a mental health professional, most veterans who have experienced traumas and have symptoms of PTSD will seek help from their doctors or chaplains and other spiritual advisors and in other settings (e.g., substance abuse treatment programs, employee assistance programs, marital and family counseling). Whatever the circumstances, veterans are unlikely to self-disclose about trauma if they are not asked. In fact, failure of providers to inquire about traumatic experiences might be viewed as a form of social constraint. To promote disclosure and subsequent discussion that can facilitate processing, it is important that explicit screening for PTSD take place in these helping encounters. In the VA and DoD healthcare systems, screening for PTSD and several other postdeployment problems occurs at multiple points in time. This is important, in that active duty personnel have been found to report more mental health concerns three to six months after return than in the first month back (Milliken, Auchterlonie & Hoge 2007; Bliese et al. 2007). Screening can increase rates of identification of PTSD and improve appropriate referrals for mental health treatment (e.g., Kimerling, Trafton & Nguyen 2006); brief screening tools are available and can be easily incorporated into intake procedures in the civilian sector (Gore et al. 2008; Prins et al. 2003).

Wherever disclosure takes place, it is important that it be received with acceptance and support to facilitate processes of recovery. This support will be more likely to occur if providers are educated about PTSD and trauma and are trained to talk to their patients about these issues. While clinicians and support staff receive some formal education regarding PTSD, this is an area of needed growth in the VA healthcare system. Some efforts are already in place. Formal training initiatives in evidence-based treatments for PTSD (Karlin et al. 2010) include the development of provider brochures and videotapes that can be used to help providers better recognize the impact of disclosure and increase appropriate referrals for treatment. Behavioral health specialists are increasingly becoming embedded in primary care medical settings (Funderburk et al. 2010; Pomerantz & Sayers 2010), which can serve to reduce barriers to trauma disclosure (e.g., time constraints on medical encounters).

Similarly, systemic efforts to educate veterans about PTSD and other mental health conditions, destigmatize mental health treatment, and improve access to care can reduce barriers to disclosure and processing. A range of educational tools has been developed to reduce barriers to participation in PTSD treatment, including educational pamphlets and videos.

Military Interventions

Though the social contexts most relevant to post-trauma recovery are likely to be dyadic (therapist-patient, veteran-partner), larger environmental contexts can also be expected to influence communication processes, likelihood of and reactions to disclosure, and perceptions of mental illness and recovery. In particular, military workplace environments will be associated with norms for behavior that facilitate or discourage disclosure and support or disparage individuals with mental health problems following deployment. Although most conceptualizations of social constraints focus on personal social networks, it may prove useful to characterize larger workplace and societal environments in terms of the degree to which they are perceived to impose constraints on disclosure. Clearly, some social environments are characterized by greater likelihood of encountering constraints to disclosure than others. For example, there have historically been significant obstacles to disclosure of sexual assault by women military personnel. Interventions to reduce social constraints on disclosure and facilitate social cognitive processing can focus on larger social environments.

Some evolving military programs are consistent with the social cognitive processing model. Large-scale educational/systems interventions in active duty military environments attempt to normalize post-traumatic stress reactions ("battlemind") (Adler et al. 2009) or redefine postdeployment stress reactions as analogous to physical injuries ("combat stress injuries") (Nash et al. in press). These efforts may help shape the larger social contexts in which disclosure occurs and that effect evolving appraisals. Disclosure by those in leadership positions about their own emotional difficulties or PTSD after difficult deployments (e.g., Dallaire 2010) can also be expected to facilitate disclosure at other organizational levels. Development of peer support initiatives during active duty (e.g., Jones, Roberts & Greenberg 2003) and for veterans with PTSD (Grenier et al. 2007) provide another, more localized way of promoting disclosure and adaptive appraisal. The Comprehensive Soldier Fitness (CSF) program (Casey 2011; Cornum, Matthews & Seligman 2011), a large-scale army prevention and resilience training program, includes several components relevant to the social cognitive processing model, such as education and skills training in emotion regulation (Algoe & Fredrickson 2011), social relationships (Cacioppo, Reiss & Zautra 2011) and family communication (Gottman, Gottman & Atkins 2011). Together, these programs may enable soldiers to more effectively identify, disclose, and receive support for emotional struggles following traumatic experiences.

Societal Interventions

In the general community, education of mental health providers and other civilians involved with veterans (e.g., employers, educators) can also facilitate social cognitive processing by improving understanding about trauma and PTSD and normalizing discussion about these problems. The establishment of state-based consortia that bring together multiple stakeholders—VA healthcare system and vet center staff, DoD personnel from all branches of service (including reserve components), TRICARE providers, state departments of veterans affairs, community-based organizations, and consumer groups—interested in the welfare of Iraq and Afghanistan war returnees and veterans of every war (e.g., Northwest Network Deployment Health Summit Regional Conference) (McFall et al. 2005) can help in this regard, as can media campaigns like the DoD's "Real Warriors" campaign (http://realwarriors.net/). Media coverage of veterans' challenges with PTSD and readjustment difficulties is especially important in shaping public perceptions of veterans and thus influencing social reactions to their problems. Educational programs for journalists can assist them in better understanding the issues and ensuring that their coverage improves public understanding (Simpson & Cote 2007).

Summary

Veterans and their families face a range of challenges following deployment. Overcoming these challenges entails, in part, cognitive emotional processing of stressors encountered in a war zone. The social cognitive processing model of adjustment following trauma exposure emphasizes that such processing occurs in a social context that can support or hinder recovery. The social context for veterans can be particularly complicated when their own reactions and beliefs about seeking help can inhibit disclosure or elicit negative responses; when family and friends are facing their own stressors and may not know how to support the veteran; and when the healthcare system, the military, and society may pose obstacles to being open about problems and receiving help. Programs are underway that seek to instill knowledge, skills, and attitudes in veterans and at all levels of their social environment that will promote disclosure, cognitive emotional processing, and engagement in services to foster post-trauma adjustment and recovery.

References

Adler, A. D., Bliese, P. D., McGurk, D., Hoge, C. W. & Castro, C. A. (2009). Battlemind debriefing and battlemind training as early interventions with soldiers returning from Iraq: Randomization by platoon. *Journal of Consulting and Clinical Psychology* 77: 928–940.

Algoe, S. B. & Fredrickson, B. L. (2011). Emotional fitness and the movement of affective science from lab to field. *American Psychologist* 66: 35–42.

Andrews, B., Brewin, C. & Rose, S. (2003). Gender, social support, and PTSD in victims of violent crime. *Journal of Traumatic Stress* 16, no. 4: 421–428.

Barrera, M. (1986). Distinctions between social support concepts, measures, and models. *American Journal of Community Psychology* 14, no. 4: 413–445.

Batten, S. V., Drapalski, A. L., Decker, M. L., DeViva, J. C., Morris, L. J., Mann, M. A. & Dixon, L. B. (2009). Veteran interest in family involvement in PTSD treatment. *Psychological Services* 6, no. 3: 184–189.

Bliese, P. D., Wright, K. M., Adler, A. B., Thomas, J. L. & Hoge, C. W. (2007). Timing of postcombat mental health assessments. *Psychological Services* 4, no. 3: 141–148.

Bonanno, G., Rennicke, C. & Dekel, S. (2005). Self-enhancement among high-exposure survivors of the September 11th terrorist attack: Resilience or social mal-adjustment? *Journal of Personality and Social Psychology* 88, no. 6: 984–998.

Borelli, J. L. & Prinstein, M. J. (2006). Reciprocal, longitudinal associations among adolescents' negative feedback-seeking, depressive symptoms, and peer relations. *Journal of Abnormal Child Psychology* 34, no. 2: 159–169.

Bowling, U. B. & Sherman, M. D. (2008). Welcoming them home: Supporting service members and their families in navigating the tasks of reintegration. *Professional Psychology: Research and Practice* 39: 451–458.

Burleson, B. R. & Goldsmith, D. J. (1998). How the comforting process works: Alleviating emotional distress through conversationally induced reappraisals. In P. A. Andersen, L. K. Guerrero, P. A. Andersen & L. K. Guerrero (Eds.), *Handbook of communication and emotion: Research, theory, applications, and contexts* (pp. 245–280). San Diego, CA: Academic Press.

Cacioppo, J. T., Reiss, H. T. & Zautra, A. J. (2011). Social resilience: The value of social fitness with an application to the military. *American Psychologist* 66: 43–51.

Carroll, E. M., Rueger, D. B., Foy, D. W. & Donahoe, C. P. (1985). Vietnam combat veterans with Posttraumatic Stress Disorder: Analysis of marital and cohabitating adjustment. *Journal of Abnormal Psychology* 94, no. 3: 329–337.

Casey, G. W. (2011). Comprehensive soldier fitness: A vision for psychological resilience in the U.S. Army. *American Psychologist* 66: 1–3.

Christensen, A., Atkins, D. C., Baucom, B. & Yi, J. (2010). Marital status and satisfaction five years following a randomized clinical trial comparing traditional versus integrative behavioral couple therapy. *Journal of Consulting and Clinical Psychology* 78: 225–235.

Christensen, A. & Jacobson, N. (2000). *Reconcilable differences.* New York: Guilford Press.

Cohen, A. N., Glynn, S. M., Murray-Swank, A. B., Barrio, C., Fischer, E. P., McCutcheon, S. J., et al. (2008). The family forum: Directions for the implementation of family psychoeducation for severe mental illness. *Psychiatric Services* 59, no. 1: 40–48.

Cohen, S. & Wills, T. A. (1985). Stress, social support, and the buffering hypothesis. *Psychological Bulletin* 98, no. 2: 310–357.

Cook, J. M., Riggs, D. S., Thompson, R., Coyne, J. C. & Sheikh, J. I. (2004). Post-traumatic stress disorder and current relationship functioning among World War II ex-prisoners of war. *Journal of Family Psychology* 18, no. 1: 36–45.

Cordova, M., Cunningham, L., Carlson, C. & Andrykowski, M. (2001). Posttraumatic growth following breast cancer: A controlled comparison study. *Health Psychology* 20, no. 3: 176–185.

Cordova, M., Giese-Davis, J., Golant, M., Kronenwetter, C., Chang, V. & Spiegel, D. (2007). Breast cancer as trauma: Posttraumatic stress and posttraumatic growth. *Journal of Clinical Psychology in Medical Settings* 14, no. 4: 308–319.

Cordova, M. J., Ruzek, J. P., Benoit, M. & Brunet, A. (2003). Promotion of emotional disclosure following illness and injury: A brief intervention for medical patients and their families. *Cognitive and Behavioral Practice* 10: 359–372.

Cordova, M. J., Walser, R., Neff, J. & Ruzek, J. I. (2005). Predictors of emotional adjustment following traumatic injury: Personal, social, and material resources. *Prehospital and Disaster Medicine* 20: 7–13.

Cornum, R., Matthews, M. D. & Seligman, M. E. P. (2011). Comprehensive soldier fitness: Building resilience in a challenging institutional context. *American Psychologist* 66: 4–9.

Creamer, M., Burgess, P. & Pattison, P. (1992). Reaction to trauma: A cognitive processing model. *Journal of Abnormal Psychology* 101, no. 3: 452–459.

Dallaire, R. (2010). Injured, not sick. Paper presented at 26th annual meeting of International Society for Traumatic Stress Studies, Montreal, Canada.

Danoff-Burg, S., Revenson, T. A., Trudeau, K. J. & Paget, S. A. (2004). Unmitigated communion, social constraints, and psychological distress among women with rheumatoid arthritis. *Journal of Personality* 72, no. 1: 29–46.

Davis, R. C. & Brickman, E. (1996). Supportive and unsupportive aspects of the behavior of others toward victims of sexual and nonsexual assault. *Journal of Interpersonal Violence* 11, no. 2: 250–262.

Davis, R. C., Brickman, E. & Baker, T. (1991). Supportive and unsupportive responses of others to rape victims: Effects on concurrent victim adjustment. *American Journal of Community Psychology* 19, no. 3: 443–451.

Dekel, R. & Solomon, Z. (2007). Secondary traumatization among wives of war veterans with PTSD. In C. R. Figley & W. P. Nash (Eds.), *Combat stress injury: Theory, research, and management* (pp. 137–157). New York: Routledge.

Department of Veterans Affairs. (2004). A comprehensive VHA strategic plan for mental health services—revised. VHA Mental Health Strategic Plan Workgroup/ Mental Health Strategic Health Care Group, Office of the Assistant Deputy Under Secretary for Health, July 9.

Department of Veterans Affairs, Office of Mental Health Services (OMHS). (2008). *VHA handbook 1160.01: Uniform mental health services in VA medical centers and clinics.* http://www1.va.gov/vhapublications/ViewPublication.asp?pub_ID=1762 (accessed January 6, 2011).

Department of Veterans Affairs, Veterans Health Administration. (2006). VHA directive 2006–041. http://www.va.gov/vhapublications/ViewPublication.asp?pub_ID=1443(accessed January 6, 2011).

Department of Veterans Affairs. Veterans Health Administration/Department of Defense. VA-DoD Clinical Practice Guideline Working Group. (2010). *Management of post-traumatic stress.* Publication no. 10Q-CPG/PTSD-04. Washington, DC: Office of Quality and Performance.

Dixon, L., Lucksted, A., Stewart, B., Burland, J., Brown, C., Postrado, L., et al. (2004). Outcomes of the peer-taught 12-week family-to-family education program for severe mental illness. *Acta Psychiatrica Scandinavica* 109: 207–215.

Epstein, S. (1991). Impulse control and self-destructive behavior. In L. P. Lipsitt & L. L. Mitick (Eds.), Self-regulatory behavior and risk-taking: Causes and consequences (pp. 273–284). Norwood, NJ: Ablex.

Evans, L., Cowlishaw, S., Forbes, D., Parslow, R. & Lewis, V. (2010). Longitudinal analyses of family functioning in veterans and their partners across treatment. *Journal of Consulting and Clinical Psychology* 78, no. 5: 611–622.

Evans, L., Cowlishaw, S. & Hopwood, M. (2009). Family functioning predicts outcomes for veterans in treatment for chronic posttraumatic stress disorder. *Journal of Family Psychology* 23, no. 4: 531–539.

Evans, L., McHugh, T., Hopwood, M. & Watt, C. (2003). Chronic posttraumatic stress disorder and family functioning of Vietnam veterans and their partners. *Australian & New Zealand Journal of Psychiatry* 37, no. 6: 765–772.

Foa, E. & Kozak, M. (1986). Emotional processing of fear. *Psychological Bulletin* 99: 20–35.

Foa, E., Steketee, G. & Rothbaum, B. (1989). Behavioral/cognitive conceptualizations of post-traumatic stress disorder. *Behavior Therapy* 20, no. 2: 155–176.

Foa, E. B., Hembree, E. A. & Rothbaum, B. O. (2007). *Prolonged exposure therapy for PTSD: Emotional processing of traumatic experiences.* New York: Oxford University Press.

Fontana, A. & Rosenheck, R. (1999). A model of war zone stressors and posttraumatic stress disorder. *Journal of Traumatic Stress* 12: 111–127.

Foy, D. W., Glynn, S. M., Schnurr, P. P., Jankowski, M. K., Wattenberg, M. S., Weiss, D. S., et al. (2000). Group therapy. In E. B. Foa, T. M. Keane & M. J. Friedman (Eds.), *Effective treatments for PTSD: Practice guidelines from the International Society for Traumatic Stress studies* (pp. 336–338). New York: Guilford Press.

Friedman, M. J. & Schnurr, P. P. (1995). The relationship between PTSD, trauma, and physical health. In M. J. Friedman, D. S. Friedman & A. Y. Deutch (Eds.), *Neurobiological and clinical consequences of stress: From normal adaptation to PTSD* (pp. 507–533). New York: Raven Press.

Funderburk, J. S., Sugarman, D. E., Maisto, S. A., Ouimette, P., Schohn, M., Lantinga, L., Wray, L., Batki, S., Nelson, B., Coolhart, D. & Strutynski, K. (2010).

The description and evaluation of the implementation of an integrated healthcare model. *Families, Systems & Health* 28: 146–160.

Galovski, T. & Lyons, J. A. (2004). Psychological sequelae of combat violence: A review of the impact of PTSD on the veteran's family and possible interventions. *Aggression and Violent Behavior* 9, no. 5: 477–501.

Goff, B., Reisbig, A. J., Bole, A., Scheer, T., Hayes, E., Archuleta, K. L., et al. (2006). The effects of trauma on intimate relationships: A qualitative study with clinical couples. *American Journal of Orthopsychiatry* 76, no. 4: 451–460.

Goff, B. & Smith, D. B. (2005). Systemic traumatic stress: The Couple Adaptation to Traumatic Stress Model. *Journal of Marital and Family Therapy* 31, no. 2: 145–157.

Gore, K. L., Engel, C. C., Freed, M. C., Liu, X. & Armstrong, D. (2008). Test of a single-item posttraumatic stress disorder screener in a military primary care setting. *General Hospital Psychiatry* 30, no. 5: 391–397.

Gottman, J. M., Gottman, J. S. & Atkins, C. L. (2011). The comprehensive soldier fitness program: Family skills component. *American Psychologist* 66: 52–57.

Grenier, S., Darte, K., Heber, A. & Richardson, D. (2007). The Operational Stress Injury Social Support Program: A peer support program in collaboration between the Canadian forces and Veterans Affairs Canada. In C. R. Figley & W. P. Nash (Eds.), *Combat stress injury: Theory, research, and management* (pp. 261–293). New York: Routledge/Taylor & Francis Group.

Haber, M. G., Cohen, J. L., Lucas, T. & Baltes, B. B. (2007). The relationship between self-reported received and perceived social support: A meta-analytic review. *American Journal of Community Psychology* 39, nos. 1–2: 133–144.

Hollon, S. D. & Kriss, M. R. (1984). Cognitive factors in clinical research and practice. *Clinical Psychology Review* 4, no. 1: 35–76.

Horowitz, M. (1986). Stress-response syndromes: A review of posttraumatic and adjustment disorders. *Hospital & Community Psychiatry* 37, no. 3: 241–249.

Huppert, J. D., Foa, E. B., McNally, R. J. & Cahill, S. P. (2009). Role of cognition in stress-induced and fear circuitry disorders. In G. Andrews, D. S. Charney, P. J. Sirovatka & D. A. Regier (Eds.), *Stress-induced and fear circuitry disorders: Advancing the research agenda for DSM-V* (pp. 175–193). Arlington, VA: American Psychiatric Publishing, Inc.

Jacobsen, L. K., Southwick, S. M. & Kosten, T. R. (2001). Substance use disorders in patients with posttraumatic stress disorder: A review of the literature. *American Journal of Psychiatry* 158: 1184–1190.

Janoff-Bulman, R. (1992). *Shattered assumptions: Towards a new psychology of trauma.* New York: Free Press.

Jewell, T. C., Downing, D. & McFarlane, W. R. (2009). Partnering with families: multiple family group psychoeducation for schizophrenia. *Journal of Clinical Psychology* 65: 868–878.

Joiner, J. E. & Metalsky, G. I. (2001). Excessive reassurance seeking: Delineating a risk factor involved in the development of depressive symptoms. *Psychological Science* (Wiley-Blackwell) 12, no. 5: 371.

Jones, N., Roberts, P. & Greenberg, N. (2003). Peer-group risk assessment: A post-traumatic management strategy for hierarchical organizations. *Occupational Medicine* 53: 469–475.

Jordan, B. K., Marmar, C. R., Fairbank, J. A., Schlenger, W. E., Kulka, R. A., Hough, R. L. & Weiss, D. S. (1992). Problems in families of male Vietnam veterans with posttraumatic stress disorder. *Journal of Consulting and Clinical Psychology* 60: 916–926.

Karlin, B. E., Ruzek, J. I., Chard, K. M., Eftekhari, A., Monson, C. M., Hembree, E. A., et al. (2010). Dissemination of evidence-based psychological treatments for posttraumatic stress disorder in the Veterans Health Administration. *Journal of Traumatic Stress* 23, no. 6: 663–673.

Keane, T. M., Zimering, R. T. & Caddell, J. M. (1985). A behavioral formulation of posttraumatic stress disorder in Vietnam veterans. *Behavior Therapist* 8, no. 1: 9–12.

Kessler, R. C., Chiu, W. T., Demler, O., Merikangas, K. R. & Walters, E. E. (2005). Prevalence, severity, and comorbidity of 12-month DSM-IV disorders in the National Comorbidity Survey Replication. *Archives of General Psychiatry* 62, no. 6: 617–627.

Kilpatrick, D. G., Veronen, L. J. & Resick, P. A. (1979). The aftermath of rape: Recent empirical findings. *American Journal of Orthopsychiatry* 49, no. 4: 658–669.

Kimerling, R., Trafton, J. A. & Nguyen, B. (2006). Validation of a brief screen for post-traumatic stress disorder with substance use disorder patients. *Addictive Behaviors* 31, no. 11: 2074–2079.

King, D. W., Taft, C., King, L. A., Hammond, C. & Stone, E. R. (2006). Directionality of the association between social support and posttraumatic stress disorder: A longitudinal investigation. *Journal of Applied Social Psychology* 36, no. 12: 2980–2992.

Kliewer, W., Lepore, S. J., Oskin, D. & Johnson, P. D. (1998). The role of social and cognitive processes in children's adjustment to community violence. *Journal of Consulting and Clinical Psychology* 66, no. 1: 199–209.

Kulka, R. A., Schlenger, W. E., Fairbank, J. A. Hough, R. L., Jordan, B. K., Marmar, C. R. & Weiss, D. S. (1990). *Trauma and the Vietnam war generation: Report of findings from the National Vietnam Veterans Readjustment Study.* New York: Brunner/Mazel.

Laffaye, C., Cavella, S., Drescher, K. & Rosen, C. (2008). Relationships among PTSD symptoms, social support, and support source in veterans with chronic PTSD. *Journal of Traumatic Stress* 21, no. 4: 394–401.

Lepore, S. (2001). A social-cognitive processing model of emotional adjustment to cancer. In *Psychosocial interventions for cancer* (pp. 99–116). Washington, DC: American Psychological Association.

Lepore, S. & Helgeson, V. (1998). Social constraints, intrusive thoughts, and mental health after prostate cancer. *Journal of Social & Clinical Psychology* 17, no. 1: 89–106.

Lepore, S. & Ituarte, P. (1999). Optimism about cancer enhances mood by reducing negative social relations. *Cancer Research, Therapy, and Control* 8: 165–174.

Lepore, S. J., Fernandez-Berrocal, P., Ragan, J. & Ramos, N. (2004). It's not that bad: Social challenges to emotional disclosure enhance adjustment to stress. *Anxiety, Stress & Coping* 17, no. 4: 341–361.

Lepore, S. J., Ragan, J. D. & Jones, S. (2000). Talking facilitates cognitive-emotional processes of adaptation to an acute stressor. *Journal of Personality and Social Psychology* 78, no. 3: 499–508.

Lepore, S., Silver, R., Wortman, C. & Wayment, H. (1996). Social constraints, intrusive thoughts, and depressive symptoms among bereaved mothers. *Journal of Personality and Social Psychology* 70. no. 2: 271–282.

Litz, B. T., Stein, N., Delaney, E., Lebowitz, L., Nash, W. P., Silva, C. & Maguen, S. (2009). Moral injury and moral repair in war veterans: A preliminary model and intervention strategy. *Clinical Psychology Review* 29, no. 8: 695–706.

MacNair, R. (2002). *Perpetration-induced traumatic stress: The psychological consequences of killing.* Lincoln, NE: Praeger/Greenwood Publishing Group.

Maguen, S. & Litz, B. T. (2006). Predictors of barriers to mental health treatment for Kosovo and Bosnia peacekeepers: A preliminary report. *Military Medicine* 171, no. 5: 454–458.

Maguen, S., Lucenko, B. A., Reger, M. A., Gahm, G. A., Litz, B. T., Seal, K. H. & Marmar, C. R. (2010). The impact of reported direct and indirect killing on mental health symptoms in Iraq War veterans. *Journal of Traumatic Stress* 23, no. 1: 86–90.

Makin-Byrd, K., Gifford, E., McCutcheon, S. & Glynn, S. (2011). Family and couples treatment for newly returning veterans. *Professional Psychology: Research and Practice.* 42, no. 1: 47–55.

Manne, S., DuHamel, K., Nereo, N., Ostroff, J., Parsons, S., Martini, R., Redd, W. H., et al. (2002). Predictors of PTSD in mothers of children undergoing bone marrow transplantation: The role of cognitive and social processes. *Journal of Pediatric Psychology* 27, no. 7: 607–617.

Manne, S., Duhamel, K. & Redd, W. (2000). Association of psychological vulnerability factors to post-traumatic stress symptomatology in mothers of pediatric cancer survivors. *Psycho-Oncology* 9, no. 5: 372–384.

Mansfield, A. J., Kaufman, J. S., Marshall, S. W., Gaynes, B. N., Morrissey, J. P. & Engel, C. C. (2010). Deployment and the use of mental health services among U. S. Army wives. *New England Journal of Medicine* 362, no. 2: 101–109.

Matsakis, A. (2007). *Back from the front: Combat trauma, love, and the family.* Baltimore, MD: Sidran Institute Press.

McCann, I. & Pearlman, L. (1990). *Psychological trauma and the adult survivor: Theory, therapy, and transformation.* Philadelphia, PA: Brunner/Mazel.

McFall, M., Hunt, S., Ruzek, J. & Klevens, M. (2005). Meeting the mental health needs of OIF and OEF veterans. Pre-meeting institute presented at annual conference of the International Society for Traumatic Stress Studies, Toronto, Canada.

McFarlane, W. R. (2002). *Multifamily groups in the treatment of severe psychiatric disorders.* New York: Guilford Press.

Milliken, C. S., Auchterlonie, J. L. & Hoge, C. W. (2007). Longitudinal assessment of mental health problems among active and reserve component soldiers returning from the Iraq war. *JAMA* 298, no. 18: 2141–2148.

Monson, C. M. & Fredman, S. J. (in press). *Cognitive-behavioral conjoint therapy for posttraumatic stress disorder: Therapist's manual.* New York: Guilford.

Monson, C. M., Schnurr, P. P., Stevens, S. P. & Guthrie, K. A. (2004). Cognitive-behavioral couple's treatment for posttraumatic stress disorder: Initial findings. *Journal of Traumatic Stress* 17: 341–344.

Monson, C. M., Taft, C. T. & Fredman, S. J. (2009). Military-related PTSD and intimate relationships: From description to theory-driven research and intervention development. *Clinical Psychology Review* 29: 707–714.

Mowrer, O. H. (1939). Stimulus response theory of anxiety. *Psychological Review* 46: 553–565.

Mueser, K. T. & Glynn, S. M. (1995). *Behavioral family therapy for psychiatric disorders.* Needham Heights, MA: Allyn & Bacon.

Nash, W. P., Krantz, L., Stein, N., Westphal, R. J. & Litz, B. (in press). Comprehensive soldier fitness, battlemind, and the stress continuum model: Military organizational approaches to prevention. In J. I. Ruzek, J. J. Vasterling, P. P. Schnurr & M. J. Friedman (Eds.), *Caring for veterans with deployment-related stress disorders: Iraq, Afghanistan, and beyond.* Washington, DC: American Psychological Association Press.

Orthner, D. K. & Rose, R. (2005). Deployment and separation adjustment among Army civilian spouses. *Army Family Deployment Report,* December 15. http://www.army.mil/cfsc/docs/saf5deployreport15dec05.pdf (accessed February 6, 2011).

Pennebaker, J. (1995). *Emotion, disclosure & health.* Washington, DC: American Psychological Association.

Pickett-Schenk, S. A., Bennett, C., Cook, J. A., Steigman, P., Lippincott, R., Villagracia, I., et al. (2006). Changes in caregiving satisfaction and information needs among relatives of adults with mental illness. *American Journal of Orthopsychiatry* 76: 545–553.

Pickett-Schenk, S. A., Lippincott, R. C., Bennett, C. & Steigman, P. J. (2008). Improving knowledge about mental illness through family-led education: The journey of hope. *Psychiatric Services* 59: 49–56.

Pietrzak, R. H., Johnson, D. C., Goldstein, M. B., Malley, J. C. & Southwick, S. M. (2009). Perceived stigma and barriers to mental health care utilization among OEF-OIF veterans. *Psychiatric Services* 60: 1118–1122.

Pomerantz, A. S. & Sayers, S. L. (2010). Primary care–mental health integration in healthcare in the Department of Veterans Affairs. *Families, Systems & Health* 28: 78–82.

Prati, G. & Pietrantoni, L. (2010). The relation of perceived and received social support to mental health among first responders: A meta-analytic review. *Journal of Community Psychology* 38, no. 3: 403–417.

Prins, A., Ouimette, P., Kimerling, R., Cameron, R. P., Hugelshofer, D. S., Shaw-Hegwer, J., et al. (2003). The primary care PTSD screen (PC-PTSD): Development and operating characteristics. *Primary Care Psychiatry* 9, no. 1: 9–14.

Renshaw, K. D., Blais, R. K. & Caska, C. M. (2011). Distress in spouses of combat veterans with PTSD: The importance of interpersonally based cognitions and behaviors. In S. Wadsworth & D. Riggs (Eds.), *Risk and resilience in U.S. military families* (pp. 69–84). New York: Springer Science + Business Media.

Resick, P. A., Monson, C. M. & Chard, K. M. (2007). Cognitive processing therapy: Veteran/military version. Washington, DC: Department of Veterans Affairs.

Resick, P. A. & Schnicke, M. K. (1992). Cognitive processing therapy for sexual assault victims. *Journal of Consulting and Clinical Psychology* 60, no. 5: 748–756.

Riggs, D. S., Byrne, C., Weathers, F. & Litz, B. (1998). The quality of the intimate relationships of male Vietnam veterans: Problems associated with posttraumatic stress disorder. *Journal of Traumatic Stress* 11, no. 1: 87–101.

Rimé, B. (1995). Mental rumination, social sharing, and the recovery from emotional exposure. In J. W. Pennebaker & J. W. Pennebaker (Eds.), *Emotion, disclosure, & health* (pp. 271–291). Washington, DC: American Psychological Association.

Ruscio, A., Weathers, F. W., King, L. A. & Kin, D. W. (2002). Male war-zone veterans' perceived relationships with their children: The importance of emotional numbing. *Journal of Traumatic Stress* 15, no. 5: 351.

Sautter, F., Glynn, S., Thompson, K., Franklin, L. & Han, X. (2009). A couple-based approach to the reduction in PTSD avoidance symptoms: Preliminary findings. *Journal of Marital and Family Therapy* 35: 343–349.

Sayer, N. A., Noorbaloochi, S., Frazier, P. A., Carlson, K. F., Gravely, A. & Murdoch, M. (2010). Reintegration problems and treatment interests among Iraq and Afghanistan combat veterans receiving VA medical care. *Psychiatric Services* 61: 589–597.

Sayers, S. L., Farrow, V. A., Ross, J. & Oslin, D. W. (2009). Family problems among recently returned military veterans referred for a mental health evaluation. *Journal of Clinical Psychiatry* 70, no. 2: 163–170.

Schmidt, J. & Andrykowski, M. (2004). The role of social and dispositional variables associated with emotional processing in adjustment to breast cancer: An Internet-based study. *Health Psychology* 23, no. 3: 259–266.

Schnurr, P. P. & Jankowski, M. K. (1999). Physical health and posttraumatic stress disorder: Review and synthesis. *Seminars in Clinical Neuropsychiatry* 4: 295–304.

Shea, M., McDevitt-Murphy, M., Ready, D. J. & Schnurr, P. P. (2009). Group therapy. In E. B. Foa, T. M. Keane, M. J. Friedman & J. A. Cohen (Eds.), *Effective treatments for PTSD: Practice guidelines from the International Society for Traumatic Stress studies,* 2nd ed. (pp. 306–326). New York: Guilford Press.

Sherman, M. D. (2006). Updates and five-year evaluation of the SAFE program. *Community Mental Health Journal* 42: 213–219.

Simpson, R. & Cote, W. (2007). *Covering violence: A guide to ethical reporting about victims and trauma.* 2nd ed. New York: Columbia University Press.

Solomon, Z. Z., Dekel, R. R. & Mikulincer, M. M. (2008). Complex trauma of war captivity: A prospective study of attachment and post-traumatic stress disorder. *Psychological Medicine* 38, no. 10: 1427–1434.

Sta. Maria, N. (2002). Facial affect recognition in post-traumatic stress disorder. *Dissertation Abstracts International* 63, no. 6–B: 3026.

Starr, L. R. & Davila, J. (2008). Excessive reassurance seeking, depression, and interpersonal rejection: A meta-analytic review. *Journal of Abnormal Psychology* 117, no. 4: 762–775.

SteelFisher, G. K., Zaslavsky, A. M. & Blendon, R. J. (2008). Health-related impact of deployment extensions on spouses of active duty army personnel. *Military Medicine* 173, no. 3: 221–229.

Substance Abuse and Mental Health Services Administration (SAMHSA). (2010). National consensus statement on mental health recovery. http://mentalhealth.samhsa.gov/publications/allpubs/sma05–4129/ (accessed January 12, 2011).

Taft, C. T., Murphy, C. M., King, L. A., Dedeyn, J. M. & Musser, P. H. (2005). Post-traumatic stress disorder symptomatology among partners of men in treatment for relationship abuse. *Journal of Abnormal Psychology* 114, no. 2: 259–268.

Tanielian, T. & Jaycox, L. (Eds.). (2008). *Invisible wounds of war: Psychological and cognitive injuries, their consequences, and services to assist recovery.* Santa Monica, CA: RAND Corporation.

Ullman, S. E. & Filipas, H. H. (2001). Predictors of PTSD symptom severity and social reactions in sexual assault victims. *Journal of Traumatic Stress* 14, no. 2: 369.

Ullrich, P., Lutgendorf, S. & Stapleton, J. (2002). Social constraints and depression in HIV infection: Effects of sexual orientation and area of residence. *Journal of Social & Clinical Psychology* 21, no. 1: 46–66.

Widows, M., Jacobsen, P. & Fields, K. (2000). Relation of psychological vulnerability factors to posttraumatic stress disorder symptomatology in bone marrow transplant recipients. *Psychosomatic Medicine* 62, no. 6: 873–882.

Wilcox, S. (2010). Social relationships and PTSD symptomatology in combat veterans. *Psychological Trauma: Theory, Research, Practice, and Policy* 2: 175–182.

Zakowski, S., Harris, C., Krueger, N., Laubmeier, K., Garrett, S., Flanigan, R., et al. (2003). Social barriers to emotional expression and their relations to distress in male and female cancer patients. *British Journal of Health Psychology* 8, no. 3: 271–286.

Zoellner, L., Foa, E. & Brigidi, B. (1999). Interpersonal friction and PTSD in female victims of sexual and nonsexual assault. *Journal of Traumatic Stress* 12, no. 4: 689–702.

Polytrauma Care and Treatment in Veterans' Healthcare

Jeanne M. Bennett

Introduction

Operation Enduring Freedom (OEF) and Operation Iraqi Freedom (OIF) produced injuries unlike those in civilian life (Lehman 2008). Devastating physical injuries such as amputations, sensory loss, and traumatic brain injuries, as well as psychological injuries (i.e., depression, post-traumatic brain disorder), had occurred in over 264,000 service members as of September 2010 (Fischer 2010). Modes of physical injury in these wars included guns and missiles, improvised explosive devices (IEDs), suicide bombers, and roadside bombs. Congress passed legislation that allowed the Department of Veterans Affairs (VA) to provide healthcare services to active duty and veteran service members (Veterans Health Programs Improvement Act of 2004). The Polytrauma System of Care was developed by VA to provide specialized treatment and rehabilitation to the combat-injured.

The development of systems for trauma care has been inextricably connected with wars. During the American Revolutionary War, trauma care was based primarily on European principles, as most of the surgeons at that time had been trained in Scottish and English (in London) schools of medicine. Surgical procedures were limited mostly to treatment of patients with mild to moderate soft tissue injuries, and amputation was the most extensive operation performed (Trunkey 2000). The magnitude of casualties during the American Civil War required surgeons to treat the injured on the battlefield (Mackenzie et al. 2003). Anesthesia was used on a regular basis by medical personnel to treat wounds and injuries.

Other accomplishments during the Civil War included the treatment of open wounds (Wagensteen 1978), the establishment of an ambulance corps, and the introduction of nursing care (Blaisdell 1988). Blood transfusions were used in the Civil War (Hess 2005), with more extensive use of blood in World Wars I and II. Fluid shifts into the cell after severe hemorrhagic shock were discovered between the Korean conflict and the Vietnam War, leading to better treatment of patients with shock (Trunkey 2000). Attention to hemorrhage control, medical evacuation, and the establishment of medical echelons of care has advanced with successive wars.

The first trauma centers for civilians were established in the United States in 1966, and by early 2000 more than 1,100 trauma centers had been established nationwide (Mackenzie et. al. 2003). Military services in the United States have drawn on the experiences of civilian trauma centers to improve combat casualty care. Many advances that have been made through wartime surgical care and military medical research have not only combined to improve combat trauma care, but have been shared symbiotically with civilian trauma care, resulting in a velocity of progress over the past century to improve the outcome of patients (Pruitt 2008).

Rehabilitation services and practices have been influenced by experience gained in treating war casualties, including spinal cord injuries, traumatic brain injuries, and limb amputations (Rusk 2003). Survivors of these war injuries are presenting for rehabilitation to the Department of Veterans Affairs, which has made significant changes in its rehabilitation system to meet the needs of the most recent population of war-injured soldiers, many of whom have survived blast injuries that may have proved fatal in previous wars. Injuries that probably would have resulted in death in past combat engagements are being survived in greater numbers due to improved military protective gear for the troops and quicker expedition of service members out of the combat arena to regional medical centers for stabilization. The Department of Veterans Affairs has become involved in treatment during acute rehabilitation to foster a seamless transition from the military facility to the VA system of care.

The Veterans Health Administration's (VHA) Polytrauma System of Care was developed to respond to the new cohort of active duty service members and veterans who received multiple injuries while serving in combat in Iraq and Afghanistan (Belanger et al. 2009). Combat survivors with complex physical injuries and emotional trauma began to be referred to VA facilities for rehabilitation services shortly after the initiation of combat operations in Iraq (Sigford 2008). The most common cause of injury in this era of modern warfare is blasts (Friedemann-Sanchez et al. 2008), and a constellation of injuries related to blasts often follows. Some injuries are more visible (i.e., amputations, burns, head trauma, gunshot wounds) than others (i.e., pain, depression, post-traumatic stress disorder), but more soldiers are surviving these injuries than in previous conflicts because of improvements in body armor and field medicine (Gawande 2004).

Blast Injuries

Explosives are classified as either high energy or low energy. High energy explosives, such as TNT, dynamite, and nitroglycerine, create supersonic, overpressurized shock waves. Low energy explosives lack the overpressurization blast wave of high energy explosives, and injuries are often due to ballistic (fragmentation), blast wind (not blast wave), and thermal sources (Centers for Disease Control and Prevention 2006). Low energy explosives burn, whereas high energy explosives detonate.

There are four basic mechanisms of blast injuries, classified as primary, secondary, tertiary, and quaternary (Centers for Disease Control and Prevention 2006). Primary blast injuries occur when there is an overpressurization wave (blast force) that passes over the body surface. Secondary injuries result from projectiles, which can cause both penetrating and blunt trauma. Tertiary injuries occur when the person is displaced by the blast wind and can result in penetrating and blunt injuries, as well as amputations. All other injuries from the blast are categorized as quaternary injuries. (See table 8.1.)

Damage is seen almost exclusively in air-containing organs such as the lungs, the gastrointestinal tract, and the auditory system (Phillips 1986). (See table 8.2.)

Traumatic brain injury (TBI) often occurs in the polytrauma spectrum in combination with other disabling conditions such as amputations, burns, auditory and visual impairments, post-traumatic stress, and other mental disorders. If a TBI exists, this impairment may dictate the initial course of rehabilitation because of the cognitive, behavioral, and emotional impairments that are secondary to the TBI. Brain injuries tend to drive the care because the severity of the head injury will affect the veteran's ability to function and to engage in other therapies.

Head injuries can be penetrating (e.g., a foreign object has pierced the skull) or closed (e.g., a blow to the head, blast or explosion force, skull fracture, blood clot, nerve damage) and are classified as mild, moderate, or severe, depending on several criteria such as length of altered or lost consciousness, Glasgow Coma Scale score, the length of post-traumatic amnesia (e.g., memory loss), and neuroimaging studies.

Table 8.1. Mechanisms of Blast Injury

Category	Characteristics	Body Part Affected	Types of Injuries
Primary	Unique to high energy explosives, results from the impact of the overpressurization wave on body surfaces.	Gas-filled structures are most susceptible: lungs, gastrointestinal tract, and middle ear.	Blast lung (pulmonary barotrauma) Tympanic membrane rupture and middle ear damage Abdominal hemorrhage and perforation: globe (eye) rupture; concussion (traumatic brain injury without physical signs of head injury)
Secondary	Results from flying debris and bomb fragments.	Any body part may be affected.	Penetrating ballistic (fragmentation) or blunt injuries Eye penetration (can be occult)
Tertiary	Results from individuals being thrown by the blast wind.	Any body part may be affected.	Fracture and traumatic amputation Closed and open brain injury
Quaternary	All explosion-related injuries, illnesses, or diseases not due to primary, secondary, or tertiary mechanisms. Includes exacerbation or complications of existing conditions.	Any body part may be affected.	Burns (flash, partial, and full thickness) Crush injuries Closed and open brain injury Asthma, chronic obstructive pulmonary disease, or other breathing problems from dust, smoke, or toxic fumes Angina Hyperglycemia, hypertension

Source: Centers for Disease Control and Prevention (2006).

Table 8.2. Overview of Explosive-Related Injuries

System	Injury or Condition
Auditory	Tympanic membrane rupture, ossicular disruption, cochlear damage, foreign body
Eye, Orbit, Face	Perforated globe, foreign body, air embolism, fractures
Respiratory	Blast lung, hemothorax, pneumothorax, pulmonary contusion and hemorrhage, A-V fistulas (source of air embolism), airway epithelial damage, aspiration pneumonitis, sepsis
Digestive	Bowel perforation, hemorrhage, ruptured liver or spleen, sepsis, mesenteric ischemia from air embolism
Circulatory	Cardiac contusion, myocardial infarction from air embolism, shock, vasovagal hypotension, peripheral vascular injury, air embolism-induced injury
CNS Injury	Concussion, closed and open brain injury, stroke, spinal cord injury, air embolism-induced injury
Renal Injury	Renal contusion, laceration, acute renal failure due to rhabdomyolysis, hypotension, and hypovolemia
Extremity Injury	Traumatic amputation, fractures, crush injuries, compartment syndrome, burns, cuts, lacerations, acute arterial occlusion, air embolism-induced injury

Source: Centers for Disease Control and Prevention (2006).

The Glasgow Coma Scale (GCS) is a commonly used system for classifying traumatic brain injury severity, grading a person's level of consciousness on a scale of 3–15 based on verbal, motor, and eye-opening reactions to stimuli (Teasdale 1974). It is generally agreed that a brain injury with a Glasgow Coma Scale of 13 or above is mild, 9–12 is moderate, and 8 and below is severe. (See table 8.3.)

Criteria for Severity of Head Injury

The majority of head injuries, particularly those that are blast-related, are classified as mild and generally resolve within one to three months with minimal, if any, long-term residual problems. Individuals with moderate to severe head injuries generally require inpatient rehabilitation and may have some permanent functional losses, although this can often be significantly reduced if timely and appropriate treatment is received. Persons with severe TBIs will often have

Table 8.3. Glasgow Coma Scale

Eye Opening Response	Spontaneous—open with blinking at baseline	4 points
	Opens to verbal command, speech, or shout	3 points
	Opens to pain, not applied to face	2 points
	None	1 point
Verbal Response	Oriented	5 points
	Confused conversation, but able to answer questions	4 points
	Inappropriate responses, words discernible	3 points
	Incomprehensible speech	2 points
	None	1 point
Motor Response	Obeys commands for movement	6 points
	Purposeful movement to painful stimulus	5 points
	Withdraws from pain	4 points
	Abnormal (spastic) flexion, decorticate posture	3 points
	Extensor (rigid) response, decerebrate posture	2 points
	None	1 point

Source: Rowlett (2001).

significant functional impairments that may require lifelong assistance with activities of daily living.

Severity of brain injury is graded by determining the initial Glasgow Coma Scale, alteration in or loss of consciousness, post-traumatic amnesia, and neuroimaging studies. After a brain injury a person may not be rendered unconscious but nonetheless experience an alteration of consciousness that involves mental confusion, disorientation, and trouble tracking events. Individuals are sometimes unaware of whether or not they have sustained loss of consciousness (Levin et al. 1987). Post-traumatic amnesia is the time interval from when the individual is able to consistently form memories of ongoing events (Whyte, Rosenthal & Zuccarelli (2000). (See table 8.4.)

The Department of Veterans and Brain Injury Center (DVBIC) (Salazar et al. 2000) searches for best treatment practices to provide active duty members and veterans with TBIs the best treatment practices (Vanderploeg et al. 2008). A review of TBI systems of care named the DVBIC network as a fully developed health system of care in brain injury (Schwab et al. 2007) with "many elements of a 'comprehensive' [health] system" (Cope, Mayer & Cervelli 2005). A longstanding agreement between the Department of Defense (DoD) and VA has provided for transfer of active duty service members who have incurred a brain injury to VA medical centers for rehabilitative care.

Table 8.4. Criteria for Severity of Traumatic Brain Injury

Mild	Alteration of consciousness, or loss of consciouness no greater than 30 minutes and with normal CT or MRI within 24 hours	Glasgow Coma Scale 13–15	Post-traumatic amnesia (memory loss): no greater than 24 hours
Moderate	Loss of consciousness no greater than 6 hours with abnormal CT or MRI	Glasgow Coma Scale 9–12	Post-traumatic amnesia: no more than 7 days
Severe	Loss of consciousness greater than 6 hours with abnormal CT or MRI	Glasgow Coma Scale less than 9	Post-traumatic amnesia: greater than 7 days

Source: Department of Veterans Affairs, Employee Education System (2010).

Mild TBI most commonly occurs following blasts, and symptoms that endure longer than usual may be complicated by a co-occurring condition, such as post-traumatic stress disorder (PTSD) (Brenner 2009). The symptoms of these two disorders overlap, and distinguishing the diagnoses can be clinically challenging (Elder 2009), According to the American Psychiatric Association's diagnostic criteria, PTSD occurs when a person has experienced, witnessed, or been confronted by a situation that involved actual or threatened death to self or others. In addition, the person responded to the event with intense fear, helplessness, or horror, and the event is persistently reexperienced in multiple ways (American Psychiatric Association 2000).

These two disorders, TBI and PTSD, share a number of symptoms, which can include irritability, depression, sleep disturbance, attention and memory problems, personality changes, and slow thought processes. Many combat veterans have both a TBI and PTSD, as well as other comorbid conditions such as depression, substance use disorder, and chronic pain. The clinical practice guidelines established by VA and the DoD recommend that treatment for these disorders should be symptom focused and evidence based (*VA/DoD Clinical Practice Guidelines* n.d.).

Combat injuries that result in amputations and residual limbs are among the most graphic reminders of the destructiveness of war. The Department of Veterans Affairs has faced several challenges in providing treatment and prosthetic fitting to this group of veterans because of associated injuries, such as burns and fractures. Numerous other combat-related physical and psychological conditions include hearing loss, vision changes, lung injuries, vestibular problems, spinal cord dysfunction, chronic pain, anxiety, and depression. Because of the number of service members who returned from Iraq and Afghanistan with multiple injuries and required specialized medical treatment and comprehensive rehabilitation, a multicomponent system of care was developed by VA to maximize the assessibility and efficacy of care for combat personnel. The objective was to provide a seamless transition through the system of care and to provide comprehensive case management that would customize and coordinate care of each individual's needs.

Polytrauma–Traumatic Brain Injury System of Care

Treatment of veterans who sustain multiple and complex injuries from combat requires involvement from providers in a wide range of specialties and disciplines. The U.S. Congress recognized the need for additional services to address the severity of injuries by passing the Veterans Health Programs Improvement Act of 2004 (§ 302) and the Consolidated Appropriations Act of 2005, which gave $30.3 billion to veteran healthcare programs. Together, these two laws required VA to treat soldiers with blast injuries, amputations, and other severe and enduring wounds. To follow the mandates of the two acts, VHA developed and implemented the Polytrauma–Traumatic Brain Injury System of Care (hereinafter referred to as the Polytrauma System of Care).

The Polytrauma System of Care was developed by drawing on established expertise at specialized VA rehabilitation programs that treated TBI, amputation care, blindness, and low vision (Pasquina & Cooper 2009). In 1986 the DoD and VA issued a memorandum of agreement for treatment of active service members by VA with TBIs, spinal cord injuries, and blindness, and the agreement was updated in 2006 (VA/DoD Health Executive Councils 2006). In 1992 VA designated four lead medical facilities for treatment of TBI, and specialized rehabilitative services were expanded to include spinal cord injury and blindness in 1996 (Veterans' Health Care Eligibility Reform Act of 1996). This mandate was followed by the creation of a TBI network of care, support, and coordinated services across the VA system of healthcare (Department of Veterans Affairs, Employee Education System 2004).

Combat service members who served in Iraq and Afghanistan (OIF and OEF) often sustained multiple injuries that not only were TBIs, spinal cord injuries, and blindness but also included multiple organ systems and mental health disorders. The Department of Veterans Affairs coined the term "polytrauma" to include these multiple sources of injury.

It has defined polytrauma as "two or more injuries to physical regions or organ systems, one of whch may be life threatening, resulting in physical,

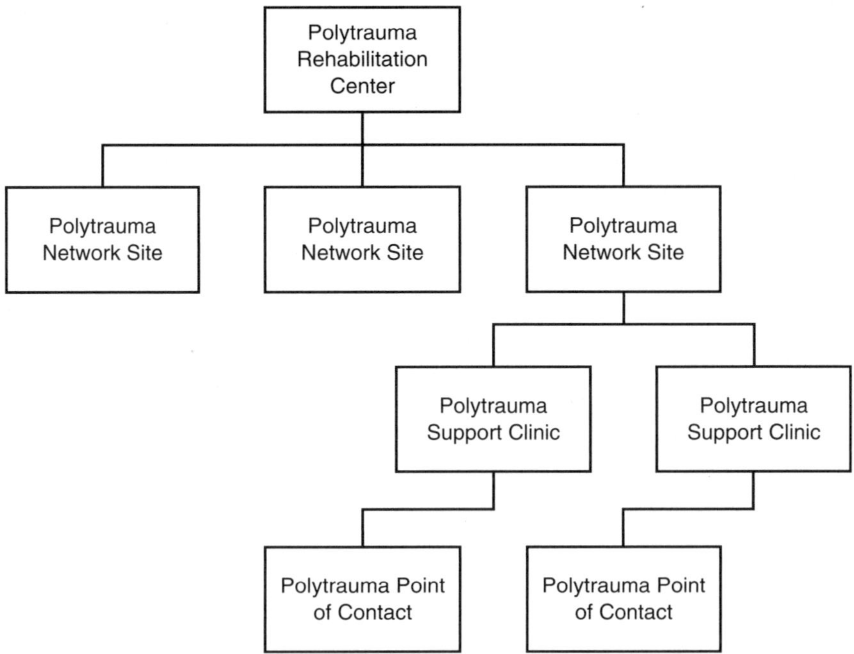

Figure 8.1. Polytrauma Four-Tiered System.

cognitive, psychological or psychosocial impairments and functional disability" (Department of Veterans Affairs, Veterans Health Administration 2005). Combat-injured service members are most likely to have moved through multiple levels of military care for treatment of injuries before being channeled into the VA system. A veteran may have initially received care in a combat theater (e.g., mobile hospital, Forward Resuscitative Surgical System) (Chambers 2005), been medically evacuated to a regional hospital, or been transferred to a DoD military medical facility that could be located outside the United States (e.g., Landstuhl, Germany). Once stabilized, service members could be transported to a military medical facility in the United States (i.e., Walter Reed Hospital, National Naval Medical Center, Bethesda Naval Hospital) before arriving at a Veterans Affairs Medical Center (VAMC).

A four-tiered system of care in VA provides specialized rehabilitation services at a facility that is closest to the veteran's home (see figure 8.1). Five VAMCs have been designated polytrauma rehabilitation centers and are the hubs of acute medical and rehabilitation care. These centers are located at the VAMCs in Richmond, Virginia; Tampa, Florida; Minneapolis, Minnesota;

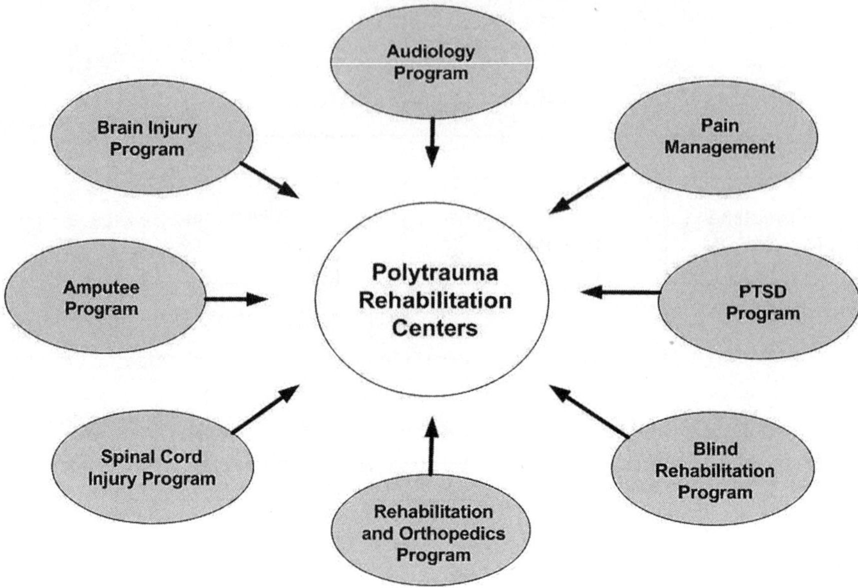

Figure 8.2. Polytrauma System of Care.

Palo Alto, California; and San Antonio, Texas. These centers are staffed with multidisciplinary teams that include rehabilitation physicians, nurses, social workers, speech-language pathologists, physical therapists, occupational therapists, recreation therapists, counseling psychologists, and neuropsychologists. The polytrauma rehabilitation centers maintain state-of-the-art equipment and techology to provide advanced rehabilitative services. The environment in each center is sensitive to particular needs of the service members that stem from age, family constellation, and the services and sacrifices that were rendered.

The next level in the tiered system involves polytrauma network sites (PNS), located in each of the Veterans Integrated Service Network (VISN) regions, where post-acute rehabilitative services are offered. Each center coordinates care within its respective VISN and serves as the regional administrative unit responsible for providing medical, surgical, mental health, and specialty services for veterans who live in that site's multistate catchment area.

Polytrauma support clinic teams are facility level teams located at eighty-one VAMCs. These facilities are often closer to the veteran's home and offer rehabilitation services, but they may not have the level of expertise or consultation that is offered at the first- and second-tier facilities. Long-term residual medical and mental health problems that stem from combat traumas are managed through direct care, case management, consultation, and use of telemedicine systems.

All other facilities that are smaller and lack the resources and expertise for rehabilitative treatment must have at least one person who can coordinate consultation, assessment, and referral for polytrauma treatment. These individuals, designated polytrauma points of contact, are people located at other VA facilities who are responsible for assisting polytrauma patients in their local area with obtaining the necessary services provided in the Polytrauma System of Care (see figure 8.2). These are usually social workers or nurses who are knowledgeable about the services offered but do not directly provide those services. They are available to assist veterans in finding the closest facility that can provide them with polytrauma care.

All facilities provide proactive case management, lifelong specialized follow-up care, telehealth, and care for veterans who are unable to return to their homes or who require extensive in-home services because of the severity of their injury. Each polytrauma veteran is assigned a case manager, who can provide more in-depth understanding of the problems and needs, not only to the individual but also to the family, during initial care as well as long-term recovery. Patients are contacted regularly to monitor the care plan and assess for new or emerging problems, as well as to identify and coordinate both VA and non-VA resources available to address the veteran's changing needs. The different facilities in the Polytrauma System of Care communicate and exchange information with each other through teleconference calls, telephone, e-mail, and a system of electronic health records, so that each person involved in the veteran's treatment can consult easily with others to provide updates and inform on changes in the patient's condition.

Scope of Services

Comprehensive Interdisciplinary Inpatient Evaluations

Injured combat veterans are admitted to inpatient rehabilitation programs for interdisciplinary evaluation by a team of highly trained specialists. These admissions generally occur at polytrauma rehabilitation centers or polytrauma network sites. Decisions for further treatment are based on results of the assessment and determine the range of services required to manage the needs of service members, who have various levels of severity in their injuries. These areas include but are not limited to neurorehabilitation, cognitive rehabilitation, state-of-the-art prosthetics and equipment, and visual rehabilitation (Pasquina & Cooper 2009).

Comprehensive Acute Interdisciplinary Inpatient Rehabilitation

Comprehensive acute inpatient rehabilitation is provided at the polytrauma rehabilitation centers by VA rehabilitation professionals who have specialized knowledge, skills, and experience. They receive additional training in their disciplines that is relevant to polytrauma and TBI. Service members are transferred to the polytrauma rehabilitation centers as soon as they are medically stable enough to tolerate the thoroughness of care. Treatment during these early months of injury focuses not only on physical rehabilitation but also on emotional problems and cognitive remediation. The patient and the patient's family are actively enlisted to participate in decisions to formulate the individualized plan of care. Progress and goals are frequently reviewed with the patient and family, and modifications are made when necessary to focus on the patient's needs. Each member of the interdisciplinary team contributes to team planning to formulate specialized goals for each patient.

The core interdisciplinary team includes but is not limited to specialists in medicine, rehabilitation, social work, psychology, speech pathology, occupational therapy, and recreation. The team consults with specialists in other areas when necessary (e.g., chaplain services, nutrition, orthopedics, neurosurgery). In addition, there is at least one full-time military liaison available to assist with questions about benefits and other military issues (Department of Veterans Affairs, Employee Education System 2007). Following are some of the specialists on the core team:

- A **physiatrist** is a rehabilitation physician who specializes in restoring optimal function to individuals with injuries to the muscles, bones, tissues, and nervous system.

- A **rehabilitation psychologist** is a specialist with a doctoral degree in psychology who assists the patient and family in coping and adjusting to traumatic injury, focusing on stress management, emotional issues, body image, and quality of life.

- A **neuropsychologist** is a person with a doctoral degree in psychology who specializes in understanding the relationship between brain functions and behavior. This person administers tests to identify an individual's cognitive strengths and weaknesses, as well as emotional functioning (box 8.1 lists specialized consultants who may be involved).

- A **rehabilitation nurse** specializes in the care of patients who are recovering from a serious illness or injury.

- An **occupational therapist** is on the team to help the service member improve motor functions and reasoning skills, perform activities of daily living, and develop compensatory strategies for loss of functioning.

Box 8.1. Specialized Consultants

Anesthesiology	Ophthalmology/Optometry
Audiology	Oral and Maxillofacial Surgery
Chaplain Services	Orthopedics
Dentistry	Otolaryngology
Gastroenterology	Pharmacy
General Surgery	Plastic Surgery
Infectious Disease	Prosthetics
Medicine	Pulmonology
Neurology	Radiology
Neurosurgery	Urology
Nutritionist	Vocational Specialist

- A **speech and language pathologist** assists the veteran with speech and language deficits, swallowing disorders, and cognitive aspects of communication.

- A **physical therapist** or **kinesiotherapist** works mainly on muscles and movement function in the area of injury. The therapist also works with the service member to help him or her learn how to use assistive devices such as aids for walking, prostheses, and wheelchairs.

- A **recreation therapist** uses sports, games, arts, crafts, and music to help the veteran build confidence to engage independently in leisure activities. The therapist guides the service member in applying practical skills to real life situations and helps the veteran function safely in environments where there are various barriers (e.g., curbs, steps, uneven surfaces).

- The **social worker/case manager** oversees all the components of the care plan to ensure they are implemented thoroughly and efficiently. This person plans the transition to the next level of care and discusses discharge options with the service member and family. Case managers help locate needed services, ensure that recommended equipment is received, and make certain that follow-up plans are implemented.

- The **military liaison** assists with the transition from military healthcare to the VA healthcare system, such as processing orders. This person also is a link between the service member and his or her chain of command as well as with the interdisciplinary team on military concerns.

Acute rehabilitation is offered when the patient has been initially medically stabilized but continues to require extensive medical and surgical support.

Approximately 90 percent of polytrauma patients in the acute rehabilitation setting have a TBI as one of their impairments (Pasquina & Cooper 2009). Treatment planning is based on medical stability, level of consciousness, other types of impairment, and cognitive status. Initial treatment might focus on level of alertness and arousal, then progress to basic skills such as orientation, bowel and bladder control, basic hygiene, and mobility. More advanced levels of functioning may be achieved to focus on activities of daily living such as money management, meal preparation, and driving.

Specialized Programs for Veterans' Healthcare

The typical course of treatment for service members and veterans begins with the comprehensive inpatient evaluations and/or acute interdisciplinary rehabilitation. Patients then reenter their community and continue with postacute care on an outpatient basis. Long-term care may be required for some veterans who are unable to return home, and the least restrictive setting possible is sought for placement (e.g., assisted living, nursing home care, long-term-care facilities). There are specialized programs offered in the Polytrauma System of Care for service members and veterans who do not follow this course of treatment.

The Emerging Consciousness Program is located at each of the polytrauma rehabilitation centers and is designed for patients who are not yet ready to participate in acute rehabilitation. Patients in this program have sustained severe brain injuries, and consciousness is impaired. Nursing and medical rehabilitation services are provided to improve responsiveness, increase consciousness, and faciitate the individual's progression to the next level of rehabilitation. In addition to the medical services, intensive case management is given, an individualized stimulation program is developed, and psychological support and education are offered to families and caregivers.

The Residential Transitional Rehabilitation Progam is available for service members and veterans with physical, cognitive, and/or behavioral management impairments who are not yet able to reintegrate effectively in the community or return to duty after acute comprehensive inpatient rehabilitation. This program is designed to guide the patient's progress to return to independent living using a milieu-based, structured program in a controlled, therapeutic setting. The focus is on restoring the person's return to home, community, and leisure activities; adaptive psychosocial functioning; and acquiring vocational skills. Individuals in this program typically engage in group therapy, individual therapy, medical care, case management, and discharge planning with follow-up services.

The Assistive Technology Program provides services to veterans and service members with severe sensory, cognitive, physical, and communication disabilities. The patient is comprehensively evaluated for individualized needs. Devices that may be provided include electronic aids for daily living, adapted automotive equipment, adapted sports and recreation equipment, cognitive prosthetic devices, wheeled mobility and seating, and alternative communication aids. Acquisition, follow-up, and maintenance of these devices are provided by the polytrauma rehabilitation centers.

Post-acute comprehensive interdisciplinary inpatient rehabilitation is offered to individuals who have progressed in acute rehabilitation and are still progressing, but who have not made rapid functional gains. This program is generally offered at the polytrauma network sites and permits the veteran to continue progressing in rehabilitation while closer to home. An interdisciplinary approach to treatment is continued to meet goals set by the patient and family and to prevent further impairment. This is a transitional service to further prepare the veteran or service member for return to the home or other care environment.

Interdisciplinary outpatient evaluation and rehabilitation are provided at the polytrauma network sites and by the polytrauma support clinic teams and are designed for individuals who can reside in the community while receiving rehabilitation services to meet individualized goals. Services offered are not limited to medical rehabilitation, but also can include psychotherapy, education, and psychosocial support.

The Veterans Health Administration requires an individualized rehabilitation and community reintegration care plan be developed for veterans and service members who receive inpatient or outpatient rehabilitation services. The care plan is developed by the interdisciplinary team with goals for continued improvement in physical, cognitive, and functional domains to maximize independence and community reintegration. The plan is reviewed periodically with the team as the individual's progress is followed. Regular follow-up is provided to meet the changing rehabilitation needs of the person and monitor progress toward goals established by the patient, family, and interdisciplinary team.

Caregiver Services with Polytrauma

Polytrauma System of Care programs make certain that families and caregivers receive the support they need to enhance the service member's rehabilitation. The polytrauma rehabilitation centers and polytrauma network sites strongly encourage family members and caregivers to be involved in the rehabilitation process. They are invited to participate in treatment decisions, be present during treatment sessions, and sit with the treatment team when treatment plans are discussed. Providing information to family members and caregivers may reduce stress and increase coping skills (Friedemann-Sanchez et al. 2008). Service members and veterans identify the individuals they consider to be a part of their caregiving network, and services are then available to those people. Social workers are assigned to each veteran and active duty service member and coordinate services to meet the needs of the extended family.

Most service members and veterans have at least one family member involved in the inpatient rehabilitation process. Initially, each polytrauma rehabilitation center developed its own methods of family education and collaboration, but no evidence-based guidelines were available to establish "best practices." To address the need to establish systemwide guidelines, the Family Care Collaborative was formed and involved clinicians, healthcare researchers, and VA operations leaders (Hall, Sigford & Sayer 2010). A Web-based tool was developed to help families understand what to expect as rehabilitation progresses and is available for families to use at the polytrauma rehabilitation center treating the service member or veteran.

Research on families of patients with polytrauma is not extant at this time on the caregiving needs of individuals who have sustained a TBI, but studies on families who care for individuals with TBI suggest that family members are significantly stressed (Fakhry et al. 2004; Verhaeghe, Defloor & Grypdonck 2005; Gordon, Zafonte & Cicerone 2006). Because the number of injuries involved in a war-related polytrauma is higher and the sequelae are more complex, caring for the service member or veteran who sustained multiple injuries while serving in Iraq or Afghanistan has been reported to be qualitatively different from caring for a person with only a TBI (Sayer et al. 2008; Friedemann-Sanchez, Sayer & Pickett 2008). There is still little known about how a family functions after a service member has sustained polytrauma. Families of those wounded in war may, in fact, face contextually different challenges due to the stigma that is often attached to disability, changing roles from military to civilian life, and the resources that are available through the Polytrauma System of Care program. The VA Health Services Research and Development Service established a Polytrauma/Blast-Related Injury (PT/BRI) Quality Enhancement Research Initiative (QUERI) Center to promote successful rehabilitation, psychological adjustment, and community reintegration for individuals with polytrauma and blast-related injuries.

President Obama signed into law the Caregivers and Veterans Omnibus Health Services Act of 2010, ensuring that family members and veterans of OEF and OIF will receive comprehensive support with needed homecare services. Passage of this legislation acknowledged the physical, psychological, emotional, and financial toll that caregiving takes on family members and caregivers of gravely injured service members. These people make great personal sacrifices to take care of their loved ones, sometimes giving up careers and putting their own lives on hold. The law designated VA as responsible for providing caregivers of severely injured veterans the help needed, including training and technical support, respite care, counseling health coverage, and modest financial support. These benefits will enhance programs for veterans' caregivers that are already available from VA:

- **In-Home and Community-Based Care:** Services offered include skilled home healthcare, community adult day healthcare, homemaker home health aide services, and home-based primary care.

- **Respite Care:** Services are designed to provide temporary relief to family caregivers tending to chronically ill, injured, or disabled veterans who are in the home. Respite services can include a short stay at a VA community living center or in-home care.

- **Family Support Services:** Services include family counseling and spiritual and pastoral care, and can be provided face-to-face or on the telephone. The polytrauma rehabilitation centers also offer recreational activities, family leisure, and temporary lodging in the Fisher Houses.

- **Caregiver Education and Training Programs:** Multiple training opportunities are provided, including predischarge care instruction, specialized caregiver programs (i.e., polytrauma and TBI), and spinal cord injuries/disorders and blind rehabilitation.

- **Other Benefits:** VA offers financial assistance to modify homes for improved accessibility and mobility; durable medical equipment and prosthetic and sensory aids; and transportation assistance for some veterans to and from medical appointments.

Polytrauma Telehealth Network

The Polytrauma Telehealth Network has been operational since 2006 (Darkins et al. 2008) and uses videoconferencing equipment to link the polytrauma sites to facilitate access to expert consultation and care among the clinical teams, veterans, and caregivers. In addition, clinical evaluation and care coordination can be provided to patients who do not have urgent inpatient needs but benefit from continuing outpatient treatment without incurring the expense of travel. The clinical videoconferencing uses of the Polytrauma Telehealth Network include connecting polytrauma rehabilitation centers (Darkins et al. 2008)

- to polytrauma sites for patient referral,
- to polytrauma sites for family and caregiver support,
- for follow-up consultation, and
- for conducting grand rounds among all polytrauma network sites.

In addition, the Polytrauma Telehealth Network can be used to make virtual referrals between military treatment facilities and the polytrauma network sites. New Polytrauma Health Network initiatives in development include home-buddy systems to maintain contact with veterans with TBI and/or amputation, as well as remote delivery of speech therapy services to veterans who live in rural areas. This systematic model of telehealth services supports the care of wounded soldiers in a clinically and cost-effective manner, permitting service members and veterans to live independently in their communities.

Current and Future Directions

The postacute polytrauma population presents with a variety of complex symptoms that likely signify the accumulation of multiple risks, injuries, and environmental conditions. Many service members and veterans who served in OEF and OIF suffered blast exposures, and a significant number coming back from the battlefield suffered multiple injuries, with many stemming from blasts. The Polytrauma System of Care was developed by VHA to provide integrated, specialized, and comprehensive service delivery to those with combat injuries. The Department of Veterans Affairs and DoD found ways to provide a "seamless transition" of care in transferring active and recently discharged military service members from a military treatment facility to a VA facility.

Specialized polytrauma rehabilitation centers are the hub for acute medical and rehabilitation care, education, and research related to polytrauma and TBI. The facilities in the four-tiered system of care are linked by the Polytrauma Telehealth Network, which provides state-of-the-art videoconferencing capabilities for consultation, team planning, case management, and treatment. Case management is a particularly critical function to provide lifelong coordination of services for the patient. As the service member or veteran progresses through the four-tiered system, the referring facility provides a "warm hand-off" of care to the case manager at the receiving facility, who manages emerging psychosocial, medical, or rehabilitation problems to meet the needs of the veteran and caregivers.

Family members bear the burden of physically caring for those injured and often assume financial, household, and family responsibilities. Caregivers may develop their own health or mental health problems, even when utilizing positive coping skills. Therefore, helping family members to adjust and providing resources to caregivers is critical. Research on caregiving has gaps that do not cover the unique circumstances of those who have served in the Gulf War on terror, and future research is critical to identify the best approaches for educating and supporting caregivers.

A potential promising intervention is the use of *peer visitors* (sometimes called "peer coaches" or "peer mentors") to assist OEF and OIF veterans and their families as they progress through various stages of rehabilitation and transition into civilian life (Uomoto & Williams 2009). Peer visitors have been reported to be beneficial to burn patients (Williams et al. 2002), combat-related amputees (Pasquina et al. 2008), and individuals with TBIs and their family members (Hibbard et al. 2002). A pilot program is underway with the DoD and VA to train and certify volunteers to be peer visitors (Uomoto & Williams 2009).

Empirically validated treatments of comorbid conditions such as PTSD, mood disorders, sleep regulation problems, and substance abuse are essential, as many of these problems also face this cohort of veterans. Modification of the treatment approaches may be necessary, however, to accommodate cognitive problems. Goals may need to be adjusted in psychotherapy as veterans work through traumatic events while continuing to recover from physical trauma.

The veterans of OEF and OIF are often young, many under thirty years of age, and face adjustments in social interactions, family relationships, and perhaps long-term disabilities. The larger, civilian population is encouraged to show compassion and appreciation for the sacrifices made by all who have served.

References

American Psychiatric Association. (2000). *Diagnostic and statistical manual of mental disorders.* 4th ed. Washington, D.C.: Author.

Belanger, H. G., Uomoto, J. & Vanderploeg R. D. (2009). The Veterans Health Administration's (VHA's) polytrauma system of care for mild traumatic brain injuries: Costs, benefits and controversies. *Journal of Head Trauma Rehabilitation* 24, no. 1: 4–13.

Blaisdell, F. (1988). Medical advances during the Civil War. *Archives of Surgery* 129, no. 9: 1045–1050.

Brenner, L. V. (2009). Assessment and diagnosis of mild traumatic brain injury, post-traumatic stress disorder and other polytrauma conditions: burden of adversity hypothesis. *Rehabilitation Psychology* 54, no. 3: 239–246.

Casualties of war—military care for the wounded from Iraq and Afghanistan. (2005). *New England Journal of Medicine* 351: 219–222.

Centers for Disease Control and Prevention. (2006). Explosions and blast injuries: A primer for clinicians. http://www.dcd.gov/masstrauma/preparedness/primer.pdf (accessed March 16, 2012).

Chambers, L. R. (2005). Initial experience of US Marine Corps forward resuscitative surgical system during Operation Iraq Freedom. *Archives of Surgery* 140, no. 1: 26–32.

Cifu, D., Cohen, S., Lew, H., Jaffee, M. & Sigford, B. (2010). The history and evolution of traumatic brain injury rehabilitation in military service members and veterans. *American Journal of Physical Medicine and Rehabilitation* 89, no. 8: 688.

Consolidated Appropriations Act of 2005. Pub. L. No. 108–447, 118 Stat. 2809 (December 8, 2004).

Cope, D., Mayer, N. & Cervelli, L. (2005). Development of systems of care for persons with traumatic brain injury. *Journal of Head Trauma Rehabilitation* 20, no. 2: 128–142.

Darkins, A., Cruise, C., Armstrong, M., Peters, J. & Finn, M. (2008). Enhancing access of combat-wounded veterans to specialist rehabilitation services: The VA Polytrauma Telehealth Network. *Archives of Physical Medicine and Rehabilitation* 89: 182–187.

Department of Veterans Affairs, Employee Education System. (2004). Traumatic brain injury. http://www1.va.gov/vhi/doc/TBI.pdf (accessed January 3, 2010).

Department of Veterans Affairs, Employee Education System. (2007). *Polytrauma rehabilitation family education manual.* http://dva.state.wi.us/Docs/TBI/Family_Ed_Manual112007.pdf (accessed November 12, 2010).

Department of Veterans Affairs, Employee Education System. (2010). *Traumatic brain injury.* Ed. R. Vanderploeg & M. Cornis-Pop. Washington, DC: Author.

Department of Veterans Affairs, Veterans Health Administration. (2005). *VHA handbook 1172.1: Polytrauma rehabilitation procedures.* Washington, DC: Author. http://www1.ga.gov/vhapublications/ViewPublicatoins.asp?pub_ID=1317 (accessed March 9, 2010).

Elder, G. A. (2009). Blast-related mild traumatic brain injury: Mechanisms of injury and impact on clinical care. *Mt. Sinai Journal of Medicine* 76, no. 2: 111–118.

Fakhry, S., Trask, A., Waller, M. & Watts, D. (2004). IRTC Neurotrauma Task Force: Management of brain-injured patients by an evidence-based medicine protocol improves outcomes and decreases hospital charges. *Journal of Trauma* 56, no. 3: 492–500.

Fischer, H. (2010). U.S. military casualty statistics: Operation New Dawn, Operation Iraqi Freedom, and Operation Enduring Freedom. September 28. http://assets.opencrs.com/rpts/RS22452_20100928.pdf (accessed March 4, 2012).

Friedemann-Sanchez, G., Griffin, J., Partin, M. & Rittman, N. R. (2008). Communicating information to families of polytrauma patients: A narrative literature review. *Rehabilitation Nursing* 5: 206–213.

Friedemann-Sanchez, G., Sayer, N. A. & Pickett, T. (2008). Provider perspectives on rehabilitation of patients with polytrauma. *Archives of Physical and Medical Rehabilitation* 89: 171–178.

Gawande, A. (2004). Notes of a surgeon: Casualties of war—military care for the wounded from Iraq and Afghanistan. *New England Journal of Medicine* 351: 2471–2475.

Gordon, W., Zafonte, R. & Cicerone K. C. J. (2006). Traumatic brain injury rehabilitation: State of the science. *American Journal of Physical Medicine and Rehabilitation* 85, no. 4: 343–382.

Hall, C., Sigford, B. & Sayer, N. (2010). Practice changes associated with the Department of Veterans Affairs' Family Care Collaborative. *Journal of General Internal Medicine* 25, supp. 1: 18–26.

Hess, J. R. & Hiipala, S. (2005). Optimizing the use of blood products in trauma care. *Critical Care* 9, supp. 5: S10–S14.

Hibbard, M., Cantor, J., Charatz, H., Rosenthal, R., Ashman, T., Gunderson, N., et al. (2002). Peer support in the community: Initial findings of a mentoring program for individuals with traumatic brain injury and their families. *Journal of Head Trauma Rehabilitation* 17: 112–131.

Lehman, C. (2008). Mechanisms of injury in wartime. *Rehabilitation Nursing* 33, no. 5: 192–205.

Levin, H., Mattis, S. R., Eisenbert, J. M., High, W. & Frankowski, R. (1987). Neurobehavioral outcome following minor head injury: A three-center study. *Journal of Neurosurgery* 66: 234–243.

Lew, H. P. (2007). Program development and defining characteristics of returning military in a VA Polytrauma Network site. *Journal of Rehabilitation Research & Development* 44: 1027–1034.

Mackenzie, E., Hoyt, D., Sacra, J., Jurkovich, G., Carlini, A. & Teitelbaum, S. (2003). National inventory of hospital trauma centers. *JAMA* 289: 1515–1522.

Pasquina, P. F. & Cooper, R. A. (Eds.). (2009). Care of the combat amputee. http://www.bordeninstitute.army.mil/published_volumes/amputee/CCAchapter03.pdf (accessed March 12, 2012).

Pasquina, P., Tsao, J., Collins, D., Chan, B., Charrow, A. & Karmarkar, A. E. (2008). Quality of medical care provided to service members with combat-related limb amputations: Report of patient satisfaction. *Journal of Rehabilitation Research and Development* 45: 953–960.

Phillips, Y. (1986). Primary blast injuries. *Annals of Emergency Medicine* 106, no. 15: 1446–1450.

Polytrauma brain injury (TBI) system of care. (2009). VHA directive 2009-028. http://www.va.gov/optometry/docs/VHA_Directive_2009-028_Polytrauma_System_of_Care.pdf (accessed March 12, 2012).

Prevention, C. F. (2006). *Explosions and blast injuries: A primer for clinicians.* http://www.bt.cdc.gov/masscasualties//explosions.asp (accessed September 4, 2010).

Pruitt, B. (2008). The symbiosis of combat casualty care and civilian trauma care: 1914–2007. *Journal of Trauma Injury, Infection and Critical Care* 64: S4–S8.

Rowlett, R. (2001). *Glasgow coma scale.* http://www.unc.edu/~rowlett/units/scales/glasgow.htm (accessed January 3, 2011).

Rusk, H. (2003). The growth and development of rehabilitation and war. *Disability Rehabilitation* 25: 1019–1023.

Salazar, A., Zitnay, G., Warden, D. & Schwab, K. (2000). Defense and Veterans Head Injury Program: Background and overview. *Journal of Head Trauma Rehabilitation* 15: 1081–1091.

Sayer, N., Chiros, C., Sigford, B., Scott, S., Clothier, B., Pickett, T., et al. (2008). Characteristics and rehabilitation outcomes among patients with blast and other injuries sustained during the global war on terror. *Archives of Physical Medicine Rehabilitation* 89, no. 1: 163–170.

Schwab, K., Warden, D., Lux, W., Shupenko, L. & Zitnay, G. (2007). Defense and Veterans Brain Injury Center: Peacetime and wartime missions. *Journal of Research and Rehabilitative Medicine* 44, no. 7: xiii–xxi.

Sigford, B. (2008). "To care for him who shall have borne the battle and for his widow and his orphan" (Abraham Lincoln): The Department of Veterans Affairs polytrauma system of care. *Archives of Physical and Medical Rehabilitation* 89: 160–162.

Teasdale, G. A. (1974). Assessment of coma and impaired consciousness: A practical scale. *Lancet* 2: 81–84.

Trunkey, D. (2000). History and development of trauma care in the United States. *Clinical Orthopaedics and Related Research* 374: 36–46.

Uomoto, J. & Williams, R. (2009). Post-acute polytrauma rehabilitation and integrated care of returning veterans: Toward a holistic approach. *Rehabilitation Psychology* 54, no. 3: 259–269.

VA and DOD health care: Efforts to provide seamless transition of care for OEF and OIF servicemembers and veterans. (2006). Government Accountability Office. June 30. http://www.gao.gov/products/GAO-06–794R (accessed January 28, 2010).

VA/DoD clinical practice guidelines. (n.d.). http://www.healthquality.va.gov/index.asp (accessed December 14, 2010).

VA/DoD Health Executive Councils. (2006). Department of Veterans Affairs (VA) and Department of Defense memorandum of agreement (MoA) regarding referral of active duty military personnel who sustain spinal cord injury, traumatic brain injury or blindness to Veterans Affairs medical facilities. http://www.tricare.mil/DVPCO/downloads/12-13-06.pdf (accessed January 3, 2011).

Vanderploeg, R., Schwab, K., Walker, W., Fraser, J., Sigford, B., Date, E., et al. (2008). Rehabilitation of traumatic brain injury in active duty military personnel and veterans: Defense and Veterans Brain Injury Center randomized controlled trial of two rehabilitation approaches. *Archives of Physical Medicine and Rehabilitation* 89: 2227–2238.

Verhaeghe, S., Defloor, T. & Grypdonck, M. (2005). Stress and coping among families of patients with traumatic brain injury: A review of the literature. *Journal of Clinical Nursing* 14, no. 8: 1004–1012.

Veterans Benefits Improvement Act of 2004. Pub. L. No. 108-422. www.smith4nj.com/laws/108-422.pdf (accessed March 12, 2012).

Veterans' Health Care Eligibility Reform Act of 1996. Pub. L. No. 104-262. http://
    bulk.resource.org/gpo.gov/laws/104/publ262.104.pdf (accessed January 3, 2011).

Veterans Health Programs Improvement Act of 2004. Pub. L. No. 108-442, 118 Stat.
    2379. www.cbo.gov/doc.cfm?index=6034&type=0 (accessed March 12, 2012).

Wagensteen, O. A. (1978). *The rise of surgery: From empiric craft to scientific discipline:
    Surgery of war*. Minneapolis: University of Minnesota Press.

Whyte, J., Rosenthal, M. & Zuccarelli, L. (2000). Altered cellular anatomy and phy-
    siology of acute brain injury and spinal cord injury. *Critical Care Nursing Clinics of
    North America* 12: 403–411.

Williams, R., Isenberg, P., Rossbach, P., Ehde, D., Bartman, M. & Engrav, L. (2002).
    Evaluations of peer consultation program for burn inpatients. *Journal of Burn Care
    and Rehabilitation* 23: 449–453.

Chapter 9

Military Traumatic Brain Injury and the Postconcussive Syndrome

Louis M. French, Victoria C. Anderson-Barnes,
Katherine Brazaitis, and Aditya A. Bhagwat

The History of Military Traumatic Brain Injury

The current nature of combat is unlike that of any war in history. Although protective gear and medical care have vastly improved, battle tactics are changing and becoming increasingly unpredictable. The use of improvised explosive devices (IEDs) and other blast-inducing weaponry has resulted in more traumatic injuries to the head and neck (Owens et al. 2008). In World War II, the Korean War, and the Vietnam War, head and neck injuries affected 21, 21.4, and 16 percent of injured service members, respectively; this percentage has increased to 30 percent in the current conflicts—and over half of these head and neck wounds were the result of IEDs (Owens et al. 2008). Similarly, more service members are surviving injuries in Operation Iraqi Freedom (OIF) and Operation Enduring Freedom (OEF) that would have been fatal in previous wars (Ling et al. 2009; Owens et al. 2008; Tanielian, Jaycox & Rand 2008). It has been suggested that the combination of improved body armor and helmets with the expertise and efficiency of field medics and combat surgeons has contributed to the higher survival rates. As a result, the number of service members sustaining what are considered the "invisible wounds of war"—namely traumatic brain injury (TBI) and post-traumatic stress disorder (PTSD)—has increased (Tanielian, Jaycox & Rand 2008).

To appreciate how the understanding of TBI in a military setting has changed, it is important to review the history of combat-related TBI in the modern era. By the time of the American Civil War, much was known about the pathophysiology of closed head injuries, as well as subdural and epidural hematomas. Likewise, there was significant knowledge on penetrating brain injuries, especially by bullets. However, surgical treatments were rudimentary and often avoided due to concern about infection. Records pertaining to the American Civil War describe in some detail almost 13,000 head injuries with over 2,700 deaths (Kaufman 1993). By the time of World War I, brain injury was receiving greater public awareness (Jones, Fear & Wessely 2007). In that war, approximately 10 percent of injured British soldiers endured amnesia, poor concentration, headache, tinnitus, hypersensitivity to noise, dizziness, and tremor following blast exposure (Mitchell & Smith 1931; Turner 1915). At that time, it was believed they had not incurred a brain injury because immediate trauma and organic lesions were not evident. Instead, these patients were given the diagnosis of "shell shock." The term "shell shock" went in and out of popularity as its etiology was debated. The symptoms were originally believed to be neurological, based on early understandings of how compression and decompression forces acted on the brain (Jones, Fear & Wessely 2007; Mott 1917). However, when soldiers presented the same somatic symptoms without any exposure to a blast, a psychological basis was suspected, and the symptoms were thought to be characterized by anxiety. Consequently, in November 1916 Director General of Army Medical Services Arthur Sloggett sanctioned two new classifications: "effects of explosion," which represented the cases more likely to be neurological because blast exposure had occurred, and "nervousness," which was diagnosed when there was no blast exposure (Jones, Fear & Wessely 2007; Sloggett 1916).

By World War II, the term "shell shock" was slowly weaned out of military medical terminology, and it was eventually banned by British authorities (Jones, Fear & Wessely 2007). "Posttrauma concussion state" and "posttraumatic psychoneurotic state" effectively replaced the terms "effects of explosion" and "nervousness" (Schaller 1939). By the early 1940s, "postconcussion syndrome" and "postconcussion neurosis" were the new terms (Jones, Fear & Wessely 2007). Due to difficulties in exact diagnosis, attention was shifted to treatment of the symptoms, rather than their causation. Occupational and vocational training were then used for the first time with this population (Jones, Fear & Wessely 2007).

Research on brain injury continued between World War II and the Vietnam War. The key feature that emerged from the Vietnam War was a significant increase in the number of "penetrating" brain injuries sustained (Sweeney & Smutok 1983). (*Penetrating brain injury* is defined as a head injury in which the dura mater, the outer layer of the meninges, is breached.) With the advent of neuroimaging in the 1970s, specifically standard CT, it was discovered that penetrating brain injuries tended to cause focal lesions, whereas closed head injuries (defined as an injury to the brain in which the dura mater is not breached) cause diffuse and nonspecific damage (Groswasser et al. 2002; Sweeney & Smutok 1983). Also during the Vietnam War, a standardized registry of head injuries incurred by U.S. soldiers serving in Vietnam was established; this effort became known as the "Vietnam Head Injury Study" (VHIS) (Sweeney & Smutok 1983). The VHIS was designed to be a longitudinal study, combining retrospective data with prospective data from service members who sustained penetrating and closed head brain injuries. The study was divided into three phases. Phase 1 encompassed a retrospective review of the data in the registry; of the 1,221 individuals whose data had been collected, 1,133 had penetrating brain injuries (Sweeney & Smutok 1983). Based on those with penetrating brain injuries, several investigators have conducted analyses pertaining to medical and surgical complications from data contained in the registry (Sweeney & Smutok 1983).

Phase 2 of the VHIS began in August 1981. This phase examined motor and functional outcomes, on average, fourteen years after injury (Sweeney & Smutok 1983). Of the 1,221 individuals in the registry, 700 patients with penetrating brain injury consented to participate. The methodology of this phase involved intensive sensory, motor, and functional evaluations. Performance findings were correlated with the location of brain lesions, demographic information, and social history. About 50 percent of the participants showed functional independence in most activities, regardless of the occurrence of persistent selective motor-control abnormalities. This was a surprising finding considering the extent of brain damage present in most of these individuals. Many participants had large focal lesions that often extended into midline regions and involved both hemispheres. Sweeney and Smutok (1983) proposed that such positive outcomes were due to the high levels of motivation typically seen in young, premorbidly healthy individuals. Children and adults with similar brain injuries who were observed in other studies did not show such high rates of functional independence (Brink et al. 1970; Jennett et al. 1981; Sweeney & Smutok 1983).

The third phase of this study, conducted in recent years, has provided some of the most detailed information correlating brain damage to cognitive, behavioral, and psychological outcomes to date. Standard CT brain scans, MRI, and functional magnetic resonance imaging (fMRI) have allowed for the close study of how damage to certain parts of the brain may affect functional outcomes, cognitive abilities, and personality. For example, the amygdala and ventromedial prefrontal cortex (vmPFC) have been shown to have a significant influence on PTSD pathogenesis (Koenigs et al. 2008). In addition, vmPFC

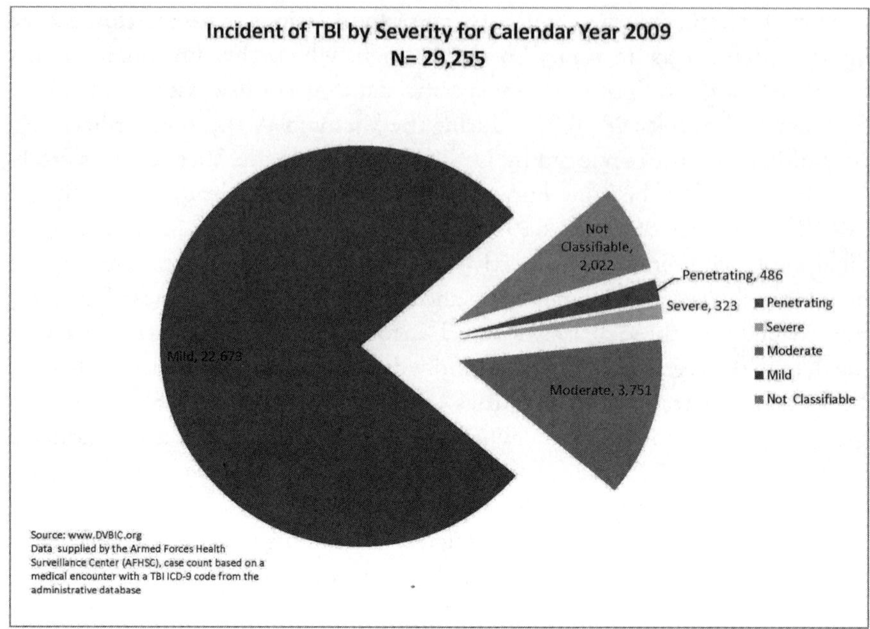

Figure 9.1. Incidence of TBI Severity for Calendar Year 2009 (n = 29,255). Case count based on a medical encounter with a TBI ICD-9 code from the administrative database. *Source:* www.DVBIC.org. Data supplied by the Armed Forces Health Surveillance Center (AFHSC).

lesions have been found to play a significant role in fatigue following penetrating brain injury (Pardini et al. 2010). Overall, the VHIS has proven to be a rich source of data about the nature of brain injuries and their outcomes (Grafman et al. 1988; Groswasser et al. 2002; Reider-Groswasser et al. 2002; Salazar, Schwab & Grafman 1995; Sweeney & Smutok 1983).

The current conflicts in Iraq and Afghanistan have triggered a new awareness of TBI. According to the Armed Forces Health Surveillance Center (AFHSC), between January 2003 and January 2010, over 135,000 military service members were diagnosed with TBI (Armed Forces Health Surveillance Center 2009). The vast majority of these have been closed, mild TBIs. Figure 9.1 represents a breakdown of the number of service members diagnosed with TBI in 2009 alone. This high incidence of TBI has led to its recognition as the "signature injury" of OIF and OEF (Hoge et al. 2008; McCrea et al. 2008). In addition to the more than 100,000 who have been diagnosed with TBI from the military medical care system, some greater number are presumed to have suffered a mild TBI (mTBI) while deployed but never sought help. Postdeployment screening and surveys of returning service members (Tanielian, Jaycox & Rand 2008; Terrio et al. 2009) have shown rates of over 20 percent. In most cases, these symptoms are time-limited and follow the expected trajectory for recovery from mTBI, even in a deployed environment. Nonetheless, given the high tempo of battle, normal combat-related stress symptoms, distraction, and sleep disturbance, the service member may be especially vulnerable to typical postconcussive symptoms such as slowed reaction times, irritability, and headache. The interaction of these symptoms may have significant implications for combat readiness. In recognition of that fact, the military has introduced numerous screening, educational, and research efforts to deal with this problem. Some of these are described later in this chapter.

Definition of TBI

Traumatic brain injury, as defined by the Department of Defense (DoD) and Department of Veterans Affairs (VA), is

> a traumatically induced structural injury and/or physiological disruption of brain function as a result of an external force that is indicated by new onset or worsening of at least one of the following clinical signs immediately following the event: any period of loss of, or a decreased level of, consciousness; any loss of memory for events immediately before or after the injury; any alteration in mental state at the time of injury (confusion, disorientation, slowed thinking, etc.); neurological deficits (weakness, loss of balance, change in vision, praxis, paresis/plegia, sensory loss, aphasia, etc.) that may or may not be transient; or intracranial lesion. (Department of Defense 2008)

Injury mechanism and injury severity play a role in characterizing and diagnosing TBI. It has been proposed that injury mechanism classification should include three categories: penetrating TBI, closed head TBI, and blast TBI (Ling et al. 2009). As described previously, penetrating TBI occurs when a foreign object enters the skull and crosses the dura mater. Closed head TBI, on the other hand, is caused by an acceleration or deceleration force applied directly to the head (or by an object striking the head), but not breaching dura mater. Blast TBI occurs when physical forces from a detonation are applied directly to the brain and may or may not breach the dura mater. For that reason it has been suggested that blast TBI shares characteristics with both penetrating and closed head TBI (Ling et al. 2009).

Although many regions of the brain are vulnerable to the pathophysiology following TBI, the anterior portions of the brain (i.e., frontal and temporal regions) are most susceptible to this insult. TBI-associated cognitive and neurobehavioral impairments are related to both primary and secondary pathophysiology (as well as multiple other factors discussed later in this chapter). Primary damage may be thought of as largely structural and involves axonal injury, contusions, hemorrhage, and vascular injury. Secondary damage is a process that arises from the endogenous evolution of cellular damage or from secondary systemic processes, such as hypotension or hypoxia. Endogenous secondary pathophysiology includes 1) ischemia, excitotoxicity, energy failure, and cell death cascades (e.g., necrosis and apoptosis); 2) edema; 3) traumatic axonal injury; and 4) inflammation (Kochanek, Clark & Jenkins 2007).

Most mTBI is thought to be associated with low levels of axonal stretching, resulting in only temporary changes in neurophysiology. Some authors (Giza & Hovda 2001) have described a model, characterized by a complex neurometabolic cascade, in which there are interwoven cellular and vascular changes following concussive forces to the brain. This includes ionic shifts, abnormal energy metabolism, diminished cerebral blood flow, and impaired neurotransmission. In most cases, this appears to be a reversible series of events (Giza & Hovda 2001; Iverson 2007; Iverson, Lange & Franzen 2005). That is, for most individuals who sustain an mTBI, it appears that the brain undergoes a process of injury and recovery, following which most individuals return to normal functioning.

Closed TBI is typically described as mild, moderate, or severe (Finkel 2006). The severity level of TBI may be determined by the initial Glasgow Coma Scale (GCS) score, duration of loss of consciousness (LOC), presence of alteration of consciousness (AOC), or duration of post-traumatic amnesia (PTA). In addition, in the DoD system, if a patient is found to have suffered any type of intracranial pathology through radiological evaluation (such as diffuse axonal injury, subdural hemorrhage, cortical contusion, etc.), the level of severity is automatically increased to at least a moderate injury regardless of the other injury characteristics. Other classification systems sometimes describe individuals with intracranial pathology and relatively brief LOC or PTA as having suffered a "complicated mild" TBI (Borgaro et al. 2003; Williams, Levin & Eisenberg 1990). An additional difference in the DoD system is that although GCS is frequently used clinically to mark severity, it is not part of the "official" classification method (see table 9.1). Finally, the term "mild traumatic brain injury" or "mTBI" is also known as concussion, and the terms can be used interchangeably.

Ideally, the injury severity classification system would be suggestive of proper rehabilitation and treatment approaches, as well as providing insight into the outcomes that can be expected after receiving such treatments. Although this is typically the case for moderate and severe diagnoses, mTBI

Table 9.1. Department of Defense TBI Injury Classification System

Criteria	Mild	Moderate	Severe
Structural imaging	Normal	Normal or abnormal	Normal or abnormal
Loss of consciousness (LOC)	0–30 mins.	> 30 mins. and < 24 hrs.	> 24 hrs.
Alteration of consciousness/ mental state (AOC)	A moment up to 24 hrs.	> 24 hours; severity based on other criteria	
Post-traumatic amnesia (PTA)	0–1 day	> 1 and < 7 days	> 7 days

does not necessarily follow such a predictable pattern (McCrea 2008). For instance, mTBI does not always result in obvious physical or neurological impairments and is considered to be "in a category by itself" (McCrea 2008).

Despite having a standardized definition in the military, accurately diagnosing mTBI remains challenging, especially as time passes after the point of injury. Diagnosis is usually done by clinical interview. However, recall of the circumstances around the injury may fade with time. Further, postconcussive symptoms are not specific to mTBI and are seen in a number of other conditions. They have been seen with equal frequency in trauma patients (Landre et al. 2006), those with chronic pain (Iverson & McCracken 1997; Smith-Seemiller et al. 2003), and even normal individuals (Mittenberg et al. 1992; Vanderploeg et al. 2007). In addition, the symptoms of TBI may overlap with PTSD, making an accurate diagnosis of either condition difficult (Elder & Cristian 2009). Finally, there is no "gold-standard" test for the detection of mTBI. Neuroimaging modalities such as standard CT or MRI may not be able to detect subtle changes in brain morphology that may be present in milder forms of brain injury. Whereas abnormalities associated with moderate and severe forms of TBI are easily visible on a CT scan, abnormalities associated with mTBI may not be visible (Maas, Stocchetti & Bullock 2008).

Symptoms of TBI and the Postconcussive Syndrome

Patients with TBI (of any severity) may experience a variety of dysfunctions that can affect behavioral, cognitive, emotional, physical, and social areas of life (Van Baalen et al. 2003). The symptoms of TBI can be organized into three categories: somatic consequences (which include headache, sleep disturbance, vision problems, fatigue, seizures, and vestibular dysfunction); cognitive dysfunction (which include attentional impairment, reduced processing speed, memory dysfunction, language difficulties, and executive function); and emotional and behavioral sequelae (which include depression, anxiety, irritability, impulsivity, and disinhibition) (Silver, McAllister & Yudofsky 2005). In general, there is a greater chance of persistent symptoms with increasing injury severity, and not all patients experience all symptoms.

Recovery after a TBI of any severity level is dependent on several factors, including the specific context in which the injuries were sustained (Warden 2006); pre-injury factors such as employment status and preexisting medical or psychological conditions; high levels of stress (McCrea 2008; Warden 2006); use of substances such as alcohol or illegal drugs (Warden 2006); social factors such as marital status, legal trouble, or poor social support systems (McCrea 2008); and other injuries sustained concomitantly with the brain injury (French et al. 2009; Stulemeijer et al. 2006). Cognitive deficits and symptoms present in the acute stage after injury typically resolve within days or weeks after the incident (Carroll et al. 2004; McCrea 2008), and full recovery is usually attained by three months postinjury (Belanger et al. 2005a; Carroll et al. 2004; McCrea 2008). Severe TBI, on the other hand, typically results in significant cognitive and functional impairments. This phenomenon is exhibited in a 2009 Institute of Medicine study, in which no associations were found between mTBI and objectively measured neurocognitive deficits, nor between mTBI and long-term adverse social functioning (unemployment, diminished social relationships, and decreases in the ability to live independently) (Institute of Medicine & Committee on Gulf War and Health 2009). However, there was an association between moderate to severe TBI and neurocognitive deficits, and between moderate to severe TBI and long-term adverse social-function outcomes (particularly unemployment and diminished social relationships). Nonetheless, a small portion of the mTBI population experiences persistent symptoms following mTBI (Belanger et al. 2009; Hartlage, Durant-Wilson & Patch 2001). For the small minority with persistent symptoms, a range of demographic, psychosocial, and situational factors have been identified in different studies. It should be further noted that analyses of the existing literature on outcomes are largely based on civilian populations. Although we can expect many similarities, there may be important differences, too.

For those with mTBI, postconcussive symptom reporting does not appear to be significantly related to injury severity markers such as duration of PTA (Ponsford et al. 2000) or GCS (Chamelian & Feinstein 2006). Counterintuitively, those with mTBI tend to experience significantly more symptoms than those with moderate to severe TBI. This has been shown in civilian (Gordon et al. 2000) and military (Belanger et al. 2009) populations. In this latter sample, these differences disappeared when the level of post-traumatic stress symptoms was controlled for, suggesting that many of the symptoms in the military population may be reflective of emotional distress. When symptoms persist for months after an mTBI, a diagnosis of "postconcussion syndrome" (PCS) is typically given (McCrea 2008). The primary criterion for being diagnosed with PCS is the occurrence of mild brain injury, followed by persistent symptoms such as headaches, dizziness, depression, and irritability (McCrea 2008; Wilde et al. 2008). Specific definitions of PCS have been published in the *Diagnostic and Statistical Manual of Mental Disorders (DSM-IV)* and the *International Classification of Diseases (ICD-10)*, and they vary slightly in inclusion requirements. However, the diagnosis of PCS is controversial, and it has been suggested that the existence of an actual syndrome is questionable (Arciniegas et al. 2005). Moreover, it has not been determined why some individuals experience persistent symptoms beyond the traditional recovery period, while others recover fully. In short, this matter is in need of further investigation.

The Polytrauma Patient

As previously mentioned, recovery after TBI is partially dependent on other injuries sustained concomitantly with the brain injury. It is common for TBI patients, especially those injured in combat, to have accompanying comorbidities, ranging from physical (such as major limb amputation and sensory dysfunctions) to psychological (PTSD, depression, and anxiety). A patient with multiple injuries is considered a "polytrauma patient." Polytrauma patients, even without brain injury, have high rates of neurobehavioral symptoms, including irritability, mood swings, suspiciousness, amotivation, feelings of guilt, and memory difficulties (Frenisy et al. 2006). There is a wide range of injuries in the polytrauma population, all of which may have repercussions for recovery.

Physical Comorbidities

Patients with TBI may have extracranial physical injuries such as limb loss or sensory dysfunction that can contribute to the patient's overall dysfunction. Major limb amputations frequently occur in combat situations and are considered to be among the most debilitating wounds sustained in combat (Stansbury et al. 2008). Limb loss alone can lead to dysfunction in the cardiovascular, endocrine, and musculoskeletal systems, as well as cause increased pain and suffering in the individual (Robbins et al. 2009). Amputee patients may have a difficult time adjusting to the missing limb, presumably due to concerns over body image, social stigma, or other related factors (Rybarczyk et al. 1995). In addition, TBI patients with comorbid limb loss often experience delays in rehabilitation, as this unique population can have difficulties remembering appointments, learning new tasks, and regaining independence (French et al. 2009).

In addition to limb loss, sensory dysfunctions such as auditory and visual impairments are common comorbidities reported in the military TBI population. In a group of polytrauma patients injured by blast, the rates of visual impairment were more than double compared to other causes of polytrauma (i.e., motor vehicle accidents, gunshot and/or shrapnel, assault, falls, or anoxia) (Goodrich et al. 2007). Overall, the rate of visual impairment in the blast-related injury was 52 percent, compared with 20 percent for all other sources of injury. In a group of patients at Walter Reed Army Medical Center (WRAMC) with TBI and combat ocular trauma (COT), explosive fragmentary munitions accounted for 79 percent of TBI-associated COT (Weichel et al. 2009). Severe TBI was more frequently associated with COT than milder TBI. Overall, TBI occurred in two-thirds of all COT, and ocular trauma was a common finding in all TBI cases. Visual problems go beyond structural damage and loss of acuity. One VA sample of polytrauma patients (Goodrich et al. 2007) suggested that self-reported vision complaints were common (74 percent) and confirmed that visual impairment occurred in 38 percent of all cases studied. The authors suggested that comprehensive eye examinations should be routinely administered, particularly when the mechanism of injury involves a blast.

Auditory impairments are also common in the military population, especially among those who have been blast-exposed. Lew and colleagues (2007) examined a group of veterans in a VA polytrauma center; in those injured by blast since the beginning of the war in Iraq, 62 percent complained of hearing loss and 38 percent reported tinnitus (with sensorineural loss being the most prevalent type of hearing loss). This compares to rates of 44 percent with hearing loss and 18 percent with tinnitus in those injured through some mechanism other than blast. In another VA polytrauma sample (Lew et al. 2009), 19 percent of the patients had hearing impairments, 34 percent had vision impairments, and 32 percent had dual (hearing and vision) impairments.

Psychological Comorbidities

Psychological comorbidities are also prevalent in the combat polytrauma population. In general, the presence of a depressive or anxiety disorder is associated with greater overall utilization of healthcare resources (Simon et al. 1995). Moreover, it is well understood that in the injured population, psychological health disorders have an effect on recovery from physical trauma (Holbrook et al. 1999; Michaels et al. 2000). Of particular concern in a combat-exposed population are PTSD and depression. Hoge and colleagues (2004) surveyed four U.S. combat infantry units and showed that those who had been deployed to Iraq reported a very high level of combat experiences, with more than 90 percent of them reporting being shot at, and a high percentage reporting handling dead bodies, knowing someone who was injured or killed, or killing an enemy combatant. In this study, the percentage of individuals whose responses met the screening criteria for PTSD, major depression, or alcohol misuse was significantly higher among soldiers after deployment than before deployment. Furthermore, the prevalence of PTSD increased with the number of firefights during deployment, with increases up to 19.3 percent for those involved in more than five firefights. Most important, the rates of PTSD in this population were significantly associated with having been wounded or injured (Hoge et al. 2004).

In a survey of a group of U.S. soldiers following a year-long deployment to Iraq (Hoge et al. 2008), service members answered questions about their deployment, including whether they sustained an mTBI or other injuries while deployed. PTSD was strongly associated with mTBI. Forty-four percent of the soldiers who had injuries with LOC met criteria for PTSD. Of those that reported an alteration in consciousness, about 27 percent met criteria for PTSD and 16 percent endorsed sustaining other types of injuries. The rate of PTSD for those having no other injuries was about 9 percent. Those soldiers who reported mTBI, especially with LOC, were more likely to report poor general health, more days of missed work, an increased number of medical visits, and a higher number of somatic and postconcussive symptoms than were soldiers with other injuries. Depression was more frequent in those with LOC than in those with other injuries. However, after adjustment for PTSD and depression, the occurrence of mTBI was no longer significantly associated with these physical concerns (except for headache in the LOC group). These findings underscore the complicated relationship between stress symptoms and TBI symptoms and how they interact to cause persistent dysfunction in some individuals.

In addition, Grieger and colleagues (2006) reported that among service members with injuries serious enough to be medically evacuated and hospitalized at WRAMC, slightly over 4 percent had PTSD and/or depression at one month postinjury. These rates increased to 12.2 percent for PTSD and 8.9 percent for depression at four months post-injury. At seven months, these rates were 12 percent and 9.3 percent, respectively. High levels of self-reported physical problems at one month postinjury were significantly predictive of PTSD and depression at seven months postinjury (Grieger et al. 2006).

The relationship between PTSD and mTBI is complex and not fully understood. It has been suggested that damage to the prefrontal cortex in TBI results in disruption of neural networks involved in the regulation of anxiety, making the affected individual more vulnerable to the effects of an emotionally traumatic event (Kochanek, Clark & Jenkins 2007). More important, TBI has been shown to complicate or prolong recovery from preexisting or comorbid conditions such as PTSD (Vanderploeg, Belanger & Curtiss 2009). The frequent co-occurrence of both conditions and the potential interactive effects have treatment implications for those injured. Postconcussive symptoms may actually increase the likelihood of developing PTSD, because these symptoms interfere with adequate adjustment to the event (Meares et al. 2008).

Unique Aspects of Military TBI

Civilian versus Military TBI

In civilian settings, many concussions are suffered secondary to sports injuries, motor vehicle accidents, and other events that may have witnesses or responders quickly at the scene. Since the diagnosis of TBI is based on the mechanism of injury, these witness reports are often very important for determining whether a TBI occurred, as well as the severity of the TBI. For example, if a patient suffers a brain injury during a football game, the individual may or may not remember with any accuracy how long he or she lost consciousness or experienced PTA. Other players, coaches, and medical personnel may be able to better characterize the events of the injury and the behaviors of the patient to determine those factors.

However, it is a different story in the military. Today the vast majority of service members who are evaluated for TBI at Walter Reed suffered their injuries during combat. Often injuries in this population occur under chaotic circumstances in which detailed descriptions of the events are impossible to put down in writing, and comprehensive medical care may not be immediately available. For these reasons, along with the complex nature of mTBI, there is a greater chance of this injury not being detected. In 2006 the Defense and Veterans Brain Injury Center (DVBIC) developed the Military Acute Concussion Evaluation (MACE) to improve the detection of TBI in theater. The MACE (French, McCrea & Baggett 2008) is a screening evaluation that was designed to take a short period of time, be easily administered, and be appropriate for use by nonclinicians in austere conditions.

Military Acute Concussion Evaluation

The MACE is composed of a brief questionnaire, followed by a cognitive evaluation. The questionnaire portion of the MACE focuses on the injury characteristics that would be necessary for a diagnosis of TBI, such as LOC, AOC,

PTA, and postconcussive symptoms. The second half of the evaluation is composed of the Standardized Assessment of Concussion (SAC) (McCrea et al. 1998). The SAC is a widely administered and well-validated tool used to assess the effects of concussion. It examines orientation to time, verbal learning and memory, concentration, and neurological symptoms. The total score of the MACE is 30; nonconcussed individuals would normally score a 28 or above. In theater, a cutoff score of 25 is found to be the most specific and sensitive to suggest cognitive impairment.

Three factors are very important to keep in mind when administering the MACE. First, it is supposed to be used acutely, soon after the event. Second, the diagnosis of TBI is based on mechanism of injury, not on the symptomology a patient experiences. Therefore, although a patient may express cognitive deficits upon testing, that alone does not suggest the patient suffered a TBI, as cognitive deficits may occur for a number of non-TBI-related reasons. Third, even if a patient does not express cognitive deficits on the MACE, the individual may have suffered a TBI but simply is not experiencing any significant sequelae, or is experiencing areas of subtle weakness that the MACE is not sensitive enough to capture. In either case, one of the uses of the MACE is to help determine a service member's readiness to return to duty; in the latter case, it is possible a person who suffered a mild concussion may be ready to return to battle if he or she is asymptomatic. Conversely, a patient who may not have suffered a TBI but is displaying areas of cognitive weakness secondary to other factors (fatigue, illness, or psychiatric issues, for example) may not be ready to return to battle and will require follow-up care. Thus, the MACE is a useful tool to evaluate a service member's TBI status and need for medical attention. Often the MACE is the initial TBI evaluation a service member will receive.

Depending on the injuries sustained, the patient may be able to receive adequate care in theater. Service members who need more comprehensive medical care for TBI or other injuries, however, are evacuated out of theater. They are taken to Landstuhl Regional Medical Center in Germany for stabilization and then transported to the United States for treatment, usually initially at the new Walter Reed National Military Medical Center (WRNMMC) in Bethesda, Maryland, or Brooke Army Medical Center in San Antonio, Texas.

The Model of Care for TBI at Walter Reed Army Medical Center

Many of the injuries requiring evacuation out of theater in OIF/OEF have been a result of the use of IEDs by the enemy. According to Warden (2006), approximately two-thirds of army war zone evacuations are due to blast. Using the

Navy–Marine Corps Combat Trauma Registry, it was determined that among the injuries sustained in battle, IEDs were the most common cause of TBI (Galarneau et al. 2008). To a large degree, as in VA, the mechanism of injury guides the approach to assessment and treatment (Belanger et al. 2005b).

As a result of the increased number of military-related TBIs, in addition to the military's commitment to addressing the needs of its service members, a comprehensive evaluation for TBI using multidisciplinary teams of providers is routine at WRAMC. These evaluations are performed on patients who are evacuated from theater and brought to the hospital on an inpatient or outpatient status, as well as on service members referred for evaluation from other clinics and services.

For patients being evacuated from theater, the evaluation process begins prior to arriving at the hospital. The initial step of the comprehensive TBI evaluation for patients returning from battle involves a close examination of the air evacuation manifest, which provides brief descriptions of injuries for all the patients who are being flown out of theater and being admitted to the hospital. A designated TBI clinician carefully reads the manifest to identify all patients with a mechanism of injury that may have resulted in a TBI. For example, any patient who is involved in a blast, was injured in a motor vehicle accident, suffered a fall, or had a gunshot wound above the neck will be flagged for evaluation.

The next step in the process is to gather whatever documentation is available regarding the event in which the patient was injured. Electronic medical records are particularly important for this step, because no matter where the initial care was delivered, the electronic record contains all of the information available on the patient's injury. After the background and history have been properly examined, a thorough clinical interview is administered to the patient. The clinical interview is the most important component of the TBI evaluative process, and thus will be described in some detail.

As previously described, patients who have suffered moderate and severe TBIs are usually easier to identify and diagnose than those suffering mTBIs. They often have findings on radiological or neurological evaluations to confirm the TBI or have suffered extended periods of LOC, AOC, or PTA that have been well documented in medical records. However, patients suffering mTBIs may have experienced very brief moments of altered consciousness that may or may not be reflected in medical records. This is why a thorough and detailed clinical interview and records review is crucial in determining TBI status. The determination of LOC is especially challenging if it is based solely on self-report. Although the patient may report an amnesic period postinjury, without outside corroboration it may be impossible to determine whether it was due to LOC, PTA, or a combination of both.

A particularly difficult aspect in accurately diagnosing mTBI is the determination of AOC. This is especially true for a military population injured in combat. Alteration of consciousness is a nonspecific construct without a good operational definition. For example, AOC is often defined as feeling "dazed," "confused," "disoriented," or as "seeing stars." However, these descriptions are far from precise and can blur the distinction between suffering an mTBI and experiencing a normal psychological reaction to a traumatic event. Feeling "dazed" for a few seconds to minutes is a common report from service members after being involved in an explosion. However, if the service member remained fully oriented to person, place, and time; had no amnesic periods; and did not suffer any postconcussive symptoms, it seems unlikely the individual suffered a TBI. On the other hand, if the patient reported feeling confused, disoriented, and unsure of his or her surroundings, this may be more suggestive of a very mild concussion. The distinction is a qualitative one to some degree, based on the report of the patient's experience immediately after the event, and despite careful questioning, it is often not definitive.

One of the most helpful questions that will allow the patient to assist in the diagnosis is whether he or she has ever suffered a concussion in the past. If a patient has suffered a concussion in the past, the individual can compare that experience to the more recent one to help determine if a concussion occurred. This can also be useful because patients can see from their own experience that concussions (for the most part) will heal, and they will likely return to baseline functioning quickly. Moreover, this can be a very reassuring notion for a patient that is diagnosed with a TBI, as the patient may not always equate the TBI diagnosis to the concussion that was suffered previously. It should be noted that some studies (Collins et al. 1999; Iverson et al. 2004) have shown a relationship between multiple concussions and persistent cognitive dysfunction.

Similarly to AOC, PTA can be challenging to diagnose. It is the period of time after the injury event for which the patient does not have any recollection and includes the time the patient may have been unconscious. It is said to resolve only after the patient begins to have clear and consistent memories for events. It is important to differentiate between what patients actually recall themselves and what they have been told by others. In addition, it is important to keep in mind that due to the emotional trauma often accompanying battlefield injuries, psychogenic amnesia (a condition wherein memory deficits are apparent but structural brain damage is absent) is a defense mechanism that may be utilized and may present as PTA. Finally, it is also interesting to note that although medical records may indicate the patient appeared intact soon after the injury event, he or she may have no recollection of that time period. In other words, although the patient may have been given a GCS of 15 and been reported to be fully oriented, if the patient is amnesic for that period he or she was likely in PTA and suffered at least an mTBI.

Thus, although the TBI severity table appears simple to use, differentiating between TBI and non-TBI, as well as the severity level of the TBI, is a complicated process that requires clinical interviewing skills and cannot be easily accomplished with the use of simple checklists or patient self-report inventories. However, such approaches may be necessary for screening purposes in nonmedically evacuated groups of service members postdeployment. This has proven to be an effective strategy (Terrio et al. 2009), but is not without controversy in itself. The question has been raised whether the TBI screening process has iatrogenic effects (Hoge, Goldberg & Castro 2009). The procedure for screening for TBI in patients who are referred from other clinics as outpatients, or from other services, is generally the same as with the WRAMC inpatient population. A specified TBI clinician (such as a social worker, physician's assistant, or psychologist) will perform a thorough medical records review and a clinical interview. The criteria for diagnosis remain the same, but the determination of an accurate diagnosis can be more challenging if the injury was not recent, as specific memories of the events can fade over time.

Once a determination has been made regarding the patient's TBI status (positive or negative), recommendations for appropriate treatment are made. If the patient has been screened as negative for TBI, yet is complaining of cognitive symptoms, it is important to explore other reasons for impaired cognition and discuss these with the patient. Some of the non-TBI factors that have been seen to affect cognitive functioning in this population are the use of narcotic pain medications, untreated pain symptoms, psychiatric symptoms (PTSD, depression, anxiety, etc.), sleep deprivation, sleep apnea, and stress. In addition, some of the difficulties patients endure arise from sensory deficits caused by hearing loss and visual disturbances. Depending on what the most salient factors appear to be, consults at the appropriate clinics are done and a treatment plan emerges. Those with mTBI are educated about typical symptoms and recovery, with the goal of encouraging the mindset of expectancy of recovery. Such interventions have been shown to be effective in reducing longer-term morbidity (Ponsford et al. 2002).

Neuropsychological testing is typically deferred until other symptoms have been better stabilized, and only if the patient continues to experience cognitive difficulties after the symptoms have been stabilized. With early and proper education, patients generally indicate understanding of the complex interrelationships between cognitive functioning and non-neurological factors, and indeed are often relieved to be told that they do not have a brain injury and can take positive steps to improve their functioning.

The treatment course for TBI positive patients depends on a number of factors, including (but not limited to) the severity of the TBI, the severity of other physical injuries, the timeframe of when the injury took place, and current duty status. Many service members who are screened for TBI as inpatients at WRNMMC have upper and/or lower limb amputations, in addition to other internal and orthopedic injuries. WRNMMC is internationally known as a premier amputee rehabilitation hospital; thus many of the patients with amputations will want to be treated at WRNMMC for long-term rehabilitation. However, in the short term, if a patient has suffered a moderate or severe TBI and is evidencing significant cognitive symptoms, he or she will likely be transferred for acute inpatient rehabilitation to one of the identified VA polytrauma hospitals. These specially designated rehabilitation hospitals are located in Palo Alto, California; Tampa, Florida; Minneapolis, Minnesota; San Antonio, Texas; and Richmond, Virginia. The length of stay in the polytrauma hospitals is determined by the patient's progress in the rehabilitation program, and may be as short as a couple of weeks or continue for months. After graduating from the inpatient rehabilitation program, patients are taken back to WRAMC for further outpatient rehabilitation, as outlined below.

Patients who are TBI positive but do not require acute inpatient rehabilitation are followed at WRNMMC in a multidisciplinary outpatient TBI clinic to ensure all pertinent issues are addressed. The TBI clinic is a unique and comprehensive entity that is composed of providers from physical medicine and rehabilitation, orthopedics, neurology, psychiatry/behavioral health, neuropsychology, audiology, optometry, ophthalmology, physical therapy, speech language pathology, occupational therapy, and case management. Patients who are positive for TBI will undergo comprehensive evaluations by each of these services to determine rehabilitative needs. Areas of deficit are identified and recommendations for treatment are implemented.

Cognitive deficits are assessed through the use of neuropsychological testing, as well as evaluations and treatment by speech language pathologists and occupational therapists. Dizziness and vestibular issues are identified and treated by physical therapists in a specially designated "Dizziness Clinic." Headaches are a complicated phenomenon and often require a multifaceted approach. Neurologists at WRNMMC have developed specialties in headache management due to the large number of patients with headache complaints. However, stress, sleep deprivation, and depressed mood can also contribute to headache onset and severity, so behavioral health interventions can also be very helpful during treatment. Chronic pain is a similar problem in that pharmacological intervention can be beneficial, but nonpharmacologic health interventions (including acupuncture and behavioral health interventions) also have been shown to be effective in pain management. Finally, tinnitus may be assessed and treated by the audiology department, and visual disturbances are assessed and treated by optometry and ophthalmology.

Most rehabilitation needs can be taken care of at WRNMMC. However, extended stays at the hospital can prove to be a financial and logistical hardship for many service members' families. To ease the burden on families, yet allow patients to continue to receive appropriate care and benefit from social support, service members may be transferred to care networks in communities closer to their homes. The military has set up "Community Based Warrior Transition Units" (CBWTUs) to meet the needs of the patients and their families. As part of this transition, each service involved in the patient's care at WRAMC will develop a set of recommendations for further treatment. Case managers will contact the CBWTU in the patient's community to ensure it has all the necessary specialties to provide adequate care, based on the recommendations of the treatment team. Only if all the required treatments are available will the service member be transferred to the CBWTU. Due to the excellent case management available for wounded service members, there is continued contact between the patient and the team at WRNMMC to ensure that all needs are being met in the CBWTU. Having an individual TBI case manager also provides the service member with one point of contact that can be used to address any needs, schedule follow-up appointments, or help with any administrative issues.

Although injured service members from the current conflicts present with very complicated conditions, this multidisciplinary approach to treatment has proven to be very effective. Service members' needs are met by utilizing providers from appropriate disciplines, and comprehensive rehabilitation plans emerge. To continue administering proper treatments and rehabilitation plans to service members, it is imperative that research in TBI continue.

Research and New Directions in TBI

The Need for Military TBI Research

To date, the majority of research on TBI has been conducted in the civilian sector, focusing on motor vehicle accidents, falls, and sports-related injuries. The information gathered from such research has greatly enhanced our knowledge of TBI; however, the findings do not always accurately reflect the type of brain injury seen in the deployed military population. Due to the unique circumstances under which combat-related TBI occurs, more research is needed to better prevent, diagnose, and treat TBI in this population.

Over the past several years, research related to military TBI has expanded, and clinical care has greatly improved. Clinicians and researchers from DVBIC, the National Capital Neuroimaging Consortium (NCNC), the Naval Medical Research Center (NMRC), the National Institutes of Health, and the Center for Neuroscience and Regenerative Medicine (CNRM) are collaborating with investigators at WRNMMC to conduct TBI-related research. These organizations have a number of ongoing research protocols involving clinical tracking of patients sustaining TBIs, the natural history of TBI, substance use associated with it, blast-related injury, and neuroimaging, in addition to the ongoing clinical management at WRNMMC.

Clinical Tracking of TBI

As part of routine care at WRNMMC, standard of care documentation such as the Clinical Tracking Form (CTF), Neurobehavioral Symptom Inventory (NBSI), and the Post-Traumatic Stress Disorder Checklist—Civilian (PCL-C) are administered and analyzed. The CTF is completed by a clinician and records demographic information including the patient's age, gender, rank, military occupation specialty (MOS), and deployment history. It also documents the nature of the injuries and includes a brief neurological exam and expected outcome. The NBSI and PCL-C are self-report measures that list a series of symptoms. The patient is directed to indicate the symptoms he or she is experiencing and to what degree, from "not at all" to "very severe." The NBSI covers somatic-based symptoms, such as headaches and dizziness, while the PCL-C covers symptoms associated with PTSD, such as avoidance of situations and nightmares.

Annual telephone interviews are another key component of routine care. These calls focus on long-term outcomes, as questions are asked regarding pain, headaches, persistent physical and cognitive symptoms, use of medication, ability to return to work and/or school, activities of daily living, and reports of overall life satisfaction. In addition, cognitive tests are administered when appropriate.

TBI Characterization Studies

In addition to the clinical tracking of TBI, several research projects are underway at WRNMMC. Each study seeks to evaluate a particular facet of TBI. The simplest of these studies strives to better define it, correlating its etiology with patient demographics, mechanisms of injury, injury severity, comorbid injuries, symptomatology, and outcomes. The primary data sources are the standard of care baseline screening documents and follow-up telephone interviews, conducted six months postconsent, twelve months postconsent, and annually thereafter.

In 2007 baseline symptom reports based on completed NBSIs and PCL-Cs of consented patients were analyzed (Bhagwat 2009). The analysis indicated symptoms across a number of categories, including physical, emotional, and cognitive domains. Difficulty falling or staying asleep was the most endorsed somatic symptom, reported by 72.8 percent of individuals. The next highest reported symptom was headaches, endorsed by 66.3 percent of the population. In addition, 54.9 and 54.8 percent of participants indicated problems with hearing and vision, respectively. Psychosocial symptoms including irritability, anxiety, frustration intolerance, and sadness received endorsements by 66.3, 64.8, 59.2, and 56.6 percent of patients, respectively. There was also endorsement of hyperviligance; 58.9 percent of subjects reported they felt jumpy or easily startled and 55.4 percent reported being super alert, watchful, or on guard. Nightmares were endorsed by 58.6 percent, who reported repeated disturbing dreams of stressful past experiences (Bhagwat 2009).

A number of other characterization studies are in process at WRNMMC, including a congressionally mandated, fifteen-year natural history follow-up study and a study of the needs and problems of family caregivers. These studies aim to prospectively follow TBI patients and their families postinjury to determine long-term outcomes, assess substance abuse, study biomarkers, and improve our understanding of vertigo and other symptoms after blast-related injury.

Neuroimaging

In addition to TBI characterization studies, a number of active protocols by DVBIC, NCNC, NMRC, and CNRM, in collaboration with WRNMMC, are utilizing recent advancements in neuroimaging techniques to further TBI research. Goals of these studies include detailing the neuroanatomical effects of blast exposure on the brain, determining the most effective modality for diagnosing brain injury, and evaluating the possible relationship between brain activity and the behavioral changes commonly seen following brain injury.

Belanger and colleagues (2009) reported that 7–33 percent of mild TBI patients endorse physical, emotional, or cognitive deficits after the time of expected recovery at one month. Diffusion tensor imaging (DTI), a new MRI application, has the ability to detect diffuse axonal injuries (DAI), which do not appear on standard CT or MRI imaging protocols, but may explain persistent symptoms. As a result, DVBIC investigators use DTI to determine the correlation between the occurrence of DAI and the prevalence of persistent symptoms as measured through the NBSI, PCL-C, and follow-up telephone interviews.

Other studies evaluate which imaging modality is best for diagnosing TBI. Participants who consent undergo an MRI, a DTI, an fMRI, a PET, and a SPECT scan, and a comprehensive neurocognitive test battery. Imaging findings are correlated with performance on cognitive testing. The cognitive test battery measures various facets of memory, concentration, attention, language, visual-spatial construction, executive functioning, and processing speed. Finally, a study utilizing fMRI attempts to classify the relationship among brain activation, cognitive control, and working memory following brain injury.

Improving Quality of Life

Quality of life studies are also essential for evaluating the TBI population. Other studies investigate interventions to improve quality of life following a TBI, including alleviating post-traumatic headaches and reducing depression type symptoms in caregivers. Post-traumatic headaches, for example, are the second most reported somatic symptom following brain injury (Bhagwat 2009). One current prospective pilot study investigates whether standardized auricular acupuncture or semistandardized traditional Chinese acupuncture (TCA) will alleviate headaches more effectively than usual care alone. The findings will be used to develop future studies and potentially modify the standard of care treatment for post-traumatic headaches.

Another quality of life study is examining the benefits of exercise for the military TBI population. Exercise has been shown to increase brain-derived neurotropic factor (BDNF) in the hippocampus and prefrontal cortex (Griesbach et al. 2004). This protein is beneficial to learning, memory, and executive functioning by supporting and strengthening synapses and assisting in the protection and growth of new neurons. Investigators propose that providing regimented aerobic exercise, in addition to standard of care occupational therapy, will improve functional outcomes. Outcomes will be measured using a battery assessing performance in cognition, motor skills, and activities of daily living.

Finally, a "Brain Fitness Center" (BFC) was recently established at WRNMMC. The BFC uses interactive computer programs to enhance brain functioning in wounded warriors. These programs were originally developed to promote neural plasticity in an effort to delay the onset of age-related dementia and Alzheimer's by promoting cognitive functioning with interactive games and tasks. Since the neuroanatomical effects of TBI have been compared to those of dementia and Alzheimer's, it is thought that these programs may be equally beneficial in the military TBI population. The randomized protocol associated with the BFC measures subjective and objective improvements resulting from weekly sessions.

Conclusion

The current conflicts, OIF and OEF, are unlike any prior war in history. Service members are surviving injuries that would have been fatal in previous military engagements, and this has resulted in an increased number of TBIs.

Patients with TBI experience a variety of dysfunctions that can affect all areas of life, and recovery is dependent on a number of factors. Patients with moderate to severe TBI typically experience persistent symptoms, whereas the majority of patients with mTBI are symptom-free within a month after the initial injury. A small portion of the mTBI population, however, experiences persistent symptoms after the expected recovery period. When symptoms persist following an mTBI, patients are said to have postconcussion syndrome.

In addition to having TBIs, many service members—especially those injured in combat—have accompanying comorbidities ranging from the physical to the psychological. Consequently, a multidisciplinary approach to treatment has been implemented at Walter Reed National Military Medical Center. Patients' needs are met by utilizing providers from a variety of appropriate disciplines, and a comprehensive rehabilitation plan is developed for each patient.

Because of the unique circumstances under which combat-related TBI occurs, more research is needed to advance our understanding of this condition. Current research tracks include better understanding the natural history of TBI and discovering why persistent symptoms exist and how to better treat them.

References

Arciniegas, D. B., Anderson, C. A., Topkoff, J. & McAllister, T. W. (2005). Mild traumatic brain injury: A neuropsychiatric approach to diagnosis, evaluation, and treatment. *Neuropsychiatric Disease and Treatment* 1, no. 4: 311–327.

Armed Forces Health Surveillance Center. (2009). TBI numbers: Department of Defense numbers for traumatic brain injury. http://www.dvbic.org/TBI-Numbers .aspx (accessed July 8, 2010).

Belanger, H. G., Curtiss, G., Demery, J. A., Lebowitz, B. K. & Vanderploeg, R. D. (2005a). Factors moderating neuropsychological outcomes following mild traumatic brain injury: a meta-analysis. *Journal of the International Neuropsychology Society* 11, no. 3: 215–227.

Belanger, H. G., Kretzmer, T., Vanderploeg, R. D. & French, L. M. (2009). Symptom complaints following combat-related traumatic brain injury: Relationship to traumatic brain injury severity and posttraumatic stress disorder. *Journal of the International Neuropsychology Society* 16: 194–199.

Belanger, H. G., Scott, S. G., Scholten, J., Curtiss, G. & Vanderploeg, R. D. (2005b). Utility of mechanism-of-injury-based assessment and treatment: Blast Injury Program case illustration. *Journal of Rehabilitation Research & Development* 42, no. 4: 403–412.

Bhagwat, A. (2009). Traumatic brain injury rehabilitation at Walter Reed: From the battlefield to the workplace. Paper presented at the Third International Conference on Vocational Outcomes in Traumatic Brain Injury, Vancouver, Canada.

Borgaro, S. R., Prigatano, G. P., Kwasnica, C. & Rexer, J. L. (2003). Cognitive and affective sequelae in complicated and uncomplicated mild traumatic brain injury. *Brain Injury* 17, no. 3: 189–198.

Brink, J. D., Garret, A. L., Hale, W. R., Woo-Sam, J. & Nickel, V. L. (1970). Recovery of motor and intellectual function in children sustaining severe head injuries. *Developmental Medicine & Child Neurology* 12: 565–571.

Carroll, L. J., Cassidy, J. D., Peloso, P. M., Borg, J., von Holst, H., Holm, L., et al. (2004). Prognosis for mild traumatic brain injury: Results of the WHO Collaborating Centre Task Force on Mild Traumatic Brain Injury. *Journal of Rehabilitation Medicine* 43, supp.: 84–105.

Chamelian, L. & Feinstein, A. (2006). The effect of major depression on subjective and objective cognitive deficits in mild to moderate traumatic brain injury. *Journal of Neuropsychiatry and Clinical Neurosciences* 18, no. 1: 33–38.

Collins, M. W., Grindel, S. H., Lovell, M. R., Dede, D. E., Moser, D. J., Phalin, B. R., et al. (1999). Relationship between concussion and neuropsychological performance in college football players. *JAMA* 282, no. 10: 964–970.

Department of Defense. (2008). Code proposals for the Departments of Defense and Veterans Affairs: ICD-9–CM Coordination and Maintenance Committee. www.cdc.gov/nchs/ppt/icd9/att1DennisSept08.pdf.

Elder, G. A. & Cristian, A. (2009). Blast-related mild traumatic brain injury: Mechanisms of injury and impact on clinical care. *Mount Sinai Journal of Medicine* 76: 111–118.

Finkel, M. F. (2006). The neurological consequences of explosives. *Journal of the Neurological Sciences* 249, no. 1: 63–67.

French, L., McCrea, M. & Baggett, M. (2008). The Military Acute Concussion Evaluation (MACE). *Journal of Special Operations Medicine* 8, no. 1: 68–77.

French, L., Mouratidis, M., Dicianno, B. & Impink, B. (2009). *Traumatic brain injury.* Washington, DC: Borden Institute.

Frenisy, M.-C., Benony, H., Chahraoui, K., Minot, D., d'Arthis, P., Pinoit, J.-M., et al. (2006). Brain injured patients versus multiple trauma patients: some neurobehavioral and psychopathological aspects. *Journal of Trauma Injury, Infection, and Critical Care* 60: 1018–1026.

Galarneau, M. R., Woodruff, S. I., Dye, J. L., Mohrle, C. R. & Wade, A. L. (2008). Traumatic brain injury during Operation Iraqi Freedom: Findings from the United States Navy–Marine Corps Combat Trauma Registry. *Journal of Neurosurgery* 108, no. 5: 950–957.

Giza, C. C. & Hovda, D. A. (2001). The neurometabolic cascade of concussion. *Journal of Athletic Training* 36, no. 3: 228–235.

Goodrich, G. L., Kirby, J., Cockerham, G., Ingalla, S. P. & Lew, H. L. (2007). Visual function in patients of a polytrauma rehabilitation center: A descriptive study. *Journal of Rehabilitation Research & Development* 44, no. 7: 929–936.

Gordon, W. A., Haddad, L., Brown, M., Hibbard, M. R. & Sliwinski, M. (2000). The sensitivity and specificity of self-reported symptoms in individuals with traumatic brain injury. *Brain Injury* 14, no. 1: 21–33.

Grafman, J., Jonas, B. S., Martin, A., Salazar, A. M., Weingartner, H., Ludlow, C., et al. (1988). Intellectual function following penetrating head injury in Vietnam veterans. *Brain* 111, pt. 1: 169–184.

Grieger, T. A., Cozza, S. J., Ursano, R. J., Hoge, C., Martinez, P. E., Engel, C. C., et al. (2006). Posttraumatic stress disorder and depression in battle-injured soldiers. *American Journal of Psychiatry* 163, no. 10: 1777–1783; quiz 1860.

Griesbach, G. S., Hovda, D., Molteni, R., Wu, A. & Gomez-Pinilla, F. (2004). Voluntary exercise following traumatic brain injury: brain-derived neurotrophic factor upregulation and recovery of function. *Neuroscience* 125, no. 1: 129–139.

Groswasser, Z., Reider, G., II, Schwab, K., Ommaya, A. K., Pridgen, A., Brown, H. R., et al. (2002). Quantitative imaging in late TBI. Part II: Cognition and work after closed and penetrating head injury: A report of the Vietnam head injury study. *Brain Injury* 16, no. 8: 681–690.

Hartlage, L. C., Durant-Wilson, D. & Patch, P. C. (2001). Persistent neurobehavioral problems following mild traumatic brain injury. *Archives of Clinical Neuropsychology* 16, no. 6: 561–570.

Hoge, C. W., Castro, C. A., Messer, S. C., McGurk, D., Cotting, D. I. & Koffman, R. L. (2004). Combat duty in Iraq and Afghanistan, mental health problems, and barriers to care. *New England Journal of Medicine* 351, no. 1: 13–22.

Hoge, C. W., Goldberg, H. M. & Castro, C. A. (2009). Care of war veterans with mild traumatic brain injury—flawed perspectives. *New England Journal of Medicine* 360, no. 16: 1588–1591.

Hoge, C. W., McGurk, D., Thomas, J. L., Cox, A. L., Engel, C. C. & Castro, C. A. (2008). Mild traumatic brain injury in U.S. soldiers returning from Iraq. *New England Journal of Medicine* 358, no. 5: 453–463.

Holbrook, T. L., Anderson, J. P., Sieber, W. J., Browner, D. & Hoyt, D. B. (1999). Outcome after major trauma: 12-month and 18-month follow-up results from the Trauma Recovery Project. *Journal of Trauma* 46, no. 5: 765–771; discussion 771–773.

Institute of Medicine & Committee on Gulf War and Health: Brain Injury in Veterans and Long-Term Health Outcomes. (2009). *Gulf War and health.* Volume 7: *Long-term consequences of traumatic brain injury.* Washington, DC: National Academies Press.

Iverson, G. L. (2007). Predicting slow recovery from sport-related concussion: The new simple-complex distinction. *Clinical Journal of Sport Medicine* 17, no. 1: 31–37.

Iverson, G. L., Gaetz, M., Lovell, M. R. & Collins, M. W. (2004). Cumulative effects of concussion in amateur athletes. *Brain Injury* 18, no. 5: 433–443.

Iverson, G. L., Lange, R. T. & Franzen, M. D. (2005). Effects of mild traumatic brain injury cannot be differentiated from substance abuse. *Brain Injury* 19, no. 1: 11–18.

Iverson, G. L. & McCracken, L. M. (1997). "Postconcussive" symptoms in persons with chronic pain. *Brain Injury* 11, no. 11: 783–790.

Jennett, B., Snoek, J., Bond, M. R. & Brooks, N. (1981). Disability after severe head injury: observations on the use of the Glasgow Outcome Scale. *Journal of Neurology, Neurosurgery, and Psychiatry* 44, no. 4: 285–293.

Jones, E., Fear, N. T. & Wessely, S. (2007). Shell shock and mild traumatic brain injury: A historical review. *American Journal of Psychiatry* 164, no. 11: 1641–1645.

Kaufman, H. H. (1993). Treatment of head injuries in the American Civil War. *Journal of Neurosurgery* 78: 838–845.

Kennedy, J. E., Jaffee, M. S., Leskin, G. A., Stokes, J. W., Leal, F. O. & Fitzpatrick, P. J. (2007). Posttraumatic stress disorder and posttraumatic stress disorder–like symptoms and mild traumatic brain injury. *Journal of Rehabilitation Research & Development* 44, no. 7: 895–920.

Kochanek, P. M., Clark, R. S. & Jenkins, L. W. (2007). *TBI: Pathobiology*. New York: Demos Medical Publications.

Koenigs, M., Huey, E. D., Raymont, V., Cheon, B., Solomon, J., Wassermann, E. M., et al. (2008). Focal brain damage protects against post-traumatic stress disorder in combat veterans. *Nature Neuroscience* 11, no. 2: 232–237.

Landre, N., Poppe, C. J., Davis, N., Schmaus, B. & Hobbs, S. E. (2006). Cognitive functioning and postconcussive symptoms in trauma patients with and without mild TBI. *Archives of Clinical Neuropsychology* 21, no. 4: 255–273.

Lew, H. L., Garvert, D. W., Pogoda, T. K., Hsu, P. T., Devine, J. M., White, D. K., et al. (2009). Auditory and visual impairments in patients with blast-related traumatic brain injury: Effect of dual sensory impairment on functional independence measure. *Journal of Rehabilitation Research & Development* 46, no. 6: 819–826.

Lew, H. L., Jerger, J. F., Guillory, S. B. & Henry, J. A. (2007). Auditory dysfunction in traumatic brain injury. *Journal of Rehabilitation Research & Development* 44, no. 7: 921–928.

Ling, G., Bandak, F., Armonda, R. A., Grant, G. A. & Ecklund, J. (2009). Explosive blast neurotrauma. *Journal of Neurotrauma* 26, no. 6: 815–825.

Maas, A. I., Stocchetti, N. & Bullock, R. (2008). Moderate and severe traumatic brain injury in adults. *Lancet Neurology* 7, no. 8: 728–741.

McCrea, M. (2008). *Mild traumatic brain injury and postconcussion syndrome: The new evidence base for diagnosis and treatment*. New York: Oxford University Press.

McCrea, M., Kelly, J. P., Randolph, C., Kluge, J., Bartolic, E., Finn, G., et al. (1998). Standardized assessment of concussion (SAC): On-site mental status evaluation of the athlete. *Journal of Head Trauma Rehabilitation* 13, no. 2: 27–35.

McCrea, M., Pliskin, N., Barth, J., Cox, D., Fink, J., French, L., et al. (2008). Official position of the military TBI task force on the role of neuropsychology and rehabilitation psychology in the evaluation, management, and research of military veterans with traumatic brain injury. *Clinical Neuropsychology*, 22(1), 10–26.

Meares, S., Shores, E. A., Taylor, A. J., Batchelor, J., Bryant, R. A., Baguley, I. J., et al. (2008). Mild traumatic brain injury does not predict acute postconcussion syndrome. *Journal of Neurology, Neurosurgery and Psychiatry* 79, no. 3: 300–306.

Michaels, A. J., Michaels, C. E., Smith, J. S., Moon, C. H., Peterson, C. & Long, W. B. (2000). Outcome from injury: General health, work status, and satisfaction 12 months after trauma. *Journal of Trauma* 48, no. 5: 841–848; discussion 848–850.

Mitchell, T. J. & Smith, G. M. (1931). *Medical services, casualties, and medical statistics of the great war*. London: His Majesty's Stationery Office.

Mittenberg, W., DiGiulio, D. V., Perrin, S. & Bass, A. E. (1992). Symptoms following mild head injury: Expectation as aetiology. *Journal of Neurology Neurosurgery and Psychiatry* 55, no. 3: 200–204.

Mott, F. W. (1917). Mental hygiene in shell shock during and after the war. *Journal of Mental Science* 63: 467–488.

Owens, B. D., Kragh, J. F., Jr., Wenke, J. C., Macaitis, J., Wade, C. E. & Holcomb, J. B. (2008). Combat wounds in Operation Iraqi Freedom and Operation Enduring Freedom. *Journal of Trauma Injury, Infection, and Critical Care* 64, no. 2: 295–299.

Pardini, M., Krueger, F., Raymont, V. & Grafman, J. (2010). Ventromedial prefrontal cortex modulates fatigue after penetrating traumatic brain injury. *Neurology* 74, no. 9: 749–754.

Ponsford, J., Willmott, C., Rothwell, A., Cameron, P., Kelly, A. M., Nelms, R., et al. (2000). Factors influencing outcome following mild traumatic brain injury in adults. *Journal of the International Neuropsychology Society* 6, no. 5: 568–579.

Ponsford, J., Willmott, C., Rothwell, A., Cameron, P., Kelly, A. M., Nelms, R., et al. (2002). Impact of early intervention on outcome following mild head injury in adults. *Journal of Neurology, Neurosurgery & Psychiatry* 73, no. 3: 330–332.

Reider-Groswasser, I. I., Groswasser, Z., Ommaya, A. K., Schwab, K., Pridgen, A., Brown, H. R., et al. (2002). Quantitive imaging in late traumatic brain injury. Part I: Late imaging parameters in closed and penetrating head injuries. *Brain Injury* 16, no. 6: 517–525.

Robbins, C. B., Vreeman, D. J., Sothmann, M. S., Wilson, S. L. & Oldridge, N. B. (2009). A review of the long-term health outcomes associated with war-related amputation. *Military Medicine* 174, no. 6: 588–592.

Rybarczyk, B., Nyenhuis, D. L., Nicholas, J. J., Cash, S. M. & Kaiser, J. (1995). Body image, perceived social stigma, and the prediction of psychosocial adjustment to leg amputation. *Rehabilitation Psychology* 40, no. 2: 95–110.

Salazar, A. M., Schwab, K. & Grafman, J. H. (1995). Penetrating injuries in the Vietnam war. Traumatic unconsciousness, epilepsy, and psychosocial outcome. *Neurosurgery Clinics of North America* 6, no. 4: 715–726.

Schaller, W. F. (1939). After-effects of head injury, the post-traumatic concussion state, and the post-traumatic psychoneurotic state. *JAMA* 113: 1779–1785.

Silver, J. M., McAllister, T. W. & Yudofsky, S. C. (2005). *Textbook of traumatic brain injury*. Arlington, VA: American Psychiatric Publishing.

Simon, G., Ormel, J., VonKorff, M. & Barlow, W. (1995). Health care costs associated with depressive and anxiety disorders in primary care. *American Journal of Psychiatry* 152, no. 3: 352–357.

Sloggett, A. (1916). Director general of Army Medical Services war diary. UK National Archives.

Smith-Seemiller, L., Fow, N. R., Kant, R. & Franzen, M. D. (2003). Presence of post-concussion syndrome symptoms in patients with chronic pain vs mild traumatic brain injury. *Brain Injury* 17, no. 3: 199–206.

Stansbury, L. G., Lalliss, S. J., Branstetter, J. G., Bagg, M. R. & Holcomb, J. B. (2008). Amputations in U.S. military personnel in the current conflicts in Afghanistan and Iraq. *Journal of Orthopedic Trauma* 22, no. 1: 43–46.

Stulemeijer, M., van der Werf, S. P., Jacobs, B., Biert, J., van Vugt, A. B., Brauer, J. M., et al. (2006). Impact of additional extracranial injuries on outcome after mild traumatic brain injury. *Journal of Neurotrauma* 23, no. 10: 1561–1569.

Sweeney, J. K. & Smutok, M. A. (1983). Vietnam head injury study: Preliminary analysis of the functional and anatomical sequelae of penetrating head trauma. *Physical Therapy* 63, no. 12: 2018–2025.

Tanielian, T. L., Jaycox, L. & Rand Corporation. (2008). *Invisible wounds of war: Psychological and cognitive injuries, their consequences, and services to assist recovery.* Santa Monica, CA: RAND.

Terrio, H., Brenner, L. A., Ivins, B. J., Cho, J. M., Helmick, K., Schwab, K., et al. (2009). Traumatic brain injury screening: preliminary findings in a US Army brigade combat team. *Journal of Head Trauma Rehabilitation* 24, no. 1: 14–23.

Turner, W. A. (1915). Cases of nervous and mental shock observed in the base hospitals in France. *Journal of the Royal Army Medical Corps* 24: 343–352.

Van Baalen, B., Odding, E., Maas, A. I., Ribbers, G. M., Bergen, M. P. & Stam, H. J. (2003). Traumatic brain injury: Classification of initial severity and determination of functional outcome. *Disability and Rehabilitation* 25, no. 1: 9–18.

Vanderploeg, R. D., Belanger, H. G. & Curtiss, G. (2009). Mild traumatic brain injury and posttraumatic stress disorder and their associations with health symptoms. *Archives of Physical Medicine and Rehabilitation* 90, no. 7: 1084–1093.

Vanderploeg, R. D., Curtiss, G., Luis, C. A. & Salazar, A. M. (2007). Long-term morbidities following self-reported mild traumatic brain injury. *Journal of Clinical & Experimental Neuropsychology* 29, no. 6: 585–598.

Warden, D. (2006). Military TBI during the Iraq and Afghanistan wars. *Journal of Head Trauma Rehabilitation* 21, no. 5: 398–402.

Weichel, E. D., Colyer, M. H., Bautista, C., Bower, K. S. & French, L. M. (2009). Traumatic brain injury associated with combat ocular trauma. *Journal of Head Trauma Rehabilitation* 24, no. 1: 41–50.

Wilde, E. A., McCauley, S. R., Hunter, J. V., Bigler, E. D., Chu, Z., Wang, Z. J., et al. (2008). Diffusion tensor imaging of acute mild traumatic brain injury in adolescents. *Neurology* 70, no. 12: 948–955.

Williams, D. H., Levin, H. S. & Eisenberg, H. M. (1990). Mild head injury classification. *Neurosurgery* 27, no. 3: 422–428.

Chapter 10

Healthcare and Issues of Racial and Ethnic Diversity

Kathleen M. McNamara

There is a shared perception that in the military/Department of Defense (DoD) during World War II and the Vietnam War, the approach to racial and ethnic minority status mirrored what occurred in society in general. During both of those wars, societal response to racial and ethnic groups was quite evident. During WWII the War Department "segregated ground forces by race . . . . Black soldiers were assigned to all-Black units, whites to all-white units, and Japanese-Americans to their own 442nd Regimental Combat Team" (Tanaka 1982, 98). In Vietnam, units were not segregated by race or ethnic background, but anecdotal stories about the conflicts among black, Hispanic, and Caucasian/white soldiers that reflected the racial divides in U.S. society at the time are pervasive, and the physical similarity of Asian American and certain Pacific Islander soldiers to the enemy in Vietnam created its own stress for those American servicemen. When the service member is no longer in the military and returns to civilian life and becomes a veteran, a critical question is: Were the military and especially the combat and war zone experiences of minority veterans different and/or perceived differently than the experiences of nonminority veterans? If so, what effects did this have on their mental health, their physical health, available treatment, attitudes of healthcare providers, and the delivery of healthcare services? This is the focus of this chapter. Race, ethnicity, and cultural differences remain salient factors for veterans of prior wars, but also for our current military personnel, who are becoming the new generation of veterans.

While what we know as the Department of Veterans Affairs (VA) already was providing services to our veterans long before 1994, it was only then that a federal statute enacted by Congress, Public Law 103-446, Section 509, established the Center for Minority Veterans to "assist the Department of Veterans Affairs to 'keep the promise' by acting as facilitator, change agent, strategic thinker, honest broker and cheerleader to the men and women of the VA in executing its mission." The Web site for the Center for Minority Veterans (2010) affirmatively states: "We acknowledge the diversity of our veterans and profoundly value the strength and unique character this diversity has contributed to our great Nation." According to the Web site, the Center's primary emphasis is on minority veterans, with the following groups specifically named: Pacific Islander, Asian American, African American, Hispanic/Latino, and Native American, including American Indian, Alaska Native, and Native Hawaiian. The Center was designed to serve as principal adviser to the Secretary (of VA) on the adoption and implementation of policies and programs affecting minority veterans, making recommendations to the Secretary, the Under Secretary for Health, the Under Secretary for Benefits, and other VA officials for the establishment or improvement of programs in VA for eligible minority veterans. However, it also was assigned a number of more active roles, such as promoting the use of VA's programs, benefits, and services for eligible minority veterans; evaluating the current programs; and making recommendations on how VA can better serve minority veterans. While these tasks alone would suggest a full agenda, the tasks taken on by the Center also suggest a more interactive role with staff across VA and with the general public. The Center also is charged with publicizing the results of medical research that is of particular significance to minority veterans, disseminating information, and serving as a resource center for the exchange of information about innovative and successful programs that improve the services available to veterans who are minorities.

Congress recognized that the Center could only accomplish this wide array of tasks if it had input from those directly served by this Center. Consequently, in Section 510 of the law that created the Center, an Advisory Committee on Minority Veterans was established. The members are appointed by the Secretary for the Department of Veterans Affairs. They are veterans who represent respective minority groups and "are recognized authorities in fields pertinent to the needs of the minority group they embody" (Center for Minority Veterans 2010).

While the Center for Minority Veterans focuses on the veterans who are served, VA also has begun to emphasize the diversity of those who serve them, acknowledging that the characteristics of the staff influence the services provided to the veteran population. In February 2009 VA issued its *Diversity and Inclusion Strategic Plan for 2009–2013* (*Strategic Plan*), which was described as supporting its strategic objective to "recruit, develop, and retain a competent, committed, and diverse workforce that provides high-quality service to veterans and their families." By way of background, the plan highlighted VA's mission and emphasized the need to be reflective of those who are served: "to fulfill President Abraham Lincoln's promise: 'To care for him who shall have borne the battle, and for his widow, and his orphan.' As a major health care and benefits provider, the Department of Veterans Affairs must maintain a workforce that is reflective of the communities it serves." Among the overarching goals delineated in the *Strategic Plan* is one that reflects this emphasis on diversity of the workforce as the foundation for the highest quality of services. The goal includes an emphasis on promoting cultural competency. Repeatedly the plan ties a diverse workforce to improved service to our veterans. In July 2009 the Advisory Committee on Minority Veterans recognized this plan's emphasis on diversity and inclusion, defining it as *critical* to supporting VA's mission and purpose.

The existence of both the Center for Minority Veterans and the *Strategic Plan* commits VA to providing services that recognize that individual differences exist, and that such factors as race and ethnicity may have to be specifically addressed. Yet a review of the minutes of the meetings included in the annual reports of the Advisory Committee on Minority Veterans from 2005 to 2009 identifies areas for improvement in VA, often with the same theme of inadequate data from VA, despite the fact that the Advisory Committee gathered information from widely divergent geographic areas. For example, in its July 2009 report, the Advisory Committee noted that in the prior year's annual report it was strongly recommended that VA formulate a plan to establish a credible set of racial and ethnic data, which included an analysis of the services and programs designed to meet the increasing needs of minority veterans and their families. This lack of reliable data was noted in the annual reports in previous years as well (Advisory Committee on Minority Veterans 2005, 2006). The Secretary of VA in 2008 directed the Veterans Benefits Administration to develop such a plan. However, in the July 2009 report, the Advisory Committee stated it had not yet received a response.

Annual site visits highlighted other areas that committee members wished to have addressed, such as describing the outreach efforts to minority veterans as "insufficient" and pointing to the underrepresentation of minorities among the senior levels of VA staff (Advisory Committee on Minority Veterans 2008). Specific to mental health, the 2008 report expressed the concern that data on the incidence among minority veterans of post-traumatic stress disorder

(PTSD) may be inaccurate. This concern was rooted in the comments offered at "town hall" meetings by minority veterans, which indicate that minority veterans were hesitant to request treatment for PTSD. These veterans appeared especially sensitive to the stigma that is still attached to receiving mental health services. They particularly questioned the effect that receiving such services would have on their ability to secure employment. Of note, the 2008 report explicitly addressed what is known or not known about the proportional representation across psychiatric diagnoses assigned to minority veterans versus what is known for majority veterans. The committee proposed ways that VA's Office of Mental Health Services might work with the DoD, the Public Health and Environmental Hazards Strategic Health Care Group, the National Center for PTSD, and the Mental Illness Research Education and Clinical Centers (MIRECC) to address the missing data. The 2008 report called for improved outreach for veterans returning from multiple deployments in Iraq and/or Afghanistan. That report highlighted the particular initiatives that had been put in place by the Veterans Health Administration's (VHA) Office of Outreach to ensure that National Guard and Reserve members receive information about VA's benefits and to encourage them to enroll for healthcare through VA.

The committee commented that during their site visits around the country, the perception among minority veterans and their families repeatedly was "that they are not being provided services by VA commensurate with those provided to majority Veterans." The intent of the Advisory Committee on Minority Veterans to address this perception by minority veterans by evaluating the research requested by the VA Secretary in 2008 is well-founded. Nonveteran studies and reports from other governmental agencies (Agency for Healthcare Research and Quality 2006) clearly identify health disparities across quality of care and access to care for minority populations in general. The Department of Veterans Affairs has made the exploration of the nature and extent of this issue among the minority veteran population a priority. In June 2007 VA's Health Services Research and Development Services issued a report, *Racial and Ethnic Disparities in the VA Healthcare System: A Systematic Review* (Saha et al. 2007). The authors concluded that health disparities existed in VA's healthcare, just as they did in the general population, even though financial barriers that might be considered as contributing in a significant way in the healthcare system for the general population are minimal within the VA healthcare system. The review was focused on studies conducted with veterans receiving care in VA and acknowledged that studies with populations outside VA were not included after considering the significant differences between healthcare systems outside VA and the model of healthcare within VA, as well as other factors that make VA a unique healthcare organization. This study of disparities stated that its intent was to use the knowledge gained to determine the best direction for future research aimed at "improving equity in DVA health care." Particularly striking was the conclusion that disparities existed in all clinical areas and were not more prevalent in one area than another. Thus, the inequity existed whether the veteran was receiving care for a range of medical diseases, such as diabetes or cardiovascular conditions, or being treated for mental health or substance abuse disorders. What were the findings regarding the sources of these disparities? Factors that emerged included differences in the degree of familiarity with and knowledge about medical interventions, which in turn may influence a veteran's perception about the necessity for, benefits from, and risks involved in certain healthcare treatments. In general, minority veterans were less informed about their care compared to white veterans, and this affected their decision making. The difference in how well informed a veteran is also involved a number of related factors, ranging from the veteran's own health literacy and understanding, to differences in how much information was shared by healthcare providers based on racial and ethnic characteristics of the patient. With a number of factors again contributing, the study also compared the trust and/or degree of skepticism found in minority veterans to white veterans. Although lack of information about or familiarity with the intervention being proposed may contribute to the reduced trust found in minority veterans, other factors were documented, such as historical or personally experienced discrimination, or a desire to seek spiritual (rather than medical) remedies. Clinician factors emerged among the potential sources for disparities, though a clearer understanding of "why" was not evident in the studies reviewed. Thus, the studies pointed to differential diagnostic and therapeutic decision making associated with racial variables, but did not support a definitive conclusion about whether clinical or nonclinical factors (e.g., racial stereotyping or bias, cross-cultural misunderstanding of symptom presentation, actual differences in coexisting disorders, etc.) were the primary deciding factors. Variables unique to the veterans were identified. Minority veterans were seen to have fewer resources and less social support to assist with disease management and decision making. Participation in their own healthcare, as demonstrated by asking fewer questions or having a lower level of adherence to a treatment plan, was found to be at a lower level among minority veterans. Finally, minority veterans had less trust in and more skepticism about a racially and culturally discordant healthcare environment. The authors questioned whether an additional influence could be an actual lower quality of care and/or fewer available services at VA medical centers that see a disproportionate number of minority veterans. With these disturbing findings, the study group called for future research to determine the sources of variation in clinician judgment, which was found to be associated with the patient's race, emphasizing evidence-based *decision making* by providers. The group called for the design of decision aids and information tools for minority veterans that take into account culture, language, and health literacy. In addition, in what would seem to be an essential response to the findings, the authors called for a determination of facility characteristics or system-level sources of disparities.

The review just described addressed the healthcare services in VA—their utilization and their quality. However, differences among ethnic and racial groups in *health* (not healthcare services), and for the purpose of this chapter specifically mental and behavioral health, have been addressed in other ways. Although significant strides have been made in attention to ethnic, racial, and cultural differences and their impact on the diagnosis and treatment of PTSD, the research addressing these same underlying differences across the broader scope of mental health diagnostic and treatment issues for veterans (as a separately identified group to be studied) has not been nearly as systematic. A sampling of available published research into the veteran population confirms that differences exist and can be documented. For example, Saha and colleagues (2007) note that clinicians more often diagnose and treat African American veterans presenting with mental health issues as having psychotic disorders, whereas white veterans are diagnosed with affective disorders. Allen (1986) noted that the diagnosis and treatment of black veterans is *complicated* (emphasis added) by a number of factors, related not only to the racial and cultural experiences of the individuals, but even to the varied ways in which PTSD presents from one individual to another. Escobar and colleagues (1983) noted the *complex symptomatology* (emphasis added) of Hispanic Vietnam veterans with PTSD, observing that the PTSD was often present amid a variety of symptoms indicative of other psychiatric diagnoses. The findings suggested that these veterans were more alienated from their cultural roots, and their social relationships more often tended to be negative. Penk and Allen (1991) addressed the clinical assessment and treatment of minority combat Vietnam veterans more broadly, clearly providing a clinical depiction consistent with the positions of the Institute of Medicine (2001) and the American Psychological Association (2005) on evidence-based practice over a decade later. Penk and Allen highlight the need to address factors such as the higher rate of PTSD among minority veterans, the differential utilization of health services, and the effect of cross-cultural interactions between patient and clinician, which might impede or even preclude the development of a therapeutic relationship. These authors cogently state that "every combat veteran, regardless of racial background, is a unique individual with his or her own unique story to tell" (1991, 41). The Institute of

Medicine report (2001) concluded that there were "significant gaps in assessing the efficacy of interventions in important subpopulations of veterans...especially...ethnic and cultural minorities, women, and older individuals." The American Psychological Association 2005 Presidential Task Force emphasized the patient focus, stating that "evidence-based practice in psychology (EBPP) is the integration of the best available research with clinical expertise in the context of patient characteristics, culture, and preferences" (2005, 7).

Though focused on the single disorder of PTSD, the large literature base relating to ethnic, racial, and cultural variables in the assessment, diagnosis, and treatment of this disorder in minority veterans potentially offers much by way of templates and frameworks for considering these same variables in the delivery of any health service, whether it is for physical, behavioral, or mental health. As the Administration for Native Americans (ANA 2009) in the U.S. Department of Health and Human Services acknowledges, "the challenges facing native veterans today are similar to those facing veterans of all ethnicities throughout the United States...access to health care, substance abuse, unemployment, homelessness, and mental health issues, including post-traumatic stress disorder (PTSD)." The research summarized in subsequent parts of this chapter illustrates a number of the areas that the Administration for Native Americans cites and supports that entity's conclusion that veterans of varying ethnicities, including our native veterans, have faced and continue to face similar challenges. What follows considers those attempts undertaken to achieve a heightened understanding of individual differences among veterans with mental and behavioral health issues. The areas of success that may be emulated by those using these volumes as a reference and a guide for delivering the highest quality of healthcare for our veterans are among the work selected for citation. However, the areas that may reflect less than the highest standard to be attained are also addressed.

The Administration for Native Americans (2009) calls attention to the differing needs of each generation of veterans based on the nature of their war and the social climate of the time regarding military service. The presence or absence and severity of PTSD is the focal point for many of its comments referencing "institutionalized racism" and stereotypes as contributory to the way native soldiers were addressed or which duties were assigned to them in combat. Johnson (1994) had previously addressed the impact of institutional racism on American Indian combat veterans. These same beliefs and attitudes influence the nature and extent of other psychological and adjustment problems upon return home for any minority veteran. That these biases continue to operate is confirmed by Loo (2007) in her finding that the services provided to our veterans of varying ethnically, racially, and culturally diverse backgrounds may be determined by a *provider's* (emphasis added) beliefs or attitudes.

One of the most significant efforts by VA to consider the needs of our ethnically diverse veterans occurred as a result of congressional action in 1983, when the National Vietnam Veterans Readjustment Study (NVVRS) was mandated. Congressional members sought a national investigation of PTSD and other post–Vietnam War psychological problems among veterans who served in that era. These supporters in Congress wanted an accurate determination of the prevalence of various disorders so that the needs of the nation's veterans could be served. Among the findings reported from the original analysis of the data from this study was one indicating that the majority of Vietnam veterans "appeared to have successfully readjusted to postwar life," but that a "substantial minority...were suffering from a variety of psychological problems and...life-adjustment problems." Vietnam theater veterans experiencing PTSD were estimated to be 15.2 percent of men and 8.5 percent of women, with 26 percent of Vietnam theater veterans overall (830,000) having "symptoms and related functional impairment associated with PTSD." This study initially considered race and ethnicity as important risk factors for developing PTSD. African American and Hispanic Vietnam veterans tended to report more mental health and life adjustment problems than white veterans, with Hispanic male veterans having the highest prevalence rate of PTSD. Recognizing the significance of the differential prevalence findings for these two groups of minority veterans, the Congress, under the leadership of the late Senator Spark Matsunaga (Hawaii), passed Public Law 101-507 in 1990, to extend the National Vietnam Veterans Readjustment Study to other minority veterans. Through this legislation, Congress mandated a follow-up study to the initial study of Vietnam veterans, which became known as the Matsunaga Vietnam Veterans Project. The Matsunaga Project was divided into two studies: (1) the American Indian Vietnam Veterans Project, which surveyed American Indian in-country Vietnam veterans residing on or near two large tribal reservations; and (2) the Hawaii Vietnam Veterans Project, which surveyed Vietnam veterans of Native Hawaiian origin and of Japanese American background residing in Hawaii. The Matsunaga study found that one of every two Native Hawaiian, one in every three Japanese American, and two out of every three American Indian veterans suffered psychological problems at some point after their service in Vietnam as a consequence of their war traumas. The Native Hawaiian and American Indian veterans received combat service medals in recognition of their hazardous combat duty more often than those in other ethnic groups, which became significant as the amount of combat emerged as a factor in PTSD. The National Center for PTSD Web site summarizes the Matsunaga Project findings as follows:

The Matsunaga Study's key finding is that exposure to war zone stress and other military danger places veterans at risk for PTSD several decades after military service. Native Hawaiian and American Indian Vietnam in-country veterans had relatively high levels of exposure to war zone stress and high levels of PTSD. Caucasian and Japanese American veterans tended to have somewhat lower levels of exposure to war zone stress and later PTSD. The unique cultural traditions, society, and family experiences of each different ethnic group played an important role in the veteran's homecoming and readjustment after Vietnam, but they do not appear to either cause or prevent PTSD. (National Center for PTSD 2007b, 2)

In a recent study of Iraq veterans, Maguen and collegaues (2010) documented that beyond combat exposure, killing or being responsible for killing during their deployment results in a greater risk for PTSD, anger, alcohol abuse, and relationship problems. Although this study did not specifically address the effects on minority veterans versus nonminority veterans, given that current military forces are more diverse and that minority veterans from prior wars experienced war traumas differently (Sutker et al. 1995; Holm 1994), these findings only serve to raise the concern that attention must be given to this aspect of the war experience as a potential predictor of more serious adjustment problems upon return home.

It is critical that healthcare providers not only acknowledge, but act in concert with, the clinical implications that follow from the reference to "unique cultural traditions" by the authors of the Matsunaga Study. This reference reaffirms the conclusion of Penk and Allen (1991) as they considered the clinical assessment of minority combat Vietnam veteran, emphasizing the uniqueness of every veteran and his or her story (41). Healthcare providers must consider whether there are parallel differences for various ethnic groups who have served in the wars since Vietnam, including our veterans from the Gulf War, our current global war on terror (GWOT) veterans, and Operation Iraqi Freedom/Operation Enduring Freedom (OEF/OIF) veterans, as well as veterans from various other conflicts where they have been exposed to traumatic events (e.g. Somalia, Dominican Republic, Panama, Bosnia, etc.).

The increasing diversity of our military since the Vietnam War and the end of the draft must be considered as the medical and psychological problems that occur during or as a consequence of military service present expanding challenges for our healthcare providers and systems. The veterans of the 1991 Gulf War are already facing the health consequences of their time in the theater of operations, with certain symptoms and illnesses (e.g., fibromyalgia, chronic fatigue syndrome, irritable bowel syndrome, and amyotrophic lateral sclerosis) now included among the presumptive disabling conditions resulting from time spent in the war zone (*Gulf War Review* 2009). The Department of Veterans Affairs was given permission by Congress in 1994 to compensate veterans for chronically disabling undiagnosed medical and neurological illnesses. The veterans of the current Iraq and Afghanistan wars will be eligible for such compensation as well. In 2008 the Institute of Medicine issued a report on the health effects associated with the Gulf War. At that time the report cited no evidence of a "Gulf War syndrome," but indicated that Gulf War veterans were experiencing a higher likelihood of anxiety, depression, PTSD, and substance abuse problems. Of note was the additional finding that, "consistent with studies of personnel who served in other armed conflicts," these veterans were more likely to sustain "transportation-related (i.e., motor vehicle accident) injuries or deaths in the first few years upon return from the war" (*Gulf War Review* 2008, 6). Much of the information in the various issues of the *Gulf War Review* focuses on long-term health issues that may be associated with exposure to environmental agents, the presence of medical and neurological symptoms that had not been there prior to deployment, and the various undiagnosed illnesses. These issues certainly carry psychological sequelae that need to be addressed as well. If the prevalence of PTSD and other mental health disorders has been found to vary among those who served in previous wars depending on their racial and ethnic group, even if the research on the most recent veterans has not been completed or is not conclusive, the quality and appropriateness of care would dictate that providers must be attentive to the potential impact of individual differences along these lines. How primary care providers, medical specialists, and mental health staff in VA healthcare facilities can best address in a culturally appropriate manner the presenting physical symptoms and their psychological sequelae will have to be determined, even as a more current and solid knowledge base is developed to address ethnic and racial differences and disparities among recent veterans. What constitutes cultural competence in practice may have to be based to whatever degree is relevant on findings for veterans of prior wars. The Administration for Native Americans' previously noted reference to the "social climate" of military service and the nature of a war as critical factors still applies. The awareness that must exist about the unique factors that make the experience of our current veterans quite different in many facets must be heightened. The summary in the 2008 *Gulf War Review* makes no reference to any evaluation that the Institute on Medicine may have considered that included possible differences across ethnic, racial, or cultural groups. It is almost as noteworthy that the *Gulf War Review* did not even mention whether these differences were controlled by the research design or considered but found noncontributory (if this were the case).

Our medical and mental health providers continue to diagnose and treat veterans of all wars. Consequently, the findings from studies of veterans of prior wars are certainly pertinent to current clinical care. If a clear description of relevant findings for cultural or ethnic differences affecting the clinical presentation of symptoms does not exist for veterans of our current wars, a review of the available literature may at least provide a template to indicate which criteria could be considered with each veteran seeking services, until a pattern emerges. The National Vietnam Veterans Readjustment Study and the Matsunaga Project yield the mostly clearly delineated findings. The sampling of studies whose findings are summarized here is presented not specifically to focus on PTSD. Rather, it addresses the intent of this chapter to provide a better understanding of the differences that exist across ethnic and cultural groups, and to emphasize how essential it is to acknowledge the diversity among veterans, which can contribute to their health and well-being.

The returning Native Hawaiian veterans seen as part of the Matsunaga Study (National Center for PTSD 2007a) struggled with the symptoms of various psychological disorders and were described as having severe adjustment problems that disrupted their lives and their relationships with families and friends. The study noted that the perception was that no one (either family or counselors) seemed able to understand or cope with the issues these veterans brought home. Symptoms identified at the time included any or all of the following:

Depression (hopelessness, loss of all interests, or suicidal impulses)

Shame (feeling embarrassed, exposed, violated, or like a misfit)

Guilt (feeling others should have lived and they should have died, or feeling that they failed or made mistakes that had terrible consequences)

Isolation and emotional emptiness (being very remote and withdrawn)

Alienation (feeling that no one understands or that everyone makes too much fuss about unimportant things and too little fuss about big problems)

Inability to relax (restless, sleepless, silently tense or on edge)

Addiction (compulsive overuse of alcohol)

Similar findings were reported for the Japanese American Vietnam veterans (National Center for PTSD 2007b). The symptoms were indicative of what has since been identified as PTSD. The symptoms that were so puzzling to families and friends of the Japanese American veterans included the following:

Unwanted, distressing memories or a feeling of reliving traumatic Vietnam experiences (flashbacks)

Nightmares and difficulty falling or staying asleep restfully

Bodily stress and tension, especially when reminded of traumatic Vietnam experiences

Loss of interest in activities and difficulty concentrating on activities or projects

Detachment or withdrawal from emotional involvement in relationships

Difficulty feeling or expressing emotions other than irritability or frustration

Feeling that there is no future or that their lives will be cut short by an untimely death

Feeling jumpy, on edge, and easily startled

Feeling constantly unsafe and unable to let down their guard (hypervigilant)

American Indians were noted to have similar symptoms. They were described as isolated and withdrawn, emotionally and often physically (i.e., homeless) distant from family and community, divorced, verbally hostile, overusing or dependent on alcohol, and displaying the poorest physical health.

As mentioned previously, the original analysis of data from the National Vietnam Veterans Readjustment Study, which included only African American and Hispanic among the minority groupings, indicated that the "majority" of Vietnam veterans had a successful adjustment. However, a reanalysis of those data, along with an analysis of data from the Matsunaga Study, produced contrary findings. Schnurr and colleagues (2003) concluded that a large majority (four out of five) of the Vietnam veterans were considered to have ongoing symptoms of chronic PTSD, even though they were interviewed twenty to twenty-five years after the war. In addition, the Vietnam veterans showed depression, generalized anxiety disorder, and alcohol dependence and abuse. The original Readjustment Study data (Price 2007) concluded that race and ethnicity appeared to be important risk factors for developing PTSD, "as African-American and Hispanic Vietnam veterans tended to report more mental health and life adjustment problems." In addition, it was reported that Hispanic male veterans had the highest prevalence rate of PTSD. Ortega and Rosenheck (2000), reexamining the data from the National Vietnam Veterans Study, also documented the Hispanic, especially Puerto Rican, Vietnam veterans' higher risk for developing PTSD and for experiencing more severe symptoms of PTSD than non-Hispanic white veterans. Acculturation did not explain the difference, and the functional impairment did not mirror the symptom severity. Consequently, the authors concluded that the differences may be a result of cultural factors not measured in the original study, and that the higher rates of PTSD among Hispanic veterans may be "more a reflection of culturally based expressive style than . . . disabling psychopathology" (619). Later studies based on the initial Readjustment Study refined the influence of race and ethnicity (Schnurr, Lunney & Sengupta 2004). These newer findings indicated that factors in addition to race and ethnicity contributed to the initial *development* of PTSD and the *maintenance* of symptoms over the longer term. In the Schnurr, Lunney, and Sengupta (2004) study, premilitary factors continued to focus on ethnicity, both as *risk factors* for developing PTSD (among veterans of Hispanic ethnicity) and as *protective factors* against both the development and maintenance of PTSD (for veterans of Japanese American and Native Hawaiian ethnicity). Military (war zone) factors associated with the risk for *developing* PTSD continued to include things such as the amount of war zone exposure and any serious injury in Vietnam. As would be logical to expect, there were no *protective* factors noted during the individual's military or war zone time. Postmilitary factors included recent stressful life events and depression for the *risk factors*, while social support at homecoming and current social support contributed to the *protective factors*. Media accounts of the effects of the Iraq and Afghanistan wars note the multiple deployments, high incidence of suicides in the war zone and at home, and documented incidence of PTSD and traumatic brain injury (TBI) among our OIF/OEF military personnel and the veterans who have returned from military service after these wars. Based on this knowledge and what we know from prior wars, more information sharing and proactive communication with our minority communities about what we know about those returning from a war zone is essential if the lack of understanding by family and counselors evident for the Vietnam veterans is to be eliminated.

This improved communication also needs to be emphasized as the makeup of our armed forces shows an increasing number of minority members, who, in turn, will increase the diversity of our veteran population seeking healthcare through VA and in our communities as they leave military service. Sutker and colleagues (1995) commented on the "more diverse ethnic and gender mix" of troops deployed for Desert Storm. They confirmed that greater levels of distress (negative mood state, somatic complaints, PTSD symptoms) were experienced by ethnic minority troops upon return from duty in that war zone. Sohn and Harada (2008) reported on data from the 2001 Veteran Identity Program Survey, examining the relationship between racism/discrimination and physical and mental health status for Asian/Pacific Islander, African American, and Hispanic veterans. Racial discrimination during military service was significantly associated with poorer physical health. In contrast, satisfaction with the health provider's sensitivity to racial/ethnic background was significantly related to better mental health.

Expecting that heightening awareness for providers of healthcare through the mental health system alone will be sufficient is shortsighted. The literature consistently shows that not only is actual physical health affected by the stress of war, but there is often a preference by veterans to seek medical services and to interpret psychological problems according to physical symptoms rather than labeling them as emotional. The Hawaiian and Japanese American Vietnam veterans certainly fit this pattern and were described as having a preference for medical clinics rather than psychiatric services. The Matsunaga Study documented how much more this was the case for the American Indian veterans, who were described as having an extremely high incidence of physical concerns and as reporting the poorest physical health and the highest level of medical care use of any of the veterans in the National Vietnam Veterans Readjustment Study or in the Matsunaga Project. Although the symptoms of PTSD (e.g., sleep disturbance, irritability, tension) may directly affect physical health, it was noted that chronic alcohol overuse, often associated with smoking and other poor lifestyle choices affecting health, also could be a contributing factor. More than 70 percent of the American Indian veterans reported current serious problems with alcohol overuse or dependence, which was over twice as many as any other group in the studies. In addition, as with the Hawaiian and Japanese American veterans, cultural determinants that focus on physical or medical complaints rather than psychological distress were acknowledged. For each of the ethnic groups, veterans presenting at medical clinics as the *preferred* treatment option were likely to be assessed and/or diagnosed by their healthcare provider with high blood pressure, stomach or bowel conditions, or chronic pain conditions, even when the presenting symptoms of restlessness, tension, irritability, or poor sleep were as likely to be a sign of a primary psychological disorder. For Hispanic veterans, especially the "less acculturated" and the Puerto Rican subgroup, "somatization is a socially common way of expressing psychological distress" (Ortega & Rosenheck 2000, 618). Thus, education and training for primary care providers and general medical staff members aimed at understanding that there are a variety of ways that mental or behavioral disorders may differ in their presentation as a function of ethnic, racial, or cultural factors is a basic first step in achieving cultural competence. Arriving at an appropriate diagnosis and subsequently selecting the best treatment will require more complex decision making. Culturally competent healthcare may require the practitioner to consider traditional healing practices, such as those more evident for American Indian, Native Hawaiian, and certain Hispanic groups, but which exist for other minority groups as well.

The Department of Veterans Affairs has begun to address cultural competence through continuing education programs. Noted in the 2009 Annual

Report of the Advisory Committee on Minority Veterans was the following statement:

> To address disparities in care that might result from cultural issues, advisory bodies have recommended that health care organizations provide continuing education on culturally and linguistically appropriate service delivery for health care providers, clinical care managers and front line clerical staff with significant responsibilities for patient interactions. Within VHA, a task force has worked to develop cultural competency training for health care providers. The stated goals for the training are: to enhance self awareness of attitudes toward people of different racial and ethnic groups; improve care by increasing knowledge about cultural beliefs and practices, attitude toward health care, and the burden of various diseases in different populations served; and improve skills such as communication. Training materials are available to health care staff across VHA. This training was developed to increase awareness of findings that both providers of health care and consumers can bring perceptions, traditions and patterns of communication based on cultural, racial and ethnic identity to the clinician-patient interactions. (8–9)

The National Center for PTSD has a series of video courses addressing cross-cultural issues in the assessment and treatment of PTSD in specific ethnic groups. The transcripts for these courses are available on the Center's Web site (http://www.ptsd.va.gov/professional/ptsd101/course-modules/course-modules.asp).

Although VA may be concerned about how to encourage veterans to seek care from the clinic or provider that has been designated to address mental and behavioral health issues, for many among the minority veteran population access to *any* care—mental, behavioral or physical—may be the larger issue. The Administration for Native Americans (2009) noted the difficulty that native veterans may have in accessing care upon their return home, with many living in areas distant from established VA healthcare facilities. They note the importance of tribes, agencies, and communities stepping in to address the problem. Tribal veterans' affairs departments have been established not only to address the "unique needs of native veterans, but also [to] recognize the ways that cultural practices can be applied in healing veterans. Language, culture, and ceremony are being revived and acknowledged as integral factors in the healing process" (Administration for Native Americans 2009). Actions by VA have included the establishment through the Veterans Benefits Administration of a network of tribal veterans' representatives, who are designated by tribal officials and trained by the Veterans Benefits Administration to serve as points of contact for tribal veterans, to serve as a resource for information and referral on benefits and services, and to provide assistance in submitting claims. To follow a broader collaborative agenda related to healthcare, in 2003 the Indian Health Service and VA entered into a memorandum of understanding (discussed further later in this chapter). This memorandum was renewed on October 1, 2010, with the intended purpose "to establish coordination, collaboration, and resource-sharing . . . to improve the health status of American Indian and Alaska Native Veterans . . . to foster an environment that brings together the strengths and expertise of each organization to actively improve the care and services provided." An additional effort by VHA to address minority veterans issues has been the appointment of a designated minority veterans program coordinator (MVPC) at each medical center. The annual report of the Advisory Committee on Minority Veterans (2009) indicates that it is the responsibility of this coordinator to develop a local plan for outreach activities to minority veterans. The duties are further described to include submitting a quarterly report for tracking and trending of outreach activity data and ethnicity data for the veterans served.

The Native Hawaiian Healthcare Improvement Act of 1988 created the oversight health board known as Papa Ola Lokahi, whose mission is stated on its Web site as "to improve the health status and well being of Native Hawaiians and others by advocating for, initiating and maintaining culturally appropriate strategic actions aimed at improving the physical, mental and spiritual health of Native Hawaiians and their 'ohana [families] and empowering them to determine their own destinies" (Papa Ola Lokahi 2011). By statute, Papa Ola Lokahi is to be the vehicle through which funds are acquired to address the healthcare needs of Native Hawaiians, with health being defined to include behavioral as well as biomedical. With funds provided by a community organization augmenting the resources of Papa Ola Lokahi itself, a separate administrative entity was established to address the needs of veterans. The mission of the Native Hawaiian Veterans Project is to assist the Native Hawaiian veteran (but efforts are not limited to veterans of Native Hawaiian ancestry) to access the relevant benefits and services of VA. In addition to the full-time director, the Papa Ola Lokahi Veterans Project has incorporated the traditional role of the elders very specifically for veterans through what is referred to as the "Uncles and Aunties Veterans Support Project"—a network of veterans and the spouses, partners, and family members of veterans on each of the main Hawaiian islands who can be available to a veteran in need, sharing their guidance and wisdom, bringing assistance and support to the veteran within his or her own cultural framework and healing practices, and connecting that veteran to the system of benefits and healthcare of VA. Since Hawaiian veterans also live on the mainland, "Uncles" and "Aunties" have been recruited in other states, and they maintain communication by e-mail or telephone with the director of the project in Hawaii.

One of the routine activities of the Advisory Committee on Minority Veterans is to conduct annual visits to medical centers or Veterans Integrated Service Network (VISN) administrative offices, and to meet with veterans in "town hall" meetings in various regions of the country. Following these annual events, the Committee prepares an annual report for submission to the Secretary of the Department of Veterans Affairs. In reviewing the annual reports for 2005 through 2009, specific areas of progress or need for further development to improve healthcare and benefits services to minority veterans are identified. Repeated themes are evident in these reports. In referencing annual reports prior to 2005, the minutes of the Committee state that "the cultural differences often prevalent between different minority groups are a recurring motif the Committee observes in its travels and discussions with minority veterans. This report addresses concerns specific to the Caribbean veterans but these concerns have been observed in other rural areas visited by the Committee as well" (Advisory Committee on Minority Veterans 2005).

The annual report in 2008 noted that since 2003, VA and the Indian Health Service have worked together under a formal agreement that "encourages cooperation and resource sharing" between the two agencies—the memorandum of understanding previously described. The Committee's report also states that the two agencies have an expressed intention to improve access and healthcare outcomes for (rural) American Indian and Alaskan Native (AIAN) veterans. Kramer and colleagues (2009c) found that American Indians and Alaskan Natives eligible to access services through both VA and the Indian Health Service under the formal agreement were similar to "all other VHA (Veterans Health Administration) users ... [having] the same three most frequent diagnoses associated with healthcare encounters: posttraumatic stress disorder, hypertension, and diabetes." The dual users were more likely to receive behavioral healthcare through VA and primary (medical) care through Indian Health Service. Twenty-five percent accessed care at facilities of both agencies, while most used either VA (28 percent) or the Indian Health Service (46 percent) facility. Though the formal agreement for collaboration has been in place for some time, a recent study (Kramer et al. 2009b) found that the collaboration in delivering healthcare was perceived by both providers and patients using the dual system as problematic, resulting in delays in care, as well as treatment conflicts and fragmentation of services. Of note was the statement that "all stakeholders (patients and providers) agreed that neither organization was fully culturally competent. IHS/tribes lacked competence about veterans' health needs and VHA lacked competence about AIAN patients' health beliefs and behaviors." On a more positive note, Kramer and colleagues (2009a) focused on the use of the two healthcare systems by American Indian/Alaska Native

(AIAN) women veterans and nonveterans, concluding that "VHA and IHS have developed specialized and complementary expertise, which might be aligned to serve the needs of female AIAN veterans."

The 2008 annual report of the Advisory Committee on Minority Veterans referenced the work of the Office of Rural Health within VHA in an effort to more adequately address the needs of rural veterans, including American Indians and Alaska Natives. In general, residents of rural areas have less access to healthcare services, creating disparities in health status in comparison to metropolitan residents. It should be noted that Secretary of Veterans Affairs Eric K. Shinseki, in referring to the 2010 memorandum of understanding with the Indian Health Service, stated that the partnership with the Indian Health Service "expands VA's capability to serve those Veterans within their communities and provides increased access for Veterans in extremely rural areas" (Office of Rural Health 2011, 1).

West and Weeks (2006) documented that issues for veterans in rural areas were an even more significant problem than for the general population. Their findings indicated that rural veterans younger than age sixty-five reported the poorest physical and mental health, with reduced access to care being a major variable. If this pattern is replicated, given the demographics of our newest generation of veterans, the issues for rural and rural minority veterans will present significant challenges for healthcare delivery systems, and in particular for VA, for many years to come.

Access to care becomes even more challenging when one is homeless. It has been reported that veterans experience homelessness at a greater rate than nonveterans in the United States (National Alliance to End Homelessness 2009). In addition, among homeless veterans a disproportionate number are minority veterans. A recent study by the Homelessness Research Institute found that minority veterans, particularly African Americans, constitute a larger share (45 percent) of the homeless veteran population (Moriarty 2009). This finding is consistent with that presented by Rossi (1989) almost twenty years before, when blacks were found to have an incidence of homelessness four times their representation in the general population, and they were again described as accounting for almost half of the homeless population in the United States. Rosenheck and colleagues (1997) looked at racial differences among black and white homeless chronically mentally ill veterans in their use of psychiatric services and the outcomes. When the veterans participated in residential treatment, no differences in improvement for psychiatric or alcohol problems existed for the African American versus white veterans. Of particular note is the observation by the researchers that "social disadvantage and racial discrimination may play an important role in the genesis of Black homelessness, while disability and illness are of greater importance among Whites" (637). Findings by VA's own Advisory Committee on Minority Veterans (2006) described the "unusually high homeless rate" among veterans during their visit to Los Angeles in 2006. The Committee commented in their annual report that not only did Los Angeles have the largest homeless population of the nation at that time, but 23 percent of those who were homeless were veterans. At that point, the members of the Advisory Committee already had identified the lack of data available specifically on veterans from minority groups, such as Native Americans, and asked that VA "remedy the lack of ethnic information immediately."

Recognizing that there are disparities in health and healthcare related to race and ethnic diversity, but more specifically that there are *provider* variables associated with these disparities, what has been the response to address this side of the healthcare equation? Marsella, Friedman and Spain (1992) asserted that many of the studies that purported to be ethnocultural studies conducted up until that time "used Western criteria and assessment instruments to diagnose the presence of PTSD. These criteria are often ethnocentric and biased." They called for cross-cultural research that considers "indigenous expressions of disorder, idioms of distress, and ethnocultural sensitivities in assessment." They concluded that though the response to a traumatic event may have some shared universal features, ethnocultural factors may play a significant role in who is more vulnerable to developing PTSD, how it is expressed, and the "treatment responsivity" of PTSD. The emphasis of their article was on the need for providers and researchers to attend to individual and cultural differences when assigning a diagnosis or making an assessment.

Loo (2007) called for clinicians working with veterans to recognize their professional responsibility to assess not only for combat exposure when evaluating a veteran for PTSD, but also "what the experience of being an ethnic minority was like for that particular veteran," referring in particular to what is known about the effect of "negative race-related events" on PTSD. Neglecting to consider race-related stressors in Asian American/Pacific Islander veterans has resulted in "missing as much as 20% of the veteran's PTSD symptoms." As did Marsella, Friedman, and Spain (1992), Loo also calls for practitioners to use "ethnically relevant measures to screen for PTSD … [to advance] the cultural-based competence level of practitioners who work with ethnic minorities."

The Department of Veterans Affairs has made some efforts to focus on culturally appropriate interventions and on education and training for providers. Although targeted materials designed to assist providers in achieving cultural competence in the delivery of services are limited, those that have been developed provide excellent resources for VA medical and benefits staff. Some of the materials are available to non-VA employees and may even have a version focused on the veteran, the family, or other non-healthcare professional. These resources range from Web-based instructional materials, to video projects with accompanying printed material, to in vivo experiences shared with veterans and their families. An example of an instructional project with both video and Web-based printed materials is *Wounded Spirits, Ailing Hearts: PTSD and the Legacy of War among American Indian & Alaska Native Veterans.* This resource, a joint project of the National Center for PTSD, the National Center for American Indian and Alaska Native Mental Health Research in the Department of Psychiatry at the University of Colorado, Denver, and the VA Employee Education System (Department of Veterans Affairs 2008a, 2008b), is designed to help medical and mental health practitioners, benefits counselors, and other staff "recognize the cultural impact on the veteran and enable them to interact with the veteran in a manner that demonstrates respect for the cultural and social values, as well as the spiritual and emotional needs of those suffering from PTSD." There are four videos, two of which are designed for primary care providers and mental health staff. The videos provide information about the native veterans' military experiences that contribute to PTSD, issues in readjustment to civilian life (including their description of problems accessing services with VA and Indian Health resources), and the clinical presentation of PTSD and its effects on native veterans and their family members.

This educational package has been available since 2000. However, recommendations for various culturally competent approaches to diagnosis and treatment can be found in previous decades. For example, the final report of the Navajo Veterans Health Needs Project (Montague 1994), a study to secure pilot data on the health needs and service utilization patterns of Navajo veterans, was issued at the conclusion of the 1992–1993 study. Participants in the study included Navajo veterans of World War II, the Korean and Vietnam Wars, Desert Storm, and peacetime. Among the goals of that project was a focus on providing information on the use of traditional healing, as well as focusing on other healthcare services, barriers to adequate healthcare, and veteran satisfaction with available resources. The diagnoses that were among the most frequently reported included mental and behavioral health problems (e.g., PTSD, depression, alcohol and other substance abuse, other mental health problems). Although almost 40 percent of the veterans surveyed sought traditional medicine and traditional healing practices for their physical concerns, 65 percent reported using a traditional healer or ceremony for "personal problems." In addition, though not quantified, the "frequent use" of protective ceremonies for the warrior prior to serving in the military was noted. Among the significant findings listed in the discussion section was that the diagnosis of mental health problems (i.e., PTSD, depression, alcohol abuse) was approximately as frequent as disgnosis of physical disorders. Also significant was the statement that "[t]raditional medicine, healing, and ceremonies play a central role in the maintenance of physical and emotional health and well-being in the majority of the Navajo veterans in this study." In addressing the implications of the findings, emphasis was placed on the need to consider "culturally adapted programs in VAMCs located outside the reservation," and the importance of "making the healing power of these traditional approaches to health more accessible to all veterans."

A unique example of efforts to "teach or sensitize VA and other practitioners who work with Indian veterans on the American Indian Traditional Methodology of Healing" is Camp Chaparral (Yakima Nation 2010). This program was begun in 1992 with the intent of using traditional healing methods to help Indian veterans suffering from PTSD, while at the same time allowing VA healthcare workers to learn about the effectiveness of traditional American Indian healing approaches. The VA staff attending Camp Chaparral are offered the opportunity to interact with Native American veterans, spiritual leaders, traditional healers, and tribal elders and family members from nine different tribes. The experience is hands-on (participatory), and among the stated goals are for VA healthcare workers to gain an improved understanding of aspects of American Indian culture, traditions, and habits and how these affect clinical outcomes, but also to demonstrate increased personal sensitivity to American Indian veterans and communicate with them about their healthcare needs. While Camp Chaparral has a long history of success in meeting its stated mission, there are at least two other Native American Indian programs through which VA staff can achieve a greater awareness of Native American culture and the unique aspects that affect healthcare for American Indians provided through the VA healthcare system. The Camp Chaparral Web site (2006) identifies the other sites as being within the Southern Arizona VA Health Care System and in the Black Hills VA area. The ongoing and increasing need for similar programs can be seen in the report of the 2007 visit by the Advisory Committee to Anchorage. The meeting included comments by the vice president for primary care of the Southcentral Foundation, who emphasized that care must be based on native values ("find roots with the Elders, their experiences and their wisdom"). The recommendation was that not only should there be "full utilization of the tribal doctor in the treatment process," but a "family warrior wellness healing approach to depression and violence" was even more important. The Anchorage Vet

Center had an identified American Indian readjustment counselor, and among the duties of that person was conducting outreach, including traveling with the National Guard during military exercises (Advisory Committee on Minority Veterans 2007).

As previously explained, VA now has designated minority veterans' program coordinators for veterans accessing services. However, a repeated concern of the Advisory Committee has been that these are often not "positions" but rather assigned duties. In the July 2008 annual report the Advisory Committee concluded that "[a]dequate outreach to minority veterans is a key cornerstone of a successful program. In that context . . . the only way of achieving success is . . . to designate the MVPCs as full time positions at the VAMC, VARO, and MSN levels." The Advisory Committee on Minority Veterans 2009 annual report continued to emphasize the need for full-time coordinators in areas with a high concentration of minority veterans. That report also concluded that "diversity and inclusion is not a secondary issue, but is critical to supporting VA's mission and purpose."

This has been a selected review of the issues, documents, and available literature and research pertaining to the uniqueness of our diverse veteran population and their healthcare. Although there is sufficient information documenting the impact of racial and ethnic differences on health and health disparities, healthcare providers and systems appear to be in their infancy in meeting criteria for cultural competency (American Psychological Association 2003).

References

Administration for Native Americans (ANA) (2009). Native American veterans: Storytelling for healing—issues facing native veterans today. http://www.acf.hhs.gov/programs/ana/veterans/issues.html (accessed July 17, 2010).

Advisory Committee on Minority Veterans. (2005). Annual report. Washington, DC: Department of Veterans Affairs. http://www.va.gov/CENTERFOR MINORITYVETERANS/docs/cmvdata/11th_acmv_annual_report_2005.pdf (accessed March 13, 2010).

Advisory Committee on Minority Veterans. (2006). Annual report. Washington, DC: Department of Veterans Affairs. http://www.va.gov/CENTERFORMINORITY VETERANS/docs/cmvdata/12th_acmv_annual_report_2006.pdf (accessed March 13, 2010).

Advisory Committee on Minority Veterans. (2007). Annual report. Washington, DC: Department of Veterans Affairs. http://www.va.gov/CENTERFOR MINORITYVETERANS/docs/cmvdata/2007finalacmvannualreport.pdf (accessed March 13, 2010)

Advisory Committee on Minority Veterans. (2008). Annual report. Washington, DC: Department of Veterans Affairs. http://www.va.gov/CENTERFOR MINORITYVETERANS/docs/cmvdata/2008finalacmvannualreport.pdf (accessed March 13, 2010).

Advisory Committee on Minority Veterans. (2009). Annual report. Washington, DC: Department of Veterans Affairs. http://www.va.gov/CENTERFOR MINORITYVETERANS/docs/cmvdata/2009finalacmvannualreport.pdf (accessed March 13, 2010).

Agency for Healthcare Research and Quality. (2006). *National healthcare disparities report*. Rockville, MD: US Department of Health and Human Services.

Allen, I. M. (1986). Posttraumatic stress disorder among black Vietnam veterans. *Hospital and Community Psychiatry* 37: 55–61.

American Psychological Association. (2003). Guidelines on multicultural education, training, research, practice, and organizational change for psychologists. *American Psychologist* 58: 377–402.

American Psychological Association. (2005). *Presidential Task Force on Evidence-Based Practice (final report)*. Washington, DC: Author.

Camp Chaparral. (2006). http://www.waterplanet.ws/cc/Site/Home.html (accessed July 17, 2010).

Center for Minority Veterans. (2010). Facts about the Center for Minority Veterans. Washington, DC: Department of Veterans Affairs. http://www.va.gov/CENTER FORMINORITYVETERANS/Fact_Sheet.asp (accessed March 13, 2010).

Department of Veterans Affairs (2008a). Wounded spirits, ailing hearts—for health care providers (DVD). http://ncptsd.va.gov/ncmain/ncdocs/videos/emv_wsah_ hcp.html (accessed July 17, 2010).

Department of Veterans Affairs (2008b). Wounded spirits, ailing hearts—for mental health care providers (DVD). http://ncptsd.va.gov/ncmain/ncdocs/videos/ emv_wsah_mhcp.html (accessed July 17, 2010).

Department of Veterans Affairs. (2009). Diversity and inclusion strategic plan for 2009–2013. Washington, DC. http://www.diversity.hr.va.gov/docs/strat.pdf (accessed June 20, 2010).

Escobar, J. I., Randolph, E. T., Puente, G., Spiwak, F., Asamen, J. K., Hill, M. & Hough, R. L. (1983). Post-traumatic stress disorder in Hispanic Vietnam veterans: Clinical phenomenology and sociocultural characteristics. *Journal of Nervous and Mental Disease* 171: 585–596.

Gulf War review newsletter. (2008). Washington, DC: Department of Veterans Affairs.

Gulf War review newsletter. (2009). Washington, DC: Department of Veterans Affairs.

Holiday, L. F., Bell, G., Klein, R. E., Wells, M. R. (2006). American Indian and Alaska Native veterans: Lasting contributions (final report). Washington, DC: Department of Veterans Affairs, Office of Policy. http://www1.va.gov/VET-DATA/docs/SpecialReports/AIANpaper9-12-06final.doc.

Holm, T. (1994). The national survey of Indian Vietnam veterans. *Journal of the National Center for American Indian and Alaska Native Mental Health Research* 6: 18–28.

Institute of Medicine. (2001). *Crossing the quality chasm: A new health system for the 21st century.* Washington, DC: National Academy Press.

Johnson, D. (1994). Stress, depression, substance abuse, and racism. *Journal of the National Center for American Indian and Alaska Native Mental Health Research* 6: 29–32.

Kramer, B. J., Jouldjian, S., Washington, D. L., Harker, J. O., Saliba, D. & Yano, E. M. (2009a). Health care for American Indian and Alaska Native women: The roles of the Veterans Health Administration and the Indian Health Service. *Women's Health Issues* 19: 135–143.

Kramer, B. J., Vivrette, R. L., Satter, D. E., Jouldjian, S. & McDonald, L. R. (2009b). Dual use of Veterans Health Administration and Indian Health Service: Healthcare provider and patient perspectives. *Journal of General Internal Medicine* 24: 758–764.

Kramer, B. J., Wang, M., Jouldjian, S., Lee, M. L., Finke, B., & Saliba, D. (2009c). Veterans Health Administration and Indian Health Service: Healthcare utilization by Indian Health Service enrollees. *Medical Care* 47: 670–676.

Loo, C. (1994). Race-related PTSD: The Asian American Vietnam veteran. *Journal of Traumatic Stress* 7: 637–656.

Loo, C. M. (2007). PTSD among ethnic minority veterans. http://www.ptsd.va.gov/professional/pages/ptsd-minority-vets.asp (accessed July 17, 2010).

Maguen, S., Lucenko, B. A., Reger, M. A., Gahm, G. A., Litz, B. T., Seal, K., Knight, S. & Marmar, C. R. (2010). The impact of reported direct and indirect killing on mental health symptoms of Iraq War veterans. *Journal of Traumatic Stress* 23: 86–90.

Marsella, A. J., Friedman, M. J. & Spain, E. H. (1992). A selective review of the literature on ethnocultural aspects of PTSD. *PTSD Research Quarterly* 3, no. 2: 1–2.

Montague, R. B. (1994). *Navajo Veterans Health Needs Project (final report).* Denver, CO: University of Colorado Health Sciences Center.

Moriarty, S. (2009). Half of homeless U.S. veterans are black. http://homelessness.change.org/blog/view/nearly_half of homeless us veterans are black (accessed July 18, 2010).

National Alliance to End Homelessness. (2009). Vital mission: Ending homelessness among veterans. http://www.endhomelessness.org/content/article/detail/2572 (accessed July 18, 2010).

National Center for PTSD. (2007a). Psychological trauma for American Indians who served in Vietnam. http://www.ptsd.va.gov/professional/pages/psych-trauma-native-american.asp (accessed June 20, 2010).

National Center for PTSD. (2007b). Psychological trauma for native Hawaiians and Americans of Japanese ancestry who served in Vietnam. http://www.ptsd.va.gov/professional/pages/psych-trauma-hawaiian-japanese.asp (accessed June 20, 2010).

Native Hawaiian Healthcare Improvement Act of 1988. Pub. L. No. 100-579.

Office of Rural Health. (2011). *The Rural Connection* 1, no. 1. http://www.rural health.va.gov (accessed January 22, 2011).

Ortega, A. N. & Rosenheck, R. (2000). Posttraumatic stress disorder among Hispanic Vietnam veterans. *American Journal of Psychiatry* 157: 615–619.

Papa Ola Lokahi (POL). (2011). Strategic plan 2007–2011. www.papaolaloka.org (accessed January 5, 2011).

Penk, W. E. & Allen, I. M. (1991). Clinical assessment of post-traumatic stress disorder (PTSD) among American minorities who served in Vietnam. *Journal of Traumatic Stress* 4: 41–66.

Price, J. L. (2007). Findings from the National Vietnam Veterans' Readjustment Study. http://www.ptsd.va.gov/professional/pages/vietnam-vets-study.asp (accessed June 20, 2010).

Rosenheck, R. A, Leda, C., Frisman, L. K. & Gallup, P. (1997). Homeless mentally ill veterans: race, service use, and treatment outcomes. *American Journal of Orthopsychiatry* 67: 632–638.

Rossi, P. H. (1989). *Down and Out in America: The Origins of Homelessness.* Chicago: University of Chicago Press.

Ruef, A. M., Litz, B. T. & Schlenger, W. E. (2000). Hispanic ethnicity and risk for combat-related posttraumatic stress disorder. *Cultural Diversity and Ethnic Minority Psychology* 6, no. 3: 235–251.

Saha, S., Freeman, M., Toure, J., Tippens, K. M. & Weeks, C. (2007). Racial and ethnic disparities in the VA healthcare system: A systematic review. Washington, DC: Department of Veterans Affairs.

Schnurr, P. P., Lunney, C. A. & Sengupta, A. (2004). Risk factors for the development versus maintenance of posttraumatic stress disorder. *Journal of Traumatic Stress* 17: 85–95.

Schnurr, P. P., Lunney, C. A., Sengupta, A. & Waelde, L. C. (2003). A descriptive analysis of PTSD chronicity in Vietnam veterans. *Journal of Traumatic Stress* 16: 545–553.

Sohn, L. & Harada, N. D. (2008). Effects of racial/ethnic discrimination on the health status of minority veterans. *Military Medicine* 173: 331–338.

Sutker, P. B., Davis, J. M., Uddo, M. & Ditta, S. R. (1995). Assessment of psychological distress in Persian Gulf troops: Ethnicity and gender comparisons. *Journal of Personality Assessment* 64: 415–427.

Tanaka, Chester. (1982). Go for broke: Legacy in Americanism. Richard, CA: Go for Broke, Inc.

West, A. & Weeks, W. B. (2006). Physical and mental health and access to care among nonmetropolitan Veterans Health Administration patients younger than 65 years. *Journal of Rural Health* 22: 9–16.

Yakima Nation. (2010). A history of Camp Chaparral. http://www.waterplanet.ws/cc/Site/History.html (accessed July 17, 2010).

Part II

Rehabilitation Care and Treatment for Veterans

Chapter 11

Trauma-focused Psychosocial Rehabilitation

Walter Erich Penk, Dolores K. Little, and Nathan D. Ainspan

Introduction

Psychosocial rehabilitation may seem new to many mental health practitioners in the Veterans Health Administration (VHA). Since the start of Operation Enduring Freedom in Afghanistan (OEF) in 2002 and Operation Iraqi Freedom (OIF) in 2003, many mental health practitioners are delivering psychosocial rehabilitation for the first time. Psychosocial rehabilitation involves clinicians providing family psychoeducation, supported employment, supported education, and supported housing; some serving as case managers; and others working with peer counselors. *VHA Handbook 1160 for Uniform Mental Health Services in VA Medical Centers and Clinics* (U.S. Department of Veterans Affairs 2009) now mandates psychosocial rehabilitation, expanding such services from inpatient units to outpatient programs in primary care settings, outpatient clinics, community-based outpatient clinics (CBOCs), vet centers, home-based care programs, peer counseling services, and partnerships with agencies and providers in communities.

A number of such policies are transforming VHA mental health services to meet the goals for recovery and resiliency that are basic in psychosocial rehabilitation, summarized as follows:

First, services and treatments must be consumer and family centered, geared to give consumers real and meaningful choices about treatment options and providers—not oriented to the requirements of bureaucracies.

Second, care must focus on increasing consumers' ability to successfully cope with life's challenges, on facilitating recovery, and on building resilience, not just on managing symptoms. (President's New Freedom Commission on Mental Health 2003, 7)

Criteria for determining efficacy and effectiveness of VHA treatments increasingly are based on principles of psychosocial rehabilitation, thus changing the VHA focus beyond reducing symptoms to creating "improvements... to live, work, learn, and participate in...communities" (President's New Freedom Commission on Mental Health 2003, 1). VHA services must improve functioning as well as reduce symptoms.

Examining how VHA was structured in the past reveals (somewhat surprisingly) that psychosocial rehabilitation has always been present. Throughout its eighty-year history, VHA has provided psychosocial rehabilitation as part of its treatment to facilitate veterans with medical and mental disorders and help them recover their capacities to live independent, productive lives in the community (e.g., Baker & Pickren 2007). These psychosocial rehabilitation mandates began in 1930 when President Herbert Hoover forever transformed delivery of services for veterans by forming a new centralized, federal agency, the Veterans Health Administration. President Hoover signed legislation that consolidated three agencies—the Veterans Bureau, the Bureau of Pensions, and the National Home for Disabled Volunteer Soldiers—into one new federal agency for veterans, now called the Department of Veterans Affairs (VA), which includes VHA.

Structuring VHA as a federal agency was done in response to both the negative consequences of the Great Depression in the 1930s and the massive buildup of the U.S. military to fight World War II in the 1940s. The first GI Bill, passed in 1944, brought education and employment services into VA medical centers. The primary author of the first GI Bill was Edith Nourse Rogers (Republican from the 5th District in the Commonwealth of Massachusetts, serving in the House of Representatives from 1927 to 1960), who crafted the bill to fund education and employment in VHA medical centers as key interventions guiding recovery of World War II military combatants returning home from war.

The GI Bill was grounded in the "Second Bill of Rights," which President Franklin D. Roosevelt presented in his Fourth Inaugural Address in 1945. President Roosevelt proposed that the federal government, including VHA, champion the following rights for all citizens, including veterans returning home from war: the right to useful and remunerative jobs in industries, shops, farms, and mines of the nation; the right to earn enough to provide food, clothing, and recreation; the right of every farmer to raise and sell products at a return that will earn the family a decent living; the right of businesses to trade in freedom from unfair competition and domination by monopolies; the right of every family to a decent home; the right of adequate protection from the economic fears of old age, sickness, accident, and unemployment; and the right to a good education.

Medical centers in VHA were structured not only to deliver medical services to assuage symptoms, but simultaneously to offer psychosocial rehabilitation to achieve these rights for effective functioning. Psychosocial rehabilitation has always been partnered with medical care in VHA. It remains central for veterans in recovery from stresses and trauma experienced while serving in the military, particularly in current times, when our nation is besieged by wars abroad and by foreclosures and unemployment at home.

The history of VHA psychosocial rehabilitation is documented in *Psychology and the Department of Veterans Affairs* (Baker & Pickren 2007) and *Stories from VA Psychology* (Baker 2007). The second book contains chapters based on autobiographical reminiscences from psychologists who designed programs to facilitate recovery and to foster resiliency among veterans returning home from war. In it, Robert Waldrop describes his work, starting in 1952, to bring vocational counseling directly into VHA medical centers, demonstrating how psychosocial rehabilitation was integrated with medical care. His story starts with an invitation from the deputy chief medical director in the VHA Central Office, Roy A. Wolford, MD, to survey how employment was provided outside VA hospitals to World War II combat veterans being treated inside VHA hospitals (Waldrop 2007). Waldrop found that vocational rehabilitation was insufficient not only because such services were "disconnected" from VA medical services, but also because providers varied in qualifications and functioned without clear organizational structures in performing duties outside VA. Dr. Wolford answered Dr. Waldrop's critique by appointing him Chief of Vocational Counseling Service to serve in the VHA Central Office, with the mission to develop a department within VHA medical centers in which PhD psychologists with expertise in counseling were to work collaboratively with PhDs in clinical psychology, as well as with other medical and mental health specialists. From 1952 to 1957 Dr. Waldrop developed vocational counseling services in 110 VHA hospitals and 10 domiciliaries across the nation. Dr. Waldrop had the further good fortune to arrive in VHA at a time when the legendary Harold Hildreth, PhD, was building up the clinical psychology programs. The two became close friends and developed strong programs in both clinical and counseling psychology throughout the VHA system inside the medical centers, further connecting psychosocial rehabilitation to psychological as well as medical clinical treatments.

Concurrently, other developments took place to change the structure of how VHA mental healthcare and rehabilitation were provided. Slowly, over time, VHA's reliance on inpatient units subsided, giving way to more outpatient programs and community-based services. With the growth of outpatient and community-based services, psychosocial rehabilitation also grew, as illustrated by the example of psychosocial rehabilitation modules, *VHA/DoD Clinical Practice Guidelines* (www.oqp.med.va.gov/cpg.htm). These guidelines were commissioned by Thomas Horvath, MD, in the mid-1990s, and a psychosocial rehabilitation module was begun in 1994, from algorithms designed and written by committees led by Miklos Losonscy, MD, and Walter Penk, PhD (Penk & Losonzcy 1997).

The history of changes in VHA from inpatient units to community-based programs is summarized in remembrances by Harold Dickman, Palo Alto's chief of psychology (Dickman 2007), detailing development of psychosocial rehabilitation in a VHA medical center. At the policy level, Charles Stenger (2007) worked to integrate clinical and psychosocial rehabilitation in the VA Central Office, based on his collaborations with Cecil Peck and Jack Davis. These, along with other chapters in Baker's (2007) book, show that reductions in inpatient units and growth in outpatient services took place across time for many different reasons: because medications were developed to reduce symptoms; because VHA faced waves of budget reductions (LaGana 2007); because VA services were facilitated by computer-assisted interventions (e.g., Gottfredson 2007); because knowledge was increasing that outpatient care was just as effective as inpatient hospitalization (e.g., Penk, Charles & Van Hoose 1978; Lips 2007; Laughlin 2007; Miller 2007); and because training has prepared clinicians to integrate clinical interventions with psychosocial rehabilitation (e.g., Moore 2007). The growth of outpatient programming is recounted in a chapter by Lee Gurel (2007), who had begun in the late 1950s to test efficacies of inpatient programs through the Psychiatric Evaluation Projects (PEP). Dr. Gurel concluded from the studies he supervised that it was essential to increase outpatient interventions for veterans with mental disorders, especially by providing support for employment. Dr. Gurel relates that, by 1969, when he left his VHA assignment, PEP had produced over 350 published studies demonstrating that interventions facilitating recovery and resiliency are central in treatment policies, as now mandated in the *VHA Health Administration Handbook 1160 for Uniform Mental Health Services in VA Medical Centers and Clinics* (U.S. Department of Veterans Affairs 2009).

It is essential to recall what treating and rehabilitating trauma in VHA has taught and continues to teach us about psychosocial rehabilitation that focuses on recovery from trauma. Providers not only treat wounds and infections but also rehabilitate the spirit, psychology, family, social, and work skills among survivors of combat (e.g., Harris & Fallot 2001). And that is why, to paraphrase VHA's mission statement from Abraham Lincoln's address at Gettysburg—to care for her and for him who shall have borne the battle, as well as widows and widowers and orphans—we must conceptualize and deliver trauma-focused treatment that is intertwined with trauma-focused rehabilitation. Psychosocial rehabilitation in VHA must center on helping veterans recover from stresses and trauma. The lessons learned from rehabilitation for and with combat veterans who have been traumatized can be applied to treat civilians who also have experienced trauma, along with military and veterans who have experienced noncombat traumas. Although psychosocial rehabilitation is not new in VHA, clinicians and consumers must recognize that such services must use trauma theory to inform, to guide, and to evaluate how healthcare is provided in VHA and in other healthcare systems for all citizens. Psychosocial rehabilitation must be informed by trauma, focused on the choices that combat veterans and traumatized citizens make and based on their strengths, to assist them in recovering from the traumas they have experienced.

Psychosocial Rehabilitation

Penk and Flannery (2000) listed seven forms of psychosocial rehabilitation as clinical practice guidelines for post-traumatic stress disorder (PTSD): 1) patient education services, including peer support; 2) self-care independent living skills training; 3) supported housing services for those who are homeless or threatened with foreclosures; 4) supported family skills services; 5) social skills training; 6) supported employment; and 7) case management. A decade later we can add to this list 8) physical health and well-being and computer-assisted self-management training in reducing PTSD and other mental disorders such as addictions and depression (see Penk & Ainspan 2009; see also Martin 2011). For self-management training, see Defense Centers of Excellence (2011).

Evidence-based research from randomized clinical trials is available to support recommending psychosocial rehabilitation when treating veterans. It should be noted that psychosocial rehabilitations are not limited to veterans with schizophrenia or other psychoses. They are recognized as efficacious in treating PTSD, major depression disorders, and addictions, especially when mental health practices are delivered through self-management manuals and the Internet integrated into supported education and supported employment (see Farkas, Jansen & Penk 2007, which examines findings on psychosocial rehabilitation for persons with severe mental disorders, as well as Glynn, Drebing & Penk 2009, a more recent review of the literature on PTSD comparing effect sizes for psychosocial rehabilitation). Such findings concur with conclusions from the Schizophrenia Patient Outcomes Research Team (PORT) (Lehman & Steinwachs 1998) that distinctions between treatment and rehabilitation must be eliminated and that psychosocial rehabilitations must be adopted in treatment planning to reduce symptoms and to increase functioning. Each of these approaches is discussed below.

Psychosocial rehabilitation mandates that veterans with medical and mental disorders must be full partners in interventions in which they choose to participate. This is the core principle of the "work cure" (Cabot 1909), long ago adopted in the practice of John Gehring, MD, of Bethel, Maine, who influenced the development of positive psychology that persists today (see also Hanson 2007, about training VA staff in the TIGER program using community partnerships, learned from the NTL groups in Bethel). This principle holds that each veteran must be a full member of his or her treatment or recovery team. Each veteran should determine services to be received, according to the "choose, get, and keep" approaches long ago stipulated by Karen Danley (Anthony 1993; Anthony, Cohen & Danley 1988). "Choose, get, keep" means that treatment and rehabilitation are not things done *to* veterans; rather, each veteran must accomplish his or her own recovery. This psychosocial rehabilitation model includes medication when needed, skills training designed to assist veterans in living productively in the community, and various forms of psychotherapy. Integrating prolonged exposure (and other trauma-centered therapies) with psychosocial rehabilitation is currently underutilized, but new interventions are being empirically validated to bring together several forms of treatment and rehabilitation for PTSD.

Evidence Supporting Psychosocial Rehabilitation

Evidence that supports psychosocial rehabilitation is now being published (Penk & Flannery 2000; Farkas, Jansen & Penk 2007; Penk & Ainspan 2009; Glynn, Drebing & Penk 2009). Comprehensive toolkits have been developed summarizing practice, providing guidelines to ensure fidelity, and specifying training for providers. (See SAMHSA evidence-based toolkits at www.samhsa.gov under the heading Mental Health System Transformation, then Evidence Based Practices Implementation Resource Kits.) (U.S. Substance Abuse and Mental Health Services Administration 2002). The Office of Academic Assistance of VHA now provides postdoctoral training in psychosocial rehabilitations. Following are summaries of psychosocial rehabilitation now practiced within VHA (see U.S. Department of Veterans Affairs 2009).

1. Assertive Community Treatment and Intensive Case Management

One of the better-known and perhaps most researched forms of psychosocial rehabilitation is assertive community treatment (ACT) and its corollary, intensive case management. Assertive community treatment (Stein & Test 1980) is a foundation upon which treatment and rehabilitation for those with serious mental illness is built. It relies on principles of intensive case management that were developed in Boston in the early 1900s. VHA began to introduce forms of ACT and intensive case management into VA medical centers in New England late in the 1980s as Intensive Psychiatric Community Care (IPCC) programs, led by Al Washkow, LICSW, and Paul Errara, MD. Outcomes for IPCCs were tracked by establishing the North East Program Evaluation Center (NEPEC), directed by Robert Rosenheck, MD. NEPEC continues to this day evaluating VHA's psychosocial rehabilitation programs (see www.nepec .org). Michael Neale, PhD, directed IPCCs in eight VHA medical centers and later reformulated IPCCs into what now is called Mental Health Intensive Case Management (MHICM). By the time of his death in 2009, Michael Neale had founded 130 MHICM centers across the country, his last efforts expanding them to the nation's rural areas.

The implementation of ACT and MHICM centers started in the late 1980s as VHA residential care for mental disorders was being reduced. Staff were discovering that many veterans were relapsing after they were discharged from inpatient care in stable condition. Readmissions took place for several reasons: 1) because types and intensity of services available to veterans were no longer available after veterans left VHA hospitals, 2) because veterans had not learned skills needed to live in the community, and 3) because veterans were particularly vulnerable to new stress associated with changes involved in moving from VA residential care to community-based lodgings.

The ACT and MHICM teams were designed to ensure veterans received services they needed to prevent relapse. The VA inpatient staff were figuratively relocated by VHA into the community to work with veterans where they lived and worked. The ACT and MHICM multidisciplinary teams provided veterans with support, treatment, and rehabilitation services for living in communities, support that varied across time. The ACT and MHICM staff responded to people in the community twenty-four hours a day, seven days a week. As veterans improved, ACT and MHICM teams decreased contacts but remained available to provide additional support as new needs arose. The range of services included resolving difficulties with basic, everyday activities like keeping themselves safe; caring for basic physical needs; maintaining safe and adequate housing; addressing unemployment, substance abuse, and homelessness; and collaborating with the criminal justice system to reduce incarcerations. Effect sizes in randomized clinical trials demonstrate that ACT and MHICM have had efficacious outcomes, becoming gold standards for treatment not only in the United States but throughout the world (Burns & Santos 1995; Solomon & Draine 1995; Latimer 1999; Bond et al. 2001). (See www .samhsa.gov for toolkits.)

Most recently, city court systems are now forming "veterans' courts" to speed service delivery and reduce incarceration. The ACT and MHICM teams consist of nurses, social workers, psychologists, and vocational specialists who collaborate in teams of five to seven members with caseloads of up to 100 veterans. Forensic Assertive Community Treatment (FACT) systems are now being developed to serve incarcerated veterans transitioning home from prison, as well as veterans who are court-referred and facing possible imprisonment. The FACTs are designed to prevent arrest and incarceration among veterans with criminal justice histories at high risk for incarceration. (See Lamberti, Weisman & Faden 2004 for guidelines for working with veterans with dual diagnoses— e.g., mental disorders coupled with substance use disorders.) Studies indicate that FACTs reduce rearrests, hospital days and hospital admissions, and overall service cost (Morrissey & Meyer 2005).

2. Supported Employment

Strong outcome data exist to support the efficacy of supported employment (SE) for veterans with medical and mental disorders (see Glynn, Drebing & Penk 2009 for a recent review of empirically validated studies). Supported employment consists of many different kinds of interventions, such as the "place-and-train" model that uses on-the-job training within and outside VA medical centers (see Penk 2000 for an analysis of therapeutic work environments in VHA; Penk, Drebing & Schutt 2002; Becker & Drake 2003). As a form of psychosocial rehabilitation, SE means that individuals with mental health disorders learn how to find and keep regular, real-world jobs in the community. In SE, vocational rehabilitation specialists provide continuous support to help veterans achieve success at work. Outcomes for SE have been shown to be much better than for traditional approaches, and this finding has been replicated in several countries (Bond et al. 1997; Latimer et al. 2006; Oldman et al. 2005; Penk et al. 2010).

Supported employment has long been used in VHA, perhaps inspired by recommendations from the Viennese neuroanatomist, Sigmund Freud, MD, who wrote in *Civilization and Its Discontents,* following World War I: "No other technique for the conduct of life attaches the individual so firmly to reality as laying emphasis upon work. For work at least gives one a secure place upon a portion of reality in the human community" (Freud 1921).

Work restoration programs were begun inside VHA medical centers shortly after the end of World War II. Favorable outcome data were published early. For example, Peter Peffer, MD, developed a model work program that employed eighty-two schizophrenic patients in positions throughout the Brockton VHA medical center. He found thirty-seven (45 percent of the patients) able to return to independent jobs in the community. Peffer (1953, 1955) attributed such high rates of return to work outside the VA medical center to the benefits of working in the medical center. It should be noted that Dr. Pfeffer's work was published in the early 1950s, before medications to treat schizophrenia were either widely used or available (see Peffer 1955). When he managed the VA medical center in Perry Point, Maryland, Dr. Peffer also studied the influence of paying veterans with schizophrenia for work performance, concluding that money was effective in rehabilitation (Peffer 1953, 1955). Such studies pioneered later use of incentives for behavioral treatments and psychosocial rehabilitation.

Implementing work therapy in VHA medical centers led to the development of incentive therapy, followed by creation of compensated work therapy (CWT) programs that have remained in effect. These CWT programs now exist in 120 VHA medical centers, paying fair wages for real jobs, involving each year well over 10,000 veterans, paying well over $32 million each year in wages to veterans in VA medical centers. The program now consists of several different kinds of interventions: incentive therapy, sheltered workshops, piecework in VHA domiciliary and medical center settings, jobs in the community; individual placement and support (IPS), job coaching, the Vet Construction Team, and veteran-owned businesses.

Cochrane Review considered eighteen randomized controlled trials among nonveteran and veteran samples, mostly those with serious mental disorders, and found SE was superior to programs that offered prevocational training (Crowther et al. 2001). It was found to be associated with fewer crises, less chaos, more structure, and ongoing support from vocational rehabilitation specialists, because consumers now focus on developing their lives in the community and managing their illnesses more independently (Bond et al. 2001). In addition, SE was found to be more effective when clinical services are integrated into services delivery (Cook et al. 2005b; O'Connor et al.

2011). Moreover, those receiving SE services secure significantly higher earnings and remain employed for longer periods (Cook et al. 2005a). The SE services delivery usually includes centering on competitive employment, participating in immediate job searches, seeking jobs tailored for specific individuals, obtaining follow-up supports, and receiving mental health services integrated with SE.

The hallmark characteristic of SE is zero exclusion criteria; that is, leaving no one out. Accordingly, SE immediately confronts one of the horrendous biases often associated with mental illness: It proceeds against the bias that those with mental disorders cannot work and assumes that every person will work. Effect sizes for treating PTSD with SE are large (Glynn, Drebing & Penk 2009; Drebing et al. 2005; Drebing et al. 2004; Rogers et al. 2006; Drebing et al. 2007; Penk et al. 2010). Evidence about SE for many different kinds of mental disorders around the world, including consumers with severe mental disorders, has demonstrated that more than 50 percent of those with serious mental illness recover or significantly improve, and close to 50 percent of those are working (Bleuler 1974; Ciompi 1988; DeSisto et al. 1995; Harding & Zahniser 1994; Harding et al. 1987a; Harding et al. 1987b; Hegarty et al. 1994; Huber, Gross & Schuttler 1975; Tsuang, Woolson & Fleming 1979). Such results for SE have been exceeded by research from Davis (2010), who is demonstrating that clinical services integrated into CWT achieve extraordinary success.

The Veterans Health Administration has developed an exceptionally complex and comprehensive approach for work restoration in VA medical centers, ranging from CWT programs operating in VA medical centers to job coaching for veterans working in the community (Penk 2000;). Recent advances for SE in VHA are concentrating on specializing in counseling on the job away from the VA hospital and training veterans to develop small businesses in the community (Penk et al. 2010; Drebing et al. 2012). One unique development is the Vet Construction Team, in which hospitalized and recently released veterans bid on construction jobs and practice building trades on real jobs in the community. Such approaches place employment among veterans hospitalized for care within the context of the recovery paradigm, making sure veterans go beyond their medical and mental disorders, supported by clinicians for whom work for consumers is a clinical concern. Work and employment specialists are integral to the clinical team (see, e.g., www.samhsa.gov or www.mentalhealth.samhsa.gov/cmhs/communitysupport/toolkits/employment/; see also Ainspan 2008 for contributions of the U.S. Department of Labor and other agencies to such efforts).

3. Family Psychoeducation

Family psychoeducation is the process of providing education and coping skills for veterans and their families about relevant medical and mental disorders. Examples of such psychosocial rehabilitation are the family interventions for PTSD developed by Shirley Glynn (2008; Glynn, Drebing & Penk 2009) at VA in West Los Angeles and manualized approaches designed by Sherman and colleagues (2005) delivered at VHA medical centers in VISN 16: Oklahoma City, Jackson, and Houston. Family psychoeducation generally takes place in multifamily groups (producing the added benefit of augmenting social support), but such techniques can also be given in single-family formats or even in books or online (Sherman & Sherman 2005; see also www.ouhsc.edu/REACHPro gram). Family psychoeducation is noted for fostering social support, challenging a key symptom in PTSD, which is characterized by social avoidance and isolation. Precautions are needed in fielding family psychoeducation among many different families, because consent of each individual is always required when information is shared about a veteran's illness and/or about families' symptoms and ways of coping. Family psychoeducation is a treatment modality in which families are a partner in providing services to each other; families are not objects in treatment. Tutorials for learning a variety of procedures for families to support military and veterans are described in *When the Warrior Comes Home* (Ainspan & Penk in press).

Family psychoeducation is effective, particularly for PTSD (Glynn, Drebing & Penk 2009), and hence is well-regarded in VHA and emphasized in mental health services. Studies from various countries over the past twenty years show that family psychoeducation reduces the rates of rehospitalization by an average of 50 percent. Further, employment rates are significantly higher among groups who have received family psychoeducation, increasing family well-being and decreasing negative symptoms and costs for medical care (Campbell 2004; Dixon et al. 2001). Meta-analyses have demonstrated that effect size in comparing family intervention with treatment-as-usual (TAU) has averaged around 0.20, with higher effect size—averaging 0.63—for treatment interventions among families participating in psychoeducation techniques for longer than six weeks. The Schizophrenia Patient Outcomes Research Team (PORT) project included family psychoeducation in its treatment recommendations (Lehman & Steinwachs 1998; Lehman et al. 2004).

Toolkits are available in the form of manualized psychosocial rehabilitation approaches (see www.samhsa.gov). These toolkits highlight family psychoeducation that promotes family relationships that provide emotional support, educational workshops, skills building for community reentry, and social skills and vocational skills development. Toolkits suggest that for family psychoeducation to be effective, it requires many sessions over several months of participation.

4. Patient Education and Illness Management

Patient education and illness management interventions are enjoying wide success in reducing symptoms and in training techniques for coping with mental disorders (Freeman, Moore & Freeman 2009; Penk & Ainspan 2009). Patient education in illness management and recovery programs consists of personal training sessions in which clinicians teach consumers manual-guided, practice-driven coping strategies for living with symptoms and coping with mental disorders. Patient education and illness management programs are offered for three to six months and consist of educational and skills-building sessions. Key to success is always practice, practice, practice. Online techniques are available (see Penk & Ainspan 2009 for a summary of online approaches improving physical adjustment, mental effectiveness, interactions at work, coping with wounds, transitioning from combat to home, and connecting with support groups). Patient education is undergoing extraordinary change because of increases in computer-assisted training courses as well as supported interactions through Twitter, Facebook, and other new forms of computer-assisted exchanges.

Research on patient education and illness management indicates efficacy based on high effect sizes (Glynn, Drebing & Penk 2009). Patient education involves behavioral skills for compliance with medication regimens, relapse prevention to prevent or reduce rehospitalization rates, and coping with symptoms (Corrigan 2005). Topics in manualized approaches include recovery strategies, practical facts about mental illness, stress-vulnerability model and treatment strategies, building social support, coping with stress, problems and symptoms, learning to use the mental health system to meet one's needs, and medication management (Dartmouth Psychiatric Research Center 2006).

Learning to improve one's physical health has the highest priority among veterans in recovery (Penk & Ainspan 2009). Just as health and exercise are central among new recruits into the military, so must taking care of the body be the major focus of attention in recovery and resiliency. Examples of self-management procedures for improving medical condition and body fitness have been emphasized by Battlemind and Re-set Training. The VHA Web site http://www.myhealth.va.gov specifies plans for physical fitness as well as measures of medical condition.

5. Social Skills Training (Including Self-care, Independent Living Skills, and Empowerment)

Social skills training is an intervention universally available in VHA for decades, although new labels may be used to describe this traditional form of psychosocial rehabilitation, such as basic communication skills, assertiveness training, self-care, independent living skills, empowerment, and training in skills associated with a variety of social and vocational settings. Social skills training in the past was designed to assist veterans with serious mental illness to function well in residential and community settings. Social skills training not only reduces symptoms, as research demonstrates, but also helps consumers function more adaptively with their medical and mental disorders. Social skills training, along with self-care, independent living skills, and empowerment techniques, is essential for success in the community. Such training is necessary for some veterans who need to learn skills for negotiating a place to live, making friends in leisure time, using public transportation, and applying for jobs.

Social skills training has a long history of use in VHA, on the basis of which rehabilitation manuals have been produced and tested for efficacy (e.g., Liberman 1992). Health services research supports social skills training in a variety of forms (Bustillo et al. 2001; Penn & Mueser 1996). One recent example of approaches adapted for veterans with PTSD can be found in the work of Frueh and colleagues—a twenty-nine-session, multicomponent behavioral treatment for chronic combat-related PTSD called "Trauma Management Therapy" (Frueh et al. 1996; Turner, Beidel & Frueh 2005). This form of social skills training involves behavioral training to improve interpersonal interactions along with anger management. Another example is STAIR (Skills Training in Affective and Interpersonal Regulation), demonstrated as efficacious for PTSD by Cloitre and colleagues (2002).

6. Peer Support

Peer support is perhaps the most traditional form of psychosocial rehabilitation for veterans (Gregory 2008). But some practitioners may not necessarily consider social support from veterans for veterans a method of psychosocial rehabilitation. Nonetheless, peer support and peer counseling have always been a valuable partner for veterans in many different ways—in volunteer services in VHA medical centers and in organizations of veterans' groups, whose purpose is to support veterans in need. A recent review of the literature on veterans' organizations reveals many Web sites offering services for veterans (see Penk & Ainspan 2009; see also Smelson et al. 2011).

A partnership with the National Alliance for the Mentally Ill (NAMI) is now growing in VHA, featuring consultation about VHA policies, sharing partnerships for delivering services in communities, and building on recommendations from those with serious mental disorders who long have advocated peer support. Several studies have confirmed the benefits of such forms of psychosocial rehabilitation (e.g., Dumont & Jones 2002; Nelson et al. 2006). Peer support groups usually are run by individuals with serious mental illness for others who have similar problems. Peers engage in active and supportive listening; share their own experiences; and offer support, hope, encouragement, and practical suggestions (Gregory 2008). Again, training in basic skills, including tutorials on VHA procedures, should be provided to ensure that peer support volunteers are skilled to offer helpful interventions (U.S. Department of Veterans Affairs 2009). Many believe that peer support programs help to normalize the experience of serious mental illness, whereas traditional treatment tends to medicalize and stigmatize it (see, e.g., Corrigan 2005).

7. Supported Education

Supported education has been a psychosocial rehabilitation resource for combat veterans since the GI Bill in 1944 and remains so in the latest version of the GI Bill that became law in 2009 (Isenwater, Lanham & Thornhill 2002; Mowbray, Collins & Bybee 1999; Unger, Pardee & Shafer 2000; Glynn, Drebing & Penk 2009). The primary aim of supported education is to provide opportunities, resources, and supports to veterans with medical and psychological disabilities so that they may gain admittance to and succeed in the pursuit of postsecondary education (Sabatier 2008). Procedures in supported education help veterans with mental disorders return to college and technical schools so they can receive the education and training they need to achieve their learning and recovery goals and/or become gainfully employed in the career of their choice (Mowbray et al. 2002). Training in learning skills is combined with teaching emotional control and coping with memories of trauma that may have become disturbing.

Current examples of exemplary approaches are those developed in Massachusetts (e.g., Ellison et al. 2012) and Texas (e.g., Smith-Osborne 2009). Critical components of these programs include the following:

Continual surveys are taken about the needs of combat veterans currently enrolled in school.

The mental health system promotes supported education.

A training-supported education team/specialist is designated to work with consumer-students.

Educational eligibility is not required for participation.

Communication and collaboration are fostered between all stakeholders.

Confidence- and knowledge-building activities are provided not only for learning skills but also in emotional and social interactions.

School enrollment is not demanded as a condition for supported education, but school attendance is encouraged.

Enrollment and support are provided to improve educational and learning skills. (Ratzlaff et al. 2005)

8. Supported Housing

It is estimated that about half of homeless persons (estimated at 150,000) in the United States are veterans. The Veterans Health Administration announced a policy in 2010 to eliminate homelessness. Although information and skills development related to obtaining and maintaining appropriate housing is generally integrated into other clinical interventions, the ability to maintain stable housing is critical to success in the community, and skills training is often needed to increase the chance for success. The greatest risks to housing arrangements and the likelihood of discontinuing rehabilitation arise from addictions (Goldfinger et al. 1999; Rog 2006; Tsemberis & Eisenberg 2000; Culhane, Metraux & Hadley 2002). Thus, interventions that provide housing supports are critical to success in rehabilitation (Mares, Kasprow & Rosenheck 2004). For decades VHA has offered support for housing through residential care programs, such as residential care in inpatient units, domiciliaries, affiliations with state and local housing resources, vouchers for single-room occupancy, and congregate housing in private homes.

One of the more successful models of supported housing recently developed in VHA is the compensated work therapy transitional residence model (CWT/TR), which requires that unemployed, homeless veterans work in CWT (and later other jobs) in order to gain access to VHA housing for a limited time before transitioning to housing on one's own or in private congregate housing with other veterans. Veterans enrolled in CWT/TR participate in managing the CWT/TR, from administration to outreach, as well as participating in CWT transitional employment before seeking jobs in the community. The CWT/TRs include staff with skills in vocational rehabilitation and in case management, with links to medical and substance abuse treatment services from the VHA medical center that hosts the CWT/TR, providing a wide array of supportive services to veterans to live as independently and productively as possible. Research on outcomes for CWT/TR has shown that such endeavors indeed are quite successful in transitioning homeless, unemployed veterans who had been hospitalized in inpatient units from VA medical centers to independent living in the community (Schutt et al. 2005).

The CWT/TR shares characteristics that have been demonstrated as successful for supported housing with Fountain House and the clubhouse model. Outcome studies show that such interventions are successful in promoting tenure in jobs and in personal living arrangements, promoting healthier styles of living, as well lowering costs due to reduced recidivism (Cook 2001; McKay et al. 2006; Cowell et al. 2003; Pelletier et al. 2005).

In Conclusion

For decades VHA policies have pioneered an extraordinary array of psychosocial rehabilitation services, currently promulgated in the latest revision of the *VHA Handbook 1160 for Uniform Health Services in VA Medical Centers and Clinics* (U.S. Department of Veterans Affairs 2009). The VHA system of trauma-informed treatment and rehabilitation centers on personal choice and strengths in recovering from medical and mental disorders. Clinicians continue to integrate treatments for PTSD in psychosocial rehabilitation, delivering services in many different community environments, accommodating interventions for varying cultural contexts. Demographics of military combatants continue to change, so VHA also changes: More women have entered the military and have become veterans; diversity in ethnicity has also increased. So VHA continues to diversify in treatment and rehabilitation to serve many different veterans in many different environments, expanding beyond inpatient units and medical center clinics and reaching out to couples and families, to colleges and training institutions, to work and to places for recreation. And VHA evaluates outcomes of such change, empirically validating benefits of using trauma theory for designing VHA service systems (Harris & Fallot 2001).

Such diversity requires that psychosocial rehabilitation be comprehensive, providing availability of many different kinds of approaches at any one time. Toward this end, clinicians and consumers together not only need to decide which psychosocial rehabilitation services will be used at which point in time during recovery, but also must know the duration of each intervention as well as when to discontinue and to move into other forms of interventions in the community. Algorithms need to be designed and validated (see algorithms for *VA/DoD Clinical Practice Guidelines* or Penk & Flannery 2000, 228: table 11.1). Now VHA needs to design approaches like those of the ASAM

(American Society of Addiction Medicine), giving a series of choice points for level of care determination, suited to the individual needs of each veteran. Each form of psychosocial rehabilitation needs clear and certain criteria for admission, discharge, and readmission. And clinicians and clients both must understand that the course of recovery requires timely and appropriate selection of which of many forms of psychosocial rehabilitation needs to be continued or discontinued.

What we learn from the rise of psychosocial rehabilitation in the history of VHA over the past eighty years is that VHA is always changing. Fortunately for veterans, that change is always toward empowering them, recovering from trauma to take command of their lives and live as fully as possible in the least restrictive environment under the influence of their hopes and spirit, to protect themselves and others. And as veterans learn upon returning home from war to cope with trauma, so they will share and teach others who experience their own forms of trauma in civilian life.

The views expressed herein are those of the authors and do not reflect the official position or policies of the U.S. Army, Department of Veterans Affairs, or Texas A&M College of Medicine.

References

Ainspan, N. D. (2008). Finding employment as a veteran with a disability. In N. D. Ainspan & W. E. Penk (Eds.), *Returning wars' wounded, injured, and ill: A reference handbook.* Westport, CT: Greenwood/Praeger.

Ainspan, N. D. & Penk, W. E. (Eds.). (2008). *Returning wars' wounded, injured, and ill: A reference handbook.* Westport, CT: Greenwood/Praeger.

Ainspan, N. D. & Penk, W. E. (Eds). (in press). *When the warrior comes home.* Annapolis, MD: Naval Institute Press.

Anthony, W. A. (1993). Recovery from mental illness: The guiding vision of the mental health system in the 1990s. *Psychosocial Rehabilitation Journal* 16: 11–23.

Anthony, W. A., Cohen, M. R. & Danley, K. S. (1988). The psychiatric rehabilitation approach as applied to vocational rehabilitation. In J. A. Ciardiello & M. D. Bell (Eds.), *Vocational rehabilitation of persons with prolonged psychiatric disorder.* Baltimore, MD: Johns Hopkins University Press, 1988.

Baker, R. R. (Ed.). (2007). *Stories from VA psychology.* Bloomington, IN: Author House. (Available for a fee from www.authorhouse.com.)

Baker, R. R. & Pickren, W. E. (2007). *Psychology and the Department of Veterans Affairs: A historical analysis of training, research, practice, and advocacy.* Washington, DC: APA Books.

Becker, D. R. & Drake, R. E. (2003). *A working life for people with severe mental illness.* New York: Oxford.

Bleuler, M. (1974). The long-term course of the schizophrenic psychoses. *Psychological Medicine* 4: 244–254.

Bond, G., Drake, R., Mueser, K. & Latimer, E. (2001). Assertive community treatment for people with severe mental illness: Critical ingredients and impact on patients. *Disease Management & Health Outcomes* 9, no. 3: 141–159.

Bond, G. R., Becker, D. R., Drake, R. E., et al. (2001). Implementing supported employment as an evidence-based practice. *Psychiatric Services* 52: 313–322.

Bond, G. R., Drake, R. E., Mueser, K. T., et al. (1997). An update on supported employment for people with severe mental illness. *Psychiatric Services* 48: 335–346.

Brady, S., Rierdan, J., Penk, W. E., Losardo, M. & Mescheda. T. (2003). Post-traumatic stress disorder in adults with serious mental illness and substance abuse. *Journal of Trauma and Dissociation* 4: 77–90.

Burns, B. J. & Santos, A.B. (1995). Assertive community treatment: An update of randomized trials. *Psychiatric Services* 46, no. 7: 669–675.

Bustillo, J., Lauriello, J., Horan, W. & Keith, S. (2001). The psychosocial treatment of schizophrenia: An update. *American Journal of Psychiatry* 158, no. 2: 163–175.

Cabot, R. C. (1909). Work cure. *Psychotherapy* 3: 24–29.

Campbell, A. S. (2004). How was it for you? Families' experiences of receiving behavioural family therapy. *Journal of Psychiatric and Mental Health Nursing* 11: 261–267.

Cather, C., Penn, D. L., Otto, M. W., et al. (2005). A pilot study of functional cognitive behavioral therapy (fCBT) for schizophrenia. *Schizophrenia Research* 74: 201–209.

Ciompi, L. (1988). *Psyche and schizophrenia*. Cambridge, MA: Harvard University Press.

Cloitre, M., Koenen, K. C., Cohen, L. R. & Han, H. (2002). Skills training in affective and interpersonal regulation followed by exposure: A phase-based treatment for PTSD related to childhood abuse. *Journal of Consulting and Clinical Psychology* 70: 1067–1074.

Cook, J. (2001). Characteristics of EIDP participants and the jobs they hold: Preliminary findings of the Employment Intervention Demonstration Program. Contact Judith Cook at www.psych.uic.edu (accessed April 20, 2012).

Cook, J. A., Leff, H. S., Blyler, C. R., et al. (2005a). Results of a multisite randomized trial of supported employment interventions for individuals with severe mental illness. *Archives of General Psychiatry* 62, no. 5: 505–512.

Cook, J. A., Lehman, A. F., Drake, R., et al. (2005b). Integration of psychiatric and vocational services: A multisite randomized, controlled trial of supported employment. *American Journal of Psychiatry* 162, no. 10: 1948–1956.

Corrigan, P. W. (Ed.). (2005). *On the stigma of mental illness: Practical strategies for research and social change*. Washington, DC: APA Press.

Cowell, A., Pollio, D. E., North, C. S., et al. (2003). Deriving service costs for a clubhouse psychosocial rehabilitation program. *Administration and Policy in Mental Health* 30: 323–340.

Crowther, R., Marshall, M., Bond, G. & Huxley, P. (2001). Vocational rehabilitation for people with severe mental illness. *Cochrane Database System Review* 2: CD003080.

Culhane, D. P., Metraux, S. & Hadley, T. (2002). Public service reductions associated with placement of homeless persons with severe mental illness in supportive housing. *Housing Policy Debate* 13: 107–163.

Dartmouth Psychiatric Research Center. (2006). www.dartmouth.edu/prc/evidence/practices/medication.

Darwin, J. (2008). Disabilities and injuries among members of the National Guard and Reserve units. In N. D. Ainspan & W. E. Penk (Eds.), *Returning wars' wounded, injured, and ill: A reference handbook*. Westport, CT: Greenwood/Praeger.

Davis, L. (2010). Supported employment in veterans with PTSD. (PowerPoint presentation available from Lori.Davis@va.gov, VA Medical Center, Tuscaloosa, Alabama, and University of Alabama Medical School, Birmingham, Alabama.)

Defense Centers of Excellence. (2011). Co-occurring conditions toolkit: Mild traumatic brain injury and psychological health: Concussion, posttraumatic stress, depression, chronic pain, headaches, and substance use disorders. Washington, DC.

DeSisto, M. J., Harding, C. M., McCormick, R. V., Ashikaga, T. & Brooks, G.W. (1995). The Maine and Vermont three-decade studies of serious mental illness. I. Matched comparison of cross-sectional outcome. *British Journal of Psychiatry* 167: 331–338.

Dickman, H. R. (2007). Recollections of a VA psychologist. In R. R. Baker (Ed.), *Stories from VA psychology* (pp. 11–18). Bloomington, IN: Author House. (Available for a fee from www.authorhouse.com.)

Dixon, L., McFarlane, W. R., Lefley, H., et al. (2001). Evidence-based services to families of people with psychiatric disabilities. *Psychiatric Services* 52: 903–910.

Drake, R. E., Mercer-McFadden, C., Mueser, K. T., et al. (1998). Review of integrated mental health and substance abuse treatment for patients with dual disorders. *Schizophrenia Bulletin* 24, no. 4: 589–608.

Drebing, C. E., Mueller, M., Van Ormer, A., Duggy, P., LePage, J., Rosenheck, R., Drake, R., Rose, G., King, K. & Penk, W. E. (2012). Pathways to vocational services: Factors affecting entry by veterans enrolled in Veterans Health Administration mental health services. *Psychological Services* 9: 49–63.

Drebing, C. E., Van Ormer, A., Mueller, L., Hebert, M., Penk, W. E., Petry, N. M., Rosenheck, R. & Rounsaville, B. (2007). Adding a contingency management intervention to vocational rehabilitation: Outcomes for dually diagnosed veterans. *Journal of Rehabilitation Research and Development* 44: 851–866.

Drebing, C., Van Ormer, A., Rosenheck, R., Rounsaville, B., Herz, L. & Penk, W. (2005). The impact of enhanced incentives on vocational rehabilitation outcomes for dually-diagnosed veterans. *Journal of Applied Behavior Analysis* 38: 359–372.

Drebing, C. E., Van Ormer, A., Schutt, R. K., Krebs, C., Losardo, M., Boyd, C., Penk, W. E. & Rosenheck, R. (2004). Client goals for participating in VHA vocational rehabilitation: Distribution and relationship to outcome. *Rehabilitation Counseling Bullteitn* 47: 162–172.

Dumont, J. & Jones, K. (2002). Findings from a consumer/survivor defined alternative to psychiatric hospitalization. *Outlook* (Spring): 4–6.

Ellison, M., Mueller, L., Smelson, D., Corrigan, P., Torres-Sloan, P., Najavits, M., Vessella, J. M. & Drebing, C. (2012). Supporting the goals of 9/11 veterans with self-reported PTSD symptoms: A needs assessment. *Psychiatric Rehabilitation Journal* 35: 209–217.

Farkas, M., Jansen, M. & Penk, W. E. (Eds.). (2007). Guest editorial: Special issue on psychosocial rehabilitation: Approach of choice for those with serious mental illness. *Journal of Rehabilitation Research and Development* 44: vii–xxi.

Freeman, S. M., Moore, B. & Freeman, A. (Eds.). (2009). *Living and surviving in harm's way: A psychological treatment handbook for pre- and post-deployment of military personnel.* New York: Routledge.

Freud, S. (1921). *Civilization and its discontents.* New York: Norton.

Frueh, B. C., Turner, S. M., Beidel, D. C., Mirabella, R. F. & Jones, W. J. (1996). Trauma management therapy: A preliminary evaluation of multicomponent behavioral treatment for chronic combat-related PTSD. *Behavioral Research and Therapy* 34: 533–543.

Glynn, S. M. (2008). Impact on family and friends. In N. D. Ainspan & W. E. Penk (Eds.), *Returning wars' wounded, injured, and ill: A reference handbook.* Westport, CT: Greenwood/Praeger.

Glynn, S., Drebing, C. & Penk, W. E. (2009). Psychosocial Rehabilitation. In E. B. Foa, T. M. Keane, M. J. Friedman & J. Cohen (Eds.), *Effective treatments for PTSD: Practice guidelines from the International Society for Traumatic Stress Studies.* New York: Guilford Press.

Goldfinger, S. M., Schutt, R. K., Tomomiczenko, G. S., Seidman, L., Penk, W. E., Turner, W., et al. (1999). Housing placement and subsequent days homeless among formerly homeless adults with mental illness. *Psychiatric Services* 50: 674–679.

Gottfredson, D. K. (2007). Computers in VA psychology. In R. R. Baker (Ed.), *Stories from VA psychology* (pp. 39–48). Bloomington, IN: Author House (Available for a fee from www.authorhouse.com.)

Gould, R. A., Mueser, K. T., Bolton, E., et al. (2001). Cognitive therapy for psychosis in schizophrenia: An effect size analysis. *Schizophrenia Research* 48: 335–342.

Gregory, W. (2008). Peer support services. In N. Ainspan & W. Penk (Eds.), *Returning wars wounded, injured, and ill: A reference handbook.* Westport, CT: Greenwood/Praeger.

Gurel, L. (2007). Reflections on the VA years. In R. R. Baker (Ed.), *Stories from VA psychology* (pp. 73–82). Bloomington, IN: Author House. (Available for a fee from www.authorhouse.com.)

Hanson, P. G. (2007). Droppings from a TIGER. In R. R. Baker (Ed.), *Stories from VA psychology* (pp. 49–56). Bloomington, IN: Author House. (Available for a fee from www.authorhouse.com.)

Haddock, G., Barrowclough, C., Tarrier, N., et al. (2003). Cognitive-behavioural therapy and motivational intervention for schizophrenia and substance misuse: 18-month outcomes of a randomised controlled trial. *British Journal of Psychiatry* 183: 377–288.

Harding, C. M., Brooks, G. W., Ashikaga, T., Strauss, J. S. & Breier, A. (1987a). The Vermont longitudinal study of persons with severe mental illness, I: Methodology, study sample, and overall status 32 years later. *American Journal of Psychiatry* 144: 718–726.

Harding, C. M., Brooks, G. W., Ashikaga, T., Strauss, J. S. & Breier, A. (1987b). The Vermont longitudinal study of persons with severe mental illness, II: Long-term outcomes of subjects who retrospectively met DSM-III criteria for schizophrenia. *American Journal of Psychiatry* 144, no. 6: 727–735.

Harding, C. M. & Zahniser, J. H. (1994). Empirical correction of seven myths about schizophrenia with implications for treatment. *ACTA Psychiatrica Scandinavica* 90, supp. 384: 140–146.

Harris, M. & Fallot, R. D. (2001). *Using trauma theory to design service systems.* San Francisco: Jossey-Bass.

Hegarty, J. D., Baldessarini, R. J., Tohen, M., Waternaux, C. & Oepen, G. (1994). The one hundred years of schizophrenia: A meta-analysis of the outcome literature. *American Journal of Psychiatry* 151: 1409–1416.

Huber, G., Gross, G. & Schuttler, R. (1975). Long-term follow-up study of schizophrenia. *ACTA Psychiatrica Scandinavica* 53: 49–57.

Isenwater, W., Lanham, W. & Thornhill, H. (2002). The College Link Program: Evaluation of a supported education initiative in Great Britain. *Psychosocial Rehabilitation Journal* 26, no. 1: 43–50.

Kavanagh, D. J. & Mueser, K. T. (2001). The future of cognitive and behavioural therapies in the prevention and early management of psychosis: Opportunities and risks. *Behavior Therapy* 32: 693–724.

LaGana, C. (2007). Musings of an "acting" leader. In R. R. Baker (Ed.), *Stories from VA psychology* (pp. 119–126). Bloomington, IN: Author House. (Available for a fee from www.authorhouse.com.)

Lamberti, J. S., Weisman, R. & Faden, D. I. (2004). Forensic assertive community treatment: Preventing incarceration of adults with severe mental illness. *Psychiatric Services* 55, no. 11: 1285–1293.

Latimer, E. (1999). Economic impacts of assertive community treatment: A review of the literature. *Canadian Journal of Psychiatry* 44: 443–454.

Latimer, E. A., Lecomte, T., Becker, D. R., et al. (2006). Generalisability of the individual placement and support model of supported employment: Results of a Canadian randomized controlled trial. *British Journal of Psychiatry* 189: 65–73.

Laughlin, P. R. (2007). A VA story from the heartland. In R. R. Baker (Ed.), *Stories from VA psychology* (pp. 29–38). Bloomington, IN: Author House (Available for a fee from www.authorhouse.com.)

Lehman, A. F., Kreyenbuhl, J., Buchanan, R. W., et al. (2004). The Schizophrenia Patient Outcomes Research Team (PORT): Updated treatment recommendations 2003. *Schizophrenia Bulletin* 30, no. 2: 193–217.

Lehman, A. F. & Steinwachs, D. M. (1998). Translating research into practice: The Schizophrenia Patient Outcomes Research Team (PORT) treatment recommendations. *Schizophrenia Bulletin* 24, no. 1: 1–10.

Liberman, R. (1992). *Handbook of psychiatric rehabilitation.* Boston: Allyn & Bacon.

Lips, O. J. (2007). Time flies (and so do pigs, sometimes). In R. R. Baker (Ed.), *Stories from VA psychology* (pp. 19–28). Bloomington, IN: Author House. (Available for a fee from www.authorhouse.com.)

Mares, A. S., Kasprow, W. J. & Rosenheck, R. (2004). Outcomes of supported housing for homeless veterans with psychiatric and substance abuse problems. *Mental Health Services Research* 6: 199–211.

Margolese, H. C., Malchy, L., Negrete, J. C., et al. (2004). Drug and alcohol use among patients with schizophrenia and related psychoses: Levels and consequences. *Schizophrenia Research* 67, nos. 2–3: 257–266.

Martin, J. J. (2011). Welcome. *Sport, Exercise, and Performance Psychology* 1: 1.

McGurk, S. R., Mueser, K. T. & Pascaris, A. (2005). Cognitive training and supported employment for persons with severe mental illness: One-year results from a randomized controlled trial. *Schizophrenia Bulletin* 31, no. 4: 898–909.

McKay, C., Johnsen, M., Banks, S. & Stein, R. (2006). Employment transitions for members of Massachusetts clubhouses. *Work: A Journal of Prevention, Assessment and Rehabilitation* 26: 67–74.

McKay, C., Yates, B. & Johnsen, M. (2007). Costs of clubhouses: An international perspective. *Administration and Policy in Mental Health and Mental Health Services Research* 34: 62–72.

Miller, T. (2007). Buffalo to the bluegrass—A VA academic career. In R. R. Baker (Ed.), *Stories from VA psychology* (pp. 57–64). Bloomington, IN: Author House. (Available for a fee from www.authorhouse.com.)

Moore, D. L. (2007). VA psychology stories. In R. R. Baker (Ed.), *Stories from VA psychology* (pp. 93–102). Bloomington, IN: Author House. (Available for a fee from www.authorhouse.com.)

Morrissey, J. & Meyer, P. (2005). *Extending assertive community treatment to criminal justice settings.* Delmar, NY: The National GAINS Center for Systemic Change for Justice-Involved People with Mental Illness.

Mowbray, C., Brown, K., Furlong-Norman, K. & Soydan, A. (Eds.) (2002). *Supported education and psychiatric rehabilitation: Models and methods.* Linthicum, MD: International Association of Psychosocial Rehabilitation Services.

Mowbray, C., Collins, M. & Bybee, D. (1999). Supported education for individuals with psychiatric disabilities: Long-term outcomes from an experimental study. *Social Work Research* 23, no. 2: 89–100.

Mueser, K. T., Corrigan, P. W., Hilton, D., et al. (2002). Illness management and recovery: A review of the research. *Psychiatric Services* 53: 1272–1284.

National Alliance for the Mentally Ill. (2005). *Dual diagnosis and integrated treatment of mental illness and substance abuse disorder.* Washington, DC: National Alliance for the Mentally Ill.

Nelson, G., Ochocka, J., Janzen, R. & Trainor, J. (2006). A longitudinal study of mental health consumer/survivor initiatives. *Journal of Community Psychology* 34, no. 3: 247–260.

O'Connor, M., Mueller, L., Van Ormer, A., Drake, R., Penk, W. E., Rosenheck, R., Semiatin, A. & Drebing, C. E. (2011). Cognitive impairment as a barrier to employment in vocational rehabilitation services among veterans with serious mental illness. *Journal of Rehabilitation Research and Development* 48: 597–608.

Oldman, J., Thomson, L., Calsaferri, K., et al. (2005). A case report of the conversion of sheltered employment to evidence-based supported employment in Canada. *Psychiatric Services* 56, no. 11: 1436–1440.

Peffer, P. A. (1953). Money: A rehabilitation incentive for mental patients. *American Journal of Psychiatry* 110: 84–92.

Peffer, P. A. (1955). The member-employee program. In VA Department of Medicine and Surgery program guide for psychiatry and neurology services, G-1, M-2, Part X, March 1955.

Pelletier, J., Ngyuen, M., Bradley, K., et al. (2005). Integrating structured physical exercise into an ICCD certified clubhouse program: Results of a pilot study. *Psychiatric Rehabilitation Journal* 29: 89–96.

Penk, W. E. (2000). Designing work environments for persons with serious mental disorders. In F. J. Frese (Ed.), *The role of organized psychology in treatment of the seriously mentally ill.* San Francisco: Jossey-Bass.

Penk, W. E. & Ainspan, N. D. (2009). Community response to returning military. In S. M. Freeman, B. A. Moore & A. Freeman (Eds.), *Living and surviving in harm's way: A psychological treatment handbook for pre- and post-deployment of military personnel* (pp. 417–436). New York: Routledge.

Penk, W. E., Charles, H. & Van Hoose, T. (1978). Comparative effectiveness of day hospital and inpatient psychiatric treatment. *Journal of Consulting and Clinical Psychology* 46: 94–101.

Penk, W. E., Drebing, C. E., Rosenheck, R., Krebs, C., Van Ormer, A. & Mueller, L. (2010). VHA transitional work experiences vs. job placement in veterans with co-occurring substance abuse and non-psychotic psychiatric disorders. *Psychiatric Rehabilitation Journal* 33: 297–307.

Penk, W. E., Drebing, C. & Schutt, R. (2002). PTSD in the workplace. In J. C. Thomas & M. Hersen (Eds.), *Handbook of mental health in the workplace.* Thousand Oaks, CA: Sage.

Penk, W. E. & Flannery, R. B. (2000). Psychosocial rehabilitation. In E. B. Foa, T. Keane & M. J. Friedman (Eds.), *Effective treatments for PTSD: Practice guidelines from the International Society for Traumatic Stress Studies.* New York: Guilford Press.

Penk, W. E. & Losonzcy, M. (1997). Psychosocial rehabilitation checklist. In T. Horvath (Ed.), *Management of persons with psychoses: Clinical guidelines.* Washington, DC: Department of Veterans Affairs.

Penn, D. L. & Mueser, K. T. (1996). Research update on the psychosocial treatment of schizophrenia. *American Journal of Psychiatry* 153, no. 5: 607–617.

President's New Freedom Commission on Mental Health. (2003). *Achieving the promise: Transforming mental health care in America: Final Report.* DHHS publication no. SMA-03-3832. Rockville, MD: DHHS.

Ratzlaff, S., McDiarmid, D., Marty, D. & Rapp, C. A. (2005). The Kansas consumer as provider program: Measuring the effects of a supported education initiative. *Community Mental Health Journal* 29, no. 3: 174–182.

Rog, D. J. (2006). The evidence on supported housing. *Psychiatric Rehabilitation Journal* 29: 334–344.

Rogers, E. S., Anthony, W., Lyass, A. & Penk, W. E. (2006). A randomized clinical trial of vocational rehabilitation among persons with serious mental disorders. *Rehabilitation Counseling Bulletin* 49: 143–156.

Sabatier, C. J. (2008). Education options. In N. D. Ainspan & W. E. Penk (Eds.), *Returning wars' wounded, injured, and ill.* Westport, CT: Greenwood/Praeger.

Schutt, R., Cournoyer, B., Penk, W., Drebing, C., Van Ormer, A., Krebs, C. & Losardo, M. (2003). Psychosocial rehabilitation with a Vets Construction Team. *Journal of Psychosocial Rehabilitation* 27: 186–189.

Schutt, R. K., Rosenheck, R. E., Penk, W. E., Drebing, C. E. & Seibyl, C. L. (2005). The social environment of transitional work and residences programs: Influences of health and functioning. *Evaluation and Programs Planning* 28: 291–300.

Schutt, R. K., Weinstein, B. & Penk, W. E. (2005). Housing preferences of homeless veterans with dual diagnoses. *Psychiatric Services* 56: 350–352.

Sherman, M. D., Sautter, F., Lyons, J. A., Manguno-Mire, G. M., Han, X., Perry, D., et al. (2005). Mental health needs of cohabiting partners of Vietnam veterans with combat-related PTSD. *Psychiatric Services* 56: 1150–1152.

Sherman, M. D. & Sherman, D. M. (2005). *Finding my way: A teen's guide to living with a parent who has experienced trauma.* Edina, MN: Beaver Pond Press.

Smelson, D. A., Sawh, L., Kane, V., Kuhn, J. & Ziedonis, D. (2011). *The Mission-VET: Treatment manual.* Washington, DC: VHA Research Development. www.research.va.gov.

Smith-Osborne, A. (2009). Does the GI Bill support educational attainment of veterans with disabilities? Implications for current veterans in resuming civilian life. *Journal of Sociology and Social Welfare* 36: 111–125.

Solomon, P. & Draine, J. (1995). One-year outcomes of a randomized trial of case management with seriously mentally ill clients leaving jail. *Evaluation Review* 19: 256–274.

Stein, L. L. & Test, M. A. (1980). Alternative to mental hospital treatment: I. conceptual model, treatment program, and clinical evaluation. *Archives of General Psychiatry* 37: 392–397.

Stenger, C. A. (2007). A view from the top. In R. R. Baker (Ed.), *Stories from VA psychology* (pp. 65–72). Bloomington, IN: Author House. (Available for a fee from www.authorhouse.com.)

Tsemberis, S. & Eisenberg, R. F. (2000). Pathways to housing: Supported housing for street-swelling homeless individuals with psychiatric disabilities. *Psychiatric Services* 51: 487–493.

Tsuang, M., Woolson, R. & Fleming, J. (1979). Long-term outcome of major psychosis. *Archives of General Psychiatry* 36: 1295–1301.

Turner, S. M., Beidel, D. C. & Frueh, B. C. (2005). Multicomponent behavioral treatment for chronic combat-related posttraumatic stress disorder: Trauma management therapy. *Behavior Modification* 29: 39–69.

Unger, K. V., Pardee, R. & Shafer, M. S. (2000). Outcomes of postsecondary supported education programs for people with psychiatric disabilities. *Journal of Vocational Rehabilitation* 14: 195–199.

U.S. Department of Veterans Affairs. (2005). *Recommendations of the Recovery Transformation Work Group to the executive committee of the Mental Health Steering Committee.* Washington, DC: Author.

U.S. Department of Veterans Affairs. (2009). *VHA Handbook 1160 for uniform mental health services in VA medical centers and clinics.* Washington, DC: Author.

U.S. Substance Abuse and Mental Health Services Administration. (2002). *Mental health system transformation, evidence based practices implementation resource kits.* Rockville, MD: Author.

Waldrop. R. S. (2007). The beginning of counseling psychology in VA hospitals. In R. R. Baker (Ed.), *Stories from VA psychology* (pp. 127–134). Bloomington, IN: Author House. (Available from www.authorhouse.com.)

Watkins, K., Hunter, S., Wenzel, S., et al. (2004). Prevalence and characteristics of clients with co-occurring disorders in outpatient substance abuse treatment. *American Journal of Drug and Alcohol Abuse* 30, no. 4: 749–764.

Psychosocial Rehabilitation and Recovery Services

Samantha Kettle, Loretta E. Braxton,
Valerie Fox, and Joshua Tiegreen

Introduction

Psychiatric rehabilitation, also known as psychosocial rehabilitation, has become a frequently cited intervention in mental healthcare, both in the community and in the Department of Veterans Affairs (VA) healthcare system. But what does it mean, and how does psychiatric rehabilitation relate to recovery? For many in the healthcare field, the term *rehabilitation* is "familiar, contested and occasionally confusing" (Roberts et al. 2006, xv), due in part to its broad application across many fields and to many different life arenas. Anthony, Cohen, and Cohen (1984) described psychiatric rehabilitation as "improving the psychiatrically disturbed person's capabilities and competence by bringing about behavioral improvement in their environment of need" (140). As described in Anthony's definition, psychiatric rehabilitation is the application of measures and interventions aimed at improving an individual's abilities; it is an act carried out by clinicians, providers, and other specialist services (Roberts et al. 2006). In contrast, recovery is individually defined and owned by the consumer and does not necessarily need specialist skills and services to occur. Per Pat Deegan (1988), rehabilitation is seen as a professional and service process and recovery as the aim and the desired outcome. In healthcare practices, there has been some difficulty separating the two terms. As a way to ensure both methods are utilized, the current movement has been to extend the terms by speaking of "rehabilitation and recovery services" when discussing these services or goals.

History of Psychiatric Rehabilitation and Recovery

The U.S. Psychiatric Rehabilitation Association (USPRA), founded in 1974 by the directors of the original thirteen psychosocial rehabilitation centers in the United States, defined psychiatric rehabilitation as rehabilitation that "promotes recovery, full community integration and improved quality of life for persons who have been diagnosed with any mental health condition that seriously impairs their ability to lead meaningful lives" (U.S. Psychiatric Rehabilitation Association 2012; Anthony et al. 1986). Its mission is to ensure that a person with a psychiatric disability can perform those skills needed to live, learn, and work as independently as possible in his or her own environment with the least amount of professional assistance or intervention. By teaching skills and modifying or adding environmental supports, individuals with psychiatric disabilities will be more adept at performing the roles and functions in their daily lives (Liberman 1988), promoting increased participation and quality of life.

Psychiatric rehabilitation had its inception in several historical events, including the moral treatment era, the inclusion of psychiatric disabilities into publicly supported vocational rehabilitation programs, the advancement of the community mental health ideology and deinstitutionalization, the psychosocial rehabilitation center movement, and the use of skills training techniques as effective mental health interventions (Anthony & Liberman 1986). Moral treatment, first introduced in 1801 by Phillippe Pinel and William Tuke, advocated humane care for individuals with mental illness (Peloquin 1989). The basic premise of moral treatment was that if people were treated with respect and dignity and given an opportunity to engage in meaningful occupations and roles, their ability to function would improve and they could regain many of their normal habits and behaviors. Consistent with present-day psychiatric rehabilitation, the moral treatment era demonstrated the importance of examining the natural contexts of those with mental illness and the premise that structured activities can have therapeutic value (Anthony & Liberman 1986). In 1943, amendments to the U.S. Vocational Rehabilitation Act extended vocational rehabilitation services and financial support to individuals with psychiatric disabilities; this legitimized the idea of rehabilitation for those with psychiatric disabilities and provided the opportunity to promote psychiatric rehabilitation in the vocational arena (Anthony & Liberman 1986). In the late 1950s and early 1960s, legislation was introduced that endorsed the idea of mental health parity, which demanded that there be equal benefits offered for physical and mental healthcare (U.S. Department of Labor 2008). With these changes, a new belief prevailed that mental illness did not necessitate removal from society to large mental institutions; rather, individuals with severe mental illness should be helped to live in the community of their choice in as normal a manner as possible (Anthony & Liberman 1986). This signified the beginning of the deinstitutionalization process, which transpired during the 1960s and 1970s.

One of the primary objectives of the deinstitutionalization movement was preparing those living within institutions for placement back into the community. In contrast with the closing of inpatient institutions, community mental health centers became the paradigm for treatment of persons with serious mental illness, with the goal that people would spend less time in the hospital and more time in the community. However, these changes faced several challenges. Funding for community resources remained scarce, and policies continued to focus on symptom management rather than improved functioning or role achievement for the consumer. Given these continued challenges, numerous advocacy groups used the opportunity to promote psychiatric rehabilitation and recovery. Anthony (1993) claimed that the failures in the implementation of the deinstitutionalization policies and the lack of community resources during this time actually sowed the seeds of recovery, because society was confronted with individuals who needed and wanted more than just symptom relief. Beginning in the 1970s, national advocacy groups and proponents of recovery proposed necessary changes to implement psychiatric rehabilitation services. In 1978 the National Conference on the Chronic Mental Client, sponsored by the American Psychiatric Association in collaboration with the President's Commission on Mental Health, was held in Washington, D.C., to address the inadequacies of care, treatment, and rehabilitation for individuals with mental illness (Liberman 1988). In the mid-1970s the National Institute on Mental Health (NIMH) held a series of meetings through which the community support system (CSS) was developed, which described how adequate services could be delivered in the community to best support individuals with long-term psychiatric disabilities. Based on this framework, the Center for Psychiatric Rehabilitation redefined the services needed to meet the fundamental needs and wants of individuals with severe mental illness, which has assisted many state and local planners and administrators in incorporating recovery-oriented, rehabilitation-focused services into their healthcare system (Anthony 2000).

Despite the many changes in both legislation and societal beliefs about psychiatric disabilities, it was not until the 1980s that psychiatric rehabilitation gained significant attention, due in large part to consumer publications and the empirical work of Harding and her associates, most notably her longitudinal recovery study (Harding 1987). Her research contrasted many of the existing beliefs that long-term mental illness and deteriorating function were the norm; instead, her three-decades-long research study examined the factors contributing to systemwide differences in consumer's recovery and revealed that recovery from mental illness was happening. In conjunction with additional publications, both research-based and first-person consumer accounts of recovery, mental health professionals began to formulate theoretical and practical models of recovery that could be adapted for use in psychiatric rehabilitation (Bleuler 1972; Ogawa et al. 1987; Jacobson & Greenley 2001). Psychiatric rehabilitation in the 1980s emphasized that mental illness was not only associated with mental impairments and symptoms, but more important, caused the person significant functional limitations, disabilities, and handicaps (Anthony 1982).

In the 1990s, described as "the decade of recovery" (Anthony 1993), psychiatric rehabilitation thrived and became a critical component utilized in numerous state and county mental health systems of care (Anthony 2000). The Boston University Center for Psychiatric Rehabilitation developed a model for designing recovery-oriented services (Jacobsen & Greenley 2001), which included four major consequences of mental illness: impairment, dysfunction, disability, and disadvantage. Through this model, recovery-oriented and rehabilitation services were able to direct services for specific reasons, such as symptom relief, case management, enrichment, and basic support, which guided rehabilitation professionals.

Policies Influencing Implementation of Rehabilitation and Recovery Services

Within the past decade, the implementation of rehabilitation services and recovery principles has become an increased focus in governmental systems, including the VA healthcare system. The earliest organization that addressed the burgeoning focus on recovery principles and psychiatric rehabilitation was the President's New Freedom Commission on Mental Health. In April 2002 President George W. Bush announced the need for improved mental healthcare services as part of his commitment to eliminate inequality for Americans with disabilities. He directed the Commission to identify policies that could be implemented by federal, state, and local governments to maximize the utility of existing resources, improve coordination of treatments and services, and promote successful community integration for adults with a serious mental illness and children with a serious emotional disturbance. The Commission articulated hope for successful recovery in their vision statement:

> We envision a future where everyone with a mental illness will recover, a future when mental illnesses can be prevented or cured, a future when mental illnesses

are detected early, and a future when everyone with a mental illness at any stage of life has access to effective treatment and supports—essentials for living, working, learning, and participating fully in the community. (President's New Freedom Commission on Mental Health 2003)

As part of the New Freedom Initiative, the president identified three primary obstacles preventing Americans with mental illness from getting appropriate care: the stigma that surrounds mental illness, unfair treatment limitations and financial requirements placed on mental health benefits in private health insurance, and the fragmented mental health service delivery system. The Commission identified the primary goal of a transformed system as recovery, which they defined as the process through which people are able to live, work, learn, and participate fully in their communities. In a transformed system, consumers would have access to accurate information, an individualized plan of care, an increased partnership in choosing their mental healthcare professionals, and shared decision making in their treatment plans. In addition, the Commission concluded that successful transformation of the mental healthcare system primarily relied on two principles: Mental health services and treatments must be consumer- and family-centered, and care must focus on increasing consumers' ability to successfully cope with life's challenges, facilitating recovery, and building resilience.

Given the complexity of mental healthcare revealed by their findings, the Commission noted the importance of making a system more seamless, convenient, consumer-driven, and based on efficacious practices. To successfully transform the mental health system, the Commission proposed the following six goals: 1) Americans must understand that mental health is essential to overall health; 2) mental healthcare should be consumer- and family-driven; 3) disparities in mental health services must be eliminated; 4) early mental health screening, assessment, and referral to services should become common practice; 5) excellent mental healthcare should be delivered and research should be accelerated; and 6) technology should be used to access mental healthcare and information.

Following the report by the New Freedom Commission, several agencies, including the Substance Abuse and Mental Health Services Administration (SAMHSA), mental health experts, researchers, consumers, and family members convened the National Consensus Conference on Mental Health Recovery and Mental Health Systems Transformation in 2004. The purpose of the conference was to more clearly define recovery. The subsequent *National Consensus Statement on Mental Health Recovery* established ten fundamental components of recovery: "Self-direction, Individualized and Person-Centered, Empowerment, Holistic, Non-linear, Strengths-based, Peer support, Respect, Responsibility, and Hope" (2004).

Shortly thereafter, the Veterans Health Administration (VHA) revised its handbooks to address the goals of the New Freedom Commission and incorporate the components of recovery as defined by the *National Consensus Statement on Mental Health Recovery* (2004). In 2007 VHA established procedures for enabling healthcare staff to support advance care planning for veterans, including psychiatric advance directives (PAD), which are written statements that allow people to declare preferences and instructions for future mental health treatment should they lose decision-making capacity, including preferences to receive or refuse certain interventions, including medications.

In 2008 the *VHA Handbook 1160.01: Uniform Mental Health Services in VA Medical Centers and Clinics* (Department of Veterans Affairs 2008) specified new requirements for VA medical centers and community-based outpatient clinics in order to ensure all veterans have access to mental health services. The guiding principle leading the change was the belief that mental healthcare is an essential component of overall healthcare. Subsequently, the primary responsibilities of mental health services, including those that address substance abuse, were revised to address the new requirements. First, mental healthcare should be integrated or coordinated with all other components of overall healthcare. In addition, every veteran seen in mental health services is provided a principal mental health provider, and this must remain clear when the veteran is seen in multiple programs. Furthermore, the principal mental health provider must ensure 1) regular contact as needed, 2) that a psychiatrist reviews psychiatric medications on a regular basis, 3) coordination of the veteran's treatment plan within a shared decision framework, 4) appropriate monitoring and documentation of treatment plans, 5) revised treatment plans when necessary, 6) that the veteran verbally consents to the treatment plan, and 7) collaboration with the suicide prevention coordinator (SCP) to support identification of veterans who are considered a high risk. Correspondingly, all VHA emergency departments (EDs) were required to have mental health coverage by an independent, licensed mental health provider (i.e., a psychiatrist, psychologist, social worker, or advanced practice nurse) either on-site or on call, on a 24/7 basis, providing greater access to services.

To address potential barriers to implementation of this new model, the *VHA Handbook* (Department of Veterans Affairs 2008) required that each Veterans Service Integrated Network (VISN) include a mental health professional as a member of its principal decision-making body. Mental health leadership at each facility was given the responsibility of building coherent, coordinated programs. To support this goal, each VA medical center was required to establish and maintain a mental health executive council, which includes representation from core professional disciplines and is responsible for proposing strategies to improve care; improve coordination among departments; and review the mental health impact of facility-wide policies, such as policies on veteran rights, restraints and seclusion, management of suicidal behavior, and management of mental health emergencies.

In addition to developing a greater mental health leadership at each facility, the new handbook promoted changes within the overall VA healthcare system to promote recovery-oriented practices. Some of these changes included improved community-based facilities, recognition of gender-specific issues, and an increased focus on utilizing recovery-based positions and programs, including local recovery coordinators, psychosocial rehabilitation and recovery centers, Mental Health Intensive Case Management (MHICM) teams, and therapeutic supported employment programs. In addition, the handbook formulated a consensus of fundamental components of recovery within the VA system, which would serve as guidelines for transforming mental health services into a recovery-oriented model.

Principles of Psychosocial Recovery in the VA System

Recovery is the idea that life has options and choices and that there is hope for the life that one wants to have despite the limitations presented by mental illness. It involves becoming expert in one's own care, regaining control over one's life, and taking responsibility for getting to where one wants to be in life. Recovery is a very individual process; however, several key concepts guide and shape the recovery process and should be considered throughout an individual's recovery. To promote the recovery process, VA adopted the ten fundamental components of recovery based on the *National Consensus Statement on Mental Health Recovery* (SAMSHA 2004) and added components relevant to VA services, to establish the following fourteen principles of recovery in VA care: "Self-direction, Individualized and Person-Centered, Empowerment, Holistic, Non-linear, Strengths-based, Peer Support, Respect, Responsibility, Hope, Privacy, Security, Honor, and Support for VA Veteran Rights." Table 12.1 contains a list of VA recovery principles and the differences between traditional medical models of care and recovery-based care.

Self-Direction

Self-direction is the idea that an individual directs his or her own life, independent of the control or influence of others. The recovery process must be self-directed by the individual, who is defining his or her own life goals and determining the path he or she will take to reach those goals.

Table 12.1. Principles of Recovery

	Provider Using a Traditional Medical Model Approach	Provider Using a Recovery-based Approach
Self-Direction	Tells the veteran what the treatment will be.	Collaborates with the veteran about treatment.
Individualized and Person-Centered	Matches diagnosis with an intervention.	Learns about the person's experience with the problem.
Empowerment	Choices ultimately made by experts.	Choices ultimately made by veteran.
Holistic	Focuses on own specialty area in treatment.	Works with interdisciplinary team to address whole person.
Nonlinear	Views progress as a steady path.	Acknowledges setbacks and relapses as part of healing.
Strengths-based	Only interested in problems people struggle with.	Includes positive aspects of the person's life.
Peer Support	Does not often acknowledge or encourage peer support; expects veteran to rely on professionals for help.	Values peers and includes them in treatment, both in VA and the larger community.
Respect	Expects it from veterans.	Expects to both give it to and receive it from veterans.
Responsibility	Often takes an all-or-nothing approach wherein it is either his/her responsibility to cure or veteran's responsibility to change.	Takes a middle ground approach wherein roles of both provider and veteran are acknowledged and appreciated.
Hope	Sometimes neglects hope due to preparing people for the chronic nature of problems.	Actively instills hope to encourage healing, while also staying realistic about potential outcomes.
Privacy	Maintains confidentiality.	Maintains confidentiality, but also actively discusses and plans with veterans.
Security	Highly values safety and protection.	Shares responsibility for safety and protection with veteran when possible.
Honor	Does not often incorporate dignity of the veteran.	Acknowledges veteran's dignity.
Support for VA Client Rights	Sometimes labels veterans "difficult," "noncompliant," or "failing treatment" when they assert personal rights.	Incorporates rights of both provider and veteran in attempt to find a treatment that works for the individual.

This is a key principle in the recovery model, because in order for an individual to recover, he or she must make choices based on what he or she values and wants in life. Providers cannot dictate a cure, but rather must encourage individuals to define their own goals and hopes for treatment. In this way, veterans are regaining control, independence, and autonomy over their own lives and taking responsibility for the choices they make. Thus when problems arise, they are viewed through the lens of the veteran's personally meaningful goals rather than as abstract or clinical definitions. Self-direction also provides a normalizing feeling, which is often missing in the lives of individuals with mental illness.

> *Example.* A veteran has been chronically depressed for twenty years. He has gotten used to being told by providers what to do and often becomes hopeless when treatment does not seem to be working. In addition, he is quick to reject suggestions from others and always has a reason why nothing will work or change in his life. Using a recovery approach, the veteran is encouraged to define his own goals for treatment and asked how he would measure success. He states that he wants to be less depressed so he can be in a meaningful relationship and not feel so lonely. His subsequent treatment incorporates his goal to have meaningful relationships and provides relevant social skills training and identifies opportunities to meet people. Thus outcomes are not measured only based on depression ratings, but also on his social network. Success is dependent upon the steps he actively takes to reach his identified goals rather than waiting for providers to "cure" him.

Individualized and Person-Centered

As stated previously, recovery is a very personal endeavor and by definition must be a journey that is self-directed by the individual. During the recovery process, the individual defines his or her life goals and designs a unique path toward those goals. There are multiple pathways to recovery, and the process will be different for every individual, based on that individual's unique strengths and resiliencies, needs, preferences, experiences, and cultural background.

As clinicians use tools to assist someone in the recovery process, it is crucial to maintain a person-centered approach to care, in which systems adapt to the person based on his or her needs and preferences rather than expecting the person to adapt to the services offered by the system. In other words, providers approach each individual where he or she is currently at in life and incorporate many aspects of that person to collaborate on the best treatment available. Evidence-based practices are used to guide treatment, but with the knowledge that one solution will not fit every person presenting for care, as each person is impacted by many dynamics in his or her life, regardless of diagnosis.

Example. A veteran is referred for post-traumatic stress disorder (PTSD) treatment due to a combat experience. She answers the clinician's questions briefly, but is hesitant to provide additional information. Using a recovery approach, the clinician asks a wide range of questions to get a sense of this veteran's life experience. Through additional questioning, it is discovered that she was also physically abused as a child, was often sexually harassed in the service, and is uncomfortable coming for treatment due to the largely male population at VA. With this knowledge, the provider is able to work with the veteran to create a treatment plan that acknowledges her experiences and addresses her concerns. Because the veteran does not want to travel and there is not a women's health clinic nearby, they decide to meet late in the day when there are fewer veterans in the clinic and to initially focus on developing safe coping skills.

Empowerment

Empowerment refers to the process of gaining or regaining the power and control over one's own life that is necessary for self-determination, dignity, autonomy, and responsibility (Peters 2003). It involves acknowledging that the individual is the expert about his or her own life and that he or she has the knowledge and experience to move toward recovery. It requires that individuals have opportunities to assume responsibility for their own lives and well-being and to freely choose their own paths to recovery and well-being. Gaining a sense of control over illness is accomplished by developing effective coping skills, use of regular medication, social supports, stable housing, collaboration with treatment team, financial resources, and access to services (Spaniol et al. 2002).

Another key component of empowerment is learning how to self-advocate. Because recovery is an individual process with the goal of promoting personal responsibility, choice, hope, empowerment, and ultimately recovery from mental illness, the ability to self-advocate is essential to helping consumers take control over their own recovery and assert their rights. Self-advocacy is also essential to rebuilding self-esteem and a sense of self-efficacy (Mead & Copeland 2000). Clinicians can help to facilitate someone's personal empowerment by reserving judgments and personal opinions, not attaching someone's choices and decisions to a symptom of mental illness, and not imposing their own expectations and ideas onto the individual (Peters 2003).

Example. A veteran has been in the VA system for thirty years. He introduces himself by saying, "Hello, My name is X and I'm a schizophrenic." He is used to others making choices for him and waits for permission from care providers rather than taking proactive steps in his life. Using a recovery approach, practitioners begin to ask him his opinion and listen to his responses. At first he is very quick to parrot what care providers have told him, but with time he begins to express his thoughts. Eventually he says he would like to live in his own apartment rather than stay in group homes. He has been waiting for ten years for someone to allow him to do this. Care providers work with him to create a list of what he would need to make this decision and encourage him to start working toward this goal. During this time, providers keep reminding him of the choices he is making and that he is ultimately responsible for his progress. For example, he is unable to save money and gets frustrated. Providers work with him to identify his various choices, such as to continue the same way, get a payee, or attend money management classes. He initially asks care providers to decide, but then chooses to use a payee to help him save money. With these choices, Mr. X also begins to talk about more aspects of his life outside of his diagnosis: his love of music, his experiences growing up as a black man in the South, and wanting to provide for his family. He starts to express himself more freely and is willing to be more assertive with people in authority roles at times, rather than remaining passive.

Holistic

Recovery encompasses an individual's whole life, including mind, body, spirit, and community, and these aspects cannot be separated out from one another. It is impossible to address a single component of an individual's life, such as substance use, without addressing all of the other areas, because all areas impact one another. Recovery requires a person to address the effects of being identified as someone with a psychiatric disability, including, but not limited to, social isolation, inadequate housing, poverty, unemployment, rejection by society, lack of purpose, and loss of control over his or her life (Davidson et al. 2005; Davidson 2003; Deegan 1996). Therefore, in recovery an individual's whole being must be considered, including past and present experiences, cultural background, the community in which the person lives, and how the individual views himself or herself as a person.

Example. A veteran has been diagnosed with schizophrenia and presents for substance abuse treatment. During the initial assessment, the veteran reported paranoia and distrust of authority. Upon further discussion, he is initially guarded but reports experiencing racism throughout his life when asked about it by the clinician. The veteran details incidents during his service in Vietnam when he felt his life was in danger from fellow soldiers due to being African American and explains that he began drinking alcohol to feel less nervous and to sleep. He states that his drinking soon became difficult to control, and he did not know how to readjust upon returning from war. The veteran spoke about having difficulties retaining employment due to his drinking and revealed that he is currently staying with various family members for housing. Within this context, the practitioner has a much better conceptualization of the veteran's experience and can address the whole person, rather than segments of different problems. The practitioner works with other services (including homeless services and vocational rehabilitation) to help the veteran reach his individual goals and not overpathologize the veteran's experience.

Nonlinear

Recovery is a lifetime process, not an outcome, and it does not always follow a linear trajectory or a step-by-step progression. It involves continual growth and occasional setbacks. It is important to understand this concept, set realistic expectations at the beginning of the journey, and realize that there are learning opportunities throughout the process.

> *Example.* A veteran has been working with her counselor for three months. She had been treated for bipolar disorder and was making steady progress. Over the past several sessions, she was reporting fewer symptoms, was working more, and was socializing more often with her friends. However, she reported having suicidal thoughts during their recent session. Fortunately, rather than viewing treatment as a failure, they had already prepared for the possibility of this recurrence. The veteran utilized her wellness recovery action plan (WRAP) (Copeland 2002) to review her daily maintenance plan and remember coping strategies for this warning sign. She applied these skills and did not require additional changes. However, she also created a psychiatric advanced directive with her counselor to be prepared in case she requires hospitalization in the future.

Strengths-based

Using strengths means that recovery focuses on valuing and building on the multiple capacities, resiliencies, talents, abilities, and inherent worth of individuals. Rather than focusing on negative aspects of the individual or how these aspects impede progress, recovery focuses on the strengths of the individual to overcome obstacles. By building on these strengths, consumers leave behind stymied life roles and engage in new ones.

It may be difficult to identify strengths at the beginning of treatment, but there is always at least one thing that is working in the veteran's favor. Similar to the practices utilized in positive psychology, focusing on what is working for the person and nurturing innate talents can allow people to thrive. Strengths are anything that helps the person move forward to lead a more fulfilling life and can vary from a love of dance to reliable transportation.

> *Example.* A veteran was depressed and anxious for several months. He was often isolated and stayed inside his house. He worried that others would judge him and he would always end up a failure. The veteran and his therapist used cognitive strategies to challenge his negative assumptions and develop more adaptive styles of thinking. The veteran often smiled when speaking about his

grandchildren, and they identified his joy in children as a strength. Utilizing this appreciation, he began to explore volunteer opportunities to spend more time with children. There were numerous options in the community and he found a program near his home. He continued to express mild feelings of depression and anxiety, but as he progressed he began to leave his house more frequently and reported that his mood improved on the days he volunteered with children.

Peer Support

Over the past three decades, peer-run services for those diagnosed with psychiatric disabilities have increasingly grown in number and diversity. Assisting in this progression was the passage of the Americans with Disabilities Act (1990), which made it illegal to discriminate based on a history of psychiatric disability. Subsequently, the mental health system is now collaborating with and incorporating more people who have been diagnosed with psychiatric disabilities.

Peer-led services fall under the category of psychosocial interventions and usually include vocational training, social support, and psychoeducation. Researchers have found that engaging in peer-led services increases an individual's feelings of hopefulness, support, confidence, and gained self-understanding (Davidson et al. 1999; Davidson et al. 2005; Mead & Copeland 2000). In addition, within peer-led services there have been findings of strong ethnic minority representation (as opposed to distrust of traditional services and support groups), informal referral sources (e.g., family, self, friends), support of local mental health services, and roles other than "mental patient" offered to consumers (Davidson et al. 1999).

> *Example.* A veteran is referred for services, but is suspicious of treatment because he was subjected to involuntary treatments while hospitalized during psychotic episodes. Upon arrival at the clinic, he is able to speak with a peer who has had similar experiences. The peer support specialist validates the veteran's concerns and assists him with identifying the pros and cons of participating in treatment. The veteran feels more at ease talking with his peer, but also feels relief that the clinic values peer involvement and respects people diagnosed with mental illness.

Respect

Respect has two meanings: respect for one another and self-respect. The respect of oneself is the kind wherein you care for yourself in healthy ways. Respect for oneself and others ensures the inclusion and full participation of consumers in all aspects of their lives. However, it is also important to note that definitions of respect can vary widely depending on cultural and personal norms. Thus it is important for providers to clarify what constitutes respect for themselves, as well as for the veterans they serve. Individual, community, and societal acceptance and appreciation of consumers, including protecting their rights and eliminating discrimination and stigma, are crucial in achieving recovery.

> *Example.* A veteran presents for services and is referred to by her first name, although she is much older than the attending doctor. The doctor does not make eye contact while talking to her, and the veteran feels rushed out the door. Furthermore, the doctor refers to her as "another borderline" while consulting with a colleague in the hallway. She does not return for treatment, but continues to utilize emergency services when needed. Eventually, during an inpatient hospitalization, she works with a provider with a recovery-focused orientation. The doctor asks her how she wants to be referred to (Mrs. X, Captain X, first name, etc.). The doctor also looks at her while she is speaking, but explains that she is in a rush and will need to leave soon. The doctor also tells her what her diagnosis is—borderline personality disorder—and describes briefly what it means. They review some treatment options, and the doctor shares her opinion about the importance of outpatient treatment. The veteran is still apprehensive, but feels respected and is more likely to engage in treatment.

Responsibility

Personal responsibility is an individual being responsible for his or her own wellness and personal recovery journey. According to Mead and Copeland (2000), personal responsibility involves a change from victimhood to actively working at one's own healing and recovery. Consumers must take responsibility for understanding and giving meaning to their experiences to promote their own wellness and recovery.

Mutual responsibility is the idea that everyone has a responsibility to aid in an individual's recovery process. Although recovery is an individual process and ultimately an individual is personally responsible for his or her own recovery, all people involved in an individual's life have a mutual responsibility to support and assist that individual on his or her recovery journey. Collaborative relationships between providers and consumers empower both parties and allow for meaningful power sharing and a more mutual assumption of responsibility (Jacobson & Greenley 2001).

> *Example.* A veteran had been actively engaged in treatment, but has missed his last two sessions. Rather than waiting for the veteran to contact the clinic, the provider places an outreach call to remind the veteran about treatment options.

The veteran admits to feeling ashamed of some recent behavior and is hesitant to return to treatment. The provider reminds the veteran that he is ultimately responsible for his life and choices, but that treatment can also be altered if necessary to help him be more successful in reaching his goals. They reschedule to meet the following week.

Hope

Hope is the belief or feeling that what we wish for or want can be had and is considered the "catalyst" of the recovery process. According to Davidson and colleagues (2005), recovery involves "incorporation of one's illness within the context of a sense of hopefulness about one's future, particularly about one's ability to rebuild a positive sense of self and social identity despite remaining mentally ill" (16). In other words, hope is the idea that people can and do overcome the barriers and obstacles confronting them to live the lives that they want to live, despite the impairments of mental illness.

Strauss (2005) also wrote about the possibility of recovery and noted the tendency for mental health professionals to ignore research about positive outcomes for those diagnosed with psychiatric disabilities. In particular, he reported being disheartened by the apparent lack of practical integration of the findings of the World Health Organization (1973), which stated that people tend to recover from severe mental illness. Strauss (2005) hypothesized that clinicians may add to the self-fulfilling prophecy that diagnoses, such as schizophrenia, are chronic and incurable, and ignore the international research literature that continues to dispute this notion.

In response, Deegan (1996) utilized case studies, and her own story as a person with a long-term mental illness, to highlight the importance of hope and the transactional nature of the individual and the environment. In addition, Harding and Zahniser (1994) recommended informing newly diagnosed patients that worldwide data show most people recover from psychiatric disabilities and that clinicians should promote hope and the self-healing capacity within patients.

> *Example.* A veteran is newly diagnosed with PTSD and has been given a service claim for disability. She has watched news reports and spoken with other veterans who have been struggling with symptoms of PTSD for decades. She has little faith that things could ever improve and is hesitant to engage in therapy due to fears about talking about her traumas. Her medical provider talks with her about her PTSD diagnosis and explains services available at VA and the local vet center. The provider explains the success rate of various talk therapies, including cognitive processing therapy (CPT) and prolonged exposure (PE). She also acknowledges that things can get worse before they get better in trauma

treatment. The doctor provides some materials for the veteran to take home and suggests watching some online videos about veterans who have received PTSD treatment. The veteran leaves the appointment feeling more hopeful about her choices.

Privacy

Self-disclosure is a controversial, highly individual decision that an individual with mental illness must make. Whether or not to disclose his or her mental illness to employers, family, friends, loved ones, and neighbors is not an easy decision. It is important for an individual to understand his or her rights related to privacy and self-disclosure and for providers to respect those decisions as much as possible. An individual with mental illness is guaranteed the same rights as others related to privacy of medical records and personal information. These factors should be taken into consideration when deciding where or when to receive treatment or care.

> *Example.* A veteran's mother calls the VA emergency department because she is worried about her son, whose behavior has become increasingly erratic. She believes he has been hospitalized at VA and wants to make sure he is safe. The provider checks his records, and there is no current release of information or psychiatric advanced directive that allows care providers to speak with family if he is incapacitated. The provider verbally sympathizes with the mother's concern and worry, but explains the limits of confidentiality.

> *Example.* A provider runs into a veteran from group therapy while they are with their respective families. The provider has already explained in sessions that he will not acknowledge clients in public unless they approach him directly. The veteran waves at the provider and smiles. The provider smiles back and says hello. When asked how they know each other, the veteran responds "from the VA" and they discuss the beautiful day. Later, the provider's wife asks if he was a client, and the provider says "I just know him from the VA."

Security

Security is defined as a state of being free of danger and injury. An important part of recovery is being safe, and VA has identified this as a specific principle in services. Not only is privacy important, but a general sense of well-being and protection is a basic right of all individuals. This principle can sometimes come into conflict with other principles, as providers may view security risks differently than veterans. These situations require shared decision making, but may also require a provider to engage in his or her expert role to ensure safety for the individual.

Example. A veteran presents to the clinic reporting suicidal thoughts with intent and a plan. The veteran clearly states that she does not want to be hospitalized, but is also unable to articulate a plan to ensure her safety in the community. The therapist wants to encourage the veteran's independence, but also has the duty to protect. The therapist petitions for an involuntary commitment, and the veteran is hospitalized. The next day, the therapist visits the veteran on the unit. The veteran is upset about being hospitalized, but also acknowledges she was not safe at home. The therapist validates the veteran's feelings and experience, and they agree to discuss the situation at more length at their next session following her discharge.

Honor

Veterans are honored for their services to our country, and they are treated in a way that acknowledges their sacrifice. In general, *honor* refers to self-dignity and a sense of integrity and good character. From a veteran's perspective, honor involves taking pride in oneself and taking steps to maintain a good sense of character, honesty, and self-respect. Furthermore, honor involves recognizing their previous struggles and their own uniqueness, and building on their strengths, including the recognition of their service to our country. From a provider's perspective, honor refers to treating our veterans with respect for their service and dignity for their personhood. Recognition of the veteran's sacrifice and service contributes to the veteran's recovery in a variety of ways, including instilling hope, empowerment, and respect.

Example. A veteran has been attending treatment for a mood disorder at his local VA for several years. Providers only asked about the veteran's service during the initial appointment. During that appointment, the veteran acknowledged earning a ranking of E-6, staff sergeant prior to his discharge, which is something of which he was very proud. Over the past several weeks the veteran has been feeling down and reported feelings of low self-esteem and self-efficacy. His provider focused on the veteran's military service and recognized that the veteran needed to possess certain skills and abilities in order to earn his ranking of staff sergeant. The veteran reported that he has been ignoring his service accomplishments or discounting them when feeling down. He reported feeling more empowered and hopeful after this discussion.

Support for VA Veteran Rights

An individual with mental health difficulties is afforded the same rights as any other VA veteran. Integral in these rights is the right to choose whether to pursue services or treatment. Recovery involves choices; it involves deciding what actions an individual is willing to take and choosing what he or she wants in life. Integral in making choices is having a variety of options to choose from.

Although treatment providers can offer options and professional opinions, it is ultimately the individual's choice how he or she proceeds on the recovery path. In recovery, an individual has the right to choose which services he or she wants to participate in, if any, and what goal(s) to pursue. It is essential to review the veteran's rights prior to treatment and to make sure that he or she fully understands them, as this is important for empowerment, self-direction, and individually centered care, which are all fundamental aspects of the recovery process.

> ***Example.*** A veteran presents for treatment of schizoaffective disorder. The therapist strongly recommends social skills training to help him reach his goal of gaining more friends. However, the veteran is reluctant due to dislike of groups. In addition, the veteran has not had a medical exam in over two years and refuses to see a PCP at this time. Rather than label this veteran "difficult" or "noncompliant." the therapist asks what type of help the veteran would like and explores potential barriers to treatment. At the same time, the therapist continues to share all treatment options and explain why she believes certain approaches might be beneficial.

Development within VA

As noted, the *VHA Handbook* (Department of Veterans Affairs 2008) propelled VA toward more fully embracing psychosocial rehabilitation and mental health recovery in services for veterans. Numerous programs and positions were generated to create and sustain these principles, including local recovery coordinator (LRC), Mental Health Intensive Case Management (MHICM) & RANGE, Psychosocial Rehabilitation & Recovery Center (PRRC), supported employment, peer services, consumer/liaison services, family services, as well as other programs within the VA system. (See table 12.2 for a brief description of programs.) All of these programs offer services fundamentally founded in the principles of psychosocial rehabilitation and recovery; however, each program offers unique services to accommodate the holistic needs of veterans.

Local Recovery Coordinator (LRC)

Deployed at each medical center to lead recovery transformation for mental health, each LRC develops a recovery plan for that center and addresses issues of stigma. The LRCs provide education and training to both veterans and VA staff and apply the recovery principles in action. Their activities may include organizing recovery-themed conferences, training staff about integrating

Table 12.2. New Recovery-based Programs

Program Name	Purpose	Number of Programs in 2009/2010
Local Recovery Coordinators (LRC)	Lead recovery transformation for mental health by providing recovery-oriented treatment, education, and training to VA staff and veterans.	Deployed at each medical center
Mental Health Intensive Case Management (MHICM)	Help veterans with severe mental illness to avoid rehospitalization and successfully live in the community.	111 teams serving over 7,500 veterans
RANGE	Focus on veterans with severe mental illness in rural areas, as well as addressing needs of homeless veterans.	19 teams serving more than 300 veterans
Psychosocial Rehabilitation & Recovery Centers (PRRC)	Outpatient programs to provide veterans with severe mental illness the skills needed to reintegrate into society.	59 designated PRRCs, with approximately 57 additional PRRCs expected
Therapeutic & Supportive Employment Services	Encourage meaningful employment, an important part of recovery through CWT, incentive therapy (IT) & vocational rehabilitation (VR).	259 work-based programs (169 CWT and 90 IT). Provided approximately 8,000 veterans with IT, 25,000 veterans with TWE, 12,000 veterans with SE. Veterans earned over $50 million through CWT.
Peer Support Services	Provide support to veterans with mental illness through shared life challenges.	All medical centers and large VA clinics have been mandated to provide counseling from peer support technicians.
Consumer/Liaison Services	Develop and maintain positive relationships with veteran consumers, mental health organizations, and veteran service organizations.	83 facility councils and 5 VISN councils
Family Services	Incorporate family members as an important element of recovery.	35 LRCs currently trained as network family education consultants

recovery into practice, engaging veterans in discussions about their care, and providing recovery-oriented services directly to veterans.

Mental Health Intensive Case Management (MHICM)

Closely aligned with an assertive community treatment (ACT) tactic, MHICM is an intensive interdisciplinary team approach to the management and treatment of veterans with severe mental illness in the community. Veterans with severe mental illness who have been repeatedly hospitalized for psychiatric concerns qualify for the program, which includes frequent contacts between the staff and veteran. The focus is on rehabilitation and successful community living. The MHICM activities may include outreach to veterans in distress, home visits with veterans and their families, case management, individual psychotherapy, medical management, crisis planning, and veteran advocacy. In addition, MHICM focuses on community integration factors such as transportation, vocation, housing, and/or budgeting issues.

RANGE

Closely aligned with MHICM, the RANGE program focuses on veterans who live in rural areas or who are currently homeless. Its activities are similar to MHICM in that they are community-based services that often offer case management and therapy directly in the home. They may also focus more on actively helping veterans locate more stable housing and establish connections in their rural communities.

Psychosocial Rehabilitation & Recovery Center (PRRC)

The PRRCs are outpatient programs designed to provide veterans with severe mental illness the skills needed to reintegrate into society. The previous day treatment/day hospital programs have been mandated to transform into recovery-oriented programs. The focus is to emphasize rehabilitation, self-determined roles, and goals for living in the community, rather than viewing the PRRC as a destination or end point in the recovery journey. The PRRC activities can include both clinic- and community-based services such as vocational skill development, case management, peer support, individual or group psychotherapy (such as cognitive restructuring or social skills training), medication management, and family education. Some PRRCs offer a wide range of services, such as yoga, veteran art shows, money management, medication education, computer tutorials, and support groups.

Therapeutic and Supportive Employment Services (TSES)

As vast research literature has shown, meaningful employment is an integral part of recovery. A wide range of vocational services is offered through VA, including incentive therapy (IT), compensated work therapy (CWT), and vocational rehabilitation (VR). Compensated work therapy incorporates sheltered workshops, transitional work experiences, and supported employment. Consultation for vocational rehabilitation is mandated at all VA facilities. The TSES activities include supported employment within VA facilities, job retraining, shadowing veterans at work, teaching job search and interview skills, and developing relationships with businesses in the community for job placement.

Peer Services

Peer support technicians provide support to veterans with severe mental illness through shared life challenges. They serve as role models and are trained to assist veterans with goal setting, problem solving, and managing symptoms. They live the principles of recovery and help staff incorporate the consumer voice. However, VA is still developing competency standards and training materials for this population. In addition, recruitment and hiring have presented some challenges in setting standards/certification as well as identifying potential candidates. Vet-to-Vet is a peer program that has been widely used in some VA sites. Peer support services include both individual and group psychoeducation; providing support; skills training; and serving as a model for advocacy, respect, and hope.

Consumer/Liaison Services

VA Medical Centers are encouraged to have consumer/liaison services to develop and maintain positive relationships with veteran consumers, mental health-related organizations (such as NAMI), and veterans' service organizations (VSO). These services should establish regular meetings between the aforementioned groups to facilitate communication and increase veteran participation. Consumer/liaison services often include monthly meetings or focus groups to gather information and inform change within the VA system.

Family Services

Another important element of recovery is the incorporation of family members into treatment. This is especially true for veterans diagnosed with severe mental illness. Mental health care providers should discuss family involvement with veterans at least annually. The Department of Veterans Affairs is rolling out training in family psychoeduation, behavioral couples therapy, behavioral family therapy, multiple family group therapy, and family consultation. In addition, some VA locations are providing family-to-family groups conjointly with NAMI. Family educational materials are also an important aspect; VA worked with *Sesame Street* to produce "Talk, Listen, Connect: Deployment, Homecomings, Changes" to help families with young children talk about the effects of deployment and parents who return home with combat-related injuries.

Other Programming

Psychosocial rehabilitation and recovery services are being implemented in established mental health clinics as well, such as inpatient units, residential programming, general mental health outpatient clinics, substance use programs, and PTSD clinics. Mental health–primary care integration is an example of holistic care with a focus on recovery toward wellness.

Case Example

A major component of successfully applying psychosocial rehabilitation hinges on interdisciplinary work and holistic collaboration across various clinics. This is not an approach that can be executed by one type of service provider or one clinic. Following is a case example that illustrates how various components and VA service can work together to provide best care for veterans while embodying these ideals.

> Robert is a forty-eight-year-old veteran who has schizophrenia, first diagnosed when he was twenty-one, while he was still actively enrolled in the military. Robert starting hearing voices telling him that bad things were going to happen to him and his family, and he thus became very paranoid about others whom he lived and worked with. Robert was immediately hospitalized, involuntarily. He did not fully understand why he was being hospitalized and forced to take medications. He also had to attend groups that he was signed up for in preparation for discharge; however, Robert was not interested in any of the groups and did not think that they related to his particular situation. Robert's family lived far away and could not visit him while he was in the hospital. He could call his family on occasion, but they did not understand what was happening to him. When Robert was discharged from the hospital, he left the military and attempted to find a job in the area. However, he could not find a job and had nowhere to live. He stayed in various homeless shelters at

night and tried to save money by panhandling during the day so he could move back home near his family.

Since his discharge, Robert had not seen a psychiatrist and had run out of medication. He also could not afford his medications because he had no job and no health insurance. He began hearing voices again and started smoking and drinking to self-medicate, as he found that they calmed him down and took his mind off his problems. Robert struggled with substance use off and on for several years and had several other psychiatric hospitalizations, both at VA and in other community hospitals. He was listed as noncompliant in many healthcare charts because he had difficulty following the verbal instructions given to him, keeping his appointments, and taking his medication consistently.

During his last hospitalization, a social worker worked with Robert to establish a psychiatric advanced directive that listed Robert's wishes related to his psychiatric illness. For example, Robert had a very bad experience at the first hospital he went to and thus did not want to go back there again if he needed to be hospitalized. Throughout the years, Robert had also tried several medications to ease his symptoms; some worked and some did not. He listed the ones that he found most helpful, as well as coping strategies that he found helpful in times of increasing stress. Robert signed himself up for two classes while in the hospital that he thought might be helpful to him: a financial management class and an employment class. Robert attended the groups as often as he could and participated in all group discussions and assignments.

The social worker also connected Robert with the MHICM program and substance use clinics at VA. With the assistance of his MHICM case manager, Robert found a one-bedroom apartment near VA so that he could ride the bus to his appointments. The MHICM case manager visited Robert weekly to assist him with filling his pillbox with his medications. The case manager also reminded Robert about his upcoming appointments and provided transportation if needed. Robert was nervous about seeing a new psychiatrist because he did not know if he would be able to remember everything he needed to tell the psychiatrist about his mental illness. The MHICM case manager helped Robert make a list of things Robert thought were important to share with the new psychiatrist and questions that he had about his mental illness and subsequent care. The MHICM case manager also offered to attend the session with Robert to make sure that the communication between Robert and the psychiatrist was clear and that Robert felt he was being heard.

Robert was so intrigued by the employment and finance classes in the hospital that he began attending a Psychosocial Rehabilitation and Recovery Center (PRRC) at his local VA. He established several goals, such as "get a job" and "manage my own money." Robert attended the finance management classes at the PRRC, as well as classes on recovery and mental illness, where he began understanding his mental illness more. Robert's MHICM case manager made an appointment with the compensated work therapy (CWT) coordinator to discuss employment opportunities and what jobs might interest Robert. The MHICM case manager and CWT coordinator assisted Robert with creating a resume, identifying job characteristics he preferred, and making initial contact with a potential employer and filling out an application. The CWT coordinator also suggested that Robert attend a ready to work group, which would help him practice interview skills, filling out applications, creating resumes, and choosing proper attire for jobs.

Although Robert has a goal of managing his own money, he developed serious financial issues due to his substance use and spending habits, so he has a VA fiduciary who manages his money for him. Robert collaborated with his MHICM case manager and PRRC clinician in establishing small steps to his overall goal of managing his own money. For example, step 1 was to remain substance-free for at least six months. Robert accomplished this step easily. For the next step, Robert and his MHICM case manager contacted his VA fiduciary and decided to try a temporary period of time for Robert to try budgeting and managing his money, for one month. With the knowledge from the PRRC groups and the help of his MHICM case manager, Robert established a budget and opened a bank account at a bank near where he lives.

Robert did well managing his money for about two months. However, he became stressed about the responsibility of paying all of his bills and began hearing the voices again. He became paranoid about his MHICM case manager and shut off communication with him. Robert stopped taking his medications and turned to substances again to self-medicate. Robert ended up back in the VA hospital. Upon his admission, the social worker obtained Robert's chart and looked at his psychiatric advanced directive. Robert began taking medications again, and his symptoms slowly began to ease. The social worker contacted Robert's MHICM case manager, who came to visit Robert in the hospital. The MHICM case manager discussed the situation with Robert and got his feedback on what happened and what could have been done differently. They revised Robert's goals for his recovery plan and established next steps after discharge. Robert still really wanted to manage his own money, but stated that he would feel better having the bills automatically drafted and having a weekly review of his budget with his case manager. The MHICM case manager agreed. With Robert's agreement, the MHICM case manager contacted his previous providers and services and reinitiated all services. His case manager also contacted his apartment landlord and confirmed that Robert still had the apartment and could return there upon discharge with no penalty.

After discharge, Robert resumed his daily activities and continued working with his MHICM case manager and attending his employment and finance groups. Although he had had a setback in his recovery, Robert continued on his recovery journey and had high hopes for obtaining his goals. He was pleased with how his psychiatric advanced directive worked when he needed to be hospitalized and felt more confident than ever that if he needed more support or treatment, he would get the care he desired. Robert still has difficult times in his life, but he is making steady progress toward his goals. He has obtained a part-time job working at a movie theater, which he really enjoys. He continues to need assistance managing his money, but with the income from his part-time job, he has begun to manage those funds independently in preparation for managing *all* of his funds.

Challenges to Implementation

Given the amount of change necessary for a transformed service, there are several challenges that prevent or deter full implementation of a recovery-oriented system. These obstacles or challenges are often divided into two categories: individual and systemic challenges.

Individual Challenges

Individual challenges are certain beliefs, behaviors, or practices that are contraindicated within a recovery model and likely have been present or reinforced through experience. Often this is expressed as a change in practice from a medical model to a recovery model. For example, during their appoinment a primary physician may not inquire about the veteran's desire for medication, or whether the veteran requires assistance from an occupational therapist to organize his or her medications. The physician is concerned about these areas, but is less likely to address them or encourage a shared decision-making practice without encouragement and training in recovery-based practices.

Correspondingly, individual challenges are also relevant for veterans who may have years of experience with non-recovery-based practices. For example, a veteran who has received psychiatric treatment for several years may hesitate to ask the doctor about a medication that doctor would like to prescribe, even if the veteran has taken the medication previously and had severe negative side effects. The responsibility of shared decision making lies with both the provider and the veteran.

Shared decision making may provide challenges for implementing evidence-based practices. For example, if a veteran presents to the VA hospital exhibiting symptoms of depression, the provider may suggest an established and efficacious treatment such as cognitive-behavioral therapy be included in the veteran's recovery plan. However, if the veteran does not desire this therapy to be included in his or her recovery plan, this may provide a challenge for the provider in determining what types of services to offer or what the provider's role should be. It may be challenging for providers trained in traditional medical models to view themselves as facilitators or collaborators rather than as experts. Although this can be a difficult balance, the impetus for shared decision making promotes a greater dialogue between veterans and providers. Subsequently, improved communication will lead to improved recovery practices.

Finally, and perhaps most important, is the difficult challenge of overcoming the stigma associated with mental illness. For providers, this stigma may include low expectations for change from the consumer. This belief may also be held by the consumer and the family. Low expectation for change can lead to poor treatment interactions, nonadherence to treatment or recovery goals, and hopelessness. To address this challenge, VA's inclusion of peer support specialist, family education programs, and education and training for staff provides both veterans and providers information that contradicts stigma often associated with mental illness and provides hope for improving the veteran's quality of life.

Systemic Challenges

If a veteran being treated for depression were to also complain of lower back pain to his or her mental health provider, the importance of collaboration between disciplines becomes paramount. This scenario often pinpoints systemic challenges when implementing recovery-based practices. Systemic challenges are often policies, programs, guidelines, or resource limitations that deter or prevent recovery-based practices. People familiar with working in a large and multidisciplinary environment understand the logistical difficulties of operating cohesively and communicating effectively with staff. Many VA hospitals are further divided into separate clinics, where integrated care becomes even more difficult. In addition, as VA continues to grow in size, the greater number of veterans requires greater expenditure of time of staff. Fortunately, through computerized medical records, e-mail and teleconferencing, and advocating for increased funding, VA continues to address these challenges.

A related challenge is implementing recovery practices when billing or crediting for services. Contrary to recovery practices, insurance billing focuses on diagnosis and what type of treatment, one that has been shown to be efficacious, was used during the session. As more insurers recognize the importance and utility of recovery-based practices, this will become less of a burden on practitioners. Though a systemic challenge, this also is associated with the previous individual challenge of overcoming stigma. Program and clinic resources may be divided for specific diagnoses, including those that are often considered more debilitating, such as schizophrenia. In addition, veterans may obtain benefits for a diagnosis if it was related to their military service. Though a systemic challenge, developing a balance between providing suitable resources and benefits and improving veterans' quality of life may often best be determined on an individual basis.

Finally, an important challenge facing implementation of recovery practices is determining the most effective way to measure recovery outcomes and results. Within the medical model, recovery is often defined as reduction of symptoms or improved functioning of the repaired area. However, recovery is not well-defined and attempts to prioritize the roles of the person rather than his or her symptoms or diagnosis. Since the concept of recovery is not concretely defined, there are variability in outcome measures and a variety of instruments that examine components of recovery rather than recovery as an individual construct. In addition, recovery is recognized as nonlinear, and components of recovery such as hope are dynamic in nature, making reliable instruments difficult to develop. In conjunction, recovery is holistic, encompassing all aspects of the person's life, making assessment multifaceted and complex. Although there are certainly limitations in evaluating recovery, recovery outcome research is still in its infancy. Additional measures continue to develop that focus on strength-based outcomes, incorporate multiple components, and account for possible dynamic changes that occur in the recovery process.

New Directions

Where do we go from here? Despite the significant developments in psychosocial rehabilitation and recovery services within the VA system, more changes need to be made. Staff and veterans continue to be unfamiliar with the concepts of recovery in mental health, and many continue to function in the traditional healthcare system that they have become accustomed to. For positive change to occur it is important for staff to be intensely trained in these concepts and to be strong advocates for these concepts throughout the VA system and the many programs and clinics that comprise the larger VA healthcare system. One such program that is being facilitated at several VA locations nationwide is the Psychosocial Rehabilitation and Recovery Fellowship (PSR).

The PSR is a one-year, post-degree, interprofessional fellowship implemented in 2003 at various VA sites throughout the United States as a result of VA's commitment to interprofessional clinical care and training in psychosocial rehabilitation and recovery for veterans with serious mental illness. The fellowship is designed to provide advanced training in the theory and practice of psychosocial rehabilitation for mental health professionals from various disciplines. This state of the art program provides individualized, mentored clinical and research training, combined with a curriculum that emphasizes a comprehensive approach to psychosocial rehabilitation to service delivery, education, and implementing positive change in mental healthcare settings (http://www4.va.gov/oaa/fellowships/psychosocial-rehab.asp).

Furthermore, as mentioned previously, numerous programs were developed specifically to assist VA in integrating rehabilitation and recovery into everyday practice. There are other VA programs that also embrace these principles. As a result of the current conflict, the Operation Enduring Freedom/ Operation Iraqi Freedom (OEF/OIF) clinics were opened across the country to address the needs of returning veterans. OEF/OIF programs work as multidisciplinary teams to smoothly transition and treat veterans with a multitude of presenting problems. The teams are active in outreach and engaging veterans in their local community. The services offered range from psychiatric medication to support groups for vocational training. The OEF/OIF programs are constantly assessing the needs of the returning veterans and developing new programming to meet their individual and unique needs. For example, some veterans have difficulty returning to school for a variety of reasons, such as adjustment issues or PTSD symptoms. As a result, some OEF/OIF clinics have developed educational and/or support groups focusing on the educational experiences of veterans to help them achieve success in the classroom. Though the OEF/OIF staff may not realize it, they are applying the principles of rehabilitation and recovery in their current practice.

In summary, it is important to remember that recovery does not refer to any specific service or intervention, but rather is the personal journey of an individual with a psychiatric disability to regain control and satisfaction in his or her life. Any assumption that service providers are responsible for someone else's recovery from mental illness is a critical error, which could not only harm an individual's recovery process, but also put an unwieldy responsibility on the clinician's shoulders. As providers, our responsibility is to provide recovery-focused and rehabilitation services, including education, support, and collaborative treatment for the individuals we serve. It is also important that clinicians take responsibility for acknowledging their own strengths and weaknesses and be willing to try new perspectives, including recovery-oriented services.

Recovery is not a brand-new concept, but rather a holistic framework that highlights values for conducting various clinical practices. It is likely that many providers will realize they are already incorporating some, if not all, of the principles into their current practice. Furthermore, using this approach systemwide, veterans are likely to reconnect with their own strengths and resources and continue to move forward on their life paths.

References

Anthony, W. (1982). Explaining "psychiatric rehabilitation" by an analogy to "physical rehabilitation." *Psychosocial Rehabilitation Journal* 5: 61–65.

Anthony, W. (1993). Recovery from mental illness: The guiding vision of the mental health service system in the 1990s. *Psychosocial Rehabilitation Journal* 16, no. 4: 11–23.

Anthony, W. (2000). A recovery-oriented service system: Setting some system level standards. *Psychiatric Rehabilitation Journal* 24, no. 2: 159–168.

Anthony, W., Cohen, M. & Cohen, B. (1984). Psychiatric rehabilitation. In J. A. Talbott (Ed.), *The chronic mental client: Five years later* (pp. 137–157). New York: Grune & Stratton.

Anthony, W., Kennard, W., O'Brien, W. & Forbess, R. (1986). Psychiatric rehabilitation: Past myths and current realities. *Community Mental Health Journal* 22, no. 4: 249–264.

Anthony, W. & Liberman, R. (1986). The practice of psychiatric rehabilitation: Historical, conceptual, and research base. *Schizophrenia Bulletin* 12, no. 4: 542–559.

Bleuler, M. (1972). *Die schizophrenen Geistesstorungen: Im Lichte langjähriger Kranken- und Familiengeschichten.* New York: Intercontinental Medical Book Corporation.

Copeland, M. (2002). *Wellness recovery action plan.* West Dummerston, VT: Peach Press.

Davidson, L. (2003). *Living outside mental illness: Qualitative studies of recovery in schizophrenia.* New York: New York University Press.

Davidson, L., Chinman, M. J., Kloos, B., Weingarten, R., Stayner, D. A. & Tebes, J. K. (1999). Peer support among individuals with severe mental illness: A review of the evidence. *Clinical Psychology: Science and Practice* 6, no. 2: 165–187.

Davidson, L., O'Connell, M. J., Tondora, J., Staeheli, M. & Evans, A. C. (2005). Recovery in serious mental illness: Paradigm shift or shibboleth? In L. Davidson, C. Harding & L. Spaniol (Eds.), *Recovery from severe mental illness: Research evidence and implications for practice* (pp. 5–26). Boston: Center for Psychiatric Rehabilitation.

Deegan, P. (1988). Recovery: The lived experience of rehabilitation. *Psychosocial Rehabilitation Journal* 11, no. 4: 11–19.

Deegan, P. (1996). Recovery as a journey of the heart. In L. Spaniol, C. Gagne & M. Koehler (Eds.), *Psychological and social aspects of psychiatric disability* (pp. 74–83). Boston: Center for Psychiatric Rehabilitation.

Department of Veterans Affairs. (2008). *VHA handbook 1160.01: Uniform mental health services in VA medical centers and clinics.* Washington, DC: Department of

Veteran Affairs. http://www1.va.gov/vhapublications/ViewPublication.asp?pub _ID=1762.

Harding, C. (1987). The Vermont Longitudinal Study of Persons with Severe Mental Illness. *American Journal of Psychiatry* 144: 727–734.

Harding, C. M. & Zahniser, J. H. (1994). Empirical correction of seven myths about schizophrenia with implications for treatment. *Acta Psychiatrica Scandinavica* 90: 140–146.

Horst, P. (2003). Introduction to empowerment and recovery in mental health: Presentation workbook. www.cmha.ca/…/1301_1183_Empowerment%20&%20 Recovery%20-%20U%20of%20Manitoba%20Presentation.ppt.

Jacobson, N. & Greenley, D. (2001). What is recovery? A conceptual model and explication. *Psychiatric Services* 52, no. 4: 482–485.

Liberman, R. (1988). *Psychiatric rehabilitation of chronic mental clients.* Washington, DC: American Psychiatric Press.

Mead, S. & Copeland, M. E. (2000). What recovery means to us: Consumers' perspectives. *Community Mental Health Journal* 36: 315–328.

Ogawa. K., Miya, M., Watarai, A., Nakazawa, M., Yuasa, S. & Utena, H. (1987). A long-term follow-up study of schizophrenia in Japan—with special reference to the source of social adjustment. *The British Journal of Psychiatry* 151: 758–765.

Peloquin, S. (1989). Moral treatment: Contexts considered. *American Journal of Occupational Therapy* 43: 537–544.

Peters, H. (2003). Introduction to empowerment and recovery in mental health: Presentation workbook. www.cmha.ca/…/1301_1183_Empowerment%20& %20Recovery%20-%20U%20of%20Manitoba%20Presentation.ppt.

President's New Freedom Commission on Mental Health. (2003). Achieving the promise: Transforming mental health care in America: Final report. DHHS publication no. SMA-03–3832. Rockville, MD: U.S. Department of Health and Human Services.

Roberts, G., Davenport, S., Holloway, F. & Tattan, T. (2006). Rehabilitation and recovery now. In G. Roberts, S. Davenport, F. Holloway & T. Tattan (Eds.), *Enabling recovery: The principle and practice of rehabilitation psychiatry* (pp. xv–xxiv). London: Cromwell Press Limited.

Spaniol, L., Wewiorski, N. J., Gagne, C. & Anthony, W. A. (2002). The process of recovery from schizophrenia. *International Review of Psychiatry* 14: 327–336.

Strauss, J. S. (2005). What is the reality about severe mental disorder? In L. Davidson, C. Harding & L. Spaniol (Eds.), *Recovery from severe mental illness: Research evidence and implications for practice* (pp. 49–56). Boston: Center for Psychiatric Rehabilitation.

Substance Abuse and Mental Health Services Administration (SAMHSA). (2004). *National consensus statement on mental health recovery.* http://mentalhealth.samh-sa.gov/publications/allpubs/sma05–4129/ (accessed September 28, 2009).

U.S. Department of Labor. (2008). Fact sheet: The Mental Health Parity Act. http://www.dol.gov/ebsa/newsroom/fsmhparity.html (accessed October 14, 2009).

U.S. Psychiatric Rehabilitation Association (USPRA). (2012). About the US Psychiatric Rehabilitation Association, 2012. https://netforum.avectra.com/eWeb/DynamicPage.aspx?Site=USPRA&WebCode=about (accessed March 22, 2012).
World Health Organization (WHO). (1973). *Report of the International Pilot Study of Schizophrenia*, volume 1. Geneva: World Health Organization.

Eradicating Mental Illness Stigma for Active Military Personnel and Veterans

Ann D. Kirkwood, Beth Hudnall Stamm,
and Chandra R. Story

History

Stigma can lead to social isolation, discrimination in housing and employment opportunities, and inadequate physical and mental health care (Bassett, Lloyd & Bassett 2001; Johnstone 2001; Watkins et al. 2001). Coupled with the challenges of transitioning from active duty to veteran status, stigma can all but control the outcome of a veteran's life. In years past, stigma was not an active part of VA policy. However, the Department of Veterans Affairs and Department of Defense (VA/DoD) Joint Executive Council Strategic Plan for fiscal years 2009–2011 (VA/DoD 2008) made reducing mental illness stigma a priority.

Stigma is defined as a mark of shame or disgrace relating to an individual's condition or status. Mental illness stigma is labeled as one of the most serious forms of stigma (Farina, Fisher & Fisher 1992; Finlay, Dinos & Lyons 2001; Fishbein 2002). Stigma is related to what a person is (involuntary) versus what a person does (voluntary). In the case of mental illnesses, mainstream American culture often perceives mental illnesses as intentional regardless of evidence to the contrary (Crocetti, Spiro & Siassi 1974). Stigma not only affects the mental health consumer and the stigmatizer, it has widespread consequences for society at large. Corrigan and Lundin (2001) note that stigma promotes injustices "that undermine some of the basic assumptions of a community" (250). They also propose that stigma "robs society of an important resource: persons with mental illness who could be gainful members of the neighborhood" (250). Leading to stigma is the individual fear that anyone could have a mental illness and thus lose cognitive control.

In the case of people with mental illnesses, stigma has created an environment wherein consumers attempt to disguise their illnesses in order to get and keep jobs, rent apartments, or gain access to an education or other activities (Kisthardt n.d.; Link et al. 1992; Link et al. 2001). When afforded a chance to give voice to their stories and how stigma affects them, people with mental illnesses may experience heightened self-esteem and self-efficacy, resulting in empowerment (Young 1990; Haghighat 2001).

Policies

Stigma

As a result of the mental health and suicide crises arising from Operation Enduring Freedom/Operation Iraqi Freedom (OEF/OIF), stigma reduction has taken a place in the forefront of VA and DoD policy. The President's Commission on Care for America's Returning Wounded Warriors (PCCWW) final report (2007) stated that stigma associated with mental health is reducing slowly but should still be combated, in particular with regard to post-traumatic stress disorder (PTSD).

Reducing stigma associated with mental health was noted as a joint priority at a Veterans Affairs–Department of Defense National Mental Health Summit held in Washington, DC, on October 26, 2009. The VA/DoD Joint Executive Council Strategic Plan for fiscal years 2009–2011 (VA/DoD 2008) required that an antistigma public education campaign be developed by November 30, 2008 and evaluated annually for the fiscal years 2009, 2010, and 2011. The annual report for 2009 extended that goal into 2012. This stigma reduction goal was linked specifically to traumatic brain injury (TBI) and psychological (PH) conditions (Carden 2010).

The PCCWW pointed to stigma as a major barrier to care and called for an extensive effort to reduce stigma (President's Commission on Care for America's Returning Wounded Warriors 2007). Stigma has been connected by military and VA officials to suicide: "We must double down on our commitment to eliminate, not just to minimize, but to eliminate stigma, that toxic, deadly hazard that all too often leads to needless suffering and loss," said Brig. Gen. Loree Sutton (Carden 2010).

Social Marketing

For veterans, seeking help may be stigmatizing in light of the "Warrior Mind" developed for battle (Norton 2010). The Warrior Mind admonishes soldiers to always place the mission first and never to quit or accept defeat (Norton 2010). It is also part of the culture to handle problems on one's own (Stecker et al. 2007). This mindset may continue past deployment and discourage soldiers from receiving mental healthcare. These barriers to care during service serve as a risk factor for psychiatric casualties and even suicide after deployment.

The VA/DoD launched a public education effort called the "Real Warrior Campaign" in May 2009. The goal of the multimedia campaign was a public education campaign fight against the stigma associated with seeking mental healthcare. Other methods have been implemented that do not utilize mass media but other approaches to attitude and behavior change. Warrior Care (http://www.warriorcare.mil/), After Deployment (www.afterdeployment.org), and Courage to Care (http://www.usuhs.mil/psy/courage.html) are some of the varied programs. Additionally, community-based interventions seem to be important to alleviate isolation and anxiety upon return from deployment (Vogt et al. 2005). Each VA medical center has a suicide prevention coordinator who has a clinical background but is also trained in evidence-based, nonclinical suicide prevention practices (*U.S. Department of Veterans Affairs' Suicide Hotline [US VA Suicide Hotline]* 2008). Their role is to ensure that veterans receive needed counseling services and to serve as a resource for VA and the community (Kemp et al. 2010). Coordinators perform various tasks regarding suicide prevention. They provide gatekeeper training, staff and patient education, and community outreach. Gatekeepers train nonclinicians to recognize suicidal ideation in veterans (Kemp 2010). Coordinators work with the National Suicide Prevention Lifeline, VA Crisis Line, and other community partners to reduce suicide among veterans (Kemp, Stephenson & Woehr 2010).

The VA Crisis Line, in partnership with the National Suicide Prevention Lifeline, began in 2007 in response to increased veteran suicide rates (*US VA Suicide Hotline* 2008). Veterans and family members are able to press "1" when calling the general number and are immediately linked to twenty-four-hour, seven-day-a-week crisis centers with trained operators (*US VA Suicide Hotline* 2008). As of 2008 Crisis Line had received approximately 32,000 calls from veterans. More than 1,628 rescues from imminent suicidal behavior are documented as a result of the hotline at that time (*US VA Suicide Hotline* 2008).

Social marketing outreach started in the District of Columbia is documented to have increased Lifeline calls by approximately 50 percent (*US VA Suicide Hotline* 2008). Outreach is also conducted by partnering with veterans' groups (*US VA Suicide Hotline* 2008). Other outreach efforts include a national media campaign and an online chat program. The online chat program allows veterans and family members to be connected with a counselor anonymously (Kemp 2010). Veterans can be connected to the suicide hotline immediately if indicated (Kemp 2010).

Mental health screenings are being conducted for OEF/OIF veterans at VA facilities during primary care appointments (Seal et al. 2007). Combining mental health services with primary care seems to reduce the stigma involved with receiving care (Seal et al. 2007). For veterans who must be hospitalized, mental health plans are made (*US VA Suicide Hotline* 2008). Safety plans include environmental safety, internal and external coping, along with environmental concerns, such as gun access (Kemp 2010). Another destigmatizing intervention is the availability of postdeployment stress clinics for everyone. In this setting, leaders can encourage everyone to pursue care if needed without singling anyone out (Associated Press 2009).

Early diagnosis and labels of mental illness also can be stigmatizing for officers. It is important to wait until they are out of active duty and severe stress environments to address these issues. Through treatment modalities, the military also has examined stigma. Military research has been examining the impact of stigma on following treatment recommendations ("treatment adherence") and family involvement in care (Murray-Swank & Dixon n.d.).

Stigma

Stigma affects various domains, including society, family, professionals, and self. Social stigma results in the inability to secure employment, for example, due to perceptions of those with mental illnesses (Henry & Lucca 2002). This could be particularly detrimental for young veterans returning to civilian life with a mental health diagnosis. Most of the veterans in a study by Pyne (2004) did not have full-time employment.

Families and caregivers of consumers perceive and receive stigma (Veltman, Cameron & Stewart 2002), with a resulting lower self-esteem in families postdeployment (Hinshaw & Cicchetti 2000; Struening et al. 2001). In a study of caregivers by Struening and colleagues (2001), caregivers reported that consumers often feel that receiving treatment is a sign of weakness, and they are perceived as being less than others if they have been patients in a hospital for psychiatric care. In fact, some consumers actually felt that having a mental illness was worse than being addicted to drugs (Struening et al. 2001).

Perceptions of mental health treatment may be an impediment to veterans. In a study by Pyne (2004), being in treatment for depression was correlated with higher levels of perceived stigma. Veterans may also perceive mental health treatment as weak and ineffective, with concern about side effects and fear of mental illness itself (Spoont et al. 2009; Brown & Bradley 2002).

Active soldiers may be concerned about location and possible costs of treatment, and that they may be treated differently by others after receiving mental healthcare. They also may be concerned that colleagues may think that they are incapable of doing their jobs, which could cause them to miss out on promotions (U.S Department of Veterans Affairs 2010; Associated Press 2009; Steckner et al. 2007; Hoge et al. 2004). This is exemplified in that soldiers needing service were twice as likely as those not needing service to worry about being stigmatized (Hoge et al. 2004). Due to stigma, many soldiers do not pay much attention to initial mental health classes postdeployment (Associated Press 2009). According to Hoge and colleagues (2002), 47 percent of soldiers diagnosed with a mental illness left the military.

Stigma also may be exacerbated by soldiers perceiving that leaders will tell them not to be honest on their mental health assessment, or that information will not be confidential (Norton 2010; Hoge et al. 2002). Soldiers could also be viewed as discipline problems instead of being encouraged to treat mental health problems during long deployments (Associated Press 2009).

Types of Stigma

For purposes of this chapter, mental illness stigma is separated into two components. Cultural and social stigma is one type, and "self-stigma" is the other.

Cultural and Societal Stigma

Stigma is a "powerful phenomenon" more severe than stereotyping, with which it is often used as a synonym. It is a social construction that involves at least two fundamental components: 1) the recognition of difference based on some distinguishing characteristic or "mark" and 2) a consequent devaluation of the person (Heatherton et al. 2003, 3). Goffman (1963) described stigma as a sign or mark that designates the bearer as "spoiled" and therefore as valued less than "normal people." Stigmatization relies on a power relation in which the stigmatizer holds control over some life aspect of the stigmatized (Falk 2001; Giddens 1990). Through stigma, then, one group "sits in judgment" of the other (Falk 2001). Stigma is influenced by powerful cultural institutions, including care providers, bureaucratic systems, and the media (Wahl 1995). It impacts the quality of life of those in the stigmatized group (Yanos, Rosenfeld & Horowitz 2001).

Stigma development in the individual is divided into specific states over the lifetime (Kirkwood 2005). First, in a continuum model developed by the lead author, "categorization" refers to the process of naming that individuals learn from their caregivers from childhood. They learn the words to describe the world around them. Prejudgment is the next developmental step when children begin attaching feelings to those items. For example, a child would categorize a dog in the initial stage and attach "good" or "bad" to the word "dog" in the prejudgment phase. The third stage is the application of stereotypes to groups, whether true or false. For example, using the dog example, a person would then stereotype all dogs as "bad." Stereotyping is a result of the previous two stages, primarily due to the experiences to which stigmatizers have been exposed (Heatherton et al. 2003). Adding a layer of culturally learned stigma at this stage results in severe negative attributions that play out in the next two stages, prejudice and discrimination.

As it relates to mental illness, a person is stigmatized through a label, such as discussing individuals with mental illnesses as dangerous and to be avoided. A social power relation corresponding to the dominance of the "in group" over the "out group" is pivotal for stigmatization. Prejudice is the next stage at which an individual or group solidifies its thinking about the stigmatized group, and it is unlikely these prejudices will be abandoned without some clear personal imperative. While "prejudice" is defined by some as an "attitude" (Heatherton et al. 2003), in this case it is far more harmful than attitude alone. Prejudice, when accompanied by stigma, as we outline here, is rigidly and inflexibly held generalizations with the threat of damage and aggression toward people with mental illnesses. Finally, the spectrum ends with overt discrimination, such as denying a person with a mental illness a livelihood, an education, or affordable housing. Discrimination is verbally articulated and readily recognizable through behaviors of the stigmatizer. Discrimination affects self-esteem and can be done by individual stigmatizers, groups of stigmatizers, and the institutions (government or private) upon which people with mental illnesses might rely (Heatherton et al. 2003; Hinshaw 2007; Falk 2001; Corrigan, Watson & Barr 2006).

Self-stigma

When a consumer accepts all or part of the messages of social stigma, the stigmas become internalized (Hinshaw 2007; Heatherton et al. 2003; Corrigan & Watson 2002). Stigma denotes an "internal 'mark' of deep degradation" for the stigmatized person (Hinshaw 2007, 25). In fact, "the demeaning attitudes of perceivers may well come to be internalized by the possessor of the devalued attribute in question" (Hinshaw 2007, 25). Hinshaw discusses the "perceiver" as a stigmatizer while the "possessor" is the person who is stigmatized. Stigma also may be internalized by groups and individuals associated with the individual who is stigmatized, resulting in forms of self-stigma similar to those a consumer experiences (Hinshaw 2007). For example, stigma is a barrier to recovery and a consumer's desire to follow treatment recommendations (Sirey et al.

2001; Struening et al. 2001; Golberstein, Eisenberg & Gollust 2008). The visibility of the stigma is related to how much effort a stigmatized person puts into concealing it. In the case of mental illness, stigmatizing conditions may be visible or invisible depending on the diagnosis, treatment, and living situation of the individual, for example, homelessness. For example, a person with schizophrenia who is homeless, psychotic, and having delusions would be a visible example of mental illness. A person with depression, however, might withdraw, possessing a condition not necessarily visible in the community. Criteria that have been outlined as determinants for levels of stigma are concealability as described above, how stigmatizers perceive future progression of the disorder (e.g., permanent or transitory), disruptiveness (e.g., how the disorder affects interpersonal communication and other events), the stigmatizers' perceived reactions to unattractiveness (e.g., how persons with mental illnesses appear), perceived origin of the disorder (e.g., is it someone's fault?), and peril to others (e.g., dangerousness). The dimensions that emerge as most central in this approach are the perceived danger, visibility, and controllability of a mental disorder (Heatherton et al. 2003). Less study is reported on the topic of why all people with mental illnesses are not affected by negative aspects and a lessening of self-esteem as a result of stigma (Heatherton et al. 2003). Heatherton and colleagues explain that self-stigma varies based on situations in which a person with a mental illness finds herself or himself. The interpretation of stigmatizing events is influenced by shared beliefs, attitudes, and values that can be inconsistent among groups and individuals (Heatherton et al. 2003).

Stigma and Race and Ethnicity

Because stigma emerges with unique differences among cultural and racial groups, it is important to address the unique concerns that must be addressed in any intervention, whether it be social marketing, Community Based Participatory Research (CBPR), education, community development, or public participation. Details of cultural issues raised here are relevant in working with or for troops and veterans. They can inform social marketing messages, address barriers to treatment seeking, and encourage training that meets individual cultural needs. A review of the literature suggests that African Americans, Asian Americans, and American Indian/Alaska Natives affected by mental illnesses face unique challenges to receiving proper mental healthcare. Stigmatizing perceptions of people with mental illnesses, access to care, and ambivalence about the use of medications are some of the issues facing these populations (Ward, Clark & Heidrich 2009; Conner, Koeske & Brown 2009). Acculturation stress is an issue as well (Gee et al. 2007; Shea 2007). A discussion of these issues follows.

Stigmatizing perceptions of mental illness among African Americans are barriers to mental health services. In a qualitative study by Alvidrez, Snowden, and Kaiser (2008), participants noted low knowledge regarding mental illness prior to their diagnosis. Low knowledge included ignorance of warning signs and where to go for help (Alvidrez, Snowden & Kaiser 2008). This may be the result of an unwillingness to discuss mental illness in many African American communities (Alvidrez, Snowden & Kaiser 2008; Ward, Clark & Heidrich 2009; Rao, Feinglass & Corrigan 2007). People are expected to handle problems on their own. For this reason, participants in several studies were fearful of being labeled "weak" for receiving help (Cruz et al. 2008; Ward, Clark & Heidrich 2009; Cooper-Patrick et al. 1997). Resulting shame and denial of mental illnesses could prohibit one from reaching out for help (Cruz et al. 2008). In addition to being weak, community members may also view those with mental illnesses as having moral deficiencies and as being dangerous (Cruz et al. 2008; Rao et al. 2007; Alvidrez et al. 2008). Some may feel that mental illness is caused by uncontrollable stressors related to being black, racism, and oppression (Ward, Clark & Heidrich 2009). Experiences with personal racism may in fact be linked to discrimination against the people with mental illnesses (Rao, Feinglass & Corrigan 2007).

Origins of mental illnesses are connected to current perceptions among American Indian/Alaska Natives. The "loss of soul," or physical illness, is synonymous with mental illness, a term not used prior to Western invasion (Grandbois 2005). Loss of soul is considered to be a lack of harmony and imbalance with the world (Grandbois 2005). This may be a result of unresolved grief from the historical trauma of boarding schools and a stripping away of culture (Shea 2007; Goldston et al. 2008). Loss of soul may actually be somatic symptoms for prolonged generational and historical distress. Nevertheless, symptoms of mental illness perceived as pathology in Western culture may be part of social culture or even supernatural possession (Shea 2007; Grandbois 2005). For example, some tribes consider symptoms of mental illness to be manifestations of a special gift (Grandbois 2005). Also, stigma may be decreased due to the connection between mind and body (Grandbois 2005). Life is considered to be circular, with spirituality as a central force that keeps everything in balance (Grandbois 2005). The body and mind are not considered as separate. This difference in perception may be a barrier to obtaining Westernized mental healthcare.

Among Asian Americans, a cultural perception that promotes stigma may be "loss of face" (Goldston et al. 2008). Loss of face is a cultural term referring to causing shame to one's family (Fogel & Ford 2005; Goldston et al. 2008). It is considered a mark of shame in some Asian communities if one must seek help by telling a mental health provider about something that should be a family secret (Goldston et al. 2008, Choi Wu, Kviz & Miller 2009; Shin & Lukens 2002). For example, Korean American women reported feelings of being weak by receiving care in a study by Choi Wu, Kviz, and Miller (2009). Also, seeking care could be perceived as selfish because there is a cultural expectation to focus on others (Choi Wu, Kviz & Miller 2009).

According to a study by Rao, Feinglass, and Corrigan (2007), Latino college students viewed people with mental illnesses as less dangerous than other races. This may be due to basic perceptions of mental illnesses by many Hispanics. Mental illnesses and other disorders are determined by a higher perceived power, or fatalism (Canino & Roberts 2001). However, this perception may lead to depression and even suicide attempts among Latina females (Zayas et al. 2005). Physical symptoms are often described to express mental distress in this population, with a reliance on healers as opposed to physicians (Bazron 2006; Shea 2007). As with Asian populations, Hispanic populations often embrace a holistic view of health, with the mind and body as one (Bazron 2006).

For youth who are of racial and sexual minority, it is thought that there may be a heightened vulnerability to discrimination leading to mental health issues (Cochran et al. 2007). Particularly, rumination over socially stressful events contributes to stigma and negative related mental health consequences (Hatzenbuehler 2009). However, there is a dearth of research around this issue.

A unique factor experienced by cultural and racial minorities is the phenomenon of acculturation. Acculturation is positively and negatively associated with perceptions of mental illness in minority populations. It is defined as "the process by which a human being acquires the culture of a particular society from infancy; merging of cultures as a result of prolonged contact" (Merriam-Webster n.d). In most populations, higher levels of acculturation are associated with lower levels of stigma associated with receiving mental health services.

Many minority groups do not have adequate access to culturally relevant mental healthcare. Discrimination, lack of culturally appropriate therapy, mistrust of providers, cultural and language limitations, and low socioeconomic status are key factors (Conner, Koeske & Brown 2009; Nadeem, Lange & Miranda 2008; Cruz et al. 2008; Ward, Clark & Heidrich 2009).

Historical trauma, embarrassment, and experiences with insensitive providers are primary reasons for the lack of trust in providers (Goldston et al. 2008). For example, African-American women may feel that a Caucasian provider cannot relate to the particular stressors that may cause mental illness, such as oppression. Minority populations are also aware of low cultural matches of providers within their communities (Ward, Clark & Heidrich 2009; Grandbois 2005).

Social Marketing

Social marketing is defined as a communication strategy designed to encourage people to voluntarily change their attitudes/behaviors to improve their or others' social and personal welfare (MacStravic 2000). Another definition includes additional factors: "Social marketing is built around the knowledge gained from business practices: the setting of measurable objectives, research on human needs, targeting products to specialized groups of consumers, the technology of positioning products to fit human needs and wants and effectively communicating their benefits, the constant vigilance to changes in the environment, and the ability to adapt to change" (Kotler & Roberto 1989, 26). It is use of technologies to affect social change in a way that increases acceptability to a social condition (Kotler & Roberto 1989; Hovland, Janis & Kelly 1953; Jaker 1998; Jones 1982). The lead author has designed a simple model for creating social marketing campaigns that supports identification of discrete target audiences, messages designed for that target audience, and communication tools to meet audience needs. This can be used by nonpractitioners in all settings to create social marketing endeavors.

Social marketing conceivably holds promise in reducing mental illness stigma. Social marketing, like traditional persuasion tenets on which it is based (Harper 1979; Infante, Rancer & Womack 1990), maintains that the right message (stimulus) will change the attitudes and/or behaviors of the target adopter (response). Change is voluntary and results from exposure to a properly positioned persuasive message. Successful social marketing is organized and collective; one group (change agent) persuades another group (target audience) to accept, change, or discard certain ideas, attitudes, practices, or behaviors (Kotler & Roberto 1989). For mental illnesses, social marketing encourages the target audience to change negative attitudes and annul stigma, thus opening up community life for people with mental illnesses.

Mental health education or social marketing campaigns are conducted to mitigate the deleterious effects of mental health stigma. Education seeks to raise awareness and knowledge gain. In juxtaposition, social marketing campaigns are the use of commercial media strategies to change behaviors for the good of individuals and society as a whole (Kotler, Roberto & Lee 2002). The two techniques can be used together, first to educate an audience and second to encourage behavior change. Educational programs can be enhanced to make behavior change more likely if trainees are engaged in meaningful conversation about stigma and empower them to make changes in their own lives (Mezirow & Associates 1990; Freire 1970, 1985). In the case of mental illness, social marketing is often merged with educational methods to raise awareness and change the attitudes/behaviors of people who are influential and provide help to those living with mental illness (gatekeepers). Social marketing campaigns should be planned with audience input, as they are used to influence discrete groups of community members. Tactics include trainings, PSAs, face to face, organizational and treatment changes and other forms of media. Campaigns often address the target audience and gatekeepers.

Gatekeepers in the military are people of authority such as commanders and psychologists, who can encourage military personnel to receive care before it is too late. Gatekeepers who have the ability to facilitate help for those living with mental illnesses are often encouraged to attend these types of gatekeeper trainings as part of joint education and social marketing campaigns. Kirkwood and Stamm (2006) noted that psychologists are an important link to decrease stigma in their communities, as their influence can affect other community members. Gatekeepers can decrease stigma through education, awareness, and advocacy for the worth of people and dignity (Brown & Bradley 2002).

New Directions in Veterans' Healthcare

This section addresses mental healthcare (also called behavioral health and psychological health, PH) and implications for its future in the military. It explores methods that can be used to reduce stigma for families, mental health consumers, and the people and institutions that serve them.

Enhance VA's Policy on Stigma Reduction

The national policies on stigma reduction are commendable, as are the goals to evaluate outcomes regularly. This chapter is designed to provide support and guidance as these policies and programs are carried out. It is important that benchmarks for stigma be developed in consultation with individuals with mental illnesses and their families, as stigma is a perceived condition in the eyes of the receiver.

Social Marketing

Social marketing programs may be appropriate to achieve attitude and behavior change in some settings. Many social marketing programs have been implemented in a variety of contexts, most of them to date in public health (Andreasen 2006). Various types of measures have been established to identify the impacts of social marketing on health initiatives, most of them linked to Healthy People 2010 (Brown & Bradley 2002; Andreasen 2006). Measuring impacts on mental illness stigma is far more complicated. For example, whether a campaign results in the target audience eating more fruits and vegetables a day is easier to measure than whether deeply held attitudes and values regarding mental illness have changed as the result of a social marketing message. "Noise" in the environment impacts results as competing messages thwart effectiveness of the selected social marketing message. Measures of social distance reveal mixed results when used as a measure for social marketing effectiveness. Social distance scales measure the physical distance a member of the wider community places between himself or herself and the stigmatized person (Antonak 1982; Kilbury, Bordieri & Wong 1996; Rousch & Klockars 1988; Stephens & Clark 1987). When people already have preconceived notions about people with mental illnesses, especially when direct contact is involved, a social marketing campaign must override those notions before it can effectively use messages to instill new, positive beliefs and behaviors. Contact communication, involving people with a mental illness interacting directly with the audience one wishes to change, can have unforeseen consequences if the interactions reinforce stereotypes (Corrigan 1997). The military has the potential to overcome these challenges due to the controlled nature of the environment and direct contact between officers and enlisted men and women. Use of social distance scales in this environment is not only possible but plausible. All social marketing campaigns must have a call to action focusing on behavioral change. Just as commercial marketing encourages the audience to buy a specific product, social marketing encourages an audience to subscribe to a social change.

Training Programs

Public Education Campaigns   Public education campaigns are different from social marketing. In a social marketing program, the goal is to encourage attitude and behavior change among the selected audience. In public education campaigns, the goal is to raise awareness about a particular issue. In a mental illness context, social marketing would change negative attitudes and encourage new specific desirable behaviors among a narrowly defined group of target adopters. An education campaign would then raise awareness about mental illnesses and stigma, but would not necessarily result in attitude or behavioral change. It is possible for an education campaign to be instituted as a precursor to social marketing. Education programs can be used in two ways. The first is to educate people with mental illnesses and their families within a military or veterans' context. The second is to provide widespread messages designed to reduce stigma among a wider audience both within the military and in the larger community. The military is uniquely suited to initiate and evaluate both social marketing and public education campaigns. As noted previously, the controlled nature of the military and the ready access to audiences can make it easier to target messages to a specific target audience and then measure whether the messages were effective in reducing stigma. In public education campaigns, evaluation is based on knowledge gain as a result of exposure to the program, and surveys can be administered pre-training, post-training, and at follow-up at one interval or more over a period of time.

Provider and Staff Education Programs (Gatekeeper Training)   Messages and content must be tailored to the specific audience, whether the goal is educational programs or social marketing. Relating to education programs, this means subgroups within the military, people with mental illnesses, and their families will require customized educational approaches. It also means that various providers, especially healthcare and mental healthcare providers, understand stigma and work to change their attitudes and behaviors. As a result of their training, mental healthcare providers often convey stigma to and about consumers (Crisp 2004). This is perceived by consumers and families as widespread in the United States and other industrialized nations (Watkins et al. 2001; Hinshaw 2007; Corrigan 1997). Currently, specific information is provided for clinicians in guides, such as the Iraq clinicians' guide (Litz & Orsillo n.d). Clinicians are advised to use terminology such as "war-zone stress reaction" instead of "combat stress reaction" so that stigmatizing effects will be minimized for returning soldiers. However, implications are more far-reaching. Regardless of how frequently people with mental illnesses are exposed to stigma by their mental health providers, even one provider can send this message to hundreds of patients over his or her career. Accordingly, trainings for providers should include more than information about stigma and how it develops. Instead, it should include a direct interaction with consumers and families who can tell their personal stories and how stigma impacts them individually (Minkler 1985). This creates a challenge to develop a cadre of trainers who not only understand mental illnesses, but also are versed in the origins and results of stigma on the consumer, family, and fellows in the military. Training people with mental illnesses and their families to serve as trainers provides authenticity and enhances learning through exposure to the very people subjected to stigma. The military should recruit people with mental illnesses and their families to lead customized trainings.

Veteran and Family Education   Special challenges exist for training veterans and their families and close others. Special suicide coordinators at VA centers are working internally and in the larger community on suicide prevention initiatives. However, upon discharge, some current OIF/OEF troops do not see themselves as "veterans" and thus do not seek out services or supports from the VA system. Those who do utilize traditional VA services receive care from staff that may not possess the requisite training in stigma and its deleterious consequences. For example, they may encourage patients to give up hope of getting a job instead of supporting consumers in job search and job retention. In addition to providing training to veterans who utilize VA services, trainings must reach into the broader civilian community. Consumers' self-esteem and self-efficacy often are improved when they are empowered to tell their stories, such as by teaching classes about stigma.

Community Campaigns　　Community campaigns can occur within the military, within the community of veterans and service providers, or within the broader civilian community. Community development and CBPR techniques can be customized for use in these three contexts (Hall 1981; Kellogg Health Scholars Program 2010). Facilitation techniques modeled after the field of public participation will provide a helpful toolkit (International Association for Public Participation 2010). Community development focuses on all community members, including people with mental illnesses, possessing equal influence in decision making (Kretzmann & McKnight 1993). Conducting these activities within the military will pose difficulties, but not impossibilities, due to the chain of command. It is possible to assign a cross-section of troops to address a specific community issue, such as stigma, and encourage development of a plan to address the concern. It becomes easier to use community development strategies as decision making moves into the veterans' and wider community. In these contexts, it is possible for groups of people with mental illnesses, their families, other veterans, and providers to identify issues relating to stigma and design community-based solutions. When working in the wider community, representatives of various civilian programs should be included (such as the National Alliance on Mental Illness). Another aspect is use of CBPR techniques to establish evaluation criteria and manage results (Kellogg Health Scholars 2010). The within-military and veterans' groups should have little difficulty establishing and measuring outcomes. It will become more difficult in the wider community, for reasons stated previously.

Increase Screening

As noted in the section on stigma, healthcare providers can have great influence on veterans with physical and/or mental disabilities, since most mental health diagnoses occur in primary healthcare settings (Seal et al. 2007; Kaplan et al. 2007). Screenings should occur immediately following deployment (Grover 2009). Additionally, screening for at-risk veterans should occur immediately post-training. Training programs and activities may allow negative feelings to surface that can harm mental health. Troops should not be exposed to these events without immediate follow-up screening. It is best to have a mental health professional on site during trainings. Others at risk are families and close others. They may also benefit from screening.

Future Issues

Utilizing the tools described here, those working with military and veterans' personnel can impact the severe negative aspects of stigma. Social marketing, CBPR, community development, education, and public participation all have potential to reduce stigma, either alone or in a group. Work toward development of methods to measure the outcome of stigma reduction education and social marketing campaigns as well as community-based approaches should be undertaken as inherent in any antistigma effort.

Culture

As noted previously, stigma in the military culture can influence help-seeking among active duty or veterans alike. Support for other methods to eradicate stigma should include broad cultural change. This is achieved by addressing discrete audiences over time. Despite significant efforts to attend to this, military personnel and veterans may still see mental healthcare as a barrier to career advancement. This must be the focus of activities through education, social marketing, and community work. Eradication of stigma, not just stigma reduction, should be the ultimate goal.

In education programs, stigma and its associated reduction in treatment-seeking should be openly and aggressively addressed. The lead author's model (categorization, prejudgment, stereotype, stigma, prejudice, and discrimination) should be explained to trainees so they understand the normal course of human language development and that they have these biases in common with the general culture. Stigma can then be normalized (not prejudice and discrimination) and tools provided to change attitudes and behaviors in concrete ways. People with mental illnesses and their families are the most suited to providing students with concrete steps that can be taken to reduce one's stigma, including development of a personal action plan designed to reduce stigma at an individual level. At the same time, military personnel must see their unique needs and vocabulary addressed in any training. Courses taught by other military personnel with mental health programs should be encouraged.

Support from Professionals

As noted previously, one critical aspect in supporting mental health treatment is reducing stigma among service providers, even mental health providers. If people with mental health problems are treated by professionals who stigmatize, the cycle of stigma will be repeated despite other attempts at training and informational outreach (Crisp 2004, 2000). Mental health and other professionals may have adopted these attitudes and behaviors as a result of their professional training, and they will be difficult to dislodge. This may be particularly difficult if the providers themselves have developed mental health challenges as a result of their work with veterans (Stamm et al. 2004; Stamm 2009). Accordingly, prior to training military personnel and their families, it is recommended that an aggressive campaign occur with mental health providers. The military's goal of eradicating stigma should be conveyed in the strongest terms. All mental health and other medical providers entering the military also should receive stigma training.

Funding

One of the most important signals the military can send is by adequately funding stigma reduction training and behavior change programs, both for professionals and for military personnel and their families. Adequate funding ensures that trainings are available widely and taught by people who understand what stigma means to military personnel and their families. Providing funds for instruction includes supporting peers with mental illnesses to teach courses at all levels. Funding should include stipends for peers to teach classes or for those participating in social marketing planning. This is especially true for veterans and families. Peers should not be penalized for time away from their normal duties. Mass media campaigns must be sufficiently resourced, but other, less-expensive approaches (CBPR, community development) will ensure troops and veterans see action behind the media messages. A critical component of any social marketing campaign is to offer a new behavior to replace an old one, then promise something will be better as a result. If a campaign cannot follow through on the "promise," the campaign will not succeed.

Create Internships to Study and Implement Antistigma Campaigns

Military leadership can offer public information staff, people with mental illnesses and their families, as well as mental health providers an opportunity to participate in educational programs through internships or on-the-job training. In addition to classroom training, on-the-job experience can illuminate issues for those involved in communication and outreach. Participation in various self-help groups can be explored. All physical and mental health providers, new to or within the military, should receive stigma training. Again, participants should prepare personal action plans to change their behaviors regarding stigma.

Fund Research into Stigma Reduction

Currently, several measures are in place for gauging effectiveness of military campaigns, although the results may not be available for some time. Whether the number of educational outreach events conducted, the number of calls to the hotline, or review of charts of those with safety plans, these measures are commendable (*US VA Suicide Hotline* 2008). However, these are process measures, not outcome measures, and will not provide data on behavioral change regarding stigma. According to Kemp (2010), National Suicide Prevention Coordinator for the Veterans Health Administration, it will take some time to measure direct impacts of the presence of suicide prevention coordinators at VA centers.

Methods of measuring outcomes of social campaigns have not been adequately studied. While social distance is widely accepted as the yardstick for measuring stigma (Corrigan & Lundin 2001), its utility for measuring social marketing efforts has not been clearly demonstrated. With the help and support of people with mental illnesses and their families, the military is suited to identify outcome measures, conduct research, and publish the results. This will serve as a significant contribution not only to military personnel and veterans, but to the entire field.

Behavioral health and suicide issues are a very complex issue for veterans. High rates of suicide in older veterans, for example, demonstrate the need for early intervention (Kaplan et al. 2007; Desai, Dausey & Rosenheck 2008; Seal et al. 2007). Stigma should be addressed before veterans return home, with support from leaders (Stecker et al. 2007; Associated Press 2009). Advantages to receiving mental healthcare should be discussed, such as better relationships and sleep (Associated Press 2009). Mindfulness training, focus on time management and peer support can decrease symptoms of depression (Brenner et al. 2008; Pyne 2004). Rehabilitation counselors may need to learn more about appropriate supports for veterans returning with polytrauma, such as social and employment assistance (Frain, Malachy & Bethel 2010). The availability of these and other services, as well as diligence to eradicate stigma, hold promise for America's troops.

Author Note: This research was supported in part by the Idaho Awareness to Action Youth Suicide Prevention Project, Substance Abuse and Mental Health Services Administration, United States Department of Health and Human Services grant no. 1U79SM059188 revised. The opinions are the authors'.

References

Alvidrez, J., Snowden, L. R. & Kaiser, D. M. (2008). The experience of stigma among black mental health consumers. *Journal of Health Care for the Poor and Underserved* 19: 874–893. http://gateway.proquest.com/openurl?url_ver=Z39.88-2004&res_dat=xri:bsc:&rft_dat=xri:bsc:ft:iibp:00371396.

Andreasen, A. R. (2006). *Social marketing in the 21st century.* Thousand Oaks, CA: Sage Publications.

Antonak, R. F. (1982). Development and psychometric analysis of the scale of attitudes toward disabled persons. *Journal of Applied Rehabilitation Counseling* 13, no. 2: 22–29.

Associated Press. (2009). Military fights mental health stigma. May 16. http://www.msnbc.msn.com/id/30782778/ns/us_news-military/page/2/.

Bassett, J., Lloyd, C. & Bassett, H. (2001). Work issues for young people with psychosis: Barriers to employment. *British Journal of Occupational Therapy* 64: 66–72.

Bazron, B. (2006). Ensuring cultural and linguistic competence. Presented at *State/Tribal/Adolescents at Risk Grantee Technical Assistance Meeting.* http://www.sprc.org/grantees/dec06mtg2.asp (accessed February 13, 2007).

Brenner, L. A., Gutierrez, P. M., Cornette, M. M., Betthauser, L. M., Bahraini, N. & Staves, P. J. (2008). A qualitative study of potential suicide risk factors in returning combat veterans. *Journal of Mental Health Counseling* 30, no. 3: 211–225. http://web.ebscohost.com.proxy.lib.utk.edu:90/ehost/pdfviewer/pdfviewer?vid=7&hid=7&sid=b5ae97ab-304e-4e36-bcfc-e8c387b66bed percent40sessionmgr11.

Brown, K. & Bradley, L. J. (2002). Reducing the stigma of mental illness. *Journal of Mental Health Counseling* 24: 81–87.

Canino, G. & Roberts, R. E. (2001). Suicidal behavior among Latin youth. *Suicide and Life-threatening Behavior* 31: 122–131.

Carden, M. J. (2010). Better mental fitness will help prevent suicide, Sutton says. *American Forces Press Service,* January 11. http://www.defense.gov/news/news-article.aspx?id=57451 (accessed July 31, 2010).

Choi Wu, M., Kviz, F. J. & Miller, A. M. (2009). Identifying individual and contextual barriers to seeking mental health services among Korean American immigrant women. *Issues in Mental Health Nursing* 30: 78–85. doi: 10.1080/01612840802595204.

Cochran, S. D., Ortega, A. N., Alegria, M. & Takeuchi, D. (2007). Mental health and bisexual adults. *Journal of Consulting and Clinical Psychology* 75, no. 5: 785–794. doi: 10.1037/0022-006X.75.5.785.

Conner, K. O., Koeske, G. & Brown, C. (2009). Racial differences in attitudes toward professional mental health treatment: The mediating effect of stigma. *Journal of Gerontological Social Work* 52, no. 7: 695–712. doi: 10.1080/01634370902914372.

Cooper-Patrick, L., Powe, N. R., Jenckes, M. W., Gonzales, J. J., Levine, D. M. & Ford, D. E. (1997). Identification of patient attitudes and preference regarding treatment of depression. *Journal of General Internal Medicine* 12: 431–438. doi: 10.1046/j.1525-1497.1997.00075.x.

Corrigan, P. & Lundin, R. (2001). *Don't call me crazy.* Tinley Park, IL: Recovery Press.

Corrigan, P. W. (1997). How clinical diagnosis might exacerbate the stigma of mental illness. *Social Work* 52, no. 1: 31–40.

Corrigan, P. W. & Watson, A. C. (2002). The paradox of self-stigma and mental illness. *Clinical Psychology: Science & Practice* 9: 35–53.

Corrigan, P. W., Watson, A. C. & Barr, L. (2006). The self-stigma of mental illness: Implications for self-esteem and self-efficacy. *Journal of Social & Clinical Psychology* 25, no. 8: 875–884. http://web.ebscohost.com.proxy.lib.utk.edu:90/ehost/ pdfviewer/pdfviewer?vid=2&hid=119&sid=001be5f2-0adb-45c6-94e3-66657b 541d2c percent40sessionmgr104.

Crisp, R. (2000). A qualitative study of the perceptions of individuals with disabilities concerning health and rehabilitation professionals. *Disability and Society* 15, no. 2: 355–367.

Crisp, R. (2004). *Every family in the land: Understanding prejudice and discrimination against people with mental illness,* rev. ed. London: The Royal Society of Medicine Press Ltd.

Crocetti, G. M., Spiro, H. R. & Siassi, I. (1974). *Contemporary attitudes toward mental illness.* Pittsburgh, PA: University of Pittsburgh Press.

Cruz, M., Pincus, H. A., Harman, J. S., Reynolds, C. F. & Post, E. P. (2008). Barriers to care-seeking for depressed African-Americans. *International Journal of Psychiatry in Medicine* 38, no. 1: 71–79. doi: 10.2190/PM.38.1.g.

Desai, R. A., Dausey, D. & Rosenheck, R. A. (2008). Suicide among discharged psychiatric inpatients in the Department of Veterans Affairs. *Military Medicine* 173, no. 8: 720–728. http://web.ebscohost.com.proxy.lib.utk.edu:90/ehost/pdfviewer/ pdfviewer?vid=4&hid=7&sid=fb0d3c6b-a7b5-4b53-8ca5-24bf194da166percent 40sessionmgr13.

Falk, G. (2001). *Stigma: How we treat outsiders.* Amherst, NY: Prometheus Books.

Farina, A., Fisher, J. D. & Fisher, E. H. (1992). Societal factors in the problems faced by deinstitutionalized psychiatric patients in stigma and mental illness. In P. J. Fink & A. Tasman (Eds.), *Stigma and mental illness* (pp. 167–184). Washington, DC: American Psychiatric Press.

Finlay, W. M., Dinos, S. & Lyons, E. (2001). Stigma and multiple social comparisons in people with schizophrenia. *European Journal of Social Psychology* 31: 579–592.

Fishbein, H. D. (2002). *Peer prejudice and discrimination: The origins of prejudice.* 2nd ed. Mahwah, NJ: Lawrence Erlbaum Associates, Publishers.

Fogel, J. & Ford, D. E. (2005). Stigma beliefs of Asian Americans with depression in an Internet sample. *Canadian Journal of Psychiatry* 50, no. 8: 470–478. http:// web.ebscohost.com.proxy.lib.utk.edu:90.

Frain, M. P., Malachy, B. & Bethel, M. (2010). A roadmap for rehabilitation counseling to serve military veterans with disabilities. *Journal of Rehabilitation 76*, no. 1: 13–21. http://web.ebscohost.com.proxy.lib.utk.edu:90/ehost/pdfviewer/pdfviewer?vid=4&hid=12&sid=b99389cb-318f-4b80-90e1-7a79350f470dpercent40sessionmgr4.

Freire, P. (1970). *Pedagogy of the oppressed.* New York: Continuum International Publishing Group Inc.

Freire, P. (1985). *The politics of education: Culture, power and liberation.* New York: Bergin and Garvey.

Gee, G. C., Spencer, M., Chen, J., Yip, T. & Takeuchi, D. T. (2007). The association between self-reported racial discrimination and 12-month DSM-IV mental disorders among Asian Americans nationwide. *Social Science & Medicine 64*: 1984–1996. doi: 10.1016/j.socscimed.2007.02.013.

Giddens, A. (1990). *Justice and the politics of difference.* Princeton, NJ: Princeton University Press.

Goffman, E. (1963). *Stigma: Notes on the management of spoiled identity.* New York: Simon & Schuster.

Golberstein, E., Eisenberg, D. & Gollust, S. E. (2008). Perceived stigma and mental health care seeking. *Psychiatric Services 59*, no. 4: 392–399. doi: 10.1176/appi.ps.59.4.392.

Goldston, D. B., Molock, S. D., Whitbeck, L. B., Murakami, J. L. & Zayas, L. H. (2008). Cultural considerations in adolescent suicide prevention and psychosocial treatment. *American Psychologist 63*, no. 1: 14–31. doi: 10.1037/0003-066X.63.1.14

Grandbois, D. (2005). Stigma of mental illness among American Indian and Alaska Native Nations: Historical and contemporary perspectives. *Issues in Mental Health Nursing 26*, no. 10: 1001–1024. doi: 1080/01612840500280661.

Grover, S. (2009). Suicidal behavior in war veterans. In L. Sher & A. Vilens (Eds.), *War and suicide* (pp. 235–248). New York: Nova Science Publishers.

Haghighat, R. (2001). A unitary theory of stigmatisation: Pursuit of self-interest and routes to destigmatisation. *British Journal of Psychiatry 178*: 207–215.

Hall, B. L. (1981). Participatory research, popular knowledge and power: A personal reflection. *Convergence xiv*, no. 3: 6–17.

Harper, N. (1979). *Human communication theory: The history of a paradigm.* Rochelle Park, NJ: Hayden Book Company Inc.

Hatzenbuehler, M. L. (2009). How does sexual minority stigma "get under the skin"? A psychological mediation framework. *Psychological Bulletin 135*, no. 5: 707–730. doi: 10.1037/a0016441.

Heatherton, T. F., Kleck, R. E., Hebl, M. R. & Hull, J. G. (2003). *The social psychology of stigma.* New York: Guilford Press.

Henry, A. D. & Lucca, A. M. (2002). Contextual factors and participation in employment for people with serious mental illness. *Occupational Therapy Journal of Research 22*: 83S–84S.

Hinshaw, S. P. (2007) *The mark of shame: Stigma of mental illness and an agenda for change*. New York: Oxford University Press.

Hinshaw, S. P. & Cicchetti, D. (2000). Stigma and mental disorder: Conceptions of illness, public attitudes, personal disclosure, and social policy. *Development and Psychopathology* 12, no. 4: 555–598. doi:10.1017/S0954579400004028.

Hoge, C. W., Castro, C. A., Messer, S. C., McGurk, D., Cotting, D. I. & Koffman, R. L. (2004). Combat duty in Iraq and Afghanistan, mental health problems, and barriers to care. *New England Journal of Medicine* 351, no. 1: 13–22. doi: 10.1056/NEJMoa040603.

Hoge, C. W., Lesikar, S. E., Guevara, R., Lange, J., Brundage, J. F., Engel, C. C., Jr., et al. (2002). Mental disorders among U.S. military personnel in the 1990s: Association with high levels of health care utilization and early military attrition. *American Journal of Psychiatry* 159, no. 9: 1576–1583. http://ajp.psychiatryonline.org/cgi/reprint/159/9/1576.

Hovland, C. I., Janis, I. L. & Kelly, H. H. (1953). *Communication and persuasion: Psychological studies of opinion change*. New Haven, CT: Yale University Press.

Infante, D. A., Rancer, A. S. & Womack, D. F. (1990). *Building communication theory*. Prospect Heights, IL: Waveland Press Inc.

International Association for Public Participation. (2010). IAP2 spectrum of public participation. www.iap2.org (accessed July 18, 2010).

Jaker, J. (1998). Social marketing: Persuasive communication of public health. *Impact* (January). http://www.emprc.org/jan98/social.html (accessed May 8, 2002).

Johnstone, M. (2001). Stigma, social justice and the rights of the mentally ill: Challenging the status quo. *Australian & New Zealand Journal of Mental Health Nursing* 10: 200–209.

Jones, S. (1982). Social marketing: Dimensions of power and politics. *The European Journal of Marketing*, 16: 46–53.

Kaplan, M. S., Huguet, N., McFarland, B. H. & Newsom, J. T. (2007). Suicide among male veterans: A prospective population-based study. *Journal of Epidemiology & Community Health* 61: 619–624. doi: 10.1136/jech.2006.054346.

Kellogg Health Scholars Program. (2010). http://www.kellogghealthscholars.org/about/community.cfm (accessed July 18, 2010).

Kemp, J., Stephenson, K. & Woehr, K. (2010). VA program for suicide prevention. Paper presented at the State and Tribal Suicide Prevention Grantees Meeting, Las Vegas, Nevada. http://www.sprc.org/grantees/statetribe/2010/6A2percent20Stephenson.pdf.

Kilbury, R., Bordieri, J. & Wong, H. (1996). Impact of physical disability and gender on personal space. *Journal of Rehabilitation* (April–June): 59–61.

Kirkwood, A. D. (2005). *Better todays better tomorrows for children's mental health*. Presentation, multiple locations. Idaho State University.

Kirkwood, A. D. & Stamm, B. H. (2006). A social marketing approach to challenging stigma. *Professional Psychology, Research and Practice* 37, no. 5: 472–476.

Kisthardt, W. (n.d.). A person and a patient. Unpublished manuscript.

Kotler, P. & Roberto, E. (1989). *Social marketing: Strategies for changing public behavior*. New York: Free Press.

Kotler, P., Roberto, N. & Lee, N. (2002). *Social marketing: Improving the quality of life*. Thousand Oaks, CA: Sage Publications.

Kretzmann, J. P. & McKnight, J. L. (1993). *Building communities from the inside out: A path toward finding and mobilizing a community's assets*. Evanston, IL: Institute for Policy Research.

Link, B. G., Cullen, F. T., Mirotznik, J. & Struening, E. (1992). The consequences of stigma on persons with mental illness: Evidence from the social sciences in stigma and mental illness. In P. J. Fink & A. Tasman (Eds.), *Stigma and mental illness* (pp. 87–96). Washington, DC: American Psychiatric Press.

Link, B. G., Struening, E. L., Neese-Todd, S., Asmussen, S. & Phelan, J. C. (2001). Stigma as a barrier to recovery: The consequences of stigma for the self-esteem of people with mental illnesses. *Psychiatric Services* 52: 1621–1626.

Litz, B. & Orsillo, S. M., III. (n.d.). The returning veteran of the Iraq war: Background issues and assessment guidelines. In *Iraq War clinician guide* (pp. 21–32). http://www.ptsd.va.gov/professional/manuals/manual-pdf/iwcg/iraq_clinician_guide_ch_3.pdf.

MacStravic, S. (2000). The missing links in social marketing. *Journal of Health Communications* 5: 255–263.

Merriam-Webster. (n.d.). http://www.merriam-webster.com/dictionary/acculturation.

Mezirow, J. & Associates (1990). *Fostering critical reflection in adulthood: A guide to transformative and emancipatory learning*. San Francisco: Jossey-Bass Publishers.

Minkler, M. (1985). Building supportive ties and sense of community among the inner-city elderly: The Tenderloin senior outreach project. *Health Education Quarterly* 12, no. 4: 303–314.

Murray-Swank, A. & Dixon, L. (n.d.). *A pilot study of the family member provider outreach intervention*. VA Capitol Health Care Network (VISN 5) Mental Illness Research, Education, and Clinical Center (MIRECC) research abstract. http://www.mirecc.va.gov/visn5/docs/murray-swank1.pdf.

Nadeem, E., Lange, J. M. & Miranda, J. (2008). Mental health care preferences among low-income and minority women. *Archives of Women's Mental Health* 11: 93–102. doi: 10.1007/s00737-008-0002-0.

Norton, K. (2010). Suicide prevention, intervention and postvention for soldiers, and family. Paper presented at the State and Tribal Suicide Prevention Grantees Meeting, Las Vegas, Nevada. http://www.sprc.org/grantees/statetribe/2010/6A1percent20Norton.pdf.

President's Commission on Care for America's Returning Wounded Warriors. (2007). Serve, support, simplify: Report of the president's commission on care for America's returning wounded warriors. July. http://www.veteransforamerica.org/wp-content/uploads/2008/12/presidents-commission-on-care-for-americas-returning-wounded-warriors-report-july-2007.pdf.

Pyne, J. M. (2004). Relationship between perceived stigma and depression severity. *Journal of Nervous and Mental Disease* 192, no. 4: 278–283. doi: 10.1097/01.nmd.0000120886.39886.a3.

Rao, D., Feinglass, J. & Corrigan, P. (2007). Racial and ethnic disparities in mental illness stigma. *Journal of Nervous and Mental Disease* 195, no. 12: 1020–1023. doi: 10.1097/NMD.0b013e31815c046e.

Rousch, S. E. & Klockars, A. J. (1988). Construct validation of two scales measuring attitudes toward persons with disabilities. *Journal of Rehabilitation* (July–September): 25–30.

Seal, K. H., Bertenthal, D., Miner, C. R., Sen, S. & Marmer, C. (2007). Bringing the war back home: Mental health disorders among 103,788 US veterans returning from Iraq and Afghanistan seen at Department of Veterans Affairs facilities. *Archives of Internal Medicine* 167: 476–482. www.archinternmed.com.

Shea, M. (2007). Cultural competence in suicide prevention. Unpublished literature review. Institute of Rural Health, Idaho State University, Meridian, ID.

Shin, S. & Lukens, E. P. (2002). Effects of psychoeducation for Korean Americans with chronic mental illness. *Psychiatric Services* 53, no. 9: 1125–1131. http://psychservices.psychiatryonline.org.

Sirey, J. A., Bruce, M. L., Alexopoulos, G. S., Perlick, D. A., Friedman, S. J. & Meyers, B. S. (2001). Stigma as a barrier to recovery: Perceived stigma and patient-rated severity of illness as predictors of antidepressant drug adherence. *Psychiatric Services* 52: 1615–1620.

Spoont, M. R., Hodges, J., Murdoch, M. & Nugent, S. (2009). Race and ethnicity as factors in mental health service use among veterans with PTSD. *Journal of Traumatic Stress* 22, no. 6: 648–653. doi: 10.1002/jts.20470.

Stamm, B. H. (2009). *The concise ProQOL manual.* Pocatello, ID: ProQOL.org.

Stamm, B. H., Tuma, F., Norris, F. H., Piland, N. F., van der Hart, O., Fairbank, J. A., Stamm, H.E., Higson-Smith, C., Barbanel, L. & Levant, R. (2004). The terror part of terrorism. *Engineering in Medicine and Biology* 23: 149–161.

Stecker, T., Fortney, J. C., Hamilton, F. & Ajzen, I. (2007). An assessment of beliefs about mental health care among veterans who served in Iraq. *Psychiatric Services* 58, no. 10: 1358–1361. doi: 10.1176/appi.ps.58.10.1358.

Stephens, K. & Clark, D. (1987). A pilot study on the effect of visible stigma on personal space. *Journal of Applied Rehabilitation Counseling* 18: 52–54.

Struening, E. L., Perlick, D. A., Link, B. G., Hellman, F., Herman, D. & Sirey, J. A. (2001). Stigma as a barrier to recovery: The extent to which caregivers believe most people devalue consumers and their families. *Psychiatric Services* 52: 1633–1638.

U.S. Department of Veterans Affairs. (2010). About VA mental health. http://www.mentalhealth.va.gov/VAMentalHealthGroup.asp.

U.S. Department of Veterans Affairs' Suicide Hotline: Hearing before the Subcommittee on Health of the Committee on Veterans Affairs, House of Representatives. (2008). 110th Cong., 2nd sess. http://frwebgate.access.gpo.gov/cgi-bin/getdoc.cgi?dbname=110_house_hearings&docid=f:44931.pdf.

U.S. Department of Veterans Affairs/U.S. Department of Defense. (2008). VA/ DOD Joint Executive Council strategic plan fiscal years 2009–2011. http:// www.health.mil/Content//docs/SIGNEDpercent20JSPpercent20FY09-11percent 2001-08-2009 percent20FINAL.pdf.

Veltman, A., Cameron, J. I. & Stewart, D. E. (2002). The experience of providing care to relatives with chronic mental illness. *Journal of Nervous & Mental Disease* 190: 108–114.

Vogt, D. S., Pless, A. P., King, L. A. & King, D. W. (2005). Deployment stressors, gender, and mental health outcomes among Gulf War I veterans. *Journal of Traumatic Stress* 18, no. 2: 115–127. doi: IO.IOO2/jts.2OOI8.

Wahl, O. F. (1995). *Media madness: Public images of mental illness.* New Brunswick, NJ: Rutgers University Press.

Ward, E. C., Clark, L. O. & Heidrich, S. (2009). African American women's beliefs, coping behaviors, and barriers to seeking mental health services. *Qualitative Health Research* 19, no. 11: 1589–1601. doi: 10.1177/1049732309350686.

Watkins, C., Carlisle, C., Whitehead, E. & Mason, T. (2001). Relationship to practice. In T. Mason, C. Carlisle, C. Watkins & E. Whitehead (Eds.), *Stigma and social exclusion in healthcare* (pp. 40–48). London: Routledge Press.

Yanos, P. T., Rosenfeld, S. & Horowitz, A. V. (2001). Negative and supportive social interactions and quality of life among persons diagnosed with severe mental illness. *Community Mental Health Journal* 37: 405–419.

Young, I. M. (1990). *Justice and the politics of difference.* Princeton, NJ: Princeton University Press.

Zayas, L. H., Lester, R. J., Cabassa, L. J. & Fortuna, L. R. (2005). Why do so many Latina teens attempt suicide? A conceptual model for research. *American Journal of Orthopsychiatry* 75, no. 2: 275–287. doi: 10.1037/0002-9432.75.2.275.

Engaging Homeless Veterans in Healthcare

Thomas P. O'Toole

Homelessness intersects with healthcare and defines health in many different contexts. In many ways it can be considered a health issue in and of itself, as well as a reflection of our social safety net and the economic realities of lower-class and underclass populations. It is also a consequence of drug and alcohol abuse, the relative paucity of addiction treatment services, and under-resourced mental health services. Many urban emergency departments are defined by the homeless populations they serve, and healthcare settings are second only to soup kitchens as the first service sites accessed by individuals upon becoming homeless (O'Toole et al. 2007b).

This chapter presents a brief synopsis of health services research on homeless persons and their healthcare needs and service use, including a discussion of how some issues and needs are unique to veterans who are homeless compared with the general homeless population. This is followed by a brief historical overview on how health services have been organized and care systems developed for homeless persons over the past twenty-five years, beginning with the original Robert Wood Johnson and Pew Charitable Trust–funded demonstration projects and the creation of Health Care for the Homeless Clinics, as well as VA-based programs and initiatives. The discussion then turns to primary care for homeless persons within the context of treatment engagement and helping homeless persons emerge to a more stable and self-sufficient state. Finally, the chapter presents empirical data on interventions that have been effective in achieving these goals, new directions for program development and research, and areas where more work is needed.

Homelessness and Health Care

In 1988 the Institute of Medicine released a report on homelessness that succinctly described the relationship between health and homelessness in three capacities. First, some health problems precede and causally contribute to homelessness. For example, mental illnesses such as depression, schizophrenia, and bipolar disorder have long been reported as precipitants of homelessness (Brickner et al. 1990). Similarly, drug and alcohol addictions, accelerated with the more ready availability of crack cocaine in the 1990s, have also been described as a pathway to homelessness for many (Jencks 1995). Second, some health problems are consequences of homelessness. Exposure to the elements resulting in frostbite, trench foot, and hypo- and hyperthermia are commonly seen, particularly in intemperate zones and when shelter demand exceeds capacity (Brickner et al. 1990). Infestations from scabies, bed bugs, and fleas are extremely common and often serve as vectors for more serious diseases (Bonilla et al. 2009). The overcrowding of shelters, especially during inclement weather, makes transmission of airborne illnesses such as tuberculosis much easier, particularly when the immune system of homeless persons is already weakened, as is often the case. Trauma is also much more common among homeless persons, with women being most vulnerable (Kushel et al. 2003). Finally, homelessness itself complicates the treatment of many illnesses. Managing insulin-dependent diabetes while living in a dusk-to-dawn emergency shelter presents significant obstacles. Not only is storing and securing medications a challenge, but also managing multiple injections in the context of an unstable, erratic, and usually suboptimal supply of food and unstable sheltering arrangements is extremely difficult. Similarly, wound care is seriously compromised by the dependent edema that results from prolonged standing and walking that unsheltered and emergency sheltered homeless persons often have to face along with inadequate hygiene in many of these sheltering arrangements.

Homeless veterans are overrepresented among the homeless on any given night, with estimates that up to one in three homeless men and one in four homeless women are veterans (Rosenheck, Frisman & Chung 1994). In a 2007 report issued by the National Alliance to End Homelessness and the Homelessness Research Institute, it was estimated that 195,827 veterans were homeless on any given night in 2006, with a total of 495,400 veterans experiencing homelessness at some point over the course of the year. Subsequent estimates have placed the number of homeless veterans in the 107,000 range (National Alliance to End Homelessness 2007), still reflecting a disproportionate share of homeless persons. As with nonveteran homeless, extreme poverty, lack of social supports, physical and mental issues, substance abuse, and lack of affordable housing typically define this population. In a community-based survey of homeless persons in Pittsburgh and Philadelphia, two-thirds of homeless veterans had a chronic medical problem; 33 percent had two or more mental health problems, both of which were significantly higher than the nonveteran homeless in the sample (O'Toole et al. 2003). Previous research did not find a correlation to combat exposure and homelessness (Mares and Rosenheck 2004), although presumably factors such as long deployments away from home contributing to the erosion of one's social support network, the development of PTSD and other injuries while on active duty, and difficulty transitioning to civilian employment all pose challenges that, when not proactively addressed, could increase a veteran's risk for becoming homeless.

Health Care Services Models for Homeless Persons over the Past Twenty-five Years

Health Care for the Homeless Program

There is a long tradition and notable history of health professionals caring for the poor. Public hospitals, free clinics, street- and soup-kitchen-based outreach programs, inebriate centers, respite programs, and others have long served as a venerable safety net for the most needy and destitute, many of whom were homeless (Institute of Medicine 1988). However, it wasn't until 1983 that the first national effort to organize health services for homeless persons emerged with the launching of the Health Care for the Homeless Program demonstration project, a collaborative effort funded by the Robert Wood Johnson Foundation, Pew Charitable Trusts, and the U.S. Conference of Mayors. In all nineteen projects with an initial focus on primary medical care and service coordination were funded and operating by 1985. Following efforts aimed to improve mental health and substance abuse treatment, provide dental care, and treat HIV/AIDS and tuberculosis-infected homeless persons. In July 1987 Congress passed the Stewart B. McKinney Homeless Assistance Act, which assumed the funding for Health Care for the Homeless programs under Section 340 of the Public Health Service Act and expanded the program exponentially. Within ten years, there were 123 Health Care for the Homeless projects in forty-eight states, the District of Columbia, and Puerto Rico (McMurray-Avila 1997).

Almost one-half of organizations receiving Health Care for the Homeless funding are federally funded community health centers. The program is built around an approach that encompasses four principles: 1) The services provided must be comprehensive and encompass the global needs of homeless persons, 2) the care must be accessible to homeless persons and work around their needs and limits, 3) the attitudes of the providers must reflect a sensitivity to cultural and ethnic diversity along with dignity and respect for the clients; and 4) the philosophy of the clinics is to ultimately help people escape homelessness (McMurray-Avila 1997). The program has been effective in both engaging homeless persons in healthcare and redirecting care away from emergency departments. Almost 450,000 individuals were served in 1995 (McMurray-Avila 1997), and in a national survey of homeless adults, those individuals with at least two Health Care for the Homeless Program visits were significantly less likely to have an inappropriate emergency department visit (odds ratio = 0.43; 95 percent CI: 0.19–0.90) (Han & Wells 2003).

Department of Veterans Affairs Homeless Programming

The Department of Veterans Affairs (VA) represents the other coordinated national effort for caring for homeless persons. In 2005, through a network of programs and initiatives, VA provided healthcare to over 100,000 homeless veterans and other services to over 60,000 veterans through specialized homeless programs run by VA. Among these programs are VA's Health Care for Homeless Veterans Program, for homeless veterans with mental illness; the Domiciliary Care for Homeless Veterans, with more than 1,800 beds at thirty-four sites; Veterans Industry/Compensated Work Therapy Program, which serves approximately 14,000 annually; the VA Grant and Per Diem Program, which provides transitional housing and service centers for homeless veterans; the HUD-VA Supported Housing Program (HUD-VASH), which grew by an additional 10,000 units in 2010; which funds public and private nonprofit organizations operating supportive housing for homeless veterans; and Operation Stand Downs, which provides respite support for homeless veterans through a variety of activities (U.S. Department of Veterans Affairs 2006).

In addition to homeless-specific programming, VA as a health system has one of the more advanced and integrated electronic medical record systems, making it possible to develop patient registries and provide population-based care. Its primary care network, which provides most general medical care to homeless veterans, is one of the most advanced in the country, with health outcomes far outpacing those of private and Medicare-based models.

Taken together, these programs have made tremendous inroads in providing both outreach and services to homeless persons. The programs are more easily accessed and delivered in ways that accommodate the needs and challenges of the homeless and assist them in efforts to exit homelessness and achieve both housing and economic security. Hundreds of thousands of homeless persons are receiving services and supports that did not exist twenty five years ago.

Homeless Outcomes

Unfortunately, despite the hundreds of millions of dollars spent on homeless programming in the United States and the advances made in both our understanding of how best to provide care for and assist homeless persons and the overall numbers served, significant health disparities and adverse outcomes persist. Homeless adults have age-adjusted mortality 3.5 times higher than their domiciled counterparts (Hibbs et al. 1994). More alarmingly, the average age of death for a homeless person is forty-seven. While younger age groups are more likely to die from infections, such as HIV/AIDS, and trauma, the most common causes of death among homeless persons in the forty-five to sixty-four age group are cancer and heart disease, a rate threefold higher than the general population (Hwang et al. 1997). This has significant implications when considering the types of healthcare, social services, and interventions needed by homeless persons, as well as the importance of strategies that ensure compliance and continuity in the care being provided.

Given the high risk for and rate of multiple morbidities, it is not surprising that homeless persons also utilize acute-level health services at very high rates. In a survey of homeless adults, over 40 percent had used the emergency department at least once for care in the previous year, and more disturbingly, 7.9 percent of those surveyed accounted for 54.5 percent of visits (Kushel et al. 2002). In a national survey of homeless persons, one out of four is hospitalized annually (Kushel, Vittinghoff & Haas 2001) and, in a study of homeless persons accessing New York City hospitals, their average length of stay was 36 percent longer per admission than nonhomeless persons (Salit et al. 1998). Those homeless in more unstable sheltering arrangements (unsheltered and emergency sheltered) were more likely to go to emergency departments for care; substance abuse, trauma, mental illness, and exacerbations of chronic disease conditions were the most common reasons for seeking care. More disconcerting, only one-quarter of eligible homeless veterans were enrolled in VA, and VA clinics were reportedly used by only 5.6 percent (Kushel, Vittinghoff & Haas 2001). Similarly, in the Pennsylvania study cited previously, almost 60 percent of homeless veterans reported needing VA benefits and were more likely to receive shelter-based care rather than go to the VA center or a community clinic despite having greater need (O'Toole et al. 2003).

How do we reconcile the abysmal data generated from community-based samples of homelessness, including homeless veterans, with the programmatic successes and evidence-based approaches shown to be effective in caring for homeless persons and facilitating their exit from homelessness? One explanation is that the demand for these services outstrips their supply and availability. Although we have clearly identified programmatic success attributed to the various efforts noted previously, it may be that there is not enough capacity to serve all the homeless veterans who might benefit from these services. With a poor economy and increasing numbers of people becoming homeless, this is a legitimate concern. Another explanation could be the relative lack of "treatment readiness" among some homeless, making them ineligible for entry into transitional programs aimed at exiting homelessness. The result is that those homeless persons most capable of taking advantage of programs are enrolled, while those most impaired and/or treatment resistant become chronically homeless and use a disproportionate amount of acute-level care. In a time series study of homeless persons in the late 1990s during a period when the economy was very robust, those homeless persons who were more "work ready" were able to reenter the labor market and exit homelessness, leaving behind those persons with more medical, mental health, and substance-abuse-related needs, who stayed homeless and continued to rely on the safety net of crisis-based and acute-level services (O'Toole et al. 2002).

A third explanation relates to the chronicity of need that persists beyond the temporal state of being homeless. Substance abuse relapses, mental illness exacerbations, increased vulnerability in the job market, unforeseen medical illnesses, and disability all place a formerly homeless person at greater risk for returning to homelessness despite completing a program and transitioning to a more stable environment. In this scenario, homelessness is a marker for more fundamental and sustained need, which requires a more longitudinal approach that persists long after housing needs are met.

The challenge then is how to engage homeless persons in these care programs. How do we keep them engaged so that they can benefit fully from the services offered? And should they have a setback, how do we intervene before they experience a return to homelessness?

Theoretical Models

Considering these questions is facilitated by applying the framework of several interrelated theoretic models that help explain 1) why homeless persons are at higher risk for the adverse health and social outcomes noted, 2) factors and considerations that help determine whether someone seeks healthcare, 3) to what extent competing demands need to be considered and how important they are for different homeless subgroups, and 4) how motivation and associated behaviors can be fluid processes subject to change based on both internal and external factors.

As shown in figure 14.1, conceptualizing the dynamics involved in engaging a homeless person in treatment is best considered within the context of how

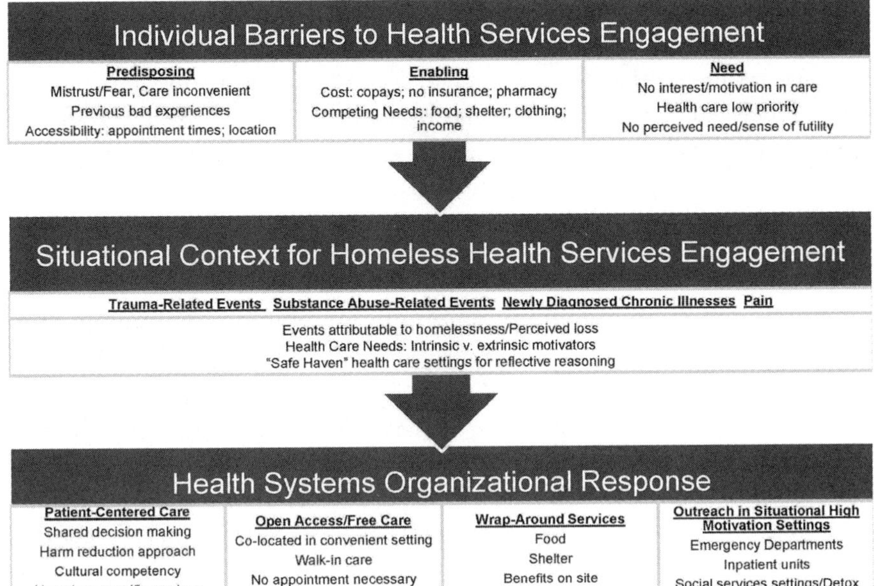

Figure 14.1. Factorial Modeling of Homeless Veteran Health Services Treatment Engagement.

four processes relate: 1) individual determents to health-seeking behavior, including predisposing, enabling, and need-based factors as well as the role of intrinsic and extrinsic motivators and situational motivation; 2) environmental factors that may include events related to becoming newly homeless and having added insight into and motivation to take actions needed to facilitate an early exit; 3) acute medical and mental health events related to one's homelessness that can prompt or precipitate an increase in motivation, as well as the capacity of one's social support network and resources; and finally, 4) organizational treatment engagement, which needs to be considered in the context of how, where, and when intervention services are made available and how responsive they are to both the immediate and long-term needs of a homeless person.

Social Determinants of Health

The first construct is based on social determinants of health, specifically the role of social deprivation and social cohesion in both the manifestations and effective treatment of mental illnesses. Dating back to the Whitehall Commission studies and others, the connection between mental and physical health and socioeconomic status is well established (Marmot et al. 1991; Wilkinson & Marmot

2003). Further research, however, has shown that social cohesion and the capacity of a low-income community to serve as an internal resource to its members can ameliorate the effects of individual social deprivation (Kawachi et al. 1996; Fone et al. 2007). The relevance to homelessness and the social support structure of homeless persons is clear and helps explain the additive impact of their environment on health status and health outcomes.

Health-Seeking Behavior

One framework for considering this dynamic is the Behavioral Model for Vulnerable Populations (Gelberg, Andersen & Leake 2002). This model has been used to describe health-seeking behavior and the receipt of health services by homeless persons in several major studies. The model posits that health-seeking behavior is determined by the relative influence of factors grouped into three domains: predisposing factors, enabling factors, and need factors. Predisposing factors include such things as education, residential stability/sheltering type, race/ethnicity, social structure, and health beliefs, including perceived efficacy of care. For homeless persons, social support has consistently been associated with receipt of health services. Those persons with stronger social support systems are more apt to receive healthcare and primary care, and also are more likely to leave homelessness earlier than those with less social support (Zlotnick, Tam & Robertson 2003). For homeless veterans, their perception of VA and the care available there is a predisposing factor that contributes to the process of treatment engagement and receipt of health services. Enabling resources include the support and assistance of family and friends, who may assist with transportation, copays, etc.; where one lives; whether he or she has insurance (which is not an issue for eligible veterans); as well as barriers to care such as competing needs (e.g. food, clothing, finding shelter), the ability to negotiate bureaucratic systems, etc.

Finally, need-based factors include both perceived and diagnosed illnesses. Perceived need for physical healthcare, defined by self-reported illnesses, has consistently been shown to be the strongest predictor of service use in both veteran and nonveteran homeless populations (Padgett, Struening & Andrews 1990; Wenzel et al. 1995). Homeless persons who had received healthcare within the previous six months were significantly more likely to report having a primary care site for usual care (O'Toole et al. 1999b). Predisposing factors including age, race, gender, veteran status, and the type of sheltering arrangement have also been identified as significant in both accessing care and having a regular provider (O'Toole et al. 1999b; Wenzel et al. 1995). Enabling factors associated with greater health service use and with having a source for usual care include having health insurance, and in the eligible veteran's case, receiving VA-based benefits (i.e. disability). For all homeless, experiencing fewer barriers to accessing care, reporting less difficulty meeting daily sustenance needs, and having a higher level of social support are all enabling factors (Padgett, Struening & Andrews 1990; O'Toole et al. 1999b; Wenzel et al. 1995).

Readiness for Change

The transtheoretical "stages of change" model (DiClemente 2003) conceptualizes readiness to change problem behaviors as occurring in stages, including *precontemplation*, in which the individual has little or no awareness of the problem behavior; *contemplation*, in which the behavior is acknowledged but there is no commitment to change; and *action*, characterized by an initiation of the behavior change. Although readiness to change behaviors is distinct from readiness to engage in substance abuse treatment, treatment is generally intended for those with high internal motivation to change their behaviors (Battjes, Onken & Delany 1999). Further, acute events such as trauma and injury have been shown in several studies to be associated with higher stages of change and a higher likelihood among injection drug users of engaging in substance abuse treatment (Bombardier, Ehde & Kilmer 1997; Apodaca & Schermer 2003).

This model has been applied extensively to drug and alcohol addictions as well as to other behaviors such as smoking cessation and dietary changes. Its applicability to homelessness becomes apparent when considering the role of substance abuse, either directly or indirectly, in causing homelessness and often in preventing an exit from homelessness.

Competing Sustenance Needs

The decision by homeless persons to seek healthcare is also based on the relative urgency and import of competing sustenance needs. In a study by Gelberg and colleagues (1997), specific needs related to food security, housing security, and safety compete with the perceived need for healthcare, particularly care needs that may not be acute or that are preventive in nature. These competing sustenance needs and the priority given to them relative to perceived or actual healthcare needs are important considerations to understanding why, where, and when homeless persons seek care. They also shape how care models can best be designed to optimize access by addressing or accommodating these needs.

Taken together, these behavioral models help explain an organizational, environmental, and individual-based context for considering treatment engagement. They also help explain why some interventions have been successful in engaging homeless persons in care while others have not and the complexity of why some approaches will work for specific subgroups of homeless persons and in specific settings or situations.

Lessons Learned

Over the past twenty-five years we have learned much about what works best in both the design and delivery of programs for homeless persons, as well as what factors need to be considered when developing interventions.

Housing Is Health Care

Previous research has consistently shown that unstable sheltering arrangements (e.g., residing in an emergency shelter or in an unsheltered arrangement) are associated with high levels of emergency department use and inappropriate emergency department use (Kushel et al. 2002; O'Toole et al. 1999a, 1999b). Homeless persons in more stable sheltering arrangements are also 2.4 times more likely to access care and receive care for chronic medical problems (O'Toole et al. 1999b). In a study of homeless persons participating in a posthospitalization medical respite intervention that included case management and housing placement, subsequent hospitalizations over the following eighteen months were reduced by 29 percent (0.5 admissions/2.7 days) and ER visits by 24 percent (1.2 episodes) (Sakowski et al. 2009).

Similarly, there is an increasing body of research demonstrating the effectiveness of "housing first" models that prioritize stable housing as a means for achieving sobriety, mental health stabilization, and economic support/self-sustainment. This is in contrast to the historic approach of making receipt of those services a requisite for obtaining stable housing, which some have argued may still be more appropriate for some homeless subgroups (Stefancic & Tsemberis 2007; Kertesz et al. 2009; Kertesz & Weiner 2009). Additional research is needed to better understand which approach to housing should be applied and when.

Social Support Is an Independent Predictor of Earlier Exits from Homelessness

Studies have consistently shown that homeless persons with higher degrees of social support are more likely to exit homelessness earlier and use fewer acute-level health services. In a community-based study of homeless in Pittsburgh, high social support scores were independently associated with receiving healthcare during a six-month period (O'Toole et al. 1999b). Similarly, in a study of homeless adults in Los Angeles, social isolation was an identified barrier to having a regular source of healthcare (Gallagher et al. 1997). Veterans experiencing longer durations of homelessness are more likely to have more mental health and substance abuse disorders and weaker levels of social support (Wenzel et al. 1995). Finally, in a sample of 397 homeless adults followed over a fifteen-month period, among those persons without a substance use disorder, having support from family or friends and engaging in service use were associated with earlier exits from homelessness (Zlotnick, Tam & Robertson 2003).

Homeless Persons Are (and Can Become) Motivated to Adopt Behaviors Necessary to Exit Homelessness

It is often assumed that homeless persons are unwilling to change and have little motivation to engage in the type of behaviors necessary for them to exit homelessness. However, several studies have identified the opposite: that homeless persons often have enhanced motivation for a behavior change, particularly in the context of an acute health or social crisis. In a study of adults admitted to an acute care hospital for complications from substance abuse, homeless persons were as likely as those domiciled to be interested in stopping their drug use and entering a treatment program. Further, 80 percent of those interested in drug treatment reported physical health concerns as a major reason for wanting to quit. Homeless respondents were also 2.5 times more likely to report their living arrangement as a major motivation for seeking treatment (O'Toole et al. 2006). In another study of homeless persons with an active history of drug and alcohol abuse, over two-thirds reported less use upon becoming homeless, citing reasons including no longer having any interest in using or pleasure from using, concerns about safety, and lack of resources. Most also were able to identify their drug or alcohol use as a precipitant to their becoming homeless (O'Toole et al. 2004).

Readiness for Change Is a Fluid Dynamic

It is often assumed that the response one gets when asking someone about his or her drug or alcohol use is set in stone and unlikely to change under any circumstances. This expectation is reflected in the limited attention often given to motivational interviewing and brief interventions when interacting with patients with addictions requiring a behavior change and the lack of follow-up typically given to negative responses. In a study of predominantly homeless individuals hospitalized for medical complications from substance abuse, it was notable that during the acute hospitalization, 42.5 percent of respondents either increased from precontemplation or contemplation to a higher stage or remained in the action stage on follow-up assessments. These findings support the idea of a therapeutic "window" occurring during an acute health event when there is an opportunity to enhance the motivation for drug and alcohol treatment among certain medical inpatients. Recent heroin and cocaine use, believing one would get sick again, and physical health concerns were all positively associated with an increase in readiness to change. Such reasons reflect the potential transience of this readiness if motivating factors are not identified and acted upon during this "window" of time (Pollini et al. 2006).

The challenge is how best to organize and align health services delivery to quickly engage a motivated homeless person, who is willing to initiate behavioral changes requisite for an exit from homelessness, and facilitate entry into the necessary services in time to take advantage of what may be a fleeting and situational motivation.

The Role of Primary Care in Homeless Healthcare

Primary care, and specifically primary care tailored to the needs of homeless persons, provides a unique opportunity to address some of the service gaps and vulnerabilities in homeless healthcare. It also provides the platform on which to engage homeless persons in an array of services over a continuum of time and needs. The role that primary care plays in caring for homeless persons has been described and discussed extensively in the literature. Shortt and colleagues (2008), in a policy analysis of care models in Canada, found that traditional primary care approaches performed poorly compared with targeted clinics, fixed outreach site-based care, and mobile outreach services for homeless persons. This is also reflected in a survey of homeless persons in which 84 percent preferred specialized homeless service for their primary care needs (Hewett 1999). However, individuals lacking or in unstable sheltering arrangements also face several homeless-specific barriers to care that need to be considered in any model or systems design. Long-term homelessness (> two years), social isolation, and competing needs, such as food, clothing, and finding shelter, are all associated with not having a regular source of care (Gallagher et al. 1997). In addition, multiple morbidities of homeless persons, including mental illnesses, substance use, and acute and chronic medical problems, often create a triaging dilemma, fragmenting and prioritizing care needs in ways that may not always reflect the priorities and preferences of the homeless patient. This also can override any opportunity to provide preventive care and engage the person in behavioral changes. In order to engage homeless veterans in healthcare, address their needs, and facilitate their exit from homelessness, the primary care model needs to incorporate five core elements/features:

1. **Accessibility:** As noted in the Health Care for the Homeless Program, health services provided to homeless persons should be consistently available when and where they are needed. Primary care clinics, when appropriately situated, urgent care centers, and emergency departments all provide immediate, just-in-time access to homeless persons without the need for referral, prior workup, or an established condition. An advantage to primary care clinics is that they are organized to provide comprehensive and continuity care incorporating social needs with an established follow-up expectation.

2. **Readiness to respond to a "treatable moment":** Several studies have demonstrated the effectiveness of brief interventions and motivational interviewing in primary care and emergency department settings. These interventions provide the means for engaging patients in behavioral changes ranging from tobacco cessation to reductions in hazardous drinking and drug abuse (Bernstein et al. 2005; Gentilello et al. 1995). The clinical staff needs the proper training and preparation to apply these interventions for engaging patients in behavioral change with the necessary resources in place to act immediately on the homeless patient's stage of readiness.

3. **Trust/relationship building:** Homeless providers consistently identify the ability to develop a trusting relationship with a patient as an integral step to engaging that person in homeless services and helping him or her exit homelessness. The longitudinal nature of primary care lends itself to capacity and is essential, particularly for those patients who are more ambivalent or precontemplative about engaging in services or a behavioral change or who have multiple competing and concurrent needs that require time and ongoing care to effectively address.

4. **Integrated delivery model/addressing competing needs:** The needs of a homeless person presenting for care are rarely, if ever, restricted to an isolated chronic or acute medical condition. Similarly, his or her decision to seek care is often made in the face of competing sustenance needs, such as securing shelter for the night, food, personal safety, finding money/seeking work, staying warm, etc. (Gelberg et al. 1997). In order to make the clinic visit more relevant to a homeless client, it is best to have as many services as possible specific to his or her medical, mental health, and social needs available on site. Primary care models that are able to incorporate mental healthcare and have social work, disability claims, food, and clothing available

on-site are generally better able to address the full spectrum of needs of a homeless person in a more comprehensive and efficient way (Blue-Howells, McGuire & Nakashima 2008; McGuire et al. 2009; O'Toole et al. 2010).

5. **Harm-reduction/housing-first approach:** Eliminating prerequisites for care and treating homeless patients on their terms are key to 1) developing the trust and relationship necessary in the care of this population and 2) supporting the longitudinal needs of these patients over time. This often requires the clinical team to encourage cutting back substance use rather than initially insisting on abstinence. It may also require spending time discussing the importance of safer sex, avoiding needle sharing, cleaning one's drug paraphernalia, or strategies to avoid injury or trauma as the initial foci for clinic visits. It also provides the homeless patient the opportunity to change his or her mind, evolve in his or her thinking, and embrace the changes necessary to leave homelessness, an opportunity that is often not possible in a one-time encounter. Again, primary care clinics tailored to the needs of homeless persons have the capacity to do this in ways that care provided in other health settings do not. Incorporating a "housing first" approach into the care model recognizes the role of housing in determining both healthcare needs and the ability to care for oneself while addressing patient priorities within a healthcare paradigm.

There are specific care models within VA that reflect these capacities and approaches to primary care for homeless persons. The Greater Los Angeles VAMC developed an integrated primary care clinic model for homeless veterans with serious mental illness and/or substance abuse with co-located clinical and social services. In a quasi-experimental design, they were able to demonstrate an increase in primary care visits and reduction in emergency-department-based care over an eighteen-month period (Blue-Howells, McGuire & Nakashima 2008; McGuire et al. 2009). At the Providence VAMC, the homeless-oriented primary care clinic combines open access on fixed days with primary care tailored to needs specific to homelessness (food, shelter security, and a special emphasis on conditions homeless persons are particularly susceptible to), care management, on-site service integration (primary care, mental health, housing, and benefits), and a harm reduction orientation (O'Toole et al. 2010). In a chart review of 316 consecutive patients seen in this clinic, each patient averaged 8.9 visits per year: 68.2 percent were for primary care/RN case management, 16.3 percent were with the regional office representative, and 15.5 percent were with the homeless veterans' housing outreach worker. Reflecting both the needs of these veterans who had previously been disconnected from a chronic care model and the benefits of an integrated care delivery approach, 70 percent of patients in this case series often had a newly diagnosed chronic disease treated, 23.6 percent were referred to mental health for ongoing care of a serious mental illness (e.g. bipolar, schizophrenia), and 17.4 percent were referred into VA substance abuse treatment programs. In addition, 38.9 percent of patients were referred to the Veterans Resource Center for supportive employment programming, 79.4 percent of veterans evaluated by the benefits officer had a claim filed (with 46 percent of those claims either granted or still under review), and 28.9 percent of veterans seen by the housing coordinator were successfully placed in either permanent VASH or transitional (VA domiciliary, per diem) housing. This model also demonstrated significant improvements in chronic disease management (diabetes, hypertension, hyperlipidemia), while simultaneously reducing emergency department visits for nonacute problems (OR 0.43; 95 percent CI: 0.2–0.8) and nonsubstance abuse/mental health hospital admissions (50 percent reduction; p < 0.01) when compared to a matched cohort of homeless veterans getting care in a traditional primary care setting.

Other models have been developed within VA facilities. The Rochester VAMC has a similar model to that in Providence and Greater Los Angeles. The Roanoke VA has implemented a unique group visit approach, with positive treatment engagement outcomes. Other VA centers have co-located primary care within grant and per diem and domiciliary settings, as well as geographically positioned community-based outpatient clinics (CBOCs) to be accessible to homeless persons residing in nearby shelters.

The Treatment Resistant Homeless Veteran

However, even with the resources and programming available for homeless services, the multiple potential "treatable moments" when homeless veterans interact with social and healthcare agencies, and the temporal, enhanced motivation among homeless veterans that represent opportunities to engage them in necessary behavioral changes, there are many whom we have not been able to engage in a health and social services model of care. While estimates vary, as noted previously, anywhere from 40 to 60 percent (and possibly more) of potentially eligible homeless veterans are not getting care at VA. These numbers may include individuals not eligible for VA services for a variety of reasons (e.g., dishonorable discharge, not enough time spent in the military) and homeless veterans who have well-established sources for primary care outside of VA and do not need services; still, there are significant numbers of veterans in need of care, support services, and housing who are not connected with VA.

From a patient perspective, competing sustenance needs often dilute the relative importance of accessing healthcare, particularly for health maintenance and monitoring of chronic, asymptomatic conditions (Gelberg et al. 1997). Further, one's perception of need for healthcare and anticipated outcomes also plays a role. Patients reporting "not caring what happens" in a survey of Pittsburgh homeless were significantly less likely to have received any healthcare, independent of self-identified comorbidities (O'Toole et al. 1999a). Similarly, patterns of healthcare avoidance were identified in over half of homeless persons with a self-described, and subsequently confirmed, acute need (typically an infectious disease complication from substance use). This cohort identified a pessimistic and fatalistic expectation of their outcome and lacked confidence in the healthcare system to adequately address their concerns (O'Toole et al. 2010).

These findings suggest that not only outreach, but outreach that educates and informs the veteran about why health services are needed, builds a sense of self-efficacy about receiving care, and educates them on how health services can be accessed and what their expectations should be, is necessary to enhance health-seeking behavior among treatment-naive homeless persons. This is also supported by several intervention and observational studies. Rumptz and colleagues (2007), in a chart review of 984 HIV-positive patients, many of whom were homeless, concluded that addressing negative health beliefs along with decreasing structural barriers to care were both key to successful treatment engagement for this population. Desai, Rosenheck, and Kasprow (2003) found that contact by an outreach worker was less effective in engaging homeless veterans in care compared to when the veteran self-referred himself or herself to a clinic. And Cabral and colleagues (2007), in a study of HIV-positive adults, found that individuals who had received one or more outreach contacts over an initial three-month period were significantly more likely to remain engaged in treatment. These findings suggest that outreach can be effective, but to be successful, it has to be both targeted and persistent.

Unfortunately, often outreach efforts to homeless persons, though well-intentioned, can become missed opportunities to engage individuals in behavioral changes and connect them to necessary resources, services, and care management. A study looking at "first access" sites among newly homeless adults found that self-reported needs (e.g., housing, healthcare) did not necessarily match the services available at the sites first accessed by those individuals (food pantry, welfare office) (O'Toole et al. 2007b). Soup kitchens were the most frequently accessed sites among persons with chronic medical conditions, followed by emergency departments, neither of which are typically outfitted or prepared to engage homeless persons in disease management or to address underlying issues that may be causal in their becoming homeless. Other studies have looked at stages of readiness for change among homeless persons encountered in soup kitchens (Nwakeze, Magura & Rosenblum 2002). Interestingly, though most homeless persons surveyed were in either a precontemplative or contemplative stage of behavioral change, perceived awareness of the problems that substance use were causing and the need for treatment were associated with higher stages of change in the study population.

In another community-based study of self-identified needs among homeless persons, housing and economic supports were the needs most commonly cited as "very important." This was followed closely by physical health needs and mental health needs, which were highly rated by 80 percent and 60 percent of the sample respectively, whereas unmet substance abuse treatment needs were reported by over one-half of the sample (O'Toole et al. 1999b). The role of physical health concerns in treatment engagement and retention was studied in the context of acute medical illnesses and substance abuse treatment. It was found to be the most common reason for treatment engagement in a cohort of predominantly homeless heroin- and cocaine-abusing adults in Baltimore, Maryland (O'Toole et al. 2006). However, this motivation was not associated with treatment retention unless the client was able to transition to more "internalized," self-empowered motivators for staying in treatment.

What Works

Much of what we know now about strategies for engaging homeless persons comes from the substance abuse literature specific to homeless persons. Several "best practices" for engaging treatment-resistant homeless persons have been studied. They can broadly be defined in four groups: 1) models that take advantage of the "situational motivation" brought on by a specific crisis (typically healthcare-related), or motivation prompted by linking an action to addressing an unmet competing need, as a means of engaging the homeless person in a care model; 2), models that work to establish a rapport and trust in a community setting and use that process to transition the homeless person to a more structured care model; 3) models that introduce pharmacologic adjuncts to facilitate engagement; and 4) models that co-link social services to create an incentive for engagement in a medical model. These strategies are not mutually exclusive, and in practice, often the most effective interventions are those that combine one or more of these approaches into an integrated, readily accessible, continuous care model.

Situational Motivation and "Treatable Moment" Interventions

Intervention studies based in emergency departments and inpatient units where this type of "situational motivation" or "treatable moment" may be present have consistently reported positive outcomes associated with brief interventions, case management, and other approaches (O'Toole et al. 2007a; Okin et al. 2000; Redelmeier, Molin & Tibshirani 1995; Sakowski et al. 2009). The rationale for this is that the personal health event or crisis creates a "treatable moment" wherein the individual is more open to considering a behavioral change because he or she can make the association between a specific behavior or action and an adverse consequence (e.g., injury, infection, trauma, becoming homeless) (Bombardier, Ehde & Kilmer 1997; Apodaca & Schermer 2003). This is often why motivational interviewing and brief interventions are most effective when based in settings where the homeless person is presenting acutely as a consequence of his or her behavior (substance use, etc.). Another advantage to placing these interventions in emergency departments and hospital settings is that the individual has already engaged in a health-seeking behavior that implies some element of help seeking. Studies in which homeless-specific interventions are based in general hospital emergency departments have demonstrated enhanced ability to redirect clients to more appropriate care settings (Okin et al. 2000; Redelmeier, Molin & Tibshirani 1995) and to engage them in care management. While interventions during acute hospitalizations have been associated with engagement in substance abuse treatment and care management, both correlate with improved housing outcomes (Sakowski et al. 2009; O'Toole et al. 2007a).

A caveat to these findings is that readiness to change can often be fleeting, within the context of an acute event. In a study of hospitalized substance-abusing adults, 40 percent of whom were homeless, serial assessments of readiness to change found that almost one-half of the study cohort regressed to a precontemplative state within several days of admission, independent of pain, withdrawal symptoms, or a change in their postdischarge housing status (Pollini et al. 2006). These findings suggest that the "treatment window" does not stay open for long and requires a timely response.

Contingency management interventions, wherein a positive behavior (e.g., abstinence, participation in a program) is reinforced by a positive feedback via positive social and/or tangible rewards (such as monetary payments, lottery drawings, and vouchers) have all been shown to improve treatment participation and abstinence rates among homeless participants (Zerger 2002). This approach does require a consistent approach to monitoring and compliance, additional resources being made available to support the behaviors needed, and a philosophical belief in the theory of contingency management and reinforcement principles, which are often viewed negatively by some as rewarding individuals for doing what they should be doing anyway (Higgins & Silverman 1999). A similar approach is the linking of housing and/or employment to abstinence among homeless participants. This has also been associated with positive and sustained outcomes (Higgins & Silverman 1999; Shumacher et al. 2000).

Establishing Rapport/Developing Trust

It is one thing to give advice and another for the person to accept that advice. Miller and Rolnick (2002), in *Motivational Interviewing*, emphasize that the first step in the process of preparing people for change is establishing a rapport. For treatment-resistant homeless persons, this is often more difficult, for several reasons. First, because of their unstable and unpredictable living arrangements, creating continuity in their encounters and interactions is often difficult, particularly when care is based in an emergency department or structured counseling sessions. Other encounters follow tight schedules that do not accommodate access challenges facing homeless persons. Second, many homeless persons have had negative experiences with the health profession in the past (Wen, Hudak & Hwang 2007) and may not be willing to readily open up to a doctor, nurse, counselor, or social worker no matter how well intentioned the practitioner.

Models that have effectively overcome this reluctance include the assertive community treatment (ACT) model, studied within the context of homeless persons with serious persistent mental illness. Street-based ACT targeted to schizophrenic homeless persons with a harm-reduction, trust-based approach to client engagement has demonstrated both reduced emergency department use and improved medication compliance (Lehman et al. 1997; Henrinckx et al. 1997).

Street outreach and street-based healthcare are other strategies for treatment and service engagement by bringing care to homeless persons and working with them on their terms (Howe, Buck & Withers 2009). In several studies, outreach initiatives were effective for targeting and contacting homeless substance abusers who are otherwise difficult to engage (Zerger 2002). Street- and shelter-based teams address the issues of transportation, fear, lack of resources, and other traditional barriers to care that typically keep homeless persons from seeking assistance when it is needed. The key to all of these approaches is to already have in place resources that homeless persons can connect with once trust has been developed and the individual is "ready" to effect a change.

Other research has shown the importance of frequent contacts and consistent outreach. In a study of difficult-to-reach persons with HIV, researchers found that when subjects received nine or more contacts during a three-month period, they were half as likely to have a treatment lapse in the first twelve months of follow-up (Cabral et al. 2007). Shelter-based outreach with weekly visits by a psychiatrist and social worker was associated with receiving subsequent care in a community mental health center and receiving substance abuse treatment (Bradford et al. 2005). Finally, a study of clients accessing a mobile needle exchange program found that a significant proportion of individuals participating ultimately entered a detoxification and/or treatment program, suggesting that harm-reduction interventions such as needle exchange programs serve as an effective "bridge" to treatment services (Strathdee et al. 1999).

Consonant with the importance of social support systems in both receipt of health services while homeless and facilitating earlier exits from homeless, several investigators have studied using family contacts and other "concerned significant others" to engage homeless persons in substance abuse treatment, with positive outcomes (Meyers et al. 2002; Slesnick et al. 2000). These approaches are typically much more labor- and resource-intensive and often require a significant amount of preplanning and family engagement to be effective, elements not always practical or affordable in the context of under-resourced substance abuse treatment services.

The Use of Pharmacologic Adjuncts

Several studies have demonstrated the effectiveness of pharmacologic modalities such as methadone maintenance, buprenorphine, and naltrexone in maintaining sobriety and treatment engagement in substance abuse treatment programs (Alford et al. 2007; Krysal et al. 2001). To the extent that substance abuse, dependence, and relapses are often the principal precipitants of becoming or staying homeless (Institute of Medicine 1988; Jencks 1995), the potential role of these agents as part of a homeless healthcare strategy is obvious. These agents act by blocking select receptors in regions of the brain associated with reward and craving, thereby reducing the urge use. Disulfiram, on the other hand, works by causing one to become acutely ill if alcohol is consumed, thus creating a negative reinforcement against continued use. Methadone maintenance, when linked to dispensing of highly active antiretroviral therapies (HAART) for patients with AIDS, has also been shown to increase antiretroviral therapy adherence, which has significant public health implications (Lucas et al. 2006). The challenge, however, with all of these agents is twofold: first, medication compliance, particularly for a drug that needs to be taken at least once a day, is challenging, especially if one is homeless; second, the effectiveness of these agents in settings where environmental triggers and stressors are heightened (e.g., when unsheltered or residing in an emergency shelter) is likely compromised and should be considered within a broader context of treatment engagement and service delivery. More research is needed on the effectiveness of these agents and possible tailoring of dosing and administration to homeless populations.

Services on Demand

The availability of services on demand is integral to all of these approaches for engaging the treatment-resistant homeless veteran. Although waiting lists and stringent prerequisites may help "weed out" those persons more ambivalent about making changes necessary to meet requirements for a program or to exit homelessness, this process of attrition also precludes treatment for many people who would otherwise benefit from the services being sought. This is the rationale behind housing-first models, which have demonstrated a capacity for service engagement once housing needs have been met (Stefancic & Tsemberis 2007; Kertesz and Weiner 2009). This is also the rationale assumed by Health Care for the Homeless Programs in colocating and linking services to create "one-stop shops" with wraparound services readily available on-site, avoiding the need to send a homeless person to multiple agencies and organizations for care. When services are not available on demand (e.g., waiting lists for supportive housing), it is critical that there be a way to effectively engage the homeless person with interim measures and supports to keep him or her engaged.

Areas for Future Research

Although VA has arguably one of the best-developed and -resourced service networks for homeless persons, at issue is how to better engage homeless veterans in those services, ideally early in their homelessness. Health services research has identified a significant proportion of homeless veterans who are not connected to VA for care, or who only receive care on an urgent or emergent basis. Other studies have identified complications from homelessness itself, arguing for the importance of early interventions (or better yet, prevention). Several more studies have noted that chronically homeless adults (including veterans) are a more challenging population to engage in health-seeking behavior and care delivery models. It is important to note that many of these studies are using data collected ten or more years ago. At the present time such findings may not necessarily capture the complete realities of veteran homelessness, which now encompasses both the aging of Vietnam-era homeless veterans and the emergence of newer populations of homeless veterans from the Iraq and Afghanistan wars. There are several related questions and issues to consider:

1. **Epidemiology:** More up-to-date information is needed regarding who the disconnected homeless veterans are, why are they not receiving care from

VA, what their needs are, and what their potential access and engagement points of contact are.

2. **Homeless typologies:** The spectrum of competing needs among homeless veteran subgroups is likely to differ by population (e.g., postdeployment, economically stressed OEF/OIF veterans doubled-up with friends, as compared to a twenty-year homeless veteran with chronic schizophrenia and alcohol dependence). Understanding motivating factors for seeking healthcare and social services among different population subgroups is critical to effectively matching services to needs.

3. **"Treatable moments" intervention studies:** Situational motivation linked to a crisis event, typically health-related (acute illness, trauma, new diagnosis) or legal-related (e.g., drug court sentencing alternative), has been shown in several studies to be an effective and efficient means of engaging homeless persons in behavioral changes necessary for exiting homelessness (such as entering substance abuse treatment). Co-locating services at first points of contact (EDs, inpatient hospital units, primary care clinics), providing on-site brief interventions, treatment on demand, and comprehensive case management have all been effective strategies in these studies. However, much less is known about how these interventions might work within VA, or how advances in VA delivery systems (the electronic medical record, patient registries, integrated primary care–mental health services, one-VA care, etc.) might facilitate such interventions. Further, we need a better understanding of what behavioral nuances (intrinsic versus extrinsic motivating factors, measures of resilience, relative roles of social support and other supportive or competing factors, etc.) are associated with these situations and how responses may vary among specific homeless veteran subgroups and their specific "treatable moments."

4. **Biologic determinants/pharmacotherapy and other adjuncts:** What is the role of naltrexone, methadone maintenance, buprenorphine, opiate-based pain relief, and other modalities as both inducements and facilitators of treatment/service engagement and retention? Do we know why they work, and for whom? Are there biological markers that can facilitate treatment matching? What are the best ways to integrate pharmacotherapy adjuncts with specific care scenarios and situations, as well as within structural and organizational care models, to optimize outcomes? As we gain a better understanding of how these agents work through functional imaging and genetic studies, the potential for designing personalized, multifaceted interventions specific to homeless persons represents a whole new frontier of care planning.

5. **Engagement versus Retention:** How can engagement be sustained, particularly when the relative stability of more structured housing can be associated with increases in substance use or when underlying high-risk behaviors have not been fully addressed? This will become increasingly important with the emphasis on housing-first approaches and the growth of the HUD-VASH program in VA.

Policy Recommendations

Service Organization and Delivery

The recent priority given to veteran homelessness by President Obama and the launching of the "Ending Veteran Homelessness in Five Years" initiative by Secretary Shinseki provide the opportunity to truly make a difference in how we organize and deliver services to homeless veterans, with the specific goal of ending homelessness. Supportive housing, community partnerships, and economic supports are all essential to veterans exiting homelessness and not returning to that state. The Department of Veterans Affairs still needs to build better pathways to these services and programs through what has been referred to as the "no wrong door" policy in Secretary Shinseki's initiative. (See box 14.1.)

Historically, VA has directed its resources to developing a programmatic approach matched to the needs of specific homeless subgroups. Strategically it has been very effective, and those veterans meeting program criteria overall have done quite well. However, it also lends itself to a "siloed" model of care that does not necessarily reflect the full scope of access points, services, needs, and stages of readiness and capacity to change among homeless veterans. Veterans need immediate access to these and other homeless-oriented programs through whatever avenue they use in accessing VA care. Outreach and intervention efforts in emergency departments; transition programs that engage patients during acute hospitalizations; and the development of homeless-specific, patient-centered medical homes in primary care all need to be put into action. They must be coordinated in ways that facilitate entry and retention in programming that stabilizes and facilitates an exit from homelessness for our veterans. Further, any comprehensive service model should be held fully accountable to the care needs of this population of homeless veterans and the continuum of services necessary to not only assist a veteran in leaving homelessness, but also prevent him or her from returning to that state. Finally, it is important to recognize that veteran homelessness affects far more than the individual. Beyond the scope and focus of the VA health system, attention also must be placed on the impact of homelessness at a community level and must be directed to the role of the

Box 14.1. Five-Year Plan to End Homelessness Among Veterans

In 2009, shortly after his appointment as Secretary of Veterans Affairs, General Eric Shinseki announced a sweeping initiative to eliminate homelessness among veterans. "The Five-Year Plan to End Homelessness among Veterans" is built on six strategic pillars: outreach and education, treatment, prevention, housing/supportive services, community partnerships, and income/employment/benefits. The plan reflects VA's "no wrong door" philosophy, whereby veterans can have ready access to VA services and programs regardless of where they are in the system.

The plan itself brings together several different departments and offices within VA as well as reaching out to local community groups to launch and coordinate a comprehensive approach linked to measurable and tangible outcomes. Altogether, nine programs are either expanded or developed as part of this initiative:

Expansion of Existing Programs

1. Health Care for Homeless Veterans (HCHV), which provides residential treatment beds through community partnerships to homeless veterans with serious psychiatric and substance use disorders, has been expanded to serve an additional 4,800 veterans.

2. The Housing Urban Development – VA Supported Housing (HUD-VASH) program is the largest national supported permanent housing initiative for veterans and will be expanded by an additional 10,000 vouchers as part of this plan.

3. The Grant and Per Diem (GPD) Program provides grants to community providers to create and operate a transitional housing program. This program will grow to serve more than 20,000 homeless veterans.

4. The Veterans Justice Outreach (VJO) Program aims to prevent homelessness by providing outreach and linkages to VA services for veterans at early stages of the justice system. This program now provides services for over 7,500 veterans.

5. VA Residential Rehabilitation Treatment Programs/Domiciliary Care for Homeless Veterans (DCHV) provide time-limited residential rehabilitation and treatment services, including medical, psychiatric, and substance abuse treatment. This program will add five new forty-bed domiciliaries to the network of sites.

(Continued)

6. Enhanced access to substance use treatment service provided services to an additional 1,400 veterans in FY 2011.

Development of New Programs

1. The HUD/VA Prevention Pilot program is designed to provide early intervention to recently discharged veterans and their families, with the goal of preventing homelessness.
2. The National Referral Call Center that will provide linkages for homeless veterans to appropriate VA and community-based resources.
3. Supportive Services for Veterans and Families will provide grants and technical assistance to community nonprofit groups to provide supportive services to veterans and their families in order to help them maintain their current housing.

Combined, this initiative represents one of the most sweeping and comprehensive efforts to address the homeless crisis among our veterans. The challenges of engaging treatment- and service-resistant veterans and ensuring the "no wrong door" policy is enacted throughout the system, including emergency department, hospital wards, and primary care encounters, will persist and will require innovative solutions. However, now there will be a much greater capacity and program options available for those homeless veterans willing to receive care and services.

veterans' families in preventing homelessness, as well as to their impact in providing support during crises and facilitating earlier exits from homelessness.

Summary and Conclusions

Homeless veterans are overrepresented among the homeless and present with unique and formidable needs that challenge the provider community; however, the human, societal, and economic price for not reaching out and making every effort to intervene with this population far outweighs any costs attributed to improving the coordination, colocation, and customization of services and interventions needed to engage this population in social services and primary and preventive healthcare.

There are several different approaches to the problem of engaging homeless veterans in care, all of which have demonstrated effectiveness. It is important to note that there is likely no one right way, but rather, what is needed is an approach that reflects the needs and priorities of homeless persons; promotes respect, autonomy, and self-determination; and meets the veteran where he or she is in terms of motivation, readiness for change, and competing needs. The other dynamic that must be emphasized is that the process of engagement is a longitudinal one, and treatment engagement and service retention are important and need to be considered in the types of care models we attempt to engage the homeless veteran in. Here, over the past twenty-five years, with Health Care for the Homeless and more recently within VA, integrated primary care models have been shown to be an effective approach for homeless persons.

Key elements and components to both treatment engagement and service retention approaches have been noted. The challenge for policy makers, healthcare administrators, and healthcare providers is how to align resources, incentivize alternative delivery approaches, and hold these models accountable to the needs and outcomes specific to this extremely vulnerable, frail, yet resilient, population. The capacity already exists within VA, as does the leadership commitment, which can serve as a model for the rest of the country.

Acknowledgments: Thanks to Ms. Erin Johnson for her assistance in proofing and editing this chapter.

References

Alford, D. P., LaBelle, C. T., Richardson, J. M., O'Connell, J. J., Hohl, C. A., Cheng, D. M. & Samet, J. H. (2007). Treating homeless opioid dependent patients with buprenorphine in an office-based setting. *Journal of General Internal Medicine* 22, no. 2: 171–176.

Apodaca, Timothy R. & Schermer, Carol R. (2003). Readiness to change alcohol use after trauma. *Journal of Trauma* 54, no. 5: 990–994.

Battjes, Robert J., Onken, Lisa S. & Delany, Peter J. (1999). Drug abuse treatment entry and engagement: Report of a meeting on treatment readiness. *Journal of Clinical Psychology* 55: 643–657.

Bernstein, J., Bernstein, E., Tassiopoulos, K., Heeren, T., Levenson, S. & Hingson, R. (2005). Brief motivational intervention at a clinic visit reduces cocaine and heroin use. *Drug & Alcohol Dependence* 77: 49–59.

Blue-Howells, Jessica, McGuire, Jim & Nakashima, John. (2008). Co-location of health care services for homeless veterans: A case study of innovation in program implementation. *Social Work in Health Care* 47, no. 3: 219–231.

Bombardier, Charles H., Ehde, Dawn & Kilmer, Jason. (1997). Readiness to change alcohol drinking habits after traumatic brain injury. *Archives of Physical Medicine & Rehabilitation* 78, no. 6: 592–596.

Bonilla, D. L., Kabeya, H., Henn, J., Karamer, V. L. & Kosoy, M. Y. (2009). Bartonella quintana in body lice and head lice from homeless persons. *Emerging Infectious Diseases* 15, no. 6: 912–915.

Bradford, D. W., Gaynes, B. N., Kim, M. M., Kaufman, J. S., Weinberger, M. (2005). Can shelter-based interventions improve treatment engagement in homeless individuals with psychiatric and/or substance misuse disorders: a randomized controlled trial. *Medical Care* 43, no. 8: 763–768.

Brickner, P. W., Scharer, L. K., Conanan, B. A., Savarese, M. & Scanlan, B. C. (Eds.). (1990). *Under the safety net.* New York: W.W. Norton Co.

Cabral, H. J., Tobias, C., Rajabium, S., Sohler, N., Cunningham, C., Wong, M. & Cunningham, W. (2007). Outreach program contacts: Do they increase the likelihood of engagement and retention in HIV primary care for hard-to-reach patients? *AIDS Patient Care and STDs* 21, supp. 1: S59–67.

Desai, Mayur M., Rosenheck, Robert A. & Kasprow, Wesley J. (2003). Determinants of receipt of ambulatory medical care in a national sample of mentally ill homeless Veterans. *Medical Care* 41, no. 2: 275–287.

DiClemente, Carlo C. 2003. *Addiction and change: How addictions develop and addicted people recover.* New York: Guilford Press.

Fone, D., Dunstan, F., Lloyd, K., Williams, G., Watkins, J. & Palmer, S. (2007). Does social cohesion modify the association between area income deprivation and mental health? A multilevel analysis. *International Journal of Epidemiology* 36, no. 2: 338–345.

Gallagher, T. C., Andersen, R. M., Koegel, P. & Gelberg, L. (1997). Determinants of regular source of care among homeless adults in Los Angeles. *Medical Care* 35, no. 8: 814–830.

Gelberg, L., Gallagher, T. C., Andersen, R. M. & Koegel, P. (1997). Competing priorities as a barrier to medical care among homeless adults in Los Angeles. *American Journal of Public Health* 87: 217–220.

Gelberg, Lillian, Andersen, Ronald M. & Leake, Barbara D. (2002). The behavioral model for vulnerable populations: Application to medical care use and outcomes for homeless people. *Health Services Research* 34, no. 6: 1273–1302.

Gentilello, L. M., Donovan, D. M., Dunn, C. W. & Rivara, F. P. (1995). Alcohol interventions in trauma centers. *JAMA* 274, no. 13: 1043–1048.

Han, Beth, & Wells, Barbara L. (2003). Inappropriate emergency department visits and use of the Health Care for the Homeless program services by homeless adults in the northeastern United States. *Journal of Public Health Management and Practice* 9, no. 6: 530–537.

Henrinckx, H. A., Kinney, R. F., Clarke, G. N. & Paulson, R. I. (1997). Assertive community treatment versus usual care in engaging and retaining clients with severe mental illness. *Psychiatric Services* 48: 1297–1306.

Hewett, Nigel C. (1999). How to provide for the primary health needs of homeless people: What do homeless people in Leicester think? *British Journal of General Practice* 49, no. 447: 819.

Hibbs, J. R., Benner, L., Klugman, L., Spencer, R., Macchia, I., Mellinger, A. & Fife, D. K. (1994). Mortality in a cohort of homeless adults in Philadelphia. *New England Journal of Medicine* 331, no. 5: 304–309.

Higgins, Stephen T. & Silverman, Kenneth (Eds.). (1999). *Motivating behavior change among illicit drug abusers: Research on contingency management interventions.* Washington, DC: American Psychological Association.

Howe, Evan C., Buck, David S. & Withers, Jim. (2009). Delivering health care on the streets: Challenges and opportunities for quality management. *Quality Management in Health Care* 18, no. 4: 239–246.

Hwang, S. W., Orav, J., O'Connell, J. J., Lebow, J. M. & Brennan, T. A. (1997). Causes of death in homeless adults in Boston. *Annals of Internal Medicine* 126, no. 8: 625–628.

Institute of Medicine/Committee on Health Care for Homeless People. (1988). *Homelessness, health, and human needs.* Washington, DC: National Academy Press.

Jencks, Christopher. (1995). *The homeless.* Cambridge, MA: Harvard University Press.

Kawachi, I., Colditz, G. A., Ascherio, A., Rimm, E. B., Giovannucci, E., Stampfer, M. J. & Willet, W. C. (1996). A prospective study of social networks in relation to total mortality and cardiovascular disease in men in the U.S.A. *Journal of Epidemiology and Community Health* 50, no. 3: 245–251.

Kertesz, S. G., Crouch, K., Milby, J. B., Cusimano, R. E. & Schumacher, J. E. (2009). Housing first for homeless persons with active addiction: Are we overreaching? *Milbank Quarterly* 87, no. 2: 495–534.

Kertesz, S. G. & Weiner, Saul J. (2009). Housing the chronically homeless: High hopes, complex realities. *JAMA* 301, no. 17: 1822–1824.

Krysal, J. H., Cramer, J. A., Krol, W. F., Kirk, G. F. & Rosenheck, R. A. (2001). Naltrexone in the treatment of alcohol dependence. *New England Journal of Medicine* 345: 1734–1739.

Kushel, M. B., Evans, J. L., Perry, S., Robertson, M. J. & Moss, A. R. (2003). No door to lock: Victimization among homeless and marginally housed persons. *Archives of Internal Medicine* 163, no. 20: 2492–2499.

Kushel, M. B., Perry, S., Bangsberg, D., Clark, R. & Moss, A. R. (2002). Emergency department use among the homeless and marginally housed: Results from a community-based study. *American Journal of Public Health* 92, no. 5: 778–784.

Kushel, Margot B., Vittinghoff, Eric & Haas, Jennifer S. (2001). Factors associated with the health care utilization of homeless persons. *JAMA* 285, no. 2: 200–206.

Lehman, A. F., Dixon, L. B., Kernan, E., DeForge, B. R. & Posrado, L. T. (1997). A randomized trial of assertive community treatment for homeless persons with severe mental illness. *Archives of General Psychiatry* 54, no. 11: 1038–1043.

Lucas, G. M., Mullen, B. A., Weidle, P. J., Hader, S., McCaul, M. E. & Moore, R. D. (2006). Directly administered antiretroviral therapy in methadone maintenance clinics is associated with improved HIV treatment outcomes compared with outcomes among concurrent comparison groups. *Clinical Infectious Diseases* 42, no. 11: 1628–1635.

Mares, Alvin S. & Rosenheck, Robert A. (2004). Perceived relationship between military service and homelessness among homeless veterans with mental illness. *Journal of Nervous and Mental Disease* 192, no. 10: 715–719.

Marmot, M. G., Smith, G. D., Stansfeld, S., Patel, C., North, F., Head, J., White, I., Brunner, E. & Feeney, A. (1991). Health inequalities among British civil servants: The Whitehall II study. *Lancet* 337, no. 8754: 1387–1393.

McGuire, J., Gelberg, L., Blue-Howells, J. & Rosenheck, R. A. (2009). Access to primary care for homeless veterans with serious mental illness or substance abuse: A follow-up evaluation of co-located primary care and homeless social services. *Administration & Policy in Mental Health* 36, no. 4: 255–264.

McMurray-Avila, Marsha. (1997). *Organizing health services for homeless people.* Nashville, TN: National Health Care for the Homeless Council.

Meyers, R. J., Miller, W. R., Smith, J. E. & Tonigan, J. S. (2002). A randomized trial of two methods for engaging treatment-refusing drug users through concerned significant others. *Journal of Consulting and Clinical Psychology* 70(5): 182–85.

Miller, William R. & Rollnick, Stephen. (2002). *Motivational interviewing: Preparing people for change.* 2nd ed. New York: Guilford Press.

National Alliance to End Homelessness. (2007). *Vital mission: Ending homelessness among veterans.* Washington, DC: National Alliance to End Homelessness.

Nwakeze, Peter C., Magura, Stephen & Rosenblum, Andrew. (2002). Drug problem recognition, desire for help, and treatment readiness in a soup kitchen population. *Substance Use & Misuse* 37: 291–312.

Okin, R. L., Boccellari, A., Azocar, F., Shumway, M., O'Brien, K., Gelb, A., Kohn, M., Harding, P. & Wachsmuth, C. (2000). The effects of clinical case management on hospital service use among ED frequent users. *American Journal of Emergency Medicine* 18, no. 5: 603–608.

O'Toole, T. P., Buckel, L., Bourgault, C., Blumen, J., Redihan, S., Jan, L. & Friedmann, P. (2010). Applying the chronic care model to homeless veterans: Effect of a population approach to primary care on utilization and clinical outcomes. *American Journal of Public Health* 100, no. 12: 2493–2499.

O'Toole, T. P., Conde-Martel, A., Gibbon, J. L., Hanusa, B. H., Freyder, P. J. and Fine, M. J. (2003). Health care for homeless veterans: Why do some individuals fall through the safety net? *Journal of General Internal Medicine* 18, no. 11: 929–933.

O'Toole, T. P., Conde-Martel, A., Gibbon, J. L., Hanusa, B. H., Freyder, P. J. & Fine, M. J. (2007b). Where do people go when they first become homeless? *Health & Social Care in the Community* 15, no. 5: 446–453.

O'Toole, T. P., Gibbon, J. L., Hanusa, B. H. & Fine, M. J. (1999a). Preferences for site of care among homeless adults. *Journal of General Internal Medicine* 14: 599–605.

O'Toole, T. P., Gibbon, J. L., Hanusa, B. H. & Fine, M. J. (1999b). Utilization of health care services among subgroups of urban homeless. *Journal of Health Politics, Policy, and Law* 24, no. 1: 91–114.

O'Toole, T. P., Gibbon, J. L., Hanusa, B. H., Freyder, P. J., Conde, A. M. & Fine, M. J. (2004). Self-reported changes in drug and alcohol use upon being homeless. *American Journal of Public Health* 94, no. 5: 830–835.

O'Toole, T. P., Gibbon, J. L., Seltzer, D., Hanusa, B. H. & Fine, M. F. (2002). Changes in urban homelessness during economic prosperity: 1995–1997. *Journal of Urban Health* 79, no. 2: 200–210.

O'Toole, T. P., Pollini, R. A., Bigelow, G. & Ford, D. E. (2007a). The effect of substance abuse treatment on health services utilization: Bidirectional results from a clinical trial. *Medical Care* 45, no. 11: 1110–1115.

O'Toole, T. P., Pollini, R. A., Ford, D. & Bigelow, G. (2006). Physical health as a motivator for substance abuse treatment: Is it enough to keep them in treatment? *Journal of Substance Abuse Treatment* 31, no. 2: 143–150.

Padgett, Deborah, Struening, Elmer L. & Andrews, Howard. (1990). Factors affecting the use of medical, mental health, alcohol, and drug treatment services by homeless adults. *Medical Care* 28, no. 9: 805–821.

Pollini, R. A., O'Toole, T. P., Ford, D. & Bigelow, G. (2006). Does this patient really want treatment? Factors associated with baseline and evolving readiness for change among hospitalized substance using adults interested in treatment. *Addictive Behaviors* 31, no. 10: 1904–1918.

Redelmeier, Donald A., Molin, Jean-Pierre & Tibshirani, Robert J. (1995). A randomised trial of compassionate care for the homeless in an emergency department. *Lancet* 345, no. 8958: 1131–1134.

Rosenheck, Robert A., Frisman, Linda & Chung, An-Me. (1994). The proportion of veterans among homeless men. *American Journal of Public Health* 84, no. 3: 466–469.

Rumptz, M. H., Tobias, C., Rajabiun, S., Bradford, J., Cabral, H., Young, R. & Cunningham, W. E. (2007). Factors associated with engaging socially marginalized HIV-positive persons in primary care. *AIDS Patient Care and STDs* 21, supp. 1: S30–39.

Sakowski, L. S., Lee, R. A., Van der Weele, T. J. & Buchanan, D. (2009). Effect of a housing and case management program on emergency department visits and hospitalizations among chronically ill homeless adults: A randomized trial. *JAMA* 301, no. 17: 1771–1778.

Salit, S. A., Kuhn, E. M., Hartz, A. J., Vu, J. M. & Mosso, A. L. (1998). Hospitalization costs associated with homelessness in New York City. *New England Journal of Medicine* 338: 1734–1740.

Shortt, S. E., Hwang, S., Stuart, H., Bedore, M., Zurba, M. & Darling, M. (2008). Delivering primary care to homeless persons: A policy analysis approach to evaluating the options. *Health Policy* 4, no. 1: 108–122.

Shumacher, J. E., Usdan, S., Milby, J. B., Wallace, D. & McNamara, C. (2000). Abstinent-contingent housing and treatment retention among crack-cocaine dependent homeless persons. *Journal of Substance Abuse Treatment* 19, no. 1: 81–88.

Slesnick, N., Meyers, R. J., Meade, M. & Segelken, D. H. (2000). Bleak and hopeless no more: Engagement of reluctant substance-abusing runaway youth and their families. *Journal of Substance Abuse Treatment* 19: 215–222.

Stefancic, Ana & Tsemberis, Sam. (2007). Housing first for long-term shelter dwellers with psychiatric disabilities in a suburban county: A four-year study of housing access and retention. *Journal of Primary Prevention* 38, nos. 3–4: 265–279.

Strathdee, S. A., Celentano, D. D., Shah, N., Lyles, C., Stambolis, V. A., Macalino, G., Nelson, K. & Vlahov, D. (1999). Needle-exchange attendance and health care utilization promote entry into detoxification. *Journal of Urban Health* 76, no. 4: 448–460.

U.S. Department of Veterans Affairs (VA). (2006). *VA programs for homeless veterans fact sheet.* Washington, DC: Department of Veterans Affairs.

Wen, Chuck K., Hudak, Pamela L. & Hwang, Stephen W. (2007). Homeless people's perceptions of welcomeness and unwelcomeness in healthcare encounters. *Journal of General Internal Medicine* 22, no. 7: 1011–1017.

Wenzel, S. L., Bakhtiar, L., Caskey, N. H., Hardie, E., Redford, C., Sadler, H. & Gelberg, L. (1995). Homeless veterans' utilization of medical, psychiatric, and substance abuse services. *Medical Care* 33, no. 11: 1132–1144.

Wilkinson, Richard G. & Marmot, Michael G. (2003). *Social determinants of health: The solid facts.* 2nd ed. Copenhagen: WHO Regional Office for Europe.

Zerger, Susanne. (2002). *Substance abuse treatment: What works for homeless people?* Nashville, TN: National Health Care for the Homeless Council.

Zlotnick, Cheryl, Tam, Tammy & Robertson, Marjorie J. (2003). Disaffiliation, substance use, and exiting homelessness. *Substance Use & Misuse* 28, nos. 3–6: 577–599.

About the Editor

Thomas W. Miller, PhD, ABPP, is Professor Emeritus and Retired Career VA Chief, Psychology Service, at the VA and University of Kentucky College of Medicine. He has been a Senior Research Scientist, Master Teacher, and University Teaching Fellow through his forty-year career and tenure at the University of Kentucky and University of Connecticut. He has served on several national and regional professional and VA task forces and committees. A graduate of the State University of New York, he is a diplomate of the American Board of Professional Psychology, and a Fellow of the American Psychological Association, the Association for Psychological Science, and the Royal Society of Medicine. He is a Distinguished Alumnus from the State University of New York and recipient of the APA Distinguished Professional Contributions to Clinical Practice Award. He honors his veteran patients and his father, William J. Miller, a veteran of Patton's Army in World War II and the Korean conflict.

About the Contributors

Nathan D. Ainspan, PhD, is a research psychologist in the Washington, D.C., area. He has conducted research, written, and spoken about psychological issues impacting returning service members and improving the situation of employment for individuals with disabilities. He edited the book *Wars' Returning Wounded, Injured and Ill: A Handbook* and *When the Warrior Comes Home: A Family Guide for Transition from the Front Line to the Home Front.* His research interests have focused on understanding the symptoms and treatment of PTSD and TBI, using employment as a form of positive psychology, and the impact and effect of disabilities on service members and their families. He has led presentations at meetings of the Society of Industrial/Organizational Psychology, the American Psychological Association, and the Department of Veterans Affairs.

Victoria C. Anderson-Barnes received her bachelor's degree in psychology from the University of Minnesota. Following graduation, she worked as a Research Assistant for the Center for Neuroscience and Regenerative Medicine at Walter Reed Army Medical Center (WRAMC) and was then a Research Coordinator for the Defense and Veterans Brain Injury Center at WRAMC. Ms. Anderson-Barnes is currently a doctoral student in clinical psychology at the Pennsylvania State University.

Bradley E. Belsher, MS, is a clinical psychology doctoral student at Palo Alto University and is completing his predoctoral internship at the Washington, D.C., VA Medical Center. Bradley completed several training experiences at the Palo Alto VA Health Care System, working with veterans presenting with a wide array of postdeployment issues. His dissertation work focused on the influence of socially constraining environments and dysfunctional cognitions on the development of PTSD.

Jeanne M. Bennett, PsyD, MBA, earned her doctorate from Spalding University in clinical psychology. She completed her internship and postdoctoral fellowship in neuropsychology at Henry Ford Hospital in Detroit, Michigan, and has a postdoctoral master's degree in psychopharmacology from Fairleigh Dickinson University. Dr. Bennett is currently lead neuropsychologist and a member of the polytrauma team at the Robley Rex Veterans Affairs Medical Center in Louisville, Kentucky. She has been adjunct faculty at the University of Louisville and Spalding University, teaching psychopharmacology, biological bases of behavior, and adult assessment.

Aditya A. Bhagwat, PhD, ABPP-CN, is currently serving as Director of Neuropsychology for the Traumatic Brain Injury Service at Walter Reed National Military Medical Center (WRNMMC) in Bethesda, Maryland. He received his doctorate from Ohio State University and completed his postdoctoral fellowship in clinical neuropsychology at the National Rehabilitation Hospital in Washington, D.C. He has served as a commissioned officer in the USAF, worked with the Defense and Veterans Brain Injury Center, and is currently a commissioned officer in the United States Public Health Service. At WRNMMC he is privileged to be able to continue serving military service members and their families.

Loretta E. Braxton, PhD, received her doctorate from the University of North Carolina at Chapel Hill. She is an assistant professor at Duke University Medical Center and a staff psychologist at the Durham VA Medical Center, where she is the Local Recovery Coordinator and directs clinical programs that are focused on recovery from serious mental illness. She also directs the psychology training program. Her particular interests include multicultural issues in clinical practice and objective personality assessment.

Katherine Brazaitis earned her BA in psychology at New York University (NYU). After NYU, Katherine was employed through the Henry M. Jackson Foundation. She was a Research Coordinator and Psychometrist for the Defense and Veterans Brain Injury Center at Walter Reed Army Medical Center. She is currently in a clinical psychology PhD program at the Catholic University of America and is a research assistant in the Suicide Prevention Laboratory. In addition, Katherine is employed as a part-time research assistant in the Laboratory for the Treatment of Suicide-Related Ideation and Behavior at the Uniformed Services University of Health Sciences.

Matthew J. Cordova, PhD, is a staff psychologist at the VA Northern California Health Care System's Martinez Outpatient Clinic and an Assistant Professor at Palo Alto University's Pacific Graduate School of Psychology. He completed his PhD at the University of Kentucky, a predoctoral internship at the VA Palo Alto, and a postdoctoral fellowship at Stanford University. He specializes in applying empirically supported interventions to assist medical and mental health patients and their families. His research focuses on adjustment to life-threatening experiences.

Valerie Fox is an occupational therapist currently working at the Durham VA Medical Center, helping veterans with the hospital-to-home transition. Valerie attended North Carolina State University as an undergraduate and received a BS in zoology. Afterward she attended graduate school at the University of North Carolina and received an MS in occupational science. After graduating in 2008, Valerie completed a one-year interdisciplinary fellowship in psychosocial rehabilitation and recovery at the Durham VA. Through this program, Valerie received intensive training and education about mental health recovery and psychosocial rehabilitation services and actively created groups and programs to facilitate veterans' recovery process.

Dr. Louis M. French received his doctorate in clinical psychology from George Washington University. He completed fellowships in clinical and experimental neuropsychology at the National Institute of Mental Health and in neuropsychology, focusing on traumatic brain injury, at the Defense and Veterans Brain Injury Center (DVBIC) at Walter Reed Army Medical Center. Dr. French is currently the TBI Service Chief at Walter Reed, Transitional Director of TBI for the National Naval Medical Center and Walter Reed, and site director for the DVBIC at Walter Reed, where he oversees operations related to the identification and treatment of individuals with TBI.

Carole A. Goguen, PsyD, is the Military Sexual Trauma Program Coordinator for the VA Greater Los Angeles Health Care System and staff psychologist at the VA Los Angeles Ambulatory Care Center. She is also in private practice. Prior to her current VA position, she was the Associate Director of Research and Education for the Executive Division of the National Center for PTSD. She received her doctor of psychology from Pepperdine University and is a member of the International Society for Traumatic Stress Studies and the National Register of Health Service Providers in Psychology.

Kim Hamlett-Berry, PhD, is the Director of Public Health Policy and Prevention in the Department of Veterans Affairs Office of Public Health and Environmental Hazards. She is responsible for national tobacco use cessation policy and programs in the Veterans Health Administration. Prior to joining VA in February 1999 as VHA's first Associate Director for HIV Prevention, she was on the faculties of the University of Virginia Children's Medical Center and Case Western University Schools of Medicine. She received her doctorate in clinical psychology from the Catholic University of America and was an intern and postdoctoral fellow in clinical psychology at Duke University Medical Center.

Nathalie Huguet, PhD, is a research associate at the Center for Public Health Studies at Portland State University. She received her doctorate in urban studies from Portland State University and holds a master's degree in social psychology. Dr. Huguet was selected for a 2010–2012 Young Investigator Award from the American Foundation for Suicide Prevention to study the epidemiology of undetermined deaths. She has collaborated with Drs. Mark Kaplan and Bentson McFarland on various projects funded by the National Institutes of Health and private foundations. Dr. Huguet's areas of expertise include healthy aging, suicide, and managing large, complex data sets.

Mark S. Kaplan, DrPH, is a professor of community health at Portland State University. He received his doctorate in public health from the University of California, Berkeley. His research focuses on using populationwide data to understand suicide risk factors among senior and veteran populations. Dr. Kaplan holds a Distinguished Investigator Award from the American Foundation for Suicide Prevention. He testified before the Senate Special Committee on Aging at its hearing on veterans' health and was a member of the Expert Panel on the VA Blue Ribbon Work Group on Suicide Prevention in the Veteran Population.

Samantha Kettle, PsyD, received her doctorate from Pacific University in Forest Grove, Oregon. After completing her degree, she participated in the VA Interprofessional Fellowship Program in Psychosocial Rehabilitation and Recovery (PSR). Dr. Kettle is currently a staff psychologist at the Durham VA Medical Center, where she works in an Intensive Outpatient Program with veterans struggling with substance use and mental health issues.

Ann D. Kirkwood, MS, received her degree in communication from Boise State University, specializing in mental illness stigma and social marketing. She has conducted social marketing campaigns for adult and children's mental health, Medicaid, child protection, disabilities, and immunizations. As project director for Idaho's Awareness to Action Youth Suicide Prevention program, she has collaborated with mental health experts at VA and National Guard. As a member of the national advisory council for the Suicide Prevention Lifeline, she reviews its support for veterans in crisis. She is a winner of a Peabody and a VOICE Award. She advises SAMHSA on stigma.

Dolores K. Little, PhD, is a Consultant in Health Care Services. She served twenty years working with the Veterans Administration, including as Associate Medical Director, Assistant Hospital Director Trainee, and Allied Health Education Coordinator. She has also been employed as an Assistant Professor of Psychology at Sam Houston State University.

Carol A. Malte, MSW, is a researcher with the Center of Excellence in Substance Abuse Treatment and Education (CESATE) at the Veterans Affairs Puget Sound Health Care System in Seattle, Washington, with a focus on healthcare utilization and health behaviors among veterans with substance use disorders and post-traumatic stress disorder. Recently she was the National Research Coordinator for the multisite cooperative study Integrating Practice Guidelines for Smoking Cessation into Mental Health Care for Posttraumatic Stress Disorder, and currently is involved in efforts to disseminate integrated care for smoking cessation nationally in the Veterans Health Administration.

Miles E. McFall, PhD, has worked as a psychologist for the VA Puget Sound Health Care System for over twenty-six years. He is Director of Psychology Service and Director of PTSD Treatment Programs at that facility. He is also a Professor in the Department of Psychiatry and Behavioral Sciences at the University of Washington School of Medicine. Dr. McFall is a funded investigator who has published extensively in health risk reduction treatment trials for veterans with PTSD. He has also collaborated on numerous pharmacological and psychotherapeutic treatment trials of innovative treatments for PTSD.

Bentson H. McFarland, MD, PhD, is Professor of Psychiatry, Public Health and Preventive Medicine at Oregon Health & Science University and Affiliate Investigator at the Kaiser Permanente Center for Health Research in Portland, Oregon. Dr. McFarland received his MD and his PhD in biostatistics from the University of Washington in Seattle. Board certified in general psychiatry, Dr. McFarland's research focuses on quality of care for people with substance abuse problems, healthcare financing, Medicaid, and pharmacoeconomics. His work has been supported by the Substance Abuse and Mental Health Services Administration, the National Institute on Drug Abuse, the National Institute on Alcohol Abuse and Alcoholism, the National Institute of Mental Health, the Robert Wood Johnson Foundation, the Food and Drug Administration, and the pharmaceutical industry. In addition to his research, Dr. McFarland maintains a clinical practice focused on psychopharmacology.

Kathleen M. McNamara, PhD, ABPP, is the Lead Professional (LP) for Psychology, holding responsibility for administrative issues that may affect the discipline of psychology and carrying ultimate responsibility for all psychology training within the VA Pacific Islands Health Care System. She presently is assigned as the staff psychologist providing services to veterans on the neighboring islands of Maui and Molokai. She served for ten years as the Assistant Chief for Psychology and the Director of Training for the Psychology Internship Program at this VA. Previously she was the Director of Training for the internship program and an Associate Professor at the Wright State University School of Professional Psychology. Dr. McNamara is a diplomate in clinical psychology from the American Board of Professional Psychology, is a Fellow of the American Psychological Association, was elected as a member of the National Academies of Practice, and is a member of the National Register of Health Service Providers in Psychology. She has been and is active in state and national professional organizations and served as the President of the Association of VA Psychologist Leaders (AVAPL). She also served on the APA Board of Directors, Board of Education Affairs, College of Professional Psychology, Committee for the Advancement of Professional Practice, Committee on Psychology and AIDS, and the Steering Committee for the APA Postdoctoral Training Conference, among other positions. Her awards include the 2011 Russell J. Bent Award for Distinguished Service and Contributions to the American Board of Professional Psychology.

Jennifer Mrnak-Meyer, PhD, is a clinical psychologist at the St. Cloud VA Medical Center. Research interests include the use of alcohol and other drugs as a method of emotion regulation and predictors and treatment of suicidality among individuals with substance use disorders. She received her PhD in 2009 from Southern Illinois University, Carbondale.

Delilah O. Noronha, PsyD, is the Program Manager of the Primary Care-Behavioral Health Program (PCBH) at the VA Palo Alto Health Care System. She completed a clinical psychology internship at the James A. Haley VA in Tampa, Florida, and a Post-Doctoral Fellowship at the University of Oklahoma Health Sciences Center–Oklahoma City VA Consortium. The focus of her pre- and postdoctoral clinical training and experience is in the areas of primary care–mental health integration, postdeployment health, and behavioral medicine. VA appointments include staff psychologist for the PCBH program and Program Manager. She has been responsible for the development and implementation of several primary care–behavioral health clinics within the VA Palo Alto Healthcare System. She also serves on the VA Palo Alto integrated postdeployment clinic leadership committee. She was appointed the clinical champion for the implementation of the *Myhealthe-Vet: My Goals* Internet protocol for patients. Dr. Noronha's major areas of interest include primary care–mental health integration, OEF/OIF post-deployment health and innovations in mental health service delivery.

Thomas P. O'Toole, MD, is the Chief of Primary Care at the Providence VAMC and directs the Homeless-Oriented Primary Care program there. He has conducted numerous studies of homeless persons and has published exten-sively on health service use, disparities in care and utilization, health-seeking preferences for different needs, motivation and treatment engagement, and primary care–based interventions and outcomes for homeless persons. He is an Associate Professor of Medicine at the Alpert Medical School at Brown University and was previously on the faculty at the University of Pittsburgh, Johns Hopkins, and Georgetown University.

Walter Erich Penk, PhD, ABPP, is Professor of Psychiatry and Behavioral Sciences at Texas A&M College of Medicine, and Consultant to Central Texas VA Health Care System, VA Center of Excellence in Stress Disorders Research, and VA Rehabilitation Research and Development, Washington, D.C. Dr. Penk completed doctoral studies in clinical psychology at the Univer-sity of Houston and subsequently was Clinical and Research Psychologist with VA medical centers in Houston, Dallas, Boston, and Bedford, Massachusetts, where he was Chief of the Psychology Service. He held clinical appointments in Dallas at the University of Texas Health Sciences Center and in Boston at Tufts, Boston University, University of Massachusetts, and Harvard Medical Schools. Dr. Penk has been funded by VA, NIDA, and NIMH to validate treatments for co-occurring PTSD, addictions, and other mental disorders. He has published more than 135 papers in peer-reviewed journals. He co-edited *Returning Wars Wounded, Injured, and Ill* (Praeger, 2008). Dr. Penk directed psychological services for the Department of Mental Health in the Commonwealth of Massachusetts and was Associate Director of New Eng-land VA (VISN 1) Mental Illness Research, Education, and Clinical Center. He has held elected offices in APA: president of Division 18 and APA's Council of Representatives (2005–2010). He is editor of *Texas Psychologist* and was recently elected to the Board of Trustees for the Texas Psychological Association (2010–2012). Awards for his health services research contribu-tions have included the APA Presidential Citation, VA Distinguished Career Award, Division 18 Harold Hildreth Award, and recognition from the

American Rehabilitation Counseling Association for randomized clinical trials conducted in vocational rehabilitation.

Josef I. Ruzek, PhD, is Associate Professor at Palo Alto University's Pacific Graduate School of Psychology and Director of the Dissemination and Training Division of the National Center for PTSD, located in the VA Palo Alto Health Care System. He is a developer of the joint VA–DOD Clinical Practice Guideline for Management of Traumatic Stress and a coeditor of three books, including *Cognitive-Behavioral Therapies for Trauma* and *Caring for Veterans with Deployment-Related Stress Disorders: Iraq, Afghanistan, and Beyond.* His current efforts are directed at disseminating evidence-based cognitive-behavioral treatments for PTSD and developing Internet- and phone-based interventions for trauma survivors.

Andrew J. Saxon, MD, is a Professor in the Department of Psychiatry and Behavioral Sciences, University of Washington; Director of the Addictions Treatment Center, VA Puget Sound Health Care System; and Director, Addiction Psychiatry Residency Program, University of Washington. Preceding his entry into psychiatry, Dr. Saxon completed an internal medicine internship and worked for four years as an emergency room physician. Subsequent to his general psychiatry residency at the University of Washington, Dr. Saxon had twenty-five years of experience as a clinical and research addiction psychiatrist and is board certified with added qualifications in addiction psychiatry by the American Board of Psychiatry and Neurology. He serves as one of five National Clinical Experts on office-based treatment of opioid dependence with buprenorphine for the Physician Clinical Support System, a national mentoring network for physicians. Dr. Saxon is also the Medical Director of the SAMHSA-funded Physician Clinical Support System for Methadone. He sits on the editorial boards of the journals *Drug and Alcohol Dependence* and *General Hospital Psychiatry.* Dr. Saxon's current research involves pharmacotherapies and psychotherapies for alcohol, cocaine, methamphetamine, nicotine, and opioid dependence as well as work in co-occurrence of substance dependence and post-traumatic stress disorder.

Beth Hudnall Stamm, PhD, holds degrees from Appalachian State University (BS, MA) and the University of Wyoming (PhD). She is a Research Professor at the Institute of Rural Health at Idaho State University. Her previous positions were at the VA National Center for Posttraumatic Stress Disorder and Dartmouth Medical School. She was recognized by the International Society for Traumatic Stress Studies for "fundamental contributions to the international public understanding of trauma." She specializes in traumatic stress, cultural trauma, and secondary traumatic stress. Stamm is a traumatic brain injury survivor.

Simona Stolpner, BA, has worked as a Health Science Specialist at the VA Program Evaluation and Resource Center (PERC) since 2005. While at PERC, she has participated in a variety of program evaluation projects centering on substance use disorder services at VA. Specifically, Ms. Stolpner has participated in monitoring the utilization of enhancement funds allocated to VA to broaden and improve substance use disorder services. In addition, she has worked with the PERC team on administering the Drug and Alcohol Program Survey, which evaluates VA's substance use disorder treatment system.

Chandra R. Story, PhD, has worked in project coordination for the Idaho Youth Suicide Prevention Intervention Project at Idaho State University and communications management for the Idaho System of Care. In both roles, Story partnered with the Regional VA Suicide Prevention Coordinator to provide information for community partners. She was employed as a Vol-Aware Project graduate assistant for one year, working alongside the project director to develop suicide prevention initiatives for student veterans. Story holds a master's of health science in health promotion and a PhD in community health education.

Susan R. Tate, PhD, is a Clinical Psychologist at the VA San Diego Healthcare System and Assistant Professor in the Department of Psychiatry at the University of California, San Diego. Dr. Tate's research interests have focused on clinical interventions for adults with substance use disorders and the role of psychiatric and medical comorbidity in addiction treatment outcomes. She conducts research at VA evaluating integrated psychotherapy interventions for substance-dependent adults with concomitant mood disorders and history of trauma. She received her PhD in 2000 from San Diego State University/University of California, San Diego Joint Doctoral Program in Psychology.

Sara Tavakoli, MPH, is a Health Science Specialist at the Program Evaluation Research Center and assisting member of the Substance Use Disorder Quality Enhancement Research Initiative. She has conducted SUD services evaluation in VA since 2006 and has worked with VA researchers and administrators in developing and delivering the 2008 and 2010 VA Drug and Alcohol Program Survey.

Joshua Tiegreen, PhD, is currently a staff psychologist at Durham VA Medical Center. After participating in the Psychosocial Rehabilitation and Recovery Fellowship at Durham VAMC, Joshua was hired as a staff psychologist to provide inpatient psychological services, with duties including recovery-based group therapy and psychological assessment. His duties also involve outpatient treatment, including individual therapy and evidence-based group therapy such as cognitive-behavioral therapy groups and skills training groups.

Stephen Tracy, MA, is a Health Science Specialist with the VA Program Evaluation and Resource Center. Since 2003 Mr. Tracy has served as the coordinator and contact person for the Drug and Alcohol Program Survey, a comprehensive evaluation of VA's substance use disorder treatment system. In addition, he has served as the overall coordinator for monitoring funds allocated to enhance VA substance use disorder treatment and has extensive experience consulting with VA staff needing assistance in implementing new treatment services.

Jodie Trafton, PhD, is Director of the VA Program Evaluation and Resource Center, a senior investigator at the VA Center for Health Care Evaluation, and a Clinical Assistant Professor (affiliated) in the Stanford University Department of Psychiatry and Behavioral Sciences. Dr. Trafton is a neurobiologist and health services researcher with expertise in chronic pain, opioid use, substance use disorders, mental health service delivery, and implementation of evidence-based mental healthcare. She has designed and conducted evaluations of VA substance use disorder treatment services since 2000.

Jessica C. Tripp, BA, is a Research Assistant at the VA San Diego Healthcare System. She received her BA in 2009 from the University of Kansas, Lawrence, and plans to continue with graduate study focused on addictive disorders.

Index

acamprosate, 60
Adams, D. P., et al. (1998), 131, 143
Administration for Native Americans
    (2009), 293
Administration for Native Americans
    (ANA 2009) report, 288
Advisory Committee on Minority
    Veterans, 295
Advisory Committee on Minority
    Veterans 2009, 300
Advisory Committee on Minority
    Veterans reports (2005 to 2009),
    281–284
Afghanistan, 127, 128
Ainspan, Nathan D., 423
alcohol and substance abuse programs,
    51–77
    Alcohol Use Disorders
      Identification Test Questions
      (AUDIT-C), 53
    attendance/retention, 62
    behavioral couple/family therapy, 58
    brief motivational interviewing
      interventions, 58

cognitive behavioral therapies,
    57–58
comorbid mental health disorders,
    62–64
comorbid physical health disorders,
    64–65
computer and web-based
    interventions, 66–67
diagnosis and assessment,
    54–55
integrated interventions, 66
introduction to, 51–52
matching and level/intensity of care
    (ASAM criteria), 61–62
pharmacotherapy for alcohol
    dependence, 59–60, 186–187
pharmacotherapy for opiate
    dependence, 60–61
pharmacotherapy interventions,
    58–59
pharmacotherapy research, 67–68
policies for, 52–61
post-traumatic stress disorder
    (PTSD) and, 63

alcohol and substance abuse programs
(*continued*)
psychotherapy interventions, 56–58
screening, 52–54
Single-Item Alcohol Screening
Question (SASQ), 53
stabilization, 55–56
suicidal thoughts, behaviors, and
attempts, 65–66
tobacco pharmacotherapies, 61
treatment, 55
Twelve-step facilitation (TSF),
56–57
alcohol pharmacotherapy, 59–60,
186–187
Alcohol Use Disorders Identification
Test Questions (AUDIT-C), 53
American Indian Traditional
Methodology of Healing, 299
American Society of Addiction
Medicine (ASAM) criteria, 179
Anchorage Vet Center, 299–300
Anderson-Barnes, Victoria C., 423
Anthony, W. (1993), 335, 361
baclofen, 67

Bagley, S. C., Munjas, B. & Shekelle, P.
(2010), 140, 143
Behavioral Health Lab, 20, 21
Belsher, Bradley E., 423–424
Bennett, Jeanne M., 424
Bhagwat, Aditya A., 424
blast injuries, 255
blasts injuries, 228–231
Blue Ribbon Work Group on Suicide
Prevention in the Veteran
Population, 131
Boston University Center for
Psychiatric Rehabilitation, 336
Braxton, Loretta E., 424
Brazaitis, Katherine, 424–425
Brief Addiction Monitor (BAM), 192
Bush, George W., 336–337

Cabral, H. J., et al. (2007), 404, 415
Camp Chaparral, 299
Caregivers and Veterans Omnibus
Health Services Act of 2010,
242–243
Center for Minority Veterans, 29, 280
Center of Excellence in Substance
Abuse Treatment and Education
(CESATE), 191
Chatterjee, S., et al. (2009), 29, 39
Chiarelli, Peter, 126, 140
*Clinical Practice Guidelines for the
Management of Substance Use
Disorders (SUD Guidelines)*, 171
Cloitre, M., et al. (2002), 319, 324
cocaine, 67–68
Cochrane Review, 315
Cognitive-behavioral conjoint therapy
for PTSD, 212
Community Based Warrior Transition
Units (CBWTUs), 268
compensated work therapy transitional
residence model (CWT/TR),
321–322
Cordova, M. J., et al. (2003), 212, 218
Cordova, Matthew J., 425
Corrigan, P. & Lundin, R. (2001),
365, 383

Danley, Karen, 312
Davidson, L., et al. (2005), 347, 361
Davis, Jack, 310
Deegan, P. (1996), 347, 361
Deegan, Pat, 333
deployment, 127–128, 129
Desai, M. M., Rosenheck, R. A. &
Craig, T. J. (2006), 22, 40
Desai, Mayur M., et al. (2003),
404, 415
*Diagnostic and Statistical Manual of
Mental Disorders* (DSM-IV;
American Psychiatric
Association 1994), 55

Dickman, Harold, 310
disulfiram, 59
Diversity and Inclusion Strategic Plan for 2009–2013 (Strategic Plan), 281
Dobscha, S. K., et al. (2009), 40
Donaldson, A. E., et al. (2006), 133, 145

Forensic Assertive Community Treatment (FACT) systems, 314
Fox, Valerie, 425
French, Louis M., 425
Freud, Sigmund, 315

Gates, Robert, 128
Gehring, John, 312
Gelberg, L., et al. (1997), 397, 415
GI Bill, 308, 320
Gifford, E., Jaszka, J. & Tracy, S. W. (2008), 177, 194
Gilbody, S., et al., 18, 41
Glasgow Coma Scale (GCS), 229, 231, 232 (table)
Goguen, Carole A., 425
Greater Los Angeles VAMC, 402
Greene-Shortridge, T. M., Britt, T. W. & Castro, C. A. (2007), 11, 47
Gulf War, 287–288
Gulf War Review, 288
Gurel, Lee, 310

Hamlett-Berry, Kim, 426
Handbook 1160.01: Uniform Mental Health Services in VA Medical Centers and Clinics, 171
Harding, C. (1987), 335, 362
Hawaii Integrated Health Care Demonstration Project, 14
Health Services Research and Development Service (HSR&D), 172

Hildreth, Harold, 309
Hispanic Vietnam veterans, 284
homeless veteran population, 296–297
homeless veterans and healthcare, 389–419
  acute hospitalizations interventions, 406
  AIDS, 408
  areas of future research, 409–411
  assertive community treatment (ACT) model, 407
  "best practices" for engaging treatment-resistant homeless persons, 405
  combat exposure and homelessness, 391
  competing sustenance needs, 397–398
  contingency management interventions, 406
  core elements/features needed in primary care model, 401–402
  "Ending Veteran Homelessness in Five Years," 411, 412–413 (box)
  establishing rapport/developing trust, 407–408
  estimated number of homeless veterans, 390
  factorial modeling of homeless veteran health services treatment engagement, 395 (fig.)
  five-year plan to end homelessness among veterans, 412–413 (box)
  Greater Los Angeles VAMC and, 402
  harm-reduction interventions, 408
  Health Care for the Homeless funding, 391–392
  health care services models for homeless persons over the past 25 years, 391–400
  healthcare avoidance, 404

homeless veterans and healthcare
(*continued*)
 healthcare for the homeless
  program, 391–392
 health-seeking behavior, 396–397
 HIV-positive people and,
  404, 407
 homeless outcomes, 393–394
 homelessness and healthcare,
  390–391
 homeless-specific barriers
  to care, 400
 housing is health care, 398
 methadone maintenance, 408
 motivation to change behaviors to
  exit homelessness, 399
 motivational interviewing and brief
  interventions, 406
 outreach, 404–405, 407–408
 percentage of potentially eligible
  veterans not getting VA
  services, 403
 policy recommendations, 411–413
 Providence VAMC and, 402
 readiness for change is a fluid
  dynamic, 399–400
 Roanoke VA and, 403
 Rochester VAMC and, 403
 role of primary care in homeless
  healthcare, 400–403
 self-identified needs, 405
 services on-demand, 409
 shelter-based outreach, 407–408
 situational motivation and
  "treatable moment"
  interventions, 405–407
 social determinants of health,
  395–396
 social support is an independent
  predictor of early exits from
  homelessness, 398–399
 Stewart B. McKinney Homeless
  Assistance Act, 391
 street outreach and street-based
  healthcare, 407
 summary and conclusions
  concerning, 413–414
 theoretical models, 394–395
 therapeutic "window," 400
 transtheoretical "stages of
  change" model (DiClemente
  2003), 397
 "treatable moments," 403, 405–407
 the treatment resistant homeless
  veteran, 403–405
 use of pharmacological adjuncts,
  408–409
 VA homeless programming, 392
homeless veterans and substance use,
 190–191
Homes for Heroes Act (H.R. 403), 191
Hoover, Herbert, 308
Housing and Urban Development and
 VA Supportive Housing
 (HUD-VASH) program, 191
Huguet, Nathalie, 426

Improving Mood-Promoting Access
 to Collaborative Treatment
 (IMPACT), 15
Indian Health Service, 294, 295, 296
Iraq, 127, 128

Jakupcak, M., et al. (2007), 128, 147

Kang, H. K. & Bullman, T. A. (2008),
 130, 147
Kaplan, F. (2006), 127, 147
Kaplan, M. S., et al. (2007), 130,
 134, 147
Kaplan, M. S., McFarland, B. H. &
 Huguet, N. (2009), 134,
 139, 147
Kaplan, Mark S., 426
Katon, W., et al. (1999), 27, 43

Kessler, R., Stafford, D. & Messier, R. (2009), 34, 43
Kettle, Samantha, 426
Kimerling, R., et al. (2008), 129, 148
Kirkwood, Ann D., 426–427
Kramer, B. J., et al. (2009a), 295, 302
Kranzler, H. R., et al., 59, 72

LaPierre, C. B., Schwegler, A. F. & LaBauve, B. J. (2007), 128, 148
Lepore, S. & Helgeson, V. (1998), 204, 221
Lepore, S. (2001), 204, 221
Little, Dolores K., 427
Loo, C. M. (2007), 285, 297, 302

MacLean, A. & Elder, G. H. (2007), 131, 148
Maguen, S., et al., 287, 302
Malte, Carol A., 427
Marsella, A. J., Friedman, M. J. & Spain, E. H. (1992), 297, 302
Matsunaga, Spark, 286
Matsunaga Vietnam Veterans Project, 286–287, 289, 290, 292
McCarthy, J. F., et al. (2009), 129, 149
McFall, Miles E., 427
McFarland, Bentson H., 427–428
McLellan, A. T., Carise, D. & Kleber, H. (2003), 182, 196
McNamara, Kathleen M., 428
Mental Health: A Report of the Surgeon General—Executive Summary, 13–14
Mental Health Awareness Project, 15
Mental Health Enhancement Initiative (MHEI), 171
Mental Health Strategic Plan (MHSP), 18–19, 171
mental illness stigma, eradication of, 365–388
    acculturation, 373
    African-Americans and, 372, 373

American Indian/Alaska Natives and, 372
Asian-Americans and, 372–373
categorization, 369
community campaigns, 378
cultural and societal stigma, 369–370
discrimination, 370, 373
funding, 380–381
future issues for, 379–381
gatekeepers and, 375
Hispanics and, 373
history of stigma, 365–366
internships, 380–381
interpretation of stigmatizing events, 371
mental health screenings, 368
military culture and, 379
new directions in veterans' healthcare, 375–379
OEF/OIF veterans, 366, 368, 378
policies and, 366–368
prejudice, 370
President's Commissionon on Care for America's Returning Wounded Warriors (PCCWW) report on, 366
provider and staff education programs (gatekeeper training), 377
public education, 367
public education campaigns, 376–377
research into stigma reduction, funding of, 381
screening, 378–379
self-stigma, 370–371
social marketing, 366–368, 374–376
stereotyping, 370
stigma affects, 368–369
stigma and race and ethnicity, 371–373

mental illness stigma, eradication
of (*continued*)
stigma development, 369–370
suicide prevention coordinator, 367
support from professionals, 380
training programs, 376–378
types of stigma, 369–373
VA Crisis Line, 367
veteran and family education,
377–378
visibility of the stigma, 371
Warrior Mind, 366–367
Military Acute Concussion Evaluation
(MACE), 262–263
military traumatic brain injury and the
postconcussive syndrome,
251–277
blast TBI, 255
civilian versus military TBI, 262
clinical tracking of TBI, 269
closed TBI, 255, 256
conclusion concerning, 271–272
definition of TBI, 255–257
diagnosing, 264–266
factors in recovery after a TBI, 258
history of military traumatic brain
injury, 251–255
incidents of TBI severity for
calendar year 2009, 254 (fig.)
Military Acute Concussion
Evaluation (MACE), 262–263
military TBI research, 268–269
model of care for TBI at Walter
Reed Army Medical Center,
263–268
mTBI (concussion), 256–257, 258,
264–265
neuroimaging, 270–271
penetrating TBI, 255
polytrauma patient and, 259–262
primary criterion for being
diagnosed with PCS, 259

quality of life, 271
research and new directions in TBI,
268–271
specific definitions of PCS, 259
Standardized Assessment of
Concussion (SAC), 263
symptoms of TBI and the
postconcussive syndrome,
257–259
TBI characterization studies,
269–270
TBI injury classification system,
257 (table)
unique aspects of military TBI,
262–263
Vietnam Head Injury Study
(VHIS), 253
Miller, M., et al. (2009), 130, 149
Miller, Thomas W., 421
Miller, William R. & Rollnick, Stephen
(2002), 407, 417
Milliken, C. S., Auchterlonie, J. L.
& Hoge, C. W. (2007),
128, 149
Mowrer, O. H. (1939), 201, 223
Mrnak-Meyer, Jennifer, 428
Multifamily Group Psychoeducation,
212
My Health*e*Vet, 192

Naltrexone, 59, 60
National Alliance for the Mentally Ill
(NAMI), 320
National Alliance for the Mentally Ill
(NAMI) Family-to-Family
Education Program, 212
National Center for PTSD video
courses, 293
*National Consensus Statement on Mental
Health Recovery*, 337
National Suicide Prevention Lifeline,
367

National Vietnam Veterans
    Readjustment Study (NVVRS),
    286, 289, 290, 292
Native American traditional healing,
    298–299
Native Hawaiian Healthcare
    Improvement Act, 294
Navajo Veterans Health Needs
    Project, 298
Neale, Michael, 313
Noronha, Delilah O., 428–429

Obama, Barack, 242, 411
Operation Enduring Freedom (OEF)
    polytrauma care, 227, 234
    psychosocial rehabilitation and
        recovery services, 360
    PTSD, 138
    rehabilitation care and
        treatment, 378
    stigma reduction, 366, 368
    substance use, 189–190
    suicide, 127
    traumatic brain injury (TBI),
        251, 254
Operation Iraqi Freedom (OIF)
    polytrauma care, 227, 234
    psychosocial rehabilitation and
        recovery services, 360
    PTSD, 138
    rehabilitation care and
        treatment, 378
    stigma reduction, 366, 368
    substance use, 189–190
    suicide, 127
    traumatic brain injury (TBI),
        251, 254
Oregon Violent Death Reporting
    System (OVDRS), 129, 134
Ortega, A. N. & Rosenheck, R. (2000),
    290, 303
O'Toole, Thomas P., 429

Papa Ola Lokahi Veterans Project, 294
Partners in Care (PIC) project, 14
Peake, James, 134
Peck, Cecil, 310
Peffer, Peter, 315
Penk, W. E. & Allen, I. M. (1991),
    284, 287, 303
Penk, W. E. (2000), 311, 329
Penk, Walter Erich, 429–430
Pfab, R., et al. (2006), 132, 150
Pignone, M. P., et al. (2002), 23, 46
Pinel, Phillippe, 334
polytrauma care and treatment,
    227–249
    acute rehabilitation, 239–240
    Assistive Technology Program, 241
    blast injury, mechanisms of,
        230 (table)
    blast injury, overview of
        explosive-related injuries,
        231 (table)
    blasts injuries, 228–231
    caregiver services with polytrauma,
        241–243
    Caregivers and Veterans Omnibus
        Health Services Act of 2010,
        242–243
    comprehensive acute
        interdisciplinary inpatient
        rehabilitation, 238–240
    comprehensive interdisciplinary
        inpatient evaluations, 237
    criteria for severity of head
        injury, 231–234
    current and future directions
        of, 244–245
    Family Care Collaborative, 242
    Glasgow Coma Scale (GCS), 229,
        231, 232 (table)
    interdisciplinary outpatient
        evaluation and rehabilitation,
        241

polytrauma care and treatment
  (*continued*)
    introduction to, 227–229
    polytrauma, definition of, 234–235
    polytrauma four tiered system,
      235–236
    polytrauma network sites (PNS),
      236–237
    Polytrauma Telehealth Network,
      243–244
    polytrauma traumatic brain injury
      system of care, 234–237
    post-acute comprehensive
      interdisciplinary inpatient
      rehabilitation, 241
    post-traumatic stress disorder
      (PTSD), 233
    rehabilitation centers, 236 (fig.)
    Residential Transitional
      Rehabilitation Progam, 240
    scope of services, 237–240
    specialized consultants, 239 (box)
    specialized programs, 240–241
    VHA individualized rehabilitation
      and community reintegration
      care plan, 241
    VHA Polytrauma System of Care,
      228, 234–237
post-trauma adjustment in veterans,
    social context of, 199–225
    cognitive models of PTSD,
      203–204
    cognitive-behavioral conjoint
      therapy for PTSD, 212
    disclosure, 214
    emotional processing theory,
      202–203
    family interventions, 211–213
    the fear network, 202
    group interventions, 213
    healthcare system interventions,
      213–214
    individual psychotherapy, 210–211
    introduction to, 199–201
    military interventions, 215
    models of intervention, 210–216
    models of post-traumatic stress
      disorder, 201–204
    Multifamily Group
      Psychoeducation, 212
    National Alliance for the Mentally
      Ill (NAMI) Family-to-Family
      Education Program, 212
    social cognitive processing, 204–208
    social cognitive processing model
      and the combat veteran,
      208–210
    societal interventions, 216
    Strategic Approach Therapy, 212
    summary, 216
    Two-Factor Conditioning Model,
      201–202
    *Uniform Mental Health Services
      Handbook* (Department of
      Veterans Affairs, OMHS
      2008), 200
post-traumatic stress disorder (PTSD),
    63, 79–80
    American Psychiatric Association's
      diagnostic criteria for, 233
    cognitive-behavioral conjoint
      therapy for PTSD, 212
    ethnic, racial, and cultural
      differences and, 284,
      290–293, 297–298
    family psychoeducation and, 317
    Hispanic Vietnam veterans and,
      284, 290, 292
    Japanese American Vietnam
      veterans, 289–290, 292
    National Vietnam Veterans
      Readjustment Study
      (NVVRS), 286, 290
    Native American veterans and, 285,
      290, 293
    Native Hawaiian veterans, 289, 292

substance use disorders and, 177
suicide and, 128, 138–139
traditional healing and, 298–299
women veterans and, 158
Wounded Spirits, Ailing Hearts: PTSD and the Legacy of War among American Indian & Alaska Native Veterans, 298
See also smoking cessation and post-traumatic stress disorder (PTSD)
President's Commission on Care for America's Returning Wounded Warriors (PCCWW) report on, 366
President's New Freedom Commission on Mental Health, 336–337
Prevention of Suicide in Primary Care Elderly: Collaborative Trial (PROSPECT), 15–16
primary care–mental health integration (PCMHI), 3–50
   access improvement, 9–11
   Alcohol Use Disorder Identification Test (AUDIT-C), 23
   anxiety, 6
   assessment, 23
   Behavioral Health Lab, 20, 21
   blended model, 21–22
   care continuance, 11–12
   care management model, 20–21
   Center for Minority Veterans, 29
   challenges and future implications, 31–37
   chronic pain, 27–28
   collaborative care medication monitoring, 26–27, 32
   co-located collaborative care model, 19–20
   depression, 6
   diagnosis (broad ICD-9 categories), 4 (table)
   diversity issues, 28–30

efficient healthcare utilization and cost effectiveness, 13
evidence base, 14–18
evidence-based psychotherapy, 33–34
frequency of possible mental disorders among OEF/OIF veterans since 2002, 5 (table)
Hawaii Integrated Health Care Demonstration Project, 14
history of, 13–18
home-based primary care (HBPC), 29–30
implementation, 32–33
Improving Mood-Promoting Access to Collaborative Treatment (IMPACT), 15
information technology (IT), 35
integration, benefits of, 9–13
interdisciplinary team approach, 12
introduction to, 3–8
journey toward integration, 18–19
key services of VHA PCMHI models, 22
leadership in sports, 36–37
Mental Health: A Report of the Surgeon General—Executive Summary, 13–14
Mental Health Awareness Project, 15
mental health screening (mandated), 23
mental health stigma, reduction of, 11
Mental Health Strategic Plan (MHSP), 18–19
nonpharmacological interventions, 25–26
outcome monitoring, quality assurance, and program evaluation, 35–36
Partners in Care (PIC) Project, 14

primary care–mental health integration
(PCMHI) (*continued*)
　Patient Aligned Care Teams
　　(PACT), 30
　Patient Health Questionnaire-2
　　item (PHQ-2), 23
　PCMHICare–mental health
　　models, 19–27
policy and, 36
post-9/11 service members, 28
President's New Freedom
　Commission on Mental
　Health, 13–14
prevalence of, 3–6
Prevention of Suicide in Primary
　Care Elderly: Collaborative Trial
　(PROSPECT), 15–16
Primary Care Research in
　Substance Abuse and Mental
　Health for Elderly
　(PRISM-E), 16
primary care setting, 9
Primary Care-Behavioral Health
　(PC-BH), 21–22
primary care–mental health brief
　interventions, 24–25
primary care–mental health
　integration, defining, 8
primary care–mental health
　integration versus specialty
　mental health, 8–9
Primary Care-Posttraumatic Stress
　Disorder (PC-PTSD), 23
psychological distress, other
　presentations of, 7–8
recruitment, 33
Re-Engineering Systems for
　Primary Care Treatment
　of Depression
　(RESPECT-Depression)
　project, 16–17
Regional Expansion of TIDES
　(ReTIDES), 17

satisfaction ratings, 12–13
screening/assessment, 22–23
special issues, 27–30
substance use, 7
suicide risk, 7
sustainability, 34–35
training, 33
Translating Initiatives in
　Depression into Effective
　Solutions (TIDES), 17
triage/referral, 24
*Uniform Mental Health Services
　Handbook*, 18
VA Palo Alto Health Care System
　(VAPAHCS), 21
Principi, Anthony, 171
Providence VAMC, 402
Psychiatric Evaluation Projects
　(PEP), 310
*Psychology and the Department of
　Veterans Affairs* (Baker &
　Pickren 2007), 309
psychosocial rehabilitation and
　recovery services, 333–363
　Boston University Center for
　　Psychiatric Rehabilitation,
　　336
　case example of, 354–357
　challenges to implementation,
　　357–359
　community support system
　　(CSS), 335
　components of recovery, 337
　consumer/liaison services, 353
　deinstitutionalization movement,
　　335
　development within the VA,
　　350–354
　empowerment component of
　　recovery, 342–343
　family services, 353–354
　history of psychiatric rehabilitation
　　and recovery, 334–336

holistic component of recovery, 343–344

honor, 349

hope as component of recovery, 347–348

individual challenges to implementation, 357–358

individualized and person-centered component of recovery, 341–342

introduction to, 333

local recovery coordinator (LRC), 350–352

mental health intensive case management (MHICM), 352

National Consensus Statement on Mental Health Recovery (2004), 337, 338

new directions in, 359–361

new recovery-based programs, 351 (table)

nonlinear component of recovery, 344

Operation Enduring Freedom/ Operation Iraqi Freedom (OEF/OIF) and, 360

other programming, 354

peer support component of recovery, 345

peer support services, 353

policies influencing implementation of rehabilitation and recovery services, 336–339

President's New Freedom Commission on Mental Health, 336–337

privacy, 348

psychosocial recovery in the VA system, principles of, 339–350

psychosocial recovery in the VA system, principles of (table), 340

Psychosocial Rehabilitation & Recovery Center (PRRC), 352

Psychosocial Rehabilitation and Recovery Fellowship (PSR), 359–360

RANGE program, 352

respect component of recovery, 345–346

responsibility component of recovery, 346–347

security, 348–349

self-advocacy, 342

self-direction component of recovery, 339, 341

self-disclosure, 348

strengths-based component of recovery, 344–345

support for VA veteran rights, 349–350

systematic challenges to implementation, 358–359

therapeutic and supported employment services (TSES), 353

U.S. Vocational Rehabilitation Act, 334

VHA Handbook 1160.01: Uniform Mental Health Services in VA Medical Centers and Clinics (2008), 338

Pyne, J. M. (2004), 368, 387

Racial and Ethnic Disparities in the VA Healthcare System: A Systematic Review (Saha et al. 2007), 282

racial and ethnic diversity, healthcare and issues of, 279–303

Administration for Native Americans (2009), 293

Administration for Native Americans (ANA 2009) report, 285, 288

Advisory Committee on Minority Veterans, 295

racial and ethnic diversity, healthcare
and issues of (*continued*)
Advisory Committee on Minority
Veterans reports (2005 to 2009),
281–284, 300
African American Vietnam
veterans, 290
American Indian and Alaskan
Native (AIAN) veterans, 295
American Psychological Association
2005 Presidential Task Force
report, 285
Anchorage Vet Center, 299–300
Annual Report of the Advisory
Committee on Minority
Veterans, 292–293
Camp Chaparral, 299
Center for Minority Veterans, 280
*Diversity and Inclusion Strategic
Plan for 2009–2013 (Strategic
Plan)*, 281
Gulf War, 287–288
Gulf War Review on, 288
Hispanic Vietnam veterans,
290, 292
homeless veteran population,
296–297
Indian Health Service, 294, 295,
296
Institute of Medicine (2001)
report, 284–285
Japanese American Vietnam
veterans, 289–290, 292
Loo, C. M. (2007) on, 285,
297, 302
Maguen, S., et al., on, 287, 302
Matsunaga Vietnam Veterans
Project, 286–287, 289, 290, 292
National Center for PTSD video
courses, 293
National Vietnam Veterans
Readjustment Study (NVVRS),
286, 289, 290, 292
Native American, 290, 293,
298–299
Native Hawaiian Healthcare
Improvement Act, 294
Native Hawaiian veterans, 289, 292
Navajo veterans, 298–299
network of tribal veterans'
representatives, 293
Papa Ola Lokahi Veterans
Project, 294
Penk, W. E. & Allen, I. M. (1991)
on, 284, 287, 303
PTSD and, 288, 290–293,
297–298
*Racial and Ethnic Disparities in
the VA Healthcare System:
A Systematic Review* (Saha et al.,
2007), 282
racial discrimination, 291
rural veterans needs, 296
traditional healing and, 298–299
Vietnam War and, 279, 286, 291
World War II and, 279
*Wounded Spirits, Ailing Hearts:
PTSD and the Legacy of War
among American Indian &
Alaska Native Veterans*, 298
Rao, D., Feinglass, J. & Corrigan, P.
(2007), 373, 387
Re-Engineering Systems for Primary
Care Treatment of Depression
(RESPECT-Depression)
project, 16–17
Regional Expansion of TIDES
(ReTIDES), 17
Reserve and National Guard service
members, 129
Roanoke VA, 403
Rochester VAMC, 403
Roosevelt, Franklin D., 308
Rosenheck, R. A., et al. (1997),
296, 303
Rosenheck, Robert, 313

Rumptz, M. H., et al. (2007), 404, 418
Ruzek, Josef I., 430

Satcher, David, 13
Saxon, Andrew J., 430
Schizophrenia Patient Outcomes
    Research Team (PORT), 317
Schnurr, P. P., et al. (2003), 290, 303
Schnurr, P. P., Lunney, C. A. &
    Sengupta, A. (2004), 291, 303
Shinseki, Eric, 189, 191, 296, 411, 412
Shortt, S. E., et al. (2008), 400, 418
Single-Item Alcohol Screening
    Question (SASQ), 53
Sloggett, Arthur, 252
smoking cessation and post-traumatic
    stress disorder (PTSD),
    79–121
    abstinence, long-term by treatment
        received, stratified by number of
        sessions attended, 102 (table)
    abstinence, primary outcome
        of twelve-month prolonged, 104
    abstinence, seven-day abstinence by
        treatment condition, 105 (fig.)
    abstinence rates, long-term,
        101 (table)
    administrative intervention, 93
    behavioral counseling, 92
    challenges to, 111–112
    clinical interventions, components
        of, 94–95
    concurrent treatment of PTSD, 98
    connection between PTSD and
        smoking, 86–87
    copayment for cessation
        counseling, 82
    defining post-traumatic stress
        disorder (PTSD), 85–86 (box)
    delivery of cessation treatment,
        90–91 (box)
    history of tobacco cessation efforts
        at the VHA, 81–84

integrate care, primary studies
    of, 98–103
integrated care, 91–103
integrated care delivery, 93–94
integrated care, dissemination of
    within the VHA, 109–111
integrated care, goals of, 91–93
integrated care sessions, breakdown
    of, 95–98
medication use by treatment
    condition, 100 (table)
motivational interventions,
    94 (box)
multisite effectiveness trial,
    103–109
national performance measures,
    83–84
national prevalence of tobacco use
    among VHA enrollees, 83 (fig.)
An Open Trial of Practice-Based
    Integrated Care (McFall et al.,
    2006), 98–100
pharmacotherapy, 93
point prevalence abstinence for
    veterans with PTSD receiving
    integrated care, 99 (fig.)
point prevalence abstinence rates for
    veterans with PTSD, 101 (fig.)
prescription restrictions, 81–82
primary studies, conclusions
    from, 102–103
psychiatric disorders and smoking,
    84–89
psychiatric symptoms, 106–108
psychiatric symptoms, change
    in, 102
A Randomized Trial of Integrated
    Care versus Specialized Smoking
    Cessation Clinic (McFall et al.,
    2005), 98–100
relapse, time in months, 106
relapse prevention and
    management, 93

smoking cessation and post-traumatic stress disorder (PTSD) (*continued*)
secondary smoking outcomes, 104–105
self-help work, 92–93
smoking as a public health problem in veterans with PTSD, 84–87
standard smoking cessation care delivery in the VHA, 88 (box)
tobacco cessation and the VHA, 80
Treating Tobacco Use and Dependence (Fiore et al., 2008), 92
treatment barriers among patients with PTSD, 87–89, 91
treatment effective mediators, 105–106
treatment implications, 89–98
treatment received from randomization to month 18, 107 (table)
VHA/DoD clinical practice guidelines, 82
Sohn, L. & Harada, N. D. (2008), 291, 303
Speer, D. C. & Schneider, M. G. (2003), 22, 47
Stahre, M. A., et al. (2009), 129, 151
Stamm, Beth Hudnall, 430–431
Standardized Assessment of Concussion (SAC), 263
Stecker, T., et al. (2007), 128, 151
Stenger, Charles, 310
Stolpner, Simona, 431
Stories from VA Psychology (Baker 2007), 309
Story, Chandra R., 431
Strategic Approach Therapy, 212
Strauss, J. S. (2005), 347, 362
Substance Abuse and Mental Health Services Administration's National Survey on Drug Use and Health, 7
substance use disorders, treatment of, 169–198
alcohol misuse screening, 172–174
American Society of Addiction Medicine (ASAM) criteria, 179
Brief Addiction Monitor (BAM), 192
brief interventions and motivational counseling, 175–176
buprenorphine, 184, 185, 186
Buprenorphine Task Group (BTG), 186
Clinical Practice Guidelines for the Management of Substance Use Disorders (SUD Guidelines), 171, 188, 189
conclusions concerning, 193
co-occurring disorders (CODs), 176–178
expansion of VA SUD, 180
Handbook 1160.01: Uniform Mental Health Services in VA Medical Centers and Clinics, 171, 182
history of specialized VA SUD treatment, 170–172
homeless veterans and, 190–191
integration and coordination of care, 176–177
introduction to, 169–170
management of substance misuse and SUDs in primary care and general mental healthcare settings, 175–178
management of SUD-related co-occurring disorders, 177–178
Mental Health Enhancement Initiative (MHEI), 171
Mental Health Strategic Plan (MHSP), 171
methadone and buprenorphine-based OAT, 184

monitoring and metrics for SUD
    treatment, 191–192
nicotine dependence Screening and
    Treatment, 174–175
OEF and OIF veterans and,
    189–190
office-based opioid treatment
    (OBOT), 184–185
opiate agonist treatment
    (OAT), 183–184
opiate agonist treatment (OAT),
    continued expansion of services
    for, 185–186
opiate agonist treatment (OAT),
    office-based versus specialty
    program treatment settings
    for, 184–185
pharmacotherapy for alcohol
    dependence, 186–187
pharmacotherapy for opioid
    dependence, 183
pharmacotherapy for substance
    dependence, 183–187
post-traumatic stress disorder
    (PTSD) and, 177
primary care and mental health
    integration, 178
residential rehabilitation
    treatment program (RRTP),
    176–177
screening and initial assessment for
    substance use, 172–175
specialty SUD care, improving the
    quality of, 181–182
specialty SUD care, increasing
    access to, 180–181
stabilization and withdrawal
    management, 187–189
SUD Quality Enhancement
    Research Initiative
    (SUDQUERI), 172
SUD treatment in VA's specialty
    SUD care settings, 178–183

SUD treatment staffing challenges,
    182–183
technology in SUD treatment,
    192–193
VA Office of Mental Health
    Services' Program Evaluation
    and Resource Center (PERC),
    172
*VA/DoD Clinical Practice Guidelines
    for Management of Tobacco Use
    (2008)*, 174–175
women veterans and, 190
On Suicide (Durkheim), 123
suicide risk among veterans of military
    service, 123–153
    addiction and dependence,
        135–136
    Afghanistan and, 127, 128
    blue ribbon work group suicide
        prevention, 142
    Centers for Disease Control
        and Prevention (CDC) data,
        131, 132
    demographic characteristics, 134
    deployment and, 127, 128–129
    epidemiology of veterans' suicides,
        131–140
    female suicide, 130
    frequency of suicides, 131
    Iraq and, 127, 128
    Joshua Omvig Veterans Suicide
        Prevention Act, 141
    male and female suicide rates per
        100,000 by methods, age, and
        veteran status, 135 (fig.)
    mental disorders, 136–137
    military suicide rates, 2001–2009,
        127 (fig.)
    misclassification of suicide
        deaths, 131–133
    Operation Enduring Freedom,
        127, 138
    Operation Iraqi Freedom, 138

suicide risk among veterans of military service (*continued*)
　Oregon Violent Death Reporting System (OVDRS) data on, 129, 134
　post-traumatic stress disorder (PTSD), 138–139
　prevention of suicide, 140–142
　psychosocial factors, 137–138
　Reserve and National Guard service members, 129
　risk factors specific to veterans, 133
　role and importance of firearms, 139–140
　stress, mental health, and the suicide of soldiers, 126–129
　suicidal ideation, 137
　suicidal ideation and suicide attempts, 125–126
　suicide in the general population, 124–125
　suicide rates per 100,000 by age and gender, 124 (table)
　suicide risk among male veterans in the general population, 130 (fig.)
　suicide risk in the military, 126
　undetermined deaths, 132–133
　Vietnam War and, 131
Sutker, P. B., et al. (1995), 291, 303

Tate, Susan R., 431
Tavakoli, Sara, 431
Tiegreen, Joshua, 431–432
tobacco, 54, 61, 79–80
　See also smoking cessation and post-traumatic stress disorder (PTSD)
Tracy, Stephen, 432
traditional healing, 298–299
Trafton, Jodie, 432
Translating Initiatives in Depression into Effective Solutions (TIDES), 17

trauma-focused psychosocial rehabilitation, 307–331
　"choose, get, and keep" approaches, 312
　assertive community treatment (ACT) and intensive case management (MHICM), 313–314
　Battlemind and Re-set Training, 318
　Cochrane Review, 315
　compensated work therapy (CWT) programs, 315
　compensated work therapy transitional residence model (CWT/TR), 321–322
　conclusion concerning, 322–323
　evidence supporting psychosocial rehabilitation, 312–322
　family psychoeducation, 317–318
　Forensic Assertive Community Treatment (FACT) systems, 314
　forms of psychosocial rehabilitation, 311
　hallmark characteristic of supported employment, 316
　history of VHA psychosocial rehabilitation, 308, 309–310
　Intensive Psychiatric Community Care (IPCC), 313
　introduction to, 307–311
　National Alliance for the Mentally Ill (NAMI) and, 320
　North East Program Evaluation Center (NEPEC), 313
　patient education and illness management, 318
　peer support, 319–320
　Psychiatric Evaluation Projects (PEP), 310
　psychosocial rehabilitation policies, 307–308

Schizophrenia Patient Outcomes
Research Team (PORT), 317
social skills training, 319
supported education, 320–321
supported employment, 314–316
supportive housing, 321–322
toolkits for family psychoeducation,
317–318
"Trauma Management Therapy,"
319
Vet Construction Team, 316
"veterans' courts," 314
*VHA Handbook 1160 for Uniform
Health Services in VA Medical
Centers and Clinics* (2009), 322
"work cure," 312
traumatic brain injury (TBI), 229,
231–233, 234, 240, 242
See also military traumatic brain
injury and the postconcussive
syndrome
tribal veterans' representatives
network, 293
Tripp, Jessica C., 432
Tuke, William, 334

Uebelacker, L. A., et al. (2009),
29, 48
*Uniform Mental Health Services
Handbook*, 18
*Uniform Mental Health Services
Handbook* (Department of
Veterans Affairs, OMHS
2008), 200
U.S. Psychiatric Rehabilitation
Association (USPRA), 334
U.S. Vocational Rehabilitation
Act, 334

VA Crisis Line, 367
VA Office of Mental Health Services'
Program Evaluation and
Resource Center (PERC), 172

VA Palo Alto Health Care System
(VAPAHCS), 21
*VA/DoD Clinical Practice Guidelines for
Management of Tobacco Use*
(2008), 174–175
Varenicline, 61
"veterans' courts," 314
*VHA Handbook 1160 for Uniform
Health Services in VA Medical
Centers and Clinics* (2009), 322
*VHA Handbook 1160.01: Uniform
Mental Health Services in VA
Medical Centers and Clinics*
(2008), 338
VHA Polytrauma System of Care, 228
Vietnam Head Injury Study
(VHIS), 253
Vietnam War, 131, 252, 279, 286

Waldrop, Robert, 309
Warden, D. (2006), 263, 277
Warrior Mind, 366–367
Watts, B.V., et al. (2007), 20, 49
West, A. & Weeks, W. B. N. (2006),
296, 303
When the Warrior Comes Home
(Ainspan & Penk in press), 317
White River Junction VA Medical
Center, 17, 20
Wolford, Roy A., 309
women veterans experiencing
trauma, VA healthcare
for, 155–168
cognitive processing therapy
(CPT), 159–161 (box)
identification and outreach,
156–161
issues related to, 161–162
military sexual trauma (MST),
156–158
military sexual trauma (MST)
related laws, directives, and
policies, 164–167

women veterans experiencing
trauma, VA healthcare
for (*continued*)
military sexual trauma (MST)
residential treatment
programs, 161
military sexual trauma (MST)
sequelae, 157
military sexual trauma
(MST) treatment,
158–159 (box)

post-traumatic stress disorder
(PTSD), 158
prolonged exposure therapy (PE),
158–159 (box)
resources for, 162
women in the military, 155–156
World War II, 279
*Wounded Spirits, Ailing Hearts: PTSD
and the Legacy of War among
American Indian & Alaska
Native Veterans*, 298

The Praeger Handbook of Veterans' Health

Volume I
History, Eras, and Global Healthcare

Volume II
Programs of Care and Groups with Special Needs

Volume III
Mental Health Treatment and Rehabilitation

Volume IV
Future Directions in Veterans' Healthcare

THE PRAEGER HANDBOOK OF VETERANS' HEALTH

History, Challenges, Issues, and Developments

Volume IV: Future Directions in Veterans' Healthcare

Thomas W. Miller, Editor

PRAEGER

AN IMPRINT OF ABC-CLIO, LLC
Santa Barbara, California • Denver, Colorado • Oxford, England

Library of Congress Cataloging-in-Publication Data

The Praeger handbook of veterans' health : history, challenges, issues, and developments / Thomas W. Miller, editor.
    v. cm.
 Includes bibliographical references and index.
 ISBN 978-0-313-38349-6 (hardcover : alk. paper) — ISBN 978-0-313-38350-2 (ebook)
1. Veterans—Health and hygiene—United States. 2. Veterans—Care—United States. 3. Veterans—United States—History. I. Miller, Thomas W., 1943– II. Title: Handbook of veterans' health.
 UB369.P73 2012
 362.1086'97—dc23
                        2012025159

ISBN: 978-0-313-38349-6
EISBN: 978-0-313-38350-2

16 15 14 13 12   1 2 3 4 5

This book is also available on the World Wide Web as an eBook.
Visit www.abc-clio.com for details.

Praeger
An Imprint of ABC-CLIO, LLC

ABC-CLIO, LLC
130 Cremona Drive, P.O. Box 1911
Santa Barbara, California 93116-1911

This book is printed on acid-free paper ∞
Manufactured in the United States of America

It is the VETERAN, not the preacher, who has given us freedom of religion.

It is the VETERAN, not the reporter, who has given us freedom of the press.

It is the VETERAN, not the poet, who has given us freedom of speech.

It is the VETERAN, not the campus organizer, who has given us freedom to assemble.

It is the VETERAN, not the lawyer, who has given us the right to a fair trial.

It is the VETERAN, not the politician, who has given us the right to vote.

It is the VETERAN, who salutes the Flag, It is the VETERAN, who serves under the Flag.

—Author Unknown

Contents

**VOLUME IV
FUTURE DIRECTIONS IN VETERANS' HEALTHCARE**

Acknowledgments ix

Foreword xi
Jacob B. Gadd

Editor's Foreword xv

Part I   Dedicated Centers for Veterans' Healthcare   1

1 Centers of Excellence in the Department of Veterans Affairs   3
Thomas W. Miller

2 Organization Development in the Department of Veterans Affairs   21
*Katerine Osatuke, Jill Draime, Scott C. Moore, Dee Ramsel,
Andrew A. Meyer, Sharon Barnes, Linda W. Belton,
and Sue R. Dyrenforth*

3 Department of Veterans Affairs National Center for Patient Safety:
First Do No Harm   77
Joseph F. Murphy and James P. Bagian

4 The National Center for PTSD   95
Matthew J. Friedman

5 Pain Management in the Veterans Health Administration   129
Kathryn LaChappelle, Samantha Boris-Karpel, and Robert D. Kerns

Part II   New Directions in Veterans' Healthcare   151

6 Achieving Clinical Integration: Observations from the Veterans'
Healthcare System   153
Kenneth W. Kizer

7 VA Healthcare System: A Potential Model for a National Plan   165
Said A. Ibrahim, David S. Macpherson, and Michael E. Moreland

8 Telehealth Applications to Underserved Veterans:
The Right Care, in the Right Place, at the Right Time   197
Jennifer A. Wood, Thomas W. Miller, and Russell Hagy

9 Suicide Prevention through a National Hotline
within the Veterans Health Administration   223
Thomas W. Miller and Janet Kemp

10 Academy of Spinal Cord Injury Professionals   235
Terrie Price

11 Ethicolegal Issues in Veterans' Healthcare   251
*Steven Nisenbaum, Thomas W. Miller, Sheila O'Keefe, and Dennis
Norman*

12 The Story of Give an Hour™   283
Barbara Van Dahlen

13 The Veterans' Healthcare System's Path to Excellence   315
Edmund J. Nightingale

About the Editor   377

About the Contributors   379

Index   387

Acknowledgments

An endeavor of this magnitude has taken several years and the efforts of numerous colleagues and friends in the Department of Veterans Affairs and others interested in the health and well-being of our veterans and their families in the general public. It is to those in the Department of Veterans Affairs Central Office in Washington, D.C., their regional Veterans Integrated Service Networks (VISNs), and regional as well as local Veteran Affairs medical centers that I am extremely grateful. Their efforts have addressed contacting the right people, gaining access to important information, manuscript preparation completion, reviews, and providing detailed guidance in the final chapters and volumes.

Special appreciation is expressed to the efforts of the Department of Veterans Affairs, Office of Communications, and in particular Mr. Daniel Bruneau, Director of Communications; Christine A. Pons, Regional Office of Public Affairs, Department of Veterans Affairs; and Charles F. Castner, Staff Attorney, Department of Veterans Affairs.

The assistance of Darlene Richardson, the Department of Veterans Affairs historian, has been helpful in completing several of the chapters, as have external organizations committed to the care and treatment of our veterans, including the American Legion, Veterans of Foreign Wars, and Paralyzed Veterans of America.

To a cadre of former and current colleagues and friends within the Department of Veterans Affairs, and to some beyond this system, for their support and encouragement, special appreciation is extended, including but

not limited to John Booss, MD; Rodney Baker, PhD; Malcolm Cox, MD; Robert Gresen, PhD; James McCormick, MD; James Holsinger, MD; Herb Spencer, MD; Robert Kraus, MD; Steve Kraman, MD; William Green, PhD; Pat DeLeon, JD, PhD; Brenda Frommer; Neil Carey, MSW; Skip Lowe, PhD; Jeffrey Fisher, PhD; Alla Moeller; Walter Penk, PhD; Ed Nighingale, PhD; Ed Kisarskis, MD; Jill Livingstone, MLB; Deborah Kessler, MLB; Desti Stimes; Joanna Hawthorne; Chesley Jaracz; Tom Martin; Ginny Hamm, JD; Joseph Fox, PhD; Donna K. Jacobs; Steve Campbell, MSW; Steve Nisenbaum, PhD, JD; Terry Clark, MSW; and Maureen Charles, ED, MSN, APRN, Military Nurse Fellow, Lieutenant Colonel, Air Force Nurse Corps.

Appreciation is extended to Praeger publishers as well and their staff and Debbie Carvalko, senior acquisitions editor, psychology, health, and social work, and Alicia S. Merritt, consultant, for their guidance and support.

I express my sincere appreciation to my family, especially my father who served our country in World War II in General Patton's army in the European theater, and friends, who have been so supportive of this effort. And I extend my sincere gratitude and appreciation to each and every contributor for the chapters in these volumes. They come from the several Department of Veterans Affairs facilities, from our major universities, and from both within and beyond our borders. The reader will meet each and every one of them in their chapters as well as in the short biographies that summarize their backgrounds, training, experiences, and expertise. May these volumes provide the reader with a detailed look at veterans' healthcare in the twenty-first century!

Foreword

For the past fifty years, the Department of Veterans Affairs (VA) has provided high-quality care to America's veterans, and it is recognized today as the largest integrated healthcare system in the United States. Its mission, as stated eloquently by President Abraham Lincoln during his second inaugural address, is "to care for him who has borne the battle, his widow and orphan." Currently there are more than twenty-five million veterans across the country. Eight million are enrolled in VA and about 5.5 million are seen at 1,300 Veterans Health Administration (VHA) facilities annually. The VHA has 153 medical centers, 800 community-based outpatient clinics (CBOCs), and 260 readjustment counseling centers (vet centers), with an operating budget of $1 billion dollars and close to 270,000 employees.

There are more than 107 VA medical centers conducting research to improve the health and wellness of veterans. Over the years, this research has led to breakthroughs including development of the CAT scan, the cardiac pacemaker, and the nicotine patch, as well as the first liver transplant. One of the VA's most successful recruitment tools is its medical school affiliations program, which helps trains thousands of medical practitioners each year.

In the 1990s the Department of Veterans Affairs began its transformation from an inpatient to an outpatient system of care. Dr. Kenneth Kizer, then under secretary of health for the VHA, and the VA leadership developed CBOCs to enable the VA to see patients closer to their communities and provide needed outpatient and primary care to veterans who were previously forced to travel hundreds of miles to receive care in veterans' medical centers. In addition, during that period the VA established a defined medical benefits

package for enrolled veterans as well as long-term care for veterans rated 70 percent or higher disabled for service-connected injuries and illnesses from their military service.

In 1998 Congress directed the VA to establish eight priority groups to prioritize and rationalize healthcare for veterans based on the most injured and poorest veterans. In 2003 then Secretary of Veterans Affairs Anthony Principi suspended enrollment for Priority Group 8 veterans due to the VA's limited budget and the increasing numbers of veterans enrolling for VA healthcare. In order to enroll, veterans were required to take a means test, or financial assessment, to determine if they qualified for one of the priority groups and if they could make copays. In 2008 the VA relaxed its enrollment by 10 percent higher than the original means test cut-off income restriction, which allowed an additional 240,000 veterans previously ineligible for VA healthcare to enroll.

Today the Priority Group 8 restriction still exists, but combat veterans who have served after September 11, 2001, in a combat theater of operations (i.e., Operation Enduring Freedom, Operation Iraqi Freedom, and Operation New Dawn), are eligible for five years of veterans' healthcare for any injury or illness related to their military service. Veteran service organizations, such as The American Legion, believe that any veteran should be entitled to use the VA, which is a system designed to meet their unique and complex war-related injuries. In 1997 the VA was given the authority to bill, collect, and retain third-party reimbursements for treatment of non-service-connected medical conditions. Veterans, regardless of level of income or injury, should be authorized to bring their private insurance to the VA for treatment of their non-service medical conditions, which would be an alternative budget stream to offset the demand for services. Another concern is that veterans are not allowed to use their Medicare benefits within the VA. Veterans pay into Medicare their entire working lives and are essentially penalized because they cannot use their earned Medicare benefits in the VA and are forced to use those benefits in the private sector. In the future, the VA must continue to try to improve access to care for any veteran and take advantage of the cost savings to the government of veterans using their Medicare benefits in the VA system rather than the private sector.

Today there is an unprecedented number of returning veterans from Iraq and Afghanistan with traumatic brain injury (TBI) and post-traumatic stress disorder (PTSD). The term *polytrauma* was coined by the VHA to describe the many returning service members with complex, multiple injuries that required a new and holistic way of providing care. Over the last several years, the VHA has developed a polytrauma system of care with four levels.

Level 1 is the lead polytrauma rehabilitation centers, network or Veteran Integrated Service Network (VISN) sites, facilities (VA medical centers), and clinic or polytrauma points of contact. The lead polytrauma centers in the country are located in Palo Alto, California; Tampa, Florida; Richmond, Virginia; and Minneapolis, Minnesota. A new center is being built in San Antonio, Texas. From the battlefield, service members are evacuated through Landshuhl, Germany, to one of the military treatment facilities in the United States. The VHA has nurse liaisons and social workers who help transition severely injured veterans from military treatment facilities to the polytrauma system of care.

If a service member is involved in an improvised explosive device (IED) blast and develops a TBI, it is very likely that the veteran will also develop PTSD. If left untreated, the TBI and PTSD symptoms could lead to substance abuse, depression, and suicide. The VA conducts mandatory screens for veterans when they first enter a VA medical facility for TBI and PTSD. If the screening is positive, those veterans are referred for a secondary evaluation. Veterans' healthcare has also developed a crisis intervention line, formerly known as the Suicide Prevention Hotline, to assist any veteran in crisis. The hotline is open 365 days a year and 24 hours a day and is staffed by licensed counselors. The hotline has been credited for saving over 16,000 lives, and the VA has suicide prevention coordinators in each VA medical center to ensure veterans in crisis receive the assistance they need. The Department of Defense (DoD) and the Department of Veterans Affairs have also led the effort to destigmatize mental health conditions in our returning service members by having mental health practitioners embedded in primary care and through antistigma campaigns such as the "Real Warriors Campaign" in the Department of Defense and "Make the Connection" campaign in the Department of Veterans Affairs.

The VA continues to work with the DoD to develop a joint medical record, which will assist transitioning veterans in obtaining their earned veterans' benefits and services. Both agencies are working on a virtual lifetime electronic record (VLER), which will help connect the DoD and the VA information technology (IT) platforms to follow a service member from the day he or she joins the service to the day that person is laid to rest. The DoD and the VA are continuing to conduct research to improve the prevention, screening, diagnosis, and treatment of TBI and PTSD.

Veteran service organizations were founded to assist veterans by helping them file claims for their earned benefits and services. Veteran service organization service officers are professionally trained and accredited by the VA to file claims for veterans. In addition, Veteran service organizations provide

advocacy and assistance to veterans as well as lobbying the administration, Congress, and senior officials in the VA to make recommendations for continuous improvements for all veterans.

The chapters that follow reflect the many contributions that have been made to veterans' healthcare as well as the key healthcare issues facing our nation's veterans in the twenty-first century. Our nation has a moral obligation to take care of our service members when they return home. George Washington once said, "The willingness with which our young people are likely to serve in any war, no matter how justified, shall be directly proportional to how they perceive the veterans of earlier wars were treated and appreciated by their nation." It is our nation's responsibility to ensure that the Department of Veterans Affairs continues to provide timely, quality healthcare for our nation's veterans.

Jacob B. Gadd
Deputy Director for Health Care,
The American Legion;
Former Hospital Corpsman Third Class,
United States Navy (1998–2003)

Editor's Foreword

This four-volume set focusing on veterans' healthcare provides a unique and valuable contribution to our understanding of veterans' healthcare in the first decade of the twenty-first century. As a professor emeritus and retired VA career service chief from Lexington Veterans Affairs Medical Center, I have enjoyed a forty-year career in veterans' healthcare. I was first contacted in 2005 by Praeger Publishers to serve as editor of a handbook on this topic and then contacted some colleagues from the Department of Veterans Affairs both past and present and several colleagues nationally to explore the level of interest in accepting the invitation from Praeger to produce a positive reference book focusing on veterans' healthcare. It is to this cadre of professionals that I am indebted; they have contributed their knowledge and expertise in the chapters comprising this handbook.

We must be reminded of not only the macro events, but also the micro transitions that have contributed to the finest model of healthcare for veterans in the world. The reader is about to begin an extraordinary journey into the spectrum of healthcare offered through the Veterans Health Administration (VHA). Volume I offers the reader an understanding of the history of veterans' healthcare. Rodney R. Baker provides an overview of the historical contributions to veterans' healthcare. James W. Holsinger Jr., the first under secretary for veterans' affairs, offers a "View from the Top," addressing the administration and VA healthcare. VHA's academic mission is presented by Stuart C. Gilman, Barbara Chang, Robert Zeiss, Mary Dougherty, William Marks Jr., Deborah Ludke, and Malcolm Cox. Recognizing the important role of legislative initiatives for veterans' healthcare, with the assistance of Corina

M. Barrow, Jacquie Rychnovsky, and Patrick DeLeon of Senator Inouye's office, I provide a historical review of key legislation that has benefited veterans' healthcare.

I also examine healthcare for veterans from various eras, covering veterans of World Wars I and II and the Korean conflict. Robert J. Fitz discusses healthcare for veterans of the Vietnam era, and Delilah O. Noronha, John Chardos, Laura Gomez, Samina Iqbal, and Steven Lindley provide a discussion of healthcare for veterans of Operations Enduring Freedom, Iraqi Freedom, and New Dawn.

In an effort to examine global healthcare for veterans, provided is a comparative look at veterans' healthcare in other countries: Australia, Canada, China, Russia, and the United Kingdom. Professor David Dunt and his team examine a critical issue for veterans, focusing on suicide in the ex-service community in Australian research and prevention efforts. Dr. David Pedlar and Stewart Macintosh provide a closer look at veterans affairs in Canada. Finally, Professor Dai Williams takes a closer look at healthcare for British veterans.

Volume II examines programs of care and veterans' special needs. James W. Anderson, a pioneer in clinical care and research, explores healthcare programs for veterans with diabetes in primary care. This is followed by a discussion of neurological healthcare for veterans by Mitchell Wallin and John Kurtzke. David Booth then examines cardiology care for veterans, followed by Philip DeSimone's acknowledgment of veterans' sacrifices made in the quest for cancer treatment. Robert C. Gresen provides a first look at mental health care in VHA. Chiropractic care in veterans' healthcare is reviewed by Bart Green and a team of colleagues from the Naval Medical Center in San Diego and at the VA medical center in Buffalo, New York. Healthcare for veterans with infectious diseases is examined by Cynthia L. Gibert, and end-of-life care for veterans in the VA healthcare system is addressed by Betty L. Gillespie, James L. Ford, and Kye Y. Kim.

Many veterans have special needs. To examine these needs, we asked Dr. Hayden B. Bosworth to assess the lifestyles and health behaviors of veterans. Noting the special needs of amputees and the guidance of Fred Downs, I examined orthotics and prosthetics healthcare for veterans. The challenges faced by Native American veterans and their solutions are addressed by Joseph Stone of the Indian Health Service, and healthcare for women military veterans is addressed by Monica Roy. Prisoners of war have always been a special population and have had special needs; Brian Engdahl and Charles Stenger take a close look at serving America's former prisoners of war. Drs. Beth Hudnall Stamm, Susan L. Blampied, and Kirstina Beck examine a

special population of caregivers in their chapter on assistance dogs and their use by veterans with disabilities.

Volume III takes a closer and more detailed look at mental health treatment and rehabilitation. Delilah O. Noronha begins by examining primary care and mental health integration in providing veterans' healthcare. This is followed by a chapter that examines alcohol and substance abuse programs, by Susan R. Tate, Jennifer Mrnak-Meyer, and Jessica C. Tripp. Smoking has been critical in veterans' healthcare, and Carol A. Malte, Andrew J. Saxon, Kim Hamlett-Berry, and Miles E. McFall investigate integrating smoking cessation into mental health care for post-traumatic stress disorder.

Clinician researchers Mark S. Kaplan, Bentson H. McFarland, and Nathalie Huguet take a close look at suicide risk among veterans. VA healthcare for women veterans experiencing trauma is the focus of Carole A. Goguen. Stephen Tracy, Sara Tavakoli, Simona Stolpner, and Jodie Trafton discuss the treatment of substance use disorders; and the social context of adjustment in combat veterans is examined by Bradley Belsher, Josef Ruzek, and Matthew Cordova. Polytrauma care and treatment in veterans' healthcare is covered by Jeanne M. Bennett. Military traumatic brain injury and the postconcussive syndrome is addressed by colleagues in the Department of Defense led by Louis M. French, Victoria C. Anderson-Barnes, Katherine Brazaitis, and Aditya Bhagwat. Healthcare and issues of racial and ethnic diversity are carefully examined by Kathleen M. McNamara.

With special attention on rehabilitation care and treatment for veterans, colleagues Walter Penk, Dolores Little, and Nathan Ainspan address trauma-focused psychosocial rehabilitation. This is followed by a chapter on psychosocial rehabilitation and recovery services by Samantha Kettle, Loretta E. Braxton, Valerie Fox, and Josh Tiegreen. Next Ann D. Kirkwood, Beth Hudnall Stamm, and Chandra R. Story address eradicating mental illness stigma for active military personnel and veterans. Finally, Thomas P. O'Toole provides an in-depth assessment of how VA is engaging homeless veterans in primary care.

Volume IV provides an examination of some of the future directions for veterans' healthcare, first examining dedicated centers for veterans' healthcare. The first chapter reviews VHA centers of excellence. Then Drs. Katerine Osatuke, Jill Draime, Scott C. Moore, Dee Ramsel, Andrew Meyer, Sharon Barnes, Linda Belton, and Sue R. Dyrenforth examine the latest in organization development in VA.

Joseph F. Murphy, public affairs officer, VA NCPS, and James P. Bagian explore for the reader the VA National Center for Patient Safety. The significance of post-trauma stress is addressed by Matthew J. Friedman, the national

director of the Department of Veterans Affairs National Center for PTSD. Leading the way in pain-related disorders, Drs. Kathryn LaChappelle, Samantha Boris-Karpel, and Robert D. Kerns provide a detailed review of the efforts to address pain management in VHA.

Dr. K. Kizer, who is responsible for a major reorganization of VHA, provides a closer view of lessons learned about clinical integration from VA's experience with VISNs. The Veterans' healthcare system is seen as a potential model for a national plan by Said A. Ibrahim, David Macpherson, and Michael E. Moreland.

New technologies are helping to create easier access to healthcare for veterans who live in rural and underserved areas of the country. Jennifer A. Wood, Thomas W. Miller, and Russell Hagy discuss telehealth applications to underserved veterans. Miller and Janet Kemp then explore the topic of suicide prevention through a national hotline. The Academy of Spinal Cord Injury is an organization outside VA that offers new directions in addressing the needs of spinal cord–injured veterans. The chapter on this topic is authored by the director, Terrie Price. VA has developed and implemented an Office for Preventative Ethics. Examining ethicolegal issues in VA healthcare are Steve Nisenbaum, Tom Miller, Sheila O'Keefe, and Dennis Norman. An organization external to VA that is meeting the needs of veterans, Give an Hour™, is described by its founder, Barbara Van Dahlen. Edmund J. Nightingale provides a very detailed and up-to-date summary of the efforts to provide quality, competent, and thorough veterans' healthcare in the final chapter, "Good to Great: The Veterans' Health Care System's Path to Excellence!"

The comprehensive nature of this four-volume set offers the reader an in-depth examination of veterans' healthcare through the first decade of the twenty-first century. More than two hundred invitations were extended to present and past members of the Department of Veterans Affairs as well as aligned agencies, veterans' organizations, and healthcare facilities associated with veterans' healthcare. What is provided are the comprehensive and dedicated work and contributions of more than one hundred scientists and practitioners, researchers, and clinicians both within the Department of Veterans Affairs and those in academically affiliated universities and public and private institutions. An effort is made to provide a glimpse of veterans' healthcare internationally. This handbook is not meant to cover every topic related to veterans' healthcare thoroughly, but rather to offer to the reader an excellent reference point from which to start a journey toward a better understanding of the complexity of providing quality healthcare to our military veterans.

This compendium provides the opportunity for dialogue on improving our understanding of veterans' healthcare, and each of the authors deals with a

part of this complex whole. As editor I trust it offers the gestalt that will increase our understanding of veterans' healthcare and the transitions we face in providing a twenty-first-century focus on healthcare for veterans worldwide.

Thomas W. Miller, PhD, ABPP,
Professor Emeritus & Senior Research Scientist,
University of Kentucky; Veterans Affairs Medical Center (Retired),
Lexington, Kentucky; Center for Prevention Research,
University of Connecticut

Part I

Dedicated Centers
for Veterans' Healthcare

Centers of Excellence in the Department of Veterans Affairs

Thomas W. Miller

In its effort to prepare for present and future needs in veterans' healthcare, the Department of Veterans Affairs (VA) has constructed a series of centers aimed at examining evidence-based decision making in providing twenty-first-century healthcare to the veterans' population. Within VA, Health Services Research and Development Service (HSR&D) provides core funding to fourteen centers of excellence (CoEs). Each CoE develops its own research agenda, is affiliated with a VA Medical Center (VAMC), and collaborates with local schools of public health and universities to carry out its mission. The research at each CoE serves to energize the facility and network with which it is affiliated and provides a constant source of innovation, creativity, and support for the VA healthcare system. These are the CoEs, which are described in the following sections:

- Ann Arbor, Michigan: Center for Clinical Management Research
- Bedford, Massachusetts: Center for Health Quality, Outcomes, and Economic Research (CHQOER)
- Boston, Massachusetts: Center for Organization, Leadership and Management Research (COLMR)
- Durham, North Carolina: Center for Health Services Research in Primary Care
- Hines, Illinois: Center for Management of Complex Chronic Care (CMC^3)

- Houston, Texas: Houston Center for Quality of Care and Utilization Studies (HCQCUS)
- Indianapolis, Indianapolis: Center of Excellence on Implementing Evidence-Based Practice (CIEBP)
- Little Rock, Arkansas: Center for Mental Healthcare and Outcomes Research (CeMHOR)
- Minneapolis, Minnesota: Center for Chronic Disease Outcomes Research (CCDOR)
- Palo Alto, California: Center for Health Care Evaluation (CHCE)
- Pittsburgh/Philadelphia, Pennsylvania: Center for Health Equity Research and Promotion (CHERP)
- Seattle, Washington: Northwest Center for Outcomes Research in Older Adults
- Sepulveda, California: Center for the Study of Healthcare Provider Behavior
- Tampa, Florida: Center for Maximizing Rehabilitation Outcomes

Center for Clinical Management Research, Ann Arbor, Michigan

The main objectives of the Center for Clinical Management Research' include improvement of the veterans' healthcare system's understanding of how to measure, monitor, and understand quality and efficiency for a patient population with substantial disease burden. It rigorously provides the examination of alternative and innovative systems and strategies for efficiently improving quality and outcomes for common, serious, and chronic illnesses. In addition, the center encourages development and applying improved methodologies for informing policymakers regarding heterogeneity in the effectiveness and safety of proposed interventions and assessing barriers to the implementation of high-priority care

At the time of writing, the center is headed by Director Eve Kerr, MD, MPH. Since the center became a full CoE in 1996, it has grown from a small group of investigators with two active VA-funded projects to an elite health services research center with more than thirty core investigators and annual funding of $16.1 million. This center is producing innovative research directed at improving the health and healthcare of veterans and the nation. In particular, this center focuses on clinical practice management issues for those conditions that account for a large proportion of the costs and preventable morbidity and mortality in the healthcare system.

Within the Ann Arbor CoE are five established research programs designed to foster intensive collaboration among groups of investigators addressing the research foci:

- VA Serious Mental Illness Treatment, Research, and Evaluation Center (SMITREC, founded 1992)
- VA Quality Enhancement Research Initiative—Diabetes Mellitus (QUERI-DM, founded 1998)
- VA/University of Michigan Center for Behavioral and Decision Sciences in Medicine (CBDSM, founded 2000)
- VA/University of Michigan Patient Safety Program (founded 2001)
- VA/University of Michigan program on Quality Improvement for Complex Chronic Conditions (QUICCC, founded 2006)

Major recent accomplishments include four new initiatives addressing the important issues of chronic back pain, suicide, schizophrenia with cardiovascular disease, and depression. All of these projects are employing innovative strategies for improving care with a focus on self-management; two (back pain and depression) are using Web-based technologies. These projects are particularly significant to veterans' healthcare because they focus on systems to improve care without major resource requirements (especially staffing). The center has also received funds from VA's Office of Rural Health to implement a Web-based program in Veterans Integrated Service Network (VISN) 11 for improving chronic disease management in rural patients, based on previous research conducted by this center's principal investigators. The program relies on "care partners" (adult family or friends) to help patients manage the symptoms associated with their chronic illnesses (depression, diabetes, and chronic heart failure). Some of the significant findings from published manuscripts addressed issues of hospital infection prevention, suicide prevention, healthier behaviors for cancer patients, and factors affecting cancer treatment decision making.

Future directions include a Health Services Research Institute, which will bring together health services researchers from multiple schools and programs across campus, including VA HSR&D. In fact, the center would be the largest group of investigators making up the institute. Consolidating the health services research resources of VA and the university into a single location would offer significant benefits, including increased opportunities for collaboration and continuing education, as well as convenience for our investigators who currently have offices at both VA and the university.

While this is an exciting opportunity, we expect that the approval and contracting requirements for both VA and the university will take some time to work out. In addition, the Ann Arbor VAMC remains committed to the improvement of the veterans' healthcare system's understanding of how to measure, monitor, and understand quality and efficiency for a patient population with substantial disease burden. It provides rigorous examination of alternative and innovative systems and strategies for efficiently improving quality and outcomes for common, serious, and chronic illnesses.

Center for Health Quality, Outcomes, and Economic Research, Bedford, Massachusetts

The Center for Health Quality, Outcomes & Economic Research (CHQOER), located at the Edith Nourse Rogers Memorial Veterans Hospital in Bedford, Massachusetts, was established on November 1, 1990. Historically, the Bedford VAMC has been a Boston University Dean's Committee Hospital, and the center has linked its structure, operations, and research themes with the health services research expertise present at Boston University, especially with the Department of Health Policy and Management at the Boston University School of Public Health. In 2007 a new academic affiliation was developed with the University of Massachusetts Medical School, and strong collaborations are developing with its Department of Psychiatry and Department of Quantitative Health Sciences. As evidence of the strength of this affiliation, CHQOER now has five recently recruited, funded (or funding-approved) investigators with appointments at the University of Massachusetts Medical School.

The CHQOER research mission continues to focus on three priority areas, each led by a senior investigator: patient-centered care, led by Susan Eisen, PhD; patient safety, led in 2011 by Amy Rosen, PhD; and medication effectiveness, led by Lewis Kazis, ScD. New VA research funding has been obtained in each of these areas. In addition, the center's focus on implementation remains strong, with CHQOER Associate Director Allen Gifford, MD, also serving as the co-director of the HIV/Hepatitis QUERI and David Smelson, PsyD, developing a program in translational mental health. This latter program has a particular emphasis on improving care for veterans with dual diagnoses and homelessness. The CHQOER has continued to recruit new faculty to work in these priority areas. In 2011 seven MD or PhD faculty members have been recruited. These recruitments have been facilitated by strong support from the medical center. Particularly noteworthy is the recruitment of Tom Houston, MD, an HSR&D-funded investigator with expertise in informatics and smoking cessation. CHQOER training programs continue to be a source of new faculty, and new HSR&D postdoctoral and physician fellows have been recruited. The

CHQOER continues to work on expanding its pool of Career Development Award (CDA) recipients. In 2011 Christine Hartmann, PhD, was funded to study safety culture in nursing homes. In addition, Keith McInnes, PhD, successfully applied for a CDA to study veterans' use of MyHealtheVet, and Eric Smith, MD, will be examining the role of medications in preventing suicide.

Center for Organization, Leadership and Management Research, Boston, Massachusetts

The Center for Organization, Leadership and Management Research (COLMR) has a unique research focus: to investigate and apply knowledge of innovative organization and management practices to improve the effectiveness and efficiency of healthcare services for our nation's veterans and the larger healthcare community. The COLMR actively supports other HSR&D activities and investigators at VA Boston, has collaborative projects with many other HSR&D centers, and has close working relationships with several VISNs and VA Central Office groups. As part of the strategic planning process for its renewal, it has made small changes to its research foci. The COLMR's three research foci are

1. organization and management practices that result in higher quality of care;
2. organization and management practices that promote successful organizational change, especially change to implement evidence-based clinical practices; and
3. organizational health and its effects on quality of care.

The COLMR is a unique partnership of the VA Boston Healthcare System, the VHA Workforce Management and Consulting Office, the National Center for Organization Development (NCOD), Boston University, and three VISNs:

- VA New England Healthcare System (VISN 1)
- VA Sunshine Healthcare Network (VISN 8)
- VA Midwest Healthcare Network (VISN 23)

The partners collaborate with COLMR investigators in conducting research to pursue the COLMR's goals and have significant, positive impact on the VA healthcare system. The work of the partners in planning and implementing research projects is coordinated through the COLMR's Collaborating Partners Council (CPC). COLMR investigators continue to have significant local and national roles in VA through which they can influence policy and practice. These include Dr. Charns's role as co-chair of the Organizational

Assessment Subcommittee of the VHA Human Resource Committee; the roles of Drs. Charns, Meterko, and Mohr, and Ms. Nealon Seibert in design, administration, and analysis of the annual VA All Employee Survey; and Dr. Meterko's role in the VA Nursing Outcomes Database, an annual national survey of all RNs in VA. These surveys are both part of the regular practice in VHA, their results have been used to address performance areas in many medical centers, and the databases have been used in several research projects. Significant accomplishments for this center have included a continuing increase in the number of funded projects for the Boston CoE.

Coordination of care measures to assess polytrauma care has been a significant focus of this CoE. This center has also been selected to conduct the national evaluation of the Office of Systems Redesign's Implementation Capability Grant program, involving approximately ninety VAMCs; this evaluation will use the Organizational Transformation Model as its conceptual framework. The framework was also used by the Office of System Redesign to formulate criteria for selecting grantees for the program.

Center for Health Services Research in Primary Care, Durham, North Carolina

The Center for Health Services Research in Primary Care is located at the Durham VAMC. The center's objective is to develop strategies that enhance the delivery, quality, and cost-efficiency of primary care among veterans. These objectives are strategically pursued through support of research investigators, funded research, and teaching programs. The center maintains close organizational ties with the Durham VAMC, primarily through Ambulatory Care, Medicine Service, and Mental Health Service. This CoE maintains academic affiliations for teaching and research collaborations with Duke University and the University of North Carolina at Chapel Hill. The center began research activities in October 1982. It supports 176 full- and part-time staff, comprised of twenty-nine core researchers (fourteen MDs, fifteen PhDs). The PhD staff provides expertise in biostatistics, epidemiology, health policy, health services, psychology, and sociology. Physician research associates provide expertise in substantive areas such as primary prevention, medical decision making, and translating evidence-based guidelines into practice, as well as provide research links to clinical disciplines such as general internal medicine, geriatrics, infectious disease, gastroenterology, psychiatry, and rehabilitative medicine. Eugene Oddone, MD, MH Sc, was named center director on July 1, 1997. Hayden Bosworth, PhD, was named the associate director of the center on May 1, 2002. Kelli Allen, PhD, was named associate director on June 1, 2009.

With the assistance of the hospital and the VISN, CoE staff and faculty moved into two contiguous floors (26,000 square feet) of leased space in a historic building in downtown Durham. For the first time in over ten years, all staff are at one site. This move has already improved communication, research meetings, and collaborations within the center. Within the broad area of primary care the CoE has specialized in five main areas of research:

1. understanding critical aspects of primary care (especially access), screening for disease, patient-provider communication, generalist-specialist interactions, and practice improvement;

2. defining and improving quality of care for patients with chronic diseases that are prevalent in primary care settings;

3. understanding and shaping patient-physician interactions;

4. understanding the influence of race/ethnicity and cultural factors on access, quality, and patient outcomes (e.g., clinical, patient-centered, healthcare utilization, costs); and

5. evaluating new technology to enhance access to, and quality of, care (e.g., telemedicine).

To support its research and training goals, the center aligned the faculty and staff into functional groups (cores) that provide scientific and operational support:

1. The Administrative Core provides broad support and human resource functions for faculty and staff.

2. The Biostatistics Core oversees all grant design and development, data analysis, storage, and access, and project management.

3. The Intervention Core provides multidisciplinary expertise to design, implement, and evaluate strategies that are feasible and pragmatic.

4. The Information Technology (IT) Core provides infrastructure support for all aspects of data acquisition and storage (including network function). This core also helps design and test IT solutions that become central components of our interventions (e.g., telemedicine connections, software for patient self-management interventions).

5. The Educational Core provides leadership and mentoring for fellowships, career development, and didactic training portions of the mission.

6. The Implementation and Dissemination Core provides support for all aspects of dissemination of research products and provides infrastructure for focused implementation of interventions discovered to be effective.

Center for Management of Complex Chronic Care, Hines, Illinois

The Center for Management of Complex Chronic Care (CMC^3) has its primary offices at Hines VA Hospital (VAH), with additional investigators and offices at Jesse Brown VAMC (JBVAMC). The CoE's strategic goals are to

- understand how management of care is affected when patients have multiple chronic conditions in which evidence or guideline-recommended care is lacking, conflicting, or complicating management;
- characterize coordination of care for patients with complex chronic conditions within and across healthcare systems, including VA, Medicare, Medicaid, and the private sector;
- assess use of patient self-management and behavioral interventions as a means of improving outcomes in patients with complex chronic conditions;
- identify and address healthcare provider and system-level factors that affect management of patients with complex chronic conditions; and
- identify, assess, and compare the effectiveness of innovative strategies and technologies for improving the care of patients with complex chronic conditions.

Dr. Fran Weaver, who had served as associate director and acting director of CMC^3, was appointed director of CMC^3 in November 2008. Dr. Saul Weiner (associate professor at University of Illinois, Chicago and research health scientist at JBVAMC) was appointed associate director of CMC^3. Dr. Marian Fitzgibbon continues in her role as assistant director of CMC^3 based at JBVAMC.

Each investigator is affiliated with one of three major universities in the Chicago area: Northwestern University (NU), University of Illinois, Chicago (UIC), or Loyola University of Chicago. New investigators joining CMC in 2011 include Dr. Timothy Hogan, who recently completed the HSR&D PhD postdoctoral fellowship; Dr. Ben Gerber, an internist at UIC trained in health informatics and hired by JBVAMC to develop health services research; Dr. David Bentrem, the newest CDA recipient; and Dr. Holly Kramer, a nephrologist and epidemiologist from Loyola University Medical Center. With respect to funded research, several CMC^3 projects had received funding, including grants for first-time principal investigators (PI). New grants included self-management strategies for preventing pressure ulcers, impacts of clinical guidelines for ESA use in cancer, healthcare use and costs for veterans with neurotrauma, management and outcomes of lower extremity fractures in spinal cord injury (SCI), evaluation of VA traumatic brain injury (TBI) screening processes, cost-effectiveness of deep-brain stimulation, development of a video to facilitate patient and provider communication, and an educational intervention to prevent contextual errors in medical decision making.

Hines VAMC is also home to the Spinal Cord Injury Quality Enhancement Research Initiative (SCI QUERI) research program. All investigators in QUERI are also investigators in CMC[3], allowing for leveraging of resources, personnel, and IT support. The QUERI programs are focused on using implementation science theories and methods to increase the use of evidence-based findings in clinical practice. Current efforts of the SCI QUERI include standardizing wound-healing assessment in pressure ulcers; increasing use of guideline-recommended strategies to prevent pressure ulcers; tailoring VA's evidence-based weight management program (MOVE!); implementing strategies to reduce the transmission of MRSA in SCI; and evaluating use of VA's personal health record, My HealtheVet, by veterans with spinal cord injury.

Houston Center for Quality of Care and Utilization Studies, Houston, Texas

The Houston Health Services Research & Development CoE capitalizes on its unique capabilities in the areas of patient-doctor communication, service delivery, outcomes assessment, health policy, and genomics, the newest focus for this center. The CoE uses available resources to 1) support, mentor, and develop outstanding research leaders and 2) produce excellent science that impacts policy, practice, and patients in the VA healthcare system. The Houston CoE was founded in 1990 and successfully renewed thereafter. It is organized in four scientific programs:

1. Members of the Health Decision-Making and Communication Program, led by Program Chief Richard Street, PhD, study the decisional and communication processes used by patients and providers as they interact in medical settings, with the goal of using this knowledge to enhance patient participation in the care process, maximize patients' ability to manage their chronic health problems, and ensure care for veterans with patients' and families' values and preferences.

2. Members of the Health Services Delivery and Organization (HSDO) Program, led by Center Associate Director Mark Kunik, MD, MPH, study innovative interventions and modes of care delivery with the goal of actively disseminating and implementing research findings into healthcare for veterans.

3. Members of the Health Policy and Quality (HPQ) Program, led by Center Director Laura Petersen, MD, MPH, FACP, study the effects of local, state,

and federal governmental policies on the health of populations, access to care, efficiency of care, and quality of care, with the goal of using this knowledge to influence health policy and improve the quality of healthcare for veterans.

4. Members of the Clinical Epidemiology and Outcomes (CEO) Program, led by Program Chief Hashem El-Serag, MD, MPH, study the distribution and determinants of health-related states, events, and outcomes in specific populations, with the goal of controlling health problems in veterans.

The members of each program seek to provide outstanding leadership and scholarship to produce the best science in their area while collaborating effectively with the other scientific programs. In addition, the Design and Analysis Program provides support to the four scientific programs for methods, statistics, and programming; and the Operations group provides finance, grants management, human resources, and administrative functions that support the center. The number of core investigators has increased, as have the total number of staff. A stable portfolio of resources maximizes the CoE's ability to reach the community, the state, and the nation.

Center of Excellence on Implementing Evidence-Based Practice, Indianapolis, Indiana

This center's mission is advancing the science of transforming the healthcare system, both within and outside the VA healthcare system, to deliver consistently high-quality care. Its vision is to become the leading national resource for studying and disseminating effective approaches to health system improvement. The center's strategy is to partner with managers, clinicians, patients, and other investigators in interdisciplinary teams to innovate, conduct research, and drive broad-scale adoption of changes to foster health system improvement.

The research priorities are to 1) develop, apply, and spread models of care that are safe, effective, relationship-centered, timely, efficient, and equitable; 2) identify and disseminate effective approaches for organizational change and redesign; 3) implement, evaluate, and disseminate systems interventions (considering individual, relational, and organizational factors) to transform care delivery; and 4) implement and integrate health informatics into improved work processes and care delivery.

Collaborating institutions include Indiana University Center for Health Services and Outcomes Research at Indiana University School of Medicine; Department of Medicine at Regenstrief Institute, Inc.; Regenstrief Center for Healthcare Engineering at Indiana University–Purdue University–Indianapolis (IUPUI); and School of Liberal Arts, School of Science at Purdue University.

The CIEBP improves the health of veterans by using implementation research methods to enhance the delivery of high-quality, cost-effective healthcare services. This CoE aspires to be the leading national VHA resource for identifying, evaluating, and implementing effective approaches to healthcare system improvement. It develops health informatics and other tools for the implementation of evidence-based practice, employs state-of-the-art methods for organizational change to improve the delivery of care, and rigorously implements and evaluates complex interventions to ensure that changes are productive and sustained. As educators and leaders in this new research domain, the CoE staff are also training the next generation of implementation researchers. The CIEBP is a local, regional, and national implementation research resource that leverages VA's investment in healthcare quality improvement, information technology, and system redesign.

Among the center's unique assets are a state-of-the-art, human-computer interaction/informatics laboratory; a productive collaboration linking VA and non-VA industrial engineers to evaluate and improve healthcare delivery; investigative synergy resulting from the co-location of the VA HSR&D Stroke Quality Enhancement Research Initiative (QUERI); expertise in de-identification and natural language text mining for the VA Consortium for Healthcare Informatics Research (CHIR); and VHA leadership for a knowledge management portal research collaborative. The center's researchers are applying implementation tools and methods to important challenges in healthcare for veterans, including cancer care survivorship, pain and burdensome symptoms, severe mental illnesses, stroke, and risks to patient safety. In its first five years of operation, the CIEBP succeeded in recruiting a full complement of investigators, establishing standard operating procedures, populating a portfolio of funded research, and maturing its organizational partnerships

This CoE's strategic goals include 1) expansion of the infrastructure of the HCI/IT laboratory to better serve its research and development activities in health information technology; 2) partnership with local VA facility staff, engineering students, and CIEBP faculty to secure funding for at least three system redesign research pilot projects; 3) conducting a pilot study to prototype a CPRS platform for general use to center investigators; 4) increasing our portfolio of other federally funded projects; and 5) solidifying a core implementation training package for fellowship participants.

Center for Mental Healthcare and Outcomes Research, Little Rock, Arkansas

This Center for Mental Healthcare and Outcomes Research (CeMHOR) is the only HSR&D research center devoted entirely to mental health services research. The CeMHOR aims to optimize quality and outcomes of mental health care for veterans. Its research targets high-priority populations: veterans in rural areas, veterans returning from Operation Iraqi Freedom (OIF) and Operation Enduring Freedom (OEF), and veterans with comorbid mental illness and physical health disorders. The center aspires to improve quality of specialty care for veterans with serious and persistent mental health disorders and substance use disorders; improve quality of mental healthcare provided in primary care settings; and improve access to and engagement in care for veterans with untreated mental health and substance use disorders in the community.

Determined to regain HSR&D CoE status for 2010, CeMHOR leaders took several steps to improve productivity during 2008–2009. They emphasized core investigators striving as PIs for continuous HSR&D funding; recruited associate investigators who would apply for HSR&D funding; strengthened annual performance appraisals by including HSR&D funding as PI and publication productivity; and reviewed and reprioritized collaborations with investigators at other centers. In response, investigators' productivity was restored to former levels by the time CeMHOR applied in spring 2009 for funding as a CoE.

The CeMHOR has eleven core investigators, two affiliate investigators, and eight associate investigators pursuing research on thirty projects and activities, three of them new HSR&D grants. They have reported sixty-four disseminated research products and held forty-nine leadership roles, many of them significant service and leadership roles in HSR&D. The center also delivered key services to veterans' healthcare as well as other national organizations and agencies, and noted several key impacts and systems improvements. One service/impact was local contributions to the Little Rock VAMC's Research Service, R&D Committee, and Institutional Review Board (IRB).

The CeMHOR's goals have included the development of innovative services and interventions to improve care for veterans with mental health and/or substance use disorders; conduct research to better understand common mental health problems and service needs of OIF/OEF veterans; pursue a research agenda to promote transformation to a recovery-oriented mental health system in VHA; promote widespread dissemination and implementation of effective interventions into routine practice; sustain a superior environment for inquiry to generate and support the highest quality mental health services research; and increase capacity in the mental health services research field by training, mentoring, recruiting, and collaborating. The center retained the last two goals for fiscal years 2010–2013 but modified the first four to reflect its mission of optimizing mental health outcomes for veterans by improving access to, engagement in, and quality of mental healthcare.

Center for Chronic Disease Outcomes Research, Minneapolis, Minnesota

The Minneapolis Center for Chronic Disease Outcomes Research (CCDOR) was established in April 1998. Its mission is to enhance, through research, education and dissemination activities, the delivery and accessibility of high-quality, cost-effective healthcare that will result in optimal clinical, psychosocial, and functional outcomes for veterans with chronic disease. The center is affiliated with the University of Minnesota Schools of Medicine and Public Health. Its primary focus is postdeployment health, with an emphasis on 1) post-traumatic stress disorder (PTSD); 2) polytrauma/blast-related injuries and other unique health issues facing veterans of Operations Iraqi and Enduring Freedom (OIF/OEF); and 3) substance use disorders (including tobacco). The center is actively developing or implementing projects in four specific areas:

1. Longitudinal studies of OIF/OEF veterans to identify those most at risk for poor mental health outcomes following deployment-related trauma.

2. Interventions that reduce barriers to obtaining and adhering to treatment for PTSD.

3. Optimizing care for the polytraumatized veteran. Specifically, the center focuses on transitions between care venues; screening for highly prevalent, "invisible" problems such as hearing loss and TBI; and facilitating the supportive care provided by family members.

4. Treatment strategies for substance users with comorbid mental health problems.

Although postdeployment health is the center's primary growth area, a significant portion of its research portfolio continues to focus on other areas of established strength. These include internationally renowned clinical research programs in osteoporosis, prostate and urological disease, and abdominal aortic aneurysm; leadership in intervention and implementation research in colorectal cancer screening; emerging strength in health disparities in disadvantaged populations; cutting edge work on methods for reducing bias in observational studies; and its strong evidence synthesis program, funded by both VA and the National Institutes of Health.

The center's major plans include reviewing current strategic planning in light of new VA priorities, reinvigorating the career development program, reorganizing its administrative infrastructure to more efficiently meet its needs, overhauling the membership of its steering committee, and sponsoring a national conference focusing on the special methodological issues associated with health services research in high-priority VA populations.

Center for Health Care Evaluation, Palo Alto, California

This CoE focuses on three critical healthcare domains for treatment of substance use and psychiatric disorders, clinical decision making, screening, and diagnostic assessment organization and delivery of healthcare services. The Center for Health Care Evaluation (CHCE) was established in fiscal year 1986 (October 1985). It now comprises thirty core investigators and has a core budget of more than $1,081,700 and an overall budget of $11,776,589. The VA Palo Alto Health Care System (VAPAHCS), the lead facility of the center, is located about three miles from Stanford University.

The Center's research focuses on three critical healthcare domains: 1) treatment of substance use and psychiatric disorders; 2) clinical decision making, screening, and diagnostic assessment; and 3) the organization and delivery of healthcare services.

Center for Health Equity Research and Promotion, Pittsburgh/Philadelphia, Pennsylvania

The mission of this CoE is to promote equity and quality in health and healthcare among veterans. Specific goals are to advance the science of health equity and health services research, improve the quality and equity of healthcare in VA through effective collaborations and dissemination of research results, support health equity and health services research training and mentoring within VA, maintain and enhance an organizational infrastructure and intellectual environment that promotes its mission and goals.

The Center for Health Equity Research and Promotion (CHERP) at the VA Pittsburgh Healthcare System (VAPHS) and Philadelphia VA Medical Center (PVAMC) continues to advance its mission to promote equity and quality in health and healthcare among veterans. CHERP research focuses on vulnerable veteran populations, including those that face potential discrimination because of race, ethnicity, or social status, and those at risk for disparities in health or healthcare due to physical and/or mental conditions.

Recent accomplishments include 1) success in procuring new intramural and extramural support for investigator-initiated research (six HSR&D Merit Review awards and six new NIH R01 grants); 2) collaboration with the local RR&D CoE on a successful RR&D Merit Review application; 3) national honors and academic promotions for CHERP faculty; 4) expansion of the Biostatistics and Informatics Core at PVAMC; and 5) a highly productive steering committee meeting focused on translating CHERP research into VISN-wide and national initiatives to improve health outcomes for veterans. CHERP investigators have launched several initiatives that enhance its local research infrastructure, extend the impact of CHERP research, facilitate access to new expertise, and provide fruitful opportunities for collaboration. As one example, Dr. Oslin is working with Vincent Kane, LCSW, director of the new National Center on Homelessness, to provide data, research, and analysis to policy makers in hopes of ending the problem of homelessness among veterans within five years.

Northwest Center for Outcomes Research in Older Adults, Seattle, Washington

The Northwest Center for Outcomes Research in Older Adults, located at Veterans Affairs Puget Sound Health Care System in Seattle, performs state-of-the-art research, generates new knowledge and research methods, provides high-caliber training in health services research, and assists VA policy makers in a rapidly changing healthcare environment. The research objectives of the center are to provide information to improve the delivery of health services to veterans and to contribute to scientific progress in the field of health services research by focusing on four emphasis areas:

- management of chronic disease in primary and specialty care
- preservation of independence in older adults
- evaluation of alternative delivery systems
- basic methodology in health services research

There are some thirty-five core and affiliate investigators who conduct health services research in association with the NW Center. This CoE currently supports eighty research projects.

Center for the Study of Healthcare Provider Behavior, Sepulveda, California

The center's principal ongoing objective is to promote better health and healthcare for veterans by gathering research evidence about healthcare provider behavior, including the organizations within which they practice, designing provider and health systems interventions to improve care, and translating such research evidence into routine practice. Its studies cover a range of VA-centric quality improvement goals through the development and application of provider behavior and organizational theories and evidence about how to change provider behavior and implement and evaluate innovative care models. The center has some thirty core investigators with a dozen affiliated investigators representing the West LA and Sepulveda VA campuses, as well as UCLA and RAND Health. Investigators bring expertise from general and subspecialty medicine, biostatistics, healthcare epidemiology, management and policy, public health, behavioral science, pharmacology, sociology, education, psychology, genetics, law, and business.

Affiliate investigators represent center partners (GRECC, MIRECC, PADRECC, CURE) and consortia at UCLA and RAND. Overall, the center has leveraged the core allocation more than tenfold, with a portfolio totaling nearly $11 million. The center's VA HSR&D funding has remained the same for the last three years, while QUERI and other VA funding has increased.

The center emphasizes observational, intervention, and implementation research studies related to provider behavior, quality improvement, collaborative care models, and assessments of VA structure and processes related to quality. In 2011 the center added the pioneering field of health services genomics and increased emphasis on acute care quality, with new projects on hospital nursing quality and emergency room care. It has also seen the culmination of a series of nationally recognized studies on the implementation and spread of collaborative care for depression and continued work on schizophrenia, in addition to VISN-level implementation studies of HIV testing and telephone counseling for smoking cessation.

The center's women veterans' research continued to grow, with the completion of the National Survey of Women Veterans and two major women veterans' health studies informing issues of access and care delivery design, in addition to the conduct of an updated systematic review. Center investigators published seventy-five peer-reviewed manuscripts and delivered eighty-eight conference presentations, including a number of briefings to VA senior leaders and managers. The center also continues to disseminate a variety of evidence reports, monographs, and intervention resource guides through traditional and Web-based means.

The training program builds on the expertise within the center as well as affiliated institutions to provide trainees with a broad array of coursework opportunities and mentoring for the study of provider behavior and implementation research. Overall, the center trained twelve VA Health Services research and associated health postdoctoral fellows and VA clinical scholars. This CoE continues to offer a VA-based seminar series and UCLA course entitled "Introduction to the Science of Implementing Evidence-based Practice," which has become the foundation for doctoral students and physician investigators seeking their master's degrees. The center continues to train local as well as other centers' researchers, who participate in monthly career development calls, cyberseminars, and the organizational theory journal club, which now draws participants from other centers.

Center for Maximizing Rehabilitation Outcomes, Tampa, Florida

The Tampa Center for Maximizing Rehabilitation Outcomes has as its mission to advance the science of rehabilitation for veterans with disabilities, including wounded warriors from Operations Enduring Freedom and Iraqi Freedom (OEF/OIF). The goals of rehabilitation are to continually reduce the burden of illness, injury, and disability, and to improve health functional status and quality of life. The advancement of these goals can be impeded by 1) rehabilitation setbacks associated with adverse events, 2) unpredictable and complex rehabilitation trajectory of war-related polytrauma, and 3) lack of measurement tools with optimal specificity and sensitivity for persons with disabilities. The Tampa center has focused on each of these barriers to rehabilitation science in addressing its five objectives.

Objective 1 is to test rehabilitation interventions designed to promote function, safety, and quality of life, while reducing healthcare utilization and cost. Research studies include wheelchair safety for persons with spinal cord injury (SCI), exit barriers for persons with dementia who wander, telerehabilitation for veterans with TBI, and TBI screening processes for OEF/OIF veterans. Two projects to improve postural instability, targeting veterans with osteoarthritis and peripheral neuropathy, have been completed. Several projects are in development, including some that focus on wheelchair skills training for persons with spinal cord injury using powered mobility devices, disaster situations and veterans with PTSD, community reintegration for OEF/OIF veterans, and two projects addressing college transition for returning OEF/OIF veterans.

Objective 2 focuses on predicting the prevalence, severity, and cost of rehabilitation-adverse events across rehabilitation care settings. Funded projects currently address adverse events associated with blast injuries, wheelchair falls in the elderly, pressure ulcers during medical evacuation for wounded warriors with SCI, and pain and fall-related injuries. Industry sponsored a small project to evaluate access to care for polytrauma patients in primary care.

Objective 3 is to develop and validate risk assessment and outcome measurement tools with optimal specificity and sensitivity for veterans with disabilities, including polytrauma. The center is currently working on a project to address quality of life measurement in TBI and has another in development for PTSD. These two studies have leveraged expertise and ongoing work of coinvestigators from two leading rehabilitation research centers: Center for Outcomes Research and Evaluation (CORE) at Northwestern University and Kessler Medical Rehabilitation Research and Education Center (KMRREC).

Objective 4 is to systematically translate research findings into clinical practice.

Objective 5 is to increase the number and quality of research trainees with a focus on rehabilitation outcomes.

The Department of Veterans Affairs has developed a strong base to yield evidence-based decision making for the future of veterans' healthcare. In its effort to prepare for present and future needs of veterans' healthcare, VA has constructed a series of centers aimed at examining evidence-based decision making in providing twenty-first-century healthcare to the veteran population. Within VA, HSR&D provides core funding for fourteen CoEs. Each center develops its own research agenda, is affiliated with a VAMC, and collaborates with local schools of public health and universities to carry out its mission. The research at each CoE serves to energize the facility and network with which it is affiliated and provides a constant source of innovation, creativity, and support for the VA healthcare system. Within these CoEs they have created the infrastructure to generate innovative programs of healthcare that will provide a leading direction for healthcare in the United States for the twenty-first century.

Chapter 2

Organization Development in the Department of Veterans Affairs

Katerine Osatuke, Jill Draime, Scott C. Moore, Dee Ramsel,
Andrew A. Meyer, Sharon Barnes, Linda W. Belton,
and Sue R. Dyrenforth

Introduction

Organization development refers to theory and practice of planned interventions aimed at understanding, developing or changing organizational culture and effectiveness, for people to be more satisfied with their work and for organizations to be more effective and efficient in reaching their goals. A decade ago, the Department of Veterans Affairs (VA) did not have an internal entity formally dedicated to the practice of organization development (OD). Today, OD is alive and well within VA, spearheaded by the Veterans Health Administration (VHA) National Center for Organization Development (NCOD). The best way of introducing ourselves may be to explain where our office originated and how it has evolved. Our growth from 1997 to the present time from a three-person office to an office of over fifty started as a story of serendipity and evolved into a decidedly strategic model to meet the challenges of a highly complex healthcare and service delivery system.

The center began as a three-employee office in a midwestern Veterans Affairs Medical Center (VAMC), in 1997 it quickly evolved to an office serving the OD needs of several VAMCs in the state, then advanced to a national center with responsibility for supporting OD work for VHA. Most recently, NCOD was recognized as the national center for OD expertise for the entire VA. The Department of Veterans Affairs is the second largest federal employer in the United States. It consists of several smaller components based in Washington, D.C., and three major subsystems: VHA, the Veterans Benefits

Administration, and the National Cemetery Administration, each with its corporate-level offices.

The OD service was expanded when it provided an intervention aimed at assisting a Veterans Integrated Service Network (VISN) through a major change management initiative. The VISN office that oversaw the VA hospital where NCOD began was reorganizing from a department-based structure to one of product or service lines. A major shift in reporting structures and the interrelationships among healthcare occupations (e.g., nurses, psychologists, social workers) was fraught with challenges. Two progressive senior leaders at the VAMC recognized the need for a systematic OD approach to facilitate the reorganization. They seized the opportunity to capitalize on the expertise of a psychologist at the local medical center to start the first OD office in the entire VA system.

The psychologist was named director of the new office. She immediately sought out interns to assist in implementing OD practices. One psychology intern and one administrative resident, along with the director, formed the OD department at the medical center. These three individuals were responsible for OD services locally and soon embarked on growing the program nationally.

The first local OD intervention involved a strategic planning and governance structure called Quorum. This body was responsible for long-range planning as well as operational and tactical planning, including monitoring the hospital's measures of performance. Quorum included facility and union leadership and met quarterly. The OD service (the future NCOD) assisted leadership in the design, facilitation, and execution of Quorum.

The second OD intervention involved measuring work environment perceptions by VA employees in the geographic region. This assessment was the first of its kind and set in motion subsequent workplace assessment work by NCOD. This second intervention became the basis for a two-year postdoctoral OD program. With initial funding of the postdoctoral fellowship for only one year, the director needed to find creative ways to finance the fellowship. In an eleventh-hour effort to secure funding, she submitted an entry describing the office's initiatives to a national contest focused on identifying exemplary initiatives for creating a high-performing workplace. The submission was successful, bringing a prize of $75,000, which secured the second year of the postdoctoral training slot. The contest application drew the attention of VHA headquarters, which had been in the planning process to seek outside contractors to do the same type of work for VHA that was being done by the local OD office. On October 1, 2001, after a two-day meeting with local and national representatives who visited the office to become acquainted with its work, the Veterans

Health Administration National Center for Organization Development (NCOD) was born.

The center was funded as a two-year pilot. Its future depended on its success in performing two tasks: developing a 360-degree assessment for VHA managers based on the national competency model and intervening at a troubled VAMC that was experiencing significant union-management issues. Within a year NCOD, in partnership with the Xavier University (Ohio) Industrial-Organizational Psychology Program, had developed and piloted a 360-degree assessment for midlevel managers, with behavioral descriptors anchored in the VHA competency model. The center then developed an executive 360-degree assessment and a nonsupervisory 180-degree assessment based on these same competencies, with the behavioral descriptors appropriate for the level of each participant group.

Staff from NCOD traveled monthly to the troubled VA facility, striving to improve the work environment and especially the conflict-laden relationship between labor and management. The structure of this intervention is shown in box 2.1. In less than one year, both the hospital and union leadership reported major progress on these problems and unanimously attributed their success to the NCOD intervention. Positive change was also evidenced by fewer filed grievances and improved hospital performance metrics. Given the success of these two initiatives, NCOD became a permanent office prior to the end of the two-year pilot period.

The creation of NCOD as an internal OD resource could not have come at a more opportune, and necessary, time. Like many healthcare organizations in the public and private sector, VHA was facing several workforce challenges. These included an aging workforce, significant budget constraints, and the need to be increasingly accountable for its use of resources. The Department of Veterans Affairs began addressing these challenges by creating NCOD to promote leadership and employee development, employee satisfaction, and workplace efficiency. The mission of NCOD mirrors that of VHA as a whole by supporting organizational interventions that improve patient care, research, and the training of healthcare professionals.

Who We Are and What We Do

The VHA National Center for Organization Development is a unique organization for several reasons. Its scope of practice is very large: NCOD provides OD services to all of VHA and is currently expanding its activities to become an internal consultant to the entire VA. The integration of practice, training,

Box 2.1. NCOD Intervention at the Veterans Affairs Medical Center

An Angry Initial Meeting. The preferred practice of NCOD is to go to a site only if invited by the hospital director and approved by the unions. However, in situations as dire as the examined hospital, administrators may view an NCOD intervention as a last chance effort to keep their jobs. In this example, even though an invitation had been extended by the national and regional leaders, the reception was less than welcoming. The initial meeting, dedicated to discussing the contract for the intervention, was tense. The hospital director expressed extreme frustration about feeling that he was being accused from all sides, feeling persecuted, and having no support in addressing the problems.

Appraisal of Initial Conditions. General background information was collected before the intervention. The intervention began with the pre-intervention assessment, designed to give the employees an outlet to voice their concerns about their work environment. The survey-feedback process fits the action science model (Argyris 1985) and represents the standard way NCOD approaches interventions. This approach carefully circumvents the negative consequences of surveys without feedback or action.

Formation of a Plan. NCOD initially worked only with the leadership team (the four top administrators at the hospital) and the union, to ensure internal commitment to the process before proceeding to work at the employee level. Internally committed individuals have a high degree of ownership and a sense of responsibility for their choices that is likely to remain strong over time (Argyris 1970). The leadership team's and the union's commitment to the intervention over time was important because the working relationships among them were poor, and NCOD wanted to ensure that their tensions would not negatively affect the progress of work in the facility over the long term. The top management and union leaders' buy-in was therefore viewed as critical to the ultimate success of the intervention. Consequently, the initial step was to support them in forming a long-term plan for jointly addressing the VAMC's problems.

Workgroup Action Planning. Similar to the leadership team, employee work groups also were enlisted as active participants in the planning process within the NCOD intervention model. This practice fits Reddy's (1994) model, wherein the clients (i.e., administrators and employees) are the content experts, and the consultants (i.e., NCOD) serve only to

(Continued)

facilitate the process. An additional strength of requiring clients to own the action planning process is increased internal commitment to the intervention, a critical component according to Argyris (1970). The specific actions taken by NCOD during the intervention were established from the data, including e-mails and minutes from the employee work group and leadership team meetings.

Getting Down to Business. After multiple interviews and feedback sessions, employees formed four action teams with the goal of addressing the majority of the voiced concerns. The work groups' names were indicative of their charge: Rewards and Recognition, Positive Possibilities, Communications, and Employee Development. The action work groups spent the next year devising initiatives to propose to the leadership team for approval and implementation. Work group members included volunteer employees, a leadership team member, and a union representative, to ensure their intimate involvement in the process as well as input into any proposed changes that they felt could affect the entire facility. The goal for each work group was to suggest changes that would ultimately improve the work environment for all employees. Throughout the process, the work groups made concerted efforts to educate and elicit feedback from all employees. At pivotal points, work group members asked for approval from all employee members, leadership, and each union before proceeding with action initiatives. Work groups met on their own schedules with NCOD dialing into their meetings by phone, and NCOD convened them approximately once every four weeks, in person, to gauge progress and reenergize the groups if necessary. Some work groups had difficulty retaining members over the year, but within each group a core of committed employees emerged that managed to push forward and develop initiatives and actions. Although the path of each work group differed, each accomplished key goals that had an immediate impact on the culture of the facility, with reverberations into the future.

Workgroup Outcomes: A Series of Small Fires. The strategy of creating a number of empowered action workgroups resulted in a series of seemingly small outcomes that affected a large number of people. These small fires provided the glimmer of hope that positive change was possible and could spread throughout the facility. Although the problems at the facility were too immense for any one group to resolve, dividing the responsibility among a few dedicated work groups made the process manageable and actionable.

Endorsement by the Leadership. In early 2003 each group presented a concise plan of action to the facility and union leadership that would

(Continued)

build on the progress they had made to date. All teams were pleased when the leadership team and union representatives unanimously approved almost every suggestion. Following approval, the list of suggestions was prioritized, and the leadership team took some immediate steps to put the plans into action. Following this successful meeting, teams continued to propose new ideas and build on existing initiatives, furthering the impact on the facility over the next few months.

Specific Successes. The employee workgroups successfully accomplished their objectives throughout the year:

- The Rewards and Recognition group developed an award tip sheet describing all available awards, placed it on the facility Web site, and distributed it to all employees. The group checked whether each service had an awards committee and encouraged the leadership to mandate one for services that did not. The group also monitored which services were using the money allotted for rewards in their budgets and provided a monthly update to the leadership. The group members visited each service and explained the tip sheet to ensure that employees would be aware of all awards and knew how to use them for peer-to-peer recognition. Finally, members attended quarterly supervisory training to educate supervisors about the awards process and how to develop an awards committee.

- The Communication Group developed a survey and distributed it hospital-wide to determine the preferred methods for receiving information (e-mail, staff meetings, etc.); how often information should be communicated (daily, weekly, etc.); what type of information employees wanted; and from whom they receive most of their information (e.g., supervisors, peers, etc.). To follow up, the group created a single monthly newsletter that combined critical elements of several other information sources in the hospital and established "Information Central," a series of bulletin boards on which employees could view and have access to the latest hospital news and happenings.

- The Positive Possibilities Group implemented strategies to celebrate the successes of the facility. Two electronic marquee boards were placed at the front and rear entrances of the hospital displaying current announcements, awards, and job openings. The group established a monthly organization-wide open house and each month highlighted a different service area, focusing on the service's functions, impact, and connection to other departments and work units. They also established an employee lounge, accessible to all employees and separate from any patient area.

(Continued)

- The Employee Development group initiated a survey to gauge employees' interests in job shadowing, coaching and mentoring, and individual development plans, all to identify career goals and paths toward them. The survey results led to establishing a job-shadowing program that allowed employees to explore jobs of interest before submitting an application. A coaching and mentoring program was initiated to recognize employees with the potential to move up the career ladder and to identify mentors to guide and support them through this process. The group also educated employees on using individual development plans and suggested that the leadership use these plans in the formal evaluation process between supervisors and employees.

Summary. By all accounts, NCOD provided a mechanism for the facility to heal. One of the key ideas espoused by Argyris (1970) and Reddy (1994), as well as others, is the goal of the interventionist. Their theories do not propose an ideal organization to be built by external consultants; rather, they advocate proposing an ideal process by which the organization (e.g., administrators, employees) can heal itself internally. The center's method of intervening at the facility effected positive change in the organization by providing such a process. In postintervention assessment, interviewee after interviewee affirmed the impact of the intervention team's actions, and from all perspectives, NCOD played a vital role in changing the nature of the organization.

and research that exists at NCOD is found in very few places. All NCOD practice work is data-driven and customized to the organizational client's needs. In addition, NCOD supports the only active psychology postdoctoral fellowship in OD and consulting of which we are aware. Its main purpose is to be a change agent in one of the largest government agencies in the country. The center is working proactively to establish evidence-based connections between key organizational processes and outcomes. Our specific goal is to increase workforce engagement, satisfaction, and productivity to improve patient satisfaction, health outcomes, and quality of care.

The five core functions of NCOD include (1) administering the All Employee Survey to the entire VA and analyzing and reporting its results to the system; (2) organizational assessments, and consulting services; (3) research into best practices of leadership (management studies); (4) pre- and postdoctoral training of OD professionals; and (5) organizational interventions directed at workplace culture in the VA system.

All Employee Survey. The All Employee Survey is an annual voluntary survey of employee satisfaction and workplace characteristics in VA. It is the key tool that supports VA efforts of assessing and learning how to manage the transformational change process (Young 2000). The survey provides a communication channel from the lowest to highest organizational levels. It allows systematic tracking of employee perceptions of the VA work environment and holding leaders accountable for articulating action plans and implementing improvements. The survey is discussed in more detail in a later section.

Organizational Assessment, Intervention, and Consulting. The NCOD practitioners provide onsite, consultative services and intensive workplace interventions at all organizational levels. After initial discussions with all appropriate parties, including labor (union) partners at a site, NCOD helps the client identify the choices available for next steps and specific measures of success. Quantitative and qualitative assessment data (including local All Employee Survey results) are used extensively to ensure that interventions are grounded in employee perceptions and ideas. This allows both the client and NCOD to measure progress on goals identified at the beginning of the intervention. (For a more detailed discussion and an example of a NCOD practice model, see Osatuke et al. 2009.)

Studies of Management Practices. Research by NCOD includes applied studies that support VA management in decision making and document best working practices in the healthcare system. This research also strives to establish and test components of an empirically derived conceptual model of optimum VA functioning, to be used proactively for recognizing and addressing various intervention needs within VHA. The overarching goal is to facilitate VA's organizational functioning by applying professional skills and tools, such as research and assessment methods, statistical techniques, conceptual understandings of organizational phenomena, and state-of-the-art workplace interventions.

Fellowship Training. The training component at NCOD combines both practice and theory/ research elements. Each year, approximately three new psychology postdoctoral fellows are selected for training in OD. The two-year fellowship includes both a research and a practitioner track. Both tracks include intensive feedback and supervision, weekly didactic sessions emphasizing consulting psychology competencies, and extensive on-the-job training, designed to help fellows integrate research findings and theoretical models with their individual characteristics and develop their personal profiles as OD professionals. The common thread in NCOD research, practice, and training is clearly its foundation in the VA context and its emphasis on the needs of the system. This does not preclude interest in and preparedness for professional functioning in other settings. In fact, NCOD fellows have been successful in academic positions, administrative and clinical roles, and private consulting.

The majority of NCOD's graduating fellows have chosen to remain in NCOD once their training was completed.

Organizational Interventions. Organizational health initiatives focus on shaping the workplace culture. They start with the executive leadership publicly supporting the culture change in a particular programmatic area (for example, in the development and training of VA executives) and articulating the main values and goals of the change. This public support for change provides the foundation for an evaluation of the current culture or a baseline assessment. This includes collecting information from relevant stakeholders, identifying problems (e.g., through surveys or group interview), defining in operational terms what the problems are and who will benefit from solving them, and setting targets for improvement. This work of evaluating the presenting needs occurs in close consultation with NCOD and is followed by action planning. Based on the results of the evaluation, strategies for next steps at the facility or program office are formulated, performance outcomes for the initiative are defined, and targets are determined, usually in the context of national norms. The execution of the action plan follows, and results are then evaluated by the stakeholders, often the next level up the leadership chain.

More generally, the concept of organizational health is the philosophical premise that informs all of NCOD's work in VA. The center defines healthy organizations as places where employees want to work and veterans want to receive their care. Organizational health is the *systemic* wellness that nurtures success in complex and chaotic organizations. It includes an awareness of and a focus on organizational processes, that is, on *how* things are done. In other words, rather than being another content area for organizations to attend to, organizational health refers to the way organizations do all that they do. In VA, organizational health initiatives serve as an incubator or supportive context for the current efforts of system transformation. This idea is further discussed later in this chapter.

Organizational health is the overarching concept that encompasses NCOD's five core functions under one umbrella to promote VA's organizational development. The following initiatives align with and expand on these core functions and serve as common denominators in promoting organizational health:

- the annual national, regional, and local planning and execution of actions based on the All Employee Survey data;
- Civility, Respect, and Engagement in the Workplace (CREW)—a nationwide initiative to increase workplace civility;
- the NCOD research program of management studies;

- organization development consulting and practice;
- developing and evaluating leadership training programs;
- training organization development professionals in the VA system; and
- supporting the current organizational transformation of VA toward becoming a veteran-centered environment through major national initiatives such as working in teams, with veterans having a place on the team.

The background of each initiative is discussed briefly in the following sections, including the initial presenting need in the organization, how the initiative addressed this need, and the outcome. Also covered is the current status of each initiative and its role in promoting organizational health in VA.

The All Employee Survey and Its Predecessors

In 1997 and 2001 VA administered the One VA Survey to assess employee satisfaction with and perceptions of the organization. The results of the survey took the vendor several months to process. Once they reached VHA organizations, the results were shared only with senior leaders, who found them insufficiently informative and expressed a desire for a different format and focus of the summary reports. Although not involved in the actual survey administration, NCOD, which had just become a national center, was asked in 2002 to play a key role in reanalyzing the 2001 results, which involved working with Web records and more than 75,000 paper surveys, making the summary reports available to the field, and coordinating the subsequent administrations of the employee survey.

In many of the survey records, employees expressed frustration over being asked to keep taking surveys, but never seeing change as a result of their input. For example, many wrote comments on the paper survey, with a typical comment being: "Why do you keep asking me to take this survey when nothing ever changes?" The NCOD staff evaluated this situation as problematic and set out to address it. Targets were set to improve the efficiency of data collection and add meaning to the collected data. Strategies were created to increase the response rate, in order to be confident that the maximum number of employees would have their voices heard. Examples of these strategies were providing results within thirty days; providing results to *all* employees; making results available at the level of any organizational unit, including work groups, as long as they had at least ten respondents; and supporting VHA leadership in the development of a performance measure that requires leaders to provide feedback to all staff and plan actions based on the results. The bottom line is that NCOD recognized that unless the survey results were actually used to improve the workplace, there was no reason to collect the data. This set the All Employee Survey apart from similar types of surveys in other organizations, as survey data are not typically used for systematically planning workplace improvements. In January 2002 NCOD formed an All Employee Survey team, which included people from several offices in VHA management: the Management Decision Research Center, the Office of Quality and Performance, the Human Resources Management Group, the Office of Equal Employment, and the High Performance Development Model Program Office. The team was given the responsibility of refining the data collection instrument, administering the survey, analyzing the data, producing reports of the results, and then assisting VISNs and VAMCs in translating results into action plans and executing those plans.

In 2003 NCOD coordinated the efforts of the All Employee Survey team to design and pilot a new instrument and administration methods. The team worked to develop a shortened and more efficient instrument and to refine the measurement of factors critical to workforce issues and patient outcomes (Warren et al. 2007), while also maintaining maximum comparability with previous survey instruments from 1997 and 2001. Two separate yet related assessment tools were developed and incorporated into the new All Employee Survey. First was the Job Satisfaction Index (Nagy 2002), in which thirteen questions assess overall job satisfaction and its specific aspects (content dimensions), such as leadership, coworker relationships, and working conditions. This survey is short and easy to administer; it can support short-term goal setting and monitoring of progress when the focus of interest is the level of individual employees' job satisfaction. The second instrument, the Organizational Assessment Index, is a refined, shortened version of the 2001 One VA Survey. Many of the questions from the previous version of the survey were kept to maintain comparability with the content dimensions included in previously reported results. Several additional content dimensions were included that proved to be important for action planning and for tracking changes over time. This survey is most useful for tracking organization-wide issues that have to do with workplace climate perceptions and influences of the organizational environment. These two instruments reflected an improved strategy of assessing the dimensions similar to those assessed by the previous survey. A third instrument, based on Zammuto and Krakower's (1991) organizational assessment model, was added to assess employees' perceptions of cultural values that characterize their entire facilities, as opposed to aspects of climate and environment in their specific work groups. In addition to psychometrically honing the instruments themselves, the All Employee Survey team tested various methods for administering them, including via the Web, paper, and IVR (telephone), to compare ease of use, response rates, and psychometric characteristics of the data. As a result, the new All Employee Survey provides reliable, valid measures that managers and researchers can use with confidence.

The pilot assessment using the new All Employee Survey was conducted with a sample of over 10,000 employees in November 2003. In the spring of 2004 it was administered to the entire organization, with 110,490 employees responding. All results were presented using content areas deemed relevant for action planning, including but not limited to rewards/recognition, planning/evaluation, diversity acceptance, employee development, cooperation, supervisory support, innovation, customer service, work-family balance, pay satisfaction, and conflict resolution. Overall results were reported as well as results by major occupational and demographic groups. The team presented the national, regional (for VISNs), and local (for medical centers) results to each regional leadership team face to face or via videoconference. The national report was made available to all, and separate reports were also created for each VHA program office (headquarters) and each VISN. Judging from the feedback of VHA leadership and regional directors, the recipients found this reporting structure and the reporting format extremely helpful. This format of feedback and reporting has continued after each All Employee Survey is administered.

Results, from national and regional down to the medical center and work group level, were made available to all employees within one month of the completion of the survey through a Web-based program called ProClarity, now mandated to be accessible at every VA location. ProClarity users are able to specify which group scores are combined and in what way. They are free to design a custom report, with results selected and displayed in any format they choose. Work group, local, regional, and national averages are available for comparison. The software provides an instant descriptive summary of results for any group of at least ten respondents. The All Employee Survey has been administered annually since 2006, and the sharing of results within one month after the survey has become an established practice, which is remarkable given that the number of respondents currently approaches 200,000. The current year's results and trended longitudinal data are both available at all organizational levels from national to the work group. The data are shared both through ProClarity and in the format of standard reports made to the national and regional leadership and then placed on the VA intranet for access by any employee. The average response rate for each administration is now 70 percent. For voluntary confidential surveys of organizational climate, to which a response rate of 30 percent would be considered average and 50 percent extremely high, 70 percent participation is unprecedented.

The All Employee Survey reports help to identify areas of strength as well as opportunities for improvement for each examined organizational unit, considering its current standing relative to its comparison group and considering its change over time. For each content area, each region's scores from the current year are statistically compared to each medical center within it, as well as to the VHA average. Longitudinal data for each VISN and VAMC are presented as well. This information enhances the action-planning process, as all units of the organization can track their performance over time. Changed scores are computed to allow statistical comparisons across years, and these scores are presented in the context of national data.

Although general summaries and interpretations of findings of survey results are shared, emphasis is placed on the importance of local interpretation of the results. Each organization develops action plans and action teams to address the locally identified opportunities for improvement and sets local goals and timelines to be subsequently evaluated based on longitudinal data. Box 2.2 describes the survey participation and action planning process at one facility. The expected outcomes identified by this facility include increasing staff awareness of how the survey results were addressed locally, improving the workplace climate at the facility, and supporting the standing of the local VAMC as an employer of choice.

The NCOD assists VA organizations in planning and implementing actions based on their local All Employee Survey results. Though specific interventions and action plans vary depending upon local needs, several initiatives (e.g., CREW) are already in place to benefit VA units. In addition, suggestions for best practices of addressing particular aspects of the survey results are freely shared and are posted on the All Employee Survey portal on the VA intranet. The center is available to conduct intensive workplace interventions, which include further assessment (via All Employee Survey measures and other assessment instruments, group interviews, or individual interviews), data feedback to the facility management and employees, and action plans (identification, implementation, and continuous follow-up over time). It has also partnered with several other program offices in VA (e.g., the Office of Resolution Management) to offer additional options for workplace intervention and improvement. All involve action learning and continuous assessment.

Addressing All Employee Survey results through action plans has become one of the measures in the VHA executives' standard performance contract, providing them with a strong motive to keep their entire organizations accountable for knowing and addressing employees' perceptions of the

Box 2.2. Local Medical Center All Employee Survey Process

- The medical center director receives a letter issued by the Under Secretary for Health (CEO of VHA) announcing the upcoming national administration of the All Employee Survey.

- The local All Employee Survey coordinator drafts a message for the director to announce the survey locally.

- The director sends the message to local managers to encourage participation of their employees in the survey.

- To market the survey, communications are directed to all employees about the role of the survey results in action planning at the facility and the importance of having their voices heard.

- The survey period begins (three weeks in the spring), and employee participation rates by work groups are publicly announced weekly throughout the survey administration period.

- The survey period closes, final work group and facility participation rates are announced, and those work groups with high response rates are incentivized and celebrated—for example, work groups with the highest participation rates are publicly acknowledged at the facility, and raffles and pizza parties are held for employees in these work groups.

- Postsurvey focus groups examine which factors supported or impeded survey participation at the facility—for example, whether all of the work groups received timely announcements of the upcoming survey, and whether access to computers was sufficient and convenient to all employees during the survey open period.

- Within a month after the survey closure, the facility receives survey results from NCOD. Key staff participate in a teleconference with NCOD representatives examining the results. The local survey coordinator and the facility's Employee Satisfaction Committee distribute the results throughout the facility to each service. Comparisons are made with the previous year's results and between local and regional results.

- Each service develops an action plan informed by the survey results and submits its plan to the Employee Satisfaction Committee and local leadership.

- Service chiefs report quarterly to executive leadership on progress with action plans.

(Continued)

- Service chiefs and assigned staff communicate progress on action plans to employees throughout the facility at monthly staff meetings.
- Additional follow-up strategies are identified for engaging employees more fully in taking ownership of the action planning process.

workplace. This alignment of rewards with desired behavior is yet another method to ensure culture change is initiated and sustained within VA. The results of these activities impact work systems, employee education and development, and employee well-being and satisfaction. All Employee Survey–based strategies and actions have become a crucial part of VHA's practice of managing the organizational culture. The positive impact of the All Employee Survey has been felt throughout VA.

Organizational Assessment Subcommittee

One by-product of the success of the All Employee Survey was the desire of many groups in VHA to survey all employees about their respective content areas. In 2006 the Organizational Assessment Subcommittee, chaired by the NCOD director, was formed to serve as a survey policy body in VHA. The subcommittee was an outgrowth of the All Employee Survey team. It included representatives from the same offices but was organized into a formal structure and given responsibility for developing policy recommendations regarding employee surveys. Its recommendations are based on evaluating the amount and content of the various survey efforts undertaken in VHA at any given time. Starting in September 2009, the Organizational Assessment Subcommittee was also charged with reviewing and approving requests for new employee surveys and serving as the clearinghouse for an inventory of existing national employee surveys. It provides advice and assistance to organizations requesting surveys, but does not serve as a warehouse for storing survey data.

To reduce the number of surveys and the burden on respondents, the Organizational Assessment Subcommittee established a process for fitting all employee surveys in the system within one of four annual windows. The All Employee Survey is administered in the spring of each year. All the other employee surveys in VHA, collectively called Voice of the VA surveys, are administered in one of the three annually announced surveying periods. Each period is open for three weeks and accommodates multiple surveys, but a respondent is invited to participate in data collection only once. Thus any respondent is asked to take no more than four national surveys annually. The All Employee Survey is a census survey of all of the VA population, whereas Voice of the VA surveys are based on a sampling approach for targeted audiences (e.g., specific demographic response, regions, or occupations).

Voice of the VA surveys are typically aligned with organizational efforts that fall under specific organizational health initiatives. For example, the Learning Organization Survey was administered as part of the winter Voice of the VA as requested by the Employee Education System. The survey provided actionable data based on assessing three important dimensions of a learning organization: being a supportive learning environment, the presence of concrete learning processes and practices, and leadership that reinforces learning (Marsick & Watkin 2003).

The Organizational Assessment Subcommittee's review and approval process benefits the system by optimally coordinating employee surveying. These benefits include better survey designs, preventing duplication of survey content, aligning survey content with organization mission, distributing and staggering surveys at optimal times, and reducing employee survey fatigue. The latter is an important strategy for preserving high survey response rates, which in turn facilitate obtaining representative results at the local level. The explicit intent of coordinating survey administration through Organizational Assessment Subcommittee oversight is to ensure that the organization "listens" to the employees by using employee responses to shape organizational change. These approved surveys are described as "Voice of the VA" because the Organizational Assessment Subcommittee expects data results to feed back into the system and be shared with all the participants.

The employee surveying process in VA promotes greater organizational accountability through eliciting regular employee feedback on the work environment (Bernstein 2004; Perlin, Kolodner & Roswell 2004; Young 2000). The Organizational Assessment Subcommittee governance of the surveying process provides a disciplined approach to assessing organizational health. This approach increases the usefulness of the organizational information that can be derived from the surveys and made available to the system. For example, for maximum participation the employees must feel that their opinions are gathered in a systematic manner, that they receive feedback on the results, and that the feedback is used to improve their workplace (Kraut 1996; Rogelberg & Stanton 2007). The Organizational Assessment Subcommittee governance helps VHA achieve these outcomes by maximizing the impact of employee surveying.

Civility, Respect, and Engagement in the Workplace (CREW)

A great deal has been written about the negative impact of incivility and its costs to organizations, but very little is known about how to address it. The NCOD designed an intervention to increase civility in the workplace and played a critical role in the establishment of this organizational health initiative, called CREW: Civility, Respect, and Engagement in the Workplace. CREW grew out of a need identified by the Human Resource Committee of the National Leadership Board, the governing body of VHA. Leadership was tracking results from several internal studies (see Osatuke et al. 2009 for a more detailed review), all pointing to an area of concern about civility, or how people treat one another in the organization. This information resulted in a pilot of an initiative aimed at improving civil and respectful interactions between management and employees and between peers. The VHA's CREW initiative was a groundbreaking effort to promote workplace civility. The overarching framework for CREW was proposed by the Human Resources Committee and NCOD and endorsed by the National Leadership Board. Civility in CREW is defined as on-stage workplace behaviors. Civil behaviors are seen as impersonal (displayed on behalf of the organization) and directed toward *everyone* at the workplace, rather than only toward people one knows (e.g., a greeting of "hello" to a passerby or holding the door open for another is a civil, rather than a personal, behavior). Civility is based on awareness of one's interpersonal impact: monitoring one's own behavior during interpersonal interactions and paying attention to how other people receive it. More specific content of civil workplace behaviors is defined locally and thus varies across sites.

Organizational support for *civility*, or employees' perceptions that the organization (e.g., policies, management) supports consistently civil workplace behaviors, is the first element of the CREW model. It is expected to impact workplace perceptions, making employees feel *respected* (the second element of the model). These perceptions, in turn, are expected to empower employee actions at the workplace, resulting in greater *engagement* (the third element) in collaborative efforts toward VHA goals. These expectations, based on National Leadership Board interpretation of results from internal studies, are generally consistent with the directions of previous OD thinking (e.g., Ostroff 1992), and extant research (e.g., Laschinger & Finegan 2005; Parker et al. 2003) and represent a broad operational context for CREW.

The literature describes incivility as unique to particular situations (e.g., Hutton 2006). Similarly, civil behaviors in the CREW framework are understood as culturally specific to each organization; a rural midwestern work group and an urban northeastern work group may each define civility differently. The CREW initiative is designed to be a customized and flexible intervention approach, whereby each site chooses its specific definitions and areas of focus related to civility. This approach supports local autonomy, increases adaptability of the interventions, and, we believe, drives their success.

The purpose of CREW is to increase awareness of the importance of civility and respect in the VA workplace. When CREW starts, the initial conversations about civility have the following aims:

1. Raise awareness of the importance of civility and respect among co-workers as well as with customers and patients.

2. Increase understanding of the relationship between civility and successful achievement of VHA's mission (i.e., the business case for civility).

3. Achieve agreement about what defines "a respectful workplace" in one's unit or team.

4. Identify barriers or bad habits that get in the way of achieving a respectful workplace.

5. Instill commitment to the common goal of "raising the bar" for acceptable behavior in the workplace.

As CREW progresses, the follow-up activities and conversations all aim at the following:

1. Maintain awareness of the climate within the unit with regard to respect and civility.

2. Recognize and reward behaviors that improve the workplace climate.

3. Link the CREW initiative to other values, priorities, and aspects of VHA's work and culture.

4. Engage all staff in striving to continuously improve the workplace climate, adopting civility as part of the organization's culture.

5. Highlight the outcomes of an improved workplace climate and celebrate them as a work group.

Groups that participate in CREW often use a "viral spread" metaphor to describe the CREW process at their sites. The perception of civil treatment by others within the organization invites more prosocial behaviors and increased collaboration, resulting in still higher perceptions of a civil environment, thus generating *more* organization-wide prosocial behaviors and collaboration at work, and so forth. Box 2.3 includes examples of the CREW impact as it was perceived by the employee participants at various VA sites.

Box 2.3. CREW Stories

- A housekeeper beginning his participation in CREW was asked what he did at the VAMC. He responded, "I mop the floors." Six months into CREW he began describing his job as "helping to keep an infection-free environment."

- A group of lab employees were ready to quit en masse. They were frustrated by a supervising pathologist who maintained a top-down, command-and-control work environment. When they approached him to initiate an "honest conversation" about their desire for a more inclusive, respectful approach, he did not respond well. A month later, the pathologist heard a presentation on CREW. It seems it was the right message at the right time. He returned to the medical center, called in the staff, apologized for not "getting it," and committed to changing his behavior. The staff contacted NCOD, stunned but delighted, to report the pathologist's "conversion."

- Food service employees involved in CREW stated that it was the first time they had been asked for their ideas. (Several had worked there for more than thirty years!) Now more fully engaged, they have renamed their function "Hospitality Services."

- The chief of residency training at a large tertiary medical center feels CREW skills are so important for staff that he now requires CREW for medical residents.

- A medical unit (which was participating in CREW) and the stat lab had a historically negative relationship: nursing staff hounded the lab for test results, and the lab staff were defensive about nursing's "unrealistic" expectations. One day the lab supervisor called the nurse manager. Instead of the complaint the nurse manager expected, the lab supervisor asked, "What's happening on your unit? Your nurses have been so courteous and respectful that my staff have noticed the change and are working twice as hard to get your test results out. What are you doing differently, and how can we get in on it?!"

- In a multidisciplinary CREW group in which a certain degree of trust had been attained, an MD complained that it took nurses too long to bring the EKG machine in an emergency. A nurse responded, "What you may not know is that we don't have one—I have to run all the way to the ER." As a result of the CREW intervention, (1) the medical staff reached a new level of understanding; 2) they requested and subsequently received their own EKG equipment, and 3) the success reinforced their desire to be part of the solution. The group is now actively engaged in process redesign.

As are all NCOD interventions, CREW is data-driven. The pre- and post-assessment of each participating site relies on the civility scale (Meterko et al. n.d.). The civility scale is part of the All Employee Survey, which allows comparison of participating sites' scores to national and local baselines. Preassessment results also provide a basis for starting the local discussion of what civility means for the group and which aspects of workplace climate they want to improve. This constitutes a typical and recommended use of survey data in the context of OD interventions (e.g., Nadler 1977; Harvey & Brown 1992).

Several aspects of the CREW intervention process remain the same at every site. The NCOD shares an educational toolkit containing ideas and experiential activities that promote exploration of CREW components. The center trains local CREW leaders (coordinators and facilitators from each site) by explaining the rationale and operational background for CREW and sharing data that support the organizational relevance of civility. A pre-intervention survey is conducted using the civility scale from the All Employee Survey. Local CREW leaders then facilitate regular on-site meetings at their medical centers. At the meetings, baseline data on civility are first shared and discussed within work groups. The work groups then decide which actions to take to improve their overall civility, thus developing their own methods for improving their work environment. Each work group chooses specific foci related to civility, based on presurvey scores and any tools in the educational kit that they see as fitting their needs. For example, some work groups with low pretest scores may focus on discussions that clarify their *definition* of civility and respect, to improve basic communication among participants. Other work groups focus on *extensive sharing* about their backgrounds and on deepening workplace relationships. Some work groups develop *action plans* for greater collaboration toward participants' shared work-related goals. Six-month follow-up assessment is conducted using the same civility scale. As additional support, NCOD facilitates monthly conference calls for all local coordinators.

One of the factors that makes CREW a success is the use of NCOD staff as CREW "companions." Companions serve a vital role in supporting CREW coordinators (those responsible for overseeing the implementation of CREW at the local site) and facilitators (those responsible for organizing and conducting local CREW meetings). Companions initiate conversations with workplace leaders to explain the rationale for CREW, help determine appropriate work groups interested in participation, and communicate facilitators' and coordinators' responsibilities and expectations. Companions check in with their sites weekly and communicate with CREW coordinators more frequently if problems or concerns arise. Companions are familiar with the CREW toolkit and research, including research in VA and the private sector. They are fluent in navigating the CREW Web site and monitor their facility's progress on the SharePoint via monthly reports. Throughout the implementation of CREW, companions remain a resource for the sites in terms of knowledge, references, maintaining connections to other participating sites, providing information about other relevant initiatives in the organization, best practices, and providing other assistance.

In 2005 NCOD supported a CREW pilot that included representatives from eight VHA organizations. As compared to comparison groups, quantitative and qualitative outcomes were positive (see Osatuke et al. 2009) and prompted an awareness of the benefits of CREW in the VHA system, followed by a rapid expansion of the initiative. Ongoing work (e.g., Osatuke et al. 2010) confirms the expected connections from higher workplace civility to positive organizational outcomes. In fall of 2010, CREW is beginning its eleventh phase of implementation. By summer 2012 more than 1,000 work units had participated or were participating in CREW. Each phase of CREW has resulted in overall statistically significant improvement in ratings of civil climate in the participating work groups. The success of CREW in VHA has made it noticeable to the broader VA system, resulting in other parts of VA as well as private-sector organizations expressing an interest in participating. The CREW approach has also been implemented in Canada (Leiter et al. 2009). The results were similar to those obtained in VHA: the intervention had a significant positive impact in the expected direction.

The CREW interventions at VA are often intertwined with systems redesign elements. Systems redesign is about thinking about work in a different way: the structure of work tasks, ways to improve it, and people who need to be involved. CREW suggests a set of tools to help coworkers relate to each other better, whereas systems redesign supports coworkers in carrying out their work tasks in a better way. These aims are mutually complementary; they serve a common purpose and enhance each other. For example, relational improvements often promote functional improvement, and vice versa. Systems redesign and CREW both promote well-being at the workplace through supporting employees in becoming leaders in relationship to their job tasks. Leadership, in its simplest definition, reflects an ability to influence other people. In a recent Gallup Healthways poll of 100,000 Americans, business owners outranked ten other occupations in overall well-being, despite working longer hours and earning slightly less on average than employed professionals and managers/executives who ranked second and third. The explanation for this apparent contradiction (longer hours and smaller wages, yet greater well-being) may be that it is much easier to be happy in jobs where people have a meaningful purpose and enhanced control of their work lives. In essence, the main focus of CREW is helping employees realize their potential of becoming leaders, by fostering engagement in work relationships and business processes and thus bringing meaning to the workplace.

Management Studies

One of the ways in which NCOD contributes to VA's functioning is by providing data analytical support for local and national planning and decision making about the workforce. This role is unique in the VA system. Most other offices that conduct research in VA focus their efforts specifically on patient care, whether on particular medical topics or on ways of managing and structuring patient care systems. Research conducted by NCOD considers questions that VA leaders face in the domains of identifying and training future leaders and developing high potential employees. The center's research also examines best practices of maintaining a healthy organizational climate in the workplace, sustaining employee engagement, and supporting organizational commitment. Other issues addressed by NCOD include workforce retention, succession planning, and workforce diversity issues. The center provides analytical support for managerial decisions in these areas by helping VA managers formulate their dilemmas in a way that can be informed by data available in the system, identifying relevant sources of data, conducting data analyses, and sharing the findings with the interested parties.

This set of activities is referred to as "management studies." Management studies and all related work with organizational data are conducted by the NCOD research team, which was established in 2005 and began with one postdoctoral fellow. Now in the process of active growth, the research team is currently made up of four health scientists, one postdoctoral fellow in research, one psychology technician, and four part-time graduate students. The responsibilities of the research team include management and analysis of data necessary for planning and executing management studies, conducting the studies, reporting results, working with the requestors to make the interpretation of results relevant to their decision-making needs, and disseminating these results to the VA system and broader professional audiences. The NCOD research team now produces more than forty management studies annually, of which ten to fifteen per year are presented at national professional conferences (see the references for examples).

On a broader scale, VA strives to encourage management practices that are empirically grounded or validated as being effective and efficient. Whereas many well-articulated models of organizational management are available in the OD literature, empirical studies examining best management practices or proposing working solutions to real-life managerial dilemmas are rare. Research by NCOD aims to make contributions toward filling this gap. For example, based on NCOD's ongoing research (e.g., Osatuke et al. 2010; Warren et al. 2008), civility and psychological safety have been established as crucial dimensions of a healthy organizational climate in VA healthcare. This work in progress substantiates the belief that these conclusions may apply to other organizational systems as well.

The NCOD research team serves as a resource for VA customers in addressing their unique data-related needs. Box 2.4 describes some of NCOD's specific, ongoing activities.

The NCOD research team disseminates findings through presentations at VA internal conferences, external professional conferences (e.g., Society of Industrial and Organizational Psychology, American Psychological Association, Association for Psychological Science, Academy of Management, Academy of Health, American Association for Public Opinion Research), and publications in the business press and research-oriented academic journals. The reference section lists selected studies that have been either organized or supported by NCOD.

The common denominator of all these activities by the NCOD research team is that it applies organizational data to analytically supporting strategic needs and everyday decision-making needs of managers at every level of VA. A longer-term aim is to take analytical support of the system to a conceptually higher level, by articulating elements of a comprehensive model that describes best practices of management within an integrated healthcare system like VHA.

Organizational Assessment, Intervention, and Consulting

Organizational assessment, intervention, and consulting services were the first contributions that NCOD provided to the VA system. The center's rapid growth reflects the recognition in VA of both the dire need for these services and the quality with which NCOD addressed this need.

The organizational assessment, intervention, and consulting activities all reflect the main tenets of NCOD's tried-and-true practice model. The center endorses the process-oriented model of working with organizational clients (Reddy 1994; Reddy & Phillips 1992; Schein 1988, 1990, 1992, 1999, 2006) and actively rejects the expert model. That is, NCOD does not tell clients what they should do. Instead, NCOD professionals add value through expert facilitation of the client's action processes. By making knowledge of the human processes and the VA system available to clients, NCOD supports their process of defining their goals, deciding on best strategies and tactics to reach these goals,

Box 2.4. NCOD Research Team Activities

Management of organizational data

  Maintain an inventory

  Update databases

  Link relevant databases for research purposes

  Data use agreement process

  Ensure proper use of VA data within and outside of VA

  Consult on uses of data:

    Internal VA staff using data

    External researchers using data

    Students using data

Reports from data for VA stakeholders

  To inform continuous improvement efforts

  All Employee Survey, CREW, Voice of the VA, 360-degree assessments

  Standardized templates

  Links between survey findings and organizational outcomes

Program evaluation

  National and regional programs and training:

    Leadership development

    Mentor training

    Other program evaluation activities on as needed

  Custom assessment measures for offices to evaluate their own programs

Custom assessment instrument (survey) development:

  2005–2006: 64 customized assessment tools

  2009–2010: 253 customized assessment tools

  Develop, host, and provide analysis support

Support for national strategic planning initiatives:

  Demographic changes in the workforce

  Workplace climate and job satisfaction

  Performance measurement for executives and medical centers

(Continued)

> Strategic research agenda:
>
> Programmatic study of VHA healthcare environment
>
> Articulate model of best leadership practices for delivering high-quality care
>
> Identify connections between VA topics and current research advances
>
> Benchmark results of VA studies with outside findings

and planning how to evaluate the outcomes and assess the need for any modifications. Rather than adopting a unified, standardized approach to implementing OD initiatives, NCOD recognizes the local conversation as a top priority in VHA medical centers. This philosophy allows NCOD to incorporate the diversity of local organizational cultures while helping implement VA national directives at the local level.

The basis of NCOD's approach to OD practice is building interpersonal relationships that embody trust and integrity. It has a well-established reputation for providing services in a strictly confidential manner, which is believed to be an important component of its success as an organizational change agent. Recognizing that system change is highly political work, NCOD provides its services with sensitivity to the national and local political contexts. For example, it is NCOD's firm principle to work at sites only by invitation from both management and labor. When working at a site, NCOD involves all employees throughout the organization in all aspects of the work: collecting data, sharing results of the organizational assessment, communicating about next steps, and so forth.

Organizational consulting is a data-based activity (Bartunek et al. 2006; Harvey & Brown 1992; Nadler 1977). Instrumentation used by NCOD includes quantitative data (e.g., workplace climate surveys, satisfaction surveys, organizational performance measures) and qualitative data (e.g., employee interviews collected as part of comprehensive assessments of organizational culture). The center uses data to provide clients with objective, valid, and reliable information to inform their decision making and action planning. It assists organizational clients in collecting, analyzing, and interpreting the data. Applying the data to planning and implementing specific changes within organizations remain the authority and responsibility of the client. As clients engage in these activities, NCOD remains available as a process consultant and offers continuous assessment, postassessment, and follow-up customized to the client's needs.

The competency model used for NCOD consulting activities is built on three overarching principles based on recommendations made by the Society of Consulting Psychologists (SCP) (American Psychological Association 2007). The first is a scientist-practitioner orientation, that is, using the skills of working with data as well as the applied skills of making the data relevant to the needs of clients. The second is recognition of OD as an evolving field, which means being open to changes in best working practices, client needs, and organizational context in which the OD work takes place. The third principle is nonexclusivity, initially defined by SCP as the ability of professionals other than consulting psychologists to deliver consulting services. The center redefined nonexclusivity to refer to the fact that NCOD services are not reserved for certain locations within the system or certain individuals of high status, but are offered on a need and priority basis to the stakeholders who request them.

These principles translate into the general competencies that outline what makes a good OD practitioner. These competencies include self-awareness; the ability to develop working relationships with clients; skills in assessment, facilitating client process, accessing, assessing, and interpreting organizational data; skills in action research and organizational intervention; knowledge of OD theories; the ability to work in the context of organizational diversity (multicultural and multidisciplinary); research skills; understanding of business operations; and professional ethics.

The center makes extensive use of quantitative and qualitative assessment data in its interventions with individuals, work units, and organizations (see box 2.5). It also conducts customized evaluations for organizational clients. The emphasis on measurement ensures that interventions are grounded in employee perceptions and ideas, providing a way for NCOD to assess the impact of its work. Its data-driven approach created its favorable reputation with VHA clients and stakeholders.

As a trusted resource, NCOD facilitates organizational change through ongoing, intensive consultative interventions as well as focused one- or two-visit consultative interventions with its stakeholders. Intensive workplace interventions and consultative services occur at all levels of the organizations in response to requests from organizational leaders. For example, if All Employee Survey data are not available (e.g., because there are fewer than ten participants per work group) or not timely (e.g., more than six months old), NCOD works with stakeholders to administer follow-up standardized assessment instruments and selected measures from the All Employee Survey. NCOD also conducts one-on-one employee interviews or group interviews as part of organizational change efforts. Data are analyzed and presented to the client (e.g., management and employees), and NCOD consultants facilitate the

> **Box 2.5. Organizational Assessment, Intervention,
> and Consulting Stakeholders**
>
> *Services to individuals*. NCOD provides services to individuals in the VA system. These services include role clarification, leadership development, participation in assessment centers, executive coaching, 360-degree assessment and feedback, vocational counseling, career development, stress management, and performance improvement consultations.
>
> *Services to work groups and teams*. NCOD provides services to groups of individuals, who usually comprise service work groups or leadership teams. These services include assessing the work environment, team building, conflict resolution, process assistance in creating vision and articulating mission and shared values for the team, process consultation to assist in meeting the team's goals, and redesign of systems and processes to help the team attain strategic goals.
>
> *Services to organizations*. NCOD provides services to organizations such as VA hospitals, specialty clinics, and program offices. These services include initiating and managing organizational change; consultation, facilitation, and support with strategic planning; planning and organization of retreats and meetings; workforce succession planning; developing effective partnerships; using workforce data in decision making; increasing employee involvement and participation; and conducting local organizational initiatives that address leadership and employee development.

organizational client's work of identifying, implementing, and continuously following up their action plans. In some cases NCOD has worked with organizations for over a year. In other cases the intervention has lasted over a period of a few months. In each case, NCOD worked with the stakeholder to assist in the development and implementation of an action plan that addressed the areas of concern revealed by the data.

Less intensive services include design and implementation of strategic planning processes, meeting and retreat design, and executive team assessment and team building. The volume of both types of services has been steadily growing in the last few years. For example, NCOD provided VHA organizations (including VISN offices, VAMCs, and program offices) with ongoing, intensive consultative services at fourteen sites in 2003, forty-five sites in 2006, seventy sites in 2008, and 67 sites in 2011. NCOD provided focused, one-time consultative services to eleven sites in 2003, fifty sites in 2006, sixty sites in 2008, and 106 sites in 2011. In 2009 the scope of consultant services expanded beyond VHA to include the entire VA system (i.e., Veterans Affairs Central Offices, Veterans Benefits Administration and National Cemetery Administration). In 2011, NCOD provided support to VHA's executive leadership in the implementation of a new organization structure. The growing demand for these services illustrates both the high organizational trust placed in NCOD and, more important, the high level of VA need for internal consultants, that is, consultants who understand and responsively address OD issues in the context of the integrated system.

Leadership Development

360-Degree Assessment and Feedback

In the context of the aging VA workforce and the approaching wave of retiring baby boomers, many of whom are senior level employees and leaders, a primary mission of NCOD is to ensure that VA will have the leadership in place today to lead the organization into the future. The importance of attracting quality professionals from outside the organization notwithstanding, it is even more crucial to identify and develop individuals of high potential within the organization.

To facilitate this process, NCOD and the High Performance Development Model Program Office, in partnership with Xavier University (Ohio), developed a Web-based 360-degree assessment. This tool provides current and potential leaders (i.e., clients) with developmental feedback in a safe and confidential format, based on their own ratings (self-survey) and ratings from their supervisors, peers, staff, and customers (external survey). The external survey respondents, who are chosen by the client, and the client answer questions about the client's work behaviors that are understood to express the core competencies at work (e.g., flexibility, interpersonal skills, systems thinking, technical skills). Several groups can be invited within each category of respondents (i.e., up to three distinct groups each of peers and of staff, and up to three bosses). This allows the client to receive separate feedback from each distinct group. Following best practices in leadership development and talent management, the survey questions are behaviorally based and represent the core competencies identified for success in the VA healthcare system. A personalized feedback report on the behavioral measures as rated by each distinct group of raters is then shared with the client. The report includes these measures for specific questions organized by areas of core competency. This feedback is designed explicitly for the purpose of professional development. Results are confidential, shared with the client only, and are not part of performance appraisals. All feedback is reported in an anonymous fashion aggregated for each group of external respondents, except for the information given by bosses (the client's supervisors). Clients are then offered an opportunity to work with an NCOD coach to design a personal development plan, to focus on two or three areas of development and track these over time.

Any interested employee can participate in the behaviorally based assessment and feedback process. Different instruments can be used depending upon the employee's position in the organization. Midlevel managers use a 360-degree assessment instrument analyzing their core competencies, while senior managers have an option of taking the senior executive 360-degree assessment. Also, any employee without formal supervisory responsibilities (up to the GS-9 level) can take the 180-degree assessment, which uses the same method and assesses the same core competency areas but does not include feedback from subordinates or staff.

Finally, NCOD provides a "living 360," which is based on the same job-related competencies, but is conducted face-to-face or by phone with NCOD staff rather than through a Web-based assessment tool. The questions for a "living 360" can be tailored to meet an individual client's needs for feedback. Typical questions include what clients do most effectively in their current position; their perceived commitment to quality, resource management, and so forth; their most positive contributions; what they could do to be more effective; and specific suggestions for changes with behavioral descriptions. The NCOD staff then interview external respondents (e.g., supervisors, peers, staff, and customers) and provide aggregated feedback to the clients (as broad reflective themes rather than individual comments). A "living 360" is often reserved for current VA executives because it is an intensive process that requires significant NCOD resources. Those who have participated in a "living 360" often comment that, although it was difficult to hear some of the feedback, it was one of the most useful experiences in their leadership development. An example of a "living 360" client's experience is shown in box 2.6.

The center also creates organizational aggregate 360-degree reports, identifying needs of leadership development in VA. The following numbers illustrate the scope of this work. The standard NCOD 360-degree assessment was provided to 900 VHA employees in 2003, 1,700 in 2006, 1,851 in 2010, and 1,615 in 2011. In 2003 NCOD developed and piloted a 360-degree assessment for senior executives. Then a 180-degree assessment was developed and piloted, thus extending developmental opportunities to all levels of VHA employees. As a result, 190 executive 360-degree assessments were provided in 2006, 565 in 2010, and 651 in 2011; 700 nonsupervisory 180-degree assessments were

Box 2.6. "Living 360" Assessment: One Participant's Story

The director (i.e., client) of a large division of administrative employees, many of them virtual, was encouraged by his supervisor to engage in executive coaching. The client was hesitant, to say the least; he did not understand his supervisor's interest in him participating in coaching. The supervisor outlined several concerns that he had about the director's communication style, urgency about addressing issues, and truly having a handle on what was happening in the director's organization, especially because many of the staff members were virtually located.

In the early stages of executive coaching, after much discussion about the best course of action, it was agreed that the client would participate in a more in-depth process to receive feedback from bosses, peers, and staff, as the most valuable course of action. This involved participating in a "living 360" assessment. Although the client had participated in several 360-degree assessments in the past and had found them useful, these assessments did not go as deep as he was hoping for, and he felt he was left guessing on some key competency issues.

The list of external feedback participants and the list of questions to ask them were mutually agreed upon by NCOD and the client. The questions centered on the client's areas of effectiveness, areas of ineffectiveness, suggestions about what he could do to be more effective, and communication issues.

Once the "living 360" assessment was completed and results were presented to the client, as is typical of many living 360-degree participants, he had difficulty hearing and accepting information on his areas of effectiveness. It was a struggle for the NCOD coach to get the client to acknowledge his strengths, as he immediately wanted to move on to areas for improvement. The discussion during the coaching session initially focused on the importance of being aware of one's areas of effectiveness, as these constitute building blocks toward addressing any areas where improvement is needed. Throughout the feedback session, as difficult as some of the feedback was to hear, the client listened to it carefully, asking thoughtful questions and working hard to fully understand what his respondents wanted him to do differently at the workplace.

During the coaching session subsequent to the "living 360" feedback session, the client had already developed a well thought out action plan to address his areas for improvement while preserving his areas of strength. Shortly afterward he held a meeting with his leadership team, openly discussing his "living 360" feedback while seeking additional feedback from them. Based on this conversation, he adjusted his action

(Continued)

plan, including how his leadership team could support him in implementing the changes outlined in his "living 360" assessment.

Within the first month after the "living 360" assessment, both the client's leadership team and the client's staff reported improvements to his NCOD coach as well as to the client himself, in the areas in which they had previously expressed the greatest concerns. His boss also reported an improved working relationship between the two of them and felt that the participant had addressed most of the expressed concerns that had prompted the boss's initial request for a coach. Improvements noted within the first month were sustained over the remainder of the coaching period (five months).

provided in 2006, 932 in 2010, and 866 in 2011. Because of this increased demand for assessment services, NCOD has expanded its staff to include employees whose full time is dedicated to supporting the 360 assessment services.

Executive Coaching

Ongoing or one-time executive coaching services to current and developing leaders within the organization are available from NCOD. Executive coaching is a relationship between an executive client and an NCOD coach focused on that client's adjustment within the organization, with the goal of helping him or her perform as effectively as possible. The coach assists the client in meeting the needs of the system while simultaneously enhancing knowledge, skills, and abilities (Ramsel, Osatuke, Brassell & Dyrenforth, 2012). Currently more than 200 leaders in VA use executive coaching services offered by NCOD. The NCOD coaches are available on-site during many of the programs offered to VHA leaders, including the VHA Health Care Leadership Development Program, as well as regional leadership programs. At these events, NCOD coaches work with current and emerging leaders in VHA to identify developmental goals, create personal development plans, and offer on-site consultation and assistance. In most cases, the VHA 360/180/360 executive assessment is used to facilitate the process. These coaching sessions are typically one-time events, but sometimes extend into longer-term coaching relationships. Many coaching relationships also develop as NCOD works intensively within VHA organizations. Ongoing executive coaching services are provided to senior leaders, high-performing supervisors, or supervisors who are struggling in their roles at all levels of the organization.

In the context of this professional coaching relationship, the client's communications are considered privileged (held in confidence). The NCOD coach may not share communications that occur within the coaching relationship with management or others in the system without the permission of the client, even though the organization, and not the client, may have initially contacted NCOD. When necessary, the NCOD coach may encourage the client to appropriately disclose some of these coaching communications with the organization, but this remains the client's choice.

The focus of the coaching relationship is the client's growth and adaptation to the responsibilities and expectations of his or her role in the organization. Observable work behaviors and the attitudes and motivations underlying these actions are examined. Although concerns from the client's personal life may be relevant, they are addressed in the context of their effect on work performance. Various work-related issues can be addressed in the coaching relationship. Coaching is most often initiated in one of three scenarios: the client may be transitioning to a new position, the client may be a high-potential leadership candidate wishing to accelerate his or her personal growth, or the client may be in danger of derailing under excessive stress and seeks coaching for assistance with those issues.

Typical foci include assisting the client in managing change, establishing core values and commitments, managing conflict, collaboration and consensus building, developing leadership skills, time management, and the development of effective teamwork skills. The coach and the client meet for a mutually agreed upon length of time. With support from the coach, the client sets goals and then develops action plans to achieve them.

The following numbers illustrate the growing demand for the NCOD executive coaching services. The center provided its one-time executive coaching services to 250 VHA employees in 2003, 400 in 2006, and 116 in 2011. Ongoing coaching services were provided to 40 VHA employees in 2003, 160 in 2006, and 230 in 2010.

Leadership Development Programs

The Executive Career Field Candidate Development Program is a national program that identifies and trains high-potential future leaders selected from top-ranked mid-managers. Executive Career Field candidates are competitively selected into the program. The two-year curriculum consists of developmental activities that aim at aligning candidates' developmental priorities with corporate growth needs. These activities are accompanied by mentoring and continuous assessment. Serving as a resource in the program activities (e.g., leadership development consultations) throughout the length of the curriculum, NCOD has sole responsibility for the design of the Executive Career Field Feedback & Critical Skills Assessment Center, which is a key evaluation event in the program.

The Assessment Center is an intensive, four-day program that uses simulations and other experiential activities to assess relevant skills and assist candidates in focusing their developmental efforts over the second year of the program. The Assessment Center includes exercises on managing one's communication inbox, conducting town hall and staff meetings, completing performance-based interviews, and more. A highlight of the Assessment Center is candidates' assignment to an executive role, with various exercises based on that role taking place throughout the week. Candidates are accompanied by an assigned mentor (outside of their work location) and a preceptor from their home medical center. The mentors and preceptors act as assessors, and NCOD staff serve as faculty, facilitators, and executive coaches. Approximately sixty-five to seventy candidates are accepted into the Executive Career Field Program and attend the Assessment Center annually. Since its inception in 2003, almost 450 candidates have attended this program. In addition to candidates, more than 100 senior leaders participate as mentors and preceptors in the program each year.

The Executive Career Field Feedback & Critical Skills Assessment Center

During the Assessment Center, candidates rotate through the following activities:

1. *Executive Coaching* is provided using the most recently completed 360-degree assessment. After reviewing their personal assessment reports, candidates meet one-on-one with NCOD staff to examine the received feedback and incorporate it into a personal development plan.

2. The *Executive Team Simulation* exercise is a comprehensive activity focused on process skills that spans the entire four days of the Assessment Center. Candidates are assigned a hospital executive role (e.g., director, chief of staff, associate director, or nurse executive) or a regional executive role in one of two mock hospital networks consisting of six medical centers each. Each "executive team" receives a packet of background information about each medical center. The summaries and data are different for each team. The executive teams each develop a strategic plan (e.g., summary white-paper and PowerPoint presentation) to be delivered on the morning of the fourth day. Several "meeting times" are scheduled throughout the week wherein the teams can spend time together working on this project.

3. The *Town Hall Meeting* exercise assesses Executive Career Field candidates' systems thinking, ethical reasoning, ability to think on their feet, and active listening skills. The mock executive team prepares to conduct a Town Hall meeting at their medical center. Candidates preside over the meeting. Mentors and preceptors play the audience (representing employees, veterans, reporters, and union officials), providing a realistic experience by introducing the types of challenges the candidates may encounter in real-life situations. The mentors and coaches then provide the candidates with feedback on their handling of the town hall meeting. The town hall meeting is videotaped; each candidate receives a DVD, along with specific suggestions.

4. The *Meeting Management/Systems Redesign* exercise assesses candidates' effectiveness in running a meeting and their understanding of basic principles and processes of systems redesign. Each candidate facilitates a mock meeting based on a scenario related to systems redesign. Candidates are instructed to lead the meeting toward resolving the problem at hand. Mentors and preceptors act as participants, playing specific roles (e.g., employees, reporters, and medical center and union), and then rate the candidates' performance.

5. The *Employee Feedback* exercise assesses interpersonal skills and understanding of basic HR processes related to providing difficult feedback to an employee. Each candidate reviews a mock personnel file for an employee with performance problems. Candidates assess the contents, potential next steps, and additional information needed. Candidates then meet with the employee of concern (played by Assessment Center staff) to discuss a resolution to the performance problems. Mentors and preceptors observe and score the candidates' skills.

6. The *Performance-Based Interview* exercise provides candidates with interview practice and generates feedback on planning, managing change, making sound decisions, negotiating, analyzing customer satisfaction data, promoting organizational health, dealing with unexpected consequences, and applying ethical standards. A panel of mentors and preceptors conducts the interview and provides feedback. The second performance-based interview is conducted with the same panel, to assess whether the candidate used the feedback received.

7. The *Inbox* exercise involves a series of e-mails, notes, and messages that might accumulate when a manager is away from the office. The exercise is designed to be challenging, with little time for completion. The purpose is to assess each candidate's approach to thinking through, prioritizing, and responding to a variety of demands that a VHA executive might face while

working under time constraints. Mentors and preceptors provide feedback on the candidates' performance and suggestions for improvement.

Each year NCOD revises Assessment Center events based on feedback from the previous year's attendees to enhance the participants' experience. Participants' competency scores improve from the first to last day of developmental activities, which reflects raters' perceptions that learning occurred. Also, mentors and preceptors tend to agree on participants' ratings; rater differences are not significant (Yanovsky et al. 2009, 2012).

Program Evaluation

Given the workforce and leadership challenges mentioned previously, in 2005 the VA leadership opted for a systematic approach to evaluating its leadership development programs, to ensure that they prepare the right number of people with the right skill sets for the appropriate executive positions in the most cost-effective manner possible. Though several methods and processes were in place to track selected workforce development and succession programs, no comprehensive strategy existed to assess their effectiveness, efficiency, and return on investment. Thus NCOD was charged with developing a model for program evaluation for all leadership development programs, beginning with the Executive Career Field Candidate Development Program. This model was presented to and endorsed by VHA senior leadership in September 2005. The model involves collecting data over time about program graduates, program candidates, program applicants, and those who have never applied to a leadership program. The data are collected at the individual level (e.g., bonuses, promotions, performance ratings, and 360-degree assessment data for the individuals of interest) and at the work group level (e.g., All Employee Survey data, Equal Employment Opportunity complaint rates, turnover, absenteeism, service-specific performance measures for work groups supervised by these individuals).

Based on preliminary results of 360-degree assessments and All Employee Survey data for candidates, applicants, and those who have never applied, candidates demonstrated significantly better results compared to both applicants and those who have never applied on most indicators (Osatuke et al. 2008a, 2008b). As more individuals complete the program and additional data become available, further analyses will be conducted to assess effects of participation in the program on additional outcomes, such as the aspiring executives' movement in the system, stretch assignments, promotions, and so forth. These findings will also be analyzed in the context of other organizational factors (e.g., organizational complexity of the medical centers where the compared individuals work) and other individual factors (e.g., demographics).

In 2010 the NCOD program evaluation strategy was deemed to be of relevance to apply to leadership development programs in the entire VA. It was charged with overseeing several contractors in the process of collecting data and conducting the evaluation of an array of leadership trainings. This work is currently ongoing. Results will help VA determine the differential impact of specific training programs and how to best use this information to promote the most effective and efficient elements of leadership development.

Postdoctoral Training

Another aspect that sets NCOD apart and has contributed significantly to its success is its postdoctoral OD fellowship program. The program began in 1999 with one fellowship slot and by 2005 had grown to ten. The fellows add tremendous value to NCOD through the amount and quality of work they complete as well as their energy, enthusiasm, and new ideas.

Goals of Training

Functioning in the real-life context of VA's large integrated system enables trainees to gain basic (predoctoral) or advanced (postdoctoral) skills as OD professionals. The structure of trainees' supervised activities and their interactions with other NCOD staff are designed to help them integrate psychological theories with applied skills in using empirical data and shape their understanding and practice of OD. Upon completion of the program, trainees are encouraged to apply their skills within VA. Many of NCOD's predoctoral trainees join the organization as postdoctoral fellows, and many of its postdoctoral fellows also choose to stay with NCOD or VA after they graduate. As of March 2012, forty-four fellows had entered the NCOD postdoctoral training, of whom seven were serving as fellows. Since the program's inception, twenty-seven postdoctoral fellows have completed the program, of whom nineteen selected employment in VHA (fourteen within NCOD).

The training provided is designed to fully prepare the graduates for a professional career in OD psychology within or outside of VA. The center strives to place graduating fellows in the VHA field to facilitate various OD activities at the local or regional levels.

Postdoctoral Fellows

Within its postdoctoral fellowship program, NCOD maintains six positions in the practitioner track (in OD consulting) and one in the research track (in management studies, program evaluation, and instrument development). Selection for these positions is competitive. Applicants typically include graduates from doctoral programs in psychology accredited by the American Psychological Association. Given the breadth of the new OD skills that the fellows acquire and the complexity of the surrounding systemic context in which these skills are applied, the postdoctoral fellowship takes two years to complete.

During the training period all fellows identify, develop, and master the advanced skills defining a competent OD practitioner or researcher. They are trained in all the domains that constitute the core of the respective specialization in OD. In particular, the practitioner track typically attracts applicants whose doctoral training was in clinical or counseling psychology. Practitioner fellows build on their previous skills in individual and group work (e.g., assessment, conceptualization of problems and strengths, intervention planning, implementation and follow-up) and add the advanced skills specific to the professional practice of OD. Research fellows come to the program from a variety of psychological disciplines (e.g., social psychology, cognitive, organizational, statistical, personality, clinical) with expertise in working with data from individuals and human systems. This variety of doctoral training prepares the research fellow with the prerequisite conceptual and technical background to learn advanced data management and data analytical techniques specific to OD research. As a result, the research fellow, in collaboration with senior staff, learns to apply the generic skills of working with data to formulate and address specific questions relevant to informing organization management in VA.

Predoctoral Training

The NCOD graduate practicum includes four half-time positions, offered on a competitive basis to students from local (Cincinnati, Ohio, metro area) graduate programs in psychology. Successful candidates have a strong interest in OD work, an appropriate academic background (e.g., statistical skills, basic training in research, OD content knowledge) and a potential to bring value to and benefit from working with a multidisciplinary team of NCOD professionals. Predoctoral trainees' participation tends to be most extensive in research and data aspects of NCOD work. Although they occasionally participate in practitioner work, predoctoral trainees are considered to be active members and contributors to the NCOD research team.

Training Model

The emphasis and balance between trainees' involvement in research and practice differ across the two fellowship tracks. Nevertheless, fellows' learning activities in either track include exposure to both data-related and applied aspects of OD. Training and exposure to the practitioner-consultant work in OD is offered to predoctoral research trainees as well. The NCOD approach to training is similar across the postdoctoral tracks (i.e., practitioner, research) and predoctoral program in that it incorporates a large experiential component: an apprentice model (i.e., learning occurs by doing). From the beginning, fellows are actively involved in ongoing projects, working side-by-side with experienced OD professionals. This provides fellows an opportunity to first learn by observation, then participate in ongoing projects and lead small projects in collaboration with other staff members, and eventually lead small, as well as complex, projects and teams independently. This developmental sequence, accompanied by a series of didactic seminars and readings along with extensive supervision, enables the fellows to gradually develop their own specific interests and skill sets in OD. The particular skills set and pace of progress through these stages of learning differ across fellows. Assignments to specific tasks account for these differences, as well as individual interests and preferences. The NCOD model of fellows' involvement balances the project needs (i.e., completing the work timely and with high quality) with the fellows' professional development goals (i.e., learning specific skills and participating at the highest level of involvement that is supported by current competencies).

The center is a feedback-rich environment. Extensive and mutual ongoing feedback on elements of professional skills, image, and presentation is routinely exchanged and extended to the staff at all levels of seniority. This aspect of the organizational culture also serves as the basis of the adopted training philosophy. Trainees who progress to the next level of professional skills are invited and expected to actively provide feedback to trainees at lower levels, to share feedback with peers, and to relay feedback to permanent staff. All permanent staff members working on joint projects with trainees regularly give them feedback on specific skill development and project management. The trainees thus receive weekly extensive input from their main supervisor as well as regular input from permanent staff and more experienced peers. In addition, the NCOD training director holds weekly group supervision meetings for postdoctoral fellows, focusing on ethical issues and thorny dilemmas in OD work, such as typical problematic situations encountered by trainees and possible solutions, as well as updates on important VA events that may impact NCOD's work. Weekly didactic seminars are also open to permanent staff, which enables NCOD staff to stay current on working methods of supervision, discuss learning needs, and track the professional progress of current fellows.

Each fellow prepares a personal development plan; box 2.7 is an example. The personal development plan serves as a guide for scheduling developmentally appropriate activities and attending to the next level of skills to be worked

Box 2.7. Sample Personal Development Plan

First-year postdoctoral fellow with a PhD in clinical psychology who entered the fellowship with no applied experience in organizations, but had presented and published on issues related to leadership.

Exposure Goals

1. Continue gaining exposure to NCOD.

   Actions:

   a. Seek out opportunities to travel.

   b. Seek diverse work assignments and find opportunities to work on ongoing projects.

   c. Learn more about NCOD initiatives such as Civility, Respect, and Engagement in the Workplace (CREW).

   d. Find opportunities to contribute to an ongoing, national project and assist the Assessment Center in scheduling and developing a new activity.

2. Acquire knowledge relating to VHA as an organization.

   Actions:

   a. Read the daily VA debriefing.

   b. Learn more about current VA policies.

   c. Learn more about roles and responsibilities of service units within VA hospitals.

3. Increase business acumen.

   Actions:

   a. Read *Harvard Business Review* and *Wall Street Journal*.

   b. Watch Consumer News and Business Channel (CNBC).

   c. Understand VHA as a business.

   d. Consult with supervisors for additional ideas.

4. Develop greater expertise in leadership and organizational dynamics.

   Actions:

   a. Read *The Leadership Challenge* by James M. Kouzes and Barry Z. Posner.

   b. Ask supervisors about other resources.

(Continued)

Personal and Professional Growth Goals

1. Seek out opportunities to work with senior management at VA.

   Actions:

   a. Offer to present during leadership debriefings.

   b. Seek out coaching opportunities with senior management.

   c. Accompany supervisor to Washington, D.C.

   d. Pursue other venues for working with senior management (e.g., team building retreats).

   e. Become more involved in the Assessment Center.

2. Increase attentiveness to administrative details.

   Actions:

   a. Check voice mail daily, even while traveling.

   b. Respond to all e-mails and phone messages within 24 hours.

   c. Maintain calendar in scheduling program.

   d. Complete all administrative forms on time.

3. Expand network of contacts within the OD field.

   Actions:

   a. Attend Society for Industrial and Organizational Psychology conferences.

   b. Find opportunities to present at professional conferences.

   c. Develop relationships with consultants both within and outside NCOD.

on. The plan is reviewed periodically in individual supervision, which includes assessment of recently developed competencies as well as a checklist for appropriate exposure to areas of work and types of projects that have been identified as relevant for that fellow's learning. Review and feedback on the developmental plan is in addition to the official VA performance appraisal that occurs annually. Evaluative feedback takes place at every on-site visit for every aspect of the intervention (for practitioner fellows) and at every phase of every project (for research fellows).

An experience checklist (see table 2.1) ensures that each fellow receives the opportunity to work with each full-time staff psychology member and is exposed to a broad range of interventions in the three major domains of

Table 2.1. Competency-Based Experience Checklist for Post-Doctoral Fellows

Date:	Fellow's Name:	Rating
Individual Level	Vocational assessment [B]	2
	Employee selection assessment [B]	4
	Job analysis (w/ individual assessment) [B]	4
	360 assessment orientation calls [A]	1
	360 assessment feedback sessions [A]	1
	Work Environment Scale interpretation [A]	1
	Maslach Burnout Inventory interpretation [A]	1
	DiSC [A]	1
	Assessment data feedback [A]	1
	Assessment center design [C]	2
	Assessment center facilitation [A]	1
	Coaching at national level [A]	1
	Executive/senior leadership coaching [C]	4
	Shadow consulting [A]	4
	Personal Development Plan assistance [A]	1
	Action plan development [A]	1
	Survey design [C]	1
	Performance-improvement counseling [B]	4
	Minority talent development [B]	4
	Leadership program design [C]	1
	Leadership program presentation [A]	1
	Leadership education/coaching [A]	1
Group Level	Team assessment [A]	1
	Team dysfunction assessment [A]	2
	Self-directed work group experience [A]	2
	Unit mission development [B]	4
	Unit objective/goals development [A]	2
	Assist meeting management [A]	4
	Facilitate interpersonal skills/communication [A]	1
	All Employee Survey action planning [A]	1
	Process consultation [A]	1
Organizational Level	Workplace assessment interviews [A]	1
	Workplace assessment theming [A]	1
	Workplace assessment feedback [A]	1
	Knowledge of All Employee Surveys [A]	1
	All Employee Survey design [C]	2
	All Employee Survey feedback presentation [A]	1
	Evaluation of corporate management philosophy [B]	4

(Continued)

Table 2.1. *(Continued)*

Date:	Fellow's Name:	Rating
	ID of aggregate performance measures [A]	3
	Change management design [A]	1
	Change management participation [A]	1
	Activity/role restructuring [B]	4
	Corporate-wide job analysis [B]	4
	Performance standards [B]	4
	De/centralizing decision making [B]	4
	Strategic planning [A]	2
	Operations research [B]	4
	Conflict resolution [A]	2
	Retreat design [A]	1
	Retreat facilitation [A]	1
	Executive teamwork [A]	2
	Transition briefing [A]	3
	Magnet work (nursing accreditation) [B]	4
	Baldrige/Carey work [B]	4
	Mission, vision [A]	2
	Responsibility charts [C]	4
	Appreciative inquiry [A]	2
	Workflow analysis [B]	4
Training	Didactic presenter [A]	1
	Conference attendance [B]	4
	VA Central Office experience w/director [A]	2
	National Committee [B]	4

A = expected to master by end of first year; B = engage as opportunity is available; C = expected to master by end of second year.

Rating scale (as defined by the fellow's role in project): 1= leading, 2= participating, 3= observing, 4= no exposure.

services (to individuals, groups, and organizations). The checklist also tracks the fellows' level of involvement for each type of activity, consistent with the developmental model used in training (from observation to participation to leading the intervention). The checklist is updated by each fellow every six months.

In addition, a mini-assessment evaluation tool is available for every type of project in which a fellow participates. It may be used as the format for providing in-depth feedback deemed relevant by fellows and their supervisors.

All evaluation tools, experience checklists, and feedback are based on the competency model developed by the Society of Consulting Psychologists (American Psychological Association 2007).

The outcomes of the training include increased trainee competency as measured by the repertoire of skills trainees can independently apply in OD contexts. Fellowship graduates are also evaluated on their readiness for independent practice; since the program's inception, all the practitioner fellows who graduated became licensed. Last, customer ratings and postintervention evaluations are assessed, which typically show clients' high satisfaction with interventions provided by NCOD fellows.

Local Organization Development Psychologists

One enhancement to the OD efforts by VA was the recent addition of OD psychologists to the staffing charts at several local medical centers. Box 2.8 shows typical activities of an organizational development psychologist at a particular VAMC. These activities illustrate how strategic national OD initiatives are implemented locally with the active involvement of these professionals.

Transformation of VA into a Veteran-Centered Care System

All three administrations within VA (Veterans Health Administration, Veterans Benefits Administration, and National Cemetery Administration) are currently deeply focused on systems transformation initiatives.

Veterans Health Administration

With the focus on the transformation of the VA healthcare system came the discovery that, although VHA leaders believed the system was patient-centered, its systems and practices were actually more centered on those delivering the care (medical model) than on those receiving it. For example, the scheduling of patient visits may be driven by schedules of clinical providers more than by patients' presenting needs. When the VHA leadership determined this model had to change, the Universal Services Task Force was chartered to identify what specific form patient-centered care would take. The membership consisted of leaders throughout the VHA system. The National Leadership Board (the governing body of VHA) and the Under Secretary for Health (the highest executive in VHA) formally endorsed and publicly supported the Task Force.

Box 2.8. Activities of an Organizational Development Psychologist in the Veterans Affairs Medical Center

Leadership Development

Individual assessment and coaching of senior leadership.

Facilitation of meetings between senior leadership members.

Leadership education using selected readings and audio books.

Development of leadership curriculum for local and regional leadership development programs.

Development and facilitation of strategic planning retreats.

Organization Development

Collaborate to elicit input, analyze, and report data and assist in the development of action plans for the All Employee Survey.

Provide train-the-trainer facilitator development for NCOD-sponsored Civility, Respect and Engagement in the Workplace (CREW) initiative.

Collaborate with chief, Education Service and others to transform facility into a "learning organization."

Assist in development of Integrated Ethics focus groups.

Work with others regarding relationship between various organizational initiatives and diversity outcomes.

Coaching and Mentoring

Provide train-the-trainer for VA Coaching and Mentoring Program.

Provide quarterly coaching and mentoring training for leadership, service chiefs, and supervisors.

Provide coaching and mentoring to members of senior leadership, service chiefs, and others on an as-needed basis.

Process Consultation

Provide process consultation to multiple programs, services, committees, and work groups. Topics include establishment of ground rules, conducting focus groups, among others.

Conduct both employee and veteran focus groups.

Organizational Health

Serve on Organizational Health Work Group.

(Continued)

Assist organization in addressing issues such as psychological safety, generational differences, diversity and inclusion, and health behaviors.

Employee Development

Serve on Employee Development Board.

Provide consultation on lifelong learning, rewards and recognition, employee satisfaction, workforce and succession planning, and professional development plans.

The main foci of transformation were outlined to include a greater emphasis on patient-centered care and employee engagement throughout the VHA system; the supportive (servant) leadership approach; strong customer service achieved through systems redesign and improved connections between organizational subsystems (such as patient care and patient family services); and operational mechanisms that support VHA as a learning organization on a routine basis. The NCOD has a major role in all of these transformational efforts.

The Task Force defined improving patient-centered care as building systems and processes around the veterans, so that no decisions about them are made without their participation (the motto is "Nothing about me without me"). A senior NCOD staff member cochaired this task force. The Task Force recommended that VHA organizations establish a consistent "line of sight" from the boardroom to the bedside, making the patients the final arbiters of the value of the services that they receive. Veteran-centered-care principles have been more specifically articulated as follows:

1. Honor the veteran's expectation of safe, high-quality, and accessible care.
2. Enhance the quality of human interactions and therapeutic alliances.
3. Solicit and respect the patient's values, preferences, and needs.
4. Systematize coordination, continuity, and integration of care.
5. Empower patients through information and education.
6. Incorporate the nutritional, cultural, and nurturing aspects of food.
7. Provide for physical comfort and management of pain.
8. Ensure emotional and spiritual support.
9. Encourage involvement of family and friends.
10. Make architectural and interior design conducive to health and healing.

11. Make creative arts part of the healing environment.

12. Support and sustain a satisfied, engaged workforce as key to the provision of patient-centered care.

To support employee engagement, the Task Force directed VHA organizations to create workplace environments that nurture both risk taking and accountability. Relationships, both among coworkers and between the employees and the organization, were stressed as fundamental at the workplace. The desired outcome of this approach is empowering employees to be creatively engaged and connected to the VA mission.

The recommended approach to leadership (supportive or servant leaders; see Greenleaf 2004) consists of adopting a culture of service as the main principle of leadership. This stance is more specifically described by the following set of premises:

1. We are all leaders, all of the time—that is, leadership is "what you do" more than "who you are" by position.

2. A leader puts people first and adopts a listening stance when facing challenges and problems; this stance can be healing for people who are led.

3. Persuasion is the preferred mode of power.

4. Whenever possible, a good leader seeks consensus, incorporates divergent points of view, and remains a compassionate collaborator.

5. Good leaders practice foresight.

6. Good leaders are skilled communicators who tempt the audience into that leap of imagination that connects verbal concepts to our own experience.

7. The art of withdrawal (going within to reorient and refresh) is important for leaders.

8. A leader shows acceptance and empathy, meeting people where they are.

9. A good leader should be a strong conceptualizer and systems thinker.

10. A leader needs to nurture the workplace community based on the unlimited sense of mutual liability ("we're all in it together"). This provides choices to lead and a ground to lead with moral authority.

Ultimately, servant leaders build and sustain a culture of service that becomes the norm in their organizations. A major component of this transformation is the patient-driven team approach to primary care delivery. Four-person teams, comprised of a physician, nurse, licensed practical nurse, and administrative support person, are designated as "teamlets," with a fifth member being the veteran. The teamlets focus on the overall health of the veteran, following the principles of holistic care, coordination of care across specialties, open access, and quality and safety. The center is heavily involved in this transformation, developing the national training module for working in teams.

Systems redesign and strengthening organizational connections for the sake of customer service are both based on the premise that those who do the work should be part of designing the work. Implementing this approach in VHA is expected to increase the effectiveness and efficiency of the system. This focus of change is expressed in the motto "Improving our work IS our work." Conducive to this is the organizational culture that promotes efforts of improvement by creating a psychologically safe environment, as expressed in the motto "Glitch hunts, not witch hunts."

Finally, the focus on organizational learning is based on instituting the processes that have been described as facilitative of new learning at the level of the individual and at the level of the organization. The VHA NCOD, VHA Employee Education System, and Harvard University School of Business currently collaborate on measuring these processes as they pertain to this system. A focus on organizational learning is an important dimension of organizational health, generally and particularly in the context of the VA transformation. It helps support an environment wherein veteran-centered practices, employee engagement, systems redesign, and supportive leadership can all occur.

There are many challenges in transforming a large bureaucracy in VA. Sustaining the impetus for the change to a patient-centered care model will involve significant efforts, given the inertia inherent in the operations of a large, complex system. Funding the infrastructure that will be needed for the move toward a patient-centered model will be an ongoing challenge as well. Despite significant funding already applied toward bolstering the primary care teamlets, there is much to be done to add or shift resources to meet the needs.

Nevertheless, because of its size and its integrated functioning as a comprehensive, "cover-all" healthcare organization, VHA also has unique strengths and resources to bring to bear on these monumental tasks. If the message in Philip Longman's *Best Care Anywhere* (2007) can be heard, the private sector would be wise to mine the wealth of experience in organizing and providing healthcare delivery that has accumulated in this government system. Indeed, the healthcare model adopted by VHA and aided by the type of expertise provided by the NCOD may currently be the only systematic approach in the United States that can set the national stage for resolving healthcare challenges for the nation. In addition, such a system provides an enormous wealth of data to be used in the service of establishing best practices in medicine, and this resource should not be underestimated.

The Veterans Benefits Administration

Fifty-eight field offices of the Veterans Benefits Administration (VBA) deliver benefits in the areas of compensation and pension, education and vocational rehabilitation, life insurance, loan guaranty, and benefits assistance. In 2010 VBA employees saw a 16 percent increase in claims for veterans' benefits, averaging 97,000 per month. The combination of ten years at war and a difficult economy are believed to be important factors in the increase in claims. A poor economy may be leading some veterans to file for benefits they earned during military service but may not have pursued in stronger economic times. Along with the sheer enormity of the number of claims, changes in the laws pertaining to eligibility further complicate VBA's challenges. For example, changes in the way VA will handle Agent Orange claims, making some conditions presumptive—that is, it may be presumed that exposure is as likely as not to have caused certain conditions—will bring in an estimated 200,000 more claims. Despite these challenges, VBA has its success stories. In 2010 almost one million compensation and pension claims were processed, and the VetSuccess and Welcome Home to Work programs were implemented to increase the number of veterans finding employment after their deployments or after completing vocational rehabilitation training.

The Veterans Benefits Administration participated in the All Employee Survey for the first time in the spring of 2010. With an extraordinary response rate of 80 percent, VBA is now data-rich for advancing its strategic initiatives. As the organization examines ways to re-engineer its business processes by automating claims, going paperless, and using technology to enhance online and self-service options for veterans, it must focus on the employee engagement that will be necessary to execute the massive culture changes that will be required. Employee education and training will be essential components of the strategy endorsed by VBA; developing uniformity of training and completing the training process before employees go into production mode will be necessary. Not only will it be necessary to build an engaged workforce, but the partnership with the Department of Defense will need to be furthered, so that the "hand-off" of military personnel from active duty to veteran status occurs smoothly. The Veterans Benefits Administration will also have to overcome some naturally expected resistance from employees and stakeholders as the organization attempts to modernize its rating structure and improve its processes.

The National Cemetery Administration

The National Cemetery Administration (NCA) oversees more than three million gravesites at 131 national cemeteries. Strict standards cover all aspects of the appearance of national cemeteries, in tribute to those who gave the ultimate sacrifice to preserve our nation's freedom and way of life.

Of the 147 national cemeteries, Department of Veterans Affairs operates all but 16. The Department of the Army operates Arlington and Soldiers' Home; the Department of the Interior operates the other 14. Of those three million gravesites, 306,000 are available for full-casket burial, 95,500 are in-ground cremation gravesites, and 92,600 are for columbaria. In fiscal year 2010 NCA provided 110,100 burials. Further developing VA-owned land could create up to six million gravesites. In developing the gravesites, cemetery leaders must adhere to this standard by law: operating veterans' cemeteries as national shrines with majestic settings in which veterans and their loved ones find a sense of serenity, historic sacrifice, and nobility of purpose.

Veterans who receive any discharge other than dishonorable are eligible for burial in a national cemetery. There are currently 24 million eligible veterans. Faced with ongoing challenges, such as ensuring a VA burial option is available within a reasonable distance (determined as seventy-five miles from the decedent's residence), NCA is hitting that target 88 percent of the time. Access to timely burial options becomes challenging with the steadily increasing numbers of families using national cemeteries. These challenges can be overcome through the engagement of NCA employees. The National Cemetery Administration has participated in the All Employee Survey since year 2007 and has an active plan for building employee satisfaction and commitment. The work of maintaining a satisfied and engaged workforce pay off in the quality of burial services provided to the families of veterans. The National Cemetery Administration enjoys a high loyalty rating from veterans. Ninety-nine percent of those polled say they would recommend a veterans' cemetery to families of veterans seeking burial options. The National Cemetery Administration is not satisfied with 99 percent loyalty, targeting 100 percent highly satisfied customers.

Future Directions

The main foci of system transformation have been publicly endorsed by the VA leadership, and the transformation is currently ongoing. "Transformational" refers to a change in organizational culture. This type of change usually takes time; VA is now in the beginning of this process. It will affect all of the major organizational initiatives. For example, leadership development programs will incorporate the notion of servant leadership. The executive 360-degree assessment will proceed based on new competencies that will include leaders' skills of supporting transformation in their organizations. CREW interventions will be grounded in the context of systems redesign in the participating medical centers, and so forth. The ongoing NCOD research program has expanded, making progress toward articulating the best working methods for maintaining organizational health and the active ingredients for successful transformational change of organizational culture.

The role of NCOD in the cultural transformation process remains that of internal OD consultant, offering research, practice, and assessment skills to the VA system in support of its change efforts. With a staff of fewer than sixty people, NCOD supports OD work in the entire VA, an organization comprised of almost 300,000 employees in all fifty states, Puerto Rico, Guam, and American Samoa, operating on an annual budget of $110 billion, and serving 5.5 million veterans. The ultimate goals of NCOD are to establish concrete options for managing the VA workplace and to continue to share these options with VA managers in specific organizations, in order to help these organizations function at their best. The most important value espoused by NCOD, upon its founding and continuing to this day, is the aspiration to see VA employees come to work every day anticipating personal growth, excitement, and the deep sense of accomplishment that results from working in the very best system functioning at the highest level of performance as it serves the most important customers: our Nation's Veterans.

References

American Psychological Association. (2007). Guidelines for education and training at the doctoral and postdoctoral levels in consulting psychology/organizational consulting psychology. *American Psychologist* 62: 980–992.

Argyris, C. (1970). *Intervention theory and method: A behavioral science view*. Reading, MA.: Addison-Wesley.

Argyris, C., Putnam, R. & Smith, D. M. (1985). *Action science*. 1st ed. San Francisco: Jossey-Bass.

Bartunek, J. M., Rousseau, D. M., Rudolph, J. W. & DePalma, J. A. (2006). On the receiving end: Sensemaking, emotion, and assessments of an organizational change initiated by others. *Journal of Applied Behavioral Science* 42: 182–206.

Benzer, J., Young, G., Caso, A., Stolzmann, K., Meterko, M., Osatuke, K., White, B. & Mohr, D. (2010). The role of primary care team climate in diabetes care. Paper presented at the annual national meeting of the Academy of Management, Montreal, Canada, August 6–10.

Bernstein, S. J. (2004). Veterans Affairs health services research: Lessons for the world's healthcare organizations. *American Journal of Managed Care* 10: 825–827.

Brassell, T., Yanovsky, B., Osatuke, K. & Dyrenforth, S. (2010). The effects of demographic dissimilarity on performance appraisal expectations. Poster presented at the annual national research meeting of the Academy of Health, Boston, MA, June 27–29.

Fishman, J., Osatuke, K. & Dyrenforth, S. (2009). Applying grounded theory to studying media coverage of veterans healthcare. Poster presented at the annual national convention of the Academy of Health, Chicago, IL, June 28.

Fishman, J., Osatuke, K., Moore, S. C., Draime, J. & Dyrenforth, S. (2009). Employee generation and workplace experience: Relationship to workplace satisfaction. Poster presented at the annual national convention of the Association for Psychological Science, San Francisco, CA, May 22.

Greenleaf, R. K. (2004). *A life of servant leadership*. San Francisco: Berrett-Koehler.

Harvey, D. F. & Brown, D. R. (1992). *An experiential approach to organizational development*. Englewood Cliffs, NJ: Prentice-Hall.

Hutton, S. A. (2006). Workplace incivility: State of the science. *Journal of Nursing Administration* 36: 22–28.

Kraut, A. I. (Ed.). (1996). *Organizational surveys*. San Francisco: Jossey-Bass.

Laschinger, H. K. S. & Finegan, J. (2005). Using empowerment to build trust and respect in the workplace: A strategy for addressing the nursing shortage. *Nursing Economics* 23: 6–13.

Leiter, M. P., Laschinger, H. K. S., Day, A. & Gilin-Oore, D. (2009). The role of civility and incivility in a model of burnout and engagement: An intervention study. Paper presented at the APA/NIOSH conference: Work, stress & health, San Juan, Puerto Rico, November.

Longman, Philip. (2007). Best care anywhere: Why VA health care is better than yours. Sausalito, CA: PoliPoint Press.

Marsick, V. J. & Watkin, K. E. (2003). Demonstrating the value of an organization's learning culture: The dimensions of the learning organization questionnaire. *Advances in Developing Human Resources* 5, no. 2: 132–151.

Meterko, M., Osatuke, K., Mohr, D., Warren, N. & Dyrenforth, S. (2007). Civility: The development and psychometric assessment of a survey measure. In M. Nagy (Moderator), Measuring and assessing workplace civility: Do "nice" organizations finish first? Panel presented at the 67th annual meeting of the Academy of Management, Philadelphia, PA, August 8.

Meterko, M., Osatuke, K., Warren, N., Benzer, J. & Mohr, D. (n.d.). Civility in the healthcare workplace: Psychometric properties of a workgroup climate measure. Unpublished manuscript.

Mohr, D., Meterko, M., Charns, M., Dyrenforth, S. & Osatuke, K. (2007). Workplace factors that increase employee satisfaction and performance. Paper presented at the Veterans Affairs HSR&D National Meeting, Boston, MA, February 21–23.

Mohr, D., Moore, S. C., Osatuke, K., Meterko, M. & Nealon Seibert, M. (2010). Primary care workload and staffing differences in Veterans Affairs urban and rural practices. Poster presented at the HSR&D national meeting on improving health care for rural veterans, Portland, Maine, May 5–6.

Mohr, D., Osatuke, K., Moore, S. C., Hodgson, M. & Warren, N. (2008). Do more civil workplaces actually have less incivility? In D. Mohr (Moderator), Workplace civility and incivility: Implications for healthcare. Panel presented at the annual conference of the Society for Industrial Organizational Psychology, San Francisco, CA, April 11.

Mohr, D. C., Warren, N., Hodgson, M., Osatuke, K., Ward, C. & Dyrenforth, S. (2007). Workplace civility, workplace incivility and employee sick leave rate usage. In Mark Nagy (Moderator), Measuring and assessing workplace civility: Do "nice" organizations finish first? Panel presented at the 67th annual meeting of the Academy of Management, Philadelphia, PA, August 8.

Moore, S. C., Osatuke, K. & Dyrenforth, S. (2009). The relationship between civility and satisfaction: An examination of three years' data from the Veterans Health Administration. Poster presented at the annual national convention of the Society for Industrial and Organizational Psychology, New Orleans, LA, April 2–4.

Moore, S. C., Osatuke, K. & Dyrenforth, S. (2010a). Factor structure and time invariance of a civility survey instrument. Poster presented at the annual national convention of the Society for Industrial and Organizational Psychology, Atlanta, GA, April 7–10.

Moore, S. C., Osatuke, K. & Dyrenforth, S. (2010b). Civility measure shows partial factorial invariance across racial and ethnic groups. Poster presented at the 22nd annual national convention of the Association for Psychological Science, Boston, MA, May 27–30.

Moore, S. C., Osatuke, K. & Howe, S. (2008). Modeling turnover and absenteeism through civility and job satisfaction scores. In D. Mohr (Moderator), Workplace civility and incivility: Implications for healthcare. Panel presented at the annual conference of the Society for Industrial Organizational Psychology, San Francisco, CA, April 11.

Moore, S. C., Willmarth, K., Osatuke, K. & Dyrenforth, S. (2009). Satisfaction increases with supervisory status in the Veterans Health Administration. Poster presented at the annual national convention of the Association for Psychological Science, San Francisco, CA, May 22.

Nadler, D. A. (1977). *Feedback and organization development: Using data-based methods.* Organization development [series]. Reading, MA: Addison-Wesley.

Nagy, M. S. (2002). Using a single-item approach to measure facet job satisfaction. *Journal of Occupational & Organizational Psychology* 75, no. 1: 77–86.

Nagy, M., Osatuke, K., Meterko, M., Scruggs, R., Mohr, D., Warren, N., Hodgson, M., Moore, S. C. & Belton, L. (2009). Exploring the boundaries of civility and incivility. Round table presented at the annual national convention of the Society for Industrial and Organizational Psychology, New Orleans, LA, April 2–4.

Nagy, M. S., Warren, N., Osatuke, K. & Dyrenforth, S. (2007). The association between civility and monetary organizational outcomes. In Mark Nagy (Moderator), Measuring and assessing workplace civility: Do "nice" organizations finish first? Panel presented at the 67th annual meeting of the Academy of Management, Philadelphia, PA, August 8.

Naimon, E. C., Mullins, M. E. & Osatuke, K. (2010). The effects of personality and spirituality on workplace incivility perceptions. Poster presented at the 22nd annual national convention of the Association for Psychological Science, Boston, MA, May 27–30.

Osatuke, K., DeLuca, N. & Dyrenforth, S. (2008). Employee versus patient perceptions of veterans healthcare: National level comparison. Poster presented at the 116th annual national convention of the American Psychological Association, Boston, MA, August 15.

Osatuke, K. & Dyrenforth, S. (2006). Civility in Veterans Affairs hospitals relates to costs and performance indicators. Paper presented at the 114th annual convention of the American Psychological Association, New Orleans, LA, August 10.

Osatuke, K. & Dyrenforth, S. (2009a). Civility, respect, engagement at the workplace (CREW): Nationwide organization development intervention at the United States Veterans Healthcare Administration. Poster presented at the 5th Australasian redesigning health care summit in Brisbane, Australia, on March 26.

Osatuke, K. & Dyrenforth, S. (2009b). Civility, respect, and engagement in the workforce (CREW): Nation-wide organization development intervention at Veterans Health Administration. Paper presented at the First World Congress on positive psychology in Philadelphia, PA, June 18–21.

Osatuke, K., Dyrenforth, S. & Belton, L. (2008). Organizational change towards greater civility: What helps intervention success? Poster presented at the 14th annual national research conference of the British Association for Counseling and Psychotherapy, Cardiff, Wales, May 9.

Osatuke, K., Fishman, J. & Dyrenforth, S. (2009). Relationship between portrayals of Veterans Affairs hospitals in the media, and employee and patient satisfaction: An exploratory analysis. Paper presented at the annual national convention of the AAPOR (American Association for Public Opinion Research), Hollywood, Florida, on May 15.

Osatuke, K., McNamara, B., Fishman, J. & Dyrenforth, S. (2010). Workplace civility perceptions relate to equal employment opportunity complaint rates. Paper presented at the 116th annual national convention by the American Psychological Association, San Diego, CA, August 12.

Osatuke, K., McNamara, B., Pohl, M., Moore, S. C., Meterko, M., Nagy, M., Charns, M. & Dyrenforth, S. (2009). Response rates and incentives in Veterans Administration All Employee Survey. Paper presented at the annual national convention of the Institute of Behavioral and Applied Management, Washington, DC, on October 1.

Osatuke, K., Mohr, D., Ward, C., Moore, S. C., Dyrenforth, S. & Belton, L. (2008a). Organization development intervention to increase civility in the workforce. In D. Mohr (Moderator), Workplace civility and incivility: Implications for healthcare. Panel presented at the annual conference of the Society for Industrial Organizational Psychology, San Francisco, CA, April 11.

Osatuke, K., Mohr, D., Ward, C., Moore, S. C., Dyrenforth, S. & Belton, L. (2008b) Organization development intervention to increase civility in the workforce: What explains variability of outcomes across participating Veterans Affairs facilities. Paper presented at the annual national conference of the Academy of Management, Anaheim, CA, August 13.

Osatuke, K., Moore, S. C. & Dyrenforth, S. (2010). Demographic and occupational characteristics as predictors of differences in workplace civility perceptions. Poster presented at the 22nd annual national convention of the Association for Psychological Science, Boston, MA, May 27–30.

Osatuke, K., Moore, S. C., Fishman, J., Draime, J. & Dyrenforth, S. (2009). Employee generation and workplace experience: Relationship to workplace climate perceptions. Poster presented at the annual national convention of the Academy of Health, Chicago, IL, on June 28.

Osatuke, K., Moore, S. C., Ward, C., Dyrenforth, S. R. & Belton, L. (2009). Civility, respect, engagement in the workforce (CREW): Nationwide organization development intervention at Veterans Health Administration. *Journal of Applied Behavioral Science* 45, no. 3: 384–410.

Osatuke, K., Yanovsky, B., Draime, J. & Dyrenforth, S. (2008). 360° ratings of managers' skill relate to workgroup satisfaction with supervision. Poster presented at the 20th annual national convention of the Association for Psychological Science, Chicago, IL, May 24.

Osatuke, K., Yanovsky, B., Naimon, E. & Dyrenforth, S. (2009). Workgroup supervisors' 360 ratings: Relationship to staff perceptions of workplace characteristics and turnover intentions. Poster presented at the annual national convention of the Association for Psychological Science, San Francisco, CA, May 22.

Osatuke, K., Yanovsky, B., Pohl, M., Draime, J. & Dyrenforth, S. (2008a). Professional development program for veterans healthcare executives: Evaluating the impact. Poster presented at the 25th annual research meeting of the Academy of Health, Washington, DC, June 9.

Osatuke, K., Yanovsky, B., Pohl, M., Draime, J. & Dyrenforth, S. (2008b). Measuring managerial competencies in veterans healthcare: An evaluation of a professional development program. Paper presented at the 32nd annual International Public Management Association Assessment Council conference, Oakland, CA, June 11.

Ostroff, C. (1992). The relationship between satisfaction, attitudes, and performance: An organizational level analysis. *Journal of Applied Psychology* 77: 963–974.

Parker, C. P., Baltes, B. B., Young, S. A., Huff, J. W., Altman, R. A., Lacost, H. A. & Roberts, J. E. (2003). Relationships between psychological climate perceptions and work outcomes: A meta-analytic review. *Journal of Organizational Behavior* 24: 389–416.

Perlin, J. B., Kolodner, R. M. & Roswell, R. H. (2004). The Veterans Healthcare Administration: Quality, value, accountability, and information as transforming strategies for patient-centered care. *American Journal of Managed Care* 10: 828–836.

Ramsel, D., Osatuke, K., Brassell, T., & Dyrenforth, S. (2012). Does executive coaching help aspiring leaders: A randomized outcome study. Paper presented at the annual national conference by the Society of Psychologists in Management (SPIM), Charleston, SC, February 24.

Reddy, W. B. (1994). *Intervention skills: Process consultation for small groups and teams.* San Diego, CA: Pfeiffer & Co.

Reddy, W. B. & Phillips, G. (1992). Traditional assessment: The way of the dinosaur. *Organization Development Practitioner* 24: 1–2.

Rogelberg, Steven G. & Stanton, Jeffrey M. (2007). Introduction: Understanding and dealing with organizational survey nonresponse. *Organizational Research Methods* 10: 195–209.

Schein, E. (1988). *Process consultation.* Vol. 1: *Its roots in organizational development.* Reading, MA: Addison-Wesley.

Schein, E. (1990). Organizational culture. *American Psychologist* 45: 109–119.

Schein, E. (1992). *Organizational culture and leadership.* San Francisco: Jossey-Bass.

Schein, E. (1999). *Process consultation revisited: Building the helping relationship.* Reading, MA: Addison-Wesley-Longman.

Schein, E. (2006). Culture assessment as an organization development intervention. In B. B. Jones & M. Brassel (Eds.), *The NTL handbook of organization development and change: Principles, practices, and perspectives* (pp. 456–465). San Francisco: Jossey-Bass.

Snell, A., Moore, S. C. & Osatuke, K. (2010). Civility score variation across ethnic groups in the Veterans Health Administration. Poster presented at the 22nd annual national convention of the Association for Psychological Science, Boston, MA, May 27–30.

Snell, A., Osatuke, K., Rickert, J. & Dyrenforth, S. (2010). Veterans Health Administration polytrauma rehabilitation: Provider perspective on patients' family involvement. Poster presented at the annual national research meeting of the Academy of Health, Boston, MA, June 27–29.

Stolzmann, K., Benzer, J., Meterko, M., Osatuke, K., Mohr, D. (2010). Primary care quality and patient satisfaction in rural and urban Veterans Health Administration settings. Poster presented at the HSR&D national meeting on improving health care for rural veterans, Portland, ME, May 5–6.

Warren, N., Hodgson, M., Craig, T., Dyrenforth, S., Perlin, J. & Murphy, F. (2007). Employee working conditions and healthcare system performance: The Veterans Health Administration experience. *Journal of Occupational and Environmental Medicine* 49: 417–429.

Warren, N. D., Mohr, D., Meterko, M., Osatuke, K., Nagy, M., Hodgson, M., Dyrenforth, S. & Charns, M. (2008). Workplace civility, verbal abuse, and employee health & safety. Paper presented at the annual work, stress & health conference, Washington, DC, March 10.

Yanovsky, B., Brassell, T., Osatuke, K. & Dyrenforth, S. (2010). An examination of the qualitative comments within a 360° performance appraisal. Poster presented at the annual national research meeting of the Academy of Health, Boston, MA, June 27–29.

Yanovsky, B., Graff-Reed, R., Kruer, K., Dyrenforth, S. & Osatuke, K. (2009). Evaluation of a developmental assessment center in veterans healthcare. Paper presented at the annual national convention of the IPMA-HR (International Public Management Association for Human Resources), Nashville, TN, September 14.

Yanovsky, B., Osatuke, K., Graff-Reed, R. & Dyrenforth, S. R. (2012). Factor structure of two different developmental assessment center rating formats. *Journal of Organizational Psychology* 11, no. 2: 70–80.

Young, G. J. (2000). Managing organizational transformations: Lessons from the Veterans Healthcare Administration. *California Management Review* 43: 66–82.

Zammuto, R. F. & Krakower, J. Y. (1991). Quantitative and qualitative studies of organizational culture. In R. W. Woodman & W. A. Passmore (Eds.), *Research in organizational change and development* (pp. 83–114). Greenwich, CT: JAI Press.

Department of Veterans Affairs National Center for Patient Safety: First Do No Harm

Joseph F. Murphy and James P. Bagian

History

In the United States, estimates of the lives lost due to factors related to patient safety exceed those lost due to motor vehicle accidents, breast cancer, and AIDS combined, as the landmark 1999 Institute of Medicine study, *To Err Is Human*, shows (Kohn, Corrigan & Donaldson 1999). That same year, the National Center for Patient Safety was established, indicating the Department of Veterans Affairs' (VA) commitment to making systemwide changes in its healthcare delivery system.

Since its inception, the National Center for Patient Safety has aggressively developed and deployed systems that are in use throughout the Veterans Health Administration (VHA) and have been adopted as a benchmark by healthcare organizations throughout the world (Heget et al. 2002).

Policy

Neither VHA nor any other healthcare system can or will ever be able to eliminate all errors. Patient safety programs focused exclusively on eliminating errors will fail. The chance of an error occurring will never disappear from human conduct. The real goal of a patient safety program should be to prevent harm to patients, by significantly improving the probability that a desired patient outcome can be achieved. This can only be accomplished by taking a systems approach to problem solving, focusing on prevention, not punishment.

Historically, those in medicine have primarily relied on people being perfect and equipment never failing. This approach never worked, and for too long most practitioners were afraid to admit it. The National Center for Patient Safety was founded on the belief that this failed approach must be abandoned, as it unrealistically requires personal perfection to make a care system succeed.

The time has come to look past the oversimplified belief that an adverse event is always someone's fault. The real cause is most often a chain of events that has gone unnoticed, leading to a recurring safety problem. It is seldom solely related to the actions of just one individual.

The National Center for Patient Safety takes a preventive approach to improving patient care by looking for ways to break that link in the chain of events that can cause a recurring problem. The focus is on building care systems that are "fault-tolerant." Such systems reduce or eliminate the possibility that harm can come to a patient, because these systems are designed to succeed even if individual components fail. The fault-tolerance principle has been used for years in high-reliability industries, such as aviation and nuclear power, industries with safety records that far surpass those of healthcare (Bagian 2002).

Initial Challenges

The National Center for Patient Safety faced many challenges that had to be addressed simultaneously following its establishment. Interlocking programs central to its goals and functions had to be launched effectively and expeditiously (Bagian et al. 2001).

Root Cause Analysis

Though root cause analyses were being performed at VA facilities, they were not being conducted in a uniform manner, and the results were not being effectively tracked nationally. The root cause analysis process is a multidisciplinary team approach used to study adverse medical events and close calls. The goal of each root cause analysis is to find out what happened, why it happened, and what must be done to prevent it from happening again (Bagian 2002).

A training program, confidential database, and cognitive aids were developed by the National Center for Patient Safety to support facility root cause analysis teams.

Safety Assessment Codes

Safety assessment codes, also developed by the National Center for Patient Safety, are used by root cause analysis teams to determine whether any further definitive action is required concerning a particular incident. The scores are based on the severity of the incident and its probability of occurrence, the combination determining the actual risk of harm to a patient. A safety assessment code score of 3 indicates a category of events with the highest risk of harm to a patient; a score of 1, the lowest. The safety assessment code scores for the severity categories comprise the extent of the injury, the length of stay, and the level of care required for remedy. The scores for probability include whether the event could reoccur frequently, occasionally, or reoccurrence is more likely to be uncommon or remote (National Center for Patient Safety 2010).

Confidential Reporting

A confidential VHA database was required to allow National Center for Patient Safety staff members to track and analyze the root causes of adverse events and close calls, as well as the corrective actions and their effectiveness. The Patient Safety Information System, nicknamed "SPOT," was developed to do just that. It provides a confidential, nonpunitive reporting system that allows users to electronically document patient safety information from across VHA so that lessons learned can benefit the entire system.

Since SPOT was first pilot-tested in 1999, nearly 20,000 root cause analysis reports and 900,000 safety reports have been placed in the system. Using specialized software, SPOT can be searched for trends, as well as for a listing and prioritization of specific events.

Following the implementation of the new root cause analysis program, a 30-fold increase in event reporting and a 1,000-fold increase in the number of root cause analyses were noted, reflecting the level of commitment to the program by VHA leaders and staff members throughout the medical system.

Close calls are given the same level of scrutiny as adverse events that result in harm to a patient; they may occur 300 times more often than actual adverse events (Heinrich & Granniss 1959). A willingness and an avenue to report problems are essential to safe care, because one can't fix what one doesn't know about.

Patient Safety Training

It was also recognized that VHA had no consistent patient safety training program. For a patient safety program to function effectively, developing a consistent method for training frontline patient safety professionals is critical. The National Center for Patient Safety developed inclusive, one- to three-day training sessions to meet this need. Attendees are presented with specific ways to enhance their patient safety efforts. For example, they are offered guidance on how best to develop and implement a root cause analysis team, provided hands-on training concerning the use of the SPOT database, and given practical applications of human factors engineering techniques (Gosbee 2002; Gosbee & Anderson 2003).

Thirty-three sessions have been conducted since 1999, which have been attended by more than 2,500 caregivers. Though attendees have been in large part VHA, the training has also drawn representatives from 12 foreign countries and 285 U.S. healthcare institutions or agencies.

Cognitive Aids and Tool Kits

The National Center for Patient Safety developed a wide range of cognitive aids and toolkits to support specific activities, such as carrying out a root cause analysis or managing escape and elopement of patients with mental health issues. The cognitive aids and kits have been used in VHA and non-VHA activities around the country, as well as by a number of foreign nations. For example, the "NCPS Triage Cards™ for Root Cause Analysis" cognitive aid has been translated into Danish, and the American Hospital Association distributed the multimedia toolkit developed by the National Center for Patient Safety, "Strategies for Leadership," to hospitals across the nation.

One of the National Center for Patient Safety's most popular products, "The Falls Toolkit," originally distributed in 2004, is a multimedia compendium that includes fall risk assessment tools, measurement and intervention strategies, and videos for analysis of balance and gait (National Center for Patient Safety 2004). Falls are a major problem, particularly for elderly veterans (Mills et al. 2003). Thousands visit the National Center for Patient Safety Internet and intranet sites annually to explore and download the electronic version.

Business Case for Patient Safety

The National Center for Patient Safety developed benefit-cost and cost-effectiveness measures that can be applied to patient safety initiatives to establish and promote sensitivity to the impact safety has on the resources available to care for patients. A benefit-cost analysis compares the amount of savings gained through an investment in patient safety and is reflected as a ratio. The numerator is the benefit, or avoided cost; the denominator the expense associated with the intervention. A ratio greater than 1 indicates a net positive return from the investment:

- Suppose an investment in hand alcohol gels cost $2,000; further, this investment results in a decrease in nosocomial infections that would have cost $10,000 in extra hospital admissions. The benefit-cost ratio would be

10,000 divided by 2,000, or five. This implies that for every $1 invested, there is a net return of $5.

Cost-effectiveness measures the cost per avoided adverse event. The numerator is the expense of the intervention; the denominator the anticipated number of avoided adverse events:

- If there were a falls intervention program that cost $40,000 per year to implement, and it avoided four fractured hips during that time period, the cost-effectiveness measure would be $10,000 per avoided hip fracture.

By using these methods, patient safety professionals can be prepared for a wide range of questions decision makers might ask, such as the following:

- Can you demonstrate that this is cost-beneficial or at least cost-neutral?
- How much will interventions and proposed actions cost in total?
- How will we know that we have made a difference in patient safety?

The financial aspects of patient safety programs are important, because this critical element of healthcare is receiving an increased investment of resources. The investment may take the form of employing new dedicated patient safety staff members, the procurement of new infrastructure or equipment, funding for training, or new root cause analysis investigations.

Patient Safety Centers of Inquiry

Patient Safety Centers of Inquiry have been managed by the National Center for Patient Safety since its establishment and are an integral part of the patient safety program. To be successful, a Patient Safety Center of Inquiry is expected to develop, disseminate, and implement clinically relevant innovations that improve patient safety in VHA facilities. Successful Patient Safety Centers of Inquiry provide specific tools for the field that can help to improve patient safety. Individual centers have tackled a wide range of problems, including

- collecting data on procedures requiring moderate sedation and developing scenarios for training nurse/physician teams using point-of-care simulation training;
- developing a number of initiatives to reduce falls, such as a multifaceted "Hip Protector Toolkit"; and
- conducting more than 5,000 medical record reviews to improve the VHA electronic medical record system and intervening in 200-plus clinical situations that prevented harm to patients.

Taking the Systems Approach

With these key programs in place, the National Center for Patient Safety began to tackle a range of issues in an effort to broaden VHA's patient safety efforts.

Healthcare Failure Modes and Effect Analysis

Making medical procedures safer was the key reason for designing the Healthcare Failure Modes and Effect Analysis process. It has a wide range of applications, from developing backup medication delivery systems to improving the way laboratory specimens are drawn. More than 1,800 analyses have been conducted since 1999.

A five-step process is used by interdisciplinary teams to proactively evaluate a healthcare process. Specifically designed for use by healthcare professionals, the process offers users analytical tools such as flow diagramming, decision trees, and prioritized scoring systems. The tools enable the user to proactively identify vulnerabilities and deal with them effectively. The process streamlines hazard analysis steps found in a traditional "Failure Mode and Effect Analysis" procedure—an analytical process often used by engineers to identify potential failures of individual components and subsystems.

Healthcare Failure Modes and Effect Analysis includes healthcare-specific definitions for severity, probability, and detectability. It is a systematic, engineering-based approach used to identify system vulnerabilities and correct problems before they occur (DeRosier et al. 2002).

Patient Safety Cultural Survey

A VHA Patient Safety Culture Survey is performed nationally every three to five years to measure changes in the patient safety culture. The first was done in 2000, followed by surveys in 2005, 2009, and 2011. A combined total of approximately 153,350 employees participated in these four surveys.

The survey questions cover fourteen patient safety dimensions. Five dimensions overlap with the Agency for Healthcare Research and Quality culture survey.

Results from 2009 show a continued overall favorable comparison between VHA and the Agency for Healthcare Research and Quality benchmarks. The Veterans Health Administration scored significantly higher in two measures:

- 80 percent (compared to 70 percent) in organizational learning and

- 70 percent (compared to 62 percent) in feedback and communication.

No significant difference was found in the three other dimensions:

- teamwork within hospital units,
- teamwork across hospital units, and
- frequency of event reporting.

One of the key sources of a patient safety program's success is management support. Measurements of senior management's awareness and actions to promote patient safety improved significantly over the first three survey periods, uniformly in nonsupervisor, supervisor, and senior management survey responders. The average responses at the national level did not go up or down significantly in the 2011 survey, a positive sign (National Center for Patient Safety 2012).

Patient Safety Curriculum for Residents

The National Center for Patient Safety began developing a patient safety curriculum in the summer of 2002 with a group of volunteers from across the country, piloting and modifying content and methods. The academicians and clinicians collaborated to improve the program via electronic communication and teleconferences, as well as attending "a summit meeting" in 2003.

Curriculum workshops are offered several times a year. During a two-day workshop, participants receive a number of resources to support future efforts: a complete toolkit that includes the workshop content, teaching materials, instructor's guides, ideas for implementation, and assessment tools. The National Center for Patient Safety also provides participants with continued mentoring on a wide range of education and patient safety issues.

A successful patient safety curriculum program is based on more than just teaching a series of modules. It is critical that instructors be committed to creating a culture of safety based on a systems approach to problem solving. Instructors must be able to deal with ethical and legal issues, conduct frank discussions with participants, and have a clear understanding of their facility's operations. They must be also willing to make a long-term commitment to both their students and patient safety.

It is particularly significant to healthcare in the United States that the National Center for Patient Safety conducts this effort. Each year more than 80,000 health professionals are trained in VHA medical centers. Nationally, more than half of the physicians practicing today received some of their professional education while in VHA. Since the program began, more than 1,100 attendees have come from more than 100 VHA hospitals and 50 university affiliates, as well as professionals from 42 states and 6 foreign nations.

Residents who have participated in the program scored more favorably in the 2005 Patient Safety Culture Survey than those who had not attended. Residents join root cause analysis teams sooner after a workshop than would otherwise be expected. They have also participated more frequently in other patient safety activities, such as patient safety modified case conferences, patient safety rotations, and rounds.

Ensuring Correct Surgery

Incorrect surgical procedures or incorrect diagnostic and therapeutic invasive procedures are relatively uncommon adverse medical events, but are often devastating when they occur. To prevent or avoid such adverse medical events, the National Center for Patient Safety developed a straightforward, five-step process to identify the correct patient, mark the correct surgical site, and ensure the correct procedure is performed.

Instituted in 2002 for surgical procedures inside the operating room, the Ensuring Correct Surgery Directive was modified in 2004 to include invasive procedures outside the operating room. The original version contributed to the development of the Joint Commission's Universal Protocol for Correct Site Surgery, which took effect in July 2004.

Analyses prior to launching the initial five-step process revealed the problem of incorrect surgery to be far more complex than previously thought. It wasn't just a series of left-right mix-ups; the National Center for Patient Safety found that 36 percent of all incorrect surgeries were conducted on the wrong patient—which is why patient identification is a major part of the five-step process.

Patient Safety Improvement Corps

Consistent with a positive assessment of the National Center for Patient Safety by the Rand Corporation, the Department of Health and Human Services (DHHS) selected the center to formulate, manage, and implement a multifaceted training program for state health officials and their hospital partners. This landmark interagency agreement between the DHHS and VA was funded by the Agency for Healthcare Research and Quality, which is part of the DHHS. The training program began in 2003 and concluded in 2008.

The goal was to provide two representatives from each state department of health and their private-sector partners with the skills required to analyze adverse medical events and close calls, as well as to identify the root causes of these events. Attendees were trained in a broad range of areas, including

- how to prepare and implement meaningful corrective actions based on their findings,
- how to conduct Healthcare Failure Modes and Effect Analysis (a proactive risk assessment) and develop and implement corresponding mitigation initiatives, and
- how to assess the effectiveness of interventions to better ensure the sustainability of effective interventions that improve patient safety.

Initial training of representatives from all fifty state departments of health and their private-sector partners was completed in 2006. Additional training sessions were offered in 2007 and completed in 2008. Twenty-two teams representing a number of states attended these sessions, as well as a group from Washington, D.C., and Puerto Rico. By its conclusion, more than 300 healthcare professionals from 210 organizations had participated in the program.

Medical Team Training

Medical Team Training was developed to improve patient outcomes through more effective communication and teamwork among providers. Since March 2005, the training program has facilitated more than 200-plus learning sessions that have involved more than 15,000 caregivers at VHA medical facilities nationwide (Mills, Neily & Dunn 2008).

The idea for Medical Team Training came from the realization that many adverse events in healthcare are related to miscommunication and teamwork failure. The aviation industry recognized this problem thirty years ago and developed Crew Resource Management to address communication failure in the cockpit. Crew Resource Management is defined as using all available sources—information, equipment, and people—to achieve safe and efficient operations (Dunn et al. 2007).

The National Center for Patient Safety began developing the Medical Team Training program in 2003. Phase I focused on operating room and surgical intensive care unit staff. The formal program, with evaluation and follow-up, started in August 2006 and ended in June 2009. Phase II extended the program to non-operating-room clinical areas and began in July 2009.

In a final Phase I update report dated August 30, 2010, teams from 121 VA Medical Centers (VAMCs) provided insight into the program's impact in the operating room:

- 69 percent reported improved teamwork and
- 66 percent indicated improved efficiency (better equipment use; improved first case on time starts).

Communication is a serious problem in healthcare, which is why the cornerstone of Medical Team Training Phase I was checklist-guided preoperative briefings and postoperative debriefings. Veterans Health Administration caregivers who received this training program "caught" 151 potentially adverse events, including problems with patient identification, lack of necessary equipment, and patient condition issues.

A VHA study in 2011 (Neily et al. 2011) analyzed data from 119,383 procedures at seventy-four VA facilities that provide care to veterans. The Medical Team Training program was implemented at forty-two facilities (57 percent). After adjusting for surgical risk, a decrease of 15 percent in morbidity rate was found for facilities in the program and a decrease of 10 percent for those not yet in the program. While the risk of surgical complications declined in both groups, the decline was 20 percent steeper in the Medical Team Training group.

Two previous studies had also indicated positive results. One showed a continued overall decrease in the number and severity of wrong site surgery in VHA (Young-Xu et al. 2011); another found an almost 50 percent greater decrease in the annual surgical mortality rate in VHA groups trained in Medical Team Training methods, as opposed to untrained groups (Neily et al. 2010).

Patient Safety Design Challenge

The Veterans Health Administration's patient safety managers could choose to participate in this voluntary challenge and have an opportunity to create a positive impact on design standards nationwide. Two categories were offered:

- architecture and design of medical care and treatment spaces and

- equipment layout, design, and procurement (such as code or medication carts).

During two challenges, held in 2006 and 2008, five teams were recognized for taking a creative approach to design.

Patient Safety Initiative

The Patient Safety Initiative was developed to stimulate creative approaches to complex patient safety issues at the local level. Participants submitted detailed proposals to the National Center for Patient Safety stating how a specific project would improve patient safety: Seventy-eight proposals were funded between fiscal year 2006 and fiscal year 2009. (U.S government fiscal years run from October 1 to September 30.)

Categories included a wide range of patient safety issues, such as education, infection prevention, and suicide prevention. Following are sample statistics from two projects:

- The fall rate decreased by 25 percent at the VAMC in Augusta, Georgia.
- The flu vaccination rate increased from 51 to 67 percent at the VAMC in Tomah, Wisconsin.

Patient Safety Fellowship Program

The VA Office of Academic Affiliations and the National Center for Patient Safety began offering one-year fellowships in patient safety in 2007. The National Center for Patient Safety manages the program, and funding is provided by the Office of Academic Affiliations. By 2011 thirty-six fellows had been selected.

The fellowships provide in-depth education in patient safety practice and leadership. The program links individualized, mentored training at a number of training sites around the nation to a state-of-the-art curriculum in the science of patient safety improvement. Participants include postresidency trained physicians and postdoctoral- or post-master's-degree-trained associated health professionals (such as nurses, psychologists, and healthcare administrators). Examples of the projects undertaken are:

- prevention of hemorrhage during dialysis,
- evaluation of falls injuries and strategies to prevent them,
- a curriculum for physician assistants, and
- evaluating root cause analysis effectiveness for patient safety improvement.

The fellowships begin with a week-long, intensive orientation to patient safety, including such topics as human factors engineering and understanding the root cause analysis and Healthcare Failure Mode Effect Analysis processes. Throughout the year, didactic and interactive learning sessions are continued using video-conferencing.

The Daily Plan®

The Daily Plan initiative enhances patient safety by involving patients in their care. A single document is provided to the patient that outlines what can be expected on a specific day of hospitalization. The plan received a positive response from patients and staff during pilot tests at five facilities, carried out in the fall of 2007 and winter of 2008, with the following results:

- Nearly 70 percent of the patients (101 evaluations) agreed or strongly agreed that having the plan made it easier for them to ask questions, increased their understanding of their hospital stay, and provided them with information that helped improve their care.
- Nurses (92 reports) were asked to reflect on assigned patients who had received the plan during their shifts and complete a single end-of-shift accumulated evaluation: 35 percent of the reports indicated one or more errors of omission were identified and corrected; 21 percent of the reports indicated prevention of other potential adverse events.

The patient is the only component of the healthcare delivery system that is always present, yet is the least likely to be used as a resource. Actively involving patients in their care is an important aspect of patient safety.

The VHA Product Recall Office

Pulling an unsafe product off the shelf and returning it to a supplier is one important way to safeguard the life or health of a patient. The National Center for Patient Safety took over the VHA product recall program in January 2008, and significant improvement has been shown in the on-time completion of Class 1 recalls. Products in this recall class can cause serious adverse health consequences or death if exposed to patients. Actions must be taken within twenty-four hours to remove these products from use. Class I recall compliance in May 2010 was 96.99 percent, up from 64 percent compliance in December 2008, following establishment of the Product Recall Office at the National Center for Patient Safety. Overall recall compliance in all classes has risen to and is holding at approximately 98 percent.

The Product Recall Office receives more than 12,500 recall notices from a variety of sources annually. Nearly 80 percent of these are not applicable. By posting only relevant recalls to the VHA Alerts and Recalls intranet site, the five-person Product Recall Office staff annually does work equivalent to more than 200 employees.

A recall can be due to a number of things, such as improper manufacturer labeling, compromised sterility, and contamination. Effective and timely response to a product recall is an important aspect of VHA's patient safety efforts.

Nursing Crew Resource Management and Clinical Crew Resource Management

Frontline nurses in multibed units deliver the majority of hands-on care and spend the most time with hospitalized patients. Nurses work in dynamic, safety-sensitive environments where they must juggle a supporting role on the medical team (partnering with physicians) with a leadership role on the patient care team (directing other nursing personnel and ancillary staff).

The ability to successfully function in this dual role is a critical challenge for nursing staff, at times demanding clinical leadership; at other times requiring an ability to practice assertive "followership."

The skills to meet this challenge may not always be present in frontline nursing staff, yet they are necessary to ensure that patient information is communicated in a timely manner among team members and that patient care is managed safely.

Patients can benefit if nurses receive training and tools that will help them succeed in their increasingly complex practice environments. The National Center for Patient Safety began providing this training through Nursing Crew Resource Management, a comprehensive program that was pilot-tested in early 2010 and was aimed specifically at VHA frontline nurses.

Whereas other team-building initiatives have focused on procedural-based areas with the physician as the primary team leader, the program takes Crew Resource Management concepts and modifies them for use in the context of an environment in which nurses routinely "touch" patients. Nursing Crew Resource Management provides nurses the core principles found in the disciplines of patient safety and human factors. It provides tangible tools that can be implemented in nursing units to build teamwork, improve performance, and manage human error.

In 2011 the National Center for Patient Safety began taking a more multidisciplinary approach to Crew Resource Management training, replacing Nursing Crew Resource Management with Clinical Crew Resource Management, which delivers the fundamental concepts of aviation's Crew Resource Management training program to all frontline VHA clinicians.

Issues

The National Center for Patient Safety faces a wide range of ongoing issues in its continuing effort to develop a "culture of safety" at VHA.

Cornerstone Recognition Program

Timely completion of root cause analyses, as well as the strength of actions developed by the teams, is an issue that the National Center for Patient Safety has addressed through the development of an incentive program. The Cornerstone

Recognition Program began in fiscal year 2008 to incentivize VHA facilities to complete stronger root cause analyses. The recognition criteria focus on timeliness and strength of actions, as well as reporting back on the impact of actions taken. Facilities can earn bronze, silver, or gold awards, based on the number of root cause analyses completed and the quality of those analyses.

One of the methods for determining whether a root cause analysis has been effective is through the concept of "strong strings," which are defined as any action with stronger or intermediate strength, a quantifiable outcome measure, and management concurrence:

- Seventy-one medical facilities achieved awards in fiscal year 2008 and 123 facilities by fiscal year 2011, indicating that nearly 80 percent of all VAMCs have achieved awards.

- The timeliness of root cause analyses has improved dramatically, from 44.5 percent completed within forty-five days in fiscal year 2006 to 97.7 percent within 45 days in fiscal year 2011.

- Facilities with at least one strong string in every root cause analysis have improved dramatically, from just 6.5 percent in fiscal year 2006 to 86.3 percent in fiscal year 2011.

Staff Publications

More than 245 articles have been published in external periodicals by National Center for Patient Safety staff members since the organization was established, on a wide range of patient safety topics. Following are two examples:

- "Teamwork and Communication in Surgical Teams: Implications for Patient Safety," *Journal of the American College of Surgeons* 206, no. 1 (2008): 207–212.

- "Using the Six Sigma Process to Implement the CDC Guideline for Hand Hygiene in Four Intensive Care Units," *Journal of General Internal Medicine* 21 (2006): S35–S42.

The first study to examine the implementation and effectiveness of a standardized checklist for mental health units, "A Checklist to Identify Inpatient Suicide Hazards in Veterans Affairs Hospitals," was published in the *Joint Commission Journal on Quality and Patient Safety* (Mills et al. 2010). The study indicated that 113 VA facilities were able to reduce the risks associated with 5,834 (76.3 percent) of the identified hazards.

Patient Safety Alerts and Advisories

The National Center for Patient Safety develops and publishes "Patient Safety Alerts" or "Advisories" online on specific issues relating to equipment, medications, and procedures that might cause harm to patients. Patient Safety Alerts communicate urgent notices that require immediate and specific action(s) by specific parties by a specified deadline. Advisories communicate recommendations and are more general in nature, and their implementation may be subject to local judgment.

Most alerts and advisories are shared with the public on the National Center for Patient Safety Web site. In some cases, when the information is only relevant to VHA employees, the information is placed on the National Center for Patient Safety intranet site. Meticulous preparation is required because of the scope and impact of actions that must be taken, in some cases, at all VAMCs (Veterans Health Administration 2010). More than 180 alerts and advisories have been published since 1999.

Reducing Adverse Drug Events

The National Center for Patient Safety received 232 medication-related root cause analysis reports and 181 aggregated review reports covering 20,724 adverse drug events reported in fiscal year 2008. The safety data analysis from these root cause analyses was used in drafting VHA's Anticoagulation Therapy Management Directive.

National Center for Patient Safety pharmacists worked collaboratively with the VHA Pharmacy Benefits Management Services in implementing the Adverse Drug Event Reporting and Monitoring Directive, published in September 2008, which established processes for reporting, monitoring, and surveillance of adverse drug events.

In 2010 pharmacists at the National Center for Patient Safety began working in conjunction with the Pharmacy Benefits Management Services to evaluate the impact of culture, age, and education on a proposed VHA evidence-based, patient-centric prescription label. The evaluation was completed through a structured in-person focus group questionnaire process. Participants were recruited from various regions around the United States to ensure broad representation by individuals of various cultural and ethnic groups. The data gathered have provided confirming evidence that the proposed standardized prescription label improves comprehension of the information on the label by veterans and caregivers independent of age, cultural background, or education level (National Center for Patient Safety 2011).

Many other drug-related safety vulnerabilities have been identified by National Center for Patient Safety pharmacists, culminating in a number of VHA Patient Safety Alerts.

Patient Safety Directives

The National Center for Patient Safety collaborates with other VA offices to develop specific guidelines for patient care efforts, such as the Ensuring Correct Surgery Directive. Like alerts and advisories, the impact of directives is felt in the day-to-day operations of VHA medical facilities around the nation (Department of Veterans Affairs 2010). Examples of other directives follow:

- Prevention of Retained Surgical Items
- Out-of-Operating-Room Airway Management
- Planning for Fire Response

Information Technology

Advocating for funds for patient-safety-related information technology projects is an important part of the National Center for Patient Safety's efforts. The center championed the creation of the VA Bar Code Resource Office and Patient Safety Office. As VA redefines excellence in the twenty-first century, the center is playing an integral part in numerous informatics initiatives, including

- use of real-time local tracking through radio frequency identification,
- bar code expansion/positive patient identification, and
- redesign of VA's pioneering Computerized Patient Record System.

The National Center for Patient Safety continues to work with the Bar Code Resource Office and Patient Safety Office to promote use of human factors engineering design principles in information technology.

Further Information

The Department of Veterans Affairs' patent safety program continues to move forward, developing new initiatives and refining past programs. Current, more detailed information is available at the National Center for Patient Safety's Web site (www.patientsafety.gov).

References

Bagian, J. (2002). Guest commentary: Patient safety: What is the goal and how do we get there? *Joint Commission Perspectives on Patient Safety* 2, no. 4: 6–6(1).

Bagian, J., et al. (2001). Developing and deploying a patient safety program in a large health care delivery system: you can't fix what you don't know about. *Journal on Quality Improvement* 27, no. 10: 522–532.

Bagian, J., et al. (2002). VA's root cause analysis system in action. *Journal on Quality Improvement* 28, no. 10: 531–545.

Department of Veterans Affairs. (2010). Directives. http://www1.va.gov/vapubs/search_action.cfm?dType=1 (accessed November 1, 2010).

DeRosier, J., Stalhandske, E., Bagian, J. & Nudell, T. (2002). Using healthcare failure mode and effect analysis: The VA National Center for Patient Safety's Prospective Risk Analysis System. *Journal on Quality Improvement* 28, no. 5: 248–267.

Dunn, E., et al. (2007). Medical team training: Applying crew resource management in the Veterans Health Administration. *Joint Commission Journal on Quality and Patient Safety* 33, no. 6: 317–325.

Gosbee, J. (2002). Human factors engineering and patient safety. *Quality & Safety in Health Care* 11: 352–354.

Gosbee, J. & Anderson, T. (2003). Human factors engineering design demonstrations can enlighten your RCA team. *Quality & Safety in Health Care* 12: 119–121.

Heget, J., Bagian, J., Lee, C. & Gosbee, J. (2002). System innovation: Veteran Health Administration National Center for Patient Safety. *Journal on Quality Improvement* 28, no. 12: 660–665.

Heinrich, H. W. & Granniss, E. R. (1959). *Industrial accident prevention: A scientific approach.* 4th ed. New York: McGraw-Hill.

Kohn, L. T., Corrigan, J. M. & Donaldson, M. S. (Eds.) (1999). *To err is human: building a safer health system.* Washington, DC: National Academy.

Mills, P., et al. (2010). A checklist to identify inpatient suicide hazards in Veterans Affairs hospitals. *Joint Commission Journal on Quality and Patient Safety* 36, no. 2: 87–93.

Mills P., Neily, J. & Dunn, E. (2008). Teamwork and communication in surgical teams: Implications for patient safety. *Journal of American College of Surgeons* 206, no. 1: 207–212.

Mills, P., Waldron, J., Quigley P., Stalhandske, E. & Weeks, W. (2003). Reducing falls and fall-related injuries in the VA system. *Journal of Healthcare Safety* 1: 25–33.

National Center for Patient Safety. (2004). Falls toolkit. http://www.patientsafety.gov/SafetyTopics/fallstoolkit/index.html (accessed March 26, 2012).

National Center for Patient Safety. Safety assessment codes. (2010). http://www4.va.gov/ncps/SafetyTopics/HFMEA/HFMEA_SAC.html (accessed March 26, 2012).

National Center for Patient Safety. (2011). Are prescription labels understood by our veterans? A snapshot of results from a new study. http://www.patientsafety.gov/TIPS/tips.html (accessed March 26, 2012).

National Center for Patient Safety. (2012). Summary of fourth National Patient Safety Survey. http://www.patientsafety.gov/TIPS/tips.html (accessed March 26, 2012).

Neily, J., et al. (2010). Association between implementation of a medical team training program and surgical mortality. *Journal of the American Medical Association* 304, no. 15: 1693–1700.

Neily, J., et al. (2011). Incorrect surgical procedures within and outside of the operating room: A follow-up report. *Archives of Surgery* 14, no.11: 1235–1239.

Veterans Health Administration. (2010). Alerts and advisories. http://www.patientsafety.gov/alerts.html (accessed March 26, 2012).

Veterans Health Administration. (2010). Directives. http://www.va.gov/vapubs/search_action.cfm?dType=1 (accessed June 27, 2012).

Young-Xu, Y., et al. (2011). Association between implementation of a medical team training program and surgical morbidity. *Archives of Surgery* 146, no. 12: 1368–1373.

Chapter 4

The National Center for PTSD

Matthew J. Friedman

The Veterans' Health Care Act of 1984 states:

> The Chief Medical Director shall establish and operate in the Department of Medicine and Surgery a National Center on Post-Traumatic-Stress Disorder. The National Center (1) shall carry out and promote the training of health care and related personnel in, and research into, the causes and diagnosis of PTSD and the treatment of Veterans for PTSD, and (2) shall serve as a resource center for, and promote and seek to coordinate the exchange of information regarding, all research and training activities carried out by the Veterans' Administration, and by other Federal and non-Federal entities, with respect to PTSD.

Although the medicalization of what is now called post-traumatic stress disorder (PTSD) can be traced back to the mid-nineteenth century, it wasn't until the late 1970s and early 1980s that the disorder demanded and received attention from the American public, the American Psychiatric Association, and the Veterans Administration. Growing public awareness of the plight of Vietnam veterans and the eloquent advocacy of the veteran community and its supporters no doubt resulted in gaining the attention of the American Psychiatric Association (APA) and the U.S. Congress. Such attention, however, occurred within a broader context of reports of psychiatric difficulties among former prisoners of war (from both World War II and the Korean conflict); concentration camp survivors of the Nazi Holocaust; and rape victims and battered women, whose cause was adopted by the feminist movement and championed by the National Organization for Women.

While the APA hotly debated the merits of including PTSD as a new diagnosis in its forthcoming revision of its *Diagnostic and Statistical Manual* (American Psychiatric Association 1980), Senator Alan Cranston and congressional colleagues, concerned about "post-Vietnam syndrome" among young veterans, passed several pieces of legislations that have had an enduring impact on VA programs, policy, and practice.

The Veterans Health Care Amendments of 1979 (P.L.96-22) established Readjustment Counseling's Vet Center program, which continues to flourish today. In 1983 Public Law 98-160 authorized the National Vietnam Veterans Readjustment Study, which demonstrated the prevalence, severity, and chronicity of PTSD among Vietnam veterans. Finally, the Veterans Health Care Act of 1984 (P.L. 98-528) stipulated that VA would establish the National Center for PTSD charged to "carry out and promote the training of health-care and related personnel in, and research into, the causes and diagnosis of PTSD and the treatment of Veterans for PTSD." The Center was created to serve as a "resource center" that "promoted and coordinated the exchange of information "regarding VA's research and training activities." It is quite significant, given subsequent history, that the Center's activities were not restricted to VA but were to "also coordinate the exchange of PTSD-related information with other Federal and non-Federal entities."

The Center's mission, based on interpretation of Public Law 98-528, has been "to promote the best clinical care and functional status of veterans through research, education and training related to the etiology, diagnosis and treatment of PTSD and stress-related disorders." From the outset, the Center has aspired to be the foremost leader in research and education on PTSD and stress. Over time it has become clear that one of the Center's highest priorities and greatest strengths has been the capacity to rapidly translate science into practice, and practice into science. With such an emphasis, Center staff have sought to develop practical clinical applications for experimental findings. The Center has also developed many rigorous laboratory protocols to test hypotheses generated by clinical observations. Primary stakeholders have been veterans and their families as well as VA clinicians, researchers, educators, program directors and policy makers. Outside of VA the Center has collaborated with many federal and academic partners, addressed many challenges with military and civilian colleagues, and helped to set the agenda for the field of traumatic stress.

This chapter reviews historical, clinical, scientific, and educational challenges the National Center has had to face since 1989. While meeting these challenges, the Center has developed a research and educational portfolio with sufficient breadth, depth, and balance to meet the needs of VA as well as the trauma field in general. The chapter also lists the Center's most significant accomplishments. The chapter concludes with speculation on the potential role of the National Center in the future.

Origin

The first National Center for PTSD was established in 1984 at a Midwestern VA Medical Center. In 1988 it was determined that this Center had not fulfilled the stipulations of Public Law 98-528. As a result, VA invited proposals for a new National Center for PTSD.

Convinced that no single VA site could meet the congressional mandate, five of us joined together and proposed that a multisite consortium was needed to actualize Senator Cranston's vision and to achieve the Act's objectives. We proposed that by integrating our different perspectives, expertise, and institutional resources, we could establish a national center in which the whole far exceeded the sum of its parts. In the same way that a group medical practice includes different specialists (e.g., internists, surgeons, pediatricians, psychiatrists, etc.) we built the National Center for PTSD around preexisting VA areas of strength that enjoyed strong local support from the affiliated medical school.

Terry Keane, a psychologist and established expert in psychological and psychophysiological assessment who had already conducted one of the first trials of cognitive-behavioral therapy for PTSD, agreed to head the Behavioral Science Division, based at VA Medical Center Boston, and affiliated first with Tufts University and later with Boston University. Dennis Charney at the VAMC in West Haven, Connecticut, and Yale University, a well-known biological psychiatrist who had made major contributions regarding pathophysiological and brain function abnormalities in depression and panic disorder, had begun to turn his attention to PTSD. He agreed to lead our Clinical Neurosciences Division. Fred Gusman, a social worker at the Menlo Park division of the VA Medical Center in Palo Alto, California (affiliated with Stanford), had established the largest inpatient PTSD program in the world. As a prominent figure in VA-wide PTSD training conferences, he agreed to lead our Educational and Clinical Laboratory (later renamed our Dissemination and Training) Division. Bob Rosenheck, a psychiatrist at both the VAMC in West Haven and at Yale, as director of VA's Northeast Program Evaluation Center was in charge of program evaluation of all specialized PTSD programs throughout the VA system; he agreed to head our Evaluation Division. This author, based at the VAMC in White River Junction, Vermont and Dartmouth College, established the National Center's Executive Division. Since Dartmouth's Baker Library was at the forefront of computerized bibliographic database technology, we also established the National PTSD Resource Center at the Executive Division.

We achieved our full complement of seven divisions in 1993. Spurred by growing interest and support for programs dedicated to female veterans, we upgraded the robust women's program in Boston, under the creative leadership of Jessica Wolfe, a psychologist, to our Women's Health Sciences Division. Finally, growing commitment to PTSD-related programs for Pacific Islander and Asian American veterans led to the establishment of our Pacific Islands Division in Honolulu under the direction of Ray Scurfield, a social worker. Ray had previously worked in the Vet Center program and later directed a specialized inpatient PTSD unit.

Historical Challenges

An unexpected fact of life for National Center staff has been that the morning headlines might determine one's work for the next days, weeks, or months. This realization became manifest six weeks after we were established, when the main hospital building and surrounding structures at the Palo Alto VA were destroyed by the Loma Prieta earthquake of 1989. Within days of this disaster, Center staff from Palo Alto had established a clinic near the earthquake's epicenter in Santa Cruz and developed collaborative initiatives with local VA and civilian authorities, the American Red Cross, and the Oakland Naval Hospital. Although we had not anticipated that the National Center would be involved in natural disasters, this event set the stage for a major emphasis on disaster mental health, described later in this chapter. Since then the Center has worked closely with a number of VA and civilian (especially the Substance Abuse and Mental Health Services Administration, and the Centers for Disease Control) authorities on a number of disasters, most notably Hurricane Katrina and its aftermath.

Our disaster mental health activities thrust us into a leadership position alongside other federal partners, culminating in a remarkable conference that we codirected with the Department of Defense in 2001, on mental health and mass violence (National Institute of Mental Health 2002). What was especially interesting was that we had been planning this event for eight months and had scheduled it for October 31, 2001, six weeks after the 9/11 attacks on the World Trade Center and Pentagon. After considering cancellation, we held the conference. It was attended by sixty international experts and produced a number of consensus recommendations that guided the national agenda in disaster mental health for many years. One of the most significant results of that conference was the determination to produce the Psychological First Aid Manual, which the National Center issued in partnership with the

National Child Traumatic Stress Network. Ironically, the Psychological First Aid manual was ready just in time for Hurricane Katrina in 2005, so we were able to post it on our Web site (www.ptsd.va.gov/professional/manuals/psych-first-aid.asp) and make it available to VA and civilian disaster mental health workers.

Because of our long-standing collaboration with the Substance Abuse and Mental Health Service's Emergency Disaster Branch in its Center for Mental Health Services, the National Center was actively involved in the mental health response to the 9/11 attacks at both the national level and in close collaboration with New York's Office of Mental Health. Since then we have done case history studies of the mental health system responses both in New York and Oklahoma City (following the bombing of the Federal Building), both of which have informed federal emergency disaster policy. We have also worked with federal partners to develop policy, produce educational material, and initiate research projects concerning both clinical and public health interventions following mass violence or natural disasters.

One final lesson from the civilian disaster response work was that it had a direct benefit to VA. All of our work on the Psychological First Aid manual and other disaster-related initiatives was funded by non-VA sources (e.g., the Substance Abuse and Mental Health Services Administration, the National Institute of Mental Health, and the Centers for Disease Control). Yet we were able to make the Psychological First Aid manual and our disaster expertise available at no cost to VA. In my opinion, this illustrates the wisdom of Senator Cranston and colleagues when they developed the Veterans' Health Care Act of 1984. Because the National Center was permitted to collaborate with non-VA federal partners, VA and veterans have gained significant and unexpected benefits.

The Persian Gulf War in 1990–1991 had an even greater impact on Center program development than the Loma Prieta earthquake. Prior to Iraq's invasion of Kuwait, our focus had been entirely on chronic PTSD among Vietnam veterans. The Gulf War turned our attention to acute post-traumatic reactions and early intervention. Before the fighting started, there was great concern that if, as some predicted, tens of thousands of American troops might be injured in Iraq, it would overwhelm the Department of Defense's (DoD) hospital capacity. Because of this concern, many VA hospitals were prepared to accept fresh casualties from the Gulf. Joint trainings were conducted between military and VA clinical staff. This included National Center staff and DoD mental health personnel. Such collaborations continued after the war, as great attention was directed to understanding "Gulf War syndrome" and whether it had anything to do with PTSD or any other psychiatric disorder.

The impact of the Gulf War experience on the National Center was profound. It turned Center attention to acute stress reactions, early intervention, and prevention. It provided the context and opportunity for us to initiate our first research on resilience at Fort Bragg, North Carolina. Expanding our scope from traumatic stress to stress in general was extremely relevant to our work in both military and disaster mental health. The Gulf War sparked our first major Center exercise in translating science into practice, because expert investigators made contributions to our Operation Desert Storm Clinicians' Packet, which provided guidance for assessment and treatment of recently returned service members and their families. Finally, it opened the door for collaborative relationships with many military colleagues that continue to this day.

The Center's growing focus on military and disaster mental health thrust us into partnership with a number of federal departments and agencies, most notably the DoD, the Substance Abuse and Mental Health Services Administration, the Centers for Disease Control and Prevention (CDC), and the National Institute of Mental Health. The Substance Abuse and Mental Health Services Administration's Emergency Disaster Branch initiated a nine-year partnership in 1999 to address the consequences of the bombing of the Oklahoma City Federal Building. Therefore, we had robust collaborations with several federal partners by the time the World Trade Center and Pentagon were attacked on September 11, 2001. As a result, we began to actively work in a consultative capacity at the federal level and with mental health officials in New York City and state. The Substance Abuse and Mental Health Services Administration, in particular, supported many National Center activities for several years, which led to the development of the Psychological First Aid manual on the one hand (in partnership with the National Child Traumatic Stress Network) and, on the other, the subsequent establishment of the National Center for Disaster Mental Health Research (involving the National Center's Executive and Clinical Neurosciences Divisions as well as the Universities of Michigan and South Carolina and Columbia University).

September 11 also affected National Center programs directly. We began to appreciate the importance of a public health approach to psycho-education when more than 45,000 individuals visited our Web site (www.ptsd.va.gov) in a single day to access the dozens of fact sheets we had posted regarding normal human stress reactions, advice to parents, guidance to clinicians, and effective early interventions. The 9/11 attacks also stimulated Center research on the acute response to traumatic stress, psychological and biological processes that mediate and moderate these reactions, and research on early interventions that might be effective. The Center played a leading role in convening national conferences on science and practice following mass violence and disasters.

The most recent events are Operation Enduring Freedom and Operation Iraqi Freedom. Drawing from our experience producing the Operation Desert Storm Clinicians' Guide to assist VA clinicians working with Gulf War veterans, we produced the Iraq War Clinicians' Guide, in partnership with Walter Reed Army Medical Center. This latter initiative was produced for our Web site so that it could be disseminated more quickly than the hard copy booklet we put together during the Gulf War. We posted the guide so that it would be immediately available to practitioners. It provided the most current information about acute and chronic post-traumatic stress responses; assessment guidelines; sections on treatment of returning veterans; and special sections on medical casualty evacuees, military sexual trauma, special problems of amputees, dealing with family issues, traumatic grief, educational materials for veterans and their families, and clinicians' self-care. We later rewrote the guide for nonprofessionals so that it was accessible to veterans and their families. This material was also posted on our Web site.

Many National Center staff have collaborated with the military directly. Most notably, Patricia Resick trained clinicians from all branches of the military in the United States and abroad in cognitive processing therapy. Steve Southwick developed resilience programs for troops as well as a research program at Fort Drum, New York. Fred Gusman provided training for marines at Camp Pendleton, California. Brett Litz and Patricia Watson worked with the army and marines, while many others participated in DoD training and research collaborations based at the Uniform Services University of Health Sciences and on national research and policy oversight committees.

What we have learned from these events is that a National Center must always be ready to drop what it is doing to support national leadership during times of war and national emergencies. Because we have adopted this stance, we have discovered that such unplanned interruptions in ongoing programs usually open up new, exciting, unimagined opportunities that have expanded and enriched the Center's portfolio, vision, and scope.

Major Accomplishments

The breadth of our research program has extended from genetic research and brain imaging, to multisite randomized clinical trials, to epidemiologic surveys, to program evaluation of every PTSD program in the VA system. Our work has identified abnormalities in behavior, sleep, cognition, memory, physiological reactivity, and hormonal regulation, as well as in brain structure and function associated with PTSD. The Center has developed some of the major instruments used in PTSD screening and assessment (see below). Our Web site (www.ptsd.va.gov) has emerged as the most comprehensive Internet source of information on PTSD; it provides information for veterans, their families, mental health practitioners, researchers, program planners, policy makers, and the general public. The site also hosts PILOTS (Published International Literature on Traumatic Stress), the largest and most comprehensive bibliographic database on traumatic stress in the world, which has indexed over 46,000 citations. Clinicians, scientists, and others have benefited from our two publications, the *PTSD Research Quarterly* and *CTU Online* (*Clinician's Trauma Update*) (see below). During its first twenty years, National Center authors published 2,500 articles, chapters, and books; made more than 4,400 scientific or educational presentations; and obtained approximately $222 million in extramural funding for over 520 peer-reviewed research projects. I focus here on major clinical, scientific, and educational challenges that we have encountered since 1989. A more comprehensive review is available through our annual reports, which are posted on our Web site.

Clinical Challenges

Unlike the National Centers for PTSD in Australia and Japan, the U.S. National Center for PTSD does not provide direct clinical care. This was stipulated in Public Law 98-528. Therefore, our best way of helping veterans with PTSD has been by supporting VA clinicians who provide their care. We have done so through the development of assessment tools and treatment manuals, provision of ongoing training programs, production and posting of Web-based materials, and direct support through mentoring of and consultation with PTSD program directors and practitioners.

Assessment Tools

When we had our first meeting in 1989, we all were concerned that there was no recognized instrument for assessing PTSD, as there were for other psychiatric diagnoses. This concern led to the development and standardization of the Clinician Administered PTSD Scale (CAPS). It is useful both for diagnostic assessment and for quantitating the severity of PTSD symptoms (Blake et al. 1990; Blake et al. 1995), has now been translated into several languages, and is universally recognized as the gold standard for the field.

Because the CAPS is a structured clinical interview, there was also need for a well-validated self-assessment tool. Again with the primary leadership coming from our Behavioral Science Division, the PTSD Checklist (PCL) was developed (Weathers et al., 1993). It has become one of the most widely used questionnaires to assess PTSD in veteran, military, and civilian settings.

Annabel Prins and colleagues (Prins et al. 2004) developed the most widely used screening tool in clinical use, the Primary Care PTSD Scale. As its name implies, this scale was originally developed as a PTSD screening instrument for use in primary care settings, and it has been utilized as such throughout VA as well as in military settings. In addition, the DoD has utilized the scale in its massive pre- and postdeployment health assessment program for troops deployed to Iraq or Afghanistan.

Finally, Dan King and Lynda King, along with Dawne Vogt, developed the most comprehensive assessment instrument for war-related stress, the Deployment Risk and Resilience Inventory. In addition to measuring combat exposure, this instrument assesses concerns about family disruptions, perceived threat in the war zone, uncomfortable living conditions, and postdeployment social support and stressors (Vogt et al. 2008). This inventory is being used in many current studies of postwar adjustment among veterans deployed to Iraq or Afghanistan, including Jennifer Vasterling's large-scale pre/postdeployment survey, The Neurocognition Deployment Health Study (Vasterling et al. 2010).

Dissemination and Training of New Treatments

The National Center has played a major role in disseminating the two most effective treatments for PTSD, prolonged exposure and cognitive processing therapy. Evidence generated by the Center's Craig Rosen showed that only 10 percent of VA practitioners were utilizing either treatment on a regular basis (Rosen et al. 2004), despite the consensus of all PTSD clinical practice guidelines that these were the two best treatments for PTSD (Forbes et al. 2010). Based on the results of our large multisite VA cooperative study demonstrating the efficacy of prolonged exposure among female veterans and active duty personnel (Schnurr et al. 2007), as well as our single site trial showing the effectiveness of cognitive processing therapy for male veterans (Monson et al. 2006), VA's Office of Mental Health Services launched a massive training program in these two treatments for VA practitioners. Patricia Resick, who developed cognitive processing therapy and directs our Women's Health Sciences Division in Boston, has led its roll-out, until recently, which (at the time of this writing) has trained approximately 5,900 VA (as well as many military and Readjustment Counseling) therapists in this treatment. In addition, 48 trainers and 514 consultants have been certified in cognitive processing therapy. Joe Ruzek, who directs the Dissemination and Training Division in Palo Alto, has led the prolonged exposure roll-out, which has trained approximately 1.330 VA clinicians and certified 16 trainers and 70 consultants.

There are other notable activities directly relevant to clinical practice. These include National Center leadership of the 2010 VA/Department of Defense Clinical Practice Guidelines for PTSD and leadership of the American Psychiatric Association's current revision of PTSD diagnostic criteria for its forthcoming fifth edition of the *Diagnostic and Statistical Manual*. Leslie Morland (Morland et al. 2010) at the Pacific Islands Division has emerged as a national leader in telemental health treatment for PTSD. Finally, the Center has recently convened two consensus conferences to identify best practices for complicated patients with PTSD, mild traumatic brain injury, and pain on the one hand and PTSD and co-occurring substance use disorders on the other.

In recent years, both VA and the DoD have promoted integrated primary/mental health models of care. This has shifted the locus of screening, diagnostic assessment, and treatment (when feasible) into the primary care setting. Besides conducting research on this model of care, the National Center has been promoting such an approach for more than a decade, having convened the first and second VA Primary Care/Mental Health Summits in 1999 and 2000. In the spirit of translating science into practice, Paula Schnurr and other investigators had shown the association between PTSD and medical illness (Schnurr & Green 2004), another reason for clinical collaborations between medical and mental health practitioners.

Mentoring and Consultation Programs

During the past five years there have been two major challenges to provision of PTSD services to veterans. First, there has been a great influx of recently deployed veterans requesting care; besides their increased demand for services, these new veterans are much younger and their PTSD is more acute than has been the case with veterans of previous wars. Second, there has been a major recruitment of thousands of new mental health personnel, many of whom were assigned to PTSD programs, often with little experience treating war-related PTSD. In its 2007 annual report, the Under Secretary for Health's Special Committee on PTSD expressed concern that the expansion of PTSD programs and greater demand for services had not been accompanied by a training component for program directors to provide them with the necessary proficiencies and management skills for implementing the best administrative and clinical practices.

In 2008 VA's Office of Mental Health Services asked the National Center to implement the Special Committee's recommendation. Under the leadership of Nancy Bernardy and with major support by the Executive, Evaluation, and Dissemination and Training Divisions, the PTSD Mentoring Program was launched in April 2008. The program has operated on two levels: mentoring for program directors and establishment of a very effective communication network.

With regard to its primary goal, two senior clinicians/administrators with experience in both PTSD treatment and program management were appointed in each of VA's twenty-two Veterans Integrated Services Networks (VISNs). The forty-four mentors meet with Dr. Bernardy at least once a month (and on an as-needed basis) to report on problems and concerns that have arisen in any of the specialized PTSD programs within their networks. Mentors also meet individually with each PTSD program director in their network to provide guidance on a wide range of clinical challenges, including assessment, referral, balancing the needs of new veterans with those of older veterans, implementation of evidence-based treatment, maintaining staff cohesion and morale, and other matters. In addition, the mentors have become a community of practice unto themselves, in which they can share problems and solutions. For example, if mentors in one network are struggling with a clinical challenge that has been effectively solved in another network, the Mentoring Program provides the infrastructure and communication network through which such exemplary practices can be disseminated throughout the system.

The Mentoring Program has also provided a conduit for two-way communication between practitioners in the field and mental health leadership in the VA Central Office through a steering committee that includes mental health leadership, network mental health liaisons, and National Center personnel involved in the program. Through this mechanism, the VA Central Office and network mental health leadership can be quickly informed about problems in the field much sooner than usual. On the other hand, Dr. Bernardy routinely provides clarification and guidance to the field regarding Central Office policies or urgent requests concerning specialized PTSD program access, treatment, administrative requirements, evidence-based treatment, and so forth.

Finally, the Mentoring Program has served an educational function. A very successful monthly psychopharmacology lecture series is regularly attended by hundreds of practitioners. This series has recently been converted to a monthly Grand Rounds format, which will utilize clinical cases to address key clinical challenges and will not be limited to medication issues. Also, educational materials are regularly posted on a VA intranet SharePoint site accessible to all VA practitioners.

A recent survey indicates that the program has been very well received in the field. Scheduled and as-needed conference calls are considered extremely beneficial. Program directors feel more connected to other PTSD programs, more supported, more in tune with the goals of Central Office leadership, more up-to-date in learning about innovations in PTSD care, and better equipped to implement best practices for PTSD treatment.

The success of the Mentoring Program prompted Central Office leadership to authorize the National Center to establish a PTSD Consultation Program to improve the quality of PTSD treatment throughout the system. Whereas the Mentoring Program provides primary administrative support for PTSD program directors, the Consultation Program will be open to any VA practitioner providing PTSD treatment in a specialized program, a mental hygiene clinic, a primary care setting, or a community-based outpatient clinic. The Center's Consultation Program began operations on February 1, 2011.

The Mentoring and Consultation Programs have ushered in a major shift in the National Center's mission. Although the Center still does not provide direct clinical care, it is now linked to first-line mental health practitioners as never before. Besides providing direct clinical consultation, the National Center will have a much greater opportunity to reach its audience of VA practitioners and equip them with the most advanced guidance on PTSD treatment through training, provision of assessment and treatment tools, and Web-based dissemination of the latest information on PTSD and related disorders.

Program Evaluation

Since 1990 the Evaluation Division (which is also a part of VA's Northeast Program Evaluation Center) has been monitoring clinical utilization of all specialized PTSD programs in its annual report, The Long Journey Home. This information has been utilized at both national and local levels for program planning and resource allocation purposes. In 1994 Dr. Rosenheck, who directed the Evaluation Division until recently, developed a methodology for producing the annual Mental Health Report Card, which made it possible to assess clinical outcomes as well as utilization of each program (Rosenheck, Fontana & Stolar 1999). Ongoing monitoring of quality of care provided the information needed by the Office of Mental Health Services to set policies on clinical practice. Furthermore, the data generated through this and other archival sources have led to a very productive series of scientific papers on mental health service delivery and practice patterns.

The Evaluation Division has also monitored inpatient PTSD care. Its data played a decisive role in clinical policy when it showed that specialized inpatient PTSD units, with long lengths of stay, had poorer outcomes than hospital programs with much briefer inpatient treatment programs (Fontana & Rosenheck 1997). Utilization of archival data sets has enabled the

Evaluation Division to address a number of critical issues. These include longitudinal studies of service utilization by veterans with chronic PTSD (Johnson et al. 2004), service utilization by racial minority veterans (Rosenheck & Fontana 2002), a twenty-year review of VA's inpatient programs for PTSD (Rosenheck, Fontana & Errera 1997), and prescribing practices of VA physicians treating PTSD (Mohamed & Rosenheck 2008).

Dr. Rosenheck and his successor, Rani Desai, have played an important role in the Mentoring Program. The Long Journey Home database and ongoing program evaluation have made it possible to provide additional supervision and assistance to struggling programs that have not met national norms. Such assistance is provided through the Mentoring Program's usual mechanisms, as well as through site visits directed by Nancy Bernardy.

Research

The National Center has helped to set the scientific agenda for the field of traumatic stress studies. Because of space limitations this section is restricted to psychophysiology research, neurobiology research, clinical trials, epidemiology research, survey research, and research on women.

Psychophysiology

Abram Kardiner (1941), impressed by physiological hyperactivity among World War I veterans with "war neurosis," called it a physioneurosis. The importance of this observation was that it suggested that PTSD was much more than a mental abnormality, as suggested by prevailing psychoanalytic theories at that time. The first large-scale study of this important insight was Cooperative Study no. 334 conducted in 1990–1992 and co-chaired by Terry Keane. This fifteen-site trial was the first large-scale study on PTSD ever funded by VA. Findings from this study showed that veterans with current PTSD were much more likely to exhibit a heightened physiological (e.g., heart rate, skin conductance, etc.) response to trauma cues (e.g., reminders of Vietnam War–related stressors) than Vietnam veterans without PTSD (Keane et al. 1998). It has also been shown that baseline (tonic) cardiovascular activity was elevated among veterans with PTSD (Buckley & Kaloupek 2001)

Neurobiology

When the National Center was established in 1989, the scant evidence for neurobiological abnormalities was based on psychophysiological, urinary neurohormonal, and sleep laboratory findings. PTSD super-suppression of cortisol following dexamethasone administration was first observed by Rachel

Yehuda and other Center investigators, thereby confirming that the hypothalamic-pituitary-adrenocortical system is dysregulated in PTSD (Yehuda et al. 1993). Initially directed by Dennis Charney and currently under the excellent leadership of John Krystal, the Clinical Neurosciences Division has opened many areas of neurobiological research for the field.

Since that time National Center investigators have been in the forefront of research demonstrating alterations in structural and brain function associated with PTSD. Historically, the most notable finding was a reduction in hippocampal volume associated with war-related PTSD (Bremner et al. 1995). This study made both scientific and lay media headlines because it suggested that traumatic stress could damage the brains of veterans with PTSD. Subsequently, National Center investigators, utilizing functional magnetic resonance imaging, observed significant reductions in anterior cingulate cortex volume (Woodward et al. 2006) as well as PTSD-related reductions in cerebrospinal fluid and cranial volumes (Woodward et al. 2007).

Abnormalities detected in cerebral blood flow, based on functional magnetic resonance imaging, indicating dysregulation of the noradrenergic system, was another key early finding (Southwick et al. 1993). Finally, the demonstration among veterans with PTSD of a significant correlation between the re-experiencing cluster and beta 2 nicotinic acetylcholine receptor availability (utilizing single photon emission computed tomography) (Czermak et al. 2008) is a more recent example of National Center brain imaging research to localize specific neurochemical disturbances in PTSD related to particular brain regions.

Other seminal neurobiological research, conducted mostly at our Clinical Neurosciences Division, includes research on gene X environment interactions and our resilience program. Joel Gelernter's laboratory has been involved in many important collaborative studies showing that a specific allele of the serotonin transporter gene was associated with increased vulnerability to PTSD among civilian hurricane survivors (Koenen et al. 2009). Joan Kaufman showed that the vulnerability to depression associated with this genotype among maltreated children could be offset by social support (Kaufman et al. 2004).

Some of the first biological studies of resilience were carried out in collaboration with the army at Fort Bragg, North Carolina, with regular and special forces troops exposed to extreme stress. In two groundbreaking studies it was shown that resilience (exhibited significantly more by special forces than by regular troops) was associated with the capacity to mobilize neuropeptide Y (Morgan et al. 2000) and dehydroepiandrosterone (DHEA) (Morgan et al. 2004).

Finally, there is an ongoing effort to establish a National PTSD Brain Bank through a partnership between the National Center and the Uniform Services

University of Health Sciences. Preliminary efforts based on postmortem examination of brains of deceased individuals with documented PTSD, coupled
with laboratory studies of animals exposed to inescapable shock, have identified a protein that may be a biomarker for PTSD (Zhang et al. 2008).

Clinical Trials

Treatment research ranks as one of the National Center's top priorities. Three
large-scale multisite VA Cooperative Studies have been undertaken by Center
investigators testing group therapy for PTSD: Cooperative Study no. 420
(Schnurr et al. 2003) on prolonged exposure therapy; Cooperative Study no.
494 (Schnurr et al. 2007) on augmentation of pharmacotherapy with the atypical antipsychotic agent, risperidone; and Cooperative Study no. 504 (Krystal
et al. 2011) The prolonged exposure study is especially noteworthy because it
exemplifies the National Center's capacity to translate science into practice. Following the successful demonstration of the efficacy of prolonged exposure on
female veteran and active duty personnel, the Office of Mental Health Services
invited the National Center to develop a training program for VA practitioners
so that they could provide this evidence-based treatment to veterans. This
became the prolonged exposure roll-out under the direction of Joe Ruzek
(described previously). Similarly, before joining the National Center to lead our
Women's Division, Patricia Resick, who had developed cognitive processing
therapy, directed the roll-out for that treatment (also described previously),
which has trained thousands of VA and DoD clinicians in this treatment.
Finally, John Krystal and Bob Rosenheck's recently published clinical trial
showing that risperidone augmentation of antidepressant pharmacotherapy for
PTSD has no beneficial effect, has resulted in a modification of the VA/DoD
clinical practice guideline for PTSD; as a result of these findings, atypical antipsychotics are no longer recommended as adjunctive treatments.

Other psychotherapies that have been investigated include cognitive behavioral couples therapy (Monson, Stevens & Schnurr 2005). Research on Seeking Safety, a treatment for comorbid PTSD and substance use disorder, is
currently ongoing (under the direction of Rachel Kimerling). Randomized
clinical trials of medication include a multisite trial of the selective serotonin
reuptake inhibitor sertraline (Friedman et al. 2007), and of naltrexone and
disulfram for comorbid PTSD and alcohol dependence (Petrakis et al. 2006).

Center investigators have also tested innovations in treatment delivery. Brett
Litz and military colleagues (2007) tested an Internet-based cognitive-behavioral
therapy approach for active duty army personnel called DE-STRESS that was
successful in a pilot study. Leslie Morland and colleagues (2010) demonstrated

that cognitive-behavioral therapy delivered via video in a telemental health format was just as effective as traditional face-to-face treatment. Craig Rosen and colleagues (2006) have tested telephone follow-up following PTSD treatment. Paula Schnurr and I are completing a comparison of integrated primary mental healthcare for PTSD delivered in a primary care setting versus treatment as usual. Finally, a number of Center investigators are participating in DoD-funded treatment research for active duty personnel as well as veterans. Most notable are clinical trials of individual versus group cognitive processing therapy, augmentation of prolonged exposure with d-cycloserine, and acceptance and commitment therapy. Medication trials for Veterans with comorbid PTSD and mild traumatic brain injury include ganaxalone (to potentiate the adrenal steroid allopregnanolone), methylphenidate (a dopamine enhancer used with traumatic brain injury alone), and galantamine (an acetylcholinesterase inhibitor).

In short, our treatment portfolio of clinical trials is diverse and relevant.

Epidemiological and Survey Research

Center investigators have been involved in several epidemiological and other large surveys. The National Vietnam Veterans Readjustment Study (Schlenger et al. 1992) was the first large-scale, rigorous epidemiological survey undertaken by any nation to assess the psychological impact of war. Its landmark findings—that 30 percent of male and 25 percent of female veterans had had PTSD at some point since deployment, and that 15 percent and 8 percent, respectively, were still symptomatic when the study was conducted in the late 1980s—had major implications for VA clinical policy and practice. Though not an investigator, Terry Keane's stewardship of this study was extremely important for its completion. He is currently working on a follow-up, the National Vietnam Veterans Lifetime Study, which promises to provide valuable longitudinal data on mental and medical health.

The National Vietnam Veterans Readjustment Study also found differences in PTSD prevalence between white, black, Hispanic, and female veterans. One result was that the National Center was mandated by Congress to carry out the Matsunaga Study (named after the former Senator from Hawaii, Spark Matsunaga), a survey of Vietnam veterans who were not included in the National Vietnam Veterans Readjustment Study, such as American Indian (Beals et al. 2002) and Asian Pacific Islander veterans (Friedman et al. 2004). The Matsunaga Study found higher PTSD prevalence (compared to Caucasians) among Northern Plains and Southwest Indian tribes as well as among Native Hawaiians. In contrast, Americans of Japanese ancestry showed lower PTSD prevalence than White veterans.

I have already mentioned the Neurocognition Deployment Health Study of recently deployed veterans led by Jennifer Vasterling (Vasterling et al. 2010) This large survey is distinctive because each active duty or military reservist was assessed prior to deployment and subsequently after demobilization. This is an extremely valuable cohort that will be followed for many years. In addition to measurement of PTSD, depression, and other psychiatric disorders, this study has monitored cognitive function. Given the prominence of traumatic brain injury due to blast injuries suffered in Iraq and Afghanistan, this will be an extremely valuable cohort to follow for decades.

Other smaller surveys have monitored the psychological health of veterans following the Gulf War (Wolfe, Keane & Young 1996) and the United Nations peacekeeping deployment to Somalia (Litz et al. 1997).

Fran Norris has support from the Substance Abuse and Mental Health Services Administration to monitor psychological health among survivors of Hurricane Katrina along the Gulf Coast. Given the diaspora of many former residents of Louisiana, Alabama, and Mississippi, her research has necessitated tracking Katrina survivors in more than thirty states. Under the dual aegis of the National Center for PTSD and the National Center for Mental Health Disaster Research (which she directs), she is currently following hundreds of survivors of Hurricane Ike, which flooded Galveston, Texas, and adjacent areas along the Texas Gulf Coast in 2008. Dr. Norris's team is measuring psychological health, cortisol levels, genotype, and clinical response to several interventions.

Research on Women

The Center has been at the forefront of research on female veterans with PTSD. In 1990 Jessica Wolfe at the Behavioral Science Division developed the Women's Military Exposure Scale. In the process, she demonstrated that some items geared for male veterans had to be modified in a scale for women (Wolfe 1996).

In 1993, when the Women's Health Sciences Division was established, Dr. Wolfe became its director. Joan Furey, who directed the Center's program for women veterans at Palo Alto, later became the first director of VA's Center for Women Veterans in the VA Central Office.

Dr. Wolfe's 1998 study on sexual harassment as a predictor of PTSD among female Gulf War military personnel (Wolfe et al. 1998) was the first of a series of articles produced by Center investigators at the Women's Division concerning military sexual trauma. The major impetus for this line of research grew out of Congress's Millennium Bill in 2000, which mandated a survey on the incidence of military sexual trauma among both female and male military reservists. Under the direction of Amy Street, 4,500 former reservists were surveyed, among whom 60 percent of women and 25 percent of men reported that they had experienced sexual trauma and/or sexual harassment during military service (Street et al. 2008). As a result of this study and subsequent work, VA has initiated military sexual trauma screening and counseling throughout the system (Kimerling et al. 2008; Kimerling et al. 2010). The National Center hosts military sexual trauma programs (funded by the Office of Mental Health Services) both at Boston and Palo Alto under the direction of Amy Street and Rachel Kimerling, respectively.

Another notable project is a longitudinal study of women and men who enlisted in the marines at Parris Island, South Carolina. Jilian Shipherd is currently assessing adaptation, retention, military sexual trauma, and psychological health among this cohort (Shipherd et al. 2009). This is a long-term follow-up of research initiated by Dr. Wolfe.

National Center investigators (Vogt et al. 2006) have conducted services research to monitor and understand women's experiences within VA, including utilization of clinical services and staff gender awareness.

A consistent finding in most epidemiological studies is that women are twice as likely to develop PTSD as men. Ann Rasmusson is conducting research to determine whether hormonal factors may contribute to such increased vulnerability (Rasmusson et al. 2006).

Finally, Dr. Resick continues her research training and dissemination efforts with regard to cognitive processing therapy. A recent, very provocative finding from a dismantling study of cognitive processing therapy was that the cognitive component alone was more effective than the (written) exposure component (Resick et al. 2008).

Educating Providers and Veterans

Public Law 98-528 mandated that the National Center should be in the forefront of research and education on the causes and treatment of PTSD. It was much easier to know how to develop research than an educational program. For research, it is pretty clear that one needs to develop a hypothesis, generate some promising pilot data, write a research grant, carry out the funded studies, and publish the results. Such a clear path was not apparent with regard to education. There were traditional approaches, to be sure, such as hands-on training programs, lectures and workshops at conferences, publication of clinical and scientific articles, and development of treatment manuals and assessment tools. We have done and continue to do all of those things with some measure of success. Most notable is the Clinical Training Program at Palo Alto, which has provided ten week-long clinical practicums per year for VA clinicians. Participants receive a thorough tutorial in assessment, treatment, and management of complex patients. This highly acclaimed program has trained approximately 140 clinicians per year since 1989, or roughly 2,300 VA practitioners.

As noted previously, during its first twenty years Center professionals produced 2,500 publications and made over 4,400 scientific or educational presentations. There was also the *PTSD Research Quarterly*, mailed to thousands of (free) subscribers, which covered specific topics of interest every three months.

Our concern, however, was how to reach a larger audience that included veterans, their families, and the lay public as well as clinicians, scientists, trainees, and others. The answer was through technology, and the process was serendipity. Although we only recognized it through hindsight, the door was the Internet and the key was our PILOTS bibliographic database.

Published International Literature on Traumatic Stress (PILOTS)

The National Center's original proposal called for the creation of a computerized bibliographic database encompassing all English-language publications on traumatic stress and PTSD. (We have since hired translators for non-English articles.) Whereas most databases of this sort are restricted to articles archived in peer-reviewed journals, PILOTS has always endeavored to include everything in this field, including books, book chapters, technical reports, and dissertations. According to Fred Lerner, the medical information scientist who created PILOTS, the PTSD literature is extremely multidisciplinary and therefore can sometimes be difficult to find. Besides the usual mental health publications, articles and chapters on trauma and PTSD appear in obstetrical, anesthesiological, forensic, sociological, and anthropological journals and books. Furthermore, there has been an explosion of attention to PTSD as the field has grown rapidly over the past two decades. Dr. Lerner has indexed 46,000 citations in PILOTS. It is now recognized as the most thorough and comprehensive bibliographic database in this field.

Web Site

In 1995 the National Center launched its Web site. The major impetus initially was to make PILOTS more accessible to the public. While accomplishing that goal, we began to experiment with this new medium by posting fact sheets on relevant topics. I became aware of the power of the Internet during the 1997

Red River floods in the Northern Plains and Manitoba, Canada, when the river crested in Fargo, North Dakota. We were able to post information on our Web site for local mental health professionals who had urgently requested clinical information on disaster mental health interventions. The clinicians were able to download our fact sheets and manuals and utilize them for dealing with distressed flood survivors. We were also able to upload materials for the public who were trying to cope with the flood on topics such as typical responses to disasters, how to help children, expectations of normal recovery, and danger signs among traumatized family and friends.

We have since utilized our Web site following other disasters and large-scale terrorist attacks such as 9/11, the Pacific tsunami, Hurricane Katrina, and the London Underground bombing. The year 2002 saw a dramatic increase in usage of our Web site, which tripled after 9/11, and spiked on 9/11/02, the first anniversary of the World Trade Center and Pentagon attacks. In fact, in FY 2002 the Web site had approximately 450,000 unique user visits from 150 different countries. It now gets more than one million visitors per year.

Over the years the Web site has emerged as the number one Internet site on PTSD and related topics. It has become a major vehicle for disseminating educational materials. Having learned that two audiences, lay and professional, were utilizing the Web site, we created two separate tracks, one for veterans, their families, and other laypersons, and one for clinicians, scientists, trainees, and other professionals. For example, the Iraq War Clinicians Guide, developed for practitioners (posted on the professional track), was transformed into Returning from the War Zone guide for recently deployed troops, veterans, and their families and posted on the nonprofessional track of our Web site.

In addition to the Internet site, we have created an intranet site on the VA network (vaww.ptsd.va.gov) that provides VA clinicians immediate access to materials not available on the Internet, restricted to VA employees. These include treatment manuals, assessment tools, and other resources.

Educational Products

A new area for the Center has been the expansion of educational resources from text-driven fact sheets to more interactive, graphics-rich products. While the Center currently maintains over 100 fact sheets on the Web site (and it is adding more all the time), over the past five years we have greatly expanded our other content. For example, we launched PTSD 101, a Web-based curriculum for clinicians. With more than twenty specialized courses, clinicians can learn about topics related to trauma and PTSD from national experts. The courses are narrated and interactive, and some contain video.

Our desire to use new technologies in our products was especially important in our goal to reach a younger veteran audience. As I write this chapter we are close to completing our third interactive course for veterans and the public. The first addressed readjustment from the war zone and featured real veterans discussing their transitions coming home. The second provided basic information about PTSD and its consequences and introduced three trauma survivors, who discussed how their PTSD symptoms interfered with their lives. The third features clinicians skilled in using evidenced-based treatments for PTSD and answers questions about how these treatments work and what to expect in treatment. As part of our AboutFace national PTSD web-based campaign, we are currently adding video profiles of individuals with PTSD who have recovered or who are starting in the process, to encourage trauma survivors to seek treatment.

Dissemination and Training

We have learned over the years that it is not enough to develop materials and wait for people to find them. The "If you build it, they will come" philosophy of education is too passive and not very effective. Consequently the National Center has come to recognize that a key to any educational initiative is effective dissemination of information. With this in mind, we have renamed our erstwhile Education Division at Palo Alto the Dissemination and Training Division. Under the vigorous and creative leadership of Joe Ruzek, the division is developing many new initiatives, such as 1) establishing SharePoint Internet sites to complement the Mentoring Program or the prolonged exposure and cognitive processing therapy roll-out initiatives, 2) developing partnerships with the DoD to reach out to recently deployed troops through afterdeployment.org, 3) working with the VA Central Office on the mental health segment of VA's My HealtheVet Web site to provide information on PTSD directly to veterans and their families; 4) disseminating information about PTSD and PTSD treatment through social media such as Facebook and Twitter; and 5) creation of mobile apps such as the very successful PTSD Coach which recently won an award from the Federal Communications Commission for helping people use technology to manage PTSD symptoms.

The Dissemination and Training Division strives to develop more interactive Web-based materials for veterans and professionals, utilize social media, and develop communities of practice. It should also be noted that both the Clinical Training Program and prolonged exposure roll-out are also managed by this division. Our Palo Alto division has also recently developed training programs for chaplains and police officers.

Periodicals

The National Center publishes two periodicals, the *PTSD Research Quarterly* and *Clinicians Trauma Update (CTU) Online*. The *Research Quarterly* has been published continuously since the Center was established. Like the *Medical Letter*, it provides a guide to the literature on a specific topic written by an expert in that area. Abstracts of major articles are presented. Topics for specific issues range from neurobiology to clinical assessment to CBT treatment to epidemiology to forensic issues. Although still published in hard copy, the *Research Quarterly* is being disseminated more and more via our Web site. Paula Schnurr, initially, and now Fran Norris, have served as scientific editors for this publication.

CTU Online is a recent development that periodically circulates summaries of five to seven current articles that are considered especially relevant to VA practitioners. The editor, Paula Schnurr, utilizes this mechanism to provide busy clinicians with the most important articles that have recently been published. Circulation is via e-mail to more than 6,000 subscribers and open to anyone who wishes to receive *CTU Online*.

Books

Despite the excitement and accessibility of Web-based fact sheets, periodicals, curricula, manuals, and interactive materials, some of us continue to write articles, chapters, and books. National Center authors have written approximately forty books. In some cases, these authors have collaborated with non-Center colleagues. Following is a list of twelve books that I consider especially important in the development of the PTSD field and the maturation of the Center.

Brymer, M. J., Layne, C. M., Jacobs, A. K., Pynoos, R. S., Ruzek, J. J., Steinberg, A. M., Vernberg, E. M. & Watson, P. J. (2006). *Psychological first aid: Field operations guide.* 2nd ed. Los Angeles: National Child Traumatic Stress Network & National Center for PTSD. Developed jointly by the National Child Traumatic Stress Network and the National Center for PTSD. It has had a major impact on mental health disaster response protocols.

Foa, E. B., Keane, T. M., Friedman, M. J. & Cohen, J. A. (2009). *Effective treatments for PTSD: Practice guidelines from the International Society for Traumatic Stress Studies.* 2nd ed. New York: Guilford. Presents practice guidelines from the International Society for Traumatic Stress. It has two National Center editors and many Center contributors.

Follett, V. M. & Ruzek, J. J. (2006). *Cognitive behavioral therapies for trauma.* 2nd ed. New York: Guilford. A comprehensive textbook that reviews the broad spectrum of cognitive behavioral therapy approaches with regard to theory, methodology, and outcome.

Friedman, M. J., Charney, D. S. & Deutch, A. Y. (1995). *Neurobiological and clinical consequences of stress: From normal adaptation to post-traumatic stress disorder.* Philadelphia: Lippincott-Raven. The first textbook to consider theoretical issues and neurobiological findings related to PTSD.

Friedman, M. J., Keane, T. M. & Resick, P. A. (2007). *Handbook of PTSD: Science and practice.* New York: Guilford. Currently considered the most comprehensive textbook on PTSD. Its editors are all from the National Center, and most of the chapters have been written by Center professionals and colleagues.

Gerrity, E., Keane, T. M. & Tuma, F. (2001). *The mental health consequences of torture.* New York: Kluwer Academic/Plenum. The results of the National Institute of Mental Health's historic 1997 international conference on torture.

Kimerling, R. E., Ouimette, P. C. & Wolfe, J. (2002). *Gender and PTSD.* New York: Guilford. The first book ever to address this crucial issue.

Marsella, A. J., Friedman, M. J., Gerrity, E. T. & Scurfield, R. M. (1996). *Ethnocultural aspects of posttraumatic stress disorder.* Washington, DC: American Psychological Association. The first book to consider PTSD from a cross-cultural perspective.

Norris, F. H., Galea, S., Friedman, M. J. & Watson, P. J. (2006). *Methods for disaster mental health research.* New York: Guilford. The authoritative textbook on methodology for research in this field.

Ritchie, E. C., Watson, P. J. & Friedman, M. (2006). *Interventions following mass violence and disasters: Strategies for mental health practices.* New York: Guilford. Updates the 2001 consensus conference on mental health and mass violence.

Schnurr, P. P. & Green, B. L. (2004). *Trauma and health: Physical health consequences of exposure to extreme stress.* Washington, DC: American Psychological Association. The authoritative text on the association between trauma and physical health.

Wilson, J. P. & Keane, T. M. (2004). *Assessing psychological trauma and PTSD.* 2nd ed. New York: Guilford. The authoritative text on the assessment of trauma and PTSD.

In addition, two recently published books should be mentioned:

Ruzek, J. J., Schnurr, P. P., Vasterling, J. J. & Friedman, M. J. (2011). *Caring for veterans with deployment related stress disorders: Iraq, Afghanistan and beyond.* Washington, DC: American Psychological Association. Summarizes scientific and clinical knowledge about psychological trauma, PTSD, and related stress reactions among troops deployed to Iraq and Afghanistan.

Southwick, S. M., Litz, B. T., Charney, D. S. & Friedman, M. J. (2011). *Comprehensive textbook on resilience.* New York: Cambridge University Press. The first attempt to consider resilience from psychobiological, psychological, and interpersonal perspectives, with specific attention to special populations.

Operational Challenges

As shown in figure 4.1, our organizational structure is based on a hub-and-spoke model, in which one division takes the lead but others join in. For all administrative matters, the Executive Division is the hub. Neurobiological initiatives are usually led by Clinical Neurosciences, assessment methodology by Behavioral Science, clinical training by our Dissemination and Training Division, military sexual trauma by our Women's Health Sciences Division, telehealth by our Pacific Islands Division, and so forth.

Although each division has major areas of specialization, there is much more cross-divisional collaboration than originally envisioned on research projects, educational initiatives, and joint authorship of scientific and educational articles. For example, the Boston and Palo Alto divisions collaborated on an investigation utilizing structural brain imaging. The Clinical Neurosciences Division led an effort to develop an assessment instrument, the Early Trauma Inventory. The Executive Division led two multisite clinical trials as well as an epidemiological survey of PTSD among American Indian and Asian Pacific Island Vietnam veterans. We have encouraged such collaboration throughout the Center from the outset.

We have put in place a number of institutional processes to sustain a vibrant, cohesive, and well-functioning center even though our seven divisions extend from New England to Hawaii. We have actively promoted a growing series of collaborative projects involving two or more divisions. Center leadership has bimonthly and as-needed director's calls. Two monthly videoconferences, devoted to ongoing research and educational projects respectively, are open to all professional staff and trainees. Quarterly all-staff meetings are attended by everyone. Our challenge has been to foster a National Center identity that transcends geography, time zones, and local VA and academic affiliations. Maintaining a

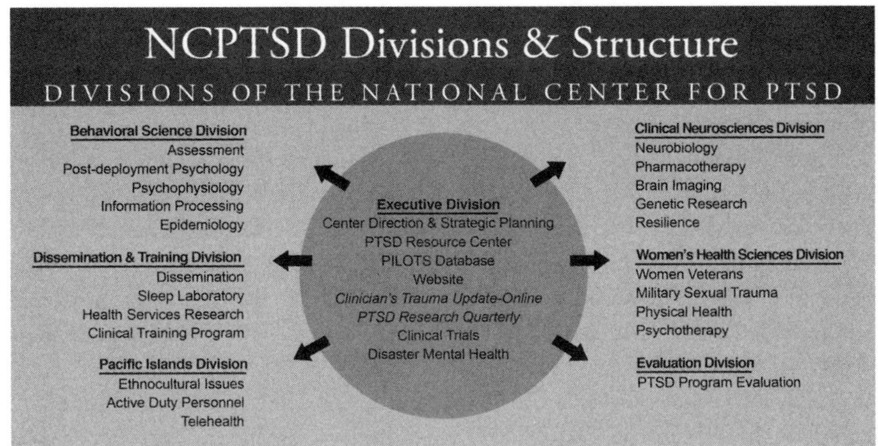

Figure 4.1. Divisions and Structure of the National Center for PTSD.

proper balance between Center priorities and local institutional (both VA and university) demands is a constant challenge, which has produced a creative and dynamic tension for all of us. After more than two decades, we believe that National Center staff are very comfortable working within this structure and feel little contradiction among their Center, VAMC, and university identities and activities.

We at the Executive Division consider ourselves the "glue" that holds the Center together by setting organizational priorities, fostering the aforementioned identity, and promoting collaborative scientific and educational initiatives. We have also been extremely fortunate that our leadership has been remarkably stable. Despite the departure, at different times, of key figures such as Dennis Charney, Jessica Wolfe, Ray Scurfield, Fred Gusman, and Bob Rosenheck, the Center has maintained its vision and momentum through the consistent contributions of a solid leadership group consisting of Terry Keane, Paula Schnurr, John Krystal, Patricia Resick, Joe Ruzek, Danny Kaloupek, Steve Southwick, Rani Desai, and Craig Rosen. Many others have provided continuity and made major contributions over the years.

Within VA, the National Center is located in the Office of Mental Health Services and reports directly to mental health leadership. We have been very fortunate to have generally received excellent support from Office of Mental Health Services directors. One of the Center's highest priorities is to support Office of Mental Health policies and activities through expert consultation and by aligning Center research and education priorities with those of the Office of Mental Health Services in particular and VA in general. This approach has enriched, rather than hampered, the National Center and prompted us to emphasize initiatives devoted to understanding the etiology or prevalence of PTSD; developing better assessment tools and treatment manuals for clinicians; conducting clinical trials to test psychotherapy and pharmacotherapy for PTSD; and, especially since 9/11, promoting a public health model that emphasizes resilience, prevention, and early intervention. As a National Center, we believe it is important to conduct practical clinical trials (Tunis, Stryer & Clancy 2003) for which the hypothesis and study design are developed specifically to answer the questions faced by decision makers. For example, our recent study comparing integrated primary and mental healthcare for PTSD in VA primary care settings was a pragmatic or practical clinical trial.

Because the first National Center failed to meet the congressional mandate stipulated in Public Law 98-528, VA insisted that there be ongoing oversight of the National Center from the start. As a result, two boards, the Scientific Advisory Board and Educational Advisory Board, have conducted an annual review of Center activities since 1989. The Scientific Advisory Board, consisting of eminent VA and non-VA scientists, has evaluated our research portfolio for quality, quantity, balance, and responsiveness to the needs of VA and the trauma field. Scientific Advisory Board recommendations have guided our strategic planning process. For example, after the Board concluded that we were not conducting enough therapeutic trials, we placed much greater emphasis on treatment research, resulting in numerous psychotherapy and pharmacotherapy trials as well as three large VA Cooperative (multisite) Studies.

The Education Advisory Board has consisted of strategic partners with whom we maintain important collaborations in order to advance our educational program. Within VA this has included the Office of Mental Health Services, Readjustment Counseling Service, and members of VA's Employee Education System. Outside of VA it has included representatives of the veteran community, the DoD, the National Institute of Mental Health, the Substance Abuse and Mental Health Administration, the CDC, and others. As with the Scientific Advisory Board, Educational Advisory Board recommendations have had a great impact on our priorities, especially as we have begun to move from traditional in-person training and hard copy publications to Web-based dissemination of information.

Looking Ahead

Our highest priority for the future is to promote the best treatment for veterans with PTSD. We will do this in a number of ways. First, we will continue to provide direct support to PTSD program directors through our Mentoring

Program and direct consultation to clinicians through our Consultation Program. Second, research to develop effective new treatments and to improve the delivery or effectiveness of current therapies is a major emphasis. This includes exploration of Internet or telehealth delivery of evidence-based treatments as well as provision of treatment within integrated primary care–mental health settings. Third, we will continue to utilize our Web site, mobile apps, social media platforms, and other dissemination and training vehicles to spread best practices and provide educational programs on the causes of and treatments for PTSD, so that clinicians will be best prepared to provide effective treatments.

Advancing understanding of the experiences and needs of female and ethno-cultural minority veterans is another key area. Such research and educational efforts include the development of strategies to promote better access to clinical care and to provide gender and culturally sensitive treatments to achieve this goal. Our strong commitment to research and education on military sexual trauma will remain a priority.

Our current strategic plan emphasizes basic and clinical research on PTSD and co-occurring conditions, especially traumatic brain injury and substance use disorders. A number of research initiatives are currently in progress in these areas. A third set of strategic initiatives concerns research on PTSD among older veterans. As with all National Center research, scientific findings will be translated into relevant clinical contexts and disseminated widely through Web-based, hard copy, and face-to-face training platforms.

Utilization of brain imaging and genetic methodologies will be an important component of all of these initiatives. It will also inform our efforts to understand resilience, although we recognize that, in addition to neurobiological and genetic factors, resilience includes psychological, interpersonal, social, and community factors. To that end, basic research on resilience will be complemented by a public health model with the goal of developing pre- and postdeployment preventive strategies. Ongoing collaborations with military colleagues will be an important component of our resilience program as we obtain pre- and postdeployment assessments of veterans with and without PTSD.

We will continue to dedicate Web-based and other dissemination efforts directly to veterans and their families. This will include information to help them understand what we know about the causes and effective treatments for PTSD. We want this information to reduce stigma and promote better understanding about PTSD among veterans, family members, professional audiences, and the nation as a whole. We are currently implementing our national web-based educational campaign, AboutFace, to improve the understanding of PTSD.

The National Center is committed to recruiting and training the next generation of PTSD clinicians, scientists, and educators. We take great pride in the growing number of National Center alumni and alumnae who occupy influential positions in VA, military, and civilian organizations.

Finally, with regard to our consultative mission, we will continue to utilize our expertise to support VA leadership, VA clinicians, the veteran community, our federal and academic partners, and the general public.

In short, although the National Center has come a long way since 1989, there is clearly much more work ahead.

Acknowledgment: The author wishes to acknowledge the valuable contribution of Jessica Hamblen, PhD, who reviewed the manuscript and made important suggestions.

References

American Psychiatric Association. (1980). *Diagnostic and statistical manual of mental disorders.* 3rd ed. Washington, DC: American Psychiatric Association.

Beals, J., Manson, S. M., Shore, J. H., Friedman, M. J., Ashcraft, M., Fairbank, J. A., et al. (2002). The prevalence of posttraumatic stress disorder among American Indian Vietnam veterans: Disparities and context. *Journal of Traumatic Stress* 15, no. 2: 89–97.

Blake, D. D., Weathers, F. W., Nagy, L. M., Kaloupek, D. G., Gusman, F. D., Charney, D. S., et al. (1995). The development of a clinician-administered PTSD scale. *Journal of Traumatic Stress* 8, no. 1: 75–90.

Blake, D. D., Weathers, F. W., Nagy, L. M., Kaloupek, D. G., Klauminzer, G., Charney, D. S., et al. (1990). A clinician rating scale for assessing current and lifetime PTSD: The CAPS-1. *Behavior Therapist* 13: 187–188.

Bremner, J. D., Randall, P. K., Scott, T. M., Bronen, R. A., Seibyl, J. P., Southwick, S. M., et al. (1995). MRI-based measurement of hippocampal volume in patients with combat-related posttraumatic stress disorder. *American Journal of Psychiatry* 152, no. 7: 973–981.

Brymer, M. J., Layne, C. M., Jacobs, A., Pynoos, R. S., Ruzek, J. I., Steinberg, A. M., et al. (2006). *Psychological first aid: field operations guide.* 2nd ed. [Los Angeles]: National Child Traumatic Stress Network and National Center for PTSD.

Buckley, T. C. & Kaloupek, D. G. (2001). A meta-analytic examination of basal cardiovascular activity in posttraumatic stress disorder. *Psychosomatic Medicine* 63, no. 4: 585–594.

Czermak, C., Staley, J. K., Kasserman, S., Bois, F., Young, T., Henry, S., et al. (2008). Beta$_2$ nicotinic acetylcholine receptor availability in post-traumatic stress disorder. *International Journal of Neuropsychopharmacology* 11, no. 3: 419–424.

Foa, E. B., Keane, T. M., Friedman, M. J. & Cohen, J. A. (Eds.). (2009). *Effective treatments for PTSD: Practice guidelines from the International Society for Traumatic Stress Studies.* 2nd ed. New York: Guilford Press.

Follette, V. M. & Ruzek, J. I. (Eds.). (2006). *Cognitive behavioral therapies for trauma.* 2nd ed. New York: Guilford Press.

Fontana, A. & Rosenheck, R. A. (1997). Effectiveness and cost of the inpatient treatment of posttraumatic stress disorder: Comparison of three models of treatment. *American Journal of Psychiatry* 154, no. 6: 758–765.

Forbes, D., Creamer, M., Bisson, J. I., Cohen, J. A., et al. (2010). A guide to "Guidelines for the Treatment of PTSD and Related Conditions." *Journal of Traumatic Stress* 23, no. 5: 537–552.

Friedman, M. J., Charney, D. S. & Deutch, A. Y. (1995). *Neurobiological and clinical consequences of stress: From normal adaptation to post-traumatic stress disorder.* Philadelphia: Lippincott-Raven.

Friedman, M. J., Keane, T. M. & Resick, P. A. (2007). *Handbook of PTSD: Science and practice.* New York: Guilford Press.

Friedman, M. J., Marmar, C. R., Baker, D. G., Sikes, C. R. & Farfel, G. M. (2007). Randomized, double-blind comparison of sertraline and placebo for posttraumatic stress disorder in a Department of Veterans Affairs setting. *Journal of Clinical Psychiatry* 68, no. 5: 711–720.

Friedman, M. J., Schnurr, P. P., Sengupta, A., Holmes, T. & Ashcraft, M. (2004). The Hawaii Vietnam Veterans Project: Is minority status a risk factor for posttraumatic stress disorder? *Journal of Nervous and Mental Disease* 192, no. 1: 42–50.

Gerrity, E. T., Keane, T. M. & Tuma, F. K. (2001). *The mental health consequences of torture.* New York: Kluwer Academic/Plenum Publishers.

Johnson, D. R., Fontana, A., Lubin, H., Corn, B. & Rosenheck, R. A. (2004). Long-term course of treatment-seeking Vietnam veterans with posttraumatic stress disorder: Mortality, clinical condition, and life satisfaction. *Journal of Nervous and Mental Disease* 192, no. 1: 35–41.

Kardiner, A. (1941). The neuroses of war. *War Medicine* 1, no. 2: 219–226.

Kaufman, J., Yang, B.-Z., Douglas-Palumberi, H., Houshyar, S., Lipschitz, D. S., Krystal, J. H., et al. (2004). Social supports and serotonin transporter gene moderate depression in maltreated children. *Proceedings of the National Academy of Sciences of the United States of America* 101, no. 49: 17316–17321.

Keane, T. M., Kolb, L. C., Kaloupek, D. G., Orr, S. P., Blanchard, E. B., Thomas, R. G., et al. (1998). Utility of psychophysiological measurement in the diagnosis of posttraumatic stress disorder: Results from a Department of Veterans Affairs cooperative study. *Journal of Consulting and Clinical Psychology* 66, no. 6: 914–923.

Kimerling, R. E., Ouimette, P. C. & Wolfe, J. (2002). *Gender and PTSD.* New York: Guilford Press.

Kimerling, R. E., Street, A. E., Gima, K. S. & Smith, M. W. (2008). Evaluation of universal screening for military-related sexual trauma. *Psychiatric Services* 59, no. 6: 635–640.

Kimerling, R., Street, A. E., Pavao, J., Smith, M. W., Cronkite, R. C., Holmes, T. H., et al. (2010). Military-related sexual trauma among Veterans Health Administration patients returning from Afghanistan and Iraq. *American Journal of Public Health* 100, no. 8: 1409–1412.

Koenen, K. C., Aiello, A. E., Bakshis, E., Amstadter, A. B., Ruggiero, K. J., Acierno, R., et al. (2009). Modification of the association between serotonin transporter genotype and risk of posttraumatic stress disorder in adults by county-level social environment. *American Journal of Epidemiology* 169, no. 6: 704–711.

Krystal, J. H., Rosenheck, R. A., Cramer, J. A., Vessicchio, J. C., Jones, K. M., Vertrees, J. E., Horney, R. A., Huang, G. D. & Stock, C. (2011). Adjunctive risperidone treatment for antidepressant-resistant symptoms of chronic military service-related PTSD: A randomized trial. *Journal of the American Medical Association* 306, no. 5: 493–502.

Litz, B. T., Engel, C. C., Bryant, R. A. & Papa, A. (2007). A randomized, controlled proof-of-concept trial of an Internet-based, therapist-assisted self-management treatment for posttraumatic stress disorder. *American Journal of Psychiatry* 164, no. 11: 1676–1683.

Litz, B. T., King, L. A., King, D. W., Orsillo, S. M. & Friedman, M. J. (1997). Warriors as peacekeepers: Features of the Somalia experience and PTSD. *Journal of Consulting and Clinical Psychology* 65, no. 6: 1001–1010.

Marsella, A. J., Friedman, M. J., Gerrity, E. T. & Scurfield, R. M. et al. (1996). *Ethnocultural aspects of posttraumatic stress disorder: Issues, research, and clinical applications.* Washington, DC: American Psychological Association.

Mohamed, S. & Rosenheck, R. A. (2008). Pharmacotherapy of PTSD in the U.S. Department of Veterans Affairs: Diagnostic- and symptom-guided drug selection. *Journal of Clinical Psychiatry* 69, no. 6: 959–965.

Monson, C. M., Schnurr, P. P., Resick, P. A., Friedman, M. J., Young-Xu, Y. & Stevens, S. P. (2006). Cognitive processing therapy for veterans with military-related posttraumatic stress disorder. *Journal of Consulting and Clinical Psychology* 74, no. 5L: 898–907.

Monson, C. M., Stevens, S. P. & Schnurr, P. P. (2005). Cognitive-behavioral couple's treatment for posttraumatic stress disorder. In T. A. Corales (Ed.), *Focus on posttraumatic stress disorder research* (pp. 245–274). Hauppage, NY: Nova Science Publishers.

Morgan, C. A., Southwick, S. M., Hazlett, G., Rasmusson, A. M., Hoyt, G., Zimolo, Z., et al. (2004). Relationships among plasma dehydroepiandrosterone sulfate and cortisol levels, symptoms of dissociation, and objective performance in humans exposed to acute stress. *Archives of General Psychiatry* 16, no. 8: 819–825.

Morgan, C. A., Wang, S., Southwick, S. M., Rasmusson, A. M., Hazlett, G., Hauger, R. L., et al. (2000). Plasma neuropeptide-Y concentrations in humans exposed to military survival training. *Biological Psychiatry* 47, no. 10: 902–909.

Morland, L. A., Greene, C. J., Rosen, C. S., Foy, D., Reilly, P., Shore, J., et al. (2010). Telemedicine for anger management therapy in a rural population of combat veterans with posttraumatic stress disorder: A randomized noninferiority trial. *Journal of Clinical Psychiatry* 71, no. 7: 855–863.

National Institute of Mental Health. (2002). *Mental health and mass violence: Evidence-based early psychological intervention for victims/survivors of mass violence: A workshop to reach consensus on best practices.* Washington, DC: U.S. Government Printing Office.

Norris, F. H., Galea, S., Friedman, M. J. & Watson, P. J. (2006). *Methods for disaster mental health research.* New York: Guilford Press.

Northeast Program Evaluation Center. (1990–2011). *The long journey home.* Washington, DC: Department of Veterans Affairs.

Petrakis, I. L., Poling, J., Levinson, C. M., Nich, C., Carroll, K. M., Ralevski, E., et al. (2006). Naltrexone and disulfiram in patients with alcohol dependence and comorbid post-traumatic stress disorder. *Biological Psychiatry* 60, no. 7: 777–783.

Prins, A., Ouimette, P. C., Kimerling, R. E., Cameron, R. P., Hugelshofer, D. S., Shaw-Hegwer, J., et al. (2004). The primary care PTSD Screen (PC-PTSD): Development and operating characteristics. *Primary Care Psychiatry* 9, no. 1: 9–14.

Rasmusson, A. M., Pinna, G., Paliwal, P., Weisman, D., Gottschalk, C., Charney, D. S., et al. (2006). Decreased cerebrospinal fluid allopregnanolone levels in women with posttraumatic stress disorder. *Biological Psychiatry* 60, no. 7: 704–713.

Resick, P. A., Galovski, T. E., Uhlmansiek, M. O. B., Scher, C. D., Clum, G. A. & Young-Xu, Y. (2008). A randomized clinical trial to dismantle components of cognitive processing therapy for posttraumatic stress disorder in female victims of interpersonal violence. *Journal of Consulting and Clinical Psychology* 76, no. 2: 243–258.

Ritchie, E. C., Watson, P. J. & Friedman, M. J. (2006). *Interventions following mass violence and disasters: Strategies for mental health practices.* New York: Guilford Press.

Rosen, C. S., Chow, H. C., Finney, J. F., Greenbaum, M. A., Moos, R. H., Sheikh, J. I., et al. (2004). VA practice patterns and practice guidelines for treating posttraumatic stress disorder. *Journal of Traumatic Stress* 17(3): 213–222.

Rosen, C. S., DiLandro, C., Corwin, K. N., Drescher, K. D., Cooney, J. H. & Gusman, F. D. (2006). Telephone monitoring and support for veterans with chronic posttraumatic stress disorder: A pilot study. *Community Mental Health Journal* 42, no. 5: 501–508.

Rosenheck, R. A. & Fontana, A. (2002). Black and Hispanic veterans in intensive VA treatment programs for posttraumatic stress disorder. *Medical Care* 40, no. 1 (supp.): I52–I61.

Rosenheck, R. A., Fontana, A. & Errera, P. (1997). Inpatient treatment of war-related posttraumatic stress disorder: A 20-year perspective. *Journal of Traumatic Stress* 10, no. 3: 407–413.

Rosenheck, R. A., Fontana, A. & Stolar, M. (1999). Assessing quality of care: Administrative indicators and clinical outcomes in posttraumatic stress disorder. *Medical Care* 37, no. 2: 180–188.

Ruzek, J. J., Schnurr, P. P., Vasterling, J. J. & Friedman, M. J. (2011). *Caring for veterans with deployment related stress disorders: Iraq, Afghanistan and beyond.* Washington, DC: American Psychological Association.

Schlenger, W. E., Kulka, R. A., Fairbank, J. A., Hough, R. L., Jordan, B. K., Marmar, C. R., et al. (1992). The prevalence of post-traumatic stress disorder in the

Vietnam generation: A multimethod, multisource assessment of psychiatric disorder. *Journal of Traumatic Stress* 5, no. 3: 333–363.

Schnurr, P. P., Friedman, M. J., Engel, C. C., Foa, E. B., Shea, M. T., Chow, B. K., et al. (2007). Cognitive behavioral therapy for posttraumatic stress disorder in women: a randomized controlled trial. *Journal of the American Medical Association* 297, no. 8: 820–830.

Schnurr, P. P., Friedman, M. J., Foy, D. W., Shea, M. T., Hsieh, F. Y., Lavori, P. W., et al. (2003). Randomized trial of trauma-focused group therapy for posttraumatic stress disorder. *Archives of General Psychiatry* 60, no. 5: 481–489.

Schnurr, P. P. & Green, B. L. (2004). *Trauma and health: Physical health consequences of exposure to extreme stress.* Washington, DC: American Psychological Association.

Shipherd, J. C., Pineles, S. L., Gradus, J. L. & Resick, P. A. (2009). Sexual harassment in the Marines, posttraumatic stress symptoms, and perceived health: Evidence for sex differences. *Journal of Traumatic Stress* 22, no. 1: 3–10.

Southwick, S. M., Krystal, J. H., Morgan, C. A., Johnson, D. R., Nagy, L. M., Nicolaou, A. L., et al. (1993). Abnormal noradrenergic function in posttraumatic stress disorder. *Archives of General Psychiatry* 50, no. 4: 266–274.

Southwick, S. M., Litz, B. T., Charney, D. S. & Friedman, M. J. (Eds.). (2011). *Resilience and mental health: Challenges across the lifespan.* Cambridge: Cambridge University Press.

Street, A. E., Stafford, J. A., Mahan, C. M. & Hendricks, A. (2008). Sexual harassment and assault experienced by reservists during military service: Prevalence and health correlates. *Journal of Rehabilitation Research and Development* 45, no. 3: 409–419.

Tunis, S. R., Stryer, D. B. & Clancy, C. M. (2003). Practical clinical trials: Increasing the value of clinical research for decision making in clinical and health policy. *JAMA* 290, no. 12: 1624–1632.

Under Secretary for Health's Special Committee on PTSD. (2007). *Annual report,* Washington, DC: Department of Veterans Affairs.

Vasterling, J. J., Proctor, S. P., Friedman, M. J., Hoge, C. W., Heeren, T., King, L. A., et al. (2010). PTSD symptom increases in Iraq-deployed soldiers: Comparison with nondeployed soldiers and associations with baseline symptoms, deployment experiences, and postdeployment stress. *Journal of Traumatic Stress* 23, no. 1: 41–51.

Veterans' Health Care Act of 1984. P.L. No. 98-528, October 19.

Vogt, D. S., Bergeron, A., Salgado, D. M., Daley, J., Ouimette, P. C. & Wolfe, J. (2006). Barriers to Veterans Health Administration care in a nationally representative sample of women veterans. *Journal of General Internal Medicine* 21, supp. 3: S19–S25.

Vogt, D. S., Proctor, S. P., King, D. W., King, L. A. & Vasterling, J. J. (2008). Validation of scales from the Deployment Risk and Resilience Inventory in a sample of Operation Iraqi Freedom veterans. *Assessment* 15, no. 4: 391–403.

Weathers, F. W., Litz, B. T., Herman, D. S., Huska, J. A. & Keane, T. M. (1993, October). The PTSD checklist (PCL): Reliabilitiy, validity and diagnostic utility. Poster presented at the 9th annual meeting of the International Society for Traumatic Stress Studies, San Antonio, TX.

Wilson, J. P. & Keane, T. M. (2004). *Assessing psychological trauma and PTSD*. 2nd ed. New York: Guilford Press.

Wolfe, J. (1996). Posttraumatic stress disorder in women veterans. *Women's Health Issues* 6, no. 6: 349–352.

Wolfe, J., Keane, T. M. & Young, B. L. (1996). From soldier to civilian: Acute adjustment patterns of returned Persian Gulf veterans. In R. J. Ursano & A. E. Norwood (Eds.), *Emotional aftermath of the Persian Gulf War: Veterans, families, communities, and nations* (pp. 477–499). Washington, DC: American Psychiatric Press.

Wolfe, J., Sharkansky, E. J., Read, J. P., Dawson, R., Martin, J. A. & Ouimette, P. C. (1998). Sexual harassment and assault as predictors of PTSD symptomatology among U.S. female Persian Gulf War military personnel. *Journal of Interpersonal Violence* 13, no. 1: 40–57.

Woodward, S. H., Kaloupek, D. G., Streeter, C. C., Kimble, M. O., Reiss, A. L., Eliez, S., et al. (2007). Brain, skull, and cerebrospinal fluid volumes in adult posttraumatic stress disorder. *Journal of Traumatic Stress* 20, no. 5: 763–774.

Woodward, S. H., Kaloupek, D. G., Streeter, C. C., Martinez, C., Schaer, M. & Eliez, S. (2006). Decreased anterior cingulate volume in combat-related PTSD. *Biological Psychiatry* 59, no. 7: 582–587.

Woodward, S. H., Schaer, M., Kaloupek, D. G., Cediel, L. & Eliez, S. (2009). Smaller global and regional cortical volume in combat-related posttraumatic stress disorder. *Archives of General Psychiatry* 66, no. 12: 1373–1382.

Yehuda, R., Southwick, S. M., Krystal, J. H., Bremner, D., Charney, D. S. & Mason, J. W. (1993). Enhanced suppression of cortisol following dexamethasone administration in posttraumatic stress disorder. *American Journal of Psychiatry* 150, no. 1: 83–86.

Zhang, L., Li, H., Su, T. P., Barker, J. L., Maric, D., Fullerton, C. S., et al. (2008). p11 is up-regulated in the forebrain of stressed rats by glucocorticoid acting via two specific glucocorticoid response elements in the p11 promoter. *Neuroscience* 153, no. 4: 1126–1134.

Chapter 5

Pain Management in the Veterans Health Administration

Kathryn LaChappelle, Samantha Boris-Karpel,
and Robert D. Kerns

Introduction and Overview

Pain management is a high priority for the Veterans Health Administration (VHA). Published data from the last decade estimate that as many as 50 percent of male VA patients in primary care report the presence of pain (Kerns et al. 2003; Clark 2002 et al.), and the prevalence may even be as high as 75 percent in female veterans (Haskell et al. 2006). Among veterans returning from deployment in Afghanistan in Operation Enduring Freedom (OEF) or Iraq in Operation Iraqi Freedom (OIF), musculoskeletal and connective tissue disorders (presumed to be painful) are known to be the most highly prevalent cluster of diagnosed medical conditions, surpassing the rates of all diagnosed mental health conditions combined. Published observational data document that pain is among the most frequent presenting complaint for OEF/OIF veterans, particularly in patients with polytrauma (Clark 2004; Gironda et al. 2006; Lew et al. 2009). Pain is also among the most costly disorders treated in VHA settings, as shown by the total estimated costs of $2.2 billion attributable to low back pain alone in fiscal year 1999 (Yu et al. 2003). Recent data document that the rates of low back pain among veterans receiving care in VHA facilities are steadily rising with each passing year (Sinnott & Wagner 2009). The presence of pain among veterans receiving primary care in VHA facilities, relative to those not reporting pain, is associated with poorer self-rated health; greater utilization of healthcare resources; greater prevalence of health risk behaviors; and factors such as tobacco use, excessive alcohol use, diet/weight concerns, decreased social and physical activity, lower social support, and greater ratings of affective distress (Kerns et al. 2003). Among women veterans, pain is associated with high rates of military and nonmilitary sexual harassment and trauma (Haskell et al. 2008).

In recognition of the high prevalence of pain among veterans and its costs in suffering and financial burden on veterans and the organization, VHA has developed a comprehensive plan for promoting systems improvements in pain care. Ultimately, VHA has established itself as a worldwide leader in these efforts and now serves as a model for promoting healthcare system improvements to address this public health crisis. This chapter provides a historical perspective on the development and implementation of the VHA National Pain Management Strategy and highlights several of VHA's most important achievements during this process.

Historical Background

It is well known that the history of the development of anesthesia and pain management has its roots in military events and military clinicians. In the United States, notable examples are the advances in acute injury anaesthesia in military theaters: Dr. Silas Weir Mitchell's identification of certain forms of chronic pain (reflex sympathetic dystrophy and phantom limb syndrome) during the U.S. Civil War and Dr. John Bonica's establishment of pain management as an interdisciplinary discipline based on his innovations in practice during World War II (Meldrum 2003; Mitchell 1872). From the latter part of the twentieth century through the present day, the veterans' healthcare system has also played a crucial role in the advancement of pain management in terms of clinical protocols, educational programs, and research.

Even as medical technology and pain care options improved over the centuries, pain care and management often seemed to fail to get the attention it deserved. This paradigm of systematic low prioritization began to reverse in 1973 when the nonprofit, nongovernmental, academic, and medical society the International Association for the Study of Pain (IASP) was founded. In 1975 the IASP began publishing the academic journal *Pain*, which further helped to bolster and create a larger network of academic and medical scholarship in pain (Holzman, Turk & Kerns 1986). In the United States, the American Pain Society was founded in 1978 as a multidisciplinary organization of basic and clinical researchers, practicing clinicians, policy analysts, and educators. These organizational efforts further cemented a commitment to integrative biopsychosocial, multidimensional, and multidisciplinary perspectives on pain and pain management.

Clinicians and researchers in the veterans' healthcare system were early contributors to these pioneering developments. By the early 1980s multidisciplinary clinical, research, and training programs had been established at numerous veterans' healthcare facilities, including those at Columbia, Missouri; Long Beach, California; West Haven, Connecticut; and White River Junction, Vermont. Clinical research at these centers was funded by the intramural research program. Three examples of the published research on veterans from this era can be cited as particularly influential examples of the impact of this early research. In 1985 Kerns, Turk, and Rudy (1985) published the West Haven–Yale Multidimensional Pain Inventory (WHYMPI), the first theoretically informed, multidimensional measure of the psychosocial impact of chronic pain. This measure was originally developed and standardized on veteran samples, and more than twenty-five years later it remains one of the most widely employed measures of chronic pain in the world. In 1986 this same group of investigators published one of the first randomized controlled trials of cognitive-behavior therapy for chronic pain, a clinical approach that continues to be recognized as a particularly effective nonpharmacological approach to the management of persistent pain (Kerns et al. 1986). Finally, in an important multisite collaboration, a team of investigators systematically examined how veterans and civilians from academic and community research centers differed on important demographic and pain-relevant descriptive characteristics (Holzman et al. 1985).

Origins of the VHA National Pain Management Strategy

By 1988 VHA's role as a leader in healthcare reform, research, and innovation in the United States was well established. Continuing reforms of policy and procedure are key elements in trying to give veterans the best care possible, and the area of pain management is no exception. Nevertheless, informal feedback and quality monitoring during the 1980s and 1990s revealed that the standard of care for pain management was inadequate and variable, especially in light of the number of veterans with different variations of chronic and acute pain across the nation. This "red flag" called for the establishment of a standardized national policy and procedure for a comprehensive approach to pain management.

In response to these observations, an eleven-member Pain Management Committee and national survey of pain management in VHA were chartered in 1997. The committee was chaired by Ms. Loretta Wasse, a nurse anesthetist at the Seattle VA Medical Center, who is arguably the most significant voice in early efforts to draw attention to the need to improve pain care for veterans. Results of the survey and a report based on these data confirmed inconsistencies in pain management services and access to treatment across VHA facilities. The data drew attention to the lack of uniformity in the standards of care in VHA, ranging from none, or consultation only services, to large multidisciplinary pain centers (Craine & Kerns 2003). The survey found that 36 percent of all facilities in VHA had no active pain management programs at all, and that although 30 percent of VHA's patient population was coming in for complaints of pain, only 2 percent of actively enrolled veterans visited a pain clinic in a given year.

From this survey it became apparent that VHA had "no centrally organized program to evaluate effectiveness, recommend therapies, or manage costs of acute and chronic pain management programs" (Acute Care Strategic Healthcare Group 1997). Findings highlighted that VHA consisted of a wide variety of treatment facilities and resources, yet there were no centrally defined pain therapy protocols or standards. There was no structure for how pain was treated, and no organized pathway for referring patients into further pain management treatment. The committee also found no standards for training and education about pain management for providers, which only perpetuated the cycle of inadequate acute and chronic pain care access and treatment. The Pain Management Committee made recommendations to appoint a permanent pain management committee and create a standardized national policy to Dr. Kenneth Kizer, then Undersecretary of Health for VHA (Acute Care Strategic Healthcare Group 1997). Dr. Kizer accepted these recommendations and formally chartered the VHA National Pain Management Strategy on November 12, 1998 (Veterans Health Administration 1998).

VHA National Pain Management Strategy

Establishment of the National Pain Management Strategy marked the recognition of pain management as a high priority for VHA. The original charter for the strategy asserted that its purpose is "to develop a system-wide approach to pain management that will reduce pain and suffering for veterans experiencing acute and chronic pain associated with a wide range of illnesses, including terminal illness." The charter further specified seven key objectives that have largely remained as guiding principles for the strategy for the first several years of its enactment:

- Provide a systemwide VHA standard of care for pain management that will reduce suffering from preventable pain.

- Assure that pain assessment is performed in a consistent manner.

- Assure that pain treatment is prompt and appropriate.

- Include patients and families as active participants in pain management.

- Provide for continual monitoring and improvement in outcomes of pain treatment.

- Provide for an interdisciplinary, multimodal approach to pain management.

- Assure that clinicians practicing in the VA healthcare system are adequately prepared to assess and manage pain effectively.

Four key elements of the national strategy were articulated, including standards for pain assessment and treatment, evaluation of outcomes and quality of pain management, clinician competence and expertise in pain management, and research.

An organizational structure was needed to promote the accomplishment of these strategic goals. It was recognized at the outset that to successfully improve pain management, the healthcare system needed guidance and tools developed at a national level for application at the facility and the caregiver level of healthcare delivery. The importance of a multidisciplinary approach was also embraced from the outset. The VHA National Pain Management Strategy Coordinating Committee (NPMSCC) was formed by Dr. Kizer to facilitate the accomplishment of these objectives. This committee was initially co-chaired by the national chief consultant of the Geriatrics and Extended Strategic Healthcare Group, Dr. Judith Salerno, and chief consultant of the Acute Care Strategic Healthcare Group, Dr. Toni Mitchell. Soon a national coordinator for pain management, Dr. Jane Tollett, was also appointed and continued to direct the strategy and the Coordinating Committee until 2004. A multidisciplinary group of ten experts from facilities throughout VHA was identified and recruited to join the NPMSCC. These members were selected to serve on the committee specifically because of their expertise in pain management or in areas of education, research, and information technology. This committee formed a core of professional resources for implementation of the national strategy. The involvement of experts from areas outside the field of pain management has been central to the success of the committee and its component working groups.

Initially, eight key responsibilities were assigned to the Coordinating Committee:

- Coordinate the systemwide implementation of "pain as the fifth vital sign."

- Coordinate the development and dissemination of state-of-the-art treatment protocols for pain management.

- Identify VHA pain management expertise and resources and facilitate a national referral system to ensure that veterans in every network have access to pain management services.

- Coordinate a national employee education initiative to assure that VHA clinicians have the expertise to provide high-quality pain assessment and treatment.

- Identify research opportunities and priorities in pain management and facilitating collaborative research efforts.

- Integrate VHA pain management standards into the curricula and clinical learning experiences of medical students, allied health professional students, interns, and resident trainees.

- Establish target goals, mechanisms for accountability, and a timeline for implementation for a comprehensive, integrated VHA Pain Management Strategy.

- Establish a communication plan for both the internal and external communication of VHA's National Pain Management Strategy.

The NPMSCC needed a well-organized infrastructure to be able to coordinate such a huge undertaking in one of the largest healthcare delivery systems in the United States (Kerns et al. 2006). So an organizational hierarchy was formed to enact and delegate the responsibilities involved in the National Pain Management Strategy. As coordinator of the strategy and eventually as chair of the NPMSCC, Dr. Tollett held programmatic responsibility for policy development, coordination, and oversight for the strategy. Working groups were formed within the committee, and they partnered with a growing number of pain management clinician members from the field and with others from the VA Central Office to encompass and achieve specific goals from the strategy. Working groups included acute pain management, education, guidelines, nursing, outcomes measurement, performance improvement, pharmacy, polytrauma, primary care, and research. Regionally, a pain point of contact (POC) was established at each of VHA's twenty-one Veterans Integrated Service Networks (VISNs) to direct responsibilities and coordinate pain management activities delegated by the NPMSCC at each local facility. In addition, many individual facilities developed their own pain management committees to oversee specific aspects of their programs at the local level (Kerns et al. 2006).

Pain as the 5th Vital Sign Initiative

In the earliest stages of implementation of the National Pain Management Strategy, VHA launched the Pain as the 5th Vital Sign Initiative. The phrase, "Pain as the 5th Vital Sign," was coined in 1996 by Dr. James Campbell of

Johns Hopkins University Medical School in his presidential address to the members of the American Pain Society. As Dr. Campbell so eloquently stated, "Vital Signs are taken seriously. If pain were assessed with the same zeal as other vital signs are, it would have a much better chance of being treated properly. We need to train doctors and nurses to treat pain as a vital sign. Quality care means that pain is measured and treated" (November 11, 1996).

The American Pain Society began this awareness campaign in response to the well-documented, widespread, and long-term neglect of pain assessment in clinical practice, especially primary care (Boris-Karpel 2011). From this, VHA established an initiative to include pain measurement in the measurement of vital signs, declaring it officially the "fifth vital sign" in clinical care. In 1999 the concept was turned into an actionable policy (Lynn et al. 2007; Boris-Karpel 2011). VHA mandated that every patient be screened for pain using a numerical rating scale. To assist in the implementation of this mandate, Loretta Wasse and her colleague from the Geriatric Strategic Healthcare Group, Bonnie Ryan, coauthored "Pain as the 5th Vital Sign Toolkit." A second version of the toolkit was published by VHA in 2000 and serves as the primary resource for a large national initiative to fully implement routine screening and comprehensive assessment of veterans presenting with pain. In conjunction with publication of the toolkit and the enactment of a comprehensive national educational campaign, VHA modified the vitals section of its Computerized Patient Record System (CPRS) to accommodate documentation of the "pain score" and to generate an automated reminder to providers when further pain assessment was indicated.

The Joint Commission on Accreditation of Hospital Organizations (Joint Commission), a widely recognized leader in the accreditation of healthcare organizations, almost simultaneously adopted the treatment of pain as the "fifth vital sign" and published its first evidence-based, pain-relevant accreditation standards. As such, the Pain as the 5th Vital Sign Initiative has had far-reaching effects, not just within VHA, but also in other public and private healthcare facilities and organizations. The initiative has helped to further the American Pain Society's campaign to raise awareness and increase the frequency of pain measurement and treatment. The original 1999 launch of the initiative has not been seen just as a major milestone for the VHA, but also has been heralded as a milestone for pain management more generally. It is considered an important step in the "long-term process to make pain management a routine part of patient care" (Schuster 1999).

Ten years since its inception, the "Pain as the 5th Vital Sign Toolkit" is still considered a principal resource for pain care providers in VHA, as well as in the outside medical community (Kerns et al. 2000). The toolkit itself is distributed as a hard copy document with posters, videotapes, reminder cards, and published articles (Joint Commission on Accreditation of Healthcare Organizations 2003). It is available online at http://www1.va.gov/painmanagement/docs/toolkit.pdf. The contents of the online toolkit are included in box 5.1.

VHA/Institute for Healthcare Improvement Pain Management Collaborative

A second early initiative designed to support the introduction of the VHA National Pain Management Strategy was its successful collaboration with the Institute for Healthcare Improvement (IHI), a nonprofit organization that works to promote change in healthcare systems. The VHA/IHI Pain Management Collaborative involved seventy teams working together from May 2000 to January 2001 to make rapid, measurable improvements in pain management throughout VHA facilities (Cleeland et al. 2003). The Collaborative Steering Committee, chaired by Dr. Charles Cleelend, a non-VHA psychologist and a leading authority in the field of pain management and efforts to promote organizational change, articulated four measurable goals:

1. Reduce the prevalence of severe pain by 25 percent.
2. Assess 100 percent of patients for pain.
3. Increase documented plans of care by at least 20 percent.
4. Assure that at least 50 percent of patients with pain receive appropriate pain management education.

Teams identified any two or more of these goals and worked in a range of clinical settings (e.g., outpatient primary or secondary care, inpatient medical or surgical, geriatric and extended care) over a nine-month cycle to promote rapid systems improvements in pain care. The IHI "Breakthrough" process was employed, which emphasized ongoing quantitative evaluation and feedback to teams to cue, monitor, and reinforce change. These efforts were supported by three national educational conferences, monthly national teleconferences with the Steering Committee and other consultants, and establishment of an electronic mail group (VA Pain List Serve). Across all teams, settings, and goals, three out of the four goals were achieved over the course of the collaboration. Only the goal of assessing 100 percent of patients for pain did not reach the target, but still showed significant improvement during the program (Cleeland et al. 2003). This VHA/IHI collaboration was another important stepping stone to the systemwide effort to improve pain management for veterans.

> **Box 5.1. Pain as the 5th Vital Sign Toolkit Contents**
>
> **Section 1: Introduction.** This section presents the objectives of the VHA National Pain Management Strategy and a synopsis of the major sections of this toolkit.
>
> **Section 2: An Overview of the VHA National Pain Management Strategy.** This section highlights the key components of the strategy and provides recommendations for implementation at individual VHA facilities (or in individual healthcare facilities if it is being used by non-VHA systems).
>
> **Section 3: Barriers to Pain Screening and Assessment.** This section reviews many of the common barriers to reliable pain screening and assessment, including barriers attributable to healthcare professionals, patients, and the healthcare system. Appreciation of the factors is critical to the development of an effective program for pain management.
>
> **Section 4: The Pain Screening Process.** This section includes information about the Numeric Rating Scale (NRS) for pain screening, a description of the tool, tips for using it reliably; guidelines for frequency of screening across diverse clinical settings; and suggestions for using the tool within the context of patient/family education on pain and pain management. This section also contains information on methods for documenting pain scores in the patient record.
>
> **Section 5: Conducting a Comprehensive Pain Assessment.** This section emphasizes the role of pain screening as an initial step in the comprehensive assessment of pain. The section discusses pain as a complex, perceptual phenomenon and provides a rationale for more comprehensive assessment. Key components and commonly employed methods of pain assessment are also described, followed by a description of common barriers to reliable pain assessment.
>
> **Section 6: Educational and Resource Information.** This section provides information to assist individuals and facilities in the successful implementation of the Pain as the 5th Vital Sign initiative.
>
> Source: Kerns et al. (2000).

Performance Improvement Monitoring

In 1999, to follow up on and monitor pain measurement and treatment outcomes, VHA implemented a series of health service quality indicators to be reviewed by a non-VHA contracted quality monitor, the External Peer Review Program (EPRP) (Halpern 1996; Joint Commission on Accreditation of

Healthcare Organizations 2003). It focused on ambulatory primary care clinics and eight specialty clinics (Halpern 1996). Per the protocol of the EPRP, the standards were based on the Joint Commission Pain Management Standards. By using these standards, healthcare outcomes could more easily be compared across VHA and other public and private sector healthcare organizations. Over the first several years of monitoring, the EPRP data provided evidence of significant increases in the frequency of pain screening, frequency of pain care plans when pain was present, and frequency of follow-up assessments when a pain plan of care was recorded. By the end of fiscal year 2004, the average rates on these three measures were noted to be 97 percent, 94 percent, and 94 percent, respectively. With evidence of sustained improvement and high rates of compliance with the standards, this monitoring process was discontinued. Similarly high ratings of compliance with these standards were also collected and reported specifically from residential geriatrics and extended care settings. Although it is not possible to determine which initiative(s) were responsible for this improvement, what is known is that there has been brisk improvement and that the trend is still continuing.

Another important metric for VHA is ratings of veteran satisfaction. The Survey of Healthcare Experiences of Patients (SHEP) continues to be used to assess the satisfaction of veterans with care received in either inpatient or outpatient settings. Although the primary tool that is used for these purposes has varied over the years, at least for inpatient surveys, pain-relevant items are included that provide valid indices of veteran satisfaction with the pain care received. By the end of fiscal year 2004, ratings for inpatient and outpatient satisfaction were continuing to rise and were as good as or better than public sector indices.

VHA Pain Management Directive

In 2003 VHA published its first pain management policy, a step that further secured the role of pain management as a high priority for VHA (VHA Directive 2003-021, Pain Management). The directive provided "policy and implementation guidance for improvement of pain management consistent with the VHA National Pain Management Strategy and accepted Pain Management Standards of Care." In a further articulation of the earlier published statement of the mission of the strategy, the directive asserted that "the overall objective of the national strategy is to develop a comprehensive, multicultural, integrated, system-wide approach to pain management that reduces pain and suffering for veterans experiencing acute and chronic pain associated with a wide range of illnesses, including terminal illness." It reasserted several more specific objectives of the strategy and reauthorized the NPMSCC as the multi-disciplinary group to provide oversight and monitoring of the strategy's implementation. Importantly, in addition to specifying the responsibilities of the NPMSCC, the directive assigned responsibilities for ensuring implementation of the strategy to VISN directors, VISN POCs, and facility directors. Three domains of pain management standards were established explicitly as VHA policy, including standards for pain assessment and treatment, evaluation of outcomes and quality of pain management, and clinician competence and expertise in pain management.

Progress from 1999 to 2005

In late 2004, after the retirement of Dr. Tollett, Dr. Robert Kerns, a psychologist and noted pain management expert, was selected to provide leadership for the next phase of implementation of the National Pain Management Strategy. Of particular significance, pain management was established as a separate organizational entity within the VA Central Office in the Office of Patient Care Services and the Medical-Surgical Strategic Healthcare Group (now the Office of Specialty Care Services [SCS]). The formal establishment of a Pain Management Program Office at the highest level of VHA is of considerable significance because it represented an explicit acknowledgment of the importance of pain management for VHA and its commitment to promoting system improvements in pain care for veterans. Dr. Kerns was appointed National Program Director for Pain Management, a senior-level position with expanded organizational authority. Within a short time, the importance of pain management within VHA was further manifested by a growth in the Program Office to include a deputy national program director and a program specialist to provide the support necessary to meet its growing list of responsibilities. Dr. Rollin Gallagher, a nationally prominent pain medicine physician, was then appointed as deputy national program director.

At a national Pain Management Leadership Conference in March 2005, Dr. Kerns provided an overview of the accomplishments of the strategy under Dr. Tollett's leadership and offered his vision for further advances. In addition to the important impacts of the Pain as the 5th Vital Sign Initiative and the VHA/IHI Pain Management Collaborative, numerous other noteworthy achievements were highlighted. By that time VHA had collaborated with the Department of Defense (DoD) in the development and dissemination of evidence-based clinical practice guidelines for the management of low back pain, acute postoperative pain, and chronic opioid therapy. An "Outcomes Measures Toolkit" was developed and published that provided a particularly comprehensive review of the domains for assessing patients and organizational level improvements in pain management. The first of an emerging list of Web-based courses for providers was published, which focused on opioid therapy.

Dr. Kerns also cited an impressive list of accomplishments focusing on provider and staff education and training, including four national pain management leadership conferences, several satellite educational seminars, the development of a process for maintaining up-to-date VISN-based libraries of pain-relevant scientific and scholarly publications, and the development of a national pain management Web site (www.va.gov/painmanagement) that continues to serve as an important resource within and outside VHA. These educational resources supplemented the VA Pain List Serve and the monthly national educational teleconferences that were initiated during the VHA/IHI Collaborative. To facilitate documentation and support standardization of pain care in VHA, a CPRS pain assessment and reassessment template and reminder system had been developed and disseminated. A consensus statement for the assessment of pain in the cognitively impaired veteran had also been developed and provided a standardized approach for addressing the challenges inherent in providing pain care for those unable to reliably report on their experiences of pain.

In delivering his first public update, Dr. Kerns took the opportunity to assert several priorities for future action. Five domains were highlighted. A continuing commitment to the objectives of the national strategy as most recently specified in the 2003 Pain Directive was emphasized as the top priority, including advancing a single standard of pain care across all VHA facilities. Second, he promised to build on the strengths of the existing infrastructure, with a focus on three specific priorities: (1) expanding the membership of the NPMSCC to include representation from important groups not previously included, such as primary care and mental health/substance abuse; (2) increasing the number of working groups, including chartering new groups focused on patient/family education, pharmacy, and primary care; and (3) focusing considerable efforts on enhancing the engagement of VISN (and facility) POCs as key pathways for communication to and from the field and the VA Central Office.

In addition, Kerns emphasized the importance of strengthening partnerships within and outside VHA. With regard to this goal, a more explicit partnership with the DoD and with public advocacy groups was highlighted. He addressed the broad scope of the National Pain Management Strategy and the importance of working toward improvements in pain care across all VHA clinical settings of care. He particularly emphasized the pain care needs of an emerging population of veterans returning from deployment in Operation Enduring Freedom and Operation Iraqi Freedom (OEF/OIF). Finally, he reasserted VHA's commitment to an interdisciplinary approach to providing pain care, including ready access to state-of-the-science pharmacological and nonpharmacological interventions, and improved access to pain medicine specialty care and to tertiary, interdisciplinary pain rehabilitation services. In this context Kerns emphasized the need to provide evidence-based and cost-effective care.

By early 2005 VHA's National Pain Management Strategy was already receiving public recognition as a model for organizational change and as a standard for excellence in pain care. In fact, overall VHA's National Pain Management Strategy has drawn international attention. Public health strategists abroad have compared it favorably with those of Australia, Canada, and France (Dobkin & Boothroyd 2008).

VHA's Commitment to Evidence-based Interdisciplinary Pain Care

Health services research in pain management overwhelmingly supports the idea that modern and comprehensive pain management is multidisciplinary and, at its best, interdisciplinary (Boris-Karpel 2011; Gatchel & Okifuji 2006; Gallagher 2005). Although there is a large and growing empirical support for multidisciplinary and interdisciplinary models of pain management, unfortunately, due to the sometimes prohibitive short-term costs of time and resources, multidisciplinary and interdisciplinary pain care are in fact the least common models of pain care found in the community.

Nevertheless, many VHA clinics offer various forms of comprehensive pain management involving interdisciplinary care. Why are VHA's clinics in the vanguard of this trend? For one thing, VHA states in its mission statement that care plans should emphasize those treatment options that have the most evidence-based support. Another likely factor is the cost-benefit analysis of lifelong patient care that takes into account, and often prioritizes, long-term outcomes over short-term outcomes (Dickinson et al. 2010). Outside VHA, third-party-payer health insurance plans will often fund and reimburse care that may be less expensive in the short term, but may be more expensive in the long term (e.g., surgery for pain management). But a care facility that treats patients for the span of their lives is more likely to value an initial higher financial cost of multidisciplinary treatment (e.g., interdisciplinary pain management that may include health psychology, physical therapy, and complementary and alternative medicine, in addition to pain medicine). This investment in the interdisciplinary approach would achieve greater health and well-being in the long term rather than a lower cost financial investment in the short term, but a poorer health outcome in the long term, as research suggests is the case with surgery and pharmacological therapy only (Boris-Karpel 2011; Martell et al. 2007).

VHA's Commitment to Pain-relevant Research

Since its implementation in 1998, an explicit component of the VHA National Pain Management Strategy has been to support and further pain-relevant research. As an indicator of the push to prioritize and improve pain-relevant research, the VHA Office of Research and Development (ORD) has more than quadrupled the pain-relevant investigator-initiated projects it has funded in the past decade. To promote collaborative research, the VHA Pain Research Working Group (PRWG) was established. The PRWG has four stated objectives (Veterans Health Administration, PRWG):

1. Establish a network of VHA pain-relevant scientists and scholars.

2. Increase the number of VHA-funded, investigator-initiated, and multisite, pain-relevant research projects.

3. Develop an agenda for health systems/health policy research designed to support the VHA National Pain Management Strategy goals.

4. Develop a research policy agenda designed to establish pain-relevant research as a priority.

This PRWG now consists of over sixty VHA and non-VHA investigators, including several from the DoD. This group in turn has generated cluster groups around common areas of research interest: diversity issues in pain management, assessment of pain in persons with cognitive impairments, pain and obesity, pain and psychiatric comorbidities, pain and medical comorbidities, pain and polytrauma, complementary and alternative medicine approaches to pain management, pain management in older adults, pain management in end-of-life care, opioid therapy, and pain and substance abuse.

Over the past decade VHA investigators have continually contributed important and original research to each of these areas, making valuable contributions to the field. In 2007 members of the PRWG published a special topic issue of VHA's *Journal of Rehabilitation Research and Development* that included an article highlighting pain-relevant research that cut across basic laboratory science, clinical science, rehabilitation, and health services research domains. At that time the editors of the special issue noted a nearly 500 percent increase in the number of pain-relevant research projects funded by ORD since 2000, and a continuing increase in the number of pain-relevant publications in peer-reviewed journals highlighting research on veterans.

In September 2007 the Rehabilitation Research and Development Service and the Polytrauma/Blast-related Injury Quality Enhancement Research Initiative (PT/BrI QuERI) provided support for the PRWG by providing funding for a Pain Research Summit, which was held in Palm Springs, California, and was attended by a group of twenty-five VA investigators, most of whom were members of the PRWG. This conference brought together leading VHA rehabilitation scientists, as well as basic laboratory and clinical scientists, with specialty interests, expertise, and ongoing research programs to foster exchange of ideas, collaboration, and networking, and to develop a cross-cutting research agenda targeting pain rehabilitation research. A specific focus of the conference was the experience of pain and psychiatric comorbidities among OEF/OIF veterans. The conference was designed to encourage translational and clinical research that is informed by contemporary theory, methodological innovation, and basic laboratory science. Several specific topics were emphasized, including

- the pathophysiology of pain and comorbid psychiatric disorders, particularly PTSD, including animal and human studies;
- implications of research on genomics, proteomics, and inflammatory markers;
- the effects of an early intervention model to prevent maintenance of pain and development of psychiatric comorbidities;
- implications of pain and occupational medicine research for understanding the experience of combat veterans and for the development of efficacious interventions;
- epidemiological studies of the effects of prolonged deployment, trauma/combat-exposure, and related factors on the risks for pain morbidity; and
- contributions of chronic pain to the maintenance of PTSD, other states of arousal, and mental health disorders.

One important outcome of the summit was the decision to pursue publication of a special issue of the journal *Pain Medicine*. This initiative was planned as an important effort to extend the discussions of the 2007 Pain Research Summit by providing an opportunity to present VHA research related either directly or indirectly to the experiences of pain among OEF/OIF veterans. The special issue was published in October 2009. A subsequent VHA-facilitated "cyberseminar" highlighted five of the sixteen contributions to emphasize the policy and practice implications of the authors' research.

The PRWG continues to meet monthly via national teleconferences and to meet in person as a Special Interest Group at an annual national meeting of ORD's Health Services Research and Development (HSR&D) Service. In 2008 HSR&D funded the Pain Research, Informatics, Medical Comorbidities, and Education (PRIME) Center at the VA Connecticut Healthcare System to help build local and national capacity for pain-relevant health services research in VHA. In late 2009 another summit was held, which focused on the comorbidities of pain; persistent post-concussive syndrome; and post-traumatic stress disorder, substance use disorders, and sleep disorders. Most recently, VHA has taken the lead on building bridges to partners in the National Institutes of Health and the DoD to further foster pain-relevant research collaboration.

Congressional Legislation and Public Law 110-387, Section 501, Pain Care Act of 2008

In every session since 2003, the U.S. Congress has attempted to ratify a pain care bill to include provisions that would affect pain management services and research throughout the nation. This bill, in its many iterations, has not yet been passed. However, in 2008 the office of Senator Daniel Akaka (D-Hawaii) took the aspects of the bill that would apply to the military and to veterans and created a bill that bolstered services and support for pain management within the military and the other supporting pain management services, education, and research for veterans. The Veterans Mental Health and Other Care Improvements Act of 2008 became Public Law 110-387. Two provisions of Public Law 110, Section 501 call upon VHA to further strengthen its commitment to providing optimal pain care to veterans. The Act specifically required VA to develop a comprehensive policy on the management of pain. As required by the law, VHA consulted with veterans' service organizations such as the Disabled American Veterans (DAV) and Veterans of Foreign Wars (VFW) as well as with representatives of non-VHA professional organizations, including the American Pain Society (APS) and American Academy of Pain Medicine (AAPM) in crafting a revised VHA Pain Management Directive, which was published in October 2009 (VHA Directive 2009-053, Pain Management). The second provision of Public Law 110-387, Section 501 called on VHA to report to Congress within 180 days of publishing the policy and annually thereafter. At the time of writing this chapter, two annual reports have been submitted.

The revised directive was significant in several important ways. It reasserted VHA's commitment to an approach that is informed by a biopsychosocial model of pain and an interdisciplinary, multidimensional, and multimodal approach to pain management. For the first time, it asserted that improved quality of life, rather than pain relief per se, is the accepted standard outcome measure of effectiveness. Improved quality of life includes improvements in physical and psychosocial (i.e., work and home) functioning and patient satisfaction. The directive further specified the organizational structure of the National Pain Management Strategy and clarified the responsibilities of various levels of the organization, including the national Pain Management Program Office, the NPMSCC, VISN and facility directors, and POCs. Perhaps most important, for the first time the directive established an evidence-based and population-based "stepped care approach" as the single standard for pain care in VHA. Some of the details of this model and approach are described later.

In its most recent report to Congress, VHA summarized its progress in implementing the strategy, including compliance with key provisions of the directive; data reflecting VHA's commitment to building capacity for pain care for veterans; updates on VHA's research, provider education, and patient education initiatives; and an update on initiatives involving collaboration with the DoD. In brief, the report documented that all VHA facilities have a pain management policy and multidisciplinary pain committee to ensure that accepted standards of pain care are met. The report documented substantial progress in building capacity for specialty pain care, with evidence of steady increases in the number of veterans receiving care from a pain medicine specialist since 2005, with nearly 100,000 veterans receiving such services in fiscal year 2009. The report also highlighted several new clinical initiatives and research efforts designed to promote innovation in pain care.

Stepped-Care Model

The Veterans Healthcare Administrartion has endorsed a stepped-care model as the single standard of pain care for veterans and has begun an aggressive process of implementing the model across its facilities. The stepped-care model begins with providing all-inclusive access to pain assessment and treatment services within the Patient Aligned Care Team (PACT), VHA's version of the Patient Centered Medical Home. The PACT team members provide assessment and management of the most common pain conditions. Partnerships with other key resources within the PACT, such as integrative primary care–mental health initiative teams work to provide evidence-based pharmacological and integrative behavioral interventions. Having built capacity for managing most painful conditions in this setting, equitable access to specialized secondary pain care resources is necessary. Thus the second step of the model involves readily accessible services, including pain medicine, behavioral health, neurology, physical medicine and rehabilitation, chiropractic, palliative care, and advanced diagnostic and medical management. For the most treatment-refractory, complex, and at-risk patients, access to highly specialized tertiary, interdisciplinary teams is necessary.

In this regard, VHA has made a commitment to building at least one tertiary pain care center in each VISN by October 2014. Services to be provided in these centers include the most advanced pain medicine, diagnostic, and intervention services, including implantable devices such as spinal cord stimulators and intrathecal medication delivery systems. Centers are also required to provide Commission for the Accreditation of Rehabilitation Facilities (CARF)–accredited chronic pain rehabilitation services. Finally, centers are expected to build capacity for managing veterans with comorbid chronic pain and substance use disorders, particularly prescription opioid abuse and dependence. There is strong empirical support for this model in the research literature, which demonstrates the efficacy of this organizational structure of care in improving pain outcomes (Dobscha et al. 2009; Kroenke, Krebs & Bair 2009; Von & Moore 2001).

A key challenge in implementation of the stepped-pain-care model is the need to build capacity with the PACT for delivering competent pain care. To support this effort, the national Pain Management Program Office and the Primary Care Program Office are collaborating on multiple fronts to develop education and training resources, clinical decision support tools, and just-in-time electronic training resources to support the developing competencies of primary care providers, nurses, and associated health professionals. Innovation in developing novel approaches to delivering team-based and patient-centered pain care are being encouraged through funding initiatives and other incentives.

Provision of equitable access to specialty pain management and other services for veterans living in rural settings or settings lacking in specialists is an important challenge for VHA. To address this challenge, another major innovation is the pending implementation of a new VHA initiative called Project SCAN (Secondary Care Access Networks), designed to build interdisciplinary teams of pain care experts who will use videoconferencing and other technologies to provide case-based learning to PACT teams in rural settings to support their development of competencies in managing complex chronic pain.

Summary and Future Directions

Since the initial stages of enacting Dr. Kenneth Kizer's vision for a VHA National Pain Management Strategy, it is apparent VHA has much to be proud of in enhancing its capacity for pain care for veterans. The evolution and maturing of the strategy has seen considerable advances in ensuring access to pain care for veterans regardless of their point of entry into the healthcare system and in increasing the likelihood that veterans will be met by a team of providers and staff who are more knowledgeable and competent to assess and manage pain than was true before the strategy was launched. The recent specification of the stepped-pain-care model holds promise as a framework for meeting VHA's mission of reducing pain and suffering and improving the quality of life for veterans experiencing pain. At the same time, it goes without saying that along with the promise are many challenges that will have to be addressed to reach VHA's strategic goals. The established infrastructure and commitment of VHA to promoting innovation in implementing and evaluating the stepped-pain-care model will likely ensure the continuing success of these efforts.

Acknowledgment: This material is based on work supported by a grant from the Department of Veterans Affairs, Veterans Health Administration, Office of Research and Development, Health Services Research and Development Service (REA 08-266).

Disclaimer: The views expressed in this chapter are those of the authors and do not necessarily reflect the position or policy of the Department of Veterans Affairs or the U.S. government.

References

Acute Care Strategic Healthcare Group. (1997). VHA Pain Management Survey. Washington, DC: Department of Veterans Affairs.

Boris-Karpel, S. (2011). Policy and practice issues in pain management. In M. H. Ebert & R. D. Kerns (Eds.), *Behavioral and psychopharmacologic pain management* (pp. 407–433). Cambridge: Cambridge University Press.

Clark, M. E. (2004). Post-deployment pain: A need for rapid detection and intervention. *Pain Medicine* 5: 333–334.

Clark, M. E., Rintala, D. H., Gironda, R. J. & Wegener, S. (2002). Spinal cord impairmentpain: Prevalence, correlates, and treatment. Symposium conducted at the 21st Annual Scientific Meeting of the American Pain Society, Baltimore, MD, March 15.

Cleeland, C. S., Reyes-Gibby, C. C., Schall, M., Nolan, K., Paice, J., Rosenberg, J. M., et al. (2003). Rapid improvement in pain management: The Veterans Health Administration and the Institute for Healthcare Improvement Collaborative. *Clinical Journal of Pain* 19: 298–305.

Craine, M. & Kerns, R. D. (2003). Pain management improvement strategies in the Veterans Health Administration. *American Pain Society Bulletin* 13: 1–9.

Dickinson, K. C., Sharma, R., Duckart, J. P., Corson, K., Gerrity, M. S. & Dobscha, S. K. (2010). VA healthcare costs of a collaborative intervention for chronic pain in primary care. *Medical Care* 48: 38–44.

Dobkin, P. L. & Boothroyd, L. J. (2008). Organizing health services for patients with chronic pain: When there is a will there is a way. *Pain Medicine* 9: 881–889.

Dobscha, S. K., Corson, K., Perrin, N. A., Hanson, G. C., Leibowitz, R. Q., Doak, M. N. et al. (2009). Collaborative care for chronic pain in primary care: A cluster randomized trial. *JAMA* 301: 1242–1252.

Gallagher, R. M. (2005). Pain science and rational polypharmacy: An historical perspective. *American Journal of Physical Medicine and Rehabilitation* 84: S1–S3.

Gatchel, R. J. & Okifuji, A. (2006). Evidence-based scientific data documenting the treatment and cost-effectiveness of comprehensive pain programs for chronic non-malignant pain. *Journal of Pain* 7: 779–793.

Gironda, R. J., Clark, M. E., Massengale, J. P. & Walker, R. L. (2006). Pain among veterans of Operations Enduring Freedom and Iraqi Freedom. *Pain Medicine* 7: 339–343.

Halpern, J. (1996). The measurement of quality of care in the Veterans Health Administration. *Medical Care* 34: MS55–MS68.

Haskell, S. G., Heapy, A., Reid, M. C., Papas, R. K. & Kerns, R. D. (2006). The prevalence and age-related characteristics of pain in a sample of women veterans receiving primary care. *Journal of Women's Health (Larchmt.)* 15: 862–869.

Haskell, S. G., Papas, R. K., Heapy, A., Reid, M. C. & Kerns, R. D. (2008). The association of sexual trauma with persistent pain in a sample of women veterans receiving primary care. *Pain Medicine* 9: 710–717.

Holzman, A. D., Turk, D. C. & Kerns, R. D. (1986). A cognitive-behavioral approach to the management of chronic pain. In A. D. Holzman & D. C. Turk (Eds.), *Chronic pain: A handbook of psychological treatment approaches.* Elmsford, NY: Pergamon Press.

Holzman, A. D., Turk, D. C., Sanders, S. H., Gerber, K. E., Zimmerman, J., Rudy, T. E. & Kerns, R. D. (1985). Chronic pain: A multiple setting comparison of patient characteristics. *Journal of Behavioral Medicine* 8: 411–422.

Joint Commission on Accreditation of Healthcare Organizations. (2003). *Pain standards for 2003.* http:/www.jcaho.org (accessed February 17, 2009).

Kerns, R. D., Booss, J., Bryan, M., Clark, M. E., Drake, A., Green-Rashad, B., et al. (2006). Veterans Health Administration national pain management strategy: Update and future directions. *American Pain Society Bulletin* 16: 1–15.

Kerns, R. D., Otis, J., Rosenberg, R. & Reid, M. C. (2003). Veterans' reports of pain and associations with ratings of health, health-risk behaviors, affective distress, and use of the healthcare system. *Journal of Rehabilitation Research and Development* 40: 371–379.

Kerns, R. D., Rosenberg, R., Jamison, R. N., Caudill, M. A. & Haythornthwaite, J. (1997). Readiness to adopt a self-management approach to chronic pain: The Pain Stages of Change Questionnaire (PSOCQ). *Pain* 72: 227–234.

Kerns, R. D., Turk, D. C., Holzman, A. D. & Rudy, T. E. (1986). Comparison of cognitive-behavioral and behavioral approaches to the outpatient treatment of chronic pain. *Clinical Journal of Pain* 1: 195–203.

Kerns, R. D., Turk, D. C. & Rudy, T. E. (1985). The West Haven–Yale Multidimensional Pain Inventory (WHYMPI). *Pain* 23: 345–356.

Kerns, R. D., Wasse, L., Ryan, B., Drake, A. & Booss, J. (2000). *Pain as the 5th vital sign toolkit.* V.2. Washington, DC: Veterans Health Administration.

Kroenke, K., Krebs, E. E. & Bair, M. J. (2009). Pharmacotherapy of chronic pain: A synthesis of recommendations from systematic reviews. *General Hospital Psychiatry* 31: 206–219.

Lew, H. L., Otis, J. D., Tun, C., Kerns, R. D., Clark, M. E. & Cifu, D. X. (2009). Prevalence of chronic pain, posttraumatic stress disorder, and persistent postconcussive symptoms in OIF/OEF veterans: Polytrauma clinical triad. *Journal of Rehabilitation Research and Development* 46: 697–702.

Lynn, J., Schuster, L. J., Wilkinson, A. & Simon, L. N. (2007). *Improving care for the end of life: A sourcebook for healthcare managers and clinicians.* 2nd ed. New York: Oxford University Press.

Martell, B. A., O'Connor, P. G., Kerns, R. D., Becker, W. C., Morales, K. H., Kosten, T. R., et al. (2007). Systematic review: opioid treatment for chronic back pain: Prevalence, efficacy, and association with addiction. *Annals of Internal Medicine* 146: 116–127.

Meldrum, M. L. (2003). A capsule history of pain management. *Journal of the American Medical Association* 290: 2470–2475.

Mitchell, S. W. (1872). *Injuries of nerves and their consequences.* Philadelphia: J.B. Lippincott & Co.

Schuster, L. J. (1999). Veterans Health Administration's addition of pain as a fifth vital sign may have far reaching effects. *Americans for Better Care of the Dying Exchange Newsletter.* (February). http://www.abcd-caring.org/newsletter.htm (accessed January 23, 2011).

Sinnott, P. & Wagner, T. H. (2009). Low back pain in VA users. *Archives of Internal Medicine* 169: 1338–1339.

Veterans Health Administration. (1998). VHA national pain management strategy. Washington, DC: Department of Veterans Affairs.

Veterans Health Administration. (2003). *VHA directive 2003-021: Pain management.* Washington, DC: Department of Veterans Affairs.

Veterans Health Administration. (2009). *VHA directive 2009-053: Pain management.* Washington, DC: Department of Veterans Affairs.

Veterans Health Administration. (n.d.). Health Services Research & Development Service (HSR&D): Pain Research Working Group (PRWG). http://www.hsrd.research.va.gov/for_researchers/sig/#pain (accessed January 23, 2011).

Veterans' Mental Health and Other Care Improvement Act of 2008. (2008). Public Law 110–387§ 501.

Von, K. M. & Moore, J. C. (2001). Stepped care for back pain: Activating approaches for primary care. *Annals of Internal Medicine* 134: 911–917.
Yu, W., Ravelo, A., Wagner, T. H., Phibbs, C. S., Bhandari, A., Chen, S., et al. (2003). Prevalence and costs of chronic conditions in the VA health care system. *Medical Care Research and Review* 60: 146S–167S.

New Directions
in Veterans' Healthcare

Achieving Clinical Integration: Observations from the Veterans' Healthcare System

Kenneth W. Kizer

Modern healthcare is one of the most complex and information-intense activities ever devised by humans. Care for all but mundane health problems is typically provided in numerous different settings by diverse types of healthcare workers who utilize an array of diagnostic and therapeutic technologies. These diverse settings of care, disparate caregivers, and multiple technologies are rarely connected in a predictable, consistent, and coherent manner, and information does not flow freely and reliably among them. In a word, clinical services are not integrated. The lack of clinical integration results in much inefficiency, waste, and frustration for patients and healthcare professionals alike, as well as causing medical errors and preventable harm.

Integrating clinical services across the continuum of care to improve the coordination and continuity of care is foundational to improving healthcare outcomes and value and will be a required core competency for healthcare organizations under the new value-driven payment and care delivery models authorized by the Patient Protection and Affordable Care Act of 2010 (ACA). However, few American healthcare organizations are designed for or have the capacity to provide integrated care.

One of the most integrated healthcare organizations in the United States is the Veterans' healthcare system, administered by the Veterans Health Administration (VHA) in the Department of Veterans Affairs (VA). Its experience integrating services offers useful insights for others seeking to achieve clinical integration.

Background and Context

The VA healthcare system is the largest healthcare system in the United States, although unusual in American healthcare insofar as it is administered centrally, is staffed by salaried government employees, and derives more than 90 percent of its operating budget from a congressional appropriation. Being a centrally administered single-payer system may provide some advantages for integrating clinical services, but these operating characteristics do not a priori lead to being integrated, as demonstrated by the severe fragmentation of care and wide variation in the availability of services that characterized the Veterans' healthcare system in the early 1990s (Kizer & Dudley 2009).

At that time, the system was viewed by many as a healthcare backwater. Care was fragmented, disjointed, expensive, difficult to access, and of unpredictable and irregular quality. The availability and predictability of services varied widely among facilities. The culture of VHA was risk-averse and punitive, in significant part due to the fishbowl-like fault-finding environment of Washington, D.C. politics. This stifled innovation, diffused accountability, discouraged individual initiative, and eroded trust. Perceptions of VA healthcare had deteriorated so much by 1994 that the system's existence was threatened.

Between 1995 and 1999, the VA healthcare system was reengineered to improve quality, increase accountability, encourage innovation, and enhance value (Kizer & Dudley 2009; Edmondson, Golden & Young 2006; Oliver 2007; Kizer 1995). This reengineering sought to transform the system from a hospital-centric, specialist-dominated healthcare delivery system providing episodic, fragmented, and reactionary care to one that provided proactive, patient-centered, continuous, coordinated high-value care (Kizer 1995). Integrating clinical services across the continuum of care was central to achieving this goal.

While achieving clinical integration in the VA healthcare system is still a work in progress, a number of observations can be made from its experience that might inform similarly intended efforts catalyzed by the Affordable Care Act. In considering the potential applicability of VHA's experience to American healthcare more broadly, however, it is important to recognize differences between VA and private-sector healthcare.

In addition to being a centrally administered, single-payer, government-operated healthcare system, the VA healthcare system differs from most private healthcare organizations in its intentional adverse selection of sick and socioeconomically disadvantaged patients, an unusually high proportion of whom have psychiatric and behavioral health conditions; its extensive involvement in health professional training and research; the broader array of services VA provides, including many social support services not typically offered in private health plans; and its important role in national emergency contingency support. The VA system is also relatively unique in being both a healthcare provider and a payer and by being subject to much greater oversight and public scrutiny than private-sector health care.

It is also noteworthy that the VA healthcare system is subject to political dynamics that sometimes impede its ability to provide services. For example, in the decade 1999–2009, VHA's operating budget was approved by Congress at the beginning of the new fiscal year only once, with the average delay being nearly four months. Among other adverse operational effects, this repeatedly delayed hiring needed staff and implementing priority programs.

Importantly, though there are differences between the VA system and private-sector healthcare in organizational structure, service population, and funding methods, the new payment and delivery models authorized by the Affordable Care Act portend greater similarities in structure and funding in the years ahead. It is also important to recognize that notwithstanding organizational and funding differences, the VA system and private-sector organizations utilize common approaches to and processes of patient care. These similarities in clinical processes should not be surprising in view of VA's extensive involvement in health professional training and the fact that some 70 percent of VA physicians hold academic positions. As one who has extensive experience in both the private sector and VA system, it has always appeared to me that the similarities in clinical practice and healthcare culture in VA and the private sector are far greater than the differences and that the barriers and strategies needed to achieve clinical integration are much the same.

Observations

Over the past fifteen years, efforts to integrate clinical services in the VA healthcare system have utilized multiple strategies and tactics. These efforts have encountered variable and sometimes strong resistance by medical staff, employee unions, and politically powerful stakeholder groups. The amount of resistance to the same intervention (e. g., implementing primary care teams and community-based clinics or using clinical guidelines) has varied among facilities in sometimes unpredictable ways, although such resistance has tended to correlate with the strength and skills of facility leadership, the history of the facility's academic affiliations (when applicable), and the composition and nature of its medical staff. Although only a few of VA's clinical integration strategies have been formally studied, a number of observations can be made from the system's accumulated experience achieving clinical integration.

The Need for an Organizational Structure That Facilitates Management and Operational Accountability

Despite being centrally administered, having volumes of operating policies and procedures, and being subject to unparalleled oversight, the VA healthcare system was paradoxically unaccountable in 1994. This stemmed in significant part from the cumbersome and dysfunctional management structure that existed at that time. Thus, one of the first steps taken to integrate clinical services to reduce fragmentation of care was to implement an organizational structure that facilitated increased management and operational accountability. This new operational structure consisted of twenty-two regional networks known as Veterans Integrated Service Networks (VISNs) (Kizer & Dudley 2009; Kizer 1995).

After obtaining stakeholder buy-in and requisite congressional approval, the reengineering of the system was officially launched in October 1995 with creation of the VISNs. Each VISN was charged with providing comprehensive care for a defined population (Kizer 1995). Empirical data at that time suggested that a population of about 250,000 patients was necessary to support a clinical services network capable of providing a continuum of primary to tertiary care services with VA assets, so each VISN was originally designed to serve a veteran population of approximately this size and included care delivery assets of seven to ten hospitals, twenty-five to thirty ambulatory care clinics, ten to fifteen nursing facilities, and one to two domiciliaries or residential care facilities, among other sites of care.

In the new operating structure a premium was placed "on improved patient services, rigorous cost management, process improvement, outcomes and 'best value' care" (Kizer 1995). Hospitals were viewed as being important but, compared to their pre-VISN status, a less central component "of a larger, more coordinated community-based network of care" in which emphasis was placed "on the integration of ambulatory care and acute and extended inpatient services so as to provide a coordinated continuum of care" (Kizer 1995). The VISNs were expected to utilize data-driven methods to manage total performance so that care was delivered "in a highly patient-centered manner that improved the overall health and functionality of the population served" (Kizer 1995). In these and other ways the intent and purposes of the VISNs appear to be strikingly similar to the goals of the new accountable care organizations authorized in the Affordable Care Act.

A Values-based Vision of the New Future

Healthcare operates as a complex adaptive system. Typical of these nonlinear, self-learning, and continually adapting systems, integrating clinical services

> **Box 6.1. The New Vision of the VA Healthcare System.**
>
> The Veterans Health Administration will provide a seamless continuum of consistent and predictable high quality patient-centered care that is of superior value.

involves innumerable unique situations and circumstances that can never be completely anticipated or addressed in policies and standardized procedures. In these ways, healthcare is distinctly different from more commonly understood linear processes such as manufacturing, in which the inputs to and component parts of the system can be specified and controlled in detail. Many healthcare improvement efforts have not understood this fundamental aspect of healthcare, especially the importance of a guiding vision, and have failed to achieve their intended effect.

Having a guiding vision of the new future to be brought about by some intentional effort is important for achieving change in any system, but is especially critical for changing complex, adaptive systems. The vision of the new future provides the critical foundation for addressing the myriad complexities of these systems. It was critical that creation of the VISNs and other steps taken to achieve clinical integration in the VA healthcare system be guided by a new vision of the future (see box 6.1). This vision needed to be clear, actionable, and based on shared values. It needed to stimulate a new organizational culture grounded on collaboration and teamwork, accountability, continuous quality improvement, and a never-ending quest for best value. Among other things, this required getting systemwide buy-in on a set of organizational core values, an iterative dialogue that took many months. Ultimately, five core values were adopted: trust, respect, excellence, compassion, and commitment. These values served as a compass for navigating through the uncertainties and complexities of integrating services across time and space.

Clinical Integration Requires an Enabling Infrastructure

Implementing the new vision for VA healthcare required instituting an enabling operational infrastructure as well as a management structure. Prominent elements of the new operational infrastructure included universal primary care; a performance management system that consistently and continuously tracked performance, analyzed results, provided feedback to frontline caregivers, and rewarded accomplishment of desired outcomes; advanced telecommunications and information management technologies, including an electronic health record having robust clinical decision support and the capacity to support health information exchange between and among diverse sites of care and telehealth; comprehensive care management tools, including multidisciplinary care teams, clinical guidelines and care protocols, an evidence-based national formulary to support appropriate medication utilization, and population health management methods; a new global funding and resource allocation methodology; a shared savings strategy; and a knowledge management system (Kizer & Dudley 2009).

Further, there needed to be a broadly participatory and structured method to balance patient and clinician freedom of choice and preferences with efforts to coordinate care and optimize resource utilization. Even though better coordinated care is likely to produce better healthcare outcomes, it will sometimes conflict with patient and provider preference and convenience, potentially leading to ill will, disharmony, and resistance to change. To amicably resolve these situations there must be structured and transparent methods for balancing freedom of choice and personal preferences with the common good.

In implementing the new operational structure, the information technology, performance management, and knowledge management systems needed to be closely aligned and linked with each other to develop organizational capacity for systems thinking and to support multidisciplinary care teams, population health management strategies, and other requisite competencies. These competencies have historically not featured prominently in physician and other health professional training, and they needed to be strengthened while being mindful of the time constraints and other demands that confront clinicians.

Achieving Clinical Integration Requires Changing Healthcare Culture

Importantly, though information management and other operational infrastructure are necessary to achieve clinical integration, they are not sufficient. The effective use of these tools requires that they be embedded in a culture of collaboration, inquiry, and continuous improvement.

Integrating clinical services in the VA healthcare system required addressing barriers deeply rooted in both VA organizational culture and healthcare culture generally. Strategies aimed at integrating clinical services in the VA system were often overtly and covertly opposed by clinicians, employee unions, and politically powerful stakeholder groups. Achieving clinical integration often required changing how clinicians and other staff thought and felt about what they did.

Many factors have contributed to the current culture of healthcare and its reactionary and piecemeal approach to providing clinical services. The history of healthcare as a cottage industry consisting of independent practitioners who were rewarded for curing acute illnesses and injuries gave rise to a healthcare culture that valued and rewarded individuality, competition, and rescue care. Physician training programs have tended to select independent thinkers, and professional societies have reinforced and steadfastly defended individual caregiver autonomy. Disdain for rules and practices that do not appear to add value to the short-term needs of individual patients and infatuation with highly technical and sometimes heroic interventions are consistent with the American ethos generally and have been glamorized both within health care and by society generally. Advances in the biomedical sciences and resultant medical specialization have progressively narrowed individual practitioners' focus and encouraged separation of clinical and managerial activities and their associated bodies of knowledge. These and other dynamics have produced a healthcare culture and generations of practitioners that are often poorly prepared to provide the coordinated, collaborative, cost-conscious, patient-centered care needed for managing the chronic conditions that are the mainstay of health care today.

The healthcare culture needed to support integrated care delivery requires new ways of thinking and intellectual competencies that currently receive little attention in graduate and postgraduate medical education or other health professional training. Prominent among the needed new competencies are systems thinking; an understanding of complexity theory; teamwork skills; and knowledge of the principles and methods of population health management, quality improvement, information management, and communication skills. In the new payment and care delivery paradigms authorized by the Affordable Care Act, hospitals need to be viewed as cost centers instead of revenue centers and preventable admissions as health system failures. Clinicians need to understand that there are limited funds for healthcare and that there is an ethical imperative to provide cost-effective care and to be prudent stewards of limited public funds. They need to understand that they are responsible for continually improving quality and removing waste from the processes of care, for the benefit of both patients and themselves. The system needs to be designed to proactively promote health, as well as treat illness, and to recognize that healthcare is but one of many determinants of health. Some progress has been made toward these ends in recent years, but much more needs to be done.

Given the importance of language to culture, attention to the nuances of language is also especially important when embarking on culture change. The words used to describe a problem may significantly shape how the problem is viewed and the strategies employed to solve it. This understanding of the importance of language has not penetrated the consciousness of healthcare as much as it has the business sector and politics. Illustrative of this is the current widespread effort to promote use of health information technology. Current efforts have tended to focus on the information technology (IT) instead of the more important knowledge transfer (KT) and process redesign that is sought from use of this technology. Conceptualizing the issue as a KT problem, instead of an IT problem, might more effectively direct attention to what is most important, as well as stimulating innovative ways of using the technology to achieve clinical integration.

Strong and Empowered Leadership Is Crucial

Strong and empowered leaders, both clinical and administrative, are needed to achieve clinical integration. The touch of the leader is felt in many ways, directly and indirectly. Leaders build trust within and outside the organization. Leaders secure resources to support new ways of providing care, and they prioritize goals and competing strategic objectives. Leaders create an environment that is conducive to learning and in which it is safe to innovate. They promote a culture of engagement and ownership and continually guide and direct individual parochial interests toward collective goals and the common good. Leaders ensure appropriate recognitions are made to reinforce and reward desired outcomes and behaviors.

Strong clinical leadership is especially important. The clinical leader must inspire caregivers with vision and compassion while also detailing the realities of the spreadsheet. The clinical leader must use both stories and statistics to explain the fine details and nuances of care delivery for nonclinician hospital trustees while wrangling funds for needed clinical upgrades. The clinical leader builds bridges between the boardroom and bedside while harmonizing and aligning the agendas of independent-minded professionals whose egos may be bruised by the new processes of integrated care.

Alignment of Finances Requires Multiple Strategies

Unquestionably, monetary awards can be useful tools to reward improved performance and reinforce desired behaviors. However, in a fundamentally altruistic profession like healthcare, payment methods may be more powerful disincentives that impede clinical integration than they are positive incentives that drive change, unlike in manufacturing or sales. Assuming that payment is reasonable, a clear and compelling purpose or mission, the opportunity for professional fulfillment, and a sense of autonomy may be more powerful incentives for improvement than modestly increased payment.

A key element in VHA's reengineering was development and implementation of a new global payment methodology for allocating funds to the VISNs. Known as the Veterans Equitable Resource Allocation (VERA) methodology, this tiered, capitation-based, global payment system was designed to incentivize administrators and clinicians to provide the right amount of care in the right setting in an efficient and patient-centered manner (Kizer & Dudley 2009).

Since first being implemented in 1997, VERA has proved to be very effective in allocating funds to the VISNs. However, it has been less effective at equitably allocating funds to operational units below the network level. Various adjustments to how funds are distributed to hospitals and clinics have been made over the years in attempts to improve the distribution of funds to more granular levels of the system, and further refinements are needed to support telemedicine and other new models of care.

Strategic Communications Plan

A strategic communications plan is an integral but frequently overlooked and undervalued enabler of implementing any type of change, including strategies to achieve clinical integration. Myriad questions and considerable confusion will arise when implementing strategies to achieve clinical integration. These uncertainties should be anticipated and addressed in advance whenever possible. Rumors and misperceptions are inherent to change and can paralyze progress if not appropriately addressed in a timely manner. Having a well-designed, strategic communications plan is one of the best ways to avoid misunderstandings.

To be effective, a strategic communications plan must have a defined message, which must be health-literate, culturally appropriate, and adaptable to local cultural and care delivery issues. The message must be designed to reach all stakeholders and must address both risks and benefits in a balanced manner. The plan must recognize the special needs of communicating with the 24/7/365 healthcare workforce; for example, the different ways needed to communicate with night and day shift workers.

As much as possible, communications to patients and community members should come from physicians and nurses, because these professionals tend to be trusted more than administrators. Both conventional and unconventional methods of communication need to be utilized. In light of the rapid evolution and widespread adoption of mobile information and communications technologies in recent years, the communications plan should devote particular attention to Internet-based social media.

Care Delivery Assets Will Probably Have to Be Restructured

The role of the hospital in an integrated delivery system will almost certainly change, and the need to increase ambulatory and home care capacities and down-size inpatient capacity should be anticipated. Illustrative of such changes, between 1995 and 1999, the VA healthcare system closed 28,986 acute care hospital beds (55 percent of its total acute care beds), reduced staffing by 25,867 full-time equivalent employees (12 percent of its workforce) while increasing the proportion of caregivers, reduced bed days of care per 1,000 patients by 68 percent, merged fifty-two medical centers into twenty-five multicampus facilities, opened 302 new community-based outpatient clinics, reduced the number of hospital admissions by 350,000 per year, and increased the number of ambulatory care visits from 24 to 37 million. The number of patients who received hands-on care per year increased by more than 700,000 (24 percent), while the average annual per patient cost per year decreased by 25.1 percent, in constant dollars.

When considering changes in care delivery assets, it is especially important to remember that hospitals are more than places where healthcare is provided. They serve as major employers in virtually every community that has one, and they are often icons of community identity. The broader social significance and potential non-healthcare impact of restructuring delivery assets (e.g., loss of jobs, travel needs, etc.) must be recognized and proactively addressed.

Conclusion

Integrating clinical services in the VA healthcare system has improved both clinical and operational outcomes. Despite serving a patient population that is older, sicker, and more socioeconomically disadvantaged (Kazis et al. 1998; Rogers et al. 2004), when VA healthcare is compared to Medicare and other health plans using standardized quality indicators, its performance over the past twelve years has been significantly better; its annual per enrollee expenditure less; and its delivery of care more predictable and consistent across facilities, geography, and patient demographics (Kizer & Dudley 2009; Trivedi et al. 2011; Trivedi & Grebla 2011; Jha et al. 2003; Congressional Budget Office n.d.; Asch et al. 2004; Keating et al. 2011). And although achieving full clinical integration in VHA is still a work in progress, especially for integrating mental health services with other clinical services and for integrating its services with those of the military healthcare system and private providers, VA's experience provides many valuable lessons for others pursuing clinical integration strategies.

References

Asch, S. M., McGlynn, E. A., Hogan, M. M., et al. (2004). Comparison of quality of care for patients in the Veterans Health Administration and patients in a national sample. *Annals of Internal Medicine* 141: 938–945.

Congressional Budget Office. (n.d.). Quality initiatives undertaken by the Veterans Health Administration. http://www.cbo.gov/ftpdocs/104xx/doc10453/08-13-VHA.pdf (accessed December 16, 2010).

Edmondson, A. C., Golden, B. R. & Young, G. J. (2006). *Turnaround at the Veterans Health Administration.* N9-607-035. Boston: Harvard Business School.

Jha, A. K., Perlin, J. B., Kizer, K. W. & Dudley, R. A. (2003). Effect of the transformation of the Veterans Affairs health care system on the quality of care. *New England Journal of Medicine* 348: 2218–2227.

Kazis, L. E., Miller, D. R., Clark, J., et al. (1998). Health-related quality of life in patients served by the Department of Veterans Affairs: Results of the Veterans Health Study. *Archives of Internal Medicine* 158: 626–632.

Keating, N. L., Landrum, M. B., Lamont, E. B., et al. (2011). Quality of care for older patients with cancer in the Veterans Health Administration versus the private sector: A cohort study. *Annals of Internal Medicine* 154: 727–736.

Kizer, K. W. (Ed.). (1995). *Vision for change: A plan to restructure the Veterans Health Administration.* Washington, DC: Department of Veterans Affairs.

Kizer, K. W. & Dudley, R. A. (2009). Extreme makeover: Transformation of the veterans health care system. *Annual Review of Public Health* 30:18. 1–18. 27.

Oliver, A. (2007). The Veterans Health Administration: An American success story? *Milbank Quarterly* 85: 5–35.

The Patient Protection and Affordable Care Act of 2010. Pub. L. No. 111-148.

Rogers, W. H., Kazis, L. E., Miller, D. R., et al. (2004). Comparing the health status of VA and non-VA ambulatory patients: The veterans' health and medical outcomes studies. *Journal of Ambulatory Care Management* 27: 249–262.

Trivedi, A. N. & Grebla, R. C. (2011). Comparison of the quality of health care in the Veterans Affairs health care system and Medicare Advantage health plans. *Medical Care* 49: 560–568.

Trivedi, A. N., Matula, S., Miake-Lye, I., Glassman, P. A., Shekelle, P. & Asch, S. (2011). Comparison of the quality of medical care in Veterans Affairs and non–Veterans Affairs settings. *Medical Care* 59: 76–88.

Chapter 7

VA Healthcare System: A Potential Model for a National Plan

Said A. Ibrahim, David S. Macpherson,
and Michael E. Moreland

Introduction

Healthcare in the United States is once again a key national issue. Most recently it received vast attention in national debates leading up to the Patient Protection and Affordable Care Act, which was passed by Congress and signed by the president in 2010. The debates reflected growing public unease about the healthcare system fueled by rising healthcare costs (Donelan et al. 1999), concerns about the quality of American healthcare, and the growing number of Americans without health insurance (*Health Insurance Coverage and the Uninsured* 1999). These concerns have been further ignited by reports that put the American healthcare system in perspective vis-à-vis the rest of the world. The World Health Organization (WHO) ranked the U.S. healthcare system at number 37 among 191 nations (*World Health Report* 2000). The Commonwealth Fund ranked the U.S. healthcare system next to last compared with the United Kingdom, Canada, New Zealand, and Australia (Davis et al. 2007). Even among insured patients, the quality and equity of healthcare delivered in the United States has been a subject of debate (Smedley, Stith & Nelson 2003). Public concern about the U.S. healthcare system shows up in public satisfaction ratings. Although most Americans still elect to receive medical care locally, patient surveys demonstrate low satisfaction rates with healthcare quality and access (Blendon et al. 2002).

The call for a national healthcare plan has been a recurring theme in the United States for almost a century. In 1916 Congress debated a draft bill proposing universal medical coverage. In 1934 Franklin Delano Roosevelt was urged to consider adding healthcare to his New Deal. The healthcare debate again returned to the national scene briefly in 1965 and then more vigorously in 1992 during the Clinton administration. Today, once again, the healthcare debate is at the forefront of national discussion.

Veterans Health Administration as a Model

In the past, when the debate about healthcare reform in the United States arose and people looked for ideas on how to improve the system, the working national healthcare models that experts often offered were based on the Canadian healthcare system or those implemented by other industrialized nations such as the United Kingdom, France, or Germany. In the present-day discussions about a domestic model for a U.S. national healthcare system, the Veterans Health Administration (VHA) is often the elephant in the room. There are several possible reasons for this. First, VHA was and still is viewed by many as a symbol of inefficient healthcare bureaucracy and poor quality (Oliver 2007); in other words, what not to do in any healthcare reform (Asch et al. 2004; Jha et al. 2003; Kerr et al. 2004; Peterson et al. 2001). Second, there is concern that politicians who would like to bring VHA into the healthcare reform discussion are fearful of the possibility that they might be accused of politicizing Department of Veterans Affairs (VA) care. Third, there is a pervasive view among Americans that the government cannot be trusted to run anything well and efficiently. This view exists even though the U.S. government runs one of the largest and most effective armies in the history of the world. Finally, for many Americans, VA is the closest the nation has ever come to socialism, and they fear its implications.

On the other hand, the recent performance of VHA compared with the private sector is starting to change attitudes toward the VA healthcare system. Studies indicate marked improvements in performance of the VA healthcare system compared to the market-based, private healthcare sector, which is increasingly seen as too costly and inadequate in quality performance. For example, diabetes care in VHA has been reported to be better than that in the private sector (Kerr et al. 2004). Patients at VA are reported to be more likely than even Medicare patients to receive life-saving treatments in cardiac care (Peterson et al. 2001). Performance by VA in many processes of care measures across a spectrum of healthcare services (screening, diagnostics, treatment, and follow-up) is better than in non-VA healthcare systems (Asch et al. 2004). Patients receiving care within VHA report higher levels of satisfaction than do their counterparts receiving care in the private sector (University of Michigan School of Business 2007).

The remarkable thing is that the VA system has achieved these quality transformations while maintaining its traditional healthcare safety net role. Compared to the private sector, the VA patient population has a disproportionately lower income and is older, sicker, and more likely to suffer from mental and behavioral illness. Veterans with disabilities that result from war-related trauma often seek medical care at VA facilities. Furthermore, in its formal affiliations with over 100 academic medical centers in 50 states, VHA continues to play an important role in educating future generations of healthcare providers.

Without intending to do so, the VA healthcare system has established itself as the largest integrated healthcare system in the United States (Evans 2005). Although it was conceived in 1930 by the Roosevelt administration as part of its national program for American war veterans, the true transformation of the VA healthcare system was not set in motion until the passage of the Veterans Health Care Eligibility Reform Act of 1996. As part of this initiative, VHA sought to reinvent itself by undergoing major structural and management reorganization, which resulted in its emergence as a national leader in healthcare within a decade (Committee on Quality of Health Care in America & Institute of Medicine 2001; Kizer, Demakis & Feussner 2000). Even more remarkable is that these achievements occurred at a time when the VA patient population was expanding. The number of VA patients accessing the system each year went up markedly, from 2.5 million in 1995 to 5.3 million in 2005 (Perlin 2005).

It is not always easy to pinpoint the factors that underlie the impressive transformation of VHA. This is in part because the broad reorganization of VHA was not designed to prospectively measure the impact of specific aspects of the reconstruction. However, an informed observation of the current VA healthcare system would note several unique elements that distinguish VHA from the private sector American healthcare system: (a) an emphasis on preventive (primary) care as the foundation of the system; (b) an affordable, evidence-based medication prescription (pharmacy) plan; (c) an automated health information system that includes a national electronic patient record system; and (d) a centralized healthcare administration. These are qualities that are clearly lacking in most American market-based private healthcare systems. The following sections briefly describe these aspects of the VA healthcare system while also outlining the financial structure and moral mission that allow the VA system to thrive and meet its obligations. The chapter concludes with a brief discussion of key challenges the VA system still faces.

Model Features of the VA Healthcare System

Quality of VA Care: The Role of Preventive/Primary Care

The VA healthcare system has focused its efforts on preventive care since the mid-1990s (Kizer 1995, 1996). This focus has resulted in dramatic gains in the proportion of VA patients receiving recommended preventive care (Asch et al. 2004; Congressional Budget Office 2007). Currently, VA patients are much more likely to receive clinically indicated preventive care than are similar-aged men and women who receive care in the private sector (see table 7.1) (Veterans Health Administration. Office of Quality and Safety 2009). Over-all, across almost all quality of care metrics commonly used in primary care, VA hospitals and facilities rank in the top 10 percent in quality performance among U.S. healthcare facilities.

Improvements in preventive care delivery in the VA system reflect real increases in the number and proportion of VA patients receiving these services. These increases also illustrate VA's success in utilizing the electronic health record to document that these preventive care services were indeed delivered to patients. Some of the key system-level factors that facilitated the transition to excellent preventive care are a) accountability throughout all levels (from head-quarters leadership through front line staff), so that incentives are aligned; b) a focus on primary care; c) frequent and accurate measurements of performance; d) diffusion of responsibility to deliver preventive care away from the physician; and e) the use of electronic health records to facilitate documentation of care.

Beginning in the mid-1990s the VA leadership began implementing a push for preventive care through enhanced primary care services. In well-articulated directives such as "Vision for Change" and "Prescription for Change," the leadership communicated the importance of measurement, improvement, and accountability in preventive care delivery. They held network directors accountable for performance in preventive care in their networks using performance contracts and end-of-year evaluations. Salary bonuses for network directors were directly linked in part to performance on preventive care metrics. Networks and facilities within networks were frequently ranked by performance. This competition encouraged sharing of best practices in preventive care among VA; thus successful approaches in preventive care diffused relatively quickly throughout the VHA organization. As a result, variation in performance among networks or Veterans Integrated Service Networks (VISNs) narrowed. The variation in performance among medical facilities also decreased, but to a lesser degree. Leadership accountability for performance in preventive care delivery moved from top management to middle management and further down to frontline providers.

Table 7.1. Quality of Care Metrics Comparing VA with Other Health Systems

Clinical Indicator	VA Average 2009*	VA Average 2008*	HEDIS Commercial 2008[†]	HEDIS Medicare 2008[†]	HEDIS Medicaid 2008[†]
Breast Cancer Screening	87%	87%	70%	68%	51%
Cervical Cancer Screening	92%	92%	80%	n/a	66%
Cholesterol Management for Patients with Cardiovascular Conditions—LDL-C Control (< v100 mg/dL)	67%	66%	60%	57%	40%
Cholesterol Management for Patients with Cardiovascular Conditions: LDL-C Screening	96%	94%	89%	89%	80%
Colorectal Cancer Screening	80%	79%	59%	53%	n/a
Comprehensive Diabetes Care—Blood Pressure Control (< 140/90)	80%	78%	66%	60%	57%
Comprehensive Diabetes Care—Eye Exams	88%	86%	57%	61%	53%
Comprehensive Diabetes Care—HbA1c Testing	98%	97%	89%	88%	81%
Comprehensive Diabetes Care—LDL-C Controlled (LDL-C < 100 mg/dL)	69%	68%	46%	49%	34%
Comprehensive Diabetes Care—LDL-C Screening	96%	95%	85%	86%	74%
Comprehensive Diabetes Care—Medical Attention for Nephropathy	95%	93%	82%	88%	77%
Comprehensive Diabetes Care—Poor HbA1c Control	16%	16%	28%	29%	45%
Controlling High Blood Pressure—Total	77%	75%	63%	59%	56%
Flu Shots for Adults (50–64)	69%	69%	50%	n/a	n/a
Medical Assistance with Smoking Cessation—Advising Smokers to Quit [‡]	96%	89%	77%	n/a	69%

(Continued)

Table 7.1. (*Continued*)

Clinical Indicator	VA Average 2009*	VA Average 2008*	HEDIS Commercial 2008[†]	HEDIS Medicare 2008[†]	HEDIS Medicaid 2008[†]
Medical Assistance with Smoking Cessation—Discussing Medications [‡]	90%	84%	54%	n/a	41%
Medical Assistance with Smoking Cessation—Discussing Strategies [‡]	96%	92%	50%	n/a	41%
Flu Shots for Adults (65 and older) [§‖]	83%	84%	n/a	71%	n/a
Immunizations: pneumococcal (note patients' age groups) [§‖]	95% (all ages)	94% (all ages)	n/a	67%	n/a

Source: Veterans Health Administration, Office of Quality and Safety (2009). Data obtained from Quality Compass, available through National Committee for Quality Assurance (www.ncqa.org).

VA = Department of Veterans Affairs; HEDIS = Healthcare Effectiveness Data and Information Set. Due to population differences and methodology variations, not all HEDIS measures are comparable to VA measures; therefore this is not a comprehensive list of indicators, but this comparison does contain those indicators that are closely aligned in content and methodology.

[*] Comparison data obtained by abstracting medical record data using *similar* methodologies to matched HEDIS methodologies.

[†] Data were obtained from the 2009 State of Health Care Quality Report, available at the National Committee for Quality Assurance Web site (www.ncqa.org).

[‡] HEDIS data are obtained by survey; VA data are obtained by medical record abstraction.

[§] Behavioral Risk Factor Surveillance System reports are available at the Centers for Disease Control and Prevention Web site (www.cdc.gov).

[‖] Behavioral Risk Factor Surveillance System (survey) scores are median scores. VA scores are averages obtained by medical record abstraction.

A Culture Shift to Preventive Care

As late as the early 1990s the VA healthcare system focused largely on inpatient care and had a fragmented and poorly organized outpatient system of care. Staff were required at that time to make a specific judgment annually for each VA patient on whether outpatient care was necessary on an ongoing basis. Although almost all veterans were judged to need outpatient care, the belief that outpatient care might not be required at all was still prevalent in the VA system. The Department of Veterans Affairs started emphasizing primary care development in the mid-1990s, at the same time that the nation as a whole was moving in that direction.

Within the VA, this shift in policy was implemented through the creation of primary care teams at each medical facility. Most if not all VA patients were assigned to primary care providers, who were based in primary care teams. The linkage between an individual veteran, his or her primary care provider, and the primary care team was solidified using sophisticated new software called Primary Care Management Module. This software interfaced with VA's electronic medical record so that the provider name and team were prominently displayed when a record was accessed.

Productivity in Preventive Care

With the shift in primary care structure and emphasis on quality of care came the movement within the VA system for productivity assessment. The decision was made to measure productivity in primary care largely through patient panel size rather than face-to-face visit production, as is commonly done in the private healthcare sector. Primary care patient panel size targets were set and adjusted by each VA medical facility based on disease severity and infrastructure support, such as support staff to provider ratios and medical examination room space. At this time VA became more active in measuring patients' experiences with VA healthcare. For example, to judge a medical facility's performance in the domain of patient satisfaction, patients were asked if they knew who their primary care provider or primary care team was (response options were "Yes" or "No"). This close and patient-centered monitoring forced most medical facilities and VA networks to invest in special efforts to make sure that patients were assigned to specific providers and primary care teams, and that patients knew which team or provider was responsible for their care.

Sources of Success in Shift to Preventive Care

Diffusion of primary care responsibility to the frontline staff is considered a key source of VA's ability to implement a successful transition to preventive care.

For example, licensed practical nurses (LPNs) became part of the healthcare team that offered and delivered preventive services such as vaccinations. This resulted in microsystem changes in workflow within the VA primary care system. In the traditional model of preventive care delivery, the physician is asked to discuss the preventive care with the patient during a primary care visit. If the patient agrees with the doctor, the doctor will then either deliver the service or request (order) that the service be delivered by support staff such as an LPN.

A key weakness of this model is that even though most physicians believe that preventive care should be a priority, other issues such as patient symptoms, diagnosis, or treatment of disease often dominate the patient-doctor encounter. As a result, preventive care discussions often don't occur and are not delivered. Furthermore, the number of recommended preventive care interventions and resultant time required to complete these tasks well exceed the usual duration of a typical office visit (Yarnall et al. 2003). VA's solution to this problem was to implement a systematic but gradual diffusion of the responsibility for offering and delivery preventive care to support staff and away from the physician. Clinical staff such as LPNs and physician assistants were trained and given responsibilities to determine, for example, whether influenza or pneumococcal vaccination was indicated for a particular patent, and if so, to offer, deliver, and document it in the VA electronic medical record. Similarly, in the area of cancer screening, nursing staff during check-in for a visit were tasked to assess whether colorectal cancer screening was indicated, and if so, to offer stool hemoccult cards to the patient: thus the health teams, rather than just the doctor, became accountable for performance on preventive care.

Pharmacy Benefits Management

One of the most challenging and costly of patient benefits in any healthcare system is access to prescription drugs. The VA healthcare system is no exception when it comes to the need to provide access to medications for its patient population. Under the Veterans' Health Care Eligibility Reform Act of 1996, VA is mandated to provide "needed care," which includes access to prescription drugs, to all its patients. One of the unique features of the VA healthcare system is that it provides a comprehensive prescription drug program to all its patients. Most veterans pay about $8 for a thirty-day supply of any one specific medication. The maximum a veteran is expected to pay out of pocket each year is about $980, and veterans with service-connected health conditions pay nothing out of pocket. In 2007 alone, VA provided 122 million prescriptions. Today more than 5.5 million veterans receive care in the VA system (Aspinall et al. 2009).

To meet this particular challenge, the visionaries of the VA's transformation recognized as early as 1995 the need to establish a standardized and centralized national formulary system (Sales et al. 2005). Before 1995 all VA facilities across the country managed their own drug coverage using local mechanisms and monitoring processes. At the time, there was a VA pharmaceutical management body located in Hines, Illinois, but this center had no direct authority for determining drug utilization; it simply managed purchasing of medications for each facility and monitored overall usage of prescription drugs. In other words, a vision for an integrated, standardized pharmacy benefits plan for all VA facilities across the nation simply did not exist before 1995.

Several factors supported the need for developing a standardized pharmacy plan. First was the issue of cost. Medications represent a significant cost in overall healthcare for the nation at large. Over the past few decades there has been a marked increase in prescription drug costs (Zuvekas & Cohen 2007). Figure 7.1 illustrates the escalating nature of prescription drug costs for VA and the savings realized over time as a result of its standardized national formulary system. Given that VA is the largest integrated healthcare system in the country, it was clear that the cost of prescription drugs had to be addressed in a systematic way. The second factor was the inefficiency associated with large-scale interfacility variation in drug access and utilization. It became apparent that to reduce that variation, the processes had to be standardized. The third factor was that VA realized it was not taking advantage of its buying power to leverage favorable prices for prescription drugs.

When the leaders of the VA's transformation proposed the establishment of a centralized pharmacy plan, Pharmacy Benefits Management, some parties had doubts. Patients expressed concerns about access to needed medications. Commercial entities such as the pharmaceutical industry expressed concern about the potential "restrictiveness" of the plan. In response to these concerns, the Senate and the House Veterans Affairs Committees called for outside reviews of the VA formulary plan. One such reviewer, the Institute of Medicine, concluded in a report released in 2001 that the VA formulary system was reasonable and that there were few patient complaints (Blumenthal & Herdman 2000). One of the more recent and perhaps lingering criticisms of the VA pharmacy policy is that it may have compromised the life expectancy of VA patients relative to the U.S. population at large (Good & Valentino 2007; Lichtenberg 2005). Figure 7.2 compares U.S. veterans' life expectancy to life expectancy at birth for all U.S. men from 1991 to 2002.

The benefits of a standardized and centralized pharmacy plan are numerous. It reduces variation in both access to and use of medications. It also diminishes risk of patient confusion, especially with generic drugs. For

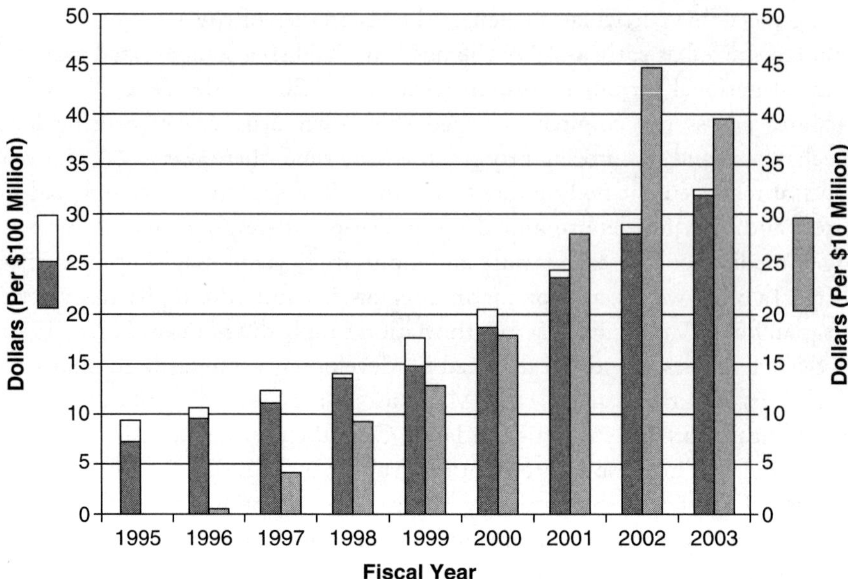

Figure 7.1. Total Drug Expenditures and Cost Avoidance. *Source:* Sales et al. (2005, 106). *Notes:* Black bars indicate expenditures classified as prime vendor purchases; white bars indicate direct purchases by individual facilities (dollars per $100 million); shaded bars indicate cost avoidance achieved with the contracting initiatives (dollars per $10 million). Total drug expenditures may include pharmaceutical expenditures for state veterans' homes or resulting from state veterans' homes' purchases, but that portion of the data is not itemized here. These data do not illustrate the influence of the increasing number of users on cost.

instance, before the establishment of Pharmacy Benefits Management, each VA facility in the country dispensed its own generic drugs, of different shapes, colors, and formulations. This is a recipe for confusion, as patients often receive care at different VA facilities. Standardization also provides the opportunity to stabilize not only the cost of drugs, but also the cost related to drug acquisition. Figure 7.3 illustrates the VA's average acquisition cost for a thirty-day-equivalent prescription from 1999 to 2003.

It is also important to note that the benefits of a centralized system of pharmacy are not only fiscal, but have implications for quality. The VA Pharmacy Benefits Management uses rigorous disease management and evidence-based drug use criteria. This is done by creating drug management guidelines that

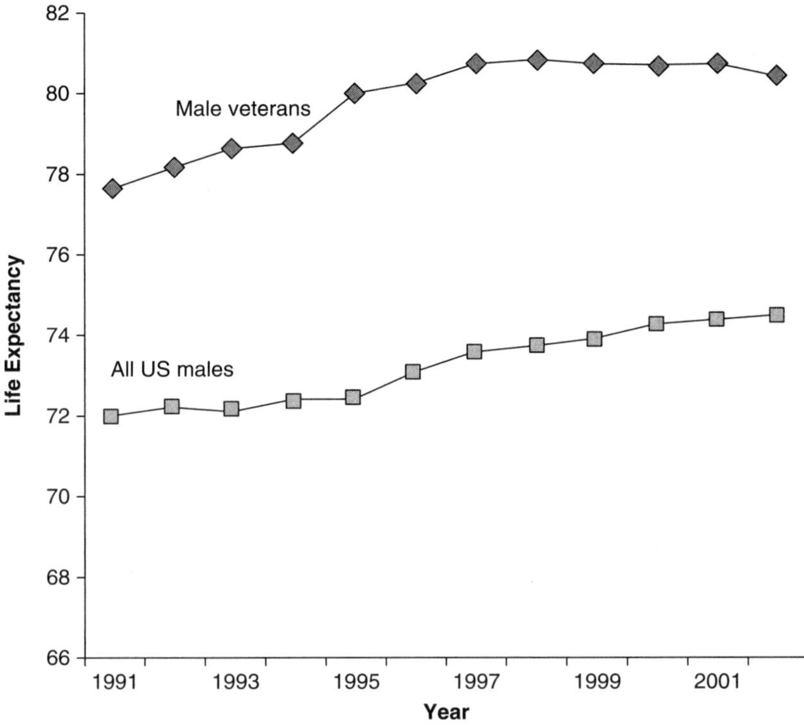

Figure 7.2. U.S. Veterans' Life Expectancy versus Life Expectancy at Birth for all U.S. Men, 1991–2002. *Source:* Good and Valentino (2007, 2130).

are informed by high-quality clinical trials and cost-effectiveness analyses, when available. Pharmacy Benefits Management acts as the overseeing entity for the VA formulary. The Veterans Affairs Medical Advisory Panel and VISN Pharmacists Executive Committee actively manage the VA formulary. The Medical Advisory Panel consists of VA practicing doctors, Pharmacy Benefits Management clinical pharmacists, and a physician from the Department of Defense. The Pharmacy Benefits Management pharmacists routinely monitor the medical literature for informative clinical trials and cost-effectiveness analyses that could be used to shape prescribing guidelines, which are then sent for peer review throughout VA before they are implemented. This process makes the VA formulary one of the most evidence-based drug prescription plans in the nation.

Standardization also allows Pharmacy Benefits Management to create a patient- and provider-specific prescription drug database and to conduct

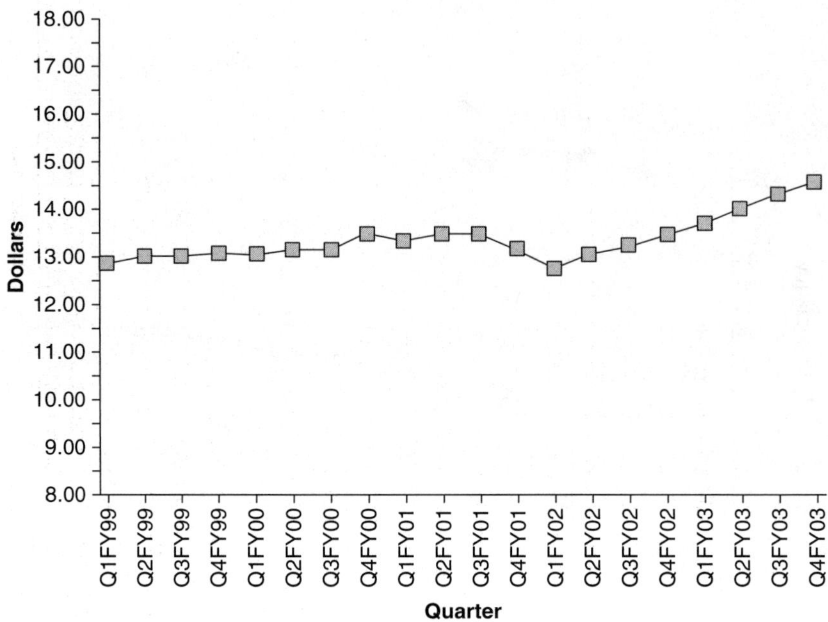

Figure 7.3. VA Average Acquisition Cost per 30-Day-Equivalent Prescriptions. *Source:* Sales et al. (2005, 109). *Notes:* These data are not broken down by the number of unique pharmacy users and therefore do not illustrate the influence of the increasing number of users on cost. Average 30-day drug ingredient cost is defined as the sum (prescription cost)/sum (day-30 prescriptions), where for each prescription, prescription cost equals quantity multiplied by unit price. Day-30 prescription = 1 for < 30 days of supply; day-30 prescription = 2 for > 30 and < 60 days of supply; day-30 prescription = 3 for > 60 days of supply. Q1 FY99 indicates quarter 1 of fiscal year 1999.

large-scale research. The VA pharmacy database, which consists of electronic information on medications, dosing, quantities, and cost, enables Pharmacy Benefits Management to evaluate patient safety and conduct quality improvement projects. The pharmacy database can be linked to VA administrative and clinical databases so that information on clinical matters such as diagnosis, hospitalization, comorbidity, and laboratory data can be used to investigate long-term patient safety and outcome assessments. Using this mechanism, Pharmacy Benefits Management has designed and published numerous studies on medication safety, appropriateness of utilization, effectiveness, and cost-effectiveness (Burk et al. 2004; Burk, Morreale & Cunningham 2004;

Charbonneau et al. 2004; Furmaga et al. 2004; Glassman et al. 2004, 2001; Hamed et al. 2004; Huang et al. 2004; London et al. 2004; Lopez et al. 2004; Ren et al. 2002; Siegel et al. 2001; Siva et al. 2003). In summary, what makes the VA pharmacy plan an important feature to consider in any national health-care policy is the robust drug formulary management process, which involves a broad spectrum of national groups such as Pharmacy Benefits Management, Medical Advisory Panel, and VISN formulary leaders, who bring to the process of formulary decision making not only the perspectives of clinicians, pharmacists, administrators, and even patients, but also a commitment to hard medical evidence.

The Veterans Affairs and the Electronic Medical Record

The VA electronic health records, here referred to as the Computerized Patient Record System, is viewed as a model system by many and has greatly aided performance on quality metrics. The history of the Computerized Patient Record System dates to the 1970s and includes a grassroots effort by frontline providers (referred to as "hardhats") who overcame bureaucratic inertia to develop the backbone of the system in the 1980s. In the early 1990s the system was somewhat rudimentary in user interface; as a result, widespread use by frontline staff who understood all of the system's components was not in place. In the mid- and late 1990s a more intuitive interface was implemented across all VA sites. From the frontline perspective, the pace of change in the interface in the late 1990s and first half of the first decade of the twenty-first century was brisk with new versions of the interface with more functions released several times each year.

The Computerized Patient Record System is viewed as a model for electronic health records for several reasons. First, its components capture nearly all information that nurses, physicians, and other clinical staff use in caring for patients. Second, it provides a comprehensive medical record that includes all progress notes, consultation reports, imaging reports (including access to actual images), laboratory results, and surgical procedure notes. In the Computerized Patient Record System, quantitative data such as vital signs or laboratory results can be organized for presentation in various ways that permit trending of results for individual patients. Third, information in VHA electronic medical records is integrated across all VA sites. Functionally, this means that clinicians have access to medical record data from other VA locations across the nation. Remote data are presented in various formats and are quickly viewable by the user, and a few clicks result in access to the full data.

The Impact of the Computerized Patient Record System on Quality

One of the key features of any electronic healthcare system is the impact it has on the delivery of high quality of care. The Computerized Patient Record System is no exception in this regard. It has assisted in improving the quality of care, as determined by common quality metrics, through three mechanisms. First, a sophisticated reminder system is in place that informs clinicians through cover sheet display what prevention and other recommended tasks are due for a patient. A by-product of this has been the proliferation of electronic reminders. This has occurred in part because most new quality measures lead to rapid reminder development. Second, the system allows reliable documentation of the implementation of specific preventive care or other healthcare quality tasks. For instance, to satisfy a quality reminder, specific documentation is required that is driven by a templated note, thus allowing standardized documentation to be created and as quickly as possible. Furthermore, many computer reminders are designed to allow the provider to order the necessary intervention from within the reminder dialogue. Third, the design of the electronic medical record allows tracking of quality performance reports by medical facility or primary care team/provider performance by showing reminder completion, a surrogate for actual performance on the metric. As a result, low-performing teams or providers can receive timely and quantitative feedback.

The Structure of the VA Healthcare System: How It Became an Integrated System

The 1990s were a difficult time for VA nationally. The system faced a number of challenges, including the fact that a quarter of hospital beds in the system were unoccupied or underutilized ("More than veterans need" 1996). One government investigation in the mid-1990s found that in about 14 percent of VA hospitals nationwide, surgeons had not operated for significant periods of time, in some cases as long as a year (*Audit of Veterans Health Administration resource allocation issues* n.d.). The Department of Veterans Affairs also faced a rapidly declining patient population. This was so in large part because of the aging and subsequent deaths of many World War II veterans. The attrition rate approached about 1,000 veterans per day. There was also a major shift in VA population demographic densities. For example, older veterans were starting to leave the northern industrial cities for warmer regions of the country such as Florida, so as large patient populations shifted from some of the northern hospitals to the hospitals in the Sunbelt, overcrowding began to occur in the latter region. These changes were not missed by the national media or U.S. Congress. In fact, there were those who advocated for the reevaluation of the need for VA hospitals and argued that it might not be a terrible idea to outsource VA care to private institutions (Kilborn 1996). These organizational challenges were further exacerbated by operational challenges, such as the need to clear with Washington, D.C., even simple expenditures that would have been best addressed at a local level ("Part III" 2000).

The VA's transformation leaders recognized these serious structural and operational challenges. However, they also saw elements of a system that although not functioning as a unit yet, could do so with the right adjustments. At the time, VA managed 159 medical centers, 375 ambulatory care clinics, 133 nursing homes, 202 readjustment counseling centers, and 39 domiciliaries offering care to disenfranchised veterans and those who suffered from drug abuse. One of the other unique dimensions of VA that was not lost on its transformation leaders was that VA has a defined patient population with which it has a long-term, perhaps lifelong, relationship. This kind of long-term commitment between the patient and a system of care provides the opportunity to envision preventive strategies in the delivery of care mechanism. Theories abound that the lack of a long-term relationship and commitment between patients and private healthcare providers underlies the lack of an organized, nationwide electronic medical record system outside the VA system. Unlike the VA system, most private healthcare systems often fail to see their patient customers as a stable population that is worthy of long-term investment; they lack the mindset necessary to invest in preventive care.

Another important difference between VA and the private healthcare systems is the unique mission of VA, which is in the business of providing healthcare for the nation's veterans. It does not see itself as an agent of profit generation responsible to shareholders. This is in part why VA has traditionally attracted a disproportionate number of healthcare providers such as physicians who are service-oriented and somewhat altruistic in their approach to the medical profession.

What did the VA transformation leaders envision? First, they saw the need for a change in perspective about healthcare delivery and management. Conceptually, they removed the patient as the unit of attention and replaced it with the population. This framework significantly altered the landscape of the VA healthcare delivery culture. It allowed for a team approach and for population-based data collection and interpretation, which was seen as essential in transforming a system as large and complex as VA. The existence of Veterans Health Information Systems and Technology Architecture, one of the well-developed national electronic medical records systems, facilitated the vision of a data-driven, fully integrated system. Another important paradigm shift was the move away from the emphasis on acute care delivery, which is dominated by specialty care, to a focus on long-term and preventive care, which placed primary care at the core.

The basic thesis of the transformation was that VA has to provide care that is comparable to or better than what private-sector healthcare can provide. One of the first issues to dog the integration concept was size. Nationally, VA had excess capacity. Several options were considered. One was to expand VA coverage to all service-connected patients who were not meeting the income criteria. Another was to outsource excess capacity and all treatments that did not meet the capacity threshold to affiliated private-sector hospitals and medical centers. The third option that was partially implemented was to close some facilities and divert saved resources to fund new primary care clinics and expand the electronic medical records system. Another key challenge the transformation faced was decentralizing the budget and policy making from the VA Central Office in Washington, D.C., to regional offices. The VISN system was created in large part to address this unique challenge. A total of twenty-two VISNs were established and were later consolidated into twenty-one networks when 13 and 14 were merged (see figure 7.4). The creation of the VISN system not only moved power and authority away from the Central

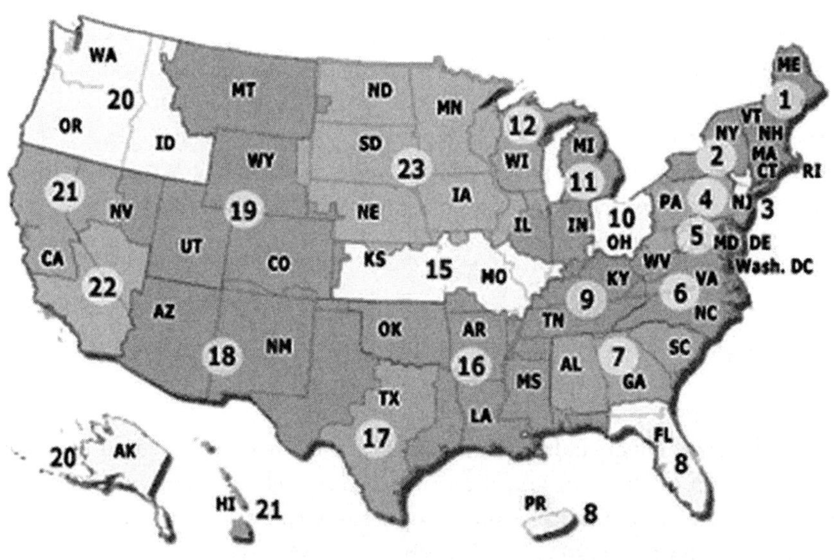

Figure 7.4. Map of Current VISNs. *Source:* Department of Veterans Affairs (n.d.).

Office, but also helped move managers closer to those they managed, thus increasing both the authority and accountability of the managers. There are unique advantages to the regionalization concept. First is the ease of communication; the leaders communicate with real people in the community as opposed to far-removed and Washington-based committees. Second is that the diffusion of authority made it feasible for VA to hold regional leaders accountable for the performance of the system, because they now have authority over resources and decision making.

In summary, the transformation of the VA system was in large part facilitated by the fact that it saw itself as a system. There were facilities in all the states. It provided longitudinal care that began with primary care, was followed by acute care and postacute care, and concluded with nursing home care. The transformation made it possible for the VA system to become the largest integrated healthcare system in the United States.

The Future of VA and Ongoing Challenges

To remain successful as a healthcare delivery system, VA faces several challenges. A few are discussed here.

Americans and Government-Run Healthcare

The Department of Veterans Affairs is a governmental entity providing healthcare. The United States, for much of the last century and currently, has been reluctant to fund the delivery of healthcare through tax dollars and government-delivered services. Most government-funded healthcare such as Medicare or Medicaid is targeted to disadvantaged populations rather than the population as a whole. Similarly, healthcare delivered by government organizations (for example, Indian Health Services, community health centers) also is targeted toward those who have limited access to care. Although care to veterans has been promised to any honorably discharged veteran, eligibility rules for VA have changed depending on political circumstances and have often excluded veterans with middle or higher income. These restrictions are driven by the relationship between Congress and the executive branch in its budgetary process. The Department of Veterans Affairs has been subject over time to variations in budgetary support. These variations are driven largely by political considerations rather than strong evidence about the quality or efficiency of the organization. In the recent past, despite evidence that VA is a model healthcare delivery system, it has not been prominently discussed in the healthcare reform debate, probably because it represents "government-run healthcare," which has been depicted in a negative light by those opposing health reform.

Public Disclosure of Quality of Care

Because VA is a public organization, problems that develop at its facilities often become a matter of public record, as stipulated by the Freedom of Information Act. In contrast, public reports of healthcare quality problems in the private sector are much less common. Therefore, from a public relations perspective VA is at a disadvantage. Recent examples include public reports of endoscope decontamination problems, brachytherapy for prostate cancer, and poor surgical outcomes. Press coverage of these incidents has been largely negative about VA. Private-sector healthcare organizations likely would not have discovered these quality problems in their own systems, as their data systems are not as sophisticated and the entities are not required to report these problems publicly. Because of the size and scope of VA facilities, problems with safety and quality are not unexpected. After all, VA is a complex healthcare system. The current VA policy of transparency, though refreshing, places it at a disadvantage in the eyes of the lay public.

Geographic Access and Virtual Care

Another challenge VA faces is size. It greatly expanded its geographic locations beginning in the last half of the 1990s by establishing over 500 new outpatient locations, called community-based outpatient clinics (CBOCs). These new sites quickly grew in number of veterans served. Approximately half of all veterans receiving VA care receive primary care at these sites. This growth allowed VA, for the most part, to meet Medicare guidelines for geographic access to primary care. Fortunately this expansion has been tempered recently by the need for congressional approval for new care sites. Changes in eligibility rules have also slowed this growth. Although VA is in a better position to provide community-based primary care than ever before, most veterans still find private healthcare closer to them. Even though every major U.S. city has a VA facility, private-sector primary care is more conveniently located for veterans living in these cities. In short, VA's ability to rapidly expand sites of care is limited, and it is unlikely to be able to provide locations of care in the future that could compete with the private sector in geographic access.

Given the limitations to providing local care, VA has begun to experiment with "virtual care," which includes many modalities, beginning with phone care but extending to remote monitoring and remote specialty care. The VA system is in a better position than most private healthcare organizations to implement virtual care, in part because the private healthcare sector reimbursement model puts limits on reimbursement for virtual care services. The VA system has already developed a successful telehealth initiative, the most comprehensive of which is the home telehealth. As of May 2010, more than 40,000 veterans with significant medical or behavioral health disorders transmit textual or physiological data on a near-daily basis to nurses who are able to intervene if necessary. Before-and-after studies (including a performance metric) demonstrate significant reduction in inpatient usage attributed to this monitoring. On the other hand, VA's telephone responsiveness is generally poor and its plans to provide e-mail and other electronic access to most veterans have been delayed by software development issues and concerns about privacy.

The Future Is Uncertain

To plan for the future, VA must consider complex issues such as demographics of the current population and predictions about future use based on current conflicts and estimates of market penetration. Current models suggest that the number of veterans using VA facilities will decrease dramatically in the next fifteen years. This is due to attrition of World War II, Korean, and Vietnam era veterans. The predicted decrease will result in a much lower need for acute inpatient care. Should these models prove accurate, VA has to consider converting or selling off capital assets at many locations across the country. But there are also other uncertainties. For example, the U.S. healthcare reform law passed by Congress in 2010 may dramatically reshape healthcare access for both veterans and nonveterans. It is conceivable that low-cost health insurance spurred by the healthcare reform could draw some veterans away from VA to the private healthcare sector. The converse is also possible; that new health insurance mandates could make VA care a preferred and more affordable option for many veterans.

Making the Business Case for the VA System

The Veterans Health Administration is a financially complex but relatively cost-effective system. To put this in perspective, in 2009 the VHA system was responsible for over 24 million veterans. In 2009 VHA provided healthcare for about 5.5 million veterans. It has a budget of $50 billion and operates more than 1,400 facilities, including 950 outpatient clinics, 153 hospitals, and 134 nursing homes. The Congressional Budget Office estimates that VHA

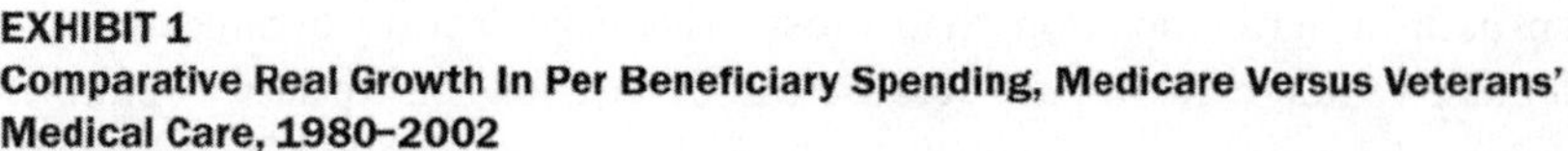

EXHIBIT 1

Comparative Real Growth In Per Beneficiary Spending, Medicare Versus Veterans' Medical Care, 1980–2002

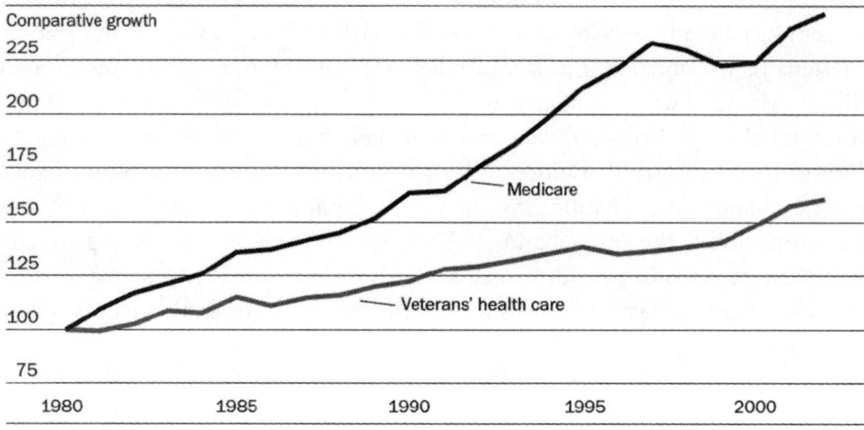

Figure 7.5. Comparative Real Growth in Per Beneficiary Spending, Medicare Versus Veterans' Medical Care, 1980–2002. *Source:* Health policy (n.d.).

healthcare cost per enrollee grew by only 1.7 percent from 1999 to 2005. This is an annual growth rate of just 0.3 percent. In contrast, Medicare's costs grew 29.4 percent per capita over that same period; that is an annual increase of 4.4 percent. In the private-sector insurance market (employer and individual plans), premiums increased by more than 70 percent between 1999 and 2005.

Another way to compare the cost of care in the VHA system to that of other systems is to examine the cost of Medicare. The VHA system is less expensive than the Medicare system, as indicated by the different growth in spending of the two systems in the period 1980–2000 (see figure 7.5). It shows that the VHA budget rose substantially, from fiscal year 1980 to fiscal year 2000. However, the growth of Medicare spending is substantially more pronounced compared to that of VHA's growth for this time period.

Although the Congressional Budget Office allocates funds for VHA, the budget development and allocation process involves many steps. In general, the office of the president of the United States annually proposes a budget for VHA, which is considered, debated, and often adjusted during the congressionally legislated budget discussions. A final budget is then forwarded to the president's office to be signed into law. The VA Central Office then distributes the approved budget to each VISN, which then distributes a budget to each medical center within the network.

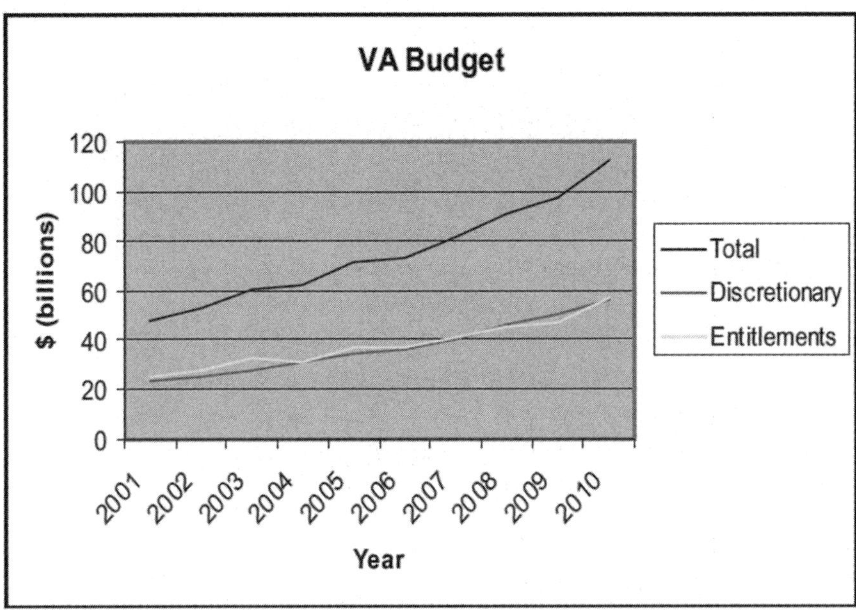

Figure 7.6. VHA Budget in Billions. *Source:* PPI policy memo (n.d.).

Figure 7.6 shows overall VHA budget including total as well as discretionary and entitlements from 2001 to 2010.

Lingering Challenges and a Summary

There are some challenges the system still faces, which must be considered in its evaluation as a worthy model for an eventual American national healthcare system. For instance, a study by Frueh and colleagues (2007) examined VA psychiatric disability and rehabilitation policies for combat-related posttraumatic stress disorder and found VHA to be antiquated and in need of reforms to bring it in line with modern demands and scientific evidence in the management of PTSD. Similarly, Himmelstein and colleagues reported in 2007 that access to care within VHA was limited to veterans with service-connected health problems and low socioeconomic status. This has left a large number of veterans with healthcare access problems unable to receive care at Veterans Affairs Medical Centers (see figure 7.7). For example, they found about 1.8 million uninsured veterans who were not receiving VA healthcare in 2004. Another report, by Helmer and colleagues (2007), found that in the many years since the first Persian Gulf War, veterans of that war have

Table 7.2. Comparison of the Major Veterans Health Administration Financing Systems

	Historical Model	Resource Allocation Management	Resource Planning and Management	Veterans Equitable Resource Allocation
Years in Use	1930–1984* 1990–1993*	1985–1989	1994–1995	1997–present
Basic Method	Incremental Change*	Procedure Reimbursement*[†]	Weak[‡] Capitation[†]/"Capitation Like" *	Strong[‡] Capitation[†]
Primary Components (as seen in the final version of each system)	Driven by historical funding patterns, with discretionary adjustments for inflation and new programs*	Two parts: 1) Three financial reimbursement models are used simultaneously, all attempting to "link resources to workload"* • Acute care (reimbursement by diagnosis price group)[†] • Ambulatory care (mixed capitation model)[†] • Long-term care (resources used)[†] All are driven by number and complexity of "incidents of care."[‡] 2) VAMCs are ranked on efficiency (average cost per "weighted work unit"), with funds directed to more	Patient number and type (49 classifications by diagnosis)*[†] • Average facility-level capitation rate (for 5 patient care groups)*[†] • Historical costs (to moderate the rate of changes)*[†] • Inflation adjustment (separate salary and nonsalary, facility specific)*[†] • Projected workload (using 4 different statistical techniques)*[†] • Proportional reduction so national budget meets appropriation[†]	Usage numbers and types[‖] • Average national capitation rate (for 54 patient-funded classes, grouped into 10 case-mix price groups, further split by patient priority)[‖¶] • Regional variance in costs (labor index)[‖] • Adjustments for highest-cost patients (in 2009 reimbursed for yearly cost over $87,000)[‖] • Education support (by number of residents)[‖] • Research support (weighted by VA involvement and if peer-reviewed)[‖]

		efficient facilities and away from less efficient ones. However, these adjustments only ever accounted for about 2% of Resource Allocation Management distributed funds.§		• Equipment (by number of patients)[‖] • Nonrecurring maintenance (by number of patients and cost of construction index)[‖] • Minimum floor on percent change (4% in 2009)[‖] • Prorated for percentage of care in any particular VISN (to account for patients receiving care in multiple VISNs)[‖]
Percent of Funding	100%	55%[*]	75%[†]	88%[‖]
Primary Unit	Veterans Affairs Medical Center (VAMC)	Veterans Affairs Medical Center	Veterans Affairs Medical Center	Veterans Integrated Service Network (VISN)
Strengths	• Predictable[*]	• VAMCs knew approximate reimbursement in advance.[†] • Budget was tied directly to treatment of patients.[†] • "Resulted in a gradual improvement in service, even though little money was used to encourage and reward performance."[**]	• Framework for integrating care across VAMCs[†] • Reduced inequities through forecasting and more highly refined patient price groups[†] • Facility-specific cost per patient reduced "adverse selection" inequities[†] • Prospective budget allowed for better planning[†] • Capitation reduces incentives for unnecessary procedures and coding gaming[†]	• Combines with rigorous performance and quality management systems to provide verification and accountability[‡] • Relatively simple and easy to understand[‡‖] • Helped correct long-standing regional inequities[‡‖] • Empowered VISNs to manage resources and maximize efficiency among VAMCs[‡]

(Continued)

Table 7.2. (*Continued*)

	Historical Model	Resource Allocation Management	Resource Planning and Management	Veterans Equitable Resource Allocation
			• National-level data, verifiable by outside reviewers[†] • Financing system linked to strategic plan for the first time[*]	• Allowed for the system to better respond to changing needs of veterans[‖] • Increased fairness of the system without harming quality and access[‖] • Increased VISN management flexibility[‖]
Weaknesses	• Funding not connected to changing needs of veterans[*] • Geographic inequalities maintained[*] • No incentive to improve access, quality, or efficiency[*]	• Complex inequities persisted.[†] • Incentive and gaming issues with treatment and coding[†] • No way of handling outliers[†] • Relies on unverifiable self-reported data[†] • "Provided open-ended incentive to expand workload," raising questions about quality[**]	• Somewhat arbitrary patient classification system[†] • Difficult to accurately classify patients prospectively[†] • Costs of comorbidity not adequately addressed[†] • Systematic inequalities remained (since capitation rates were made at the facility level)[†][††] • Called for a radical redistribution of funds, which made it not politically viable short-term (never fully implemented for this reason)[‡] • Too complex and difficult to understand[‡]	

Intended Incentives	• Reward efficiency[‡‡] • Reward maximum production[‡‡]	• Reduce inappropriate diagnosis, coding, and treatment (gaming)[†] • Increase ambulatory and preventive care[†] • Reward efficiency[‡]	• Reduce inappropriate diagnosis, coding, and treatment (gaming)[‖] • Increase efficiency, quality, and access[‖]
Unintended Incentives	• Increasingly complex (and expensive) procedures favored over simple ones[‡] • Incentivized quantity without checks on quality[**]	• Creaming (focusing on only the most highly priced portion of a patient's needs)	• Greater transparency and comparability of metrics increases competition for improvement between VISNs and VAMCs.

* General Accounting Office (1996).

† Lehner et al. (1996).

‡ Oliver (2007).

§ General Accounting Office (1989).

‖ Department of Veterans Affairs (2009).

¶ Department of Veterans Affairs (2010).

** Gore (1993).

†† Department of Veterans Affairs (1998).

‡‡ General Accounting Office (1987).

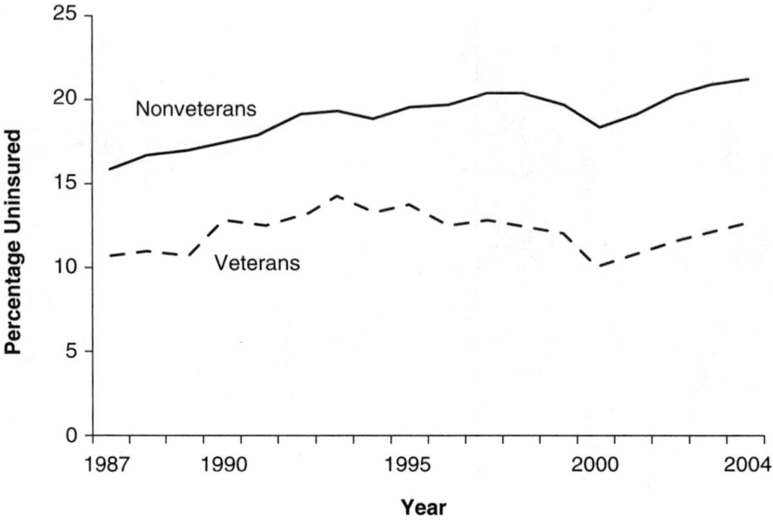

Figure 7.7. Percentage of Veterans and Nonveterans Ages 18–64 Who Lacked Coverage, 1987–2004. *Source:* Himmelstein et al. (2007, 2203).

continued to seek emergency department services for problems related to that war, suggesting that the healthcare needs of those veterans may not have been fully met.

Although the VHA system has undergone extensive improvements in quality in the last fifteen years, there is still a general agreement that further transformation is necessary before it can be viewed as a solution to the nation's overall healthcare crisis. Specifically, there is a need to demonstrate success in each of the three domains of the "triple aim": high satisfaction, high quality, and controlled costs. To achieve higher customer satisfaction, VHA will have to continue to move the interface between the veteran (patient) and the system away from a government/patient tone and closer to a customer/service provider tone. To achieve this, personal relationships with stable providers or teams of healthcare workers are needed. It is with this goal in mind that VHA is now investing heavily in the patient-centered medical home model of healthcare. One of the objectives of the patient-centered medical home model is to foster more trusting relationships between patients and healthcare system employees.

In current measures of quality, VHA is doing relatively well. However, the measurement of quality is evolving. VHA's current data systems and focus on quality make it well positioned to lead the nation in innovating healthcare quality metrics. The Veterans Health Administration has done a relatively good job in controlling healthcare costs, but the exact nature of the cost savings remains a matter of debate. This is in part because patients in the VA system often rely on multiple sources of healthcare insurance. The conundrum of the veteran receiving both VA and non-VA care remains a challenge. To overcome this challenge, the VA system needs to make itself more accessible to patients. Although it currently lacks the geographic prevalence of the private healthcare sector, investment in technology such as telehealth may allow VA to improve access.

In summary, the improvements in structural organization and quality performance have resulted in VHA's emergence as a serious player in the American healthcare sector. Elements of VHA such as centralized administration; emphasis on preventive (primary) care; electronic medical records; and the provision of an affordable, evidence-based medication prescription plan provide models to consider in any discussion on the merits and the feasibility of a national healthcare system. Finally, VHA's shift from a focus on acute care medicine to preventive care and outpatient care has paid a huge dividend in keeping the cost of care in the VA system down relative to other federally funded healthcare plans such as Medicare. The success of healthcare reform will in large part depend on how well VA controls cost of care without compromising quality of care. This is a challenge that the VA system faced in the 1990s, and there are lessons from that period that should be considered in shaping a national healthcare agenda.

References

Asch, S. M., McGlynn, E. A., Hogan, M. M., Hayward, R. A., Shekelle, P., Rubenstein, L., et al. (2004). Comparison for quality of care for patients in the Veterans Health Administration and patients in a national sample. *Annals of Internal Medicine* 141: 938–945.

Aspinall, S. L., Banthin, J. S., Good, C. B., Miller, G. E. & Cunningham, F. E. (2009). VA pharmacy users: How they differ from other veterans. *American Journal of Managed Care* 15, no. 10: 701–708.

Audit of Veterans Health Administration resource allocation issues: Physician staffing levels. 5R8–A19–113. Washington, DC: Department of Veterans Affairs, Office of the Inspector General.

Blendon, R. J., Schoen, C., DesRoches, C. M., Osborn, R., Scoles, K. L. & Zapert, K. (2002). Inequities in health care: A five-country survey. *Health Affairs* 21, no. 3: 182–191.

Blumenthal, D. & Herdman, R. (Eds.). (2000). *Formulary Analysis Committee, Division of Health Care Services, Institute of Medicine: Description and analysis of the VA National Formulary.* Washington, DC: National Academy Press.

Burk, M., Furmaga, E., Dong, D. & Cunningham, F. (2004). Multicenter drug use evaluation of tamsulosin and availability of guidance criteria for nonformulary use in the veterans affairs health system. *Journal of Managed Care Pharmacy* 10, no. 5: 423–432.

Burk, M., Morreale, A. P. & Cunningham, F. (2004). Conversion from troglitazone to rosiglitazone or pioglitazone in the VA: A multicenter DUE. *Formulary* 39: 310–317.

Charbonneau, A., Rosen, A. K., Owen, R. R., Spiro, A., III, Ash, A. S., Miller, D. R., et al. (2004). Monitoring depression care: In search of an accurate quality indicator. *Medical Care* 42, no. 6: 522–531.

Committee on Quality of Health Care in America & Institute of Medicine. (2001). *Crossing the quality chasm: A new health system for the 21st century.* Washington, DC: National Academy of Sciences.

Congressional Budget Office. (2007). The health care system for veterans: An interim report. http://www.cbo.gov/ftpdocs/88xx/doc8892/MainText.3.1.shtml#1070090.

Davis, K., Schoen, C., Schoenbaum, S. C., Doty, M. M., Holmgren, A. L., Kriss, J. L., et al. (2007). *Mirror, mirror on the wall: An international update on the comparative performance of American health care.* The Commonwealth Fund.

Department of Veterans Affairs. (1998). *Veterans equitable resource allocation 1998.* Washington, DC: Department of Veterans Affairs.

Department of Veterans Affairs. (2009). *Veterans equitable resource allocation 2009.* Washington, DC: Department of Veterans Affairs.

Department of Veterans Affairs. (2010). *Veterans equitable resource allocation 2010.* Washington, DC: Department of Veterans Affairs.

Department of Veterans Affairs. (n.d.). Map of Veterans Health Administration. http://www.va.gov/sta/guide/map.asp?divisionid=1 (accessed August 25, 2003).

Donelan, K., Blendon, R. J., Schoen, C., Davis, K. & Binns, K. (1999). The cost of health system change: Public discontent in five nations. *Health Affairs (Millwood)* 18: 206–216.

Evans, L. (2005). *Recognizing the 75th anniversary of the establishment of the Veterans Administration.* Washington, DC: U.S. Government Printing Office.

Freedom of Information Act, Pub. L. No. 89-487, Pub. L. no. 104-2310.

Frueh, B. C., Grubaugh, A. L., Elhai, J. D. & Buckley, T. C. (2007). US Department of Veterans Affairs disability policies for posttraumatic stress disorder: Administrative trends and implications for treatment, rehabilitation, and research. *American Journal of Public Health* 97, no. 12: 2143–2145.

Furmaga, E. M., Glassman, P. A., Cunningham, F. E. & Good, C. B. (2004). Using a national pharmaceutical database to reduce prescribing of short-acting nifedipine in patients with hypertension. In *Advances in Patient Safety: From Research to Implementation.* Rockville, MD: Agency for Healthcare Research and Quality.

General Accounting Office. (1987). *VA health care: Resource allocation methodology should improve VA's financial management.* Washington, DC: General Accounting Office.

General Accounting Office. (1989). *VA health care: Resource allocation methodology has had little impact on medical centers' budgets.* Washington, DC: General Accounting Office.

General Accounting Office. (1996). *Veterans' health care: Facilities' resource allocations could be more equitable.* Washington, DC: General Accounting Office.

Glassman, P. A., Good, C. B., Kelley, M. E., Bradley, M. & Valentino, M. (2004). Physician satisfaction with formulary policies: Is it access to formulary or nonformulary drugs that matters most? *American Journal of Managed Care* 10, no. 3: 209–216.

Glassman, P. A., Good, C. B., Kelley, M. E., Bradley, M., Valentino, M., Ogden, J., et al. (2001). Physician perceptions of a national formulary. *American Journal of Managed Care* 7, no. 3: 241–251.

Good, C. B. & Valentino, M. (2007). Access to affordable medications: The Department of Veterans Affairs pharmacy plan as a national model. *American Journal of Public Health* 97, no. 12: 2129–2131.

Gore, Al. (1993). *Department of Veterans Affairs: Accompanying report of the national performance review.* Washington, DC: White House.

Hamed, A., Lee, A., Ren, X. S., Miller, D. R., Cunningham, F., Zhang, H., et al. (2004). Use of antidepressant medications: Are there differences in psychiatric visits among patient treatments in the Veterans Administration? *Medical Care* 42, no. 6: 551–559.

Health insurance coverage and the uninsured 1990–1998. (1999). Washington, DC: Health Insurance Association of America.

Health policy: A journey through policy, progress, and being a patient by Kate Steadman. (n.d.). http://healthypolicy.typepad.com/blog/veterans_affairs/ (accessed April 4, 2012).

Helmer, D. A., Flanagan, M. E., Woolson, R. F. & Doebbeling, B. N. (2007). Health services use among Gulf War veterans and Gulf War era nondeployed veterans: A large population-based survey. *American Journal of Public Health* 97, no. 12: 2145–2148.

Himmelstein, D. U., Lasser, K. E., McCormick, D., Bor, D. H., Boyd, J. W. & Woolhandler, S. (2007). Lack of health coverage among US veterans from 1987 to 2004. *American Journal of Public Health* 97, no. 12: 2199–2203.

Huang, J. V., Casebeer, A. W., Plomondon, M. E., Shroyer, A. L., McDonald, G. O., Fullerton, D., et al. (2004). Prescription-filling rates for key medications in Veterans Affairs patients after coronary artery bypass grafting. *American Journal of Health System Pharmacy* 61, no. 12: 1248–1252.

Jha, A. K., Perlin, J. B., Kizer, K. W. & Dudley, R. A. (2003). Effect of the transformation of the Veterans Affairs health care system on the quality of care. *New England Journal of Medicine* 348: 2218–2227.

Kerr, E. A., Gerzoff, R. B., Krein, S. L., Selby, J. V., Piette, J. D., Curb, J. D., et al. (2004). Diabetes care quality in the Veterans Affairs health care system and commercial managed care. *Annals of Internal Medicine* 141, no. 4: 272–281.

Kilborn, P. T. (1996). Veterans expand hospital system in face of cuts. *New York Times,* January 14, 1.

Kizer, K. W. (1995). Vision for change. http://www4.va.gov/HEALTHPOLICY PLANNING/VISION/2CHAP1.pdf.

Kizer, K. W. (1996). Prescription for change. http://www4.va.gov/HEALTH POLICYPLANNING/rxweb.pdf.

Kizer, K. W., Demakis, J. G. & Feussner, J. R. (2000). Reinventing VA health care: Systematizing quality improvement and quality innovation. *Medical Care* 38, supp.1: I7–I16.

Lehner, L., Burgess, J., Hults, D. & Stefos, T. (1996). Data and information requirements for the Department of Veterans Affairs Resource Allocation Systems. *Medical Care* 34, no. 3: MS21–MS30.

Lichtenberg, F. R. (2005). Older drugs, shorter lives? An examination of the health effects of the Veterans Health Administration formulary. Medical progress report no. 2. http://www.manhattan-institute.org/pdf/mpr_02.pdf (accessed July 20, 2007).

London, M. J., Itani, K. M., Perrino, A. C., Jr., Guarino, P. D., Schwartz, G. G., Cunningham, F., et al. (2004). Perioperative beta-blockade: A survey of physician attitudes in the Department of Veterans Affairs. *Journal of Cardiothoracic and Vascular Anesthesia* 18, no. 1: 14–24.

Lopez, J., Meier, J., Cunningham, F. & Siegel, D. (2004). Antihypertensive medication use in the Department of Veterans Affairs: A national analysis of prescribing patterns from 2000 to 2002. *American Journal of Hypertension* 17, no. 12, pt. 1: 1095–1099.

More than veterans need. (1996). *St. Petersburg Times,* January 16, 10A.

Oliver, A. (2007). The Veterans Health Administration: An American success story? *Milbank Quarterly* 85, no. 1: 5–35.

Part III: The VHA transformation as viewed by Dr. Kenneth W. Kizer, former undersecretary for health, U.S. Department of Veterans Affairs. (2000). In *Transforming government: The revitalization of the Veterans Health Administration.* Retrieved 3/15/2010, from http://www.businessofgovernment.org/pdfs/ Young_Report.pdf.

Patient Protection and Affordable Care Act of 2010, Pub. L. No. 111-148.

Perlin, J. B. (2005). *Transformational strategies of the U.S. Veterans Health Administration.* London: Health Foundation, International Health Care Quality Exchange Conference.

Peterson, L. A., Normand, S. L., Leape, L. L. & McNeil, B. J. (2001). Comparison of use of medications after acute myocardial infarction in the Veterans Health Administration and Medicare. *Circulation* 104, no. 24: 2898–2904.

PPI policy memo. (n.d.). http://www.progressivefix.com/wp-content/uploads/2010/01/The-Pentagons-Most-Expensive-Weapon.pdf (accessed April 4, 2012).

Ren, X. S., Kazis, L. E., Lee, A. F., Hamed, A., Huang, Y. H., Cunningham, F., et al. (2002). Patient characteristics and prescription patterns of atypical antipsychotics among patients with schizophrenia. *Journal of Clinical Pharmacy and Therapeutics* 27, no. 6: 441–451.

Sales, M. M., Cunningham, F. E., Glassman, P. A., Valentino, M. A. & Good, C. B. (2005). Pharmacy benefits management in the Veterans Health Administration: 1995 to 2003. *American Journal of Managed Care* 11, no. 2: 104–112.

Siegel, D., Lopez, J., Meier, J. & Cunningham, F. (2001). Changes in the pharmacologic treatment of hypertension in the Department of Veterans Affairs 1997–1999: Decreased use of calcium antagonists and increased use of beta-blockers and thiazide diuretics. *American Journal of Hypertension* 14, no. 9, pt. 1: 957–962.

Siva, C., Eisen, S. A., Shepherd, R., Cunningham, F., Fang, M. A., Finch, W., et al. (2003). Leflunomide use during the first 33 months after food and drug administration approval: experience with a national cohort of 3,325 patients. *Arthritis & Rheumatism* 49, no. 6: 745–751.

Smedley, B. D., Stith, A. Y. & Nelson, A. R. (Eds.). (2003). *Unequal treatment: Confronting racial and ethnic disparities in health care.* Washington, DC: National Academy Press.

University of Michigan School of Business. (2007). American customer satisfaction index, 2000–2006. http://www.theacsi.org/index.php?option=com_content&task=view&id=27&Itemid=62 (accessed August 24, 2007).

Veterans Health Administration. Office of Quality and Safety. (2009). 2009 VHA facility quality and safety report. http://www1.va.gov/vetdata/docs/Datagov/DataGov_VHA_FY09_Hospital_Final_Report.pdf.

The Veterans' Health Care Eligibility Reform Act of 1996, Pub. L. No. 104-262.

The World Health Report 2000—health systems: Improving performance. (2000). Geneva, Switzerland: World Health Organization.

Yarnall, K. S., Pollak, K. I., Ostbye, T., Krause, K. M. & Michener, J. L. (2003). Primary care: Is there enough time for prevention? *American Journal of Public Health* 93, no. 4: 635–641.

Zuvekas, S. H. & Cohen, J. W. (2007). Prescription drugs and the changing concentration of health care expenditures. *Health Affairs (Millwood)* 26, no. 1: 249–257.

Telehealth Applications to Underserved Veterans: The Right Care, in the Right Place, at the Right Time

Jennifer A. Wood, Thomas W. Miller, and Russell Hagy

Introduction

As one of the first institutions to establish and implement telehealth technologies, the Department of Veterans Affairs (VA) has served as a pioneer in telehealth development and research since the 1970s. At present VA is the largest single medical system in the United States, providing care to an estimated 5.5 million veterans each year. Approximately one-quarter of the nation's population is potentially eligible for VA benefits via status as a veteran, family member, or survivor of a veteran. Given its mission to provide world-class healthcare to U.S. veterans, VA is tasked with delivering medical and behavioral services to a geographically, economically, and culturally diverse population. This is traditionally accomplished via a network of approximately 1,649 healthcare facilities, including 153 VA Medical Centers (VAMCs), 135 nursing homes, and over 800 outpatient clinics (U.S. Department of Veterans Affairs 2010).

Considering the significant diversity inherent in the VA healthcare system, getting care via traditional clinic or hospital-based services is often challenging for veterans living in remote or underserved areas. Factors such as geographic location, socioeconomic challenges, lack of transportation infrastructure, inhospitable weather, and variations in the availability of specialty providers have all been cited as barriers to care. Fortunately, telehealth has served as a means of enhancing access to healthcare by transcending these obstacles. This chapter outlines the development of telemedicine and telehealth technologies within

VA, provides an overview of the organizational structure of telehealth services, shares current training initiatives and program evaluation standards, discusses applications of telehealth technology across a broad array of healthcare disciplines, and outlines future directions for telehealth within VA.

Telehealth: Definitions and Technical Applications

The discipline of telehealth has developed a vernacular all its own to refer to the use of technology to deliver healthcare services. Literature reviews reveal a host of terms such as *telehealth*, *telemedicine*, and *telecare*, as well as numerous *tele*-specialty terms that are utilized to describe this growing field of practice. Prior to delving into the history and evolution of telehealth, a brief discussion of the telehealth vocabulary will assist in clarifying these seemingly interchangeable descriptors. The prefix *tele* is Greek for "distant" or "over a distance" (*An Introduction to Telehealth in the VA* 2010). Terms such as *telecommute*, *telephone*, and *telegram* clearly illustrate the implication of this prefix and help to demonstrate how this meaning is also applied within the realm of telehealth. *Telemedicine* and *telehealth* are two of the most frequently used terms to describe the practice of utilizing technology to deliver healthcare services. Of the two, *telehealth* is generally recognized as being the broader term and is defined by Nickelson (1998) as the use of telecommunication technology to provide access to health assessment, diagnosis, intervention, consultation, supervision, education, and information across distance. It encompasses telemedicine as well as other healthcare-related activities, including health education, administrative activities, and training. In turn, *telemedicine* is a more specific term falling under the umbrella of telehealth; it refers to the use of electronic communications and information technology to provide or support clinical care at a distance (U.S. Department of Commerce 1997). A number of terms also exist to describe the use of telecommunications to deliver specialty healthcare services, such as *telemental health*, *telepsychiatry*, *teleretinal services*, *teledermatology*, *teleradiology*, etc.

In addition to an array of lingo, many forms of technology are also included under the umbrella of telehealth applications. Telehealth relies on a wide range of technologies to connect individuals and transmit information. Most types of telecommunication can be classified as either synchronous or asynchronous. Asynchronous communication occurs through store-and-forward technology, which allows professionals to compile information, which can then be sent to another party for retrieval. In other words, the sender and receiver need not be present at the same time in order to access the information. Common asynchronous health care applications include e-mail, fax, digital messaging, and digital imaging techniques. For instance, teleretinal and teleimaging programs often rely heavily on asynchronous technology whereby a technician captures an image of a specimen (e.g., retinal images, MRI of the brain, etc.), which is then digitized and sent to a remote specialist for interpretation.

In contrast, synchronous applications provide for real-time or live communication between parties. Examples of interactions using synchronous communication include standard telephone conversations, Internet chat rooms, and interactive videoconferencing. With advances in videoconferencing technology, this mode of communication has practically become synonymous with telehealth. Videoconferencing applications are ideal for clinical interactions in that they transmit real time audio-video data, which allows for technology-mediated face-to-face contact between geographically distant parties. Several types of videoconferencing applications currently exist. These include, but are not limited to, dedicated videoconference systems, PC-based videoconferencing, and retrofit units. Dedicated videoconference units are those that utilize digital phone lines (T1 lines) to transmit information. They are "dedicated" in that specific lines are designated for client-provider services only, and transmission of data is typically encrypted for security purposes. These systems are usually composed of at least two TV monitors and a codex. An alternative to the dedicated unit is desktop PC videoconferencing. In this medium, computer-based programs can transmit data either through standard telephone lines or by way of the Internet. These types of systems require the purchase and use of a computer with a webcam at each site and may require specific videoconferencing software. A third, less commonly used, alternative is the retrofit unit, which works by using existing televisions and telephones to transmit video and audio data. The unit, similar to a cable box, is connected to both the television and phone line, allowing audio-video feed to be transmitted through the television. Other similar applications include videophones and cell-phone-based video chat capabilities. Given this range of technology, great potential exists for implementing telehealth applications across a wide variety of clinical domains in a manner that can accommodate variations in budget and technological infrastructure.

Telehealth: History and Evolution

The concept of utilizing technology to overcome barriers to healthcare delivery is not a novel one. In its earliest form, telehealth can be traced back to the late 1880s, during which time the telephone was first introduced as a tool to link medical professionals to their patients. Documented examples of physician-patient telephone interactions with the purpose of relaying medical advice first occurred around this time. Shortly after the turn of century, in 1906, William Einthoven, the father of electrocardiography, first investigated electrocardiogram (ECG) transmission via telephone lines. During the course of this project, he successfully relayed ECG data from a local hospital to his laboratory 1.5 km away (Einthoven 1906). It is noteworthy that in 1924 Einthoven was awarded the Nobel Prize for Medicine for his discovery of the electrical properties of the heart through his ECG instrument. Other early uses of telehealth include efforts in the 1920's to deliver healthcare via radio transmissions to ships at sea (Telemedicine 2010).

In 1924 the cover of *Radio News* magazine featured a futuristic depiction of a doctor interacting with a patient via television. Thirty-five years later this concept became a reality with the formal debut of telepsychiatry/telemedicine. In 1959, researchers at the Nebraska Psychiatric Institute devised a two-way television connection for the purpose of enhancing classroom instruction. With this modality, medical students seated across campus were able to observe and interact with professors performing neurological exams at the institute (Brown 1998; Wittson & Benschoter 1972). After observing the usefulness of this approach with students, the institute sought to apply this technology within a working psychiatric setting by creating a video link between it and the Nebraska State Mental Hospital, approximately 100 miles away. The project was considered to be a significant milestone in that it demonstrated the feasibility of teleconferencing for consultation, research, education, and administrative purposes and helped to set in motion the first wave of telehealth demonstration projects in the United States. Subsequent projects focused primarily on telemedicine and telepsychiatry services. For instance, in 1968 a video link between Massachusetts General Hospital and the Logan Airport Medical Station was established, allowing the small airport clinic to benefit from the expertise of medical specialists at Massachusetts General. More specifically, physicians at the hospital were able to provide medical assessment to airport employees as well as emergency care to travelers. This project further demonstrated that video links could be effectively utilized for medical consultation, triage, and interpretation of images (Dwyer 1973; Puskin, Mintzer & Wasem 1997). Likewise the Department of Psychiatry at Dartmouth Medical School established video links with several physicians in Claremont, New Hampshire, in an effort to afford physicians with specialty consultations. At an agreed upon time, independent physicians and their patients could request the assistance of a psychiatrist from Dartmouth. Participating psychiatrists reported that the television medium presented almost no difficulties in establishing rapport or in perceiving emotional nuances (Solow et al. 1971). During the 1960s NASA also took part in implementing video technology by supporting satellite-transmitted medical services. Initial efforts included monitoring physiological data telemetered from astronauts' space suits and spacecraft equipment. NASA's contributions to telemedicine continued in the 1970s, when it sponsored the Space Technology Applied to Rural Papago

Advanced Health Care (STARPAHC) project. The STARPHAC project allowed for the delivery of medical care to the Papago Indian Reservation in Arizona via two-way microwave audiovisual transmissions. This connection facilitated the direct provision of medical services and transmission of X-rays and ECG data for residents in some of the most remote areas in the United States (Brown 1998; Puskin, Mintzer & Wasem 1997). In 1971 VA debuted its first telemedicine project, during which a video link was utilized to connect the Nebraska Medical Center to the Omaha Veterans Administration Hospital as well as to two other VA clinical sites.

As illustrated by these examples, many of the early telemedicine projects sought to utilize technology to deliver care to remote or very distant populations. In a novel attempt to reach urban but underserved areas, in 1976 an interactive television system was used to link the Mount Sinai School of Medicine to a child health station in East Harlem. Results of the collaboration showed that children were more likely to receive needed healthcare and to follow up with their plan of care with the introduction of the telemedicine service (Straker, Mostyn & Marshall 1976). That same year, the U.S. military began implementing telemedicine to allow Army Special Forces dentists to utilize a digital tooth identification system to transmit images of soldiers' teeth to distant sites. Throughout the 1960s and 1970s continued research demonstrated that telecommunication technology could be successfully utilized for a variety of clinical applications, including neurological assessments, group therapy, medical consultations, patient interviews, and observation (Brown 1998; Wittson & Benschoter 1972; Wittson, Affleck & Van Johnson 1961; Solow et al. 1971; Puskin, Mintzer & Wasem 1997; Straker, Mostyn & Marshall 1976).

Unfortunately, these efforts, which began with such promise, eventually faded from public view. The decline in attempts to implement telecommunication systems was most likely due to the high cost of equipment and lack of unobtrusive, high-quality technology. As a result, telehealth and its applications remained relatively obscure for almost two decades (Graham 1996; Puskin, Mintzer & Wasem 1997). Although substantial, such limitations were merely products of a lag in technological innovation.

During the 1990s advances in telecommunications, combined with the decreasing costs of technology, served to spark a renewed interest in the application of videoconferencing in the healthcare field. Complementing these technological advances were other factors such as heightened consumer awareness, state and federal policy changes, and an increased marketplace demand for innovative and cost-effective methods of service delivery (Jerome et al. 2000). This revival was further fueled by the ever-present imperative to increase access to health services in underserved populations (Puskin, Mintzer & Wasem 1997).

Table 8.1. Milestones in the First-Wave Development of Telehealth

Date	Event
1880s	The telephone is first used to relay medical advice to patients.
1906	William Einthoven successfully transmits ECG data via telephone lines.
1924	The concept of videoconferencing is first depicted on the cover of *Radio News*.
1959	Two-way television is used to allow medical students to observe neurological exams.
1959	First telemental health project is conducted between Nebraska State Mental Hospital and the Nebraska Psychiatric Institute.
1968	Video link is established between Massachusetts General Hospital and Logan Airport Medical Station.
1960s	NASA begins remote monitoring of astronauts' vital signs.
1970s	NASA's STARPHAC telemedicine project takes place.
1971	Telemedicine link is established between Omaha VA hospital and two VA outpatient clinics.
1976	Telepsychiatry link is established between Mount Sinai School of Medicine and East Harlem pediatric clinic.
1976	U.S. Army uses store-and-forward technology to transmit dental images.

Today, telehealth applications are one of the fastest growing modes of service delivery among a variety of healthcare specialties. In 1993 there were ten telemedicine programs in the United States. Since that time, the number of telehealth programs has almost doubled each year (Maheu, Whitten & Allen 2001). Recent estimates indicate that nearly all states and provinces in the United States and Canada have now implemented telehealth programs (Stamm 1998). This exponential growth has been due in large part to increased state and federal funding for telehealth systems. During the 1994–1996 fiscal years, federal and independent agencies invested approximately $646 million to support telehealth projects. In 1998 the Rural Telemedicine Grant program, established by the Health Resources and Services Administration, provided $13.6 million to fund forty-one telehealth grants for projects in twenty-nine states (Maheu, Whitten & Allen 2001). Expansion of telehealth services in VA has followed a similar trajectory, with the number of active projects increasing throughout the 1990s. In 1997 VA began to systematically implement telehealth and boasted over 300,000 telemedicine episodes a year by 1999 (*An Introduction to Telehealth in the VA* 2010).

By 2004 telehealth had expanded to include projects at twenty of VA's twenty-one Veterans Integrated Service Networks (VISNs). In fiscal year 2008, more than 230,000 telehealth encounters took place in VA, a substantial increase from the 83,500 encounters conducted just two years before (What Is Care Coordination Services? 2010). At present, more than forty specialty areas in VA utilize telehealth, including areas such as telemental health, teleradiology, teledermatology, teleretinal imaging, telesurgery, and telerehabilitation (Darkins 2008a).

Paralleling this growth is an expansion in both clinical and nonclinical telehealth applications. Telehealth systems are currently used by a variety of healthcare professionals, including cardiologists, endocrinologists, dermatologists, psychiatrists, psychologists, nurses, and orthopedists. In addition to utilizing this technology for specialist consultations, other applications such as management of chronic illnesses, surgical follow-up, correctional facility care, home healthcare, crisis intervention, monitoring of patient progress, and medication support are becoming increasingly common. Telehealth systems are also used to support a variety of nonclinical services, including consumer health education, continuing education for professionals, administrative meetings, and staff training (Maheu, Whitten & Allen 2001).

Organizational Structure of VA Telehealth

Given VA's commitment to providing world-class care to a diverse veteran population and the use of telehealth technology to extend services to VA enrollees, the Office of Telehealth Services (formerly known as the Office of Care Coordination Services) was created in 2003 with a mission to support VA in "implementing information, telehealth and disease management technologies to extend and enhance care and case management" (Darkins 2010, 1). It is the goal of the Office of Telehealth Services (OTS) to create and sustain telehealth services that will enable the delivery of the right care in the right place at the right time to veterans at their preferred site of care, whether that be at home or in the community. In other words, the needs of the veteran drive care priorities, with the application of telehealth technology complementing this goal by enhancing access, convenience, and continuity of care. A recent study conducted by the North Florida/South Georgia Veterans Health Care System supports this notion. Researchers found that the utilization of telehealth resulted in decreased travel for veterans, improved provider communication and continuity of care, and enhanced compliance with the veteran's plan of care (*An Introduction to Telehealth in the VA* 2010).

The OTS consists of three divisions: Clinical Video Telehealth, Care Coordination Home Telehealth, and Store-and-Forward Telehealth. Clinical Video

Telehealth (CVT) encompasses those services that deliver telehealth care via synchronous telecommunication technology (Darkins 2010). This involves a wide range of clinical applications, including, but not limited to, telemental health, telemedicine for spinal cord injury patients, and mobile medical units. Often these interactions involve a veteran located at his or her local VA clinic interacting with a specialist from another VA clinic or medical center via video-conference. All communications are encrypted and relayed via a closed network system. For instance, in telemental health, telecommunication technology is utilized to link a veteran at one site to a mental health specialist at another site. Services delivered via this mode have included psychiatric assessment, triage services, empirically based psychotherapy (e.g., cognitive processing therapy, cognitive behavioral therapy for depression, prolonged exposure, etc.), as well as group therapy. In the same manner, virtual linkages are also used in telerehabilitation to link speech pathologists and rehabilitation specialists to veterans in need of such care. This has proven to be effective for veterans in need of post-stroke rehabilitation as well as for monitoring functional status and equipment needs of veterans in the home (What Is Care Coordination Services? 2010). In an effort to foster the development of VA CVT programs and their staff, the Rocky Mountain Telehealth Training Center, described in further detail later, was created to provide training and support to VA staff involved in CVT (Durham 2008).

Care Coordination Home Telehealth (CCHT) is the branch of the OTS concerned with "remote monitoring telehealth" wherein telehealth technology is used to capture biometric data and transmit the information back to the veteran's healthcare team. This customarily works by issuing a home monitoring device to the veteran, which he or she then uses to enter data regarding health status. These devices are particularly well suited for veterans with chronic diseases such as diabetes, heart failure, or chronic pulmonary disease, or those with mental health conditions such as depression or anxiety (Darkins 2010). Data from CCHT programs have shown that remote monitoring is an effective intervention for promoting self-management and patient education, reducing hospitalizations, and allowing veterans to remain in their homes, resulting in improved quality of life. To date, thousands of veterans have been enrolled in CCHT across VA (What Is Care Coordination Services? 2010). The Sunshine Telehealth Training Center, described in further detail later, serves as the training and support center for CCHT programs.

The Store-and-Forward division focuses on clinical situations in which digital images, video, audio, and/or clinical data are captured and securely transmitted to a specialist at another location for evaluation (Darkins 2010). In this manner, store-and-forward programs allow specialists at a central location to assist with evaluation and treatment planning for veterans at remote or distant sites. Within VA, the three most robust areas in which this technology is currently utilized are teledermatology, teleradiology, and teleretinal imaging. Given that dermatological conditions are quite common and are often a source of discomfort for veterans, teledermatology allows for increased access to specialty care for veterans in remote areas. This system typically works by having an onsite technician or clinical provider take a digital picture of the area of concern, which is then uploaded and transmitted to a dermatologist. The dermatologist reviews the data and makes a diagnosis or treatment recommendation, which is communicated back to the referring provider. Data from teledermatology clinics have shown that for approximately 20 percent of patients, teledermatology significantly decreases time to initiation of treatment while effectively avoiding the need for a face-to-face appointment. It has also proven to be a cost-effective measure for patients by reducing the time and financial burden incurred by the need to travel long distances to see a specialist. Likewise, with teleradiology, X-ray images can be transmitted over telecommunication lines to a radiologist for expert review and recommendation. Teleradiology is now a routine element of care in many VA hospital and clinical settings. Teleretinal programming has also become a standard of care in providing early detection and treatment of diabetic retinopathy. Utilizing a specialized camera, pictures of the retina can be taken at the patient's local clinic and then sent to an eye-care specialist for review. A report is sent back to the patient's primary care provider, who can initiate treatment if needed (What Is Care Coordination Services? 2010). The Boston Store-and-Forward Telehealth Training Center provides training and support to VA staff involved in store-and-forward programs (Boston Telehealth Training Center 2010). In addition to online training, resources, and subject matter experts, the Boston Training Center also offers a master preceptor training program, which has trained more than seventy teleretinal imagers throughout VA, bringing the number of imagers to more than 300 nationwide. Thus far more than 300 teleretinal cameras have been deployed throughout VA, which have screened more than 400,000 veterans with diabetes (Rocky Mountain Telehealth Training Center 2009).

Telehealth Training Initiatives

To support staff in developing and sustaining telehealth programs in VA, several initiatives have been devised to provide employees with needed training and development opportunities. These include general training modules available to all staff, national and regional conferences, monthly conference calls, and journal clubs, as well as activities and support coordinated through the three aforementioned formal training centers associated with the three divisions. Each of these three training centers is described in further detail here.

In 2005 the Rocky Mountain Telehealth Training Center (RMTTC) was developed to provide training and support to VA staff involved in CVT (Rocky Mountain Telehealth Training Center 2009). It is a "one-stop shop" for resources and training for staff engaged in CVT throughout VA. Among the many valuable resources available at the RMTTC Web site is a collection of comprehensive documents such as the General Telehealth Resource Guide, Operations Manual, sample documents, marketing tools, and a virtual library of best practice materials. Personalized just-in-time training is available to CVT staff as well as consultation tailored to small group needs, in addition to a host of Web-based training modules and videos. Individual CVT staff may access RMTTC staff by phone or e-mail with questions or requests for training assistance. Just as telehealth is intended to bring healthcare to veterans in a personalized and accessible manner, so is the training available from the RMTTC. In an effort to expand the number of telehealth experts in the field, a master preceptor program is available to provide additional leadership at the field level. The RMTTC also hosts a variety of specialized SharePoint sites to bridge providers from like programs and facilitate group meetings. The RMTTC also works closely with the Telehealth Clinical Field groups as well as the General Telehealth VISN Leads across VA. For fiscal year 2008, the RMTTC reported more than 135 training events, ranging from national conference forums to individualized training. Almost 2,400 hours of training were provided to over 2,000 staff via the various modalities referenced above. Plans are under way to enhance training with a series of data gathering and management tools to assist CVT programs in evaluating and developing their programs (Rocky Mountain Telehealth Training Center 2009).

The Care Coordination Home Telehealth (CCHT) National Training Center, also known as the Sunshine Training Center, was similarly developed to provide training and support to staff involved in home telehealth programs. The Sunshine Training Center offers a variety of Web-based training modules and videos available via its Web site, in addition to an expert collection of toolkits and resource documents. It also operates a master preceptor program, which enrolls a new class of preceptors annually. Routine virtual meetings and satellite broadcasts are conducted for field staff.

To support store-and-forward programs, the Boston Store-and-Forward Telehealth Training Center was developed to provide training and assistance to staff involved in the delivery of store-and-forward telehealth services. More specifically, the center's mission has been to provide quality training and educational programs to staff in direct support of multiple store-and-forward telehealth initiatives. Since March 2006 the Boston Training Center has established more than fifty-five educational programs, including training materials accessed through Web-based courses, continuing education programs, general training modules available to all staff, national and regional conferences, and monthly conference calls. A SharePoint site has also been established to facilitate collaboration and information exchange. The Boston Training Center initiated and maintains a Master Preceptor program in teleretinal imaging, which now has more than sixty trained teleretinal preceptors. The intent of developing this program was to create a cadre of experts to facilitate training efforts within each VISN and to promote personal and professional development. Since the inception of the first program in May 2008, preceptors have trained more than 130 imagers in the field throughout VA, bringing the total number of teleretinal imagers involved in the program to more than 370 nationwide. Boston's Training Center Master Preceptors play an important role in the operation of teleretinal training programs in the field by mentoring and training prospective imagers and serving as an extension of the Boston Training Center. The preceptors also interact with clinic managers, physicians, and VISN telehealth coordinators and serve as liaisons to the diabetic retinopathy screening program. In addition to direct support to staff, the center conducts routine patient satisfaction surveys to assess veteran satisfaction with store-and-forward services and monitors ongoing competency assessments for readers.

In addition to developing a cadre of highly trained telehealth professionals and clinicians, VA has also implemented a standardized quality management tool, the Conditions of Participation (CoP), applicable to all three branches of its telehealth program. The CoP serves as an internal certification and evaluation process intended to address the system elements of individual telehealth programs and proactively assess for possible points of failure that are inherent in any systems design. Through routine monitoring, the CoP seeks to ensure that the necessary structures are in place to support telehealth programs and that telehealth staff receive appropriate training, and to identify best practices that might be shared with others in the field (Darkins 2008b). For instance, the CoP for CVT systematically tracks identification of specialty providers participating in telehealth, each provider site and corresponding patient sites of care, how telehealth programs are aligned in the organization, workload validation procedures, local telehealth policies and procedures, documentation of training in telehealth and subsequent maintenance of competencies for each provider, outcome data for each telehealth project, as well as completion of a comprehensive self-assessment tool.

Telehealth Applications

At present, VA operates a wide variety of telehealth programs. These currently include, but are not limited to, telemental health, teleretinal imaging, telepharmacy, telesurgery, teledermatology, telepulmonology, telerehabilitation, teleradiology, home-based telehealth monitoring, and polytrauma telehealth. The following review represents a sampling of such programs. It is not meant to be exhaustive, but rather to be a snapshot of the current types of telehealth activity occurring in this ever-evolving field.

Telemental Health

Numerous telemental health applications have been employed in VA, many of which aim to address geographic barriers to care or shortages of specialty providers. These programs offer a variety of services, including telepsychiatry, individual psychotherapy, group psychotherapy, specialty mental health services, screening for cognitive impairment, and crisis intervention. As of 2007 there were over 300 telemental health sites of care in VA, from which more than 50,000 veterans were provided with mental health services (Darkins 2007). An example is the Women's Telemental Health Clinic for trauma treatment and recovery, based at the VA Outpatient Clinic in Austin, Texas. Through this program women trauma survivors are able to participate in psycho-educational groups offered by a VA psychologist. The VA psychologist is based at the Austin clinic, and women at several outlying clinics (some as far as 180 miles away) are able to participate via videoconferencing (New Women's Telemental Health Clinic 2008). Extensive telemental health services are also employed in the VA Texas Valley Coastal Bend Health Care System, which provides service to the southernmost part of Texas. Barriers to care in this region include difficulty recruiting specialty providers, rural and highly rural populations, geographic dispersion, and lack of a comprehensive public transportation infrastructure. Several unique programs have been developed to address these challenges, including a telemental health substance abuse intensive outpatient program, telepsychiatry specialists who provide coverage to areas that are short of providers, as well as the system's Mobile Medical Unit, which serves veterans from the area's most rural counties, and teletherapy services (Wood 2010; Wood & Vega 2010). These activities have been incorporated into the training of rotating medical students and psychology interns, which offers a unique opportunity for future healthcare professionals to receive training in telehealth modalities (Wood 2010). Programs such as this have become commonplace throughout VA, to the extent that funding was allocated to hire dedicated telemental health program support staff for each VISN. These individuals assist in the implementation and sustainability of telemental health programs by monitoring the purchase and installation of telehealth equipment, assisting telemental health staff, tracking telemental health workload, and serving as liaisons between the Telemental Health Lead and the mental health service at the facilities within their VISN (New Telemental Health Field Staff Meet 2008). Paralleling the expansion of telemental health services is also an increase in VA telemental health research initiatives, the majority of which have indicated that telemental health is comparable to face-to-face care (Darkins 2008b).

Home Telehealth

Care Coordination Home Telehealth utilizes home-based telehealth technology to link veterans to VA staff from the comfort and convenience of their homes. This mode of communication is ideal for individuals with chronic diseases such as diabetes, heart failure, and chronic pulmonary disease, in that home-based care can significantly prevent or delay the need for long-term institutional care, thus promoting quality of life and the highest level of independence possible. As of 2007 more than 30,000 veterans were enrolled in CCHT (Over 30,000 Veterans Enrolled in CCHT 2007). Home telehealth may utilize several types of equipment to connect veterans to their treatment team. One frequently used modality is messaging devices, which may be programmed to deliver a standard set of questions regarding health behaviors or symptoms to the veteran at set intervals. The veteran enters his or her responses and/or vital signs, which are electronically transmitted to a member of the care coordination team, usually a nurse. These data are screened and entered into the veteran's medical record for tracking. If the data indicate an unhealthy increase in symptoms, immediate intervention can take place to better manage the condition. Videophones may also be employed as part of a home telehealth treatment program. These typically utilize a standard land line and allow for real-time interactions between the veteran and his or her provider. In other instances, computers may be used to allow the veteran to connect with online support groups (What Is Care Coordination Services? 2010).

Electronic Medical Records

Complementing its progressive implementation of telehealth applications is VA's utilization of electronic medical records. As early as the mid-1980s VA began to implement automated data processing systems to facilitate both administrative and clinical aspects of care through its VistA package.

These efforts culminated in the development of the Decentralized Hospital Computer Program information system (DHCP). In 1995 the DHCP was the recipient of the Smithsonian Award for best use of information technology in medicine, one of the most prestigious honors in the computer world. In 1997 the Computerized Patient Record System (CPRS) was released. The CPRS program was developed to provide clinicians with a user-friendly platform for reviewing and updating the electronic medical record. Features of CPRS include the ability to place orders; enter prescriptions; request specialty consults; order X-rays; enter alerts for critical information, which display as pop-up windows when the chart is accessed; view digital images (e.g., MRI, CT, scanned documents such as advanced directives); and request and track laboratory tests. Thus a veteran's electronic medical record can be accessed by his or her provider at any VA facility, which ensures continuity of care for patients who may need services while traveling or upon relocation, or prefer to receive healthcare at multiple VA sites. For its development of the CPRS, VA was named the recipient of the Innovations in American Government Award, presented by the Ash Institute of the John F. Kennedy School of Government at Harvard University in July 2006. In addition to improving continuity of care, the implementation of an electronic medical records system has improved efficiency by 6 percent per year and allowed VA to achieve a pharmacy prescription accuracy rate of 99.997 percent, and VA currently outperforms most public-sector hospitals on a variety of criteria (Veterans Health Administration 2010).

In concert with these efforts, VA has also developed a secure portal at which veterans may access their personal health information, called MyHealtheVet. By registering for and logging onto a personalized MyHealtheVet secure Web site, veterans may access certain information from their medical records, refill their prescriptions online, graph changes in their lab values or vital signs, and print certain portions of their health information. MyHealtheVet also provides access to educational materials and behavioral support for lifestyle changes, and allows veterans to send secure messages to their treatment team. Future plans for development of MyHealtheVet include the ability to schedule appointments online.

Research Initiatives

Paralleling VA's large-scale expansion of telehealth services, VA providers are also engaged in ongoing, cutting-edge research associated with telehealth activity. This activity ranges from program evaluation projects, to local demonstration pilots, to funded controlled research trials. An area particularly ripe for research is telemental health. Several VA studies have demonstrated that telemental health interventions are comparable to face-to-face treatment in terms of efficacy, therapeutic rapport, cost-effectiveness, and patient and provider satisfaction. For instance, demonstration projects have shown that telehealth interventions for smoking cessation are equally as effective in terms of degree of behavioral change and quit rates as traditional face-to-face smoking cessation programs. Veterans enrolled in telehealth smoking cessation programs also report high levels of satisfaction with the service, high degrees of therapeutic rapport, and no significant discomfort with the technological medium. Similarly, satisfaction surveys among both veterans engaged in telepsychiatry services and VA psychiatrists delivering such care revealed high degrees of satisfaction with the telehealth mode, no significant technological difficulties, and adequate therapeutic rapport (Wood 2006). Other similar studies have demonstrated the feasibility of delivering intensive outpatient services for veterans with substance abuse/dependence diagnoses (Wood & Vega 2010). Several innovative uses of home messaging devices among veterans diagnosed with depression and/or anxiety have shown that at-home monitoring after psychiatric hospitalization is effective at reducing the need for future psychiatric hospitalizations, improving the veteran's understanding of his or her condition, and providing insight into the fluctuation of symptomatology and early intervention to prevent crises.

In addition to these demonstration projects, several large-scale research have been initiated by VA. These include a four-year, prospective, randomized clinical trial comparing the effectiveness of behavioral activation delivered via in-home videoconferencing with traditional face-to-face services. The sample included 224 elderly veterans who received an eight-session, manualized behavioral activation treatment. Participants were followed for twelve months to ascertain treatment outcomes with regard to clinical variables (i.e., symptom severity, functional status), process variables (i.e., patient satisfaction, treatment adherence), and economic factors (i.e., cost and resource use) (Egede et al. 2009). Pilot programs are also under way to provide telemental health treatment for PTSD to returning soldiers by combining resources and expertise to create joint VA–Department of Defense (DoD) collaborations. Given the resources of these two agencies, the need for effective delivery of PTSD treatment to returning veterans, and general familiarity with technology-mediated communication among this veteran cohort, future studies aim to evaluate creative methods of service delivery (Nieves et al. 2009). At present, VA is effectively delivering several empirically supported PTSD treatments via telemental health, including cognitive processing therapy and prolonged exposure. Other proposed projects include the use of telemental health for neuropsychological testing, videoconferencing technology as an outreach mechanism for Mental

Health Intensive Case Management, and telehealth coaching as a training tool for primary care providers conducting suicide risk assessments.

Telehealth Practice Considerations

Although a detailed discussion is beyond the scope of this chapter, a brief review of practice considerations is in order. Before initiating any telehealth project, is it important to be aware of the following facets of telehealth service delivery. Adequate assessment and preplanning to address these factors is, at a minimum, necessary to the success of telehealth interactions.

Technological Infrastructure

Facilities seeking to implement telehealth programming should carefully assess the technological infrastructure required to support the requirements of the equipment that is to be deployed. This includes careful examination of bandwidth requirements, security of data transmissions, and start-up as well as maintenance costs of telehealth equipment. Fortunately, numerous options exist for creating virtual connections, many of which will accommodate variations in budget and bandwidth. For facilities outfitted with Internet capabilities, e-mail and chat rooms may serve as acceptable media of communication. Data can be sent on secure, closed intranets or encrypted to ensure confidentiality. Equipment needs are minimal; only a computer and Internet access at each location are required. The cost of a new computer may range from $1,000 to $3,000, and Internet fees typically vary from $15 to $40 per month. Although costs range depending on local rates and sophistication of equipment, start-up investment for this type of system will range from $3,500 to $5,000 (Stamm 1998).

For sites interested in incorporating technology-mediated, face-to-face contact, several types of videoconferencing applications exist. As a general rule of thumb, the quality of these units can be measured in frames per second (fps). Broadcast quality is usually 30 fps, but fairly clear resolution can be achieved at speeds of 15–20 fps. Thus, as fps increases, so does the quality of the transmission as well as the cost of the system. In choosing the appropriate system for a treatment site, it is important to consider the clinical demands on the system. For example, if the ability to see movement clearly is important, a system with higher fps would be most suitable. On the other hand, slower frames might be more appropriate when movement is not an important factor or when the cost of higher frame rates is prohibitive. Dedicated videoconference systems, the most expensive option, can range from $7,000 to $50,000 per site. These units typically transmit data via digital telephone lines at up to

30 frames per second. Computer-based desktop units that utilize telephones typically have a maximum transfer rate of 15 fps and cost between $1,000 and $5,000 per unit (excluding the cost of the computer). Internet-based computer models are less expensive, ranging from $100 to $500 (sans computer) and vary from 15 to 30 fps, depending on Internet traffic and computer processing speed. Finally retrofit units, which utilize existing televisions and telephone lines, can transmit data at 20 fps. Per unit costs range from $350 to $500. In addition to their low cost, because these units can operate on analog phone lines, they may be ideal for areas without access to digital phone lines (Stamm 1998). Ironically, the cost of developing and maintaining telehealth systems tends to be the highest in the regions where telehealth would be most beneficial (e.g., rural areas) (Nickelson 1998). Fortunately, federal programs such as the Universal Service Program for Rural Health Providers may help to defray the operating costs of telehealth systems (Smith & Allison 1998).

Licensure and Competence to Provide Telehealth Services

Given that VA is a national healthcare organization, in order to practice within VA clinicians may hold an active, unrestricted license in a U.S. state, territory, commonwealth of the United States (e.g., Puerto Rico), or the District of Columbia. Generally, this license to practice includes care delivered within the federal healthcare system even if such care crosses state lines. Therefore, within VA licensure is typically not a prohibitive factor in the delivery of telehealth services. Providers must, however, be credentialed and hold clinical privileges for the VA facilities within which they provide clinical care, whether such care is delivered face-to-face or via telehealth. Current VA policy requires that providers undertaking teleconsultation be appointed, credentialed, and privileged only at the site at which the practitioner is physically located. These credentials must be shared with the facility receiving the teleconsultation. In contrast, when telemedicine services are being delivered, providers must be appointed, credentialed, and privileged at both the facility from which the practitioner delivers such care (e.g., the provider site) and at the facility that receives such care (e.g., the patient site).

It is useful for clinicians outside the federal system to be knowledgeable about their local state licensing regulations, because the majority of states require that a practitioner providing care to residents of the state possess an active license for such state. To address the unique issues of telecare and virtual practice, several states have begun to develop specific regulations regarding telehealth and/or reciprocity agreements that allow licensure in one state to be recognized in other states. It is advised that clinicians in the private sector with questions about licensure as it relates to the practice of telehealth contact their local state licensing board to inquire about appropriate and applicable regulations. In addition, as alluded to previously, practitioners would be wise to inquire about credentialing or privileging requirements at the telehealth recipient site of care. In some cases formal memoranda of understanding (MOUs) may have to be established in order to formalize and approve telehealth practice between care locations.

Competency to perform telehealth interventions is a separate but related issue. In general, telehealth services are recognized as the delivery of established skills via an alternative modality. In VA, at present local VISNs and healthcare systems may exercise discretion as to the specific competency required for practitioners engaged in telehealth. In general, the majority of VA healthcare systems require clinicians and administrative personnel involved in the use of telehealth to complete a series of training modules developed by their respective training centers (i.e., training modules from the RMTTC for personnel involved in CVT, training from the Boston Store-and-Forward Training Center for staff engaged in store-and-forward telehealth activity). In addition to didactic training, most systems also require staff to complete hands-on training in the use of the telehealth equipment and basic troubleshooting. This may be accomplished via demonstration training with the associated national training center or through hands-on training with local, experienced practitioners.

Contingency Plans

Related to competency requirements is the need for established contingency plans designed to address technological failures or emergent situations. In the event of a technological failure or disruption, such as a power outage or dropped transmission, both the provider and patient should be aware of the contingency plan to continue or reschedule the session. For videoconference interactions, VA protocol requires that each videoconference unit be equipped with user-friendly troubleshooting tips as well as emergency contact numbers for technological support. In addition, it is recommended that the patient and provider rooms be equipped with telephones so that sessions may be continued by phone or at a minimum contact can be made with the patient to reschedule the interaction. Clear protocols must also be in place in the event of a medical or psychiatric emergency at the patient site. These protocols clearly identify onsite staff at the patient location who are predetermined to respond to either a medical emergency (e.g., cardiac arrest, seizure) or a psychiatric emergency (e.g., when immediate assistance might be needed to triage a patient with homicidal or suicidal ideation/intent). The establishment of these protocols requires clear communication and collaboration with staff at the distal sites. It is recommended that the protocols be periodically tested to ensure efficient and effective response patterns.

Security of Telehealth Communications

As with face-to-face exchanges, diligence must exercised in protecting the confidentiality of information exchanged during telehealth interactions. This includes adherence to Health Insurance Portability and Accountability Act of 1996 (HIPAA) regulations, state and local law, as well as agency regulations. In addition, telehealth requires particular attention to security of data transmission, privacy at the patient and provider sites, as well as continual updating of security software.

According to Stamm (1999), security risks fall into two basic categories: 1) risks directly from people and 2) risks from technology. Risks from people may come in the form of criminal and malevolent intent or from accident or curiosity. One of the most serious compromises to security is unauthorized access to confidential information. Fortunately these risks may be reduced by utilizing secure or closed networks, through the use of encryption programs, and by adhering to the standards set forth in HIPAA, which provides national standards to reduce healthcare inefficiencies by encouraging the use of information technology to better secure and protect patient information. HIPPA helps to assure patients that applicable federal and state laws will be applied to maintain the privacy of health-related information. Typically, a notice of privacy practices is provided to all patients related to their healthcare services by their provider. Under HIPAA, and as a part of the informed consent process, patients should be advised of uses and disclosures of health information, including healthcare operations that involve quality assessment, evaluating practitioner and provider performance, conducting training programs, clinical supervision, accreditation, certification, and credentialing activities. Telehealth practitioners should also take care to ensure that the telehealth room at the patient site provides adequate privacy and has adequate sound barriers, and should work with staff at the distant site to clearly identify the room when a session is in progress so as to prevent staff from entering the telehealth room during clinical interactions. Likewise, the provider should ensure that he or she is not interrupted during sessions, as such interruptions by other staff may compromise the patient's confidentiality.

In addition to risks that come directly from people, there are also technological risks that originate from software or computer systems. For example, computer viruses may be designed to destroy data or disrupt computer systems.

To avoid these dangers, system managers must continually update their virus scan programs, be alert for system glitches, and work to ensure compatibility of all system components (Stamm 1999). Another area of possible concern is the use of "bridge services," which connect multiple sites. Some networks may purchase this service from a contracted systems integrator or national telephone company. Companies that provide bridge services have access to and can record network activity. Providers can require the bridging company to sign a written agreement detailing its efforts to protect confidentiality.

Selection of Telehealth Candidates

As with most treatment modalities, telehealth is not intended to serve as a panacea applicable to all patients. Providers must exercise caution in evaluating patients for telehealth interventions and screen out those for whom this modality may not be appropriate. Contraindications for telehealth will vary according to the service being delivered; thus a universal set of criteria is not appropriate, and contraindications should be based on research literature, clinical judgment, and patient preference. All patients should be provided with sufficient information to provide informed consent to participate in telehealth. Information regarding the nature of the telehealth interaction, other options for care, security of data transmission, and so forth should be discussed in lay terms, and questions about the telehealth interaction should be adequately addressed. In general, the literature suggests that telehealth is a viable option for adults across the lifespan, even those with little to no exposure to technology. Among psychiatric populations, studies suggest that telehealth may be successfully utilized for patients with psychotic features, for crisis intervention, as well as for those with a variety of psychological and behavioral conditions. Nevertheless, clinical judgment must be exercised to determine a candidate's suitability for the telehealth modality and whether face-to-face care might be more suitable given factors such as psychological stability, acuity of symptoms, personality factors, hearing and visual impairments, and cognitive functioning.

Future Directions in Veterans' Telehealth Care

Within VA, telehealth applications are now considered mainstream, mission-critical services because of their ability to negate many traditional obstacles to healthcare delivery. More specifically, telehealth approaches are especially well suited for underserved populations and areas that are short of providers and have proven to be effective in delivering a variety of specialty care services.

Research overwhelmingly supports the efficacy, efficiency, and acceptance of telehealth services in many areas of specialty care. Given the significant advantages of telehealth in delivering care to veterans in underserved areas, VA has incorporated telehealth into routine practice and established nationally recognized training centers to support each area of the system's telehealth activity. As one of the early leaders in telehealth development VA, through its continued support and enhancement of telehealth activities, remains a leader in telehealth implementation. Extensive efforts to ensure quality implementation of telehealth services, proper training for telehealth providers, quality management of telehealth activity, and ongoing evaluation and research have culminated in an advanced virtual system of care. Although VA has developed robust procedures to address many of the issues inherent in telehealth practice, such as provider credentialing and privileging, licensure, security of telehealth transmissions, and quality of telehealth care, future technological developments will continue to necessitate continuous quality improvement and attention to technological innovation. The future of telehealth in VA will likely expand to meet the needs of the newest generation of veterans, for whom video chats and twenty-four-hour access to information have become the norm, as well as the needs of established generations of veterans, for whom access to high-quality care becomes a priority as retirement approaches. Virtual access to care, information, and education will become the norm rather than the exception. Innovation in melding the use of technology for health data collection, tracking, and synthesis at the micro- and macro-levels will serve to enhance providers' ability to further develop personalized medical care tailored to the needs and desires of the patient. Through attention to technological developments and incorporation of new technology into routine healthcare, VA will continue to further its telehealth mission to deliver the right care, in the right place, at the right time.

Telehealth both within VA and in the public and private sectors is a rapidly changing arena for healthcare. Research involving ever greater distances is continuously being conducted, and new technologies for conveying even more health-related information are constantly being developed. New models of monitoring and delivering medical, surgical, and a variety of health-related options for patients and their providers continue to evolve at a rapid pace.

Healthcare practitioners and patients have benefited from telehealth in various ways since its inception. However, how much early telemedicine could have grown and delivered to its recipients remains unclear, as hindrances arose from the start and prohibited and/or created hurdles to its development. It has faced barriers such as legal issues, patient privacy concerns, interjurisdictional dilemmas, and limited certified providers.

Telediagnosis, Consultation, and Treatment Interventions

The utilization of telehealth is only limited by the speed with which new applicable and appropriate technologies develop and are incorporated into healthcare practice. At present several emerging technologies have the potential to further revolutionize the standard of practice in healthcare, such as advanced data synthesis for telediagnosis, online informatics, and advanced telesurgery. Telediagnosis involves the healthcare professional making an assessment without physical examination, based on data transmitted from a distant site through telehealth technology. This can be as simple as transmitting X-rays, an MRI or CT scan, or more advanced computer data fused with real-time video for expert collaboration and diagnostic accuracy. An example of the latter is the Advanced Real Time Motion Analysis (ARTMA) project, which involves the integration of live video data with overlaid virtual data (such as bone structure). The virtual data are computed and generated sixty times per second, seamlessly merging with the video footage. The composite image or video can aid the surgeon by providing more than simple visual cues, which would otherwise be the only source of information. This also allows the surgeon to prescribe treatments to patients who cannot be examined and treated on site.

A tremendous wealth of information has benefited veterans and the public through well-respected Internet-based Web sites, including WebMD.com, Medlineplus.gov, Medscape.com, MayoClinic.com, ClevelandClinic.com, and Mentalhelp.net. The accuracy of information is a crucial issue for consumers when it comes to the distribution of healthcare information on the Internet, and veterans as well as the general public should be cautious about which Web sites they visit for information. The availability of information, online self-help programs, and self-assessments increases exponentially each year. At present both VA and the DoD offer specialized, online mental health self-assessment tools, self-help programs for behavioral modification, online coaching, and 24/7 access to live chats for those in crisis.

Telesurgery technology will someday offer robotic operations on a patient completely unsupervised. The leading edge of the surgical field at this writing combines human skill and information technology in ways never before thought possible with distance telemedicine applications. At issue now is what is termed *cooperative telesurgery*. This modality involves medical associates who are local to the patient, and a surgeon in a remote location, providing healthcare treatment to a patient at the remote site. Also finding its way into twenty-first-century healthcare is *telepresence surgery*. This offers even more sophisticated precision, wherein the surgeon is no longer spatially constrained. The tip of the instrument is equipped with a lens to relay visual information at a distance.

The surgeon's hands are effectively inside the patient's body, situated at the tip of the probe. This technology makes the process known as telepresence invaluable in cases where extreme precision is required, such as in eye surgery. It offers the surgeon effective hand precision of a few microns, previously impossible using conventional surgical techniques.

It is likely that in the future telehealth technologies and the information provided through this medium will be designed to allow computers and technology to facilitate healthcare delivery, monitoring, and recovery. The Office of Telehealth Services has been established in VA to utilize health informatics and disease management. Telehealth technologies are targeting care and case management to improve access to care and improving the continuity of healthcare for veterans.

This twenty-first century technology addresses access to care and improves healthcare services for veterans who have been underserved and had difficulty accessing care for some time. For technology to work it must do so for the people it is meant to help: patients and the professionals providing care. The VA Office of Telehealth Services vision sees telehealth services within VA helping to ensure veteran patients get the right care, in the right place, at the right time and aims to make the home into the preferred place of care, whenever possible.

If the home or place of residence is the preferred site of care, the caregiver in the home and caregiver support in the local community are very important and change the location where healthcare services have been routinely provided. The value VA derives from telehealth is not in implementing telehealth technologies alone, but in how it uses health informatics, disease management, and technologies to target veterans' healthcare and case management, thereby facilitating veterans' access to quality healthcare and improving the healthcare available to them. If telehealth can bring benefits to these sensitive healthcare areas, there is a strong chance that these technologies will be more widely accepted and used in veterans' healthcare.

References

Boston telehealth training center. (2010). *VHA Telehealth Quarterly* 9 (January): 4.

Brown, F. W. (1998). Rural telepsychiatry. *Psychiatric Services* 49: 963–964.

Darkins, A. (2007). Coordination of emergency and disaster recovery plans for VHA telehealth programs. *VHA Care Coordination & Telehealth Newsletter* 7 (August): 2.

Darkins, A. (2008a). Telehealth development and quantum changes in quality measurement. *Office of Care Coordination Services Newsletter* 8 (September): 2.

Darkins, A. (2008b). Care coordination services. *VHA Telehealth Quarterly* 3 (December): 2.

Darkins, A. (2010). The office formerly known as Care Coordination Services. *VHA Telehealth Quarterly* 9 (January): 1–2.

Durham, C. (2008). Care coordination general telehealth CCGT national training center: More than just training. *Office of Care Coordination Services Newsletter* 8 (June): 4.

Dwyer, T. F. (1973). Telepsychiatry: Psychiatric consultation by interactive television. *American Journal of Psychiatry* 130: 865–869.

Egede, L. E., Frueh, C. B., Richardson, L. K., Acierno, R., Mauldin, P. D., Knapp, R. G. & Lejuez, C. (2009). Rationale and design: Telepsychology service delivery for depressed elderly veterans. *Trials* 10: 22–39.

Einthoven, W. (1906). Le telecardiogramme. *Archives Internationales Physiologie* 4: 132.

Graham, M. (1996). Telepsychiatry in Appalachia. *American Psychologist* 46: 232–239.

Health Insurance Portability and Accountability Act of 1996, Pub. L. No. 104-191.

An introduction to telehealth in the VA. (2010). EES training module. https:www.lms.va.gov (accessed October 20, 2010).

Jerome, L. W., DeLeon, P. H., James, L. C., Folen, R., Earles, J., & Gedney, J. J. (2000). The coming age of telecommunications in psychological research and practice. *American Psychologist* 55: 407–421.

Maheu, M., Whitten, P., & Allen, A. (2001). *E-health, telehealth, and telemedicine: A guide to start-up and success.* San Francisco: Jossey-Bass.

New telemental health field staff meet. (2008). *Office of Care Coordination Services Newsletter* 8 (September): 1.

New women's telemental health clinic. (2008). *Office of Care Coordination Services Newsletter* 8 (June): 1.

Nickelson, D. (1998). Telehealth: Rural Medicare reimbursement, reduced telecom rates and grant funding opportunities. *Rural Health Bulletin* 6 (Summer): 3–4.

Nieves, J. E., Candelario, J., Short, D. & Briscoe, G. (2009). Telemental health for our soldiers: A brief review and a new pilot program. *Military Medicine* 174: xxi–xxii.

Over 30,000 veterans enrolled in CCHT. (2007). *VHA Care Coordination & Telehealth Newsletter* 7 (November): 1.

Puskin, D., Mintzer, C., & Wasem, C. (1997). *Information networks for community health.* New York: Springer.

Rocky Mountain telehealth training center. (2009). *VHA Telehealth Quarterly* 9 (September): 3.

Smith, H. A., & Allison, R. A. (1998). *Telemental health: Delivering mental health care at a distance.* http://telehealth.hrsa.gov/pubs/mental/home.htm (accessed August 1, 2003).

Solow, C., Weiss, R., Bergen, B., & Sanborn, C. (1971). 24-hour psychiatric consultation via TV. *American Journal of Psychiatry* 127: 1684–1687.

Stamm, B. H. (1998). Clinical applications of telehealth in mental health care. *Professional Psychology: Research and Practice* 29: 536–542.

Stamm, B. H. (1999). Creating virtual community: Telehealth and self-care updated. In B. H. Stamm (Ed.), *Secondary traumatic stress: Self-care issues for clinicians, researchers, and educators* (pp. 179–208). Lutherville, MD: Sidran Press.

Straker, N., Mostyn, P., & Marshall, C. (1976). The use of two-way TV in bringing mental health services to the inner city. *American Journal of Psychiatry* 133: 1202–1205.

Telemedicine. (2010). http://users.forthnet.gr/ath/giovas/telemed/ (accessed September 9, 2010).

U.S. Department of Commerce. (1997). Telemedicine report to Congress. http://www.ntia.doc.gov/reports/telemed/index.htm (accessed September 10, 1998).

U.S. Department of Veterans Affairs. (2010). *Health care A–Z index: Medical centers.* http://www1.va.gov/health/MedicalCenters.asp (accessed November 15, 2010).

Veterans Health Administration. (2010). http://en.wikipedia.org/wiki/Veterans_Health_Administration (accessed August 24, 2010).

What Is Care Coordination Services? (2010). http://www.carecoordination.va.gov/activity/index.asp (accessed August 24, 2010).

Wittson, C. L., Affleck, D. C., & Van Johnson. (1961). Two-way television in group therapy. *Mental Hospitals* 2: 22–23.

Wittson, C. L. & Benschoter, R. (1972). Two-way television: Helping the medical center reach out. *American Journal of Psychiatry* 129: 136–139.

Wood, J. A. (2006). Patient and provider satisfaction with telemental health services. Poster presented at the VA psychology leadership conference, Dallas, TX, April.

Wood, J. A. (2010). Training our newest generation: Incorporating telemental health training into post-doctoral residency programs. Poster presented at the VA national telehealth leadership forum, St. Louis, MO, May.

Wood, J. A. & Vega, S. (2010). Utilization of telemental health to provide intensive outpatient substance use disorder treatment. Poster presented at the VA national telehealth leadership forum, St. Louis, MO, May.

Suicide Prevention through a National Hotline within the Veterans Health Administration

Thomas W. Miller and Janet Kemp

Introduction

The Department of Veterans Affairs (VA) Veterans Health Administration (VHA) has founded the Veterans Crisis Line (formerly the Veterans Suicide Prevention Hotline) to ensure veterans and families in emotional crisis have free, 24/7 access to trained counselors. To operate the Veterans Hotline, VHA partnered with the Substance Abuse and Mental Health Services Administration (SAMHSA) and the National Suicide Prevention Lifeline.

The Office of Mental Health Services

The Office of Mental Health Services has as its mission to maintain and improve the health and well-being of veterans through excellence in healthcare, social services, education, and research. The Office of Mental Health Services Internet site is intended to serve veterans, their family members, mental health clinicians, VHA staff, affiliated mental health associations, and the community.

Mental Health Services Overview

The Veterans Health Administration provides specialty inpatient and out-patient mental health services at its medical centers and community-based outpatient clinics (CBOCs). In addition, readjustment counseling services are available for veterans and their families at vet centers across the nation.

All mental health care provided by VHA supports recovery, striving to enable a person with mental health problems to live a meaningful life in the community and achieve his or her full potential.

The Department of Veterans Affairs delivers state-of-the-art behavioral health services to our nation's veterans. The Veterans Health Administration has established a Web site for mental health providers (http://www.mental health.va.gov/) to ensure that VHA's knowledge base in behavioral health can reach the broadest possible audience. The Veterans Health Administration encourages all behavioral healthcare providers who work with veterans to utilize these resources.

Mental Health Services for Veterans and Families

Veterans, veterans' family members, members of a veterans' service organization, and members of other groups interested in mental healthcare can use the mental health Web site previously mentioned to learn what mental health services a local or regional healthcare facility has pledged to provide to veterans. The Department of Veterans Affairs National Suicide Prevention Lifeline is on track to record its 10,000th rescue in 2012. That's 10,000 veterans who would not be here today had they not called the VA Lifeline and talked to a trained responder—a responder who deemed it necessary to take immediate action to save the caller's life.

VHA's Lifeline crisis center, which opened in July 2007, is staffed every day around the clock by national coordinator Jan Kemp and more than twenty responders, social workers, health technician assistants, and counselors who handle some fifteen telephone lines and three chat lines. The center received about 260,000 calls in three years and is located at the Canandaigua Veterans Affairs Medical Center in upstate New York. The phone number for VHA's Prevention Lifeline is 800-273-TALK (8255). The chat line address is www.suicide preventionlifeline.org.

Who Has Used the VHA Lifeline?

It is clear that this hotline is a valuable tool for healthcare access for veterans and their families who are in crises and need help. Recent data reveal that 431,970 have used this resource during the most recent report period. Of the number of calls received by the hotline, 240,611 were directly from veterans, 28,857 were from family or friends, 58,612 were from suicide prevention crisis centers recognizing that the caller was a veteran, and 15,580 were identified as rescues. Some 11,792 were identified as warm transfers and 5,640 were calls from active duty service personnel (http://www.mentalhealth.va.gov/).This information is summarized in table 9.1.

Table 9.1. VA National Suicide Prevention Hotline Call Report 2011 Totals YTD

Months/Years	Total Calls	Identified as Veteran	Identified as Family/ Friend of Veteran	SPC Referrals	Rescues	Warm Transfers	Active Duty
Oct. 1–31	12,514	7,528	795	1,964	527	296	185
Nov. 1–30	12,566	7,425	796	1,893	524	291	209
Dec. 1–31	12,091	7,200	750	1,863	512	250	181
Jan. 1–31	12,345	7,422	798	2,051	513	256	162
Feb. 1–28	10,525	6,646	698	2,088	486	236	178
Mar. 1–31	12,905	8,071	888	2,424	538	314	177
Apr. 1–30	14,236	8,720	1,010	2,649	558	380	164
May 1–31	14,547	9,063	1,127	2,747	593	361	178
FY 11 YTD	101,729	62,075	6,862	17,679	4,251	2,384	1,434
FY 10 Totals	134,528	81,805	9,925	19,970	5,732	2,428	1,744
FY 09 Totals	118,984	63,934	7,553	13,960	3,709	3,021	1,589
FY 08 Totals	67,350	29,879	4,517	6,264	1,749	3,466	780
FY 07 Totals	9,379	2,918	not avail.	739	139	493	93
Totals to Date	431,970	240,611	28,857	58,612	15,580	11,792	5,640

Source: http://www.mentalhealth.va.gov/.

Table 9.2. Veterans Chat Report Totals 2011 YTD

Month/Yr	Total	Active	Transfer to SHL	Transfer to Backup	Mentioned Suicide
Oct. 10	847	819	85	112	395
Nov. 10	950	856	128	125	473
Dec. 10	1,038	977	95	154	422
Jan. 11	1,412	1,348	136	198	460
Feb. 11	1,102	943	85	145	408
Mar. 11	1,081	1,051	98	158	433
Apr. 11	939	912	112	82	510
May 11	1,448	1,448	230	150	778
FY 11 YTD	8,817	8,354	969	1,124	3,879
FY 10 Totals	8,471	7,570	878	1,036	3,433
FY 09 Totals	864	675	73	29	328
Total to Date	18,152	16,599	1,920	2,189	7,640

Source: Kemp (2012).

Table 9.2 provides the most recently reported information on the usage of the chat line by veterans and their family and friends. It shows that 18,152 veterans had used this form of service through the hotline services of this National Center through 2011.

Veterans' Healthcare and the Privacy Act

The Veterans Health Administration follows the requirements of the Privacy Act of 2009, which protects the personal information that VA maintains in a "systems of records" database or program from which personal information is retrieved by name or other personal identifier. The Privacy Act provides a number of protections for personal information. These typically include how information is collected, used, disclosed, stored, and disposed. The VHA System of Records Notices is available at Department of Veterans Affairs Privacy Act Systems of Records (http://www.rms.oit.va.gov/sor_records.asp). The Veterans Health Administration will not disclose personal information to third parties outside the system without the consent of the person whose records are being sought, except to facilitate that person's transaction, to act on that person's behalf at his or her request, or as authorized by law.

When VHA does collect personal information online, it informs users in advance that it will do so in the Limited Privacy Policy's Privacy Act

Statement. The Privacy Act Statement will contain any additional privacy policies that apply to the information collected on a particular official VA Web page. The Web pages that collect personal information will have a hyperlink to the Limited Privacy Policy that applies to that particular Web page. Providing such information is generally voluntary, but if it is not provided, VHA may not be able to process the transaction. When information is required to process a veteran's request, the Lifeline program will advise the veteran or family member of this fact in the appropriate Limited Privacy Policy.

Services for Families In Crisis

Friends and family members of veterans in crisis are welcome to call the Veterans Hotline. They can also give the number (1-800-273-TALK) to the veteran. If the veteran is having a medical emergency, of course 911 should be called. All calls to the Veterans Hotline are confidential. It is the veteran caller's decision whether he or she wants to use VHA services, receive care after the call, or provide personal information.

When a veteran is in an emotional crisis and can't figure out the VHA mental healthcare system, the veteran or a family member can call the Veterans Hotline, and counselors will help the caller locate the best service and facility for his or her needs as well as provide crisis counseling. Callers dial 1-800-273-TALK, then press 1 to indicate that they are veterans, and are routed to the Veterans Hotline. Crisis counselors answer the hotline 24/7. Some counselors are veterans, and all counselors are trained to counsel veterans specifically. If all the VA counselors are busy talking to other callers, the call is routed to a backup center in the National Suicide Prevention Lifeline network. Counselors at the backup centers are also trained to help veterans.

Why Should a Veteran Enroll for Healthcare Benefits?

A veteran should enroll to ensure that he or she will receive the comprehensive benefits package offered through VHA's national healthcare system. The Department of Veterans Affairs offers comprehensive medical care, including any necessary medical outpatient and inpatient services. Veterans can apply for healthcare enrollment by completing VA Form 10-10EZ, which takes approximately fifteen minutes. It will take the VA approximately a month to process Web and mail-in applications. The 10-10EZ can be obtained by visiting, calling, or writing any VA healthcare facility or VA benefits office. Facilities can be located by visiting the Resource Locator at http://www.veteranscrisisline

.net/GetHelp/ResourceLocator.aspx. Veterans may also call toll-free 1-877-222-VETS (1-877-222-8387) or access the form on the Internet at www.va.gov, and click on "Online Applications." Veterans can receive only emergency services until their enrollment has been processed.

Mental Health Services Available to Veterans

The Mental Health Strategic Healthcare Group provides general inpatient psychiatric services at 132 medical centers as well as mental health outpatient services in 689 medical centers and community-based outpatient clinics. In addition, readjustment counseling services are available for veterans and their families at 209 vet centers across the nation. Mental health services are available in primary care clinics, VHA nursing homes, and residential care facilities where veterans receive healthcare. Veterans with serious mental illness are seen at facilities and clinics where specialized programs, such as mental health intensive case management, day centers, work programs, and psychosocial rehabilitation, are provided. Veterans can find the nearest facility at the Resource Locator.

Suicide Prevention Resources for Veterans

Veterans can contact their local suicide prevention coordinator (SPC) for more information on suicide prevention and veterans. Local SPCs can be found using the Resource Locator. The National Suicide Prevention Lifeline Web site is updated periodically with current information relevant to suicide prevention. Veterans may also visit the Suicide Prevention Resource Center at http://www.sprc.org. Veterans can chat with a VHA counselor live at any time through the Confidential Veterans Chat tab, available at www.suicidepreventionlifeline.org/veterans.

Veterans and their family members who dial 800-SUICIDE are helped through the National Suicide Prevention Lifeline's network of more than 140 crisis centers across the nation, the same network that responds to 800-273-TALK callers in crisis. The "Press 1" option to be routed to the Veterans Hotline is also available by dialing 800-SUICIDE. Recently the Federal Communications Commission assigned 800-SUICIDE and two other related toll-free numbers to the Substance Abuse and Mental Health Services Administration (SAMHSA). SAMHSA has directed that 800-SUICIDE calls be assisted through the federally funded Lifeline network of crisis centers, a process which began on February 22, 2007. For more information about how 800-SUICIDE callers are being efficiently assisted through this network, consult the FAQ page at http://www.mentalhealth.va.gov/ or the hotline telephone option at 1-800-SUICIDE.

Additional Resources for Veterans in Need of Mental Healthcare

- **American Association of Suicidology (AAS):** The goal of AAS is to understand and prevent suicide by promoting research, public awareness programs, public education, and training for professionals and volunteers.

- **American Foundation for Suicide Prevention:** The American Foundation for Suicide Prevention is dedicated to preventing suicide, including groundbreaking research, new educational campaigns, innovative demonstration programs, and critical policy work.

- **The American Legion:** The American Legion is committed to mentoring and sponsorship of youth programs, advocating patriotism and honor, promoting strong national security, and continued devotion to our fellow service members and veterans.

- **American Psychiatric Association:** The American Psychiatric Association is a medical specialty society recognized worldwide. Its over 35,000 U.S. and international member physicians work together to ensure humane care and effective treatment for all persons with mental disorders.

- **American Psychiatric Nurses Association (APNA):** APNA is a professional membership organization of more than 6,000 members committed to the specialty practice of psychiatric mental health nursing, health and wellness promotion through identification of mental health issues, prevention of mental health problems, and the care and treatment of persons with psychiatric disorders.

- **American Psychological Association (APA):** Based in Washington, D.C., APA is a scientific and professional organization that represents psychology in the United States.

- **American Veterans (AMVETS):** AMVETS is dedicated to leadership, advocacy, and service for America's veterans on issues such as employment and training, mandatory funding for government-provided health care and other benefits to which they are entitled.

- **Depression and Bipolar Support Alliance (DBSA):** DBSA is dedicated to improving the lives of people with mood disorders through education and support.

- **Disabled American Veterans (DAV):** DAV is dedicated to building better lives for America's disabled veterans and their families.

- **International Nurses Society on Addictions** (IntNSA): IntNSA is a professional specialty organization founded in 1975 for nurses committed to the prevention, intervention, treatment, and management of addictive disorders, including alcohol and other drug dependencies, nicotine dependencies, eating disorders, dual and multiple diagnoses, and process addictions such as gambling.

- **Iraq and Afghanistan Veterans of America (IAVA)**: IAVA is dedicated to improving the lives of Iraq and Afghanistan veterans and their families by addressing critical issues facing new veterans, including mental health, the VA system, healthcare for female veterans, and GI Bill education benefits.

- **Mental Health America (MHA)**: MHA is dedicated to helping ALL people live mentally healthier lives by addressing the full spectrum of mental and substance use conditions and their effects nationwide, working to inform, advocate, and enable access to quality behavioral health services for all Americans.

- **National Alliance on Mental Illness (NAMI)**: NAMI is a mental health advocacy organization that is dedicated to improving the lives of individuals and families affected by mental illness through support, education, advocacy, and research.

- **National Association of Social Workers (NASW)**: NASW is the largest membership organization of professional social workers in the world, with 150,000 members. It works to enhance the professional growth and development of its members, to create and maintain professional standards, and to advance sound social policies.

- **National Institute on Alcohol Abuse and Alcoholism (NIAAA)**: NIAAA is an organization dedicated to reducing alcohol-related problems through research and practice.

- **National Institute of Mental Health**: NIMH is the lead federal agency for research on mental and behavioral disorders. Its mission is to reduce the burden of mental illness and behavioral disorders through research on mind, brain, and behavior.

- **National Strategy for Suicide Prevention (NSSP)**: NSSP is a coordinated effort by both the public and private sectors to prevent and reduce suicide and suicidal behavior. The National Strategy lays out a framework for action and guides development of an array of services and programs.

- **Paralyzed Veterans of America (PVA)**: PVA works to enhance the quality of life for veterans of the armed forces who have experienced spinal cord injury/dysfunction (SCI/D), advocating for quality healthcare, research and education, veterans' benefits and rights, accessibility and the removal of architectural barriers, sports programs, and disability rights.

- **Substance Abuse and Mental Health Services Administration (SAMHSA):** SAMHSA's vision is "A Life in the Community for Everyone," which is based on the premise that all people with or at risk for mental or substance use disorders should have the opportunity for a fulfilling life that includes a job/education, a home, and meaningful personal relationships with friends and family. SAMHSA works to achieve this goal by building resilience and facilitating recovery.

- **Student Veterans of America (SVA):** SVA is an association of student veteran groups from college campuses across the United States. The organization works to develop new student groups; coordinate between existing groups; and advocate on behalf of student veterans at the local, state, and national levels.

- **Vet to Vet (Peer Support):** Vermont Vet to Vet is a volunteer organization dedicated to helping veterans recover from mental illness.

- **Vietnam Veterans of America (VVA):** VVA is dedicated to promoting and supporting the full range of issues important to Vietnam-era veterans and their families.

Veterans of the U.S. armed forces may be eligible for a broad range of programs and services provided by VHA. Eligibility for most VHA benefits is based on discharge from active military service under other than dishonorable conditions, and certain benefits require service during wartime. Veterans or family members new to VHA should consult the booklet *Federal Benefits for Veterans, Dependents and Survivors* (U.S. Department of Veterans Affairs 2011). As the nation's largest integrated healthcare system, VHA operates more than 1,400 sites of care, including hospitals, community clinics, community living centers, domiciliaries, readjustment counseling centers, and various other facilities.

Resources

Emergency Contacts (24 Hour)

National Suicide Prevention Lifeline, 1-800-273-8255

911

Suicide Prevention Hotlines (Available 24/7) and Related Publications

National Hopeline Network, 1-800-784-2433 or 1-800-SUICIDE

http://www.mentalhealth.va.gov/providers/index.asp

SAMHSA's Support of Behavioral Health Systems Serving Service Members, Veterans, and Their Families Fact Sheet: Provides support through technical assistance and the promotion of ongoing interagency collaboration.

Veteran Suicide Prevention Hotline: Founded to ensure veterans in emotional crisis have free, 24/7 access to trained counselors. To operate the Veterans Hotline, VA partnered with the Substance Abuse and Mental Health Service Administration and the National Suicide Prevention Lifeline. Veterans can call the Lifeline number, 1-800-273-TALK (8255), and press "1" to be routed to the Veterans Suicide Prevention Hotline.

Jail Diversion and Trauma Recovery—Priority to Veterans: Supports states, territories, and tribes to divert persons with behavioral health disorders, prioritizing veterans from jail to community services.

Publications and Multimedia

- Addressing Suicidal Thoughts and Behaviors in Substance Abuse Treatment—A Treatment Improvement Protocol (TIP 50) (SAMSHA 2011): Provides guidelines to help substance abuse treatment counselors' work with suicidal adult clients. Covers risk factors and warning signs for suicide, core counselor competencies, clinical vignettes, and information for administrators and clinical supervisors.

- Video Companion to Addressing Suicidal Thoughts and Behaviors in Substance Abuse Treatment (TIP 50) (SAMSHA 2011): Offers guidance to substance abuse treatment counselors working with persons with suicidal behaviors. Developed through SAMSHA and the Department of Veterans Affairs.

- *Handbook for Family & Friends of Service Members Before, During and After Deployment* (Defense Centers of Excellence 2012): Prepares family and friends of military service members with information to better understand and cope with the range of emotions and stress that often accompany deployment. Covers before, during, and after deployment and includes referrals to tools and resources.

- Kaplan, M.S., McFarland, B. & Huguet, N. (2012). Suicide risk among veterans of military service. In T. W. Miller (Ed.), *Veterans' healthcare*. Volume III. *Mental Health: Treatment & Rehabilitation*. New York: Praeger Publishers.

References

Defense Centers of Excellence. (2012). *Handbook for family & friends of service members before, during and after deployment*. Washington, DC: Defense Centers of

Excellence.   http://www.dcoe.health.mil/blog/article.aspx?id=1&postid=171 (accessed March 22, 2012).

Kaplan, M. S., McFarland, B. & Huguet, N. (2012). Suicide risk among veterans of military service. In T. W. Miller (Ed.), *Veterans' healthcare*. Volume III. *Mental health: Treatment & rehabilitation*. New York: Praeger Publishers.

Kemp, J. (2012) Annual report for the VA National Suicide Prevention Hotline Call & Chat Line: Report totals for 2011. Canandaigua, NY: Department of Veterans Affairs Medical Center.

Substance Abuse and Mental Health Services Administration (SAMSHA). (2011). Addressing suicidal thoughts and behaviors in substance abuse treatment/ SMA09-4381. TIP 50. Substance Abuse and Mental Health Services Administration. http://store.samhsa.gov/product/TIP-50-Addressing-Suicidal-Thoughts-and-Behaviors-in-Substance-Abuse-Treatment/SMA09-4381 (accessed March 22, 2012).

U.S. Department of Veterans Affairs. (2011). *Federal benefits for veterans, dependents and survivors*. Washington DC: Department of Veterans Affairs. http://www.va .gov/opa/publications/benefits_book.asp (accessed March 22, 2012).

U.S. Department of Veterans Affairs. (2012) Mental health services for veterans. Department of Veterans Affairs. http://www.mentalhealth.va.gov/ (accessed March 22, 2012).

Chapter 10

Academy of Spinal Cord Injury Professionals

Terrie Price

Introduction

The Christopher and Dana Reeve Foundation (2010), citing a Centers for Disease Control and Prevention (CDC)–sponsored grant, reports that 1,275,000 individuals live with paralysis associated with spinal cord injury. A Department of Veterans Affairs (VA) QUERI Fact Sheet (2011) notes that 225,000 to 296,000 individuals in the United States live with some type of spinal cord injury or disease (SCI/D) affecting their ability to participate in a spectrum of life activities. The VA HSR&D's Quality Enhancement Research Initiative (QUERI) currently focuses on nine conditions that are prevalent and high risk among veterans: Among these is spinal cord injury. The other eight conditions are chronic heart failure, diabetes, HIV/hepatitis, ischemic heart disease, mental health, polytrauma and blast-related injuries, stroke, and substance use disorders.

QUERI utilizes a six-step process to diagnose gaps in performance and identify and implement interventions to address them:

1. Identify priority conditions and opportunities for improving the health of veterans.

2. Put in place effective practices for improving outcomes for priority conditions.

3. Examine variations in existing practices, the sources of variation, and their relation to health outcomes.

4. Identify and test interventions to improve the delivery of best practices.

5. Evaluate the feasibility, adoption, and impact of coordinated improvement programs to spread best practices.

6. Evaluate the effects of improvement programs on veterans' health outcomes, including quality of life.

SCI Healthcare Services for Veterans

The VA QUERI Fact Sheet (2011) indicates that an estimated 25,000 individuals living with SCI/D are treated through the integrated veterans' healthcare system. Spinal cord injury/disease presents with dynamic and long-term challenges in every aspect of one's life throughout the lifespan. Medical treatment and rehabilitation of such a catastrophic injury/disease requires the skills of a unified and dedicated multidisciplinary rehabilitation team. To meet the challenge, the Veterans Health Administration (VHA) has grown to include twenty-four acute care spinal cord injury centers in the existing veterans' healthcare system and five spinal cord injury long-term-care facilities tasked to provide quality acute and long-term healthcare, assist in preventing complications, and educate the veteran on self-management. There are fourteen federally sponsored "Model Spinal Cord Injury Systems" of care across the country in major medical facilities.

Challenges Faced by Veterans with Spinal Cord Injury

Many advances have been made in spinal cord injury medicine and rehabilitation for veterans. However, challenges remain. Many veterans are challenged in their ability to access such services. Although a local VA may provide certain care, a veteran may be referred to a facility with greater expertise well outside of his or her home community. Such challenges impact the veteran, his or her family, and the caregiving community. Subsequently, veterans may defer critical annual checkups and care because of access problems. Though community resources may be available within a more accessible distance, veterans may not be informed about their availability or how to use their healthcare benefits for the services. When families are required to provide transportation, there is an economic impact as well as a social/family impact. Veterans face vocational placement challenges just as their community counterparts do. Although VA is beginning to expand resources for vocational assessment and placement, these resources pale in comparison to the need. State agencies provide a wealth of resources through state vocational rehabilitation services. Liked politics, all jobs are local. The veteran faces the challenge of identifying what vocational resources are available through VA, the state, and the local community. Individuals with SCI face an increased risk of complications, including skin breakdown, urinary tract infections, and pulmonary illnesses. However, hypertension and diabetes are concerns for the entire aging population. Veterans may find themselves managing their healthcare through a labyrinth network of community care and VA care specialists. This poses a challenge for their medical and rehabilitation treatment team to ensure that adequate communication occurs about medications, interventions, and referrals. Veterans are at increased risk of post-traumatic stress disorder (PTSD), depression, and general anxiety disorders. Adjustment concerns are as vital as healthcare concerns, calling for a local network of mental healthcare professionals available to provide emergent care and treatment to the veteran and his or her family or caregiving network.

The challenges of living with SCI include physical access to buildings and transportation, access to adequate public transportation, vocational training and placement, and physical access in the workplace. Finding expertise in SCI care is especially challenging in more rural regions, comprising much of the center of the country. Women with SCI are doubly challenged in finding expertise in reproductive care, modified childcare equipment, and homecare assistance. Women with SCI are at increased risk of abuse and neglect, and accessible and available domestic violence services may be scarce.

The following sections provide information on the development of professional groups that are concerned with every aspect of the challenges presented. Medical and rehabilitation professionals in the Academy of Spinal Cord Injury have been largely responsible for the SCI medical and rehabilitation research and clinical guidelines and standards of care, advocating for access to expert care, and annual education to professionals who gather to expand their expertise in SCI care.

In September 2009, at the Congress on Spinal Cord Medicine and Rehabilitation, the Academy of Spinal Cord Injury Professionals (ASCIP) was launched as a national multidisciplinary professional organization that brings together the breadth of professional expertise in spinal cord injuries or illness. The Academy is the result of a merger of three established and esteemed professional associations—the American Association of Spinal Cord Injury Nurses, the American Association of Spinal Cord Injury Psychologists and Social Workers, and the American Paraplegia Society—and the newest professional group, the Therapy Leadership Council. The ASCIP brings together physicians, nurses, psychologists, social workers, and rehabilitation therapists dedicated to spinal cord treatment and rehabilitation.

Organizational Structure

The genesis of each of the professional associations begins in the VA system and groups of SCI/D medical and rehabilitation providers concerned with ensuring the highest level of care and opportunities for community integration for veterans living with SCI/D. However, recognizing the prevalence and magnitude of SCI/D, each professional association and the Academy are composed of members from public and private healthcare. Members of the Academy represent centers of excellence such as the VA healthcare system, Model SCI Systems, and Commission on Accreditation of Rehabilitation Facilities (CARF)–accredited centers across the nation. A primary benefit of membership includes networking; continuing education opportunities; a peer-reviewed, research-based journal; and publications for professionals in the field.

Historically, conference themes include presenting state-of-the-art research in SCI/D medicine and rehabilitation and advocating better quality of life through comprehensive lifelong healthcare, community access, and employment for all people with SCI/D. A necessary component is promoting awareness of the challenges facing people with SCI/D and professionals alike and advancing public policy that enhances the life of individuals with SCI/D.

Respecting the importance of each discipline and the value of collaboration, the new Academy is grounded in a key principle of mandated equal representation of each association, now referenced as sections, in the governance of the Academy and its committees. The inaugural leadership comprises President Terrie Price, PhD, ABPP-PSW; Vice President William Bockenek, MD, APS;; Treasurer Elaine Rogers, PT, TLC; and Secretary Mary Ann Reilly, RN.

A second key principle is professional autonomy. Professional disciplines look to their section for discipline-specific education and networking

Table 10.1. ASCIP Governance Board

Section Boards	Academy Committees	Sponsors
APS	Program	Acad. Industrial
ASCIN	Nominating	Roundtable
AASCIPSW	Membership	
TLC	Electronic Communication	
	Clinical Practice	
	Finance	

opportunities. Each section retains committees and activities that promote section initiatives and the larger mission and vision of the Academy.

Chronological Development

The ASCIP is grounded in the history of the four professional organizations, now referenced as sections by the acronyms APS (American Paraplegia Society), SCIN (Spinal Cord Injury Nurses), PSW (Psychologists and Social Workers), and TLC (Therapeutic Leadership Council). Each organization has written a history, and their stories are briefly summarized in their own words in the following subsections. Each association owes a debt of gratitude to James J. Peters, former executive director and member of Eastern Paralyzed Veterans Association (EPVA) a chapter of Paralyzed Veterans of America. Mr. Peters was a veteran who had experienced a spinal cord injury during his military service and benefited from the quality treatment provided through VA. Under his direction, EPVA was driven to provide the highest possible level of assistance to the rehabilitation medicine community in SCI care. With a goal of ensuring the highest quality of care for individuals who have experienced a spinal cord injury, EPVA poured its resources not only into funding and managing the annual meetings of the associations, but also into developing the growing professional associations. The association provided unparalleled financial and human resource support in an effort to ensure that all professionals in the field of SCI/D medicine received the highest quality training. Mr. Peters also worked to ensure that each of the professional groups became independent and worked collectively to foster vital new research on all aspects of SCI/D care, including quality of life, ongoing education of the medical rehabilitation team members in SCI care, developing clinical standards of care, and developing a rich network of well-trained professionals. The EPVA separated from Paralyzed Veterans of America in 2004 and became the United Spinal Association. Subsequent to Mr. Peters's untimely death, the associations were privileged to have the ongoing support and assistance of the newly formed United Spinal Association under the leadership of Chief Executive Officer Gerard Kelly then succeeded by Paul Tobin. The PVA provided financial support and the management role of the associations in 2008 until November 2010, when the ASCIP became a fully independent organization.

Until the merger of the associations in October 2009, the professional associations functioned in a parallel manner, focusing their efforts on their association's mission and goals. In the history of the associations an overlap in mission and goals appears: ongoing education in quality SCI care, exceptional research in SCI medicine and rehabilitation, and the development of a network of specialty-trained treatment providers. From the beginning of each association, an annual conference was held concurrently with that of the other associations. In recent years efforts were made to identify educational opportunities of mutual interest and benefit in recognition of their shared goals and work. In addition, the three established groups had separate professional publications and research activities.

In 2008 the three associations and representatives from the newest professional group (TLC) began meeting with representatives of United Spinal and Paralyzed Veterans Associations, collaboratively discussing the many challenges faced by the unwieldy and fiscally imprudent structure of four separate associations and the untenable financial resources on which it depended. With the support and guidance of the PVA and United Spinal Association, the four associations deliberated and elected to move toward a merger. The PVA generously extended financial and organizational support in the legal transition and development of a new organizational infrastructure, including a viable business plan. In November 2010 the Academy and PVA ended their collaboration, leading to the Academy forging ahead with the stated mission and vision, with Futures in Rehabilitation Management providing management support for Academy activities and Denny O'Malley serving as executive director.

Over the course of the three years leading to the merger decision, representatives of each professional group worked together tirelessly in many hours of teleconferences and face-to-face meetings, leading to the development of a new mission and vision statement and a sense of renewed excitement as they considered the new opportunities that existed in working together in an integrated effort. Each section participates equally and collaboratively in Academy-level membership, program, nominating, finance, electronic communication, and clinical practice committees toward the accomplishment of their stated goals. The primary goal of the Membership Committee is to identify professionals engaged in providing medical and rehabilitation services to individuals with SCI. It is the members' core belief that SCI care requires specialty training to ensure the highest degree of care. The committee is dedicated to reaching to the VA/DoD and larger community. The organization includes professionals from the Model SCI systems of care across the United States as well as CARF-accredited agencies with specialty SCI care. The Program Committee is tasked with developing the annual conference of the Academy, ensuring timely and foundational scientific and clinical presentations across all of the professional groups represented. The Program Committee secures continuing medical and educational credit from major accrediting bodies. The Electronic Communication Committee (ECC) manages information posted on the Web site, encouraging the development of useful links to SCI information, providing information about the ASCIP and the sections, and promoting various activities occurring in the committee. The ECC ensures that members have access to a listserv for sharing information and identifying member SCI specialists across the country. The Finance Committee prepares and monitors the Academy budget and identifies grants and sponsorship opportunities to fund the activities of ASCIP. The Nominating Committee oversees the call for award nominations across all of the sections and awards specific to ASCIP. Their second duty is to secure nominations for section boards and committees, appreciating that sections are the ladders of professional development. Section boards and committees provide nominations for the Governance Board and Academy-level committees. Finally, the newest committee, Clinical Practice, will be called upon to review standards of care, identifying professionals to serve on standards guideline committees, providing members with information on clinical-based Internet links, seminal reading material, and current discussions on evidence-based care. All of the committees work in collaboration to support and promote their goals and activities. As each section is equally represented on every Academy-level committee and the Governance Board, together they strive toward the goal of working together as a fully integrated team.

American Paraplegia Society

The following short history is taken from the full historical review "American Paraplegia Society 1954–2004" (2004). The American Paraplegia Society (APS) was founded in post–World War II America by a group of dedicated Veterans Administration physicians and scientists. Caring for wounded veterans made these professionals acutely aware of the need to understand the implications of spinal cord injury. To meet this need, in 1954 they founded the APS. A guiding tenet was that physicians who know and understand all aspects of SCI are best equipped to provide a continuum of quality care, from the acute phase to community integration. Sharing knowledge and experience is essential to the growth of spinal injury medicine and to ongoing research. This process continues to be the driving force of the APS.

In 1977 the APS launched the *Journal of the American Paraplegia Society*, which was renamed the *Journal of Spinal Cord Medicine* in 1992. With the merger and inauguration of the ASCIP, the four professional associations adopted the *Journal of Spinal Cord Medicine* (*JSCM*) as their official journal, moving to expand the editorial board to include all disciplines. In March 2010 the *JSCM* was transferred to the ownership of the ASCIP as a final step to endorsing it as the representative professional publication.

In and before 1954, few physicians were experienced in the medical management of patients with SCI. Dr. Donald Munro, a neurosurgeon, is heralded as one of the pioneers of spinal cord medicine. Dr. Munro served in the U.S. Army Medical Corps in World War I. He developed important techniques for routine management of individuals with SCI. Because of his experience, Dr. Munro became a consultant for the Veterans Administration, which eventually developed a network of SCI treatment centers. After the war, the Veterans Administration recognized the need for specialized multidisciplinary care for complex injuries and established specialized centers at U.S. Army medical facilities. These centers were the rudimentary core of the modern SCI unit. At these centers, physicians were encouraged to explore better ways to care for individuals with SCI.

Dr. Ernest Bors. a pioneer in the early treatment of SCI, was in the army when he was appointed chief of the SCI Service at Hammond General Hospital, an army facility in Modesto, California. The lack of treatment options spurred Dr. Bors to develop an organized approach to the management of SCI complications.

The need for a professional society was fully appreciated. The first organized meeting of physicians involved in SCI care was held in Washington, D.C., in 1948, with the support of the Veterans Administration. The presiding chairman was Dr. Paul Budd Magnuson, chief medical director of the Veterans Administration. After a short business meeting, attendees delivered papers on a variety of medical issues related to spinal cord injuries. Because the medical conferences were not providing sufficient information on SCI treatment, the Veterans Administration established the Annual Spinal Cord Injury Conferences, to be hosted at one of the SCI centers. By 1953 there were six Veterans Administration SCI centers, and three more were soon added. The first annual meeting was held at the Memphis, Tennessee, Veterans Administration hospital in 1952. The conference was very well received, and it was decided to record all future clinical sessions and publish the proceedings.

The Third Annual Spinal Cord Injury Conference was held in 1954 at the Veterans Administration hospital in West Roxbury. Massachusetts. During this meeting Dr. Comarr first proposed the formation of a society "to give identity to those physicians who would choose to make SCI medicine a career," who in turn, "would eventually offer the best possible care to those afflicted." Dr. Comarr's proposal was approved by a unanimous vote. The new society was named the American Paraplegia Society, and Dr. Comarr was elected as the founding president. The APS was incorporated on May 6, 1977. In 1978 James Peters, the executive director of the Eastern Paralyzed Veterans Association, was elected as the executive director of the APS.

The purpose of APS, as well summarized in its corporate charter, remains "for scientific, charitable and educational purposes to advance, foster, encourage, promote, and improve spinal cord injury patient care: to develop and promote research and education related to spinal cord injury: and to recognize physicians and doctoral trained researchers whose careers are devoted to the problems of spinal cord injury and to promote the exchange of ideas between such persons" (APS bylaws).

Among its many accomplishments, the APS was instrumental in the development of an SCI subspecialty designation and certification under the American Board of Medical Specialties.

To honor those who have been foundational to quality SCI medicine, each year the society sponsors the Donald Munro Lecture Series; the A. Estin Comarr Award for Distinguished Clinical Service; the Ernest Bors Award for Scientific Development, awarded each year to the junior investigator who published the best original research article in the *Journal of Spinal Cord Medicine*; the Excellence Award; and the James J. Peters Lectureship (established in 2003).

American Association of Spinal Cord Injury Nurses

The American Association of Spinal Cord Injury Nurses (AASCIN) began in 1983 through the collaboration of James Peters and a small group of Veterans Administration–based nurses. Following a dynamic discussion of their experiences, ideas, and expertise, plans were put into place to convene a meeting in Washington, D.C. Those in attendance had an opportunity to discuss the unique challenges facing nursing and the vital importance of specialty training in SCI care. A formal planning committee met in Las Vegas within the year and included representatives from nineteen Veterans Administration SCI centers as well as nursing representatives from the Central Office. In planning for the new organization, each attendee was given a task for the preliminary development of the new organization's, committees, reflecting needs for training, in education, editorial, publicity, program, and research. The newly founded organization formed its first board of directors and elected officers. The AASCIN distributed a professional journal of nursing-related research and clinical practice–based articles. The program committee convened an annual meeting and grew to well over a hundred members.

The mission and vision of the AASCIN, now referred to as Spinal Cord Injury Nurses (SCIN), is to advance spinal cord injury nursing practice through education, research, and networking. The organization's mission statement embodies its true mission: "We promote excellence in meeting the nursing care needs of individuals with spinal cord injury." Goals identified to carry out this mission include the following:

- Promote advancement in nursing care of individuals with spinal cord injury and related diseases.
- Provide education related to SCI nursing practice.
- Report research findings.
- Disseminate scientific information to achieve optimal healthcare outcomes.
- Recognize nurses whose careers are devoted to enhancing the outcomes of individuals with SCI.
- Afford members an opportunity to participate in activities.
- Provide an educational forum for nurses to network.
- Introduce nursing students to the specialized field of SCI nursing.

Historically, the AASCIN has promoted professional development in SCI nursing care through publications, presentations, and awards. Recognizing the advancement and accomplishment of nurses in SCI care is vital to establishing quality standards of care. Annually, SCIN recognizes individuals in categories for outstanding contributions to SCI nursing:

1. **Staff Nurse Award for Excellence in SCI Nursing:** awarded for knowledge and expertise in SCI/D nursing practice, creativity in providing nursing care to individuals with SCI/D and supporting significant others, and collaboration with healthcare professionals in providing optimal care.

2. **Expanded Role Award for Excellence in SCI Nursing:** Awarded to the nurse who contributes to SCI/D nursing practice through outstanding clinical performance in SCI/D care, as evidenced by knowledge and expertise in SCI/D nursing practice, creativity in providing nursing care to individuals with SCI/D and professional support to others, and collaboration with other healthcare professionals in providing optimal care to achieving excellence in the healthcare of persons with SCI/D.

American Association of Spinal Cord Injury Psychologists and Social Workers

In 1985, during a meeting of Veterans Administration SCI–home care coordinators in San Francisco, Irene Saperstein, from Palo Alto, brought up the idea of forming a psychosocial association dedicated to issues related to SCI. The idea was discussed at a subsequent meeting, and in 1986 Joan Sheldon, working in the Veterans Administration Central Office, provided a list of psychologists and social workers in SCI centers to James Peters, who invited them to a planning meeting in Atlanta hosted by the EPVA. Helen Bosshart, a founding member, writes that Jim met with a group in Richmond in 1985:

> The focus was increasing patient participation in the rehab process, and we talked with Jim informally about an additional association to focus on the allied health components of rehabilitation. A PVA member survey published at about that same time rated psychosocial services, i.e. those provided by psychologists and social workers, as the least beneficial in their rehabilitation. Mr. Peters felt strongly that members of PVA needed psychosocial services. Although Mr. Peters was reluctant to fund a new ancillary services association, he strongly felt there was a need for psychosocial services to address the psychological/social issues facing veterans with SCI. As a result, he agreed to support this new organization. (personal communication).

Following two days of meetings, the group readily recognized the critical need for an organization addressing psychosocial needs of persons with spinal cord injury, leading to the beginning of the American Association of Spinal Cord Injury Psychologists and Social Workers (AASCIPSW). From its inception the founding group agreed to the importance of including professionals from the public sector and began reaching out to psychologists and social workers in SCI centers across the country. Their initial goals and efforts were directed toward three tasks: plan an annual conference, begin a professional publication, and develop a research program. The first annual program began in November 1986 at the Union Plaza Hotel in Las Vegas.

Five committees were created and operational by the beginning of the conference: membership, research, publications, programming, and nominating. The organization's work has grown tremendously since its founding, including developing and revising standards for psychologists and social workers in SCI care and maintaining a comprehensive reading list of critical articles and books in SCI psychosocial concerns. Through the years, the committees developed goals of promoting quality practice standards, education in the science and practice of psychosocial rehabilitation, public policy advocacy on behalf of the profession and those it serves, and promoting the importance of specialty training in SCI rehabilitation. Research grants led to research indicating the critical importance of psychological adjustment to the outcomes for individuals with SCI and their families and caregiving system.

The American Association of Spinal Cord Injury Psychologists, now known as the Psychology and Social Worker (PSW) section of ASCIP, strives to promote research, education, and clinical services to meet the cognitive, social, emotional, and behavioral care needs of persons affected by spinal cord impairment. The members have the opportunity to work collaboratively with many of the finest leaders specializing in spinal cord injury/dysfunction (SCI/D), developing their own skills through active participation in the Academy. Their mission statement declares: "Organized and operated for scientific and educational purposes, we provide the highest quality educational and training opportunities in SCI/D; promote the use of empirically-based psychosocial interventions; develop research and scientific inquiry into improving the quality of life for persons affected by SCI/D; and recognize credentialed health care professionals devoted to treating the psychosocial problems of SCI/D." (Academy of Spinal Cord Injury Professionals webpage: www.academyscipro.org/psychologists andsocial workers, 2010)

The strength of the mission is reflected in the organization's goals:

- Establish standards of care for psychologists and social workers working in the field of SCI.
- Publish educational materials for professionals and persons with SCI.
- Publish a quarterly electronic journal, the *SCI Psychosocial Process.*

The PSW recognizes individuals who have demonstrated outstanding accomplishments in the field of SCI rehabilitation:

1. **Clinical Performance Award:** Given to a psychologist or social worker who has demonstrated outstanding performance in the area of clinical skill related to the psychosocial adjustment and rehabilitation of persons with SCI/D. This includes outstanding clinical contributions and expertise and exceptional performance in the nominee's work environment as well as in the community.

2. **Essie Morgan lectureship:** An invited lecture by a member recognized for his or her clinical or research activities in psychosocial rehabilitation.

Therapeutic Leadership Council

The ASCIP therapist section, the Therapy Leadership Council (TLC) in Spinal Cord Injury, is a professional network for therapists who work with individuals with SCI/D. The United Spinal Association recognized the importance of developing an association of physical therapists, occupational therapists, and kinesiotherapists in acute SCI rehabilitation, given their integral role on the SCI rehabilitation team. The first meeting was held in Seattle in 2004 with a group of VA therapists. Noting the unique management issues within the SCI healthcare system faced by rehabilitation therapists, the newest professional group was launched as an informal group. They began planning a conference tract, which was in place by 2006. The group attended the Tri-Association conference in 2006, where membership was opened to all SCI therapists. The group has steadily grown in number and in the depth of the presentations at the annual meetings. During the initial discussions about collaboration among the three existing professional associations, it was uniformly agreed to invite the TLC leadership for full inclusion in discussions of an evolutionary process. The TLC was formally adopted as a section of the ASCIP in September 2009.

The TLC history states that their members

> are challenged to provide quality rehabilitation in an increasingly complex and diverse health-care setting. Rehabilitation of persons with spinal cord injury has grown in complexity and scope as advances in the field of applied technologies and rehabilitation science have been translated into clinical practice. Unique rehabilitation issues and durable equipment needs are common to persons with SCI/D who have lifelong challenges in maintaining their independence and quality of life. We promote research, education, and the development of clinical practice guidelines, as well as identifying professional mentors. We strive to improve clinical skills and encourage standardized evidence-based practice methods throughout the continuum of care in order to maximize functional outcomes in individuals with SCI/D. (Academy of Spinal Cord Injury Professionals 2010).

To this end, the TLC's goals are to

1. provide an advanced level educational experience for SCI therapists and
2. promote continuing education, essential to professional growth and excellence in clinical practice.

The TLC recognizes excellence among members through two awards:

1. **Clinical Service Award:** Given to a member who has demonstrated outstanding clinical contributions in the area of SCI/D. This may include demonstration of clinical application of evidenced-based medicine and/or translational research.
2. **Excellence Award:** Given to a member who has demonstrated outstanding qualities of leadership in the clinical application of SCI/D.

Future Directions

The ASCIP is a historical extension of the work of many in the field of SCI medical treatment and rehabilitation. Few areas enjoy the extensive, multifaceted study realized in the advancement of SCI treatment initiatives. The three core groups (APS, AASCIN, AASCIPSW) have launched journals featuring sentinel research in every area of SCI medicine, science, and psychosocial care. With the merger in 2009, the Academy adopted the *Journal of Spinal Cord Medicine* as its official journal and the APS transferred ownership of the *JSCM* to the Academy. A future goal is to expand the reach of the journal to fully represent all areas of SCI/D medicine and rehabilitation. The editorial board has grown to include representatives of each of the Academy sections. As of January 1, 2011, the *JSCM* is published by Maney Publishing, substantially extending its subscription to include international distribution. Recognizing its value, the American Spinal Injury Association (ASIA) identified the *JSCM* as its official journal.

This chapter cannot readily encapsulate the breadth of research published by the three associations. It has consistently spanned research in VA, SCI model systems of care, state agencies, earlier CDC SCI surveillance data, education, and community-based research. Scientific exploration includes stem cell research, neuroprotective agents, and foundational care to minimize early damage and promote recovery. Members have contributed expertise in a consortium model of developing clinical practice guidelines, under PVA sponsorship, in SCI care from acute care management through care issues related to complications and common challenges and psychosocial concerns of depression and sexuality, and there are more guidelines forthcoming. Therapeutic literature evidences the benefit of individualized therapeutic rehabilitation not only directed toward recovery but for critical functional gains in living independently and hopefully preparing the individual to be a recipient of future care options. Adjustment to disability has grown to embrace self-advocacy at every level of life, such as hiring personal care attendants, directing one's care, participating fully in community activities, and gaining access to an ever-growing range of recreational activities, including extreme sports.

Future directions revolve around the recognized importance of specialized and cross education in SCI/D treatment. The annual conference stands as the crown jewel of the associations and now the ASCIP. The Academy has enjoyed the unparalleled financial support of two advocacy agencies (United Spinal and PVA) in the development of the professional organizations and in hosting an annual conference that is noted for providing superior education in SCI-based research, outcomes-based clinical practice, and professional networking spanning the public and private sectors. The ASCIP recognizes the importance of communication among professionals involved in treatment and care activities. The annual conference has evolved to allow attendees to obtain continuing education in their fields from the full range of presentations. Practitioners in the VA/DoD and community have an opportunity to share information on resources. Professionals working with individuals with SCI recognize the enormous challenges. The conference is an outstanding opportunity to learn about new developments within and outside of the VA system for veterans while community-based professionals learn about resources available in VA for their eligible veterans. The Academy's future directions expand on past goals, accomplishments, and values:

- Publishing and presenting cutting-edge scientific research leading toward improvement in care and future cure.

- Publishing and presenting research on evidence-based care in nursing, medical therapy, psychosocial care, and medicine.

- Establishing standards of care across specific areas, populations, and settings.

- Promoting equal access and community participation.

- Identifying and providing critical education for new practitioners in SCI care.

- Promoting student development across the professional groups.

- Reaching out to the international community toward international development of quality SCI care and rehabilitation.

- Working collaboratively with sister professional agencies in cross education and networking.

- Promoting and encouraging specialty and board certification in SCI rehabilitation and medicine.

- Serving as the central agency for evaluating national standards of SCI care through regulating agencies such as CARF and TJC (The Joint Commission; formally JCAHO, Joint Commission on Accreditation of Healthcare Organizations).

- Participating in public advocacy for research dollars, access to affordable and appropriate healthcare, and policy that removes barriers impeding community participation.

- Providing access to a directory of professionals and vetted agencies with expertise in SCI care and rehabilitation.

- Providing cross education among professionals, appreciating that knowledge of care and research in an allied field adds to the overall understanding of the challenges and care needs of those with SCI/D.

Acknowledgments: Professional organization movements that began in the Veterans Administration and DoD system have been matched by the initiative of community-based counterparts and found a meeting place in the Academy of Spinal Cord Injury. It is fitting to close with a nod to the many individuals who have also worked tirelessly for the associations and ASCIP. Vivian Beyda, DrPH, worked alongside Jim Peters through much of the early history and then served as a consultant to PVA. Thomas Stripling, former PVA director of education and research, was pivotal during the early meetings with PVA on the collaboration and merger. Maurice Jordan, former deputy executive director of PVA, was fully involved in the early merger discussions and served as ASCIP's executive director during the collaborative relationship with PVA. Finally, Academy members come from the breadth of rehabilitation and medical treatment facilities in the private and public sectors. The strength of the association remains in the membership. The board members of all the sections and the Academy are actively involved in and fully committed to their professional sections and the Academy.

I am thankful to the section presidents for their assistance in the writing of this abbreviated history (APS, Bill Bockenek, MD, SCIN; Laura Johnson, RN, MSN, PSW; Sigmund Hough, PhD, ABPP, TLC; Amy Icarangal, PT, NCS), along with Helen Bosshart, ACSW/LCSW, a former PSW president and founding PSW member; Larry Vogel, MD, past president of APS; and Lester Butt, PhD, ABPP, past president of AASCIPSW. For additional information on the sections and Academy; a list of awardees, publications, and activities; the *Journal of Spinal Cord Medicine*; and information on the annual conference, see the web site atwww.academyscipro.org. The Academy remains immensely grateful to the leadership and boards of United Spinal and PVA for years of commitment, financial support, and ongoing guidance, all of which have been nothing short of pivotal to our growth, expansion, and maturity.

References

Academy of Spinal Cord Injury Professionals. (2010). www.academyscipro.org/therapy (URL no longer accessible).

American Paraplegia Society 1954–2004: Our legacy, our future. (2004). *Journal of Spinal Cord Medicine* 27: 287–303.

The Christopher and Dana Reeve Foundation. (2010). Paralysis and SCI in the U.S. Available at: http://www.christopherreeve.org (URL no longer accessible).

Department of Veterans Affairs. Office of Research and Development. Health Services Research and Development Service. (2011). Spinal cord injury, Hines, Illinois and Seattle, Washington. QUERI fact sheet. (June). http://www.queri.research.va.gov/about/factsheets/sci_factsheet.pdf (accessed March 16, 2012).

Chapter 11

Ethicolegal Issues in Veterans' Healthcare

Steven Nisenbaum, Thomas W. Miller,
Sheila O'Keefe, and Dennis Norman

Introduction

The veterans' healthcare arena has developed and maintained a bioethical framework for providing a legal and ethical approach to ensuring patients and their families ethical care, treatment, and follow-up. Ethical standards of practice have always been a goal of the Department of Veterans Affairs (VA). The Veterans Health Administration (VHA) Handbook 1004.06, first issued in 2009 (U.S. Department of Veterans Affairs 2009), addresses the concept of "preventive ethics." Preventive ethics refers to activities performed by an individual or group on behalf of a healthcare organization to identify, prioritize, and address systemic ethics quality gaps. It is one of the three core functions of integrated ethics. Closely linked to it is a value-oriented environment in all healthcare activities and in the process of healthcare delivery. Values-oriented healthcare has become the focus of ethical and responsible healthcare delivery. In the healthcare setting, values are strongly held beliefs, ideals, principles, or standards that inform ethical decisions or actions.

Ethicolegal Issues in Veterans' Healthcare

The Institute of Medicine (IOM) report *Informing the Future: Critical Issues in Health* (2009) prioritized "increasing effectiveness and efficiency of the health care system" as vitally important for the nation to cure flaws in a system marked by rising costs and lack of evidence of effectiveness and comparative value of medical interventions and procedures, preventive and treatment technologies, and methods of organizing and delivering care." Already the Patient Protection and Affordable Care Act of 2010 has initiated changes by extending coverage for young adults, expanding free preventive care, prohibiting rescinding of certain health insurance coverage, eliminating lifetime coverage limits, and preventing denials for preexisting conditions. These and other projected changes have generated controversy and calls for continued revisions and refinements, but it is widely accepted that improvements in the healthcare sector, which represents fully one-sixth of the economy and is disproportionately inflationary and contributing to the federal deficit, are required in development of healthcare methods and technologies; selection, training, and coordination among care providers; continuously improved quality and effectiveness of care; and quality control in service delivery through monitoring and corrective action.

VA is already a national healthcare program for one large segment of the populace, and in many ways it occupies a special place as a venue for innovation and leadership by example. Among these critical changes is improvement in the quality of healthcare practices through effective oversight and remedial interventions, and key to that is an initiative for building a culture of patient-oriented ethical and legal commitments to care by replacing the traditional apparatus of prescriptive rule enforcement throughout the private and public sectors. If successful, such an effort may overcome a mostly retributive system that is commonplace but encourages an adversarial relationship between the providers of healthcare and the recipients, breeds distrust, and probably undermines precisely the treatment alliance that is most conducive to optimal healthful lifestyles and adherence to treatment recommendations.

What is the typical framework of the ethical and legal environs for healthcare delivery in hospitals, clinics, and healthcare facilities in the United States? The sources of ethical healthcare practice are mainly a combination of mores based on religio-cultural values, often shared but also based in private beliefs and moral conscience, along with a pastiche of declared pronouncements from professional guilds, hospitals, and healthcare accreditation agencies, whose binding authority and influence is reinforced by statutory and regulatory laws and policies. The professionalization of healthcare disciplines and specialties in the progressive industrialization of healthcare delivery throughout the twentieth century has given rise to a plethora of national professional guilds, which create codes of ethical conduct and standards of practice for their particular professionals. Licensure of professionals is primarily done at the state level through boards of registration intended to protect the public interest and safety by encouraging consensual standards of practice within that profession. Very often the state boards of registration explicitly adopt the guild codes of conduct and apply these to enforce correct service delivery and professional conduct.

The virtue of this arrangement is that the professional codes are often the product of careful consideration by a broad array of leading practitioners who have the experience needed to articulate essential guidance that hopefully is practical and also furthers the ideals of the profession. The influence of this arrangement is also generalized, so that it creates public perceptions of right and wrong professional behavior and also tends to control even practices of nonmembers and nonlicensed practitioners in that field of healthcare. Usually academics subscribe to and participate in the code-creating process, so the training of newcomers to the field involves socialization to these ethical standards through formal classroom and laboratory instruction and supervision by more senior members of the profession.

Closely related are the "accepted" approaches or "best-evidence practices" incorporated simply by assent or into promulgated guidelines and premises of leading practitioners. These also exercise a steering function regarding what will be rewarded for advancement and to convince the uninformed consumer public what is best for them.

However noble and laudatory the aspirational standards of practice or recommended best methods, it should be recognized that there are also competitive and marketing implications that are unstated ulterior motives, some of which may have little to do with ethics per se. In other words, the professional guilds are operating somewhat like medieval craft guilds. They are certifying to the public that the practitioners who are bound by their codes of ethical practice meet at least certain recognized minimum standards for training and accountability and thereby are protecting the public, which otherwise may lack the expertise to choose among healthcare providers. In this manner the codes promote professionalism. But they also serve a marketing purpose, in that the guilds are sometimes competing for market share with other providers of the same or similar services, so the certification of the guild is a seal of approval meant to enhance consumer flow. The pretense of serving the public is also a public relations gimmick that is helpful for positioning and control, regulating excessive competition among members of the profession, alerting the membership to liability risks, and lobbying for advantages and group purchasing power, as well as limiting outsiders from imposing burdensome duties or interfering by regulating, since the profession is ostensibly self-monitoring and self-regulating practice. The guilds and boards of registration do attempt to identify impaired, unethical, or incompetent colleagues in order to limit their practice, provide supervision, or provide rehabilitative assistance. Of course weeding out problematic practitioners reinforces the perception of assiduously protecting the public as a noble commitment, but it also helps to lower overall malpractice insurance coverage rates for all other practitioners and to ward off outside scrutiny, further empowering the already more competitively dominant providers in their market share relative to newcomers, weaker colleagues, novel treatment practitioners, and others whom the public otherwise would have the prerogative to decide for itself to choose, in a sort of "legally sanctioned restraint of trade," delegating authority to the big fish for patrolling the pond.

Very often the codes of professional conduct and dominant-group-sanctioned "best practices" guidelines are also convenient for third-party payers (health insurance and managed care, as well as federal and state welfare programs) to simply adopt as a logical method for verifying competence in lieu of empirically measurable criteria, which often do not exist or are not available for all particular specificities.

In addition to these formal codifications of best practices and codes of conduct, individual practitioners are also guided by their own values and moral conscience, which is largely a reflection of personal life experience, religious and cultural values and beliefs, and other societal contextual factors. Aside from ethical parameters for professional practice, there also are important legal constraints. As noted previously, the guild codes of conduct very often receive explicit sanction in statutes and in administrative law regulating the profession. But there are three other major sources of legal regulation of practice that supplement ethics throughout the healthcare delivery system.

First, and perhaps foremost, is litigation. It is widely remarked that America is a highly litigious society, and the healthcare sector of the economy is no exception. The provision of healthcare services by a practitioner is a legal transaction. There is a contractual obligation, in that the professional is forming an agreement with the consumer in exchange for payment to provide services that are competent and skillful and within the bounds of that practitioner's training, experience, and ability; deficiencies may be the subject of a lawsuit for breach of contract. Our legal system also allows people who feel they are victims of poor or inappropriate professional services to recover damages for tortious wrongs, both negligent breach of a duty owed to the patient to perform within a certain standard of care (usually the standard to which a reasonable practitioner in that profession of that service would adhere), which results in proximate harm, and certain intentional torts that may take the form of legal causes of action in defamation, assault and battery, false imprisonment, invasion of privacy, and so forth. The collective wisdom embodied in codes of ethics and recommended best practices is at least some measure of a sanctioned seal of approval, so even the courts defer to these when passing judgment on what a reasonable practitioner in that field of specialized expertise would be expected to do, especially when no other evidence is available or easy to interpret as applied to specific facts.

A large segment of the legal profession is devoted to medical malpractice, and lawsuits may generate spectacular jury awards of damages. This continual threat is a major force to discipline healthcare practitioners by encouraging concerted efforts and detailed risk management procedures to avoid accusations, founded or not, that can impoverish practices through expensive attorneys' fees and costs of litigation, drive up the prohibitive costs of or even access to professional liability insurance, and impair or destroy professional reputations and destroy practices.

The massive and detailed standards imposed by accreditation agencies are the second source of legal regulation. Surely the most prominent and influential of these agencies is the Joint Commission for Accreditation of Healthcare Organizations (JCAHO), recently renamed The Joint Commission (TJC). The Joint Commission accredits more than 17,000 healthcare organizations and programs in the United States. A majority of state governments have come to recognize TCJ accreditation as a condition of licensure and the receipt of Medicaid reimbursement. The declared mission of the organization is "To continuously improve health care for the public, in collaboration with other stakeholders, by evaluating health care organizations and inspiring them to excel in providing safe and effective care of the highest quality and value" (Joint Commission for Accreditation of Healthcare Organizations 2012).

The Joint Commission, from its inception in 1951, was granted "deeming" power for hospitals: "Under 42 U.S.C. §§ 1395bb(a),(b), a hospital that meets Joint Commission accreditation is deemed to meet the Medicare Conditions of Participation" (which is a requirement for Medicaid). Section 125 of the Medicare Improvements for Patients and Providers Act of 2008 (MIPPA) removed TJC's statutorily guaranteed accreditation authority for hospitals, effective July 15, 2010. At that time TJC's hospital accreditation program was made subject to Centers for Medicare & Medicaid (CMS) requirements for accrediting organizations seeking deeming authority. To avoid a lapse in deeming authority, TJC must submit an application for hospital-deeming authority consistent with these requirements and within a time frame that will enable the CMS to review and evaluate the submission. The CMS will make the decision to grant deeming authority and determine the term.

Nevertheless, TJC has achieved great hegemony in conducting survey inspections and certifying that standards of care are met. The Joint Commission and various other similar accreditation agencies impose requirements that greatly influence what are considered to be the legal (and ethical) standards for practice. Again, the courts do also look to the professional codes of ethics and the standards of such accrediting agencies to ascertain what the prevailing custom of practice for a reasonable practitioner in that profession is. Many of these quasi-public organizations also develop and issue guidelines for care provision that set standards for actual healthcare service delivery and related operational practices, such as record keeping, privacy and confidentiality, handicapped access, nondiscrimination, and so forth.

Another important development was the Health Insurance Portability and Accountability Act (HIPAA), which promulgated new standards in the storage, transmission, and access to healthcare records and the continuation of services.

The third source of legal regulation are the myriad laws and governmental agencies that also greatly affect healthcare practice. Many of these are general consumer protection laws (e.g., Federal Fair Debt Collection Practices Act, Fair Credit Billing Act, Federal Trade Commission, Food and Drug Administration rules), special rights laws (e.g., Federal Title IX and disabled persons legislation, Americans with Disabilities Act), workplace rules (Family Medical and Leave Act), benefits-related laws (e.g., Consolidated Omnibus Budget Reconciliation Act or COBRA, and Employment and Retirement Income Security Act or ERISA, Old Age Survivors and Disability Insurance, or Social Security, Supplemental Security Income), labor laws (e.g., Equal Employment Opportunity Commission, National Labor Relations Board), and workplace conditions regulations (Occupational Safety and Health Administration, Centers for Disease Control and Prevention, National Fire Protection Association). These also interface with local labor relations issues in unionized facilities and with institutional policies and procedures of hospitals and healthcare facilities that establish requirements for conformity to practice.

Identification of existing or potential problems and the areas that need corrective action begins with routine operational management monitoring systemic needs and performance, and by response to complaints. These are typically largely separate processes and fairly bifurcated structures with limited feedback, often mainly dependent on administrator operational skill in forecasting and balancing of budgetary limitations against many different competing demands. The overlap of decision makers with the seriousness of consideration of patient complaints is a factor in how much spread of learning and change takes place. Corrective action has blinders pointing backward, so changes are often applying bandages after the damage is done.

In the traditional ethicolegal system of monitoring and reactive intervention, deficiencies and violations of ethical and legal rules and requirements rely principally on response to patient complaints. The scope and modes of review and enforcement of professional practice are varied, encompassing mainly privileging and credentialing of professional healthcare providers; training and regular supervisory oversight; informal peer feedback and peer pressure; procedures for complaints and processes for peer reviews of care and sanctions; and assistance for impaired, unethical, or incompetent colleagues. This is a risk management focus with a retrospective gaze at the historical record, premised on certain standard goals and objectives, including dissemination of knowledge of legal and ethical standards; comprehensive prior informed consent; practice in areas of competence in relation to training, types of patients and conditions, and realistic treatment objectives; appropriate caution for high-risk situations; avoidance of role conflicts; competent and thorough record keeping; maintenance of confidentiality and advance explanation of the limits thereof; professional consultation and supervision; and managing the treatment alliance and satisfaction.

In both private and public sectors professional liability insurance coverage creates litigation as an avenue of recourse to compensate patients for professional failures and impropriety, breaches of confidentiality, violations of civil rights, contractual breaches and tortious negligence injury, and intentional wrongful behavior. Allegations are often made about incorrect diagnosis; incorrect treatment or failure to treat properly; improper methods resulting in poor outcomes, such as injury or death; failure to adequately supervise; abandonment or failure to treat; and failure to warn or to refer.

This approach has both merits and disadvantages. Insurance coverage may allow certain claims to be disposed of relatively expeditiously, but not when the expectations of the alleged victim are very divergent from routine, the cause or degree of fault is debatable, or the claim is seen as extravagant or simply potentially worth the risk of denial because the cost of recovery may deter the plaintiff from pursuing it or pressure the plaintiff into accepting far less.

Where insurance is not forthcoming, litigation is spawned to seek compensation for injury, pain and suffering, and other damages. The most common malpractice claims are for misdiagnosis, exceeding area of competence, lack of informed consent, negligent or improper treatment, physical contact or sexual behavior with a patient, failure to prevent harm or to protect others, improper discharge, failure to seek consultation or refer out, failure to supervise, abandonment, breach of confidentiality, defamation or invasion of privacy, undue influence, breach of contract, assault and battery, false imprisonment, violation of civil rights, and wrongful billing or insurance fraud.

But the avenues of litigation through the courts are long and difficult, and the results are often speculative, or the costs of pursuing a claim consume much of the award. Litigation is expensive because the process is cumbersome and highly technical, so fees for lawyers can seem inordinate. The process of preparing for trial is arduous and expensive, and the backlogs of cases and grounds for delay mean that resolution is slow. Complaint processes to boards of registration against licensed professionals or to professional guild ethics committees are also frustratingly slow and result in penalties against the wrongdoer but not compensation to a victim. Indeed, this avenue is often simply a means to an end meant to leverage negotiations about insurance coverage or seek vindication or protection of potential future victims, but not immediately or directly leading to compensatory damages to the actual victim for injury or suffering.

Institutional review procedures such as hospital patient complaint processes and peer review committees also may not be seen as actually compensatory to the alleged victim. These forums are also sometimes seen as suspect due to bias and self-protective agendas. There is another problem, which perhaps looms even larger. The mechanics of the system, organized around insurance bureaucracies and legal responses, depends on the initiative of a complainant, but even more important, it is frequently off-putting, defensive, and alienating to the person who feels victimized, and the process further exacerbates injury and suffering.

Certainly alternatives to such a highly prescriptive and proscriptive, rule-oriented ethicolegal environment for healthcare practice are worth considering. Some have argued that the costs of such a cumbersome system, which fosters adversarial attitudes and defensive secrecy, may outweigh the benefits. The argument is made that it may be possible to create a much less expensive and arbitrary enforcement mechanism by cultivating a proactive, more trusting, and patient-oriented, consumer-friendly healthcare service delivery environment. That is what VA has tried to accomplish in revamping its approach to ethicolegal parameters of care provision, and this may be an experiment that can guide change elsewhere in the private and public sectors, especially as national healthcare appears to be on the horizon. Potentially, preventive ethics integrated with the healthcare delivery system could supplant the reactive and retributive approach.

A Model of Integrated Preventive Ethics for Veterans' Healthcare

At the end of the twentieth century VA developed a bold effort to incorporate a program aimed at preventive ethics. Its model and the scope of this initiative empower each VA healthcare facility in the identified Veterans Integrated Serviced Networks (VISNs) to develop and maintain an active Integrated Ethics (IE) Program that is organized and managed through VA.

Integrated ethics targets three levels of individual and organizational practices: decisions and actions, systems and processes, and environment and culture: This is accomplished through three core functions:

1. **Ethics consultation:** The consultation service at each facility must respond to requests for both consultation about ethical questions pertaining to an active clinical case and general information, policy clarification, document review, discussion of hypothetical or historical cases, and ethical analysis of organizational ethics questions.

2. **Preventive ethics (PE):** The preventive ethics team at each facility must use a systematic approach for proactively identifying, prioritizing, and addressing ethics quality gaps on a systems level. The goal of the preventive ethics function is to reduce disparities between actual practices and best or preferred practices by implementing systems-level changes.

3. **Ethical leadership:** The ethical leadership function requires that leaders make clear through their words and actions that ethics is a priority, as well as communicate clear expectations for ethical practice, practice ethical decision making, and support their organization's ethics program.

Ethics in today's healthcare encompasses the following domains within the structure of VA:

1. Shared decision making with patients
2. Ethical practices in end-of-life care
3. Patient privacy and confidentiality
4. Professionalism in patient care
5. Ethical practices in business and management
6. Ethical practices in government service
7. Ethical practices in the everyday workplace
8. Ethical practices in research
9. Ethical practices in resource allocation

What Is Meant by Ethics Consultation?

Ethics consultation refers to the process wherein each of the 173 VA Medical Centers (VAMCs) has the responsibility of developing within that facility an "ethics consultation service" with the purpose of responding to ethics issues, situations, or questions that emerge in that facility. The ethics consultation service assists individuals and groups in resolving uncertainty or conflict about values. Issues involving allegations of misconduct, violations of rules, or intentional unsafe acts should be referred to other appropriate VHA or VA programs or offices, such as the Office of the Medical Inspector, the Office of Compliance and Business Integrity, the Office of Research Oversight, the Office of the Inspector General, and the Office of General Counsel (Council on Ethical and Judicial Affairs 2002).

The ethics consultation service is led by the ethics consultation coordinator (ECC). In addition to strong management skills, this individual must be an experienced ethics consultant and have the specific knowledge, skills, and character traits requisite for successful ethics consultation, as delineated in "Ethics Consultation: Responding to Ethics Questions in Health Care" (U.S. Department of Veterans Affairs 2007a).

The ECC designates members of the ethics consultation service, regularly assesses their proficiency, and facilitates appropriate education to enhance their consultation skills. Ethics consultation activities are conducted according to the procedures outlined in "Ethics Consultation: Responding to Ethics Questions in Health Care" and in "Ethics Consultation Toolkit: A Manual for the Ethics Consultation Coordinator" (U.S. Department of Veterans Affairs 2007a, 2007b). Ethics consultation activities are conducted using the CASES approach and are documented in ECWeb (accessible at http://vaww.ecweb.ethics.va.gov/).

At each VHA facility, one or more individuals function as an ECWeb administrator consultant, responsible for managing ECWeb. Individuals provided with access to ECWeb by the administrator consultant may be identified as consultants, evaluators, or both. The administrator consultant is also responsible for indicating who is permitted to generate reports on the facility's consultation activity.

Within this model of management, ECWeb security is implemented as follows: 1) only staff members who have been explicitly granted access are able to log into the ECWeb application. ECWeb user names and passwords are included in the user profile; 2) users are able to access only data for consultations that occur at their facility; 3) information in ECWeb is used and released only in accordance with the provisions of all applicable federal laws and regulations, including the Privacy Act and applicable VA and VHA policies.

Within this structure, ECWeb is used for the following consultation functions: 1) case consultation, when the consultation involves an active clinical case; 2) noncase consultation, when the consultation does not involve an active clinical case; and 3) evaluation by the consultation evaluator to record requests for, and results of feedback from, the individual who requested the consultation and others, as appropriate.

Final summary notes for ethics consultations pertaining to active clinical cases are generated by ECWeb and entered into the electronic medical record using the "cut and paste" function in accordance with VHA Handbook 1907.01. **Note:** It is possible to delete consultation records, but this can only be done by special request to consultation staff at the National Center for Ethics in Health Care.

What Is Preventive Ethics?

Preventive ethics refers to decisions or actions consistent with widely accepted ethics standards, norms, or expectations for a healthcare organization and its staff. Within the model advocated by VA, each facility has a preventive ethics (PE) committee or team. Each VHA facility's PE team identifies, prioritizes, and addresses ethics quality gaps on a systems level. Furthermore, the PE team is led by the preventive ethics coordinator (PEC). The PEC needs to be knowledgeable about organizational change strategies and quality improvement principles, methods, and practices (e.g., quality manager, patient safety officer, compliance officer). The PEC needs to have thorough knowledge of the local organizational environment, skills in moral reasoning and systems thinking, and some experience in ethics consultation.

The PEC selects members of the PE team. Preventive ethics activities are conducted according to the procedures outlined in "Preventive Ethics: Addressing Ethics Quality Gaps on a Systems Level" (U.S. Department of Veterans Affairs 2007c) and the "Preventive Ethics Toolkit: A Manual for the Preventive Ethics Coordinator" (U.S. Department of Veterans Affairs 2007d). Team members are encouraged to use the ISSUES process to ensure that their efforts are of high quality, or to use an alternative standardized approach that is well-accepted in the quality improvement field, such as Healthcare Failure Mode and Effects Analysis (HFMEA).

Developing Ethical Leadership within Each Facility

Within each VA facility there is an ethical leadership coordinator (ELC). The facility director serves as the ELC and is ultimately responsible for the success of the facility's Integrative Ethics Program. The ELC chairs the Integrative Ethics Council. The ELC models ethical practices, champions the program, and works to create and sustain a strong ethical environment and culture.

The integrative ethics program officer (IEPO) serves as executive director of the Integrative Ethics Council and is responsible for the day-to-day operations of the facility's Integrative Ethics Program. The IEPO must have strong administrative and management skills and be a trusted, well-respected member of the staff. The IEPO reports facility ethics activities to the VISN Integrative Ethics Advisory Board (IEAB), the VISN Integrative Ethics Point of Contact (POC), and the National Center for Ethics in Health Care. The IEPO reports directly to the facility director on matters related to IE.

Role of the Integrated Ethics (IE) Council

As defined by VA, each VAMC facility Integrated Ethics Council is responsible for the following: 1) overseeing the integration of ethics activities at the facility, 2) directing ethics activities, 3) coordinating assignments for subcommittees or workgroups, 4) ensuring communications with relevant programs across the organization, and 5) supporting staff education regarding ethics activities and the facility's Integrative Ethics Program.

Integrative Ethics Councils do not provide legal advice. If there is a question about whether the issue before them involves legal matters, they are always to consult with regional counsel. Members of the Integrated Ethics Council include VAMC leaders and senior staff who regularly encounter ethics concerns and are invested in improving ethics quality at the facility. Membership, which may vary according to the existing governance structure and needs of the facility, includes the ELC, the IEPO, the ECC, the PEC, and senior leaders of the facility (e.g., associate director, nurse executive, chief of staff, associate chief of staff for research, chief of quality management, patient safety officer, compliance officer, privacy officer, equal employment opportunity manager, chief of medicine, chief of human resources, chief of fiscal service).

Integrative Ethics Program Evaluation and Improvement

On an annual basis, the Integrative Ethics Facility Workbook is used at each facility to assess the structure and functions of its IE program and to identify strengths and opportunities for improvement. Based on the results of this assessment, facilities develop and carry out quality improvement plans.

On a biennial basis, the Integrative Ethics Staff Survey is used at each facility to assess employees' perceptions about specific ethical practices, their knowledge of concepts in ethics and policies related to ethical practices, and their views about how well the organization supports ethical practices. Based on the results of this assessment, facilities develop and carry out quality improvement plans.

Oversight Provided by the VISN Integrative Ethics Advisory Board

Within the conceptual framework of IE is the VISN Integrative Ethics Advisory Board (IEAB), chaired by the VISN senior lead, who provides visible leadership and executive oversight and guidance in IE at the VISN level. This individual needs to be the VISN director, quality management officer, facility director, facility chief of staff, or other senior or facility-level official.

The VISN point of contact for IE serves as the executive director of the IEAB and is responsible for the day-to-day operations of IE at the VISN level. The point of contact must have strong administrative and management skills and be trusted and well respected. He or she may be either a member of the VISN staff or a member with assigned VISN-level duties and responsibilities.

The IE point of contact is responsible for 1) promoting and tracking the operation of facility IE programs; 2) facilitating the identification of ethical issues that cut across facility lines; 3) managing IE activities undertaken at the VISN level; 4) coordinating the flow of information; and 5) serving as the contact between the National Center for Ethics in Health Care and the facility IEPO and other IE staff. The point of contact is responsible for facilitating the identification of ethical issues that cut across facility lines.

The Integrative Ethics Advisory Board membership typically includes the IEPO from each facility in the VISN, representatives from each of the three core functions of IE, and representatives of various areas that contribute to the VISN's ethics culture and environment (e.g., Compliance and Business Integrity, Contracting/Procurement/Logistics, Finance/Business, Medical Care Cost Recovery, Human Resources, Research Compliance, Equal Employment Opportunity, Quality Management, regional counsel, patient advocate, privacy officer, union representative, information security officer).

The Integrative Ethics Advisory Board meets regularly and has processes and systems to ensure that ethics questions and ethics quality gaps at the VISN level or that cross facility boundaries are identified, prioritized, and addressed. The Integrative Ethics Advisory Board assists facilities with IE program development and builds connections between facilities to provide support for ethics in the VISN. Ethics quality gaps involving factors outside the scope of the Integrative Ethics Advisory Board are reported to the VISN director.

Integrative Ethics Responsibilities and Roles

Responsibilities of the Facility Director

It is the responsibility of the medical center or facility director to

1. develop and maintain an active IE program that is organized and managed according to the provisions of Handbook 1004.06 (U.S. Department of Veterans Affairs 2009);

2. establish an ethics consultation service and a preventive ethics team, serve as the ELC, and ensure the overall success of IE in the facility;

3. establish and chair the Integrative Ethics Council;

4. designate or hire staff to serve as IEPO, ECC, and on the Preventive Ethics Council;

5. establish clear lines of authority and accountability for IE;

6. ensure that performance plans for employees who participate in the facility's IE program include clear delineation of their ethics-related responsibilities;

7. ensure that the IE leaders have the knowledge, skills, and time they need to succeed in their roles;

8. provide needed resources to support and ensure the success of IE in the facility (e.g., budget, space, clerical support, library materials, and ongoing training);

9. monitor performance to determine whether the IE program is meeting its goals to evaluate and improve ethics quality;

10. establish a process by which facility leaders receive ethical leadership training to assist them in understanding their role in creating and sustaining an ethical environment;

11. champion IE and support other facility leaders in doing so; and

12. establish a facility level IE policy that is consistent with Handbook 1004.06 (U.S. Department of Veterans Affairs 2009) and published IE guidance and material.

Responsibilities of the Program Officer

The responsibilities of the IEPO are to

1. direct the implementation and development of IE at the facility level;

2. coordinate educational activities with the facility and the designated learning officer at the local level, and if appropriate, link local activities with VISNs and the VHA Central Office;

3. serve as executive director for the Integrative Ethics Council;

4. collaborate with the Integrative Ethics Council and ELC to champion IE and ensure continuous program improvement by

    a. creating awareness and support for IE throughout the facility,

    b. ensuring that appropriate communication and educational materials are available to all employees, including information about how to contact the IE program, and

    c. identifying the resources required for each function to succeed (e.g., dedicated time, educational materials, or workspace) and communicating these needs to the facility director or designee responsible for the allocation of resources;

5. monitor the progress of the program, including achievement of implementation and performance goals, and report to facility leadership, the Integrative Ethics Council, and the VISN IE point of contact;

6. serve as a member of the VISN IE advisory board;

7. serve as the primary liaison for the facility to the VISN IE point of contact and to the National Center for Ethics in Health Care; and

8. collaborate with the Ethics Leadership Council and Preventive Ethics Council to develop the facility IE policy, ensuring that it describes the structure of the program and includes, at a minimum,

    a. the goals and core functions of IE,

    b. IE program management, responsibilities, and delegation of authority,

    c. Integrative Ethics Council membership, meetings, activities, and minutes,

    d. the relationship between the facility and VISN IE structures,

    e. education, proficiency, and training requirements of staff responsible for IE functions or duties in the facility.

Role of the Ethics Consultation Coordinator

The responsibilities of the ECC are to

1. manage the facility's ethics consultation service, identifying ethics consultants, assessing consultant proficiency, and ensuring that consultants are

    a. appropriately trained in the IE approach to ethics consultation and

    b. engaged in appropriate skills development;

2. implement and manage the use of ECWeb, serving as ECWeb administrator consultant;

3. ensure horizontal and vertical integration with other groups in the organization, establishing relationships with stakeholders, including facility leaders, who may bring ethics questions to the service;

4. serve on the Integrative Ethics Council;

5. build visibility and support for ethics consultation by working closely with the IEPO to create awareness of and support for the ethics consultation function;

6. participate in forums and training hosted by the National Center for Ethics in Health Care to ensure that information and best practices in ethics consultation are shared across VHA; and

7. collaborate with the Ethics Leadership Council, IEPO, and Preventive Ethics Council to develop the facility's IE policy, ensuring that the ethics consultation of the policy is consistent with VHA Handbook 1004.06 (U.S.

Department of Veterans Affairs 2009), reflects local practices, and includes, at a minimum,

a. the goals of ethics consultation,

b. who may perform ethics consultations,

c. who may request an ethics consultation,

d. how ethics consultants may be contacted,

e. who must be notified when an ethics consultation has been requested,

f. which consultation model(s) may be used and when (e.g., individual consultants, a team of consultants, or committee of consultants),

g. how the confidentiality of participants is protected,

h. how ethics consultations are performed (i.e., the CASES approach);

i. how ethics consultations are documented (i.e., ECWeb);

j. who is responsible for the management of the ethics consultation service;

k. the membership and meeting schedule of the ethics consultation service; and

l. how the quality of ethics consultations is assessed and ensured (e.g., use of the evaluation function of ECWeb).

Responsibilities of the ECWeb Administrator and Ethics Consultants

The responsibilities of ECWeb administrator consultants are to

1. create and maintain a user profile for each ECWeb user at the facility;

2. assign roles to each ECWeb user within the application, including ECWeb Consultant, ECWeb Evaluator, or both;

3. assist users in creating and maintaining ECWeb passwords;

4. control which users are able to generate ECWeb reports at the facility; and

5. act as a liaison with National Center for Ethics in Health Care staff for ECWeb concerns.

The responsibilities of ethics consultants are to

1. conduct ethics consultations using the CASES approach;

2. designate ethics consultations as case or noncase consultations; and

3. document ethics consultations by entering and maintaining pertinent information in the ECWeb database.

The responsibilities of ethics consultation evaluators are to

1. obtain customer feedback on completed ethics consultations and
2. document customer feedback in the ECWeb database.

Responsibilities of the Preventive Ethics Coordinator

The responsibilities of the PEC are to:

1. manage the facility's PE team, selecting one to four individuals to be members of the PE team and ensuring that they are appropriately trained in the IE approach;
2. ensure horizontal and vertical integration with other groups in the organization by establishing relationships with stakeholders, including facility leaders, who help identify issues for the PE team to address;
3. serve on the Integrative Ethics Council;
4. build visibility and support for PE by working closely with the IEPO to create awareness of and support for the PE function;
5. participate in forums and training hosted by the National Center for Ethics in Health Care to ensure that information and best practices in PE are shared across VHA;
6. collaborate with other PECs in the VISN to identify cross-cutting ethics quality gaps. (These ethics quality gaps and actions taken to address them must be brought to the attention of the Integrative Ethics Advisory Board.);
7. collaborate with the IEPO, ELC, and ECC to develop the facility's IE policy, ensuring that the PE section is consistent with Handbook 1004.06 (U.S. Department of Veterans Affairs 2009), reflects local practices, and includes, at a minimum,

    a. the goals of PE;
    b. who may perform PE activities;
    c. what issues are appropriate for the ethics team to consider;
    d. how the PE team may be contacted;
    e. how ethics issues are identified, prioritized, and addressed;
    f. what methods are used to address PE issues (i.e., the ISSUES approach);
    g. how the confidentiality of participants is protected;
    h. how PE activities are documented (e.g., PE log, PE storyboards, summary reports);

   i. who is responsible for the management of the PE team;

   j. membership and the meeting schedule of the PE team; and

   k. how the quality of PE activities is assessed.

Responsibilities of the VISN Director

The responsibilities of the VISN director are to

1. develop and maintain an active IE program that is organized and managed according to the provisions of VHA Handbook 1004.06 (U.S. Department of Veterans Affairs 2009);

2. establish clear lines of authority and accountability for IE in the VISN;

3. establish the VISN IE Advisory Board;

4. serve as the VISN IE senior lead, or designate staff to do so;

5. designate a staff member to serve as the VISN IE point of contact;

6. ensure that the VISN IE leaders have the knowledge, skills, and time they need to succeed in their roles;

7. ensure that the VISN IE leaders have access to the VISN director for purposes of

   a. reporting on progress and

   b. discussing ethical issues and concerns of importance to the VISN;

8. provide resources IE needs to succeed (e.g., budget, space, clerical support, reference materials, and ongoing training; and

9. champion IE and support other VISN leaders in doing so.

Role of the VISN Integrative Ethics Senior Lead

The responsibilities of the VISN IE senior lead are to

1. act as a spokesperson and leader for IE in the VISN, providing overall vision and direction for the implementation, development, and management of IE in the VISN;

2. champion IE within the VISN and support facility directors as they champion IE in their facilities; and

3. chair the VISN IE Advisory Board.

Responsibilities of the VISN Integrated Ethics Point of Contact

The responsibilities of the VISN IE point of contact are to

1. monitor facility efforts to develop and maintain IE programs, ensuring accountability for achieving milestones and supporting IE development in facilities and the VISN;

2. facilitate communication among facilities regarding IE, enabling facilities in the VISN to share ethics knowledge and solutions to common ethics problems and facilitating identification of cross-cutting ethics quality gaps;

3. coordinate efforts among facilities to promote consistent standards for IE quality;

4. educate VISN staff about ethics and IE activities;

5. manage IE activities undertaken at the VISN level with guidance and support from the VISN IE senior lead; and

6. act as the executive officer of the Integrative Ethics Advisory Board.

Responsibilities of All VHA Leaders

The responsibility of all VHA leaders is to foster an ethical environment and culture in VHA by incorporating the following four elements into their leadership behaviors:

1. Demonstrate that ethics is a priority by talking about ethics, proving that ethics matters to them, and encouraging discussion of ethical concerns.

2. Communicate clear expectations for ethical practice by recognizing when expectations need to be clarified, stating expectations explicitly, using examples to clarify expectations, and explaining the values underlying their decisions. Veterans Health Administration leaders must ensure their expectations are reasonable and attainable and anticipate and address barriers to meeting those expectations.

3. Practice ethical decision making by identifying decisions that raise ethical concerns, addressing those ethical decisions systematically, and explaining their decisions.

4. Support the local ethics program by knowing what their ethics program is and what it does, championing the program, and supporting participation in that ethics program.

Responsibilities of VHA Employees

The responsibilities of all VHA employees are to

1. support IE by using the ethics consultation service to address ethical concerns encountered on the job and contacting the IEPO or Integrative Ethics Council when systems-level ethics quality gaps are recognized, and complete required education provided through IE;

2. consider participating in the IE staff survey; and

3. contribute to ethical environment and culture by striving to "do the right things for the right reasons" and by encouraging others to do the same.

Resources Provided at Each Facility for Program Effectiveness

The Department of Veterans Affairs Central Office and Center for Ethics in Health provide a spectrum of resources for program implementation and use. Resources to assist facilities and VISNs with IE development, assessment, and improvement can be found at the National Center for Ethics in Health Care IE Web site (http://vaww.ethics.va.gov/IntegratedEthics/Healthcare).

Is the Ethicolegal System in Veterans' Healthcare a "Field of Dreams"?

However laudable VA's noble intentions, the question remains whether or not the prospect of the new healthcare model is actually the kind of "Field of Dreams" memorialized in the 1989 Kevin Costner movie: "If you build it, they will come." Whether or not the new model works will take many years to determine, but even now one can wonder whether the VHA approach is generalizable as an example to inform and guide national trends in the rest of the healthcare sector. Are the premises of fostering openness, involvement, and transparency likely to be liberating and constructive? There is reason to doubt.

Can There Be Integrated Ethics and Transparency?

The underlying premise of the latest revision in the VHA ethicolegal apparatus is that "values oriented healthcare" is more virtuous and more effective, so it should be an essential ingredient and animating ethos for ethical and responsible healthcare delivery. This is said to be optimally accomplished not by isolating ethics as a retributive enforcement mechanism for prescriptive standards and methods, but rather by an "integrated" ethics in which a more "preventive ethics" posture not only engages all individuals and groups to identify, prioritize, and address systemic ethics quality gaps, but also is linked closely to a value-oriented environment in all healthcare activities and in the process of healthcare delivery. It is assumed that better results and satisfaction will be accomplished by encouraging truth and understanding through openness and dialogical processes in which the patient is given maximum information and authority equivalent to that of healthcare professional providers for collaborative planning, consideration of options, participation in treatment, and reviews of outcomes, including discouraging or very negative results and even mistakes and medical errors, blunders, or blameworthy behavior.

Indeed, Kraman and Hamm (1999), though admitting that the real financial implications of the policy are not yet known, staunchly support such a "humanistic risk management policy" that includes early injury review, steadfast maintenance of the relationship between the hospital and the patient, proactive full disclosure to patients who have been injured because of accidents or medical negligence, and fair compensation for injuries. They point out that one VA medical center, which has been using humanistic risk management since 1987, has had encouragingly moderate liability payments. They suggest that "extreme honesty" may be the "best policy." They have also questioned the conclusions of David Studdert and colleagues (2007), who constructed a mathematical model to predict the financial outcome if disclosures of medical errors became widespread and concluded there would be "a high likelihood of increased cost."

Kraman and Hamm (1999) found highly suspect the methodology of Studdert and colleagues, which was based on a large group of anonymous "experts" making judgments on the basis of their own disclosure experiences with a Monte Carlo procedure to "correct for uncertainty." The procedure of Studdert and colleagues (2007) appears to Kraman and Hamm (1999) to be highly speculative rather than empirically based, and therefore of dubious validity as a sound predictive model. Furthermore, it was impossible to readily evaluate in the absence of disclosure who these "experts" were and whether their judgments reflected any actual experience of financial outcome of medical errors and what the amounts were (Schroder 2004)

Kraman and Hamm (1999) go so far as to accuse Studdert and colleagues (2007) of "irresponsible and bad science" for publishing a "flawed study," which is "apt to encourage risk managers to stay the deny-and-defend course because of the (unfounded) fear of doubling or tripling their liability exposure," even though they concede that Studdert and colleagues (2007) stated that "disclosure is the right thing to do; so is compensating patients who sustain injury as a result of substandard care."

There are also other possible considerations that may make healthcare providers less likely to be transparently honest (Smith & Forster 2000). Logically, to provide fully informed consent in advance, a patient needs full knowledge of all possibilities, including the risks of failure and the unknowns. But the potential for being sued for medical malpractice or having an ethical complaint filed with a licensing board makes healthcare providers wary about an admission of error, especially if the harm might be portrayed as having been preventable. Often medical malpractice insurance policies contain a "cooperation" clause requiring insureds to cooperate with the insurer's efforts to defend the insured against a claim. Commonly this clause also stipulates that the insured is forbidden to "admit liability" to an injured or harmed party or in any manner undermine the litigation strategy of the insurer. In fact, an admission of error by the insured or anything that can be construed as a failure to cooperate with the insurer's lawyers will void coverage for the related claims. It may also make medical insurance coverage unavailable in the future. Credentialing for the staff of most hospitals typically requires evidence of effective medical malpractice coverage, so hospital staff appointments may be dropped and future opportunities may be jeopardized.

Whether these assumptions hold up in actual practice in a healthcare system such as VHA remains to be seen. Even if implemented and operationalized, it remains to be seen whether or not these assumptions hold up in actual practice so that the goals of "integrated care" are substantially achieved for such an ambitious and sweeping project in a healthcare system such as VHA. But VHA also is a different environment than the rest of the healthcare sector in the country, and such differences may not be merely incidental and inconsequential.

Is Transparency Respected by Patients and Medical Practitioners Alike?

Although it is tempting to assume that "transparency" contributes value in medical care service delivery and in ethicolegal practices, this is a far more complicated matter for both patients and medical practitioners than it may seem. What might be considered "scientific" medicine is largely a recent historical phenomenon and could not have existed before many modern scientific methods of experimental measure and empirical study, including powerful technologies that have opened many previously unknowable worlds in molecular and subatomic biochemistry: medical technologies and equipment, DNA and genomic mechanisms, and so forth. What was considered "medicine" before was far more infiltrated with pseudoscientific, philosophical, religious, and superstitious views and assumptions. As Torrey (2002) has demonstrated, modern physicians and psychiatrists derive much of their mystique and influence from the worldwide cultural roles of shamans and witch doctors, because by analogy and in practice what they do is shrouded (for the layperson and even for the practitioner) in mystery and as much an art form as it is a scientific endeavor. This contributes to ambivalence about "transparency."

In Western nations, the danger of transparency that accords more perfect knowledge has been regarded as a potent challenge to religious faith, and this tradition can be traced back to Genesis. The bold attempt by Adam and Eve to defy divine prohibitions and instructions simply to accept eternal bliss and the health of paradise without eating from the fruit of the tree of knowledge, thereby aspiring to emulate the wisdom of the gods, was met with unleashed perils and banishment from the Garden of Eden. Intrinsic to the power of religion and its long tradition of prayer and clergy-provided healing arts has been the protective veil of secrecy from real scrutiny in the aftermath of the original temptation and a strong tradition of simple acceptance based only on faith. In many ways, modern patients and their healthcare providers, who are descendants in the functional sociological role of clergy, share this disposition to accord a wide berth to matters of such profound human wonderment as life and death decisions. Furthermore, the advent of scientific medicine actually tends to render the layperson less confident and less in possession of adequate knowledge or even the desire to diminish the scope of medical authority, preferring instead the security of hope and trust in what feels like the superiority of divine providence.

If science must always fight a rearguard action against encroaching sentiments favoring faith, it is also indisputable that there is robust scientific evidence to suggest that significant healing power resides in things not readily susceptible to scientific explanation. No healthcare practitioner can perfectly predict disease and injury trajectories and outcomes, or many end-of-life scenarios in terminal illnesses. Placebos are widely used in medical research and practice, and the placebo effect is a pervasive phenomenon; in fact, it is part of the response to any active medical intervention.

Since the publication of Henry K. Beecher's "The Powerful Placebo" (1955), the placebo phenomenon has been considered to have clinically important effects. A *placebo* is "a substance or procedure ... that is objectively without specific activity for the condition being treated." Under this definition, a wide variety of things can be placebos and exhibit a placebo effect, including pharmacological substances, medical devices, sham surgeries, and so forth. The physician can even be called a placebo: studies have found that patient recovery can be increased by words that suggest the patient "would be better in a few days," and if the patient is given treatment, that "the treatment would certainly make him better" rather than negative words such as "I am not sure that the treatment I am going to give you will have an effect." Placebos do not work on everyone. Beecher's article suggested placebo effects occurred in about 35 percent of people. However, the response rate is wide, ranging from zero to nearly everyone (Beecher 1955).

But if the reason placebos can be so effective in so many diverse situations is the trust that accompanies idealization of the healer and trust in the care and special skill, then arguably full transparency could well be at the expense of efficacy of healthcare treatment procedures and outcomes. Furthermore, whatever the hypothesized value of informing consumers to help guide treatment decisions, there is reason to doubt that doctors share this confidence. For example, a recent *Consumer Reports* survey indicated that although 61 percent of patients said they researched healthcare information on the Internet to assist their medical care, only 8 percent of physicians said that Internet research by patients was helpful. Among doctors, 47 percent said information about whether the physician has been involved in a malpractice lawsuit was "of little value." Only 17 percent felt information about disciplinary actions by medical licensing boards was "very valuable" (What doctors wish 2011).

The recent national healthcare reform law calls for a public Web site (Physician Compare, www.medicare.cov/find-a-doctor) that is supposed to include information on physician quality, patient outcomes, continuity and coordination of care, efficiency, and safety. But that tool is not expected to come online until at least 2015 (Medicare Improvement for Patients and Providers Act 2008).

Consumerism in Healthcare and the "Balance of Power" in Medicolegal Ethics

Another way to think about this topic is in terms of "balance of power." The special doctor-patient relationship, based on trust, privacy, and confidentiality, is a reflection of the iconic archetype of the healer physician, selflessly devoting his (in the past most doctors were male) energy and skills to the best care for patients. Embodied in the layperson's understanding of the Hippocratic oath and the legendary image of a country doctor visiting sick patients on horseback or buggy, the healer role acquired a saintly eminence in the folk psyche that imbued physicians with considerable status, and a popular reputation that grew as medicine emerged as a profession and into industrialized healthcare over the twentieth century.

In the mental health arena, the notion of the interests of the patient as a "consumer" emerged first with the publication of *Client-Centered Therapy* (Rogers 1951). To some extent that idea was derived from a fierce debate in the field about whether psychoanalysis was a "medical" procedure and could be practiced only by someone trained as a physician, or "lay analysis" was possible, as Sigmund Freud himself believed. By the 1970s during deinstitutionalization the terms "consumer" and "survivor" came into use by such groups as the Mental Patients Liberation Front and other consumer movement leaders.

This patient-as-consumer perspective continued to broaden beyond the field of psychiatry into all of healthcare and has become intrinsic in many statutory declarations of "patient rights." Rights to confidentiality of medical information, specified patient complaint formal review procedures, and medical staff credentialing were expectations of private insurance and government third-party payers (Gallagher, Waterman & Ebers 2003). The ethical codes of professional guilds and the standards and guidelines of influential healthcare facility accreditation organizations like TJC incorporated this trend, and this viewpoint is fairly ubiquitous now. It has been alleged that this trend was also a product of the growth of a medical malpractice lawsuit "industry" in which attorneys pursue extraordinary damages to be awarded for care (e.g., medical and hospital bills, prescription drugs and healthcare procedures, nursing home care), compensation for lost earnings, and damages for emotional harm (pain and suffering, loss of consortium) or even punitive damages (for intention, ill will, or fraud). This is said to drive up insurance costs for healthcare facilities and providers and promote "defensive medicine," in which procedures and referrals are ordered primarily as a protection against possible lawsuits rather than for prudent and reasonable treatment of the condition. Insurance costs for defensive medicine are stated to range from $50–60 billion yearly to as high as $150+ billion, and estimates of the proportion of total healthcare costs range from 3 to 10 percent. The issue is a matter of intense debate about national healthcare reform and whether caps on malpractice claims are necessary to control costs.

Over the past century, health insurance in the United States became a common job benefit so that costs were primarily the product of group coverage rates negotiated by employers with the more than 700 health insurance companies that existed by the 1960s, when Medicare and Medicaid came into being and created a major federal responsibility, subsidized by tax revenues. Healthcare costs rose at double the rate of inflation for many years. Still, a sizable portion (16 percent) of the population had no health insurance, and free care available through emergency rooms prompted many to use these facilities, at a disproportionately higher than necessary overhead cost.

But the VHA system is quite separate and differs from the rest of the U.S. healthcare system in that eligibility is standardized nationwide rather than varying widely by locale, and categories of care are far more uniform and consistent.

Can VHA Be a Model for a National Healthcare System?

Certain important comparison criteria raise doubts about generalizing to national healthcare on the basis of the VHA model and experience. National healthcare policy must consider the full scope of patients and their healthcare service needs, including all demographics of age, race, gender, nationality and linguistic culture, socioeconomic status, literacy and education, marital status, religion, and many other variables. Of course, in making decisions about investment in and allocation of healthcare resources, planners must also consider the vast array of medical epidemiological "conditions," settings for treatment and access to care, and availability of technologies.

One obvious reservation about basing plans on the VA model is that VHA serves patients with varying statistical distribution of population demographic characteristics and needs. Although female veterans and families of veterans increasingly are significant recipients of healthcare services, adult males have always been the mainstay of the system because of the composition of the military. Also, the physical health conditions requiring treatment include disproportionately higher battle-related injuries, such as head trauma, amputations, residual wound care, and other results of vital organ and peripheral organ damage, disability, and pain. In World War II there were approximately two wounded soldiers for every person who died, and that number jumped to three to one in Vietnam. In Iraq and Afghanistan, improved medical care and protective body armor yield proportionately fewer deaths and more casualties. In the ten years of U.S. combat in Vietnam, 2.7 million people were deployed, and currently in Iraq and Afghanistan 2.2 million have been deployed. The death toll in Vietnam was 58,000; in Iraq and Afghanistan it has been 5,000, but the ratio of casualty wounded to combat deaths has increased. By comparison, casualties were far greater in the World Wars, and if one considers the Civil War, the number of casualties was even greater. In the single Battle of Gettysburg, which lasted four days, almost 8,000 soldiers were killed (3,155 Union and 4,708 Confederate)—greater than the combined totals from Iraq and Afghanistan—and over 27,000 wounded (14,531 Union and 12,693 Confederate), excluding more than 10,000 combined forces captured or missing.

There have been dramatic changes in the mental health conditions requiring treatment in VHA. Just having body armor or helmets hit by bullets or shrapnel can inflict traumatic brain injury (TBI), and even without physical injury, this exposure can lead to mental health sequelae such as depression, post-traumatic stress disorder (PTSD), and cognitive impairments. One Department of Defense study identified a 30 percent lifetime incidence of PTSD among Vietnam combat veterans, often protracted over many years. Furthermore, comorbidity with alcohol and drug abuse has increased. Findings from various studies suggest that among veterans with PTSD, up to 84 percent meet the criteria for comorbidity with alcohol abuse, and up to 44 percent for lifetime drug use disorder (including nicotine), with concomitant very high rates of depression. Since September 11, 2001, VA has seen 167,000 new cases of PTSD, 195,000 cases of depressive conditions and affective psychoses, and 103,000 cases of anxiety disorders. The suicide rate in the army and marines has for the first time reached that of the civilian population (Stetka et al. 2011).

Of course, what is recognized as a condition deserving treatment and how it is handled in the field have also changed dramatically. The history of modern medical study of war-related traumatic stress disorders began with research by a cardiologist named Da Costas in the Civil War, who considered the symptoms of anxiety, shortness of breath, palpitations, inability to work, and so forth to be cardiac problems, termed irritable heart syndrome, effort syndrome, Da Costa syndrome, or soldier's heart. In World War I, what was then termed "shell shock" and early in the war believed to be a physical disorder caused by the vibration of the brain and disruption of nerve cells due to artillery explosions and noxious gases, by the end of the war was mostly seen as a psychological response to war stress not related to shell concussions. But even in World War I, what was known as shell shock was primarily gross functional problems like not being able to speak or walk, along with moderate to severe TBI. What is now recognized as more subtle, mild TBI was not noticed. During World War II, to reduce the skyrocketing number of psychiatric casualties, the PIE (Proximity, Immediacy, and Expectancy) model developed by Army Medical Officer Thomas Salmon in World War I was reinstituted. Psychological issues during war (i.e., the "thousand-yard stare," social or emotional withdrawal, irritability, dissociation, and conversion disorders) were treated in close proximity to the battlefield, included high immediacy access to sleep and nutrition ("three hots and a cot"), remaining in uniform and being given jobs, with a high expectancy of improvement, and 95 percent returned to combat. In Vietnam, PIE was supplemented with S (simplicity) and was the broadly employed approach, but by the late 1970s and early 1980s a Vietnam stress syndrome among veterans was getting attention. The *Diagnostic and Statistical Manual-I* diagnosis of "gross stress reaction" in 1952 was based on the work of General William Menninger in World War II, had been dropped in *Diagnostic and Statistical Manual-II* in the 1960s, then returned in *Diagnostic and Statistical Manual-III* in the diagnosis of PTSD. In Iraq and Afghanistan, vigilance is higher and the available psycho-diagnostic system defines the problem in a manner that focuses attention on the problem.

There have been dramatic changes in other possibly important corollary factors. Notably, public approval and acceptance of returning war veterans plunged in Vietnam from the World War levels, but recovered during the Reagan presidency, Operation Desert Storm, and in the aftermath of September 11, 2001, terrorist attacks and the "Shock and Awe" assault on Baghdad, so that public approval has been much higher for Operation Iraqi Freedom and in Afghanistan for Operation Enduring Freedom. Also, there has been increased reliance on the Reserve and National Guard units, comprised of "volunteer" citizen-soldiers, and increased patterns of systematic multiple deployments, with far-reaching implications for stress and burnout, complicated by family stresses and the implications of older soldiers having family dependents and jobs at home.

Furthermore, the premorbid characteristics of military servicemen are very likely a different profile now than in the past. Among regular military in particular, the proportion of individuals who would not have been drafted or enlisted before is much higher now in Iraq and Afghanistan than in the past, and in some cases simply going off medications for a six-month period may restore eligibility. Therefore, the proportion of the military with vulnerability to PTSD due to pre-existing psychiatric conditions (including serious diagnoses of anxiety, depression, bipolar disorder, and other disorders), abuse during childhood, limited educational achievement, and so forth is greater now than ever before. These complexities make it difficult to generalize about both direct patient care and ethicolegal issues from the current experience in the VHA system to a national healthcare system.

Financing Healthcare and Systemic Operational Features

The implications are varied, but in numerous ways conditions are distinctly different in VHA than elsewhere in the nation's healthcare sector. On the one hand, VHA has been the lead innovator for uniform healthcare information technology and medical records, as well as case management. On the other hand, VHA is encumbered by a restricted pharmaceutical formulary (less than one-third of the drugs available to Medicare beneficiaries), more rationing in specialized areas, and decision making susceptible to outside political clout, resulting in distorted resource allocation, backlogs, and other complications. The Veterans Health Administration has a pervasive residual permeating "military" ethos, which interacts and reverberates with the medical hierarchical chain of command culture.

The Veterans Health Administration is a "single payer" healthcare system that controls costs by a "global budget," which sets a limit to what it can spend on healthcare provision. Such year-to-year funding according to the whims of politics in Congress is not according to what consumers want or are willing to spend, so the VHA system differs inherently from what is being called "Obamacare" and from any systems that may try to retain marketplace and private sector health industry care and insurance coverage. Furthermore, federal workers by law cannot bargain for wages or benefits, so VHA does not face the same vulnerability to labor union pressures, strikes, and other leverage that drive up overhead costs. Also, there are limitations by law on government exposure to tort liability and on many aspects of healthcare service providers, so the playing field is not the same for the VHA system in delivering healthcare and the threat of malpractice claims against facilities and staff.

The differences between the VHA system and the rest of the U.S. healthcare system are sufficiently substantial to make generalizing on the basis of a model of "integrated care" difficult. Much depends on the final shape of changes in the healthcare delivery system.

In Medicolegal Ethics, Does One Size Fit All?

An absolute rule that forces an all-or-nothing response and a standard approach to all ethicolegal choices has the underlying premise that all possible situations are sufficiently uniform in the determinative dimension so that nuances and differences do not justify discriminations among the possible options. This may indeed be true if the value asserted is so paramount that it ought never to be attenuated for any reason. But that begs the question of whether simply categorizing the decision as ethicolegal supersedes all important distinctions.

Perhaps the concerns raised are more disparate, so that a single wrench is not automatically the solution for all. To some extent this depends on what might be categorized among the ethicolegal situations. A recent Medscape survey of physician ethics posed questions spanning a diverse range of ostensibly "ethical" and "legal" choices and implications. In some cases, it seemed to respondents to matter whether the physician's role involved the implementation of some procedure or the discontinuation of care, such as recommending or giving life-sustaining therapy when the physician judged it futile, contrasted with halting care because of family demands even if the doctor felt that was premature (Reese 2010).

Whose decision should take priority when reasonable people might differ, and what are the implications for others not present or for other reasons not being considered? What about assisting in patient suicide for an elderly person in pain with a terminal condition whose quality of life is minimal? Likewise, prescribing a treatment that is a placebo or performing a treatment that isn't medically warranted simply because the patient wanted it might be different than doing one of those things as a hedge against a medical liability complaint. Undertreating pain because the patient might become addicted, affecting the patient's future health, is different than being concerned about other repercussions. Not revealing a mistake might be viewed differently if there was more potential for causing or preventing harm if it were revealed. Reporting a colleague to a superior or a licensing board for impairment (e.g., drug or alcohol use or mental illness) or for no longer being competent may be a matter of judgment that seriously affects that person's livelihood and professional relationships, but it might have different significance depending on the kind and conditions of the practice and the availability of alternatives. Referring a patient to someone not considered to be the very best qualified might involve professional courtesies, logistics of healthcare payment and access, as well as ongoing professional relationships and business. A practitioner dropping an insurer that doesn't pay well might force some longtime patients to stop seeing that practitioner. A condition might be overstated to get the patient access to vital treatment that would not otherwise be covered.

In many instances there are considerations other than the bilateral relationship of the patient and the doctor affecting choice of care, and sometimes these factors affect others, including even colleagues and family members of the patient, personal values, and the patient's confidence in subjective impressions when information is ambiguous and susceptible to multiple interpretations or variables. An absolute policy such as total honesty between the patient and the doctor discounts certain implications or opportunities for judgment.

Future Directions

The Veterans Health Administration has adopted a plan to transform its system of healthcare provision into an "integrated care model," which prioritizes informed patient involvement in decision making. This envisions a fundamental change in the relationship between healthcare providers and the patients who receive these services, with important impacts on the cost of care and choices among investment in technologies and training, allocation of resources, and access to and distribution of scarce and costly services. The domain of healthcare is a huge sector of the national economy and currently is undergoing serious scrutiny for potential changes that will have powerful, enduring implications for the delivery of services; this will affect the overall health and quality of life for citizens. Regardless of the outcome, a national healthcare system may well be realized by VHA, and the extent to which it may become a model for the rest of the U.S. healthcare system depends on critical features and the degree of comparability that may emerge over the next several years.

References

Beecher, H. K. (1955). The powerful placebo. *JAMA* 159, no. 17: 123–143.

Council on Ethical and Judicial Affairs. (2002). *Code of medical ethics: Current opinions.* Chicago: American Medical Association Press, 217–218.

Gallagher, T. H., Waterman, A. D. & Ebers, A. G. (2003). Patients' and physicians' attitudes regarding the disclosure of medical errors. *JAMA* 289, no. 8: 1001–1007.

Institute of Medicine (IOM). (2009). *Informing the future: Critical issues in health.* http://www.The+Institute+of+Medicine+%28IOM%29+report+Informing+the+Future%3A+Critical+Issues+in+Health (accessed April 2012).

Joint Commission for Accreditation of Healthcare Organizations (JCAHO). (2012). Joint Commission for Accreditation of Healthcare Organizations handbook. http://www.Joint-Commission-on-Accreditation-of-Healthcare-Organizations/135834383114842 (accessed April 2012).

Kraman, S. S. & Hamm, G. (1999). Risk management: Extreme honesty may be the best policy. *Annals of Internal Medicine* 131: 963–967.

Medicare Improvement for Patients and Providers Act of 2008, Pub. L. No. 110-275.

Patient Protection and Affordable Care Act of 2010, Pub. L. No. 111-148.

Reese, S. M. (2010). Exclusive ethics survey: "Should I keep this patient alive?" *Medscape Medical Ethics* (November 16). www.medscape.com/viewarticle/731856.

Rogers, Carl. (1951). *Client-centered therapy: Its current practice, implications and theory.* London: Constable.

Schroder, J. (2004). Disclosing medical errors: Practical, ethical and legal considerations. Paper delivered at the Hospitals and Health Systems Law Institute, Hollywood, FL, February 12.

Smith, M. L. & Forster, H. P. (2000). Morally managing medical mistakes. *Cambridge Quarterly Health Ethics* 9, no. 1: 38–53.

Stetka, B., Kudler, H., Weisler, R. H. & Nasrallah, H. A. (2011). At war with mental illness: Caring for troops and veterans. *Medscape Psychiatry & Mental Health.* (February). www.medscape.com/viewarticle/737039_print.

Studdert, D., Mello, M., Gawande, A. & Brennan, T. (2007). Disclosure of errors: The right thing to do. *Health Affairs* 26, no. 3: 904–905.

Torrey, E. F. (2002). The going rate on shrinks: Big pharma and the buying of psychiatry. *The American Prospect*, July 14.

U.S. Department of Veterans Affairs. (2007a). Ethics consultation: Responding to ethics questions in health care. http://www.ethics.va.gov/docs/integratedethics/Ethics_Consultation_Responding_to_Ethics_Questions_in_Health_Care_20070808.pdf (accessed May 7, 2012).

U.S. Department of Veterans Affairs. (2007b). Ethics consultation toolkit: A manual for the ethics consultation coordinator. www.ethics.va.gov/docs/integratedethics/Ethics_Consultation_Toolkit–20070228.pdf (accessed May 7, 2012).

U.S. Department of Veterans Affairs. (2007c). Preventive ethics: Addressing ethics quality gaps on a systems level. www.ethics.va.gov/docs/integratedethics/Preventive_

Ethics_Addressing_Ethics_Quality_Gaps_on_a_Systems_Level–20070808.pdf (accessed May 7, 2012).

U.S. Department of Veterans Affairs. (2007d). Preventive ethics toolkit: A manual for the preventive ethics coordinator. www.ethics.va.gov/docs/integratedethics/ Preventive_Ethics_Toolkit–20070228.pdf (accessed May 7, 2012).

U.S. Department of Veterans Affairs. (2009). Veterans Health Administration handbook 1004.06. www.ethics.va.gov/docs/policy/VHA_Handbook_1004-06_ IntegratedEthics_20090616.pdf (accessed April 2012).

What doctors wish their patients knew: Surprising results from our survey of 660 primary-care physicians. (2011). *Consumer Reports* (March): 20–23.

Chapter 12

The Story of Give an Hour™

Barbara Van Dahlen

The idea that led to the development of a national nonprofit organization that provides free mental health services to U.S. returning troops, their families, and their communities evolved over several months as events in the world signaled the need for a creative response to the mental health consequences of the wars in Iraq and Afghanistan. The story of Give an Hour™ (GAH) is really a story of dedication and determination on the part of the many people who answered Barbara Van Dahlen's call for civilians to give their time, expertise, and compassion to the men, women, and families who serve our country.

The Inspiration

It was the summer of 2005, and the Iraq war was in its third year. Stories about soldiers coming home with post-traumatic stress (PTSD) and traumatic brain injuries (TBIs) were beginning to make their way into mainstream media. For many in the mental health community, the fact that the war was taking a psychological toll on service members and their families was not surprising. They had seen this before: Vietnam left an entire generation of veterans psychologically damaged as a result of their service. What was surprising was the lack of resources in place to respond to the clear and growing need within the military community. As would become clear later, few in the Department of Defense (DoD) expected that the war would last three years, let alone seven. Few anticipated the significant impact on the men and women who were deployed two, three, four, or more times. Few anticipated the highest suicide rate among military personnel since such data have been recorded.

National Public Radio and other media outlets were beginning to run stories about the effects of war. One such story, aired on NPR in June 2005, described an Iraq veteran who returned home with severe symptoms of post-traumatic stress. It was clear from the story that he had served honorably and was highly regarded by his peers and superiors. Soon after the veteran returned home, however, he began experiencing difficulties. Unfortunately, no one recognized that his symptoms resulted from his experience in combat. He was intensely depressed and anxious, irritable, and at times aggressive and had trouble controlling his impulses. He described walking into a convenience store and having an argument with the owner. He described feeling an urge to kill the owner and the horror he felt at the intensity of that urge. His marriage fell apart—he lost his wife and kids. Unable to work, he lost his home and was living out of his car.

Fortunately, this story had a happy ending. A program in New York identified the veteran as suffering from PTSD and began helping him rebuild his life. Once he received a proper diagnosis and appropriate treatment, he was better able to manage his symptoms. He reunited with his wife and kids. The story concluded with the man's caseworker commenting on the need for additional services for returning troops and their families.

The NPR story haunted Dr. Van Dahlen, as she reflected about how much those in the mental health profession had learned from the experiences of veterans. Whereas psychology classes used to mention "shell shock" and "combat fatigue," they now address PTSD. Whereas the plight of Vietnam veterans was once ignored, we now recognize that having come home to an unsupportive and hostile country, for too many of those veterans the war never ended and their wounds never healed.

As a mental health professional, Dr. Van Dahlen sensed that veterans from the current conflicts were failing to receive adequate care for their psychological injuries, and that American society was not ready for the onslaught of those coming home with the invisible wounds of war. As a child psychologist, she was also bothered by the impact that these invisible injuries—if left untreated— would have on the spouses and children of service personnel. And as the daughter of a World War II veteran, she began to think about possible solutions to the growing crisis.

Many civilians, including Dr. Van Dahlen, assumed that the Departments of Defense and Veterans Affairs (VA) were on top of these issues and that the military community was well equipped to care for its own. Terms like "reintegration" began appearing in articles about the government's response to the needs of those coming home. This suggested that there was a growing awareness that military personnel and military families were being strained by repeated deployments and that these individuals and families needed support to ensure proper reintegration and reunification. Later, many would realize these assumptions were naïve, and they would learn about the complexity of the issues that affect our ability to care for the mental health needs of returning troops and their families.

At the time the complexities were hidden, but the occasional hints of the starker realities were not. Driving in suburban Washington, D.C., one summer day, Dr. Van Dahlen and her elementary-school-aged daughters saw a homeless veteran on a street corner. He was wearing fatigues and holding a sign that read, "Homeless Vietnam veteran. Please help. God Bless." One of her daughters reacted with outrage and compassion, asking how American society could let this happen to men who had served their country.

It was a question that led Dr. Van Dahlen to do a little research and ask a few additional questions, namely, how many men and women had been deployed. How were they faring with respect to the challenges that all who go to war face when they come home? The numbers were disturbing. Hundreds of thousands of men and women had been deployed, and many had already done multiple tours of duty. The early reports on the consequences of combat experience were of concern as well (Hoge et al. 2004; Hoge, Auchterlonie & Milliken 2006).

It seemed clear that even if the war were to end immediately, millions of military personnel and family members had already been affected, and the need for care would continue for the foreseeable future. In addition, the government would be unable to adequately care for all of those in need. The civilian mental health community would have a role to play—if it could be harnessed.

The Concept

As a busy mental health professional and single mother of two, Dr. Van Dahlen wasn't about to leave her successful clinical practice and go to work for VA. She didn't even know whether VA would accept her help if offered. She just knew she would have been happy to see someone from the military in her practice as a pro bono service. She also figured that many mental health professionals probably felt the same way she did—bothered by the reports they heard, aware that a tidal wave of need was coming, aware that they had important skills to offer, unsure of how to help.

She suspected that many of her colleagues would donate their time if there was an easy and effective way to do so. An idea began to percolate—a mechanism to connect mental health professionals interested in helping this population directly to those in the military community who were in need of assistance and expertise. Though mental health professionals with experience in military mental health and trauma would be critical to this effort, all mental health professionals had important skills to offer. Not only were soldiers, marines, airmen, and sailors affected by the current conflicts, family members were suffering as well because of the impact of war on their loved ones.

Americans believe in volunteerism—and the data are clear that volunteering provides tremendous benefits for those who donate their time to a worthy cause. Though not all citizens volunteer at the same rate or with the same frequency, many volunteer in their communities, at their children's schools, and in their houses of worship. Some serve on boards of nonprofit organizations, and some volunteer with organizations such as the Red Cross or the United Way.

Many wonderful volunteer-based organizations are serving those in need in the United States, but few offer the opportunity for professionals to use their specific skills and expertise to assist a group or community on a regular basis. The organization Doctors without Borders is an example of such an opportunity. The mental health consequences of the conflicts in Iraq and Afghanistan to returning troops and their families demand a similar response, namely, an organization that could harness the nearly 400,000 civilian mental health professionals in the United States. Give an Hour™ was created to offer a mechanism for all mental health professionals—psychologists, psychiatrists, social workers, pastoral counselors, marriage and family therapists, licensed professional counselors, substance abuse counselors, and psychiatric nurses—to offer their specific skills to the military community during this time of growing need.

Many volunteer opportunities offer the potential to make an important difference in the lives of others. Those who have volunteered in soup kitchens or in homeless shelters know the satisfaction of providing assistance to those who are less fortunate. Give an Hour™ providers have expressed similar satisfaction when reporting back on their work with the military community. Some had experience with the military—either a family member had served or they themselves are veterans. Others had no prior experience with military culture but felt a calling to join the effort to support those coming home. Many GAH providers have written to express gratitude for the opportunity to serve this worthy community. Some tell of their unsuccessful efforts to volunteer their time at their local VA. Many share heartwarming—and some heart-wrenching—stories of those they are providing care for. A common theme has been deep satisfaction at using skills in new and different ways to assist individuals, families, and communities. Many providers write about their newfound respect and admiration for the military community, a culture they previously knew little about. Others share a profound sense of accomplishment as they reflect on how they have helped save lives and families by giving of themselves.

Components of the Model

The mechanism for connecting providers to those in need grew out of Dr. Van Dahlen's experience with the popular Internet site Craig's List. She had used the site to successfully find a number of wonderful childcare providers and was amazed at how simply and effectively the system connected those offering a service to those with a specific need. It occurred to her that an organization could use this model to directly link mental health professionals willing to donate their time with military personnel and family members seeking care.

Delivery System

The vast majority of mental health professionals who are accepted into the Give an Hour™ network are licensed mental health professionals who carry their own malpractice insurance. There are two exceptions to this standard: pastoral counselors and supervised graduate students. In many states pastoral counselors are not required to be licensed. These professionals offer a valuable and unique service, and many want to offer their services to military families. One of the first professional associations that offered its support to GAH was the American Association of Pastoral Counselors. This organization has excellent standards of professional conduct and is a recognized and respected organization in the mental health community. Pastoral counselors who are members of the AAPC are welcome to join GAH even if they are not required to be licensed in the state where they practice.

Some graduate students are also allowed to join GAH, now that it has developed relationships with a number of clinical training programs across the country. The organization only accepts students whose supervisors are GAH providers. Fortunately, some in the mental health profession are beginning to recognize the need to train students in the area of military mental health. Clearly students in all disciplines should be properly prepared to work with this community, given the growing demand for services beyond what the government can provide. This is an exciting area for further development—one that will benefit those who serve as well as the next generation of mental health professionals. Give an Hour™ will continue to work to ensure that those who care for the military community are trained to meet the specific needs of those who serve and their families.

Unlike other mental health efforts to provide services for underserved populations, GAH does not operate as a clinic or treatment facility. It does not screen those who seek care, nor does it attempt to "match" providers with those seeking service. Staff members regularly assist military visitors in their efforts to locate a provider for themselves or a loved one, but many returning troops and family members also locate a provider on their own through the GAH Web site.

Give an Hour™'s approach is to create a mechanism whereby mental health professionals register and list their skills and areas of expertise. Once their licensure is verified, they are added to the network. Although providers are asked to agree to a set of professional guidelines, GAH does not dictate the type of treatment they provide or monitor the care that they deliver. Although some treatment approaches have been shown to have promise when treating post-traumatic stress, it is clear that there is no silver bullet in this area and one size does not fit all. Even in situations where the individual is clearly suffering from post-traumatic stress—and a form of exposure therapy might be indicated as a likely treatment approach—the clinician is free to provide a mixture of education, support, relaxation, and family involvement, all of which have been known to help, according to feedback GAH has received from service members. There certainly are incompetent mental health professionals in the United States, but most providers who join GAH do so because they feel called to help the men, women, and families who serve. They care about the impact of these conflicts on service members, and they want to help. They use their skills, resources, and compassion to develop relationships with those who are suffering. They provide relief and understanding. They provide a tremendous service.

An early criticism of the GAH concept and organization came from VA and DoD. Officials in both organizations questioned the qualifications of GAH providers and suggested that only DoD- or VA-trained mental health professionals could provide the services the military community needs. Give an Hour™ was asked to require that all of its mental health professionals join the TRICARE system, to become healthcare providers through DoD. Dr. Van Dahlen's response to the criticism and the request has remained the same. Mental health professionals vary in their level of skill, expertise, competence, and effectiveness across settings within and outside VA and DoD. Indeed, this is true of all professions across all settings. As a former TRICARE provider and the colleague of countless others who still provide service under TRICARE, she can attest to the fact that joining a network of any kind does nothing to ensure the quality of care that mental health professionals provide. There are wonderful counselors in VA; there are also some who are mediocre at best. The professionals who join GAH do so because they want to give their services, and their efforts and the quality of their care are valued and appreciated.

Although GAH doesn't monitor or dictate care, it does provide as much training to providers as possible. During focus groups Dr. Van Dahlen and her team learned that providers do not want to be paid for this work—nor do they want to join some bureaucratic entity like TRICARE in order to care for those who need their assistance. They do want a little recognition for their generosity, and they want to be adequately prepared. Give an Hour™ thus offers as much training literature through its Web site as possible, while continuously sending out notices to providers regarding other training opportunities in their regions or through the Internet.

Give an Hour™ also educates those who visit its Web site about seeking proper care. Educating the military community about mental healthcare increases the likelihood that military members and their families will have a good experience with a mental health professional. Give an Hour™ ensures they receive information that will lead to realistic expectations about the benefits of mental healthcare. Just as the mental health professionals who join the GAH network need cultural education, so the military community needs education about those who provide mental healthcare. Give an Hour™'s job is to create the opportunity for healing by bringing together someone in need with someone who possesses the skill to help. Of course, the one variable GAH cannot control is the goodness of fit—how well the relationship works. It must trust military personnel, their family members, and mental health professionals to know what is helpful, what is effective, and when a relationship fits.

So how do those in need of care find GAH? A tremendous amount of time and effort goes into outreach and education campaigns. Give an Hour™'s director of public relations, herself a military spouse, joined GAH as a volunteer in the early days of the organization. She has done a tremendous job in publicizing its efforts through major media outlets such as *Time, Newsweek, USA Today*, NBC, ABC, CNN, and so forth. As a result, many service members and their family members hear or see a mention of GAH and visit the site (www.giveanhour.org) for more information. Once they find the site, they can search for a provider by using their zip code or can reach a GAH staff member by clicking on the "contact us" tab. Many returning troops and their family members are referred to GAH by some of its partner organizations, such as TAPS (Tragedy Assistance Program for Survivors), the Red Cross, and the American Legion Auxiliary. Friends in the National Guard also routinely refer individuals and families to GAH, as do other mental health providers in VA and DoD. Dr. Van Dahlen is proud of GAH's reach thus far but knows there are many who would benefit from mental health services who do not yet know that GAH exists. Clearly there is much more to be done.

Giving Back

Once the service delivery mechanism was identified, it was time to think through other aspects of the organization. Dr. Van Dahlen found inspiration for a critical component in the life story of her father, who served in World War II long before she was born. He joined the U.S. Navy because the world was at war and he wanted to protect his country. A first-generation American, her father—whose mother was German and father was Dutch—was the third born of eight. His life was similar to the lives of many of the young men who joined the military to protect the United States. His parents, who had sacrificed a great deal to come to America, instilled in him a sense of honor, integrity, and patriotism that went far beyond loving his country. This brand of patriotism included a willingness to die for his country if necessary.

Dr. Van Dahlen's father died in 1986, before she was old enough and wise enough to question him about the details of his military experience. As a result, what she knows about his experience is limited. He did see combat and was injured and received care for his wounds in a military hospital in Washington State. And he told his children many great stories about his escapades with buddies while on leave in the Philippines. But he never spoke about the battles, the lives lost, or the horror of war.

As the plan for GAH began to crystallize, Dr. Van Dahlen wondered how her father would advise someone to build an organization to address the invisible wounds of war—the wounds he certainly had but never discussed. She instinctively knew that he would have urged her to create a mechanism for those seeking service to give back—to pay it forward, so to speak. Her father preferred to serve. He resisted offers of help from others. Like many in the U.S. military community, his focus was always on what he could do for his family, friends, community, and country. Thus she was certain he would have stressed the need to ensure that those who received services be given the opportunity to give back and serve others. He would have known the importance of building this philosophy into the organization, and he would have been right. Since launching GAH in 2005, Dr. Van Dahlen has had the opportunity to interact with numerous men and women in the armed forces, as well as their loved ones. Invariably, as service members learn about GAH and its mission, they express deep gratitude and ask what they can do in return.

So from the beginning GAH has offered those who receive services the opportunity to give back in their communities. This isn't required for someone to receive services, but it is something that many have chosen to do. Some offer to become spokesmen for GAH, speaking to media and at events to encourage others in need to seek services. Some give back by volunteering with veterans' service organizations in their community. A fruitful partnership with The Mission Continues is developing along these lines, as that organization recognizes the need to provide returning service members with opportunities to continue their commitment to service by linking them with ways to serve in their communities.

Interestingly, providing the opportunity for those receiving services to give back to their communities had an unintentional benefit. When Dr. Van Dahlen began discussing the concept of GAH with the mental health community, she found that many in the profession believed that for counseling or therapy to be successful, the individual receiving care must be invested in the process. One way to ensure that someone is invested in the process is to require him or her to pay for it. As a result, many in the mental health community are reluctant to provide their services for free. As the concept of GAH began to spread, it was met with resistance from some mental health professionals. Although they were very sympathetic to the cause, they questioned the model—until they learned about the opportunity for those receiving services to give back in their communities. The notion of "giving back" satisfied their concern that those receiving services must pay in order to benefit.

Although Dr. Van Dahlen was trained in this tradition—and in general agrees with the principle—she sees providing mental health services to the military community as very different from offering mental healthcare to other populations. The men, women, and families who serve the United States have already given a great deal; in many instances they have paid a very high price for the honor of serving. Many have sustained physical injuries, while others come home struggling with the invisible injuries of war. Families are affected by the strain of deployment as well as the challenge of reintegration. In essence, military families have already "paid" for any service they receive. Offering compassion and expertise is the least the civilian population can do to ease their transition to home.

In addition, most of the individuals in need of mental healthcare and support upon return from war would not have needed these services had they not joined the military. They are experiencing service-related injuries that must be addressed if they are to successfully return to the lives they left behind. Just as communities rally around the survivors of natural disasters (floods, earthquakes, hurricanes), civilians must rally around the men and women who have chosen to risk their lives and their mental health by doing things that most of us would never be willing to do. Everyone must be willing to do his or her part and be willing to serve by supporting those who are on the front lines of these wars.

Finally, most of those in the military community live by the values of the military, including honor, integrity, and loyalty. The vast majority of the men and women who serve our country are extremely appreciative of any assistance that civilians provide. These are individuals who value hard work, responsibility, punctuality, and competence. They pride themselves on these qualities and respect dedication and commitment from others. If they are unable to participate in their own program of care—unable to keep appointments or follow recommendations—it is likely that these behaviors are the result of the mental health issues affecting them and not a matter of resistance or a lack of respect for the provider. Recall the important work of Jonathan Shay described in his book *Achilles in Vietnam*, which chronicled his observations of and work with Vietnam veterans. Dr. Shay described severe damage to these veterans—to their sense of self, their ability to trust, and their sense of morality. These men who had served their country honorably were often shells of their prior selves. They were extremely difficult to care for, self-destructive, and hopeless. But as Dr. Shay pointed out, all of this was quite understandable—even predictable—given the horrors of war they had experienced.

Those in the mental health field must understand the nature of the injuries they are tasked to treat: how they differ from other injuries caused by trauma as well as the impact on those who serve and the potential damage to the identity and soul of those who wear the uniform. Mental health professionals must develop an informed perspective if they are to be successful in their efforts to assist. They must be called on to adjust their treatment approaches to better fit the men, women, and families in need of care.

Defining the Military Community

Give an Hour™ provides mental healthcare and support to returning troops, their families, and their communities. How each of these entities is defined is an important consideration within the organization and one that guides its efforts in the areas of outreach and education.

From the beginning, GAH has provided mental healthcare and support to service personnel—active duty, National Guard, Reservists, veterans—and their families. It does not differentiate between those veterans honorably discharged and those who were not. All served and all are at risk for suffering the consequences of war. "Family" is defined very broadly as well, to include anyone who loves someone who has been affected by military service since September 11, 2001. In addition to providing services to spouses and children, GAH providers give support and assistance to parents, siblings, grandparents, aunts, uncles, cousins, and nonmarried partners. By providing effective care for the families of those who serve, GAH ensures that the U.S. military community remains strong and resilient. As one wise retired army officer told Dr. Van Dahlen, "treat a family, heal a soldier."

An important change occurred in the focus of these efforts soon after GAH began providing mental health services to military families. As Dr. Van Dahlen traveled throughout the country discussing GAH with community leaders, it became clear that many in the United States knew little about the real issues coming home with returning troops and their families. Not only were communities ill prepared in terms of coordinating services for those coming home, many did not have the proper information necessary to develop programs or facilitate care. Give an Hour™ began offering education and information to communities. It also began consulting with other organizations and entities to assist in their understanding of the mental health consequences of war on those who fight and their loved ones.

Providing education and information to local communities has become an important element of GAH's mission. Many GAH providers give presentations at community events, while others consult with organizations that provide additional services (employment, education, medical care, financial support) to the military community. The mental health issues coming home with military personnel are significant and affect all aspects of reintegration. By harnessing the mental health community, GAH is providing far more than the opportunity to offer direct service to those immediately affected. It is harnessing wisdom, expertise, and knowledge.

Providing therapy and counseling is critical, but it is only one part of the solution to a growing public health crisis. All citizens must learn about and be mindful of the needs of those who bear the burden of the fight. If GAH is successful in launching an effective public awareness campaign, community leaders and citizens in every region will step up to assist those coming home. Vietnam veterans suffered terribly because they were blamed for the war and then turned away in their time of need. This is no longer the case: Americans no longer blame veterans for the country's foreign policy, but a sustained and effective commitment to them and their families has yet to be demonstrated. Sticking a yellow ribbon on a car means little if there is no action behind it.

Assumptions and Realities

Like any voyage into the unknown, starting GAH involved a set of assumptions—some accurate, many not. Dr. Van Dahlen proceeded with a fair amount of ignorance and naiveté, which somewhat protected her from the harsh realities she would later confront, as she set to work formulating and founding her nonprofit.

The Mission

Thankfully, some of Dr. Van Dahlen's impressions and expectations were correct. For example, she assumed that the mental health needs of the military exceed the capabilities of DoD and VA. Indeed, this was and still is the case, for a number of reasons. Although much has been written about the significant number of military personnel suffering from mental health symptoms as a result of their combat experience (Rand Corporation 2008), it is still difficult for service members to acknowledge the need for help. Soldiers, airmen, sailors, and marines are trained to be tough, resilient, and self-reliant. They are supposed to be able to handle war and all that it entails, including taking fire, killing, seeing dead bodies, and seeing buddies injured and killed. Countless men and women in the military—individuals who have performed honorably and often heroically—report feeling shame and disgrace because they are unable to "handle" the stress of war.

Compounding this issue is the reaction of others to their pain and trauma. In general, our society does a poor job of supporting individuals with mental health concerns. It is fear that pushes us away from those who struggle with depression, anxiety, or trauma. Afraid of getting too close to darkness and despair, we too often look the other way and reassure ourselves that it is a weakness or a character flaw that leads to mental illness—something that we surely don't have to be concerned about in ourselves.

In addition, even if a service member acknowledges that he or she needs assistance, it isn't always easy to get help. There are still many in the military, at all levels, in all units, who continue to believe that if you are strong enough or brave enough, you won't need a "shrink" to solve your problems. They see those suffering from depression and anxiety as "whiners" who need to suck it up, shut up, and get back to duty. The leadership in DoD is aware of this issue and is doing a great deal to address the problem. Still, these internal obstacles make seeking care within the system difficult.

Even if someone acknowledges he or she needs help and receives support from superiors and loved ones for seeking help, adequate and accessible care is not always easy to find within the military or VA. As reported in numerous articles since the Iraq War began, the sheer number of returning troops in need of care has overwhelmed the system. Several officers in DoD have expressed frustration about their inability to hire enough mental health professionals to fill the need. Many mental health professionals in DoD report being overwhelmed by the demands on the system. Sadly, the Walter Reed scandal taught us about the failures of care that can occur.

Not surprisingly, similar stories have come from colleagues at VA: too many cases and not enough resources to meet the growing demands for services. One senior level official at a New England VA sadly noted, "this generation is lost." He was convinced that we are too far behind the curve, that it will be impossible to catch up to the growing demands of those coming home while attempting to continue to serve those who have already returned.

Further, numerous articles have quoted service members who have reported long waits to see a counselor (Reno 2009). Finally assigned a counselor, these veterans tell their story to one mental health professional and are told to return for follow-up in three months, only to be assigned a completely different counselor at the return visit. Commonly, veterans report that they receive only medication in response to their symptoms, because there are no counselors available. Vet centers are trying to keep up with the demand but are overwhelmed as well. For many veterans who live in rural or remote areas, neither a VA hospital nor a vet center is available. They have few options.

The Military, VA, and the Administration

Other assumptions made by Dr. Van Dahlen proved not quite as accurate. She had assumed that DoD and VA would welcome GAH's efforts to harness the civilian mental health community and assist those agencies by providing additional services that would complement their efforts. So she was surprised to discover that the gift she believed she was offering was neither trusted nor, initially, wanted.

Dr. Van Dahlen began her efforts to reach officials at DoD and VA in the late fall of 2005. She used her professional network to locate mental health professionals who had a military or VA background or connection and began making calls. Having a "PhD" after her name helped ensure people would return her phone calls. The conversations in those early months were interesting and informative. Many in DoD and VA thanked her for her interest, efforts, and patriotism. Most indicated that they had the issue well in hand. Others politely wondered about her ability to create such an organization. Some challenged the concept that nonmilitary mental health professionals would be able to understand and treat military personnel. Only a few questioned her motivation or integrity. Those skeptics actually suggested that her "liberal" mental health colleagues would try to convince the troops that they were misguided and that they should lay down their arms and refuse to fight.

Fortunately, a few military and VA mental health professionals considered GAH a valid and worthy concept. Some actually offered to assist by introducing Dr. Van Dahlen to other professionals and by helping her work her way up the chain of command. The best advice came from a DoD psychologist, who said, "You don't need our permission to build this organization." He went on to say that he could see the need for such an entity and that if she was successful in her efforts, DoD would eventually find a way to make use of GAH. These were wise words indeed.

Although Dr. Van Dahlen continued her campaign to spread the word about her efforts, she stopped caring about receiving support or endorsement from the military establishment or VA. Instead, she focused on building a credible and viable organization that could offer additional mental healthcare to returning troops and their families. Over time she developed relationships with several colleagues at DoD and a few at VA (though far fewer, as discussed later), who trusted her and saw the potential for collaboration. She learned how to work within the system.

Eventually GAH began to receive requests from DoD-sponsored reintegration programs in all branches of the military for brochures and sometimes for speakers. Camp Liberty in Baghdad sent a request for materials to distribute to troops coming home from deployment. Over time it became apparent that GAH was respected and valued by those within DoD and that GAH services were being utilized.

Clearly DoD is evolving and doors are opening. Give an Hour™ doesn't need to be endorsed in order to accomplish its mission. Does DoD want the organization's help? It seems so. Can the organization assist the men, women, and families who serve? Yes, it can and does.

Give an Hour™'s relationship with VA has been slower to develop. Dr. Van Dahlen has attended many many high-level meetings and has been invited to brief various officials and dignitaries on several occasions. She was invited to present a white paper to President Obama's transition team for VA. Yet until early 2012 little collaboration or coordination occurred.

Many GAH supporters have assumed that a relationship with VA would be easy to develop, unencumbered by the security issues that often are raised by individuals in DoD. One might expect VA to welcome the assistance and work to spread the word about additional services available to veterans and family members. This was not the case until recently. A major threshold was crossed when Give an Hour™ and VA signed a memorandum of agreement for GAH providers to provide counseling services to callers to the Veterans Crisis Line in need of ongoing services rather than crisis management. The polite interest of officials at VA has developed into a partnership of increasing substance as it moves forward.

Relationships with some very talented folks at the Pentagon are another matter. Dr. Van Dahlen has established good working relationships with top officials in the Chairman of the Joint Chief's office, the Vice Chief of the Army's office, and the DoD Center of Excellence (DCoE). She meets regularly with staff members in these offices to share information, develop strategies, and solve situations that arise for service members and their families.

The Obama administration has been consistent and enthusiastic in its support of the military community and of efforts by organizations like GAH and others to assist those who serve. Mrs. Obama and Dr. Biden hosted a gathering at the White House in May 2008. Give an Hour™ and approximately twenty-five other organizations participated in an event that lasted for several hours and included presentations by White House and administration staff on their efforts to support returning troops and their families. More important, the event provided a key opportunity for those working in this area to be heard, to share observations, concerns, and visions with administration officials. That meeting launched several efforts and initiatives and led to the development of relationships with White House staff that have proved very important in GAH's efforts to improve care for the military community.

The Mental Health Providers

Dr. Van Dahlen's assumption that mental health professionals would want to donate time to assist returning troops and their families was correct. Indeed, the mental health community has stepped up in an impressive manner. Though many have wanted to help, the task of harnessing and coordinating this outpouring of generosity has not been easy.

Many of the mental health professionals who joined GAH held a set of beliefs—their own assumptions—about working with the military community. They also had expectations about joining GAH. Specifically, many believed that as soon as they joined, they would receive a call from someone in the military who needed assistance. They thought that GAH would serve as a referral source. Some providers have expressed frustration or irritation that their services have yet to be utilized. If they are ready to give, why have they not immediately been asked to do so?

Philosophically, GAH holds the position that all mental health professionals have something to give during this time of crisis in the military community. Thus, they have been asked to give what they can, when they can—their time, their expertise, their willingness to help. They have been asked to stand ready, while GAH continues the process of getting the word out to those in need about the services they are so kindly offering. They have been asked to provide public education, that is, to give in ways that are a bit outside their comfort zone, by getting out in communities to educate and inform. They have been sent templates and toolkits to assist them in these efforts. They have been encouraged to offer talks to their local chambers of commerce, schools, and other organizations that need to understand the mental health issues facing returning troops and their families.

They have also been asked to understand that military personnel and their family members may be reluctant to accept services, even when freely given.

Those who live and breathe the military culture may be uneasy sharing personal details or information they believe reflects weakness. Give an Hour™ providers have been asked to be patient and realize that some members of the military may make several attempts before they engage in counseling. The mental health professional's job is to be available, encouraging, understanding, and ready to assist when military folks are ready to receive.

Training the mental health professionals who want to provide care has become an important part of GAH's program. It is what providers have said they want: background so that they can be well prepared for the task at hand. And it is what GAH wants to give them.

Contrary to expectation, it is not easy to locate and develop training for those who have stepped up to give their time to this critical effort. Although training is provided to DoD mental health professionals and VA clinicians, GAH has not been able to coordinate efforts with these agencies to provide quality information to its providers. The military community has not yet welcomed the opportunity to equip community clinicians with the skills necessary to provide quality care to service personnel and their families. Though some within DoD and VA have tried to make this happen, nothing has yet come to pass.

Give an Hour™ has thus found other ways to bring training to its network of providers. The organization has developed its own primers for clinicians working with this population. Through newsletters, e-mail messages, and Web site announcements, GAH keeps its mental health professionals apprised of the training opportunities in their geographic regions. Funding has been requested to develop a comprehensive training program for civilian mental health professionals. And partnerships are developing with other nonprofit organizations that will focus on the training and preparation of community mental health professionals who will be assisting the military community for the foreseeable future.

The Mental Health Associations

Dr. Van Dahlen's next assumption was that the major mental health associations would be excited about the concept of harnessing the civilian mental health community to assist those who serve. She assumed that these associations would see assisting troops and their families as a priority, as something the mental health community could do to support those who serve. And this turned out to be true. Give an Hour™ now has the support of all the major mental health associations in the country: the American Association for Marriage and Family Therapy, the American Association of Pastoral Counselors, the American Mental Health Counselors Association, the American Psychiatric Association, the American Psychiatric Nurses Association, the American Psychological

Association, the Anxiety Disorders Association of America, Mental Health America, the National Association of Social Workers, and Therapeutic Communities of America. But this support was not easy to come by, and the associations have been limited in their ability to translate support into action. Still, many individuals within the associations stepped up to help, providing valuable assistance and wisdom along the way.

As a psychologist, Dr. Van Dahlen's first stop on the tour of mental health associations was her own national organization, the American Psychological Association. She assumed APA would be responsive and eager to get involved in this effort, given its long relationship with VA as a primary training site for many clinical psychologists across the country. After a few calls she was connected to an executive at APA who was genuinely interested in the concept and the opportunity to enlist mental health professionals for this cause. He was generous with his time and honest about the political landscape of the mental health association universe. He offered to help where he could, to make introductions and open doors within APA, but he also cautioned her about expectations. His message was clear. In essence he told her, "you don't need the associations to succeed. You are unlikely to get much assistance, but what you are doing is sorely needed."

This was a sobering and liberating conversation that forced Dr. Van Dahlen to accept responsibility for her organization's destiny. If GAH was going to be successful, it would be because of its initiative and innovation, not because it was riding the coattails of any of the major mental health associations. The APA executive was true to his word, and his assistance has been instrumental in helping GAH connect some important dots. More important, however, he challenged Dr. Van Dahlen to make her vision a reality and to accept her role as a leader in the movement to help returning troops and their families. He provided a gentle but necessary push.

The executive director of the American Association of Pastoral Counselors was also quite receptive to a request that AAPC endorse GAH. Its leaders allowed GAH to list them on its first Web site and have been quick to respond to requests for posting announcements and calls to action. Understandably, they don't have the resources to do much more than this. Similarly, once the National Association of Social Workers came on board, its leadership became quite eager to work with GAH to increase membership and expand awareness. Though they have given more time and energy to this initiative than any other association, they are working to address many important mental health issues in our society and cannot focus their attention exclusively on GAH's efforts. The National Association of Social Workers has been a good partner and will no doubt develop additional areas of collaboration with GAH in the future, but GAH must drive the movement. And this is as it should be.

Interestingly, it was the philanthropic arm of the American Psychiatric Association that GAH partnered with to receive a $1 million grant from the Eli Lilly & Company Foundation. Dr. Van Dahlen met the current executive director of the American Psychiatric Foundation (APF) in the fall of 2007, before he was even working for the foundation. He is a veteran and a man of great vision and integrity. They worked together briefly that fall, putting together a screening of a movie that focused on the impact of the Iraq war on soldiers coming home. Later that winter they spoke again. He had recently taken the helm at the APF and was interested in partnering with GAH. He introduced Dr. Van Dahlen to the leadership of the American Psychiatric Association and thus began what has become a long and very productive partnership.

As a result of its relationship with the APF and a generous grant from the Eli Lilly Foundation, GAH has become a major voice in the conversation about the mental healthcare of returning troops and their families. Dr. Van Dahlen regularly participates in high-level meetings at the White House, VA, and DoD. Give an Hour™ has engaged in public education efforts across the country, creating educational materials and public service announcements and generally building awareness about the impact of war on those who serve. Fortunately, GAH has found leaders within the mental health community and beyond who have stepped up to do their part to push this organization—and this movement—forward.

The Veterans' Service Organizations and Nonprofit Organizations

Like most Americans, Dr. Van Dahlen knew very little about veterans' service organizations (another indication of the gulf between the military and civilian communities). She knew some of the larger ones by name, such as the American Legion and the Veterans of Foreign Wars, but had no idea what they did or how they operated. Upon learning a little more, she assumed they would welcome GAH's assistance and be eager to partner and collaborate. As it turns out, she had much more to learn about the world of the veterans' service organizations (VSOs).

There are many many VSOs. Some have existed for decades; others have cropped up since the start of the Iraq War in 2003. Each war has seen the establishment of VSOs specifically focused on veterans from those conflicts, such as the Vietnam Veterans of America and the Gulf War Resource Center. The VSOs are typically established and headed by veterans or military family members. They tend to have a strong lobbying component and are instrumental in pushing legislators to ensure proper care for veterans and their families.

There are also a number of nonprofit organizations and nongovernmental organizations that have a focus—within their larger efforts—on responding to the needs of those who serve. The Red Cross is an excellent example, with its Service to the Armed Forces initiative. Another wonderful effort is the Mission Serve initiative of Service Nation, which links those coming home with opportunities to continue to serve in their communities. Many of these efforts provide valuable services within the context of the larger organizations; some are less successful. And then there are organizations like GAH, which is not a veterans' service organization. It is a nonprofit that provides services to the military community. Although several members of the military community either work or volunteer for GAH, the organization was founded by a civilian and is an effort to harness civilian resources to assist those who serve.

Many nonprofits of all sizes sprang up after the start of the Iraq War. Some provided free airfare for service members, others free cell phone hours, and many others free care packages to the men and women serving overseas. A few regional mental health efforts also developed—most notably SoFar in Massachusetts and the Soldiers Project in California. As far as Dr. Van Dahlen knows, GAH is the only national nonprofit providing free mental health services to returning troops, their families, and their communities.

Soon after the start of the Iraq War, DoD attempted to develop a mechanism to coordinate the myriad VSOs and nonprofits that claimed to be responding to the needs of troops and families. Corporations and individuals were stepping up with offers of financial support and asking DoD to indicate which VSOs were worthy of such assistance. As a government entity, DoD is unable to recommend, suggest, or otherwise indicate preference for a veterans' service organization. In an effort to provide some information about available support to potential funders, interested volunteers, and those who might benefit from the services offered, DoD created the America Supports You program and Web site. Originally ASY was simply a directory of organizations that purported to provide care and support to the military community. Although an application of sorts was required, there was little oversight and even less coordination of efforts. The result was an unwieldy collection of organizations—some that did excellent work, others that did not. Ultimately ASY failed, having garnered little respect for the effort and provided little assistance to those in need of services or funders in need of guidance. The DoD has revamped the project with more oversight and more restrictions, but the effort is still not generally perceived as having much value to the military community or those attempting to support it.

Other attempts to evaluate and coordinate the efforts of VSOs and nonprofits have emerged. The Veterans Innovation Center (VIC)—itself a nonprofit—is an organization whose mission is to improve the lives of veterans and their families by working with the government, VSOs, NGOs, and nonprofit organizations to improve programs, support initiatives, and remove obstacles. The VIC is hoping to develop and support metrics that will allow consumers to offer and receive feedback about available VSOs. Metrics can also provide critical information to potential funders for helping them choose organizations that will best utilize the financial resources they are given.

The VSOs and nonprofits are like corporations and government agencies in one important way: leadership is key. The VSOs come in all shapes, sizes, missions, and ages. Regardless of the size of the budget or the reach of the effort, the organization is only as good as the leader whose vision guides it. Many of the "old guard" VSOs have little interest in working with GAH. They curse the impact of post-traumatic stress on the men and women who serve and acknowledge the need for mental healthcare, but they are not interested in joining forces or coordinating efforts. Many of the old guard VSOs are uninterested in partnering with any other organization.

Some VSOs have wanted to enlist GAH's assistance. They have recognized the value of its services and have accepted its consultants and providers, but then do little to actually partner with the organization. They do not list GAH on their Web sites, do not invite GAH to events they host, and certainly do not include GAH in possible funding opportunities as potential partners. If everyone could move beyond territorialism and ego, much more care could be provided to those who serve, but many of the leaders in this area are not there yet.

There are, of course, wonderful leaders in the VSO, NGO, and nonprofit communities. Give an Hour™ would not have succeeded if not for the support of many bright and capable visionaries who share its passion and the vision that American society can do a better job of caring for those who serve.

The Philanthropic Community

Prior to launching GAH, Dr. Van Dahlen had no experience with the philanthropic community, erroneously assuming, for example, that it would be relatively easy to get funding for her organization. Although everyone she spoke with was enthusiastic about the concept and eager to offer suggestions and recommendations, no one offered funding. Consultants offered to work for a fee on grant applications and proposals, but of course GAH had no budget to hire anyone. It had a board and a handful of part-time volunteers. It had the beginnings of a Web site, built with open source software by a handful of dedicated and generous IT wizards. In other words, it had a great idea but no funding to support it.

A few foundations invited GAH to apply for grants, only to turn it down. As untested organization with an unproven concept, GAH was a nontraditional organization. It had no office—and there were no plans for one. The team worked out of individual homes; board meetings were held in Dr. Van Dahlen's dining room. The "product" was providing free mental healthcare to members of the military community, and those who sought and received services remained anonymous, as the services they received were confidential. There were few opportunities to provide "testimonials" from the population being served.

At one board meeting in the winter of 2007 the conversation focused on how GAH might go about getting some basic operating money. One well-intentioned board member suggested Dr. Van Dahlen solicit donations from the handful of mental health professionals who had agreed to join the GAH network. The organization wasn't actually providing services to any service members at the time, but it had succeeded in getting a handful of providers to sign up. The idea was to begin recruiting them in an effort to build an appropriate "pool" of mental health professionals who would be ready to someday provide services to those in need. Dr. Van Dahlen respectfully disagreed with the board member who made the suggestion—a good friend who was trying to be creative. (Indeed, in those early days, all initial board members were friends or acquaintances who had agreed to join her on this unusual journey.) In this instance she explained that GAH's providers were giving their time and that their time was valuable and in fact the same as a cash donation. Give an Hour™ couldn't seek donations from those who visited the site for services or from those who provided them. That night, as many realized that it would be very difficult for such a young and inexperienced organization to secure funding, GAH's future looked rather bleak.

Dr. Van Dahlen persevered. In the summer of 2007 she met the executive director of an organization called the Coalition to Salute America's Heroes (CSAH). This organization's mission was to provide support for military personnel and their families. Its executive director was impressed with GAH's mission and vision. He recognized the critical need for additional mental health services in the military community and championed GAH's cause to his board. The board awarded GAH a grant of $330,000 for infrastructure development and operating expenses. The money was promised in three equal installments at three-month intervals. The GAH board was thrilled, and Dr. Van Dahlen was amazed: GAH would now be able to begin the actual work she had envisioned. She made her first hire—an administrative assistant—and GAH was off and running. Unfortunately, GAH received only the first installment on the grant; CSAH had some serious internal difficulties, and the founder refused to honor the agreement between GAH and the executive director, who was no longer with the organization. Give an Hour™ had no funds to pursue legal action and so accepted the disappointment and moved on.

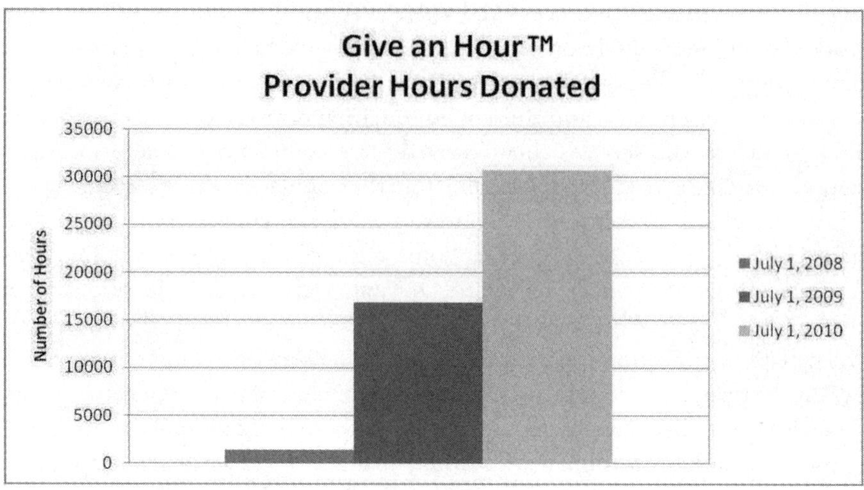

Figure 12.1. Number of Hours Donated by GAH Providers. *Source: Surveys taken on July 1, 2008, July 1, 2009, and July 1, 2010. Note:* Given that survey response rates average 25 percent, actual hours donated are probably several times higher.

Receiving this initial grant made GAH a legitimate—though fledgling—organization. The contacts Dr. Van Dahlen had cultivated began to lead to invitations to meetings at the Pentagon and VA. The organization now had materials to distribute, a Web site, and a small staff. To Dr. Van Dahlen's great pride, it began offering free mental health services to returning troops and their families in July 2007.

If the original grant of $110,000 made GAH legitimate, the grant the organization received from the Lilly Foundation in May 2008 made it significant—and allowed GAH to grow in concept and organization. In the spring of 2008 the GAH network had approximately 1,200 providers who had given approximately 1,000 hours of service to returning troops, their families, and their communities. By May 2010 the GAH network had grown to over 5,000 mental health professionals who had given nearly 28,000 hours of service (see figures 12.1 and 12.2). Because of the Lilly Foundation's generous funding, GAH became one of the leading organizations harnessing the resources in our communities to assist those who serve.

As previously mentioned, Dr. Van Dahlen was introduced to the Lilly Foundation by the executive director of the American Psychiatric Foundation. Her colleague at APF believed that Lilly might be interested in funding a project

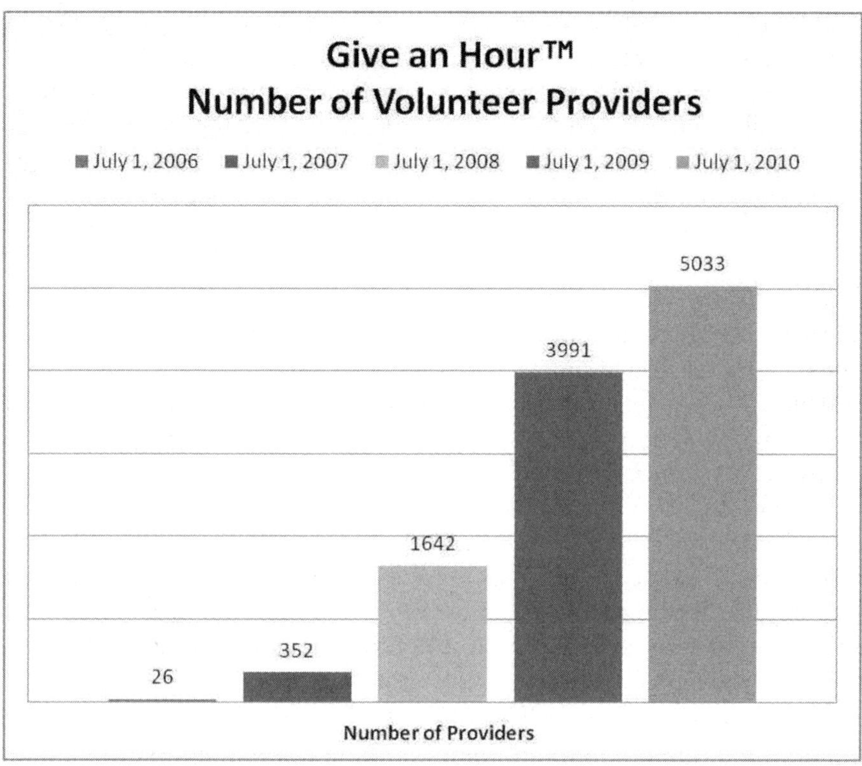

Figure 12.2. Number of Give an Hour™ Volunteer Providers. *Source: Provider Registration Database, July 1, 2006–July 2, 2010.*

developed by APF and GAH together. In early spring of 2008 they began having conversations with the president of the Lilly Foundation, who turned out to be a gentle man with great vision and compassion. These conversations quickly led to a plan to launch a public education campaign aimed at adding mental health professionals to the GAH network and raising awareness throughout the country about the mental health issues affecting the military community. The president of the Lilly Foundation believed in GAH's vision and ability to inspire others to join the movement, and Dr. Van Dahlen will always be deeply grateful for his confidence and commitment to GAH's mission.

Once the Lilly grant was announced, GAH was able to successfully apply for and receive funds from other sources. This meant staff could be hired and projects and initiatives could be supported. Like all nonprofits, however,

GAH must constantly work to locate those in the philanthropic community who believe in its goals and who have the means and willingness to support its efforts. At some point, GAH will develop a division that generates income to support all its projects. For now, it is gratifying to have found a few foundations, corporations, and individuals who share GAH's belief that the military community needs and deserves respect, appreciation, and assistance.

The Give an Hour™ "Family"

There is clearly something powerfully appealing about GAH's vision and mission that draws talented and dedicated people to this organization. They seem to share a sense of urgency—that lives are at stake—and a desire to bring hope and assistance to those who serve in the military. They step up to give, to work, to create.

Early on Dr. Van Dahlen had to get over her reluctance to solicit friends and colleagues for help. There was so much to do, and so much she had never done before, that she needed to recruit folks to fill gaps in her knowledge and expertise. She became less reluctant and more impassioned as she read story after story about the suffering of those who were fighting in Iraq and Afghanistan and the long-term consequences for the families who love them.

Not only did friends and colleagues agree to join the board, they actually gave up precious free time to work on mundane but necessary tasks like creating bylaws and policies and filling out pages and pages of IRS materials. They reached out to their friends to fill additional gaps: attorneys to review GAH materials, graphic artists to create the logo, and IT gurus to build the Web site. One of GAH's current board members has been with Dr. Van Dahlen from the beginning. He sat around her dining room table in the fall of 2005 developing a strategic plan for an organization they weren't sure had a chance of becoming a reality. He believed in her, the concept, and the mission. He brought resources, enthusiasm, and leadership to a board that knew little about governance, oversight, or fundraising. He didn't know much about these areas either but was determined to do his part to give GAH a chance at success.

The story of the woman who would later become the executive vice president for GAH is typical of the stories of those who have joined the effort. She has had a profound effect on the development and growth of GAH and on Dr. Van Dahlen's development as well. They met at the pool where their kids swam and hit it off immediately. While their girls swam, they passed the time in conversation—about life, kids, and the world. When Dr. Van Dahlen developed the concept for GAH, she knew she wanted this friend to help build the organization. The friend was supportive and intrigued but direct in her uncertainty about how she might help. She was an editor, from neither the military nor the mental health community. How could she contribute?

For three years the friend worked as a volunteer for GAH. She edited everything Dr. Van Dahlen wrote and helped with the development of the organizational structure and the design and implementation of the Web site. Dr. Van Dahlen credits her friend with making her a better writer and making GAH the well-organized, efficient, and successful organization it has become. In the winter of 2008, GAH received a generous grant from the Woodruff Foundation. Finally, her volunteer editor became the vice president of a growing national nonprofit effort caring for the military community.

And then there is GAH's public relations director, whom Dr. Van Dahlen also met at her girls' pool. Her husband is a physician in the navy and was actually the first member of the family Dr. Van Dahlen met. As he sat wearing fatigues and reading the paper at a practice one day, she approached him to tell him about GAH. She wanted him to know about its services in the event that he knew of anyone in need. He was enthusiastic and supportive but wanted to tell her about his wife, whose expertise was in public relations. They had recently had their third child, he noted, and she was itching to get involved in something meaningful on a part-time basis. When Dr. Van Dahlen told him that GAH couldn't pay for his wife's services, he said he knew she would want to volunteer. When the two women met, Dr. Van Dahlen was immediately impressed, and the PR expert was instantly drawn to the concept, understood the need, and was excited about the opportunity to "pitch" such a great story.

The PR director volunteered for over a year—and is responsible for the impressive coverage the organization has received. She has been successful in convincing *Time* magazine to run GAH's full-page ad, not once but four times. The ad has also appeared in *USA Today* and numerous military and mental health publications. Dr. Van Dahlen has been interviewed by CNN, ABC, NBC, NPR, the *Washington Post*, the *New York Times*, the *Wall Street Journal*, *Army Times*, *Stars and Stripes*, numerous regional newspapers, and many other military and mental health magazines. *Ladies Home Journal* and *Family Circle* have published feature articles about her and her work with GAH. *Women's Day* named her one of the "50 Women Changing the World." Clearly, this PR director has done a tremendous job in spreading the word, both before and after being officially hired in May 2008.

In addition to these two extraordinary women, Give an Hour™ has been blessed to find several other talented and industrious individuals for this important work. Many have been veterans or family members, and all have been dedicated, passionate, and committed individuals who work tirelessly to reach and serve those in need of care. For example, GAH's development director—who came to GAH with neither experience nor prior knowledge of the issues the organization addresses—has become as passionate and driven to accomplish GAH's mission as those with a more direct link to the suffering in the military community. Finally, Dr. Van Dahlen's first executive assistant, now GAH's program specialist, is probably the most dedicated, detail-oriented young woman in the world. She has become intensely committed to GAH's mission and cares deeply for the families the organization serves. She is conscientious and extremely capable. She is ever present behind the scenes, making sure that Give an Hour™ runs smoothly.

The Troops and Their Families

The one area Dr. Van Dahlen didn't have many assumptions about is the military community. She had a wish that they would accept her efforts to assist them with the burdens they carry for all. And she had a sense that she didn't know much about them—their culture or their day-to-day lives. She also knew she felt uncomfortable, and even awkward, in her ignorance.

Her experience with her father (the World War II veteran) could do little to inform her about this generation of service members and their families. He did, however, teach her a fair amount about shared values in the military—values that are as important today as they were in the 1940s, such as honor, integrity, loyalty, and service. Dr. Van Dahlen thus reasoned that the only way to win the trust of those in the military community would be to acknowledge her ignorance, avoid promising more than she could deliver, and follow through on promises made and commitments offered. People tell her she has accomplished all that and more; she now has many dear friends in the military community who trust her and value GAH's efforts.

What she did not realize is how gracious and appreciative members of the military are for the services they receive. It is clear that the men, women, and families who serve do so not for the recognition they might receive but for the satisfaction they feel in serving their country and doing what they believe is right. They are typically surprised that a civilian organization wants to provide assistance and almost embarrassed to accept the support it offers. And yet when they do accept services, they are quick to acknowledge the value and eager to express their gratitude. Often Dr. Van Dahlen has encountered service men and women who, upon learning about GAH, quickly respond with some version of, "Ma'am, thank you for taking care of my buddies [or family members]. What can I do for you, how can I help?" The United States has a tremendously valuable resource in these families and must do a better job of bridging the gap between the civilian and military communities so as to honor their willingness and harness their potential.

Unintended Consequences

When Dr. Van Dahlen started out on her "simple" mission to assist those who serve, she could not have known what the journey would entail and what wonderful, unintended consequences would ensue. Some of these unintended consequences will shape the next chapter of GAH's story. Some may even inform a much larger and more important dialogue about the country's relationship with the military community.

The Community Blueprint

As Dr. Van Dahlen began to travel the country to discuss GAH and efforts to provide critical mental healthcare to returning troops and their families, she became aware of a developing pattern. Efforts were under way in communities across the country to assist military personnel and their families. Most of these efforts, however, were poorly organized, with little coordination of care. Organizations were often unaware of available resources in their own communities, let alone at the state or federal levels. Citizens, foundations, and corporations wanted to help the men and women in uniform, but they had neither understanding of the needs nor a clear vision of how they could provide meaningful assistance.

Dr. Van Dahlen began to imagine a comprehensive and integrated system of care for service personnel and their families. She entered into conversations with colleagues in the nonprofit and VSO worlds as well as individuals at DoD, VA, and the White House. In December 2007 she was invited to submit a white paper to President Obama's Transition Team on Veterans Affairs, which gave her a chance to write about the importance of coordinating care across agencies and organizations and of community-based resources. In May 2008 she was invited to testify before the House Committee on Veterans Affairs, where she spoke about an emerging public health crisis and addressed the need for a comprehensive and integrated system of care that utilized community-based resources. Others were also expressing the need to address this issue. The chairman of the Joint Chiefs of Staff, Admiral Mike Mullen, began speaking about the "Sea of Goodwill" that exists across the United States and the need for collaboration among organizations providing care.

In January 2010 Dr. Van Dahlen attended a gathering called "America Joins Forces with Military Families," in White Oak, Florida. At this event, a group representing fifty-five nonprofit organizations; veterans and military family service organizations; government agencies; faith-based groups; and senior VA, Department of Labor (DOL), and DoD offices came together to discuss the challenges facing America's military families. She was encouraged to present the idea of a guide for community leaders—a tool to assist them in their efforts to coordinate care for the military community. The support for the concept was overwhelming, and the organizers of the event adopted the idea as the main initiative to come out of the White Oak gathering. Leaders from four nonprofit organizations—the American Red Cross, Service Nation, America's Promise Alliance, and the Veterans Innovation Center—stepped up and offered to help make the concept a reality.

The Community Blueprint Initiative, as it is now called, has received support from numerous organizations, including the American Legion Auxiliary, American Psychiatric Association, American Red Cross, America's Promise Alliance, Blue Star Families, Boys and Girls Clubs of America, Cause and Effect, GAH, HandsOn Network, Lions Clubs International, Military Child Education Coalition, Military Officer Association of America, Mission Serve, NASW, National Military Family Association, Student Veterans of America, The Mission Continues, Veterans Innovation Center, United Way, USO, and Warrior Gateway. The White House has hosted meetings to support the initiative and is following its progress closely. If it is successful, the Community Blueprint will mark the beginning of a new era of support for those who serve and their families. The following is from a document summarizing the goals and philosophy of this initiative:

- There is universal support for our warriors and families, and nonprofit services have grown and improved in communities across America. Still, there remain significant gaps that can only be filled by more focused planning and coordination.

  - Supporting veterans, warriors, and families is about ensuring that communities are prepared to provide the services and supports that help military families lead healthy, successful lives.

  - Many solutions can only be handled by communities, but too often communities lack a full understanding of the services that help veterans, warriors, and their families.

  - Additional support is needed in many areas, including behavioral health, physical health, education, employment, financial/legal problems, homelessness, and more.

- To address these gaps, volunteers from several leading nonprofits are creating an online Community Blueprint that will help local leaders assess and improve their community's support for military families.

  - Our vision is to create a blueprint that will allow each community to assess and fulfill its role in supporting those who have borne the price of battle—service members, veterans, and military families.

- The blueprint will help community leaders and citizens understand exactly how they can contribute to an improved support matrix for local veterans and their families, to include providing opportunities for civilians, service members, veterans, and their families to volunteer and serve alongside each other.

- The blueprint will provide community leaders with information about the primary challenges veterans and military families face upon returning home.

- The blueprint will offer advice based on best practices and experience about setting priorities, adopting strategies that work, and building coalitions to implement those strategies.

In the summer of 2010, the Bristol Myers-Squibb Foundation (BMSF) became interested in supporting GAH and its efforts to provide critical mental healthcare to those who serve and their families. They were particularly interested in supporting GAH's work on the Community Blueprint. After several meetings in an amazingly short period of time, BMSF invited GAH to apply for a large two-year grant that would allow GAH to implement the Blueprint in two demonstration sites. The concept was quite simple: Give an Hour™ would be given funding to lead a team into two communities to engage stakeholders (community leaders, military and VA personnel, military families, nonprofit organizations, VSOs, and business leaders), introduce the Blueprint, identify and address obstacles that interfere with coordination and effective care, and evaluate the process over the two years of the grant. By engaging those in need and those with an interest in providing services, the project provided a rare opportunity to create a model of change that could be replicated across the country in communities looking to support our military community.

There was tremendous excitement—on the part of the Blueprint partners and friends in DoD, VA, and the Obama administration—and a flurry of activity associated with the development of this proposal. BMSF has funded extraordinary efforts in the past—in the United States and Africa—to assist communities as they struggle to respond to social issues. If funded, this project would provide a tremendous opportunity. The Community Blueprint would be used to marshal existing resources—initially in two communities and ultimately nationwide—to improve care for those who serve and their families. In addition, this effort could help to narrow the gap that has existed for decades between the military and civilian communities. The two communities might better learn to communicate with each other, understand each other, and appreciate each other—to the benefit of both. Along the way, the stigma associated with seeking and receiving mental health care would diminish and understanding of the impact of trauma and traumatic brain injuries would increase dramatically.

On October 29, 2010, GAH was awarded a $2 million, two-year grant to implement the Community Blueprint in two communities, Norfolk, Virginia, and Fayetteville, North Carolina. Work began immediately to coordinate the announcement of this historic opportunity with the official launch of the Community Blueprint as well as complementary efforts by the chairman of the Joint Chief's office and the White House. The actual work in the two demonstration sites began in earnest in early 2011.

Time Magazine's 100

One of the more surprising unintended consequences of Dr. Van Dahlen's work was her selection in April 2012 as one of *Time* magazine's 100 Most Influential People in the World. Dr. Van Dahlen sees this incredible honor as an amazing gift that will allow Give an Hour™ to do even more great work to assist those who serve and their families. In addition, her selection by *Time* for this recognition reflects a growing interest in and support for the philosophy that remains at the heart of Give an Hour™'s efforts and success—that the only way our society can truly care for our returning service members, our veterans, and their families is by harnessing the resources of all of our citizens. We must collaborate more frequently and coordinate more effectively if we are to prevent those who have given so much from suffering when they come home.

Future Directions

In GAH Dr. Van Dahlen has created an organization that allows civilian mental health professionals to provide critical care to returning troops, their families, and their communities. As the organization grows, it will find new and innovative ways to provide this assistance. For example, GAH is currently exploring telehealth strategies as another form of service delivery. With this technology, those who are unable to meet with a counselor in his or her office can use a Web camera to "meet" with the counselor. Similarly, virtual technologies are demonstrating promise in the area of treating post-traumatic stress, especially when used in conjunction with traditional care offered by a trained mental health professional.

When it comes to treatment for mental health conditions, we know that one size does not fit all. Clearly this is true when developing options for the men, women, and families who serve. We must develop a variety of options for individuals and their loved ones if we are to create a comprehensive system of care that effectively supports our military community. For example, yoga has been found to be very effective for treating some of the symptoms of post-traumatic stress; many veterans of war report it is the only way that they are able to establish an internal experience of quiet and calm. Similarly, acupuncture is hailed as one of the only effective forms of treatment for chronic muscle and joint pain—a frequent complaint of returning troops.

Further research is needed to help us understand how best to prepare our military community for the strain and psychological injury they may experience. By determining how to better prepare military personnel and their families for the challenges they will face as a result of their service, we will save resources, time, money and, most important, lives.

Additional investigation is also needed to better understand those factors that help to identify individuals at risk for the development of mental health concerns. Though we do have broad-brush ideas about this area of inquiry—we know that the more often someone deploys to a combat zone, the more likely he or she is to develop significant mental health difficulties—we must continue to refine our knowledge base so that those who serve are armed with knowledge and information they will need to protect themselves from the potentially devastating consequences of war.

As GAH continues work on the BMSF grant to implement the Community Blueprint in Fayetteville and Norfolk, it is endeavoring to develop a model for assisting communities in their efforts to effectively coordinate care for those who serve and their families. For the first time, tremendous energy is being poured into a focused effort to harness available resources, first in two communities and then in all of the communities across our nation that choose to support our military families. The Community Blueprint initiative will provide fertile ground for evaluation and will allow partnerships with individuals and organizations that have expertise in this critical arena. Give an Hour™ will learn valuable information and share much with the broader community, as it joins forces with its partners in the military and nonprofit communities in the service of caring for our armed forces.

As GAH grows, it will also continue to learn how best to support those who are volunteering to provide their services to the military community. Information gathered from GAH providers will inform further organizational developments and initiatives. The organization also expects to continue to develop and expand its relationships with DoD and VA, perhaps collaborating on training and initiatives like the Community Blueprint.

Give an Hour™ is one of a handful of efforts that harness the skills and generosity of professionals to help solve some of society's most difficult problems. As it grows and evolves, Dr. Van Dahlen expects to apply its model to other populations of professionals and to other acute and chronic conditions that affect the world.

Note: This history of the nonprofit Give an Hour™ was written by the founder in the third person to follow scientific conventions.

References

Hoge, C. W., Castro, C. A., Messer, S. C., et al. (2004). Combat duty in Iraq and Afghanistan, mental health problems, and barriers to care. *New England Journal of Medicine* 351: 13–22.

Hoge, C. W., Auchterlonie, J. L. & Milliken, C. S. (2006). Mental health problems, use of mental health services, and attrition from military service after returning from deployment to Iraq or Afghanistan. *JAMA* 295: 1023–1032.

Rand Corporation. (2008). Invisible wounds of war: Psychological and cognitive injuries, their consequences, and services to assist recovery. Edited by T. Tanielian & L. H. Jaycox. Santa Monica, CA: RAND Corporation, 2008. http://www.rand.org/pubs/monographs/MG720.

Reno, J. (2009). "PTSD: New war on an old foe." *Newsweek*, September 30. http://www.thedailybeast.com/newsweek/2009/09/30/ptsd-new-war-on-an-old-foe.html.

The Veterans' Healthcare System's Path to Excellence

Edmund J. Nightingale

Introduction

The U.S. Department of Veterans Affairs healthcare system has been recognized many times as the premier example of successful integrated healthcare delivery. It was not always so. Subject to the vagaries of congressional funding, pounded by the twin needs of an aging veterans' population and increased demand for acute care services by younger veterans, the balkanized system of quasi-independent fiefdoms long struggled to operate with limited resources. Individual hospitals and clinics competed with one another for resources from the VA Central Office and from congressional patrons eager to earmark dollars for the local facility, currying favor with veterans in their constituencies.

The eventual confluence of three major processes over a score of years, having originated independently of one another, together transformed the old Department of Medicine and Surgery (DM&S) into the modern Veterans Health Administration (VHA) that we know today.

The first of these elements was the transformation of how healthcare data were conceived and managed, moving from a centralized batch processing system focused on the creation of clinical and financial statistics to a patient-centered, decentralized, hospital-based program, which came to be known as the Decentralized Hospital Computing Program (DHCP). The DHCP evolved over time to become the national clinical information system now known as the Computerized Patient Record System (CPRS), the flagship component of the Veterans Information System & Technology Architecture

(VistA) introduced in 1996. VistA also hosts the Decision Support System (DSS) and other VHA databases.

The second element was the development over time of successive approximations to what is today arguably the best medical econometric model for distribution of medical care resources in a semiclosed, prospectively funded revenue system.

The third element was the visionary leadership of the VA healthcare system. General George C. Marshall had created the partnership of VA hospitals and medical schools to improve care and ensure that the post–World War II expansion of facilities would be driven by the most advanced medical science. A second visionary era occurred under Dr. Kenneth Kizer's incumbency as Under Secretary for Health. Like General Marshall, Dr. Kizer came to VA at a time of crisis and had the wisdom to surround himself with talented people. Kizer also had the advantage of bringing his vision to VA at a time when creative, sometimes maverick, elements of the VA bureaucracy were developing the tools necessary to make that vision a reality. Ironically, they were iconic examples of what would later become known as the "new VA."

Part I: From Data Management to a Computerized Patient Record System (CPRS) and Decision Support System (DSS)

AMIS: The Early Automated VA Medical Information System

Until the early 1980s, the infrastructure for data management in VA hospitals and clinics was overseen by the Office of Data Management and Telecommunications (ODM&T). The very name is evocative of a system in which data would be entered in remote terminals connected to a central switchboard or computer center: "It was necessitated by the high cost of computer equipment, the scarcity of trained personnel, and the need for expensive space. The model was complicated in the VA by the very long chain of command up through the Department of Medicine and Surgery and back down to the ODM&T which served other departments as well" (Nesbitt 2010).[1]

In that era there were generally no computers permitted in the healthcare facilities unless they were authorized to support research data collection and analysis or were processors built into medical devices. Authorized exceptions were extremely difficult to obtain from Central Office. Even requests for PCs in the field, supported by clinical management centers in Central Office, had to obtain approval from the Office of Data Management and Telecommunications. For some two decades there had been high-level controversy about whether the future of clinical computing in VA health facilities would lie in a central system with several large data centers sited around the country or should be hospital-based. The dispute was more than an intellectual exercise because of its local impact:

> The issue comes down to propinquity.... [I]n my opinion, a multitude of healthcare information systems have failed because neither the complexity nor the need to resolve the complexities near their source were recognized.... With decentralization you gain local control of the resource and its costs, perhaps some autonomy and the ability to adapt the resource to local needs. With a centralized system you gain the ability to maintain consistency across facilities, the ability to more easily share the data across facilities, and (perhaps) reduced costs. (Nesbitt 2010)

A second issue involved the underlying architecture that the centralized office chose for VA's data management. In that system the data were arrayed hierarchically, with all data points predefined and subsumed within ever-narrowing higher level categories, such that the data could be summarized and analyzed in predefined "buckets." This architecture made the process of updating or modifying the data points rather laborious. Hence requests for changes always had to be "justified" at a number of levels in the DM&S before being forwarded to a less than welcoming Office of Data Management and Telecommunications, serving not only DM&S, but also the Department of Veterans Benefits (DVB) and the National Cemetery System, now known as the VA's National Cemetery Administration.

At that time, the DM&S was seen primarily as a hospital system, rather than a healthcare system. For the most part, outpatient care was seen as adjunctive follow-up to hospitalization. The Medical Administration Service at each facility had responsibility for keeping track of the numbers and kinds of admissions and discharges. Over time, paper admissions and discharges were created to enable outpatient care that might avoid a hospitalization. These transactions were the primary targets of the AMIS (Automated Medical Information System). This paper trail of admissions and discharges, along with census counts and tallies of bed days of care, formed the basis for determining local and national workload, part of the formula for determining future funding.

Medical Administration also coordinated counting the instances of care denominated by the preset descriptors provided by and for each clinical and administrative department, or "service" as they were known in VA's organizational structure. These figures were used by the clinical "services" or management centers in Central Office to keep track of trends and to make a case for their portion of the VA healthcare budget. For example, in mental health, episodes of individual, group, family psychotherapy, and psychological testing would be reported; in dentistry, routine examinations or amalgams or extractions of various types would be collected through paper and pencil reports authored by individual clinicians. The reports were filled out and filed retrospectively, then transferred to punch cards later transmitted to the central VA data processing center at Austin, Texas (DPC).[2] The Austin center, dating to 1967, primarily serviced the DVB insurance, compensation and pension, home loan, and veterans' education financing. However, its large mainframe computers serviced the DM&S as well. Eventually the tallied reports from individual facilities were returned in the form of computer printouts of data, aggregated by facility and by service information sources.

These results were pored over by national and facility "management analysts," who looked for deviations from national averages or changes in these internal reports quarter after quarter. The analysts in turn asked local clinical managers and department leaders to "justify" (explain or defend) any deviations upward or downward. Inpatient workload was measured in terms of admissions, discharges, bed occupancy rates, and turnover rates. Outpatient workload, with the exception of the "specialized programs," which had their own funding stream or target allowance, was measured rather crudely by the number of "visits." A single visit was defined as one or more patient care contacts at a single facility during a single day. Hence a veteran patient might see the ophthalmologist for an eye refraction, the podiatrist for treatment of plantar flexion, and the dentist for an extraction on the same day and be counted once in the Medical Administration tally, as one "visit" for workload purposes, even though the various clinical services logged much more work for that day. New congressionally funded (earmarked) clinical programs, then called "specially funded programs" (e.g., drug dependency treatment, cardiac catheterization, Special Diagnostic Treatment Units, etc.), also reported their workload and expenses to the same system. For these specialized programs, funding came in the form of a special "target allowance," which projected expected workload and funding for the associated full-time employee equivalents for the coming year.

The Decentralized Hospital Computing Program: VA's First Integrated Clinical Information System

I am indebted to George Timson's *History of the Hard Hats* (2009) and to Martin Johnson's recollections (1981), as well as to those of Rick Nesbitt (2010) for this history of the foundations and early development of the DHCP system, upon which this section has liberally drawn. As early as 1977, the winds of change began to blow when clinicians in the then Veterans Administration hospitals worked on clinical applications to provide more efficient care and record keeping. That same year Joseph (Ted) O'Neill worked with the National Bureau of Standards to have the MUMPS (**M**assachusetts **G**eneral **H**ospital **U**tility **M**ulti-**P**rogramming **S**ystem) certified as meeting the ANSI standards, rendering ANSI MUMPS available in a standardized manner as a high-level language and operating system. Previously the "Mass General" language had existed in several "dialects" and as such would have been difficult to orchestrate for use in a large decentralized system. O'Neill and Johnson soon became the core of a small DM&S unit called the Computer Adapted Systems Staff (CASS). They subsequently located others out in the field who were also working on programming clinical systems, people such as "Gordon Moreshead and Wally Fort at Salt Lake, developing a clinical psychology data system" (Timson 2009). They found Bob Luschene in St. Petersburg, Florida (Bay Pines VA), running patients through batteries of online psychodiagnostic tests; Richard Davis at the Lexington, Kentucky VA, writing a nutrient analysis program for treatment of diabetics; and Joe Tatarczuk in Albany, computerizing nuclear medicine. These folks and others were the first targets for proselytization by O'Neill and Johnson, and each in time became a convert to the use of the Massachusetts General programming language. A growing number of programmers and clinicians from different disciplines, working on clinical routines in other languages, were soon converted to MUMPS by the joint efforts of CASS and George Timson. The Massachusetts General programming language (now known as "M") used a data architecture known as an "inverted file" system, in which core data elements had "pointers" to other elements so they could be associated with one another without being limited to the point in time when the database was originally conceived and implemented. For example, added information categories could be linked with basic building blocks like a patient's social security number. Reports could be generated from as many points of view as there were elements to associate with one another. Data could be entered in real time and summarized instantly because the online database was updated as new information was entered. Given the limited capacity of the early computers out in the field, systems slowed considerably unless the reports were generated at night, when the demand for computer processing time for clinical activities was minimized. Data were backed up locally on a daily basis, allowing for security of data and simple restoration in case of system corruption or breakdown. In practice, data summary reports would be produced overnight locally without using the Austin center, yet could be and were transmitted to Austin at the end of the month, responding to the information needs of Central Office. The Massachusetts General system was friendly to other operating systems and languages, able to accept their data and incorporate them into its own datasets, making it possible to import information from medical devices into the database easily.

The chosen language and associated operating system ran initially on Digital Equipment Corporation computers. Fortuitously, a number of these machines were available at select locations in the field, in support of research projects or as a result of placement through a strategic purchase (by CASS in late 1978). Hence they could be found at Albany, Bay Pines, Bronx, Loma Linda, Oklahoma City, Palo Alto, Salt Lake City, Seattle, Tucson, Washington, D.C., and many other sites (Johnson 1981). At Bay Pines and Salt Lake City, psychologists were initially interested in developing a system for computerized administration and scoring of psychological tests and interview instruments, along with a means of tracking patient care. A group of pathologists at Albany were intrigued by the possibilities of a nuclear medicine package. They later produced a laboratory package pulling together the data from many different tests into a single report. In Tucson, pharmacists were developing a more accessible system for clinicians to process prescriptions; furnish summary information to providers; and track single patient drug records for poly pharmacy, reactions, allergies, etc. Many of these clinicians either schooled themselves in the Massachusetts General system or found sympathetic research programmers to help them develop "packages" that would respond to their needs. Eventually through various encounters, especially at the annual MUMPS conferences, people working independently began to share information and agree on some basic rules of the road. George Timson, from the San Francisco VAMC, wrote the first "Kernel," the central interface that allowed the new VA system to "nest" in any of several MUMPS hardware or software implementations. Timson, along with David Wilson at the Tulsa VAMC, with input from many others, developed "FileMan" (abbreviation for file manager), which set the parameters for internal software pathways:

> This utility created consistent mechanisms for defining new pieces of data (adding to the data dictionary) and for manipulating data that was defined by the dictionary (for example, report writing). FileMan is a data base management system which imposes an easily understood data structure over the more complex and less easily understood MUMPS data structure. Its great advantage was that it allowed programmers working in disparate locations and on disparate applications to be consistent, using existing data elements and creating new ones as needed. (Nesbitt 2010)

The efforts of this larger group coalesced into a network of highly talented and passionate software engineers who became known as the "hard hats." They drove the developmental work in consultation with their clinician colleagues. Some of the "hard hats" were clinicians as well (Robert Luschene, Marina Bates, Richard Davis, and others). Their efforts did not go unnoticed.

When Office of Data Management and Telecommunications officials discovered what was going on out in the field, they viewed CASS as an unauthorized rival within the VA system and moved swiftly to have the unit dismantled (Timson 2009).

The next three years were characterized by what Timson labeled "a conspiracy." Ironically, the dispersal of the DM&S's computer staff, and the fact that many of the original developers were already in diaspora, enabled a covert effort to continue the work: "In Salt Lake, a comprehensive Clinical Lab System was brought into being, in Palo Alto, a Clinic Scheduling System. Pharmacy record-keeping was built in no fewer than four separate sites: Salt Lake, Fresno, Washington, and finally Birmingham, with each analyst or group of analysts sharing and passing on his work to the others" (Timson 2009).

Although computers were generally proscribed in the medical centers, "word processors" were permitted, so the conspirators equipped themselves with computers bought as "word processors." Of course these lacked tape drives and vastly complicated the covert work of task sharing among the hard hats.

In spite of efforts to squelch the new developments (including an order from Chief Medical Director Dr. Donald Custis to turn off these rogue computers), the demand for these useful, nascent systems persisted. The physicians at the Washington, D.C., VAMC were said to have "rebelled" at this Central Office directive. Dr. Custis decided to respond to these pressures with a trip across town to the recalcitrant medical center. When he arrived he found a system of coherent clinical "packages." Some had been developed there, others at dispersed sites across the country. He was later quoted as having remarked "it sounds like an 'underground railway' has been at work—and doing good work" (Timson 2009).

In the fall of 1981 the Symposium on Computer Applications in Medical Care was pivotal. Dr. Custis attended a demonstration of an integrated system with components brought in from all over the country by a number of these "renegade" clinicians who had brought mini-computers to the Washington conference. They had also arranged a demonstration for members of the House and Senate Veterans Affairs Committees to view their handiwork. The solons were quite impressed and decided to hold hearings on the issue. Dr. Custis soon rescinded his order barring the use of DM&S computers for the purpose of software development in the hospitals.

Against this backdrop of the underground railway, it is of note that the Office of Data Management and Telecommunications had actually begun work on a clinical laboratory system in 1968. By 1982 it had been implemented at only eight VA medical centers. The Office produced a paper in 1980 delineating a transactional Patient Treatment File and promised a future product by 1990. When a batch pharmacy program could not meet the workload demands at the Minneapolis VA facility, Central Office approved implementation there of a program known as **Automated Pharmacy Profiling and LabEling System** (APPLES), developed elsewhere in VA (Nesbitt 2010). Over a six-year period ten sites had been put online as a trial. Five of these sites were in the Chicago VA Medical Centers (Brown et al. 2003). APPLES was intended to unify pharmacy record keeping, print prescription labels, and allow the pharmacist to be aware of other drugs prescribed for individual patients. It was also capable of keeping track of inventory. It was too little, too late, and ultimately could not compete with what had been developed by the hard hats.

In early 1982 the new administrator for Veterans Affairs, Robert P. Nimmo, issued a directive authorizing what was then to be called the Decentralized Hospital Computing System (DHCP). In a relatively brief period of time, the reach of the Office of Data Management and Telecommunications was altered. Computer programmers and data management personnel were added slowly by local VA healthcare facilities, too slowly in some instances, creating implementation problems. Special interest user groups (SIUGs) were created for the various clinical disciplines and eventually for administrative departments as well. Information Service Centers (ISCs) were created in strategic locations across the country and empowered to serve as resources for software development to the medical centers.

In 1985 an initial rollout of $65 million worth of computers was provided to 169 hospitals to support the packages initially authorized and "validated." Congress also required that VA test commercially available systems in the three remaining facilities. Eventually the costs at those three test facilities required 20 percent of VA's information technology budget (Brown et al. 2003). For comparison purposes, the Department of Defense (DoD) spent over $200 million in 1987 on a contract to "study the feasibility" of providing a medical information system for the three hospital systems of that department. This author was told that George Timson was later hired by that corporation to develop TRIMIS (the Tri-military Medical Information System) for the hospitals of the army, navy, and air force. Elements of that system came from the public domain, VA-developed "packages" (Gottfredsen 1990; Kolodner 1997). Not surprising! For other accounts of these early developmental years, read Martin E. Johnson's memo to Dr. Kenneth J. Dickie at the Washington, D.C., VAMC (Johnson 1981), and Robert Kolodner's chapter, "Creating a Robust Multi-facility Healthcare Information System" (Kolodner 1997), in the book he co-edited with Judith Douglas, *Computerizing Large Integrated Health Networks: The VA Success* (Kolodner & Douglas 1997). Martin Johnson's memo is unique in that it provides not only a brief history of the developmental years

(1976–1981) but also lays out a prescient national programmatic path for VA to follow.

Over time a completely integrated medical information system was developed, embracing everything from patient scheduling, to medical record generation, to workload collection based on real-time, clinician-entered information for an episode of care. Due to fiscal considerations ("dumb" terminals were less expensive than "smart" units), the original DHCP had a "roll and scroll" presentation of data and information. As such it required backing out of one package to access information in another. Each clinical package had its own output, which was originally intended to be printed out and simply placed in the corresponding section of the existing paper clinical chart. There was not yet a fully integrated clinical record.

Different classes of software existed, with some approved for use and maintained nationally, and others developed, implemented, and maintained by field facilities. Some of this latter, "class three" software was later validated for use nationwide and became a part of the overall "package," while other routines remained local and were made available to other facilities if they desired to use them. Though this entrepreneurial spirit continued to produce great "products," it also created problems later when the Veterans Integrated Service Networks (VISNs) were introduced. The new "networks" found that the data routines used by the various facilities were diverse enough to make regionalized integration of some databases problematic. Up to now this had not been an issue, because the information required by Central Office was still maintained separately in the old AMIS. The DHCP was quite capable of "talking" to that system and of providing information extracted from local activity records. The new networks were interested in seeing the development of real-time management information systems, similar to the real-time clinical information systems that existed in the DHCP.

From the DHCP to the CPRS

In 1994 VA migrated its DHCP system to VistA and rolled out the graphic user interface, the CPRS, in 1997. The new patient record system provided a much improved interface for the end-user. The "Order Entry Results Reporting" utility allowed access to any of the different "packages" from a single point of entry and pulled together the information from the different packages for reporting and charting purposes. It sported graphics with the look and feel of the traditional paper record, with tabs that could be selected and pop-ups that could display changes in vital signs and lab results over periods of time selected by the clinician user, all in a single, integrated view. Later improvements made it possible to integrate radiologic, sonographic, MRI, and EKG images as well as independent documents and reports (from external providers or signed patient consents) into the system. These images could be tied to the patient record notes for a visit and be instantly available to the clinician in the patient care chart. The system has clinical reminders for tests or procedures needing to be done for a particular patient. Alerts are provided for allergies, potential drug interactions, and other patient-relevant information. A barcode system is built into the pharmacy package so that a social security number affixed to the prescription ordered by the physician, in the CPRS system, may be matched with the code on a wristband or other VA patient ID so as to avoid medication errors and other problems related to patient misidentification. These barcodes on patient wristbands are used to double-check patient identity in numerous clinical venues, even the operating room:

> Presently VistA [Veterans Information System & Technology Architecture] is composed of 99 packages. . . . Of these, there are 16 infrastructure applications, 28 administrative and financial applications, and 55 clinical applications. VistA applications perform functions in common with other HIS's [health information systems] such as laboratory, pharmacy, radiology, ADT, and scheduling. VistA functions less commonly found in other HIS's [health information systems] include police and security, library, and missing patient registry applications. These applications are built upon a common database using common tools and techniques. . . . The reader is referred to the VA website (www.va.gov/vista) for [complete] application descriptions, user and programmer manuals, and the software source code. (Brown et al. 2003, 7)

The system is very comprehensive and is available as public domain open source material for other governmental and nongovernmental institutions to use. It has been the basis of the DoD and Indian Health System (IHS) medical information systems in the federal sector. As of 2003 it was known to have been in use at twenty-seven institutions across the globe, circulated as public domain software (Brown et al. 2003). It had been adapted for use in Colombia, Iceland, Germany, Nigeria, and Uganda, to name only a few of these foreign sites:

> In 1995, the Veterans Administration's patient Admission/Tracking/Discharge system, Decentralized Hospital Computer Program (DHCP) was the recipient of the Computerworld Smithsonian Award for best use of Information Technology in Medicine. A decade later (July, 2006), the Department of Veterans Affairs (VA)/Veterans Health Administration (VHA) was the recipient of the Innovations in American Government Award presented by the Ash Institute of the John F. Kennedy School of Government at Harvard University for

its extension of DHCP into the Veterans Health Information Systems and Technology Architecture (VistA) in July, 2006. (Wikipedia 2009b)

The most recent VA patient informatics initiative is "My HealtheVet," a Web-based interface with the patient record system. Patients may now access key portions of their own medical records from home, have access to current literature on their own conditions and recommended care, and even enter data collected at home to assist physicians monitoring their care. The details of this program are beyond the scope of this chapter. Readers wishing to pursue an overview may wish to consult Dr. Robert M. Kolodner's testimony before a congressional committee (Kolodner 2005).

During the first decade of the current millennium a new VA CIO began the process of recentralizing VA's automated system, moving toward an enterprise system, much like that favored by the old Office of Data and Telecommunications, with software development conceived, developed, and implemented centrally. "VA's future infrastructure will focus upon Integrated Network Services and Regional Data Processing with integrated, standardized COOP capabilities, in the future" (Department of Veterans Affairs. Office of Information Technology 2009). Programmers and technical personnel at local sites no longer report locally, but rather centrally through their own chain of command. Only time will tell if the system remains as creative and responsive to frontline clinical experience and needs as it did in the era of DHCP, SIUGs, and third-class software. The history of its forerunner, the Office of Data Management and Telecommunications, may not augur well for this kind of arrangement. Lessons learned from the past can ensure that VistA remains the premier healthcare informatics system.

Cost Distribution Report (CDR) to Decision Support System (DSS): Static Accounting to Dynamic Decision Support

The financial management and accounting offices of the DM&S facilities were called "Fiscal Services." The fiscal offices of the facilities transmitted financial data collected from the various clinical and administrative departments. Each department estimated the percentage of staff effort expended by its personnel in support of inpatient programs (medicine, surgery, psychiatry, rehabilitation medicine, etc.) and of its outpatient components. This report was known as the Records Control System (RCS) 14-4 Cost Distribution Report, or CDR. This tool was also a retrospectively collected data source, with the clinician managers asking their clinical and technical staff for a quarterly estimate of the percent of their time spent on inpatient services versus outpatient services.

Though the CDR's categories were well-defined, like those in AMIS, they were wooden, constrained by the requirements of a predefined hierarchical database written in a computer language that was becoming increasingly obsolete. The CDR was able to incorporate data from other administrative data sources such as the PAID (Personnel and Accounting Integrated Data) report, which also tracked time and attendance for the Personnel Service (now Human Resources), and COINS (Customer Online Information Network), which tracked payments to outside vendors at the behest of the Supply Service (now Acquisition & Material Management Service). The resulting report would array these figures against the Medical Administration Service's workload reports and provide "costs" for these services: for bed days of care in each of the facility bed sections and for outpatient "visits" in departmental clinics.

The RCS 14-4 gave clinician managers in various departments the putative costing of their services provided as inpatient days of care in the "bed sections" and as outpatient visits in clinic venues. These figures were based on their own estimates of the percent of time devoted by their administrative and clinical assets to inpatient and outpatient work. The methodology was crude at best and subject to intended or unintended error by department heads. In some cases department heads did not bother to input their own figures into the system, and functionaries in the fiscal service simply assigned values they thought reasonable. Many clinical service chiefs paid little attention to the quarterly output unless there were questions from the management analysts about why they appeared to deviate so much from the national average or historical precedent.

The AMIS and the CDR shared weaknesses: (1) data were gathered retrospectively rather than in real time; (2) data entry personnel depended on paper and pencil reports of past activities based on clinician memories and/or clinician manager "guestimates" rather than being event-driven; (3) the data points sought by Medical Administration and Fiscal were increasingly irrelevant to the manner in which services were being delivered (note the example of the counting of a "visit" and the oddity that the statistic, "patients treated," referred only to inpatient discharges, ignoring the fact that the vast majority of patient care services were moving to an outpatient basis); (4) there was a disconnect between the clinical event data gathered on most types of patient contacts and the cost accounting system's inability to distribute costs to these discrete clinical activities; and finally, (5) information gathered was lumped together in such a manner that it was not possible to determine the true cost of an episode of care or of any single patient care contact. However, the CDR did allow for capture of resources devoted to research and teaching, as distinct from direct patient care, but required that it be attributed as an adjunct to either inpatient or outpatient care, an increasingly awkward task. It also allowed for the tracking of time allocated to examinations requested by Veterans Benefits Administration to service its compensation and pension programs. Clearly managing resources in a modern healthcare system required something better, an event-driven system, one in which the inputs were tied to the clinical information system, itself driven by episodes of patient care.

In the decade of the 1980s, consensus conferences were held by the Health Services Research & Development Office and by Central Office's Medical Administration Service in collaboration with the Boston Development Center (now the Allocation Resource Center) and the Resource Management Office in Central Office. The major thrust of a 1985 meeting sponsored by the Health Services Research & Development Office was the development of decision support systems: systems for the collection and utilization of patient care data in support of clinical decision making. A 1987 conference was primarily focused on the development and implementation of Resource Allocation Methodology (RAM), but also provided an opportunity for reports on two pilot management information systems projects (described later in this section). In an era of tight budgets and keen competition for resources, there were serious concerns over how costs of care were determined through the use of the CDR and its resultant products. Efforts were underway to try to understand hospital costs by the nature of the facility (metropolitan, urban, rural neuropsychiatric, university affiliated, unaffiliated, tertiary care, and higher versus lower levels of complexity). The CDR system, which initially compared bed day of care costs to a national average, had to be modified to compare to "like facilities" as well. Even then, the patient care services provided at each facility might have a different "case-mix." These complexities were poorly reflected by the existing system. It was time to implement a more sophisticated clinical accounting process.

In the mid- to late 1980s two VA pilot projects were run. The first was sited in two locations: the Edward J. Hines Hospital, outside of Maywood, Illinois, and the Boston VA Medical Center. The second was sited at White River Junction, Vermont.

The Decentralized Medical Management System dual pilot at the Hines VA Hospital was overseen by John R. Fears, the medical center director, and the work at Boston by its director, Barbara Small (Fears & Small 1985a).

The Decentralized Medical Management System effort was reminiscent of so much of innovative VA software development at the time. It was a program developed collaboratively in the field by the Hines Verification and Development Center and the Boston Development Center, with input from clinician panels and administrators alike. The resulting product could incorporate financial data with information from other VA information systems, including that collected by the various modules or packages in the contemporary

DHCP. One of its major strengths was the ability to characterize different groupings of inpatients within each DRG, the major driver of the RAM described in the next main section of this chapter. In that era, the main factor explaining facility costs was inpatient care and the associated DRG case-mix. The summation of the frequency and weights of these DRGs and their associated values was used to calculate prospective payment to the VA facilities. Fears and Small reported that where their system was being piloted, "the process of defining patterns of care has helped physicians to demonstrate what resources are needed to provide quality care … producing important information for developing department budgets … [and monitoring] the performance of resident physicians" (1985b):

> DMMS [Decentralized Medical Management System] also provided managers and clinicians with information to make decisions regarding quality assurance, utilization review, budgeting, performance assessment, planning and staff recruitment … [and provided] comparison data to aid in setting performance criteria, the analysis of variance by case mix groups, special reports to highlight problem areas, and up to three years of historical information for trend analysis. (Fears & Small 1985a)

The second pilot project, at White River Junction VA Medical Center, affiliated with Dartmouth in Vermont, was directed by Dr. Howard Green, the chief of staff, and his wife, Dr. Elisabeth McSherry, both well-known figures in VA (Green & McSherry 1985). Drs. Green and McSherry approached the task from the point of view of a management control system, much like that which might be found in any industrial plant, producing intermediate products from raw materials and end products through combining intermediate products. In this view, the costs of labor and materials of various kinds could be assigned to each of the intermediate products produced (e.g., lab and X-ray findings) as well as to final products (e.g., a surgical procedure or treated myocardial infarction):

> In a job order costing system, input costs are determined and tallied for all aspects of the end product production. The final cost of the product (in this case, the patient encounter or DRG) equals the sum of the *direct costs* (those costs directly attributable to the production of product, including labor, supplies, specific capital equipment, and such direct overhead as supervisors and space) of all of the inputs plus the *indirect costs* (those costs not directly attributable to the production of the product including building management, administrative, engineering, fiscal, and supply departments). (Green & McSherry 1985, 49)

As with Fears and Small's DMMS, Green and McSherry viewed the method they were testing as a powerful management tool for tracking and eliminating undue cost variances. Exact measures of productivity and of capacity would assist managers in intelligently planning for expansion of capacity, finding and utilizing the margins in the production process.

Officials at VA selected the White River Junction option, dubbed "Decision Support System" or DSS. It was an adaptation of an "off-the-shelf" product used in the private sector (Department of Veterans Affairs. Information Resource Center 2009), later rumored to have had an expected purchase cost of $9 million. A contract was signed with the vendor to commence work in 1991. Over the course of the next eight years the original contract purchase price ballooned to over $24 million. The increase was reportedly due to the cost of modifications needed to tailor the product to the changing requirements of the Veterans Health Administration (VHA). Another estimated $175 million in VHA staff costs were incurred in the process of implementation, maintenance, and development (Green 2000). As may be inferred from the soaring costs and from the tenor of Dr. Green's testimony, the development and implementation of the DSS was not a straight-line course. In the field it seemed as though it was many years before any data usable on the local level were available (this author's personal recollection). Unlike the old CDR, which pulled from other batched databases such as the Patient Treatment File, the Out Patient File, Personnel and Accounting Integrated Data (PAID), and Customer Online Information Network (COINS), already in Austin at the Data Center, the DSS required taking that same data; loading it into servers dedicated to the DSS task; and reassigning those costs to clinics, bed sections, and individual clinicians. During the ever-increasing developmental period, national and facility reports for the DSS and CDR often arrived at different figures for the dollars spent at medical centers. In Dr. Green's later testimony in support of the DSS initiative before a congressional committee, he bitterly complained about his critics and questioned their motives, providing clues to some of those difficulties (Green 2000). However, in fairness to Dr. Green's detractors, the DSS did have its own peculiar problems and questionable assumptions, about which more will be discussed later in this section.

The Decision Support System was intended to cost episodes of care accurately, be they hospital episodes or outpatient clinician-patient encounters. However such a system was envisioned by VA decision makers as much more than a clinical accounting system. It was also to be a tool for quality improvement of clinical work, enabling managers to study all of the components of care provided for individual patients, the order in which that care was provided, and even the level of provider involved at various stages. Once again, clinical and administrative service line directors were to render an accounting for the time of their personnel across clinical areas served (specific bed sections or clinics identified), teaching activities performed, and research projects supported.

Therein lay the single great weakness of the system. Though the DSS can cost every single procedure or other clinical service identified by the various departments, it depends for its accuracy on the labor mapping process completed by managers and upon the relative value units (measures of units of work relative to a standard unit value, expressed as a decimal fraction) assigned by them or Central Office to each intermediate "product." Inpatient care episodes are assigned (ICD-9 CM) codes to identify the main diagnosis that best accounted for hospitalization. These codes were grouped into the DRGs first developed for Medicare for the billing and payment of inpatient services. These same groups were later "weighted" with known VHA costs. Since 1996, VHA has routinely used the Current Procedural Terminology codes (CPT-4 codes) to identify or classify outpatient clinical encounters. Relative value units for outpatient encounters are already built in for use without resorting to managerial estimates of clinician effort. The use of standardized encounter information based on the assigned CPT-4 codes for outpatient care can ensure the correct assignment of measured workload units. The Decision Support System adopted is unable to utilize this information in a straightforward manner. Ironically, instead, the encounter information system is essentially stripped of its externally established values. These workload proxies (CPT-4 encounter tallies) are assigned back to their "location codes" (clinics and bed sections), where the manager's estimate of an individual clinician's time is parceled out over the locations and then to the products via relative value units (RVUs), also set by managers. "A great deal of time is spent at each VistA site mapping 'DSS Extracts' of local files such as lab, pharmacy, and clinic names to the standard DSS forms. Despite the time invested, the DSS system still suffers from mapping errors and non-comparability of results" (Brown et al. 2003, 19).

Replacing the use of "location codes" and the associated labor mapping for clinical encounters in favor of the built-in clinician labor calculus of the CPT-4 codes could result in a world-class system on a par with VistA's Computerized Patient Record System. The Decision Support System admirably incorporates information from a myriad of sources. Financial data are collected from the record of fees paid to external contractors, from the VA Financial Management System, from the adjusted labor information both of clinical providers and of support staff, pharmacy and prosthetic costs, facility and equipment capital costs, maintenance, and depreciation, utilities, and the administrative overhead found at all levels of management ranging from the local clinic, to the medical centers, to VISNs, and finally, to Central Office. Patient care information is provided by the National Patient Care Data set (NPCD)—Patient Treatment File and PCE (Patient Care Encounter, formerly the OPF, or Outpatient File) for acute care; the Resident Assessment Instrument and Patient Assessment

Instrument for extended care sites; the Census File; and finally the Fee File for episodes of care in non-VA facilities provided to eligible veterans (Kussman 2009; Veterans Affairs Allocation Resource Center 2004–2007).

The Decision Support System will produce "products" specific to individual patients, types of services, clinical providers, clinical programs, and patient service lines (PSLs). It will also, most valuably, provide "indicators" identifying information for comparison of individual cases or groups of cases to clinical or financial benchmarks, enabling swift and sure identification of problems in care delivery patterns, efficacy, or the efficiency with which care is delivered. Thus the system will answer questions such as: "What does a medical bed day of care for a heart attack cost?" "What are the clinical components of that episode of care?" "Were best practices utilized and were clinical reminders followed up?" "Was the sequence of care recommended in 'best practice' benchmarks appropriately followed?" "What is the local readmission rate for this condition, and how does it compare to peer facilities in the VISN or nationally?" Outpatient care may be studied patient by patient or clinician by clinician. Similarly, episodes of extended care may be analyzed.

Thus in the DSS the VA medical care system has developed an extraordinarily powerful tool for understanding and managing its costs, for building local department budgets, and for heuristic monitoring of care quality. Such oversight in turn may lead to changes in or affirmation of the value of practices or processes. Although the method for the assignment of labor costs is not yet optimal, the seeds of its optimization already exist within the databases. In the opinion of this author, the DSS would be an even more powerful management tool if these changes were embraced.[3]

Part II: Resource Allocation in a "Closed" System: Rational Distribution of Limited Dollars across a System of Competing Missions, Needs, and Priorities

Overview

Medical econometrics, the process of rationalizing the costs of medical care and subsequently pricing that care for reimbursement by patients or third-party payers, has never been an exact science. The infamous "$10" aspirin given in a healthcare facility may be considered a poster child for that effort and an indicator of its pitfalls.

The VA healthcare system, like others, is a third-party payer system. Unlike most other third-party payers, Congress determines the entire budget upfront. Changes in demand for care; advances in care technology; increases in the costs of pharmaceuticals, prosthetics, utilities; and other support costs must be absorbed elastically within the relatively inelastic annual appropriation for VA's healthcare. Historically the appropriation was distributed based on each facility's prior year allocation. Add-ons were provided annually in proportion to any increases in the overall VA budget and for the initiation of new programs or facilities. Some VA medical centers benefited from time to time from the actions of congressional allies in positions that made it possible to earmark funds for facilities. In the years following World War II and the Korean conflict, the numbers of veterans occupying seats in the House and Senate were high. Indeed the unofficial alliance among VA, the veterans' service organizations (VFW, American Legion, Disabled Veterans of America, Paralyzed Veterans of America, etc.), and the House and Senate Veterans Affairs Committees was known as the "Iron Triangle." At a time when half of the male populace in the World War II age cohort had served in uniform, taking care of veterans was good politics as well as good citizenship. From time to time "supplemental appropriations" were passed to alleviate impending budget shortages. However, such supplemental appropriations were never a given, and often VAMCs short on funds would institute hiring lags or freezes and postpone purchases in order to stay within budget. Nationally, VA recognized that its priority was to serve the "service-connected" veterans, those whose conditions or disabilities were directly related to their military service. All other veterans were to be seen on the basis of available capacity, and their care was seen as "discretionary." This policy led to a number of anomalies at medical centers, such as non-service-connected veterans being seen in some clinics, but being ineligible in others, creating a nightmare for coordination of care.

As more and more high technology became available, the VA system was often under pressure from its university medical school affiliates to obtain and use such advances in the training of their medical students and residents. Ultimately this was helpful to VA in terms of maintaining a high standard of care. However, it was a budget breaker in the short term because congressional appropriations had not kept up with these changes and the costs associated with them. Medicare at that time faced no such challenge because it was a "fee-for-service program," with no cap on the payments to any single facility or provider. Medicare has long since faced fiscal challenges and responded with econometric adjustments for equitable distribution of dollars, but that is another story.

When new medical centers were built and activated after World War II, or during the major expansion of the Korean era, standards developed in Central Office by the various clinical and administrative departments established the size of the facility, the staffing required by its mission and size, its equipment, the capacity of its wards, and the size of its startup budget. Subsequently the primary method of determining recurring allocations to the medical centers was historical, past allocations supplemented for new programs and equipment or expanded or replaced physical facilities. Attention was also paid to the number of bed days of care (BDOC) provided to patients. An inpatient census was conducted annually to take a snapshot of the "in-house" occupancy, as a proxy for care demand. As time went on it became obvious that administrators could enhance their budgets at the expense of those at other facilities by delaying discharges, especially at the time of the annual bed census. To discourage such manipulations, Central Office officials introduced another statistic, the turnover rate, to measure the intensity of throughput in patient workload. Always short of funds, embattled local officials found incentives to transfer patients between bed sections (medicine, neurology, surgery, psychiatry, intermediate medicine, etc.) in an effort to increase bed section turnover rates, for an apparent efficiency of throughput. Clearly a better system was needed, and a number of alternate methods from outside the VA were examined.

DRGs and RAM

Beginning in 1980, the DRGs were developed by Yale professors Fetter and Thompson, under contract from the Health Care Financing Administration (HCFA, now known as Centers for Medicare and Medicaid Services or CMS). Medicare made plans to introduce the DRGs for the reimbursement of acute hospital stays for FY 1983 (Wikipedia 2009a). Fetter and Thompson had conducted a three-year trial, beginning with a few New Jersey hospitals and eventually including them all. The system consisted of 13 medical diagnostic categories (MDCs), subdivided into 470 DRGs, which embraced the range of diagnostic and procedural codes found in the ICD-9 CM that might be applied for inpatient care (Wikipedia 2009a). The system was based on the assumption that each of the DRGs was homogeneous and on average descriptive of the resources required for the care of a person with a diagnosable condition or who had undergone a particular procedure. Closer inspection of the underlying statistics, however, revealed multiple problems with the underlying assumption. Some of the DRG categories appeared to explain very little about the costs of the individual cases contained therein, having standard deviations almost as large as their mean. In fact, the DRGs explained surgical procedures best, because they were built around a fairly standard procedure. They explained the inpatient costs of medical conditions less well, because initially there was no way to adjust for severity of illness. A receiving hospital with a severe case might very shortly transfer a very ill patient to a tertiary care facility. Each hospital would have been credited with one instance of treatment for the same DRG even though the resource intensity of each episode of care was very different. Medicare handled other anomalies attributable to economies of scale by making different payments to different classes of hospitals based on geography. In psychiatry, the DRGs explained little of the differences among groups in costs of care for hospitalizations and were not predictive of the resources to be required for the inpatient treatment of such patients in facilities ranging from affiliated acute care hospitals to long-term psychiatric facilities. For this reason initially HCFA did not utilize the psychiatric DRGs outside of psychiatry units in general medical and surgical facilities.

About the same time, Central Office's Health Services Research and Development Office was also funding a demonstration project at its Great Lakes Region field station. The study would model distribution of funds to VA medical care facilities in Michigan using the DRGs, in an effort to apply "science" to the process. In 1981 the system was used to distribute acute care dollars for the hospitals in VA's Medical District 14 (Zamberlan & Moore 1984). In the following year the entire region was modeled. What appealed to HCFA administrators about the system also appealed to a number of high-ranking executives in the VA system. It appeared to pay for services based on the average cost of an inpatient episode for a particular condition or for a particular procedure, thus encouraging facility costs in the direction of the mean. It also moved away from concepts of reimbursement (or in VA, of prospective payment) viewed as more diffuse, such as BDOC. Although some critics noted problems in taking a model developed using private sector facilities, with insured patient populations, and applying it to large uninsured public facilities and marginally employed populations (Nightingale 1984), VA went ahead. In 1985 the DM&S introduced RAM to the field, a joint effort of the national Health Services Research and Development Office, the Resource Management Office in Washington, D.C., and the Boston Development Center.

Whereas Medicare paid for the costs of medical education (residencies) with a separate payment, VA initially classified its hospitals as "affiliated" or resident teaching hospitals and "unaffiliated" and created a dual track payment scheme. Unlike the manner in which Medicare handled freestanding psychiatric facilities by exempting them, all psychiatric units were included in the system. Some econometric modelers in VA took the position that the problems evident in test runs of the DRGs for psychiatric care were due to differing practice patterns across the country, rather than shortcomings in the model. The modelers noted that lengths of stay were longer in parts of the country with neuropsychiatric facilities that could provide longer-term care and shorter in parts of the country without such facilities (Holden 1989). Modelers reasoned that disincentivizing longer-term hospitalizations would shorten the VA system's average length of stay to be more in line with those found in the private sector, especially in psychiatry. At the time of adoption of the new method, 40 percent of the beds occupied in VA were psychiatric beds, many in the longer-term hospitals. Other bed sections were affected negatively as well, most notably neurology and physical medicine and rehabilitation.

A secondary, less overt policy agenda involved a massive shift of monies from VA mental healthcare to support the demands of high-tech developments in DM&S. The words of the then chief medical director, Dr. Donald Custis, as he introduced the new methodology gave a hint of this shift in policy. He stated that the psychiatric bed sections had previously consumed the largest portion of available resources, and that the new methodology would mean finding alternative arrangements for those psychiatric patients "whom we have hosted for these many years" (Custis 1984).

As RAM was first implemented, the DRG model was applied to acute care bed sections, to the longer term psychiatric and rehabilitation bed sections, and to NP hospitals, but not to extended care (nursing homes and what were termed "intermediate medicine" bed sections). The latter units were originally treated as "pass-throughs" (funded at cost) until their coverage could be modeled. Under the initial RAM methodology, days of care beyond the range allotted for each DRG grouping would be reimbursed at progressively more restrictive "disincentive rates." Those officials and staff in VA who were alarmed at these trends pointed to the fact that DRG length of stay standards were developed in studies of private facilities. Lengths of stay in those facilities were often limited by insurance contracts. Rarely did patients stay beyond the limits of their insurance. Under Medicare inpatient bills were reimbursed in a "bundled" manner with a single payment for an episode of care. The impact was to shorten lengths of stay. Bed days of care were funded to the average of national usage. If fewer days were allowed locally, profits increased for the private hospitals. Patients with insurance were most often in a different socioeconomic group than VA's chronically ill, often disabled, patients. The insured were insured because they held employment. Those who lost their insurance due to extensive or extended illness went to the public sector hospitals not included in the initial Fetter and Thompson data. Hence the lengths of stay and the purported resources consumed by patients assigned the various DRGs were not generalizable beyond the population selected for study.

In 1985 some VA service chiefs took on the challenge of identifying characteristics of psychiatric patients that would reliably predict their resource utilization (Errera et al. 1985). The data from that work and a follow-up study of the same patients in long-term care facilities were later cross-analyzed. Two markers were subsequently identified (from factors in the first study) as predictive of the intensity of resource utilization by the same individuals in the later time period (personal recollection of this present author of an informal data run requested of the Boston Development Center in 1990). Both markers were related to prior employment or planning for vocational reintegration. The details of that work go beyond the scope of the present chapter.

In response to the immediate outcry from clinicians that RAM was a blunt instrument, with a negative impact on funding for acute outpatient care and for the care of the chronically ill in rehabilitation medicine and mental health, Marjorie M. Quandt convened the DM&S Physician and Dentists Expert Review Panel—Re-weighting of DRGs to VA Costs under the auspices of the Health Services Research and Development Office, with participation from the Boston Development Center and the Resource Management Office, also in Central Office. Miss Quandt was then the associate chief medical director for administration in the DM&S. Both the health services research group and the Boston Development Center reported to her office. The current author's participation in this convened work group was invited by Ms. Quandt. Previously, Dr. Paul Errera (then chief of psychiatry at West Haven VA, later director of the Mental Health and Behavioral Sciences Service in Central Office) and this author had been summoned to Central Office to explain a white paper authored by the latter, and disseminated by Dr. Errera, detailing the negative impact of the 1985 implementation of RAM on chronically ill mental patients. The long-term impact of these meetings was to sensitize the econometric modelers to serious issues in the field, including homelessness for those displaced from neuropsychiatric facilities or discharged from the psychiatric wards of general medical and surgical hospitals without adequate outpatient support. The practical short-term consequence was the introduction of some payment stratification, by age and utilization, among psychiatric outpatients. New DRG weights were derived from VA data for use in 1987 and replaced those taken from Medicare data. The affiliation differential was replaced by a resident-based education supplement. Other FY 1987 changes were detailed in the October 1986 issue of *VA Practitioner* (Nightingale 1986).

Some facility administrators complained that the system rewarded a high frequency of hospital episodes of care and procedures. As noted previously, some others attempted to maximize their financial advantage through excessive transfers between bed sections, thus generating additional "discharges." Still others attempted to improve their outpatient balance sheet through a loophole that paid more money for an outpatient surgical encounter than for a standard encounter to enhance local revenue by using an obscure outpatient surgical code that could be interpreted to include vaccinations. Inflating the number of "surgeries" by inclusion of preventive flu shots became a way of gaming the system. The perverse incentive inherent in RAM was to produce workload far beyond normal facility and staff capacity in order to reap the financial rewards in later years. At the 1987 HSR&D Resource Allocation Methodologies National Consensus Conference convened by Central Office, the tone from the field was frustration. The then chief of staff of the Boston VAMC rose to state that "flagship Boston VAMC was now sunk in Boston Harbor" (personal recollection of this author). Problems with RAM were identified. Ideas were solicited about alternative methods that might be used. Some participants opined that correctives for "severity of illness" would lead to more equitable distribution. Others noted that the allocation methods then available did not reduce the variation enough to explain the massive funding dislocations being experienced across VA:

> Creating this open-ended expansion of workload with VA's fixed funding ultimately led to a budget crisis in 1989. Local VA Medical Center management was faced with trying to make short term budget compromises to increase workload on the gamble that future RAM allocations would make up any shortfall. However, since the whole VHA system was doing the same thing, the expected payoff, in many cases, did not occur. (Veterans Affairs Allocation Resource Center 1997, 1)

In a closed, zero-sum system, such machinations and efforts at suboptimization were threatening the integrity of fair resource distribution. The Resource Allocation Methodology was also noted to use financial and workload data that were two years old by the time new allocations were distributed. Facility leaders found the time lag to be particularly problematic in an era of increasing workloads and aging veterans.

By 1989 the modelers at the Boston Development Center were clear on the fact that RAM was too crude to account for the various levels of care found in an integrated medical care system that encompassed acute general medical and surgical facilities (both medical school–affiliated and unaffiliated), neuropsychiatric hospitals, intermediate medicine and intermediate psychiatry units, physical rehabilitation units, and nursing homes. It was recognized that HCFA had proceeded with much more caution in these areas, using a different model of reimbursement for freestanding psychiatric and rehabilitation facilities as well as for extended care. Technical advisory groups were named for mental health and other stakeholders to assist the econometric modelers in analyzing and understanding the cost and discharge data available to them. It was recognized that though "large bucket" versus "small bucket" analyses of the same data made no difference in the national roll-up of costs, finer-grained analyses and the development of more discrete, data-based buckets could make huge differences in allocations to many facilities.

Resource Planning Methodology (RPM)

In 1990 the Boston Development Center introduced a new funding model, the Resource Planning Management (RPM), a patient-based system recognizing seven facility groupings in the hopes of comparing apples to apples and of moving facilities in the direction of a mean cost for services judged to be comparable. There were now sixteen pricing groups embracing the Medical Diagnostic Categories (wherein the DRGs were grouped) and the Resource User Groups (RUGs) method of accounting for extended care patient costs, and finally, a new approach to better characterize outpatient care. These pricing groups contained some forty-nine subgroupings encompassing the full range of ICD-9 CM codes (U.S. General Accounting Office 1996). Medical centers were to be "paid prospectively" at a rate that reflected their historical costs plus any additional increase authorized to the entire system by Congress. There was an effort to recognize the unique circumstances of individual medical centers, with course corrections during the fiscal year to accommodate special situations:

> In the end, the model and the process to negotiate final budget allocations proved to be too complex and onerous to effectively and credibly allocate resources. In addition, RPM [Resource Planning Management] was not created to hold all facilities to a nationally adjusted average cost. This perpetuated the inequities in funding, efficiency, and access that existed in the VHA healthcare system. (Veterans Affairs Allocation Resource Center 1997, 2)

By 1995 the initial impact of Dr. Kenneth Kizer's reorganization of VHA was felt, with the creation of vertically integrated networks of facilities and line authority decentralized to the network directors. Along with such authority came responsibility for meeting the budgets of facilities large and small, affiliated and unaffiliated, relatively new and long established, within each VISN. "Silos" were out, whether they were intrafacility disciplinary silos competing for local resources or facility silos, competing with nearby VAMCs for patients and dollars. The extant method of distributing resources did not fit the new realities.

In 1996 an effort was undertaken to move toward a national pricing strategy, with a single price for any given unit of care. The prior year's method, based as it was upon local or peer group historical costs, was not flexible enough to allow for the shifting of resources across the country to correct imbalances. In the first year of the revised RPM method, the rate structure was heavily weighted toward historical facility costs (70 percent), then 20 percent at the national rate, and finally 5 percent each for peer group and network rates. Had the methodology been fully implemented, the shift in dollars across the country would have amounted to $150 million. A system of caps was put in place to limit the shifts to more sustainable levels for individual centers. The magnitude of the shift in 1996 was approximately $23 million. Had the prior RPM been allowed to continue unchecked, the shift would have been in the neighborhood of $200 million. Each succeeding year, these percentages were to change so as to gradually move medical care disbursement across the country to a more equitable and defensible method (Veterans Affairs Allocation Resource Center 1997).

But even this revised RPM was viewed by clinicians and administrators alike as too complex, unpredictable, and insufficiently addressing the issue of equity across the nation.

Veterans Equitable Resource Methodology (VERA) and Its Revisions

In 1997 a fundamental change in VA's resource allocation system was introduced. Simply stated, the overarching goals of the Veterans Equitable Resource Methodology (VERA) were (1) to use national unit pricing for care, thus providing equitable access to care nationally; (2) to have veterans receiving care be enrolled in one network; (3) to have the numbers of patients seeking care drive the determination of which patient priority levels would be accepted for care, ranging from the various classes of the "service-connected" to the lowest priority "space available" groups; (4) to link the dollars paid to the VISNs to the individual patient no matter where the person received care; and finally (5) to comply with the provisions and intent of Public Law 104-204 (1996), which simplified the heretofore arcane and complex relationships among priority classes for eligibility and the kinds of care that could be provided. Now, for the first time, all veterans admitted to the system could be provided care across a spectrum of services offered without regard for priority level. The Department of Veterans Affairs would determine how many priority levels it could support given its budget, and the president would make the decision about any group(s) from which additional veterans would no longer be accepted, or in a worst case scenario, designate those no longer eligible for care.

The tactical objectives for VERA included aligning systemwide management and operational incentives with best practices; ensuring understanding, credibility, and predictability in the field; providing appropriate support for VA's research and education missions; promoting managerial flexibility in the implementation of VISNs' strategic plans and initiatives; and finally, encouraging increases in alternative revenue collections (third-party insurance and sales of excess capacity).

In the 1997 version of VERA, fifty-three "patient classes" were rolled up into two national price groups, Basic Care (twenty-five patient classes funded at $2,995 per pro-rated person) and Special Care (twenty-eight patient classes funded at $35,707 per pro-rated person). The "pro-rated person" (PRP) was a new concept introduced with VERA to track the care of persons who receive care in different VISNs due to a move, travel, or "snowbird" sojourning. For patients qualifying in one or another funding group, the VISNs are credited with a partial person, insofar as the cost of that person's entire care for a base year can be apportioned between or among networks. Each patient is classified at the end of a base year and assigned to the highest patient class for which he or she qualifies, based on the kinds of procedures performed, diagnoses treated, or chronic condition managed. Some conditions were recognized to be so catastrophically costly that patients so classified remained in the class over multiple years as long as they required care. Stability was introduced into these numbers by using a three-year rolling count as the basis for the annual determination of "enrollees" in the system. These head counts of PRPs were credited annually to each network in proportion to the portion of the entire care provided by each facility for each veteran. For 1997, only "mandatory" patients were included in these patient counts, and the new VA networks were expected to provide appropriate care to other categories of patients (lower priority, "discretionary") from the resources allocated, using the mandatory patients as proxies for the entire workload.

Once again caps were introduced to prevent the magnitude of shifts in funding from destabilizing any given network. Uncapped, some networks would have gained or lost up to 15 percent over their prior year's allocation. With the caps no network had its base reduced more than 1.6 percent below its 1996 level prior to having the 1997 systemwide increase applied to its final allocation. Further adjustments were made for the cost of labor, above or below that experienced nationally.

It was expected that VERA would provide VISNs with adequate resources to carry out their mission, based as it was on a national price and applied to the projected workload (the three-year rolling count) of veterans served. "It is important to note that networks receiving relatively fewer funds [than baseline] will adjust by becoming more efficient—not by reducing services or numbers of veterans served" (Veterans Affairs Allocation Resource Center 1997, 4).

Changes to the new system for 1998 were minimal, with the national price for a Basic Care PRP rising to $2,604 and that for Special Care rising to $36,960. Pro-rated persons for the latter group were removed from the Basic Care three-year count and placed in their own five-year count group. Education support dollars continued to be distributed based on the number of medical residents in a VISN, and research support dollars (other than the grants them-selves) were distributed in a manner adjusted for VA/non-VA grant sources, favoring the former or other peer-reviewed grants administered through VA research corporations. These monies were derived from those identified in the new accounting system as salary dollars spent in support of implementing a research grant. This became the VA version of "indirect support" found in National Institutes of Health or other federal agancy research grants, though not directly comparable because the direct grants of other federal agencies con-tain salary dollars. In VA these dollars represent the portion of the medical care salary appropriation spent in support of research activity rather than patient care. Since the basic budget of a facility is based on its patient care work, this method allows for segregating the personnel costs of supporting research and of funneling the dollars back to productive research sites. Caps introduced in 1998 limited the overall negative exposure of any network to 5 percent of its prior year's allocation, prior to adding the systemwide increase intended by Congress to cover increases in the cost of care (Veterans Affairs Allocation Resource Center 1998).

In the following year there were few changes. "Special Care" became "Com-plex Care." A new class of patients, with a single outpatient visit in the three-year base period, was placed in a category by itself to reflect the low intensity of care provided. Veterans who came to the VA medical care facility only to receive a disability examination were not counted in this group. Hence in 1999 there were three care groups: Complex Care (funded at $36,995), Basic "Vested" Care (funded at $2,857), and Single Outpatient [visit] (funded at $66). The "vested" qualification on the Basic Care group was an innovation both to account for resource intensity and to move the system in the direction of providing more complete medical involvement with its enrolled patients. Vesting required that the patient have a complete physical examination by a physician or other quali-fied practitioner at least every three years during enrollment (Veterans Affairs Allocation Resource Center 1999).

Refinements were added to the model for supporting research to distin-guish peer-reviewed, non-VA-funded research from that which was not VA funded and not peer reviewed, such as pharmaceutical research. The impact of these tiers may be viewed as especially intended to discourage using VA salary dollars in support of drug or medical device company research (Veterans Affairs Allocation Resource Center 1999).

The Veterans Equitable Resource Allocation Method continued through fiscal year 2002, with minor tweaking and annual changes in the dollar value assigned to each of the care groups (Veterans Affairs Allocation Resource Center 2000, 2001, 2002). Studies were undertaken in 2001 by the Rand

Corporation (Wasserman et al. 2003), the GAO (U.S. General Accounting Office 2002), and Price, Waterhouse Coopers (Price Waterhouse LLP and the Lewin Group Inc. 1998), all of which examined the underlying data and concluded that three care groups were not sufficient to represent the complexity of the underlying clinical activities and their costs. A number of other recommendations were made by the General Accounting Office (GAO), including provision for a reserve to offset the costs of catastrophic complex care cases requiring resources well beyond what is provided by their current group, paying attention to facility and geographic factors, measuring and funding the actual workload and not simply the mandatory workload (the GAO suggested funding category 7 at 50 percent of the mandatory workload), and the updating of the inpatient case-mix weights with the best available data. The GAO used the figures provided by Boston's Allocation Resource Center, with each of the forty-seven patient classes, and concluded that more major funding groups would likely better represent the range of care and allow better discrimination between high cost and intermediate cost care.

The Under Secretary for Veterans Affairs, responding to the findings of these three reports in his testimony before Congress in 2002 (Roswell 2002), agreed to make changes for FY 2003, when the Boston group was to roll out "Veterans Equitable Resource Allocation-10" or VERA-10 (Veterans Affairs Allocation Resource Center 2003). Now there were ten secondary funding groups across the Basic Vested Care and Complex Care major groups, each with its own national price. Once again caps were utilized to ease the transition for networks. Provision was made for catastrophic cases as well, with the introduction of a high-cost patient deductible, after which the remainder of costs would be paid. A second analysis by the RAND Group noted improvements with the newer model, but also observed that the Rand regression analyses found the five variables that still accounted for the largest portion of monetary shifts across the nation were "[patient] health status, research costs per unique patient, the VA labor indices, [degree of] Medicare reliance [by enrolled veteran patients], and the square feet of building space per patient" (Wasserman et al. 2004).

For 2003, the aims of the revised model were described as follows, and they were retained unchanged in succeeding years:

- Improve equity of allocation process and decisions
- Be responsive to the GAO and RAND recommendations
- Recognize price and cost differences in "core mission" patients (those veterans with service-connected disabilities or those with incomes below the current income threshhold or special needs patients, e.g., homeless)

- Require minimal education for VERA users
- Eliminate the need to provide networks with supplemental funding (Veterans Affairs Allocation Resource Center 2008)

A further refinement was made to the model in 2004, in line with the recommendations of the GAO and the RAND group, to improve accounting for workload by including the two "discretionary" priority groups (known as priority groups 7 and 8) in the allocations. Previously they were modeled but not included in funding distribution. The analysis of costs for these two groups showed that they were for the most part much less expensive than their mandatory cohorts. VERA 10+ was so named to account for the fact that each of the ten care groups now had two prices set prospectively, one for the mandatory patients and another for the discretionary patients. For the first four of ten groups, the difference is nearly a 50 percent reduction in pricing for the discretionary workload. In groups 5 through 7, the reduction ranged from 25 to 30 percent. Smaller differences were observed for the last three groups, those who were the most severely ill or required the most extensive care (Veterans Affairs Allocation Resource Center, 2004–2007).

The model has remained quite stable since 2004, and the 2004 VERA Handbook was so little changed over the next three fiscal years that the ARC archives list only a single handbook for 2004 through 2007. Changes for 2008 and 2009 mainly reflected the manner in which shifts in the adjustments were made to the prior year's base funding figure prior to adding newly appropriated monies. In 2008 the appropriation for medical care was significantly increased; hence no network was adjusted to below its prior year's base prior to receiving the annual increase, even where the model would have called for such an adjustment. In 2009 the adjustments were back in place, as were caps on dollar growth on those networks with the largest growth, in order to make up deficits below the lower cap set for declining growth networks (Veterans Affairs Allocation Resource Center 2008, 2009).

The impact of all of these changes over the years has been to provide more equitable access to healthcare for veterans across the nation, create incentives for accepting and treating patients with serious or chronic illness, support reasonable local growth within the parameters of systemwide growth, and emplace disincentives for the kind of "skimming [accepting only healthy patients] and dumping [getting rid of chronically ill patients]" sometimes observed in other sectors of American healthcare.

The joint impact of the new computerized hospital patient record system, cost accounting system, and resource allocation system in giving VA managers at all levels an ability to improve the equity, efficacy, and efficiency with which care is delivered cannot be overestimated. Fortuitously, the development of these tools created the basis of a synergy that supported the larger structural changes to come during the years in which Dr. Kenneth Kizer served as Under Secretary for Health in the U.S. Department of Veterans Affairs.

Part III: The Kizer Revolution: The Vision, the Prescription, and the Journey

VHA Vision Statement

> Healthcare VAlue [sic] begins with VA. The new veterans [sic] healthcare system supports innovation, empowerment, productivity, accountability and continuous improvement. Working together, we provide a continuum of high quality healthcare in a convenient, responsive, caring manner—and at a reasonable cost. (Kizer 1996)

Overview

The position of Under Secretary for Health for the Veterans Health Administration of the U.S. Department of Veterans Affairs is highly visible, subject to presidential appointment and senate confirmation. The predecessor office was known as the Chief Medical Director (CMD) of the Department of Medicine and Surgery of the Veterans Administration. During the period covered by this chapter there have been ten CMDs or Under Secretaries for Health, from Dr. Donald L. Custis (1980–1984) to Dr. Robert A. Petzel (2010–). Some have served as little as a year. Dr. Kenneth Kizer (1994–2000) was an exception in that he served a full six-year term, and he brought about extraordinary structural change in a huge federal government department over a relatively brief period of time.

Vision for Change

Dr. Kizer was named to the office in April 1994, and less than a year later he presented his *Vision for Change* (Kizer 1995). The backdrop for this scenario was the healthcare reform proposals of the Clinton administration, which were expected to foster the concept of vertically integrated healthcare systems accountable for the full range of their enrollees' medical care:

> The proposed structure optimizes VHA's ability to function as both an integrated and a virtual health care organization; it provides structural incentives for efficiency, quality and improved access; it builds in a formal means of ensuring a high degree of stakeholder involvement; and it provides for a level of accountability

not typical of government agencies. Once operational, it should be apparent to our patients, Congress and the public that this is not only a better model than the present structure, but that it is also better than the various alternatives that call for doing away with VHA.

Important to note, however, is that in and of itself, the planned organizational structure merely provides a template upon which new attitudes and behavior will be encouraged and rewarded, and around which a new organizational culture can grow. This transformation will take time, and the difficulty of changing a decades-old culture in the second largest bureaucracy in the Federal government should not be underestimated. The change will be neither easy nor painless. Nonetheless, if the veterans health care system is to remain viable it must fundamentally change its approach to providing care. (Kizer 1995, 7)

The focus of the reorganization was to be "Patients First," not only as applied to patient care, the first of VA's traditonal fourfold missions, but also to its teaching, research, and DoD emergency preparedness functions. This mantra's impact on VA structural redesign would have a wide-ranging effect: increased outpatient care points of access, reemphasized primary care, and decentralized management decision making. He called for "integrating the delivery assets to provide an interdependent, interlocking system of care" (Kizer 1995, 14) through the creation of twenty-two VISNs. Field leaders were to be held responsible for "meeting defined levels of patient satisfaction, access, quality, and efficiency," while Central Office officials' "purview . . . [was to] include the development of systemwide policies, clinical protocols and critical pathways, definition of expected levels of performance and monitoring of outcomes" (Kizer 1995, 15):

[T]he basic concept of an integrated health care organization is that it is one which will be accountable for providing a coordinated range of physician, hospital and other medical care services for a defined population, and generally for a fixed amount. The assumption is that it will be easier and more efficient to provide for all the needs of the population if all the pieces of the healthcare system needed to provide the care are integrated into and under the control of a single entity.

In an integrated healthcare system, physicians, hospitals and all other components share the risks and rewards and support one another. In doing so they blend their talents and pool their resources; they focus on delivering "best value" care. To be successful, the integrated health care system requires management of total costs; a focus on populations rather than individuals; and a data-driven, process-focused customer orientation. (Kizer 1995, 16–17)

In addition to the vertical integration model for the networks, Dr. Kizer planned to use elements of a model known as the "virtual health care organization." He meant to foster collaborations within VA and with community and other federal partners based on the sharing of patient care protocols, information systems, and provider incentives. He described both the vertical integration and the virtual organization as "learning systems" that self-correct with experience in providing care and managing resources (Kizer 1995). "The Veterans Health Administration has the relatively unique advantage of being able to function as both an integrated and a virtual health care organization, although it has not been organizationally aligned and managed as such in the past" (Kizer 1995, 18). With these few powerful concepts, Dr. Kenneth Kizer, like the proverbial Archimedes, placed a lever in the exact location required to move VHA into a new orbit.

Prescription for Change

"Our business is healthcare, not hospital care" (Kizer 1996).

VHA Mission Statement

> The mission of the Veterans Healthcare System is to serve the needs of America's veterans by providing primary care, specialized care and related medical and social support services. To accomplish this mission, VHA needs to be a comprehensive, integrated healthcare system that provides excellence in healthcare value, excellence in service as defined by its customers, and excellence in education and research, and needs to be an organization characterized by exceptional accountability and by being an employer of choice. (Kizer 1996)

In the mid-1990s Dr. Kizer began his blueprint for the transformation of VHA by reviewing the external healthcare environment within which VA found itself and the assumptions derived therefrom. Among the national trends listed were (1) increased competition for federal funding; (2) continued predomination in healthcare of the private sector; (3) consolidation of healthcare facilities, systems, and HMOs; (4) managed care in integrated systems becoming the modal manner of healthcare provision; (5) increased use of nonphysician providers in these new systems; (6) the continued growth of medical scientific knowledge, leading to new advances in heretofore untreatable conditions; (7) technological advances in clinical practice, with concomitant acceleration of expense for new drugs and devices; (8) improvement in healthcare delivery through application of new communications and information technology; (9) increased emphasis on disease prevention and health promotion in addition to traditional individual treatment of illness; (10) more focus on accountability of providers and systems for improved healthcare outcomes, along with systematic measurement; (11) increased emphasis on customer service and quality of care, along with cost containment; and (12) the advanced aging of the eligible veteran population, driving an increased demand for service, both acute and chronic, out of proportion to the age-related decrease in enrollees. Local and regional issues were also expected to have an impact on networks and their component facilities. Finally, Dr. Kizer assumed that "the future is unpredictable and that VA must be flexible enough to rapidly respond to unforeseen circumstances" (1996, 4) He then outlined what he called the five missions of the transformation: excellence in healthcare; excellence in customer satisfaction as defined by customers; excellence in teaching and research; being an organization characterized by exceptional accountability; and being an employer of choice. In four major sections of *Prescription for Change*, Dr. Kizer outlined very specific objectives and the means to arrive at these goals. It was fortunate that the infrastructure that success required in information systems, cost accounting, and patient care information was already underway, only awaiting an overarching vision to create synergy.

Excellence in Healthcare

Prescription for Change noted the environmental pressures of the time and the place of VA's historical missions in that situation. Dr. Kizer enunciated principles that characterize high-level healthcare value and delineated the strategic objectives to achieve the goals contained within those principles. He called for implementing the organizational restructuring described in *Vision for Change*, embraced continuity of care and its management; fostered disease prevention and health promotion; emphasized primary care for all enrollees; directed that all components of care and clinicians providing care be working as teams; mandated the alignment of all these elements with VA's goals and objectives; and called for minimizing errors, promoting quality improvement, and for measuring the quality of care, along with the effectiveness of its outcomes and the efficiency with which it is delivered (Kizer 1996).

To follow these principles and accomplish these objectives, Dr. Kizer recognized that it was not enough to restructure Central Office and to implement the twenty-two new VISNs. At all levels, VA would have to recruit managers with the expert skills required to transform the vision into reality. Staff training and education programs would have to be developed to teach and train the skills needed to facilitate the vision's implementation. This was no longer "your father's VA," but the "new VA" (Kizer 1996).

Operating costs would have to be reduced by continuing to transfer VA healthcare to ambulatory care from bed care. Where this process was impeded by law or regulation, VA would seek relief. During Dr. Kizer's first eighteen months in office, nearly 5,000 beds were closed across the country. From 1980 to mid-1996, nearly 35,000 beds had been closed, leaving better than 48,000 acute care beds in the system, along with more than 22,000 extended care beds. During that same period of time, outpatient workload increased nearly 10 percent. Ambulatory surgical capacity was to be expanded, along with homecare, promoting alternatives to hospital care whenever possible. The use of "hoptels" (hospital hotels) and state veterans' homes was also encouraged for convalescence or residential care. Renewed emphasis on preadmission screening and discharge planning was aimed at decreasing length of stay for the hospitalized. Cohorts who could benefit from disease management protocols were to be identified and treated using best practices. Call centers for triage and telephone care were to be implemented systemwide (Kizer 1996).

Administrative changes were called for as well, such as altering the manner in which VA collected and denominated ambulatory care data, changing from using "clinic stops" to using the Current Procedural Terminology codes (CPT-4). Interestingly, although this change was swiftly implemented throughout the clinical system, it never penetrated the DSS in the same manner, as noted previously. Variations in staffing patterns for facilities having similar missions and workloads were to be reduced. Databases on personnel workload and productivity, along with quality indicators, were to be developed and implemented at facility, network, and systemwide levels. The restructuring of facilities, or the grouping of them or of their management structures, was to be explored to reduce administrative overhead and to place those dollars at the service of direct patient care. The allocation of resources needed to be overhauled so that the manner of their distribution would be equitable and would encourage the use of the right setting for each care episode, all the while maintaining support of the VHA special emphasis programs. The manner in which fee basis care was reimbursed was to be changed, using the available Medicare fee schedules for payment. Other sources of revenue were to be aggressively pursued: increased third-party collections for non-service-connected care and exploration of Medicare subvention for non-service-connected, elderly patients (Kizer 1996).

The Department of Veterans Affairs would now be a player on a larger stage, as the principal of a virtual organization, contracting with the private sector for veterans' care where that might be more cost-effective, negotiating for the sale of excess capacity to the private sector. Also in the picture was increased sharing with VA's university affiliates and with federal partners so as to reduce duplication of highly expensive equipment and facilities. Telemedicine was to assist the process of becoming an effective virtual organization. For example, one facility might read radiological images for a distant facility, transmitting images and reports back and forth in a seamless and transparent manner. Interoperability and linkages of VA's medical information systems with the DoD, Medicare, and Medicaid was seen as a goal. The DHCP was to move to the more user-friendly graphic user interface (GUI), later to be known as the Computerized Patient Record System (CPRS), the successor to the old roll and scroll presentation found in the Decentralized Hospital Computer Program, and the electronic patient record was to be made available system-wide, so that any veteran seeking care at any VA facility could be seen in the presence of the complete medical record. Purchasing and contracting processes were to take advantage of VA's sheer size to obtain the best prices and conditions. The Department of Veterans Affairs was to move more aggressively into electronic commerce, with the use of purchase cards and smart cards for identifying staff and patients (Kizer 1996).

Continuing quality improvement was to become a hallmark of the culture, along with strong aspirations to become the very best in the nation. The VAMCs participated in national organizational excellence competitions such as VA's Kerry Award and the Department of Commerce's Baldridge Award. Performance measures common in the private sector were to be imported and implemented so that VA could be meaningfully compared with the best in the nation's medical care. A culture of reporting and learning from mistakes rather than minimizing or covering them was encouraged. Lessons learned at one facility or in one network were to be shared. A VHA Center for Dissemination of Innovations and Best Practices was to be developed. A physician safety expert from NASA was brought into Central Office to develop a systems approach to patient and provider safety. Clinical Centers of Excellence were to be identified and fostered to recognize and propagate best practices and optimal organizational strategies. Performance measures for programs, facilities, networks, and the overall system were to be tied to the identified "four domains of value, (1) Cost/price, (2) Technical quality, (3) Customer Satisfaction, and (4) Access" (Kizer 1996, 25).

Excellence in Service as Defined by Customers

To paraphrase the late Speaker of the House, Tip O'Neill, "All healthcare is local." The Under Secretary was determined that care be accessible geographically and temporally, that it be delivered and communicated in a manner that was user-friendly, with participation of the patient and family in decision making. To ensure these aims were met he recommended the formation of consumer advisory groups, the use of focus groups and patient surveys, and the development of VISN patient newsletters with invitations to patients to relate their concerns to their caregivers and management. The assignment of one key provider to each patient; care coordination; the elimination of red tape, complex and redundant forms, and unnecessary reports; and the training and empowering of frontline staff on service recovery were seen as means to increase consumer satisfaction. Attention was to be paid to the physical comfort of patients. The cross-training of staff was also recommended as a way to eliminate shuffling patients back and forth among clinicians and administrative staff. Staff courtesy and timeliness were to be hallmarks of their relationships with their "consumers." Accessibility and timeliness were vastly improved within current resources through the use of strategies such as consultation with the Institute for Healthcare Improvement and the subsequent training staff in the theory and practice of "Advanced Clinic Access." Over a two-year period, the latter initiative cut patient waiting times for appointments in primary care nationwide by more than 53 percent, all the while increasing the number of unique individuals served by 23 percent, with a minimal 2.3 percent increase in resources (Parlier 2003). As more medical centers have adopted these changes, the statistics have improved even more. The process has been replicated beyond primary care and has evidenced dramatic changes in mental health clinic accessibility as well. The aim was "to provide quality service that meets the customer's needs the 'first time, every time'" (Kizer 1996, 55).

Providing Excellence in Education and Research

"The organization and structure of medical education activities shoud be driven by the clinical delivery system" (Kizer 1996, 56). Education and research activities of VA were to be accountable, with performance and outcome measures similar to those instituted for clinicians and clinical care. Training in VA should be responsive to both VA and national needs. The numbers and kinds of health professionals trained would now be determined by those needs. Training in primary care was to be reemphasized. Relationships with affiliated medical and professional schools were expected to be a true partnership, "fair and equitable, and VA personnel should have recognition and influence in affiliated universities commensurate with the contributions of their educational services" (Kizer 1996, 56).

The research agenda would now turn its attention, and considerable research funding, to translational research, fostering projects related to conditions having the most significance for VA, while maintaining a "balance among basic, applied, and outcomes research" (Kizer 1996, 57). A VHA research strategy, aligned with the organizational principles and objectives of the "new VA," would be developed to drive VA's research agenda, ensuring that the dollars spent would advance the overall mission of the organization. Research collaboration with universities and private enterprise in the service of VA's agenda would be promoted. There would be more emphasis on health outcomes research. Experiments with alternative administrative structures were to be conducted, the findings to be shared throughout the system. Emblematic of the latter goal was an ongoing study of the new Patient Service Line organizational structures as compared with more traditional entities. These new entities were cross-disciplinary, with authority vested in the team leader at every level.

An Organization Characterized by Exceptional Accountability, and an Employer of Choice

A constant theme of the Kizer renaissance is the notion of accountability, from the highest officials to the frontline staff. The decentralization of authority and the empowerment of upper, middle, and lower level employees to make the decisions required to obtain the desired outcomes came at a price. Wherever the power to solve a problem lay, there was found the obligation to be accountable to the highest of standards. The new informatics capability made it possible to link every clinical encounter to a provider and every administrative transaction to the person who effected it in the system. Performance-based pay was recommended for high level executives, clinical providers, and support staff alike. The development of other incentives for innovation, teamwork, and high performance was encouraged as well. All of this involves a recognition that an organization's most valuable resource is its workforce. "The more desirable an institution is to work for, the more likely it is to have a highly motivated staff that is focused on accomplishing the organization's mission" (Kizer 1996, 7). Hence it follows that the factors that contribute to employee satisfaction or dissatisfaction and defection need to be identified, the former enhanced and the latter eliminated. Employee education, opportunities for self-betterment and promotion, elimination of "turf" issues in favor of collaboration, along with mutual respect and absence of harassment and discrimination, a safe environment, and union management partnerships were all viewed as elements favoring employee recruitment, retention, and most of all, "buy-in" to the principles and objectives of the "new VA" (Kizer 1996).

Journey of Change

VHA Strategy Statement

VHA's strategy is to provide excellent healthcare value and customer satisfaction to veterans through the integration of performance measurement, strategic planning, and financial goals and targets to achieve a patient-oriented, ambulatory care-based, results-driven, organized system of coordinated health-care delivery focused on continuous quality improvement. (Kizer 1996)

Dr. Kizer's last publication in this series, *Journey of Change*, appeared in 1997. It incorporated the strategic plans of the twenty-two new VISNs as the basis for an on-the-ground implementation of a national strategy for the next five years. In a special note in the cover section of the document, the very bright and ambitious Under Secretary acknowledged the barriers:

> While any organization can change or reduce its costs, it is much more difficult to change systematically in a way that produces clear, measurable, improved performance that readily translates into improved services and products at a reduced cost. This is an even more compelling challenge when the service provided is health care, the organization is a large government agency, and the customers are veterans of military service. (Kizer 1997)

At the outset he invited his leadership colleagues, line employees, and potential critics to evaluate the document's contents, even including an evaluation form in an appendix for readers to use for providing feedback and further input. In keeping with his call for accountability, *Journey of Change* sets out ten systemwide targets with annual performance measures to be monitored for progress to be fully achieved by 2002. "The key VHA policy impacting network operations strategies is the Veterans Equitable Resource Allocations system implemented in the second half of FY 1997" (Kizer 1997, 4). Dr. Kizer intended to use the system that funded the networks as a management tool to incentivize the changes required to meet the 2002 targets, christened "Ten for 2002." The ten targets were quite bold in their reach:

- Decrease the system-wide average cost (expenditure) per patient by 30 percent
- Increase the number of users of the veterans' healthcare system by 20 percent
- Increase the percent of the operating budget obtained from non-appropriated sources to 10 percent of the total
- Exceed by 10 percent the proportion of patients of other large healthcare providers who achieve maximal functional potential
- Increase to 90 percent the proportion of patients reporting VA healthcare as very good or excellent
- Increase to 90 percent the proportion of patients who rate the quality of VHA healthcare as equivalent to or better than what they would receive from others

- Increase to 99 percent the proportion of research projects that are demonstrably related to the healthcare of veterans or to other missions of the Department of Veterans Affairs

- When asked, 95% of physician house staff and other trainees would rate their VA educational experience as good or superior to their other academic training

- Increase to 2 percent, or 40 hours per year, the amount of an employee's paid time that is spent in continuing education to promote and support quality improvement or customer service

- Increase to 100 percent the number of employees who, when queried, are able to appropriately describe how their work helps meet the mission of the "new VHA" (Kizer 1997).

As with all of the Under Secretary's initiatives, these were built into his own performance contract, those of Central Office officials, VISN and facility directors, chiefs of staff, and eventually, as applicable, local service line directors and their employees. Building the performance measures into individual performance contracts was a very powerful way to move the system in the desired direction. The national performance measures for 1997 called for decreases in BDOCs and in overall bed capacity; expanded use of outpatient surgery and of clinical practice guidelines; increases in mandatory workload, patients, primary care enrollment, and total funding for peer-reviewed research; implementation of and improvement in Chronic Disease Index and Prevention Index Scores; improvement in customer satisfaction in spinal cord injury patients, and in all patients, with timeliness of access and overall service; improvement in VHA's management of the Veterans Benefits Administration's (VBA) requests for disability examinations; documentation of the use of the Addiction Severity Index with substance abuse patients and end-of-life planning for all patients; and measured improvement in the knowledge of the VHA mission by rank and file employees.

In 1996 BDOCs were reduced 21 percent. It was estimated that the continuing emphasis on reducing BDOCs and consequently, bed capacity, coupled with the shift in venue to ambulatory care, would literally reverse the 60/40 relationship of inpatient expenditures to outpatient expenditures over the period 1994–2002. Monies gained from the efficiencies would help to fund the continuing growth in patient workload and associated expenses for expanded outpatient access in community-based outpatient clinics (CBOCs). Staffing was also projected to decrease overall in the transition from one venue to the other (Kizer 1997). The decrease in staff numbers would also fund the change in staff mix required by expanded ambulatory care capacity.

A uniform benefits package was proposed to Congress, passed, and implemented so that veterans would receive a consistent quality of medical care regardless of location. Disabled veterans, in six special groups, were singled out for attention. The system's success in meeting their needs would first be measured by VA's capacity, in terms of workload and resources, to support their needs. However, quality of care outcome measures were to be developed and implemented over two years, to replace the proxy measures of workload and resources expended (Kizer 1997).

Just as VERA 10+ became a key driver of change by incentivizing the desired clinical and management behaviors in the VISNs and their components, so now the DSS also became a key player in measuring progress toward achievement of the strategic plan.

> The ... DSS is a management information system that integrates cost, quality, and clinical information in a patient-centered data base ... used to improve strategic and operational decision making, ... the information infrastructure for data driven management decision making in the "new VHA." It enables accurate determination of the results of performance measurements.... In FY 1999, the DSS database will become the principal management tool for decision making on performance, budget, and resource allocation. (Kizer 1997, 40)

The CPRS was expected to integrate predefined and personalized order sets, integrating them with "progress notes, results, procedures, diagnosis, and problem lists" (Kizer 1997, 42).

Patients would be linked to their teams, primary care providers, and attending physician, to the scheduling process, and to the functions that automatically accommodate changes in scheduling, rebooking not only the patient, but all the tests and procedures to be associated with the visit. The introduction of electronic signature codes truly completed the transformation of the system into a paperless record.

The education and research offices, both in Central Office and in the field, were provided with their own targets for realignment with the spirit and letter of the "new VA." Methods for empowering employees were described in *Journey of Change*. Finally, the programs that address conditions specific to VA's core mission population, the service-connected, were designated as "Special Programs." Twelve programs were identified: blind rehabilitation, geriatrics and long-term care, homelessness, Persian Gulf veterans, post-traumatic stress disorder, preservation of amputation care and treatment, prosthetics and orthotics, readjustment counseling, seriously mentally ill, spinal cord dysfunction, substance abuse, and women veterans. The Under Secretary recognized that the list would likely change over time. Each program was to have special management attention in

Central Office and in the field. Monitoring of the allocation of resources, performance, and customer satisfaction for and in these programs was already undertaken by the office of the Under Secretary for Health. (Kizer 1997).

Dr. Kizer, upon learning that his renomination as Under Secretary for Health would be opposed in the Senate, did not submit a request for renewal of his appointment and thus left VA in 2000. Though he did not stay to oversee the complete fulfillment of his vision, the vector of change he set in motion has continued to this day.

The "Proof Is in the Pudding"

There is no better evidence of the success of the Kizer revolution than that contained in Phillip Longman's account of what he found upon investigating VHA healthcare. In recent years VA has been singled out for its excellence by no less than the *New England Journal of Medicine* (*NJM*) and the *Harvard Business Review* (Young 2000). The *NJM* published a study

> that compared veterans health facilities on 11 meaures of quality with fee-for service Medicare. On all 11 measures the quality of care in veterans facilities proved to be "significantly better".... The *Annals of Internal Medicine* recently published a study that compared veterans health facilities with commercial managed-care systems in their treatment of diabetes patients. In seven out of seven measures of quality, the VA provided better care ... [and finally] the National Committee for Quality Assurance today [which] ranks health-care plans on 17 different performance measures ... [including] how well the plans manage high blood pressure or how precisely they adhere to standard protocols of evidence-based medicine such as prescribing beta blockers for patients recovering from a heart attack ... [found that] in every single category, the VHA system outperforms the highest rated non-VHA hospitals. (Longman 2005)

Longman, who had set out to write a piece on the failings of the VA sytem, finished by authoring a book after his magazine expressed no further interest in his findings. The article cited here and the book *The Best Care Anywhere: Why VA Health Care Is Better Than Yours*, were an instant sensation in healthcare circles. "The quality of care is outstanding," says Peter Gayton, deputy director for veterans affairs and rehabilitation at the American Legion; ".... eighty-one percent of VHA hospital patients express satisfaction with the care they receive, compared to 77 percent of Medicare and Medicaid patients" (as cited in Longman 2005):

> Outside experts agree that the VHA has become an industry leader in its safety and quality measures. Dr. Donald M. Berwick, president of the Institute for

Health Care Improvement and one of the nation's top health-care quality experts, praises the VHA's information technology as "spectacular." The venerable Institute of Medicine notes that the VHA's "integrated health information system, including its framework for using performance measures to improve quality, is considered one of the best in the nation." (Longman 2005)

One might reasonably ask about costs. Between 1999 and 2003, the number of VHA-enrolled patients increased 70 percent, but funding (unadjusted for inflation) went up only 41 percent. "So the VHA has not only become the health care industry's best quality performer, it has done so while spending less and less on each patient" (Longman 2005). One could argue that the sources of such improvements and economies rest with VHA's lifetime involvement with its patients, leading it to make up-front investments in health promotion and chronic disease management to receive long-term dividends; or one might cite the fact that most VA providers, including physicians, are salaried rather than paid fee-for-service; or one could focus on the regimentation inherent in a system with its roots in the military (Longman 2005). However, all of these factors were true twenty years ago. A Google search in November 2009 targeting "VHA healthcare" and the "Harvard Business Review" revealed that the turnaround that Kizer energized has continued to inspire academic studies of the VHA healthcare system's sustained success. The fact is that the contributions of hundreds, if not thousands, of dedicated and caring VA employees, known and unknown, developing and implementing systems for improving care and its management, along with the charismatic leadership of Dr. Kenneth Kizer, have resulted in a healthcare system second to none. VHA has truly become a "learning system," one in which the cultures of creativity and self-correction have become embedded.

Part IV: Current Trends and Future Directions

Current Progress: Performance and Accountability

When President Barack Obama took office, he pledged to ensure that VA healthcare would be twenty-first-century healthcare. As previously noted, VA had already become the benchmark for innovations in both clinical practice and its supporting infrastructure. The president had appointed General Eric Shinseki to serve as his Secretary for Veterans Affairs in recognition of his administrative abilities, integrity, and devotion to duty. Since World War II other former flag rank officers have been appointed to head VA; however, only two were four-star generals, Omar Bradley and Eric Shinseki. Like his post–World War II predecessor, General Shinseki has planned a major reorganization of the Department of Veterans Affairs. Early in 2009 Secretary Shinseki announced the initial steps of a plan that was to drive VA's fiscal year 2010 budget. He titled it "Transformation 21." It has come to be known as "T21":

> [It] focused on a series of focused initiatives:
>
> - Creating a "virtual lifetime electronic record" to ensure uniform registration of all military service members in conjunction with the defense department
> - Accelerating a "telehealth" and home care initiative, primarily for older, chronically ill veterans in order to keep them out of hospitals
> - Eliminating homelessness among veterans
> - Self-service devices so veterans can improve interactions with VA staff, and an integrated "veterans relationship management system"
> - Developing a human capital plan for strategically managing VA's staff of nearly 300,000 (IBM Center 2010)

By the end of the first fiscal year, there was already evidence of some success. The Performance and Accountability Report for Fiscal Year 2009 was released in mid-November 2009. The section of the "Executive Summary" devoted to the activities of VHA was titled "Medical Services: Delivering High-Quality Health Care," and began by asserting that

> VA maintained its status as the largest integrated health care system in America. Throughout the year, VA implemented new innovative practices to improve Veterans access to health care, such as telemedicine and mobile clinics, to provide care to more than 5.6 million unique patients. Our commitment to delivering timely, high-quality care to America's Veterans while controlling costs remains a top priority. (Department of Veterans Affairs 2009a, 1)

Each year VHA has identified key performance measures for the system, aligning incentives for personnel ranging from the Under Secretary for Health down through the layers of management to the frontline service providers and their support teams. For fiscal 2009 (October 1, 2008 through September 30, 2009) VA reported that 99 percent of primary care appointments were completed within the target thirty days of the desired appointment date. Performance of VHA measured by "nationally recognized industry standards" (Department of Veterans Affairs 2009a) continued to increase beyond the levels described previously as already leading the healthcare field. The Clinical Practice Guidelines Index, measuring the degree to which care episodes followed best practices, increased from 84 to 86 percent, and the Prevention Index, measuring the degree to which care included interventions known to reduce the instance of complications or of poor health, increased from 88 to 89 percent.

The "Executive Summary" reported that VHA continued its Rural Mobile Health Care Clinics and supported "studies and analyses on a wide range of health care issues relevant to rural and highly rural Veterans including studies on telehealth technology and implementation, the unique needs of the Native American population, and older Veterans" (Department of Veterans Affairs 2009a, 2).

Other programs highlighted in the summary of the Performance and Accountability Report were the Suicide Hotline and Suicide Prevention Programs, developed by VHA in response to an observed increase in suicides among returning veterans of the current conflicts. Many of these veterans had had no prior VHA mental health contacts. Expansion of this hotline during 2009 allowed VHA to field about 350 calls per day and to assist over 5,000 callers who had already begun to hurt themselves or were at immediate risk of suicide, dispatching local first responders to the scene. A joint partnership with the Department of Housing and Urban Development placed more than 6,300 formerly homeless veterans in permanent homes. In addition, more than 20,000 units of supportive housing were provided to homeless veterans. The VHA telehealth programs were reported to be "the largest and most sophisticated in the nation, providing care for over 230,000 patients in more than 144 VA medical Centers and 450 community-based outpatient clinics" (Department of Veterans Affairs 2009a, 2). The telehealth programs involve not only direct access to veterans for health promotion, habit management, and mental healthcare through such equipment as Web cameras and closed circuit television, but also the use of the technology to provide access to specialists for consultation with primary care providers, hence tele-radiology, tele-pathology, tele-dermatology, etc.

Finally, VA announced the establishment of five new partnerships with prestigious schools of nursing as part of VHA's Nursing Academy, which now numbers fifteen such collaborations. These partnerships differ from the historic standard affiliations with nursing schools, which enabled student nurses and their professors access to VHA sites for training in patient care. This initiative provides the partner with enhanced resources for increasing faculty numbers and for support for the faculty's continuing professional development. The aim is to increase nursing enrollment and therefore the pool of well-trained nurses from which VHA and other facilities may draw. The increased enrollment is targeted primarily at the baccalaureate nursing program; however, some graduate nurse education is supported as well. The program is also expected to pay dividends in recruitment and retention at VHA medical centers where the nursing staff will have an enhanced role in teaching and training (Department of Veterans Affairs 2010).

Future Strategic Moves: VA/DoD Joint Executive Council Strategic Plan Fiscal Years 2009–2011 and the Department of Veterans Affairs Strategic Plan: FY 2010–2014

Since the publication of the transformative documents authored by Dr. Kenneth Kizer, VA has increased its emphasis on partnerships with other federal agencies (Department of Defense, Indian Health Service, Public Health Service, etc.) as well as with other governmental and nongovernmental bodies and facilities. The hallmark of that era, continued through the present, has been the use of "sharing agreements," which spell out the rights and obligations of each member of the partnership. Funds, bricks and mortar, equipment, and human resources have been shared in pursuit of common goals. Collaborations have been initiated to ensure continuity of care between VAMCs and state veterans' homes and mental health facilities.

In early 2009, during the last days of the presidency of George W. Bush, representatives of the DoD and VA inked a joint two-year strategic plan. The document is fifty pages in length and can only be summarized in these pages; however it is worth reading in its entirety (Department of Veterans Affairs/ Department of Defense 2009). The mission of the partnership was "to improve the quality, efficiency, and effectiveness of the delivery of benefits and services to veterans, service members, military retirees, and their families through an enhanced Department of Veterans Affairs and Department of Defense partnership" (Department of Veterans Affairs/Department of Defense 2009, 4). The agreement's vision statement set forth the goal of developing "a world-class partnership that delivers seamless, cost-effective, quality services to beneficiaries and value to our nation" (Department of Veterans Affairs/Department of Defense 2009, 4). Six goals were enunciated, each with its own set of objectives, strategies for realizing those objectives, and performance measures for subsequent oversight:

- Leadership, Commitment, and Accountability
- High Quality Health Care
- Seamless Coordination of Benefits
- Integrated Information Sharing
- Efficiency of Operations
- Joint Medical Contingency/Readiness Capabilities (Department of Veterans Affairs/Department of Defense 2009, 5)

The second of these goals is most relevant to this chapter. The first objective of this goal aimed at VA and DoD becoming joint "leaders in developing and delivering innovative clinical processes and programs that enhance the quality of health care" (Department of Veterans Affairs/Department of Defense 2009, 10). Strategic work groups were expected to focus on (1) patient safety concerns in clinical settings, (2) issues of traumatic brain injury and psychological health concerns, (3) soldiers and veterans at risk of suicide, (4) collaboration in the education and training of health professionals, and (5) health risks surveillance for service members and veterans exposed to toxic agents or traumatic brain injury.

Since the document was signed, the Obama administration has succeeded that of the former president. This author has been told that VA has made a commitment to carrying out those strategies that fall within its purview (Zeiss 2010). Given that many of the political appointees to VA have Pentagon backgrounds, it would be surprising not to see continuity from the DoD.

The Shinseki VA Initiatives

The DoD underwent its own major transformation around the turn of the twenty-first century. A number of executives involved in that reform effort are now at VA and taking a hard look at its administrative infrastructure in the light of lessons learned at the Pentagon. One area of change revisited was information technology (IT) reorganization, which took place earlier in the last decade, described previously. Authority for IT spending had been centralized to the Departmental Chief Information Officer, and by extension, away from the various facilities of VHA, a move that required congressional action. When the new IT arrangement was later scored on the White House Information Technology Scorecard, it was rated as failing on a number of projects. Hence a second look was deemed warranted. Subsequently a transition began to take place from "a series of disconnected projects to a set of portfolios around major initiatives. For example, one portfolio is to be created around a veteran-centric benefit system where there will be a 'single face' to the veterans" (IBM Center 2010, 2).

A major overhaul of VA's procurement systems has been envisioned as well, with different contract vehicles for different purposes rather than a "one-size-fits-all" approach. Hence there could be one vehicle for IT solutions, another for purchasing various bulk commodities, and still another for procuring software licenses. The aim of this streamlining of the administrative support processes is financial, with the expectation of saving millions of dollars that could be better spent on direct services to the veterans. Similarly, VA's overall financial management system and its human resources office have been similarly targeted so as to provide better support for its mission delivery functions. Four strategic goals, outlined on the Web site of VA's Office of Acquisition and Logistics, have guided these interventions, with the intent to

- Improve the quality and accessibility of healthcare, benefits, and memorial services while optimizing value.
- Increase Veteran client satisfaction with health, education, training, counseling, financial, and burial benefits and services.
- Raise readiness to provide services and protect people and assets continuously and in time of crisis.
- Improve internal customer satisfaction with management systems and support services to make VA an employer of choice by investing in human capital." (Department of Veterans Affairs 2009b)

These goals have been operationalized in a series of initiatives under the rubric "The Thirteen Greatest Challenges." Each of these challenges is to be engaged by a clear and specific tactical plan with an aggressive timeline. The process is to be "people-centric ... Results-driven ... and Forward-Looking" (Department of Veterans Affairs. Office of Policy and Planning 2010, 21):

1. "Eliminate Veteran Homelessness": A 2009 estimate of veterans homeless on any given night was 131,000, recognizing, however, that at some points in time over the year the number may be double this estimate. The goal set has been the elimination of such homelessness by 2014. The methods have included the use of empirically proven mental health treatments and active clinical trials of other available interventions to alleviate suffering; establishment of a national homeless veterans' registry to enable better tracking of individuals and coordination of efforts among VA sites; and application of handheld technology to enable staff to more easily enter and retrieve information about the veteran client in an accurate and timely manner while in the field. (Department of Veterans Affairs 2009c)

2. "Enable 21st Century Benefits Delivery and Services (e.g., Backlog Reduction)": There are benefits and services that VA provides to veteran clients and in other cases, to their families (life insurance, disability and pension benefits, and memorial services). The aging of the veteran population and the press of new veterans from the Afghani and Iraqi conflicts have severely stressed the Veterans Benefits Administration (VBA), creating a backlog that has been targeted for elimination. VBA has announced its intention to improve the information technology underlying the various benefits systems, increasing their ability to exchange information in a more seamless manner; to provide a more transparent process for veterans to monitor their claims status throughout the process, thus improving service and

client satisfaction; and finally, to streamline the claims process, rendering it more efficient to enable better utilization of staff resources by rebalancing workload across functions and localities (Department of Veterans Affairs 2009c). The target performance measure is to be 125 days or less by 2015. (Department of Veterans Affairs. Office of Policy and Planning 2010)

3. "Automate GI Bill Benefits": The most recent GI bill was enacted after the 9/11 engagement of our military in the war on terror. Among other provisions were those giving education benefits to active duty service members and to Reserve and National Guard members provided they were on active duty ninety days or more since 9/11. Due to the complexity of administering these benefits to these groups with previously disparate entitlements, new processing systems were required, along with the underlying computerized support capable of managing high volumes of work. A twelve-month timeline (2010) was put in place for this target (Department of Veterans Affairs 2009c). The 2011 processing target for these benefit claims had been initially set at eighteen days, and later nineteen days, a major reduction from the baseline of fifty-six days in 2009. The ultimate target is now set at ten days. Over that same period the accuracy of the processed education claims is to increase from 94 to 95 percent. The strategic plan target will be 97 percent. Similarly ambitious targets have been set for completion of supplemental education benefits (Department of Veterans Affairs. Office of Policy and Planning 2010; 2011).[4]

4. "Implement Virtual Lifetime Electronic Records (VLER)": About 150,000 active duty members of the armed forces are released to civilian life each year, now in veteran status. To ensure the continuity of the health record and of the services provided, the VA and the Department of Defense (DoD) have set out to create a completely integrated set of electronic personal health and personal benefits records. The plan is to create a single, unified record that would follow the service member/veteran seamlessly throughout his or her service tenure and later life. To arrive at such a goal VA is "seeking solutions to help

   - Develop and Implement common standards and processes to be used by VA, DoD, and private sector providers for collecting, publishing, transmitting and reconciling medical and administrative information while ensuring privacy and security are not compromised.

   - Ensure system interoperability between Federal and private sector partners.

   - Develop IT interfaces required to make the system user-friendly.

- Integrate DoD/VA initiative with Beacon Communities program to create a comprehensive Electronic Health Records (EHR) environment in several locations across the U.S." (Department of Veterans Affairs 2009c, 1)

The current date targeted for prototyping and piloting of the initiative is 2012. (Department of Veterans Affairs. Office of Policy and Planning 2010). In the recent update of the plan, another goal is for bidirectional interchange of medical information between VA, DoD, and the private sector among at least three sites (Department of Veterans Affairs. Office of Policy and Planning 2011).

5. "Improve Veteran Mental Health": More than 1.5 million of the 5.5 million veterans seen in the prior fiscal year carried a mental health diagnosis, often along with other medical issues. The identified mental health clientele has become increasingly numerous. VHA seeks ideas "to help . . .

   - Identify and test new comprehensive approaches to improve mental health through prevention, diagnosis, and treatment.

   - Identify specific measures to track their effectiveness so we can allocate resources more efficiently.

   - Develop and test new treatment models to remove stigma associated with admitting problems and seeking help." (Department of Veterans Affairs 2009c)

Performance targets for this initiative (Department of Veterans Affairs. Office of Policy and Planning 2010) include 97 percent of veteran patients being screened at regular intervals for alcohol issues (2010) and 96 percent screened for depression; by 2011, 97 percent of patients regularly screened for PTSD; and the percent of OEF/OIF veterans with a primary diagnosis of post-traumatic stress disorder who have received at least eight psychotherapy sessions within a fourteen-week timeframe will be raised from a 2009 baseline of 20 to 35 percent in 2010 (altered to 15 percent in the 2011 update), with a strategic target of 60 percent. Also added in 2011 was a requirement to provide 96 percent of patients with a full evaluation within fourteen days of their first formal encounter with mental health service staff (Department of Veterans Affairs. Office of Policy and Planning 2011).

6. "Build Veteran Relationship Management (VRM) Capability to Enable Convenient, Seamless Interactions": This capability will enable on-demand access to the full range of VA services and benefits in a consistent, user-friendly manner. This client-centered access will be characterized by multichannel accessibility so there will never be a "wrong door" approach by the

client. The desired VA service will be able to be accessed whether the approach would be by phone, e-mail, letter, or in person. New processes will be needed to make this happen, and VA has solicited help from within and without to make it occur, all the while intending to protect privacy and observe security requirements (Department of Veterans Affairs 2009c). By June 2011 the full range of VA benefits and services were to have been included in this initiative, and by the close of 2011 customer satisfaction on this issue was targeted to become an 8 on a scale of 1 to 10 (Department of Veterans Affairs. Office of Policy and Planning 2010). The plan update altered both of these goals, with the 2011 VRM rollout moved back to June 2012, and the customer satisfaction measure changed to increasing the effectiveness of the National Call and Health Resource centers by decreasing the rate of abandoned calls to 5 percent for 2011 (Department of Veterans Affairs. Office of Policy and Planning 2011).

7. "Design a Veteran-Centric Healthcare Model and Right-Sized Infrastructure to Help Veterans Navigate the Healthcare Delivery System and Receive Coordinated Care": The changing needs of the veteran population along with changes in healthcare nationally have required "a more fundamental reassessment of VA's approach to healthcare delivery, funding, and coordination" (Department of Veterans Affairs 2009c, 1). The Office of Patient Centered Care and Cultural Transformation, in Arlington, VA, is to work toward building patient-centered healthcare plans for recipients of VA healthcare services focused on a personalized approach to care. In our nation's current, rapidly developing healthcare environment, VA is in a unique position to transform modern healthcare culture. This new office is expected to be nimble, a "living, learning organization" (Miller 2011).

As new models of care are developed, their results and impact will be measured to determine what initiatives will be made available nationwide at all VA medical centers, as well as assist in their implementation. There will be 4 regional satellite locations of this new office, and they are scattered across the country. The locations were chosen because of their strong history of providing localized patient-centered care. These locations have been given the responsibility of taking the VA's new model of health care and working out the kinks so to speak before the programs go nationwide. (Miller 2011)

Two examples of the kinds of initiatives that Dr. Miller referenced are (1) the development of patient-centered primary care medical homes, and (2) the My HealtheVet program, described as the "Gateway to Veteran Health and Wellness." The former are intended to offer coordinated, comprehensive care from the first contact to the most recent and utilize a team approach working "collaboratively to improve access, communication, coordination, quality, and safety" (Miller 2011, 48). The latter program is a computer-based, patient- and care-provider-accessible program that combines elements of the medical record with patient education modules and personal health record keeping.

VA has reported itself to have sought input on how to track and analyze patient demand and outcome trends so as to understand better the variability seen in the VA system; on how to implement a better control system over third-party contracts to discover any instances of fraud or abuse; and on how to transform the "organizational culture within the . . . [VHA] healthcare system to be [even] more patient-centered" (Department of Veterans Affairs 2009c); the integration of the new telehealth models with comprehensive home-based treatment for patients with chronic conditions such as heart disease, diabetes, pulmonary dysfunction, and others; and finally, the design of an R&D path to improve rates of innovation and of adoption of these innovations in support of the client-centric model (Department of Veterans Affairs 2009c).

Specific measures developed for this veteran-centric model initiative include developing a baseline (2010) and setting a target of 84 percent for customer satisfaction on the Consumer Assessment of Health Care Providers and Systems (CAHPS) survey; improving the American College of Physicians Home Builder Score from a 2009 baseline of 69 percent to 79 percent in 2010 with an ultimate target of 100 percent; increasing the utilization of telehealth programs from a 2009 baseline of 14,921 average daily utilizers to a 2010 target of 28,084; and increasing the percentage of VA facilities with "interdisciplinary health promotion/disease prevention committees" (Department of Veterans Affairs. Office of Policy and Planning 2010, 28) from a 2009 baseline of 59 percent to 75 percent in 2010, with an ultimate goal of 100 percent. In 2011 the target for telehealth average daily census is set at 59,800 patients; and the target of 84 percent for customer satisfactions on the Consumer Assessment of Health Care Providers and Systems (CAHPS) survey was moved to the following section (Department of Veterans Affairs. Office of Policy and Planning 2011).

8. "Expand Healthcare Access for Veterans, Including Women and Rural Populations":[5] Demographic changes in the veteran cohorts and population shifts in where veterans reside require VA to continuously realign its delivery of services with the changes observed in the target population. Help has been solicited in identifying any gaps in services or in the quality of services through more aggressive collection and analysis of data at the market level, as well as through the development of a model for efficient integration of third-party service provision to help meet these objectives (Department of Veterans Affairs 2009c).

Two performance measures were set for this goal: increasing the percentage of female veterans utilizing vet centers with a target, based on the proportion of the OEF/OIF population that is female, from a 2009 baseline of 9.6 percent to 11.9 percent in 2010 with an ultimate target of 13 percent and raising the percentage of appointments completed "within 30 days of desired date" from the 2009 baseline of 91 percent to 95 percent in 2010, with a final target of 100 percent (Department of Veterans Affairs. Office of Policy and Planning 2010). The revised plan of 2011 does not mention the target for services to female veterans in vet centers; however, it proposes raising the bar on the other measure to "within 14 days of the desired date" (Department of Veterans Affairs. Office of Policy and Planning 2011, 29).

9. "Ensure Preparedness to Meet Emergent National Needs (e.g., Hurricanes, H1N1 Virus)": To ensure VA's viability in its adjunctive role to the DoD's healthcare system in wartime or national emergency, as well as to other federal agencies in following up on disaster or terror attack, VA will undertake a full inventory of its various clinical and logistical capacities in a manner that can be easily accessed. VA planned to create a system that can efficiently be kept up to date. All frontline clinicians are to be trained to participate in such adjunctive efforts through teaching, training, and simulations (Department of Veterans Affairs 2009c).

   Performance measure: Response time for Integrated Operations Center (IOC) to receive Serious Incident Report. Provide leadership with timely, accurate, and credible information, while providing predictive analysis for better decision making. Strategic Target: 2 hours. (Department of Veterans Affairs. Office of Policy and Planning 2010)

10. "Develop Capabilities and Enabling Systems to Drive Performance and Outcomes": Dr. Kizer (1996) had insisted that VHA become value-oriented, measuring performance in all of what he termed "the domains of value," that is, (1) cost/price, (2) technical quality, (3) customer satisfaction, and (4) access. The new direction places much of its emphasis on the first aspect, return on investment. The document went on to state:

   The best run organizations in the world vigorously manage to value, to ensure efficiency and effectiveness, and to appropriate allocation of scarce resource. By value, we mean outputs that are measurable and that show return on inputs (e.g. people, time, and funding) for a task or process. VA seeks ideas to help the organization:

   • Develop a shared enterprise-wide framework for assessing value, to which all parts of the organization will contribute commonly denominated metrics, to ensure that corporate and organizational leaders have the information they need to evaluate performance and allocate resources. (Department of Veterans Affairs 2009c, 2)

The performance measure for this goal was to measure the percentage of internal customers (staff) who are satisfied with the cost accounting data they are given upon which to base decisions. A baseline was to be determined during 2010, with an expected future goal of 95 percent (Department of Veterans Affairs. Office of Policy and Planning 2010).

11. "Establish VA Management Infrastructure and Integrated Operating Model": Local field operations were to be strengthened by providing the means of sharing information on best practices, improving communications throughout and across all levels of the organization, taking advantage of economies of scale in acquisitions and personnel recruitment, improving allocation of resources, and more consistent deployment of talent across the entire VA. Specifically, VA was to solicit ideas on "how to:

- Identify opportunities to pool resources and benefit from economies of scale and skill [sic].
- Develop the following capacities:

  - Financial and Logistics Integrated Technology Enterprise (FLITE)
  - Strategic Capital Investment Planning (SCIP)
  - Use of purchase organization
  - IT [Information Technology] PMAS [Property Management Accountability Software] support and enhance project management capability." (Department of Veterans Affairs 2009c, 2)

In the Strategic Plan 2010–2014, customer service performance measure targets were set for the Office of Acquisition, Logistics, and Constructions services (a 2010 baseline to be determined, with a later target of 95 percent); the Office of Human Resources and Administration (from a 2009 baseline of 3.37 on a 5-point scale to 4.5 percent); the Office of Information Technology (baseline to be developed in 2010, with a 2011 target of 80 percent); and for Financial Management a performance measure required the implementation of a Web-based time and attendance system to better track and assess the costs of labor in delivering VA services (Department of Veterans Affairs. Office of Policy and Planning 2010).

Here again, the 2011 Strategic Plan revises the targets: the baseline for the Office of Acquisitions, Logistics, and Construction Services was moved from

2010 to 2014, with a new strategic target of 75 percent; the strategic target for the Office of Human Resources and Administration was lowered from 4.5 to 3.81; the Office of Information Technology was assigned a new target of 100 percent by 2013; the Financial Management performance measure was extended to 2013 from 2011; and the Office for Policy and Planning was assigned a customer satisfaction measure for the first time, with a target date of 2011 and a performance target of 80 percent (Department of Veterans Affairs. Office of Policy and Planning 2011).

12. "Transform Human Capital Management": Since Dr. Kizer's assertion that VA should aim to be the "employer of choice," attention has been given to improving the work environment, empowering employees at all levels, and providing proper recognition for high performance. Now VA was to seek to "invest in developing our people and helping them reach their full potential . . . [making managers accountable] for the development and well-being of their people" (Department of Veterans Affairs 2009c, 2) and ensuring that their employees have the skillsets and managerial support they need to do so. VA actively solicited ideas "to help [the Department]

- Develop and Implement high-quality surge-training for 20,000 people in 12 months on project management, change management, and supervisory skills improvement.

- Develop a Talent Management Tool so that VA can track and develop the talents of its employees and match them with the right opportunities.

- Assess and address gaps in leadership capabilities among frontline managers.

- Develop enterprise management solution for workforce management, training and development." (Department of Veterans Affairs 2009c, 2)

The performance measures for this initiative included the "percentage of VA Title 5 employees hired within 60 calendar days. Baseline [2009]: 46%; Strategic Target: 80%"; and measuring

> the number of managers and employees trained in leadership competencies and employee technical training to establish a more robust leadership competency model and address gaps in leadership capabilities [set at 16,500 in 2011]. Percentages and measures TBD. Baseline: TBD; Strategic Target: TBD. (Department of Veterans Affairs. Office of Policy and Planning 2010, 30)

In 2011 another measure was appended to this initiative, setting a goal for the number of employees given technical/competency-based training to raise the level of their professional proficiency in core competencies as well as those specific to their jobs. The 2011 baseline was set at 135,000, and a 2015 strategic target was set at 148,500 (Department of Veterans Affairs. Office of Policy and Planning 2011).

13. "Perform Research and Development to Enhance the Long-Term Health and Well-Being of Veterans": The theme of this "challenge" echoed the intention of Dr. Kizer's increased emphasis on clinical research, with special attention being given to those conditions found to be primarily associated with military service. The development of the evidence basis for innovations in clinical care and improvements in clinical service delivery was once again underscored as critical to the "long-term health and well-being of Veterans. With these goals in mind, VA sought ideas to assist the organization to:

- Define a research and development agenda that focuses on filling in the data and knowledge gaps for the most high-priority areas (e.g., mental health, aging Veterans with multiple conditions).

- Adjust model to favor process of unique VA needs." (Department of Veterans Affairs 2009c, 2)

For this initiative two performance measures had been published at the time of this writing (2011): continuation of the National Research Advisory Council's assessment of the quality and balance of the VA research portfolio (baseline rating A-level in 2009, with a goal of maintaining that rating) and fostering wide recognition of VA research (first-quarter baseline of 2,139 VA research publications and an FY 2010 target of 8,500).

The VA Approach to Implementation

The Department of Veterans Affairs intends to move beyond analysis and planning and has developed a five-point program for ensuring focused attention and execution of its goals:

1. A "behaviorally-oriented communication with employees ... will ensure that employees throughout the organization—the people who will actually implement the strategy—understand the need for change and what is expected of them." (Department of Veterans Affairs. Office of Policy and Planning 2010, 26).

2. "Coordination and Accountability" are fostered by mechanisms created to review performance against annual planned implementation, ensuring close managerial alignment and identifying risks, challenges, and outstanding performance to enable the sharing of best practices. The major management efforts in this regard will target the initiatives with the highest priorities as contained in this strategic plan (Department of Veterans Affairs. Office of Policy and Planning 2010, 26).

3. "Performance management" is a theme running throughout the entirety of the strategic plan for 2010–2014. The measures developed will continue to evolve and raise the bar to achieve or maintain excellence (Department of Veterans Affairs. Office of Policy and Planning 2010, 26).

4. "Program evaluation" is key to strategic management, helping "VA's strategy, operations and results to improve over time by leveraging learning from past experience." VA Oncology programs were evaluated in 2010 and found to provide a quality of care comparable or better than that found in patients treated under Medicare (Department of Veterans Affairs 2011). Treatment of the seriously mentally ill seen in the VA mental health program was similarly evaluated and the results made available in 2011. Once again VA's outcomes were comparable or superior to those reported for other healthcare systems, but not yet at the performance levels targeted by VA (Watkins et al. 2011). The request for proposals for the evaluation of the Medical Research Program was issued in FY 2011 and Harvard University's Department of Health Care Policy has been awarded the contract to conduct the study (McNeil 2012).

5. "Risk Management . . . [must] involve monitoring and adjusting the strategy according to developments outside the Department's control, including:

    a. Global and national socioeconomic conditions [which] will influence competitive salary levels, labor availability, program demand, and health insurance coverage.

    b. Continued interagency collaboration between VA and DoD, as well as with other federal, . . . state and local . . . [bodies], . . . [veterans service organizations], and the private sector. . . .

    c. DoD recruitment and retention variables. . . .

    d. Emerging technologies and advances in medicine are likely to change the scope of Veterans' needs. . . .

    e. VA's preparedness role and the outlook for national security both have bearing on the requirements of VA programs" (Department of Veterans. Affairs Office of Policy and Planning 2010, 32).

Epilogue

The VA "Path to Excellence" began within what is now VHA and before that, the DM&S. What has continued to impress this author is the continuous process of self-correction and improvement in that group. Further, it appears that management of the overall VA, embracing not only the clinical services delivery portions of VHA and its administrative infrastructure, along with the

Departments of Veterans Benefits and Memorial Affairs, appears to have been swept up in the culture of veteran-centered delivery of services. Some of the more recent initiatives of the current Secretary of Veterans Affairs call for VA-wide actions, a number of which have long been embedded in VHA. Unlike many of his predecessors, Secretary Eric Shinseki exercises the kind of "command and control" from the top that characterizes successful military operations. That single-mindedness, along with the concomitant solicitation of ideas from VA employees, veteran beneficiaries, the private sector, and the American public, bode well for continued organizational transformation and cost-beneficial, high-quality services to our nation's veterans.

Endnotes

1. Richard (Rick) Nesbitt retired as Director of Information Resource Management Service at the Minneapolis VA Medical Center early in 1998. His VA information technology career spanned the era of ODM&T and VA's transition to the decentralized system. His comments have been most helpful to the author.
2. Today the facility is called the Corporate Data Center Operations (CDCO) –Austin Information Technology Center. It is a now a federal franchise fund operation providing IT enterprise services to various federal entities.
3. Special mention should also be made of the KLF, named after its initiator, Kathy Lee Frisbee, who developed a number of standard SAS shells and a methodology that can be used to display available administrative and clinical data in a host of ways, ranging from appointment wait times to provider prescribing patterns. A full description is beyond the scope of this chapter.
4. Note that the order of initiatives 3 and 4 was inverted in the 2010 plan from that found in 2009.
5. Reworded slightly in 2010 to read "Enhance the Veteran experience and access to healthcare."

References

Brown, S., Lincoln, M. J., Groen, P. J. & Kolodner, R. M. (2003). VistA-US Department of Veterans Affairs national scale HIS. *International Journal of Medical Informatics* 69, nos. 2–3: 135–156.

Custis, D. (1984). *Chief medical director's letter: Resources allocated and VA national health policy.* IL 10-84(5). Washington, DC: VACO.

Department of Veterans Affairs. (2009a). *FY 2009 performance & accountability report: Executive summary.* Office of Budget. http://www.va.gov/budget/report/ (accessed March 24, 2012).

Department of Veterans Affairs. (2009b). *Office of acquisition and logistics—supplier relationship transformation.* Office of Acquisition and Logistics. http://www.docstoc.com/docs/37496917/Veterans-Health-Administration (accessed March 24, 2012).

Department of Veterans Affairs. (2009c). *Office of acquisition and logistics—supplier relationship transformation: The 13 greatest challenges.* Office of Acquisitions & Logistics. http://www.theambitgroup.com/vasrt/challenges.html (accessed March 24, 2012).

Department of Veterans Affairs. (2010). VA Nursing Academy. Office of Academic Affiliations. http://www.va.gov/oaa/vana/default.asp (accessed March 24, 2012).

Department of Veterans Affairs. Information Resource Center (VIREC). (2009). VHA decision support system (DSS): Introduction. http://www.virec.research.va.gov/DataSourcesName/DSS/DSSintro.htm. (accessed March 24, 2012).

Department of Veterans Affairs. Office of Information Technology. (2009). Enterprise architecture future vision. http://www.ea.oit.va.gov/extdocs/Practice_Guidance_20090812.pdf (accessed March 24, 2012).

Department of Veterans Affairs. Office of Policy and Planning. (2010). Department of Veterans Affairs strategic plan: FY 2010–2014. http://www.va.gov/op3/Docs/StrategicPlanning/VA_2010_2014_Strategic_Plan.pdf. (accessed March 24, 2012).

Department of Veterans Affairs. Office of Policy and Planning. (2011). Department of Veterans Affairs strategic plan refresh: FY 2011–2015. http://www.va.gov/VA_2011–2015_Strategic_Plan_Refresh_wv.pdf. (accessed March 24, 2012).

Department of Veterans Affairs/Department of Defense. (2009). VA/DoD Joint Executive Council strategic plan fiscal years 2009–2011. Department of Veterans Affairs/Department of Defense. http://prhome.defense.gov/docs/2009%20VA%20DoD%20Joint%20Executive%20Council%20Annual%20Report%20and%20Joint%20Strategic%20Plan.pdf. (accessed March 24, 2012).

Errera, P. E., Nightingale, E. J., Lipkin, J. O. & Ashcraft, M. E. (1985). DRGs and psychiatry: A work in progress. *General Hospital Psychiatry* 7: 316–320.

Fears, J. R. & Small, B. F. (1985a). A medical management information system—part I. *VA Practitioner* no. 11: 78–82.

Fears, J. R. & Small, B. F. (1985b). A medical management information system—part II. *VA Practitioner* no. 12: 43–44.

Gottfredsen, Douglas. (1990). Personal communication to author.

Green, H. H. (2000). *Testimony of Howard H. Green, M.D., concerning the Veterans Health Administration decision support system (DSS) to the Subcommittee on Oversight and Investigations, September 21.* http://democrats.veterans.house.gov/hearings/schedule106/sept00/9-21-00/hgreen.htm (accessed March 24, 2012).

Green, H. H. & McSherry, E. (1985). New case mix management tools for the DRG era. *VA Practitioner* (February): 44–57.

Holden, Dr. Frank. (1989). Personal communication to author, July.

IBM Center for the Business of Government blog. (2010). Veterans Affairs: "Transformation 21" and beyond. Department of Veterans Affairs. http://bizgov.wordpress.com/tag/eric-shinseki/ (accessed March 24, 2012).

Johnson, M. E. (1981). *Memo: DM&S medical information systems.* http://vistaexpertise.net/docs/1981-memo.pdf (accessed March 24, 2012).

Kizer, K. W. (1995). *Vision for change: A plan to restructure the Veterans Health Administration.* Washington, DC: U.S. Department of Veterans Affairs.

Kizer, K. W. (1996). *Prescription for change: The guiding principle and strategic objectives underlying the transformation of the Veterans Healthcare System.* Washington, DC: U.S. Department of Veterans Affairs.

Kizer, K. W. (1997). *Journey of change.* Washington, DC: U.S. Department of Veterans Affairs. http://www.va.gov/HEALTHPOLICYPLANNING/JourneyofChange.pdf. (accessed March 24, 2012).

Kolodner, R. M. (1997). Creating a robust multi-facility healthcare information system. In R. Kolodner & J. V. Douglas (Eds.), *Computerizing large integrated health networks* (pp. 39–56). New York: Springer Verlag.

Kolodner, R. M. (2005). *Statement of Robert M. Kolodner, MD, chief health informatics officer, Veterans Health Administration, Department of Veterans Affairs before the U.S. House of Representatives Committee on Government Reform, September 29.* http://www.va.gov/OCA/testimony/hgrc/050929RK.asp (accessed March 24, 2012).

Kolodner, R. M. & Douglas, J. V. (Eds.). (1997). *Computerizing large integrated health networks: The VA success.* New York: Springer.

Kussman, M. J. (2009). *Patient care data capture.* VHA Directive. Washington, DC: U.S. Department of Veterans Affairs, Veterans Health Administration.

Longman, P. (2005). The best care anywhere. *Washington Monthly* (January/February). http://www.washingtonmonthly.com/features/2005/0501.longman.html. (accessed March 24, 2012).

McNeil, B. (2012). *Evaluation of research structure.* Harvard Medical School Department of Health Care Policy. http://www.hcp.med.harvard.edu/node/2848. (accessed March 24, 2012).

Miller, Thomas W. (2011). Personal communication to author, July 25.

Nesbitt, Rick. (2010). Personal communication to author, April 30.

Nightingale, E. J. (1984). Here come the DRG's. *The VA Psychologist.* (Special issue).

Nightingale, E. J. (1986). Reviewing prospective payment of VA mental health services. *VA Practitioner* no. 10: 67–71.

Parlier, R. (2003). *Improvement report: Advanced Clinic Access Initiative.* U.S. Department of Veterans Affairs, VHA Advanced Clinic Access Initiative. http://www.ihi.org/knowledge/Pages/ImprovementStories/MemberReportAdvancedClinicAccessInitiative.aspx. (accessed March 24, 2012).

Price Waterhouse LLP and the Lewin Group Inc. (1998). *Veterans equitable resource allocation assessment final report.* Department of Veterans Affairs prime contract no. V101 (93) P-1444, task order 24, March. Price Waterhouse LLP.

Roswell, R. H. (2002). *Statement of the Honorable Robert H. Roswell, M.D., under secretary for health, Department of Veterans Affairs, before the Committee on Veterans Affairs, U.S. House of Representatives, on the veterans equitable resource allocation (VERA) model.* Washington, DC: http://democrats.veterans.house.gov/hearings/schedule 107/sept02/9-19-02/rroswell.pdf. (accessed March 24, 2012).

Timson, G. (2009). The history of the hardhats. http://www.hardhats.org/history/ hardhats.html. (accessed March 24, 2012).

U.S. General Accounting Office. (1996). Veterans' health care: Facilities' resource allocations could be more equitable. Letter report 02/07/96, GAO/HEHS-96–48. http://www.fas.org/man/gao/gao9648.htm. (accessed March 24, 2012).

U.S. General Accounting Office. (2002). Allocation changes would better align resources with workload. http://www.gao.gov/new.items/d02338.pdf. (accessed March 24, 2012).

Veterans Affairs Allocation Resource Center. (1997). *Resource allocation handbook.* Boston: Veterans Affairs Allocation Resource Center. http://vaww.arc.med.gov/ references/handbook/chap1.html. (accessed on VA intranet October 14, 2009).

Veterans Affairs Allocation Resource Center. (1998). *Resource allocation handbook: Overview.* Boston: Veterans Affairs Allocation Resource Center. http://vaww.arc .med.va.gov/references/VERA98_overview_tech_man.html. (accessed on VA intranet October 14, 2009).

Veterans Affairs Allocation Resource Center. (1999). *VERA handbook 1999: Executive overview.* Boston: Veterans Affairs Allocation Resource Center. http://vaww .arc.med.va.gov/references/handbook99/VERA_1999_Executive_Overview.html. (accessed on VA intranet October 14, 2009).

Veterans Affairs Allocation Resource Center. (2000). *VERA handbook 2000: Executive summary.* Boston: Veterans Affairs Allocation Resource Center. http://vaww .arc.med.va.gov/references/handbook00/Exec_Summary.html. (accessed on VA intranet October 14, 2009).

Veterans Affairs Allocation Resource Center. (2001). *VERA handbook 2001: Executive overview.* Boston: Veterans Affairs Allocation Resource Center. http://vaww .arc.med.va.gov/references/handbook01/toc.html. (accessed on VA intranet October 14, 2009).

Veterans Affairs Allocation Resource Center. (2002). *VERA handbook 2002: Executive overview.* Boston: Veterans Affairs Allocation Resource Center. http://arc.med .va.gov/references/handbook02/exec_summary.html. (accessed on VA intranet October 14, 2009).

Veterans Affairs Allocation Resource Center. (2003). *VERA handbook 2003: Executive overview.* Boston: Veterans Affairs Allocation Resource Center. http://arc.med.va.gov/ references/VERA2003/VERA_2003_Ex_Ov2_html. (accessed on VA intranet October 14, 2009).

Veterans Affairs Allocation Resource Center. (2004–2007). *VERA handbook 2004, 2005, 2006, 2007: Executive summary: overview.* Boston. http://arc.med.va.gov/ archive/references/archive_arc-tech_manuals_html. (accessed on VA intranet October 14, 2009).

Veterans Affairs Allocation Resource Center. (2008). *Veterans equitable resource allocation handbook 2008: Executive summary.* Boston: Veterans Affairs Allocation

Resource Center. http://vaww.arc.va.gov/references/VERA08_book/2008_vera_book.pdf. (accessed on VA intranet October 14, 2009).

Veterans Affairs Allocation Resource Center. (2009). *Veterans equitable resource allocation handbook 2009: Executive summary.* http://vaww.arc.va.gov/references/VERA09_book/vera09_book.pdf. (accessed on VA intranet October 14, 2009).

Wasserman, J., Ringel, J., Ricci, K., Malkin, J., Schoenbaum, M., Wynn, B., et al. (2003). *An analysis of the Veterans Equitable Resource Allocation (VERA) System.* Santa Monica, CA: RAND National Defense Research Institute/RAND Health.

Wasserman, J., Ringel, J., Ricci, K., Malkin, J., Wynn, B., Zwanziger, J., et al. (2004). *Understanding potential changes to the Veterans Equitable Resource Allocation (VERA) System: A regression-based approach.* Santa Monica, CA: RAND National Defense Research Institute and Rand Health.

Watkins, K. E., Pincus, H. A., Smith, B., Paddock, S. M., Mannle, T. E., Woodroffe, A., et al. (2011). *Veterans Health Administration mental health program evaluation: Capstone report.* Santa Monica, CA: RAND Corporation. http://www.rand.org/pubs/technical_reports/TR956 (accessed May 7, 2012).

Wikipedia. (2009a). Diagnosis related group. http://en.wikipedia.org/wiki/Diagnosis-related_group.

Wikipedia. (2009b). MUMPS: Current users of MUMPS applications. http://en.wikipedia.org/wiki/MUMPS#Current_users_of_MUMPS_applications.

Young, G. J. (2000). Managing organizational transformation: Lessons from the Veterans Health Administration. Product #: CMR 187–PDF-ENG. Harvard Business Publishing, October 1.

Zamberlan, A. & Moore, J. (1984). A novel methodology for VA resource allocation. *VA Practitioner* no. 9: 42–45.

Zeiss, Antonette. (2010). Remarks made after a formal address, May 14.

About the Editor

Thomas W. Miller, PhD, ABPP, is Professor Emeritus and Retired Career VA Chief, Psychology Service, at the VA and University of Kentucky College of Medicine. He has been a Senior Research Scientist, Master Teacher, and University Teaching Fellow through his forty-year career and tenure at the University of Kentucky and University of Connecticut. He has served on several national and regional professional and VA task forces and committees. A graduate of the State University of New York, he is a diplomate of the American Board of Professional Psychology, and a Fellow of the American Psychological Association, the Association for Psychological Science, and the Royal Society of Medicine. He is a Distinguished Alumnus from the State University of New York and recipient of the APA Distinguished Professional Contributions to Clinical Practice Award. He honors his veteran patients and his father, William J. Miller, a veteran of Patton's Army in World War II and the Korean conflict.

About the Contributors

James P. Bagian, MD, PE, is the director of the University of Michigan's Center for Healthcare Engineering and Patient Safety, as well as being a professor at the Medical School and College of Engineering. From 1999 to 2010 he served as the founding director of the VA National Center for Patient Safety and the first Chief Patient Safety Officer for the Department of Veterans Affairs, where he developed numerous patient safety–related tools and programs that have been adopted nationally and internationally. Dr. Bagian was a NASA astronaut for fifteen years and is a veteran of two space shuttle missions. He has also been elected to membership in the National Academy of Engineering and the Institute of Medicine.

Sharon Barnes joined NCOD as the Director of Special Projects in January 2009. She is the NCOD liaison for departmental activities, including team development, leadership development, learning organization transformation, systems redesign, healthcare transformation, succession planning, and workforce development. Since joining VA in 1985, she has served in field and VACO positions in the Veterans Health Administration, Office of Congressional and Legislative Affairs, and Office of the Secretary. Prior to joining NCOD she served as VA Deputy Chief of Staff. She is a graduate of Auburn University and completed the Harvard Business School General Management Program.

Linda W. Belton, FACHE, joined NCOD as Director in Organizational Health in 2008. Her primary interests are Civility, Respect and Engagement in the Workplace (CREW); patient-centered care; servant leadership; and organizational transformation. Prior to her current position, she served as Director, Veterans Integrated Service Network (VISN) 11; Administrator of the Division of Care and Treatment Facilities, Department of Health and Social Services, State of Wisconsin; and vice president, Mercy Medical Center Oshkosh, Wisconsin. Ms. Belton holds a master's degree in administration and completed the program for Senior Executives in Government, Harvard University.

Samantha Boris-Karpel, PhD, MPH, LMT, is a clinical research psychologist and Education Coordinator at the Pain Research, Informatics, Medical Comorbidities, and Education (PRIME) Center. She also serves as Clinical Health Psychology Faculty at the VA Connecticut Healthcare System and as a Staff Associate at the Department of Psychiatry, Yale School of Medicine. Dr. Boris-Karpel's professional activities include clinical work and research as well as work in program planning, policy, and education. Her chief areas of interest are health psychology, pain management, tinnitus management, IM/CAM, medical anthropology, and public health.

Jill Draime, PsyD, is a Supervisory Program Analyst for the Veterans Health Administration National Center for Organization Development. She serves as the Supervisory Psychologist for OD Practice, directly supervising the consultative practice of organization development across the Department of Veterans Affairs. Her interests include large-scale systems change, process consultation, executive coaching, and the interface between organizational research and practice. She has coauthored six publications and national conference presentations.

Sue R. Dyrenforth, PhD, began her VA career in 1989 as a Clinical Psychologist in Mental Health. She quickly progressed to the Director in Substance Abuse Rehabilitation, then Assistant Chief of Psychology, and finally Director, NCOD. She is active in workplace enrichment programs: the Civility, Respect, Engagement in the Workplace (CREW) initiative; the All Employee Survey administration; analysis; and action planning. She provides executive coaching to VA leaders and maintains a private practice (psychotherapy, executive coaching, and organizational consultation). She has been involved in psychological research, practice, and education for over thirty years and has served as a consultant to organizations for more than twenty years.

Matthew J. Friedman, MD, PhD, is Executive Director of the U.S. Department of Veterans Affairs National Center for Post-Traumatic Stress Disorder (PTSD) and Professor of Psychiatry and of Pharmacology and Toxicology at Dartmouth Medical School. He has worked with PTSD patients as a clinician and researcher for thirty-five years and has over 200 publications, including nineteen books and monographs. Listed in *The Best Doctors in America*, he is a Distinguished Lifetime Fellow of the American Psychiatric Association, past president of the International Society for Traumatic Stress Studies (ISTSS), and a member of the American Psychiatric Association's DSM-5 Anxiety Disorders Work Group.

Russell Hagy, CRA, COA, works with the Texas VA Healthcare System.

Said A. Ibrahim, MD, MPH, is a tenured professor of medicine and Vice Chair, Department of Medicine, for the University of Pennsylvania, School of Medicine. He is also Associate Chief of Staff for Medicine at the Philadelphia VA Medical Center. In 2001 he joined the VA Center for Health Equity Research and Promotion (CHERP) in Pittsburgh. He is also an Associate Editor of the *American Journal of Public Health*. Dr. Ibrahim has been a member of the SGIM council and served on the National Advisory Board for the Robert Wood Johnson Foundation national program "Finding Answers: Health Disparities."

Janet Kemp, RN, PhD, has twenty years' experience working with veterans. She currently serves as National VA Mental Health Director for Suicide Prevention. She is responsible for providing provider and patient education in the areas of suicide awareness and prevention, current assessment and treatment strategies and new findings in the area of suicide, and assisting in the implementation of Suicide Prevention Programs throughout the VA system. Dr. Kemp directs and advises the suicide prevention coordinators at each local VA and is the national program manager for the VA Suicide Hotline. Dr. Kemp has done extensive qualitative research in the area of war experiences and effects. Her current projects include suicide attempt and completion database development as well as studies involving veteran suicide attempt experiences and the experiences of veterans with traumatic brain injuries who have attempted suicide.

Robert D. Kerns, PhD, is VHA National Program Director for Pain Management; Director of the Pain Research, Informatics, Medical Comorbidities, and Education (PRIME) Center at the VA Connecticut Healthcare System; and Professor of Psychiatry, Neurology, and Psychology at Yale University. As National Program Director for Pain Management he has programmatic responsibility for policy development, coordination, and oversight of the VHA National Pain Management Strategy. He was recently awarded a VA Health Services Research and Development grant to establish the PRIME Center, which will build capacity for pain-relevant health services research at VA Connecticut and Yale University.

Kenneth W. Kizer, MD, MPH, is Distinguished Professor, University of California Davis School of Medicine and Betty Irene Moore School of Nursing, and Director, Institute for Population Health Improvement, UC Davis Health System. Dr. Kizer served for five years as the Under Secretary for Health in the U.S. Department of Veterans Affairs (VA). In this capacity he was the highest ranking physician in the federal government and the CEO of the veterans' healthcare system, the largest integrated healthcare system in the nation. Dr. Kizer's professional experience includes a variety of positions in both the public and private sectors. Dr. Kizer is a Fellow of the American College of Emergency Physicians, the American College of Preventive Medicine, the American College of Occupational and Environmental Medicine, the American College of Medical Toxicology, the American Academy of Clinical Toxicology, the American College of Physician Executives, the American Academy of Medical Administrators, the Royal Society of Health, and the Royal Society of Medicine.

Kathryn LaChappelle received her BA in psychology from Fairfield University in 2009. She is currently a research assistant in the Pain Research, Informatics, Medical Comorbidities, and Education (PRIME) Center of the VA Connecticut Healthcare System in West Haven. Her role within the PRIME Center includes recruitment of participants, data collection, material development, and study coordination and maintenance. Her research interests include health services research and chronic conditions. Kathryn is currently a graduate student at the University of Massachusetts, Amherst, working toward her MPH.

David S. Macpherson, MD, MPH, is the Chief Medical Officer for the 4th Veterans Integrated Service Network and Professor of Medicine at the University of Pittsburgh. Dr. Macpherson received his medical degree from Northwestern University School of Medicine and his Masters in Public Health from the University of Pittsburgh, Graduate School of Public Health. Prior to his appointment as Chief Medical Officer, Dr. Macpherson served as Vice President of the Primary Care Service Line and as Section Chief of General Internal Medicine for the VA Pittsburgh Healthcare System.

Andrew A. Meyer, PhD, currently serves as the Organizational Development Psychologist with the Robley Rex (Louisville, KY) Veterans Affairs Medical Center. Prior to this he was the Director of the Business Solutions Group and a Senior Organizational Consultant with Innovative Productivity, Inc. He previously served as Chair of the School of Professional Psychology, Dean of the College of Social Sciences and Humanities, and was the founding Director of the Health Psychology Emphasis Area at Spalding University. He was the inpatient and outpatient Clinic Chief for the Harry S Truman (Columbia, MO) Veterans Affairs Medical Center Substance Abuse Treatment Programs.

Scott C. Moore, PhD, is a Health Science Specialist with the VHA National Center for Organization Development. He earned his doctorate in organizational consultation and program evaluation from the University of Cincinnati in 2009. He completed several graduate-level practicum experiences with the NCOD prior to becoming a full-time staff member. His primary foci are survey-related research and development, program evaluation, and statistical methodology.

Michael E. Moreland is network director, Veterans Integrate Services Network (VISN4), directing operations and clinical programs serving 1.5 million veterans across Pennsylvania, Delaware, and parts of West Virginia and New Jersey. VISN4 has ten medical centers, forty-five outpatient clinics, and a budget over $2.5 billion. Prior to his service at VISN4, Mr. Moreland was director, VA Pittsburgh Healthcare System. Mr. Moreland is a Fellow, American College of Healthcare Executives and recipient of the Presidential Rank Award for Meritorious Achievement from President Bush in 2002 and President Obama in 2010. Mr. Moreland is Adjunct Professor, Graduate School of Public Health, Department of Health Services Administration, University of Pittsburgh.

Joseph F. Murphy, MS, is the public affairs officer for the VA National Center for Patient Safety. He has twenty-four years' experience in public affairs for government, private sector organizations, and the military. Murphy is a graduate of the University of California, Berkeley, and has a master's degree in human resources management from Golden Gate University, San Francisco, California. He is accredited by the Public Relations Society of America and is a Commander, retired, U.S. Naval Reserve.

Edmund J. Nightingale, PhD, ABPP, retired from the Minneapolis VA Medical Center as Chief Psychologist, a role he enjoyed, at Danville, Illinois, and Minneapolis, Minnesota, for twenty-six of his thirty-two plus years with Veterans Affairs. He served on numerous national and regional professional and VA task forces and committees, including seven years on the DM&S Resource Planning Management Technical Advisory Group on Chronic Mental Illness. Dr. Nightingale has held clinical or adjunct appointments in family practice at the University of Illinois (Chicago and Champaign/Urbana), in psychology at Purdue, Loyola University of Chicago (which awarded his doctorate), and in psychiatry and psychology at the University of Minnesota.

Steven Nisenbaum, PhD, JD, holds a Medical Staff appointment in psychiatry at Massachusetts General Hospital/Harvard Medical School and as Assistant Clinical Professor in Pediatrics at Tufts Medical School. He is a past president of the Massachusetts Psychological Association and of Division 18 (Public Service) Psychology of the American Psychological Association, as well as the Massachusetts Chapter of the Association of Family and Conciliation Courts. He has also been Clinical Director and Director of Psychology for the Massachusetts Department of Mental Health at Danvers State Hospital and Tewksbury Hospital.

Dennis Norman, EdD, ABPP, is Chief of Psychology, Massachusetts General Hospital, and Faculty Chair at the Harvard University Native American Program. He is board-certified in clinical and child and adolescent psychology.

Sheila O'Keefe, EdD, is the Director of Psychology Training for the APA-accredited Psychology Internship Program at Massachusetts General Hospital and Assistant Professor in the Psychiatry Department at Harvard Medical School. She is a former chairperson of the Massachusetts Board of Registration for Psychologists. Dr. O'Keefe has published articles in the area of psychological and neuropsychological assessment and evaluation in inpatient psychiatric units.

Katerine Osatuke, PhD, is a Supervisory Health Scientist and Research Director at the Veterans Health Administration National Center for Organization Development (NCOD). She provides data analytic support to management initiatives, conducts research studies, and participates in designing nationwide organizational intervention programs. She has conceptual and empirical background and research interests in models of psychological change, including how change is defined, empirically measured and tracked through time. She is a licensed clinical psychologist experienced at working with diverse individuals and groups. She has coauthored twenty-seven publications and over four dozen national and international conference presentations on aspects of clinical and organizational change.

Terrie Price, PhD, ABPP, served as president of the Academy of Spinal Cord Injury Professionals from 2009 to 2011. She previously cochaired the Tri-Association Strategic Planning Committee and was president of the American Association of Spinal Cord Injury Psychologists and Social Workers. Dr. Price is the Director of Neuropsychology and Family Services at The Rehabilitation

Institute of Kansas City, Missouri. She is a coauthor of *Traumatic Head Injury: Cause, Consequence and Challenge*, 3rd ed. (2010).

Dee Ramsel, PhD, MBA, is a clinical psychologist who began her career as director of a 200-bed mental health rehabilitation (domiciliary) program and regional mental health coordinator. In 2003 she became director of the Healthcare Analysis & Information Group in the Office of Policy and Planning at the VA. She earned her MBA in 1999 and in 2008 joined the VHA National Center for Organization Development as the director of training. She is an Associate Professor in the Department of Psychiatry and Behavioral Sciences at the Medical College of Wisconsin. Her interests include leadership development, executive coaching, and systems change.

Barbara Van Dahlen, Ph.D., president of Give an Hour™, is a licensed clinical psychologist practicing in the Washington, D.C., area for 20 years. A specialist in children's issues, she served as an adjunct faculty member at George Washington University. She received her Ph.D. in clinical psychology from the University of Maryland in 1991. Concerned about the mental health implications of the Iraq War, Dr. Van Dahlen founded Give an Hour™ in 2005. Dr. Van Dahlen frequently participates in panels, conferences, and hearings on issues facing veterans. She also writes a monthly column for *Veterans Advantage* and has contributed to a book on post-traumatic stress and traumatic brain injuries.

Jennifer A. Wood, PhD, serves as the Associate Chief of Staff for Mental Health for the VA Texas Valley Coastal Bend Health Care System. In her current role, she oversees mental health programming for four VA outpatient clinics (Harlingen, McAllen, Corpus Christi, and Laredo). Prior to her current appointment she served as the Clinical Psychologist for the Lower Rio Grande Valley OEF/OIF Program. Her primary clinical duties involved the provision of individual and group therapy for PTSD, depression, and postdeployment readjustment, neuropsychological testing for patients with traumatic brain injury, psychological assessments, and conducting outreach to local National Guard and Reserve units as well as community organizations and institutions of higher education. Wood also coordinates and provides telemental healthcare to veterans located throughout the Valley Coastal Bend Health Care System. In addition to her clinical duties, Wood is an Assistant Professor for the Department of Psychiatry, University of Texas Health Science Center. Her clinical and research interests include evaluation of telemental health interventions, service delivery systems in rural settings, geriatric assessment, treatment for OEF/OIF veterans, and evaluation of group interventions.

Index

Academy of Spinal Cord Injury
    Professionals (ASCIP),
    235–250
  American Association of Spinal
    Cord Injury Nurses (AASCIN),
    243–244
  American Association of Spinal
    Cord Injury Psychologists and
    Social Workers, 244–246
  American Paraplegic Society (APS),
    241–243
  Annual Spinal Cord Injury
    Conferences, 242
  chronological development of,
    239–241
  Clinical Practice Committee, 241
  Electronic Communication
    Committee (ECC), 240–241
  formation of, 237–238
  future directions of, 247–249
  governance board of, 238 (table)
  HSR&D's Quality Enhancement
    Research Initiative (QUERI),
    235–236
  inaugural leadership of, 238
  introduction to, 235–236
  Journal of Spinal Cord Medicine
    (JSCM), 241, 248
  Membership Committee, 240
  Nominating Committee, 241
  organizational structure,
    238–239
  Program Committee, 240
  SCI healthcare services for
    veterans, 236
  spinal cord injury challenges,
    236–238
  Therapeutic Leadership Council
    (TLC), 246–247
Achilles in Vietnam (Shay), 292
Agent Orange claims, 68
Akaka, Daniel, 144
All Employee Survey, 28, 30–35
Allen, Kelli, 8
America Supports You program
    (ASY), 301
American Association for Marriage and
    Family Therapy, 298

American Association of Pastoral
    Counselors, 299
American Association of Suicidology
    (AAS), 229
American Legion, 229
American Mental Health Counselors
    Association, 298
American Pain Society, 135
American Psychiatric Association, 95,
    96, 229
American Psychiatric Foundation
    (APF), 300
American Psychiatric Nurses
    Association (APNA), 229, 298
American Psychological Association
    (APA), 229, 298–299
American Veterans (AMVETS), 229
Anxiety Disorders Association of
    America, 299
assessment and feedback (Web-based
    360-degree), 48–49, 50–51 (fig.)
Automated Pharmacy Profiling
    and LabEling System
    (APPLES), 322

Bagian, James P., 379
Bar Code Resource Office and
    Information Technology
    Patient Safety Office, 92
Barnes, Sharon, 379
Belton, Linda W., 379–380
Bentrem, David, 10
Bernardy, Nancy, 105
Best Care Anywhere (Longman), 67
Boris-Karpel, Samantha, 380
Bors, Ernest, 242
Bosshart, Helen, 245
Bosworth, Hayden, 8
Bristol Myer Squibb Foundation
    (BMSF), 311

Campbell, James, 134–135
centers of excellence (CoEs)

Arkansas, Little Rock, Center
    for Mental Healthcare and
    Outcomes Research
    (CeMHOR), 13–14
California, Palo Alto,
    Centerpoint Health Care
    Evaluation, 16
California, Sepulveda, Center for
    the Study of Healthcare
    Provider Behavior, 17–19
Florida, Tampa, Center for
    Maximizing Rehabilitation
    Outcomes, 19–20
Illinois, Hines, Center for
    Management of Complex
    Chronic Care (CMC^3), 10–11
Indiana, Indianapolis, Center of
    Excellence on Implementing
    Evidence-Based Practice
    (CIEBP), 12–13
Massachusetts, Bedford, Center for
    Health Quality, Outcomes,
    and Economic Research
    (CHQOER), 6–7
Massachusetts, Boston, Center
    for Organization, Leadership
    and Management Research
    (COLMR), 7–8
Michigan, Ann Arbor, Center
    for Clinical Management
    Research, 4–6
Minnesota, Minneapolis, Center for
    Chronic Disease Outcomes
    Research, 15
North Carolina, Durham, Center for
    Health Services Research, 8–9
Pennsylvania, Pittsburgh/
    Philadelphia, Center for Health
    Equity Research and Promotion
    (CHERP), 16–17
Texas, Houston, Center for Quality
    of Care and Utilization Studies,
    11–12

Washington, Seattle, Northwest
    Center for Outcomes Research
    in Older Adults, 17
Charney, Dennis, 97
"A Checklist to Identify Inpatient
    Suicide Hazards in Veterans
    Affairs Hospitals," 90
Christopher and Dana Reeve
    Foundation, 235
Civility, Respect, and Engagement in
    the Workplace (CREW), 37–42
  civility scale, 40
  "companions" factor in, 40–41
  CREW stories, 40 (fig.)
  purpose of, 38
  success of, 38, 41
  system redesign and, 41–42
Cleelend, Charles, 136
Client-Centered Therapy (Rogers), 274
clinical integration, 153–163
  background and context, 154–155
  care delivery assets, 162
  conclusion concerning, 162
  enabling infrastructure, 157–158
  finances and, 160–161
  health information technology, 160
  healthcare culture, 158–160
  hospitals, 162
  language and, 159–160
  leadership, 160
  management and operational
    accountability, 156
  new competencies, 159
  the new vision of the VA healthcare
    system, 157 (box)
  observations, 155–162
  Patient Protection and Affordable
    Care Act of 2010 (ACA) and,
    153, 154, 155, 159
  political dynamics and, 155
  strategic communications plan, 161
  a values-based vision of the new
    future, 156–157

Collaborating Partners Council
    (CPC), 7
Computerized Patient Record System
    (CPRS), 178, 210, 315, 349, 354
*Computerizing Large Integrated Health
    Networks: The VA Success*
    (Kolodner & Douglas), 322
Consumer Assessment of Health
    Care Providers and Systems
    (CAHPS), 365
Consumer Reports, 274
Cornerstone Recognition Program,
    89–90
Cranston, Alan, 96, 99
Curtis, Donald, 321, 335

Daily Plan®, The, 87–88
Decentralized Hospital Computer
    Program information system
    (DHCP), 210, 315
Deployment Risk and Resilience
    Inventory, 103
Depression and Bipolar Support
    Alliance (DBSA), 229
Desai, Rani, 107
Digital Equipment Corporation, 320
Disabled American Veterans
    (DAV), 229
Draime, Jill, 380
Dyrenforth, Sue R., 380

Einthoven, William, 199
electronic medical records, 177
Eli Lilly & Company Foundation,
    300, 304–305
El-Serag, Hashem, 12
ethicolegal issues in veterans'
    healthcare, 251–282
  benefits-related laws, 256
  consumer protection laws, 256
  consumerism in health care and the
    "balance of power" in medicolegal
    ethics, 274–275

ethicolegal issues in veterans'
healthcare (*continued*)
corrective action, 256
defensive medicine, 275
ECWeb administrator consultants
responsibilities, 266–267
ethical consultation, 258, 259–260
ethical leadership, 258, 261
ethics consultation coordinator, role
of, 265–266
facility director responsibilities,
263–264
financing healthcare, 278–279
future directions of, 280
Health Insurance Portability
and Accountability Act
(HIPAA), 256
institutional review procedures, 258
Integrated Ethics (IE) Council, role
of, 261–262
integrated ethics program evaluation
and improvement, 262
integrated ethics responsibilities and
roles, 263–270
introduction to, 251
Joint Commission (TJC), 255–256
labor laws, 256
legal regulation, 254–256
liability insurance coverage, 257
litigation, 254, 257–258
medical malpractice, 255
medicolegal ethics, 279–280
a model of integrated preventive
ethics, 258–261
monitoring and reactive
intervention, 256–257
National Center for Ethics in
Health Care IE Web site, 270
overview of, 251–258
Patient Protection and Affordable
Care Act of 2010 (ACA), 252
Physician Compare Web site, 274
placebo phenomena, 273–274
preventive ethics, 258, 260–261
preventive ethics coordinator
responsibilities, 267–268
program officer responsibilities,
264–265
resources for program
effectiveness, 277
sources of ethical healthcare
practice, 252–254
special rights laws, 256
transparency, medical practitioners
and patients, 272–274
transparency and integrated ethics,
270–272
VHA as a model for national
healthcare system, 276–278
VHA employees responsibilities,
270
VHA leaders responsibilities, 269
VISN director responsibilities, 268
VISN IE point of contact
responsibilities, 269
VISN IE senior lead
responsibilities, 268
VISN Integrative Ethics Advisory
Board oversight, 262–263
workplace rules, 256
Executive Career Field Candidate
Development Program, 52–53
External Peer Review Program
(EPRP), 137–138

"The Falls Toolkit," 80
Fears, John R., 327
*Federal Benefits for Veterans, Dependents
and Survivors*, 231
Fitzgibbon, Marian, 10
Friedman, Matthew J., 380–381
Frueh, B. C., et al. (2007), 185, 193
Furey, Joan, 111

Gayton, Peter, 355
Gelernter, Joel, 108

Gerber, Ben, 10
Gifford, Allen, 6
Give an Hour™ (GAH), 283–314
    assumptions and realities in,
        293–308
    Bristol Myer Squibb Foundation
        (BMSF), 311
    Community Blueprint initiative,
        309–312
    components of the model, 287–293
    concept of, 285–286
    delivery system, 287–289
    early criticism of, 288
    education and information, 293
    education and training, 288–289
    Eli Lilly & Company Foundation
        and, 300, 304–305
    the "family" of, 306–308
    future directions, 312–313
    giving back, 289–292
    inspiration for, 283–285
    mental health associations
        and, 298–300
    mental health providers and,
        297–298
    military, VA, and the
        administration, 295–297
    military community, defining,
        292–293
    mission of, 293–295
    National Public Radio
        report, 284
    number of hours donated by
        providers, 304 (fig.)
    number of volunteer providers,
        305 (fig.)
    partner organizations, 289
    philanthropic community and,
        302–306
    the troops and their families, 308
    veterans' service organizations and
        nonprofit organizations,
        300–302
    volunteerism and, 286
    website address, 289
Green, Howard, 328
"Gulf War syndrome," 99–100
Gusman, Fred, 97, 101

Hagy, Russell, 381
Hartmann, Christine, 7
Harvard Business Review
        (Young 2000), 355
Health Insurance Portability and
        Accountability Act of 1996
        (HIPAA), 215, 256
Helmer, D. A., et al. (2007),
        185, 193
Himmelstein, D. U., et al. (2007), 194
"Hip Protector Toolkit," 81
Hogan, Timothy, 10
HSR&D's Quality Enhancement
        Research Initiative
        (QUERI), 235–236

Information Service Centers
        (ISCs), 322
Informing the Future: Critical Issues in
        Health (2009), 251
International Nurses Society on
        Addictions (IntNSA), 230
Iraq and Afghanistan Veterans of
        America (IAVA), 230
Iraq War Clinicians' Guide, 101

Jail Diversion and Trauma Recovery—
        Priority to Veterans, 232
Johnson, Martin, 319, 322
Joint Commission Journal on Quality
        and Patient Safety (Mills et al.
        2010), 90
Joint Commission on Accreditation of
        Hospital Organizations, 135
Journal of Spinal Cord Medicine
        (JSCM), 241, 248
Journey of Change (Kizer), 352, 354

Kardiner, A. (1941), 107, 123
Kaufmans, Joan, 108
Keane, Terry, 97, 107, 110
Kemp, Jan, 224
Kemp, Janet, 381
Kerns, R. D., Turk, D. C. & Rudy, T. E. (1985), 131, 149
Kerns, Robert D., 139–141, 381
Kerr, Eve, 4
Kimerling, Rachel, 112
King, Dan, 103
King, Lynda, 103
Kizer, Kenneth W., 132, 316, 338, 344–345, 347, 355, 382
Kraman, S. S. & Hamm, G. (1999), 271, 281
Kramer, Holly, 10
Krystal, John, 108, 109
Kunik, Mark, 11

LaChappelle, Kathryn, 382
The Leadership Challenge (Kouzes and Posner), 59
leadership development, 48–56
    360-Degree Assessment and Feedback, 48–51, 50–51 (fig.)
    Executive Career Field Candidate Development Program, 52–53
    leadership development programs, 52–56
    program evaluation, 55–56
Lerner, Fred, 113
Limited Privacy Policy's Privacy Act Statement, 227
Litz, B. T. et al. (2007), 109, 124
Litz, Brett, 101
"Living 360" Assessment: one participant's story, 50–51 (fig.)
Longman, Phillip, 355
Luschene, Bob, 319

Macpherson, David S., 382
management studies, 42–43
Marshall, George C., 316
Massachusetts General programming language, 319
McInnes, Keith, 7
McSherry, Elisabeth, 328
Medicare, 334, 335
Menninger, William, 277
Mental Health America, 299
Mental Health America (MHA), 230
Mental Health Strategic Healthcare Group, 228
Meyer, Andrew A., 382–383
Miller, Thomas W., 377
Mitchell, Toni, 133
Moore, Scott C., 383
Moreland, Michael E., 383
Morland, Leslie, 104
Mullen, Mike, 309
Munro, Donald, 242
Murphy, Joseph F., 383
MyHealtheVet, 210, 325, 364

National Alliance on Mental Illness (NAMI), 230
National Association of Social Workers (NASW), 299, 230
National Cemetery Administration (NCA), 68–69
National Center for Ethics in Health Care IE Web site, 270
National Center for Organization Development (NCOD), 21–22
National Center for Patient Safety, 77–94
    adverse drug events, reducing, 91–92
    Bar Code Resource Office and Information Technology Patient Safety Office, 92

business case for patient safety,
    80–81
cognitive aids and tool kits, 80
confidential reporting, 79
Cornerstone Recognition
    Program, 89–90
correct surgery, ensuring, 84
the Daily Plan®, 87–88
healthcare failure modes and
    effective analysis, 82
history of, 77
information technology and, 92
initial challenges to, 78–81
issues, 89–92
Medical Team Training, 85–86
nursing crew resource management
    and clinical crew resource
    management, 88–89
patient safety alerts and
    advisories, 91
Patient Safety Centers of
    Inquiry, 81
Patient Safety Culture Survey,
    82–83
patient safety curriculum for
    residents, 83–84
patient safety design challenge, 86
patient safety directives, 92
Patient Safety Fellowship
    Program, 87
Patient Safety Improvement Corps,
    84–85
Patient Safety Initiative, 86–87
patient safety training, 79–80
policy, 77–78
root cause analysis, 78
safety assessment codes, 78–79
staff publications, 90
VHA Product Recall Office, 88
National Center for PTSD, 95–127
    9/11 attacks and, 100
    American Psychiatric Association
        (APA), 95, 96
    assessment tools, 102–103
    books, 116–118
    civilian disaster response work,
        98–99
    clinical challenges, 102–106
    Clinical Training Program at Palo
        Alto, 113
    clinical trials, 109–110
    Clinician Administered PTSD
        Scale (CAPS), 102–103
    Deployment Risk and Resilience
        Inventory, 103
    dissemination and training,
        103–104, 115–116
    divisions and structure of, 119 (fig.)
    educating providers and veterans,
        112–113
    educational products, 114–115
    epidemiological and survey research,
        110–111
    future work, 120–122
    "Gulf War syndrome," 99–100
    historical challenges, 98–101
    Iraq War Clinicians' Guide, 101
    The Long Journey Home report,
        106, 107
    major accomplishments of,
        101–102
    medicalization of, 95
    mentoring and consultation
        programs, 104–106
    mission of, 96
    National PTSD Brain Bank,
        108–109
    National Vietnam Veterans
        Readjustment Study, 110
    neurobiology, 107–109
    Operation Desert Storm Clinicians'
        Packet, 100
    Operation Enduring Freedom
        (OEF), 101
    operational challenges, 118–120
    origin of, 97–98

National Center for PTSD (*continued*)
    partnerships, 100
    periodicals, 116
    program evaluating, 106–107
    prolonged exposure and cognitive processing therapy, 103
    Psychological First Aid Manual, 98, 99
    psychophysiology, 107
    PTSD research, 107–112
    PTSD research on women, 111–112
    PTSD Research Quarterly, 113
    Public Law 98-528, 112
    publications of, 102
    Published International Literature on Traumatic Stress (PILOTS), 113
    Readjustment Counseling's Vet Center program, 96
    Substance Abuse and Mental Health Services Administration, 100
    Veterans' Health Care Act of 1984 and, 95
    Veterans Health Care Amendments of 1979 (P.L.96-22), 96
    Web site, 113–114
    Web site of, 102
    Women's Military Exposure Scale, 111
National Hopeline Network, 231
National Institute of Mental Health (NIMH), 230
National Institute on Alcohol Abuse and Alcoholism (NIAAA), 230
National Public Radio, 284
National Strategy for Suicide Prevention (NSSP), 230
National Suicide Prevention Lifeline, 231
National Vietnam Veterans Readjustment Study, 110

NCPS Triage Cards™ for Root Cause Analysis, 80
Neurocognition Deployment Health Study, 103
New England Journal of Medicine (NJM), 355
Nightingale, Edmund J., 383–384
Nimmo, Robert P., 322
Nisenbaum, Steven, 384
Norman, Dennis, 384
Norris, Fran, 111
nursing crew resource management and clinical crew resource management, 88–89

Obama, Barack, 356
Oddone, Eugene, 8
O'Keefe, Sheila, 384
O'Neill, Joseph (Ted), 319
Operation Desert Storm Clinicians' Guide, 101
Operation Desert Storm Clinicians' Packet, 100
Operation Enduring Freedom (OEF), 19, 101, 129
Operation Iraqi Freedom (OIF), 19, 101, 129
organizational assessment, intervention, and consulting, 28, 43–48
    basis of NCOD's approach to, 45
    competencies measured, 46
    competency model of, 46
    instrumentation used, 46
    NCOD research team activities, 44–45 (fig.)
    services provided, 47–48
    stakeholders, 47 (fig.)
organizational development (OD) in the VA, 21–76
    All Employee Survey, 27–28, 30–35

assessment and feedback
(Web-based 360-degree),
48–49, 50–51 (fig.)

basis of NCOD's approach to, 45

Civility, Respect, and Engagement
in the Workplace (CREW),
37–42

Civility, Respect, and Engagement
in the Workplace (CREW)
stories, 39 (fig.)

competency-based experience
checklist for postdoctoral fellows,
61–62 (table)

Executive Career Field Candidate
Development Program,
52–53

executive coaching, 51–52

fellowship training, 28–29

first and second local OD
interventions, 22

future directions, 69–70

introduction to, 21–27

leadership development, 48–56

leadership development
programs, 52–56

local medical center All Employee
Survey process, 34–37 (fig.)

local organization development
psychologists, 63

management practices, studies
of, 28

management studies, 42–43

National Cemetery Administration
(NCA), 68–69

National Center for Organization
Development (NCOD),
21–22

NCOD, core functions of, 27, 29

NCOD, work of, 23–27

NCOD initiatives, 29–30

NCOD interventions at the
Veterans Affairs Medical Center,
24–27 (fig.)

NCOD research team activities,
44–45 (fig.)

organizational assessment,
intervention, and consulting,
28, 43–48

Organizational Assessment
Subcommittee, 35–36

organizational interventions, 29

postdoctoral fellowship program,
56–57

postdoctoral training, 56–63

predoctoral training, 57

sample personal development
plan, 59–60 (fig.)

training goals, 56

training model, 57–63

transformation of the VA into
a veteran-centered care
system, 63–70

Veterans Benefits Administration
(VBA), 68

Veterans Health Administration,
63–67

Osatuke, Katerine, 384

pain management, 129–150

Congressional legislation and Public
Law 110-387, Section 501,
Pain Care Act of 2008,
144–145

evidence-based interdisciplinary
pain care commitment,
141–142

historical background, 130–131

introduction and overview,
129–130

OEF/OIF and, 129

Pain as the 5th Vital Sign
initiative, 134–136

Pain as the 5th Vital Sign toolkit
contents, 137 (fig.)

Pain Management Program
Office, 139

pain management (*continued*)
　Pain Research Working Group
　　(PRWG), 142–144
　pain-relevant research commitment,
　　142–144
　Patient Aligned Care Team
　　(PACT), 145–146
　performance improvement
　　monitoring, 137–138
　progress from 1999 to 2005,
　　139–141
　Project SCAN (Secondary Care
　　Access Networks), 146
　stepped care model, 145–146
　summary and future directions
　　of, 146–147
　VHA National Pain Management
　　Strategy Coordinating
　　Committee (NPMSCC),
　　133–134
　VHA pain management directive,
　　138–139
　VHA/Institute for Healthcare
　　Improvement Pain Management
　　Collaborative, 136
　VVHA National Pain
　　Management Strategy,
　　132–134
　VVHA National Pain
　　Management Strategy, origins
　　of, 131–132
　West Haven-Yale
　　Multidimensional Pain
　　Inventory (WHYMPI), 131
Paralyzed Veterans of America
　(PVA), 230
Patient Aligned Care Team (PACT),
　145–146
Patient Protection and Affordable Care
　Act of 2010 (ACA), 153, 154,
　155, 159, 165, 252
Patient Safety Information System
　(SPOT), 79–80

Peters, James J., 239
Petersen, Laura, 11
PIE (Proximity, Immediacy, and
　Expectancy) models, 277
postdoctoral training, 56–63
　competency-based experience
　　checklist for postdoctoral
　　fellows, 61–62 (fig.)
　goals of training, 56
　local organization development
　　psychologists, 63
　mini-assessment evaluation tool, 62
　personal development plan, 58–60
　personal development plan sample,
　　59–60 (fig.)
　postdoctoral fellows, 56–57
　training model, 58–63
　training outcomes, 63
The Powerful Placebo (Beecher), 273
Price, Terrie, 384
Primary Care Management
　Module, 171
Prins, A., et al. (2004), 103, 125
Privacy Act and veterans' healthcare,
　226–227
Project SCAN (Secondary Care Access
　Networks), 146
Psychological First Aid Manual, 98, 99
PTSD, 19, 237, 363
　chronic pain and, 143
　pre-existing psychiatric conditions
　　and, 278
　telehealth and, 211
　VHA management of, 185
　See also National Center for PTSD
Published International Literature
　on Traumatic Stress
　(PILOTS), 113

Quandt, Marjorie M., 336

Ramsel, Dee, 385
RAND Corporation, 84

Rasmusson, Ann, 112
Readjustment Counseling's Vet Center
        program, 96
regional VSOs, 301
Resick, Patricia, 101, 103, 109
Rosen, Amy, 6
Rosen, Craig, 103
Rosenheck, Bob, 97
Rosenheck, R. A., 106, 107, 109, 112
Rural Mobile Health Care Clinics, 358
Ruzek, Joe, 103
Ryan, Bonnie, 135

Salerno, Judith, 133
Schnurr, Paula, 104
Scurfield, Ray, 98
Seibert, Nealon, 8
Serag, Hashem El-, 12
Service to the Armed Forces
        initiative, 301
Shay, Jonathan, 292
Shinseki, Eric, 356–357, 360–369
Shipherd, Jilian, 112
Small, Barbara, 327
Smelson, David, 6
Smith, Eric, 7
Spinal Cord Injury Quality
        Enhancement Research
        Initiative (SCI QUERI), 11
Stamm, B. H. (1999), 215, 220
Street, Amy, 112
Street, Richard, 11
Studdert, D., et al. (2007), 271, 281
Student Veterans of America
        (SVA), 231
Substance Abuse and Mental Health
        Services Administration
        (SAMHSA), 231
Suicide Hotline and Suicide
        Prevention Programs, 358
suicide prevention, 223–233
    hotlines for, 231–232
    introduction to, 223

Limited Privacy Policy's Privacy Act
        Statement, 227
mental health services available to
        veterans, 228
mental health services for veterans
        and families, 224–226
mental health services overview,
        223–224
Mental Health Strategic Healthcare
        Group, 228
Office of Mental Health
        Services, 223
phone numbers for, 224, 227,
        228–229, 231–232
Privacy Act and veterans'
        healthcare, 226–227
publications and multimedia, 232
resources for veterans, 228–232
services for families in crisis, 221
VA Form 10-10EZ, 227
VA national suicide prevention
        hotline call report 2011 totals
        YDT, 225 (table)
Veteran Suicide Prevention
        Hotline, 232
veterans chat report totals 2011
        YDT, 226 (table)
VHA national healthcare system
        enrollment enrollment,
        227–228
VHA National Suicide Prevention
        Lifeline, 224
VHA System of Records
        Notices, 226
websites for, 224, 228–229
Survey of Healthcare Experiences of
        Patients (SHEP), 138

Tatarczuk, Joe, 319
telehealth applications, 197–221
    Advanced Real Time Motion
        Analysis (ARTMA) project, 218
    asynchronous technology, 199

telehealth applications (*continued*)
  Boston Store-and-Forward
    Telehealth Training Center,
    205, 206–207
  Care Coordination Home
    Telehealth (CCHT) National
    Training Center, 204, 206, 209
  common asynchronous health care
    applications, 198
  Computerized Patient Record
    System (CPRS), 210
  Conditions of Participation (CoP)
    tool, 207
  contingency plans, 214–215
  Decentralized Hospital Computer
    Program information system
    (DHCP), 210
  definitions and technical
    applications, 198–199
  demonstration projects, 211
  electronic medical records, 209–210
  expansion of in the VA, 202–203
  future directions in veterans'
    telehealth care, 216–270
  Health Insurance Portability and
    Accountability Act of 1996
    (HIPAA), 215
  history and evolution of, 199–203
  home messaging, 211
  home telehealth, 209
  introduction to, 197–198
  licensure and competence to provide
    telehealth services, 213–214
  Master Preceptor program, 207
  milestones in the first-wave
    development of telehealth,
    202 (table)
  NASA and, 200–201
  Office of Telehealth Services
    (OTS), 203–204
  organizational structure of VA
    telehealth, 203–205
  PTSD and, 211
  research initiatives, 210–212
  Rocky Mountain Telehealth
    Training Center (RMTTC),
    204, 206
  Rural Telemedicine Grant
    program, 202
  security of telehealth
    communications, 215–216
  selection of telehealth candidates,
    216
  Sunshine Telehealth Training
    Center, 204, 206
  synchronous applications, 199
  technological infrastructure,
    212–213
  telediagnosis, consultation, and
    treatment interventions,
    218–219
  telehealth practice considerations,
    212–216
  telemental health, 208–209
  telepresence surgery, 218–219
  training initiatives, 205–207
  uses of, 203
  videoconferencing, 199, 212
  Women's Telemental Health
    Clinic, 208
telehealth programs, 358
Therapeutic Communities of
  America, 299
Timson, George, 319, 320, 322
Tollett, Jane, 133, 134
Torrey, E. F. (2002), 272, 281
transformation of the VA into a
  veteran-centered care
  system, 63–70
  focus on organizational learning, 67
  future directions, 69–70
  infrastructure funding, 67
  National Cemetery Administration
    (NCA), 68–69
  patient-driven team approach to
    primary care delivery, 66–67

recommended approach to
leadership, 66
Task Force for, 65–66
Veterans Benefits Administration
(VBA), 68
Veterans Health Administration,
63–67

Universal Service Program for Rural
Health Providers, 213
Universal Services Task Force, 65–66
U.S. healthcare system ranking, 165

VA care delivery assets, 162
VA Form 10-10EZ, 227
VA healthcare system: a potential
model for a national plan,
165–195
Americans and government-run
healthcare, 181–182
comparative real growth in per
beneficiary spending, Medicare
versus veterans' medical care
(1980–2002), 184 (fig.)
comparison of the Major Veterans
Health Administration financing
systems, 186–189 (table)
Computerized Patient Record
System, 178
cost-effectiveness, 184
electronic medical records, 168, 177
future of VA and ongoing
challenges, 181–184
geographic access and virtual
care, 182–183
introduction, 165–166
leadership accountability, 168
licensed practical nurses
(LPNs), 172
life expectancy of U.S. veterans
versus life expectancy at birth
for all U.S. men, 1991–2002,
175 (fig.)

lingering challenges, 185–191
map of current VISNs, 180 (fig.)
maximum veteran drug costs, 172
model features of the VA healthcare
system, 168–181
Patient Protection and Affordable
Care Act of 2010 (ACA), 165
percentage of veterans and
nonveterans ages 18–64 who
lacked coverage, 1987–2004,
190 (fig.)
pharmacy benefits management,
172–177
preventive care, a cultural shift
to, 171
preventive care, productivity
and, 171
preventive care, sources of success
in, 171–172
Primary Care Management
Module, 171
quality of care metrics comparing
VA with other health systems,
169–170 (table)
quality of care, public disclosure
of, 182
quality of VA care: the role
of preventive/primary care,
168–170
standardized and centralized
pharmacy plan, 173–177
structure of the VA healthcare
system, 178–181
summary of, 191
total drug expenditures and cost
avoidance, 174 (fig.)
transformation of the VA
healthcare system, 167,
179–181
U.S. healthcare system ranking, 165
VA average acquisition cost per
30-day-equivalent prescriptions,
176 (fig.)

VA healthcare system: a potential
model for a national plan
(*continued*)
VA system versus private sector,
166–167, 179
Veterans Health Administration as
a model, 166–167
VHA budget in billions, 185 (fig.)
virtual care, 183
VA healthcare system, the new vision
of, 157 (box)
VA Practitioner (Nightingale), 336
Van Dahlen, Barbara, 284–285, 289,
290, 295–296, 300, 303,
306–307, 312, 385
Vasterling, Jennifer, 103
Vet to Vet (Peer Support), 231
Veteran Suicide Prevention
Hotline, 232
Veterans Benefits Administration
(VBA), 68
Veterans Health Administration,
63–67
Veterans' Health Care Act of
1984, 95
Veterans Health Care Amendments
of 1979 (P.L.96-22), 96
Veterans' Health Care Eligibility
Reform Act (1996), 167, 172
veterans' healthcare system's path to
excellence, 315–375
AMIS: the early automated VA
medical information system,
316–318, 326
ANSI MUMPS, 319, 320
Automated Pharmacy Profiling
and LabEling System
(APPLES), 322
bed days of care (BDOC), 333,
334, 335
benefits delivery and services,
361–362
Boston Development Center, 327

Computer Adapted Systems Staff
(CASS), 319
Computerized Patient Record
System (CPRS), 315, 349, 354
*Computerizing Large Integrated
Health Networks: The VA Success*
(Kolodner & Douglas), 322
Cost Distribution Report (CDR)
to Decision Support System
(DSS), 325–331
Current Procedural Terminology
codes (CPT-4), 348
current progress: performance and
accountability, 356–358
current trends and future directions,
356–369
decentralized hospital computing
program, 318–323
Decentralized Hospital Computing
System (DHCP), 315,
322–323, 324
Decentralized Medical Management
System, 327–328
Decision Support System (DSS),
329–331, 348, 354
DHCP to the CPRS, 323–325
DRGs and RAM, 333–338
emergent national needs
preparedness, 366
evidence of success, 355–356
excellence in education and research,
350–351
excellence in service as defined by
customers, 349–350
financial management system
overhaul, 360–361
four domains of value, 349
future strategic moves, 359–369
GI Bill benefits, automation
of, 362
health care access for veterans,
including women and rural
populations, 365–366

Hines Verification and
    Development Center, 327
human capital management,
    368–369
Information Service Centers
    (ISCs), 322
information technology (IT)
    reorganization, 360
introduction to, 315–316
Kizer revolution, 344–356
long-term health and well-being of
    veterans, 369
management infrastructure and
    integrated operating model
    establishment, 367–368
Massachusetts General
    programming language, 319
Medicare and, 334, 335
My HealtheVet and, 325, 364
"Order Entry Results Reporting,"
    323
overview of resource allocation,
    331–333
"Patients First" and reorganization,
    345
performance and outcomes
    capabilities and systems,
    366–367
procurement systems, 360
resource allocation in a "closed"
    system, 331–344
Resource Planning Management
    (RPM), 338–339
Right-Sized Infrastructure, 364
Shinseki VA initiatives, 360–369
"The Thirteen Greatest
    Challenges," 361–369
VA approach to implementation,
    369–370
veteran homelessness, 361
veteran mental health, 363
Veteran Relationship Management
    (VRM), 363–364

Veteran-Centric Healthcare
    Model, 364
Veterans Equitable Resource
    Allocations system, 352
Veterans Equitable Resource
    Methodology (VERA) and its
    revisions, 339–344
VHA mission statement, 346–347
VHA strategy statement, 351–355
Virtual Lifetime Electronic Records
    (VLER), 362–363
VistA (Veterans Information
    System & Technology
    Architecture), 315–316,
    324, 325
White River Junction VA Medical
    Center, 327, 328, 329
Veterans Innovation Center (VIC),
    301–302
Veterans Integrated Service Networks
    (VISNs), 5, 156, 181 (fig.)
VHA as a model for national
    healthcare system, 276–278
VHA national healthcare system
    enrollment, 227–228
VHA Product Recall Office, 88
VHA System of Records Notices,
    226
VHA's Nursing Academy, 358
Vietnam Veterans of America
    (VVA), 231
virtual care, 183
Vision for Change (Kizer), 344, 347
VistA (Veterans Information System
    & Technology Architecture),
    315–316, 324, 325
Vogt, Dawne, 103
Voice of the VA surveys, 35

Wasse, Loretta, 135
Watson, Patricia, 101
Weaver, Fran, 10
Weiner, Saul, 10

Welcome Home to Work
    programs, 68
Wilson, David, 320
Wolfe, Jessica, 98, 111
Women's Military Exposure Scale, 111
Wood, Jennifer A., 385

Xavier University (Ohio),
    48
    Industrial-Organizational
    Psychology Program, 23

Yehuda, Rachel, 107–108